HARRAP'S
SLANG
DICTIONARY

HARRAP'S

SLANG

French-English

DICTIONARY

DICTIONNAIRE

Anglais-Français

---

by Georgette A. Marks
and Charles B. Johnson

completely revised and edited
by Jane Pratt

HARRAP

London

First published in Great Britain 1984
by HARRAP Ltd
19–23 Ludgate Hill, London EC4M 7PD

© HARRAP Ltd 1984

ISBN 0 245-54047-4

Reprinted 1984 (twice), 1985, 1986, 1987

Dépôt légal : novembre 1983

Cover design by Brooke Calverley
Keyboarded by Aylesbury Keyboarding
Typeset by Alexander Typesetting Inc.
Printed and bound in Great Britain
by Mackays of Chatham Ltd, Kent

PREFACE

Informal language is both ephemeral and subject to rapid change and no dictionary can claim to contain an exhaustive record of everyday slang and colloquialisms. The aim of this dictionary is to allow greater access to the daily languages of English and French speaking cultures. We hope that the work will be of interest to academics and the general public whilst, at the same time, providing an entertaining selection of the more light-hearted and racy aspects of the English and French languages.

The dictionary features a broad selection of terms and expressions ranging from the almost standard and colloquial to the *very* vulgar. In order to make the text as readable as possible, the layout has been simplified and abbreviations and other such devices have been kept to a minimum. Many examples of usage are given. Readers are referred to the section on *'How to use this dictionary'* for any guidance they may need.

One of the major features of the dictionary is the inclusion of the Indexes of Slang Synonyms, to be found at the end of each section. Each contains a comprehensive list of slang and colloquial synonyms for each of the key words asterisked in the text, and several other sections, which it was not possible to indicate in the text, but which should prove of interest to the reader.

This dictionary is a revised edition of *Harrap's Dictionary of Slang and Colloquialisms* and the Editor owes a great debt to the care and attention which Marks and Johnson gave to their work on the previous editions. Their work has been continued by many contributors from various parts of the world.

Grateful thanks are due to the following people who, in many different ways, gave advice and assistance during the compilation of this edition:

Fabrice Antoine
J. P. Bean
Fiona Clarke
Françoise Clarke
Peter Collin
Karen George
Diana Giese
Anne Gruneberg
Paul Janssen
Janet Kernachan
Helen Knox
Gabriel Otman
Geneviève Talon
Jef Tombeur
Elisabeth Turner
Sarah Wallis
Edward Wilson

J.E.P.

PRÉFACE

La langue familière est à la fois éphémère et sujette à une évolution rapide: aucun dictionnaire ne peut donc prétendre offrir une compilation exhaustive des expressions familières et de l'argot communément employés. L'objectif de ce dictionnaire est de permettre un meilleur accès à la langue quotidienne de la culture parlée anglaise et française. Nous souhaitons que l'ouvrage intéresse les linguistes professionnels aussi bien que le grand public, tout en montrant la langue anglaise et la langue française sous leur jour le plus amusant et le plus savoureux.

On trouvera dans le dictionnaire un large choix de termes et d'expressions variant de l'acceptable et du familier au *très* vulgaire. Pour rendre le texte aussi lisible que possible, la mise en pages a été simplifiée et le recours aux abréviations et autres procédés similaires a été réduit au minimum. L'usage est largement illustré par l'exemple. Les lecteurs peuvent se reporter à la section *'Comment utiliser ce dictionnaire'* s'ils ont besoin de conseils quelconques.

L'une des principales caractéristiques du dictionnaire, ce sont les Répertoires de synonymes populaires qui se trouvent à la fin de chaque section. Chaque index offre une liste complète de synonymes familiers et argotiques pour chacun des mots-clefs marqués d'un astérisque dans le texte, ainsi que quelques autres sections qu'il n'était pas possible de mentionner dans le texte, mais qui devraient intéresser le lecteur.

Ce dictionnaire est une édition revue et corrigée du *Harrap's Dictionary of Slang and Colloquialisms* et la tâche de l'Editeur a été grandement facilitée par le soin et l'attention que Marks et Johnson ont apportés aux éditions précédentes. Leur travail a été poursuivi par de nombreux collaborateurs venus de divers pays.

Nous tenons à exprimer notre reconnaissance aux personnes suivantes, dont l'aide et les conseils, de façon très variée, ont été précieux lors de la compilation de cette édition:

Fabrice Antoine
J. P. Bean
Fiona Clarke
Françoise Clarke
Peter Collin
Karen George
Diana Giese
Anne Gruneberg
Paul Janssen
Janet Kernachan
Helen Knox
Gabriel Otman
Geneviève Talon
Jef Tombeur
Elisabeth Turner
Sarah Wallis
Edward Wilson

J.E.P.

How to use this dictionary

headword in bold sans serif

toerag ['touræg] *n P* (*term of abuse*) salaud*/con *m*/couillon *m*: **you little toerag!** petit morveux!/petit trou du cul!

entrée en Linéales grasses

transcription phonétique selon l'API

phonetics in IPA

asterisk indicates that a word is included as a headword in the Index of Slang Synonyms

archaic expression

Rhyming Slang

gender of French nouns

cross references

daisy ['deizi] **I** *a F* excellent*/super; **a daisy day**, une belle journée/une sacrée journée **II** *n* **1.** *F* qn/qch d'excellent*/d'épatant/d'impec; **she's a daisy**, c'est une perle; elle est sensass **2.** *A P* pot *m* de chambre/Jules **3.** *F* **to be kicking/pushing up the daisies**, être enterré/bouffer les pissenlits par la racine **4.** *P* (*RS = boots*) **daisy roots/daisies**, chaussures*/godillots *mpl*/godasses *fpl* **5.** *P* **daisy chain**, partouze *f* à la bague **6.** *F* **as fresh as a daisy**, frais comme une rose/frais et dispo. (*See* **oops-a-daisy!**; **ups-a-daisy!**; **upsy-daisy!**; **whoops-a-daisy!**)

l'astérisque indique que ce mot figure comme entrée dans le Répertoire de synonymes populaires

archaïsme

argot dont les mots ont leur sens non pas en eux-mêmes mais dans le mot avec lequel ils riment

genre des noms communs

renvois

plural noun
Australianism

daks [dæks] *npl Austr P* pantalon*/falzar *m*/futal *m*.

nom pluriel
mot australien

Americanism
superior numbers distinguish nouns from verbs
P: slang expression
V: vulgar expression
F: colloquial expression

field label

hammer[1] ['hæmər] *n* **1.** *NAm P* belle fille*/belle nana/beau petit lot **2.** *P* (*CB*) accélérateur *m*/champignon *m*/ **3.** *NAm V* pénis*/défonceuse *f*/sabre *m*.
hammer[2] ['hæmər] *vtr* **1.** *F* (*Stock Exchange*) déclarer (un agent) en défaut **2.** *P* **to hammer s.o. into the ground**, battre qn à plate(s) couture(s)/tailler qn en pièces **3.** *F* **to hammer a play/a film**, démolir/bousiller/éreinter une pièce/un film **4.** *P* (*RS = trail*) **to hammer (and nail)**, traîner/suivre/filer le train (à qn).

américanisme
chiffres supérieurs distinguant le nom du verbe
P: expression argotique
V: expression vulgaire
F: expression familière

champ sémantique

phrasal verb

hammer back ['hæmər'bæk] *vi P* (*CB*) ralentir/lever le pied.

verbe à particule

adverb

licketysplit ['likəti'split] *adv NAm F* très vite*/à pleins gaz/à fond de train.

adverbe

old-fashioned/dated expression

fab [fæb] *a O F* excellent*/terrible: *excl* **fab!** chouette!/sensass!/super!

emploi vieilli

Comment utiliser ce dictionnaire

I II III etc indicate parts of speech	**coincer** [kwɛse] **I** *vi P* to stink*/ to pong **II** *vtr* **1.** *F* **coincer qn** (*i*) to corner s.o. (*ii*) to arrest* s.o./to nick s.o./to nab s.o. **III** *vpr* **se coincer** *V* **se coincer les couilles,** to get one's balls in a twist (esp by wearing tight trousers). (*Voir* **bulle II 1**)	I II III etc distinguant les catégories grammaticales
intransitive verb		verbe intransitif
transitive verb		verbe transitif
pronominal verb		verbe pronominal
(*i*) (*ii*) (*iii*) etc for expressions with more than one meaning		(*i*) (*ii*) (*iii*) etc pour les expressions ayant plus d'un sens
French Canadianism	**quétaine** [ketɛn] *a FrC P* **1.** old-fashioned/dated; past it **2.** cheap and nasty/rubbishy.	canadianisme
masculine noun	**coco** [koko, kɔ-] **I** *nm* **1.** *P* head*/nut; **avoir le coco fêlé/ détraqué,** to be mad*/to be off one's nut/to be as nutty as a fruit-cake **2.** *P* stomach*; **se remplir le coco,** to eat* heartily/to stuff one-self/to have a good blow-out; **en avoir plein le coco,** to have a bel-lyful **3.** *P* throat/gullet; **dévisser le coco à qn,** to strangle s.o. **4.** *F* (*mot enfantin*) (*a*) cock/hen/chicken (*b*) egg/eggie **5.** *F* communist; **les cocos,** the commies/the reds **6.** *F* (*a*) (*type*) **un drôle de coco,** a strange fellow/an odd bod/a queer customer; **un vilain coco/un sale coco,** a nasty piece of work; (*iron et péj*) **c'est un gentil/un beau/un joli coco!** he's a nice one! (*b*) **mon (petit) coco,** my darling*/my pet **7.** *P* petrol; **mettre le coco,** to hurry* up/to step on the gas **II** *nf P* (*drogues*) cocaine*/coke/snow/ flake **III** *a F* old-fashioned/out of date.	nom masculin
1. 2. 3. etc indicate differences in meaning		1. 2. 3. etc indiquant les différents sens
example in bold type translation in light face		exemple en caractères gras traduction en caractères maigres
explanations in italics		gloses en italiques
(*a*) (*b*) (*c*) etc show different uses		(*a*) (*b*) (*c*) etc indiquant les différents usages
feminine noun		nom féminin
adjective		adjectif
dialect	**fada** [fada] *F* (*esp dial du midi*) **I** *a* stupid*/dumb/(a bit) nutty/nuts **II** *nm* fool*/nutter/crackpot.	dialecte
proper noun	**Étienne** [etjɛn] *Prnm F* **à la tienne, Étienne!** cheers!*/good health!	nom propre

ABBREVIATIONS - ABRÉVIATIONS

a	adjective	adjectif
A	archaic; in former use	archaïque; vieux
abbr	abbreviation	abréviation
abs	absolute use	emploi absolu
adv	adverb	adverbe
adv phr	adverbial phrase	locution adverbiale
anat	anatomy	anatomie
a phr	adjectival phrase	locution adjective
attrib	attributive	attributif
Austr	Australianism	expression australienne
aut	motoring; motoring industry	automobiles; industrie automobile
Belg	Belgian	mot belge
CB	Citizens Band Radio	jargon des cibistes
coll	collective	collectif
conj	conjunction	conjonction
dial	dialect	dialecte
ecc	ecclesiastical	ecclésiastique
eg	for example	par exemple
esp	especially	surtout
etc	et cetera	et cetera; et cætera
euph	euphemism	euphémisme
excl	exclamation	exclamation
f	feminine	féminin
F	familiar; colloquial	familier
fig	figurative	figuratif
fin	finance	finances
FrC	French Canadian	franco-canadien
hist	historical	historique
hum	humorous	humoristique
impers	impersonal	impersonnel
indef	indefinite	indéfini
int	interjection	interjection
interr	interrogative	interrogatif
inv	invariable	invariable
iron	ironical	ironique
journ	journalism	journalisme
m	masculine	masculin
mil	military	militaire

mus	music	musique
n	noun	nom
NAm	North American	de l'Amérique du Nord
naut	nautical	terme nautique; terme de marine
O	obsolescent; old fashioned	vieilli
occ	occasionally	parfois
P	popular; slang	populaire; argotique
pej	pejorative	péjoratif
pers	person	personne
phot	photography	photographie
pl	plural	pluriel
pol	politics	politique
poss	possessive	possessif
pp	past participle	participe passé
prep	preposition	préposition
Prn	proper noun	nom propre
pron	pronoun	pronom
qch		quelque chose
qn		quelqu'un
qv	quod vide; which see	se reporter à ce mot
rel	relative	relatif
RS	Rhyming slang	mots composés qui ont leur sens non pas en eux-mêmes mais dans le mot avec lequel ils riment
RTM	registered trade mark	marque déposée
scol	school	scolaire
sing	singular	singulier
s.o.	someone	
sth	something	
typo	typography	typographie
usu	usually	d'ordinaire
v	verb	verbe
V	vulgar	trivial
vi	intransitive verb	verbe intransitif
vpr	reflexive verb	verbe pronominal
vtr	transitive verb	verbe transitif
VV	very vulgar; taboo	obscène; ordurier
WWI	World War One	première guerre mondiale
WWII	World War Two	seconde guerre mondiale

PART 1

ENGLISH-FRENCH

TABLE OF PHONETIC SYMBOLS

VOWELS AND VOWEL COMBINATIONS

[æ]	bat gander	[ə]	china goner balon(e)y bolony
[aː]	cart bar nark hooha	[əɪ]	burn learn nerd whirl
[e]	get dead belly	[ai]	aisle high kite fly hypo
[i]	bit undies system dimwitted	[au]	down mouse kraut
[iː]	bee peter tea spiel	[ei]	mate lay fey bait weight
[ɔ]	hot what-for Aussie Oz cough	[ɛə]	bear spare there airy-fairy
[ɔː]	all haul rorty jaw war walk	[iə]	queer gear real
[u]	wool bull pussy	[ɔi]	boil boy
[uː]	loo move shoes	[ou]	go snow soap dope dough
[ʌ]	nut bun ton some cover rough	[uə]	poorly sure

CONSONANTS AND SEMI-CONSONANTS

[b]	bat boob job nabbed
[d]	dab bad fiddle
[f]	fat fifty syph rough
[g]	gherkin gag guy egg agony
[h]	hat behind
[k]	cat chronic kittens make tick plonk
[l]	lid all tumble dildo chisel
[m]	mug jammy ram jism
[n]	nab bun tenner knob gnashers pancake
[p]	pan crap napper
[r]	rat around jerry
[ɾ]	drooper gear reefer (sounded only when final as in later on)
[s]	sausage scene mouse sassy psycho ceiling
[t]	top pot batter Thames trip
[v]	ever rave savvy vibes
[z]	zip buzz lousy pansy breeze tizwas business eggs
[dz]	reds odds
[dʒ]	ginger age edge juice
[ks]	extras expect accident mixer
[kʃ]	ructions
[lj]	million
[nj]	onion
[tʃ]	chick bitch rich chunder
[θ]	meths
[ð]	feather with that
[ʃ]	shark dish chassis machine
[ʒ]	usual
[ŋ]	bang sing conk anchors
[ŋg]	finger angle danglers
[j]	yack yob used putrid euchre few queue
[w]	wire wank sweep away
[(h)w]	white whistle whiz(z)

A

A [ei] *abbr P* **1.** (*drugs*) (= *amphetamine*) amphétamine* **2.** = **acid 2** **3. A over T** (= *arse over tip or tit(s)*) cul par-dessus tête. (*See* **arse 4**)

ab [æb], **AB** ['ei'biː] (*abbr* = *abscess*) *P* (*abscess caused by an unsterilized needle or by impure drugs*) caramel *m*/fondant *m*/puant *m*. (*See* **ABC 3**)

ABC ['eibiː'siː] *n* **1.** *F* (as) easy as ABC, simple comme bonjour/c'est l'enfance de l'art. (*See* **easy I 6**) **2.** *F* the ABC of sth, le B.A. ba de qch **3.** *P* = **ab, AB.**

abdabs ['æbdæbz] *npl P* to have the screaming abdabs, piauler à la bit(t)ure/voir les rats bleus.

abo, Abo ['æbou] *n Austr F* (= *aborigine*) aborigène *mf*.

about [ə'baut] *adv F* that's about the size of it, c'est à peu près ça/ça se résume à peu près à ça.

above board [ə'bʌv'bɔːd] *a F* it's all above board, c'est réglo.

absoballylutely! ['æbsou-'bæli'l(j)uːtli] *excl O F* ça colle, Anatole!/naturellement et comme de bien entendu!

absobloodylutely! ['æbsou-'blʌdi'l(j)uːtli] *excl O P* = **absoballylutely!**

abysmal [ə'bizməl] *a F* affreux/exécrable; **abysmal ignorance,** ignorance *f* crasse; **an abysmal memory,** une mémoire épouvantable.

ACAB ['eisi:'eibiː] *abbr P* (= *all coppers are bastards*) (*approx*) = mort aux vaches!

accident ['æksidənt] *n F* (*euph*) **1.** to have an accident, s'oublier; he's had an accident, il a fait pipi dans sa culotte **2.** their first child was an accident, leur premier enfant n'était pas prévu au programme.

accidentally [æksi'dentəli] *adv F* (*often hum*) accidentally on purpose, exprès.

AC-DC, ac-dc, ac/dc ['eisiːdiːsiː] *a P* ambivalent/bisexuel; he's a bit AC-DC, il marche à voile et à vapeur.

ace [eis] **I** *a F* excellent*/formid(able)/super/hyper; we had an ace time, on s'est drôlement amusés; he's an ace guy, c'est un chic type/ça c'est qn; an ace idea, une idée super chouette **II** *adv & excl F* d'accord*/dac/OK **III** *n* **1.** *F* as *m*/crack *m* **2.** *F* to have an ace up one's sleeve, avoir un as dans sa manche/avoir plus d'un tour dans son sac **3.** *F* to hold all the aces, avoir tous les atouts (en main) **4.** *NAm P* billet* d'un dollar **5.** *F* (*a*) individu* loyal/bon/généreux (*b*) individu* chouette **6.** *A P* (*drugs*) cigarette* de marijuana/stick *m*.

acid ['æsid] *n P* **1.** (*not common*) to put the acid on/to come the acid, la faire à la pose/se payer la tête de qn **2.** *P* (*drugs*) LSD*/sucre *m*/acide *m*; **acid freak/acid head,** habitué(e) du LSD*/acidulé(e); **acid cube,** dose de LSD* déposée sur un morceau de sucre; **acid funk,** dépression due au LSD*/trouille acidulée; **to drop/to take/to use acid,** prendre du LSD*/de l'acide.

ack-ack ['æk'æk] *n F* (*mil*) défense contre-avions (DCA); **ack-ack guns,** canons anti-aériens.

ack-emma ['æk'emə] *adv O F* (*mil*) avant midi.

ackers ['ækəz] *npl P* argent*/fric *m*/pézettes *fpl.*

across [ə'krɔs] *prep F* **to get sth across,** se faire comprendre; **did you get it across to him?** il t'a compris?/il a pigé?

act [ækt] *n F* **1. to put on an act/a big act,** frimer/faire du cinéma; **it's his little act,** c'est son petit numéro **2. to get in on the act,** se mettre dans le bain; **to let s.o. in on the act,** mettre qn dans le coup; **he wanted to be in on the act,** il a voulu être dans le coup/y être pour qch. (*See* **sob-act**)

actress ['æktris] *n F* (*catchphrase*) **as the actress said to the bishop,** comme dit l'autre.

ad [æd] *n F* **1.** (*abbr = advertisement*) annonce *f*/pub *f*; **small ads,** petites annonces. (*See* **advert**) **2.** *P* = **AD.**

AD ['ei'diː] *n P* (*abbr = (drug) addict*) drogué(e)*/camé(e) *mf*/toxico *mf.*

ad-agency ['ædeidʒənsi] *n F* agence *f* de pub.

Adam ['ædəm] *Prn F* **1. I don't know him from Adam,** je ne le connais ni d'Adam ni d'Ève **2. the old Adam,** le mal; le vieil Adam **3. Adam's ale,** eau*/Château-la-Pompe *m* **4. Adam and Eve on a raft,** œufs servis sur du toast.

Adam and Eve ['ædəməniːv] *vtr P* (*RS = believe*) **you'll never Adam and Eve it!** tu ne le croirais jamais!

addict ['ædikt] *n F* mordu *m*/fana *mf*; **he's a real comic addict,** c'est un fana de BD; **jazz addict,** dingue *m* du jazz.

add up ['æd'ʌp] *vi F* **it (just) doesn't add up,** ça n'a ni queue ni tête/ça n'a ni rime ni raison/ça ne tient pas debout.

ad-lib[1] ['æd'lib] *a F* (*a*) à volonté/à discrétion (*b*) improvisé/impromptu; **all his jokes were ad-lib,** toutes ses blagues étaient improvisées/spontanées.

ad-lib[2] ['æd'lib] *vi F* improviser; **I just had to ad-lib in the meeting,** j'ai dû improviser dans la réunion.

ad-man ['ædmæn], *pl* **ad-men** *n F* agent *m* de publicité/de pub.

admirer [əd'maiərər] *n O F* soupirant *m.*

adrift [ə'drift] *adv F* **1. to be (all) adrift,** dérailler/perdre le nord; **the project went adrift,** le projet est tombé à l'eau **2. the button has come adrift,** le bouton a lâché/s'est décousu.

advert ['ædvəːt] *n F* (*abbr = advertisement*) annonce *f*/pub *f*. (*See* **ad 1**)

aer(e)ated ['ɛər(i)eitid] *a P* fâché/vexé; **don't get (all) aer(e)ated,** ne prends pas la pique!/te fâche pas!

after ['ɑːftər] *prep F* **1.** *O* (*catchphrase*) **after you, Claude. – no, after you, Cecil,** après vous, Marquis. – non, après vous, Prince **2. what are you after?** qu'est-ce que tu cherches?/où veux-tu en venir? **3. after a fashion,** tant bien que mal.

afterbird ['ɑːftərbəːd] *n P* **to do (some) afterbird,** boire après la fermeture du pub/du bar.

afters ['ɑːftəz] *npl F* dessert *m.*

afto ['ɑːftou, 'æftou] *n F* (*regional*) après-midi; **this afto,** cet aprèm'.

age [eidʒ] *n F* **1. act your age!** (ne) fait pas l'enfant! **2. it took us an age/ages to get there,** ça nous a pris un temps fou pour y arriver; **I saw that film ages ago,** il y a une éternité que j'ai vu ce film **3. the age to catch 'em:** *see* **bingo 17;** **my age?:** *see* **bingo 21.** (*See* **awkward**)

aggravate ['ægrəveit] *vtr&i F* exaspérer/assommer/taper sur le système à (qn).

aggravating ['ægrəveitiŋ] *a F* exaspérant/assommant; **it's really aggravating!** c'est exaspérant à la fin!

aggravation ['ægrə'veiʃ(ə)n] *n F* agacement *m*/exaspération *f*.

aggro ['ægrou] *n P* (= *aggravation*) (*i*) (*mental, emotional strain*) tracas *mpl*; **leave out the aggro!** laisse tomber!/écrase! **I can't stand all this aggro you're giving me!** tu m'épuises à la fin! (*ii*) (*physical violence*) **I never go there because of all the aggro,** y a tellement de grabuge que j'y mets jamais les pieds; **there'll be some aggro tonight,** ça va barder/y aura du grabuge ce soir.

agin [ə'gin] *prep & adv O F* contre; **I'm not agin it,** je ne suis pas contre/je ne dis pas non.

agony ['ægəni] *n F* **1. it was agony!** j'en ai bavé! **2. to pile on the agony,** forcer la dose **3.** (*journ*) **agony column,** courrier *m* du cœur.

agriculture ['ægrikʌltʃər] *n P* (*police slang*) le fait de cacher des drogues, de l'argent, etc sur un suspect/fabriquer de faux témoignages contre qn.

agro ['ægrou] *n P* = **aggro.**

ahead [ə'hed] *adv F* **1. to be one jump ahead (of s.o.),** avoir un mètre d'avance (sur qn) **2.** (*sport*) **to be ahead on points,** mener aux points. (*See* **go-ahead**)

aid [eid] *n F* **what's all this in aid of then?** à quoi ça rime?

AIDS [eids] *abbr F* (= *acquired immune deficiency syndrome*) syndrome immuno-déficitaire acquis/ SIDA.

ain't [eint] *P* = am not, is not, are not; **ain't got** = has not (got), have not (got); **I ain't seen it,** je l'ai pas vu, moi.

air [ɛər] *n* **1.** *F* **to go up in the air,** se mettre en colère*/se mettre en rogne; **he flew straight up in the air**

when he heard of it, il a sauté au plafond/ça l'a fait bondir quand il l'a su **2.** *F* **to float/to tread/to walk on air,** être au septième ciel/ voir les anges; planer **3.** *F* **to live on (fresh) air,** vivre d'amour et d'eau fraîche/vivre de l'air du temps **4.** *P* **to give s.o. the air,** se débarrasser* de qn/envoyer promener qn/envoyer paître qn **5.** *F* **hot air,** platitudes *fpl*/foutaises *fpl*; **that's all hot air,** tout cela n'est que du vent **6.** *P* (*RS* = *faces*) **airs and graces,** visages* **7.** *F* **to put on airs and graces/to give oneself airs,** faire sa poire/faire l'intéressant/minauder/frimer.

airy-fairy ['ɛəri'fɛəri] *a F* vasouillard/du bidon; **he's full of airy-fairy ideas,** il déborde d'idées farfelues.

aisle [ail] *n* **1.** *F* **to walk down the aisle,** se marier/se marida **2.** *P* **that'll have 'em rolling in the aisles,** ça fera crouler la baraque/ça fera un malheur.

akkers ['ækəz] *npl P* = **ackers.**

alarming [ə'lɑːmiŋ] *adv O F* **she went off at me something alarming,** elle m'est tombée dessus comme une furie.

Alec, alec(k) ['ælik] *n* **1.** *F* **smart alec** (*i*) finaud *m*/combinard *m* (*ii*) bêcheur, -euse/m'as-tu-vu *m*/ je-sais-tout *m*; **he's a smart alec,** c'est un petit malin **2.** *Austr F* dupe *f*/cave *m*/navet *m*; **you big aleck!** espèce d'andouille!

alive [ə'laiv] *a F* **1. alive and kicking,** en pleine forme; **I'm still alive and kicking,** je ne suis pas mort/je suis bien en vie **2. look alive!** réveille-toi!/secoue-toi!/grouille-toi! (*See* **dead-and-alive; Jack 12**)

alkie, alky ['ælki] *n P* ivrogne*/ alcoolique *mf*/alcolo *mf*/poivrot *m*.

all [ɔːl] **I** *adv F* **1. to be all for sth,** être tout à fait en faveur de qch; **I'm all for it,** je ne demande que ça **2. to go all out for sth** (*i*) être emballé par qch (*ii*) mettre toute son énergie à faire qch/se donner corps et âme pour faire qch **3. that's him all over,** c'est lui tout craché; je le reconnais bien là! **4. to be all in,** être fatigué*/à bout/à plat **5. to be all there,** avoir les yeux en face des trous; **he's not quite all there,** il lui manque une case. (*See* **there 2**) **6. to be all over s.o.,** faire de la lèche à qn. (*See* **all right**) **II** *n F* **1. it's all over/up with him** (*i*) il est fichu (*ii*) il est pigé. (*See* **up¹ II 3**) **2. I'm tired. – aren't we all?** je suis fatigué.* – (il n')y a pas que toi! **3. all but one:** *see* **bingo 89.** (*See* **bugger-all**; **damn-all**; **fuck-all**; **know-all**; **sod-all**)

all-American ['ɔːlə'merikən] *a F* américain jusqu'au bout des ongles/cent pour cent américain; **the all-American hero,** le héros américain par excellence.

all-clear ['ɔːl'kliər] *n F* **to give the all-clear,** donner le feu vert.

alley ['æli] *n F* **that's right up my alley,** c'est tout à fait mon rayon/truc. (*See* **doodle-alley**; **street 2**; **tin-pan alley**)

alley cat¹ ['æli'kæt] *n P* prostituée*/racoleuse *f*; **she's a bit of an alley cat,** elle est un peu pute par les bords/elle couche à droite et à gauche.

alley cat² ['æli'kæt] *vi esp NAm P* **to alley cat around,** draguer/faire du racolage/racoler*.

alligator ['æligeitər] *n F* (*catch-phrase*) **see you later, alligator!** – **in a while, crocodile!** à tout à l'heure, voltigeur! – à bientôt, mon oiseau.

all-nighter ['ɔːl'naitər] *n P* **1.** (spectacle, boum, etc) qui dure toute la nuit/qui se fait jusqu'au petit matin **2.** (*prostitutes*) client *m*/clille *m* de nuit; couché *m* **3.** *NAm* (*students*) **to pull an all-nighter,** passer la nuit à étudier.

all right ['ɔːl'rait] **I** *a* **he's all right**/*esp NAm* **he's an all(-)right**

guy, il n'est pas mal/c'est un brave type **II** *adv F* **1.** d'accord*/OK; ça va **2. it's all right for you, you don't have to get up early,** ça t'est bien égal, t'es pas obligé de te lever de bonne heure **3. don't worry about him, he's all right,** t'en fais pas pour lui **4. to see s.o. all right** (*i*) veiller à ce que qn ait son dû (*ii*) donner un coup de main à qn (*iii*) payer qn grassement **III** *n P* **a bit of all right,** qn qui a du chien/qui jette du jus; *esp* une fille* séduisante/un beau petit lot; **she's a bit of all right,** elle est bien bandante/elle est mettable; **he's a bit of all right,** il est beau mec/il est mettable/il en jette.

all star ['ɔːl'staɪr] *a F* **an all star cast,** rien que des têtes d'affiche/des vedettes.

all-time ['ɔːl'taim] *a F* sans précédent/inouï; **all-time high,** record le plus élevé; **his sex life had reached an all-time low,** les temps n'avaient jamais été aussi durs dans sa vie sexuelle. (*See* **great III**)

almighty [ɔːl'maiti] *a* **1.** *F* formidable; **an almighty row,** un boucan de tous les diables **2.** *P* **God Almighty!** Bon Dieu de Bon Dieu!

Alphonse [æl'fɔns] *Prn P* (*RS = ponce*) souteneur*/mac *m*.

alright ['ɔːl'rait] *adv & n F =* **all right.**

also-ran ['ɔːlsəuræn] *n F* (*a*) perdant *m*; **to be an also-ran,** être dans les choux (*b*) nullité *f*/nullard *m*.

altogether ['ɔːltə'geðər] *n F* **in the altogether,** nu*/à poil; dans le costume d'Adam/d'Ève.

ambidextrous ['æmbi'dekstrəs] *a P* ambivalent/bisexuel/qui marche à voile et à vapeur/qui joue sur les deux tableaux.

ammo ['æmou] *n F* (*abbr = ammunition*) munitions *fpl*/bastos *f*.

amscray ['æm'skrei] *vi A P* (= *scram*) partir*/décamper/se débiner; **amscray!** décampe!

amster ['æmstər] *n Austr O P* = **shill(aber)**.

amy ['eimi] *n P* (*drugs*) nitrite *m* d'amyle* (en capsule); *pl* **amys**, poppers *mpl*.

amy-john ['eimi'dʒɔn] *n P* lesbienne*/gougnot(t)e *f*/gouine *f*.

amyl ['æmiːl] *n P* (*drugs*) = **amy**.

anchors ['æŋkəz] *npl F* **to put the anchors on**, mettre les freins *mpl*.

ancient ['einʃənt] *a F* **1**. croulant; **she's ancient**, elle est croulante/elle croule **2**. antédiluvien; **that's ancient history**, c'est du réchauffé/c'est de l'histoire ancienne.

Andrew ['ændruː] *Prn A P* (*navy*) **Andrew (Miller)**, la marine nationale.

angel ['eindʒəl] *n* **1**. *F* **you're no angel!** ne te prends pas pour un enfant de chœur!/tu n'es pas un prix de vertu! **2**. *P* (*nurse who provides drug addicts with unprescribed drugs*) **white angel**, ange blanc **3**. *P* (*a*) (*esp theatre*) commanditaire *m* (*b*) *NAm* commanditaire *m*/ sponsor *m* d'un parti politique **4**. *P* victime *f* d'un voleur *ou* d'un escroc* **5**. *P* homosexuel*/pédé *m*/homo *m* **6**. *P* (*drugs*) cocaïne*/ (fée) blanche/coco *m*. (*See* **hell 15**)

angel dust ['eindʒəl'dʌst] *n P* (*drugs*) phéncyclidine/PCP*.

angel-face ['eindʒəlfeis] *n F* (*term of affection*) (*to woman*) ma toute belle/ma gueule; (*to man*) mon chéri/mon chou/mon lapin.

angie ['eindʒi] *n P* = **angel 6**.

angle ['æŋgl] *n F* **1**. **what's your angle?** quel est ton point de vue?/ comment vois-tu la chose? **2**. **to know all the angles**, connaître la musique.

Anne [æn] *Prn F* **Queen Anne's dead** (*a*) ta combinaison dépasse/tu cherches une belle-mère? (*See*

Charl(e)y 2) (*b*) *O* c'est du réchauffé.

anno domini ['ænou'dɔminai] *n F* (*hum*) vieillesse *f*; **he's suffering from anno domini**, il souffre de ses artères.

another [ə'nʌðər] *pron F* **tell me another!** allez! va conter ça ailleurs! **ask me another**, tu me fais rigoler; et après?

AN Other ['ei'enəðər] *n F* (*occ hum*) un illustre inconnu.

answer ['ɑːnsər] *n F* **the answer to a maiden's prayer** (*i*) le mari/ l'homme rêvé (*ii*) un homme qui fait bien l'amour/une affaire.

ante ['ænti] *n esp NAm F* **to up/to raise the ante** (*i*) (*poker*) forcer la mise (*ii*) augmenter le prix/donner le coup de pouce/allonger le tir.

ante (up) ['ænti('ʌp)] *vi F* payer*/ les lâcher/cracher.

anti ['ænti, *NAm* 'æntai] *adv & prep F* **to be anti s.o./sth**, être contre; **I'm rather anti that sort of thing**, je suis plutôt contre.

antics ['æntiks] *npl F* **to be up to one's antics again**, refaire le même cinéma/le même cirque.

ants [ænts] *npl F* **to have ants in one's pants**, avoir la bougeotte/ avoir le feu au cul.

antsy ['æntsi] *a NAm F* énervé/ agité/sur des charbons ardents.

any ['eni] **I** *a F* **1**. **any more for any more?** qui veut du rab? **2**. **any day**, n'importe quand; **I can do better than that any day**, je peux faire mieux quand ça me chante **II** *pron F* **he wasn't having any**, il n'a pas marché; **I'm not having any!** rien à faire!/ça ne prend pas! **III** *adv F* **that didn't help it any**, ça ne nous a pas servi à grand-chose.

anybody ['enibɔdi], **anyone** ['eniwʌn] *pron & n F* **it's anybody's/ anyone's guess**, qui sait?/vous en savez autant que moi!

anyhow ['enihau], **anyoldhow** ['eni'ouldhau] *adv F* n'importe comment/tant bien que mal; **to do sth all anyhow,** faire qch n'importe comment/à la six-quatre-deux; **they left the bedroom all anyoldhow,** ils ont laissé la chambre en pagaille.

anyplace ['enipleis] *adv esp NAm F* n'importe où.

anyroad(s) ['eniroud(s)] *adv F* (= *anyway*) de toute façon/quand même; **that's what I think anyroad,** c'est ce que je pense de toute façon.

Anzac ['ænzæk] *n F* soldat* australien *ou* néo-zélandais.

ape [eip] **I** *a NAm P* **to go ape** (*i*) perdre les pédales (*ii*) se déchaîner; **to go ape over s.o.,** s'enticher/se toquer de qn **II** *n F* **you big ape!** grosse brute!/espèce de gorille!

apology [ə'pɔlədʒi] *n F* **an apology for ...,** un vague semblant d'excuse pour....

apoth ['eipəθ] *n F* = **ape II.**

apple ['æpl] *n P* **1.** (*RS = stairs*) **apples (and pears),** escalier *m* **2.** *NAm* individu*/type *m*/mec *m*; **smooth apple,** individu* suave/ girofle *m* **3.** *NAm* **to polish the apple,** flatter*/faire de la lèche. (*See* **apple-polish**; **apple-polisher**) **4.** **the Big Apple,** New York *m* **5.** *pl Austr* OK*; **she'll be apples/it'll be apples,** ça/tout ira bien.

apple-cart ['æplkɑɪt] *n F* **to upset s.o.'s apple-cart,** chambarder les plans de qn; **that's upset the apple-cart,** ça a tout chamboulé/ça a tout fichu en l'air.

apple-pie ['æpl'pai] **I** *a attrib F* **1. apple-pie bed,** lit *m* en portefeuille **2. in apple-pie order,** en ordre parfait/soin-soin **II** *n F* **as American as apple-pie,** amerloc comme l'oncle Sam.

apple-polish ['æpl'pɔliʃ] *vi NAm P* flatter*/lécher les bottes à (qn). (*See* **apple 3**)

apple-polisher ['æpl'pɔliʃər] *n NAm P* flatteur *m*/lèche-bottes *m*.

apple-sauce ['æpl'sɔːs] *n NAm P* **1.** bêtises*/foutaises *fpl*/bidon *m* **2.** flatterie *f*/pommade *f*.

apple-tree ['æpltriː] *n P* (*not common*) (*girl*) **to fall off the apple-tree,** perdre sa virginité/voir le loup/ casser sa cruche.

appro ['æprou] *n F* (*abbr = approval*) **on appro,** à condition/à l'essai.

apron-strings ['eiprənstrinz] *npl F* **tied to his mother's apron-strings,** dans les jupons de sa mère.

arf [ɑɪf] *a & adv P* = **half.**

arf-an'-arf ['ɑɪfən'ɑɪf] *adv & n P* = **half and half.** (*See* **half[1] 5**; **half[2]**)

Argie ['ɑɪdʒi] *n P* Argentin(e) *m(f)*.

argie-bargie ['ɑɪdʒi'bɑɪdʒi] *n F* = **argy-bargy.**

argle-bargle ['ɑɪgl'bɑɪgl] *n F* = **argy-bargy.**

argufy ['ɑɪgjuːfai] *vi P* discuter le bout de gras.

Argy ['ɑɪdʒi] *n P* = **Argie.**

argy-bargy ['ɑɪdʒi'bɑɪdʒi] *n F* chicane *f*/prise *f* de bec; discutailleries *fpl*; **they had a bit of an argy-bargy,** ils ont eu une prise de bec.

aris ['æris] *n P* = **Aristotle.**

Aristotle [æri'stɔtl] *n P* (*RS = bottle and glass = arse*) fesses*; anus*; cul *m*.

arm [ɑɪm] *n* **1.** *F* **to chance one's arm,** tenter le coup **2.** *NAm P* **to put the arm on s.o.,** mettre le grappin sur qn **3.** *NAm P* **on the arm** (*i*) à crédit/à la gagne/à croum(e) (*ii*) gratuit*/gratis/à l'œil **4.** *r'* **the long arm of the law,** la justice. (*See* **short I 3**; **shot II 3**; **strong-arm[1,2]**)

army ['ɑɪmi] *n P* **1.** (*in defiance of a threat*) **... you and whose army?** toi et qui encore? **2.** *O* **the (old)**

army game, escroquerie*/coup *m* d'arnac. (*See* **Fred**)

around [ə'raund] *adv* F **1.** I've **been around,** je connais la vie/j'ai roulé ma bosse **2. she around?** elle est là?

arse [aɪs], *NAm* **ass** [æs] *n V* I **1.** cul; anus*/trou *m* du cul **2. my arse!** mon cul! **twenty-five my arse! she's forty if she's a day,** vingt ans je t'en fiche, elle a quarante ans et mèche! **3. he doesn't know whether he's on his arse or his elbow** (*i*) il ne sait pas où il en est (*ii*) c'est un vrai cul **4. to go arse over tip/tits,** faire tête à cul. (*See* **A 3**) **5. arse about face,** sens devant, sens derrière **6. to sit on one's arse (and do nothing),** ne pas se magner le cul; **get up off your arse!** tire ton cul de là! **7. you can kiss my arse!/you can stick it up your arse!** tu peux te le foutre au cul! (*See* **shove**) **8. to be out on one's arse/***Austr* **to get the arse,** être flanqué/foutu à la porte **9. to shag one's arse off** (*i*) faire l'amour* fréquemment/baiser non-stop (*ii*) se crever au boulot **10. to work one's arse off,** travailler* dur/se crever au boulot. (*See* **ass¹**; **kick¹ 5**; **lead¹ 4**; **pain** (*c*); **shit arse**; **short arse**; **split-arse**; **tear-arse**) II idiot*/ imbécile*; **he's a stupid arse,** c'est un vrai cul/connard; il est complètement bouché. (*See* **ass II**)

arse about, arse around ['aɪsə'baut, 'aɪsə'raund], *NAm* **ass about, ass around** *vi V* faire le con/déconner; **don't go arsing about in there!** va pas faire le con là-dedans! **stop arsing about!** déconne pas!

arse-bandit ['aɪsbændit], *NAm* **ass-bandit** *n V* homosexuel* actif/bourrin *m*.

arse crawl ['aɪskrɔɪl], *NAm* **ass crawl** *vi V* = **arse lick.**

arse crawler ['aɪskrɔɪlər], *NAm* **ass crawler** *n V* = **arse licker.**

arsehole ['aɪs(h)ouɪl] *n V* **1.** anus*/anneau *m*/trou *m* du cul/ trou de balle/troufignon *m* **2.** (*term of abuse*) **(you) arsehole!** trouduc!/enculé!/connard! **3. pissed as arseholes,** ivre* mort/ bourré à zéro/rond comme une bille.

arseholed ['aɪshould] *a V* ivre* mort/bourré à zéro.

arse kisser ['aɪskisər], *NAm* **ass kisser** *n V* = **arse licker.**

arse lick ['aɪslik], *NAm* **ass lick** *vi V* faire de la lèche.

arse licker ['aɪslikər], *NAm* **ass licker** *n V* lèche-cul *mf*.

arse licking ['aɪslikiŋ], *NAm* **ass licking** *n V* la lèche.

arse-man ['aɪsmæn], *NAm* **ass man** *n V* = **arse-bandit.**

arse up ['aɪs'ʌp] *vtr V* (*a*) mettre en désordre/chambouler; **he completely arsed it up,** il y a foutu le merdier/ il a tout foutu en l'air (*b*) abîmer*/ amocher.

artic ['aɪtik] *n F* (= *articulated (lorry)*) (camion *m*) semi-remorque *m*; poids lourd *m*.

artillery [aɪ'tiləri] *n P* **1.** (*drugs*) **(light) artillery,** attirail* de camé/kit *m*/artillerie *f* **2.** (*i*) revolver* (*ii*) couteau* (*iii*) armes *fpl* à main.

arty ['aɪti] *a F* **to be arty,** se piquer de talent artistique; **he's very arty,** il fait très bohème.

arty-crafty ['aɪti'kraɪfti] *a F* artiste/bohème.

arvo ['aɪvou] *n Austr F* après-midi *mf*/aprèm *m*.

asap, ASAP ['æsæp] *abbr F* (= *as soon as possible*) aussitôt que possible/dès que possible/le plus tôt possible.

ashes ['æʃiz] *npl* **1.** F (*cricket*) **the Ashes,** trophée symbolique des matchs Angleterre–Australie **2.** *NAm P* **to get one's ashes hauled,**

faire l'amour*/se l'envoyer/tirer un coup. (*See* **green I 1**)

ask [ɑːsk] *vtr&i* **1. to ask for it,** chercher des embêtements *mpl*; **you asked for it!** tu l'as cherché!/tu l'as voulu! **you're asking for it, and you'll get it if you're not careful!** tu me cherches, et tu vas me trouver! **2.** *F* **don't ask me!** est-ce que je sais, moi? **he wasn't asking you!** il ne t'a pas sonné! **I ask you!** je vous demande un peu! **3.** *F* (*catchphrase*) **ask a silly/daft question and you'll get a silly/daft answer,** à question idiote, réponse idiote. (*See* **another**)

ass [æs] *n NAm V* **I 1.** (= **arse**) **to chew s.o.'s ass out,** engueuler qn/passer un savon à qn. (*For all compounds of* **ass** *see* **arse**) **2. piece of ass** (*a*) acte sexuel*/partie *f* de jambes en l'air (*b*) (*pej*) (*considered sexually*) femme*/gonzesse *f*/fendue *f* (*c*) (*occ*) sexe de la femme*; **to peddle ass,** racoler*/faire le tapin **3. big ass man,** coureur *m* de jupons/cavaleur *m* **4. to do sth ass backwards,** faire qch à rebours/brider l'âne par la queue **5. to have one's ass in a sling,** avoir le cafard/broyer du noir **6. on one's ass,** dans la gêne/dans le besoin. (*See* **green-ass**; **kiss-ass**; **lead¹ 4**; **ream out**; **shit ass**; **suck-ass**) **II** *P* (you) **silly ass!** espèce d'idiot!/espèce de nouille!

association [əsousi'eiʃ(ə)n] *n P* (*prisons*) (l'heure *f* de) la récréation/récré *f*.

assy ['æsi] *a NAm P* **1.** radin; vil; méchant; entêté **2.** (*seat of trousers, etc*) reluisant.

at [æt] *prep F* **1. where it's at,** où ça boume/où ça ronfle **2. to be at it** (*a*) être au boulot (*b*) (*crime*) être sur un coup (*c*) être en train de faire l'amour*; (*prostitute*) être avec un client.

attaboy ['ætəbɔi] *excl F* vas-y, fiston!

attagirl ['ætəgəːl] *excl F* vas-y, fifille!/vas-y, nénette!

attic ['ætik] *n F* **he's a bit queer in the attic,** il est un peu fou*/il a une araignée au plafond. (*See* **bat¹ 7**)

aunt, Aunt [ɑːnt] *n* **1.** *F* **my Aunt Fanny!** et ta sœur! **2.** *O F* **Aunt Jane,** WC*/goguenots *mpl* **3.** *P* patronne* d'un bordel/taulière *f*/mère-maquerelle/mère-maca *f* **4.** *P* vieux homosexuel*/tante *f*/tantouse *f* **5.** *P* (*drugs*) **Aunt Emma,** morphine* **6.** *P* (*RS* = *fire*) **Aunt Maria,** feu *m*/conflagration *f*.

auntie¹, aunty¹ ['ɑːnti] *n P* homosexuel* vieillissant/tantouse *f*.

Auntie², Aunty² ['ɑːnti] *n F* **Auntie (Beeb),** la BBC (British Broadcasting Corporation). (*See* **Beeb**)

Aussie ['ɔzi] **I** *a F* (*abbr* = *Australian*) australien(ne) **II** *n F* (*abbr* = *Australian*) Australien(ne)/kangourou *m*.

away [ə'wei] *adv F* **1.** (*euph*) en prison*/au bloc; **they put him away,** ils l'ont flanqué en taule **2. well away,** ivre*/pompette/parti **3. he's well away,** le voilà lancé/il est bien parti. (*See* **have 1, 2, 3**)

awful ['ɔːful] *a F* terrible/affreux; **an awful bore,** (*thing*) qch d'ennuyeux/d'assommant/de canulant; (*pers*) casse-burettes *m*/casse-pieds *m*; **he's an awful bore,** il est vachement rasoir; **it's an awful bore!** c'est une vraie barbe!/ce que c'est rasoir! **awful weather,** un temps de chien/de cochon. (*See* **god-awful**)

awkward ['ɔːkwəd] *a F* **1. the awkward age,** l'âge ingrat **2. an awkward customer,** un type pas commode/un mauvais coucheur.

AWOL ['ei'dʌbljuː'ou'el, 'eiwɔl] (*abbr* = *absent without leave*) *F* (*mil*) absent sans permission/avec fausse-perm(e).

axe¹ [æks], *NAm* **ax** [æks] *n* **1.** *F*

(*expenditure, personnel, etc*) coupe *f* sombre; **to get the axe/ax,** se faire vider; **to give s.o. the axe/ax,** se débarrasser* de qn/sacquer qn/vider qn/balancer qn **2.** *F* **to have an axe/ax to grind,** prêcher pour son saint **3.** *NAm P* instrument *m* de musique.

axe² [æks], *NAm* **ax** [æks] *vtr F* **to axe/to ax expenditure,** faire des coupes *fpl* sombres dans le budget; **to axe/to ax s.o.,** porter la hache à qn.

B

b [biː] *abbr P* **1.** = **bloody**; **BF** = **bloody fool 2.** = **bastard 3.** (*drugs*) Benzédrine *f* (*RTM*) **4. B flats,** poux*/punaises *fpl*/morpions *mpl*.

b & b [ˈbiːənˈbiː] (*abbr = bed and breakfast*) *F* chambre *f* avec petit déjeuner.

babbling [ˈbæblɪŋ] *a F* **babbling brook,** jacteuse *f*/pie *f* borgne.

babe [beib] *n P* **1.** *esp NAm* pépée *f*/poupée *f*/poule *f*; petite amie; **hi babe!** salut beauté/bébé! **2.** *NAm* **a hot babe,** une chaude de la pince/une chaude lapine/une bandeuse.

baby [ˈbeibi] *n* **1.** *P* = **babe 1 2.** *P* un homme*/un mec; **this baby's really tough,** c'est un dur à cuire **3.** *F* **to be left holding the baby,** porter le chapeau/payer les pots cassés/rester en plan **4.** *F* **that's my baby,** c'est mon affaire/c'est mon blot; **that's your baby,** c'est ton business/c'est tes oignons *mpl*; débrouille-toi tout seul **5.** *P* **to (nearly) have a baby** (*a*) avoir peur*/chier dans son froc (*b*) être en colère*/être à cran **6.** *P* (*drugs*) marijuana*/douce *f*. (*See* **bathwater**; **cry-baby**; **jelly-baby**; **scare-baby**)

baby factory [ˈbeibiˈfæktəri] *n F* (*hum*) maternité *f*/clinique *f* d'accouchement.

baby-juice [ˈbeibidʒuːs] *n P* sperme*/jus *m* de cyclope/purée *f*.

baby-kisser [ˈbeibikisər] *n F* (*hum*) député *m ou* candidat *m* en période électorale.

baby-snatcher [ˈbeibisnætʃər] *n* (*a*) *F* kidnappeur, -euse (d'enfants) (*b*) *P* (*i*) vieux marcheur/vieux barbeau (*ii*) femme* qui épouse *ou* qui sort avec un homme* beaucoup plus jeune qu'elle; **he/she is a baby-snatcher,** il/elle les prend au berceau. (*See* **cradle-snatcher**)

baccy [ˈbæki] *n F* tabac*/pétun *m*.

back [bæk] **I** *a* **1.** *F* **to take a back seat,** être la cinquième roue du carrosse/passer au second plan/céder le pas aux autres. (*See* **backseat**) **2.** *F* **the back end,** l'automne *m* **3.** *P* **back door,** anus*/trou *m* du cul/trou de balle. (*See* **fed up** (*a*) **II** *n* **1.** *F* **to get s.o.'s back up,** mettre qn en colère*/prendre qn à rebrousse-poil/braquer qn **2.** *P* **to get off s.o.'s back,** cesser de harceler qn; **get off my back!** fous-moi la paix! **3.** *F* **to be on s.o.'s back (about sth),** harceler qn/tomber sur le dos de qn **4.** *F* **you scratch my back and I'll scratch yours,** passe-moi la rhubarbe, je te passe le séné. (*See* **backscratcher**) **5.** *F* **to put one's back into sth,** en mettre un coup; **come on, put your back into it!** allons, un peu d'effort! **6.** *F* **to have one's back to the wall,** avoir le dos au mur/tirer ses dernières cartouches **7.** *F* **he's at the back of all our problems,** il est l'auteur/il est à l'origine de tous nos ennuis **8.** *F* **the back of beyond,** en plein bled/au diable (vau)vert; **he lives at the back of beyond,** il habite au-delà des poules/dans un trou perdu. (*See* **boondocks**) **9.** *F* **to be (laid) on one's back,** être malade*/être mal fichu **10.** *F* **to break the back of sth,** faire le plus dur de qch **11.** *F* **I'll be glad to see the back of him,** ça me ferait plaisir d'être débarrassé de lui **12.** *F* **I know it like the back of my hand,** je le connais comme le fond de ma poche **13.** *F* **she's got a face like the back of a bus,** c'est une mocheté/elle est belle comme un camion **14.** *P* **she earns her living on her back,** elle fait l'horizontale. (*See* **greenback**; **greybacks**; **piggyback**; **shellback**)

backasswards [bæk'æswədz] *adv NAm P* = **ass backwards** (**ass I 4**).

backchat ['bæktʃæt] *n F* insolence *f*/impertinence *f*; **less of this backchat!** assez de mauvais esprit!

back down ['bæk'daun] *vi F* caler/caner/lâcher pied; se dégonfler.

back-end ['bækend] *n F* **she looks like the back-end of a bus,** c'est une mocheté/elle est belle comme un camion. (*See* **back II 13**)

backfire ['bæk'faiər] *vi F* rater/mal tourner/faire fausse route; **his plan backfired,** son projet a foiré.

backhanded ['bæk'hændid] *a F* **backhanded compliment,** compliment *m* équivoque/à double tranchant.

backhander ['bæk'hændər] *n P* graissage *m* de patte/pot-de-vin *m*.

backlash ['bæklæʃ] *n F* retour *m* de flamme/effet *m* de boumerang.

back-number ['bæknʌmbər] *n F* (*a*) objet démodé (*b*) (*pers*) croulant *m*/périmé *m*/PPH *m*.

back off ['bæk'ɔf] *vi P* **back off!** fiche-moi la paix!

back out ['bæk'aut] *vi F* (*a*) se dédire/se dérober/se dégonfler (*b*) sortir d'une position difficile/faire marche arrière.

backpack ['bæk'pæk] *vi F* (*i*) faire de l'autostop/du stop (en emportant son matériel de

couchage, etc sur le dos) (*ii*) faire de la randonnée (avec son sac à dos).

backpacker [bæk'pækər] *n F* (*i*) autostoppeur, -euse/stoppeur, -euse (*ii*) personne qui fait de la randonnée (avec son sac à dos).

backpacking ['bæk'pækiŋ] *n F* **to go backpacking** (*i*) faire de l'autostop (*ii*) faire de la randonnée (avec son sac à dos).

back-pedal ['bæk'pedl] *vi F* faire marche arrière/faire machine arrière.

backroom ['bækruːm] *a F* confidentiel/secret; **the backroom boys,** les experts *mpl*/les techniciens *mpl*, etc qui restent dans les coulisses.

backscratcher ['bækskrætʃər] *n F* flatteur *m*/lèche-cul *m*/lèche-bottes *m*/lécheur *m*. (*See* **back II 4**)

backscratching ['bækskrætʃiŋ] *n F* flagornerie *f*/lèche *f*.

backseat ['bæksiːt] *a attrib F* **backseat driver,** passager *m* qui donne des conseils au chauffeur.

backside [bæk'said] *n F* fesses*/postérieur *m*.

backslang ['bækslæŋ] *n F* = verlan *m*/code *m* verlan.

backslapper ['bækslæpər] *n F* **he's a bit of a backslapper,** il est à tu et à toi avec tout le monde.

backslapping ['bækslæpiŋ] *n F* bruyante démonstration d'amitié.

backstairs ['bæksteəz] *a F* **backstairs gossip,** cancan *m* de domestiques; **backstairs politics,** intrigues *fpl* politiques/politique *f* de sous-main.

backtrack ['bæktræk] *vi* **1.** *F* (*a*) rebrousser chemin (*b*) faire machine arrière/faire marche arrière/se dégonfler **2.** *P* = **back up 2** (*b*).

back-up ['bækʌp] *n* **1.** *F* appui *m*/soutien *m*/aide *f*; **media back-up,** supports-média *mpl* **2.** *P* (*drugs*) (*a*) piqûre* (dans une veine déjà gonflée) (*b*) tirette *f* et poussette *f* **3.** *O P* enculage (hétérosexuel).

back up ['bæk'ʌp] *vtr&i* **1.** *F* **to back s.o. up**, seconder qn/prendre les patins de qn **2.** *P* (*drugs*) (*a*) dilater la veine avant une piqûre de drogues (*b*) aspirer le sang dans la seringue pendant une piqûre pour le mélanger à la drogue avant de le réinjecter **3.** *F* faire machine arrière/faire marche arrière.

backward ['bækwəd] *a F* **he's not backward in coming forward**, il ne se fait pas prier/il n'a pas froid aux yeux.

backwards ['bækwədz] *adv F* **1. to bend/to fall/to lean over backwards for s.o.**, se mettre en quatre pour qn/se décarcasser. (*See* **fall 3**) **2. to know sth backwards**, comprendre qch parfaitement; savoir/connaître qch par cœur; **I know the way home backwards**, je connais mon chemin sur le bout du doigt/les yeux fermés.

backwoodsman ['bækwudzmən] *n F* **1.** rustre *m*/péquenaud *m*/plouc *m* **2.** (*pol*) un pair qui fréquente peu la Chambre des Lords.

bacon ['beikən] *n F* **1. to bring home the bacon** (*a*) faire bouillir la marmite/gagner sa croûte/gagner son bifteck (*b*) remporter le pompon **2. to save one's bacon**, sauver sa peau.

bad [bæd] **I** *a* **1.** *F* **that's too bad** (*i*) dommage!/manque de pot! (*ii*) c'est un peu fort! **that's not half bad**, c'est pas mal du tout; **that's not so bad**, c'est pas si mal que ça **2.** *F* **she's not bad!** c'est pas mal!/elle est bien roulée!/elle est bien foutue! **3.** *F* **he's in a bad way** (*i*) il est dans le pétrin/dans de mauvais draps (*ii*) il file un mauvais coton **4.** *F* **I'm in his bad books**, il ne m'a pas à la bonne/je ne suis pas dans ses petits papiers **5.** *F* **she's bad news**, il faut se méfier d'elle **6.** *F* **to turn up like a bad**

penny, venir comme un cheveu/des cheveux sur la soupe **7.** *F* **a bad lot**/*O* **bad egg**/*O* **bad hat**/*O* **bad 'un**, une canaille/un salaud; **he's a bad lot**, c'est un sale type/une canaille **8.** *P* **to give someone the bad eye**, regarder qn avec méfiance; regarder qn d'un œil noir **9.** *F* **I feel bad about it**, ça m'embête **10.** *F* (*film, etc*) **the bad guys and the good guys**, les bons *mpl* et les méchants *mpl* **11.** *NAm P* (*negro use*) excellent*/super/sensass **II** *adv F* (= *badly*) **1. to have it bad for s.o.**, aimer qn/avoir le béguin pour qn/être dingue de qn **2. I need it real bad**, j'en ai vachement besoin **3.** (*obsession*) **he's got it bad**, c'est une manie chez lui/il en est dingue **III** *n F* **1. to go to the bad**, être sur la mauvaise pente/mal tourner; **he's gone to the bad**, il a mal tourné **2. to the bad**, en arriérages; **£5 to the bad**, en être de £5.

bad eye ['bædai] *vtr P* **to bad eye s.o.**, regarder qn avec méfiance; regarder qn d'un œil noir.

baddie, baddy ['bædi] *n F* (*in films, etc*) le vilain/le méchant. (*See* **goodies 2**)

badge [bædʒ] *n O P* (*drugs*) quantité de drogues insuffisante pour le prix payé.

badger ['bædʒər] *n* **1.** *esp NAm P* **the badger game** (*a*) moyens employés pour compromettre un homme avec une femme afin de lui tirer de l'argent (*b*) escroquerie*/chantage *m*/tromperie (*esp* dans un but personnel ou politique) **2.** *NAm F* habitant *m* de l'état de Wisconsin.

bad-looking ['bæd'lukiŋ] *a F* **she's not bad-looking**, elle n'est pas mal/elle n'est pas désagréable à regarder/elle est bien balancée.

bad-mouth ['bædmauθ] *vtr NAm F* dire du mal de (qn/qch)/casser du sucre sur le dos de (qn).

bag¹ [bæg] *n* **1.** *P* (*pej*) femme* laide/acariâtre; (**you**) **old bag!** vieille chouette!/vieille bique!/ vieille pouffiasse! **2. bag of wind** (*a*) vantard*/hâbleur *m* (*b*) bavard*/baratineur *m* **3.** *F* **there's bags of it,** il y en a en abondance*/ il y en a à gogo; **there's bags of room,** la place ne manque pas **4.** *F* **it's in the bag,** c'est dans le sac/ c'est du tout cuit **5.** *F* **the whole bag of tricks,** tout le Saint-Frusquin et tout le bataclan **6.** *V* (*rare*) **bag** (**of tricks**), testicules*/bijoux *mpl* de famille **7.** *F* **he's got huge bags under his eyes,** il a des valises sous les yeux **8.** *F* **she's nothing but a bag of bones,** elle est maigre* comme un clou/elle n'a que la peau sur les os **9.** *pl F* pantalon*/ falz(ar) *m*/froc *m* **10.** *P* (*drugs*) une certaine quantité de drogue (esp héroïne*) contenue dans un sac en plastique *ou* un sachet de papier **11.** *NAm F* **to be left holding the bag** = **to be left holding the baby** (**baby²** 4) **12.** *NAm O P* (*a*) préservatif*/capote (anglaise) (*b*) diaphragme *m* **13.** *esp NAm F* penchant *m*/goût *m*; **rock's not my bag,** le rock, c'est pas mon genre/ mon truc. (*See* **cat 13; doggy bag; fag 2** (*c*); **fleabag; gasbag; moneybags; nosebag; ragbag; ratbag; scumbag; shagbag; shitbag**)

bag² [bæg] *vtr P* **1.** arrêter*/ agrafer **2.** mettre le grappin sur (qch); **to bag the best seat,** rafler la meilleure place **3.** voler*/piquer/ chauffer **4.** *WWII* descendre/piffer (un avion) **5. bags I go first!** à moi/pour bibi le premier tour!

baggage ['bægidʒ] *n O F* **1.** fille* effrontée/garce *f*/coquine *f*/gis- quette *f* **2.** prostituée*/traînée *f*/ roulure *f*.

bagged [bægd] *a NAm P* ivre*/ blindé/chargé.

bagman ['bægmæn] *n P* **1.** *A* commis voyageur *m* **2.** (*drugs*)

revendeur *m*/trafiquant *m* de drogues/dealer *m*/fourmi *m*.

bag-snatcher ['bægsnætʃər] *n F* piqueur *m*/faucheur *m* de sacs à main.

bail out ['beil'aut] *vtr F* **to bail s.o. out** (*i*) aider qn à remonter le cou- rant (*ii*) tendre une main secourable à qn.

bait [beit] *n P* homme* beau et efféminé qui attire des homosex- uels*. (*See* **jail-bait**)

ball¹ [bɔːl] *n* **1.** *F* **to be on the ball** (*i*) être dans le coup/savoir nager/ connaître la musique (*ii*) être à la page/à la coule (*iii*) être capable/ être malin*/être dégourdi; **get on the ball, kid!** à l'attaque, mon vieux! **2.** *P* **to have (oneself) a ball,** s'en payer une tranche/se fen- dre la gueule/prendre son pied; **we're gonna have our- selves a ball!** on va s'en payer! **3.** *F* **to play ball with s.o.,** coopérer avec qn/entrer dans le jeu de qn **4.** *F* **to set the ball rolling,** mener la danse/mettre en branle **5.** *P* pilule *f ou* dose *f* de drogue. (*See* **goof- ball 3, 4; speedball**) **6.** *F* **ball of fire,** individu* dynamique/plein d'énergie. (*See* **fireball**) **7.** *NAm F* (*hum*) **ball and chain,** épouse*/ bourgeoise *f*/bobonne *f* **8.** *F* **the ball is in your court,** (c'est) à vous de jouer **9.** *O P* **that's the way the ball bounces,** c'est la vie, que veux- tu? (*See* **cookie 2; mop; onion 1**) **10.** *V* testicule*/bille *f*/balloche *f*. (*See* **balls¹; chalk 4; eight 2; fly- ball; oddball; patball; pinball; screwball; snowball¹**)

ball² [bɔːl] *vtr* **1.** *P* = **to have (oneself) a ball** (**ball 2**) **2.** *V* faire l'amour* avec qn/baiser qn/ s'envoyer qn/se faire qn. (*See* **jack 6; snowball 2**)

ball-breaker ['bɔːlbreikər], **ball- buster** ['bɔːlbʌstər] *n NAm P* boulot *m* extrêmement difficile/ casse-gueule *m*.

ball game ['bɔːl'geim] *n esp NAm F* it's a whole new ball game, c'est une autre paire de manches/ce n'est plus la même histoire/le vent a changé de direction.

balling-out ['bɔːliŋ'aut] *n esp NAm P* = **bawling out.**

ballocking ['bɔləkiŋ] *n V* = **bollocking.**

ballock-naked ['bɔlək'neikid] *a V* = **bollock-naked.**

ballocks[1] ['bɔləks] *npl V* = **bollocks.**

ballocks[2] ['bɔləks] *vtr V* = **bollocks (up).**

ball-off ['bɔːlɔf] *n V* branlage *m*; to have a ball-off, se masturber*/se branler.

ball off ['bɔːl'ɔf] *vi V* se masturber*/se branler/s'astiquer.

balloon [bə'luːn] *n* 1. *F* when the balloon goes up ..., quand on découvrira le pot aux roses.../ quand la chose éclatera 2. *P* (*drugs*) petit sac contenant de l'héroïne*/ballon *m*.

ball out ['bɔːl'aut] *vtr esp NAm P* = **bawl out.**

ball-park ['bɔːlpaːk] *a esp NAm F* a ball-park figure, un chiffre approximatif.

ball park ['bɔːl'paːk] *n esp NAm F* in the right ball park, bien placé.

balls[1] [bɔːlz] *npl V* 1. testicules*/ couilles *fpl*/balloches *fpl*; he kicked him in the balls, il lui a flanqué un coup de pied aux couilles 2. balls! merde! balls to you! je t'emmerde! balls to that! quelle couillonade! that's a load of balls/that's all balls! c'est de la couille!/que de conneries! 3. he's got a lot of balls, il a un de ces culots!/il a des couilles au cul 4. it's enough to freeze the balls off a brass monkey, on (se) caille/on se les gèle/on se caille les miches/on pète de froid. (*See* brass monkey(s)) 5. he made a real balls of it, il y a foutu un de

ces merdiers 6. to have s.o. by the balls, avoir qn à la pogne; she's got him by the balls, elle le tient par la queue/par là 7. to chew s.o.'s balls off, réprimander* qn/engueuler qn/ passer un savon à qn 8. to work one's balls off, bosser comme un dingue/se crever au boulot 9. I'll have his balls for this, j'aurai sa peau.

balls[2] ['bɔːlz], *NAm* **ball** [bɔːl] *vtr V* to balls sth/*NAm* to ball sth, saloper qch/se foutre dedans; he ballsed it/*NAm* he balled it, il s'est foutu dedans/il a tout foutu en l'air.

balls-ache ['bɔːlzeik] *n V* you give me balls-ache, tu me casses les couilles/tu me fais chier.

ballsey ['bɔːlzi] *a NAm P* agressif/ impulsif.

balls-up ['bɔːlzʌp], *NAm* **ball-up** ['bɔːlʌp] *n V* to make a balls-up of sth, foutre la merde dans qch; he made a real balls-up of that, il y a foutu le merdier/il a tout foutu en l'air/il a foutu une de ces salades.

balls up ['bɔːlz'ʌp], *NAm* **ball up** ['bɔːl'ʌp] *vtr V* to balls sth up/*NAm* to ball sth up, foutre la merde/le bordel dans qch; he ballsed it up/ *NAm* he balled it up, il a foutu le merdier; it's all ballsed up/*NAm* it's all balled up, c'est complètement foutu.

bally ['bæli] *a O F* (*euph for* bloody) satané/sacré.

ballyhoo ['bælihuː] *n F* 1. publicité tapageuse/battage *m*/ramdam *m*/tamtam *m* 2. balivernes *fpl*/ bourrage *m* de crâne/boniments *mpl*.

balmy ['baːmi] *a P* = **barmy.**

balon(e)y [bə'louni] *n F* = **boloney.**

bam [bæm] *n A P* (*drugs*) 1. amphétamine* 2. mélange *m* de stimulant et de calmant.

bambalacha ['bæmbə'laıtʃə] n A P (drugs) marijuana*.

bamboo [bæm'buː] n **1.** P pipe f à opium*/bambou m; **to suck the bamboo,** sucer le bambou **2.** Pol F **the bamboo curtain,** le rideau de bambou.

bamboozle [bæm'buːzl] vtr F duper*/empaumer/embobiner/ rouler.

banana [bə'nɑːnə] n **1.** V (rare) to **have one's banana peeled/to have a banana (with s.o.),** faire l'amour* (avec qn)/arracher son copeau **2.** F **I haven't just come in on the banana boat,** je ne suis pas né d'hier/je ne sors pas de l'œuf/je ne suis pas tombé de la dernière pluie **3.** NAm O F comédien m/acteur m de burlesque; **top banana,** vedette f **4.** F **banana republic,** république bananière **5.** NAm P (turf) course (de chevaux) truquée.

bananas [bə'nɑːnəz] a P fou*/ maboul/toqué/cinglé; **I'll go bananas in here on my own,** je vais devenir dingue à rester seul ici; **she drives me bananas,** elle me rend dingue.

band [bænd] n O F **Big Band,** grand orchestre de jazz comportant vingt musiciens au maximum. (See **one-man)**

bandit ['bændit] n F **one-armed bandit,** machine f à sous. (See **arse-bandit; beef-bandit)**

bandwagon ['bændwægən] n F **to jump/to climb/to get on the bandwagon,** prendre le train en marche/ se mettre du côté du manche.

bang¹ [bæŋ] **I** a F **the whole bang lot/the whole bang shoot,** et tout le tremblement/et tout le reste/et tout le bataclan **II** adv F **1. to arrive bang on time,** arriver pile **2. to be bang up-to-date,** être à jour/à la dernière heure; (pers) être à la coule/à la page **3. to be caught bang to rights,** être pris sur le fait/ être pris en flagrant délit **4.** int

bang went another fiver! et voilà un autre (billet* de) cinq livres de perdu; **bang goes that idea,** cette idée est (tombée) à l'eau. (See **dead II 10; slap-bang(-wallop); wallop) III** n **1.** P l'acte sexuel*/ baise f/coup m; **she's a good bang,** elle baise bien/c'est une sacrée baiseuse. (See **gang bang) 2.** F coup*/gnon m; **he gave it a bang with the hammer,** il lui a donné un coup de marteau **3.** F **to go with a bang** (i) aller comme sur des roulettes (ii) être une réussite sensationnelle; **the party went with a real bang,** ce fut une boum du tonnerre/ça a chauffé à la boum **4.** P **I got a real bang out of it,** ça m'a vraiment fait qch/j'ai trouvé ça vachement chié **5.** P = **bhang 6.** esp NAm P **to have a bang at sth,** tenter/risquer le coup **7.** P (drugs) piqûre*/piquouze f/shoot m/fixe m **8.** P impression f de plénitude ou sensation f de plaisir intense qui suit une injection intraveineuse de drogue/flash m. (See **whizz-bang)**

bang² [bæŋ] vtr V **1.** (usu of a man) faire l'amour* (avec qn)/ s'envoyer (qn)/bourrer (qn); **they banged all night,** ils ont baisé toute la nuit **2.** F **to bang into s.o.,** se taper dans qn; **I banged into Charlie in town,** je suis tombé sur Charlie en ville **3. it's like banging your head against a brick wall, trying to talk to him!** inutile d'essayer de lui parler, c'est à se taper la tête contre les murs! **4.** P (drugs) se piquer*/piquouser/se shooter.

banged up ['bæŋd'ʌp] a P en prison*/en taule/bouclé.

banger [bæŋər] n F **1.** (vieille) voiture*/guimbarde f/caisse f; **my old banger,** ma vieille bagnole/tire f/chiotte f **2.** saucisse f; **bangers and mash,** saucisses à la purée (de pommes de terre).

bang-on ['bæŋ'ɔn] adv F **bang-on!** recta!/au poil!

bang-up ['bæŋ'ʌp] *a F* excellent*/
soin-soin; **a bang-up meal,** un repas
fameux/un balthazar. (*See* **slap-up**)

banjax ['bændʒæks] *vtr P* (*not common*) démolir/bousiller/foutre en
l'air; **that's banjaxed that,** ça a tout
fait foirer.

bank on ['bæŋk'ɔn] *vtr F* compter
sur (qch); **don't bank on it!** compte
pas dessus!

bankroll ['bæŋkroul] *vtr esp NAm
F* fournir les frais d'une entreprise;
financer/parainer (qch); **he bankrol-
led that film,** il a financé ce film.

bar [bɑːr] *n* **1.** *F* **to be behind bars,**
être emprisonné*/être bouclé/être
en taule **2.** *A P* billet* d'une livre
3. *V* **to have a bar (on),** être en
érection*/avoir la trique. (*See* **handlebar**)

barbies ['bɑːbiz] *npl P* = **barbs.**

barbs [bɑːbz] *n P* (*abbr* = *barbiturates*) (*drugs*) barbituriques*/
barbitos *mpl*/barbis *mpl*.

bare-arsed ['bɛər'ɑːst], *NAm*
bare-ass(ed) ['bɛər'æɪst] *a P*
nu*/le cul à l'air.

bareback ['bɛəbæk] *adv P* (*not
common*) **to ride bareback,** cracher
dans le bénitier/jouer sans blanc.

barf [bɑːf] *vi NAm P* vomir*/
dégueuler/gerber.

bar-fly ['bɑːflai] *n esp NAm F* **1.**
pilier *m* de bistrot **2.** ivrogne* qui
se fait offrir des tournées.

barge in ['bɑːdʒ'in] *vi F* **1.** **to
barge in on a party,** s'introduire
dans une réception/une boum sans
invitation **2.** **to barge in on s.o.'s
conversation,** mettre son grain de
sel **3.** **to barge in where you're not
wanted** (*i*) se mêler de ce qui ne
vous regarde pas (*ii*) piétiner les
plate-bandes (à qn)/marcher sur les
pieds de qn.

barge into ['bɑːdʒ'intu] *vtr F* **to
barge into s.o.,** se taper dans qn/
bousculer qn/entrer dans qn.

barge-pole ['bɑːdʒpoul] *n F* I

wouldn't touch it with a barge-pole,
je ne le prendrais pas avec des
pincettes.

bar-girl ['bɑːgəɪl] *n P* hôtesse *f*/
entraîneuse *f*.

bar-happy ['bɑː'hæpi] *a NAm F*
(légèrement) ivre*/éméché.

barhop ['bɑːhɔp] *vi esp NAm F*
faire la tournée des bars.

barhopping ['bɑːhɔpiŋ] *n esp
NAm F* **to go barhopping,** faire la
tournée des bars.

bark [bɑːk] *vi F* **to bark up the
wrong tree,** se tromper d'adresse/
faire fausse route/se mettre le doigt
dans l'œil.

barker ['bɑːkər] *n A P* revolver*/
pétard *m*/flingue *m*.

barmpot ['bɑːmpɔt] *n P* individu
bête*/cruche *f*/balluche *m*/bas *m*
de plafond.

barmy ['bɑːmi] *a P* fou*/toqué*/
loufoque.

barn [bɑːn] *n F* **were you born/
NAm raised in a barn?** t'es né sous
les ponts?

Barnaby Rudge ['bɑːnəbi'rʌdʒ]
Prn P (*RS* = *judge*) juge *m*/gerbe
m/curieux *m*.

barnet ['bɑːnit] *n P* (*RS* = *Barnet
Fair* = *hair*) cheveux*/tifs *mpl*/
cresson *m*.

barney¹ ['bɑːni] *n P* **a bit of a barney,** querelle*/prise *f* de bec/
accrochage *m*.

barney² ['bɑːni] *vi P* avoir une
prise de bec (avec qn).

baron ['bærən] *n* **1.** *O P* prisonnier *m* qui a de l'argent, du tabac,
etc; baron *m*. (*See* **snout 2**) **2.** *F*
(*in industry, business*) magnat *m*/
gros bonnet; **the press barons,** les
grands manitous de la presse.

barrack-room ['bærəkruːm] *a F*
barrack-room lawyer, chicaneur *m*/
râleur *m*/mauvais coucheur/
emmerdeur *m*.

barrel¹ ['bærəl] *n P* **1. to be over a barrel,** être dans le pétrin/dans la merde **2. to get/to have s.o. over a barrel,** avoir qn dans sa poche/à sa pogne **3.** beaucoup/en abondance*; **to have a barrel of money,** être riche*/plein aux as; **he's a barrel of fun** (*i*) il est rigolo/il est marrant (*ii*) (*iron*) quel rabat-joie! (*See* **scrape²** 1)

barrel² (**ass**) ['bærəl(æs)] *vi NAm O P* aller vite*/rouler à plein(s) tube(s)/gazer.

barrelhouse ['bærəlhaus] *n NAm O P* cabaret *m* populaire qui sert aussi d'hôtel dans un quartier pauvre.

barrelled up ['bærəld'ʌp] *a P* (*not common*) ivre*/bit(t)uré.

base [beis] *n F* **1. he won't even make first base,** il claquera au départ; **he couldn't get to first base with her,** il a raté son coup avec elle **2. base over apex,** cul par-dessus tête; **he went base over apex,** il a fait une belle culbute **3.** *NAm* **to be off base,** se tromper/se gour(r)er/se fourrer le doigt dans l'œil.

bash¹ [bæʃ] *n* **1.** *P* coup*/châtaigne *f* **2.** *F* **to have a bash at sth/to give sth a bash,** tenter le coup/sa chance; **I'll have a bash at it,** je vais essayer un coup **3.** *F* réjouissances*/boum *f*/surboum *f*/fête *f*.

bash² [bæʃ] *vtr P* **1.** battre*/cogner; **to bash s.o. about,** passer qn à tabac/tabasser qn **2.** *P* (*rare*) **to bash it = to hit the bottle** (**bottle** 1). (*See* **bishop; square-bash**)

basher ['bæʃər] *n P* (*See* **pak(k)i-basher; queer-basher; spud-basher; square-basher**)

bash in ['bæʃ'in] *vtr P* **to bash s.o.'s head/face in,** abîmer le portrait à qn/passer qn à tabac.

bashing ['bæʃiŋ] *n P* **1.** coups*/raclée *f*/trempe *f*; **Spurs took a bashing from Liverpool,** Spurs furent battus par Liverpool; **the platoon took a bashing,** la section s'est fait amocher **2.** la prostitution/le truc/le trottoir. (*See* **pak(k)i-bashing; queer-bashing; spud-bashing; square-bashing**)

bash on ['bæʃ'ɔn] *vi F* **to bash on regardless,** aller envers et contre tout.

bash out ['bæʃ'aut] *vr F* **to bash out a tune,** tapoter un air.

bash up ['bæʃ'ʌp] *vtr P* battre*/filer une avoine à qn/passer qn à tabac/tabasser qn.

basinful ['beisnful] *n P* **to have (had) a basinful,** en avoir assez*/en avoir marre/en avoir par-dessus la tête; **I've had a basinful,** j'en ai ras le bol.

basket ['bɑ:skit] *n P* (*euph for* **bastard**) vaurien*/salaud*; **you silly basket!** espèce de con, va! (*See* **bread-basket**)

bastard ['bɑ:stəd, 'bæstəd] *n V* **1.** vaurien*/canaille *f*/saligaud *m*; **you bastard!** salaud!/t'es un salaud, toi! **2. lucky bastard!** le veinard! **3.** emmerdement *m*; **that's a bastard!** ça c'est couille!/quelle chiotte! **that job's a real bastard!** ce boulot est vraiment chiant!

bat¹ [bæt] *n* **1.** *P* **an old bat,** une vieille bique/une vieille chouette; **you daft bat,** espèce de nouille! **2.** *NAm P* prostituée*/grue *f* **3.** *F* **like a bat out of hell,** vite*/à tout berzingue/comme un zèbre **4.** *F NAm* **right off the bat,** du premier coup/illico-presto **5.** *F* **off one's own bat,** de son propre chef **6.** *NAm P* réjouissances*/noce *f*/bombe *f* **7.** *F* **to have bats in the belfry/attic,** être fou*/avoir une araignée au plafond.

bat² [bæt] *vtr* **1.** *O P* battre*/frapper/rosser **2.** *F* **he didn't bat an eyelid/***NAm* **an eye,** il n'a pas sourcillé/bronché/pipé **3.** *F* **to bat first,** tirer le premier. (*See* **sticky 4**)

batch [bætʃ] *vtr NAm F* **to batch it,** vivre en célibataire.

bathwater ['baɪθwɔɪtər] *n F* **to throw the baby out with the bathwater,** envoyer tout promener/ balancer le manche après la cognée/jeter le bébé avec l'eau du bain.

bats [bæts] *a P* **1.** fou*/timbré; **to go bats,** devenir fou*/perdre la boule **2. to be bats about s.o./sth,** aimer*/être toqué de qn/qch; **he's bats about it,** il en est fou*/dingue.

batter ['bætər] *vtr F* battre*/cogner qn; **I'll batter you if you don't stop!** arrête, ou je t'assomme! **battered baby,** enfant martyr.

battleaxe ['bætlæks] *n F* femme* acariâtre aux manières autoritaires/ harpie *f*/dragon *m*/virago *f*.

battle cruiser ['bætl'kruːzər] *n P* (*RS* = **boozer**) (*pub*) café*/bistrot *m*/troquet *m*.

battler ['bætlər] *n A P* bagarreur *m*.

batty ['bæti] *a P* fou*/timbré/ toqué/givré.

bawling out ['bɔːlɪŋ'aut] *n P* engueulade *f*/savon *m*.

bawl out ['bɔːl'aut] *vtr P* injurier*/ engueuler qn.

bayonet ['beɪənɪt] *n P* pénis*/ arbalète *f*; **to have bayonet practice,** faire l'amour*/tirer un coup/filer un coup d'arbalète.

bazoo [bə'zuː] *n NAm P* bouche*/ bec *m*.

bazooka [bə'zuːkə] *n P* **1.** pénis*/ arbalète *f* **2.** *pl* seins*/doudounes *fpl*.

bazookaed [bə'zuːkəd] *a O P* sabordé/bousillé.

bazooms [bə'zuːmz] *npl O P* = **bazookas** (**bazooka 2**).

beach [biːtʃ] *n NAm F* **1. to be on the beach,** être chômeur/chômer **2. you're not the only pebble on the beach,** tu n'es pas unique dans ton genre.

beak [biːk] *n P* **1.** magistrat *m*/ chat *m*/curieux *m*; **to be up before the beak,** paraître devant le juge/au parquet **2.** nez* (crochu)/pif *m*/ tarin *m*. (*See* **stickybeak**)

beam [biːm] *n F* **1. on the beam** (*i*) sur la même longueur d'ondes (*ii*) dans la bonne direction/sur la bonne voie **2. to be off (the) beam** (*a*) ne pas comprendre/ne rien piger (*b*) faire fausse route/se tromper; **you're way off beam,** tu t'es gour(r)é sur toute la ligne/tu débloques (à pleins tubes) **3. to be broad in the beam,** être large des hanches *fpl*/joufflu du pétard.

beam-ends ['biːm'endz] *npl F* **to be on one's beam-ends,** être pauvre*/être dans la dèche.

bean [biːn] *n* **1.** *P* tête*/caboche *f* **2.** *O F* (*usu hum*) **old bean,** mon vieux pote/ma vieille branche **3.** *F* **he hasn't got a bean,** il n'a pas le sou*/il n'a pas un radis **4.** *F* **it's not worth a bean,** ça ne vaut pas grand-chose/ça ne vaut pas tripette **5.** *F* **to spill the beans** (*i*) vendre/ éventer la mèche (*ii*) avouer*/man- ger le morceau **6.** *F* **to be full of beans,** être d'attaque; être plein d'entrain/péter le feu **7.** (*drugs*) Benzédrine* (*RTM*) **8.** *P* (*drugs*) **jolly beans,** amphétamine* **9.** *NAm P* (*pej*) Mexicain *m*. (*See* **string-bean**)

beanery ['biːnəri] *n NAm P* restau- rant *m* de mauvaise qualité/gargote *f*.

beanfeast ['biːnfiːst] *n F* (*i*) (*meal*) gueuleton *m*/balthazar *m* (*ii*) bombe *f*/fête*.

beano ['biːnou] *n O P* réjouis- sances*/bombe *f*/fête*.

bean-pole ['biːnpoul] *n F* (*pers*) une grande perche/une asperge (montée).

bear-garden ['bɛə'gɑɪdn] *n F* pétaudière *f*; **to turn the place into a bear-garden,** mettre le désordre partout/foutre la pagaille.

beastly ['biːstli] *a&adv F* abominable/infect; **what beastly weather!** quel sale temps!/quel temps de cochon!/quelle putain de temps!

beat¹ [biːt] **I** *a F* **1.** (dead) beat, très fatigué*/claqué/vanné/crevé **2.** découragé/lessivé/vidé **3.** the **beat generation**, la génération des beatniks. (*See* **downbeat**; **upbeat**) **II** *n* **1.** *O P* beatnik *m* **2.** *F* (*jazz*) le rythme/le beat **3.** *F* that's off my beat, ce n'est pas mon rayon **4.** *V* to have a beat on, être en érection*/avoir le gourdin/bander. (*See* **dead-beat**)

beat² [biːt] *vtr* **1.** *P* to beat it, s'enfuir*/se tirer; **beat it!** file!/ décampe!/tire-toi!/fous le camp! **2.** *F* that beats everything/that takes some beating, c'est le comble/c'est le bouquet **3.** *F* can you beat it! ça alors!/faut le faire! **4.** *F* (it) beats me, ça me dépasse/*P* j'en sais foutre rien! **it beats me how you can do that!** je ne comprends pas que tu puisses faire ça! **5.** *F* to beat about the bush, s'égarer/tourner autour du pot; **let's not beat about the bush!** ne nous égarons pas; allons droit au but/aux faits. (*See* **dummy 5**; **meat 4**)

beat off ['biːt'ɔf] *vi V* se masturber*/se branler.

beat-up ['biːtʌp] *a F* usé jusqu'à la corde; **a beat-up old car**, une vieille bagnole/une guimbarde.

beat up ['biːt'ʌp] *vtr F* **1.** battre*/ rosser/tabasser (qn); **he was beaten up by the cops**, les flics l'ont passé à tabac **2.** to beat it up, faire les quatre cents coups.

beaut [bjuːt] **I** *a Austr F* beau*/ bath; **the weather was beaut**, il faisait beau; **it's been beaut**, ça a été génial/merveilleux **II** *n esp Austr F* (= *beauty*) **1.** qch de beau*; **she's a beaut!** quelle belle poupée! **it's a beaut!** c'est chouette/sensass! **2.** coup* bien employé par un boxeur.

beauty ['bjuːti] *n F* **1.** what a beauty! quelle merveille! that's a beauty of a black eye, c'est un beau coquard qu'il a **2.** the beauty of this job is that..., le plus beau de l'affaire c'est que...; that's the beauty of it, c'est ça le plus beau/ c'est ça qui est formidable **3.** *O* (*form of address*) my beauty! ma beauté!/ma jolie! (*often hum*) well, my old beauty! eh bien, vieux pote! **4.** (*euph hum*) a pair of beauties, une belle paire de seins*/des nénés *mpl* superbes.

beaver ['biːvər] *n* **1.** *F* barbe*/ barbouze *f* **2.** *esp NAm V* (*of woman*) poils *mpl* du pubis/barbu *m*. (*See* **eager**)

bed¹ [bed] *n F* **1.** bed of roses, la vie de château; **it's not exactly a bed of roses**, ce n'est pas tout miel/ ce n'est pas de la tarte **2.** you got out of bed on the wrong side this morning, tu t'es levé du pied gauche ce matin **3.** to go to bed with s.o., coucher/faire l'amour* avec qn; **all he ever thinks of is bed**, il ne pense qu'à faire l'amour*/il ne pense qu'à ça **4.** bed and breakfast: *see* **bingo 26.** (*See* **feather-bed**)

bed² [bed] *vtr O P* to bed s.o., faire l'amour* avec qn; **she's all right for bedding**, c'est une sacrée baiseuse.

bed-house ['bedhaus] *n esp NAm* (*rare*) *P* bordel*/boxon *m*.

bed-sit ['bed'sit] *n F* (= *bed-sitter*) garni *m*/meublé *m*; studio *m*.

bedworthy ['bedwɔːði] *a O P* she's bedworthy, elle est bonne à baiser/ elle est baisable.

bee [biː] *n* **1.** *F* he thinks he's the bee's knees, il ne se prend pas pour de la petite bière/pour de la crotte/ pour de la merde. (*See* **cat 8**) **2.** *P* (*RS* = *money*) bees and honey, argent*/fric *m*/flouse *m* **3.** *F* to have a bee in one's bonnet (*a*) avoir une idée fixe/une marotte (*b*) *O* être un peu timbré/avoir une araignée au plafond **4.** *A P* **to put the bee on s.o.,** taper qn pour de l'argent. (*See* **bird 7**; **queen¹ 3**)

Beeb [biːb] *n F* **the Beeb,** la BBC (*British Broadcasting Corporation*). (*See* **Auntie²**)

beef¹ [biːf] *n* **1.** *F* **to have plenty of beef,** être fort* comme un bœuf/ être costaud **2.** *P* réclamation *f*/ rouspétance *f*; **he had a beef about the bill,** il se plaignait de l'addition.

beef² [biːf] *vi P* grogner*/rouspéter/ ronchonner; **stop beefing and get on with it!** arrête de râler et remets-toi au boulot.

beef-bandit ['biːfbændit] *n V* = **arse-bandit.**

beefcake ['biːfkeik] *n P* pin-up masculin. (*See* **cheesecake**)

beefer ['biːfər] *n F* rouspéteur *m*/ râleur *m*.

beef up ['biːf'ʌp] *vtr F P* corser (qch).

beefy ['biːfi] *a F* (*a*) costaud/fort/ balaise/solide (*b*) bien en chair.

beer [biər] *n* **1.** *P* **to go on the beer,** boire*/picoler **2.** *F* **small beer,** peu de chose/de la petite bière; **he's small beer, really,** il compte pour rien/pour du beurre, celui-là.

beer belly ['biər'beli], **beer gut** ['biər'gʌt] *n F* gros ventre*/grosse brioche; **what a huge beer gut he's got!** qu'est-ce qu'il tient comme bide!

beer joint ['biər'dʒɔint] *n NAm F* débit *m* de bière/brasserie *f*.

beer-up ['biərʌp] *n P* beuverie *f* (de bière)/soûlerie *f*.

beeswax ['biːzwæks] *n P* (*turf*) (*RS = betting tax*) taxe *f*/impôt *m* sur les paris.

Beetle ['biːtl] *n F* (*RTM*) (*small car manufactured by Volkswagen*) coccinelle *f*.

beetle-crushers ['biːtl'krʌʃəz]

npl F grosses chaussures*/écrase-merde *mpl.*

beetle off ['biːtl'ɔf] *vi F* partir*/ déguerpir/ficher le camp.

beezer ['biːzər] *n A P* **1.** nez*/ blair *m*/pif *m* **2.** visage*/tête*/ fiole *f.*

beggar ['begər] *n* (*euph for* **bugger**) *F* individu*; **silly beggar!** espèce d'imbécile/d'abruti! **poor beggar!** pauvre type!/pauvre con! **lucky beggar!** le veinard!

beggar-my-neighbour ['begə-mi'neibər] *n P* (*RS = Labour (Exchange)*) **on the beggar-my-neighbour,** au chômage.

begorra! [bi'gɔrə] *interj F* (*considered to be characteristic of Irishmen = by God*) sacrebleu!/bon Dieu!/ nom de Dieu!

behind [bi'haind, bə'haind] *n F* fesses*/postérieur *m*; **to sit on one's behind (and do nothing),** ne pas se manier/se magner le cul; **come on, get up off your behind!** allez, magne-toi le train/le popotin!

bejabbers [bi'dʒæbəz], **beja-bers** [bi'dʒeibəz] *interj Irish F* = **begorra!**

bejesus! [bi'dʒiːzəs, bi'dʒeizəs] **I** *interj Irish F* = **begorra! II** *n NAm P* **to knock the bejesus out of s.o.,** battre* qn comme plâtre/ envoyer dormir qn.

belch [beltʃ] *vi esp NAm P* avouer*/dégorger/roter.

bell¹ [bel] *n F* **1. that rings a bell,** ça me dit quelque chose/ça me rappelle quelque chose **2.** (*catchphrase*) **pull the other one** (= *leg*), **it's got bells on!** à d'autres! cela ne prend pas! **3.** coup de téléphone*; **give me a bell in the morning,** passe-moi un coup de fil demain matin. (*See* **dumb-bell**)

bell² [bel] *vtr F* **to bell s.o.,** téléphoner qn/passer un coup de fil à qn.

bell-bottoms ['belbɔtəmz] *npl F*

(= *bell-bottomed trousers*) pantalon*
à pattes d'éléphant.

belly ['beli] *n* F ventre*/panse *f*/
bedaine *f*. (*See* **beer belly**; **yellow-
belly**)

belly-ache¹ ['belieik] *n* F mal *m*
au ventre/au bide.

belly-ache² ['belieik] *vi* P
grogner*/réclamer/ronchonner/
rouspéter; **he's always belly-aching,**
il râle toujours.

belly-acher ['belieikər] *n* P
ronchonneur, -euse/rouspéteur, -
euse/râleur, -euse.

belly-aching ['belieikiŋ] *n* P
rouspétance *f*.

belly-button ['beli'bʌtn] *n* F nombril *m*.

belly-flop ['beliflɔp] *n* F (*swimming*) **to do a belly-flop,** faire un
plat (ventre).

bellyful ['beliful] *n* P **to have had a
bellyful,** en avoir assez*/en avoir
marre/en avoir ras le bol; **I've had
a bellyful of your advice,** j'en ai
plein le dos/le cul de tes conseils.
(*See* **gutful**)

belly-laugh ['belilɑːf] *n* F gros
rire.

belt¹ [belt] *n* **1.** P **to give s.o. a
belt,** battre* qn/donner une raclée
à qn/flanquer un coup à qn **2.** F
(*a*) **to hit s.o. below the belt,** donner
un coup bas à qn (*b*) **his tactics
were a bit below the belt,** ses tacti-
ques étaient très injustes; **that's a
bit below the belt,** c'est une dure
critique **3.** F **to tighten one's belt,**
se serrer la ceinture/se l'accrocher
4. P (*not common*) l'acte sexuel*/
baise *f*/baisage *m* **5.** P (*not common*) **endless belt,** fille* *ou* femme*
de mœurs faciles/qui fait de
l'abattage **6.** P **to have a belt at
sth,** s'attaquer à qch/tenter
l'aventure.

belt² [belt] *vtr* **1.** P attaquer* (qn)/
sauter dessus **2.** P battre*/filer
une raclée à (qn) **3.** P faire

l'amour* avec (qn)/bourrer (qn) **4.**
V (*rare*) **to belt one's batter,** se
masturber*/se taper la colonne **5.**
NAm P **to belt the grape,** boire*
abondamment/picoler.

belt along, down ['beltəlɔŋ,
dɑun] *vi* F aller à toute vitesse; **to
belt down the motorway,** rouler à
pleins gaz sur l'autoroute.

belting ['beltiŋ] *n* P **1.** volée *f* de
coups*/raclée *f*/dérouillée *f* **2.**
défaite écrasante.

belt off ['belt'ɔf] *vi* P s'enfuir*/se
tirer/se carapater.

belt out ['belt'aut] *vtr* F **to belt out
a song,** gueuler une chanson;
chanter à pleins poumons.

belt up ['belt'ʌp] *vi* P se taire*/la
boucler/la fermer; **belt up, will you!**
la ferme!/boucle-la!/ta gueule!

bend¹ [bend] *n* P **1. to go round
the bend,** devenir fou*/perdre la
boule; **that kid drives me round the
bend,** ce gosse me rend fou*; **I'm
driven round the bend by her inces-
sant chatter,** son bavardage inces-
sant me fait perdre la boule **2. to
go on a bend** = **to go on a bender**
(**bender 1**).

bend² [bend] *vtr* F **1. to bend the
rules,** faire un passe-droit **2. to
bend over backwards to please s.o.,**
se mettre en quatre/se décarcasser
(pour plaire à qn). (*See* **bent¹**;
elbow 3)

bender ['bendər] *n* P **1.** soûlerie *f*;
to go on a bender, aller se cuiter/se
soûler; **he went on a real bender,** il
a pris une sacrée cuite **2.** (*jur*) **six
month bender,** condamnation à six
mois de prison avec sursis. (*See*
hell-bender; **mind-bender**)

bennie, benny ['beni] *n* P
(*drugs*) cachet *m*/pilule *f* de Benzédrine* (*RTM*).

bent [bent] *a* P **1.** malhonnête/vé-
reux; **a bent copper,** un flic véreux
2. homosexuel; **did you know he
was bent?** tu savais qu'il était pédé,
toi?

benz [benz] *n P* (*abbr = Benze-drine*) (*drugs*) Benzédrine* (*RTM*). (*See* **bennie**)

berk [bɜːk] *n P* (*also abbr of* **Berk-eley Hunt**) individu bête*/gourde *f*/andouille *f*; **what a berk!** quel crétin!/quelle nouille! (*See* **Berkeley Hunt**)

Berkeley Hunt ['bɜːkli, 'bɑːkli'hʌnt] *n P* (*RS =* **cunt**) individu bête*/crétin *m*/con *m*/connasse *f*.

bernice ['bɜːnis] *n*, **bernies** ['bɜːniz] *npl P* (*drugs*) cocaïne*/topette *f*.

berth [bɜːθ] *n* 1. *F* **to give s.o. a wide berth,** passer au large de qn/éviter qn à tout prix 2. *P* **soft/safe berth,** boulot *m* pépère/planque *f*/filon *m*.

best ['best] *n F* (*catchphrase*) **and the best of British (luck) (to you),** je te souhaite (bien) du plaisir.

bet [bet] *vtr&i F* 1. **you bet!** pour sûr!/tu parles!/(il) y a des chances!/un peu! 2. **I bet you don't!** chiche (que tu ne le feras pas)! 3. **bet you I will!** chiche (que je le fais)! 4. **you can bet your boots/your bottom dollar/your life,** tu peux y aller/je te fous mon billet que...; **I'll bet anything you like that...,** je te parie tout ce que tu veux que.../je te fous mon billet que... 5. **I bet!** je t'en fiche mon billet! 6. **want to/wanna bet?** tu t'alignes? (*See* **sweet 2**)

better ['betər] *a F* **better half** (*i*) épouse*/moitié *f* (*ii*) mari*/moitié.

betty¹ ['beti] *n A P* passe-partout *m*/crochet *m*/rossignol *m*.

Betty² ['beti] *n O F* **that's all my eye and Betty Martin,** tout ça c'est des foutaises/de la blague. (*See* **eye 2**)

betwixt [bi'twikst] *adv F* **betwixt and between,** ni l'un ni l'autre/ni chèvre ni chou/mi-figue, mi-raisin.

bevvied up ['bevid'ʌp] *a P* **to get**

bevvied up, boire* beaucoup/se soûler/se cuiter.

bevvy ['bevi] *n P* (*beer, wine, etc*) pot *m*/verre *m*/coup *m*; **we had a bevvy in the pub,** on a été boire un coup/prendre un pot au bistrot; **he had a few bevvies first,** d'abord, il a bu un bon coup.

b.f., BF ['biː'ef] *abbr F euph for* **bloody fool** (*see* **bloody I**)

B.-girl ['biːgɜːl] *n NAm P =* **bar-girl.**

bhang [bæŋ] *n P* (*drugs*) **baby bhang/bhang ganjah,** marijuana*.

bi [bai] *a P* (*= bisexual*) ambivalent/à voile et à vapeur. (*See* **ambidex-trous**)

bib [bib] *n F* **in one's best bib and tucker,** sur son trente et un/tiré à quatre épingles.

bible-basher ['baiblbæʃər], **bible-puncher** ['baiblpʌntʃər] *n F* évangéliste *m* de carrefour/prêcheur agressif.

biccy, bicky ['bikiː] *n F* (*= bis-cuit*) gâteau sec/biscuit *m*.

biddy ['bidi] *n* 1. *F* **an old biddy,** une vieille poule/une vieille chipie/une vieille bique 2. *P* **red biddy,** vin rouge additionné d'alcool à brûler.

biff¹ [bif] *n F* coup* de poing/gnon *m*/beigne *f*/baffe *f*.

biff² [bif] *vtr F* **to biff s.o.,** battre* qn/flanquer un gnon à qn; **to biff s.o. on the nose,** flanquer un coup de poing sur la figure de qn/abîmer le portrait à qn.

big [big] **I** *a F* 1. **big bug/cheese/gun/hitter/noise/shot,** personnage important/caïd *m*/grosse légume/gros bonnet/(grosse) huile; **he's the big man around here,** c'est lui la grosse tête/le cerveau du coin; **Mr Big/the big white chief,** le grand manitou; **Big Brother,** grand frère 2. **big mouth,** gueulard *m*/grande gueule; **why can't you keep your big mouth shut?** pas moyen que tu la fermes? **3. he's a big name in the music industry,** il est très connu dans le monde de la musique **4. she's hit the big time,** elle y est arrivée/elle a bien réussi; **she's made it big,** elle a fait un triomphe/un succès **5. to give s.o. a big hand,** applaudir qn; **they gave him a big hand,** ils ont applaudi bien fort/ils l'ont acclamé **6. what's the big idea?** à quoi ça rime?/ça ne va pas, non? **7. to earn big money,** gagner gros/se faire plein de fric **8. big deal!** et alors! **that's no big deal,** c'est pas dramatique/c'est pas bien difficile; **that's big of you!** on nous a gâtés, hein? **9. you big dummy/stiff/twit!** gros bêta, va! **10. to be too big for one's boots,** péter plus haut que son derrière. (*See* **bloke** 3; **chief** 1; **smoke**[1] 2; **stick**[1] 2; **stink**[1] 1; **way** II 2) II *adv F* **1. to talk big,** faire l'important/se faire mousser/crâner **2. to go down big/to go over big,** réussir/avoir un succès fou; **his idea went down big with the boss,** le patron a été emballé par son idée/a trouvé son idée géniale **3. to think big,** viser haut/voir grand.

Big C ['big'siː] *n P* (*drugs*) cocaïne*/coco f/neige f.*

Big D ['big'diː] *n P* (*drugs*) LSD*/acide m.*

biggie, biggy ['bigi] *n F* **1.** *NAm* **that's a biggie,** c'est vachement dur **2.** *NAm* **he's a biggy,** c'est un type important/un gros bonnet **3. he's got a biggy,** il est en érection*/il bande/il a la trique.

Big H ['big'eitʃ] *n P* (*drugs*) heroïne*/H.*

bighead ['bighed] *n P* crâneur *m*; **he's such a bighead,** il ne se prend pas pour de la merde.

big-headed ['big'hedid] *a P* prétentieux*/vaniteux/suffisant/crâneur.*

big-note[1] ['big'nout] *a Austr F* **1. big-note man,** richard *m*/rupin *m*

2. big-note artist (*i*) baratineur *m* (*ii*) déconneur *m.*

big-note[2] ['big'nout] *vtr Austr F* louanger/vanter/passer de la pommade; **to big-note oneself,** se vanter/se faire mousser.

big P ['big'piː] *n P* (= *parole*) (*jur*) liberté conditionnelle.

big-time ['big'taim] *a F* **1. big-time operator,** gros trafiquant **2. big-time racketeer,** chef *m* de bande/caïd *m*. (*See* **big** I 6; **small-time**)

big-timer ['big'taimər] *n F* **1.** = **big noise** (**big** I 1); **to be a big-timer,** être sur la lancée. (*See* **small-timer**) **2.** (*sport, etc*) joueur professionnel/pro *m.*

bigwig ['big'wig] *n F* personnage important/gros bonnet/grosse légume.

big Z's ['big'ziːz] *npl P* (*sleep*) sommeil *m*; **time for the big Z's,** l'heure d'aller au dodo/au pieu.

bike [baik] *n* **1.** *F* bicyclette *f*/vélo *m* **2.** *F* motocyclette *f*/moto *f*/meule *f* **3.** *P* **on your bike!** (*i*) tiretoi!/fiche le camp!/casse-toi!/barretoi! (*ii*) magne-toi!/grouille-toi! **4.** *Austr P* grue *f*/salope *f*/Mariecouche-toi-là *f.*

biker ['baikər], **bikie** ['baiki] *n P* loubard *m*/loulou *m*/blouson noir.

bilge [bildʒ] *n P* **1.** bêtises*/foutaises fpl/eau f de bidet/sornettes fpl* **2. to talk bilge,** dire des bêtises; **you do talk a lot of bilge,** tu débloques **3.** boisson *f* insipide/pipi *m* de chat/bibine *f.*

bilge-water ['bildʒwɔːtər] *n P* = **bilge** 3.

bill[1] [bil] *n* **1.** *F* **to top the bill/to be top of the bill,** être en vedette **2.** *F* **to fit/to fill the bill,** remplir toutes les conditions/faire l'affaire **3.** *NAm P* nez*/pif m/blair m.* (*See* **foot**[2] 1)

Bill[2] [bil] *Prn P see* **old Bill.**

billet ['bilit] *n F* **1.** (*wartime*) to get a safe billet, s'embusquer **2.** (*not common*) emploi *m*; to get a cushy billet, décrocher une bonne planque.

Billingsgate ['biliŋzgeit] *Prn F* (*London fish market*) langage *m* de poissarde; to talk Billingsgate, parler comme une poissarde.

billio ['biliou] *n F* = billy-o.

billy ['bili] *n* **1.** *A P* mouchoir*/blave *m* **2.** *Austr F* (*a*) (= billy-can) gamelle *f*/bouilloire *f* (à thé).

billy-o, billy-oh ['biliou] *n O F* like billy-o, très fort; avec acharnement; it's raining like billy-o, il pleut à seaux; he's rushing around like billy-o, il court çà et là comme un dératé.

bin [bin] *n P* = loony-bin.

bind [baind] *n F* **1.** (*pers*) crampon *m*/casse-pieds *m*/scie *f* **2.** (*thg*) scie *f*; what a bind! quelle corvée! it's an awful bind having to do that, c'est casse-pieds/quelle barbe d'avoir à faire ça **3.** to be in a bit of a bind, être dans le pétrin.

bindle ['bindl] *n NAm A P* **1.** baluchon *m* (de clochard*) **2.** (*drugs*) sachet *m ou* paquet *m* d'héroïne* **3.** bindle stiff, clochard*/clodo(t) *m*.

bing [biŋ] *n NAm A P* cachot *m* (de prison*)/mitard *m*.

binge [bindʒ] *n F* réjouissances*/bombe *f*; to go on a binge, faire la foire/la bombe.

bingo ['biŋgou] *n* sorte de loto public. *The following terms are used in this game:* Kelly's eye/*or* Little Jimmy = 1; buckle my shoe/dirty old Jew/Little Boy Blue = 2; dearie me! = 3; knock at the door = 4; Jack's alive = 5; Tom Mix = 6; lucky seven = 7; one fat lady = 8; doctor's orders = 9; Downing Street = 10; legs eleven = 11; one doz = 12; unlucky for some = 13; she's lovely *or* never been kissed = 16; the age to catch 'em = 17; key of the door = 21; all the twos/dinky-doo = 22; bed and breakfast/half-a-crown = 26; you're doing fine = 29; all the threes = 33; dirty whore = 34; all the steps = 39; life begins = 40; life's begun = 41; all the fours/droopy-drawers = 44; half-way = 45; bullseye/bunghole = 50; all the varieties/Heinz = 57; Brighton line = 59; old-age pension = 65; clickety-click = 66; any way round = 69; was she worth it? = 76; sunset strip = 77; two fat ladies = 88; all but one/nearly there = 89; top of the shop/as far as we go = 99; bingo! jeu!/gagné!

bins [binz] *npl P* lunettes*/bernicles *fpl*.

bint [bint] *n P* **1.** (*pej*) femme*/gonzesse *f*; she's a silly bint, c'est une connasse, celle-là **2.** *A* (*pej*) petite amie/poule *f*.

bird [bəːd] *n* **1.** *F* individu*/type *m*/oiseau *m*/moineau *m*; who's that old bird? qu'est-ce que c'est que ce vieux type? he's a queer old bird, c'est un drôle de vieux numéro **2.** *F* (*a*) jeune femme*/nana *f*/gonzesse *f* (*b*) compagne *f*/petite amie; minette; who was that bird I saw you with? qui c'était la nana avec qui je t'ai vu/qui t'accompagnait? **3.** *F* to get the bird (*i*) être renvoyé/sacqué (*ii*) (*theatre*) se faire siffler **4.** *F* to give s.o. the bird (*i*) envoyer promener qn/envoyer qn au bain (*ii*) renvoyer qn/sacquer qn (*iii*) (*theatre*) huer qn/siffler qn **5.** *P* to do bird, faire de la prison*/faire de la taule; he's done bird, il a fait de la taule/c'est un ancien taulard **6.** *F* it's (strictly) for the birds, c'est seulement pour les cruches **7.** the birds and the bees, éléments sexuels de base; to learn all about the birds and the bees, apprendre que les enfants ne naissent pas dans les choux **8.** *F* a little bird told me, mon petit doigt me l'a dit **9.** *F* the bird has flown, l'oiseau s'est envolé. (*See* dicky-bird; dolly-bird;

early; **feather**[1] **1**; **gallows-bird**;
home-bird; **jail-bird**; **jay-bird**;
lovebird; **night-bird**; **snowbird**;
whirly-bird; **yardbird**)

bird-brain ['bɜːdbreɪn] *n F*
individu bête*/tête de linotte.

bird-brained ['bɜːdbreɪnd] *a F*
1. bête*/farfelu **2.** écervelé/
évaporé.

bird-cage ['bɜːdkeɪdʒ] *n P* cellule
f de prison*/cellote *f*.

bird-fancier ['bɜːdfænsɪər] *n P*
juponnard *m*/coureur *m* de filles/
dragueur *m*.

birdie ['bɜːdi] *a P* (*for photograph*)
watch the birdie! un beau sourire!/
attention le petit oiseau va sortir!

birdie-powder ['bɜːdipaʊdər] *n O
P* (*drugs*) héroïne* *ou* morphine* en
poudre.

bird-lime ['bɜːdlaɪm] *n P* (*RS =
time*) **1.** *O* **how's the bird-lime?**
quelle heure est-il? **2.** = **bird 5.**

bird's-eye ['bɜːdzaɪ] *n P* (*drugs*)
petite quantité de drogue.

bird-watcher ['bɜːdwɒtʃər] *n P* =
bird-fancier.

bird-wood ['bɜːdwʊd] *n A P*
(*drugs*) cigarettes* de marijuana.

birthday ['bɜːθdeɪ] *n F* **to be in
one's birthday suit,** être nu*/être à
poil/être dans le costume d'Adam.

biscuit ['bɪskɪt] *n* **1.** *F* **you take
the biscuit,** à toi le pompon; **that
takes the biscuit!** ça c'est le com-
ble/le bouquet! **2.** *NAm P*
revolver*/flingue *m*/pétard *m*.

bish [bɪʃ] *n O F* bévue*/bourde *f*/
gaffe *f*.

bishop ['bɪʃəp] *n V* **to flog/to bash
the bishop,** se masturber*/se
secouer le bonhomme/faire sauter
la cervelle de Charles-le-Chauve.
(*See* **actress**)

bit [bɪt] **I** *a F* (*films, theatre*) **a bit
part,** un rôle secondaire/une panne;
a bit player, un figurant **II** *n* **1.** *P*
a (nice) bit of all right/crumpet/

fluff/skirt/stuff/tail (*i*) un beau brin
de fille/un beau petit lot/un prix
de Diane (*ii*) l'acte sexuel*/baisage
m; **he's only after a bit of crumpet/
tail,** il ne s'intéresse qu'à baiser **2.
to have a bit on the side** (*i*) avoir
une maîtresse/un amant quelque
part (*ii*) tromper sa femme/son
mari **3.** *F* **a bit much** (*a*) un peu
cher* (*b*) un peu exagéré/un peu
fort; **it was a bit much, all the
same!** c'était un peu fort, tout de
même!/faut pas charrier, quand
même! **it was all a bit of a laugh
really,** c'était plutôt une rigolade
4. *F* **he's a bit of an idiot,** il est un
peu bête/ce n'est pas une lumière;
he's a bit of a lad, c'est un chaud
lapin/un sacré dragueur **5.** *NAm
F* **two bits,** pièce *f* de 25 cents. (*See*
two-bit) **6.** *NAm F* condamnation* à la prison/purge *f* **7.** *F* **to
be thrilled to bits,** être ravi/être aux
anges; **I was thrilled to bits by it,** je
trouvais ça extra/génial. (*See* **side
1, 2; spare II; stray; threepenny-
bits; trey-bits**)

bitch[1] [bɪtʃ] *n P* **1.** (*pej*) femme*/
salope *f*/garce *f*/ordure *f*/chameau
m/peau *f* de vache; **you bitch!**
salope!/garce! **what a bitch she can
be!** ce qu'elle peut être vache! **his
mother is a real bitch!** sa mère est
une vraie peau de vache! **2. this
job is a real bitch!** cette saloperie
de boulot! **that bitch of a car!** cette
putain de bagnole! (*See* **s.o.b.; son
of a bitch**)

bitch[2] [bɪtʃ] *vi&tr P* **1.** grogner*/
rouspéter/râler; **stop bitching!** arrête
de rouspéter! **2.** tromper*/
entuber/rouler (qn); **to bitch s.o.
out of sth,** roustir qn à propos de
qch **3.** = **bitch up**.

bitchiness ['bɪtʃɪnɪs] *n P*
saloperie *f*/coup *m* en vache/
vacherie *f*.

bitch up ['bɪtʃ 'ʌp] *vtr P* saboter/
bousiller (qch); **you've bitched that
up nicely!** tu l'as joliment salopé!/

c'est du joli travail!/c'est du beau travail!

bitchy ['bitʃi] *a P* (*a*) rouspéteur/râleur (*b*) moche/rosse/vache; **a bitchy remark**, une vanne/une pique.

bite¹ [bait] *n* **1.** *O P* **to put the bite on s.o.** (*a*) emprunter* à qn/taper qn (*b*) faire chanter qn **2.** *F* **to have a bite to eat**, manger* un morceau/casser la croûte. (*See* **cherry 2**; **fleabite**)

bite² [bait] *vtr* **1.** *F* (*fig*) **to get bitten**, se faire avoir; **I've been badly bitten** (*i*) j'ai été roulé (*ii*) on m'a mis dedans; (*catchphrase*) **once bitten twice shy**, chat échaudé craint l'eau froide **2.** *F* **what's biting you?** quelle mouche te pique?/qu'est-ce qui te chiffonne? **3.** *P* **to bite s.o. for money**, taper/torpiller qn. (*See* **dust¹ 4**)

bite off ['bait'ɔf] *F* **1. to bite s.o.'s head off**, injurier* qn/rembarrer qn **2. to bite off more than one can chew**, avoir les yeux plus grands que le ventre.

bitser ['bitsər] *n Austr F* chien* bâtard/corniaud *m*.

bitsy-witsy ['bitsi'witsi] *n F* = **itsy-bitsy**.

bitty ['biti] *a F* (*book, play, etc*) décousu/hétéroclite/de bric et de broc.

bivvy ['bivi] *n P* (= *bivouac*) (*not common*) bivouac *m*.

biz [biz] *n* **1.** *P* (= *business*) **the biz**, le bis(e)ness/le truc. (*See* **show-biz**) **2.** (*drugs*) artillerie *f*/kit *m*.

blab (off) ['blæb('ɔf)] *vtr&i P* **1.** (*esp*) **to blab one's mouth off**, révéler un secret/lâcher le morceau **2.** bavarder*/jaser/jacter.

blabbermouth ['blæbə'mauθ] *n F* (*a*) qui laisse échapper un secret cafardeur (*b*) bavard*/jaspineur *m*.

black¹ [blæk] **I** *a* **1.** *F* **a black mark**, un mauvais point **2. black**

spot (*a*) *F* (*on the roads*) endroit dangereux/point noir (*b*) *A P* fumerie *f* d'opium* **3.** *P* **black stuff** (*a*) (*drugs*) opium* *m*/noir *m* (*b*) macadam (goudronné) **4. black and tan** (*a*) *F* panaché *m* de bière brune et blonde (*b*) (*drugs*) *P* amphétamine* (*c*) *Hist F* **Black and Tans**, milice chargée de l'ordre en Irlande (*c.* 1920) **5.** *F* **black diamonds**, charbon *m* **6.** *P* (*pej*) **as black as a nigger**/*Austr* **as black as an abo's arsehole** = noir comme dans le trou du cul d'un nègre. (*See* **book¹ 2**; **velvet 2**) **II** *n* **1.** *F* (*occ pej*) Noir(e)*/nègre *m*/bougnoul *m* **2.** *A P* chantage *m*; **to put the black on s.o.**, faire du chantage **3.** *F* **in the black**, à l'actif *m*; **my account is in the black**, mon compte est en crédit **4.** *F* **in black and white**, en noir et blanc.

black² [blæk] *vtr F* = **blacklist**.

blackbirding ['blækbə:diŋ] *n Hist P* trafic *m* d'esclaves noirs.

blackbirds ['blækbə:dz] *npl P* **1.** *Hist* esclaves noirs **2.** (*drugs*) amphétamines*/speed *m*.

black box ['blæk'bɔks] *n F* (*aviation*) (= *flight recorder*) enregistreur *m* de vol/boîte noire.

blackleg¹ ['blækleg] *n F* briseur *m* de grève/jaune *m*.

blackleg² ['blækleg] *vi F* briser la grève.

blacklist ['blæklist] *vtr F* mettre sur la liste noire.

Black Maria ['blækmə'raiə] *n F* car* de police/panier *m* à salade.

black-out ['blækaut] *n F* **1.** évanouissement *m* **2.** (*a*) panne *f* d'électricité (*b*) (*wartime*) camouflage *m* des lumières/black-out *m*.

black out ['blæk'aut] *vtr&i F* **1.** s'évanouir*/tourner de l'œil/tomber dans les pommes **2.** couper l'électricité (dans un quartier, un immeuble, etc); **to be blacked out,**

être en panne d'électricité; se trouver dans le noir.

blag[1] [blæg] *n P* (*armed robbery*) vol* à main armée/braquage *m*/hold-up *m*.

blag[2] [blæg] *vtr P* (*to rob with violence*) voler* à main armée/braquer.

blagger ['blægər] *n P* (*armed robber*) braqueur *m*.

blah(-blah) ['blɑɪ('blɑɪ)] *n F* blabla(bla) *m*/boniment *m*/baratin *m*.

blank [blæŋk] *n F* **to draw a blank,** échouer/faire chou blanc; **we've looked, but up to now we've drawn a complete blank,** on a bien cherché, mais jusqu'à présent c'est le bide complet.

blankety(-blank) ['blæŋkiti-('blæŋk)] *a&n O F euph for* **damn-(ed), bloody,** *etc.*

blarney[1] ['blɑɪni] *n F* flatterie*/cajolerie *f*/boniment *m*; **he's full of the blarney/he's kissed the blarney stone,** il a la langue bien pendue/il sait baratiner.

blarney[2] ['blɑɪni] *vi F* flatter*/cajoler/bonimenter/passer de la pommade.

blast[1] [blɑɪst] *n P* **1.** (*drugs*) piqûre*/piquouse *f*/shoot *m*/fixe *m* **2.** longue bouffée d'une cigarette* de marijuana/taffe *f*; **here, have a blast of this joint,** tiens, tire-toi une bouffée de ce joint **3.** effet puissant d'une drogue/flash *m* **4.** (*a kick, a thrill*) **we had a blast at that party!** on s'est vachement bien marrés à cette boum!

blast[2] [blɑɪst] *vtr&i P* **1.** (*esp sport*) battre à plate(s) couture(s) **2.** (*drugs*) (*a*) se piquer*/se shooter (*b*) **to blast (on) a joint,** fumer de la marijuana*/tirer sur un stick **3. blast (it)!** zut!/la barbe!/merde! **blast you!** va te faire voir! **blast him!** il est empoisonnant! **damn and blast!** merde (alors)!/bordel!

blasted ['blɑɪstid] *a P* **1.** fichu/

sacré/maudit; **it's a blasted nuisance,** c'est un fichu embêtement/la poisse/la barbe; **he's a blasted nuisance,** il est enquiquinant; **a blasted idiot,** le roi des imbéciles **2.** drogué*/envapé/défoncé.

blather[1] ['blæðər] *n F* bêtises*/fadaises *fpl*/blablabla *m*.

blather[2] ['blæðər] *vi F* dire des bêtises*/débloquer; **to go blathering on,** raconter n'importe quoi; débloquer à pleins tubes.

blazes ['bleiziz] *npl O F* **1. go to blazes!** aller au diable!/va te faire voir! **2. what the blazes ...!** que diable ...! **3. to run like blazes,** courir très vite*/comme si on avait le feu au derrière.

bleed ['bliːd] *vi F* (*iron*) **my heart bleeds (for you)!** tu me fais pleurer!/tu me fends le cœur!

bleeder ['bliːdər] *n P* **1.** salaud; **poor bleeder!** pauvre type! **silly bleeder!** espèce de con! **2. wait till I catch the little bleeder!** le petit morveux ne perd rien pour attendre!

bleeding, bleedin' ['bliːdiŋ, 'bliːdn] *a P* (*intensifier*) **1. don't be a bleeding fool!** ne fais pas le con! **2. it's bleeding/bleedin' beautiful,** c'est vachement beau/c'est super chouette **3. it's bleeding marvellous, isn't it!** super, hein! **4. that bleeding car!** cette putain de bagnole!

blessed ['blesid] *a F* **what a blessed nuisance!** quel fichu embêtement! **that blessed boy!** il est enquiquinant/empoisonnant, ce gamin! **the whole blessed day,** toute la sainte journée.

blest [blest] *pp F* **well I'm blest!** ça par exemple!/ça alors! **I'm/I'll be blest if I know,** comment veux-tu que je le sache!

blether ['bleðər] *n & v* (*Scottish*) *F* = **blather**[1,2].

blighter ['blaitər] *n F* individu*/type *m*/zèbre *m*; **poor blighter!**

pauvre type!/pauvre diable!; **lucky blighter!** le veinard!; **you rotten blighter!** ce que t'es vache!

Blighty ['blaiti] *n F (mil wartime)* l'Angleterre *f*/le pays.

blimey! ['blaimi] *excl P* zut alors!/ mince alors!/merde alors! (*See* **cor!** (*b*); **gorblimey!**)

blimp [blimp] *n (also Colonel Blimp) F* vieille culotte de peau.

blind [blaind] **I** *a* **1.** *F* **blind date,** rendez-vous*/rancart *m* avec qn qu'on ne connaît pas **2.** *F* **blind (drunk),** complètement ivre*/rétamé **3.** *F* **to turn a blind eye (to sth),** fermer les yeux (sur qch) **4.** *F* **he didn't take a blind bit of notice,** il n'a même pas fait attention/il n'a même pas remarqué. (*See* **eye 9**) **II** *n* **1.** *F* couverture*/couverte *f*/ couvrante *f* **2.** *P* soûlerie *f*; **to go on a blind,** aller se soûler **3.** *P* **to put the blinds on s.o.,** mettre un bandeau sur les yeux de qn.

blind² [blaind] *vi P* **1.** jurer/sacrer **2.** conduire avec insouciance; **blind and brake driver,** chauffard *m*.

blinder ['blaindər] *n* **1.** *P (i)* réjouissances*/bamboche *f (ii)* soûlerie *f* **2.** (*turf*) cheval dopé.

blinders ['blaindəz] *a O P* **(Harry) blinders,** complètement ivre*/ rétamé/bituré.

blink [bliŋk] *n F* **on the blink,** qui ne marche pas/qui foire; **my phone is on the blink,** mon téléphone est détraqué.

blinkers ['bliŋkəz] *npl O F* yeux*/ quinquets *mpl*.

blinking ['bliŋkiŋ] *a F (euph for bloody I, II)* **1. blinking idiot!** espèce d'idiot!/de crétin! **2. blinking heck!** mince alors! **3. a blinking cheek/nerve,** un sacré culot **4. a blinking good film,** un film vachement chouette.

blister ['blistər] *n NAm A P* prostituée*/pute *f*. (*See* **skin¹ 11**)

blithering ['bliðəriŋ] *a F* **you blith-ering idiot!** bougre d'idiot!/espèce de connard!

blob [blɔb] *n P (cricket)* zéro *m*; **to score a blob,** ne pas marquer/de points.

block [blɔk] *n P* **1.** tête*/caboche *f*; **to knock s.o.'s block off,** casser la figure à qn; **I'll knock your block off if you do that!** je te casserai la gueule si tu fais ça! **2.** *Austr* **to do one's block,** se mettre en colère*/en rogne/en pétard **3.** *O (drugs) (a)* paquet *m* de morphine* (*b*) semelle *f* de haschisch* **4.** *V* **block and tackle,** sexe de l'homme*/service *m* trois pièces. (*See* **chip 6**)

blockbust ['blɔkbʌst] *vi NAm P (real estate)* persuader les Blancs dans un quartier résidentiel de vendre leurs propriétés de peur que des Noirs s'y installent.

blockbuster ['blɔk'bʌstər] *n P* **1.** bombe très puissante/marmite *f* **2.** (*a*) (*pers*) personne très efficace et pleine de dynamisme; **she's a real blockbuster,** elle est d'un dynamisme à tout casser/c'est un véritable ouragan, cette femme (*b*) (idée, discours) qui a un succès fou/qui est très puissant(e); film *ou* spectacle réalisé à grands frais; **'Brideshead Revisited' is ITV's latest blockbuster,** 'Brideshead Revisited' – la dernière superproduction de la ITV **3.** *NAm* agent immobilier qui achète des propriétés des Blancs dans un quartier résidentiel pour les revendre ensuite à des Noirs qui cherchent à s'y installer.

blocked [blɔkt] *a P* drogué*/ camé/défoncé.

blockhead ['blɔk'hed] *n F* imbécile*/crétin *m*; **you blockhead!** espèce de nouille!

bloke [blouk] *n* **1.** *F* individu*/ type *m*/mec *m*; **a good bloke,** un brave type/un bon zigue; **he's a great bloke,** c'est un type sensass/ génial **2.** *O F (Navy)* **the Bloke,** le

Patron **3.** *O P* (*drugs*) **big bloke,** cocaïne*.

blood [blʌd] *n* **1.** *F* **to be after s.o.'s blood,** vouloir la peau de qn **2.** *F* **to get s.o.'s blood up/to make s.o.'s blood boil,** mettre qn en colère*/faire fulminer qn; **to have one's blood up,** être en colère*/voir rouge; **it gets my blood up/it makes my blood boil,** ça me rend furax **3.** *F* **to make s.o.'s blood run cold,** glacer le sang à qn **4. to sweat blood,** suer sang et eau/avoir des sueurs froides; travailler* dur **5.** *P* = **soul-brother.** (*See* **Nelson**)

bloody ['blʌdi] **I** *a P* fichu/foutu; **you bloody fool!** espèce de couillon! **to play the bloody fool,** faire le con; **he's a bloody nuisance,** il est vachement chiant; **stop that bloody row!** arrêtez ce bordel!/arrêtez ce ramdam! **the bloody car's broken down again!** cette putain de bagnole est encore tombée en panne; **bosses are all the bloody same!** ces foutus patrons/ces putains de patrons, c'est toujours la même histoire!/c'est toujours le même tabac! **the bloody limit,** la fin des haricots. (*See* **Mary 4**) **II** *adv P* vachement; **I feel bloody,** j'ai pas la frite!/j'ai pas la pêche! **not bloody likely!** pas de danger!/tu te fous de ma gueule? **it's bloody hot!** il fait une chaleur à crever!

bloody-minded ['blʌdi'maindid] *a P* pas commode; **he's a bloody-minded sod,** c'est un mauvais coucheur/c'est un emmerdeur/il emmerde tout le monde.

bloody-mindedness ['blʌdi'-maindidnis] *n P* sale caractère *m*/ caractère de cochon; **he did it out of sheer bloody-mindedness,** il ne l'a fait que pour emmerder/faire chier le monde.

bloomer ['bluːmər] *n F* bévue*/ gaffe *f*/bourde *f*; **he's made a real bloomer,** il s'est complètement gour(r)é/il s'est complètement fichu dedans.

blooming ['bluːmiŋ] *a & adv F* (*euph for* **bloody I, II**) **you're a blooming genius!** t'est super doué, toi!

blotto ['blɔtou] *a F* complètement ivre*/rétamé; **he's completely blotto,** il est complètement paf/bourré à zéro/beurré comme un petit lu.

blow [blou] *vtr&i* **1.** *F* (*euph for* **blast² 3**) **blow the expense!** au diable l'avarice! **blow me!/well I'm blowed!** ça par exemple!/ça alors! (*See* **blest**); **generous be blowed,** he's as mean as they come! généreux, mon œil! il est radin comme tout! **I'll be blowed if I'll do it!** pas question que je le fasse! **blow it!** zut!/la barbe!/merde! **2.** *P* s'enfuir*/se barrer/se tirer; **let's blow!** allez, on se tire!/tirons-nous les gars! **3.** *F* **to blow one's own trumpet/horn,** se vanter/se faire mousser/s'envoyer des fleurs **4.** *F* **to blow hot and cold,** souffler le chaud et le froid/n'être ni chair ni poisson **5.** *P* **to blow one's top/ lid/stack/a fuse,** se mettre en colère*/piquer une crise/sortir de ses gonds **6.** *P* **to blow the gaff,** vendre la mèche; **to blow the gaff on s.o.,** dénoncer*/donner/balancer (qn); **to blow the gaff on sth,** exposer publiquement (un scandale, etc)/lâcher le morceau **7.** *P* dépenser*/gaspiller de l'argent; **he blew fifty quid on that,** il a claqué cinquante livres pour ça **8.** *P* bousiller/saboter/louper; **we should have won but we blew it,** on aurait dû gagner mais on a tout raté/on s'est planté **9.** *P* priser une drogue/(s)chnouffer; **to blow a joint,** fumer un joint **10.** *P* **to blow one's mind** (*a*) (*esp under hallucinogenic drug*) faire planer qn (*b*) donner à qn une sensation de plaisir et d'euphorie (*c*) secouer qn; **their new album will really blow your mind!** leur nouvel album c'est le super-pied! **11.** *P* se masturber*/se branler **12.** *V* faire une fellation* à qn/sucer qn/tailler une pipe à qn. (*See* **gaff 3**; **lid 2**; **stack 2**; **tank 1**; **top**[1] **2**)

blow away ['blouǝ'wei] *vtr esp NAm P* tuer*/descendre/flinguer (qn); ficher/flanquer/foutre (qn) en l'air.

blower ['blouǝr] *n P* téléphone*/ronfleur *m*/tube *m*; **to get on the blower to s.o.**, passer un coup de bigophone à qn. (*See* **mind-blower**)

blowhard ['blouhɑːd] *n NAm P* vantard*/crâneur *m*; gueulard *m*.

blow in ['blou'in] *vtr&i P* arriver* en coup de vent/s'amener à l'improviste; **look what the wind's blown in!** regarde ce qui s'est amené!

blow-job ['blou'dʒɔb] *n V* fellation*/pipe *f*; **she gave him a blow-job**, elle lui a fait une pipe/elle lui a taillé une plume/elle lui a fait un pompier.

blow off ['blou'ɔf] *P* **I** *vi* péter*/cloquer **II** *vtr* **to blow one's mouth off**, parler* trop/dégoiser/dévider. (*See* **steam 1**)

blow-out ['blouaut] *n F* gueuleton *m*/ripaille *f*/balthazar *m*/grande bouffe; **to have a good blow-out**, manger* abondamment/gueuletonner.

blow-up ['blouʌp] *n F* **1.** (accès *m* de) colère*/engueulade *f*/prise *f* de bec **2.** (*photo*) agrandissement *m*.

blow up ['blou'ʌp] *F* **I** *vi* se mettre en colère*/exploser **II** *vtr* **1.** réprimander*/passer un savon à qn/engueuler qn **2.** (*photo*) faire un agrandissement.

blub [blʌb] *vi F* pleurer*/chialer/pleurnicher.

bludge [blʌdʒ] *Austr P* **I** *vi* flâner/fainéanter/tirer au flanc **II** *vtr* taper/chiper (qch à qn).

bludger ['blʌdʒǝr] *n Austr P* **1.** fainéant *m*/flemmard *m*/tire-au-flanc *m* **2.** souteneur*/mangeur *m* de blanc/jules *m*.

blue[1] [bluː] **I** *a* **1.** *F* **blue film/movie**, film *m* porno/film de cul **2.** *F* **to scream blue murder**, crier*/gueuler au charron **3.** *F* **you can talk till you're blue in the face, I'm not going**, cause toujours, j'irai pas **4.** *F* **(the) boys in blue**, agents *mpl* de police* (en uniforme)/les habillés **5.** *P* **blue house**, bordel*/maison *f* de passe **6.** *F* **once in a blue moon**, la semaine des quatre jeudis/tous les 36 du mois **7.** *F* triste/cafardeux; **to feel blue**, avoir le cafard. (*See* **devil**[1] **17**) **8.** *A P* **blue ruin**, alcool*/tord-boyaux *m* **9.** *F* (*politics*) **true blue**, Conservateur/de la droite. (*See* **funk**[1] **1**; **velvet 1**) **II** *n* **1.** *P* (*drugs*) bleue *f*; **double blue**, mélange *m* d'amphétamine* et de barbiturique*; *pl* **blues**, préparation artisanale d'amphétamines*/bleues *fpl*; **heavenly blues**, graines *fpl* de volubilis (employées comme drogues). (*See* **pearly**) **2.** *F* **to turn up out of the blue**, arriver* à l'improviste/venir comme un cheveu sur la soupe **3.** *pl F* **to have the blues**, avoir le cafard/broyer du noir **4.** *A P* agent* de police/poulet *m*. (*See* **bluebottle**) **5.** *pl F* le blues; **to sing the blues**, chanter le blues **6.** *Austr P* querelle*/prise *f* de bec **7.** *Austr P* rouquin(e)/poil *m* de carotte.

blue[2] [bluː] *vi P* **1. to blue one's money**, dépenser*/bouffer/claquer son argent **2. he blued his lot**, il a tout paumé/il a mangé la ferme.

blue balls ['bluː'bɔːlz] *npl NAm VV* **to have blue balls**, avoir une blennorragie*/la chaude-pisse.

bluebottle ['bluːbɔtl] *n O P* agent* de police/flic *m*/poulet *m*.

blue-eyed ['bluːaid] *a F* innocent/candide; **to be s.o.'s blue-eyed boy**, être le chouchou de qn.

blue heaven ['bluː'hevǝn] *n P* (*drugs*) (*a*) LSD*/acide *m* (*b*) *pl* **blue heavens**, barbituriques*/amytal *m*/barbital *m*.

bluey ['bluːi] *n P* billet* de cinq livres.

B.O. ['biː'ou] *n F* (*abbr* = *body odour*) odeur corporelle; **she's got B.O.**, elle ne connaît pas le savon/ le déodorant.

bo [bou] *n NAm F* clochard*/clodot *m.*

boat [bout] *n* **1.** *F* **to push the boat out** (*a*) payer* une tournée (*b*) faire la fête*/la noce/la foire **2.** *F* **to miss the boat**, passer à côté/manquer le coche **3.** *F* **to be in the same boat**, être sur le même bateau/être logé(s) à la même enseigne **4.** *F* **I haven't just got off the boat = I haven't just come in on the banana boat (banana 3) 5.** *pl F* grandes chaussures*/bateaux *mpl* **6.** *P* (*RS* = *boat-race* = *face*) visage*/gueule *f.* (*See* **dream-boat**; **pig-boat**; **rock² 2**)

bob¹ [bɔb] *n F* cinq pence; **ten bob**, cinquante pence. (*See* **fly-bob**)

Bob² [bɔb] *Prn P* **Bob's your uncle**, ça y est/c'est dans le sac; **take the next right and, Bob's your uncle, there it is staring you in the face!** prends la première rue à droite, et le voilà, juste devant ton nez.

bobby ['bɔbi] *n F* agent* de police/ flic *m.*

bobby-dazzler ['bɔbidæzlər] *n O F* (*a*) qch de voyant/de tapageur (*b*) beau brin de fille*/beau petit lot.

bobbysocks ['bɔbisɔks] *npl P F* socquettes *fpl.*

bobbysoxer ['bɔbisɔksər] *n O F* jeune fille*/minette *f.*

bo-bo ['boubou] *n P* (*drugs*) marijuana*/kif *m.* (*See* **bush 2**)

bod [bɔd] *n F* individu*; **he's a bit of an odd bod**, c'est un drôle de type/de zèbre.

bodge-up ['bɔdʒʌp] *n F* gâchis *m/* bousillage *m/*bâclage *m;* **to make a right bodge-up (of sth)**, tout

saloper; foutre le bordel/la merde (dans qch).

bodge (up) ['bɔdʒ('ʌp)] *vtr F* gâcher/bousiller/saloper.

bodgie ['bɔdʒi] *n Austr P* jeune voyou *m.*

boffin ['bɔfin] *n F* chercheur *m* scientifique.

bog [bɔg] *n P* **1.** WC*/gogues *mpl/* chiottes *fpl;* **to go to the bog**, aller aux chiottes **2. to make a bog of sth**, bousiller/saloper qch.

bogey, bogie ['bougi] *n P* **1.** (*a*) policier* en civil/perdreau *m* (*b*) agent* de police/poulet *m* **2.** (= *snot*) morve *f/*loulou *m/*bête *f/* crotte *f.*

bogue [boug] *a P* (drugs) (*rare*) (*a*) en l'état de manque (*b*) souffrant d'un sevrage.

bog(up) ['bɔg('ʌp)] *vtr P* bousiller/ saloper (qch); **he really bogged it**, il a tout salopé; il y a foutu le bordel/la merde.

bogy ['bougi] *n P* = **bogey 1, 2.**

bohunk ['bouhʌŋk] *n P* **1.** immigrant *m* d'Europe centrale **2.** individu *m* bête* et gauche/empoté *m/*patate *f.*

boiled [bɔild] *a esp NAm P* ivre*/ rétamé. (*See* **hard-boiled**; **shirt 5**)

boiling ['bɔiliŋ] **I** *a & adv F* **I'm absolutely boiling**, je crève de chaleur **II** *n O P* **the whole boiling**, (et) tout le bazar/(et) tout le bataclan/(et) tout le tremblement. (*See* **caboodle**; **shebang 1**; **shoot¹ 1**; **shooting-match**)

boing! [bɔiŋ] *excl F* boum!/pan!/ vlan!

boko ['boukou] *n A P* grand nez*.

bollix ['bɔliks] *n V* = **bollocks**.

bollix (up) ['bɔliks('ʌp)] *vtr V* = **bollocks (up).**

bollocking ['bɔləkiŋ] *n V* engueulade *f/*savon *m;* **to get a bollocking**, se faire engueuler; **to give s.o. a bollocking**, en faire voir des vertes et des pas mûres à qn; passer un savon à qn.

bollock-naked ['bɔlək'neikid] *a* V nu*/à poil/le cul à l'air.

bollocks ['bɔləks] *npl* V **1.** testicules*/balloches *fpl*/couilles *fpl*; **he kicked him in the bollocks,** il lui a flanqué un coup de pied aux couilles **2. bollocks!/what a load of bollocks!** quelles conneries!/quelle couillonnade!/c'est de la couille! **3. bollocks to you!** je t'emmerde!/va te faire foutre! **4. to make a bollocks of sth,** saloper qch/foutre le bordel dans qch; **he made a right bollocks of it,** il a tout foutu en l'air/il y a foutu le merdier.

bollocks (up) ['bɔləks('ʌp)] *vtr* V foutre le bordel dans qch/saloper qch; **he really bollocksed it (up),** il s'est complètement foutu dedans.

boloney [bə'louni] *n* F bêtises*/foutaises *fpl*; **that's a lot of boloney!** c'est du flan!

bolshie, bolshy ['bɔlʃi] **I** F *a* **1.** bolcho/communo **2.** râleur/enquiquineur; **he's a bolshy sod,** c'est un mauvais coucheur/il emmerde le monde; **don't get bolshy with me!** ne la remène pas avec moi!/commence pas à me gonfler!/m'emmerde pas! **II** *n* coco *m*/bolcho *m*. (*See* **commie**)

bolted up ['boulted'ʌp] *a* P en prison*/en taule/bouclé.

bomb¹ [bɔm] *n* **1.** F **to cost a bomb,** coûter cher*/coûter les yeux de la tête **2.** F **to make a bomb,** gagner* beaucoup d'argent/faire du fric/tomber sur un champ d'oseille **3.** F **to go like a bomb,** ronfler/gazer/boumer; **his car goes like a bomb,** sa voiture, c'est une petite bombe; **it went like a bomb last night,** ça a été un grand succès hier soir **4.** *NAm* P échec*/fiasco *m*/four *m* **5.** *Austr* F vieille voiture*/guimbarde *f.* (*See* **sex-bomb**; **stink-bomb**)

bomb² [bɔm] *vi NAm* F échouer*;

the play bombed on Broadway, la pièce a été/a fait un four complet à Broadway.

bombed (out) ['bɔmd('aut)] *a* P = drogué*/camé; **he was bombed out of his mind,** il était complètement défoncé.

bomber ['bɔmər] *n* P (*drugs*) (*a*) **black bomber,** bonbon *m*; **brown bomber,** panaché *m* de bière brune et blonde. (*See* **black¹** 4) (*b*) cigarette* de marijuana/joint *m*/bomb *f.*

bombida [bɔm'biːdə], **bombido** [bɔm'biːdou] *n* P (*drugs*) mélange *m* d'amphétamines* pour injection.

bombshell ['bɔmʃel] *n* F **1. a blonde bombshell,** une blonde sensass **2. the news hit us like a bombshell,** la nouvelle est tombée comme une bombe.

bonce [bɔns] *n* P tête*/caboche *f.*

bondage ['bɔndidʒ] *n NAm* P **in bondage,** endetté/déficitaire/dans le rouge.

bone¹ [boun] *n* **1.** F **to make no bones about sth,** ne pas y aller par quatre chemins; **she made no bones about it,** elle y est allée carrément/elle n'a pas fait de difficultés **2.** F **to pick a bone with s.o.,** chercher querelle* à qn/chercher noise à qn; **to have a bone to pick with s.o.,** avoir maille à partir avec qn **3.** F (*esp joke*) **close to/near the bone,** risqué; **that's a bit near the bone!** ça, c'est un peu osé/salé! **4.** *pl* F dés*; **to roll the bones,** pousser les bobs **5.** *pl* F (*not common*) médecin *m*/toubib *m* **6.** V **to have a bone,** être en érection*/avoir la trique/bander. (*See* **bone-on**; **boner** 2; **dry** 1; **marrow-bones**; **sawbones**)

bone² [boun] *vtr&i* P **1.** (*not common*) voler*/chiper **2.** *NAm* ennuyer*/barber/canuler (qn) **3.** *esp NAm* **to bone (up on) a subject,** piocher/potasser un sujet.

bonehead ['bounhed] *n F* imbécile *m*/crétin *m*/bûche *f*.

bone-on ['bounɔn] *n V* érection*/ bandaison *f*/trique *f*. (*See* **bone**¹ 6)

bone-orchard ['bounɔitʃəd] *P* cimetière*/le boulevard des allongés.

boner ['bounər] *n NAm* **1.** *F* bévue*/bourde *f*/gaffe *f* **2.** *V* (*rare*) = **bone**¹ 6; **bone-on**.

bone-shaker ['bounʃeikər] *n F* (*a*) vieille voiture*/vieille guimbarde/tape-cul *m* (*b*) (*bike*) vélocipède *m*.

bone-yard ['bounjaid] *n P* = **bone-orchard**.

bonk¹ [bɔŋk] *n F* coup*/gnon *m*.

bonk² [bɔŋk] *vtr F* **to bonk s.o. on the head**, donner un coup* sur la tête de qn/assommer qn.

bonkers ['bɔŋkəz] *a P* dingue/cinglé; **stark raving bonkers**, fou* à lier.

bonzer ['bɔnzər] *a Austr A F* excellent*/sensass/super.

boo [buɪ] *n P* (*drugs*) marijuana*/kif *m*.

boob¹ [buɪb] *n* **1.** *F* (*i*) individu bête*/ballot *m*/crétin *m* (*ii*) nigaud *m*/benêt *m* **2.** *F* bévue*/gaffe *f* **3.** *pl P* **boobs**, seins*/nénés *mpl*/ nichons *mpl*/lolos *mpl*; **she's got huge boobs**, elle a de gros nénés **4.** *P* (*a*) prison* (*b*) = poste *m* de police/gendarmerie *f*.

boob² [buɪb] *vi F* faire une bévue*/ une gaffe; **I really boobed there**, je m'y suis gouré/je me suis foutu dedans.

booboo ['buɪbuɪ] *n* **1.** *F* bévue*/ bourde *f*/gaffe *f* **2.** *pl A P* testicules*/clopinettes *fpl*.

boob tube ['buɪb'tjuɪb] *n F* **1.** *NAm* télévision *f*/télé *f*/téloche *f*. (*See* **tube** 3) **2.** bustier *m*.

booby ['buɪbi] *n* **1.** *O F* imbécile*/ nigaud *m* **2.** *pl A P* seins*/ doudounes *fpl*.

booby-hatch ['buɪbihætʃ] *n P* **1.** *NAm* maison *f* de fous/cabanon *m* **2.** *esp Austr* = **boob**¹ 4.

boodle ['buɪdl] *n esp NAm P* butin*/fade *m*.

boofhead ['buɪfhed] *n Austr A F* individu *m* bête*.

boogie ['buɪgi] *n* **1.** *esp NAm P* sorte de blues sur lequel on danse; **to dance to the boogie**, danser/faire le boogie-woogie **2.** *NAm A P* (*pej*) Noir(e)*/nègre *mf*/bougnoul(e) *m(f)*.

book¹ [buk] *n F* **1. to throw the book at s.o.** (*i*) donner la peine maximum à qn; **the judge threw the book at him**, le juge l'a fadé; **he got the book thrown at him**, il a attrapé le maxi (*ii*) engueuler qn; **my mother threw the book at me**, ma mère m'a fait un amphi **2. to be in s.o.'s good books**, être dans les petits papiers de qn; **I'm not in his good books**, il ne m'a pas à la bonne **3. it suits my book**, ça me va/ça me botte. (*See* **cook**² 2; **turn-up** 1)

book² [buk] *vtr F* **to book s.o.**, dresser une contravention à qn/ mettre/coller un PV (= procès-verbal) à qn; **to get booked** (*i*) (*speeding, parking*) se faire coller un PV (*ii*) (*sport*) recevoir un avertissement; **the ref booked him**, l'arbitre a pris son nom.

bookie ['buki] *n F* book *m*.

booky ['buki] *n F* = **bookie**.

boom box ['buɪm'bɔks] *n P* lecteur *m* de cassettes stéréo portable. (*See* **ghetto blaster**)

boomer ['buɪmər] *n Austr F* qch d'énorme/de géant/de maousse.

boondocks ['buɪndɔks], **boonies** ['buɪniz] *npl NAm P* le bled/le trou.

boondoggle¹ ['buɪndɔgl] *n NAm P* objet *m* ou *esp* travail *m* sans grande valeur.

boondoggle² ['buːndɔgl] *vi NAm P* perdre son temps à faire des choses inutiles et sans importance; peigner la giraffe.

boong [buŋ] *n Austr F* (*pej*) aborigène *mf*.

boot [buːt] *n* **1.** *P* **to give s.o. the (order of the) boot,** congédier qn/ flanquer qn à la porte; **he got the boot from his job,** il s'est fait sacqué de son boulot **2.** *P* **to put the boot in,** donner un coup de pied vicieux (à qn)/tabasser (qn)/ passer(qn) à tabac **3.** *F* **to be too big for one's boots,** péter plus haut que son derrière **4.** *F* **to lick s.o.'s boots,** flatter* qn/lécher les bottes/ lécher le cul à qn/faire de la lèche à qn **5.** *P* **to splash one's boots,** uriner*/lancequiner/mouiller une ardoise. (*See* **bet 4**; **bovver-boots**; **slyboots**)

bootlicker ['buːtlikər] *n F* lèche-bottes *m*/lèche-cul *m*.

boot out ['but'aut] *vtr P* se débarrasser* de/sacquer/vider/virer (qn); **he got booted out of the army,** il a été viré de l'armée.

booze¹ [buːz] *n P* alcool*/pinard *m*; **to be on the/to hit the booze,** boire* beaucoup/picoler/se biturer; **must cut down on the booze,** faut que j'arrête de boire.

booze² [buːz] *vi P* boire*/lever le coude/picoler/biberonner.

boozed (up) ['buːzd('ʌp)] *a P* ivre*/soûl/bourré.

boozer ['buːzər] *P* **1.** ivrogne*/ poivrot *m*/soûlaud *m* **2.** (*pub*) café*/bistrot *m*/troquet *m*.

booze-up ['buːzʌp] *n P* soûlerie *f*; **let's have a booze-up!** on va se payer une bonne cuite!

boozy ['buːzi] *a P* ivrogne/soûlard; **we had a boozy evening,** on a passé la soirée à boire.

bo-peep ['bou'piːp] *n P* (*RS = sleep*) dodo *m*.

boracic [bə'ræsik, 'bræsik] *a P* (*RS*

= *boracic lint* = *skint*) très pauvre*/dans la dèche/sans un/ fauché/raide. (*See* **skint**)

born [bɔːn] *a&pp F* **1. in all my born days,** de toute ma vie; **never in all my born days have I heard so much rubbish!** jamais je n'ai entendu tant de conneries! **2. I wasn't born yesterday,** je ne suis pas né d'hier/je ne suis pas tombé de la dernière pluie. (*See* **one 7**)

bosh [bɔʃ] *n F* bêtises*/boniments *mpl*/sornettes *fpl*; **what bosh!** des bêtises!

boss¹ [bɔs] **I** *a NAm P* excellent*/ chouette; **we had a boss time,** on s'est rudement amusés **II** *n F* patron*/singe *m*/boss *m*/chef *m*; **he's the boss around here,** c'est lui qui commande ici.

boss² [bɔs] *vtr P* **1.** mener/diriger; **to boss the show,** être le manitou de l'affaire/tenir la barre/faire marcher la machine.

boss about ['bɔsə'baut], **boss around** ['bɔsə'raund] *vtr F* **to boss s.o. about,** mener qn par le bout du nez/faire marcher qn/faire la loi à qn.

boss-eyed ['bɔsaid] *a P* qui louche*/qui a un œil* qui dit merde à l'autre.

boss-man ['bɔsmæn] *n F* = **boss¹ II.**

bossy ['bɔsi] *a F* autoritaire; **he's (too) bossy,** c'est un Monsieur Jordonne.

bossy-boots ['bɔsibuts] *n F* individu* autoritaire/grand manitou; **she's a real bossy-boots,** c'est un vrai gendarme, celle-là.

bother ['bɔðər], **botheration** [bɔðə'reiʃ(ə)n] *excl F* zut!/flûte!/la barbe!

bottle¹ ['bɔtl] *n P* **1. to hit/to be on the bottle,** caresser la bouteille/ biberonner/picoler **2.** (*i*) (*courage*) sang-froid *m*/cran *m* (*ii*) (*cheek, nerve*) culot *m*/toupet *m*; **lost your**

bottle? t'as le trac? **he lost his bottle?** t'as le trac? **he lost his bottle,** il s'est dégonflé. (*See* **bluebottle**; **milk-bottles**; **titty-bottle**)

bottle² ['bɔtl] *P* **I** *vtr* (*not common*) taper (qn) à coups de bouteille **II** *vtr&i* avoir peur*/se dégonfler/avoir le trouillomètre à zéro.

bottled ['bɔtld] *a P* **1.** ivre*/bourré **2.** lâche*/peureux/froussard; **he bottled it,** il s'est dégonflé/il a la frousse; il a la chiasse/les chocottes.

bottler ['bɔtlər] *n P* voiture *f* difficile à vendre. (*See* **palm-tree**; **square-wheeler**)

bottle-washer ['bɔtlwɔʃər] *n see* **cook¹** **2.**

bottom ['bɔtəm] **I** *a F* **to bet one's bottom dollar,** risquer le paquet; **you can bet your bottom dollar that** ..., je te fiche/fous mon billet que .... (*See* **bet 4**) **II** *n F* **1.** fesses*/derrière *m*/postérieur *m* **2.** **bottoms up!** videz vos verres!/cul sec! (*See* **bell-bottoms**; **heap 2**; **rock¹ 4**; **scrape² 1**)

botty ['bɔti] *n F* (*esp child's language*) = **bottom² 1.** (*See* **smack-botty**)

bounce [bauns] *vtr* **1.** *P* congédier*/flanquer (qn) à la porte (d'une boîte de nuit, etc)/vider **2.** *F* **to bounce a cheque,** renvoyer un chèque sans provision; **he paid with a cheque that bounced,** il m'a filé un chèque en bois.

bouncer ['baunsər] *n P* **1.** videur *m* (d'une boîte de nuit, etc) **2.** *pl* (*not common*) seins*/rotoplots *mpl* **3.** chèque *m* en bois.

bovver ['bɔvər] *n P* (= *bother*) bagarre *f*/grabuge *m*; **don't give us any bovver!** pas d'histoires, hein!/pas de grabuge ici!

bovver-boots ['bɔvə'buːts] *npl P* chaussures* des **bovverboys**/= Dr Martens *mpl* (*RTM*). (*See* **DMs**)

bovver-boy ['bɔvəbɔi] *n P* jeune

voyou *m esp* aux cheveux tondus ras/= skinhead *m*.

bowl over ['boul'ouvər] *vtr F* **1.** épater/sidérer; **he was bowled over by our present,** notre cadeau l'a rendu tout chose/l'a sidéré; **I was bowled over by that,** j'en ai été soufflé **2.** chambouler.

box¹ [bɔks] *n* **1.** *V* sexe de la femme*/boîte *f* à ouvrage **2.** *F* télé *f*/téloche *f*; **what's on the box?** qu'est-ce qu'il y a la téloche? (*See* **goggle-box**; **idiot-box**) **3.** *P* cercueil*/boîte *f* à dominos; **to go home in a box,** mourir*/partir les pieds en avant **4.** *P* coffre-fort *m*/coffiot *m* **5.** *P* (*RS* = *box of fruit* = *suit*) costume *m*/complet *m*. (*See* **brain-box**; **jack-in-the-box**; **saucebox**; **squeezebox**; **thinkbox**)

box² [bɔks] *vtr P* mettre (qn) en prison*/en taule; coffrer (qn).

boxed [bɔkst] *a P* **1.** (*a*) ivre*/rétamé*/bourré (*b*) drogué*/camé/défoncé **2.** emprisonné*/bloqué/bouclé/coffré.

boy [bɔi] **I** *excl F* **1.** oh boy!/boy oh boy! chouette alors!/oh là là! **2.** **boy, did she tear me off a strip!** mes enfants! qu'est-ce qu'elle m'a passé! **II** *n F* **1.** *F* **hello, old boy!** salut, vieille branche/vieux pote! **2.** *P* (*drugs*) héroïne*/héro *f*/boy *m*. (*See* **backroom**; **bovver-boy**; **bum-boy**; **doughboy**; **glamour-boy**; **jay-boy**; **J-boy**; **jewboy**; **job 11**; **K-boy**; **lover-boy**; **old-boy**; **playboy**; **sandboy**; **wide 1**)

boyo ['bɔijou] *n P* fiston *m*; **listen boyo!** écoute mon gars!

bracelets ['breislits] *npl F* menottes*/bracelets *mpl*/cadènes *fpl*.

bracer ['breisər] *n F* (*drink*) remontant *m*/tonique *m*.

braille [breil] *n Austr P* (**bit of) braille,** renseignement*/tuyau *m*/info *f*.

brain¹ [brein] *n F* **1.** **to have brains,** être intelligent*/une grosse tête/un crac/une lumière **2. he's the brains of the outfit**, il est le cerveau de la bande **3. to have s.o./sth on the brain**, être obsédé par qn/qch; **he's got it on the brain**, il ne pense qu'à ça **4. to beat/to rack one's brains**, se creuser la cervelle/les méninges. (*See* **birdbrain**; **featherbrain**; **lame-brain**; **scatter-brain**)

brain² [brein] *vtr* F battre*/rosser/ casser la figure (à qn); **if you don't shut up I'll brain you!** ferme-la ou je t'assomme!

brain-box ['breinbɔks] *n* O F crâne *m*/ciboulot *m*.

brainchild ['breintʃaild] *n* F idée originale; **this model is his brainchild**, c'est son invention(, ce modèle).

brain drain ['brein'drein] *n* F fuite *f*/exode *m*/drainage *m* des cerveaux.

brainwave ['breinweiv] *n* F inspiration *f*/idée *f* de génie; **and then he had a real brainwave**, et alors, il a eu l'inspiration.

brainy ['breini] *a* F intelligent*/ doué/calé/débrouillard.

brass [brɑːs] **I** *a* F **to get down to brass tacks**, se concentrer sur l'essentiel/en venir aux faits. (*See* **balls¹** 4) **II** *n* **1.** *P* argent*/ pognon *m*/pèze *m*; (*catchphrase*) **where there's muck there's brass**, il y a toujours du fric dans les ordures **2.** *P* toupet *m*/culot *m*; **he's got the brass to do it**, il est assez culotté pour le faire **3.** *F* **top brass**, les huiles *fpl* **4.** *P* prostituée*/pute *f*/tapineuse *f*. (*See* **half-brass**)

brassed off ['brɑːst'ɔf] *a* P de mauvaise humeur/de mauvais poil.

brass-hat ['brɑːs'hæt] *n* F (*mil*) galonné *m*/galonnard *m*.

brass monkey(s) ['brɑːs'mʌŋki(z)] *n* P **it's brass monkey weather/it's a bit brass monkeys**, on

se les caille/on se les miches/on pèle (de froid). (*See* **balls¹** 4)

brassy ['brɑːsi] *a* P effronté/culotté.

bread [bred] *n* **1.** *P* argent*/ galette *f*/blé *m*/oseille *f* **2.** *P* **to be on the bread line**, être sans le sou/ claquer du bec/danser devant le buffet **3.** *F* **that's his bread and butter**, c'est son gagne-pain/c'est avec ça qu'il gagne sa croûte.

bread-and-butter ['bred-ən(d)'bʌtər] *a* F **1.** (*politics*) **bread-and-butter issues**, le prix du bifteck **2. bread-and-butter letter**, lettre de remerciement/de château. (*See* **bread** 3)

bread-basket ['bredbɑːskit] *n* F ventre*/bedaine *f*/brioche *f*; **to get one in the bread-basket**, recevoir un coup* dans le gésier.

breadhooks ['bred'huks] *npl* P mains*/croches *fpl*. (*See* **hooks**; **meathooks**)

break [breik] *n* F **1.** de la chance*/coup *m* de pot; **that was a lucky break for us**, on a eu de la veine/du pot/du cul. (*See* **tough I** 4) **2. to give s.o. a break** (*i*) donner sa chance à qn (*ii*) tendre la perche à qn; **come on, give me/us a break!** arrête ton char!/laisse-moi souffler un peu! **3.** récréation *f*/ récré *f*/repos *m*; **a break for lunch**, une pause pour le déjeuner; **coffee break**, pause-café *f* **4.** évasion *f* de prison*/cavale *f*; **to make a break for it**, se faire la malle.

break up ['breik'ʌp] *vtr* F **break it up!** arrêtez/finissez de vous battre!

breather ['briːðər] *n* F moment *m* de répit/de repos; **give me a breather**, laisse-moi tranquille; laisse-moi souffler un peu; arrête ton char! **to go out for a breather**, sortir prendre l'air.

breeze [briːz] *n* P **1.** O querelle*; **there was a bit of a breeze when he got home**, il y a eu du grabuge quand il est rentré **2. it was a**

breeze, c'était facile/c'était l'enfance de l'art. (*See* **shoot**[2] **7**)

breeze in, out ['briːz'in, aut] *vi F* **1.** entrer/sortir (*i*) en coup de vent (*ii*) d'une façon désinvolte **2.** *esp NAm* (*racing*) **to breeze in,** arriver dans un fauteuil.

breeze off ['briːz'ɔf] *vi NAm F* (*not common*) partir*/se barrer/se débiner.

breezy ['briːzi] *a F* (**all**) **bright and breezy,** plein d'entrain/d'attaque.

brekker ['brekər] *n,* **brekky** ['breki] *n F* (= *breakfast*) petit déjeuner.

brick [brik] *n F* **1. he's been a (real) brick,** c'est le meilleur des potes; **be a brick!** sois sympa! **2. to drop a brick,** faire une bévue*/lâcher le pavé dans la mare **3.** *P* (*drugs*) kilo *m* de marijuana* *ou* haschisch* présenté sous forme compressée. (*See* **come down 3; drop**[2] **1; goldbrick**[1]; **wall 4, 5, 6**)

bride [braid] *n A P* **1.** jeune fille*/gamine *f* **2.** petite amie *f*/nénette *f.*

bridewell ['braidwel] *n P* commissariat *m* de police/quart *m.*

brief [briːf] *n P* (*i*) = avocat *m* (*ii*) = notaire *m.*

Brighton line ['braitn'lain] *F see* **bingo 59.**

bring down ['briŋ'daun] *vtr&i P* déprimer/attrister/rendre cafardeux; **the news really brought him down,** la nouvelle ne lui a pas remonté le moral/lui a foutu le cafard. (*See* **brought down; house 3**)

bring off ['briŋ'ɔf] *vtr P* masturber*/branler (qn); faire jouir qn; **he brings himself off like that,** il se branle comme ça/c'est comme ça qu'il prend son pied.

bring up ['briŋ'ʌp] *vi P* = **back up 2.**

brinkmanship ['briŋkmənʃip] *n F* politique *f* du bord de l'abîme.

briny ['braini] *n O F* **the briny,** l'océan *m*/la Grande Tasse.

bristlers ['brisləz] *npl A P* seins*/nichons *mpl*/nénés *mpl.*

Bristol-fashion ['bristəlfæʃən] *adv F* (**ship-shape and**) **Bristol-fashion,** bien rangé/en ordre/impec/parfaitement comme il faut.

Bristols, bristols ['bristəlz] *npl P* (*RS* = *Bristol City's* = *titties*) seins*/nichons *mpl*/lolos *mpl*; **a nice pair of Bristols,** une belle paire d'amortisseurs. (*See* **fit**[1] **II 3; tale 3; threepenny-bits; trey-bits**)

bro [brou] *n esp NAm F* frère*/frangin *m*/frèrot *m.*

broad [brɔːd] *n NAm P* **1.** (*a*) fille*/femme*/gonzesse *f*/nana *f*; **she's just a dumb broad,** c'est une vraie connasse (*b*) prostituée*/pute *f*/grue *f* **2.** *pl A* cartes* à jouer; **to fake the broads,** truquer les cartes/maquiller les brèmes.

brodie, brody ['broudi] *n NAm P* (*not common*) échec*/four *m*/fiasco *m*; gaffe *f.*

broke [brouk] *a F* **1. to be broke/dead broke/flat broke/stony broke,** être pauvre*/être sans un/être sans le sou/dans la dêche/sans un radis; **to be broke to the wide,** être fauché (comme les blés) **2.** (*gambling*) **to go for broke,** risquer tout/risquer le paquet.

broker ['broukər] *n P* trafiquant *m*/fourgue *m.*

brolly ['brɔli] *n F* **1.** parapuie*/pépin *m*/riflard *m*/pébroque *m* **2.** parachute*/pépin *m.*

bronco ['brɔŋkou] *n NAm F* cheval sauvage/non dressé.

bronco-buster ['brɔŋkoubʌstər] *n NAm F* cowboy *m* (qui dresse des chevaux sauvages).

brought down ['brɔːt'daun] *pp P* (*drug addicts*) déprimé après le flash. (*See* **bring down**)

brown[1] [braun] **I** *a* **to be done brown,** se faire entuber/se faire enculer; **brown job,** coït anal*/ baisage *m* à la riche **II** *n A V* anus*/trou *m* de balle.

brown² ['braun] *vtr V* (*i*) sodomiser*/enculer (qn) (*ii*) se faire enculer.

brown-hatter ['braun'hætər] *n V* homosexuel*/tante *f*/pédé *m*.

brownie ['brauni] *n O V* anus*/ trou *m* du cul.

brown-nose ['braunnouz] *vtr V* lécher le cul à (qn).

brown off ['braun'ɔf] *vtr P* décourager (qn); **to be browned off,** avoir le cafard/broyer du noir; **that really browns me off,** ça me fiche la déprime/le cafard/le noir.

bruiser ['bruɪzər] *n F* (*i*) boxeur *m* (*ii*) cogneur *m*.

Brum [brʌm] *Prn F* Birmingham.

brumby ['brʌmbi] *n Austr F* cheval *m* sauvage.

Brummie ['brʌmi] *n F* habitant *m* de Birmingham.

brunch [brʌntʃ] *n F* repas *m* tenant lieu de *breakfast* et *lunch*.

brush [brʌʃ] *n* **1.** *P* = **brush-off 1** **2.** *Austr P* jeune femme*/ minette *f*/nana *f* **3.** *V* pubis féminin/barbu *m*. (*See* **tar²**; **tarbrush**)

brush-off ['brʌʃɔf] *n F* **to give s.o. the brush-off,** se débarrasser* de qn/envoyer promener qn/envoyer balader qn; **he gave her the brush-off,** il l'a envoyée chier.

brush off ['brʌʃɔf] *vtr F* **to brush s.o. off** (*i*) snober qn (*ii*) se débarrasser* de qn; **he brushed her off with no excuse,** il l'a envoyée sur les roses.

bubbies ['bʌbiz] *npl A P* (*rare*) seins*/nichons *mpl*.

bubble-and-squeak ['bʌbl-ən(d)'skwiːk] *n* **1.** *F* réchauffé *m* (en friture) de pommes de terre et de choux **2.** *P* (*RS* = *Greek*) un

Grec **3.** *P* (*RS* = *beak* = *magistrate*): *see* **beak 1.**

bubbly ['bʌbli] *n F* champagne *m*/ champ(e) *m*; **a bottle of bubbly,** une roteuse. (*See* **champers**)

bubs [bʌbz] *npl A P* (*rare*) seins*/ nichons *mpl*.

buck¹ [bʌk] *n* **1.** *NAm F* dollar *m*; **to make a fast buck,** obtenir/gagner de l'argent rapidement et sans faire de scrupules; **to make a few bucks on the side,** se faire un peu de fric (au noir)/se faire un petit à-côté **2.** *F* **to pass the buck,** filer la responsabilité à qn/faire porter le chapeau à qn.

buck² [bʌk] *vi F* **to buck against sth,** résister à/s'opposer à/regimber devant qch.

bucked [bʌkt] *a O F* ragaillardi/ content; enchanté.

bucket ['bʌkit] *n F* **1. to kick the bucket,** mourir*/lâcher la rampe/ casser sa pipe/avaler son bulletin de naissance **2. it's raining buckets,** il pleut à seaux.

bucket down ['bʌkit'daun] *vi F* **it's bucketing down out there,** il pleut à seaux/il tombe des hallebardes dehors.

bucket shop ['bʌkit'ʃɔp] *n F* agence *f* de voyages à prix réduits.

buckle ['bʌkl] *vtr&i P* **1. buckle my shoe:** *see* **bingo (2)** **2. to buckle down to sth,** s'appliquer à qch; **buckle down to your work, lads!** au boulot, les gars!

bucko ['bʌkou] *a P Irish* (*term of address*) **(me) bucko!** mon vieux!

buckshee¹ ['bʌk'ʃiː] *a F* gratuit*/ gratis/à l'œil.

buck up ['bʌk'ʌp] *F* **1.** remonter le moral à (qn); **come on, buck up! it's not so bad!** allons, du courage! c'est pas si mal que ça! **2.** se dépêcher*/se grouiller **3.** he'd **better buck up his ideas a little,** il ferait bien de se débrouiller un peu.

bud [bʌd] *n F* **1.** *NAm* **listen, bud!** écoute, mon vieux!/écoute, mec! (*See* **buddy 1**) **2. to nip sth in the bud,** tuer/étouffer qch dans l'œuf.

buddy ['bʌdi] *n F* ami*/copain *m*/pote *m*; **they're great buddies,** ils sont comme cul et chemise.

buddy-buddy ['bʌdibʌdi] *a F* **to be buddy-buddy,** être amis comme cochons/s'entendre comme des larrons en foire.

buddy up ['bʌdi'ʌp] *vi NAm F* (*esp university/faculty*) partager une chambre avec qn.

buff [bʌf] *n F* **1. in the buff,** tout nu*/à poil **2.** (*enthusiast*) **film buff,** mordu *m*/fana *mf* du ciné.

buffalo ['bʌfəlou] *vtr NAm F* intimider/entortiller/entourlouper (qn).

bug¹ [bʌg] *n* **1.** *F* micro clandestin **2.** *F* accroc *m*/pépin *m*; **a bug in the works,** un défaut dans la machine **3.** *F* obsession *f*/marotte *f*; **he's been bitten by the jogging bug,** c'est un mordu/un dingue du jogging **4.** *F* (*infection*) microbe *m*/bactérie *f*; **I must have picked up a bug,** j'ai dû attraper quelque chose **5.** *F* (*catchphrase*) **as snug as a bug in a rug,** tranquille comme Baptiste **6.** *P* **love bugs = crabs** (*see* **crab¹ 2**). (*See* **big I 1**; **doodle-bug**; **fire-bug**; **jitterbug**; **litterbug**)

bug² [bʌg] *vtr&i* **1.** *F* installer des micros clandestins (dans une salle, etc); **the phone's bugged,** le bigophone est branché sur la table d'écoute **2.** *P* **to bug s.o.,** ennuyer* qn/embêter qn/casser les pieds à qn; **stop bugging me!** m'emmerde pas!/écrase! **what's bugging you?** qu'est-ce qui te chiffonne?/qu'est-ce qui te turlupine?

bug-eyed ['bʌgaid] *a F* **1. to be bug-eyed** (*i*) avoir les yeux* en boules de loto (*ii*) avoir les yeux à fleur de tête **2. bug-eyed monster,** monstre atomique.

bugger¹ ['bʌgər] *n V* **1.** saligaud *m*; **he's a filthy bugger!** c'est un salaud*/un sale type **2.** con *m*/couillon *m*; **don't play silly buggers with me!** (ne) te paye pas ma tête!/(ne) fais pas le con avec moi!/arrête de déconner! **3.** (*affectionately*) individu*/type *m*; **a cute little bugger,** une gentille petite fripouille; **poor little bugger!** pauvre petit bonhomme! **a silly (old) bugger,** un pauvre (vieux) con/une (vieille) andouille; **what a lucky bugger!** le veinard!/il a eu du cul! **4. that's a real bugger!** ça c'est couillon!/ça c'est couille! **a bugger of a job,** une saloperie/un putain de boulot **5. I don't give a bugger!** je n'en ai rien à foutre!

bugger² ['bʌgər] *vtr V* **1. bugger (it)!** merde (alors)! **bugger you!** va te faire foutre!/je t'emmerde! **2. that's buggered it!** ça a tout foutu en l'air! **3. it's buggered,** c'est foutu **4. it's got me buggered,** j'en suis bien baisé **5. well, I'm buggered!** ça c'est trop fort!

bugger about, around ['bʌgərə'baut, ə'raund] *vi V* **1.** perdre son temps/se la couler douce/ne rien foutre **2.** manier/tripoter qch; **stop buggering about with that!** arrête de tripoter ça! **to bugger about with s.o.,** peloter qn/mettre la main au panier **3. to bugger s.o. about,** faire tourner qn en bourrique.

bugger-all ['bʌgə'rɔːl] *n V* rien*/des clous/que dalle.

buggeration! ['bʌgə'reiʃən] *excl O* tonnerre de Dieu!/bordel de Dieu!

buggered ['bʌgəd] *a V* fatigué*/foutu; **I'm buggered,** je suis crevé. (*See* **bugger² 3, 4**)

bugger off ['bʌgə'rɔf] *vi V* partir*/foutre le camp; **I told him to bugger off,** je lui ai dit de foutre le camp.

bugger up ['bʌgə'rʌp] *vtr V* bousiller/saboter; **you've buggered**

it up again! tu l'as encore salopé!/ tu nous refais les mêmes conneries!

buggery ['bʌgəri] *n O V* **1.** **like buggery!** mon œil!/mon cul! **can she cook? can she buggery!** et pour la bouffe? mon cul!/rien à faire!/ que dalle!/zéro! **2. (all) to buggery,** complètement/jusqu'au trognon/en brise-tout **3.** *esp Austr* **go to buggery!** va te faire voir!/va te faire foutre!

buggy ['bʌgi] *a* **1.** *NAm P* fou*/timbré/louftingue **2.** *F* (= *beach buggy, dune buggy*) bagnole *f.*

bug-house ['bʌghaus] **I** *a NAm P* fou*/cinglé **II** *n P* asile *m* de fous/maison *f* de dingues/cabanon *m.*

bug out ['bʌg'aut] *vi NAm P* **1.** se dégonfler/retirer ses marrons du feu **2.** s'enfuir*/déguerpir; **bug out, kid!** tire-toi, mon vieux!

bugs [bʌgz] *a NAm P* fou*/cinglé/dingue.

bulge [bʌldʒ] *n F* **1.** (*hum*) **the battle of the bulge,** la bataille du bide/la lutte pour la ligne **2.** (*euph*) **he's got a nice bulge,** il est bien équipé/bien monté.

bull [bul] *n P* **1.** policier*/flic *m*/condé *m.* (*See* **fly-bull**) **2.** (= *bullshit*) foutaises *fpl*/conneries *fpl*; **don't give me all that bull!** arrête de déconner!/déconne pas!/arrête ton baratin! **bull!** quelles conneries!/mon cul! **3.** (*RS* = *row*) **bull and cow,** querelle*. (*See* **rag¹** 4; **shoot²** 7)

bulldagger ['buldægər] *n P* = **bull-dyke.**

bulldoze ['buldouz] *vtr F* intimider (qn) (pour lui faire faire qch).

bull-dyke ['buldaik] *n P* lesbienne* qui tient le rôle de l'homme/vrille *f.* (*See* **dyke**)

bullet ['bulit] *n P* **1.** capsule *f* contenant de la drogue **2. to give s.o. the bullet,** se débarrasser* de qn/sacquer qn/virer qn; **he got the bul-**

let, on l'a flanqué/il s'est fait flanquer à la porte **3.** *pl* sperme*/semoule *f;* **to give s.o. the bullets,** envoyer le paquet.

bullion-fringe ['buljən'frindʒ] *n F* (*mil*) feuilles *fpl* de chêne/graine *f* d'épinards. (*See* **egg 3**)

bull session ['bʌl'seʃ(ə)n] *n NAm F* **they were having a bull session,** il se taillaient une bavette entre hommes.

bullseye ['bulzai] *n F see* **bingo 50.**

bullshine ['bulʃain] *n F euph for* **bullshit¹.**

bullshit¹ ['bulʃit] *n P* bêtises*/foutaises *fpl*/conneries *fpl*; **to talk bullshit,** déconner; **that's bullshit,** c'est des conneries/c'est de la couille/c'est du baratin; **bullshit!** mon cul! **bullshit artist** = **bulshitter 1, 2.**

bullshit² [bulʃit] *vi P* (*a*) baratiner/dévider/jaspiner (*b*) déconner.

bullshitter ['bulʃitər] *n P* **1.** baratineur *m*/jaspineur *m* **2.** con *m*/connard *m.*

bully ['buli] **I** *a F* **bully for you!** bravo!/chapeau! **II** *n A P* (*rare*) souteneur*/maquereau *m*/Alphonse *m.*

bum¹ [bʌm] **I** *a esp NAm F* piètre/minable/moche; **a bum deal,** un sale coup/un coup en vache; **bum steer,** faux renseignement*/tuyau crevé; (*drugs*) **a bum trip,** un mauvais voyage. (*See* **kick¹** 3) **II** *n P* **1.** fesses*/postérieur *m*/cul *m;* **a kick up the bum,** un coup de pied au cul **2.** paresseux*/fainéant *m*/feignant *m;* **he's a lazy bum,** c'est un tire-au-cul; **beach bum/ski bum,** fana *mf* de la plage/du ski **3.** *esp NAm* clochard*/clodo *m.* (*See* **bum's rush; touch-your-bum**)

bum² [bʌm] *vtr P* **1.** emprunter* (qch)/taper (qn); **can I bum a fag/a cig (off you)?** t'as une clope à me filer? **to bum a lift,** faire de l'autostop/du stop; **to bum a meal off s.o.,** se faire payer à dîner par qn **2.** vivre aux crochets de qn **3.** = **bum around 4.** vivre en clochard*/faire le clodo.

bum around ['bʌmə'raund] *vi P* paresser*/fainéanter/tirer au cul.

bum-boy ['bʌmbɔi] *n P* (*not common*) homosexuel*/pédé *m*/enculé *m*.

bumf [bʌmf] *n F* (= **bum-fodder**) **1.** papier *m* hygiènique/papier-cul *m*/P-cul *m* **2.** paperasserie *f*; **the taxman sent me all this bumf,** le percepteur m'a envoyé toutes ces paperasseries/tout ce papier-cul.

bum-fodder ['bʌmfɔdər] *n O P* = **bumf.**

bum-freezer ['bʌmfriːzər] *n P* (*jacket*) pet-en-l'air *m*/rase-pet *m*.

bum-hole ['bʌm(h)oul] *n V* anus*/ anneau *m*/rond *m*.

bummer ['bʌmər] *n P* **1.** bousillage *m* **2.** (*i*) fainéant *m*/feignant *m*/écornifleur *m* (*ii*) clochard*/ clodo *m* **3.** déception *f*/sale expérience *f*; **that party was a real bummer!** quelle poisse/quelle barbe cette boum! **4.** (*drugs*) mauvais voyage; **he was on a bummer,** il flippait **5.** homosexuel*/pédé *m*/ tante *f*.

bumper ['bʌmpər] *n Austr F* mégot* (de cigarette)/clope *m*.

bumph [bʌmf] *n F* = **bumf.**

bump off ['bʌmp'ɔf] *vtr F* tuer*/ descendre/liquider (qn).

bum-rubber ['bʌmrʌbər] *n P* (*not common*) homosexuel*/pédé *m*.

bum's rush ['bʌmz'rʌʃ] *n P* **to give s.o. the bum's rush,** congédier* qn/balancer qn; **he got the bum's rush,** il a été flanqué à la porte.

bum-sucker ['bʌmsʌkər] *n P* lèche-cul *m*/lécheur *m*.

bun [bʌn] *n* **1.** *P* **to have a bun in the oven,** être enceinte*/avoir un polichinelle dans le tiroir **2.** *NAm*

O P **to have a bun on,** être ivre*/ être soûl. (*See* **currant-bun**)

bunch [bʌntʃ] *n* **1.** *F* **a bunch of idiots,** une bande* d'idiots **2.** *P* **a bunch of fives,** poing *m*/pogne *f*. (*See* **honeybunch**; **pick**)

bunco ['bʌŋkou] *vtr P* rouler (qn) au jeu (*surtout* aux cartes).

bundle ['bʌndl] *n* **1.** *F* grande somme d'argent*/liasse *f*/paquet *m*; **to make a bundle,** faire sa pelote/ son beurre **2.** *P* **to go a bundle,** s'enthousiasmer/s'emballer; **I don't go a bundle on that,** ça me m'emballe pas/ça ne me botte pas tellement **3.** *F* **a bundle of nerves,** un paquet de nerfs **4. this kid is a bundle of joy,** ce gosse est un amour.

bung [bʌŋ] *vtr&i P* **1.** jeter*/ envoyer; **bung it over here!** jette-moi ça! **2. my nose is bunged up,** j'ai le nez bouché/j'ai un gros rhume **3. to bung s.o.,** donner un pot de vin à qn/graisser la patte à qn.

bungalow ['bʌŋgəlou] *n P* individu bête*/bas *m* de plafond/andouille *f*.

bung-ho! ['bʌŋ'hou] *excl A F* **1.** au revoir!/ciao!/salut! **2.** à la tienne!

bung-hole ['bʌŋ(h)oul] *n* **1.** *A V* anus*/anneau *m* **2.** *F see* **bingo 50.**

bunk [bʌŋk] *n* **1.** *F* = **bunkum 2.** *P* **to do a bunk,** s'enfuir*/filer/se tirer/se faire la malle.

bunkum ['bʌŋkəm] *n F* bêtises*/ blagues *fpl*/foutaises *fpl*; **that's all bunkum!** tout ça c'est du bidon!/de la blague!

bunk-up ['bʌŋkʌp] *n P* **to give s.o. a bunk-up,** faire la courte échelle à qn.

bunny¹ ['bʌni] *n* **1.** *P* **bunny(girl),** hôtesse *f*/entraîneuse *f* **2.** *P* (*rare*) prostituée* pour lesbiennes*/chatte *f* jaune **3.** (*rare*) prostitué pour homosexuels*/micheton *m* **4.** *F* lapin *m*/Jeannot Lapin **5.** *P* bavardage *m*/bavette *f* **6.** *Austr P* dupe *f*/cave *m*/navet *m*. (*See* **dumb 1** (*b*); **jungle 3**)

bunny² ['bʌni] *vi P* bavarder*/(se) tailler une bavette. (*See* **rabbit²**)

bunny-fuck ['bʌnifʌk] *vi VV* faire l'amour* avec rapidité/fourailler à la une/tirer un coup vite fait.

burk(e) [bɜːk] *n P* individu bête/ gourde *f*/andouille *f*. (*See* **berk**)

burn¹ [bɜːn] *n A P* (*a*) cigarette*/ cibiche *f*; **to twist a burn**, rouler une cigarette* (*b*) (*drugs*) cigarette* de marijuana/joint *m*.

burn² [bɜːn] *vtr&i* **1.** *P* (*a*) escroquer*/arnaquer (*b*) voler*/ chaparder **2.** *NAm P* être exécuté par électrocution **3.** *P* (*a*) se mettre en colère*/en boule/en pétard; **that really burns me!** ça me fout vraiment en rogne! (*b*) mettre en colère*/énerver **4.** *F* conduire très vite*/foncer/gazer **5.** *O P* fumer*/ bombarder/bouffarder **6.** *F* **to burn the candle at both ends**, brûler la chandelle par les deux bouts **7.** *F* **to burn one's fingers/to get one's fingers burnt**, se brûler les doigts/se faire échauder **8.** *F* **to burn one's bridges/boats**, brûler les ponts/ses vaisseaux.

burned out ['bɜːnd'aut] *a&pp P* **1.** fatigué*/pompé **2.** (être) épuisé/dans un état d'apathie après avoir cessé de prendre des drogues **3.** ennuyé*/embêté.

burn-up ['bɜːnʌp] *n P* **to have a burn-up**, conduire très vite*/foncer/ brûler la route.

burn up ['bɜːn'ʌp] *vtr P* **to burn up the tarmac**, aller très vite*/brûler le pavé/brûler la route.

burp¹ [bɜːp] *n F* rot *m*.

burp² [bɜːp] *vi F* roter.

burp-gun ['bɜːpgʌn] *n NAm P* mitraillette*/sulfateuse *f*.

burton ['bɜːtn] *n F* **to go for a bur-**ton (*i*) disparaître (*ii*) (*aviation*) faire un trou dans l'eau (*iii*) mourir* (*iv*) tomber (par terre); **he's gone for a burton**, il a eu son compte/il est fichu; **he went for a burton**, il est tombé sur le nez.

bus [bʌs] *n F* **1.** (*a*) vieille bagnole/guimbarde *f* (*b*) (*plane*) (vieux) coucou *m* **2. to miss the bus**, manquer le coche/rater l'occasion. (*See* **back II 13**; **back-end**)

bush [buʃ] *n* **1.** *V* poils *mpl* du pubis féminin/cresson *m*/gazon *m*/ barbu *m* **2.** *P* (*drugs*) marijuana *f* **3.** *F* **bush telegraph**, téléphone *m* arabe **4.** *Austr F* **what do you think this is, bush week?** arrête ton char!/ne la ramène pas avec moi! (*See* **mulberry-bush**)

bushed [buʃt] *a P* **1.** désorienté/ interdit **2.** fatigué*/claqué/crevé.

bushel and peck ['buʃələn(d)- 'pek] *n P* (*RS = neck*) cou*.

bush-whacker ['buʃwækər] *n Austr F* qn qui habite au fin fond du bled/péquenot *m*/plouc *m*.

business ['biznis] *n* **1.** *F* **to mean business**, prendre les choses au sérieux/ne pas rigoler **2.** *F* **to do one's business**, déféquer*/débourrer **3.** *F* affaire *f*/histoire *f*; **what a filthy business!** quelle sale affaire! **4.** *F* **why he ever married her is nobody's business**, Dieu seul sait pourquoi il l'a épousée! **5.** *NAm* (*not common*) **the business** (*a*) *P* (*i*) traitement brutal (*ii*) réprimande *f*/ savon *m* (*b*) *V* (*i*) pénis* (*ii*) sexe de la femme* (*iii*) l'acte sexuel*/ baisage *m* (*c*) *P* attirail* de camé/ popote *f*/kit *m* **6.** (= *show business; music business, etc*) **his father was in the business**, son père faisait du show-biz **7.** *P* la prostitution/le bisness **8.** *P* **to look the business**, être très élégant/être sur son trente-et-un/être tiré à quatre épingles. (*See* **funny I 2**)

busk [bʌsk] *vi* **1.** *F* (*music*) jouer/ chanter dans la rue/dans le métro/

dans les bars (pour se faire de l'argent) **2.** *F* (*theatre*) jouer dans une troupe ambulante.

busker ['bʌskər] *n* **1.** *F* musicien *m*/chanteur *m* qui se fait de l'argent dans la rue/dans le métro/ dans les bars **2.** *F* comédien ambulant.

busman ['bʌsmən] *n F* **to take a busman's holiday,** faire du métier en guise de congé ou de loisirs.

bust¹ ['bʌst] **I** *a F* **1.** cassé/ esquinté; **my watch is bust,** ma montre est fichue/foutue **2.** (*a*) sans le sou/fauché (*b*) **to go bust,** faire faillite/boire un bouillon **II** *n P* **1.** échec*/fiasco *m*/four *m* **2.** réjouissances*/bamboche *f*/bringue *f* **3.** arrestation *f*/rafle *f* de police; **marijuana bust,** arrestation par la police pour usage de marijuana*.

bust² *vtr P* **1.** casser (un racket, etc) **2.** arrêter*/agrafer; **the club was busted for drugs,** la police a fait une descente dans le club pour chercher des stupéfiants; **he got busted for possession of cannabis,** il fut (*i*) arrêté (*ii*) mis en taule pour avoir été en possession de canna- bis* **3.** battre*/rosser; **to bust s.o.'s ass,** casser la gueule à qn **4. to bust a gut,** se décarcasser. (*See* **shit²** 3)

buster ['bʌstər] *n esp NAm F* homme*/type *m*; **listen, buster!** écoute, mec! mon gars!/écoute (*See* **ball-buster; blockbuster; bronco- buster; jaw-buster**)

bust in ['bʌst'in] *vtr&i P* **1. to bust s.o.'s face in,** casser la figure* à qn/ abîmer le portrait à qn **2. to bust in (on s.o.),** arriver* comme un chien dans un jeu de quilles **3. to bust in on s.o.'s conversation,** s'injecter dans la conversation.

bust open ['bʌst'oupən] *vtr P* **to bust open a safe,** casser un coffre- fort.

bust out ['bʌst'aut] *vi P* **1.** s'évader/faire sa malle **2. she's**

busting out all over, elle a des seins* plantureux/il y a du monde au balcon.

bust-up ['bʌstʌp] *n F* **1.** quer- elle*/engueulade *f*; **to have a bust- up with s.o.,** avoir une prise de bec avec qn/s'engueuler avec qn **2.** rupture *f*/mallette *f* et paquette *f*; **they've had a bust-up,** ils ont rompu.

bust up ['bʌst'ʌp] *vtr F* **1.** esquinter **(une pièce de machine, etc) 2.** rompre (une amitié)/briser (un mariage).

busty ['bʌsti] *a F* à la poitrine proéminente; **she's a rather busty lady,** il y a du monde au balcon.

butch [butʃ] *a&n P* **1.** (*a*) homme* fort et viril/dur *m*/macho *m* (*b*) homosexuel* actif/macho *m*/butch *m* **2.** femme*, *esp* lesbienne*, d'apparence *ou* de caractère mascu- lin/viriliste *f*.

butchers ['butʃəz] *n P* (*RS* = *butcher's hook* = *look*) coup d'œil*; **to take a butchers at sth,** regarder* qch/reluquer qch; **let's have a butchers,** fais voir.

butt [bʌt] *n NAm F* fesses*/derrière *m*; **get your butt out of here!** tire ton cul d'ici!

butter ['bʌtər] *n F* **she looks as though butter wouldn't melt in her mouth,** elle fait la Sainte-Nitouche/ elle fait la sucrée/on lui donnerait le bon Dieu sans confession. (*See* **bread 3; bread-and-butter**)

butterfingers ['bʌtəfiŋgəz] *n F* malagauche *mf*/malapatte *mf*; **to have butterfingers/to be a butterfin- gers,** avoir la main malheureuse/ être brise-tout; **butterfingers!** espèce d'empoté!

butterflies ['bʌtəflaiz] *npl F* **to have butterflies (in one's stomach/in one's tummy),** avoir peur*/avoir le trac/avoir les jetons.

butter up ['bʌtə'(r)ʌp] *vtr F* flatter*/pommader/passer de la pommade à (qn).

button[1] ['bʌtn] *n esp NAm* **1.** *P* menton *m*/bichonnet *m* **2.** *V* clitoris*/bouton *m* **3.** *F* **on the button,** à point/recta. (*See* **belly-button**; **panic 2**)

button[2] ['bʌtn] *vtr P* **button your mouth/lip!** (ferme) ton bec!

buttoned up ['bʌtnd'ʌp] *a&pp P* **1.** peu communicatif/constipé **2.** **it's all buttoned up,** c'est dans le sac/c'est du tout cuit.

buttonhole ['bʌtnhoul] *vtr F* accrocher/agrafer/cramponner (qn).

button men ['bʌtn'men] *npl P* agents *mpl* de police* (en uniforme)/habillés *mpl*.

butty ['bʌti] *n P* (*esp N. England*) **jam butty,** sandwich *m* à la confiture; **chip butty,** sandwich aux (pommes) frites.

buy [bai] *vtr* **1.** *F* (**go on,**) **I'll buy it,** vas-y, déballe! je donne ma langue au chat; **I'll buy that,** je marche/je suis d'acc/dac! **2.** *P* **he bought it/a packet** (*i*) il a écopé (*ii*) il a passé l'arme à gauche.

buyer ['baiər] *n P* receleur*/fourgue *m*.

buzz[1] [bʌz] *n* **1.** *F* **to give s.o. a buzz,** donner/passer un coup de fil à qn **2.** *P* plaisir violent/transport *m*; **rock gives me a real buzz,** le rock, ça me branche.

buzz[2] [bʌz] *vtr F* **1.** **to buzz s.o.,** passer un coup de fil à qn **2.** *F* (*aircraft*) coller/frôler/harceler un autre avion.

buzzer [bʌzər] *n* **1.** *P* (*pickpocket*) voleur* à la tire/fourche *f*/tireur *m*/fourchette *f* **2.** *F* téléphone*/ronfleur *m*/bigophone *m*.

buzz off ['bʌz'ɔf] *vi F* s'enfuir*/décamper/filer; **buzz off!** débarrasse!/fiche le camp!/casse-toi!

bye(-bye)! ['bai('bai)] *excl F* salut!/ciao!

bye-byes ['baibaiz] *npl F* (*child's talk*) dodo *m*; **go (to) bye-byes for mummy!** fais dodo pour maman!

BYO ['biwaiou] *abbr F* (= **bring your own**) apporter sa bouteille.

C

C, c [siː] *abbr* **1.** *P* (*drugs*) (= *cocaine*) **big c,** cocaïne*/coco *f*/ neige *f*; **C habit,** passion *f* d'un toxico pour la cocaïne **2.** (= *cancer*) **his fight against the Big C,** sa lutte contre le cancer.

cabbage ['kæbidʒ] *n F* (*pej*) **he's a real cabbage,** c'est un vrai crétin.

cabbage-head ['kæbidʒhed] *n NAm F* individu bête*/gourde *f*/ cornichon *m*.

cabbie, cabby ['kæbi] *n F* chauffeur *m* de taxi*/rongeur *m*/taxi *mf*.

caboodle [kə'buːdl] *n F* **the whole (kit and) caboodle,** et tout le Saint-Frusquin/et tout le bataclan/tout le fourbi. (*See* **boiling II; shebang 1; shoot¹ 1; shooting-match**)

cack¹ [kæk] *n A P* (*not common*) étron*/caca *m*.

cack² [kæk] *vi A P* (*rare*) déféquer*/caguer/faire caca.

cackhanded ['kæk'hændid] *a F* (*a*) balourd/empoté (*b*) gaucher.

cackle ['kækl] *n P* **cut the cackle!** assez bavardé!/assez jacté!

cacky ['kæki] *a O P* merdeux.

cactus ['kæktəs] *n P* (*drugs*) mescaline *f*/cactus *m* du Mexique.

caddy ['kædi] *abbr esp NAm F* (*aut*) Cadillac *m* (*RTM*).

cadge¹ [kædʒ] *n F* **he's always on the cadge,** c'est un tapeur chronique/professionnel.

cadge² [kædʒ] *vtr F* emprunter*/ taper/repasser le burlingue; faire la manche; **to cadge a thousand francs from s.o.,** taper/torpiller qn de mille francs; **to cadge a lift,** se faire emmener en voiture/faire du stop.

cadger ['kædʒər] *n F* tapeur *m*/ torpilleur *m*.

cadie ['keidi] *n A P* chapeau*.

cafe [kæf, keif], **caff** [kæf] *n P* = café*/troquet *m*; cafèt *m*.

cag(e)y ['keidʒi] *a F* malin*/futé; **to be/to act cagey,** se boutonner/ jouer serré; **he's very cagey about his salary,** il n'aime pas avouer combien il gagne.

cahoot(s) [kə'huːt(s)] *n F* (*a*) **to be in cahoots with s.o.,** être de mèche/ en cheville avec qn (*b*) *NAm* **to go cahoots with s.o.,** partager avec qn.

Cain [kein] *Prn P* **1. to raise Cain,** faire du bruit*/faire un boucan de tous les diables **2.** (*RS = table*) **Cain and Abel,** table *f*.

cake [keik] *n* **1.** *F* **it's a piece of cake,** c'est du gâteau/de la tarte **2.** *F* **that takes the cake,** ça c'est le comble/le bouquet **3.** *NAm P* **to grab a piece of cake,** faire l'amour*/faire un carton **4.** *F* **you can't have your cake and eat it,** on ne peut être et avoir été/on ne peut pas tout avoir **5.** *F* **the workers are asking for a bigger slice of the cake,** les ouvriers revendiquent une augmentation. (*See* **beefcake; cheesecake; fruitcake; hot 17; pancakes**)

cakehole ['keik(h)oul] *n P* bouche*/bec *m*; **shut your cakehole!** ferme ça!/la ferme!/ferme ton bec!

calaboose, calaboosh

[kælə'buːs, kælə'buːʃ] n NAm P prison*/bloc m/violon m/taule f.

call¹ [kɔːl] n F 1. **to pay a call,** uriner*/aller faire sa petite commission 2. **it was a close call,** il était moins une. (See **shave**)

call² [kɔːl] vtr F 1. **to call it quits,** abandonner/s'arrêter; **let's cut our losses and call it quits,** arrêtons les frais et n'insistons pas 2. **to call it a day,** mettre fin à qch/s'en tenir là 3. **to call the shots,** faire/dicter la loi.

call down ['kɔːl'daun] vtr NAm F réprimander*/attraper.

call girl ['kɔːl'gəːl] n F (a) prostituée*/pute f (b) prostituée* qui prend ses rendez-vous par téléphone/call-girl f.

calling-down ['kɔːliŋ'daun] n NAm F attrapade f/savon m.

camp¹ [kæmp] I a F 1. (a) affecté/poseur (b) qui fait preuve de mauvais goût/de vulgarité (c) chichiteux 2. (a) efféminé (b) homosexuel; **he's very camp,** il fait très pédé/tapette; c'est une affiche (c) lesbienne II n F manières efféminées (esp d'homosexuel)/tantouserie f.

camp² [kæmp] vi P être homosexuel* ou lesbienne*; être de la pédale ou de la maison tire-bouton.

camp up ['kæmp'ʌp] vtr F **to camp it up** (a) jouer la comédie (b) se montrer efféminé/faire la persilleuse/faire l'affiche.

can¹ [kæn] n 1. P prison*/taule f/bloc m; **to put s.o. in the can,** fourrer qn au bloc 2. (recording, etc) **in the can,** en boîte; **it's in the can,** c'est dans le sac 3. pl F casque m (à écouteurs) 4. F **to carry/to take the can for s.o.,** écoper pour qn/porter le chapeau; **I had to carry the can for that,** c'est moi qui ai dû payer les pots cassés 5. P (drugs) (a) opium*/noir m (b) deux grammes de n'importe quelle drogue 6. NAm P WC*/chiottes

fpl/pissotière f 7. NAm P fesses*/pétrousquin m; **to kick s.o. in the can,** donner à qn un coup de pied au cul 8. NAm F **can of worms,** problème m difficile à résoudre/sac m de nœuds 9. pl NAm A P seins*/boîtes fpl à lait. (See **oil-can**)

can² [kæn] vtr 1. P emprisonner*/fourrer dedans 2. esp NAm P se débarrasser* de (qn)/sacquer/flanquer à la porte 3. F (music) enregistrer/mettre en conserve. (See **canned** 2) 4. P **can it!** ferme ça!/la ferme!

canapa ['kænəpə] n P (drugs) marijuana*/canapa f.

canary [kə'nɛəri] n P dénonciateur*/chevreuil m/donneur m; **to sing like a canary,** tout avouer*/vendre la mèche.

cancer-stick ['kænsəstik] n P cigarette*/cibiche f/cancérette f.

candle ['kændl] n F 1. (spark plug) bougie f 2. **she can't hold a candle to you,** elle n'est rien à côté de toi 3. **the game's not worth the candle,** le jeu n'en vaut pas la chandelle 4. **to burn the candle at both ends,** brûler la chandelle par les deux bouts. (See **Roman 1**)

candy ['kændi] n P (drugs) (a) cocaïne*/neige f (b) haschisch* (c) LSD*/sucre m (d) drogues* en général; **candy man,** fourgueur m/passeur m de drogues. (See **needle-candy; nose-candy; rock-candy**)

cane¹ [kein] n P pince-monseigneur*/rossignol m. (See **varnish²**)

cane² ['kein] vtr P **to cane s.o.** (a) faire payer* trop cher à qn/fusiller qn (b) battre* qn à plate(s) couture(s).

canful ['kænful] n P **to have (had) a canful,** être ivre*/prendre une cuite.

caning ['keiniŋ] n F victoire f facile/les doigts dans le nez; **he got a real caning,** il a été battu à plates coutures.

canned [kænd] *a* **1.** *P* (*a*) ivre*/ soûl; **he was completely canned,** il était bourré à zéro/beurré comme un petit lu (*b*) drogué*/camé/ défoncé **2.** *F* **canned music,** musique en conserve **3.** *NAm P* balancé/viré.

cannibal ['kænibəl] *n V* (*esp Black Sl*) qn/qui pratique la fellation* *ou* le cunnilinctus*.

cannibalism ['kænibəlizm] *n V* (*esp Black Sl*) (*a*) fellation* (*b*) cunnilinctus*.

cannon ['kænən] *n NAm P* voleur *m* à la tire/fourchette *f*/tireur *m*.

canoe [kə'nuː] *n F* **to paddle one's own canoe,** mener seul sa barque/ voler de ses propres ailes/se débrouiller.

canoodle [kə'nuːdl] *vi O F* (se) bécoter/(se) peloter/se faire des mamours.

canoodling [kə'nuːdliŋ] *n O F* pelotage *m*/mamours *mpl*.

Canuck [kæ'nʌk] *n F* Canadien(ne) (*esp* français(e)).

cap¹ [kæp] *n* **1.** *P* capsule *f* de narcs **2.** *F* diaphragme *m* (contraceptif). (*See* **Dutch I 3**; **feather¹ 2**; **red-cap**; **thinking-cap**)

cap² [kæp] *vtr* **1.** *P* ouvrir *ou* consommer une capsule contenant de la drogue **2.** *P* acheter des stupéfiants **3.** *F* **to cap it all,** pour comble; **that just about caps it all,** il ne manquait plus que ça.

caper ['keipər] *n F* (*a*) escapade *f*/ farce *f* (*b*) **... and all that caper,** entourloupe et compagnie/et tout ça.

carby ['kɑːbi] *n Austr F* carburateur *m*/carbu *m*.

carcass ['kɑːkəs] *n F* **drag your carcass over here!** radine!/amène ta viande! **shift your carcass!** (*i*) bouge-toi!/remue ta graisse!/pousse ton cul! (*ii*) débarrasse (le plancher)!

card [kɑːd] *n O F* **1. he's a real card,** c'est un drôle d'individu*/ drôle de numéro/de phénomène **2. to get one's cards,** être renvoyé/se faire virer; **to give s.o. his cards,** renvoyer qn/sacquer qn/virer qn **3. to put one's cards on the table,** jouer cartes sur table **4. it's on the cards**/*NAm* **it's in the cards that ...,** il se peut fort bien que ... **5. to play one's trump card,** jouer sa meilleure carte/son atout; **to hold the trump card,** avoir les atouts en main **6. to throw in one's cards,** abandonner la partie. (*See* **close**; **mark² 1**)

cardy ['kɑːdi] *n F* (*abbr* = *cardigan*) gilet *m*/cardigan *m*.

carhop ['kɑːhɔp] *n NAm F* (*in drive-in*) personne qui sert les repas aux clients (dans leurs voitures)/ carhop *m*.

carpet¹ ['kɑːpit] *n* **1.** *F* (*a*) (*under consideration*) **on the carpet,** sur le tapis (*b*) (*reprimanded*) **to have s.o. on the carpet,** tenir qn sur la sellette **2.** *P* (*RS* = *carpet bag* = *drag*) trois mois de prison*/de taule. (*See* **dirt 4**; **drag¹ 7**; **red I 2**)

carpet² ['kɑːpit] *vtr F* **to carpet s.o.** = **to have s.o. on the carpet** (**carpet¹ 1** (*b*))

carpetbagger ['kɑːpitbægər] *n NAm F* candidat parachuté; aventurier *m*/profiteur *m* politique.

carrier ['kæriər] *n F* **1.** (*drugs*) contact *m*/intermédiaire *m*/passeur *m* **2.** (= *carrier bag*) sac *m* (en plastique).

carrot(s) ['kærət(s)], **carrot- top** ['kærəttɔp] *n F* rouquin(e)/poil *m* de carotte.

carry ['kæri] *vtr F* **1.** avoir/posséder de la drogue **2. to carry s.o.,** garder du bois mort **3. he's had as much as he can carry,** il a son compte/il en a tout son soûl. (*See* **can¹ 4**)

carryings-on ['kæriiŋz'ɔn] *npl F*
(*a*) simagrées *fpl*/pitreries *fpl*/
chichis *mpl*/clowneries *mpl* (*b*) ébats
amoureux/zizi pan-pan *m*.

carry off ['kæri'ɔf] *vtr F* **to carry it
off (well)**, bien s'en tirer/réussir son
coup.

carry-on ['kæri'ɔn] *n P* **what a
carry-on! quel cirque!/quelle
comédie!/que d'histoires!**

carry on ['kæri'ɔn] *vi F* **1.** (*a*) **to
carry on with s.o.**, fréquenter qn/
sortir avec qn/flirter (*b*) avoir une
liaison avec qn **2.** faire une scène;
don't carry on like that! ne fais pas
l'idiot! (*See* **alarming**)

cart [kɑɪt] *n F* **to land s.o. (right) in
the cart,** mettre qn dans le pétrin.
(*See* **apple-cart; dog-cart**)

cart about, around ['kɑɪtə'baut,
ə'raund] *vtr F* trimbal(l)er (qn/qch).

cart off ['kɑɪt'ɔf] *vtr F* **to get carted
off to hospital,** être transbahuté à
l'hosto *m*.

cartwheels ['kɑɪtwiɪlz] *npl P*
(*drugs*) amphétamines*/amphés *fpl*.

carve up ['kɑɪv'ʌp] *vtr P* **1.** mas-
sacrer/charcuter (qn) (à coups de
couteau) **2.** partager/décarpiller/
aller au fade.

carzy ['kɑɪzi] *n P* = **karzy.**

Casanova [kæsə'nouvə] *n F*
débauché *m*/Casanova *m*/cavaleur
m/don Juan.

case[1] [keis] *n* **1.** *F* individu excentrique; **he's a hard case,** c'est un
dur (à cuire); **he's a head case,** c'est
un fou/un cinglé **2.** *P* casse *f*/fric-
frac *m*; **to have/to do a case,**
voler*/faire un fric-frac. (*See* **nutcase**)

case[2] [keis] *vtr P* **1. to case the
joint,** aller examiner (une maison,
une banque, etc) avant de la cambrioler*/se rencarder sur la boîte
3. to get cased, être inculpé/fargué.

cashed up ['kæʃd'ʌp] *a Austr F*
être riche*/avoir plein de fric/être
plein aux as.

cash in ['kæʃ'in] *vtr&i* **1.** *P* **to
cash in one's chips,** mourir*/lâcher
la rampe/poser sa chique **2.** *F* **to
cash in on sth,** tirer profit de qch.

casting couch ['kɑɪstiŋ'kautʃ] *n
F* (*euph*) **she used the casting couch
to get a good rôle in the film,** elle a
dû coucher avec le directeur pour
avoir un beau rôle dans le film.

cast-iron ['kɑɪst'aiən] *a F* (*a*) **cast-
iron case,** affaire *f* inattaquable (*b*)
cast-iron constitution, santé *f* de fer;
cast-iron stomach, estomac *m*
d'autruche; **cast-iron alibi,** alibi *m*
irréfutable; **cast-iron jaw,** boxeur *m*
difficile à mettre KO.

cast-offs ['kɑɪstɔfs] *npl F* **1.** vieux
vêtements*/vieilles frusques **2.**
laissés-pour-compte *mpl*; **he's one
of her old cast-offs,** c'est une de ses
anciennes conquêtes.

casual ['kæzjuəl] *n F* **1.** client *m*
de passage **2.** *pl* chaussures* *ou*
vêtements* de sport.

cat [kæt] *n* **1.** *P* (*esp Black Sl*) mec
m/type *m*; **cool cat,** baba *m* cool;
he's a real cool cat, c'est un chic
type/un type cool; **hey, you cats!**
eh, les mecs! **2.** *P* musicien *m* de
jazz **3.** *F* (*pej*) femme*
(malicieuse)/rosse *f* **4.** *F* (= *cat
o'nine tails*) fouet *m*/chat *m* à neuf
queues **5.** *F* **he thinks he's the
cat's whiskers,** il ne se prend pas
pour la crotte/de la merde. (*See*
bee 1) **6.** *F* **to lead a cat and dog
life,** vivre comme chien et chat **7.**
F **it's raining cats and dogs,** il pleut
des hallebardes/à seaux; il tombe
des cordes **8.** *F* **to play cat and
mouse with s.o.,** jouer au chat et à
la souris avec qn **9.** *F* **not enough
room to swing a cat,** pas la place
de se retourner **10.** *F* **(has) the cat
got your tongue?** tu as perdu ta
langue? **11.** *F* **you look like something the cat's brought in!** t'as l'air
dégueulasse!/tu en as une touche!
12. *F* **not a cat in hell's chance!**
rien à faire! **13.** *F* **to let the cat
out of the bag,** éventer la mèche

14. *F* **that's put the cat among the pigeons,** ça a été le pavé dans la mare. (*See* **copycat**; **fat I 5**; **fraidy**; **hell-cat**; **hip cat**; **holy 1**; **piss¹ 5**; **scaredy-cat**; **shoot² 6**)

catch¹ [kætʃ] **I** *a F* **a catch question,** une question-piège/une colle **II** *n* **1.** *F* (*husband*) prise *f*/chopin *m*; **he's a good catch,** c'est un beau parti **2.** *P* homosexuel* passif/ chouquette *f* **3.** *F* entourloupette *f*; **what's the catch?** quel est le truc/le hic? **4.** *F* **it's (a) catch 22 (situation),** (il n')y a pas moyen de s'en tirer/de s'en sortir.

catch² [kætʃ] *vtr F* **1. you won't catch me doing that!** pas de danger qu'on m'y prenne! **don't let me catch you at it again!** que je t'y reprenne! **2. you'll catch it!** tu en prendras pour ton grade! **3. caught napping/with one's trousers down,** pris au pied levé/au dépourvu/sans vert **4. to be caught short,** s'oublier/faire pipi dans son froc **5. the age to catch 'em:** *see* **bingo 17 6. to catch s.o. off base,** prendre qn au dépourvu. (*See* **cold II 1**; **packet 1**)

catch on [ˈkætʃɔn] *vi F* **1.** comprendre/piger/entraver; **he catches on quick,** il pige vite, lui **2.** prendre/être en vogue/être dans le vent; **it'll never catch on!** ça ne prendra/ne marchera jamais!

catch out [ˈkætʃaut] *vtr F* prendre en défaut; **he got caught out,** il s'est fait prendre/coincer/pincer; il s'est fait avoir.

cathouse [ˈkæthaus] *n NAm P* bordel*/claque *m*/boxon *m*.

cat-lap [ˈkætlæp] *n F* bibine *f*/jus *m* de chaussette.

catlick [ˈkætlik] *n F* bout *m*/brin *m* de toilette/toilette *f* de chat.

cattle [ˈkætl] *vtr P* duper*/tromper/ avoir/rouler (qn).

catty [ˈkæti] *a F* rosse/vache; **a catty remark,** une vanne/une pique.

cauliflower [ˈkɔliflauər] *n F* **cauliflower ear,** oreille *f* en chou-fleur.

cause [kɔːz] *n F* (*hum*) **all in a good cause!** c'est pour le bien de tout le monde!

caution [ˈkɔːʃ(ə)n] *n O F* **a proper caution,** un drôle de numéro/un drôle de phénomène.

cave [ˈkeivi] *n O P* (*school*) **cave!** vingt-deux!/pet! pet!

cave-man [ˈkeivmæn] *n O* grosse brute; **caveman stuff,** brutalités *fpl*.

Cecil, cecil [ˈsesl] *n P* (*drugs*) cocaïne*/cecil *m*. (*See* **after 1**)

cee [siː] *n O P* (*drugs*) cocaïne*/C *f*.

ceiling [ˈsiːliŋ] *n F* **to go through the ceiling/to hit the ceiling,** se mettre en colère*/sortir de ses gonds/sauter au plafond.

century [ˈsentʃuri, ˈsentʃəri] *n P* **1.** cent livres sterling **2.** *NAm* **century note,** cent dollars.

cert [səːt] *n F* (*abbr = certainty*) **it's a dead cert,** c'est du tout cuit/c'est affiché; (*horse racing*) c'est un gagnant sûr/c'est couru.

cha [tʃɑː] *n F* = **char 1.**

chain-gang [ˈtʃeingæŋ] *n P* partouze *f* à la bague/enculage *m* en rond. (*See* **daisy II 6**).

chair [ˈtʃɛər] *n NAm F* **1.** chaise *f* électrique; **to go to the chair,** être grillé **2. chair warmer,** rond-de-cuir *m*/gratte-papier *m* **3.** (*in pub*) **to be in the chair,** être celui qui offre une tournée.

chalk [tʃɔːk] *n* **1.** *F* **better by a long chalk,** de bien loin le meilleur; **not by a long chalk,** il s'en faut de beaucoup **2.** *F* **they're like/as different as chalk and cheese,** c'est le jour et la nuit **3.** (*drugs*) amphétamines*/amphés *fpl* **4.** *P* (*RS = walk*) **ball/penn'orth of chalk,** promenade *f* **5.** *P* (*RS = arm*) **chalk farm,** bras*/aile *f*.

chalk up [tʃɔːkˈʌp] *vtr&i* **1.** *F*

porter sur l'ardoise **2.** *P* **to chalk up a score** = **score**[2] **1, 2.**

champ [tʃæmp] (*abbr* = *champion*) *F* **I** *n* as *m*/crack *m* **II** *a* = **champion I.**

champers ['ʃæmpəz] *n* *F* champagne *m*/champ(e) *m*.

champion ['tʃæmpjən] **I** *a* *F* (*esp Northern dial*) **(right/proper) champion,** excellent*/de première/du tonnerre/impec. (*See* **gate-crasher**) **II** *adv* *F* (*esp Northern dial*) excellemment/soin-soin.

chancy ['tʃɑːnsi] *a* *F* chanceux/glandilleux; **it's a chancy business,** c'est risqué.

change [tʃeindʒ] *n* *F* **1. you won't get much change out of him,** tu n'en tireras pas grand-chose/tu perds tes peines avec lui **2. it makes a change,** ça change un peu **3. the change of life,** la ménopause/le retour d'âge. (*See* **ring**[2] **2**)

channel ['tʃæn(ə)l] *n* *P* (*drugs*) veine dans laquelle un drogué injecte le stupéfiant.

chap [tʃæp] *n* (*slightly O*) *F* individu*/type *m*; **poor chap,** pauvre type; **he's a queer chap,** c'est un drôle de bonhomme; **hello, old chap,** salut, vieux pote/vieille branche! **listen old chap!** écoute, mon vieux!

char[1] [tʃɑːr] *n* *F* **1.** thé *m*; **a cup of char,** une tasse de thé **2.** (= *charwoman, charlady*) femme *f* de ménage/torche-pot *m*/bonniche *f*.

char[2] [tʃɑːr] *vi* *F* **to char/to go out charring (for s.o.),** faire des ménages.

character ['kærɪktər] *n* *F* **he's quite a character,** c'est un drôle d'individu*/de numéro.

charas [tʃæ'ræs], **charash** [tʃæ'ræʃ] *n* *P* (*drugs*) cannabis*/marijuana*/dagga *m*.

charge [tʃɑːdʒ] *n* *P* **1.** (*drugs*) piquouse *f*; **to go on the charge,** se camer/se charger **2.** plaisir *m*/

émotion *f*; **to get a charge out of sth,** tirer plaisir de qch/s'en payer une tranche; **I got a charge out of it,** ça m'a fait quelque chose.

charged (up) ['tʃɑːdʒd('ʌp)] *a* *P* drogué*/bourré/défoncé/chargé; **to get charged (up),** se camer.

Charl(e)y, charl(e)y, Charlie, charlie ['tʃɑːli] *n* *P* **1. a right/proper Charley,** un vrai gugusse **2. Charley's dead,** ton jupon dépasse; tu pavoises. (*See* **Anne**) **3.** *A* (*drugs*) **Charley (coke)** (*i*) cocaïne*/*C* *f* (*ii*) cocaïnomane *mf* **4.** *NAm* (*i*) soldat *m* du Viêt Cong (*ii*) armée *f* Viêt Cong **5.** lesbienne*/gougnotte *f* **6.** (*Black Sl*) blanc *m* **7.** *NAm* dollar *m* **8.** *NAm* **Charley Horse,** crampe *f* dans les muscles des bras ou des jambes. (*See* **good-time 2**)

charms [tʃɑːmz] *npl* *F* seins*/appas *mpl*/doudounes *fpl*.

chart [tʃɑːt] *n* *F* (*usu pl*) palmarès *m*/hit-parade *m*; **number one in the charts,** numéro un au palmarès.

charver ['tʃɑːvər] *n* *V* l'acte sexuel*/tringlage *m*.

chase around ['tʃeisə'raund] *vi* *F* **to chase around after women,** courir les filles/les jupons/cavaler.

chaser ['tʃeisər] *n* *F* rince-cochon *m*/rince-gueule *m*. (*See* **petticoat-chaser; skirt-chaser; woman-chaser**)

chassis ['ʃæsi] *n* *F* (*woman's body*) châssis *m*/académie *f*.

chat up ['tʃæt'ʌp] *vtr* *F* baratiner; draguer; **to chat up a bird,** faire du rentre-dedans/du gringue à une fille*; draguer une nana.

cheapie ['tʃiːpi] *n* *F* **1. it's a cheapie,** c'est de la camelote **2.** *pl* **cheapies,** billets *mpl* d'avion à prix réduits.

cheapjack ['tʃiːpdʒæk] *n* *F* camelot *m*; **cheapjack goods,** de la camelote.

cheapskate ['tʃiːpskeit] *n NAm F*
1. avare*/grippe-sou *m*/radin *m* **2.**
vaurien*/bon-à-rien *m*.

cheat [tʃiːt] *vtr esp NAm F*
cocufier/doubler/faire porter des
cornes (à); **he's cheating (on) his
wife,** il trompe sa femme.

check! [tʃek] *excl esp NAm* oui*/
d'acc!/dac!/banco!

check out ['tʃek'aut] *vtr&i* **1.** *P*
mourir*/déposer le bilan/plier
bagage **2.** *P* partir*/filer **3.** *F* to
check s.o./sth, out, vérifier qch/se
rencarder sur qn/qch.

check-up ['tʃekʌp] *n F* examen
médical/bilan *m* de santé/check-up
m.

cheddar ['tʃedər] *n F* **hard cheddar
= hard cheese (cheese 1)**

cheek[1] [tʃiːk] *n F* **1.** toupet *m*/
culot *m*; **he's got a hell of a cheek/
the cheek of the devil,** il a un culot
monstre/il en a un souffle/il est
vachement culotté; **bleeding cheek!**
sacré culot! **don't give me any of
your cheek!** (ne) te fiche pas de
moi! **it's a damned cheek!** ça c'est
se fiche(r) du monde! **2.** *pl*
fesses*/fessier *m*/joufflu *m*.

cheek[2] [tʃiːk] *vtr F* se moquer* de
(qn)/se payer la tête de (qn)/faire
l'insolent avec (qn)/narguer (qn).

cheeky ['tʃiːki] *a F* effronté/
culotté/soufflé; **cheeky little sod!**
petit effronté!

cheerio! ['tʃiəri'ou] *excl F* **1.** =
cheers! 2. à bientôt!/bon courage!/salut!/ciao!

cheers! [tʃiəz] *excl F* (*a*) à la
bonne vôtre!/à la tienne (Étienne)!
(*b*) merci (*c*) salut!/bon courage!

cheerybye! ['tʃiəri'bai] *excl F* au
revoir!/salut!

cheese [tʃiːz] *n* **1.** *F* **hard cheese!**
pas de chance*!/manque de pot!/
quelle guigne! **2.** *P* (*RS = missis*)
cheese and kisses, épouse*/
bourgeoise *f*/légitime *f* **3.** *F* **say
cheese!** souriez!/regardez le petit

oiseau!/un beau sourire! **4.** *VV*
smegma *m*/fromage *m*. (*See* **big 1
1**; **chalk 2**; **cream**[1] **2**)

cheesecake ['tʃiːzkeik] *n F* pin-
up *f*.

cheesed off ['tʃiːzd'ɔf] *a P* **to be/
to feel cheesed off,** avoir le cafard/
en avoir marre.

cheese it ['tʃiːzit] *P* partir*/se
calter; **cheese it!** (*i*) ça va!/c'est
marre! (*ii*) fiche le camp!

cheesy ['tʃiːzi] *a* **1.** *NAm F*
miteux/moche/à la manque/toc
2. *VV* (gland du pénis) recouvert de
smegma/de fromage **3.** *F* (*pieds*)
qui sentent mauvais/qui tapent.

chef [ʃef] *n P* (*drugs*) **1.** opium*/
boue verte **2.** chef *m*/caïd *m*.

chemist ['kemist] *n P* personne qui
falsifie/qui maquille des prescrip-
tions pour un drogué.

cherry ['tʃeri] *n* **1.** *P* virginité*/
pucelage *m*/fleur *f*/coquille *f*; **to
lose one's cherry,** perdre sa fleur; **to
pick a girl's cherry,** déflorer/
dépuceler une fille **2.** *F* **to take
two bites at the cherry/to have
another bite at the cherry,** s'y prendre à deux fois/y remordre **3.**
NAm F **cherry pie,** chose *f* facile/
jeu *m* d'enfant.

cherry-ripe ['tʃeri'raip] *n O P* (*a*)
(*RS = pipe*) pipe *f* (*b*) (*RS =
tripe*) bêtises*/sornettes *fpl*.

chest [tʃest] *n F* **to get sth off one's
chest,** déballer ce qu'on a sur le
cœur/vider son sac. (*See* **close**;
hair 5)

chestnut ['tʃesnʌt] *n* **1.** *F* **old
chestnut,** histoire rabâchée/rengaine
f; vieille blague/blague éventée **2.**
pl O P testicules*/olives *fpl*.

chesty ['tʃesti] *a F* **1.** délicat des
bronches **2.** *NAm* vaniteux/faraud.

chevy (chase) ['tʃevi('tʃeis)] *n P*
(*RS = face*) visage*/bouille *f*.

Chevvy ['ʃevi] *n NAm F* (*aut*)
Chevrolet *m* (*RTM*).

chew [tʃuː] P **to chew the fat/the rag**, bavarder*/se tailler une bavette/jacter/discuter le bout de gras. (*See* **bite off 2**)

chewbacon ['tʃuːbeikən] n F paysan*/cul-terreux m.

chew off ['tʃuːˈɔf] vtr F **to chew s.o.'s head/**NAm **ears off**, réprimander* qn/passer un savon à qn. (*See* **balls¹ 7**)

chew out ['tʃuːˈaut] vtr NAm P **to get (one's ass) chewed out**, se faire engueuler.

chew over ['tʃuːˈouvər] vtr F **to chew it over**, réfléchir/ruminer.

chewie, chewy ['tʃuːwi] n esp Austr F chewing gum m.

chiack ['tʃaiæk] n Austr F = **chyack.**

chick [tʃik] n F **1.** (*child*) môme mf/coco m **2.** fille*/poulette f/pépée f; **a good-looking chick**, une jolie nana/minette; **his chick**, sa petite amie.

chickabiddy ['tʃikəbidi] n F cocotte f; **my little chickabiddy**, mon petit coco/poulet.

chicken ['tʃikin] **I** a P lâche*; **to turn chicken**, se dégonfler **II** n **1.** F **she's no (spring) chicken!** elle n'est pas de première jeunesse!/c'est pas un poulet de grain! **2.** NAm F **to get up with the chickens**, se lever avec les poules. (*See* **lark 3**) **3.** F **to count one's chickens (before they are hatched)**, vendre la peau de l'ours (avant de l'avoir tué) **4.** P lâche*/caneur m/dégonfleur m/flubard m/froussard m **5.** P mineur(e)/gamin(e)/poulet m de grain/poulette f; **to have a chicken dinner**, faire l'amour avec un(e) mineur(e)/déplumer le poulet **6.** NAm F **chicken shit**, rien*/pet m de lapin.

chicken-feed ['tʃikinfiːd] n F **1.** quelques sous*/bagatelle f/mitraille f; **we work there for chicken-feed**, on y travaille pour des clous **2.** rien*/des clopinettes fpl; **it's just**

chicken-feed, c'est de la gnognot(t)e.

chicken out ['tʃikinˈaut] vi F se dégonfler; **he chickened out at the last moment**, il s'est dégonflé à la dernière minute.

chicken-roost ['tʃikinruːst] n F (*theatre*) poulailler m. (*See* **pigeon-roost**)

chickie ['tʃiki] adv NAm F **to lay chickie**, faire le guet/faire gaffe.

chief [tʃiːf] n **1.** F patron*/chef m; **the big (white) chief**, le patron*/le grand manitou/le grand chef **2.** O P (*drugs*) **the chief** (a) LSD* (b) mescaline f.

chill [tʃil] n NAm P **1. to put the chill on s.o.**, battre froid à qn/faire la gueule à qn **2. to have the chills**, avoir peur*/avoir la tremblote/avoir le trac.

chimbley ['tʃimbli] n F (= *chimney*) cheminée f/bouffardière f.

chime in ['tʃaimˈin] vi F (i) couper la parole/placer son mot/mettre son grain de sel (ii) faire chorus.

chimney ['tʃimni] n F **to smoke like a chimney**, fumer comme un pompier.

chin [tʃin] n **1.** F **to take it on the chin**, encaisser un sale coup/ne pas se laisser abattre **2.** F **to keep one's chin up**, tenir bon/tenir le coup; **chin up!** du courage! **3.** P lame f de rasoir.

china ['tʃainə] n P (*RS* = *china plate* = *mate*) ami(e)*/pote m/copain m/copine f; **my old china**, ma vieille branche.

Chinaman ['tʃainəmən] n P **to have a Chinaman on one's back**, souffrir des symptômes du sevrage de drogues/être en manque/être cold turkey.

chinch [tʃintʃ] n P punaise f.

Chinese ['tʃainiːz] a P (*drugs*) **Chinese needlework**, piqûre*/piquouse f/shoot m; **chinese tobacco**, opium*.

chin-chin! ['tʃin'tʃin] *excl F* **1.** au revoir!/à bientôt! **2.** à la vôtre/à la tienne!

chinfest ['tʃinfest] *n esp NAm P =* **chinwag¹**.

chink¹ [tʃiŋk] *n A P* argent*/fric *m.*

Chink² [tʃiŋk] *n P* (*pej*) Chinois *m*/ Chinoise *f*/Chinetoque *m*; *NAm* **Chink joint** (*i*) boîte chinoise (*ii*) restaurant Chinois.

chinky, Chinky ['tʃiŋki] *a&n P* chinois/chinetoque; **chinky (takeaway)**, bouffe *f* chinetoque (à emporter).

chinless ['tʃinles] *a F* **chinless wonder**, imbécile*/idiot *m* de la haute.

chino ['tʃainou] *n A P* Chinois *m* forgueur *m* de drogues.

chinwag¹ ['tʃinwæg] *n P* bavette *f*/ causette *f*; **to have a chinwag**, (se) tailler une bavette.

chinwag² ['tʃinwæg] *vi P* bavarder*/jaboter/tailler une bavette.

chip [tʃip] *n* **1.** *O P* cinq pence **2.** *esp NAm P* **to be in the chips**, être plein aux as **3.** *F* **he's had his chips**, il est cuit/fichu **4.** *F* **when the chips are down**, quand les dés sont jetés/en cas de coup dur **5.** *F* **to have a chip on one's shoulder**, chercher la bagarre/des crosses *fpl*; **she's always had a chip on her shoulder**, elle en veut à tout le monde **6.** *F* **he's a chip off the old block**, c'est bien le fils de son père **7.** *F* (*computers*) puce *f*/pastille *f*. (*See* **cash in** 1; **chips**)

chip at ['tʃipæt] *vtr O* **1.** *F* critiquer* (qn/qch) **2.** se ficher de qn.

chip in ['tʃip'in] *vtr&i F* **1.** payer* sa part **2.** dire son mot/y aller de son grain de sel.

chipper ['tʃipər] *adv esp NAm P* **to feel chipper**, être en forme.

chippy ['tʃipi] *n P* **1.** (= (*fish and*) *chip shop*) friterie *f*; **let's get sth from the chippy tonight**, si on

mangeait des fish and chips, ce soir? **2.** *NAm A* (*a*) prostituée*/ grue *f*/radeuse *f* (*b*) allumeuse *f*/ dragueuse *f* **3.** *O* (*drugs**) (*a*) (= *mild narcotic*) herbe *f* (*b*) usager *m* occasionnel de drogues **4.** menuisier *m*/copeau *m.*

chips [tʃips] *n P =* **chippy 4.**

chirpy ['tʃəːpi] *adj F* gai/de bonne humeur; **you're very chirpy today**, tu es gai comme un pinson, aujourd'hui.

chisel ['tʃiz(ə)l] *vtr P* voler*/rouler/ carotter (qn).

chiseller ['tʃiz(ə)lər] *n P* escroc*/ carotteur *m*/filou *m.*

chit [tʃit] *n F* petit enfant*/mioche *mf*/bout *m* de zan; (*esp in phrase*) **(she's) a mere chit of a girl**, ce n'est qu'une gosse.

chiv¹ [ʃiv] *n P* **1.** couteau*/surin *m* **2.** rasoir*/rasibe *m.*

chiv² [ʃiv] *vtr P* **1.** taillader/larder/ suriner (qn) **2.** marquer/faire la croix des vaches à (qn).

chive [ʃiv] *n&v P =* **chiv¹,².**

chiv(e)-man ['(t)ʃivmæn, 'tʃaivmæn], **chiv(e)-merchant** ['(t)ʃivməːtʃənt, 'tʃaivməːtʃənt] *n P* surineur *m.*

chivey ['ʃivi] *n P =* **chiv¹** 1, 2.

chivvy up, along ['tʃivi'ʌp, ə'lɔŋ] *vtr F* relancer/poursuivre/harceler (qn).

chock-a-block ['tʃɔkə'blɔk] *a F* plein à craquer/archi-plein/plein comme un œuf.

chocker ['tʃɔkər] *a* **1.** *F =* **chock-a-block**. *F* **to be chocker**, en avoir assez*/en avoir marre. (*See* **dead II 3**)

chock-full ['tʃɔk'ful] *a F =* **chock-a-block**.

chocolate ['tʃɔklit] *n P* **chocolate lover**, homosexuel* blanc qui s'accouple de préférence avec des Noirs. (*See* **queen¹ 2**; **coal-burner**)

choke 54 chuck in

choke¹ [tʃouk] *n P* = **chok(e)y 2.**

choke² [tʃouk] *vi P* mourir*/lâcher la rampe.

choke off ['tʃouk'ɔf] *vtr F* (*not common*) se débarrasser* de/ envoyer balader (qn).

chok(e)y ['tʃouki] *n P* **1.** prison*/ clou *m*/taule *f* **2.** mitard *m*/trou *m.*

choo-choo ['tʃuːtʃuː] *n F* (*child's word*) teuf-teuf *m.*

chook(ie) ['tʃuk(i)] *n Austr F* poule *f*/poulet *m.*

choosy ['tʃuːzi] *a F* chipoteur; **I'm not choosy,** je ne suis pas difficile/ chiant.

chop¹ [tʃɔp] *n* **1.** (*a*) **to give s.o. the chop,** se débarrasser* de qn/ sacquer qn. (*See* **sack¹ 1**) (*b*) **to get the chop,** être viré/flanqué à la porte; **he's for the chop!** qu'est-ce qu'il va prendre!/son affaire est bonne! **2. to smack s.o. round the chops,** donner une bonne claque à qn **3.** *Austr* part *f*/fade *m* **4.** *Austr* **no chop,** minable; **not much chop,** qui ne vaut pas grand'chose. (*See* **lamb 1; lick² 5; slobber-chops**)

chop² [tʃɔp] *vi* **1.** *P* (*sports*) donner un coup de pied dans les jambes à (qn) **2.** *F* **to chop and change,** changer d'idée comme de chemise.

chop-chop ['tʃɔp'tʃɔp] *adv F* vite*/presto/dare-dare; **chop-chop!** et que ça saute!/grouille-toi!

chopper ['tʃɔpər] *n* **1.** *V* pénis*/ défonceuse *f* **2.** *esp NAm P* mitraillette*/moulin *m* à café **3.** *P* hélicoptère *m*/hélico *m*/banane *f* **4.** *pl P* dents*/croquantes *fpl*/crocs *mpl* **5.** *P* moto *ou* vélo modifié(e) à la 'Easy Rider'/chopper *m.*

chow [tʃau] *n F* nourriture*/bouffe *f*/becquetance *f*/boustifaille *f*; **chow time,** l'heure *f* de la bouffe.

chowderhead ['tʃaudəhed] *n NAm O F* = **chucklehead.**

Chrissie, chrissie ['krisi] *n F* (= *Christmas*) Noël *m*; **chrissie present,** cadeau *m* de Noël.

Christ [kraist] *Prn P* **1. Christ (Almighty)!** bon Dieu (de bon Dieu)!/merde alors! **2. for Christ's sake!** pour l'amour de Dieu!/du ciel! (*See* **Jesus (Christ)!**)

Christmas-tree ['krisməstriː] *n P* (*drugs*) drinamyl *m*/arbre *m* de Noël.

chromo ['kroumou] *n Austr A P* prostituée*/pute *f*/racoleuse *f.*

chronic ['krɔnik] **I** *a F* affreux; insupportable/empoisonnant/rasoir; **she's chronic!** elle est imbuvable! **she's got chronic taste in men,** question mecs, elle n'a vraiment pas de goût **II** *adv P* à haute dose; **I've got the guts-ache something chronic,** j'ai un mal de ventre carabiné.

chuck¹ [tʃʌk] *n P* **1.** *NAm* nourri-ture*/becquetance *f*/bouffe *f* **2.** (*of drug addicts during withdrawal period*) **chuck habit,** gavage *m*; **chuck horrors,** dégoût *m* de la nourriture **3. to give s.o. the chuck,** se débarrasser* de qn/bal-ancer qn/flanquer qn à la porte; **she gave her bloke the chuck,** elle a plaqué son petit ami.

chuck² [tʃʌk] *vtr* **1.** *F* jeter*/ lancer (qch); **chuck it to me!** jette-moi ça! **2.** *P* se débarrasser* de (qn); **he chucked her,** il l'a plaquée **3.** *P* **he's chucked the habit,** il a réussi à se faire décrocher **4.** *F* **chuck it!** en voilà assez*!/ça va comme ça!/écrase! (*See* **dummy 4**)

chuck about, around ['tʃʌkə'baut, 'tʃʌkə'raund] *vtr F* **1. to chuck one's money about/around,** jeter son argent* par les fenêtres **2. to chuck one's weight about/ around,** faire l'important/faire du volume/de l'esbrouf(f)e *f.*

chucker-out ['tʃʌkə'raut] *n F* videur *m.*

chuck in ['tʃʌk'in] *vtr F* **1. to chuck in one's job,** lâcher son travail*/son boulot 2. **to chuck it in,** y renoncer/quitter la partie/lâcher les dés.

chucking-out ['tʃʌkiŋ'aut] *a F* **chucking-out time,** l'heure de la fermeture (des pubs).

chucklehead ['tʃʌklhed] *n NAm F* individu bête*/andouille *f*/patate *f*.

chuckleheaded ['tʃʌklhedid] *a NAm F* bête*/bas de plafond.

chuck out ['tʃʌk'aut] *vtr F* se débarrasser* de (qn)/flanquer (qn) à la porte/balancer/vider (qn).

chuck up ['tʃʌk'ʌp] *vi & tr* **1.** *F* = **chuck in 1, 2 2.** *F* **to chuck s.o. up,** lâcher qn/plaquer qn **3.** *P* vomir*/dégobiller.

chuff [tʃʌf] *n P* (*esp regional*) individu bête*/gourde *f*/cruche *f*; **to make s.o. look a chuff,** se moquer de qn/se payer la tête de qn.

chuffed [tʃʌft] *a F* **to be chuffed** (*i*) être ravi(e)/être aux anges; **I was really chuffed about it,** j'en étais tout content/ravi (*ii*) avoir le cafard/en avoir marre/en avoir ras le bol.

chum [tʃʌm] *n F* ami*/pote *m*/copain *m*/copine *f*; **you said it, chum!** comme de juste, Auguste!/c'est toi qui le dis! (*See* **have 4**)

chummy ['tʃʌmi] **I** *a F* amical/bon copain; **they were very chummy,** ils étaient copains comme cochons **II** *n P* (*police slang*) suspect *m*.

chump [tʃʌmp] *n* **1.** *P* tête*, caboche *f*; **he's off his chump,** il perd la boule **2.** *F* individu bête*/nigaud *m*/cruche *f*; **he's a silly chump,** c'est un crétin.

chum up ['tʃʌm'ʌp] *vi F* copiner.

chunder ['tʃʌndər] *vi Austr P* vomir*/dégueuler.

chunks [tʃʌŋks] *npl P* (*drugs*) haschisch*/griffs *mpl*.

chunky ['tʃʌŋki] *a F* trapu; **she's a bit on the chunky side,** elle est un peu rondelette/elle se porte bien.

Chunnel ['tʃʌnəl] *n F* (= *Channel Tunnel*) le tunnel sous la Manche.

chunter on ['tʃʌntər'ɔn] *vi F* grogner*/radoter.

churn out ['tʃəːn'aut] *vtr F* produire beaucoup de (qch); **this author churns out books by the dozen,** il les pond en série, cet auteur.

chute [ʃuːt] *n* **1.** *P* **to go up the chute,** ne servir à rien/partir en fumée; **up the chute,** perdu/fichu/foutu **2.** *F* (= *parachute*) parachute *m*/pépin *m*.

chyack ['tʃaijæk] *vtr Austr P* se montrer très insolent envers (qn)/narguer (qn). (*See* **chiack**)

cig(gy) ['sig(i)] *n F* cigarette*/cibiche *f*/clope *mf*; **ciggy break,** pause *f* pour fumer une clope au boulot.

cinch [sintʃ] *n F* certitude *f*; **it's a cinch** (*i*) c'est certain/c'est couru d'avance/c'est du tout cuit (*ii*) c'est facile/c'est de la tarte.

circs [səːks] *npl F* (*abbr = circumstances*) **in/under the circs,** dans ce cas-là.

circus ['səːkəs] *n F* cirque *m*/rigolade *f*; **it's just like a circus in here!** qu'est-ce que c'est que ce bordel/ce cirque! (*See* **Piccadilly Circus**)

cissy ['sisi] *n F* = **sissy.**

civvies ['siviz] *npl F* **in civvies,** en civelot/en bourgeois; (*police*) en pékin. (*See* **civvy II**)

civvy ['sivi] **I** *a F* civil/pékin; **in civvy street,** dans le civil **III** *n F* bourgeois *m*/civil *m*. (*See* **civvies**)

clack¹ [klæk] *n O P* caquet *m*/jacasserie *f*.

clack² [klæk] *vi P* bavarder*/caqueter/jacasser; **this will stop their tongues clacking,** ça empêchera les gens de jaser.

clackety-clack ['klækəti'klæk] *n*
O F caquetage *m*/jacasserie *f*. (*See*
yackety-yack)

clamp-down ['klæmpdaun] *n F*
contrainte *f*/vissage *m*; **there's been
a clamp-down on spending,** on a mis
un frein aux dépenses.

clamp down ['klæmp'daun] *vi F*
contraindre par la force/freiner/
restreindre; **to clamp down on sth/
s.o.,** serrer la vis à qch/qn.

clam up ['klæm'ʌp] *vi F* se taire*/
la boucler; **she clammed up,** elle l'a
bouclée.

clanger ['klæŋər] *n F* **to drop a
clanger,** faire une bévue*/une gaffe.

clap [klæp] *n P* blennorragie*/
gonorrhée *f*/chaude-pisse *f*/coulante
f; **to have the clap,** pisser des lames
de rasoir/avoir des gonos.

clapped out ['klæpt'aut] *a F*
(*pers*) fatigué*/crevé; (*car, etc*)
crevé; **a clapped-out old banger,** un
vieux tas (de ferraille)/un vieux
machin.

clapper ['klæpər] *n F* **1.** langue*/
clapette *f* **2. to go like the clappers,** filer comme un zèbre; **to work
like the clappers,** travailler dur*/
comme un fou/comme une bête.

claptrap ['klæptræp] *n F* bêtises*;
what a lot of claptrap! c'est un tas
de foutaises!

claret ['klærət] *n A P* sang *m*/résiné
m; **to have one's claret tapped,**
saigner du nez.

class [klɑːs] *n F* **to have class,** avoir
de la classe.

classic ['klæsik] *a F* **you should
have seen him, it was absolutely
classic,** tu aurais dû le voir, c'était
le coup classique.

classy ['klɑːsi] *a F* (*a*) chic/bon
genre (*b*) beau*/badour; **that's
really classy,** ça c'est de la classe.

clean [kliːn] **I** *a F* **1. to be clean**
(*a*) être sans condamnation*/être
blanc (*b*) être pauvre*/être à blanc
(*c*) être sans arme (*d*) ne pas pren-

dre de drogues/se tenir clean (*e*) ne
pas avoir de drogues sur soi; **the
pusher was clean when the cops
searched him,** le dealer était clean/
n'avait rien sur lui quand les flics
l'ont fouillé **2. to make a clean
breast of it,** tout avouer*/se mettre
à table **3. to come clean,** avouer*/
lâcher le paquet. (*See* **nose 3**;
sweep¹ 2) **II** *adv F* **it went clean
out of my head,** ça m'est complètement sorti de la tête.

cleaners ['kliːnəz] *nfpl P* **to take
s.o. to the cleaners,** mettre qn à
sec/nettoyer qn.

clean-out ['kliːnaut] *n F* lessive *f*/
coup *m* de balai.

clean out ['kliːn'aut] *vtr F* (*a*) **to
clean s.o. out,** prendre l'argent* à
qn/lessiver qn/nettoyer qn; **to get
cleaned out,** perdre son argent*/
boire un bouillon/se faire plumer
(*b*) **to be cleaned out,** être fauché
comme les blés/à sec.

clean-up ['klinʌp] *n F* **1. clean-
up campaign,** campagne *f* contre la
porno(graphie) **2.** *esp NAm* **to
make a clean-up,** faire un gros
profit.

clear [kliər] **I** *a F* **it's (as) clear as
mud,** c'est la bouteille à l'encre;
c'est clair comme du jus de
boudin/de chique **II** *n F* (*a*) **to be
in the clear** (*i*) être tiré d'affaire/
sorti de l'auberge (*ii*) être blanc (*b*)
to put s.o. in the clear (*i*) tirer qn
d'affaire (*ii*) défarguer qn. (*See* **all-
clear**)

clear off ['kliər'ɔf] *vi F* partir*/
prendre le large; **clear off!** casse-
toi!/fiche le camp!

clear-out ['kliəraut] *n* **to have a
clear-out** (*a*) *F* faire du triage/
désencombrer (*b*) *P* déféquer*/
déflaquer.

clear out ['kliər'aut] *vi F* **1. to
clear s.o. out of sth,** débarrasser qn
de qch/nettoyer qn **2.** s'en aller/se
tirer; **come on, let's clear out!** allez,
on change de crémerie!

cleavage ['kliːvidʒ] *n F* naissance *f* des seins*; **her blouse showed a lot of cleavage,** sa chemise était très décolletée/laissait voir la naissance des seins/avait un décolleté plongeant.

cleft [kleft] *n V* sexe de la femme*/crac *m*/fente *f.*

clever-clever ['klevəklevər] *a F* malin*/débrouillard.

cleverclogs ['klevəklɔgz], **cleverguts** ['klevəgʌts] *n P* petit/gros malin; un Monsieur je-sait-tout. (*See* **dick 4**)

click [klik] *vi F* (a) **to click with s.o.** (*i*) sympathiser/accrocher avec qn (*ii*) faire une touche (*b*) **and then, suddenly it clicked,** et puis tout d'un coup ça a fait tilt.

clickety-click ['klikəti'klik] *F see* **bingo 66.**

cliffhanger ['klifhæŋər] *n F* feuilleton *m*, etc à suspense; suspense *m.*

climber ['klaimər] *n P* (*cat burglar*) monte-en-l'air *m.*

clinch¹ [klintʃ] *n F* étreinte amoureuse/enlacement *m.*

clinch² [klintʃ] *vtr F* **that clinches it!** ça coupe court à tout!/c'est le mot de la fin!/ça met un point final!

clincher ['klintʃər] *n F* argument définitif; **that's a clincher** (*i*) ça lui a fermé le bec (*ii*) c'est le mot de la fin.

clinger ['kliŋər] *n F* (*pers*) crampon *m.*

clink [kliŋk] *n P* prison*/taule *f*/violon *m*; **to be in clink,** faire de la grosse caisse; **to put s.o. in clink,** mettre qn au bloc.

clip¹ [klip] *n F* **1.** coup*/beigne *f*/taloche *f*; **to give s.o. a clip round the ear,** flanquer une taloche à qn **2.** pas *m* rapide.

clip² [klip] *vtr* **1.** *F* flanquer une taloche à (qn) **2.** *P* voler*/écorcher/plumer/estamper (qn).

clip-game ['klipgeim] *n P* escroquerie*/filouterie *f.*

clip-joint ['klipdʒɔint] *n F* boîte *f*/tripot *m* (qui exploite les clients); maison *f* tire-pognon.

clippie ['klipi] *n F* receveuse *f* d'autobus.

cliquey ['kliːki] *a F* (*pej*) qui a l'esprit de clan *ou* de petite chapelle.

clit [klit] *n V* clitoris*/clicli *m*/bouton *m*; (*pej*) **you stupid clit!** espèce de conne!/connasse!

cloak-and-dagger ['klouk-(ə)n'dægər] *a F* clandestin; **a cloak and dagger novel,** un roman d'intrigue et d'espionnage.

clobber¹ ['klɔbər] *n P* (*a*) vêtements*/frusques *fpl*/hardes *fpl* (*b*) (*belongings*) barda *m.*

clobber² ['klɔbər] *vtr P* **1.** battre*/matraquer/rosser; **to get clobbered,** être rossé/se faire arranger **2. the taxi driver clobbered me for £50,** le chauffeur de taxi m'a tapé/torpillé de £50.

clock¹ [klɔk] *n* **1.** *P* visage*/poire *f* **2.** *F* compteur *m*; **this car's got 50,000 (miles) on the clock,** cette bagnole a 80,000 au compteur **3.** *F* **to beat the clock,** arriver* avant l'heure **4.** *F* **round the clock,** vingt-quatre heures sur vingt-quatre; **round the clock protection,** surveillance permanente.

clock² [klɔk] *vtr P* **1.** battre*/calotter (qn)/abîmer le portrait à (qn) **2.** guetter*/mater (qn); **clock that bloke!** vise-moi/zyeute-moi ce mec-là! **3.** prendre une photo (de qn/qch) **4.** remettre à zéro (le compteur d'une voiture).

clock up ['klɔk'ʌp] *vtr F* **to clock up the miles,** rouler vite*/avaler les kilomètres.

clock-watcher ['klɔkwɔtʃər] *n F* (*esp*) employé qui ne fait que guetter l'heure de la sortie/tire-au-flanc *m*.

clod [klɔd] *n F* = **clodhopper 1.**

clodhopper ['klɔdhɔpər] *n P* **1.** paysan*/plouc *m* **2.** lourdaud *m*/baloud *m* **3.** *pl* grosses chaussures*/tatanes *fpl.*

clogging ['klɔgiŋ] *n (football)* *F* jeu déloyal/barbouillage *m*.

cloghead ['klɔghed] *n O P* individu bête*/gourde *f*.

clomp about ['klɔmpə'baut] *vi F* = **clump about.**

clonk [klɔŋk] *vtr P* battre*/frapper; **to clonk s.o. on the head,** assommer qn/envoyer dormir qn.

clonk about ['klɔŋkə'baut] *vi F* = **clump about.**

close [klous] *adv F* **to play it/one's cards close to the chest,** y aller mollo/jouer serré.

close-fisted ['klous'fistid] *a F* avare*/radin/pingre/dur à la détente.

clot [klɔt] *n F* personne bête*/gourde *f*/patate *f*; **you clumsy clot!** espèce d'empoté! **what a clot!** quelle andouille!

cloth cap ['klɔθ'kæp] *a F* (= *working class*) **cloth cap ideas,** mentalité ouvrière.

cloth-ears ['klɔθiəz] *n F* sourd*/dur *m* de la feuille; **listen, cloth-ears!** écoute, sourdingue!

clothes-horse ['klouðzhɔːs] *n P* femme* tape-à-l'œil/mannequin ambulant.

cloth-head ['klɔθhed] *n F* = **clot.**

cloud [klaud] *n F* **1. to have one's head in the clouds,** être dans la lune **2. to be on cloud nine,** être au septième ciel/être aux anges.

cloud-cuckoo-land ['klaud-'kukuːlænd] *n F* pays *m* des rêves/pays des Châteaux en Espagne; **you're living in cloud-cuckoo-land,** tu siphonnes complètement.

clout[1] [klaut] *n* **1.** *F* coup*/calotte *f*; **to give/fetch s.o. a clout,** filer une calotte à qn **2.** *F (influence)* **to have a lot of clout,** avoir le bras long **3.** *A V* sexe de la femme*/motte *f*. *(See **dishclout**)*

clout[2] [klaut] *vtr F* filer une calotte à (qn).

clover ['klouvər] *n F* **to be/live in clover,** être comme un coq en pâte.

club [klʌb] *n* **1.** *F* **to join the club,** s'acoquiner avec qn; **join the club!** tu n'es pas le seul!/tope-là! **2.** *P* **to join the (pudding) club,** être enceinte*.

cluck [klʌk] *n esp NAm P* **dumb cluck,** individu bête*/gourde *f*/cruche *f*.

clucky ['klʌki] *a Austr P* enceinte*/en cloque.

clue [kluː] *n F* **he hasn't a clue** (*i*) il n'a pas la moindre idée (*ii*) il n'est bon à rien; **(I) haven't (got) a clue!** aucune idée!

clue in ['kluː'in] *vtr F* **to clue s.o. in,** mettre qn au courant/au parfum.

clueless ['kluːlis] *a F* (*a*) qui n'a pas la moindre idée/qui est dans le noir (*b*) qui n'a pas trouvé le joint.

clue up ['kluː'ʌp] *vtr F* **to clue s.o. up,** mettre qn sur la piste/au parfum/à la page; **he's very clued up on insurance,** il est très calé en assurance.

clump[1] [klʌmp] *n F* coup*/beigne *f*.

clump[2] [klʌmp] *vtr F* battre*/tabasser (qn).

clump about ['klʌmpə'baut] *vi F* marcher lourdement/comme un éléphant.

clutch up ['klʌtʃ'ʌp] *vi NAm (not common)* s'énerver/se monter le ciboulot.

cly [klai] *n A P* poche*/fouille *f*.

coal-burner ['koulbɜːnər] *n P* homosexuel* blanc qui s'accouple

de préférence avec des Noirs. (*See*
chocolate; **queen**[1] 2)

coalie, **coaly** ['kouli] *n F*
charbonnier *m*/carbi *m*.

coast ['koust] *n F* **the coast's clear**,
la voie est libre.

coast along ['koustə'lɔŋ] *vi F* se
la couler douce/ne pas se fouler.

coating ['koutiŋ] *n P* réprimande
f/savon *m*; **to give s.o. a coating**,
sonner les cloches à qn.

cob [kɔb] *n P* miche *f* de pain*/
demi-boule *f*.

cobber ['kɔbər] *n Austr O F* ami*/
copain *m*/pote *m*.

cobbler ['kɔblər] *n P* faussaire *m*/
homme *m* de lettres. (*See* **cobblers**)

cobblers ['kɔbləz] *npl P* (*RS =
cobblers' awls = balls*) (*a*) testicules*/balloches *fpl* (*b*) **(that's a
load of) cobblers!** c'est de la couil-
lonnade/de la couille/des conneries.
(*See* **balls**[1])

cock [kɔk] *n* 1. *V* (*a*) pénis*/queue
f/bite *f* 2. *P* bêtises*/conneries
fpl; **to talk cock**, déconner/déblo-
quer. (*See* **load 2**; **poppy-cock**)
3. *P* **all to cock**, de traviole 4. *P*
ami*/pote *m*; **well, old cock, eh
bien, mon colon! watcher cock!**
comment ça gaze, vieille branche?
5. *P* (*RS = ten*) **cock and hen**, billet* de dix livres. (*See* **half-cock**)

cock-a-hoop ['kɔkə'huːp] *a F* fier
comme Artaban.

cocked [kɔkt] *a F* **to knock s.o.
into a cocked hat** (*i*) battre* qn à
plate(s) couture(s)/pulvériser qn (*ii*)
abasourdir qn.

cocker ['kɔkər] *n P* ami*/pote *m*;
me old cocker, ma vieille branche.
(*See* **cock 4**)

cockeyed ['kɔkaid] *a P* 1. (*idea,
etc*) très bête/dingue/à la noix 2.
ivre*/rétamé à bloc 3. de travers/
de guingois/de traviole 4. qui
louche*/qui a un œil qui dit zut à
l'autre.

**cockeye bob, cock-eyed
bob** ['kɔkai(d)'bɔb] *n Austr P*
tempête *f ou* cyclone *m* inat-
tendu(e).

cock-handler ['kɔkhændlər],
cock-pusher ['kɔkpuʃər] *n V*
homosexuel*/pédé *m*.

cock rag [kɔk'ræg] *n Austr P*
cache-sexe *m* que portent les
Aborigènes.

cock-shy ['kɔkʃai] *a V* (*woman*)
qui a peur des rapports sexuels/
frustrée.

cock-sparrow ['kɔk'spærou,
'kɔk'spærə] *n P* **wotcher, me old
cock-sparrow!** salut, vieille branche!
(*See* **cock 4**)

cock-sucker ['kɔksʌkər] *n V* 1.
homosexuel*/pédé *m*/enculé *m* 2.
personne qui fait une fellation* à
une autre/suceur, -euse 3. *esp
NAm O* salaud*/fumier *m* 4.
lèches-bottes *m*/lèche-cul *m*.

cock-sucking ['kɔksʌkiŋ] *n V*
fellation*/prise *f* de pipe.

cock-teaser ['kɔktiːzər] *n V*
allumeuse *f*/bandeuse *f*/aguicheuse
f. (*See* **CT**; **prick teaser**; **PT**)

cock-up ['kɔkʌp] *n V* **it was one
almightly cock-up**, c'était un vrai
bordel/une belle salade; **he made a
real cock-up of it**, il y a foutu le
merdier/il a tout salopé. (*See* **balls-
up**)

cock up ['kɔk'ʌp] *vtr V* 1. foutre
la merde/foutre le bordel/tout foutre en l'air; **they've cocked it (up)
again**, ils y ont refoutu la merde/le
bordel 2. *Austr* (*woman*) s'offrir à
un homme.

cocky ['kɔki] *a F* culotté/qui a du
toupet; **he's a cocky little sod**, il a
un sacré culot.

coco(a) ['koukou] *vtr A P* (*RS =
coffee and cocoa = I should say so*)
I should coco(a)! et comment
donc!/tu parles!

cod [kɔd] *vtr O P* duper*/emmener (qn) en bateau/faire marcher (qn).

codger ['kɔdʒər] *n F* **old codger,** (drôle de) vieux bonhomme/vieux décati.

cods [kɔdz] *npl A P* testicules*/ burettes *fpl*/burnes *fpl*.

codswallop ['kɔdzwɔləp] *n F* bêtises*/foutaises *fpl*; **that's a load of codswallop,** c'est un tas de foutaises.

co-ed ['kou'(w)ed] *n F* (*abbr = co-educational*) (*a*) école *f*/lycée *m*, etc, mixte (*b*) *NAm* étudiante dans un établissement mixte.

C of E ['siːɔviː] *abbr.* **1.** *F* (= *Church of England*) l'Église anglicane **2.** *P* (= *customs and excise*) la douane.

coffin ['kɔfin] *n* **1.** *NAm P* (*disciplinary cell*) mitard *m*/(s)chtard *m* **2.** *F* **coffin nail,** cigarette*/cibiche *f*/sèche *f*.

coin [kɔin] *vtr F* **1. to coin it in,** devenir riche*/faire des affaires d'or **2.** (*iron*) **to coin a phrase,** si je puis m'exprimer ainsi.

coke [kouk] *n* **1.** *F* Coca(-Cola) *m* (*RTM*) **2.** *P* (*drugs*) cocaïne*/coco *f*/coke *f*.

coked (up) ['koukt('ʌp)] *a P* drogué*/défoncé (à la cocaïne).

cokehead ['koukhed] *n P* cocaïnomane *mf*/chnouffard *m*.

cokey, cokie ['kouki], **cokomo** [kou'koumou] *n P* cocaïnomane *mf*/ chnouffard *m*.

cold [kould] **I** *a F* **1. to be out (stone) cold,** être dans les pommes/ être KO; **to knock s.o. out cold,** mettre qn sur le tapis/mettre qn KO **2. that leaves me cold,** ça me laisse froid **3. to give s.o. the cold shoulder,** battre froid à qn/faire la tête à qn. (*See* **cold-shoulder**) **4. cold feet,** peur*/frousse *f*; **to get cold feet,** caner/avoir la trouille/ avoir le trac/avoir les jetons **5. cold fish,** pisse-froid *m* **6.** (*fig*) **to**

put in cold storage, mettre au frigidaire. (*See* **blood 3**; **meat 4**; **stone-cold**; **sweat**[1] **4**; **turkey 1**; **water 1**) **II** *n F* **1. to catch a cold,** écoper; (*business, etc*) faire faillite; aller à vau-l'eau **2. to be left out in the cold,** être mis de côté/rester en carafe/rester sur le carreau.

coldies ['kouldiːz] *npl Austr F* canettes *fpl* de bière (froide).

cold-shoulder ['kould'ʃouldər] *vtr F* battre froid à (qn)/snober qn. (*See* **cold I 3**)

collar[1] ['kɔlər] *n P* arrestation*.

collar[2] ['kɔlər] *vtr F* **1.** arrêter*/ cravater **2.** saisir/pincer/mettre la main sur (qn/qch).

collywobbles ['kɔliwɔblz] *npl F* **to have the collywobbles** (*a*) avoir mal au ventre/avoir des borborygmes *mpl* (*b*) avoir la diarrhée*/avoir la chiasse (*c*) avoir peur*/avoir la frousse.

colour, *NAm* **color** ['kʌlər] *n F* **let's see the colour of your money,** fais voir la couleur de ton fric/où est l'auréole de ton Saint-Fric? (*See* **horse**[1] **3**; **off IV 1**)

column-dodger ['kɔləm'dɔdʒər] *n F* tire-au-flanc *m*. (*See* **dodge**[2] **1**)

combo ['kɔmbou] *n* **1.** *F* orchestre *m* de jazz **2.** *Austr P* un Blanc qui cohabite avec une Aborigène.

come[1] [kʌm] *n P* sperme*/jus *m*. (*See* **cum**)

come[2] [kʌm] *vtr&i* **1.** *P* avoir un orgasme*/jouir/juter/prendre son pied; **she never comes when they make love,** elle ne jouit jamais quand ils font l'amour **2.** *F* **as dim/daft as they come,** bête* comme un pied/comme tout **3.** *F* **you'll get what's coming to you!** tu ne perds rien pour attendre!/tu l'as bien cherché! **4.** *F* **to come it a bit strong,** exagérer*/y aller un peu fort/attiger (la cabane) **5.** *F* jouer un rôle; **to come the heavy husband,** faire le mari autoritaire; **to**

come the innocent with s.o., faire l'innocent avec qn; **don't you come it with me!** ne charrie pas avec moi! **6.** *F* **to come over (all) funny/(all) queer,** se sentir tout chose **7.** *P* **come again?** répète un peu?/comment?/pardon? **8.** *F* **how come?** comment (que) ça se fait? (*See* **acid 1**; **clean I 3**; **raw prawn**; **soldier¹ 3**; **think¹**)

come-at-able [kʌm'ætəbəl] *a F* accessible/abordable.

come-back ['kʌmbæk] *n F* (*actor*) retour *m* à la scène/à l'écran; (*politician*) retour au pouvoir; **to make a come-back,** se remettre sur pied/se retaper; **he has made several come-backs,** il est remonté plusieurs fois sur la scène.

come-down ['kʌmdaun] *n* **1.** *F* **what a come-down!** quelle dégringolade!/quelle douche!/quelle déchéance! **2.** *P* (*drugs*) retour *m* à l'état hors drogue/descente *f*.

come down ['kʌm'daun] *vi* **1.** *P* revenir à l'état hors drogue/redescendre **2.** *V* **to come down on s.o.** (*i*) faire une fellation* à qn/faire un pompier à qn/tailler une pipe à qn (*ii*) pratiquer le cunnilinctus sur qn/brouter le cresson **3.** *F* **to come down on s.o. (like a ton of bricks),** réprimander qn/enguirlander qn/tomber sur le dos à qn **4.** *F* **to come down in the world,** déchoir/descendre plusieurs échelons. (*See* **peg 2** (*b*))

comedy ['kɔmidi] *n F* **cut (out) the comedy!** finie la comédie!/arrête ton char!

come good ['kʌm'gud] *vi F* réussir/tenir bon; **he's come good,** il a apporté la marchandise/il a tenu bon.

come-hither ['kʌm'hiðər] *a F* **a come-hither look,** les yeux* doux/un regard aguichant/des yeux couleur besoin.

come off ['kʌm'ɔf] *vtr F* **1.** *P* avoir un orgasme*/s'envoyer en

l'air/prendre son pied **2.** *F* **come off it!** (*i*) change de disque!/arrête ton char!/mon œil! (*ii*) pas tant de manières!

come-on ['kʌmɔn] *n P* **to give s.o. the come-on,** encourager les avances sexuelles de qn/flirter avec qn/allumer qn/aguicher qn.

come on ['kʌm'ɔn] *vi P* **1.** commencer à ressentir les effets d'une drogue/partir **2.** flirter/faire des avances sexuelles/aguicher/allumer; **he comes on really strong,** il en impose **3. come on!** (*i*) = **come off it!** (**come off 2**) (*ii*) courage!

come on ['kʌm'ɔn] *vi P* avoir ses règles*/ses affaires.

come out ['kʌm'aut] *vi P* (*homosexuals*) **to come out (of the closet),** oser dire qu'on est homosexuel/sortir du placard/faire son comeout.

come up ['kʌm'ʌp] *vi P* gagner/affurer; **to come up on the pools,** gagner/prendre un paquet en pariant sur les matchs de foot.

come-uppance ['kʌm'ʌpəns] *n F* **to get one's come-uppance,** recevoir ce qu'on mérite/se faire dire ses quatre vérités.

comfy ['kʌmfi] *a* (= *comfortable*) *F* confortable/douillet. (*See* **nice II 1**)

comic ['kɔmik] *a A F* **comic cuts,** bandes dessinées.

commie, commy ['kɔmi] *a&n F* (*pej*) communiste (*mf*)/coco (*m*)/bolcho (*m*); **commie bastard,** salaud *m* de communiste; **commie hunt,** chasse *f* aux communistes.

commission [kə'miʃən] *n P* (*protection money*) **he pays them commission,** il leur verse du fric pour qu'ils le laissent en paix.

compree! ['kɔm'priː] *excl F* compris!/pigé!

con¹ [kɔn] *n* **1.** *F* (= *convict*) taulard *m*. (*See* **ex**) **2.** *F* escroquerie*/arnaque *f*/carottage *m*; **con game,** combine *f* louche/attrape-couillons *m*; **con man/con artist,**

escroc*/arnaqueur m/estampeur m;
it was all a complete con, c'était de
l'arnaque patentée. (*See* **pro 3**)

con² [kɔn] *vtr F* escroquer*/
empaumer/rouler (qn); **to con s.o.
into doing sth,** entortiller qn; **I was
conned,** je me suis fait avoir/baiser.

conchie, conchy ['kɔntʃɪ] *n O F*
(= *conscientious objector*) objecteur
m de conscience.

confab ['kɔnfæb] *n F* bavette *f/*
causette *f;* **there's a confab going on
in there,** on discutaille là-dedans.

confab(ulate) [kɔn'fæb(juleit)] *vi
F* bavarder*/tailler une bavette;
discutailler.

conflab ['kɔnflæb] *n F* = **confab.**

congrats! [kən'græts] *interj F*
félicitations!/bravo!

conk¹ [kɔŋk] *n P* **1.** nez*/pif *m/*
blair *m* **2.** tête*/caboche *f.*

conk² [kɔŋk] *vtr P* **to conk s.o.,**
flanquer un gnon à qn/matraquer
qn; **she conked him on the head,**
elle lui a flanqué un coup sur la
tête.

conker ['kɔŋkər] *n F* (*a*) marron *m*
(*b*) *pl* jeu *m* de marrons.

conk out ['kɔŋk'aut] *vi* **1.** *F*
tomber en rade/claquer/caler; **my
car conked out,** ma bagnole m'a
claqué dans les doigts/m'a lâché
2. *P* mourir*/caner/casser sa pipe
3. *F* s'endormir tout d'un coup; **he
was so tired he conked out on the
sofa,** il était tellement crevé qu'il
s'est effondré sur le canapé.

connect [kə'nekt] *vi P* trouver une
source de drogue/se mettre en contact avec un fourgueur afin de lui
acheter des drogues.

connection [kə'nekʃ(ə)n], **connector** [kə'nektər], **connexion** [kə'nekʃ(ə)n] *n F* (*esp drugs*)
contact *m/*inter *m/*fourgue *m/*
dealer *m.*

conshie, conshy ['kɔnʃɪ] *n O F*
= **conchie, conchy.**

contract ['kɔntrækt] *n P* engagement *m* à tuer* qn/dessoudage *m;*
to have a contract on s.o., s'être
engagé à tuer* qn; **contract killing,**
meurtre *m* sur commande/contrat
m.

coo! [kuː] *excl F* tiens!/ça alors!

cook¹ [kuk] *n* **1.** *F* **to be head/
chief cook and bottle-washer,** être
l'homme à tout faire/être le
lampiste **2.** *P* =**chef 2.**

cook² [kuk] *vtr&i* **1.** *F* **what's
cooking?** quoi de neuf?/qu'est-ce
qui se mijote?/qu'est-ce qui se
goupille? **2.** *F* **to cook the books,**
truquer/cuisiner/maquiller les
comptes **3.** *F* **to cook s.o.'s goose,**
faire son affaire à qn/régler son
compte à qn **4.** *P* = **cook up 2.**

cooked [kukt] *a* **1.** *F* très
fatigué*/exténué **2.** *F* (*pers*) **to be
cooked,** cuire dans son jus **3.** *P*
=**cooked up.**

cooked up ['kukt'ʌp] *a P* (*not
common*) drogué*/camé/défoncé.
(*See* **cook up 2**)

cookie ['kuki] *n* **1.** *F* **that's the
way the cookie crumbles!** c'est la
vie (que veux-tu)! **2.** *esp NAm F*
individu*/type *m;* **a tough cookie,**
un dur (à cuire) **3.** *P* **hot cookie
= hot babe** (**babe 2**) **4.** *NAm V*
sexe de la femme*.

cook up ['kuk'ʌp] *vtr&i* **1.** *F* **to
cook up an excuse/a story,** combiner une excuse **2.** *P* préparer
une drogue en la diluant et en la
chauffant/se préparer un fixe. (*See*
cooked up)

cool¹ [kuːl] **I** *a* **1.** *F* (*a*) détendu/
relax/coolos (*b*) beau*/bien/satis-
faisant (*c*) passionnant (*d*) avant-
garde; **that's really cool,** c'est super
cool/c'est le (super-)pied **2.** *F* **a
cool £1000,** rien moins que £1000
3. *F* distant/peu émotif/de glace; **a
cool customer,** qui a du culot/qui a
la tête froide **4.** *F* (*jazz*) sobre/
relax. (*See* **cat 1, 2; hot 7**) **5.** *P*
(*drug addict*) **to be cool,** planer

calmement **II** *adv* F (*a*) **to play it cool**, ne pas s'énerver/y aller la tête froide; **play it cool!** pas de panique! (*b*) *esp NAm* **stay cool!** (*i*) pas de panique!/t'énerve pas! (*ii*) bon courage!/salut! (*iii*) tiens bon! **III** *n* F **1.** sang-froid *m*; **to keep one's cool**, ne pas s'énerver/y aller la tête froide **2. to lose one's cool/to blow one's cool** (*i*) se mettre en colère*/piquer une crise (*ii*) paniquer; se dégonfler **3.** P (*sort of jazz*) cool *m*.

cool² [kuːl] *vtr* **1.** F **to cool it**, se calmer; **cool it!** t'énerve pas!/ t'emballe pas! **2.** (*relationship, etc*) **let's cool it/let's cool things down for a while**, attendons que les choses se calment un peu/si on prenait une certaine distance pendant quelque temps?

cooler ['kuːlər] *n* P prison*/taule *f* **2.** mitard *m*/chtard *m*.

coon [kuːn] *n* P **1.** (*pej*) Noir(e)*/ nègre *mf*/bougnoul *m* **2.** *NAm* **a coon's age**, longtemps/belle lurette.

co-op ['kou(w)ɔp] *n* F (*abbr = co-operative stores*) société coopérative/ coopé *f*.

coot [kuːt] *n* **1.** P individu bête*/ gourde *f*; **he's a silly old coot**, c'est un vieux con/une vieille andouille **2.** F **bald as a coot**, chauve* comme un genou/un œuf/une bille.

cootie ['kuːti] *n esp NAm* P pou*/ morbac *m*.

cooze [kuːz], **coozie** [kuːzi] *n NAm* V **coït*/coup *m* de tringle/ baise *f* **2.** sexe de la femme*/baba *m*.

cop¹ [kɔp] *n* **1.** F flic *m*/poulet *m*; **bent cop**, flic véreux; **speed/courtesy cop**, motard *m*. (*See* **copper 1; fly-cop**) **2.** P arrestation *f*; **it's a fair cop**, on est fait, rien à dire **3.** P **it's not much cop/it's no great cop**, ça ne vaut pas grand-chose/ c'est de la camelote/c'est de la pacotille **4.** *Austr* P (bon) filon/ affure *f*.

cop² [kɔp] *vtr* P **1.** arrêter*/pincer (qn); **to get copped**, se faire pincer/ alpaguer **2. to cop it** (*i*) écoper (*ii*) être réprimandé*/recevoir un savon **3. to cop hold of sth**, choper/ attraper le bout de qch; **here, cop hold of this!** tiens, attrape ça! **4.** (*to listen or to see*) **cop a load of this!** (*i*) écoute-moi ça! (*ii*) vise-moi ça! **5.** obtenir *ou* acheter (des drogues)/se fournir. (*See* **dose 1; needle¹ 1** (*e*); **packet 1; plea; spike¹ 2**)

copilots ['koupailəts] *npl* P (*drugs*) Benzédrine* (*RTM*).

cop-out ['kɔpaut] *n* P **it's just one big cop-out**, c'est de l'arnaque; c'est pour se défiler tout simplement.

cop out ['kɔp'aut] *vi* P **1.** se retirer/se dégager/se défiler **2.** éviter/éluder (une question, la responsabilité, etc) **3.** ne pas tenir une promesse.

copper ['kɔpər] *n* **1.** P agent* de police/flic *m*; **copper's nark**, indic *m*/mouchard *m*. (*See* **bent 1**) **2.** P **to come copper**, devenir indicateur* de police/y aller du coup de casserole **3.** F gros sou*/de la petite monnaie; **he gave the busker a few coppers**, il a donné quelques sous au type qui jouait dans la rue.

cop-shop ['kɔpʃɔp] *n* P commissariat *m* de police/quart *m*; **he's still down the cop-shop**, il est toujours au quart.

cop-wagon ['kɔpwægən] *n* P car* de police/panier *m* à salade/poulailler ambulant. (*See* **Black Maria**)

copycat ['kɔpikæt] *n* F **to be a copycat**, faire le singe/singer; **copycat!** espèce de singe!

cor! [kɔr] *excl* (*a*) F ça alors! **cor, she's a knockout!** merde! ce qu'elle est belle!/elle n'est pas pourrie! **cor love a duck!** grands dieux! (*b*) P **cor blimey!** = **gorblimey!**

corine ['kɔːrin] *n* P (*drugs*) cocaïne*.

corked [kɔːkt] *a P* ivre* mort.

corker [ˈkɔːkər] *n F* **1.** (*a*) individu* formidable/chic type (*b*) belle fille/beau morceau **2.** gros mensonge*/bourrage *m* de crâne; craque *f*; **that's a corker,** ça vous a la bouche/ça vous en bouche un coin.

corking [ˈkɔːkiŋ] *a O F* excellent*/épatant/foutral/formid(able).

corn [kɔːn] *n F* **1.** (*a*) vieille rengaine/vieux jeu (*b*) guimauve *f*; **it's pure corn,** c'est de la guimauve/c'est une histoire à l'eau de rose **2. to step/tread on s.o.'s corns,** toucher qn à l'endroit sensible/marcher sur les pieds de qn; froisser qn. (*See* **popcorn**)

cornhole[1] [ˈkɔːnhoul] *n NAm V* (*rare*) anus*/trou *m* de balle; (*homosexual use*) **cornhole palace,** WC* pour hommes/tasses *fpl*.

cornhole[2] [ˈkɔːnhoul] *vtr NAm V* (*to have anal sex*) sodomiser*/empaffer/enculer.

cornholer [ˈkɔːnhoulər] *n NAm V* (*rare*) homosexuel*/bourrin *m*.

corny [ˈkɔːni] *F* (*a*) banal/rebattu (*b*) vieux jeu/vioque (*c*) à l'eau de rose; **this film is so corny,** ce film est tellement cul-cul (la praline).

'cos [kɔz] *conj F* (= *because*) parce que/pasque/bicause.

cosh[1] [kɔʃ] *n F* matraque *f*/assommoir *m*/cigare *m*.

cosh[2] [kɔʃ] *vtr F* matraquer/assommer (qn).

cost [kɔst] *vtr F* **I can get it but it'll cost you,** je peux l'avoir mais ça sera chérot/ça vous coûtera cher. (*See* **earth 2**)

cottage[1] [ˈkɔtidʒ] *n P* (*homosexual use*) WC*/tasses *fpl*.

cottage[2] [ˈkɔtidʒ] *vi P* (*homosexuals*) **to cottage/to go cottaging,** draguer dans les toilettes/dans les tasses; faire les tasses.

cotton[1] [kɔtn] *n P* (*drugs*) morceau de coton utilisé pour filtrer

l'héroïne avant de se piquer; **cotton freak,** camé(e) qui prépare sa piquouse de cette façon.

cotton[2] [kɔtn] *vi F* (*a*) **to cotton to s.o.,** être attiré par qn/avoir qn à la bonne (*b*) **to cotton to sth,** approuver/apprécier qch; **he doesn't cotton to it much,** ça ne le botte pas tellement.

cotton on [ˈkɔtnˈɔn] *vi F* **1.** comprendre/piger/entraver; **he cottons on quickly,** il pige vite **2. I can't cotton on to him,** sa tête ne me revient pas/ça ne biche pas avec lui.

cotton-picking [ˈkɔtnˈpikiŋ] *a NAm* (*a*) commun/vulgaire (*b*) sacré/satané (*c*) niais/navet; **you cotton-picking idiot,** tête de nœud!/quelle nouille!

cotton-wool [ˈkɔtnˈwul] *n F* **1. to wrap s.o. in cotton-wool,** mettre qn dans du coton/garder qn sous cloche **2. my legs were like cotton-wool,** j'avais les jambes en coton/en laine.

couch doctor [ˈkautʃˈdɔktər] *n F* (*hum*) psychanalyste *mf*/psy *mf*.

cough [kɔf] *vtr&i P* avouer*/accoucher/manger le morceau.

cough up [ˈkɔfˈʌp] *vi F* **1.** payer*/cracher/abouler **2.** parler*/dévider/dégoiser **3.** avouer*/accoucher/manger le morceau.

count [kaunt] *n F* **to be out for the count** (*a*) avoir son compte/être KO (*b*) être profondément endormi.

counter [ˈkauntər] *n F* **to sell sth under the counter,** vendre qch en cachette. (*See* **under-the-counter**)

count in [ˈkauntˈin] *vtr F* **you can count me in,** je marche/je suis partant/je suis de la partie.

count out [ˈkauntˈaut] *vtr F* **you can count me out,** je ne marche pas/je ne suis pas partant/ne comptez pas sur moi/rayez moi de vos tablettes.

county ['kaunti] *a F* **the county set,** l'aristocratie provinciale/la haute bourgeoisie provinciale; **she's terribly county,** elle fait très aristo/elle fait très snob.

coupon ['kuːpɔn] *n P* visage*/frime *f*/tronche *f*.

courage ['kʌridʒ] *n P* (*drugs*) courage pills, comprimé *m* d'héroïne.

cove [kouv] *n O F* individu*; **a queer cove,** un drôle de pistolet/un drôle de numéro.

Coventry ['kɔvəntri] *n F* **to send s.o. to Coventry,** mettre qn en quarantaine.

cover ['kʌvər] *n F* couverture*/couverte *f*/prétexte *m*; **you're my cover,** tu es mon alibi.

cover-girl ['kʌvəgəːl] *n F* pin-up *f*/cover-girl *f*.

cover up ['kʌvər'ʌp] *vi F* **to cover up for s.o.,** couvrir qn/prendre les patins pour qn.

cow [kau] *n* **1.** *P* (*pej*) (*disagreeable woman*) vache *f*/chameau *m*/garce *f*/salope *f*/peau *f* de vache; **an old cow,** une vieille bique; **silly cow!** espèce de conne!/connasse! **poor cow!** pauvre pute! **what a cow she is at times,** ce qu'elle peut être garce/vache des fois; c'est une vraie peau de vache **2.** *Austr* (*disagreeable thing*) **it's a fair cow!** ce que c'est moche! **he's a fair cow!** qu'il est moche! **3.** *A P* une livre sterling **4.** *F* **till the cows come home,** jusqu'à la Saint-Glinglin/quand les poules auront des dents; **to wait until the cows come home,** attendre la semaine des quatre jeudis. (*See* **bull 3; holy 1; moo-cow**)

cow-juice ['kaudʒuːs] *n F* lait *m*/lolo *m*.

cow-poke ['kaupouk], **cow-puncher** ['kaupʌntʃər] *n NAm F* cowboy *m*.

crab[1] [kræb] *n F* **1.** grognon *m*/rouscailleur *m*; **she's an old crab,** c'est une vieille emmerdeuse **2.** *pl*

poux* du pubis/morpions *mpl*/morbacs *mpl* **3.** *Austr* **to draw the crabs,** se faire repérer.

crab[2] [kræb] *vtr&i P* **1.** grogner*/râler **2. to crab the act/deal,** mettre des bâtons dans les roues.

crack[1] [kræk] *n* **1.** *V* sexe de la femme*/fente *f*/crac *m* **2.** *F* blague *f*/vanne *f*; **he made a crack about my mother,** il s'est moqué de ma mère/il s'est payé la tête de ma mère **3.** *F* **to have/to take a crack (at sth),** tenter le coup/sa chance **4.** *F* **to have a crack at s.o.** (*i*) filer une taloche à qn (*ii*) se moquer de qn **5.** *F* (*pers who excels*) as *m*/crack *m*; **crack shot,** tireur *m* d'élite **6.** renseignement*/tuyau *m*/info *f*; **to give s.o. the crack,** tuyauter qn/mettre qn dans le parfum; **what's the crack?** quoi de neuf? (*See* **paper**[2] **2; whip**[1] **1; wisecrack**[1])

crack[2] [kræk] *vtr&i* **1.** *P* filer/flanquer un coup* à qn **2.** *F* **to get cracking** (*i*) commencer/se mettre au boulot; **let's get cracking!** au boulot! (*ii*) aller vite*/se grouiller; **get cracking!** magne-toi! **3.** *F* **to crack a safe,** cambrioler/faire un coffre-fort **4. to crack it** (*a*) *F* réussir/l'avoir belle (*b*) *P* (*man*) faire l'amour*/se l'envoyer/tringler. (*See* **crib**[1] **1; fat II 4; nut**[1] **7; whip**[1] **4; wisecrack**[2])

crack down ['kræk'daun] *vi F* **1. to crack down on s.o.** (*i*) tomber sur le paletot à qn/tomber à bras raccourcis sur qn (*ii*) serrer la vis à qn **2. to crack down on sth,** mettre le frein à qch.

cracked [krækt] *a F* fou*/cinglé/toqué.

cracker ['krækər] *n F* **1.** mensonge*/craque *f* **2. she's a cracker,** elle est formid(able)/c'est un beau morceau/elle n'est pas pourrie **3.** *Austr* **not worth a cracker,** qui ne sert à rien/qui ne vaut pas grand-chose/qui ne vaut pas tripette. (*See* **crib-cracker**)

cracker-barrel ['krækə'bærəl] *a* *NAm* *F* **cracker-barrel philosopher,** philosophe *m* en chambre.

crackerjack ['krækədʒæk] **I** *a* *O* *F* excellent*/formid(able)/sensass **II** *n* *O* *F* **1.** (*pers*) as *m*/crack *m* **2.** (*thing*) qch d'excellent*/du tonnerre.

crackers ['krækəz] *a* *P* fou*/cinglé/timbré.

cracking ['krækiŋ] *a* *F* **1. to be in cracking form,** être en super forme/avoir la frite/avoir la pêche **2. at a cracking pace,** très vite*/en quatrième vitesse.

crackpot ['krækpɔt] *a & n F* fou*/loufoque (*m*)/cinglé (*mf*).

cracksman ['kræksmən] *n P* (*esp safecracker*) cambrioleur*/casseur *m*.

crack-up ['krækʌp] *n F* **1.** (*thing*) (*i*) *esp NAm* accident très grave (*esp* d'un avion) (*ii*) effondrement *m*/écroulement *m* **2.** (*of pers*) dépression nerveuse.

crack up ['krækʌp] *vi F* **1.** perdre la boule/perdre les pédales/être au bout (du rouleau); **I must be cracking up!** ça ne tourne pas rond chez moi!/je perds la tête! **2.** faire une dépression nerveuse **3. it's not all it's cracked up to be,** ce n'est pas aussi bien qu'on le dit/c'est pas aussi sensationnel qu'on le prétend.

cradle ['kreidl] *n F* **to rob the cradle,** les prendre au berceau.

cradle-snatcher ['kreidlsnætʃər] *n F* vieux marcheur; **he/she is a cradle-snatcher,** il/elle les prend au berceau. (*See* **baby-snatcher**)

crafty ['krɑːfti] *a F* **to have a crafty smoke,** en griller une en douce/en loucedoc; **he's a crafty little beggar,** c'est un petit malin/futé. (*See* **arty-crafty**)

cram [kræm] *vi F* **to cram for an exam,** chauffer/bachoter.

cramp [kræmp] *vtr F* **to cramp s.o.'s style,** ennuyer/gêner qn; **does**

that **cramp your style?** est-ce que ça te défrise?

crank [kræŋk] *n F* (*a*) excentrique *m*/original *m*/loufoque *m* (*b*) *esp NAm* grognon *m*/rouspéteur *m* (*c*) fanatique *mf*.

crank up ['kræŋkʌp] *vi P* (*drugs*) se piquer/se faire un fixe.

cranky ['kræŋki] *a F* **1.** excentrique/original **2.** *esp NAm* grincheux/rouspéteur.

crap¹ [kræp] *n V* **1.** étron*/merde *f*; **to have a crap,** chier **2.** bêtises*/conneries *fpl*/couillonnades *fpl*; **don't give me that crap!** ne me sers pas ces conneries! **I don't have to take that sort of crap from you,** si tu crois que je vais encaisser ce genre de conneries de ta part; **cut the crap!** déconne pas!/écrase!/fais pas chier! **3. it's a load of crap,** tout ça c'est de l'eau de bidet/de la merde/de la saloperie **4. he's full of crap,** il est fort en gueule; c'est un couillon/un connard **5.** (*drugs*) héroïne* de qualité inférieure/merde *f*. (*See* **shoot²** 7)

crap² [kræp] *vi V* **1.** déféquer*/chier **2.** déconner/faire le con; **don't crap about like that!** fais pas le con!/arrête de déconner! **3. to crap on (about sth),** dire des conneries/débloquer.

craphouse ['kræphaus], **crapper** ['kræpər] *n V* WC*/chiottes *fpl*/gogues *mpl*.

crappy ['kræpi] *a V* sale*/cracra/crado/cradingue/merdique/ dégueulasse; **he's got a really crappy job,** il a un boulot vraiment merdique.

crash [kræʃ] *F* **I** *vtr* = **gatecrash** **II** *vi* **to crash (down),** s'endormir*/pioncer/en écraser/coincer la bulle.

crashed [kræʃt] *a NAm P* ivre*/rétamé.

crashing ['kræʃiŋ] *a F* **crashing bore,** casse-pieds *m*/raseur *m* de première (classe).

crash out ['kræʃaut] *vi P* **1.**
s'endormir*/en écraser **2.**
s'endormir *ou* s'effondrer (de façon
désagréable) sous l'effet de la
drogue/crasher.

crash-pad ['kræʃpæd] *n P* asile *m*
temporaire.

crate [kreit] *n F* (*a*) (*plane*) zinc *m*/
coucou *m* (*b*) (*car*) vieille voiture*/
guimbarde *f*/tacot *m*.

crawl [krɔːl] *vi F* **1.** s'aplatir; **to
crawl all over s.o.**, faire de la lèche
à qn **2. the place was crawling
with cops**, l'endroit grouillait de
flics. (*See* **arse crawl**; **pub crawl²**)

crawler ['krɔːlər] *n F* **1.** lécheur *m*
de bottes **2.** tortillard *m*. (*See*
arse-crawler; **kerb crawler**)

crazy ['kreizi] *a F* **1.** fou*/cinglé;
are you crazy? t'es pas fou*?/ça ne
va pas, la tête? **2.** terrible/
formid(able) **3.** enthousiaste/pas-
sionné/fana(tique); **she's crazy
about it**, elle en est dingue; **he's
crazy about her**, il en est toqué.
(*See* **man-crazy**; **sex-crazy**; **stir-
crazy**; **woman-crazy**)

crazyhouse ['kreizihaus] *n P* maison *f* de fous/asile *m* de dingues.

cream¹ [kriːm] *n* **1.** *P* sperme*/
blanc *m*/jus *m* **2.** *V* **cream cheese**,
smegma *m*/fromage *m*. (*See*
cheese 4; **ice-cream**)

cream² [kriːm] *vtr esp NAm P* **1.**
battre*/filer une raclée à (qn) **2.**
tuer*/repasser/descendre (qn) **3.**
éjaculer*/cracher son venin; **to
cream one's jeans**, juter dans son
froc.

cream off ['kriːm'ɔf] *vtr P* masturber* (qn)/branler (qn) (pour le
faire jouir).

creampuff ['kriːm'pʌf] *n P* homme
efféminé/folle *f*.

crease¹ [kriːs] *n V* sexe de la
femme*/fente *f*.

crease² [kriːs] *vtr P* **1.** ennuyer*;
you crease me, tu me cours **2. to
feel creased** (*i*) être déprimé/avoir

le cafard (*ii*) être fatigué*/crevé **3.
you crease me!** tu me fais (tordre
de) rire!

create [kriː'eit] *vi P* (*a*) grogner*/
rouscailler (*b*) faire une scène/faire
du foin. (*See* **hell 3**)

creek [kriːk] *n F* **to be up the
creek**/*V* **to be up shit creek (without a paddle)**, être dans le pétrin;
être embêté/emmouscaillé; *V* être
emmerdé/être dans les emmerde-
ments/avoir des emmerdes.

creep¹ [kriːp] *n* **1.** *F* vaurien*/
salaud*/fripouille *f*; **he's a real
creep**, c'est un vrai salaud/saligaud
2. *F* lèche-bottes *m*/lèche-cul *m*/
flagorneur *m* **3.** *P* cambrioleur *m*
qui travaille de nuit. (*See* **creeps**)

creep² [kriːp] *vi F* ramper (devant
qn)/s'aplatir/lécher les bottes à qn.

creepers ['kriːpəz] *npl O F*
(brothel) creepers, chaussures* à
semelle souple. (*See* **jeepers!**)

creeps [kriːps] *npl F* **he gives me
the creeps**, il me fait peur*/il me
donne la chair de poule/*P* il me
fout les boules; **it gives me the
creeps**, ça me met les nerfs en
pelote.

creepy-crawly ['kriːpi'krɔːli] **I** *a
F* **creepy-crawly feeling** (*i*) fourmil-
lement *m* (*ii*) chair *f* de poule **II** *n
F* vermine *f*; petite bestiole
(rampante).

cretin ['kretin] *n F* (*pej*) imbécile*/
crétin *m*/gland *m*; **what a cretin!**
espèce de nœud!/quel con!

cretinous ['kretinəs] *a F* (*remark,
etc*) bête*/crétin(e).

crib¹ [krib] *n* **1.** *O P* **to crack a
crib**, cambrioler/faire un fric-frac/
casser un coffiot. (*See* **crib-cracker**) **2.** *F* antisèche *f* **3.** *P* rouspétance *f*.

crib² [krib] *vtr F* tricher/bidocher.

crib-cracker ['kribkrækər] *n O P*
cambrioleur*/casseur *m*. (*See* **crib¹
1**)

crib-cracking ['krɪbkrækɪŋ] *n O P* cambriolage *m*/casse(ment) *m*.

cricket ['krɪkɪt] *n F* that's not cricket, c'est pas de jeu/ça ne se fait pas.

crikey! ['kraɪki] *excl F* crikey! mince alors!/fichtre!

crim [krɪm] *n Austr P* (= *criminal*) criminel *m*/taulard *m*.

crimp¹ [krɪmp] *n NAm F* to put a crimp in s.o.'s style, couper les effets à qn; mettre des bâtons dans les roues de qn.

crimp² [krɪmp] *vtr F* to crimp s.o.'s style, couper les effets à qn; mettre des bâtons dans les roues de qn.

cripes! [kraɪps] *excl F* = crikey!

cripple ['krɪpəl] *n F* (*pej*) idiot(e)*/imbécile *mf*/crétin(e) *m(f)*; you bloody cripple! espèce d'andouille!

crippler ['krɪplər] *n P* to slip s.o. a crippler, filer un coup bas à qn.

croak [krouk] *vtr&i P* **1.** tuer*/descendre (qn)/liquider (qn) **2.** mourir*/cronir/claquer/clamser.

croaker ['kroukər] *n P* médecin *m*/toubib *m*; *esp* médecin qui prescrit sans scrupules des stupéfiants pour un drogué.

crock [krɔk] *n* **1.** *P* pipe *f* à opium*/bambou *m* **2.** *F* old crock (*a*) vieille voiture*/tacot *m*/guimbarde *f* (*b*) (*pers*) croulant *m*/vieux birbe/vieux jeton **3.** *F* cheval* fourbu/rosse *f* **4.** *NAm F* individu* peu sympathique/arsouille *m*/sale coco *m* **5.** *NAm P* crock of shit (*a*) mensonges*/boniments *mpl* (*b*) (*pers*) menteur *m*/fumiste *m*.

crocked ['krɔkt] *a P* **1.** blessé/amoché **2.** *esp NAm* ivre*/rétamé.

crockery ['krɔkəri] *n NAm F* dentier *m*/tabourets *mpl*.

crocodile ['krɔkədaɪl] *n F* élèves marchant deux à deux/en rang(s) d'oignons/à la queue leu-leu. (*See* **alligator**)

crook [kruk] **I** *a Austr F* **1.** (*a*) (*also dial*) malade*/patraque (*b*) de mauvaise qualité/de la camelote (*c*) (*unpleasant*) désagréable/fâcheux **2.** to go off crook, se mettre en colère*/piquer une crise; to go crook at s.o./on s.o., réprimander* qn/engueuler qn/passer un savon à qn **II** *n F* **1.** escroc*/arnaqueur *m*/filou *m* **2.** voleur*/chapardeur *m*/faucheur *m*.

cropper ['krɔpər] *n F* to come a cropper (*a*) tomber*/ramasser une pelle/se casser la figure (*b*) tomber sur un bec/faire un bide/faire un four.

crop up ['krɔpʌp] *vi F* survenir à l'improviste/surgir; ready for any problems that might crop up, paré à toute éventualité.

cross¹ [krɔs] *n P* escroquerie*/arnaque *f*; on the cross, malhonnêtement/en filouterie. (*See* **white I 1**)

cross² [krɔs] *vtr F* **1.** tromper*/trahir/posséder (qn). (*See* **double cross**) **2.** to cross one's heart, jurer ses grands dieux; (*esp child's language*) cross my heart (and hope to die), croix de bois, croix de fer (, si je mens je vais en enfer) **3.** to cross one's fingers, faire une petite prière; let's keep our fingers crossed, touchons du bois.

crow [krou] *n* **1.** *F* (*pej*) old crow, (vieille) femme*/vieille bique **2.** *NAm F* to eat crow, faire des excuses humiliantes/avaler des couleuvres **3.** *F* stone the crows! ça alors!/merde alors! (*See* **Jim Crow**)

crowd [kraud] *vtr P* casser les pieds à (qn)/s'en prendre à (qn)/chercher noise à (qn); don't crowd me! fiche-moi la paix!

crown¹ [kraun] *n P* crown jewels, sexe de l'homme*/service *m* de trois pièces/bijoux *mpl* de famille.

crown² [kraun] *vtr F* **1.** flanquer un coup* à la tête de (qn)/assom-

crud [krʌd] *n* **1.** *P* salaud*/fumier *m*; **you stupid crud,** espèce d'andouille!/tête de nœud! **2.** *O P* **Bombay cruds,** diarrhée*/riquette *f* **3.** *V* sperme* séché/foutre *m*.

cruise ['kruːz] *vi P* (*esp homosexuals*) chercher un partenaire sexuel *ou* un(e) prostitué(e)/draguer.

cruiser ['kruːzər] *n P* **1.** homosexuel* qui drague/dragueur *m* **2.** *O* prostituée*/marcheuse *f*. (*See* **kerb cruiser**)

cruising ['kruːzɪŋ] *n P* (*esp homosexuals*) la drague; **they go there to do some cruising,** ils y vont pour draguer les mecs.

crumb [krʌm] *n P* (*a*) vaurien*/ salaud* (*b*) pauvre type *m*.

crumbs [krʌmz] *excl F* ça alors!/ zut!

crummy ['krʌmi] *F* (*a*) sale*/ miteux (*b*) moche/minable.

crumpet ['krʌmpit] *n* **1.** (*a*) *V* sexe de la femme*/abricot *m*; **to have a bit of crumpet/to get one's crumpet,** faire l'amour* avec/ baiser/s'envoyer une femme (*b*) *P* (*coll* = *women*) **there's some crumpet around,** il y a de la fesse (*c*) *F* **a piece/a nice bit of crumpet,** un beau petit lot/un beau morceau/ une roulée au moule **2.** *F* tête*/ caboche *f* **3.** *Austr P* **not worth a crumpet,** qui ne vaut rien* du tout/ que dalle.

crunch [krʌntʃ] *n F* **the crunch,** le moment critique; **when it comes to the crunch...,** quand on est au pied du mur.../au moment critique.

crush [krʌʃ] *n F* béguin *m*; **to have a crush on s.o.,** en pincer pour qn/ se toquer de qn.

crust [krʌst] *n F* **1.** **the upper crust,** la haute/le gratin/le dessus du panier **2.** *Austr P* **to earn a crust,** gagner sa vie.

crutch [krʌtʃ] *n P* (*drugs*) béquille *f* (*allumette fendue qui permet de fumer une cigarette de marijuana jusqu'au bout*).

crutch merchant ['krʌtʃ 'mɜːtʃənt] *n Austr P* tombeur *m* de femmes/draguer *m*/chaud lapin.

cry-baby ['kraibeibi] *n F* chialeur, -euse/pleurnicheur, -euse.

cry out ['krai'aut] *vi F* **for crying out loud!** pour l'amour du ciel!

crystals ['kristəlz] *npl P* (*drugs*) méthédrine cristallisée/cristal *m*.

CT, ct ['siː'tiː] *abbr P* = **cock-teaser.** (*See* **prick-teaser; PT**)

cube [kjuːb] *n P* **1.** (*drugs*) un gramme de haschisch*/cube *m*. (*See* **acid 2**) **2.** *pl esp NAm* (*dice*) dés*/bobs *mpl*.

cubehead ['kjuːbhed] *n O P* (*drugs*) consommateur *m* de morceaux de sucre imprégnés de LSD*.

cuckoo ['kukuː] *a P* fou*/ loufoque/cinglé; **you're cuckoo!** tu perds la boule!

cuddly ['kʌdli] *a F* qu'on aimerait caresser; (*woman*) gironde/ rondelette.

cuff[1] [kʌf] *n* **1.** *NAm P* **to buy sth on the cuff,** acheter qch à crédit/à croume **2.** *F* **to say sth off the cuff,** dire qch au pied levé/à l'improviste **3.** *F* coup*/beigne *f*/ taloche *f* **4.** *pl* (= *handcuffs*) menottes*/bracelets *mpl*.

cuff[2] [kʌf] *vtr* **1.** *F* **to cuff s.o. round the ear,** flanquer une taloche/une beigne à qn **2.** *P* mettre/passer les menottes à qn.

cum [kʌm] *n P* = **come**[1].

cunt [kʌnt] *n V* **1.** sexe de la femme*/con *m*/chatte *f* **2.** (*pej*) femme*/femelle *f*/salope *f*; **a nice**

bit of **cunt**, une nana qui a du chien **3.** con *m*/connasse *f*; **he's a prize/first-class cunt**, il est archicon; **you silly cunt!** espèce de con!/ connard! **she's just a dumb cunt**, ce n'est qu'une connasse **4. cunt talk**, histoires *fpl* de cul/de fesses.

cunt-lapper ['kʌntlæpər] *n V* (*cunnilingus*) brouteur *m* de cresson.

cunt-struck ['kʌntstrʌk] *a O V* queutard/porté sur la bagatelle.

cup [kʌp] *n* **1.** *F* **that's not my cup of tea**, ce n'est pas à mon goût; **that's just her cup of tea**, c'est exactement ce qui lui convient; **that isn't everyone's cup of tea**, ça ne plaît pas à tout le monde **2.** *O P* (*homosexuals*) **to have a cup of tea**, faire l'amour* dans des toilettes publiques/dans les tasses **3.** *F* **in one's cups**, dans les Vignes du Seigneur.

cuppa, cupper ['kʌpə] *n F* tasse *f* de thé.

curl up ['kəɪl'ʌp] *vi F* **I just wanted to curl up and die**, j'avais envie de tout lâcher/de tout planter là/de rentrer sous terre/de tout bazarder.

curlies ['kəɪliz] *npl P* **to have s.o. by the short and curlies**, avoir qn à sa merci/à sa pogne.

currant-bun ['kʌrənt'bʌn] *n P* (*RS = son*) fils *m*/fiston *m*.

curse [kəɪs] *n F* **to have the curse**, avoir ses règles*/ses affaires *fpl*.

curtains ['kəɪtnz] *npl F* **it'll be curtains for you if...**, votre compte est bon si...; **it was curtains for him**, il était fichu.

curvaceous [kəɪ'veiʃəs] *a F* (*woman*) bien balancée/carrossée/roulée.

cushy ['kuʃi] *a F* **a cushy time/number**, une planque/un filon; **to have a cushy time**, se la couler douce; **a cushy life**, une vie pépère; **cushy job**, sinécure *f*/fromage *m*.

cuss¹ [kʌs] *n F* **1.** individu*; **an awkward cuss**, un type pas com-

mode/un mauvais coucheur **2. it's not worth a (tinker's) cuss**, ça ne vaut pas un clou; **I don't give a tinker's cuss**, je m'en fiche pas mal/ je m'en moque comme de l'an quarante. (*See* **tinker 2**)

cuss² [kʌs] *F* **I** *vi* jurer **II** *vtr* réprimander*/enguirlander/sonner les cloches à (qn).

cussed ['kʌsid] *a F* damné/sacré.

customer ['kʌstəmər] *n F* **1.** individu*/type *m*; **a queer customer**, un drôle de client/de numéro; **an awkward customer**, un type pas commode/un mauvais coucheur. (*See* **rough I 4; tough I 2**) **2.** (*of prostitute*) clille *m*/ micheton *m*.

cut¹ [kʌt] **I** *a* **1.** *P* (légèrement) ivre*/éméché. (*See* **half-cut**) **2.** *F* **cut and dried**, tout fait/tout taillé **II** *n F* **1.** fade *m*/taf(fe) *m*; **to get one's cut**, toucher son fade/avoir sa gratte **2. he's a cut above the rest**, il vaut mieux que les autres **3.** (*cards*) **to slip the cut**, faire sauter la coupe.

cut² [kʌt] *vtr&i* **1.** *P* **to cut and run**, se tirer **2.** *P* adultérer/couper (une drogue) **3.** *F* **to cut it fine** (*i*) compter/calculer trop juste (*ii*) arriver*/faire qch à la dernière minute **4.** *F* **to cut no ice (with s.o.)**, demeurer sans effet; **that doesn't cut any ice with me**, ça ne me fait ni chaud ni froid **5.** *F* **to cut s.o. dead**, snober qn/tourner le dos à qn **6.** *F* **to cut a class**, sécher un cours **7.** (*car, etc*) *F* **to cut a corner**, prendre un virage à la corde **8.** *F* **to cut corners**, économiser*/faire des raccourcis/ couper un sou en quatre **9.** *F* **it cuts both ways**, c'est à double tranchant **10.** *O F* **to cut a dash**, faire de l'épate **11.** *F* **to cut loose**, s'émanciper/couper les amarres **12.** *F* **to cut one's teeth on sth**, se faire des dents sur qch **13.** *P* mettre fin à qch; **cut the crap!** arrête de déconner!/déconne pas! (*See* **cackle**; **comedy**; **throat 2**)

cute [kjuːt] *a F* **1.** (*pers*) (*a*) charmant/gentil; **what a cute little baby!** quel mignon petit bébé! (*b*) malin*/futé; **he's a cute one,** il a le nez creux **2.** (*thing*) mignon/gentil/chouette; **what a cute idea!** quelle idée originale/géniale*/quelle chouette idée! **3. to play a cute trick on s.o.,** faire une entourloupette à qn.

cutey, cutie ['kjuːti] *n F* **1.** jolie fille/mignonne *f*/poupée *f* **2.** malin, -igne/rusé(e) *m(f)*.

cut in ['kʌt'in] *vtr F* **to cut s.o. in,** mettre qn dans le coup; **we cut him in on the deal,** on l'a mis dans le coup.

cut out ['kʌt'aut] *vtr&i* **1.** *F* **cut it out!** ça suffit!/basta! **2.** *F* **to have one's work cut out (to do sth),** avoir de quoi faire/avoir du pain sur la planche **3.** *F* **I'm not cut out for that sort of job,** je ne suis pas taillé pour ce genre de boulot **4.** *F* souffler la place à (qn)/couper l'herbe sous les pieds de (qn). (*See* **fancy**[1] **4**)

cut up ['kʌt'ʌp] *vi F* **1. to be/to feel cut up,** être affecté/affligé; **I was very cut up by his death,** sa mort m'a beaucoup secoué **2.** éreinter/mettre en morceaux (un livre, etc) **3. to cut up nasty/ rough/ugly** (*i*) se mettre en colère*/ en rogne; se rebiffer/regimber (*ii*) faire le méchant/être vache.

cylinder ['silindər] *n F* **to fire on all cylinders,** rouler très vite*/à pleins tubes/à pleins gaz/sur les chapeaux de roue.

D

d [diː] (abbr = decent) F gentil/chic/chouette; **that's jolly d of you,** c'est sympa de ta part. (See **decent 1**)

D [diː] (abbr) P **1.** (drugs) (= LSD*) D m/acide m **2.** (= diamond) diamant*/diam m/caillou m **3.** (= detective) agent* de la Sûreté/condé m **4.** Austr agent* de la brigade des stupéfiants/stup m. (See **dog 21**; **D-racks**)

DA ['diː'ei] abbr **1.** P (= drug addict) drogué*/toxico(mane) mf/camé m **2.** NAm F (= district attorney) = procureur m de la République **3.** F (= duck's arse) coiffure des années 50 (esp portée par des **Teddy Boys**)/ = banane f.

da [daː] n F père*/papa/dab m; **my da,** mon vieux/mon vioc. (See **dar**)

dab¹ [dæb] **I** a F capable/calé/fort(iche); **a dab hand,** un expert/un as/un crack; **he's a dab hand at that,** il est doué en ça **II** n **1.** O F expert m/as m/crack m **2.** pl P empreintes digitales; **to have one's dabs taken,** passer au piano. (See **mug**¹ **1**)

dab² [dæb] vtr F **to dab one's nose,** se poudrer le nez/se refaire une petite beauté.

dabble ['dæbl] vi F se droguer* irrégulièrement/(s)chnouffailler.

dabbler ['dæblər] n F drogué* par intermittence/drogué* du samedi soir/(s)chnouffailleur m.

dab down ['dæb'daun] vi O P (regional) donner* de l'argent*/les allonger/abouler son fric.

dabster ['dæbstər] n O F = **dab**¹ **II 1.**

dad [dæd] n F **1.** père*/papa; **my dad,** mon vieux/mon vioc **2.** un vieux/un pépère/un croulant.

dad(d)a ['dædə] n F (child's word) père*/papa/papy.

daddio ['dædiou] n O P **1.** = **dad 2 2.** (beatnik term) (a) chef m d'un groupe de beatniks (b) un vieux/un pépère/un croulant.

daddle ['dædl] n A P main*/paluche f/pince f/louche f.

daddy ['dædi] n F **1.** = **dad 1 2. the daddy (of them all),** l'ancien/le maestro; **he's the daddy of them all,** il les coiffe tous **3.** (esp prisons) meneur m/chef m; **I'm the daddy,** c'est moi le patron **4.** = **sugar-daddy.**

daff [dæf] n F (abbr = daffodil) **a nice bunch of daffs,** un joli bouquet de jonquilles.

daffodil ['dæfədil] n O P jeune homme* efféminé/minet m.

daffy ['dæfi] a P **1.** (a) bête*/cruche/dingue (b) fou*/timbré/toqué **2. to be daffy about s.o.** = **to be daft about s.o.** (**daft I 2**).

daft [daːft] **I** a F **1.** idiot/dingue; **he's as daft as a brush/as they come/as they make 'em,** il est bête* comme ses pieds/il est fou* à lier; **that's a daft idea,** c'est ridicule/c'est stupide; **c'est une idée à la con/à la noix 2. to be daft about s.o.,** être toqué de qn/en pincer pour qn. (See **plain**) **II** adv P **don't talk daft!** ne raconte pas de salades!

daftie, dafty ['dɑːfti] *n P* individu bête*/cruche *f*/crétin *m*/cloche *f*.

dag [dæg] *n Austr F* **1.** rigolo *m*/ excentrique *m*; un gai luron/un joyeux drille **2.** (*square*) fils *m* à papa/baba *m* cool/bab *m*.

dagga ['dægə] *n P* (*drugs*) canna-bis*/dagga *m*.

dagged [dægd] *a NAm O P* ivre*/ soûl.

dago ['deigou] *n P* (*pej*) métèque *m* (*esp* d'origine espagnole *ou* italienne).

daily ['deili] *n F* femme *f* de journée/de ménage.

dairies ['dɛəriz] *npl A P* (*not common*) seins*/boîtes *fpl* à lait/lolos *mpl*.

daisy ['deizi] **I** *a F* excellent*/ super; **a daisy day**, une belle journée/une sacrée journée **II** *n* **1.** *F* qn/qch d'excellent*/d'épatant*/ d'impec; **she's a daisy**, c'est une perle; elle est sensass **2.** *A P* pot *m* de chambre/Jules **3.** *F* **to be kicking/pushing up the daisies**, être enterré/bouffer les pissenlits par la racine **4.** *P* (*RS = boots*) **daisy roots/daisies**, chaussures*/godillots *mpl*/godasses *fpl* **5.** *P* **daisy chain**, partouze *f* à la bague **6.** *F* **as fresh as a daisy**, frais comme une rose/frais et dispo. (*See* **oops-a-daisy!**; **ups-a-daisy!**; **upsy-daisy!**; **whoops-a-daisy!**)

daks [dæks] *npl Austr P* pantalon*/ falzar *m*/futal *m*.

dam [dæm] *n F* **1.** = **damn¹ III 2. that's a lot of water over the dam since . . .**, il est passé beaucoup d'eau sous les ponts depuis . . . .

damage ['dæmidʒ] *n F* **what's the damage?** ça fait combien? **to stand the damage**, payer* l'addition/régler la douloureuse.

damaged ['dæmidʒd] *a P* **damaged goods**, ex-vierge *f*/cruche cassée/ fille* qui a vu le loup.

dame [deim] *n esp NAm F* femme*/

fille*/nana *f*/baronne *f*/gonzesse *f*. (*See* **dizzy 2**)

damfool ['dæm'fuːl] **I** *a F* bête*/ stupide/idiot; **damfool idea**, idée *f* à la noix/à la con; **that damfool driver!** ce fichu conducteur! **II** *n F* individu bête*/imbécile *m*/crétin *m*/connard *m*; **he's a damfool**, c'est un sacré idiot.

damfoolery ['dæm'fuːləri], **damfoolishness** ['dæm'fuːliʃnis] *n F* sacrée imbécil-lité/foutaises *fpl*/sottises *fpl*/con-neries *fpl*.

dammit! ['dæmit] *excl F* **1.** zut!/ flûte!/nom d'un chien!/merde! **2. it was as near as dammit**, il était moins une; **as quick as dammit**, aussi sec/illico.

damn¹ [dæm] **I** *a & adv* = **damned II** *excl* **damn!** zut!/flûte!/ bon sang!/merde! (*See* **damn² 4, 5, 6**) **III** *n F* **1. I don't give a damn/I don't care a damn/I don't give a tinker's damn**, je m'en moque comme de l'an quarante/je m'en fiche pas mal/je m'en soucie comme de ma première chemise/je m'en tamponne le coquillard **2. it's not worth a damn**, ça ne vaut pas un clou/ça ne casse rien. (*See* **tuppenny**)

damn² [dæm] *vtr F* **1. damn you!/ you be damned!** va te faire voir (chez les grecs)!/je t'emmerde! **damn him!** qu'il aille se faire fiche! **2. well I'm damned/I'll be damned!** ça c'est trop fort!/ça c'est le com-ble! **3. I'll be damned if I'll do it!** il est hors de question que je le fasse! **4. damn it!** zut!/flûte!/ merde! **5. damn and blast!/damn it all!** nom de nom!/nom d'un chien!/ bon sang!/bordel (de merde)! **6. damn this car!** (il) y en a marre de cette bagnole!

damnable ['dæmnəbl] *a F* maudit*/ exécrable.

damnably ['dæmnəbli] *adv F* bigrement/rudement/vachement.

damn-all ['dæm'ɔːl] *n F* rien*; he's doing damn-all, il ne fiche rien/il n'en fout pas une rame; **he's done damn-all today,** il n'a fichu que dalle aujourd'hui/il n'a rien foutu de la journée; **I know damn-all about it,** je n'en sais fichtre rien/je n'en sais que dalle.

damnation ['dæmneiʃ(ə)n] *excl F* zut!/flûte!/merde! **what in damnation are you doing here?** que diable fais-tu ici?

damned [dæmd] **I** *a F* **1.** sacré/satané/fichu; **these damned taxes,** ces fichus impôts! **that damned car,** cette foutue bagnole! **2. what a/it's a damned nuisance!** quel empoisonnement!/quelle poisse!/(c'est) la barbe! **3. he's a damned nuisance!** quel enquiquineur!/quel emmerdeur!/quel casse-pieds! **4. it's a damned shame,** c'est une sacrée honte **5. a damned good idea,** une idée hyper chouette/une idée sensass **6. a damned sight better than . . . ,** fichtrement mieux que . . . /vachement mieux que . . . /salement mieux que . . . **7. it's one damned problem after another,** quand ce n'est pas une chose . . . **8. a damned fool = damfool II** **II** *adv F* **1.** diablement/vachement; **it's damned hard,** c'est vachement coton/c'est salement dur **2.** . . . **and a damned good job too!** . . . et c'est pas malheureux! **3. you're damned right there!** tu as carrément raison/tu as fichtrement raison! **4. pretty damned quick,** au trot!/et que ça saute! (*See* **pdq**) **5. it'll be damned useful,** ça va nous rendre salement service.

damnedest ['dæmdist] *n F* **to do/to try one's damnedest,** se décarcasser/travailler d'achar/travailler d'arrache-pied.

damned-well, damn-well ['dæmnd'wel, 'dæm'wel] *adv F* **1. it damned-well serves you right,** c'est bien fait pour ta gueule **2. you can do what you damned-well like!**

fais ce que tu veux, je m'en fous/je m'en contrefous! **3. I should damned-well think so!** et (il) y a intérêt!/et j'espère bien!

damp [dæmp] *n F* **to keep the damp out,** boire* un alcool/se rincer le gosier.

damper ['dæmpər] *n F* **1.** douche *f* (froide); **to put the damper(s) on sth,** jeter un froid sur qch; donner un coup de frein à qch; refroidir l'enthousiasme **2. to put the damper on s.o.,** faire taire* qn/clouer le bec à qn/rabattre le caquet à qn.

dance [dɑːns, dæns] *n NAm F* **to lead s.o. a dance,** donner du fil à retordre à qn/en faire voir de toutes les couleurs à qn. (*See* **song 1**)

dander ['dændər] *n F* **to get one's dander up,** se mettre en colère*/s'emballer/sortir de ses gonds.

dandruff ['dændrʌf] *n P* **walking dandruff,** poux*/morpions *mpl.*

dandy ['dændi] **I** *a esp NAm F* (*slightly O*) excellent*/sensas/super; **that's (fine and) dandy,** c'est chouette **II** *adv esp NAm F* excellemment; **to get along (just) dandy with s.o.,** s'entendre à merveille avec qn/être copain comme cochon (avec qn) **II** *n esp NAm F* chose excellente*/une perle.

dang[1] [dæŋ] *n esp NAm F* = **damn**[1] **III.**

dang[2] [dæŋ] *vtr esp NAm F* = **damn**[2].

danglers ['dæŋgləz] *npl V* testicules*/balloches *fpl.*

dar [dɑːr] *n F* père*/dab *m*/vieux *m*/vioc *m.* (*See* **da**)

darb [dɑːb] *n NAm O P* chose excellente* *ou* remarquable/une perle.

darbies ['dɑːbiz] *npl P* menottes*/fichets *mpl*/bracelets *mpl.*

Darby and Joan ['dɑːbiən(d)-dʒoun] *Prn* **1.** *F* vieux ménage;

Darby and Joan club, club *m* du troisième âge **2.** *P* (*RS* = *telephone*) téléphone*/bigophone *m* **3.** *P* (*RS* = *alone*) **on one's Darby and Joan,** seulâbre.

dare [dɛər] *vtr F* **I dare you!** chiche!

dark [dɑːk] **I** *a F* **to keep it dark,** cacher*/étouffer qch; **keep it dark!** motus et bouche cousue! (*See* **horse¹** 1) **II** *n* **1.** *F* **to be in the dark about sth,** ne pas être dans le coup **2.** *P* (*mil*) **in the dark,** au cachot/au violon/à l'ombre. (*See* **shot II** 8)

darkey, darkie, darky ['dɑːki] *n* (*pej*) Noir(e)*/nègre *mf*/moricaud(e) *m(f)*.

darling ['dɑːliŋ] *a F* **that's darling of you!** c'est chouette/c'est sympa/c'est chic de ta part.

darn¹ [dɑːn] **I** *a & adv F* (*euph for* **damned I, II**) **that darn car,** cette foutue bagnole; **it's a darn nuisance,** quelle poisse!/c'est la barbe! (*See* **darned**) **II** *excl F* (*euph for* **damn¹ II**) zut!/flûte!/merde!

darn² [dɑːn] *vtr F* (*euph for* **damn²**) **1. darn it!** flûte!/merde!/bordel! **2. well I'll be darned!** ça c'est trop fort!/c'est le bouquet!/c'est (un peu) fort de café!

darnation [dɑːˈneiʃ(ə)n] *excl O F* (*euph for* **damnation**) zut!/flûte!/merde! (*See* **tarnation**)

darned [dɑːnd] *a & adv F* (*euph for* **damned I, II**) **1. he's a darned nuisance!** quel emmerdeur!/quel casse-pieds! **2. you darned idiot!** espèce de nouille!/espèce de con! **3. he made a darned good job of it,** il a fait du bien beau travail. (*See* **darn¹ I**)

darnedest ['dɑːndist] *n F* (*euph for* **damnedest**) **to do one's darnedest,** faire de son mieux/se décarcasser.

dash¹ [dæʃ] *n F* **1.** (= *dashboard*) tableau *m* de bord **2.** tentative *f*/ essai *m*; **to have a dash at sth,** tenter le coup. (*See* **cut² 10**)

dash² [dæʃ] *vtr&i F* **1.** partir* rapidement/filer/se débiner; **(I) must dash,** (il) faut que je me tire **2.** (*euph for* **damn²**) **dash it all!** flûte!/zut!

dashed ['dæʃt] *a & adv F* (*euph for* **damned I, II**) **dashed bad luck, old man!** pas de veine, petit gars!/ quelle poisse, mon vieux!

dasher ['dæʃər] *n A F* individu élégant*/m'as-tu-vu *m*/frimeur *m*.

date¹ [deit] *n F* **1.** (*esp with s.o. of the opposite sex*) rendez-vous*/rencard *m*; **I've got a date with him,** j'ai rencard avec lui; **to break a date,** poser un lapin **2.** personne (du sexe opposé) avec qui on a rendez-vous*; **my date didn't show up,** mon copain/ma copine ne s'est pas amené(e)/m'a posé un lapin. (*See* **blind I** 1; **heavy I** 2)

date² [deit] *vtr F* **to date s.o.,** donner rendez-vous*/rencard *m* à qn; sortir (regulièrement) avec qn; **he's dating her,** il sort avec elle.

daughter ['dɔːtər] *n P* (*RS* = *quarter*) 25 livres sterling; **four and a daughter,** 425 livres.

day [dei] *n F* **1. that'll be the day!** on fera une croix à la cheminée!/ on plantera un arbre! **2. to name the day,** fixer le jour du mariage **3. to pass the time of day,** bavarder*/jacasser/(se) tailler une bavette **4. to call it a day,** s'arrêter de travailler/s'en tenir là; **let's call it a day,** ça suffira pour aujourd'hui **5. this coat's seen better days,** ce manteau a fait son temps **6. it's not my day,** je me suis levé du pied gauche/c'est un jour à rester couché **7. at the end of the day,** au bout du compte/en fin de compte **8. that really made my day!** (*i*) (*iron*) il ne manquait plus que ça! (*ii*) ça a transformé ma journée/ça m'a remonté le moral **9. she's thirty if she's a day!** elle a ses trente printemps bien sonnés! (*See* **rainy-day**)

daylight ['deilait] **I** *a* F it's daylight robbery! c'est de l'arnaque patentée!/on se fait arnaquer! **II** *n* F **1.** to be able to see daylight, commencer à en voir le bout/voir la lumière au bout du tunnel **2.** *pl* to knock/to beat/to bash the living daylights out of s.o., battre* qn comme plâtre/flanquer une dérouillée à qn/donner une roustée à qn.

dazzler ['dæzlər] *n* F **1.** diamant*/diam *m*/caillou *m* **2.** (*pers*) m'as-tu-vu *m*/flambard *m*/frimeur *m*/qn qui en jette.

dead [ded] **I** *a* F **1.** (*a*) (*pers*) dead loss, nullité *f*/nullard *m*/crêpe *m*/zéro *m* (*b*) that concert was a dead loss, quel bide/four ce concert!/c'était pas fameux, ce concert; his idea was a dead loss, c'était une idée à la noix/à la con **2.** dead cert/dead cinch, certitude absolue/du sûr et certain; he's a dead cert for the job, il est exactement ce qu'il nous faut pour ce boulot/il est fait pour ce boulot; that horse is a dead cert, ce cheval c'est un tuyau dur comme fer/c'est du sûr **3.** dead man/dead soldier, bouteille* vide/cadavre *m*/macchabée *m* **4.** dead duck, échec *m*/faillite *f*/bide *m*; that play is a dead duck, cette pièce a fait un four; he's a dead duck, il est cuit/il est foutu/il est fichu **5.** he's dead from the neck up, il est bête/il n'a rien dans la tête/il est con comme un balai **6.** dead to the world (*i*) profondément endormi/dans les bras de Morphée/complètement KO (*ii*) ivre* mort/bourré/beurré/rétamé à zéro **7.** he's the dead spit of his father, c'est son père tout craché/c'est tout le portrait de son père **8.** to be waiting for dead men's shoes, attendre la mort de qn (pour lui prendre sa place) **9.** (you'll do that) over my dead body! pas question que tu le fasses! **10.** I wouldn't be seen dead wearing that! je ne le porterai pas à aucun prix! I wouldn't be seen dead with him!

plutôt rester vieille fille que sortir avec ce type! **11.** drop dead! écrase!/va te faire voir!/va te faire foutre! (*See* **Anne**; **Charley 2**; **cut²** 5; **dead-and-alive**; **horse¹** 4; **ringer 1**; **set¹** II) **II** *adv* F **1.** dead boring, très ennuyeux*/barbant/rasant/rasoir au possible **2.** dead broke, fauché comme les blés/sans le sou/sans un/dans la dèche **3.** I was dead chuffed (*i*) j'étais tout content/aux anges (*ii*) j'en avais marre/ras le bol **4.** dead drunk, ivre* mort/bourré à zéro/schlâss **5.** dead easy, facile comme bonjour; de la tarte **6.** I was dead lucky, j'ai eu un sacré pot **7.** dead on, dans le mille **8.** dead right mate! tout juste Auguste/mon pote! **9.** dead scared, mort de peur*/de frousse; to be dead scared, avoir peur*/les mouiller/avoir les foies/avoir les chocottes/fluber **10.** dead to rights, absolument; to catch s.o. dead to rights, prendre qn la main dans le sac/épingler qn sur le fait **11.** to be dead set against sth, être braqué/buté contre qch; to be dead set against s.o., en avoir après qn; to be dead set on doing sth, vouloir faire qch à tout prix/à tout crin.

dead-and-alive ['dedəndə'laiv] *a* F a dead-and-alive place, un endroit mort *ou* triste; un trou perdu/un bled.

dead-beat ['dedbiːt] *n esp NAm* F **1.** paresseux*/fainéant *m*/flemmard *m*/parasite *m* **2.** mauvais payeur/filou *m*.

dead-end ['ded'end] *a* F **1.** travail*/boulot *m* sans avenir **2.** dead-end kid, jeune délinquant *esp* des quartiers pauvres qui est sans avenir/voyou *m*/loubard *m*/blouson noir.

deadhead ['dedhed] *NAm* F **I** *n* **1.** individu bête*/sot *m*/cruche *f* **2.** personne possédant un billet de faveur pour le théâtre, le train, etc **3.** train, etc roulant à vide **II** *a* (*a*) libre/disponible (b) abandonné; laissé en plan.

deadly ['dedli] **I** a F ennuyeux*/ rasoir/casse-pieds **II** adv F **deadly boring/dull,** mortellement ennuyeux*/à mourir d'ennui/ mortellement rasoir.

deadneck ['dednek] n O P = **deadhead 1.**

deal [diːl] n **1.** F to **clinch a deal,** s'assurer une vente/signer une vente/boucler une affaire; **to make a deal,** décrocher une affaire; **it's a deal!** d'accord!/marché conclu! **a new deal,** un nouveau départ; **a phoney deal,** une affaire véreuse; **dirty deal,** mauvais tour/coup bas/ sale coup m/vacherie f. (See **raw I 1; square¹ I 1**) **2.** F **big deal!** et mon œil! **no deal!** pas moyen!/rien à faire! **3.** P (drugs) petite dose (d'une drogue)/fixe m.

dealer ['diːlər] n F (drugs) trafiquant m/dealer m/revendeur m. (See **wheeler-dealer**)

dear [diə] a F **Dear John letter,** lettre f de rupture d'une jeune fille à son fiancé (qui est à l'armée).

dearie, deary ['diəri] n F **1.** (mon petit) chéri/(ma petite) chérie/mon chou/ma puce/mon lapin **2. (oh) dearie me!** (a) douce Mère! (b) see **bingo 3.** (See **hello-dearie**)

death [deθ] n F **1. to feel like death (warmed up),** être crevé/se sentir flagada; **to look like death (warmed up),** avoir l'air d'un cadavre ambulant/être plus mort que vif/être tout patraque **2. his plan died a death,** son projet a fait un four/est mort dans l'œuf **3. to bore s.o. to death,** faire mourir* qn d'ennui/barber qn jusqu'à la gauche/raser qn à mort **4. I'm frozen to death,** je meurs/je crève de froid **5. we're sick to death of all that,** on en a marre/on en a pardessus la tête/on en a ras le bol de tout ça **6. that car will be the death of me,** cette voiture me rendra fou/me donnera des cheveux gris **7.** (in car) **death seat,** siège m à côté du conducteur/place f du mort. (See **flog 2; hang on 2; tickle² 3**)

deb [deb] n F (abbr = debutante) débutante f.

debag ['diːˈbæg] vtr F déculotter/ défroquer.

debug ['diːˈbʌg] vtr F **1.** réparer/ mettre au point/réviser **2.** désonoriser/neutraliser des micros clandestins.

debunk ['diːˈbʌŋk] vtr F faire descendre (qn) d'un cran; déboulonner.

decent ['diːs(ə)nt] a F **1.** (kind, generous) **a decent chap,** un brave type/un bon gars **2. to be decent,** être habillé décemment/être convenable.

deck [dek] n **1.** F **to hit the deck** (a) sortir du lit/sortir du plumard/ se dépagnoter (b) tomber à plat ventre **2.** F **to clear the decks,** tout préparer/se préparer à agir/ être sur le point d'attaquer **3.** F jeu m de cartes*; **to play with a stacked deck,** jouer avec des cartes biseautées/maquillées **4.** P (drugs) (i) petite quantité de drogues/prise f (ii) petite dose d'héroïne* ou de cocaïne*.

deck man ['dek'mæn] n P (drugs) trafiquant m/revendeur m de cocaïne*.

decorators ['dekəreitəz] npl P **to have the decorators in,** avoir ses règles*/repeindre sa grille en rouge. (See **painter 2**)

dee-jay n F (abbr = disc-jockey) = **DJ.**

deep [diːp] **I** a F **1.** malin*/fin/ roublard/retors **2. to put sth in the deep freeze,** mettre qch au frigo/ mettre qch sur la planche. (See **end 5, 12; jump² 12**) **II** n P (RS = to sleep) **to plough the deep,** dormir*/pioncer.

degree [di'griː] *n F* **1.** **to be/to feel one degree under,** être légèrement malade*/être patraque/ne pas être dans son assiette **2.** (*esp by police, etc*) **to give s.o. the third degree,** cuisiner qn/griller qn; passer qn à tabac.

dekko ['dekou] *n P* **let's have a dekko!** fais(-moi) voir!/juste un coup d'œil*! **have/take a dekko out of the window!** jette un coup d'œil* par la fenêtre!

delicate ['delikət] *a F* **to be in a delicate condition,** être enceinte*/avoir un polichinelle dans le tiroir.

demo ['demou] *n F* manifestation *f* politique/manif *f*.

demob¹ ['diː'mɔb] *n F* (*abbr = demobilization*) libération *f* militaire/la quille; **to be due for demob,** être de la classe/attendre la quille.

demob² ['diː'mɔb] *vtr F* (*abbr = demobilize*) démobiliser/libérer/renvoyer dans ses foyers.

demolish [di'mɔliʃ] *vtr F* manger*/dévorer; **she demolished the whole cake,** elle a bâfré tout le gâteau.

den [den] *n F* repaire *m*/clandé *m*.

dense [dens] *a F* bête*/bouché.

dent [dent] *n F* **to make a dent (in sth),** commencer à mordre; **buying the car made a big dent in his savings,** avec l'achat de cette voiture, ses économies ont en pris une sacrée claque/un sacré coup.

Derby Kel(l) or **Kelly** ['dɑːbi'kel(i)] *n P* (*RS = belly*) ventre*/bide *m*/bidon *m*.

derry ['deri] *n P* (= *derelict (house)*) (*esp used by tramps, drug addicts, etc*) baraque *f*/cambuse *f*/turne *f*.

deuce [djuːs] *n* **1.** *A F* (= *devil*) diable *m*; **to raise the deuce** = **to raise the devil** (**devil¹** 15) **2.** *A F* (= *devil*) (*expression of annoyance*) zut!/flûte! **3.** *O F* (= *devil*) **what the deuce!** que diable! **who the deuce are you?** qui diable êtes-vous? **4.** *P* deux livres sterling/*NAm* deux dollars.

deuced [djuːst] **I** *a O F* satané/sacré; **he's a deuced idiot,** c'est un sacré imbécile; **deuced bad luck old chap!** fichue déveine, mon gars! **II** *adv O F* diablement/diantrement.

devil¹ ['devl] *n F* **1.** **poor devil!** pauvre diable!/pauvre bougre! **he's a lucky devil!** il a du pot, celui-là! **2.** **go on, be a devil and have another!** allez! laisse-toi tenter et reprends un verre! **3.** **he's an absolute devil!** il est infernal! **he's a devil with the ladies,** il est terrible avec les femmes/c'est un tombeur de 1ère classe **4.** **what the devil!** que diable! **how the devil did you get in?** comment diable es-tu entré? **how the devil should/would I know?** comment veux-tu que je (le) sache? **who the devil do you think you are?** pour qui diable te prends-tu? **why the devil didn't you say so?** pourquoi diable ne l'as-tu pas dit?/mais alors! pourquoi ne l'as-tu pas dit? **5.** **we had the devil of a job/the devil's own job to find it,** c'était la croix et la bannière pour le trouver/a eu un mal fou à le trouver; **it's the devil of a job/it's the very devil to wake him up in the morning,** c'est la croix et la bannière pour le réveiller le matin; **he has the devil of a temper,** il a un sale caractère/un caractère de cochon; c'est un mauvais coucheur **6.** **there'll be the devil to pay,** ça va nous coûter cher; ça va barder **7.** *O* **the devil you will!** (il n'en est) pas question!/pas moyen! **the devil take it!** merde alors! **8.** **to send s.o. to the devil,** envoyer qn au diable/envoyer qn paître; **go to the devil!** va te faire voir!/va te faire foutre! **9.** **to go to the devil,** mal tourner/tomber dans la merde; **his work has gone to the devil,** son travail ne vaut pas grand-chose **10.** **to play the devil with sth,** mettre la confusion dans qch/semer la pagaille; **this strike will play the**

devil with trains to London, cette grève va mettre la pagaille dans les trains pour Londres **11. to work like the devil,** travailler* avec acharnement/travailler* comme une bête/bûcher comme un noir **12. to have the luck of the devil,** avoir une veine de pendu/de cocu **13. to give the devil his due,** rendre justice à (qn) **14. between the devil and the deep blue sea,** entre l'enclume et le marteau/entre Charybde et Scylla **15. to raise the devil/to make a devil of a row,** faire du bruit/faire du foin/faire du ramdam **16.** *O* **the Devil's Bible/playthings,** cartes* à jouer/brêmes *fpl* **17. blue devils,** le cafard/le bourdon/le blues **18. red devils = reds (red II 5).**

devil² ['devl] *vtr F* **to devil the life out of s.o.,** tourmenter qn/faire suer qn/empoisonner qn/casser les pieds à qn.

devil-dodger ['devldɔdʒər] *n A F* prêtre*/ratichon *m.*

devilish(ly) ['devliʃ(li)] *adv F* diablement/diantrement/extrêmement/vachement.

devo ['diːvou] *n Austr P* (a) perverti *m* (b) voyeur *m.*

dewdrop ['djuːdrɔp] *n F* (*euph*) goutte *f* au nez/chandelle *f.*

dex [deks], **dexie** ['deksi], **dexo** ['deksou], **dexy** ['deksi] *n P* (*drugs*) cachet *m* de dexamphétamine; *pl* **dexies/dexos,** amphétamines *fpl*/amphés *fpl.*

diabolical [daiə'bɔlik(ə)l] *a F* diabolique/satané/affreux/atroce/épouvantable; **it's a diabolical liberty!** c'est un sacré culot!

dial(-piece) ['daiəl(piːs)] *n P* visage*/museau *m*/margoulette *f*/bobine *f*/gueule *f.*

diarrhoea, *NAm* **diarrhea** [daiə'riə] *n F* **verbal diarrhoea,** discours *m*/bavardage *m* sans fin/diarrhée verbale.

dibs [dibz] *n P* argent*/fric *m*; **to have the dibs,** être riche*/avoir du fric/être au pèze/être plein aux as.**

dice¹ [dais] *npl F* **1. no dice!** pas mèche!/je ne marche pas!/rien à faire! **2. to throw in the dice,** lâcher les dés/jeter l'éponge.

dice² [dais] *vi F* **to dice with death,** faire la course à la mort/jouer avec la mort.

dicey ['daisi] *a F* hasardeux; **it's a bit dicey,** c'est du risqué/c'est pas du tout cuit/c'est pas de la tarte.

dick [dik] *n P* **1.** pénis*/Charles-le-Chauve/Popaul *m* **2.** individu bête*/andouille *f*/crétin *m*; **what a dick!** quel nœud!/quel gland! **3.** policier*/détective *m*/bourre *m*; **a private dick,** un privé. (*See* **fly-dick**) **4. clever Dick,** un petit/gros malin; affranchi *m* **5. dirty Dick,** sale dégoûtant *m*/sale coco *m* **6.** *pl* poux*/morpions *mpl* **7.** *O* dictionnaire *m*/dico *m* **8.** *NAm* **to buy the dick** (a) s'attirer des ennuis/s'amocher (b) mourir*/dévisser son billard. (*See* **Tom 1**)

dickens ['dikinz] *n F* (*euph for* **devil**) **1. they were making the dickens of a noise,** ils faisaient un bruit/un potin du diable **2. we had the dickens of a job to finish it,** on a eu un mal fou pour le finir.

dickhead ['dik(h)ed] *n P* individu bête*/crétin *m*/tête *f* de nœud.

dick licker ['dik'likər] *n V* **1.** homosexuel*/pédé *m*/enculé *m* **2.** personne qui fait une fellation* à qn/qui taille une pipe à qn; suceur, -euse *mf*/pipeur, -euse *mf.*

dickory dock ['dikəri'dɔk] *n P* **1.** (*RS = clock*) horloge *f*/pendule *f*/tocante *f* **2.** (*RS = cock*) pénis*/queue *f*/bite *f*. (*See* **cock 1**)

dicky ['diki] **I** *a F* (a) malade*/patraque/pas dans son assiette; **I feel a bit dicky today,** je suis (un peu) mal foutu aujourd'hui; **he's got a dicky heart,** il a le cœur qui flanche. (*See* **ticker 1**) (b) (*object, chair, ladder, etc*) pas solide (c) (*finances*) pas solide/frisant la faillite; dans la dèche/fauché **II** *n* **1.** **P = dick 1** **2.** *F* = **dicky-bird.**

dicky-bird ['dikibəːd] *n* *F* **1.** oiseau *m*/zozio *m*/zoziau *m*/piaf *m* **2.** (*RS* = *word*) mot *m*; **not a dicky-bird!** pas un mot!/motus (et bouche consue)!

dicky dirt ['diki'dəːt] *n* *P* (*RS* = *shirt*) chemise*/liquette *f*/sac *m* à viande.

diddies ['didiz] *npl* *A* *P* seins*/ nénés *mpl*.

diddle ['didl] *vtr* **1.** *F* voler* **2.** *F* duper*/rouer/carotter (qn); **I've been diddled,** je me suis fait avoir **3.** *NAm* *P* (*a*) faire l'amour* (avec qn)/calcer qn/se faire qn (*b*) se masturber*/se branler **4.** *F* (*rare* = **piddle**) uriner*/faire pipi. (*See* **piddle²**)

diddle around ['didlə'raund] *vi* *A* *P* flânocher/baguenauder.

diddle away ['didlə'wei] *vtr* *A* *F* **to diddle away one's time,** flâner.

diddler ['didlər] *n* *F* **1.** voleur* **2.** escroc*/carotteur *m*/estampeur *m*.

diddling ['didliŋ] *n* *F* **1.** vol *m*/ estampage *m* **2.** escroquerie*/ arnaque *f*.

diddly (shit) ['didli'(ʃit)] *a* *NAm* *P* qui ne vaut pas grand-chose; merdique.

diddums ['didʌmz] *excl* *F* (*to a child or ironic*) **diddums hurt himself then?** on s'est fait bobo, mon petit?

diddy ['didi] *a* *F* petit/tout petit/ minuscule.

didekei, didikai ['didikai], **didlo** ['didlou] *n* *P* (*not common*) romanichel *m*/romano *m*/rabouin *m*.

dig¹ [dig] *n* **1.** *F* fouilles *fpl* (archéologiques) **2.** *P* (*RS* = *shave*) **dig in the grave,** rasage *m*/ raclage *m* **3.** *pl* *F* logement*/ chambre meublée/meublé *m*/piaule

f **4.** *F* **to have a dig at s.o.,** lancer/filer une vanne/des piques *fpl*/un coup de patte à qn **5.** *P* (*drugs*) piqûre*/piquouse *f*/shoot *m*.

dig² [dig] *vtr* **1.** *F* (*a*) **I dig that!** ça me plaît!/ça me botte!/ça me branche! **I really dig rock (music),** le rock, ça me branche (*b*) comprendre/entraver/piger; **you dig?** tu piges? (*c*) remarquer; **dig that!** vise-moi ça!/mate-moi ça! **2.** aimer* (qn)/avoir qn à la bonne **3.** *P* (*not common*) taper sur les nerfs/sur le système à qn; **what's digging you?** qu'est-ce qui te turlupine? **4.** *P* (*rare*) faire l'amour* avec/fourrer (une femme) **5.** *esp NAm* *F* travailler* dur (*esp* en vue d'un examen)/bachoter/bûcher **6.** *F* (*not often used*) habiter*/crécher; **I dig in Hampstead,** je crèche à Hampstead.

digger ['digər] *n* *F* (*a*) Australien *m* *ou* Néo-Zélandais *m*; kangourou *m*; kiwi *m* (*b*) (*as modifier*) **a digger accent,** un accent australien *ou* néozélandais. (*See* **gold-digger**)

diggings ['digiŋz] *npl* *A* *F* = **digs** (**dig¹ 3**).

dig in ['dig'in] *vtr&i* *F* **1.** manger*/ s'empiffrer/bouffer; **he dug into a pile of sausages,** il attaqua une montagne de saucisses **2.** travailler* soigneusement **3.** **to dig in (one's heels),** rester sur ses positions/ne pas broncher/ne pas moufter/se tenir peinard.

dig up ['dig'ʌp] *vtr* *F* dégoter qch; **where did you dig that up?** où l'as-tu déniché/pêché? (*often humorous*) **I wonder where they dug him up from!** je me demande où ils ont déniché ce type!

dike [daik] *n* *P* **1.** *A* WC*/chiottes *fpl*; urinoir*/pissotière *f* **2.** = **dyke.**

dikey ['daiki] *a* *P* = **dykey.**

dildo ['dildou] *n* *P* gode(miché) *m*/ jacquot *m*.

dill [dil] *n Austr P* imbécile*/navet *m*/andouille *f*.

dilly ['dili] **I** *a Austr P* bête*/ gourde/frappé **II** *n esp NAm F* **1.** she's a dilly, elle est mignonne (à croquer) **2.** qch de chouette/de super.

dilly bag ['dili'bæg] *n P* (*Aboriginal word for small bag or basket*) cabas *m*/lacsé *m*.

dilly dally ['dili'dæli] *vi O F* perdre son temps/flanôcher/traînasser/ glander.

dim [dim] *a F* **1.** to take a dim view of sth, avoir une piètre opinion de qch **2.** bête*/idiot; he's a bit dim, il est bouché/il est un peu con.

dime [daim] *n NAm F* pièce *f* de dix cents; **dime novel**, roman feuilleton/de deux sous; **it's a dime a dozen**, ça ne vaut pas cher/ça ne vaut pas tripette/ça ne vaut pas un pet; **dime-a-dance palace**, bal *m* musette/bastringue *m*/guinche *f*/le balajo; **dime store**, magasin *m* pas cher/ = Prisu *m*; (*drugs*) **dime bag**, paquet *ou* quantité d'une drogue qui vaut 10 dollars.

dimmock ['dimɔk] *n A P* argent*/ artiche *m*.

dimwit ['dimwit] *n F* individu bête*/andouille *f*/ballot *m*/zozo *m*; **what a dimwit!** quel crétin!

dimwitted ['dimwitid] *a F* bête*/ bas de plafond/baluche/ballot.

din-dins ['dindinz] *npl F* (*child's language*) repas *m*/dinette *f*/niamniam *m*.

ding [diŋ] *n P Austr* **1.** (*pej*) (*a*) Italien* (-ienne)/rital *m* (*b*) Grec(que) *mf* (*c*) métèque *m* **2.** = **dinger**.

dingbat ['diŋbæt] *n P* **1.** *Austr NAm* imbécile*/andouille *f*/crétin *m*; **you dingbat!** espèce de nouille! **2.** *pl Austr* **to have the dingbats/to be dingbats**, avoir le délirium tremens/avoir le trac (quand un

alcoolique s'arrête de boire)/voir les rats bleus; **to give s.o. the dingbats**, énerver qn/filer le trac à qn.

ding-dong ['diŋdɔŋ] *a&n F* **a real ding-dong (of a) battle**, une lutte acharnée/une vraie luttanche/un vrai pétard.

dinge [dindʒ] *n esp NAm P* (*pej*) Noir(e)*/nègre *mf*/négro *m*/moricaud *m*. (*See* **queen 2**)

dinger ['diŋər] *n Austr P* fesses*/ pétrousquin *m*/baba *m*; anus*/ anneau *m*; **a kick in the dinger**, un coup de pied au cul.

dink [dink] *n NAm* (*pej*) Vietnamien, -ienne/Viet *m*.

dinkum ['diŋkəm] *a Austr F* **1.** **(fair) dinkum**, régulier/régló/aux petits oignons/vrai de vrai **2.** **the dinkum article** (*i*) de l'authentique/ du vrai (*ii*) l'homme qu'il faut **3.** **a dinkum Aussie**, Australien *m* de naissance/kangourou *m*.

dinky ['diŋki] *a F* **1.** mignon/ chouette/croquignole **2.** *NAm* petit/insignifiant/sans importance.

dinky-di ['diŋki'dai] *a Austr F* vrai de vrai/pur/authentique; **he's a dinky-di Aussie**, c'est un australien à 100%/jusqu'au bout des ongles.

dinky-doo ['diŋki'duɪ] *F See* **bingo 22.**

dip[1] [dip] *n* **1.** *P* voleur* à la tire/ voleur* à la fourche/fourchette *f*; cambuteur *m*/tireur *m* **2.** *O P* drogué/camé *m*/toxico *m* **3.** *F* to **take a dip**, faire une petite baignade/faire trempette/se mettre au jus. (*See* **skinny dip**)

dip[2] [dip] *vtr&i P* **1.** mettre en gage/mettre au Mont de Piété/mettre au clou **2.** voler* à la tire/à la fourche/barboter. (*See* **lid 1**; **wick 2**)

dippy ['dipi] *a P* **1.** fou*/timbré/ toqué/louf(oque)/dingo **2.** **to be dippy about s.o.**, aimer* qn/avoir le béguin pour qn/en pincer pour qn.

dipshit ['dipʃit] *n NAm V* malappris *m*; connard *m*/ducon-la-joie *m*.

dipso ['dipsou] *n F* (*abbr = dipsomaniac*) ivrogne*/soûlot *m*/soûlard *m*/poivrot *m*/alcolo *mf*.

dirt [dəːt] *n* **1.** *F* pornographie *f*/porno *m*/obscénité *f*/du cul/de la fesse **2.** *P* ragots *mpl*/potins *mpl*/merde *f*; **to dig up the dirt about s.o.**/**to dish out the dirt**, fouiller la merde de qn; **to throw dirt at s.o.**/**to spread the dirt about s.o.**, déblatérer contre qn/débiner qn; **to have the dirt on s.o.**, savoir des choses peu relevées sur qn **3.** *F* **to treat s.o. like dirt**, traiter qn plus bas que terre/traiter qn comme de la merde **4.** *F* **to sweep the dirt under the carpet/the rug**, couvrir la vérité/tirer le rideau **5.** *F* **to eat dirt**, avaler son amour-propre/avaler des couleuvres **6.** *O P* **to do dirt on s.o.**/**to do s.o. dirt**, faire un sale coup/une crasse/des saloperies *fpl* à qn. (*See* **dirty II**) **7.** *A P* argent*/braise *f*/pèze *m*. (*See* **dicky-dirt**)

dirt cheap ['dəːt'tʃiːp] *a & adv* à vil prix/pour rien*/pour des clopinettes/pour des clous; **I got it dirt cheap**, je l'ai eu très bon marché/pour une bouchée de pain/pour trois fois rien.

dirt track rider ['dəːt'træk'raidər] *n P* homosexuel* actif/bourrin *m*.

dirty ['dəːti] **I** *a* **1.** *F* **a dirty business** (*i*) un sale métier (*ii*) une sale affaire/histoire; **dirty crack**, vacherie *f*; **dirty rat/dirty dog**, un sale type/un sale mec/un salaud; (*sport*) **a dirty player**, un joueur salaud; **dirty trick**, sale coup *m*/sale tour *m*; **dirty weather**, temps pourri/temps de chien; **I leave all the dirty work to him**, à lui la sale besogne; **she gave me a dirty look**, elle m'a regardé d'un sale œil **2.** (*lewd*) **dirty joke**, blague porno; **dirty old man**, vieux barbeau/vieux marcheur; **dirty weekend**, un week-end de débauche/de partouze; **to**

have a dirty mind, avoir l'esprit mal tourné/avoir l'esprit cochon; **he's got a dirty mind**, il ne pense qu'à ça; **she's really dirty-minded/she's got a really dirty mind!** comme elle est cochonne!/quelle salope! **to have a dirty mouth**, jurer comme un charretier/comme un sapeur; être mal embouché **3.** *P* **dirty money**, argent* mal acquis/gratte *f*/tour *m* de bâton **4.** *P* (*intensifier*) **a dirty great lorry**, un camion maous(se)/un gros bahut; **a dirty big suitcase**, une valoche comme un camion **5.** *P* **dirty old Jew**: *see* **bingo 2**; **dirty whore**: *see* **bingo 34**. (*See* **linen 1**; **mac²**) **II** *n P* **to do the dirty on s.o.**, jouer un tour de cochon à qn/faire des crasses à qn/chier dans les bottes à qn. (*See* **dirt 6**)

disappearing [disə'piəriŋ] *a F* **to do a disappearing act** (*i*) partir*/s'esquiver/se casser (*ii*) déménager à la cloche de bois.

disco ['diskou] *n F* (*abbr = discotheque*) discothèque *f*/disco *f*/boîte *f*; **disco music**, musique *f* disco/musique de boîte; **to go disco dancing**, (aller) danser disco; **to go to a disco**, aller en boîte/sortir en boîte.

dish¹ [diʃ] *n* **1.** *F* individu* beau/joli/qui a du chien/qui jette du jus; **he's a real dish**, il en jette/il dégage; **what a dish!** quelle beauté! (*See* **dishy**) **2.** *P* (*rare*) fesses*/pétard *m*/derche *m*.

dish² [diʃ] *vtr&i* **1.** enfoncer (ses adversaires)/couper l'herbe sous le pied à (qn) **2.** duper*/rouler (qn) **3.** confondre/dérouter/frustrer; **he dished his chances of getting promoted**, il a gâché/il a foutu en l'air ses possibilités d'avancement **4.** *NAm* bavarder*/potiner/se tailler une bavette.

dishclout ['diʃklaut] *n A P* salope *f*/souillon *f*.

dish out ['diʃaut] *vtr F* **1. to dish out money/the lolly**, payer*/casquer/cracher de l'argent* **2. to**

dish it out, réprimander*/enguirlander/passer un savon **3. to dish out punishment,** assener des coups* à son adversaire/envoyer un marron/envoyer une pêche à qn. (*See* **dirt 2; porridge 2**)

dish up ['diʃʌp] *vtr* **1.** *F* bien arranger/bien trousser/requinquer; **he dished up some excuse or other,** il a sorti une excuse quelconque; **they just dished up a load of old info in a new form,** ils ont fait un réchauffé de faits bien connus **2.** *P* **to be dished up,** être fatigué*/être pompé/être sur les rotules.

dishwater ['diʃwɔːtər] *n F* **1.** lavasse *f*; bibine *f*; (*food*) **to taste of dishwater,** sentir la graille; **this coffee's like dishwater,** ce café c'est du jus de chaussettes **2. dull as dishwater,** ennuyeux*/chiant comme la pluie. (*See* **ditchwater**)

dishy ['diʃi] *a F* qui a du chien/qui jette du jus; **she's rather dishy,** elle est plutôt sexy/elle on jette/elle a de la classe; **he's a very dishy guy,** il a de la gueule/il dégage, ce mec. (*See* **dish¹ 1**)

distance ['dist(ə)ns] *n F* (*sport, esp boxing*) **to go the distance,** aller à la limite.

ditch¹ [ditʃ] *n F* **the Ditch** (*a*) la Manche *ou* la mer du Nord; **the big ditch,** l'océan *m*/la Grande Tasse/la baille/la grande bleue (*b*) Shoreditch (dans la banlieue est de Londres). (*See* **last-ditch**)

ditch² [ditʃ] *vtr F* **1.** jeter par-dessus bord/larguer/balancer/bazarder **2. to ditch a car** (*i*) verser une dans un fossé/aller dans le décor (*ii*) abandonner*/bazarder une bagnole **3. to ditch a plane,** amerrir en catastrophe/faire un amerrissage de fortune **4.** (*a*) abandonner* (une idée); plaquer/larguer (une gonzesse) (*b*) se débarrasser* de qn; balancer/sacquer/virer qn.

ditchwater ['ditʃwɔːtər] *n F* **dull as ditchwater,** ennuyeux*/chiant comme la pluie; **he's as dull as ditchwater,** c'est un robinet d'eau tiède.

dither ['diðər] *n F* **to be all of a dither/to be in a dither,** être dans tous ses états/ne plus savoir où donner de la tête.

dithery ['diðəri] *a F* agité/nerveux/tout chose.

ditto¹ ['ditou] *n F* idem; **to say ditto,** opiner du bonnet/du chef.

ditto² ['ditou] *vi F* faire *ou* dire la même chose.

dive¹ [daiv] *n F* **1.** (*seedy bar or club*) café*/bouge *m*/tripot *m*/gargote *f*/boui-boui *m*; **it's a bit of a dive, but the music's really good,** ça fait un peu tripot mais il y a de la bonne musique **2.** (*esp boxing*) **to take a dive,** aller au tapis. (*See* **nosedive¹**)

dive² [daiv] *vi V* (*cunnilingus*) **to dive (into the bushes),** faire minette/brouter le cresson. (*See* **muff² 3; nosedive²; pearl-dive**)

divi ['divi] *n F* = **divvy.**

divine [di'vain] *a F* excellent*/divin*/merveilleux/ravissant.

divvy ['divi] *n F* (= *dividend*) intérêt *m*/divi(dende) *m*/fade *m*.

divvy up ['divi'ʌp] *vi F* partager/aller au fade/faire la motte.

dizzy ['dizi] *a F* **1.** étourdi/écervelé/à tête de linotte **2. a dizzy blonde,** une blonde tape-à-l'œil/platine/vaporeuse; **a dizzy dame,** une femme* bête*/(*pej*) une connasse **3.** *O* **it's the dizzy limit,** c'est le comble/c'est la fin des haricots.

DJ, d.j., ['diːˈdʒei] *n F* (*abbr = disc jockey*) présentateur, -trice de disques/animateur, -trice/disque-jockey *m*/disc-jockey *m*.

DMs ['diːˈemz] *npl F* (*abbr = Dr Martens*) = **Doc Martens.** (*See* **bovver-boots**)

do¹ [duː] *n* **1.** *F* réjouissances*/

boum *f*/bombance *f*; **there's a big do on at the Palace tonight**, il va y avoir une grande fête au Palais ce soir **2.** *P* escroquerie *f*/filouterie *f*/ attrape *f*/roublardise *f* **3.** *pl F* **do's**, partage *m*/fade *m*/taf *m*; **fair do's**, une juste part; **to give s.o. fair do's**, jouer franc jeu avec qn/donner à chacun son dû **4.** **the do's and dont's**, ce qu'il faut faire et ne pas faire **5.** **it's a poor do**, c'est minable; c'est pas terrible/ça ne casse rien. (*See* **hair-do**)

do² [duː] *vtr* **1.** *P* (*man*) faire l'amour* avec/sauter/tomber (qn) **2.** *P* sodomiser*/enculer/bourrer (qn) **3.** *F* **to do sth no one else can do for you**, déféquer*/déposer un bronze/aller où le Roi va à pied **4.** *P* escroquer*/arnaquer/refaire/ rouler; **to be/to get done**, se faire avoir **5.** *P* cambrioler*/caroubler; **to do a place**, faire un casse **6.** *P* battre*/flauper/tabasser; **they did him**, ils l'ont passé à tabac; **if you don't shut up I'll do you!** la ferme! ou je te casse la gueule! **7.** *P* arrêter*/épingler; **to get done by the police**, se faire alpaguer/se faire agrafer par la police **8.** *P* (*serve a prison term*) **he's doing ten years for GBH**, il fait dix ans pour coups et blessures **9.** *F* (*to imitate*) **he does a very good Groucho Marx**, il fait très bien/il imite bien Groucho Marx **10.** *F* visiter; **to do Europe**, faire l'Europe **11.** *F* **that'll do!** assez!*/ça suffit!/c'est marre!/y en a marre! **he'll do me**, il me va/ça fait mon blot **12.** *F* **that just won't do!** ça ne se fait vraiment pas! **13.** *F* **have nothing to do with it!** n'y touchez pas!/mettez pas le doigt dans cet engrenage! **nothing doing!** rien à faire!/pas question!/que dalle! **lend me a fiver? nothing doing!** tu me prêtes cinq livres? rien à faire!/tu peux toujours courir! **14.** *F* **done!** d'accord*!/dac!/tope-là! **15.** *F* **that's done it!** ça a tout gâché!/ça a tout bousillé! (*See* **tear²**) **16.** *F* **do or die**, marche ou

crève **17.** *P* **I'm absolutely done**, je suis complètement à plat/à bout/ crevé. (*See* **do down; do for; do in; do-it-yourself; do-it-your-selfer; do out; do over; do up; do with; do without; proud 1, 2; thing 10**)

DOA ['diːouˈeiː] *a&n F* (*abbr = dead on arrival*) **he was (a) DOA**, il était mort avant d'arriver à l'hôpital.

dob in ['dɔbˈin] *vtr Austr F* dénoncer*/trahir/moucharder/balancer; vendre la mèche.

dobbo ['dɔbou] *n Austr P* individu bête*/andouille *f*.

doc [dɔk] *n F* (*abbr = doctor*) docteur *m*/toubib *m*.

dock¹ [dɔk] *n F* **in dock** (*a*) à l'hôpital/à l'hosto (*b*) (*car, etc*) au garage/en réparation/en rade. (*See* **dickory dock**)

dock² [dɔk] *vtr F* **to dock s.o.'s pay**, rogner le salaire de qn; **to dock £5 off s.o.'s wages**, retenir/rogner £5 sur le salaire de qn.

Doc Martens ['dɔkˈmɑːtinz] *npl F* (*= Dr Martens*) bottes *ou* chaussures portées par des bovver-boys *ou* des skinheads/Dr Martens (*RTM*). (*See* **DMs**)

doctor¹ ['dɔktər] *n F* **1.** **just what the doctor ordered**, exactement ce qu'il (me) faut **2.** **doctor's orders:** *see* **bingo 9.** (*See* **couch doctor; horse doctor**)

doctor² ['dɔktər] *vtr F* **1.** châtrer/ couper; **my cat's been doctored**, mon chat a été châtré **2.** (*wine*) frelater; (*text, etc*) tripatouiller **3.** (*accounts*) truquer/maquiller.

doddle¹ [dɔdl] *n F* **it's a doddle**, c'est simple comme bonjour/c'est facile comme tout; **that exam was a real doddle**, j'ai passé cet examen sur une jambe; cet exam, c'était du nougat.

doddle² [dɔdl] *vtr F* (*rare*) **to doddle it**, gagner les doigts dans le nez/gagner les mains dans les poches.

dodge[1] [dɔdʒ] *n* F ruse *f*/astuce *f*/combine *f*; **a clever dodge/a good dodge,** un bon truc/un filon; **the old, old dodge,** le coup classique; **to be up to all the dodges,** connaître tous les trucs/toutes les ficelles; **he knows all the tax dodges there are,** il connaît toutes les combines *fpl*/les échappatoires *fpl* pour payer moins d'impôts.

dodge[2] [dɔdʒ] *vtr* F **1. to dodge the column,** tirer au flanc/se défiler/couper à qch/tirer au cul. (*See* **column-dodger**) **2. to dodge the draft** (*a*) éviter d'être envoyé outre-mer/se défiler (*b*) faire chibis à la grive/se faire la belle. (*See* **column-dodger**; **devil-dodger**; **draft-dodger**)

dodger [dɔdʒər] *n* (*resourceful*) malin(, -igne) *m(f)*/débrouillard(e) *m(f)*/dégourdi(e) *m(f)*; (*trickster*) roublard *m*/filou *m*; (*shirker*) tire-au-flanc *m*/tire-au-cul *m*; **he's a bit of an artful dodger,** il n'a pas les deux pieds dans le même sabot (*b*) P (*RS = lodger*) **artful dodger,** locataire *mf*. (*See* **column-dodger**; **devil-dodger**; **draft-dodger**)

dodgy [dɔdʒi] *a* F **1.** malin*/débrouillard/roublard **2.** douteux; **it's a dodgy business,** c'est une affaire louche/fumeuse/qui sent mauvais **3.** délicat/difficile; **the whole thing's rather dodgy, we'll have to tread carefully,** l'affaire m'a l'air fumeuse, regardons bien où nous mettons les pieds **4.** (*unsafe, dangerous*) **that chair's a bit dodgy, don't sit on it,** cette chaise est bancale, ne vous asseyez pas dessus.

dodo [doudou] *n* F (*old-fashioned or reactionary pers*) vieux rabâcheur/vieux croûton/vieux birbe/vieux débris; **dead as a dodo,** mort et enterré.

do down [duːˈdaun] *vtr* F l'emporter sur (qn)/rouler (qn)/refaire (qn).

do for [duːˈfɔːr] *vtr* **1.** F faire le ménage pour (qn) **2.** P tuer*/descendre/envoyer (qn) en l'air/se faire (qn) **3.** P **to be done for** (*a*) être ruiné/fauché/dans la dèche/sans un (*b*) fini/fichu/cuit; **he's done for,** les carottes sont cuites pour lui (*c*) être mort/fichu; **he's done for,** il a écopé (*d*) être fatigué*/sur les genoux/sur les rotules; **I'm done for,** je suis crevé.

dog [dɔg] *n* F **1.** (*pers*) vaurien*/sale type *m*/canaille *f*/saligaud *m*; *O* **you dog!** canaille!/espèce de salaud! **a gay dog,** un gai luron/un joyeux drille/un fêtard; **a lucky dog,** un veinard; **a sly dog,** un fin renard **2.** *pl* **dogs,** pieds*/nougats *mpl*/arpions *mpl*; **my dogs are killing me,** j'ai les pieds qui me rentrent dans le ventre **3.** = **dog-end 4.** *pl* **the dogs,** courses *fpl* de lévriers **5. it's a dog's life,** c'est une vie de chien; **she's leading him a dog's life,** elle lui fait une vie de chien **6. dressed up/got up like a dog's dinner,** en grand tralala/sur son trente-et-un/sapé comme un milord **7. you need some/the hair of the dog (that bit you),** ce qu'il te faut faire c'est de reprendre du poil de la bête **8. he doesn't stand a dog's chance,** il n'a pas l'ombre d'une chance **9. to go to the dogs,** aller à sa ruine/filer un mauvais coton; **his business is going to the dogs,** son affaire part à vau-l'eau **10. he's top dog around here,** c'est lui qui mène la danse/qui fait la pluie et le beau temps **11. dog in the manger,** le chien du jardinier; **don't be such a dog in the manger!** ne fais pas le rabat-joie! **12.** (*proverb*) **let sleeping dogs lie,** ne réveillez pas le chat qui dort **13.** *NAm* **to put on the dog,** en étaler/poser pour la galerie/frimer/en jeter **14. to see a man about a dog,** aller aux WC*/uriner*/arroser les fleurs/se payer une ardoise **15. to work like a dog,** travailler dur*/trimer/travailler d'arrache-pied **16.**

in a dog's age, il y a belle lurette/ ça fait des plombes 17. to call off the dogs, cesser les hostilités/enterrer la hâche de guerre 18. there's life in the old dog yet, il n'est pas près de sa fin/il est encore vert 19. love me love my dog, qui m'aime aime mon chien 20. (*RS* = *dog and bone* = *phone*) téléphone*/bigophone *m*/grelot *m*/ cornichon *m* 21. *Austr P* (= *drug observation group*) brigade *f* des stupéfiants/stups *mpl*. (*See* **cat 6**, **7**; **dirty I 1**; **dumb 2**; **hot 25**; **hound-dog**; **shaggy-dog**; **sheep-dog**; **yard-dog**)

dog-cart ['dɔgkɑɪt] *n Austr P* = **trawler**.

dog-collar ['dɔgkɔlər] *n F* faux-col *m* d'ecclésiastique/col romain; **the dog-collar brigade**, le clergé/les prêtres*/la ratiche/la curetaille.

dog-end ['dɔgend] *n F* mégot*/ clope *m*.

dog-fashion ['dɔgfæʃ(ə)n] *adv P* (*anal sex*) **to have it/to do it dog-fashion** (*i*) sodomiser*/enculer (qn) (*ii*) se faire enculer (par qn). (*See* **doggy-fashion**; **dogways**)

doggie ['dɔgi] *n F* = **doggy**.

doggo ['dɔgou] *F* caché*/planqué; **to lie doggo**, faire le mort/se tenir peinard/se garer des voitures.

doggone ['dɔgɔn] *NAm F* (*euph for damn*) **I** *a* sacré/satané/fichu/ maudit **II** *excl* **doggone it!** zut!/ merde!

doggy ['dɔgi] *n F* (*esp child's word*) chien*/chien-chien *m*/toutou *m*/ azor *m*.

doggy bag ['dɔgi'bæg] *n F* (*in restaurant*) petit sac pour emporter les restes; **could you put this in a doggy bag for me?** pourriez-vous me faire un petit paquet de ces restes pour mon chien/chat?

doggy-fashion ['dɔgi'fæʃ(ə)n] *adv P* = **dog-fashion**.

dog-house ['dɔghaus] *n F* **in the** dog-house, mis de côté/en quarantaine/mal en cour; **I'm in the dog-house because I forgot his birthday**, il me snobe/il me fait la gueule parce que j'ai oublié son anniversaire.

do-gooder ['duɪ'gudər] *n F* (*pej*) redresseur *m* de torts/dame patronesse/faiseur, -euse de bonnes œuvres.

dogsbody ['dɔgzbɔdi] *n F* subordonné(e)/sous-fifre *m*/lampiste *m*; **I'm the general dogsbody around here**, je suis la bonne à tout faire.

dog-tag ['dɔgtæg] *n F* (*mil*) plaque *f* d'identité.

dog-tired ['dɔg'taiəd] *a F* très fatigué/crevé/claqué/lessivé.

dogways ['dɔgweiz] *adv P* = **dog-fashion**.

do in ['duɪ'in] *vtr P* **1.** tuer/ assassiner*/liquider/supprimer; **to do oneself in**, se suicider*/se buter/ s'envoyer en l'air/se flanquer en l'air **2.** fatiguer/éreinter; **done in**, très fatigué*/claqué/crevé.

doing! ['dɔiŋ] *excl F* boum!/pan!/ vlan! (*See* **doink!**)

doings ['duiŋz] *npl F* **1.** machin *m*/truc *m*/fourbi *m*/bidule *m*; **doings over there**, machin là-bas **2. the doings**, tout le bataclan/tout le bazar; **I've got the doings**, j'ai de quoi/j'ai ce qu'il faut.

doink! [dɔiŋk] *excl F* = **doing!**

do-it-yourself ['duitjə'self] *n* **1.** *F* (*a*) bricolage *m*/bricole *f* (*b*) attirail *m* de bricoleur **2.** *V* masturbation*/branlette *f* maison.

do-it-yourselfer ['duitjə'selfər] *n F* bricoleur *m*.

dojee, dojie ['doudʒi] *n P* (*drugs*) héroïne*/cheval *m*/blanche *f*.

doldrums ['dɔldrəmz] *npl F* **to be in the doldrums** (*a*) avoir le cafard/ broyer du noir/avoir le blues (*b*) être dans le marasme.

doll [dɔl] *n F* **1.** (*esp attractive girl*) fille* *ou* jeune femme*/nana *f*/ poupée *f*/pépée; **hi doll!** salut bébé! **2.** tête *f* de linotte/petite tête/tête en l'air.

dollop ['dɔləp] *n F* morceau *m* informe/flanquée *f*/plâtrée *f*; **a good dollop of jam,** une bonne tapée/ cuillerée de confiture; **a dollop of beans,** une porcif de haricots.

doll up ['dɔl'ʌp] *vtr F* **to doll oneself up,** se pomponner/se bichonner; se badigeonner; **to get all dolled up,** se mettre sur son trente et un.

dolly ['dɔli] *n* **1.** *F* poupée *f*/pépée *f*. (*See* **doll 1**) **2.** *F* = **dolly-bird 1 3.** *P* (*drugs*) méthadone *f* (dolphine).

dolly-bird ['dɔlibəɹd] *n* **1.** *F* (*attractive and fashionable girl*) (belle) nana *f*/(belle) poupée/une nana roulée au moule **2.** *P* fille facile/à la cuisse hospitalière.

dome [doum] *n F* tête*/caboche *f*/ boule *f*. (*See* **ivory**)

dominoes ['dɔminouz] *npl P* **1.** *O* **it's dominoes with/for him,** il est fichu **2.** *A* dents* jaunies/dominos *mpl*; **box of dominoes,** bouche*/ boîte *f*.

dona(h) ['dounə] *n A P* petite amie/régulière *f*/particulière *f*.

done up ['dʌn'ʌp] *a & pp F* **1.** très fatigué*/crevé **2.** ruiné*/ fauché/nettoyé **3.** (*a*) maquillé/ emplâté/badigeonné (*b*) habillé avec élégance/bien sapé/bien fringué/tiré à quatre épingles. (*See* **do up**)

dong [dɔŋ], **donker** ['dɔŋkər] *n V* (gros) pénis*/gros bout. (*See* **donkey 4**)

donkey ['dɔŋki] *n* **1.** *F* **to talk the hind leg off a donkey,** être bavard* comme une pie/être un moulin à paroles/l'avoir bien pendue **2.** *F* **donkey work,** travail *m*/turbin *m* de routine **3.** *F* **I haven't seen him in/for donkey's years,** ça fait/il y a

une éternité/une paye/des plombes que je (ne) l'ai vu; **donkey's years ago,** il y a belle lurette **4.** *V* (gros) pénis*/gros bout; **to flog one's donkey,** se masturber*/s'astiquer la colonne/se taper une pignole.

donnybrook ['dɔnibruk] *n NAm F* querelle*/bagarre *f*/rififi *m*/corrida *f*.

doo-da, doodah ['duːdɑɪ] *n F* **1.** truc *m*/machin *m*/fourbi *m*/ bidule *m*/zinzin *m* **2.** agitation *f*/ énervement *m*; **to be all of a doo-da,** être énervé/dans tous ses états.

doodle¹ ['duːdl] *n* **1.** *A P* pénis*/ verge *f*/queue *f* **2.** *F* griffonnage *m*.

doodle² ['duːdl] *vtr F* griffonner (d'un air distrait ou en pensant à autre chose).

doodle-alley ['duːdl'æli] *a O P* (*a*) qui a une case de vide (*b*) fou*/ cinoque/timbré.

doodle-bug ['duːdlbʌg] *n A F* **1.** vieille voiture*/tacot *m*/guimbarde *f* **2.** (*WWII*) bombe volante.

doofer ['duːfər] *n P* = **doo-da 1.**

doohickey ['duːhiki] *n NAm F* = **doo-da 1.**

doojee ['duːdʒi], **doojer** ['duːdʒər], **dooji** ['duːdʒi] *n P* = **dojee.**

doojigger ['duːdʒigər] *n NAm O F* = **doo-da 1.**

dooks [duːks] *npl P* = **dukes.**

doolally (tap) ['duː'læli('tæp)] *a P* = **doodle-alley.**

door [dɔːr] *n F* **1. to show s.o. the door,** mettre/flanquer qn à la porte; virer/balancer qn **2.** (*a*) **knock at the door:** see **bingo 4** (*b*) **key of the door:** see **bingo 21.** (*See* **back I 3**)

doormat ['dɔːmæt] *n F* individu* qui se laisse marcher dessus/paillasson *m*.

door-nail ['dɔːneil] *n F* **dead as a door-nail,** mort et enterré.

doorstep ['dɔːstep] *n F* quignon *m* de pain.

do out ['duː'aut] *vtr F* **to do s.o. out of sth,** escroquer* qn/arnaquer/rouler/carotter qn.

do over ['duː'ouvər] *vtr* **1.** *F* (*redecorate*) refaire/retaper **2.** *P* (*a*) voler* (qn) (*b*) tromper*/rouler (qn) **3.** *P* battre* (qn)/passer (qn) à tabac/tabasser (qn) **4.** *P* (*burgle/ NAm burglarize*) **to do a place over,** cambrioler*/faire un fric-frac/faire un casse; ratisser/nettoyer un endroit.

dope¹ [doup] *n* **1.** *F* (*a*) renseignement*/tuyau *m*/tubard *m*; **the latest dope,** les dernières nouvelles/les derniers renseignements*; **to give s.o. the latest dope,** mettre qn à la page/affranchir qn/mettre qn au parfum (*b*) faux renseignements*/bourrage *m* de crâne (*c*) tuyaux sur les courses de chevaux; **dope sheet,** journal *m* hippique/le turf **2.** *F* individu bête*/andouille *f*/nouille *f*; **what a dope he is!** quel crétin que ce type! **3.** *F* (*administered to a horse*) doping *m*/dopant *m*; **dope test,** contrôle *m* anti-doping/antidopage **4.** *P* (*drugs*) stup(éfiant) *m*/narc(otique) *m*/drogue *f*/came *f*; **dope addict,** camé(e) *m(f)*/toxico *mf*/junkie *m*/accrochée *m(f)*; **dope fiend,** morphinomane *mf*; **dope pusher/peddler,** fourgueur *m*/trafiquant *m*/dealer *m* (en stupéfiants); **dope racket,** trafic *m* de drogues*; **dope ring,** bande *f* de trafiquants; **to be on dope/to use dope,** se droguer*/se camer/se schnouffer; **to push/to peddle dope,** revendre de la came/trafiquer.

dope² [doup] *vtr* **1.** *F* (*a*) administrer un narcotique à (qn)/droguer/doper (*b*) mêler un narcotique à (un verre de vin)/narcotiser (une cigarette)/doper (*c*) **to dope oneself,** prendre des stupéfiants *mpl*/se droguer*; **doped (up) to the eyeballs/eyebrows,** schnouffé à bloc/camé jusqu'à l'os **2.** *F* doper (un

cheval) **3.** *F* ajouter de l'alcool à une boisson non alcoolisée/corser **4.** *P* tromper*/refaire/rouler/couillonner (qn).

dopehead ['douphed] *n NAm P* = **doper.**

dope out ['doup'aut] *vtr NAm P* (*a*) découvrir*/dénicher (*b*) trouver le joint.

doper ['doupər] *n NAm P* drogué*/camé *m*/toxico *mf*/junkie *m*.

doperie ['doupəri] *n A P* (*drugs*) fumerie *f* d'opium*/repaire *m* de drogués.

dopester ['doupstər] *n P* **1.** = **doper 2.** (*horse racing*) marchand *m* de tuyaux/tuyauteur *m*/tubardeur *m*.

dope up ['doup'ʌp] *vtr&i P* (*a*) se droguer*/se camer (*b*) droguer/schnouffer (qn).

dopey ['doupi] *a F* **1.** bête*/bêta empoté/con/cruche **2.** abruti (de fatigue) **3.** stupéfié/hébété (par un narcotique).

dopium ['doupiəm] *n A P* (*drugs*) opium*/op *m*/noir *m*.

dopy ['doupi] *a F* = **dopey.**

do-re-mi ['dou'rei'miː] *n esp NAm P* argent*/fric *m*/oseille *f*/pépettes *fpl*/picaillons *mpl*.

dorm [dɔːm] *n F* (*abbr = dormitory*) dortoir *m*/dorto *m*.

Dorothy Dixer ['dɔrɔθi'diksər] *n Austr F* question *f* à un membre du gouvernement, posée par un parlementaire de la majorité.

dose [dous] *n* **1.** *P* **to get/to catch/to cop a dose,** attraper une maladie* vénérienne/ramasser la (s)chtouille; **to have caught/copped a dose of the clap,** être (s)chtouillard/pisser des lames de rasoir/se faire poivrer/se faire fader **2.** *F* **like a dose of salts,** comme une lettre à la poste.

dose up ['dous'ʌp] *vtr&i P* contaminer (qn) avec une maladie* vénérienne/fader (qn)/plomber (qn)/refiler sa vérole (à qn); **to be dosed up (to the eyeballs/eyebrows)** (*a*) souffrir d'une maladie* vénérienne/être (bien) fadé/être naze (*b*) être drogué*/camé/chargé jusquelà; être défoncé.

dosh [dɔʃ] *n O P* (*rare*) argent*/fric *m*/pèze *m*.

doss[1] [dɔs] *n P* **1.** lit* (*esp* dans une pension peu relevée)/boîte *f* à puces/pucier *m*/pieu *m* **2.** somme *m*/dorme *f*/roupillon *m*; **to have a doss,** dormir*/piquer un roupillon/en écraser.

doss[2] [dɔs] *vi P* dormir*/pioncer/en écraser.

doss down ['dɔs'daun] *vi P* (*a*) se coucher*/se lâcher/se plumer (*b*) crécher (quelque part); **we can doss down at his place,** on peut crécher/pieuter chez lui.

dosser ['dɔsər] *n P* (*down-and-out*) (*a*) clochard*/clodo *m* (*b*) sans le sou *m*/fauché *m*/déchard *m* (*c*) ivrogne*/alcoolique *mf*/alcolo *m* (*d*) drogué*/junkie *m*/camé *m*.

doss-house ['dɔshaus] *n F* asile *m* de nuit/dorme *f*/piaule *f* à clodos; **their place looks like a real doss-house,** c'est un vrai foutoir chez eux.

dot[1] [dɔt] *n* **1.** *F* **on the dot,** à l'heure/à pic/pile/recta **2.** *F* **in the year dot,** il y a longtemps/une paye; **it goes back to the year dot,** ça remonte au déluge/à Mathusalem.

dot[2] [dɔt] *vtr* **1.** *P* **to dot s.o. (one),** battre* qn/flanquer un gnon à qn/balancer une pêche à qn **2.** *F* **to dot and carry one,** boîter (en marchant)/aller clopin-clopant/faire cinq et trois font huit **3.** *F* **to dot one's i's and cross one's t's,** mettre les points sur les i; **it's just a case of dotting the i's and crossing the t's,** il ne reste qu'à y mettre la dernière touche.

dottiness ['dɔtinis] *n F* folie

douce/toquade *f*/loufoquerie *f*/détraquage *m*.

dotty ['dɔti] *a F* fou*/cinglé/toqué/maboule; **she's gone a bit dotty,** elle a perdu la boule/elle travaille du chapeau.

double ['dʌbl] *a F* **1. to do a double take,** y regarder* à deux fois **2. double talk,** propos *mpl* ambigus *ou* trompeurs/boniment *m*/double parler *m* **3. double think,** croyance *f* au pour et au contre **4. to do the double act,** se marier/signer le bail. (*See* **Dutch III 1**)

double-cross ['dʌbl'krɔs] *n F* entubage *m*/roustissure *f*/arnaque *f*.

double cross ['dʌbl'krɔs] *vtr F* tromper*/entuber/doubler; **to get double-crossed,** se faire faire marron/se faire rouler.

double-crosser ['dʌbl'krɔsər] *n F* faux jeton/entubeur *m*/carambouilleur *m*/roustisseur *m*.

double-decker ['dʌbl'dekər] *n F* **1.** autobus *m* à impériale **2.** sandwich *m* à deux étages.

double-quick ['dʌbl'kwik] *adv F* au pas de course/en cinq secs; **to do (sth) double-quick/in double-quick time,** faire (qch) fissa/se magner le popotin. (*See* **quick**)

double up ['dʌbl'ʌp] *vi F* **1. to double up/to be doubled up with laughter/pain,** se tordre (de rire*)/se gondoler/se fendre la pêche **2. to double up on a horse,** doubler la mise **3. to double up with s.o.,** partager une chambre avec qn.

douche [duʃ] *n F* surprise *f* désagréable/douche froide.

dough [dou] *n F* argent*/galette *f*/fric *m*/pognon *m*; **to be in the dough,** être riche*/être au pèze/être bourré à bloc; **he throws his dough around,** il dépense sans compter/il jette son argent* par les fenêtres/il fait valser ses ronds.

doughboy ['doubɔi], **dough-foot** ['doufut] *n NAm F* (*esp*

WW1) soldat* (de 2ème classe) de l'infanterie américaine/biffin *m*/ troufion *m*.

doughnut ['dounʌt] *n Austr V* **golden doughnut**, sexe de la femme*/abricot *m*/moule *f*.

doughy ['dou(w)i] *a F* (*rare*) riche*/galetteux/bourré aux as.

do up ['duːʌp] *vtr* **1.** *P* battre* (qn)/arranger le portrait (à qn)/ tabasser qn/passer (qn) à tabac **2.** *F* raccommoder/remettre en état. (*See* **done up**)

dove [dʌv] *n F* (*pol*) qn qui s'oppose à la guerre/pacifiste *mf*/ colombe *f*/mou *m* (*See* **hawk**)

do with ['duːwið] *vtr F* **I could do with a drink,** je m'en jetterais bien un derrière la cravate/un verre ne serait pas de refus.

do without ['duːwið'aut] *vi F* se l'accrocher/se serrer la ceinture/se taper.

down¹ [daun] **I** *a F* **down drugs,** drogues tranquillisantes/sédatifs *mpl*/calmants *mpl*. (*See* **up¹**) **II** *adv F* **1. to be down and out,** être très pauvre*/être dans la dèche/ être sans le sou **2. to be down on s.o.,** en avoir après qn **3. to be down on one's luck,** avoir de la malchance*/de la guigne/de la poisse; avoir la cerise **4. down under,** aux antipodes **5.** (*a*) (*drugs*) **to be down,** redescendre (*b*) (*depressed*) **to be (feeling) down,** avoir le cafard/broyer du noir; avoir le moral à zéro. (*See* **ground 2**; **mouth 2**) **III** *n F* **1. to have a down on s.o.,** avoir une dent contre qn/avoir qn dans le nez/en avoir après qn **2.** = **downer 1, 2.**

down² [daun] *vtr F* **1.** faire tomber/descendre (qn)/envoyer (qn) au tapis **2.** boire*; **to down a pint,** s'envoyer un coup/s'en jeter un derrière la cravate/se rincer la dalle **3. to down tools** (*i*) cesser le travail (*ii*) se mettre en grève.

down-and-out ['daunənd'aut] **I** *a O F* **a down-and-out cad,** une canaille achevée; **a down-and-out liar,** un fichu menteur. (*See* **down¹ II 1**) **II** *n F* (*a*) déchard *m*/bat-la-dèche *m* (*b*) clochard*/clodo *m* (*c*) ivrogne*/alcoolique *mf*/alcolo *m*.

downbeat ['daunbiːt] *a F* **1.** calme/tête froide/coolos/sans avoir l'air d'y toucher; **he was rather downbeat about it,** il n'avait pas l'air d'y toucher **2.** (*pers*) déprimé. (*See* **upbeat**)

downer ['daunər] *n F* **1.** (*drugs*) tranquillisant *m*/sédatif *m*/calmant *m*. (*See* **up III 2**; **upper**) **2.** situation déprimante/déconfiture *f*; déprime *f*; **to be on a downer,** être dans la panade. (*See* **up-and-downer**)

downhill ['daunhil] *adv F* **to go downhill,** dégringoler/être sur le déclin/être sur la mauvaise pente/ filer un mauvais coton.

downie ['dauni] *n P* = **downer 1.**

Downing Street ['dauniŋstriːt] *Prn F see* **bingo 10.**

down market ['daunmɑːkit] *a F* bas de gamme. (*See* **up market**)

downy [dauni] *a O F* malin*/ marloupin/roublard.

doxy ['dɔksi] *n A P* (*pej*) (*a*) prostituée*/pute *f*/roulure *f* (*b*) maîtresse *f*.

doz [dʌz] *n F* (*abbr* = *dozen*) **one dozen: see bingo 12.**

dozen ['dʌzn] *n F* **1. a baker's dozen,** treize à la douzaine **2. daily dozen,** culture *f* physique **3. dozens of...,** une abondance* de.../ une flop(p)ée de.../une tripotée de.../une tapée de... (*See* **dime**; **nineteen**; **six 3**)

dozy ['douzi] *a F* **1.** abruti/ballot/ demeuré; **you dozy twit!** espèce d'abruti! **2.** paresseux*/flemmard/ cossard/feignant.

dozy-arsed ['douziɑːst] *a P* bête*;
what a dozy-arsed bastard! quel
connard!/quel trouduc!

drac(k) [dræk] *a Austr F (unattrac-
tive)* moche; **a drack sort** (*i*) une
mocheté (*ii*) un mocheton.

D-racks ['diːræks] *npl O P* cartes*
à jouer/brêmes *fpl.*

draft-dodger ['drɑːftdɔdʒər] *n F*
tire-au-flanc *m*/insoumis *m*; (*mil*)
déserteur *m.* (*See* **dodge²** 2)

drag¹ [dræg] *n* **1.** *F* vêtements* de
travelo; **in drag,** en travelo; **drag
club,** club *m* de travelos; **drag
queen,** travelo *m*/trav *m* **2.** *F (a)*
(*pers*) individu ennuyeux*/casse-
pieds *m*/raseur *m*/emmerdeur *m*/
casse-bonbons *m* (*b*) (*thing*)
ennuyeux*/rasoir/embêtant; **what a
drag!**/**it's a real drag!** quelle
barbe!/c'est la barbe! **3.** *P* voiture*/tire *f*/tank *m*; **drag race,**
course *f* de vieilles voitures* **4.** *P*
(*a*) cigarette*/cibiche *f*/sèche *f*/
clope *mf.* (*See* **spit** 2) (*b*) bouffée *f*
de tabac; **to take a drag,** tirer une
bouffée/une taf(fe); **give us a drag,**
donne une bouffée **5.** *NAm P* piston *m*/pistonnage *m* **6.** *NAm P*
rue *f*/strasse *f*; **the main drag,** la
grand-rue **7.** *P* (*RS = carpet bag*)
trois mois de taule. (*See* **carpet¹** 2)

drag² [dræg] *vtr F* **to drag one's
feet,** se faire tirer l'oreille/renâcler/
traîner les pieds.

drag-ass ['drægæs] *vi NAm P* **1.**
être abattu/être à plat **2.** partir*/
se barrer/se carapater.

dragged out ['drægd'aut] *a NAm
P* fatigué*/crevé/éreinté. (*See* **drag
out**)

draggy ['drægi] *a P* ennuyeux*/
canulant/rasoir/chiant.

drag in ['dræg'in] *vtr F* amener
(qch) comme un cheveu sur la
soupe.

drag on ['dræg'ɔn] *vtr&i F* tirer en
longueur/allonger la sauce.

dragon ['drægən] *n* **1.** *F (fierce*

person; usu (old) woman) dragon *m*
2. *F* **dragon's teeth,** défenses *fpl*
anti-tank **3.** *P (drugs)* **green
dragon,** amphétamine*/amph(é) *f*;
to chase the dragon, respirer la
fumée d'un mélange héroïne-barbi-
turiques/chasser le dragon **4.**
Austr P **to drain the dragon,**
uriner*/égoutter son cyclope.

drag out ['dræg'aut] *vtr&i F* **1.**
faire traîner/tirer en longueur/
allonger la sauce **2. to drag sth
out of s.o.,** extirper qn/tirer les vers
du nez à qn. (*See* **dragged out**)

dragsman ['drægzmən] *n A P*
voleur* de train.

drag up ['dræg'ʌp] *vtr* **1.** *F* **to
drag up s.o.'s past,** faire ressortir le
passé de qn/sortir le squelette du
placard/fouiller la merde **2.** *P*
where were you dragged up? où as-
tu été élevé?/d'où sors-tu?/de quel
trou est-ce que tu sors? **dragged
up,** élevé à la va-comme-je-te-pousse.

drain¹ [drein] *n F* **1. to go down
the drain,** échouer*/tomber dans le
lac/tomber à l'eau; **money down
the drain,** c'est jeter l'argent* par
les fenêtres **2. to laugh like a
drain,** rire* de bon cœur/se
boyauter/se bidonner **3. up the
drain,** dans le pétrin/dans la
mouise. (*See* **brain drain**)

drain² [drein] *vtr F* **to drain s.o.
dry,** saigner qn à blanc/plumer qn/
tondre la laine sur le dos à qn.

drainpipe ['dreinpaip] *n F* **1.**
individu* grand et mince/asperge
f/un grand sifflet **2.** *pl* (= *drainpipe trousers*) pantalon* étroit/
fuseau *m*/(pantalon) tuyau de
poêle.

drape [dreip] *vtr F* **to drape oneself
(all over sth)** (*i*) poser pour la
galerie/frimer (*ii*) en étaler (sur
qch).

drappie, drappy ['dræpi] *n A F*
a wee drappie, un petit verre/une
goutte d'alcool*; un remontant/un
schnaps.

drat [dræt] *excl F* (*expression of annoyance, euph for* **damn**) **drat (it)!** nom de nom!/bon sang! **drat the child!** au diable ce gosse!/sale môme!

dratted ['drætid] *a F* maudit/sacré; **this dratted weather!** ce fichu temps!/ce temps pourri!

draw¹ [drɔɪ] *n F* **to be quick on the draw** (*a*) être rapide à dégainer son arme/avoir la détente facile (*b*) piger au quart de poil/avoir de bonnes reprises.

draw² [drɔɪ] *vtr F* **1. to draw s.o.,** faire parler* qn/tirer les vers du nez à qn **2.** taquiner/faire enrager **3. to draw the line,** fixer une limite/mettre fin (à qch); **I draw the line at that,** je n'irai pas jusque là/je me refuse à faire ça. (*See* **blank**)

drawers ['drɔɪz] *npl P* (*women's*) culotte *f*/slip *m*; **to let one's drawers down/to drop one's drawers,** permettre des rapports sexuels/laisser tomber la culotte; **she'll drop her drawers for anyone,** elle couche avec n'importe qui/elle a la cuisse hospitalière. (*See* **droopy-drawers**)

dreadlocks ['dredlɔks] *npl P* (*Black Slang*) coiffure *f* rasta/dreadlocks *mpl*.

dream [driːm] **I** *a F* rêvé/de rêve; **to live in a dream world,** nager dans le bleu **II** *n* **1.** *F* **she's a dream,** c'est la femme rêvée; **it goes like a dream,** ça marche à merveille/comme dans un rêve **2.** *F* **he goes about in a dream,** il est toujours à rêvasser/à gamberger **3.** *F* **wet dream,** carte *f* (de France) **4.** *P* (*drugs*) (*pl*) **dreams/dream wax,** opium*/noir *m*.

dream-boat ['driːmbout] *n F* (*for a girl/a woman*) l'homme rêvé.

dream up ['driːm'ʌp] *vtr F* imaginer/inventer/gamberger.

dreamy ['driːmi] *a F* exquis/charmant/ravissant.

dreck [drek] *n A P* **1.** camelote *f*/

gnognot(t)e *f* **2.** clinquant *m*/tape-à-l'œil *m*.

dress down ['dres'daun] *vtr F* **1.** battre*/filer une raclée à (qn) **2.** réprimander* (qn)/enguirlander (qn)/assaisonner (qn)/engueuler (qn) comme du poisson pourri. (*See* **dressing-down**)

dressed [drest] *a&pp F* **dressed (fit) to kill,** élégant*/habillé sur son trente et un/en grand tralala/bien bâché/tiré à quatre épingles. (*See* **dress up 2**)

dressing-down ['dresiŋ'daun] *n F* **1.** volée *f* de coups*/raclée *f*/avoine *f* **2.** réprimande *f*/savon *m*. (*See* **dress down**)

dress up ['dres'ʌp] *vi F* **1. all dressed up and nowhere to go,** laissé(e) pour compte/laissé(e) (sur le carreau)/resté(e) en carafe **2. dressed up to the nines/to the teeth/to the knocker,** élégant*/habillé sur son trente et un/tiré à quatre épingles. (*See* **dressed**)

dressy ['dresi] *a F* élégant*/chic/ridère/rider.

dribs [dribz] *npl F* **in dribs and drabs,** petit à petit/au compte-gouttes.

drift [drift] *n F* **to catch the drift,** tenir le fil/piger/entraver/saisir; **I get your drift,** je pige.

drifter ['driftər] *n F* (*a*) personne qui se laisse aller (*b*) vagabond*/clochard*/clodo *m*.

drill [dril] *n F* **to know the drill,** connaître les rouages/connaître la musique/s'y connaître. (*See* **packdrill**)

drin [drin] *n P* (*drugs*) comprimé *m* de Benzédrine* (*RTM*).

drink [driŋk] *n* **1.** *F* **the drink,** la mer/la Tasse/la Grande Grande Bleue/la flotte **2.** *P* (*cut*) fade *m*/taffe *m*.

drinkies ['driŋkiz] *npl F* boissons *fpl*/consommations *fpl*/godets *mpl*;

to have **drinkies** before lunch, prendre l'apéro.

drip [drip] *n F* individu bête*/ nouille *f*/empoté *m*/andouille *f*/ cornichon *m*; **what a drip!** quelle nouille!/tête de nœud!

dripper ['dripər] *n F* goutte-à-goutte *m* (*seringue faite avec un compte-gouttes et une épingle*).

drippy ['dripi] *a F* 1. bête*/ empoté/cloche/gland 2. fadasse/ larmoyant/à l'eau de rose.

driver ['draivər] *n* 1. *F* **to be in the driver's seat**, être en position de force/tenir les rênes/diriger les opérations/mener la barque 2. *pl P* (*drugs*) amphétamines*/amphés *fpl*. (*See* **backseat**; **nigger-driver**; **pile-driver**; **slave-driver**; **truck-driver**)

drizzle-puss ['drizlpus] *n NAm O F* rabat-joie *m*/peau *f* de vache/ vieux chameau.

drome [droum] *n* (= *aerodrome*) *F* aérodrome *m*/terrain *m* (d'aviation).

drongo ['drɔŋgou] *n Austr F* individu bête*/buse *f*/gourde *f*/ poire *f*.

droob [druːb] *n Austr F* 1. un chouia/une larme; **he didn't get a droob**, il n'a rien* eu/il n'a eu que dalle/il n'a eu que peau de balle 2. = **drube.**

drool [druːl] *vi F* **to drool over sth/ s.o.**, baver (d'admiration, de plaisir) sur qch/qn.

droop [druːp] *n P* 1. = **drip** 2. **brewer's droop**, affaissement *m* du pénis* dû à l'alcool/le six heures de l'alcoolique; **to get brewer's droop**, faire queue de rat/ s'endormir sur le rôti.

drooper ['druːpər] *n* 1. *F* moustache* tombante/ramasse-miettes *m*/bacchantes *fpl* 2. *pl P* seins* tombants/blagues *fpl* à tabac/pendants *mpl*/tétasses *fpl*/gants *mpl* de toilette.

droopy-drawers ['druːpidrɔː(ə)z]

n P 1. individu dont la culotte tombe/nu-fesses *f*/cul-nu *m* 2. *see* **bingo 44.**

drop¹ [drɔp] *n* 1. *P* = **dropsy 1, 2** 2. *F* **at the drop of a hat**, tout de suite/illico/en un rien de temps/ aussi sec 3. *P* cache *f*/planque *f*/ planquouse *f* 4. *P* **to get the drop on s.o.**, dégainer plus vite que qn; tenir qn à merci/tenir le bon bout 5. *F* **a drop in the ocean**, une goutte d'eau dans la mer 6. *P* **to have a drop in the eye/to have had a drop too much**, être ivre*/être dans le cirage/avoir un verre dans le nez/être chargé 7. *F* petit verre d'alcool*/une goutte/un doigt/un chouia.

drop² [drɔp] *vtr* 1. *F* **to drop s.o. like a hot potato/a hot brick**, abandonner* qn/lâcher qn/plaquer qn/laisser tomber qn comme une vieille chaussette 2. *P* abattre/ descendre/buter (qn) 3. *F* donner un pourboire* (à qn); **we dropped him something**, on lui a graissé la patte/refilé la pièce 4. *P* (*gambling*) perdre/paumer de l'argent*; prendre une veste/une culotte 5. *F* **fit to drop**, très fatigué*/crevé/ éreinté/flagada; **he's fit to drop**, il a le coup de barre 6. *F* **to drop s.o. a line**, envoyer/mettre/griffonner un mot à qn 7. *F* **to drop sth/to let it drop**, laisser courir/laisser tomber/ laisser pisser (qch); **drop it!** c'est marre!/y en a marre!/écrase!/laisse pisser! 8. *P* **to drop one's load**, éjaculer*/arracher son copeau/ envoyer la purée 9. *P* prendre une drogue par voie buccale; **to drop acid**, prendre de l'acide 10. *Austr P* battre* (qn)/passer (qn) à tabac. (*See* **brick 2**; **clanger**; **dead I 11**; **shit III 2**; **stumer 3**)

drop in ['drɔp'in] **I** *vi F* **to drop in on s.o.**, rendre visite à qn en passant/passer chez qn/faire un saut chez qn **II** *vtr P* **to drop s.o. in it**, mettre qn dans la merde.

drop off ['drɔp'ɔf] *vtr&i* F **1.** s'endormir/piquer un roupillon/pioncer/écraser la bulle **2. to drop s.o. off,** déposer qn quelque part.

drop-out ['drɔpaut] *n* F **1.** qn qui refuse la société/le système; qn qui vit en marge de la société; hippie *mf*/drop-out *mf*/punk *mf* **2.** qn qui se retire d'un jeu; (*when winning*) qn qui fait Charlemagne.

drop out ['drɔp'aut] *vi* F **1.** refuser la société/le système; vivre en marge de la société; être un(e) hippie/un(e) drop-out **2.** se retirer de qch/abandonner qch; tirer son épingle du jeu/reprendre ses billes; (*when winning*) faire Charlemagne.

dropper ['drɔpər] *n* **1.** F seringue *f*/shooteuse *f*/hypo *f* **2.** P passeur *m* de faux chèques/pastiqueur *m*. (*See* **name-dropper**)

dropsy ['drɔpsi] *n* O P **1.** pot-de-vin *m*/dessous-de-table *m* **2.** pourboire*/pourliche *m*/pièce *f*.

dross [drɔs] *n* F **1.** O argent*/fric *m*/flouze *m*/pèze *m* **2.** vaurien*/saligaud *m*/salaud *m*.

drown [draun] *vtr* F **1. to drown a drink,** mettre trop d'eau dans une boisson/noyer une boisson **2. to drown in a teacup,** se noyer dans un verre d'eau **3. to drown one's sorrows,** noyer ses chagrins.

drube [druːb] *n Austr* F individu bête*/nouille *f*/andouille *f*/trouduc *m*.

druggie, druggy ['drʌgi] *n* P drogué*/camé(e) *m(f)*/toxico *mf*.

drum [drʌm] *n* **1.** P logement*/cambuse *f*; **to have one's drum done** (*i*) avoir une perquisition/avoir une descente dans sa piaule (*ii*) être cambriolé/en être d'un baluchonnage. (*See* **screw²** 3) **2.** P un paradis pour les voleurs/un casse de première **3.** F **to beat the drums/the big drum for s.o.,** faire du battage pour qn/faire du tam-tam/battre la grosse caisse pour qn

4. P route*/tire *f*/trime *f*/ruban *m* **5.** P NAm (= *eardrum*) tympan *m*.

drummer ['drʌmər] *n* O P commis voyageur/roulant *m*/hirondelle *f*.

drumstick ['drʌmstik] *n* F **1.** pilon *m* (de poulet) **2.** *pl* jambes* maigres/allumettes *fpl*/flûtes *fpl*/échasses *fpl*/échalas *mpl*.

drum up ['drʌm'ʌp] *vtr* F **to drum up business,** faire de la réclame/chauffer une affaire.

drunk [drʌŋk] *n* F (*abbr* = *drunkard*) ivrogne*/soûlard *m*/soûlaud *m*/alcolo *mf*/poivrot *m*.

dry [drai] *a* **1.** F **to be dry,** avoir soif*/avoir le gosier sec/la sécher; **dry as a bone,** sec comme un clou **2.** F **not dry behind the ears,** blanc-bec/morveux. (*See* **wet I** 5) **3.** F **dry run** (*a*) P coït* avec emploi d'un contraceptif/dérouillage *m* à sec (*b*) F (*theatre*) répétition *f* d'essai (*c*) F (*aviation*) manœuvre *f* d'essai **4.** V **dry fuck/dry hump,** dérouillage *m* à sec; **to have a dry hump,** jouir tout habillé. (*See* **drain²**; **high¹** 2; **home** 1; **suck** 2)

dry out ['drai'aut] *vi* P **1.** cuver son vin/déboiser sa gueule/se dépoivrer **2.** (*drugs*) se désintoxiquer/faire une cure.

dry up ['drai'ʌp] *vi* F **1. dry up!** tais-toi!/écrase!/ta gueule!/la ferme! **2.** (*theatre*) oublier son rôle/sécher/avoir un trou.

DT's ['diː'tiːz] *npl* F délirium *m* tremens/les rats bleus.

dub [dʌb] *n* **1.** F (*theatre*) doublure *f*/double *m* **2.** NAm A P nourriture*/boustifaille *f* **3.** *pl* A WC*/chiottes *fpl*.

dubee ['d(j)uːbiː] *n* P (*drugs*) cigarette* de marijuana/joint *m*/bomb *f*.

duby ['d(j)uːbiː] *n* P = **dubee**.

duchess ['dʌtʃis] *n* F **1.** grande dame/marquise *f* **2. my old duchess** = **my old Dutch** (**Dutch III** 2).

duck¹ [dʌk] *n F* **1.** (*term of affection*) mon poulet/mon chou/mon canard/mon lapin. (*See* **ducks**; **ducky II**) **2.** (**Lord**) **love a duck!** grands dieux!/mazette! **3. a sitting duck,** une cible facile **4. to behave like a dying duck (in a thunderstorm),** faire la carpe pâmée/faire des yeux de merlan frit **5. lame duck** (*a*) un canard boiteux/une épave/un(e) éclopé(e) (*b*) *NAm* fonctionnaire public qui arrive à terme sans être réélu; **lame duck president,** président pendant les derniers mois de sa présidence (quand son successeur a déjà été élu) **6.** véhicule *m* amphibie **7. it's like water off a duck's back,** c'est comme si on chantait **8. to play ducks and drakes with one's money,** jeter son argent* par les fenêtres **9. like a duck takes to water,** comme un poisson dans l'eau **10.** (*cricket*) zéro (pointé)/chou blanc **11.** *NAm* **duck soup,** qch de très facile/du cousu-main/du gâteau **12. a nice day for ducks/lovely weather for ducks,** beau temps pour les grenouilles **13. one little duck, two little ducks:** *see* **bingo 2, 22.** (*See* **dead I 4; fuck² 4**)

duck² [dʌk] *vtr F* éviter (qn/qch); passer (qch) à l'as. (*See* **duck out**)

duck egg ['dʌk'eg] *n F* (*cricket*) zéro (pointé)/chou blanc.

duckie ['dʌki] *n F* = **ducky II.**

duck out ['dʌk'aut] *n F* **to duck out of (doing) sth,** s'esquiver/se tirer/se débiner/se dérober/sécher/se défiler. (*See* **duck²**)

ducks [dʌks] *n F* mon chéri/ma chérie/mon chou *m.* (*See* **duck¹ 1; ducky II**)

ducky ['dʌki] **I** *a O F* excellent*/chouette/bath **II** *n F* **1.** mon poulet/ma poupoule/ma cocotte/mon chou **2.** (*catchphrase*) **hello ducky! = hello sailor!** (**sailor 2**)

dud [dʌd] **I** *a F* mauvais*/ toc(ard)/à la manque **II** *n F* **1.** obus non éclaté **2.** échec*/four *m*/bide *m*/qch à la manque **3.** faux billet/faux talbin; chèque *m* sans provision/chèque en bois **4.** un raté/un zéro/une nullité/un cancre **5.** *pl* vêtements*/frusques *fpl*/nippes *fpl*/sapes *fpl*/loques *fpl.*

dude [d(j)uːd] *n NAm F* **1.** gommeux *m*/miché *m*/freluquet *m* **2.** individu*/mec *m*/type *m*/gars *m* **3. dude ranch,** ranch-hôtel *m* de vacances (pour vacanciers).

dud up ['dʌd'ʌp] *vtr&i F* **1.** maquiller (la marchandise, la vérité) **2.** se bichonner/se pomponner.

duff¹ [dʌf] **I** *a F* faux/truqué/à la manque/gnognot(t)eux; **a duff idea,** une idée à la noix **II** *n* **1.** *P* dessert *m*/pouding *m* (de prison) **2.** *Austr F* **up the duff,** enceinte*/en cloque.

duff² [dʌf] *vtr F* **1.** (*golf*) cogner une balle de travers/louper une balle **2.** rater/bousiller/louper **3.** maquiller/camoufler **4.** truquer/frauder.

duffer ['dʌfər] *n F* individu bête*/cancre *m*/nullard *m*; **he's a duffer at maths,** c'est une nullité/il est nul en maths.

duff up ['dʌf'ʌp] *vtr P* battre* (qn)/tabasser (qn)/passer (qn) à tabac.

dugout ['dʌgaut] *n P* **1.** *A* drogué*/junkie *m* **2.** officier *m* à la retraite rappelé en service/rempilé *m.*

duke [djuːk] *vi esp NAm P* boxer/faire de la boxe; perloter.

dukes [djuːks] *npl P* mains*/poings *mpl*/paluches *fpl*/pognes *fpl.*

dullsville ['dʌlzvil] *n F* ennuyeux/mortel; chiant comme la pluie; **this record is really dullsville,** ce disque, c'est le comble de l'ennui.

dumb [dʌm] *a* **1.** (*a*) *F* bête*/bouché/stupide/cloche (*b*) *P* **dumb ass/bunny/cluck/jerk,** individu bête*/cruchon *m*/gourde *f*/nigaud *m* (*c*) F **to act/to play dumb**, faire l'idiot (*d*) F **dumb blonde/Dora**, blonde vaporeuse/blonde platine. (*See* **plain**) **2.** F **dumb dog**, personne *f* taciturne/bonnet *m* de nuit.

dumb-bell ['dʌmbel] *n* F individu bête*/baluche *f*/andouille *f*/qn con comme ses pieds.

dumbdumb, dumdum ['dʌm-'dʌm] *n* individu bête*/andouille *f*/patate *f*/gourde *f*.

dumbo ['dʌmbou] *n* P = **dumb-bell.**

dummy ['dʌmi] *n* **1.** P sourd-muet *m*/sourde-muette *f* **2.** P individu bête*/ballot *m*/empoté *m*/empaillé *m* **3.** P = **flash Harry** (**flash**[1] I 1) **4.** P **to chuck a dummy** (*a*) s'évanouir*/tomber dans le cirage/tomber dans les vapes (*b*) simuler un évanouissement dans une foule pour faciliter le travail des pickpockets **5.** V **to beat/to flog the dummy**, se masturber*/se secouer le bonhomme/se taper la Veuve Poignet/se branler.

dummy up ['dʌmi'ʌp] *vi esp NAm* P se taire*/boucler la trappe/la boucler/ne pas piper.

dump[1] [dʌmp] *n* F **1.** endroit *m* sordide/taudis *m* **2.** gargote *f*/boui-boui *m*/bouge *m* **3.** **to be fit for the dump**, être bon pour la casse/bon à mettre au rencart **4.** **to be (down) in the dumps**, avoir le cafard/être dans le cirage/avoir le noir/avoir le bourdon.

dump[2] [dʌmp] *vtr* F **1.** abandonner*/larguer/laisser choir/bazarder **2.** délaisser/planter/plaquer.

dumpling ['dʌmpliŋ] *n* **1.** F patapouf *m*/pot *m* à tabac/bouboule *m*/boulot(te) *m(f)* **2.** *pl* P seins*/rondins *mpl*/miches *fpl* **3.** P individu bête*.

dunno [də'nou] P (= *don't know*) **dunno!** sais pas!/j'sais pas!/chépa!

dunny ['dʌni] *n Austr* F WC*/chiotte *f*/cabinet *m*.

duros ['duːrɔs] *n NAm* P (*drugs*) marijuana*.

dust[1] [dʌst] *n* **1.** F **you couldn't see him for dust**, il courait comme s'il avait le feu au derrière/il a pris la poudre d'escampette **2.** P (*drugs*) (*a*) **foo-foo/happy/heaven/ reindeer dust**, narcotiques *mpl* en poudre/poudrette *f*/narcos *mpl* (*b*) **gold/heaven dust**, cocaïne*/coco *f*/talc *m*/neige *f* **3.** P argent*/pépettes *fpl*/pèze *m*/blé *m* **4.** F **to bite/to kiss the dust**, mordre la poussière **5.** F **to lick the dust**, s'aplatir/lécher les bottes à qn **6.** F **to shake the dust off one's feet**, secouer la poussière de ses souliers **7.** F **to throw dust in s.o.'s eyes**, jeter de la poudre aux yeux de qn **8.** F (*in a car or figuratively*) **to make s.o. eat one's dust**, dépasser qn/faire sentir ses gaz/faire la pige à qn/gratter qn. (*See* **kick up 2**(*b*))

dust[2] [dʌst] *vtr* F **to dust s.o.'s jacket for him**, battre* qn/flanquer une raclée à qn/tanner le cuir à qn.

dustbin ['dʌs(t)bin] *n* P (*RS* = *kids*) **dustbin lids/dustbins**, enfants*/mioches *mpl*/chiards *mpl*. (*See* **godfer**)

duster ['dʌstər] *n* P **1.** (= *knuckle-duster*) coup-de-poing américain/sortie *f* de bal **2.** *pl Austr* testicules*/roupignolles *fpl*/valseuses *fpl*.

dusting ['dʌstiŋ] *n* F coups*/raclée *f*/tabassée *f*/trempe *f*/avoine *f*.

dustman ['dʌs(t)mən] *n* O F **the dustman**, sommeil *m*/le marchand de sable. (*See* **sandman**)

dust-off ['dʌstɔf] *n NAm* F (*Vietnam War*) hélicoptère *m* d'évacuation.

dust off ['dʌst'ɔf] *vtr* F **1.** **to dust s.o. off**, abandonner* qn/se débarrasser* de qn/laisser qn en carafe/poser un lapin à qn **2.** **to dust sth off**, faire qch rapidement/enlever un travail; bâcler/torcher qch **3.**

NAm (*Vietnam War*) évacuer (des blessés) par hélicoptère.

dust-up ['dʌstʌp] *n* F bagarre*/ coup *m* de chien/corrida *f*/cognage *m*.

dust up ['dʌst'ʌp] *vtr* F battre* (qn)/passer (qn) à tabac/filer une avoine à (qn).

Dutch [dʌtʃ] I *a* F 1. Dutch courage, courage puisé dans la bouteille 2. Dutch auction, enchère *f* au rabais/vente *f* à la baisse 3. Dutch cap, diaphragme *m* 4. Dutch comfort, consolation qui n'en est pas une/piètre consolation 5. to talk to s.o. like a Dutch uncle, dire ses quatre vérités à qn 6. Dutch treat, sortie où chacun paye sa part/sortie en Suisse. (*See* Dutch II) 7. to do the Dutch act, se suicider*/se faire sauter la caisse/ s'envoyer en l'air/se buter 8. to take Dutch leave, filer à l'anglaise II *adv* F to go Dutch, payer sa part/partager les frais III *n* 1. F to talk double Dutch, baragouiner/ parler une langue inintelligible/ parler en javanais; that's double Dutch to me, pour moi c'est de l'hébreu/du chinois 2. F my (old) Dutch, mon épouse*/ma

bourgeoise/ma régulière/ma bergère 3. F that beats the Dutch! c'est le comble!/c'est le bouquet!

Dutchman ['dʌtʃmən] *n* F 1. if that's so then I'm a Dutchman, si c'est ainsi je mange mon chapeau/ je veux bien être pendu 2. O to have a Dutchman's headache, avoir la gueule de bois/la GDB.

duty ['djuːti] *n* F to do one's duty, déféquer*/faire la grande commission/poser un colombin.

dyke [daik] *n* P lesbienne*/gouine *f*/gousse *f*/vrille *f*/goudou *f*. (*See* bull-dyke)

dykey ['daiki] *a* P lesbienne*/ gavousse/qui aime l'ail.

dynamite ['dainəmait] *n* 1. P (*drugs*) (*a*) stupéfiant très fort/ dynamite *f* (*b*) stupéfiant *m* de haute qualité/du max (*c*) marijuana* (*d*) héroïne*/cheval *m*/ blanche *f* 2. F she's dynamite! elle est explosive! 3. F his idea's really dynamite, c'est une idée sensass/du tonnerre qu'il a eue 4. F don't touch it, it's dynamite! n'y touche pas, c'est de la dynamite/c'est explosif/c'est jouer avec le feu!

E

eager ['iːgər] *a* **1.** *F* **eager beaver,** bourreau *m* de travail*/turbineur *m*/bûcheur *m*/dingue *m* du boulot; **to be an eager beaver,** faire du zèle **2.** *P* (*CB*) **eager beaver,** fille* à la voix sensuelle.

ear [iər] *n* **1.** *F* **to be all ears,** être tout oreilles/être tout ouïe **2.** *F* **up to one's ears,** jusqu'au cou/par-dessus la tête; **up to one's ears in work,** accablé/débordé/submergé de travail* **3.** *F* **to play it by ear,** jouer d'oreille/y aller d'instinct/aller au pif(f)omètre/aller au pif **4.** *P* **to throw s.o. out on his ear,** se débarrasser* de qn/flanquer qn dehors; **to get thrown out on one's ear,** se faire flanquer/foutre dehors **5.** *F* **to give s.o. a thick ear,** donner des coups* à qn/abîmer le portrait à qn/refaire le portrait à qn **6.** *F* **to pin s.o.'s ears back,** réprimander* qn/enguirlander qn/pincer l'oreille à qn/passer un savon à qn **7.** *F* **to turn a deaf ear to sth,** faire la sourde oreille à qch **8.** *F* **to keep one's ear to the ground,** être/se tenir aux écoutes **9.** *pl P* (*CB*) **ears,** récepteur CB. (*See* **blow 12**; **cloth-ears**; **dry 2**; **flea**; **pig¹ 4**; **wet I 5**)

earbash ['iəbæʃ] *vi Austr P* parler* incessamment/jacasser.

earful ['iəful] *n P* **to give s.o. an earful** (*i*) réprimander* qn/enguirlander qn (*ii*) dire ses quatre vérités/vider son sac à qn; **get an earful of this,** écoute(-moi) bien/écoute-moi ça.

earhole ['iəroul] *n P* **to clip s.o. round the earhole,** abîmer le portrait à qn/flanquer une paire de gifles à qn. (*See* **plug¹ 2**)

early ['əːli] *a F* **1. to be an early bird,** se lever tôt/avec les poules; être matinal **2. it's early days yet,** c'est trop tôt pour dire.

earner ['əːnə] *n P* **1.** (*bribe*) pot *m* de vin/graissage *m* de patte **2.** *pl* **earners,** argent*/pognon *m*/fric *m*.

earth [əːθ] *n F* **1. to come back/down to earth,** revenir sur terre/(re)tomber des nues **2. to cost the earth,** coûter cher*; **to pay the earth for sth,** payer les yeux de la tête pour qch **3. to be down to earth,** avoir les pieds sur terre/avoir la tête sur les épaules **4. where on earth...?** où diable...? **why on earth...?** pourquoi diable...? (*See* **end 4**)

earthly ['əːθli] **I** *a F* **no earthly use,** sans aucune/sans la moindre utilité; comme un vélo à un poisson; **for no earthly reason,** à propos de bottes **II** *n F* **he hasn't an earthly,** il n'a pas l'ombre d'une chance; **haven't (got) an earthly!** aucune idée!

earwig¹ ['iəwig] *n F* qn qui écoute aux portes/esgourdeur *m* de lourdes.

earwig² ['iəwig] *vi F* écouter aux portes.

easy ['iːzi] **I** *a F* **1. to be on easy street,** être riche*/rouler sur l'or **2. easy money,** argent* gagné facilement/affure *f* **3. easy mark,** personne bête* et crédule/dupe *f*/jobard *m*/andouille *f* **4. to take the easy way out** (*i*) ne pas s'en faire/s'en tirer à bon compte (*ii*) se suicider*/se balancer (dans la Seine) **5. easy meat** (*i*) individu* complaisant/facile (*ii*) adversaire peu dangereux **6. easy as pie,** simple comme bonjour/du billard. (*See* **ABC** 1) **7.** *A* **easy rider,** souteneur*/mangeur *m* de brioche **8.** (*woman*) **to be easy on the eye,** être bien balancé(e)/bien roulé(e) **9. I'm easy,** ça m'est égal **10.** (*usu woman*) **an easy lay,** qui couche à droite et à gauche/avec n'importe qui; **she's an easy lay,** elle a la cuisse légère/hospitalière **II** *adv F* **1. to take it easy,** ne pas se fouler la rate/se la couler douce; **take it easy,** (ne) te tracasse* pas/(ne) t'en fais pas **2. easy now!** doucement!/ piano! **3. easy does it!** vas-y doucement!/vas-y mollo! **4. easy come, easy go,** vite gagné, vite perdu; ce qui vient avec le flot s'en retourne avec la marée **5. to go easy on s.o./sth,** ménager qn/qch; **go easy on him!** vas-y doucement avec lui.

easy-going ['iːzi'gouiŋ] *a F* facile à vivre); **he's very easy-going,** il ne se fait pas de la bile/il n'est pas compliqué/il est super-relax.

eat [iːt] *vtr* **1.** *F* **what's eating him?** quelle mouche l'a piqué?/qu'est-ce qui le chiffonne?/qu'est-ce qui le turlupine?/qu'est-ce qu'il lui prend? **2.** *F* **to eat one's words,** se rétracter/revenir sur ses paroles **3.** *F* **to eat one's heart out,** se ronger le cœur/se faire du mouron/sécher sur pied **4.** *F* **he's eating us out of house and home,** il nous dépouille/ il nous enlève jusqu'à nos chaussettes; il mange comme un ogre **5.** *F* **to eat out of s.o.'s hand,** manger dans la main de wn; **she had him eating out of her hand,** il faisait tout ce qu'elle voulait **6.** *F* **to eat s.o.('s head off),** réprimander* qn; **she won't eat you!** elle ne va pas te manger/bouffer/mordre **7.** *V* (*i*) faire une fellation* à qn/sucer qn (*ii*) pratiquer un cunnilinctus* sur

qn/brouter le cresson/sucer qn. (*See* **dirt 5; shit**[1] **III 5**)

eatery ['iːtəri] *n NAm P* café*/bistroquet *m.*

eats [iːts] *npl P* nourriture*/bouffe *f*/boustifaille *f.*

ecofreak ['iːkou'friːk] *n esp NAm F* écolo *mf* (ramolli)/fana *mf* d'écologie.

edge [edʒ] *n* **1.** *NAm P* **to have an edge,** être légèrement ivre*/être éméché **2.** *Austr F* **over the edge,** qui dépasse les limites **3.** *F* **to have the edge over s.o.,** avoir le dessus/l'emporter sur qn.

edged [edʒd] *a NAm P* ivre*/ rétamé/blindé.

edgeways ['edʒweiz], **edgewise** ['edʒwaiz] *adv F* **I couldn't get a word in edgeways,** j'arrivais pas à placer mon mot/impossible d'en placer une.

edgy ['edʒi] *a F* crispé/les nerfs en pelote.

eff [ef] *vi P* (*euph for* **fuck**) **1. eff off** = **fuck off 2. she was effing and blinding all over the place,** elle jurait comme un charretier.

effer ['efər] *n P* (*euph for* **fucker**) **you silly effer,** espèce de con/ d'enculé/d'enfoiré.

effing ['efiŋ] *a P* (*euph for* **fucking**) **1. an effing bastard,** (un) espèce de salaud **2. effing this and effing that,** une saloperie après l'autre **3. it's an effing nuisance,** c'est chiant/ c'est emmerdant.

egg [eg] *n* **1.** *O F* individu*/mec *m*; **bad/rotten egg,** vaurien*/sale type *m*/bon à rien; **he's a good egg,** c'est un chic type/un bon zigue **2.** *O F* **good egg!** épatant!/bravo! **3.** *F* (*military*) **scrambled eggs,** feuilles *fpl* de chêne/sardines *fpl* **4.** *F* **as sure as eggs is eggs,** couru d'avance/aussi vrai qu'il fait jour/ comme deux et deux font quatre **5.** *F* **don't put all your eggs in one basket,** ne mettez pas tous vos œufs dans le même panier **6.** *F* **don't try to teach your grandmother to suck eggs,** ce n'est pas aux vieux singes qu'on apprend à faire les grimaces **7.** *esp NAm P* **to lay an egg,** avoir un échec*/faire un four/ foirer **8.** *F* **to have egg on one's face,** avoir l'air ridicule; **he was left with egg on his face,** il avait l'air d'un con. (*See* **nest-egg**)

egghead ['eghed] *n F* intellectuel *m*/grosse tête/tête d'œuf.

ego trip ['iːgou'trip] *n F* fête pour soi; **he's on an ego trip,** il se fait mousser/il croit que c'est arrivé.

ego-trip ['iːgoutrip] *vi F* (*i*) être égoïste (*ii*) se faire mousser/se gober/se monter le job/le faire à la pose.

eight [eit] *n F* **1. to have had one over the eight,** être ivre*/boire un coup de trop/en avoir un de trop dans le nez. (*See* **one** 1) **2. to be behind the eight ball,** être en mauvaise posture/dans le pétrin/ mal en point.

eighteen-pence ['eitiːn'pens] *n P* (*RS = (common) sense*) bon sens/ sens commun/du chou.

eighty-eights ['eiti'eits] *npl P* (*CB*) (*= love and kisses*) salut!/au revoir!/(grosses) bises!

elbow ['elbou] *n F* **1. to rub elbows with s.o.,** fréquenter qn/ s'acoquiner avec qn **2. elbow grease,** huile *f* de coude/de bras **3. to lift/to bend the elbow; to get some elbow practice,** boire*/lever le coude.

elbow out ['elbou'aut] *vtr F* écarter/évincer qn; **to be elbowed out,** être délogé.

electric [i'lektrik] *a P* (*drink*) **electric soup,** mélange *m* d'alcool dénaturé et de cidre.

elephant ['elifənt] *n* **1.** *F* **white elephant,** possession inutile et coûteuse/attrape-poussière *m*; rossignol *m* **2.** *O F* **pink elephants,** rats bleus/éléphants *mpl* roses (vus par

les alcooliques) **3.** *NAm P* (*drugs*) héroïne*.

elephant and castle ['elifəntn'kɑːsl] *n O P* (*RS = arsehole*) anus*.

elephants ['elifənts] *a P* (*RS = elephant's trunk = drunk*) ivre*.

elevenses [i'levnziz] *npl F* pause-café *f*.

'em [əm] *pron F = them.* (*See* **aisle** 2; **daft** 1; **lick**[2] 3 (*c*); **make**[2] 2; **set up** 1; **stick up** 2)

emcee ['em'siː] *vtr F* **to emcee a show,** présenter/animer un spectacle. (*See* **MC**)

empty ['em(p)ti] *a F* **to feel empty,** avoir faim*/avoir un creux/claquer du bec/crever la dalle.

end [end] *n* **1.** *P* fesses*/arrière-train *m.* (*See* **rear (end)**) **2.** *V* pénis*/queue *f*/le (gros) bout; **to get one's end away/in,** faire l'amour*/mettre la cheville dans le trou/tremper son baigneur **3.** *F* (*i*) **to the bitter end,** jusqu'au bout des bouts; **that's just the absolute end!** il ne manquait plus que cela!/ça c'est le comble!/c'est la fin des haricots! (*ii*) **he's the (bitter) end,** il est plus que minable **4.** *F* **to go to the ends of the earth (to do sth),** se mettre en quatre/se décarcasser (pour faire qch) **5.** *F* **to go off the deep end,** se mettre en colère*/sortir de ses gonds/piquer une crise/ monter sur ses grands chevaux **6.** *F* **to keep one's end up,** résister/se défendre/tenir bon **7.** *F* **to be at a loose end,** se tourner les pouces/ avoir du temps à perdre/se la couler douce **8.** *F* **to make ends meet,** joindre les deux bouts/ boucler son budget **9.** *F* **no end of ...,** une abondance* de .../une flopée de .../une tapée de ...; **it'll do you no end of good,** ça vous fera un bien fou/énormément de bien; **he thinks no end of himself,** il est prétentieux*/il se gobe/il s'en croit **10.** *F* **three weeks on end,** trois

semaines d'affilée **11.** *F* **to get hold
of the wrong end of the stick,** prendre qch à contre-sens/saisir le mauvais bout/comprendre de travers/
prendre le problème à l'envers **12.**
F **to be thrown in at the deep end,**
être mis en pleine eau/faire son
baptême du feu **13.** *F* **he'll come
to a sticky end,** il finira mal/cela
finira mal pour lui. (*See* **back I 2**;
back-end; **beam-ends**; **dead-end**;
dog-end; **fag-end**; **jump² 12**; **tab-
end**; **tail-end**)

enders ['endəz] *n A P* (*rare*) **to go
enders with a woman,** faire l'amour*
avec une femme*.

enemy ['enəmi] *n A F* **the enemy,**
l'heure *f* qui tourne; **how's the
enemy?** t'as l'heure?

enforcer [infɔːsər] *n esp Austr P*
tueur professionnel/à gages;
voyou*/loubard *m*.

Enzed [en'zed] *n Austr & NZ F* **1.**
Nouvelle-Zélande *f* **2.** Néo-
Zélandais(e) *m(f)*.

Enzedder [en'zedər] *Austr & NZ F*
Néo-Zélandais(e) *m(f)*.

erase ['iːreiz] *vtr P* tuer*/liquider/
effacer (qn).

erk [əːk] *n O F* conscrit *m*/bleu *m*/
recrue *f*.

Esky ['eski] *n Austr RTM F* glacière
f.

ethno ['eθnou] *n Austr F* (= *ethnic*)
migrant(e) *m(f)*.

euchre ['juːkər] *vtr P* **1.** *NAm*
duper*/entuber (qn) **2.** *Austr* **to
be euchred,** être dans le pétrin/être
fichu.

even ['iːvən] **I** *a P* **even(s)
Steven(s)/Stephen(s),** quitte; **to call
it even(s) Steven(s),** être quitte; **to
go even(s) Steven(s),** partager fifty-
fifty **II** *adv F* **to get even (with
s.o.),** se venger/rendre la pareille à
qn; **I'll get even with him for that,**
je lui revaudrai/rendrai ça; il ne
perd rien pour attendre.

ever ['evər] *adv F* **1. ever so...,**

tellement...; **ever so much,**
beaucoup*/vachement **2. did you
ever!** époustouflant!/par exemple!/
ça alors!/sans blague!

ex [eks] *prefix & n F* **1.** (*former
boyfriend/girlfriend/husband/wife*)
her ex, son ex **2. ex-con,** ex-
prisonnier *m*/relargué *m*/guéri *m*.

exhibition [eksi'biʃ(ə)n] *n F* **to
make an exhibition of oneself,** faire
la comédie/se donner en spectacle/
se défoncer pour la galérie.

expect [eks'pekt] *vtr F* **to be
expecting,** être enceinte*/être dans
une situation intéressante.

experience [eks'piəriəns, iks-
'piəriəns] *n F* (*drugs*) voyage *m*/trip
m.

extras ['ekstrəz] *npl F* (*a*) à-côtés
mpl (*b*) (*food*) (du) rab(iot).

eye [ai] *n* **1.** *F* **easy on the eye,**
agréable à regarder/de quoi se
rincer l'œil. (*See* **easy 8**) **2.** *F* **all
my eye (and Betty Martin),**
bêtises*/foutaises *fpl*/balivernes *fpl*
3. *F* **my eye!** (*i*) mon œil!/mon
zob!/mon cul! (*ii*) mince alors! **4.**
F **glad eye,** œillade*; **to give s.o.
the (glad) eye,** faire de l'œil à qn/
lancer une œillade à qn/allumer qn
5. *F* **to keep an eye on s.o.,** surveiller qn/avoir qn à l'œil **6.** *F* **to
keep one's eyes open/skinned/
peeled,** ouvrir l'œil (et le bon)/ne
pas avoir ses yeux dans sa poche;
keep an eye out for the car, essaie
de repérer la bagnole **7.** *F* **sheep's
eyes,** des yeux de carpe; **to make
eyes at s.o.,** couver qn des yeux/
faire les yeux doux à qn **8.** *F* **to
see eye to eye (with s.o.),** être du
même avis (que qn)/être d'accord
(avec qn)/voir du même œil; **they
never see eye to eye (with each
other),** ils ne sont jamais d'accord
9. *F* **to turn a blind eye (to sth),**
fermer les yeux (sur qch)/garder les
yeux dans le tiroir **10.** *F* **to be up
to one's eyes in sth,** être plongé
jusqu'aux yeux/par-dessus les yeux;
he's in it up to his eyes, il est dans

la merde jusqu'au cou. (*See* **ear 2**)
11. *F* **a sight for sore eyes,** un régal
pour les yeux **12.** *F* **there's more
in/to this than meets the eye,** il y a
quelque anguille sous roche **13.** *F*
private eye, détective privé/fileur *m*
14. *P* **that's one in the eye for him!**
il a été mouché de belle façon!/
c'est bien fait pour sa poire! **15.**
NAm F (*on a letter*) **'eyes only',**
'confidentiel'/'personnel' **16.** *V*
round eye, anus*/œil de bronze.
(*See* **bird's-eye**; **drop¹ 6**; **four-
eyes**; **Kelly**; **mud 1**; **red-eye**;
shuteye; **slap¹ II 1**; **snake-eyes**)

eyeball¹ ['aibɔːl] *n P* **1.** (*esp CB*)
(*a*) rencontre *f*/visite *f*/rendez-
vous*/visu *m* (*b*) **to lay an eyeball
on s.o.,** voir qn/regarder qn/avoir
qn à l'œil **2. eyeball to eyeball,**
face *f* à face/tête *f* à tête; (*CB*)
visu *m*. (*See* **dope² 1**; **dose up**;
poxed (up))

eyeball² ['aibɔːl] *vtr P* (*esp CB*) (*a*)
rencontrer (qn) (*b*) voir/regarder
(qn) dans le blanc des yeux; avoir
(qn) à l'œil.

eyebrows ['aibrauz] *npl A F* **he's
hanging on by his eyebrows,** il se

maintient tout juste/il est sur la
corde raide/il tient à un fil. (*See*
dope² 1; **dose up**; **poxed (up)**)

eye-eye! ['ai'(j)ai] *excl P* ouvre
l'œil!/fais gaffe!

eyeful ['aiful] *n P* (*i*) qch de très
beau*/de très intéressant (*ii*) jolie
fille*/belle pépée; **to get an eyeful,**
se rincer l'œil; **here, get an eyeful
of this!** vise-moi ça un peu!/mate-
moi ça!

eye-opener ['ai(j)oup(ə)nər] *n F*
1. révélation *f*/surprise *f*; **it was a
real eye-opener for me,** ça m'a vraiment ouvert les yeux/ça m'a
déclenché un déclic/ça m'a enlevé
la merde des yeux **2.** (*a*) boisson
forte prise à jeun/rince-cochon *m*/
réveil-matin *m* (*b*) (*drugs*) la première piqûre de la journée.

Eyetie ['ai'tai, 'aitai] *n P* Italien*/
rital *m*/macaroni *m*.

eyewash ['aiwɔʃ] *n F* **1.** flatterie
f/bourrage *m* de crâne/frime *f* **2.**
baratin *m*/boniment *m*; **that's just a
load of eyewash!** ce ne sont que des
foutaises/c'est du bidon!

F

f.a., FA ['efʼei] *abbr* = **fuck-all**; **sweet f.a./FA** = **sweet fuck-all** *or* **sweet Fanny Adams** (**sweet 4**).

fab [fæb] *a* O F excellent*/terrible; *excl* **fab!** chouette!/sensass!/super!

face¹ [feis] *n* **1.** F **shut your face!** ferme ta gueule!/la ferme!/ta gueule! **2.** F **to have the face to do sth**, avoir le culot/le toupet de faire qch **3.** F **to show one's face**, montrer (le bout de) son nez; **he won't show his face here again**, il ne remettra plus les pieds ici **4.** F **to feed one's face**, manger*/s'empiffrer **5.** F **to paint one's face**, se maquiller*/se badigeonner **6.** P célébrité *f*/vedette *f*/personnage important (*esp* appartenant au **milieu**). (*See* **angel-face**; **back II 13**; **fungus 2**; **laugh² 2**; **pudding-face**; **pushface**; **slap¹ II 1**; **stare**)

face² [feis] *vtr* F **1. let's face it/ let's face facts**, regardons les choses en face/faut bien le dire **2.** *Austr* = **dud up 1.** (*See* **music**)

face-ache ['feiseik] *n* P tête *f* à claques; **hello, face-ache!** salut, minable!

face out ['feisʼaut] *vtr* F **to face it out** = **to face the music** (**music**).

face-paint ['feispeint] *n* F badigeon *m*. (*See* **face¹ 5**; **warpaint**)

facer ['feisər] *n* F **1.** pépin *m*/tuile *f* **2.** coup* au visage/torgnole *f* **3.** carte* (à jouer) qui baisse.

face up ['feisʼʌp] *vi* F **to face up to s.o./sth**, affronter qn/qch; tenir tête à qn/qch.

fack [fæk] *vi* P (*Black Sl*) dire la vérité/dire vrai.

facings ['feisiŋz] *npl* F **to put s.o. through his facings** (*a*) éprouver le savoir de qn/voir ce qu'il dans le crâne (*b*) injurier* qn/dire son fait à qn.

factory ['fæktəri] *n* P commissariat *m* de police/la (grande) maison. (*See* **glue-factory**)

fad [fæd] *n* F marotte *f*/lubie *f*; **health food fad**, manie *f* des aliments biologiques/naturels.

fade¹ [feid] *n* P **1.** (*Black Sl*) (*a*) Blanc, Blanche (*b*) Noir(e)* qui mène la vie d'un Blanc *ou* qui préfère choisir ses ami(e)s parmi les Blancs **2.** *esp NAm* **to do a fade**, s'enfuir*/en jouer un air.

fade² [feid] *vi* P s'enfuir*/s'éclipser/ en jouer un air.

fag [fæg] *n* **1.** F cigarette*/sèche *f*/ cibiche *f*/clope *mf* **2.** P (*a*) homosexuel*/pédé *m*/fiotte *f*/ lope(tte) *f* (*b*) homme efféminé/ chouquette *f* (*c*) **fag bag/fag hag**, femme* qui recherche la compagnie des homosexuels*/pouf(-molle) *f* **3.** F **what a fag!** quelle corvée!

fag-end ['fægend] *n* F mégot*/ clope *m*.

fageroo [fægəʼruː] *n* P = **fag 1.**

fagged (out) ['fægd('aut)] *a* F très fatigué*/vanné/crevé.

faggot ['fægət] *n* **1.** P homosexuel*/pédé *m*/tante *f* **2.** F (*pej*) **old faggot**, vieille femme*/vieille pouffiasse/vieille bique.

faggotry ['fægətrı] *n esp NAm P* les homosexuels*/la famille tuyau de poêle/la pédale.

fainites! ['feinaits] *excl O F (child's language)* pouce!

fair ['fɛər] **I** *a F* **1. fair enough!** ça va!/d'accord!* **2. fair's fair,** ce n'est que juste/(il) faut dire ce qui est **3.** *Austr* **fair go!** *(i)* jouer à la loyale!/jouer sans coups fourrés! *(ii)* change de disque! *(See* **cop¹ 2**; **cow 2**; **dinkum 1**; **do¹ 3**; **middling**; **shake¹ 3**; **whip¹ 1**) **II** *adv P* très/absolument/bougrement; **I'm fair knackered,** je suis complètement à plat/crevé; **this fair stumped me,** du coup je n'ai su que répondre **III** *n F* **to arrive the day after the fair,** arriver trop tard/manquer le coche/arriver après la course.

fair-haired ['fɛə'hɛəd] *a NAm F* = **blue-eyed.**

fair-weather ['fɛəweðər] *a F* **fair-weather friends,** amis des beaux jours.

fairy ['fɛərı] *n P* **1.** homosexuel*/pédé *m*/tapette *f*; **fairy hawk,** chasseur *m*/casseur *m* de pédés; **fairy lady/queen,** lesbienne*/vrille *f*/gougnotte *f*; **I look a right fairy dressed up like this,** j'ai l'air d'une vraie tapette avec ces frusques **2.** *(football)* joueur ramollo/mou *m*. *(See* **airy-fairy**)

fairyland ['fɛərılænd] *n P* le monde des homosexuels*/la famille tuyau de poêle/la pédale; **does he come from fairyland?** il en est? *(See* **pansyland**)

fake off ['feik'ɔf] *vi NAm P* s'esquiver/traîner le cul/tirer au flanc/se la couler douce.

fake out ['feik'aut] *vtr NAm F* **to fake s.o. out,** tromper/duper/avoir qn.

falconer ['fɔlkənər] *n P (con artist)* escroc*/arnaqueur *m*/estampeur *m*.

fall [fɔl] *vi F* **1. to fall for a trick,** gober/tomber dans un piège; **he fell for it,** il s'est fait avoir **2. to fall**

for s.o., se toquer de qn/s'amouracher de qn **3. to fall all over oneself to please s.o.,** se mettre en quatre/se décarcasser pour plaire à qn **4. it's like falling off a log,** c'est du billard. *(See* **backwards 1**)

fall down ['fɔl'daun] *vi F* **to fall down on a job,** échouer*/louper/foirer; rater son coup.

fall-guy ['fɔlgai] *n F* bouc *m* émissaire/âne *m* de moulin/dindon *m* de la farce/pigeon *m*.

fall out ['fɔl'aut] *n NAm P* = **flak.**

fall through ['fɔl'θruː] *vi F (plan, etc)* foirer; **it fell through at the last moment,** ça m'a claqué dans les doigts/c'est tombé à l'eau (tout d'un coup).

falsies ['fɔlsiz] *npl F* seins* artificiels/faux nénés/roberts *mpl* de chez Michelin/flotteurs *mpl*.

family ['fæm(i)lı] *a attrib* **1.** *F* **in the family way,** enceinte*/cloquée/dans une situation intéressante/en chemin de famille **2.** *P* **family jewels,** testicules*/bijoux *mpl* de famille/précieuses *fpl*.

famished ['fæmiʃt] *a F* **to be famished,** avoir très faim*/avoir la dent; **I'm absolutely famished,** je crève de faim.

famous ['feiməs] *a (a) F* excellent*/sensass/fameux *(b)* **famous last words!** on verra bien!

famously ['feiməslı] *adv F* fameusement/rudement; **to get on famously,** s'entendre à merveille.

fan [fæn] *n F* fanatique *mf*/fan *mf*/fana *mf*/mordu *m*; **fan club,** club *m* des fanas; **fan mail,** courrier *m* des fanas; **film fan,** cinéphile *mf*/fana de ciné.

fancy¹ ['fænsı] *a* **1.** *P* **fancy man** *(i)* amant *m*/gigolo *m*; petit ami *(ii)* souteneur*/julot *m* **2.** *P* **fancy woman/fancy piece** *(i)* prostituée*/pute *f (ii)* maîtresse *f*/petite amie **3.** *P* **fancy pants,** (joli) coco *m*/

minet *m* **4.** *F* **cut out the fancy stuff!** (raconte) pas de bêtises!/ épargne-moi les détails, fumeux!

fancy² ['fænsi] *vtr F* **1. fancy!/ fancy that!** figurez-vous ça!/ça par exemple! **2. fancy meeting you!** quelle bonne rencontre! **3. to fancy oneself,** être infatué de sa petite personne/se gober/s'en croire/faire sa poire; **she really fancies herself,** elle ne se prend pas pour de la crotte **4.** (*catchphrase*) **a little of what you fancy does you good,** un chouia de ce qui ragaillardit, ça fait du bien par où ça passe **5. do you fancy her?** elle te dit? **I really fancy him,** je le trouve pas mal du tout/vachement bien; j'ai un faible pour lui.

fanny ['fæni] *n* **1.** *V* sexe de la femme*/chatte *f*/minet *m*; **fanny tickler,** lesbienne*/gouine *f*/ gougnotte *f* **2.** *NAm P* fesses*/ baba *m*/pétrousquin *m*; **to park one's fanny,** s'asseoir/poser son cul **3.** *P* bêtises*/sornettes *fpl*; **a load of fanny,** un tas de foutaises. (*See* **aunt 1; sweet 4**)

fantastic [fæn'tæstik] *a F* excellent*/super/sensass; **that was fantastic,** c'était chouette; **a fantastic concert,** un concert sensationnel/ superbe/génial.

fanzine ['fænziːn] *n esp NAm F* magazine *m* des fans/fanzine *m*.

far [faːr] *adv F* **far gone** (*a*) fou* à lier (*b*) ivre* mort. (*See* **gone 1**)

far-out ['faːr'aut] *a F* **1.** bizarre/ avant-garde; (*esp music*) extramoderne/progressif/super-branché **2.** emballant/enthousiasmant/bottant; **far out!** (c'est) génial!/(c'est) le pied! **that song is really far-out,** elle est (vachement) cool/super/ dingue, cette chanson!

fart¹ [faːt] *n V* **1.** pet*/vesse *f*/ perle *f*/perlouze *f* **2. I don't care a fart,** je m'en fous complètement/je n'en ai rien à foutre/je n'en ai rien à branler **3. to stand as much**

chance as a fart in a wind-storm, ne pas avoir la moindre chance de réussir/avoir autant d'effet que pisser dans la mer **4. like a fart in a bottle,** agité/nerveux **5.** saligaud *m*; **old fart** (*i*) vieux cochon/vieux schnoque (*ii*) croulant *m*/ringard *m*/vieux rocker; **he's a silly (old) fart,** c'est un petit con/un trouduc. (*See* **sparrow-fart**)

fart² [faːt] *vi V* péter*/lâcher un pet/en écraser un.

fart(-arse) around, about ['faːt(aːs)ə'raund, ə'baut] *vi V* **1.** traîner son cul **2.** faire le con/ déconner.

fart-catcher ['faːtkætʃər] *n V* homosexuel*/pédé *m*/enculé *m*.

fart-hole ['faːt(h)oul] *n V* anus*/ trou *m* de balle/trou du cul/rondelle *f*/troufignon *m*.

fast [faːst] **I** *a F* **1.** dévergondé/ rapide; **to lead a fast life,** faire les quatre cents coups; **he's a fast worker/a fast one with the girls,** c'est un tombeur de filles/de femmes; c'est un Don Juan/un chaud lapin **2. fast talk,** boniment *m*/ baratin *m*. (*See* **buck¹ 1; one 4**) **II** *adv F* **to play fast and loose,** jouer double jeu.

fast food ['faːst'fuːd] *n F* (*hamburgers, pizzas, etc*) fast food(e) *m*; **we ate in a fast food place,** nous avons pris un truc dans un fast food.

fast talk ['faːst'tɔːk] *vtr P* bonimenter/baratiner/faire du baratin à (qn).

fat [fæt] **I** *a* **1.** *P* bête*/ballot/ enflé **2.** *P* **a fat lot,** rien*/des clous; **a fat lot of good that'll do you!** cela vous fera une belle jambe! **a fat lot I care!** je m'en fiche pas mal!/je m'en moque comme de l'an quarante!/je m'en soucie comme de ma première chemise! **a fat lot you know about it!** comme si vous en saviez quelque chose! **a fat lot of difference it**

makes to you! pour ce que ça vous coûte! **3.** *P* **fat chance!** y a pas de danger! **a fat chance he's got!** il n'a pas l'ombre d'une chance **4.** *F* **a fat salary,** un gros salaire/de gros émoluments **5.** *esp NAm P* **fat cat** (*i*) huile *f*/cacique *m*/gros bonnet *m* (*ii*) commanditaire *m*/sponsor *m* (d'un parti politique, etc) **6.** *NAm P* **in fat city,** en super-forme/en pleine santé; **he was in fat city,** ça marchait terrible pour lui; il pétait la forme **7.** *F* **one fat lady, two fat ladies:** *see* **bingo 8, 88** II *n F* **1.** (*a*) (*theatre*) rôle *m* en or (*b*) bonne réplique/une percutante **2.** *F* **the fat is in the fire,** il y a le feu aux poudres; le torchon brûle **3.** *F* **to live off the fat of the land,** vivre grassement/mener la vie de château/vivre comme un coq en pâte **4.** *Austr V* **to crack a fat,** être en érection*/bander/redresser le gland/se mettre les couilles en joie. (*See* **chew; puppy 1**)

fathead ['fæthed] *n F* individu bête*/imbécile *m*/enflure *f*/empaqueté *m*/patate *f*/andouille *f*.

fatheaded ['fæthedid] *a F* bête*/ballot/baluche.

fatherfucker ['fɑːðərfʌkər] *n NAm VV* = **motherfucker.**

fatso ['fætsou], **fatty** ['fæti] *n P* personne grosse*/bouboule *mf*/patapouf *m*/gravos(se) *m(f)*/gros plein de soupe.

faze [feiz] *vtr NAm F* gêner (qn)/casser les pieds à (qn)/courir sur le haricot à qn.

fear ['fiər] *n F* **no fear!** pas de danger!/jamais de la vie!

fearful ['fiəful] *a F* terrible/formidable; **fearful bore,** emmerdeur *m*/casse-pieds *m*.

feather¹ ['feðər] *n* **1.** *F* **birds of a feather,** du pareil au même/du même acabit **2.** *F* **a feather in one's cap,** une perle à sa couronne/un bon point; **that's a feather in her cap,** elle peut en être fière **3.**

F **in fine feather,** en pleine forme **4.** *F* **to show the (white) feather,** laisser voir qu'on a peur*/caner/caler **5.** *F* **you could have knocked me down with a feather!** j'ai pensé tomber de mon haut! **6.** *pl P* lit*/plumard *m*; **to hit the feathers,** se coucher*/se plumer.

feather² ['feðər] *vtr F* **to feather one's nest,** faire ses choux gras/faire sa pelote/faire son beurre/mettre du foin dans ses bottes.

feather-bed ['feðəbed] *n F* traitement *m* de faveur/fromage *m*/combine juteuse.

featherbrain ['feðəbrein] *n F* individu bête*/tête *f* de linotte; **she's a real featherbrain,** c'est une petite évaporée.

featherbrained ['feðəbreind] *a F* bête*/à tête de linotte/écervelé/évaporé; **to be featherbrained,** avoir une cervelle de moineau.

feature ['fiːtʃər] *vtr* **1.** *NAm F* s'imaginer; **I can't feature that,** je n'arrive pas à me l'imaginer **2.** *esp Austr P* **to feature with s.o.** (*i*) faire l'amour* avec qn (*ii*) draguer qn.

fed, Fed [fed] *n NAm F* (*abbr* = *Federal Agent*) **1.** fonctionnaire fédéral de l'ordre judiciaire; agent *m*/inspecteur *m* des services régionaux de la police judiciaire (SRPJ) **2.** agent *m* de la Brigade fédérale des Stupéfiants/= inspecteur *m* des Stups.

fed up ['fed'ʌp] *a F* (*a*) **to be fed up (to the back teeth),** en avoir assez*/en avoir ras le bol/en avoir (plus que) marre (*b*) **I'm fed up with him,** il me tape sur le système/j'ai soupé de lui; **I'm bloody fed up with it,** j'en ai plein le cul (de ce truc).

feed [fiːd] *n F* **1. to be off one's feed,** être malade*/n'être pas dans son assiette **2.** *P* (*NAm* **feeder**) (*theatre*) comparse *m*/faire-valoir *m*. (*See* **chicken-feed**)

feel¹ [fiːl] *n P* attouchement *m*/tripotage *m*/pelotage *m*; **to have a**

quick feel, aller aux renseigne-
ments/mettre la main au panier.
feel² [fiːl] *vtr* 1. P caresser/peloter
qn; aller aux renseignements/mettre
la main au panier 2. *F* do you feel
like it? est-ce que ça te chante?/est-
ce que ça te dit?/ça t'irait? 3. *P*
(*Black Slang*) to feel a draft, flairer
le racisme chez qn.
feel up ['fiːl'ʌp] *vtr P* to feel s.o. up
= **feel²** 1.
feet [fiːt] *npl see* **foot¹**.
feisty ['faisti] *a NAm F* hargneux/
grincheux/de mauvais poil.
fella ['felə], **feller** ['felər] *n F* (=
fellow) (*a*) individu*/type *m*/mec *m*
(*b*) amoureux *m*/petit ami; she
brought her latest fella, elle a
ramené le dernier en date/elle s'est
pointée avec sa dernière conquête.
fem [fem] *n esp NAm O P* 1.
femme* 2. lesbienne* (qui tient le
rôle de la femme)/gavousse *f*.
female ['fiːmeil] *n F* (*a*) femme*/
fille*; (*often pej*) femelle *f*/fumelle *f*
(*b*) (*girlfriend*) petite amie/nana *f*.
fence¹ [fens] *n F* 1. receleur*/
fourgue *m*/fourgat *m*/lessiveur *m*
2. to sit on the fence, ménager la
chèvre et le chou/nager entre deux
eaux 3. *Austr* over the fence, qui
dépasse les limites/qui n'est pas du
tout raisonnable. (*See* **edge¹** 2)
fence² [fens] *vtr F* receler/fourguer.
fence hanger ['fenshæŋər] *n
NAm F* (*a*) personne indécise (*b*)
bavard *m*/commère *f*.
fencing ['fensiŋ] *n F* recelage *m*/
fourgage *m*/lessivage *m*/fourgue *f*.
ferret ['ferit] *n Austr P* to exercise
the ferret, faire l'amour*/emmener
le petit au cirque.
fest [fest] *n esp NAm F* fête *f*/festi-
val *m*/gala *m*/réunion *f*. (*See*
chinfest; **gabfest**; **gayfest**; **slugfest**)
fetch [fetʃ] *vtr F* 1. (*esp idea*)
séduire/emballer/taper dans l'œil

2. to fetch a blow at s.o., flanquer
un coup à qn. (*See* **clonk**; **clout¹**
1; **one** 3)
fetching ['fetʃiŋ] *a F* (*clothes, personality, etc*) charmant/séduisant/
ravissant.
fetch up ['fetʃʌp] *vtr&i F* vomir*/
dégobiller.
few [fjuː] *npl F* to have (had) a few,
être ivre*/avoir un verre dans le
nez; he's had a few too many, il a
pas mal bu/il en a un de trop
(dans le nez).
fey ['fei] *a F* efféminé; he's a bit fey,
il est un peu pédé sur les bords.
fib¹ [fib] *n F* mensonge*/craque *f*/
bobard *m*; that's a big fib, tu
racontes des bobards.
fib² [fib] *vi F* mentir*/en conter/
raconter des bobards.
fibber ['fibər] *n F* menteur *m*/cra-
queur *m*; you big fibber! (espèce
de) menteur!
fiddle¹ ['fidl] *n F* 1. violon *m*/crin-
crin *m*/plumier *m* 2. (*i*) combine
f/truc *m* (*ii*) fricotage *m*; it was all
a bit of a fiddle, tout ça c'était une
combine/du fricotage/du magouil-
lage; she's on the/a fiddle, elle
fricote/elle traficote/elle est de la
combine. (*See* **work²** 1) 3. to be
as fit as a fiddle, se porter comme
un charme 4. to play second fiddle, jouer en sous-fifre/en sous-
main/en deuxième couteau.
fiddle² ['fidl] *vtr&i F* 1. violoner/
racler du violon 2. to fiddle the
tax, rouler le percepteur/maquiller
sa feuille d'impôts 3. combiner/
fricoter/trafiquer/traficoter.
fiddle about, around
['fidlə'baut, ə'raund] *vi F* (*a*)
traînasser/flânocher (*b*) to fiddle
about/around with sth, tripoter qch.
fiddle-arse about ['fidl-
'ɑːsə'baut] *vi P* = **fiddle about,
around.**
fiddlede(e)dee! ['fidldi(ː)'diː]
excl A F = **fiddlesticks.**

fiddle-faddle¹ ['fidlfædl] *excl F* **fiddle-faddle!** quelle bêtise*!/quelle blague!

fiddle-faddle² ['fidlfædl] *vi A F* musarder/baguenauder/tatillonner.

fiddler ['fidlər] *n F* **1.** racleur *m* de violon **2.** fricoteur *m*/combinard *m* **3.** (*a*) flâneur *m*/musardeur *m* (*b*) bricoleur *m*/tripoteur *m*.

fiddlestick ['fidlstik] *n F* **1.** archet *m*/baguette *f* de violon **2.** *pl* balivernes *fpl*; *excl* **fiddlesticks!** quelle bêtise*!/quelle blague!

fiddling ['fidliŋ] **I** *a F* insignifiant; **fiddling little queries,** questions oiseuses/futiles/embêtantes **II** *n F* **1.** raclage *m* de violon **2.** combine *f*/fricotage *m*/truc *m* **3.** tripotage *m*; **there's been a lot of fiddling going on,** il y a eu beaucoup de fricotage/magouillage/coups fourrés là-dessous.

fiddly ['fidli] *a F* délicat/minutieux; **a fiddly job,** un travail délicat; un sac de nœuds.

fidgets ['fidʒits] *npl F* **to have the fidgets,** avoir la bougeotte/être comme une pile électrique.

field day ['fiːld'dei] *n F* **umbrella sellers had a field day,** c'était un jour béni pour les vendeurs de parapluie.

fiend [fiːnd] *n F* emballé *m*/mordu *m*/fana *mf*; *O* **dope fiend,** drogué*/esp* morphinomane *mf*/toxico *mf*; **sex fiend,** obsédé sexuel/queutard *m.*

fifty-fifty ['fifti'fifti] *a & adv F* moitié-moitié/afanaf/fifti-fifti; **to go fifty-fifty,** se mettre de moitié/partager fifti-fifti; **a fifty-fifty chance,** une chance sur deux. (*See* **half¹ 5** (*b*))

fig¹ [fig] *n* **1.** *V* sexe de la femme*/figue *f* **2.** *F* **I don't care a fig,** je m'en moque pas mal/je m'en fiche éperdument **3.** *O F* **in full fig,** habillé avec élégance; sur son trente et un.

fig² [fig] *vtr P* doper (un cheval de course).

figure [figə, *NAm* figjər] *vtr&i esp NAm F* **1.** compter sur qch/penser; **they don't figure he'll live,** on ne pense pas le sauver **2.** **that figures,** ça va de soi/ça s'explique **3.** **I figure that's OK,** ça m'a l'air OK/ça a l'air d'aller.

figure out ['figər'aut] *vtr F* **1.** calculer/chiffrer; **I've figured out how much I need,** j'ai calculé combien j'en ai besoin **2.** comprendre; **he can't figure it out,** ça le dépasse.

file [fail] *n O P* (*rare*) malin *m*/roublard *m*/matois *m.*

fill-in ['filin] *n F* **1.** *esp NAm* sommaire *m*/tuyautage *m*/mise *f* au courant **2.** suppléant *m*/intérim *m*/volant *m.*

fill in ['fil'in] *vtr&i F* **1.** **to fill s.o. in (on sth),** mettre qn au courant/au parfum; parfumer qn **2.** **to fill in for s.o.,** suppléer/remplacer qn au pied levé.

filly ['fili] *n F* (*not common*) jeune fille* fringante/jolie pouliche.

filth [filθ] *n P* (= *CID*) police judiciaire/PJ; **then the filth arrived,** et puis les flics/les poulets/les bourres se sont amenés; **he's filth,** c'est un détective/un flic/un poulet.

filthy ['filθi] *a F* **1.** (*a*) sale*/cradingue/crado; **filthy weather,** temps *m* pourri/temps de cochon/bougre *m* de temps (*b*) ordurier/obscène; **don't be filthy!** pas d'obscénités, s'il te plaît! **to have a filthy mind,** avoir l'esprit mal tourné; **he's got a filthy mind,** il ne pense qu'à ça; **filthy sod** (*i*) saligaud *m*/salaud *m*/sale cochon (*ii*) obsédé sexuel/queutard *m*; (*sport*) **filthy player,** joueur salaud **2.** **filthy rich,** les (sales) rupins/les pleins aux as; **he's filthy rich,** il est pourri de fric. (*See* **lucre**)

fin [fin] *n P* **1.** main*/pince *f*/patte *f.* (*See* **flipper**) **2.** bras*/aile *f*/

nageoire *f* 3. *NAm P* billet* de cinq dollars.

finagle [fin'eigl] *vtr F* manigancer/resquiller.

finagler [fin'eiglər] *n F* fricoteur *m*/resquilleur *m*/combinard *m*/magouilleur *m*.

finals ['fain(ə)lz] *npl F* (*university*) examens *mpl* de fin d'année.

fine [fain] I *a F* 1. chic/parfait; it's all very fine but…, tout cela est bien joli/bien beau mais… 2. one fine day, un beau jour II *adv F* 1. I'm doing fine! je me débrouille bien!/ça va bien! 2. you're doing fine: see **bingo** 29. (*See* **cut²** 3)

finest ['fainest] *n NAm F* (= *New York City Police Department*) New York's Finest, sûreté urbaine New Yorkaise.

finger¹ ['fiŋgər] *n* 1. *P* indicateur*/mouchard *m*/donneur *m*; to put the finger on s.o. (*i*) balancer qn/enfoncer qn (*ii*) dénoncer* qn/donner qn à la police/balanstiquer qn 2. *F* to pull one's finger out, se secouer/se dégrouiller; get/pull your finger out! secoue tes puces!/grouille-toi!/magne-toi! 3. *F* to put one's finger on it, mettre le doigt dessus 4. *F* to keep one's fingers crossed, toucher du bois 5. *F* to lift the little finger, boire*/lever le coude 6. *F* to have a finger in every pie, être mêlé à tout; to have a finger in the pie, y être pour qch 7. *F* not to lift a little finger (to help s.o.), ne pas lever le petit doigt (pour aider qn) 8. *F* to lay a finger on s.o., lever la main sur qn/amocher qn; I didn't (even) lay a finger on him! je ne l'ai même pas touché! 9. *F* to twist s.o. round one's little finger, entortiller qn/faire de qn ce qu'on veut 10. *NAm O P* to give s.o. the finger (*i*) faire une crasse à qn (*ii*) snober qn/bazarder qn; she was giving me the polite finger, elle me snobait 11. *P* two fingers!/fingers to you! je

t'emmerde! (*See* **fingers-up**) 12. *P* finger artist, lesbienne*/gougnotte *f*/gouine *f* 13. *pl P* (*CB*) fingers, cibiste *mf* changeant incessamment de canal/cibiste *mf* tripotant les boutons de fréquence. (*See* **butterfingers**; **fruit-basket**; **green I** 5; **sticky** 3; **thumb** 1)

finger² ['fiŋgər] *vtr* 1. *P* (*a*) fouiller (qn) (*b*) dénoncer*/moucharder/balancer (qn) 2. *P* to finger sth, chaparder/chiper qch 3. *V* (*esp of woman*) to finger oneself, se masturber*/se filer une gerbe/s'astiquer le boilton.

finger-fuck ['fiŋgəfʌk], **finger-job** ['fiŋgədʒɔb] *n VV* 1. (*woman*) masturbation *f*/gerbe *f* 2. (*esp lesbian and homosexual use*) insertion d'un doigt dans l'anus* (de son partenaire).

finger-fuck ['fiŋgəfʌk] *vtr VV* (*esp lesbian and homosexual use*) (*a*) se masturber* (*b*) mettre la main au panier (*c*) insérer/mettre/enfiler un doigt dans l'anus* (de son partenaire).

finger popper ['fiŋgər'pɔpər] *n NAm P* (*jazz*) personne *f* qui part en jouant/qui se défonce en improvisant/qui part sur son tempo.

fingers-up ['fiŋgəz'ʌp] *n V* geste *m* obscène de défi et de mépris/basane *f*.

finisher ['finiʃər] *n F* (*boxing*) knockout *m*/coup d'assommoir.

finish off ['finiʃ'ɔf] *vtr P* (*prostitutes*) to finish off a client, faire jouir/finir un client.

fink¹ [fiŋk] *n esp NAm P* 1. briseur *m* de grèves/jaune *m* 2. clochard*/clodo *m* 3. vaurien*/fripouille *f*/ordure *f*/fumier *m*. (*See* **ratfink**) 4. détective privé/policier*/poulet *m*/perdreau *m* 5. indicateur*/indic *m*/donneur *m*.

fink² [fiŋk] *vi esp NAm P* 1. dénoncer* (à la police)/cafarder/

balancer 2. se dégonfler/se déballonner/foirer.

fire¹ ['faɪər] n F 1. to play with fire, jouer avec le feu 2. running fire, feu roulant (de questions) 3. under fire, sur la sellette 4. where's the fire? il y a le feu sur le pont? 5. to set the world on fire, inventer la poudre. (See sure-fire; Thames)

fire² ['faɪər] vtr 1. F balancer/sacquer/vider (qn) 2. V éjaculer*; to fire in the air/to fire blanks, éjaculer dans le vide/tout balancer sur le ventre/décharger devant la porte.

fire away ['faɪərə'weɪ] vi F commencer (à parler)/se lancer; fire away! allez-y!/dites toujours!/racontez!

fireball ['faɪəbɔːl] n F individu* dynamique. (See ball¹ 6)

fire-bug ['faɪəbʌg] n F incendiaire m/bouteleu m.

fire up ['faɪə'rʌp] vi P (drugs) fumer de la marijuana*.

fire-water ['faɪəwɔːtər] n F alcool*/tord-boyaux m.

fireworks ['faɪəwɜːks] npl F if you do that again there'll be fireworks! si tu recommences, ça va barder/il y aura du grabuge!

firm [fɜːm] n P bande f/gang m de criminels/de voleurs, etc.

first [fɜːst] I a F NAm to get to first base = base 1 II n F hot coffee! that's a first for British Rail! du café chaud! c'est l'événement/une grande première pour British Rail!

first-class ['fɜːst'klɑːs], **first-rate** ['fɜːst'reɪt] F I adv au poil/de première; it's going first-class/first-rate, ça marche à merveille II a extra/super; first-class!/first-rate! très bien!/superbe!

first-timer ['fɜːst'taɪmər] n F prisonnier m pour la première fois/un nouveau de la lourde.

fish¹ [fɪʃ] n 1. F individu*/zèbre

m; a queer fish, un drôle d'oiseau/de numéro; a poor fish, un paumé 2. F to feed the fishes (a) avoir le mal de mer/donner à manger aux poissons (b) se noyer/boire le bouillon 3. F to have other fish to fry, avoir d'autres chats à fouetter 4. F to be like a fish out of water, ne pas être dans son élément/être comme un poisson hors de l'eau 5. F to drink like a fish, boire* comme un trou 6. P a fresh fish (a) un nouveau/un bleu (b) qn arrêté pour la première fois/un ramassé de preu 6. P (lesbian and homosexual use) femme* hétérosexuelle/une hétéro. (See cold I 5; jellyfish; kettle 2; tin I 4)

fish² [fɪʃ] vi F 1. aller à la pêche/tirer les vers du nez à qn; to fish for compliments, quêter des compliments 2. to fish in troubled waters, pêcher en eau trouble.

fish-bowl ['fɪʃboʊl] n NAm P = fish-tank.

fish-pond ['fɪʃpɒnd], **fish-shop** ['fɪʃʃɒp] n P sexe de la femme*/boîte f à ouvrage/bénitier m.

fish-tank ['fɪʃtæŋk] n NAm P 1. cellule f où l'on met les nouveaux prisonniers. (See tank 2) 2. sexe de la femme*/boîte f à ouvrage.

fish-wrapper ['fɪʃræpər] n F journal*/canard m.

fishy ['fɪʃi] a F douteux/louche/véreux; it looks a bit fishy, ça ne dit rien de bon/ça n'a pas l'air très catholique.

fist [fɪst] n P main*/pogne f/paluche f. (See hand¹ 2)

fist fuck ['fɪst'fʌk] vtr VV (esp homosexual use) insérer le poing dans l'anus* ou le rectum (de son partenaire)/bourrer le cul avec le poing/faire le fist-fucking.

fist fucker ['fɪst'fʌkər] n VV (homosexual use) homosexuel* qui pratique le fist-fucking/fist-fucker m.

fist-fucking ['fist'fʌkiŋ] *n VV* (*homosexual use*) fist-fucking *m*.

fistful ['fistful] *n NAm P* peine *f* de prison de cinq ans.

fit¹ [fit] **I** *a F* **are you fit?** t'es prêt?/tu te sens d'attaque? (*See* **dressed**; **drop² 5**; **dump¹ 3**) **II** *n* **1.** *F* **to have/to throw a fit,** piquer une colère*/se mettre à cran/piquer une crise **2.** *F* **to have s.o. in fits,** faire rire* qn/donner le fou rire à qn **3.** *P* (*RS* = *tits*) **fainting fits,** seins*/tétons. (*See* **Bristols**; **tale 3**; **threepenny-bits**; **trey-bits**) **4.** *P* attirail*/artillerie *f* de camé.

fit² [fit] *vtr&i F* **that fits/that fits the bill,** ça cadre dans le tableau/ça s'explique.

fit-up ['fitʌp] *n P* complot *m*/coup monté.

fit up ['fit'ʌp] *vtr P* **to fit s.o. up,** donner de faux témoignages/monter un coup contre qn; faire porter le bada à qn; **they fitted him up,** il est victime d'un coup monté.

five [faiv] *num a&n F* **1. to take five,** faire la pause/souffler un brin; **(just) take five!** arrêt buffet!/pause-café!/dételer un peu!/relax(e)! **2. to give five,** en écraser cinq/y aller de cinq. (*See* **bunch 2**) **3.** *NAm* (*i*) cinq dollars (*ii*) billet* de cinq dollars.

five finger ['faiv'fiŋgər] *n NAm O P* **1.** voleur*/filou *m* **2.** *pl* **five fingers,** peine *f* de prison* de cinq ans.

fiver ['faivər] *n F* (*a*) cinq livres *fpl* sterling (*b*) billet* de cinq livres *ou NAm* cinq dollars.

five-spot ['faivspɔt] *n NAm F* **1.** billet* de cinq dollars **2.** *A* emprisonnement *m* de cinq années/cinq berges *fpl*.

fix¹ [fiks] *n* **1.** *P* (*drugs*) (*a*) fixe *m*/piquouse *f*; **to take a fix,** se piquer/se faire un shoot/se shooter (*b*) quantité de drogue vendue en paquet/dose *f*/fixe *m*/shoot *m* **2.**

P **the fix** (*i*) pot-de-vin *m*/dessous-de-table *m* (*ii*) graissage de patte (de la police, etc); **it's a fix,** ça a été truqué/c'est une magouille **3.** *F* difficulté *f*/embêtement *m*; **to be in a fix,** être dans une situation embarrassante; **he's got himself into a real fix,** il s'est complètement fourré dans le pétrin; il s'est mis dans une très sale affaire/passe.

fix² [fiks] *vtr* **1.** *F* (*a*) arranger/mettre en ordre; réparer/rabibocher; **don't worry, I'll fix it,** ne t'en fais pas, je vais m'en occuper/je vais arranger ça; **fix me a drink!** donne-moi un verre! **how are you fixed moneywise?** (comment) es-tu paré côté argent? (*b*) préparer/décider; **I'm fixing to go to London,** je compte aller à Londres **2.** *P* rendre la pareille à qn/régler son compte à qn; **I'll fix him!** je lui ferai son affaire!/je l'aurai au tournant! **3.** *F* soudoyer/suborner qn; truquer qch; **the fight was fixed,** le match était truqué/la rencontre etait truqué **4.** *P* s'injecter une drogue/se faire une piquouse/se shooter/se faire un fixe.

fixer ['fiksər] *n P* (*a*) avocat véreux; combinard *m* (*b*) (*drugs*) revendeur *m*/trafiquant *m* (*c*) fourgue *m*.

fixture ['fikstʃər] *n F* (*pers*) **to be a fixture,** faire partie des meubles; **he's a permanent fixture,** il fait partie du mobilier/du décor.

fizz [fiz] *n F* champagne *m*/champ *m*.

fizzer ['fizər] *n F* **1.** *A* qch d'excellent*/du tonnerre **2.** *A* (*cricket*) balle rapide lancée à toute vitesse **3.** (*mil*) **to be on a fizzer,** être consigné au rapport.

fizzle ['fizl] *n P* échec*/bide *m* (complet).

fizzle out ['fizl'aut] *vi F* échouer*/ne pas aboutir/finir en queue de poisson/foirer/s'en aller en eau de boudin.

flabbergast ['flæbəɡɑɪst] *vtr F* abasourdir/stupéfier; **I was flabbergasted,** j'ai été sidéré/j'en suis resté baba/j'en suis resté comme deux ronds de flan.

fladge, flag¹ [flædʒ] *n P* (*esp homosexual, sado-masochistic use*) flagellation *f*; **fladge/flag party,** partie *f* de flagellation.

flag² [flæɡ] *n* **1.** *F* **to show the flag,** faire acte de présence **2.** *P* faux nom*/blaze *m*/alias *m* **3.** *F* **to keep the flag flying,** tenir bon/se défendre **4.** *P* **to fly the flag** (*a*) avoir ses règles*/repeindre sa grille en rouge (*b*) être (très) patriote/être chauvin **5.** *P* billet* de cinq livres.

flag-wagger ['flæɡwæɡə*r*], **flag-waver** ['flæɡweɪvə*r*]*n F* patriote exalté/cocardier *m*/chauvin *m*.

flag-wagging ['flæɡwæɡɪŋ], **flag-waving** ['flæɡweɪvɪŋ] *n F* patriotisme *m*/chauvinisme *m*/ cocarde *f*.

flak [flæk] *n F* censure *f* (défavorable); **he had to take a lot of flak from the board,** il a été beaucoup critiqué/censuré par le conseil.

flake [fleɪk] *n P* (*drugs*) cocaïne*/ poudrette *f*.

flaked (out) ['fleɪkt('aut)] *a F* (*a*) sans connaissance/KO (*esp* sous l'effet d'une drogue) (*b*) très fatigué*/pompé/crevé. (*See* **flakers**)

flake out ['fleɪk'aut] *vi F* **1.** s'évanouir*/tourner de l'œil; perdre connaissance sous l'effet d'une drogue **2.** être très fatigué*/avoir le coup de pompe/être crevé.

flakers ['fleɪkəz] *a O P* (**Harry**) **flakers,** très fatigué*/crevé/ esquinté/claqué.

flam [flæm] *n F* **1.** (*esp dial*) histoire *f*/chiqué *m*/trompe-l'œil *m*/ salades *fpl* **2.** *NAm* = **flimflam¹.**

flame [fleɪm] *n F* béguin *m*; **an old flame,** une de mes anciennes (conquêtes). (*See* **shoot down**)

flaming ['fleɪmɪŋ] *a F* (*a*) furax/ furibard; **a flaming temper,** un caractère infernal/un sale caractère; **a flaming row,** un barouf de tous les diables (*b*) (*euph for* **bloody**) sacré/fichu/foutu; **a flaming idiot,** un sacré crétin/le roi des imbéciles; **it's a flaming nuisance,** c'est un putain d'emmerdement/c'est vraiment la merde; **flaming hell!** merde alors!

flannel¹ ['flæn(ə)l] *n F* flatterie *f*/ pommade *m*/lèche *f*/eau bénite.

flannel² ['flæn(ə)l] *vtr F* acheter les bonnes grâces de (qn); passer de la pommade.

flanneller ['flænələr] *n F* flatteur *m*/bonimenteur *m*/lèche-bottes *m*.

flap¹ [flæp] *n* **1.** *F* affolement *m*/ panique *f*; **to be in a flap,** être dans tous ses états; **to get into a flap,** paniquer/s'affoler **2.** *pl O P* oreilles*/pavillons *mpl*/anses *fpl*.

flap² [flæp] *vi F* paniquer/s'affoler; **stop flapping!** (ne) panique pas!

flapdoodle ['flæp'duːdl] *n F* bêtise*/bidon *m*/salades *fpl*.

flapjaw ['flæpdʒɔː] *n esp NAm F* **1.** bavardage *m*/bavette *f*/papotage *m* **2.** (*pers*) bavard*/jacteur *m*.

flapper ['flæpər] *n* **1.** *F* (*1920's use*) jeune fille*/gamine *f*/mignonne *f* **2.** *esp NAm P* = **fin 1.** (*See* **flipper**)

flare-up ['flɛərʌp] *n F* (*a*) colère bleue (*b*) altercation *f*/scène *f* (*c*) bagarre*/grabuge *m*.

flare up ['flɛə'rʌp] *vi F* se mettre en colère*/piquer une crise.

flash¹ [flæʃ] **I** *a* **1.** *F* voyant/ tapageur; **his watch is a bit flash, isn't it?** sa montre, c'est un peu tape-à-l'œil, non? *O* **Flash Harry,** Fredo l'Esbrouf(f)e/un m'as-tu-vu/ frimeur *m* **2.** *P* contrefait/toc/ bidon **3.** qui est du milieu/de la pègre **II** *n* **1.** *F* pensée-éclair *f*/ idée-éclair *f*/éclair *f* (de génie) **2.** *F* œillade*/clin *m* d'œil **3.** *F* a

flash in the pan, un feu de paille **4.** P argot* des voleurs/arguemuche m du milieu/jars m **5.** P (*drugs*) sensation f de plaisir au moment d'une piqûre/flash m/rush m/boum m. (*See* **rush¹**)

flash² [flæʃ] *vtr&i* P **1.** crâner/ plastronner/frimer **2.** exhiber ses organes génitaux/exhiber ses parties *fpl*/s'exhiber/sortir ses précieuses.

flashback ['flæʃbæk] n P (*drugs*) répétition f des effets d'une drogue sans nouvelle administration de celle-ci.

flasher ['flæʃər] n P exhibitionniste m/satyre m.

flashy ['flæʃi] a F (a) voyant/ tapageur/tape-à-l'œil (b) qui jette du jus.

flat [flæt] **I** a F net/catégorique; **that's flat!** c'est clair et net!/c'est mon dernier mot!/un point c'est tout! (*See* **spin** 1) **II** adv F **1.** entièrement/tout à fait/carrément; **flat broke,** fauché comme les blés/à sec raide **2.** exactement/au poil; **in three minutes flat,** en trois minutes pile **3. to go flat out** (i) se mettre en quatre/se décarcasser (ii) aller bille en tête/mettre le paquet (iii) aller à fond de train/à pleins gaz/à tout berzingue **4. to be flat out,** (*exhausted*) être éreinté/à plat/KO **5. to fall flat (on its face)** (i) (*joke*) manquer son effet/rater (ii) (*play*) faire un four. (*See* **nothing** 2) **III** n F pneu m à plat/crevé.

flat-backer ['flætbækər] n A P prostituée*/pute f.

flatfoot ['flætfut] n O F agent* de police/poulet m.

flatfooted ['flæt'futid] a P **1.** (i) bête*/lourdaud (ii) maladroit/ empoté **2. to be caught flatfooted,** être pris la main dans le sac/être piqué sur le tas.

flathead ['flæthed] n NAm P individu m bête*/nouille f.

flatheaded ['flæt'hedid] a NAm P bête*/bas de plafond.

flatten ['flætn] vtr F **1.** mettre (qn) knock-out/KO **2.** aplatir (qn)/ déconfire (qn)/clouer le bec (à qn).

flattener ['flætnər] n F coup* d'assommoir/knock-out m/un KO.

flattie, flatty ['flæti] n P **1.** A = **flatfoot 2.** F femme* à la poitrine plate; (qui est) plate comme une planche à pain/une planche à repasser **3.** pl F **flatties,** chaussures fpl à talons plats/ballerines fpl.

flea [fliː] n F **to send s.o. away with a flea in his ear,** secouer les puces à qn/dire à qn ses quatre vérités.

fleabag ['fliːbæg] n P **1.** (i) sac m de couchage (ii) lit*/matelas m/ pucier m **2.** personne f malpropre/ pouilleux m; **she's an old fleabag,** c'est une vieille cradingue/un sac à puces **3.** mauvais cheval* de course/tocard m/canasson m/rosse f **4.** NAm hôtel m borgne/asile m de nuit.

fleabite ['fliːbait] n F un rien/une bagatelle/une vétille/une broutille.

fleabitten ['fliːbitn] a F sale*/ pouilleux/miteux/crassouillard; **fleabitten moggy,** chat m de gout- tière/greffier m miteux.

flea-house ['fliːhaus] n NAm P hôtel m borgne/hôtel des Trois Canards/taule miteuse.

flea-market ['fliːmɑːkit] n F marché m aux puces.

fleapit ['fliːpit] n F cinéma m miteux; **let's go to the local fleapit!** si on allait au ciné du quartier?

flea powder ['fliːpaudər] n P (*drugs*) stupéfiant m/drogue f de mauvaise qualité.

fleatrap ['fliːtræp] n NAm F hôtel m borgne/asile m de nuit.

fleece ['fliːs] vtr F estamper/ plumer/écorcher (qn).

flesh-peddler ['fleʃpedlər] n F **1.** souteneur*/mangeur m de blanc/ maquereau m/julot m **2.** prosti- tuée*/raccrocheuse f/pute f.

flick [flik] n F (a) O film m/ciné m/ cinoche m (b) cinéma m/ciné m/ cinoche m; **to go to the flicks,** aller au ciné/se payer une toile. (See **skin-flick**)

flier ['flaiər] n F **1. to take a flier** (a) risquer le paquet (b) tomber*/ ramasser une bûche/prendre une pelle **2.** imprimé m publicitaire. (See **high-flier**)

flimflam¹ ['flimflæm] n F (not common) escroquerie*/filouterie f/ entubage m.

flimflam² ['flimflæm] vtr F (not common) escroquer*/filouter/ entuber.

flimflammer ['flimflæmər] n F (not common) escroc*/entôleur m/ filou m.

flimsy ['flimzi] n **1.** F papier-pelure m **2.** F billet* de banque m/faffe m **3.** O P télégramme m/ petit bleu.

fling [fliŋ] n F **1.** réjouissances*/ boum f/bamboche f/foire f; **to have a fling,** faire la noce/faire la foire **2. to take a fling,** tenter sa chance; **to have a fling at sth,** tenter le coup/s'essayer la main à qch **3. to have one's fling,** jeter sa gourme.

flip¹ [flip] **I** a **1.** NAm P impu-dent/culotté/qui a du toupet; **a flip remark,** une saillie osée/une imper-tinence **2.** F (record) **flip side,** revers m/face f B/flip m **II** n P (a) (drugs) état m d'angoisse/de délire subi par des drogués pendant un voyage (b) déprime f/déveine f.

flip² [flip] vtr&i **1.** P s'emballer; **he flipped when he heard the group,** il a flippé quand il a entendu le groupe **2.** P **to flip one's top/lid/** NAm **noodle/raspberry,** être très en colère*/piquer une crise/sortir de ses gonds **3.** P faire une dépres-sion (nerveuse)/être claqué/sombrer dans la déprime **4.** NAm P rouler dans un train sans payer/brûler le dur **5.** NAm P **to flip one's lip** (i)

bavarder*/jacasser/baver (ii) dire des bêtises*/dégoiser/radoter.

flip out ['flip'aut] vi P = **freak out 1, 2, 3.**

flipper ['flipər] n NAm P main*/ pince f/patte f.

flipping ['flipiŋ] a F satané/fichu; **it's a flipping nuisance,** c'est un sacré embêtement; **flipping hell!** merde alors! **what a flipping idiot!** quel abruti!/quel sombre crétin.

flit¹ [flit] n **1.** F **to do a moonlight flit,** déménager à la cloche de bois **2.** F (elopement) fuite f/enlèvement m **3.** NAm P homosexuel*/pédé m/chouquette f.

flit² [flit] vi F **1. = to do a moon-light flit (flit¹1) 2.** (elope) s'enfuir* (avec un amant)/se faire enlever.

fliv [fliv] n P = **flivver 1.**

flivver ['flivər] n O P **1.** vieille voi-ture*/guimbarde f/tacot m **2.** échec*/bide m/fiasco m/four m.

float¹ [flout] n **1.** P client m qui sort pendant que le marchand cherche l'article; volant m **2.** F prêt m d'argent/emprunt m.

float² [flout] vtr O P **to float (one)** (i) toucher un chèque (ii) prêter de l'argent*. (See **air I 2**)

float about, around ['floutə'baut, ə'raund] vi F **to float names about,** balancer des noms*; **there's a rumour floating about (that . . .),** on dit que . . . /le bruit court que . . . .

floater ['floutər] n esp NAm F **1.** prêt m d'argent/emprunt m/tapage m **2.** (a) vagabond* (b) ouvrier itinérant **3.** (a) électeur indécis (b) personne indécise. (See **fence hanger**)

floating ['floutiŋ] a F **floating on air/on cloud nine** (i) ivre*/dans les vapes (ii) (drugs) high/flippé/dans les vapes.

flog [flɔg] vtr **1.** P bazarder/trafi-quer/troquer; **I flogged it for fifty quid,** je l'ai fourgué/je l'ai refilé (pour) cinquante balles 2. *F* (*esp idea*) **to flog sth to death,** éreinter qch; rabâcher qch; **to flog oneself to death,** se fatiguer à l'extrême; **he's flogging himself to death,** il se tue/se crève au boulot. (*See* **bishop**; **donkey 4**; **dummy 5**; **horse¹ 4**)

flogger ['flɔgər] *n Austr P* agent* de police/poulet *m*.

floor¹ [flɔɪr] *n* **1.** *F* **to take the floor** (*a*) (*dance*) ouvrir le bal (*b*) (*speech*) prendre la parole **2.** *F* **to hold the floor,** tenir le crachoir **3.** *F* (*driving*) **he had his foot on the floor,** il appuyait sur le champignon. (*See* **wipe² 1**)

floor² [flɔɪr] *vtr F* **1.** terrasser (qn)/ envoyer (qn) à terre/mettre (qn) KO **2.** (*i*) réduire (qn) à quia/au silence; clouer le bec (à qn) (*ii*) secouer (qn)/laisser (qn) baba; **that floored you!** ça te l'a coupé!

floosie, floosy, floozie, floozy ['fluːzi] *n esp NAm P* (*a*) femme* *ou* fille* de mœurs légères/ pouffiasse *f*/marie-salope *f* (*b*) aguicheuse *f* (*c*) prostituée*/roulure *f*.

flop¹ [flɔp] **I** *adv F* **to go flop** = **flop² 1, 2 II** *n* **1.** *F* (*i*) (*thing*) échec*/bide *m* (*ii*) (*pers*) raté *m*/ laissé *m* pour compte; **it was a complete flop,** c'était le bide complet/un four total **2.** *NAm F* (*a*) asile *m* de nuit (*b*) lit*/bâche *f* **3.** *P* (*hide-out*) cachette *f*/planque *f*. (*See* **belly-flop**)

flop² [flɔp] *vi F* **1.** échouer*/faire faillite/ramasser une veste; **his film flopped,** son film a fait un four **2.** s'affaisser/s'affaler; **to be ready to flop,** être fatigué*/claqué/crevé. (*See* **mop 1**)

flop-house ['flɔphaus] *n esp NAm P* **1.** hôtel *m* borgne/hôtel des Trois Canards **2.** (*doss-house*) asile *m* de nuit/piaule *f* à clodos/repaire *m* de pouilleux.

flopperoo ['flɔpə'ruː] *n P* = **flop¹ II 1.**

floral ['flɔɪrəl] *a P* **floral arrangement = daisy chain** (**daisy II 5**).

flossie, flossy ['flɔsi] *a NAm F* (*of dress*) (*i*) très élégant* (*ii*) tape-à-l'œil/tapageur.

flounder ['flaundər] *n P* (*RS = (taxi)cab*) **flounder (and dab),** taxi*/ rongeur *m*/tac *m*.

flower ['flauər] *n* **1.** *F* (*late 1960s*) **flower children/people,** enfants-fleur *mpl*/hippies *mpl*; **Flower power,** pouvoir *m* des fleurs/flower power *m* **2.** *pl P* règles*/affaires *fpl* anglaises *fpl* **3.** *P* homosexuel*/ tapette *f*. (*See* **wallflower**)

flowery (dell) ['flau(ə)ri('del)] *n P* (*RS = (prison) cell*) cellule *f*/bloc *m*/trou *m*.

flu [fluː] *n F* (= *influenza*) **he's got (the) flu,** il a la grippe.

flue [fluː] *n* **1.** *V* sexe de la femme*/cheminée *f*/bonbonnière *f* **2.** *V* **you can stick it up your flue,** tu peux te le mettre quelque part **3.** *P* (*RS = screw*) gardien* de prison/maton(ne) *m(f)*/gaffe *m*/ matuche *m* **4.** *F* **to go up the flue,** échouer*/foirer.

fluence ['fluːəns] *n F* **to put the fluence on s.o.** (*i*) persuader qn (*ii*) hypnotiser qn.

fluff¹ [flʌf] *n* **1.** *F* (*i*) jeune femme*/une jeunesse/mousmé(e) *f* (*ii*) gonzesse *f*/nénette *f*/nana *f*; **she's a nice bit of fluff,** elle est bien roulée/c'est un beau petit lot/c'est un morceau de choix **2.** *F* (*a*) cuir *m*/pataquès *m* (*b*) boulette *f*/gaffe *f* **3.** *NAm P* **to give s.o. the fluff,** remettre qn à sa place/snober qn/ rabattre le caquet à qn.

fluff² [flʌf] *vtr F* **1.** (*theatre*) rater/ louper son entrée; bouler (son rôle) **2.** saboter/bousiller/louper; **I fluffed it,** j'ai raté mon coup.

fluke [fluːk] *n F* coup *m* de chance*/veine *f*/bol *m*/pot *m*; **it**

was (a) sheer fluke, c'était un coup de veine extraordinaire.

fluky ['fluːki] *a F* par raccroc; **he won a fluky victory,** il a gagné par un hasard extraordinaire.

flummery ['flʌməri] *n F* bêtises*/ balivernes *fpl*/blagues *fpl*/sornettes *fpl.*

flummox ['flʌməks] *vtr F* démonter/épater/éberluer (qn); **I was completely flummoxed by his directions,** après ses explications, j'étais totalement dans le brouillard.

flunk [flʌŋk] *vtr&i esp NAm F* **1.** se dérober/se défiler/tirer au flanc **2.** être recalé/collé/étendu à un examen; **he flunked high school** (*a*) il a été recalé à l'examen de passage/il a raté son bac (*b*) il a abandonné/laissé tomber ses études **3.** recaler/coller/étendre.

flunk out ['flʌŋk'aut] *vi esp NAm F* **to flunk out of high school** (*a*) rater son bac (*b*) abandonner/laisser tomber ses études.

flush¹ [flʌʃ] *a F* riche*/plein aux as; **I'm feeling a bit flush today,** j'ai plein de fric/je suis à l'aise aujourd'hui.

flush² [flʌʃ] *vtr P* (*drugs*) faire monter du sang dans la seringue pour la mélanger à la drogue avant une piqûre. (*See* **four-flush**)

flute [fluːt], **fluter** ['fluːtər] *n P* homosexuel*/tapette *f*/lope(tte) *f.* (*See* **whistle¹ 2**)

flutter ['flʌtər] *n F* **1. to be all of a flutter,** être tout chose/être dans tous ses états **2. to have a flutter on the gee-gees,** jouer aux courtines/risquer qch sur les chevaux. (*See* **ring¹ 1**)

fly¹ [flai] **I** *a* **1.** *F* malin*/rusé/ futé/roublard **2.** *P* (*Black Slang*) élégant/qui a du chic **II** *n F* **1. there are no flies on him,** c'est un malin/il n'est pas né d'hier/il n'est pas tombé de la dernière pluie **2.** (*sing or pl*) braguette *f*; **your flies are undone,** ta braguette est ouverte

3. there's a fly in the ointment, il y a un cheveu/un hic **4.** *Austr* **to have a fly at sth,** faire un essai/ tenter le coup. (*See* **bar-fly**)

fly² [flai] *vi* **1.** (*a*) *F* **to fly high,** voler/viser haut (*b*) *P* (*drugs*) **flying high,** camé/planant/high/envapé **2. to let fly** (*a*) *F* lâcher une volée/ une bordée d'injures (*b*) *P* cracher*/glavioter (*c*) *P* uriner*/ lâcher l'écluse. (*See* **flag² 4**; **fur**; **handle 1**)

fly-ball ['flaibɔːl], **fly-bob** ['flaibɔb] *n NAm A P* policier* en civil/hambourgeois *m*/perdreau *m*/ civil *m.*

flyboy ['flaibɔi] *n P* malin* *m*/ mariol(le) *m.*

fly-bull ['flaibul] *n NAm A P* = **fly-ball.**

fly-by-night ['flaibainait, 'flaibənait] **I** *a F* (*pers*) irréfléchi/ évaporé; (*company, etc*) véreux **II** *n F* **1.** déménageur *m* à la cloche de bois **2.** évaporé *m*/tête *f* de linotte/écervelé *m* **3.** noctambule *m*/oiseau *m* de nuit.

flychick ['flaitʃik] *n NAm O P* belle fille*/joli lot.

fly-cop ['flaikɔp], **fly-dick** ['flaidik], **fly-mug** ['flaimʌg] *n P* = **fly-ball.**

fly-pitch ['flaipitʃ] *vi O F* vendre à la sauvette/cameloter.

fly-pitcher ['flaipitʃər] *n F* camelot *m* à la sauvette.

fly-pitching ['flaipitʃiŋ] *n O F* vente *f* à la sauvette.

fob [fɔb] *vtr A P* duper*/rouler.

fob off ['fɔb'ɔf] *vtr F* **to fob sth off on s.o./to fob s.o. off with sth,** refarcir qch à qn; **to get fobbed off with sth,** se faire refiler qch.

fog [fɔg] *n F* **to be in a fog,** être dans le brouillard/ne plus savoir où l'on est/se perdre en conjectures.

fogey ['fougi] *n F* (**old**) **fogey,** vieille

baderne/croulant *m*/périmé *m*/ vieux schnoque.

foggiest ['fɔgiist] *a&n* F **I haven't the foggiest (idea)**, je n'en ai pas la moindre idée; **not the foggiest!** aucune idée!

fog up ['fɔg'ʌp] *vtr* F brouiller (les cartes)/embrouiller.

fogy ['fougi] *n* F = **fogey.**

fold ['fould] *vi* F (*company, project, etc*) échouer*/faire faillite; tomber à l'eau.

folding ['fouldiŋ] *a* P **folding stuff**, billets *mpl* de banque/talbins *mpl*.

folks [fouks] *npl* F **1. the (old) folks**, les parents*/les vieux/les dab(e)s *mpl*; **my folks**, mes viocs **2. hi, folks!** salut tout le monde!/ salut la compagnie!

folksy ['fouksi] *a* F (*a*) campagnard/à la bonne franquette/ sans prétentions (*b*) sociable/populaire/sympa.

font [fɔnt] *n* P billet* d'une livre..

fooey! ['fuːi] *excl* O F la barbe!/ flûte alors! (*See* **phooey**)

foo-foo ['fuːfuː] *a* P **foo-foo dust = dust**[1] **2** (*a*). (*See* **fu**)

fool[1] [fuːl] **I** *a* F bête*/idiot/ridicule. (*See* **damfool I**) **II** *n* F **stupid fool!** espèce d'idiot!/espèce d'imbécile! **bloody fool!** espèce de con! **to play/to act the fool**, faire l'idiot/P faire le con.

fool[2] [fuːl] *vtr&i* F **1.** faire l'idiot/ faire l'imbécile/faire des bêtises* **2. to fool s.o.** (*a*) se payer la tête de qn (*b*) escroquer* qn/empiler qn.

fool about, around ['fuːlə'baut, ə'raund] *vi* F **1.** flânocher/ traînasser/glander/baguenauder **2.** taquiner/asticoter/faire enrager qn; se payer la tête de qn **3. to fool about/around with s.o.**, flirter/faire des avances à qn; avoir une liaison sexuelle avec qn.

foot[1] [fuːt] *n* F **1. my foot!** quelle blague!/et ta sœur! **2. to fall on**

one's feet, (re)tomber sur ses pieds **3. to find one's feet**, voler de ses propres ailes/se retrouver de l'aplomb **4. to have one foot in the grave**, avoir un pied dans la tombe **5. to put one's foot down** (*a*) faire acte d'autorité/mettre bon ordre **6. to put one's best foot forward** (*a*) allonger/presser le pas (*b*) faire de son mieux **7. to put one's foot in it**, mettre les pieds dans le plat; **he's always putting his foot in it!** il n'en rate pas une! **8. to put one's feet up**, se reposer/se relaxer/ poser ses fesses **9. to be carried out feet first**, mourir*/partir les pieds devant **10. to be dead on one's feet**, être très fatigué*/être à plat **11. to get off/to start off on the wrong foot**, être mal parti; partir/se lever du pied gauche. (*See* **cold I 4**; **doughfoot**; **drag**[2]; **flatfoot**; **pussyfoot**[1]; **six 1**; **sweep**[2] **1**; **tanglefoot**)

foot[2] [fuːt] *vtr* F **1. to foot the bill**, payer* la note/payer la douloureuse/casquer **2. to foot it**, marcher*/aller à pattes/arquer. (*See* **hotfoot**; **pussyfoot**[2])

football ['futbɔːl] *n* P (*drugs*) mélange *m* de dextroamphétamine et amphétamine/football *m*.

footer ['futər] *n* F football *m*; **let's have a game of footer**, allons jouer au foot/taquiner le ballon.

footle ['fuːtl] *n* F (*rare*) bêtise*/ fadaise *f*.

footle about ['fuːtlə'baut] *vi* F **1.** traînasser/flemmarder/ baguenauder/glander **2.** (*a*) faire des bêtises* (*b*) dire des sornettes *fpl*.

footling ['fuːtliŋ] *a* F futile/ insignifiant; mesquin.

footsie, footsy ['futsi] *n* F **to play footsie/footsy with s.o.**, faire du pied avec qn. (*See* **kneesies**)

foot-slog ['futslɔg] *vi* F marcher* péniblement/arquer/trimarder/battre le bitume.

foot-slogger ['futslɔgər] *n F* marcheur *m*/pousse-cailloux *m*; (*mil*) biffin *m*.

for [fɔɪr] *prep F* (*a*) **to be (all) for it,** être pour ...; **I'm all for it,** je suis tout à fait pour/j'en suis très partisan (*b*) **to be for it,** être bon pour ...; **you're for it!** ton affaire est bonne!/qu'est-ce que tu vas prendre! (*See* **free**; **real I 1**; **what-for**)

force [fɔɪrs] *n F* (*abbr = police force*) **the force,** la police; **then the force arrived,** et puis les flics se sont ramenés.

fork [fɔɪk] *n A P* (*a*) main*/grappin *m* (*b*) *pl* doigts*/fourchettes *fpl*.

fork out ['fɔɪk'aut] *vi F* payer*/les allonger/les aligner/cracher.

fork up ['fɔɪk'ʌp] *vi F* payer*/les allonger/cracher.

form [fɔɪm] *n F* **1. to know the form,** savoir ce qu'il faut faire **2.** casier *m* judiciaire/case *m*/pédigrée *m*; **he's got form,** il a fait de la taule **3. to be off form,** ne pas tenir la forme/ne pas avoir la frite/ne pas avoir la pêche.

forrader ['fɔrədər] *adv F* plus en avant; **that doesn't get us any further forrader,** ça ne nous avance guère.

fort [fɔɪt] *n F* **to hold the fort,** garder la baraque/tenir la position.

forty ['fɔɪti] *num a F* **to have forty winks,** dormir*/faire un petit somme/piquer un roupillon.

forty-four *n* **1.** *NAm P* (*RS = whore*) prostituée*/putain *f* **2.** *P* (*CB*) salut!/bises!/bye!

forwards ['fɔɪwəds] *npl P* (*drugs*) amphétamines*/speeds *mpl*.

fossick ['fɔsik] *vi esp Austr F* **1.** fureter/fouiller/farfouiller **2.** marauder dans les mines d'or.

fossil ['fɔsl] *n F* croulant *m*/vieux fossile/vieux schnoque; **you old fossil!** vieux croûton!/vieux con!/vieux birbe!

foul [faul] *a F* **1.** dégueulasse/dégoûtant/infect; **what a foul dump!** quel merdier!/quelle pétaudière!/quel gourbi!

foul up ['faul'ʌp] *vtr F* amocher/bousiller/saloper; **that's really fouled everything up,** ça a tout fichu/foutu en l'air; tout a filé en quenouille. (*See* **snafu**[1,2])

four-by-two ['fɔɪrbai'tuɪ] *n P* (*RS = Jew*) (*pej*) Juif*/Youtre *m*/Youde *m*.

four-eyes ['fɔɪraiz] *n P* qn qui porte des lunettes*/binoclard *m*/bésiclard *m*.

four-flush ['fɔɪflʌʃ] *vi P* **1.** bluffer*/se gonfler/se monter le job **2.** ne pas payer ses dettes/ne pas essuyer l'ardoise **3.** écornifler/vivre aux crochets de qn.

four-flusher ['fɔɪ'flʌʃər] *n P* vantard*/bluffeur *m*.

four-letter ['fɔɪletər] *a F* **four-letter word,** les cinq lettres/le mot de Cambronne (*= merde*)/gros mot.

fourpenny ['fɔɪpni] *a P* **to give s.o. a fourpenny one,** donner un coup* de poing/un gnon/un marron à qn; filer une châtaigne maison à qn.

four-ten ['fɔɪten] *n P* (*CB*) (*= 10-4*) je reçois.

fox[1] [fɔks] *n esp NAm P* (*also CB*) belle femme*/fille*; un beau petit lot/une chouette nana.

fox[2] [fɔks] *vtr F* (*a*) duper*/avoir/rouler (qn) (*b*) rendre perplexe/mystifier (qn).

foxy ['fɔksi] *a esp NAm P* (*also CB*) **foxy lady,** belle femme*/fille; beau petit lot/prix *m* de Diane/beau morceau; fille bien balancée/bien roulée.

fracture ['fræktʃər] *vtr P* **you fracture me!** tu me fais tordre de rire*! (*b*) tu m'écœures!

fractured ['fræktʃəd] *a O P* ivre*/rétamé.

frag [fræg] *vtr NAm P* (*mil*) tuer*/

assassiner (*esp*) un supérieur à la grenade (à fragmentation) défensive/descendre dans le dos (à qn) à la grenade.

fragging ['frægiŋ] *n NAm P* (*mil*) meurtre déguisé (*esp*) d'un supérieur à la grenade (à fragmentation) défensive.

fraidy ['freidi] *a esp NAm F* (*esp child's word*) **to be a fraidy cat**, être lâche/avoir peur*/avoir les jetons. (*See* **scaredy-cat**)

frail [freil] *a P* **frail job** (*a*) femme* de petite vertu/femme facile/nénette *f*/gonzesse *f* (*b*) coït*/partie *f* de jambes en l'air.

frame¹ [freim] *n P* (*rare, homosexual use*) hétérosexuel *m* qui plaît aux homosexuels/une amorce. (*See* **bait**)

frame² [freim] *vtr F* **to frame s.o.**, farguer qn/faire porter le bada à qn/monter un coup contre qn; **to be framed**, être victime d'un coup monté; **I've been framed**, on m'a roulé/on a monté un coup contre moi.

frame-up ['freimʌp] *n F* complot *m*/machination *f*/coup monté. (*See* **fit-up**; **set-up 3**)

frat [fræt] *n NAm F* **1.** (= *fraternity*) association *f*/confrérie *f* d'étudiants **2.** étudiant conforme/rangé/typique; **clean** *m*/fils *m* à papa.

frazzle ['fræzl] *n F* **1. to be done to a frazzle**, être trop cuit/être carbonisé **2. to be worn to a frazzle**, être très fatigué/à plat/à bout **3. to beat s.o. to a frazzle**, battre qn à plate(s) couture(s).

freak [friːk] *n* **1.** *F* drôle *m* de numéro/original *m*/phénomène *m* **2.** *P* fervent *m*/fana *mf*/branché *m*/mordu *m*; **jazz freak**, fana de jazz **3.** *P* hippie/hippy *mf*/marginal *m*/marjo *m* **4.** *P* usager *m* d'une drogue/camé *m*. (*See* **acid 2**) **5.** *P* homosexuel*/tapette *f*.

freak-out ['friːk'aut] *n P* **1.** (*drugs*) mauvais trip **2.** (*esp with drugs*) boum *f*/surboum *f*/partie *f*; hash-partie *f*/coke-partie *f*.

freak out ['friːk'aut] *vi P* **1.** se dévergonder/se débaucher **2.** vivre en marge de la société **3.** devenir fou*/perdre les pédales **3.** (*drugs*) perdre tout contrôle mental sous l'effet d'un hallucinogène/flipper/se défoncer/divaguer.

freaky ['friːki] *a F* bizarre/saugrenu/marjo; dingue/dingo/barjo(t).

Fred [fred] *Prn O F* **Fred Karno's army**, cafouillis *m*/gâchis *m*/loufoquerie *f*.

Freddy ['fredi] *n P* (*drugs*) comprimé *m* d'éphédrine/Freddie *m*.

free [friː] *a F* (*a*) **for free**, gratuit*/gratis/à l'œil/pour la peau (*b*) **feel free!** je t'en prie!/vas-y!/te gêne pas!/sers-toi! (*See* **show**¹ **1**)

freebie ['friːbi] *n P* (*esp journ*) (*a*) cadeau, etc, gratuit; **freebie trip**, reportage *m* grand luxe (*b*) *pl* **freebies**, à-côtés *mpl*/bénefs *mpl*/gratte *f*.

free-for-all ['friːfərɔːl] *n F* mêlée générale/barouf *m*/corrida *f*/castagne *f*.

free-load ['friːloud] *vi esp NAm P* écornifler/vivre aux crochets de qn.

free-loader ['friːloudər] *n esp NAm P* parasite *mf*/écornifleur *m*/tapeur *m*.

free-loading ['friːloudiŋ] *n esp NAm P* le fait de boire/de manger/de vivre aux frais *ou* aux dépens d'autrui; vie *f* de pique-assiette.

free-wheeling ['friː(h)wiːliŋ] *a F* **1.** qui dépense* sans compter/qui jette de l'argent par les fenêtres **2.** sans contrainte/sans gêne/en roue libre.

freeze¹ [friːz] *n P* **to put the freeze on s.o.**, battre froid à qn/faire la gueule à qn. (*See* **deep I 2**)

freeze² [friːz] *vi* F **1.** (*a*) avoir peur*/avoir le sang qui gèle (*b*) être figé sur place/se figer **2.** it's freezing cold, ça caille. (*See* **balls¹ 4**)

freeze out ['friːz'aut] *vtr esp NAm* F (*a*) mettre en quarantaine/boycotter (*b*) supplanter (un rival)/évincer (qn).

freeze-up ['friːzʌp] *n* F gel *m* à pierre fendre; the big freeze-up of '76, le grand hiver de '76.

French¹ [frentʃ] **I** *a* **1.** F French kiss, baiser profond sur la bouche/patin *m*/saucisse *f*; **to give s.o.** a French kiss, faire une langue fourrée à qn/rouler un patin à qn/rouler une saucisse à qn **2.** F French letter/*NAm* French safe, capote anglaise/imperméable *m* à Popaul **3.** F to take French leave, filer à l'anglaise **4.** V the French way (*i*) fellation* (*ii*) cunnilinctus*; to do it the French way (*i*) tailler une pipe/faire un pompier à qn (*ii*) brouter le cresson/lécher la chatte **II** *n* F that bloody idiot... −pardon/'scuse my French! ce sacré... −excusez mon latin!

french² [frentʃ] *vtr&i* V (*i*) faire une fellation* (à qn)/tailler une pipe (à qn) (*ii*) pratiquer le cunnilinctus*/brouter le cresson.

frenchie, frenchy ['frentʃi] *n* P = French letter (**French¹ 2**).

fresh [freʃ] **I** *a* F **1.** O légèrement ivre*/émèché/paf **2.** (*a*) effronté/culotté; don't get fresh with me! ne la ramène pas avec moi! (*b*) flirteur/coureur/dragueur; he got fresh with me, il a essayé de me draguer. (*See* **air 3**) **II** *adv* F to be fresh out of sth, être complètement vidé de qch.

fresher ['freʃər] *n* F étudiant de première année/bizut *m*.

friar ['fraiər] *n* P (RS = liar) holy friar, menteur *m*.

fridge [fridʒ] *n* F (*abbr* = refrigerator*) réfrigérateur *m*/frigo *m*.

frig¹ [frig] *n* V **1.** coït*/baisage *m*/

bourre *f* **2.** masturbation*/branlage *m*/branlette *f*.

frig² [frig] *vtr&i* **1.** V faire l'amour* (avec qn)/baiser/bourrer/niquer; **frig off!** fous(-moi) le camp!/va te faire foutre!/va te faire enculer! **2.** V se masturber*/se branler **3.** NAm P escroquer*/carotter/entuber.

frigger ['frigər] *n* **1.** V baiseur *m*/tringleur *m*/troncheur *m* **2.** V masturbateur*/branleur *m* **3.** NAm P escroc*/empileur *m*/carotteur *m*.

frigging [frigin] **I** *a* F sacré*/fichu/foutu; that frigging idiot! ce foutu imbécile!/ce connard!/cet espèce d'enculé!; it's a frigging nuisance, c'est vachement chiant; frigging hell! putain (alors)!/bordel (de merde)! **II** *n* **1.** V coït*/baisage *m*/bourre *f* **2.** V masturbation*/branlage *m* **3.** NAm P escroquerie*/entubage *m*/filouterie *f*.

fright [frait] *n* F individu laid*/moche *f*/tarte *f*; you look a fright! t'as l'air dégueulasse!

frightful ['fraitful] *a* F affreux/effroyable; a frightful bore, un casse-pieds.

frill [fril] *n* **1.** A P jeune fille*/jeune femme*/mousmée *f*/gisquette *f* **2.** F without any/no frills, sans façons.

frippet ['fripit] *n* O P = talent.

frisk [frisk] *vtr* F fouiller (un suspect, etc).

Fritz [frits] *Prn* P (esp WWII) Allemand*/fritz *m*/fridolin *m*/frizou *m*/frisé *m*.

frog¹ [frɔg] *n* P (RS = road) frog (and toad), route*/rue *f*/strasse *f*.

Frog² [frɔg], **Froggie, Froggy** ['frɔgi] *a&n* P Français *m*/Fransquillon *m*.

front [frʌnt] **I** *a* F **1.** front runner, candidat *m* en tête/la tête de liste/coureur *m* de tête **2.** front man, homme* de paille; (drugs, etc) intermédiaire *m*/agent *m* **3.** to

have a front seat, être aux premières loges II *n F* **1.** activité *ou* individu* qui sert à cacher des activités illicites/couverture *f*/façade *f*/paravent *m*/parapluie *m*; homme *m* de paille **2. to put on a front,** faire le prétentieux*/crâner/faire de l'esbrouffe/frimer **3. to put on a bold front,** faire bonne contenance/faire bonne figure/affronter avec panache.

frost [frɔst] *n F* échec*/four *m*/bide *m*/fiasco *m*.

frowst [fraust] *n F* renfermé *m*/odeur *f* de renfermé.

frowsty ['frausti] *a F* qui sent le renfermé.

frowsy, frowzy ['frauzi] *n F* femme* mal torchée/souillon *f*.

fruit [fruːt] *n* **1.** *F* **hello, old fruit!** salut, mon pote!/salut, vieille branche! **2.** *P* homosexuel*/pédé *m*; **frozen fruit,** homosexuel* frigide; **fruit fly,** femme* qui recherche la compagnie des homosexuels*/pouf(-molle) *f*; **fruit picker,** hétérosexuel qui, de temps en temps, fait l'amour* avec des homosexuels* **3.** *NAm P* prostituée*/grue *f*/morue *f*.

fruit-basket ['fruːtbɑːskit] *n V* sexe de la femme*/boîte *f* à ouvrage/bonbonnière *f*; **to have one's fingers in the fruit-basket,** mettre la main au panier.

fruit-cake ['fruːtkeik] *n* **1.** *NAm P* homosexuel*/tapette *f* **2.** *F* **nutty as a fruit-cake,** fou* à lier/complètement dingue.

fruit-salad ['fruːt'sæləd] *n* **1.** *F* rangée *f* de médailles et décorations/batterie *f* de cuisine/bananes *fpl* **2.** *P* (*drugs*) mélange *m* de plusieurs drogues; = cocktail *m*.

fruity ['fruːti] *a* **1.** *F* (*voice*) de gorge/moelleux **2.** *F* salace/pimenté/corsé; **a fruity joke,** blague *f* un peu raide **3.** *P* excité/allumé; **he was feeling fruity,** il bandait/il

avait la trique **4.** *esp NAm* homosexuel*/de pédé/de tapette.

fruity-pie ['fruːtipai] *n P* **listen, fruity-pie!** écoute, mon bonhomme/mon pote!

fry [frai] *vtr esp NAm* **1.** électrocuter qn (dans la chaise)/griller qn/faire rôtir qn **2.** (*Black Slang*) défriser les cheveux. (*See* **fish¹** 3)

FTA! ['eftiei] *excl NAm V* (*abbr = Fuck the Army*) à bas l'Armée/aux chiottes l'Armée (générale).

fu [fuː] *n P* (*drugs*) marijuana* *f*/marie-jeanne *f*. (*See* **foo-foo**)

fuck¹ [fʌk] *n V* coït*/baisage *m*/bourre *f*/baise *f*; **a good fuck** (*i*) un bon coup/une sacrée baise (*ii*) (*pers*) une sacrée baiseuse/un sacré baiseur; **a quick fuck,** un coup rapide **2. I don't give a fuck,** je m'en fous (et m'en contrefous)/j'en ai rien à branler; **who gives a fuck!** on s'en fout!/rien à branler! **3. what the fuck!** qu'est-ce que c'est que cette connerie? **what the fuck is going on?** qu'est-ce que c'est que ce bordel? **4. get the fuck out of here!** casse-toi rapide!/fous le camp! **5. how the fuck did you do that?** comment as-tu réussi ce coup foireux? **how the fuck should I know?** j'en sais rien, moi, bordel!/j'en ai rien à branler! **6. like fuck!** et mon cul!/tiens, mes deux! **7.** *NAm* **fuck film,** film *m* porno/porno *m*/film de cul. (*See* **finger-fuck; honey-fuck(ing)**).

fuck² [fʌk] *vtr V* **1.** faire l'amour* (avec qn)/baiser (qn)/niquer (qn)/tringler (qn)/enfiler (qn); **he'd fuck anything on two legs/with a hole in it,** il baiserait n'importe quelle pouffiasse/tout lui est bon pour piner/il s'enverrait même une chèvre **2. fuck me!** mon cul!/merde alors! **fuck you!/go fuck yourself!** je t'emmerde!/va te faire enculer! **fuck it!** (*i*) merde alors!/et merde! (*ii*) c'est marre!/y en a marre! **3. (I'm) fucked if I know,** je n'en sais foutre rien **4. fuck a**

duck! nom de Dieu de putain!/bordel de merde! **5.** (=**fucked up**) **it's really fucked!** c'est vraiment la merde! **6.** (*tired*) **I feel fucked,** je suis crevé/vanné **7.** *esp NAm* escroquer*/rouler/carotter; **I got fucked by that shopkeeper,** j'ai été baisé par ce vendeur/je me suis fait baisé en beauté par ce type. (*See* **finger fuck; fist fuck; mind fuck**)

fuckable ['fʌkəbl] *a V* bon(ne) à baiser/baisable/mettable.

fuck about, around ['fʌkə'baut, ə'raund] *vi V* **1. to fuck about/around,** traîner (son cul)/traînasser/merdoyer **2. to fuck s.o. about/around,** emmerder qn; **he's always fucking me about/around,** il est toujours en train de me faire chier **3.** déconner; **to fuck about/around with sth,** tripatouiller qch; **stop fucking about/around!** arrête de déconner!/fais pas le con!

fuck-about ['fʌkəbaut] *n V* **it's a real fuck-about** (*i*) c'est vraiment un sale gag/un mauvais tour (*ii*) c'est une vraie histoire de cons/un vrai tour de cochon (*iii*) c'est une sacrée rigolade/une sacrée marrade/une franche rigolade/une bonne tranche de rire.

fuck-all [fʌk'ɔːl] *n V* **1.** rien*/que dalle/peau de balle/des prunes; **we get fuck-all out of that,** on peut rien en tirer de ce merdier; **there's fuck-all to drink here,** y'a rien a siffler/avaler dans cette taule miteuse. (*See* **f.a., FA; sweet 4**)

fuck arse ['fʌkɑːs], *NAm* **fuck ass** ['fʌkæs] *n V* (petit) con/connard *m*; merdeux *m*/ordure *f*.

fucker ['fʌkər] *n V* **1.** baiseur, -euse **2.** (*a*) salaud*/saligaud *m*/crapule *f* (*b*) **you silly fucker!** espèce de connard/d'enculé/d'enfoiré!(*See* **fist fucker**)

fucking ['fʌkiŋ] **I** *a V* **1.** sacré/foutu; **it's a fucking nuisance,** c'est vraiment chiant/emmerdant; **he's a fucking cunt/bastard,** (c'est un)

espèce de salaud/d'enflure/de dégueulis! **you fucking idiot!** (espèce de) connard!/quel crétin!/enculé! **this fucking job is a real pain!** ce putain de boulot/ce job à la con me fout la chiasse/m'emmerde à crever! **I'll knock your fucking head off!** je vais te rectifier le portrait! **2. fucking hell!** bordel de Dieu!/bordel de merde! **II** *adv V* **a fucking awful film,** un sacré navet/une vraie connerie de film; **fucking dreadful weather,** saloperie *f*/saleté *f* de temps; une pourriture de temps; **we had a fucking amazing time/a fucking ace time,** on s'en est payé une bonne tranche; *NAm* **fucking A!** c'est vrai/(je suis) d'accord; banco!/je marche! **III** *n V* coït*/baisage *m*/baise *f*/dérouillage *m*. (*See* **fist-fucking; honey-fuck(ing)**)

fuck off ['fʌk'ɔf] *vi V* **1.** s'enfuir*/mettre les bouts/se tirer; **I'll just fuck off then,** bon, je n'ai plus qu'à me barrer; **tell him to fuck off,** dis-lui de se barrer/se calter; **fuck off!** va te faire foutre! **2.** (*rare*) se masturber*/se branler (la colonne) **3.** *NAm* (*not common*) faire le con/déconner.

fuck over ['fʌk'ouvər] *vtr V* (*a*) (*police*) fouiller qn (*b*) chambouler/bordéliser/retourner; **the cops fucked the place over,** les flics y ont foutu le merdier/mis le bordel.

fuckster ['fʌkstər] *n A V* baiseur *m*/qn porté sur l'article/porté sur la bagatelle.

fuckstress ['fʌkstris] *n A V* baiseuse *f*/chaude lapine/chaude *f* de la pince.

fuck up ['fʌk'ʌp] *vtr V* saloper/cochonner/bousiller; foutre la merde/le merdier/le bordel (dans qch); foutre (qch) en l'air; **to fuck s.o. up,** emmerder qn/faire chier qn; **he fucked it up,** il s'est foutu dedans/il y a foutu le merdier. (*See* **snafu**)

fuddy-duddy ['fʌdidʌdi] *n F* vieux croulant/périmé *m*/vieux schnoque.

fudge [fʌdʒ] *vtr&i* **1.** *F* raconter des blagues *fpl*/des craques *fpl* **2.** *V* faire jouir au toucher/faire mousser/envoyer (qn) aux anges.

fug [fʌg] *n F* forte odeur de renfermé; **what a fug in here!** ça schlingue ici!

full [ful] *a P* **1.** ivre*/plein (comme une bourrique)/rond **2.** intoxiqué par la drogue/chargé/bourré. (*See* **chock-full**)

fun [fʌn] **I** *a F* marrant/rigolo; **it's the fun thing to do,** c'est ce qu'il y a de plus marrant/c'est la chose à faire; **he's a fun person,** il est rigolo, lui; c'est un marrant/c'est pas un triste **II** *n F* **1. like fun,** pas du tout; **did you enjoy yourself? like fun I did!** tu t'es bien amusé? tu parles! **2. fun (and games)** (*i*) (*difficulty*) **I had fun (and games) getting the car going this morning,** j'ai eu du mal/un mal de chien à la faire démarrer ce matin, la bagnole (*ii*) (*trouble*) **there'll be fun and games if we don't get a rise this year,** ça va barder/il y aura du grabuge si l'on ne reçoit pas d'augmentation cette année (*iii*) (*euph*) **to have fun and games with one's secretary,** s'amuser avec sa secrétaire/s'envoyer la secrétaire en douce.

funeral ['fjuːnərəl] *n F* **that's your funeral,** c'est ton affaire/mêle-toi de tes oignons/tant pis pour toi; **it's not my funeral!** ça ne me regarde pas/c'est pas mes oignons.

fungus ['fʌŋgəs] *n P* **1. (face) fungus,** barbe*/moustache*/poils *mpl* au menton **2. fungus face,** barbu *m*; moustachu *m*.

funk¹ [fʌŋk] *n F* **1.** peur*/frousse *f*/trac *m*/trouille *f*; **to be in funk/in a blue funk,** avoir une peur* bleue/ avoir la frousse/avoir la trouille. (*See* **acid 2**) **2.** froussard(e) *m(f)*/ trouillard(e) *m(f)*.

funk² [fʌŋk] *vtr&i F* **to funk it,** caner/se dégonfler/les mouiller; **he funked it,** il s'est dégonflé.

funked out ['fʌŋkt'aut] *a P* sous l'influence des drogues/défoncé/ high/camé.

funky ['fʌŋki] *a* **1.** *F* froussard/ trouillard **2.** *P* (*jazz, rock, etc*) funky.

funny ['fʌni] **I** *a* **1.** *F* **don't (try to) be funny!** c'est pas le moment de plaisanter!/fais pas l'imbécile!/ fais pas le con! **2.** *F* **funny business,** affaire *f* louche/fricotage *m*; **no funny business/none of your funny tricks!** pas d'histoires, hein!/ pas de blagues! **3.** *F* (*ill*) **to feel funny,** se sentir tout chose; **I came over all funny,** ça m'a fait tout drôle **4.** *P* **funny farm**/*esp NAm* **funny house,** asile *m* (d'aliénés)/ maison *f* de fous **II** *n F* **1.** plaisanterie *f*/blague *f*; **to make a funny,** plaisanter/blaguer **2.** *pl esp NAm* **funnies** (*i*) bandes dessinées/ bédés *fpl* (*ii*) dessins animés.

fur [fɔːr] *n F* **to make the fur fly** (*i*) se battre* avec acharnement (*ii*) se quereller* avec fracas; **this will make the fur fly,** ça fera du grabuge; **the fur was flying,** ça bardait/il y avait du grabuge.

furburger ['fɔːbɔːgɔr] *n esp NAm VV* sexe de la femme*/le barbu. (*See* **fur pie**; **hair burger**)

furniture ['fɔːmitʃər] *n F* **1. to be part of the furniture,** faire partie du mobilier/des meubles. (*See* **fixture**) **2.** *NAm O* **a nice little piece of furniture,** un beau brin de fille/un beau petit lot.

furphy ['fɔːfi] *n Austr P* fausse rumeur/canulard *m*/ragots *mpl*/ bruit *m* de chiottes.

fur pie ['fɔː'pai] *n V* sexe de la femme*/barbu *m*/chagatte *f*.

fury ['fjuːri] *n F* **like fury** (*i*) déchaîné/en fureur (*ii*) très vite*/à toute pompe; **to work like fury,**

travailler comme un dératé/comme un nègre/comme une bête.

fuse [fjuːz] *n F* **to blow a fuse,** se mettre en colère*/piquer une crise.

fuss [fʌs] *n F* chichis *mpl*/chinoiseries *fpl*; **to make a fuss/to kick up a fuss,** faire des arias/faire des histoires/en faire tout un plat; **it's nothing to make a fuss about,** il n'y a pas de quoi fouetter un chat.

fusspot ['fʌspɔt], *NAm* **fuss budget** ['fʌsbʌdʒit] *n F* (*i*) individu* qui fait des histoires/des embarras; chichiteux *m* (*ii*) enquiquineur, -euse *mf*.

future ['fjuːtʃər] *n* **1.** *F* **there's no future in it,** ça n'a pas d'avenir *m*/ça ne servira à rien/ça ne mènera à rien **2.** *P* testicules*/bijoux *mpl* de famille/roupettes *fpl*.

futz¹ [fʌts] *n V* sexe de la femme*/fente *f*/chagatte *f*.

futz² [fʌts] *vtr NAm* faire l'amour*/baiser/tringler.

fuzz [fʌz] *n P* **1.** policier*/détective *m*/flic *m*/roussin *m* **2.** (*coll*) la police*/flicaille *f*/rousse *f*; **here's the fuzz,** voilà les flics **3.** gardien* de prison/matuche *m*/maton(ne) *m*.

fuzzled ['fʌzld] *a P* ivre*/pompette/chargé.

fuzzy ['fʌzi] *a F* (*i*) désorienté (*ii*) un peu ivre*; **my head's a bit fuzzy,** j'ai la tête qui tourne/je ne me sens pas très bien.

G

G [dʒiː] P **1. to put in the G** (a) serrer la vis/les pouces à qn (b) dénoncer*/cafarder/moucharder/donner qn **2.** (i) mille livres (sterling) (ii) mille dollars; = mille balles. (See **G-man**; **grand**)

gab¹ [gæb] n **1.** P blabla m/jactage m **2.** F **to have the gift of the gab** (i) avoir du bagou(t)/savoir baratiner/avoir une bonne tapette (ii) savoir vendre sa salade; **she's got the gift of the gab**, elle a la langue bien pendue **3.** P = **gob¹ 1.**

gab² [gæb] vi P bavarder*/bavasser/blablater/jacter/jaser/tenir le crachoir; **they spend the day gabbing away**, ils/elles passent la journée à jacasser.

gabber ['gæbər] n P bavard*/baratineur m/jacteur m/tapette f.

gabby ['gæbi] a P bavard/qui a la langue bien pendue.

gabfest ['gæbfest] n esp NAm P bavette f/(brin m de) causette f.

gad, Gad [gæd] n A F **by gad!** sacrebleu!/sapristi!/mes aïeux!

gadabout ['gædəbaut] n F vadrouilleur, -euse mf; glandeur m.

gad about ['gædə'baut] vi F **1.** vadrouiller/baguenauder/se balader/aller par voies et par chemins/aller par monts et par vaux **2.** courir les filles/le jupon.

gadie ['geidi] n P gadjé m (celui qui n'est pas bohémien ou manouche).

gaff [gæf] n P **1.** logement*/piaule f/taule f/crèche f; **they did him in his gaff**, ils l'ont arrêté/piqué dans sa piaule. (See **drum 1**; **screw² 3**) **2. gambling gaff**, maison f de jeu/tripot m **3. to blow the gaff**, vendre la mèche; **to blow the gaff on s.o.**, dénoncer* qn/donner qn **4.** NAm **to stand the gaff**, être courageux*/encaisser les coups durs/en avoir dans le ventre **5.** bêtises*/blagues fpl/foutaises fpl. (See **guff**) **6.** café-concert m/beuglant m **7.** champ m de foire; **gaff waller**, légrier m.

gaffe [gæf] n F bévue*/gaffe f; **that was a bit of a gaffe you made there**, tu t'es gour(r)é un peu/tu as gaffé/tu t'es foutu dedans.

gaffed [gæft] a NAm P **gaffed dice**, dés truqués.

gaffer ['gæfər] n **1.** F patron*/chef m/taulier m/singe m **2.** F vieil homme/vieux bonhomme **3.** NAm P (films, TV) le chef électricien.

gag¹ [gæg] n F **1.** plaisanterie f/blague f; **he did it for a gag**, il l'a fait histoire de rigoler/pour blaguer **2.** canular m; **to pull a gag on s.o.**, faire une entourloupette à qn/rouler qn/mener qn en bateau **3.** (cinema, etc) gag m.

gag² [gæg] vi F **1.** (theatre) enchaîner **2.** dire des plaisanteries fpl/blaguer; faire des gags.

gaga ['gɑːgɑː] a F **1.** gaga; **the old man's completely gaga**, c'est un vieux gâteux **2.** fou*/cinglé/timbré **3. to go gaga over s.o.**, s'enticher de qn/se toquer de qn/être complètement gaga de qn.

gage [geidʒ] n esp NAm P **1.** whisky m/alcool* bon marché/tord-boyaux m **2.** tabac*/cigarettes*/

cigares*/chique *f*; **stick of gage**, cigarette* (tabac *ou* marijuana*) **3.** (*drugs*) marijuana* **4. to get one's gage up** (*a*) se mettre en colère*/sortir de ses gonds (*b*) être ivre*/se piquer le nez/se bit(t)urer/avoir sa cuite/prendre sa cuite.

gaged [geidʒd] *a NAm P* ivre*/bit(t)uré/noir/rond/schlass.

gal [gæl] *n F* jeune fille*/môme *f*/gonzesse *f*/nana *f*/minette *f*.

galah ['gɑːlə] *n Austr F* individu bête*/buse *f*/doux dingue *m*.

gall [gɔːl] *n F* culot *m*/toupet *m*; **he had the gall to do that!** il a eu le culot de faire ça!

gallery ['gæləri] *n F* **to play to the gallery**, faire de l'esbrouffe/de l'épate; poser pour la galerie.

gallows-bird ['gæləʊzbɜːd] *n F* gibier *m* de potence.

galluses ['gæləsiz] *npl A P* bretelles *fpl*.

galoot [gə'luːt] *n esp NAm P* **1.** individu*/type *m*/mec *m*/client *m* **2.** lourdaud *m*/empoté *m*/godiche *m*.

galumph [gə'lʌmf] *vi F* caracoler/galoper lourdement; **to go galumphing around**, marcher comme un éléphant/charrier sa viande/déambuler avec ses gros godillots.

gam¹ [gæm] *n* **1.** *pl P* jambes*/guibolles *fpl*/gambettes *fpl* **2.** *F* bavette *f*/causette *f*.

gam² [gæm] *vi NAm* **1.** *P* se vanter/esbrouffer/en jeter/en installer **2.** *P* flirter.

game [geim] **I** *a F* **1. I'm game!** OK!/dac!/ça me botte!/je suis pour! **2.** crâne; **to be dead game**, être très courageux*/en avoir dans le ventre **3.** = **gammy II** *n* **1.** *P* **to be on the game**, racoler*/turfer/turbiner/faire le trottoir **2.** *F* travail/boulot; **he hasn't been in this game very long**, il fait ça depuis très peu **3.** *F* **I know your little game!** je vois votre mani-

gance!/je vois votre petit jeu!/je te vois venir! **4.** *F* **to have the game sewn up**, avoir la partie belle/en main; tenir le bon bout **5.** *F* **to play the game**, jouer le jeu. (*See* **army 2**; **badger 1**; **clip-game**; **fun II 2**; **play² 2**; **sack¹ 4**; **skin¹ 5** (*a*); **up¹ I 3**)

gamesmanship ['geimzmənʃip] *n F* l'art *m* de gagner.

gammer ['gæmər] *n A F* grand-mère/la vieille/la matronne.

gammon¹ ['gæmən] *n O P* bobards *mpl*/boniments *mpl*.

gammon² ['gæmən] *vtr O P* **1.** duper*/monter un bateau à (qn)/emmener (qn) en bateau **2.** emberlificoter.

gammy ['gæmi] *a F* boiteux/bancal/banban/béquillard; **he's got a gammy leg**, il a une patte folle.

gamp [gæmp] *n O F* parapluie*/riflard *m*/pébroc *m*.

gander¹ ['gændər] *n P* **to have/to take a gander**, jeter un coup d'œil*/bigler/zyeuter; **just take a gander (at that)!** mate-moi ça!/zyeute-moi ça!

gander² ['gændər] *vtr P* (*rare*) regarder*/lorgner/reluquer.

gang [gæŋ] *n* **1.** *P* **gang-bang/gang-shag**, viol collectif/barlu *m*/rodéo *m* **2.** *F* **gangland**, le milieu/la pègre.

ganga ['gændʒər] *n P* (*drugs*) marijuana*/gania *m*.

gang bang ['gæŋ'bæŋ], **gang shaf** ['gæŋ'ʃæg] *vtr P* violer (qn) à tour de rôle/passer (qn) à la casserole.

gangster ['gæŋstər] *n P* (*drugs*) (*a*) marijuana* (*b*) habitué(e) de la marijuana* (*c*) cigarette* de marijuana/joint *m*/stick *m*.

gang up ['gæŋ'ʌp] *vi F* **to gang up on s.o.**, former équipe/se liguer contre qn; s'acoquiner pour tomber qn; **they all ganged up on me**, ils se sont tous montés contre moi.

ganjah ['gændʒɑɪ], **ganji** ['gændʒi] *n P* (*drugs*) marijuana*. (*See* **bhang**; **ganga**; **gunji**)

gannet ['gænit] *n F* goinfre*/ bouffe-tout *m*/bec *m* à tout grain.

garbage ['gɑːbidʒ] *n* **1.** *F* camelote *f*/rossignols *mpl*/came *f* **2.** *P* bêtises*/boniments *mpl*/ bobards *mpl*/bidon *m*; **don't give me all that garbage!** ne me sers pas des conneries!/arrête de déconner! **that's a load of garbage!** ce ne sont que des conneries!/c'est de la merde! **3.** *P* mauvaise nourriture*/ ragougnasse *f* **4.** *P* drogue *f* de mauvaise qualité/foin *m* **5.** *P* résidu *m* après cuisson d'une drogue/fond *m* de culot **6.** *P* (*drugs*) amphétamines*/amphés *fpl* **7.** *P* (*computers*) erreur *f*/bévue*/ gaffe *f*.

garbo ['gɑːbou] *n Austr F* éboueur *m*/boueux *m*/boueur *m*.

garden ['gɑːdn] *n F* **1. to lead s.o. up the garden path**, faire marcher qn/faire voir des étoiles en plein midi/(em)mener qn en bateau **2. everything in the garden is lovely**, tout va comme sur des roulettes/ tout baigne dans l'huile/tout baigne dans le beurre. (*See* **bear-garden**)

gas[1] [gæs] **I** *a P* **1.** excellent*/ter- rible/super **2.** très amusant*/à crever de rire*/marrant/boyautant/ astap **II** *n* **1.** *F* bavardage *m* vide/palas(s) *m*/baratinage *m*/bidon *m*; **he's all gas**, il parle pour ne rien dire/tout ça c'est du vent; **to have a gas**, tailler une bavette **2.** *esp NAm F* (= *gasoline*) essence *f*/ jus *m*; **to step on the gas** (*i*) appuyer sur le champignon/donner plein gaz/foncer (*ii*) se dépêcher*/ se grouiller/se magner; **come on, step on the gas!** allez, magne-toi! **to run out of gas**, devenir fatigué*/être à bout de souffle **3.** *P* (*a*) qch d'excellent*/du tonnerre/de foutral; **what a gas!** c'est le (super-)pied!/ c'est génial (*b*) rigolade *f*; **it was a real gas!** c'était une sacrée mar-

rade/une franche rigolade/une bonne tranche (de rire)! **we had a real gas**, on s'en est payé une bonne tranche **4.** *P* **a gas meter bandit**, un faisandier/un escroc de bas étage.

gas[2] [gæs] *vi* **1.** *F* bavarder*/bara- tiner/jacter; **he never stops gassing**, il n'arrête pas de jacasser/bavasser **2.** *P* bonimenter/bourrer le crâne/ avoir (qn) au baratin **3.** *P* entourlouper/épater/époustoufler.

gasbag ['gæsbæg] *n F* moulin *m* à paroles/beau parleur/phraseur *m*.

gash [gæʃ] **I** *a P* de rechange/en surplus/en rab(iot) **II** *n* **1.** *P* rab(iot) *m* **2.** *P* femme*/fendue *f*/ fumelle *f* **3.** *V* sexe de la femme*/ fente *f*/crevasse *f* (*b*) coït*/giclée *f*.

gash-hound ['gæʃhaund] *n O P* coureur *m* de jupons/cavaleur *m*/ chaud lapin.

gasket ['gæskit] *n F* **to blow a gas- ket**, se mettre en colère*/sortir de ses gonds/piquer une crise.

gasp [gɑːsp] *n F* **to be at one's last gasp**, être à bout/être au bout du rouleau.

gasper ['gɑːspər] *n P* cigarette*/ cibiche *f*/sèche *f*/pipe *f*.

gassed [gæst] *a P* **1.** ivre*/ asphyxié/allumé **2.** tordu de rire*/ époustouflé/renversé/plié en deux.

gasser ['gæsər] *n P* **1.** baratineur *m*/fort *m* en gueule **2.** *O* une merveille/du bath/du badour.

gassy ['gæsi] *a P* **1.** bavard/bara- tineur/jacasseur **2.** = **groovy**.

gas up ['gæs'ʌp] *vi NAm* **1.** *F* faire le plein (d'essence) **2.** *P* animer/ exciter/stimuler/émoustiller.

gat [gæt] *n NAm O P* revolver*/pis- tolet *m*/calibre *m*.

gate-crash ['geitkræʃ] *vtr F* se rendre à une réception, une boum, une fête, etc, sans être invité/ resquiller/se glisser à une fête.

gate-crasher ['geitkræʃər] *n F* passe-volant *m*/resquilleur *m*; **champion gate-crasher**, roi *m* des resquilleurs.

gate-post ['geitpoust] *n F* **between you and me and the gate-post**, entre quat'zyeux/entre quat'murs/de toi z'à moi.

gauge [geidʒ] *n P* = **gage 3.**

Gawd [gɔːd] *n P* (= *God*) **oh my Gawd!** ah mon Dieu!/bon Dieu! **Gawd 'elp us!/Gawd love us!** Dieu merci!/bon diou!/grands dieux!

gawk [gɔːk] *n O F* **1.** godiche *mf*/niais *m*/navet *m* **2. big gawk**, grand escogriffe/asperge montée.

gawky ['gɔːki] *a F* degingandé.

gay [gei] **I** *a F* **1. gay deceivers**, seins* artificiels/flotteurs *mpl* **2.** homosexuel/pédale/gai/pédé; **gay bar**, boîte homo; **he's as gay as a coot**, c'est une pédale/une folle affichée. (*See* **dog¹ 9**) **II** *n P* homosexuel*/homo *m*/pédé *m*/pédalo *m*.

gayfest ['geifest] *n F* réunion d'homosexuels/de pédés.

gazump [gə'zʌmp] *vtr F* **1.** escroquer* en faisant monter le prix d'une propriété au dernier moment; faire valser les prix **2.** escroquer*/arnaquer/carotter.

gazumper [gə'zʌmpər] *n F* escroc* en propriétés immobilières.

gear [giər] **I** *a P* (*esp regional*) excellent*/du tonnerre/super **II** *n* **1.** *F* biens *mpl*/possessions *fpl*. (*See* **marriage**) **2.** *F* attirail *m*/barda *m*/bataclan *m*; **he leaves his gear out everywhere**, il laisse traîner ses affaires partout **3.** *F* (*esp fashionable*) vêtements*/nippes *fpl*/frusques *fpl*/fringues *fpl* **4.** *P* attirail* de drogué/popote *f*/artillerie *f*/kit *m* **5.** *P* butin*/rafle *f*/fade *m* **6.** *F* **to be in high gear**, être survolté/péter le feu; **to be in low gear**, ne pas avoir la forme/ne pas avoir la frite/ne pas avoir la pêche **7.** *Austr P* fausses dents*/

râtelier *m* **8.** *P* **gear stick**, pénis*/manche *m*/arbalète *f*.

geared up ['giəd'ʌp] *a&pp F* **to be all geared up for sth**, être fin prêt/être conditionné pour qch.

gee [dʒiː] **I** *excl esp NAm F* **gee (whiz(z))!** ah, dis donc!/mince!/eh ben!/ben mon vieux! **II** *P* **1.** = **G 1, 2 2.** *NAm O* individu*/mec *m*; **front gee**, homme *m* de paille/couverture *f*; **a hip gee**, un mec à la coule; un pote/un régulier.

geed up ['dʒiːd'ʌp] *a P* **1.** sous l'effet des drogues*/chargé/camé/high/défoncé **2.** fin prêt/conditionné pour faire qch.

gee-gee ['dʒiːdʒi] *n F* **1.** (*esp child's language*) cheval*/dada *m* **2. to follow the gee-gees**, jouer aux courtines/suivre les gails/les canassons. (*See* **flutter 2**)

geek¹ [giːk] *n P* **1.** *Austr* coup d'œil*; **give us a geek**, fais voir ça **2.** *NAm* individu bête *ou* désagréable/crétin *m*/nœud *m*/con *m*/enculé *m*.

geek² [giːk] *vtr Austr P* regarder*/mater/zyeuter qch.

gee up ['dʒiː'ʌp] *vtr&i* **1.** *F* (*to a horse*) **gee up!** hue!/au trot! **2.** *O* **he gee-ed them up** (*a*) *P* il les a montés l'un contre l'autre (*b*) *F* il les a fait se dégrouiller. (*See* **geed up**)

Geez(e)! [dʒiːz] *excl P* (= *Jesus*) bon Dieu!/eh ben ça alors! (*See* **Jeeze!**)

geezed up ['dʒiːzd'ʌp] *a NAm P* **1.** ivre*/bit(t)uré/blindé/rétamé **2.** drogué*/camé/high.

geezer ['giːzər] *n P* **1.** homme*/type *m*/mec *m*; **he's a silly old geezer**, c'est un vieux schnock/un vieux débris **2.** (*drugs*) piqûre*/shoot *m*/fixe *m*/piquouse *f*.

gel [gel] *n F* = **gal.**

gelt [gelt] *n P* argent*/pognon *m*/soudure *f*/fric *m*/flouse *m*.

gen [dʒen] *n F* renseignements*/ tuyaux *mpl*/info *f*; **to give s.o. the gen,** tuyauter qn/mettre qn à la page/rencarder qn; **I need some gen on that business,** il faut me tuyauter sur cette affaire/je veux connaître le papier à propos de cette affaire.

genned up ['dʒend'ʌp] *a&pp F* **to get genned up,** se mettre au courant/se rencarder; **to be all genned up,** être rencardé/être à la page/ être au parfum.

gent [dʒent] *n F* (*abbr = gentleman*) **1. a real gent,** un monsieur/un type bien **2.** *pl* **the gents,** WC* pour hommes; **to go to the gents,** aller aux chiottes/aller se faire une vidange/aller faire sa goutte.

genuine ['dʒenjuin] *a F* **1.** régulier; **a genuine guy,** un type réglo **2. the genuine article,** du vrai/de l'authentique; **it's your genuine article,** c'est pas de la camelote/c'est du vrai de vrai/c'est pas du toc.

gen up ['dʒen'ʌp] *vtr F* **to gen s.o. up,** tuyauter qn/mettre qn au parfum/rencarder qn.

Geordie ['dʒɔːdi] *a&n F* **1.** originaire *mf* de la région de Tyneside **2.** dialecte parlé dans la région de Tyneside.

George [dʒɔːdʒ] *Prn F* **1.** *O* **by George!** sapristi!/mince alors! **2.** (*avions*) pilote *m* automatique/ Georges *m*.

gerdoing! gerdoying! [gə'dɔiŋ] *excl F* boum (badaboum)!/pan!/ vlan! (*See* **doing!**; **kerdoing!**)

gertcha! gertcher! ['gɔːtʃə(r)] *excl P* (*cockney*) = (*i*) va te promener! (*ii*) arrête ton char!

get¹ [get] *n P* = **git II.**

get² [get] *vtr* **1.** *F* comprendre/ piger/entraver; **I don't get you,** je (ne) pige pas/je n'entrave que dalle; **get me?/get my drift?/get what I mean?** tu y es?/tu saisis?/tu piges?/compris? **2.** *F* **I'll get you for that!** j'aurai ta peau/je t'aurai

au tournant/je te louperai pas/tu me le paieras! **I've got him,** je le tiens **3.** *F* **it gets me when . . . ,** ça m'énerve/ça me crispe/ça m'agace/ je supporte pas quand . . . ; **he really gets my goat/my back up,** il me court/tape sur le système **4.** *F* **to get it in the neck,** écoper/en prendre pour son grade **5.** *P* **we got trouble** (= *we have trouble*), on a des emmerdes; **I got rhythm** (= *I have rhythm*), j'ai du swing; **(you) got a light?** (= *do you have a light?*), t'as du feu? **6.** *F* **to get ten years,** attraper/piger dix berges/ (s')en prendre pour dix ans **7.** *F* **you've got me there,** là tu me la coupe/tu me colles; je donne ma langue au chat **8.** *F* émouvoir/ secouer/emballer; **this film gets you right there,** ce film te prend aux tripes; ce film te retourne l'estomac **9.** *F* tuer*/bousiller/zigouiller; **he always gets his man,** il ne rate jamais son homme/il met toujours dans le mille **10.** *F* arrêter*/épingler **11.** *F* **to get there,** réussir/ arriver/se débrouiller; **we're getting there,** on arrive à la fin; **not to get anywhere,** n'aboutir à rien **12.** *F* **to get going,** (*a*) se dépêcher*/se magner/se dégrouiller; **get going!** allez, en route! (*b*) se mettre au travail*/se mettre en branle **13.** *P* **to get behind it,** (*drugs*) être défoncé/être high **14.** *P* **to get with it,** se mettre à la mode/dans le vent/à la coule **15.** *P* **to get shot of sth,** se débarrasser de* qch/ larguer qch.

get about ['getə'baut] *vi F* = **get around.**

get across ['getə'krɔs] *vtr&i F* faire comprendre/faire piger/ éclairer; **I just can't get this across to him,** pas moyen de lui faire piger ce truc.

get along ['getə'lɔŋ] *vi F* **1. I must be getting along,** il faut que je m'en aille/je me tire **2. get along with you!** (*i*) va te promener!/ débarrasse (le plancher)! (*ii*) vas-y

voir!/tu charries!/arrête ton char!
(*iii*) je n'en crois rien/allons donc!/
tu me prends pour qui? **3. to get
along with s.o.,** bien s'entendre avec
qn **4.** se défendre; **I'm getting
along fine,** je me défends/je me
débrouille.

get around ['getə'raund] *vi F* **1.**
it's getting around that.... le bruit
court que... **2.** rouler sa bosse/
circuler/faire son temps **3.** = **get
round 1 4. get around to doing
sth,** arriver à faire qch **5.** circon-
venir/surmonter (une difficulté, etc).

get at ['get'æt] *vtr F* **1.** acheter/
soudoyer/graisser la patte à (qn)
2. what are you getting at? où
voulez-vous en venir? **3.** asticoter/
chercher des crosses à (qn); **stop
getting at me, will you?** arrête de
me les casser/de me courir! **4.** tri-
poter/tripatouiller/trifouiller.

get-at-able ['get'ætəbl] *a F* acces-
sible/d'accès facile; **our boss is very
get-at-able,** notre patron n'est pas
enfermé dans sa tour.

getaway ['getəwei] *n F* évasion *f*/la
belle/la cavale; **to make a quick
getaway,** s'évader*/s'éclipser/se
faire la belle/faire un plongeon;
getaway car, voiture* de fuite/
bagnole *f* de cavale.

get away ['getə'wei] *vi* **1.** *F* **get
away (with you)!** (*i*) laisse tomber!/
fiche-moi la paix!/barca!/écrase! (*ii*)
je ne mords pas!/ça ne prend pas!
2. *F* **to get away with it,** s'en tirer à
bon compte; **he won't get away with
it,** il ne l'emportera pas au paradis/
il ne s'en sortira pas comme ça **3.**
F **there's no getting away from it,** il
n'y a pas moyen d'en sortir **4.** *P*
**to get it away = to get it off (get
off 4** (*b*)). (*See* **end 2**)

get by ['get'bai] *vi F* s'en tirer/en
être quitte/s'en contenter; **I get by,**
je me débrouille.

get down ['get'daun] *vtr F* **1. to
get s.o. down,** irriter/déprimer/
déconcerter qn; taper sur le sys-

tème à qn; foutre le cafard/le noir
à qn; **what gets me down is his attitude,** ce qui me fout en l'air c'est
son attitude; **don't let it get you
down!** ne te laisse pas abattre! **2.
to get down to it,** s'y mettre/en
mettre un coup; **come on, get down
to some work,** allez, au boulot!

get off ['get'ɔf] *vtr&i* **1.** *F* **to get
off lightly,** s'en tirer à bon compte/
bien s'en sortir **2.** *P* **get off!** fous-
moi la paix!/arrête ton char! **3.** *F*
to get off with s.o., faire une touche
4. *V* **to get (it) off** (*a*) avoir un
orgasme*/prendre son pied/
s'envoyer en l'air/lâcher le jus (*b*)
faire l'amour*; **to get (it) off with a
bird/a chick,** s'envoyer/se faire une
nana (*c*) se masturber*/se branler
5. *P* se doper/se défoncer; **heroin
really gets him off/he gets off on
heroin,** il se défonce à l'héroïne/
l'héro c'est son truc pour s'envoyer
en l'air **6.** *F* **get it off your chest!**
vide ton sac!/accouche! **7.** *F* **to
tell s.o. where to get off,** réprimander* sévèrement qn/dire à qn
ses quatre vérités/envoyer qn
promener **8.** *P* **to get off on sth,**
être transporté par qch; **I really get
off on their music,** leur musique
c'est le (super-)pied/ça me branche.

get on ['get'ɔn] *vi F* **get on with
you!** (*i*) arrête ton char! (*ii*) je n'en
crois rien!/tu me prends pour qui?
(*iii*) débarrasse (le plancher)!

get on to ['get'ɔntuː] *vtr F* **1.**
découvrir*; **I got on to sth really
interesting,** j'ai mis la main sur un
truc vraiment intéressant **2.** se
mettre en rapport avec (qn)/con-
tacter (qn) **3.** (*drugs*) **to get on to
heroin,** passer à l'héroïne/à l'héro.

get-out ['getaut] *n F* **1.** esquive *f*/
moyen *m* de sortie **2.** = **get-up.**

get out ['get'aut] *vi F* **1. to get out
from under,** se tirer d'affaire/se
dépatouiller **2. to get out while the
going's good,** se ranger tant que les
affaires marchent.

get over ['get'ouvər] *vtr F* **1. I can't get over it!** je n'en reviens pas/j'en reste baba!/ça m'a coupé le souffle **2. let's get it over with,** finissons-en!

get-rich-quick ['get'ritʃ'kwik] *a F* véreux; **get-rich-quick plan/scheme,** projet qui promet la lune.

get round ['get'raund] *vtr&i F* **1.** cajoler/enjôler; **you can't get round me like that,** tu ne m'auras pas comme ça **2. = get around 4.**

get through ['get'θruː] *vtr&i* **1.** *F* **to get through to s.o.,** faire comprendre qch à qn/faire piger qn **2.** *F* **to get through the month,** boucler son mois/joindre les deux bouts **3.** *P* obtenir des drogues*/se garnir/ trouver la cheville/trouver le joint **4.** *F* **to get through some work,** abattre du travail*; **to get through a lot of money,** dépenser* beaucoup d'argent*/bouffer du pognon.

get-together ['getəgeðər] *n F* réunion amicale/retrouvaille *f.*

get together ['get(t)ə'geðər] *vtr F* **to get it together** (*i*) se ressaisir/ s'éclaircir les idées/éclairer sa lanterne (*ii*) se magner le train/se grouiller.

get-up ['getʌp] *n F* vêtements*/ fripes *fpl*/nippes *fpl*/loques *fpl*; **he was wearing some decidedly peculiar get-up,** il portait des fringues vraiment bizarres/il avait des sapes vraiment pas banales.

get up ['get'ʌp] *vtr V* **to get it up** (*a*) faire l'amour*/s'envoyer en l'air (*b*) avoir une érection*/la trique; marquer midi; **he can't get it up,** il bande mou/il débande.

get-up-and-go ['getʌpən(d)'gou] **I** *a F* plein d'allant/plein d'entrain/ dynamique **II** *n* **to be full of get-up-and-go,** péter le feu/la santé; avoir la frite/la pêche.

ghastly ['gɑːstli] *a F* abominable/ hideux; **the weather's ghastly,** il fait un putain de temps/un temps pourri; **what a ghastly woman!**

quelle femme* abominable!/quelle sale chipie!

gherkin ['gəːkin] *n P* pénis*/ gourdin *m*/gourde *f* à poils; **to jerk one's gherkin,** se masturber*/tirer son coup/se taper la colonne.

ghetto blaster ['getou'blæstər] *n NAm* lecteur *m* de cassettes stéréo portable/magnéto (stéréo) portatif.

ghost [goust] *vi F* **to ghost (for)** s.o., remplacer qn/faire le nègre.

GI ['dʒiː'ai] *abbr US F* **1.** (= *government issue*) ce qui vient de l'intendance militaire américaine **2.** soldat* américain; **GI Joe,** le type du biffin américain pendant la deuxième guerre mondiale.

giddy up! ['gidi'ʌp] *excl F* (*esp child's language*) (*to a horse*) hue!/ au trot! (*See* **gee up 1**)

gift [gift] *n F* qch de pas difficile*/ du beurre; **it was a real gift,** c'était du nougat.

gig¹ [gig] *n esp NAm* **1.** *F* joujou *m* quelconque/sucette *f* **2.** *V* (*rare*) anus*/rondibé *m*/trou *m*; **up your gig!** je t'emmerde! **3.** *V* sexe de la femme*/baba *m*/crac *m* **4.** *O F* réjouissances*/surboum *f*/bamboche *f* **5.** *F* (*jazz, rock, etc*) engagement *m* d'un soir/gig *m*; **to do/to play a gig,** jouer/faire un gig **6.** *Austr F* coup *m* d'œil **7.** *Austr P* individu bête*/gourde *f*/crétin *m.*

gig² [gig] *vi* **1.** *F* jouer dans un groupe (de jazz, de rock) **2.** *F* regarder*/reluquer/zyeuter **3.** *P* taquiner/tourmenter/faire enrager (qn).

giggle ['gigl] *n* **1.** *F* **we did it (just) for a giggle,** c'était pour rigoler/on l'a fait histoire de rigoler un peu; **it was all a bit of a giggle,** on s'est bien marré/on s'en est payé une bonne tranche; **what a giggle!** quelle bonne rigolade! **2.** *F* **to get the giggles,** attraper le fou rire **3.** *P* (*drugs*) **giggle smoke/ weed,** cigarette* de marijuana/joint *m*/stick *m* **4.** *NAm F* **giggle water,** champagne *m*/champ' *m*.

gild [gild] *vtr P* (*of police*) **to gild the lily,** exagérer/en rajouter/noircir le tableau/mettre le paquet.

gills [gilz] *npl* **1.** *P* **to be stewed to the gills,** être complètement ivre*/ avoir sa cuite/être bourré à bloc **2. to be a bit green about the gills** (*i*) avoir peur*/avoir les jetons (*ii*) être sur le point de vomir*/avoir envie de dégueuler.

gimme ['gimi] *abbr F* (= *give me*) donne!/aboule! (*See* **skin**[1] **10**)

gimmick ['gimik] *n* **1.** *F* attrape *f*/tour *m*/combine *f*/astuce *f*/truc *m* **2.** *P* attrape-couillons *m*/truc *m* publicitaire **3.** *F* gadget *m*/truc *m*/ machin *m* **4.** *pl P* (*drugs*) attirail* de camé/artillerie *f*/popote *f*/kit *m*.

gimmicky ['gimiki] *a F* rempli de trucs *mpl*.

gin [dʒin] *n Austr P* femme aborigène.

ginger ['dʒindʒər] *n F* **1.** rouquin(e) *m(f)*/poil *m* de carotte **2. to have (a lot of) ginger,** avoir de l'entrain *m*/péter la santé/péter le feu **3. ginger group,** groupe *m* de pression **4.** (*RS* = *ginger beer* = **queer**) homosexuel*; **he's a bit ginger,** il fait très pédé/tapette.

ginger up ['dʒindʒər'ʌp] *vtr F* émoustiller/mettre de l'entrain dans/donner un coup de fouet à.

gink [giŋk] *n esp NAm P* (*a*) drôle *m* de paroissien/de zèbre (*b*) pauvre type *m*/couillon *m*/salaud*.

gin-mill ['dʒinmil] *NAm*, **gin-palace** ['dʒinpæləs] *n A F* bar mal famé/boui-boui *m*/bouge *m*/ assommoir *m*.

ginormous [dʒai'nɔːməs] *a F* colossal/maous(se)/babylonien/ (h)énaurme.

gip [dʒip] *n F* **1. to give s.o. gip,** tomber sur qn à bras raccourcis/ tomber sur le paletot à qn **2. my rheumatism is giving me gip,** mes

rhumatismes me font voir trente-six chandelles/m'en font déguster.

gippo ['dʒipou] *n P* romanichel *m*/ romani *m*/manouche *m*.

girl [gəːl] *n P* **1.** (*drugs*) cocaïne*/ fillette *f*/coco *f* **2.** homosexuel*/ chouquette *f*/tante *f* **3. working girl,** prostituée*/persilleuse *f*/ gagneuse *f*. (*See* **bar-girl**; **B-girl**; **call girl**; **cover-girl**; **glamour-girl**; **yes-girl**)

girlie ['gəːli] *n* **1.** *attrib F* fillette *f*/ girl *f*; **girlie show,** spectacle *m* de girls; **girlie magazines,** presse *f* de charme; revues *fpl* de fesses/de cul **2.** *P esp NAm* prostituée*/fille *f*.

gis [giz] *abbr P* = **giz.**

git [git] **I** *excl P* file!/fiche le camp!/décolle! **II** *n P* individu*/ type *m*/mec *m*; **you stupid git!** espèce de con!/espèce de nœud!

give [giv] *vtr F* **1. don't give me that!** (ne) me raconte pas d'histoires!/ne me la fais pas! **2. to give it to s.o.,** réprimander* qn/ passer un savon à qn/sonner les cloches à qn **3. give it all you've got!** fais le maxi(mum)!/donne un (bon) coup de collier! **4. to know what gives,** être à la page/dans le vent/à la coule; **what gives?** (*i*) salut! (*ii*) qu'est-ce qui se fricote? (*iii*) quoi de neuf? **5.** avouer*; **give!** accouche! (*See* **vocals**)

give-away ['givəwei] **I** *a F* **to sell sth at a give-away price,** vendre qch à un prix défiant toute concurrence/pour trois fois rien **II** *n F* **1.** article sacrifié **2. a (dead) give-away,** geste *m* (mot, etc) qui en dit long.

give over ['giv'ouvər] *vi F* renoncer à (qch)/dételer/remiser; **give over, will you?** laisse tomber, veux-tu?/ écrase!

giz [giz] *abbr P* (= *give us* = *give me*) donne(-moi); **giz a/gizza hand with this!** tu me donnes un coup de main?

gizzard ['gizəd] *n F* **that sticks in my gizzard**, je ne digère pas ça/ça me reste en travers du gosier; ça me fout en rogne.

glad [glæd] *a F* **glad rags**, les plus beaux vêtements* de sa garde-robe/des nippes *fpl* du dimanche; **to put on one's glad rags**, se mettre sur son trente et un. (*See* **eye 4**)

glamour-boy ['glæməbɔi] *n F* (*a*) séducteur *m*/joli cœur/jeune premier (*b*) un beau mâle/un beau mec.

glamour-girl ['glæməgəːl] *n F* (*a*) ensorceleuse *f*/vamp *f* (*b*) beau morceau/prix *m* de Diane/joli lot.

glamour-puss ['glæməpus] *n O F* pin-up *f*/ensorceleuse *f*.

glass[1] [glɑːs] *a F* (*boxer*) **to have a glass jaw**, avoir la mâchoire en verre.

glass[2] [glɑːs] *vtr P* taillader (qn) avec du verre cassé (dans une rixe).

glasshouse ['glɑːshaus] *n P* (*mil*) prison*/ militaire/grosse lourde.

glassy-eyed ['glɑːsi'aid], **glazed** [gleizd] *a F* ivre*/blindé/bituré/dans les vapes.

glim [glim] *n P* lampe *f* de poche/lampe-poche *f*/loupiot(t)e *f*.

glims [glimz] *npl O P* **1.** yeux*/quinquets *mpl*/lanternes *fpl* **2.** lumières/ca(le)bombe *f*/calbiche *f*; **to douse the glims**, étouffer la ca(le)bombe **3.** phares *mpl* (d'une voiture) **4.** lunettes*/bernicles *fpl*/carreaux *mpl*.

globes [gloubz] *npl P* seins*/globes *mpl*/ballons *mpl*.

glory ['glɔːri] *n F* **1.** **he's got the glory**, il tombe dans la bondieuserie **2.** **to go to glory** (*a*) mourir* (*b*) se délabrer/dégringoler/aller à dame **3.** **to get all the glory**, récolter toute la gloire/décrocher le pompon **4.** **glory be!** grand Dieu!/Seigneur!

glory-hole ['glɔːrihoul] *n F* capharnaüm *m*/cagibi *m*.

glossies ['glɔsiz] *npl F* **the glossies**, des revues *fpl*/des magazines *mpl* (sur papier couché) de luxe.

glow [glou] *n NAm F* **to have/to get a glow on**, être légèrement ivre*/être gris/pompette/éméché.

glue-factory ['gluːfæktəri], **glue-pot** ['gluːpɔt] *n V* (*rare*) sexe de la femme*/baveux *m*.

glue sniffer ['gluːsnifər] personne, esp adolescent, qui se drogue en respirant de la colle/sniffeur, -euse.

glue-sniffing ['gluːsnifiŋ] *n P* **to go glue-sniffing**, aller sniffer de la colle. (*See* **sniff**; **sniffer**)

G-man ['dʒiːmæn] *n NAm F* agent *m* du Deuxième Bureau américain.

gnashers ['næʃəz] *npl P* dents*/crocs *mpl*/croquantes *fpl*.

gnat [næt] *n F* **1.** **gnat's piss**, mauvaise boisson (*esp* bière de qualité inférieure)/bibine *f*/jus *m* de chaussettes/pipi *m* de chat **2.** **gnat bites**, petits seins*/mandarines *fpl*/œufs *mpl* sur le plat.

go[1] [gou] **I** *a F* en bon ordre/OK; **all systems are go/it's all systems go**, on a le feu vert **II** *n F* **1.** (*a*) **no go!** rien à faire!/ça ne marche pas!/pas mèche! (*b*) **it's no go**, rien à faire/cela ne prend pas/c'est nib/c'est midi (sonné) **2.** **to have a go at s.o.**, s'en prendre à qn/dire deux mots à qn/sonner les cloches à qn **3.** **to be always on the go**, avoir la bougeotte/être toujours sur la brèche/avoir toujours un pied en l'air; **it's all go!** on n'a pas une minute à soi!/ça n'arrête pas! **4.** **have a go!** tente la chance!/à toi de jouer! **have another go!** remets ça! **5.** **he's got no go in him**, il est ramollo/il est mou comme une chiffe; il n'a pas la frite **6.** **to put some go into it**, y mettre de l'entrain/du piment **7.** **to give sth a go**, tenter le coup/s'attaquer à qch **8.** **at/in one go**, d'un seul coup/trait; tout d'une haleine **9.** **to be all the go**, faire rage/faire

fureur **10. (right) from the word
go,** dès le départ/tout au début.
(*See* **bag² 5; touch¹ 2**)

go² [gou] *vtr&i* **1.** *F* **how goes it?**
comment ça va? **2.** *F* **go it!** lance-
toi!/fonce! **3.** *P* (*drugs*) **to be
gone,** être défoncé/planer/être high
4. *F* mourir; **when you've got to go,
you've got to go,** quand faut y aller,
faut y aller.

go-ahead ['gouəhed] **I** *a F* **a go-
ahead young man with go-ahead
ideas,** un garçon entreprenant qui
voit loin; un jeune loup **II** *F* **to
get the go-ahead,** avoir le feu vert.

goalie ['gouli] *n F* (*abbr* = *goal-
keeper*) gardien *m* de but/goal *m*.

go along with ['gouə'lɒŋwið] *vtr*
F accepter (qch) en tout et pour
tout; **I'll go along with that,** je suis
tout à fait d'accord/je suis partant;
I can't go along with that, je ne suis
pas d'accord; je ne marche pas.

goat [gout] *n F* **1. to get s.o.'s
goat,** ennuyer*/irriter/ahurir qn;
he gets my goat, il me tape sur le
système/il me fait chier **2. old
goat,** vieux* birbe/vieille bique/
vieille baderne/vieux schnock.

gob¹ [gɒb] *n P* **1.** bouche*/gueule
f; **to keep one's gob shut,** se taire*/
la boucler/ne pas piper; **shut your
gob!** la ferme! **stick that in your
gob and shut up!** fourre-toi ça dans
ton clapoir et boucle-la! **2.**
crachat*/glaviot *m*/mollard *m* **3.**
NAm marin*/cachalot *m*/mataf *m*.

gob² [gɒb] *vi P* cracher*/mollarder.
(*See* **gob¹ 2**)

gobble ['gɒbl] *vtr V* (*not common*)
faire une fellation* à (qn)/sucer
(qn)/faire un pompier à (qn).

gobbledegook ['gɒbldiguːk] *n F*
jargon *m*/charabia *m*/baragouin *m*.

gobbler ['gɒblər] *n V* **1.** homosexuel*/pédé *m*/pédalo *m*/tante *f* **2.**
(*cocksucker*) suceur *m*/pipeur *m*.

gobble up ['gɒbl'ʌp] *vtr Austr P*
arrêter*/agrafer/coffrer (qn).

gobstopper ['gɒb'stɒpər] *n F* bonbon dur.

goby ['goubi] *n P* (= *go-between*)
messager *m*/matignon *m*.

go-by ['goubai] *n F* **to give s.o. the
go-by,** battre froid à qn/snober qn/
faire grise mine à qn; **to give sth
the go-by,** dépasser qch/esquiver
qch.

God, god [gɒd] *n* **1.** *F* **by God!**
(sacré) nom de Dieu!/grands dieux!
my God!/good God! bon Dieu (de
bon Dieu)! **God Almighty!** Dieu
Tout-Puissant! **God only knows,**
Dieu seul le sait **2.** *P* **(the) God
man,** prêtre*/l'homme du bon
Dieu/cureton *m* **3.** (*theatre*) *F* **the
gods,** le poulailler/la poulaille/le
paradis/le paradou/les titis *mpl*.
(*See* **tin I 3**)

god-awful ['gɒd'ɔːful] *n P* répu-
gnant/dégueulasse/puant/ infect;
**stuck out here in this god-awful
place,** bloqué dans ce trou perdu/
de merde.

goddam ['gɒdæm], **goddamned**
['gɒdæmd] *a P* sacré/satané; **that
goddam idiot,** ce putain de con; **the
goddamned car's broken down
again,** cette saloperie de bagnole est
encore tombée en panne/en rade.

goddammit! ['gɒd'dæmit] *excl P*
sacré nom (de nom)!/merde!/
putain!

godfer ['gɒdfər] *n* (*RS* = *God forbid* = *kid*) *P* enfant*/gosse *mf*/
môme *mf*. (*See* **dustbin**)

God forbid ['gɒdfəbid] *n* (*RS* =
kid) *P* = **godfer**.

go down ['gou'daun] *vi* **1.** *F* (*uni-
versities, etc*) (*a*) finir ses études
universitaires (*b*) partir en vacances
2. *F* tomber malade*; **to go down
with sth nasty,** attraper/choper la
crève **3.** *F* **my dinner won't go
down,** mon dîner a du mal à
passer/ne descend pas **4.** *F* **if it goes
down well with the public,** le public
l'avale tout rond; **that won't go
down with me,** ça ne prend pas

avec moi; **my idea went down like a ton of bricks,** mon projet est tombé à l'eau/a fait un bide total/s'est complètement cassé la gueule **5.** *esp NAm F* **what's going down?** que se passe-t-il?/quoi de neuf? **it's going down tonight,** c'est prévu pour ce soir **6.** *F* être mis en prison*/aller en taule; **he went down for ten,** il a chopé dix ans de prison* **7.** *V* **to go down on s.o.** (*i*) faire une fellation* à qn/sucer qn/ tailler une pipe à qn (*ii*) pratiquer un cunnilinctus* à qn/sucer qn/ brouter le cresson.

goer ['gouər] *n P* **1.** she's a real **goer,** c'est une chaude de la pince/ c'est une chaude lapine; elle est bien bandante; elle a la cuisse légère **2.** expert *m*/calé *m*/fortiche *m*.

gofer ['goufər] *n F* larbin *m*/ lampiste *m*/bonniche *f*.

go for ['goufɔːr, 'goufər] *vtr F* **1. to go for s.o.** (*a*) rentrer dans le chou à qn/tomber sur le poil à qn (*b*) avoir une prise de bec avec qn **2.** aller chercher/essayer d'obtenir; **let's go for it!** allons-y! **3.** être entiché de/se toquer de; **I don't go for that,** cela ne m'emballe pas/ça ne me dit pas grand-chose/ça me botte pas tellement **4. everything's going for him/he's really got something going for him,** tout va très bien pour lui. (*See* **way II**)

go-getter ['gougetər] *n F* arriviste *mf*/personne qui a les dents longues.

go-getting ['gougetiŋ] *a F* opportuniste/ambitieux/arriviste.

goggle-box ['gɔglbɔks] *n F* télé *f*/ boîte *f* à images/téloche *f*/ (*See* **box¹ 2**; **idiot-box**; **lantern**)

goggle-eyed ['gɔgl'aid] *a F* avec les yeux en boules de loto/qui sortent de la tête.

goggles ['gɔglz] *npl P* lunettes*/ pare-brise *m*/bernicles *fpl*.

going ['gouiŋ] *n F* **to get out while**

the **going's good,** partir* pendant que c'est possible/que la voie est libre/qu'on a le vent en poupe/ qu'on en a l'occase; **we made good going on that journey,** on a bien roulé pendant ce voyage; **his speech was a bit heavy going,** son discours traînait en longueur/était plutôt rasoir.

going-over ['gouiŋ'ouvər] *n F* **to give s.o. a going-over** (*a*) battre* qn/passer qn à tabac/tabasser qn/ amocher qn; **the cops gave him a good going-over,** les flics lui ont filé une bonne tabassée/l'ont passé à tabac (*b*) réprimander* qn/passer un savon à qn/sonner les cloches à qn (*c*) fouiller qn/faire la barbote à qn.

goings-on ['gouiŋz'ɔn] *npl F* conduite *f*/manège *m*/manigances *fpl*; **such goings-on!** en voilà des façons!; **I've heard of your goings-on,** j'en ai appris de belles sur vous; **there were some strange goings-on at the cemetery,** il se passait des trucs plutôt bizarres/il s'en passait de drôles/il faisait un drôle de cinéma au cimetière.

gold [gould] *n P* **1.** argent*/pèze *m*/flouze *m* **2.** (*drugs*) **(Acapulco) gold,** marijuana* de bonne qualité/ gold *m*. (*See* **dust¹ 2** (*b*))

goldbrick¹ ['gouldbrik] *n NAm P* **1.** paresseux*/tire-au-flanc *m*/ ramier *m* **2.** une fille* tartignole/ une mocheté.

goldbrick² ['gouldbrik] *vtr&i NAm P* **1.** paresser à son travail/tirer au cul/tirer au flanc/se défiler **2.** duper*/estamper/arnaquer (qn).

goldbricker ['gouldbrikər] *n NAm P* **1.** = **goldbrick¹1 2.** escroc*/ estampeur *m*/arnaqueur *m*.

gold-digger ['gould'digər] *n F* aventurière *f*/croqueuse *f* de diamants/gigolette *f*.

golden ['gould(ə)n] *a* **1.** *F* **golden disc,** disque *m* d'or (le millionième) **2.** *F* **golden opportunity,** affaire *f*

d'or/occasion rêvée **3.** *F* doré/
beurré/en or **4.** *F* excellent*/
superbe/doré sur tranche; **he's our
golden boy,** c'est notre chéri/le
chouchou à tous; c'est la
coqueluche (du bureau, de l'atelier,
etc) **5.** *P* (*homosexuals*) **golden
shower,** urine *f*/pipi *m*/pisse *f*. (*See*
handshake; **queen¹ 2**)

goldfish-bowl ['gouldfiʃboul] *n F*
maison *f* de verre/place *f* publique;
it's like living in a goldfish bowl,
c'est comme vivre dans une maison
de verre.

goldmine ['gouldmain] *n F* situation lucrative/mine *f* d'or/filon *m*;
**the MD doesn't realise he's sitting
on top of a goldmine,** le P-DG ne
se rend pas compte qu'il est assis
sur une mine d'or.

gollion ['gɔliən] *n Austr P*
crachat*/graillon *m*.

golly! ['gɔli] *excl O F* **(by) golly!**
mince alors!/flûte!

goma ['goumə] *n P* (*drugs*) opium
brut/vert; goma *m*.

gone [gɔn] *a P* **1.** parti (sous
l'influence de l'alcool* ou du
hachisch*, etc; **he's really gone,** il
est complètement défoncé/il plane.
(*See* **go² 3**) **2. to be gone on s.o.,**
être toqué/entiché de qn; en pincer
pour qn **3.** (*pregnant*) **six months
gone,** enceinte de six mois. (*See*
far; **go on 6**)

goner ['gɔnər] *n F* **1.** (*a*) type fini/
foutu (*b*) chose perdue **2.** crevard
m/crevetant *m*; **he was almost a
goner,** il a failli mourir/avoir son
compte; il revient de loin.

gong [gɔn] *n* **1.** *F* médaille *f*/pas-
tille *f*/banane *f*/méduche *f* **2.** *P*
(*drugs*) pipe *f* à opium*/bambou *m*;
to kick the gong around, tirer sur le
bambou.

gonga ['gɔngə] *n P* anus*/anneau
m/troufignon *m*; **(you can) stick it
up your gonga!** tu peux te le met-
tre/te le fourrer quelque part!/tu

peux te le foutre là où je pense!
(*See* **stick² 3**)

gonif ['gɔnif] *n O P* **1.** voleur*/
chapardeur *m* **2.** homosexuel*/
pédé *m*/tante *f*.

gonna ['gənə, -gɔ] *P* = *going to*.

gonof, gonoph ['gɔnɔf] *n P* =
gonif.

goo [guː] *n F* **1.** sentimentalité
excessive/à la guimauve/à l'eau de
rose **2.** bouillabaisse *f*/ratatouille
f/colle *f*; **how do I get this goo off
my hands?** cette saleté de mélasse
me colle aux pattes, je ne peux pas
m'en débarrasser **3.** flatterie *f*/
pommade *f*/lèche *f*. (*See* **gooey**)

good [gud] *a F* **1. good God!/good
Lord!** bondieu! **2. good heavens!**
ciel! **3. good grief!** zut alors!/
merde alors! **4. good gracious!**
fichtre!/eh ben! **5. good egg!**
bath!/super!/bravo! **6.** (*prostitute,
etc*) **to give s.o. a good time,** faire
jouir qn/régaler qn/faire voir les
anges à qn/faire une gâterie à qn.
(*See* **hiding 1**; **job 5**; **no-good**;
thing 9)

goodies ['gudiz] *npl F* **1.** gour-
mandises *fpl*/du nanan **2.** les bons
mpl/les bien-pensants; **in his films
the goodies always win,** les bons ne
perdent jamais dans ses films. (*See*
baddie) **3.** argent*/fric *m*/flouse
m.

goodish ['gudiʃ] *a F* **1.** assez bon
2. a goodish while, assez longtemps;
**it's been a goodish time since we
met,** ça fait des siècles/une paye
depuis qu'on s'est vus; **it's a goodish way from here,** c'est à un bon
bout de chemin d'ici.

goodness ['gudnis] *n & excl F*
goodness! Dieu!/bigre!; **goodness
me!** bonté divine!; **goodness gracious (me)!** miséricorde!; **for goodness sake!** pour l'amour de Dieu/
du ciel! **thank goodness!** heureusement!/Dieu merci!; **goodness (only)
knows what I must do,** Dieu sait ce

que je dois faire. (*See* **honest-to-goodness**)

goodo! ['gudou] *excl F* chic alors!/parfait!/épatant!/chouette (alors)!

goods [gudz] *npl P* **1.** (*a*) **a nice bit/piece of goods,** une fille* bien balancée/un beau petit châssis/une jolie poupée (*b*) les parties sexuelles/la marchandise; **I like to see the goods before I buy,** j'aime voir la marchandise avant d'acheter. (*See* **damaged**) **2. the goods,** du vrai de vrai/de la bonne marchandise; **it's the goods,** c'est ce qu'il faut/ça tombe pile **3.** (*a*) **to deliver the goods,** remplir ses engagements/tenir parole; **she delivered the goods,** elle s'est couchée avec lui/elle a livré la marchandise **4.** chose promise/chose due; **he came up with the goods,** il a apporté la marchandise/il a payé ses dettes **5. to have the goods,** être capable **6.** preuves *fpl* de culpabilité; **to have the goods on s.o.,** tenir le bon bout contre qn **7.** drogues *fpl* en général/stups *mpl*/came *f*. (*See* **sample**)

good-time ['gud'taim] *a P* **1. good-time girl,** fille* rigolote/qui en prend une bosse **2. good-time guy/Charley,** (joyeux) viveur *m*/noceur *m*/bambocheur *m*/joyeux drille.

goody ['gudi] *n F see* **goodies.**

goody-goody ['gudigudi] **I** *a F* bien-pensant; d'une vertu suffisante; **to be all goody-goody,** faire le saint/faire sa Sophie/recevoir le bon Dieu sans confession **II** *excl F* oh, **goody-goody!** chic de chic!/chic alors! **III** *n F* **he's/she's a little goody-goody,** c'est un petit saint (de bois)/une sainte-Nitouche.

gooey ['guːi] *a F* **1.** collant/visqueux/poisseux **2.** mièvre/à l'eau de rose.

goof¹ [guːf] *n esp NAm* **1.** *F* individu bête*/couillon *m*/cave *m*/empoté *m* **2.** *F* fou *m*/timbré *m* **3.** *F* homme*/mec *m*/type *m* **4.** *P*

drogué(e)*/camé(e) *m*(*f*)/toxico *m*(*f*) **5.** *F* bévue*/boulette *f*/gaffe *f*/bourde *f*.

goof² [guːf] *vi* **1.** *F* gaffer/faire une bourde/mettre les pieds dans le plat/se gour(r)er; dire une connerie **2.** *F* se trahir/se vendre/se couper **3.** *F* rêvasser/être dans les nuages **4.** *F* duper*/endormir/engourdir (qn) **5.** *P* (*drugs*) rater/louper une piquouse **6.** *P* (*drugs*) se droguer*/se camer. (*See* **goofed (up)**)

goof at ['guːf'æt] *vtr P* regarder*/reluquer/mirer/mater/zieuter.

goofball ['guːfbɔːl] *n esp NAm P* **1.** individu bête*/con *m*/andouille *f*/empoté *m* **2.** individu bizarre/drôle d'oiseau/drôle de paroissien **3.** (*drugs*) barbituriques*/barbis *mpl*. (*See* **ball¹** 5) **4.** (*drugs*) mélange *m* de barbituriques* et d'amphétamines **5.** drogué*/camé *m*/toxico *m* **6.** calmant *m*/tranquillisant *m*.

goofed (up) ['guːft(ʌp)] *a P* sous l'influence d'un narcotique ou d'un barbiturique; bourré/chargé/défoncé/envapé. (*See* **goof up**)

goofer ['guːfər] *n P* (*drugs*) **1.** qn qui prend des pilules **2.** barbituriques *mpl*/barbis *mpl*.

go off ['gou'ɔf] *vtr&i* **1.** *F* détériorer/s'abîmer/tourner; **his ideas have gone off recently,** depuis quelques temps ses idées ne font plus moudre/tombent à plat **2.** *F* (*a*) **to go off s.o.,** ne plus aimer* qn; **I've gone off him,** je ne veux plus sortir avec lui/je l'ai plaqué (*b*) **to go off sth,** ne plus apprécier qch/perdre le goût de qch **3.** *P* avoir un orgasme*/décharger/jouir/prendre son pied **4.** *F* **how did it go off?** comment cela s'est-il passé? (*See* **alarming; end 5; rails; rocker 2**)

goof off ['guːf'ɔf] *P* **1.** *O* faire une bévue*/gaffer/mettre les pieds dans le plat/se gour(r)er. (*See* **goof²** 1) **2.** traînasser/flemmarder/ne rien

goof up faire de ses dix doigts/tirer au flanc; se la couler douce.

goof up ['guːfʌp] *vtr esp NAm P* mal exécuter/rater/saboter/ louper/ bousiller/saloper. (*See* **goofed (up)**)

goofy ['gufi] *a F* **1.** bête*/stupide/ sot/ballot/cruche; **he's a bit goofy,** il est un peu dingue **2. to be/to go goofy over s.o.,** être toqué de qn/en pincer pour qn; **to be goofy over sth,** être mordu pour qch; **he's goofy over it,** il en est dingue.

goog [gug] *n Austr F* **1.** œuf *m* **2.** individu bête*/ballot *m*.

googly ['gugli] *n F* **to bowl s.o. a googly,** doubler qn/coincer qn/ embobiner qn/rouler qn (dans la farine)/pigeonner qn.

goo-goo ['guːguː] *a F* **to make goo-goo eyes at s.o.,** faire les yeux doux à qn.

gook [guk] *esp NAm n P* **1.** du toc/de la camelote/de la came **2.** saleté*/saloperie *f*/crasse *f* **3.** sauce *ou* assaisonnement visqueux; graille *f* **4.** (*pej*) (*a*) moricaud *m*/ café *m* au lait (*b*) chinetoque *m*/ jaune *m* (*c*) vietnamien *m*/viet *m*.

gooky ['guki] *a esp NAm P* gras/ collant/poisseux/visqueux.

gool(e)y ['guːli] *n P* testicule*. (*See* **goolies**)

goolies ['guːliz] *npl P* testicules*/ balloches *fpl*/pendeloques *fpl*; **to kick s.o. in the goolies,** filer un coup de pied aux couilles à qn.

goon [guːn] *n* **1.** *F* individu bête*/ clown *m*/cornichon *m*/enflé *m* **2.** *NAm P* anti-gréviste *m*/jaune *m*/ renard *m* **3.** *NAm P* (*thug*) gorille *m*/cogneur *m*/casseur *m* de gueules **4.** *NAm P* un(e) laissé(e) pour compte.

go on ['gou'ɔn] *vi F* **1. that's enough to go on with/to be going on with,** voilà du pain sur la planche/assez pour le quart d'heure **2. I don't go much on that,** ça ne

me dit rien/ça ne me chante pas/je ne suis pas d'accord **3. go on!** (*a*) dis toujours! (*b*) **go on (with you)!** à d'autres!/n'en jetez plus (la cour est pleine)!/et ta sœur! **4.** discuter le bout de gras; **she does go on!** impossible de la lui boucler! **to go on and on (about sth),** déblatérer (sur qch) **5. to be going on (for) forty,** friser la quarantaine/aller sur ses quarante piges **6. to be gone on s.o.,** aimer* qn/s'enticher de qn/ en pincer pour qn.

goop [guːp] *n esp NAm F* individu bête*/couillon *m*/empoté *m*.

goose[1] [guːs] *n F* **1.** individu bête*; **she's a silly little goose,** c'est une petite dinde **2. all his geese are swans,** tout ce qu'il fait tient du prodige. (*See* **cook**[2] 3)

goose[2] [guːs] *vtr P* **1.** faire des papouilles/des pattes d'araignée à (qn) **2.** pincer les fesses* à (qn); mettre la main au panier **3.** duper*/faisander/pigeonner/ englander (qn).

gooseberry ['guzb(ə)ri] *n* **1.** *F* **to play gooseberry,** faire le chaperon/ tenir le chandelier **2.** *P* les fils barbelés/les barbelouses *fpl*.

goosegog ['guzgɔg] *n* (= *gooseberry*) *F* groseille (verte *ou* à maquereau).

gooser ['guːsər] *n A P* homosexuel*/empapaouté *m*.

go out ['go'aut] *vi F* **to go out like a light** (*i*) s'évanouir*/tourner de l'œil/tomber dans les pommes (*ii*) s'endormir/pioncer.

go over ['gou'ouvər] *vtr&i* **1.** passer la rampe/faire son petit effet; **that didn't go over too well,** ça n'a pas été tellement apprécié **2.** *P* battre* (qn); **they went over him with an iron bar,** ils lui ont arrangé le portrait avec une barre à mine.

GOP ['dʒiːouːpiː] *abbr NAm F* (= *Grand Old Party*) le parti républicain.

gorblimey! ['gɔːˈblaimi] *excl P* sacré nom (de nom)!/merde (alors)! (*See* **blimey!**)

Gordon Bennett! ['gɔːdnˈbenit] *excl P* doux Jésus!/mercredi!/merde (alors)!/putain!

gorgeous ['gɔːdʒəs] *a F* excellent*/super(be)/terrible/extra; **gorgeous weather,** un temps superbe; **hi, gorgeous!** salut ma beauté!/t'as de beaux yeux, tu sais!

gorilla [gəˈrilə] *n* **1.** *F* (*esp bodyguard*) brute *f*/gorille *m* **2.** *P* gangster *m*/tueur *m*/malfrat *m* **3.** *P* mille livres sterling. (*See* **monkey 2**)

gormless ['gɔːmlis] *a F* bouché/gourde; **you gormless jerk!** espèce d'empoté/d'andouille!

gosh! [gɔʃ] *excl F* mince!/zut!

gospel ['gɔspəl] *n F* **that's gospel/it's the gospel truth,** c'est la vérité pure/parole d'évangile; croix de bois, croix de fer (si je mens, je vais en enfer).

gospeller ['gɔspələr] *n F* **hot gospeller,** évangéliste outré/bigot *m* à tous crins.

go through ['goˈθruː] *vtr* **1.** *F* **he's gone through a lot,** il en a vu des vertes et des pas mûres/il en a vu de toutes les couleurs **2.** *Austr P* s'enfuir*/filer.

gotta ['gɔtə] *P* **1.** (= **got to**) **when you've gotta go you've gotta go,** quand l'heure est venue il faut partir **2.** (= **got a**) **you've gotta lot to go through,** t'en verras des vertes et des pas mûres/ce sera pas de la tarte/t'as du chemin à faire.

gov [gʌv], **governor** ['gʌvnər] *n F* **1.** **(the) gov/(the) governor,** le patron*/le singe; dirlot *m* **2.** **(the) gov/(the) governor,** père*/le vieux/le paternel **3.** (*respectful form of address*) **thanks gov!** merci chef!

gow [gau] *n NAm P* (*drugs*) **1.** opium *m* **2.** came *f* **3.** cigarette*

de marijuana/stick *m*/joint *m* **4.** voyage *m*/trip *m*. (*See* **hoosegow**)

gowed up ['gaudˈʌp] *a NAm P* **1.** drogué*/camé **2.** survolté.

goy, Goy [gɔi] *n F* non-Juif *m*/Gentil *m*/goy(e) *m*.

grab¹ [græb] *n P* **1.** paye *f*/salaire *m*; **grab day,** jour *m* de paye/la Sainte-Touche **2.** **up for grabs,** sur le marché/à vendre.

grab² [græb] *vtr* **1.** *F* accrocher (qn)/prendre (qn) aux entrailles **2.** *F* **how does that grab you?** qu'est-ce que tu en dis?/ça te branche? **3.** *F* **to grab a bite,** avaler un casse-croûte/un morceau sur le pouce; prendre un petit en-cas **4.** *P* arrêter*/agrafer/agriffer (qn).

grabber ['græbər] *n P* **1.** qch qui accroche/accroche *f* **2.** qn qui intéresse et stimule/accrocheur *m*.

grade [greid] *n F* **to make the grade,** réussir/être à la hauteur.

graft¹ [grɑːft] *n* **1.** *F* pot-de-vin *m*/graissage *m* de patte/gratte *f*/tour(s) *m(pl)* de bâton **2.** *F* (**hard**) **graft,** travail*/boulot *m*/turbin *m*; **to put in a bit of hard graft,** travailler dur/comme un nègre/comme une bête; donner un coup de collier **3.** *P* logement* et nourriture*/pension *f*; **good graft,** bon gîte/bonne bouffe.

graft² ['grɑːft] *vtr P* voler*/chaparder/chouraver.

grafter ['grɑːftər] *n F* **1.** tripoteur *m*/trafiquant *m* **2.** politicien véreux/affairiste *m*/politicard *m* **3.** bûcheur *m*/turbineur *m*.

grafting ['grɑːftiŋ] *n P* **grafting bloomers,** des dessous bouffants portés par des voleurs à la tire; **to wear grafting bloomers,** faire du vol au kangourou.

grand [grænd] *n F* (*a*) mille livres (sterling) (*b*) mille dollars.

grannie, granny ['græni] *n* **1.** *F* grand-mère *f*/mémé(e) *f*/mémère *f*/mamie *f* **2.** *P* négoce légal qui couvre des activités condamnables; couvert *m*/couverture *f*/paravent *m* **3.** *P* **to strangle one's grannie,** se masturber*/s'astiquer la colonne/ étrangler Popaul.

grapes [greips] *npl P* hémorroïdes *fpl*/grappillons *mpl.*

grapevine ['greipvain] *n F* renseignements* (de vive voix)/téléphone *m* arabe; **I heard it on the grapevine,** mon petit doigt me l'a dit.

grappler ['græplǝr] *n* **1.** *F* lutteur *m*/catcheur *m*/tombeur *m* **2.** (*pl*) *P* mains*/agrafes *fpl*/grappins *mpl.*

grappling ['græpliŋ] *a attrib* **1.** *F* **grappling fan,** amateur *m* de lutte/ du catch **2.** *P* **grappling hooks =** **grapplers** (**grappler 2**).

grass¹ [grɑɪs] *n* **1.** *P* dénonciateur*/mouchard *m*/donneur *m.* (*See* **supergrass**) **2.** *P* (*drugs*) marijuana*/herbe *f*/mariejeanne *f*; **to smoke grass,** fumer de l'herbe **3.** *Austr P* **to be on the grass,** être en liberté/profiter de la fraîche **4.** *F* **to be put out to grass,** être mis à la retraite.

grass² [grɑɪs] *vi P* cafarder/ moutonner; **to grass on s.o.,** dénoncer*/balancer/donner qn.

grasser ['grɑɪsǝr] *n P* dénonciateur*/mouchard *m*/ cafardeur *m*/mouton *m*/donneur *m*/indic *m.*

grasshopper ['grɑɪshɔpǝr] *n P* **1.** (*a*) usager *m* de la marijuana* (*b*) habitué(e) de la marijuana*. (*See* **grass¹ 2**) **2.** (*RS = copper*) agent* de police/perdreau *m*/flic *m.* (*See* **knee-high**)

grassroots¹ ['grɑɪs'ruɪts] **I** *a F* qui vient de la masse/d'en bas; **grassroots political movement,** mouvement *m* politique populaire; **grassroots democracy,** le populisme **II** *npl F* **1.** région *f* agricole/la brousse **2.** le gros (de la troupe)/ la masse/la base (d'un parti, d'une société, etc) **3.** raisonnements *mpl*

de grosse caisse **4.** fondation *f*/ source *f*/base *f.*

grass-widow ['grɑɪs'widou] *n F* **1.** femme* dont le mari est absent pendant un laps de temps **2.** femme* séparée ou divorcée.

grass-widower ['grɑɪs'widouǝr] *n F* mari dont la femme est absente pendant un laps de temps; divorcé/ homme séparé de sa femme; veuf *m* de cœur.

graveyard ['greivjɑɪd] *a F* **1.** **a graveyard cough,** toux *f* qui sent le sapin **2.** **graveyard shift,** équipe *f* (de travailleurs) de nuit.

gravy ['greivi] *n P* **1.** bénéfice*/ butin*/bénef *m*/affure *f*/gratte *f*; **the gravy train,** l'assiette *f* au beurre/le bon filon; **to ride the gravy train,** taper dans l'assiette au beurre **2.** l'Atlantique *m*/la Grande Tasse **3. to dish out the gravy** (*a*) ne pas y aller avec le dos de la cuiller/y aller carrément (*b*) (*prison sentence*) condamner au maximum.

grease [griɪs] *n P* **1.** (*a*) petit cadeau/glissage *m* de pièce/dessous *m* de table (*b*) achat *m* de conscience/prix *m* du silence/amende *f.* (*See* **palm-grease**) **2. grease monkey,** garagiste *m*/mécanicien *m*/ mécano *m.*

greaseball ['griɪsbɔɪl] *n esp NAm P* individu* sale/malpropre; souillon *mf.*

greased [griɪst] *a F* **like greased lightning,** très vite/(rapide) comme l'éclair/à toute pompe.

greaser ['griɪsǝr] *n P* **1.** soudoyeur *m*/graisseur *m*/chien couchant **2.** *NAm* (*pej*) Mexicain *m*/Sud-Américain *m*/café au lait **3.** jeune homme/jeune voyou au blouson noir et aux cheveux longs (*esp* en moto); blouson noir *m*/ loubard *m*/loulou *m.*

greasy ['griɪsi, griɪzi] *a P* **1.** flagorneur/lèche-bottes; **he's a greasy old slob,** c'est un vieux lécheur 2. **greasy spoon**, bistrot m/gargote f/boui-boui m.

great [greit] I a F 1. excellent*/ terrible/super/génial/sensass; **it's great to be alive**, c'est bon d'être au monde et d'y voir clair; **that's really great**, c'est le (super-)pied; **to have a great time**, s'en payer une bonne tranche (de rire); **he's a great guy**, c'est un chic type/un type sensass/ un mec extra; **he's great at tennis**, il se débrouille vachement bien au tennis/c'est un as du tennis 2. **great Scott!** bondieu!/bon sang! (*See* **gun**[1] 3; **shake**[1] 5) II adv F 1. **I feel great**, je suis bien dans ma peau/j'ai la forme 2. **it was working just great**, ça marchait à merveille/comme sur des roulettes III n F **he's one of the all-time greats**, il est un des grands de toujours/un des plus fameux de tous les temps.

greatest ['greitist] n F **he's the greatest!** c'est le plus grand/le champion/l'as des as!

greedy-guts ['griːdigʌts] n P goinfre*/glouton m/(béni-)- bouftou(t) m.

greefa ['griːfə] n P (*drugs*) ciga- rette* de marijuana/joint m/stick m.

greefo ['griːfou] n P (*drugs*) mari- juana/kif m/herbe f.

Greek[1] [griːk] I a P **the Greek way**, coït* anal/baisage m à la riche; **to do it Greek style/to do it like the Greeks**, pratiquer le coït* anal/prendre du petit/tourner la page II n F **it's all Greek to me**, c'est de l'hébreu/c'est du chinois pour moi.

Greek[2] [griːk] vtr&i P pratiquer le coït* anal/prendre du chouette/ prendre l'escalier de service.

green [griːn] I a 1. P (*drugs*) **green mud/ashes**, opium*/dross m/ boue verte 2. P **green and blacks**, capsules fpl barbituriques/vert et noir 3. F **to give s.o. the green**

light, donner le feu vert à qn 4. F (*i*) novice/inexpérimenté (*ii*) crédule/naïf/béjaune/blanc-bec; **he's not as green as he looks**, il n'est pas né d'hier/de la dernière pluie 5. F **to have green fingers/** *NAm* **a green thumb**, être un bon jardinier/avoir la main verte. (*See* **dragon** 3) II n 1. F **do you see any green in my eye?** tu ne m'as pas regardé?/je ne suis pas né d'hier! 2. P (*drugs*) marijuana* de mauvaise qualité. (*See* **greens**)

green-ass ['griːnæs] a *NAm* P = **green** I 4.

greenback ['griːnbæk] n F (a) bil- let* d'une livre sterling (b) billet* de banque américain.

greenie ['griːni] n P 1. novice m/ bleu m/blanc-bec m/serin m 2. = **green dragon** (**dragon** 3).

greenies ['griːniz] npl P billets mpl de banque/talbins mpl/faf(f)iots mpl.

greens [griːnz] npl 1. F légumes verts 2. P **to like one's greens**, être porté sur l'article/la bagatelle 3. F **the Greens**, les écolos.

grefa ['griːfə] n P = **greefa**.

gremlin ['gremlin] n F 1. lutin m de malheur/pépin m/eau f dans le gaz; **the gremlins must have got into my watch, it's ten minutes fast**, il doit y avoir des fourmis dans ma toccante, elle cavale de dix minutes 2. crampon m/casse-pieds m/enqui- quineur m.

greta ['griːtə] n P = **greefo**.

greybacks ['greibæks] npl P poux*/grains mpl de blé/mies fpl de pain.

griddle[1] ['gridl] n P (*theatre*) cabo- tin m/théâtreux m.

griddle[2] ['gridl] vi P faire du théâ- tre ambulant/cabotiner.

griffa ['griːfə] n P = **greefa**.

griff(in) ['grif(in)] n F **the griff(in)**, renseignement* utile/bon tuyau/ bon rencart; **to get the griff(in) on**

sth, être affranchi/s'être rencardé sur qch.

griffo ['griːfou] n P = **greefo.**

grift [grift] vtr esp NAm P escroquer*/empiler/estamper.

grifter ['griftər] n esp NAm P escroc*/estampeur m/empileur m.

grill[1] [gril] n F (on fruit machine) **mixed grill,** embrouillamini m. (See **fruit-salad** 2)

grill[2] [gril] vtr F **to grill s.o.,** serrer les pouces mpl à qn (pour obtenir un aveu)/cuisiner qn.

grilled [grild] a NAm P ivre*/noir/noircicot.

grim [grim] a F mauvais*/désagréable/de mauvais augure; **things look grim,** ça la fout mal/ça s'annonce mal; **he's feeling a bit grim,** il a le moral à zéro/il n'a pas la frite/il n'a pas la pêche. (See **hang on** 2)

grind[1] [graind] n 1. F travail* dur et monotone; **the daily grind,** la routine/le train-train quotidien/le métro-boulot-dodo; **to go back to the old grind,** reprendre le collier/se remettre au turbin; **to get down to a bit of hard grind,** travailler dur/comme un nègre/comme une bête 2. F (a) course f difficile (b) steeple m 3. P coït*/baisage m/fouraillage m/dérouillade f; **to have a grind,** faire l'amour*/faire un carton/tringler.

grind[2] [graind] vtr&i 1. F travailler* dur/boulonner/trimer/bûcher/en abattre 2. P faire l'amour*/fourailler/dérouiller. (See **axe**[1] 2)

grinder ['graindər] n F 1. **to put s.o. through the grinder,** faire passer un mauvais quart d'heure à qn 2. (pl) dents*/croquantes fpl/crocs mpl.

grip[1] [grip] n 1. **to get a grip on oneself** (a) F se contenir/se retenir/se contrôler/se ressaisir (b) V se masturber*/se faire une pogne/se taper la colonne 2. F **to lose one's grip,** perdre la tête/les pédales fpl.

grip[2] [grip] vtr V **to grip (oneself),** se masturber*/se taper la colonne/se pogner.

gripe[1] [graip] n F 1. plainte f/rouspétance f; **he's always got a gripe about sth,** il est toujours à rouspéter contre qch; **what gripes does he have against you?** qu'est-ce qu'il te reproche? **to have/to get the gripes** (a) se mettre en rogne/en boule; rouspéter/ronchonner (b) avoir la diarrhée*/la courante 2. geignard m/râleur m/bâton merdeux.

gripe[2] [graip] vi F 1. grogner*/rouspéter/ronchonner/râler; **he was griping about the bill,** la note lui a fait perdre le sourire/la note trop salée le faisait râler 2. ennuyer*/tourmenter/barber/raser (qn).

griper ['graipər] n F râleur m/rouspéteur m; mauvais coucheur.

grit [grit] n F 1. cran m/battant m; **he's full of grit,** il en a dans le ventre 2. (in Canada) (politique) Libéral(e).

gritty ['griti] a F qui est brave*/qui a du cran/qui a du cul/qui en a dans le ventre.

grizzle ['grizl] vi F 1. pleurnicher/geindre 2. grogner*/rouspéter.

grizzler ['grizlər] n F 1. pleurnicheur m/chialeur m 2. geignard m/chignard m.

grody ['groudi] a NAm P répugnant/dégueulasse/débectant.

grog [grɔg] n esp Austr P alcool* (en général); **to be on the grog,** boire* (beaucoup)/caresser la bouteille/biberonner/picoler.

groggy ['grɔgi] a F 1. un peu malade*/patraque/mal fichu; **to feel a bit groggy,** n'avoir pas la pêche/la frite 2. (boxing) groggy/sonné 3. ivre*/paf/éméché/parti 4. **a groggy old table,** une vieille table bancale.

grog shop ['grɔg'ʃɔp] *n F Austr* (= *off licence*) = débit *m* de boissons/magasin de vins et spiritueux.

groin [grɔin] *n P* bande* noire de parieurs sur un champ de courses.

groove [gruːv] *n F* **1.** spécialité *f*/ dada *m*/rayon *m*; **that's my groove,** ça, c'est mon blot **2.** *O* **it's a groove,** c'est chic **3.** *O* **in the groove,** en pleine forme/en plein boum; (*jazz*) (orchestre) donnant son plein/faisant des étincelles; **it's in the groove** (*i*) c'est à la mode/à la coule/dans le vent (*ii*) ça marche comme sur des roulettes/tout baigne dans l'huile **4. to get into a groove,** s'encroûter/être dans l'ornière/s'enroutiner.

groovy ['gruːvi] *a O F* excellent*/ super/génial; **that's really groovy,** c'est vachement bien; c'est très cool.

grope¹ [group] *n P* tripotage *m*/ pelotage *m*; **to have a quick grope,** aller aux renseignements/mettre la main au panier/tripoter qn.

grope² [group] *vtr P* palper les parties de qn sous ses vêtements/ peloter (qn); mettre la main au panier; faire du rentre-dedans.

gross [grous] *a F* répugnant/ dégueulasse/débectant.

grotty ['grɔti] *a F* **1.** laid*/moche/ tocard/tarte **2.** outré et inutile.

grouch¹ [grautʃ] *n F* **1.** ronchonnage *m*/rouspétance *f* **2.** râleur *m*/ ronchonneur *m*.

grouch² [grautʃ] *vi F* grogner*/ râler/ronchonner.

groucher ['grautʃər] *n F* = **grouch¹ 2.**

ground [graund] *n F* **1. to run s.o. into the ground,** débiner/démolir qn **2. that suits me down to the ground,** cela me convient parfaitement/ça me botte/ça fait mon blot **3. to get a scheme off the ground,** faire démarrer un projet; **it'll never get off the ground,** cela ne verra jamais

le jour/cela ne démarrera jamais. (*See* **stamping-ground**)

groupie ['gruːpi] *n* **1.** *F* fervente des pop-groups/groupie *f* **2.** *P* fille* qui aime faire l'amour en groupe.

grouse¹ [graus] *n F* **1.** plainte *f*/ rouspétance *f*; grogne(rie) *f*/ bougonnement *m* **2.** rouscailleur *m*/marronneur *m*.

grouse² [graus] *vi F* grogner*/marronner/rouscailler; **he's always grousing about something or other,** il n'arrête pas de rouspéter/il a toujours qch à râler.

grouser ['grausər] *n F* rouspéteur *m*/râleur *m*.

grub [grʌb] *n P* **1.** nourriture*/ boustifaille *f*/mangeaille *f*/bectance *f*; **grub up!/grub's up!** à la bouffe!/ à la soupe! **2.** enfant sale*/petite vermine/petit morveux.

grubby ['grʌbi] *a F* sale*/pouilleux/cracra/crado; **grubby hands,** mains douteuses.

gruel ['gruːəl] *n F* **1.** réprimande *f*/ attrapade *f*/engueulade *f*/trempe *f* **2. to give s.o. his gruel** (*a*) battre* qn (comme plâtre) (*b*) éreinter/ échiner qn **3. to take/to get one's gruel,** avaler sa médecine/encaisser/ avaler la pilule.

gruelling ['gruːəliŋ] *n F* (*a*) passage *m* à tabac/dérouillée *f*/raclée *f* (*b*) épreuve éreintante.

Grundy ['grʌndi] *Prn A F* **not to care about Mrs Grundy/not to care what Mrs Grundy says,** se moquer du qu'en-dira-t-on.

grunt-and-groan ['grʌnt-ən(d)'groun] *n F* la lutte/le catch.

grunt-and-groaner ['grʌnt-ən(d)'grounər] *n F* lutteur *m*/ catcheur *m*.

grunter ['grʌntər] *n F* porc *m*.

G-string ['dʒiːstriŋ] *n F* cache-sexe *m*/feuille *f* de vigne/cache-fri-fri *m*/ cache-truc *m*.

gubbins ['gʌbinz] *n F* **1.** *O* nourriture*/becquetance *f* **2.** gadget *m*/bidule *m*/truc *m*/machin *m* **3.** (*rare*) = **muggins.**

guess [ges] *vi F* croire/penser; **I guess,** je suppose; **I guess that**..., il y a des chances pour que...; **you're right, I guess,** oui, il me semble que vous avec raison/tu as sans doute raison; **guess what?** devine!/imagine!

guesstimate¹ ['gestimət] *n F* conjecture *f*/estimation bien pesée.

guesstimate² ['gestimeit] *vtr F* estimer/évaluer soigneusement/ calculer au pifomètre.

guest [gest] *n F* **be my guest!** c'est à toi!/prends!/emporte!/fais comme chez toi!

guff [gʌf] *n F* **1.** bêtises*/blagues *fpl*/foutaises *fpl* **2.** (*a*) renseignements *mpl*/information(s) *f(pl)*; **have you got all the guff?** t'as les infos? (*b*) paperasserie *f*/papelards *mpl*.

guide [gaid] *n P* drogué* endurci qui entraîne les autres/guide *m* de neufs.

guinea ['gini] *n O F* **it's a guinea a minute,** c'est très amusant*/c'est impayable.

guiver¹ ['gaivər] *n Austr F* baratin *m*; **to sling the guiver,** baratiner.

guiver² ['gaivər] *vi Austr F* baratiner/faire du baratin.

gum [gʌm] *n F* **by gum!** mince alors!/nom d'un chien! (*See* **gumtree**)

gump [gʌmp] *n A F* individu bête*/ nouille *f*/andouille *f*.

gumption ['gʌm(p)ʃ(ə)n] *n F* bon sens/débrouillardise *f*/entregent *m*; **to have gumption,** avoir de la jugeot(t)e; **he's got plenty of gumption,** c'est un débrouillard/un démerdard; il se débrouille bien.

gumshoe ['gʌmʃuː] *n NAm F* agent* de police habillé en civil/ poulet *m*/ham(bourgeois) *m*/condé *m*.

gum-tree ['gʌmtriː] *n F* **(stuck) up a gum-tree,** dans une impasse/dans le pétrin/dans de beaux draps.

gum up ['gʌm'ʌp] *vtr F* **to gum up the works,** encrasser les rouages/ mettre des bâtons dans les roues/ mettre HS/(tout) foutre en l'air.

gun¹ [gʌn] *n* **1.** *P* seringue* hypodermique/poussette *m*/hypo *f*/ shooteuse *f* **2.** *F* **to jump the gun,** brûler le feu/marcher avant les violons **3.** *F* **to go great guns,** prospérer/faire un boum; **his business is going great guns,** son commerce marche à merveille/à plein gaz; **the party was going great guns,** ça chauffait à la boum/c'était une boum du tonnerre/la boum faisait un tabac monstre **4.** *F* **to stick to one's guns,** s'accrocher/tenir bon/ ne pas en démordre **5.** *NAm P* (*a*) voleur*/caroubleur *m*/casseur *m*; voleur à la tire (*b*) **(hired) gun,** bandit *m*/gangster *m*/malfrat *m*/porteflingue *m* **6.** *F* **to give sth the gun,** accélérer qch/mettre les gaz/mettre la gomme **7.** *P* **to get behind the gun,** risquer la prison*/la taule **8.** *P* (*euph*) pénis*. (*See* **big I 1**; **burp-gun**; **spike² 3**)

gun² [gʌn] *vi F* **to be (out) gunning for s.o.,** pourchasser qn pour se venger de lui/aller à la rebiffe; **I'm gunning for you,** je t'aurai au tournant/je te revaudrai ça/j'aurai ta peau/je te mettrai à mon tableau de chasse.

gun down ['gʌn'daun] *vtr F* fusiller/flinguer/descendre (qn).

gunge [gʌndʒ] *n F* saleté*/saloperie *f*/merde *f*.

gunji ['gʌndʒi], **gunny** ['gʌni] *n P* (*drugs*) marijuana*/kif *m*. (*See* **ganjah**)

gunsel ['gʌnzl] *n NAm P* **1.** gangster *m*/malfrat *m*/dur *m* **2.** faux jeton/faux frère/bordille *f* **3.** mignon *m*/giton *m*/lopette *f* **4.** blanc-bec *m*/béjaune *m*/dadais *m*.

gunslinger ['gʌnsliŋər] *n F* vaurien* armé/porte-flingue *m/* loubard *m*.

gurk [gəɪk] *vi A P* roter.

gussie ['gʌsi] *n P* (*not common*) homosexuel*/lopaille *f*.

gut [gʌt] *n P* **to bust a gut to do sth,** se sortir les tripes/se décarcasser pour faire qch. (*See* **guts**; **rot-gut**)

gutful ['gʌtful] *n P* (*a*) ventrée *f/* gavée *f* (*b*) **to have (had) a gutful,** en avoir ras le bol/en avoir son compte/en avoir plein le cul. (*See* **bellyful**)

gutless ['gʌtlis] *a P* **to be gutless,** être lâche/ne rien avoir dans le bide; **a gutless character,** un type mou/une chiffe molle/un trouillard/une lavette.

gut-rot ['gʌtrɔt] *n F* **1.** = **rot-gut 2.** mal *m* au ventre.

guts [gʌts] *npl* **1.** *F* **to have guts,** être brave*; avoir du cul/du cran/ de l'estomac; en avoir dans le bide; **to have no guts,** avoir les foies/les jetons; ne pas en avoir dans le bidon; **he's got no guts,** il n'a rien dans le ventre; **she's got guts,** elle a du cran; **it takes a lot of guts to do that,** il faut beaucoup d'estomac pour faire ça; il faut avoir des couilles/en avoir pour le faire **2.** *P* **to hate s.o.'s guts,** détester* qn/ avoir qn dans le nez/ne pas pouvoir blairer qn/ne pas pouvoir piffrer qn **3.** *V* **to drop one's guts,** péter*/en lâcher un/vesser **4.** *P* **to knife s.o. in the guts,** éventrer qn/ mettre les tripes à l'air à qn/crever la paillasse à qn **5.** *P* **put some guts into it!** mets-en un (bon) coup!/magne-toi le train! **6.** *P* **to sweat one's guts out,** travailler* dur/en foutre un coup/se casser les reins/pisser du sang/se crever le cul **7.** *P* **to heave/to spew one's guts up,** vomir*/dégueuler/aller au refil(e)/dégoupillonner **8.** *Austr P* **to hold one's guts,** se taire*/poser sa chique **9.** *Austr P* **to spill one's**

guts, avouer*/vider son sac **10.** *P* **I'll have your guts for garters!** j'aurai ta peau!/je me ferai un porte-monnaie avec tes couilles! **11.** *P* du charnu/de l'étoffe *f/*de la substance; **the real guts of the problem,** l'essentiel/le cœur du problème **12.** *P* engrenages *mpl/* rouages *mpl/*boyaux *mpl/*entrailles *fpl*; **my gut reaction is to say yes,** d'instinct, je dis/je dirais oui; par réflexe viscéral, je dirais oui **13.** *P* = **greedy-guts.** (*See* **cleverguts**; **gut**; **worryguts**)

guts-ache ['gʌtseik] *n P* **1.** mal *m* au ventre* **2.** casse-pieds *m/* casse-burettes *m*.

gut-scraper ['gʌtskreipər] *n P* racleur *m* de cordes/joueur *m* de crincrin.

gutsy ['gʌtsi] *a P* **1.** qui a du cran/qui en a dans le ventre; qui a du cul(ot) **2.** goinfre*/goulu.

gutted ['gʌtid] *a P* très déçu*/ chagriné; **to feel/to be gutted,** l'avoir saumâtre; **he was gutted,** ça lui en a foutu un coup/ça lui a sappé le moral.

gutter ['gʌtər] *n F* **1.** **the gutter press,** la presse à scandales **2.** *esp NAm* **to have one's mind in the gutter,** être obsédé(e)/ne penser qu'à ça/avoir l'esprit mal tourné.

gutty ['gʌti] *a P* **1.** qui prend aux entrailles/aux tripes; qui empoigne **2.** fondamental/substantiel/qui vient du tréfonds.

gutzer ['gʌtsər] *n Austr P* **to come a gutzer** (*a*) tomber*/se casser la figure (*b*) tomber sur un bec/faire un bide.

guv [gʌv], **guv'nor** ['gʌvnər] *n F* = **gov.**

guy [gai] *n* **1.** *F esp NAm* (*a*) homme*/type *m/*mec *m/*zigoto *m*; **he's a nice guy,** c'est un chic type/ un mec réglo; **a wise guy** (*i*) un crâneur/un je-sais-tout (*ii*) un roublard/un mariol(e); **a gay guy,** un gai/un homo; **hi, you guys!**

salut (, tout le monde)! (*b*) (*boy-friend, husband*) **her guy,** son mec/ son jules **2.** *P* **to do a guy** (*a*) s'enfuir*/se tirer/se casser (*b*) donner un faux nom*/filer le faux blaze. (*See* **fall-guy; great I 1; right I 3; tough I 1**)

guzunder [gǝ'zʌndǝr] *n A F* pot *m* de chambre/Jules *m*/Thomas *m*/ Colin *m.*

gyp¹ [dʒip] *n* **1.** *F =* **gip 2.** *NAm* *P* escroc*/filou *m*/carotteur *m* **3.** *NAm* escroquerie*/tromperie *f/* arnaque *f*/carottage *m* **4.** *P* **gyp joint** = **clip-joint.**

gyp² [dʒip] *vtr NAm P* **to gyp s.o.** (*a*) escroquer* qn/estamper qn/ empiler qn (*b*) écorcher qn; **to be gypped,** être pigeonné.

gyve [dʒaiv] *n P* (*drugs*) cigarette* de marijuana*/stick *m*/joint *m.*

H

H [eitʃ] *n P* (*drugs*) héroïne*/H *f*/ blanche *f*.

habit ['hæbit] *n* **1.** *F* usage *m* des drogues; **to kick the habit,** décrocher/lâcher le pied; **off the habit,** décamé/désintox(iqué) **2.** *P* dose (habituelle de drogues).

hack¹ [hæk] *n* **1.** *F* journaliste *mf*; **hack writer,** nègre *m* **2.** *NAm F* taxi *m*/bahut *m* **3.** *NAm P* (*Black Slang*) Blanc *m*.

hack² [hæk] *vi NAm F* conduire un taxi/faire le taxi.

hack around ['hækə'raund] *vi NAm F* flâner/flânocher.

hacked (off) ['hækt('ɔf)] *a P* (*not common*) **1.** en colère*/à cran **2.** qui en a assez*/qui en a soupé; qui en a ras le bol/plein le dos.

hagbag ['hæg'bæg] *n P* (*CB*) fille* *ou* femme* laide/boudin *m*/ mocheté *f*; vieille femme laide/ vieille harpie.

Haggis land ['hægislænd] *n P* (*CB*) Écosse *f*.

hair [hɛər] *n* **1.** *F* **to get in s.o.'s hair,** taper sur les nerfs/sur le système à qn **2.** *F* **to let one's hair down,** se laisser aller/ne pas faire de chichis/ne pas se formaliser **3.** *P* **keep your hair on!** calme-toi!/ (ne) t'emballe pas! **4.** *F* **to split hairs,** couper les cheveux en quatre **5.** *F* **get some hair on your chest!** conduis-toi en homme!/sors de tes langes! (*medicine, whisky, etc*) **this'll put hair(s) on your chest!** ça te fera du bien/te remontera (le moral)! **6.** *P* **to have s.o. by the short hairs**

= to have s.o. by the short and curlies (**curlies**). (*See* **dog¹ 7**)

hairburger ['hɛəbəɪgər] *n esp NAm V* sexe de la femme*/barbu *m*/chatte *f*. (*See* **furburger**)

haircut ['hɛəkʌt] *n P* courte période en prison*.

hair-do ['hɛəduɪ] *n F* **I'm going to have a hair-do,** je vais chez le coiffeur/je vais me faire couper les douilles *fpl*.

hairpie ['hɛə'pai] *n NAm V =* **hairburger.**

hairy ['hɛəri] *a P* (*a*) (*difficult*) épineux/duraille/trapu (*b*) (*frightening*) horrible/à vous faire dresser les cheveux sur la tête; **it was a bit of a hairy experience,** ça m'a donné une sacrée pétoche/j'en ai eu des suées/j'ai failli en pisser dans mon froc.

half [haɪf] **I** *adv F* **1. not half!** et comment!/tu parles!/une paille!/à peine! **2. she didn't half laugh,** elle s'est bien tordue de rire **3. you won't half catch it!** qu'est-ce que tu vas prendre! **4. he hasn't half changed,** il a drôlement décollé **5.** (*a*) **half and half,** moitié-moitié (*b*) **to go half and half,** marcher à cinquante-cinquante/faire moit'-moit'/ faire fifty-fifty/faire afanaf. (*See* **fifty-fifty**) **6. to be only half there,** être un peu fou*/être toqué/être un peu touché. (*See* **shift² 1**) **II** *n* **1.** *F* (*beer*) demi *m* **2. half and half** (*a*) *P* panaché *m* de bière brune et blonde (*b*) *P* (*esp prostitutes*) fellation* suivie d'un coït* conventionnel **3.** *F* **you haven't heard the half**

of it (yet), faut que je te dise le meilleur!/attends, il y a mieux! **4.** F **my better/other half,** ma (douce) moitié.

half-a-crown ['hɑɪfə'kraun] n F see **bingo 26.**

half-a-dollar ['hɑɪfə'dɔlər] n O P (= *half-a-crown*) demi-couronne f.

half-assed ['hæf'æst] a NAm V **1.** margoulin/sabré/d'arabe **2.** mal fait/salopé/bousillé.

half-baked ['hɑɪf'beikt] a F (a) inexpérimenté/blanc-bec (b) bête*/ niais/bêta (c) à la noix; **that half-baked idea of yours,** ton idée à la con.

half-brass ['hɑɪf'brɑɪs] n O P femme* facile qui ne fait pas payer ses faveurs. (*See* **brass II 4**)

half-century ['hɑɪf'sentʃuri] n P cinquante livres.

half-cock ['hɑɪf'kɔk] n F **to go off at half-cock,** mal partir/mal démarrer/rater.

half-cut ['hɑɪf'kʌt] a P légèrement ivre*/gris/pompette. (*See* **cut¹ I 1**)

half-dead ['hɑɪf'ded] a F fatigué*/ à moitié mort/éreinté.

half-inch ['hɑɪf'intʃ] vtr P (RS = pinch) voler*/chiper/chaparder.

half-iron ['hɑɪf'aiən] n P qn qui fréquente les homosexuels sans en être. (*See* **hoof¹ 2**)

half-pint ['hɑɪf'paint] n F petit* individu/avorton m; demi-portion f.

half-pissed ['hɑɪf'pist] a P (légèrement) ivre*/paf/parti. (*See* **pissed**)

half-seas-over ['hɑɪf'siz'ouvər] a F (légèrement) ivre*/paf/parti.

half-squarie ['hɑɪf'skwɛəri] n Aust P fille* ou femme* de petite vertu/ Marie-couche-toi-là f.

half-stewed ['hɑɪf'stjuɪd] a O P = **half-pissed.**

half-way ['hɑɪf'wei] adv F **1. to meet s.o. half-way,** couper la poire en deux **2.** see **bingo 45.**

halls [hɔɪlz] npl F **the halls,** théâtres mpl vaudeville.

halves ['hɑɪvz] adv F **to go halves,** y aller moitié-moitié.

ham¹ [hæm] a F **1.** amateur **2.** inférieur/de basse qualité; NAm **ham joint,** gargote f.

ham² [hæm] n F **1.** (*theatre*) **pure ham,** pièce pleine de clichés et d'emphase/cagnade f **2.** (a) acteur amateur (b) mauvais acteur/cabotin m **3.** radio-amateur.

ham³ [hæm] vtr F (*theatre*) **to ham up** (i) mal jouer un rôle/cabotiner (ii) déclamer/jouer pour la galerie.

ham-fisted ['hæm'fistid], **ham-handed** ['hæm'hændid] a F maladroit/empoté/qui a les mains nickelées.

hammer¹ ['hæmər] n **1.** NAm P belle fille*/belle nana/beau petit lot **2.** P (CB) accélérateur m/champignon m/ **3.** NAm V pénis*/ défonceuse f/sabre m.

hammer² ['hæmər] vtr **1.** F (Stock Exchange) déclarer (un agent) en défaut **2.** F **to hammer s.o. into the ground,** battre qn à plate(s) couture(s)/tailler qn en pièces **3.** F **to hammer a play/a film,** démolir/ bousiller/éreinter une pièce/un film **4.** P (RS = trail) **to hammer (and nail),** traîner/suivre/filer le train (à qn).

hammer back ['hæmər'bæk] vi F (CB) ralentir/lever le pied.

hammer down ['hæmər'daun] vi P (CB) accélérer/appuyer sur le champignon/mettre le pied au plancher.

hammered ['hæmərd] a NAm P ivre*/défoncé/refait.

hammering ['hæməriŋ] n F **1.** volée f de coups* **2.** (sports) défaite f/raclée f/dérouillée f **3. the play took a hammering,** la pièce s'est fait esquinter/éreinter.

hammer up ['hæmər'ʌp] vi P (CB) ralentir/lever le pied.

hammocks ['hæməks] *npl P* seins* opulents/du monde au balcon.

hammy ['hæmi] *a F* outré/chargé/ exagéré.

Hampton ['hæmptən] *n V (RS = prick)* **Hampton Wick**, pénis*. (*See* **wick 1, 2**)

hand¹ [hænd] *F* **1. to keep one's hand in**, garder le pied à l'étrier **2. to make money hand over fist**, gagner* beaucoup d'argent*/se faire un pognon fou/ramasser du fric à la pelle **3. old hand**, vieux *m* de la vieille/vieux routier/ficelard *m*; **he's an old hand (at it)**, il connaît la musique **4. to be hand in glove with s.o.**, être comme larrons en foire/comme cul et chemise avec qn. (*See* **big 1 5**; **dab¹ I**)

hand² [hænd] *vtr* **1.** *F* **you've got to hand it to him!** devant lui, chapeau! **2.** *P* **don't hand me that!** raconte pas d'histoires!/arrête tes salades!/arrête ton char(re)! (*See* **plate¹ 3**; **sweet 3**)

hand artist ['hænd'ɑːtist] *n P* masturbateur *m*/branleur *m*/pignoleur *m*.

handful ['hændful] *n* **1.** *P* (condamnation* à) cinq ans* de prison*; cinq piges *fpl*/cinq longes *fpl* (de taule) **2.** *P* cinq livres sterling **3.** *F* (*esp child, animal*) **to be a handful**, donner du fil à retordre/être une peste/être infernal.

hand-job ['hænddʒɔb] *n V* **to give s.o. a hand-job**, masturber* qn/branler qn.

handle ['hændl] *n F* **1. to fly off the handle**, se mettre en colère*/sortir de ses gonds **2.** *F* **to have a handle**, avoir un titre/avoir un nom à rallonge **3.** *F* nom* de famille/prénom *m*/surnom *m*/blaze *m* **4.** *P (CB)* identification personnelle du cibiste/indicatif *m*.

handlebar ['hændlbɑːr] *a attrib F* **handlebar moustache**, moustache* à la gauloise/bacchantes *fpl* en guidon.

hand-me-downs ['hænd-midaunz] *npl O F* vêtements* usagés *ou* d'occasion; frusques *fpl*; décrochez-moi-ça *m*; **my brother's hand-me-downs**, les fringues que j'ai héritées de mon frère. (*See* **reach-me-downs**)

hand-out ['hændaut] *n F* **1.** prospectus *m*/circulaire *m* publicitaire **2.** aumône *f*/charité *f*.

handshake ['hændʃeik] *n F* **golden handshake**, cadeau *m* d'adieu/indemnité *f* de départ.

handsome ['hænsəm] *a F* généreux; honorable; **to do the handsome thing**, se conduire comme il faut/avec générosité; avoir un beau geste.

handwriting ['hændraitiŋ] *n F* style particulier d'un criminel; **it's got his handwriting all over it**, c'est bien de chez lui.

hang¹ [hæŋ] *n F* **1. to get the hang of sth**, saisir le truc pour faire qch; **when you've got the hang of things**, quand vous serez au courant/dans le bain/dans le coup **2. I don't give a hang**, je m'en fiche/je m'en fous; j'en ai rien à foutre/à glander; **it's not worth a hang**, cela ne vaut pas un pet de lapin.

hang² [hæŋ] *vtr F* **1. hang it!** flûte!/mince alors! **2. hang the expense!** au diable l'avarice! **3. I'll be hanged if I'll do that!** pas question que je le fasse!/ça me ferait mal de faire ça! (*See* **hung**)

hang about, around ['hæŋə'baut, ə'raund] *vi* **1.** *F* flâner/flânocher/rôdailler; **to keep s.o. hanging about**, faire/laisser poireauter qn **2.** *P* **hang about!** minute! (*See* **hang on 1** (*a*))

hanger-on ['hæŋə'rɔn] *n F* **1.** dépendant *m*/parasite *m* **2.** crampon *m*/pique-assiette *m*.

hang in ['hæŋ'in] *vi esp NAm P* **hang in (there)!** tiens bon!

hang loose ['hæŋ'lus] *vi NAm P* se la couler douce; **hang loose!** ne vous en faites pas!

hang on ['hæŋ'ɔn] *vi* **1.** *F (a)* attendre*; **hang on!** une seconde!/ minute! (*telephone*) ne quitte pas! (*b*) poireauter **2.** *F* **to hang on like grim death**, se cramponner/ s'accrocher/ne pas lâcher le morceau **3.** *F* tenir bon **4.** *NAm P* **to hang one on**, s'enivrer/se piquer le nez.

hang-out ['hæŋaut] *n* **1.** *F* logement*/chez-soi *m* **2.** *F* rendez-vous*/lieu *m* de réunion; repaire *m* de gangsters **3.** *NAm P* **hang-out (road)**, déballage (de la vérité).

hang out ['hæŋ'aut] *vi* **1.** *F* **to hang out for sth**, réclamer/contester qch **2.** *F* habiter*/crécher/nicher; **where do you hang out?** où perchez-vous? **3.** *F* traînailler/glander/ glandouiller; **those yobs were hanging out in the bar**, ces petits loulous glandaient dans le troquet **4.** *P (a)* **let it all hang out!** fais ta vie!/fais (tout) ce qui te chante! (*b*) *NAm* tout déballer/tout sortir/accoucher. (*See* **hang-out 3**)

hangover ['hæŋouvər] *n F* **to have a hangover**, avoir la gueule de bois/ la GDB.

hang tough ['hæŋ'tʌf] *vi NAm P* persister/s'obstiner; **hang tough!** tiens bon!/accroche-toi, Jeannot!

hang-up ['hæŋʌp] *n F* **1.** ennui mental/trouble *m* psychique/complexe *m* **2.** dada *m*/combine *f* **3.** embêtement *m*/enquiquinement *m*/ emmerde *f*.

hang up ['hæŋ'ʌp] *vtr F* **1.** (*telephone*) raccrocher **2.** **to hang up one's hat**, se marier/se marida **3.** **to hang s.o. up**, planter qn **4.** *NAm* **hang up!** ça suffit!/ça va comme ça! (*See* **hung up**)

hank¹ [hæŋk] *n esp NAm P* **to play with hank**, se masturber*/se branler/se secouer le bonhomme.

hank² [hæŋk] *vi esp NAm P* se masturber*/se branler/se pignoler.

hankie, hanky ['hæŋki] *n F (= handkerchief)* F mouchoir*/blave *m*; tire-jus *m*.

hanky-panky ['hæŋki'pæŋki] *n F* **1.** entourloupe(tte) *f*/coup fourré **2.** (*i*) adultère*/carambolage *m* en douce (*ii*) flirt *m*; **to go in for a bit of hanky-panky with one's secretary**, s'envoyer la secrétaire en douce **3.** manigance *f*.

happen¹ ['hæp(ə)n] *adv F (regional)* peut-être; **happen he will, happen he won't**, peut-être bien que oui, peut-être bien que non.

happen² ['hæp(ə)n] *vi F* **it's all happening**, tout est en marche/tout roule.

happen along ['hæp(ə)nə'lɔŋ] *vi F* arriver* au hasard/entrer en passant.

happening ['hæp(ə)niŋ] *n* **1.** *pl A P* drogues *fpl*/narcotiques *mpl*/came *f* **2.** *F* spectacle/événement imprévu *ou* spontané; happening *m*.

happenstance ['hæp(ə)nstæns] *n NAm F* événement fortuit.

happy ['hæpi] *a F* **1.** légèrement ivre*/paf/pompette **2.** **happy days!** à la (bonne) vôtre! **3.** **a happy event**, un heureux événement. (*See* **bar-happy**; **dust¹ 2** (*a*); **shag-happy**; **slap-happy**; **trigger-happy**)

hard [hɑːd] **I** *a* **1.** *F* **a drop of the hard stuff**, une goutte d'alcool*/un petit coup de gnôle **2.** *F* **hard drugs**, drogues dures. (*See* **soft I 4**) **3.** *F* **hard lines**, malchance*/poisse *f*; **hard lines!/hard luck!** manque de bol!/pas de pot! (*See* **cheddar**; **cheese 3**) **4.** *F* **hard tack**, biscuits *mpl* de marin **5.** *F* **hard sell**, battage *m* publicitaire/vente *f* au sabot. (*See* **soft I 5**) **6.** *F* **to play hard to get**, faire la difficile/faire la Sainte-Nitouche **7.** *A P* excellent*/super **8.** *Austr P* **to put the hard word on** (*i*) (*man*) (essayer de) persuader une femme de faire l'amour/faire du rentre-dedans/ baratiner (*ii*) (essayer de) persuader qn de faire qch (de difficile, de désagréable)/baratiner. (*See* **case**¹ 1; **hat** 6; **nut**¹ 4) **II** *n* **1**. *P* (= *hard labour*) travaux forcés; **fifteen years' hard**, quinze piges *fpl* des durs **2**. *V* = **hard-on**.

hard-baked ['hɑːd'beikt] *a F* endurci/dur(aille).

hard-bitten ['hɑːd'bitn] *a F* = **hard-boiled 2**.

hard-boiled ['hɑːd'bɔild] *a F* **1**. malin*/coriace; **a hard-boiled businessman**, un homme d'affaires qui n'est pas né de la dernière pluie **2**. dur (à cuire) **3**. peu susceptible/ sans scrupules.

hard-liner ['hɑːd'lainər] *n F* **1**. intransigeant *m* (en politique)/dur *m* (d'un parti) **2**. toxicomane majeur (opium et dérivés).

hard-nosed ['hɑːd'nouzd] *a esp NAm F* réaliste/dur à cuire; qui n'est pas né de la dernière pluie.

hard-on ['hɑːdɔn] *n V* **to have a hard-on**, être en érection*/bander.

hard up ['hɑːd'ʌp] *a F* pauvre*/ dans la dèche/fauché/à sec; **to be hard up**, être raide (comme un passe-lacet).

hardware ['hɑːdwɛər] *n F* armes *fpl*/quincaillerie *f*.

hardy ['hɑːdi] *a F* **hardy annual**, vieille histoire/question *f* qui revient régulièrement sur le tapis.

hare (off) ['hɛər('ɔf)] *vi F* s'enfuir*/se tailler/se carapater; **to hare back home**, regagner la maison à toutes jambes/ventre à terre.

hark [hɑːk] *vi F* **hark at her!** écoute-moi celle-là!

harp¹ [hɑːp] *n* **1**. *A F* Irlandais **2**. *F* harmonica *m*. (*See* **jew's-harp**)

harp² [hɑːp] *vi F* **he's always harping on the same string**, il récite toujours la même litanie/il rabâche

toujours la même chose; **stop harping on about that!** change de disque!/change de refrain!

Harry ['hæri] *Prn* **1**. *O F* **old Harry**, le diable; **it's giving me old Harry**, cela me fait un mal du diable **2**. *F* **to play old Harry with s.o.**, engueuler qn/sonner les cloches à qn **3**. *O P* **Harry bonkers** = **bonkers**; **Harry flakers** = **flakers**; **Harry preggers** = **preggers**; **Harry starkers** = **starkers 3**. *P* (*drugs*) héroïne*/ héro *f*/Henriette *f*. (*See* **flash**¹ **I** 1; **Tom** 1)

has-been ['hæzbiːn] *n F* **1**. individu* vieux-jeu; vieux ramolli; **he's a has-been**, c'est un croulant; **it's better to be a has-been than a never-was**, il vaut mieux ne plus être que n'avoir jamais été **2**. vieillerie *f*/vieux machin.

hash¹ [hæʃ] *n F* **1**. nourriture*/ boustifaille *f*/bectance *f*/bouffe *f* **2**. *NAm* râgots *mpl*/potins *mpl*/cancans *mpl* **3**. (*drugs*) hachisch*; **to smoke hash**, fumer du hasch **4**. pagaille *f*/gâchis *m*; **to make a hash of it**, tout foutre en l'air/tout faire foirer **5**. du rebattu/du rabâché; **don't give me that hash!** garde tes salades!/arrête ton char(re)! **6**. **to settle s.o.'s hash** (*a*) régler son compte à qn (*b*) clouer le bec à qn.

hash² [hæʃ] *vtr F* gâcher/bousiller/ saloper/bâcler.

hashery ['hæʃəri], **hash-house** ['hæʃhaus] *n NAm F* gargote *f*.

hash over ['hæʃ'ouvər] *vi NAm F* discuter/ressasser/rabâcher (un problème, une difficulté, etc).

hash-slinger ['hæʃsliŋər] *n NAm F* **1**. serveur, -euse de gargote/ loufiat *m* **2**. mauvais(e) cuisinier, -ière **3**. marmiton *m*/gargot *m*.

hash-up ['hæʃʌp] *n F* réchauffé *m*/ ripopée *f* (de vieux contes, etc).

hash up ['hæʃʌp] *vtr F* = **hash**².

hassle¹ ['hæsl] *n F* querelle*/ bagarre*; (*confusion*) pagaille *f*; **it's a real hassle!** c'est toute une histoire!/c'est vraiment la barbe!

hassle² ['hæsl] *vtr F* **1.** se quereller*/se battre*/se bagarrer **2.** se tracasser*/se faire du mauvais sang/se ronger/se faire de la bile; **don't hassle me!** (ne) m'embête pas!/fiche-moi la paix!/arrête tes salades!

hassle-free ['hæsl'friː] *a F* sans problème(s)/pas compliqué.

hat [hæt] *n F* **1. old hat,** vieux jeu; **that's old hat,** c'est du déjà vu/c'est vieux comme le monde **2. to talk through one's hat,** parler* à tort et à travers/délirer **3. to keep it under one's hat,** garder qch pour soi; **keep it under your hat!** motus (et bouche cousue)!/mets-le dans ta poche avec ton mouchoir dessus! **4. to pass the hat round,** faire la quête **5. my hat!** (*i*) mince alors!/ mes aïeux! (*ii*) mon œil! **6. hard hat,** casque *m* de chantier; **the hard hats,** les gens du bâtiment **7. high hat,** cymbale *f.* (*See* **brass-hat; cocked; drop¹ 2**)

hatch [hætʃ] *n F* **down the hatch!** à la vôtre! **to put one down the hatch,** s'en jeter un (derrière la cravate)/en mettre un à l'abri de la pluie. (*See* **booby-hatch**)

hatchet ['hætʃit] *n F* **1. to bury the hatchet,** se réconcilier/se rabibocher **2. hatchet man** (*a*) tueur *m* (à gages)/homme *m* de main (*b*) celui qui arrange les sales affaires des autres; qui est payé pour laver le linge sale des autres.

haul¹ [hɔːl] *n F* **a good haul,** un bon/un beau coup de filet; une bonne récolte.

haul² [hɔːl] *vtr F* **to haul s.o. over the coals,** réprimander* qn/ engueuler qn; **to get hauled over the coals,** se faire passer un savon. (*See* **ashes 2**)

haul-ass ['hɔːlæs] *vi NAm P* partir* en vitesse/se tailler/déhotter/ changer de crémerie.

hauler ['hɔːlər] *n NAm F* voiture très rapide/bolide *m*.

haul in [hɔːl'in] *vtr F* arrêter*/ agrafer/épingler/coffrer (qn).

haul off ['hɔːl'ɔf] *vi NAm F* lever le bras/faire une pause avant de cogner qn; **I hauled off before I hit him,** je me suis préparé pour le cogner.

haul up ['hɔːl'ʌp] *vi F* critiquer* (qn)/débiner (qn)/dénigrer (qn)/ casser du sucre sur le dos (à qn).

have [hæv] *vtr* **1.** *P* **to have it,** faire l'amour*; **to have s.o./to have it away with s.o./to have it off with s.o.,** s'envoyer qn/se faire qn **2.** *O F* **to have it away with sth,** voler* qch/chiper qch **3.** *O F* **to have it away,** s'échapper; **he's had it away over the wall,** il a fait la belle/il s'est fait la paire **4.** *F* **to have had it** (*i*) rater sa chance/rater son coup; rater le coche (*ii*) mourir*/ claquer (*iii*) être fatigué*/crevé (*iv*) être ruiné*; **I've had it,** je suis vanné; **you've had it, chum!** tu es fait, mon vieux!/tu es foutu, mon vieux!; **my car's had it,** elle est foutue, ma bagnole; **I've had it (up to here),** j'en ai assez/j'en ai ras le bol/j'en ai plein le cul **5.** *F* **to let s.o. have it** (*i*) battre* qn/filer une avoine à qn (*ii*) critiquer* qn (*iii*) réprimander* qn/sonner les cloches à qn (*iv*) dire ses quatre vérités à qn (*v*) régler son compte à qn **6.** *F* duper*/avoir (qn)/rouler (qn); **I've been had,** je me suis fait avoir/ on m'a eu **7.** *F* vaincre (qn); **there you have me,** là, tu me la coupes/ ça va, je ne dis plus rien/ça va, je me tais **8.** *F* **to have it out with s.o.,** vider une querelle* avec qn/ s'expliquer avec qn **9.** *F* **to have it in for s.o./to have a down on s.o.,** en vouloir à qn/avoir une dent contre qn. (*See* **any; down¹ III 1**)

have-nots ['hæv'nɔts] *npl F* les dépourvus *mpl*/les déshérités *mpl*;

the haves and the have-nots, les riches* et les pauvres*/les rupins *mpl* et les purotins *mpl.*

have on ['hæv'ɔn] *vtr F* **1.** duper*/faire marcher (qn); **he's having you on,** il te fait marcher **2. to have sth on,** être occupé; **I've got nothing on tomorrow,** je ne suis pas pris/je n'ai rien demain.

have up ['hæv'ʌp] *vtr F* traduire (qn) en justice; **to be had up,** passer en jugement; **he was had up before the beak,** le magistrat l'a convoqué.

hawk [hɔːk] *n* **1.** *F (pol)* qn qui pousse à la guerre et au chauvinisme; partisan *m* des solutions de force *esp* dans une guerre; faucon *m.* (*See* **dove**; **fairy 1**; **newshawk**) **2.** *P (drugs) (a)* LSD* *(b)* trafiquant *m*/dealer *m* en LSD.

hawkish ['hɔːkiʃ] *a F (pol)* qui pousse à la guerre et au chauvinisme; **hawkish policies,** politique *f* belliciste/agressive.

hay [hei] *n* **1.** *F* **to hit the hay,** se coucher*/se pieuter **2.** *P* **to have a roll in the hay with s.o.,** faire une partie de jambes en l'air avec qn. (*See* **roll¹ 2**) **3.** *P (drugs)* **(Indian) hay,** marijuana*/chanvre (indien) **4.** *F* peu d'argent*/gnognot(t)e *f* **5.** *F* **to make hay (while the sun shines),** battre le fer pendant qu'il est chaud **6.** *F* **to make hay of sth,** chambarder/bouleverser/démolir qch.

hay-eater ['heiiːtər] *n P (Black Slang)* Blanc(he) *m(f).*

hayhead ['heihed] *n O P (drugs) (a)* usager *m* de la marijuana* *(b)* habitué(e) de la marijuana*. (*See* **hay 3**)

haymaker ['heimeikər] *n P (boxing)* coup* puissant (mettant l'adversaire hors de combat)/knockout *m.*

hayseed ['heisiːd] *n NAm F* paysan*/cul-terreux *m*/cul-pailleux *m*/bouseux *m.*

haywire ['heiwaiər] *a F (machine,* *etc)* détraqué; *(situation)* embrouillé; *(pers)* emballé/excité/cinglé; **to go haywire,** *(pers)* ne pas tourner rond/perdre la boule/déconner; *(plan, project)* être loupé/finir en queue de poisson/en os de boudin; *(machine)* se détraquer.

haze [heiz] *vtr NAm F (scol)* brimer; faire des brimades *fpl* à/bizut(h)er (un nouvel élève).

head [hed] *n* **1.** *F* mal *m* de tête; **to have a (bad) head/to have a head on (one)** *(i)* avoir mal au crâne *(ii)* avoir la gueule de bois/la GDB **2.** *F* **to yell one's head off,** gueuler comme un sourd/crier à tue-tête; **to talk one's head off,** ne pas s'arrêter de parler **3.** *F* **to be head over heels in love,** aimer* qn/être toqué de qn/avoir le béguin pour qn/en pincer pour qn **4.** *O P* usager *m* de drogues; drogué(e)*/camé(e) *(b)* (= *high*) **to get a head,** planer. (*See* **acid 2**; **cokehead**; **cubehead**; **dopehead**; **hayhead**; **hophead**; **juicehead**; **methhead**; **pillhead**; **pothead**; **teahead**; **weedhead**) **5.** *F* **to go off one's head,** devenir fou*/perdre la boule; **to be soft in the head,** être bête*/ramolli **6.** *usu pl P* WC*/chiottes *fpl* **7.** *F* **I need it like (I need) a hole in the head!** c'est aussi souhaitable qu'une jambe cassée!/il ne me manque que ça!/il ne manquait plus que ça! **8.** *F* **not to (be able to) make head nor tail of sth,** ne comprendre goutte à qch; **I can't make head nor tail of it,** je n'y pige que dalle/que couic/que chti; **you couldn't make head nor tail of it,** une truie n'y retrouverait pas ses petits **9.** *F* **I could do it (standing) on my head,** c'est simple comme bonjour **10.** *F* **to talk s.o.'s head off,** étourdir qn/casser les oreilles* à qn **11.** *F* **to talk off the top of one's head,** dire n'importe quoi; **I just said that off the top of my head,** j'ai dit ça comme ça/j'ai dit ça sans savoir exactement **12.** *F* **heads will roll,** les têtes vont tomber/ce sera le coup de balai/ça va saigner **13.** *V* fellation*; **head job,** prise *f* de pipe/taillage *m* de plume; **to give s.o. head/to give s.o. a head job,** tailler une pipe/une plume à qn; sucer qn. (*See* **big-head; bonehead; boofhead; cab-bage-head; chew off; chowderhead; chucklehead; cloghead; deadhead; eat 6; egghead; fathead; flathead; jughead; knock² 2; knothead; knucklehead; lughead; lunk-head; meathead; muscle-head; muttonhead; nail¹ 2; pea-head; pinhead; puddinghead; pumpkinhead; redhead; sap(head); screw² 6; shithead; skinhead; sleepyhead; sore 2; sorehead; squarehead; thick-head; turniphead; water 2)**

headache ['hedeik] *n* **1.** *F* ennui *m*/embêtement *m*/casse-tête *m*; **what a headache you are!** ce que tu peux être casse-pieds! **2.** *NAm P* épouse*/bourgeoise *f*. (*See* **Dutch-man 2) 3.** *P* **to give s.o. a serious headache,** tuer* qn d'une balle dans la tête/faire sauter la cervelle à qn.

headbanger ['hed'bæŋər] *n P* **1.** fana(tique) *mf* de rock **2.** individu bête* *ou* fou*/cinglé/dingo *m*/barjot *m*.

headbone ['hedboun] *n NAm P* (*Black Slang*) crâne *m*.

headcase ['hedkeis] *n F* fou*/cin-glé *m*/dingue *m*/dingo *m*/barjot *m*.

header ['hedər] *n F* **to take a header,** tomber* par terre/ramasser une pelle; (*esp motorbike*) se viander.

headhunter ['hedhʌntər] *n F* **1.** (*media*) chasseur *m* de têtes **2.** tueur *m* à gages/meurtrier profes-sionnel.

headlights ['hedlaits] *npl P* (*not common*) **1.** seins*/amortisseurs *mpl*/pare-chocs *mpl* **2.** gros dia-mants*/bouchons *mpl* de carafe.

headlines ['hedlainz] *npl F* **to hit the headlines,** devenir célèbre/faire la une/faire les gros titres.

head-merchant ['hedmərtʃ(ə)nt] *n F* = **head-shrinker.**

head-piece ['hedpiːs] *n F* tête*/cerveau *m*/ciboulot *m*/cigare *m*.

head-shrinker ['hedʃriŋkər] *n F* psychiatre *mf*/psychanalyste *mf*; psy *mf*. (*See* **shrink**)

health [helθ] *n F* **I don't do that for my health,** je ne fais pas cela pour mon plaisir/pour m'amuser.

heap [hiːp] *n F* **1. to be (struck) all of a heap,** rester comme deux ronds de flan; **he was struck all of a heap,** ça l'a sidéré/soufflé/laissé baba **2.** (*winner*) **to come out at the top of/on top of the heap,** être au premier rang/tenir le haut du pavé; (*loser*) **to stay at the bottom of the heap,** être le dernier des derniers/être le des ders/être la super crasse **3. a whole heap of nonsense,** un tissu d'âneries **4.** vieille voiture*/bagnole *f*; vieux clou/guimbarde *f* **5. heaps of...,** une abondance* de.../un tas de.../une tripotée de.../une flopée de.../un rab' de...; **there's heaps of things to do,** il y a tout un tas de choses à faire; **we've got heaps of time,** on a tout le temps qu'il faut/on n'est pas aux pièces; **he's in heaps of trouble,** il est dans le pétrin/la merde; **heaps better,** beaucoup mieux. (*See* **scrap-heap**)

heart [hɑːt] *n F* **have a heart!** (ne) parle pas de malheur!/pitié! (*iron*) **my heart bleeds for you!/you're breaking my heart!** tu vas me faire pleurer!/tu me fends le cœur! (*See* **purple**)

heart-throb ['hɑːtθrɔb] *n F* objet *m* d'amour/béguin *m*; idole *m*.

heart-to-heart ['hɑːttu'hɑːt] *n F* **to have a heart-to-heart with s.o.,** parler à cœur ouvert avec qn.

hearty ['hɑːti] *n F* **1.** athlète (opposé à un esthète) **2.** *pl* camarades *mpl*/copains *mpl*/potes *mpl*; O (*nau*) **me hearties!** les gars!

heat [hiːt] *n* **1.** F pression *f*/feu *m*; **to turn on the heat,** s'enflammer/s'échauffer; **to put the heat on s.o.,** faire pression sur qn/lui mettre le feu au derrière; (*police*) aller à la recherche d'un criminel; **the heat is on,** ça commence à chauffer/ça va barder **2.** F (*police*) interrogatoire* poussé/saignement *m* de nez **3.** *NAm* P fonctionnaire *m* de l'ordre judiciaire **4.** *NAm* P = **heater.**

heater ['hiːtər] *n NAm* P revolver*/feu *m*/pétard *m.*

Heath Robinson ['hiːθ'rɔbinsən] *a attrib* (*machine, contraption*) construit d'une façon très compliquée pour remplir une fonction très limitée *ou* très simple; construit n'importe comment; (*gadget*) à la noix; **the plumbing's a bit Heath Robinson,** la plomberie laisse beaucoup à désirer.

heave-ho ['hiːv'hou] *n* P **to get the (old) heave-ho,** être congédié*/être flanqué à la porte/être lourdé; être plaqué; **to give s.o. the heave-ho,** se débarrasser* de qn/larguer/sacquer/virer qn; plaquer qn.

heaven ['hevn] *n* F **1. it's heaven to relax,** c'est super de pouvoir se reposer/c'est bath de pouvoir se reposer **2. good heavens!** juste ciel!/bonté divine!/zut alors! **heavens above!** nom d'une pipe! **for heaven's sake!** pour l'amour de Dieu! **heaven forbid!** surtout pas! (*See* **dust**[1] **2** (*a*), (*b*))

heavenly ['hevnli] *a* F ravissant/merveilleux; super/le pied/pas dégueu. (*See* **blue**[1] **II 1**)

heaves [hiːvz] *npl* F **to have the heaves,** avoir des nausées *fpl.*

heavy ['hevi] **I** *a* **1.** F passionné; impudique/vicieux; **heavy necking,** pelotage *m*/tripotage *m* **2.** F **heavy date,** rendez-vous* sentimental important **3.** F **to make heavy weather of sth,** faire toute une affaire de qch/faire tout un plat de qch **4.** P (*butin*) de valeur; **the heavy mob,** bande* de voleurs* de grande envergure **5.** F **heavy stuff,** renforts motorisés dans une descente de police **6.** F (*theatre, etc*) **heavy rôle,** rôle *m* du méchant de la pièce **7.** P (*a*) sale*/dégueulbif (*b*) **it was a (really) heavy scene** (*i*) (*drugs*) c'était la grande défonce (*ii*) (*violence*) il y avait de la bagarre dans l'air **8.** P (*rock, etc*) super-beat/maxi-beat; **heavy metal,** métal lourd **9.** P excellent*/très agréable; **that's really heavy!** c'est le (super-)pied!/c'est vachement cool! **II** *adv* P **things started to get heavy,** ça allait barder/chier/saigner; il y avait de la bagarre dans l'air; **he started to get a bit heavy,** il avait l'air de chercher la bagarre; **don't get heavy with me!** (ne) me faites pas chier! **III** *n* **1.** F (*boxing*) (= *heavyweight*) poids lourd **2.** P (*a*) apache *m*/bandit *m* (*b*) assassin* **3.** F le méchant dans une pièce *ou* un film **4.** *NAm* P **to be in the heavy,** avoir beaucoup d'argent*/être riche*/rouler sur l'or **5.** F dur *m*/balaise *m*; garde *m* du corps/gorille *m*; videur *m* (d'une boîte de nuit); **to come the heavy,** faire l'autoritaire; faire le méchant/jouer au dur.

hebe ['hiːbi] *n NAm* P Juif*/Youpe *m*/youpin *m*/youtre *m.* (*See* **heeb**)

heck [hek] *n* F (*euph for* **hell**) **1. heck!** sapristi!/zut!/flûte!/la barbe! **what the heck...!** que diable...! **2. a heck of a lot,** une abondance*/une grande quantité; un sacré paquet/un tas de.

hedge [hedʒ] *vtr* F **1. to hedge one's bets,** étaler *ou* protéger ses paris **2.** chercher des échappatoires *fpl*/des faux-fuyants *mpl*; s'échapper par la tangente/tourner autour du pot; **stop hedging,** dis-le carrément!/allez, accouche!

heeb [hiːb] *n NAm P* = **hebe.**

heebie-jeebies ['hiːbi'dʒiːbiz] *npl F* **1.** délirium *m* tremens/les rats bleus **2.** angoisse *f*/frousse *f*/trac *m*/peur bleue; **to give s.o. the heebie-jeebies,** filer la trouille/les chocottes *fpl* à qn; **it gives me the heebie-jeebies** (*i*) cela me donne la chair de poule (*ii*) ça me dégoûte/ça me débecte.

heel [hiːl] *n* **1.** *F* individu* méprisable/cave *m*/salaud *m*; **to be a (bit of a) heel,** friser la canaille; **he's a real heel,** c'est une vraie canaille **2.** *A P* **to have round heels,** avoir la cuisse hospitalière. (*See* **roundheel(s)**) **3.** *F* **to cool/to kick one's heels,** se morfondre/faire le pied de grue/poireauter. (*See* **head 3; kick up 3; shitheel**)

heeled [hiːld] *a NAm P* **1.** = **well-heeled 2.** armé d'un revolver*/enfouraillé.

heft [heft] *vtr F* soulever/soupeser (qch).

hefty ['hefti] *a F* **1.** fort*/costaud/malabar/balaise **2.** gros/important; **a hefty bill,** une note de taille/une sacrée douloureuse; **a hefty chunk,** un morceau imposant.

he-ing and she-ing ['hiːiŋ'ʃiːiŋ] *n P* partie *f* de jambes en l'air/baisage *m*.

Heinie, heinie ['haini] *n A P* (*esp WWI & II*) (*a*) Allemand*/boche *m* (*b*) soldat allemand/hun *m*/doryphore *m*/Fritz *m*.

Heinz 57 ['hainz'fifti'sevn] *n F* chien* bâtard/corniaud *m*. (*See* **bingo 57**)

heist¹ [haist] *n esp NAm F* **1.** (*a*) cambriolage *m*/casse *m*/fric-frac *m* (*b*) hold-up *m*/braquage *m*. *A* = **heister.**

heist² [haist] *vtr esp NAm F* **1.** cambrioler*/faire un casse **2.** voler qch.

heister ['haistər] *n esp NAm O F*

cambrioleur*/casseur *m*/braqueur *m*.

hell [hel] *n* **1.** *P* (*a*) **go to hell!** va te faire voir (chez les Grecs)/va te faire foutre; **to hell with it!** ras le bol de tout cela!/y'en a marre de tout cela! **get the hell out of here!** (nom de Dieu) débarrasse le plancher!/fiche-moi le camp! **oh hell!** (*i*) (oh,) bordel! (*ii*) et merde!/putain! **bloody hell!** bordel de merde! **hell's bells (and buckets of blood)!** sacré nom de nom! **would he go? would he hell!** partir, lui? penses-tu!/tu parles! **hell, I don't know,** je n'en sais foutre rien/qu'est-ce que j'en sais moi? **like hell!** tu parles!/ça va la tête?/mon œil, oui!/et puis quoi encore?/pas si con! (*b*) **what the hell does it matter?** qu'est-ce que ça peut bien faire/foutre? **what the hell has that got to do with me?** qu'est-ce que ça peut bien me foutre? **who the hell are you?** mais qui êtes-vous donc, à la fin? **who the hell do you think you are (anyway)?** pour qui te prends tu, à la fin? **what the hell do you think you're doing/playing at?** tu maquilles quoi, au juste?/dis donc, tu te crois où? **what in hell/in hell's name is that?** qu'est-ce que c'est que ce putain de truc? **where the hell did you put it?** où diable l'as-tu fourré? **why the hell doesn't he belt up?** (est-ce qu')il va la boucler, oui ou merde! **2.** *F* **to give s.o. hell,** faire passer un mauvais quart d'heure à qn/en faire voir (de toutes les couleurs) à qn; **to get hell/to have hell to pay,** être réprimandé*; se faire engueuler/incendier; en prendre pour son grade; **there'll be hell to pay!** ça va barder!/ça va chauffer!/il va y avoir du grabuge! **3.** *F* **like (all) hell let loose,** comme les damnés en enfer; **to create/to raise (merry) hell** (*i*) faire du boucan/faire un chambard du diable (*ii*) rouscailler/râler (comme un enragé) **4.** *P* **in a/in one hell of a mess/state,** dans une pagaille infernale/du tonnerre; **a hell of a/one hell of a nice bloke/** *esp NAm* **guy,** un (super) chic type/ un mec super; **you've got a hell of a nerve/cheek!** tu manques pas d'air!/tu as un sacré culot! **it's a hell of a bore/bind,** c'est drôlement embêtant; **a hell of a row** (*i*) un bruit* d'enfer/un vacarme infernal (*ii*) une engueulade maison; **we had a hell of a good time,** on s'en est payé une bien bonne **5.** *F* **to do sth for the hell of it,** faire qch histoire de rire/pour s'en payer une tranche **6.** *F* **to play hell with s.o./ sth,** en faire voir à qn/cabosser qch; **this weather's playing hell with my leg,** avec ce temps-là, j'ai la jambe qui déguste/qui me fait jongler! **7.** *F* **to feel like hell,** se sentir drôlement pas bien/complètement vaseux/complètement patraque **8.** *P* **sure as hell,** sûr et certain/dans la fouille **9.** *P* **to knock hell out of s.o.,** battre* qn comme plâtre **10.** *P* **all to hell,** démoli/gâché/coulé **11.** *F* **to go hell for leather,** galoper ventre à terre/courir avec le feu au derrière **12.** *F* **till hell freezes over,** jusqu'à la Saint-Glinglin **13.** *NAm F* **from hell to breakfast,** entièrement/ totalement/de A à Z **14.** *NAm F* **to hell and gone** (*i*) disparu/passé à l'as (*ii*) aux antipodes/chez les damnés **15.** *F* **hell's angels,** jeunes voyous *mpl* (en moto)/blousons noirs/loubars *mpl*/loulous *mpl* **16.** *F* **come hell or high water,** advienne que pourra. (*See* **fucking I** 2; **hell-cat; kick up** 3; **snowball¹** 2; **sodding; stink¹** 1)

hell-bender ['helbendər] *n P* bamboche infernale. (*See* **bender** 1)

hell-cat ['helkæt] *n F* (*a*) fille* *ou* femme* pleine d'entrain et de témérité/qui n'a pas froid aux yeux (*b*) mégère *f*/chipie *f*.

hell-hole ['helhoul] *n F* endroit mal famé/coupe-gorge *m*; bouge *m*.

hellion ['heljən] *n NAm F* **1.** vaurien*/sale type *m*/fripouille *f* **2.** enfant* terrible/petit diable/(un) gosse infernal.

hellishly ['heliʃli] *adv F* diablement/vachement.

hello-dearie ['həlou'diəri] *n A P* prostituée*/frangipane *f*.

helluva ['heləvə] *P* (= *hell of a*) *see* **hell 4.**

he-man ['hiːmæn] *n* (*pl* **he-men**) *F* (*a*) homme fort* et viril/malabar *m*/un mâle/un mec/un macho (*b*) un beau mâle.

hemp [hemp] *n F* (*drugs*) **(Indian) hemp,** cannabis*/chanvre (indien).

hen [hen] *n F* (*a*) (*pej*) femme*/ vieille dinde (*b*) jeune femme*/une petite poule; **hen party,** réunion *f* de femmes/volière *f* (*c*) (*form of address*) (*regional*) ma chère/mon chou. (*See* **stag¹** 1)

Henry, henry ['henri] *n F* (*drugs*) héroïne*.

hep [hep] *a A F* = **hip.**

hep-cat ['hep'kæt] *n A F* = **hip-cat.**

herb [həːb] *n F* (*drugs*) **(the) herb,** cannabis*/herbe *f*.

Herbert ['(h)əːbət] *Prn O F* **he's a right little Herbert,** c'est un vrai connard/un vrai crétin.

here ['hiər] *adv F* **1. that's neither here nor there,** cela ne fait ni chaud ni froid/cela n'a aucune importance **2. here goes!** ça démarre!/allons-y!/c'est parti (mon kiki)! **3. here you are,** tenez/ prenez-le/et voilà **4. from here on in,** à partir de ce moment.

heron ['herən] *n A P* (*drugs*) héroïne*.

herring ['heriŋ] *n F* **1. red herring,** procédé servant à brouiller les pistes/diversion *f* **2. the Herring Pond,** l'océan *m* Atlantique/la Grande Tasse.

het up ['het'ʌp] *a F* **1.** énervé/
agité/tracassé **2.** en colère*/en
rogne.

hex[1] [heks] *n NAm F* (*a*)
malchance*/poisse *f* (*b*) porte-
guigne *m*.

hex[2] [heks] *vtr NAm F* porter la
guigne/la poisse à (qn).

hi! [hai] *excl F* salut!/bonjour!

hick [hik] **I** *a NAm P* **1.** rus-
tique/campagnard; **a hick town,** un
patelin/un bled/un trou **2.** igno-
rant/rustaud **II** *n NAm P* **1.**
paysan*/péquenaud *m*/plouc *m* **2.**
innocent *m*/couillon *m* **3.**
cadavre*/croni *m*/macchab(ée) *m*
4. *NAm* (*pej*) Portoricain(e) *m(f)*.

hickey ['hiki] *n NAm F* suçon *m*.

hide [haid] *n F* **1.** (*skin*) peau *f*/
cuir *m*/couenne *f*; **to tan the hide
off s.o.,** battre* qn/tanner le cuir à
qn **2. to have a thick hide,** avoir la
peau dure. (*See* **thick-skinned**)

hiding ['haidiŋ] *n F* **1. (good)** hiding, volée *f* de coups*/tannée *f*/dér-
ouillée *f*/passage *m* à tabac **2. to
be on a hiding to nothing,** avoir
tout à perdre sans rien à gagner.

hi-fi ['hai'fai] *abbr F* (= *high fidelity*)
(de) haute fidélité/hi-fi.

high [hai] **I** *a F* **1. to be for the
high jump,** en être pour de la
casse/être dans de mauvais draps;
he's for the high jump, qu'est-ce
qu'il va prendre!/son compte est
bon **2. to leave s.o. high and dry,**
laisser qn en plan/laisser tomber
qn comme une vieille chaussette **3.
to be high** (*a*) être ivre*/parti/
rétamé/schlass (*b*) (*drugs*) être dans
un état d'euphorie/être high/
planer/voyager. (*See* **fly**[2] **1** (*b*); **kite
4**) **4.** *NAm* **high on sth/s.o.,** qui a
une haute opinion de qch/de qn
5. to have a high old time, faire la
fête*/la noce; s'en payer une
(bonne) tranche. (*See* **hat 7;**
horse[1] **5; jinks; knee-high**) **II** *n
F* **to be on a high,** être high/
planer/voyager.

highbinder ['haibaindər] *n NAm
F* **1.** gangster *m*/assassin*/bandit
m **2.** escroc*/filou *m*/empileur *m*
3. politicien corrompu/véreux.

highbrow ['haibrau] **I** *a F* intel-
lectuel/calé **II** *n F* intellectuel *m*/
mandarin *m*/grosse tête.

highfalutin(g) ['haifə'luːtin, -iŋ] *a
F* prétentieux*/ronflant/ampoulé/
esbroufeur.

high-flier ['hai'flaiər] *n F* ambitieux *m*/qn qui va aux extrêmes.
(*See* **fly**[2] **1** (*a*))

high-muck-a-muck ['hai-
'mʌkəmʌk] *n F* personnage impor-
tant/grosse légume/huile *f*/ponte *m*.

highspots ['haispɔts] *npl F* **to hit
the highspots** (*a*) exceller/toucher
les hauteurs *fpl*/toucher sa bille à
qch (*b*) s'en payer une tranche/faire
la foire/faire la noce.

hightail ['haiteil] *vi F* **to hightail it,**
se dépêcher*/se magner le train;
let's hightail it out of here! allez, on
se tire!/allez, on change de
crémerie!

high-ups ['haiʌps] *npl F* hauts
fonctionnaires/gros bonnets.

highway ['haiwei] *a attrib F* **it's
highway robbery!** c'est du vol
manifeste!/c'est de l'arnaque patentée!

hillbilly ['hil'bili] *n NAm F* **1.**
petit fermier de montagne **2.** rustre *m*/rustaud *m*/péquenaud *m* **3.**
hillbilly (music), musique
montagnarde et rustique.

hinnie ['hini] *n F* (*regional*) = **hen**
(*c*).

hip [hip] *a O F* (*up-to-date*) branché/
à la coule/dans le vent/à la page;
qui apprécie la musique moderne;
to get hip, suivre la mode; se mettre à la coule/à la page; être
branché.

hip cat ['hip'kæt] *n O F* (*jazz,
swing, etc*) (*a*) admirateur *m*/
fana(tique) *mf* du jazz (*b*) individu

branché/dans le vent/à la coule. (*See* **cat 1**)

hipped [hipt] *a NAm P* **1.** enthousiaste/passionné/fanatique **2.** *A* ivre*.

hippie, hippy ['hipi] *n F* hippie *mf*/hippy *mf*.

hipster ['hipstər] *n O* **1.** *F* = **hipcat 2.** *F* membre d'un groupe de cools **3.** *F* membre de la génération beat **4.** *P* initié(e) à la drogue. (*See* **hip**)

hister ['haistər] *n NAm F* = **heister**.

hit[1] [hit] *n* **1.** *F* pièce *f*/chanson *f* à succès/tube *m*; **summer hit,** tube de l'été **2.** *F* succès *m* populaire; **to make a hit,** faire un boum/faire un tabac; **she made/scored a big hit with him,** elle a fait une grosse impression sur lui/elle lui a tapé dans l'œil **3.** *P* réussite sexuelle/partie *f* de piquet **4.** *P* rendezvous* de contrebande; moyens *mpl* de contrebande **5.** *P* plaquette *f* de drogues **6.** *P* injection *f* de drogues/piquouse *f*/shoot *m* **7.** *P* (*esp contract killing*) meurtre prémédité/meurtre sur commande/contrat *m*; **to make a hit,** remplir un contrat; tuer*/buter/descendre qn sur commande. (*See* **smash-hit**)

hit[2] [hit] *vtr* **1.** *F* **to hit the hundred mark,** (*car, etc*) taper le 160 **2.** *P* (*drugs*) (*a*) provoquer une forte réaction (*b*) **to hit s.o.,** pourvoir un usager avec de la drogue **3.** *F* toucher/taper qn pour de l'argent; **he hit me for four quid,** il m'a tapé/torpillé de quatre livres **4.** *esp NAm P* assassiner qn; **the hit man hit his man,** le tueur a buté sa victime/a rempli son contrat/a descendu son client **5.** *P* (*music*) commencer à jouer; **let's hit it!** bon, allez, en avant!/en avant la musique! (*See* **bottle**[1] **1**; **ceiling; deck 1; feather**[1] **6; hay 1; highspots; jackpot; pad**[1] **2; panic 2; pipe 2; road 2; sack**[1] **3; sauce**[1] **2; track**[1] **1; trail**)

hitch [hitʃ] *vtr F* **1. to hitch one's wag(g)on to a star,** être dévoré d'ambition/viser très haut **2. to get hitched** (*i*) se marier/se marida/s'entifler (*ii*) se maquer. (*See* **unhitched**) **3. to hitch (a ride),** se faire emmener en voiture/faire de l'auto-stop/faire du stop.

hitching ['hitʃiŋ] *n F* auto-stop *m*/stop *m*; **to go hitching,** faire du stop.

hit man ['hit'mæn] *n esp NAm P* tueur *m* (à gages)/meurtrier professionnel.

hit off ['hit'ɔf] *vi F* **to hit it off with s.o.,** bien s'entendre avec qn; **they don't hit it off,** il y a du tirage entre eux.

hit-parade ['hitpəreid] *n F* hit-parade *m*.

hive off ['haiv'ɔf] *vtr&i F* **1.** mettre de côté/mettre à l'écart **2.** s'enfuir*/se cavaler/se débiner.

hiya! ['haijə] *excl F* salut! (*See* **hi!**)

hock[1] [hɔk] *n F* **in hock** (*a*) en gage/chez ma tante/au clou (*b*) en prison*/en taule.

hock[2] [hɔk] *vtr F* mettre en gage/mettre au clou.

hockshop ['hɔkʃɔp] *n F* mont-de-piété *m*/chez ma tante/le clou.

hocky ['hɔki] *n NAm P* **1.** mensonges*/blagues *fpl*/salades *fpl*/craques *fpl* **2.** merde *f*/caca *m* **3.** sperme*/blanc *m* **4.** nourriture* peu appétissante/boustifaille *f*.

ho-dad(dy) ['hou'dæd(i)] *n NAm F* **1.** individu* farfelu/m'as-tu-vu *m* **2.** (*esp hanger-on*) individu* qui aime fréquenter les sportifs sans en être un lui-même; parasite *m* **3.** pète-sec *m*/collet monté/constipé *m* **4.** individu bête*/crétin *m*/gland *m*/nœud *m*.

hoedown ['houdaun] *n NAm F* **1.** danse *f* rustique; bal animé/guinche *f* de pedzouille **2.** querelle*/engueulade *f* **3.** bagarre*/rixe *f*/rififi *m*/baston *m*.

hog¹ [hɔg] *n* **1.** *F* goinfre*/porc *m*
2. *F* **to go the whole hog,** aller
jusqu'au bout/tout risquer/mettre le
paquet. (*See* **whole-hogger**;
whole-hoggism) **3.** *NAm P*
(*motorbike*) grosse moto/gros cube
4. *P* (*drugs*) phéncyclidine/PCP*.
(*See* **road-hog**; **speed-hog**)

hog² [hɔg] *vtr F* **1.** to hog oneself,
goinfrer/bâfrer **2.** monopoliser; **to
hog the limelight,** accaparer la
vedette **3. to hog the road,** conduire au milieu de la route/con-
duire comme un âne. (*See* **road-
hog**) **4. to hog it,** vivre comme un
cochon.

hog-tie ['hɔgtai] *vtr esp NAm F*
réduire à l'impuissance.

hogwash ['hɔgwɔʃ] *n F* **1.** bibine
f/lavasse *f*/pisson *m* d'âne **2.**
bêtise*/sottise *f*/du pipeau; **that's
just hogwash!** c'est des foutaises!
3. boniments *mpl*/baratinage *m*.

hoi polloi ['hɔipə'lɔi] *n F* (*pej*) **the
hoi polloi,** le peuple/le popu(lo).

hoist¹ [hɔist] *n esp NAm P* **1.** vol
m/braquage *m*/hold-up *m*. (*See*
heist 1)

hoist² [hɔist] *vtr esp NAm P* **1.**
cambrioler*/voler*/caroubler. (*See*
heist² 1, 2) **2.** voler* à l'étalage/
chouraver/acheter à la foire
d'empoigne **3.** *Austr* procéder à
une arrestation/coffrer/alpaguer.

hokey-pokey ['houki'pouki] *n F*
1. = **hokum 1** **2.** *NAm* glace *f ou*
bonbon *m* de mauvaise qualité.

hokum ['houkəm] *n esp NAm F* **1.**
bêtises*/blagues *fpl*/foutaises *fpl*
2. sentimentalité niaise (dans une
pièce, un film, etc); guimauve *f*/
mélo *m*.

hokus ['houkəs] *n P* (*drugs*) drogues
fpl/came *f*/narcs *mpl*.

hold [hould] **I** *vtr* **1.** *F* **hold
everything! / hold your horses! / hold
it!** arrêtez!/attendez!/(ne) bougez
plus!/(ne) faites rien!/minute! **2.**
P **to hold (oneself),** se masturber*/
se branler/se pogner/se palucher

II *vi* (*a*) fourguer des drogues (*b*)
posséder des drogues.

hold out for ['hould'autfɔɪr] *vtr F*
he's holding out for more money, il
tient bon pour avoir plus de fric/il
ne veut pas lâcher le morceau, pour
ce qui est de la question fric.

hold out on ['hould'autɔn] *vtr F*
faire des cachotteries *fpl* (à qn);
he's holding out on us, il nous fait
des cachotteries/il nous cache qch.

hole [houl] *n* **1.** *F* bouge *m*/bas-
tringue *m*/boui-boui *m*/caboulot *m*
2. *F* (*room, house*) taudis *m*/gourbi
m/piaule *f*; (*town, village*) bled *m*/
trou *m* **3.** *F* embarras *m*/pétrin
m/impasse *f*; **to be in a hole,** être
dans une situation difficile/être en
rade/être dans le caca **4.** *F* **to
make a hole in one's capital,**
écorner son capital; taper dans/sur
ses économies *fpl* **5.** *F* **to pick
holes in sth,** trouver à redire à qch/
chercher la petite bête **6.** *V* sexe
de la femme*/fente *f*. (*See* **manhole**) **7.** *V* anus*/trou *m* de balle.
(*See* **arsehole**; **bum-hole**; **bung-
hole 1**; **cornhole¹**; **fart-hole**; **shit-
hole**) **8.** *P* the hole, cachot *m*
(disciplinaire)/mitard *m*/trou *m* **9.**
F **hole in the wall,** petite maison *ou*
lieu *m* de commerce/trou *m* **10.** *F*
to burn a hole in one's stomach,
manger* *ou* boire* qch de très fort/
se brûler l'estomac *m* **11.** *NAm P*
to go in the hole, s'endetter/
s'encroumer **12.** *F* **to put a hole
through s.o./to drill holes in s.o.,**
assassiner* qn/flinguer qn/trans-
former qn en passoire/trouer la
peau à qn. (*See* **cakehole**;
earhole; **glory-hole**; **head 7**; **hell-
hole**; **keyhole**; **lugholes**; **nineteenth**; **square¹ I 7**; **top-hole**)

hole-and-corner ['houl-
ən(d)'kɔɪnər] *a F* fait en douce/sous
la table; **hole-and-corner work,**
manigances *fpl*.

hole up ['houl'ʌp] *vi F* se cacher*/
se terrer/se planquer.

holier-than-thou ['houliə-ðæn'ðau] n F Sainte-Nitouche f/Tartuffe m/bon apôtre.

holler ['hɔlər] vi P 1. crier*/gueuler/beugler 2. moucharder/cafarder.

holler-wag(g)on ['hɔləwægən] n P voiture-radio f de la police.

hollow ['hɔlou, 'hɔlə] adv F to beat s.o. hollow, battre qn à plate(s) couture(s).

holly-golly ['hɔli'gɔli] n NAm A F 1. bêtises*/sornettes fpl/fadaises fpl 2. tintamarre m/vacarme m/ramdam m/boucan m.

hols [hɔlz] npl F (abbr = holidays) vacances fpl/vacs fpl.

holy ['houli] a 1. F holy cow!/holy cats!/holy mackerel!/holy Moses!/holy smoke! sapristi!/saperlipopette!/crénom de nom! V holy fuck!/holy shit! merde (alors)!/vingt dieux! 2. P (pej) holy Joe (a) prêtre*/pasteur m; étudiant m en théologie/ratichon m (b) personne dévote/grenouille f de bénitier 3. F holy terror (a) enfant* malicieux/petit diable (b) individu* bassinant/colique f (c) individu* qui fait peur/épouvantail m 4. (RS = winning post) Holy Ghost, poteau m (d'arrivée). (See friar)

home [houm] adv F 1. home and dry, à bon port/sain et sauf 2. my suit is going home, mon costume commence à rendre l'âme 3. it's nothing to write home about, ça ne casse rien/ça ne casse pas des briques/ça ne casse pas trois pattes à un canard.

home-bird ['houmbəɪd] n F he's a home bird, il est casanier; she's a home-bird, elle est casanière/popote/pot-au-feu.

homestretch ['houm'stretʃ] n F dernière étape/dernière ligne droite.

homework ['houmwəɪk] n 1. to do one's homework (a) F faire une préparation attentive (b) P (euph) remplir ses obligations conjugales

2. P (a) pelotage m/baisage m (b) a nice bit of homework, une fille* à la cuisse hospitalière.

homo ['houmou] I a P homo(sexuel) II n P homosexuel*/homo m/pédé m.

hon [hʌn] n esp NAm F (= honey) listen hon! écoute chéri(e)!

honcho ['hɔntʃou] n NAm P (mil) chef m.

honest to goodness ['ɔnist(t)ə'gudnis] F I a vrai/réel/authentique II excl honest to goodness! je te jure!/j't'assure!

honey ['hʌni] n F (a) petit(e) ami(e)/chéri(e)/bien-aimé(e); yes, honey! oui, ma puce! (b) qch d'excellent*/de bath/de chouette; it's a (real) honey! c'est du nanan! he's a real honey, c'est un vrai chou/un amour; that's a honey of a car, cette bagnole, c'est un petit bijou. (See bee 2)

honeybunch ['hʌnibʌntʃ] n F = honey (a).

honey fuck ['hʌnifʌk] vi V 1. faire l'amour* d'une manière romantique/à la douce 2. faire l'amour* avec une fille très jeune/baiser la petite fleur.

honey-fuck(ing) ['hʌnifʌk(iŋ)] n V 1. coït*/crampette f/baisage m à la douce 2. coït* lent et agréable/soupe délayée à la quéquette 3. coït* avec une fille très jeune/baisage m de petite fleur.

honk [hɔŋk] vtr&i 1. P to honk (one's chuff), vomir*/dégobiller/faire renard/aller au refil(e) 2. A P to get honked, s'enivrer 3. Austr F sentir* mauvais/puer/schlinguer.

honkers ['hɔŋkəz] a A P (Harry) honkers, ivre*/rétamé/soûl.

honkey, honkie, honky ['hɔŋki] n (esp NAm) P (originally Black Slang) Blanc(he) m(f).

honky-tonk ['hɔŋki'tɔŋk] n NAm F 1. cabaret m de basse classe/caboulot m/boui-boui m 2. petit théâtre de province **3.** bordel*/ claque *m*/bobinard *m*.

hooch [huːtʃ] *n F* **1.** *esp NAm* (*a*) alcool*/gnôle *f* (*esp* de contrebande) (*b*) alcool* très fort/cassegueule *m*/tord-boyaux *m* **2.** *NAm P* hutte *f*/cabane *f*/baraque *f*.

hood [hud] *n P* **1.** = **hoodlum 2.** religieuse *f*/bonne sœur/cornette *f*.

hoodlum ['huːdləm] *n esp NAm F* (*gangster*) voyou*/loubard *m*/loulou *m*.

hooey ['huːi] *n P* bêtises*/foutaises *fpl*; **that's a lot of hooey!** c'est du bidon!

hoof[1] [huːf] *n* **1.** *F* pied*/panard *m*/pinceau *m* **2.** *P* (*RS = poof*) homosexuel*/pédale *f*.

hoof[2] [huːf] *vtr F* **to hoof it**, aller à pied/à pattes/à pinces; aller pedibus (cum jambis).

hoo-ha(a) ['huːhɑː] *n F* (*i*) bruit *m*/ramdam *m*/boucan *m* (*ii*) chichis *mpl* (*iii*) pagaïe *f*; **it wasn't worth all the hoo-ha(a),** ça valait pas tout ce tapage/c'était vraiment pas la peine d'en faire tout un plat.

hook[1] [huk] *n* **1.** *F* **on the hook,** dans une mauvaise passe/dans le pétrin **2.** *F* **to get off the hook,** se débrouiller*/se tirer d'embarras/ d'affaire; **that lets me off the hook,** cela me tire d'affaire; **to get s.o. off the hook,** tirer qn d'affaire/sortir qn de mauvais draps **3.** *P* **to go off the hooks** (*a*) devenir fou*/dérailler/décrocher (*b*) mourir*/passer l'arme à gauche/décrocher/lâcher la rampe **4.** *F esp NAm* **on one's own hook,** sans appui/à son (propre) compte **5.** *F* **he swallowed it hook line and sinker,** il a tout avalé/il a tout gobé **6.** *P* **to sling one's hook,** partir*/s'enfuir/mettre les bouts **7.** *pl F* mains*/croches *fpl*; **to get one's hooks on s.o./sth,** mettre le grappin sur qn/qch. (*See* **grappling 2; meat-hooks**) **8.** *P* drogue narcotique (*esp* héroïne*)/accroche *f*

9. *NAm V* **to put the hooks to s.o.,** faire l'amour* avec qn/fourrer qn/ sabrer qn/calecer qn **10.** *P* voleur*/leveur *m*.

hook[2] [huk] *vtr* **1.** *P* voler*/grappiner/enquiller **2.** *P* arrêter*/ agrafer/alpaguer/épingler **3.** *P* **to get hooked for a few quid**/*NAm* **a few dollars,** être estampé/se faire tondre de quelques talbins/quelques sacs (au jeu) **4.** *F* **to be hooked (on drugs),** se droguer*/se camer/se (s)chnouffer/être accroché **5.** *F* **to be hooked on s.o.,** être épris de qn/ avoir le béguin pour qn/en pincer pour qn **6.** *F* **to hook a husband,** crocheter/mettre le grappin sur un mari **7.** *P* s'enfuir*/se tailler/mettre les bouts.

hooker ['hukər] *n P* **1.** *esp NAm* prostituée*/raccrocheuse *f*/racoleuse *f*/pute *f* **2.** *NAm* verre *m* d'alcool* (*esp* whisky)/godet *m*.

hook(e)y ['huki] *n esp NAm F* **to play hook(e)y,** faire l'école buissonnière.

hook-shop ['hukʃɔp] *n A P* bordel*/clandé *m*/maison bancale.

hook up ['hukʌp] *vi F* **to be hooked up with s.o.** (*a*) être le complice* de qn; être de mèche/en cheville avec qn (*b*) se marier/se caser/se marida avec qn.

hoop [huːp] *n F* **to go through the hoop** (*i*) passer un mauvais quart d'heure (*ii*) être puni/en prendre pour son grade.

hoop-la ['huːplɑː] *n NAm F* **1.** tapage *m*/chahut *m*/boucan *m* **2.** publicité exagérée.

Hooray Henry ['huːrei'henriː] *n F* imbécile *m* de la haute/idiot *m* bcbg.

hoosegow ['huːsgau] *n NAm F* **1.** commissariat *m* de police/ (burlingue *m* de) quart *m* **2.** prison*/bloc *m*/taule *f*.

hoot[1] [huːt] *n F* **1.** rigolade *f*/ blague *f*; **it's a real hoot,** c'est vachement marrant/c'est tordant;

he's a real **hoot**, c'est un marrant/ un rigolo **2. I don't care a hoot/I couldn't give two hoots**, je m'en moque/je m'en balance/j'en ai rien à glander/je m'en bats l'œil **3. it's not worth a hoot**, ça ne vaut rien*/ ça ne vaut pas un pet de lapin.

hoot² [huːt] *vi F* **1. to hoot (with laughter)**, rire* aux éclats/se bidonner/se tordre de rire **2.** *Austr* sentir* mauvais/puer/schlinguer.

hootch [huːtʃ] *n NAm F* = **hooch.**

hooter ['huːtər] *n P* grand nez*/ nez* en trompette/tasseau *m*/tarin *m*.

hop¹ [hɔp] *n* **1.** *F* danse *f*/sauterie *f*/surboum *f* **2.** *F* **a short hop**, une courte distance/un pas/un saut; **it's only a hop, skip and a jump away**, c'est à deux pas d'ici **3.** *F* **to catch s.o. on the hop**, surprendre qn/ prendre qn au pied levé/tomber sur qn au débotté **4.** *F* **to be on the hop**, être toujours en mouvement/ avoir la bougeotte **5.** *P* (*drugs*) opium*/noir *m*; **hop fiend** = **hophead.**

hop² [hɔp] *vtr&i* **1.** *F* **hop in!** allez hop!/monte!/saute dedans! **2.** *F* **hop it!** file!/fiche le camp!/casse-toi! **3.** *F* **to hop on a bus**, sauter dans un autobus; **to hop off a bus**, sauter d'un autobus **4.** *F* **hopping mad**, très en colère*/en rogne/ furax/furibard **5.** *P* **to hop into bed with s.o.**, se foutre au lit avec qn. (*See* **lorry-hop; wag¹**)

hophead ['hɔphed] *n A P* morphinomane *mf*.

hop-joint ['hɔpdʒɔint] *n A P* **1.** gargote *f*/boui-boui *m* **2.** (*drugs*) fumerie *f* d'opium*.

hopped up ['hɔptʌp] *a P* **1.** stimulé par la drogue/dopé/chargé **2.** *NAm* (moteur) gonflé/bricolé **3.** surexcité/survolté/remonté.

horn [hɔːn] *n* **1.** *V* érection *f*; **to have the/a horn**, être en érection*/ avoir la trique/bander **2.** *F* (*jazz*) trompette *f* **3.** *NAm F* téléphone*;

to get on the horn, passer un coup de bigophone/de biniou. (*See* **blow 3**)

horn in ['hɔːn'in] *vi esp NAm F* **to horn in on s.o.'s conversation**, ramener sa fraise/mêler son grain de sel.

hornswoggle ['hɔːnswɔgl] *vtr NAm F* duper/entuber qn; mener qn en bateau.

horny ['hɔːni] *a V* **to be horny** (*a*) être en érection*/avoir le bambou/ avoir la canne/avoir le gourdin (*b*) être excité (sexuellement) (*c*) être obsédé/ne penser qu'à ça.

horror ['hɔrər] *n F* **1.** qch de laid* et ridicule/horreur *f*/monstruosité *f*; individu* abominable/monstre *m*; **horrors!** quelle horreur! **2. to have the horrors** (*a*) grelotter de peur*/ avoir la chair de poule (*b*) être en proie au délirium tremens (*c*) avoir des troubles mentaux dus aux amphétamines (*d*) faire une dépression due au manque de drogues/ être cold-turkey (*e*) avoir des symptômes dûs au sevrage d'héroïne/être cold-turkey/être poulet froid. (*See* **chuck¹ 2**)

horse¹ [hɔːs] *n* **1.** *F* **he's a dark horse**, il cache son jeu/il n'a pas l'air d'y toucher **2.** *F* **it's straight from the horse's mouth** (*i*) (ça vient) de source sûre (*ii*) c'est un tuyau increvable/de première; c'est un chocolat; **to have it straight from the horse's mouth**, ne pas l'envoyer dire **3.** *F* **a horse of another colour**, une autre paire de manches **4.** *F* **to flog a dead horse**, enfoncer des portes ouvertes **5.** *F* **to get on one's high horse**, monter sur ses grands chevaux/le prendre de haut **6.** *F* **hold your horses!** (*i*) (ne) t'emballe pas!/mollo!/doucement les basses! (*ii*) attendez!/arrêtez!/ minute! **7.** *NAm F* **horse opera**, (film *m*) western (*m*) **8.** *P* (*drugs*) héroïne*/cheval *m*/horse *m*. (*See* **Charl(e)y 8**) **9.** *P* **to water the horses**, uriner*/changer les poissons d'eau. (*See* **clothes-horse; one-horse; switch²; war-horse**)

horse² ['hɔːs] *vi NAm* **1.** *F* = **horse about 2.** *P* faire l'amour* (en adultère)/pinocher/piner.

horse about ['hɔːsə'baut], **horse around** ['hɔːsə'raund]*vi F* faire l'imbécile; chahuter/faire le zouave.

horse doctor ['hɔːsdɔktər] *n F* **1.** vétérinaire *mf*/véto *mf* **2.** médecin peu compétent/toubib *m* marron.

horseplay ['hɔːsplei] *n F* jeu brutal/chahut brutal/badinerie grossière.

horse-shit ['hɔːsʃit] *n esp NAm V* **1.** mensonges*/craques *fpl* **2.** foutaises *fpl*/conneries *fpl*; **that's horse-shit!** c'est des bobards!/c'est des conneries!

horse-trading ['hɔːstreidiŋ] *n F* manigance *f*/maquignonnage *m*.

hose [houz] *vtr NAm* **1.** *V* faire l'amour* avec (qn); enfiler/tringler (qn) **2.** *P* duper* (qn)/entuber (qn)/mener (qn) en bateau.

hoss [hɔs] *n esp NAm F* (= *horse*) cheval *m*/canasson *m*/bourrin *m*.

hostie ['hɔusti] *n Austr F* (= *air hostess*) hôtesse *f* de l'air.

hot [hɔt] *a* **1.** *P* chaud(e) de la pince/de la pointe; **to have hot pants** (*i*) avoir le feu aux fesses*/au cul (*ii*) avoir le feu au pantalon; **to be hot for s.o.,** en pincer pour qn/bander pour qn; **hot mama/hot lay/hot piece/hot stuff,** femme* passionnée/sexy; chaude lapine; (*film, book, etc*) **that's really hot stuff!** ça fait bander!/c'est super bandant! (*See* **babe 2; cookie 3; number 3; patootie; red-hot 1**) **2.** *F* **hot pants,** short *m* **3. hot stuff** (*a*) *P* un(e) chaud(e) lapin(e) (*b*) *P* jeux provocants (*c*) *P* butin* (*d*) *F* **she's really hot stuff,** elle est sensass/terrible; **he's hot stuff at tennis,** c'est un as du tennis/un joueur de première **4.** *F* expert/as/crack **5.** *F* **to be hot under the collar,** être en colère*/être furibard/l'avoir mauvaise **6.** *F* (*a*) énervé/excité/qui a les nerfs en pelote (*b*) agité/effaré/dans tous ses états; **to get all hot and bothered,** s'échauffer/se faire du mauvais sang **7.** *F* (*jazz*) improvisé avec passion/joué avec chaleur/hot; **hot music,** le jazz/le swing **8.** *F* très récent/à la une/sensationnel; **hot tip,** renseignement* sûr/tuyau *m* increvable/tuyau de première/chocolat *m*; **hot from the press,** dernier cri/de dernière minute **9.** *P* (*a*) (*stolen goods*) recherché par la police/difficile à écouler; **hot money,** argent* volé; **hot rock,** bijou fauché (*b*) criminel recherché par la police pour crime. (*See* **hot 3** (*c*)) **10.** (*a*) *NAm P* **hot seat/hot squat,** chaise *f* électrique (*b*) *F* **to be in the hot seat,** être dans le fauteuil directorial/être sur la sellette **11.** *F* **to make it hot for s.o.,** faire des difficultés *fpl* à qn/être vache avec qn; **I'll make it hot for him!** ça va chauffer pour lui!/ça va barder pour son matricule! **12.** *F* **to give it to s.o./to let s.o. have it hot (and strong),** passer un bon savon à qn/sonner les cloches à qn/donner une belle engueulade à qn **13.** *F* **to be in hot water,** être dans de mauvais draps/dans la mélasse; **to get into hot water,** se mettre dans le pétrin **14.** *F* **that's not so hot!** c'est pas formidable!/c'est pas fameux! **15.** *F* (*iron*) **she's had more boyfriends than I've had hot dinners!** elle change de mec plus souvent que moi de chemise! **16.** *F* (*esp guessing games*) **you're getting hot,** tu brûles **17.** *F* **to sell like hot cakes,** se vendre comme des petits pains **18.** *F* **to hold a hot hand,** avoir de bonnes cartes*/un bon jeu/un jeu du tonnerre; **to have a hot streak,** avoir une veine dingue **19.** *F* **hot war,** la guerre sanglante (*contraire de* la guerre froide) **20. hot rod** (*a*) *F* (*souped-up racing car*) bolide *m*; voiture gonflée/bricolée (*b*) pénis*/

bite *f*. (*See* **rod 1**) 21. *F* **hot spot** (*i*) cabaret *m*/boîte *f* de nuit (*ii*) mauvaise passe/pétrin *m* 22. **hot shot** (*a*) *F* = **big shot** (**big I 1**) (*b*) *P* injection *f* de drogues qui devient fatale/overdose *f* 23. *V* (*a*) *NAm* **he thinks he's hot shit**, il ne se prend pas pour de la merde (*b*) *Austr* **hot cack**, (qch) d'excellent*; **it's hot cack**, c'est pas dégueu/c'est pas pourri 24. *F* radio-actif; **hot lab(oratory)**, labo(ratoire) *m* traitant des matières radio-actives 25. *NAm F* **hot dog!** hourra!/bravo! (*See* **air 5**; **blow 4**; **drop² 1**; **gospeller**; **potato 3**; **red-hot**)

hotfoot ['hɔt'fut] *vtr F* **to hotfoot it**, se dépêcher*/mettre les bouts.

hothouse ['hɔthaus] *a attrib F* **hothouse plant**, personne délicate/petite nature.

hot-rod ['hɔtrɔd] *vi NAm V* se masturber*/faire cinq contre un. (*See* **hot 20**; **rod 1**)

hots [hɔts] *npl NAm P* **the hots** (*i*) amour *m* (*ii*) désir sexuel; **he had the hots for her**, il bandait pour elle/il en pinçait dur pour elle/il marquait midi pour elle.

hotsie-totsie, hotsy-totsy ['hɔtsi'tɔtsi] *a NAm O F* = **hunky-dory**.

hotted up ['hɔtid'ʌp] *a F* **hotted up car**, voiture* au moteur poussé/gonflé/bricolé.

hottie, hotty ['hɔti] *n F* (= *hot-water bottle*) bouillotte *f*.

hound-dog ['haund(d)ɔg, *NAm* 'haund(d)ɔːg] *n F* **1.** tombeur *m* de femmes/coureur *m* de jupons/cavaleur *m*/juponneur *m* **2.** vaurien *m*/salaud*.

house [haus] *n F* **1.** (*a*) **like a house on fire**, vite*/à toute pompe/à pleins gaz (*b*) **to get on like a house on fire**, sympathiser/s'entendre comme des larrons en foire/être copains comme cochons/être comme ꞔul et chemise **2. on**

the house, gratuit*/à l'œil/aux frais *mpl* de la princesse/offert par la maison **3. to bring the house down**, faire crouler la salle (sous les applaudissements)/casser la baraque/faire un malheur **4.** *A* (*RS* = *bet*) **house to let**, pari *m*. (*See* **barrelhouse**; **blue¹ I 5**; **bughouse¹,²**; **cathouse**; **craphouse**; **crazyhouse**; **dog-house**; **dosshouse**; **flea-house**; **flop-house**; **glasshouse**; **hash-house**; **hothouse**; **jag-house**; **joy-house**; **kip-house**; **madhouse**; **meathouse**; **nut-house**; **pisshouse**; **power-house**; **rough-house**; **shithouse**; **whore-house**)

how [hau] **I** *adv F* **1. any old how**, n'importe comment/à la va-comme-je-te-pousse **2. how come?** comment est-ce possible?/comment ça?/comment ça se fait? **3. and how!** et comment! (*See* **nohow**) **II** *excl F* (*hum, supposedly used by North American Indians*) **how!** comment va?/ça va?

how-do-you-do ['haudjuːduː, 'haudjəduː] *n F* **here's a fine old/a right old how-do-you-do** (*i*) c'est une mauvaise passe/une sale affaire (*ii*) en voilà du joli!/nous voilà propres!/on a les cuisses propres!

howdy! ['haudi] *excl NAm F* comment va?/ça va?/ça gaze?

how-d'ye-do ['haudjəduː] *n F* = **how-do-you-do**.

how's-your-father ['hauzjə-'faːðər] *n F* (*euph*) **a bit of how's-your-father**, une partie de jambes en l'air/une partie d'écarté.

hubba-hubba ['hʌbə'hʌbə] *adv & excl esp NAm F* vite*/à toute barde/à tout berzingue. |

hubby ['hʌbi] *n F* (= *husband*) mari *m*/le légitime.

huddle ['hʌdl] *n F* **1.** séance secrète; **to go into a huddle**, tenir une séance secrète **2.** période *f* de réflexion personnelle.

hully-gully ['hʌli'gʌli] *n NAm F* = **holly-golly 1, 2.**

hum [hʌm] *vi F* **1.** s'animer/chauffer; **to be humming,** être en pleine activité/boumer **2.** sentir* mauvais/schlinguer.

humdinger ['hʌm'diŋər] *n F* qn *ou* qch d'excellent*/du tonnerre; **that was a real humdinger!** c'était le (super-)pied!/c'était (super) sensass!

hummy ['hʌmi] *a NAm F* **1.** excellent*/épatant **2.** heureux/insouciant/relax/à l'aise **3.** puant/cocotant.

hump¹ [hʌmp] *n* **1.** *F* **to get over the hump,** surmonter le plus dur (d'un problème, etc) **2.** *F* **to have the hump,** être de mauvaise humeur/broyer du noir; **to give s.o. the hump,** donner le cafard à qn; **that gives me the hump,** ça me fout le cafard/ça me fiche le moral à zéro **3.** *V* (*a*) coït*/baise *f*; **to like one's hump,** aimer la crampette (*b*) *O esp NAm* femme* (*esp* prostituée)/garce *f*; **she's good hump,** c'est une sacrée baiseuse **4.** *NAm F* **to get a hump on,** se dépêcher*/se dégrouiller/se magner (le train).

hump² [hʌmp] *vtr&i* **1.** *V* **to hump s.o.,** faire l'amour* avec qn/pinocher qn/faire la bête à deux dos avec qn **2.** *F* porter sur le dos (avec difficulté)/se coltiner/trimbal(l)er; **it's not easy humping this case around,** c'est pas de la tarte, de se coltiner cette valoche! **3.** *NAm F* = **to get a hump on** (**hump¹ 4**).

humpy ['hʌmpi] *a F* (*a*) en colère* (*b*) grognon/grincheux.

Hun, hun [hʌn] **I** *a F* allemand*/boche **II** *n F* (*a*) Allemand*/boche *m* (*b*) soldat* allemand/hun *m*/doryphore *m*.

hunch [hʌntʃ] *n F* intuition *f*/pressentiment *m*; **to have a hunch that** ..., soupçonner que .../avoir des gourances *fpl*; **I've got a hunch that** ..., j'ai comme une petite idée que

...; **to play a hunch,** agir par intuition/aller au pifomètre.

hundred ['hʌndrəd] *n num F* **1. a hundred,** cent livres sterling; **half a hundred,** cinquante livres sterling **2. a hundred proof,** le meilleur/vrai/authentique/cent pour cent/garanti pur sucre.

hundred-percenter ['hʌndrədpə'sentər] *n F* = **whole-hogger.**

hung [hʌŋ] *a P* **1.** *NAm A* fâché/irrité/embêté **2.** (*man*) **hung (like a bull),** bien monté/bien équipé/bien outillé/monté comme un âne. (*See* **well-hung**)

hunger ['hʌŋgər] *n NAm F* **from hunger,** miteux/pouilleux/toc/moche.

hung over ['hʌŋ'ouvər] *a F* **to be hung over,** avoir la gueule de bois/la GDB. (*See* **hangover**)

hung up ['hʌŋ'ʌp] *a F* **1.** (*i*) collet monté/vieux jeu (*ii*) obsédé/frustré/agité; **he's really hung up about it,** il en fait tout un complexe **2.** avoir un béguin pour qn; **he's hung up on her,** il en pince pour elle **3.** tombant sur un os/sur un bec **4.** (*drugs*) en manque. (*See* **hang up**)

hunk ['hʌŋk] *n* **1.** *P* bel homme; **he's a (real) hunk,** il en jette/il jette du jus **2.** *pl F* (*rare*) (*a*) vieux birbe (*b*) avare* *m*/(vieux) rat/radin *m*.

hunkers ['hʌŋkəz] *npl F* (*esp dial*) **on one's hunkers,** accroupi/à croupetons.

hunky ['hʌŋki] **I** *a* **1.** *P* (*homme*) beau/qui a du chien/qui jette du jus; **he's really hunky,** il a de la gueule/c'est un beau mec **2.** *F* = **hunky-dory II** *n NAm P* immigrant *m* de l'Europe centrale. (*See* **bohunk 1**)

hunky-dory ['hʌŋki'dɔːri] *a F* parfait/ronflant/au poil; **everything's hunky-dory,** ça marche comme sur des roulettes/ça gaze au poil.

hurry ['hʌri] *n F* **he won't do that again in a hurry,** il ne recommencera pas de sitôt/il (n')est pas prêt de recommencer.

hurry-up ['hʌri'ʌp] **I** *a attrib O F* **hurry-up wag(g)on,** car* de police/panier à salade/poulailler ambulant **II** *n P* **to have it away for the hurry-up,** partir* en hâte/décamper.

hush-hush ['hʌʃ'hʌʃ] *a F* très secret/confidentiel; **it's all very hush-hush!** c'est ultra-secret!/pas un mot, là-dessus!/c'est top-secret!

hush money ['hʌʃ'mʌni] *n P* pot *m* de vin/graissage *m* de patte; **to give (s.o.) hush-money,** acheter le silence (de qn); **he got £50 hush money to keep him quiet,** on lui a acheté son silence (avec) £50.

hush up ['hʌʃ'ʌp] *vtr F* étouffer/supprimer (par la censure).

hustle¹ ['hʌsl] *n esp NAm F* **1.** tromperie *f*/entourloupe *f*/arnaque *f* **2.** bousculade *f*/grouillement *m*; **to get a hustle on,** se dépêcher*/se grouiller.

hustle² ['hʌsl] *vtr&i esp NAm P* **1.** mendier*/faire la manche **2.** (*prostitutes and homosexuals*) racoler*/faire le trottoir/faire le business **3.** vendre (qch)/bazarder **4.** gagner sa vie par des méthodes louches; fourguer/lessiver de la marchandise.

hustler ['hʌslər] *n P* **1.** qn qui gagne sa vie par des moyens louches/débrouillard *m*/brasseur *m* d'affaires **2.** (*a*) prostituée*/biseneusseuse *f* (*b*) (*homosexual prostitute*) tapette *f* **3.** souteneur*/marlou *m*/maq(uereau) *m*/proxo *m*.

hyp(e) [haip] *n P* **1.** (= *hypodermic needle*) aiguille *f* hypodermique/hypo *m* **2.** (*drugs*) piqûre*/piquouse *f*/shoot *m* **3.** (*drug addict*) drogué*/camé(e) *m(f)*/toxico *mf* **4.** (*drugs*) fourgueur *m*/passeur *m* fourmi **5.** (*advertising*) opération publicitaire, souvent mensongère, avant la mise sur le marché; **a big hype,** un grand/gros coup de pub; un matraquage/battage publicitaire monstre.

hyped up ['haipd'ʌp] *a P* stimulé par la drogue/drogué*/camé.

hype-stick ['haipstik] *n P* = **hyp(e) 1.**

hypo ['haipou] *n P* **1.** (*a*) (= *hypochondria*) hypocondrie *f* (*b*) (= *hypochondriac*) hypocondriaque *mf* **2.** (*drugs*) (*a*) (= *hypodermic needle*) aiguille *f* hypodermique/hypo *m* (*b*) piqûre *f*/piquouse *f*/shoot *m*/fixe *m*. (*See* **hyp(e) 1, 2**) **3.** (*drug addict*) drogué*/camé *m*/toxico *mf*.

hysterics [his'teriks] *npl F* **to have/to be in hysterics,** se tordre de rire/se marrer/rire à faire pipi dans sa culotte/rire à en pisser dans son froc.

I

I-am [ai'(j)æm] *n* F **he thinks he's the big I-am,** il se croit le bon Dieu en personne; il se prend pour Dieu le Père.

ice¹ [ais] *n* **1.** P diamant(s)*/diam *m*; **green ice,** émeraude(s) *f(pl)*; **ice palace,** bijouterie *f*/brocaillerie *f* **2.** F **to break the ice,** rompre la glace; (*prostitute*) faire le premier client de la journée/dérouiller **3.** F **to cut no ice with s.o.,** ne pas impressionner qn/ne pas faire d'effet sur qn; **that doesn't cut any ice with me** (*i*) ça me laisse froid/de glace (*ii*) ça (ne) marche pas avec moi (ce genre de truc) **4.** F **to put on ice,** mettre au frigidaire/au frigo **5.** F **to skate on thin ice,** marcher sur des œufs/sur des lames de rasoir **6.** P **to be on ice** (*a*) être assuré d'avance/être du tout cuit/être affiché (*b*) **= to be iced** (**ice²** 4) **7.** P **to have ice in one's shoes,** avoir peur de s'adonner à la drogue/avoir la hantise des drogues.

ice² [ais] *vtr&i* P **1.** tuer*/refroidir (qn) **2.** feindre d'ignorer qn/ne pas s'occuper de qn/négliger qn/mettre qn en quarantaine **3.** se taire*/la boucler **4. to be iced,** être emprisonné* au secret/être quasi-mort.

iceberg ['aisbɔig] *n* F **1.** (*pers*) glaçon *m*/bloc *m* de glace/marbre *m* **2.** *Austr* F individu* qui nage/qui fait du surf/qui prend des douches froides en hiver.

ice-cream ['ais'krixm] *n* P (*drugs*) opium*/boue *f*.

iceman ['aismæn, 'aismən] *n* P

voleur* de bijoux/chopeur *m* de joncaille. (*See* **ice¹** 1)

icing ['aisiŋ] *n* F **icing on the cake,** profit *m*; **the rest is just icing on the cake,** le reste, c'est tout bénéf.

icky ['iki] *a esp NAm* P **1.** vieux jeu/rococo **2.** d'une sentimentalité excessive/de la guimauve **3.** poisseux/visqueux.

ID¹ ['aidiï] *n* P (= *identity (card)*) brèmes *fpl*/faffes *fpl*; **got any ID on you?** fais voir tes faffes!

ID² ['ai'di] *vtr* P **to ID s.o.,** identifier/cerner/repérer qn.

idiot-board ['idiətbɔid] *n* F (*TV*) pancarte cachée des caméras qui souffle aux acteurs/dérouleur *m*; = téléprompteur *m*; = pense-bête *m*.

idiot-box ['idiətbɔks] *n* F (*a*) télévision *f*/téloche *f* (*b*) téléviseur *m*/télé *f*.- (*See* **box¹** 2; **goggle-box**; **lantern**)

iffy ['ifi] *a* F douteux/plein de si/avec des si et des mais; **it's all a bit iffy,** c'est pas du tout cuit/du nougat.

Ikey (Mo) ['aiki('mou)] *Prn* P (*pej*) Juif*/Youpin *m*/Youpe *m*/Youtre *m*.

in [in] **I** *a attrib* F **1. in joke,** plaisanterie *f* de coterie **2.** à la coule/dans le vent; **it's the in thing to do,** c'est très à la mode de faire ça; **it's the in place to go,** c'est l'endroit où se faire voir/c'est le dernier endroit chic; **it's the in place to eat,** c'est le resto où aller **II** *adv* **1.** P **to get (it) in,** faire l'amour*/mettre la cheville dans le trou/(se l')enfoncer 2. *F* to be (well) in with s.o., être bien avec qn/être dans les petits papiers de qn 3. *F* to be in (*a*) être dans le vent/à la page/à la coule (*b*) être accepté dans la bonne société/ savoir nager 4. *F* to have it in for s.o. (*a*) en vouloir à qn/avoir une dent contre qn (*b*) détester* qn/ avoir qn dans le nez 5. *F* to be in on sth, être dans le bain/dans le coup 6. *F* he's in for it! son affaire est bonne!/le voilà dans de beaux draps!/il va écoper!/il va en prendre pour son grade! 7. *F* to be all in, être fatigué*/claqué/vidé III *n F* 1. to have an in, avoir de l'influence/avoir le bras long 2. the ins and outs, les coins et recoins (d'une affaire)/les tenants et les aboutissants.

incy(-wincy) ['insi('winsi)] *a F* an incy(-wincy) bit of..., un petit peu* de.../un chouia de.../une pincée de.../une larme de....

indeedy [in'didi] *adv NAm O F* yes indeedy! bien sûr (que oui)!

India, india ['indiə] *n O P* (*drugs*) cannabis*/chanvre indien.

Indian ['indiən] *a* 1. *NAm P* Indian gift, cadeau-hameçon *m*/ cadeau-bidon *m*; Indian giver, donneur *m* de cadeaux-hameçons 2. *P* Indian hay/hemp, cannabis*/chanvre indien. (*See* India) 3. *F* too many chiefs and not enough Indians, c'est une armée de généraux.

indigo ['indigou] *a esp NAm F* indigo mood, idées noires/cafard *m*/ bourdon *m*; to be in an indigo mood, avoir les boules.

influence ['influəns] *n F* under the influence, sous l'empire de la boisson/dans les vignes (du Seigneur).

info ['infou] *n F* (*abbr = information*) renseignements*/info *f*/tuyau *m*; he gave me the info, il m'a filé un tuyau/il m'a rencardé/il m'a tuyauté; got any info? t'as du neuf?/t'as une piste?

infra dig ['infrə'dig] *adv phr F* indigne/au-dessous de soi.

Injun ['indʒən] *n* 1. *esp NAm F* Indien (d'Amérique) 2. *P* (*excl*) honest Injun! mais, c'est vrai!/vraiment!/sans blague!/je t'assure!

ink-slinger ['iŋksliŋər] *n F* (*bureaucrat*) gratte-papier *m*/rond-de-cuir *m*.

in-laws ['inlɔːz] *npl F* belle-famille *f*; les beaux-parents *mpl*/les (beaux-)dabs *mpl*.

innards ['inədz] *npl F* ventre*/ boyaux *mpl*/tripes *fpl*/tuyaux *mpl*/ cimetière *m* à poulets.

inner ['inər] *a F* the inner man, appétit *m*/ventre*; to look after the inner man, se remplir le buffet/la panse.

innings ['iniŋz] *n F* 1. to have (had) a good innings, vivre vieux*; he's had a good innings, il a couvert pas mal de chemin/il a fait un bon tour de terrain/il s'est bien défendu 2. your innings! à vous de jouer!/à vous le tour!

inside ['insaid] I *a F* 1. inside information/dope, tuyaux confidentiels/infos *fpl* de première bourre/ tuyaux de première main 2. the inside story, l'histoire *f* authentique/véridique (racontée par l'un des participants); l'histoire dans l'histoire; témoignage vécu 3. inside job, vol, etc, attribué à un membre du personnel (de l'entreprise)/coup monté par qn de la maison 4. an inside man, quelqu'un de la maison qui aide à monter un coup de l'intérieur; taupe *f* II *adv F* 1. en prison*/à l'ombre/au frais; he's been inside, il a fait de la taule 2. inside out (*a*) à fond; to know s.o./sth inside out, connaître qn/qch comme sa poche/ sur le bout du doigt/de fond en combles; to know Paris inside out, s'y retrouver dans Paris les yeux fermés (*b*) to turn everything inside out, mettre tout sens dessus dessous

3. **to be inside on sth,** connaître les dessous d'une affaire/être bien tuyauté/savoir même les relents *mpl* de placard **III** *n F* **1.** (= **innards**) **I laughed so much my insides were all sore,** j'ai ri jusqu'à en avoir mal aux côtes/j'ai ri à m'en retourner les tripes **2. to be on the inside,** être dans le coup/ être du bâtiment **IV** *prep F* **to do sth inside (of) an hour,** faire qch en moins d'une heure/en un tour d'horloge.

instrument ['instrumənt] *n P* pénis*/instrument *m*/outil *m*; **to play (with) one's instrument,** se masturber*/jouer de son instrument/se tripoter les couilles *fpl*.

intended [in'tendid] *n O F* un(e) futur(e)/promis(e).

intestinal [intes'tainəl] *a NAm F* (*euph*) **to have intestinal fortitude,** avoir du cran/en avoir dans le bide/avoir les tripes *fpl* solides.

into ['intuɪ] *prep F* absorbé par (qch); en proie à (qch); **I'm into Russian novels this week,** je suis plongé dans les romans russes cette semaine; **she's heavily into health foods at the moment,** elle s'est totalement branchée sur/elle est accro à la bouffe-bio; son truc maintenant, c'est la bouffe-bio.

invite ['invait] *n F* invitation *f*/ invite *f*/appât *m*.

Irish ['airiʃ] **I** *a F* **1.** biscornu; **the whole sentence sounds a bit Irish,** toute la phrase ne tient pas debout **2. Irish confetti,** briques *fpl* **3. Irish banjo,** pelle *f* **4. Irish grape,** pomme *f* de terre/patate *f* **5. Irish wedding,** beuverie générale/soûlographie *f* **II** *n F* **to get one's Irish up,** se mettre en colère*/se mettre en rogne/voir rouge.

iron ['aiən] **I** *n* **1.** *P* **to carry iron,** être armé/enfouraillé. (*See* **shooting-iron**) **2.** *F* (**eating**) **irons,** couteau *m* fourchette *f* et cuiller *f*; les couverts *mpl*. (*See* **cast-iron**; **half-**

iron; **hoof**[1] **2**) **II** *a A P* **iron horse,** locomotive *f*.

it [it] *pron* **1.** *F* du sex-appeal/du chien; **he's got it!** il jette du jus!/il en a! **2.** *F* vermouth (italien); **gin and it,** gin-vermouth *m* **3.** *F you've had it!* t'as ton compte!/tu l'as voulu!/tu es fichu! **4. to give it to s.o.** (*a*) *P* faire l'amour* avec qn/ baiser qn/tringler qn/défoncer qn/ en donner à qn (*b*) *F* battre* qn/ tabasser qn (*c*) *F* réprimander* qn/ sonner les cloches à qn **5.** *P* **to make it with s.o.** (*a*) faire l'amour* avec qn/s'envoyer qn (*b*) plaire à qn/faire une touche/avoir un ticket **6.** *F* **he thinks he's really it,** il se prend pour le nombril du monde; il ne se prend pas pour de la crotte/pour de la merde **7.** *F* **to step on it,** accélérer/appuyer sur le champignon. (*See* **bad II; gas**[1] **II 3; in II 4, 6; with 1** (*a*), (*b*); **with-it**)

itch[1] [itʃ] *n F* **1. the seven-year itch,** l'écueil *m* des sept ans* de mariage/la démangeaison de la sep-tième année*; le démon de midi **2. to have an itch to do sth,** mourir/crever d'envie de faire qch; **I've (got) an itch to do it,** j'en bande d'envie.

itch[2] [itʃ] *vi F* **to itch to do sth/to be itching to do sth,** être démangé par l'envie de faire qch; bander (d'envie) pour qch; **he's itching for trouble,** la peau lui démange/ça le démange (de se battre); ça le gratte.

itchy ['itʃi] *a F* **1.** qui brûle de faire qch **2. to have itchy feet,** avoir la bougeotte **3. to have itchy fingers,** être voleur/chapardeur; avoir les doigts collants. (*See* **palm 2**)

itsy-bitsy ['itsi'bitsi] *a F* minus-cule/tout petit/riquiqui.

ivories ['aivəriz] *npl F* **1.** dents*/ clavier *m*. (*See* **sluice**[2]) **2.** boules *fpl* de billard **3.** dés*/doches *mpl*/ bobs *mpl* **4.** touches *fpl* d'un piano/clavier *m*; **to tickle the ivories,** jouer du piano/taquiner les ivories.

ivory ['aivəri] *a F* **1.** *NAm* ivory dome, intellectuel *m*/grosse tête/tête *f* d'œuf/mandarin *m* **2.** ivory tower, tour *f* d'ivoire.

J

J [dʒei] = **jay 1.**

jab¹ [dʒæb] *n F* (*a*) inoculation*f*/vaccin *m*/piqûre *f*; **have you had your jabs?** tu les a eues, tes piqûres? (*b*) (*drugs*) piqûre* (*esp* héroïne)/piquouse *f*/shoot *m*.

jab² [dʒæb] *vtr* **1.** *F* (*a*) inoculer/faire une piqûre à (qn) (*b*) piquer/piquouser/shooter **2.** *P* donner un coup de poing (à qn).

jabber ['dʒæbər] *n F* (*drugs*) aiguille* hypodermique/hypo *f*; shooteuse *f*.

jab-off ['dʒæbɔf] *n P* (*a*) piqûre*/piquouse *f* (de narcotique) (*b*) effet *m* de la piqûre/le bang/le flash.

jaboney ['dʒæbouni] *n NAm P* **1.** (*a*) (*greenhorn*) blanc bec *m*/bleu *m* (*b*) immigrant(e) *m(f)* (sans expérience)/nouveau *m* **2.** garde *m* du corps/gorille *m*.

jack¹, Jack [dʒæk] **I** *n* **1.** *P* **on one's jack,** tout seul/seulabre/esseulé **2.** *F* **every man jack,** tout un chacun **3.** *F* **I'm all right Jack,** ça tourne rond pour bibi; *V* **fuck you, Jack, I'm all right!** je t'emmerde, en tous cas moi ça va! (*See* **ladder**) **4.** *V* pénis*; **to get the jack,** être en érection*/avoir le bambou/avoir la canne **5.** *P* (*drugs*) cachet *m* d'héroïne/cheval *m* **6.** *NAm P* **to ball the jack** (*a*) se dépêcher*/s'activer/se magner (*b*) jouer son va-tout/mettre le paquet **7.** *F* **jack/Jack Tar,** marin*/matelot *m*/mathurin *m* **8.** *F* **before you can say Jack Robinson,** en un clin d'œil/en moins de deux/avant de pouvoir dire ouf/en deux coups de cuillère à pot **9.**

NAm P argent*/galette *f*; **a nice piece of jack,** un bon petit paquet/pacson **10.** *P* (*RS* = *kipper*) **Jack the Ripper,** hareng saur/kipper *m* **11.** *A P* policier*/condé *m* **12.** *P* (*RS* = *five*) **Jack's alive** (*a*) *A* (billet* de) cinq livres sterling (*b*) *see* **bingo 5 13.** *A F* **yellow jack,** fièvre *f* jaune/godiche *f* jaune **14.** *Austr V* anus*/trou *m* du cul **II** *a Austr P* (*fed up*) **to be jack of (sth),** en avoir marre/en avoir ras le bol (de qch).

jack² [dʒæk] *vtr P* **1.** = **jack in 1 2.** = **jack up 3.**

jackaroo ['dʒækə'ruː] *n P* **1.** *Austr* colon immigrant sans expérience **2.** (*a*) *Austr* jeune homme inexperimenté qui fait son apprentissage sur un ranch (*b*) *NAm* = cowboy *m*.

jack around ['dʒækə'raund] *vi P* **1.** traîner/flemmarder/glander **2.** faire le zouave/faire le con/déconner.

jacked up ['dʒækt'ʌp] *a P* **1.** stimulé par la drogue/drogué/camé **2.** excité/tendu/énervé/remonté/à cran. (*See* **jack up 1**)

jackeroo ['dʒækə'ruː] *n P* = **jackaroo.**

jacket ['dʒækit] *vtr A P* battre*/sauter sur le paletot à. (*See* **dust²**)

jack in ['dʒæk'in] *vtr P* **1.** abandonner*/lâcher/balancer/plaquer/laisser tomber; **he's jacked his job in,** il a plaqué/largué son boulot **2. to jack it in,** se taire*/la boucler/la fermer.

jack-in-office n F (pej) fonctionnaire plein de son importance/petit chef/Sa Suffisance.

jack-in-the-box ['dʒækinðəbɔks] n F 1. diablotin m/qn qui a un ressort au derrière 2. fantoche m.

jack off ['dʒæk'ɔf] vi V se masturber*/s'astiquer le manche/se taper la colonne/se tirer son coup.

jackpot ['dʒækpɔt] n F **to hit the jackpot,** gagner le gros lot/décrocher la timbale/taper dans le mille.

jacksie ['dʒæksi] n A P fesses*/postérieur m.

jack up ['dʒæk'ʌp] vtr&i 1. P (drugs) se faire une piquouse/se piquouser/se shooter. (See **jacked up** 1) 2. P = **jack in** 1 3. P **to jack up the price,** corser le prix/saler la note; faire valser les étiquettes 4. F **to jack s.o. up,** encourager qn/donner du cœur au ventre à qn/remonter le moral à qn 5. Austr F protester/piaffer 6. Austr P plaider innocent/se dire blanc/se blanchir.

jacky ['dʒæki] n Austr P aborigène m/indigène m.

jade [dʒeid] n F (pej) **she's a real/right jade,** c'est une vraie rosse/une vraie peau de vache.

jag [dʒæg] I n P 1. (drugs) piqûre*/piquouse f/shoot m 2. état prolongé d'intoxication par une drogue 3. **to have a jag on** (a) être drogué*/camé (b) être ivre*/rond/noir/rétamé 4. **to go on a jag** (i) se camer à bloc (ii) faire la noce/la bombe; se soûler/prendre une cuite (iii) faire une orgie de . . . ; **to go on a culture jag,** prendre une indigestion de culture/faire sa ration de culture/faire une cure de culture 5. coup m de chance*; du pot/du cul/du bol II n F (aut) Jaguar f (RTM)/Jag.

jagged [dʒægd] a P 1. ivre*/rond/noir/rétamé 2. drogué*/camé/(s)chnouffe.

jag-house ['dʒæghaus] n P bordel* d'homosexuels*/musée m à jocondes.

jag off ['dʒæg'ɔf] vi V = **jack off.**

jail-bait ['dʒeilbeit] n P fille* de moins de seize ans/faux-poids m/laitue f.

jailbird ['dʒeilbəːd] n F individu* qui est souvent en prison*/cheval m de retour/bois dur; **an old jailbird,** un vieux taulard.

jake [dʒeik] I adv NAm P 1. d'accord*/dac/OK; **things are/everything is jake,** ça marche bien/ça gaze/ça roule 2. excellent*/impec/de première II n 1. F NAm (cards) valet m/valdingue m. (See **jock** 5) 2. pl A P WC*/goguenots mpl/chiottes fpl 3. P alcool à brûler additionné de cidre.

jalopy [dʒə'lɔpi] n F (vieille) voiture* (esp en mauvais état ou hum)/tacot m/guimbarde f.

jam¹ [dʒæm] I a P (homosexual use) hétéro(sexuel)/sexuellement normal II n F 1. **it's money for jam,** c'est de l'argent* facile/c'est donné/c'est du nanan 2. **to be in a jam,** être dans le pétrin/dans la mélasse/dans la mouise 3. **a bit of jam,** un coup de chance*; du pot/du bol/du cul 4. **do you want jam on it?** tu veux (pas) que je te le dore sur tranches, en plus?/tu voudrais pas que je te le mâche, des fois?/la mariée est peut-être pas assez belle pour toi? 5. = **jam session** (**session** 1). (See **jim-jams**)

jam² [dʒæm] vi F (jazz) improviser/faire un bœuf.

jam-jar ['dʒæmdʒaːr] n P 1. (RS = car) voiture f/bagnole f/caisse f 2. œillet m (des fleuristes).

jammed up ['dʒæmd'ʌp] a NAm P ayant dépassé une dose normale de drogue.

jammer ['dʒæmər] n F musicien qui participe à une séance de jazz improvisée/à un bœuf.

jammy ['dʒæmi] *a P* **1.** simple comme bonjour/du gâteau **2.** qui a de la chance*/qui a du cul/ veinard; **what a jammy devil!** quel veinard, celui-là! **3.** de premier ordre/de prem(ière).

jam-packed ['dʒæm'pækt] *a F* au grand complet/archi-plein/archi-comble/bourré à craquer.

jam roll ['dʒæm'roul] *n* (*prisons*) (*RS* = *parole*) liberté condition-nelle/parole *f*.

jam sandwich ['dʒæm'sændwidʒ] *n P* car* de police/bagnole *f* de flics/panier *m* à salade.

jam-sheet ['dʒæmʃiːt] *n P* (*rare*) = **shit-list.**

jam up ['dʒæm'ʌp] *vtr F* **to jam up the works** = **to gum up the works** (**gum up**).

jane, Jane [dʒein] *n* **1.** *F esp NAm* fille*/femme*/nénette *f*/nana *f*; **a plain Jane,** une laidasse/une pas-jolie; **she's a bit of a plain Jane,** ce n'est pas une beauté/c'est pas Raquel Welch **2.** *P* la petite amie/la nénette **3.** *P* WC* pour femmes/chiottes *fpl* à poules. (*See* **john 1; lady**)

jankers ['dʒænkəz] *npl F* (*mil*) punitions *fpl*/la pelote/le bal; **to be on jankers,** être au piquet des punis.

Jap [dʒæp] **I** *a F* japonais*/nippon **II** *n F* Japonais* *m*/Nippon *m*/jap *mf*/jaune *mf*.

jar¹ [dʒɑːr] *n* **1.** *F* **to have/to down a few jars,** boire*/s'envoyer quelques verres; **let's go and have a jar down the pub,** allons prendre un pot au bistrot/allons s'en jeter un au troquet (du coin) **2.** *P* faux diamant*/faux diam(e)/caillou *m*. (*See* **jam-jar; jargoon**)

jar² [dʒɑːr] *vtr P* vendre de faux diamants (à qn).

jargoon [dʒɑːrguːn] *n P* = **jar¹ 2.**

jasper ['dʒæspər] *n O P* **1.** les-

bienne*/gavousse *f* **2.** puce *f*/sauteuse *f*.

java ['dʒɑɪvə] *n NAm O P* café*/caoua *m*/jus *m*.

jaw¹ [dʒɔː] *n* **1.** *P* bavardage *m*; **to have a good jaw,** tailler une bonne bavette; **hold your jaw!/not so much of your jaw!** ta gueule!/la ferme! **2.** *P* **pi jaw,** bondieuseries *fpl*/sermon *m*/paroles *fpl* de curé/prêchi-prêcha *m* **3.** *F* **his jaw dropped,** il a fait/tiré une drôle de tête/bobine.

jaw² [dʒɔː] *P* **I** *vi* bavarder*/tailler une bavette **II** *vtr* engueuler (qn)/enguirlander (qn)/sonner les cloches (à qn).

jawbone ['dʒɔː'boun] *vi NAm P* persuader/insister; **to jawbone (s.o.) into paying,** faire cracher (qn) au bassinet.

jawboning ['dʒɔːbounɪŋ] *n NAm P* **he needed some jawboning before he paid up,** il a fallu insister lourde-ment pour qu'il raque.

jaw-breaker ['dʒɔːbreikər], **jaw-buster** ['dʒɔːbʌstər] *n F* **1.** nom *m* à coucher dehors/mot *m* à vous décrocher la mâchoire **2.** bonbon dur.

jawing ['dʒɔːɪŋ] *n P* **1.** bavardage *m*/bavette *f* **2.** **to give s.o. a jaw-ing,** réprimander* qn/passer un savon à qn/sonner les cloches à qn.

jaw out ['dʒɔː'aut] *vtr NAm P* **to jaw s.o. out,** engueuler qn/passer un savon à qn.

jaw queen ['dʒɔːkwiːn] *n V* (*homo-sexual use*) qn qui pratique la fella-tion*/suceur *m*/pipeur *m*.

jaw-twister ['dʒɔːtwistər] *n F* = **jaw-breaker.**

jay [dʒei] *n* **1.** *P* (*drugs*) cigarette* de marijuana/joint *m*/stick *m* **2.** *NAm F* individu bête*/nouille *f*; plouc *m*/cloche *f*.

jaybird ['dʒeibəːd] *n NAm* **1.** *P* paysan*/plouc *m*/péquenaud *m* **2.** *F* = **jailbird 3.** *P* Juif*/Youpin *m*.

jayboy ['dʒeibɔi] *n NAm F (cards)* valet *m. (See* **jake II 1**)

jaywalk ['dʒeiwɔːk] *vi F* traverser en dehors des clous/marcher sur la chaussée.

jaywalker ['dʒeiwɔːkər] *n F* piéton imprudent.

jazz¹ [dʒæz] *n* **1.** *F (i)* mensonges*/foutaises *fpl*/craques *fpl*/bourres *fpl (ii)* baratin *m*; ...**and all that jazz,** et tout et tout/et tout ce qui s'ensuit/et tout le fourbi/et tout le tremblement **2.** *NAm A V (a)* coït* *(b)* sexe de la femme*/chatte *f* **3.** *NAm P* emballement *m*/entrain *m*.

jazz² [dʒæz] *vi* **1.** *NAm A V* coïter*/tirer un coup **2.** *NAm P* mettre en train/donner le branle à (qch)/aiguillonner **3.** *F (a)* mentir*/bourrer le crâne *(b)* exagérer*/en rajouter.

jazzed up ['dʒæzd'ʌp] *a* **1.** *F* élégant*/endimanché/sur son trente-et-un **2.** *P* animé/survolté **3.** *A P* drogué*/camé/chargé/bourré.

jazz up ['dʒæz'ʌp] *vtr F* émoustiller/échauffer/ravigoter/requinquer. *(See* **jazzed up**)

jazzy ['dʒæzi] *a* **1.** *F* tapageur/tape-à-l'œil **2.** *P* vieux-jeu/périmé.

J-boy ['dʒeibɔi] *n NAm F (cards)* valet *m. (See* **jake II 1**; **jayboy**)

jeepers (creepers)! ['dʒiːpəz-('kriːpəz)] *excl NAm O F* mon Dieu!/sapristi!

jeez(e)! Jeez(e)! [dʒiːz] *excl P (euph for* **Jesus!**) mon Dieu!/bon sang!/(oh) pute!/putain!

jell [dʒel] *vi F* **1.** *(ideas, etc)* (se) concrétiser **2.** bien s'entendre/sympathiser/être sur la même longueur d'ondes/avoir des atomes crochus (avec qn).

jelly ['dʒeli] *n F* **1.** gélignite *f*/gelée *f* **2. to pound s.o. into a jelly,** battre* qn comme plâtre/faire de la bouillie de qn.

jelly-baby ['dʒelibeibi] *n P (drugs)* amphétamine*.

jellyfish ['dʒelifiʃ] *n F* larve *f*/mollasson *m*.

jelly-roll ['dʒeliroul] *n NAm* **1.** *V* sexe de la femme*/baveux *m*/millefeuille *m* **2.** *P* homme *m* à femmes/obsédé *m*/queutard *m* **3.** *P* amant *m*.

jemima [dʒi'maimə] *n F* pot *m* de chambre/Jules *m*/Thomas *m*.

jerk¹ [dʒɜːk] *n* **1.** *P* individu bête*/(petit) con/enflé *m*/connard *m*/enculé *m*/pauvre type *m*; **you stupid jerk!** espèce de con! *(See* **dumb 1** *(b))* **2.** *P* novice *m*/bleu *m* **3.** *F* **put a jerk in(to) it!** et que ça saute! **4.** *F* **physical jerks,** mouvements *mpl* de gym(nastique). *(See* **soda**)

jerk² [dʒɜːk] *vi NAm V* faire l'amour* avec (qn)/bourrer (qn)/niquer (qn).

jerk off ['dʒɜːk'ɔf] *vi V* se masturber*/se branler/se taper la colonne.

jerkwater ['dʒɜːkwɔːtər] *n NAm* trou paumé/bled *m*/coin perdu. *(See* **one-horse**)

jerky ['dʒɜːki] *a NAm F* bête*/cave/cruche.

jerry, Jerry ['dʒeri] *n F* **1.** pot *m* de chambre/Thomas *m*/Jules *m* **2.** soldat* allemand*/Fritz/fridolin *m*/frizou *m* **3.** les Allemands*/les boches *mpl*.

jerry built ['dʒeribilt] *a F* inférieur/à la manque/à la noix; (construit) en papier carton/en papier mâché.

Jesus (Christ)! ['dʒiːzəs('kraist)] *excl P* nom de Dieu! *VV* **Jesus fucking Christ!** putain de merde!/bordel de Dieu!/bordel de merde!/putain de bordel de merde! *(See* **jeez(e)!**; **Christ**)

Jesus freak ['dʒiːzəs'friːk] *n F* membre *m* d'un groupe de chrétiens fervents qui mène la vie collective des hippies/un illuminé (de Jésus).

jet [dʒet] *a attrib F* **1. the jet set,** les bringueurs *mpl* cosmopolites/le jet-set **2.** (*souped-up car*) **jet job,** bolide *m*.

Jew¹ [dʒuː] *n P* **dirty old Jew:** *see* **bingo 2.**

jew² [dʒuː] *vtr A P* (*pej*) duper* (qn)/mettre (qn) dedans/faire marcher (qn).

jewboy, Jewboy ['dʒuːbɔi] *n P* (*pej*) Juif*/Youpin *m*.

jew down ['dʒuː'daun] *vtr esp NAm P* marchander/chipoter/regratter (qn).

jewish, Jewish ['dʒuːiʃ] *a P* (*pej*) avare/radin/grippe-sou; **he's so jewish, he never buys drinks,** il est tellement juif/rat qu'il ne paye jamais un coup.

jew's harp ['dʒuːz'hɑːp] *n F* peigne recouvert de papier de soie qui sert d'harmonica; guimbarde *f*.

jiff [dʒif], **jiffy** ['dʒifi] *n F* **in (half) a jiffy,** dans un instant/en un clin d'œil/en moins de deux; **I'll be back in a jiffy,** je reviens dans un instant/une seconde. (*See* **mo; sec; shake¹ 1, 2; tick¹ 3**)

jig [dʒig] *n* **1.** *P* gigolo *m*/lustucru *m*/frère mironton **2.** *P* (*pej*) (*a*) Noir*/bougnoul(e) *m*/bamboula *m* (*b*) moricaud *m*/café au lait **3.** *F NAm* **the jig is up,** c'est fichu/ c'est dans le lac/c'est rapé.

jigaboo [dʒigə'buː] *n NAm P* (*pej*) Noir(e)*/nègre *mf*/bougnoul(e) *m*.

jig-a-jig ['dʒigə'dʒig] *n P* = **jig-jig.**

jigger ['dʒigər] *n* **1.** *P* prison*/ bloc *m* **2.** *P* pénis*/queue *f* **3.** *NAm F* (*gadget*) truc *m*/machin *m*/ bidule *m*.

jigger (up) ['dʒigər('ʌp)] *vtr F* abîmer*/bousiller.

jiggered ['dʒigəd] *a F* étonné*/ estomaqué/baba; **well I'm jiggered!** j'en suis comme deux ronds de flan!/je n'en reviens pas!/ça me scie!

jiggered (up) ['dʒigəd'ʌp] *a F* fatigué*/à bout/claqué/vanné/HS.

jiggery-pokery ['dʒigəri'poukəri] *n F* manigance *f*/attrape *f*/tour *m* de passe-passe; **there was a bit of jiggery-pokery going on there,** il y avait qch de louche/de pas clair/de pas catholique là-dedans.

jiggumbob ['dʒigəmbɔb] *n F* (*rare*) = **thingamy.**

jig-jig ['dʒig'dʒig] *n P* coït*/cri-quon-criquette *m*/partie *f* de jambes en l'air.

Jim Crow ['dʒim'krou] *n NAm F* (*a*) (*pej*) Noir(e)*/nègre* *mf*/ bamboula *m* (*b*) la ségrégation raciale et tout ce qui s'y rapporte.

jiminy! ['dʒimini] *excl F* (**by) jiminy!** mince (alors)!

jim-jams ['dʒimdʒæmz] *npl F* (*a*) les nerfs *mpl* en boule/la chair de poule; **he's got the jim-jams,** il a les chocottes/les copeaux (*b*) délirium tremens *m*/les rats bleus.

Jimmy ['dʒimi] *Prn P* **1.** (*RS = piddle*) **Jimmy Riddle,** pipi *m*; **to have a Jimmy Riddle,** uriner*/faire pipi; **he's gone for a Jimmy Riddle,** il est allé faire une vidange/faire sa goutte **2. Little Jimmy:** *see* **bingo 1 3.** (*navy*) **Jimmy (the one),** officier *m* qui commande en second à bord d'un navire (de guerre) **4.** *F* Écossais *m*; **listen Jimmy!** écoute, mon pote!/écoute, mec!/écoute, mon gars!

jing-jang ['dʒiŋdʒæŋ] *n NAm A V* **1.** pénis*/zizi *m* **2.** sexe de la femme* **3.** coït*/zizi-panpan *m*.

jingo ['dʒiŋgou] *excl F* **by jingo!** nom d'une pipe!

jinks [dʒiŋks] *npl F* **high jinks,** réjouissances*/noce *f*/bamboche *f*.

jinx¹ [dʒiŋks] *n F* **1.** malchance*/ guigne *f*/poisse *f* **2.** porte-poisse *m*/porte-guigne *m*.

jinx² [dʒiŋks] *vtr F* porter malchance*/la guigne/la poisse à (qn).

jism ['dʒizm], **jissom** ['dʒis(ə)m] *n esp NAm* **1.** *V* sperme*/jus *m*/ purée *f* **2.** *P* dynamisme *m*/tonus *m.*

jitney ['dʒitni] **I** *a NAm O P* camelote/piètre/piteux **II** *n NAm* **1.** *A F* pièce *f* de cinq cents **2.** minibus *m* **3.** *A* **jitney bag,** porte-monnaie*/morlingue *m.*

jitter¹ [dʒitər] *n F* **1. to be all of a jitter,** être dans tous ses états **2.** *pl* **to have the jitters,** avoir les nerfs à fleur de peau; avoir la tremblote/la frousse; **to give s.o. the jitters,** flanquer la trouille à qn.

jitter² ['dʒitər] *vtr F* (*a*) **to jitter s.o.** = **to give s.o. the jitters** (**jitter¹** 2) (*b*) se trémousser/s'exciter/se démener.

jitterbug ['dʒitəbʌg] *n O F* défaitiste *mf*/paniquard *m*/trouillard *m*/dégonflé *m.*

jittery ['dʒitəri] *a F* crispé/à cran; **to feel jittery,** avoir les nerfs en pelote/à fleur de peau; **I feel really jittery,** j'ai la trouille/le trac.

jive¹ [dʒaiv] *n* **1.** *F* (*i*) baratin *m* (*ii*) mensonges*/foutaises *fpl*/con-neries *fpl*; **don't give me all that jive!** arrête de déconner!/arrête ton char(re)!/garde tes salades! **jive talk,** jargon des amateurs de jazz (surtout les Noirs). (*See* **jazz 1**) **2.** *P* (*drugs*) marijuana*; **jive stick,** cigarette* de marijuana/joint *m*/ stick *m.*

jive² [dʒaiv] *P* **I** *vi* **1.** trouver le maillon/éclairer la lanterne **2.** bavarder*/bavasser/jacter/dévider le jars **II** *vtr* **to jive s.o.** (*i*) taquiner/blaguer/faire marcher qn (*ii*) injurier/insulter qn (*iii*) duper/ avoir qn; rouler qn dans la farine.

jizz [dʒiz] *n esp NAm V* = **jism 1.**

joanna [dʒou'ænə] *n P* (*RS* = *piano*) (vieux) piano/chaudron *m*/ commode *f*/bastringue *m.*

job [dʒɔb] *n* **1.** *F* tout article façonné/manufacturé *ou* fabriqué; **that new car is a really nice job,**

cette nouvelle bagnole, c'est du beau travail/c'est pas de la camelote. (*See* **jet 2**) **2.** *P* (*a*) réparation *f*;‖ **he made a good job of it,** il a fait du beau boulot (*b*) boulot *m*; **what a dreadful job! quelle sale boulot! 3.** *P* (*a*) vol *m*/ coup *m*/fric-frac *m*; **to do/to pull a job,** faire un fric-frac; **they did that bank job/that job on the bank,** ils ont monté le coup de la banque (*b*) crime *m*/méfait *m*/coup *m*/combine *f* **4. to be on the job** (*a*) *F* être au boulot (*b*) *P* être en train de faire l'amour*/de besogner; (*prostitute*) être avec un client/sous l'homme **5.** *F* (*a*) **it's a good job that . . . ,** heureusement que . . . ; **. . . and a good job too!** c'est pas malheureux! **just the job!** juste ce qu'il faut!/ c'est au poil!/c'est pas dommage! (*b*) **to give sth up as a bad job,** laisser tomber qch! **6.** *F* (*esp child's language*) **to do small jobs,** faire la petite commission; **to do big jobs,** faire la grosse commission. (*See* **number 6**) **7.** *P* colis *m* de drogues*/la charge **8.** *F* **to lie/to lay/to fall down on the job,** paresser*/tirer au flanc/s'endormir sur ses lauriers **9.** *P* **the blonde job sitting over there,** la petite blonde assise là-bas **10.** *P* (*taxi*) client *m* **11.** *F* **jobs for the boys,** l'assiette *f* au beurre/distribution *f* des planques/partage *m* du même gâteau **12.** *F* **to have a job to do sth,** avoir du mal à faire qch; **I had a dreadful job to do that!** j'en ai chié/sué pour faire ça; ça (n')a pas été de la tarte. (*See* **blow-job; brown¹ I; finger-job; frail** ; **hand-job; head 13; one-night job; pipe-job; put-up; shack-up; skull-job; snow-job; soup up** (*a*))

jock [dʒɔk] *n P* **1.** (*rare*) homosex-uel*/emmanché *m* **2.** (*i*) pénis* (*ii*) *pl* testicules*/roustons *mpl*; **jock itch,** la gratte **3.** *F* = **jock-strap 4.** *NAm F* (*i*) athlète *mf*/sportif, -ive *m(f)* (*ii*) enthousiaste *mf*/fana *mf* des sports **5.** *F* (*cartes*) valet

m. (*See* **jake II 1**) 6. *F* Écossais
m.

jocker ['dʒɔkər] *n P* = **jock 1.**

jockey ['dʒɔki] *n P* **1.** = **jock 1**
2. (*regional*) homme*/gars *m*/type
m **3.** *pl Austr* caleçon *m*/slip *m*/
calcif *m.*

jock-strap ['dʒɔkstræp] *n F* sus-
pensoir *m*/soutien-couilles *m*/
trousse-couilles *m.*

jodie ['dʒoudi] *n P* **1.** *NAm* (*mil*)
(*pers rejected or deferred from the
draft*) planqué *m*/embusqué *m* **2.**
homosexuel* passif.

joe, Joe [dʒou] *n O P* **1.** *NAm*
café*/caoua *m*/jus *m* **2.** *NAm*
homme*/un Julot/un bon zigue **3.**
NAm soldat*/pioupiou/troufion *m.*
(*See* **GI 2**) **4.** (*a*) prêtre*/cureton
m/sanglier *m.* (*See* **holy 2**) (*b*)
aumônier *m* militaire **5. Joe Soap,**
Père Tartempion **6.** *O* (*RS =
cake*) **Joe Blake,** gâteau *m* **7.** (*RS
= stir = prison*) **Joe Gurr,**
prison*/bloc *m* **8.** *F* **Joe Bloggs/
Joe Public**/*NAm* **Joe Blow,**
l'homme* moyen; l'Anglais/
l'Américain moyen; = M. Dupont.
(*See* **John 5; sloppy 2**)

joey ['dʒoui] *n* **1.** *F* clown *m*/pier-
rot *m* **2.** *Austr F* fraude *f*/tar-
tignole *f*/carotte *f* **3.** *P* règles*/
anglais *mpl* **4.** *Austr F* jeune
kangourou *m* **5.** *P* jeune homosexuel*.

john, John [dʒɔn] *n* **1.** *F esp*
NAm **the john,** WC* pour hommes/
chiottes *fpl*/gogues *mpl.* (*See* **jane
3**) **2.** *P* **John Thomas,** pénis*/
Popaul/Charles-le-Chauve **3.** *F*
John Barleycorn, whisky *m* **4.**
NAm & Austr P (*RS = cop*) **John
(hop),** policier*/flic *m*/condé *m* **5.**
NAm F **John Doe,** l'Américain
moyen; = Monsieur Blot/Monsieur
Dupont-Durand **6.** *P* **John
Hancock,** signature *f*/griffe *f* **7.** *F*
long johns, caleçon long/calecif *m*
8. *P* client d'une prostituée*/miché
m/micheton *m* **9.** *P* (*homosexuals*)

to go **john** cruising, draguer dans
les tasses/faire les tasses/draguer
les tasseuses. (*See* **amy-john**)

**johnnie, Johnnie, johnny,
Johnny** ['dʒɔni] *n* **1.** *P* jeune
homme*/petit gars/zigoto *m*/zigue
m **2.** *P* homme élégant*/minet *m*
3. *P* (**rubber**) **johnnie,** préservatif*/
capote (anglaise)/chapeau *m* **4.** *P*
(*RS = corner*) **Johnnie Horner,**
coin *m* (*esp* un coin de rue et
souvent le bistrot du coin) **5.** *F*
Johnnie Raw, bleu *m*/morveux *m*
6. *F* = **john 1 7.** *NAm F* **Johnny
Reb** (*i*) soldat sudiste (guerre de
Seécession) (*ii*) rebelle *m*/révolté *m.*

Johnny-come-lately ['dʒɔni-
kʌm'leitli] *n F* blanc-bec *m*/bleu *m*/
serin *m.*

Johnny-on-the-spot ['dʒɔni-
ɔnðə'spɔt] *n NAm F* **1.** qn qui
tombe à pic **2.** qn qui arrive au
poil.

joint [dʒɔint] *n P* **1.** logement*/
cambuse *f*/piaule *f*; **a nice joint,** un
beau petit coin. (*See* **case² 1**) **2.**
(*dive*) café/bar mal famé; bouge *m*/
foutoir *m*; **gambling joint,** tripot *m*
3. (*drugs*) cigarette* de marijuana/
joint *m*/stick *m* **4.** (*drugs*) attirail*
pour s'injecter des drogues/popote
f/kit *m* **5.** pénis*/queue *f*/gourdin
m. (*See* **clip-joint; hop-joint**)

joke¹ [dʒouk] *n F* **1. it's no joke/
it's getting beyond a joke,** ça commence à ne plus être rigolo/ce n'est
plus rigolo/ça commence à me (les)
chauffer **2. he must have his little
joke,** il aime à plaisanter.

joke² [dʒouk] *vi F* **you must be/
you've got to be joking!** c'est pas
vrai!/sans blague!/tu charries!/tu
rigoles, ou quoi?

joker ['dʒoukər] *n F* **1.** homme*/
type *m*/client *m*/zigue *m*/zèbre *m*
2. malin *m*/loustic *m*/lascar *m.*

jollies ['dʒɔliz] *npl F* tout ce qui
emballe et passionne (*esp* les
plaisirs sexuels).

jolly ['dʒɔli] *F* **I** *a* **1.** légèrement ivre*/gris/éméché **2. Jolly Roger,** drapeau *m* des pirates/le pavillon noir. (*See* **bean 8**) **II** *adv F* **1.** it's a jolly good job that..., bien heureusement que...; **he's jolly glad about it,** il en est drôlement/rudement content; **it serves him jolly well right!** c'est rudement bien fait pour lui! **she's jolly nice,** elle est rudement/vachement bien; **I should jolly well think so!** c'est bien ce qui me semble!/je ne te le fais pas dire!/à qui le dis-tu? **III** *n* **1.** (*journ*) visite *f* de presse où on s'amuse beaucoup et où on fait très peu de travail. (*See* **jolly-up**) **2.** (*marine*) fusilier marin.

jolly along ['dʒɔliə'lɔŋ] *vtr F* (*a*) dérider/ragaillardir (qn) (*b*) faire marcher (qn) (pour en obtenir qch).

jolly-up ['dʒɔliʌp] *n F* réjouissances*/bombe *f*/boum *f*.

jolt¹ [dʒoult] *n P* **1.** (*drugs*) cigarette* de marijuana/stick *m* **2.** effets *mpl* primaires d'une drogue *ou* d'une cigarette* de marijuana **3.** (*i*) piqûre* d'un narcotique (*ii*) piqûre* d'héroïne; fixe *m*/shoot *m* **4.** un petit coup d'alcool*/une lampée. (*See* **overjolt**)

jolt² [dʒoult] *vi P* (*drugs*) se faire une piqûre d'héroïne (dans le bras)/se piquer*/se shooter/se faire un fixe.

jonah ['dʒounə] *n F* porte-guigne *m*/porte-poisse *m*/bonnet *m* de nuit.

Jones [dʒounz] *Prn P* (*drugs*) usage *m*/habitude *f* des drogues; l'accroche *f*.

Joneses ['dʒounziz] *Prnpl F* **to keep up with the Joneses,** ne pas se laisser doubler par ses voisins/vivre au-dessus de ses moyens pour donner l'illusion d'un standing élevé.

jordan ['dʒɔːdn] *n P* pot *m* de chambre/Jules *m*/Thomas *m*.

josh¹ [dʒɔʃ] *n NAm F* plaisanterie *f*/blague *f*.

josh² [dʒɔʃ] *vtr NAm F* taquiner/chiner/blaguer/mettre (qn) en boîte.

josher ['dʒɔʃər] *n NAm F* blagueur *m*/chineur *m*.

joskin ['dʒɔskin] *n A F* (*a*) fermier *m*/cul-terreux *m* (*b*) paysan*/plouc *m*.

josser ['dʒɔsər] *n O P* individu*/type *m*/mec *m*.

Jove [dʒouv] *n O F* **by Jove!** bon sang!/sacrebleu! **by Jove it's cold!** bon Dieu, qu'il fait froid!

joy [dʒɔi] *n F* chance*/veine *f*/pot *m*; **any joy?** ça a marché? **no joy!** pas de chance!/tant pis!/manque de bol!

joy-girl ['dʒɔigəːl] *n A P* prostituée*/fille *f* de joie.

joy-house ['dʒɔihaus] *n A P* bordel*/maison *f* de passe/maison bancale.

joy-pop¹ ['dʒɔipɔp] *n P* (*drugs*) emploi occasionnel (*esp* pour le plaisir) d'une drogue par un non-initié; piqûre* de remonte-pente. (*See* **pop¹ 5**)

joy-pop² ['dʒɔipɔp] *vi P* (*drugs*) prendre des stupéfiants à volonté (*esp* pour le plaisir) sans s'y habituer.

joy-popper ['dʒɔipɔpər] *n P* (*drugs*) **1.** qn qui se drogue* (*esp* marijuana*) pour la première fois; un neuf **2.** qn qui prend des stupéfiants (à volonté) (*esp* pour le plaisir) sans s'y habituer; saccadeur *m*.

joy-powder ['dʒɔipaudər] *n P* (*drugs*) morphine*.

joy-ride ['dʒɔiraid] *n* **1.** *F* (*a*) promenade *f* en voiture sans la permission du propriétaire; balade *f* à la sauvette (*b*) promenade *f* à toute vitesse (*c*) partie *f* de plaisir **2.** *P* expérience de drogues faite par un non-initié; saccade *f*.

joy-rider ['dʒɔiraidər] *n* **1.** *F* qn qui se promène en voiture (*i*) sans la permission du propriétaire (*ii*) en allant à toute vitesse (*iii*) pour son plaisir **2.** *P* =**joy-popper 1, 2.**

joy-smoke ['dʒɔismouk] *n P* (*drugs*) (*a*) marijuana* (*b*) haschisch*.

joystick ['dʒɔistik] *n P* **1.** pénis*/ cigare *m* à moustache/instrument *m* **2.** (*drugs*) (*a*) pipe *f* à opium/ bambou *m* (*b*) = **joint 3.**

juana [dʒuˈaɪnə, 'hwaɪnə], **juane** [dʒuˈaɪn, hwaɪn], **juanita** [djuə-ˈniːtə, hwɑːˈniːtə] *n P* (*drugs*) mari-juana*/marie-jeanne *f*/juana *f*.

judy ['dʒuːdi] *n P* **1.** fille*/femme*/ nénette *f*/nana *f* **2. to make a judy of oneself,** faire le guignol/le polichinelle.

jug¹ [dʒʌg] *n P* **1.** (*RS* = *jug and pail* = *jail*) prison*/taule *f*/coffre *m*; **to go to jug,** aller en tôle/au coffre; **he's in jug,** il s'est fait ench-tiber **2.** *pl* seins*/boîtes *fpl* à lait; **juicy jugs,** rotoplots *mpl* **3.** récip-ient *m* contenant une drogue liquide/flacon *m*/fiole *f* **4.** banque *f*; **to screw a jug,** monter un coup contre une banque/braquer une banque.

jug² [dʒʌg] *vtr P* emprisonner*/cof-frer/mettre en taule *f*/boucler.

juggins ['dʒʌginz] *n F* individu* bête/cruche *f*/nigaud *m.* (*See* **mug-gins 1**)

jughead ['dʒʌghed] *n NAm F* individu bête*/cruche *f*/cruchon *m.*

juice [dʒuːs] *n* **1.** *F* courant *m* électrique/jus *m* **2.** *F* essence *f*/ coco *m*; **to step on the juice,** mettre les gaz **3.** *P* (*a*) sperme*/jus *m*/ sauce *f*; **to jet the juice,** envoyer la purée/balancer la sauce (*b*) sperme *m* de la femme/jus *m.* (*See* **baby-juice**) **4.** *F* **the Juice,** la mer du Nord/le Bouillon **5.** *P* alcool*/ gnôle *f* **6.** *P* tonus *m*/force *f*/ vigueur *f.* (*See* **cow-juice; jungle 4; stew²**)

juiced (up) ['dʒuːstˈʌp] *a* **1.** *P* (*a*) ivre*/chargé/fadé (*b*) aiguil-lonné/survolté **2.** *F* (*car engine*) gonflé/poussé/bricolé **3.** *P* (*woman*) excitée sexuellement/le haricot à la portière/qui mouille.

juicehead ['dʒuːshed] *n NAm P* ivrogne*/soûlard *m*/poivrot *m.*

juicer ['dʒuːsər] *n NAm F* (*theatre*) électricien *m*/électro *m.*

juicy ['dʒuːsi] *a* **1.** *F* juteux/ savoureux/risqué **2.** *F* lucratif/qui rapporte/bien beurré **3.** *P* sexy/ séducteur; **she's a juicy bit of stuff,** elle est bien bandante **4.** *V* (*female genitals*) mouillé/baveux/ humide.

juju, ju-ju ['dʒuːdʒuː] *n P* (*drugs*) cigarette* de marijuana/juju *f.*

jumbo¹ ['dʒʌmbou] *a F* de grande taille/maouss(e)/mastodonte; **jumbo jet,** (avion) gros porteur/jumbo(-jet) *m.*

Jumbo, jumbo² ['dʒʌmbou] *n F* **1.** nom donné à un éléphant/Babar **2.** jumbo(-jet) *m.*

jumbuck ['dʒʌmbʌk] *n Austr F* mouton *m*/bêlant *m.*

jump¹ [dʒʌmp] *n* **1.** *P* coït*/partie *f* de jambes en l'air; **to have a jump/to give s.o. a jump** = **jump**² **1** (*a*) **2.** *P* **go (and) take a running jump (at yourself)!** va te faire voir/ va te faire foutre! (*See* **jump**² **6**) **3.** *F* **to have the jumps,** avoir les nerfs à fleur de peau; avoir la bougeotte/ne pas tenir en place/ avoir la danse de Saint-Guy **4.** *NAm P* **on the jump,** en plein coup de feu; **to be on the jump,** être très affairé. (*See* **ahead 1; high I 1**)

jump² [dʒʌmp] *vtr* **1.** *P* (*a*) faire l'amour*/faire une partie de jambes en l'air/faire zizi-panpan (*b*) faire l'amour* avec (qn)/sauter (qn) **2.** *P* voler*/faire sauter/faucher; **to jump a drag,** voler* une voiture*/ faucher une tire **3.** *F* **to jump bail,** se dérober à la justice **4.** *F* **to jump ship,** tirer une bordée **5.** *F* **to**

jump the queue, passer avant son tour. (*See* **queue-jumper**) **6.** *F* **go (and) jump in the lake!** va te faire voir! (*See* **jump¹ 2**) **7.** *F* **jump to it!** et que ça saute! **8.** *F* **to jump on s.o.,** réprimander* qn/sonner les cloches à qn/passer un savon à qn **9.** *F* **to jump down s.o.'s throat,** rabrouer qn/bouffer le nez à qn/rentrer dans la gueule à qn **10.** *P* attaquer*/sauter sur le paletot à (qn)/agrafer **11.** *F* (*party, etc*) boumer/être en plein boum/ronfler/gazer **12.** *F* **to jump off the deep end,** y aller d'autor/foncer **13.** *F* **to jump the broomstick/the hurdle,** se marier/sauter le pas/se passer la corde au cou **14.** *F* (*car, driver*) **to jump the lights,** brûler/griller le (feu) rouge. (*See* **bandwagon; gun¹ 2**)

jumped up ['dʒʌmpt'ʌp] *a F* **1.** prétentieux*/crâneur/esbrouffeur **2.** parvenu/nouveau-riche **3.** bâclé/fait à la six-quatre-deux.

jumper ['dʒʌmpər] *n P* **(you can) stick it up your jumper!** fous ça dans ta poche (et ton mouchoir par-dessus)!/tu sais où tu peux te le mettre! (*See* **queue-jumper; stick² 3**)

jumping ['dʒʌmpiŋ] *a F* (*party, etc*) en plein boum. (*See* **jump² 11**)

jungle ['dʒʌŋgl] *n* **1.** *F* la jungle/endroit *m* de mauvaises mœurs **2.** *P* lieu *m* de refuge des vagabonds/la zone/la cloche **3.** *esp NAm P* (*pej*) **jungle bunny,** Noir(e)*/nègre *mf*/bougnoul(e) *m* **4.** *P* **jungle juice,** alcool*/gnôle *f*/tord-boyaux *m*.

junk¹ [dʒʌŋk] *n* **1.** *F* (*a*) articles variés sans grande valeur/pacotille *f*/gnognote *f*; **this shop sells a load of junk,** ce magasin ne vend que de la camelote; **junk food,** fast food *m* (*b*) effets *mpl* personnels/affaires *fpl*/barda *m*; **get your junk out of here!** enlève ton bazar/ton fourbi de là! **2.** *P* (*hard drugs*) (*a*) drogues *fpl*/stupéfiants *mpl*/stups *mpl*; **to be on the junk,** se droguer*/se camer (*b*) héroïne*/héro *f* **3.** *F* bêtises*/balivernes *fpl*; **you do talk a lot of junk!** tu déblogues!/tu délires pas mal, toi! **4.** *F* ferraille *f*; **heap of junk,** vieille voiture*/guimbarde *f*/tas *m* de ferraille **5.** *P* ordures *fpl*/de la cochonnerie **6.** *P* bijoux *mpl* (comme butin*)/joncaille *f*/broquille *f*.

junk² [dʒʌŋk] *vtr NAm P* mettre au rebut/au rencart/à la casse/à la poubelle; balancer.

junked up ['dʒʌŋkt'ʌp] *a P* drogué*/camé/junké/junkie. (*See* **junk¹ 2**)

junker ['dʒʌŋkər] *n P* = **junkie, junky¹ 1, 2.**

junkie, junky¹ ['dʒʌŋki] *n P* (*drugs*) **1.** drogué*/toxico(mane) *mf*/junkie *mf*/camé(e) **2.** trafiquant *m* de drogues/fourgueur *m*/dealer *m*.

junky² ['dʒʌŋki] *a F* qui n'a pas de valeur/bon à foutre en l'air/de la camelote/(du) toc.

K

K [kei] *abbr F* (= *1,000*) mille; **salary (of) 10K,** salaire de dix mille (livres, dollars, etc).

kale [keil] *n NAm P* argent*/blé *m*.

kangaroo [kæŋgəˈruː] *n F* **1. kangaroo court,** tribunal illégal/guignol *m* à l'estoc **2.** *pl* titres *mpl* de bourse australiens/mous *mpl*.

kaput(t) [kæˈput, kə-] *a F* cassé/fichu/kaput; **my watch is kaput,** ma montre est fichue/foutue; **all my plans have gone kaput,** tous mes projets sont tombés à l'eau.

karzy [ˈkɑːzi] *n P* WC*/chiottes *fpl*/gogues *mpl*; **karzy paper,** papier *m* hygiénique/torche-cul *m*/p(apier)-cul *m*.

Kate and Sidney [ˈkeitənˈsidni] *n F* (*hum*) (*RS* = *steak and kidney*) **Kate and Sidney pie,** tourte *f* à la viande de bœuf et aux rognons/= contre-pèterie *f*.

kayo[1] [ˈkeiˈjou] *n F* (*esp boxing*) = **k.o.**[1].

kayo[2] [ˈkeiˈjou] *vtr F* (*esp boxing*) = **k.o.**[2].

K-boy [ˈkeibɔi] *n NAm P* (*cards*) roi *m*/le papa.

kecks [keks] *npl P* pantalon*/falzar(d) *m*/fut(al) *m*.

keef [kiːf] *n P* (*drugs*) marijuana*/kif *m*.

keen [kiːn] *a NAm P* excellent*/chouette/bath/super.

keep [kiːp] *vtr F* **1. to keep oneself to oneself,** faire bande à part **2. to keep at it,** persévérer/s'accrocher à qch/prendre le mors aux dents; **to**

keep s.o. at it, serrer les côtes/la vis à qn. (*See* **hat 3**)

keep in [ˈkiːpˈin] *vi F* **to keep in with s.o.,** rester bien avec qn/peaufiner (une relation); **to keep in with both sides,** ménager la chèvre et le chou/nager entre deux eaux/jouer sur tous les tableaux.

keep on [ˈkiːpˈɔn] *vi F* **to keep on at s.o.,** harceler qn/être sur le dos de qn.

keep out [ˈkiːpˈaut] *vi F* **you keep out of this!** mêle-toi de ce qui te regarde!/occupe-toi de tes oignons!

keeps [kiːps] *npl F* **for keeps,** pour de bon/pas pour la frime/à perpète/pas pour de rire.

keep up [ˈkiːpˈʌp] *vtr F* **keep it up!** vas-y!/continue!/tu l'auras! **keep your pecker up!** tiens bon!/te laisse pas abattre! (*See* **end 6; Joneses; pecker 2**)

keester [ˈkiːstər] *n NAm P* **1.** fesses*/postérieur *m*/derche *m* **2.** poche* arrière de pantalon/fouille *f*/profonde *f* **3.** valise *f* de camelot/valdingue *f*/valoche *f* **4.** coffre-fort *m*/coffiot *m*/jacquot *m* **5.** *A V* sexe de la femme*/boîte *f* à ouvrage.

kef [keif, kef] *n P* = **keef.**

kefuffle [kəˈfʌfl] *n F* = **kerfuffle.**

keister [ˈkiːstər] *n NAm P* = **keester.**

keks [keks] *npl P* = **kecks.**

Kelly, kelly [ˈkeli] *n* **1.** *NAm P* (*hat*) chapeau*/galurin *m*/doulos *m*/toiture *f* **2.** *F* **Kelly's eye:** *see* **bingo 1.** (*See* **Derby Kelly**)

kerb crawl ['kɜːb'krɔːl], **kerb cruise** ['kɜːb'kruːz] *vi F* chercher un partenaire sexuel *ou* une prostituée en voiture/draguer en voiture.

kerb crawler ['kɜːb'krɔːlər], **kerb cruiser** ['kɜːb'kruːzər] *n F* qn qui cherche un partenaire sexuel *ou* une prostituée en voiture/dragueur *m* en voiture/maraudeur *m*.

kerdoing, kerdoying! [kə'dɔiŋ] *excl F* boum!/pan!/vlan! (*See* **gerdoing!**)

kerflooie [kɜː'fluːi] *adv NAm F* **to go kerflooie,** échouer*/foirer/finir en queue de poisson/faire un bide total.

kerfuffle [kə'fʌfl] *n F* commotion *f*/agitation *f*/chienlit *f*; histoire *f*/affaire *f*; **there was all this kerfuffle,** c'était toute une histoire.

kerplunk [kə'plʌŋk] *adv F* **to go kerplunk,** tomber*/ramasser un gadin/mordre la poussière.

kettle ['ketl] *n* **1.** *esp NAm P* montre* (en or*); **kettle and piece,** montre et chaîne/toccante et pendante **2.** *F* **here's a nice/fine/pretty kettle of fish!** (*a*) en voilà une affaire!/en voilà des histoires!/quelle salade! (*b*) nous voilà dans de beaux draps/dans un beau gâchis!

key [kiː] *n F* **key of the door:** *see* **bingo 21.**

keyed up ['kiːd'ʌp] *a&pp F* gonflé à bloc.

keyhole ['kiːhoul] *n P* **to play Keyhole Kate,** faire le voyeur/fouiner à la serrure/faire le fouineur.

keyster ['kiːstər] *n NAm P* = **keester.**

khazi ['kɑːzi] *n P* = **karzy.**

Khyber ['kaibər] *n P* (*RS = Khyber Pass = arse*) **he can stick it up his Khyber,** il peut se le mettre quelque part/il peut se le fourrer (là) où il le pense. (*See* **stick² 3**)

ki [kai] *n P* **1.** cacao *m ou* chocolat *m* de prison **2.** (*drugs*) kilo *m* de marijuana*.

kibitz ['kibits] *vi F* **1.** suivre/regarder une partie de cartes en donnant son avis **2.** se mêler de ce qui ne vous regarde pas/mettre son grain de sel/ramener sa fraise.

kibitzer ['kibitsər] *n F* individu *m* qui donne des conseils non sollicités/qui se mêle de tout; canule *f*/canulard *m*.

kibosh ['kaibɔʃ] *n F* **1. to put the kibosh on sth,** mettre fin/mettre son veto/mettre le holà à qch; **that's put the kibosh on that,** ça a tout foutu en l'air/ça a tout salopé **2.** (*rare*) = **bosh.**

kick¹ [kik] *n* **1.** *F* (*a*) frisson *m* (de plaisir)/piquant *m* (d'une chose); **to get a kick out of sth,** prendre/éprouver du plaisir à qch; **prendre son pied/son fade; that's how he gets his kicks,** c'est comme ça qu'il prend son pied; **he doesn't get much of a kick out of that,** ça ne le botte pas tellement; **to do sth for kicks,** faire ce qui botte/ce qui chante (*b*) marotte *f*/manie *f*; **to be on a health food kick,** être accro à la bouffe-bio **2.** *F* (*drink*) **it's got a kick in it,** ça vous remonte/ça vous requinque/ça vous donne un coup de fouet **3.** *F* (*drugs*) le pied/l'extase *f*; **to go on a kick,** prendre son pied/aller à la défonce/se défoncer; **bum kicks,** mauvaise expérience d'un drogué*/flippage *m*/mauvais voyage **4.** *F* **he's got no kick left in him,** il est vidé/lessivé/pompé **5.** (*a*) *F* **that's better than a kick in the pants,** ça vaut mieux qu'un coup de pied au derrière/ça vaut mieux que de se casser la jambe/il vaut mieux entendre ça qu'être sourd (*b*) *P* **he's had a kick in the pants/the arse/*NAm* the ass,** il s'est fait botter le cul/il s'est fait asseoir; **that was a kick in the pants/the teeth for my idea,** mon idée a été un bide total/je me suis ramassé avec cette idée. (*See* **pants**

3) **6.** *F* **the kick,** sacquage *m*; **to get the kick,** recevoir son paquet/ être boulé/se faire mettre sur le carreau **7.** *A P* poche* (de pantalon)/fouille *f* **8.** *P* grogne *f*/ rouspétance *f* **9.** *A P* pièce de six pence; **two and a kick,** (pièce de) deux shillings et six pence/demi-couronne *f*. (*See* **sidekick**)

kick² [kik] *vtr&i* **1.** *P* grogner*/ bougonner/rouspéter/ronchonner/ râler **2.** *F* résister/ruer dans les brancards **3.** *P* (*drugs, etc*) **he's kicked it,** il a décroché **4.** *F I* **could have kicked myself,** je me serais flanqué des claques/des coups. (*See* **alive 1**; **bucket 1**; **habit 1**)

kick around ['kikə'raund] *vtr F* **1.** retourner/ruminer; **to kick a few ideas around,** lancer quelques idées **2. to kick s.o. around,** mener qn à la trique/à la baguette; **he kicks his kids around,** il mène ses gosses à la baguette/ses gosses lui obéissent au doigt et à l'œil **3.** rouler sa bosse/ bourlinguer; **there are lots of people like that kicking around,** des gens comme ça, ce n'est pas ça qui manque; **I've lost my gloves, but they must be kicking around somewhere,** j'ai perdu mes gants, mais ils doivent traîner quelque part. (*See* **gong 2**)

kickback ['kikbæk] *n* **1.** *F* réaction violente/coup *m* de boome-rang/retour *m* de manivelle **2.** *P* ristourne *f*/dessous-de-table *m*/pot *m* de vin/graissage *m* de patte **3.** *P* récidive *f* dans la drogue/rechute *f*.

kicker ['kikər] *n NAm P* piège *m*/ hic *m*/os *m*. (*See* **shitkicker**)

kick in ['kik'in] *F* **I** *vi* payer sa part/payer son écot **II** *vtr* **to kick s.o.'s head in,** battre* qn/passer qn à tabac.

kickman ['kikmæn] *n P* (*drugs*) dealer *m*/fourgueur *m*.

kick-off ['kikɔf] *n F* coup *m* d'envoi/démarrage *m*; **and you can**

stop doing that for a kick-off, et pour commencer tu vas m'arrêter ça/tu vas m'arrêter ce cinéma.

kick off ['kikɔf] *vi* **1.** *F* donner le départ/le coup d'envoi/démarrer **2.** *P* partir*/lever l'ancre/se tirer/se tailler **3.** *P* mourir*/claquer/ clamser.

kick out ['kik'aut] *vtr F* (*a*) flan-quer (qn) à la porte/balancer/ larguer (qn) (*b*) congédier* (qn)/ sacquer (qn); **I got kicked out of that job,** je me suis fait virer/ba-lancer de ce boulot-là.

kick-stick ['kikstik] *n P* (*drugs*) cigarette* de marijuana/stick *m*/ joint *m*.

kick-up ['kikʌp] *n esp NAm F* chahut *m*/tapage *m*/chambard *m*.

kick up ['kik'ʌp] *vtr* **1.** *F* **to kick up a fuss,** faire des chichis *mpl*/ faire des histoires/faire tout un plat **2.** (*a*) *F* **to kick up a row/a racket/ a shindy/a hullabaloo,** faire beaucoup de bruit*/faire du bou-can/faire du ramdam (*b*) *F* **to kick up a dust,** mener grand bruit*/faire une scène/faire un scandale/faire du foin (*c*) *P* **to kick up hell,** faire un scandale du diable **3.** *F* **to kick up one's heels,** sauter de joie. (*See* **stink¹ 1**)

kick upstairs ['kikʌp'stɛəz] *vtr F* **to kick s.o. upstairs,** donner de l'avancement à qn/catapulter qn à un poste supérieur pour s'en débar-rasser*; donner un titre de noblesse/faire un limogeage doré.

kid¹ [kid] **I** *a F* **1.** jeunet/cadet; **my kid sister,** ma sœur cadette **2.** enfantin/puéril; **kid stuff,** enfantil-lage *m*/gaminerie *f*; **it's kids' stuff,** c'est simple comme bonjour/c'est un jeu d'enfant **3. to handle/to treat s.o. with kid gloves** (*i*) ménager qn/manier qn comme du verre cassé/prendre des gants avec qn (*ii*) dorloter/chouchouter qn **II** *n F* enfant*/gosse *mf*/môme *mf*/ moutard *m*; **when I was a kid,**

quand j'étais gosse; **our kid,** le ben-jamin/le cadet/la cadette de la famille; mon petit frangin/ma petite frangine. (*See* **whiz(z)¹** I)

kid² [kid] *F* **I** *vtr* **1.** en conter à (qn)/faire marcher (qn); **don't kid yourself!** ne te fais pas d'illusion!/ ne te montes pas le bourrichon! **who are you trying to kid?/who do you think you're kidding?** tu te fiches de moi?/tu me prends pour qui? **no kidding!** sans blague!/ blague à part!/sans déconner! **II** *vi* plaisanter/charrier; **are you kidding?/no kidding?** tu me fais marcher?/tu veux me mener en bateau?/tu veux rire ou quoi? **stop kidding!** arrête ton char!/arrête tes salades!/arrête tes conneries!

kid along ['kidə'lɔŋ] *vtr F* bourrer le crâne à (qn)/envelopper (qn)/ monter un bateau (à qn).

kidder ['kidər] *n F* plaisantin *m*/ farceur *m*/blagueur *m*/loustic *m*.

kiddie ['kidi] *n F* = **kiddy.**

kiddy ['kidi], **kiddywink** ['kidiwiŋk] *n F* petit enfant*/mioche *mf*/chiard *m*/gniard *m*. (*See* **kid¹** II)

kief [ki:f], **kif** [kif] *n P* = **keef.**

kike [kaik] *n P* (*pej*) Juif* *m*/Youpe *m*/Youpin *m*/Youtre *m*.

kill¹ [kil] **I** *a NAm F* excellent*/ super/extra/génial **II** *n F* **1.** assassinat *m*/butage *m*/saignage *m*/ mise *f* en l'air/zigouillage *m* **2.** (*a*) descente *f* (d'avion ennemi)/inscrip-tion *f* au tableau de chasse (*b*) cou-lée *f* (d'un navire ennemi) **3.** **kill or cure,** remède *m* de cheval **4. to be in at the kill,** assister au dénoue-ment. (*See* **set up 2**)

kill² [kil] *vtr F* **1. to kill a bottle,** étrangler/sécher/siffler une bouteille; faire cul sec **2.** ruiner/ enfoncer/couler (qn *ou* qch) **3.** (*theatre*) **to kill an audience,** brûler les planches/casser la baraque/faire un tabac **4.** (*cigarette*) éteindre/ écraser; (*motor*) arrêter; **kill those lights!** (*headlights*) coupe ces

phares! (*lightbulbs*) éteins ces loupi-otes! **5. to kill time,** tuer le temps/ paresser*/flemmarder/tirer sa flemme/se la couler douce **6. to kill oneself (with work),** se tuer/se crever de travail; (*iron*) **don't kill yourself!** ne te fais pas de mal! **7. to kill oneself laughing,** se tordre de rire/se boyauter; **his jokes really kill me,** ses plaisanteries sont tordantes **8. my feet are killing me,** j'ai les pieds en compote/je ne sens plus mes cannes. (*See* **dressed**)

killer ['kilər] *n P* **1.** flambard *m*/ frimeur *m* **2.** (*joke*) **it was a real killer!** c'était crevant/à se rouler par terre/à mourir de rire! **3. that job's a real killer!** c'est tuant/cre-vant, ce boulot!/on se crève avec ce boulot-là! **4.** (*drugs*) cigarette* de marijuana/stick *m*.

killing ['kiliŋ] **I** *a F* **1.** très amusant*/tordant/crevant/à se rouler par terre/boyautant; **it's too killing for words,** c'est à mourir de rire **2.** fatigant/tuant/crevant; **this job is really killing!** c'est crevant/ chiant, ce boulot! **II** *n F* **to make a killing,** faire de gros profits/ affurer/faire son beurre/se faire un sacré velours.

kind [kaind] *n F* **1. I don't have that kind of money,** je n'ai pas des sommes pareilles **2. these kind of things annoy me,** ce genre de choses m'agace **3. she's not my kind (of woman),** cette femme, ce n'est pas mon genre **4. I'm not that kind (of person),** je ne mange pas de ce pain-là. (*See* **kind of**)

kinda ['kaində] *adv F* = **kind of.**

kind of ['kaindəv] *adv F* **1. he's kind of careful with money!** il est plutôt près de ses sous! **2. I kind of expected it/I had a kind of feel-ing,** j'avais comme un pressenti-ment/je le sentais venir/je m'en doutais presque **3. it's kind of chil-ly,** il fait plutôt frisquet.

kingdom-come ['kɪŋdəm'kʌm]
1. *F* le paradis/le paradouze **2.** *P*
to knock s.o. to kingdom-come, battre* qn/envoyer qn dans l'autre
monde/foutre une trempe à qn;
**shut your face or I'll knock you to
kingdom-come!** ferme ta gueule ou
je te fais une tête au carré! **3.** *P*
(*RS* = *rum*) rhum *m*. (*See* **Tom 4**;
touch-your-bum)

king-size(d) ['kɪŋsaiz(d)] *a F*
géant/énorme/maousse; baby-
lonien; **it was a king-size(d) problem,** on était dans une sacrée
parade.

kink [kɪŋk] *n F* truc *m*/lubie *f*/
manie *f*/dada *m*; **he's got a kink,** il
est un peu timbré/il travaille du
citron; **he's got a kink for young
boys,** les jeunes mecs, c'est son
truc.

kinky ['kɪŋki] **I** *a* **1.** *F* fantasque/
excentrique/fada **2.** *F* bizarre/
équivoque; **she wears really kinky
clothes,** elle porte des fringues complètement dingues; **he asked me to
do some very kinky things,** il m'a
demandé de faire des trucs plutôt
bizarres **3.** *P* homosexuel/qui a
des goûts spéciaux; **he's a bit kinky,**
il est un peu pédé sur les bords/il
fait très tapette **II** *n P* (*not common*) **1.** homosexuel*/pédé *m*/
pédale *f*/tante *f* **2.** lesbienne*/
goudou *f*/gouine *f*/vrille *f*.

kip¹ [kɪp] *n P* **1.** lit*/pieu *m*/
plumard *m*; **he had to find a kip for
the night,** il a dû se dénicher un
paddock pour la nuit **2.** (*not common*) pension *f* (de famille)/chambre meublée/crèche *f* **3.** sommeil
m; **to have a kip,** dormir*/piquer
un roupillon/pioncer/écraser la
bulle; **did you get enough kip?** t'as
écrasé la bulle?

kip² [kɪp] *vi P* **1.** se coucher*/se
pieuter/se bâcher; **he was kipping
on the floor,** il s'était couché par
terre/il pionçait par terre **2.**
dormir*/pioncer/roupiller/écraser la
bulle/faire une partie de traversin

3. coucher à la dure/compter les
étoiles.

kip down ['kɪp'daun] *vi P* se
coucher/se bâcher/se pieuter; **you
can kip down at my place,** tu peux
pioncer à ma taule.

kip-house ['kɪphaus] *n P* =
doss-house.

kipper ['kɪpər] *n P* **1.** *A*
individu*/type *m*/client *m* **2.**
(*horse racing, etc*) **kipper season,**
morte-saison *f*.

kipper-feast ['kɪpərfiːst] *n VV*
cunnilinctus*/langue fourrée;
gougnottage *m*.

kip-shop ['kɪpʃɔp] *n A P* bordel*/
boxon *m*.

kiss¹ [kɪs] *n F* **1. the kiss of death,**
le coup de grâce **2. the kiss of life,**
le bouche-à-bouche. (*See* **French¹ I
1**; **tongue-kiss**)

kiss² [kɪs] *vtr F* **1. to kiss sth
goodbye,** faire ses adieux à qch/en
faire son deuil/faire une croix sur
qch; **you can kiss goodbye to your
holidays!** tu peux faire une croix
sur tes vacances **2. never been
kissed:** *see* **bingo 16** **3. to kiss
and be friends/to kiss and make up,**
se réconcilier/se rebonneter/faire
ami-ami/se rabibocher. (*See* **arse I
7**; **dust¹ 4**)

kiss-ass ['kɪsæs] *n NAm V* **1.**
(*pers*) lèche-cul *mf* **2.** lèche *f*/boniments *mpl*. (*See* **ass-kisser**)

kiss ass ['kɪs'æs] *vi NAm V* faire
de la lèche.

kisser ['kɪsər] *n P* **1.** bouche*/bec
m/museau *m*/margoulette *f* **2.**
lèvres*/baiseuses *fpl*/babines *fpl* **3.**
visage*/fiole *f*/trombine *f*/fraise *f*;
**he socked him one right in the
kisser,** il lui a flanqué une pêche en
pleine poire. (*See* **arse-kisser**;
baby-kisser)

kiss-off ['kɪsɔf] *n NAm P* **1.** mort
f/crève *f*/crevaison *f*/saignage *m*
2. sacquage *m*/limogeage *m*/vidage
m.

kiss off ['kis'ɔf] *vtr NAm P* **1.** tuer*/buter/crounir (qn) **2.** se débarrasser* de/sacquer/balancer/expédier (qn).

kissy ['kisi] *a P* (*not common*) flagorneur/lèche-cul/lèche-botte.

kit [kit] *n* **1.** *F* barda *m*/bataclan *m*/Saint-Frusquin *m*. (*See* **caboodle**) **2.** *P* (*drug addict's instruments*) artillerie *f*.

kitchen-sink¹ ['kitʃin'siŋk] *a attrib F* **kitchen-sink novel/play**, roman *m/ou* pièce *f* naturaliste/réaliste/boîte à ordures.

kitchen-sink² ['kitʃin'siŋk] *n F* **everything but the kitchen-sink**, tout sans exception/y compris la cage aux serins.

kite¹ [kait] *n* **1.** *F* avion *m*/coucou *m* **2.** *F* **to fly a kite** (*a*) mettre une fausse traite en circulation (*b*) tâter le terrain/lancer un ballon d'essai (*c*) (*finance*) tirer en l'air/tirer en blanc **3.** *P* chèque *m*; **kite man**, faussaire *m*/mornifleur *m* **4.** *F* **high as a kite** (*a*) ivre*/parti/beurré/rétamé (*b*) drogué/chargé/envappé/bourré à zéro/défoncé; **he's as high as a kite**, il a du vent dans les voiles/il est dans les vapes.

kite² [kait] *vtr P* **to kite s.o.**, donner/filer un chèque sans provision à qn.

kittens ['kitnz] *npl F* **to (nearly) have kittens** (*a*) être très en colère*/piquer une crise/avoir un coup de sang; **he had kittens when he saw how much she had spent**, il a piqué une crise quand il a vu combien elle avait dépensé (*b*) avoir peur*/avoir les foies *mpl*/avoir chaud aux fesses *fpl*/avoir le trouillomètre à zéro. (*See* **sex-kitten**)

kitty ['kiti] *n* **1.** *F* chaton *m*/petit(e) chat(te)/mistigri *m* **2.** *F* (*a*) cagnotte *f* (*b*) magot *m*/galette *f* **3.** *P* prison*/trou *m*/taule *f*/gnouf *m*.

Kiwi, kiwi ['kiːwiː] *n F* **1.** Néo-Zélandais *m*/Kiwi *m* **2.** employé

d'un aéroport affecté à terre; rampant *m*.

klink [kliŋk] *n P* = **clink**.

klutz [klʌts] *n NAm P* individu bête*/navet *m*/poire *f*.

klutzy ['klʌtsi] *a NAm P* bête/con/balluche.

k-man ['keimæn] *abbr P* = **kickman**.

knacker ['nækər] *vtr P* **1.** châtrer **2.** réduire à quia/démonter **3.** éreinter/crever (qn); **this job will really knacker you**, ce boulot va vous crever. (*See* **knackered**)

knackered ['nækəd] *a&pp P* **to be knackered** (*a*) être fatigué*/éreinté/vanné; **I'm really knackered after that**, je suis complètement sur les genoux (*b*) se trouver en mauvaise posture/être emmerdé/ne pas savoir sur quel pied danser; **all our ideas are knackered now**, tous nos projets sont à l'eau/se sont cassés la gueule.

knackers ['nækəz] *npl P* **1.** testicules*/balloches *fpl*/noisettes *fpl*/joyeuses *fpl* **2.** *excl* **knackers to that!** mon cul!/je t'emmerde!/et mon œil c'est du poulet!

knee [niː] *n F* **housemaid's knee**, épanchement *m* de synovie/genou *m* en compote. (*See* **bee 1**)

knee-high ['niːˈhai] *a F* **to be knee-high to a grasshopper**, être une courte-botte/être un petit poucet/être un rase-mottes/être bas-du-cul/avoir le cul près du trottoir; **when I was knee-high to a grasshopper**, quand j'étais gosse.

kneesies ['niːziz] *npl F* **to play kneesies with s.o.**, faire du genou/du pied. (*See* **footsie**)

knees-up ['niːzʌp] *n F* gambade *f*/cabriole *f*; (*lively dance or party*) **they were having a real knees-up in there**, c'était une fête à tout casser/ils s'éclataient carrément là-haut.

knee-trembler ['niːtremblər] *n V* **to do a knee-trembler**, faire l'amour* debout/sabrer à la verticale.

knickers ['nikəz] *npl* **1.** *P* **don't get your knickers in a twist,** ne te mets pas dans tous tes états/ne prends pas ta chique **2.** *excl* **knickers!** des foutaises!/des conneries!/mon cul!

knife [naif] *n F* **1. to get one's knife into s.o./to have one's knife in s.o.,** avoir une dent contre qn/s'acharner sur qn/en avoir après qn; **she's really got her knife into me,** elle en a après moi/elle m'en veut.

knob [nɔb] *n* **1.** *V* pénis*/(gros) bout/zob *m*/nœud *m*/gourdin *m*; **knob job,** fellation*/taillage *m* de plume/pompier *m*; **knob rot** (*i*) blennorragie*/chaude-pisse *f* (*ii*) syphilis*/syphlotte *f*/naze *f* **2.** *P* tête*/caboche *f*/ciboulot *m*/coco *m* **3.** *P* **with knobs on,** et le pouce/et mèche/et le rab; **and the same to you with brass knobs on,** et ta sœur!/va te faire voir!

knob-gobbler ['nɔbgɔblər] *n V* **1.** homosexuel*/pédé *m*/enculé *m* **2.** qn qui fait une fellation* à qn/suceur *m*/pipeur *m*.

knobstick ['nɔbstik] *n P* (*not common*) ouvrier non-syndiqué/jaune *m*.

knock¹ [nɔk] *n* **1.** *F* critique *f*/éreintement *m*/abattage *m* **2.** *F* ennui *m*/pépin *m*; revers *m*; **to take a knock,** essuyer un échec* *ou* une déception/recevoir un coup dans les gencives **3.** *F* (*cartes*) **it's your knock,** c'est ton tour/c'est ta passe **4.** *P* **on the knock,** à crédit/à croume.

knock² [nɔk] *vtr* **1.** *F* critiquer*/trouver à redire à (qn, qch)/éreinter/débiner; **don't knock the film before you've even seen it!** ne descends pas ce film en flammes avant de l'avoir vu! **2.** *F* **to knock sth on the head,** battre qch en brèche/mettre le holà; arrêter les

frais; **that's knocked his little idea on the head,** son projet est tombé à l'eau/il a coupé court à son projet **3.** *F* **to be knocking 60,** friser la soixantaine **4.** *P* = **knock off 4 5.** *P* **that'll knock 'em cold,** cela va leur en boucher un coin **6.** *P* (*a*) faire l'amour* avec/baiser/bourrer/caramboler (qn) (*b*) *Austr* violer/baptiser (qn); passer (qn) à la casserole **7.** *F* **to knock s.o. silly/for six,** battre qn à plate(s) couture(s)/donner une tabassée à qn/démolir qn/filer une purge à qn **8.** *F* **knock at the door:** *see* **bingo 4.** (*See* **feather¹ 5; sideways; spot 3; wall 4; week**)

knock about, around ['nɔkə'baut, ə'raund] *vi F* **1.** vadrouiller/rouler sa bosse/bourlinguer; **he's knocked about a bit,** il a roulé sa bosse **2. to knock about with s.o.,** s'acoquiner avec qn/sortir avec qn/fréquenter qn; **he knocks about with that gang of hooligans,** il fréquente cette bande de voyous.

knock back ['nɔk'bæk] *vtr F* **1. to knock back a drink,** boire*/lamper un verre/écluser un godet/s'en jeter un derrière la cravate; **knock it back!** cul sec! **2.** coûter/peser; **it knocked him back a packet,** ça lui a pesé un sac/il en a aligné un paquet **3.** renvoyer/faire rebondir; **he knocked it back at me,** il me l'a balanstiqué/il m'a refilé le bébé.

knock-down ['nɔkdaun] *n Austr & NAm P* présentation *f* (d'une personne à une autre); **will you give me a knock-down to him?** tu me présenteras?

knocked off ['nɔkt'ɔf] *a&pp P* volé/fauché. (*See* **knock off 4**)

knocked out ['nɔkt'aut] *a&pp P* **1.** fatigué/vanné/lessivé; **I'm really knocked out,** je suis vraiment foutu **2.** épaté/estomaqué/médusé; **I'm really knocked out by that idea,** cette idée m'a coupé le sifflet **3.**

(*a*) ivre*/rétamé/beurré (*b*) drogué*/camé/bourré. (*See* **knock out**)

knocked up ['nɔkt'ʌp] *a&pp P* **1.** malade*/patraque/flapi/flagada **2.** très fatigué*/claqué **3.** *esp NAm* enceinte*/engrossée/en cloque; **she's knocked up,** elle a un polichinelle dans le tiroir/elle a le ballon. (*See* **knock up**)

knocker ['nɔkər] *n* **1.** *F* critique *m* sévère/éreinteur *m*/esquinteur *m*/ abatteur *m* **2.** *P* personne importante (ou qui se croit telle)/ gros bonnet/grosse légume/huile *f* **3.** *pl P* seins*/nichons *mpl*/rondins *mpl*/nénés *mpl*/tétons *mpl*; **what a huge pair of knockers!** quel balcon!/quelle belle paire de melons! **4.** *P* **on the knocker,** à crédit/à tempérament/au croum(e)/au crayon. (*See* **dress up 2**)

knocking ['nɔkiŋ] *a* **1.** *P* **knocking company,** maison *f* de ventes à crédit/croumiers *mpl* **2.** *P* **knocking shop,** bordel*/maison *f* d'abattage/claque *m* **3.** *F* **knocking copy,** publicité qui critique un concurrent/publicité comparative.

knock-kneed ['nɔk'niːd] *a F* (*euph*) poltron*/froussard/péteux.

knock off ['nɔk'ɔf] *vtr* **1.** *P* **to knock s.o. off,** caramboler/baiser/ tringler/s'envoyer qn; **he's knocking off his secretary,** il s'envoie sa secrétaire en cinq à sept **2.** *P* **knock it off (will you)!** basta!/ écrase!/ferme-là!/boucle ton égout! **3.** *F* = **knock back 1 4.** *P* voler*/faucher; **to knock off a bank,** faire/monter un coup contre une banque; **did you buy it or did you knock it off?** tu l'as acheté ou piqué? **5.** *F* finir de travailler/ débrayer/boucler/dételer; **he knocks off at 5pm,** il détèle à 5 heures **6.** *F* finir vite/exécuter avec rapidité/ liquider/expédier; **she knocked off her letters in no time,** elle a bâclé ses lettres en deux temps trois mouvements **7.** *P* arrêter*/agrafer

8. *P* tuer*/démolir/zigouiller/refroidir (qn) **9.** *F* **I'll knock two quid off the price for you,** je vous fais une remise de vingt balles/je vous fais vingt balles sur le prix. (*See* **block 1**)

knockout ['nɔkaut] **I** *a F* **1.** **knockout drops,** stupéfiant *m* qu'on met dans la boisson de la victime pour lui faire perdre connaissance (dans le but de la dépouiller)/coup *m* d'assommoir **2.** mirobolant/ transcendant; **what a knockout idea!** quelle chouette idée/quelle idée géniale! **II** *n F* **1.** une merveille/ un phénomène/qch *ou* qn de mirifique; **he's a knockout,** il en jette; il roule des mécaniques **2.** (*esp woman*) prix *m* de Diane/ femme roulée au moule/belle mécanique. (*See* **k.o.[1]**)

knock out ['nɔk'aut] *vtr F* **1.** **to knock oneself out,** travailler* dur/ s'éreinter/s'esquinter; **that work really knocked me out,** ce boulot m'a bouché un coin/m'a vraiment épaté **2.** époustoufler/éblouir/ épater/en boucher un coin à qn; **it really knocked me out when he gave me the flowers,** j'en suis restée baba quand il m'a donné ces fleurs. (*See* **knocked out; k.o.[2]**)

knock-over ['nɔkouvər] *n P* cambriolage *m*/fric(-)frac *m*/caroublage *m*/mise *f* en l'air.

knock over ['nɔk'ouvər] *vtr O P esp NAm* **1.** cambrioler*/ caroubler/mettre en l'air/faire un fric(-)frac/faire un casse **2.** faire une descente (de police) dans . . . / rafler.

knock together ['nɔktə'geðər] *vtr F* = **knock up 1.**

knock up ['nɔk'ʌp] *vtr* **1.** *F* préparer/concocter/combiner/ bricoler à la hâte; **they've knocked up some sort of an alibi,** ils se sont bricolés/montés un alibi quelconque **2.** *F* (*a*) réveiller/secouer (*b*) tambouriner à une porte à une heure tardive **3.** *esp NAm P* rendre enceinte*/engrosser/mettre en cloque/mettre un polichinelle dans le tiroir **4.** *P* (*a*) abîmer*/amocher/saboter (*b*) fatiguer/éreinter/crever (qn); **that work really knocks you up,** ce boulot est vachement crevant/tuant **5.** *F* **to knock up £100 a week,** se faire/ramasser cent livres par semaine.

knot [nɔt] *n F* **1. to tie the knot,** se marier/se mettre la corde au cou/signer un bail/s'entifler **2. to get tied (up) in knots,** s'embrouiller/s'emberlificoter/ne pas s'en sortir/se faire des nœuds; perdre les pédales. (*See* **top-knot**)

knothead ['nɔthed] *n NAm F* = **knucklehead.**

knotted ['nɔtid] *a&pp P* **get knotted!** va te faire voir!/va te faire foutre!

know[1] [nou] *n F* **to be in the know,** être affranchi/être au parfum/être dans le coup; **to put s.o. in the know,** affranchir/parfumer/tuyauter qn.

know[2] [nou] *vtr&i F* **1. I don't want to know,** rien à faire/je ne marche pas **2. not that I know of,** pas que je sache; **for all I know,** autant que je sache **3.** (*a*) **what do you know?** quoi de neuf? (*b*) **well, what do you know!** sans blague!/sans char!/sans déconner! **4. don't I know it!** à qui le dites-vous! **5. not if I know (anything about) it!** pour rien au monde!/pas pour tout l'or du monde! **6. I wouldn't know,** je ne saurais dire **7. he knows a good thing when he sees one/it,** c'est un connaisseur/il sait ce qui est bon/il sait reconnaître un bon cheval **8. you know what you can do with that/where you can put that/where you can stick that/where you can shove that!** tu peux te le mettre quelque part/là où je pense! **9. to know a thing or two/to know what's what,** être malin*/être à la coule/être fortiche/être à la hauteur; **he knows a thing or**

two, il n'a pas les deux pieds dans le même sabot.

know-all ['nouwɔ:l] *n F* je-sais-tout *mf*; **he's a real Mr Know-all,** c'est un vrai Monsieur Je-sais-tout.

know-how ['nouhar] *n F* (*a*) savoir-faire *m*/habileté *f* (*b*) savoir-faire (technique)/connaissances *fpl* techniques/mise *f* en pratique.

know-it-all ['nouwitɔ:l] *n esp NAm F* = **know-all.**

knuckle[1] ['nʌkl] *n F* **near the knuckle,** scabreux/grivois; **that joke was a bit near the knuckle,** cette plaisanterie n'était pas de la dentelle/n'était pas à mettre sous toutes les oreilles.

knuckle[2] ['nʌkl] *vtr P* battre* (qn)/passer (qn) à tabac/amocher (qn).

knuckle down ['nʌkl'daun] *vi F* se ranger des voitures/s'y mettre/avoir du plomb dans la tête; **come on, knuckle down to some work!** allez, mets-toi au travail!

knucklehead ['nʌklhed] *n F* individu bête*/niguedouille *m*/empoté *m*/andouille *f*/ballot *m.*

knuckle sandwich ['nʌkl'sændwidʒ, -tʃ] *n P* coup *m* de poing/châtaigne *f*/bourre-pif *m.*

knuckle under ['nʌkl'ʌndər] *vi F* se soumettre/filer doux/baisser pavillon.

k.o., KO[1] ['kei'jou] *F* (*abbr* = *knockout*) (*esp boxing*) KO *m*/knock-out *m.*

k.o., KO[2] ['kei'jou] *vtr F* (*abbr* = *knock out*) **1.** (*esp boxing*) mettre KO/knockouter/envoyer au tapis **2.** = **to knock on the head (knock**[2] **2).**

Kojak ['koudʒæk] *n P* (*aut*) (*hum*) pneu *m* lisse.

kokomo [kou'koumou] *n P* (*drugs*) = **cokomo.**

kook [ku:k] *n NAm P* (*weirdo*)

excentrique *m*/braque *m*/bran-
quignol(le) *m*/louftingue *m*.

kooky ['kuɪki] *a NAm F* **1.** un peu
fou*/braque/louftingue **2.** (*clothes*)
sophistiqué/raffiné.

kosher ['kouʃər] *a F* au poil/
impec/réglo; **it doesn't look very
kosher to me,** ça n'a pas l'air très
catholique.

kowtow ['kautau] *vi F* **to kowtow to
s.o.,** s'aplatir/se mettre à genoux

devant qn; lécher les bottes à qn/
passer de la pommade à qn.

kraut,   Kraut   [kraut],
krauthead ['krauthed] *n P* (*pej*)
Allemand*/fridolin *m*/frizou *m*/
fritz *m*/boche *m*.

kudos ['kjuɪdɔs] *n F* panache *m*/
gloriole *f*; **to get all the kudos,**
récolter toute la gloire/décrocher le
pompon.

L

lab [læb] F (*abbr = laboratory*) labo m.

lace [leis] *vtr* F corser/arroser/faire champoreau; **laced coffee,** café* au rhum/bossu m.

lace curtains ['leis'kɔːtnz] *npl* VV (*homosexuals*) prépuce m d'un homme non circoncis.

lace into ['leis'intuː] *vtr* F **1.** to lace into s.o. (*a*) battre*/rosser qn **2. to lace into sth,** y aller de tout son cœur/y mettre toute la sauce/ s'y mettre à fond.

lace ups ['leis'ʌps] *npl* F chaussures *fpl*/bottes *fpl* à lacets.

lacy ['leisi] *a* P efféminé/homosexuel sur les bords/un peu folle.

lad [læd] *n* F **1. he's a bit of a lad (with the women),** c'est un tombeur de filles/c'est un chaud lapin/c'est un sacré dragueur **2. one of the lads,** un gai luron/un joyeux compère; qui fait partie de la bande; **to go for a quick drink with the lads,** aller prendre un pot avec les potes.

ladder ['lædər] *n* F (*catchphrase*) **pull the ladder up (, Jack)/take the ladder away (, Jack),** après nous le déluge/la fin du monde.

laddie ['lædi] *n* F (petit) gars/ gamin m; **listen, (my) laddie!** écoute bien, mon petit bonhomme/mon petit gars!

la-de-da, la-di-da, ladidah ['lɑːdi'dɑː] *a* F **1.** élégant*/(super-)chic/très classe/à grand tralala; **it was a very la-di-da gathering,** tout le gratin se trouvait là **2.** (*pej*) **she's so la-di-da!** elle fait la préten-

tieuse*; **she's got such a la-di-da accent,** elle parle avec affectation/ elle prend le ton intello-snob/elle parle avec l'accent des beaux quartiers.

ladies ['leidiz] *n* F **1. the ladies, WC*** pour dames; **where's the ladies?** où sont les toilettes/où est le pipi-room? **2.** (*euph*) **he's not really a ladies' man/he's never been one for the ladies,** il préfère les mecs.

Lady ['leidi] *n* P **Lady Jane,** sexe de la femme*/chatte *f*/pâquerette *f*. (*See* **fat I 7; lollipop-lady; old 3**)

lady-killer ['leidikilər] *n* F bourreau m des cœurs/tombeur m de filles/play-boy *m*/cavaleur m.

lag[1] [læg] *n* F (*a*) forçat *m*/bagnard m (*b*) forçat libéré/fagot affranchi; **old lag,** cheval m de retour/forçat chevronné.

lag[2] [læg] *vtr* F (*a*) arrêter*/épingler (*b*) emprisonner*/bloquer/boucler.

lagging ['lægiŋ] *n* P peine de prison de trois ans au minimum; **lagging station,** prison*.

lah-di-dah ['lɑːdi'dɑː] *a* F = **la- de-da.**

laid back ['leid'bæk] *a* P détendu/ relax/rilax/coolos/peinard(os).

laid up ['leid'ʌp] *a&pp* F malade*/ alité/mal fichu.

lair ['lɛər] *n Austr* F élégant *m*/tape- à-l'œil *m*/m'as-tu-vu m frimeur m.

lairy ['lɛəri] *a esp Austr* F voyant/ tapageur.

lake [leik] *n* F **go (and) jump in the**

lake! va te faire pendre!/va te faire voir!/va voir ailleurs si j'y suis!

lam¹ [læm] *n NAm P* **on the lam** (*i*) en fuite/en cavale (*ii*) en déplacement/en voyage/par monts et par vaux.

lam² [læm] *vtr&i P* **1.** battre*/rosser/étriller **2.** *NAm* partir* précipitamment/mettre les bouts/se calter/se trisser.

lamb [læm] *n* **1.** *P* **lamb (chop),** piqûre* de narcotique/piquouse *f*/fixe *m*/shoot *m* **2.** *F* (*a*) (*child*) lapin *m*/agneau *m*; **poor little lamb,** mon pauvre petit (*b*) **my little lamb,** mon petit poulet/coco/poussin/trésor **3.** *NAm F* individu* crédule/gobeur *m*/cave *m*/pigeon *m* **4.** *F* **he took it like a lamb,** il s'est laissé faire/il n'a pas rouspété/il l'a pris sans broncher/il l'a encaissé sans rien dire.

lambaste ['læm'beist] *vtr F* (*a*) battre*/dérouiller (*b*) critiquer*/éreinter (*c*) engueuler/sonner les cloches à/passer un savon à (qn).

lambasting ['læm'beistiŋ] *n F* (*a*) raclée *f*/frottée *f* (*b*) critique *f*/éreintage | *m* (*c*) engueulade *f*/savon *m*/attrapade *f*.

lame-brain ['leim'brein] *n esp NAm F* individu bête*/imbécile *m*/sot *m*/abruti *m*.

lam into ['læm'intuɪ] *vtr P* = **lam²** **1.**

lamming ['læmiŋ] *n P* = **lambasting.**

lam out ['læm'aut] *vi NAm P* = **lam²** 2.

lamp [læmp] *vtr P* regarder*/zyeuter/reluquer/mater.

lamp-post ['læmppoust] *n F* **between you (and) me and the lamp-post,** tout à fait entre nous/de vous à moi/entre nous et la Gare Saint-Lazare. (*See* **gate-post**)

lamps [læmps] *npl P* (*a*) yeux*/clignotants *mpl*/quinquets *mpl*/lanternes *fpl*/lampions *mpl* (*b*) yeux*

pochés/au beurre noir; coquards *mpl*.

land [lænd] *vtr F* **1.** gagner/obtenir/dénicher/dégot(t)er; **he landed himself a really good job,** il s'est dégotté un boulot tout ce qu'il y a de bien **2.** arriver*/débarquer/s'abouler **3. to land s.o. a blow,** flanquer/balancer un coup*/une taloche/une baffe à qn **4. that will land you in prison,** cela vous vaudra de la prison*/vous ne couperez pas à la taule. (*See* **muck 3**; **shit¹ III** 2)

landed ['lændid] *a&pp F* dans le pétrin; **to be landed with s.o.,** avoir qn sur les bras/avoir qn aux basques/se faire retenir par la jambe par qn; **I got landed with the washing-up,** c'est moi qui ai dû me coltiner toute la vaisselle/qui me suis retrouvé avec la vaisselle.

land up ['lænd'ʌp] *vi F* (*a*) **to land up with nothing,** n'aboutir à rien/finir en queue de poisson/finir en eau de boudin (*b*) **to land up somewhere,** aboutir quelque part; aboutir à qch; **to land up nowhere,** déboucher sur rien/dans une impasse/dans un cul-de-sac (*c*) **to land up in a bar,** atterrir finalement dans un bar.

language ['læŋgwidʒ] *n F* **to speak s.o.'s language,** parler la même langue/être sur la même longueur d'ondes.

lantern ['læntən] *n F* **idiot's lantern,** télé *f*/téloche *f*. (*See* **box¹ 2**; **goggle-box**; **idiot-box**)

lap [læp] *n F* **1. to lay sth in s.o.'s lap,** coller qch sur le dos de qn/faire porter le chapeau à qn/refiler le morceau à qn; **it fell right into his lap,** ça lui est tombé tout rôti/tout cru dans la bouche **2. in the lap of luxury,** en plein luxe/au sein de l'abondance **3. it's in the lap of the gods,** c'est impossible à prévoir/c'est pas sûr/Dieu seul sait. (*See* **cat-lap**)

lap it up ['læpit'ʌp] *vi F* **1.** gober/avaler qch/boire du petit lait; **he was lapping up all these compliments,** il buvait tous ces compliments comme du petit lait/on aurait dit qu'il buvait du petit lait, à écouter ces compliments **2.** boire* beaucoup/picoler/biberonner.

lark [lɑːk] *n F* **1.** une franche rigolade/une tranche de rire; **talk about a lark!/what a lark!/it was a real lark!** quelle rigolade!/quelle bonne blague! **2. he did it for a lark,** il l'a fait pour rigoler/histoire de rigoler. (*See* **skylark**)

lark about ['lɑːkə'baut] *vi F* faire le zouave/rigoler/faire le pitre; **stop larking about and get on with the job!** arrête de glandouiller et (mets-toi) au boulot!

larrikin ['lærikin] *n Austr F* gavroche *m*/gamin *m* des rues; petit voyou.

larrup ['lærəp] *vtr F* **1.** battre*/rosser **2.** battre (un adversaire) à plate(s) couture(s).

larruping ['lærəpiŋ] *n F* (*a*) volée *f* de coups*/rossée *f*/raclée *f*/roulée *f* (*b*) victoire *f* facile/les doigts dans le nez.

lash¹ [læʃ] *n Austr F* **to have a lash at sth,** tenter sa chance/tenter le coup.

lash² [læʃ] *vtr F* (*esp journ*) critiquer*/éreinter/démolir (qn).

lashings ['læʃiŋz] *npl F* une abondance* de.../des tas *mpl* de .../une flopée de...; **lashings of cream,** une tapée/une ventrée/une platrée de crème fraîche.

lash out ['læʃaut] *vi F* **1.** lâcher un coup*/décocher des coups* **2.** dépenser/larguer son fric; les lâcher/les allonger; **I lashed out on a new coat,** je me suis fait une petite folie: j'ai acheté un manteau neuf **3.** invectiver/se déchaîner; lancer (ses quatre vérités) à la figure de (qn).

lash-up ['læʃʌp] *n P* (*a*) expédient *m*/échappatoire *f*/moyen *m* de fortune; bouts *mpl* de ficelle (*b*) réunion *f* intime/à la bonne franquette; soirée *f* entre copains.

last [lɑːst] *a F* **the last word in socks,** des chaussettes dernier cri. (*See* **leg¹ 9**; **straw 1, 2**)

last-ditch ['lɑːst'ditʃ] *a F* **a last-ditch effort,** un dernier effort/un baroud d'honneur/le coup de collier final/le dernier coup de pelle.

latch on ['lætʃɔn] *vi F* comprendre/saisir/piger/entraver.

latch onto, on to ['lætʃɔntuː] *vtr F* obtenir/agrafer/mettre le grappin sur (qch).

latest ['leitist] *n F* **to be up on the latest,** être à la page/au courant/à la coule/dans le vent/dans le coup.

lather¹ ['lɑːðər] *n F* **to work oneself (up) into a lather** (*a*) se mettre en colère*/fulminer/sortir de ses gonds/piquer une crise (*b*) s'inquiéter/se faire du mauvais sang/se faire du mouron.

lather² ['lɑːðər] *vtr F* battre*/rosser/tabasser/passer à tabac.

laugh¹ [lɑːf] *n F* **1. that's a laugh!** quelle bonne blague!/c'est marrant!/c'est une valse! **2. to do sth for laughs,** faire qch pour rigoler/faire qch à la rigolade **3. he's good for a laugh,** il nous fait toujours rire **4. the laugh's on you,** c'est toi qui as l'air d'une andouille dans l'histoire. (*See* **belly-laugh**)

laugh² [lɑːf] *vi F* **1. don't make me laugh!** ne me fais pas rire*/marrer/rigoler! **2. to laugh on the other side of one's face,** rire* jaune/rire* de travers; **I soon made him laugh on the other side of his face,** je lui ai bientôt fait passer son envie de rire* **3. to be laughing,** se la couler douce/vivre pépère/se les tourner; **if you win the pools you'll be laughing,** si vous gagnez à la loterie vous aurez le filon/les poches bien garnies **4. to**

laugh to oneself, rire* aux anges 5. to laugh one's head off, rire* à se faire mal aux côtes/à en crever; se gondoler/se marrer comme une baleine. (*See* drain¹ 2)

launching-pad ['lɔɪntʃɪŋpæd] *n F* = shooting-gallery.

launder [lɔːndər] *vtr P* lessiver (de l'argent volé); receler.

lav [læv] *n F* (*abbr = lavatory*) WC*/cabinets *mpl*/cabinces *fpl*; to go to the lav, aller aux vécés *mpl*/ aux chiottes *fpl*.

lavatorial [lævə'tɔːriəl] *a F* ordurier/cochon; lavatorial humour, humour scatologique/des chiottes.

law, Law [lɔː] *n F* the law (*i*) la police*/la rousse (*ii*) policier*/flic *m*; here comes the law! voilà les flics! I'll have the law on you, je vais vous traîner en justice/devant les tribunaux.

lay¹ [lei] *n* 1. *P* coït*/baise *f*/ baisage *m*; to have a lay, coucher avec qn/baiser qn/se faire qn; he's a really good lay, c'est un sacré baiseur; she's an easy lay, elle a la cuisse hospitalière/c'est une coucheuse/c'est une qui y va (au lit) 2. *F* pari *m*/mise *f* 3. *F* to get the lay of the land, tâter le terrain/se rencarder sur qch.

lay² [lei] *vtr P* 1. to lay s.o., faire l'amour* avec qn/coucher avec qn/ baiser qn 2. to lay one on s.o., battre* qn/flanquer une taloche à qn 3. to lay for s.o., attendre qn au tournant/avoir qn dans sa ligne de mire.

lay down ['lei'daun] *vtr P* renvoyer (qn) en détention provisoire.

lay-in ['lei'in] *n F* = lie-in.

lay into ['lei'intuː] *vtr F* (*a*) atta-quer*/agrafer/serrer (qn) (*b*) criti-quer*/éreinter (qn); he really laid into me, il m'a filé une engueulade maison.

lay off ['lei'ɔf] *vtr&i* 1. *P* lâcher/ larguer/plaquer (qn) 2. *P* lay off,

will you? laisse tomber!/c'est marre!/écrase! 3. *F* (*football*) to lay a ball off to s.o., faire une passe à qn 4. *P* to lay off s.o. (*a*) ficher/ foutre la paix à qn; lay off my girl-friend! bas les pattes, c'est ma copine! (*b*) congédier*/bouler/virer qn 5. *Austr P* to lay off with s.o. = to lay s.o. (lay² 1).

lay on ['lei'ɔn] *vtr F* 1. to lay it on thick/with a shovel/with a trowel (*i*) flatter*/passer la pommade/casser le nez à coups d'encensoir/caresser dans le sens du poil (*ii*) exagérer*/ y aller fort/charrier/forcer la dose/ en rajouter 2. arranger/préparer/ amarrer/arnaquer; it's all laid on, tout est bien branché/tout est en règle/tout est en bonnes mains.

layout ['leiaut] *n P* 1. to be sick of the whole layout, en avoir assez*/en avoir ras le bol/en avoir sa claque 2. (*drugs*) attirail* de camé/artillerie *f*/kit *m*.

lay out ['lei'aut] *vtr F* 1. assom-mer/étendre (qn) sur le carreau/ mettre qn KO/envoyer qn au tapis 2. to lay oneself out (to do sth), se mettre en quatre/se démener/se décarcasser (pour faire qch) 3. dépenser* de l'argent/les allonger/ cracher.

lay up ['lei'ʌp] *vi F* se la couler douce/se prélasser/se rouler les pouces/se les rouler. (*See* laid up)

lazybones ['leizibounz] *n F* pares-seux*/cossard *m*/feignant *m*; je m'en fichiste *m*; bâcleur *m*.

lead¹ [led] *n* 1. *F* to fill s.o. with lead/to pump s.o. full of lead, fusil-ler qn/flinguer qn/truffer qn de plomb/transformer qn en passoire. (*See* lead-poisoning) 2. *F* to swing the lead, tirer au flanc/au cul. (*See* lead-swinger) 3. to have lead in one's pencil (*a*) *P* être en érection*/avoir la canne/avoir le bambou/avoir le sexe en majesté/ être au garde à vous (*b*) *P* être prêt à faire l'amour/à (ouvrir) l'allumage (*c*) *F* avoir de l'allant/péter le feu/

péter la santé **4.** *P* (*a*) **to get the lead out of s.o.'s arse**/*NAm* **ass**/ *NAm* **pants**, se dépêcher*/se magner le train/l'arrière-train; se démerder (*b*) **to have lead in one's arse**/*NAm* **ass**, paresser*/tirer au cul/tirer au flanc.

lead² [liːd] *n F* (*a*) **to have a lead on sth**, avoir des renseignements* sur qch/avoir un tuyau sur qch; **I've got a lead on that stolen car**, j'ai un tuyau sur cette bagnole volée (*b*) **to have a lead on s.o.**, avoir barre sur qn/tenir qn.

lead-off ['liːdɔf] *n F* démarrage *m*/ point *m* de départ.

lead off ['liːd'ɔf] *vi F* **to lead off at s.o.**, passer un savon à qn/redresser qn.

lead-poisoning ['ledpɔizniŋ] *n F* **to have lead-poisoning**, être fusillé/ être bourré de plomb. (*See* **lead¹** 1)

lead-swinger ['ledswiŋər] *n F* paresseux*/feignant *m*/tire-au-flanc *m*. (*See* **lead¹** 2)

league [liːg] *n F* **not to be in the same league as s.o.**, ne pas être dans la même catégorie/ne pas être dans la même panier/ne pas arriver à la cheville de qn.

leak¹ [liːk] *n* **1.** *P* **to go for a leak**/ *NAm* **to spring a leak**, uriner*/ (aller) pisser un coup/(aller) se faire une vidange/lansquiner/égoutter sa sardine **2.** (*a*) *P* donneur *m*/macaron *m*/passoire *f* (*b*) *F* (*secrets, etc*) fuite *f*/divulgation *f*.

leak² [liːk] *vtr F* (*secrets, etc*) divulguer/laisser filtrer/cabasser/ faire du ragoût.

lean and lurch ['liːnən'lɜːtʃ] *n P* (*RS* = *church*) église *f*.

lean on ['liːnɔn] *vtr F* faire pression sur (qn)/serrer la vis à (qn)/passer (qn) à la moulinette.

leap [liːp] *n F* **to take the big leap**, se marier/se marida/se mettre la corde au cou.

leaper ['liːpər] *n P* (*drugs*) amphétamine*/amph *f*.

learn [lɜːn] *vtr P* **I'll learn you!** je vais t'apprendre! **that'll learn you!** ça t'apprendra!

leary ['liəri] *a F* = **leery**.

leather¹ ['leðər] *n P* **1. to put the leather in**, flanquer un coup de pied (à qn). (*See* **boot** 2) **2.** voleur* à la tire/à la fourche; **to snatch leather**, voler*/piquer un portefeuille à la tire/décrocher un portefeuille **3.** (*esp homosexuals*) **leather boys/leather brigade/leather merchants**, ceux qui portent le cuir/ cuirs *mpl*; **he's heavily into leather**/ **he's a leather fetishist**, c'est un fétichiste du cuir. (*See* **hell** 11; **queen¹** 2)

leather² ['leðər] *vtr F* battre*/tanner le cuir à (qn).

leather-man ['leðəmæn] *n P* = **leather¹** 2.

leatherneck ['leðənek] *n NAm F* fusilier marin/marsouin *m*.

lech¹ [letʃ] *n P* **1.** (= *lecher*) obsédé *m*/débauché *m*/paillard *m*/ noceur *m*/cavaleur *m*. **2.** (*a*) (= *lechery*) paillardise *f*/lubricité *f* (*b*) désir ardent et obsédant.

lech² [letʃ] *vi P* **to lech after/for s.o.**, en pincer pour qn/en mouiller pour qn/en baver pour qn.

leery ['liəri] *a F* méfiant; **to be leery of s.o.**, se méfier de qn/faire gaffe à qn.

leftfooter ['left'futər] *n P* catholique *mf*.

left-handed ['left'hændid] *a P* homosexuel/emmanché.

left-hander ['left'hændər] *n F* gifle donnée de la main gauche.

leftover ['leftouvər] *n F* **1.** laissé(e) pour compte **2.** *pl* restes *mpl*/arlequins *mpl*/rogatons *mpl*; rab(iot) *m*.

lefty ['lefti] *n F* **1.** gaucher *m* **2.** gauchiste *mf*/gaucho *mf*.

leg[1] [leg] *n* **1.** *F* **to show a leg,** se lever/sortir du lit/se dépieuter/se dépagnoter **2.** *F* **leg show,** spectacle *m* avec de la fesse/de la cuisse **3.** *F* **to shake a leg** (*a*) danser*/gambiller (*b*) se dépêcher*/se grouiller (*c*) jouer des guibolles *fpl* **4.** *F* **he hasn't a leg to stand on,** on lui a rivé son clou/on l'a coincé **5.** *F* **to pull s.o.'s leg,** faire marcher qn/mettre qn en boîte/monter un bateau à qn/faire avaler une bourre à qn. (*See* **leg-pull**) **6.** *F* **to have leg room,** être au large **7.** *F* **to give s.o. a leg up** (*i*) faire la courte échelle à qn (*ii*) dépanner qn/donner un coup de main à qn **8.** *F* **to get (up) on one's hind legs,** se mettre debout **9.** *F* **to be on one's last legs** (*a*) être très malade*/filer un mauvais coton/avoir un pied dans la tombe/battre de l'aile; **my car's on its last legs,** ma bagnole est pas loin de rendre l'âme/va pas tarder à rendre l'âme (*b*) être très fatigué*/être à bout de course/être au bout du rouleau/tirer à sa fin/être crevé **10.** *F* **to have a leg up on s.o.,** avoir barre sur qn **11.** *F* **to stretch one's legs,** se dérouiller/se dégourdir les jambes **12.** *P* **middle/third leg,** pénis*/jambe *f* du milieu **13.** *P* (*man*) **to get one's leg over/to be in a leg over position,** faire l'amour*/enjamber/baiser/tirer un coup **14.** *F* **legs eleven:** *see* **bingo 11.** (*See* **donkey 1; open**[2] **1; peg-leg; show**[1] **1**)

leg[2] [leg] *vtr F* **1.** faire trébucher (qn) **2. to leg it,** marcher*/courir*/s'enfuir*/se cavaler/jouer des flûtes.

leggo! ['le'gou] *excl F* (= *let go!*) lâche (tout)!/bas les pattes!

legit [le'dʒit] *a F* (= *legitimate*) vrai/authentique/légitime; **on the legit,** officiel/légal; **he's legit,** on peut lui faire confiance.

legless ['leglis] *a P* ivre*/dans le cirage/bourré à bloc; **he was completely legless,** il était rétamé à zéro.

legman ['legmæn] *n F* **1.** reporter *m*/envoyé spécial **2.** celui qui travaille activement/turbineur *m*/bosseur *m*. (*See* **legwork**)

leg-pull ['legpul] *n F* blague *f*/canular *m*/mise *f* en boîte. (*See* **leg**[1] **5**)

legshake ['legʃeik] *n Austr P* **legshake artist,** voleur* à la tire/tireur *m*/fourchette *f*.

legwork ['legwɔːk] *n F* travail* actif/turbin *m*. (*See* **legman 2**)

lemon ['lemən] *n* **1.** *F* **the answer's a lemon,** rien à faire!/des clous! **2.** *F* **to feel a (right) lemon,** se sentir un peu bête*/se sentir tout con; rester comme deux ronds de flan **3.** *P* femme* laide/tartignole *f*/mocheté *f*/remède *m* d'amour **4.** *P* coup monté/doublage *m*/fumisterie *f* **5.** *P* **to squeeze the lemon,** uriner*/ouvrir les écluses *fpl*/égoutter sa sardine/faire pleurer le petit Jésus **6.** *P* (*RS* = *wash*) **to have a lemon squash,** se laver.

length [leŋ(k)θ] *n P* **1. to go one's length,** chercher des embêtements; **you're going your length!** tu le cherches! **2. to give/to slip (a woman) a length,** faire l'amour* (avec une femme)/filer un coup (d'arbalète) (à une femme). (*See* **wavelength**)

lergi ['lɔːdʒi] *n P* (= *allergy*) allergie *f*. (*See* **lurgy**)

les [lez] **I** *a P* (= *lesbian*) lesbienne/qui aime l'ail/qui tape l'ail **II** *n P* (= *lesbian*) lesbienne*/gouine *f*/gougnote *f*/goudou *f*.

lesbie ['lezbi], **lesbo** ['lezbou], **lessie** ['lezi] *n P* lesbienne*/gouine *f*/vrille *f*; **they're a couple of lesbies/lesbos,** c'est deux marchandes d'ail/c'est deux gouines.

letch [letʃ] *n&v P* = **lech**[1,2].

let-down ['letdaun] *n F* déception *f*/déboire *m*.

let down ['let'daun] *vtr F* **1.** décevoir (qn)/laisser (qn) en panne/laisser (qn) en rade/faire faux bond à (qn) **2. to let s.o. down gently/lightly,** contrecarrer qn avec ménagement. (*See* **hair 2)**

let in on ['let'inɔn] *vtr F* **to let s.o. in on sth,** mettre qn dans le coup/ mettre qn au parfum/rencarder qn.

let off ['let'ɔf] *vtr&i P* **to let (one) off,** péter*/en lâcher un/en écraser un/coincer une bulle. (*See* **steam 1)**

let on ['let'ɔn] *vi F* **1. to let on (about sth) to s.o.,** mettre qn au courant/à la page; **don't let on!** motus!/bouche cousue! **2.** faire semblant/frimer/chiquer.

let-out ['letaut] *n F* (*a*) porte *f* de sortie (*b*) alibi *m*/parapluie *m*.

lettuce ['letis] *n P* argent*/blé *m*/ galette *f*; billets* (de banque)/ faf(f)iots *mpl*. (*See* **kale)**

letty ['leti] *n A P* lit*/plumard *m*.

let-up ['letʌp] *n F* **with no let-up,** sans cesse/sans pause/sans relâche/ sans débrider; **there was no let-up in the rain,** la pluie ne s'arrêtait pas.

let up ['let'ʌp] *vi* **1.** *F* cesser/ diminuer/relâcher/ralentir; **he just doesn't let up talking,** il n'arrête pas/il n'en finit pas de jacasser **2.** *P* **to let up on s.o.,** ficher/foutre la paix à qn; oublier qn.

level[1] ['levəl] **I** *a F* **to do one's level best,** faire de son mieux/en mettre un bon coup/mettre le paquet. (*See* **pegging) II** *n F* **on the level,** honnête/régulier/réglo; **he's on the level,** c'est un mec réglo.

level[2] ['levəl] *vi F* **to level with s.o.** (*a*) parler franchement/vider son sac; s'expliquer avec qn; **look, I'm going to level with you,** tenez, je vais être franc avec vous/je vais vous parler franchement (*b*) rendre la pareille/garder un chien de sa chienne.

lez [lez], **lezo** ['lezou], **lezzie** ['lezi] *n P* =**les II.**

lick[1] [lik] *n* **1.** *F* démarrage *m*/ coup *m* de vitesse; **we were going at a fair old lick,** on allait à pleins gaz/à toute blinde **2.** *P* coup*/ torgnole *f*/raclée *f* **3.** *F* **a lick and a promise,** un bout/un brin de toilette; une toilette de chat. (*See* **cat-lick) 4.** *F* **to get a lick at sth,** tenter de faire qch/tâter de qch/se faire la main à qch/se frotter à qch.

lick[2] [lik] *vtr F* **1.** venir à bout de (qch)/vaincre/enfoncer/maîtriser/ surmonter (un problème, une difficulté, etc); **it's got me licked,** ça me dépasse **2. to lick s.o.** (*a*) battre* qn/rosser qn/passer qn à tabac (*b*) vaincre qn; **they had us licked,** il nous ont battu à plates coutures **3.** (*catchphrase*) **if you can't lick them/'em join them/'em,** si tu ne peux pas les mettre pattes en l'air, serre-leur la pince/il faut les battre ou s'allier avec eux **4. to lick sth into shape,** finir un travail/boucler une affaire; **to lick s.o. into shape,** former qn/dégrossir qn **5. to lick one's chops,** s'en lécher/pourlécher les babines *fpl*. (*See* **arse lick; boot 4; dust**[1] **5; pants 6)**

licketysplit ['likəti'split] *adv NAm F* très vite*/à pleins gaz/à fond de train.

licking ['likiŋ] *n F* **to give s.o. a licking** (*a*) donner une volée de coups*/une rossée/une raclée à qn (*b*) vaincre/écraser/griller qn; **they gave us a dreadful licking,** ils nous ont battus à plate(s) couture(s)/ils nous ont écrasés. (*See* **arse licking)**

lid [lid] *n* **1.** *F* chapeau*/galurin *m*/ casquette*/bâche *f*; **to dip one's lid,** soulever son feutre **2.** *F* **to take/to blow the lid off sth,** faire éclater/ exposer un scandale **3.** *F* **to put the lid on sth,** interdire qch/mettre le holà à qch; mettre qch au placard; **that puts the lid on it!** c'est le comble! **4.** *P* (*drugs*) deux grammes de marijuana* **5.** *F* capote *f* (d'une voiture). (*See* **dustbin**; **flip² 2**; **skid-lid**; **tin I 1, 2**)

lid-popper ['lidpɔpər] *n P* (*drugs*) amphétamines*/amphés *fpl*.

lie-in ['lai'in] *n F* **to have a lie-in**, faire la grasse (matinée).

life [laif] *n F* **1. for the life of me I can't remember**, j'ai beau chercher à me souvenir, je n'y arrive pas **2. to worry the life out of s.o.**, tourmenter/asticoter qn; **to frighten/to scare the life out of s.o.**, faire très peur* à qn; foutre les jetons/la trouille/les chocottes à qn **3. he turned up the next day as large as life**, il reparut le lendemain comme si de rien n'était; **as large as life and twice as natural**, dans toute sa beauté/grandeur nature **4. to see life**, rouler sa bosse; en voir des vertes et des pas mûres/être passé par là/en avoir vu de toutes les couleurs **5. not on your life!** pas de danger!/rien à faire! **6. to get life**, être condamné* à perpétuité/être gerbé à perpète **7. to get another life**, repartir à zéro/recommencer à zéro/refaire sa vie **8. I couldn't do it to save my life**, même si on me payait, je pourrais pas le faire **9.** (*a*) **life begins:** *see* **bingo 40** (*b*) **life's begun:** *see* **bingo 41**. (*See* **dog¹ 5, 18**; **Riley**; **sweet 2**)

lifer ['laifər] *n F* (*a*) prisonnier *m* à perpétuité/ench(e)tibé *m* à perpète/mis en taule à perte de vue (*b*) gerbement *m* à perpète.

lifesaver ['laifseivər] *n F* planche *f* de salut/bouée *f* de sauvetage/dernier bateau; **that cup of coffee was a lifesaver**, ça m'a sauvé la vie, ce café.

lift¹ [lift] *n F* **to give s.o. a lift** (*a*) raccompagner/emmener/faire monter qn (en voiture) avec soi; prendre qn en (auto-)stop; **can you give me a lift home?** tu peux me ramener chez moi (en voiture)? (*b*)

remonter le moral à qn; (*drugs*) **lift pill**, amphétamines*/amphés *fpl*.

lift² [lift] *vtr F* **1.** voler*/chiper/faucher **2.** plagier/démarquer **3.** augmenter/hausser **4.** arrêter*/embarquer/lever (qn). (*See* **elbow 3**)

lifter ['liftər] *n F* voleur*/faucheur *m*. (*See* **shirt-lifter**)

light [lait] **I** *a F* **to be sth light** (*a*) avoir qch qui manque (*b*) être à court d'argent*/dans la dèche/sans un **II** *n* **1.** *F* (*a*) **to be out like a light** (*i*) être ivre*/être éteint/avoir sa cuite/en tenir une (bonne) (*ii*) dormir*/en écraser (*b*) **to go out like a light**, s'évanouir*; tomber dans les pommes/dans les vapes/dans le cirage; ...**and then the lights went out**, ...et puis je me suis évanoui*/j'ai tourné de l'œil **2.** *pl P* yeux*/lanternes *fpl*/quinquets *mpl*/clignotants *mpl* **3.** *F* **the light**, compréhension *f*/comprenette *f*; **to see the light**, comprendre/saisir/entraver/piger, **4.** *F* **to see the red light (flashing)**, flairer le danger/voir le voyant passer au rouge **5.** *F* **the light of my life** (*i*) (*RS = wife*) épouse* (*ii*) bien aimé(e)/chéri(e). (*See* **green I 3**; **headlights**; **red-light**; **strike 1**)

light-fingered ['lait'fiŋgəd] *a P* qui vole avec facilité/qui a les doigts crochus.

light-footed ['lait'futid] *a P* homosexuel/chochotte/chouquette.

light into ['lait'intuː] *vtr F* **to light into s.o.** (*a*) attaquer* qn/tomber (à bras raccourcis) sur qn/agrafer qn (*b*) réprimander* sévèrement/passer un bon savon à/enguirlander/engueuler qn.

lightning ['laitniŋ] *n F* **like (greased) lightning**, très vite*/à plein(s) tube(s)/à toute barre/en quatrième vitesse.

lightweight ['laitweit] *n F* individu* qui ne fait pas le poids/un minus/demi-portion *m*.

like¹ [laik] **I** *adv F* **1.** comme qui dirait; **you're one of the family, like,** vous êtes comme qui dirait de la famille **2. very like/(as) like as not/like enough,** probablement/vraisemblablement **II** *conj F* **1.** (= *as if*) **he treated me like I was dirt/a piece of shit,** il m'a traité comme si j'étais de la crotte/de la merde; **seems like it works,** on dirait que ça marche **2.** (= *as*) **like I said,** comme je l'ai (si bien) dit **III** *n F* **the likes of us,** des (gens) comme nous/nos semblables/nos pareils.

like² [laik] *vtr F* **(well,) I like that!** elle est bien bonne, celle-là!/en voilà une bonne!/ça par exemple!

likely ['laikli] *a F* **1. a likely lad,** un joyeux gaillard/un gars qui promet/un joyeux drille/un gai luron **2. (as) like as not,** il y a beaucoup de chance (que...); sans doute **3. not likely!** pas de danger!/jamais de la vie! (*See* **bloody II**)

lily ['lili] *n NAm P* homosexuel*/tapette *f*.

lily-livered ['lililivəd] *a F* lâche; froussard/trouillard/foireux.

lily-white ['liliwait] *a F* blanc(he) comme neige; **she's not so lily-white!** ce n'est pas un prix de vertu!

limb [lim] *n F* **out on a limb,** en plan/sur la corde raide/le bec dans l'eau.

limey ['laimi] *n P* **1.** Anglais *m*/Angliche *m*/rosbif *m* **2.** matelot *m* britannique/angliche.

limit ['limit] *n* **1.** *F* **that's the limit!** c'est le comble!/c'est le bouquet! **she's the absolute limit!** (*i*) elle est marrante/impayable! (*ii*) elle est chiante! **2. to go the limit** (*a*) *F* y aller à fond/mettre le paquet (*b*) *P* (*girl, woman*) se laisser séduire/céder/lever la jambe **3.** *F* **the sky's the limit,** y a rien d'impossible/tout est possible.

limmo, limo ['limou] *n F* (*aut*) limousine *f*.

limp-wristed ['limp'ristid] *a P* homosexuel/tapette/pédé sur les bords/folle.

limy ['laimi] *n P* = **limey 1, 2.**

line [lain] *n F* **1. what's your line (of business)?** quel est votre genre d'affaires?/quelle est votre partie?/vous faites dans quoi? **that's not in my line/that's not my line (of country),** ce n'est pas mon rayon; **that's more in his line,** c'est plus dans son genre/dans ses cordes/dans son boulot/dans son style; **something in that line,** quelque chose dans ce genre-là/ce goût-là; **all in the line of duty!** ça fait partie du boulot! **2.** renseignement*/tuyau *m*/rencard *m*; **to get a line on sth,** reconnaître*/retapisser/reconnobler qch; **to get a line on s.o.,** se renseigner* sur qn/se rencarder sur qn **3. to win all along the line,** gagner sur toute la ligne **4. to toe the line,** rentrer dans les rangs/marcher au pas **5. to read between the lines,** lire entre les lignes **6. to put it on the line,** dire en toutes lettres/ne pas mâcher les mots **7. to be out of line,** être rebelle/se distinguer; **you're way out of line!** tu es complètement à côté de la plaque! **8. to come to the end of the line,** mourir*/lâcher la rampe. (*See* **drop² 6; hard I 3; headlines; main-line¹; pipeline; punch-line; shoot² 5; sweet 3; top-line**)

linen ['linin] *n* **1.** *F* **to wash one's dirty linen in public,** laver son linge sale en public **2.** *P* (*RS = newspaper*) **linen draper,** journal*/canard *m*.

line-shooter ['lainʃuːtər] *n F* vantard*/esbrouf(f)eur *m*/baratineur *m*/rambineur *m*. (*See* **shoot² 5**)

line-shooting ['lainʃuːtiŋ] *n F* rambin *m*/esbrouf(f)e *f*/baratin *m*. (*See* **shoot² 5**)

lingo ['lingou] *n* **1.** *F* langue
étrangère/baragouin *m*; **I shall
never get the hang of their lingo,** je
n'arriverai jamais à parler ce
baragouin **2.** *P* argot*; **to shoot/to
sling the lingo,** parler l'argot*;
dévider/bagouler/rouler le jars.

lip [lip] *n* **1.** *P* effronterie *f*; **don't
give me/I don't want any of your
lip!** ne te fiche pas de moi!/ne te
paye pas ma tête!/ne la ramène
pas! **2.** *F* **to keep a stiff upper lip,**
ne pas broncher/garder son courage
et faire contre mauvaise fortune
bon cœur/serrer les dents. (*See*
flip² 5)

lippy ['lipi] *a P* **1.** effronté/culotté/
gonflé **2.** bavard*/bavasseur/jacas-
seur.

liquidate ['likwideit] *vtr F* tuer*/
liquider/effacer.

liquidator ['likwideitər] *n esp NAm
P* **1.** assassin*/tueur *m* à gages/
buteur *m* **2.** revolver*/flingue *m*/
pétard *m*.

liquored up ['likəd'ʌp] *a&pp F*
ivre*/cuité/bit(t)uré.

liquorice ['likəris] *n P* **liquorice
stick,** clarinette *f*.

listed ['listid] *a P* aliéné.

lit [lit] *a&pp F* = **lit up.**

litter-bug ['litəbʌg], **litter-lout**
['litəlaut] *n F* qn qui fait des
ordures *fpl*/ordurier *m*/cochon *m*.

little ['litl] *a F* **the little woman,**
mon épouse*/ma moitié.

lit up ['lit'ʌp] *a&pp F* (*a*) légèrement
ivre*/émêché; **well lit up,** ivre*/
noir/beurré (comme un petit lu) (*b*)
drogué*/camé/bourré.

live it up ['livit'ʌp] *vi F* faire la
noce/mener une vie de bâton de
chaise/faire les quatre cents coups/
faire bombance/s'en payer une
tranche.

lively ['laivli] *a F* **look lively (about
it)!** et que ça saute!/mets-y de
l'entrain!/grouille-toi!

liver ['livər] *n F* **to have a liver** (*a*)
être malade* du foie (*b*) être de
mauvaise humeur/d'humeur massacrante; être en rogne.

liverish ['livəriʃ] *a F* qui a le foie
dérangé; **to feel liverish,** se sentir
mal en train/détraqué/barbouillé.

livid ['livid] *a F* blême de colère*/à
cran.

lizard ['lizəd] *n NAm P* pénis*/fré-
tillard *m*; **to stroke the lizard,** se
masturber*/s'astiquer le manche.

lizzie ['lizi] *n F* **1.** **(tin) lizzie,**
vieille voiture*/tinette *f* **2.** *P*
homosexuel*/tantouse *f*.

load [loud] *n* **1.** *P* **get a load of
that!** (*i*) écoute-moi ça!/écoute un
peu ça! (*ii*) vise-moi ça!/mate-moi
ça!/zyeute-moi ça! **2.** *P* **a load of
baloney/balls/cobblers/cock/cod-
swallop/crap,** un tas de foutaises
fpl/de conneries *fpl*; **you do talk a
load of balls at times,** ce que tu
peux déconner/débloquer des fois.
(*See* **muck 2; swill¹ 3**) **3.** *P* **to
drop one's load,** déféquer*/lâcher
un colombin/couler un bronze **4.**
P stock illégal de drogues/charge *f*
5. *F* **loads of...,** une abondance*
de.../une bardée de.../une
flopée de.../une tapée de... **6.**
F **take the load off your feet!**
assieds-toi!/pose tes fesses!/pose un
cul! **7.** *F* **he's a load of wind,** il
parle pour ne rien dire/il la ramène
pour pas grand'chose **8.** *P*
sperme*/jus *m*; **to shoot one's load,**
éjaculer*/lancer son jus/lâcher la
purée. (*See* **tie on**)

loaded ['loudid] *a* **1.** *P* riche*/
plein aux as; **to be loaded,** être à
l'as/avoir du foin dans ses bottes/
en avoir plein les poches **2.** *P* (*i*)
ivre*/beurré/bourré (*ii*) drogué/
chargé/défoncé.

loaf [louf] *n F* (*RS* = *loaf of bread*
= *head*) tête*/caboche *f*; **use your
loaf!** fais travailler tes méninges!

lob¹ [lɔb] *n P* **1.** pénis/zob *m* **2.**
oreille*/pavillon *m*.

lob[2] ['lɔb] *vtr P* **1.** jeter/envoyer dinguer; **lob it over!** balance-moi ça!/fous-ça ici! **2.** *Austr* **to lob somewhere**, arriver*/s'abouler/ débouler quelque part; **to lob back**, revenir/rabouler/radiner.

local ['loukəl] *n F* café* de quartier/bistrot *m* du coin/troquet *m.*

lock-up ['lɔkʌp] *n F* (*a*) prison*/ taule *f* (*b*) mitard *m*/violon *m.*

lock up ['lɔk'ʌp] *vtr F* emprisonner*; mettre au violon.

loco ['loukou] *a F* fou*/maboul/ dingo.

locoweed ['loukou'wiːd] *n P* (*drugs*) cannabis*/herbe *f.*

lofty ['lɔfti] *n F* **1.** individu* grand/une grande perche/une asperge montée **2.** (*iron*) petit* individu/astèque *m.*

lollie ['lɔli] *n F* = **lolly**[1] **4.**

lollipop-man, lady ['lɔlipɔp-'mæn, -'leidi] *n F* contractuel(le) qui fait traverser la rue aux enfants aux sorties d'école.

lollop ['lɔləp] *vi F* **1.** marcher* lourdement/comme un éléphant **2.** sauter/rebondir/faire des sauts de carpe **3. to lollop around**, paresser*/flânocher.

lolly[1] ['lɔli] *n* **1.** *F* argent*/fric *m*/ flouze *m*; **lay off the lolly!** touchez pas au grisbi! **2.** *Austr P* un timide/un tiède/un frileux **3.** *Austr P* **to do the/one's lolly**, se mettre en colère/se fâcher **4.** *F* (= *lollipop*) sucette *f*; **ice(d) lolly**, sucette glacée.

lolly[2] ['lɔli] *vtr P* dénoncer*/balancer/balanstiquer (qn) (pour de l'argent).

loner ['lounər] *n F* personne *f* qui fait bande à part/qui fait cavalier (seul); solitaire *mf.*

lonesome ['lounsəm] *n F* **(all) on one's lonesome**, (tout) seulâbre. (*See* **ownsome**)

long [lɔŋ] **I** *a F* **to be long on sth**, avoir des masses *fpl* de qch/ déborder de qch. (*See* **shot II 5**; **tooth 2**; **vac**) **II** *n F* **the long and short of it is ...**, le fin mot de l'histoire c'est que ....

long-tailed ['lɔŋteild] *a P* **long-tailed 'uns**, billets* de banque.

loo [luː] *n F* WC*/ouatères *mpl*/ gogues *mpl*/chiottes *fpl*; **he's gone to the loo**, il est allé au petit coin; **loo paper**, papier-cul *m*/pécu *m.*

look[1] [luk] *n F* **to take a long, hard look at sth**, examiner qch sur toutes les coutures.

look[2] [luk] *vi F* **1. to look like a million (dollars)**, être très élégant*/ être très chic/avoir la grande classe **2. here's looking at you!** à la tienne!/à la bonne vôtre! **3. look here!** dis donc! (*See* **nose 7**)

looka ['luːkər] *n P* = **lucre.**

looker ['lukər] *n F* **a (good) looker**, une belle fille/un beau brin de fille/un prix de Diane/un joli lot; **he's a really good looker**, il est beau mec.

look-in ['luk'in] *n F* **1.** belle occasion/beau jeu **2.** chances *fpl* de succès; **he won't get a look-in**, il n'a pas la moindre chance **3.** coup *m* d'œil rapide/coup de sabord **4.** visite-éclair *f*; **to give s.o. a look-in**, faire un saut chez qn.

look-out ['lukaut] *n F* **1.** guetteur *m*/gaffe *m* **2. that's your look-out!** c'est ton affaire!/c'est tes oignons!/ c'est ton truc!

look-see ['luk'siː] *n F* coup *m* d'œil*/coup de sabord; **let's have a look-see**, jetons un coup d'œil/ regardons ça un peu.

look up ['luk'ʌp] *vi F* **business is looking up**, les affaires reprennent; **things are looking up with him**, ses affaires s'améliorent/ses actions remontent.

looloo ['luːluː] *n F* = **lulu.**

loony ['luːni] **I** *a* fou*/toqué/cinglé; **he's gone completely loony,** il travaille de la tête/il a perdu la boule/il dévisse du cigare **II** *n* cinglé(e) *m(f)*/dingue *mf*; **are you a complete loony, or what?** ça (ne) va pas la tête?/t'es fou ou quoi?/t'es complètement siphonné?

loony-bin ['luːnibin] *n* P maison *f* de fous/cabanon *m*/asile *m* de dingues; **to be fit for the loony-bin,** être bon/mûr pour Sainte-Anne/pour Charenton.

looped [luːpt] *a* P ivre*/plein/ rond; **looped to the eyeballs,** plein comme une bourrique.

loop-the-loop ['luːpðə'luːp] *n* P (*RS* = *soup*) soupe *f*/rata *m*.

loopy ['luːpi] *a* F fou*/dingo/tapé/ cinglé/maboul/jeté; **to go completely loopy,** perdre la boule/ travailler du chapeau.

loose [luːs] *n* F **to be (out) on the loose** (*i*) être déchaîné/faire les quatre cents coups (*ii*) être en bordée/en virée; mener une vie de bâtons de chaise.

loosen up ['luːsən'ʌp] *vi* F se détendre/se relaxer.

loot [luːt] *n* P (*a*) argent*/artiche *m*/flouse *m*/pognon *m*/fric *m* (*b*) bénéfice* financier/bénef *m*/gratte *f*/gratouille *f* (*c*) butin*/fade *m*/ taf(fe) *m*.

lorry ['lɔri] *n* F **it fell off the back of a lorry,** c'est volé/fauché.

lorry-hop ['lɔrihɔp] *vi* F faire de l'auto-stop *m* (dans les camions)/ faire du pouce aux routiers.

lose [luːz] *vtr* **1.** P **get lost!** va te faire fiche!/va te faire foutre!/va te faire voir!/au bout du quai les ballots! **2.** F **you've lost me!** je n'y suis plus/j'ai perdu le fil.

lose out ['luːz'aut] *vi* F perdre/ paumer; être perdant.

loud [laud] *adv* F **for crying out loud!** (sacré) nom d'un chien!/nom de nom!

loudmouth ['laudmauθ] *n* F gueulard *m*/va-de-la-gueule *m*/grande gueule *f*.

loudmouthed ['laudmauðd] *a* F gueulard/fort en gueule.

louse [laus] *n* F vaurien*/saligaud *m*/salope *f*; **what a louse!** (quelle) peau de vache!

louse up ['laus'ʌp] *vtr* P bousiller/ gâcher/saloper/louper; **I've gone and loused it up again,** j'ai encore mis les pieds dans le plat/j'ai tout foutu en l'air/j'y ai refoutu le merdier.

lousy ['lauzi] *a* **1.** F mauvais*/ moche; miteux/pouilleux; ringard; **lousy weather,** temps pourri/ dégueulasse; **a lousy film,** un film merdique/à la con; **to feel/to look lousy,** être mal fichu/n'avoir pas la frite; **to play a lousy trick on s.o.,** jouer un sale tour/jouer un tour de cochon/faire une vacherie à qn **2.** P **lousy with...,** plein de...; **the place was lousy with cops,** ça grouillait de flics **3.** F **I'm lousy at it,** je suis nul/zéro; j'en touche pas une.

love [lʌv] *n* F **1. hello, love!** salut! **thanks love!** merci mon pote!/merci chéri(e)!/merci (mon) coco! **2. for the love of Mike!** pour l'amour du ciel! (*See* **bug¹** 6; **puppy 2**)

lovebird ['lʌvbɜːd] *n* F amoureux *m*/amoureuse *f*/soupirant(e) *m(f)*; **young lovebirds,** des tourtereaux *mpl*.

love-in ['lʌvin] *n* O F festival *m* hippie.

lovely ['lʌvli] *n* F belle* fille*/une vénus/beau brin de fille/prix *m* de Diane.

lover-boy ['lʌvəbɔi] *n* F **1.** beau* gars/un Adonis/un Apollon/un jeune premier **2.** un don Juan/ coureur *m* de jupons/cavaleur *m*/ tombeur *m* de filles/dragueur *m*.

love juice ['lʌv'dʒuːs] *n* V sperme*/jus *m*.

love-weed ['lʌvwiːd] *n P* (*drugs*) marijuana*/herbe douce.

lovey ['lʌvi] *n F* chéri(e)/petit chou/ petit cœur.

lovey-dovey ['lʌvi'dʌvi] *a F* **1.** (trop) affectueux/amoureux/senti- mental; **to be all lovey-dovey,** être comme des tourtereaux **2.** à la guimauve/à l'eau de rose.

low [lou] *n F* **1. to be on a low,** avoir la déprime/broyer du noir **2.** (*drugs*) (*i*) déprime due à la drogue (*ii*) mauvaise réaction à une drogue; **to be on a low,** redescen- dre; flipper.

lowbrow ['loubrau] **I** *a F* (*a*) sans prétentions intellectuelles/terre à terre (*b*) faubourien/populo **II** *n F* (*a*) prolétaire *m*/prolo *m*/inculte *mf*/simplet *m* (*b*) qn qui ne s'intéresse pas aux choses intellec- tuelles/individu* peu relevé.

lowdown¹ ['lou'daun] **I** *a F* méprisable/moche/dégueulasse; **a lowdown trick,** un sale tour/une vacherie/un coup fourré **II** *n* **1.** *F* renseignements*; **to get the low- down on s.o.,** se tuyauter/se ren- carder sur qch; **he gave him the lowdown on it,** il l'a tuyauté/il l'a mis au parfum/il l'a mis au courant **2.** *P* tour *m* de cochon/coup fourré/sale coup.

lube [luːb] *n P* huile *f* de graissage.

lubricate ['luːbrikeit] *vtr F* **1.** graisser la patte à (qn) **2.** (*a*) enivrer/soûler (qn) (*b*) boire*/se rincer la dalle.

lubrication [luːbri'keiʃən] *n F* alcool*/gnôle *f*/goutte *f*.

luck [lʌk] *n F* **1. you never know your luck,** on ne sait jamais ce qui vous pend au nez **2. no such luck!** ç'aurait été trop beau!/tu parles, Charles!/et ben, penses-tu! (*See* **pot-luck; push² 2**)

lucre ['luːkər] *n F* argent*/flouse *m*; bénéfice*/bénef *m*; **filthy lucre** (*i*) gain *m*/gratte *f* (*ii*) argent*/carbure

m; **to do sth for filthy lucre,** faire qch rien que pour le fric.

lucy ['luːsi] *n P* (*drugs*) **sweet lucy,** marijuana*/herbe *f*/kif *m*.

lug¹ [lʌg] *n P* **1.** (*a*) oreille*/ esgourde *f*. (*See* **lugholes**) (*b*) *NAm* visage*; gueule *f* (*c*) *pl NAm* mains*/paluches *fpl* **2.** (*a*) homme*/mec *m* (*b*) ballot *m*/ baluchard *m* **3.** *NAm* (*a*) demande *f* d'argent*/botte *f* (*b*) dessous-de- table *m*/gratte *f*/tour *m* de bâton.

lug² [lʌg] *vtr Austr P* **to lug s.o. for money,** emprunter* de l'argent à qn/taper qn/bottiner qn.

lughead ['lʌghed] *n P* individu bête*/ballot *m*/cruche *f*.

lugholes ['lʌg(h)oulz] *npl P* oreil- les*; **pin back your lugholes!** dessale tes portugaises!/écarquille tes esgourdes! (*See* **lug¹ 1** (*a*))

lulu ['luːluː] *n F* (*a*) belle fille*/beau brin de fille/joli lot (*b*) qch de sen- sass/de super (*c*) *NAm* qch d'énorme.

lumber¹ ['lʌmbər] *n P* **to be in lumber,** être dans le pétrin/dans de beaux draps.

lumber² ['lʌmbər] *vtr&i* **1.** *P* arrêter*/agrafer/épingler; **to get lumbered,** se faire agrafer/alpaguer **2.** *F* **to get lumbered with s.o./sth,** être chargé/encombré de qn/de qch; **I got lumbered with the wash- ing up,** je me suis tapé/je me suis farci/j'ai dû me coltiner la vaisselle.

lumme! ['lʌmi] *excl O F* nom de Dieu!/mince alors!

lummox ['lʌməks] *n NAm P* individu bête*/cornichon *m*/ niguedouille *m*.

lummy! ['lʌmi] *excl O F* = **lumme!**

lump¹ [lʌmp] *n F* **1.** individu bête*/crétin *m*/cruche *f*; **you great lump!** espèce d'empoté! **2. a big lump of a girl,** une grosse dondon/ une godiche.

lump² [lʌmp] *vtr F* **1.** porter/ trimbal(l)er **2. like it or lump it,**

que ça plaise ou non, c'est le même prix; **you'll have to lump it,** il faudra l'avaler/il faut passer par là/tu peux mettre ça dans ton mouchoir et le remettre dans ta poche.

lungs [lʌŋs] *npl P* seins*/rotoplots *mpl*/doudounes *fpl*; **she's got huge lungs,** il y a du monde au balcon.

lunkhead [lʌŋkhed] *n P* = **lughead.**

lurgy ['ləːgi] *n F* **the dreaded lurgy,** la crève; **he's got the lurgy,** il a attrapé/chopé la crève.

lush¹ [lʌʃ] **I** *a F* chouette/badour; **she's a lush piece,** c'est un beau brin de fille/un beau morceau/un joli lot **II** *n espNAm F* **1.** ivrogne*/poivrot *m*/soûlard *m* **2.** soûlerie *f*/bringue *f* **3.** alcool*/ gnôle *f*.

lush² [lʌʃ] *vi NAm F* boire* de l'alcool*/biberonner/siffler/picoler/ siroter.

lush-hound ['lʌʃhaund] *n NAm F* = **lush II 1.**

lush-roller ['lʌʃroulər] *n NAm P* voleur* d'ivrognes/voleur* au poivrier.

lush-rolling ['lʌʃroulinŋ] *n NAm P* vol *m* au poivrier.

lush up ['lʌʃʌp] *vi NAm F* soûler/ charger/bourrer.

luv [lʌv] *n F* = **love 1.**

M

M [em] *abbr* P (*drugs*) (*a*) morphine*/morph *f*/M (*b*) marijuana*/ Maria *f*/Marie *f*/Marie-Jeanne *f*.

ma [mɑɪ] *n* F mère*/m'man.

Ma Bell ['mɑɪ'bel] *n* F (surnom de la) compagnie américaine des téléphones/ = les Télécoms *fpl*.

Mac, mac [mæk] **I** *n* **1**. F Écossais *m* **2**. P individu*/mec *m*/ gonze *m*. (*See* **mack¹** 3) **II** *n* (*abbr* = *mackintosh*) **1**. F imper(méable) *m*; **the dirty mac brigade**, individus qui vont voir des films pornos, etc **2**. P préservatif*/imperméable à Popaul.

macaroni [mækə'rouni] *n* **1**. P Italien*/macaroni *m*/Rital *m* **2**. F fil *m*/câble *m* (*esp* électrique) **3**. P (*prisons*) excrément *m*/merde *f*.

mace [meis] *vi* A P obtenir (qch) pour rien/faire de la resquille/avoir (qch) à l'œil.

machine [mə'ʃiːn] *n* P (*drugs*) seringue *f* hypodermique/hypo *m*/ poussette *f*/shooteuse *f*.

machinery [mə'ʃiːnəri] *n* P (*drugs*) attirail* de camé/artillerie *f*/kit *m*/ popote *f*.

macho ['matʃou] F **I** *a* macho/ phallo(crate); (*iron*) **he's terribly macho**, c'est un petit macho **II** *n* macho *m*/phallo(crate) *m*/butch *m*.

mack¹ [mæk] *n* **1**. F = **mac II** **2**. P souteneur*/maquereau *m*/mac *m* **3**. P mec *m*/zigoto *m*/gonze *m*.

mack² [mæk] *vi* P rabattre le client (pour une prostituée*)/maquereauter.

Mackay [mə'kai] *n* F = **McCoy**.

mackerel ['mækərəl] *n* P = **mack¹** 2. (*See* **holy** 1)

macking ['mækiŋ] *n* A P maquereautage *m*.

mackman ['mækmən] *n* P = **mack¹** 2.

maconha [mə'kɔnə] *n* P (*drugs*) cannabis*.

mad [mæd] **I** *a* F **1**. en colère*; **to be mad at s.o.**, être à cran contre qn/être remonté contre qn **2**. **to be mad about s.o./sth**, raffoler de qn/de qch/être dingue de qn/qch **3**. **like mad** (*a*) comme un enragé/ un perdu/un paumé; **to shout like mad**, crier comme un dingue (*b*) très vite*; **to run like mad**, foncer/ gazer/courir comme un dératé. (*See* **man-mad**; **sex-mad**; **woman-mad**) **II** *adv* F **mad keen on sth/ s.o.**, emballé par qch/qn; **he's mad about her**, il en pince sec pour elle.

madam¹ ['mædəm] *n* **1**. P (*rare*) **don't come the old madam with me!** ne monte pas sur tes grands chevaux!/(ne) la ramène pas!/pas la peine de prendre tes (grands) airs avec moi! **2**. F patronne* (de maison de tolérance)/madame *f*/taulière *f*/maquerelle *f*.

madam² ['mædəm] *vi* A P **1**. mentir*/bourrer le crâne/bourrer le mou **2**. faire du baratin.

madame [mæ'dɑɪm] *n* F patronne* (de maison de tolérance)/madame *f*/taulière *f*/maquerelle *f*.

madhouse ['mædhaus] *n* F maison *f* de fous/Charenton; **this place is like a madhouse**, on se croirait à

Charenton/à Sainte-Anne/chez les fous.

mag [mæg] *abbr F* (= *magazine*) magazine *m*/revue *f*; **porny/porno mag**, revue porno.

magic ['mædʒik] *a P* excellent*/super/sensass; **magic!** sensass!/super!/le pied!/formid(able)! **he's really magic, isn't he?** il est super, non?

main-line¹ ['mein'lain] *n P* veine apparente (pour piqûre intraveineuse).

main-line² ['mein'lain] *vi P* se faire une injection intraveineuse/se piquer/se piquouser/se shooter/se faire un fixe.

main-liner ['mein'lainər]*n P* drogué* qui se fait des piqûres intraveineuses/piquouseur *m*/piquomane *mf*/fixer *m*/junkie *m*.

mainman ['mein'mæn] *n P* patron*/chef *m*/boss *m*.

make¹ [meik] *n* 1. *P* **easy make**, femme* facile/à la cuisse hospitalière; une chaude lapine. (*See* **lay¹** 2) 2. **on the make** (*a*) *F* âpre au gain/chercheur d'affure; **he's on the make**, il cherche à se faire des petits à-côtés (*b*) *P* en quête d'aventures amoureuses/dragueur; **he's always on the make**, c'est un dragueur/un chaud lapin 3. *P* **to get a make on a criminal**, identifier/détrancher/tapisser un criminel; **we got a make on the stolen car**, on a repéré la bagnole volée 4. *P* butin*/fade *m*/bouquet *m*/taf *m*.

make² [meik] *vtr* 1. (*a*) *F* **to make it**, réussir/gagner le cocotier; **he's made it**, il se la fait belle (*b*) *P* **to make (it with) a woman**, lever une fille*; **he's always trying to make (it with) some chick or other**, il est sans arrêt en train de chercher à s'envoyer/lever une poupée; **they make it two or three times a week**, ils font l'amour/ils baisent deux ou trois fois par semaine 2. *F* **he's as sharp as they make 'em**, pour un

malin, c'est un malin 3. *F* gagner*; **how much do you make?** qu'est-ce que/combien tu te fais? 4. *P* voler*/faire/fabriquer (qch) 5. *P* = **to get a make on** (**make¹** 3) 6. *P* comprendre/piger/entraver (qn/qch) 7. *F* arriver* à/débarquer à (un endroit) 8. *F* **do you want to make sth (out) of it?** tu veux chercher noise, ou quoi?/tu cherches des histoires, ou quoi?/tu vas pas en faire un plat, non? 9. *F* **to have it made**, se la couler douce/avoir le filon 10. *F* **I just made my train**, j'ai eu mon train mais ça a été moins une 11. *P* (*drugs*) se ravitailler en drogue/se garnir/trouver le joint; **to make speed**, obtenir du speed. (*See* **daft I** 1; **side** 1)

make like ['meik'laik] *vi esp NAm F* faire semblant; **make like you're sick**, fais comme si tu étais malade.

make out ['meik'aut] *vi* 1. *F* prospérer/faire des progrès; aller/marcher (bien *ou* mal); **how do your children make out at school?** comment vos enfants se débrouillent-ils à l'école? **we're making out**, on se débrouille/on se démerde 2. *F* subsister; **I can make out on bread and water**, je peux vivre de pain et d'eau; **he earns enough to make out**, il se débrouille avec ce qu'il gagne 3. *F* faire semblant/chiquer 4. *P* s'étreindre/s'enlacer passionnément 5. *P* **to make out with a girl** (*i*) faire une touche (à une nana) (*ii*) se faire/s'envoyer une nana.

make up ['meik'ʌp] *vi F* **to make up to s.o.** (*i*) flatter qn/lécher les bottes à qn (*ii*) faire des avances *fpl* à qn/flirter avec qn/draguer qn.

malark(e)y [mə'lɑiki] *n F* 1. flatteries *fpl*/boniment *m*/baratin *m* 2. balivernes *fpl*; **a lot of malarkey**, du pipeau.

male [meil] *n F* **male chauvinist pig**, (sale) phallocrate *m*/phallo *m*.

mallee ['mælii] *n Austr F* **to take to the mallee**, prendre le maquis.

mam(m)a ['mæmə] *n esp NAm P*
1. fille*/femme*/nana *f*/poupée *f*/
chouquette *f*/gonzesse *f* **2.** une
fille bandante.

mammie, mammy ['mæmi] *n*
NAm F **1.** mère*/maman **2.**
nourrice/nounou noire **3. mammy**
boy, homme faible/femmelette *f*/
chiffe molle/hommelette *f*.

man [mæn] *n* **1.** *F* **(why) man,**
you're crazy! mais mon pauvre
vieux, tu es fou*/tu dérailles! **2.** *F*
he's a big man (*i*) c'est quelqu'un
(*ii*) il est bien équipé/membré **3.**
F **her man,** son mari/son homme/
son mec **4.** *O F* **my young man** (*i*)
mon copain (*ii*) mon futur/mon
fiancé **5.** *P* **the man/the Man** (*a*)
la police*/ces Messieurs *mpl* (*b*)
(*drugs*) fourgueur *m*/dealer *m*; **to**
make the man, acheter des drogues/
brancher; **to be waiting for the man,**
être en manque/être crevard (*c*)
patron*/dab *m*/chef *m*. (*See* **ad-**
man; **arse-man**; **boss-man**; **bus-**
man; **cave-man**; **chiv(e)-man**;
dead I 3, 8; **dog¹ 14**; **dustman**;
G-man; **he-man**; **ice-man**;
kickman; **k-man**; **leather-man**;
legman; **lollipop-man**; **mackman**;
mainman; **middleman**; **muscle-**
man; **old 1, 2**; **one-man**; **pen-**
man; **peterman**; **prop-man**; **rod-**
man; **sandman**; **screwsman**;
showman; **sideman**; **spiderman**;
swagman; **swordsman**; **tail-man**;
trigger-man; **yes-man**)

manage ['mænidʒ] *vtr F* **can you**
manage a bit more? vous avez bien
encore une petite place? **I couldn't**
manage another drop, je ne pourrais
plus avaler une seule goutte.

man-crazy ['mæn'kreizi] *a F* =
man-mad. (*See* **woman-crazy**)

manhole ['mænhoul] *n V* sexe de
la femme*/fente *f*/con *m*.

manicure ['mænikjuə] *n P* (*drugs*)
cannabis*.

manky ['mænki] *a P* sale et moche/
cradingue/crado.

man-mad ['mæn'mæd] *a F*
nymphomane; **she's man-mad,** elle
est nympho. (*See* **woman-mad**)

manor ['mænər] *n P* (*a*) territoire
m/champ *m* d'action (d'un
criminel)/chasse gardée (*b*) secteur
couvert par un commissariat de
police; **morguey manor,** quartier
farci/pourri de flics. (*See* **mystery**;
patch 2)

man-size(d) ['mænsaiz(d)] *a F* (*a*)
gros*/de taille/comaque (*b*) cos-
taud/maousse; **a man-sized meal,**
un repas copieux/abondant; un
balthazar.

map [mæp] *n* **1.** *F* **to put on the**
map, populariser/mettre en vedette;
this will put London back on the
map, ça va remettre Londres sous
les projecteurs **2.** *F* **off the map,**
inaccessible/au diable vauvert/à
Trifouillis-les-Oies **3.** *Austr P* **to**
throw a map, vomir*/aller au refile/
balancer un renard **4.** *P* visage*/
boule *f*/bobine *f* **5.** *NAm P*
chèque *m*.

maracas [mə'rækəz] *npl P* **1.**
seins*/rotoplots *mpl*/roploplots
mpl/roberts *mpl* **2.** (*RS = knack-*
ers) testicules*/noisettes *fpl*/val-
seuses *fpl*.

Marble Bar ['mɑːbl'bɑː] *n Austr F*
till it rains in Marble Bar, jusqu'à
la Saint-Glinglin.

marbles ['mɑːblz] *npl P* **1. to pass**
in one's marbles, mourir*/passer
l'arme à gauche/lâcher la rampe
2. to tell s.o. to go and play mar-
bles, envoyer paître qn; **go and play**
marbles! va te faire cuire un œuf!/
va te faire voir (chez les Grecs)!
3. to lose one's marbles, devenir
fou*/perdre le nord/perdre la
boule/déménager; **he's lost (all) his**
marbles, il a perdu la boule/il
dévisse du cigare; **he's still got all**
his marbles, il a encore toute sa
tête **4.** testicules*/billes *fpl*/burnes
fpl.

marching ['mɑːtʃiŋ] *n F* **to give**

s.o. **his marching orders,** se débarrasser* de qn/flanquer qn à la porte; envoyer paître qn/envoyer qn dinguer.

mare ['mɛər] *n P* **femme*** méprisable/carne *f*/vache *f*.

marge [mɑːdʒ] *n* **1.** *F* (= *margarine*) margarine *f* **2.** *P* lesbienne*/goudou *f*.

maricon ['mærikən] *n NAm P* homosexuel*/tapette *f*/lope *f*; **maricon! pédé!/tante!/emmanché!**

Marine [məˈriːn] *n F* **(go) tell that to the Marines!** à d'autres!/et ta sœur!/arrête ton char(, Ben Hur)!

marjie ['mɑːdʒi], **marjorie** ['mɑːdʒəri] *n P* (*drugs*) marijuana*/kif *m*/Marie-Jeanne *f*. (*See* **juana**)

mark[1] [mɑːk] *n F* **to feel up to the mark,** être en train/tenir la forme/péter la santé/avoir la frite; **I don't feel up to the mark,** je ne suis pas dans mon assiette. (*See* **easy I 3**; **tide-mark**)

mark[2] [mɑːk] *vtr P* **1. to mark s.o.'s card,** mettre qn sur ses gardes/faire ouvrir l'œil à qn **2.** chercher *ou* trouver (*i*) un cave (*ii*) un bon casse.

marker ['mɑːkər] *n P* reconnaissance *f* de dette.

mark up ['mɑːkʌp] *vtr F* donner un bon point pour (qch); **to mark it up to s.o.,** mettre (qch) au crédit de qn.

marriage ['mærɪdʒ] *a attrib P* **marriage gear/prospects,** testicules*/bijoux *mpl* de famille/joyeuses *fpl*.

married ['mærɪd] *a P* **to be married to the five-fingered widow,** se masturber*/se taper la Veuve Poignet.

marrow-bones ['mæroubounz, 'mærəbounz] *npl P* genoux *mpl*/coussinets *mpl*.

marshmallows ['mɑːʃmælouz] *npl P* **1.** seins* **2.** testicules*.

marvellous ['mɑːv(ə)ləs] *a F* excellent*/super; **marvellous, isn't**

it?/**bloody marvellous!** ça, c'est la meilleure!/voilà bien le bouquet!

Mary, mary ['mɛəri] *n* **1.** *P* homosexuel* passif/joconde *f*/tapette *f* **2.** *P* lesbienne*/gouine *f* **3.** *P* = **Mary Ann(e) 4.** *F* **bloody Mary,** cocktail *m* de vodka et jus de tomate/Marie-Salope *f*.

Mary Ann(e) ['mɛəri'æn], **Mary Jane** ['mɛəri'dʒein], **Mary Warner** ['mɛəri'wɔːnər] *n P* (*drugs*) (*a*) marijuana*/Marie-Jeanne *f*/Marie-Warner *f* (*b*) cigarette* de marijuana/juju *f*/joint *m*/bomb *f*.

masher ['mæʃər] *n F* **1.** *A* gigolo *m*/gommeux *m*/coco-bel-œil *m* **2.** *pl* dents*/croquantes *fpl*/ratiches *fpl*.

massage ['mæsɑːʒ] *n F* (*euph for brothel*) **massage parlour,** salon *m* de massages thaïlandais/spéciaux.

master ['mɑːstər] *n F* (*sado-masochism*) partenaire dominant/dominateur *m*/maître *m*. (*See* **slave**)

mat [mæt] *n F* **on the mat** = **on the carpet** (**carpet**[1] **1**). (*See* **doormat**; **welcome-mat**)

mate [meit] *n F* **1.** ami*/copain *m*/pote *m*; **to go for a drink with one's mates,** (aller) prendre un pot avec les potes **2.** mec *m*/type *m*/zigoto *m*; **that's too bad, mate!** tant pis pour toi, vieux frère!

matey ['meiti] **I** *a F* **to be matey,** être à tu et à toi/copiner; **they've got all matey now,** ils sont copains comme cochons maintenant **II** *n F* = **mate 1, 2.**

mateyness ['meitinis] *n F* copinage *m*.

Matilda [məˈtildə] *n Austr F* (*bushman's swag*) balluchon *m*.

matlo(w) ['mætlou] *n F* marin*/matelot *m*.

mattress ['mætris] *n P* **to hit the mattress,** se cacher*/se planquer/se planquouser.

mauler ['mɔːlər] n P (a) main*/ patte f/paluche f (b) poing m/ pogne m.

maybe ['meibiː] adv F ...and I don't mean maybe! ...et je ne plaisante pas!/je ne rigole pas!

mazuma [mə'zuːmə] n P argent*/ pognon m/fric m/flouse m.

MC ['em'siː] vtr P to MC a show, présenter/animer un spectacle. (See emcee)

McCoy [mə'kɔi] n F the real McCoy (a) boisson f de bonne qualité/de la vraie (de vraie) (b) de l'authentique/du vrai de vrai; de la marchandise irréprochable/du garanti pur sucre; it's the real McCoy, c'est pas de la camelote.

MCP ['em'siː'piː] abbr P = male chauvinist pig (male).

MDA ['em'diː'ei] n P (drugs) (abbr = methyl diamphetamine) MDA m.

meal [miːl] n F to make a meal out of sth, faire toute une histoire/tout un plat de qch.

meal-ticket ['miːltikit] n (prostitute) F gagne-pain m/vache f à lait/gagneuse f/bifteck m.

mean [miːn] a 1. F mauvais/ méchant/sale; mean weather, sale temps/temps pourri; mean job, travail* désagréable/boulot m dégueulasse 2. P a mean bastard/ esp NAm a mean son of a bitch, un vrai salaud/une vraie peau de vache 3. F to feel mean about sth, avoir honte de qch; I feel really mean about it, ça m'embête 4. P formid(able)/du tonnerre; he plays a mean guitar, il touche (sa bille) à la guitare.

meanie, meany ['miːniː] n F grigou m/rat m/radin m/rapiat m; he's a real meany, ce qu'il est moche/vache (avec nous).

measly ['miːzli] a F 1. misérable/ insignifiant/de rien du tout; a measly five quid, cinq malheureuses livres 2. avare*/constipé du

morlingue/qui a des mites dans son crapaud.

meat [miːt] n 1. F fond m/moelle f/substance f 2. (sex) P to love one's meat, être porté à la chose 3. V (a) pénis*; small meat, un petit pénis*/petit bout; to beat the meat, se masturber*/se secouer le bonhomme/se tirer son coup/se l'agiter (b) meat and two veg, sexe de l'homme*/service m trois pièces 4. P jouissance f d'un homosexuel* 5. F to make cold meat of s.o., tuer* qn/refroidir qn 6. Austr F as Australian as a meat pie, typiquement australien/on ne peut plus australien. (See apple-pie II; easy1 6; mincemeat; pig-meat; plate1 2)

meathead ['miːthed] n P individu bête*/gourde f/andouille f/nouille f.

meat-hooks ['miːthuks] npl P grandes mains*/battoirs mpl/ croches fpl/paluches fpl. (See hook1 7)

meat-house ['miːthaus] n P bordel*/maison f d'abattage/claque m.

meat rack ['miːt'ræk] n P lieu m où les homosexuels se retrouvent/ = les Tuileries fpl.

meat-show ['miːtʃou] n P spectacle m de nu/parade f de fesses/ spectacle de cul.

meat-wag(g)on ['miːtwægən] P 1. ambulance f 2. corbillard*/roulante f à refroidis/trottinette f à macchabs 3. car* de police/panier m à salade/familiale f.

mebbe ['mebi] adv P (= maybe) ça se peut/des fois/p'têt ben.

mechanic [miː'kænik] n P tricheur m aux cartes/maquilleur m.

medals ['med(ə)lz] npl F your medals are showing, ta braguette est ouverte; n'expose pas tes bijoux.

medic(o) ['medik(ou)] n F 1. médecin m/toubib m 2. étudiant m en médecine/carabin m.

meemies ['miːmiz] *npl NAm P* the screaming meemies, angoisse *f* extrême/peur bleue; to get the screaming meemies (*i*) avoir les jetons/les chocottes (*ii*) piauler à la bit(t)ure.

meet [miːt] *n P* 1. gig¹ 5 2. rendez-vous*/rancart *m*; let's arrange a meet, on se donne rancart/on prend date 3. (*drugs*) to make a meet, avoir rendez-vous avec son fourgueur/acheter des drogues/brancher.

mental ['ment(ə)l] *a F* to go mental, devenir fou*; you must be mental! t'es pas dingue/ça va la tête, oui?; mental eunuch, imbécile*/nigaud *m*/ducon la joie.

merchant ['mɔːtʃənt] *n F* individu*/type *m*/mec *m*/péquin *m*/paroissien *m*. (*See* chiv(e)-merchant; speed-merchant)

merino [məˈriːnou] *n F Austr* pure merino, Australien de sang pur (sans lien avec les anciens déportés ou leurs descendants); = aristo *mf*.

merry ['meri] *a F* légèrement ivre*/pompette/éméché; to get rather merry/a bit merry, avoir un verre dans le nez. (*See* hell 3)

mesc [mesk] *n P* (*drugs*) (*abbr* = *mescaline*) mescaline*/mesc *f*.

mess [mes] *n* 1. *F* isn't she a mess! ce qu'elle est tarte/tartignolle! 2. *F* the house is in a real mess, la maison est un vrai foutoir; what a mess! quel gâchis!/quelle pagaille! his life is in a dreadful mess, il a gâché sa vie/il a fait un vrai gâchis de sa vie 3. *F* to be in a (bit of a) mess, être dans le pétrin/dans de mauvais draps/dans le caca; to help s.o. out of a mess, tirer qn d'un mauvais pas 4. *P* to make a mess of s.o., battre* qn/tabasser qn/amocher qn; faire de la bouillie de qn; the accident made a dreadful mess of her face, l'accident lui a bousillé la figure 5. *F* to make a mess of things/it, tout gâcher/tout bousiller/tout foutre en l'air; he always makes a mess of things, il n'en rate pas une. (*See* right I 1)

mess about, around ['mesə'baut, ə'raund] *vtr&i* 1. *F* patauger/patouiller (dans la boue) 2. *F* traîner/bricoler/lambiner/glander 3. *F* to mess s.o. about, tourmenter/turlupiner qn 4. *P* to mess about with s.o. (*a*) peloter/pelotailler qn; amuser/stop messing around with my wife! pas de jeux de mains avec ma femme! (*b*) s'acoquiner avec qn.

message ['mesidʒ] *n F* to get the message, comprendre/piger/entraver; I get the message, je vous reçois cinq sur cinq; get the message? tu piges?

mess-up ['mesʌp] *n F* 1. gâchis *m*/méli-mélo *m*/pagaille *f* 2. malentendu *m*/embrouillamini *m*/cafouillage *m*.

mess up ['mesʌp] *vtr F* 1. salir/bousiller/saloper 2. abîmer*/amocher/saboter; he's messed his face up, il s'est abîmé le portrait; we're gonna mess your face up, on va vous arranger joliment le portrait.

metal ['met(ə)l] *n P* (*motor trade*) to move the metal, vendre des voitures/écouler la marchandise.

metal-spiv ['met(ə)lspiv] *n O P* marchand *m*/trafiquant *m* en ferraille; cribleur *m* de ferraille. (*See* spiv)

meth [meθ] *abbr* 1. *P* (*drugs*) (= *methedrine*) méthédrine *f*/meth *f* 2. *pl F* (= *methylated spirits*) alcool *m* à brûler; meths drinker, alcolo *mf*/clodo *m* qui se soûle à l'alcool à brûler.

methhead ['meθhed] *n P* (*drugs*) habitué *m* de la méthédrine.

metho ['meθou] *n Austr P* alcool *m* à brûler; metho drinker, alcolo *mf*/clodo *m* (qui se soûle à l'alcool à brûler); alcolo au dernier degré;

to go on the metho, se soûler à l'alcool à brûler. (*See* **meth 2**)

Mexican red ['meksikən'red] *n P* (*drugs*) marijuana* du Mexique/de la Mexicaine.

mezz [mez] *n esp NAm P* (*drugs*) cigarette* de marijuana/stick *m*/bomb *f*/joint *m*.

MF ['em'ef] *abbr P* = **motherfucker.**

Michael ['maik(ə)l] *n F* **1.** (*hum*) Michael Flyn = Mick(e)y Finn (**Mick(e)y 4**) **2.** to take the Michael = to take the mick(e)y (**mick(e)y 2**).

mick, Mick [mik] *n P* **1.** (*a*) Irlandais *m* (*b*) qn d'origine irlandaise. (*See* **Paddy**) **2.** to take the mick = to take the mick(e)y (**mick(e)y 2**).

mick(e)y, Mick(e)y ['miki] *n* **1.** *P* = **mick, Mick 1 2.** *F* to take the mick(e)y out of s.o., faire marcher qn/se payer la tête de qn; **stop taking the mick(e)y!** ne charrie pas!/n'attige pas! (*See* **mick(e)y-taker**) **3.** *P* pomme *f* de terre/patate *f* **4.** *F* Mick(e)y (Finn) (*a*) boisson droguée; **to slip s.o. a Mick(e)y Finn,** refiler à qn une boisson droguée (*b*) casse-pattes *m* **5.** *P* to do a mick(e)y, s'enfuir*/se barrer/déguerpir **6.** *Austr F* jeune taureau *m*.

Mickey Mouse ['miki'maus] **I** *a P* **1.** inférieur/du toc; à la noix; **that firm's a real Mickey Mouse outfit,** cette boîte, c'est un truc de rigolos **2.** simple/facile/pas dif; **he settled for a Mickey Mouse job instead,** il s'est décidé pour un boulot pépère/un job à la con **3.** routinier/train-train **4.** louche/toc **II** *n P* (*RS* = *house*) maison *f*.

mick(e)y-taker ['mikiteikər] *n F* moqueur *m*/charrieur *m*/railleur *m*/lardeur *m*/gouailleur *m*; **he's a real mickey-taker,** il n'arrête pas de se payer la tête des gens. (*See* **Mick(e)y 2**)

middleman ['midlmæn] *n F* (*drugs*) contact *m*/intermédiaire *m*/passeur *m*.

middle-of-the-road ['midl-əvðəroud] *a F* modéré; **the Party has a middle-of-the-road policy,** le parti poursuit une politique modérée *ou* centriste.

middling ['midliŋ] *adv F* fair to middling, pas mal/couci-couça/entre les deux.

middy ['midi] *n F* (*naut* = *midshipman*) midship *m*/aspi *m*.

miff[1] [mif] *n F* (*a*) mauvaise humeur/cran *m*/rogne *f* (*b*) pique *f*/brouille *f*.

miff[2] [mif] *vtr&i F* **1.** offenser/vexer; prendre la mouche; **he was a bit miffed by it,** ça l'avait un peu vexé/il avait pas trop apprécié/il appréciait pas trop **2.** rater/louper.

mighty ['maiti] *a F* bigrement/bougrement/fichtrement/vachement; **it's mighty cold,** il fait sacrément froid; **I'm mighty glad to see you,** je suis vachement content de te voir.

mike[1] [maik] *n* **1.** *P* = **mick 1 2.** *F* to take the mike = to take the mick(e)y (**mick(e)y 2**) **3.** *F* (= *microphone*) micro *m* **4.** *P* to take a mike at sth, regarder*/lorgner/mater/tapisser qch **5.** *P* to do a mike = to do a mick(e)y (**mick(e)y 5**) **6.** *P* to have a mike = **mike**[2] **7.** *P* (*RS* = *telephone*) Mike Malone, téléphone*/biniou *m* **8.** *P* (*drugs*) (*abbr* = *microgram*) dose *f* d'un microgramme (de drogue). (*See* **love 2**)

mike[2] [maik] *vi P* paresser*/se les tourner/glander/branler les mouches/tirer sa cosse.

mile [mail] *n F* **1.** you're a mile out/you're miles out/you're miles off course, tu en es à mille lieues/tu es complètement à côté (de la plaque)/ **you're miles too slow,** tu es mille fois trop lent **2.** I'd go a mile (*or* miles) for that, je ferais des kilomètres pour cela/j'irais au bout

213

du monde pour ça **3. a miss is as good as a mile,** à côté, c'est à côté **4. to be miles away,** être ailleurs/ rêvasser/décoller/gamberger **5. it sticks out a mile/you can see it a mile off/you can see it a mile away,** ça se voit d'une lieue/ça saute aux yeux/ça se voit comme le nez au milieu de la figure. (*See* **thumb 4**)

milk [milk] *vtr* **1.** *F* traire (qn/qch) **2.** *V* masturber*/allonger (qn)/ écrémer (qn)/faire mousser le créateur.

milk-bottles ['milkbɔtlz] *npl P* seins*/boîtes *fpl* à lait/lolos *fpl*.

milko ['milkou] *n esp Austr F* laitier *m*.

milk run ['milkrʌn] *n F* (*aviation*) vol *m* de routine/vol pépère.

milk-shop ['milkʃɔp] *n P* = **milk-bottles.**

milk-train ['milktrein] *n F* **to catch the milk-train,** rentrer au petit matin.

milk-wag(g)on ['milkwægən] *n P* car* de police/panier *m* à salade.

milky ['milki] *a F* foireux/trouillard; **to turn milky,** avoir peur*/avoir la trouille/avoir les foies.

mill[1] [mil] *n F* **1.** bagarre*/baston *m*/rififi *m* **2. to go through the mill,** en voir de toutes les couleurs/ en voir des vertes et des pas mûres/en baver; **to put s.o. through the mill,** faire passer qn par la filière. (*See* **run-of-the-mill**)

mill[2] [mil] *vtr F* bourrer de coups*/ tabasser/dérouiller/encadrer.

milling ['milin] *n F* **to give s.o. a milling,** donner une raclée à qn/ passer qn à la machine à bosseler/ filer une toise à qn.

million ['miljən] *n F* **1. thanks a million!** merci mille fois! **2. to feel like a million (dollars),** être au septième ciel/être aux anges; **to look like a million dollars,** être tiré à quatre épingles; jeter du jus **3.**

Austr **gone a million,** dans de mauvais draps/dans le pétrin.

min [min] *n A P* agent* de police/ poulet *m*/cogne *m*/flic *m*.

mince [mins] *n A F* **at a fast mince,** vite*/à toute barde/à tout berzingue.

mincemeat ['minsmiːt] *n F* **to make mincemeat (out) of s.o.,** faire de la bouillie de qn/mettre qn dans sa poche.

mince-pies ['mins'paiz] *npl P* (*RS* = *eyes*) yeux*/mirettes *fpl*/calots *mpl*/clignotants *mpl*.

mincers ['minsəz], **minces** ['minsiz] *npl P* = **mince-pies.**

mind [maind] *vtr P* protéger/surveiller (qn).

mind-bender ['maindbendər] *n P* **1.** drogue *f* qui affine l'intelligence; euphorisant *m* **2.** qn *ou* qch qui élargit l'esprit et l'approfondit.

mind-blower ['maindblouər] *n P* (*a*) expérience inaccoutumée (*b*) choc soudain/coup *m* de massue (*c*) drogue *f* hallucinogène extatique/ bonbon *m* à kick.

mind-boggling ['maindbɔglin] *a P* renversant/à vous couper le souffle; **it was a mind-boggling experience,** j'en suis resté baba.

mind-bogglingly ['maindbɔglinli] *a P* remarquablement; **that film was mind-bogglingly awful,** c'était une vraie connerie de film.

minder ['maindər] *n P* garde *m* du corps/ange gardien; gorille *m*.

mind fuck ['maindfʌk] *vtr P* endoctriner qn/bourrer le crâne à qn/laver le cerveau à qn.

minge [mindʒ] *n V* sexe de la femme*/barbu *m*; **minge fringe,** poils *mpl* du pubis/paquet *m* de tabac/persil *m*/mouron *m*.

mingy ['mindʒi] *a F* = **measly 1, 2.**

mink [miŋk] *n NAm* **1.** *P* fille*/gis-

quette *f*; nana bien roulée/mettable
2. *V* sexe de la femme*/chatte *f*/
petit chat.

minstrel ['minstrəl] *n P* (*drugs*)
black and white/nigger minstrel,
amphétamine*/cranck *m*/amph *m*.

mint [mint] *n F* to cost a mint (of
money), coûter les yeux de la tête/
coûter bonbon; to make a mint,
gagner un paquet/faire fortune/
faire du blé.

mintie, minty ['minti] **I** *a P* **1.**
homosexuel/tata/chochotte **2.**
intéressant/curieux/spécial; he's a
bit minty, c'est un drôle d'oiseau
II *n P* lesbienne* masculine et
agressive.

mischief ['mistʃif] *n F* enfant*
espiègle/petit diable/phénomène *m*.

mish-mash ['miʃmæʃ] *n F* méli-
mélo *m*.

mishugah [mi'ʃugə] *a NAm F*
fou*/barjot/cinglé.

miss [mis] *n* **1.** *F* to give sth a
miss, laisser passer qch/laisser
courir qch; sécher (un cours); I
think I'll give your plonk a miss, je
crois que je vais pas me laisser
tenter par ton petit vin/ta piquette.
(*See* **mile 3**) **2.** *P* (*drugs*) Miss
Emma, morphine*.

missis ['misiz] *n F* the/my missus,
mon épouse*/la bourgeoise/la
patronne; I'll have to ask the missus, faut demander à mon
gouvernement.

miss out on ['mis'autən] *vtr F*
manquer/louper/rater (qch); I
missed out on my best chance, j'ai
raté ma meilleure occasion; he
doesn't miss out on a thing, il n'en
rate pas une.

missus ['misiz] *n F* = missis.

missy ['misi] *n O F* mademoiselle/
mam'zelle.

mistake [mis'teik] *n F* ...and no
mistake/make no mistake! ...et tu
peux en être sûr!/...je t'en
réponds.

mitt [mit] *n P* **1.** main*/patte *f*;
keep your mitts off! bas les pattes!
2. gant *m* de boxe/mitaine bourrée
3. *pl* menottes*/poucettes *fpl*/brace-
lets *mpl* **4.** to put one's mitts on
sth, voler* qch/faire main basse sur
qch/griffer qch/se faire la main sur
qch.

mitten ['mitn] *n O F* to give s.o. the
mitten, abandonner qn/plaquer qn.

mitt-reader ['mitriːdər] *n P* diseur
m/diseuse *f* de bonne aventure;
chiromancien *m*/chiromancienne *f*.

mix [miks] *vtr&i F* **1.** to mix it with
s.o., se battre* avec qn/s'expliquer
avec qn/se castagner **2.** to mix
things up, remuer les eaux troubles/
semer la merde.

mixer ['miksər] *n F* **1.** he's a good
mixer, il est sociable/il se lie facilement; he's a bad mixer, c'est un
ours/il est sauvage **2.** (*trouble-
maker*) mauvais coucheur.

mix-up ['miksʌp] *n F* **1.** confusion
f/pagaille *f* **2.** bagarre*/mêlée *f*/rif
m.

miz(z) [miz] *a O P* malheureux/
tout chose/cafardeux.

mizzers ['mizəz] *npl O P* to have
the mizzers, avoir le cafard/avoir
au bourdon/être le 36ème dessous.

mizzle ['mizl] *vi P* **1.** s'enfuir*/se
cavaler/mettre les bouts **2.** rous-
péter/râler/renauder.

mizzler ['mizlər] *n P* geignard *m*/
pleurnicheur *m*.

mo [mou] *n F* (= *moment*) half a
mo! une seconde!/minute! (*See*
jiff(y); sec; shake[1] 1, 2; tick[1] 3)

m.o. ['em'ou] *abbr P* (= *modus oper-
andi*) = handwriting.

moan[1] [moun] *n F* to have a (good)
moan = moan[2].

moan[2] [moun] *vi F* to moan (and
groan), grogner*/ronchonner/rous-
cailler.

moaner ['mounər] *n F* ronchonneur
m/rouscailleur *m*/râleur *m*.

moaning ['mouniŋ] *a F* **a moaning Minnie,** une geignarde/une rouspéteuse.

mob [mɔb] *n F* bande* de criminels/flèche *f*/gang *m*/soce *f*. (*See* **heavy I 4**; **swell I 3**)

mobile ['moubail] *a F* **to get mobile** (*i*) travailler* plus vite/se décarcasser/se démancher/se magner le train (*ii*) se dépêcher*/se magner/se grouiller/se secouer.

mobster ['mɔbstər] *n NAm F* homme* du milieu/membre *m* de la pègre/dur *m*/truand *m*/arcan *m*.

mockers ['mɔkəz] *npl F* **to put the mockers on s.o./sth** (*i*) jeter un sort sur qn/qch; enguignonner qn/qch; porter la poisse à qn/qch (*ii*) mettre des bâtons dans les roues à qn.

mockie, mocky ['mɔki] *n P* (*pej*) Juif*/Youpin *m*.

mod [mɔd] *n F* scootériste *m*/mod *m*. (*See* **rocker 1**)

mog [mɔg], **moggie, moggy** ['mɔgi] *n F* chat *m*/matou *m*/greffier *m*.

mojo ['moudʒou] *n P* (*drugs*) stupéfiant(s) *m(pl)* (en poudre)/stups *mpl*.

moke [mouk] *n F* âne *m*/bourricot *m*/martin *m*/branque *m*/oreillard *m*.

mola ['moulə] *n NAm P* homosexuel*/pédé *m*/lope *f*.

moll [mɔl] *n* **1.** *P* jeune femme*/gonzesse *f*/mousmé(e) *f*/nana *f* **2.** *P* prostituée/catin *f* **3.** *F poule f*/môme *f* d'un gangster.

molly-dooker ['mɔliduɪkər] *n Austr F* gaucher *m*.

molly-shop ['mɔliʃɔp] *n P* = **meat-house.**

Molotov cocktail ['mɔlɔtɔv-'kɔkteil] *n F* cocktail *m* molotov.

mom [mɔm] *n esp NAm F* mère*/mam(an).

moments ['moumənts] *npl F* **I've had my moments,** j'ai eu mes bons

moments; moi aussi, j'ai été jeune/j'ai fait les 400 coups.

monarch ['mɔnək] *n Austr F* la police*/les flics *mpl*/les cognes *mpl*/les poulets *mpl*.

Monday ['mʌndi] *n F* **that Monday morning feeling,** l'humeur *f* du lundi/l'après-weekend *m*.

Mondayish ['mʌndiiʃ] *F* **I** *a* **that Mondayish feeling = that Monday morning feeling (Monday) II** *adv* **to feel Mondayish,** être dans les vapes du lundi/avoir le cafard du lundi.

money ['mʌni] *n F* **1. to be in the money,** être riche*/rouler sur l'or/être plein aux as **2. he's the man for my money,** c'est juste l'homme qu'il me faut; il a tous mes suffrages **3. to throw good money after bad** (*a*) jouer à quitte ou double (*b*) jeter/balancer/foutre l'argent* par les fenêtres **4. I'm not made of money,** je ne suis pas cousu d'or; je ne roule pas sur l'or/je ne suis pas Crésus. (*See* **big I 7**; **rope 1**)

moneybags ['mʌnibægz] *n F* individu très riche*/rupin *m*/richard *m*.

moniker ['mɔnikər] *n P* nom*/blaze *m*/centre *m*.

monkey ['mʌŋki] *n* **1.** *F* **to get one's monkey up,** se mettre en colère*/piquer une rogne/prendre la mouche; **to get s.o.'s monkey up,** mettre qn en colère/en rogne **2.** *P* billet*/faf(f)iot *m* de cinq cents livres; un gros talbin **3.** *P* **I don't give a monkey's (toss)!** je m'en fous et contrefous!/je n'en ai rien à glander!/je n'en ai rien à foutre! **4.** *F* **to make a monkey (out) of s.o.,** se payer la tronche de qn; **he made me look a right monkey,** il s'est bien foutu de ma poire **5.** *F* **monkey business** (*a*) affaire peu sérieuse/peu loyale; rocambouille *f* (*b*) conduite *f* malhonnête/procédé irrégulier (*c*) coup fourré/

entourloupe *f* (*d*) fumisterie *f*; **no monkey business!** pas de blagues! **6.** *F* **to stand there like a stuffed monkey,** rester planté là **7.** *F* **right monkey!** à bon entendeur, salut! **8.** *P* habitude *f* de la drogue/la guêpe/la guenon; **to get the monkey off,** désintoxiquer/chasser la guenon; **to have a monkey on one's back** (*a*) être drogué*/camé (*b*) avoir une dent contre qn **9.** *F* **monkey jacket,** veste courte/spencer *m*/rase-pet *m* **10.** *F* **monkey suit,** uniforme *m* de gala; **to be in one's monkey-suit,** être sur son trente-et-un **11.** *Austr O F* mouton *m*/bêlant *m* **12.** *Austr V* sexe de la femme*/chatte *f*/chagatte *f*. (*See* **balls**[1] **4**; **grease 2**)

monkey about, around ['mʌŋkiə'baut, ə'raund] *F* **to monkey about with s.o./sth,** tripoter/tripatouiller qn/qch.

monniker ['mɔnikər] *n P* = **moniker.**

Montezuma [mɔnti'zymə] *n NAm F* **Montezuma's revenge,** diarrhée*/chiasse *f*/courante *f*.

monthlies ['mʌnθliz] *npl F* **the monthlies,** les règles*; **to have the monthlies,** avoir ses affaires *fpl*/ses trucs *mpl*.

moo [muː] *n P* **1. she's a (right old) moo,** c'est une belle vache; **silly (old) moo!** espèce de vieille bique!/vieille peau de vache! **2.** = **moola(h).**

moocah ['muːkaɪ, 'muːkə] *n P* (*drugs*) marijuana*/Marie-Jeanne *f*.

mooch [muːtʃ] *vtr&i P* **1.** mendier*/faire la manche **2.** voler*/chouraver **3. to mooch about/around,** flâner/traîner ses lattes *fpl*/traîner ses guêtres *fpl*; glander **4.** emprunter*/taper/sonner.

moocher ['muːtʃər] *n P* **1.** mendiant*/mendigot *m* **2.** voleur*/chapardeur *m* **3.** baguenaudeur *m*/traîne-savates *m*/glandeur *m* **4.** tapeur *m*/torpilleur *m*.

moo-cow ['muːkau] *n* **1.** *F* (*child's word*) vache *f*/meu-meu *f* **2.** *P* = **cow 1.**

moody ['muːdi] **I** *n P* flatterie *f*/boniment *m*/brosse *f à reluire;* **cut out the moody!** assez de baratin!/suffit les boniments! **II** *a P* (*i*) dangereux/épineux/risqué (*ii*) faux/suspect/véreux; **a moody blag,** un braquage dangereux/une sale affaire; **moody licence,** faux permis/permis maquillé.

moola(h) ['muːlaɪ, 'muːlə] *n P* argent*/pognon *m*/fric *m*/flouse *m*.

moon[1] [muːn] *n* **1.** *P* **a moon,** un mois de prison/un marqué **2.** *F* **over the moon!** au septième ciel/aux nues. (*See* **blue**[1] **I 6**; **shoot**[2] **9**)

moon[2] [muːn] *vi NAm P* montrer ses fesses*/son cul à qn; faire voir la lune en plein jour.

moon about, around ['muːnə'baut, ə'raund] *vi F* lambiner/musarder/cueillir les pâquerettes.

moonie [muːni] *n F* = **moony II.**

moonlight ['muːnlait] *vi F* faire du travail (au) noir/travailler au noir.

moonlighter ['muːnlaitər] *n F* qn qui travaille au noir/travailleur au noir; **he's a moonlighter,** il fait du noir.

moonshine ['muːnʃain] *n F* **1.** *esp NAm* alcool* illicitement distillé ou en contrebande/gnôle *f* sous les fagots **2.** bêtises*/foutaises *fpl*.

moony ['muːni] **I** *a P* un peu fou*/toqué/jeté/touché **II** *n F* (*after cult of Reverend Moon*) mooniste *mf*.

moosh [muʃ] *n P* **1.** = **mush II 1, 2 2.** *Austr* (mauvaise) nourriture*/rata *m*/ragougnasse *f*.

mooters ['muːtəz] *npl P* = **muggles 3.**

mop [mɔp] *n F* **that's the way the mop flops,** c'est comme ça que tombent les dés; c'est ainsi que la roue tourne; c'est comme ça et pas autrement. (*See* **cookie 1**; **onion 1**)

mopping ['mɔpiŋ] *n F* (*police, etc*) **mopping-up operations,** (opération *f* de) nettoyage *m*; opération coup de poing.

mop up ['mɔp'ʌp] *vtr* **1.** *F* exterminer/nettoyer/liquider **2.** *P* aplatir/rouler/estamper (qn).

MOR ['em'ou'ɑr] *abbr F* (= *middle of the road (music)*) musique pépère/douce/pas trop braillante.

moreish ['mɔːriʃ] *a F* **these sweets are very moreish,** ces bonbons ont un goût de revenez-y.

morf [mɔːf] *n P* (*drugs*) (= *morphine*) morphine*/morph *f*.

moron ['mɔːrɔn] *n P* individu bête*/crétin *m*; **you moron!** petit trouduc!/espèce d'enculé!

mosey along ['mouziə'lɔŋ] *vi F* aller son petit bonhomme de chemin/aller mollo.

mosey off ['mouzi'ɔf] *vi F* s'enfuir*/décamper/se barrer.

mosquito [mɔs'kitou] *n P* (*drugs*) **mosquito bite,** piqûre* (*esp* de morphine)/fixe *m*/shoot *m*.

moss [mɔs] *n P* cheveux*/crins *mpl*/cresson *m*/gazon *m*.

mossback ['mɔsbæk] *n NAm P* paysan*/péquenot *m*/cul-terreux *m*.

mossie ['mɔzi] *n Austr F* moustique *m*.

most(est) ['moust(est)] *n F* **the most(est),** le super/l'archi (bien)/le plus mieux; **he's the most,** il est super/sensass; **she's got the mostest,** elle est vachement bien roulée.

mota ['moutɑɪ, 'moutə] *n P* (*drugs*) marijuana* de haute qualité.

mote [mout] *vi Austr F* filer à toute allure/brûler le pavé/décaniller.

mother ['mʌðər] *n* **1.** *F* **shall I be mother?** je vous sers? **2.** *P* (*RS* = *gin*) **mother's ruin,** gin *m* **3.** *P* a **(father and) mother of a row,** un sacré barouf/un foin de tous les diables **4.** *V* = **motherfucker.**

motherfucker ['mʌðəfʌkər] *n NAm VV* **1.** (belle) saloperie/(espèce de) con *m*/empaffé *m*/fumier *m*/belle ordure; **this motherfucker!** cette saloperie! **2.** con *m*/connard *m*/enculé *m* (de sa mère)/enfouaré *m*; **you motherfuckers!** bande d'enculés! **3.** (*jocular term of address*) **listen, (you) motherfucker!** écoute, mon con!

motherfucking ['mʌðəfʌkiŋ] *a NAm VV* **1.** charognard/pourri/saligaud/chiasseux **2.** emmerdant/chiant (comme la pluie).

mother-in-law ['mʌðərinlɔː] *n F* mélange *m* de *stout* (bière brune forte) et de *bitter* (bière amère); panaché *m* nègre.

motor [moutər] *n F* voiture*/bagnole *f*/tire *f*/caisse *f*.

motser, motza ['mɔtsə(r)] *n Austr P* (*gambling*) le gros lot.

moula ['muɪlɑɪ, 'muɪlə] *n P* = **moola(h).**

mouldy ['mouldi] *a F* moche(ton)/toc(ard)/tarte/tartignol(l)e; **mouldy old rubbish,** du toc/de la came.

mountain ['mauntin] *n F* **1. to make a mountain out of a molehill,** faire d'un œuf un bœuf/se noyer dans un verre d'eau/faire d'une merde de chien un pain de sucre **2. a mountain of a man,** un homme* fort/bien baraqué; une armoire à glace **3. a mountain of work,** un tas de travail*; un boulot du diable.

mounties ['mauntiz] *npl P* **to join the mounties,** faire l'amour*/grimper/pousser sa pointe/tremper le goupillon.

mourning ['mɔːniŋ] *n F* **to have one's (finger-)nails in mourning,** avoir les ongles sales/en deuil.

mouse [maus] *n F* **1.** (*catchphrase*) **are you a man or a mouse?** t'en as ou t'en as pas? **2.** fille* *ou* jeune femme* séduisante/gisquette *f*/gosseline *f*. (*See* **cat 8**; **Mickey Mouse**; **rat¹ 10**)

mouth [mauθ] *n* **1.** *F* **to have a big mouth**, être une grande gueule/être fort en gueule. (*See* **big I 2**; **blow off II**; **loudmouth**; **shoot off 2**) **2.** *F* **to be down in the mouth**, avoir le cafard/être abattu/être défrisé/ être au 36ème dessous **3.** *P* indicateur*/indic *m*/balance *f*. (*See* **horse¹ 2**)

mouthful ['mauθful] *n F* **1. you've said a mouthful!** tu l'as dit bouffi! **2. to give s.o. a mouthful**, en dire à qn de toutes les couleurs/traiter qn de noms d'oiseaux.

mouth off ['mauð'ɔf] *vi F* **1. to mouth off at s.o.** = **to give s.o. a mouthful** (**mouthful 2**) **2.** *NAm* (*i*) parler/l'ouvrir (*ii*) bavasser/tailler une bavette.

mouth on ['mauð'ɔn] *vi F* discutailler/pinailler.

mouthpiece ['mauθpiːs] *n* **1.** *F* porte-parole *m* **2.** *P* avocat*/ débardot *m*/bavard *m*/babillard *m*/ débarbotteur *m*.

move¹ [muːv] *n F* **1. to get a move on**, se dépêcher*/se magner; **get a move on!** grouille-toi! **2. to be up to every move**, connaître la musique/la connaître dans les coins.

move² [muːv] *vtr O P* voler*/lever/ piquer.

mover ['muːvər] *n P* femme* à la démarche séduisante; **she's a lovely mover**, c'est une belle mécanique.

movie ['muːvi] *n esp NAm F* film *m*; **the movies**, le cinéma; **to go to the movies**, aller au cinoche/se payer une toile.

mozz [mɔz] *n Austr F* **to put the mozz on s.o./sth** (*i*) jeter un sort à qn/qch; ensorceler qn/qch (*ii*) porter la poisse à qn/qch.

much [mʌtʃ] *adv F* **1. that's a bit much!** (*i*) c'est un peu beaucoup/ faut pas pousser (mémère dans les orties)!/c'est un peu fort de café!

(*ii*) c'est le comble!/c'est le bouquet!/faut pas charrier! **2. it's much of a muchness**, c'est kif-kif (bourricot)/c'est blanc bonnet et bonnet blanc/c'est jus vert et verjus/c'est du pareil au même.

muck [mʌk] *n P* **1. to make a muck of sth**, abîmer*/gâcher/ bousiller qch **2. it's a load of muck** (*a*) c'est un tas de conneries (*b*) c'est de la saleté*/de la cochonnerie/de la rocambouille **3. to land/to drop s.o. in the muck**, mettre qn dans le pétrin/dans la mouscaille/dans la merde **4. common as muck** = **common as mud** (**mud 6** (*b*)) **5. dog muck**, crotte *f* de chien/sentinelle *f* **6.** confusion *f*/ pagaille *f* **7. Lord Muck**, Monsieur J'en-fous-plein-la-vue; **she thinks she's Lady Muck**, elle ne se prend pas pour de la crotte/de la merde. (*See* **brass II 1**; **high-muck-a-muck**)

muck about, around ['mʌkə'baut, ə'raund] *vtr&i* **1.** *F* traîner/lambiner/bricoler **2.** *F* flâner/flânocher/traîner ses lattes/ glandouiller **3.** *F* **to muck s.o. about**, faire tourner qn en bourrique **4.** *P* **to muck about with s.o.**, peloter qn; **stop mucking around, will you?** (*i*) bas les pattes!/jeux de mains, jeux de vilains! (*ii*) arrête de déconner!/fais pas le con!

mucker ['mʌkər] *n P* **1.** qn qui est sale*/crasseux **2.** ami*/copain *m*/ pote *m*/aminche *m* **3.** rustre *m*/ grossier personnage **4.** chute *f*/ culbute *f*/bûche *f*; **to come a mucker**, tomber*/ramasser un billet de parterre/se viander. (*See* **cropper**)

muck in ['mʌk'in] *vi F* **1. to muck in with s.o.**, chambrer avec qn/faire gourbi ensemble **2. to muck in together** (*a*) partager/fader/ décarpiller (*b*) s'actionner/ s'escrimer/se dépatouiller ensemble.

muck-raker ['mʌkreikər] *n F* (*journ*) fouille-merde *m*.

muck up [ˈmʌkˈʌp] *vtr F* **1.** emberlificoter **2.** abîmer*/gâcher/ bousiller/cochonner; **that's mucked up all our plans,** ça fout tout en l'air/ça gâche tout.

mucky [ˈmʌki] *a F* **1.** a mucky eater, qn qui mange comme un cochon **2. a mucky pup,** un enfant qui fait des saletés/qui se tient mal; **you mucky (little) pup!** petit goret!/petit cochon!

mud [mʌd] *n* **1.** *F* **here's mud in your eye!** à votre santé!/à la bonne vôtre! **2.** *P* (*drugs*) (*i*) opium* brut (*ii*) opium*/noir *m*/chandoo *m*. (*See* **green I 1**) **3.** *NAm P* café*/ petit noir/jus *m* (de chaussette)/ caoua *m* **4.** *NAm P* pudding *m* au chocolat **5.** *NAm P* signes télégraphiques brouillés/brouillage *m* **6.** *F* **common as mud** (*a*) du tout-venant/chemin battu (*b*) qui traîne partout/dans les ornières; qui sent le pavé **7.** *F* cancan *m*/ déblatérage *m*/débinage *m*; **to throw/to sling mud at s.o.,** éclabousser qn/traîner qn dans la boue **8.** *F* **his name is mud,** sa réputation est moins que rien. (*See* **clear I**; **stick-in-the-mud**)

muddler [ˈmʌdlər] *n F* brouillon *m*/pagailleur *m*.

mudslinger [ˈmʌdsliŋər] *n F* calomniateur *m*/médisant *m*/ débineur *m*/casseur *m* de sucre.

mudslinging [ˈmʌdsliŋiŋ] *n F* attaque calomnieuse/médisance *f*/ bêche *f*.

muff¹ [mʌf] *n* **1.** *F* échec*/loupage *m*/coup raté **2.** *V* sexe de la femme*/barbu *m*/chatte *f*/chagatte *f*.

muff² [mʌf] *vtr&i* **1.** *F* faire une erreur/commettre une faute/louper; **I muffed it,** j'ai raté mon coup/je l'ai loupé **2.** *F* bousiller/bâcler/ rater/gâcher **3.** *V* (*cunnilingus*) faire minette/brouter (le cresson). (*See* **pearl-dive**)

muff-diver [ˈmʌfdaivər] *n V* (*cun-*

nilingus) buveur *m* de bénitier/ lécheur *m* de minette. (*See* **pearl-diver**)

mug¹ [mʌg] *n* **1.** *P* visage*/fiole *f*; **ugly mug,** gueule *f* d'empeigne; **get your ugly mug out of here!** tire ta sale gueule d'ici! **mug shot,** photo d'un criminel prise par la police *ou* en prison; cliché *m* anthropométrique; **mug and dabs,** photo et empreintes digitales; **to have one's mug and dabs taken,** passer au pied et au sommier **2.** *F* dupe *f*/cavé *m*/bonnard *m*/jobard *m*/vache *f* à lait; **mugs wanted,** on cherche des poires; **to be a mug,** être poire; **to be the mug,** être le couillon/l'avoir dans le baigneur; **what sort of a mug do you take me for?** tu me prends pour un con? **it's a mug's game,** c'est un piège à cons/c'est un attrape-couillon; **mug's tax,** impôt *m* sur le revenu/l'impôt des poires. (*See* **thunder-mug**)

mug² [mʌg] *vtr F* attaquer* (les passants) (à main armée)/agresser/ tabasser/voler*.

mugger [ˈmʌgər] *n F* **1.** voleur* (à main armée)/agresseur *m*/cogneur *m* **2.** *NAm* acteur *m* qui grimace pour faire rire; farineux *m*.

mugging [ˈmʌgiŋ] *n F* attaque *f* (de passants) (à main armée)/agression.

muggins [ˈmʌginz] *n P* **1.** individu bête*/gourde *f*/cruche *f*/ balourd *m* **2.** (*oneself*) **muggins, here, had to do it,** c'est encore ma pomme/mézigue qui a dû le faire; c'est encore ma pomme qui s'est fait avoir/qui l'a eu dans le dos.

muggles [ˈmʌglz] *n P* (*drugs*) **1.** (*a*) marijuana* (*b*) cigarette* de marijuana/kif *m*/bomb *f* **2.** habitué(e) de la marijuana* **3.** haschisch*/hasch *m*/shit *m*/merde *f*.

mug up [ˈmʌgˈʌp] *vi F* bûcher/ piocher/potasser.

muh-fuh ['mǝfǝ] *n NAm P* = motherfucker.

mularky [mǝ'lɑːki] *n F* = malark(e)y.

mulberry-bush ['mʌlbǝribuʃ] *n F* **to go (all) round the mulberry-bush,** tourner en rond/tourner autour du pot.

mule [mjuːl] *n P (drugs)* passeur *m* fourmi/mule *f* (à came).

mulga ['mʌlgǝ] *n Austr F* cambrousse *f*; **the mulga wire,** le téléphone arabe.

mullarky [mǝ'lɑːki] *n F* = malark(e)y.

mullet ['mʌlit] *n Austr F* **like a stunned mullet,** ahuri/médusé/baba.

mulligans ['mʌligǝnz] *npl Austr P* cartes* à jouer/brèmes *fpl*/cartons *mpl*.

mull over ['mʌl'ouvǝr] *vtr F* ruminer/ressasser/gamberger.

mum [mʌm] **I** *a F* **to keep mum,** se taire*/ne pas moufter/la boucler/ l'écraser; **mum's the word!** motus et bouche cousue! **II** *n esp Austr P* **to have mum nature,** avoir ses règles*/ses ours.

mump [mʌmp] *vtr P* mendier*/faire la manche/aller à la mangave.

murder¹ ['mǝːdǝr] *n F* **1.** **it's (sheer) murder in the rush-hour,** c'est (absolument) épouvantable/un cauchemar aux heures de pointe **2. to get away with murder,** s'en tirer à bon compte/tirer les marrons du feu; **he could get away with murder,** on lui donnerait le bon Dieu sans confession. *(See blue¹ I 2)*

murder² ['mǝːdǝr] *vtr* **1.** *P* battre* (qn) comme plâtre/tabasser (qn); **I'll murder you if you don't shut up!** je vais te bousiller, si tu la boucles pas! **2.** *F* massacrer/écorcher/ estropier (un morceau de musique, etc) **3.** *F* **I could murder a drink/a fag,** je meurs de soif/j'ai une envie folle de fumer une clope.

musak ['mjuːzæk] *n F* = muzak.

muscle-head ['mʌslhed] *n F* individu bête*/bûche *f*/truffe *f*.

muscle in ['mʌsl'in] *vi F* **1.** se pousser/jouer des coudes **2.** **he muscled his way in,** il s'est introduit de force/il a forcé la porte **3. to muscle in on a conversation,** s'injecter dans une conversation.

muscle-man ['mʌslmæn] *n F* homme fort*/malabar *m*/costaud *m*/homme* à pogne.

mush [mʌʃ] **I** *n F* **1.** propos *mpl* bêtes*/conneries *fpl* **2.** flatterie *f* **3.** cafouillage *m* **4.** amourette *f* **II** *n P* **1.** *(a)* visage*/frime *f* *(b)* bouche*/goule *f* **2.** *(a)* individu*/ type *m*/mec *m*; **listen, mush!** écoute, petit mec! *(b)* corniaud *m*/ cornichon *m*/con *m*/trouduc *m* **3.** parapluie*/pébroc *m*/riflard *m*.

mushy ['mʌʃi] *a F* à l'eau de rose/à la guimauve/gnan-gnan.

music ['mjuːzik] *n F* **to face the music** *(a)* tenir le coup/payer d'audace *(b)* braver l'orage/avaler la pilule; **he was left to face the music,** c'est lui qui a payé les pots cassés.

mustard ['mʌstǝd] *a F* capable/ malin/dégourdi.

mutah [mʌtǝ, mjuːtaɪ] *n P (drugs)* cannabis*.

mutt [mʌt] *n P* **1. poor mutt!** le pauvre/pauv' mec!/pauv' con! **2.** chien* (bâtard)/clébard *m*/clebs *m*/ cabot *m* **3.** *(RS = deaf)* **Mutt'n Jeff,** sourd*/dur de la feuille.

mutton ['mʌtn] *n F* **mutton dressed (up) as lamb,** vieux tableau/vieille poupée.

mutton-fancier ['mʌtnfænsiǝr] *n P* homosexuel*/enviandé *m*.

muttonhead ['mʌtnhed] *n F* individu bête*/andouille *f*/tête *f* de nœud.

muvver ['mʌvǝr] *n F* mère*/dabesse *f*/vieille *f*.

muzak ['mjuːzæk] *n F* (*pej*) musique *f* de fond/facile à écouter/musiquette *f*.

muzzle[1] ['muzl] *n P* **1.** chance*/ veine *f*/pot *m*/fion *m* **2.** visage*/ museau *m*/frimousse *f*/carafe *f*.

muzzle[2] ['mʌzl] *vtr P* **to muzzle s.o.**, gifler/torgnoler qn; foutre une tarte dans la gueule à qn.

muzzy ['mʌzi] *a F* légèrement ivre*/ paf/éméché.

mystery ['mist(ə)ri] *n P* femme* inconnue dans le pays; **a mystery in the manor,** une nouvelle venue dans le coin.

myxo ['miksou] *n Austr F* (*abbr* = *myxomatosis*) myxomatose *f*/myxo *f*.

N

nab¹ [næb] *n P* (*rare*) agent* de police/flic *m*.

nab² [næb] *vtr P* **1.** (*a*) arrêter*/pincer/agrafer/cueillir (qn); **the police nabbed the lot of them**, la police les a tous ratissés/cueillis/embarqués; **to get nabbed**, se faire pincer/se faire faire (*b*) prendre (qn) sur le fait/la main dans le sac **2.** (*a*) voler*/chiper/chaparder/chouraver (qch) (*b*) saisir/escamoter (qch).

nadgers ['nædʒəz] *npl P* (*not common*) **to put the nadgers on s.o.**, donner la malchance* à qn/foutre la poisse à qn; **to give s.o. the nadgers**, ennuyer qn/casser les pieds à qn/courir sur le haricot à qn/scier le dos à qn.

naff [næf] *a P* vieux jeu/ringard; tocard/moche; **that's a bit naff**, c'est du toc/de la came.

naff off ['næf'ɔf] *vi P* (*euph for* **fuck off!**) **naff off!** tire-toi!/taille-toi!/casse-toi!/fous le camp!

nag [næg] *n F* cheval*/bidet *m*/canasson *m*; **to follow the nags** = **to follow the gee-gees** (**gee-gee 2**).

nagsbody ['nægzbɔdi] *n P* rouspéteur *m*/rouscailleur *m*.

nail¹ [neil] *n* **1.** *F* **to pay (cash) on the nail**, payer cash/payer recta/payer rubis sur l'ongle **2.** *F* **to hit the nail on the head**, mettre le doigt dessus/taper dans le mille/tomber juste **3.** *P* (*drugs*) aiguille *f* hypodermique/hypo *m*. (*See* **coffin 2; door-nail; tooth 6**)

nail² [neil] *vtr P* **1.** filer un coup* à (qn)/frapper **2.** (*a*) intercepter

(qn) (*b*) arrêter*/agrafer (qn); **I got nailed**, je me suis fait pincer **3.** demander un prix exorbitant à (qn)/fusiller (qn)/extorquer de l'argent* à (qn) **4.** faire l'amour* avec (qn)/aiguiller (qn). (*See* **hammer¹ 4**)

nailer ['neilər] *n A F as m*/épée *f*/crack *m*.

'Nam, Nam [nɑːm] *n NAm P* Vietnam.

namby-pamby ['næmbi'pæmbi] *F* **I** *n* chiffe molle **II** *a* gnangnan/à l'eau de rose.

name¹ [neim] *n F* **1. to call s.o. names**, injurier* qn/traiter qn de tous les noms **2. that's the name of the game** (*i*) c'est la vie! (*ii*) c'est ça la grande attraction **3. not a penny to one's name**, sans le sou/sans un/pas un radis **4. what in the name of God/of Heaven are you doing?** mais nom d'un petit bonhomme/nom d'un chien/sacré nom d'une pipe/nom de Dieu, qu'est-ce que tu fais? (*See* **pack-drill; what's-(h)er-name; what's-(h)is-name; what's-its-name**)

name² [neim] *vtr F* **you name it, he's got it!** il a tout ce que tu peux imaginer; **you name it, he's done it**, tout ce que tu peux imaginer, il l'a fait.

name-drop ['neimdrɔp] *vi F* truffer sa conversation de noms de gens connus/passer son temps à faire mention des célébrités qu'on connaît.

name-dropper ['neimdrɔpər] *n F* qn qui passe son temps à faire mention des gens connus qu'il connaît.

name-dropping ['neimdrɔpiŋ] *n* *F* **she's always name-dropping**, à l'entendre on dirait qu'elle connaît le monde entier.

nana ['nɑɪnə] *n* **1.** *P* **he's a right nana!** c'est un vrai gugusse! **to feel a right/a proper nana**, se sentir tout bête*; **you silly great nana!** espèce de grande gourde!/espèce de nouille! **2.** *F* ['nænə] = **nanna.**

nance [næns], **nancy(-boy)** ['nænsi(bɔi)] *n* *P* **1.** homosexuel* passif/empaffé *m*/chochotte *f*/joconde *f*/chouquette *f*; **he's a bit of a nancy-boy**, il fait très tapette/il est un peu pédé sur les bords **2.** homme* efféminé/femmelette *f*/mauviette *f*.

nanna ['nænə] *n* *F* grand-mère/mémé *f*.

nap[1] [næp] *n* *F* **to go nap on sth**, être sûr et certain de qch/en mettre sa main au feu/foutre son billet.

nap[2] [næp] *vi* *F* **to be caught napping** (*a*) être pris au dépourvu (*b*) être pris en faute.

napper ['næpər] *n* *P* tête*/caboche *f*.

narc(o) ['nɑɪk(ou)] *n* *NAm* *P* agent *m* de la Brigade fédérale des Stupéfiants/des Stups.

nark[1] [nɑɪk] *n* *P* **1.** qn qui sert de piège/coqueur *m* **2.** indicateur* de police/indic *m*/bordille *m*/mouchard *m*. (*See* **copper 1**) **3.** = **narc(o).**

nark[2] [nɑɪk] *vtr* *P* **1.** mettre en colère/braquer/mettre en rogne/prendre à rebrousse-poil; **it really narks me**, ça me fout en rogne/ça me met en pétard/ça me met en boule **2.** **to get narked**, se faire arrêter* / agrafer / pincer **3.** moucharder/en croquer/en manger **4.** **nark it!** écrase!/la ferme!/fous-moi la paix!

narky ['nɑɪki] *a* *P* **1.** en colère*/en

rogne/de mauvais poil **2.** = **sarky.**

nasties ['nɑɪstiz] *npl* *P* (*drugs*) drogues *fpl*/came *f*/dope *m*/stups *mpl*/stuff *m*.

nasty ['nɑɪsti] *n* *F* **video nasty**, vidéo *m* d'épouvante (souvent porno-graphique).

natch! [nætʃ] *excl* *P* naturellement!/naturliche!

natter[1] ['nætər] *n* *F* baratinage *m*/jactage *m*/tapette *f*; **to have a nat-ter**, tailler une bavette.

natter[2] ['nætər] *vi* *F* bavarder*/jacter/jacasser/tailler une bavette.

natty ['næti] *a* *F* chic/coquet/pimpant; **a natty little outfit**, un beau petit ensemble/costard.

natural ['nætʃrəl] *n* *F* **1.** **never/not in all my natural**, jamais de la vie **2.** **a natural**, qui est né pour ça/tout trouvé pour . . . /qui va comme un gant.

naughty ['nɔɪti] *n* *Austr* *P* coït*/partie *f* de jambes en l'air; **to go naughty/to do the naughty**, faire l'amour* avec (qn)/godiller avec (qn).

nbg, NBG ['en'biɪ'dʒiɪ] *abbr* *P* (= *no bloody good*) bon à rien*/bon à nib.

nearly ['niəli] *adv* *F* **nearly there:** *see* **bingo 89.**

neat [niɪt] *a* *P* formid(able)/chouette/super; **that's real neat!** c'est extra/sensass/super!

neb(bish) ['neb(iʃ)] *a* *NAm* *P* nullard *m*; nouille *f*/cloche *f*/péteux *m*.

necessary ['nesəsəri] *n* *F* **the nec-essary**, argent*/galette *f*/beurre *m*/blé *m*; **to do the necessary**, payer* la note/casquer; **have you got the necessary?** t'as le fric?

neck[1] [nek] *n* *F* **1.** **to get it in the neck**, écoper/en avoir pour son compte/trinquer; **he got it in the neck for that**, il en a pris pour son grade **2.** **you've got a neck!** quel toupet!/quel culot! **3. to stick one's neck out**, prendre des risques/ se mouiller/se jeter à l'eau **4. it's neck or nothing**, il faut risquer/ jouer le tout pour le tout **5. to be up to one's neck in work**, être débordé de travail*/en avoir jusque-là **6. to be in sth up to one's neck**, être submergé/y être jusqu'au cou **7.** *(a)* **to break one's neck to do sth**, se décarcasser/se couper en quatre pour faire qch *(b)* **I'll break your neck if you touch it!** si tu y touches, je te casse la tête/ je te fais une tête au carré **8. to breathe down/to be on s.o.'s neck**, être sur le dos de qn/être aux trousses de qn; **to get off s.o.'s neck**, ficher/foutre la paix à qn **9. to talk through the back of one's neck**, dire des bêtises*/débloquer. *(See* **dead I 5; deadneck; leatherneck; pain; roughneck; rubberneck**[1]; **stiffneck; wood 3**)

neck[2] [nek] *vi* F s'embrasser/se bécoter; se peloter; rouler une pelle; **to neck with s.o.**, peloter qn. *(See* **rubberneck**[2])

necking ['nekiŋ] *n* F bécotage *m*/ pelotage *m*; **to get down to some serious necking**, faire un pelotage poussé.

necktie ['nektai] *n NAm* F corde *f* du gibet/cravate *f*; **to throw a necktie party**, lyncher/pendre/béquiller.

needful ['niːdful] *n* F **the needful** = the necessary (**necessary**).

needle[1] ['niːdl] *n P* **1.** *(a)* **to give s.o. the needle** *(i)* agacer/enquiquiner qn *(ii)* aiguillonner/inciter qn *(iii)* harceler qn *(iv)* taquiner qn; **he really gives me the needle**, il me tape sur le système/j'en ai soupé de lui; il arrête pas de me charrier *(b)* **to have the (dead) needle for s.o.**, avoir une (sacrée) dent contre qn *(c)* **to get/to cop the needle**, se mettre en colère*/piquer une crise; **I really got the needle**, ça m'a vraiment foutu en rogne **2. to be on the needle** *(i)* être de la piquouse/

tenir à la poussette *(ii)* être drogué*/camé/toxico **3.** *(RS = gin)* **needle and pin**, gin *m*. *(See* **pins 2; piss**[2] **2**)

needle[2] ['niːdl] *vtr* **1.** F *(a)* agacer/asticoter/enquiquiner (qn); **to be needled**, être de mauvais poil *(b)* aiguillonner/inciter/tanner *(c)* harceler/bassiner; **to needle s.o. into doing sth**, pomper l'air à qn jusqu'à ce qu'il fasse qch/casser les pieds à qn pour qu'il fasse qch *(d)* taquiner/canuler/chiner **2.** P inoculer/vacciner **3.** P extirper des renseignements* de (qn)/pomper (qn).

needle(-)candy ['niːdlkændi] *n P (drugs)* stupéfiant pris par injection/liqueur *f* de shooteuse **2.** héroïne*/cheval *m*/jus *m*.

nellie, Nellie, nelly, Nelly ['neli] *n* **1.** P homosexuel*/tante *f*/ tata *f*/persilleuse *f* **2.** F **not on your nellie!** jamais de la vie!/rien à faire!/tu peux toujours courir!/(il y a) pas de danger!

Nelson ['nelsən] *Prn* F **Nelson's blood**, rhum *m*. *(See* **tear**[1] **2**)

nerd [nəːd] *n P* = **nurd**.

nerve [nəːv] *n* F **1. to get on s.o.'s nerves**, courir/taper sur le système à qn; courir sur le haricot à qn **2. you've got a nerve!** quel culot!/quel toupet! **what a nerve you've got!** t'as un sacré toupet! **I like your nerve!** t'es culotté/gonflé! **that takes a lot of nerve**, faut être gonflé! **3. to have the nerve to do sth**, avoir de l'audace/du ventre/du poil au cul pour faire qch. *(See* **bundle 3**)

nervy ['nəːvi] *a* F **1.** énervé; **he's terribly nervy**, il a les nerfs en boule/à fleur de peau **2.** *esp NAm* culotté/gonflé.

nest-egg ['nesteg] *n* F économies *fpl*/argent* mis de côté; **to have a nice little nest-egg (tucked away)**, avoir un bas de laine bien garni.

never ['nevər] *adv* F **1. well I never!** pas possible!/ça par exemple!/je n'en reviens pas! **2. never been kissed:** see **bingo 16 3.** (RS = beer) **never fear,** bière f.

never-never ['nevər'nevər] n F **to buy sth on the never-never,** acheter qch à crédit/à croume/à l'œil.

neves [niːvz], **nevis** ['nevis] n O P (backslang = seven) sept.

new [njuː] a F **1.** (employee, politician, etc) **new boy,** novice m/bleu m **2. that's a new one on me!** ça vient de sortir/je ne suis pas au courant! **3. what's new?** quoi de neuf?

Newfie ['njuːfi] Prn NAm F (a) Terre-neuvien(ne) m(f) (b) Terre-Neuve f.

news-hawk ['njuːzhɔːk], **news-hound** ['njuːzhaund] n F (pej) journaliste mf/reporter m/chasseur m de copie.

newt [njuːt] n F **tight/pissed as a newt,** ivre* mort/complètement paf/beurré comme un petit lu/bit(t)uré.

newy ['njuːi] n Austr F **1.** novice m/bleu m **2.** qch de nouveau/nouveauté f.

next [nekst] adv P **1. to get next to s.o.,** se mettre bien avec qn/se mettre dans les petits papiers de qn **2. next off,** puis/après/alors.

Niagaras ['naiæg(ə)rəz] npl P (RS = Niagara Falls = balls) testicules*/balloches fpl/couilles fpl.

nibble ['nibl] n P **to have a nibble,** faire l'amour*/faire un carton.

nibs, Nibs [nibz] n F (a) gros bonnet/grosse légume/milord m (b) cézig(ue) m; **his nibs,** son altesse.

nice [nais] F **I** a (iron) **nice work!** félicitations!/bravo!/chapeau! **II** adv **1. nice and handy,** bien commode; **nice and comfy,** bien à l'aise/tout bien **2. nice as pie,** très poli/trop poli pour être honnête/gentil comme un cœur.

nick¹ [nik] n **1.** P (a) prison*/bloc m/taule f; **he's in the nick,** il est en taule/au violon (b) commissariat m de police/le quart; **they took him down the nick,** ils l'ont emmené au quart **2. P in good nick** (i) en bon état/impec; aux petits oignons (ii) en forme/d'attaque; **he's in quite good nick for a sixty-year old,** il est encore vert pour un vieux de soixante berges **3.** F **Old Nick,** le diable/le Malin/le barbet.

nick² [nik] vtr P **1.** voler*/faucher/chiper; **s.o.'s nicked my wallet,** on m'a piqué mon portefeuille **2.** arrêter*/agrafer/cravater/épingler; **to get nicked,** se faire pincer; **the cops nicked him for that bank job,** les flics l'ont mis en cabane pour ce coup de la banque **3.** faire payer*/extorquer/étriller; **you were nicked,** tu t'es fait avoir **4.** Austr s'enfuir*/se calter/se trisser; **he nicked off,** il a mis les voiles/les bouts.

nickel ['nikl] n NAm **1.** F pièce f de cinq cents; **it's not worth a nickel,** ça ne vaut pas tripette **2.** P (drugs) **nickel bag,** quantité de drogues qui vaut cinq dollars/dose f à cinq dollars.

nicker ['nikər] n P **1.** (billet* ou pièce d')une livre sterling; **fifty nicker,** cinquante balles/demi-livre f/demi-jambe f **2.** mégot*/clope m.

niff¹ [nif] n P **1.** (a) puanteur f/(s)chlingage m (b) odeur f/effluve m; **to catch a niff of perfume,** prendre une bouffée de parfum **2.** reniflette f; **take a niff at that,** renifle-moi ça.

niff² [nif] vi P puer/(s)chlinguer/cocoter.

niffy ['nifi] a P = **nifty 3.**

nifty ['nifti] a **1.** F beau*/pimpant/bath/choucard **2.** P malin*/débrouillard/dégourdi; **a nifty little motor,** un beau petit bolide; **it's a nifty idea,** c'est génial/c'est super/c'est une idée du tonnerre **3.** P qui sent* mauvais/puant.

nig [nig] n P (pej) = **nigger 1.**

nigger ['nigər] *n P* (*pej*) **1.** nègre*/bougnoul(e) *m*/bamboula *m* **2. there's a nigger in the woodpile,** il y a anguille sous roche; **that's the nigger in the woodpile,** voilà le fin mot de l'histoire **3. to work like a nigger,** travailler* comme un nègre/comme une brute/comme une bête; pisser du sang/suer sang et eau. (*See* **minstrel**)

nigger-driver ['nigədraivər] *n P* négrier *m*/garde-chiourme *m.*

nigger-lover ['nigəlʌvər] *n NAm P* (*pej*) anti-ségrégationiste *mf*/protecteur *m* du noir.

niggly ['nigli] *a F* de mauvaise humeur/ronchonnard.

night-bird ['naitbəɪd] *n F* = **fly-by-night II 3.**

night hawk ['nait'hɔɪk] *n F* = **night owl.**

nightie ['naiti] *n F* = **nighty.**

night-night! ['naitnait] *excl F* = **nighty-night!**

night owl ['nait'aul] *n F* couche-tard *mf*/oiseau *m* de nuit.

nights [naits] *npl F* **to do/to work nights,** être de nuit/faire les trois huits/être nuitard.

nightspot ['naitspɔt] *n F* night-club *m*/boîte *f* (de nuit).

nighty ['naiti] *n F* (= *night-dress*) chemise *f*/liquette *f* de nuit.

nighty-night! ['naiti'nait] *excl F* bonne nuit!/'soir!

nignog ['nignɔg] *n P* **1.** individu bête*/niguedouille *mf*; **you silly nignog!** espèce de nouille! **2.** (*pej*) Noir(e)*/nègre *mf*/bougnoul(e) *mf.*

nineteen ['naintiɪn] *n F* **to talk nineteen to the dozen** (*i*) parler* vite/faire couler le crachoir (*ii*) bavarder*/bavasser/jaser comme une pie borgne.

nineteenth ['naintiɪnθ] *a F* (*hum*) **the nineteenth hole,** le bar d'un club de golf.

nine-to-five¹ ['naintəfaiv] *n F*

nine-to-five job, travail*/boulot *m* à plein temps; métro, boulot, dodo *m.*

nine-to-five² ['naintəfaiv] *vi F* travailler de neuf à cinq (heures)/travailler à plein temps/avoir des horaires de bureau.

nine-to-fiver ['naintəfaivər] *n F* qn qui travaille à plein temps/qui a des horaires de bureau/qui fait le métro, boulot, dodo.

ninnies ['niniz] *npl A P* seins*/tétons *mpl*/nénés *mpl.*

nip¹ [nip] **I** *n F* **1. there's a nip in the air,** ça pince **2.** goutte *f*; **a nip of gin,** une rincette de gin **3. to make a nip for it,** décaniller/prendre la poudre d'escampette **4.** = **nipper 1 II** *n P* Nip, Japonais(e) *m(f)*/Jap *mf.*

nip² [nip] *vtr&i* **1.** *F* **to nip round/over to s.o.'s house,** faire un saut chez qn **2.** *P* **to nip s.o. for money,** emprunter* de l'argent à qn/taper qn **3.** *P* voler*/barboter/faucher **4.** *P* prendre (qn) la main dans le sac/prendre (qn) en flag/faire marron sur le tas.

nip along ['nipə'lɔŋ] *vi F* se dépêcher*/se décarcasser/s'activer; **nip along to the shops for me,** fonce/file à l'épicerie pour moi.

nip in ['nip'in] *vi F* **1.** entrer (lestement); **I nipped in to see her,** j'ai fait un saut chez elle **2. to nip in (smartly),** tirer avantage d'une situation.

nip off ['nip'ɔf] *vi F* partir*/jouer des flûtes/prendre le large; **he nipped off with the takings,** il a mis les bouts avec la caisse/la recette.

nipper ['nipər] *n* **1.** *F* gamin *m*/gosse *mf*/mioche *f*/moutard *m*/loupiot *m*; **I've got two nippers,** j'ai deux gosses **2.** *pl P* menottes*/bracelets *mpl.*

nippy ['nipi] **I** *a F* **1.** froid/frisquet/frisco **2.** rapide/alerte/vif; **to be nippy,** se dépêcher*/se grouiller; **that's a nippy little car,** c'est une

voiture nerveuse/un petit bolide **II**
n O P serveuse *f*/loufiate *f*.

nips [nips] *npl Austr P* **to put in the
nips/to put the nips into** (s.o.),
taper/torpiller (qn) (de qch).

nishte ['niʃtə] *n P* rien*/nib.

nit [nit] *n F* **1.** individu bête*/cré-
tin *m*; **a steaming nit,** un couillon
fini/un duschnock achevé/un triple
crétin/le roi des crétins **2.** *Austr* **to
keep nit,** monter la garde/faire le
pet. (*See* **nit-nit!**; **nitwit**)

nitery ['naitəri] *n NAm F* = **nightspot.**

nit-nit! ['nit'nit] *excl A P* boucle-
la!/gare!/vingt-deux!/acré!

nit-pick ['nitpik] *vi F* ergoter/
couper les cheveux en quatre/
enculer les mouches/chinoiser/être
chinois.

nit-picker ['nit'pikər] *n F* ergoteur,
-euse/enculeur, -euse de mouches.

nitty-gritty ['niti'griti] *n F* **the
nitty-gritty,** le (fin) fond/le tréfonds
(d'une affaire)/le substratum; les
faits *mpl* sans fioritures/l'essentiel
m sans le baratin; **let's get down to
the real nitty-gritty,** venons-en aux
faits; **no small talk, give me the
nitty-gritty!** pas de baratin, du
solide!

nitwit ['nitwit] *n F* = **nit 1.**

nix [niks] *NAm P* **I** *excl P* **nix!** pas
mèche!/rien à faire! **II** *n* **1.**
rien*/nib/que dalle/peau *f* de balle
2. to keep nix, monter la garde/
faire le pet/faire gaffe.

no [nou] **I** *a F* **long time no see!** ça
fait un bail qu'on s'est vu! (*See*
fear; **go II 1**) **II** *adv F* **no can do,**
compte pas sur bibi.

nob¹ [nɔb] *n* **1.** *P* tête*/coco *m*/
caboche *f*/nénette *f*; **so much a nob,**
tant par tête de pipe **2.** *P*
aristo(crate) *m*; **the nobs,** les rupins
mpl/les gens *mpl* de la haute/le
dessus du panier **3.** *V* = **knob 1.**

nob² [nɔb] *vtr P* assommer/étourdir
(qn).

nobble ['nɔbl] *vtr* **1.** *F* doper/
écloper (un cheval); acheter/
soudoyer (qn); donner un dessous-
de-table (à qn)/donner un pot-de-
vin (à qn) **2.** *P* duper*/entôler **4.**
P enlever/kidnapper.

nobody ['noubədi] *n F* **a nobody,**
une nullité/un zéro/un rien-du-
tout/un minable/un minus. (*See*
business 4)

nod [nɔd] *n P* **1. on the nod** (*a*)
ahuri par la drogue/envapé (*b*)
NAm à crédit/à croume/à la
gagne/à l'œil **2. to get the nod,**
être choisi/élu **3. to give the nod,**
donner le feu vert; **it went through
on the nod,** la proposition a été
adoptée sans discussion.

noddle ['nɔdl] *n F* tête*/ciboulot
m/caboche *f*; **use your noddle!** fais
travailler tes méninges!

nod off ['nɔd'ɔf] *vi F* s'endormir/
piquer un roupillon/coincer la
bulle.

nog [nɔg] *n F* = **noggin 2.**

noggin ['nɔgin] *n F* **1.** tête*/
caboche *f* **2.** verre *m* (d'alcool)/
pot *m*/démi *m*; **to have a noggin,**
prendre un pot.

no-good ['nou'gud] *a F* bon à rien;
esp NAm **he's a no-good son of a
bitch,** c'est un bon à rien de connard.

no-gooder ['nou'gudər], **nogoodnik** ['nou'gudnik] *n F* vaurien*/bon-à-rien *m*/loquedu *m*/
minable *m*.

no-hoper ['nou'houpər] *n Austr P*
= **nobody.**

nohow ['nouhau] *adv P* en aucune
façon.

noise [nɔiz] *n F* **to make the right
noises,** savoir se tirer d'affaire/
savoir s'en sortir. (*See* **big¹ I 1**)

nonce [nɔns] *n P* (*prisons*) **1.**
violeur *m* **2.** = **nance 1, 2.**

non-com ['nɔn'kɔm] *n F* (*abbr =
non-commissioned officer*) (*mil*) sous-
off *m*/sous-officier *m*.

nong [nɔŋ] *n Austr P* individu
bête*/truffe *f*/andouille *f*/patate *f*.

no-no ['nounou] *n F esp NAm* **1.**
= **nobody 2.** qch d'interdit;
that's a no-no, ça ne se fait pas/pas
touche à ça; **politics, that's a no-no
around here!** la politique, alors là,
pas touche!

noodle ['nuːdl] *n F* **1.** individu
bête*/nouille *f*/andouille *f* **2.**
NAm tête*/tronche *f*. (*See* **flip² 2**)

nookie, nooky ['nuki] *n P* coït*/
crampe *f*/crampette *f*; **a bit of
nookie,** une partie d'écarté **2.** *O*
nookie bookie, souteneur*/jules *m*.

nope [noup] *adv P* (= *no*) non*.

norgies ['nɔɪgiz], **norgs** [nɔɪgz],
norkers ['nɔɪkəz], **norks** [nɔɪks]
npl Austr P seins*/rotoplots *mpl*/
roberts *mpl*/nichons *mpl*.

north and south ['nɔɪθən(d)-
'sauθ, 'nɔɪfən'sauf] *n P* (*RS =
mouth*) bouche*/goule *f*/trappe *f*.

nose [nouz] *n* **1.** *F* **to poke one's
nose in (where it's not wanted),**
fourrer son nez*/mettre son grain
de sel/ramener sa fraise **2.** *F* **to
pay through the nose for sth,** payer*
les yeux de la tête pour qch/
acheter qch au poids de l'or **3.** *P*
to keep one's nose clean, se tenir à
carreau/ne pas se mouiller/se
ranger des voitures **4.** *P* indica-
teur* de police/indic *m*/mouchard
m/mouton *m* **5.** *F* **to put s.o.'s
nose out of joint,** faire une contrecarre à qn/contrer qn **6.** *F* **to turn
one's nose up (at sth),** faire le
dégoûté/faire la petite bouche **7.**
F **to look down one's nose at s.o./
sth,** toiser qn/qch/regarder* qn/qch
de haut (en bas) **8.** *F* **to have a
nose (for sth),** avoir le nez creux/
avoir du pif **9.** *F* **he gets up my
nose,** il me fait monter la moutarde
au nez **10.** *F* **the parson's nose,** le
croupion (d'une volaille)/as *m* de
pique **11.** *esp NAm P* **on the nose,**
à pic/à poil **12.** *P* **to rub s.o.'s
nose in it,** mettre le nez (à qn)

dedans **13.** *F* **he can't see any further than/beyond the end of his
nose** (*i*) il est myope (*ii*) il ne peut
pas voir plus loin que le bout de
son nez/il a les idées courtes. (*See*
skin¹ 2, 3; **toffee-nose**)

nose about, around ['nouz-
ə'baut, ə'raund] *vi F* fureter/fouiner.

nosebag ['nouzbæg] *n P* **to put/to
tie on the nosebag,** manger*/casser
la croûte/se remplir le bocal. (*See*
trough)

nose-candy ['nouzkændi] *n P*
(*drugs*) cocaïne*/neige *f*.

nosedive¹ ['nouzdaiv] *n F* baisse *f*
(de prix, etc)/plongeon *m*; **oil
(prices) took a nosedive,** les prix
pétroliers se sont effondrés.

nosedive² ['nouzdaiv] *vi F* (*prices,
etc*) tomber à pic/dégringoler/
s'effondrer.

nose job ['nouzdʒɔb] *n F* **she's had
a nose job,** elle s'est fait refaire/
retaper le nez/le pif/le tarin.

nose on ['nouzɔn] *vi P* dénoncer*/
moutonner/bourdiller/caf(e)ter (qn).

nose-rag ['nouzræg], **nose-
wipe** ['nouzwaip], **nose-wiper**
['nouzwaipər] *n P* mouchoir*/tire-
jus *m*.

nosey ['nouzi] *a F* = **nosy**.

nosh¹ [nɔʃ] *n P* **1.** nourriture*/
bouffe *f*/boustifaille *f* **2.** repas *m*/
boulottage *m*.

nosh² [nɔʃ] *vi P* **1.** manger*/
boulotter/bouffer/croûter **2.** mettre la main sur (qch).

nosher ['nɔʃər] *n P* mangeur *m*/
bouffeur *m*.

nosherie ['nɔʃ(ə)ri] *n P* restaurant
m/café *m*/bistroquet *m*.

nosh-up ['nɔʃʌp] *n P* bon repas/
noce *f*/bombe *f*.

nostrils ['nɔstrilz] *npl F* **he gets up
my nostrils** = **he gets up my nose**
(**nose 9**).

nosy ['nouzi] *a F* fureteur/fouinard;

nosy parker, fouine *f*/fouille-merde *mf*.

nothing ['nʌθiŋ] *n* **1.** *F* **nothing doing!** rien à faire!/macache!/tu peux toujours courir! **2.** *F* **to do sth in nothing flat,** faire qch très vite*/presto illico/en cinq secs; **nothing to it!** du nougat!/du gâteau!/du tout cuit! **3.** *P* **you don't know nothing,** t'es ignorant*; t'es en retard d'une rame/d'un métro; tu n'y piges que dalle. (*See* **sweet 5**; **write**)

nowt [naut] *n F* rien*/nib/que dalle. (*See* **owt**)

nud [nʌd], **nuddy** ['nʌdi] *n F* **in the nud/in the nuddy,** tout nu*/à poil/cul nu/le cul à l'air/dans le costume d'Adam *ou* d'Ève.

nudie ['njuːdi] *n P* (*a*) film *m*/pièce *f*/revue *f* porno/de cul (*b*) **nudie (show),** spectacle *m* de striptease/de fesses/de cul (*c*) danseuse nue.

nukes [njuːks] *npl F* armes *fpl*/missiles *mpl* nucléaires; **no nukes!** non au nucléaire!/à bas le nucléaire!/nucléaire: non merci!

number ['nʌmbər] *n F* **1. your number's up,** ton compte est bon **2. to look after number one,** penser à mézigue/soigner bibi/tirer la couverture à soi **3. a hot number** (*a*) une chaude lapine/une chaude de la pince; **she's a hot number,** elle est bandante/excitante à mort; c'est un beau sujet/elle est roulée au moule (*b*) morceau de musique enlevé avec fougue (*c*) article *m* qui se vend bien/article-réclame *m* **4. to have s.o.'s number,** en savoir long sur qn/être rencardé sur qn **5. to have the wrong number,** être sur la mauvaise piste/se gour(r)er **6.** (*child's language*) **to do number one = to do small jobs** (**job 9**); **to do number two = to do big jobs** (**job 9**) **7.** (*Marine*) **number one,** officier *m* qui commande en second à bord d'un navire (de guerre). (*See* **back-number**; **cushy**)

nunky ['nʌŋki] *n F* **1.** (*child's word*) oncle *m*/tonton *m* **2.** = **uncle 5.**

nurd [nəːd] *n esp NAm P* individu bête*/crétin *m*/(petit) con/enculé *m*/connard *m*; **he's a real nurd,** c'est un vrai connard/un pauv'type.

nut¹ [nʌt] *n* **1.** *P* tête*/caboche *f*/ciboulot *m*; **use your nut!** fais travailler tes méninges! *Austr* **to nod the nut,** plaider coupable; **off one's nut,** fou*/dingue/dingo; **to go off one's nut,** devenir fou*/perdre la boule; **he's off his nut,** il a le coco fêlé. (*See* **nuts I 1**) **2.** *P* = **nutcase 3.** *P* **to do one's nut,** se mettre en colère*/sortir de ses gonds/piquer une crise/se mettre en rogne **4.** *F* **he's a hard nut (to crack),** c'est un têtu/un cabochard/une tête de mule; **it's a hard nut to crack,** c'est un casse-tête chinois/c'est une colle **5.** *F* **she can't play/sing for nuts,** elle joue/chante comme un pied; **he can't drive for nuts,** il conduit comme un manche. (*See* **toffee**) **6.** *F* **nuts and bolts,** l'essentiel/les bases *fpl*; **he's a very nuts and bolts sort of person,** il a les pieds sur terre/il ne plane pas **7.** *pl V* testicules*/noix *fpl*; **to get hot nuts,** être en érection*/bander; **to get one's nuts off,** éjaculer*/vider ses burettes; **to have one's nuts cracked,** faire l'amour*/tirer sa chique **8.** *P* **to talk nuts,** dire des bêtises*/des conneries *fpl*; **to talk like a nut,** dérailler/déconner/débloquer. (*See* **peanut**)

nut² [nʌt] *vtr* **1.** *P* donner un coup de tête*/de caboche/de ciboulot à (qn) **2.** *V* faire l'amour* avec (qn)/buriner (qn).

nutcase ['nʌtkeis] *n P* fou *m*/cinglé *m*; **he's a real nutcase,** il est fou*/cinglé/dingue/toqué; il a perdu la boule.

nut chokers ['nʌt'tʃoukəz] *npl Austr P* caleçon *m*/slip *m*/calbard *m*/calcif *m*.

nut-house ['nʌthaus] *n P* maison *f* de fous/asile *m* de dingues/cabanon *m*/Charenton/Sainte-Anne.

nuts [nʌts] **I** *a P* **1.** fou*/cinglé/ dingue; **he's completely nuts,** il est complètement frappé/fêlé; **you're driving me nuts with all these questions,** tu me rends dingue avec toutes ces questions **2. to be nuts about/on s.o./sth,** être toqué/fana de qn/de qch; être mordu pour qn/ qch; **he's nuts about basket-ball,** c'est un mordu du basket/il est dingue de basket; **he's nuts about her,** il en est dingue/il en pince pour elle. (*See* **nutty 2**) **II** *excl* **nuts!** zut!/merde! **nuts to you!** des clous!/flûte!

nutter ['nʌtər] *n P* = **nutcase.**

nuttiness ['nʌtines] *n P* folie *f*/ loufoquerie *f*/maboulisme *m*.

nutty ['nʌti] *a P* **1.** loufoque/ maboul(e) **2.** fou* (à lier)/cinglé. (*See* **fruit-cake 2**) **3. to be nutty about s.o./sth = to be nuts about s.o./sth** (**nuts I 2**).

nymphet [nim'fet] *n F* petite poule/nénette *f*.

nympho ['nimfou] *n F* (= *nymphomaniac*) nymphomane *f*/femme* à passions/chaude lapine/nympho *f*.

O

O [ou] *abbr P* (= *opium*) (*drugs*) opium*/op *m*/boue *f*.

oak [ouk] *n P* (*RS* = *oak and ash*) **1.** (= *cash*) argent*/fric *m* **2.** (= *flash*) = **oakey.**

oakey [ouki] *a P* (*from RS* = *oak and ash* = *flash*) tapageur/voyant/ tape-à-l'œil.

oats [outs] *npl* **1.** *P* **to get one's oats**, être satisfait sexuellement/ne pas mettre ses chaussettes à la fenêtre **2.** *esp NAm F* **to feel one's oats** (*a*) se sentir important/se monter du collet (*b*) avoir de l'entrain/avoir la pêche/avoir la frite **3.** *F* **to be off one's oats**, se sentir patraque/tout chose/pas dans son assiette.

obbo ['ɔbou] *n F* (*mil, police, etc*) (= *observation*) surveillance *f*; **to be on obbo duty**, être/se mettre en planque; surbiner/planquer qn/qch.

obstropolous [ɔb'strɔpələs] *a F* bruyant/tapageur.

ochre ['oukər] *n esp NAm P* argent*/osier *m*/blanc *m*.

ocker ['ɔkər] *Austr F* **I** *a* grossier/ malotru/malpoli **II** *n* branquignol *m*/plouc *m*.

OD ['ou'diː] *n F* (*abbr* = *overdose*) dose trop forte (de narcotiques)/ overdose *f*.

OD ['ou'diː] *vi F* prendre une over- dose; **he OD'd on heroin,** il a fait une overdose d'héroïne.

oddball ['ɔdbɔːl] **I** *a P* **1.** excen- trique/loufoque/farfelu **2.** gaffeur **II** *n P* **1.** excentrique *mf*/drôle *m* de zigoto/drôle d'oiseau/farfelu *m*

2. flagorneur *m* **3.** dissident(e) *m(f)* **4.** homosexuel*/pédé; **he's a bit of an oddball,** il a des goûts spéciaux.

odds [ɔdz] *npl* **1.** *P* **odds and sods**, petits bouts/bibelots *mpl*/bribes et morceaux; **there were a few odds and sods at the meeting,** il (n')y avait pas la foule/il y avait quatre pelés et un tondu à la réunion **2.** *F* **over the odds**, beaucoup trop/ bien plus **3.** *F* **what odds does it make?/what's the odds?** qu'est-ce que ça fait?/et après? **4.** *P* **to shout the odds**, se vanter/en rajouter/se faire mousser **5.** *F* **to be within the odds**, être bien possi- ble; **that's well within the odds**, ça se peut fort bien **6.** *F* volumes dépareillés; livres *mpl* supplé- mentaires.

odds-on ['ɔdzɔn] *a F* **to have an odds-on chance**, jouer gagnant; **it's an odds-on chance he'll get arrested,** à tous les coups, il va se faire arrêter.

off¹ [ɔf] *F* **I** *a* **to have an off day**, se sentir un peu malade*/ne pas être en train/ne pas avoir la pêche/ne pas être dans un bon jour **II** *adv* **1.** **that's a bit off** (*a*) c'est un peu de travers/ce n'est pas tout à fait ça (*b*) ça dépasse les bornes/c'est un peu fort de café; c'est moche; **his attitude was a bit off,** il n'y allait pas avec le dos de la cuillère (*c*) ça commence à être mauvais **2.** (*drugs*) **to be off it/off the stuff,** s'arrêter de prendre des drogues **III** *n* **ready for the off,** prêt à par- tir*/sur le départ **IV** *prep* **1.** *F* **off colour** (*a*) un peu malade*/

patraque/mal fichu (b) NAm
scabreux/osé/salé/pimenté 2. P
off (of)..., de...; I got it off (of)
my brother, je le tiens de mon
frère. (See go off 2)

off² [ɔf] vtr NAm P tuer*/éliminer/
descendre/crounir (qn).

off chance ['ɔftʃɑɪns] n F on the
off chance, à l'imprévu; he did it on
the off chance, il l'a fait pour le cas
où.../parce qu'on ne sait jamais.

office ['ɔfis] n P signal particulier/
œillade f. (See jack-in-office)

offish ['ɔfiʃ] a F (a) distant/
hautain/snobinard; bêcheur; she
was very offish with me, elle me
snobait/elle me faisait la gueule (b)
mal en train/mal fichu; to feel a bit
offish, ne pas avoir la frite.

off-putting ['ɔfputiŋ, 'ɔf'putiŋ] a F
déconcertant/déroutant; I find all
this talk about redundancies rather
off-putting, je trouve toutes ces histoires de chômage déprimantes/
démoralisantes.

off-the-wall ['ɔfðəwɔɪl] a NAm P
(a) bizarre/excentrique/loufoque; he
has an off-the-wall sense of humour,
il a un humour à tailler à la hache/
son humour, c'est pas de la dentelle
(b) fou*/dérangé/tapé/toqué; she
was off-the-wall, elle avait perdu la
boule.

offy ['ɔfi] n F (= off-licence) débit m
(où on vend des boissons à
emporter).

oh-be-joyful ['oubɪ'dʒɔɪfəl] n A F
bouteille f de rhum.

oil [ɔil] n F 1. flatterie f/boniment
m/pommade f. (See palm-oil) 2.
pot-de-vin m/dessous-de-table m
3. to strike oil, gagner* beaucoup
d'argent/trouver filon 4. Austr
renseignement* sûr/tuyau m de
première/tuyau de plomb.

oil-can ['ɔilkæn] n NAm P échec*/
four m/fiasco m.

oiled [ɔild] a F (well) oiled, ivre*/
bituré/cuit/dans le cirage.

oil-painting ['ɔilpeintiŋ] n F she's
no oil-painting, elle est laide*/c'est
un vieux tableau/elle est belle
comme un camion.

oily ['ɔili] a F (pej) onctueux/miel-
leux. (See rag¹ 9)

oink [ɔiŋk] n NAm P policier*/
condé m.

OK¹, ok, okay ['ou'kei] a F OK/
impec/au poil; an OK guy, un type
bien/un chic type/un mec sympa/
un mec réglo.

OK², ok, okay ['ou'kei], oke
[ouk], okey-doke ['ouki'douk],
okey-dokey ['ouki'douki] adv F
d'accord*/dac/OK/banco; it's OK
by me, ça me va; pour moi, ça
marche/ça colle.

OK³, ok, okay ['ou'kei] n F
accord m/conciliation f/approba-
tion f/OK m; to give s.o. the OK,
donner le feu vert à qn.

OK⁴, ok, okay ['ou'kei] vtr F être
d'accord avec/approuver; opiner du
bonnet; he OK'd it, il a fait signe
qu'il marchait/qu'il acceptait.

old [ould] a 1. the old man (a) F
mari m/l'homme m/le vieux/le
patron (b) F le père*/le paternel;
my old man, mon homme/mon
vieux/mon vioc (c) F le patron*/le
singe/le chef (d) F the Old Man, le
capitaine d'un navire (e) P pénis*/
le petit frère 2. F hello, old man!
salut, vieille branche/vieux pote!
(See thing 8) 3. F old woman/old
lady (a) épouse*/la moitié/la
patronne/la bourgeoise (b) mère*/la
vieille/la mater(nelle) (c) individu*
qui fait des manières/chichiteux m
4. F it's the same old story/tune,
c'est toujours la même histoire/la
même rengaine 5. F I met old
Smith the other day, j'ai rencontré
l'ami Smith l'autre jour 6. F
(catchphrase) it's a funny old world
(we live in), tout est bizarre autant
qu'étrange/c'est la vie, que veux-tu?
7. F put them down any old where,
pose-les n'importe où. (See army 2;

bean 2; boy II 1; chap; crock¹ 2; fogey; fruit 1; Harry 1, 2; hat 1; high I 5; how I 1; how-do-you-do; nick¹ 3; rare; school 2; soldier¹ 3; stick¹ 8 (b); thing 8)

old Bill ['ould'bil] n P (a) agent* de police ou policier*/flic m/poulet m (b) la police*/la flicaille/les flics.

old-boy ['ould'bɔi] n F **the old-boy network,** la clique des anciens élèves; **he got his job through the old-boy network,** il a obtenu son boulot grâce au réseau des anciens.

oldie ['ouldi] n F **1.** vieux*/viocard m/vioque m **2.** vieillerie f/antiquaille f; (record, film, etc) **an oldie but goodie/a golden oldie,** une vieillerie/une vieille cire; un vieux disque qui gratte.

old-timer [ould'taimər] n F un vieux de la vieille/un vieux routier.

oldy ['ouldi] n = **oldie.**

Oliver (Twist) ['ɔlivə('twist)] n P (RS = fist) poing*.

on [ɔn] **I** a **1.** V (pénis) en érection*/en l'air/qui marque midi **2.** P (a) euphorisé par la drogue/high (b) habitué des drogues/branché. (See **switched on** 2) **II** adv F **1.** it's on, ça marche/ça va; it's not on, rien à faire/pas mèche **2.** I'm on, j'en suis **3. to be always on at s.o.,** être toujours sur le dos de qn **III** prep F **1. the drinks are on me/this one's on me,** j'offre la tournée/c'est moi qui régale **2.** Austr **to be on it,** boire*/caresser la bouteille/biberonner/picoler; he's on it again, il est (encore) chargé/dans le cirage.

once [wʌns] adv P (RS = cheek) **once a week** (i) toupet m/culot m (ii) faire l'insolent/se payer la tête (de qn).

once-over ['wʌnsouvər] n F **to give sth/s.o. the once-over** (a) regarder*/reluquer/mirer qch/qn (b) battre* qn/passer qn à tabac/abîmer le portrait à qn.

oncer ['wʌnsər] n P (billet* ou pièce d')une livre.

one [wʌn] pron **1.** F un verre/un coup; **to have (had) one too many,** avoir (pris) un coup de trop/en avoir un dans le nez; **one for the road,** le coup du départ/de l'étrier. (See **eight** 1; **quick** 1) **2.** F (joke) **that's a good one!** elle est bien bonne celle-là! **3.** F (blow) **he landed/fetched him one on the nose,** il lui en a allongé un (ramponneau)/une (avoine) (sur le nez). (See **fourpenny**) **4.** F **he pulled a fast one on me,** il m'a eu/fait/roulé; il m'a joué un tour de cochon **5.** F **you are a one!** tu me la copieras! **6.** F **to be a one for sth,** être un fana/un mordu de qch; **he's a right one for the ladies,** c'est un chaud lapin/un chaud de la pince; il est porté sur la chose **7.** F (catchphrase) **there's one born every minute,** on pend les andouilles sans les compter. (See **mother** 5; **sucker** II 1) **8.** F **it's/that's a new one on me!** ça m'en bouche un coin! **9.** P (RS = shoes) **ones and twos,** chaussures*/godasses fpl **10.** NAm P **one thou(sand),** pire que le plus mauvais/plus que pire. (See **eye** 14; **number** 2, 6, 7; **stick²** 10)

one-eyed ['wʌnaid] a P insignifiant/de rien du tout/pitoyable/piètre; **a one-eyed town,** un patelin/un bled/un trou perdu. (See **trousersnake**)

one-horse ['wʌnhɔːs] a F **a one-horse town,** une petite ville de province/un trou (perdu)/un patelin/un bled.

one-liner ['wʌnlainər] n esp NAm F (one-line joke) un bon mot.

one-man ['wʌn'mæn] a F **one-man band,** homme-orchestre m (= amant parfait ou qn qui fait tout lui-même).

one-nighter ['wʌn'naitər, **one-night job** ['wɔn'nait'dʒɔb] n P (a) (jazz, rock, etc) représentation f d'un soir; gala *m*; bœuf *m* (*b*) rendez-vous sentimental d'un soir (*c*) client *m* d'une prostituée qui passe la nuit avec elle/clille *m* de nuit/couché *m*; **to have/to do a one-nighter**, faire un couché.

one-off ['wʌnɔf] *a F* (*a*) (*TV*) **one-off film**, film *m* en exclusivité (*b*) **one-off title**, livre qui ne fait pas partie d'une série/livre à tirage limité.

oner ['wʌnər] *n F* **1.** sommité *f*/ongle *m*/as *m*/crack *m* **2.** un expert/un calé **3.** coup* de la fin/assommoir *m* **4.** (billet* *ou* pièce d')une livre.

one-two ['wʌn'tuː] *n F* **the old one-two**, coup* sec de gauche suivi d'un direct de droite.

one-up ['wʌnʌp] *vtr NAm* **to one-up (s.o.)** = **to practise one-upmanship** (**one-upmanship**).

one-upmanship ['wʌnʌpmənʃip] *n F* refus *m* de se laisser jeter la poudre aux yeux/l'escalade *f*/l'art *m* des raménoïdes; **to practise one-upmanship**, renchérir/avoir la dragée haute; en rajouter/en remontrer aux autres.

onion ['ʌnjən] *n* **1.** *F* **that's the way the onion peels** = **that's the way the mop flops** (**mop**) **2.** *F* **to know one's onions**, connaître son sujet à fond/connaître son affaire; être à la coule/à la hauteur **3.** *P* (*rare*) tête*/poire *f*; **off one's onion**, fou*/maboul(e).

oodles ['uːdlz] *npl F* **oodles of...**, beaucoup de.../une abondance* de.../des tas de.../un paquet de .../un rab de....

oojamaflip ['uːdʒəməflip], **oojie** ['uːdʒi] *n F* truc *m*/machin *m*/chose *mf*/machin-chose *m*.

oo-la-la! ['uːlɑː'lɑː] *excl F* ho-là-là!

oomph [umf] *n F* charme *m*/personnalité *f*/sex-appeal *m*/chien *m*; **he's got oomph**, il jette du jus/il en jette.

oops-a-daisy! ['upsə'deizi] *excl F* hop-là!/youp-là (boum)!

op [ɔp] *n F* (*abbr* = *operation*) opération *f*/opé *f*.

open¹ ['oup(ə)n] *a F* **it's an open and shut case**, c'est sûr et certain/c'est du tout cuit/c'est dans le sac/c'est du tout vu/c'est couru d'avance.

open² ['oup(ə)n] *vtr P* (*woman*) **to open one's legs (for s.o.)**, faire l'amour*/faire une partie d'écarté.

openers ['oup(ə)nəz] *npl F* **for openers**, pour commencer/comme hors-d'œuvre.

open up ['oup(ə)nʌp] *vi F* **1.** (*a*) avouer*/manger le morceau (*b*) parler franchement/vider son sac **2.** se déchaîner/y aller de tout son soûl/y aller à fond les manettes **3.** (*gun*, *rifle*) tirer*/flinguer/envoyer la purée.

operator ['ɔpəreitər] *n P* **1.** voleur* (à la tire)/escroc*/filou *m*/empileur *m* **2.** fourgueur *m*/pourvoyeur *m* de drogues. (*See* **smooth**)

orchestras ['ɔːkestrəz] *npl P* (*RS* = *orchestra stalls* = *balls*) testicules*/couilles *fpl*/balloches *fpl*/roubignolles *fpl*.

organ ['ɔːgən] *n P* **1.** pénis*/machin *m*/outil *m*/arbalète *f* **2.** **organ grinder**, sexe de la femme*/boîte *f* à ouvrage/grippette *f*.

organize ['ɔːgənaiz] *vtr P* = **wangle²**.

ornery ['ɔːnəri] *a NAm F* d'humeur maussade/de mauvais poil/en rogne.

Oscar ['ɔskər] *vtr V* sodomiser*/empaffer/enculer (qn).

other ['ʌðər] *n P* **to have a bit of the other**, faire l'amour*/faire ça/faire un peu de truc. (*See* **pull 3**; **tother**)

ounce man ['aunsmæn] *n NAm P* (*drugs*) petit revendeur (*esp* d'héroïne)/dealer *m*/fourmi *f*.

out [aut] **I** *adv* **1.** *F* **out on one's feet**, fatigué/flapi/flagada **2.** *F* (*a*) **to be out of it** (*i*) ne pas être de connivence (*ii*) être laissé à l'écart; **you're well out of it**, par bonheur, tu n'es pas dans le coup; tu ne connais pas ton bonheur (*b*) **to feel out of it** (*i*) se sentir dépaysé (*ii*) se sentir de trop **3.** *P* **out of sight**, bœuf/du tonnerre; **that's out of sight!** c'est sensass!/c'est le (super-)pied! **4.** *NAm P* **out to lunch** (*a*) bizarre/excentrique/loufoque (*b*) dans les nuages/sur sa planète; **to be out to lunch**, être sur sa planète/ailleurs. (*See* **light II 1**) **II** *n F* **to find an out**, se tirer d'affaire/se débrouiller*/se dépatouiller/trouver une porte de sortie. (*See* **get out**; **in III 2**)

outer ['autər] *n Austr F* **to be on the outer** (*i*) (*pers*) être pauvre*/dans la dèche; ne pas avoir la moindre chance/ne pas être verni (*ii*) (*horse, in races*) ne pas avoir la moindre chance; être un mort/une chèvre.

outfit ['autfit] *n F* **1.** équipe *f*/groupement *m* **2.** firme *f*/(maison *f* de) travail *m*; **what an outfit!** quelle boîte!/quelle taule!

outside ['aut'said] **I** *n F* **to be on the outside looking in**, ne pas faire partie d'une société *ou* d'un groupe; être un outsider **II** *prep F* **get outside that!** enfile-toi ça!

overcoat ['ouvəkout] *n F* **wooden/pine overcoat**, cercueil*/redingote *f* de sapin/pardessus *m* sans manches; **to fit s.o. with a concrete overcoat**, tuer*/assassiner* qn et l'enterrer dans du béton (armé); bétonner qn.

overjolt ['ouvədʒoult] *n F* dose trop forte (d'une drogue)/overdose *f*.

overspill ['ouvəspil] *n F* ville *f* satellite.

ownsome ['ounsəm], **owny-o** ['ouniou] *n F* **on one's ownsome**, tout seul/seulâbre. (*See* **lonesome**)

owt [aut] *n F* quelque chose; **I don't do owt for nowt**, je ne fais rien pour rien. (*See* **nowt**)

oyster ['ɔistər] *n P* **1.** crachat*/glaviot *m*/huître *f* (bien grasse) **2.** bouche*/boîte *f*.

Oz ['ɔz] *n Austr P* Australie *f*/pays *m* des kangourous.

ozzy, Ozzy ['ɔzi] *n P* **1.** hôpital*/host(e)au *m*/hosto *m* **2.** *Austr* Australien(ne) *m(f)*. (*See* **Aussie I, II**)

P

p [piː] *F* **1. to mind/to watch one's p's and q's** (*a*) se tenir convenablement/être dans ses petits souliers; se tenir à carreau (*b*) s'occuper de ses affaires/de ses oignons **2. to know one's p's and q's,** être débrouillard/démerdard.

pa [pɑː] *n F* père*/papa *m*.

pace [peis] *n F* **to go the pace,** mener une vie de bâton de chaise/ mener un train d'enfer.

pack[1] [pæk] *n* **1.** *P* (*drugs*) pochette *f* d'héroïne* **2.** *F* **pack of lies,** tissu *m*/tas *m* de mensonges* **3.** *Austr* **to go to the pack,** détériorer/aller mal; aller à vau-l'eau.

pack[2] [pæk] *vtr F* **1. to pack a gun/a piece,** être armé/enfouraillé **2. to pack a punch** (*a*) boxer dur/ perloter (*b*) (*drink*) être corsé **3. to send s.o. packing,** envoyer qn dinguer/paître/promener/sur les roses.

pack-drill ['pækdril] *n F* (*catch-phrase*) **no names, no pack-drill,** pas de nom, pas de démon.

packet ['pækit] *n* **1.** *P* **to catch/to cop a packet** (*a*) écoper/en prendre pour son grade (*b*) être bouclé/être envoyé en villégiature (*c*) = **to get a dose** (**dose** 1) **2.** *F* **to cost a packet,** coûter cher*/être salé; **it cost me a packet,** ça m'a fait un paquet/ça m'a coûté chaud **3.** *F* (*a*) **to make a packet,** gagner* beaucoup d'argent/prendre le paquet/en ramasser/se sucrer/faire son beurre (*b*) **to lose a packet,** perdre beaucoup d'argent*/perdre un paquet/en être d'un paquet/ ramasser une culotte/être paumard **4.** *F* un sale coup/une bonne dose. (*See* **buy 2**)

pack in ['pæk'in] *vtr* **1.** *P* **to pack s.o. in,** cesser de voir qn/débarquer/plaquer/envoyer bouler qn **2.** (*a*) *F* **to pack sth in,** cesser de faire qch/larguer/laisser choir qch; **he's packed his job in,** il a plaqué/largué son boulot (*b*) *P* **pack it in!** (*i*) arrête!/laisse tomber!/écrase! (*ii*) ta gueule!/la ferme! **3.** *F* (*theatre, etc*) **to pack them in,** faire salle comble.

pack up ['pæk'ʌp] *vtr&i* **1.** *P* **to pack s.o. up** = **to pack s.o. in** (**pack in 1**) **2.** *F* **to pack sth up** = **to pack sth in** (**pack in 2** (*a*), (*b*)) **3.** *F* arrêter le travail/ débrayer; **come on, let's pack up for today,** allez, on boucle pour aujourd'hui **4.** *F* se détraquer/ sombrer/s'effondrer **5.** (*a*) *F* partir*/plier bagage/prendre ses cliques et ses claques (*b*) *P* mourir*/ lâcher la rampe/se laisser glisser **6.** *F* tomber en panne/en rade; **my car's packed up again,** ma bagnole est encore tombée en rade.

pad[1] [pæd] *n* **1.** *F* logement*/ piaule *f*; **your pad or mine?** je monte à ta strasse ou tu viens à ma turne? (*See* **crash-pad**; **pill-pad**) **2.** *P* lit*/pieu *m*; **to hit the pad,** se coucher*/se pieuter/se pagnoter. (*See* **launching-pad**)

pad[2] [pæd] *vtr&i F* marcher* (péniblement)/trimarder; **to pad it,** aller à pied/affûter des pinceaux/

prendre le train onze. (*See* **hoof**[1] **1**;
hoof[2])

paddler ['pædl*ə*r] *n Austr A P*
agent* de police/tige *f*.

paddles ['pædlz] *npl Austr F*
pieds*/péniches *fpl*/ripatons *mpl*.

pad down ['pæd'daun] *vi F*
dormir*/roupiller.

paddy, Paddy ['pædi] *n* **1.**
F (a) mauvaise humeur; **he was in a right
old paddy**, il s'est foutu en rogne/il
était en pétard (*b*) éclat *m* de
colère/coup *m* de sang/coup de raisin **2.** *P* cellule matelassée/caba-
non *m* **3.** (*a*) Irlandais *m* (*b*) qn
d'origine Irlandaise.

paddy-wag(g)on ['pædiwagən] *n
esp NAm F* car* de police/panier *m*
à salade/poulailler ambulant.

paddywhack ['pædi(h)wæk] *n F*
1. = **paddy 1 2.** (*child's word*)
fessée *f*/pan-pan (cucul) *m*.

pain [pein] *n F* **a pain in the neck**,
individu ennuyeux* *ou*
antipathique/raseur *m*/casse-pieds
m; **he gives me a pain in the neck**,
il me tape sur le système; *P* **a pain
in the arse**, un emmerdeur; **that girl
is a real pain**, c'est une
emmerdeuse/une julie pot de colle.

paint [peint] *vtr F* **to paint a picture**,
faire le point; **do you want me to
paint a picture for you?** je te fais un
dessin?/faut te faire un dessin? (*See*
red I 3)

painter ['peintər] *n* **1.** *F* **to slip
the painter**, mourir*/lâcher la
rampe **2.** *P* **to have the painters
in**, avoir ses règles*/repeindre sa
grille en rouge. (*See* **decorators**)

Pak(k)i ['pæki] *n P* (*pej*) Pakis-
tanais(e) *m(f)*.

pak(k)i-basher ['pækibæʃər] *n P*
chasseur *m* de Pakistanais.

pak(k)i-bashing ['pækibæʃiŋ] *n
P* chasse *f* aux Pakistanais/ =
ratonnade *f*.

pal [pæl] *n F* ami*/copain *m*/pote
m; **they're great pals**, ils sont

copains comme cochon. (*See* **pal
up**)

palaver[1] [pə'lɑivər] *n F* **1.**
bavardages *mpl*/palabres *fpl* **2.**
embarras *mpl*/chichis *mpl*; **what a
palaver! quelle histoire! 3.** baratin
m.

palaver[2] [pə'lɑivər] *vi F* **1.**
parler*/palabrer **2.** baratiner.

pal in ['pæl'in] *vi F* = **pal up**.

pally ['pæli] *a F* **to be pally with
s.o.**, être très copain/lié avec qn;
être copain comme cochon avec
qn/être comme cul et chemise avec
qn.

palm [pɑim] *n F* **1. to grease/to oil
s.o.'s palm**, graisser la patte à qn
2. to have an itchy/itching palm,
être grippe-sou/les avoir crochues.

palm-grease ['pɑimgriis] *n P*
graissage *m* de patte.

palm off ['pɑim'ɔf] *vtr F* **to palm
sth off on to s.o.**, colloquer/refiler/
pastiquer/coller qch à qn.

palm-oil ['pɑimɔil] *n P* = **palm-
grease**.

palm-tree ['pɑimtrii] *n P* voiture *f*
difficile à vendre/rossignol *m*. (*See*
bottler; **square-wheeler**)

palooka [pə'luikə] *n esp NAm P*
(*a*) (*boxing, etc*) joueur peu compé-
tent (*b*) nullité *f*/nouille *f*.

pal out ['pæl'aut] *vi F* se brouiller/
se fâcher (avec qn); snober (qn)/
faire la gueule (à qn).

palsy-walsy ['pælzi'wælzi] *a esp
NAm F* **to be (all) palsy-walsy (with
s.o.)**, être bons amis*/être à tu et à
toi/être comme cul et chemise.

paluka [pə'luikə] *n P* = **palooka**.

pal up ['pæl'ʌp] *vi F* **to pal up with
s.o.**, copiner/se lier avec qn.

pan[1] [pæn] *n* **1.** *P* **to go down the
pan**, échouer*/tomber dans le lac/
tomber à l'eau **2.** *P* visage*/
burette *f*/fiole *f* **3.** *F* compte-rendu
m défavorable/éreintage *m*/abattage
m. (*See* **drain**[1] **1**; **flash**[1] **II 3**)

pan² [pæn] *vtr F* **1.** critiquer*/
éreinter/démolir (qn/qch) **2.**
panoramiquer (une vue).

Panama red ['pænəmɑː'red] *n P*
(*drugs*) marijuana* de Panama.

pancake ['pænkeik] *vi F* (*aviation*)
atterrir en crash/sur le gésier.

pancakes ['pænkeiks] *npl P* seins*
aplatis/œufs *mpl* sur le plat.

panhandle ['pænhændl] *vi NAm F*
mendier*/pilonner/torpiller/taper.

panhandler ['pænhændlər] *n
NAm F* mendiant*/mendigot *m*/
torpilleur *m*/tapeur.

panic ['pænik] *n* **1.** *F* **panic sta-
tions,** postes *mpl* de combat/garde-
à-vous *m*; **it was panic stations,**
c'était la grande panique **2.** *F* **to
push/to hit the panic button** (*i*)
appuyer sur l'accélérateur/mettre
les gaz (*ii*) être pris de panique/
paniquer/avoir les foies/se dégon-
fler/perdre les pédales **3.** *P* manque *m* (de drogues).

panicky ['pæniki] *a F* paniqué/
paniquard; **don't get panicky,** ne
t'affole pas!/pas de panique!

panning ['pæniŋ] *n F* = **pan¹ 3.**

pan out ['pæn'aut] *vi* **1.** *F* finir/se
terminer/aboutir **2.** *P* rapporter
(de l'argent)/donner **3.** *P* **to pan
out about sth,** s'étendre sur un
sujet.

pansified ['pænzifaid], **pansy¹**
['pænzi] *a F* (*a*) homosexuel/pédé
(*b*) efféminé; **he's a bit pansified,** il
fait un peu tapette.

pansy² ['pænzi] *n F* **1.** homosexuel*/tante *f*/pédé *m*/lopette *f* **2.**
homme efféminé/chochotte *f*/fem-
melette *f*/mauviette *f*.

pansyland ['pænzilænd] *n F* **1.** le
monde des homosexuels*/la
jaquette/la pédale/les tuyaux *mpl*
de poêle. (*See* **fairyland**) **2. in
pansyland,** au pays des contes de
fées.

panties ['pæntiz] *npl F* slip *m*/
culotte *f* (de femme); culbute *f*.

pants [pænts] *npl* **1.** *F* (*a*)
pantalon*/falzar *m*/fut(al) *m* (*b*)
caleçon *m*/slip *m*/slibard *m* (*c*) =
panties 2. *P* **to be caught with
one's pants down,** être pris au
dépourvu/la main dans le sac/sur
le tas; se trouver en mauvaise posture **3.** *F* **to get a kick in the
pants,** être réprimandé* sévèrement;
recevoir un coup de pied aux
fesses*/quelque part. (*See* **kick¹ 5**)
4. *P* **to scare the pants off s.o.,** faire
peur* à qn/donner la pétoche à
qn/foutre les jetons à qn **5.** *P* **to
tear the pants off s.o.,** prendre qn à
partie/habiller qn/secouer les puces
à qn **6.** *P* **to beat/lick the pants
off s.o.,** battre qn à plate(s) cou-
ture(s)/écraser qn **7.** *F* **she wears
the pants around here,** c'est elle qui
porte la culotte **8.** *P* **to get into
s.o.'s pants,** faire l'amour* avec qn/
se faire qn. (*See* **ants; fancy¹ 3;
hot 1, 2; lead¹ 4; smarty(-pants);
trousers**)

pantsman ['pæntsmən] *n Austr P*
violeur *m*.

paper¹ ['peipər] *n P* **1.** (*theatre*)
billets *mpl* de faveur/bif(fe)tons *mpl*
2. (*drugs*) prescription *f*/ordonnance
f **3.** (*police*) **to put in the papers,**
démissionner.

paper² ['peipər] *vtr* **1.** *P* (*theatre*)
to paper the house, jouer à la
bif(fe)tonnade **2.** *F* **to paper over
the cracks,** replâtrer/essayer de
rafistoler les choses.

paper-hanger ['peipəhæŋər],
paper-pusher ['peipəpuʃər] *n
P* faux-monnayeur *m*/faux-
mornifleur *m*.

parakeet ['pærəkiːt] *n NAm P* (*pej*)
Portoricain(e) *m(f)*.

paralytic [pærə'litik] *a F* ivre*
mort/bituré; **he was completely
paralytic,** il était rond comme une
bille/plein comme une bourrique.

pard [pɑːd], **pardner** ['pɑːdnər] *n
NAm F* (*a*) associé *m*/assoce *m*/
baron *m* (*b*) ami*/pote *m*.

park [pɑːk] *vtr F* **to park oneself somewhere**, se mettre/s'installer quelque part; **park your backside down next to me**, pose ton cul à côté de moi; **park it over there! mets-le/colle-le là!** (*See* **ticket 2**)

parky ['pɑːki] *a F* (*weather*) frais/frisco/frisquet; **it's right parky today**, on se les gèle/il fait un froid de canard aujourd'hui.

parlour ['pɑːlə] *n Austr P* bordel*/maison de passe. (*See* **massage**)

parney ['pɑːni] *n A P* pluie*/flotte *f*/saucée *f*.

party ['pɑːti] *n F* **a certain party**, un certain individu*/un loustic/un numéro. (*See* **hen**; **stag 1**; **tea-party**)

pash [pæʃ] *n F* **to have a pash on s.o.**, aimer* qn/avoir le béguin pour qn/en pincer pour qn/être mordu pour qn.

pass [pɑːs] *n F* **to make a pass at s.o.**, flirter/faire du boniment à qn/draguer qn; faire du rentre-dedans.

passenger ['pæsindʒər] *n F* poids mort.

pass up ['pɑːs'ʌp] *vtr F* se passer de/sauter/supprimer (qch); **he passed up the opportunity**, il a raté l'occase.

past [pɑːst] *prep F* **1. I wouldn't put it past him**, il en est bien capable; **he's past it**, il est plus cap(able)/il est fichu/il est foutu.

paste [peist] *vtr F* battre*/rosser/dérouiller/étriller.

pasting ['peistiŋ] *n F* **to give s.o. a pasting** (*a*) coller une raclée à qn/passer une peignée à qn (*b*) (*sport, etc*) battre qn à plate(s) couture(s).

pasture ['pɑːstjər] *n F* **to be put out to pasture**, être mis à la retraite/au vert.

pat [pæt] *n F* **1.** *Austr* **on one's pat**, tout seul/seulâbre **2. Pat** (*a*) Irlandais *m* (*b*) qn d'origine irlandaise.

pat-ball ['pætbɔːl] *n F* tennis mal joué/jeu *m* à la raquette.

patch [pætʃ] *n* **1.** *F* **she's not a patch on him**, elle n'est pas de taille/elle ne lui arrive pas à la cheville **2.** *P* (*underworld slang*) territoire *m*/champ *m* d'action/chasse gardée. (*See* **manor**; **plot**) **3.** *F* **bad patch**, malchance*/guigne *f*/pétrin *m*; **we're going through a bad patch**, on est dans une mauvaise passe **4.** *P* devise inscrite sur le dos des blousons de cuir des "Hell's Angels".

patch up ['pætʃ'ʌp] *vtr F* **to patch up a quarrel/to patch it up**, se rabibocher/se raccommoder; **they've patched things up**, ils ont recollé les pots cassés.

pathetic [pə'θetik] *a F* **1. it's pathetic!** c'est lamentable!/c'est à pleurer! **2. you're really pathetic!** t'es minable!/t'es en dessous de tout!/t'es pitoyable!

patootie [pə'tuːti] *n NAm O P* **hot patootie**, petite amie; blonde incendiaire.

patsy ['pætsi] *n P* **1.** dupe *f*/victime *f*/gogo *m*/jobard *m*/cave *m* **2.** poule mouillée/trouillard *m*.

patter ['pætər] *n F* (*i*) bavardage *m*/causette *f*/jaserie *m* (*ii*) baratin *m*/boniment *m*/bagou *m*.

paw¹ [pɔː] *n P* main*/patte *f*/paluche *f*; **paws off!/keep your paws to yourself!** bas les pattes!/pas touche! (*See* **southpaw**)

paw² [pɔː] *vtr F* peloter/tripoter (une femme); patouiller (qn/qch).

pax! [pæks] *excl F* (*scol*) pouce! **end of pax**, pouce cassé.

pay [pei] *vtr P* battre*/rosser/tabasser/étriller. (*See* **call¹ 1**; **visit**)

pay dirt ['pei'dɔːt] *n Austr F* **to strike (bottom on) pay dirt**, réussir/toucher au but/décrocher le pompon.

pay-off ['peiɔf] *n F* **1.** règlement *m* de comptes **2.** le bouquet/le comble (qch de tout à fait inattendu) **3.** pot-de-vin *m*/dessous-de-table *m* **4.** (*a*) facteur décisif (*b*) le fin mot (de l'histoire).

pay off ['pei'ɔf] *vi* F avoir du succès/être rentable/faire un boum/boumer.

payola [pei'joulə] *n* F (*esp for a disc jockey*) ristourne *f*/gratte *f*/gant *m*/pot *m* de vin/dessous *m* de table/pourliche *m*.

payroll ['peiroul] *n* F **to be on the payroll**, faire partie de la bande*/être du même bâtiment/émarger.

PCP ['piːsiːpiː] *n* P (= *phencyclidine*) (*drugs*) phéncyclidine *m*/PCP*.

pdq ['piːdiːkjuː] P (*abbr* = *pretty damn quick*) très vite*/en cinq secs/dare-dare.

peacenik ['piːsnik] *n* F marcheur *m*/manifestant *m* pour la paix.

peach¹ [piːtʃ] *n* **1.** F belle* fille/jolie pépée/beau petit lot; **she's a peach of a girl**, c'est un beau brin de fille **2.** F qch de super/de sensass; un délice; **it's a peach of a party**, c'est une super boum; **a peach of an idea**, une idée chouette/sensass **3.** P (*drugs*) amphétamine*/amph *m*.

peach² [piːtʃ] *vi* P dénoncer*/moucharder/cafarder/bourdiller; **to peach on s.o.**, vendre/balancer/donner qn.

peachy ['piːtʃi] *a* F agréable/jojo/juteux.

pea-head ['piːhed] *n* NAm P individu bête*/tête *f* de nœud.

peanut ['piːnʌt] *n* **1.** P (*drugs*) barbiturique* **2.** *pl* F presque rien*/des clous/des clopinettes/des prunes; **that's peanuts!** ça vaut des clopinettes/ça ne vaut pas un rond; **he pays peanuts**, il paie en monnaie de singe/il paie des clous/il les lâche avec un élastique **3.** NAm F (*theatre*) **peanut gallery**, poulailler *m*.

pearl-dive ['pəːldaiv] *vi* V = **muff² 3.**

pearl-diver ['pəːldaivər] *n* V = **muff-diver.**

pearlies ['pəːliz] *npl* F dents*/dominos *mpl*.

pearls [pəːlz] *npl* P (*drugs*) nitrite *m* d'amyle.

pearly ['pəːli] *a* P **pearly gates**, graines *fpl* de volubilis (drogue hallucinogène)/de gloire du matin. (*See* **blue¹ II 1**)

pea-shooter ['piːʃuːtər] *n* P revolver*/rigolo *m*/soufflant *m*. (*See* **shooter**)

pea-souper ['piː'suːpər] *n* F brouillard *m* (à couper au couteau)/purée *f* de pois.

peck [pek] *vi* F manger* du bout des dents; **to peck at one's food**, pignocher/mangeotter son repas.

pecker ['pekər] *n* **1.** P pénis*/goupillon *m*/chibre *m*; **to play with one's pecker**, se masturber*/s'amuser tout seul/se taper une pignole **2.** F courage *m*/cran *m*; **to keep one's pecker up**, ne pas se laisser abattre/tenir bon/tenir le coup.

pecking ['pekiŋ] *a* F **pecking order**, hiérarchie (sociale).

peckish ['pekiʃ] *a* F **to be/feel peckish**, avoir faim*/claquer du bec/avoir la dalle.

pedigree ['pedigriː] *n* P casier *m* judiciaire d'un criminel/pédigrée *m*.

pee¹ [piː] *n* P urine *f*/pipi *m*/pisse *f*; **to have a pee**, uriner*; **to go for a pee**, aller faire pipi/aller pisser un coup.

pee² [piː] *vi* P **1.** uriner*/pisser **2.** pleuvoir à torrent/flotter/pisser; **it's peeing down**, il pleut comme une vache qui pisse.

peed off ['piːd'ɔf] *a* P = **pissed off.**

peek [piːk] *n* P **the peek** = **peep 1.**

peeker ['piːkər] *n P* curieux *m*/ indiscret *m*/voyeur *m*.

peel (off) ['piːl('ɔf)] *vtr&i F* **to peel off** (one's clothes), se déshabiller*/ se décarpiller/se dénipper. (*See* **banana 1**; **onion 1**)

peeler ['piːlər] *n* **1.** *NAm P* strip-teaseuse *f*/effeuilleuse *f* **2.** *A F* agent* de police.

peenie ['piːni] *n A P* pénis*/pine *f*.

pee off ['piː'ɔf] *vi P* = **piss off**.

peep [piːp] *n* **1.** *P* **the peep**, cellule *f*/cellot(t)e *f* de remouchage; cage *f* à poules **2.** *F* **I don't want to hear another peep out of you**, tâche de ne pas piper.

peepers ['piːpəz] *npl F* yeux *mpl*/ mirettes *fpl*/châsses *mpl*/calots *mpl*.

peep freak ['piːp'friːk] *n NAm F* voyeur *m*/individu qui se rince l'œil.

peeping Tom ['piːpiŋ'tɔm] *n F* voyeur *m*/individu qui se rince l'œil.

pee-slit ['piːslit] *n V* sexe de la femme*/fente *f*.

peeve¹ [piːv] *n F* ennui *m*/barbe *f*/ emmerdement *m*; **pet peeve**, barbe *f* de premier ordre/super-emmerde *f*; **it's a pet peeve of mine**, ça me fout toujours en rogne.

peeve² [piːv] *vtr F* ennuyer*/bar-ber/empoisonner/faire chier/mettre en rogne.

peeved [piːvd] *a F* fâché/irrité/ ennuyé; **he was really peeved about it**, ça l'a vraiment mis en rogne/ça lui a donné un coup de sang.

peg [peg] *n F* **1.** **off the peg**, prêt-à-porter *m*/confection *f* **2.** (*a*) **to take s.o. down a peg (or two)**, rabattre le caquet à qn/rogner les ailes à qn/faire déchanter qn (*b*) **to come down a peg**, en rabattre/ baisser le ton/baisser d'un cran **3.** doigt *m* (de whisky, etc) **4.** *pl* jambes*/bâtons *mpl*/cannes *fpl*. (*See* **square¹ I 7**)

peg away ['peg'wei] *vi F* travail-ler* dur/turbiner/piocher/trimer.

pegging ['pegiŋ] *n F* **(on) level pegging**, à égalité; **it's level pegging**, ils sont à égalité.

peg-leg ['pegleg] *n F* (*a*) jambe *f* de bois/pilon *m* (*b*) pilonneur *m*.

peg out ['peg'aut] *vi F* **1.** mourir*/lâcher la rampe/casser sa pipe **2.** **to be pegged out**, être très fatigué*/vanné/crevé/claqué.

pellet ['pelit] *n P* (*drugs*) capsule *f*/ comprimé *m*.

pen [pen] *n NAm F* (= *penitentiary*) prison*/taule *f*/ballon *m*.

pen and ink ['penənd'iŋk] *vi P* **1.** (*RS* = *to stink*) puer/schlinguer/ taper **2.** (*not common*) (*RS* = *to drink*) boire*.

pencil ['pensl] *n P* pénis*/bout *m*/ pointe *f*. (*See* **lead¹ 3**)

penguin ['peŋgwin] *n F* **1.** (*avia-tion*) = **ground walla(h)** (**walla(h) 2**) **2.** **penguin suit**, habit *m* (de soirée)/queue *f* de pie; **wearing a penguin suit**, déguisé/habillé en pingouin.

penman ['penmən] *n P* faussaire *m*/homme *m* de lettres/maquilleur *m*.

penny ['peni] *n F* **1.** **then the penny dropped**, alors on a compris/ pigé; et puis, ça a fait tilt **2.** **to spend a penny**, aller aux WC*/aller au petit coin **3.** (*catchphrase*) **a penny for your thoughts**, à quoi penses-tu? **4.** **she cost me a pretty penny**, elle m'en a fait écosser. (*See* **bad I 6**)

penny-pincher ['penipintʃər] *n F* avare *m*/radin *m*/rapiat *m*/rat *m*.

penny-pinching ['penipintʃiŋ] *F* **I** *a* avare*/constipé du morlingue **II** *n* avarice *f*/radinerie *f*; **I'm fed up with all this penny-pinching**, j'en ai ras le bol de ces radineries/de ces pingreries/de ces histoires de grippe-sous.

pen-pusher ['penpuʃər] *n F* gratte-papier *m*/rond-de-cuir *m*.

pension ['penʃ(ə)n] *n* **1.** *F* old-age pension: *see* **bingo 65 2.** *P* argent versé à un criminel/un racketteur pour qu'il vous protège; **to put s.o. on a pension,** mettre qn à l'amende.

pen-yen ['pen'jen] *n NAm P (drugs)* opium*/op *m*/toufiane *f*/noir *m*.

people ['piːpl] *npl F* **1.** the income-tax people, les gens du fisc/les dégraisseurs *mpl* **2.** to know the right people, avoir le bras long **3.** famille *f*/parents*; **his people live in the country,** ses vieux/ses dabs habitent à la campagne.

pep [pep] *n F* **1. to be full of pep,** être plein d'entrain/péter le feu/péter la santé/avoir la pêche **2. pep pill,** stimulant *m*/topette *f*/remontant *m*/excitant *m* **3. pep talk,** paroles encourageantes qui remontent le moral et émoustillent; **she gave me a little pep talk,** elle m'a fait un petit discours*/d'encouragement/son baratin m'a requinqué.

peppermint ['pepəmint] *a P (RS = skint)* très pauvre*/dans la dèche/raide.

peppy ['pepi] *a F* plein d'allant et de vitalité.

pep up ['pep'ʌp] *vtr F* **1.** émoustiller/ravigoter (qch) **2.** remonter/ragaillardir (qn).

Perce [pɜːs], **Percy** ['pɜːsi] *n P* pénis*/cyclope *m*/Popaul; **to point Percy at the porcelain,** uriner*/égoutter son cyclope/faire pleurer le costaud.

perch [pɜːtʃ] *n F* **to knock s.o. off his perch/to make s.o. come down from his perch,** faire descendre qn de son perchoir/déboulonner qn; **to come off one's perch,** jeter du lest.

perfect ['pɜːfikt] *a F* vrai/absolu; **he's a perfect idiot,** c'est un idiot fini; **he's a perfect menace,** c'est un véritable danger public.

perform [pə'fɔːm] *vi P* **1.** déféquer*/déballer **2.** faire l'amour*/niquer; **he performs very well,** c'est une sacrée affaire/un sacré baiseur.

period ['piəriəd] *n F* I'm not going, period! j'y vais pas, un point c'est tout!

perished ['periʃt] *a F* exténué de froid/rétamé/plombé; **I'm perished,** je crève de froid/ça caille.

perisher ['periʃər] *n F* the little perisher! petite peste!/petit morveux!

perishing ['periʃiŋ] *a F* **1.** it's perishing, il fait un froid de canard; I'm perished, je crève de froid/je suis gelé **2.** sacré/maudit/fichu; a perishing nuisance, un fichu embêtement; you perishing idiot! espèce de triple idiot!/foutu connard!

perks [pɜːks] *npl F (= perquisites)* gratte *f*/affure *f*/grinche *f*/tour *m* de bâton; les petits à-côtés/les petits bénefs; **the job does have a few perks,** ce boulot présente des à-côtés intéressants/des avantages non négligeables.

perk up ['pɜːk'ʌp] *vi F (a)* ravigoter/requinquer (qn) *(b)* se ravigoter/se requinquer.

perm¹ [pɜːm] *n F* **1.** *(= permanent wave)* indéfrisable *f*/permanente *f* **2.** *(= permutation)* permutation *f* (au tiercé du football).

perm² [pɜːm] *vtr F* **1. to have one's hair permed,** se faire faire une permanente **2.** *(football pools)* faire une permutation; permuter.

pernickety [pə'nikəti] *a F* tâtillon/pointilleux; **to be pernickety about one's food,** être difficile/délicat sur la nourriture*.

persuader [pə'sweidər] *n P* **1.** pénis*/baïonnette *f* **2.** arme *f*/flingue *m*.

perv(e)¹ [pɜːv] *n P* **1.** perverti *m*; inverti *m* **2.** voyeur *m*.

perv(e)[2] [pəɪv] *vi P* **to perv(e) on s.o.**, se rincer l'œil (en regardant qn).

pesky ['peski] *a NAm F* ennuyeux*/scie/rasoir; **a pesky brat**, un petit morveux/un chiard.

pest [pest] *n F* enquiquineur *m*/poison *mf*/plaie *f*.

pet [pet] *vi F* se caresser/se peloter. (*See* **petting**)

Pete [piːt] *Prn F* **for Pete's sake!** pour l'amour de Dieu!/pour l'amour du ciel!/bon sang!

peter ['piːtər] *n P* **1.** coffre-fort *m*/coffiot *m* **2.** (*RS = (prison) cell*) **Peter (Bell)**, cellule *f* de prison/celot(t)e *f*. (*See* **flowery (dell)**) **3.** pénis*/Charles-le-Chauve/Popaul.

peterman ['piːtəmən] *n P* perceur *m*/casseur *m* de coffre-fort.

petticoat-chaser ['petikoutʃeisər] *n O F* coureur *m* de jupons/cavaleur *m*.

petting ['petiŋ] *n F* badinage amoureux/pelotage *m*; **heavy petting**, pelotage poussé; **petting party**, party *f* de pelote maison; **petting session**, séance *f* de bécotage *m*/de pelotage *m*. (*See* **pet**)

pew [pjuː] *n F* **to take a pew**, s'asseoir/poser ses fesses/se poser; **take a pew!** pose ton cul!/gare ta graisse!

pewter ['pjuːtər] *n P* argent *m* (métal).

peyote ['peijouti] *n P* (*drugs*) mescaline*/mesc *f*.

p.g. ['piːˈdʒiː] *abbr P* (*drugs*) (*= paregoric*) (élixir *m*) parégorique *m*/parégo *m*.

phenie ['fiːni] *n F* (*drugs*) phénobarbital *m*; barbiturique *m*.

phiz [fiz], **phizog** ['fizɔg] *n P* visage*/frime *f*/frimousse *f*; **an ugly phiz**, une gueule d'empeigne/une gueule de raie/une sale gueule/une face de rat.

phon(e)y ['founi] **I** *a* **1.** *F* faux*/bidon/toc(ard); **it's phon(e)y**, c'est du toc **2.** (*a*) *F* contrefait/falsifié (*b*) *P* **phon(e)y white**, fausses pièces d'argent*/mornifle truquée **II** *n* **1.** *F* (*a*) charlatan *m*/bluffeur *m*/chiqueur *m* (*b*) (*insincere*) **what a phon(e)y he was!** quel baratineur! **2.** *P* qn qui fait des appels téléphoniques obscènes.

phooey! ['fuːi] *excl F* flûte!/mince alors!

phut [fʌt] *adv F* **to go phut**, échouer*/rater/louper/s'en aller en eau de boudin/claquer.

phy [fai] *P* (*abbr = physeptone*) (*drugs*) physeptone *f*.

pi [pai] *a P* (*= pious*) papelard/bondieusard. (*See* **jaw**[1] **2**)

Piccadilly Circus ['pikədiliˈsəɪkəs] *Prn F* **it's like Piccadilly Circus!** quel embouteillage!/on se croirait à l'Étoile!/c'est pire que l'Étoile!

pick [pik] *n F* **the pick of the bunch**, le dessus du panier/la fleur des petits pois.

picker ['pikər] *n NAm P = peeker*. (*See* **winkle-pickers**)

pickle ['pikl] *n F* **1. to be in a pickle**, être dans le pétrin/dans de mauvais draps/dans la mouise; **he's got himself into a right old pickle**, il s'est complètement fourré dans le pétrin/il s'est mis dans une très sale passe **2.** petit diable/diablotin *m*.

pickled ['pikld] *a F* ivre*/rétamé.

pick-me-up ['pikmi(ɪ)ʌp] *n F* remontant *m*/stimulant *m*/coup *m* de fouet.

pick on ['pikɔn] *vtr F* chercher noise à (qn)/chercher des poux dans la tête à (qn)/être sur le dos à (qn); **stop picking on me!** lâche-moi les baskets!/arrête de me courir sur le haricot!

pick-up ['pikʌp] *n* **1.** *F* (*a*) rencontre *f* de fortune/femme dont on fait connaissance dans la rue (*b*) client* de prostituée/clille *m*/ micheton *m* **2.** *F* **to have a pick-up,** être conduit quelque part en voiture **3.** *F* redressement *m*/ relèvement *m*/reprise *f* **4.** *P* drogues* obtenues d'un pourvoyeur; **to make a pick-up,** se garnir/trouver le contact.

pick up ['pik'ʌp] *vtr* **1.** *F* arrêter*/ agrafer/pincer/coffrer **2.** *F* (*prostitute*) ramasser/emballer/lever (un client); faire (un levage) **3.** *F* ramasser/récolter; **to pick up sth nasty,** attraper/choper la crève **4.** *F* **to pick up the pieces,** repartir à zéro/recoller les restes **5.** *F* reprendre/corriger (qn) **6.** *F* **to pick up with s.o.,** faire la connaissance de qn **7.** *P* obtenir des drogues d'un pourvoyeur **8.** *F* **to pick up on sth,** assimiler/digérer qch **9.** *F* (*physically, financially*) se rebecter/se rebecqueter/se remplumer/se refaire/reprendre du poil de la bête.

picky ['piki] *a F* méticuleux/chichiteux; **to be picky,** chercher la petite bête.

picnic ['piknik] *n P* **1.** occupation *f* agréable et facile/partie *f* de plaisir; **it was no picnic, I can assure you,** ce n'était pas du gâteau/de la tarte, je vous le promets **2.** rigolade *f*/un vrai cirque.

picture ['piktʃər] *n F* **1. to put s.o. in the picture,** mettre qn au courant/à la page; affranchir qn **2. she's a real picture!** c'est une beauté!/elle est ravissante! **3.** (*a*) **to step into the picture,** se montrer/ se manifester (*b*) **to step out of the picture,** s'effacer/se retirer **4. get the picture?** compris?/pigé?/tu piges? (*See* **paint**)

piddle¹ ['pidl] *n F* urine *f*/pipi *m*/ pisse *f*; **I need a piddle,** j'ai envie de faire pipi; **he's gone for a piddle,** il est allé faire sa goutte/faire une vidange.

piddle² ['pidl] *vi F* uriner*/faire

pipi/pisser **2.** *P* pleuvoter/ pleuvasser/tomber un pipi de chat.

piddle about, around ['pidlə'baut, ə'raund] *P* (*a*) paresser*/flânocher/glander/ glandouiller (*b*) faire le con/déconner; **stop piddling about over there and come here!** arrêtez de vous les tourner et ramenez-vous ici!

piddling ['pidliŋ] *a F* insignifiant/ futile; négligeable; **a piddling amount,** que dalle/peau de balle/ des clous; **you piddling little idiot!** espèce de petit con/de trou du cul!

pidgin ['pidʒin] *n F* **1.** = **pigeon 2 2. to talk pidgin,** parler petit nègre.

pie [pai] *n F* **pie in the sky,** le miel de l'autre monde. (*See* **apple-pie**; **easy I 6; finger¹ 6; fruity-pie; furpie; hairpie; mince-pies; resurrection pie; sweetie-pie; tongue-pie; tweety(-pie)**)

piece [piːs] *n* **1.** *P* fille*/femme*; **she's a sexy piece,** c'est un beau morceau/un beau brin de fille/un beau petit lot; une chaude lapine/ une chaude de la pince **2.** *F* (*pers*) **to go to pieces,** s'effondrer/ s'écrouler; perdre les pédales **3.** *P* deux grammes d'héroïne *ou* de stupéfiant **4.** *F* **to pull s.o. to pieces,** démolir qn/mettre qn en bouillie **5.** *NAm F* arme *f*/ revolver*/flingue *m* **6.** *F* **to give s.o. a piece of one's mind,** sonner les cloches à qn/passer un (bon) savon à qn. (*See* **ass I 2; cake 1, 3; headpiece; kettle 1; mouth-piece; pick up 4; piss 9; ring-piece; sky-piece; tail¹ 4; think-piece; two-piece; work¹**)

pie-eyed ['paiaid] *a F* ivre*/gris/ éméché.

piffle ['pifl] *n F* bêtises*/futilités *fpl*/balivernes *fpl*/conneries *fpl*; **to talk piffle,** dire des conneries/débloquer/déconner.

piffling ['pifliŋ] *a F* = **piddling.**

pig¹ [pig] *n* **1.** *F* goinfre*/gueulard *m*/morfalou *m*; **to make a pig of oneself**, se goinfrer/s'empiffrer/bâfrer **2.** *F* salaud *m*/saligaud *m*/vache *f*; **you pig!** la vache!/salaud!/sale type! **he's a real pig towards women**, c'est un (sale) phallocrate/un phallo **3.** *P* agent* de police/perdreau *m*/flic *m*/vache *f*; **the pigs**, la flicaille/les vaches **4.** *P* (*a*) (*RS = beer*) **pig's ear**, bière *f* (*b*) **pig's ear**, désordre *m*/pagaille *f*/gâchis *m*; **he made a real pig's ear of it**, il en a fait un beau gâchis **5.** *P* **in pig**, enceinte*/en cloque **6.** *F* **to buy a pig in a poke**, acheter chat en poche **7.** *F* **pig's breakfast**, méli-mélo *m*/fouillis *m*/salade *f*; **it looked like a pig's breakfast**, c'était un sacré bazar/chantier.

pig² [pig] *vtr&i* *P* **1.** se goinfrer/s'empiffrer/bâfrer/manger comme un cochon **2.** **to pig it**, vivre comme un cochon/vivre dans une écurie **3.** **to pig together**, partager la même chambre.

pig-boat ['pigbout] *n* *P* sous-marin *m*/plongeant *m*.

pigeon ['pidʒin] *n* *F* **1.** dupe *f*/dindon *m*/poire *f*/pigeon *m* **2.** **it's not my pigeon**, ça ne me regarde pas/c'est pas mes oignons; **that's your pigeon**, ça te regarde/c'est ton rayon/ton affaire **3.** jeune fille*/caille *f*. (*See* **stool-pigeon**)

pigeon-roost ['pidʒinruːst] *n* *F* le poulailler/le paradis. (*See* **chicken-roost**)

piggish ['pigiʃ] *a* *F* **1.** sale/grossier/cochon **2.** têtu/entêté.

piggy ['pigi] *F* **I** *a* goinfre*/goulu; **piggy eyes**, de petits yeux de cochon **II** *n* (*child's word*) **1.** cochonnet *m*/cochon *m* de lait/porcelet *m* **2.** petit goret/petit goulu **3.** (*a*) doigt *m* (*b*) doigt de pied.

piggyback ['pigibæk] *n* *F* **to give s.o. a piggyback**, porter qn sur le dos *ou* sur les épaules.

piggy-bank ['pigibæŋk] *n* *F* tire-lire *f*/boîte *f* à sous (en forme de cochon).

pig-meat ['pigmiːt] *n* *P* **1.** prostituée*/bourrin *m* **2.** la Veuve Montre-tout/une vieille paillasse **3.** fille bête*/andouille *f*.

pigwash ['pigwɔʃ] *n* *F* (*not common*) = **hogwash 1**.

pike¹ [paik] *n* **1.** *O* *P̂* route*/trime *f* **2.** *NAm* *F* (= *turnpike*) autoroute *f* à péage.

pike² [paik] *vi* *O* *P* marcher*/trimarder/aller à pattes.

piker ['paikər] *n* *P* **1.** avare *m*/grigou *m* **2.** débiteur *m*/qn qui part sans payer.

pikestaff ['paikstæf] *n* *F* **it's as plain as a pikestaff**, c'est clair comme le jour.

pile [pail] *n* *F* **1.** (*a*) **to make a pile (of money)**, gagner* beaucoup d'argent/en amasser/faire sa pelote (*b*) **to make one's pile**, devenir riche*/faire son beurre **2.** **a pile of work**, un tas/un monceau/une pile de travail* **3.** **piles of...**, des masses de.../tout un tas de....

pile-driver ['paildraivər] *n* *F* coup* d'assommoir/direct *m*/marron *m*.

pile in ['pail'in] *vi* *F* s'empiler dans un véhicule; **they all piled into the bus**, ils se sont tous empilés/entassés dans le bus.

pile into ['pail'intuː] *vtr* *F* **to pile into s.o.**, attaquer* qn/rentrer dedans/agrafer qn.

pile on ['pail'ɔn] *vtr* *F* **to pile it on**, exagérer*/y aller fort/charrier. (*See* **agony 2**)

pile-up ['pailʌp] *n* *F* carambolage *m*/emboutissage *m*; **a fifty car pile-up on the motorway**, un carambolage de cinquante voitures sur l'autoroute.

pill [pil] *n* **1.** *F* balle *f*/ballon *m* **2.** *pl* *P* testicules*/billes *fpl*/roupettes *fpl* **3.** *F* **(bitter) pill**, personne *f*

ou chose *f* désagréable/pilule *f*/
poison *mf*; **it was a bitter pill to
swallow**, c'était dur à avaler/une
pilule difficile à avaler **4.** *P (drugs)*
(a) capsule *f* de Nembutal *(b)*
boulette *f* d'opium*. (*See* **pill-pad**)
5. *F* **to be on the pill**, prendre la
pilule.

pillhead ['pilhed] *n P* habitué(e)
des opiacés/opiomane *mf*.

pillock ['pilək] *n F* imbécile*/
andouille *f*/tête *f* de nœud.

pillow-talk ['piloutɔ:k] *n F*
semence conjugale/discours *m* sur
l'oreiller/engueulade *f* entre deux
draps.

pill-pad ['pilpæd] *n P* fumerie *f*
d'opium; repaire *m*/turne *f* de
drogués.

pimple ['pimpl] *n P* **1.** (*RS =
Scotch (whisky)*) **pimple and blotch,**
whisky *m* **2.** *pl* **pimples,** petits
seins*/mandarines *fpl*.

pin [pin] *vtr F* **1. to pin sth on s.o.**,
rendre qn responsable/mettre qch
sur le dos de qn; **they pinned it on
me**, j'ai dû porter le chapeau pour
eux **2.** *NAm* draguer/faire du plat
à/faire du gringue à (qn).

pinball ['pinbɔ:l] *n F* flipper *m*/flip
m.

pinch¹ [pintʃ] *n F* **1. to feel the
pinch**, tirer le diable par la queue
2. at a pinch, au besoin.

pinch² [pintʃ] *vtr F* **1.** voler*/
chiper/chaparder **2.** arrêter*/
alpaguer/agrafer; **to get pinched**, se
faire épingler/pincer **3. to be
pinched for time/money**, être à
court de temps/d'argent.

pinchers ['pintʃəz] *npl P* menottes*/pinces *fpl*/poucettes *fpl*/brace-
lets *mpl*.

pinching ['pintʃiŋ] *n F* vol *m*/
chapardage *m*. (*See* **penny-pinch-
ing²**)

pine [pain] *n F* **pine overcoat =
wooden overcoat** (**overcoat**).

pineapple ['painæpl] *n F* grenade
f à main/poire *f*/ananas *m*.

ping [piŋ] *n P* piqûre* de drogue;
ping in the wing, piquouse *f* dans
l'aile.

pinhead ['pinhed] *n P* **1.** petite
tête*/tête d'épingle **2.** qn
d'ignorant*/nouille *f*.

pink [piŋk] *F* **I** *a* **1.** à tendances
socialistes; rose sur les bords **2.**
NAm **to get the pink slip**, être
renvoyé/se faire virer. (*See* **elephant 2; strike 1; tickle² 2**) **II** *n*
F **to be in the pink**, se porter à
merveille/comme un charme.

pink-eye ['piŋkai] *n Austr P* lèche-
bottes *m*/lèche-cul *m*.

pinkie ['piŋki] *n* **1.** *F* le petit
doigt/le riquiqui/le petit didi **2.** *P*
un blanc.

pink lint ['piŋklint] *a P* (*RS =
skint*) pauvre*/raide.

pinko ['piŋkou] *n NAm F (pej)* personne *f* à tendances socialistes/à
tendances roses; gauchiste *mf*/
gaucho *mf*.

pinky ['piŋki] *n F & P* = **pinkie**.

pinny ['pini] *n F* (= *pinafore*) tablier *m*/bavette *f*.

pin-pricks ['pinpriks] *npl F* tracas-
series *fpl*/asticotages *mpl*.

pins [pinz] *F* **1.** jambes*/fusains
mpl/quilles *fpl*; **he's not very steady
on his pins**, il ne tient pas sur ses
cannes **2. to be on pins and needles**, être sur des charbons ardents.
(*See* **piss² 2**)

pinta ['paintə] *n F* bouteille *f* de
lait; demi-litre *m* (de lait).

pint-size(d) ['paintsaiz(d)] *a F* **a
pint-size(d) person**, individu *m* de
petite* taille/courte-botte *f*/demi-
portion *f*/rase-bitume *m*.

pin-up ['pinʌp] *n F* **1.** belle fille*/
pin-up *f*/prix *m* de Diane; **pin-up
mag**, magazine *m* de pin-up.

pip¹ [pip] *n F* **1. to give s.o. the
pip** *(a)* déprimer qn/flanquer le

cafard à qn (b) embêter qn/casser les pieds à qn 2. (mil) galon m/ficelle f; to get one's pip, recevoir ses galons/arborer la ficelle; he's just got his third pip, il vient d'avoir sa troisième ficelle.

pip² [pip] vtr 1. P blackbouler (qn) 2. F the horse was pipped at the post, le cheval a été battu au poteau (d'arrivée) 3. F to pip an exam, être recalé/se faire coller à un examen 4. P tuer* ou blesser (qn) avec une arme à feu/flinguer (qn).

pipe [paip] n 1. F put that in your pipe and smoke it! mets ça dans ta poche et ton mouchoir par-dessus! 2. P to hit the pipe, fumer de l'opium/y aller du chilom. (See drainpipe; stove-pipe)

pipe down ['paip'daun] vi P (a) faire moins de bruit*; mettre un bémol/une sourdine (à la clef); pipe down, will you! baisse un peu ta musique! (b) se taire*/la boucler.

pipe-job ['paipdʒɔb] n V fellation*/prise f de pipe; to give s.o. a pipe-job, tailler une pipe/faire un pompier à qn. (See blow-job)

pipeline ['paiplain] n F 1. to be in the pipeline, être en cours/en voie/en train 2. to have a pipeline, avoir une filière/une combine.

pipe up ['paip'ʌp] vi F se faire entendre/l'ouvrir tout d'un coup.

pip out ['pip'aut] vi P mourir*/faire couic/clamser.

pippins ['pipinz] npl A P (euph) seins*/nénés mpl.

pipsqueak ['pipskwiːk] F I a petit/minuscule/insignifiant II n gringalet m/minus m/minable m; a little pipsqueak like you, un petit bout de rien comme toi.

piss¹ [pis] n P 1. urine f/pipi m/pisse f; I need a piss, j'ai envie de faire pipi; he's gone for a piss, il est allé faire sa goutte/pisser un coup 2. to take the piss (out of s.o.), faire marcher qn/se payer la

tête de qn; stop taking the piss, will you? arrête de te foutre de ma gueule! (See piss-taker) 3. a long streak of piss (a) une perche/un échalas/un individu long comme un jour sans pain (b) un gros plein de soupe 4. bêtises*/foutaises fpl/conneries fpl 5. cat's/gnat's piss, pipi m de chat/bibine f/jus m de chaussettes 6. to be full of piss and wind, être comme une bulle de savon 7. to be full of piss and vinegar, être plein d'entrain/péter le feu/avoir la frite 8. to beat the piss out of s.o., battre* qn comme plâtre/tabasser qn/passer qn à tabac 9. a piece of piss, qch de très facile/du nougat.

piss² [pis] vtr&i P uriner*/pisser/lansquiner 2. to piss pins and needles, être atteint de gonorrhée*/avoir la chaude-pisse/pisser des lames de rasoir (en travers) 3. to piss oneself laughing, se tordre les côtes de rire/rire* à s'en mouiller/pisser dans sa culotte (de rire) 4. to piss blood, suer sang et eau/s'échiner 5. = piss down.

piss-about ['pisəbaut] n P bonne rigolade/franche marrade/une bonne tranche de rire.

piss about, around ['pisə'baut, -ə'raund] vi V (a) glander/glandouiller (b) faire le con/déconner; foutre la merde; stop pissing about, will you! arrête de déconner, veux-tu!

piss-all ['pisɔːl] n P rien/peau de balle/balpeau; there's piss-all to do at night round here, il n'y a rien de lâché/il n'y a rien à secouer, ici la nuit; there's piss-all to drink in the cupboard, il y a pas une goutte/rien à licher dans le buffet.

piss-artist ['pisɑːtist] n P 1. ivrogne*/poivrier m/poivrot m 2. fouteur m de merde; connard m/con m.

piss away ['pisə'wei] vi P dépenser* sans compter/bouffer/

claquer (de l'argent*)/flamber son fric.

piss down ['pis'daun] *vi* P pleuvoir*/pisser; **it's pissing down,** il pleut comme une vache qui pisse.

pissed [pist] *a* P ivre*; **to get pissed (up),** s'enivrer/prendre une cuite/prendre une bit(t)ure; **they were pissed out of their minds/completely pissed,** ils étaient bourrés à zéro. (*See* **arsehole 2**)

pissed off ['pist'ɔf] *a* P **1. to be pissed off,** en avoir assez*/ras le bol/plus que marre; **I was really pissed off with it all,** j'en avais plein le cul de tout ça **2.** très en colère*/en rage/en boule.

pisser ['pisər] *n* P **1.** pénis*/queue *f*/pine *f* **2.** WC*/pissotière *f*/pissoir *m* **3.** con *m*/connard *m* **4. to pull s.o.'s pisser,** faire marcher qn/monter un bateau à qn/faire monter qn à l'échelle.

pisshouse ['pishaus] *n* P WC*/pissotière *f*/tasse *f*.

pissing ['pisiŋ] *a* V **1.** (*intensifier*) **it's pissing cold,** ça caille les miches; **he's a pissing nuisance,** c'est un raseur/un emmerdeur de première; **that was a pissing awful film,** c'était un sacré navet, ce film **2. pissing hell!** bordel de merde!

piss off ['pis'ɔf] *vi* P s'enfuir*/se tirer/se trisser; **piss off!** fous le camp!/je t'envoie chier!/va te faire voir! **the little bugger's pissed off,** le petit merdeux s'est carapaté/a mis les bouts. (*See* **pissed off**)

piss on ['pisɔn] *vtr* P dénigrer (qn)/débiner (qn)/traiter (qn) comme du poisson pourri; pisser à la raie à qn.

piss-poor ['pis'pɔːr] *a* P **1.** très pauvre*/purotin/déchard/dans la purée noire **2.** de mauvaise qualité/tocard/de la camelote/du toc.

pisspot ['pispɔt] *n* P **1.** pot *m* de chambre/Jules/Thomas **2.** saligaud *m*/salaud *m* **3.** ivrogne*/sac *m* à vin/poivrot *mf*/alcolo *mf*.

piss-taker ['pisteikər] *n* P blagueur *m*/persifleur m. (*See* **mick(e)y-taker; piss¹ 2**)

piss-tank ['pistæŋk] *n* P = **pisspot 3.**

piss-up ['pisʌp] *n* P **1.** beuverie (générale); boum *f* **2. he couldn't organise a piss-up in a brewery,** il est pas capable de/il pourrait pas monter une beuverie générale à la brasserie.

pit [pit] *n* P **1.** lit*/pageot *m* **2.** poche* intérieure d'un vêtement/profonde *f* **3.** *pl* **the pits,** le pire (de tout); **this place is the pits of the Earth,** c'est un des coins les plus perdus/les plus moches/les plus minables du globe. (*See* **fleapit**)

pitch¹ [pitʃ] *n* P **1.** paroisse *f* d'une prostituée/chasse gardée **2.** le "mâle" dans un couple homosexuel/chauffeur *m* **3.** discours*/boniment *m*/speech *m*; laïus *m*; **to make a pitch,** bonimenter/pleurer misère **4.** *esp NAm* **to make a pitch for s.o.,** draguer qn; faire du rentre-dedans à qn. (*See* **queer² 1**)

pitch² [pitʃ] *vi* F **to be in there pitching,** y aller de tout son soûl/se décarcasser. (*See* **fly-pitch; yarn¹**)

pitcher ['pitʃər] *n Austr* F bavard*/jacasseur m. (*See* **fly-pitcher**)

pitch in ['pitʃ'in] *vi* F **1.** s'empiffrer/s'en mettre plein la lampe **2.** se mettre au travail*/embrayer/rentrer dans le mastic/s'y mettre **3.** donner de l'argent*/les abouler.

pitch into ['pitʃ'intuː] *vtr* F **1.** attaquer*/tomber sur le poil de (qn)/rentrer dans le lard à (qn) **2.** réprimander*/attraper/secouer les puces à (qn).

pix [piks] **1.** *n NAm* P (*not common*) homosexuel*/lopette *f* **2.** *pl* F (= *pictures*) (*a*) film *m*; cinéma *m*/cinoche *m* (*b*) images *fpl*/illustrations *fpl*; photos *fpl*.

pixil(l)ated ['piksileitid] *a esp NAm F* **1.** un peu fou*/cinglé/ barjot **2.** ivre*/bit(t)uré/rétamé.

place¹ [pleis] *n F* **1. to go places** (*a*) voir du pays et du monde/ rouler sa bosse (*b*) réussir dans la vie/monter les échelons/faire un boum **2.** piaule *f*; **come and lunch at our place,** venez déjeuner chez nous.

place² [pleis] *vtr F* **I can't place him,** je ne le remets pas.

plague¹ [pleig] *n F* (*pers*) plaie *f*/ peste *f*/poison *mf*.

plague² [pleig] *vtr F* **to plague (the life out of)** s.o., harceler qn/rendre la vie impossible à qn.

plain [plein] *adv F* **plain daft/dumb,** bête* comme chou/complètement borné/con comme la lune.

plant¹ [plɑint] *n P* **1.** faux-frère *m*/pisteur *m*/chevilleur *m* **2.** piège *m*/amarre *f*/duperie *f*/roustissure *f* **3.** fabrication *f* de faux témoignage/boucanade *f*; coup monté **4.** planque (voulue *ou* délibérée) **5.** cachette*/lieu sûr/ planque *f*/planquouse *f* **6.** (*drugs*) marijuana*/herbe *f*.

plant² [plɑint] *vtr* **1.** *F* **to plant sth,** cacher* qch/mettre qch en planque; **the cops planted a gun/the drugs on him,** les flics lui ont collé un canon/de la drogue sur le dos **2.** *P* donner/flanquer/foutre (un coup* à qn) **3.** *F* **to plant oneself in front of** s.o., se planter devant qn; **to plant oneself on** s.o., s'installer chez qn **4.** *Austr P* faire l'amour*/pousser sa pointe/planter.

plaster ['plɑistər] *vtr P* **1.** battre*/ rouer de coups*/filer une dérouillée à (qn) **2.** battre (un adversaire) à plate(s) couture(s) **3.** (*mil*) bombarder/pilonner.

plastered ['plɑistəd] *a P* ivre*/ rétamé/blindé/fadé; **he was completely plastered,** il était bourré à zéro.

plastering ['plɑistəriŋ] *n F* **1.**

volée *f* de coups*/pâtée *f*/raclée *f*/ dérouillée *f* **2.** défaite *f*/raclée *f*/ déculottage *m* **3.** (*mil*) bombardement *m* d'artillerie lourde/artiflottage *m*/pilonnage *m* **4.** (*mil*) bombardement *m* de saturation.

plate¹ [pleit] *n* **1.** *F* **to have plenty/a lot on one's plate,** avoir du pain sur la planche/avoir de quoi faire; **I've got far too much on my plate,** j'ai du boulot par-dessus les oreilles; j'en ai plus que ma part **2.** *P* (*RS = feet*) **plates (of meat),** pieds*/panards *mpl*/nougats *mpl*/ arpions *mpl* **3.** *F* **to give/hand** s.o. **sth on a plate,** le servir sur un plateau/l'offrir tout rôti.

plate² [pleit] *vtr V* (*oral sex*) faire une fellation à (qn)/faire un pompier à (qn)/manger (qn)/sucer (qn).

play¹ [plei] *n F* **to make a play for** s.o./sth, user de tout son talent pour obtenir qch *ou* pour séduire qn; faire du gringue/du palass/du charme. (*See* **horseplay**)

play² [plei] *vtr&i F* **1. to play with oneself,** se masturber*/jouer de la mandoline/s'amuser tout seul/faire cinq contre un **2. don't play games with me!** ne te paye pas ma tête!/ ne me fais pas marcher!/ne me fais pas tourner en bourrique!/n'essaie pas de me rouler! (*See* **ball**¹ **3**; **cool**¹ **II**; **fool**¹ **II**; **Harry 2**; **safe II**; **sucker II 1**)

play about, around ['pleiə'baut, -ə'raund] *vi F* **1. to play about with women,** courir le jupon/juponner; **stop playing about with my wife,** arrête de tourner autour de ma femme/de faire de l'œil à ma femme **2. don't play about with me! = don't play games with me!** (**play**² **2**).

playact ['pleiækt] *vi F* (*fig*) faire du théâtre/jouer la comédie.

playacting ['pleiæktiŋ] *n F* comédie *f*; **it's only playacting,** c'est de la comédie/c'est du cinéma.

playboy ['pleibɔi] *n F* homme riche* qui aime s'amuser/grand viveur/noceur *m*/playboy *m*.

played out ['pleid'aut] *a* **1.** *F* très fatigué*/vanné/éreinté **2.** *F* vieux jeu/démodé **3.** *F* banal/usé/rebattu **4.** *P* très pauvre*/sans le sou/dans la purée/décavé/à sec.

play up ['pleiˈʌp] *vtr&i F* **1.** my rheumatism is playing me up, mes douleurs me font mal **2.** ennuyer*/asticoter/enquiquiner **3.** to play sth up, monter qch en épingle/faire ressortir qch **4.** to play up to s.o. (*a*) flatter* qn/lécher les bottes à qn/pommader qn (*b*) collaborer avec qn/baronner qn.

plea [pliː] *n NAm F* (*law*) **to cop a plea,** plaider coupable afin de recevoir une peine plus légère.

pleb¹ [pleb], **plebby** ['plebi] *a P* vulgaire*/popu(lo)/populmiche; **he lives in a very plebby area,** il y a du peuple, là où il crèche; il habite un quartier prolo.

pleb² [pleb] *n P* faubourien *m*/prolo *m*; **you're such a pleb!** t'es un drôle de péquin/de prolo!

plenty ['plenti] *adv F* **it's plenty good enough,** ça suffit largement; **it's plenty big enough,** c'est bien assez gros.

plonk¹ [plɔŋk] *n F* vin* ordinaire/gros rouge/vinasse *f*/décapant *m*.

plonk² [plɔŋk] *vtr F* (*a*) mettre/flanquer/coller/ficher; **to plonk money on a horse,** miser sur un cheval* (*b*) laisser tomber lourdement; **plonk it down over there,** flanque-moi ça dans ce coin.

plonker ['plɔŋkər] *n P* pénis*/défonceuse *f*/dardillon *m*/zob *m*; **to pull one's plonker,** se masturber*/s'astiquer (la colonne); **he got his plonker out,** il a sorti sa chose/son petit frère.

plonko ['plɔŋkou] *n esp Austr P* ivrogne*/sac *m* à vin/poivrot *mf*/alcolo *mf*. (*See* **wino**)

plonk out ['plɔŋk'aut] *vi P* (*a*) payer*/les allonger/les abouler (*b*) placer de l'argent*.

plot [plɔt] *n P* (*criminals, police*) territoire *m*/champ *m* d'action/chasse gardée. (*See* **manor**; **patch 2**)

plough¹ [plau] *n F* échec *m* (à un examen)/recalade *f*/recalage *m*.

plough² [plau] *vtr F* **to plough an exam/to be ploughed in an exam,** échouer*/être recalé/se planter/être collé à un examen. (*See* **deep II**)

ploughed, *NAm* **plowed** [plaud] *a P* ivre*/blindé/bourré (à zéro).

plough into, *NAm* **plow into** ['plau'intuː] *n F* **to plough into s.o.,** attaquer* qn/tomber sur le dos/le paletot à qn; **to plough into a parked car,** emboutir une voiture en stationnement.

ploy [plɔi] *n F* stratagème *m*/roublardise *f*/ruse *f* du sioux.

pluck [plʌk] *vtr Austr P* arrêter*/agrafer/cueillir (qn).

plug¹ [plʌg] *n* **1.** *F* publicité *f*/battage *m*/postiche *f*/coup *m* de pouce; pub gratuite **2.** *P* **to give s.o. a plug (in the earhole),** donner*/foutre une beigne/une baffe à qn **3.** *P* balle*/bastos *f*/pastille *f* **4.** *F* cheval* médiocre/canasson *m*/bourrin *m*/trottinette *f* **5.** *F* **to pull the plug on sth,** abandonner l'idée de qch; faire échouer* qch; **to pull the plug on s.o.,** couler qn (à fond).

plug² [plʌg] *vtr&i* **1.** *F* (*a*) faire de la réclame/du battage (*b*) promouvoir/pousser (qch) **2.** *P* faire l'amour* avec (une femme)/fourrer **3.** *P* battre*/frapper/rosser (qn) **4.** *F* = **plug away 5.** *P* fusiller/flinguer/flingoter (qn).

plug away ['plʌgə'wei] *vi F* **1.** travailler* dur/turbiner/bûcher **2.** s'acharner/s'obstiner; **he was still plugging away at it,** il se décarcassait toujours sur ce travail.

plugger ['plʌgər] *n F* **1.** agent *m*

de publicité/posticheur *m*/ promoteur *m* de vente **2.** trimeur *m*/turbineur *m*/bûcheur *m*/coltineur *m*.

plug-ugly ['plʌg'ʌgli] *n NAm F* (*a*) canaille *f*/affreux *m*/dur *m*/crapule *f* (*b*) gueule *f* d'empeigne/de raie.

plum [plʌm] *n F* **1. plum (job),** travail* facile et bien rétribué/ boulot *m* en or/filon *m*/fromage *m* **2.** assiette *f* au beurre/vache *f* à lait.

plumb [plʌm] *adv F* **plumb crazy,** fou* à lier/complètement siphonné.

plumbing ['plʌmiŋ] *n F* **to have a look at the plumbing,** aller aux WC*/au petit coin; faire pipi.

plummy ['plʌmi] *a F* **1.** (travail, etc) agréable/bien payé/en or **2.** (voix) (*i*) profonde/caverneuse (*ii*) de la haute.

plunge[1] [plʌndʒ] *n F* **to take the plunge** (*a*) prendre le taureau par les cornes/se jeter à l'eau/plonger au large (*b*) se marier/se marida/ signer un bail.

plunge[2] [plʌndʒ] *vi F* jouer gros jeu/se mouiller.

plunger ['plʌndʒər] *n F* joueur *m* de grosse mise/ponte *m*.

plunk [plʌŋk] *n NAm P* **1.** A dollar *m* **2.** coup* bien asséné/une bonne beigne.

plush [plʌʃ], **plushy** ['plʌʃi] *a F* riche*/rupin/somptueux; **his place is a bit plush,** elle est chic, sa turne; il pète dans la soie.

plute [pluːt] *n F* (*abbr* = *plutocrat*) plutocrate *m*/rupin(os) *m*.

po [pou] *n F* pot *m* de chambre/ Jules. (*See* **po-faced**)

pocket ['pɔkit] *n F* **to have short arms and deep pockets/to have a death adder in one's pocket,** être avare*/être constipé du morlingue/ être dur à la détente.

pod [pɔd] *n P* **1.** (*drugs*) (*a*) marijuana*/thé vert (*b*) cigarette* de marijuana/stick *m*/bomb *f* **2. to be in pod,** être enceinte*/être en cloque/avoir un polichinelle dans le tiroir **3.** ventre*/bidon *m*/bide *m*. (*See* **podge 2** (*b*))

podge [pɔdʒ] *n F* **1.** individu gros*/bouboule *m*/patapouf *m* **2.** (*a*) graisse *f*/gras-double *m*/pneu *m* Michelin (*b*) bedaine *f*/panse *f*/bide *m*.

podgy ['pɔdʒi] *a F* rondelet/gras-souillet/plein de soupe.

poet's day ['pouitsdei] *abbr F&P* (= *push off/piss off early tomorrow's Saturday*) vendredi *m*.

po-faced ['poufeist] *a P* avec une tête d'enterrement/de bedeau.

point [pɔint] *n P* (*drugs*) shooteuse *f*/aiguille*/hypo *f*.

pointy(-)head ['pɔintihed] *n NAm F* intellectuel *m*/mandarin *m*/ tête *f* d'œuf.

poison ['pɔizn] *n F* **1. name your poison!** qu'est-ce que tu veux boire?/qu'est-ce que tu prends? **2. to put the poison in,** empoisonner l'esprit de qn (contre qn)/semer le venin. (*See* **rat**[1] **5**)

poke[1] [pouk] *n P* **1.** coït*/baise *f*/ bourre *f*/coup *m* (d'arbalète); **to have a quick poke,** faire l'amour*/ tirer un coup vite fait/une petite crampette **2. to take a poke at s.o.,** sonner/filer/coller une taloche à qn **3.** portefeuille*/lazingue *m* **4. it's better than a poke in the eye,** c'est mieux que rien/il vaut mieux entendre ça que d'être sourd. (*See* **cow-poke**; **pig**[1] **6**; **slowpoke**)

poke[2] [pouk] *vtr P* **1.** faire l'amour* avec/bourrer/filer un coup d'arbalète à (qn) **2. to poke s.o.** = **to take a poke at s.o.** (**poke**[1] **2**). (*See* **nose 1**)

poke about, around ['poukə'baut, ə'raund] *vi F* fouiller/ farfouiller.

poker ['poukər] *n A P* pénis*/ gourdin *m*.

pokey ['pouki] *n NAm F* prison*/ trou *m*/coffre *m*/placard *m*. (*See* hokey-pokey)

pole [poul] *n F* **1.** to go up the pole, devenir fou*/partir du ciboulot/perdre la boule **2.** to drive s.o. up the pole, rendre qn fou*/faire perdre la boule/le ciboulot à qn **3.** to be up the pole, avoir tort/se tromper; you're completely up the pole, tu t'es gour(r)é complètement/tu as mis les pieds dans le plat **4.** I wouldn't touch it with a ten-foot pole, je ne le prendrais pas avec des pincettes. (*See* barge-pole; bean-pole)

polisher ['pɔliʃər] *n Austr P* échappé *m* de prison*/gibier *m* de potence. (*See* apple-polisher)

polish off ['pɔliʃ'ɔf] *vtr F* **1.** tuer*/dégommer/démolir/liquider **2.** terminer/liquider/boucler **3.** achever/solder/nettoyer (un plat, une bouteille).

pom [pɔm] *n* **1.** *F* (*abbr* = Pomeranian) loulou *m* (de Poméranie) **2.** *Austr P* (*pej*) = **pommy.**

pommy, Pommy ['pɔmi] *Austr F* (*pej*) **I** *a* anglais/engliche; pommy bastards, salauds *mpl* d'engliches **II** *n* Anglais*/Engliche *mf*/rosbif *m*/britiche *m*.

ponce¹ [pɔns] *n P* **1.** souteneur*/ marle *m*/marlou *m*/mac *m*/julot *m* **2.** homme efféminé; he's a bit of a ponce, il fait très tapette.

ponce² [pɔns] *vtr&i P* **1.** se conduire comme un souteneur*/faire le maquereau/être julot/faire le mac/ relever les compteurs **2.** mendier*/ taper*/torpiller/pilonner; to ponce a smoke from s.o., taper qn d'une cigarette*.

ponce about, around ['pɔnsə'baut, -ə'raund] *vi P* **1.** être efféminé/faire des airs (de pédé)/se conduire comme une lopette **2.** (*a*) glander/glandouiller (*b*) faire le con/déconner.

ponce off [pɔns'ɔf] *vi P* partir*/

dégager/les mettre; ponce off! fous le camp!/file!

ponce up ['pɔns'ʌp] *vtr&i P* to get ponced up/to ponce oneself up, se mettre sur son trente et un.

poncy ['pɔnsi] *a* **1.** *P* a poncy individual, un individu* qui semble se faire entretenir par les femmes/ maquereau *m* sur les bords **2.** *F* efféminé; a poncy little man, une lopette; a poncy little car, une vraie bagnole de pédé/de tapette.

pond, Pond [pɔnd] *n F* the Pond = the Herring Pond (herring 2). (*See* fish-pond)

pong¹ [pɔŋ] *n P* ce qui sent* mauvais; puanteur *f*/(s)chlingage *m*; what a dreadful pong! ça cocotte/ça schlingue ici!

pong² [pɔŋ] *P* sentir* mauvais; puer/(s)chlinguer/cocoter/sentir la caque; your feet really pong! tu chasses des arpions!

pongo ['pɔŋgou] *n P* (*navy*) soldat*/bidasse *m*; fusilier marin/ chie-dans-l'eau *m*.

pontoon [pɔn'tuːn] *n P* 21 mois de prison.

pony ['pouni] *n P* **1.** 25 livres sterling; it cost me a pony, ça m'a coûté 250 balles **2.** petit verre de liqueur/bourgeron *m* **3.** *NAm* (*scol*) traduc *f*.

pony (and trap) ['pouniən'træp] *P* (*RS* = crap) **I** *a* that's a bit pony, c'est merdique/c'est de la merde **II** *n* to go for a pony, aller déféquer*/chier.

poo¹ [puː] *n F* (*child's language*) excrément *m*/caca *m*; to do a poo, faire caca.

poo² [puː] *vi F* déféquer*/faire caca.

pooch [puːtʃ], **poochy** ['puːtʃi] *n P* (*a*) chien* (bâtard)/cabot *m*/clebs *m*/clébard *m* (*b*) chien* favori/ toutou *m*/chien-chien *m*.

poodle on ['puːdl'ɔn] *vi F* (*not common*) bavasser/jacasser/jaspiner.

poof [puf, puːf], **pooftah, poofter** ['puftər] n P (a) homosexuel*/pédé m/empaffé m/ tante f; **he's a poof,** il en est/il est de la bague/c'est une pédale (b) efféminé m; **I look a right poofter wearing this,** j'ai l'air d'une vraie tapette fringué comme ça.

poofy ['pufi, 'puːfi] a P à tendance homosexuelle/pédé sur les bords/ qui fait tapette; **he was wearing a very poofy looking outfit,** ses fringues lui donnaient l'air d'un travelo/d'un pédé.

pooh! [puː] excl F 1. ça pue! 2. peuh!/quelle affaire!/la belle affaire!

pool [puːl] vtr Austr F dénoncer* (qn)/moucharder (qn)/balancer (qn).

poon [puːn] n Austr P individu bête*/niais m/ballot m/baluchard m/ducon-la-joie m.

poonce [puːns] n Austr P 1. individu bête*/gourde f/andouille f 2. homosexuel*/tapette f/pédale f.

poon up ['puːn'ʌp] vi Austr P **to get pooned up,** s'habiller avec élégance/se mettre sur son trente-et-un.

poop [pup, puːp] n NAm 1. P excrément m/merde f; **poop chute,** anus*/pot m d'échappement/tuyau m à gaz 2. F renseignement*/rencard m; **to know the (latest) poop,** être dans le vent/à la coule; **poop sheet,** formulaire m de renseignements/rencardage m.

pooped (out) ['puːpt('aut)] a F très fatigué*/éreinté/vanné.

poorly ['puəli, 'pɔəli, 'pɔːli] a F malade*/patraque/pas dans son assiette. (See **proper**)

poove [puːv] n P = **poof.**

poovy ['puːvi] a P = **poofy.**

pop¹ [pop] n 1. F (a) pop (music), musique f pop/yé-yé m; **pop singer,** chanteur m pop; **top of the pops,** palmarès m/hit-parade m; **pop art,** le pop'art 2. F (a) père*/papa; vieux m/croulant m (b) vieil homme; **listen pop!** écoute grand'père/pépé! 3. F boisson pétillante/gazeuse 4. P = **poppy 1** 5. P (drugs) piqûre intermittente ou pour le plaisir/piquouse f/shoot m. (See **joy-pop; joy-popper**) 6. Austr F **to give sth a pop,** s'attaquer à qch/faire un essai 7. F **to be in pop,** être chez ma tante/au clou.

pop² [pop] vtr&i 1. P (drugs) se faire une piqûre/se piquer/se shooter. (See **joy-pop; skin-pop**) 2. P (drugs) **to pop pills,** prendre des pilules (de LSD*) 3. F **to pop the question,** proposer le mariage* (à qn) 4. P avoir un orgasme*/ décharger/dégorger 5. F mettre en gage/chez ma tante/au clou.

pop along ['popə'lɔŋ] vi F 1. aller voir qn/faire un saut (chez qn) 2. = **pop off 1.**

popcorn ['popkɔːn] n P homosexuel*/tante f; **a raving popcorn,** une folle affichée.

pop-eyed ['popaid] a F (a) aux yeux protubérants/saillants (b) aux yeux en boules de loto.

pop in ['pop'in] vi F (a) entrer en passant (b) entrer à l'improviste.

pop off ['pop'ɔf] vi F 1. partir*/ filer/déguerpir 2. mourir* (subitement)/claquer; **he just popped off,** il n'a pas fait couic 3. tuer*/ but(t)er/estourbir; **to get popped off,** se faire tuer* 4. **to pop off a gun,** lâcher un coup de fusil.

pop out ['pop'aut] vi F faire un saut dehors/aller faire un petit tour; **I saw him pop out of the house,** je l'ai vu sortir.

pop outside ['popaut'said] vi uriner*/aller faire pipi/aller arroser les marguerites.

poppa ['popə] n NAm F père*/ papa. (See **pop¹ 2** (a))

popper ['popər] n 1. P (drugs) ampoule de nitrite d'amyle*. (See **amy**) 2. F bouton m (à) pression.

(*See* **joy-popper**; **lid-popper**; **skin-popper**)

poppet ['pɔpit] *n F* (*a*) petit(e) chéri(e)/petit chou (*b*) enfant* adorable/chérubin *m*/trésor *m*.

popping ['pɔpiŋ] *n P* (**skin**) **popping**, piqûre* souscutanée de drogue.

poppy ['pɔpi] *n P* **1.** (*drugs*) opium*/pavot *m*/fée brune **2.** argent*/fric *m*.

poppycock ['pɔpikɔk] *n F* bêtises*/idioties *fpl*/fadaises *fpl*; **that's poppycock!** c'est des salades/des conneries!

pop round ['pɔp'raund] *vi F* faire une petite visite à qn/faire un saut chez qn.

popsy ['pɔpsi] *n* **1.** *F* petite amie/petite chérie **2.** *P* = **popper 1.**

pop up ['pɔp'ʌp] *vi F* apparaître/surgir/émerger.

porky ['pɔːki] **I** *a F* **1.** gros* et gras/gravos **2.** *NAm* très mauvais*/blèche/loquedu **3.** *NAm* en colère*/ronchonnant/en rogne **II** *n P* (*RS = pork pie = lie*) mensonge *m*/bateau *m*/bourrage *m* de crâne.

porn [pɔːn], **porno** ['pɔːnou] *n F* porno(graphie) *f*; **hard porn**, porno *m* hard/porno dur/hard *m*; **soft porn**, porno *m* soft/soft *m*; **porn merchant**, qn qui vend *ou* fabrique des produits pornographiques; pornographe *m*; **porno mags**, revues *fpl* pornos/de cul.

porn-shop ['pɔːnʃɔp] *n F* boutique* érotique/porno; sex(e)-shop *f*.

porny ['pɔːni] *a P* porno(graphique); **porny books**, livres *mpl* pornos; **porny film**, film porno/de cul; porno *m*.

porridge ['pɔridʒ] *n P* **1. to dish out the porridge**, ne pas y aller avec le dos de la cuiller/y aller carrément **2.** condamnation *f* à la prison; **to dish out the porridge**, condamner au maximum; **to do/to eat porridge**, purger sa peine en prison*/être mis au frais.

port [pɔːt] *n Austr F* valise *f*/valoche *f*.

posh [pɔʃ] *F* **I** *a* élégant*/chic/rupin/de la haute; **posh car**, voiture *f* de luxe; **posh accent**, accent *m* snob/accent de la haute/accent pointu **II** *adv* **to talk posh**, faire des phrases/parler avec un petit accent de la haute/parler pointu.

posh up ['pɔʃʌp] *vtr F* **to posh oneself up**, se pomponner/se bichonner; **all poshed up**, sur son trente et un.

poss [pɔs] *a F* (= *possible*) **it's just poss**, c'est pas impossible/ça se peut bien/on sait jamais; **if poss**, si possible.

possodeluxe ['pɔsodiluks] *a Austr P* homosexuel*/gai/pédé.

possum ['pɔsəm] *n* **1.** *F* (= *opossum*) **to play possum** (*i*) faire le mort (*ii*) se tenir coi **2.** *Austr P* prostituée*/pute *f* '3. *Austr P* voleur*/chapardeur *m*.

posted ['poustid] *pp F* **to keep s.o. posted**, tenir qn au courant/au parfum.

pot¹ [pɔt] *n F* **1.** *P* (*drugs*) (*a*) marijuana*/pot *m* (*b*) cigarette* de marijuana/joint *m*/kif *m* (*c*) haschisch*; **pot party**, séance collective au haschisch* *ou* à la marijuana* **2.** *F* (= *pot-belly*) ventre*/bide *m*/bedaine *f*/brioche *f* **3.** *F* **to go to pot**, tomber en décrépitude/aller à la ruine/aller à la dérive/aller à vau-l'eau; **he's gone to pot**, il est fichu; **his plans went (all) to pot**, ses projets sont tombés à l'eau/sont fichus **4.** *F* **pots of money**, une abondance*/une tapée d'argent*; **to make pots of money**, gagner gros/gagner des mille et des cents **5.** *F* trophée *m*/coupe *f* **6.** *F pl* (= *potatoes*) pommes *fpl* de terre/patates *fpl* **7.** *F* = **kitty 2** (*a*) **8.** *F* verre *m* de bière; **to go**

for a pot, aller prendre un pot. (*See*
**fusspot; glue-pot; jackpot; piss-
pot; sexpot; shitpot; stinkpot;
tinpot**)

pot² [pɔt] *vtr F* **1. to pot a child,**
asseoir/mettre un enfant sur le pot
(de chambre) **2. to pot at sth,** tirer
sur une cible peu éloignée.

potato [pəˈteitou, pəˈteitə] *n* **1.** *P*
trou *m* dans une chaussette/patate *f*
2. *F* **small potatoes** (*a*) de la petite
bière (*b*) personnes *ou* choses
insignifiantes/racaille *f*/gnognot(t)e
f **3.** *NAm* **hot potato** (*a*) *F* casse-
tête (chinois) (*b*) *F* affaire épineuse
(*c*) *P* = **hot patootie** (**patootie**) **4.**
Austr P (*RS* = *sheila*) **potato
peeler,** fille*/femme*/nana *f*/
gonzesse *f*. (*See* **drop²** 1; **sack¹** 2)

pot-boiler [ˈpɔtbɔilər] *n F* abattage
m/œuvre *f* alimentaire/ticket *m* de
pain.

pothead [ˈpɔthed] *n P* habitué(e)
de la marijuana*; amateur *m* de
haschisch*. (*See* **pot¹** 1)

pot-luck [ˈpɔtˈlʌk] *n F* **to take pot-
luck,** choisir au hasard/à
l'aventure/au pif/au fion; y aller au
petit bonheur.

pot-pot [ˈpɔtˈpɔt] *n F* motocyclette
f; vélomoteur *m*/pétrolette *f*/meule
f/tasse *f* à café.

pot-shot [ˈpɔtʃɔt] *n F* (*a*) **to take a
pot-shot at sth,** faire qch au petit
bonheur (*b*) **to take a pot-shot at
sth/s.o.,** lâcher à l'aveuglette un
coup de fusil à qch/qn/tirer au
pif(omètre).

potted¹ [ˈpɔtid] *a F* abrégé; **I gave
him a potted version of (the) events,**
je lui ai fait un raccourci/un con-
densé des événements.

potted² (up) [ˈpɔtid(ˈʌp)] *a NAm
P* **1.** ivre*/rond/rondibé/rétamé
2. drogué*/camé/chargé.

pottie [ˈpɔti] *n F* = **potty** II.

potty [ˈpɔti] *F* **I** *a* **1. to go potty,**
devenir fou*/maboul(e); perdre les
pédales/la boule **2. to be potty**

about/on s.o./sth, être mordu pour/
toqué de qn/qch; en pincer pour
qn/qch **3.** minable/insignifiant **II**
n pot *m* de chambre (d'enfant).

pouch [pautʃ] *n Austr V* sexe de la
femme*/grippette *f*/boîte *f* à
ouvrage.

poufdah [ˈpufdɑi], **pouff** [puf] *n
P* (*not common*) = **poof.**

pound [paund] *vtr P* **1.** (*a*) faire
l'amour*/aller à la bourre/bourri-
quer (*b*) faire l'amour* avec (une
femme)/bourrer/dérouiller **2. to
pound (off)/to pound the meat,** se
masturber*/se taper sur la colonne/
se secouer le bonhomme.

powder [ˈpaudər] *n P* **1. to do/to
take a powder** (*a*) déserter (de
l'armée)/faire chibis (*b*) s'enfuir*/
prendre la poudre d'escampette **2.**
(*drugs*) cocaïne*/neige *f*/talc *m*;
powder monkey, trafiquant *m*/dealer
m/pusher *m* (d'héroïne). (*See*
birdie-powder; joy-powder)

powder-room [ˈpaudəˈruːm] *n F*
WC*/toilette *f*/pipi-room *m*.

power-house [ˈpauəhaus] *n F*
individu* dynamique.

pow-wow [ˈpauwau] *n F* tête-à-tête
m.

pox [pɔks] *n P* **(the) pox,** syphilis*/
la (s)chtouille/la naze/la vérole.

poxed off [ˈpɔksdˈɔf] *a P* **to be
poxed off with sth/s.o.,** en avoir
assez*/ras le bol/plein le cul de
qch/qn.

poxed (up) [ˈpɔkstˈʌp)] *a P* **poxed
(up) (to the eyeballs/eyebrows),**
naze(broque)/poivré/plombé.

poxy [ˈpɔksi] *a P* (de la) camelote/
tocard; nazebroque/vérolé; **it's none
of your poxy rubbish,** c'est pas de
la marchandise naze.

prance about, around [ˈprɑinsəˈbaut, -əˈraund] *vi F*
caracoler; se pavaner/poser; faire le
beau/le m'as-tu-vu; rouler sa
caisse; **to prance around in the nud,**
se balader à poil/cul nu.

prang¹ [præŋ] *n F* **1.** exploit *m*/coup fumant **2.** raid *m* de bombardement **3.** collision *f*/crash *m*/emboutissage *m*.

prang² [præŋ] *vtr F* **1.** bombarder/tabasser **2.** emboutir/bousiller (un avion, une auto); **he pranged his car,** il a embouti/cabossé sa tire.

prat [præt] *n P* **1.** fesses*/derche *m*/derjeot *m*/pétard *m* **2.** sexe de la femme*/con *m*/conasse *f*/cramouille *f* **3.** individu bête*/couillon *m*; **you prat!** espèce de nœud!/enculé!

prawn [prɔːn] *n P* **1.** individu bête/gourde *f*/andouille *f*; **to look a prawn,** avoir l'air bête/con **2.** *Austr* **to come the raw prawn** (*i*) tromper*/rouler/avoir (qn) (*ii*) la ramener; **don't come the raw prawn!** faut pas me la refaire!/(ne) la ramène pas avec moi!

preachify ['priːtʃifai] *vi F* sermonner/faire la morale.

preachy ['priːtʃi] *a F* sermonneur/prêchi-prêcha.

preggers ['pregəz] *a P* **(Harry) preggers,** enceinte*/en cloque; **she's preggers,** elle a un polichinelle dans le tiroir/elle est en cloque.

preppie, preppy ['prepi] *F NAm* **I** *a* = khâgneux/en prépa **II** *n* = khâgneux, -euse *mf*.

press ['pres] *vtr NAm P* **to press the flesh,** serrer la main (à qn)/y aller de cinq.

pressie ['prezi] *n F* (= *present*) cadeau *m*.

pretty-pretty ['pritipriti] *a F* fanfreluché/mignon tout plein.

previous ['priːvjəs] **I** *adv F* trop tôt/trop vite*; **you're a bit previous, aren't you?** tu y vas un peu fort, non? **II** *n* (= *previous convictions*) casier *m* judiciaire/pédigrée *m*; **he's got no previous,** il a un casier judiciaire vierge; **he's got a lot of previous,** il a un casier judiciaire

bien rempli/il a eu plusieurs condamnations/son pédigrée est bien noir.

prezzie ['prezi] *n F* = **pressie.**

priceless ['praislis] *a F* **1.** très amusant*/impayable **2.** très bête*/unique.

pricey ['praisi] *a F* cher*/chérot/coûteux/salé.

prick [prik] *n V* **1.** pénis*/pine *f*/queue *f* **2.** vaurien*/sale coco *m*/couillon *m* **3. a spare prick,** un pas grand-chose/un bon à rien; **to feel like a spare prick at a wedding,** être un onguent miton mitaine **4.** individu bête*/con *m*/connard *m*; **silly prick!** espèce d'enculé! (*See* **pin-pricks**)

prick-tease ['priktiːz] *n V* allumeuse *f*/bandeuse *f*/aguicheuse *f*. (*See* **cock-teaser**; **tease**; **teaser** **2**)

prick tease ['prik'tiːz] *vi V* aguicher/allumer/faire bander (qn).

prick-teaser ['prik'tiːzər] *n V* = **prick-tease.**

printed ['printid] *pp P* **to get printed,** se faire prendre les empreintes digitales/jouer du piano/passer au piano.

prissy ['prisi] *a F* bégueule/collet monté/guindé/chochotte.

privates ['praivits] *npl F* sexe de l'homme*/parties *fpl*/service *m* trois-pièces; **a kick in the privates,** un coup de pied aux couilles/dans les bijoux de famille.

prize [praiz] *a F* **a prize idiot,** un ballot de premier ordre/une andouille enracinée/le roi des cons. (*See* **swill¹ 3**)

pro [prou] *n* **1.** *P* (= *prostitute*) prostituée*/catin *f*/pute *f* **2.** *F* (= *professional*) professionnel *m*/pro *m*; **he's a real pro,** il n'a rien d'un amateur **3.** *F* **the pros and cons,** le pour et le contre.

prob [prɔb] *abbr F* (= *problem*) **no prob!** pas de problème!

pronto ['prɔntou] *adv F* vite*/illico/ presto.

proper ['prɔpər] *adv F* vraiment/ extrêmement; **proper poorly,** vraiment malade*. (*See* **champion** I)

prop-man ['prɔpmæn] *n F* = **props 2.**

proposition ['prɔpə'ziʃ(ə)n] *vtr F* **1.** proposer un plan *ou* un projet à (qn) **2. to proposition a woman,** faire des propositions indécentes à une femme/proposer la botte à une femme/faire du rentre-dedans à une femme.

props [prɔps] *n F* **1.** *pl* (*theatre*) accessoires *mpl*/bouts *mpl* de bois **2.** *sing* accessoiriste *mf.*

prop up ['prɔp'ʌp] *vtr F* **to prop up the bar,** boire dans un bar/être accoudé au zinc/être un pilier de bistrot.

pross [prɔs], **prossie, prossy** ['prɔsi], **prostie, prosty** ['prɔsti] *n P* prostituée*/pute *f*/ putain *f.*

proud [praud] *adv F* **1. to do s.o. proud** (*a*) recevoir qn comme un roi/traiter qn à la hauteur (*b*) se mettre en frais pour qn **2. to do oneself proud** (*a*) faire un bon travail*/se montrer à la hauteur (*b*) bien se soigner/ne se priver de rien/ne rien se refuser.

prowl [praul] *n F* **to be on the prowl,** chercher les aventures (amoureuses)/chercher les bonnes fortunes/être en maraude.

prowl-car ['praulkɑr] *n F* voiture *f* de police/voiture-pie *f.*

pseud [sjuːd] *n P* (*i*) individu hypocrite/faux; faux jeton (*ii*) prétentieux, -euse *mf*/crâneur, -euse *mf*/ bêcheur, -euse *mf*/frimeur, -euse *mf*; **he's a real pseud** (*i*) c'est un faux cul/un faux derche (*ii*) c'est un type qui cherche à en jeter.

pseudo ['sjuːdou] *a F* (*i*) pseudo/ insincère/faux (*ii*) prétentieux/ bêcheur/crâneur/frimeur/poseur.

pseudy ['sjuːdi] *a P* = **pseudo.**

psych [saik] *F* **I** *vtr* **to psych s.o.,** tourner qn en bourrique **II** *vi* péter le feu.

psycho ['saikou] **I** *a P* fou*/ dérangé/détraqué/dévissé; **to go psycho,** perdre la boule/battre la breloque/débloquer **II** *n F* **1.** psycho(pathe) *mf* **2.** (*a*) psychanalyste *mf* (*b*) psychiatre *mf.*

psych out ['saik'aut] *vtr&i F* (*a*) perdre les pédales/perdre la tête/ débloquer (*b*) avoir peur*/caner/se dégonfler (*c*) ébranler la détermination de (qn).

psych up ['saik'ʌp] *vtr F* **to psych oneself up,** se préparer psychologiquement/se brancher sur qch/se brancher à faire qch.

pt, PT ['piː'tiː] *abbr P* = **pricktease(r).** (*See* **CT**)

pub [pʌb] *n F* bistro(t) *m*/pub *m.*

pubbing ['pʌbiŋ] *n F* **to go pubbing,** faire la tournée des bistro(t)s/ godailler.

pub-crawl[1] ['pʌbkrɔːl] *n F* tournée *f* des bistro(t)s.

pub-crawl[2] ['pʌbkrɔːl] *vi F* faire la tournée des bistrots.

pub-crawler ['pʌbkrɔːlər] *n F* coureur *m* de bistro(t)s/vadrouilleur *m*/pilier *m* de bistrot.

pubes [pjuːbz] *npl P* poils *mpl* du pubis/gazon *m*/cresson *m.*

public ['pʌblik] *n P* (*homosexuals*) **to go public,** oser dire qu'on est homosexuel/sortir du placard.

pucker-assed ['pʌkər'æst] *a NAm V* peureux/froussard/ pétochard/qui a le trouillomètre à zéro.

pud [pud] *n F* (*abbr* = *pudding*) **1.** pudding *m* **2.** dessert *m.*

pudding ['pudiŋ] *n P* **to pull one's pudding,** se masturber*/se l'allonger/s'astiquer (la colonne). (*See* **club 2**)

pudding-face ['pudiŋfeis] *n O F* visage* empâté/pleine lune.

puddinghead ['pudiŋhed] *n F* individu bête*/gourde *f*/empoté *m*.

puddled ['pʌdld] *a F* bête*/ballot/empoté.

puff¹ [pʌf] *n* 1. *F* to be out of puff, être hors d'haleine/être essoufflé 2. *F* critique *f* favorable/battage *m*/puffisme *m* 3. *P* = **poof**. (*See* **creampuff**)

puff² [pʌf] *vtr F* 1. prôner/vanter 2. faire la promotion/faire l'article.

puffer(-train) ['pʌfər(trein)], **puff-puff** ['pʌfpʌf] *n F* (*child's word*) teuf-teuf *m*.

pug [pʌg] *n P* pugiliste *m*/boxeur *m*.

puka ['puːkə] *n NAm P* sexe de la femme*/fente *f*/crac *m*/craque *m*.

puke¹ [pjuːk] *n P* vomissement *m*/dégobillade *f*/fusée *f*/dégueulis *m*/*Belg* dégobillotte *f*.

pukeish ['pjuːkiʃ] *a P* = **pukey**.

puke² (**up**) ['pjuːk('ʌp)] *vi P* vomir*/aller au refil(e)/dégobiller; it makes me want to puke, ça me débecte/ça me fait gerber.

pukey ['pjuːki] *a P* gerbant/débectant/à dégueuler; it's really pukey, c'est dégueulasse/débectant/à dégueuler.

pukka ['pʌkə] *a F* authentique/du vrai de vrai; pukka sahib [saɪb], un vrai monsieur/un vrai gentleman.

pull¹ [pul] *n* 1. *P* coït*/carambolage *m* 2. *F* influence *f*/piston *m*/bras long. (*See* **leg-pull**)

pull² [pul] *vtr&i* 1. *P* faire l'amour* avec (une femme)/caramboler; to try to pull a bird, draguer une nana. (*See* **train**) 2. *F* to pull a gun, sortir un revolver*/dégainer. (*See* **bell¹** 2; **leg¹** 5; **one** 4; **plonker**; **pudding**; **rank**; **wire** 2, 8; **yarn¹**)

pull-in ['pulin] *n F* café* des routiers/routier *m*.

pull in ['pul'in] *vtr F* 1. arrêter*/

embarquer/choper; the cops pulled him in, les flics l'ont embarqué/pincé 2. s'arrêter/faire une étape.

pull off ['pul'ɔf] *vtr* 1. *F* to pull off a deal, réussir une opération/boucler une affaire 2. *P* se masturber*/s'astiquer (la colonne).

pull out ['pul'aut] *vtr&i F* 1. partir*/se (re)tirer 2. *NAm* se dérober/tirer son épingle du jeu 3. to pull out all the stops, donner un coup de collier/donner le maximum/mettre le paquet. (*See* **finger¹** 2)

pump¹ [pʌmp] *n F* cœur *m*/battant *m*/palpitant *m*.

pump² [pʌmp] *vtr F* to pump s.o., pomper qn (pour avoir des renseignements*)/tirer les vers du nez à qn. (*See* **lead¹** 1)

pumpkinhead ['pʌmpkinhed] *n NAm F* individu bête*/nouille *f*/andouille *f*.

punch¹ [pʌntʃ] *n F* 1. allant *m*/énergie *f*/dynamisme *m* 2. he didn't pull his punches, il n'a pas ménagé son adversaire/il n'a pas pris de gants. (*See* **pack²** 2)

Punch² [pʌntʃ] *Prn F* (*a*) (as) proud as Punch, fier comme Artaban (*b*) (as) pleased as Punch, heureux comme un roi/aux anges.

punch-drunk ['pʌntʃ'drʌŋk] *a F* ivre de coups/ahuri/hébété (par des coups reçus)/groggy.

punch-line ['pʌntʃlain] *n F* phrase-clef *f* (dans une histoire)/astuce *f*/mot *m* de la fin/chute *f*.

punch-up ['pʌntʃʌp] *n F* bagarre *f*/baston *f*/raclée *f*/tabassée *f*; to have a punch-up, se bagarrer.

pundit ['pʌndit] *n F* ponte *m*.

punk [pʌŋk] *P* **I** *a* de basse qualité/moche/tocard/tarte **II** *n* 1. tordu *m*/tête *f* de lard/face *f* de rat/bille *f* de clown 2. débutant *m*/novice *m*/bleu *m*/blanc-bec *m* 2. *A* homosexuel*/lopette *f*/fiotte *f*/tapette *f* 4. (*a*) jeune vaurien*/

loulou *m*/loubard *m*/zonard *m* (b)
punk (rocker), punk *mf* **5.** qch de
toc(ard) *ou* de moche/pacotille *f*/
camelote *f*.

punk out ['pʌŋk'aut] *vi* O P se
dégonfler/caner.

punter ['pʌntər] *n* P **1.** (*horse racing, etc*) parieur, -euse *mf* **2.** (*i*)
client(e) *m(f)* (*ii*) client d'une pros-
tituée/clille *m*/micheton *m* **3.**
individu* quelconque/type *m*/
numéro *m*.

pup [pʌp] *n* F **to sell s.o. a pup,**
escroquer*/entuber/rouler qn. (*See*
mucky 2)

puppy ['pʌpi] *a attrib* F **1. puppy
fat,** grassouille *f* du bébé **2. puppy
love,** premier amour/amour juvé-
nile.

purler ['pəɪlər] *n* F **to come a
purler,** tomber*/ramasser une
bûche/prendre un gadin.

purple ['pəɪpl] *a* P (*drugs*) **purple
hearts,** barbituriques*/mélange bar-
bituré.

purty ['pəɪti] *a NAm* F joli/mignon.

push¹ [puʃ] *n* **1.** F **to give s.o. the
push,** flanquer qn à la porte/sac-
quer qn; laisser tomber (son/sa
petit(e) ami(e)); **she gave him the
push,** elle l'a plaqué **2.** F **at a
push,** au moment critique/en cas de
besoin; **when it comes to the push,**
quand il est question d'agir/au
moment de l'exécution; **we could do
it at a push,** à la rigueur, ça pourrait se faire/c'est pas impossible/ça
se peut bien **3.** *Austr* P bande*/
gang *m*.

push² [puʃ] *vtr* F **1. to push drugs,**
fourguer des drogues **2. to push
one's luck,** pousser/aller trop loin/
attiger/aller un peu fort; **don't push
your luck (too far)!** vas-y mollo! **3.**
she must be pushing forty, elle doit
aller sur ses quarante printemps/
elle a ses quarante berges bien son-
nées **4. shut up or I'll push your
face in!** la ferme ou je te cogne/ou

je te casse la gueule/ou je t'écrase
le museau! (*See* **queer II 4**)

push around ['puʃə'raund] *vtr* F
to push s.o. around, malmener/mal-
traiter qn; être vache/chien avec
qn.

pushed [pʌʃd] *a* F **to be a bit
pushed for money/time,** manquer
d'argent/de temps; **he's a bit
pushed today,** il est débordé (de
travail) aujourd'hui.

pusher ['puʃər] *n* F **1.** (*drugs*)
fourgueur *m*/pourvoyeur *m*/
revendeur *m*/pusher *m*/dealer *m*.
(*See* **push² 1**) **2.** ambitieux *m*/
arriviste *m*/joueur *m* de coudes.
(*See* **cock-pusher; paper-pusher;
pen-pusher**)

pushface ['puʃfeis] *n* P gueule *f* en
coin (de rue)/gueule de raie/tête *f*
de pipe.

push off ['puʃ'ɔf] *vi* P partir*/
déguerpir/décamper; **push off!** file!/
débarrasse (le plancher)!/fous le
camp!/dégage!

push on ['puʃ'ɔn] *vi* F **1.** pousser
en avant/activer/faire avancer **2.**
pousser/exciter (qn) **3. to push on
with sth,** chauffer une affaire.

pushover ['puʃouvər] *n* **1.** F qch
de facile/du tout cuit/du tout rôti/
du gâteau **2.** P femme* facile/à la
cuisse hospitalière/qui donne dans
le panneau; une chaude lapine.

pushy ['puʃi] *a* F arriviste/plastron-
neur/poseur; **he's a pushy little sod!**
c'est un crâneur de première!/c'est
un type qui cherche à en jeter/à en
mettre plein la vue!

puss [pus] *n* **1.** F chat *m*/minou
m/minet *m* **2.** P visage*/frime *f*/
frimousse *f* **3.** P bouche*/gueule
f/goule *f*/margoulette *f* **4.** P =
pussy 2. (*See* **drizzle-puss; glamour-puss; sourpuss**)

pussy ['pusi] *n* **1.** F = **puss 1 2.**
P sexe de la femme*/chat *m*/chatte
f/chagatte *f*/minou *m*; **to chase
pussy,** chercher de la fesse; **he's
after a bit of pussy,** il ne cherche

qu'à baiser/qu'à tringler **3.** *F* (=
cat-o'-nine-tails) fouet *m* (à neuf
cordes)/chat *m* à neuf queues **4.** *F*
fourrure(s) *f(pl)*.

pussycat ['pusikæt] *n NAm F*
individu agréable; chou *m*/cœur *m*.

pussyfoot¹ ['pusifut] *n NAm F*
prohibitionniste *m*/partisan *m* du
sec.

pussyfoot² ['pusifut] *vi F* **1.**
marcher* à pas étouffés/sur la
pointe des pieds **2.** faire patte de
velours **3.** ne pas se mouiller/
ménager la chèvre et le chou/nager
entre deux eaux/zigzaguer.

pussyfooter ['pusifutər] *n esp
NAm F* qn qui ne veut pas se com-
promettre/qui tourne autour du
pot; ennemi *m* du oui et du non;
normand *m*.

pussyfooting ['pusifutiŋ] *n esp
NAm F* l'art *m* de ne pas se mouiller.

pussywhipped ['pʌsi'wipd] *a
NAm F* (homme) dominé par sa
femme *ou* sa petite amie/dont la
femme porte la culotte/mené par le
bout du nez.

puta ['putə] *n NAm P* prostituée*/
pute *f*.

put across ['putə'krɔs] *vtr F* **1.**
to put it across s.o., tromper*/
refaire/rouler qn; **they put one
across on me**, on m'a roulé/je me
suis fait avoir **2. to put it across
to s.o.**, faire comprendre/piger à
qn; éclairer la lanterne à qn.

put away ['putə'wei] *vtr* **1.** *P*
(*boxing*) mettre (qn) knock-out **2.**
F **to put it away**, boire/manger à
s'en mettre derrière la cravate; **he
can't half put it away**, ce qu'il peut

engloutir/avaler! **3.** *F* emprisonner*/faire enfermer/boucler/blo-
quer; **they put him away**, ils l'ont
mis au bloc **4.** *P* tuer*/descendre/
dessouder/dézinguer **5.** *F* mettre
(de l'argent, etc) de côté. (*See*
rainy)

put-down ['putdaun] *n F* jugement
m défavorable/éreintage *m*/sabrage
m.

put down ['pʌt'daun] *vtr F* critiquer*/éreinter/démolir (qn).

put-on ['putɔn] *n F* bateau *m*/boni-
ment *m*; **it was all a put-on**, c'était
du boniment/de la blague/du
chiqué.

put on ['put'ɔn] *vtr F* **1. to put it
on** (*a*) prétendre/en installer/faire
de la graisse/faire sa poire (*b*)
exagérer*/charrier/y aller fort; **he
puts it on a bit**, il est un peu
crâneur **2. to put s.o. on**, mener
qn en bateau/pigeonner qn/rouler
qn **3.** interloquer (qn)/brouiller les
idées à (qn) **4. who put you on to
it?** qui vous a donné le tuyau? (*See*
ritz)

put out ['put'aut] *vtr* **1.** *F* décon-
certer/décontenancer/embarrasser
(qn) **2.** *NAm P* (*woman*) avoir la
cuisse hospitalière/être tombeuse/
être une chaude lapine.

putrid ['pjutrid] *a F* dégueulasse/
dégueulbif/débectant.

put-up ['putʌp] *a F* **a put-up job**,
un coup monté/une affaire
bricolée/un micmac.

putz [puts] *n NAm P* pénis*/pine *f*/
paf *m*.

python ['paiθ(ə)n] *n P* **to siphon the
python**, uriner*/égoutter son
cyclope.

Q

q.t., QT ['kjuːˈtiː] *abbr F* **1.** (= *quiet time*) petite prière/méditation *f* **2. on the (strict) q.t.** (= *quiet*), en douce/discrètement/en catimini/ en lousdoc/en loucedé; **to do sth on the q.t.,** faire qch en cachette/à la dérobée; **I am telling you on the q.t.,** je vous dis ça entre nous/entre quat'zyeux; **he fixed it on the QT,** il a arrangé ça en lousdoc.

quack [kwæk] *n P* médecin *m*/charlatan *m*/mécano *m*/marchand *m* de mort; **I went to see the quack,** je suis allé chez le toubib.

quack-quack ['kwæk'kwæk] *n F* (*child's word*) canard *m*/coin-coin *m*.

quad [kwɔd] *n* **1.** *F* (= *quadrangle*) cour carrée (d'une école, université, etc) **2.** *P* prison*/boîte *f*/bloc *m*/taule *f*/gnouf *m*; **in quad,** au bloc/à l'ombre/au frigo **3.** *F* (= *quadruplet*) quadruplé(e) **4.** *NAm P* auto *f* à quatre phares *mpl*; *pl* les quatre phares d'une auto.

quail [kweil] *n P* **1.** (*not common*) femme*/fille*/mousmée *f*/souris *f* **2.** *NAm* élève (fille) d'une école mixte.

quandong ['kwændɔŋ] *n Austr P* (*a*) individu louche/voyou *m*/ apache *m* (*b*) qn de dessalé/qn qui est ficelle.

quarter ['kwɔːtər] *n NAm F* pièce *f* de 25 cents.

quean [kwiːn] *n A P* = **queen¹ 1, 2.**

queen¹ [kwiːn] *n* **1.** *F* fille* *ou* femme* séduisante/une beauté/prix *m* de Diane/beau sujet **2.** *P*

homosexuel* qui joue le rôle de femme/persilleuse *f*/folle *f*/tante *f*; **an old queen,** une vieille pédale; **dinge queen,** homosexuel* blanc qui s'accouple de préférence avec des noirs; paillasse *f* à négros/tapette *f* à bougnouls; **golden shower queen,** homosexuel* qui aime qu'on lui pisse dessus; **leather queen,** fétichiste *m* du cuir/cuir *m*; **size queen,** homosexuel*/pédé *m* qui aime les mecs virils; **xerox queen,** clone *m* **3.** *F* **queen bee,** femme* active/maîtresse-femme **4.** *F* **Queen Anne's dead!** (*a*) (*iron*) ce n'est pas une nouvelle!/c'est pas tout neuf! (*b*) ton jupon dépasse! **5.** *F* (*dial, form of address*) ma petite dame.

queen² [kwiːn] *vtr F* **to queen it (over s.o.),** faire la grande dame (avec qn).

queenie ['kwiːni] *n P* = **queen¹ 2.**

queer¹ [kwiər] **I** *a* **1.** *F* homosexuel/pédé; **he's a bit queer,** il fait très tapette/il est un peu pédé sur les bords **2.** *F* **to be in queer street,** être dans la mélasse/tirer le diable par la queue/être dans la mouise/être dans la panade **3.** *F* un peu fou*; **queer in the head,** maboul(e) / loufoque / toqué / siphonné/jobard. (*See* **attic; fish¹** 1) **4.** *P* criminel/suspect/louche; **it's all a bit queer,** ça n'a pas l'air très catholique **5.** *P* faux/contrefait **6.** *O F* **to feel queer,** se sentir tout chose/patraque; **he's feeling a bit queer,** il marche à côté de ses pompes/il n'est pas dans son assiette **II** *n* **1.** *F* (*pej*) (*a*) pédé *m*/homo *m*/pédale *f*/tante *f* (*b*) lesbienne*/gouine *f*/vrille *f*. (*See* **quim**) **2.** *P* **in queer,** dans le pétrin/dans la mélasse/dans la mouise/dans de beaux draps **3.** *P* **on the queer,** par des moyens louches/peu honnêtes **4.** *P* monnaie contrefaite/fausse mornifle; **to push the queer,** passer de la fausse monnaie/faire la fournaise.

queer² [kwiər] *vtr&i* *P* **1.** déranger/détraquer; **to queer the pitch,** mettre des bâtons dans les roues/savonner la pente/jambonner (qn); **to queer s.o.'s pitch,** contrecarrer qn/couper l'herbe sous les pieds de qn/mettre qch dans les dents de qn **2. to queer oneself with s.o.,** se brouiller avec qn/ne plus être dans les petits papiers de qn/être en suif après qn **3.** **to queer for sth,** aimer* qch/en mordre pour qch/en pincer pour qch.

queer-basher ['kwiəbæʃər] *n* *P* chasseur *m*/casseur *m* de pédés.

queer-bashing ['kwiəbæʃɪŋ] *n* *P* chasse *f* aux pédés/ratonnade *f* contre les pédés.

queue-jumper ['kjuːdʒʌmpər] *n* *F* qn qui passe avant son tour/resquilleur *m*.

quick [kwik] *a* *F* **1. a quick one** = **quickie 1, 2 2. to do sth in quick order,** faire qch vite*/fissa/à toute vapeur/en moins de deux/en cinq secs. (*See* **double-quick**; **draw¹**; **pdq**; **uptake** (*a*))

quickie, quicky ['kwiki] *n* **1.** *F* un (petit) verre/un (petit) coup bu en vitesse; **to have a quickie,** s'en envoyer un/s'en jeter un vite fait; **have a quickie?** tu prendras vite qch? **2.** *P* coït* hâtif; **to have a quickie,** s'en envoyer un petit coup **3.** *P* prostituée* rapide/qui fait de l'abattage; pute *f* à la grouille **4.** *F* qch fait rapidement/à la six-quatre-deux/en quatrième vitesse/ en deux temps, trois mouvements; du vite-fait **5.** *F* question-éclair *f* (*esp* dans un jeu de devinette) **6.**

NAm *F* grève soudaine et irrationnelle/grève sauvage.

quid [kwid] *n* *F* **1.** une livre sterling; **I paid forty quid for that,** je l'ai payé/j'ai craché quarante balles **2. to be quids in,** avoir de la marge/marcher comme sur des roulettes; **he's quids in,** il a de la chance*/du pot/du bol/de la bagouse; **I'm quids in,** tout baigne dans l'huile pour moi **3.** *Austr* **he's not the full quid,** il n'était pas derrière la porte le jour de la distribution (d'intelligence)/il n'est pas à la hauteur.

quiet ['kwaiət] *F* **I** *a* **anything for a quiet life!** tout ce que tu voudras, mais fiche-moi la paix/fous-moi la paix/lâche-moi les baskets! **II** *n* **on the quiet,** en douce/en lousdoc/en loucedé. (*See* **q.t.**)

quiff [kwif] *n* *A* **1.** *P* argent*/pèze *m* **2.** *P* prostituée* bon marché/pute *f* de la basse/morue *f* d'eau douce/colis *m* **3.** *P* bon tour/tour de passe-passe **4.** *V* sexe de la femme*/baba *m*/didi *m* **5.** *P* conseil *m*/avis *m*/tuyau *m*.

quill [kwil] *vi* *O* *P* s'efforcer de gagner les bonnes grâces de (qn)/lécher les bottes à (qn)/passer la brosse à reluire à (qn).

quim [kwim] *n* *V* sexe de la femme*/grippette *f*/millefeuille *m*/ berlingot *m*/panier *m*; **quim queer,** lesbienne*/goudou *f*/gouine *f*/ gousse *f*/gavousse *f*.

quin [kwin] *n* *F* (= *quintuplet*) quintuplé(e).

quince [kwins] *n* *P* fiotte *f*/lopette *f*/joconde *f*.

quit [kwit] *vtr&i* **1.** *F* abandonner*/lâcher/débarquer/ déposer; **he quit while the going was good,** il a laissé tomber/il a mis la clef sous la porte, au bon moment/alors que ça marchait bien **2.** *P* **to quit it,** mourir*/se laisser glisser **3.** *P* **to quit the scene** (*a*) mourir*/lâcher la rampe (*b*) partir*/lever l'ancre.

quitter ['kwitər] *n P* lâcheur *m*/tire-au-flanc *m*/tire-au-cul *m.*

quod [kwɔd] *n P* = **quad 2.**

quote [kwout] *n F* **1.** (= *quota-* *tion*) citation *f* **2.** *pl* (= *quotation marks*) guillemets *mpl*; **you can put that in quotes,** à mettre entre guillemets/n'oubliez pas les guillemets.

R

rab [ræb] *n P* tiroir-caisse *m*.

rabbit¹ ['ræbit] *n* 1. *P* salade *f*/ crudités *fpl*/verdure *f* 2. *P* (*RS = rabbit and pork = talk*) bavardage *m*/jactance *f*/jaspinage *f*; **I never heard anyone with so much rabbit,** je n'ai jamais entendu une telle tapette 3. *F* **rabbit punch,** le coup du lapin.

rabbit² ['ræbit] *vi P* **to rabbit (on),** avoir la langue bien pendue/jacter/ avoir avalé son transistor; **she does go rabbiting on,** elle (n')arrête pas de jacasser.

rabbity ['ræbiti] *a P* insignifiant/ toc/tocard/camelote.

race off ['reis'ɔf] *vtr Austr P* séduire/draguer/faire du gringue à/ faire de l'œil à qn.

rack [ræk] *n NAm P* lit*/pieu *m*.

racket ['rækit] *n F* 1. **to make a racket,** faire du bruit*/du tapage/ du ramdam; **they were making one hell of a racket,** ils faisaient un boucan du diable. (*See* **kick up** 2) 2. coup fourré/combine *f*/trafic *m* louche; **the drugs racket,** le trafic de la drogue; **protection racket,** racket *m* 3. **to stand the racket** (*a*) payer* les frais/casquer/essuyer le coup de fusil/payer les pots cassés/ cracher au bassinet (*b*) tenir le coup/tenir bon 4. escroquerie*/ carambouille *f*/arnaque *f*; **what's your racket?** à quoi/comment faistu ton beurre? 5. **to go on the racket** = **to go on the razzle** (**razzle**).

rack (out) ['ræk'aut] *vi NAm* se coucher*/se pieuter/se pagnoter.

Rafferty rules ['ræfə(r)ti'ruːlz] *n*

Austr P la loi de la jungle/la loi du plus fort; (jouer) sans règles/(jouer) de manière sauvage.

rag¹ [ræg] *n* 1. *F* vêtement*; **I haven't a rag to wear,** je n'ai rien à me mettre/je n'ai plus de sapes; **the rag trade,** l'industrie *f* du vêtement/ la nipperie/la fripe/la sape. (*See* **glad**) 2. *P* serviette *f* hygiénique/ tampon *m*; **to be on the rag/to have the rag on/to have the rag out,** avoir ses règles*/avoir la rue barrée/avoir ses ragnagnas/repeindre sa grille en rouge/avoir les ours 3. *F* journal*/canard *m*/torchon *m*/ baveux *m*; **local rag,** la feuille de chou du pays 4. *F* **like a red rag to a bull,** comme le rouge pour les taureaux 5. *P* **to lose one's rag/to get one's rag out,** se mettre en colère*/voir rouge/prendre un coup de sang/prendre un coup de rouge 6. *P* langue*/chiffe *f*/chiffon *m* rouge 7. *F* **rag, tag and bobtail,** la canaille/la merdaille/la chienlit 8. *F* carnaval *m*/monôme *m* d'étudiants/canular *m* 9. *P* (*RS = fag = cigarette*) **oily rag,** cigarette*/cibiche *f*/sèche *f*/pipe *f* 10. *F* **to feel like a wet rag,** se sentir mou comme une chiffe/comme une chiffe molle; se sentir tout ramollo 11. *NAm F* (*aut*) décapotable *f* 12. *P* (*horse racing*) (*outsider*) canasson *m*/mort *m*/lapin *m* à roulettes. (*See* **chew; nose-rag; snitch-rag; snot-rag**)

rag² [ræg] *vtr F* 1. (*a*) brimer (un camarade) (*b*) chahuter (un professeur) (*c*) charrier (qn)/faire du chahut/du chambard/du raffut.

ragbag ['rægbæg] *n F* individu* mal vêtu/mal ficelé/mal fagoté/ fringué comme un as de pique; souillon *mf*/loqueteux *m*.

raggle ['rægl] *n NAm A P* pin-up *f*/allumeuse *f*/belle mécanique.

rag-top ['rægtɔp] *n esp NAm F* voiture *f* décapotable.

railroad ['reilroud] *vtr esp NAm F* **1.** bousculer/tarabuster/houspiller (qn) **2.** se débarrasser* de (qn)/ faire dinguer (qn) à la boucanade **3.** pousser/bouler (qch).

rails [reilz] *npl F* **to go off the rails,** dérailler/être détraqué/perdre les pédales.

rain [rein] *vi F* (*catchphrase*) **it never rains but it pours,** un malheur n'arrive jamais seul.

rainbows ['reinbouz] *npl P* (*drugs*) tuinal *m*/barbiturique*/tricolore *m*.

raincheck ['reintʃek] *n NAm F* invitation remise/partie remise; **let's take a raincheck (on that),** ce sera partie remise.

rainy ['reini] *a F* **to put sth away/by for a rainy day,** garder une poire pour la soif/mettre qch de côté pour ses vieux jours.

rainy-day ['reinidei] *a attrib P* (*drugs*) **rainy-day woman,** cigarette* de marijuana/joint *m*/stick *m*/ bomb *f*.

raise¹ [reiz] *n V* **to get a raise,** avoir une érection*/bander/l'avoir en l'air/marquer midi.

raise² [reiz] *vtr V* **to raise it/to raise a beam,** être en érection*/ bander/marquer midi.

rake in ['reik'in] *vtr F* **to rake it in,** gagner* beaucoup d'argent/(le) ramasser à la pelle/faire du pèze/ faire son beurre/se bourrer/prendre le paquet; **he's raking it in,** il ramasse un pognon fou.

rake-off ['reikɔf] *n F* commission *f*/ristourne *f*/pot-de-vin *m*/dessous *m* de table.

raker ['reikər] *n Austr F* **to go a raker,** tomber*/ramasser une bûche/ramasser un gadin/se casser la figure.

ralph (up) ['rælf('ʌp)] *vi NAm P* vomir*/gerber/dégobiller/dégueuler (tripes et boyaux).

ram¹ [ræm] *n P* **1.** *Austr* = **shill(aber) 2.** individu* porté sur le sexe/chaud lapin.

ram² [ræm] *vtr V* **1.** faire l'amour* avec (une femme)/égoïner/bourrer/ sabrer **2.** avoir un coït* anal avec (qn)/empaffer/enculer (qn). (*See* **throat 1**)

rambunctious [ræm'bʌŋkʃəs] *a F* tapageur/chahuteur.

ramp [ræmp] *n F* (*not common*) combine *f*/coup fourré; escroquerie *f*; **it's a ramp,** c'est de l'arnaque.

ramrod ['ræmrɔd] *n V* pénis*/ défonceuse *f*/gourdin *m*.

r & b, R & B ['aırən'biː] *n F* (= *rhythm and blues*) musique populaire qui dérive du blues/rhythm and blues *m*/R & B *m*.

R & R ['aırən'aır] *n F* **1.** (= *rock-and-roll*) rock (-and-roll) *m*/rock-'n-roll *m* **2.** *NAm* (*mil*) (= *rest and recreation*) récréation *f*/récré *f*.

randy ['rændi] *a P* sexuellement très excité(e); **to be randy,** éprouver un désir *ou* une excitation sexuelle intense; (*man*) bander/l'avoir en l'air/avoir la trique/avoir le gourdin; (*woman*) bander/mouiller/ avoir le haricot à la portière; **he was really randy for her,** il bandait pour elle/il l'avait en l'air pour elle/elle l'excitait à mort.

rangoon [ræn'guın] *n P* (*drugs*) cannabis* naturel.

rank [ræŋk] *n F* **to pull rank (on s.o.),** user et abuser de son rang *ou* de sa position.

rap¹ [ræp] *n F* **1.** réprimande *f*/ punition *f*/savon *m*/attrapage *m*/ engueulade *f*; **to take the rap,** payer les pots cassés; **he had to take the**

rap, il a dû porter le chapeau 2.
condamnation*/gerbage *m*/gerbe-
ment *m*/sape(ment) *m*/sucrage *m*;
murder rap, accusation *f* de meur-
tre/dévidage *m* de but(t)e; **to beat
the rap,** se faire acquitter (en justice)/se soustraire à une amende/
déjouer la loi/faire un coup de nib;
to square a rap, faire enlever/faire
sauter une punition *ou* une
amende/défarguer 3. **not to care a
rap,** s'en ficher éperdument/s'en
ficher comme de l'an quarante 4.
not to be worth a rap, ne rien*
valoir/ne pas valoir tripette/ne pas
valoir un pet de lapin 5. *NAm*
conversation *f*/bavardage *m*/con-
verse *f* 6. *NAm* **rap club/parlour/
studio,** bar *m* à hôtesses
(montantes).

rap² [ræp] **I** *vtr* **1.** *F* **to rap (s.o.)
(over the knuckles),** critiquer*/
tancer/bêcher (qn) **2.** *P* arrêter*/
épingler/agrafer/pincer **3.** *P*
tuer*/but(t)er/bousiller/descendre
II *vi esp NAm P* tailler une
bavette/baver/dégoiser/jaspiner.

rare [rɛər] *a F* **we had a rare old
time,** on s'en est payé une sacrée
tranche/on s'en est donné à cœur
joie.

rarin' ['rɛərin], **raring** ['rɛəriŋ] *a
F* **to be rarin' to go,** piaffer
d'impatience/être prêt à ruer/atten-
dre le gong/avoir le feu au derrière.

raspberry ['rɑːzb(ə)ri] *n P* **1.** (*RS
= raspberry tart = fart*) (*a*) pet*/
pastille *f*/perlouse *f* (*b*) bruit fait
avec les lèvres imitant un pet **2.**
désapprobation *f*/engueulade *f*/
savon *m* **3.** rebuffade *f*/défargage
m/vidage *m* **4.** (*a*) **to give s.o. a/
the raspberry,** dire zut à qn/
envoyer qn paître/envoyer chier qn;
his idea was given the raspberry,
on envoya son idée balader (*b*) **to get
a raspberry (from s.o.),** se faire
rabrouer/se faire remballer. (*See*
flip² 2)

rat¹ [ræt] *n* **1.** *F* salaud*/sale type
m/salopard *m*/peau *f* de vache; **you

rat!** espèce de salaud!/sale type!
(*See* **dirty II 1**) **2.** *F* indicateur*/
chevreuil *m*/donneur *m*/mouchard
m **3.** *F* briseur *m* de grève/jaune
m/faux frère **4.** *F* **to smell a rat,**
sentir qch de louche/soupçonner
anguille sous roche/avoir la puce à
l'oreille **5.** *F* **rat poison,** alcool* de
mauvaise qualité/casse-gueule *m*/
tord-boyaux *m*/mort-aux-rats *f* **6.**
F **the rat race,** la jungle/la course
au bifteck; foire *f* d'empoigne **7.** *F*
to have the rats (*a*) être en colère*/
en rogne/en suif (*b*) être en proie
au delirium tremens/voir les rats
bleus **8.** *F* **rats!** flûte!/zut!/merde!
rats to you! va donc!/sans blague!/
mon œil!/va te faire voir! **9.** *F*
(*mil, WWII*) **the Desert Rats,** les
Rats du Désert (7ᵉ division blindée
en Afrique du Nord) **10.** *P* (*a*)
logement*/piaule *f*/nid *m*/taule *f*
(*b*) (*RS = house*) **rat and mouse,**
maison *f*.

rat² [ræt] *vi F* **1. to rat on s.o.** (*a*)
revenir sur un marché (*b*)
dénoncer*/cafarder/bourdiller/ba-
lancer qn; casser le morceau **2.**
abandonner* ses complices/les
lâcher/les plaquer/les laisser en
carafe/les laisser en frime; renarder.

ratbag ['rætbæg] *n P* **1.** vaurien*/
sale coco *m*/ordure *f*/salaud *m*; **you
ratbag!** espèce de salaud!/sale
type!/ordure! **2.** *Austr* excentrique
mf/original *m*.

rate [reit] *vtr F* **1.** avoir un dû/
recevoir son dû/empocher la monnaie de sa pièce **2.** être coté/
estimé/bien vu; avoir la cote auprès
de (qn); **I really rate him,** je lui
donne le tableau d'honneur/il me
botte.

ratfink ['rætfiŋk] *n P* sale mouchard
m/saligaud *m*/sale type *m*/lavette *f*.
(*See* **fink¹ 3**)

rat out ['ræt'aut] *vi P* partir*/
déguerpir/détaler/calter.

ratter ['rætər] *n F* = **rat¹ 2, 3.**

rattle ['rætl] *vtr F* consterner/
bouleverser/retourner/souffler (qn);
it rattled him, il en est resté baba;
he never gets rattled, il ne se laisse
pas démonter/il ne s'épate jamais.

rattle on ['rætl'ɔn] *vi F* **she does
rattle on!** c'est un moulin à
paroles/elle a la langue bien
pendue/elle a avalé un transistor!

rattler ['rætlər] *n F* **1.** train *m*/dur
m **2.** (= *rattlesnake*) serpent *m* à
sonnettes **3.** personne *ou* chose
excellente*/épatante/super/de pre-
mière/champion.

rattling ['rætliŋ] *a O F* **1.** vif/
déluré/d'attaque **2.** excellent*/du
tonnerre; **a rattling good book/film,**
un film/livre génial/de première **3.**
at a rattling pace, au grand trot/au
galop/au pas de course.

rat-trap ['ræt træp] *n P* bouche*/
trappe *f*/évier *m*/clapoir *m*. (*See*
trap 1)

ratty ['ræti] *a* **1.** *F* méchant*/
teigneux/chameau **2.** *F* râleur/
ronchonneur/grincheux/rouspéteur/
rouscailleur; **he gets really ratty at
times,** ça lui arrive d'être de mauvais poil/d'être mal vissé/de l'avoir
sec **3.** *NAm P* (*a*) moche/tarte (*b*)
mal soigné/loquedu (*c*) délabré/
croulant.

raunchy ['rɔːntʃi] *a NAm F* **1.**
moche/toc/tocard/blèche/tartignol
2. salingue/cracra/cradingue **3.**
ivre*/rondibé/jeté/gelé/givré **4.**
grossier/ordurier/grivois/scabreux/
risqué. (*See* **ronchie, ronchy**)

rave[1] [reiv] *n F* **1.** louange *f*
enthousiaste/concert   *m*   de
louanges/coup *m* d'encensoir; **rave
review,**critique élogieuse/dithy
rambique; **it's the latest rave,** c'est
la chose in (à faire) **2.** béguin *m*/
tocade *f*.

rave[2] [reiv] *vi F* s'extasier/être
mordu/être pincé; en rester baba
(d'admiration).

raver ['reivər] *n F* **1. a (little)
raver,** une beauté/un prix de

Diane/un beau petit lot; **she's a bit
of a raver,** elle est bien bandante;
c'est une chaude lapine **2.** personne à la mode/dans le vent/à la
coule.

rave-up ['reivʌp] *n F* boum *f*/
surboum *f*; **to have a rave-up,** se
déchaîner/s'en payer une sacrée
tranche.

raw [rɔː] **I** *a F* **1. raw deal,** sale
coup/coup *m* en vache/vacherie *f*;
it's a raw deal, il y a de l'abus/c'est
dur à avaler; **to give s.o. a raw deal**
(*i*) en faire voir de dures à qn/en
faire voir des vertes et des pas
mûres à qn/faire un sale coup à qn
(*ii*) être vache/moche avec qn **2.**
esp NAm risqué/scabreux/cru **3. a
raw hand/a raw recruit,** un novice/
un bleu/un mal dégrossi **II** *n* **1.**
to catch s.o. on the raw, piquer qn
au vif/toucher le point sensible de
qn **2. in the raw** (*a*) à poil/en costume d'Adam/d'Ève (*b*) fruste/brut.

ray [rei] *n F* **to be s.o.'s little ray of
sunshine,** être le rayon de soleil de
qn.

razz[1] [ræz] *n NAm F* dérision *f*/
ridicule *f*; charriage *m*/mise *f* en
boîte.

razz[2] [ræz] *vtr NAm F* taquiner
(qn)/narguer (qn)/se moquer* de
(qn)/se payer la tête de (qn)/mettre
(qn) en boîte/emboîter (qn).

razz(a)matazz ['ræz(ə)mə'tæz] **I**
a vieux jeu/rococo/à l'eau de rose/
ringard **II** *n* tape-à-l'œil *m*/clin-
quant *m*/chiqué *m*; **the razzamatazz
of show business,** les feux de la
rampe/le strass et les paillettes du
show-biz.

razzle ['ræzl] *n F* **on the razzle,** en
réjouissances*/en bringue; **to go on
the razzle,** faire la bringue/la
ribouldingue/la noce/la tournée des
grands ducs/les 400 coups.

razzle-dazzle ['ræzldæzl] *n esp
NAm F* **1.** bouleversement *m*/
chambard(ement) *m*/remue-ménage
m/chienlit *f* **2.** embrouillamini *m*/

micmac (voulu) **3.** fraude *f*/
supercherie *f*/filouterie *f*/
carambouille *f* **4.** agitation *f*/éclat
m/clinquant *m*/tape-à-l'œil *m* **5.**
réjouissances*/bombe *f*/nouba *f*.

reach [riːtʃ] *n F* **to have a reach
impediment**, être avare*/être constipé du morlingue/avoir un cactus
dans la poche.

reach-me-downs ['riːtʃmidaunz]
npl F prêt-à-porter *m*/décrochez-
moi-ça *m*. (*See* **hand-me-downs**)

read [riːd] *vtr F* **1. I can read him
like a book**, je le connais comme
(le fond de) ma poche/je le lis
comme un livre **2.** comprendre/
piger/entraver.

reader ['riːdər] *n P* **1.** (*in prisons*)
livre *m*/revue *f*/journal *m*/de la lecture **2.** (*drug addicts*) ordonnance *f*
pour ces drogues. (*See* **mitt-reader**)

ready ['redi] *n F* **the ready**, argent*/
pèze *m*/fric *m*/trèfle *m*/pépettes *fpl*;
have you got the readies? t'as le
fric/les ronds/les talbins/le blé?

ready-eye, ready-I ['rediai] *n P*
(*police*) (*i*) guet-apens *m* (*ii*) planque
f.

real [riəl] *F* **I** *adv* **1. for real** (*a*)
réel/vraisemblable/authentique; **it's
for real**, c'est du vrai de vrai/c'est
pas de la came(lote) (*b*) trop beau
pour y croire/incroyable **2.** réelle-
ment/véritablement/vraisemblable-
ment/effectivement; **that's real nice
of you**, c'est vraiment gentil/c'est
très gentil de votre part **II** *a*
(*intensifier*) **he's a real jerk**, c'est un
vrai con/il est con à 100%.

ream [riːm] *vtr P* **to ream s.o.** (*a*)
rentrer qch dans le rectum de qn
(*b*) avoir un coït anal* (avec qn);
enculer/embaguer (qn); tourner la
page/prendre l'escalier de service
(*c*) lécher l'anus* de son partenaire
(avant de faire un coït anal*)/faire
feuille de rose.

ream out ['riːm'aut] *vtr NAm P* **to
ream s.o. out/to ream s.o.'s ass out**,
réprimander* qn sévèrement/passer

un savon à qn/enguirlander qn/
engueuler qn.

rear(-end) ['riər(end)] *n F* fesses*/
postérieur *m*/popotin *m*/derche *m*/
pétard *m*/valseur *m*. (*See* **end 1**)

recap[1] ['riːkæp] *n F* (= *recapitula-
tion*) résumé *m*/récapitulation *f*.

recap[2] ['riː'kæp] *vi F* (= *recapitu-
late*) récapituler/faire un résumé (de
qch).

recce[1] ['reki] *n F* (*esp mil*) (=
reconnaissance) exploration *f*/inves-
tigation *f*.

recce[2] ['reki] *vtr F* (*esp mil*) (= *rec-
onnoitre*) faire une reconnaissance/
éclairer le terrain/ouvrir la route.

red [red] **I** *a* **1.** *F* communiste/
communo/rouge/coco **2.** *F* **to roll
out the red carpet for s.o.**, faire les
honneurs à qn/mettre les petits
plats dans les grands/dérouler le
tapis rouge **3.** *F* **to paint the town
red**, être en réjouissances*/faire les
quatre cents coups/faire la noce/
faire la tournée des grands ducs/
faire la bringue **4.** *P* **red birds/
devils/jackets = reds** (**red II 5**) **5.**
P (*drugs*) **red leb**, haschisch du
Liban/Liban *m* **6.** *V* (*Hell's
Angels*) **to get/to earn one's red
wings**, pratiquer le cunnilinctus sur
une femme pendant ses règles/avoir
ses ailes rouges **7.** *P* (*prisons*) **red
band**, prisonnier à qui l'on donne
certains privilèges/sûr *m*/tenancier
m/garçon *m* de famille. (*See* **her-
ring 1**; **light II 4**; **rag**[1] **4**; **tape**[1];
wing 2) **II** *n* **1.** *F* communiste
mf/communo *m*/rouge *mf*/coco *m*
2. *P* or*/joncaille *f*/jonc *m*/dorure
f **3.** *F* **in the red**, déficitaire/dans
le rouge **4.** *F* **to see red**, voir
rouge/piquer une colère* **5.** *pl P*
(*drugs*) barbituriques*/diables
rouges/barbis *fpl*. (*See* **red I 4**) **6.**
P **to have the reds**, avoir ses
règles*/avoir ses affaires/mettre le
drapeau rouge/repeindre sa grille
en rouge.

red-cap ['redkæp] *n F* **1.** (*mil*) soldat *m* de la police militaire **2.** *NAm* porteur *m* (dans une gare).

red-assed ['redæsd] *a NAm P* en colère*/en rogne/en pétard; **to be red-assed,** être rouge de colère/ prendre un coup de rouge.

reddite ['redait] *n A P* **1.** bijoutier *m*/brocandier *m*/joncailler *m* **2.** qn qui s'occupe d'or*/marchand *m* de jonc. (*See* **red II 2**)

red-eye ['redai] *n NAm P* **1.** whisky *m* de contrebande/casse-pattes *m* **2.** alcool*/tord-boyau(x) *m*/gnôle *f*/antigel *m*/schmic *f*.

redhead ['redhed] *n F* rouquin(e)/ poil *m* de carotte/poil *m* de brique; (*woman*) rouquemonte *f*/rouquemotte *f*.

red-hot ['red'hɔt] *a F* **1.** (*a*) plein de sève/d'allant; qui pète le feu/qui a du mordant (*b*) avec du sex-appeal; **a red-hot mam(m)a** (*i*) une chaude lapine/une chaude de la pince (*ii*) vocaliste plantureuse/ chanteuse de jazz **2. a red-hot communist,** un communiste à tous crins/un stal **3.** très récent/tout chaud/tout brûlant/de dernière heure; **a red-hot tip,** un tuyau sensationnel/de première; **it's red hot,** ça vient de sortir.

red-lamp ['red'læmp] *a attrib F* = **red-light.**

red-letter ['red'letər] *a attrib F* **red-letter day,** jour *m* de fête/jour mémorable/jour à marquer d'une pierre blanche.

red-light ['red'lait] *a attrib F* **a red-light district,** un quartier à prostituées/un quartier chaud.

redneck ['rednek] *n F* paysan*/ plouc *m*/cul-terreux *m*/bouseux *m*/ péquenot *m*.

reef [riːf] *vi Austr P* prendre/ chaparder/faucher/ratiboiser/ barboter.

reefer ['riːfər] *n* **1.** *F* (*drugs*) cigarette* de marijuana/reefer *m* **2.** *P*

fumeur *m* de marijuana/chat *m* **3.** *Austr P* complice *m* (d'un pick-pocket)/baron *m*/trimballeur *m*/ cheville *f*.

Reekie ['riːki] *n F* **Auld Reekie,** Édimbourg.

re-entry [riː'entri] *n P* fin *f* de voyage d'un drogué/redescente *f*.

ref¹ [ref] *n F* (*sports*) (= *referee*) arbitre *m*.

ref² [ref] *vtr F* (*sports*) (= *referee*) arbitrer (un match).

refusenik [ri'fuːznik] *n esp NAm* qn à qui on refuse le droit de s'expatrier (surtout en parlant des dissidents qui veulent quitter l'URSS).

regs [regz] *npl F* (= *regulations*) règlements *mpl*.

reign [rein] *vi Austr P* être en liberté/profiter de la fraîche.

rent [rent] *n P* prostitué mâle/tru-queur *m*/lopaille *f*/garçon *m*.

rep [rep] *abbr F* **1.** (= *representative*) commis voyageur *m*/gaudissard *m*/hirondelle *m*/pilier *m* **2.** (= *reputation*) réputation *f* **3.** (= *repertory (theatre)*) théâtre *m* de province/théâtre municipal; **to be in rep,** être acteur/actrice au théâtre municipal.

repeaters [ri'piːtəz] *npl P* dés* truqués/balourds *mpl*/matuches *mpl*/dés pipés/bouts *mpl* de sucre.

result [ri'zʌlt] *n F* bon résultat; **to get results,** obtenir de bons résultats/arriver à quelque chose; **we got results,** ça a marché/ça a gazé.

resurrection pie [rezə-'rekʃ(ə)n'pai] *n F* nourriture* réchauffée; **to eat resurrection pie,** manger des arlequins.

retard ['riːtaːd] *n NAm F* (= *retarded*) arriéré *m*/handicapé mental/débile *m*.

retread ['riːtred] *n NAm F* rappelé

m au service militaire; naphtalinard *m*.

revamp [riː'væmp] *vtr F* renouveler/remettre à neuf/retaper; **they've revamped the menu,** ils ont rajeuni le(ur) menu.

reviver [ri'vaivər] *n F* remontant *m*/apéritif *m*/apéro *m*/tonique *f*.

rhino ['rainou] *n* **1.** *F* (*abbr* = *rhinoceros*) rhino(céros) *m* **2.** *P* argent*/galette *f*; paie *f*/salaire *m*/ sonnettes *fpl*.

rhubarb ['ruːbɑːb] *n NAm P* querelle*/chahut *m*/grabuge *m*/rif *m*; prise *f* de bec.

rib [rib] *vtr F* taquiner/mettre en boîte/chiner/mener en bateau (qn); **he was ribbing me,** il se payait ma tronche.

ribbing ['ribiŋ] *n F* **to give s.o. a ribbing,** taquiner qn/mener qn en barque.

rib-tickler ['ribtiklər] *n F* plaisanterie *f*/rigolade *f*/vanne *f*.

rich [ritʃ] **I** *F* **1.** *a* **1.** très amusant/rigolo/marrant **2.** scabreux/osé/cochon; (*iron*) **that's a bit rich!** ça c'est le comble/c'est un peu fort de café! (*See* **filthy 2**) **II** *adv* **to strike it rich,** décrocher le gros lot.

Richard, richard ['ritʃəd] *n P* **1.** (*RS = Richard the Third =*) (*a*) (*not common*) (*word*) mot *m*. (*See* **dicky-bird 2**) (*b*) (*bird*) oiseau *m*/ piaf *m* (*c*) (*turd*) étron*/colombin *m*/rondin *m* **2.** *NAm O* détective *m*/policier*/poulet *m* **3.** *esp Austr* **Richard Cranium = dickhead**.

rick [rik] *n P* bévue*/gaffe *f*/bourde *f*/gour(r)ance *f*.

riddance ['ridəns] *n F* **good riddance (to bad rubbish)!** bon débarras!/fous-moi le camp!/débarrasse-moi le plancher!

ride¹ [raid] *n* **1.** *P* coït*/dérouillage *m*/grimpage *m* **2.** *F* **to take s.o. for a ride** (*a*) entraîner et tuer qn/mettre qn en l'air/faire la peau

à qn (*b*) tromper* qn/jouer un sale tour à qn/mener qn en bateau/faire marcher qn/rouler qn **3.** *F* **to go along (just) for the ride,** suivre le gros de la troupe/suivre le courant/ y aller pour y aller. (*See* **joy-ride**)

ride² [raid] *vtr* **1.** *P* faire l'amour* avec (une femme)/faire un carton/ enfiler/dérouiller/grimper **2.** *esp NAm F* asticoter/canuler/enquiquiner/courir sur les haricots **3.** *F* **to let sth ride,** laisser courir qch; **let it ride!** laisse pisser!

riff [rif] *n P* court motif mélodique de jazz *ou* de rock.

rig¹ [rig] *n* **1.** *P* pénis*/colonne *f*/ marteau *m*/dard *m* **2.** camion *m*/ (*esp*) poids lourd.

rig² [rig] *vtr F* arranger/manigancer/ magouiller (à son avantage); **to rig an election,** truquer une élection.

right [rait] **I** *a* **1.** *P* (*a*) **to make a right mess of it,** tout gâcher/tout bousiller/foutre une vraie pagaille/ semer la merde; **she made a right cock-up,** elle a tout mis en l'air/elle y a foutu le merdier (*b*) **he's a right jerk,** c'est un con fini/un idiot intégral (*c*) **she's a right (old) cow,** c'est une vraie peau de vache/une salope intégrale/une vache à 100%. (*See* **balls-up**; **nana**; **so-and-so 2**; **sucker²** 1). **2.** *F* **as right as rain,** en parfait état; **to feel as right as rain,** se porter comme un charme/ avoir la frite **3.** *NAm F* **a right guy** (*a*) un chic type/un mec bien (*b*) un vrai de vrai/un réglo **4.** *F* **to get on the right side of s.o.,** être bien vu de qn/se mettre dans les petits papiers de qn/se mettre à la bonne avec qn. (*See* **noise; people 2**) **II** *adv Austr F* **she'll be right,** tout ira bien/ça ira, mon gars/t'en fais pas, mon gars/on verra bien.

righthander ['rait'hændər] *n P* coup *m*/crochet *m* du droit; **to give s.o. a couple of righthanders,** filer une pêche à qn/casser la gueule à qn/passer qn à tabac.

right-ho! ['rait'hou], **right-o(h)!** ['rait'ou] *excl F* oui*/d'ac(cord)/ OK/entendu!.

right on ['rait'ɔn] *adv F* au poil/ impec; *esp NAm P* **right on!** c'est sûr!/c'est vrai!/pas de doute!/vas-y!

righty-(h)o! ['raiti'(h)ou] *excl F* = **right-ho!**

rigid ['ridʒid] *a P* **1. to bore s.o. rigid**, ennuyer* qn au plus haut point/emmerder qn jusqu'à la moelle/scier le dos à qn/taper sur le système à qn/casser les couilles à qn **2.** *NAm* ivre* mort/bit(t)uré/ jeté.

rig-out ['rigaut] *n F* toilette *f*/tenue *f*/attifage *m*; pelure *f*; nippes *fpl*.

rig out ['rig'aut] *vtr F* habiller*/ fringuer/harnacher/frusquer/loquer/ fagoter.

rig-up ['rigʌp] *n F* appareil impro-visé/installation *f* de fortune/zinzin *m*.

rig up ['rig'ʌp] *vtr F* **1.** apprêter/ préparer/concocter (un repas, une excuse, etc) **2.** = **rig out.**

Riley ['raili] *n F* **to live the life of Riley,** se la couler douce/se la faire belle/vivre comme un coq en pâte.

rim [rim] *vtr P* = **ream.**

ring¹ [riŋ] *n* **1.** *P* anus*/anneau *m*/bague *f*/bagouse *f*/rondelle *f*; **ring twitter/flutter,** peur*/frousse *f*/ jetons *mpl*/chocottes *fpl* **2.** *F* **to run rings round s.o.,** l'emporter sur qn/surpasser qn/remporter la palme/décrocher la timbale.

ring² [riŋ] *vtr* **1.** *F* **it rings a bell,** cela me dit/me rappelle quelque chose **2.** *F* **to ring the changes** (*a*) escroquer*/arnaquer/empiler; faire du vol au rendez-moi/marcher au rendez/marcher au rendème (*b*) écouler de la fausse monnaie/faire la fournaise (*c*) ressasser (un sujet, etc) **3.** *F* substituer un cheval pour un autre dans une course/aller de cheval à canasson **4.** *P* maquiller des objets volés.

ringer ['riŋər] *n F* **1.** sosie *m*; **to be a (dead) ringer for s.o.,** être qn tout craché/être le portrait (tout) craché de qn/être tout le portrait de qn/sortir du même moule que qn **2.** qn qui substitue un cheval pour un autre dans une course **3.** *Austr F* champion *m*/as *m*.

ring-piece ['riŋpiːs] *n P* = **ring¹ 1.**

ringtail ['riŋteil] *n Austr F* (*a*) lâche *m*/caneur *m*/frileux *m*/déballonné *m* (*b*) faux frère/macaron *m*/ mouton *m*/cafard *m*.

rinky-dink ['riŋki'diŋk] *n NAm O F* **1.** camelote *f*/pacotille *f*/ saloperie *f* **2.** guinche *f*/boui-boui *m*/bastringue *m*/pince-fesses *m*.

riot ['raiət] *n F* **1.** grand succès/ boum *m* (du tonnerre)/fureur *f*; **that film's a riot,** ça a fait un tabac (monstre), ce film; **it was a real riot,** on s'en est payé une sacrée tranche/ça déménageait à fond **2.** boute-en-train *m*/rigolo *m*/ rigolboche *m*; **he's a real riot, that guy,** c'est un rigolo/il est impaya-ble, ce type/il est à mourir de rire **3.** déchaînement *m*/tapage *m*/ débauche *f*/chahut *m*/barouf *m* **4.** **to read the Riot Act to s.o.** (*a*) avertir/menacer qn (*b*) répri-mander* qn/passer un savon à qn/ faire un amphi à qn.

rip [rip] *vtr F* **to let rip,** exploser/ vider son sac; (*motorbike*) mettre la poignée dans le coin; **let it rip!/let her rip!** fonce!/appuie sur le cham-pignon!/mets les pleins gaz! **the band let rip,** le groupe a arraché; **the drummer really let it rip,** le bat-teur a dégagé comme une bête/le batteur s'est défoncé.

rip into ['rip'intu] *vtr F* attaquer* (qn)/rentrer dans le lard à (qn)/ tomber sur le paletot (à qn).

rip-off ['ripɔf] *n P* (*a*) vol *m*/escro-querie *f*/arnaque *f* (*b*) entourloupe *f*/pigeonnage *m*.

rip off ['rip'ɔf] *vtr P* **1.** (*a*) voler*/
faucher; **to get ripped off,** être
ratiboisé/être pigeonné/être mené
en bateau; **you were ripped off,** tu
t'es fait voler/tu t'es fait avoir (*b*)
to rip s.o. off, exploiter/arnaquer/
rouler (qn); **I was really ripped off
there,** je m'y suis fait baisé en
beauté **3.** (*rare*) tuer*/zigouiller.

ripped [ript] *a P* (*a*) (*drugs*)
défoncé/très high/planant (*b*) très
ivre*/rétamé/schlass.

ripping ['ripiŋ] *a O F* excellent*/
formid(able)/super.

rip-roaring ['riprɔɪriŋ] *a P* endi-
ablé/piaffant; **a rip-roaring success,**
une réussite du tonnerre/un succès
fulgurant/un tabac (monstre)/un
boum du tonnerre.

ripsnorter ['rip-snɔɪtər] *n F* personne *ou* chose remarquable/crack
m/as *m*; type *m* fortiche.

ripsnorting ['ripsnɔɪtiŋ] *a F* excellent*/bœuf/du tonnerre.

rise[1] [raiz] *n F* **to take a/the rise
out of s.o./to get a rise out of s.o.,**
mettre qn en pétard/faire monter
qn au plafond.

rise[2] [raiz] *vi* **1.** *F* (*catchphrase*)
rise and shine! debout les morts!
2. *P* **to rise to the occasion,** avoir
une érection*/bander.

ritz [rits] *n F* **to put on the ritz,** être
prétentieux*/se donner des airs/
crâner/faire du vent/rouler des
mécaniques/rouler des épaules.

ritzy ['ritsi] *a F* **1.** tape-à-l'œil/
voyant/clinquant; **a ritzy tart,** une
pépée qui en jette/une (femme)
roulée au moule/un beau châssis
2. élégant*/fastueux/ultra-chic **3.**
crâneur/esbrouf(f)eur/plastronneur.

river ['rivər] *n F* **1. to sell s.o.
down the river,** trahir/vendre/
moutonner/donner qn **2. to send
s.o. up the river** = **to send s.o. up
(send up 2).**

roach [routʃ] *n P* (*drugs*) mégot* de
cigarette de marijuana.

road [roud] *n F* **1. to be on the
road,** vivre sur les grands chemins/
vagabonder/trimarder/rouler sa
bosse **2. to hit the road,** partir*/se
mettre en route/prendre le large/
lever l'ancre **3. you're in my road,**
tu es dans mon chemin; **get out of
the road!** dégage!/gadget! (*See* **middle-of-the-road; one 1**)

road-hog ['roudhɔg] *n F* chauffeur
m qui conduit au milieu de la
chaussée/chauffard *m*/écraseur *m*.

roadie ['roudi] *n P* (*rock music*)
homme à tout faire qui accom-
pagne un groupe en tournée/roadie
m.

roast[1] [roust] *n F* (*a*) critique *f*
défavorable/éreintage *m*/bêchage *m*
(*b*) calomnie *f*/débinage *m*/cassage
m de sucre.

roast[2] [roust] *vtr F* critiquer*/
éreinter/bêcher/jardiner.

roasting ['roustiŋ] *n F* **to give
(s.o.) a roasting** = **roast**[2].

rock[1] [rɔk] *n* **1.** *F* (*jazz*) rock *m*.
(*See* **rock-'n-roll**) **2.** *F* **on the
rocks** (*a*) (boisson) servie avec de la
glace (*b*) ruiné*/fauché/nettoyé/
passé (*c*) (mariage) en échec*/à
(vau-)l'eau (*d*) (*commerce*) en fail-
lite/dans le bouillon **3.** *pl P* diamants*/diames *mpl*/pierres *fpl*/cail-
loux *mpl*. (*See* **hot 9**) **4.** *F* **to
touch rock bottom,** être arrivé au
fin fond/être tout à fait à plat/être
dans la dèche **5.** *P* **to get one's
rocks off** (*i*) avoir un orgasme/
s'envoyer en l'air/prendre son pied
(*ii*) s'en payer une tranche/prendre
son pied **6.** *pl P* (*drugs*) héroïne*/
héro *f*.

rock[2] [rɔk] *vtr* **1.** *F* secouer/
ébranler/alarmer **2.** *F* **to rock the
boat,** secouer la barque/la baraque;
ruer dans les brancards; secouer les
puces/faire du grabuge **3.** *P* faire
l'amour* avec (une femme)/biquer/
niquer/sauter.

rock-candy ['rɔk'kændi] *n P* =
rocks (rock[1] **3**).

rocker ['rɔkər] *n F* **1.** blouson noir sur grosse moto/loubard *m*/loulou *m*/rocker *m*. (*See* **mod**) **2.** off one's rocker, fou*/timbré/loufoque/maboul(e)/ échappé de Charenton/ de Sainte-Anne **3.** rocking-chair *f*.

rocket ['rɔkit] *n F* to give s.o. a rocket, réprimander* qn/passer un savon à qn/engueuler qn/sonner les cloches à qn. (*See* **sky-rocket**)

rock-'n-roll[1] ['rɔkən'roul] *n F* rock-and-roll *m*/rock-'n-roll *m*/rock *m*. (*See* **rock**[1] 1)

rock-'n-roll[2] ['rɔkənroul] *vi F* faire du rock-and-roll/danser le rock.

rocky ['rɔki] *a F* (*a*) vacillant/flageollant; a rocky marriage, un mariage qui s'effiloche (*b*) chancelant/titubant (de boisson *ou* de fatigue).

rod [rɔd] *n P* **1.** pénis*/canne *f*/os *m* à moëlle/poireau *m*/gourdin *m*. (*See* **hot 20** (*b*); **hot-rod**) **2.** revolver*/calibre *m*/flingue *m*/pétard *m* **3.** pardessus*/lardosse *m*/lardingue *m*/pardaf *m*.

rod-man ['rɔdmæn] *n NAm P* gangster *m*/bandit *m*/voleur* armé/braqueur *m*.

Roger! roger![1] ['rɔdʒər] *excl F* oui*/d'ac!/OK!

roger[2] ['rɔdʒər] *vtr P* faire l'amour*/baiser/tirer un coup/égoïner.

roll[1] [roul] *n* **1.** *F* liasse *f* de billets* (de banque)/matelas *m* (de faf(f)iots)/mille-feuille *m* **2.** *P* coït*/culbute *f*/troussage *m*; a roll in the hay, une partie de jambes en l'air. (*See* **hay 2**; **jelly-roll**; **payroll**; **rock-'n-roll**[1])

roll[2] [roul] *vtr&i* **1.** *P* voler*/rouler/roustir/ratiboiser/ arnaquer/pigeonner **2.** *F* to be rolling in it, être très riche*/être plein aux as/rouler sur l'or/être rupin/avoir le matelas **3.** *F* to get rolling, partir*/se déhotter/démarrer/décaniller/mettre les voiles **4.** *P* faire

l'amour* avec (une femme)/envoyer (une femme) en l'air/faire un carton. (*See* **aisle 2**; **rock-'n-roll**[2])

roll along ['roulə'lɔŋ] *vi F* avancer tranquillement/suivre son petit bonhomme de chemin/aller cahin-caha.

Roller ['roulər] *n P* = **Rolls**.

rollicking ['rɔlikiŋ] *n P* engueulade *f*/savon *m*.

roll on ['roul'ɔn] *vtr F* roll on Christmas! vivement Noël!

roll-on ['roulɔn] *n F* (*woman's*) gaine *f* (élastique)/béton *m*/pansement *m* à brioche.

roll out ['roul'aut] *vi F* they rolled out of the pub at closing time, à la fermeture ils sont sortis du café en titubant. (*See* **red I 2**)

Rolls ['roulz] *n F* (*aut*) Rolls Royce *f RTM*/Rolls *f*.

roll-up ['roulʌp] *n P* cigarette* roulée (main)/cibiche *f* maison/une cousue main/*FrC* rouleuse *f*. (*See* **roll up 2**)

roll up ['roulʌp] *vi* **1.** *F* arriver*/s'abouler/débouler/débarquer/se pointer **2.** *P* faire une cigarette* de marijuana/rouler un reefer/(se) rouler un joint. (*See* **roll-up**)

roll-your-own ['rouljə'roun] *n F* (*a*) machine *f* à rouler les cigarettes* (*b*) = **roll-up**.

roly-poly ['rouli'pouli] *n F* individu* rondouillard/patapouf *m*/bouboule *m*/dondon *m*/gros lard.

Roman ['roumən] *a P* **1.** Roman candle, catholique *mf*/catho *m* **2.** (= *roaming*) (*a*) Roman hands, mains caressantes/baladeuses; mains qui vont aux renseignements (*b*) Roman eyes, yeux farfouilleurs.

romp[1] [rɔmp] *n F* **1.** to have a romp on the sofa, prendre ses ébats/culbuter (qn) sur le canapé **2.** chose facile à réaliser/du beurre/du nougat/du gâteau/du cousu main.

romp² [rɔmp] *vi F* (*horse*) **to romp home,** gagner facilement/arriver dans un fauteuil/gagner haut la main.

ronchie, ronchy ['rɔntʃi] *a NAm F* = **raunchy.**

roof [ruːf] *n* **1.** *F* **to go through/to hit the roof,** piquer une colère/monter sur ses grands chevaux/sortir de ses gonds/prendre un coup de sang **2.** *F* **to raise the roof,** faire du chahut/du chambard/du grabuge **3.** *P* **to fall off the roof,** avoir ses règles*/repeindre sa grille (en rouge)/avoir sa rue barrée/recevoir ses cousins.

rook [ruk] *vtr F* escroquer*/faisander/pigeonner/rouler/mener en bateau; **he got rooked,** il s'est fait avoir/arnaquer.

rookie ['ruki] *n F* (*esp mil*) recrue *f*/débutant *m*/blanc-bec *m*.

rooking ['rukiŋ] *n F* **to get a rooking,** payer* trop cher/se faire empiler/être faisandé/se faire écorcher/payer bonbon.

rooky ['ruki] *n F* = **rookie.**

room [ruːm] *n F* **1.** **the smallest room/the little boys' room/the little girls' room,** WC*/le petit endroit/le petit coin **2.** (*horse racing*) **to go to the rooms,** gagner par décision des commissaires à la photo-finish. (*See* **barrack-room; throne-room**)

roost [ruːst] *n F* **1.** logement*/niche *f*/guitoune *f*/cambuse *f* **2.** **to hit the roost,** se coucher*/se zoner/aller au paddock/se plumarder/mettre sa viande dans le torchon. (*See* **chicken-roost; pigeon-roost**)

root¹ [ruːt] *n P* **1.** cigarette*/cibiche *f*/clope *mf* **2.** (*drugs*) amphétamines*/amphés *fpl*/bombita *f* **3.** pénis*/bout *m*/queue *f* **4.** fellation*/pipe *f*/pompier *m* **5.** *Austr* coït*/coup *m*/baise *f*.

root² [ruːt] *vi* **1.** *Austr P* faire l'amour* avec (une femme)/fourrer/tringler **2.** *P* faire une fellation* (à qn)/faire un pompier (à qn)/tailler

une pipe (à qn) **3.** *Austr P* **get rooted!** va te faire voir! **4.** *F* **to root for s.o.,** applaudir/encourager qn.

rooted ['ruːtid] *a Austr P* très fatigué*/vanné/sur les rotules/lessivé.

rooter ['ruːtər] *n* **1.** *F* partisan *m*/fana(tique) *mf*/supporter *m* (d'une équipe, etc) **2.** *P* qn qui fait une fellation*/suceur, -euse/pipeur, -euse.

rootin'-tootin' ['ruːtin'tuːtin] *a NAm F* bruyant/chahuteur/pétardier.

rope [roup] *n* **1.** *F* **it's money for old rope,** c'est donné pour une bouchée de pain **2.** *P* tabac* fort/perlot *m*/trèfle *m*/percale *f* **3.** *P* (*drugs*) (a) marijuana*/chanvre *m* (b) cigarette* de marijuana/stick *m*/bomb *f* **4.** *F* **to know the ropes,** être au courant/à la coule/au parfum/affranchi; savoir nager/connaître la combine/les tenants et les aboutissants **5.** *F* **to give s.o. plenty of rope,** lâcher la bride/la jambe à qn; **give him enough rope and he'll hang himself,** laissez-le faire et il se passera lui-même la corde au cou.

rope in ['roup'in] *vtr F* **to rope s.o. in,** s'assurer le concours de qn; **they've roped me in on it,** ils m'ont mis dans le coup.

rop(e)y ['roupi] *a F* camelote/toc/tocard/ordurier; **it's a bit rop(e)y,** c'est du toc.

rort [rɔːt] *n Austr F* **1.** coup monté/fourré; combine bien cuisinée **2.** boniment *m*/baratin *m* **3.** fiesta *f*/beuverie *f*/nouba *f*.

rorter [rɔːtər] *n Austr F* escroc*/fourgueur *m*/faisan *m*.

rorty ['rɔːti] *a P* **1.** réjoui/de bonne humeur/guilleret/folichon/jouasse **2.** = **randy.**

Rory (O'Moore) ['rɔːri(ou'mɔər)] *Prn P* **1.** (*RS* = *door*) porte *f*/

lourde *f* 2. (*RS* = *floor*) **on the Rory,** pauvre*/fauché/sans le sou.

Roscoe, roscoe ['rɔskou] *n* *NAm F* revolver*/pétoire *m*/rigolo *m*.

rosy ['rouzi] *n P* 1. = **claret** 2. vin* rouge/pinard *m*/rouquin *m*/ picrate *m* 3. **ring around the rosy** = **daisy chain** (**daisy II 5**) 4. (*RS* = *tea*) Rosy Lee, thé *m*.

rot [rɔt] *n F* bêtises*/sottises *fpl*/ salades *fpl*/bobards *mpl*; **what rot!** c'est de la blague!/c'est des foutaises! **to talk (utter) rot/a load of rot,** dire des bêtises*/des conneries; débloquer/déconner. (*See* **tommy-rot**)

rot-gut ['rɔtgʌt] *n F* alcool* de mauvaise qualité/tord-boyau(x) *m*/ gnôle *f*.

rotten ['rɔtn] *a F* 1. désagréable/ dégueulasse/débectant/ moche/ merdique/loquedu; **rotten weather,** temps *m* de chien/temps pourri/ saloperie *f* de temps; **a rotten business,** une sale affaire; une affaire véreuse/fumeuse; **rotten luck!** quelle poisse!/quelle déveine!/pas de veine! 2. toc/tocard/camelote/ ordurier 3. malade*/patraque 4. ennuyeux*/barbant/emmerdant 5. *Austr* ivre*/chargé/bourré; **to get rotten,** se noircir/se beurrer/se givrer. (*See* **sod¹ 2**)

rotter ['rɔtər] *n O F* vaurien*/fri- pouille *f*/charogne *f*/ordure *f*.

rough [rʌf] **I** *a F* 1. **rough dia- mond,** personne aux dehors grossiers mais bon enfant/un dia- mant dans sa gangue 2. **that's rough!** c'est vache!/c'est dur à avaler!/c'est un coup dur! 3. **he's had a rough deal,** il en a bavé/il a bouffé de la vache enragée/il en a vu (des vertes et des pas mûres); il en a encaissé/il en a chié 4. **they're a rough lot,** c'est une bande* de sales types/c'est une fine équipe; **a rough customer,** un mau- vais coucheur/un dur à cuire 5.

rough and ready (*a*) **a rough and ready person,** une personne nature (pas très fine ni distinguée)/un péquenot sur les bords (*b*) **a rough and ready method,** une méthode peu précise mais pratique (*c*) **a rough and ready piece of work,** un ouvrage grossièrement fait/fait à la va-vite/à la va-comme-je-te-pousse 6. **rough stuff,** brutalités *fpl*/ vacheries *fpl*; **there'll be some rough stuff tonight,** ça va barder/il va y avoir de la bagarre/il y aura du grabuge/il y aura du baston, ce soir 7. **to give s.o. a rough time,** mal- traiter qn/être chien avec qn/être vache avec qn/en faire voir à qn **II** *adv F* 1. **to sleep rough,** coucher* à la dure/à la belle étoile; compter les étoiles 2. **to feel rough** (*a*) se sentir malade*/patraque; être mal fichu (*b*) se sentir moulu/en avoir sa claque (*c*) avoir la gueule de bois/avoir mal aux cheveux. (*See* **cut up 3**) **III** *n* 1. *F* **to take the rough with the smooth,** prendre le bien avec le mal/à la guerre comme à la guerre/prendre la vie comme elle vient 2. *P* = **rough- neck** 3. *P* **to have a bit of rough** = **to have a bit on the side** (**side 2**).

rough-house ['rʌfhaus] *n F* (*a*) conduite *f* de vaurien*/voyouterie *f* (*b*) bagarre* générale/badaboum *m*/ barouf(fe) *m*/ramdam(e) *m*/cognage *m*/sonnage *m*; **it was all a bit of a rough-house,** ça cognait dur.

rough it ['rʌfit] *vi F* vivre à la dure.

roughneck ['rʌfnek] *n F* vaurien*/ canaille *f*/voyou *m*/dur *m*/casseur *m*/loubard *m*.

rough-trade ['rʌftreid] *n P* homosexuel* sadique/sado; empaleur *m*/tapette *f* qui aime se faire mettre.

rough-up ['rʌfʌp] *n P* violente querelle*/cognage *m*/tabassage *m*/ dérouillée *f*/avoine *f*.

rough up ['rʌf'ʌp] *vtr P* battre* (qn)/tabasser (qn)/bourrer (qn) de coups/avoiner (qn); **the cops roughed him up a bit,** les flics l'ont passé à tabac.

roundabouts ['raundəbauts] *npl F* (*catchphrase*) **what you lose on the roundabouts you gain on the swings/it's all swings and roundabouts,** il y a des hauts et des bas/ à tout prendre on ne gagne ni ne perd/on récupère à droite ce qu'on perd à gauche.

roundheel(s) ['raundhiːl(z)] *n NAm P* **to be a roundheel,** être une femme facile/avoir les talons courts/être une groseille à maquereaux. (*See* **heel 2**)

round robin ['raund'rɔbin] *n* **1.** *F* pétition *f* (où les signatures sont disposées en rond) **2.** *P* (*horse racing*) (*accumulative bet*) paroli *m*.

round-up ['raundʌp] *n F* **1.** rassemblement *m*/compilation *f*/ résumé *m* (des dernières nouvelles, etc) **2. to be heading for the last round-up,** être près de mourir*/sentir le sapin/graisser ses bottes.

rouser ['rauzər] *n P* **1.** qch de sensationnel/de saisissant/un boum **2.** gros mensonge*/bobard *m*/ bateau *m*.

roust out ['raust'aut] *vtr F* **to roust s.o. out,** se débarrasser* de qn/ flanquer qn à la porte/balancer qn/ envoyer balader qn.

row¹ [rau] *n* **1.** *F* querelle*/rififi *m*/baston *m*/cognage *m* **2.** (*a*) *F* chahut *m*/charivari *m* (du diable)/ barouf *m* (*b*) *P* **hold/shut your row!** la ferme!/la boucle!/ta gueule!/ mets-la en veilleuse!

row² [rau] *vi F* se quereller/ s'attraper/pétarder/s'engueuler/se voler dans les plumes.

royals ['rɔiəlz] *npl* **1.** *F* la famille royale **2.** *P* (*to turn Queen's Evidence*) **to do the royals,** dénoncer ses complices (souvent en échange d'une peine plus légère/déballer le morceau/se mettre à table.

rozzer ['rɔzər] *n P* agent* de police/flic *m*/poulet *m*/poulaga *m*.

rubadub ['rʌbə'dʌb] *n P* (*RS*) (*a*) (= *club*) club *m*/boîte *f* de nuit/ tripot *m* (*b*) (= *pub*) bar *m*/bistrot *m*/rade *m*.

rubber ['rʌbər] *n* **1.** *P* préservatif*/capote anglaise/imper *m* à Popaul/chapeau *m* **2.** *pl F* galoches *fpl*/caoutchoucs *mpl* **3.** *P* (*RS* = *rubber dub*) = **rubadub**. (*See* **bum-rubber**)

rubberneck¹ ['rʌbənek] *n NAm P* touriste *mf*/badaud *m*/glaude *f*.

rubberneck² ['rʌbənek] *vi NAm F* excursionner/visiter (des monuments, etc).

rubber-stamp¹ ['rʌbə'stæmp] *n F* (*a*) fonctionnaire *m* qui exécute aveuglément les ordres de ses supérieurs/rond-de-cuir *m* (*b*) béni-oui-oui *m*/lèche-bottes *m*.

rubber-stamp² ['rʌbərstæmp] *vtr F* approuver (qch) sans discussion.

rubbity ['rʌbiti] *n Austr F* (= *pub*) rade *m*/troquet *m*/bistrot *m*.

rube [ruːb] *n NAm F* (*a*) fermier *m*/ cul-terreux *m* (*b*) paysan*/pétrousquin *m*/plouc *m*/péquenot *m*/ glaiseux *m*.

rub in ['rʌb'in] *vtr F* **to rub it in,** insister/remuer le couteau dans la plaie; **don't rub it in/there's no need to rub it in,** pas la peine d'en rajouter.

rub off ['rʌb'ɔf] *vtr&i P* **1.** faire l'amour* **2. to rub (it) off,** se masturber*/s'astiquer/se pignoler/se frotter le chinois.

rub-out ['rʌbaut] *n P* **1.** assassinat *m*/tuerie *f*/but(t)age *m*/dessoudage *m*/mise *f* en l'air/dégommage *m* **2.** coït*/baisage *m*/frottage *m*/ carambolage *m*.

rub out ['rʌb'aut] *vtr P* **1.** tuer*/ but(t)er/dessouder/démolir/zigouiller/refroidir **2.** battre*/bourrer de

rub-up 277 **run-out**

coups*/dérouiller/filer une avoine
à/carder le cuir à (qn).

rub-up ['rʌbʌp] *n P* (acte *m* de)
masturbation *f*/moussage *m*/
branlette *f*/astiquage *m*. (*See* **rub
up** 2)

rub up ['rʌb'ʌp] *vtr* 1. *F* to rub s.o.
up the wrong way, prendre qn à
rebrousse-poil 2. *P* se masturber*/
s'astiquer/se faire mousser/jouer à
cinq contre un 3. *P* caresser
activement (qn)/faire mousser (qn);
allumer les gaz; aller aux renseigne-
ments/mettre la main au panier/
peloter/papouiller.

ruck¹ [rʌk] *n P* querelle*/prise *f* de
bec/prise de gueule.

ruck² [rʌk] *vtr&i P* 1. agacer/
énerver/ronchonner/taper sur le
système 2. faire beaucoup de
bruit*/faire du chahut/faire un
barouf (de tous les diables)/faire un
boucan à réveiller les morts.

ruckus ['rʌkəs] *n P* chahut *m*/
barouf *m*; grabuge *m*. (*See* **ruck¹**)

ructions ['rʌkʃənz] *npl F* bagarre*/
tapage *m*/vacarme *m*/rébecca *m*/
scène *f*; if you come home late
there'll be ructions, si tu rentres
tard, tu te feras incendier/tu te
feras tirer les oreilles.

ruddy ['rʌdi] *a & adv P* (*euph for*
bloody) a ruddy liar, un sacré
menteur/un bourreur de mou; he's
a ruddy nuisance, il est vachement
casse-pieds/il est casse-bonbons/il
nous les casse; you ruddy fool!
espèce de nœud/d'andouille/
d'enfoiré/de laveduc/de branque!

rug [rʌg] *n* 1. *NAm P* perruque *f*/
moumoute *f* 2. *F* to pull the rug
from under s.o.('s feet), couper
l'herbe sous les pieds de qn. (*See*
dirt 4)

rugger ['rʌgər] *n F* le rugby.

rum [rʌm] *a F* bizarre; a rum one,
un drôle de type/de zèbre/
d'oiseau/de paroissien; it was a rum
do, c'était un truc plutôt bizarre/
c'était un drôle de cinéma.

rumble¹ ['rʌmbl] *n P* bagarre*/rixe
f/cognage *m*; bataille arrangée
entre bandes* de voyous.

rumble² ['rʌmbl] *vtr F* flairer/se
douter de (qch)/se gourrer/voir
venir (qn); he's rumbled us, il nous
a mis à jour/il a découvert le pot
aux roses.

rumbustious [rʌm'bʌstiəs] *a F*
tapageur/chahuteur.

rumdum ['rʌmdʌm], **rumhound**
['rʌmhaund] *n A P* ivrogne*/poivrot
m/soûlot *m*/soûlard *m*.

rummy ['rʌmi] I *a F* = **rum** II *n*
esp NAm P = **rumdum**.

rump [rʌmp] *vi P* (*drugs*) se droguer
à l'héroïne*.

rumpot ['rʌmpɔt] *n A P* =
rumdum.

rumpus ['rʌmpəs] *n F* querelle*/
chahut *m*/vacarme *m*; to kick up a
rumpus, faire une scène; there's
gonna be a rumpus, ça va ronfler/
barder.

run [rʌn] *n F* 1. to have a run for
one's money, en avoir pour son
argent*/pour ses sous 2. the runs,
diarrhée*/courante *f*/chiasse *f* 3.
to be on the run, être recherché par
la police/être en cavale/faire la
belle 4. dry run, essai *m*/répétition
f.

run-around ['rʌnəraund] *n F* to
give s.o. the run-around, donner le
change à qn/faire marcher qn/
mener qn en bateau.

run-down ['rʌndaun] *n F* résumé
m/récapitulation *f*/topo *m*.

run down ['rʌn'daun] *vtr F* criti-
quer*/éreinter/débiner.

run in ['rʌn'in] *vtr F* arrêter*/
embarquer/ramasser/coffrer.

run-of-the-mill ['rʌnəvðə'mil] *a*
F ordinaire/quelconque/banal.

run-out ['rʌnaut] *n P* to have a
run-out, uriner*/se l'égoutter/jeter
sa goutte.

run out ['rʌn'aut] *vi F* **to run out on s.o.**, se défiler/prendre la poudre d'escampette/se débiner.

runt [rʌnt] *n F (a)* nain *m*/nabot *m (b)* avorton *m*/crapoussin *m*/ crapaud *m*/foutriquet *m*/bas-du-cul *m (c) (pej)* **you little runt!** (espèce de) nabot!/trouduc!/basduc!

runty ['rʌnti] *a F* rabougri/riquiqui.

rush¹ [rʌʃ] *n P (drugs)* impression *f* de plénitude physique et psychique avec une drogue; flash *m*/boum *m*/ le pied. (*See* **bum's rush**)

rush² [rʌʃ] *vtr F* **to rush s.o. for sth,** pratiquer le coup de fusil sur qn/ écorcher qn.

Russky ['ruski, 'rʌski] *n F* Russe*/ roscof *m*/popof *m*.

rust bucket ['rʌstbʌkit] *n Austr P* vieille voiture*/guinde *f*/guimbarde *f*/tacot *m*.

rustle up ['rʌsl'ʌp] *vtr F* dénicher/ concocter/dégotter (qch); **she can always rustle up a little something,** elle sait toujours se débrouiller pour faire de quoi bouffer.

Ruth [ru:θ] *Prn Austr P* **to cry Ruth,** vomir*/dégueuler/aller au refil(e).

S

sack¹ [sæk] *n* **1.** *F* **to get the sack,** être congédié*; se faire congédier/ renvoyer/sacquer/lourder; **to give s.o. the sack,** se débarrasser* de/ sacquer/virer/balancer qn; **he got (given) the sack,** il s'est fait foutre à la porte **2.** *F* **to look like a sack of potatoes,** avoir une drôle de touche; **he looks like a sack of potatoes,** on dirait l'as de pique **3.** *F* **to hit the sack,** se coucher*/ dormir*/se pieuter/se bâcher/se pager; **sack time** (*a*) temps passé au lit*/temps de pieutage/dorme *f* (*b*) heure *f* du coucher/du plumard **4.** *P* **sack game,** cour amoureuse/jeux amoureux/fleurette *f*.

sack² [sæk] *vtr F* **to sack s.o.** = **to give s.o. the sack (sack¹ 1)**

sack out, up ['sæk'aut, 'ʌp] *vi P* se coucher*/se pieuter.

saddle ['sædl] *vtr&i F* **to be saddled with s.o./sth,** avoir qn/qch sur le dos; se coltiner qn/qch; **I got saddled with all the washing-up,** j'ai dû me coltiner toute la vaisselle.

safe [seif] **I** *a F* **to be safe/to be on the safe side** (*a*) être du bon côté (*b*) agir pour plus de sûreté; **I'll take an extra £1 (just) to be on the safe side,** je prendrai une livre de plus pour plus de sûreté **II** *adv F* **to play (it) safe,** agir à coup sûr/ jouer serré/ne pas prendre de risques/jouer sur le velours **III** *n NAm P* préservatif*/capote (anglaise).

safety ['seifti] *n P* préservatif/ capote (anglaise)/doigt *m* de sécurité.

sail [seil] *n F* **to take the wind out of s.o.'s sails,** couper l'herbe sous les pieds de qn.

sailing ['seiliŋ] *n F* **to be (all) plain sailing,** aller tout seul/ne pas faire un pli; **it's going to be all plain sailing from now on,** ça va aller comme sur des roulettes.

sail into ['seil'intuɪ] *vtr F* (*a*) attaquer*/assaillir/agrafer/rentrer dans (la gueule de) (qn) (*b*) sonner les cloches à/passer un savon à (qn) (*c*) entamer/attaquer (un travail) avec élan.

sailor ['seilər] *n* **1.** *V* **sailor's bride** = poupée *f* gonflable; planche *f* à trou; poisson suceur **2.** *F* (*catchphrase*) **hello sailor!** salut tata!/salut chocotte!/coquine va!

sail through ['seil'θruɪ] *vtr F* terminer (un travail, etc) en moins de deux/faire (qch) (illico) presto/ liquider (qch) en deux coups de cuillère à pot; **to sail through an exam,** réussir un examen les doigts dans le nez/haut la main.

sale [seil] *n P* **no sale!** pas mêche!/ rien à faire!/que dalle!

Sally Army ['sæli'ɑɪmi] *n F* (= *Salvation Army*) l'Armée *f* du Salut.

salt [sɔɪlt] *n* **1.** *F* **(old) salt,** marin*/vieux loup de mer **2.** *P* (*drugs*) héroïne* (en poudre)/poudre *f*/neige *f*/blanche *f* **3.** *P* (*drugs*) **salt and pepper,** marijuana* de mauvaise qualité/chiendent *m* **4.** *F* **to be worth one's salt,** gagner bien son pain/sa croûte; **he's not worth his salt,** il ne vaut pas grand-chose. (*See* **dose 2**)

salt-cellar ['sɔːltselər] *n F* salière *f* (derrière les clavicules).

sam, Sam [sæm] *n P* **1. to stand sam**, payer la tournée/liquider l'ardoise **2.** *NAm* agent *m* de la Brigade fédérale des Stupéfiants. (*See* **Uncle 6**)

sambo, Sambo ['sæmbou] *n P* (*pej*) Noir(e)*/nègre *mf*/bamboula *m*.

sample ['sɑːmpl] *vtr F* **to sample the goods**, mettre/coller la main au panier (à qn).

sand [sænd] *n NAm F* courage *m*/cran *m*/estome *m*. (*See* **grit 1**)

sandboy ['sæn(d)bɔi] *n F* **(as) happy as a sandboy**, gai comme un pinson/heureux comme un poisson dans l'eau.

sandman ['sæn(d)mæn, 'sæn(d)mən] *n* **1.** *F* **the sandman is coming**, le marchand de sable va passer **2.** *P* (*drugs*) trafiquant *m*/dealer *m* (d'héroïne).

sanger ['sæŋgər] *n Austr F* sandwich *m*/croustille *f*.

sao [sau] *n NAm P* salaud*/fumier *m*/ordure *f*/connard *m*.

sap(head) ['sæp(hed)] *n P* individu bête*/niguedouille *mf*/œuf *m*.

sappy ['sæpi] *a F* **1.** bête*/ballot/baluchard/cruche **2.** sans expérience/nigaud/bleu.

sarge [sɑːdʒ] *n F* (= *sergeant*) (*mil*) sergent *m*/serpied *m*/sergot *m*.

sarky ['sɑːki] *a F* sarcastique/mordant/ironique/caustique/persifleur; **to be sarky with s.o.**, mettre qn en boîte/chambrer qn; **no need to be so sarky!** ça va, c'est pas la peine de me chambrer comme ça!

sarny ['sɑːni] *n F* sandwich *m*; **I forgot my sarnies**, j'ai oublié mon casse-croûte.

sass¹ [sæs] *n NAm F* = **sauce¹ 1.**

sass² [sæs] *vtr NAm F* = **sauce².**

sassy ['sæsi] *a NAm F* = **saucy 1.**

satch [sætʃ], **satchelmouth** ['satʃəlmauθ] *n F* qn qui a une grande bouche*/grande gueule.

Saturday ['sætədi] *n NAm F* **Saturday night special**, revolver*/feu *m*/soufflant *m*/calibre *m*.

sauce¹ [sɔːs] *n F* **1.** effronterie *f*/toupet *m*/culot *m*; **I'll have none of your sauce!** pas d'impertinences! **2.** *NAm* alcool*/goutte *f*; **to hit the sauce**, boire* beaucoup/tomber sur la bouteille/biberonner; **to be off the sauce**, ne plus prendre d'alcool*/suivre la croix bleue/être au régime sec. (*See* **apple-sauce**)

sauce² [sɔːs] *vtr F* faire l'insolent avec/se payer la tête de (qn).

saucebox ['sɔːsbɔks] *n F* effronté(e) *m(f)*/mufle *m*/butor *m*/malotru *m*.

saucepan ['sɔːspæn] *n P* (*RS* = *kids*) **saucepan lids**, enfants*/mioches *mpl*/morpions *mpl*. (*See* **dustbin**)

saucy ['sɔːsi] *a F* **1.** impertinent/effronté/gonflé/culotté/qui n'a pas froid aux yeux/qui ne manque pas d'air **2.** aguichant/coquet/chic **3.** scabreux/osé/épicé/vert/salé.

sausage ['sɔsidʒ] *n* **1.** *F* **not a sausage**, rien* du tout/que dalle **2.** *F* **(you) silly sausage!** gros bête!/gros ballot!/espèce de nouille! **3.** *F* **sausage dog**, teckel *m*/saucisse *f* à pattes **4.** *P* (*drugs*) cigarette* de marijuana/stick *m*/bomb *f* **5.** *P* (*RS* = *cash*) **sausage and mash**, argent*/fric *m*/pognon *m* **6.** *P* (*euph*) pénis*/chipolata *f*/berdouillette *f*; **sausage grappler**, branleur *m*.

save [seiv] *vtr F* **save it!** arrête ça!/arrête ton char!/écrase!

saver ['seivər] *n F* (*horse racing*) pari *m* de protection/pari caisse d'épargne/pari micheton. (*See* **life-saver**)

savvy¹ ['sævi] *n F* bon sens/jugeot(t)e *f*.

savvy² ['sævi] *vi O F* savoir/connaître/piger/con(n)obler; **you savvy?** tu piges?

sawbones ['sɔːbounz] *n F* chirurgien *m*/charcuteur *m*/coupe-toujours *m*/tranche-lard *m*.

sawder ['sɔːdər] *n NAm F* **soft sawder** = **soft soap (soap¹ 1).**

sawney ['sɔːni] *n* **1.** *F* Écossais *m*/kiltie *m* **2.** *P* individu bête*/baluchard *m*.

sawn-off ['sɔːnɔf] **I** *a F* petit* (individu)/demi-portion/inachevé/(individu) rase-bitume **II** *n P* (= *sawn-off shotgun*) fusil *m* à canon scié.

sax [sæks] *n F* (*abbr* = *saxophone*) *F* saxo(phone) *m*.

say [sei] *vtr* **1.** *F* **I'll say!** vous avez raison!/et comment donc! **2.** *F* **you don't say!** ça par exemple!/pas vrai! **3.** *P* **says you!** que tu dis! (*See* **sez you!**) **4.** *P* **says who?** chiche!

say-so ['seisou] *n F* **1. to have the say-so,** avoir voix au chapitre; **I did it on his say-so,** je n'ai fait qu'obéir/j'ai fait ce qu'il m'a dit **2.** parole *f*/mot *m*/dire *m*.

scab¹ [skæb] *n F* briseur *m* de grève/jaune *m*.

scab² [skæb] *vi F* briser une grève.

scabby ['skæbi] *a P* minable/mesquin/pouilleux.

scag [skæg] *n P* (*drugs*) héroïne*/chnouf *m*/jules *m*.

scale [skeil] *vtr&i Austr P* **1.** voler*/carotter (qch) **2.** ne pas payer (sa part)/passer à l'as; (*trains, etc*) brûler le dur.

scalper ['skælpər] *n F* **(ticket) scalper,** qn qui pratique le coup de fusil/empileur *m*/arnaqueur *m*/entubeur *m*.

scallywag ['skæliwæg] *n F* petit polisson/petit galopin.

scam [skæm] *n NAm F* **1.**

scandale *m* **2.** canular *m*; coup monté/carambouille *f*/estampage *m*.

scamp [skæmp] *n F* **you young/little scamp!** petit galopin!/petit polisson!

scanties ['skæntiz], **scants** [skænts] *npl F* cache-truc *m*/vignette *f*/minislip *m*.

scarce [skɛəs] *a F* **to make oneself scarce,** partir*/prendre le large/prendre la tangente/se faire oublier.

scare-baby ['skɛəbeibi], **scaredy-cat** ['skɛədikæt] *n F* poltron*/lâche *m*/poule mouillée/vessard *m*/dégonflé *m*/trouillard *m*/pétochard *m*.

scare up ['skɛər'ʌp] *vtr esp NAm F* chercher et trouver (qch); **to scare up a quick snack,** se dégotter un truc à bouffer.

scarper ['skɑːpər] *vi P* s'enfuir*/déguerpir/se tailler.

scary ['skɛəri] *a F* qui fait peur*/effroyable; **a really scary film,** un super film d'épouvante.

scat [skæt] **I** *excl P* **scat!** décampe!/détale!/file!/barre-toi! **II** *n P* **1.** (*a*) chantonnement *m*/fredonnage *m* (*b*) baragouin *m*/charabia *m* **2.** (*drugs*) héroïne*/jus *m*.

scatterbrain ['skætəbrein] *n F* Jean-de-la-lune *m*/étourdi *m*/écervelé *m*/tête *f* de linotte.

scatterbrained ['skætəbreind] *a F* étourdi/écervelé/évaporé/à tête de linotte/à cervelle *f* de moineau.

scatty ['skæti] *a F* **1.** un peu fou*/toqué/maboul(e) **2.** farfelu.

scene [siːn] *n* **1.** *F* **behind the scenes,** en coulisses **2.** *F* action *f*/pratique *f*; **it's all part of today's scene,** c'est ce qui se fait maintenant; **it's a really heavy scene,** c'est une galère **3.** *P* endroit *m* où les drogués se réunissent/le lieu **4.** *F* **to make a scene,** faire une scène/renauder/rouscailler **5.** *F* **to make the scene** (*a*) arriver*/s'abouler/se

pointer; faire acte de présence (b)
réussir/arriver/y avoir la main **6.**
F **bad scene,** mauvaise posture **7.**
F **it's not my scene,** ce n'est pas
mon genre/c'est pas mon truc.

schiz(o) ['skits(ou)] a&n F
schizo(phrène) (mf).

schlemiel, schlemihl [ʃləˈmiːl,
ʃleˈmiːl] n NAm P nullité f/zéro m;
ballot m/gourde f; **he's a schlemiel,**
ce n'est pas une lumière.

schlenter ['ʃlentər] a P toc/de
camelote.

schlep [ʃlep] vtr P tirer/hâler/
remorquer/trimballer.

schlimazel [ʃliˈmaːzl] n NAm P
qn qui a de la malchance*/poissard
m/guignard m/qn qui a la
scoumoune.

schliver ['ʃlivər] n P = **chiv**[1] **1.**

schlong [ʃlɒŋ] n NAm P pénis*/
trique f.

schmal(t)z [ʃmælts, ʃmɔːlts,
ʃmɔlts] n F (musique, etc) très sen-
timental(e); guimauve f.

schmal(t)zy ['ʃmæltsi, 'ʃmɔːltsi,
'ʃmɔltsi] a F à l'eau de rose; **it's
rather smaltzy,** c'est de la
guimauve.

schmeck [ʃmek], **schmee** [ʃmiː]
n P = **shmeck.**

schmeer ['ʃmiər] n P **1.** = **dope**[1]
1 2. pot-de-vin m/dessous m de
table **3.** calomnie f/bêche f.

schmier [ʃmiər] n P ristourne f/
commission f/dessous-de-table m/
bakchich m.

schmo [ʃmou], **schmock** [ʃmɔk],
schmoe [ʃmou] n P **1.** individu
bête*/nigaud m/baluchard m/
duschmol m **2.** individu
ennuyeux*/raseur m/casse-pieds m.

schmoose, schmooze [ʃmuːz]
vi P bavarder*/papoter/ragoter/
bavasser.

schmuck [ʃmuk] n P = **prick 1,
2.**

schnide [ʃnaid] n P = **snide II 1,
2.**

schnook [ʃnuk, ʃnuːk] n P =
schmo 1, 2.

schnorrer ['ʃnɔːrər] n P mendiant*/mangav(eur) m.

schnozz [ʃnɔz], **schnozzle**
['ʃnɔzl], **schnozzola** [ʃnɔˈzoulə]
n P nez*/pif m/naze m/tarin m.

schnuk [ʃnuk] n P = **schmo 1, 2.**

school [skuːl] n F **1.** personnes
réunies pour jouer de l'argent* **2.**
the old school tie, la clique des
anciens élèves.

schoolboy ['skuːlbɔi] n P (drugs)
codéine f.

schoolie ['skuːli] n Austr F (=
school teacher) prof mf/instit mf.

schoolmarm ['skuːlmaːm] n F
maîtresse f d'école; **she's a real
schoolmarm,** c'est une vraie prude/
elle fait sa julie.

schoolmarmish ['skuːlmaːmiʃ] a
F (pej) **she's very schoolmarmish,**
elle fait très maîtresse d'école/elle
fait très institutrice (en retraite).

schpieler ['ʃpiːlər] n P = **spieler.**

schtuck ['ʃtuk] n P **to be in
schtuck,** être dans le pétrin/dans de
mauvais draps/dans la mélasse/
dans la panade.

schtumm ['ʃtʌm] a P (a) mort/
clam(p)sé (b) peinard/qui (ne)
moufte pas/qui la boucle.

schwar(t)z [ʃwɔːts] n NAm P (pej)
Noir(e)*/nègre mf/bamboula m/
bougnoul(e) m.

scoff[1] [skɔf] n P nourriture*/bous-
tifaille f/graille f.

scoff[2] [skɔf] vi P (a) se goinfrer/
s'en foutre plein la lampe (b) manger*/bouffer/boulotter/grailler.

scoop[1] [skuːp] n F **1.** coup m de
chance*/de bol/de fion **2.** (press)
nouvelle sensationnelle (que l'on est
seul à publier)/rafle f/scoop m.

scoop[2] [skuːp] vtr F **1.** avoir un

droit exclusif de publication/faire un scoop **2.** rafler/ratiboiser (qn) **3.** déjouer les intentions de (qn)/ dépasser (qn) en finesse.

scoot [skut] *vi F* **1.** s'enfuir*/ déguerpir (en quatrième vitesse); **scoot!** détale!/file!/dégage! **2.** filer à toute vitesse/aller à fond la caisse.

scorch¹ [skɔːtʃ] *n F* allure effrénée/ bride abattue.

scorch² (along) ['skɔːtʃ(əˈlɔŋ)] *vi F* conduire comme un fou/aller à un train d'enfer/aller à fond de train/brûler le bitume.

scorcher ['skɔːtʃər] *n F* **1.** journée *f* torride; vague *f* de chaleur; **it's a scorcher,** on se croirait dans un four **2.** amateur *m* de vitesse/avaleur *m* de kilomètres **3.** remarque/réplique coupante *ou* sarcastique; riposte cinglante.

score¹ [skɔːr, skɔər] *n* **1.** *F* **to know the score,** être au courant/à la page/dans le coup; **what's the score?** quoi de neuf? **2.** *P* vingt livres sterling **3.** *P* **to make a score = score²** 1, 2 **4.** *P* butin*/ affure *f* **5.** *P* affaire réussie/bien enlevée **6.** *esp NAm* meurtre (prémédité)/but(t)age *m*/dessoudage *m*; contrat *m*.

score² [skɔːr, skɔər] *vi P* **1.** (*drugs*) s'approvisionner/se ravitailler en drogue; se garnir/trouver le joint **2.** (*a*) (*prostitute*) faire un levage/ lever un miché (*b*) (*to find sexual partner for the night, etc*) faire une touche/lever qn/emballer qn **3.** être au mieux avec qn/être dans les petits papiers de qn/avoir la cote avec qn **4.** réussir/se tailler un succès/épater la galerie **5.** *esp NAm* tuer*/but(t)er/dessouder/mettre en l'air (qn).

scot [skɔt] *n P* (*drugs*) héroïne*.

Scotch [skɔtʃ] *a F* **to see through Scotch mist,** avoir des visions/être comme Jeanne d'Arc.

Scouse [skaus] *n F* **1.** habitant *m* de Liverpool **2.** patois *m* de Liverpool.

Scouser ['skausər] *n F* habitant *m* de Liverpool. (*See* **Scouse** 1)

scout [skaut] *n F* **(good) scout,** brave homme*/chic type.

scrag¹ [skræg] *n* **1.** *F* cou décharné/cou de grue/mince collier **2.** *P* femme* efflanquée/décharnée; sac *m* d'os.

scrag² [skræg] *vtr* **1.** *P* pendre/ garrotter (qn) **2.** *F* (*a*) tuer*/tordre le cou à (qn)/donner le coup de pouce à (qn) (*b*) saisir (un adversaire) au collet.

scram [skræm] *vi P* partir*/gicler/ ficher le camp/détaler; **scram!** fous le camp!/dégage!

scran [skræn] *n P* restes *mpl* (de nourriture*)/rogatons *mpl*.

scrap¹ [skræp] *n F* (*a*) querelle*/ rixe *f* (*b*) bagarre*/baston *m* (*c*) (*boxing*) match *m*; **to have a scrap,** se battre/se bagarrer.

scrap² [skræp] *vtr F* **1.** mettre (qch) au rancart; bazarder; envoyer/jeter à la casse **2.** (*a*) se quereller*/avoir une prise de bec (*b*) se battre*/se bagarrer.

scrape¹ [skreip] *n* **1.** *F* **to get into a scrape,** se mettre dans un mauvais pas/dans le pétrin; **to get out of a scrape,** se tirer d'affaire **2.** *F* mince couche *f* de beurre, etc, sur une tartine/raclage *m* **3.** *P* **to have a scrape,** se raser*/se racler/se gratter la couenne.

scrape² [skreip] *vtr* **1.** *F* **to scrape the (bottom of the) barrel,** faire les fonds de tiroir **2.** *F* **to scrape clear of prison,** friser la prison* **3.** *Austr P* faire l'amour*/baiser/sauter/ niquer/tringler.

scrape along ['skreipəˈlɔŋ] *vi F* s'en tirer péniblement/vivoter/à peine joindre les deux bouts/tirer le diable par la queue.

scrap-heap ['skræphiːp] *n F* (*a*) (*pers*) **to be thrown on the scrap-heap,** être mis au rebut/être mis au placard (*b*) **it's fit for/it's only good for the scrap-heap,** c'est bon à mettre à la poubelle/c'est bon pour la caisse. (*See* **wind up**)

scratch[1] [skrætʃ] *n* **1.** *P* argent*/pognon *m*/fric *m* **2.** *F* **to come up to scratch,** être à la hauteur **3.** *V* sexe de la femme*/craque(tte) *f*/cicatrice *f* **4.** *F* **to start from scratch,** partir de zéro/rien.

scratch[2] [skrætʃ] *vi P* chasser la drogue. (*See* **back II 4**)

scratcher ['skrætʃər] *n P* **1.** faussaire *m*/"homme de lettres" **2.** allumette *f*/bûche *f*/souffrante *f*/grattante *f*/frotte *f*. (*See* **backscratcher**)

scream[1] [skriːm] *n F* **1.** (*a*) **she's a scream,** elle est rigolotte/désopilante/marrante/impayable (*b*) **it's a scream,** c'est à se tordre/à mourir de rire; c'est à se rouler par terre (de rire) **2.** clameur *f*/chambard *m*/barouf *m*; **wait for the scream to die down,** laisse le ramdam se calmer.

scream[2] [skriːm] *vi F* rire* aux éclats/à ventre déboutonné/à gorge déployée/se rouler par terre; **he made us scream,** il nous a fait tordre.

screamer ['skriːmər] *n P* **1.** client jamais satisfait/rouspéteur *m*/mauvais coucheur **2.** gros titre(s)/grande manchette/cinq colonnes à la une **3.** *pl* **the screamers,** diarrhée*/chiasse *f*/courante *f*.

screaming ['skriːmiŋ] *a Austr O F* **screaming on s.o./sth,** monté contre qn/qch. (*See* **abdabs**; **meemies**)

screamingly ['skriːmiŋli] *adv F* **screamingly funny,** tordant/crevant/à se rouler par terre.

screaming-match ['skriːmiŋmætʃ] *n F* coups *mpl* de gueule/engueulade *f* maison.

screw[1] [skruː] *n* **1.** *P* gardien* de prison/gaffe *m*/gâfe *m*/matuche *m*/maton(ne) *m*(*f*) **2.** *V* (*a*) coït*/baisage *m*/baise *f*/bourre *f*; **to have a quick screw,** tirer un coup vite fait; **have a good screw!** (à la) bonne bourre! (*b*) femme*/fendue *f* (*c*) **he's/she's a good screw,** il/elle baise bien; c'est un sacré baiseur/une sacrée baiseuse; c'est une sacrée affaire **3.** *P* gages *mpl*/salaire *m*; **to get a good screw,** être bien payé/avoir un bon fromage **4.** *F* **to have a screw loose,** être un peu fou*/être un peu fêlé; **she's got a screw loose,** il lui manque une case **5.** *F* **to put the screw(s) on s.o.,** forcer qn/serrer la vis à qn **6.** *F* cheval*/bidet *m*/canasson *m* **7.** *P* (*a*) clef* (*b*) passe-partout *m*/caroube *f*/crochette *f*/rossignol *m* **8.** *P* coup *m* d'œil*/coup *m* de sabord; **take a screw at this!** zyeute ça!/vise un peu ça!

screw[2] [skruː] *vtr* **1.** *V* faire l'amour* avec (qn)/baiser/niquer/tringler **2.** *V* sodomiser*/enculer/endauffer/encaldosser; **he likes screwing men,** il aime bien baiser les mecs/il aime bien prendre du petit chouette **3.** *P* **to screw a gaff/a drum,** casser une crèche/caroubler une baraque; **to go screwing,** cambrioler*/faire un casse; **to do a screwing job,** faire un fric-frac/caroubler. (*See* **screwing 3**) **4.** *F* **to screw money out of s.o.,** extorquer/soutirer de l'argent* à qn; taper/torpiller qn **5.** *esp Austr P* regarder*/lorgner/gaffer **6.** *F* **to have one's head screwed on (the right way),** avoir la tête* solide/sur les épaules **7.** *NAm P* s'enfuir*/décamper/se barrer/se débiner **8.** *P* duper*/tromper/empiler/entuber **9.** *V* **screw you!/get screwed!/screw that!** va te faire foutre!/va te faire voir (chez les Grecs)! **10.** *P* gâcher/cafouiller.

screwable ['skruːəbl] *a V* baisable/mettable/enfournable.

screw about, around ['skruːə'baut, ə'raund] *vi* **1.** *P* faire le con/déconner **2.** *V* faire l'amour*/baiser avec n'importe qui; être très porté sur la chose/ne penser qu'à ça.

screwball[1] ['skruːbɔːl] *NAm F* **I** *a* fou*/tapé/dingue **II** *n F* personne étrange/bizarre/excentrique/ cinglée; personne excessivement capricieuse; **he's a bit of a screwball,** c'est un drôle de zèbre/ de phénomène.

screwed [skruːd] *a P* ivre*/ rétamé/rondibé/schlass **2.** dupé/ roulé/entubé.

screwing ['skruːiŋ] *n* **1.** *V* coït*/ carambolage *m*/dérouillage *m* **2.** *V* enculage *m*/encaldossage *m* **3.** *P* cambriolage *m*/cambriole *f*/fric-frac *m*. (*See* **screw**[2] **3**)

screw off ['skruː'ɔf] *vi V* se masturber*/se branler/s'astiquer (la colonne).

screwsman ['skruːzmən] *n P* cambrioleur*/casseur *m*/fracasseur *m*.

screw-up ['skruːʌp] *n esp NAm P* erreur *f*/gaffe *f*/gourrance *f*/bide *m*.

screw up ['skruː'ʌp] *vtr* **1.** *P* fermer/boucler/brider **2.** *P* bousiller/rater (qch); **he's screwed it all up again,** il a tout refoutu en l'air; il y a refoutu le merdier **3.** *F* **to be all screwed up** (*i*) se tromper/se ficher dedans/se mettre le doigt dans l'œil (*ii*) avoir des idées confuses/être embarbouillé/être dans le brouillard; **she's really screwed up about it,** elle y pige que dalle/elle est complètement paumée.

screwy ['skruːi] *a* **1.** *F* fou*/cinglé/dingue/barjot **2.** *P* louche/suspect.

scrimshank ['skrimʃæŋk] *vi P* tirer au flanc/au cul.

scrimshanker ['skrimʃæŋkər] *n P* tireur *m* au flanc/au cul.

scrip(t) [skrip(t)] *n P* (*from a doc-*

tor) ordonnance *f* de complaisance (pour obtenir des drogues).

scrounge[1] [skraundʒ] *n F* **1.** = **scrounger 1, 2 2.** **he's always on the scrounge,** c'est un vrai pique-assiette; il ne cherche qu'à vivre aux crochets des autres; **I'm on the scrounge, can you lend me £5,** je suis dans la panade, tu peux pas me refiler cinq livres?

scrounge[2] [skraundʒ] *vtr F* **1.** écornifler; taper/torpiller (qn); **to scrounge £5 off s.o.,** taper/torpiller qn de £5 **2.** voler*/chiper/ chaparder/barboter.

scrounge around ['skraundʒə'raund] *vi F* (*a*) rabioter à la ronde (*b*) **to scrounge around for sth,** aller à la recherche de qch/ fouiner.

scrounger ['skraundʒər] *n F* **1.** pique-assiette *m*/parasite *m*/torpilleur *m*/tapeur *m* **2.** voleur*/ chapardeur *m*/barboteur *m*.

scrub [skrʌb] *vtr F* (*a*) **let's scrub it,** passons l'éponge là-dessus (*b*) effacer/démagnétiser (une bande).

scrubber ['skrʌbər] *n P* (*pej*) **1.** femme* *ou* fille* laide* *ou* peu appétissante/mocheté *f*/boudin *m* **2.** fille* *ou* femme* de mœurs légères/roulure *f*/salope *f*/pute *f*.

scruff [skrʌf] *n F* (*a*) individu* mal soigné *ou* mal fichu/débraillé *m*; **he looks a real scruff,** il est fringué comme l'as de pique (*b*) clodo(t) *m*.

scrum [skrʌm] *n F* mêlée *f*/bousculade *f*.

scrump [skrʌmp] *vi F* chaparder/ piquer des pommes à l'arbre.

scrumptious ['skrʌmpʃəs] *a F* (*a*) excellent*/épatant/fameux/remarquable (*b*) délicieux/bon.

scrumpy ['skrʌmpi] *n F* cidre *m*/ gaulé *m*.

scuffer ['skʌfər] *n P* (*regional*) agent *m* de police/flic *m*/condé *m*.

scum [skʌm] *n P* **1.** *NAm*

sperme*/purée *f*/venin *m* **2.** =
scumbag 1.

scumbag ['skʌmbæg] *n* P **1.**
vaurien *m*/salaud*; **you scumbag!**
espèce de salaud!/ordure!/salopard!
2. *NAm* préservatif*/capote
anglaise.

scummy ['skʌmi] *a* P méprisable/
sans valeur; de salaud; de la
saloperie/de merde.

scunner ['skʌnər] *n* F (*dial*) **to take
a scunner to s.o.,** prendre qn en
grippe/avoir qn dans le nez.

scupper ['skʌpər] *vtr* F couler/
abîmer/massacrer; **that's scuppered
all my plans,** ça a fichu en l'air tous
mes projets/ça m'a tout foutu en
l'air.

sea [siː] *n* F **to be all at sea,** être
dérouté/désorienté; perdre le nord;
nager (complètement). (*See* **half-
seas-over**)

search [sɜːtʃ] *vtr* F **search me!** je
n'en ai pas la moindre idée!/je n'en
ai pas la queue d'une!/mystère et
boule de gomme!/sais pas, moi!

sec [sek] *n* F (*abbr* = *second*) **just a
sec!/half a sec!** un moment!/min-
ute! (*See* **jiff(y)**; **mo**; **shake¹ 1**;
tick¹ 3)

secko ['sekou] *Austr* P **I** *a* perverti
II *n* perverti *m*/vieux salaud/
queutard *m*/obsédé sexuel.

seconds ['sekəndz] *npl* F **1.** articles défectueux/démarqués **2.**
portion *f* (de nourriture*) supplé-
mentaire/rab(iot) *m*.

see [siː] *vtr* F **see you!** au revoir!/
salut!/ciao!/à la revoyure!/à la
prochaine! (*See* **dog 14**; **thing 7**)

seed [siːd] *n* **1.** F (*pers*) **to go to
seed,** se décatir/s'avachir **2.** P =
roach. (*See* **hayseed**)

seedy ['siːdi] *a* F **1.** pauvre*/mi-
nable/râpé/usé/élimé **2.**
malade*/patraque/pas dans son
assiette/mal fichu.

see off ['siːɒf] *vtr* F (*a*) **to see s.o.
off,** régler son compte à qn (*b*) **to**

see sth off, régler/liquider/conclure
qch.

see out ['siːaut] *vtr* F survivre à
(qn).

sell¹ [sel] *n* F **1.** attrape *f*/carotte
f/blague *f*/fumisterie *f* **2.** déception *f*. (*See* **hard I 5**; **soft I 5**)

sell² [sel] *vtr* F **1.** duper* (qn)/
avoir (qn)/amener (qn) à la
balançoire/monter le cou à (qn)/
entuber (qn) **2. to sell s.o. short,**
sous-estimer qn **3.** convaincre/per-
suader; **to sell sth to s.o.,** faire
accepter qch à qn; **to be sold on
s.o./sth,** être amené vers qn/qch;
he's really sold on it, il en est
dingue/emballé; il (ne) jure que par
ça **4. to sell oneself,** se faire
accepter/se faire valoir. (*See* **river
1**)

sell-out ['selaut] *n* F **1.** trahison
f/judasserie *f*/macaronage *m* **2.**
vente *f* de tous les billets pour un
spectacle; séance *f* à guichet(s)
fermé(s) **3.** vente *f* de liquidation.

sell out ['sel'aut] *vtr* F **1.** (*a*)
dénoncer*/vendre (qn) (*b*) trahir/
balancer/judasser/lessiver/
macaroner (qn) **2.** (*pers*) se vendre. (*See* **sold out**)

semi ['semi] *n* F (= *semi-detached
house*) maison jumelée.

send [send] *vtr* F **1.** emballer/
transporter (qn); **she sends me!**
elle me botte!/elle me fait flipper!; **that
really sends me!** ça c'est le pied!/ça
me botte! **2.** (*pers*) faire partir/
faire voyager/faire flipper (qn).

send-off ['sendɒf] *n* F **1.** fête *f*
d'adieu/souhaits *mpl* de bon voyage; **we gave him a good send-off,**
on a bien fêté son départ **2.** inau-
guration réussie **3.** enterrement.

send-up ['sendʌp] *n* F satire *f*/
éreintage *m*/mise *f* en boîte.

send up ['send'ʌp] *vtr* **1.** F
satiriser/parodier/se moquer de/
ridiculiser/éreinter; **to send s.o. up,**
mettre qn en boîte **2.** P **to send**

s.o. up, emprisonner*/boucler/coffrer qn/mettre qn en taule.

septic ['septik] *a P* **1.** désagréable/puant **2.** (*RS = Yank*) **septic tank,** Américain*/Amerlo *m*/Yankee *m*/Ricain *m*.

serve [səːv] *vtr F* **(it) serves you right!** (c'est) bien fait (pour toi)!

sesh [seʃ] *n F* (*abbr = session*) séance *f*. (*See* **session**)

session ['seʃ(ə)n] *n F* **1. jam session,** réunion *f* de musiciens qui improvisent collectivement; bœuf *m* **2.** longue séance. (*See* **petting**)

set [set] **I** *a&pp F* **to be all set,** être fin prêt/être paré **II** *n F* **1. to make a dead set at s.o.** (*a*) attaquer furieusement qn (à la tribune) (*b*) se jeter à la tête de qn/relancer qn/poursuivre qn de ses avances **2.** (*Navy*) **full set,** barbe* et moustaches*.

set about ['setə'baut] *vtr F* **1. to set about s.o.,** attaquer* qn/tomber sur le paletot à qn **2. to set about (doing) sth,** entreprendre qch/se mettre à qch/s'atteler à qch.

set back ['set'bæk] *vtr F* coûter/peser; **the round of drinks set him back five quid,** la tournée lui a pesé cinq livres.

set-to ['set'tuː] *n F* bagarre*/lutte *f*/torchage *m*/baston *m*.

set-up ['setʌp] *n* **1.** *F* structure *f*/organisation *f*/fonctionnement *m*; **it's a peculiar set-up at their place,** c'est bizarrement organisé, chez eux **2.** *F* édifice *m*/installation *f*; **a nice set-up you have here,** vous êtes pas mal installé ici/c'est gentil, chez vous **3.** *P* coup monté. (*See* **frame-up**)

set up ['set'ʌp] *vtr F* **1. to set 'em up again,** remplir les verres de nouveau/remettre ça/faire une autre tournée/rhabiller les gamins **2. to set s.o. up for the kill,** conditionner qn pour le coup de massue **3. to set s.o. up,** duper*/rouler qn; monter un coup contre qn; **they set**

me up, on a monté un coup contre moi/ils m'ont eu.

sew up ['sou'ʌp] *vtr F* **it's all sewn up,** c'est tout fixé/c'est tout arrangé/c'est dans le sac/c'est du tout cuit.

sex [seks] *n F* **the third sex,** homosexuels *mpl*/le troisième sexe/la jaquette.

sexation ['seksəθən] *n P* partouze *f* qui dure très longtemps/partouze monstre.

sex-bomb ['seksbɔm] *n O F* allumeuse *f*/blonde incendiaire.

sex-crazy ['seks'kreizi] *a F =* **sex-mad.**

sexed up ['sekst'ʌp] *a F* excité/allumé/aguiché.

sex-kitten ['sekskitn] *n F* fille* aguichante/jeune pin-up alléchante/nénette ronronnante.

sex-mad ['seks'mæd] *a F* **he's sex-mad,** il ne pense qu'à ça/c'est un chaud lapin/il est porté sur la chose.

sexo ['seksou] *a Austr P =* **secko.**

sexpot ['sekspɔt] *n P* femme* qui a du sex-appeal/aguicheuse *f*/allumeuse *f*.

sex-ridden ['seksridn] *a F* porté sur la chose.

sex-starved ['sekstɑːvd] *a F* en manque (sexuel)/victime de diète sexuelle/frustré/refoulé.

sexy ['seksi] *a F* sensuel/chaud/sexy/sexe; **she's sexy,** elle est bien bandante.

sez you! ['sez'juː] *excl P =* **says you!** (**say 3**).

SF ['es'ef] *abbr F* (*= San Francisco*) San Francisco.

shack [ʃæk] *n F* (*a*) taudis *m*/cambuse *f*/bouge *m* (*b*) guitoune *f*/cabane *f*.

shack-up ['ʃækʌp] *a attrib P* **a shack-up job** (*a*) nuit passée avec n'importe quelle femme*/one-nighter/one-night job (b) femme* d'un soir.

shack up ['ʃæk'ʌp] vi P to shack up with s.o., vivre ensemble/se coller avec qn/s'entifler/se maquer.

shade ['ʃeid] n 1. F to put s.o. in the shade, laisser qn dans l'ombre/ éclipser qn 2. pl P lunettes* de soleil/vitraux mpl.

shadow[1] ['ʃædou] n F 1. to put a shadow on s.o., faire suivre qn/faire filer qn/faire faire la filoche à qn. (See tail[1] 5) 2. five-o'clock shadow, la barbe du soir/le foin de la journée.

shadow[2] ['ʃadou] vtr F suivre qn/ filer (le train à qn)/faire la filoche à (qn).

shady ['ʃeidi] a F louche/équi-voque/trouble/véreux; shady deal, affaire f louche/truc m pas catholique.

shaft[1] [ʃɑɪt] n V pénis*/colonne f.

shaft[2] [ʃɑɪt] vtr&i 1. V faire l'amour* (esp avec une femme)/ pinocher 2. P escroquer*/carotter (qn) 3. P congédier*/sacquer/ dégommer (qn).

shag[1] [ʃæg] n 1. V coït*/dérouill-age m/baisage m 2. V she's a good shag, c'est une sacrée baiseuse/c'est une Marie-jambe(s)-en-l'air 3. P it's a (bit of a) shag, c'est ennuyeux*/emmerdant/rasoir.

shag[2] [ʃæg] vtr 1. V (a) faire l'amour* (esp avec une femme)/dér-ouiller/égoïner (b) faire l'amour*/ faire un carton/baiser/se dérouiller. (See arse I 9) 2. P fatiguer*/ vider/pomper; to feel completely shagged, être vanné.

shag-ass ['ʃægæs] vi NAm V s'enfuir*/se carapater/mettre les bouts/foutre le camp.

shagbag ['ʃægbæg] n V vieille femme*/vieille rombière patte-en-l'air.

shaggable ['ʃægəbl] a V baisable/ mettable/enfournable.

shagged (out) ['ʃægd('aut)] a P très fatigué/éreinté/crevé/HS.

shagger ['ʃægər] n V habitué(e) du baisage/baiseur, -euse mf.

shaggy-dog ['ʃægi'dɔg] a attrib F shaggy-dog story, histoire f de fous/ histoire farfelue/histoire à dormir debout.

shag-happy ['ʃæg'hæpi] a V qui pratique avec entrain le baisage/ chaud de la pince.

shag-nasty ['ʃæg'nɑɪsti] a P très désagréable/emmerdant/chiant (comme la pluie).

shag off ['ʃæg'ɔf] vi V partir*/ décamper; shag off! déguerpis!/ file!/dégage!/va te faire chier!

shake[1] [ʃeik] n 1. F half a shake! un moment!/une seconde!/minute! 2. F in two shakes (of a lamb's tail), en moins de deux/en deux temps trois mouvements/en deux coups de cuiller à pot 3. F to give s.o. a fair shake, agir loyalement envers qn/être régul(ier) avec qn; we got a fair shake, on a été régló avec nous 4. F to have the shakes (a) avoir peur*/les foies/les jetons/les chocottes (b) avoir le délirium tremens 5. F no great shakes, rien d'extraordinaire/quelconque/qui ne casse pas des briques/qui ne casse pas trois pattes à un canard 6. P to put the shake on s.o., faire chanter qn/faire casquer qn. (See handshake; shake down 4)

shake[2] [ʃeik] vi F 1. that'll shake him! ça va lui en boucher un coin!/ ça va le faire tiquer! 2. shake on it! tope là! 3. Austr shook on s.o., entiché de qn; to be shook on sth, être fou*/mordu/dingue de qch 4. Austr voler*/chaparder/chouraver. (See leg[1] 3)

shakedown ['ʃeikdaun] n 1. F lit* de fortune; hébergement m d'une nuit 2. P chantage m/ran-çon f 3. P (search, frisk) fouille f.

shake down ['ʃeik'daun] vtr 1. F être vache avec (qn)/mener (qn) à la baguette **2.** *P* fouiller (*esp* un prisonnier)/fourober **3.** *F* se coucher*/se pieuter/se pagnoter/se pager **4.** *P* faire chanter qn/faire casquer (qn)/faire cracher (qn).

shakers ['ʃeikəz] *npl P* seins*/ flotteurs *mpl*/nénés *mpl*/roberts *mpl.*

shake-up ['ʃeikʌp] *n F* **1.** remaniement *m*/réorganisation *f* (du personnel) **2.** commotion *f*/bouleversement *m* **3.** mélange *m* d'alcool* et de whisky.

shamateur ['ʃæmə'təɪr] *n F* (athlète) professionnel qui prétend être amateur.

shambles ['ʃæmblz] *n F* **a shambles,** une pagaille; **it's a real shambles, their place,** c'est un vrai foutoir, leur baraque.

shambolic [ʃæm'bɔlik] *a P* en pleine pagaille/bordelique; merdique.

shammy ['ʃæmi] *n F* **shammy (leather),** peau *f* (de chamois).

shampers ['ʃæmpəz] *n F =* **champers.**

shanghai [ʃæŋ'hai] *vtr* **1.** *F* forcer (qn) à un travail désagréable; **I was shanghaied into doing it,** on m'a forcé à le faire/on m'a forcé la main **2.** *P* transférer un prisonnier d'une prison à une autre (dans les plus brefs délais).

shanks [ʃæŋks] *npl F* **1.** jambes*/ gambilles *fpl* **2.** **to ride Shanks's pony**/*esp NAm* **mare,** voyager à pied/aller à pinces/prendre le train onze/prendre la voiture de Saint-Crépin/y aller pedibus (cum jambis).

shapes [ʃeips] *npl NAm P* dés* truqués/balourds *mpl.*

shark [ʃɑɪk] *n F* **1.** escroc*/arnaqueur *m*/requin *m* **2.** *NAm* as *m*/ champion *m*/crack *m.*

sharp¹ [ʃɑɪp] **I** *a NAm A F* élégant*/coquet/chic/jojo **II** *n F*

escroc*/arnaqueur *m*; **card sharp = sharper.**

sharp² [ʃɑɪp] *vi P* escroquer*/arnaquer/roustir/entuber.

sharper ['ʃɑɪpər] *n F* tricheur* (aux cartes)/maquilleur *m.*

sharpie ['ʃɑɪpi] *P* **1.** *=* **shark 1 2.** *NAm* minet *m* **3.** malin *m*/ dégourdi *m*/débrouillard *m.*

sharpish ['ʃɑɪpiʃ] *adv F* **(a bit) sharpish,** vite*/(illico) presto/ rapidos.

shave [ʃeiv] *n F* **to have a close/ narrow shave,** l'échapper belle/ échapper à un cheveu près; **it was a close/narrow shave,** ça a été moins une/c'est pas passé loin.

shaved [ʃeivd] *a NAm F* ivre*/ bourré/rétamé. (*See* **half-shaved**)

shaver ['ʃeivər] *n O F* **young shaver,** gamin *m*/gosse *m*/môme *m*/ moutard *m.*

shebang [ʃi'bæŋ] *n* **1.** *F* **the whole shebang,** tout le bataclan/ tout le tremblement. (*See* **boiling II; caboodle; shoot¹ 1; shooting-match**) **2.** *P* cabane *f*/cambuse *f* **3.** *P* bordel*/clandé *m*/volière *f.*

shee [ʃiː] *n P =* **yen-shee.**

sheenie, sheeny ['ʃiːni] *n P* (*pej*) Juif*/Youpin *m.*

sheepdog ['ʃiːpdɔg] *n F* chaperon *m*/chien *m* de garde.

sheet [ʃiːt] *n* **1.** *F* **to be three/four sheets in/to the wind,** être ivre*/ avoir du vent dans les voiles/en rouler une **2.** *P* une livre sterling; **half a sheet,** 50 pence **3.** *P* journal*/feuille *f* (de chou) **4.** *P* casier *m* judiciaire (d'un criminel)/pédigrée *m.* (*See* **swindle-sheet**)

sheila ['ʃiːlə] *n Austr F* (jeune) fille*/(jeune) femme*/nénette *f*/ nana *f*/gonzesse *f*/meuf *f.* (*See* **potato 4**)

shekels ['ʃekəlz] *npl P* argent*/fric *m*/pognon *m*/artiche *f.*

shelf [ʃelf] *n F* **on the shelf** (*i*)

célibataire/laissé(e) pour compte (ii) mis(e) de côté/resté(e) dans les cartons/mis(e) au placard.

shelf-kit ['ʃelfkit] n P seins*/avant-scène f/balcon m.

shellac(k) [ʃe'læk] vtr NAm F **1.** battre*/rosser (qn)/passer (qn) à tabac **2.** vaincre/écraser/griller (qn).

shellacked [ʃe'lækt] a NAm P ivre*/rétamé/culbuté.

shellacking [ʃe'lækiŋ] n NAm P **1.** rossée f/tournée f **2.** (sports) défaite f/raclée f.

shellback ['ʃelbæk] n F vieux marin*/vieux loup de mer.

shell out ['ʃel'aut] vtr&i P payer*/(les) abouler/casquer/banquer.

shemozzle¹ [ʃi'mɔzl] n P (a) bruit*/boucan m/chahut m/chambard m (b) difficultés fpl/ennuis mpl/emmerdement m/emmerde f.

shemozzle² [ʃi'mɔzl] vi P = **ske-daddle.**

shenanagins [ʃə'nænəginz] npl F fumisterie f/truquage m/mystification f.

shice [ʃais] vtr P **1.** trahir/plaquer/planter **2.** = **welsh.**

shicker ['ʃikər] n Austr P (a) alcool*/gnôle f; **to go on the shicker,** biberonner/picoler (b) boisson alcoolisée/antigel m.

shickered ['ʃikəd] a Austr P ivre*/paf/éméché/schlass.

shield ['ʃiəld] n NAm F (police) insigne m/badge m.

shift¹ [ʃift] n F **1.** échappatoire f/faux-fuyant m/biaisement m **2. to get a shift on,** se dépêcher*/se magner le train/faire vinaigre.

shift² [ʃift] vtr&i **1.** P shift! file! bouge-toi! shift your arse/NAm ass! pousse ton cul! he didn't half shift! il s'est calté en moins de deux! **2.** F **to shift a pint,** écluser un verre/en étrangler un/s'en jeter un (der-

rière la cravate) **3.** F **to shift for oneself,** se débrouiller/se dépatouiller/se démerder.

shiksa ['ʃiksə] n P (pej) fille* non-juive/goyette f.

shill(aber) ['ʃil(əbər)] n P compère m dans un tripot de jeux/jockey m; baron m/appeau m.

shimmy ['ʃimi] n O F chemise f/liquette f/limace f.

shindig ['ʃindig] n F **1.** querelle*/chambard m/raffut m/ramdam m; **to kick up a shindig,** faire un boucan du diable/faire du ramdam **2.** réunion bruyante/boum f; partouze f.

shindy ['ʃindi] n F = **shindig 1.**

shine [ʃain] n **1.** F **to take a shine to s.o.** (i) s'éprendre de qn/s'amouracher de qn/s'enticher de qn/attraper le béguin pour qn (ii) avoir qn à la bonne; **he's taken a shine to me,** je suis dans ses petits papiers **2.** NAm P (pej) Noir(e)*/nègre mf/bougnoul(l)e m/cireur m **3.** NAm A P pièce f d'or **4.** NAm P = **moonshine 1 5.** P = **shindig 1, 2 6.** F **to take the shine out of s.o.,** éclipser/dépasser qn. (See **bullshine**)

shiner ['ʃainər] n **1.** F œil* poché/au beurre noir; coquard m **2.** NAm P (pej) = **shine 2 3.** F voiture neuve **4.** F diamant*/diam m **5.** F pièce (d'argent*) neuve.

shine up to ['ʃain'ʌptuː] vtr F **to shine up to s.o.,** chercher à se faire bien voir de qn/faire de la lèche auprès de qn/lécher les bottes à qn.

shin(ny) up ['ʃin(i)'ʌp] vtr F grimper/escalader.

ship [ʃip] n F **when my ship comes home,** quand il m'arrivera de l'argent*/quand mes galions seront arrivés/quand j'aurai décroché le gros lot/quand j'aurai décroché la timbale.

ship out ['ʃip'aut] vi P s'enfuir*/se calter/décamper.

shirt [ʃɜːt] *n F* **1. to put one's shirt on sth,** miser le tout pour le tout/ parier sa chemise **2. to lose one's shirt** (*a*) tout perdre/être lessivé (*b*) *NAm* s'emporter/prendre la mouche **3. keep your shirt on!** (ne) t'énerve pas!/ne t'emballe pas! **4. to have one's shirt out,** être de mauvais poil/être à rebrousse-poil **5. stuffed/boiled shirt,** crâneur *m*/plastronneur *m*/collet monté.

shirt-lifter [ˈʃɜːtlɪftər] *n P* homosexuel*/pédé *m*/enculé *m*; **he's a shirt-lifter,** il est de la jaquette/il met sa chemise en véranda.

shirty [ˈʃɜːti] *a F* **to be shirty,** être de mauvaise humeur/faire la gueule/être de mauvais poil; **to get shirty,** se mettre en colère*/en rogne/en pétard.

shit[1] [ʃit] **I** *adv V* extrêmement/ complètement/tout à fait; **to be shit poor,** être vachement pauvre*/être dans la purée; **to be shit out of luck,** avoir une poisse noire/être dans la merde (jusqu'au cou); **to be shit hot at sth,** être vachement calé sur qch **II** *excl V* **shit!/shit me!/ shit a brick!** merde (alors)!/bordel (de merde)! **III** *n V* **1.** merde*/ caca *m*/chiasse *f*; **to have/to go for a shit,** (aller) déféquer*/chier/couler un bronze **2. to land/to drop s.o. in the shit,** mettre/foutre qn dans la merde **3. to be (right) in the shit,** être emmerdé/dans les emmerdes jusqu'au cou **4.** (*a*) **to scare the shit out of s.o.,** rendre qn foireux/donner la chiasse à qn; foutre les boules/les jetons/les chocottes à qn. (*See* **shit-scared**) (*b*) **to beat the shit out of s.o.,** battre* qn comme plâtre/passer qn à tabac/passer qn à la machine à bosseler **5. to eat shit,** traîner dans la merde; **eat shit!** va te faire enculer! **6. don't talk shit!/that's a load of shit!** ne dis pas de conneries!/arrête de déconner! **don't give me that shit!** fais pas chier! **7. I don't give a shit,** j'en ai rien à

foutre/à glander/à branler **8. full of shit,** mal renseigné/chiasseux; **he's full of shit,** c'est un déconneur/ il déconne à pleins tubes **9. (it's) no shit,** c'est la vérité/c'est pas de la merde **10.** individu méprisable/ salaud*/trou *m* du cul/trouduc; **he's a real shit!** tu parles d'un enculé! (*See* **shitbag**) **11.** emmerdeur *m*/mauvais coucheur/ fouteur *m* de merde/casse-couilles *m* **12.** came(lote) *f*/de la merde **13.** (*drugs*) (*i*) héroïne*/shit *m* (*ii*) haschisch*/merde *f* (*iii*) drogues* en général/came *f* **14. the shits,** diarrhée*/chiasse *f*/courante *f* **15. when the shit hits the fan,** ça va barder/il va y avoir du grabuge **16. to work like shit,** travailler* comme un nègre/pisser du sang; **to run like shit,** courir comme un dératé/avoir le feu au cul. (*See* **bullshit**[1]; **creek**; **crock**[1] **5**; **horseshit**)

shit[2] [ʃit] *vtr&i V* **1.** déféquer*/ chier/débourrer/couler un bronze **2.** exagérer*/chier dans la colle; **don't shit me!** ne me bourre pas le crâne!/ne me bourre pas le mou!/ (ne) me prends pas pour un con! **3. shit or bust,** tout ou rien/marche ou crève/pisse ou fais-toi éclater la vessie. (*See* **bullshit**[2])

shit-ass [ˈʃitæs] *n V* = **shitbag**.

shitbag [ˈʃitbæg] *n V* merdaillon *m*/enculé *m*/enfoiré *m*/merdeux *m*/ merde *f*; **you shitbag!** petit trou du cul!

shitcan [ˈʃitkæn] *vtr V* **1.** *Austr* casser/enfoncer (qn) **2.** *NAm* se défaire de/balancer/larguer (qch).

shite[1] [ʃait] *n V* = **shit**[1] **II, III.**

shite[2] [ʃait] *vi V* = **shit**[2] **1.**

shit-faced [ˈʃitfeisd] *a NAm V* ivre*/rétamé/dans le cirage.

shithead [ˈʃithed], **shitheel** [ˈʃithiːl] *n V* = **shitbag**.

shit-hole [ˈʃithoul] *n V* **1.** anus*/ trou *m* du cul/trou de balle/ rondibé *m* **2.** endroit *m* sordide/ taudis *m*/foutoir *m*.

shit-house ['ʃithaus] *n V* WC*/ chiottes *fpl*/débourre *f*/gogues *mpl*/ vécés *mpl*.

shitkicker ['ʃitkikər] *n NAm V* **1.** traîne-la-merde *m* **2.** paysan*/culterreux *m* **3.** but(t)eur *m*/katangais *m*.

shitless ['ʃitlis] *a V* foireux/chiasseux; **to be scared shitless,** avoir les jetons/la chiasse/les chocottes.

shit-list ['ʃitlist] *n V* tableau *m* des mal-vus/liste *f* des hors-petits-papiers/liste noire. (*See* **stink-list**)

shit off ['ʃit'ɔf] *vi V* s'enfuir*/mettre les bouts; **shit off!** calte-toi!/va te faire chier!

shitpot ['ʃitpɔt] *n V* = **shitbag.**

shit-scared ['ʃit'skɛəd] *a V* chiasseux/foireux; **to be shit-scared = to be scared shitless** (**shitless**). (*See* **shit¹ III 4**)

shitstick ['ʃitstik] *n NAm V* = **shitbag.**

shitters ['ʃitəz] *npl V* **the shitters,** diarrhée*/la chiasse/la courante.

shitty ['ʃiti] *a V* **1.** méprisable/débectant/dégueulasse/merdique; **they live in some shitty little hole,** ils habitent dans un petit truc merdique/zonard; **what a shitty idea!** tu parles d'une idée à la con/ à la mords-moi-le-nœud! **2.** *NAm* douteux/plein de gourance/foireux.

shiv [ʃiv] *n P* = **chiv(e)¹ 1, 2.**

shive [ʃaiv] *vtr P* = **chiv(e)² 1, 2.**

shivers ['ʃivəz] *npl F* **to give s.o. the shivers,** donner la tremblote/le frisson à qn.

shivoo ['ʃai'vuː] *n Austr F* réjouissances*/bamboula *f*/raout *m*.

shliver ['ʃlivər] *n P* = **chiv(e)¹ 1, 2.**

shlonger ['ʃlɔŋər] *n NAm P* = **schlong.**

shmeck [ʃmek], **shmee** [ʃmiː] *n P* (*drugs*) héroïne*/chnouf *f*.

shmo(e) [ʃmou] *n P* = **schmo 1, 2.**

shnockered ['ʃnɔkəd] *a P* hébété par un narcotique/bourré à bloc/ dans les vapes.

shocker ['ʃɔkər] *n F* (*pers or thing*) horreur *f*/affreux *m*; **you're a shocker!** tu es impossible!

shoes [ʃuːz] *npl F* **that's another pair of shoes,** c'est une autre paire de manches. (*See* **dead I 8; ice¹ 7**)

shoestring ['ʃuːstriŋ] *n F* **to do business on a shoestring,** faire des affaires avec des moyens financiers très limités; tirer sur la corde/être sur la corde raide.

shonk [ʃɔŋk] *n P* (*pej*) Juif*/ Youpin *m*.

shook ['ʃuk] *a Austr F* **to be shook on sth,** être emballé par qch; **he was shook on her,** il était amoureux fou d'elle/il en était dingue.

shook up ['ʃuk'ʌp] *a P* (**all**) **shook up,** secoué/émotionné/remué.

shoot¹ [ʃuːt] *n* **1.** *F* **the whole** (**bang**) **shoot,** tout le bataclan/tout le tremblement. (*See* **boiling II; caboodle; shebang¹ 1; shooting-match**) **2.** *P* (*drugs*) piqûre*/ fixe *m*/shoot *m*.

shoot² [ʃuːt] *vtr&i* **1.** *P* **shoot!** vas-y!/rentre dedans!/accouche!/ déballe! **2.** *P* éjaculer*/arroser/ décharger. (*See* **load 8**) **3.** *F* filmer/photographier/tourner **4.** *P* **to get shot of s.o./sth,** se débarrasser* de qn/de qch; défarguer/ larguer qn/qch **5.** *F* **to shoot a line,** exagérer*/blouser/se vanter/en installer/esbrouf(f)er; **to shoot s.o. a line,** jeter de la poudre aux yeux de qn/bourrer le mou à qn. (*See* **line-shooter; line-shooting**) **6.** *P* **to shoot the cat,** vomir*/évacuer le couloir/faire renard **7.** *NAm P* **to shoot the bull/the crap/the breeze,** bavarder*/tailler une bavette **8.** *P* **to shoot the works** (*a*) dilapider son argent*/jeter son fric par les fenêtres (*b*) avouer*/manger le morceau/se mettre à table (c) jouer/ miser/risquer le tout pour le tout; jouer sa chemise (d) y aller de tout son soûl/donner un coup de collier **9.** *P* **to shoot the moon,** déménager à la cloche de bois **10.** *F* **he has shot his bolt,** il a vidé son carquois/il a jeté tout son feu/il n'a plus de dents pour mordre **11.** *P* (*drugs*) se piquer*/se shooter/se fixer. (*See* **lingo 2**; **wad 4**)

shoot down [ʃuːt'daun] *vtr F* **to shoot s.o. down (in flames),** rabattre le caquet à qn/torcher le bec à qn/ ramener qn à ses justes propor- tions/moucher qn; **to get shot down in flames,** l'avoir dans l'os.

shooter [ʃuːtər] *n P* arme *f* à feu/ flingue *m*/pétard *m*/soufflant *m*. (*See* **line-shooter**; **pea-shooter**; **six-shooter**)

shoot-flier [ʃuːtflaiər] *n P* voleur* à l'arrachée/décrocheur *m*.

shooting-gallery [ʃuːtiŋgæləri] *n P* endroit où on se pique à la drogue/shooterie *f*.

shooting-iron [ʃuːtiŋaiən] *n F* revolver*/flingot *m*/pétard *m*.

shooting-match [ʃuːtiŋmætʃ] *n F* **the whole shooting-match** = **the whole (bang) shoot** (**shoot¹ 1**).

shoot off [ʃuːt'ɔf] *vtr&i* **1.** *P* = **shoot² 2 2.** *P* **to shoot one's mouth/face off** (*a*) révéler un secret/vendre la mèche/se mettre à table (*b*) bavasser/être atteint de diarrhée verbale **3.** *F* partir*/se tirer/se barrer.

shoot through [ʃuːt'θruː] *vi Austr F* partir*/se tirer/se casser/mettre les bouts.

shoot up [ʃuːt'ʌp] *vi P* se piquer*/ se shooter/se fixer/se faire une piquouse.

shop¹ [ʃɔp] *n* **1.** *F* **all over the shop** (*i*) en vrac/en pagaille/bordé- lique (*ii*) partout/dans tous les coins **2.** *P* **you've come to the wrong shop,** vous n'êtes pas au bon

guichet/il y a erreur d'aiguillage/ vous vous êtes trompé d'adresse **3.** *F* **to talk shop,** parler affaires/parler boutique. (*See* **shop-talk**) **4.** *F* **to shut up shop** (*sport*) fermer le jeu; (*entreprise, affaires*) fermer boutique **5.** *P* prison*/boîte *f* **6.** *F* **top of the shop:** *see* **bingo 99.** (*See* **cop- shop**; **hock-shop**; **hook-shop**; **kip-shop**; **knocking 2**; **milk-shop**; **molly-shop**; **porn-shop**; **slop- shop**; **sweat-shop**; **whore-shop**)

shop² [ʃɔp] *vtr P* **1.** dénoncer*/ trahir/balancer/moutonner **2.** traduire (qn) en justice **3.** emprisonner*/mettre en boîte **4.** (= *shoplift*) voler* dans les magasins/piquer/chouraver/gauler.

shop-talk [ʃɔptɔːk] *n F* jargon *m* de métier/d'un groupe profession- nel, etc. (*See* **shop¹ 3**)

short [ʃɔːt] **I** *a* **1.** *F* **to be a bit short,** être à court (d'argent*)/être à sec **2.** *P* (*prostitutes*) **short time,** courte séance; passe *f* rapide; coup *m* vite fait **3.** *P* **short arm,** pénis*/ troisième jambe; (*homosexuals*) **short arm bandit,** bourrin *m*; **short arm heist,** viol collectif. (*See* **cur- lies**; **hair 6**) **II** *adv F* **to be caught short** (*a*) être pris d'un besoin pres- sant; avoir envie de pisser/de chier (*b*) être pris de court. (*See* **sell² 2**) **III** *n F* **1.** un petit verre d'alcool*/de goutte *f* **2.** *NAm* petite voiture de sport/petit bolide.

short-arse [ʃɔːtɑːs] *n V* bas-du- cul *m*/basduc *m*/rase-bitume *m*. (*See* **shorty**)

shortchange¹ [ʃɔːtʃeindʒ] *a F* **shortchange artist,** escroc*/filou *m*/ estampeur *m*/arnaqueur *m*.

shortchange² [ʃɔːtʃeindʒ] *vtr F* **to shortchange s.o.,** voler* qn en lui rendant la monnaie (lui rendre moins qu'il ne lui revient); rouler/ arnaquer qn au rendème.

shortweight [ʃɔːt'weit] *vtr F* estamper sur le poids de qch.

shorty ['ʃɔːti] *n F* petit individu*/homme de petite taille/courte-botte *m*/rase-bitume *m*.

shot [ʃɔt] *F* **I** *a* **1.** ivre*/bituré/rétamé/rond **2.** très fatigué*/vanné **II** *n F* **1.** (*drugs*) piqûre *f*/piquouse *f*. (*See* **hot 22** (*b*)) **2.** une mesure d'alcool*/un dé/une rincette/une goutte **3. a shot in the arm,** un remontant/un stimulant/un coup de fouet **4. to have a shot at sth,** essayer qch/tenter le coup **5.** (*a*) **a long shot** (*i*) un gros risque (*ii*) (*horse*) un gros risque; une chance sur mille (*b*) **not by a long shot** = **not by a long chalk** (**chalk 1**) **6. like a shot** (*a*) très vite*/comme l'éclair (*b*) volontiers/de bon cœur **7.** *Austr F* **that's the shot!** voilà une idée!/à la bonne heure! **8. to make a shot in the dark,** deviner au hasard/y aller au pifomètre **9.** dada *m*/habitude *f*/manie *f*. (*See* **pot-shot; shoot² 4**)

shotgun ['ʃɔtgʌn] *a attrib F* **1. shotgun agreement,** convention signée sous la contrainte **2. shotgun wedding,** mariage forcé/régularisation *f* **3.** (*on motorcycle*) **to ride shotgun,** monter sur le siège arrière.

shoulder ['ʃouldər] *n F* **1. to rub shoulders with s.o.,** frayer avec qn/se frotter à qn **2. straight from the shoulder,** carrément/sans mettre de gants; **he let me have it straight from the shoulder,** il ne me l'a pas envoyé dire. (*See* **cold I 3; cold-shoulder**)

shouse [ʃaus] *n Austr P* WC*/chiottes *fpl*/tasses *fpl*/gogues *mpl*.

shout [ʃaut] *n F* **1. it's my shout,** c'est ma tournée **2. give me a shout when you're ready,** fais signe quand tu es prêt.

shouting ['ʃautiŋ] *n F* **it's all over bar the shouting,** c'est dans le sac/les applaudissements suivront/c'est du tout cuit.

shove [ʃʌv] *vtr* (*a*) *P* **you know where you can shove that!** tu sais où tu peux te le mettre!/tu peux te le mettre quelque part! (*b*) *V* **you can shove that (right) up your arse!** tu peux te le foutre/carrer au cul!

shove around ['ʃʌvə'raund] *vtr F* bousculer/ballotter (qn)/faire marcher (qn).

shovel ['ʃʌvəl] *n P* **1.** prison*/taule *f*/bloc *m* **2.** (*aut*) **shovel and brush job,** (vieille) voiture bonne à mettre à la ferraille/tas *m* de ferraille.

shove off ['ʃʌ'ɔf] *vi* (*a*) *F* partir*/décamper (*b*) *P* **shove off!** fiche le camp!

shovel it down ['ʃʌvəlit'daun] *vi F* se goinfrer/se gaver.

show¹ [ʃou] *n F* **1. a show of leg,** un étalage de cuisses; **free show,** striptease *m* à l'œil; **it's a free show,** elle a soulevé son capot, on voit le moteur **2. good show!** bravo!/c'est au poil! **it's a poor show!** c'est lamentable!/c'est minable!/c'est moche!/c'est zonard! **3. to give the show away,** vendre/éventer la mèche; débiner le truc **4.** (*theatre*) **to stop the show,** casser la baraque/faire crouler la baraque **5. to steal the show,** capter l'attention/magnétiser l'assemblée/tirer à soi la couverture **6. to run the whole show,** faire marcher l'affaire/faire tourner la baraque. (*See* **boss² 1; leg¹ 2; meat-show**)

show² [ʃou] *vi F* = **show up 1.** (*See* **leg¹ 1**)

showbiz ['ʃoubiz] *n F* l'industrie *f* du spectacle/le showbiz.

showdown ['ʃoudaun] *n F* **1.** confrontation *f*/déballage *m* (de ses intentions) **2.** révélation *f* d'adversité/mise *f* au point; mise *f* à jour.

shower ['ʃauər] *n P* (*a*) nullité *f*/nouille *f*; **he's a right shower!** quelle andouille! (*b*) **what a shower!** quelle bande*/quel tas de crétins!

showman ['ʃoumən] *n F* (*jazz*) musicien *m* spectaculaire/showman *m*.

show-off ['ʃouɔf] *n F* individu* qui fait de l'épate *f*/esbrouf(f)eur *m*/ poseur *m*/m'as-tu-vu *m*/plastron- neur *m*/frimeur *m*.

show off ['ʃou'ɔf] *vi F* parader/ plastronner/se donner des airs/ chercher à épater/frimer/faire le m'as-tu-vu.

show up ['ʃou'ʌp] *vtr&i F* **1.** arriver/faire acte de présence/se pointer **2.** (*a*) révéler/dévoiler/ démasquer (*b*) attirer l'attention sur (qn); **he's been shown up,** il est grillé.

shrewdie ['ʃruːdi] *n Austr F* (*shrewd person*) **a shrewdie,** un petit futé/un marlou/un malin/un ma- riole.

shrift [ʃrift] *n F* **to give s.o. short shrift,** traiter qn sans ménagement; **I got short shrift from him,** il m'a envoyé patre/promener.

shrimp [ʃrimp] *n F* petit individu*/ crapoussin *m*/avorton *m*/rase- bitume *m*.

shrink [ʃriŋk] *n P* psychiatre *mf*/ psychanalyste *mf*/psy *mf*. (*See* **head-shrinker**)

shtup [ʃtʌp] *vtr NAm P* = **tup**.

shuck¹ [ʃʌk] *n NAm F* **1.** mystifi- cation *f*/supercherie *f* **2.** **it's not worth shucks,** ça ne vaut pas chipette.

shuck² [ʃʌk] *vtr&i NAm F* **1.** faire marcher (qn)/mystifier (qn) **2.** dire des bêtises*/déconner.

shucks! [ʃʌks] *excl esp NAm F* mince!/zut alors!

shudders ['ʃʌdəz] *npl F* **to give s.o. the shudders = to give s.o. the shivers** (**shivers**).

shuffles ['ʃʌflz] *npl P* cartes* à jouer/brèmes *fpl*/cartons *mpl*.

shufty ['ʃufti] *n F* regard *m*/coup d'œil*/coup *m* de châsse/clinc *m*;

to have a quick shufty at sth, filer un coup de sabord/de saveur à qch.

shush [ʃuʃ] *vtr F* faire taire* (qn)/ river le clou à (qn)/clouer le bec à (qn).

shut [ʃʌt] *vtr P* **to shut it,** se taire*/ fermer sa boîte/fermer; son clapet/ la fermer **shut it!** ta gueule!/la ferme! (*See* **face¹ 1; gob¹ 1; trap**)

shuteye ['ʃʌtai] *n F* sommeil *m*/ somme *m*; **to get/to grab some shuteye,** dormir*/piquer un roupil- lon/roupiller.

shutters ['ʃʌtəz] *npl F* **to put the shutters up,** se retirer en soi-même/ baisser la vitrine/faire le hibou.

shut up ['ʃʌt'ʌp] *vtr* (*a*) *F* faire taire* (qn)/clouer le bec à (qn) (*b*) *P* **shut up!** la ferme!/ferme ça! (*c*) assassiner*/effacer/liquider (qn).

shy [ʃai] *n F* **1.** jet *m*/lancement *m* **2.** tentative *f*/essai *m*.

shyster ['ʃaistər] *n F* homme d'affaires, etc véreux; marron *m*.

sick [sik] *a* **1.** *F* furieux/furibard/ furax **2.** *F* déçu/chocolat **3.** *F* **sick joke,** plaisanterie *f* macabre **4.** *F* **I'm sick (and tired) of it,** j'en ai plein le dos/j'en ai marre/j'en ai ma claque **5.** *P* (*drugs*) en man- que* **6. sick as a parrot,** malade comme un chien.

sickener ['sikənər] *n F* **1.** aven- ture écœurante **2.** spectacle écœurant.

sick-making ['sikmeikiŋ] *a F* écœurant/navrant/débectant.

sick up ['sik'ʌp] *vi F* vomir* (qch)/ dégobiller/dégueuler.

side [said] *n* **1.** *F* **to make sth/a bit on the side,** se faire des petits à- côtés **2.** *P* **to have a bit on the side,** dérouiller sa crampette hors du ménage/prendre un petit à-côté **3.** *F* **to split one's sides (with) laughing,** se tordre de rire*. (*See* **side-splitting**) **4.** *F* crânerie *f*/ esbrouf(f)e *f*; **to put on side,** faire sa poire (anglaise). (*See* **bed¹ 2; right I 4; safe I**)

sideboards ['saidbɔːdz], **sideburns** ['saidbəːnz]*npl F* favoris *mpl*/pattes *fpl* de lapin/côtelettes *fpl*.

sidekick ['saidkik] *n F* **1.** ami*/copain *m* **2.** associé *m*/assistant *m*/sous-fifre *m*.

sideman ['saidmæn] *n P* (*jazz*) musicien *m* de pupitre.

side-splitting ['saidsplitiŋ] *a F* tordant/désopilant/marrant/crevant/fendant/à se rouler par terre (de rire). (*See* **side 3**)

sideways ['saidweiz] *adv F* **to knock s.o. sideways**, époustoufler qn/ébahir qn/mettre qn sur le cul/asseoir qn.

siff [sif] *n P* = **syph**.

siffo ['sifou] *n P* = **sypho**.

siffy ['sifi] *n P* = **syphy**.

sight [sait] *n F* **1. I can't bear/stand the sight of him**, je ne peux pas le voir en peinture **2.** (*a*) **you (do) look a sight!** te voilà bien arrangé!/tu es fichu comme l'as de pique!/tu en as une touche! (*b*) **his face was a sight**, si vous aviez vu son visage! **3. a sight of...**, énormément de...; **he's a (damn(ed)) sight too clever for you**, il est beaucoup trop malin* pour vous. (*See* **damned I 6; out I 3**)

sign off ['sain'ɔf] *vi F* conclure/terminer/finocher.

silly ['sili] *n F* individu bête*/ballot *m*/baluchard *m*/nouille *f*.

silvertail ['silvəteil] *n Austr F* personnage important/gros bonnet/grosse légume.

simmer down ['simə'daun] *vi F* se calmer/ne pas s'emballer.

simp [simp] *n P* nigaud *m*/niguedouille *mf*.

simply ['simpli] *adv F* absolument/complètement; **you look simply lovely!** vous êtes absolument ravissante! **it's simply ghastly weather**, il fait un temps de chien.

sing [siŋ] *vi* **1.** P (*a*) avouer*/accoucher/manger le morceau (*b*) moucharder/vendre la mèche **2.** P payer du chantage **3.** F **to sing small**, se conduire avec humilité/baisser pavillon.

sing out ['siŋ'aut] *vi F* **sing out if you need me**, appelez si vous avec besoin de moi.

sink [siŋk] *vtr&i F* **1. sink or swim!** au petit bonheur! **2. to sink a pint**, s'envoyer un (demi).

sinker ['siŋkər] *n NAm F* (= *doughnut*) beignet *m*.

sin-shifter ['sinʃiftər] *n Austr P* aumônier *m* militaire/radis-noir *m*.

sirree ['sərˈriː] *n NAm F* **no sirree!** non, monsieur!/non, mon cher! **yes sirree!** mais oui, mon brave!/ça colle, Anatole!

sissy ['sisi] *n F* (*a*) (*coward*) poltron*/caneur *m*/dégonflard *m* (*b*) homme efféminé/chochotte *f*/femmelette *f*/tapette *f*.

sit [sit] *vi F* **to be sitting pretty** (*a*) tenir le bon bout/le filon; avoir la vie belle/se la couler douce (*b*) rouler sur l'or. (*See* **behind; duck¹ 3; fence¹ 2; tight II**)

sit-in ['sitin] *n F* occupation *f* (des locaux)/sit-in *m*.

sit-me-down ['sitmidaun] *n F* fesses*/arrière-train *m*/pont-arrière *m*.

sit on ['sitɔn] *vtr F* **1. to sit on sth**, ne pas s'occuper de qch/laisser dormir qch/faire des conserves avec qch/garder qch sous le coude **2. to get sat on**, être réprimandé*/recevoir un abattage; **to sit on s.o.**, rabrouer qn/rabaisser le caquet à qn; **he won't be sat on**, il ne se laisse pas marcher sur les pieds.

sitter ['sitər] *n F* **1.** = **sitting duck (duck¹3) 2.** une certitude/du tout cuit/la loi et les prophètes.

sit up ['sit'ʌp] *vi F* **to sit up and take notice,** se réveiller/se secouer; **I'll make you sit up!** tu auras de mes nouvelles!

sit-upon ['sitəpɔn] *n F =* **sit-me-down.**

six [siks] *n F* **1. to be six feet/foot under,** être enterré/être dans le royaume des taupes/bouffer les pissenlits par la racine **2. at sixes and sevens,** sens dessus dessous/en pagaille **3. it's six of one and half a dozen of the other,** c'est blanc bonnet et bonnet blanc/c'est kif-kif (bourricot)/c'est du quès. (*See* knock² 7)

six-footer ['siks'futər] *n F* homme* (haut) de six pieds/homme très grand/double-mètre *m.*

six-shooter ['siks'ʃuɪtər] *n F* revolver* (à six coups)/six coups *m*/flingue *m*/pétard *m.*

sixty-four ['siksti'fɔɪr] *n F* **the sixty-four (thousand) dollar question** (*a*) la questin du gros lot/la question super-banco (*b*) la question vitale/qui compte le plus.

sixty-nine¹ ['siksti'nain] *n P* (*mutual oral sex between two people*) six-à-neuf *m*/soixante-neuf *m*/69.

sixty-nine² ['siksti'nain] *vi P* faire soixante-neuf.

size [saiz] *n F* **1. to cut s.o. down to size,** rabaisser qn/rabattre le caquet à qn/rogner les ailes à qn **2. that's about the size of it** (*i*) c'est à peu près cela (*ii*) c'est ainsi (et pas autrement). (*See* king-size(d); man-size(d); pint-size(d); queen)

sizzler ['sizlər] *n F =* **scorcher 1.**

skag [skæg] *n P* **1.** (*drugs*) héroïne*/chnouf *m* **2.** *NAm* individu ennuyeux*/raseur *m*/casse-couilles *m.*

skate [skeit] *n* **1.** *NAm P =* **cheapskate 2** **2.** *NAm P* canasson *m*/bidet *m* **3.** *F* **to put/to get one's skates on,** se dépêcher*/se grouiller/se magner le train.

skating-rink ['skeitiŋriŋk] *n F* tête chauve*/mouchodrome *m*/boule *f* de billard.

skedaddle [ski'dædl] *vi F* s'enfuir*/ficher le camp/filer/s'esquiver/se tailler.

skelp [skelp] *vtr F* (*regional*) battre* (qn)/talocher.

skerrick ['skerik] *n Austr F* **a skerrick,** un peu* (de...)/un chouia; **not a skerrick...,** nib de.../pas lourd de.../pas une miette de....

skewer ['skjuɪər] *n F* (*a*) épée *f* (*b*) baïonnette *f.*

skew-eyed ['skjuɪaid] *a F* **to be skew-eyed,** loucher*; avoir un œil qui dit merde/zut à l'autre; bigler/être bigleux.

skew-whiff ['skjuɪ'wif] **I** *a F* tordu/biscornu **II** *adv F* en biais/de traviole/de travers.

skid-lid ['skidlid] *n F* casque *m* de moto.

skid marks ['skid'maɪks] *npl P* taches *fpl* d'excrément/de merde sur le slip/sur le calecif.

skid-row ['skid'rou] *n esp NAm F* quartier mal famé; bas-fonds *mpl*/zone *f*; **a skid-row joint,** un bouiboui de la plus basse catégorie.

skids [skidz] *npl F* **1.** *NAm* **on the skids,** sur la pente savonneuse/en train de perdre prestige, etc/en perte de vitesse **2.** (*a*) **to put the skids under s.o./sth,** faire échouer* qn/qch; huiler la pente (*b*) **to put the skids under s.o.,** congédier* qn/flanquer qn à la porte/vider qn.

skin¹ [skin] *n* **1.** *F* **to get under s.o.'s skin,** ennuyer*/barber/raser qn; **he's getting under my skin,** il me court sur le(s) haricot(s)/il me tape sur le système **2.** *F* **it's no skin off my nose,** ce n'est pas mon affaire/ça ne me touche pas/c'est pas mes oignons **3.** *O F* (*toast*) **skin off your nose!** à la bonne vôtre! **4.** *F* **to have s.o. under one's skin,** être entiché de qn/avoir qn dans la peau **5.** *P* (*a*) **skin game,** escroquerie*/arnaquage *m* (*b*) **skin artist,** escroc*/arnaqueur *m* **6.** *NAm P* billet *m* de un dollar **7.** *P* préservatif*/capote (anglaise)/chapeau *m* **8.** *pl P* (*jazz, rock*) batterie *f*/caisses *fpl*/drums *mpl* **9.** *P* pneu *m* de voiture (usé)/pneu lisse/boudin *m* **10.** *P* **gimme some skin!** touche là!/tope là! **11.** *P* (*RS = sister*) **skin and blister,** sœur *f*/frangine *f* **12.** *P* = **skinhead.** (*See* **popping**; **thick 4**)

skin² [skin] *vtr F* **1.** carotter/dépouiller/écorcher/plumer (qn) **2.** anéantir/écraser. (*See* **eye 6**)

skin-flick ['skinflik] *n esp NAm F* film *m* porno(graphique)/film de cul/film de fesses/porno *m*.

skinful ['skinful] *n P* **1.** **to have (had) a skinful,** être ivre*/avoir une cuite/en tenir une **2.** = **bellyful.**

skinhead ['skinhed] *n F* homme* à la tête rasée/individu* qui a une perruque en peau de fesses; jeune voyou *m*/skinhead *m*.

skinner ['skinər] *n P* (*horse racing*) cheval mal côté/délaissé *m*.

skinny dip¹ ['skini'dip] *n esp NAm F* baignade *f* tout nu*/à poil.

skinny dip² ['skini'dip] *vi esp NAm F* se baigner tout nu*/à poil/à loilpé.

skin-pop ['skinpɔp] *vi P* (*drugs*) se faire une piqûre* intramusculaire. (*See* **popping**)

skin-popper ['skinpɔpər] *n P* (*drugs*) qn qui se fait lui-même des piqûres *fpl* de drogues/piquouseur *m* maison.

skint [skint] *a P* très pauvre*/fauché/raide/sans un.

skip [skip] *vi* **1.** *P* (*not common*) faire l'amour* avec/sauter (une femme) **2.** *F* **to skip the country,** fuir le pays; **to skip school,** sécher les cours/faire l'école buissonnière **3.** **skip it!** (*a*) *F* laisse courir! (*b*) *P* file!/décampe! **4.** **F** = **skipper.**

skipper ['skipər] *n F* patron*/chef *m*.

skip off ['skip'ɔf] *vi F* s'enfuir*/décamper/filer.

skippering ['skipəriŋ] *n P* **to be skippering,** dormir à la dure/compter les étoiles.

skippy ['skipi] *n P* (*a*) homosexuel*/lopette *f* (*b*) homme efféminé.

skirt [skɔɪt] *n P* femme*/jeune fille*/poupée *f*; **a nice bit of skirt,** une jolie pépée/un beau petit lot; de la fesse; **to go out looking for skirt,** courir les femmes/cavaler/chercher de la fesse. (*See* **hot 1, 3**)

skirt-chaser, skirt-hunter ['skɔɪttʃeisər, 'skɔɪthʌntər] *n P* cavaleur *m*/coureur *m* de jupons/chaud lapin.

skite¹ [skait] *n Austr F* vantard*/bluffeur *m*/poseur *m*; baratineur *m*.

skite² [skait] *vi Austr F* se vanter/esbrouf(f)er/en jeter plein la vue/en rajouter/en installer.

skive [skaiv] *n F* **there's nothing wrong in having a bit of a skive on Friday afternoons,** c'est tout à fait normal de vouloir tirer au flanc/au cul le vendredi après-midi.

skive (off) ['skaiv'ɔf] *vi F* s'esquiver/tirer au flanc/tirer au cul; **to skive (off) from school,** sécher les cours; **he's skiving,** il sèche les cours; il tire au flanc.

skiver ['skaivər] *n F* tire-au-flanc *m*/tire-au-cul *m*; **what a skiver!** quel feignant!/quel feignasse!

skiving ['skaiviŋ] *n F* tirage-au-flanc *m*/tirage au cul.

skivvy ['skivi] *n F* **1.** bonne *f* à tout faire/bonniche *f* **2.** *NAm* (*a*) sous-vêtement *m* d'homme/tee-shirt *m* (*b*) caleçon *m*/calcif *m* (en coton).

skivy ['skaivi] *a P* (*a*) malhonnête/filou (*b*) renâcleur/tire-au-flanc.

skulduggery [skʌl'dʌgəri] *n F*

maquignonnage *m*/trafic *m* louche/ combine *f* louche.

skull [skʌul] *n* P (*pej*) = **egghead**.

skull-job ['skʌldʒɔb] *n* V fellation*/prise *f* de pipe/pompier *m*.

skunk [skʌŋk] *n* F chameau *m*/ mufle *m*/rossard *m*/salopard *m*.

sky [skai] *n* P **to see the sky through the trees**, faire l'amour* à la campagne; voir les feuilles/la feuille à l'envers. (*See* **limit 3**)

skyjack ['skaidʒæk] *vtr* F détourner (un avion).

skyjacker ['skaidʒækər] *n* F pirate *m* de l'air.

skylark ['skailɑːk] *vi* P batifoler/ chahuter/plaisanter.

sky-piece ['skaipiːs] *n* P chapeau*/galure *m*/galurin *m*/bada *m*.

sky-pilot ['skaipailət] *n* P prêtre*/ pasteur *m*/chapelain *m*/corbeau *m*.

sky-rocket ['skairɔkit] *n* P (*RS* = *pocket*) poche*/fouille *f*.

slab [slæb] *n* F **1.** table *f* d'opération/billard *m* **2.** dalle *f* funéraire/pierre *f* de macchab(e).

slag [slæg] *n* P **1.** vieille prostituée*/tarderie *f* **2.** fille* *ou* femme* de mœurs légères/roulure *f*/pute *f* **3.** (*general insult*) individu* méprisable/ordure *f*/ trouduc *m*; **you slag!** ordure!/peau de vache!/duchnoque!/enculé!

slag (off) ['slæg'ɔf] *vtr* P critiquer*/éreinter/descendre en flammes; **parents are always slagging off their kids**, les vioques bavent toujours sur les jeunes.

slam [slæm] *vtr* F **1.** vaincre/battre avec conviction; écraser **2.** frapper avec violence/flanquer par terre **3.** critiquer* sévèrement/éreinter/ débiner.

slammer ['slæmər] *n* P **in the slammer**, en prison*/en taule/au violon/au trou. (*See* **slams**)

slams [slæmz] *npl NAm O* P **the slams**, prison*/taule *f*.

slanging-match ['slæŋiŋmætʃ] *n* F prise *f* de bec/engueulade *f* maison; **to have a slanging match with s.o.**, traiter qn de tous les noms.

slant[1] [slɑːnt] *n* **1.** F (*a*) point *m* de vue/manière *f* de voir (*b*) préjugé *m*/biais *m*/point de vue détourné **2.** P coup d'œil*; **take a slant at that!** jette un coup de châsse!/vise-moi un peu ça!

slant[2] [slɑːnt] *vtr* F donner un biais/un tournant à (une question, etc); **slanted article**, article orienté/ qui n'est pas objectif.

slanter ['slɑːntər] *n Austr* P tour *m*/ruse *f*/astuce *f*.

slap[1] [slæp] **I** *adv* F (*a*) directement/tout droit; **slap (bang) in the middle**, en plein (dans le) milieu/en plein dans le mille/en plein mitan (*b*) brusquement/brutalement/rudement; **she put it slap on the table**, elle l'a flanqué sur la table. (*See* **slap-bang(-wallop); smack**[1]; **wallop**[1]) **II** *n* F **1.** slap in the eye/ face, affront *m*/camouflet *m*/rebuffade *f* **2.** **slap and tickle**, partie *f* de pelotage *m*; **we were having a bit of (the old) slap and tickle**, on était en train de se peloter/de se faire des mamours.

slap[2] [slæp] *vtr* F **slap it on the bill!** colle-le sur l'addition!

slap-bang(-wallop) ['slæp-'bæŋ('wɔləp)] *adv* F (*a*) tout à coup/de but en blanc/hâtivement (*b*) brusquement (*c*) **the car went slap-bang(-wallop) into a lamp-post**, la voiture a emplafonné un réverbère. (*See* **wallop**[1] **I 2**)

slap down ['slæp'daun] *vtr* F réprimander*/rabrouer rudement.

slap-happy ['slæp'hæpi] *a* F **1.** plein d'entrain/d'allant/d'humeur joyeuse **2.** farfelu/téméraire/insouciant **3.** (*boxing*) ivre de coups.

slap together ['slæptə'geðər] *vtr* F préparer hâtivement/bâcler.

slap-up ['slæpʌp] *a F* chic/dernier cri/prodigue; **a slap-up meal**, un balthazar. (*See* **bang-up**)

slash [slæʃ] *n P* **to have a slash**, uriner*/faire sa goutte/lancequiner; **to go for a slash**, aller aux WC*/ aller quelque part/aller pisser un coup.

slate¹ [sleit] *n F* **1. on the slate**, sur la note/sur le compte/sur l'ardoise **2. to have a slate loose**, être un peu fou*/onduler de la toiture.

slate² [sleit] *vtr F* (*a*) réprimander* (qn) vertement/attraper (qn)/passer un savon à (qn)/sonner les cloches (à qn) (*b*) critiquer*/éreinter (un livre, etc).

slater ['sleitər] *n F* critique *m* sévère/abatteur *m*/éreinteur *m*.

slating ['sleitiŋ] *n F* (*a*) verte réprimande/savon *m* (*b*) éreintement *m*.

slats [slæts] *npl NAm P* côtes *fpl*/ côtelettes *fpl*.

slaughter¹ ['slɔːtər] *n* **1.** *F* victoire décisive/coup *m* de Trafalgar/hécatombe *f* **2.** *P* cachette *f* *ou* lieu sûr; planque *f*/placard *m*/ planquouse *f*.

slaughter² ['slɔːtər] *vtr F* battre à plate(s) couture(s)/écrabouiller; **I'll slaughter you!** je vais un peu te tuer!

slave [sleiv] *n P* (*sado-masochism*) partenaire passif/esclave *m*. (*See* **master**)

slave (away) ['sleiv(ə'wei)] *vi F* travailler* dur/se crever/s'échiner/ bosser comme une bête.

slave-driver ['sleivdraivər] *n F* garde-chiourme *m*.

slavey ['sleivi] *n F* = **skivvy 1**.

slay [slei] *vtr F* **you slay me!** tu me fais rigoler!/tu me fais tordre!

sleazy ['sliːzi] *a F* sordide/répugnant/dégueulasse/débectant/cradingue; **a sleazy little joint**, un bouiboui/un gargote.

sleep around ['sliːpə'raund] *vi F* coucher avec n'importe qui/fréquenter les lits/coucher à droite et à gauche; (*man*) être un chaud lapin/un chaud de la pince; (*woman*) être une chaude lapine/ une fille à la cuisse hospitalière.

sleeper ['sliːpər] *n F* **1.** (*drugs*) somnifère *m*/barbiturique*/barbitos *mpl* **2.** (*wrestling, judo*) prise *f* qui abasourdit l'adversaire **3.** film *m* qui rapporte beaucoup plus qu'on n'escomptait **4.** livre *m* qui se vend couramment pendant une longue période sans publicité spéciale **5.** (*commerce*) article auquel on découvre soudainement une plus-value jusque-là ignorée **6.** wagon-lit *m* **7.** (*espionage*) dormant *m*.

sleep off ['sliːp'ɔf] *vtr F* **to sleep it off**, cuver son vin.

sleepy-byes ['sliːpibaiz] *n F* (*child's language*) dodo *m*. (*See* **bye-byes**)

sleepyhead ['sliːpihed] *n F* individu* (*esp* enfant) à moitié endormi/(bon) client du marchand de sable.

slewed [sluːd] *a P* ivre*/blindé/ bourré.

slice [slais] *n P* (*not common*) **to knock a slice off (a woman)**, faire l'amour* avec (une femme)/filer un coup d'arbalète. (*See* **tongue-pie**)

slick [slik] *a F* **1.** (*a*) malin*/rusé/ marle/roublard/filouteur; **a slick customer**, un faisan/un carambouilleur/un arnaqueur (*b*) habile/adroit **2.** beau parleur **3.** séduisant/ aguichant/désirable.

slicker ['slikər] *n F* escroc* adroit/ combinard *m*; **city slicker**, roustisseur *m* de ville/affranchi *m*/mec *m* du milieu.

slide off ['slaid'ɔf] *vi F* partir* (sans bruit)/se défiler/se débiner.

slime¹ [slaim] *n P* **1.** flatterie *f*/ lèche *f*/pommade *f* **2.** personnage grossier/rustaud *m* **3.** calomnie *f*/

diffamation f/débinage m/médisance f/bave f du crapaud.

slime² [slaim] vtr P flatter*/cirer/pommader.

slim(e)y ['slaimi] n P lèche-cul m/lèche-bottes m.

slimy ['slaimi] a F servile/obséquieux/mielleux/sirupeux/lécheur; **slimy little creep**, lèche-bottes m/lèche-cul m.

sling [sliŋ] vtr NAm P **to sling it/the bull = to shoot the bull** (**shoot²** 7). (See **hook¹** 5; **lingo** 2; **mud** 7)

slinger ['sliŋər] n P individu* qui écoule la fausse monnaie/fournaise f/fourgueur m. (See **gunslinger**; **hash-slinger**; **ink-slinger**; **mud-slinger**)

sling in ['sliŋ'in] vtr P **to sling in one's job**, lâcher son travail/rendre son tablier.

sling off ['sliŋ'ɔf] vi Austr P **to sling off at s.o.**, charrier qn/mener qn en bateau/monter un bobard à qn.

sling out ['sliŋ'aut] vtr P faire déguerpir/flanquer dehors/balancer/vider.

slinky ['sliŋki] a F 1. élégant*/mince 2. qui se meut avec élégance/gandin 3. (vêtement) collant/moulant.

slinter ['slintər] n Austr P = **slanter**.

slip¹ [slip] n F **to give s.o. the slip**, fausser compagnie à qn.

slip² [slip] vtr&i F 1. glisser/faufiler (qch à qn); **he slipped the waiter a couple of quid**, il a (re)filé vingt balles au garçon 2. **you're slipping**, tu perds les pédales/tu baisses/tu te laisses aller/tu dérapes 3. **to slip one over on s.o.**, duper* qn/tirer une carotte à qn. (See **cut¹** II 3)

slippy ['slipi] a F (a) glissant (b) rapide/presto.

slipslop ['slipslɔp] n F 1. O = **slops** 2 2. sensiblerie f/fadeur sentimentale/guimauve f.

slip-up ['slipʌp] n F erreur f/gaffe f/accident m/bourre f.

slip up ['slip'ʌp] vi F faire une erreur/gaffer/faire une bourre; **you slipped up there**, tu t'es planté sur toute la ligne.

slit [slit] n V sexe de la femme*/fente f/crac m. (See **pee-slit**)

slob [slɔb] n P 1. (a) **a big (fat) slob**, un gros (sac à) lard/un gros patapouf (b) individu* sale/cracra/cradingue/dégueulasse 2. = **slouch** 3. rustaud m/plouc m; **he's a real slob**, c'est un sacré connard; **you rotten slob!** espèce de schnock!

slobber ['slɔbər] vi F 1. faire du sentimentalisme / larmoyer / s'attendrir 2. baver/avoir la bouche* souillée de nourriture* 3. **to slobber over s.o.**, flatter qn/lécher les bottes à qn 4. (kiss) **to slobber (all) over s.o.**, sucer la pêche à qn/faire un baveux à qn.

slobberchops ['slɔbətʃɔps] n F individu* aux bajoues baveuses.

slog¹ [slɔg] n F 1. coup* violent/ramponneau m/gnon m 2. travail* dur/turbin m/boulot m 3. marche f pénible.

slog² [slɔg] vtr&i F 1. battre* violemment (qn)/tabasser (qn)/passer (qn) à tabac 2. (cricket) marquer des points en frappant fort sur la balle 3. travailler* dur/turbiner/bosser; **to slog away (at sth)**, travailler comme un dingue/bosser comme une bête/se crever au boulot 4. = **foot-slog**.

slogger ['slɔgər] n F 1. (boxing) cogneur m 2. travailleur* acharné/turbineur m/bosseur m/bûcheur m. (See **foot-slogger**)

slop [slɔp] n P 1. A agent* de police/poulet m 2. sensiblerie f. (See **slipslop**; **slops**)

slop about, around ['slɔpə'baut, -ə'raund] *vi F* patauger/barboter.

slope [sloup] *n P* **to do a slope = slope off.**

slope off ['sloup'ɔf] *vi P* s'enfuir*/se barrer/déguerpir.

slop out ['slɔp'aut] *vtr&i P (esp en prisons)* vider les seaux hygiéniques/vider les tinettes.

sloppy ['slɔpi] *a* **1.** *F* sale*/souillon/désordonné/cradingue; merdique/ pagailleux **2.** *O F* **sloppy joe,** paletot *m* de laine vague **3.** *NAm P* ivre*/éméché **4.** *F* mièvre/sirupeux; **sloppy sentimentality,** sensiblerie *f*/guimauve *f* **5.** *F* avec du laisser-aller/sans soin; **sloppy English,** anglais mal parlé/anglais débraillé; **sloppy work,** travail bâclé.

slops [slɔps] *npl F* **1.** *(Navy)* vêtements*/uniforme *m*/harnais *m* **2.** *(i)* aliments *mpl* liquides/bouillie *f* *(ii)* restes *mpl*/rabiot *m*.

slopshop ['slɔpʃɔp] *n P* **1.** braderie *f*/décrochez-moi-ça *m* **2.** *(Navy)* boutique *f* à bord d'un bateau de guerre/bouterne *f*/cambuse *f*.

slosh¹ [slɔʃ] *n P* **1.** sensiblerie *f*/sentimentalité *f* fadasse/guimauve *f* **2.** coup*/gnon *m*/marron *m* **3.** *(a)* (le) boire *(b)* boisson *f*/pictance *f*.

slosh² [slɔʃ] *vtr* **1.** *P* flanquer un coup* à (qn)/tabasser (qn) **2.** *F* **to slosh paint on/all over the place,** flanquer de la peinture partout/barbouiller.

sloshed [slɔʃt] *a P* ivre*/gris*/pompette/refait; **completely sloshed,** gelé à mort/plein comme un boudin/poivré.

slot [slɔt] *n* **1.** *P (a)* emploi *m*/situation *f*/job *m (b)* place *f*; **to finish in third slot,** finir en troisième place **2.** *Austr P* cellule *f* de prison*/cellotte *f* **3.** *V* = **slit.**

slouch [slautʃ] *n F* bousilleur *m*/gâte-métier *m*; **he's no slouch,** il est malin*/il n'est pas empoté.

slow [slou] *adv F* **1. to go slow,** marcher/fonctionner au ralenti; faire la grève du zèle **2. to take it slow,** aller doucement/y aller mollo/ne pas agir à la hâte.

slowcoach ['sloukoutʃ] *n F* flâneur *m*/traînard *m*/lambin *m*.

slowpoke ['sloupouk] *n NAm F* = **slowcoach.**

slug¹ [slʌg] *n P* **1.** balle* (de revolver)/bastos *f*/dragée *f*/valda *f* **2.** pièce fausse/mornifle *f* **3.** coup*/triquée *f*/taloche *f* **4. to have a slug,** boire* un coup **5.** *NAm* dollar *m*.

slug² [slʌg] *vtr P* **1.** battre*/frapper/tabasser/cogner **2.** boire*/avaler/ingurgiter **3.** tirer un coup (de fusil *ou* de revolver*) à qn/fusiller qn.

slugfest ['slʌgfest] *n NAm P* match *m* de boxe (entre boxeurs qui frappent dur).

slugger ['slʌgər] *n F* boxeur *m* (qui frappe dur)/cogneur *m*.

slug it out ['slʌgit'aut] *vi F* se battre* en frappant de grands coups*/se rentrer dedans.

slug-up ['slʌgʌp] *n Austr P* = **frame-up.**

sluice¹ [sluːs] *n P* trempette *f*/débarbouillage *m*.

sluice² [sluːs] *vtr P* **to sluice one's ivories,** boire*/se rincer la dalle/s'humecter le gosier.

slum [slʌm] *vtr&i* **1.** *F* **to go slumming,** fréquenter les bars des bas quartiers/faire la zone **2.** *P* **to slum it,** vivre comme un cochon; s'encanailler/se taper de la vache enragée.

slush [slʌʃ] *n* **1.** *F* sensiblerie *f* **2.** *P* fausse monnaie/mornifle *f*; **slush fund,** caisse noire (servant à payer des pots de vin/des dessous de table).

slushy ['slʌʃi] *a* F sentimental/fadasse; à l'eau de rose.

sly [slai] *n* F **on the sly,** à la dérobée/en cachette/en loucedoc/en loucedé.

slyboots ['slaibuːts] *n* F **1.** cachottier *m*/sournois *m* **2.** malin *m*/finaud *m* **3.** vaurien*/coquin *m*.

SM ['es'em] *P* (*abbr* = *sado-masochism*) **I** *n* sado-masochisme *m* **II** *a* sado-maso.

smack¹ [smæk] **I** *adv* F **1. to hit s.o. smack between the eyes,** frapper qn en plein entre les deux yeux **2. smack in the middle,** au beau milieu/en plein dans le mille. (*See* **slap¹** I)) **II** *n* **1.** F **smack in the eye/face = slap in the eye/face** (**slap¹** II 1) **2.** F **to have a smack at sth,** essayer de faire qch/tenter le coup **3.** F **to have a smack at s.o.,** donner un coup de patte à qn **4.** F = **smacker 1 5.** P (*drugs*) héroïne*/héro *f*. (*See* **shmeck**)

smack² [smæk] *vtr* P donner un coup de poing/des coups de poing à (qn); cogner (qn).

smack-bang(-wallop) ['smæk'bæŋ('wɔləp)] *adv* F = **slap-bang(-wallop).**

smack-botty ['smæk'bɔti] *n* F (*child's language*) panpan-culcul *m*; **to give a kid a smack-botty,** filer/flanquer une fessée à un gosse. (*See* **botty**)

smack down [smæk'daun] *vtr* F = **slap down.**

smacker ['smækər] *n* **1.** F gros baiser/bizou(t) *m* **2.** P (*a*) une livre sterling (*b*) NAm un dollar **3.** P **to rub smackers,** embrasser*/se sucer le caillou/se lécher la poire.

small [smɔːl] *a* F **the small print,** les petits caractères/l'important du bas de la page. (*See* **potato 2**; **room**)

smalls [smɔːlz] *npl* F sous-vêtements *mpl*/lingerie *f*/dessous *mpl*/fringues *fpl* de coulisse.

small-time ['smɔːltaim] *a* F insignifiant/médiocre/tocard/au petit pied; **a small-time crook,** un petit escroc*. (*See* **big-time**)

small-timer ['smɔːltaimər] *n* F individu* insignifiant/minus *m*/gagne-petit *m*. (*See* **big-timer**)

smarm [smɑːm] *vtr&i* F **1. to smarm (all) over s.o.,** flatter* qn/passer la main dans le dos de qn **2. to smarm one's hair down,** s'aplatir/se pommader les cheveux*.

smarmer ['smɑːmər] *n* F flagorneur *m*/lèche-bottes *m*/lèche-cul *m*.

smarmy ['smɑːmi] *a* F tout sucre tout miel/mielleux/flagorneur; **a smarmy little sod,** un lèche-cul.

smart [smɑːt] *a* F **1. don't get smart with me!** ne fais pas le malin avec moi!/ne la ramène pas! **2. smart guy,** malin *m*/fortiche *m*/roublard *m* **3. smart arse!/**NAm **smart ass!** petit malin! (*See* **Alec 1**)

smart-arsed ['smɑːtaɪst], NAm **smart-assed** [smɑːtæst] *a* P malin*/fortiche/démerdard.

smarty(-pants) ['smɑːti(pænts)] *n* F cuistre *m*/savantas(se) *m*/Je-sais-tout *m*.

smash [smæʃ] **I** *adv* F **to go smash** (*a*) se briser (*b*) faire faillite/mettre la clef sous la porte **II** *n* **1.** F = **smash-hit 2.** P petite monnaie*/ferraille *f*/mitraille *f*.

smashed [smæʃt] *a* P (*a*) ivre*/bit(t)uré/blindé (*b*) défoncé par la drogue*/bourré/stone/(raide) def.

smasher ['smæʃər] *n* F **1. she's a smasher,** c'est une jolie pépée/un beau petit lot; **what a smasher!** ce qu'elle est belle*/bien roulée! **he's a smasher,** il est beau mec/il a de la classe **2.** qch d'excellent*/de super*/de sensass/de génial **3.** coup* violent/châtaigne *f*/marron *m*.

smash-hit ['smæʃhit] *n* F réussite *f*/grand succès; **it was a smash-hit,** ça a fait un boum (terrible); **their**

album was a smash-hit, leur album a fait un tabac monstre.

smash in ['smæʃin] *vtr P* **to smash s.o.'s face in,** casser la gueule à qn/arranger le portrait à qn.

smashing ['smæʃiŋ] *a O F* excellent*/formid(able)/du tonnerre.

smash up ['smæʃʌp] *vtr P* **1.** battre* (qn)/filer une avoine à (qn)/passer (qn) à tabac **2. he's smashed his car up,** il a amoché/bousillé sa bagnole.

smell [smel] *vi F* sembler louche/ne pas avoir l'air catholique/sentir mauvais; **I won't do it, your idea smells,** je ne marche pas; ton idée est foireuse. (*See* **rat¹ 4**)

smelly ['smeli] *a F* suspect/louche.

smidgen ['smidʒən] *n esp NAm F* un peu*/un chouia/une miette.

smithereens ['smiðə'riːnz] *npl F* morceaux *mpl*/miettes *fpl;* **to smash sth to smithereens,** briser qch en mille morceaux/mettre qch en miettes.

smizz [smiz] *n NAm P* = **shmeck.**

smoke¹ [smouk] *n* **1.** *F* **to go up in smoke,** ne servir à rien/partir en fumée **2.** *F* **the Smoke,** une grande métropole; **the (Big) Smoke,** Londres; *Austr* **the big smoke,** Sydney **3.** *F* **a smoke** (*a*) cigarette*/cibiche *f;* **want a smoke?** tu veux un(e) clope? (*b*) (*drugs*) cigarette* de marijuana*/stick *m.* (*See* **giggle 3**) **4.** *Austr P* **in smoke,** en cachette/planqué **5.** *NAm P* (*pej*) Noir(e)*/nègre *mf.* (*See* **holy 1**; **joy-smoke**)

smoke² (off) ['smouk('ɔf)] *vi Austr P* partir*/déguerpir/lever le pied.

smoke-o(h) ['smoukou] *n Austr F* pause-café *f*/pause-thé *f;* récré *f;* break *m.*

smoker ['smoukər] *n* **1.** *F* compartiment *m* fumeur **2.** *P* voiture *f* à haut kilométrage **3.** *P* pot *m* de chambre **4.** *V* (*fellator*) suceur, -euse *mf*/pipeur, -euse *mf.*

smoko ['smoukou] *n Austr P* = **smoke-o(h).**

smoky ['smouki] *a P* en colère*/en rogne/à cran/en pétard.

smooch [smuːtʃ] *vi F* s'embrasser*/se bécoter/se baisoter/se faire des mamours *mpl* (*esp* en dansant).

smoocher ['smuːtʃər] *n F* embrasseur *m*/peloteur *m.*

smooching ['smuːtʃiŋ] *n F* caressage *m*/pelotage *m*/fricassée *f* de museaux (*esp* en dansant).

smoodge [smuːdʒ] *vi,* **smoodger** ['smuːdʒər] *n,* **smoodging** ['smuːdʒiŋ] *n Austr F* = **smooch, smoocher, smooching.**

smooth [smuːð] *a F* malin*/débrouillard/fortiche; **smooth operator,** individu malin*/démerdard *m;* bonimenteur/beau parleur.

smoothie, smoothy ['smuːði] *F* **1.** homme* doucereux/papelard; beau parleur **2.** homme* qui se prend pour un don Juan.

smother ['smʌðər] *n A P* (*a*) pardessus*/pardosse *m*/pardingue *m* (*b*) imperméable *m*/imper *m.*

smudge [smʌdʒ] *n P* photo *f*/cliché *m*/portrait *m.*

snack [snæk] *n Austr F* qch de facile/du gâteau/du nougat/de la tarte.

snaffle ['snæfl] *vtr P* voler*/barbot(t)er/chiper.

snafu¹, SNAFU ['snæ'fuː] *P* (*abbr* = *situation normal, all fucked up/fouled up*) **I** *a* en désordre/en pagaille/confus; amoché/bousillé **II** *n* désordre *m*/pagaille *f.*

snafu², SNAFU ['snæ'fuː] *vtr P* mettre/foutre le désordre/la pagaille dans qch; semer la merde.

snags [snægz] *npl Austr F* saucisses *fpl.*

snakebite ['sneikbait] *n P* (*drink*) mélange *m* de bière blonde et de cidre.

snake-eyes ['sneik-aiz] *npl F* (*dice game*) double un.

snake-hips ['sneikhips] *n F* qn de souple et flexible/danseur *m* (-euse *f*) de corde.

snake off ['sneik'ɔf] *vi F* s'esquiver/jouer rip.

snak(e)y ['sneiki] *a F* malin*/ficelle/marle.

snap¹ [snæp] *n F* **1.** vigueur *f*/entrain *m*/allant *m*/dynamisme *m* **2.** qch de facile/du nougat/du tout cuit **3.** (*workman's packed lunch*) sachet repas *m*/panier repas *m*.

snap² [snæp] *vtr&i F* **1.** s'exprimer avec aigreur/parler* d'un ton sec; **to snap at s.o./to snap s.o.'s head off,** manger le nez à qn/avaler qn **2.** (*pers*) avoir une maladie mentale/perdre la raison; **I just snapped,** j'ai flippé/j'ai débloqué **3. to snap into it,** agir avec énergie et rapidité **4. to snap out of it,** se secouer/se remettre d'aplomb/reprendre du poil de la bête.

snaped [sneipt] *a esp NAm F* ivre*/bourré/soûl.

snapper ['snæpər] *n* **1.** *V* sexe de la femme*/grippette *f*/abricot *m* **2.** *P* = **amy 3.** *A P* contrôleur *m* d'autobus **4.** *pl P* dents*/croquantes *fpl*. (*See* **whipper-snapper**)

snappy ['snæpi] *a F* **1.** acariâtre/hargneux/bourru **2. look snappy!/make it snappy!** dépêchez*-vous!/grouille-toi!/au trot!/et que ça saute! **3.** élégant*/flambard/badour **4.** sarcastique/mordant/spirituel.

snap up ['snæp'ʌp] *vtr F* **1. to snap up a bargain,** enlever une affaire/saisir une occasion **2. to snap it up,** activer le mouvement; **snap it up!** grouille-toi!/et que ça saute!

snarl [snɑil] *n F* = **snarl-up**.

snarled up ['snɑild'ʌp] *a F* embouteillé/encombré/coincé.

snarl-up ['snɑilʌp] *n F* embouteillage *m*/bouchon *m*.

snatch¹ [snætʃ] *n* **1.** *V* (*a*) sexe de la femme*/grippette *f*/cramouille *f* (*b*) coït*/baise *f* **2.** *P* (*a*) arrestation *f*/épinglage *m*/agrafage *m* (*b*) enlèvement *m*; **to put the snatch on s.o.** (*i*) arrêter* qn (*ii*) enlever qn **3.** *F* vol *m*/cambriolage *m*/casse *m*; **wages snatch,** ratissage *m* de la paye.

snatch² [snætʃ] *vtr* **1.** *P* arrêter*/alpaguer/épingler/agrafer **2.** *P* enlever/kidnapper **3.** *P* voler*/barbot(t)er **4. to snatch a quick one** (*a*) *F* boire* un coup/s'en jeter un vite fait (*b*) *P* faire l'amour* rapidement/s'envoyer un petit coup/tirer un coup vite fait.

snazzy ['snæzi] *a F* (*a*) élégant*/chic (*b*) criard/voyant/clinquant/tape-à-l'œil.

sneak¹ [sniːk] **I** *a F* **sneak attack,** attaque sournoise/en dessous; coup *m* en vache; (*film*, play, etc) **sneak preview,** banc *m* d'essai/séance privée; **sneak thief,** chapardeur *m*/chipeur *m*/barbot(t)eur *m* **II** *n F* indicateur*/indic *m*/mouchard *m*/rapporteur *m*.

sneak² [sniːk] *vtr&i F* **1.** voler*/furtivement/barbot(t)er/chaparder **2.** dénoncer*/moucharder/cafarder **3.** se conduire en pleutre/caner.

sneak in ['sniːk'in] *F* **I** *vtr* inclure/glisser furtivement (qch dans qch) **II** *vi* se glisser furtivement/se faufiler; entrer à la dérobée/en douce/en catimini.

sneak on ['sniːkɔn] *vtr F* dénoncer*/cafter/cafarder/moutonner.

sneak out ['sniːk'aut] *vi F* partir* furtivement/s'éclipser/se défiler.

sneaky ['sniːki] *a F* **1.** sournois/dissimulé; **that was a really sneaky thing to do,** c'était vraiment un coup de vache/un coup fumant à faire **2.** rampant/servile.

sneeze at ['sniːz'æt] *vtr F* **it's not**

to be sneezed at, ce n'est pas de la petite bière/ce n'est pas à cracher dessus.

sneezer ['sni:zər] *n P* **1.** nez*/tarin *m* **2.** prison*/block *m*/frigo *m*.

snicket ['snikit] *n P* passage *m*/ruelle *f*/allée *f*.

snide [snaid] **I** *a F* **1.** faux/tocard/à la manque **2.** roublard/ficelle **3.** sarcastique/persifleur **II** *n P* **1.** voleur*/filou *m*/truqueur *m* **2.** fausse monnaie/fausse mornifle; bijouterie *f* factice/toc *m*.

snidy ['snaidi] *a P* malin*/astucieux/rusé.

sniff [snif] *vtr* **1.** *P* inhaler une poudre narcotique/prendre une reniflette/sniffer; **to sniff glue,** sniffer de la colle **2.** *F* **it's not to be sniffed at** = **it's not to be sneezed at (sneeze at).**

sniffer ['snifər] *n P* **1.** nez*/reniflant *m*/blair *m* **2.** mouchoir*/blave *m*/tire-jus *m* **3.** (*drugs, glue*) (*pers*) sniffeur, -euse *mf*.

sniffles ['sniflz] *npl F* **to have the sniffles,** être enchifrené.

sniff rag ['snif'ræg] *n P* mouchoir*/blave *m*/tire-jus *m*.

sniffy ['snifi] *a* **1.** *F* arrogant/hautain/pimbêche **2.** *P* = **niffy.**

snifter ['sniftər] *n P* petit verre d'alcool*/goutte *f*; **to have a quick snifter,** s'en jeter un vite fait.

snip [snip] *n F* **1.** affaire* avantageuse/trouvaille *f*/occasion *f*; **it's a snip,** c'est une occase **2.** certitude *f*/affaire* certaine; du nougat/du tout cuit; (*horse racing*) gagnant sûr/une grosse cote **3.** tailleur *m*/fringueur *m* **4.** enfant*/gamin *m*/gavroche *m*/titi *m*/moutard *m*.

snipe[1] [snaip] *n P* (*a*) mégot*/clope *m*/orphelin *m* (*b*) mégot* de cigarette de marijuana/roach *m*.

snipe[2] [snaip] *vtr P* voler*/faucher.

sniper ['snaipər] *n P* mégot(t)ier *m*/mégot(t)eur *m*. (*See* **snipe**[1])

snippy ['snipi] *a P* insolent/effronté/culotté/gonflé.

snitch[1] [snitʃ] *n P* **1.** vol *m*/filouterie *f* **2.** indicateur* de police/mouchard *m* **3.** un tout petit peu* (de qch)/un chouia **4.** nez*/tarin *m*/pif *m* **5.** *Austr* aversion *f*/dégoût *m*.

snitch[2] [snitʃ] *vi P* = **sneak**[2] **1, 2.**

snitcher ['snitʃər] *n P* **1.** | indicateur*/indic *m*/rapporteur *m*/cafteur *m* **2.** *pl* menottes*/cadènes *fpl*/bracelets *mpl*/poucettes *fpl*.

snitch-rag ['snitʃræg] *n P* mouchoir*/tire-jus *m*/tire-moelle *m*.

snob [snɔb] *n P* cordonnier *m*/bouif *m*/ribouis *m*/gnaf *m*.

snoddy ['snɔdi] *n P* soldat*/bidasse *m*/troufion *m*.

snodger ['snɔdʒər] *n Austr O P* délectation *f*/agrément *m*.

snog[1] [snɔg] *n P* embrassage *m*/pelotage *m*/fricassée *f* de museaux.

snog[2] [snɔg] *vi P* s'embrasser*/se bécoter/se baisoter/se sucer le caillou/se lécher la poire; **snogging session,** pelotage *m*.

snogger ['snɔgər] *n P* embrasseur, -euse/peloteur *m*; flirteur *m*/juponneur *m*.

snook [snu:k] *n F* **to cock a snook at s.o.,** faire un pied de nez à qn.

snooker ['snu:kər] *vtr F* **to snooker s.o.,** mettre qn dans une impasse; **to be snookered,** se trouver en mauvaise posture/être réduit à l'impuissance.

snooks [snu:ks], **snookums** ['snu:kəmz] *n NAm F* chéri(e)/cocotte *f*.

snoop[1] [snu:p] *n F* **1.** fureteur *m*/fouineur *m* **2.** (*a*) investigateur *ou* inspecteur officiel (*b*) détective privé/privé *m*/limier *m*.

snoop[2] [snu:p] *vi F* fureter/fouiner/fourrer le nez* partout.

snooper ['snuːpər] *n F* = **snoop**[1] 1, 2.

snoopy ['snuːpi] *a F* curieux/ fouineur/fureteur.

snoot [snuːt] *n P* 1. nez*/pif *m* 2. grimace *f*/grigne *f*.

snootful ['snuːtful] *n NAm P* **to have (had) a snootful**, être ivre*/ avoir une cuite/en tenir une/en avoir un dans le nez.

snootiness ['snuːtinis] *n F* morgue *f*/crânage *m*/pose *f*.

snooty ['snuːti] *a F* hautain/orgueil-leux/dédaigneux; gommeux; **to be snooty**, se donner de grands airs/ croire que c'est arrivé.

snooze[1] [snuːz] *n F* petit somme; **to have a snooze**, piquer un roupil-lon.

snooze[2] [snuːz] *vi F* dormir*/ roupiller/pioncer.

snoozer ['snuːzər] *n F* roupilleur *m*/pionceur *m*.

snort[1] [snɔːt] *n P* 1. petit verre d'alcool*/goutte *f*; **to have a snort**, s'en jeter un (derrière la cravate) 2. (*drugs*) dose *f*.

snort[2] [snɔːt] *vtr&i P* (*drugs*) renifler/respirer/priser/sniffer (de la cocaïne*, etc).

snorter ['snɔːtər] *n* 1. *P* = **snort**[1] 1 2. *F* qch qui donne du fil à retordre 3. *F* réponse *f* ou lettre *f* qui assoit; lettre carabinée. (*See* **ripsnorter**)

snot [snɔt] *n P* 1. morve *f*/chan-delle *f* 2. morveux *m*/merdeux *m*.

snot-rag ['snɔtræg] *n P* mouchoir*/blave *m*/tire-moelle *m*/ tire-jus *m*.

snotty ['snɔti] **I** *a P* 1. qui a le nez* enchifrené 2. prétentieux*/ culotté/gonflé 3. sale*/salingue/ cradigue 4. avare*/radin 5. méprisable/vache; **you snotty little git!** petit morveux!/petite ordure! **II** *n F* aspirant *m* de Marine/aspi *m*.

snotty-nosed ['snɔtinouzd] *a P* 1. morveux 2. hautain/ dédaigneux/gommeux; **she's terribly snotty-nosed**, elle joue les grandes dames/elle pète plus haut que son cul.

snout [snaut] *n P* 1. nez*/blair *m* 2. (*a*) tabac*/perlot *m* (*b*) ciga-rette*/sèche *f*; **snout baron**, prison-nier *m* qui vend du tabac aux autres détenus 3. indicateur* de police/indic *m*/mouchard *m*/ mouton *m*.

snow[1] [snou] *n* 1. *P* (*drugs*) (*a*) cocaïne* en poudre/neige *f* (*b*) morphine* *ou* autre narcotique 2. *P* pièce *f* *ou* article *m* en argent; blanc *m*/blanquette *f* 3. *F* points blancs mobiles sur écran de télévi-sion/neige *f* 4. *F* **snow bunny**, jeune fille* qui fréquente les sta-tions de sports d'hiver (et sort avec les skieurs).

snow[2] [snou] *vtr&i* 1. *P* duper*/ rouler dans la farine/mystifier 2. *F* **it's snowing down south**, ta com-binaison dépasse; tu cherches une belle-mère? (*See* **Charl(e)y 2**)

snowball[1] ['snoubɔːl] *n P* 1. *NAm* (*pej*) Noir(e)*/nègre *mf*/ bougnoul(l)e *m*/boule *f* de neige 2. **he doesn't stand a snowball's chance in hell**, il n'a pas l'ombre d'une chance 3. = **snowbird**.

snowball[2] ['snoubɔːl] *vi F* (*problems, debts, etc*) faire boule *f* de neige.

snowbird ['snoubəːd] *n P* drogué*/ cocaïnomane *mf*/occ héroïnomane *mf*.

snow-dropping ['snoudrɔpiŋ] *n A P* vol *m* de linge séchant dans les jardins.

snowed [snoud] *a* 1. *P* drogué* à la cocaïne*/enneigé 2. *F* **snowed under**, accablé de travail*/abruti.

snow-job ['snoudʒɔb] *n* 1. *NAm F* flatterie intéressée/pommade *f*; **to give s.o. a snow-job**, jeter de la poudre aux yeux à qn/bourrer le mou à qn **2.** *V* (*homosexuals*) fellation*/prise *f* de pipe; **to give s.o. a snow-job,** tailler une pipe à qn/ faire un pompier à qn.

snow-white ['snou'wait] *a F* innocent/blanc (comme la neige). (*See* **lily-white**)

snuff [snʌf] *n F* **up to snuff** (*a*) à la hauteur/à la coule (*b*) malin*/dessalé/dégourdi.

snuff it ['snʌf'it] *vi P* mourir*/ éteindre son gaz/avaler sa chique.

snuffles ['snʌflz] *npl F* **to have the snuffles,** être enchifrené/un peu enrhumé. (*See* **sniffles**)

snuff out ['snʌf'aut] *vtr&i P* **1.** = **snuff it** **2.** tuer*/zigouiller/ estourbir/effacer.

so [sou] *adv & conj F* **1. so long!** à bientôt!/à tout à l'heure! **2. so what?** et après?/et alors?

soak[1] [souk] *n P* **1.** ivrogne*/ poivrot *m*/(vieille) éponge **2.** ivrognerie *f*/soûlerie *f*/ribote *f*/cuite *f*.

soak[2] [souk] *vtr&i* **1.** *P* boire* beaucoup/pomper/s'ivrogner/boire* comme un trou; **to get soaked,** s'enivrer/prendre une cuite **2.** *F* (*a*) faire payer* trop cher/écocher/ estamper (*b*) taxer à haute dose/ assaisonner.

soaker ['soukər] *n F* **1.** = **soak**[1] **1 2.** pluie* forte/averse *f*/bouillon *m*.

so-and-so ['souənsou] *n F* **1. Mr So-and-so/Mrs So-and-so,** Monsieur un tel/Madame une telle; Monsieur/Madame Machin(-truc) **2.** (*pej*) salaud*/sale mec *m*/peau *f* de vache; **she's a right old so-and-so,** c'est une vraie salope/une vieille bique.

soap[1] [soup] *n* **1.** *F* (**soft**) **soap,** flatterie *f*/eau bénite/pommade *f* **2.** *P* argent*/fric *m* de chantage **3.** *F* **no soap!** = **no dice! (dice**[1] **1**) **4.** *F* **soap opera,** feuilleton *m* à l'eau de rose.

soap[2] [soup] *vtr P* = **soft-soap.**

soapy ['soupi] *a F* doucereux/mielleux/tout sucre tout miel.

s.o.b. ['esou'biː] *abbr P* **1.** = **shit or bust (shit**[2] **3**) **2.** = **son-of-a-bitch.**

sob-act ['sɔbækt] *n P* **to put on a/ the (big) sob-act,** pleurer des larmes de crocodile; la faire aux larmes.

sobs [sɔbz] *npl P* livres *fpl* sterling.

sob-sister ['sɔbsistər] *n esp NAm F* **1.** journaliste spécialisée dans le mélodrame **2.** actrice *f* qui joue le mélo(drame)/chialeuse *f*.

sob-story ['sɔbstɔːri] *n F* histoire larmoyante/au jus de mirettes; **he came out with this long sob-story about his low wages,** il s'est amené avec une histoire à faire pleurer/à nous faire chialer sur son bas salaire.

sob-stuff ['sɔbstʌf] *n F* sensiblerie *f*/eau *f* de guimauve/mélo *m*.

sock[1] [sɔk] *n* **1.** *P* **put a sock in it!** passe la main!/la ferme!/ta gueule! **2.** *P* coup* de poing/gifle *f*/taloche *f* **3.** *F* **to pull one's socks up,** se remuer/remonter la pente/faire mieux que ça. (*See* **bobbysocks; wet I 6**)

sock[2] [sɔk] *vtr P* **1.** donner un coup* à (qn)/flanquer une raclée à (qn)/en allonger une à (qn); **I'll sock you (one), if you don't shut up!** la ferme, ou je te refais le portrait! **2. sock it to me!** (*a*) passe-moi ça!/flanque-moi ça! (*b*) fais-moi la cour!/fais-moi du plat! (*c*) continue, tu te débrouilles bien! (*d*) vas-y!/donne!/déballe!

sod[1] [sɔd] *n V* **1.** homosexuel*/ pédé *m*/pédalo *m*/enculé *m* **2. poor sod!** pauv'con!/pauvre enculé! **silly sod!** espèce d'andouille!/espèce de con! **rotten sod!** peau *f* de vache!/salaud!/ordure!/la vache! **you sods!** bande d'enculés!/tas de salauds! **3. I don't give/care a sod,** je m'en fous (comme de l'an quarante); j'en ai rien à branler/à foutre. (*See* **odds** 1)

sod² [sɔd] *vtr V* **1.** sodomiser*/enculer/empaffer **2. sod you!** va te faire foutre!/va te faire voir (chez les Grecs)!/va te faire enculer! **sod it!** merde alors!/bordel de Dieu!/bordel de merde!

sod about, around ['sɔdə'baut, -ə'raund] *vtr&i V* **1.** faire le con/déconner; **stop sodding about!** arrête de déconner! **2.** ennuyer/emmerder (qn); **you're sodding me about!** tu me fais chier! **this car is sodding about again,** cette bagnole déconne à nouveau **3.** paresser*/glander/glandouiller/traînasser.

sod-all ['sɔd'ɔil] *n V* rien*/que dalle/peau *f* de balle.

sodding [sɔdiŋ] *a V* (*intensifier*) sacré/foutu; **that's a sodding nuisance!** c'est vraiment chiant! **you sodding bastard!** (espèce de) salaud!/pauv' type!/enculé; **the sodding car,** cette saloperie de bagnole/cette putain de bagnole; **sodding hell!** bordel de Dieu!/bordel de merde!

sod off ['sɔd'ɔf] *vi V* partir*/foutre le camp; **he just sods off whenever there's work about,** il fonce/il se carapate/il met les bouts dès qu'il est question de travailler; **sod off, will you!** va te faire voir!/va te faire foutre!/va te faire enculer!

soft [sɔft] **I** *a F* **1.** (*a*) crédule/sentimental (*b*) bête*/niais/nigaud; **soft in the head,** faible d'esprit (*c*) poltron*/lâche/caneur; **to go soft,** se dégonfler **2. a soft job,** un filon/un bon fromage/une planque; **to have a soft time (of it),** se la couler douce. (*See* **berth** 2) **3. to be soft on s.o.,** être épris/entiché de qn; **he's soft on her,** il en est toqué **4. soft drugs,** drogues* douces. (*See* **hard I** 2) **5. soft sell,** publicité discrète. (*See* **hard I** 5) **6. soft porn,** porno *m* soft/soft *m.* (*See* **sawder; soap¹** 1; **spot** 4; **touch¹** 3) **II** *adv F* **1. don't talk soft!** ne

dis pas de bêtises*! **2. to have it soft,** se la couler douce.

soft-pedal ['sɔft'pedl] *vi F* y aller mollo/ne pas trop insister/garder le secret/mettre la pédale douce.

soft-soap ['sɔft'soup] *vtr F* flatter*/passer de la pommade à/pommader/flagorner (qn); bonimenter/baratiner.

softy ['sɔfti] *n F* (*a*) homme* mou *ou* efféminé/hommelette *f* (*b*) lavette *f*/poule mouillée/dégonflé *m*/trouillard *m* (*c*) personne *f* frêle/mauviette *f*; chiffe molle/mollasson(ne) *m(f)* (*d*) individu* sentimental à l'excès; **you big softy!** mon gros bébé!

soldier¹ ['souldʒər] *n* **1.** *P* gendarme*/sauret *m* **2.** *F* (*a*) cigare* (*b*) bouteille *f* de bière *ou* de whisky; **dead soldier** (*a*) mégot* froid (*b*) bouteille* vide/cadavre *m.* (*See* **dead I** 3) **3.** *F* **old soldier,** soudard *m*/brisquard *m*; **to come the old soldier,** la faire au vieux sergent/poser au vieux brisquard.

soldier² ['souldʒər] *vi P* **to soldier on the job,** renâcler à la besogne/flémarder.

soldier on ['souldʒə'ɔn] *vi F* continuer à se maintenir/se défendre/se débattre.

sold out ['sould'aut] *a P* très fatigué*/vanné/crevé.

solid ['sɔlid] *F* **I** *a* **five solid hours,** cinq heures pleines; **six solid weeks I had to wait,** six bonnes semaines que j'ai dû poireauter **II** *adv* **to be in solid with s.o.,** être dans les petits papiers de qn/avoir la cote avec qn.

solitary ['sɔlitəri] *n F* **in solitary,** en réclusion *f*/dans les bondes *fpl.*

some [sʌm] **I** *a F* **1.** excellent*/formid(able); **she's some girl!** elle est sensas(s)!/c'est une fille* formidable!/elle a de la classe!/elle est classe! **2. some hope!** quelle illusion!/tu parles! **II** *adv F* (*a*) dans une certaine mesure (*b*) considérablement; **to go some,** y aller en plein/gazer; **that's going some, getting there in two hours!** y arriver en deux heures, faut le faire! **III** *pron* *F* ... **and then some,** ... et le reste/ ... et encore plus.

somebody ['sʌmbɔdi, 'sʌmbədi] *n* *F* **he's a somebody,** c'est vraiment quelqu'un/c'est un personnage. (*See* **nobody**)

something ['sʌmθiŋ] **I** *adv* *F* très/beaucoup*; **she went off at him something awful,** elle lui a passé un bon savon. (*See* **chronic II**) **II** *n* *F* **1. that's something like it!** voilà qui est bien!/voilà qui est mieux!/ ça au moins, ça vaut le coup! **2. isn't that something!/that really is something!** n'est-ce pas super!/ça se pose là!

song [sɔŋ] *n* **1.** *F* **to make a song (and dance) about sth,** faire des histoires/des tas d'histoires au sujet de qch; **no need to make a big song and dance over it,** pas de quoi en faire tout un plat **2.** *F* **to buy sth for a song,** acheter qch pour une bouchée de pain **3.** *P* aveu *m*/ déboutonnage *m*/accouchage *m*.

sonk [sɔŋk] *n* *Austr O P* homosexuel*/lope *f*.

sonny (Jim) ['sʌni('dʒim)] *n* *F* (mon) petit/(mon) fiston/mon gars.

sonofabitch, son of a bitch, sonovabitch ['sʌnəvə'bitʃ] *n* *P* **1.** salaud*/ peau *f* de vache / fils *m* de pute/ fils de garce; **you sons of bitches!** bande d'enculés! / tas de salauds! **2.** (*thing*) **this car is a real son of a bitch,** c'est une vrai saloperie/une vache/une putain de bagnole.

soppiness ['sɔpinis] *n* *F* mollesse *f*/fadasserie *f*.

soppy ['sɔpi] *a* *F* (*a*) bête*/ baluchard; **you soppy twit!** gros bêta! (*b*) mou/fadasse (*c*) à l'eau de rose/gnian-gnian.

sore [sɔːr] *a* *F* **1.** en colère*/fâché/ à cran; **to get sore with s.o.,** en

vouloir à qn; **he was really sore about it,** ça l'a foutu en rogne/en pétard **2. to be like a bear with a sore head,** être d'une humeur massacrante. (*See* **eye 11**; **thumb¹ 4**)

sorehead ['sɔːhed] *n* *P* rancunier *m*/qn plein de ressentiment.

sort [sɔːt] *n* **1.** *F* **a good sort,** un brave homme*/un chic type **2.** *F* **out of sorts,** malade*/patraque/pas dans son assiette.

sort of ['sɔːtəv] *adv* *F* = **kind of.**

sort out ['sɔːt'aut] *vtr* *F* **to sort s.o. out** (*i*) remettre qn à sa place/régler son compte à qn (*ii*) battre* qn/ passer qn à tabac.

so-so ['sousou] *adv* *F* couci-couça/ entre les deux.

soul [soul] *n* *F* **poor soul!** pauvre créature!/pauvre bonhomme!/ pauvre bonne femme! le/la pauvre! **she's a good soul,** c'est une bien brave femme/c'est une bonne pâte.

soul brother ['soulbrʌðər] *n* *F* (*a*) frère *m* (*esp* terme employé par un Noir américain en parlant d'un autre Noir) (*b*) Noir*/négro *m*.

soul sister ['soul'sistər] *n* *F* (*a*) (*Black Slang*) sœur*/frangine *f* (*b*) (*esp pej*) Noire*/négresse *f*/boule *f* de neige.

sound ['saund] *a* *F* **sound as a pound,** bon/solide; valable; régulier/réglo.

sound off ['saund'ɔf] *vi* *F* **to sound off at s.o.,** réprimander* qn/ engueuler qn/sonner les cloches à qn; **to sound off about sth,** déblatérer contre qch/rouspéter à propos de qch.

soup [suːp] *n* **1.** *F* **in the soup,** dans le pétrin/la panade **2.** *P* (*a*) nitroglycérine *f* (pour faire sauter les coffres-forts)/jus *m* (*b*) dynamite *f*. (*See* **duck¹ 11**; **electric**)

soup up ['suːp'ʌp] *vtr* *F* (*a*) gonfler (un moteur); **a souped-up job** (*i*) bagnole gonflée (*ii*) (*fig*) une affaire survoltée (b) exagérer*/épicer (une publicité, etc); en rajouter.

soupy ['suːpɪ] *a esp NAm F* (a) sentimental/à l'eau de rose (b) (voix) larmoyante.

sourpuss ['sauəpus] *n F* individu* morose/revêche/renfrogné; bonnet *m* de nuit/rabat-joie *m*.

souse¹ [saus] *n P* (*not common*) **1.** = **sozzler 2.** ivresse*/cuite *f*/ soûlerie *f*.

souse² [saus] *vi P* = **sozzle**.

soused [saust] *a P* = **sozzled**.

southpaw ['sauθpɔː] *n F* gaucher *m*.

sov [sɔv] *n P* (*abbr* = *sovereign*) livre *f* sterling.

sozzle ['sɔzl] *vi P* **1.** boire* beaucoup/picoler **2.** s'enivrer/se charger.

sozzled ['sɔzld] *a P* ivre*/soûl/ chargé.

sozzler ['sɔzlər] *n P* ivrogne*/soûlard *m*/poivrot *m*/alcolo *mf*.

sozzling ['sɔzlɪŋ] *n P* ivresse*/ poivrade *f*.

SP ['es'piː] *n P* (*abbr* = *starting price*) **1.** (*horse racing*) prix *m* de départ **2.** information*/info *f*/ tuyau *m*; **to give s.o. the SP**, mettre qn au parfum/tuyauter qn; **give me the SP on this bloke**, fais-moi le papier sur ce type.

spaced out ['speisdaut] *a P* (*drugs*) camé/envapé/chargé; **he's really spaced out**, il est défoncé/sur sa planète; il s'éclate.

spade [speid] *n* **1.** *P* (*pej*) Noir(e)*/nègre *mf*/bougnoul(l)e *m* **2.** *F* **to call a spade a spade**, appeler un chat un chat.

spank along ['spæŋkə'lɔŋ] *vi O F* aller vite*/filer/foncer/gazer.

spanker ['spæŋkər] *n O F* **1.** beau spécimen/qch d'épatant/qch de super **2.** cheval* rapide/crack *m*.

spanking ['spæŋkɪŋ] **I** *a F* **1.**

rapide/à pleins tubes **2.** grand/ énorme/maousse **3.** excellent*/ épatant **II** *adv F* **spanking new**, flambant neuf.

spanner ['spænər] *n F* **to put/to throw a spanner in the works**, mettre des bâtons dans les roues.

spare ['spɛər] **I** *a F* **1.** (*a*) **to go spare**, être furieux/fulminer; **to drive s.o. spare**, rendre qn furieux/ faire marronner qn; **he'll go spare when he finds out**, il va monter au plafond/il va prendre son bœuf quand il (le) découvrira (c) **there's a glass going spare here**, il y a un verre qui traîne par ici **2. spare tyre**/*NAm* tire, bourrelet *m* (de graisse)/pneu *m* Michelin. (*See* **prick 3**) **II** *n P* **1. to have a bit of spare** = **to have a bit on the side** (**side 2**) **2.** individu bête*/ andouille *f*/nouille *f*; **he's a real spare!** c'est une vraie cloche/un vrai gland!

spare-part ['spɛə'paɪt] *attrib F* **spare-part surgery**, chirurgie *f* de greffage.

spark [spaɪk] *n F* **bright spark**, qn de très intelligent/lumière *f*; (*iron*) andouille *f*/tête *f* de nœud; **who's the bright spark who did that!** qui c'est, le petit malin qui a fait ça?

sparkle plenty ['spaɪkl'plenti] *n P* (*drugs*) amphétamine*/bombita *f*/amph *m*.

sparklers ['spaɪkləz] *npl F* diamants*/diames *mpl*.

sparks [spaɪks] *n F* (*boats, planes*) opérateur *m* de TSF/radio *m*.

sparring-partner ['spaɪrɪŋpaɪtnər] *n F* épouse*/ (chère) moitié.

sparrow-fart ['spæroufaɪt] *n P* **at sparrow-fart**, aux aurores/dès potron-ja(c)quet/dès potron-minet.

spastic ['spæstik] *n P* (*pej*) **you spastic!** espèce d'enfoiré/quel nœud!

spat [spæt] *n NAm F* petite querelle*/bisbille *f*/prise *f* de bec.

speakeasy ['spiːkiːzi] *n NAm O F* bar clandestin.

spec [spek] *n* F (*abbr* = *speculation*) **on spec,** à tout hasard. (*See* **specs**)

specimen ['spesimən, 'spesimin] *n F* individu*/type *m*; **an odd/a queer specimen,** un drôle de numéro/de client/d'oiseau/de zèbre.

specs [speks] *npl F* (*abbr* = *spectacles*) lunettes*/bernicles *fpl*/carreaux *mpl*/pare-brise *m*.

speed[1] [spiːd] *n P* (*drugs*) amphétamine*/speed *m*; **he's on speed,** il est speedé/défoncé.

speed[2] ['spiːd] *vi P* (*drugs*) prendre des amphétamines*/du speed; **to be speeding,** être speedé.

speedball ['spiːdbɔːl] *n P* (*drugs*) 1. mélange *m* d'amphétamines* et de barbituriques* 2. mélange *m* d'héroïne* et de cocaïne* 3. drogué(e)*/camé(e) *mf*/toxico *mf*.

speed-cop ['spiːdkɔp] *n F* motard *m*.

speedfreak ['spiːdfriːk] *n P* (*drugs*) usager habituel d'amphétamines*/speedé *m*.

speed-hog ['spiːdhɔg] *n F* chauffard *m*.

speed-merchant ['spiːdmɜːtʃənt] *n F* 1. passionné *m* de la vitesse/fou *m* du volant 2. chauffard *m*.

speedo ['spiːdo] *n F* (*aut*) (= *speedometer*) compteur *m*.

speed-up ['spiːdʌp] *n F* allure accélérée.

spellbinder ['spelbaindər] *n F* orateur entraînant/fascinant.

spell out ['spel'aut] *vtr&i F* expliquer dans le langage le plus simple/comme a, b, c/mâcher la besogne.

SPG ['es'piː'dʒiː] *n P* (*abbr* = *Special Patrol Group*) (*police*) Brigade spéciale.

spiced [spaist] *a P* **done up like a spiced pig,** élégant*/tiré à quatre épingles/sur son trente et un.

spiderman ['spaidəmæn] *n F* ouvrier *m* qui travaille au sommet des édifices/homme-mouche *m*.

spiel[1] [spiːl, ʃpiːl] *n F* boniment *m*/baratin *m*.

spiel[2] [spiːl, ʃpiːl] *vi* 1. *F* avoir du bagou(t); baratiner/pérorer 2. *P* jouer de l'argent (aux jeux, aux cartes, etc).

spieler ['spiːlər, 'ʃpiːlər] 1. *P* tricheur* (aux cartes)/maquilleur *m* 2. *P* escroc*/arnaqueur *m* 3. *P* tripot *m* de jeux 4. *P* embobineur *m* 5. *F* beau parleur/baratineur *m*/bonimenteur *m*.

spiel off ['spiːl'ɔf, 'ʃpiːl'ɔf] *vtr F* **to spiel off a whole list of names,** débiter/dégoiser toute une liste de noms.

spiffing ['spifiŋ] *a O F* ravissant/charmant/délicieux.

spifflicate ['spiflikeit] *vtr F* écraser/aplatir/fracasser/démolir/écrabouiller (un adversaire).

spifflicated ['spiflikeitid] *a P* ivre*/rétamé.

spike[1] [spaik] *n P* 1. (*drugs*) aiguille* hypodermique/hypo *m*; shooteuse *f*/poussette *f* 2. *O* **to get/to cop the spike,** se mettre en colère*/prendre la mouche 3. (*hostel for tramps, etc*) = l'Armée du Salut/la soupe pop(ulaire).

spike[2] [spaik] *vtr* 1. *P* (*drugs*) injecter/piquer*/piquouser/shooter 2. *F* **to spike a drink,** ajouter de l'alcool* *ou* une drogue à une boisson non alcoolisée; **to spike coffee with cognac,** corser du café avec du cognac/faire champoreau/faire gloria 3. *F* **to spike s.o.'s guns,** contrarier/contrecarrer qn; **I spiked his guns for him,** je lui ai damé le pion.

spiked [spaikt] *a P* (a) drogué*/

high; défoncé (b) **spiked drink,** boisson droguée/mickey m.

spiky ['spaiki] a F susceptible/
chatouilleux.

spin¹ [spin] n F **1. to be in a flat
spin,** être paniqué/affolé **2. to go
for a spin,** aller se balader (en voiture)/aller faire une virée **3.** station f de taxis **4. to give sth a
spin,** prendre qch à l'essai; **let's
give it a spin!** on tente le coup!
(See **tail-spin**)

spin² [spin] vtr P **1.** fouiller/
vaguer (qn); (prison) faire la
barbote; (house) faire une perquise
2. démolir/bousiller/casser/fra-
casser.

spin-off ['spinɔf] n F **spin-offs,**
produits mpl secondaires; dérivés
mpl.

spit¹ [spit] n **1.** F **spit and polish,**
astiquage m/fourbissage m; **to give
sth a spit and polish,** faire reluire
qch/astiquer qch **2.** P (RS = fag)
spit and drag, cigarette*/cibiche f/
sèche f **3.** P **spit and sawdust,** (bar
m ou restaurant m) sans chichis/
sans fioritures/à la bonne franquette; le troquet du coin/un petit
boui-boui sympa **4.** Austr P **to go
for the big spit/to do a big spit,**
vomir*/dégueuler/gerber/aller au
refil(e). (See **dead I 7**)

spit² [spit] vtr Austr P **1.** avoir
(très) soif/cracher blanc/avoir la
pépie **2.** être en colère*/voir
rouge/être en pétard.

spit out ['spit'aut] vtr F **to spit it
out,** dire/accoucher/vider son sac;
come on, spit it out! allez, déballe!/
accouche!

spiv [spiv] n O F trafiquant m/che-
valier m d'industrie. (See **metal-
spiv**)

spivvy ['spivi] a F louche/parasite.

splash¹ [splæʃ] n F **1. to make a
(big) splash** (a) faire sensation/jeter
du jus (b) = **splash out 2.**
étalage m/déploiement m **3.** jet m

de siphon; **a whisky (and) splash,**
un whisky-soda.

splash² [splæʃ] vtr F **1.** annoncer
en grande manchette **2. to splash
one's money about** = **splash out.**
(See **boot 5**)

splash out ['splæʃ'aut] vtr&i F
dépenser* sans compter/claquer du
fric/jeter son fric par les fenêtres;
faire une folie; **we splashed out on
a bottle of plonk,** on a claqué notre
fric sur une bouteille de pinard/de
gros rouge.

splay [splei] n P (drugs) marijuana*.

splendiferous [splen'difərəs] a O
F splendide/rutilant.

spliced [splaist] a&pp F **to get
spliced,** se marier/s'entifler/se
marida.

spliff [splif] n P (drugs) cigarette*
de marijuana*/stick m/bomb f.

split¹ [split] n **1.** F = **splitter 1
2.** P détective m/condé m **3.** P
part f (de butin)/gratte f **4.** P
allumette f/bûche f **5.** F (a) demi-
bouteille/petite bouteille* d'eau
gazeuse (b) demi-verre m de
liqueur.

split² [split] vi **1.** F (a) vendre la
mèche (b) **to split on s.o.,**
dénoncer*/cafarder/vendre/donner
qn **2.** P partager (bénéfices, butin,
etc)/aller au fade **3.** P partir*/
ficher le camp/mettre les bouts;
come on, let's split! allez, on
change de crémerie! **4.** F **splitting
headache,** mal m de tête de première; **my head is splitting,** j'ai un
super mal au crâne. (See **side 3**)

split-arse ['splitɑis] adv P **to run
split-arse,** courir avec le feu au derrière.

split beaver ['split'birvər] n NAm
V sexe de la femme*/mille-feuille
m/abricot m/barbu m. (See **beaver**)

split out ['split'aut] vi P (a) partir*/ficher le camp (b) s'enfuir*/se
carapater/mettre les bouts.

split tail ['split'teil] n NAm V = **split beaver**.

splitter ['splitər] n F 1. dénonciateur*/cafard m/donneur m/mouchard m 2. mal m de tête de première.

split-up ['splitʌp] n F 1. querelle*/brisure f 2. divorce m/séparation légale.

split up ['split'ʌp] vi F 1. rompre avec qn 2. divorcer/se démaquer.

splodge¹ [splɔdʒ] n F tache f (de couleur, etc).

splodge² [splɔdʒ] vtr F flanquer/asperger.

sploff [splɔf] n P (rare) = **spliff**.

splonk [splɔŋk] n P (horse racing) favori m/increvable m.

splurge¹ [splɜːdʒ] n F esbrouf(f)e f; démonstration bruyante; **to make a splurge = splurge²**.

splurge² [splɜːdʒ] vi F faire de l'esbrouf(f)e f/de l'épate f/de la chique.

spon [spɔn] n P = **spondulic(k)s**.

spondulic(k)s [spɔn'djuːliks] npl P argent*/fric m/oseille f.

sponge¹ [spʌndʒ] n F = **sponger**. (See **throw in**)

sponge² [spʌndʒ] vtr&i F (a) écornifler/écumer les marmites (b) **to sponge a drink**, se faire offrir une tournée; **to sponge on/off s.o.**, vivre aux dépens/aux crochets de qn.

sponger ['spʌndʒər] n F écornifleur m/tapeur m/torpille f/pique-assiette mf.

sponging ['spʌndʒiŋ] n F écorniflage m/tapage m.

spoof¹ [spuːf] n F plaisanterie f/blague f/tour m/canular m.

spoof² [spuːf] vtr&i 1. F dire des bêtises*/sortir des sornettes fpl/débiter des conneries fpl 2. F tromper*/filouter/empiler; **you've been spoofed**, tu t'es fait avoir 3.

F duper*/faire marcher/mener en bateau/mettre en boîte.

spook¹ [spuːk] n 1. F fantôme m/revenant m/apparition f 2. NAm P espion m/agent (secret).

spook² [spuːk] vtr F faire peur* à (qn)/ficher la frousse à (qn).

spooky ['spuːki] a F (a) hanté (b) sinistre/étrange/surnaturel.

spoon [spuːn] vi O F se faire des mamours mpl/des cajoleries fpl.

spooner ['spuːnər] n A F = **spoon(e)y** II.

spoon(e)y ['spuːni] A F I a qui fait des mamours mpl/cajoleur/caressant II n cajoleur m/peloteur m.

sport [spɔːt] n 1. F a (**good**) **sport**, individu* sympa(thique)/bon type/bonne nature; **be a sport!** sois chic! 2. P fille*/petite amie 3. esp Austr ami*/copain m/pote m; **hullo/g'day sport!** salut, mon pote!/salut, vieille branche!

sporting ['spɔːtiŋ] a 1. F qui a bon caractère/d'un bon naturel 2. P **sporting woman**, femme* facile/qui a la cuisse légère; chaude de la pince/Marie-couche-toi-là.

sporty ['spɔːti] a F 1. sportif 2. **the sporty set**, les (bons) viveurs.

spot [spɔt] n 1. F **to be in a spot**, être dans une situation difficile/être dans le pétrin; **he's in a bit of a tight spot**, il est dans une mauvaise passe 2. F **to get into a spot of bother**, avoir des ennuis mpl/être dans de mauvais draps 3. F **to knock spots off s.o.**, exceller sur qn/rendre des points à qn/battre qn à plate(s) couture(s) 4. F **to have a soft spot for s.o./sth**, avoir un faible pour qn/qch 5. P cinq ans mpl de prison*/gerbement m de cinq longes fpl 6. F a **spot**, un (petit) peu*; **a spot of whisky**, un petit coup de whisky/une jectouse de whisky; **how about a spot of lunch?** si on cassait une petite graine?/si on mangeait un petit qch? **7.** *F* **on the spot** (*a*) en danger/sur la corde raide (*b*) mis à tâche (*c*) alerte/vif/éveillé (*d*) immédiatement/sur-le-champ/illico presto **8. to put s.o. on the spot** (*a*) *P* assassiner* qn/descendre qn (*b*) *F* mettre qn dans une situation difficile/handicaper qn **9.** *F* (*TV*) message *m*/spot *m* publicitaire. (*See* **five-spot; highspots; hot 21; Johnny-on-the-spot; nightspot; ten-spot**)

spotlight ['spɔtlait] *vtr F* mettre en vedette/en relief; souligner.

spot-on ['spɔt'ɔn] *a F* dans le mille/qui fait mouche.

spout¹ [spaut] *n P* **1. up the spout,** en gage/chez ma tante **2. up/down the spout,** perdu/raté/fichu/foutu **3. to put a girl up the spout,** rendre une fille enceinte*/mettre une fille en cloque.

spout² [spaut] *vi F* dégoiser/déblatérer/débiter.

spread¹ [spred] *n F* **1.** repas copieux/gueuleton *m*/balthazar *m* **2. middle-age(d) spread,** l'embonpoint *m* de la maturité/pneu *m* Michelin de la quarantaine.

spread² [spred] *vtr P* violer (qn)/passer (qn) à la casserole.

spring [spriŋ] *vtr* **1.** *P* faire libérer (qn) de prison*/cautionner **2.** *P* faire échapper (qn) de prison*/faire larguer (qn) **3.** *F* annoncer à l'improviste/révéler à brûle-pourpoint; **to spring sth on s.o.,** prendre qn au dépourvu avec qch **4.** *F* **where did you spring from?** d'où sortez-vous? (*See* **leak¹ 1**)

sprog [sprɔg] *n P* **1.** recrue *f*/conscrit *m*/bleu *m* **2.** enfant*/mioche *mf*/moutard *m*.

sprout [spraut] *vtr F* **to sprout wings** (*a*) faire une bonne action/se faire pousser des ailes (*b*) mourir*/aller au paradis.

spruik ['spruːik] *vi Austr P* (*street traders, etc*) faire l'article/faire du baratin/faire la postiche.

spruiker ['spruːikər] *n Austr P* **1.** (*street trader*) batouseur *m* **2.** (*talkative person*) baratineur *m*/jaspineux *m*/jacteur *m*.

sprung [sprʌŋ] *a esp NAm F* ivre*/raide/rondibé. (*See* **half-sprung**)

spud [spʌd] *n F* pomme *f* de terre/patate *f*.

spud-basher ['spʌdbæʃər] *n F* (*mil*) éplucheur *m* de pommes de terre.

spud-bashing ['spʌdbæʃiŋ] *n F* (*mil*) corvée *f* de patates/pluches *fpl*.

spug [spʌg], **spuggy** ['spʌgi] *n F* moineau *m*/piaf *m*.

spunk [spʌŋk] *n* **1.** *V* sperme*/jus *m* **2.** *P* courage *m*/cran *m*/estomac *m*; **he's got no spunk,** il n'a pas de couilles/il n'a rien dans le ventre **3.** *P* **to put fresh spunk into sth,** ravigoter qch **4.** *NAm P* colère *f*/emportement *m*/coup *m* de raisin.

spunkless ['spʌŋklis] *a P* **1.** amorphe/larveux **2.** poltron/froussard/sans couilles.

spunky ['spʌŋki] *a F* courageux*/qui en a dans le bide/dans le ventre; qui a quelque chose dans la culotte.

spur [spəːr] *vtr Austr A F* contre-carrer/mettre des bâtons dans les roues de (qn).

squad-car ['skwɔdkaːr] *n F* car* de police/porte-poulaille *m*/poulailler *m*.

squaddie, squaddy ['skwɔdi] *n F* (*mil*) (*a*) recrue *f*/conscrit *m* de l'escouade/bleu *m*/blaireau *m* (*b*) soldat*/bidasse *m*.

square¹ [skweər] **I** *a* **1.** *F* **a square deal,** une affaire* honnête/un coup réglo **2.** *F* **a square meal,** un bon repas **3.** *F* **to be all square,** être quitte/être à égalité/être réglo **4.** *F* (*a*) vieux jeu/croulant/périmé (*b*) honnête/régulier/

régul/réglo **5.** *P* sexuellement normal. (*See* **straight I 2**) **6.** *F* **to get square with s.o.** (*a*) se venger de qn (*b*) être quitte envers qn **7.** *F* **to be a square peg in a round hole,** être inapte à qch. (*See* **faire¹ 2**) **II** *n F* **1. to be back to square one,** repartir à zéro/revenir à la case départ **2.** (*a*) bourgeois démodé/croulant *m*; **he's a square,** il est tout à fait vieux jeu (*b*) individu* honnête/réglo **3. on the square,** droit/honnête/comme il faut.

square² [skwɛər] *vtr F* (*a*) suborner/soudoyer/acheter/graisser la patte à (qn) (*b*) obtenir la complicité de (qn); **I've squared it with the boss,** j'ai arrangé ça avec le patron; **it won't be difficult to square things with him,** je l'ai dans la manche. (*See* **rap¹ 2**)

square-bash ['skwɛəbæʃ] *vi F* faire l'exercice *m* (militaire).

square-basher ['skwɛəbæʃər] *n F* soldat* à l'exercice.

square-bashing ['skwɛəbæʃiŋ] *n F* exercices *mpl*/manœuvres *fpl* militaires; l'exercice *m*.

squarehead ['skwɛəhed] *n P* **1.** Allemand*/boche *m* **2.** *Austr* criminel *m* en liberté.

square off ['skwɛərˈɔf] *vi Austr P* se tirer d'un mauvais pas.

squaresville ['skwɛəzvil] *n P* société conformiste et bourgeoise.

square up ['skwɛərˈʌp] *vi F* **1.** être prêt à se battre/se mettre en quarante **2. to square up to the facts,** faire face à la réalité/regarder les choses en face **3.** régler une affaire avec qn.

square-wheeler ['skwɛəˈ(h)wiːlər] *n P* voiture *f* difficile à vendre/rossignol *m*. (*See* **bottler**; **palm-tree**)

squarie ['skwɛəri] *n Austr P* = **squarehead 2.** (*See* **half-squarie**)

squawk¹ [skwɔːk] *n P* **1.** appel *m* d'une condamnation/rappel *m* **2.** plainte *f*/réclamation *f*.

squawk² [skwɔːk] *vi P* **1.** faire des aveux *mpl* (à la police)/se mettre à table **2.** se plaindre/rouspéter/ronchonner/rouscailler/renauder.

squawker ['skwɔːkər] *n P* rouspéteur *m*/ronchonneur *m*.

squeak¹ [skwiːk] *n* **1.** *P* = **squeal¹ 2.** *P* = **squealer 1, 3 3.** *F* **to have a narrow squeak,** l'échapper belle/revenir de loin **4.** *F* **I don't want to hear another squeak out of you,** je ne veux pas entendre le moindre murmure (de ta part)/je ne veux plus t'entendre. (*See* **bubble-and-squeak**; **pip-squeak**)

squeak² [skwiːk] *vi P* = **squeal² 1, 2.**

squeaker ['skwiːkər] *n P* **1.** = **squealer 1, 3 2.** résultat serré/aboutissement *m* à un fil.

squeal¹ [skwiːl] *n P* plainte *f* (à la police); **to put the squeal in,** moutonner/cafarder.

squeal² [skwiːl] *vi P* **1.** avouer*/manger le morceau/accoucher/vider son sac **2.** moucharder/vendre la mèche; **to squeal on s.o.,** dénoncer*/balancer/cafarder/donner qn.

squealer ['skwiːlər] *n P* **1.** dénonciateur*/cafardeur *m*/mouton *m*/donneur *m* **2.** (*not common*) voiture-radio *f* de la police **3.** rouspéteur *m*/ronchonneur *m*.

squeeze¹ [skwiːz] *n* **1.** *F* **to put the squeeze on s.o.,** forcer la main à qn **2.** *F* (*a*) **tight squeeze,** presse *f*/cohue *f* (*b*) **it was a tight squeeze,** on tenait tout juste **3.** *P* empreinte *f* d'une clef*/douce *f* **4.** *P* **main squeeze,** épouse*/légitime *f* **5.** *P* soie *f*.

squeeze² [skwiːz] *vtr F* **to squeeze s.o.** = **to put the squeeze on s.o.** (**squeeze¹ 1**). (*See* **lemon 5**)

squeezebox ['skwiːzbɔks] *n F* **1.** concertina *f* **2.** accordéon *m*.

squelch[1] [skweltʃ] *n* F = **squelcher**.

squelch[2] [skweltʃ] *vtr* F faire taire* (qn)/river le clou à (qn).

squelcher ['skweltʃər] *n* F réplique cinglante/riposte *f* qui vous rive le clou.

squiffy ['skwifi] F **1.** légèrement ivre*/paf **2.** de travers/biscornu/ tordu **3.** bête*/nigaud.

squint[1] [skwint] *n* P coup d'œil*/ coup de châsse; **let's have a squint at it!** fais voir! **take a squint at that!** zyeute-moi ça!/vise-moi ça!

squint[2] [skwint] *vi* P (*a*) regarder*/ jeter un coup d'œil* (*b*) **to squint at sth,** regarder* qch de côté/furtive- ment; zyeuter/mater qch.

squirt [skwəit] *n* P **1.** (*a*) freluquet *m*/merdaillon *m*; **little squirt!** petit morveux! (*b*) rapiat *m*/rat *m* **2.** rafale *f* de mitraillette/purée *f* **3.** **to have a squirt,** uriner*/lance- quiner.

squirter [skwəitər] *n* P revolver*/ flingue *m*/calibre *m*/pétard *m*.

squish [skwiʃ] *n* **1.** F boue *f*/ bouillabaisse *f*/pulpe *f*/gadoue *f* **2.** P marmelade *f* d'orange.

squishy ['skwiʃi] *a* F détrempé/ pulpeux/bourbeux/gadouilleux.

squit [skwit] *n* P **1.** = **squirt 1** (*a*), (*b*) **2.** (*a*) camelote *f*/saleté *f* (*b*) bêtises*/conneries *fpl*/balivernes *fpl* **3.** *pl* diarrhée*/courante *f*.

squitters ['skwitəz] *npl* P **1.** diar- rhée*/courante *f*/chiasse *f* **2. to have the squitters,** avoir peur*/avoir les foies *mpl*/avoir les jetons *mpl*.

squitty ['skwiti] *a* P connard/ loqudu.

stab [stæb] *n* F **to have a stab (at sth),** faire un essai/tenter le coup.

stable-companion ['steibl- kəm'pænjən] *n* F membre *m* d'une même société, bande*, etc.

stack [stæk] *n* **1.** F (*a*) **to have a stack/stacks of money,** être très riche*/être cousu d'or/avoir le sac (*b*) **to have a stack/stacks of work,** avoir beaucoup de travail*/avoir du pain sur la planche **2.** *P* **to blow one's stack** = **to blow one's top** (**top**[1] 2) **3.** F (*aut*) **twin stacks,** double tuyau *m* d'échappement **4.** P quantité *f ou* lot *m* de cigarettes*/ de marijuana*.

stacked [stækt] *a* P = **well- stacked 1, 2**.

stag [stæg] *n* F **1.** célibataire *m*/ vieux garçon; **stag party,** réunion *f ou* sortie *f* entre hommes (*esp* la veille au soir d'un mariage) **2.** (*Stock Exchange*) loup *m*.

stager ['steidʒər] *n* F **an old stager,** un vieux routier/un vieux de la vieille.

staggers ['stægəz] *npl* F **to have the staggers,** chanceler/tituber/être zigzag.

stakeout ['steikaut] *n* P **1.** lieu sûr/planque *f*/cachette *f*/plan- quouse **2.** maison de criminel, etc, surveillée/embusquée par la police.

stake out ['steik'aut] *vtr* P surveil- ler/embusquer/faire la planque.

stalk [stɔik] *n* P pénis*/queue *f*.

stall [stɔil] *n* P complice *m* d'un pickpocket/cheville *f*.

stallion ['stæljən] *n* F = **stud 1**.

stamping ground ['stæmpiŋ- graund] *n* F lieu *m* que l'on fré- quente/coin favori; **that's my old stamping ground,** c'est ici que j'ai usé mes fonds de culotte/c'est mon terrain de chasse/j'ai mes racines dans le coin.

stand[1] [stænd] *n* **1.** F (*jazz, rock, etc*) (**one-night**) **stand,** représenta- tion *f* d'un soir. (*See* **one-nighter**) **2.** P **to have a stand,** être en érec- tion*/avoir le bambou **3.** *NAm* F barre *f* (de témoins).

stand[2] [stænd] *vtr* F **1. to stand s.o. a drink,** offrir un verre/une tournée à qn; **I'm standing this one,** c'est ma tournée/c'est moi qui paie

2. = **stick²** **8.** (*See* **gaff 4**; **racket 3**)

standover ['stændouvər] *n Austr P*
1. standover man, garde *m* du corps/gorille *m*/dur *m*/balèze *m* **2. standover merchant,** extorqueur *m*/racketteur *m*.

stand over ['stænd'ouvər] *vtr&i Austr F* **1.** manier rudement/mener à la baguette/être vache avec (qn) **2.** extorquer de l'argent/faire cracher/faire casquer/mettre qn à l'amende.

stand up ['stænd'ʌp] *vtr F* **1.** faire attendre* (qn)/faire poireauter (qn) **2.** lâcher (qn)/planter là/poser un lapin à (qn) **3.** tromper*/rouler/refaire (qn) **4. to take it standing up,** ne pas broncher/encaisser le coup.

star [stɑːr] *n F* **1. to see stars,** voir trente-six chandelles **2. there's a star in the east,** ta braguette est déboutonnée; on voit le moteur.

stardust ['stɑːdʌst] *n* **1.** *F* illusion *f*/vision *f* **2.** *P* = **snow¹ 1.**

stare [stɛər] *vtr&i F* **it's staring you in the face,** ça vous saute aux yeux/ça se voit comme le nez au milieu de la figure.

starkers ['stɑːkəz] *a P* **starkers**/*O* **Harry starkers,** tout nu*/à poil/à loilpé/cul nul/défrusqué.

starry-eyed ['stɑːri'aid] *a F* idéaliste/inexpérimenté/ingénu/songe-creux.

stash¹ [stæʃ] *n P* (*drugs*) **1.** cachette *f*/lieu sûr/carre *f*/planque *f*; **stash man,** homme* de carre/carreur *m* (pour des marchandises volées, des drogues, etc) **2.** provision *f* (de drogues)/sac *m*.

stash² [stæʃ] *vtr P* **1.** cacher*/planquer/planquouser **2.** arrêter/finir/finocher; **stash it!** arrête!

stash away ['stæʃə'wei] *vtr P* **1.** = **stash²** **1 2.** accumuler/amasser/entasser (de l'argent, etc).

stashed [stæʃt] *a F* (**well**) **stashed,** riche*/plein aux as/galetteux/rupin.

state [steit] *n F* **to be in a (bit of a) state,** être dans tous ses états; **to get into a terrible state** (*a*) se mettre dans tous ses états (*b*) se trouver dans un état lamentable.

statistics [stə'tistiks] *npl F* **vital statistics,** les trois mesures essentielles de la femme (poitrine, taille, hanches)/(beau) châssis/(belle) mécanique.

stay [stei] *vi P* (*maintain an erection*) garder la trique en l'air/rester au garde-à-vous/marquer midi.

steady ['stedi] *F* **I** *adv* **to go steady,** se fréquenter/sortir ensemble **II** *n* petit(e) ami(e)/l'attitré(e)/-ière.

steam [stiːm] *n F* **1. to let/to blow off steam** (*a*) dépenser son superflu d'énergie (*b*) épancher sa bile **2. to get up steam** (*a*) rassembler son énergie/se mettre sous pression (*b*) s'exciter/s'emballer/péter le feu **3. steam radio,** la TSF des familles/la vieille radio/la radio de papa.

steamed up ['stiːmd'ʌp] *a&pp F* **to get (all) steamed up** (*a*) = **to get up steam** (**steam 2** (*b*)) (*b*) se mettre en colère*/mousser/se mettre en pétard.

steamer ['stiːmər] *n P* **1.** (*from: RS* = *steam jug* = *mug*) individu bête*/con *m*/couillon *m* **2.** homosexuel*/pédé *m.*

steaming ['stiːmiŋ] *a F* **1.** *F* a **steaming idiot/twit,** un crétin/un couillon achevé/fini **2.** *P* **to be steaming,** être ivre*/avoir un coup dans l'aile/être chargé.

steep [stiːp] *a F* **1.** trop cher*/exorbitant/excessif/salé **2.** abusif/incroyable; **that's a bit steep!** c'est un peu fort de café!/c'est la fin des haricots!

steer¹ [stiər] *n NAm* **1.** *F* renseignement*/tuyau *m.* (*See* **bum¹ I**) **2.** *P* = **steerer.**

steer² [stiər] *vi P* amorcer les clients (pour tripot, casino, etc).

steerer ['stiərər] *n P* rabatteur *m*/racoleur *m* de clients (pour bordels, etc).

stem [stem] *n P* pipe *f* à opium/chilom *m*.

step¹ [step] *n* 1. *P* up the steps, renvoyé aux Assises/devant le comptoir 2. *F* all the steps: *see* **bingo 39**. (*See* **doorstep**)

step² [step] *vi F* 1. to step outside, sortir pour se battre* 2. (*aut*) to step on it, accélérer/appuyer sur le champignon. (*See* **gas¹ II 2**)

step in ['step'in] *vi F* intervenir; s'interposer.

step-up ['stepʌp] *n F* promotion *f*/avancement *m*.

step up ['step'ʌp] *vtr F* 1. to step up the pace, accélérer le pas/allonger la sauce 2. avoir une promotion/monter d'un échelon.

stern [stəːn] *n F* fesses*/postérieur *m*/arrière-train *m*.

stew¹ [stjuː] *n* 1. *F* in a stew (*i*) sur des charbons ardents/sur le gril/dans tous ses états (*ii*) *NAm* en colère*/à cran; to work oneself (up) into a stew, se mettre en colère/en rogne 2. *Austr P* = **jacky** 3. *P* bordel*/claque *m*/baisodrome *m*/maison close.

stew² [stjuː] *vi F* to stew in one's own juice, cuire/mijoter dans son jus.

stewed [stjuːd] *a P* ivre*/rétamé. (*See* **gills 1**; **half-stewed**)

stick¹ [stik] *n* 1. *F* to give s.o. stick, réprimander* qn/engueuler qn/sonner les cloches à qn; to take a lot of stick, être pilonné/recevoir une dégelée 2. *F* to wave the big stick, faire les gros yeux (à qn)/mener (qn) à la trique 3. *F* over the sticks, steeplechases *mpl*/course *f* d'obstacles 4. *F* the sticks (*a*) la campagne*/le bled/la cambrousse (*b*) la banlieue 5. *P* (*drugs*) stick (of tea), cigarette* de marijuana*/stick *m*/bomb *f*. (*See* **cancer-stick**) 6. *P* pince-monseigneur*/jacques *m* 7. *V* pénis* en érection*/canne *f*/trique *f* 8. *F* (*a*) a queer stick, un drôle de type/de zigoto/de zèbre (*b*) old stick, père tartempion; he's a good old stick, c'est un brave zigue. (*See* **drumstick**; **end 11**; **fiddlestick**; **hype-stick**; **joystick**; **kick-stick**; **knobstick**; **shitstick**; **up² 1**)

stick² [stik] *vtr* 1. *F* mettre/placer/coller; stick it in your pocket, fourre-toi ça dans la poche 2. *F* to stick at sth, persévérer/s'accrocher à qch 3. *P* you know where you can stick that, tu sais où tu peux te le mettre!/tu peux te le mettre (là) où je pense! stick it! va te faire enculer!/et mon cul c'est du poulet! (*See* **arse I 7**; **flue 2**; **gonga**; **jumper 1**; **Khyber**) 4. *F* to get stuck with s.o., avoir qn de collé à soi/avoir qn sur le dos 5. *F* to be stuck on s.o., être amoureux de qn/en pincer pour qn/être entiché de qn 6. *F* to stick with s.o., se cramponner à qn/soutenir qn 7. *F* to make sth stick, faire obéir (un ordre, etc) 8. *F* supporter/endurer/tenir; I can't stick him (at any price), je ne peux pas le sentir/le blairer 9. *F* to stick to sth, garder qch pour soi 10. *P* to stick one on s.o., battre* qn/fosser qn/passer une peignée à qn. (*See* **bill 3**; **gun¹ 4**)

stick around ['stikə'raund] *vi F* attendre* sur place/poireauter; to stick around the house all day, traîner dans la maison toute la journée; stick around! I'll be back in five minutes, bouge pas! je reviens dans cinq minutes.

stick down ['stik'daun] *vtr F* 1. stick it down anywhere, collez-le n'importe où. (*See* **stick² 1**) 2. to stick sth down in a notebook, inscrire qch sur un carnet.

sticker ['stikər] *n F* **1.** article *m* invendable/rossignol *m* **2.** travailleur* appliqué/bûcheur *m* **3.** problème *m* difficile/colle *f*/casse-tête *m* **4.** (*pers*) crampon *m*/pot *m* de colle.

stick in ['stik'in] *vtr&i* **1.** *F* to get stuck in, se cramponner/se maintenir **2.** *V* to stick it in, faire l'amour*/casser la canne/se baguer le nœud.

stick-in-the-mud ['stikinðəmʌd] **I** *a F* conservateur/immobiliste/casanier **II** *n F* vieux croûton/vieille perruque.

stick out ['stik'aut] *vi F* **1.** to stick out for higher wages, demander avec insistance une augmentation de salaire **2.** to stick it out, tenir jusqu'au bout **3.** she sticks out in all the right places, elle est bien carrossée/c'est une belle mécanique/c'est un beau numéro/elle a ce qu'il faut. (*See* neck¹ 3; thumb 4)

stick-up ['stikʌp] *n F* vol *m* à main armée/braquage *m*/hold-up *m*.

stick up ['stik'ʌp] *vtr F* **1.** attaquer* *ou* voler à main armée/braquer; **stick 'em up!** haut les mains! **2.** to stick up for s.o., prendre la défense/le parti de qn.

sticky ['stiki] *a F* **1.** peu accommodant/difficile **2.** mauvais*/tocard/désagréable **3.** to have sticky fingers, voler* avoir facilité/chiper/avoir de la poix aux mains/ne rien laisser traîner. (*See* sticky-fingered) **4.** to bat/to be on a sticky wicket, agir lorsqu'il y a peu de chance de réussir/marcher sur un terrain glissant; être dans le pétrin/être dans de mauvais draps.

stickybeak ['stikibiːk] *n Austr F* curieux *m*/fouinard *m*/fouineur *m*; fouille-merde *m*.

sticky-fingered ['stiki'fiŋgəd] *a F* qui a les doigts crochus. (*See* sticky 3)

stiff [stif] **I** *a* **1.** *P* mort/raide **2.** *P* ivre*/raide **3.** *F* that's a bit stiff! c'est un peu raide! (*See* lip 2) **II** *adv F* **1.** to bore s.o. stiff, scier (le dos à) qn/taper sur le système à qn **2.** to be scared stiff, avoir une peur* bleue **III** *n P* **1.** cadavre*/macchabé(e) *m*/refroidi *m* **2.** ivrogne*/poivrot *m* **3.** working stiffs, travailleurs*/ouvriers*/salariés *mpl* **4.** lettre de prisonnier passée en fraude **5.** cheval* certain de perdre/fer *m* à repasser/mort *m* **6.** *NAm* clochard*/clodot *m*. (*See* big I 9; bindle 3)

stiffener ['stif(ə)nər] *n F* boisson alcoolisée/apéritif *m*/remontant *m*.

stiffneck ['stifnek] *n F* individu* entiché de sa personne.

stiffy ['stifi] *n P* (pénis* en) érection*/canne *f*/trique *f*.

stilts [stilts] *npl P* jambes*/pinceaux *mpl*/béquilles *fpl*.

sting¹ [stiŋ] *n P* entourloupe *f*/arnaque *f*.

sting² [stiŋ] *vtr F* to sting s.o. for sth, faire payer qch à qn à un prix exorbitant; to be/to get stung, attraper/essuyer le coup de fusil; faire écorcher/estamper/arnaquer; he stung me for a quid, il m'a tapé/torpillé d'une livre.

stinger ['stiŋər] *n F* **1.** coup* cinglant/coup raide/torgnole *f* **2.** (*a*) méduse *f* (*b*) torpille *f*.

stink¹ [stiŋk] *n* **1.** *P* to raise/to kick up a stink, faire de l'esclandre *m*/rouspéter; there's going to be a hell of a stink, il va y avoir du grabuge/ça va chauffer/ça va chier; a big stink (*i*) chahut *m*/ramdam *m* (*ii*) scandale *m* **2.** *P* to work like stink, travailler* dur/bûcher/se fouler la rate/bosser comme une bête.

stink² [stiŋk] *vi* **1.** *P* être un vrai salaud*; he (positively) stinks! c'est un type infect! **2.** *F* être puant/infect; schlinguer **3.** *F* sembler louche/ne pas avoir l'air très catholique/sentir mauvais; **it stinks (to high heaven)!** ça schlingue!/ça fouette!

stinkador ['stiŋkədɔɪr], **stinkaduro** ['stiŋkə'd(j)uɪrou] *n P* (*cigar*) crapulos *m*.

stinkaroo ['stiŋkə'ruɪ] *n esp NAm P* article *m* de mauvaise qualité/ peau *f* de zèbre.

stink-bomb ['stiŋkbɔm] *n F* boule puante.

stinker ['stiŋkər] *n F* **1.** individu* méprisable/sale type *m* **2.** individu* qui sent* mauvais/qui pue **3. to write s.o. a stinker** (*a*) écrire une verte réprimande à qn (*b*) écrire une lettre carabinée à qn **4.** rhume carabiné **5. the English paper was a stinker,** on a eu une sale/rosse composition d'anglais **6.** cigare* *ou* cigarette* bon marché **7.** (*sport*) **to play a stinker,** jouer comme un pied **8.** camelote *f*/ navet *m*/toc *m* **9.** *Austr* = **scorcher 1**.

stinking ['stiŋkiŋ] *a* **1.** *F* **stinking (rich)/stinking with money,** très riche*/plein aux as **2.** *P* ivre*/ blindé **3.** *F* puant/nauséabond/ infect **4.** *F* **stinking weather,** temps *m* de cochon/de chien; **a stinking cold,** un sale rhume.

stink-list ['stiŋklist] *n P* **to have s.o. on one's stink-list,** avoir qn dans le nez/ne pas pouvoir blairer qn. (*See* **shit-list**)

stinko ['stiŋkou] *a P* = **stinking 2**.

stinkpot ['stiŋkpɔt] *n P* saligaud *m*/salopard *m*.

stir¹ [stəɪr] *n P* prison*/bloc *m*/ taule *f*; **in stir,** en prison/à l'ombre; **stir crazy,** fou* à force d'être en taule.

stir² [stəɪr] *vtr F* **to stir it** = **to stir it up** (**stir up**). (*See* **stumps**)

stirrer ['stəɪrər] *n F* agitateur *m*/ fomenteur *m* de difficultés/mauvais coucheur/fouteur *m* de merde.

stir up ['stəɪ'rʌp] *vtr F* **to stir it up,**

fomenter la dissension/remuer les eaux troubles/mettre sa merde (quelque part)/semer la merde.

stitch up ['stitʃʌp] *vtr P* farguer (qn)/monter un coup contre (qn)/ faire porter le chapeau (à qn).

stodge¹ [stɔdʒ] *n F* **1.** aliment bourratif/étouffe-chrétien *m* **2.** qch de difficile à retenir/de dur à digérer.

stodge² [stɔdʒ] *vi F* manger* abondamment/se goinfrer/se caler les joues *fpl*/s'empiffrer.

stoke up ['stouk'ʌp] *vi F* manger* de bon cœur/bouffer.

stomach ['stʌmək] *vtr F* endurer/ supporter/tolérer/digérer; **I can't stomach that guy,** je (ne) peux pas le gober, ce mec/il me fait gerber, ce mec.

stone-cold ['stoun'kould] *adv F* **I've got him stone-cold,** je le tiens (à ma merci)/il me mange dans la main. (*See* **cold I 1**)

stoned [stound] *a P* (*a*) ivre*/raide (*b*) drogué*/camé/chargé.

stones [stounz] *npl P* **1.** testicules*/burettes *fpl*/roubignolles *fpl* **2.** bijoux *mpl*/cailloux *mpl*/joncaille *f*.

stone's throw ['stounzθrou] *n F* **just a stone's throw from here,** à deux pas d'ici.

stonewall ['stoun'wɔl] *vi F* donner des réponses évasives; faire de l'obstruction/répondre à côté; faire la politique de l'escargot.

stonkered ['stɔŋkəd] *a Austr P* **1.** fatigué/claqué/crevé **2.** fini/foutu; **I'm stonkered,** je suis cuit/foutu/ naze; c'est râpé pour moi.

stony ['stouni] *a F* **stony (broke),** archi-pauvre*/à sec/dans la dèche/ fauché comme les blés.

stooge¹ [stuɪdʒ] *n* (*esp pej*) **1.** *F* délégué *m*/remplaçant *m*/nègre *m* **2.** *F* individu* trop serviable/ ramasse-boulot *m* **3.** *F* (*theatre*) comparse *m*/faire-valoir *m* **4.** *P* indicateur*/bourdille *m*.

stooge² [stuːdʒ] *vi F* **1.** faire le nègre **2.** servir de comparse *m*/de faire-valoir *m* (à un acteur).

stooge about, around ['stuːdʒə'baut, -ə'raund] *vi P* **1.** faire un tour/flâner **2.** bricoler.

stoolie ['stuːli], **stool-pigeon** ['stuːlpidʒin] *n F* (*a*) indicateur*/indic *m*/mouchard *m* (*b*) compère *m* (d'un escroc).

stop [stɔp] *n P* receleur *m*/fargue *m*. (*See* **pull out 3**)

stop by ['stɔp'bai] *vtr F* rendre visite (à qn)/entrer en passant/passer chez qn/faire un saut chez qn.

stop-off ['stɔpɔf] *n F* étape *f*/(point *m* d')arrêt *m*/halte *f*.

stop off ['stɔp'ɔf] *vi F* faire une halte/un arrêt; **to stop off in London,** faire étape à Londres.

stopover ['stɔpouvər] *n F* arrêt *m* (au cours d'un voyage).

stop over ['stɔp'ouvər] *vi F* interrompre son voyage/s'arrêter/faire étape.

stopper ['stɔpər] *n F* **1. to put the stopper on sth,** mettre fin à qch **2.** (*boxing*) coup* knock-out/KO *m*.

stoppo ['stɔpou] *n P* **to take stoppo,** s'en aller*/se casser/mettre les bouts/chier du poivre.

stork [stɔːk] *n F* **a visit from the stork,** l'arrivée *f* d'un bébé/une visite de la cigogne.

story ['stɔːri] *n F* mensonge*/conte *m*; **to tell stories,** mentir*/raconter des blagues *fpl*. (*See* **sob-story; tall I 2**)

storyteller ['stɔːritelər] *n F* menteur *m*/batteur *m*/chiqueur *m*.

stoush¹ [stauʃ] *n Austr P* bagarre *f*/castagne *f*/rififi *m*/baston *m*.

stoush² [stauʃ] *vtr Austr P* battre* (qn)/casser la gueule à (qn)/arranger le portrait à (qn).

stove [stouv] *n P* (*aut*) chauffage *m*.

stove-pipe ['stouvpaip] *n* **1.** *A F* chapeau* haut de forme/tuyau *m* de poêle/huit-reflets *m* **2.** *NAm P* avion *m* de chasse à réaction.

stow [stou] *vtr P* **stow it!** c'est marre!/y en a marre!/ferme ça!/arrête ton char!

strafe [strɑːf] *vtr F* réprimander*/passer un savon à (qn)/engueuler (qn).

strafing ['strɑːfiŋ] *n F* réprimande *f*/verte semonce/engueulade *f*.

straight [streit] **I** *a* **1.** *F* (cigarettes, tabac) ordinaire (sans narcotiques); (*alcoholic drink*) sec/sans eau **2.** *P* (sexuellement) normal/hétéro **3.** *P* qui ne se drogue pas **4.** *F* **straight man = stooge¹ 3**. (*See* **ticket 3**) **II** *adv* **to go straight** (*a*) *F* marcher droit/suivre le droit chemin (*b*) *P* se désintoxiquer (de drogues)/se décamer/lâcher la guenon (*c*) *P* cesser d'être homosexuel. (*See* **horse¹ 2; shoulder 2; straight up**) **III** *n F* **1. to act on the straight,** agir loyalement **2. to follow the straight/to go on the straight and narrow,** se conduire honnêtement; marcher droit.

straighten ['streit(ə)n] *vtr P* soudoyer/acheter/graisser la patte à (qn).

straightened out ['streitnd'aut] *a P* véreux. (*See* **bent**)

straightener [streit(ə)nər] *n P* pot-de-vin *m*/dessous *m* de table/enveloppe *f*/graissage *m* de patte.

straighten out ['streit(ə)n'aut] *vtr* **1.** *P* **to straighten s.o. out = to put s.o. wise (wise 2)** **2.** *F* **to** straighten things out, arranger les choses; **I expect that things will straighten out,** je pense que ça va s'arranger.

straight up ['streit'ʌp] *a F* honnête/régulier/réglo; **straight up!** c'est du vrai!/sans blague!

strain [strein] *n O P* **to have a strain,** uriner*/lancequiner; **to go for a strain,** aller quelque part.

strap [stræp] *n P* **on the strap,** à crédit/à croum(e)/à l'œil. (*See* **jock-strap**)

strap-hanger ['stræphæŋər] *n F* voyageur *m* debout (dans le métro, le train, etc).

straw [strɔː] *n F* **1. that's the last straw,** c'est le coup de grâce!/c'est le comble!/c'est la fin des haricots!/il ne manquait plus que cela! **2.** (*catchphrase*) **it's the last straw that breaks the camel's back,** c'est la dernière goutte (d'eau) qui fait déborder le vase.

stray [strei] *n P* **to have a bit/piece of stray** = to have a bit on the side (**side 2**).

streak¹ [striːk] *n F* **1. a losing streak,** une série de malchance*/série noire aux jeux; **a winning streak,** une série de chance* **2.** promenade *f* tout nu*/à poil en public. (*See* **piss¹ 3; yellow 1**)

streak² [striːk] *vi F* se promener *ou* courir tout nu*/à poil en public.

streak (along) ['striːk(əˈlɔŋ)] *vi F* aller à toute vitesse/gazer.

streaker ['striːkər] *n F* qn qui se promène/se balade tout nu* en public; nudiste galopant(e)/streaker *mf*.

street [striːt] *n F* **1. to be streets ahead of s.o.,** avoir plusieurs rames d'avance sur qn **2. it's right up your street,** cela te connaît/c'est ton rayon/c'est ton truc. (*See* **alley 1**) **3. the horse won by a street,** le cheval a gagné dans un fauteuil **4. it's not in the same street,** ce n'est pas du même acabit/du même tonneau **5. to be on the streets,** racoler*/faire le trottoir. (*See* **easy I 1; sunny 1**)

stretch¹ [stretʃ] *n P* **to do a stretch,** faire de la prison*/faire une longe/être à l'ombre/être au ballon; **he was given a stretch,** on

l'a mis au trou; **to get a twenty year stretch,** tirer vingt longes. (*See* **homestretch**)

stretch² [stretʃ] *vtr* **1.** *F* **that's stretching it a bit,** c'est un peu tiré par les cheveux **2.** *P* être pendu/béquillé.

strewth! [struːθ] *excl P* (*abbr* = *God's truth*) sacrebleu!/saprisiti!/mince (alors)!

strides [straidz] *npl P* pantalon*/falzar(d) *m*/grimpant *m*/futal *m*.

strike [straik] *vtr F* **1. strike a light!** morbleu! **strike me pink!** tu m'assois! **2. to get struck on s.o.,** aimer* qn/s'enticher de qn/en pincer pour qn/être dingue de qn. (*See* **cunt-struck; heap 1; rich II**)

Strine [strain] *n F* la langue australienne.

string [striŋ] *n F* **1. to have s.o. on a (piece of) string,** mener qn par le bout du nez **2. no strings attached,** sans obligations/sans à-côtés/sans os **3. to pull (the) strings,** faire jouer le piston. (*See* **apron-strings; G-string; shoestring**)

string along ['striŋəˈlɔŋ] *vtr&i F* **1.** tenir (qn) en suspens/mener (qn) en bateau **2. to string along (with s.o.),** filer le train à qn.

string-bean ['striŋˈbiːn] *n NAm F* = **bean-pole**.

string out ['striŋˈaut] *vtr&i* **1.** *F* faire durer (qch) **2.** *P* (*drugs*) (*a*) être drogué*/camé/chargé; **to be strung out,** être défoncé (*b*) être en manque*/être cold turkey/être crevard.

string up ['striŋˈʌp] *vtr F* pendre (un condamné). (*See* **strung up**)

strip¹ [strip] *n F* **1. to tear s.o. off a strip,** réprimander* qn/passer un rude savon à qn/sonner les cloches à qn **2. strip show,** spectacle *m* de nus/striptease *m*; **strip poker,** poker *m* de déshabillage/strip-poker *m*.

strip² [strip] vtr F (mil) faire perdre ses galons mpl/dégrader/faire passer chez le dernier tailleur.

strip off ['strip'ɔf] vi F se déshabiller*/se mettre à poil/se désaper.

stripper ['stripər] n F stripteaseuse f/effeuilleuse f.

stroke [strouk] n P sale coup/coup m (en) vache/coup en traître; **to pull a stroke,** faire une vacherie/un coup en vache.

strong-arm¹ ['strɔŋaɪm] a attrib F **strong-arm man** (i) homme fort/fortiche m/balèze m (ii) battant m/dur m; **strong-arm tactics,** manœuvres fpl à la matraque/la politique du gros bâton.

strong-arm² ['strɔŋaɪm] vtr F manier rudement/mener à la baguette/mener à la trique.

stroppy ['strɔpi] a P de mauvaise humeur/à cran/de mauvais poil; **don't get stroppy with me!** ne la ramène pas avec moi!

struck [strʌk] a&pp F **to be struck on sth,** être frappé/impressionné par qch; **to be struck on s.o.,** être toqué de qn; **I'm not all that struck on it,** ça ne me dit pas grand chose. (See **strike**)

strung up ['strʌŋ'ʌp] a&pp **1.** F **to be strung up,** être pendu/béquillé. (See **string up**) **2.** F **to be (all) strung up,** être tendu/énervé **3.** P malade par le manque de drogues; en manque*/cold-turkey/crevard.

struth! [struɪθ] excl P = **strewth!**

stubby ['stʌbi] n Austr P petite bouteille de bière/cannette f.

stuck [stʌk] **I** a F en panne/en rade. (See **stick²** 4, 5; **stick in** 1) **II** n P **to be in stuck** [ʃtʌk], être dans une mauvaise posture/dans de mauvais draps/dans une mauvaise passe.

stuck-up ['stʌk'ʌp] a F prétentieux*/crâneur/plastronneur; **she's a stuck-up bitch,** c'est une

crâneuse/une bêcheuse; elle se croit sortie de la cuisse de Jupiter.

stud [stʌd] n esp NAm F **1.** mâle m/mec m/macho m/caïd m; **he's a real stud,** c'est un tireur d'élite/une sacrée pointure **2.** malin m/roué m **3.** homme m dans le vent/minet m.

stuff¹ [stʌf] n **1.** F **to know one's stuff,** être capable/s'y connaître/être à la hauteur **2.** F **that's the stuff (to give the troops)!** voilà ce qu'il faut (pour remonter la République)! **3.** P **a nice bit of stuff,** une belle pépée/une môme bath/une nana roulée au moule; **he's a nice bit of stuff,** il est classe; **his bit of stuff,** sa petite amie **4.** P (drugs) (a) héroïne*/héro f (b) drogues*/stups mpl/came f/marchandise f/stuff m **5.** P butin*/contrebande f/pluc m/marchandise f **6.** F **to do one's stuff,** faire ce qu'on doit/faire son boulot; **go on, do your stuff!** allez, au turbin! (See **heavy I** 5; **rough I** 6; **sob-stuff; white I** 1)

stuff² [stʌf] vtr F **1.** V faire l'amour* avec (qn)/bourrer/égoïner **2.** P **get stuffed!** va te faire voir!/va te faire foutre! **3.** F **to stuff oneself/one's face,** manger* abondamment/se goinfrer/s'empiffrer. (See **shirt** 5)

stuffing ['stʌfɪŋ] n F **to knock the stuffing out of s.o.** (a) battre qn à plate(s) couture(s)/flanquer une tripotée à qn/étriper qn (b) désarçonner/démonter/dégonfler qn; mettre qn à plat.

stuffy ['stʌfi] a F collet monté/constipé.

stum [stʌm] n P **1.** (drugs) marijuana*/kif m **2.** = **stumbler.**

stumbler ['stʌmblər] n P (drugs) somnifère m/barbiturique*/barbitos mpl.

stumer ['stjuɪmər] n P **1.** chose f qui ne vaut rien **2.** chèque m sans provision/chèque m en bois **3.** bévue*/boulette f/bourde f; **to drop a stumer,** faire une gaffe **4.** (esp horse) perdant *m*/paumé *m*/toquard *m* **5.** raté *m*/paumé *m* **6.** faillite *f*/banqueroute *f*/binelle *f*.

stump [stʌmp] *vtr* F coller (qn)/ réduire (qn) à quia/laisser (qn) baba; **to stump s.o. on sth**, faire sécher qn sur qch; **that really stumped me**, sur le coup je n'ai su que répondre/ça m'a cloué le bec.

stumps [stʌmps] *npl* F jambes*/ guibolles *fpl*; **to stir one's stumps** (*i*) se dépêcher*/se décarcasser (*ii*) se remuer.

stump up ['stʌmp'ʌp] *vi* F payer*/ les abouler/cracher/casquer.

stun [stʌn] *vtr* F **1.** emballer/combler **2.** abasourdir/abrutir/laisser baba. (*See* **stunned**)

stunned [stʌnd] *a NAm* P ivre*/ fadé.

stunner ['stʌnər] *n* F (*a*) qn d'irrésistible *ou* de formidable/prix *m* de Diane/Apollon *m*; **she's a real stunner**, c'est un morceau de choix (*b*) chose épatante.

stunning ['stʌniŋ] *a* F (*a*) excellent*/formid(able)/épatant (*b*) très beau*/ravissant/irrésistible.

stupe [stuːp] *n NAm* P individu bête*/cruche *f*/cruchon *m*.

stymie, stymy ['staimi] *vtr* F entraver/gêner/contrecarrer; **I'm completely stymied**, je suis dans une impasse/je suis coincé.

sub¹ [sʌb] *n* F **1. to get a sub from/off s.o.**, emprunter* à qn/faire un emprunt; taper qch à qn **2.** (= *sub-editor*) secrétaire *mf* de rédaction **3.** (= *submarine*) sous-marin *m* **4.** (= *subaltern*) subalterne *mf* **5.** (= *substitute*) substitut *m*/remplaçant *m* **6.** (= *subscription*) abonnement *m*/cotisation *f*.

sub² [sʌb] *vtr* F **1. to sub s.o.**, prêter de l'argent* à qn/financer qn **2.** (= *sub-edit*) corriger/mettre au point (un article/des épreuves) **3.** (= *substitute*) **to sub for s.o.**, remplacer qn.

suck [sʌk] *vtr* **1.** F (*catchphrase*) **suck it and see**, essaie et tu verras; suce et tu goûteras **2.** F **to suck s.o. dry**, saigner qn à blanc/tondre la laine sur le dos à qn **3.** V **to suck s.o.**, (*fellatio*) sucer qn/tailler une pipe/faire un pompier à qn; (*cunnilinctus*) sucer/brouter qn. (*See* **egg 6**)

suck around ['sʌkə'raund] *vtr NAm* P **to suck around s.o.** = **to suck up to s.o. (suck up)**.

suckass ['sʌkæs] *n NAm* P lèche-cul *m*/lèche-bottes *m*.

sucker ['sʌkər] **I** *a attrib* F (*boxing*) **sucker punch**, coup* de pré-attaque **II** *n* F **1.** dupe *f*/poire *f*/ dindon *m*; (*catchphrase*) **there's a sucker born every minute**, les poires se cueillent tous les jours/on pend les andouilles sans les compter; **to make a (right) sucker of s.o.**, faire tourner qn en bourrique; **to be played for a sucker**, être escroqué*/ entubé; **he made a right sucker out of you!** il t'a eu jusqu'à la gauche! **2.** admirateur *m*/fana*/mordu *m*; **he's a sucker for a beautiful blonde**, il est porté vers les belles blondes. (*See* **bum-sucker**; **cock-sucker**; **one 7**)

suck in ['sʌk'in] *vtr* P escroquer*/ carotter/empiler.

suck off ['sʌk'ɔf] *vtr* V **to suck s.o. off**, (*fellatio*) sucer qn/faire une pipe à qn/ronger l'os; (*cunnilinctus*) sucer qn/brouter le cresson.

suck up ['sʌk'ʌp] *vi* F **to suck up to s.o.**, flatter* qn/faire de la lèche à qn/lécher le cul à qn.

sugar¹ ['ʃugər] *n* **1.** P (*a*) argent*/ galette *f* (*b*) bénéfices*/affure *f*/ gâteau *m* **2.** F (*a*) belle* fille* (*b*) petite amie/fiancée **3.** P (*drugs*) (*a*) héroïne*/cocaïne*/morphine*/ sucre *m* (*b*) **sugar (lump)**, LSD*/ acide *m*. (*See* **acid 2**) **4.** F flatterie *f*/pommade *f* **5.** P pot-de-vin *m*/dessous-de-table *m*.

sugar[2] [ˈʃugər] *vtr* **1.** *F* flatter*/pommader **2.** *P* soudoyer/acheter.

sugar-daddy [ˈʃugədædi] *n F* vieux protecteur (envers une maîtresse)/papa-gâteau *m*; **she's got a sugar-daddy,** elle s'est trouvé un vieux.

sugar-hill [ˈʃugəˈhil] *n NAm P* quartier *m* des bordels* dans une région habitée par les noirs.

summat [ˈsʌmət, ˈsumət] *adv & n P* = **something.**

Sunday [ˈsʌndi] *a attrib F* **1.** Sunday driver, chauffeur peu expérimenté/chauffard *m* du dimanche **2.** (*boxing*) **Sunday punch,** coup* meurtrier/KO.

sundowner [ˈsʌndaunər] *n F* **1.** boisson alcoolisée (prise le soir) **2.** *Austr* clochard*/cloche *m*/clodo *m* **3.** *NAm* pète-sec *m*/garde-chiourme *m*/gendarme *m*.

sunk [sʌŋk] *a F* ruiné*/perdu/fichu.

sunny [ˈsʌni] *a F* **1.** the sunny side of the street, la vie en rose **2.** sunny side up, (un œuf) sur le plat.

sunset strip [ˈsʌnsetˈstrip] *n F see* **bingo 77.**

super [ˈs(j)uːpər] **I** *a O F* excellent*/super/épatant **II** *n F* (= *Superintendent* (*of Police*)) commissaire *m* de police/quart *m* (d'œil).

super-duper [ˈs(j)uːpəˈd(j)uːpər] *a O F* excellent*/formid(able)/bœuf.

superfly [ˈs(j)uːpəflai] *a NAm P* (*esp Black Slang*) excellent*/extra/génial/super/class.

supergrass [ˈs(j)uːpəgræs] *n P* indicateur* de police (qui livre plusieurs criminels à la police)/balance *f*/chacal *m*. (*See* **grass**[1] **1**)

sup up [ˈsʌpˈʌp] *vi F* lamper son verre.

sure [ʃuər, ʃɔər, ʃɔɪr] *F* **I** *a* (it's a) sure thing, c'est une certitude/c'est sûr et certain/c'est du tout cuit; sure thing! = sure! **II.** (*See* **egg 4**)

II *excl* **sure!**/for sure! naturellement!/bien sûr!/pour sûr!

sure-fire [ˈʃuəˈfaiər, ˈʃɔəˈfaiər, ˈʃɔɪˈfaiər] *a F* sûr et certain.

surfie [ˈsɔrfi] *n Austr F* **1.** fana *mf* du surf **2.** habitué(e) de la plage.

suss[1] [sʌs] *n P* **1.** to have the suss (*a*) se gourrer de qch/de qn (*b*) être à la coule/dans le vent/à la page **2.** (*police, etc*); sus law, loi *f* qui permet à la police d'arrêter quiconque lui paraît suspect *ou* qui semble sur le point de commettre un délit; to get picked up on suss, être arrêté sur des présomptions/se faire pincer par gourance.

suss[2] [sʌs] *vtr P* soupçonner/avoir à l'œil/avoir des gourances (à propos de qn/qch).

suss out [ˈsʌsˈaut] *vtr P* to suss s.o. out, cataloguer qn/mettre qn en fiche; to suss sth out, classifier qch/éclairer sa lanterne; he sussed that out pretty quick, il a vite pigé le truc.

swab [swɔb] *n O P* rustre *m*/lourdaud *m*/andouille *f*/propre à rien *m*.

swacked [swækt] *a P* ivre*/blindé.

swaddie, swaddy [ˈswɔdi] *n F* = **squaddie, squaddy.**

swag [swæg] *n F* butin*/fade *m*/taf *m*.

swagger [ˈswægər] *a F* (*rare*) élégant*/chic/riflo.

swagman [ˈswægmæn] *n Austr F* clochard*/vagabond *m*.

swallow[1] [ˈswɔlou] *n F* to have a big swallow, avoir un bon avaloir/avoir la dalle en pente.

swallow[2] [ˈswɔlou] *vtr F* **1.** I can't swallow that, je ne peux pas l'avaler/je ne peux pas le gober; hard to swallow, difficile à avaler **2.** croire*; he won't swallow that, il ne va pas gober ça/il ne va pas donner dans ce panneau.

swank [swæŋk] **I** *a NAm F* =

swanky (*b*) **II** *n F* **1.** élégance *f*/ chic *m*/coquetterie *f* **2. to put on (the) swank,** prendre des airs *mpl*/ faire de l'esbrouf(f)e *f*/frimer **3.** prétention *f*/gloriole *f*/épate *f* **4.** épateur *m*/poseur *m*/crâneur *m*/ frimeur *m*.

swank² [swæŋk] *vi F* se donner des airs *mpl*/crâner/faire de l'épate *f*/ frimer.

swanker ['swæŋkər] *n F* = **swank II 4.**

swanky ['swæŋki] *a F* (*a*) prétentieux*/poseur (*b*) élégant*/ flambard/ridère.

swap¹ [swɔp] *n F* (*a*) échange *m*/ troc *m* (*b*) article *m* que l'on échange/troc *m*; *pl* doubles *mpl*.

swap² [swɔp] *vtr F* échanger/troquer.

swear [swɛər] *n F* **to have a good swear,** lâcher une bordée de jurons/ jurer comme un charretier.

sweat¹ [swet] *n F* **1.** travail* pénible/corvée *f*/turbin *m*; **it's no sweat,** c'est du tout cuit/c'est pas du durillon; **no sweat!** pas de problème!/c'est tout vu! **2.** (*mil*) **an old sweat,** un vieux troupier/un vétéran **3. to work oneself (up) into a sweat = to work oneself (up) into a lather (lather¹** (*a*), (*b*)) **4. to be in a cold sweat,** s'inquiéter/avoir le trac.

sweat² [swet] *vi F* **1. to be sweating on the top line,** être agité/ excité/emballé; être sur des charbons ardents **2.** *NAm* se tracasser*/se casser la tête/se casser la nénette/se faire de la bile. (*See* **blood 4**)

sweat out ['swet'aut] *vtr F* **to sweat it out,** attendre* patiemment/ compter les pavés. (*See* **guts 6**)

sweat-shop ['swetʃɔp] *n F* usine *f* où les ouvriers sont exploités/vrai bagne.

swedey ['swiːdi] *n P* **1.** (*police*) agent* de police/gendarme *m*/

flicaillon *m* de province **2.** paysan*/plouc *m*/bouseux *m*.

Sweeney ['swiːni] *n P* **1.** (*RS = Flying Squad*) **Sweeney Todd/the Sweeney,** la brigade mobile (de la police) **2.** = **holler-wag(g)on.**

sweep¹ [swiːp] *n F* **1.** sweepstake *m* **2. to make a clean sweep,** faire table rase/faire rafle/rafler le tout/ ramasser.

sweep² [swiːp] *vtr F* **1. to be swept off one's feet** (*a*) être emballé/s'emballer/se montrer chaud pour qn (*b*) être débordé/ inondé de travail* **2. to sweep the board,** emporter tout/nettoyer le tapis. (*See* **dirt 4**)

sweeper ['swiːpər] *n F* **1.** (*football*) arrière *m* de défense **2. leave it for the sweeper,** ne ramassez rien/laissez pousser.

sweep up ['swiːp'ʌp] *vi F* (*football*) jouer en arrière de défense.

sweet [swiːt] *a* **1.** *F* **to be sweet on s.o.,** être amoureux de qn/avoir le béguin pour qn/en pincer pour qn **2.** *F* **you can bet your sweet life!** tu peux en mettre la main au feu **3.** *F* **to hand s.o. a sweet line,** flatter*/ qn/faire marcher qn/faire de la lèche à qn **4.** *P* **sweet Fanny Adams**/*P* **sweet FA**/*V* **sweet fuck-all,** rien*/moins que rien/peau de balle (et balai de crin)/que dalle/ des prunes/peau de zébi **5.** *F* **to whisper sweet nothings,** murmurer des mots d'amour/conter fleurette **6.** *F* **sweet talk,** flatterie *f*/lèche *f*/ pommade *f* **7.** *F* facile/lucratif; **a sweet job,** une planque **8.** *F* aimable/accueillant/gentil; (*pers*) **sweet as a nut,** doux comme un agneau/ bon comme la romaine **9.** *P* homosexuel/chouquette/pédé. (*See* **tooth 1**)

sweeten ['swiːtn] *vtr F* (*a*) soudoyer/acheter (qn)/graisser la patte à (qn) (*b*) flatter*/cajoler/ pommader (qn).

sweetener ['swiːtnər] n F (a) pot-de-vin m (b) pourboire*/pourliche m; **I had to give him a sweetener,** j'ai dû lui graisser la patte/lui refiler la pièce.

sweeten up ['swiːtnʌp] vtr F = **sweeten**.

sweetie ['swiːti] n **1.** F bonbon m **2.** F chéri(e) m(f)/cocotte f; **he's a real sweetie,** c'est un cœur/un ange/une chochotte **3.** P (drugs) Préludine f (RTM).

sweetie-pie ['swiːtipai] n F = **sweetie 2**.

sweets [swiːts] npl P (drugs) amphétamines*/bonbons mpl.

sweet-talk ['swiːtɔːk] vtr F cajoler/enjôler (qn).

sweet-talker ['swiːtɔːkər] n F cajoleur m/enjôleur m.

sweety ['swiːti], **sweety-pie** ['swiːtipai] n F = **sweetie, sweetie-pie**.

swell [swel] I a **1.** O F élégant*/flambard **2.** O excellent*/chouettos/épatant **3.** A P swell mob, pickpockets bien fringués II n O F **1.** élégant m/suiffard m; **the swells,** les gens chics/le grand monde **2.** grand personnage/grosse légume.

swellhead ['swelhed] n NAm F prétentieux m/crâneur m/esbrouf(f)eur m.

swift [swift] a P malin*/ficelle/marle; **swift copper** (i) fin limier/super-condé m (ii) flic véreux.

swig¹ [swig] n F grand trait/lampée f (de bière, etc); **to take a swig from the bottle,** boire à même la bouteille.

swig² [swig] vi F boire à grands traits/à grands coups; lamper.

swill¹ [swil] n P **1.** nourriture*/bouftance f/bectance f **2.** (a) alcool* de mauvaise qualité/gnôle f (b) lampée f/rasade f **3.** bêtises*/foutaises fpl; **a prize load of swill,** un vrai tissu d'âneries.

swill² [swil] I vtr **1.** P to swill one's food, s'empiffrer de la nourriture* **2.** F to swill beer, s'entonner de la bière II vi P **1.** manger* abondamment/s'empiffrer/goinfrer **2.** boire* beaucoup/picoler.

swim [swim] n F in the swim, dans le bain/dans le vent/à la coule; **to get back in/into the swim of things,** se remettre dans le bain; **out of the swim,** hors du coup/pas à la page.

swimmingly ['swimiŋli] adv F à merveille/comme sur des roulettes.

swindle-sheet ['swindlʃiːt] n P indemnité f pour frais professionnels/frais de la princesse.

swine [swain] n F salopard m/salaud*/saligaud m; **you swine!** espèce de dégueulasse/de voyou/d'ordure!

swing¹ [swiŋ] n F **1.** to get into the swing of it/of things, se mettre dans le mouvement **2.** everything went with a swing, tout a très bien marché **3.** in full swing, en pleine activité/en plein boum/en plein coup de feu **4.** to take a swing at s.o., lancer un coup de poing à qn. (See **roundabouts**)

swing² [swiŋ] vtr&i **1.** F bien marcher/gazer/ronfler **2.** P to swing it/a fast one on s.o., duper* qn/(re)faire qn/tirer une carotte à qn/jouer un tour de cochon à qn **3.** F être pendu/béquillé; **I'll swing for him,** je me vengerai quitte à y aller du caillou **4.** F prendre du plaisir à (qch) **5.** F faire balancer (qch) en sa faveur **6.** P to swing both ways, être ambivalent/marcher à voile et à vapeur/jouer sur les deux tableaux **7.** Austr P to swing a bag, racoler*/faire le trottoir. (See **lead¹ 2**)

swinger ['swiŋər] **1.** F qn dans le vent/à la coule **2.** pl P seins*/flotteurs mpl. (See **lead-swinger**)

swinging ['swiŋiŋ] a F (a) plein d'allant/de ressort (b) dans le vent/à la coule; avant-garde.

swipe¹ [swaip] *n F* **1.** (*a*) coup*/ taloche *f*; **to take a swipe at s.o.**, flanquer une raclée/une torgnole à qn (*b*) **to have/to take a swipe at sth**, se lancer à faire qch **2.** *pl A* la petite bière.

swipe² [swaip] *vtr F* **1.** battre* (qn)/flanquer une raclée (à qn)/ gifler (qn) **2.** voler*/chiper/ chaparder (qch à qn).

swish¹ [swiʃ] **I** *a F* élégant*/chic **II** *n P* homosexuel*/lopette *f*/ joconde *f*/lopaille *f*.

swish² [swiʃ] *vi P* être efféminé/ faire pédé.

switch¹ [switʃ] *n F* **to do/to pull a switch**, échanger/troquer/chanstiquer.

switch² [switʃ] *vtr F* **to switch horses (in midstream)**, changer son fusil d'épaule (au milieu du combat).

switched on ['switʃt'ɔn] *a&pp F* **1.** faux*/forcé/artificiel **2.** euphorique/chargé/allumé/branché (par les drogues) **3.** à la mode/ dernier cri/dans le vent/dans le coup. (*See* **switch on**)

switch-hitter ['switʃhitər] *n P* bisexuel *m*/qn qui marche à voiles et à vapeur.

switch off ['switʃ'ɔf] *vi F* se détacher (de qch)/couper l'allumage *m*.

switch on ['switʃ'ɔn] *vtr* **1.** *F* **to switch s.o. on** (*a*) éveiller l'intérêt *m ou* la curiosité de qn/brancher qn (*b*) exciter/émoustiller qn (sexuellement); allumer/aguicher/brancher (qn) **2.** *P* (*drugs*) fumer de la marijuana* **3.** *P* (*drugs*) initier (par une première piqûre) à la drogue. (*See* **switched on**)

swizz [swiz] *n F* (= **swizzle¹ 1, 2**) **what a swizz!** c'est de l'arnaque!

swizzle¹ ['swizl] *n F* **1.** escroquerie*/filoutage *m*/doublage *m*/ estampage *m*/arnaque *f* **2.** déception *f*/déboire *m* **3.** *NAm* cocktail *m*/mélange *m*.

swizzle² ['swizl] *vtr F* escroquer*/ filouter/doubler/arnaquer.

swop [swɔp] *n&v F* = **swap**.

swordsman ['sɔːdzmən] *n P* **1.** receleur*/fourgue *m* **2.** *NAm* libertin *m*/cavaleur *m*.

swot¹ [swɔt] *n F* (*a*) bûcheur *m*/ potasseur *m* (*b*) fort *m* en thème.

swot² [swɔt] *vi F* étudier/bûcher/ potasser.

swot up ['swɔt'ʌp] *vtr F* rabâcher par cœur/potasser.

syph [sif] *n P* (*a*) syphilis*/syphilo *f*/syphlote *f*/vérole *f* (*b*) syphilitique *mf*/naze *mf*/nazebroque *mf*/ vérolé(e) *m(f)*.

syphed up ['sift'ʌp] *a&pp P* atteint de syphilis/syphilitique/vérolé/nazi.

sypho ['sifou], **syphy** ['sifi] *n P* (*pers*) syphilitique *mf*/nazebroque *mf*/vérolé(e) *m(f)*.

syrupy ['sirəpi] *a F* sirupeux/sentimental/gnan-gnan.

system ['sistəm] *n F* **1. the system**, le Système/la République **2. it's all systems go!** ça gaze! on démarre!/c'est parti(, mon kiki)!

T

T [tiː] **1.** *F* **that suits me (down) to a T,** cela me va parfaitement/cela me va comme un gant; cela me botte **2.** *P* =**tea 1.**

ta [taɪ] *excl F* merci.

tab [tæb] *n* **1.** *P* cigarette*/cibiche *f*/clop(e) *mf*/sèche *f* **2.** *P* oreille*/étiquette *f* **3.** *NAm F* note *f*/facture *f*/addition *f* **4.** *F* **to keep tabs on s.o.,** surveiller qn/avoir l'œil sur qn/avoir qn à l'œil **5.** *P* (*abbr* = *tablet*) comprimé *m*/cachet *m.*

tab-end ['tæb'end] *n F* mégot*/clope *f.*

table ['teibl] *n F* **to be under the table,** être ivre*/rouler sous la table.

tack [tæk] *n F* **1.** (*a*) **soft tack,** pain*/bricheton *m* (*b*) **hard tack,** biscuits *mpl* de marin **2.** nourriture*/fricot *m*/rata *m.* (*See* **brass l**)

tacky ['tæki] *a NAm F* minable/moche.

Taffy ['tæfi] *n F* habitant *m* du pays de Galles/Gallois *m.*

tag¹ [tæg] *n F* **1.** nom* *ou* surnom *m*/blaze *m* **2.** (*aut*) plaque *f* (d'immatriculation) **3.** =**ticket 2 4.** (*theatre*) **tag line,** mot *m* de la fin. (*See* **dog-tag**)

tag² [tæg] *vtr&i* **1.** *P F* suivre (qn)/être sur les talons de (qn)/filer le train à (qn)/faire la filoche à (qn) **2.** *P* arrêter*/choper/ceinturer **3.** *F* (*boxing*) mettre knockout/mettre KO/knockouter (qn).

tag along ['tægə'lɔŋ] *vi F* suivre/être à la traîne de qn.

tag around ['tægə'raund] *vi F* **to tag around with s.o.,** être accroché à qn/rouler sa bosse avec qn.

tag on ['tæg'ɔn] *vi F* **1.** se joindre à qn/s'accrocher à qn **2.** apposer/fixer.

tail¹ [teil] *n* **1.** *P* fesses*/pont-arrière *m*/arrière-train *m*; **get your tail out of here!** débarrasse le plancher!/tire ton cul de là! **2.** *P* pénis*/queue *f*/bite *f*/pine *f* **3.** *P* sexe de la femme*/chagatte *f*/cramouille *f*/conasse *f* **4.** *P* **a piece of tail,** un bout de fesses/de cuisse; **he's after a piece of tail,** il faire de la fesse/il cherche à planter son panard **5.** *F* policier*/détective *m* en filature/limier *m*; **to be on s.o.'s tail** (*i*) filer le train à qn/faire la filoche à qn (*ii*) être sur le dos de qn; **to put a tail on s.o.,** faire suivre qn/faire filer qn/faire la filoche à qn **6.** *F* **to go top over tail,** faire une culbute **7.** *F* **habit** *m* à queue/queue-de-pie *f*; **to wear tails,** porter l'habit **8.** *F* **to turn tail,** s'enfuir*/tourner le dos **9.** *F* **to have one's tail up** (*a*) se sentir très heureux/se sentir pousser des ailes (*b*) être très optimiste/être en pleine forme **10.** *F* **to keep one's tail up,** ne pas se laisser abattre. (*See* **ringtail**)

tail² [teil] *vtr F* suivre/épier/filer (qn). (*See* **hightail**)

tail-end ['teil'end] *n F* **the tail-end,** la fin/le bout.

tail-ender ['teil'endər] *n F* dernier *m*/lanterne *f* rouge/der *m* (des ders).

tailgate ['teilgeit] *vtr NAm F* coller au train/au cul (d'une voiture, etc).

tail-man ['teilmæn] *n P* coureur *m* (de jupons)/cavaleur *m*/juponneur *m*.

tail-spin ['teilspin] *n F* to go into a tail-spin, être saisi de panique/paniquer.

take¹ [teik] *n F* the take, la recette/les revenus *mpl*/le beurre; to be on the take (*i*) affurer/faire son beurre (*ii*) (*bribe*) en toucher.

take² [teik] *vtr* 1. *F* to have what it takes (*a*) avoir du courage*/du battant; he's got what it takes, il a des couilles/il en a dans le calcif (*b*) être capable/être à la hauteur 2. *F* endurer/encaisser; we can take it, on peut tenir le choc/le coup 3. *F* I'm not taking any of that! je ne gobe rien de tout cela!/on ne me fera pas croire ça! 4. *P* (*drugs*) tirer sur une cigarette* de marijuana* *ou* de haschisch 5. *P* (*bribe*) to take one, en toucher. (*See* lamb 4; plunge¹)

take apart ['teikə'paɪt] *vtr F* réprimander* fortement/passer un bon savon à (qn).

take in ['teik'in] *vtr F* 1. comprendre/piger/entraver 2. he takes it all in, il prend tout ça pour argent comptant 3. tromper*/ficher dedans/avoir (qn); I've been taken in, je me suis fait rouler/avoir.

take-off ['teikɔf] *n F* 1. départ *m*/décollage *m* 2. imitation *f*/mimique *f*/pastiche *m*.

take off ['teik'ɔf] *vtr&i* 1. *F* s'enfuir*/s'en aller/se barrer; take off! fiche le camp!/déguerpis! 2. *F* imiter/copier/singer 3. *P* (*drugs*) (*a*) se faire une piquouse/se fixer/se shooter (*b*) être high/être défoncé par la drogue 4. *P* voler*/chiper; to get taken off, être empilé 5. *P* mourir*/lâcher la rampe.

take-on ['teikɔn] *n F* farce *f*/canular(d) *m*.

take on ['teik'ɔn] *vi F* 1.

s'émotionner/se retourner 2. devenir populaire/prendre.

take out ['teik'aut] *vtr P* tuer*/descendre/éliminer/expédier (qn).

talc [tælk] *n P* (*drugs*) cocaïne*/talc *m*.

tale [teil] *n* 1. *F* to tell the tale, raconter des boniments *mpl*/faire du baratin 2. *F* to live to tell the tale, survivre/être là pour en parler 3. *P* (*RS = titties*) Tale of Two Cities, seins*. (*See* Bristols; fit¹ II 3; threepenny-bits; tit 1; titty; trey-bits) 4. *P* (*RS = jail*) sorrowful tale, prison*. (*See* tall I 2)

talent ['tælənt] *n P* (*women or men considered sexually*) the local talent, les nénettes *fpl*/les types *mpl* bien du coin; he's looking for talent, il cherche de la fesse/du cul.

talk [tɔːk] *vi F* 1. now you're talking! maintenant tu y es/tu y viens!/voilà qui devient intéressant! 2. money talks, l'argent* peut tout dire 3. talk about luck! tu parles d'une veine! 4. look who's talking! tu peux toujours parler, toi! (*See* Dutch I 5; hat 2; head 10, 11; sweet-talk)

talkie ['tɔːki] *n F* (*cinema*) film parlant/talkie *m*.

talking-to ['tɔːkiŋtuː] *n F* réprimande *f*/attrapade *f*/savon *m*; to give s.o. a good talking-to, sonner les cloches à qn.

tall [tɔːl] I *a F* 1. a tall order, un travail* dur/un sacré boulot 2. a tall story/NAm tale, un mensonge*/un bateau; une histoire à dormir debout; that's a bit of a tall story! elle est bonne, celle-là! II *adv F* avec jactance *f*/avec fanfaronnade *f*; to walk tall, crâner/se gonfler/se monter le cou.

tammy ['tæmi] *n F* (= *tam-o'-shanter*) béret écossais.

tampi ['tæmpi] *n P* (*drugs*) marijuana*/tampi *m*.

tangle ['tæŋgl] *vi F* **to tangle with s.o.** (*a*) se brouiller avec qn/se frotter à qn (*b*) embrasser* qn/étreindre qn/serrer qn dans ses bras.

tanglefoot ['tæŋglfut] *n NAm F* whisky *m* (de mauvaise qualité)/casse-pattes *m*/tord-boyaux *m*.

tank [tæŋk] *n P* **1.** coffre-fort *m*/coffio(t) *m*; **to blow a tank,** faire sauter un coffiot **2.** *NAm* (*a*) prison*/coffre *m* (*b*) cellule *f*/cage *f* à poules. (*See* **fish-tank**) **3.** ivrogne*/sac *m* à vin/poivrot *m* **4. to go in the tank,** se laisser battre volontairement. (*See* **piss-tank**; **septic 2**; **think tank**)

tanked up ['tæŋkt'ʌp] *a P* ivre*/bourré/chargé/blindé; **to get tanked up,** se soûler la gueule/se noircir/se bourrer/se piquer le nez.

tank up ['tæŋk'ʌp] *vi P* boire* beaucoup d'alcool*/picoler/pinter.

tanner ['tænər] *n F* ancienne pièce *f* de six pennies *ou* 2½ nouveaux pennies.

tanning ['tæniŋ] *O F* volée *f* de coups*/raclée *f*/peignée *f*. (*See* **hide 1**)

tap[1] [tæp] *n F* **to be on tap,** être disponible/être à la disposition.

tap[2] [tæp] *vtr F* demander de l'argent* à/taper/torpiller (qn). (*See* **claret**)

tape[1] [teip] *n F* **red tape,** bureaucratie *f*/paperasserie *f*/chinoiseries administratives.

tape[2] [teip] *vtr F* **to have s.o./sth taped,** avoir qn/qch bien catalogué/étiqueté/pointé.

tapped out ['tæpt'aut] *a NAm P* ruiné*/paumé/dans la dèche.

tapper ['tæpər] *n P* mendiant*/frappeur *m*/tapeur *m*.

tar[1] [tɑːr] *n P* (*drugs*) opium*/noir *m*. (*See* **Jack 7**)

tar[2] [tɑːr] *vtr F* **to be tarred with the same brush,** être du pareil au

même/être dans le même panier/faire la paire.

tar-brush ['tɑːbrʌʃ] *n F* **to have a touch of the tar-brush,** avoir du négrillon dans les veines/avoir du sang noir.

tarnation! [tɑːˈneiʃən] *excl NAm F* (*euph for* **damnation**) mince!/mercredi!

tart [tɑːt] *n P* **1.** prostituée*/fille *f*/cocotte *f*/grue *f*/pute *f* **2.** jeune fille* *ou* femme*/donzelle *f*/gonzesse *f* **3.** petite amie; **his tart,** sa nana.

tart up ['tɑːt'ʌp] *vtr P* (*a*) décorer (qch) avec du tape-à-l'œil; rajeunir/retaper (*b*) **to tart oneself up,** s'affubler/s'attifer de clinquant/faire le carnaval/se mettre sur son trente-et-un.

tarty ['tɑːti] *a P* qui a l'air d'une prostituée*/à la pute.

tash [tæʃ] *n F* moustache*/bacchante *f*.

tassel ['tæs(ə)l] *n O P* **1.** pénis*/goupillon *m* **2. don't get your tassel in a twist,** ne te mets pas dans tous tes états/ne t'en fais pas. (*See* **knickers 1**)

taste [teist] *n* **1.** *P* bénéfice* *ou* partie *f* d'un bénéfice/fade *m* **2.** *F* boisson *f* alcoolique; **would you like a taste?** tu veux boire* un coup? **3.** *P* **to have a taste,** faire l'amour*/s'en payer un petit coup.

tasty ['teisti] *a P* élégant*/chic; **a tasty piece,** une belle nana/une nana bien balancée/une roulée au moule/un joli morceau; **a tasty villain,** un voleur*/un escroc qui a de la classe.

ta-ta ['tæ'tɑː, tæ'tɑː] *F* **I** *excl* au revoir/r'voir **II** *n* (*child's word*) **to go ta-ta's,** faire une petite promenade/sortir en promenade.

tater ['teitər], **tatie** ['teiti] *n P* pomme *f* de terre/patate *f*.

taters ['teitəz] *a P* **to be taters,** avoir froid/être frisco/cailler; **it's**

bleeding taters in here! ça caille les miches!

Tattersalls ['tætəsɔɪlz, 'tætəsəlz] n F la pelouse.

tatty ['tæti] a F défraîchi; délabré; miteux/moche; **that's a bit tatty,** c'est toc(ard)/c'est moche; **a tatty old pair of jeans,** un vieux jean délavé/moche/ringard.

tatty-bye ['tæti'bai] excl P au revoir/au'voir/salut.

taurus [tɔːrəs] n P (= **bullshit**) **taurus excretus,** bêtises*/foutaises fpl/conneries fpl.

tea [tiː] n P 1. marijuana*/thé m; **bush tea,** concoction f d'herbes et de marijuana* 2. (homosexuals) urine f/pisse f. (See **cup 1, 2; stick¹ 5; weed-tea**)

tea blower ['tiːblouər] n P = **teahead.**

teach [tiːtʃ] vtr F **that'll teach you!** ça t'apprendra! **that'll teach him a thing or two!** ça va le dégourdir un peu.

teach-in ['tiːtʃin] n F colloque m/ teach-in m/table ronde.

tead-up ['tiːd'ʌp] a&pp P (not common) drogué* à la marijuana*.

teahead ['tiːhed] n P (drugs) habitué(e) de la marijuana*/fumeur, -euse de thé.

tea house ['tiːhaus] n P (homosexuals) WC*/tasses fpl/théière f.

tea-leaf ['tiːliːf] n P (RS = thief) voleur*.

tea-party ['tiːpaːti] n P réunion f pour fumer la marijuana*.

tear¹ [tiər] n 1. P perle f/perlouse f 2. F **to shed a tear for Nelson,** uriner*/changer son poisson d'eau/ égoutter sa sardine.

tear² [tɛər] vtr F **that's torn it!** ça a tout gâché/ça a tout bousillé. (See **pants 5**)

tear along ['tɛərə'lɔŋ] vi F aller très vite*/foncer/brûler le pavé.

tear apart ['tɛərə'paːt] vtr F **to tear s.o. apart,** écharper qn/engueuler qn.

tear-arse ['tɛəraɪs], **tearaway** ['tɛərəwei] n P braillard m/grande-gueule f/fort m en gueule.

tearing ['tɛəriŋ] a F **to be in a tearing hurry,** avoir le feu au derrière/ filer dare-dare.

tear-jerker ['tiədʒɜːkər] n F mélo-(drame) m/histoire larmoyante; **that film's a real tear-jerker,** ce film vous arrache les larmes/sortez vos mouchoirs si vous allez voir ce film.

tear off ['tɛər'ɔf] vtr P **to tear it off/to tear off a piece of ass,** faire l'amour*/tirer un coup/faire un carton.

tea room ['tiːruːm] n P (homosexuals) = **tea house.**

tease [tiːz] n P aguicheuse f/ allumeuse f. (See **prick tease**)

teaser ['tiːzər] n 1. F casse-tête (chinois) 2. P aguicheuse f/ allumeuse f. (See **cock-teaser; prick-teaser**)

tea-stick ['tiːstik] n P = **stick of tea (stick¹ 5).**

tec [tek] n F (abbr = detective) détective m/condé m.

tech [tek] n F (abbr = technical college) collège m technique.

technicolour ['teknikələr] n P **to have a technicolour yawn,** vomir*/ rendre ses comptes/gerber/piquer un renard.

Ted, ted [ted], **Teddy-boy, teddy-boy** ['tedibɔi]n F (a) zazou m/zaz m (b) voyou m/ loubard m/blouson noir.

teed off ['tiːd'ɔf] a&pp P **to be teed off,** en avoir par-dessus la tête/en avoir ras le bol/en avoir jusque-là.

teed up ['tiːd'ʌp] a&pp P ivre*/ rétamé.

teeny ['tiːni] a F = **teeny-weeny.**

teeny-weeny ['tiːni'wiːni] a F minuscule/archi-petit/rikiki.

teeth [tiːθ] *npl see* **tooth.**

telegraph ['teligrɑːf] *vtr F* (*boxing*) **to telegraph a punch,** annoncer un direct.

telephone ['telifoun] *n F* **to talk in telephone numbers,** exagérer*/en rajouter/gonfler le mou/faire de la graisse.

tell [tel] *vtr F* **you're telling me!** tu l'as dit bouffi!/et comment! (*See* **another**; **Marine**; **tale 1, 2**)

telling-off ['teliŋ'ɔf] *n F* réprimande *f*/engueulade *f*/savon *m*.

tell off ['tel'ɔf] *vtr F* réprimander*/ enguirlander/passer un savon à (qn).

tell on ['telɔn] *vtr F* dénoncer*/ cafarder/bourdiller; **I'll tell mum on you!** je (m'en) vais le dire à maman!

telly ['teli] *n F* (*a*) la télé(vision) (*b*) (poste *m* de) télé *f*/téloche *f*.

ten [ten] *n F* **1. the upper ten,** l'aristocratie *f*/les aristos *mpl*/les cent familles **2. the top ten,** le palmarès.

tenderloin ['tendəlɔin] *n NAm F* quartier *m* louche/bas-fonds *mpl*/ quartier chaud.

tenner ['tenər] *n F* (*a*) dix livres *fpl* sterling (*b*) billet* de dix livres *ou* de dix dollars; **it'll cost you a tenner,** faudra cracher/allonger dix sacs/cent balles.

ten-spot ['tenspɔt] *n NAm F* **1.** billet* de dix dollars **2.** emprisonnement *m* de dix années/dix longes *fpl*/dix berges *fpl*.

terrible ['teribl] *a F* excessif/formidable; **terrible prices,** des prix exorbitants/formidables; **a terrible talker,** un bavard du diable.

terribly ['teribli, 'terəbli] *adv F* extrêmement/vachement; **terribly rich,** excessivement riche.

terrific [tə'rifik] *a F* **1.** excellent*/ sensass/du tonnerre **2. a terrific bore,** un sacré casse-pieds.

terrifically [tə'rifik(ə)li] *adv F* terriblement/énormément; **I'm terrifically impressed,** cela m'a fait une énorme impression; **it's terrifically nice of you,** c'est extrêmement gentil de votre part.

terror ['terər] *n F* fléau *m*/ cauchemar *m*/peste *f*; **he's a real terror,** c'est une vraie peste. (*See* **holy 3**)

Thames [temz] *Prn F* **he'll never set the Thames on fire,** il n'a pas inventé la poudre/le fil à couper le beurre; il est passé à côté de la distribution; il n'a jamais cassé trois pattes à un canard.

that [ðæt] *F* **I** *adv* jusque-là/si; **he's not that clever** ['ðætklevər], il n'est pas si malin* (que ça) **II** *pron* **1.** ...and that's that! un point, c'est tout! **and that was that,** plus rien à dire **2.** ...and all that, ...et tout le reste/...et patati et patata.

thatch [ðætʃ] *n F* **to lose one's thatch,** devenir chauve*/être dégazonné/perdre ses plumes/se dégarnir.

them [ðem] **I** *a P* = (*those*) **get up them stairs!** grimpe cet escalier! **give me them pencils!** donne-moi ces crayons! **I know them people,** je connais ces gens-là. (*See* **there 5**) **II** *pron P* (= *those*) **them's my sentiments,** voilà ce que je pense, moi.

there [ðɛər] *adv F* **1.** ...so there! ...et voilà! **2. all there,** malin*/ débrouillard; **not all there,** bête*/un peu fou*/loufoque; **he's not quite all there,** il est un peu demeuré/il lui manque une case. (*See* **all I 5**) **3. there you are!** je te l'avais bien dit! **4. there you go (again)!** te voilà reparti!/tu recommences!/tu remets ça! **5. them there sheep,** ces moutons-là **6. there you have me,** ça me dépasse **7. nearly there:** *see* **bingo 89.**

thick [θik] *a F* **1.** bête*/ballot*/ gourde; **he's as thick as a plank/as two short planks,** il est bête* ⟩

comme ses pieds; **to have a thick
head** (*a*) être bête*/être bouché à
l'émeri (*b*) avoir la gueule de bois/
la GDB **2. that's a bit thick** (*a*)
cela coûte les yeux de la tête (*b*)
cela dépasse les bornes/c'est un peu
raide/c'est un peu fort de café **3.**
amical/bon copain; **they're as thick
as thieves,** ils s'entendent comme
des larrons en foire/ils sont copains
comme cochons **4. to have a thick
skin,** avoir une peau
d'hippopotame/de rhinocéros; avoir
le cuir tanné. (*See* **ear 5**).

thickhead ['θikhed] *n F* individu
bête*/andouille *f*/bas-de-plafond *m*.
(*See* **thick¹**)

thickheaded ['θik'hedid] *a F*
bête*/bas de plafond/lourdingue.

thick-skinned ['θik'skind] *a F* **to
be thick-skinned,** n'avoir pas
l'épiderme *m* sensible/avoir une
peau de rhinocéros/avoir le cuir
tanné. (*See* **hide 2**; **thick¹ 4**)

thick-skulled ['θik'skʌld] *a F* =
thickheaded.

thigh sandwich ['θai'sændwitʃ] *n
P* **to give s.o. a thigh sandwich,** faire
éjaculer* qn (en frottant le sexe
contre les cuisses).

thin [θin] *a F* **1. thin on top,**
presque chauve*/sans mousse sur le
caillou; **to be going a bit thin on
top,** se dégarnir/perdre ses plumes
2. to have a thin time (of it),
s'ennuyer*/s'embêter/se morfondre
3. that's a bit thin! c'est peu con-
vaincant! (*See* **ice¹ 5**; **thin-
skinned**)

thing [θiŋ] *n* **1.** *F* **to have a thing
about s.o./sth,** trotte sur le ciboulot; **he's got a
thing about her,** il en est dingue **2.**
F **it's not the (done) thing,** ça ne se
fait pas/c'est peu conforme aux
règles/ce n'est pas canonique **3.** *F*
the thing is..., le fait est... **4.**
F **just the thing,** exactement ce qu'il
faut **5.** *F* **it's just one of those
things,** on ne peut rien y faire **6.**

F (*a*) **to know a thing or two,** être
malin*/avoir plus d'un tour dans
son sac (*b*) **I could tell you a thing
or two,** je pourrais vous en conter/
je pourrais vous en dire des vertes
et des pas mûres **7.** *F* **to see
things,** avoir des visions **8.** *F*
individu* quelconque; **hello, old
thing!** bonjour mon vieux!/salut
mon pote! **he's a nice old thing,**
c'est un bien brave type; **you poor
old thing!** mon/ma pauvre!/le/la
pauvre! **9.** *F* (*a*) **to be on(to) a
good thing,** avoir le filon/être sur
un bon filon (*b*) **he makes a good
thing out of it,** ça lui rapporte pas
mal; il en fait ses choux gras **10.**
F **do your (own) thing!** fais ta vie!/
fais (tout) ce qui te chante! **11.** *P*
pénis*/outil *m*/chose *f* **12.** *F*
how's things? comment ça va?

thingamy ['θiŋəmi], **thingamybob** ['θiŋəmibɔb], **thingamyjig** ['θiŋəmidʒig],
thingum(e)bob ['θiŋəm(ə)bɔb],
thingummy ['θiŋəmi], **thingy**
['θiŋi] *n F* chose *f*/machin *m*/
machin-chose *m*/machin-chouette
m/truc *m*/bidule *m*/trucmuche *m*.

think¹ [θiŋk] *n F* **you've got another
think coming!** tu peux toujours
courir!/tu te mets le doigt dans
l'œil!

think² [θiŋk] *vi F* **I don't think!**
sûrement pas!/et mon œil!/et ta
sœur!

think-box ['θiŋkbɔks], **thinker**
['θiŋkər]*n F* cerveau *m*/ciboulot *m*;
to use one's think-box, faire travailler ses méninges/agiter ses
neurones/se remuer la cervelle.

think-in ['θiŋkin] *n F* colloque *m*/
séminaire *m*/groupe *m* d'études.

thinking-cap ['θiŋkiŋkæp] *n F* **to
put one's thinking-cap on,** aviser à
ce qu'on doit faire/réfléchir sur
qch; se creuser le cerveau/se
remuer la cervelle.

think-piece ['θiŋkpiːs] *n F* =
think-box.

think tank ['θɪŋktæŋk] *n F* **1.** (*a*) comité-conseil *m*/réunion *f* d'une société savante (*b*) réservoirs *mpl* d'idées; cercle *m* de réflexion **2.** *Austr* cellule *f* (de prison)/cachot *m*/mitard *m*.

thin-skinned ['θɪn'skɪnd] *a F* **to be thin-skinned,** avoir l'épiderme *m* sensible/être susceptible/être chatouilleux.

thrash¹ [θræʃ] *n O P* **1.** coït*/dérouillage *m* **2.** réjouissances*/boum *f*/noce *f*/nouba *f*.

thrash² [θræʃ] *vtr F* **1.** battre*/rosser/tabasser (qn) **2.** battre (un adversaire) à plate(s) couture(s).

thrashing ['θræʃɪŋ] *n F* **1.** volée *f* de coups*/raclée *f*/tabassée *f* **2.** défaite *f*/raclée *f*.

thread [θred] *vtr P* (*rare*) faire l'amour* avec (une femme)/enfiler.

threads [θredz] *npl P* vêtements*/fringues *fpl*/sapes *fpl*/frusques *fpl*.

three [θriː] *n P* **packet of three,** préservatifs* (vendus en paquet de trois).

threepenny-bits ['θrʌpni'bits, 'θrepni'bits] *npl P* (*RS* = **tits**) seins*/nénés *mpl*. (*See* **Bristols; fit**¹ **II 3; tale 3; trey-bits**)

three-piece ['θriːpiːs] *n P* **three-piece suite,** sexe de l'homme*/service *m* trois pièces/bijoux *mpl* de famille/panoplie *f*/boutique *f*.

thrill [θril] *n P* (*drugs*) spasme provoqué par l'héroïne*.

throat [θrout] *n F* **1. to ram/to shove sth down s.o.'s throat,** rabattre les oreilles à qn de qch; **we're always having it rammed down our throats that we've never had it so good,** on nous rabat les oreilles en nous répétant que tout est au mieux **2. he's cutting his own throat,** il travaille à sa propre ruine; il creuse sa tombe. (*See* **jump**² **9**)

throne [θroun] *n P* siège *m* de WC*/trône *m*.

throne-room ['θrounruːm] *n P* WC*/cabinets *mpl*/chiottes *fpl*.

through [θruː] *F* **I** *adv* **1. to get through to s.o.,** faire comprendre qch à qn/faire piger; **am I getting through to you?** faut te faire un dessin?/tu piges? **2. to be through** (*a*) avoir terminé qch/en avoir vu la fin (*b*) être fichu/foutu/au bout du rouleau **3. to be through with s.o.,** rompre avec qn/couper les ponts; **she's through with him,** elle l'a plaqué **II** *prep* **he's been through it,** il en a vu de dures/il en a vu des vertes et des pas mûres/il en a bavé/il en a vu de toutes les couleurs.

throw¹ [θrou] *n F* **the tickets cost £5 a throw,** les billets coûtent £5 chaque.

throw² [θrou] *vtr F* **1. I trust him as far as I can throw him,** je n'ai pas la moindre confiance en lui **2.** étonner/estomaquer/laisser baba; **that threw you!** ça te l'a coupé!/ça t'en a bouché un coin! **3.** (*sport, etc*) perdre (une course, etc) exprès **4.** (*esp boxing*) to throw a fight, se laisser battre volontairement/se coucher. (*See* **bathwater; book**¹ **1; mud 7**)

throw about, around ['θrouə'baut, -'raund] *vtr F* **to throw (one's) money about,** dépenser* sans compter/faire valser le fric/jeter son fric par les fenêtres; **he doesn't throw his money about/he throws his money about like a man with no arms,** il n'attache pas son chien avec des saucisses/il est plutôt près de ses sous.

throw in ['θrou'in] *vtr F* **to throw in the towel/the sponge** (*a*) (*sport*) abandonner la lutte/la partie; jeter l'éponge (*b*) s'avouer vaincu/quitter le dé. (*See* **end 12**)

throw up ['θrou'ʌp] *vi F* vomir*/dégobiller/aller au refil(e)/faire renard; **to throw up after a party,** renvoyer la came/dégueuler tripes et boyaux après s'être bituré à une bamboula.

thrust [θrʌst] *n P* (*drugs*) amphétamine*.

thumb¹ [θʌm] *n F* **1. to be all thumbs,** être lourdaud/pataud; **his fingers are all thumbs,** il a la main malheureuse/il est gauche/c'est un brise-tout **2. thumbs up!** bravo!/ victoire! **to give s.o. (the) thumbs up (sign),** faire signe à qn que tout va bien; donner le feu vert à qn; **he gave me the thumbs down,** il m'a fait signe que ça ne marchait pas **3. to twiddle one's thumbs (and do nothing),** se tourner les pouces **4. it stands/sticks out like a sore thumb,** ça saute aux yeux/ça crève les yeux. (*See* **green ĺ 5; Tom 4**)

thumb² [θʌm] *vtr F* **to thumb (a lift/a ride),** faire de l'auto-stop/du stop; **he thumbed it,** il y est allé en stop.

thunderbox ['θʌndəbɔks] *n P* cuvette *f* (de cabinets).

thundering ['θʌndəriŋ] *a F* du tonnerre; **to win with a thundering majority,** l'emporter avec une majorité écrasante; **he's a thundering nuisance,** il est assommant au possible; **it's a thundering good book,** c'est un bouquin à tout casser.

thunder-mug ['θʌndəmʌg] *n P* pot *m* de chambre.

tich [titʃ] *n P* = **titch**.

tichy ['titʃi] *a P* = **titchy**.

tick¹ [tik] *n* **1.** *P* individu* méprisable/salaud *m*/saligaud *m* **2.** *F* crédit *m*/croum(e) *m*; **on tick,** à crédit/à croum(e); **I'm buying it on tick,** je l'achète à croume **3.** *F* moment *m*/instant *m*; **hang on a tick!** (attends) une seconde!/minute! (*See* **jiff(y); mo; sec; shake¹ 1, 2**)

tick² [tik] *vi F* **I'd like to know what makes him tick,** je voudrais bien savoir ce qui le pousse/ce qui le fait courir.

ticker ['tikər] *n F* **1.** cœur*/palpitant *m*; **to have a dicky ticker,** avoir le cœur branlant/qui flanche **2.** montre*/pendule *f*/tocante *f*.

ticket ['tikit] *n* **1.** *F* **that's (just) the ticket!** c'est exactement ce qui colle!/c'est juste ce qu'il nous faut! **2.** *F* contravention *f*/PV *m*/papillon *m*; **to get a parking ticket,** se faire coller un biscuit/une contredanse **3.** *esp NAm F* liste électorale; **to vote a straight ticket,** voter pour toute la liste; **to vote a split ticket,** faire du panachage; **the Republican ticket,** le programme du parti républicain **4.** *F* **to give s.o. a round ticket,** donner carte blanche à qn **5.** *P* peine *f* de prison* **6.** *Austr F* **to have tickets on oneself,** se mettre en avant/se gonfler/ crâner. (*See* **meal-ticket**)

tickety-boo ['tikiti'buː] *a F* excellent*/parfait*/bœuf*/au poil*/aux pommes; **everything's just tickety-boo,** tout baigne dans l'huile.

ticking-off ['tikiŋ'ɔf] *n F* réprimande *f*/savon *m*/engueulade *f*; **to give s.o. a good ticking-off,** passer un bon savon/sonner les cloches à qn. (*See* **tick off**)

tickle¹ ['tikl] *n F* de la chance*/ coup *m* de pot; **to make a tickle,** faire une touche. (*See* **slap¹ II 2**)

tickle² ['tikl] *vtr F* **1. to tickle s.o./to tickle s.o.'s fancy,** amuser qn **2. to be tickled pink,** être ravi/être aux anges **3. to be tickled to death,** se tordre de rire*/se boyauter. (*See* **ivories 4**)

tickler ['tiklər] *n F* **1.** moustache*/charmeuses *fpl* **2.** martinet *m*/fouet *m*. (*See* **rib-tickler**)

tick off ['tik'ɔf] *vtr F* réprimander*/ attraper/enguirlander; **to get ticked off,** être réprimandé*/écoper/ recevoir un savon. (*See* **ticking-off**)

tick over ['tik'ouvər] *vi F* **1.** (*business, etc*) suivre son petit bonhomme de chemin **2.** (*aut, etc*) bien marcher/tourner rond.

tiddle¹ ['tidl] *n F* (*child's word*) urine *f*/pipi *m*; **to have a tiddle,** faire pipi.

tiddle² ['tidl] *vi F* (*child's word*) uriner*/faire pipi.

tiddler ['tidlər] *n F* **1.** petit poisson/friture *f* **2.** petit(e) enfant*/ mioche *mf*/gosse *mf*/môme *mf*/ moutard *m* **3.** *O* pièce *f* d'un demi-penny.

tiddl(e)y ['tidli] *F* **I** *a* **1.** légèrement ivre*/pompette/éméché **2.** très petit/minuscule **II** *n* **a drop of tiddl(e)y,** un petit coup d'alcool*/ une goutte de gnôle.

tide-mark ['taidmɑɪk] *n F* ligne *f* de crasse autour du cou *ou* sur la baignoire.

tide over ['taid'ouvər] *vtr F* **I borrowed ten quid to tide me over,** j'ai emprunté cent balles pour me dépanner.

tidy ['taidi] *a F* **a tidy sum,** une somme rondelette; **a tidy fortune,** une jolie fortune.

tie on ['tai'ɔn] *vtr P* **to tie one on/to tie on a load,** s'enivrer/se biturer/ prendre une cuite/se piquer le nez/ se charger.

tie up ['tai'ʌp] *vtr F* **1. I'm rather tied up at the moment,** pour le moment je suis pas mal occupé/j'ai pas mal à faire **2. that ties up with what I've just said,** cela correspond à ce que je viens de dire.

tight [tait] *F* **I** *a* **1.** ivre*/soûl/ rétamé/raide; **to get tight,** prendre une cuite. (*See* **newt**) **2.** avare*/ serré/dur à la détente; **he's a bit tight with his cash,** il est plutôt près de ses sous **3.** à court; **things are a bit tight at the moment,** c'est pas du gâteau/ça baigne pas dans le beurre. (*See* **squeeze¹** 2) **II** *adv* **to sit tight** (*a*) voir venir/serrer les fesses/se tenir à carreau (*b*) ne pas bouger/ne pas se laisser ébranler.

tight-arse ['taitɑɪs], *NAm* **tight-ass** ['taitæs] *n P* avare *m*/rat *m*/ grippe-sou *m*.

tight-arsed ['taitɑɪst], *NAm* **tight-assed** ['taitæst] *a P* avare*/radin; **he's a tight-arsed old sod,** il est plutôt constipé du morlingue/il les lâche avec un lance-pierres.

tight-fisted ['tait'fistid] *a F* = **tight I 2**.

tightwad ['taitwɔd] *n F* avare *m*/ radin *m*/grigou *m*/grippe-sou *m*.

tike [taik] *n P* = **tyke**.

tile [tail] *n F* **1.** chapeau*/bitos *m*; haut-de-forme *m* **2. to have a tile loose,** être un peu fou*/onduler de la toiture **3. to be out on the tiles,** faire la fête/la bombe/la noce; **he spends his nights on the tiles,** il traîne dehors toute la nuit.

time [taim] *n.* **1.** *F* **to do time,** être en prison*/purger sa peine; **he's done time,** il a fait de la taule **2.** *NAm P* **to make time with s.o.,** séduire/tomber/sauter qn. (*See* **all-time; big-time; day 3; good-time; short I 2; small-time**)

timothy ['timəθi] *n Austr A P* bordel*/boxon *m*.

tin [tin] **I** *a F* **1. tin hat/lid,** casque *m* (de soldat) **2. that puts the tin lid on it,** c'est le comble/ c'est la fin des haricots **3. little tin god,** individu* qui se croit sorti de la cuisse de Jupiter/esbrouf(f)eur *m*/poseur *m* **4. tin fish,** torpille *f* **II** *n P* argent*/galette *f*/pognon *m*/ fric *m*/braise *f*.

tin-arse ['tinɑɪs] *n Austr P* qn qui a de la chance*/veinard *m*.

tin-arsed ['tinɑɪst] *a Austr P* qui a de la chance*/du pot/du cul.

tincture ['tiŋktjər] *n P* petit verre d'alcool*/goutte *f*.

tinker ['tiŋkər] *n* **1.** *F* (*esp child*) petit diable/vilain *m*/polisson(ne) *m(f)*/peste *f* **2.** *P* **I don't care/give a tinker's/a tinker's cuss/a tinker's toss,** je m'en fiche/je m'en bats l'œil/je m'en soucie comme de l'an quarante/j'en ai rien à fiche.

tinkle¹ ['tiŋkl] *n F* **to give s.o. a tin-kle,** téléphoner/passer un coup de fil à qn.

tinkle² ['tiŋkl] *vi F* (*child's word*) uriner*/faire pipi.

tinkler ['tiŋklər] *n P* pot *m* de chambre/Jules/Thomas.

tinned [tind] *a F* **tinned music,** musique *f* en conserve. (*See* **canned 2**)

tin-pan alley ['tin'pæn'æli] *n F* **1.** quartier *m* des éditeurs de musique populaire **2.** les compositeurs *mpl* de musique populaire.

tinpot ['tin'pɔt] *a F* inférieur/de second ordre/camelote; **tinpot ideas,** des idées à la noix/à la manque.

tin-tack ['tin'tæk] *n P* (*RS = sack*) **to get the tin-tack,** être congédié/se faire flanquer à la porte/être balancé.

tiny ['taini] *a F* **you must be out of your tiny mind,** tu es en train de perdre le peu de raison que tu as/tu es complètement siphonné.

tip [tip] *n F* endroit désordonné *ou* sordide/taudis *m*; **what a tip!** quel pagaille!/quel fouillis!/quel foutoir! (*See* **A 3**)

tip-off ['tipɔf] *n F* renseignement*/avertissement *m*/tuyau *m*/info *f*.

tip off ['tip'ɔf] *vtr F* avertir/affranchir/mettre dans le coup; **he tipped me off,** il m'a mis au parfum/il m'a rencardé.

tipple ['tipl] *n P* boisson corsée/très alcoolisée; **whisky is his favourite tipple,** whisky est sa gobette préférée.

tippler ['tiplər] *n P* ivrogne*/picoleur, -euse *m(f)*.

tip-top ['tip'tɔp] *a F* excellent*/extra/super; **in tip-top condition,** qui pète la santé/le feu.

tit [tit] *n* **1.** *V* sein*/nichon *m*/téton *m*/néné *m*; **to have huge tits,** avoir du monde au balcon **2.** *V* **to get on s.o.'s tits,** taper sur le système à

qn; **he really gets on my tits,** il me court sur les haricots/il me les casse **3.** *P* individu bête*/idiot *m*/crétin *m*; **you big tit!** espèce de connard/de nœud! **I must have looked a real tit standing there!** qu'est-ce que je devais avoir l'air con/l'air d'un gland planté là! (*See* **arse I 4; Tom 3**)

titch [titʃ] *n P* petit* individu/bas-du-cul *m*/astèque *m*/rase-bitume *m*/avorton *m*.

titchy ['titʃi] *a P* petit/crapoussin.

titfer ['titfər] *n P* (*RS = tit-for-tat = hat*) chapeau*.

titholder ['tithouldər] *n P* soutien-gorge *m*/soutien-loloches *m*.

titty ['titi] *n V =* **tit 1**.

titty-bottle ['titibɔtl] *n P* biberon *m*.

tizwas ['tizwɔz] *n F* **to be all of a tizwas,** être aux cent coups/être démonté/être affolé/être dans tous ses états. (*See* **doodah; tizzy**)

tizzy ['tizi] *n F* (*a*) affolement *m*/remue-ménage *m*/débandade *f* (*b*) panique *f*/bile *f*/mauvais sang; **to be in a tizzy,** être affolé/dans tous ses états.

toast [toust] *n F* **to have s.o. on toast,** avoir qn à sa merci/tenir qn.

toby ['toubi] *n P* **1.** *A* **the toby,** la grande route*/le grand trimard **2.** (*a*) territoire *m*/champ *m* d'action (d'un criminel); chasse gardée (*b*) secteur couvert par un commissariat de police.

tod, Tod [tɔd] *n P* (*RS = Tod Sloan = alone*) **to be on one's tod,** être tout seul/être seulabre.

toddle¹ ['tɔdl] *n F* petite promenade/balade *f*; **to go for a toddle,** aller faire un petit tour/se dérouiller les pinceaux.

toddle² ['tɔdl] *vi F* **1.** se balader/se baguenauder/déambuler.

toddle along, off ['tɔdlə'lɔŋ, -'ɔf] *vi F* partir*/se trotter/se carapater/

décarrer; (*pej*) **toddle off now, there's a good boy!** tire-toi/casse-toi petit gars!

to-do [tə'duː] *n F* remue-ménage *m*; **what a to-do!** quelle affaire!/quelle histoire! **to make a great to-do about sth,** faire tout un plat de qch.

toe [tou] *n F* **1. to tread on s.o.'s toes,** marcher sur les pieds de qn/offenser qn/froisser qn **2.** (*a*) **to be on one's toes,** être alerté/être sur le qui-vive/ouvrir l'œil (*b*) être en fuite *ou* recherché par la police/être en cavale **3. to turn up one's toes,** mourir*/casser sa pipe/avaler sa chique **4.** (*aut*) **to put one's toe down,** accélerer/appuyer sur le champignon/mettre les gaz.

toehold ['touhould] *n F* **to get a toehold,** avoir une prise précaire.

toerag ['touræg] *n P* (*term of abuse*) salaud*/con *m*/couillon *m*; **you little toerag!** petit morveux!/petit trou du cul!

toe-ragger ['tourægər] *n Austr P* prisonnier *m* de courte durée/enchtibé *m* d'une courte.

toey ['toui] *a Austr P* inquiet/anxieux/bileux.

toff [tɔf] *n F* rupin(os) *m*/cossu *m*/milord *m*; **the toffs,** le grand monde/le gratin/la haute.

toffee [tɔfi] *n F* **he can't play for toffee,** il joue comme un pied.

toffeenose ['tɔfinouz] *n F* snob *m*/crâneur *m*/poseur *m*.

toffee-nosed ['tɔfinouzd] *a F* prétentieux*/bêcheur/pincé.

together [tə'geðər] *a & adv F* sans mousse/peinard/coolos; **he's got it (all) together/he's a very together person/he's got his act together,** il est bien peinard/c'est un père peinard/il se fait jamais de la mousse.

tog out [tɔg'aut] *vtr F* **to tog (oneself) out,** se mettre sur son trente et un/se saper.

togs [tɔgz] *npl F* vêtements*/nippes *fpl*/frusques *fpl*.

tog up [tɔg'ʌp] *vtr F* **to tog (oneself) up = to tog (oneself) out** (**tog out**).

toilet ['tɔilit] *n P* **1.** endroit *m* sordide/taudis *m*/trou *m*; **what a toilet!** quelle sale baraque!/quel foutoir! **2.** (*homosexuals*) **toilet queen,** homosexuel* qui drague dans les WC*/tasseuse *f*.

toke [touk] *n P* **1.** pain*/bricheton *m*/larton *m* **2.** bouffée (*esp* d'une cigarette* de marijuana*).

toke up ['touk'ʌp] *vi P* allumer (une cigarette* de marijuana*).

tokus ['toukəs] *n P* **1.** fesses*/pétrus *m*/pétrousquin *m* **2.** anus*/troufignon *m*.

Tom, tom [tɔm] *n* **1.** *F* **any Tom, Dick, or Harry,** Pierre et Paul/n'importe qui/le premier venu **2.** *P* **Tom Mix** (*a*) (*drugs*) (*RS = fix*) piqûre* de narcotique/piquouse *f*/fixe *m* (*b*) *see* **bingo 6 3.** *P* (*a*) (*RS = shit*) **to go for a tom tit,** aller déféquer*/aller faire caca/aller couler un bronze (*b*) *Austr* (*RS = shits*) **the tom tits,** la diarrhée*/la coulante/la chiasse **4.** *P* (*RS = rum*) **Tom Thumb,** rhum *m* **5.** *P* prostituée*/pute *f*/gagneuse *f*. (*See* **kingdom-come 3; touch-your-bum; Uncle 9**)

tomato [tə'meitou] *n NAm* **1.** *F* jolie fille*/fleur *f*/pépée *f*/poulette *f* **2.** *P* prostituée*/pute *f*.

tommy[1] ['tɔmi] *n F* tommy/Tommy (Atkins), soldat* anglais/Tommy *m*.

tommy[2] ['tɔmi] *vi Austr A P* s'enfuir*/décamper/filer.

tommy-rot ['tɔmirɔt] *n F* bêtises*/tissu *m* d'âneries; **that's tommy-rot,** c'est de la foutaise/du pipeau.

ton [tʌn] *n* **1.** *F* **to do a ton,** bomber/aller à toute pompe. (*See* **ton-up**) **2.** *F* **tons of ...,** une abondance*/une tripotée/une pleine brassée/des tas de ...; **to have tons**

of money, avoir beaucoup d'argent*/avoir des masses d'argent*/avoir de l'argent* à gogo; **to have tons of time,** avoir tout son temps devant soi **3.** *F* cent livres *fpl* sterling **4.** *F* **to weigh a ton,** peser lourd/peser des mille et des cents **5.** *P* (*drugs*) cannabis*. (*See* **come down 3**)

tongue [tʌŋ] *vtr V* (*a*) (*cunnilingus*) **to tongue** (**a woman**), sucer/brouter/lécher (une femme); faire minette/faire une langue fourrée (*b*) (*fellatio*) sucer/faire une pipe/tailler une plume (*c*) (*anilingus*) **to tongue s.o.** (**out**), faire feuille de rose/faire une langue fourrée (à qn).

tongue-kiss ['tʌŋkis] *n F* patin *m*/saucisse *f*/langue fourrée. (*See* **French¹ I 1**).

tongue-pie ['tʌŋ'pai] *n F* **to get a slice of tongue-pie,** se faire dire ses (quatre) vérités/en prendre pour son grade.

tonk [tɔŋk] *n P* **1.** pénis*/tringle *f* **2.** *Austr* (*a*) homosexuel*/pédé *m*/tapette *f* (*b*) efféminé *m*/lopette *f*. (*See* **honky-tonk**)

ton-up ['tʌnʌp] *n F* **to do a ton-up,** faire cent milles (160 km) à l'heure (*esp* en moto); **the ton-up boys,** les motards *mpl*/les dingues *mpl* de la moto.

toodle-oo ['tuːdl'uː] *excl F* au revoir/ciao.

toodle-pip ['tuːdl'pip] *excl F* = **toodle-oo.**

tool [tuːl] *n P* **1.** pénis*/outil *m*/chose *f*/machin *m* **2.** individu bête*/crétin *m*; **you tool!** espèce de nœud! **he's a real tool!** quel connard/quel gland, ce mec! **3.** pickpocket *m*/tire *m*/tireur *m*/fourche *f*/fourchette *f* **4.** *pl* (*drugs*) attirail *m* de camé/artillerie *f*/kit *m* **5.** *P* revolver*/flingue *m*.

tool along ['tuːlə'lɔŋ] *vi F* se balader/se baguenauder/glander.

tool off ['tuːl'ɔf] *vi P* partir*/se barrer.

tool up ['tuːl'ʌp] *vi P* se munir d'une arme à feu/s'outiller/se charger; **to be tooled up,** être outillé/chargé/enfouraillé.

tooth [tuːθ] *n F* **1. to have a sweet tooth,** aimer les sucreries *fpl* **2. to be long in the tooth,** n'être plus jeune/avoir de la bouteille **3.** *Austr* **on the tooth** (*a*) affamé (*b*) de bon goût/savoureux/succulent **4. to get one's teeth into sth,** se mettre pour de bon à qch/s'acharner à faire qch/se mettre à l'ouvrage/se plonger dans qch **5. to knock s.o.'s teeth in,** battre* qn/rentrer dans le chou à qn/amocher le portrait à qn **6. to go at it tooth and nail,** travailler* d'acharnement. (*See* **dress up 2; fed up** (*a*))

toothy-peg ['tuːθipeg] *n F* (*child's word*) petite dent* d'enfant/quenotte *f*.

tootle ['tuːtl] *vi F* corner/klaxonner.

tootle along ['tuːtlə'lɔŋ] *vi F* suivre son petit bonhomme de chemin.

toots [tuts] *n F* chéri(e)/mon petit/ma petite; **hi toots!** salut coco/cocotte!

tootsie ['tutsi] *n* **1.** *F* = **toots 2.** *P* lesbienne*/gouchotte *f*/gouine *f* **3.** (*pl*) *F* = **tootsie-wootsies.**

tootsie-wootsies ['tutsi'wutsiz] *npl F* (*child's language*) pieds*/petons *mpl*/paturons *mpl*.

tootsy ['tutsi] *n F* = **toots; tootsie.**

tootsy-footsy ['tutsi'futsi] *n F* = **footsy.**

top¹ [tɔp] *n F* **1. to go over the top,** exagérer*/y aller fort/charrier/forcer la dose **2. to blow one's top,** se mettre en colère*/éclater/sortir de ses gonds/piquer une rage. (*See* **flip² 2**) **3. the top of the morning to you!** je vous souhaite le meilleur des bonjours! **4. off the top,** la première réaction/(le mouvement) d'instinct **5. top of the shop:** *see* bingo 90. (*See* **heap 2; rag-top; tail**[1] **6; thin 1**)

top[2] [tɔp] *vtr P* pendre/exécuter/ agrafer; **topped (and chopped),** pendu/exécuté.

top-flight ['tɔp'flait], **top-hole** ['tɔp'houl] *a F* excellent*/foutral/le dessus du panier/le bouquet.

top-knot ['tɔpnɔt] *n P* tête*/ bobèche *f*/plafond *m*.

top-line ['tɔp'lain], **top-notch** ['tɔp'nɔtʃ] *a F* = **top-flight**.

top-off ['tɔpɔf] *n Austr P* dénonciateur*/indic *m*/mouton *m*/ donneur *m*/balance *f*.

top off ['tɔp'ɔf] *vtr Austr P* **1. to top s.o. off,** rabrouer qn/remettre qn à sa place **2.** (*a*) dénoncer*/ servir d'indicateur* de police/en croquer (*b*) balancer/moutonner/ vendre (qn).

topper ['tɔpər] *n F* **1.** le dessus du panier/le bouquet/la crème/la fleur des petits pois/le gratin **2.** chapeau* haut de forme/gibus *m*.

topping ['tɔpiŋ] *a O F* excellent*/ formid(able)/épatant.

topping-out ['tɔpiŋ'aut] *n F* cérémonie *f* qui marque la terminaison de la construction de la grosse œuvre d'un bâtiment.

tops [tɔps] *n F* **the tops,** le dessus du panier/la crème/la haute/le gratin; **he's the tops,** il est champion/ c'est un as.

top shop ['tɔp'ʃɔp] *n P* (= *Crown Court*) les Grands Carreaux.

torch [tɔːtʃ] *n F* **1. to carry a torch for s.o.,** aimer* qn qui ne vous aime pas/soupirer en vain **2.** pyromane *m*/incendiaire *m*/ pétroleur *m*.

torch up ['tɔːtʃ'ʌp] *vi P* = **toke up**.

tosh [tɔʃ] *n* **1.** *P* (*regional*) individu*/mec *m*/type *m* **2.** *F* bêtises*/sornettes *fpl*/blague *f*; **that's tosh!** c'est du bidon!

tosher ['tɔʃər] *n P* (*regional*) = **tosh 1**.

toss [tɔs] *n P* **I couldn't give a toss!** je n'en ai rien à branler/à glander/ à foutre.

toss-off ['tɔsɔf] *n V* acte *m* de masturbation/moussage *m* maison.

toss off ['tɔs'ɔf] *vtr* **1. to toss (oneself) off** (*i*) *V* se masturber*/se faire mousser/s'en taper une/ s'astiquer (*ii*) se vanter/s'en croire/ se faire mousser/ne pas se prendre pour de la merde **2.** *F* **to toss off a pint,** boire*/écluser un godet/s'en jeter un (derrière la cravate).

toss-up ['tɔsʌp] *n F* une chance sur deux/chance égale/pile ou face/kif-kif; **it was a toss-up between his car and mine,** entre sa tire et la mienne, c'était fifti-fifti.

total ['tout(ə)l] *vtr NAm P* **1.** démolir/bousiller/amocher (qch) **2.** battre*/mettre KO/amocher (qn).

tote[1] [tout] *n F* (*turf*) totaliseur *m*/ totalisateur *m* (des paris)/le pari mutuel/le PMU.

tote[2] [tout] *vtr F* **1.** porter/trimballer/transbahuter; **to tote a gun,** être armé/flingué **2. to tote for business/custom,** chercher à faire des affaires/quémander du travail; (*prostitute*) racoler/tapiner/faire le tapin.

tother, t'other ['tʌðər] *a & pron F* (= *the other*) l'autre; **you can't tell one from tother,** ils sont du pareil au même/on ne peut les distinguer l'un de l'autre/ils se ressemblent comme deux gouttes d'eau.

touch[1] [tʌtʃ] *n* **1.** *P* **to make a touch/to put the touch on s.o.,** emprunter* de l'argent à qn/taper qn/torpiller qn **2.** *F* **it was touch and go/it was a near touch,** cela ne tenait qu'à un fil. (*See* **touch-and-go**) **3.** *F* **soft touch,** personne bête* et crédule/dupe *f*/jobard *m*; **he's a really soft touch,** c'est un vrai cave/pigeon.

touch² [tʌtʃ] *vtr* **1.** *P* **to touch s.o. for money,** emprunter*/taper de l'argent à qn; **he touched me for a tenner,** il m'a tapé/pompé cent balles **2.** *F* **to touch lucky,** avoir de la chance*/être veinard/avoir du pot/ tirer le bon numéro **3.** *P* arrêter*/ épingler/alpaguer. (*See* **rock¹** 4; **wood** 1)

touch-and-go ['tʌtʃən'gou] *a F* (*a*) très incertain/douteux/dans la balance (*b*) hasardeux/chanceux/ aléatoire. (*See* **touch¹** 2)

touched [tʌtʃt] *a F* **touched (in the head),** fou*/toqué/timbré/cinoque.

touch up ['tʌtʃ'ʌp] *vtr P* **to touch up a girl,** peloter/palper une nana; mettre la main au panier/aller aux renseignements.

touch-your-bum ['tʌtʃjə'bʌm] *n* (*RS = rum*) *P* rhum *m.* (*See* **kingdom-come** 3; **Tom** 4)

tough [tʌf] *F* **I** *a* **1. a tough nut/ guy/cookie,** un dur (à cuire)/un coriace/un balaise **2. he's a tough customer,** il est peu commode/c'est pas un rigolo/c'est un mauvais coucheur **3.** difficile* **4. tough luck/(a) tough break,** malchance*/ déveine *f*/guigne *f*; **that's tough,** c'est moche/c'est vache; **tough shit!** manque de pot!/quel merdier! **II** *n* **1.** vaurien*/voyou *m*/loubard *m* **2.** brute *f*/crapule *f*/fripouille *f*/sale type *m* **3.** gangster *m*/criminel *m*/ saigneur *m.*

toughie ['tʌfi] *n F* **1.** = **tough II 1, 2, 3 2.** problème *m* difficile à résoudre/casse-tête *m.*

towel [taul, 'tauəl] *vtr P* battre*/ rosser/dérouiller.

towelling ['tau(ə)liŋ] *n P* raclée *f*/ peignée *f*/dérouillée *f.*

towel up ['tauəl'ʌp] *vtr Austr P* = **towel.**

town [taun] *n F* **1. to go to town** (*a*) faire la bombe/la foire/la noce (*b*) dépenser* sans compter/mettre le paquet (*c*) aller jusqu'au bout/ mettre le paquet **2. to go on the**

town = **to go to town** (*a*) **3. to go to town on s.o.,** réprimander* qn/ engueuler qn/passer un savon à qn. (*See* **red I 3**)

townified ['taunifaid], **towny** ['tauni] *a F* urbain/citadin.

track¹ [træk] *n* **1.** *F* **to hit the track/to make tracks,** partir*/se mettre en route/plier bagage/mettre les bouts/se tailler; **to make tracks for home,** rentrer chez soi/regagner le bercail; **right, must make tracks!** bon, faut que je me sauve! **2.** *P* trous *mpl* (de piqûres hypodermiques). (*See* **dirt track rider**)

track² [træk] *vi Austr O F* **to track with a girl** (*i*) faire la cour à une fille/draguer une nana (*ii*) se mettre en ménage avec une fille/se maquer. (*See* **backtrack**)

trad [træd] *F* **I** *a* (= *traditional*) traditionnel; **trad jazz,** jazz Nouvelle-Orléans et ses dérivés **II** *n* (= *traditional jazz*) jazz traditionnel.

trade¹ [treid] *n* **1.** *F* **to take it out in trade,** se faire payer en nature plutôt qu'en argent **2.** *P* clientèle *f* (d'une prostituée* *ou* d'un homosexuel*); miché *m*/micheton *m*/clille *m* **3.** *F* **he knows all the tricks of the trade,** il la connaît dans les coins/il connaît toutes les ficelles/c'est un vieux singe.

trade² [treid] *vtr&i* **1.** *F* **to trade punches,** échanger des coups*/se crêper le chignon **2.** *P* chercher des rapports sexuels/faire le trottoir/tapiner.

trade-in ['treidin] *n F* (article *m* de) reprise *f.*

trail [treil] *n F* **to hit the trail,** partir*/mettre les bouts/se tailler.

train [trein] *n P* (*woman*) **to pull a train,** faire l'amour* avec une succession de garçons/caramboler à la file/faire un petit train/tringler à la chaîne. (*See* **gravy 1; milk-train; puffer(-train)**)

tramp [træmp]*n P* femme* facile/ chaude lapine/baiseuse *f*/tringleuse *f*.

trannie, tranny ['træni] *n F* (= *transistor*) transistor *m*/poste *m*.

trap [træp] *n P* bouche*/gueule *f*; **shut your trap!** tais-toi!/ferme-la!/ ferme ton clapet! **to keep one's trap shut**, taire sa gueule/la fermer. (*See* **fleatrap**; **rat-trap**)

trash [træʃ] *n NAm P* **1.** mendiant*/clodo *m*/mangav *m* **2. white trash**, petits blancs pauvres.

travel-agent ['trævəl'eidʒənt] *n P* (*drugs*) fournisseur *m* de LSD/ dealer* d'acide/agent *m* de voyage.

traveller ['træv(ə)lər] *n F* romanichel *m*/manouche *mf*/ romano *m*.

trawler ['trɔːlər] *n Austr P* car* de police/panier *m* à salade/fourgon *m*/poulailler *m*.

treacle ['triːkl] *n P* **1.** (*drugs*) opium *m*/noir *m* **2.** homosexuel*/ chochotte *f*/tapette *f*.

tree [triː] *n F* **1. up a tree**, dans le pétrin/dans de beaux draps/dans la mélasse **2. they don't grow on trees**, on n'en trouve pas comme ça si facilement/ça ne se trouve pas sous le sabot d'un cheval. (*See* **apple-tree**; **Christmas-tree**; **gum-tree**; **palm-tree**)

tremble ['trembl] *n F* **to be all of a tremble**, avoir la tremblote.

tremendous [tri'mendəs, trə'mendəs] *a F* **1.** énorme/immense; **a tremendous decision**, une décision très importante **2.** passionnant/ palpitant; **a tremendous time was had by all**, on s'est drôlement/follement amusés.

tremendously [tri'mendəsli, trə'mendəsli] *adv F* énormément/drôlement/vachement.

trendy ['trendi] **I** *a F* à la mode/ dans le vent/du dernier chic; **a really trendy restaurant**, le dernier cri en matière de resto **II** *n* qn à

la mode/à la page; dandy *m*/minet *m* beau linge.

trey [trei] *n A P* (*drugs*) colis *m ou* paquet *m ou* sachet *m* de stupéfiants.

trey-bits ['treibits] *npl Austr P* = **threepenny-bits**.

tribe [traib] *n F* smala(h) *f*; (toute) une kyrielle/une ribambelle (d'enfants).

trick¹ [trik] *n* **1.** *F* **how's tricks?** quoi de neuf?. **2.** *F* **he doesn't miss a trick**, rien ne lui échappe/il est roublard/il est malin comme pas deux **3.** *F* **that should do the trick**, ça fera l'affaire **4.** *P* client *m* (d'une prostituée)/clille *m*/micheton *m*/miché *m*; **to turn a trick**, trouver un client/faire une passe **5.** *F* **to be up to all sorts of tricks**, faire les quatre cents coups. (*See* **bag¹** 5, 6; **funny I** 2; **trade¹** 3)

trick² [trik] *vi P* **1.** *A* faire l'amour* (avec une femme)/godiller/pinocher **2.** *esp NAm* (*prostitutes*) racoler*/faire le truc; **to trick a john**, monter un client/un micheton; faire une passe.

trick-cyclist ['trik'saiklist] *n P* psychiatre *mf*.

trigger-happy ['trigəhæpi] *a F* **to be trigger-happy**, être rapide à la gâchette/avoir la gâchette facile.

trigger-man ['trigə(r)mæn] *n F* (*a*) assassin*/professionnel *m* de la gâchette (*b*) but(t)eur *m*/flingueur *m* (*c*) garde *f* du corps/gorille *m*.

trip¹ [trip] *n P* **1.** (*drugs*) (*a*) dose *f* de LSD* (*b*) voyage *m*/trip *m*; **to take/to go on a trip**, être sous l'effet du LSD*/être en voyage/partir/tripper; faire/prendre un trip **2. to take/to make a trip**, purger sa peine de prison/faire sa taule.

trip² [trip] *vi P* être sous l'effet du LSD*/être en voyage/partir/tripper.

tripe [traip] *n F* **1.** bêtises*/sornettes *fpl*/fichaises *fpl*; **that's tripe,**

c'est du flan/du pipeau 2. camelote *f*/quincaillerie *f*/toc *m*.

tripehound ['traiphaund] *n A P* vaurien*/charogne *f*/sale type.

trip out ['trip'aut] *vi P* (*drugs*) être sous l'effet du LSD*/tripper; **to be tripped out,** être envapé/être sur sa planète/planer.

trizzer ['trizər] *n Austr A P* WC*/chiottes *fpl*.

trolley ['trɔli] *n NAm F* **off one's trolley** = **off one's rocker (rocker 2).**

troppo ['trɔpou] *a Austr P* (*mentally affected by a tropical climate*) **he's gone troppo,** le soleil lui a trop tapé sur le citron/il a pris un coup de bambou.

trot [trɔt] *n* **1.** *F* **on the trot** (*a*) à la suite/coup sur coup; **to win four times on the trot,** gagner quatre fois de suite (*b*) (*prison*) en fuite/en cavale **2.** *F* **to keep s.o. on the trot,** faire trotter qn/actionner qn **3.** *P* prostituée*/marcheuse *f*/roulure *f* **4.** *P* **the trots,** diarrhée*/courante *f*/chiassée *f* **5.** *P* (*pol*) (= *trotskyite*) gauchiste *mf*/gaucho *mf* = stal *m*.

trot artist ['trɔt'ɑitist] *n Austr P* avare*/grippe-sou *m* (qui s'en va aux toilettes au lieu d'offrir une tournée).

trotter ['trɔtər] *n P* **1.** déserteur *m*/franc-fileur *m* **2.** individu* recherché par la police/décarreur *m* **3.** *pl* pieds*/trottinets *mpl* **4.** = **trot artist.**

trouble ['trʌbl] *n* **1.** *F* **to get a girl into trouble,** rendre une fille enceinte*/mettre une fille en cloque **2.** *P* (*RS* = *wife*) **trouble and strife,** épouse*.

trough [trɔf] *n F* (*hum*) (= *feeding trough*) assiette *f*/auge *f*.

trousers ['trauzəz] *npl F* **his wife wears the trousers at home,** c'est sa femme qui porte la culotte chez eux. (*See* **pants 7**)

trouser-snake ['trauzəsneik] *n Austr P* **one-eyed trouser-snake,** pénis*/anguille *f* de calecif.

trout [traut] *n P* vieille femme*/vieille savate/vieux trumeau; **she's a real old trout,** c'est une vieille bique.

truck-driver ['trʌkdraivər] *n P* (*drugs*) amphétamine*/amph *m*. (*See* **driver 2**)

truckie ['trʌki] *n Austr F* camionneur *m*/routier *m*.

trump [trʌmp] *n F* **1.** brave homme*/chic type *m*/brave mec *m* **2. to turn up trumps** (*a*) réussir mieux que l'on espérait/avoir de la chance* (*b*) rendre service/donner un bon coup de main; **he really turned up trumps that time,** il nous a rendu salement service/il a fait des merveilles. (*See* **card 7**)

trusty ['trʌsti] *n F* prisonnier *m* à qui l'on donne certains privilèges/un sûr/un prévot.

try-on ['traiɔn] *n F* **1.** ballon *m* d'essai **2.** (coup *m* de) bluff *m*; **it's a try-on,** c'est du bluff/de l'esbrouffe.

try on ['traiɔn] *vtr F* **don't (you) try it on with me!** (ne) cherche pas à me bluffer! (il ne) faut pas me la refaire!/(ne) la ramène pas avec moi! **just (you) try it on!** chiche!/vas-y qu'on voit!/essaye pour voir! **to try it on with a woman,** aller aux renseignements/faire du rentrededans.

tub [tʌb] *n F* **1.** gros ventre*/bedaine *f* **2.** (*boat*) **old tub,** raf(f)iot *m*.

tube [tjuːb] *n F* **1. it's my tubes** [mi'tjuːbz], c'est mes bronches **2. the Tube,** le Métro; **we came by Tube,** nous avons pris le Métro **3.** *NAm* **the tube,** la télé/la téloche. (*See* **boob tube**) **4.** *Austr* bouteille *f ou* boîte *f* de bière/cannette *f*.

tuck [tʌk] *n F* (*scol*) friandises *fpl*/sucreries *fpl*; boustifaille *f*. (*See* **tuckshop**)

tuck away ['tʌkə'wei] *vtr F* **1.** cacher/mettre à gauche **2. to tuck it away,** boire* *et/ou* manger*; s'en mettre derrière la cravate/s'en mettre jusque-là/se caler les côtes/se taper la cloche.

tucker ['tʌkər] *n Austr F* nourriture*/mangeaille *f*/boustifaille *f*. (*See* **bib**)

tuckered ['tʌkəd] *a P* fatigué*/éreinté/vanné/lessivé.

tuck-in ['tʌk'in] *n F* repas faramineux/gueuleton *m*/bombance *f*/balthazar *m*; **to have a good tuck-in,** s'en mettre plein la lampe.

tuck in ['tʌk'in] *vi F* manger* de bon cœur/s'en mettre jusqu'au menton/s'en mettre plein la lampe/se taper la cloche; **tuck in!** vas-y, mange!/attaque!

tuck into ['tʌk'intuː] *vtr F* **to tuck into a meal,** manger* un repas à belles dents/faire bonne chère.

tuckshop ['tʌkʃɔp] *n F* (*scol*) boutique *f ou* annexe *f* de la cantine où se vendent les friandises *fpl*. (*See* **tuck**)

tuck up ['tʌk'ʌp] *vtr P* **1.** entuber/rouler/avoir/pigeonner (qn) **2.** tuer*/zigouiller/faire la peau à (qn).

tumble[1] ['tʌmbl] *n F* **to have a tumble with s.o.,** faire l'amour* avec qn/avoir une partie de jambes en l'air avec qn.

tumble[2] ['tʌmbl] *vtr&i F* **1.** *O* **to tumble (a woman),** culbuter/sauter (une femme) **2. to tumble to sth,** comprendre qch tout à coup/entraver qch; **then he tumbled to it,** puis, il a pigé.

tummy ['tʌmi] *n F* (*a*) ventre*/bide *m*/bidon *m* (*b*) bedaine *f*.

tummy-ache ['tʌmieik] *n F* mal *m* au ventre.

tune [tjuːn] *n F* **1. to the tune of ...,** pour la somme (pas mal salée) de ... **2. to change one's tune,** changer de ton/changer de langage/chanter sur une autre note/en rabattre d'un ton. (*See* **old 4**)

tune in ['tjuːn'in] *vi F* se mettre au diapason; **she isn't tuned in,** elle n'est pas sur la même longueur d'ondes.

tune up ['tjuːn'ʌp] *vi F* se conditionner/s'entraîner.

tup [tʌp] *vtr A P* faire l'amour* avec (une femme)/calecer/caramboler/sch(e)nailler.

tuppence ['tʌp(ə)ns] *n F* (= *twopence*) **I don't care tuppence,** ça m'est bien égal/je m'en fiche pas mal; **it's not worth tuppence,** ça ne vaut pas deux sous/tripette/deux rondelles de carotte/un pet de lapin.

tuppenny ['tʌp(ə)ni] *a F* (= *twopenny*) **I don't give/care a tuppenny damn/***V* **a tuppenny fuck,** je m'en fiche complètement/je m'en contrefiche/*V* je m'en fous pas mal/je m'en branle complètement. (*See* **damn**[1] **III**)

tuppenny-ha'penny ['tʌp(ə)ni'heip(ə)ni] *a F* (= *twopenny-halfpenny*) insignifiant/piètre/de quatre sous/de rien du tout.

tupp'ny ['tʌpni] *a F* = **tuppenny**.

turd [təːd] *n P* **1.** étron*/colombin *m*/merde *f* **2.** saligaud *m*/salaud *m*/fumier *m*/ordure *f*; **he's a real turd,** c'est un vrai con/un sale type; **you turd!** (espèce de) salaud! **3. to skin a turd,** être avare*/être constipé du morlingue.

turd-burglar ['təːdbəːglər], **turd-snipper** ['təːdsnipər] *n V* homosexuel*/qn qui est de la bague/pédoque *m*/amateur *m* de rosette.

turf [təːf] *n NAm P* **to be on the turf,** racoler*/faire le bitume/faire le trottoir/aller au turf/tapiner.

turf out ['təːf'aut] *vtr F* flanquer dehors/balancer/envoyer dinguer.

turistas ['turistəz] *n NAm P* the

turistas, la diarrhée*/la courante/la chiassée.

turkey ['tɜːki] *n* **1.** *P* (*drugs*) cold turkey, sevrage *m* de drogues; **to be cold turkey,** être en manque/être cold turkey/être poulet froid **2.** *F esp NAm* **to talk turkey,** parler* sérieusement/en venir au fait **3.** *esp NAm P* homme*/mec *m*/type *m*/zigoto *m*.

turn [tɜːn] *n F* **1.** (*a*) it gave me quite a (nasty) turn, (tout) mon sang n'a fait qu'un tour/ça m'a fait quelque chose (*b*) you gave me such a turn! vous m'avez fait une belle peur*!/vous m'avez retourné le sang! **2.** she had one of her turns yesterday, hier elle a eu une de ses crises/ses attaques.

turned on ['tɜːnd'ɒn] *a&pp* **1.** *F* dans le vent/à la coule **2.** *P* (*drugs*) allumé/chargé/branché par la drogue; **to be turned on,** être envapé/planer/être sur sa planète **3.** *P* (*sexually*) allumé/excité/branché; **he gets turned on by black leather,** le cuir noir c'est son truc/le cuir noir le fait bander.

turn in ['tɜːn'in] *vtr&i F* **1.** se coucher*/se pieuter **2.** rendre/rapporter (qch); **to turn oneself in (to the police),** se constituer prisonnier/se faire coffrer/se livrer.

turniphead ['tɜːniphed] *n P* individu bête*/cruche *f*/ballot *m*/naveton *m*.

turn-off ['tɜːnɒf] *n P* qch de déplaisant/de débectant/de répugnant; **it was a real turn-off,** c'était comme une douche froide; ça m'a foutu les boules.

turn off ['tɜːn'ɒf] *vtr P* **1.** ennuyer/emmerder/casser les pieds à (qn) **2.** déplaire à (qn)/rebuter (qn); **that sort of thing turns me off completely,** ces trucs-là, ça me fout les boules; **you really turn me off!** tu me débectes!

turn-on ['tɜːnɒn] *n P* **1.** (*drugs*) une séance particulière de drogues **2.** qch d'excitant/d'emballant; **that was a real turn-on!** c'était le pied!/ça m'a vraiment emballé!/c'était l'éclat!

turn on ['tɜːn'ɒn] *vtr* **1.** *F* emballer/botter/brancher (qn); **that turns me on,** ça me botte/ça me branche/c'est comme ça que je prends mon pied **2.** *P* (*drugs*) allumer/brancher (qn); **LSD turns him on,** le LSD* c'est son truc **3.** (*sexually*) exciter/faire bander (qn); **she really turns him on,** elle le fait bander à mort.

turnout ['tɜːnaut] *n* **1.** *F* assemblée *f*/foule *f*/assistance *f*/auditoire *m*/public *m*; **they had a good turnout at the meeting,** il y avait du monde à la réunion **2.** *F* vêtements*/tenue *f*/uniforme *m* **3.** *P* coït* d'un groupe avec une seule fille *ou* femme; dérouillage *m* à la une/petit train; rodéo *m*/barlu *m*.

turnover ['tɜːnouvər] *n P* perquisition *f*/fouille *f*.

turn over ['tɜːn'ouvər] *vtr P* **1.** to turn s.o. over, voler*/refaire qn/rouler qn; **to turn a place over,** faire un cambriolage/un fric-frac/un casse **2.** to turn over a cell, fouiller une cellule.

turn-up ['tɜːnʌp] *n P* **1.** that's a turn-up (for the book), c'est une sacrée/une belle surprise **2.** chahut *m*/tapage *m*/boucan *m*/chambard *m*.

turn up ['tɜːn'ʌp] *vtr&i F* **1.** arriver* (à l'improviste)/débarquer/faire une apparition **2.** arriver/se passer/se produire **3.** découvrir*/trouver/dégot(t)er **4.** that turns me up, ça m'écœure/ça me soulève le cœur **5.** turn it up! arrête (les frais)!/c'est marre!/écrase! (*See* nose 6; toe 3)

turps [tɜːps] *n F* **1.** (= *turpentine*) (essence *f* de) térébenthine *f* **2.** *Austr* alcool* de mauvaise qualité/tord-boyaux *m*/gobette *f*/gnôle *f*; **to hit the turps,** écluser/picoler.

twack [twæk], **twam(my)** ['twæm(i)] n P = **twat 1**.

twang [twæŋ] n P (drugs) opium*/ toufiane f/noir m.

twat [twɔt] n 1. V sexe de la femme*/con m/con(n)asse f 2. P individu bête*/idiot m/con m/connard m; **you great twat!** espèce de nœud/d'andouille/d'enculé!

twee [twiː] a F (a) gentil/mignon (b) (pej) maniéré/mignard; **that's terribly twee,** ça fait très cucul (la praline).

tweetie(-pie) ['twiːti('pai)] n F = **sweetie-pie.**

twenty-five ['twenti'faiv] n P (drugs) LSD*/vingt-cinq m.

twerp [twɔːp] n F individu bête*/ ballot m/crétin m; **what a twerp!** quelle andouille!/quelle nouille!

twig [twig] vtr&i P comprendre/ saisir/piger/entraver; **now I twig it!** j'y suis maintenant! **and then he twigged!** et puis, ça a fait tilt!

twink [twiŋk] n P homosexuel* ou efféminé m/chochotte f/chouquette f/fofolle f.

twinkle ['twiŋkl] n P 1. pénis* (d'enfant)/zizi m/quéquette f 2. **to have a twinkle,** uriner*/pisser.

twirl [twɔːl] n P 1. gardien* de prison/maton m/matuche m 2. clef*/passe-partout m/carouble f 3. (rare) cigarette*/cibiche f.

twirp [twɔːp] n F = **twerp.**

twist¹ [twist] n P 1. **to go round the twist,** devenir fou*/perdre la boule/déménager; **he drives me round the twist,** il me rend fou/ dingue. (See **bend¹** 1) 2. (drugs) cigarette* de marijuana*/stick m/ joint m. (See **knickers 1; tassel 2**)

twist² [twist] vtr F 1. escroquer*/ frauder/filouter/arnaquer 2. **to twist s.o.'s arm,** persuader qn/forcer la main à qn; **he likes to have his arm twisted,** il aime se faire prier; **go on! twist my arm!** vas-y

toujours!/insiste un peu! je ne dirais pas non. (See **burn¹**(a); **finger¹ 9**)

twisted ['twistid] a P (drugs) chargé/défoncé/camé (jusqu'aux yeux).

twister ['twistər] n F 1. escroc*/ faux jeton/fripouille f/filou m/arnaqueur m 2. casse-tête (chinois).

twit [twit] n F individu bête*/ballot m/con(n)ard m; **he's a hopeless twit,** il en a une couche; **you silly twit!** espèce de nœud!/pauvre con, va!

twitter ['twitər] n F 1. **to be all of a twitter/in a twitter,** être sens dessus dessous/être dans tous ses états 2. **to have the twitters,** avoir la tremblote/la trouille. (See **ring¹ 1**)

two [tuː] n F 1. **to put two and two together,** tirer/en déduire ses conclusions; tirer la leçon de la chose; **he's capable of putting two and two together and getting five,** chez lui deux et deux font cinq, c'est dire s'il est con/il est con comme un balai 2. **all the twos: see bingo 22**. (See **one-two; thing 6**)

two-bit ['tuːbit] a NAm F insignifiant/à la manque/à la gomme.

twopenny-halfpenny ['tʌp(ə)ni'heip(ə)ni] a F = **tuppenny-ha'penny.**

two-piece ['tuːpiːs] n P testicules*/paire f.

twot [twɔt] n P = **twat 1, 2**.

two-time ['tuː'taim] vtr F 1. tromper (qn) (en amour)/être infidèle/doubler qn 2. duper*/ tromper.

two-timer ['tuː'taimər] n F mari m qui trompe sa femme ou femme infidèle.

tyke [taik] n P 1. (often pej) natif m du comté du Yorkshire 2. malotru m/rustre m/rustaud m 3. vilain chien*/sale cabot m/clébard m.

typo ['taipou] *n F* (=*typographical error*) typo *m*/coquille *f.*

U

U [juː] *a F* (= *upper class*) **his accent is very U,** il a un petit accent de la haute; **that's not a terribly U thing to do,** ça (ne) fait pas très distingué, ça.

udders [ˈʌdəz] *npl P* seins*/boîtes *fpl* à lait/roploplots *mpl*.

umpteen [ˈʌmptiːn, ʌmpˈtiːn] *a F* je ne sais combien; **they have umpteen kids,** ils ont je ne sais combien de gosses/ils ont une ribambelle de gosses; **to have umpteen reasons for doing sth,** avoir trente-six raisons de faire qch; **I've told you umpteen times,** je vous l'ai dit x [iks] fois.

umpteenth [ˈʌmptiːnθ, ʌmpˈtiːnθ] *a F* trente-sixième/ennième/xième [ˈiksjɛm].

umpty [ˈʌm(p)ti] *a P* un peu malade*/mal fichu/pas dans son assiette.

'un [ən] *pron F* (= *one*) individu*/quelqu'un/type *m*/mec *m*; **a little 'un,** un petiot; **a wrong 'un,** un fripon/un coquin/un chenapan/un zigoto.

unchubb [ʌnˈtʃʌb] *vi A P* ouvrir*/la serrure/débloquer/débrider (la lourde)/délourder (la porte). (*See* **unmiln**)

Uncle, uncle [ˈʌŋkl] *n* **1.** *P* agent* de police/flic *m*/ange gardien/cogne *m* **2.** *P* indicateur* (de police)/indic *m*/balance *f* **3.** *P* (*RS*) **Uncle Dick,** (*a*) (= *prick*) pénis*. (*See* **dick¹**) (*b*) (= *sick*) malade* **4.** *P* (*RS*) **Uncle Ned,** (*a*) (= *bed*) lit* (*b*) (= *head*) tête* **5.** *F* prêteur *m* (sur gages)/tante *f*; **at (my) uncle's,** chez ma tante/au

clou/chez mon oncle **6.** *F* **Uncle Sam,** l'oncle Sam/les États-Unis *mpl* (d'Amérique)/les ricains *mpl* **7.** *P* receleur*/fourgue *m* **8.** *NAm P* = **Sam 2 9.** *NAm F* **Uncle Tom,** noir *m* qui s'insinue dans les bonnes grâces des blancs/Oncle Tom **10.** *NAm P* **Uncle Sugar** = Federal Bureau of Investigation (FBI). (*See* **Bob²**; **Dutch 5**)

uncool [ˈʌnˈkuːl] *a P* (*a*) passionnant/palpitant (*b*) dans tous ses états/énervé; **he felt terribly uncool about the whole thing,** ça l'a mis dans tous ses états/ça l'a tout retourné.

uncut [ˈʌnkʌt] *a P* **1.** (*drugs*) (*esp heroin*) pur(e) **2.** (*homosexuels*) non circoncis.

under [ˈʌndər] *prep F* **to be under the doctor,** être en traitement/être sous surveillance médicale. (*See* **weather**)

underdaks [ˈʌndədæks] *npl Austr P* caleçon *m* (d'homme)/slip *m*/calcif *m*/calbard *m*.

undergrad [ˈʌndəˈgræd] *n F* (= *undergraduate*) étudiant(e) (qui n'a pas encore ses diplômes).

under-the-counter [ˈʌndə-ðəˈkauntər] *a F* au marché noir/en sous-main. (*See* **counter**)

undies [ˈʌndiz] *npl F* sous-vêtements féminins/lingerie *f*/dessous *mpl*/falbalas *mpl*/fringues *fpl* de coulisse.

unearthly [ʌnˈəːθli] *a F* **at an unearthly hour,** à une heure indue/à une heure pas permise. (*See* **ungodly**)

unflappable ['ʌn'flæpəbl] *a F* flegmatique/calme/qui ne s'affole pas/nonchalant/cool.

un-get-at-able ['ʌnget'ætəbl] *a F* inaccessible.

unglued ['ʌn'gluːd] *a NAm P* **1.** frénétique/forcené/affolé **2.** fou*/loufoque/piqué.

ungodly [ʌn'gɔdli] *a F* **at an/some ungodly hour,** à une heure indue/à une heure pas permise.

unhitched ['ʌn'hitʃt] *a&pp F* **to get unhitched,** divorcer/se séparer/se démaquer/casser/rompre. (*See* **hitch 2**)

uni [juːni] *n Austr F* université *f*/fac *f*.

unlucky ['ʌn'lʌki] *a F* **unlucky for some:** *see* **bingo 13**.

unmiln ['ʌnmiln] *vi A P* = **unchubb**.

unscramble ['ʌn'skræmbl] *vtr F* (*a*) débrouiller (un message)/déchiffrer/mettre au clair (*b*) **I'll try and unscramble my appointments,** j'essaierai de remanier mes rendez-vous*.

unscrewed [ʌn'skruːd] *a NAm P* = **unglued 1, 2**.

unstuck [ʌn'stʌk] *a&pp F* **to come unstuck** (*a*) (*project, etc*) s'effondrer/s'écrouler/tomber à l'eau/partir à vau l'eau (*b*) (*pers*) (*i*) tomber sur un bec/tomber sur un os; faire un bide (*ii*) s'effondrer/se planter/faire la culbute.

unwashed [ʌn'wɔʃt] *a&pp F* **the Great Unwashed,** les prolétaires *mpl*/les prolos *mpl*/les pouilleux *mpl*.

up¹ [ʌp] **I** *a F* **1.** euphorique dû à la drogue/high/défoncé/planant; **to be up,** planer/voyager/être sur sa planète **2. up drugs,** drogues stimulantes psychiques/stimulants *mpl*/dopants *mpl*. (*See* **down¹ I**; **upper²**) **3.** heureux/en pleine forme/qui pète la santé **II** *adv* **1.** *F* **to be up against it,** avoir la malchance*/la guigne/la déveine/la poisse; **we're really up against it now,** on a la super-poisse maintenant **2.** *F* **to be up to sth,** fabriquer/mijoter/manigancer qch; **what's he up to now?** qu'est-ce qu'il mijote? **3.** *F* **it's all up/the game's up,** c'est fichu/c'est cuit/c'est râpé/c'est à l'eau. (*See* **all II 1**) **4.** *F* **what's up?** que se passe-t-il?/qu'y a-t-il?/ça ne va pas? **5.** *P* en coït* (avec une femme)/en mise/en prise; **to have it up,** être en érection*/l'avoir en l'air. (*See* **move¹ 2**) **III** *n* **1.** *F* **to be on the up and up** (*a*) être en bonne voie/prospérer/faire son beurre; **his career is on the up and up,** il fait son chemin/il grimpe les échelons (*b*) être honnête/correct/réglo **2.** *P* = **upper²** **3.** *F* **to give s.o. a quick up and down,** jauger qn/se faire une idée de qn. (*See* **high-ups**) **IV** *prep P* **1. up yours!** fous ça dans ta poche (et ton mouchoir par-dessus)!/tu peux te le foutre quelque part!/tu peux te l'accrocher! (*See* **arse I 7**; **flue 2**; **gonga**; **jumper**; **Khyber**) **2.** en coït* avec (une femme). (*See* **creek**; **spout¹ 1, 2, 3**)

up² [ʌp] *vtr&i* **1.** *F* **to up sticks,** déménager/décaniller/bouger ses bois/plier bagages **2.** *P* (*a*) se lever d'un bond; **then he upped and left,** puis d'un bond il s'est mis debout et s'est cassé (*b*) agir avec élan; **so I ups and tells him what I think,** et je me suis lancé et lui ai dit exactement ce que je pensais/ses quatre vérités.

up-and-downer ['ʌpən'daunər] *n F* (*not common*) querelle*/prise *f* de bec/engueulade/suif *m*.

upbeat ['ʌpbiːt] *a F* (*a*) pétillant/fringant/pimpant/euphorique (*b*) optimiste. (*See* **downbeat**)

upholstery [ʌp'houlstəri] *n P* seins*/avant-scène *f*/balcon *m*. (*See* **well-upholstered**)

up market ['ʌp'mɑːkit] *a F* (de) haut de gamme/qui a de la classe;

qui vaut très cher. (*See* **down market**)

upper¹ ['ʌpər] *a F* **1. upper storey**, tête*/cerveau *m*/ciboulot *m*/cafetière *f*; **to be weak in the upper storey**, avoir une araignée au plafond/travailler du citron **2. upper bracket**, tête *f* de liste **3. upper crust**, les huiles *fpl*/les grosses légumes/la crème/le gratin/le dessus du panier/la haute. (*See* **lip 2**; **ten 1**)

upper² ['ʌpər], **uppie** ['ʌpi] *n P* (*drugs*) amphétamine*/amph *m*/cranck *m*; **to be on uppers**, prendre des amphés. (*See* **downer 1**; **downie**; **uppers**)

upper-and-downer ['ʌpə(r)-æn'daunər] *n F* = **up-and-downer**.

uppers ['ʌpəz] *npl F* **to be down on one's uppers**, être très pauvre*/être dans la purée noire/être dans la dèche. (*See* **upper²**)

uppish ['ʌpiʃ] *a F* = **uppity 1**.

uppity ['ʌpiti] *a F* **1.** prétentieux*/arrogant/crâneur/hautain; **to act uppity**, en installer **2.** féroce; dédaigneux/bêcheur; **to get uppity with s.o.**, traiter qn de haut.

ups-a-daisy! ['ʌpsə'deizi] *excl F* hoop-là!

upset ['ʌpset] *n F* querelle*/remueménage *m*; **they had a bit of an upset**, ils ont eu une prise de bec.

upsides ['ʌpsaidz] *adv F* **to be upsides with s.o.**, être quitte avec qn/rendre la monnaie de sa pièce à qn.

upstage¹ [ʌp'steidʒ] *a F* prétentieux*/snob/bêcheur/crâneur.

upstage² [ʌp'steidʒ] *vtr F* **1.** (*theatre*) mettre (un autre acteur) à l'ombre du public/retirer le haut des planches à (un autre acteur)/décrocher (qn) **2.** remettre (qn) à sa place/faire semblant de ne pas voir (qn)/snober (qn).

upstairs [ʌp'stɛəz] *adv F* **to have sth upstairs**, avoir le ciboulot bien

rempli/être intelligent/en avoir dans le cigare; **he's got it all upstairs!** il en a dans le citron!/il en a, là-dedans! (*See* **kick upstairs**)

upsy-daisy! ['ʌpsi'deizi] *excl F* = **ups-a-daisy!**

uptake ['ʌpteik] *n F* (*a*) **to be quick on the uptake**, comprendre vite/avoir l'esprit vif/avoir la comprenette facile (*b*) **to be slow on the uptake**, avoir la comprenette difficile/être dur à la détente.

uptight ['ʌp'tait] *a F* **1.** tendu/ému/agité; **don't get uptight about it!** te fais pas toute cette bile pour ça!/t'en fais donc pas comme ça! **2.** survolté **3.** *NAm* connu à fond/sur le bout du doigt **4.** complexé/inhibé/bloqué/coincé **5.** fielleux/rancunier.

us [ʌs, əs] *pron F* (= *me*) moi; **give us a kiss!** alors, on m'embrasse/fais-moi une bise! **let's have a look!** laisse-moi regarder!/fais voir!

use [juːs] *vtr* **1.** *F* exploiter/tirer parti de (qn)/abuser de (qn) **2.** *F* prendre plaisir à/ profiter de (qch); **I could use a cup of tea**, je ne dirais pas non à une tasse de thé; **I could use a week's holiday**, une semaine de vacances ne me ferait pas de mal **3.** *P* se droguer*/se camer.

used up ['juːzd'ʌp] *a&pp P* très fatigué*/crevé/claqué/vanné/lessivé.

useful ['juːsful] *a F* efficace/habile/cap(able); **he's pretty useful with his fists**, il sait bien jouer des poings/il sait se servir de ses poings.

user ['juːzər] *n P* drogué*/camé *mf*/toxico *mf*/junkie *mf*.

usual ['juːʒu(ə)l] *n F* **the usual**, ce que l'on a *ou* prend d'habitude/l'ordinaire; **he had his usual, a bottle of red wine**, il siffla son litron quotidien; **the usual?** comme d'habitude?

V

vac [væk] *n F* (*abbr = vacation*) vacances *fpl*; **the Long Vac,** les grandes vacances.

vamoose [vəˈmuːs] *vi P* s'enfuir*/ décamper / riper / s'arracher; **vamoose!** file!/casse-toi!/fiche le camp!

varieties [vəˈraiətiz] *npl F* **all the varieties:** *see* **bingo 57.**

varmint [ˈvɑːmint] *n F* (*a*) vermine *f* (*b*) **young varmint,** petit polisson/ jeune morpion *m*/mioche *m*.

varnish¹ [ˈvɑːniʃ] *n P* (*not common*) mauvais alcool*/camphre *m*/cogne *f*/tord-boyaux *m*.

varnish² [ˈvɑːniʃ] *vtr P* **to varnish the cane,** se masturber*/s'astiquer la colonne/s'allonger la couenne.

varsity, Varsity [ˈvɑːsiti] *n O F* l'Université *f*/la Faculté/la Fac.

veep [viːp] *n NAm F* vice-président *m*.

vegetable [ˈvedʒtəbl] *n F* handicapé(e) mental(e)/épave *f*/crétin *m*; **she's just a vegetable,** elle n'a pas toutes ses facultés.

velvet [ˈvelvit] *n* **1.** *P* **blue velvet,** drogues* (parégorique et antihistamine) **2. black velvet** (*a*) *F* mélange *m* de champagne et de stout (*b*) *P* noire*/négresse *f*/ bougnoul(l)e *f* **3.** *F* **to be on velvet** (*a*) jouer sur le velours/sur du velours (*b*) vivre comme un prince/ mener la vie de château/se la couler douce **4.** *F* (*a*) bénéfice*/ velours *m*/gâteau *m*/affure *m* or *f* (*b*) argent*/galette *f*/galtouze *f*.

Vera Lynn [ˈvirəˈlin] *n P* (*RS = gin*) gin *m*.

verbal¹ [ˈvɜːbəl] *n P* **1. the verbal,** bavardage *m*/bavette *f*; **they were having a bit of a verbal,** ils taillaient une bavette. (*See* **diarrhoea**) **2.** *pl* (*underworld, etc*) **verbals,** témoignage basé sur l'aveu (oral) de culpabilité d'un accusé (et fait à la police).

verbal² [ˈvɜːbəl] *vtr P* (*of police*) déclarer qu'un criminel, etc, a fait des aveux oraux; **the cops will verbal you,** les flics vont déclarer que tu leur as tout dit.

vet¹ [vet] *abbr F* **1.** (*= veterinary surgeon*) vétérinaire *mf*/véto *m* **2.** *NAm* (*US Army*) (*= veteran*) ancien combattant.

vet² [vet] *vtr F* revoir/corriger/mettre au point.

vibes [vaibz] *npl F* **1.** (*jazz*) vibraphone *m*; **he's on vibes,** il joue du vibraphone **2.** (*= vibrations*) vibrations *fpl*; **the vibes are all wrong,** ça ne gaze pas; c'est craignos/c'est galère; **good vibes!** ça déménage!/c'est le pied!

vice [vais] *n F* **1.** (*= vice-president, vice-chairman*) vice-président *m*/ sous-Mec *m* **2.** (*= vice-chancellor*) recteur *m* (d'une université)/recto *m* **3.** (*= deputy*) substitut *m*/délégué *m*/sous-Mec *m*.

villain [ˈvilən] *n F* **1.** bandit *m*/ scélérat *m*/malfrat *m*; **a small-time villain,** un petit truand/un truand à la mie de pain **2.** coquin *m*/garnement *m*; **you little villain!** petit polisson!/sacré brigand!/petit garnement!

villainy ['vilǝni] *n F* **to do a villainy** (*a*) cambrioler*/faire un fric-frac/ monter en l'air/faire un casse (*b*) commettre un crime/un acte criminel.

vim [vim] *n F* vigueur *f*/force *f*/ énergie *f*/vitalité *f*; **to be full of vim,** avoir de la vitalité à revendre/ péter le feu.

vine [vain] *n* **1.** *P* **the vine = the grapevine (grapevine) 2.** *pl P* vêtements*/fringues *fpl*/frusques *fpl* **3.** *F* **clinging vine,** femme* possessive/pot *m* de colle/julie *f* pot de colle.

vino ['viːnou] *n P* vin*/gros rouge/ pinard *m*/picrate *m*/pivois *m*.

VIP ['viːaɪ'piː] *abbr F* (= *very important person*) personnage important/ grosse légume/huile *f*; **to give s.o.**

(the) VIP treatment, recevoir qn avec tambour et trompettes; dérouler le tapis rouge pour qn.

viper ['vaipǝr] *n NAm P* (*drugs*) (*a*) drogué* à la marijuana* (*b*) fourgueur *m*/dealer* de marijuana*.

visit ['vizit] *n F* **to pay a visit,** aller faire pipi/aller faire sa petite commission; (*man*) jeter sa goutte/ changer l'eau des poissons.

vocab ['voukæb, vǝ'kæb] *n F* (*abbr* = *vocabulary*) vocabulaire *m*/ voc(ab) *m*; **vocab book,** carnet *m* de voc(ab).

vocals ['voukǝlz] *npl P* **to give with the vocals,** chanter*/pousser une goualante/y aller de sa goualante/ goualer.

voyager ['vɔiǝdʒǝr] *n P* drogué(e)* au LSD*/voyageur *m*/tripeur *m*/ planeur *m*. (*See* **trip**[1] **1**)

W

wack [wæk] *n P* **1.** *esp NAm* fou *m*/fêlé *m*/cinglé *m*/détraqué *m*/fada *m* **2.** *esp NAm* excentrique *m*/original *m*/farfelu *m* **3.** (*dial*) ami*/pote *m*/copain *m*/poteau *m*.

wacker ['wækər] *n P* (*dial*) = **wack 3.**

wacky ['wæki] *a P* **1.** fou*/fêlé/cinglé/détraqué/fada **2.** excentrique/original/farfelu **3.** de qualité inférieure/de camelote/(du) toc.

wad [wɔd] *n F* **1.** (*a*) petit pain (*b*) sandwich *m*; **tea and a wad,** casse-croûte *m* **2.** liasse *f* de billets* de banque/matelas *m* de faf(f)iots/mille-feuille(s) *m*/épingle *f* **3.** abondance*/une chiée (de...)/un tas (de...)/une flop(p)ée (de...) **4. to shoot one's wad,** risquer le tout pour le tout/parier sa chemise/mettre le paquet. (*See* **tightwad**)

wade in ['weid'in] *vi F* s'attaquer à qch/intervenir/s'interposer.

wade into ['weid'intuɪ] *vtr F* **1. to wade into s.o.** (*a*) attaquer* qn/tomber sur le dos à qn/tomber sur le paletot à qn (*b*) critiquer* qn sévèrement/éreinter qn; descendre qn en flammes **2. to wade into sth,** se plonger dans un travail/s'atteler à qch/s'y mettre.

waffle¹ ['wɔfl] *n F* verbosité *f*/verbiage *m*/fariboles *fpl*; **it's just waffle,** c'est du jaspinage/du pallas.

waffle² (on) ['wɔfl('ɔn)] *vi F* **1.** épiloguer/parlot(t)er/écrire *ou* parler dans le vague **2.** dire des bêtises*/sortir des niaiseries *fpl* **3.**

bavarder*/dégoiser/jaboter/tenir le crachoir.

waffler ['wɔflər] *n F* **1.** baratineur *m*/bagouleur *m*/jacteur *m* **2.** épilogueur *m*/individu* verbeux.

wag¹ [wæg] *n F* **to hop the wag,** vagabonder/faire l'école buissonnière/zoner.

wag² [wæg] *vtr F* **to wag it** = **to hop the wag** (**wag¹**).

wag(g)on ['wægən] *n F* **1. to be on the (water) wagon,** s'abstenir de boissons alcooliques/être buveur d'eau/être au régime sec/grenouiller/risquer d'avoir des joncs aux fesses; **to be off the wagon,** s'adonner à la boisson/bibéronner/lichailler **2.** *NAm* **to fix s.o.'s wagon,** se venger sur qn/avoir qn au tournant/garder un chien de sa chienne. (*See* **bandwagon; copwagon; holler-wag(g)on; meatwag(g)on; milk-wag(g)on; paddy-wag(g)on**)

wag out ['wæg'aut] *vi P* (*drugs*) devenir défoncé par la drogue/glisser dans le high/monter sur sa planète/se mettre à planer.

wake-up ['weikʌp] *n P* (*drugs*) **1.** première piqûre de drogues du matin **2.** (*drugs*) amphétamine*/amph *m* **3.** dernier jour de prison*; jour *m* de décarrade/de décambutage *m*.

wakey(-wakey)! ['weiki('weiki)] *excl F* **1.** réveille-toi!/debout les morts! **2.** secoue-toi!/secoue tes puces!/dégrouille-toi!

walk [wɔːk] *vtr F* **1.** (*sports*) **to walk it,** arriver dans un fauteuil/

gagner les mains dans les poches/ gagner les doigts dans le nez **2.** disparaître/passer à l'as. (*See* **jay-walk**)

walk-about ['wɔːkəbaut] *n F* bain *m* de foule.

walk-away ['wɔːkəwei] *n F* = **walkover**.

walk away ['wɔːkə'wei] *vi F* **1.** to walk away with sth, voler*/faucher/ chiper/barboter qch **2.** to walk away (with it)/to walk away with the first prize, gagner les mains dans les poches/arriver dans un fauteuil; to walk away from a competitor, semer un concurrent/laisser un concurrent sur place.

walk into ['wɔːk'intuː] *vtr F* attaquer* (qn)/rentrer dans le lard à (qn).

walk off ['wɔːk'ɔf] *vi F* to walk off with sth, voler* qch/faucher qch/ ratiboiser qch.

walk-out ['wɔːkaut] *n F* grève *f* (surprise)/débrayage *m*.

walk out ['wɔːk'aut] *vi F* **1.** se mettre en grève/débrayer **2.** to walk out on s.o., abandonner* qn/ lâcher qn/plaquer qn/laisser qn en plan.

walkover ['wɔːkouvər] *n F* victoire *f* facile/dans un fauteuil/les doigts dans le nez; promenade *f* de santé; it was a walkover, c'était du tout cuit/du nougat.

walk over ['wɔːk'ouvər] *vtr F* to walk all over s.o., agir abominablement envers qn; traiter qn par-dessus la jambe/comme du poisson pourri/plus bas que terre; if you don't watch him, he'll walk all over you, si tu fais pas gaffe, il va te marcher sur le ventre.

wall [wɔːl] *n F* **1.** to be up the wall, être fou*/cinglé/dingue/barjot; to drive s.o. up the wall, rendre qn fou*/taper sur le système à qn/ courir sur le haricot à qn/scier le dos à qn; the neighbour's baby drives me up the wall, la voisine me

jambonne avec son bébé **2.** to go to the wall (*a*) succomber/frapper au monument (*b*) faire faillite/mettre la clé sous la porte **3.** to go over the wall, s'échapper de prison*/faire le mur/faire la belle/ jouer rip(e) **4.** to hit/to knock/to run one's head against a (brick) wall; to come up against a blank wall, ne rien tirer de qn; se heurter contre une porte de prison/se buter à l'impossible; it's like hitting your head against a brick wall, ça vaut vraiment pas la peine **5.** he can see through a brick wall, il a le nez fin/il a le nez creux/c'est un marlou **6.** it's like talking to/you might just as well talk to a brick wall, autant parler à un sourd/c'est pire que de parler à un mur. (*See* **back II 6**)

walla ['wɔlə] *n F* = **wallah**.

wallaby ['wɔləbi] *n F* Australien *m*.

wallah ['wɔlə] *n F* **1.** *O* individu*/ homme*/type *m*/zèbre *m*/coco *m* **2.** (*aviation*) ground wallah, rampant *m*; ground wallahs, personnel *m* au sol.

wall-eyed ['wɔːl'aid] *a P* ivre*/ raide/rétamé/pistaché.

wallflower ['wɔːlflauər] *n* **1.** *F* personne (*esp jeune fille*) qui, à un bal, n'est pas invitée à danser; to be a wallflower, faire tapisserie **2.** *NAm P* = **bar-fly 2**.

wallop¹ ['wɔləp] **I** *adv F* **1.** slap, bang, wallop! pan, vlan, boum! (*See* **slap-bang(-wallop)**) **2.** the car went wallop into the lamp-post, et boum, la voiture s'est encadrée le lampadaire **II** *n* **1.** *F* gros coup*/ torgn(i)ole *f*/pain *m*/gnon *m* **2.** *F* and down he went with a wallop! et patatras, le voilà par terre! **3.** *P* bière *f*/mousse *f*/moussante *f*. (*See* **codswallop**)

wallop² ['wɔləp] *vtr F* **1.** battre* (qn)/rosser (qn)/flanquer une tannée à (qn)/filer une rouste à (qn) **2.** vaincre/écraser/battre (qn).

walloping ['wɔləpiŋ] I *a* F énorme/fantastique/phénoménal; **he got a walloping good rise,** il a eu une super augmentation II *n* F **to give s.o. a walloping** (*a*) donner une volée de coups*/une raclée/une avoine/une peignée à qn (*b*) battre qn à plate(s) couture(s)/battre qn sur toute la ligne.

wally ['wɔli] *n* P **1.** pénis*/frétillard *m*/flûte *f* **2.** individu bête*/andouille *f*/nœud *m*; **you wally!** espèce de nœud!/espèce d'enflé! **he's a real wally,** c'est un vrai con(nard)/une tête de nœud.

waltz off ['wɔːls'ɔf] *vi* F partir*/déhotter/jouer ripe/mettre les adjas; **he's waltzed off with my biro again,** il a encore embarqué mon Bic.

wampum ['wɔmpəm] *n NAm* P argent*/fric *m*/pèze *m*/flouse *m*.

wanger [wæŋ(g)ər] *n* P pénis*. (*See* **whang, whanger**)

wangle[1] ['wæŋgl] *n* F truc *m* malhonnête/manigance *f*/magouille *f*/coup *m* fourré.

wangle[2] ['wæŋgl] *vtr* F **1.** cuisiner/resquiller **2.** obtenir par subterfuge/manigancer/carotter/magouiller; **he wangled 20 quid out of me,** il m'a refait/estampé de 20 livres **3.** pratiquer le système D/se débrouiller/se démerder/savoir nager.

wangler ['wæŋglər] *n* F fricoteur *m*/carotteur *m*/resquilleur *m*/roublard *m*/marlou *m*.

wangling ['wæŋgliŋ] *n* F fricotage *m*/resquille *f*/roublardise *f*.

wank[1] [wæŋk] *n* V **to have a wank,** se masturber*/se l'astiquer/se branler/s'allonger la couenne.

wank[2] [wæŋk] *vtr* V **to wank (one-self off),** se masturber*/se branler/se secouer le bonhomme/se faire mousser le créateur.

wanker ['wæŋkər] *n* V **1.** masturbateur *m*/branleur *m*/pignoleur

m **2. wanker's doom,** masturbation excessive **3.** (*pej*) **you wanker!** espèce d'enculé! **what a wanker!** quel branleur!

wanna ['wɔnə] *vtr* F (= *want to*) vouloir.

want [wɔnt] *vtr* F (*iron*) **1. you don't want much, do you!** tu ne doutes de rien!/tu n'as pas froid aux yeux!/tu ne manques pas d'air! **2.** (*a*) **to want in,** vouloir participer à qch/vouloir être dans le coup; **he wants in,** il veut être dans la course (*b*) **to want out,** vouloir se retirer/retirer ses marrons du feu; **I want out,** je ne suis pas partant.

war [wɔː] *n* F **to be in the wars,** être malmené/être tarabusté; **you really have been in the wars, haven't you!** t'en as vu de toutes les couleurs, hein?

warb [wɔːb] *n Austr* P **1.** ouvrier *m*/prolétaire *m*/prolo *m* **2.** personne sale* *ou* désordonnée/souillon *m*/salope *f*/cochon *m*.

warby ['wɔːbi] *a Austr* P sale*/salingue/crado/craspignol.

warehouse ['wɛərhaus] *n* P commissariat *m* de police/quart *m*.

war-horse ['wɔːhɔːs] *n* F **an old war-horse** (*i*) un vieux soldat* (*ii*) un vétéran de la politique; un vieux de la vieille.

warm [wɔːm] *a* F **1. to be (getting) warm,** être sur le point de trouver qch/brûler/chauffer **2. to make things warm for s.o.,** punir qn/en faire baver à qn/en faire voir de toutes les couleurs à qn **3.** riche*/galetteux/rupin/plein aux as.

war-paint ['wɔːpeint] *n* F maquillage *m*/badigeon(nage) *m*; **to put on the war-paint,** se maquiller*/se ravaler le portrait/se peinturlurer la façade/se badigeonner.

war-path ['wɔːpɑːθ] *n* F **to be on the war-path,** être sur le sentier de la guerre/chercher noise/déterrer la hache de guerre; **the boss is on the war-path,** le patron* est d'une humeur massacrante/est très mal vissé.

wash¹ [wɔʃ] *n F* **1. to hold up in the wash,** tenir à l'usage **2. to come out in the wash** (*a*) être dévoilé un jour ou l'autre/se montrer sous son vrai jour; **don't worry, it'll all come out in the wash,** t'en fais pas, ça se saura un jour ou l'autre (*b*) se tasser. (*See* **eyewash; hogwash; pigwash; whitewash¹**)

wash² [wɔʃ] *vi F* **it won't wash with me,** cela ne prend pas/cela ne passe pas/je ne marche pas. (*See* **linen 1; whitewash²**)

washed out [wɔʃt'aut] *a F* **1.** fatigué*/lessivé **2.** annulé/supprimé; **all our plans are washed out,** tous nos projets sont tombés à l'eau.

washed up [wɔʃt'ʌp] *a F* **1.** fatigué*/exténué/vanné/lessivé **2.** mis au rancart/fichu en l'air/bazardé; **they're all washed up,** tout est fini entre eux.

washer-upper [wɔʃə'rʌpər] *n F* qn qui fait la vaisselle/plongeur *m*.

washout [wɔʃaut] *n F* **1.** échec*/fiasco *m*/bide *m*; **the party was a complete washout,** la soirée a été un fiasco complet **2.** raté *m*/propre *m* à rien/nullité *f*/zéro *m*; **he's a real washout,** c'est un vrai nullard/un raté de première.

wasp [wɔsp] *n NAm P* (= *white Anglo-Saxon Protestant*) parpaillot *m*.

wasted ['weistid] *a P* (*drugs*) drogué*/camé/envappé.

watch [wɔtʃ] *vtr F* **watch it!** attention!/fais gaffe!

watcher! ['wɔtʃə] *excl P* = **wotcher!**

water ['wɔːtər] *n F* **1. to pour cold water on sth,** jeter une douche froide sur qch **2. to keep one's head above water,** réussir tant bien que mal/ramer/maintenir la tête hors de l'eau **3. to hold water,** avoir du sens/tenir debout; **that idea really does hold water,** ce projet se tient/a de la gueule **4. to be in low water** (*a*) être sans le sou/être dans la dèche/avoir les eaux basses/rouler sur la jante (*b*) être déprimé/être dans le troisième dessous. (*See* **bathwater; bilge-water; dishwater; ditchwater; duck¹ 7; fire-water; hell 16; hot 13; jerkwater; wag(g)on 1**)

watering hole ['wɔːtəriŋhoul] *n P* (*hum*) bar *m*/café*/troquet *m*/abreuvoir *m*.

waterworks ['wɔːtəwɜːks] *npl F* **to turn on the waterworks** (*a*) se mettre à pleurer*/ouvrir les écluses *fpl*/gicler des mirettes *fpl*; chialer (*b*) uriner*/faire pipi/lisbroquer.

wavelength ['weivleŋθ] *n F* **on the same wavelength,** sur la même longueur d'ondes. (*See* **beam 1**)

wax [wæks] *n O F* accès *m* de colère*/crise *f*/rage *f*/coup *m* de raisin; **to be in a wax,** être en pétard.

waxy ['wæksi] *a O F* en colère/en rogne/en pétard/en boule.

way [wei] **I** *adv F* (= *away*) **it was way back in 1900,** cela remonte à 1900 **II** *n* **1. all the way** (*a*) complètement/sans réserve/à bloc/à fond (la caisse); **I'll go all the way with you on that,** là-dessus, je te soutiendrai jusqu'à la gauche (*b*) jusqu'à une complète satisfaction sexuelle/jusqu'au septième ciel; **to go all the way,** casser la canne jusqu'au bout; **she wouldn't let him go all the way,** elle voulait pas de ça qu'est bon/elle voulait pas se faire mettre **2.** (*a*) **to go for s.o./sth in a big way,** s'emballer follement pour qn/qch; **he's gone for it in a big way,** il en est toqué/dingue/fana (*b*) **to do sth in a big way,** mettre les petits plats dans les grands **3. to know one's way about/around,** être malin*/roublard/démerdard/marlou **4. to put s.o. out of the way,** se débarrasser* de qn/virer qn/vider qn **5. down our way,** chez nous/chez nozigues **6. no way,** balpeau/des clous/que dalle/que pouic/peau de balle **7. any way round:** see **bingo 69.** (*See* **family 1**)

way off ['wei'ɔf] *a* & *adv F* dans l'erreur; **you're way off (the mark),** tu es complètement à côte de la plaque.

way out ['wei'aut] *a F* **1.** anticonformiste/outré **2.** original/excentrique **3.** dans l'erreur/gour(r)é/fichu dedans; **he was really way out there,** il était complètement à côté de la plaque/il s'est planté sur toute la ligne.

weapon ['wepən] *n P* pénis*/carabine *f*/pistolet *m* à eau chaude.

wear [wɛər] *vtr F* admettre/tolérer/fermer les yeux sur; **he won't wear it,** il ne sera pas d'accord/il ne marchera pas.

weasel out ['wiːzl'aut] *vi F* se défiler/se rétracter; **I won't let him weasel out of it,** je ne le laisserai pas prendre la tangente.

weather ['weðər] *n F* **under the weather** (*a*) malade*/patraque/dans les vapes (*b*) déprimé/qui n'a pas le moral. (*See* **fair-weather**; **heavy I 3**)

weave [wiːv] *vi F* **to get weaving,** s'y mettre/se lancer; **get weaving!** vas-y!/roule, fonce!

wee [wiː] *n&v F* = **wee-wee[1,2]**.

weed [wiːd] *n F* **1.** (*a*) cigare*/long *m* (*b*) cigarette*/sèche *f* (*c*) tabac*/perlot *m*/trèfle *m* **2.** marijuana*/chiendent *m*/herbe *f*; **to be on the weed,** être accro à/branché sur la marijuana*. (*See* **giggle 3**; **loveweed**) **3.** personne étique/malingre/chétive; chiffe (molle); **what a weed!** quelle nouille!

weedhead ['wiːdhed] *n P* (*drugs*) habitué(e) de la marijuana*/fumeur *m* de marijuana*.

weed-tea ['wiːd'tiː] *n P* (*drugs*) marijuana*/thé (vert).

week [wiːk] *n F* **to knock s.o. into the middle of next week,** donner à qn un fameux coup* / envoyer valdinguer qn / mettre un pain à qn/rentrer dans le portrait à qn.

weekend ['wiːkend] *n P* (*drugs*) **to have the weekend habit,** toucher de la drogue de temps en temps.

weener ['wiːnər] *n P* = **weeny II**.

weeny ['wiːni] **I** *a F* minuscule/minus/menu. (*See* **teeny-weeny**) **II** *n NAm P* pénis*/petit frère/petit bout/flageolet *m*.

weeping ['wiːpiŋ] *a P* (*RS = pillow*) **weeping willow,** oreiller *m*/femme *f* du pauvre.

weepy ['wiːpi] *n F* (film/livre, etc) larmoyant/à vous arracher des larmes/à faire pleurer; mélo *m*.

wee-wee[1] ['wiːwiː] *n F* (*child's word*) pipi *m*; **to do a wee-wee/to do wee-wees,** uriner*/faire pipi.

wee-wee[2] ['wiːwiː] *vi F* (*child's word*) **to (go) wee-wee,** uriner*/faire pipi.

weigh in ['wei'in] *vi F* arriver*/s'amener/ramener sa fraise.

weight [weit] *n* **1.** *F* **to take the weight off (one's feet),** s'asseoir/poser ses fesses* **2.** *F* **to throw one's weight around,** faire l'important/rouler les mécaniques/les rouler **3.** *P* (*drugs*) livre *f* (½ kg) de drogue (*esp* cannabis*). (*See* **chuck about 2**; **lightweight**)

weirdie ['wiədi], **weirdo** ['wiədou], **weirdy** ['wiədi] *n F* individu* étrange/excentrique *m*/olibrius *m*/drôle *m* de coco/drôle d'oiseau/zigomar *m*.

welcome-mat ['welkəm'mæt] *n F* **to put out the welcome-mat for s.o.,** accueillir qn à bras ouverts.

well-endowed ['welen'daud], **well-equipped** ['weli'kwipt] *a F* **1.** (*man*) fortement membré/bien monté/bien outillé. (*See* **well-**

hung) 2. (*woman*) aux seins*
développés/à la belle devanture/qui
a du monde au balcon. (*See* **well-
stacked 2**; **well-upholstered 1**)

well-fixed ['wel'fikst], **well-
heeled** ['wel'hiːld] *a F* riche*/
plein aux as/rupin/qui est au sac/
qui a le matelas.

well-hung ['wel'hʌŋ] *a P* (*man*)
fortement membré; monté comme
un âne/un cheval/un taureau; qui a
un gros paquet; **she likes her men
well-hung**, elle les aime bien montés.

wellies ['weliz] *npl F* bottes *fpl* en
caoutchouc.

well-lined ['wel'laind] *a F* = **well-
fixed**.

well-off ['wel'ɔf] *a F* **1. to be well-
off**, être riche*/avoir de quoi/être
au pèze **2. you don't know when
you're well off**, vous ne connaissez
pas votre bonheur **3. to be well-off
for sth**, être bien pourvu de qch/
être à l'aise de qch.

well-stacked ['wel'stækt] *a F* **1.**
= **well-fixed 2.** = **well-
endowed 2.**

well-upholstered
['welʌp'houlstəd] *a F* **1.** = **well-
endowed 2.** (*See* **upholstery**) **2.**
grassouillet/bien rembourré.

welsh [welʃ] *vi F* partir* sans
payer/se refuser à payer une dette/
poser une ardoise/planter un
drapeau/laisser une feuille de chou/
faire jambe de bois; **to welsh on
s.o.**, manquer à une obligation/faire
faux bond à qn/chier dans les
doigts à qn.

welsher ['welʃər] *n F* tire-au-cul
m/tire-au-flanc *m*.

welt [welt] *vtr P* (*rare*) battre*/
rosser/flanquer une raclée à (qn).

wench [wentʃ] *n F* **1.** fille*/môme
f/gonzesse *f* **2.** *A* prostituée*/
traînée *f*/roulure *f*.

west [west] *adv F* **to go west** (*a*)
mourir*/casser sa pipe/passer

l'arme à gauche (*b*) s'user/être
fichu/rendre l'âme (*c*) (*business, etc*)
faire faillite/mettre la clé sous la
porte/couler (*d*) **that's another fiver
gone west**, encore un faf(f)iot de
claqué/encore un dont je ne rever-
rai pas la couleur.

wet¹ [wet] **I** *a* **1.** *F* bête*/crétin;
don't talk so wet! arrête de lâcher
des conneries! **he's a bit wet**, il est
plutôt bête*/c'est une vraie nouille/
il en tient une sacrée couche **2.** *F*
wet blanket, rabat-joie *m* **3.** *F* à
l'eau de rose **4.** *NAm F* qui a la
permission de vendre de l'alcool*
5. *F* **to be wet behind the ears**, être
né d'hier/être né de la dernière
pluie; **she's still a bit wet behind
the ears**, il y a du lait qui sort
quand on lui pince le nez. (*See* **dry
2**) **6.** *F* **wet sock**, main* molle et
flasque **7.** *F* **to be all wet**, se fourrer le doigt dans l'œil/se gourrer
8. *P* **the wet season**, règles*/ours
mpl/coquelicots *mpl*. (*See* **dream II
3; rag¹ 10**) **II** *n F* **1.** individu
bête*/nouille *f*/andouille *f* **2.**
(*politics*) **the wets and drys in the
cabinet**, les mous et les durs du
gouvernement/les mous et les purs
et durs.

wet² [wet] *vtr&i F* **to wet one's
pants/to be wetting oneself**, avoir
peur*/pisser dans son froc/les
mouiller.

whack¹ [(h)wæk] *n* **1.** *F* coup*/
taloche *f*/torgnole *f*/pain *m*/beigne
f **2.** *F* **to have a whack**, tenter le
coup/faire un essai **3.** *F* **to get a
good whack**, avoir un bon salaire/
toucher un bon paquet/faire son
beurre **4.** *P* = **wack 1, 2 5.** *F*
part *f*/fade *m*/blot *m*; **to get one's
whack**, toucher son taf.

whack² [(h)wæk] **1.** *F* battre*/
rosser/bourrer de coups*/avoiner
2. *F* battre/vaincre/écraser (un
adversaire) **3.** *P* partager/répartir/
fader/décarpiller.

whacked [(h)wækt] *a F* fatigué*/
éreinté/vanné/pompé/lessivé.

whacker ['(h)wækər] *n F* = **whopper**. (*See* **bush-whacker**)

whacking ['(h)wækiŋ] *F* **I** *a* énorme/(h)énaurme/maousse/bœuf **II** *n* raclée *f*/volée *f* de coups*/fricassée *f*/avoine *f*.

whacko! ['(h)wækou] *excl O F* magnifique!/épatant!/formid!/super!

whack up ['(h)wæk'ʌp] *vtr* **1.** *F* **to whack up the pace**, aller plus vite*/forcer le pas/accélérer la cadence **2.** *F* augmenter (les prix, etc) **3.** *P* diviser et partager en parts égales **4.** *P* distribuer un butin* *ou* un gain/fader le barbotin/décarpiller.

whacky ['(h)wæki] *a P* = **wacky 1, 2, 3**.

whale [(h)weil] *n F* **we had a whale of a time**, on s'est drôlement amusé/on a pris notre pied.

wham [(h)wæm] *vtr P* (*not common*) faire l'amour* avec une femme/s'envoyer en l'air.

wham-bam ['(h)wæm'bæm] *n NAm P* coït* rapide et sans tendresse; bourre *f*; **to have a wham-bam**, faire criquon-criquette/tirer un coup rapide.

whammy ['(h)wæmi] *n NAm F* **1.** **to put the whammy on**, mettre des bâtons dans les roues **2.** = **whopper 1**.

whang [(h)wæŋ], **whanger** [(h)wæŋ(g)ər] *n esp NAm A P* pénis*/berdouillette *f*.

whank [(h)wæŋk] *n&v V* = **wank**[1,2].

whatcha(ma)callit ['(h)wɔtʃə(mə)'kɔːlit], **what-do-you-call-it** ['(h)wɔtdjuːˈkɔːlit] *F* machin *m*/chose *f*/machin-chose *m*/machin-chouette *m*/trucmuche *m*.

what-for ['(h)wɔt'fɔːr] *n F* **to give s.o. what-for**, réprimander* qn/laver la tête à qn/flanquer une bonne raclée à qn/passer un savon à qn.

what-ho! ['(h)wɔt'hou] *excl O F* **1.** eh bien!/eh alors! **2.** salut!

whatnot ['(h)wɔtnɔt] *n F* = **whatcha(ma)callit.**

what's-(h)er-name ['(h)wɔtsəneim] *n F* machin *m*/Madame Machin-Truc/Madame Trucmuche.

what's-(h)is-name ['(h)wɔtsizneim] *n F* machin *m*/Monsieur Machin-Truc/M. Trucmuche.

whatsit ['(h)wɔtsit] *n F* = **whatcha(ma)callit.**

what's-its-name ['(h)wɔt-sitsneim] *n F* = **whatcha(ma)callit**.

what-you-may-call-it ['(h)wɔtʃəmə'kɔːlit] *n O F* = **whatcha(ma)callit.**

wheel[1] [(h)wiːl] *n F* **1.** **there are wheels within wheels**, les rouages (de la chose) sont très compliqués/c'est un sac de nœuds **2. big wheel** = **big shot** (**big 1**) **3. to take (over) the wheel**, prendre la barre/prendre les rênes **4. it greases the wheels**, cela fait marcher les affaires **5.** *pl* (= car) tire *f*/chignole *f*; **nice wheels**, belle bagnole. (*See* **cartwheels**; **wheels(man)**)

wheel[2] [(h)wiːl] *vi F* **to wheel and deal**, brasser des affaires plus ou moins louches/manigancer/magouiller (dans des affaires louches).

wheeler-dealer ['(h)wiːlə'diːlər] *n F* brasseur *m* d'affaires louches/magouilleur *m*/grenouilleur *m*.

wheels(man) ['wiːlz(mæn)] *n P* conducteur *m* d'une voiture de fuite/d'une bagnole de cavale.

wheeze [(h)wiːz] *n F* ruse *f*/artifice *m*/truc *m*; **that was a good wheeze**, c'était une bonne ruse de sioux.

whelk [welk] *n P* crachat*/glaviot *m*/huître *f*/mollard *m*.

wherewithal ['(h)wɛəwiðɑːl] *n F* **the wherewithal**, argent*/le Saint-Fric.

whiffy ['(h)wifi] *a P* qui sent mauvais/qui pue; **it's a bit whiffy in here**, ça schlingue/ça cocotte là-dedans.

whing-ding ['(h)wiŋdiŋ] *n NAm P* = **wing-ding**.

whinge [(h)windʒ] *vi Austr F* grogner*/bougonner/râler/grinchonner.

whingy ['(h)windʒi] *a F* geignard/grincheux/grognon/rouscailleur.

whip¹ [(h)wip] *n F* **1.** to get a fair crack of the whip, avoir sa (bonne) part/en tirer un bon parti **2.** to hold the whip hand/*NAm* handle, avoir le dessus **3.** *Austr* whips of ... = tons of... (**ton 2**) **4.** to crack the whip, montrer le fouet/faire preuve d'autorité/taper sur la table.

whip² [(h)wip] *vtr* **1.** *F* battre*/rosser/dérouiller/passer à tabac **2.** *P* voler*/faucher/piquer/barboter/chouraver **3.** *F* vaincre/battre à plate(s) couture(s)/tailler en pièces.

whipped [(h)wipt] *a F* très fatigué*/vanné/sur les rotules/HS.

whipper-snapper ['(h)wipəsnæpər] *n F* freluquet *m*/paltoquet *m*; **you young whipper-snapper!** petit malappris!/petit malotru!

whip-round ['(h)wip'raund] *n F* to have a whip-round, faire une collecte; **let's have a whip-round for his widow,** faisons passer une enveloppe pour sa veuve.

whip through ['(h)wip'θruɪ] *vtr F* faire (qch) rapidement/bâcler/liquider; bazarder un boulot.

whip up ['(h)wip'ʌp] *vtr F* to whip up a meal, préparer un repas rapidement; faire à manger/faire un morceau à la va-vite.

whirl [(h)wəɪl] *n F* to give sth a whirl, essayer qch/faire l'essai de qch/tenter le coup.

whirly-bird ['(h)wəɪlibəɪd] *n NAm F* hélicoptère *m*/battoir *m* (à œufs)/hélico *m*.

whisker ['(h)wiskər] *n F* **1.** to win (a race) by a whisker, arriver dans

un mouchoir de poche/gagner d'un cheveu. (*See* **cat 5**)

whistle¹ ['(h)wisl] *n* **1.** *F* gorge*/avaloir *m*/gargoulette *f*/sifflet *m*; **to wet one's whistle,** boire*/s'humecter le gosier/se rincer la dalle **2.** *P* (*RS* = *suit*) whistle (and flute), complet *m*/costard *m*/ridère *m* **3.** *P* to blow the whistle on s.o., dénoncer* qn/vendre la mèche/casser le morceau/balancer qn **4.** *P* clean as a whistle = **clean I 1.** (*See* **wolf-whistle**)

whistle² ['(h)wisl] *vi* **1.** *F* you can whistle for it! tu peux te fouiller!/tu peux te l'accrocher! **2.** *V* to whistle in the dark, faire un cunnilingus (à qn)/faire minette/brouter (le cresson).

whistle-stop ['(h)wislstɔp] *n F* **1.** *NAm* (a) halte *f* de chemin de fer (b) patelin *m*/trou *m*/bled *m* **2.** (*politics*) arrêt bref/visite *f* éclair (dans une campagne électorale); **a whistle-stop tour,** une tournée marathon/une tournée éclair.

white [(h)wait] **I** *a* **1.** *P* (*drugs*) white cross/stuff (a) cocaïne*/coco *f*/(fée) blanche *f*/neige *f*/bigornette *f*/talc *m* (b) héroïne*/héro *m*/chnouf *f* (c) morphine*/morph *f*/mousseline *f*. (*See* **white II 4**) **2.** *P* (*drugs*) white lightning, cocktail *m* de LSD* et methédrine **3.** *F* honnête/intègre; **to play the white man,** se bien conduire/agir en honnête homme; **come on, play the white man!** allez, sois chic!/allez, fais un bon geste! (*See* **angel 2**; **lily-white**; **snow-white**) **II** *n P* **1.** *A* cinq livres *fpl* sterling et au-dessus **2.** platine *m*/blanc *m*/blanquette *f* **3.** pièces *fpl* d'argent*/blanchettes *fpl*. (*See* **phon(e)y I 2** (*b*)) **4.** (*drugs*) (old lady) white (a) héroïne*/blanche *f* (b) amphétamine*/amph *f*/bombita *f* (c) Benzédrine*.

white-slaver ['(h)wait'sleivər] *n F* souteneur*/mangeur *m* de blanc/marchand *m* de barbaque/marlou *m*/mac *m*.

whitewash[1] ['(h)waitwɔʃ] *n F* (*sport*) défaite *f* à zéro.

whitewash[2] ['(h)waitwɔʃ] *vtr F* **1.** blanchir/disculper/réhabiliter **2.** (*sport*) **to whitewash one's opponents,** battre ses adversaires (sans qu'ils aient marqué un point)/écraser ses adversaires.

whitey, whitie ['(h)waiti] *n P* **1.** blanc *m* **2.** (*drugs*) amphétamine*.

whittled ['(h)witld] *a Austr P* ivre*/rétamé.

whiz(z)[1] [(h)wiz] **I** *a attrib* **1.** *F* **whiz kid,** jeune cadre *m* qui monte en flèche/prodige *m*/jeune coq *m*/jeune loup *m* (aux dents longues) **2.** *P* **whiz mob,** bande* de pickpockets/flèche *f* de tireurs **II** *n* **1. to be a whiz at sth,** être un as/un crack à qch **2.** dynamisme *m*/entrain *m*/vitalité *f*.

whiz(z)[2] [(h)wiz] *vi* **1.** *F* aller très vite*/bomber/gazer/filer à plein tube **2.** *NAm P* voler* à la tire/décrocher.

whizz-bang ['(h)wiz'bæŋ] *n P* **1.** (*a*) *A* obus *m* à vitesse accélérée (*b*) feu *m* d'artifice **2.** (*drugs*) mélange *m* de morphine et de cocaïne*; bang *m*; piquouose-bang *f*.

whizzer ['(h)wizər] *n NAm P* voleur* à la tire/fourchette *f*/tireur *m*.

whizzing ['(h)wiziŋ] *n P* vol *m* par une bande de pickpockets.

whodunit [huːˈdʌnit] *n F* roman policier/polar *m*.

whole-hogger ['houl'hɔgər] *n F* (*a*) qn qui s'engage à fond/jusqu'au-boutiste *mf*/qn qui fonce tête baissée/fonceur *m* (*b*) partisan *m*/supporte(u)r acharné/fan *mf*. (*See* **hog**[1] 2)

whole-hoggism ['houl'hɔgizm] *n F* jusqu'au-boutisme *m*.

whoomph [wumf] *n F* = **oomph.**

whoopee ['wuˈpiː] **I** *excl F* **whoopee!** youpi!/youp!/hourrah! **II** *n* **to make whoopee** (*a*) fêter

bruyamment/faire du chahut/faire la noce/faire la fête (*b*) bien s'amuser/se marrer.

whoops-a-daisy! ['(h)wupsə-deizi] *excl F* oup-là (boum)!/debout!

whoosh [(h)wuʃ] *vi F* conduire très vite*/rouler *ou* voler à plein(s) gaz.

whop [(h)wɔp] *vtr P* **1.** battre*/rosser/avoiner (qn) **2.** vaincre/écraser (un adversaire).

whopper ['(h)wɔpər] *n F* **1.** qch d'énorme/de colossal; mastodonte *m* **2.** gros mensonge*/bateau *m*/paquebot *m*; **what a whopper!** elle est un peu forte/grosse, celle-là!

whopping ['(h)wɔpiŋ] **I** *a F* **1.** = énorme/(h)énaurme/maousse/bœuf; **a whopping great sandwich,** un sandwich comaque **2. whopping lie** = **whopper 2 II** *n P* volée *f* de coups*/rossée *f*/raclée *f*/dérouillée *f*/trempe *f*.

whore[1] [hɔər, hɔır] *n P* **dirty whore:** see **bingo 34.** (*See* **forty-four 1**)

whore[2] [hɔər, hɔır] *vi P* putasser/courir la gueuse.

whore-house ['hɔı(ə)haus] *n P* bordel*/boxon *m*/lupanar *m*/claque *m*.

whoring ['hɔı(ə)riŋ] *n P* putasserie *f*/dragage *m*.

whore-shop ['hɔı(ə)ʃɔp] *n P* = **whore-house.**

wick [wik] *n P* **1. to get on s.o.'s wick,** taper sur le système à qn/courir sur le haricot à qn/casser les noix à qn/casser les bonbons à qn **2. to dip one's wick,** faire l'amour*/mouiller le goupillon/tremper le biscuit. (*See* **Hampton**)

wicked ['wikid] *a P* excellent*/bath/du tonnerre.

widdle ['widl] *n&v F* = **piddle**[1,2].

wide [waid] *a* **1.** *F* malin*/roublard/marlou/fortiche; **a wide boy,** un affranchi/un débrouillard/

un fortiche **2.** *P* (*turf*) **wide world,** la pelouse/le champ. (*See* **berth 1**)

wife [waif], **wifey** ['waifi] *n F* **the wife,** l'épouse*/la bourgeoise/la ménagère/la bergère/la régulière/la patronne.

wig [wig] *n P* **1.** *NAm* fou*/cinglé(e) *m(f)*/dingue *m*/toqué(e) *m(f)* **2. to blow one's wig,** être très en colère*/piquer une crise/monter au plafond/être en pétard. (*See* **bigwig**)

wigging ['wigiŋ] *n F* réprimande *f*/engueulade *f*/coup *m* de semonce/savon *m*; **to get a good wigging,** se faire réprimander*/se faire laver la tête/se faire passer un savon.

wiggle ['wigl] *n esp NAm F* **to get a wiggle on,** se dépêcher*/se dégrouiller/faire vinaigre/faire fissa.

wiggy ['wigi] *n F* (*child's word*) pénis*/zizi *m*/kiki *m*/quéquette *f*.

wig out ['wig'aut] *vi NAm P* **1.** être très en colère/être en pétard/piquer une crise **2.** perdre la tête/les pédales.

wild [waild] *a F* **1.** en colère*/furibard/en pétard **2. to be wild about s.o.,** être emballé pour qn/en pincer pour qn/en mordre pour qn/avoir qn dans la peau/être dingue de qn **3.** passionnant/palpitant/captivant; **it'll drive you wild,** ça va t'emballer. (*See* **woolly**)

willie, Willie, willy ['wili] *Prn P* **1.** pénis*/petit frère/quéquette *f* **2. to get on s.o.'s willy,** taper sur le système à qn/casser les bonbons à qn. (*See* **wick 1**)

Willies ['wiliz] *npl F* **to give s.o. the willies,** donner la chair de poule à qn; foutre la trouille/les jetons à qn; **to have the willies,** avoir peur*/avoir la trouille/avoir les foies/avoir les chocottes.

wimp [wimp] *n F* = **weed 3.**

win [win] *vtr&i* **1.** *F* (*catchphrase*) **you can't win (can you)!** tu auras toujours tort! **2.** *F* (*catchphrase*)

you can't win them all, on ne peut pas plaire à tout le monde/on ne peut pas contenter tout le monde **3.** *P* voler*/rouler/soulever.

wind [wind] *n F* **1. to raise the wind,** se procurer de l'argent*/ramasser les fonds/récolter le blé **2. to get the wind up,** avoir peur*/avoir les foies/les mouiller; **to put the wind up s.o.,** faire peur* à qn/ficher la frousse à qn/flanquer la trouille à qn **3. to be all wind (and water),** être comme une bulle de savon **4. to be full of wind,** mentir*/mener en bateau/monter un bateau **5. to sail close to the wind** (*a*) friser l'illégalité/l'insolence/l'indécence, etc (*b*) faire des affaires* douteuses/magouiller **6. there's something in the wind,** il y a anguille sous roche/il se manigance quelque chose. (*See* **bag**[1] **2**; **load 7**; **sail**; **sheet 1**)

wind up ['waind'ʌp] *vi F* **to wind up on the scrap-heap,** finir sur la paille/dans le caniveau; **to wind up in prison,** finir en prison*.

windy ['windi] *a* **1.** *F* **to be windy,** avoir peur*/avoir la trouille/avoir les foies **2.** *NAm* **(the) Windy City,** Chicago.

wing [wiŋ] *n* **1.** *P* bras*/aile *f*/aileron *m* **2.** *V* (*Hell's Angels*) **to get/to earn one's black wings,** faire l'amour* avec un(e) noir(e)/gagner ses ailes noires; **to earn one's brown wings,** sodomiser* qn/gagner ses ailes brunes. (*See* **ping**; **red I 6**; **sprout**)

wing-ding ['wiŋdiŋ] *n esp NAm P* **1.** attaque *f*/crise *f* d'épilepsie/digue-digue *f* (*esp* prétendue crise pour s'attirer de la sympathie) **2.** accès *m* de folie dû aux drogues/flip *m* **3.** coup *m* de colère*/rage *f*/coup de raisin **4.** réjouissances* bruyantes/réunion pleine de bruit*/chahut *m*/ramdam(e) *m*/barouf *m*.

wing(e)y ['windʒi] *a F* = **whingy.**

wink [wiŋk] *n F* **to tip s.o. the wink,**
avertir qn/faire signe de l'œil à qn/
lancer une œillade à qn/faire le
châsse à qn. (*See* **forty**)

winkers ['wiŋkəz] *npl F* clignotants
mpl.

winking ['wiŋkiŋ] *n F* **1. (as) easy
as winking,** simple comme bonjour
2. like winking, en un clin d'œil/en
(un) rien de temps/en cinq secs/
rapidos.

winkle ['wiŋkl] *n P* pénis*/frétillard
m/frétillante *f.*

winkle-pickers ['wiŋklpikəz] *npl
F* chaussures *fpl* à bout pointu.

winner ['winər] *n F* (*a*) réussite
certaine/succès assuré; tabac *m* (*b*)
roman, pièce, etc à grand succès.

wino ['wainou] *n P* ivrogne*/sac *m*
à vin/poivrot *m*/alcolo *m*/nez *m*
sale.

win out ['win'aut] *vi F* surmonter
les difficultés *fpl*/arriver au but.

wipe[1] [waip] *n P* **1.** mouchoir*/
tire-jus *m*/blave *m* **2.** coup*/
taloche *f.*

wipe[2] [waip] *vtr P* **1. to wipe the
floor with s.o.** (*a*) fermer le bec/
clouer le bec/river le clou à qn (*b*)
battre qn à plate(s) couture(s)/n'en
faire qu'une bouchée (*c*) réprimander* qn/agonir qn d'injures/
incendier qn/passer un savon à qn
2. battre*/flanquer une raclée à
(qn)/filer une purge à (qn).

wipe out ['waip'aut] *vtr F* tuer*/
nettoyer/ratatiner/lessiver/effacer
(qn); **the whole lot were wiped out,**
toute la bande a été zigouillée.

wire[1] ['waiər] *n* **1.** *F* **to give s.o.
the wire,** donner un tuyau à qn/
mettre qn dans le coup/tuyauter
qn/mettre qn au parfum **2.** *P* **to
pull one's wire,** se masturber*/se
l'allonger/s'allonger la couenne.
(*See* **wire-puller**; **wire-pulling** 2)
3. *F* **a live wire,** un malin/un
dégourdi/un débrouillard **4.** *F*
télégramme *m*/petit bleu **5.** *F* **to**

get in under the wire, arriver* au
dernier moment/s'abouler pile/
arriver sur le fil **6.** *F* **to get one's
wires crossed,** se tromper/se
gour(r)er/s'embrouiller/se mettre le
doigt dans l'œil/s'emmêler les crayons **7.** *P* pickpocket *m*/fourlineur
m/fourchette *f*/tireur *m* **8.** *F* **to
pull (the) wires,** tirer les ficelles *fpl*/
faire jouer le piston **9.** *P* enregis-
trement *m* (au magnétophone); **to
run a wire,** enregistrer une conversation (téléphonique).

wire[2] ['waiər] *vtr&i P* (*a*) (*to bug*)
installer des micros clandestins/
brancher sur la table d'écoute (*b*)
enregistrer (une conversation) au
magnétophone.

wired ['waiəd] *a P* (*drugs*) (*a*)
adonné/accroché/accro à une
drogue (*b*) défoncé/high.

wire-puller ['waiəpulər] *n* **1.** *F*
intrigant *m*/magouilleur *m*/gre-
nouilleur *m* **2.** *P* masturbateur *m*/
branleur *m.* (*See* **wire**[1] 2)

wire-pulling ['waiəpuliŋ] *n* **1.** *F*
l'art *m* de tirer les ficelles *fpl*/
intrigues *fpl* de couloir *m*/mani-
gances *fpl*/magouilles *fpl* **2.** *P*
masturbation *f*/astiquage *m*/
branlette *f.* (*See* **wire**[1] 2)

wise [waiz] *a F* **to get wise,** se mettre à la coule/se dessaler; se
dégourdir; se mettre à la page; **to
get wise to sth,** s'apercevoir de la
vérité/ouvrir les yeux; piger/saisir
qch; **to put s.o. wise,** affranchir qn/
mettre qn à la page/tuyauter qn;
put me wise about it, expliquez-moi
ça. (*See* **guy 1**)

wisecrack[1] ['waizkræk] *n F* bon
mot/mot spirituel/boutade *f*; vanne
f; **to make a wisecrack,** lâcher/
lancer/sortir une vanne.

wisecrack[2] ['waizkræk] *vi F* faire
de l'esprit/lancer des boutades/
lâcher des vannes/vanner.

wise up ['waiz'ʌp] *vi F* (*a*) = **to
get wise** (**wise**) (*b*) **to wise s.o. up**
= **to put s.o. wise** (**wise**).

wish [wiʃ] *vi* F **it's been wished on me,** c'est une chose que je n'ai pas pu refuser/on me l'a collé.

wishing well ['wiʃiŋ'wel] *n Austr P (RS = (prison) cell)* cellule *f* de prison/cachet *m*/mitard *m*.

wishy-washy ['wiʃiwɔʃi] *a* F fade/insipide/lavasse; **wishy-washy coffee,** jus *m* de chaussette; **wishy-washy beer,** pisse *f* de chat.

with [wið] *prep* F **1.** (*a*) **to be with it,** être dans le vent/être in/être à la page (*b*) **to get with it,** se mettre dans le bain/se mettre au diapason/se mettre au parfum **2. I'm not with you,** je ne comprends pas/je ne pige pas/je n'y suis pas/je ne suis pas sur la même longueur d'onde que vous.

with-it ['wiðit] *a attrib* F **with-it gear,** des vêtements* dernier cri.

wizard ['wizəd] *a* F excellent*/épatant/au poil/super/classe.

wodge [wɔdʒ] *n* F (*a*) gros morceau/bloc *m*/quartier *m* (*b*) liasse *f* (de papiers).

wog [wɔg] *n* P (*pej*) **1.** Levantin *m*/Égyptien *m*/Arabe*/bico(t) *m*/bougnoul(l)e *m*/noraf *m*/arbi *m*/bic *m* **2.** un étranger.

wolf[1] [wulf] *n* **1.** F coureur *m* de jupons/tombeur *m* de femmes/don Juan *m*/dragueur *m* **2.** F **to keep the wolf from the door,** se mettre à l'abri du besoin (de nourriture) **3.** P homosexuel* actif/loup *m* de Sibérie/chien *m* jaune. **4.** F **lone wolf** (*a*) homme* qui fait bande à part/qui fait cavalier seul; solitaire *m*. (*See* **loner**) (*b*) célibataire endurci/vieux bouc/vieux garçon.

wolf[2] [wulf] *vtr&i* **1.** F manger* abondamment/s'empiffrer/se goinfrer/se bâfrer **2.** P séduire la femme d'un autre.

wolf-whistle ['wulf(h)wisl] *n* F sifflement admiratif à l'adresse d'une femme*; **to give a girl a wolf-whistle,** siffler une fille*.

wolly ['wɔli] *n* P = **wally 2.**

woman-chaser ['wumən tʃeisər] *n* F coureur *m* de jupons/tombeur *m* de femmes/dragueur *m*.

woman-crazy ['wumən kreizi], **woman-mad** ['wumən mæd] *a* F qui a les femmes dans la peau/qui est porté sur la chose/queutard/qui est chaud de la pince. (*See* **man-crazy**; **man-mad**)

wonder[1] ['wʌndər] *n* F **1.** (*catchphrase*) **wonders will never cease!** il y a toujours des miracles!/c'est un prodige!/tu m'étonneras toujours! **2. no wonder!** pas étonnant!

wonder[2] ['wʌndər] *vi* F **I shouldn't wonder,** cela ne me surprendrait pas/ça serait pas étonnant!

wonk [wɔŋk] *n Austr P* homosexuel*/empapaouté *m*/enculé *m*/empaffé *m*.

wonky ['wɔŋki] *a* P **1.** titubant/chancelant/branlant/zigzaguant **2.** hésitant/vacillant/oscillant **3.** mal fichu/patraque **4.** *Austr* homosexuel*/pédé.

wood [wud] *n* F **1. touch wood/** *NAm* **knock on wood!** touche du bois! **2.** (*catchphrase*) **you can't see the wood for the trees,** on se perd dans les détails; les arbres empêchent de voir la forêt/les arbres cachent la forêt **3. he's wood from the neck up,** il est bouché à l'émeri/il a une tête de bûche. (*See* **bird-wood**)

woodbine ['wudbain] *n* P (*drugs*) **African woodbine,** cigarette de marijuana*.

wooden [wʌdn] *a* P **wooden one,** peine *f* de prison d'un mois.

woodentop ['wʌdntɔp] *n* P agent* de police en uniforme/habillé *m*/pèlerin *m*.

woodshed ['wudʃed] *n* F **there's something nasty in the woodshed,** on nous cache quelque chose/il y a anguille sous roche.

wool [wul] *n* **1.** *F* **to lose one's wool**, se mettre en colère*/ s'emballer/se mettre en boule; **keep your wool on!** (ne) te frappe pas!/ calme-toi! **2.** *F* **to pull the wool over s.o.'s eyes**, jeter de la poudre aux yeux de qn. (*See* **cotton-wool**)

woolly ['wuli] *a F* **(wild and) woolly** (*a*) ignare/inculte/mal léché (*b*) hirsute/hérissé.

woozy ['wuɪzi] *a* **1.** *F* étourdi/qui a le vertige/dont la tête tourne; **to feel a bit woozy**, être dans le coltar/naviguer dans le potage **2.** *P* ivre*/blindé/chargé.

wop [wɔp] *n P* Italien*/macaroni *m/* rital *m.*

work¹ [wɜɪk] *n F* **a nasty piece of work**, un sale type/une peau de vache/un salopard/une ordure. (*See* **cut out** 2; **homework**; **legwork**; **works**)

work² [wɜɪk] *vtr* **1.** *F* arranger/ manigancer/machiner/trafiquer; **to work a fiddle**, manigancer une combine/magouiller un sale coup/ traficoter **2.** *A F* faire l'amour* avec (une femme)/bourrer.

workaholic [wɜɪkə'hɔlik] *n F* bourreau *m* de travail; abatteur *m* de besogne.

working over ['wɜɪkiŋ'ouvər] *n P* **to give s.o. a working over** = **to work s.o. over** (**work over**).

workout ['wɜɪkaut] *n* **1.** *F* essai *m/*tentative *f/*ébauche *f* **2.** *P* volée *f* de coups*/raclée *f/*tabassée *f/* avoine *f/*peignée *f.*

work over ['wɜɪk'ouvər] *vtr P* **to work s.o. over**, battre* qn/passer une peignée à qn/passer qn à la machine à bosseler; **he got worked over by some yobs**, il s'est fait bastonner/dérouiller par des loubards.

works [wɜɪks] *npl* **1.** *P* **to give s.o. the works** (*a*) battre* qn/tabasser qn/passer qn à tabac/donner une dérouillée à qn (*b*) tuer* qn/zigouiller qn/faire son affaire à qn/faire

la peau à qn **2.** *P* **the works**, attirail *m* de camé/popote *f/*kit *m* **3.** *F* **the whole works**, tout le bataclan/tout le bazar. (*See* **boiling** II; **caboodle**; **gum up**; **shebang** 1; **shoot¹** 1; **shoot²** 8; **spanner**; **waterworks**)

work up ['wɜɪk'ʌp] *vtr* **1.** *P* exciter sexuellement/émoustiller/chauffer **2.** *F* mettre (qn) en colère/échauffer/affoler; **don't get worked up (about it)**, (ne) t'emballe pas/(ne) te monte pas le bourrichon/t'excite pas. (*See* **lather¹**; **sweat¹** 3)

world [wɜɪld] *n F* **1.** **to feel on top of the world**, être en pleine forme/ être au septième ciel/avoir la frite/ péter le feu **2.** **out of this world**, mirifique/génial/transcendant/sensass; **it was out of this world**, c'était le pied! **3.** **to think the world of s.o.**, estimer hautement qn/porter qn aux nues; **she thinks the world of him**, elle ne jure que par lui. (*See* **come down** 4; **dead I** 6; **wide** 2)

worm [wɜɪm] *n F* (*pers*) (*a*) lavette *f/*mollasson *m/*chiffe molle (*b*) raté *m/*minable *m* (*c*) saligaud *m.*

worry ['wʌri] *vi F* **1.** **not to worry!** faut pas s'en faire! **2.** **I should worry!** ce n'est pas mon affaire!/ c'est le cadet de mes soucis!/je m'en fiche comme de l'an quarante!

worryguts ['wʌrigʌts], *NAm* **worry wart** ['wʌriwɔɪt] *n P* bileux, -euse/qn qui se fait des cheveux/qn qui se fait de la bile; flubard *m/*péteux *m.*

worth [wɜɪθ] *a F* **1.** **for all one is worth**, de toutes ses forces **2.** **was she worth it?**: *see* **bingo** 76.

wotcher! ['wɔtʃə] *excl P* **wotcher mate!/wotcher cock!** comment ça gaze, vieille branche!

wow [wau] **I** *excl F* wow! oh là là!/wouah!/wow! **II** *n F* succès *m* formidable/du tonnerre; tabac *m* (monstre). (*See* **pow-wow**)

wow² [wau] *vtr F* stupéfier/époustoufler/en mettre plein la vue/en boucher un coin à qn/laisser qn baba.

wowser ['wauzər] *n Austr F* rabat-joie *m*/trouble-fête *m*.

wrap¹ [ræp] *n P* **to be under wraps** (*i*) être en planque/être au vent (*ii*) (*thing, project, etc*) être secret/en cachette.

wrap² [ræp] *vtr F* **1. wrap yourself round that!** mange* *ou* bois* ça!/tape-toi ça!/mets-toi ça derrière la cravate! **2. he wrapped his car round a tree,** il a encadré un arbre/il s'est payé un arbre.

wrap-up ['ræpʌp] *n P* **1.** résumé *m*/topo *m* **2.** colis *m* contenant des drogues/sac *m*.

wrap up ['ræp'ʌp] *vtr&i* **1.** *P* se taire*/la fermer/la boucler; **wrap up!** ta gueule!/la ferme!/boucle la!/écrase (ta chique)! **2.** *F* terminer/achever/boucler; **it's all wrapped up,** tout est arrangé/bouclé; c'est dans le sac.

wringer ['riŋər] *n P* **to put s.o. through the wringer,** en faire voir des vertes et des pas mûres à qn/faire passer qn à la casserole/faire passer un sale quart d'heure à qn.

wrinkle ['riŋkl] *n F* **1.** tuyau *m*/truc *m*/combine *f*; **to know all the wrinkles,** la connaître dans les coins/connaître toutes les ficelles/en connaître un rayon **2.** nouveauté *f*/idée originale/novation *f*; **that's a new wrinkle,** c'est du neuf.

wrist [rist] *n V* **1. limp wrist,** homosexuel*/chouquette *f*/chochotte *f*/minot *m*. (*See* **limp-wristed**) **2. one off the wrist,** masturbation *f*/un astiquage maison/une branlette.

write [rait] *vi F* **it's nothing to write home about,** cela n'a rien d'extraordinaire/cela ne casse rien/ça ne casse pas des briques.

write-off ['raitɔf] *n F* individu* désemparé/épave *f*/loque *f*.

write off ['rait'ɔf] *vtr F* **to write s.o. off,** congédier* qn; ne tenir aucun compte de qn/éloigner qn de ses pensées; rayer qn.

wrong [rɔŋ] *I a F* **to get on the wrong side of s.o.,** se faire mal voir de qn/ne pas être dans les petits papiers de qn. (*See* **bed¹ 2; end 11**) *II adv* **1. to get s.o. in wrong with s.o.,** disgracier qn aux yeux de qn d'autre/griller qn **2. to be in wrong with s.o.,** ne pas être dans les bonnes grâces/les petits papiers de qn; être mal vu.

wrongheaded ['rɔŋ'hedid] *a F* bête*/demeuré/cloche/con comme un balai.

Y

yabber¹ ['jæbər] *n* F bavardage *m*/ bavasse *f*/jactage *m*/bavette *f*.

yabber² ['jæbər] *vi* F bavarder*/ bavasser/jacter/faire causette; **they were yabbering away as usual,** ils taillaient leur bavette habituelle.

yack¹ [jæk] *n* F = **yackety-yack**.

yack² [jæk] *vi* F (*a*) bavarder*/ jacasser (*b*) ragoter/papoter (*c*) caqueter/dévider.

yackety-yack ['jækəti'jæk] *n* F caquetage *m*/jacasserie *f*/bla-bla *m*. (*See* **clackety-clack**)

yak¹ [jæk] *n* F = **yackety-yack**.

yak² [jæk] *vi* F = **yack²**.

yammer ['jæmər] *vi* F **1.** bavarder*/bavasser/dégoiser **2.** grogner*/râler/rouscailler/bougonner.

yancy ['jænsi] *a* NAm F = **antsy**.

yang [jæŋ] *n* NAm P pénis*/zob *m*/ zébi *m*.

yank¹ [jæŋk] *n* F secousse *f*/saccade *f*/coup sec.

yank² [jæŋk] *vtr* **1.** F tirer d'un coup sec; **to yank the bedclothes off s.o.,** découvrir qn brusquement **2.** NAm P arrêter*/agrafer/alpaguer.

Yank³ [jæŋk], **Yankee¹** ['jæŋki] **I** *a* F américain/amerlo(que)/yankee/ricain **II** *n* F **1.** habitant *m* de la Nouvelle Angleterre *ou* d'un des états du nord des États-Unis **2.** Américain*/Amerlo/ Amerloque *m*/Yankee *m*/Ricain *m*.

Yankee² ['jæŋki] *n* P (*turf*) pari (cumulatif)/paroli *m*.

yankeeism ['jæŋkiːiz(ə)m] *n* F (*a*) mot américain (*b*) américanisme *m*/ amerloche *m*.

yantsy ['jæntsi] *a* NAm F = **antsy**.

yap¹ [jæp] *n* P **1.** (*a*) bavardage bruyant/caquetage *m* (*b*) bouche*/ goule *f*/bec *m*/clapet *m* **2.** NAm A individu bête*/gourde *f*/navet *m*.

yap² [jæp] *vi* P **1.** grogner*/ bougonner/rouspéter **2.** parler* beaucoup/déblatérer/en dégoiser/ japper/bavasser/bagouler.

yapper ['jæpər] *n* P bavard*/jacasseur *m*/jaspineur *m*/bagouleur *m*.

yapping ['jæpiŋ] *n* P bavardage *m*/ dévidage *m*/jactage *m*/pallas *m*/jaspinage *m*.

yard¹ [jɑɪd] *n* **1.** F words a yard long, mots longs d'une toise/longs comme ça/qui n'en finissent pas; **he pulled a face a yard long,** il a fait une tête de six pieds de long **2.** F (= *Scotland Yard*) **the Yard,** (*approx*) = le Quai (des Orfèvres) **3.** P pénis* **4.** NAm P cent dollars. (*See* **bone-yard**)

yard² [jɑɪd] *vtr* A P **to yard s.o.,** faire l'amour* avec qn de tout à fait étranger.

yardbird ['jɑɪdbɜɪd] *n* NAm F = **jailbird**.

yard-dog ['jɑɪddɔg] *n* NAm P malappris *m*/chien galeux.

yarn¹ [jɑɪn] *n* F (*a*) histoire *f*/conte *m* de matelot (*b*) histoire *f* à dormir debout/bateau *m*/bobard *m*; **to spin/to pitch/to pull a yarn,** mentir*/raconter des histoires/bourrer le crâne (à qn); **he spun me this long yarn about being short of cash,**

il m'a fait son charre, soit disant qu'il était raide.

yarn² [jɑɪn] *vi F* débiter des histoires *fpl*.

yarra ['jærə] *a Austr F* (stone) yarra, fou*/loufoque.

yatter¹ ['jætər] *n P* bavardage *m*/baratin *m*/déblatérage *m*.

yatter² ['jætər] *vi P* bavarder*/baratiner/déblatérer/tenir le crachoir.

yawny ['jɔɪni] *a F* ennuyeux*/rasoir/qui fait bâiller (à s'en décrocher la mâchoire)/bassinant/chiant (comme la pluie).

yawp [jɔɪp] *vi NAm F* grogner*/râler/rouspéter/renauder.

yeah ['jɛə, 'jɛəɪ] *adv & excl F* (a) oui*/gy/gygo (*b*) **oh yeah?** et alors?/et après?

year [jiər, jɔɪr] *n F* **to put years on s.o.,** donner du mal à qn/donner des cheveux blancs à qn. (*See* **donkey 3; dot¹ 2**)

yegg [jeg] *n NAm P* **1.** déboucleur *m*/casseur *m* de coffiot **2.** voleur*/caroubleur *m*/faucheur *m*.

yellow ['jelou, 'jelə] *a F* **1.** lâche/couard; **to have a yellow streak,** être poltron*/froussard/dégonflé; avoir les foies *mpl*/les chocottes *fpl*; ne rien avoir dans le ventre/dans la culotte **2. the Yellow Press,** presse *f* qui vise à la sensation/journaux* à scandales. (*See* **jack¹ 13**)

yellow-bellied ['jeloubelid, 'jeləbelid] *a F* qui a peur*/déballonné/flubard; **to be yellow-bellied,** avoir les foies (blancs)/les chocottes/la chiasse/les copeaux.

yellow-belly ['jeloubeli, 'jeləbeli] *n F* froussard *m*/trouillard *m*/foie blanc/flubard *m*.

yellow-jacket ['jeloudʒækit, 'jelədʒækit]*P* (*drugs*) pilule *f* à base de barbital/barbiturique*.

yellow-livered ['jeloulivəd, 'jeləlivəd] *a F* =**yellow-bellied**.

yen¹ [jen] *n* **1.** *F* désir ardent et obsédant/appétit *m*; **to have a yen for sth,** ne rêver que de qch/avoir une super envie de qch **2.** *P* = **yen-yen.** (*See* **pen-yen**)

yen² [jen] *vi F* (*not common*) désirer ardemment/en vouloir.

yen-shee ['jen'ʃiɪ] *n P* (*drugs*) opium*/touf(f)iane *f*/op *m*/noir *m*.

yen sleep ['jen'sliɪp] *n P* (*drugs*) état de manque.

yen-yen ['jenjen] *n P* (*drugs*) besoin *m* de la drogue/guêpe *f*/guenon *f*.

yep [jep] *excl P* = **yeah** (*a*).

yer [jər] *pron P* (= *you*) tu/vous; **will yer or won't yer?** tu veux ou tu veux pas?

yesca ['jeskə] *n P* (*drugs*) marijuana*/Marie-jeanne *f*.

yes-girl ['jesgəɪl] *n P* fille* facile/Marie-couche-toi-là/fille qui se couche quand on lui dit de s'asseoir.

yes-man ['jesmæn] *n F* individu* qui dit oui à tout/béni-oui-oui *m*.

Yid [jid] *n P* (*pej*) Juif*/Youtre *m*/Youpin *m*/Youde *m*.

yike¹ [jaik] *n Austr F* querelle*/engueulade *f*/prise *f* de bec.

yike² [jaik] *vi Austr F* s'engueuler (avec qn)/avoir une prise de bec (avec qn)/s'accrocher (avec qn).

ying-yang ['jinjæŋ] *n NAm P* = **yang**.

yippee! [ji'piɪ] *excl F* bravo!/hourrah!

yob(bo) ['jɔb(ou)] *n P* (jeune) voyou*/loubard *m*/loulou *m*/blouson noir; **they're just a load of yobs,** c'est rien que des petits loulous.

yonks [jɔŋks] *npl F* longtemps/des années*/des berges; **it's been yonks since I saw you,** ça fait une paye qu'on s'est vus.

york ['jɔɪk] *vi NAm P* vomir*/faire renard/dégueuler.

you-and-me [ˈjuən'miː] *n P* (*RS* = *tea*) thé *m*.

yours [jɔːz, jɔəz] *pron F* **1.** what's yours? qu'est-ce que tu prends? **2.** yours truly, moi-même/mézigue/bibi/ma pomme. (*See* **up IV 1**)

yow [jau] *n Austr F* to keep yow = to keep nit (**nit 2**).

yowly [ˈjauli] *a F* pleurnicheur/geignard.

yo-yo¹ [ˈjouyou] *n NAm F* **1.** idiot *m*/individu bête*/gourde *f*/crétin *m* **2.** pigeon *m*/poire *f*/gobeur *m*.

yo-yo² [ˈyouyou] *vi NAm F* changer d'opinion très souvent/changer d'avis comme de chemise.

yuck!, yuk! [jʌk] *excl F* pouah!/berk!

yucky, yukky [ˈjʌki] *a F* **1.** odieux/dégueulasse/débectant **2.** à l'eau de rose//gnan-gnan.

Yugo [ˈjuːgou] *n F* Yougoslave *mf*.

yummy [ˈjʌmi] *a F* très bon/délicieux/du nanan.

yum-yum! [ˈjʌm'jʌm] *excl F* du nanan!/miam-miam!

Z

Z [zed, *NAm* ziː] *n esp NAm P*
(*drugs*) = gramme *m* de drogue/
dose(tte) *f*.

zany ['zeini] *a F* bouffon/gugusse/
toqué/cinglé/loufoque; **a really
zany idea,** une idée complètement
loufoque/farfelue.

zap [zæp] *vtr P* **1.** tuer* d'un coup
de feu/zigouiller/flinguer/mettre en
l'air **2.** battre à plate(s) cou-
ture(s)/anéantir; écraser **3.** se
dépêcher*/se décarcasser; **to zap
along,** aller à tout berzingue/à
pleins tubes.

zazzle ['zæzl] *n NAm A P* désir
sexuel/tracassin *m*.

zazzy ['zæzi] *a F* appétissante/bien
roulée/qui a du chien.

Z car ['zedkɑr] *n F* voiture *f* de
police/voiture pie.

Zen [zen] *n P* (*drugs*) **instant Zen,**
LSD*.

zilch [ziltʃ] *n esp NAm F* **1.** rien*/
zéro/nib/que dalle **2.** (*pers*) zéro
m/nullard *m*.

zing [ziŋ] *n F* vitalité *f*/vigueur *f*/
énergie *f*/dynamisme *m*/ressort *m*.

zingy ['ziŋi] *a F* plein d'entrain *m*/
qui pète le feu.

zip [zip] *n F* énergie *f*/entrain *m*; **put
some zip into it!** mets-y du nerf!/
secoue-toi!/grouille-toi!

zip along ['zipə'lɔŋ] *vi F* aller très
vite*/aller à toute pompe.

zipper ['zipər] *n P* (*homosexual use*)
zipper dinner/zipper sex, fellation*;
pipe vite faite/vite taillée.

zippy ['zipi] *a F* vif/plein d'allant/
dynamique; **look zippy!** grouille-
toi!/magne-toi (le train)!

zit [zit] *n NAm P* (*pimple*) bouton
m/bourgeon *m*; **zit doctor,**
dermato(logue) *mf*.

zizz¹ [ziz] *n F* (petit) somme *m*/
roupillon *m*.

zizz² [ziz] *vi F* dormir*/faire un
somme/piquer un roupillon.

zombi(e), zomby ['zɔmbi] *n F*
1. individu* sans force de
caractère/lavette *f*/chiffe (molle)/
avachi *m*; **what a zombie!** tu parles
d'un macchabée! **2.** individu
bête*/duschnock *m* **3.** individu*
ennuyeux/rasoir; scie *f*.

zoned [zound] *a P* = **zonked
(out)**.

zonk [zɔŋk] *vtr P* = **zap 1, 2, 3**.

zonked (out) ['zɔŋkt('aut)] *a P*
(*a*) ivre* mort/cuit/rétamé/bourré
(*b*) (*drugs*) drogué*/défoncé à zéro/
camé jusqu'aux os; **he was completely zonked,** il était complètement défoncé/il était défoncé à
mort.

zoom [zuːm] *n P* (*drugs*) amphétamine*/speed *m*.

zoom up ['zuːm'ʌp] *vi F* **to zoom
up/to come zooming up,** arriver en
trombe.

zoot [zuːt] *a O F* (*a*) voyant/criard/
tapageur (*b*) à la mode/(au) dernier
cri; **zoot suit,** complet *m* d'homme
avec veston long et pantalon étroit;
costume *m* zazou.

Répertoire alphabétique
de synonymes
populaires français

abandonner: balancer; balanstiquer; bouler; débarquer; foutre à la
porte; foutre dehors; lâcher; laisser
choir/courir/glisser/tomber; laisser
en carafe/en frime/en panne/en
plan/en rade; laisser quimper;
larguer; plaquer; scier; semer; virer.
(*Voir* **débarrasser de, se**)

abîmer: amocher; bousiller;
esquinter; fusiller; saboter.

abject: *voir* **sale.**

abondance *f*: des bottes *fpl*;
charibotée *f*; chiée *f*; flo(p)pée *f*;
flottes *fpl*; foul(e)titude *f*; des
masses *fpl*; des mille et des cents;
muffée *f*; palanquée *f*; potée *f*;
ribambelle *f*; secouée *f*; tapée *f*; tas
m; tassée *f*; tinée *f*; tirée *f*; tripotée
f.

accord, d': banco; ça biche; ça
boume; ça colle; ça gaze; ça
marche; dac; d'ac(c); gy; ji; jy;
OK.

accoucher: chier *ou* faire un
lard/un lardon/un môme/un salé;
faire un doublé; pisser sa/une côtelette; pisser son os; pisser un
môme; pondre.

adultère *m*: carambolage *m* en
douce; char *m*; coup *m* de canif
(dans le contrat); doublage *m*;
galoup *m*; impair *m*; mise *f* en
double; paille *f*; paillons *mpl*;
queues *fpl*.

adversité *f*: cerise *f*; cirage *m*;
choux *mpl*; confiture *f*; emmerde *f*;

emmerdement *m*; emmouscaillement
m; guigne *f*; limonade *f*; marmelade *f*; mélasse *f*; merde *f*; merdier
m; mouise *f*; mouscaille *f*; panade
f; pétrin *m*; purée *f*; scoumoune *f*;
skoumoune *f*.

affaire *f*: balle *f*; blot *m*; boulot
m; combine *f*; coup *m*; filon *m*;
flanche *m*; oignons *mpl*; parcours
m; truc *m*.

agent *m* **de police:** bédi *m*;
bourrin *m*; cognard *m*; cogne *m*;
condé *m*; flic *m*; flicard *m*; fliquesse
f; fliquette *f*; maton *m*; matuche *m*;
pèlerin *m*; pèlerine *f*; poulaga *m*;
poulet *m*; schmit *m*; sergot *m*; tige
m or f.

agent cycliste: cyclo *m*;
hirondelle *f*; roulette *f*; tige *m or f*;
vache *f* à roulettes.

agent *m* **en moto:** mobilard *m*;
motard *m*.
(*Voir* **policier**)

agression *f*: accrochage *m*; braquage *m*; colletage *m*; cravate *f*;
mise *f* en l'air; serrage *m*.

aiguille *f*: *voir* **seringue.**

aimer: s'amouracher de; avoir à la
bonne/à la chouette; avoir dans la
peau; avoir un/le béguin pour;
avoir un/le pépin pour; avoir une
toquade pour; bander pour; se coiffer de; en croquer pour; en pincer
pour; en tenir pour; s'enticher de;
être chipé pour; être pincé/toqué
de; être mordu pour; gober; goder

pour; l'avoir en l'air pour; raffoler de.

alcool *m*: antigel *m*; blanche *f*; camphre *m*; casse-gueule *m*; casse-pattes *m*; cric *m*; élixir *m* de hussard; fil *m* en quatre/six/trois; gn(i)ole *f*; gnôle *f*; goutte *f*; pousse-au-crime *m*; raide *f*; schnaps *m*; schnick *m*; tafiat *m*; tord-boyau(x) *m*; vitriol *m*.
(*Voir* **vin**)

alibi *m*: berlanche *f*; berlue *f*; chauffeuse *f*; *coupure f*; couverte *f*; couverture *f*; couvrante *f*; parapluie *m*; pébroc *m*; pébroque *m*.

Allemand *m*: boche *m*; chleu(h) *m*; doryphore *m*; fridolin *m*; frisé *m*; fritz *m*; frizou *m*; haricot vert; prusco(t) *m*.

aller, s'en: *voir* **partir**.

amant *m*: coquin *m*; dessous *m*; gigolo *m*; gigolpince *m*; jules *m*; julot *m*; matou *m*; matz *m*; mec *m*; miché *m*; micheton *m*; régulier *m*.

Américain *m*: amerlo *m*; amerloc *m*; amerloque *m*; amerlot *m*; ricain *m*; yankee *m*.

ami *m*: aminche *m*; cop(a)in *m*; frangin *m*; pote *m*; poteau *m*; social *m*; vieille branche; zig(ue) *m*.

amour, faire l': abattre la quille; aiguiller; aller à la bourre/au cul/au joint; amener le petit au cirque; s'appuyer qn; arracher son copeau/son pavé; asperger le persil; baiser; baisouiller; besogner; biquer; bit(t)er; bourrer; bourriner; bourriquer; brosser; calecer; caramboler; caser; casser la canne; chevaucher; chibrer; coller; coucher avec; cracher dans le bénitier; cramper; culbuter; défoncer; se dégraisser; dérouiller; dérouiller son petit frère/Totor; effeuiller la marguerite; égoïner; enfiler; enjamber; s'enfoncer; (s')envoyer en l'air; le faire; se faire qn; faire la bête à deux dos; faire ça; faire des cabriolets/un carton/criquon-criquette; faire une partie de balayette/

d'écarté/de jambes en l'air; faire zizi-panpan; se farcir; filer un coup d'arbalète/de brosse/de patte/de sabre/de tromblon; fourailler; fourrer; foutre un coup d'arbalète/de brosse/de manche; frotter; godiller; goupillonner; grimper; limer; se mélanger; le mettre; mettre la cheville dans le trou; miser; niquer; s'en payer un petit coup; pinailler; piner; pinocher; planter; planter le mai; pointer; pousser sa pointe; prendre du mâle; quener; ramer; ramoner; sabrer; sauter; sch(e)nailler; se taper; tirer sa chique/son coup/sa crampe/sa crampette; tomber; torcher; torpiller; tremper son biscuit; tringler; trombiner; troncher; verger; voir la feuille à l'envers; yenser; z(a)iber.

amphétamine(s) *f(pl)*: amph *f*; amphé(s) *f(pl)*; bonbons *mpl*; speed *m*.

(très) amusant: à se crever de rire; astap(e); bidonnant; bolant; boyautant; crevant; drôlichon; fendant; gondolant; gonflant; impayable; marrant; pilant; pissant; poilant; rigolard; rigolboche; rigouillard; roulant; tire-bouchonnant; tordant; torsif.

an *m*, **année** *f*: balai *m*; berge *f*; carat *m*; gerbe *f*; longe *f*; pige *f*; pigette *f*.

Anglais *m*: angliche *m*; engliche *m*; rosbif *m*.

anus *m*: anneau *m*; baba *m*; bagouse *f*; bague *f*; boîte *f* à pâté; borgne *m*; chevalière *f*; chouette *m*; cul *m*; derge *m*; entrée *f* de service; fias *m*; fignard *m*; fignarès *m*; figne *m*; figneð *m*; fignolet *m*; fion(ard) *m*; foiron *m*; luc *m*; lucarne *f*; motte *f*; œil *m* de bronze; œillet *m*; oignard *m*; oigne *m*; oignon *m*; pastille *f*; pot *m* (d'échappement); petit *m*; petit guichet; rond *m*; rondelle *f*; rondibé *m*; rosette *f*; terre *f* jaune; trèfle *m*; trou *m* (de balle/du cul); troufignard *m*; troufignon *m*;

troufion *m*; turbine *f* à chocolat; tutu *m*; tuyau *m* à gaz.

Arabe *m*: arbi *m*; arbicot *m*; bic *m*; bicot *m*; crougnat *m*; crouillat *m*; crouille *m*; crouilledouche *m*; melon *m*; rat *m*; raton *m*; sidi *m*; tronc *m* (de figuier).

argent *m*: (*monnaie*) artiche *m*; aspine *f*; auber *m*; aubère *m*; beurre *m*; blanc *m*; blanquette *f*; blé *m*; boules *fpl*; braise *f*; bulle *m*; caire *m*; carbi *m*; carburant *m*; carbure *m*; carme *m*; dolluche *m*; douille *f*; ferraille *f*; fifrelin *m*; flouse *m*; flouze *m*; fraîche *f*; fric *m*; galette *f*; galtouze *f*; ganot *m*; grisbi *m*; japonais *m*; kope(c)ks *mpl*; lovés *mpl*; mitraille *f*; mornifle *f*; oseille *f*; osier *m*; nerf *m*; pécune *f*; pépètes *fpl*; pépettes *fpl*; pèse *m*; pésètes *fpl*; pésettes *fpl*; pèze *m*; picaillons *mpl*; plâtre *m*; pognon *m*; quibus *m*; radis *mpl*; rond *m*; rotin *m*; Saint-Fric *m*; soudure *f*; thune *f*; trèfle *m*.
(*Voir* **billet(s)**)

argot *m*: argomuche *m*; jar(s) *m*; javanais *m*; largonji *m*; loucherbem *m*; verlan *m*.

arrêter: agrafer; agricher; agriffer; alpaguer; argougner; arquepincer; baiser; ceinturer; chauffer; choper; coffrer; coincer; cravater; crever; croquer; cueillir; emballer; embarquer; embastiller; emboîter; embourremaner; empaqueter; emporter; enchtiber; enchrister; engerber; entoiler; envelopper; épingler; fabriquer; faire (marron); gaufrer; gauler; grouper; harponner; lever; mettre/jeter/poser le grappin sur; mettre la main sur l'alpague de; paumer; pincer; pingler; piper; piquer; poisser; quimper; rafler; ramasser; ratisser; saucissonner; sauter; secouer; serrer; servietter; sucrer; tomber.
être arrêté: être baisé/bon/ bondi/bonnard/bourru/crevé/ fabriqué/fait/marron/têtard; se

faire bondir; se faire faire; se faire piger.
(*Voir* **emprisonner**)

arriver: s'abouler; amener sa graisse; amener sa viande; s'amener; débarquer; radiner; rappliquer; se pointer.

assassin *m*: but(t)eur *m*; flingueur *m*; metteur *m* en l'air; rectifieur *m*; repasseur *m*; saigneur *m*; scionneur *m*; surineur *m*; tueur *m*.

assassiner: arranger; bousiller; but(t)er; canner; chouriner; crever; cronir; crounir; décoller; dégringoler; démolir; descendre; dessouder; dézinguer; ébouser; effacer; escoffier; estourbir; expédier; faire avaler son bulletin de naissance à; faire la peau à; ficher/flanquer/foutre en l'air; flingoter; flinguer; lessiver; liquider; mettre en l'air; nettoyer; percer; planter; plomber; ratatiner; rectifier; refroidir; repasser; sacailler; saigner; sécher; suriner; zigouiller.

assez (en avoir): arrêter les frais; en avoir sa claque; en avoir jusque-là; en avoir par-dessus la tête; en avoir plein les bottes/le cul/les couilles/le dos/les endosses; en avoir (plus que) marre; en avoir quine; en avoir ras le bol; en avoir ras le cul; en avoir soupé; se faire chier.

assez!: arrête les frais! barca! basta! ça va comme ça! c'est class(e)! c'est marre! écrase! flac! la jambe! n'en jetez plus!(, la cour est pleine)! quine! ras-le-bol! ras-le-cul! rideau! y en a marre!

attaquer: braquer; chabler; harponner; râbler; rentrer dans le lard/le mou à; rentrer dedans; sauter dessus; tomber dessus; tomber sur l'alpague/le paletot/le poil de; voler dans les plumes.

attendre: arracher le chiendent; faire le pied de grue; faire le poireau; se faire poser un lapin; mariner; moisir; poireauter, poser;

prendre racine; rester en carafe/en frime/en plan.

attirail *m* **(d'un drogué):** arsenal *m*; artillerie *f*; kit *m*; popote *f*.

avare (être): avoir un cactus dans la poche/dans le portefeuille; avoir un oursin dans la fouille; avoir des mites dans son crapaud; être chien; être dur à la desserre/ dur à la détente; être duraille; grigou/grippe-sou/pignouf/pingre/ radin/rapiat/rat; être constipé du morlingue; être large du dos; les lâcher avec un élastique/un lance-pierre; les planquer; ne pas les attacher avec des saucisses; ne pas les sortir; tondre les œufs.

avocat *m*: bavard *m*; baveux *m*; cravateur *m*; débarbot *m*; débarbot-teur *m*; perroquet *m*.

avouer: accoucher; s'affaler; s'allonger; blutiner; casser (le mor-ceau); cracher (dans le bassin); déballer ses outils; déballonner; se déboutonner; dégueuler; lâcher le paquet; manger le morceau; se met-tre/passer à table; ouvrir (les van-nes); vider son sac.

bagarre *f*: badaboum *m*; baroud *m*; barrabille *f*; baston *m*; bigorne *f*; castagne *f*; chambard *m*; chambardement *m*; châtaigne *f*; cognage *m*; cogne *f*; corrida *f*; crêpage *m* de chignon(s)/de tignasse(s); crochetage *m*; grabuge *m*; rif *m*; rififi *m*; sonnage *m*; suif *m*; suiffée *f*; torchée *f*.

balle *f*: (*armes à feu*) bastos *f*; dra-gée *f*; pastille *f*; praline *f*; prune *f*; pruneau *m*; valda *f*.

bande *f*: (*groupe d'individus*) soce *f*; tierce *f*.

barbe *f*: bacchante *f*; barbouze *f*; foin *m*; piège *m*.

barbituriques *mpl*: balle *f* de copaille; barbis *mpl*; barbitos *mpl*.

battre: abîmer (le portrait à); amocher; aplatir; aquiger; arranger;

assaisonner; astiquer; attiger; avoiner; bastonner; battre comme plâtre; bigorner; bosseler; botter (le cul à); bourrer de coups; brosser; carder le cuir à; casser la gueule à; chabler; cogner; crêper (le chignon/ la tignasse à); démolir; dérouiller; emplafonner; emplâtrer; encadrer; étriller; filer *ou* foutre une avoine/ une danse/une pâtée à; se frotter; moucher; passer à la machine à bosseler; passer à tabac; passer une peignée/une raclée/une trempe à; ramponner; rentrer dans le chou/la gueule/le lard/le portrait à; rentrer dedans; rosser; rouster; sataner; satonner; scionner; sonner; tabasser; tamponner; tarter; tatouil-ler; tisaner; tomber sur le paletot/ le poil à; torgnoler.

battre, se: s'accrocher; s'amocher; se bagarrer; se bigorner; se bouffer le blair; se bûcher; se châtaigner; se colleter; se coltiner; se crêper le chignon/la tignasse; se crocheter; échanger des politesses; escagasser; s'expliquer; se filer des toises; se flanquer/se foutre sur la gueule, se flanquer/se foutre une peignée; se frotter; se peigner; se riffer; secouer la poêle à marrons à; se torcher.

bavard *m*: baratineur *m*; bavacheur *m*; bavasseur *m*; jacasse *f*; jacasseur *m*; jacassier *m*; jacteur *m*, jaspineur *m*; mitrailleuse *f*; pie *f*; tapette *f*; vacciné *m* avec une aiguille de phono.

bavarder: avoir une platine; bara-tiner; bavacher; bavasser; baver; blablater; caqueter; dégoiser; dépenser beaucoup de salive; dévider; jaboter; jacasser; jacter; jasper; jaspiner; palasser; papoter; pomper de l'air; potiner; rouler; tailler une bavette; en tailler une; tenir le crachoir; user sa salive. (*Voir* **parler**)

beau, belle: badour; bath; baveau; bavelle; bien balancé(e); chbeb; choucard; chouettard; chouette; chouettos; girofle; girond(e); jojo; juteux; laubé;

leaubé; lobé; ridère; riflo; roulé(e) au moule; schbeb; du tonnerre; urf.

beaucoup: bézef; bigrement; bougrement; lerche; lerchem; lerchot; (un) rien; vachement.

bébé *m:* criard *m;* gluant *m;* morceau *m* de salé; ourson *m;* petit salé; têtard *m.*

bénéfice *m:* affure *f;* bénef *m;* beurre *m;* gants *mpl;* gâteau *m;* gras *m;* gratouille *f;* gratte *f;* rab(e) *m;* rabiot *m;* velours *m.*

Benzédrine *(RTM) f: voir* **amphétamine(s).**

bête: andouille; ballot; baluchard; baluche; bas de plafond; bébête; bec d'ombrelle; bêta; bidon; bille; bouché (à l'émeri); bourrique; branque; branquignol; buse; carafon; cave; cavé; cavillon; cloche; con; con comme un balai/comme un comptoir sans verre/comme ses pieds; con(n)ard; con(n)asse; conne; con(n)eau; corniaud; cornichon; couillon; crétin; cruche; cruchon; cul; culcul; déplafonné; ducon(-la-joie); duschnock; empaillé; empaqueté; emplâtré; emplumé; empoté; enflé; fada; (fleur de) nave; gland; gourde; gourdiflot; jobard; lavedu; lourdingue; melon; moule; navet; niguedouille; noix; nouille; oie; panard; patate; pied; plat de nouilles; pocheté; poire; pomme; qui n'était pas derrière la porte (le jour de la distribution); qui en tient une couche; saucisse; schnock; serin; à tête de linotte; (tête de) nœud; tourte; tronche; trouduc; truffe; veau.

bêtise *f:* de la balançoire; des balançoires *fpl;* bidon *m;* blague *f;* bourdes *fpl;* connerie *f;* couillonnade *f;* eau bénite de cour; eau *f* de bidet; fadaise *f;* faribole *f;* fichaise *f;* focard(e) *f;* focardise *f;* focardité *f;* foutaise *f;* pommade *f;* salades *fpl;* sornettes *fpl;* sottise *f;* trouducuterie *f.*

bévue *f:* boulette *f;* bourde *f;* cagade *f;* caraco *m;* char *m;* connerie *f;* gaffe *f;* galoup(e) *f;* impair *m.*

billet(s) *m(pl):* biffeton *m;* faf *m;* faf(f)iot *m;* la grosse artillerie; image *f;* papier *m;* talbin *m.* (*Voir* **argent**)

blennorragie *f:* castapiane *f;* chaude-lance *f;* chaude-pince *f;* chaude-pisse *f;* chtouille *f;* coulante *f;* schtouille *f.*

avoir une blennorragie: pisser des lames de rasoir.

transmettre la blennorragie: attiger.

blesser: abîmer; amocher; aquiger; aquijer; arranger; attiger; jambonner; maquiller; moucher.

blesser au couteau: faire des boutonnières à; faire la croix des vaches à; mettre les tripes à l'air/au soleil à; piquer; poser un portemanteau dans le dos de; rallonger; saigner.

bluffer: *voir* **exagérer.**

boire: s'arroser l'avaloir/la dalle; biberonner; chauffer le four; chopiner; écluser (un godet); s'enfiler un verre; entonner; s'envoyer un coup; en étouffer un; en étrangler un; se gargariser; gorgeonner; se graisser le toboggan; s'humecter les amygdales/le gosier; se jeter une jatte; s'en jeter un (derrière la cravate); lamper; se laver les dents; lever le coude; lécher; lichailler; licher; lipper; se mouiller la dalle/la meule; picoler; pictancher; picter; pictonner; pinter; se piquer le nez/la ruche; pitancher; pomper; se rincer les amygdales/le bec/le cornet/la dalle/le fusil/le sifflet; se salir le nez; sécher un verre; siffler; siroter; soiffer; sucer; se taper un gorgeon; téter.

bordel *m:* baisodrome *m;* bobi *m;* bobinard *m;* bocard *m;* bocsif *m;* bouic *m;* boxon *m;* bric *m;* cabane *f;* casbah *m;* chabanais *m;* clac *m;*

clandé *m*; claque *m*; claquedent *m*; foutoir *m*; maison d'abattage/à gros numéro/de passe; pinarium *m*; pouf *m*; taule *f*; tringlodrome *m*; volière *f*.

bouche *f*: accroche-pipe *m*; bec *m*; boîte *f*; clapet *m*; claque-merde *m*; dalle *f*; déconnophone *m*; égout *m*; gargoulette *f*; gargue *f*; goule *f*; goulot *m*; gueule *f*; malle *f*; margoulette *f*; micro *m*; museau *m*; porte-pipe *m*; respirante *f*; saladier *m*; salle *f* à manger; tirelire *f*; trappe *f*.

bourreau *m*: charlot *m*; faucheur *m*; grand coiffeur; rectifieur *m*.

bouteille *f*: boutanche *f*; chopine *f*; chopotte *f*; rouillarde *f*; rouille *f*.
bouteille de champagne: roteuse *f*.
bouteille de vin rouge: kil *m*; kilbus *m*; kilo *m*; légionnaire *m*; litron *m*; négresse *f*; pieu *m*.
bouteille vide: cadavre *m*; macchabée *m*.

boutique *f*: bouclard *m*; boutanche *f*; estanco *m*; magase *m*; magaze *m*.

bras *m*: abattis *m*; aile *f*; aileron *m*; anse *f*; balancier *m*; bradillon *m*; brandillon *m*; nageoire *f*.

brave (être): avoir des couilles/ du cran/de l'estomac/du poil; avoir quelque chose dans le calbar(d)/ dans le slip; en avoir au cul/dans les bal(l)oches/dans le bide/dans le ventre; n'avoir pas froid aux yeux; être accroché/culotté; être d'attaque; être gonflé; être un peu là; ne pas manquer d'air.

bruit *m*: bacchanal *m*; barouf *m*; bastringue *m*; boucan *m*; bousin *m*; chabanais *m*; chahut *m*; chambard *m*; foin *m*; grabuge *m*; musique *f*; pet *m*; pétard *m*; potin *m*; raffut *m*; rafût *m*; ramdam(e) *m*; schproum *m*; tamtam *m*; zinzin *m*.

butin *m*: barbotin *m*; bouquet *m*; fade *m*; pied *m*; taf *m*; taffe *m*.

cacher: car(r)er; mettre à l'ombre/ en planque/en veilleuse; passer au bleu; placarder; planquer; plan- quouser; plonger.

cacher, se: se carrer; se pla- carder; se planquer; se planquouser.

cachette *f*: placarde *f*; planque *f*; planquouse *f*; trou *m*.

cadavre *m*: allongé *m*; can(n)é *m*; croni *m*; macchab *m*; macchabé(e) *m*; refroidi *m*; viande froide.

café *m*: (*boisson*) caoua(h) *m*; cahoua *m*; jus *m* de chapeau/de chaussette/de chique; kawa *m*; noir *m*.

café *m*: (*débit*) abreuvoir *m*; bar *m*; bistre *m*; bistro *m*; bistroc *m*; bis- troquet *m*; bistrot *m*; caboulot *m*; cafèt *f*; cafeton *m*; estanco(t) *m*; tapis *m*; troquet *m*.

cambrioler: baluchonner; caroubler; faire une cambriole/un casse/un fric-frac; faire du bois; fracasser; fricfraquer; mettre/ monter en l'air; travailler au bec de canne.

cambrioleur *m*: baluchonneur *m*; cambrio *m*; caroubleur *m*; casseur *m*; chevalier *m* de la lune; fracas- seur *m*; fric(-)frac *m*; lourdeur *m*; marcheur *m*; monte-en-l'air *m*.
(*Voir* **voleur**)

campagne *f*: bled *m*; brousse *f*; cambrousse *f*; parpagne *f*; patelin *m*; trou *m*.

cannabis *m*: voir **marijuana**.

car *m* **de police:** familiale *f*; panier *m* à salade; poulailler ambu- lant; voiture *f* de mariée.

caresses *fpl*: chatouilles *fpl*; chouteries *fpl*; mamours *mpl*; papouilles *fpl*; patouilles *fpl*; pattes *fpl* d'araignée; pelotage *m*.

cartes *fpl* **à jouer:** bauches *fpl*; biffetons *mpl*; brèmes *fpl*; cartons *mpl*; papiers *mpl*.

casquette *f*: bâche *f*; deffe *f*; gapette *f*; gaufre *f*; gribelle *f*; grivelle *f*; guimpe(tte) *f*.

cercueil *m*: boîte *f* à dominos;

caisse *f*; paletot *m*/redingote *f* de sapin; pardessus *m* sans manche(s).

chambre *f*: bocal *m*; cambuse *f*; carrée *f*; case *f*; crèche *f*; garno *m*; gourbi *m*; guitoune *f*; piaule *f*; strasse *f*; taule *f*; turne *f*.

chance (avoir de la): avoir du baraka/de la bague/de la bagouse/du bol/du cul/du fion/du flambeau/du gluck/du pot/du proze/du vase/de la veine; avoir l'oignon qui décallotte; l'avoir large/en or; être bidard/chançard/cocu/doré/veinard/verjot/verni. (*Voir* **malchance**)

chanter: goualer; la pousser; envoyer/pousser la goualante; y aller de sa goualante.

chapeau *m*: bada *m*; bibi *m*; bitos *m*; bloum *m*; capet *m*; doul(e) *m*; doulos *m*; galure *m*; galurin *m*; papeau *m*; pétase *m*.

chapeau haut de forme: huit-reflets *m*; lampion *m*; tube *m*; tuyau *m*; de poêle.

chaussures *fpl*: bateaux *mpl*; boîtes *fpl* à violon; crocos *mpl*; croquenots *mpl*; écrase-merde *mpl*; flacons *mpl*; godasses *fpl*; godilles *fpl*; godillots *mpl*; grôles *fpl*; grolles *fpl*; lattes *fpl*; pompes *fpl*; ribouis *mpl*; rigadins *mpl*; savates *fpl*; sorlots *mpl*; targettes *fpl*; tartines *fpl*; tatanes *fpl*; tiges *fpl*.

chauve (être): avoir une bille de billard/un billard/une boule de billard/le caillou déplumé/le melon déplumé/un mouchodrome/la tête nickelée/un vélodrome à mouches; avoir la casquette en peau de fesse/une perruque en peau de fesse/avoir nib de tif(fe)s; être chauve comme un genou; être jambonneau/zigué; n'avoir plus d'alfa sur les hauts plateaux; n'avoir plus de cresson sur la cafetière/sur le caillou/sur la fontaine/sur la truffe; n'avoir plus de gazon sur la plate-bande/sur la prairie/sur la terrasse;

ne plus avoir de mouron sur la cage.

chemise *f*: bannière *f*; limace *f*; limasse *f*; lime *f*; limouse *f*; limouze *f*; panais *m*; sac *m* à viande.

cher, chère: chaud; chéro(t); grisol(e); lerche; lerchem; lerchot; salé.

cheval *m*: bique *f*; bourdon *m*; bourrin *m*; canasson *m*; carcan *m*; carne *m*; dada *m*; gail(le) *m*; hareng *m*; rossard *m*; rosse *f*; tréteau *m*.

cheveux *mpl*: crayons *mpl*; cresson *m*; crins *mpl*; douillards *mpl*; douilles *fpl*; gazon *m*; mourons *mpl*; plumes *fpl*; tiffes *mpl*; tifs *mpl*; tignasse *f*; toison *f*.

couper les cheveux: couper les roseaux; déboiser la colline; tiffer; varloper la toiture.

chien *m*: azor *m*; bougnou(le) *m*; cabot *m*; cador *m*; chien-chien *m*; clébard *m*; clebs *m*; klébard *m*; klebs *m*; oua(h)-oua(h) *m*; toutou *m*.

cigare *m*: barreau *m* de chaise; clou *m* de cercueil; crapulos *m*.

cigarette *f*: baluche *f*; cibiche *f*; clope *mf*; cousue *f*; goldo *f*; grillante *f*; périodique *f*; pipe *f*; pipette *f*; roulée *f*; sèche *f*; taf *f*; taffe *f*; tampax. (*Voir* **cigarette de marijuana**)

cimetière *m*: boulevard *m* des allongés; champ *m* de navets; champ *m*/jardin *m*/parc *m* des refroidis; chez les têtes en os; jardin *m* des claqués; parc *m* des cronis.

clé *f*: caroube *f*; tournante *f*.

clitoris *m*: berlingot *m*; berlingue *f*; bouton *m* (d'amour/de rose); boutonneau *m*; clicli *m*; cliquette *f*; clito(n) *m*; flageolet *m*; framboise *f*; grain *m* de café; haricot *m*; noisette *f*; praline *f*; soissonnais *m* (rose).

clochard *m*: cloche *f*; clodomir *m*; clodo(t) *m*; traîne-pattes *m*; traîne-sabots *m*; traîne-savates *m*; traîne-semelles *m*; trimard *m*; trimardeur *m*; zonard *m*.
(*Voir* **vagabond**)

cocaïne *f*: bigornette *f*; blanche *f*; C *f*; Caroline *f*; cécil(e) *m*; coco *f*; coke *f*; colombine *f*; dynamite *f*; fée blanche; Jules *m*; Julie *f*; naph(taline) *f*; naphte *m*; neige *f*; poudrette *m*; respirante *f*; respirette *f*; talc *m*; topette *f*.

cœur *m*: battant *m*; horloge *f*; palpitant *m*; grand ressort; tocant *m*; toquant *m*.

coït *m*: baisage *m*; baise *f*; bourre *f*; café *m* du pauvre; carambolage *m*; carton *m*; chique *f*; cinq *m* à sept; coup *m*; coup d'arbalète/de tringle; crampe *f*; crampette *f*; partie *f* de balayette/d'écarté/de jambes en l'air; passe *f*; pinette *f*; politesse *f*; queutage *m*; radada *m*; tringlette *m*; truc *m*; vite-fait *m*; zizi-panpan *m*.
(*Voir* **faire l'amour**)
coït anal: *voir* **sodomiser**.
coït buccal: *voir* **cunnilinctus**; **fellation**.
coïter: *voir* **faire l'amour**.

colère *f* **être en**: attraper le coup de raisin/le coup de sang; attraper une crise; l'avoir à la caille; s'emballer; être à cran/à ressaut; être en boule/en fumasse/en pétard/en renaud/en rif/en rogne/en suif; être furax/furibard; exploser; fumer; marronner; monter à l'échelle/sur ses grands chevaux; mousser; piquer une crise; (en) prendre un coup de raisin/de sang; râler; rogner; (en) roter; sortir de ses gonds; voir rouge.

complice *m*: baron *m*; cheville *f*; gaffeur *m*.

concierge *mf*: bignole *mf*; cloporte *m*; concepige *mf*; lourdier *m*; lourdière *f*; pibloque *mf*; pipelet *m*; pipelette *f*.

condamnation *f*: balancement *m*; gerbage *m*; gerbement *m*; sape *m*; sapement *m*; sucrage *m*.
condamné être: cascader; écoper; être bon(nard); être sucré; gerber; morfler; payer; plonger; quimper; saper; tomber; trinquer.

congédier: balancer; balanstiquer; balayer; bordurer; bouler; débarquer; dégommer; envoyer dinguer/paître; envoyer à Chaillot; flanquer/mettre à la porte; lourder; raousser; raouster; sa(c)quer; scier; sortir; valouser; vider; virer.
(*Voir* **débarrasser de, se**)

corbillard *m*: corbi *m*; trottinette *f* (à macchabs).

cou *m*: colbac *m*; colbaque *m*; kiki *m*; sifflet *m*; vis *f*.

coucher, se: aller au dodo/à la dorme/au paddock/au page/au pageot/au pieu/au plumard/au schlaf/au schloff; (se) bâcher; (se) borgnot(t)er; (se) crécher; faire banette; se filer/se glisser/se mettre dans les toiles; se fourrer au plumard; se grabater; se mettre dans les bâches/dans les bannes; se paddocker; se pageoter; se pager; se pagnot(t)er; se pajoter; se pieuter; se plumarder; se plumer; se sacquer; se zoner.

coup(s) *m(pl)*: atout *m*; avoine *f*; baffe *f*; baffre *f*; beigne *f*; bourre-pif *m*; calotte *f*; châtaigne *f*; danse *f*; emplâtre *m*; fricassée *f*; frictionnée *f*; frottée *f*; gnon *m*; jeton *m*; marron *m*; pain *m*; passage *m* à tabac; pâtée *f*; pêche *f*; peignée *f*; pile *f*; prune *f*; pruneau *m*; purge *f*; raclée *f*; ramponneau *m*; ratatouille *f*; rincée *f*; rossée *f*; roulée *f*; tabassage *m*; tabassée *f*; talmouse *f*; taloche *f*; tampon *m*; tamponnage *m*; tannée *f*; taquet *m*; tarte *f*; tatouille *f*; tisane *f*; toise *f*; torchée *f*; torgn(i)ole *f*; tournée *f*; trempe *f*; trempée *f*; tripotée *f*; triquée *f*; valse *f*.
(*Voir* **battre**; **recevoir (des coups)**)

381

courageux: *voir* **brave.**

courir: se carapater; cavaler; (se) drop(p)er; jouer des flûtes/des guibolles; mettre les bâtons; se tirer des gambettes; tricoter des bâtons/des gambettes.

couteau *m*: coupe-lard *m*; cure-dent *m*; eustache *m*; lame *f*; lardoir *m*; lingre *m*; outil *m*; pointe *f*; rallonge *f*; rapière *f*; ratiche *f*; saccagne *f*; sorlingue *m*; surin *m*; yatagan *m*.

couverture *f*: *voir* **alibi.**

crachat *m*: glaviot *m*; gluau *m*; graillon *m*; huître *f*; mol(l)ard *m*; postillon *m*.

cracher: glavioter; graillonner; mollarder.

crâne *m*: caillou *m*; plafond *m*; plafonnard *m*; toiture *f*.

crier: beugler; braire; charronner; goualer; gueuler (au charron); péter; piailler; piauler; pousser des gueulements.

critiquer: abîmer; aquijer; assassiner; bêcher; carboniser; charrier; chiner; débiner; dégrainer; déshabiller; donner un coup de dent à; éreinter; faire un abattage de; faire du jardin; faire une tinette sur; griller; jardiner; jeter la pierre à; vanner.

croire: avaler; couper dedans; donner dedans; encaisser; gober; marcher.

cunnilinctus *m*: gâterie *f*; langue fourrée; pèlerinage *m* aux sources; politesse *f*.
faire un cunnilinctus: bouffer la chatte; brouter le cresson; descendre au panier; donner sa langue au chat; faire mimi/minette; faire une langue fourrée/un pèlerinage aux sources; se gougnotter; se gouiner; (se) gousser; manger; morfier; morfiler; morfiller; sucer.

danser: dansotter; frotter; gambiller; gigoter; guincher; en suer une; tricoter des jambes/des gambettes/des pincettes.

débarrasser de, se: balancer; balanstiquer/se décramponner de; se défarguer de; dégommer; envoyer chier/dinguer/paître/promener; laisser choir; larguer; lessiver; sa(c)quer; scier; vider; virer.
(*Voir* **abandonner; congédier**)

débrouiller, se: avoir la combine; la connaître (dans les coins); se débarboter; se défendre; se démerder; se démieller; se démouscailler; se dépatouiller; savoir s'expliquer/nager/se retourner.

découvrir: dégauchir; dégommer; dégot(t)er; dénicher; faire tilt; piger; repérer.

déféquer; aller où le Roi va à pied; caguer; chier; couler un bronze; débloquer; débonder; déboucher son orchestre; débourrer (sa pipe); déflaquer; déposer sa pêche/une prune; faire caca; faire sa grande commission; faire ses affaires; faire ses grands besoins; faire son gros; flaquer; flasquer; foirer; poser un colombin/sa pêche/une prune/un rondin/une sentinelle; planter une borne; pousser le bouchon; tartir.

dénoncer: balancer; balanstiquer; brûler; cafarder; cafeter; cafter; donner; en croquer; fourguer; griller; moucharder; moutonner; vendre la mèche.
(*Voir* **avouer**)

dénonciateur *m*: balance *f*; balanceur *m*; balanceuse *f*; bordille *m*; bourdille *m*; bourrique *f*; cafard *m*; cafarde *f*; cafardeur *m*; casserole *f*; chevreuil *m*; coqueur *m*; donneur *m*; fileur *m*; indic *m*; mouchard *m*; mouche *f*; mouton *m*.

dents *fpl*: chailles *fpl*; chaillottes *fpl*; chocottes *fpl*; crochets *mpl*; crocs *mpl*; doches *fpl*; dominos *mpl*; pavés *mpl*; piloches *fpl*; quenottes *fpl*; ratelier *m*; ratiches

382

fpl; tabourets *mpl*; touches *fpl* de piano.

dépêcher, se: s'activer; se dégrouiller; se déhotter; se démerder; se dérouiller; faire fissa; se grouiller; se magner le cul/le derche/le derrière/le popotin/le proze/la raie/la rondelle/le train; en mettre/en filer un rayon; se trotter.

dépenser: bouffer/claquer/croquer de l'argent; casquer; cigler; décher; les écosser; les faire valser; les lâcher.

dépensier *m*: claque-fric *mf*; décheur *m*; décheuse *f*.

dés *mpl*: bobs *mpl*; doches *mpl*.

dés truqués: artillerie *f*; balourds *mpl*; bouts *mpl* de sucre; matuches *mpl*; pipés *mpl*; plateaux *mpl*; plats *mpl*.

déshabiller: décapoter; décarpiller; défringuer; défrusquer; déharnacher; délinger; déloquer; dénipper; désaper; (se) dépiauter; (se) foutre à poil.

détester: avoir à la caille; avoir dans le blair/dans le cul/dans le nez; ne pas avoir à la bonne; ne pas pouvoir blairer/encadrer/encaisser/sentir; ne pas pouvoir voir en peinture.

diamant *m*: bauche *m*; bouchon *m* de carafe; caillou *m*; diam(e) *m*; pierre *f*.

diarrhée *f*: chiasse *f*; cliche *f*; courante *f*; foirade *f*; foire *f*; riquette *f*.

difficile: coton; cottard; duraille; duraillon; durillon; duringue; glandilleux; merdique.

discours *m*: baratin *m*; boniment *m*; palas(s) *m*; parlote *f*; postiche *f*; salade *f*.

doigt *m*: (*main*) fourchette *f*; phalangette *f*; piloir *m*; salsifis *m*; (*pied*) haricot *m*; racine *f*; radis *m*.

donner: abouler; allonger; balancer; balanstiquer; coller; ficher;

filer; flanquer; foutre; lâcher; refiler.

dormir: aller à la ronfle; dormailler; dormasser; en écraser (dur); faire dodo/schloff; faire un coup de traversin/une partie de traversin; faire une ronflette; pioncer; piquer un chien; piquer/pousser une ronflette/un roupillon; ronfler; roupiller; roupillonner; schloffer; zoner.

dormir dehors: compter les étoiles; coucher à la belle étoile/sur la dure; dormir à la dure; la refiler; refiler la comète.

drap *m*: bâche *f*; banne *f*; toile *f*.

drogué: accroché; bourré; branché; camé; chargé; dans les vapes; défoncé; dynamite; enneigé; envappé; en voyage; flippé; high; parti; planant; raide (def); speedé; stoned; sur sa planète.

drogué, ee *mf*: acidulé, -ée; accroché, -ée; branché, -ée; camé. -ée; chevalier *m* de la piquouze; chnouffé, -ée; dynamité, -ée; enragé, -ée de la shooteuse; fixer *m*; junkie *mf*; priseur *m*; sniffeur *m*; toxico *m*.

droguer, se: se camer; se charger; se chnouffer; se défoncer; faire un trip/un voyage; se faire un fixe/un shoot; se fixer; se piquer; se piquouser; prendre un trip/un voyage; se schnouffer; se shooter; tirer sur le bambou; tripper; voyager.

drogues *fpl*: came *f*; chnouff *m*; junk *m*; marchandise *f*; narcs *mpl*; schnouff(e) *m*; stuff *m*; stups *mpl*.

duper: *voir* **escroquer.**

eau *f*: baille *f*; bouillon *m*; Château-la-Pompe *m*; flotte *f*; jus *m* de grenouille; jus *m* de parapluie; lance *f*; lancequine *f*; lansquine *f*; limonade *f*; sirop *m* de canard/de grenouille/de parapluie.

échec *m*: bec *m* de gaz; bide *m*; black-boulage *m*; bouchon *m*; bûche *f*; chou blanc; fiasco *m*;

foirage *m*; four *m*; gamelle *f*; loupage *m*; pelle *f*; veste *f*.

échouer: boire la tasse; cafouiller; se casser le nez; claquer; se cogner le nez; culbuter; s'en aller en eau de boudin; être dans le lac; être en plein baccara; être râpé; faire chou blanc; faire la culbute; faire un bide/un four; finir dans les choux/en eau de boudin/en queue de poisson; foirer; louper; partir en couille; péter dans la main; ramasser un bouchon/une bûche; ramasser/remporter une pelle/une veste; tomber à l'eau; tomber en couille; tomber dans le lac.

économiser: arrondir sa pelote; car(r)er; faire son beurre/sa pelote; garer; en mettre à gauche; mettre en petite; planquer; planquouser.

éjaculer: arracher son copeau/son pavé; balancer la/sa purée; balancer la sauce; cracher son venin; décharger; dégorger; égoutter son cyclope; envoyer sa came/la purée/la sauce/la semoule; faire pleurer le cyclope; jeter la purée/son venin; juter; lâcher sa came/une giclée/le jus/sa purée/la semoule/son venin; tirer une giclée; vider ses burettes/les burnes; y aller du/de son voyage.
(*Voir* **orgasme (avoir un)**).

élégant: badour; chic; chicard; class(e); eulpif; flambard; en grand tralala; holpif; qui en jette; qui jette du jus; juteux; minet; rider; ridère; riflo(t); sur son trente et un; tiré à quatre épingles; urf(e).

embrasser: bécoter; coquer un bécot; faire un bec/un bécot/une bise à; faire une galoche/une langue fourrée à; se lécher; se lécher la gueule; rouler une galoche/un patin/des saucisses à; (se) sucer la poire.

emploi *m*: *voir* **travail.**

emprisonner: bloquer; boucler; coffrer; emballer; emplatarder; enchetarder; enchetiber; enchrister; enchtiber; ficher au clou; fourrer au bloc; fourrer dedans; mettre au bloc/à l'ombre/au trou; mettre en cage/en taule.

emprunter (de l'argent) à: bottiner; latter; pilonner; relancer; taper; tartiner; torpiller.

enceinte (être): s'arrondir; attraper/avoir le ballon; avoir avalé le pépin; avoir sa butte; avoir un moufflet/un petit polichinelle dans le tiroir; être dans une situation intéressante; être en cloque; être engrossée; être tombée sur un clou rouillé; se faire arrondir le devant/le globe; gondoler de la devanture; travailler pour Marianne.

mettre enceinte: enceintrer; enchoser; encloquer; engrosser; flanquer le ballon à; mettre en cloque.

enfant *m*: bout *m* de chou/de zan; bouture *f*; chiard *m*; crapaud *m*; gamin *m*; gamine *f*; gluant *m*; gnard *m*; gniard *m*; gosse *mf*; graine *f* de bois de lit; lardon *m*; loupiau *m*; loupiot *m*; loupiotte *f*; marmaille *f*; marmot *m*; marmouset *m*; mignard *m*; mignarde *f*; minot *m*; mioche *mf*; momaque *f*; môme *mf*; momichon *m*; mômichon *m*; momignard *m*; mômignard *m*; morbac *m*; morbaque *m*; morceau *m* de salé; morpion *m*; moucheron *m*; moucheronne *f*; moufflet *m*; moufflette *f*; moujingue *m*; moustique *f*; moutard *m*; niston *m*; nistonne *f*; ourson *m*; petiot *m*; petiote *f*; petit salé *m*; pisseuse *f*; têtard *m*.

enfuir, s': *voir* **partir.**

ennuyer: assassiner; assommer; barber; bassiner; baver sur les burettes/sur les burnes à; caner; casser les bonbons/les burettes/les burnes/les couilles/les noix/les pieds/la tête à; la casser à; les casser à; cavaler; courir qn; courir sur le haricot/sur le système à; cramponner; emmerder; emmieller; emmouscailler; empoisonner; encchariboter; enquiquiner; faire

chier; faire mal aux noix à; faire suer; râper les burettes/les burnes à; raser; rompre la tête à; tanner; taper sur le haricot/sur le système à.
(*Voir* **assez (en avoir)**)

ennuyeux: assommant; barbant; barbe; barbifiant; bassin; bassinant; canulant; canule *f*; casse-bonbons *m*; casse-burettes *m*; casse-burnes *m*; casse-couilles *m*; casse-cul *m*; casse-noisettes *m*; casse-olives *m*; casse-pieds *m*; chiant; chiasse *f*; chierie *f*; chiotte *f*; colique *f*; collant comme la glu; colle *f*; crampon; emmerdant; emmerdement *m*; emmerdeur *m*; emmerdeuse *f*; gluant; pot *m* de colle; rasant; raseur; rasoir; sciant; scie; tannant.

épouse *f*: baronne *f*; bergère *f*; bonbonne *f*; boulet *m*; bourgeoise *f*; gouvernement *m*; légitime *f*; ma (chère) moitié; particulière *f*; patronne *f*; vieille *f*.

érection *f*, **être en:** arquer; avoir le bambou/le bâton/la canne/la gaule/le manche/le mandrin/l'os/le tracassin/le tricotin/la tringle/la trique; avoir du gourdin; avoir les coliques bâtonneuses/cornues; l'avoir dur; l'avoir en l'air; avoir une balle dans le canon; avoir une bandaison; bander; bandocher; être au garde-à-vous; être triqué; godailler; goder; godiller; lever; marquer midi; redresser; tenir la canne; triquer.

escroc *m*: arnaqueur *m*; arrangemane *m*; arrangeur *m*; cambuteur *m*; carabin *m* de la comète; carambouilleur *m*; carotteur *m*; carotteuse *f*; carottier *m*; carottière *f*; combinard *m*; embrouilleur *m*; embrouilleuse *f*; empileur *m*; empileuse *f*; entôleur *m*; entôleuse *f*; estampeur *m*; estampeuse *f*; faisan *m*; faisandier *m*; faiseur *m*; faux jeton; filou *m*; floueur *m*; floueuse *f*; fripouillard *m*; fripouille *f*; musicien *m*; pipeur *m*; pipeuse *f*; poseur *m*; rangemane *m*; rangeur *m*; requin *m*; resquilleur *m*; rouleur *m*; rouleuse *f*; roustisseur *m*.

escroquer: arnaquer; arrangemaner; arranger; avoir; baiser; échauder; écorcher; empaumer; empiler; endormir; enfiler; englander; entuber; estamper; fabriquer; faisander; farcir; filouter; flouer; mener en bateau/en double; monter le coup à; opérer; piper; posséder; pigeonner; rangemaner; refaire; repasser; rouler; roustir; souffler; tirer une carotte à.

escroquerie *f*: arnac *f*; arnaquage *m*; arnaque *f*; carambouillage *m*; carambouille *f*; carottage *m*; carotte *f*; coup *m* (d'arnac/d'arnaque); doublage *m*; entôlage *m*; entourloupe *f*; entourloupette *f*; entubage *m*; estampage *m*; estampe *f*; fripouillerie *f*; repassage *m*; resquillage *m*; resquille *f*.

estomac *m*: boîte *f* à fressures/à ragoût; buffecaille *m*; buffet *m*; burelingue *m*; burlingue *m*; caisse *f*; coco *m*; cornet *m*; estom' *m*; estom(m)e *m*; fanal *m*; fusil *m*; garde-manger *m*; gésier *m*; jabot *m*; lampe *f*; lampion *m*; tube *m*.
(*Voir* **ventre**)

étonner: aplatir; asseoir; en boucher un coin/une surface à; cisailler; clouer (le bec à); couper la chique à; épater; époustoufler; esbloquer; escagasser; estomaquer; souffler.

étonné, être: en avoir la chique coupée; demeurer/être/en rester baba; être/en rester comme deux ronds de flan/comme une tomate.

étrangler: dévisser le coco/le trognon à; serrer le kiki/la vis à.

étron *m*: borne *f*; bronze *m*; caca *m*; colombin *m*; déflaque *f*; factionnaire *m*; merde *f*; orphelin *m*; pêche *f*; prune *f*; rondin *m*; sentinelle *f*.

385

évader, s': *voir* **partir.**

évanouir, s': tomber dans le
cirage/les frites/les pommes/le
sirop/les vapes; tomber en digue-
digue; tourner de l'œil.

exagérer: attiger (la cabane);
blouser; charrier/cherrer (dans les
bégonias); chier dans la colle;
chiquer; cravater; se donner des
coups de pied (dans les chevilles);
envoyer le bouchon; épicer;
esbrouf(f)er; faire de l'esbrouf(f)e/
de la graisse/du pallas; en faire une
tartine; forcer la dose; se gonfler;
gonfler le mou; graisser; en
installer; se monter le job; pousser;
en pousser une; se pousser du col;
pousser le bouchon trop loin; en
rajouter; en remettre; vanner; y
aller fort.

excellent: à tout casser; aux
pommes; baisant; bath; bœuf;
champion; chié; chouette; chouettos; de première; doré sur tranche;
du tonnerre; épatant; époustouflant; extra; fameux;
faramineux; formid(able); formide;
foutral; génial; hyper; impec; meumeu; nickel; pas piqué des hannetons; au poil; pommé; sensass;
soin-soin; super; terrible; trans.

faim (avoir): avoir un creux;
avoir les crochets/les crocs/la dent;
avoir l'estomac dans les talons;
avoir les dents longues; les avoir
longues; bouffer des briques; se
brosser; claquer du bec; la crever;
crever la faim/la dalle; danser
devant le buffet; se mettre la ceinture; la péter; péter la faim; la
sauter; se sentir l'estomac dans les
talons; la serrer; (se) serrer la ceinture; se taper.

fatigué, être: avoir le coup de
bambou/de barre/de pompe; avoir
son compte; en avoir plein sa
botte; être à plat/brisé/claqué/
crevé/éreinté/esquinté/flagada/
flapi/fourbu/ foutu/hachès/
hachesse/HS/lessivé/mal fichu/
pompé/raplapla/vanné/ vaseux/
vidé; être à ramasser à la petite
cuiller; être sur le flanc; être sur les
dents/les genoux/les rotules.

fellation *f*: boule *f* de gomme;
pipe *f*; plume *f*; politesse *f*;
pompier *m*; turlutte *f*.
faire une fellation: brouter
la tige; dévorer; faire boule de
gomme; faire une asperge/une
pipe/un pompier/un pomplard/une
turlutte; se le faire allonger; se
faire croquer; se laver les dents;
manger; pomper (le dard à); prendre en poire; rogner l'os; souffler
dans la canne/le mirliton; sucer;
tailler une pipe/une plume.

faux: bidon; chinetoque; toc;
tocard.

femme *f* (*péj*): boude *m*; boudin
m; bougresse *f*; chipie *f*; créature *f*;
donzelle *f*; fatma *f*; fatmuche *f*;
femelle *f*; fendue *f*; fumelle *f*;
frangine *f*; garce *f*; gendarme *m*;
génisse *f*; gisquette *f*; goncesse *f*;
gonsesse *f*; gonzesse *f*; greluche *f*;
grognasse *f*; guenipe *f*; harpie *f*;
hourrie *f*; lamdé *f*; lamedé *f*; lamfé
f; largue *f*; lièvre *m*; limace *f*;
mémé *f*; ménesse *f*; meuf *f*; mistonne *f*; moukère *f*; mousmé(e) *f*;
nana *f*; nénesse *f*; nénette *f*; paillasse *f*; paillasson *m*; peau *f* (de
vache); pépée *f*; pétasse *f*; polka *f*;
pouffiasse *f*; poule *f*; poulette *f*;
pouliche *f*; poupée *f*; rombière *f*;
souris *f*; tarderie *f*; tartavelle *f*;
typesse *f*; vache *f*.
belle femme: beau châssis;
beau linge; beau (petit) lot; belle
mécanique; bien balancée; bien
roulée; pépée *f*; poulette *f*; pouliche
f; prix *m* de Diane; roulée au
moule.

jeune femme: bergère *f*;
frangine *f*; garce *f*; gisquette *f*;
gonzesse *f*; greluche *f*; grimbiche *f*;
Julie *f*; lamdé *f*; lamedé *f*; lamfé *f*;
meuf *f*; mistonne *f*; môme *f*;
mousmé(e) *f*; nana *f*; nénette *f*;
palombe *f*; pépée *f*; poule *f*;
poulette *f*; pouliche *f*.

(vieille) femme laide: bique *f*; grognasse *f*; guenon *f*; guenuche *f*; mémée *f*; mocheté *f*; prix *m* à réclamer; remède *m* d'amour; rombière *f*; saucisson *m*; tarderie *f*; tardingue *f*; tartavelle *f*; vieille bique/chèvre/rombière/toupie/vache; vieux trumeau.

fesses *fpl*: arrière-train *m*; as *m*; baba *m*; bernard *m*; ballon *m*; brioches *fpl*; cadran *m* (solaire); croupe *f*; croupillon *m*; cul *m*; dédé *m*; derche *m*; derge *m*; derrière *m*; dossière *f*; faubourg *m*; fessier *m*; fouaron *m*; fouettard *m*; fouignedé *m*; foiron *m*; griottes *fpl*; joufflu *m*; jumelles *fpl*; luc *m*; lune *f*; meules *fpl*; miches *mpl*; mouilles *fpl*; moutardier *m*; noix *fpl*; panier *m* à crottes; pastèque *f*; pendule *f*; père-fouettard *m*; pétard *m*; petits pains; pétouler *m*; pétrousquin *m*; pétrus *m*; pont-arrière *m*; popotin *m*; postère *m*; postérieur *m*; pot *m*; prose *m*; prosinard *m*; proze *m*; prozinard *m*; radada *m*; tafanard *m*; tal *m*; tapanard *m*; train *m*; valseur *m*; vase *m*.

fête *f*: *voir* **réjouissances.**

figure *f*: *voir* **visage.**

(jeune) fille *f*: caille *f*; gamine *f*; gisquette *f*; gosse *f*; jeunesse *f*; jeunette *f*; minette *f*; mômaque *f*; môme *f*; nistonne *f*; pisseuse *f*; quille *f*; tendron *m*.

flatter: baratiner; bonimenter; bourrer la caisse/le crâne/le mou à; caresser dans le sens du poil; casser le nez à coups d'encensoir à; cirer; faire de la lèche à; faire du baratin/du boniment/du flan/du plat à; fayoter; jeter de la pommade à; lécher les bottes/le cul à; passer la main dans le dos à; passer (de) la pommade à; peloter; pommader.

fort, être: être balaise/balès/baleste/balèze/bien balancé/bien baraqué/costaud/fortiche/mailloche/malabar/maousse; être fort comme un bœuf; être un homme à

pogne; être un mec/un macho; se poser là.

fou: azimuté; ballot; barjo(t); branque; branquignol; braque; chabraque; cinglé; cinoque; cintré; détraqué; dingo; dingot; dingue; fada; farfelu; fêlé; focard; follingue; fondu; frappadingue; frappé; givré; gland; jeté; locdu; loquedu; loubac; louf; loufoque; louftingue; maboul(e); malade; marteau; percuté; piqué; ravagé; sinoc; sinoque; siphonné; sonné; synoque; tapé; timbré; tocbombe; toctoc; toqué; tordu; touché.

devenir fou: décrocher; déménager; dérailler; partir du ciboulot; perdre la boule/la boussole/la carte/le nord/les pédales; recevoir un coup de bambou.

être fou: avoir une araignée/une chauve souris/un hanneton au plafond; avoir reçu un coup de bambou; avoir une fêlure/une fissure/un grain; battre la breloque; se décarcasser le boisseau; être bon/fait/mûr pour Sainte-Anne; être cucul (la praline); être dérangé du cigare; être fou à lier; onduler de la toiture/de la touffe; travailler du bigoudi/du chapeau/du ciboulot du cigare de la touffe; yoyoter de la mansarde.

foule *f*: populo *m*; tref *m*; trèfle *m*; trèpe *m*; trèple *m*.

frère *m*: frangibus *m*; frangin *m*; frelot *m*; frérot *m*; moré *m*.

fromage *m*: frome *m*; fromegi *m*; frometon *m*; fromgi *m*; fromgom *m*; fromjo *m*; fromtegomme *m*; fromton *m*; puant *m*.

fumer: bombarder; bouffarder; en griller une; faire la loco; piper; sécher.

gagner (de l'argent): afflurer; affurer; arrondir sa pelote; en amasser; se bourrer; en ramasser; faire du pèse; faire sa pelote; faire son beurre; faire son oseille; se faire un pognon fou; ferrer la mule; ramasser du fric (à la pelle); se remplir (les poches); se sucrer; tomber sur un champ d'osier; trouver le filon; toucher un joli paquet.

gain *m*: afflure *f*; affure *f*; bénef *m*; beurre *m*; bonus *m*; paquet *m*; velours *m*.

gardien *m* **(de prison):** gâfe *m*; gaffe *m*; maton *m*; matuche *m*.
gardien-chef *m*: doublard *m*.

gendarme *m*: bédi *m*; pandore *m*; pèlerin *m*; pèlerine *f*; sansonnet *m*; sauret *m*; schmit *m*.

goinfre *(m)*: bâfreur *(m)*; (béni-)-bouffe-tout *(m)*; (béni-)bouftou(t) *(m)*; bouffe-la-balle *(m)*; bouffe-tout *(m)*; bouftou(t) *(m)*; crevard *(m)*; goulu *(m)*; gueulard *(m)*; morfal *(m)*; morfalou *(m)*; piffre *(m)*; porc *m*.

gonorrhée *f*: *voir* **blennorragie.**

gorge *f*: avaloir *m*; cornet *m*; corridor *m*; couloir *m*; courgnole *f*; dalle *f*; entonnoir *m*; garga *f*; gargamelle *f*; gargane *f*; garganelle *f*; gargoine *f*; gargoulette *f*; gargue *f*; goule *f*; goulette *f*; goulot *m*.

gras: *voir* **gros.**

gratuit: au châsse; à l'œil; pour des clous; pour du beurre; pour la peau; pour que dalle.

grogner: chialer; être en boule/à cran/comme un crin/en rogne/en suif; groumer; marronner; râler; la ramener; renâcler; renauder; rogner; ronchonner; rouscailler; rouspéter; tousser.

gros: bouboule; boulot(te); dondon; gravos; mailloche; malabar; maousse; patapouf; plein de soupe; rondouillard.

guetter: avoir à l'œil; borgnotter; faire le gaffe/le pet/la planque; gaffer; gafouiller; mater; zyeuter.

guillotine *f*: abbaye *f* de Monte-à-regret; bascule *f* (à charlot); bécane *f*; coupante *f*; coupe-cigare

m; faucheuse *f*; le Grand Hachoir; machine *f* à raccourcir; Veuve *f*.

être guillotiné: y aller du gadin; cracher dans le panier; épouser la Veuve; éternuer dans le sac/le son; se faire couper le cigare; se faire raccourcir; mettre le nez/la tête à la fenêtre; tirer sa crampe avec la Veuve.

habile (être): *voir* **malin.**

habiller: fagoter; ficeler; fringuer; frusquer; harnacher; linger; loquer; nipper; (se) sabouler; saper.

mal habillé: fichu comme quat' sous; la jeter mal; mal fagoté; mal ficelé; fringué comme l'as de pique.

habiter: crécher; nicher; percher; pioger.

habits: *voir* **vêtements.**

haschisch *m*: fée verte; H *m*; hasch *m*; merde *f*; shit *m*.

héroïne *f*: antigel *m*; blanche *f*; boy *m*; cheval *m*; chnouf(fe) *f*; H *f*; héro *mf*; jules *m*; junk *m*; jus *m*; merde *f*; naphtaline *f*; naphte *f*; niflette *f*; poudre *f*; schnouf(fe) *f*; shit *m*.

homme *m*: artiste *m*; asticot *m*; birbe *m*; bougre *m*; client *m*; coco *m*; fias *m*; frangin *m*; frelot *m*; gars *m*; gazier *m*; gnace *m*; gniasse *m*; gnière *m*; gonce *m*; goncier *m*; gonse *m*; gonsier *m*; gonze *m*; gonzier *m*; gugusse *m*; gus *m*; guss(e) *m*; Jules *m*; Julot *m*; lascar *m*; loulou *m*; loustic *m*; matz *m*; mec *m*; mecqueton *m*; mecton *m*; mironton *m*; moineau *m*; numéro *m*; oiseau *m*; paroissien *m*; pékin *m*; péquin *m*; pétrousquin *m*; piaf *m*; pierrot *m*; pistolet *m*; tartempion *m*; type *m*; zèbre *m*; zig *m*; zigomar(d) *m*; zigoteau; zigoto *m*; zigue *m*.

homosexuel *m*: bourrin *m*; caroline *f*; chochotte *f*; chouquette *f*; emmanché *m*; empaffé *m*; empapaouté *m*; empétardé *m*; emp-

rosé *m*; encaldossé *m*; enculé *m*; enfifré *m*; enfoiré *m*; englandé *m*; enviandé *m*; fagot *m*; fiotte *f*; gazier *m*; girond *m*; jésus *m*; joconde *f*; lopaille *f*; lopart *m*; lope *f*; lopette *f*; papaout *m*; p.d. *m*; PD *m*; pédé *m*; pédéro *m*; pédoc *m*; pédoque *m*; pointeur *m*; poulette *f*; qui en est; qui est de la bague; qui est de la famille tuyau de poêle; qui en prend; qui file de la jaquette; rivette *f*; schbeb *m*; sœur *f*; tante *f*; tantinette *f*; tantouse *f*; tantouze *f*; tapette *f*; travelo(t) *m*.
être homosexuel: donner du dos/du rond; en être; en donner; en lâcher; en prendre; être de la bague/de la famille tuyau de poêle/ de la jaquette flottante/de la rondelle; filer du chouette/du dos/de la jaquette; mettre sa chemise en véranda; prendre du dos/du petit; travailler de la jaquette.
(*Voir* **sodomiser**)

hôpital *m*: castre *m*; host(e)au *m*; hosto *m*; planque *f* aux attigés.

idiot (*m*); **ignorant** (*m*); **imbécile** (*mf*): *voir* **bête**.

indicateur *m*: *voir* **dénonciateur**.

individu *m*: *voir* **homme**.

information *f*: *voir* **renseignement**.

injurier: agoniser; baptiser; engueuler; enguirlander; incendier; rembarrer; traiter de tous les noms. (*Voir* **réprimander**)

intelligent: calé; débrouillard; démerdard; doué; fort (en tête); grosse tête; tête *f* d'œuf.

interrogatoire *m*: blutinage *m*; cuisinage *m*; cuisine *f*; musique *f*; saignement *m* de nez.

Italien *m*: macaroni *m*; rital *m*.

ivre (être): s'arrondir; avoir du vent dans les voiles; avoir pris une bit(t)ure/une cuite; avoir sa cuite/ son plumet; avoir un coup dans l'aile; avoir un verre dans le nez; se barrer; se bit(t)urer; être au pays noir; être allumé/arrondi/beurré/ bit(t)uré/blindé/bourré (à bloc)/ brindezingué/chargé/chicoré/cuit/ culbuté (à zéro)/fabriqué/fadé/ gelé/givré/mâchuré/mûr/mur-dingue/noir/ noircicot/ourdé/paf/ parti/ pinté/ pion/ pionnard/pis-taché/poivré/raide/ rétamé (à zéro)/rond/rondibé/saoul/schlass/ soûl/teinté; être dans les brinde-zingues/dans le cirage/dans les vapes; être plein comme un boudin/une bourrique/un fût/une huître/un œuf/une outre; être rond comme une barrique/une bille/un boudin/une boule; se murdinguer; se mûrir; se pionner; se piquer le nez; se pistacher; prendre la/sa cuite; prendre une bit(t)ure/une pistache; ramasser une beurrée/une bit(t)ure; en tenir une bit(t)ure/une cuite; tenir une (bonne) ourdée/son plumet.
être légèrement ivre: avoir chaud aux plumes; avoir sa pointe; être ébréché/émeché/gris/parti/ pompette.

ivresse *f*: beuverie *f*; bit(t)ure *f*; buverie *f*; caisse *f*; cuite *f*; cuvée *f*; pistache *f*; pocharderie *f*; poivrade *f*; saoulerie *f*; saoulographie *f*; soû-lardise *f*; soûlographie *f*; soûlerie *f*.

ivrogne *m*: alcolo *m*; bibard *m*; bibart *m*; biberon *m*; biberonne *f*; licheur *m*; licheuse *f*; picoleur *m*; picoleuse *f*; pionnard *m*; pochard *m*; pocharde *f*; poivrot *m*; poivrote *f*; qui a la dalle en pente; riboteur *m*; riboteuse *f*; sac *m* à vin; saou-lard *m*; saoularde *f*; saouloir *m*; saoulot *m*; soiffard *m*; soiffarde *f*; soiffeur *m*; soiffeuse *f*; soûlard *m*; soûlarde *f*; soûlaud *m*; soûlaude *f*; soûlographe *m*; soûlot *m*.

jambes *fpl*: baguettes *fpl*; bâtons *mpl*; bégonias *mpl*; béquilles *fpl*; bouts *mpl* de bois; brancards *mpl*; cannes *fpl*; compas *mpl*; flubards *mpl*; fusains *mpl*; fuseaux *mpl*; gambettes *fpl*; gambilles *fpl*; gigots *mpl*; gigues *fpl*; guibolles *fpl*;

guisots *mpl*; nougats *mpl*; pattes *fpl*; piliers *mpl*; pilons *mpl*; pivots *mpl*; quilles *fpl*.

jambes maigres: allumettes *fpl*; crayons *mpl*; échalas *mpl*; échasses *fpl*; flûtes *fpl*; fumerons *mpl*; pinceaux *mpl*; pincettes *fpl*.

Japonais *m*: jap *m*; jaune *m*; nippon *m*.

jeter: balancer; balanstiquer; envoyer dinguer; ficher/foutre en l'air.

journal *m*: babillard *m*; baveux *m*; canard *m*; feuille *f* de chou; torchon *m*.

Juif, Juive: Youde *mf*; Youpe *mf*; Youpin *m*; Youpine *f*; Youtre *mf*; Youvance *m*.

laid: belle comme un camion; bléchard; blèche; blèchecaille; miteux; mochard; moche; mochetingue; mocheton; pas jojo; roupie; tarde; tartavelle; tarte; tartignol; tartouille; tartouse; toc; tocard. (*Voir* **(vieille) femme laide**)
personne laide: boudin *m*; caricature *f*; carnaval *m*; gueule *f* à coucher dehors; gueule d'empeigne/ de raie; hideur *f*; mocheté *f*; qui a une sale/vilaine gueule; roupie *f*; tarderie *f*; tardingue *f*; tartavelle *f*.

langue *f*: battant *m*; bavarde *f*; baveuse *f*; clapette *f*; langouse *f*; lavette *f*; membrineuse *f*; menteuse *f*; mouillette *f*; patin *m*; platine *m*; râpeuse *f*; tapette *f*.

lesbienne *f*: éplucheuse *f* de lentilles; gavousse *f*; godo *f*; gouchotte *f*; goudou *f*; gougne *f*; gougnette *f*; gougnot(t)e *f*; gouine *f*; gousse *f* (d'ail); mangeuse *f* de lentilles; marchande *f* d'ail; qui aime/qui tape l'ail; vrille *f*.
être lesbienne: aimer l'ail; être de la bottine/de la maison tire-bouton; (se) gougnotter; (se) gouiner; (se) gousser; manger/sentir/taper l'ail; travailler de la bottine.

lèvre *f*: babine *f*; babouine *f*;

badigoince *f*; bagougnasse *f*; baiseuse *f*; limace *f*; pompeuse *f*.

lit *m*: bâche *f*; banette *f*; boîte *f* à puces; champ *m* de manœuvre; dodo *m*; matelas *m*; nid *m*; paddock *m*; page *m*; pageot *m*; pagne *m*; pagnot *m*; panier *m*; pieu *m*; plumard *m*; plume *f*; pucier *m*; sac *m* à puces.

logement *m*: bahut *m*; baraque *f*; bocal *m*; cabane *f*; cagna *f*; cambuse *f*; carrée *f*; casba(h) *f*; case *f*; crèche *f*; garno *m*; gourbi *m*; guitoune *f*; niche *f*; nid *m*; piaule *f*; planque *f*; strasse *f*; taule *f*; tôle *f*; turne *f*.

loucher: avoir un œil qui dit merde/zut à l'autre; bigler (en biais); boîter des calots.

LSD *m*: acide *m*; D *m*; sucre *m*.

lunettes *fpl*: bernicles *fpl*; carreaux *mpl*; carrelingues *mpl*; faux quinquets; pare-brise *mpl*.

maigre: désossé; long comme un jour sans pain; maigre comme un clou; maigrichon; maigrot; que la peau sur les os; sec comme un coup de trique; séco; sécot.
personne maigre: asperge *f*; échalas *m*; fil *m* (de fer); planche *f* à pain; sac *m* d'os; séco.

main *f*: agrafe *f*; battoir *m*; croche *f*; cuiller *f*; grappin *m*; grattante *f*; griffe *f*; louche *f*; mimine *f*; palette *f*; paluche *f*; papogne *f*; patte *f*; pat(t)oche *f*; pince *f*; pogne *f*; quintuplée *f*.

malade (être): amoché; avoir un pet de travers; n'avoir pas le moral; être dans les vapes/flagada/ flapi/mal fichu/mal foutu/mal vissé; ne pas avoir la frite/la pêche; ne pas être dans un bon jour; pas dans son assiette; pas en train; patraque.

(être) très malade: avoir un pied dans la tombe; battre de l'aile; être cuit/fichu/flambé/foutu/fricassé/frit/paumé; filer un mauvais coton; marcher à côté de ses pompes; sentir le sapin.

maladie vénérienne: *voir* **blennoragie; syphilis.**

malchance *f*: bouillabaisse *f*; bouscaille *f*; cerise *f*; confiture *f*; déveine *f*; guigne *f*; guignon *m*; manque *m* de bol/de pot/de vase; marmelade *f*; masque *m*; pestouille *f*; pétrin *m*; poisse *f*; pommade *f*; scoumoune *f*; sirop *m*.

malin: affranchi; à la coule; à la hauteur; à la page; dans le train; débrouillard; dégourdi; démerdard; dessalé; ficelle; filou(teur); fortiche; fute-fute; mariole; marle; marloupin; roublard.

manger: aller à la graille; s'appuyer (un repas); becqueter; becter; becqueter; bouffer; boulotter; boustifailler; briffer; casser la croûte/la graine; claper; cléber; croquer; croustiller; croûter; dévorer; effacer; s'envoyer; grailler; grainer; jaffer; lipper; mastéguer; mastiquer; morfier; morfiler; morfiller; morganer; recharger les accus; se remplir le bocal/le cornet/le garde-manger/la lampe; se taper la cloche; tortorer.

manger abondamment: bâfrer; bouffer (à crever); se bourrer; se caler les amygdales/les babines / les babouines / les badigoinces/les côtes/les joues; se la caler; se les caler; s'empiffrer; se faire péter la sous-ventrière; s'en fourrer jusque-là; s'en foutre plein la lampe; s'en jeter/s'en mettre derrière la cravate; s'en mettre jusqu'au menton/jusque-là; s'en mettre plein le fusil/plein la lampe; se goinfrer; gueuletonner; morphaler; prendre une bonne ventrée; se remplir le buffet.

maquiller, se: se badigeonner; faire un raccord; faire son ravalement; se plâtrer le visage; se (re)faire la façade; se sucrer la fraise/la gaufre.

marchandise *f*: came *f*; camelote *f*; lamedu *f*.

marcher: affûter des pinceaux; aller à pattes; aller par le train d'onze heures; arpenter le bitume; arquer; bagoter; prendre le train onze; prendre la voiture de Saint-Crépin; ripatonner; se trimballer.

mariage *m*: antiflage *m*; conjungo *m*; entiflage *m*; marida *m*; maridat *m*.

se marier: aller au marida; s'antifler (de sec); s'entifler (de sec); se marida; prononcer le conjungo; signer un bail.

divorcer: casser le bail.

marijuana *f*: chanvre *m*; chiendent *m*; douce *f*; foin *m*; herbe (douce); kif *m*; Marie-Jeanne *f*; pot *m*; thé *m*.

cigarette *f* **de marijuana:** bomb *f*; drag *m*; fumette *f*; joint *m*; reefer *m*; stick *m*.

marin *m*: col bleu; loup *m* de mer; marsouin *m*; mataf *m*; matave *m*; mathurin *m*; pompon *m* rouge.

masturber, se: (*homme*) s'achever à la manivelle; s'agiter le poireau; se l'agiter; s'allonger la couenne; se l'allonger; s'astiquer; s'astiquer la colonne/le manche; se l'astiquer; se battre le chinois; s'en battre une; se branler; se chatouiller le poireau; se coller un rassis; épouser la veuve Poignet; étrangler Popaul/Popol; faire cinq contre un; se faire écrémer; faire glouglouter le poireau; se faire malice tout seul; se faire mousser (le créateur); se faire reluire; faire sauter la cervelle à Charles-le-Chauve; se faire une pogne; se fréquenter; fréquenter la veuve Poignet; se griffer; se palucher; se polir le chinois/la colonne; se pogner; se secouer le bonhomme; se soulager; se taper la veuve Poignet; se taper (sur) la colonne; se taper une pignole/un rassis/une sègue; s'en taper une; se tirer son/un coup; se toucher; se tripoter (les couilles).

se masturber: (*femme*) s'astiquer le boilton/le bouton; se branler; se compter les poils; se filer une gerbe; jouer de la mandoline; secouer son grain de café; se soulager; se toucher.

masturbation *f*: branlage *m*; branlée *f*; branlette *f*; branlette maison; branlure *f*; paluche *f*; pignole *f*; pogne *f*; secouette *f*; sègue *f*; veuve Poignet.

masturbateur *m*: branleur *m*; branleuse *f*.

mauvais: à la manque; à la noix; bidon; blèche; locdu; loquedu; moche; raté; tarte; tartouse; toc; tocard.

méchant *m*: *voir* **salaud.**

mégot *m*: clope *m*; meg *m*; orphelin *m*.

mendiant *m*: clodo(t) *m*; frappeur *m*; manchard *m*; mangav *m*; mégot(t)eur *m*; mégot(t)euse *f*; mégot(t)ier *m*; mégot(t)ière *f*; mendiche *m*; mendigot *m*; pilon *m*; pilonneur *m*; tapeur *m*; tapeuse *f*; torpille *f*; torpilleur *m*.

mendicité *f*: manche *f*; mangave *f*; mégotage *m*; pilon *m*; sonnage *m*; tapage *m*; tape *f*; torpille *f*.

mendier: aller à la mangave; faire la manche/le pilon; frapper; marcher à la torpille; mendigoter; pilonner; taper; tirer le pied de biche; torpiller.

menottes *fpl*: bracelets *mpl*; brides *fpl*; cabriolets *mpl*; cadènes *fpl*; cadenettes *fpl*; cadennes *fpl*; cannelles *fpl*; chapelet *m*; ficelles *fpl*; fichets *mpl*; manchettes *fpl*; pinces *fpl*; poucettes *fpl*.

mensonge *m*: balançoire *f*; bateau *m*; bidon *m*; blague *f*; bobard *m*; boniment *m*; bourde *f*; bourrage *m* (de crâne/de mou); du bourre-mou; char(re) *m*; connerie *f*; craque *f*; cravate *f*; doublage *m*; frime *f*; histoire *f* à dormir debout; histoire raide; van(n)e *m*.

mentir: bourrer la caisse/le

crâne/le mou; en conter; monter une galère; raconter des bobards/des histoires.

merde *f*: *voir* **étron.**

mère *f*: dabe *f*; dabesse *f*; dabuche *f*; daronne *f*; doche *f*; mater *f*; matère *f*; (la) maternelle; vieille *f*.

mescaline *f*: mesc *f*.

mitraillette *f*: arroseuse *f*; arrosoir *m*; lampe *f* à souder; machine *f* à coudre/à percer/à secouer le paletot; mandoline *f*; moulin *m* à café; moulinette *f*; sulfateuse *f*; tititine *f*; vaporisateur *m*.

monnaie *f*: ferraille *f*; menouille *f*; mitraille *f*; mornifle *m*; vaisselle *f* de fouille.

montre *f*: dégoulinante *f*; montrouze *f*; pendule *f*; tocante *f*; toquante *f*.

moquer de, se: acheter; blaguer; chambrer; charrier; chiner; jardiner; se ficher de; se foutre de; mettre en boîte/en caisse; se payer la cafetière/la gueule/la poire/la tête/la tronche de.

morphine *f*: lili-pioncette *f*; M *f*; morph *f*.

mouchoir *m*: blave *m*; tire-jus *m*; tire-moelle *m*.

mourir: avaler son acte/son bulletin/son extrait de naissance; avaler sa chique; l'avaler; boucler sa malle; bouffer du pissenlit/des pissenlits par la racine; cadancher; calancher; calencher; caner; casser sa pipe; la casser; cirer ses bottes; claboter; clam(e)cer; clam(p)ser; clapoter; clapser; claquer; cram(p)ser; crever; cronir; la déchirer; déposer le bilan; dépoter son géranium; déramer; (la) dessouder; (la) dévisser; dévisser son billard; éteindre sa bougie/son gaz; faire couic; fermer son gaz/son parapluie; glisser; graisser ses bottes; lâcher la rampe; se laisser glisser; oublier de respirer; passer l'arme à gauche; perdre le goût du pain; plier bagage; quimper; remercier son boulanger; sentir le sapin; sortir les pieds devant; souffler sa veilleuse.

moustaches *fpl*: bac(c)antes *fpl*; bacchantes *fpl*; bacchantes en guidon (de course); baffe *f*; baffi *mf*; balai *m* (à chiottes); charmeuses *fpl*; ramasse-miettes *m*.

nègre *m*: *voir* **Noir(e)**.

nez *m*: baigneur *m*; blair *m*; blaireau *m*; blase *m*; blaze *m*; boîte *f* à morve; cep *m*; naze *m*; pif *m*; piffard *m*; piton *m*; pivase *m*; priseur *m*; reniflant *m*; step *m*; tarbouif *m*; tarin *m*; trompette *f*.

nez épaté: patate *f*; pied *m* de marmite; truffe *f*.

grand nez: éteignoir *m*; fer *m* à souder; quart *m* de brie; step *m* (à trier les lentilles/à repiquer les choux); tasseau *m*; tassot *m*.

nez rouge: aubergine *f*; piment *m*; tomate *f*.

Noir(e) *m(f)*: bamboula *m*; bougnoul(le) *m*; boule *f* de neige; gobi *m*; mal blanchi(e) *m(f)*; négro *m*; noyama *m*; radis noir.

nom *m*: blaze *m*; centre *m*.

non!: balpeau! bernique! des clopes! des clopinettes! des clous! macache (et midi sonné)! mon œil! mon zob! nib! nibe! la peau! la peau de mes burnes! peau de balle (et balai de crin)! peau de balle et variété! peau de nœud! peau de zob! que dalle!

nourriture *f*: avoine *f*; becquetance *f*; bectance *f*; bouffe *f*; bouftance *f*; boustifaille *f*; boustiffe *f*; briffe *f*; casse-dalle *m*; cassegraine *m*; croustance *f*; croustille *f*; croûte *f*; frichti *m*; fricot *m*; frip(p)e *f*; graille *f*; graine *f*; grinque *f*; jaffe *f*; mangeaille *f*; mastègue *f*; tambouille *f*; tortore *f*.

mauvaise nourriture: graillon *m*; ragougnasse *f*; rata *m*; ratatouille *f*.

nu: à loilpé; à loilpuche; à poil; comme un savon; (le) cul à l'air; dans le costume d'Adam/d'Eve; en Jésus.

nuit *f*: borgne *f*; borgniot *m*; borgno *m*; borgnon *m*; neuille *f*; noie *f*; noille *f*; sorgue *f*.

œil *m*: bille *f*; calot *m*; carreau *m*; châsse *m*; clignotant *m*; coquillard *m*; lampion *m*; lanterne *f*; lentille *f*; loupe *f*; lucarne *f*; mire *f*; mirette *f*; mironton *m*; œillet *m*; quinquet *m*; yakas *m*.

coup d'œil: coup *m* de sabord; coup de saveur.

œil poché: coquard *m*; coquart *m*; coquelicot *m*; œil au beurre noir; œil pavoisé; œil poché.

œillade (faire une): donner/faire un appel/un coup de châsse/un coup de sabord; jouer des châsses; reluquer.

opium *m*: boue verte; chandoo *m*; dross *m*; fée brune; noir *m*; op *m*; pavot *m*; touffiane *f*.

or *m*: jonc *m*; joncaille *f*.

oreille *f*: anse *f*; cliquette *f*; écoute *f*; écoutille *f*; escalope *f*; esgourde *f*; étagère *f* à mégot; étiquette *f*; feuille *f* (de chou); manette *f*; pavillon *m*; portugaise *f*; soucoupe *f*; zozore *f*.

orgasme (avoir un): se balancer; briller; s'envoyer en l'air; jouir; juter; prendre son fade/son panard/son pied; rayonner; se régaler; reluire; vider ses burettes; y aller du/de son voyage.

oui!: banco! ça botte! ça colle! c'est bon! dac! d'acc! entendu! gy! je marche! gi! gy!

ouvrier *m*: *voir* **travailleur**.

ouvrir: débâcler; déboucler; débrider; mettre en dedans.

pain *m*: bricheton *m*; briffeton *m*; brignole *f*; brignolet *m*; brignoluche *m*; larton *m*.

pantalon *m*: bénard *m*; bénouse *m*; bénouze *m*; cotte *f*; culbutant *m*; culbute *m*; false *m*; falzar(d) *m*; fendant *m*; fendard *m*; fendart *m*; froc *m*; fut *m*; futal *m*; grimpant *m*; montant *m*; valseur *m*.

pantalon étroit: fourreau *m*; tuyau *m* de poêle.

papier *m*: balourd *m*; faf(f)e *m*; faf(f)iot *m*; papelard *m*; pelure *f*.

parapluie *m*: paralance *m*; pare-flotte *m*; pare-lance *m*; pébroc *m*; pébroque *m*; pèlerin *m*; pépin *m*; riflard *m*.

pardessus *m*: lardeusse *m*; lardingue *m*; lardosse *m*; pardaf *m*; pardess *m*; pardeuss(e) *m*; pardingue *m*; pardosse *m*; pelure *f*.

parents *mpl*: dabs *mpl*; dabes *mpl*; darons *mpl*; vieux *mpl*; viocards *mpl*; vioques *mpl*.

paresser: avoir les bras à la retourne; avoir la cosse/la flème/la flemme/la rame; avoir les pieds en cosses de melon; les avoir à la retourne; les avoir palmées; se branler les couilles; se les branler; se la couler douce; s'endormir sur le mastic; enfiler des perles; feignasser; ne pas en faire/en ficher/en foutre un coup/une rame; flânocher; flémarder; flemmarder; ne pas se fouler la rate; glander; glandocher; glandouiller; tirer au cul/au flanc; tirer sa cosse/sa flemme; se tourner les pouces; se les tourner; traîner ses patins/les savates.

paresseux *m*: cagnard *m*; cagnarde *f*; cossard *m*; faignant *m*; faignante *f*; fainéasse *mf*; feignant *m*; feignante *f*; feignasse *mf*; flânocheur *m*; flânocheuse *f*; flemmard *m*; flemmarde *f*; ramier *m*; tire(ur)-au-cul *m*; tire(ur)-au-flanc *m*; vachard *m*.

parler: bagouler; baratiner; bonnir; déblatérer; dégoiser; dévider; jacasser; jacter; jaspiner; l'ouvrir; tailler une bavette; tenir le crachoir. (*Voir* **bavarder**)

partir: les agiter; s'arracher; se barrer; (se) caleter; (se) calter; se carapater; se casser; se cavaler; changer de crémerie; chier du poivre; se criquer; débarrasser le plancher; se débiner; déblayer le terrain; décambuter; décamper; décaniller; décarrer; décharger le plancher; se défiler; déguerpir; (se) déhotter; dériper; se donner de l'air; s'éclipser; s'esbigner; s'esbrousser; escamper; s'évaporer; faire la valise; se faire la belle/la revue/la malle; se faire oublier; ficher le camp; filer; foncer dans le brouillard; foutre le camp; les jouer; jouer des flûtes; jouer la fille de l'air; jouer rip; jouer ripe; en jouer un air; larguer les amarres/les voiles; lever l'ancre; lever le camp/le pied/les voiles; mettre les adjas/les baguettes/le bouts/les cannes/les loubés/les voiles; les mettre; se mettre en cavale; se natchaver; plier bagage; prendre la clef des champs/le large/la poudre d'escampette/la tangente; prendre ses cliques et ses claques; ripatonner; riper; se tailler; se tirer (des flûtes/des ripatons); se tracer; (se) trisser; se trissoter; se trotter; valiser.

partir sans payer: faire jambe de bois; faire une queue; laisser une feuille de chou; laisser une queue; planter un drapeau; poser une ardoise.

patron *m*: boss *m*; chef *m*; dab(e) *m*; daron *m*; direlot *m*; dirlingue *m*; dirlot *m*; le grand manitou; latronpem *m*; pompe-la-sueur *m*; singe *m*; taulier *m*; tôlier *m*.

patronne *f* **(de maison de tolérance):** bordelière *f*; maqua *f*; maquerelle *f*; maquesée *f*; marquise *f*; mère-maca *f*; mère-maquerelle *f*; rombière *f*; taulière *f*; tôlière *f*.

pauvre: à la côte; à sec; cisaillé; crève-la-faim; dans la dèche/la mélasse/la purée; décavé; déchard; fauché; comme les blés;

fauchemane; lavé; lessivé; miteux; mouisard; nettoyé; pané; panné; paumé; purotin; qui traîne les patins/la savate; raide; raqué; rincé; rôti; sans le sou; sans un; sans un radis; sec; sur la paille/le pavé; tondu; vacant; vidé; de la zone.

pauvreté *f*: bouillabaisse *f*; débine *f*; dèche *f*; mélasse *f*; mistoufle *f*; mouise *f*; mouscaille *f*; panade *f*; purée *f*.

payer: les abouler; les aligner; aller au refil/au rembour; les allonger; arroser; banquer; carburer; carmer; casquer; cigler; cracher (dans le bassin); décher; douiller; éclairer; envoyer la valse; essuyer le coup de fusil; s'exécuter; se fendre; lâcher les valses lentes; les lâcher; mouiller; raquer; régaler; régler la douloureuse; les sortir; valser.

paysan *m*: boueux *m*; bouseux *m*; cambroussard *m*; croquant *m*; culterreux *m*; glaiseux *m*; pécore *m*; péd(e)zouille *m*; peigne-cul *m*; péquenaud *m*; péquenot *m*; pétrousquin *m*; petzouillard *m*; petzouille *m*; plouc *m*.

pénis *m*: andouille *f* à col roulé; anguille *f* de calecif; arbalète *f*; asperge *f*; baigneur *m*; baïonnette *f*; baisette *f*; balayette *f*; baveuse *f*; berdouillette *f*; berloque *f*; biroute *f*; bit(t)e *f*; (gros) bout *m*; bra(c)quemard *m*; canne *f*; carabine *f*; Charles-le-Chauve; chibre *m*; chinois *m*; chipolata *mf*; chose *f*; cigare *m* à moustache; clarinette *f*; colonne *f*; cyclope *m*; dard *m*; dardillon *m*; défonceuse *f*; fifre *m* à grelots; flageolet *m*; frétillante *f*; frétillard *m*; gaule *f*; gland *m*; goupillon *m*; gourde *f* à poils; gourdin *m*; guignol *m*; guise *m*; guiseau *m*; guisot *m*; guizot *m*; instrument *m*; jambe *f* du milieu; macaroni *m*; machin *m*; mandrin *m*; marsouin *m*; mohican *m*; morceau *m*; nœud *m*; os *m* à moelle; outil *m*; paf *m*; panais *m*; le père frappart; petit frère; pine *f*; pointe

f; poireau *m*; polard *m*; Popaul *m*; Popol *m*; quéquette *f*; queue *f*; quille *f*; quiquette *f*; quiqui *m*; sabre *m*; Totor; tracassin *m*; tringle *f*; trique *f*; verge *f*; vié *m*; vier *m*; zeb *m*; zigouigoui *m*; zizi *m*; zob(i) *m*.

père *m*: dab *m*; dabuche *m*; daron *m*; pater *m*; paternel *m*; vieux *m*.

pet *m*: cloque *m*; flousse *m*; fusant *m*; louffe *f*; louise *f*; pastoche *f*; perle *f*; perlouse *f*; perlouze *f*; vesse *f*.

péter: cloquer; déchirer son false/son froc/la toile; en écraser un; flouser; flouzer; fuser; en lâcher un; lâcher les gaz/une louise/une perle/une perlouse; louffer; vesser.

petit individu: astec *m*; astèque *m*; avorton *m*; aztèque *m*; basduc *m*; bas-du-cul *m*; courte-botte *m*; crapaud *m*; crapoussin *m*; demi-portion *f*; fabriqué *m* au compte-gouttes; inachevé *m*; microbe *m*; puce *f*; qui est haut comme trois pommes; ras-de-bitume *m*; ras-de-mottes *m*; rasduc *m*; ras-du-cul *m*; rase-bitume *m*; rikiki *m*; riquiqui *m*.

peu (un): un (petit) bout; un chouia; pas bésef, pas bézef; des clopinettes; pas gras; pas lerche; pas lourd; pas lourdingue; une larme; une miette.

peur *f*: chiasse *f*; chocottes *fpl*; colombins *mpl*; flubes *mpl*; frousse *f*; grelots *mpl*; pétasse *f*; pétoche *f*; pétouille *f*; peur bleue; taf *m*; taffe *m*; trac *m*; tracsir *m*; traczir *m*; traquette *f*; traquouse *f*; tremblote *f*; trouille *f*.

avoir peur: avoir chaud aux fesses; avoir les boules/les chocottes/la colique/les colombins/les copeaux/les flubes/les foies/les jetons/les moules; avoir les miches/les noix qui font bravo; avoir le pétoulet/le trouillomètre à zéro; se l'avoir à zéro; caler; caner; chier dans son froc; se déballonner; se dégonfler; être flubard/trouillard;

fluber; foirer; les mouiller; serrer les fesses/les miches.

pieds *mpl*: argasses *mpl*; arpions *mpl*; artous *mpl*; nougats *mpl*; panards *mpl*; patins *mpl*; pattes *fpl*; paturons *mpl*; péniches *fpl*; petons *mpl*; pinceaux *mpl*; pinglots *mpl*; pingots *mpl*; pingouins *mpl*; raquettes *fpl*; ribouis *mpl*; ripatons *mpl*; trottinants *mpl*; trottinets *mpl*.

pince-monseigneur *f*: clarinette *f*; dauphin *m*; dingue *f*; dombeur *m*; dur *m*; jacques *m*; jacquot *m*; plume *f*; sucre *m* de pomme.

piqûre *f*: fixe *m*; piquouse *f*; piquouze *f*; shoot *m*.
(se) piquer: (se) faire un fixe/une piquouse/une piquouze/un shoot; (se) fixer; (se) piquouser; (se) piquouzer; (se) shooter.
(*Voir* **seringue**)

pleurer: baver des clignotants; chialer; gicler des mirettes/des œillets; miter; ouvrir les écluses; pisser des châsses.

pluie *f*: bouillon *m*; flotte *f*; lancequine *f*; rincée *f*; saucée *f*.

poche *f*: bacreuse *f*; ballade *f*; farfouillette *f*; fouille *f*; fouillette *f*; glaude *f*; profonde *f*; vague *f*; valde *f*.

poing *m*: *voir* **main.**

poitrine *f*: armoire *f*; caisse *f*; caisson *m*; coffre *m*; plastron *m*.

police *f*: bourre *f*; bourrique *f*; flicaille *f*; guignols *mpl*; la maison Bourreman(e)/Bourremann/Cognedur/Parapluie/Pébroc/Poulaga/Poulardin/Poulemane/Pouleminche; ces Messieurs; poulaille *f*; poule *f*; raclette *f*; renifle *f*; rousse *f*; volaille *f*.
policier *m*: argousin *m*; bourre *m*; bourrin *m*; chaussette *f*; cogne *m*; condé *m*; drauper *m*; bourgeois *m*; flic *m*; flicaillon *m*; flicard *m*; guignol *m*; hambourgeois *m*; lardu *m*; maton *m*; mec *m* de la

rousse; perdreau *m*; poulaga *m*; poulardos *m*; poulet *m*; roussin *m*.

poltron *m*: baisse-froc *m*; caneur *m*; capon *m*; chiasseur *m*; chiasseuse *f*; déballonné *m*; déballonnée *f*; dégonflard *m*; dégonflarde *f*; dégonflé *m*; dégonflée *f*; dégonfleur *m*; dégonfleuse *f*; flubard *m*; foireux *m*; foireuse *f*; froussard *m*; froussarde *f*; grelotteur *m*; grelotteuse *f*; péteux *m*; péteuse *f*; pétochard *m*; pétocharde *f*; poule mouillée; taffeur *m*; taffeuse *f*; traqueur *m*; traqueuse *f*; trouillard *m*; trouillarde *f*.

portefeuille *m*: lasagne *m*; lasane *f*; lazagne *f*; lazane *f*; lazingue *m*.
portefeuille plein: matelas *m*.

porte-monnaie *m*: artichaut *m*; artiche *m*; crapaud *m*; lasagne *m*; lazingue *m*; morlingue *m*; morniflard *m*; porte-biffetons *m*; porte-faf(f)iots *m*.

pou *m*: crabe *m*; galopard *m*; gau *m*; grain *m* de blé; mie *f* de pain mécanique; morbac *m*; morbaque *m*; morfic *m*; morpion *m*; piocre *m*; toto *m*.

pourboire *m*: pourliche *m*; poursoif *m*.

préservatif *m*: capote (anglaise); chapeau *m*; imper(méable) *m* à Popaul; scaphandre *m* de poche.

prétentieux, être: bêcher; crâner; croire que c'est arrivé; se croire sorti de la cuisse de Jupiter; s'en croire; épater; esbrouf(f)er; être bêcheur/crâneur/esbrouffeur/plastronneur/poseur/snob; faire des chichis de l'épate/de l'esbrouf(f)e/des magnes; faire du vent; frimer; se gober; se gonfler; en installer; se monter le job; ne pas se prendre pour la crotte/pour de la merde; plastronner; pontifier; rouler les épahules/les épaules/les mécaniques.

prêtre *m*: calotin *m*; coin-coin *m*; corbeau *m*; cureton *m*; radis noir;

rase *m*; ratiche *m*; ratichon *m*; sac *m* à carbi/à charbon; sanglier *m*.

prison *f*: ballon *m*; bigne *f*; bing *m*; bloc *m*; boîte *f*; cabane *f*; carlingue *f*; carluche *f*; centrouse *f*; centrouze *f*; chetard *m*; ch'tar *m*; chtard *m*; clou *m*; coffre *m*; coquille *f*; gn(i)ouf *m*; grande marmite; grosse *f*; jettard *m*; lazaro *m*; mitard *m*; ombre *f*; ours *m*; placard *m*; ratière *f*; schib *m*; schtard *m*; schtib *m*; schtilibem *m*; séchoir *m*; taule *f*; tôle *f*; trou *m*; violon *m*.
en prison: à l'ombre; au ballon; au bloc; au frais; au frigo; au trou; au violon; bouclé; dedans; en taule; en tôle.
(*Voir* **emprisonner**)

prostituée *f*: amazone *f*; béguineuse *f*; bisenesseuse *f*; boudin *m*; bourrin *m*; catin *f*; chamelle *f*; chèvre *f*; essoreuse *f*; étoile filante; fille *f*; fin *f* de mois; frangine *f*; frangipane *f*; gagneuse *f*; garce *f*; girelle *f*; gisquette *f*; gonzesse *f*; grue *f*; guenon *f*; langouste *f*; marcheuse *f*; mistonne *f*; morue *f*; moukère *f*; mousmé(e) *f*; nana *f*; pépée *f*; persilleuse *f*; ponette *f*; pouffiasse *f*; poule *f*; putain *f*; pute *f*; raccrocheuse *f*; racoleuse *f*; radeuse *f*; respectueuse *f*; rouchie *f*; roulure *f*; souris *f*; tapin *f*; tapineuse *f*; traînée *f*; truqueuse *f*; turfeuse *f*; volaille *f*; zigouince *f*.
client de prostituée: branque *m*; cave *m*; clille *m*; miché *m*; micheton *m*.
prostituer, se: *voir* **racoler.**

querelle *f*: accrochage *m*; asticotage *m*; attrapade *f*; attrapage *m*; badaboum *m*; barabille *f*; baroud *m*; barouf *m*; barouffe *m*; baroufle *m*; bigorne *f*; bisbille *f*; corrida *f*; crosse *f*; engueulade *f*; pétard *m*; prise *f* de bec/de gueule; rif *m*; rififi *m*; rogne *f*; salade *f*; savon *m*; suif *m*; tabac *m*; tapage *m*; torchée *f*.

quereller: avoir une prise de bec/de gueule; chercher la cogne/des crosses/des patins/du rif/des rognes/du suif; chercher noise; crosser; s'expliquer (avec).
querelleur: asticoteur; crosseur; mauvais coucheur; pétardier; péteur; râleur; renaudeur; rouspéteur; saladier; suiffeur.

racoler: aller aux asperges; aller au turf; arpenter le bitume; chasser le mâle; dérouiller; se défendre; draguer; emballer; s'expliquer; faire le business/le bitume/la grue/un levage/le macadam/le pavé/le quart/le raccroc/le rade/la retape/le ruban/le tapin/le tas/le trottoir/le truc/le turbin/le turf; faire son persil; lever un client; michetonner; en moudre; persiller; raccrocher; en retourner; tapiner; truquer; turbiner; turfer.

raser, se: se gratter; se gratter la couenne; se racler.

rasoir *m*: coupe-chou *m*; racloir *m*; rasibe *m*; rasife *m*; razif *m*.

receleur *m*: fourgat *m*; fourgue *m*; fourgueur *m*; franquiste *m*; laveur *m*; lessiveur *m*.

recevoir (*des coups ou des insultes*): déguster; dérouiller; écoper; effacer; encaisser; étrenner; palper; en prendre pour son grade/pour son rhume; en prendre plein la gueule/la tronche; morfler.

recommencer: rebiffer; remettre ça; (y) remordre; repiquer (au truc).

reconnaître: reconnobler; reconnobrer; redresser; retapisser.

regarder: allumer; bigler; borgnoter; châsser; frimer; gaffer; lorgner; loucher sur; mater; matouser; mirer; mordre; rechâsser; reluquer; remoucher; tapisser; viser; zyeuter.

règles *fpl*: affaires *fpl*; anglais *mpl*; arcagnasses *mpl*; arcagnats *mpl*; argagnasses *mpl*; cardinales *fpl*;

carlets *mpl*; coquelicots *mpl*; doches *fpl*; histoires *fpl*; ours *mpl*; ragnagnas *mpl*.

avoir ses règles: les Anglais débarquent; faire relâche; pavoiser; recevoir ses cousins; repeindre sa grille en rouge.

réjouissances *fpl*: bamboche *f*; bamboula *f*; bombe *f*; bordée *f*; boum *f*; bringue *f*; faridon *f*; fiesta *f*; foire *f*; foiridon *f*; java *f*; noce *f*; nouba *f*; renversée *f*; ribote *f*; ribouldingue *f*; riboule *f*; surboum *f*; vadrouille *f*; virée *f*.

rendez-vous *m*: rambour *m*; rancart *m*; rembo *m*; rembour *m*; rencart *m*; rendève *m*.

renseignement *m*: duce *m*; info *f*; rancard *m*; rencard *m*; rencart *m*; tubard *m*; tube *m*; tuyau *m*.

renseigner: affranchir; éclairer la lanterne à; embrayer sur; mettre à la page/au parfum/dans le coup; parfumer; rancarder; tuyauter.

réprimander: agonir; agrafer; assaisonner; attraper; casser; dire ses quatre vérites à; donner le bal à; doucher; engueuler; engueuler comme du poisson pourri; enguirlander; faire un amphi à; faire voir des vertes et des pas mûres (à); filer/flanquer un savon à; habiller; incendier; laver la tête à; lessiver; mettre sur le tapis; moucher; passer une bonne engueulade/un (bon) savon à; ramasser; ramoner; sabouler; secouer (les puces à); sonner les cloches à.

être réprimandé: écoper; en prendre pour son grade; recevoir un abattage/une saucée/une savonnée.

revolver *m*: azor *m*; bagaf *m*; brelica *m*; brûle-parfum(s) *m*; calibre *m*; feu *m*; flingot *m*; flingue *m*; pétard *m*; pétoire *f*; pistolache *m*; remède *m*; ribarbère *m*; riboustin *m*; rifle *m*; riflette *f*; rigolo *m*; rigoustin *m*; soufflant *m*; tic-tac *m*.

riche: bourré (à bloc); calé; cousu d'or; flambant; au fric; galetteux;

gonflé; gros; oseillé; péseux; au pèze; plein aux as; qui a du foin dans ses bottes; qui a le matelas; qui a le sac; qui roule dans le fric/ sur l'or; rempli; richard; rupin; rupinos; tombé sur un champ d'oseille.

rien: balpeau; des clopinettes; des clous; des prunes; macache; de la merde; négatif; nib; niente; nix; la peau; peau de balle/de zébi; pet *m* de lapin; que dalle; que pouic; que t'chi; du vent; zéro.

rire: se bidonner; se boler; se boyauter; se crever; se fendre le bol/la gueule/la pêche/la pipe; se gondoler; se marrer; s'en payer une tranche; pisser dans sa culotte (de rire); se poiler; se pouffer; rigoler; rire à se faire mal aux côtes/à en crever/à s'en mouiller/à ventre déboutonné; se rouler; se tenir les côtes; se tirebouchonner; se tordre (comme une baleine).

route *f*: antif(fe) *f*; bitume *m*; ruban *m*; tire *f*; trimard *m*; trime *f*.

ruiné: *voir* **pauvre.**

rupture *f*: lâchage *m*; largage *m*; malle *f*; mallouse *f*; plaquage *m*; valise *f*; valoche *f*.

Russe *m*: Popof *m*; Ruscoff *m*; Ruskoff *m*.

salaud *m*: affreux *m*; apache *m*; bon-à-rien *m*; bordille *f*; (sale) bougre *m*; bourdille *f*; canaille *f*; casseur *m*; charognard *m*; charogne; con *m*; connard *m*; connasse *f*; copaille *f*; couillon *m*; crapule *f*; dur *m*; fils *m* de garce; fils de pute; fripouillard *m*; fripouille *f*; fumier *m*; gale *f*; gouape *f*; locdu *m*; loquedu *m*; loubard *m*; loulou *m*; malfrappe *m*; malfrat *m*; mauvaise graine; minable *m*; mufle *m*; ordure *f*; pauvre type; peau *f* de vache; pourriture *f*; raclure *f*; rien-du-tout *m*; sale coco/mec/type; saligaud *m*; salopard *m*; salope *f*;

trou *m* du cul; trouduc *m*; vache *f*;
vicelard *m*; zonard *m*.

sale: cochon; cracra; cradingue;
crado; crapoteux; crasp; craspec;
craspèque; craspet; craspignol;
craspouette; craspouillard;
débectant; dégueu; dégueulasse;
dégueulbif; dégueulpif; merdeux;
merdique; minable; miteux; moche;
pouilleux; saligaud; salingue.

saleté *f*: cochonnerie *f*; crotaille *f*;
crotte *f*; merde; merdoie *f*;
merdouille *f*; saloperie *f*.

seins *mpl*: amortisseurs *mpl*;
ananas *mpl*; avantages *mpl*; avant-
postes *mpl*; avant-scène *f*; balcon
m; ballons *mpl*; blagues *fpl* à tabac;
boîtes *fpl* à lait/à lolo; devanture *f*;
doudounes *fpl*; flotteurs *mpl*; globes
mpl; loloches *mpl*; lolos *mpl*;
mandarines *fpl*; mappemondes *fpl*;
melons *mpl*; miches *fpl*; du monde
au balcon; montgolfières *fpl*; nénés
mpl; nibards *mpl*; niches *mpl*;
nichons *mpl*; œufs *mpl* sur le plat;
oranges *fpl*; pare-chocs *mpl*; pelotes
fpl; roberts *mpl*; rondins *mpl*;
ropoplots *mpl*; rotoplots *mpl*;
rototos *mpl*; tétasses *fpl*; tétés *mpl*;
tétines *fpl*; tétons *mpl*.

sentir: blairer; renifler.

sentir mauvais: boucaner;
cocot(t)er; cogner; cornancher; corner; foisonner; fouetter; plomber;
polker; puer; refouler; renifler;
rougnotter; (s)chlinguer; taper.

**sentir mauvais de la
bouche:** plomber du goulot;
puer du bec; refouler; repousser (du
goulot); taper du saladier; tuer les
mouches à quinze pas.

seringue *f*: hypo *mf*; lance *f*;
poussette *f*; shooteuse *f*.

sexe *m* **de la femme:** abricot
m; baba *m*; barbu *m*; baveux *m*;
bénitier *m*; berlingot *m*; bijou *m* de
famille; boîte *f* à ouvrage; bonbonnière *f*; bréviaire *m* d'amour; centre
m; chagatte *f*; chat *m*; chatte *f*;
cheminée *f*; cicatrice *f*; con *m*;
con(n)asse *f*; crac *m*; cramouille *f*;

craque *f*; craquette *f*; crevasse *f*;
didi *m*; didine *f*; étau; fente *f*; figue
f; fri-fri *m*; grippette *f*; mille(-)
feuille *m*; mimi *m*; minet *m*; minou
m; moniche *f*; motte *f*; moule *f*;
nénuphar *m*; panier *m* (d'amour);
pâquerette *f*; pince *f*; portail *m*;
tabernacle *m*; tire-lire *f*.

sexe *m* **de l'homme:** bazar *m*;
bijoux *mpl* de famille; boutique *f*;
devant *m*; histoire *f*; marchandise *f*;
panoplie *f*; paquet *m*; service *m*
trois pièces.
(*Voir* **pénis; testicules**)

sodomiser: baiser à la riche;
caser; casser coco; casser le pot/la
rondelle; dauffer; défoncer la pastille; emmancher; empaffer;
empaler; empapaouter; empétarder;
emproser; encaldosser; enculer;
enfifrer; entigner; englander; goûter
la terre jaune; miser; planter;
pointer; prendre de l'oignon/du
petit/du sonore; tourner la page;
tremper la soupe; troncher.

sœur *f*: fraline *f*; frangine *f*; frangipane *f*; frelotte *f*.

soif (avoir): avoir la dalle en
pente; avoir le gosier sec; avoir la
pépie; cracher blanc; la péter; la
sécher.

soldat *m*: bidasse *m*; biffin *m*;
deuxième pompe *m*; gribier *m*;
grif(e)ton *m*; griveton *m*; grivier *m*;
pioupiou *m*; tourlourou *m*;
troubade *m*; trouf(f)ion *m*.

sou *m*: bourgue *m*; croque *m*;
fléchard *m*; kope(c)k *m*; pelot *m*;
radis *m*; rond *m*; rotin *m*.

sourd: constipé/dur de la feuille;
ensablé des portugaises; sourdingue
(comme un pot).

souteneur *m*: Alphonse *m*; barbeau *m*; broche *f*; brochet *m*;
brocheton *m*; dos fin/vert;
estaf(f)ier *m*; hareng *m*; Jules *m*;
Julot *m*; mac *m*; mangeur *m* de
blanc/de brioche; maquereau *m*;
marchand *m* de barbaque/de
bidoche/de viande; marle *m*;

marlou *m*; marloupin *m*; méc *m*; mecton *m*; merlan *m*; poiscaille *m*; poiscal *m*; poisson *m*; proxémac *m*; proxo *m*; rabat *m*; rabatteur *m*; sauré *m*; sauret *m*.

être souteneur: être julot; faire le mac/le maquereau; relever les compteurs.

sperme *m*: blanc *m*; came *f*; foutre *m*; jus *m* de corps/de cyclope; purée *f*; sauce *f*; semoule *f*; venin *m*.

stupéfait: asphyxié; assis; baba; bleu; comme deux ronds de flan; époustouflé; estomaqué; sidéré; soufflé.

suicider, se: se balancer dans la Seine; se but(t)er; se déramer; s'envoyer en l'air; se faire sauter la caisse/le caisson; se flanquer/se foutre en l'air.

syphilis *f*: chtouille *f*; daube *f*; lazziloffe *f*; naze *m*; nazebroque *m*; schtouille *f*; sigma *m*; syphilo *f*; syphlotte *f*; vérole *f*.

tabac *m*: herbe *f*; percale *m*; perle *m*; perlot *m*; pétun *m*; tref *m*; trèfle *m*.

taire, se: avoir la bouche cousue; bonnir lap(e); ne pas en casser une; la boucler; écraser; s'éteindre; s'étouffer; fermer sa boîte/son clapet/sa gueule; la fermer; la mettre en veilleuse; ne pas moufter; ne pas piper; poser sa chique; rengracier; taire sa gueule; tirer sa fermeture éclair.
faire taire: boucler la trappe à; brider; clouer (le bec à); museler; rabattre le caquet à; rembarrer; river le clou à.
tais-toi! ta bouche! boucle-la! boucle ton égout! ferme-la! la ferme! ferme ta gueule! ta gueule!

taxi *m*: bahut *m*; hotte *f*; loche *mf*; rongeur *m*; sapin *m*; tac *m*; taquemard *m*; tire *f*.

téléphone *m*: bigophone *m*; bigorneau *m*; biniou *m*; cornichon *m*; escargot *m*; grelot *m*; phonard *m*; ronfleur *m*; télémuche *m*; tube *m*; turlu *m*.

testicules *fpl*: balloches *fpl*; balustrines *fpl*; bijoux *mpl* de famille; billes *fpl*; blosses *fpl*; bonbons *mpl*; burettes *fpl*; burnes *fpl*; claoui(e)s *mpl*; clopinettes *fpl*; couilles *fpl*; couillons *mpl*; croquignoles *fpl*; joyeuses *fpl*; montgolfières *fpl*; noisettes *fpl*; noix *fpl*; olives *fpl*; paire *f*; pendantes *fpl*; pendeloques *fpl*; précieuses *fpl*; rognons *mpl*; roubignolles *fpl*; rouleaux *mpl*; roupes *fpl*; roupettes *fpl*; roupignolles *fpl*; roustons *mpl*; valseuses *fpl*.

tête *f*: baigneur *m*; balle *f*; bille *f*; binette *f*; bobèche *f*; bobéchon *m*; bobine *f*; bougie *f*; bouille *f*; bouillotte *f*; boule *f*; bourrichon *m*; boussole *f*; burette *f*; caberlot *m*; caboche *f*; cabochon *m*; cafetière *f*; caillou *m*; carafe *f*; carafon *m*; cassis *m*; chou *m*; ciboulot *m*; cigare *m*; citron *m*; citrouille *f*; coco *m*; fiole *f*; frite *f*; gadin *m*; gourde *f*; nénette *f*; patate *f*; pêche *f*; plafond *m*; poire *f*; pomme *f*; sinoquet *m*; siphon *m*; terrine *f*; têtère *f*; téterre *f*; théière *f*; tirelire *f*; tomate *f*; toupie *f*; tranche *f*; trogne *f*; trognon *m*; trombine *f*; tronc *m*; tronche *f*.

tirer (*une arme à feu*): défourailler; envoyer/lâcher la fumée/la purée/la sauce; flingot(t)er; flinguer.

tomber: aller à dame; aller valser dans les décors; se casser la figure; chuter; faire une valdingue; se ficher/se foutre la gueule en l'air/par terre; partir à dame; prendre/ramasser une bûche/un gadin/une pelle/une valdingue; quimper; valdinguer.

tracasser, se: se biler; se cailler; se casser la tête; s'en faire; se faire de la bile/des cheveux/(blancs)/des crins/du mauvais sang/du mouron/de la mousse; se monter le bourrichon; se turlupiner.

travail *m*: bis(e)ness *m*; boulot *m*; bricolage *m*; charbon *m*; coltin *m*; coltinage *m*; flambeau *m*; flanche *f*; gâche *f*; gratin *m*; job *m*; placarde *f*; truc *m*; turbin *m*.

travailler dur: bosser; boulon- ner; bûcher; buriner; se cailler; se casser (le cul); se décarcasser; en donner (une secousse); s'échiner; s'éreinter; s'esquinter; s'expliquer; en ficher/en foutre/un coup/une secousse; se fouler la rate; gratter; marner; pinocher; piocher; pisser du sang; suer (sang et eau); taper dans la butte; travailler comme un nègre/une bête/un chien; trimer; turbiner; usiner.

travailleur *m*: bosseur *m*; boulot *m*; bûcheur *m*; piocheur *m*; prolo *m*; pue-la-sueur *m*; turbineur *m*.

tricher: arnaquer; arrangemaner; avoir; biseauter; doubler; échauder; empalmer; entuber; étriller; faisander; maquiller; quiller; rangemaner.

tricheur *m*: arnaqueur *m*; arrangeman *m*; biseauteur *m*; empalmeur *m*; entôleur *m*; faisan *m*; faisandier *m*; faiseur *m*; maquil- leur *m*; rangemane *m*; rangeur *m*.

tromper: arnaquer; arranger; avoir; bidonner; blouser; carotter; charrier; doubler; empiler; endormir; enfiler; enfler; enfoncer; entôler; entuber; faire (à l'oseille); ficher/foutre dedans; gour(r)er; jobarder; maquiller; mettre dedans; posséder; quiller; ranger; refaire; rouler; roustir.

trottoir *m*: bitume *m*; pavé *m*; ruban *m*; turf *m*.

trouver: *voir* **découvrir**.

tuer: *voir* **assassiner**.

uriner: aller faire sa petite commis- sion; arroser les marguerites; changer son poisson d'eau; égoutter son colosse/son cyclope/sa sardine; se l'égoutter; faire pipi; faire pleurer le colosse/le costaud/le petit Jésus; faire sa goutte; se faire une vidange; jeter de la lance; jeter sa goutte; lâcher l'eau/l'écluse/un fil; lancecailler; lancequiner; lan- squiner; lisbroquer; lispoquer; mouiller une ardoise; ouvrir les écluses; pisser; pisser son coup; prendre une ardoise à l'eau; renverser la vapeur; tenir l'âne par la queue; verser de l'eau; *(femme)* arroser le persil; humecter sa four- rure; mouiller son gazon.

urinoir *m*: ardoises *fpl*; lavabe *m*; pissoir *m*; pissotière *f*; pissotoire *f*; tasse *f*; théière *f*.

vagabond *m*: cloche *f*; clodo *m*; clodomir *m*; clodot *m*; grelotteux *m*; mouisard *m*; refileur *m* de comète; traîne-lattes *m*; traîne- patins *m*; traîne-pattes *m*; traîne- sabots *m*; traîne-savates *m*; trimard *m*; vacant *m*; zonard *m*.
(*Voir* **clochard**)

vantard *m*: baratineur *m*; blagueur *m*; bluffeur *m*; bourreur *m* de crâne; chiqueur *m*; cracheur *m*; cravateur *m*; esbrouf(f)eur *m*; fort *m* en gueule; frimeur *m*; fumiste *m*; grande gueule; gueulard *m*; musicien *m*; rambineur *m*.

ventre *m*: ballon *m*; balourd *m*; baquet *m*; battant *m*; bedaine *f*; bedon *m*; bide *m*; bidon *m*; bocal *m*; boîte *f* à ragoût; brioche *f*; buf- fecaille *m*; buffet *m*; bureau *m*; burlingue *m*; caisse *f*; fusil *m*; gras- double *m*; panse *f*; sac *m* à tripes; tiroir *m*.
(*Voir* **estomac**)

veste *f*: alezingue *f*; alpague *f*; al- pingue *f*; pelure *f*; vestouse *f*.

vêtements *mpl*: fringues *fpl*; frip(p)es *fpl*; frusques *fpl*; harnais *mpl*; linges *mpl*; loques *fpl*; nippes *fpl*; pelure *f*; sapes *fpl*; vêtures *fpl*.

viande *f*: barbaque *f*; bidoche *f*; carne *f*; charogne *f*.

vieillir: avoir de la bouteille/du flacon; être bon pour la casse; faire d'occasion; se fossiliser; prendre de la bouteille/du flacon; prendre un coup de vieux; sentir la fin de saison; vioquer.

vieux: bibard; bléchard; blèche; croulant; périmé; viocard; vioque.

vieux *m*: bonze *m*; croulant *m*; fossile *m*; périmé *m*; vestige *m*; vieille baderne/noix; vieux birbe/croûton/jeton/rococo; vioc *m*; viocard *m*; vioquard *m*; vioque *m*.

vin *m*: brouille-ménage *m*; brutal *m*; décapant *m*; gingin *m*; gobette *f*; gorgeon *m*; du gros (qui tache); gros bleu; gros *m* rouge; jaja *m*; petit velours; pichetegorne *m*; pichtogorme *m*; pichtegorne *m*; picolo *m*; picrate *m*; picton *m*; pinard *m*; pive *m*; piveton *m*; pivois *m*; reginglard *m*; reglinguet *m*; rouquemoute *mf*; rouquin *m*; rouquinos *m*; sens *m* unique; tutu *m*.

visage *m*: balle *f*; bille *f*; binette *f*; bobine *f*; bougie *f*; bouille *f*; bouillotte *f*; boule *f*; burette *f*; cerise *f*; fiole *f*; fraise *f*; frime *f*; frimousse *f*; frite *f*; gaufre *f*; gueule *f*; hure *f*; margoulette *f*; museau *m*; poire *f*; pomme *f*; portrait *m*; terrine *f*; tire-lire *f*; trogne *f*; trognon *m*; trombine *f*; trompette *f*; tronche *f*.

vite: à bride abattue; à fond de train; à plein(s) tube(s); à tout bersingue/berzingue; à toute blinde; à toute barre; à toute bombe; à toute(s) pompe(s); comme un zèbre; dare-dare; en cinq secs; en moins de deux; en quatrième vitesse; fissa; presto; quatre à quatre; rapidos.

aller vite: bomber; bousculer les bornes; brûler le pavé/la route; filocher; foncer; gazer; se magner le train; pédaler; rajouter de la sauce; rouler à plein(s) gaz/à toute pompe; tracer.

(vieille) voiture *f*: bagnole *f*; bahut *m*; berlingot *m*; caisse *f*; chiotte *f*; guimbarde *f*; guinde *f*; hotte *f*; tacot *m*; tape-cul *m*; tinette *f*; tire *f*; tombereau *m*.

voler: accrocher; acheter à la foire d'empoigne; arranger; barbot(t)er; bichotter; calotter; chaparder; chauffer; chiper; choper; chouraver; dégraisser; doubler; écorcher; empiler; emplafonner; emplâtrer; engourdir; enquiller; escan(n)er; estamper; étouffer; étourdir; fabriquer; faire; faire sauter; faucher; gauler; grapper; grappiner; griffer; grincher; lever; pégrer; piquer; plumer; poirer; poisser; raboter; ratiboiser; ratisser; refaire; rincer; roustir; secouer; soulever; sucrer; tirer.
(*Voir* **cambrioler**)

voleur *m*: barbot(t)eur *m*; carotteur *m*; chapardeur *m*; chipeur *m*; chopeur *m*; doubleur *m*; encanneur *m*; faucheur *m*; filou *m*; gauleur *m*; grinche *m*; leveur *m*; pégriot *m*; piqueur *m*; roustisseur *m*.
(*Voir* **cambrioleur**)

vomir: aller au refil(e)/au renard; bader; débagouler; dégobiller; dégoupillonner; dégueuler; évacuer le couloir; gerber; lâcher une fusée; refiler; renarder.

voyou *m*: *voir* **salaud**.

WC *mpl*: azor *m*; cabinces *mpl*; chiards *mpl*; chiottes *fpl*; débourre *f*; débourroir *m*; garde-manger *m*; gogs *mpl*; goguenots *mpl*; gogues *mpl*; lieux *mpl*; ouatères *mpl*; petit coin; pipi-room *m*; tartiss(es) *mpl*; tartissoires *mpl*; téléphone *m*; tinettes *fpl*; vécés *mpl*.

yeux *mpl*: *voir* **œil**.

PART 2

FRENCH-ENGLISH

VOYELLES

[i]	pignoler snif zizi
[e]	chez étriller légume
[ɛ]	chèvre perle pelle resto terre maison
[a]	patte chat tape toile phare
[ɑ]	gâche paille pâté sable
[ɔ]	mort bol Popaul
[o]	pot môme chérot taule
[u]	tout goût genou coup roue
[y]	cruche mur ruban truc usine
[ø]	peu feu nœud queue
[œ]	peur œuf sœur feuille
[ə]	le ce quenotte premier
[ɛ̃]	plein machin chien crin
[ɑ̃]	enfance arranger temps branche sans vent
[ɔ̃]	bon tonton monte plomb compte
[œ̃]	un lundi parfum

CONSONNES ET SEMI-CONSONNES

[p]	père pain soupe type
[b]	beau bol roberts
[m]	trumeau main femme
[f]	feu bref neuf phrase photo
[v]	voyage grève vrille voir
[t]	attigé table thune ticket vite
[d]	dondon danse rondelle coude
[n]	nougat canne ananas nègre
[s]	sou cirer six scier dessous
[z]	zéro zézette cuisine basane deuxio
[l]	lait clille aile facile
[ʃ]	chat moche miche schnock
[ʒ]	gilet manger gingin cage jeune
[k]	quart coup klebs fac
[g]	gare bague gueule
[ɲ]	campagne gnôle figne niard
[ŋ]	frotting skating
[r]	arbre rhume rubis tenir rancart terre
[ks]	accident action
[gz]	exister examen
[j]	yeux voyager travailler pied piano
[w]	noir waters nouer oui
[ɥ]	huile reluire aiguille

A

abattage [abataʒ] *nm* **1.** *O F*
recevoir un **abattage,** to get told
off/to get ticked off **2.** *F* rushed
work/rush job/quickie; (*livre*) pot-
boiler **3.** *F* dynamism; **avoir de
l'abattage,** to be full of go; **elle a
de l'abattage,** she's very dynamic/
she's got plenty of go **4.** *P* (*prostituée*) **faire de l'abattage,** to get
through a succession of clients
quickly. (*Voir* **maison 1**)

abatteur, euse [abatœr, -øz] *n F*
abatteur de besogne, hard worker/
slogger; workaholic.

abattis [abati] *nm P usu pl* arms*;
legs*; **tu risques de te casser les
abattis si tu sautes,** you'll break
your legs if you jump; **numérote tes
abattis!** I'll break every bone in
your body! (*Voir* **aile 1**)

abattre [abatr] *vtr F* **en abattre,** to
get through a lot of work; to be a
glutton for work; to be a
workaholic; (*distance; fig*) to cover
a lot of ground. (*Voir* **bois 1**)

abbaye [abei] *nf P* **aller à l'abbaye
de Monte-à-regret,** to go to the
scaffold/the guillotine.

abîmer [abime] *vtr F* **abîmer qn** (*a*)
(*dans la presse, etc*) to run s.o.
down/to slate s.o. (*b*) to beat s.o.
up*/to knock s.o. about/to work
s.o. over; **se faire abîmer,** to get
beaten up/to get worked over/to
get knocked about. (*Voir* **portrait**
(*b*))

ablette [ablɛt] *nf F* **taquiner
l'ablette,** to do a spot of fishing (for
information).

abouler [abule] **I** *vtr P* (*a*) to

give/to hand over; **aboule ça (ici)!**
give it here!/let's have it! (*b*) to
pay* up/to fork out/to cough up
II *vi P* (*argot policier*) to give oneself up to the police **III** *vpr*
s'abouler *P* to arrive*/to come
along; **alors, tu t'aboules?** well, are
you coming?/come on!

aboyeur [abwajœr] *nm O* **1.** *F*
(*théâtre, cirque, etc*) tout/spieler/
barker **2.** *P* revolver*/shooter.

abreuvoir [abrœvwar] *nm P* bar/
pub; hostelry.

abricot [abriko] *nm V* female genitals*/fruit basket.

abruti [abryti] *nm F* **1.** drunk/
drunkard*/drunken bum **2.** fool*/
idiot/blockhead; **quel abruti!** what a
clot!/what a moron!

abus [aby] *nm F* **(il) y a de l'abus!/
y a un peu d'abus!** that's going a
bit too far!/that's a bit much!

acabit [akabi] *nm F* (*souvent péj*)
des gens de son acabit, people of
his sort/people like him; **ils sont du
même acabit,** they're birds of a
feather/they're all tarred with the
same brush.

académie [akademi] *nf F* (*esp
femme*) body; **avoir une belle
académie,** to have an attractive
body/a shapely figure; to have
curves in all the right places; **elle a
une belle académie,** she's well-
stacked.

accident [aksidã] *nm F* (*a*) miscarriage, unplanned pregnancy, etc;
ma petite sœur, c'était un accident,
my little sister was an afterthought
(*b*) any delicate or embarrassing sit-

uation (eg bankruptcy, imprisonment, etc) (c) (enfant) avoir un accident, to wet one's pants.

accidenter [aksidɑ̃te] vtr F to damage (another car, etc)/to injure (s.o.) in an accident.

s'accointer [sakwɛ̃te] vpr F (péj) s'accointer avec qn, to take up with s.o.; to become chummy/pally with s.o.; il s'accointe avec cette femme, he's knocking around with that woman.

accommoder [akɔmɔde] vtr F 1. (= accoutrer) je vais l'accommoder, I'll soon sort him out/fix him (up) 2. (a) accommoder qn à toutes les sauces, to use s.o. as an odd-job man/as a general factotum (b) accommoder qch à toutes les sauces, to use sth for just about everything 3. accommoder qn au beurre noir, to give s.o. a black eye*.

accordéon [akɔrdeɔ̃] nm 1. F en accordéon, (vêtements) crumpled/creased/wrinkled; (pare-chocs, etc) bashed-in/dented/crumpled 2. F (aut, cyclisme) string of (racing) cars, bikes which close up in a bunch and then become strung out again; faire l'accordéon, to get bunched up/to concertina 3. P (argot policier) heavy police record/form.

accoucher [akuʃe] vi F to confess*/to come clean; mais accouche donc! come on, out with it!/spit it out!/give!/shoot! faire accoucher un prisonnier, to make a prisoner talk/grass.

accoutrer [akutre] I vtr F accoutrer qn de toutes pièces (i) to tell s.o. off (in no uncertain fashion)/to give s.o. what-for/to come down on s.o. like a ton of bricks (ii) to run s.o. down/to tear s.o. to pieces II vpr s'accoutrer F (péj) to dress badly or in a bizarre fashion; on n'a pas idée de s'accoutrer comme ça! you'd have to be crazy to get rigged out in that sort of thing!

accro [akro] a F (abbr = accroché) (a) être accro à une drogue, to be hooked/strung out on a drug (b) être accro de/sur qn/qch, to be infatuated* with s.o./sth; to be hung up on s.o./sth.

accrochant [akrɔʃɑ̃] a F un air accrochant, a catchy tune.

accroche [akrɔʃ] nf 1. F (publicité) hook; gimmick 2. P l'accroche (i) (drogues) habit/hook (ii) the drug scene/drug addicts (in general) 3. F avoir l'accroche de qn, to be loved by s.o.

accroche-cœur [akrɔʃkœr] nm F kiss-curl/love-lock.

accroche-pipe [akrɔʃpip] nm P mouth*/cakehole.

accroché [akrɔʃe] a P être accroché (a) to be in debt/in the red (b) to be arrested*/held for questioning (c) to be brave*/to have guts/to have balls (d) (drogues) to be addicted/hooked/strung out (e) to be infatuated* (with s.o.)/to be hung up on (s.o.).

accrocher [akrɔʃe] I vtr 1. F essayer d'accrocher un mari, to look for a husband 2. F accrocher qn, to buttonhole s.o./to corner s.o. 3. F (marketing) (a) to capture a market (b) accrocher une affaire, to clinch a deal 4. P se l'accrocher, to go hungry/to tighten one's belt; tu peux te l'accrocher! you can whistle for it!/you can say goodbye to it! 5. P to steal* (sth) II vi P 1. to have problems/trouble; la géo, ça accroche, I'm having trouble with geography; les maths, j'accroche pas encore, I'm not getting anywhere with maths; les négociations entre les deux pays accrochent, the negotiations between the two countries aren't going smoothly 2. accrocher avec qn, to hit it off with s.o. III vpr s'accrocher F s'accrocher avec qn (a) (courses, etc) to catch up with s.o./to draw level with s.o. (b) to have a row with s.o./to pitch into s.o.

accrochette [akrɔʃɛt] *nf F =* **accroche 2** (*i*).

accrocheur, -euse [akrɔʃœr, -øz] *F* **I** *n* (*a*) wangler (*b*) tenacious bore*/leech/clinger **II** *a* (*a*) stubborn/pig-headed; **un vendeur très accrocheur,** a very persistent/persuasive salesman (*b*) eye-catching; **une pub accrocheuse,** an eye-catching ad.

accu [aky] *nm F* **1.** (*abbr =* *accumulateur*) accumulator; **recharger les accus** (*i*) to have another drink (*ii*) to have a bite more to eat (*iii*) to have a snooze.

accueil [akœj] *nm P* (*argot policier*) **comité d'accueil,** welcoming committee.

accuser [akyze] *vtr F* **accuser le coup,** to react strongly; **il a mal accusé le coup,** it really hit him hard/the blow really went home.

achar,d' [d'aʃar] *adv phr P* (*abbr = acharnement*) **travailler d'achar,** to work* hard/like mad; to go at it hammer and tongs. (*Voir* **autor, d'**)

acheter [aʃte] *vtr F* **1.** (*i*) to bribe* (s.o.) (*ii*) to buy (s.o.) off; **le flic s'est laissé acheter,** the cop didn't object to being bought/bribed **2.** to hoax* (s.o.)/to take s.o. for a ride; **on vous a acheté!** you've been had!

acid(e) [asid] *nm F* LSD*/acid; **prendre de l'acid(e),** to take/to drop acid.

acidulé, -ée [asidyle] *P* (*drogues*) **I** *n* **1.** (habitual) user of LSD*/acid head/acid freak **II** *a* **trouille acidulée,** depression due to LSD*/acid funk.

acompte [akɔ̃t] *nm* **1.** *F* **tiens, mange, c'est un petit acompte,** this'll give you a taste of what's to come **2.** *P* **prendre un acompte,** to have sex* before marriage/to sample the goods.

à-côté [akote] *nm* **1.** *P* **prendre un petit à-côté,** to indulge in extramarital sex*/to have a bit (of fluff/stuff) on the side **2.** *pl F* **à-côtés,** (little) extras/perks; a bit on the side; **son boulot lui donne la possibilité de faire des petits à-côtés,** his job gives him the chance to make a little bit on the side.

acrais! [akrɛ], **acré!** [akre] *int O P* look out!/watch it!/careful!/mind out! **acrais! v'là les flics!** beat it! here come the cops!

acteuse [aktøz] *nf P* (*péj*) actress devoid of talent.

action [aksjɔ̃] *nf F* **ses actions sont en hausse/en baisse,** things are looking up/aren't looking too good for him.

activer [aktive] *vi F* to hurry* up/to get a move on; **activons!** let's get cracking!/let's make it snappy! **activez!** get moving!/move it!

Adam [adɑ̃] *Prnm F* (*homme*) **dans le/en costume d'Adam,** naked*/in the altogether/in one's birthday suit. (*Voir* **Ève; fourchette 2; pomme 2**)

adieu, *pl* **-ieux** [adjø] *nm & int F* **1. faire ses adieux à qch,** to kiss sth goodbye; **tu peux lui dire adieu!** you can kiss it goodbye!/you can say goodbye to that!/you can forget it! **2. adieu Berthe!/adieu la valise!** it's all up!/it's curtains!

adja [adʒa] *nm or f P* (*usu pl*) **mettre les adjas,** to run away*/to beat it/to clear off/to do a bunk.

adjudant [adʒydɑ̃] *nm F* (*a*) (*mil*) **coucher avec la femme de l'adjudant,** to be put in the guardroom (*b*) domineering person; **cette femme, c'est un vrai adjudant,** that woman's a real bully.

adjupète [adʒypɛt] *nm P* (*a*) (*mil*) warrant officer (*b*) authoritarian/domineering person.

adresse [adrɛs] *nf F* **vous vous êtes trompé d'adresse!** you've got the wrong place (mate)!

aéro [aero] *nm* F (*abbr* = *aérogramme*) air letter.

afanaf [afanaf] *adv* P half and half/ fifty-fifty; **faire afanaf,** to go halves/ to go fifty-fifty/to go even steven/ to split (it) down the middle.

affaire [afɛr] *nf* **1.** *F* **il a fait ses affaires,** he has made his pile, his fortune **2. faire son affaire à qn** (*i*) *F* to give s.o. what-for (*ii*) *P* to kill* s.o./to do s.o. in/to bump s.o. off **3.** *F* **la belle affaire!** so what?/ big deal! **4.** *F* **ce n'est pas une affaire d'État!** it's not a National Emergency! **5.** *F* **faire/aller à ses affaires,** to defecate*/to go to the loo/to do one's duty **6.** *F* **elle a ses affaires,** she's got her period*/ she's got the curse/it's the wrong time of the month **7.** *F* **son affaire est claire** (*i*) I'll settle him/ I'll sort him out (*ii*) I've settled him **8.** *F* (*esp enfant*) **montrer son affaire,** to show one's 'private property'/ = to play mummies and daddies **9.** *F* **c'est une affaire,** it's a (real) bargain/it's a snip **10.** *F* **être à son affaire,** to be in one's element; to be on the job **11.** *P* man *or* woman who is good in bed/a good lay; **c'est une affaire, ce type,** that bloke's a really good lay/ that guy's fantastic in bed.

s'affaler [safale] *vpr* **1.** *F* to flop/ to slump/to sag; **s'affaler dans un fauteuil,** to flop into an armchair; (*à un élève*) **ne vous affalez pas!** sit up (straight)! **2.** *P* to confess*/to come clean/to grass.

affection [afɛksjɔ̃] *nf* *F* **être en retard d'affection,** to be hard up (sexually).

affiche [afiʃ] *nf* *F* **faire l'affiche** (*i*) to show off*/to flaunt oneself (*ii*) (*homosexuel*) to camp it up/to limp-wrist it; **c'est l'affiche,** it's just for show.

affiché [afiʃe] *a* *F* **c'est affiché!** it's in the bag!/it's a (dead) cert!

affirmatif! [afirmatif] *int* F (*esp mil*) affirmative!/roger!

afflure [aflyr] *nf* P = **affure.**

afflurer [aflyre] *vtr&i* P = **affurer.**

affranchi, -ie [afrɑ̃ʃi] *a&n* **1.** *F* (*a*) totally unscrupulous (person)/ nasty piece of work (*b*) (person) who has nothing to learn about sex, vice, etc **2.** *P* (person) who sticks to the code of honour of the underworld. (*Voir* **cicatrice**)

affranchir [afrɑ̃ʃir] *vtr* **1.** *F* **affranchir qn,** to put s.o. in the picture/to gen s.o. up/to give s.o. the low-down/to put s.o. in the know/ to tip s.o. off* **2.** *P* to corrupt/to get at/to nobble (s.o.). (*Voir* **couleur**)

affreux [afrø] *nm* **1.** *F* objectionable person/nasty piece of work; creep **2.** *P* (*esp* white) mercenary. (*Voir* **jojo II 1**)

affure [afyr] *nf* P **1.** profit/gain; **faire de l'affure,** to find it profitable **2. avoir de l'affure,** to have the edge (on/over s.o.).

affurer [afyre] *P* **I** *vtr* **1.** to make a profit out of (sth); **faire affurer son fric,** to put one's money to good use/to make one's money work **2.** to reach/to arrive at; **mon fiston affure ses quinze berges,** my lad's coming up to fifteen **3.** (*courses*) **en affurer une,** to win a race **II** *vi* to make money; to wheel and deal; **affurer gros,** to make money hand over fist/to rake it in.

affûter [afyte] *vtr* **1.** *F* (*sport*) **affûter la forme,** to get down to some serious training **2.** *P* (*voleurs, etc*) to persuade/to recruit (an accomplice) by offering a share of the loot/haul. (*Voir* **pinceau 1** (*b*))

affutiaux [afytjo] *nmpl* P tools.

afghan [afgɑ̃] *nm* P (*drogues*) hashish* from Afghanistan/afghan.

afro [afro] *a inv* F **elle se coiffe à l'afro,** she's got an afro cut.

afnaf [afnaf] *adv* P = **afanaf.**

agace-cul [agasky] *nm* V penis*/prick.

agace-machin [agasmaʃɛ̃] *nm* P itching/itchiness.

agacer [agase] *vtr* V **agacer le sous-préfet,** to masturbate*/to flog the bishop/to flog the dummy.

agates [agat] *nfpl* P eyes*.

agiter [aʒite] *vtr* **1.** P **les agiter,** to run away*/to scarper/to beat it **2.** V **se l'agiter,** to masturbate*/to wank/to jerk (oneself) off.

agobilles [agɔbij] *nfpl* V testicles*/balls/ballocks.

agoniser [agɔnize] *vtr* F **agoniser qn d'injures,** to hurl abuse at s.o./to let s.o. have it (good and proper)/to eff and blind at s.o.

agrafe [agraf] *nf* A P hand*/(meat) hook.

agrafer [agrafe] *vtr* F **1.** to buttonhole (s.o.)/to corner s.o. **2.** to arrest*/to nab/to nick; **il s'est fait agrafer par les flics,** he got nicked by the cops **3.** to steal*/to hook/to nick.

agreg [agrɛg] *nf,* **agrég** [agreg] *nf* F (*abbr* = *agrégation*) competitive State exam for teaching posts in France.

agri [agri] *nm* F student at an agricultural college.

agricher [agriʃe] *vtr,* **agriffer** [agrife] *vtr* P **1.** to grab (hold of) (s.o.) **2.** to arrest*/to nick (s.o.)/to run (s.o.) in.

agro [agro] *nm* F (*a*) = *Institut national agronomique* (*b*) student at this college.

aguichant [agiʃɑ̃] *a* F seductive/inviting/alluring/sexy.

aguicher [agiʃe] *vtr* F **1.** to excite*/to arouse (s.o.)/to lead (s.o.) on/to give (s.o.) the come-on/to prick-tease **2.** to excite the curiosity of (s.o.).

aguicheur, euse [agiʃœr, -øz] F **I** *a* seductive/alluring/arousing/sexy **II** *nf* aguicheuse, tease/prick-teaser/cock-teaser.

aidé [ede] *a* F (*pers*) **pas aidé** (*i*) plain/ugly (*ii*) stupid*/dim/dumb.

aiguiller [egɥije] *vtr* V **aiguiller une femme,** to have sex* with a woman/to screw a woman.

ail [aj] *nm* P **aimer/sentir/taper l'ail; manger/vendre/de l'ail,** to be a lesbian*; **marchandes d'ail,** lesbians*/gay women/lesbos/lezzies. (*Voir* **gousse**)

aile [ɛl] *nf* **1.** P arm/fin/flipper; **battres des ailes,** to flail one's arms about **2.** F **battre de l'aile/ne battre que d'une aile,** to be in a bad way; **l'entreprise ne bat que d'une aile,** the business is very shaky/in a bad way **3.** F **voler de ses propres ailes,** to stand on one's own two feet **4.** F **avoir un coup dans l'aile,** to be a bit drunk*/tipsy **5.** F (*voiture*) **prendre un virage sur l'aile,** to take a corner on two wheels **6.** P (*Hell's Angels*) **avoir ses ailes brunes,** to have anal sex* (with s.o.); **avoir ses ailes noires,** to have sex* with a Black* (girl); **avoir ses ailes rouges,** to have sex* with a girl during her period. (*Voir* **plomb 2; rogner II**)

aileron [ɛlrɔ̃] *nm* P arm*/fin/flipper.

aimer [eme] **I** *vtr* **1.** F **j'aime mieux pas,** I'd rather not; **j'aime autant ça,** that sounds more like it; **j'aime mieux te dire que tu ne réussiras pas comme ça!** I'm warning you, you won't make it like that! **2.** P **va te faire aimer!** get lost!/take a running jump!/get stuffed! **II** *vpr* **s'aimer** F **il s'aime à la campagne,** he likes living in the country.

air [ɛr] **I** *nm* **1.** F **autant cracher en l'air,** it's a sheer waste of time;

c'est comme si je crachais en l'air, it's like (I was) talking to a brick wall/I might as well be talking to myself. (*Voir* **cracher**) **2.** *F* **jouer la fille de l'air/se donner de l'air,** to run away*/to clear off. (*Voir* **air III 1**) **3.** *F* **ne plus tenir en l'air,** to be fit/ready to drop (with tiredness) **4.** *F* **ne pas manquer d'air** (*i*) to have guts/to have nerve (*ii*) to have the cheek of the devil; **il ne manque pas d'air!** he's a cheeky little sod!/ he's got a nerve! **5.** *P* **fiche(r)/flanquer/foutre (qch) en l'air** (*i*) to chuck (sth) away/to chuck (sth) up (*ii*) to ruin/to mess sth up; **ça a fichu en l'air toutes mes idées,** that's completely scuppered/screwed up all my plans (*iii*) to kill* (s.o.)/to bump (s.o.) off/*esp NAm* to blow (s.o.) away. (*Voir* **fiche(r) 2**; **foutre II 7** (*c*)) **6.** *P* **se flanquer/se foutre en l'air,** to commit suicide/to do oneself in **7.** *P* **mettre en l'air** (*i*) to kill* (s.o.)/*esp NAm* to blow s.o. away (*ii*) to steal*/to nick (sth) (*iii*) to wreck (a place)/to turn (somewhere) upside down/to mess up (a place) **8.** *V* **l'avoir en l'air,** to have an erection*/to get it up; **l'avoir en l'air pour qn,** to have the hots for s.o./to be horny/to be randy. (*Voir* **courant 1, 2, 3**; **envoyer 3**; **s'envoyer 3** (*b*); **jambe 18**; **pomper 3, 4**) **II** *nm F* **1.** (*a*) **elle n'a pas l'air d'y toucher,** she looks as though butter wouldn't melt in her mouth (*b*) **ça n'a l'air de rien, mais c'est très important,** you wouldn't think so to look at it, but it's really very important **2. de quoi j'ai l'air maintenant?** I look a right chump now! **il a l'air fin/l'air con,** he looks a right idiot/a complete arse/*NAm* ass **3. il vous a dit non, ça en a tout l'air,** he said no by the look of things **4. ce vase-là prend un petit air penché,** that vase looks as though it's going to go any moment **III** *nm* (*mélodie*) *F* **1. en jouer un air,** to run away*/to beat it/to scarper. (*Voir* **air I 3**) **2. air**

connu! I've heard that one before! **3. il en a l'air et la chanson,** he not only looks it, he is.

alcolo [alkɔlo] *nm P* drunkard*/ alkie/boozer/wino.

alfa [alfa] *nm F* **il n'a plus d'alfa sur les hauts plateaux,** he's as bald* as a coot/he's a bit thin on top.

algèbre [alʒɛbr] *nf F* **c'est de l'algèbre pour moi,** it's all Greek to me.

aligner [aliɲe] *P* **I** *vtr* **les aligner,** to pay* up/to fork out/to cough up **II** *vpr* **s'aligner** (*a*) **s'aligner avec qn,** to take s.o. on/to face up to s.o. (*b*) **tu peux (toujours) t'aligner,** you're no match for him!/ just you try and beat that! (*c*) **tu t'alignes?** (do) you want to bet?/is it a bet?

aller [ale] *vi* **1.** *P* **aller au boucher,** to go to the butcher's **2.** *P* **aller en bicyclette,** to cycle/to bike (it) **3.** *F* **faire aller qn** (*i*) to order s.o. about (*ii*) to lead s.o. on (*iii*) to dupe* s.o./to take s.o. in **4.** *F* to defecate*; **qch qui fait aller,** laxative/sth that clears you out **5.** *F* (*i*) **(comment) ça va?/comment va la santé?** how are you?/how's life?/ how's things?/how's tricks? **ça va,** I'm OK/I'm fine/not so bad/keeping my end up; **ça (ne) va pas (la tête)?** you're mad*!/you're round the bend!/you've off your head! (*ii*) **ça va! all right!/OK! ça va, ça va!** all right! all right!/don't go on! **ça ira comme ça,** we'll leave it at that; **ça va comme ça!** it's all right as it is! (*iii*) **rancard dans une heure? — ça me va,** see you in an hour? — suits me/OK with me (*iv*) **ça te va mal de faire une chose pareille!** you've got a nerve doing something like that! **6.** *F* **aller mal,** to be mad*; **elle va mal,** she's not quite all there/she's a bit touched **7.** *F* **y aller de ...,** to contribute sth/to put up (a sum of money)/to pay* up (a sum of money); **il y est allé de ses cent francs,** he put in a hundred francs; **il y est allé d'une tournée**, he stood us a round; **elle y est allée de sa petite larme**, she had a little cry **8.** *F* **on y va?** all set?/ (are) we off then? **allez-y doucement!** go easy!/gently does it! **il y va un peu fort**, he's going a bit far **9.** *F* **aller avec une femme**, to have sex* with a woman **10.** *F* **ça n'a pas l'air d'aller**, you look as if there's something wrong; what's the matter?/what's up? (*Voir* **chagrin**; **charbon**; **chemin 2**; **cri 2**; **dame I 6** (*a*); **fort II**; **mal I 3**; **malva**; **mollo(-mollo)**; **pape**; **se promener 1** (*a*); **renseignements**; **se rhabiller 1, 2**; **roi 3**)

aller et retour [aleerətur] *nm F* double slap on the face (first with the back of the hand and then the front)/a right and a left.

allezingue [alzɛ̃g] *nm A P* jacket.

allocs [alɔk] *nfpl P* = **alloques**.

allongé, -ée [alɔ̃ʒe] *n P* corpse*/ stiff; (*à l'hôpital*) **être aux allongés**, to be in the mortuary; **le boulevard des allongés**, the cemetery/bone-yard/bone orchard.

allonger [alɔ̃ʒe] **I** *vtr* **1.** *F* **allonger un coup à qn**, to hit out at s.o.; **allonger une taloche à qn**, to slap s.o. round the face/to clout s.o.; **allonger qn par terre**, to knock s.o. to the ground/to knock s.o. flat on his/her face **2.** *F* (**les**) **allonger**, to pay* up; **il va falloir que tu les allonges**, you've got to/you'd better cough up/fork out; **allonger le tir**, to increase/to raise/to up the price/the stake; to raise the ante **3.** *V* (*a*) **se l'allonger**, to masturbate*/to jack off (*b*) **se le faire allonger** (*i*) to be masturbated/to be jerked off (*ii*) (*fellation*) to be sucked off. (*Voir* **sauce 2**) **II** *vpr* **s'allonger** *P* **1.** to confess*/to come clean/to grass **2.** (*boxe*) to take a dive.

alloques [alɔk] *nfpl P* (*abbr* = *allocations*) **1.** family allowance

2. unemployment benefit/dole/*NAm* unemployment compensation.

allouf [aluf] *nf P* = **alouf**.

allumage [alymaʒ] *nm F* **1. avoir du retard à l'allumage**, to be slow on the uptake **2.** (*pers*) **couper l'allumage**, to switch off (completely).

allumé [alyme] *a* **1.** *F* drunk*/ stoned **2.** *P* sexually excited*/ turned on/randy/horny **3.** *P* (*drogues*) high/stoned/turned on.

allumer [alyme] *vtr* **1.** *P* to excite* (s.o.) sexually/to turn s.o. on; (*femmes*) to tease/to prick-tease/to cock-tease **2.** *P* to look out for/to watch out for; **allume les flics!** keep an eye out for the fuzz! **3.** *P* to shoot (s.o.)/to fill (s.o.) full of lead **4.** *abs P* **allume!** hurry* up! **5.** *F* **se faire allumer** (*i*) to attract attention/to make oneself conspicuous (*ii*) (*mil*) to fall into an ambush.

allumettes [alymɛt] *nfpl F* (*a*) long skinny legs*/matchsticks (*b*) (narrow slalom) skis.

allumeur [alymœr] *nm P* associate (of gambler/swindler, etc)/decoy (man).

allumeuse [alymøz] *nf P* **1.** flirt/ vamp **2.** dance/nightclub hostess; bar-girl **3.** tease/prick-teaser/cock-teaser/PT/CT.

alors [alɔr] *adv F* (*a*) **alors, tu viens?** are you coming, then? **et (puis) alors?/alors quoi?** and what then?/ so what?/what now? (*b*) **ça alors!/ non, mais alors!** well I'm blowed!/ you don't say!/cor!

alouf [aluf] *nf P* match.

alpague [alpag] *nf P* **1.** jacket/ coat **2.** (*a*) (*dos*) back; **mettre la main sur l'alpague à qn**, to arrest* s.o./to collar s.o. (*b*) **l'avoir sur l'alpague**, to be saddled/lumbered (with a crime, etc) (*c*) **les avoir sur l'alpague**, to have s.o. breathing down one's neck; **avoir les flics sur**

l'**alpague,** to have the cops on one's back.

alpaguer [alpage] *vtr P* to arrest* (s.o.); **se faire alpaguer,** to get arrested/nabbed/nicked.

alphonse [alfɔ̃s] *nm F* pimp*/ ponce.

alpingue [alpɛ̃g] *nf P* jacket/coat.

Alsaco [alzako] *nm & f F* person from Alsace/Alsatian.

alu [aly] *nm F* aluminium.

amarrer [amare] *vtr P* to seize/to get hold of/to collar/to nab.

amarres [amar] *nfpl F* **larguer les amarres,** to go/to leave/to shove off/to push off.

amazone [amazon] *nf P* high-class prostitute*.

ambivalent [ãbivalã] *a P* bisexual/bi/AC-DC/ambidextrous.

âme [ɑm] *nf F* (*a*) **errer comme une âme en peine,** to wander about like a lost soul (*b*) **la mort dans l'âme,** desperate; with a heavy heart (*c*) **je n'ai pas vu âme qui vive,** I haven't seen a soul.

amen [amɛn] *adv F* **dire toujours amen,** to be a yes-man.

amende [amɑ̃d] *nf P* **mettre qn à l'amende,** to take/to force protection money from s.o.

amener [amne] **I** *vtr P* (= *apporter*) to bring (along); **amène une boutanche,** bring a bottle. (*Voir* **fraise 6**) **II** *vpr* **s'amener** *F* **1.** to turn up/to put in an appearance/to show one's face; **amène-toi!** come along!/come on! **il va s'amener dans quelques minutes,** he'll be along in a few minutes; **elle s'est amenée avec trois heures de retard,** she waltzed in/breezed in three hours late **2. il peut toujours s'amener!** just let him try it on!

amère [amɛr] *af F* **1. l'avoir amère,** to be indignant/annoyed **2. je la trouve amère,** I don't see

what's so funny about that/I don't get the joke.

Amerloc(k), Amerloque [amɛrlɔk], **Amerlo(t)** [amɛrlo], **Amerluche** [amɛrlyʃ] *P* **I** *nm* American/Yank/Yankee **II** *a* American; **amerloc(k) comme l'oncle Sam,** as American as apple pie. (*Voir* **ricain**)

ami, -e [ami] *n F* man*(friend*) *or* boyfriend; *f* woman*(friend*) *or* girlfriend; lover; sweetheart; **sa bonne amie,** his sweetheart; **petit ami,** boyfriend/bloke/guy; **petite amie,** girlfriend/woman*/chick/ bird. (*Voir* **cochon 4**)

aminche [amɛ̃ʃ] *nm O P* friend*/ mate/pal/buddy.

amocher [amɔʃe] **I** *vtr P* **1. amocher qch,** to make a mess of sth/to arse sth up; (*bagnole*) to smash up/to wreck **2. amocher qn,** to beat s.o. up*/to knock s.o. about/to spoil s.o.'s beauty; **se faire amocher,** to get beaten up/to get done over **3. il a une patte amochée,** he's got a gammy leg **II** *vpr* **s'amocher, s'amochir** [samɔʃir] *P* (*pers*) to become weak; to be/to look the worse for wear; to look a wreck.

amortis [amɔrti] *nmpl F* **les amortis,** the not so young/the past-its/ the has-beens/the old fogeys.

amortisseurs [amɔrtisœr] *nmpl P* breasts*/boobs/knockers; **une belle paire d'amortisseurs,** a nice pair of Bristols.

amour [amur] *nm* **1.** *F* **amour vache,** cave-man stuff/rough stuff **2.** *P* **y'a plus d'amour,** it just won't work any longer/it's no good, we just can't make a go of it **3.** *F* **quel amour de gosse!** what a cute (little) kid! **tu es un amour (d'avoir fait ça pour moi),** you're an angel/a darling/a love (to have done that for me); **quel amour de robe!** that's a great dress!/that's a dream of a dress! **4.** *F* **à vos amours!** (*i*) bless you! (*ii*) cheers!* **5.** *F* **vivre d'amour et d'eau fraîche,** to live on love. (*Voir* **gueule II 7**; **remède 2**)

amph [ãf] *nf,* **amphés** [ãfe] *nfpl F* (*abbr* = *amphétamine(s)*) amphetamine(s)*.

amphi [ãfi] *nm F* (*a*) (*abbr* = *amphithéâtre*) lecture room/hall (*b*) lecture; paper (on a subject); **faire un amphi à qn,** to give s.o. a lecture/a talking to (*c*) (*aviation, mil*) briefing (*d*) (*à l'hôpital*) mortuary/ morgue.

ampli [ãpli] *nm F* (*abbr* = *amplificateur*) amplifier.

ampoule [ãpul] *nf F* **il ne se fait pas d'ampoules aux mains,** he doesn't overtax himself/he doesn't put himself out much.

amusette [amyzɛt] *nf P* small-time racket.

amuse-gueule [amyzgœl] *nm F* (*a*) *pl* appetizers/nibbles (*b*) (*théâtre*) warm-up act.

amygdales [ami(g)dal] *nfpl F* **1.** **lécher les amygdales à qn,** to give s.o. a French kiss **2.** **s'humecter/se rincer les amygdales,** to have a drink*/to wet one's whistle/to have a (quick) snifter. (*Voir* **caler II 2**)

amyl(e) [amil] *nm P* (*drogues*) amyl nitrite*/amys.

ananas [anana(s)] *nm* **1.** *F* hand grenade/pineapple **2.** *pl P* breasts*/melons.

anar [anar], **anarcho, -ote** [anarʃo, -ɔt] *a&n F* (*abbr* = *anarchiste*) anarchist.

Anastasie [anastazi] *Prnf A F* = the censor/ = (*WWI*) DORA/ = (the man with) the blue pencil.

Anatole [anatɔl] *Prnm O F* (*locution populaire*) **ça colle, Anatole!** absobllylutely!/absobloodylutely! **ça colle, Anatole?** how's tricks, old man?/how goes it, Joe?/how's it going, buster?

ancêtre [ãsɛtr] *nm F* (*a*) old man/

grandad (*b*) *pl* **mes ancêtres,** my parents/my (old) folks.

ancre [ãkr] *nf F* **lever l'ancre,** to leave*/to make tracks.

andosses [ãdos] *nfpl P* **1.** shoulders; back **2.** **en avoir plein les andosses** (*i*) to be exhausted*/to be dead beat (*ii*) to be sick (and tired) of sth/to have had a bellyful of sth.

andouille [ãduj] *nf* **1.** *P* fool*/ twerp/twit/clot/nurd; **faire l'andouille,** to play the fool; **arrête de faire l'andouille!** stop acting the goat!/stop arsing about! **sacrée andouille!/espèce d'andouille!** (you) bloody fool!/(you) silly twit!/(you) stupid idiot. (*Voir* **terrine 2** (*b*)) **2.** *F* **il est ficelé comme une andouille,** his clothes are so tight he can hardly move **3.** *F* **s'en aller en brouet d'andouille,** to fizzle out **4.** *F* **faire son andouille,** to show off*/ to swank/to swagger **5.** *V* **andouille à col roulé** penis*/meat. (*Voir* **dépendeur**)

âne [ɑn] *nm P* **1.** **tenir l'âne par la queue,** to urinate*/to point Percy at the porcelain **2.** (*homme*) **être monté comme un âne,** to be well-endowed/to be well-equipped/to be well-hung/to be hung like a bull. (*Voir* **bougre**; **brider**; **peau 11**; **pet 1**; **pied 13**; **son II 3**)

ange [ãʒ] *nm* **1.** *F* **faire l'ange,** to procure an abortion; **faiseur, -euse d'anges** (*i*) abortionist/angel-maker (*ii*) baby-farmer **2.** *F* **un ange passe/un ange a passé,** there is/was an awkward/embarrassing silence *or* lull in the conversation **3.** *F* **rire aux anges** (*i*) to have a huge grin on one's face (*ii*) to smile in one's sleep **4.** *F* **parler aux anges,** to talk to oneself **5.** *F* **être aux anges,** to be in the seventh heaven/ to be on cloud nine/to walk on air **6.** *F* **les anges** (*a*) motor-cycle cops (*b*) hell's angels **7.** *F* **veux-tu être un ange et me passer le pain?** be an angel and pass me the bread **8.** *P*

voir les anges, to have an orgasm*/ to come; **mettre qn aux anges,** to give s.o. sexual pleasure/to screw s.o. well/to be a good lay **9.** *P (infirmière qui fait passer des drogues à un toxicomane)* **ange blanc,** white angel **10.** *F* **ange gardien** (*i*) policeman* guarding a prisoner (*ii*) bodyguard/guardian angel/gorilla.

Anglais [ɑ̃glɛ] *nmpl F* **avoir les Anglais,** to have one's period(s)*/to come on; **les Anglais ont débarqué/elle a ses anglais,** she's got her period/she's got the curse/she's on the rag. (*Voir* **capote**)

anglaise, à l' [alɑ̃glɛz] *adv phr F* **filer à l'anglaise,** to take French leave.

anglaiser [ɑ̃glɛze] *vtr* **1.** *P* to rob/ to fleece/to rook (s.o.) **2.** *V* to have anal sex* with (s.o.)/to bugger s.o./to screw s.o.'s ass **3.** *V* to rape (s.o.).

angliche [ɑ̃gliʃ] *P* **I** *a* English **II** *n* **un/une Angliche,** an Englishman/ an English woman; a limey/a Brit.

anguille [ɑ̃gij] *nf V* **anguille de cal(e)cif,** penis*/prick.

anneau, -eaux [ano] *nm V* **1.** anus*/ring/ring-piece/round eye **2. anneau de queue,** cock ring.

annexe [anɛks] *nf F* **l'annexe,** the local (pub).

anse [ɑ̃s] *nf* **1.** *P* ear*/lughole/flap **2.** *P* arm/fin **3.** *F* **faire danser l'anse du panier,** to make a bit on the side.

antif(fe) [ɑ̃tif] *nm P* **battre l'antif(fe),** to bum around.

antiffer [ɑ̃tife] *vi P* to enter/to drop in; to barge in.

antifle [ɑ̃tifl] *nf P* church.

antifler [ɑ̃tifle] *P* **I** *vi* = **antiffer** **II** *vpr* **s'antifler s'antifler (de sec),** to get married*/hitched/spliced.

antigel [ɑ̃tiʒɛl] *nm P* **1.** strong spirits*/antifreeze **2.** (*drogues*) hero- in*.

antigrippe [ɑ̃tigrip] *nm F* (*pousse-café*) (*i*) chaser (*ii*) (after-dinner) liqueur.

antisèche [ɑ̃tisɛʃ] *nm or f F* (*à un examen*) crib/*NAm* pony.

ap' [ap] *nm F* (*abbr* = *appétit*) **bon ap'!** (*i*) have a nice meal!/bon appetit! (*ii*) get stuck in!/*NAm* eat hearty!

apaiser [apeze] *vtr P* to kill*.

apé [ape] *nm,* **apéro** [apero] *nm P* aperitif/cocktail; **l'heure de l'apéro,** cocktail time; **venez prendre l'apéro,** come for drinks/for cocktails.

aplatir [aplatir] **I** *vtr F* **1. aplatir qn,** to knock (s.o.) down/to flatten (s.o.) **2.** to flabbergast* (s.o.)/to floor (s.o.) (by a rebuff, etc); **la nouvelle l'a aplati,** the news knocked him out/he was floored by the news **II** *vpr* **s'aplatir** *F* **1.** to fall flat on one's face/to come a cropper **2. s'aplatir devant qn,** to grovel at s.o.'s feet/to crawl to s.o. **3.** not to insist; **dans ces cas-là, il vaut mieux s'aplatir,** when that happens it's best to drop it.

app' [ap] *nm F* = **appart.**

appareil [aparɛj] *nm F* (*hum*) **dans le plus simple appareil,** stark naked*/in the altogether/in one's birthday suit.

appart [apart] *nm,* **appe** [ap] *nm F* flat/*esp NAm* apartment/pad.

appel [apɛl] *nm F* **1. faire des appels à qn** (*i*) to give s.o. the glad eye/to give s.o. the once over/to give s.o. the come-on (*ii*) to make a pass at s.o. **2. faire des appels du pied à qn,** to play footsie with s.o. **3. faire des appels de phare,** to flash one's headlights at another car.

s'apporter [saporte] *vpr P* **apporte-toi ici!** get yourself over here!

s'appuyer [apɥije] *vpr P* **1. s'appuyer un bon dîner,** to treat oneself to a good dinner **2.** to put up with sth/to get landed with sth;

s'appuyer qn, to get stuck with s.o. **3.** s'appuyer (une gonzesse/un mec), to have sex* with/to make it with (a woman/a bloke).

aprèm [aprɛm] nm P (= après-midi) cet aprèm, this afternoon/this afto.

après [aprɛ] adv F et (puis) après? what of it?/what about it?/so what?

aquiger, aquijer [akiʒe] vtr P **1.** to criticize* (s.o.)/to pull (s.o.) to pieces/to run (s.o.) down **2.** to hurt/to injure; les pinceaux m'aquigent, my feet are killing me.

araignée [areɲe] nf F avoir une araignée au/dans le plafond, to have a screw loose/to be touched in the head. (Voir **patte 6**)

arbalète [arbalɛt] nf **1.** V penis*/prick/cock; filer un coup d'arbalète, to have sex*/to (have a) screw **2.** O P (religious) cross.

arbi [arbi] nm, **arbico(t)** [arbiko] nm P (péj) Arab/wog. (Voir **bicot**)

arbre [arbr] nm **1.** F faire grimper/faire monter qn à l'arbre, to hoax* s.o./to play a practical joke on s.o./to have s.o. on; grimper à l'arbre, to have/to get one's leg pulled **2.** F monter à l'arbre, to get angry*/to fly off the handle/to hit the roof **3.** P human body.

arcagnasses [arkaɲas], **arcagnats** [arkaɲa] nmpl P period(s)*/the curse. (Voir **argagnasses; ragnagnas**)

arcan [arkɑ̃] nm P (a) hooligan*/tough guy/thug (b) crook/shady character.

arche [arʃ] nm P buttocks*; tu me fends l'arche, you give me a pain in the arse/NAm ass.

archer [arʃe] nm O P (a) policeman* (b) detective.

archi [arʃi] nm F (a) architect (b) student of architecture.

archi- [arʃi] prefix O F (très/extrêmement); archicon, too bloody stupid (for words); archiconnu, overfamous/tremendously well-known; archicomble/archiplein, chock-a-block/chocker; archifou, stark staring mad; je suis archifauché, I'm completely skint/cleaned right out.

archicube [arʃikyb] nm F former student of the Ecole Normale Supérieure.

archimillionnaire [arʃimiljɔnɛr] n & a F multimillionaire/millionaire many times over.

archipointu [arʃipwɛ̃ty] nm P archbishop.

archiriche [arʃiriʃ] a F tremendously rich*/rolling in it/stinking rich.

archisec, -sèche [arʃisɛk, -sɛʃ] a F bone-dry.

archisecret, -ète [arʃisəkrɛ, -ɛt] a F top secret/very hush-hush.

arcpincer, arcquepincer [arkpɛ̃se] vtr P = **arquepincer**.

ardillon [ardijɔ̃] nm V penis*/shaft.

ardoise [ardwaz] nf F **1.** avoir une ardoise chez ..., to have credit with .../to get (things on) tick from ...; inscrire les consommations à l'ardoise, to chalk up the drinks/to put the drinks on the slate; liquider une ardoise, to pay off a debt/to wipe the slate clean; liquider une vieille ardoise, to settle an old score; poser une ardoise, to leave without paying **2.** prendre une ardoise à l'eau/se payer une ardoise/mouiller une ardoise, to urinate*/to have a slash/to splash one's boots (in a public urinal).

arêtes [arɛt] nfpl P ribs.

argagnasses [argaɲas] nmpl P period(s)*; elle a ses argagnasses, she's got the curse. (Voir **arcagnasses; ragnagnas**)

argasses [argas] nfpl P feet*/plates of meat/dogs.

argenté [arʒɑ̃te] a F rich*/in the money; on n'est pas très argenté en ce moment, we're a bit broke at the moment; **se trouver bien argenté,** to be flush. (*Voir* **cuiller 4**)

argomuche [argɔmyʃ] *nm P* slang; **jacter/jaspiller/jaspiner l'argomuche,** to talk slang.

argougner, argougnier [arguɲe], **argouiner** [argwine] *vtr P* **1.** to get hold of/to grab/to collar **2.** to arrest*/to nick.

argousin [arguzɛ̃] *nm O F* policeman*/rozzer/bobby.

aria [arja] *nm F* fuss/bother; **faire des arias,** to kick up a fuss; **ne faites pas tant d'arias!** don't make such a song and dance about it!

aristo [aristo], **aristoche** [aristɔʃ] *nm P* aristocrat/nob/toff.

arlequins [arləkɛ̃] *nmpl F* resurrection pie; leftovers.

arme [arm] *nf F* **passer l'arme à gauche,** to die*/to peg out/to kick the bucket.

armé [arme] *a* **1.** *V* **être armé,** to have an erection*/to have a hardon **2.** *P* **être armé,** to have some cash (on one)/to be in funds.

Arménouche [armenuʃ] *a&n P* Armenian.

armoire [armwar] *nf F* **armoire (normande)/armoire à glace,** hefty fellow/hulking great brute; **c'est une vraie armoire à glace,** he's built like a battleship/he's a giant of a man.

arnac, arnaque [arnak] *nf P* swindle*/con; **c'est de l'arnaque,** it's a con; **monter une arnac,** to pull a fast one; **faire de l'arnacque,** to go in for swindling/to be a con merchant.

arnaquer [arnake] *vtr P* **1.** to swindle*/to do/to diddle/to rook (s.o.) **2.** to arrest*/to nab (s.o.); **se faire arnaquer par les flics,** to get nicked by the cops.

arnaqueur, -euse [arnakœr, -øz] *n P* cheat/swindler*/crook/con artist.

arnau, arno [arno] *a P* very angry*/in a vile temper/hopping mad/*NAm* bummed out.

arpète, arpette [arpɛt] *nf P* milliner's apprentice/errand-girl.

arpinche [arpɛ̃ʃ] *nm P* miser*/skinflint.

arpion [arpjɔ̃] *nm P* **1.** foot*/hoof; **j'ai mal aux arpions,** my dogs are killing me; **taper des arpions,** to have smelly feet **2.** toe.

arquepincer [arkpɛ̃se] *vtr P* to arrest*; **se faire arquepincer,** to get nabbed. (*Voir* **J't'arquepince**)

arquer [arke] *vi* **1.** *P* to walk*/to hoof it/to go by Shanks's pony; **je ne pouvais plus arquer,** I couldn't go a step further **2.** *V* to have an erection*/a hard-on; to get it up/ *esp NAm* to get it on.

arquin [arkɛ̃] *nm P* safe-cracker/peterman/crib-cracker.

arquinche [arkɛ̃ʃ] *a P* mean*/tight-fisted/stingy/mingy.

arracher [araʃe] **I** *vtr F* **1.** ça lui **arrache le cœur de** ..., it breaks his heart to ... **2. on se l'arrache,** he/she/it is in great demand/is all the rage **3.** *V* (*homme*) **arracher son copeau/son pavé,** to have an orgasm*/to come **II** *vi P* **1.** (*disque, livre, etc*) to be very successful; **son dernier simple, il arrache!** his latest single is a run-away/smash hit! **2.** (*bagnole, moto*) to be very powerful **3.** (*chanteur, etc*) to give a powerful performance; **le groupe a arraché,** the band let rip/pulled all the stops out **III** *vpr* **s'arracher** *P* to run away*/to clear off/to beat it.

arrangemane [arɑ̃ʒman] *nm P* swindler*/cheat/con artist.

arrangemané [arɑ̃ʒmane] *a P* (*pers*) who has VD*/the clap.

arrangemaner [arɑ̃ʒmane] *vtr P* **1.** to swindle* (s.o.)/to cheat/to con **2.** to beat (s.o.) up*/to knock (s.o.) about/to work (s.o.) over.

arranger [arɑ̃ʒe] I *vtr* **1.** *F* **je l'ai arrangé (de la belle manière)** (*i*) I told him where to get off (*ii*) I fixed him/I sorted him out **2.** *F* to swindle*/to cheat/to rook (s.o.) **3.** *F* to cook/to doctor (the books, etc) **4.** *P* to steal*/to walk off with (sth) **5.** *P* to assault/to beat up*; **ils l'ont bien arrangé, tes mecs,** your blokes gave him a right working over **6. se faire arranger** (*i*) *F* to be swindled/diddled/overcharged (*ii*) *P* to get hurt/to get wounded/to cop a packet (*iii*) *F* to get told off/ticked off (*iv*) *P* to get killed/to get done in (*v*) *P* to catch VD*/to cop a dose/to get the clap II *vpr* **s'arranger** *F* **ça s'arrangera,** it'll turn out all right/it'll sort itself out/it'll all work out; **ça s'arrange pas au Moyen Orient,** things are getting worse in the Middle East; **laisse-les s'arranger tous les deux,** let them sort it out between themselves (*b*) **tu t'es bien arrangé!** that's a fine mess you've got yourself into; **tu pourrais t'arranger un peu!** you could try to smarten yourself up a little!

arrangeur [arɑ̃ʒœr] *nm P* swindler*/cheat/con artist.

arrière-saison [arjɛrsɛzɔ̃] *nf F* **sentir l'arrière-saison,** to get old/to be getting past it.

arrière-train [arjɛrtrɛ̃] *nm F* buttocks*/behind/rear.

arriver [arive] *vi F* **1. il croit que c'est arrivé** (*i*) he takes it all in/he takes it all as gospel (*ii*) he thinks he's the cat's whiskers/he really fancies himself **2. c'est arrivé,** the penny's dropped **3. il arrive de son pays,** he's a bit green/he's easily taken in; he's a sucker.

s'arrondir [sarɔ̃dir] *vpr P* **1.** to get drunk* **2.** to get pregnant*/to have a bun in the oven **3. tu peux te l'arrondir!** you can whistle for it! **4. se l'arrondir,** to go without food/to tighten one's belt.

arrosage [arozaʒ] *nm F* celebration drinks (to celebrate sth).

arroser [aroze] *vtr F* **1.** (*i*) to bomb(ard)/to shell (a town, etc) (*ii*) to spray/to pepper with bullets **2. arroser ses créanciers,** to pay small sums on account to one's creditors **3. se faire arroser,** to get soaked to the skin/to get wet through **4.** to hand out bribes/hush-money to (s.o.) **5. s'arroser la gorge,** to wet one's whistle; (*mil*) **arroser ses galons,** to wet/to christen one's stripes; **arroser un client,** to keep in with a customer by buying him lots of drinks; **c'est moi qui arrose,** it's my round/my shout; the drinks are on me; **ça s'arrose,** this calls for a drink!/let's drink to that! **courage arrosé,** Dutch courage; **café arrosé,** laced coffee. (*Voir* **dalle²**)

arroseuse [arozøz] *nf*, **arrosoir** [arozwar] *nm P* sub-machine-gun; sten gun; tommy-gun.

arsouille [arsuj] I *a P* **1.** given to drink/boozy **2.** vulgar/scruffy/tatty; **malgré son air arsouille, il n'est pas si mauvais,** he's not so wild as he looks II *n P* **1.** *m* crook/cheat/swindler* **2.** *m* hooligan*/yob(bo) **3.** *f* trollop/tart.

s'arsouiller [sarsuje] *vpr P* **1.** to be a crook/a scoundrel **2.** to be debauched **3.** to drink* to excess.

Arthur [artyr] *Prnm F* **se faire appeler Arthur,** to get reprimanded*/told off/ticked off.

arti [arti] *nf F* (= **artillerie**) artillery.

artichaut [artiʃo] *nm O P* purse; wallet/*NAm* pocketbook. (*Voir* **cœur**)

artiche [artiʃ] *nm P* **1.** purse; wallet/*NAm* pocketbook **2.** money*/bread **3.** buttocks*/behind.

article [artikl] *nm* **1.** *F* **faire l'article,** to promote/to plug sth **2.** *P* **être porté sur l'article,** to be fond of sex*/to like it; to have a one-track mind/to be obsessed; (*femme*) to be a (bit of a) nympho **3.** *P* knife/shiv/chiv **4.** revolver*/shooter/*esp NAm* gat/piece.

artiflot [artiflo] *nm P* (*mil*) artilleryman/gunner.

artiller [artije] *vtr P* to have sex* with (s.o.)/to bang (s.o.).

artillerie [artijri] *nf P* **1.** loaded dice **2.** (*i*) revolver*/shooter (*ii*) firearms; **balader son artillerie dans ses fouilles,** to carry a gun **3.** (*drogues*) **artillerie d'un camé,** drug addict's instruments*/artillery/arsenal **4.** stodgy food **5. la grosse artillerie,** paper money/notes/the big stuff **6. sortir la grosse artillerie,** to take strong measures/to bring out the big guns.

artiste [artist] *nm F* character/joker/artist; **c'est triste la vie d'artiste!** life's no joke!

artou, *pl* **-ous** [artu] *nm P* foot*.

Arverne [arvɛrn] *nm P* = **Auverpin.**

as [as] *nm* **1.** *F* (*sports, etc*) star (performer)/ace/whiz(kid); **as du volant,** crack (racing) driver; **ce mec-là, c'est pas un as,** this bloke/guy isn't what you'd call an expert/doesn't seem to know what he's doing **2. as de pique** (*i*) *F* (*volaille*) parson's nose/*esp NAm* pope's nose; (*pers*) buttocks* (*ii*) *F* **fichu comme l'as de pique,** dressed like a scarecrow/dressed (up) anyoldhow (*iii*) *P* female genitals* **3.** *P* **as de carreau** (*i*) (*esp mil*) pack/knapsack (*ii*) ribbon of the Legion of Honour **4.** *P* **aller à l'as,** to come a cropper* **5.** *P* **être (plein) aux as/être (plein) à l'as,** to be rich*/to be rolling in it **6.** *F* **passer à l'as,** to vanish into thin air; **passer qch à l'as,** to spirit something away; **3000 francs passés à l'as,** 3000 francs down the drain **7.** (*dans un restaurant*) *F* table no. 1/no. 1 table **8.** *F* **veiller à l'as,** to keep a sharp look-out/to keep one's eyes peeled **9.** *P* alibi*/let-out. (*Voir* **tref 5**)

ascenseur [asɑ̃sœr] *nm F* **renvoyer l'ascenseur,** to return a favour.

asperge [aspɛrʒ] *nf* **1.** *F* **une asperge montée/une (grande) asperge,** a tall, thin person*/a beanpole **2.** *V* penis*; *O* **faire une asperge à qn,** to fellate* s.o./to suck s.o. off **3.** *pl V* prostitution; **aller/être aux asperges,** to be a prostitute*/to solicit*/to be on the game/to walk the streets.

asphyxier [asfiksje] *vtr F* to steal*/to pinch. (*Voir* **perroquet**)

aspi [aspi] *nm F* (*abbr* = *aspirant*) (*a*) (*marine*) midshipman/middie (*b*) (*mil*) officer cadet (*c*) young hopeful.

aspine [aspin] *nf P* money*/dough/lolly.

aspirateur [aspiratœr] *nm P* **aspirateur à pépées,** kerb crawler (looking for women).

aspirine [aspirin] *nf F* **blanc comme un cachet d'aspirine,** white as a ghost/sheet.

assaisonner [asɛzɔne] *vtr P* **1. assaisonner qn** (*a*) to beat (s.o.) up*/to clobber s.o. (*b*) to reprimand* s.o. severely/to give s.o. a piece of one's mind/to give s.o. what for (*b*) to give s.o. VD*/the clap **2. se faire assaisonner** (*i*) to get beaten up/to get worked over (*ii*) to get a stiff sentence/to get the book thrown at one. (*Voir* **assassiner 3**)

assassiner [asasine] *vtr F* **1.** (*a*) to ruin/to make a mess of (sth); **elle assassine cette chanson,** she's murdering that song (*b*) to bore* (s.o.) to death (**de**, with) **2.** to overcharge (s.o.) (exorbitantly)/to rip (s.o.) off; **ses créanciers l'assassinent,** his creditors are bleeding him (to death) **3. se faire assassiner = se faire assaisonner** (**assaisonner 2**).

asseoir [aswar] **I** *vtr F* **1.** to snub/to sit on (s.o.); to take the wind out of (s.o.'s) sails **2.** to flabbergast*/to floor (s.o.); **sa grossièreté m'assoit,** I'm staggered by his coarseness. (*Voir* **assis**) **II** *vpr* **s'asseoir 1.** *F* **s'asseoir sur qn,** to sit on s.o./to take the wind out of s.o.'s sails **2.** *F* **va t'asseoir!** get lost!*/go take a running jump!/go jump in a lake! **3.** *P* **moi, je m'assieds/je m'assois dessus!** I don't give a damn about it!/you know what you can do with it! (*Voir* **se coucher 3**)

assiette [asjɛt] *nf* **1.** *F* **il n'est pas dans son assiette,** he's feeling out of sorts/below par/one degree under/off colour **2.** *F* **l'assiette au beurre,** plum (government) jobs/cushy jobs/jobs for the boys; **taper dans l'assiette au beurre,** to ride the gravy train **3.** *pl P* **les Assiettes,** = the Crown Courts (formerly the Assizes) **4.** *F* **piquer dans l'assiette de qn** (*i*) to steal from s.o.'s plate (*ii*) to sponge off s.o. (*Voir* **casseur 2**)

assis [asi] *a F* **en être/en rester assis,** to be flabbergasted/to be struck all of a heap; **j'en suis resté assis,** it completely staggered/stunned me; that floored me. (*Voir* **asseoir 2**)

assommant [asɔmɑ̃] *a F* deadly boring/deadly dull.

assommer [asɔme] **I** *vtr F* **assommer qn** (*i*) to bore* s.o. to death/rigid (*ii*) to annoy* s.o./to pester s.o. to death **II** *vpr* **s'assommer** *F* to be bored* stiff/rigid.

assommeur, -euse [asɔmœr, -øz] *n F* crashing bore*/pain in the neck.

Assottes, les [lezasɔt] *nfpl P* = the Crown Courts (formerly the Assizes).

astap(e) [astap] *a P* (*abbr de* **à se taper le derrière par terre**) (*Voir* **taper I 5**) **c'est astap!** it's hilarious!/it's a scream!/it's a riot!

astec [astɛk], **astèque** [astɛk] *nm P* = **aztèque.**

asteure [astœr] *adv P* (= **à cette heure**) at that moment/then; now.

astibloc [astiblɔk], **astibloche** [astiblɔʃ] *nm P* (*pêche*) maggot/worm.

astic [astik] *nm F* = **astique.**

asticot [astiko] *nm F* **1. engraisser les asticots,** to be dead and buried/to be pushing up the daisies/to be food for worms **2. un drôle d'asticot,** an odd character/a queer fellow; a (bit of a) worm.

asticotage [astikɔtaʒ] *nm F* teasing/worrying/pestering/plaguing.

asticoter [astikɔte] **I** *vtr* (= **astiquer 2, 3**); **arrête d'asticoter ton frère!** stop nagging/pestering your brother! **II** *vpr* **s'asticoter** *P* to quarrel*/to bicker/to squabble.

astique [astik] *nf F* (*esp mil*) **passer à l'astique,** to polish (buttons, etc)/to do fatigues/to do bull.

astiquer [astike] **I** *vtr* **1.** *F* **homme bien astiqué,** well-groomed/well-turned out man **2.** *F* to tease*/to worry/to pester/to plague (s.o.); **j'ai qch qui m'astique sous le pied,** I've got an itch under my foot **3.** *P* to thrash/to beat (s.o.) up* **4.** *V* (*homme*) **s'astiquer la colonne/le manche,** to masturbate*/to flog the bishop/to flog the dummy; (*femme*) **s'astiquer le boilton/le bouton,** to masturbate*/to finger-fuck; **astiquer la motte à une nana,** to feel up/to touch up/to finger a girl **II** *vpr* **s'astiquer 1.** *F* to tidy/to smarten oneself up **2.** *P* (*a*) to fight/to have a set-to (**avec,** with) (*b*) to quarrel*/to bicker/to squabble.

astuce [astys] *nf F* **1.** joke/wisecrack/pun; **une astuce vaseuse,** a weak pun/a lousy joke; **je ne saisis pas l'astuce,** I don't get it **2.** gadget/gimmick; **voilà l'astuce!** that's the trick!/that's how it's done!

atout [atu] *nm F* blow*/knock; **prendre/recevoir un atout**, (*pers*) to get clouted; (*voiture*) to get a bash/a knock.

attaque, d' [datak] *adv phr F* (*i*) vigorously; **il y va d'attaque,** he goes at it like a bull at a gate/he goes at it hammer and tongs; **travailler d'attaque,** to work like mad (*ii*) on form; **être/se sentir d'attaque,** to be full of beans/to be on top form; **je ne suis pas d'attaque,** I don't feel up to it/I feel out of sorts.

attaquer [atake] *vtr F* **attaque-moi vers dix plombes,** give me a buzz about ten.

attelé [atle] *a P* (*souteneur*) **être attelé à deux,** to live off two women.

atteler [atle] *vi P* (*souteneur*) to live off the earnings of one or more prostitutes.

attention [atɑ̃sjɔ] *nf F* **attention aux épluchures!** watch out for the consequences!

attifer [atife] **I** *vtr F* **vise un peu comme elle est attifée!** take a look at her get-up!/her outfit! **ce gosse est vraiment mal attifé,** this kid is really badly dressed **II** *vpr* **s'attifer** *F* to get oneself up in/to doll oneself up in (sth).

attigé, -ée [atiʒe] *a&n P* (*a*) (person) infected with VD*; **planque aux attigés,** VD* clinic (*b*) bashed up/knocked about; **être attigé,** to get beaten up/done in.

attiger [atiʒe] *P* **I** *vtr* **1.** (*a*) to hit/to wound; **il s'est fait attiger,** he got hit/he copped it (*b*) to beat (s.o.) up*/to knock (s.o.) about; (*parfois*) to kill (s.o.) **2.** to give (s.o.) VD*/a dose/the clap **3.** **attiger la cabane,** to exaggerate*/to shoot a line/to go a bit far **II** *vi* to exaggerate*/to spin a yarn; **n'attiges pas!** come off it!/stop having me on!

attrapade [atrapad] *nf,*

attrapage [atrapaʒ] *nm F* **1.** quarrel*/set-to **2.** reprimand*/ticking-off.

attrape-cons, attrape-couillons [atrapkɔ̃, -kujɔ̃] *nm inv P* swindle*/hoax*/con.

attrape-gogos, attrape-nigauds [atrapgogo, -nigo] *nm inv F* = **attrape-cons.**

attrape-pèze, attrape-pognon [atrappɛz, -poɲɔ̃] *nm inv P* = **attrappe-cons.**

attrape-poussière(s) [atrappusjɛr] *nm F* useless object that collects dust/white elephant.

attraper [atrape] *vtr F* **1.** to reprimand* (s.o.); to come down on (s.o.) like a ton of bricks; **se faire attraper,** to get told off/to catch it **2.** to cheat/to swindle*; **se faire attraper,** to be diddled/to be taken for a ride; **je me suis laissé attraper,** I was (well and truly) had/done **3.** **attrape!** take that!/put that in your pipe and smoke it! **4.** **il en a attrapé pour cinq ans,** he got/he copped five years. (*Voir* **crève**)

attrape-touristes [atrapturist] *nm inv F* tourist trap.

attributs [atriby] *nmpl P* testicles*/family jewels/marriage prospects.

attriquer [atrike] *vtr P* **1.** to appropriate/to acquire (sth) (*esp* illegally) **2.** to buy (*esp* stolen goods).

auber, aubère [obɛr] *nm P* money*/lolly/dough.

auberge [obɛrʒ] *nf F* **1. sortir de l'auberge,** to get out of a tight corner; **on n'est pas sorti de l'auberge,** we're not out of the wood yet **2. il se croit à l'auberge,** he treats this place like a hotel.

aubergine [obɛrʒin] *nf P* **1.** red nose (from excessive drinking)/bottlenose **2.** woman traffic warden/

esp NAm meter maid. (*Voir* **pervenche**)

aubert [obɛr] *nm P* = **auber.**

auge [oʒ] *nf P* plate; **passe-moi ton auge que je te serve,** hand me your plate/dish so I can serve you.

Auguste [ogyst] *Prnm F* **comme de juste, Auguste!/tout juste, Auguste!** you('ve) said it, mate!

autiche [otiʃ] *nf P* **faire de l'autiche,** to raise a rumpus/to kick up a fuss/to stir up trouble.

auticher [otiʃe] **I** *vtr P* to excite* (s.o.) sexually/to turn (s.o.) on **II** *vpr* **s'auticher** *P* to become sexually excited*; to get turned on/to become randy.

auto [oto, ɔto] *nm F* (*abbr* = *autographe*) autograph.

autobus [otɔbys] *nm P* casual prostitute*/pick-up.

autor, d' [dɔtɔr, dot-] *adv phr P* **faire qch d'autor** (*i*) to do sth off one's own bat (*ii*) to do sth on the spur of the moment; **y aller d'autor,** to go it alone; **travailler d'autor et d'achar,** to work* hard (**à qch,** at sth); to put one's back into sth; **d'autor et de rif/de rif et d'autor,** without more ado.

autre [otr] *pron F* **comme dit l'autre,** as the saying goes/as they say; as the actress said to the bishop; **à d'autres!** pull the other one (it's got bells on)! (*Voir* **chat**)

Auverpin [overpɛ̃], **Auverploum** [overplum] *nm P* (*péj*) native of Auvergne/Auvergnat.

auxi [ɔksi] *nm F* (*abbr* = *auxiliaire*) auxiliary.

auxico [ɔksiko], **auxigo** [ɔksigo] *nm F* **1.** (*mil*) auxiliary **2.** (*prison*) trusty.

auxipatte [ɔksipat] *nm F* (*mil*) = **auxico 1.**

avaler [avale] *vtr* **1.** *F* **avaler les kilomètres,** to eat up the miles **2.** *P* **avaler son acte/son bulletin/son** extrait de naissance; avaler sa chique/l'avaler, to die*/to kick the bucket/to give up the ghost. (*Voir* **canne 3; consigne; crapaud 1; cuiller 3; fumée 2; langue 2; parapluie**)

avaloir *nm,* **avaloire** [avalwar] *nf P* throat/gullet; **s'arroser l'avaloir,** to have a drink*/to wet one's whistle.

avantage [avɑ̃taʒ] *nm* **1.** *F* **faire un avantage à qn,** to be nice to s.o.; **fais-moi un avantage,** do me a favour **2.** *F* **à qui ai-je l'avantage?** to whom do I have the pleasure of speaking? **3.** *pl P* breasts*/charms.

avant-postes [avɑ̃pɔst] *nmpl P* breasts*/bristols.

avant-scène [avɑ̃sɛn] *nf P* breasts*; (**il**) **y a du monde à l'avant-scène/elle est bien pourvue en avant-scène,** she's well stacked/she's a big girl; *pl* **avant-scènes,** breasts*.

avaro [avaro] *nm P* **1.** accident/mishap **2.** trouble/worry.

avec [avɛk] **I** *prep P* **nous l'avons fait avec mon frère,** my brother and I did it **II** *adv F* **elle a pris mon portefeuille et s'est sauvée avec,** she took my wallet and ran off with it; **il faudra faire avec,** you'll have to make do with what you've got. (*Voir* **ça 3**)

aveux [avø] *nmpl P* **passer à la chambre des aveux spontanés,** to be put through the third degree/to get the rough stuff.

avocat [avɔka] *nm P* **faire l'avocat,** to act as an accomplice/a decoy. (*Voir* **bêcheur I 4**)

avoine [avwan] *nf P* **1.** food*/grub/chow **2.** **coller/filer/refiler une avoine à qn** (*i*) to give s.o. a good hiding/a thrashing (*ii*) to beat s.o. up*/to work s.o. over (*iii*) (*prostituée*) to flagellate/to whip (a client).

avoiner [avwane] *vtr* P **avoiner qn** = **avoine 2**.

avoir [avwar] *vtr* **1.** *F* to fool (s.o.)/to pull a fast one on (s.o.); **se faire/se laisser avoir,** to be taken in/to be had/to be conned; **on vous a eu!** you've been had!/you've been taken for a ride!/you've been done! **on ne m'a pas comme ça!** you can't fool me!/you won't catch me that way! **il a été bien eu!** he's been well and truly had! **on les aura!** we'll beat them yet!/we'll get them! **2.** *F* **en avoir,** to have guts/*esp NAm* to have balls **3.** *F* **tu en auras!** you've got it coming to you! **4.** *F* **je l'ai eu!** I passed (my exam)!/I got it! **5.** *F* **en avoir par-dessus la tête/plein le dos/assez,** to be fed up*/cheesed off/browned off; **j'en ai jusque-là!** I'm fed up to the (back) teeth! **6.** *F* **avoir qn à la pitié/à la sympathie, etc,** to play on s.o.'s pity, sympathy, etc **7.** *P* **avoir une femme,** to have (sex* with) a woman **8.** *P* **l'avoir,** to have syphilis*. (*Voir* **air I 8; sec I; tournant**)

avorton [avɔrtɔ̃] *nm F* (*péj*) (*pers*) (little) runt/shorty/shrimp/weed.

azimut [azimyt] *nm F* **dans tous les azimuts,** in all directions/all over the shop; left, right and centre; **direction tous azimuts,** facing all ways/*esp NAm* every which way.

azimuté [azimyte] *a P* mad*/barmy/crazy*/bonkers.

azor [azɔr] *nm O* **1.** *F* dog*; (*nom donné aux chiens*) Fido/Rover **2.** *P* (*mil*) knapsack/pack **3.** *P* revolver*/pistol **4.** *P* WC*/bog/shithouse **5.** *P* (*théâtre*) **appeler Azor,** to boo/to hiss.

aztèque [aztɛk] *nm P* (*péj*) undersized* man/shrimp of a man/short-arse/(little) runt.

B

baba [baba] I *nm* 1. *P* (*a*) buttocks*; **le mettre dans le baba à qn,** to do the dirty on s.o.; **l'avoir dans le baba/se le faire mettre dans le baba,** to be badly let down/to get the thin end of the wedge/to get screwed up (*b*) anus* 2. *V* female genitals* 3. *P* **baba (cool),** (peaceloving) dropout/hippy/groovy. (*Voir* **carrer 3**) II *a inv F* flabbergasted; **en être/en rester/en demeurer baba,** to be dumbfounded/to be flabbergasted.

babafier [babafje] *vtr A F* to flabbergast*/to dumbfound.

babillard [babijar] *nm* 1. *F* notice board 2. *P* newspaper/daily rag/scandal sheet 3. *O P* = **babillarde 4.** *P* lawyer/brief 5. *P* chaplain/padre.

babillarde [babijard] *nf P* 1. letter/line/note 2. (wrist-)watch.

babillarder [babijarde] *vi A P* to write a letter/to drop a line.

babille [babij] *nf P* = **babillarde.**

babin [babɛ̃] *nm O P* mouth*/chops.

babines [babin] *nfpl* (*a*) *F* lips; **vous vous en (pour)lécherez les babines,** you'll lick your lips/smack your chops over it (*b*) *V* (*sexe de la femme*) lips.

babouin [babwɛ̃] *nm F* pimple on the lip.

babouines [babwin] *nfpl F* = **babines.**

baby-foot [babifut] *nm F* (pin-)table football.

babylonien [babilɔnjɛ̃] *a P* (*esp CB*) gigantic/fabulous/giant/ginormous.

bac [bak] *nm F* 1. (*abbr = baccalauréat*) French school-leaving examination (*approx* = A level) 2. (= **baccara(t)**) baccara(t); **tailler un bac,** to have a game of baccara(t).

bacantes, baccantes [bakɑ̃t] *nfpl F* = **bacchantes.**

baccara [bakara] *nm P* 1. **avoir baccara,** to be on a hiding to nothing/to be sure to lose 2. **être en plein baccara** (*i*) to have a run of bad luck/to have nothing going right (*ii*) to be down in the dumps.

bacchanal [bakanal] *nm F* uproar*/row/din/racket; **faire un bacchanal de tous les diables,** to kick up a hell of a row/to make the dickens of a noise.

bacchanale [bakanal] *nf O F* drunken revel.

bacchantes [bakɑ̃t] *nfpl F* moustache*; **bacchantes en guidon (de course),** handlebar moustache.

bâche [baʃ] *nf P* 1. (*casquette*) cap 2. (bed) sheet; **se mettre dans les bâches,** to go to bed*/to hit the sack.

se bâcher [səbaʃe] *vpr P* to go to bed*/to hit the sack.

bâcheuse [baʃøz] *nf P* landlady (of a lodging-house).

bachot [baʃo] *nm F* (*a*) = **bac 1** (*b*) **boîte à bachot,** crammer's/cramming school.

bachotage [baʃotaʒ] *nm F* cramming/swotting.

bachoter [baʃɔte] *F* **I** *vtr* to cram (up) (a subject)/to swot for the *baccalauréat* or other exam **II** *vi* (*i*) to cram/to swot (*ii*) to sit the *baccalauréat* exam.

bachoteur, euse [baʃɔtœr, -øz] *n F* student cramming/swotting (up) for an exam (*esp* the *baccalauréat*); student who works hard/swot.

bâclage [baklaʒ] *nm F* botching (of work).

bâclé [bakle] *a F* travail bâclé, slap-dash/slipshod work; un travail bâclé, a botch(ed) job.

bâcler [bakle] *vtr F* to botch (work)/to do (sth) hurriedly and carelessly/to make a hash of sth.

bacreuse [bakrøz] *nf P* pocket.

bada [bada] *nm P* **1.** (*a*) hat/titfer (*b*) le petit bada rouquinos, Little Red Riding Hood **2.** porter le bada (*i*) to be wrongly accused/to take the rap/to carry the can (*ii*) to have a bad reputation (*iii*) to be (suspected of being) a police informer*.

badaboum [badabum] *nm P* brawl/scuffle/shindy/free-for-all.

badaf [badaf] *nm P* = bat' d'af.

baderne [badɛrn] *nf F* (*péj*) une (vieille) baderne, an old fog(e)y*/an old stick-in-the-mud/an old fuddy duddy; (*mil*) a blimp/a Colonel Blimp.

badigeon [badiʒɔ̃] *nm F* make-up/face-paint/war-paint. (*Voir* ripolin)

badigeonner [badiʒɔne] *vtr F* to paint/to make up (one's face).

badigoinces [badigwɛs] *nfpl P* lips; jouer des badigoinces, to eat* heartily/to nosh.

badines [badin] *nfpl O P* legs*/pins.

Badingue [badɛ̃g], **Badinguet** [badɛ̃gɛ] *Prnm F* (*hist*) (nickname for) Napoleon III.

Badingues, les [lɛbadɛ̃g] *Prnmpl* (*hist*) Batignolles (district of Paris).

badour [badur] *a F* **1.** (*pers*) attractive/good-looking/handsome/pretty **2.** nice/pleasant.

bâdrage [badraʒ] *nm FrC P* nuisance/annoyance.

bâdrant [badrã] *a FrC P* annoying/bothersome.

bâdrer [badre] *vtr FrC P* to bother/to annoy.

baffe [baf] **I** *nf P* **1.** blow*; slap; coller/flanquer une baffe à qn, to slap s.o. (round the face)/to clip s.o. round the ear **2.** (*fig*) j'ai pris une de ces baffes à ce concert! I got a real buzz out of that concert! (*Voir* java 2 (*a*)) **II** *nf P* moustache*/tache/tickler.

baffer [bafe] *vtr P* to give (s.o.) a slap (round the face).

baffi [bafi] *nm or f O P* = baffe II.

baffre [bafr] *nf O P* = baffe I.

baffrer [bafre] *vtr&i P* = bâfrer.

bafouillage [bafujaʒ] *nm F* (*a*) incoherent speech/babbling (*b*) swallowing of one's words (*c*) nonsense/rubbish/gibberish (*d*) stammering/spluttering/stuttering (*e*) (*moteur*) misfiring/sputtering.

bafouillarder [bafujarde] *vtr A P* to write (a letter)/to drop (a line) (to s.o.).

bafouille [bafuj] *nf P* letter/note/line.

bafouiller [bafuje] *vtr&i F* (*a*) to babble (*b*) to swallow one's words (*c*) to talk nonsense/gibberish (*d*) to stammer/to splutter; bafouiller quelque chose, to stutter out something (*e*) (*moteur*) to miss/to misfire/to sputter.

bafouillette [bafujɛt] *nf P* short letter.

bafouilleur, euse [bafujœr, -øz] *n F* (*a*) stammerer/stutterer (*b*) someone who talks nonsense/rubbish.

bafouillis [bafuji] *nm F* = **bafouillage.**

bâfre [bɑfr] *nf P* **1.** *A* feed/tuckin/blow-out **2.** = **baffe I 3.** moustache and beard/full set.

bâfrée [bɑfre] *nf P* feed/tuck-in/blow-out.

bâfrer [bɑfre] *P* **I** *vi* to stuff oneself (with food) **II** *vtr* to wolf/to gobble (one's food) (down); **bâfrer sa mangeaille,** to stuff one's face **III** *vpr* **se bâfrer** *P* to stuff oneself (with food).

bâfrerie [bɑfrəri] *nf P* gluttony/gorging/guzzling.

bâfreur, euse [bɑfrœr, -øz] *n P* hog/pig/greedy-guts/guzzler.

bagage [bagaʒ] *nm F* **plier bagage** (*i*) to (pack up and) clear out/to do a bunk (*ii*) to die*/to pop off/to snuff it.

bagali [bagali] *nm P* mud.

bagarrer [bagare] **I** *vi F* to fight/to battle (**pour,** for) **II** *vpr* **se bagarrer** *F* to fight/to brawl/to have a set-to/to have a punch-up.

bagarreur [bagarœr] *nm F* brawler/rowdy; **c'est un bagarreur,** he's always ready for a fight.

bagasse! [bagas] *excl A F* nonsense!/rubbish!

bagatelle [bagatɛl] *nf P* (*hum*) sex*/love-making; **être porté sur la bagatelle,** to be fond of sex*/to like *it* a lot/to have a one-track mind; **les bagatelles de la porte,** foreplay/heavy petting.

bagne [baɲ] *nm F* (*fig*) one's place of work (factory, office, etc); **quel bagne!** (*i*) it's sheer slavery! (*ii*) what a grind! **un vrai bagne,** a sweatshop.

bagnole [baɲɔl] *nf F* car*/motor/wheels; **c'est une belle bagnole,** she's a nice job/that's a nice motor; **une vieille bagnole,** an old banger/a jalopy/an old heap.

bagot [bago] *nm P* luggage; **faire les bagots,** to steal luggage (from parked cars, railway stations, etc).

bagot(t)er [bagɔte] *vi P* **1.** to walk quickly **2. comment vont les affaires? – ça bagot(t)e,** how's business? – not so bad.

bagou [bagu] *nm F* **avoir du bagou,** to have a smooth tongue/to have the gift of the gab/to have a touch of the Blarney.

bagougnasses [baguɲas] *nfpl P* lips.

bagouler [bagule] *vi P* to talk/to jabber away nineteen to the dozen.

bagouse [baguz] *nf* **1.** *P* ring (worn on finger) **2.** *P* **avoir de la bagouse,** to be lucky **3.** *P* **l'avoir dans la bagouse,** to get the thin end of the wedge **4.** *V* anus*/ring; **être de la bagouse,** to be a homosexual*/to be one of them.

bagout [bagu] *nm F* = **bagou.**

bagouze [baguz] *nf P V* = **bagouse.**

bague [bag] *nf P* anus*/ring(-piece); **être de la bague,** to be a homosexual*/to be one of them.

baguenaudage [bagnodaʒ] *nm F* mooching about/loafing around; fooling about/larking about.

baguenaude [bagnod] *nf P* pocket.

baguenauder [bagnode] *vi & pr F* (**se**) **baguenauder,** to mooch about/to loaf around; to fool about/to lark about.

baguenauderie [bagnodri] *nf F* **1.** = **baguenaudage 2.** small talk/idle gossip.

baguette [bagɛt] *nf* **1.** *P* **avoir de la baguette,** to be lucky **2.** *V* **filer un coup de baguette à une femme,** to have sex* with/to screw/to lay a woman **3.** *F* **cheveux raides comme des baguettes de tambour,** dead straight hair **4.** *F* **commander/faire marcher/mener qn à la baguette,** to rule s.o. with a rod of iron **5.** *P pl* legs*; **baguettes de**

tambour, thin legs/drumsticks; **mettre les baguettes,** to run away*/to beat it/to scarper **6.** *V* penis*/prick; **s'astiquer la baguette,** to masturbate*/to jack off.

bahut [bay] *nm P* **1.** (*a*) school/lycée (*b*) place of work **2.** (*a*) car* (*b*) taxi (*c*) lorry/truck.

bahutage [baytaʒ] *nm P* (*scol*) (*a*) ragging (*b*) noisy behaviour.

bahuter [bayte] **I** *vi P* (*scol*) (*a*) to rag (*b*) to behave noisily **II** *vpr* **se bahuter** *V* to masturbate*.

bahuteur, -euse [baytœr, -øz] *n P* (*scol*) **1.** rowdy pupil **2.** schoolfriend/schoolmate.

bahutien [baytjɛ̃], **bahutier** [baytje] *nm P* (*scol*) = **bahuteur 2.**

baigner [beɲe] *vi* **1.** *F* **baigner dans le beurre/dans l'huile/dans la margarine,** to be functioning perfectly/to go very smoothly/to go like a dream; **tout baigne (dans l'huile)/ça baigne,** everything's fine/hunky-dory **2.** *P* **envoyer qn baigner,** to tell s.o. to go (and) jump in the lake.

baigneur [beɲœr] *nm* **1.** *P* head*; **se casser le baigneur,** to rack one's brains **2.** *P* nose*; **claquer le baigneur à qn,** to punch s.o. on the nose/to sock s.o. in the kisser **3.** *V* penis*/plonker; **tremper son baigneur,** to have sex* (with s.o.)/to get one's end away/to dip one's wick.

bail [baj] *nm* **1.** *F* **il y a un bail/ça fait un bail qu'on ne s'est pas vus!** it's ages/yonks since we met!/we haven't seen each other in donkey's years! **2.** *P* **casser le bail,** to get a divorce.

baille [baj] *nf P* **1.** water (of sea, river, etc); **la (grande) Baille,** the sea/the drink; **tomber à la baille,** to fall in(to) the drink **2.** rain **3. la Baille,** the *Ecole navale* **4.** dilapidated ship/old tub.

bailler [baje] *vtr F* **je n'en baille**

pas un mot, I won't breathe/say a word.

bain [bɛ̃] *nm* **1.** *F* (*a*) **être dans le bain** (*i*) to be implicated/mixed up in sth (*ii*) to be in the know/to be with it (*iii*) to get the hang of things/to pick it up (*b*) **se mettre dans le bain** (*i*) to get down to it/to get into the swing of things (*ii*) to get in on the act (*iii*) to get into the mood/to get the hang of things/to get warmed up (*c*) **mettre qn dans le bain** (*i*) to implicate s.o. (*ii*) to let s.o. in on a deal (*d*) **se remettre dans le bain,** to return to work/to pick up where one left off/to get back into the swim (of things) **2.** *F* **envoyer qn au bain,** to send s.o. packing*/to send s.o. off with a flea in his ear/to tell s.o. where he gets off **3.** *F* **il a pris tout le bain,** he's been blamed for everything **4.** *F* **plaisanterie de garçon de bains,** senseless/stupid joke **5.** *F* **c'est un bain qui chauffe,** there's trouble ahead/there's a storm brewing **6.** *P* (*a*) **flanquer qn dans le bain,** to accuse s.o./to put s.o. on the spot (*b*) **sortir qn du bain,** to get s.o. out of a fix (*c*) **tremper dans le bain,** to be in it up to one's neck/to be in dead trouble. (*Voir* **lézard**)

bain-marie [bɛ̃mari] *nm P* bidet.

baïonnette [bajɔnɛt] *nf V* penis*/bayonet/chopper.

baisage [bezaʒ] *nm V* sex*/lovemaking.

baisant [bezɑ̃] *a P* first-rate/fantastic/super; **peu baisant,** lousy.

baise [bɛz] *nf* **1.** *V* sex*/screw/fuck/lay; **une bonne baise,** a good fuck/screw **2.** *P* (*scol*) detention.

baise-à-l'œil [bezalœj] *nf P* (*prostituées*) straight woman/woman not on the game.

baise-en-ville [bezɑ̃vil] *nm P* **1.** small overnight bag **2.** (*rare*) (vaginal) douche.

baiser [beze] *vtr* **1.** *V* to have

sex*/to have it off/to have it away
with (s.o.); to screw/to fuck/to lay
(s.o.); to knock (s.o.) off; abs **il
baise vachement bien,** he's a bloody
marvellous lay; he's a good screw/a
good fuck. (Voir **bourgeoise 2;
canard; couille 6; cygne; épicier
2; hussard; hussarde; levrette;
papa 1; riche**) **2.** P (a) to catch
(s.o.) red-handed/in the act; **se
faire baiser,** to be caught with one's
pants down (b) to arrest* (s.o.); **se
faire baiser,** to get nabbed/nicked
3. P to steal (sth)/to knock (sth)
off **4.** P (a) to deceive/to fool*
(s.o.); **se faire baiser,** to be taken
in/to be taken for a ride/to be had
(b) to swindle*/to cheat (s.o.); **se
faire baiser,** to be done/to get
rooked **5.** P **je n'y baise rien,** I
don't get it/I can't make head nor
tail of it.

baisette [bɛzɛt] nf V penis*/willy.

baiseur, -euse [bɛzœr, -øz] n V
s.o. who is fond of sex*; fucker;
c'est une sacrée baiseuse! she's a
terrific lay!/she's a fucking good
screw!

baiseuses [bɛzøz] nfpl P lips.

baisodrome [bɛzɔdrom] nm V
(lieu où l'on fait souvent l'amour) (a)
brothel* (b) bedroom; bed (c) lovers' lane, etc.

baisoir(e) [bɛzwar] nf V female
genitals*/cunt.

baisoter [bɛzɔte] vtr F (i) to kiss
(s.o.) (ii) to give (s.o.) a peck on
the cheek.

baisouiller [bɛzuje] vi V to have
sex* with/to screw (s.o.) (perfuncto-
rily/badly).

baisse-froc [bɛsfrɔk] nm P cow-
ard*/chicken/yellowbelly. (Voir
froc 3)

bak(h)chich [bakʃiʃ] nm F gratu-
ity/tip (as a bribe); backhander.

balade [balad] nf F (a) stroll/ram-
ble (on foot); **on se fait une petite
balade?** come on! let's go for a

walk! (b) drive/spin/run (in car,
etc).

balader [balade] F **I** vi envoyer
balader qn, to tell s.o. to clear off/
to send s.o. packing*; (amant) to
jilt/to chuck; **envoyer balader son
boulot,** to chuck one's job **II** vtr to
take (s.o.) out/to drag s.o. around;
balader son chien, to take one's dog
for a walk **III** vpr **se balader** F
(a) to go for a walk/to take a stroll
(b) to traipse about/to swan
around.

baladeur, -euse [baladœr, -øz]
a F **avoir les mains baladeuses,** to
have wandering/roaming hands.

balai [balɛ] nm **1.** F (a) **donner un
(bon) coup de balai,** to make a
clean sweep (of one's staff) (b) **faire
balai neuf,** to start off well/to get
off to a good start (in a new job,
etc) (c) **il fait balai neuf,** a new
broom sweeps clean **2.** F **rôtir le
balai,** to lead a fast life/to live it
up **3.** F last bus, tube, etc (at
night). (Voir **voiture-balai**) **4.** F
ramasser les balais, to be overtaken
(in a yacht race, etc); **être du balai,**
to be the last to arrive **5.** P **du
balai!** clear off!/hop it! **6.** P con
comme un balai, as daft as a brush;
sacré balai! you bloody fool! **7.** P
balai à chiottes, moustache* **8.** P
year; **il a 50 balais,** he is fifty. (Voir
balayette; manche I; peau 19)

balaise [balɛz] P **I** a hefty/beefy
II nm (a) strong/powerfully built/
hefty man (b) (iron) clever; **t'es un
balaise, toi!** you're a bright one!/a
bright spark!

balançage [balɑ̃saʒ] nm P
denouncing/informing/grassing.

balance [balɑ̃s] nf P dismissal/
sacking.

balancé [balɑ̃se] a **1.** F (pers)
bien balancé, well-built/well-propor-
tioned/well set-up; **elle est bien
balancée,** she's got a good figure;
she's got curves in all the right
places; she's well-stacked **2.** P ça,

c'est balancé! that's got him!/that's floored him!

balancement [balɑ̃smɑ̃] *nm P* prison sentence*.

balancer [balɑ̃se] **I** *vtr F* **1.** (*a*) to throw/to chuck (stones, etc) (*b*) to throw (sth) away/out; to get rid of (sth)/to chuck sth away **2.** ba-lancer un coup de pied à qn, to kick out at s.o. **3.** (*a*) to throw (s.o.) out/to chuck s.o. out/to give s.o. the push (*b*) to dismiss* (s.o.)/to fire (s.o.)/to sack (s.o.)/to give (s.o.) the boot **4.** to swindle*/to con (s.o.) **5.** en balancer une, to sing a song **6.** to denounce* (s.o.)/to put the finger on (s.o.); balancer la cavalerie, to blow the gaff on one's accomplices. (*Voir* décor; fumée 1; grouille; purée 2) **II** *vi F* (*musique*) to swing; ça balance! that's really cool! **III** *vpr* se ba-lancer **1.** *P* je m'en balance! I don't give/care a damn!; il se ba-lance bien de tout ça, he doesn't give a toss for all that **2.** *V* to have an orgasm*/to come.

balanceur, -euse [balɑ̃sœr, -ǿz] *n F* informer*/squealer/grass.

balancier [balɑ̃sje] *nm P* arm.

balançoire [balɑ̃swar] **1.** *nf O F* de la balançoire/des balançoires, nonsense*/rubbish; je ne coupe pas dans tes balançoires, you can't kid me/I'm not falling for that **2.** *F* envoyer qn à la balançoire, to send s.o. packing*/to give s.o. the boot **3.** *P* balançoire à Mickey/à minouche, sanitary towel/*NAm* sanitary napkin.

balanstiquer [balɑ̃stike] *vtr P* = balancer I 1, 3, 5.

balarguer [balarge] *vtr P* = ba-lancer I 1, 2, 3.

balaud [balo] *nm P* = ballot.

balayer [baleje] *vtr F* to dismiss*/ to fire/to sack; balayer tout le per-sonnel, to make a clean sweep of the staff. (*Voir* planche 2)

balayette [balɛjɛt] *nf* **1.** *V*

penis*; faire une partie de balayette, to have sex*/to have it off **2.** *P* balayette à chiottes, moustache/ tache.

balcon [balkɔ̃] *nm P* (il) y a du monde au balcon, she's well-stacked/she's got big knockers; quel balcon! what a pair of beauts/ knockers!

baleine [balɛn] *nf F* **1.** se marrer comme une baleine, to laugh uproariously/to fall about (laugh-ing) **2.** (*cirque*) big top.

balès [balɛs], **baleste** [balɛst], **balèz(e)** [balɛz] *a&nm P* = balaise.

baliser [balize] *vi O P* to be afraid*/to have the wind up.

ballade [balad] *nf P* pocket; faire les ballades à qn, to go through s.o.'s pockets.

balle [bal] *nf* **1.** *P* head*/nut **2.** *P* face*/mug **3.** *P* franc; dix bal-les, ten francs **4.** *P* c'est ma balle, that's my affair/my business **5.** *P* ça fait ma balle, that suits me down to the ground **6.** *F* raide comme (une) balle, like a shot/like (greased) lightning; without beating about the bush **7.** *F* (*a*) renvoyer la balle à qn, to give s.o. tit for tat/ to give s.o. as good as he gave; to turn the tables on s.o. (*b*) se renvoyer la balle, to pass the buck **8.** *F* à vous la balle (*i*) (it's) your turn (*ii*) that (remark, etc) was aimed at you **9.** *F* faire (la) balle, to score a bull's-eye/to hit the bull **10.** *F* enfant de la balle, s.o. (*esp* actor, circus performer) born into a profession/following in his father's footsteps **11.** *F* balle perdue, wasted effort **12.** *P* balle de copaille, barbiturates*/barbs. (*Voir* peau 19; trou)

baller [bale] *vi P* envoyer baller qn, to send s.o. packing*/to give s.o. the push.

balleste [balɛst] *a&nm P* (*rare*) = balaise.

ballet [balɛ] *nm V* **ballet rose,** (sexual) orgy involving girls under age; **ballet bleu,** (sexual) orgy involving young boys.

ballochards [balɔʃar] *nmpl P* breasts*.

balloches [balɔʃ] *nfpl V* testicles*/ balls/bollocks.

ballon [balɔ̃] *nm P* **1.** buttocks*; **enlever le ballon à qn,** to give s.o. a kick up the bum/*NAm* butt **2.** stomach*; **se remplir le ballon,** to have a good blow-out/to tuck into one's food **3.** **faire ballon** (*i*) to go without food (*ii*) to tighten one's belt/to go without (*iii*) to be disappointed; to come away empty-handed **4.** **faire souffler dans le ballon,** to breathalyse (s.o.)/to get (s.o.) to blow into the bag **5.** **attraper le ballon,** to become pregnant*/to get in the family way; **avoir le ballon,** to be pregnant*/to be in the family way/to be in the club; **flanquer le ballon à qn,** to get s.o. pregnant*/up the spout; to knock s.o. up **6.** prison*/nick; **faire du ballon,** to do time/to do a stretch/to do bird; **mettre qn au ballon,** to send s.o. to prison*/to put s.o. inside. (*Voir* **marqué II** (*b*)) **7.** *pl* (large) breasts*/(big) tits/ (huge) knockers.

ballonner [balɔne] *vtr P* to imprison*/to put (s.o.) in clink.

ballot [balo] *nm P* fool*/clot/twit/ dolt; **tu parles d'un ballot!** he's a prize idiot!/what an ass! **t'es pas ballot?** are you mad*?/have you gone crazy? **les bons ballots,** the mugs. (*Voir* **bout 8**)

ballot(t)er [balɔte] *vtr O P* to pay* up/to fork out; to hand over/ to give.

balluches [balyʃ] *nfpl P* (*esp forçats*) (pack of) cigarettes/fags.

balluchon [balyʃɔ̃] *nm P* = **baluchon.**

ballustrines [balystrin] *nfpl V* testicles*/balls.

balmuche [balmyʃ] *excl O P* = **balpeau 1.**

balochard [balɔʃar] *nm P* idler/ layabout.

balocher [balɔʃe] *vi P* (*a*) to mooch about (*b*) to laze about/to hang about/to bum around.

baloches [balɔʃ] *nfpl V* testicles*/ balls/bollocks; **en avoir dans les baloches,** to have balls/to have guts.

balocheur [balɔʃœr] *nm P* idler/ layabout.

balourd [balur] *P* **I** *a* false/fake/ sham; imitation (jewels, etc); phon(e)y **II** *nm* **1.** fool*/idiot/ twerp/twit **2.** *pl* **balourds** (*a*) false banknotes (*b*) false identity papers (*c*) loaded dice.

balpeau [balpo] *P* **I** *excl* (*verlan de peau de balle!*) (*i*) nothing*!/ damn all!/sweet FA! (*ii*) nothing doing!*/no dice! **II** *nm* **faire balpeau,** to be disappointed; to come away empty-handed.

Balthazar [baltazar] *nm P* good meal/tuck-in/blow-out/nosh-up.

baltringue [baltrɛ̃g] *a&nm P* (*rare*) good-for-nothing.

baluchard, arde [balyʃar, -ard] *n P* = **baluche.**

baluche [balyʃ] *P* **I** *nm&f* fool*/ twit/twerp/nurd **II** *nf* cigarette*/ fag.

baluchon [balyʃɔ̃] *nm P* = **baluchard.**

baluchonner [balyʃɔne] *vtr P* to pack away (stolen goods) in a bag, etc (during a robbery).

baluchonneur [balyʃɔnœr] *nm P* (small-time) burglar/housebreaker.

bamban [bãbã] *nm&f & adv P* (*péj*) = **banban.**

bambochade [bãbɔʃad] *nf F* **une bambochade,** a bit of a spree.

bambochard [bãbɔʃar] *nm F* = **bambocheur.**

bamboche [bɑ̃bɔʃ] *nf F* **1.**
spree*/good time/bender/binge.
(*Voir* **bamboula II**) **2.** undersized*
person/half-pint/short-ass/shrimp.

bambocher [bɑ̃bɔʃe] *vi F* to go
on a spree*/to paint the town red/
to live it up/to have a good time*/
to have a ball.

bambocheur, euse [bɑ̃bɔʃœr,
-øz] *n F* reveller/hell-bender/hell-
raiser/fast liver.

bambou [bɑ̃bu] *nm* **1.** *F* sucer/
tirer sur le bambou, to smoke
opium*/to suck the bamboo **2.** (*a*)
F coup de bambou (*i*) sunstroke (*ii*)
sudden attack of madness (*b*) P il a
reçu un/le coup de bambou (*i*) he's
gone mad*/he's gone off his rock-
er/he's lost his marbles (*ii*) he's
exhausted*/(dead) beat/whacked (*c*)
P donner un coup de bambou à qn,
to stun s.o. (with bad news) (*d*)
c'est le coup de bambou! it's
daylight robbery! **3.** *P* (*forçat*)
aller aux bambous, to be buried **4.**
P être sous le bambou, to be
banned/to be persona non grata
somewhere. (*Voir* **bâton I 4**) **5.** *V*
avoir le bambou, to have an erection*/a hard-on.

bamboula [bɑ̃bula] **I** *nm P* (*péj*)
negro* **II** *nf F* spree*/bender/
good time*/binge; faire la
bamboula, to have a good time/to
live it up/to have a ball/to go out
on the town. (*Voir* **bamboche 1**)

bambouter [bɑ̃bute] *vtr P*
bambouter qn, to stun s.o. (with
bad news). (*Voir* **bambou 2** (*c*))

banal [banal] *a O F* c'est pas banal,
ça! well, that's the limit!

banane [banan] *nf* **1.** *P* military
decoration/gong; *pl* bananes, chest
hardware/fruit salad **2.** *P* (big)
military helicopter*/chopper **3.** *P*
(*cyclisme*) porter la banane, to wear
the leader's yellow jersey in the
Tour de France **4.** *F* (*coiffure*)
rock and roll hairstyle of the
1950s/Teddy-boy cut; duck tail/

duck's arse/DA **5.** *V* avoir la
banane, to have an erection*/to
have a hard-on/to get it up. (*Voir*
peau 12)

banban [bɑ̃bɑ̃] *P* (*péj*) **I** *nm&f*
lame/gammy-legged person **II** *adv*
with a limp.

banc [bɑ̃] *nm* **1.** *F* il faut vous
remettre sur les bancs, you'd better
go back to school **2.** *P* (*en parlant
de la tenancière d'un bordel*) avoir
commencé/débuté sur le banc, to
have begun as a practising prostitute; to have started off on the
streets/in a brothel. (*Voir* **pied 21**)

bancal, *pl* -als [bɑ̃kal] *nm F*
(*mil*) light curved cavalry sword/
sabre.

banco! [bɑ̃ko] *int P* agreed!*/OK!/
you're on!

bancuche [bɑ̃kyʃ] *nf P* **1.** bank
2. cash-desk.

bandaison [bɑ̃dɛzɔ̃] *nf V* erection*/horn/hard-on.

bandant [bɑ̃dɑ̃] *a V* (*a*) (*esp fille,
femme*) desirable/sexually exciting;
elle est bandante, she's (a bit of)
hot stuff/she's a bit of all right/she
really gets me going/she's a cracker
(*b*) thrilling/stimulating; c'est pas
bien bandant, that's not exactly
earth-shattering/that won't set the
world on fire.

bande [bɑ̃d] *nf* **1.** *F* par la bande,
indirectly/in a roundabout way;
apprendre qch par la bande, to hear
sth on the grapevine **2.** *F* crowd/
group/gang; une bande de motards,
a gang of bikers/hell's angels **3.** *P*
(*insulte*) bande de ..., bunch of
...; bande de cons/bande
d'enculés! load of cretins/cunts/
piss-artists!

bander [bɑ̃de] *vi V* **1.** (*a*) to have
an erection*/to have a hard-on/to
get it up; il ne bandait pas, he
couldn't get it up; il bandait comme
un cerf/un Turc, he had a huge
erection*/hard-on; he was really
horny/randy (*b*) to feel fruity/

horny/randy/turned on (*c*) **bander pour qn,** to desire s.o. sexually/to be turned on by s.o./to be horny for s.o. **2. bander mou/ne bander que d'une,** to be afraid*/to have the wind up/to have the willies **3.** (*hum*) (= *faire bande à part*) **bander à part,** to keep (oneself) to oneself. (*Voir* **zéro 6**)

bandeur, -euse [bɑ̃dœr, -øz] *n V* sexually obsessed person/s.o. with a one-track mind/s.o. who can't get enough; (*homme*) randy bugger/devil/sod; a bit of a lecher; (*femme*) a goer/a nympho; **quel bandeur,** he's continually randy/he's always trying to get his end away.

bandocher [bɑ̃dɔʃe] *vi V* to feel sexually excited*/randy/horny.

bandocheur [bɑ̃dɔʃœr] *nm V* coward*/timid person/chicken.

banette [banɛt] *nf P* bed; **faire banette,** to go to bed*.

bang [bɑ̃g] *nm P* (*drogues*) **1.** cannabis* **2.** injection*/fix.

banlieusard, -arde [bɑ̃ljøzar, -ard] *F* **I** *n* (*a*) suburbanite (*b*) commuter **II** *a* suburban.

bannes [ban] *nfpl P* (bed-)sheets; **se mettre dans les bannes,** to get between the sheets/to hit the sack.

bannière [banjɛr] *nf P* **être en bannière,** to be in one's shirt(-tails). (*Voir* **croix 2**)

banque [bɑ̃k] *nf* **1.** *P* (**jour de**) **banque,** pay day; **aller/passer à la banque,** to draw one's wages **2.** *P* **tailler une banque,** to be bet at cards **3.** *F* (*a*) (showman's, etc) patter/spiel (*b*) **la banque,** the circus world (*c*) travelling show.

banquer [bɑ̃ke] *vtr&i P* to pay* (up)/to shell out.

banquettes [bɑ̃kɛt] *nfpl F* (*théâtre*) **jouer devant les banquettes (vides),** to play to an empty house.

banquezingue [bɑ̃kzɛ̃g] *nm P* banker.

baptême [batɛm] *nm O P* (collective) rape/gang bang.

baptiser [batize] *vtr* **1.** *F* to water down (wine, milk, etc) **2.** *O P* to rape.

Baptiste [batist] *Prnm F* **1. être tranquille comme Baptiste** (*i*) to be as cool as a cucumber; to feel quite calm and collected (*ii*) (*enfant*) to be as quiet as a mouse **2.** (*cartes, esp belote*) **petit Baptiste,** trump nine.

se baquer [səbake] *vpr P* to have/to take a bath.

baquet [bakɛ] *nm* **1.** *P* stomach*/bread-basket; **en avoir dans le baquet,** to have guts **2.** *V* female genitals*/fruit-basket; **descendre au baquet,** to practise cunnilingus*/to go down on s.o.

barabille [barabij] *nf P* **mettre la barabille,** to stir up trouble/to stir it up.

baraka [baraka] *nm F* (good) luck.

baraque [barak] *nf* **1.** *F* (*a*) hole (of a place)/dump; **quelle baraque!** what a dump! (*b*) place/pad; **à la baraque,** at home/at my place **2.** *F* (*a*) **cela fera casser/crouler la baraque,** that'll bring the house down/that'll have 'em rolling in the aisles (*b*) **casser la baraque à qn,** to ruin s.o.'s plans **3.** *F* **toute la baraque** (*i*) the whole bag* of tricks/the whole bang shoot (*ii*) the whole damn lot of them.

baraqué [barake] *a P* **bien baraqué,** (*homme*) well-built/hefty/beefy; (*femme*) well-built; well-stacked.

barat(t)in [baratɛ̃] *nm F* patter/spiel/sales talk; smooth talk/sweet talk(ing); **faire du barat(t)in (à qn)** (*a*) to sweet talk (s.o.)/to chat (s.o.) up (*b*) to spin a yarn/to shoot a line; **avoir du baratin,** to be a smooth talker/to be a fast-talker.

barat(t)iner [baratine] *F* **I** *vtr* (*bonimenter; draguer*) to sweet talk (s.o.)/to chat (s.o.) up/to fast talk

II vi (a) to dish out the sales talk/ the patter/the spiel; to fast talk (b) to shoot a line/to spin a yarn.

barat(t)ineur, euse [baratinœr, -øz] n F glib talker/smooth talker/fast talker.

barbacque [barbak] nf P = barbaque.

barbant [barbɑ̃] a F boring/tedious/deadly dull; **ce qu'il est barbant!** what a bore!/he's a real drag!

barbaque [barbak] nf P **1.** (poor-quality) meat **2.** (human) skin/ flesh; (human) body. (Voir **marchand 1**)

barbe [barb] **I** a F = **barbant II** nf F **1. faire qch (au nez et) à la barbe de qn,** to do sth (right) under s.o.'s nose **2. faire la barbe,** to win at cards **3.** (chose ou pers) bore*; **quelle barbe!** what a bore!/what a nuisance!/what a drag!/what a pain! **c'était la barbe et les cheveux!** it was deadly boring!/it was a real drag!/it was the bitter end! **4. la barbe avec ...!** to hell with ...! **5. la barbe!** (i) shut up*!/shut your mouth!/give it a rest! (ii) damn it!/blast!/hell! **6. prendre une barbe,** to get drunk*/to get pissed.

barbeau [barbo] nm P pimp*/ ponce; **barbeau à la mie de pain,** small-time pimp*. (Voir **barbiflard**)

barbelouzes [barbəluz] nfpl barbed wire.

barber [barbe] **I** vtr F to bore* (s.o.) to tears; **barber tout le monde,** to bore everyone stiff **II** vpr **se barber** F to be bored* (stiff); **se barber à cent sous de l'heure,** to be bored to tears/to be bored rigid.

barbette [barbɛt] nf P **coucher à barbette,** to sleep (on a mattress) on the floor.

barbichonner [barbiʃɔne] vi P to win at cards.

barbifiant [barbifjɑ̃] a F boring/ draggy/dullsville.

barbifier [barbifje] **I** vtr O F **1.** to shave (s.o.) **2.** to bore (s.o.) **II** vpr **se barbifier** O F **1.** to (have a) shave **2.** to be bored*.

barbiflard [barbiflar] nm, **barbillon** [barbijɔ̃] nm P (a) young pimp* (b) small-time pimp*. (Voir **barbeau**)

barbiquet [barbikɛ] nm P **1.** = **barbiflard 2.** juvenile delinquent; (young) hooligan*.

barbiset [barbizɛ] nm P = **barbiflard.**

barbot [barbo] nm P pimp*.

barbotage [barbɔtaʒ] nm P stealing/petty thieving/scrounging/ pinching/pilfering.

barbote [barbɔt] nf P **1.** medical examination (of prostitute) **2.** frisking/body search (of prisoner in custody).

barboter [barbɔte] P **I** vtr **1.** to steal*/to swipe/to scrounge/to pinch/to nick (sth) **2.** to frisk (a prisoner) **II** vi to pick pockets.

barboteur, euse [barbɔtœr, -øz] n P (petty) thief*/pilferer/ scrounger; **c'est un barboteur,** he's got light fingers.

barbotier [barbɔtje] nm P prison officer who searches/frisks prisoners taken into custody.

barbotin [barbɔtɛ̃] nm P proceeds of a theft; loot/haul.

barbottage [barbɔtaʒ] nm P = **barbotage.**

barbotte [barbɔt] nf P = **barbote 1, 2.**

barbotter [barbɔte] vtr&i P = **barboter.**

barbotteur, euse [barbɔtœr, -øz] n P = **barboteur, euse.**

barbouille [barbuj] nf P **1. la barbouille,** painting (as an art or a hobby) **2. être dans la barbouille,**

to be in a fix*/to be in a mess/to be up the creek.

barbouillé [barbuje] *a F* **1.** avoir l'estomac barbouillé, to have an upset stomach; to feel queasy/funny **2.** avoir le cœur barbouillé/se sentir tout barbouillé (*i*) to feel sick (*ii*) to be squeamish.

barbouiller [barbuje] **I** *vtr F* **1.** barbouiller une affaire, to make a botch(-up) of sth/to botch sth up **2.** ça me barbouille le cœur, that turns my stomach (over)/that makes me feel sick **3.** to mess about with paints and things/to be a bit of an amateur artist **II** *vpr* se barbouiller *P* **1.** to make up (one's face) **2.** je m'en barbouille! I don't give a damn!/I couldn't give a monkey's!

barbouillette [barbujɛt] *nf V* faire barbouillette, to practise cunnilingus*.

barbouilleur, -euse [barbujœr, -ǿz] *n P* (*péj*) artist/painter.

barbouse [barbuz] *P* **I** *nf* beard **II** *nm ou f* (*a*) secret agent/undercover agent (*b*) member of the secret police.

barbouseux [barbuzǿ] *a P* (*homme*) bearded.

barbouze [barbuz] *nm&f P* = barbouse.

barbu [barby] *nm* **1.** *V* (*a*) female genitals*/pussy/beaver (*b*) pubic hair. (*Voir* descente 3) **2.** *pl F* (*cartes*) les barbus, (the) four kings.

barca! [barka] *int P* **1.** that's enough!/cut it out! **2.** nothing doing!*

barda [barda] *nm P* **1.** (*mil*) kit/pack **2.** things/belongings/gear/stuff **3.** (*i*) ten-franc note (*ii*) hundred-franc note (*iii*) thousand-franc note.

bardane [bardan] *nf P* bed-bug.

barde [bard] *nf F* à toute barde, at full speed/at full tilt/flat out.

barder [barde] *vi P* to take a turn

for the worse; ça barde! things are warming/hotting up! ça va barder! watch out (for trouble)!/things are going to get rough!/there's trouble brewing!/there'll be some aggro! ça va barder pour toi! you're in for it!/you'll cop it! c'est là que ça a commencé à barder! and then the fun started! ça a dû barder! I bet the fur was flying! il faut que ça barde! jump to it!/look lively!/make it snappy! (*Voir* matricule 2)

barjo(t) [barʒo] *P* (*verlan de* jobard) **I** *a.* **1.** gullible/easily taken in **2.** mad*/bonkers; t'es pas barjo(t)? have you lost your marbles? **II** *nm* **1.** mug/sucker **2.** fool*/nut/nutter.

barlu [barly] *nm P* (*régional*) rape (of a woman) by several men in succession/group rape/gang bang. (*Voir* rodéo)

barnum [barnɔm] *nm P* **1.** uproar/din/racket **2.** (*enfants*) montrer tout son barnum, to show one's 'private property'/= to play mummies and daddies **3.** big top (at circus).

baron [barɔ̃] *nm P* **1.** accomplice/confederate/decoy; faire le baron, to act as decoy **2.** prostitute's protector; pimp*; (sugar)daddy.

baronne [barɔn] *nf P* la baronne, the wife*/the missis/the old lady.

baronner [barɔne] *vi P* to act as an accomplice/a confederate/a decoy.

baroud [barud] *nm P* **1.** (*esp mil*) fight(ing); baroud d'honneur, face-saving last stand/last ditch attempt **2.** uproar*/bedlam/(hell of a) racket.

barouder [barude] *vi P* (*esp mil*) to fight.

baroudeur [barudœr] *nm P* fighter/brawler.

barouf(fe) [baruf] *nm,* **baroufle** [barufl] *nm P* **1.** uproar*/din/racket; un barouf du diable, a hell of a row **2.** faire du

barouf, to kick up a fuss/to cause a rumpus/to make a stink.

barque [bark] *nf F* **mener qn en barque,** to hoax* s.o./to lead s.o. up the garden path.

barrabille [barabij] *nf P* = **barabille.**

barraqué [barake] *a P* = **baraqué.**

barre [bar] *nf F* **1.** avoir le coup de barre, to be exhausted*/to be fit to drop **2.** c'est le coup de barre, it's daylight robbery **3.** manger à la barre fixe, to eat (next to) nothing. **4.** à toute barre, at top speed/at full tilt **5.** avoir barre/ avoir barres sur qn, to have an advantage over s.o./to be one up on s.o./to have the edge on s.o. **6.** homme de barre, staunch friend; trustworthy associate; **c'est un homme de barre,** he's straight up **7.** se rincer les barres, to (have a) drink* **8.** avoir la barre, to make a hit (with s.o. of the opposite sex)/ to hit it off with s.o.

barreau, *pl* **-eaux** [baro] *nm P* **barreau de chaise,** (large) cigar.

se barrer [səbare] *vpr P* to beat it/to run away*/to scram/to clear off; **je me barre,** I'm making myself scarce.

bas [ba] *nm F* **bas de laine,** savings; **avoir un bas de laine bien garni,** to have a nice little nest-egg (stashed away).

basane [bazan] *nf* **1.** *O F* (*mil*) être dans la basane, to be in the cavalry **2.** *P* (human) skin/hide; **tanner la basane à qn,** to tan s.o.'s hide **3.** *P* tailler une basane à qn, to make an obscene gesture of contempt/ = to put two fingers up at s.o.

bascule [baskyl] *nf P* **la bascule (à Charlot),** the guillotine. (*Voir* **botte II 1; Charlot 1**)

basculer [baskyle] *vtr P* **basculer un godet,** to knock back a drink.

bas-de-plafond [badəplafɔ̃] *nm inv F* fool*/prize idiot/thickhead.

basduc [badyk] *nm,* **bas-du-cul** [badyky] **I** *nm inv P* under-sized* person/short-arse **II** *a P* (*aut*) extra-low/underslung (chassis, etc).

baskets [baskɛt] *nfpl* **1.** *F* sneakers/basketball boots/baseball boots **2.** *P* à l'aise dans ses baskets, relaxed/cool (*esp* when in a tight spot) **3.** *P* lâcher les baskets à qn, to leave s.o. alone; **lâche-moi les baskets!** lay off!/get lost!*

basoche [bazɔʃ] *nf F* (*péj*) the legal fraternity; **termes de basoche,** legal jargon.

basset [base, base] *nm A P* revolver*/gat.

bassin [basɛ̃] **I** *nm P* **1.** cracher au/dans le bassin = cracher au bassinet (**bassinet**) **2.** (*pers*) bore*/pain in the neck **II** *a P* (*pers*) boring; **ce qu'il est bassin!** what a bore*/what a pain (he is)!

bassinant [basinɑ̃] *a P* **1.** boring **2.** persistent/pestering.

bassiner [basine] *vtr P* **1.** to bore* (s.o.) **2.** to pester/to badger (s.o.).

bassinet [basinɛ] *nm P* **cracher au/dans le bassinet** (*i*) to pay* up/ to cough up/to fork out (*ii*) to con-fess*/to come clean/to blow the gaff.

bassinoire [basinwar] *nf* **1.** *F* (*chose ou pers*) (*a*) bore* (*b*) pest/ nuisance **2.** *P* large (old-fashioned) watch.

basta! [basta] *excl P* that's enough (of that)!/cut it out!/give it a rest!

Bastaga, la [labastaga], **Bastoche, la** [labastɔʃ] *Prn P* the Bastille (district) (in Paris).

baston [bastɔ̃] *nm P* fight*/scuffle/ brawl/free-for-all/punch-up.

bastonner (se) [səbastɔne] *vi & pr P* to fight/to brawl/to have a punch-up.

bastos [bastɔs] *nf P* bullet/slug.

bastringue [bastrɛ̃g] *nm P* **1.** (*a*) seedy dance-hall/sleasy joint/dive/hole (*b*) = pub **2.** (*a*) juke-box (*b*) noisy dance band **3.** uproar*/din/racket/shindy **4.** paraphernalia/junk; **tout le bastringue,** the whole bag* of tricks/the (whole) works.

bastringuer [bastrɛ̃ge] *vi O P* **1.** to frequent second-rate/seedy dance-halls **2.** to make a din/a racket/a hell of a noise.

bataclan [bataklɑ̃] *nm F* **1.** paraphernalia/belongings/junk/gear/stuff **2. tout le bataclan,** the whole lot/the whole works/the whole shooting-match; ... **et tout le bataclan,** ... and all the rest of it.

bataillon [batajɔ̃] *nm F* **inconnu au bataillon,** never heard of him.

bâtard [bɑtar] *a F* **c'est un peu bâtard, ton truc,** your idea's a bit cockeyed.

bat' d'Af [batdaf] *nm P* **1.** (= *bataillon d'Afrique*) disciplinary batallion (formerly stationed in North Africa) **2.** (= *bataillon-naire*) young criminal serving in a *bataillon d'Afrique*.

bateau [bato] **I** *nm F* **1. monter un bateau à qn,** to hoax* s.o./to have s.o. on/to take s.o. in/to play a practical joke on s.o. **2. mener/emmener qn en bateau,** to con s.o.; **se laisser mener en bateau,** to allow oneself to be taken in/played for a sucker **3. du même bateau,** of the same kidney/tarred with the same brush; **des gens du même bateau,** birds of a feather **4. être du dernier bateau,** to be bang up to date **5. arriver en trois/en quatre bateaux,** to arrive in style/with a great flourish **6.** *pl* **bateaux** (*a*) big feet* (*b*) big boots*/clodhoppers **II** *a inv P* banal/trite; **un sujet bateau,** a hackneyed subject/the same old thing.

bateaux-mouches [batomuʃ] *nmpl F* = **bateau 6** (*a*), (*b*).

bath [bat] *F* **I** *a* first-rate/first-class/super/classy; **une bath gonzesse,** a peach of a girl*/a bit of all right; **un bath pantalon,** a snazzy pair of trousers; **t'es bath,** you're a good sort/a great guy; you're straight up/you're all right; **huit jours de congé, c'est bien bath,** a week's leave – that can't be bad; **bath aux pommes,** tip-top/super-duper. (*Voir* **pieu 1**) **II** *nm* **c'est du bath,** it's the real thing; it's the genuine article.

bath(e)ment [batmɑ̃] *adv F* fabulously/splendidly/terrifically.

bathouse [batuz] *a P* = **bath I.**

batifolage [batifɔlaʒ] *nm F* **1.** playing around/larking about **2.** flirting; necking/smooching.

batifoler [batifɔle] *vi F* **1.** to play around/to lark about **2.** to flirt; to neck/to smooch.

batifoleur, euse [batifɔlœr, -øz] *n F* **1.** s.o. who enjoys larking about/who enjoys having a bit of a lark **2.** flirt.

batifouiller [batifuje] *vi P* to get muddled; to be all at sixes and sevens; to be all at sea.

bâtiment [bɑtimɑ̃] *nm F* **il est du bâtiment** (*i*) he's in the trade/he's in the same line (of business) (*ii*) he knows all the tricks of the trade (*iii*) he's one of us/he's one of the lads.

bat-la-dèche [baladɛʃ] *nm inv P* down-and-out.

bâton [bɑtɔ̃] **I** *nm* **1.** *F* **tours de bâton,** illicit gains/graft/pickings; **savoir le tour du bâton,** to know how to spirit things away (dishonestly) **2.** *F* **vie de bâton de chaise,** life of pleasure/fast life; **mener une vie de bâton de chaise,** to live it up/to have a wild time/to have a ball **3.** *P* **un bâton merdeux,** a contemptible and untrustworthy individual; a bastard*/a shit **4.** *F* **être sous le bâton** = **être sous le bambou** (**bambou 4**) **5.** *F* **sauter**

le bâton, to suffer an ordeal/to go through it **6.** *pl P* **bâtons,** legs*; **mettre les bâtons,** to run away*/to beat it/to scarper **7.** *V* **avoir le bâton,** to have an erection*/a hard-on. (*Voir* **jus 17; merde 10; roue 1**) **II** *nm P* (*mil*) (= *bataillon*) battalion.

bâtonné [batɔne] *a P* être bâtoné = être sous le bambou (**bambou 4**).

batousard [batuzar] *nm P* = **batouseur.**

batouse [batuz] *nf P* textiles; **faire la batouse** (*i*) to sell textiles door to door *or* in open-air markets; to work the markets in textiles (*ii*) to cheat on the price of textiles.

batouseur [batuzœr] *nm,* **batouzard** [batuzar] *nm,* **batouzeur** [batuzœr] *nm P* door-to-door salesman in textiles.

battage [bataʒ] *nm F* publicity; ballyhoo; hard sell; **faire du battage autour d'un livre,** to plug/to push a book; to give a book the hard sell.

battant [batã] *nm P* **1.** heart/ticker **2.** tongue/clapper **3.** dynamic/go-ahead individual; **avoir du battant,** to have plenty of drive/of (get-up-and-)go **4.** stomach*; **se remplir le battant,** to have a blow-out/a tuck-in **5.** money put by for a rainy day; nest-egg **6.** *pl* **battants,** hours.

battante [batãt] *nf P* clock; watch; ticker/tick-tock.

batterie [batri] *nf F* **batterie de cuisine** (*i*) percussion instruments; percussion band (*ii*) array of medals and ribbons (on uniform)/gongs/chest hardware/fruit salad.

batteur [batœr] *nm F* **1.** (*a*) liar (*b*) hypocrite **2. batteur (de pavé),** idler/loafer.

batteuse [batøz] *nf P* car battery.

battoir [batwar] *nm* **1.** *F* **battoir à œufs,** helicopter*/chopper **2.** *pl P*

battoirs, large/clumsy hands*; hams.

battre [batr] *vtr V* **s'en battre une,** to masturbate*/to beat the dummy/to flog the dummy/to beat the meat/to flog the bishop. (*Voir* **campagne 2; Niort**)

bauche [boʃ] *nf P* **1.** diamond/sparkler **2.** *pl* **bauches,** playing cards; **jeu de trois bauches,** three-card trick.

bavacher [bavaʃe] *vi F* = **bavasser 1.**

bavacheur, euse [bavaʃœr, -øz] *P* **I** *a* talkative **II** *n* talkative* person/windbag/gasbag.

bavard [bavar] *nm P* **1.** defending counsel/lawyer/mouthpiece **2.** (*mil*) service record **3.** buttocks*/bottom/behind/bum.

bavarde [bavard] *nf P* **1.** tongue/clapper **2.** mouth* **3.** letter/note/line.

bavasser [bavase] *vi F* **1.** (*a*) to talk without thinking/to go rabbiting on/to natter/to gas; **bavasser comme un perroquet,** to chatter away like a parrot/to rattle on (nineteen to the dozen) (*b*) to talk nonsense*/to talk a lot of hot air **2.** to gossip about (s.o.)/to sling mud at (s.o.).

bave [bav] *nf P* **avoir les baves,** to be speechless (with admiration)/to be knocked out (by sth/s.o.)/to be drooling over s.o./sth.

baveau, elle [bavo, -ɛl] *a P* (*javanais de* **beau, belle**) beautiful/good-looking.

baver [bave] **I** *vi* **1.** *F* to talk drivel/rubbish; **qu'est-ce que tu baves?** what on earth are you going on about? **2.** *F* (**en) baver,** to be furious/fuming; **faire baver qn** (*i*) to make s.o. furious/to get s.o. all steamed up (*ii*) to make s.o. jealous/green with envy (about sth) **3.** *F* **en baver** (*i*) to have a rough time of it (*ii*) to work* hard/to slave away; **j'en ai bavé,** it was (sheer)

bavette   33   **bébête**

hell/agony; **en faire baver à qn,** to put s.o. through it/to give s.o. a hard time/to make s.o. sweat (blood) **4.** *P* **baver dans les fils de fer,** to exaggerate* **II** *vtr P* **en baver des ronds de chapeau/des ronds de citron,** to be flabbergasted/to be knocked sideways. (*Voir* **burnes; clignotants; rouleau 2; roustons**)

bavette [bavɛt] *nf F* **tailler une bavette,** to have a (little) chat* with s.o./to have a natter.

baveuse [bavøz] *nf* **1.** *P* tongue/clapper **2.** *V* penis*.

baveux [bavø] *nm* **1.** *P* talkative* person/gasbag **2.** *P* lawyer/brief **3.** *P* soap **4.** *P* newspaper/rag **5.** *V* female genitals*.

bavocher [bavɔʃe] *vi P* to talk drivel.

bavocheur [bavɔʃœr], **bavocheux** [bavɔʃø] *nm P* = **bavard 1.**

bavour [bavur] *a P* (*pers*) good-looking/attractive.

bavure [bavyr] *nf F* **1.** regrettable error/unfortunate mistake (*esp* made by the police) **2. sans bavure(s)/net et sans bavure(s)** (*i*) *a* clear/precise; impeccable/flawless (*ii*) *adv* clearly/precisely; impeccably.

baz [baz] *nm P* school; **le Baz Grand,** the Louis-le-Grand *lycée*, in Paris.

bazar [bazar] *nm* **1.** *P* (= **baz**) **le Bazar,** the Saint-Cyr military school **2.** *F* **tout le bazar** (*i*) everything/the whole works/the whole bag* of tricks; **vous allez fusiller tout le bazar,** you're going to mess up the whole show/thing (*ii*) everyone/the whole lot of them **3.** *P* untidy flat, room, etc; hole (of a place)/dump; **quel bazar!** what a mess!/what a shambles! **4.** *P* belongings/things/gear/stuff/junk; **il a tout son bazar dans sa valoche,** he's got all his

clobber stuffed in his suitcase **5.** *P* **l'avoir dans le bazar,** to be badly let down/to get a raw deal **6.** *V* (*a*) female genitals*/fanny (*b*) pubic hair.

bazarder [bazarde] *vtr P* **1.** to sell (sth) (cheaply); to flog; **j'ai bazardé ma bagnole,** I've got rid of/I've flogged my car **2.** to give (s.o.) the sack/to give (s.o.) the push **3.** to denounce* (s.o.)/to sell out on (s.o.)/to shop (s.o.).

baze [baz] *nm P* = **baz.**

bcbg [besebeʒe] *abbr F* = **bon-chic-bon-genre.**

BD [bede] *nf F* (*abbr de bande(s) dessinée(s)*) comic strip/comic(s)/cartoon(s)/*NAm* funny/*NAm* funnies; **c'est un fana de BD,** he's nuts about comics. (*Voir* **bédé**)

beau, *pl* **beaux** [bo] *a* **1.** *P* **être beau,** to be in a fix*/a mess/a pickle; **nous voilà beaux!** here's a fine mess! (*Voir* **drap**) **2.** (*intensif*) (*a*) *F* **il se démène comme un beau diable,** he's like a cat on hot bricks/on a hot tin roof (*b*) *P* **un beau salaud,** a right bastard*/a real sod. (*Voir* **belle; jeu**)

beau-dab(e) [bodab] *nm P* father-in-law. (*Voir* **dab(e)**)

beauf, beauffe [bof] *nm P* (= *beau-frère*) brother-in-law.

beaujol [boʒɔl] *nm,* **beaujolpif** [boʒɔlpif] *nm P* Beaujolais (wine).

beauté [bote] *nf F* **1. se (re)faire une beauté,** to make up (one's face)/to do one's face/to powder one's nose **2. finir en beauté,** to end in a blaze of glory.

beaux-dab(e)s [bodab] *nmpl P* parents-in-law. (*Voir* **dab(e)s**)

beaux-vieux [bovjø] *nmpl P* parents-in-law.

bébête [bebɛt] *a F* silly/babyish/childish; **des rires bébêtes,** giggling/silly giggles; **je ne suis pas si bébête!** I'm not such a fool*.

bec [bɛk] *nm* **1.** *P* mouth*/gob/ kisser/cakehole; **un fin bec,** gourmet; **avoir bon bec/être fort en bec,** to have the gift of the gab; **boucler/clore/clouer/river le bec à qn,** to reduce s.o. to silence/to shut s.o. up*; **ça lui clouera le bec,** that'll settle his hash; **claquer du bec,** to be hungry/starving/ravenous; **donner du bec,** to kiss; **faire un bec à qn,** to give s.o. a peck on the cheek; **se refaire le bec,** to have a good meal; **rincer le bec à qn,** to stand s.o. a drink; **se rincer le bec,** to have a drink*/to wet one's whistle; **tenir son bec,** to keep quiet/to keep one's trap shut; **ferme ton bec!** shut up!*/shut your gob!/put a sock in it! **2.** *P* nose*/beak; **ils se sont rencontrés bec à bec,** they met face to face **3.** *F* (*a*) **laisser qn le bec dans l'eau,** to leave s.o. in the lurch/to ditch s.o./to run out on s.o. (*i*) **rester le bec dans l'eau** (*i*) to be left stranded/to be left in the lurch/to be left high and dry/to be stood up (*ii*) to be stuck for a reply/to be tongue-tied (*c*) **tenir qn le bec dans l'eau,** to keep s.o. in suspense/to keep s.o. on a string **4.** *F* **donner un coup de bec à qn,** to have a dig/a poke at s.o. **5.** *F* **faire le bec à qn,** to prime s.o. (with what he should say) **6.** *F* **se prendre de bec avec qn/avoir une prise de bec avec qn,** to have a (violent) quarrel* with s.o./to have an argy-bargy with s.o./to have a slanging match with s.o. **7.** *F* **tomber sur un bec (de gaz),** to come up against a snag; to come a cropper*. (*Voir* **ch(e)linguer**; **pisser 13; schlinguer; vesser**)

béca [beka] *nm P* bacillus/germ.

bécamel [bekamɛl] *nm P* (*WWII*) (= *bec à mélasse*) grocer.

bécane [bekan] *nf* **1.** *F* (*a*) bicycle/bike (*b*) motorcycle/motorbike **2.** *F* locomotive/engine **3.** *F* (*a*) (old-fashioned) typewriter (*b*) printing press **4.** *P* guillotine.

bécasse [bekas] *nf F* silly girl/woman.

bécassine [bekasin] *nf F* silly young girl/(silly) goose.

because [bikoz] *P* **I** *prep* because of/on account of; **je reste ici because le mauvais temps,** I'm staying here because of the bad weather; **pourquoi ne viens-tu pas?** – Because. – Because quoi? – Because d'à cause, why aren't you coming? – Because. – Because what? – Because I'm not **II** *conj* **because que,** because/'cause/cos; **faut pas faire ça because que ça me chatouillerait,** you mustn't do that (because) it tickles.

bec-de-cane [bɛkdəkan] *nm P* **travailler au bec-de-cane,** to burgle/ *NAm* to burglarize.

bêchage [bɛʃaʒ] *nm F* **1.** knocking/running down (of s.o.) **2.** showing off/posing.

béchamel(le) [beʃamɛl] *F* **I** *nf* **être dans la béchamel(le),** to be in a fix*/in a jam **II** *nm* **être béchamel,** to be pretentious/to show off*/to pose.

bêche [bɛʃ] *nf F* **faire de la bêche sur qn,** to run s.o. down/to criticize s.o.*/to pick s.o. to pieces; to look down one's nose at s.o.

bêcher [beʃe] *vtr F* **1.** to criticize* (s.o.)/to run (s.o.) down/to knock (s.o.)/to get at s.o. **2.** to show off*.

bêcheur, euse [beʃœr, -øz] **I** *n F* **1.** (*a*) supercilious person/toffee-nosed person/stuck-up person/snob/toffee-nose (*b*) show-off*/poser **2.** hard worker/slogger/plodder **3.** backbiter/carping critic **4.** (l'avocat) **bêcheur** = the Public Prosecutor/*NAm* the District Attorney (DA) **II** *a F* **1.** disparaging/carping/critical **2.** supercilious/snobbish/stuck-up/toffee-nosed.

béchigne [beʃiɲ] *nf P* (*rugby*) **la béchigne,** the ball.

bécif [besif] *adv P* **1.** under coercion/under compulsion/forced **2.** quickly and forcibly.

bécot [beko] *nm F* little kiss; peck; **gros bécot,** big kiss/smacker; **coquer un bécot à qn,** to give s.o. a kiss.

bécotage [bekɔtaʒ] *nm F* kissing/necking/smooching.

bécoter [bekɔte] **I** *vtr F* to give (s.o.) a kiss/a peck **II** *vpr* **se bécoter** *F* to neck/to smooch; **ils étaient en train de se bécoter,** they were snogging away.

becquetance, bectance [bɛktɑ̃s] *nf P* food*/grub/nosh/chow.

becqueter, becter [bɛkte] *vi P* **1.** to eat*/to nosh (away). (*Voir* **clarinette 3; fayot 2**) **2. en becqueter,** to be a police informer*/a grass; to grass (on s.o.)/to shop (s.o.) (*Voir* **lapin 5**)

bedaine [bədɛn] *nf F* (*a*) stomach*/belly (*b*) **(grosse) bedaine,** paunch/pot-belly/beer-belly/(beer-)gut.

bédé [bede] *nf F* (= *bande(s) dessinée(s)*) = **BD.**

bédi [bedi] *nm P* gendarme.

bedon [bədɔ̃] *nm F* (= **bedaine**) **un gros bedon,** a big fat man.

bedonnant [bədɔnɑ̃] *a F* paunchy/pot-bellied/beer-bellied.

bedonner [bədɔne] *vi F* to develop a paunch/to grow paunchy/to get a (beer-) gut.

bédouin [bedwɛ̃] *nm F* **il n'y avait pas un bédouin,** there wasn't a soul (about).

bégonias [begɔnja] *nmpl P* **1. charrier dans les bégonias,** to exaggerate*/to lay it on thick/to shoot a line **2. piétiner les bégonias** (*i*) to put one's foot in it/to drop a clanger (*ii*) to barge in (where you're not wanted) **3.** legs*.

béguin [begɛ̃] *nm F* (*a*) sweetheart/

boyfriend/girlfriend; heart-throb; **c'est mon béguin,** I've got a crush on him/her (*b*) **avoir le béguin pour qn/avoir qn au béguin,** to be infatuated* with s.o./to have a thing on s.o./to be sweet on s.o./to be crazy about s.o.

béguinage [beginaʒ] *nm F* excessive piety/excessive devotion.

béguine [begin] *nf F* (*péj*) very devout woman.

béguineuse [beginøz] *nf P* prostitute*.

béhème [beɛm] *nf F* BMW (*RTM*) motorbike.

beigne [bɛɲ] *nf P* blow*/clout/slap; **donner/filer/flanquer une beigne à qn,** to hit s.o./to clout s.o.; to beat s.o. up*.

beigner [beɲe] *vtr P* to hit s.o./to clout s.o.

beignet [beɲɛ] *nm P* face*; **claquer/tarter le beignet à qn,** to sock s.o. on the jaw.

bêlant [bɛlɑ̃] *nm P* sheep.

bêler [bɛle] *vtr P* (*péj*) to sing (badly).

Belgico [bɛlʒiko] *nm P* Belgian.

belle [bɛl] *a&n* **1.** *P* **(se) faire la belle,** to escape from prison/to break out of prison/to go over the wall; **il s'est fait la belle,** he did a bunk/he bust out (of prison) **2.** *P* (*gangsters, etc*) **mener/emmener qn en belle,** to kill*/to bump off/to do away with/to knock off (an accomplice, etc) **3.** *F* **l'avoir belle,** to find it easy going **4.** *F* **se la faire belle** (*i*) to have a cushy time/to take it easy (*ii*) to go on the spree/to have a good time **5.** *F* **elle est belle femme,** she's a big/fat woman; she's a large lady **6.** *F* (= *à la belle étoile*) **coucher à la belle,** to sleep in the open/to sleep rough **7.** *F* **en faire voir de belles à qn,** to put s.o. through the mill/to put s.o. through it/to give s.o. a hard time (of it) **8.** *F* **il en a fait**

de belles! he's been up to some pretty funny things! **en conter/en dire de belles,** to say outrageous things; **j'en ai entendu de belles sur ton compte!** I've been hearing some pretty funny things about you! **tu en as fait une belle!** you've put your foot right in it!/you've dropped a real clanger there!/you've done it now! **en voici une belle!** here's a fine how-do-you-do!/we're in a right (old) mess now! (*Voir* **beau**; **décarrer**)

belle-dabesse [bɛldabɛs] *nf*, **belle-doche** [bɛldɔʃ] *nf P* mother-in-law. (*Voir* **dabesse 1**) (*pl* **belle-dabesses, -doches**)

belle-de-nuit [bɛldənɥi] *nf F* prostitute*. (*pl* **belles-de-nuit**)

belle-frangine [bɛlfrãʒin] *nf P* sister-in-law. (*pl* **belles-frangines**)

belle-mère [bɛlmɛr] *nf F* **1. tu cherches une belle-mère?** your slip's showing/Charley's dead/Queen Anne's dead/it's snowing down south **2.** BMW (*RTM*) motorbike.

bellot, -otte [bɛlo, -ɔt] *O F* I *a* pretty/dainty/cute II *n* **mon bellot/ma bellotte,** my little cherub.

ben [bɛ̃] *adv P* (= *bien*) **eh ben!** well!/why! **ben oui!** why, yes! **ben quoi?** so what?

bénard [benar] *nm P* (men's) trousers/*esp NAm* pants.

bénarès [benarɛs] *nm O P* opium*.

bénédiction [benediksjɔ̃] *nf F* **il pleut que c'est une bénédiction!** it's raining cats and dogs!/it's bucketing down!

bénéf [benɛf] *nm P* profit/gain; **c'est tout bénéf,** it's all profit; **petits bénéfs,** perks.

Ben Hur [bɛnyr] *Prn F* **t'as vu ça où? dans Ben Hur en couleurs?** what do you think you're doing?

béni-bouffe-tout, béni-bouftou(t) [benibuftu] *nm inv P* glutton*/hog/greedyguts.

béni-coco [benikoko] *nm inv P* fool*/idiot/clot/nit/twit.

béni-mouff-mouff [benimufmuf] *nm inv P* Parisian.

béni-oui-oui [beniwiwi] *nm inv F* yes-man/rubber stamp.

bénissage [benisaʒ] *nm F* blarney/soft soap.

bénisseur, -euse [benisœr, -øz] *a&n F* glib (individual); oily/greasy/slippery (person); (s.o.) who pays empty compliments.

bénit [beni] *a F* **1. c'est pain bénit,** it serves him/her/you/them right **2. eau bénite de cour,** fair promises/empty words.

bénitier [benitje] *nm V* female genitals*; **cracher dans le bénitier,** to have sex*.

benne [bɛn] *nm P* = **bénard**.

bénouse, bénouze [benuz] *nm P* **1.** = **bénard 2.** (men's or women's) briefs.

benzine [bɛ̃zin] *nf F* petrol/*NAm* gas.

béqueter [bekte] *vi P* = **becqueter**.

béquille [bekij] *nf* **1.** *F* **vieille béquille,** silly old fool; driveller **2.** *pl P* **béquilles,** legs*/stumps **3.** *V* penis*/middle leg/third leg.

berceau [bɛrso] *nm F* **les prendre au berceau** (*i*) to like (very) young boys/girls; to cradle snatch/to go in for cradle-snatching (*ii*) to have a young(er) lover; **il/elle les prend au berceau,** he's/she's a cradle snatcher.

berdouillette [bɛrdujɛt] *nf V* penis*.

bérésina [berezina] *nf P* calamity/disaster/catastrophe.

berge [bɛrʒ] *nf P* (*usu pl*) year; **tirer dix berges à l'ombre,** to do a ten-year stretch; **avoir trente berges,** to be thirty (years old).

bergère [bɛrʒer] *nf* **1.** *F* last card in the pack **2.** *P* (*a*) woman* (*b*)

béton

girl* **3.** *P* **ma bergère,** my wife*/
my old lady/my old woman.
berlanche [bɛrlɑ̃ʃ] *nf P* blanket.
berlingot [bɛrlɛ̃go] *nm* **1.** *F* (old)
banger/jalopy/old crock **2.** *P*
pimple/boil/*NAm* zit **3.** *V* virgin-
ity/maidenhead/cherry **4.** *V* clitoris; **allonger le berlingot,** to practise
cunnilingus*.
berlingue [bɛrlɛ̃g] *nm* =
berlingot 2, 3, 4.
berloque [bɛrlɔk] *nf* **1.** *F* **battre
la berloque = battre la breloque
(breloque) 2.** *V* penis*.
berlue [bɛrly] *nf* **1.** *F* illusion;
avoir la berlue, to have hallucina-
tions/to be deluded/to be seeing
things; **j'ai cru avoir la berlue en le
voyant revenir,** I thought my eyes
were deceiving me when I saw him
returning; **se faire des berlues,** to
labour under a delusion/to kid oneself **2.** *P* blanket **3.** *P* front (for
some illegal activity); cover-up.
se berlurer [səbɛrlyre] *vpr F* to
delude oneself/to kid oneself/to
imagine things.
bernard [bɛrnar] *nm P* buttocks*/
backside/behind/bum/*NAm* butt.
bernicles [bɛrnikl] *nfpl O F* spec-
tacles/specs.
bernique! [bɛrnik] *excl F* nothing
doing!*/not a chance!/no dice!
bersingue [bɛrzɛ̃g] *nm P* = **berzingue.**
Bertha [bɛrta] *Prnf* **la grosse Bertha**
(*a*) *F* Big Bertha (the German
heavy gun that shelled Paris in
WWI) (*b*) (*péj*) a fat woman*.
berzingue [bɛrzɛ̃g] *nm P* **à tout
berzingue,** at top speed/at full tilt;
donner à tout berzingue, to go flat
out.
bésef(f) [bezɛf] *adv P* much/a lot/
many; **y en a pas bésef,** there's not
much of it.
bésiclard [beziklar] *nm F* man/
boy wearing glasses; four-eyes.

besicles [bəzikl] *nfpl F* spectacles/
specs.
besogner [bəzɔɲe] *vi P* (*a*) (*pour
un homme*) to have sex* (*b*) (*en
parlant d'un homme qui masturbe
une femme*) to finger fuck.
besoins [bəzwɛ̃] *nmpl F* (*a*) **faire
ses besoins,** to defecate* (*b*) **faire
ses petits besoins,** to urinate*/to
spend a penny (*c*) (*chien, chat, etc*)
faire ses besoins, to do its business.
bessif [besif] *adv P* = **bécif.**
bêta, -asse [beta, -ɑs] *F* **I** *a* stupid*/dim/gormless; **elle est jolie
mais bêtasse,** she's pretty but clueless **II** *n* fool*/dimwit/dope; **gros
bêta,** you silly twit!/you big stiff!
c'était pour te taquiner, gros bêta! I
was only teasing, stupid!
bête [bɛt] **I** *nf* **1.** *F* (*pers*) **une
bonne bête,** a good sort; **une
mauvaise bête,** a spiteful character
2. *F* **chercher la petite bête,** to be
over-critical/to pick holes/to keep
finding fault **3.** *F* **bête à bon Dieu**
(*i*) ladybird (*ii*) harmless individual/
simple soul **4.** *F* **faire la bête** (*i*) to
act/to behave like a fool* (*ii*) to
pretend to be stupid **5.** *P* **faire la
bête à deux dos,** to have sex*/to
hump. (*Voir* **poli 9**; **tour I 5**) **II** *a*
**1. bête à manger du foin/bête à
pleurer/bête comme un âne/bête
comme une oie/bête comme ses
pieds,** very stupid*/thick (as two
short planks) **2. bête comme
chou/comme tout,** very easy*/dead
easy*/simple as pie; **c'est bête
comme chou,** I could do it standing
on my head **3. pas si bête!** (*i*) I'm
not such a fool* (as all that)! (*ii*)
not likely!/not if I can help it!/no
chance! **4. ses bêtes d'idées,** his
daft/silly ideas; **ce bête de voyage,**
that stupid journey. (*Voir* **chou 10**;
pleurer 2)
béton [betɔ̃] **I** *nm F* **faire du béton**
(*i*) to become established (in a
place, etc) (*ii*) (*football*) to pack the
defence/to play defensively **II** *vi P*
(*verlan de tomber*) **laisse**

béton! lay off!/drop it!/give it a rest!

betterave [bɛtrav] *nf* P **1.** bottle of red wine **2.** dupe/mug/sucker.

beuglant [bøglɑ̃] *nm* P seedy/sleazy music-hall, night-club, etc; dive/dump.

beuglante [bøglɑ̃t] *nf* P (pop) song.

beugler [bøgle] P **I** *vi* to yell/to holler **II** *vtr* to sing loudly and badly.

beurre [bœr] *nm* **1.** *F* **comme dans du beurre,** with the greatest of ease; **c'est rentré comme dans du beurre,** it went in with no trouble at all **2.** *F* **c'est du beurre!/c'est un (vrai) beurre!** it's very easy* (to do)!/it's dead simple!/it's a cinch! **3.** *F* money*; profit*; **y aller de son beurre,** to spend (one's money) freely/to throw one's money about; **faire son beurre,** to make stacks of money*/to make one's pile/to make a packet/to feather one's nest **4.** *F* **ça fait mon beurre,** that suits me down to the ground **5.** *F* **ça mettra du beurre dans les épinards,** that'll make life (a bit) more comfortable (for me)/that'll make life easier (for me) **6.** *F* **au prix où est le beurre,** the way things are going these days; with the cost of living today **7.** *F* **compter pour du beurre,** to count for nothing **8.** *F* **promettre plus de beurre que de pain,** to make exaggerated promises **9.** *P* **pas plus de ... que de beurre en broche/que de beurre en branche/que de beurre dans la cuisine/que de beurre au cul/que de beurre aux fesses,** nothing at all/damn all/sweet FA in the way of ... **10.** *F* **jouer pour du beurre,** to play for nothing/for love **11.** *V* **battre le beurre,** to have sex*. (*Voir* **accommoder** 3; **assiette** 2; **baigner** 1; **bique I** 1 (*b*); **œil; pédaler** 2)

beurré [bœre] *a* P drunk*/smashed/plastered/canned; **beurré**

comme un coing/comme une huître, to be dead drunk*/to be pissed as a newt.

beurrée [bœre] *nf* P **ramasser/en avoir une beurrée,** to be dead drunk*; **il a pris une sacrée beurrée,** he's had a skinful.

se beurrer [səbœre] *vpr* **1.** *F* to make one's pile/to make a packet/to feather one's nest. (*Voir* **beurre** 3) **2.** *P* to get drunk*/canned/pissed.

beuverie [bøvri] *nf* F drinking bout/drinking session/binge.

bézef(f) [bezɛf] *adv* P = **bésef(f).**

bi [bi] *nm* F **1.** = **bise 2.** O (= *bicyclette*) **(grand) bi,** penny-farthing.

bibard, bibart [bibar] *nm* P **1.** old soak/old boozer/old wino **2.** old fog(e)y*/old fuddy-duddy.

bibelot [biblo] *nm* P **1.** skeleton key **2.** *pl* testicles*.

biber [bibe] *vtr* F to cheat*/to swindle* (s.o.).

biberon, onne [bibrɔ̃, -ɔn] F **I** *a* tippling/boozing **II** *n* **1.** drunkard*/heavy drinker/wino/alky/boozer/soak **2.** bottle **III** *nm* F **je ne les prends pas au biberon,** I'm not a baby-snatcher/I don't go in for cradle-snatching. (*Voir* **berceau**)

biberonner [bibrɔne] *vi* F to drink*/to tipple/to booze/to go on the booze/to hit the bottle.

bibi [bibi] *nm* **1.** *F* (*à un enfant*) **fais bibi à pépère!** give daddy a kiss! **2.** *F* (woman's) hat **3.** *P* **un simple bibi,** a private (soldier) **4.** *P* I/me/myself/yours truly; **pour bibi ça!** that's mine!/bags I (that)! **pas pour bibi!** not for me! **ça tourne rond pour bibi, bibi lui s'en tire,** I'm all right Jack **5.** *P* skeleton key.

bibiche [bibiʃ] *nf* P (*terme d'affection*) **ma bibiche!** my darling*!/my sweetie!/honey!/my pet!

bibine [bibin] *nf P* tasteless drink/ dishwater/gnat's piss.

bibli [bibli] *nf*, **biblio** [biblio] *nf F* (= *bibliothèque*) library.

bic [bik] *nm P* (*péj*) Arab/wog. (*Voir* **bico(t)**)

bica [bika] *nm*, **bicarré** [bikare] *nm F* fourth-year student in a class preparing for the *grandes écoles* or in a *grande école*.

bicause [bikoz] *prep P* = **because**.

Bicêtre [bisɛtr] *Prnm O F* c'est un échappé de **Bicêtre**, he's mad/ bonkers; he's escaped from the loony-bin. (*Voir* **Sainte-Anne**)

biche [biʃ] *nf F* (*terme d'affection*) **ma biche!** my darling*!/my pet!/my love! (*Voir* **pied 20**)

bicher [biʃe] *vi* **1.** *F* **ça biche?** how goes it?/how's tricks?/how's things?/everything OK? **ça biche!** (*i*) everything's fine/OK; not so bad (*ii*) agreed!/it's a deal! **ça biche entre eux**, they get on very well together/they hit it off well **2.** *P* to be delighted; **ça me fait bicher**, that does my heart good; **bicher comme un pou (dans la crème fraîche)**, to be as pleased as Punch.

bichette [biʃɛt] *nf F* (*terme d'affection*) **ma bichette!** my (little) darling*!/my (little) pet!

bichon, -onne [biʃɔ̃, -ɔn] *n F* = **bichette**.

bichonner [biʃɔne] *vtr F* **bichonner sa bagnole**, to take great care of one's car; to be nuts/daft about one's car.

bichonnet [biʃɔnɛ] *nm P* chin.

bichot(t)er [biʃɔte] **I** *vi F* = **bicher 1 II** *vtr P* to steal*/to swipe/to pinch.

biclo [biklo] *nm*, **biclou** [biklu] *nm P* bicycle/bike.

bico [biko] *nm P* (*péj*) = **bicot**.

bicoque [bikɔk] *nf F* (*a*) poky little house; shanty/shack/dump (*b*) **nous avons une bicoque à la campagne**, we've got a small place in the country.

bicot [biko] *nm P* (*péj*) Arab/wog. (*Voir* **arbico(t)**)

biçoteaux [bisoto] *nmpl P* = **biscot(t)eaux**.

bidard, -arde [bidar, -ard] *a&n P* lucky (blighter).

bidasse [bidas] *nm P* private (soldier)/squaddie.

bide [bid] *nm* **1.** *P* (*a*) stomach*; **gras du bide**, fat/pot-bellied; **avoir du bide**, to be paunchy; **prendre du bide**, to get a pot-belly/to get a beer-gut; **s'en mettre plein le bide/ se remplir le bide**, to stuff oneself (*b*) **en avoir dans le bide**, to have guts/to have what it takes; **il n'a rien dans le bide**, he's got no guts/ no balls **2.** *F* (*esp théâtre*) **faire un bide**, to be a flop/a washout.

bidet [bidɛ] *nm F* **eau de bidet**, something worthless/cheap/contemptible; **il ne se prend pas pour de l'eau de bidet**, he thinks he's really something/he thinks he's the cat's whiskers/he thinks no small beer of himself.

bidochard [bidoʃar] *nm P* pimp*/ ponce/mack.

bidoche [bidoʃ] *nf P* **1.** (*i*) (poor-quality) meat (*ii*) human flesh **2. sac à bidoche**, sleeping-bag **3. vider son sac à bidoche**, to get it off one's chest/to make a clean breast of it. (*Voir* **marchand 1**)

bidon [bidɔ̃] *P* **I** *a* false/fake/ phon(e)y; **une maladie bidon**, a fake illness **II** *nm* **1.** **c'est du bidon** (*i*) it's a fake/a phon(e)y (*ii*) it's (a load of) rubbish/codswallop/crap/ balon(e)y; **c'est pas du bidon**, it's the gospel truth **2.** (= **bide 1**) **se remplir le bidon**, to fill one's belly/ to stuff one's face.

bidonnant [bidɔnɑ̃] *a P* very comical/screamingly funny; **c'est bidonnant!** it's a real scream!

bidonner [bidɔne] **I** *vtr P* to deceive/to take (s.o.) in/to trick (s.o.) **II** *vpr* **se bidonner** *P* to laugh* uproariously/to split one's sides laughing/to be doubled up (with laughter)/to crease oneself.

bidonneur [bidɔnœr] *nm P* cheat/swindler*/crook; liar.

bidule [bidyl] *nm P* **1.** (*a*) gadget*/contraption/thing (*b*) thingamy/whatsit/what-do-you-call-it/thingamybob (*c*) what's-his-name*/thingy; **quel bidule!** what a strange bloke! **2.** (policeman's, etc) truncheon.

biduleur [bidylœr] *nm P* potterer/tinkerer/do-it-yourselfer.

bière [bjɛr] *nf F* **1.** **ce n'est pas de la petite bière** (*i*) he's a big shot/a VIP (*ii*) it's not to be sneezed at **2.** **ne pas se prendre pour de la petite bière**, to have a high opinion of oneself/to think no small beer of oneself.

bif [bif] *nm P* **1.** banknote/flimsy **2.** beefsteak.

bifeton [biftɔ̃] *nm P* = **biffeton**.

biffe [bif] *nf P* (*coll*) **la biffe** (*a*) (*i*) the junk business (*ii*) junk collectors (*b*) (*mil*) the infantry.

biffeton [biftɔ̃] *nm P* **1.** (railway, theatre, etc) ticket **2.** (short) letter/note **3.** banknote. (*Voir* **porte-bif(f)etons**) **4.** (doctor's, etc) certificate; **piquer un biffeton**, to inflict injuries on oneself in order to obtain discharge from the armed forces, to claim insurance, etc **5.** *pl* playing cards.

biffin [bifɛ̃] *nm P* **1.** rag-and-bone man/junk collector/junk dealer **2.** (*mil*) infantryman/footslogger.

bifteck, biftèque [biftɛk] *nm* **1.** *F* **faire du bifteck**, to get saddlesore **2.** *P* **gagner son bifteck**, to earn one's living; **la lutte/la course au bifteck**, the rat race; **défendre son bifteck**, to look after one's own bread and butter/to look after number one **3.** *P* prostitute* profitable to her pimp*/good earner/good meal-ticket **4.** *P* the human body **5.** *P* **les Biftecks**, the English*/the British/the Brits. (*Voir* **Rosbifs**) **6.** *F* **il est bifteck moins cinq**, it's nearly dinnertime.

bifton [biftɔ̃] *nm P* = **biffeton**.

biftonner [biftɔne] *vtr P* to write (a letter); to scribble (a few lines).

bigarrée [bigare] *a f F* **elle n'est pas mal bigarrée**, she's not so dusty/not so bad.

bigler [bigle] *vtr P* (*a*) to (have a) squint at (s.o./sth); to take a gander/a butcher's at (s.o./sth) (*b*) **bigler qn en biais**, to give s.o. the glad eye/to eye s.o. up.

bigleux, euse [biglø, -øz] *a&n P* **1.** squint-eyed/cock-eyed (person) **2.** short-sighted (person).

bigne [biɲ] *nm P* prison*; **au bigne**, in prison.

bignol(l)e [biɲɔl] *nm&f P* concierge.

bignolon [biɲɔlɔ̃] *nm P* **1.** detective **2.** prison guard/warder/screw.

bigophone [bigɔfɔn] *nm F* (tele)phone*/blower; **donner/filer/passer un coup de bigophone à qn**, to give s.o. a ring/a buzz/a bell; to get on the blower to s.o.

bigophoner [bigɔfɔne] *vi F* **bigophoner à qn**, to (tele)phone s.o./to give s.o. a buzz.

bigorne [bigɔrn] *nf P* **1.** fight*/battle **2.** slang; **jaspiller bigorne**, to speak slang.

bigorneau, *pl* **-eaux** [bigɔrno] *nm F* = **bigophone**.

bigorner [bigɔrne] **I** *vtr P* **1.** to beat (s.o.) up*/to work (s.o.) over **2.** to damage/to injure; **il s'est fait bigorner sa bagnole**, s.o.'s smashed up/into his car **II** *vpr* **se bigorner** *P* to fight/to come to blows/to have a set-to.

bigornette [bigɔrnɛt] *nf O P* (*drugs*) cocaine*/coke/nose candy.

bigoudi [bigudi] *nm P* **travailler du bigoudi**, to be slightly mad*/to be touched (in the head)/to have a screw loose.

bigre! [bigr] *excl F* gosh!/my goodness!

bigrement [bigrəmã] *adv F* very/extremely/awfully; **il fait bigrement froid**, it's jolly cold; **c'est bigrement embêtant**, it's a blessed nuisance; **vous avez bigrement raison!** you're dead right!

bijou, oux [biʒu] *nm* **1.** *F* **mon bijou**, my darling*/my precious/my pet **2.** *A V* **bijou de famille**, female genitals* **3.** *V* **bijoux de famille** (*i*) testicles*/family jewels (*ii*) male genitals*/bag of tricks.

bilan [bilã] *nm P* **déposer son bilan**, to die*/to cash in one's chips.

bile [bil] *nf F* **se faire de la bile**, to worry/to fret/to get into a tizzy; to get all hot and bothered; **ne te fais pas de bile!** don't worry! **épancher sa bile**, to let off steam.

se biler [səbile] *vpr F* (= **se faire de la bile**) **il ne se bile pas**, he doesn't get worked up/he's not easily upset; **ne te bile pas!** (*i*) don't worry! (*ii*) easy does it!/take it easy!

bileux, euse [bilø, -øz] *F* **I** *a* (addicted to) worrying/fretting; **il n'est pas bileux** (*i*) he's a cool one/a cool customer (*ii*) he's easygoing/happy-go-lucky **II** *n* worrier/worryguts/fretter.

billancher [bijãʃe] *vi P* to pay* (up).

billard [bijar] *nm* **1.** *F* **c'est du billard**, it's very easy*/it's a pushover/it's a piece of cake; it's all plain sailing; **c'est pas du billard**, it's no cinch/it takes a lot of doing **2.** *F* operating table; **monter/passer sur le billard**, to have an operation/to be operated on **3.** *F* (*WWI*) **monter sur le billard**, to go over the top **4.** *F* bald* head/billiard ball

5. *P* **dévisser son billard**, to die*/to snuff it.

bille [bij] *nf* **1.** *F* head*/nut; **il a une bille de billard**, he's as bald* as a coot **2.** *F* face*/mug; **il a une bonne bille**, he looks pleasant enough **3.** *pl V* testicles*/balls.

billet [bijɛ] *nm F* **1.** ten-franc note **2.** **je te donne/fiche/flanque/fous mon billet que ...**, (you can) take my word for it that ... /(you can) take it from me that ...; you can bet your boots/your bottom dollar/your life that ...; I'll bet you what you like that ... **3.** **prendre/ramasser un billet de parterre**, to come a cropper/to fall flat on one's face/to take a header.

billot [bijo] *nm P* fool*/idiot/imbecile/dope.

binaise [binɛz] *nf P* (= **combinaison** (*louche*)) shady scheme/crooked deal/fiddle/racket. (*Voir* **combine**)

binette [binɛt] *nf F* **1.** face* **2.** head*.

bing [biŋ] *nm P* prison*; **descendre au bing**, to be put away/inside; **bing à perpète**, life sentence.

bingre [bɛ̃gr] *nm P* executioner.

biniou [binju] *nm* **1.** *P* musical instrument **2.** *P* automatic (pistol); **jouer un air de biniou**, to fire an automatic **3.** *P* (tele)phone*; **filer un coup de biniou**, to make a phone call **4.** *V* (*rare*) (*a*) female genitals* (*b*) penis*; **jouer un air de biniou/souffler dans le biniou**, to have oral sex*/a blow-job.

binoclard, arde [binɔklar, -ard] *n F* person who wears glasses/four-eyes.

binôme [binom] *nm F* (school) room-mate.

bique [bik] **I** *nf* **1.** (*a*) *F* she-goat/nanny-goat (*b*) *P* **c'est du beurre de bique**, it's worthless*/useless/not much cop/no great shakes; **crotte(s) de bique**, rubbish/tripe;

c'est de la crotte de bique, it's rubbishy/trashy 2. P old horse/nag 3. P une vieille bique, an old hag/an old cow/an old trout 4. P passive homosexual*. (Voir bouc 3) II nm P (péj) Arab/wog.

biquer [bike] vtr V to have sex*.

biquet [bikɛ] nm F 1. (a) (chevreau) kid (b) fawn 2. (terme d'affection) mon biquet, my darling*/my pet.

biquette [bikɛt] I nf F (terme d'affection) ma biquette, my darling*/my pet II nf P (péj) = bique II.

birbasse [birbas] nf P old hag/old bag/old bat.

birbe [birb] nm, birbon [birbɔ̃] nm P old man; vieux birbe, old fogey*/old fuddy-duddy.

biribi [biribi] nm (mil) P = bat'd'Af.

biroute [birut] nf V penis*.

bisbille [bisbij] nf F petty quarrel/tiff; être en bisbille avec qn, to be at odds/at loggerheads with s.o.

Biscaille [biskaj] Prn P = Bicêtre.

biscotte [biskɔt] prep & conj P = because.

biscot(t)eaux, biscot(t)os [biskoto] nmpl P biceps; rouler les/des biscot(t)eaux, to swagger/to throw one's weight around.

biscuit [biskɥi] nm 1. F ne pas s'embarquer sans biscuit(s), to get clued up in advance/to do one's homework; avoir des biscuits, to be clued up/to know the score 2. P (parking) ticket; coller un biscuit à qn, to book s.o./to give s.o. a ticket; choper un biscuit, to get booked/to get a ticket 3. V tremper son biscuit, to have sex*/to dip one's wick.

bise [biz] nf F kiss (on the cheek); (à un enfant) fais la/une bise à ..., (go and) kiss ...; fais bise à

maman, give mummy a kiss; grosse bise, big kiss/smacker; se faire la bise, to kiss each other on both cheeks.

bis(e)ness [biznɛs] nm P 1. work; job 2. (shady) business/job/racket 3. en faire tout un bis(e)ness, to make a big fuss/a song and dance about it 4. (prostituée) faire son/le bis(e)ness, to solicit*/to be on the game.

bis(e)nesseuse [biznɛsǿz] nf P prostitute*/hooker/tart.

bisou [bizu] nm F = bise.

bisquant [biskɑ̃] a F annoying/irritating; ce que c'est bisquant! what a nuisance!

bisque [bisk] nf F bad temper*/irritation; avoir la bisque, to be peeved; to be in a bad mood; prendre la bisque, to take umbrage.

bisquer [biske] vi F to be in a bad mood; to be annoyed/irritated/riled; to sulk; faire bisquer qn, to rub s.o. up the wrong way; (écoliers) bisque! bisque! rage! yah boo sucks!

bistouille [bistuj] nf P 1. coffee laced with brandy (or some other spirit) 2. poor-quality spirits/rotgut 3. nonsense*/rot/tripe.

bistouquette [bistukɛt] nf V penis*.

bistre [bistr] nm, bistro [bistro] nm, bistroc [bistrɔk] nm, bistroquet [bistrɔkɛ] nm, bistrot [bistro] nm F 1. = public house/pub/bar (esp where snacks are served); le bistrot du coin, the local. (Voir troquet) 2. O (a) = publican/bartender (b) wine merchant.

bistrote [bistrɔt] nf F (a) = landlord's wife (b) = landlady (of a pub).

bistrouillage [bistrujaʒ] nm P manufacture of bad quality wine.

bistrouille [bistruj] nf P 1. = bistouille 2. bad quality wine.

bistrouiller [bistruje] *vi P* to manufacture bad quality wine.

bisut(h) [bizy] *nm*, **bisut(h)age** [bizytaʒ] *nm*, **bisut(h)er** [bizyte] *vtr F* = **bizut(h), bizut(h)age, bizut(h)er.**

bitard [bitar] *nm*, **bitau,** *pl* **-aux** [bito] *nm P* hat*/titfer. (*Voir* **bitos**)

bite [bit] *nf V* **1.** penis*/prick/ cock; **il a une grosse bite,** he's well-endowed/well-hung; he's got a huge tool **2. bite à Jean-Pierre,** (policeman's) truncheon; cosh **3. con à bouffer de la bite,** very stupid*/ completely bonkers **4. rentrer la bite sous le bras,** to return empty-handed.

biter [bite] *vtr* **1.** *V* to have sex* with/to have it off with (s.o.) **2.** *P* **se laisser biter,** to be cheated/diddled **3.** *P* **je n'y bite rien,** I can't make head nor tail of it; it's all Greek to me.

bitonner [bitɔne] *vi P* to be undecided/to be in two minds.

bitos [bitos] *nm P* hat*/titfer; **bitos à la reculette,** hat tilted at the back of the head.

bitte [bit] *nf V* = **bite.**

bitter [bite] *vtr V & P* = **biter.**

bitture [bityr] *nf P* **1.** booze; **prendre/ramasser une bitture,** to get drunk*/canned/plastered; **une bonne bitture,** a skinful; **qu'est-ce qu'il tient comme bitture!** he's had a skinful!/he's blind drunk!/he's completely plastered! **2. à toute bitture,** at top speed/flat out/at full blast.

bitturer [bityre] **I** *vtr P* to make (s.o.) drunk*/to get (s.o.) pissed **II** *vpr* **se bitturer** *P* to get drunk*; **se bitturer au pastis,** to get pissed on pastis.

bitume [bitym] *nm P* pavement; (*a*) **rasser le bitume,** to be very short/ to be a short-arse (*b*) **arpenter/faire le bitume,** to be a prostitute*/to walk the streets; **elle arpente le bitume du Boul' Mich,** her beat is the Boulevard St Michel. (*Voir* **calouser**)

biture [bityr] *nf,* **(se) biturer** [(sə)bityre] *vtr & pr P* = **bitture, (se) bitturer.**

biveton [bivtɔ̃] *nm P* = **biffeton.**

bizet [bizɛ] *nm P* (*a*) young pimp* (*b*) small-time pimp*.

biz(e)ness [biznɛs] *nm,* **biz(e)nesseuse** [biznɛsøz] *nf P* = **bis(e)ness, bis(e)nesseuse.**

bizut(h) [bizy] *nm F* freshman/ fresher (*esp* first-year student in preparatory class for the *grandes écoles,* or in the *grandes écoles* themselves).

bizut(h)age [bizytaʒ] *nm F* initiation (of freshman); ragging.

bizut(h)er [bizyte] *vtr F* to rag (a freshman).

bla-bla(-bla) [blabla(bla)] *nm F* (*a*) blah(-blah)/yackety-yack/clackety-clack/claptrap (*b*) padding (of a speech, etc)/waffle.

blablater [blablate] *vi P* to talk nonsense*; to blather/to blether; **ces politiciens passent leur temps à blablater,** politicians do talk a lot of bilge.

blackboulage [blakbulaʒ] *nm F* blackballing/rejection.

blackbouler [blakbule] *vtr F* to blackball/to reject; to fail (examinee); to turn down (candidate); **je me suis fait blackbouler à l'oral,** I failed my oral.

blafarde [blafard] *nf P* **la blafarde** (*i*) death (*ii*) the moon.

blague [blag] *nf* **1.** *F* tall story/ hoax/humbug/bunkum; **tout ça c'est de la blague!** that's all bunkum!/that's all rot!/that's a load of nonsense! **ne raconte pas de blagues!** don't tell cock-and-bull stories!/pull the other one! **quelle bonne blague!** my Aunt Fanny! **2.** *F* joke; **sans blague!/blague à part!** (*i*) no kid(ding)!/seriously!/joking apart!/honest(ly)! (*ii*) you don't say! **quelle blague!** what a joke! **faire une blague à qn,** to fool* s.o.; **prendre qch en blague/à la blague,** to take sth as a joke; **il prend tout à la blague,** he's always got his tongue in his cheek; he's never serious about anything; **raconter des blagues à qn,** to pull s.o.'s leg 3. *P* **blagues à tabac,** (woman's) flabby breasts*/droopers.

blaguer [blage] *F* **I** *vi* (*a*) to talk nonsense*/to talk through one's hat (*b*) to talk with one's tongue in one's cheek (*c*) **blaguer avec qch,** to make light of sth/not to take sth seriously; **ne blague pas avec ce canon,** don't fool around with that gun (*d*) to joke; **(c'est) assez blagué!** that's enough of that! **II** *vtr* **blaguer qn,** to make fun of s.o./ to pull s.o.'s leg/to tease s.o.

blagueur, -euse [blagœr, -øz] *F* **I** *a* bantering/ironical/mocking **II** *n* (*a*) joker/leg-puller; tease(r); **c'est le blagueur de la bande,** he's the joker of the group.

blair [blɛr] *nm P* **1.** nose*/hooter; **bouffer/jambonner le blair à qn,** to bash s.o.'s face in/to hit s.o. on the nose; **se bouffer le blair,** to have a fight/a scrap **2. je l'ai dans le blair,** I can't stand him/he gets up my nose **3. en avoir un coup dans le blair,** to be drunk*/to have (had) a skinful.

blaireau, -eaux [blɛro] *nm P* nose*.

blairer [blɛre] *P* **I** *vtr* (*a*) to sniff at (sth) (*b*) **je (ne) peux pas le blairer,** I can't stand/stick/stomach him; **je le blaire bien,** I don't dislike him **II** *vi* to smell bad/off.

blanc, *f* **blanche** [blɑ̃, blɑ̃ʃ] **I** *a* **1.** *F* **dire tantôt blanc tantôt noir,** to say first one thing and then another **2.** *P* **être blanc,** to have a clean (police) record **3.** *P* **ne pas être blanc,** to be in a (bit of a) spot **4.** *F* (*innocent*) **je ne te vois pas blanc,** you're (in) for it. (*Voir* **bon-**

net; foies) **II** *nm* **1.** *F* **se bouffer le blanc des yeux,** to have a terrific row **2.** *F* **chauffer qn à blanc,** to bring s.o. up to scratch **3.** *F* **s'en jeter un coup de blanc/un petit blanc,** to knock back a glass of white wine **4.** *P* (*a*) silver (*b*) platinum (used for jewellery)/white **5.** *P* cocaine*/snow **6.** *V* sperm/ semen*/spunk. (*Voir* **raide**; **saigner**) **III** *nf P* (*drogues*) **1.** cocaine*/snow **2.** heroin*/H.

blanc-bec [blɑ̃bɛk] *nm F* greenhorn/rookie. (*pl* **blancs-becs**)

blanc-casse [blɑ̃kas], **blanc-cassis** [blɑ̃kasis] *nm P* (*boisson*) blackcurrant syrup *or* liqueur with white wine. (*Voir* **kir**)

blanchecaille [blɑ̃ʃkaj] *nf P* **1.** (*a*) laundress (*b*) washerwoman **2.** laundry; washing.

blanchi [blɑ̃ʃi] *nm P* (*péj*) **un mal blanchi,** a negro*.

blanchir [blɑ̃ʃir] *vtr* **1.** *F* to clear (s.o.) (of an accusation, etc)/to whitewash (s.o.) **2.** *F* **blanchir un manuscrit,** to touch up/to revise a manuscript (belonging to s.o. else) **3.** *P* to cure (s.o.) of VD*, etc.

blanchisseur [blɑ̃ʃisœr] *nm P* (prisoner's) counsel/lawyer/brief. (*Voir* **blanchir 1**)

blanchisseuse [blɑ̃ʃisøz] *nf P* customer who doesn't buy and says 'I'll come again' (*je repasserai*); **cette blanchisseuse a une ardoise dans tous les bistrots,** he's got a slate in every pub.

blanchouillard [blɑ̃ʃujar] *a P* **1.** white **2.** = **blanc I 2, 3, 4.**

blanco [blɑ̃ko] *P* **I** *a* (*a*) pale; **la frousse l'a fait tourner blanco,** he went white with fear/he was scared shitless (*b*) innocent (of a crime) **II** *nm* glass of white wine

blanquette [blɑ̃kɛt] *nf O P* **1.** (*a*) silver (*b*) platinum (used for jewellery) **2.** laundress.

blanquiste [blɑ̃kist] *nm P* = **blanco II.**

blard [blar] *nm P* shawl.

blase [blɑz] *nm P* = **blaze.**

se blaser [səblɑze] *vpr P* to be called/named; to call oneself.

blavard [blavar] *nm*, **blave** [blav] *nm*, **blavec** [blavɛk] *nm* handkerchief*.

blavin [blavɛ̃] *nm P* 1. = **blave** 2. scarf.

blaze [blɑz] *nm P* 1. (*a*) name/mon(n)icker (*b*) nickname 2. nose*.

blé [ble] *nm F* 1. être pris comme dans un blé, to be caught like a rat in a trap 2. money*; manger son blé en herbe/en vert, to spend one's wages before one gets them/to blow one's pay in advance. (*Voir* fauché)

bléchard [bleʃar], **blèche** [blɛʃ], **blèchecaille** [bleʃkaj] *a P* 1. ugly; elle est rien blèche! isn't she a fright! (*Voir* gerber 1) 2. old 3. (*a*) shameful/scabby/mean/nasty (*b*) bad/rotten.

bled [blɛd] *nm* 1. *F* (*a*) God-forsaken place/hole/dump/*NAm* boondocks; quel bled! what a dump! en plein bled, at the back of beyond (*b*) home town; mon bled c'est Nantes, I come from Nantes 2. *P* (*mil, WWI*) no-man's-land; monter sur le bled, to go over the top.

bleu [blø] I *a F* 1. une colère bleue, a dreadful rage; piquer/se mettre dans une colère bleue, to flare up/to hit the roof 2. avoir une peur bleue, to be scared stiff; ça m'a donné une peur bleue, it frightened the life out of me/it scared me to death 3. une envie bleue, an overwhelming desire 4. j'en suis resté bleu, I was flabbergasted. (*Voir* rat 1 (*b*)) II *nm F* 1. bruise; je ne suis qu'un bleu/je suis couvert de bleus, I'm a mass of bruises/I'm black and blue all over

2. (*a*) passer au bleu, to vanish into thin air (*b*) passer qch au bleu, to conceal sth; to hush sth up 3. n'y voir que du bleu (*i*) to be puzzled/flummoxed (*ii*) to be unaware of sth/blind to sth; le flic n'y a vu que du bleu, the cop didn't twig/was none the wiser/didn't smell a rat 4. (*a*) (*f* bleue) beginner/novice; greenhorn (*b*) (*esp mil*) raw recruit/rookie 5. gros bleu, coarse/poor quality red wine 6. *O* petit bleu, express letter transmitted by pneumatic tube, in Paris 7. (= *bleu caporal*) un paquet de bleu, a packet of cheap pipe tobacco 8. un bleu/des bleus (de travail/de chauffe), overalls/dungarees/boiler suit.

bleubite [bløbit] *nm P* (*a*) beginner/novice/greenhorn (*b*) (*esp mil*) raw recruit/rookie.

bleues [blø] *nfpl F* un paquet de bleues, a packet of Gauloises (*RTM*) (cigarettes).

bleusaille [bløzaj] *nf P* (*mil*) (*a*) raw recruit/rookie (*b*) la bleusaille, the young recruits/the awkward squad.

blinde [blɛ̃d] *nm P* share (of loot)/cut/whack/split; après le coup chacun a reçu son blinde, we all got our cut after we'd pulled the job.

blindé [blɛ̃de] *a* 1. *F* blindé contre qch, immune/impervious to sth; je suis blindé contre les injures, you can't insult me 2. *P* blindé, drunk*/plastered/blotto; il était blindé à zéro du matin au soir, he was completely pissed from morning to night 3. *P* under the influence of drugs/stoned 4. *P* être blindé, to have syphilis*/syph.

blinder [blɛ̃de] I *vtr* 1. to get s.o. drunk*/plastered/canned 2. to give s.o. VD*; cette pute m'a blindé, that whore gave me a dose/I copped a dose from that tart II *vpr* se blinder *P* to get blind drunk*/to get pissed.

bloblot(t)e [blɔblɔt] *nf P* avoir la

bloblot(t)e (*i*) to be all of a tremble/to have the jitters (*ii*) to have the shivers/the shakes (*iii*) to have a fever/to be feverish.

bloc [blɔk] *nm* **1.** *P* (*a*) prison*/clink/jug; **mettre/flanquer/fourrer qn au bloc,** to send s.o. to prison*/to put s.o. in the nick (*b*) (*mil*) guardroom; cells; **flanquer sept jours de bloc à qn,** to sentence s.o. to seven days in the glasshouse **2.** *P* **bourré à bloc,** very rich*. (*Voir* **bourré 1, 2**) **3.** *F* **gonflé à bloc** (*i*) keyed up (*ii*) full of zip/full of vim; **les joueurs étaient gonflés à bloc avant le match,** the players were full of beans before the match (*iii*) cocksure (*iv*) self-confident **4.** *F* **ça gaze à bloc,** things are going like a house on fire.

bloche [blɔʃ] *nm P* maggot.

blonde [blɔ̃d] *nf P* **1.** (bottle of) white wine **2.** lager **3.** *FrC* girlfriend.

bloquer [blɔke] *vtr* **1.** *P* to send (s.o.) to prison*/to put (s.o.) inside **2.** *P* **bloquer une pêche,** to receive a blow*/to get one in the kisser.

blosses [blɔs] *nfpl A V* testicles*.

blot [blo] *nm* **1.** *F* (agreed, contract) price; **acheter qch à bas blot,** to buy sth on the cheap; **faire un blot à qn,** to knock sth off the price for s.o. **2.** *P* personal business/job/work; **c'est mon blot** (*i*) it's my business; it's in my line (of business) (*ii*) that's my affair; **ce n'est pas ton blot,** it's none of your business; **c'est pas mon blot,** it's not my cup of tea; **ça fait mon blot,** that suits me fine **3.** *P* **en avoir son blot,** to have had enough/one's fill (of sth) **4.** *P* **c'est le même blot,** it makes no odds/it's as broad as it's long/it's much of a muchness; **que ça te plaise ou pas, c'est le même blot,** like it or lump it.

bloum [blum] *nm,* **bloumard** [blumar] *nm O P* (outlandish) hat.

blouse [bluz] *nf P* **blouse de plâtrier,** (priest's) surplice.

blouser [bluze] **I** *vtr F* to fool*; to cheat*/to deceive; to take (s.o.) in/to put one over on (s.o.); **se faire blouser,** to be taken in/to be had/to be conned **II** *vpr* **se blouser** *F* to be mistaken; to be wide of the mark.

blouson [bluzɔ̃] *nm F* **blouson noir** (*a*) teenage delinquent/young hooligan*/teddy-boy/yobbo (*b*) biker/hell's angel.

blutinage [blytinaʒ] *nm P* questioning (of prisoner); third degree.

blutiner [blytine] *vi P* to confess*/to come clean.

bob [bɔb] *nm* **1.** *F* (= **bobsleigh**) bobsleigh **2.** *P* brothel*/knocking shop. (*Voir* **bobi(nard**))

bobard [bɔbar] *nm F* (*a*) nonsense*/bosh/rot; **des bobards (à la noix/à la gomme),** rubbish/balderdash/bilge (*b*) tall story; *O* **bobards dans le coin!** no kid(ding)!/you don't say! **envoyer des bobards à qn,** to make a dirty crack about s.o.; **monter un bobard,** to shoot a line; **monter un bobard à qn,** to pull s.o.'s leg.

bobèche [bɔbɛʃ] *nf O P* head*/nut; **se monter la bobèche,** to kid oneself; **se payer la bobèche de qn,** to fool* s.o./to have s.o. on.

bobéchon [bɔbeʃɔ̃] *nm O P* head*; **monter le bobéchon à qn,** to fool* s.o./to have s.o. on; **perdre le bobéchon,** to lose one's head/one's cool.

bobi [bɔbi] *nm,* **bobinard** [bɔbinar] *nm P* brothel*/whorehouse/knocking shop.

bobine [bɔbin] *nf P* **1.** head* **2.** face*; **il a une drôle de bobine,** I don't like his face/I don't like the look of him **3.** **il n'a plus de fil sur la bobine,** he's bald*/he's lost his thatch.

bobinette [bɔbinɛt] *nf P* = **bobine 3**.

bobino [bɔbino] *nf P* watch/ticker.

bobo [bobo] *nm F (mot enfantin) (a)* pain/sore/sore spot; **avoir (du) bobo,** to have a pain/a bump/a bruise, etc; **ça fait bobo,** it hurts/it aches; **ça t'a fait bobo?** diddums? *(b)* **avoir un bobo au doigt,** to have a swollen finger *(c)* **y a pas de bobo,** no harm's been done; nothing's broken.

bobonne [bɔbɔn] *nf F (épouse)* the missus/the old lady/the trouble and strife; *(terme d'affection)* **oui ma bobonne,** yes (my) love/(my) pet/honeybunch/ducky.

bobs [bɔb] *nmpl P* **1.** dice; **piper les bobs,** to cheat at dice; to load/to stack the dice; **manier les bobs,** to play dice; **pousser les bobs,** to throw the dice/to roll the bones **2.** **lâcher les bobs,** to cry off/to drop out/to quit/to call it quits.

boc [bɔk] *nm P* = **boc(c)ard 1.**

bocal, -aux [bɔkal, -o] *nm P* **1.** *(= local)* premises/building; room; house/place/pad; **les flics l'ont cueilli à son bocal,** the cops/the fuzz picked him up at his place **2.** **un échappé de bocal,** undersized* person/little squirt/short-arse **3.** **faire/nager/mettre/tremper le poisson dans le bocal,** to have sex*/to dip one's wick.

boc(c)ard [bɔkar] *nm P* **1.** brothel* **2.** anger.

boche [bɔʃ] *a & nm&f P (péj)* German*/jerry/kraut.

bocsif [bɔksif], **bocson** [bɔksɔ̃] *nm P* brothel*/whorehouse/knocking shop. *(Voir* **boxif, boxon)**

bœuf *(f occ* **bœuve)** [bœf, bœv] **I** *a F* tremendous/colossal/fantastic (success, impudence, etc); **faire un effet bœuf,** to have a great/fantastic effect; **c'est bœuf** *(i)* it's great/super *(ii)* it's stupid **II** *nm F* **1.** **travailler comme un bœuf,** to work like a horse/a Trojan **2.** **(on fait ce qu'on peut,) on n'est pas des bœufs!** we're only human! **3.** **avoir un bœuf sur la langue,** to (have been paid to) keep one's mouth shut **4.** **faire du bœuf à la mode,** to get saddle-sore **5.** **faire/gagner son bœuf** *(i)* to earn one's living/one's bread and butter *(ii)* to carve out a lucrative career for oneself **6.** *(musiciens)* **faire un bœuf,** to have a jam (session)/to jam.

bœuffer [bœfe] *vi F (musiciens)* to have a jam(session)/to jam.

B.O.F., bof¹ [beɔɛf, bɔf] *nm F* spiv/black marketeer (originally, in WWII, the French profiteers in *beurre, œufs, fromages*).

bof² [bɔf] *int F (pour exprimer le mépris, l'indifférence, l'ironie, la lassitude, le doute, etc) (i)* pooh!/pah!/bah! *(ii)* who cares!/you don't say!/big deal!

boilton [bwaltɔ̃] *nm V (peu usuel)* clitoris*; *(pour une femme)* **s'astiquer le boilton,** to masturbate*/to finger oneself/to fingerfuck.

boire [bwar] *vtr F* **il y a à boire et à manger (là-dedans)** *(i) (vin, etc)* it's got bits in it/it's food as well as drink *(ii) (film, livre, etc)* it has its good points and its bad points/there's a bit of everything in it. *(Voir* **lait 1; tasse; trou)**

bois [bwa] *nm* **1.** *F* **abattre du bois,** to work* hard/to slog away. *(Voir* **abattre) 2.** *F* **homme de bois,** dull/lifeless man **3.** *F* **je leur ferai voir de quel bois je me chauffe,** I'll show them what sort of stuff I'm made of **4.** *F* **ils ne se chauffent pas du même bois,** they've got nothing in common **5.** *F* **il est du bois dont on fait les flûtes,** you can twist him round your little finger **6.** *F (avions)* **casser du bois** *(i)* to crash on landing *(ii)* to crash-land/to make a crash-landing **7.** *F* **on n'est pas de bois,** I'm not made of wood/I'm only human **8.** *F* **touche(z) du bois!** touch wood!/

NAm knock on wood! **9.** *F* **chèque en bois,** dud/rubber cheque **10.** *F* **bouts de bois,** sticks of furniture; **être dans ses bois,** to have a place of one's own; **se mettre dans ses bois,** to set up home/to buy one's own furniture **11.** *P* **mettre les bois,** to run away*/to clear off/to beat it **12.** *P* **tirer sur le bois mort,** to row **13.** *P* **faire du bois,** to burgle/*NAm* to burglarize/to break in **14.** *P* (*cocu*) **il lui pousse du bois/des bois,** his horns are sprouting **15.** **scier du bois,** to play the cello. (*Voir* **gueule 4** (*a*); **sirop 2**; **visage 2**)

boisseau, -eaux [bwaso] *nm* **1.** *F* **se remuer comme un boisseau de puces,** to fidget/to have the fidgets **2.** *P* **se décarcasser le boisseau,** to be slightly mad*/to have a screw loose.

boissonner [bwasɔne] *vi F* (*rare*) to drink* heavily/to (go on the) booze.

boîte [bwat] *nf* **1.** *P* (*a*) uncomfortable/poky little room; **quelle boîte!** what a dump!/what a hole! (*b*) place of work, etc (*eg* school, office, shop, factory, café); **je travaille dans cette sale boîte,** I work in that rotten hole/crummy dump **2.** *F* **boîte (de nuit),** nightclub/nightspot; **aller/sortir en boîte,** to go night-clubbing/to go out on the town/to go down the clubs **3.** *P* prison*; (*mil*) guardroom/cells; **mettre qn à la boîte,** to put s.o. inside/in the can; **bouffer de la boîte,** to be put away **4.** *P* mouth*; **ferme ta boîte!** shut your trap! **5.** *F* (*a*) **mettre qn en boîte,** to pull s.o.'s leg/to take the mickey (out of s.o.) (*b*) (*musique, cinéma, TV*) **mettre en boîte,** to record/to can; **c'est dans la boîte,** it's in the can **6.** *P* **boîte à asticots/à dominos/à violon,** coffin/box; *F* **boîte à cancans** (*i*) gossip/chatterbox (*ii*) gossip-shop; *P* **boîte aux claqués/aux dégelés/aux refroidis,** mortuary/morgue; *P* **boîte à fressures/à ragoût,** stomach*/bread-box; *P* **boîtes à lait/à lolo,** breasts*/milk bottles/jugs. (*Voir* **lolo 3**); *P* **boîte à morve,** nose*/snot-box; *V* **boîte à ouvrage,** vagina*/box; *V* **boîte à pâté,** anus*; *F* (*théâtre*) **boîte à sel,** box office; *F* **boîte à vice,** sly dog/sly customer; *P* **boîtes à violon,** big boots*/clodhoppers.

boitout [bwatu] *nm*, **boit-sans-soif** [bwasɑ̃swaf] *nm*, **boit-tout** [bwatu] *nm* drunkard (who drinks all his earnings); lush/alky.

bol [bɔl] *nm* **1.** *F* **prendre un bon bol d'air pur,** to fill one's lungs with fresh air **2.** *P* luck; **un coup de bol,** a bit of luck/a stroke of luck; **avoir du bol,** to be lucky/in luck; to have a lucky break; **manquer de bol,** to be unlucky/out of luck; **manque de bol!** bad luck!/hard luck!/rotten luck! **3.** *F* **cheveux coupés au bol/une coupe-au-bol,** pudding-basin haircut **4.** *P* **j'en ai ras le bol,** I'm fed up (to the back teeth) with it/I've had a basinful of it/I've had it up to here **5.** *P* **il en fait un drôle de bol,** it's boiling hot **6.** *P* **il ne se casse pas le bol,** he's not worried.

bolant [bɔlɑ̃] *a P* very funny*/too funny for words/priceless; **elle est bolante, cette histoire belge,** it's a real killer, that Belgian joke.

bolcho [bɔlʃo] *F* **I** *a* communist/commie/red/leftist **II** *nm & f* communist/commie/red/lefty.

se boler [səbɔle] *vpr* to laugh* uproariously/to crease oneself with laughter.

bomb [bɔ̃(b)] *nf P* (*drogues*) marijuana cigarette*/joint.

bombance [bɔ̃bɑ̃s] *nf O F* feast(ing)/carousing; beanfeast.

bombarder [bɔ̃barde] *vtr* **1.** *F* to pitchfork (s.o.) into a job; **on l'a bombardé ministre,** he's been made a minister out of the blue **2.** *P* to smoke (a lot); **il bombarde toute la journée,** he chain-smokes all day

long; **qu'est-ce qu'elle bombarde!**
she smokes a hell of a lot!/she's a
heavy smoker! **3.** *P* (*boxe*) to give
(one's opponent) a pasting/to hit
(one's opponent) all over the ring.

bombe [bɔ̃b] *nf* F **1.** (*a*) **arriver
comme une bombe,** to turn up
unexpectedly/out of the blue (*b*)
entrer comme une bombe, to come
bursting in **2.** feast/spree/binge/
good time; **faire la bombe,** to go
out on a spree/on a binge; **s'offrir
une bombe carabinée/une bombe à
tout casser,** to have a rare old
time/to have a ball/to have a wild
time; **passer la nuit en bombe,** to
make a night of it; **un lendemain de
bombe,** the morning after the night
before.

bomber [bɔ̃be] **I** *vi* P to drive
fast/to bomb along; **on a bombé
pour arriver à l'heure,** we had to
step on it/to belt along/to do a ton
to get there in time **II** *vpr* **se
bomber** *P* **1.** to go without food
2. se bomber de qch, to do without
sth **3. tu peux (toujours) te
bomber!** nothing doing!*/get lost!*/
go (and) jump in the lake!/go take
a running jump!

bombido [bɔ̃bido] *nm,* **bombita**
[bɔ̃mbita] *nf P* (*drogues*) (*a*)
amphetamine* (*b*) mixture of
amphetamine* and heroin* for
injection.

bon, *f* **bonne** [bɔ̃, bɔn] *a* F **1.**
être bon (*i*) to be duped/hoaxed/
swindled/conned; to be done/to be
had (*ii*) to be done for/to be a
goner (*iii*) to be arrested/to get
nicked/to get done (*iv*) to be in for
it; **être bon pour ...,** to be due for
(sth unpleasant)/to be in for ...;
on est bon pour rentrer à pied (*i*)
we're in for walking home/we're
stuck with walking back (*ii*) we're
game for walking home **2. ne pas
être bon,** to refuse/not to agree; **j'
suis pas bon!** I'm not having any
(of it/that)! **3.** (*pers*) **être bon à
rien/à tuer,** to be a dead loss/a

hopeless case **4. y a bon!** OK! **5.
avec dix minutes de bon,** with ten
minutes to spare/in hand **6. une
bien bonne,** a good joke; a good
story; **elle est (bien) bonne, celle-là!**
that's a good one, that is!/I like
that! **en voilà une bonne!** that's a
good 'un! **tu en as de bonnes!** (*i*)
you've got some funny ideas! (*ii*)
you've got a weird sense of
humour! (*iii*) it's all very well for
you to talk! **7. avoir qn à la
bonne,** to like s.o./to have a liking
for s.o./a soft spot for s.o.; to take
a shine to s.o.; **ne pas avoir qn à la
bonne,** to have a down on s.o.; **la
garder bonne à qn,** to have a
grudge against s.o./to have it in for
s.o. **8. prendre qch à la bonne,** to
take sth in good part. (*Voir* **ferte;
lap(e); romaine**)

bona [bɔna] *nm,* **bonap** [bɔnap]
nm, **bonaparte** [bɔnapart] *nm A
P* 500-franc note.

bonbon [bɔ̃bɔ̃] *nm* **1.** *pl P*
(*drogues esp* amphetamines* *ou*
LSD*)/candy/sweets **2.** *pl V* testicles*; **casser les bonbons à qn,** to
bore* s.o. to death/to give s.o. a
pain in the arse/to get on s.o.'s tits.

bonbonnière [bɔ̃bɔnjɛr] *nf V*
female genitals*.

bon-chic-bon-genre [bɔ̃-
ʃikbɔ̃ʒɑ̃r] *F* **I** *a phr* well-bred/
high-class **II** *nm&f* = bright
young thing/BYT; *pl* = the smart
set.

bondieu [bɔ̃djø] *P* **I** *int* **bondieu
(de bondieu)!** God almighty!/good
God! **II** *nm* **quel bondieu
d'imbécile!** what a bloody fool!

bondieusard, -arde [bɔ̃djøzar,
-ard] *P* **I** *n* sanctimonious/churchy
person **II** *a* sanctimonious/
churchy/pi.

bondieuserie [bɔ̃djøzri] *nf P* **1.**
churchiness/sanctimonious devotion
2. *pl* (*péj*) church ornaments/devo-
tional objects (in bad taste)/reli-
gious frippery.

bondir [bɔ̃dir] *vi* **1.** *P* **se faire bondir**, to be arrested/to get run in **2.** *F* to get angry*/crazy/mad; **ça va le faire bondir!** he'll go nuts/he'll hit the roof!

bonheur [bɔnœr] *nm F* **1.** **faire qch au petit bonheur**, to do sth in a slapdash manner; **il fait les choses au petit bonheur**, he's slap-happy **2.** **au petit bonheur la chance!** here's chancing it!/here's trusting to luck!

bonhomme [bɔnɔm], *pl* **bonshommes** [bɔ̃zɔm] *nm* **1.** *F* (*a*) man*/chap/fellow/bloke/guy; **connaître son bonhomme**, to have s.o. sized up/weighed up (*b*) (*mari*) old man/bloke/guy **2.** *F* soldier **3.** *F* **il va son petit bonhomme de chemin** (*i*) he's just going/trundling/footling along in his own little way (*ii*) (*en voiture*) he's just tootling along **4.** *F* **nom d'un petit bonhomme!** gosh!/wow!/good heavens! **5.** *F* (*théâtre*) **entrer dans la peau du bonhomme**, to get into the skin of the character **6.** *F* **salut, (mon) bonhomme!** hello, old man!/wotcher, cock! **7.** *V* erect penis*; **se secouer le bonhomme**, to masturbate*.

boniche [bɔniʃ] *nf*, **bonichonne** [bɔniʃɔn] *nf P* (*péj*) = **bonniche**.

boniment [bɔnimɑ̃] *nm F* **1.** patter/sales talk/spiel/fast talk(ing) (of showman, tout, etc) **2.** **du boniment** *ou* **des boniments** (**à la graisse (d'oie)/à la graisse de chevaux de bois/à la graisse de hareng saur/à la noix/à la peau de toutou**), nonsense*/rubbish/twaddle/claptrap/piffle/bilge **3.** **avoir qn au boniment**, to get round s.o./to talk s.o. into it **4.** (*a*) **faire du boniment à qn**, to try to get round s.o./to try to coax s.o.; to fast-talk s.o./to sweet-talk s.o. (*b*) **faire du boniment à une femme**, to chat a woman up/to sweet-talk a woman.

bonimenter [bɔnimɑ̃te] *F* **I** *vi & tr* to kid (s.o.) **II** *vtr* **bonimenter**

qn = faire du boniment à qn (**boniment 4** (*a*)).

bonimenteur, -euse [bɔnimɑ̃tœr, -øz] *n F* **1.** tout/spieler **2.** flatterer*/soft-soap artist.

bonir [bɔnir] *P* **I** *vi & tr* to talk/to speak/to tell/to say; **personne n'en a boni une**, no one uttered a word **II** *vtr* to disclose/to reveal (a secret, etc); **il a tout boni à la police**, he blabbed/shot his mouth off to the police. (*Voir* **salade 3**)

bonisseur [bɔnisœr] *nm P* tout; **il a un p'tit job de bonisseur aux Galeries Lafayette**, he makes a living touting outside the *Galeries Lafayette*.

bonjour [bɔ̃ʒur] *nm* **1.** *F* **c'est simple comme bonjour**, it's as easy* as ABC/as pie **2.** *F* **avoir le bonjour**, to come too late/to arrive when it's all over **3.** *P* **bonjour d'Alfred** (*i*) (*pourboire*) tip (*ii*) **si tu crois ça t'auras le bonjour d'Alfred**, if you believe that then you're more stupid than I thought.

bonnard [bɔnar] *P* **I** *nm* simpleton/softie; dupe/sucker **II** *a* (*a*) simple-minded/soft (*b*) **être (fait) bonnard/se faire faire bonnard = être bon** (**bon 1**).

bonne [bɔn] *a & nf Voir* **bon**.

bonnet [bɔnɛ] *nm* **1.** *F* **c'est bonnet blanc et blanc bonnet**, it's six of one and half a dozen of the other/it's as broad as it's long **2.** *F* **avoir la tête près du bonnet**, to be quick-tempered/to fly off the handle easily **3.** *F* **parler à son bonnet**, to talk to oneself **4.** *F* **bonnet de nuit**, wet blanket; **c'est une histoire triste comme un bonnet de nuit**, that story's as dull as ditchwater **5.** *F* **jeter son bonnet par-dessus les moulins**, to have one's fling **6.** *F* **gros bonnet**, important person*/big shot/big noise/bigwig **7.** *F* (*cuisine*) **bonnet d'évêque**, parson's nose **8.** *P* (= **bonneteau**) three-card trick **9.** *P* **il ne se casse pas le bonnet,** he doesn't put himself out/ he doesn't exactly overwork himself **10.** *V* **bonnet à poils,** female genitals*/pussy.

bonniche [bɔniʃ] *nf P* (*péj*) maid/ skivvy.

bonnir [bɔnir] *vtr&i P* = **bonir.**

bonsoir [bɔ̃swar] *nm* **1.** *F* **tout est dit, bonsoir!** there's nothing more to be said!/that's (all there is to) it! **2.** *P* **dire bonsoir aux amis/aux voisins,** to die*.

bonze [bɔ̃z] *nm F* **1.** high priest/ bigwig (of political party, etc) **2. vieux bonze,** old fog(e)y*/old dodderer/old fossil.

book [buk] *nm F* bookmaker/ bookie; **book marron,** welsher.

boom [bum] *nf F* (young people's) party; (*scol*) end-of-term/end-of-year party. (*Voir* **boum II**)

boquillonner [bɔkijɔne] *vi P* to limp.

bord [bɔr] *nm F* **1. être du (même) bord de qn,** to be in the same boat as s.o. **2. ... sur les bords,** slightly, a bit of a ...; **menteur sur les bords,** a bit of a liar; **il est un peu empaffé/pédé/tapette sur les bords,** he's a bit camp/a bit of a poofter/a bit poofy.

bordée [bɔrde] *nf F* (*marins*) **faire/ courir/tirer une bordée,** to go on a spree*/on a binge/on a bender; to go out on the town.

bordel [bɔrdɛl] *nm* **1.** *F* brothel*/ whorehouse/knocking shop **2.** *P* shambles; **quel bordel!** what a bloody mess! **ça va être le bordel,** it's going to be hell; **semer le bordel,** to raise hell; **foutre le bordel (quelque part),** to bollocks sth up/ to cock sth up/to balls sth (up) **3.** *P* **tout le bordel,** the whole (bloody) lot **4.** *P* **bordel (de Dieu)!/bordel de merde!** damn and blast it!/bloody hell!/sodding hell!

bordelaise [bɔrdəlɛz] *nf P* **une partie de bordelaise,** a heavy petting session.

bordéleux [bɔrdelø] *a P* = **bordélique.**

bordelier, -ière [bɔrdəlje, -jɛr] *n F* brothel-keeper.

bordélique [bɔrdelik] *a P* messy/ in a mess/in a shambles; **c'est bordélique, ce truc,** this thing's a real bastard*/a real sod; it's a real cock-up.

bordille [bɔrdij] *nf P* **1.** (*pers*) nasty piece of work/(rotten) bastard*/(real) sod/son of a bitch **2.** police informer*/stoolie/grass **3.** trash/rubbishy goods/crap/junk.

bordurer [bɔrdyre] *vtr P* **se faire bordurer/être borduré** (*i*) to be prohibited (by the police or by the underworld) from frequenting certain specified places; **le patron l'a borduré de son établissement,** the landlord's banned him from the premises (*ii*) (*médecin*) to be struck off (the register).

borgne [bɔrɲ] **I** *nm* **1.** penis* **2.** anus*/arsehole/*NAm* asshole **II** *nf* night; **profiter de la borgne pour disparaître,** to slip off into the night.

borgnesse [bɔrɲɛs] *nf P* (*péj*) one-eyed girl *or* woman.

borgnio(t) [bɔrɲo] *nm,* **borgno** [bɔrɲo] *nm,* **borgnon** [bɔrɲɔ̃] *nm P* night.

borgnot(t)er [bɔrɲɔte] *P* **I** *vtr* **borgnot(t)er qn** (*i*) to gaze intently at s.o. (*ii*) to keep a sharp lookout for s.o. **II** *vi* to go to bed*.

borne [bɔrn] *nf* **1.** *F* kilometre; **bousculer les bornes,** to speed along; = to eat up the miles **2.** *P* **planter une borne,** to defecate*.

bosco, boscot, -ot(t)e [bɔsko, -ɔt] *P* **I** *a* hunchbacked/ humpbacked **II** *n* (*a*) hunchback (*b*) **rigoler/rire/se tordre comme un bosco,** to roar with laughter*.

boss [bɔs] *nm F* **1.** boss/guv'nor/

chief **2.** leader (of gang, etc)/big shot/top man.

bossant [bɔsã] *a F* very funny*/priceless.

bosse [bɔs] *nf F* **1.** avoir la bosse de qch, to have a knack/a flair for sth **2.** (*a*) rouler sa bosse (un peu partout), to knock about/to be a rolling stone; j'ai roulé ma bosse, I've been around (*b*) allons, roule ta bosse! come on, get a move on! **3.** (*cyclisme*) hill/slope/incline. (*Voir* demander 1)

bosseler [bɔsle] *vtr P* to beat up*/to lay into (s.o.)/to set about (s.o.); machine à bosseler, fist/bunch of fives; passer qn à la machine à bosseler, to beat s.o. up*/to work s.o. over.

bosser [bɔse] I *vi P* to work* hard/to slave/to slog (away); bosser comme un nègre, to work like a Trojan/to slog one's guts out/to work like a nigger II *vpr* se bosser *O F* to have lots of fun/to have a whale of a time.

bosseur [bɔsœr] *nm P* hard worker/swot/plodder/slogger.

bossoirs [bɔswar] *nmpl P* (large prominent) breasts*.

bossu [bɔsy] *nm P* petit bossu, coffee laced with brandy.

botte [bɔt] I *nf F* (*a*) wad of 100 ten-franc notes (*b*) (il) y en a des bottes, there's stacks/heaps/loads of them II *nf* **1.** *P* avoir les bottes à bascule/à rouleaux, to be drunk* **2.** *F* j'en ai plein les bottes (*i*) I'm exhausted* (*ii*) I'm fed up (to the back teeth)/I'm pissed off (with it, them) **3.** *P* filer un coup de botte à qn, to tap s.o. for a loan **4.** *F* cirer/graisser ses bottes, to prepare (*i*) for a journey (*ii*) for the next world **5.** *F* cirer/lécher les bottes de qn, to toady to s.o./to suck up to s.o./to lick s.o.'s boots **6.** proposer la botte à qn (*i*) *P* to challenge s.o. to a fight (*ii*) *P* to make amorous advances to s.o./to try to

get off with s.o.; dès la première rencontre il leur proposait la botte, he used to try and get them into bed right from the word go **7.** *F* sortir dans la botte, to graduate brilliantly from the *Ecole polytechnique*. (*Voir* bottier) **8.** *F* y laisser ses bottes, to die* with one's boots on **9.** *V* chier dans les bottes de qn, to play a dirty trick on s.o./to do the dirty on s.o. **10.** *P* faire dans les bottes de qn, to disturb/to interfere with s.o.; to be a nuisance to s.o./to get in s.o.'s hair **10.** *F* à propos de bottes, apropos of nothing at all; without rhyme or reason; chercher querelle à qn à propos de bottes, to pick a quarrel with s.o. over nothing/over a trifle. (*Voir* foin 1)

botter [bɔte] *vtr F* **1.** botter (le derrière/les fesses/*P* le cul à) qn, to kick s.o.'s buttocks/to give s.o. a boot up the behind/to give s.o. a kick in the pants **2.** to suit; ça me botte (*i*) that suits me fine, down to the ground/to a T (*ii*) I really like/fancy/dig that. (*Voir* fouettard 2)

bottier [bɔtje] *nm F* s.o. who graduates brilliantly from the *Ecole polytechnique*. (*Voir* botte II 7)

bottine [bɔtin] *nf P* **1.** lesbians* (in general); travailler dans/être de la bottine, to be a lesbian*/a les/a dyke **2.** filer un coup de bottine à qn, to tap/to touch s.o. for money; to be on the cadge.

bottiner [bɔtine] *vtr P* bottiner qn, to tap/to touch s.o. (for money, etc); to cadge off s.o.

bouboule [bubul] *nm&f F* fat person/fatso/(fat) slob.

bouc [buk] *nm P* **1.** = boulc **2.** planquer son bouc, to take shelter **3.** homosexual* **4.** puer le bouc, to stink*/to smell to high heaven. (*Voir* bique I 4)

boucan [bukã] *nm F* uproar/din/hullabaloo; faire un boucan infernal/du tonnerre/de tous les diables, to make a hell of a noise/to make the devil of a row; to kick up a fuss.

boucaner [bukane] I *vi A F* to make a lot of noise/to kick up a row/a shindy II *vi A P* to stink*.

bouche [buʃ] *nf* 1. *F* en avoir à bouche que veux-tu, to have plenty/to have one's fill 2. *F* être sur sa bouche/être porté sur la bouche, to be fond of one's food 3. *F* faire la bouche en cœur, to give oneself airs/to put on airs 4. *F* il en avait la bouche pleine/plein la bouche, he could talk of nothing else/he was full of it 5. *F* (motus et) bouche cousue! mum's the word!/don't breathe a word! 6. *P* ta bouche (bébé, t'auras une frite)! shut up!*/belt up!/give it a rest!/put a sock in it! (*Voir* cul 12; palissandre)

bouché [buʃe] *a F* être bouché, to be stupid*; être bouché à l'émeri, to be as thick as two short planks.

bouchée [buʃe] *nf F* 1. ne faire qu'une bouchée de ..., to make short work of (s.o., sth)/to make mincemeat of (s.o.)/to wipe the floor with (s.o.) 2. mettre les bouchées doubles, to work at double speed; to do a job in double quick time 3. pour une bouchée de pain, for a trifle/for a song/for a mere nothing.

bouchon [buʃ ɔ̃] *nm* 1. *P* the youngest child in a family/the baby of the family 2. *P* un petit bouchon, a mere wisp of a man 3. (*marine*) bouchons gras, engine-room artificers 4. *P* prendre du bouchon, to age/to be getting on in years 5. *F* traffic jam; hold-up/tailback 6. *F* bouchon de carafe, large diamond/sparkler 7. *F* c'est plus fort que de jouer au bouchon (avec des queues de radis), that's the (absolute) limit!/that beats everything! 8. *P* envoyer le bouchon/pousser le bouchon trop loin, to boast/to exaggerate* 9. *P* mets-y

un bouchon! shut* up!/put a sock in it! 10. *F* ramasser un bouchon, to come unstuck/to come a cropper 11. *F* être torché comme un bouchon, to be got up like a guy 12. *V* pousser le bouchon, to defecate*/to have a crap.

bouclage [buklaʒ] *nm P* imprisonment.

bouclard [buklar] *nm P* shop.

bouclarès [buklarɛs] *a inv P* closed.

boucle [bukl] *nf* 1. *F* se serrer la boucle, to tighten one's belt/to go without (food) 2. *P* = bouclage 3. *F* la grande Boucle, the Tour de France (cycle race).

boucler [bukle] *vtr* 1. *F* se boucler la ceinture/se la boucler, to tighten one's belt/to do without 2. *P* to send s.o. to prison*/to lock (s.o.) up; se faire boucler, to get put inside 3. *F* boucler son budget, to make ends meet 4. (*a*) *F* to close; bouclez la lourde! shut the door! (*b*) *P* boucle-la! shut up!*/belt up!/shut your trap! la boucler, to keep quiet/to keep one's trap shut; ça vous la boucle! that's got you! (*c*) *F* boucler une affaire, to settle/to clinch a matter; c'est une affaire bouclée, it's all sewn up (*d*) *F abs* il n'y a plus qu'à boucler, we'll have to close down/to shut up shop.

boude [bud] *nm O P* ugly woman/fright. (*Voir* boudin)

bouder [bude] *vi F* 1. bouder à la besogne, to be workshy 2. bouder contre son ventre, to cut off one's nose to spite one's face.

boudin [budɛ̃] *nm* 1. *P* (pneu) tyre 2. *P* (*a*) woman of easy virtue/easy lay/pushover (*b*) prostitute* (*c*) prostitute's earnings (*d*) ugly/frumpish woman 3. *P* girl(friend) 4. *pl F* fat/podgy fingers 5. *P* (*au jeu*) avoir du boudin, to have the master cards 6. *P* être plein/rond comme un boudin, to be blind

bouffarde drunk*/to have had a skinful **7.** **faire du boudin** (*i*) *F* to have the sulks (*ii*) *P* to spill blood **8.** *P* **boudin blanc,** penis*/sausage. (*Voir* **eau 5; os 8**)

bouffarde [bufard] *nf F* (old) pipe; **téter sa bouffarde,** to smoke one's pipe.

bouffarder [bufarde] *vtr F* to smoke (a pipe)/to puff at (one's pipe).

bouffe [buf] *nf P* **1.** food*/grub/ nosh/chow; **faire la bouffe,** to do the cooking **2.** gluttony/gorging; **une grande bouffe,** a big nosh-up.

bouffe-la-balle [buflabal] *nm&f inv P* glutton/greedyguts.

bouffer [bufe] **I** *vtr&i* **1.** *P* (*a*) to eat* (*b*) to eat greedily; **bouffer à en crever,** to stuff oneself/one's face (with food); **j'ai bien bouffé,** that was a super meal (*c*) (*voiture*) **bouffer de l'essence,** to be heavy on/to drink petrol **2.** *P* to spend (freely)/to blow/to run through/to get through a lot of money **3.** *V* **bouffer la chatte,** to practise cunnilingus*/to eat hair-pie **II** *vpr* **se bouffer** *F* **se bouffer le nez,** to quarrel*/to have a row; to have a go at each other. (*Voir* **bite 3; blair; boîte 3; brique 2; clarinette 3; clou 7; curé 1; foie 3; lion; morceau 2; rat 10; vache**)

bouffetance [buftɑ̃s] *nf P* **1.** food*/grub/nosh **2.** gluttony/gorging.

bouffi [bufi] *nm P* (*locution*) **tu l'as dit, bouffi!** you've said a mouthful there!

bouftou(t) [buftu] *nm P* glutton/ greedyguts.

bougeotte [buʒɔt] *nf F* **avoir la bougeotte,** to be restless/to have the fidgets/to have ants in one's pants.

bougie [buʒi] *nf* **1.** *F* **éteindre sa bougie,** to die*/to snuff it **2.** *P*

face*; **tirer une drôle de bougie,** to look astonished.

bougna(t) [buɲa] *nm F* **1.** native of Auvergne/Auvergnat **2.** coalman/coal merchant **3.** keeper of a small bistrot.

bougnou [buɲu] *nm,* **bougnoul(e)** [buɲul] *nm P* (*péj*) **1.** Arab/wog **2.** *O* negro* **3.** half-breed **4.** mongrel (dog).

bougnoulle [buɲul] *nm P =* **bougnou.**

bougre, *f* **bougresse** [bugr, bugrɛs] *P* **I** *n* **1.** person/individual; **un bon bougre,** a good sort/a nice guy; **un mauvais bougre,** an ugly customer; **un sale bougre,** a rotter/a rotten sod/a bastard*; **un pauvre bougre,** a poor devil; **pauvre bougre!** poor sod! **bougre d'imbécile!/bougre d'âne!** (you) bloody fool! **2.** **bougre de temps,** filthy weather **3.** *f* **bougresse,** big/ strapping woman **II** *int* **bougre!** hell!/heck! **bougre que ça fait mal!** Christ, that hurts!

bougrement [bugrəmɑ̃] *adv P* damn(ed)/darn(ed)/damnably/devil- ishly/hellishly/bloody; **il fait bougrement froid,** it's bloody cold.

boui-boui [bwibwi] *nm P* (low, sleazy) dive (for eating or entertain- ment); dump; honky-tonk joint. (*pl* **bouis-bouis**)

bouic [bwik] *nm O P* **1.** brothel* **2.** = **boui-boui.**

bouif [bwif] *nm P* cobbler.

bouillabaisse [bujabɛs] *nf P* **être dans la bouillabaisse,** to be in a fix*/in a pickle.

bouille [buj] *nf P* **1.** face*/mug; **avoir une bonne bouille,** to have a friendly face/to look like a friendly sort of person **2.** head* **3.** victim (of a confidence trick, etc)/mug/ sucker **4.** old steam locomotive.

bouillie [buji] *nf F* (*a*) **être comme de la bouillie,** to have no back- bone/to be spineless (*b*) **c'est de la**

bouillie **pour les chats,** it's a worthless jumble/a hopeless muddle/a dog's dinner (c) **mettre qn/qch en bouillie,** to smash s.o./sth to pieces; to beat s.o./sth to a pulp.

bouillon [bujɔ̃] *nm* **1.** *P* water; **tomber dans le/au bouillon,** to fall into the water/into the drink; **avaler/boire un bouillon,** to swallow/to get a mouthful (when swimming) **2.** *P* **boire/prendre un bouillon,** to sustain a heavy financial loss; to come unstuck (in a business venture)/to be ruined **3.** *P* heavy downpour (of rain) **4.** *F* cheap, popular restaurant **5.** *F* un **bouillon de onze/d'onze heures** (*i*) a poisoned drink (*ii*) a Mickey Finn **6.** *pl F* **bouillons,** unsold copies (of a newspaper, a book)/returns/remainders.

bouillonner [bujɔne] *vi F* (*journaux, etc*) to remain unsold; **ce canard bouillonne à 15% (de son tirage),** 15% of this newspaper's print run remains unsold. (*Voir* **couvercle**)

bouillotte [bujɔt] *nf P* = **bouille** 1, 2, 4.

bouisbouis [bwibwi] *nm P* = **boui-boui.**

Boulange [bulɑ̃ʒ] *nf P* **1.** la **Grande Boulange/la Boulange aux faffes,** the Bank of France **2.** **faire dans la boulange,** to make counterfeit money/to forge money.

boulanger [bulɑ̃ʒe] *nm* **1.** *F* le **Boulanger,** the devil/Old Nick **2.** *P* **remercier son boulanger,** to die*.

boulangère [bulɑ̃ʒɛr] *nf P* prostitute* supporting a fancy-man; meal ticket.

boule [bul] *nf* **1.** *P* head*/nut; **perdre la boule,** to go mad*/to go round the bend/to go off one's head; **un coup de boule,** a (head-)butt (in the chest or stomach); **boule de billard,** bald head; **il a une boule de billard,** he's as bald as a coot **2.** *P* face*/mug/dial; **boule** de son, freckled face **3.** *O F* (*mil*) **boule de son,** ration loaf **4.** *P* (clenched) fist **5.** *F* **boule (dans la gorge),** lump in one's throat **6.** *F pl* **boules,** money*; **rentrer dans ses boules,** to get one's money/one's outlay back **7.** *F* **avoir les yeux en boules de loto,** to be goggle-eyed/bug-eyed; to have eyes like saucers **8.** *F* **boule de feu, boule de fer,** cross my heart (and hope to die). (*Voir* **croix** 6) **9.** *P* **avoir des boules de gomme dans les zozos/dans les portugaises,** to be deaf **10.** *F* **se mettre en boule,** to get angry*/to blow one's top; **ça me met (les nerfs) en boule,** that gets my goat/that makes me livid; **il me met en boule,** he gets my back up **11.** *P* **avoir les boules,** to be afraid*/to be scared shitless **12.** *P* **se serrer la boule,** to go hungry*/to tighten one's belt **13.** *F* **la boule noire lui tombe toujours,** nothing ever turns out well for him; he is dogged by bad luck **14.** *V* **faire boule de gomme,** to have oral sex*. (*Voir* **maboul(e)**; **mystère**)

boule-de-neige [buldəneʒ] *nm P* (*péj*) negro*/black/nigger.

boulé [bule] *a P* hooked (on drugs).

bouler [bule] *vtr F* **1.** **envoyer bouler qn,** to send s.o. packing/to tell s.o. where he gets off **2.** (*a*) to make a mess of (sth)/to mess (sth) up (*b*) (*théâtre*) to fluff (one's lines, an entrance).

boulet [bulɛ] *nm* **1.** *P* wife*/ball and chain **2.** *F* **mettre qn sur les boulets,** to wear s.o. out **3.** *F* **traîner le boulet,** to have one's nose to the grindstone **4.** *P* (*péj*) **boulet** Bernot, negro*.

boulette [bulɛt] *nf F* mistake*/blunder/boob; **grosse boulette,** howler; **faire une boulette,** to boob/to drop a brick/to drop a clanger.

bouleux, euse [bulø, -øz] *a&n F* hard-working but unimaginative (person); **un bon bouleux,** a plodder.

boulevard [bulvar] *nm* F **les événements du boulevard,** life in town; **faire un boulevard,** to wander/to stroll up and down a boulevard/an avenue. (*Voir* **allongé)**

boullé [bule] *a* P hooked (on drugs).

Boul'Mich', le [ləbulmiʃ] *Prnm* F = le Boulevard Saint-Michel (in the Latin quarter of Paris).

boulonner [bulɔne] *vi* F to work* hard/to slog away.

boulot¹ [bulo] *nm* **1.** F work; job; drudgery/grind/slog; **quel est son boulot?** what's his job? **quel sale boulot!** what a crummy job! **s'atteler au boulot,** to pitch in/to get down to it; **au boulot!** get cracking! **du boulot tout cuit,** an easy* job, a cushy number; **parler boulot,** to talk shop **2.** F worker **3.** P business; **c'est ton boulot,** that's your business!/that's your look-out! **4.** P burglary/job.

boulot², boulot-boulot [bulobulo] *a* F **être boulot(-boulot),** to be fond of work/to be dead keen; to be a grafter.

boulot³, otte [bulo, -ɔt] *a&n* F podgy/dumpy/plump (person); **petit boulot (d'enfant),** little dumpling.

boulotter [bulɔte] P **I** *vtr* **1.** to eat* **2.** to squander/to spend money freely/to blow money **II** *vi* O **ça boulotte! ça boulotte?** = **ça biche! ça biche? (bicher 1).**

boum [bum] **I** *nm* **1.** F **en plein boum,** in full swing; **être en plein boum** (*i*) to be in full swing (*ii*) to be up to one's neck in work/to have plenty on one's plate **2.** F **faire un boum** (*i*) to cause a sensation (*ii*) to be a success/a hit; to be going great guns **3.** V (*a*) **faire boum,** to have sex* (*b*) **se faire boum,** to masturbate*. **II** *nf*

(young people's) party. (*Voir* **surboum)**

boumer [bume] *vi* F **1.** to go well; **ça boume?** how's tricks?/ how's it going? **2. où ça boume,** where it's at.

bouniol [buɲɔl] *nm* P (*péj*) = **bougnou.**

bouquet [bukɛ] *nm* **1.** F (ça) **c'est le bouquet!/v'là le bouquet!** that's the absolute limit!*/that's the last straw!/that takes the cake! **2.** (*a*) F gift/present/tip (*esp* to a prostitute*) (*b*) P payoff (to police informer*, etc) (*c*) P share of the spoils; cut/whack **3.** V **mettre les pieds en bouquet de violettes,** to have an orgasm*/to climax.

bouquin [bukɛ̃] *nm* F book.

bouquiner [bukine] *vi* F to read (for pleasure)/to browse through books.

bouquineur, euse [bukinœr, -øz] *n* F bookworm.

bourbier [burbje] *nm* F **être dans le bourbier,** to be in a fix*/to be in a mess/to be in a pickle; **se tirer d'un bourbier,** to get out of a scrape/a mess.

bourde [burd] *nf* F **1.** lie/fib/ story; **débiter des bourdes,** to tell fibs/stories **2.** mistake*/boob/ bloomer; **faire une bourde,** to put one's foot in it/to drop a clanger **3.** *pl* nonsense*/humbug; **faire avaler des bourdes à qn,** to take s.o. in/to get s.o. to swallow a load of nonsense.

bourdille [burdij] *nf* P = **bordille.**

bourdon [burdɔ̃] *nm* P **1.** old horse/old nag **2. avoir le bourdon,** to be/to feel depressed*; to have the blues/to feel down in the mouth/to be down in the dumps.

bourgeois [burʒwa] *nm* P **1.** boss; **et le pourboire, mon bourgeois?** what about something for myself, guv'nor? **2. les en bour-**

geois (i) plain-clothes detectives (ii) the Vice Squad.

bourgeoise [burʒwaz] *nf* **1.** *P* **ma bourgeoise,** my wife*/the missis/the old lady **2.** *V* **baiser à la bourgeoise,** to have sex* in the missionary position.

bourgeron [burʒərɔ̃] *nm A P* (priest's) surplice.

bourgue¹ [burg] *nm A P* **1.** sou (*coin*) **2.** minute.

bourgue² *nm A*, **bourguignon** [burgiɲɔ̃] *nm P* the sun.

bourguignotte [burgiɲɔt] *nf F* (*mil*) steel helmet; tin hat.

bourin [burɛ̃] *nm P* = **bourrin.**

bourlingue [burlɛ̃g] *nf F* wandering from place to place; journey with no set destination.

bourlinguer [burlɛ̃ge] *vi F* (*a*) to live a hard life/to rough it (*b*) to be a rolling stone; **bourlinguer de par le monde/un peu partout,** to knock about the world.

bourrage [buraʒ] *nm F* **bourrage de crâne/de mou** (*i*) eyewash (*ii*) brainwashing (*iii*) cramming/swotting. (*Voir* **crâne**)

bourratif, ive [buratif, -iv] *a F* very filling/stodgy (food).

bourre [bur] **I** *nm P* policeman*/cop/copper **II** *nf P* **1.** *coll* **la bourre,** the police*/the fuzz **2.** *pl* lies **3. être à la bourre,** to be late (for an appointment, etc) **4. de première bourre,** excellent*/first-rate/top-quality/super **5.** sex*/screw*/ **bonne bourre!** have a good fuck! **6.** struggle/rivalry; hassle; **tirer la bourre à qn,** to compete with s.o.; **se tirer la bourre,** to compete with one another; to have a set-to.

bourré [bure] *a P* **1.** rich*; **bourré aux as,** loaded/stinking rich **2.** drunk*/sloshed/tight; **bourré à bloc/à zéro; bourré comme un cochon,** dead drunk*/stewed to the

eyeballs/pissed as a newt **3.** under the influence of a drug/stoned.

bourrée [bure] *nf F* thrashing/beating* up.

Bourreman(e), Bourremann [burman] *nm P* **la maison Bourreman(e),** the police*/the cops/the boys in blue.

bourre-mou [burmu] *nm P* nonsense*/eyewash.

bourre-pif [burpif] *nm inv P* punch on the nose*.

bourrer [bure] **I** *vtr* **1.** *F* **bourrer un élève de latin,** to cram a pupil with Latin **2.** *F* **il est bourré de complexes,** he's one mass of complexes **3.** *F* to thrash (s.o.)/to beat (s.o.) up*; **bourrer qn de coups,** to give s.o. a (good) hiding/to give s.o. a belting; **bourrer la gueule à qn,** to bash s.o.'s face in; (*boxe*) **il le bourrait de coups de gauche,** he was plugging away at him with his left **4.** *V* to have sex* (with s.o.)/to screw (s.o.) **II** *vi F* **bourrer sur qch,** to jib at sth **2. bourrer (à tout berzingue),** to speed along/to belt along. (*Voir* **crâne; mou**) **III** *vpr* **se bourrer** *F* **1.** to stuff/to gorge/to pig oneself **2.** to make a packet (of money).

bourre-toujours [burtujur] *nm inv P* road-hog/speed merchant.

bourreur [burœr] *nm F* **bourreur de crâne(s),** s.o. who fills people full of lies/propaganda; brainwasher.

bourriche [buriʃ] *nf P* = **bourrichon.**

bourrichon [buriʃɔ̃] *nm P* head*; **monter le bourrichon à qn,** to work on s.o.'s feelings/to poison s.o.'s mind; **on lui a monté le bourrichon contre nous,** they've set him against us; **avoir le bourrichon monté,** to have one's blood up; **se monter le bourrichon** (*i*) to get excited/to work oneself up (into a state) (*ii*) to imagine things/to kid oneself

bourrin [burɛ̃] **I** *nm P* **1.** (*a*) horse/nag **2.** (*a*) prostitute* (*b*) woman of easy virtue/easy lay **3.** detective* from the vice squad **II** *a P* **être bourrin,** to be fond of sex*/to like it a lot.

bourriner [burine] *vi P* to chase after women/to chase skirt.

bourrique [burik] *nf* **1.** *F* idiot*/ ass/ignoramus **2.** *F* stubborn/pig-headed person **3.** *P* **la bourrique,** the police*/the fuzz **4.** *P* police informer*/copper's nark; grass **5.** *F* **faire tourner qn en bourrique,** to drive s.o. crazy; **il m'a fait tourner en bourrique avec ses questions,** he drove me up the wall with his questions **6.** *P* **plein/soûl comme une bourrique,** dead drunk*/(as) pissed as a newt.

bourriquer [burike] *vi & tr V* to have sex* (**avec qn,** with s.o.); **bourriquer à gogo,** to shag one's arse off.

bourru [bury] *a P* **1.** **être bourru,** to be arrested* **2.** **faire qn bourru,** to catch s.o. in the act/red-handed.

bouscaille [buskaj] *nf O P* mud; **être dans la bouscaille,** to be in a fix*/to be in a mess/to be in a pickle. (*Voir* **mouscaille**)

bouseux [buzø] *nm P* (*péj*) peasant*/country bumpkin/yokel/hick.

bousillage [buzijaʒ] *nm* **1.** *F* bungling/botching **2.** *F* bungled/botched work; bungle/botch-up/cock-up **3.** *F* smashing up/wrecking **4.** *P* (*a*) killing/murdering (*b*) **bousillage en série,** war **5.** *P* tattooing.

bousille [buzij] *nf P* (*a*) **la bousille,** tattooing (*b*) *pl* **bousilles,** tatoos/tattoo marks.

bousiller [buzije] *vtr* **1.** *F* **bousiller qch,** to bungle*/to botch sth; **du travail bousillé,** a botched job/a botch-up; **tu vas tout bousiller,** you're going to louse everything up **2.** *F* to smash up/to wreck/to crash/to prang (a car, a plane, etc);

il l'a complètement bousillée, sa **bagnole,** he's written off his car/his car's a complete write-off **3.** *P* to adulterate (drugs) **4.** *P* **bousiller qn,** to kill* s.o./to do s.o. in/to bump s.o. off; **se bousiller le portrait,** to blow one's brains out **5.** *P* to tatoo; **bousillé à zéro,** (completely) covered in tattoos.

bousilleur, -euse [buzijœr, -øz] *n* **1.** *F* bungler/botcher **2.** *P* tattooist.

bousin [buzɛ̃] *nm O P* **1.** seedy/ sleazy café *or* pub **2.** brothel*/ knocking shop **3.** (*a*) bear-garden/ bedlam (*b*) uproar*/racket/shindy/ rumpus.

bousiner [buzine] *vi O P* **1.** to frequent brothels/to do the round of the whorehouses **2.** to kick up a row/to make a (hell of a) racket.

boussole [busɔl] *nf F* **perdre la boussole** (*i*) to lose one's bearings/ to be all at sea (*ii*) to go mad*/ dotty; to lose one's head.

boustifaille [bustifaj] *nf P* **1.** food*/grub/nosh **2.** blow-out/ tuck-in/nosh-up.

boustifailler [bustifaje] *vi P* to eat* (and drink) (greedily).

boustiffe [bustif] *nf P* = **boustifaille.**

bout [bu] *nm* **1.** *F* **c'est le bout du monde,** it's a god-forsaken hole/a dump; **c'est pas le bout du monde,** it's not impossible/it's not the end of the world; **s'il a huit mille francs c'est (tout) le bout du monde** (*i*) he's got eight thousand francs at the outside/at the very most (*ii*) he's lucky if he's got eight thousand francs to his name **2.** *F* **faire un bout de conduite à qn,** to set s.o. on his way/to go part of the way with s.o. **3.** *F* **tenir le bon bout** (*i*) to hold the whiphand (*ii*) to be on the right track **4.** *F* **en connaître un bout,** to know a thing or two/to know the score **5.** *F* **prendre le bout de bois,** to take the wheel (of a vehicle) **6.** *F* **mettre les bouts (de bois),** to run away*/to skedaddle/to scarper **7.** *F (a)* **un petit bout de femme,** a mere slip of a woman *(b)* **un petit bout de chou/ un petit bout de zan,** a little mite/a little nipper **8.** *P* **au bout du quai les ballots!** get lost!*/go jump in the lake! **9.** *P* **bouts de sucre,** loaded dice **10.** *V* **le (gros) bout/le bout de viande,** penis*/end/knob; **se l'envoyer sur le bout/se mettre sur le bout,** to have sex*/to have it off/to get one's end away. (*Voir* **discuter**)

boutanche [butɑ̃ʃ] *nf P* **1.** bottle **2.** shop.

bouteille [butɛj] *nf F* **1. prendre de la bouteille,** to be getting on/to be past one's prime/to be long in the tooth **2. c'est la bouteille à l'encre,** it's a hopeless mess/muddle; it's as clear as mud **3. aimer la bouteille,** to be fond of the bottle/to like a drink.

boutéon [buteɔ̃] *nm P* = **bouthéon.**

bouthéon [buteɔ̃] *n P (mil)* **1.** dixie **2.** (*WWII*) cookhouse rumour.

boutique [butik] *nf* **1.** *F* (seedy, crummy) place/hole; **quelle boutique!** what a dump! **2.** *F* **parler boutique,** to talk shop **3.** *F* **toute la boutique,** the whole bag of tricks/the whole works **4.** *P (homme)* **montrer (toute) sa boutique,** to expose oneself/to flash; *(femme)* **ouvrir la boutique,** to have sex*/to give oneself to a man.

bouton [butɔ̃] *nm* **1.** *V (sexe de la femme)* **bouton (d'amour/de rose),** clitoris/clit; **arroser le bouton,** to ejaculate*/to come outside; **s'astiquer/se chatouiller le bouton,** to masturbate*/to play with oneself; **se lécher le bouton,** to indulge in cunnilingus* **2.** *P* **bouton (de rose),** nipple; **mangeuse de boutons,** lesbian*/dyke/les **3.** *F* **donner les boutons (à qn),** to irritate/to aggra-

vate s.o.; to get on s.o.'s nerves; **ça me fout les boutons,** that gets on my wick **4.** *F* **s'en jeter un derrière le bouton de col,** to knock back a drink/to knock one back **5.** *F* **cirer toujours le même bouton,** to be always harping on the same string. (*Voir* **tire-bouton**)

boutonnière [butɔnjɛr] *nf F* **faire une boutonnière à qn,** to slash s.o. (with knife, razor, etc) **2.** *V (rare)* female genitals*/slit/hole.

boutonneau [butɔno] *nm V* **boutonneau d'amour** = **bouton 1.**

bouture [butyr] *nf F* child*/brat/kid.

bouzillage [buzijaʒ] *nm F P* = **bousillage.**

bouzille [buzij] *nf P* = **bousille.**

bouziller [buzije] *vtr F P* = **bousiller.**

bouzin [buzɛ̃] *nm P* = **bousin.**

bouzine [buzin] *nf P* **1.** old car*/old banger/old jalopy **2.** computer.

boxif [bɔksif] *nm,* **boxon** [bɔksɔ̃] *nm P* **1.** brothel*/whorehouse/knocking shop **2.** shambles/mess; **quel boxon!** what a shambles!

boy [bɔj] *nm P (drogues)* heroin*/H.

boyau, *pl* **-aux** [bwajo] *nm P* **1. aimer qn comme ses petits boyaux,** to love s.o. dearly **2. avoir le boyau de la rigolade/avoir le boyau rigolard,** to want to burst out laughing **3.** *(mil)* communication trench.

boyautant [bwajotɑ̃] *a P* screamingly funny*; **c'est boyautant!** it's a real scream!

se boyauter [səbwajote] *vpr P* to laugh* uproariously/to crease oneself (with laughter)/to piss oneself (laughing).

brac [brak] *a F* = **braque I.**

bracelets [braslɛ] *nmpl P* handcuffs*/cuffs.

braco [brako] *nm P* poacher.

bracquemard, bracquemart
[brakmar] *nm O V* penis*; **dérouiller son bracquemard,** to have sex*.

bradillon [bradijɔ̃] *nm P* arm/fin.

braire [brɛr] *vi F* 1. to weep/to cry/to bawl 2. to shout/to bawl 3. to protest loudly/to complain.

braise [brɛz] *nf P* money*/cash/ dough.

bran [brɑ̃] *nm A P* shit/muck.

brancards [brɑ̃kar] *nmpl* 1. *P* legs*/pins 2. *F* **ruer dans les brancards,** to protest*/to kick out/to rebel/to refuse to do sth 3. *P* **sortir des brancards,** to leave one's wife*/to walk out on one's wife.

branchant [brɑ̃ʃɑ̃] *a F* exciting/ fantastic; **c'est un album très branchant,** it's an album that really knocks you out.

branche [brɑ̃ʃ] *nf* 1. *F* **avoir de la branche,** to have a distinguished, aristocratic, air 2. *P* **ma vieille branche,** my old friend*/my old pal; **salut, vieille branche!** hello, old bean!/wotcher cock! (*Voir* **beurre 9**)

branché [brɑ̃ʃe] *a F* **être branché,** to be with it/to be up-to-date/to be in/to be trendy; (*drogues, etc*) addicted/hooked/turned on; **Londres est une ville branchée,** London's a with-it place/the in-place/a turned-on place.

brancher [brɑ̃ʃe] I *vtr F* 1. **brancher qn avec qn,** to put s.o. in touch with s.o. 2. **brancher qn sur qch,** to inform s.o. about sth/to give s.o. the low-down about sth 3. to turn s.o. on; **le Reggae, ça me branche mais le Disco, ça ne me branche pas du tout!** Reggae really turns me on but Disco's not my scene at all; **elle le branche,** she excites him/she turns him on; (*drogues*) **ça le branche énormément,** that really gets him going/that really turns him on/he's really hooked II *vpr* **se brancher** 1. *F* **se brancher avec qn,** to get in touch/in contact with s.o. 2. *P* (*musique, drogues*) to get turned on/switched on/knocked out.

branco [brɑ̃ko] *nm P* stretcher bearer.

brandillon [brɑ̃dijɔ̃] *nm P* arm*/ fin.

branlage [brɑ̃laʒ] *nm V* (act of) masturbation/tossing off/wanking.

branlantes [brɑ̃lɑ̃t] *nfpl P* teeth*.

branlée [brɑ̃le] *nf V* 1. (*raclée*) **attraper/prendre une branlée,** to take a beating*/a hiding/a thrashing 2. = **branlage.**

branler [brɑ̃le] I *vi F* **ça branle dans le manche,** it's a bit dicey/a bit tricky II *vtr* 1. *F* **qu'est-ce qu'il branle?** what's he up to? 2. *P* **ne pas en branler une,** not to give a damn/a monkey's (about sth); **qu'est-ce que j'en ai à branler?** what the hell/what the fuck has it got to do with me? 3. *V* **se les branler/se branler les couilles,** not to work at all/to do damn all/to do fuck all/ to sit on one's arse and do nothing 4. *V* **se branler la colonne,** to masturbate*/to toss off/to jerk off; **elle a dû le branler dans la bagnole,** she had to toss him off in the car. (*Voir* **nez 2**) III *vpr* **se branler** 1. *P* **s'en branler/se branler de qch,** not to give a damn/a monkey's (about sth); **je m'en branle,** I don't give a toss/a fuck 2. *V* to masturbate*/to toss off/to wank/to jerk off.

branlette [brɑ̃lɛt] *nf*, **branlure** [brɑ̃lyr] *nf V* **se faire une petite branlette,** to masturbate*/to have a quick toss.

branleur [brɑ̃lœr] *nm V* (a) masturbator/wanker (b) (*fig*) **c'est un branleur de 1ère,** he's a real wanker/ jerk.

branleuse [brɑ̃løz] *nf V* masturbator/wanker; **c'est une bonne branleuse,** she's got a good wrist action/she tosses off well.

branlocher [brɑ̃lɔʃe] *vtr&i* = **branler.**

branque [brɑ̃k] **I** *nm P* **1.** fool*/simpleton/dope **2.** eccentric/crackpot **3.** prostitute's client/punter/john **II** (*also* **branquignol(le)** [brɑ̃kiɲɔl]) *a P* **1.** mad*/crazy/bonkers/round the twist **2.** eccentric/way-out.

braquage [brakaʒ] *nm F* armed attack/armed robbery/hold-up/stick-up/heist.

braque [brak] **I** *a F* hare-brained/feather-brained/crackers/nutty **II** *nm P* clapped-out engine (of car, etc).

braquemard, braquemart [brakmar] *nm O V* penis*; **dérouiller son braquemard,** to have sex*.

braquer [brake] *vtr F* **1.** to hold (s.o.) up (at gunpoint) **2. braquer qn,** to antagonize s.o./to get s.o.'s back up; **être braqué contre qn,** to be stubbornly opposed to s.o.

braqueur [brakœr] *nm F* armed robber/hold-up man/blagger.

bras [bra] *nm F* **1. avoir les bras cassés/retournés/à la retourne,** to be lazy/to be a layabout. (*Voir* **retourne, retourné**) **2. gros bras** (*i*) strong man (*ii*) influential man; **avoir le bras long,** to be very influential/to have friends in the right places **3. être le bras droit de qn,** to be s.o.'s right-hand man **4. avoir des yeux qui se croisent les bras,** to be cross-eyed/to (have a) squint **5. faire un bras d'honneur à qn,** to make an obscene gesture at s.o./ = to put two fingers up at s.o. (= up yours!). (*Voir* **lourd I; pâté 1; tomber II 1**)

bravo [bravo] *int P* **faire bravo,** to be dead scared. (*Voir* **miches 1** (*b*) (*iii*))

bredi-breda [brədibrəda] *adv phr O F* in a hurried/slapdash manner.

brêle [brɛl] *nm P* (*mil*) mule.

brelica, brélica [brelika] *nm P*

(*verlan de* **calibre**) revolver*/pistol/shooter.

brelique-breloque [brəlik-brəlɔk] *adv F* higgledy-piggledy/anyoldhow/anywhichway.

breloque [brəlɔk] *nf F* **battre la breloque** (*i*) (*montre, etc*) to keep bad time (*ii*) (*cœur, machine*) to be on the blink.

brème, brême [brɛm] *nf P* **1.** playing card; **manier/taper/taquiner les brèmes,** to play cards; **maquiller les brèmes,** to mark/to fake the cards **2.** (*i*) identity card (*ii*) policeman's card (*iii*) business card (*iv*) prostitute's card; **fille en brème,** registered prostitute. (*v*) (*informatique*) punched/perforated card **3.** telegram.

Bretagne [brɔtaɲ] *Prnf F* **neveu/nièce/oncle/tante à la mode de Bretagne** (*i*) first cousin once removed (*ii*) distant relative.

bretelles [brətɛl] *nfpl F* **en avoir jusqu'aux bretelles/par-dessus les bretelles** (*i*) to be up to one's neck in trouble (*ii*) to be very drunk*.

Breton [brətɔ̃] *nm P* **un coup de tête de Breton,** a head-butt (in the chest or stomach).

brevet [brəvɛ] *nm P* **faire passer le brevet colonial à qn,** to introduce s.o. to sodomy/to initiate s.o.

bréviaire [brevjɛr] *nm P* **1. bréviaire d'amour,** female genitals* **2.** book **3.** (Paris) street guide.

bric [brik] *nm P* (licensed) brothel*.

bricard [brikar] *nm P* (*mil*) lance-sergeant.

brich(e)ton [briʃtɔ̃] *nm P* bread.

bricolage [brikɔlaʒ] *nm F* pottering about/tinkering/doing odd jobs; **un mordu du bricolage,** a do-it-yourself/DIY enthusiast; a keen do-it-yourselfer.

bricole [brikɔl] *nf F* **1.** (*a*) trifle (*b*) *pl* odd jobs; **s'occuper à des bricoles,** to potter about/to do odd jobs **2.** (*mil*) Sam Browne (belt)

3. faire des bricoles à qn, to treat s.o. brutally; to give s.o. a good hiding (with a strap).

bricoler [brikɔle] **I** *vtr* **1.** *F* to knock together (a piece of furniture, etc); to tinker with (a car engine, etc) **2.** *P* **bricoler une femme,** to feel a woman (up)/to touch up (a woman) **3.** *P* **bricoler le chemin,** to lurch along the road (in a drunken state) **II** *vi* *F* to potter about/to do odd jobs.

bricoleur, -euse [brikɔlœr, -øz] *F* **I** *a* handy (person) **II** *n* handyman/potterer/tinkerer/do-it-yourselfer.

bride [brid] *nf* *P* **1.** (*a*) (watch-)-chain (*b*) chain lock **2.** se mettre la bride, to tighten one's belt/to go without **3.** *pl* **brides,** handcuffs*.

brider [bride] *vtr* **1.** *F* to check/to restrain (s.o.); to keep a tight rein on (s.o.); to clamp down on (s.o.) **2.** *P* to close (a door) **3.** *P* se faire **brider,** to be tattooed.

brif(f)e [brif] *nf* *P* (*a*) brif(f)e de pain, chunk of bread (*b*) food*/grub/chow; aller à **briffe,** to (go and) eat*.

brif(f)ée [brife] *nf* *P* square meal; blow-out/tuck-in/nosh-up.

brif(f)er [brife] *vtr & i* *P* to eat* (greedily).

brif(f)eton [briftɔ̃] *nm* *P* (*a*) bread (*b*) snack.

brif(f)eur, -euse [brifœr, -øz] *n* *P* greedy eater/greedyguts.

brigadier [brigadje] *nm* **1.** *F* (*théâtre*) the stick with which one gives the three knocks (just before the curtain rises) **2.** *P* **brigadier d'amour,** middle finger.

brignol(e) [brinɔl] *nm,* **brignolet** [brinɔlɛ] *nm,* **brignoluche** [brinɔlyʃ] *nm* *P* bread.

brillant [brijɑ̃] *a* *F* **pas brillant, ça!** that's not too good!/that's not so hot!/it's not up to much!

briller [brije] *vi* *V* to have an orgasm*.

brin [brɛ̃] *nm* *F* **1.** un brin de causette, a bit of a chat; un brin de toilette, a quick wash/a catlick/a lick and a promise; aller prendre un brin d'air, to go for a breather **2.** un beau brin de fille, a nice-looking girl. (*Voir* **salade 4**)

brindes [brɛ̃d] *nfpl,* **brindezingues** [brɛ̃dzɛ̃g] *nfpl* *P* être dans les brindes, to be drunk*.

brindezingue [brɛ̃dzɛ̃g] *a* *P* drunk*.

bringue [brɛ̃g] **I** *a* *P* mad*/bonkers/nuts **II** *nf* *F* **1.** bit/piece; en bringues (*i*) in shreds/in tatters (*ii*) at sixes and sevens **2.** grande bringue (de femme), big gawk (of a woman) **III** *nf* *P* faire la bringue, to be/to go on a spree*/on a bender.

bringuer [brɛ̃ge] *vi* *P* = faire la bringue (**bringue III**).

bringueur [brɛ̃gœr] *nm* *P* reveller/hell-raiser.

brioche [bri(j)ɔʃ] *nf* **1.** *F* mistake*/blunder/boob **2.** *F* paunch; avoir de la brioche, to be paunchy/pot-bellied; prendre de la brioche, to develop a paunch/a corporation/a pot-belly/a beer-belly **3.** *F* partir en brioche, to neglect oneself/to go to pieces/to go to pot **4.** *F* tortiller (de) la brioche, to dance **5.** *pl* *P* brioches, buttocks* **6.** *P* pansement à brioche, corset.

brique [brik] *nf* *P* **1.** ten thousand (new) francs **2.** bouffer des briques, to go without food/to live on air. (*Voir* **poil 10**)

briquer [brike] **I** *vtr* *F* to clean thoroughly; to polish; to scrub **II** *vpr* se briquer *F* to have a wash (and brush-up).

briquet [brikɛ] *nm* *F* battre le briquet, to knock one's ankles together in walking.

briqueuse [brikøz] *nf P* laundress.

brisant [brizɑ̃] *nm P* wind.

briscard [briskar] *nm F* = **brisquard**.

brisé [brize] *a F* **1.** exhausted*/tired out **2. être tout brisé,** to be sore/aching all over.

briser [brize] *vtr P* **1. il me les brise,** he gets on my bloody nerves; **ça me les brise,** it gets on my tits **2. se la briser,** to run away*/to clear off/to scarper.

brisquard [briskar] *nm F* old soldier/old campaigner/veteran.

brisque [brisk] *nf F* (*mil*) **1.** long-service badge/stripe; war-service chevron **2. une vieille brisque,** an old campaigner.

bristol [bristɔl] *nm F* visiting card.

Britiche [britiʃ] *a&n F* British (person); Brit.

briveton [brivtɔ̃] *nm P* = **brif(f)eton.**

broc [brɔk] **I** *nf P* **ça ne vaut pas une broc,** it's utterly worthless/it's not worth a brass farthing **II** *nm P* (= *brocanteur*) second-hand/antique dealer.

brocasse [brɔkas] *nf P* (*a*) second-hand goods (*b*) junk/scrap.

broche [brɔʃ] *nm P* pimp*/ponce.

broches [brɔʃ] *nfpl P* **se gratter les broches,** to clean one's teeth.

brochet [brɔʃɛ] *nm P* pimp*.

brocheton [brɔʃtɔ̃] *nm P* young pimp*.

broco [brɔko] *nm P* = **broc II.**

bronze [brɔ̃z] *nm P* turd; **mouler un bronze,** to defecate*/to have a shit. (*Voir* **œil**)

broque [brɔk] *nf P* **de la broque,** dud/worthless* stuff; junk/trash.

broquette [brɔkɛt] *nf F* **ça ne vaut pas une broquette,** it's absolutely worthless*/it's not worth a toss.

broquille [brɔkij] *nf P* minute.

brosse [brɔs] *nf P* (*mil*) moustache*. (*Voir* **reluire 1**)

brosser [brɔse] **I** *vtr* **1.** *P* **se brosser le ventre,** to go hungry/to have an empty belly **2.** *V* to have sex* with (s.o.) **II** *vpr* **se brosser** *P* to have to go without (food, etc); **tu peux te brosser!** you can whistle for it!/go screw yourself!

broue [bru] *nf FrC P* froth; **faire de la broue,** to show off*/to talk big.

brouet [bruɛ] *nm F* nasty-looking stew/soup.

brouillamini [brujamini] *nm F* confusion/disorder/tangle.

brouillard [brujar] *nm* **1.** *F* **je suis dans le brouillard/je n'y vois que du brouillard,** I'm very hazy about it/I can't make head nor tail of it **2.** *P* (*a*) **être dans le brouillard/dans les brouillards,** to be tipsy/sozzled/fuddled (*b*) **abattre/chasser le brouillard,** to clear one's head/to brush away the cobwebs (with an alcoholic drink); to take (a) hair of the dog (that bit you) **3.** *P* **s'évanouir/foncer dans le brouillard,** to run away*/to skedaddle/to clear off. (*Voir* **foncer 3**)

brouillé [bruje] *a F* **être brouillé avec les dates,** to be unable to remember dates/to be hazy about dates; **être brouillé avec les chiffres,** to be hopeless at figures.

brouille-ménage [brujmenaʒ] *nm P* red wine.

brousse [brus] *nf F* **au fin fond de la brousse,** at the back of beyond/*NAm* out in the boondocks.

brouter [brute] **I** *vtr&i V* **1. brouter (le cresson),** (*cunnilinctus*) to have oral sex*/to eat hair-pie **2. brouter (la tige),** (*fellation*) to have oral sex*/to suck cock/to give (s.o.) a blow-job **II** *vpr* **se brouter** *V* (*entre femmes*) to indulge in mutual cunnilingus*; **elles se broutent,** they're a couple of lesbians*/they're sucking each other off.

brouteur [brutœr] *nm V* **brouteur de cresson**, cunt-lapper/cunt sucker.

brouteuse [brutøz] *nf V* lesbian*.

broutille [brutij] *nf F* trifling matter/trifle/(mere) fleabite; *pl* chickenfeed; **c'est de la broutille**, it's not worth worrying about.

brûlé [bryle] *a F* **il est brûlé** (*i*) he has lost his reputation/his credit/his influence; he's done for/he's ruined (*ii*) he has been betrayed (*iii*) (*espion*) his cover's been blown.

brûle-gueule [brylgœl] *nm inv F* short clay pipe/cutty(-pipe)/nose-warmer.

brûle-parfum(s) [brylparfœ̃] *nm P* firearm/revolver*/rifle/gun/shooter.

brûler [bryle] *vtr* 1. **brûler qn** (*i*) *F* to ruin s.o.'s reputation/credit (*ii*) *P* to kill* s.o. 2. *F* **brûler un espion**, to expose/to blow (the cover of) a spy; **se laisser brûler**, to give oneself away 3. *F* **brûler le pavé/la route**, to go along the road at full speed/to burn up the road/to do a ton. (*Voir* **dur** 1; **planche** 2)

brutal [brytal] *nm P* 1. strong wine 2. black bread 3. gun.

bu [by] *a P* **il est bu**, he's drunk*.

bûche [byʃ] I *nf* 1. *F* fool*/blockhead/prize idiot; **ne reste pas planté là comme une bûche**, don't just stand there like a lemon 2. *P* (safety) match 3. *P* bad card (in gambling games) 4. *F* **ramasser une bûche**, to fall/to come a cropper II *nf F* hard work/swotting/slogging (away).

bûcher [byʃe] I *vtr&i F* to work* hard (at)/to slog away (at); to swot (at); **bûcher un examen**, to swot/to mug up for an exam; **bûcher toute la journée**, to slave away/to slog away all day II *vtr P* to thrash/to beat (s.o.) up* III *vpr* **se bûcher** *P* to fight/to come to blows/to have a set-to/to scrap.

bûcheur, -euse [byʃœr, -øz] *n F* hard worker; swot.

bucolique [bykɔlik] *nf P* prostitute* who picks up her clients in parks.

buffecaille [byfkɑj] *nm P* = **buffet 1**.

buffet [byfɛ] *nm* 1. *P* stomach*/belly; **piquer qn au buffet**, to knife s.o. in the guts; **se remplir le buffet**, to have a good tuck-in/a good nosh(-up); **en avoir dans le buffet**, to have guts/balls; **n'avoir rien dans le buffet** (*i*) to have an empty belly (*ii*) to have no guts 2. *F* **danser devant le buffet**, to have nothing to eat/to go hungry.

buis [bɥi] *nm P* 1. **avoir reçu un coup de buis**, to be exhausted*/to be bushed 2. **recevoir/prendre un coup de buis**, to be the victim of circumstances 3. **une patte de buis**, a wooden leg.

buissonnière [bɥisɔnjɛr] *af O F* **faire l'école buissonnière**, to play truant/*esp NAm* hook(e)y.

bulle [byl] I *nm O P* money* II *nf P* 1. **coincer la/sa bulle** (*i*) to be idle/to laze about/to take it easy/to skive (off) (*ii*) to go to bed; to have a rest 2. (*scol*) **attraper une bulle**, to get nought (in an exam, etc). (*Voir* **chier 4**)

bureau, *pl* **-eaux** [byro] *nm* 1. *F* **bureau des pleurs**, complaints office, department 2. *P* stomach*; **en avoir dans le bureau**, to have guts.

burelingue [byrlɛ̃g] *nm P* = **burlingue**.

burette [byrɛt] *nf* 1. *P* face* 2. *P* head* 3. *pl V* testicles*/balls (*a*) **vider ses burettes**, to ejaculate*/to come/to get one's nuts off (*b*) **casser/râper les burettes à qn**; **baver sur les burettes à qn**, to give s.o. a pain in the arse/to get on s.o.'s tits.

buriner [byrine] *vi P* to work* hard; to swot.

burineur 65 **buvoter**

burineur [byrinœr] *nm* *P* hard worker; swot.

burlain [byrlɛ̃] *nm* *P* office worker.

burlingue [byrlɛ̃g] *nm* *P* **1.** stomach* **2.** office **3.** desk.

burnes [byrn] *nfpl* *V* testicles*/balls/nuts; **casser/râper les burnes à qn; baver sur les burnes à qn,** to bore s.o. to death/to give s.o. a pain in the arse/to get on s.o.'s tits/to get on s.o.'s wick; **se vider les burnes,** to ejaculate*/to come off/to shoot one's load.

burnous [byrnu(s)] *nm* *F* **faire suer le burnous,** to slavedrive/to exploit/to sweat (cheap labour).

bus [bys] *nm* *F* (= *autobus*) bus.

buse [byz] *nf* *F* fool*/idiot/dimwit; **triple buse,** extremely stupid* person/a real thickie.

business [biznɛs] *nm* *P* = **bis(e)ness.**

butage [bytaʒ] *nm* *P* murder.

buter [byte] **I** *vtr* *P* to kill* (s.o.); **se faire buter,** to get bumped off **II** *vpr* **se buter** *P* to commit suicide/to do oneself in.

buteur [bytœr] *nm* *P* killer/murderer.

butte [byt] *nf* **1.** *P* **avoir sa butte,** to be pregnant* **2.** *P* killing/murdering/bumping off **3.** *F* (a) **la Butte,** Montmartre (b) **les Buttes,** les Buttes-Chaumont (district in Paris).

butter [byte] *vtr,* **butteur** [bytœr] *nm* *P* = **buter, buteur.**

buvable [byvabl] *a* *F* bearable/tolerable/acceptable/passable; **un type pas buvable,** an impossible character/an insufferable individual. (*Voir* **potable**)

buverie [byvri] *nf* *F* drinking session/binge/bender/piss-up.

buveton [byvtɔ̃] *nm* *F* blotter/blotting pad; blotting paper.

buveur [byvœr] *nm* *F* (*écrivain, journaliste, etc*) **buveur d'encre,** ink-slinger; pen-pusher.

buvoter [byvɔte] *vi* *F* to drink* heavily/to tipple.

C

C [se] *nf* P (*drogues*) cocaine*/(big)
C.

ça [sa] *dem pron neut* **1.** *F* **rien que
ça?** is *that* all? **rien que ça!** no kidding! **2.** *F* **les gonzesses, il faut
que ça jase!** these birds will natter!
c'est ça ta bagnole? (is) that your
car?/these your wheels? **3.** *P* **avec
ça!** get along with you!/(a load of)
rubbish!/tell that to the marines!
4. *F* (*a*) **elle est grande et mince
avec ça,** she's tall, and, what's
more, slim (*b*) **avec ça que ...,** as
if ...; **avec ça qu'on vous le
permettrait!** as if they'd let you!
avec ça qu'il n'a pas triché! don't
say he didn't cheat! **5.** *F* **avoir de
ça,** to have what it takes (*i*) to have
plenty of money* (*ii*) (*femme*) to
have sex appeal (*iii*) *O* to have
intelligence*/courage, etc **6.** *P* (*a*)
comme ça tu déménages? so you're
moving out, are you? **il a dit
comme ça qu'il regrettait bien,** he
said just like that (that) he was
very sorry (*b*) **les avoir comme ça,**
to be scared*/to have the wind up
7. *F* **allons, pas de ça!** now then,
none of that! **8.** *P* **c'est pas tout
ça,** that's all very well ... **9.** *P*
faire ça, to have sex*/to make
love/to do it; **ne penser qu'à ça,** to
be obsessed by it/to have a dirty
mind/*NAm* to have one's mind in
the gutter. (*Voir* **aller** 5; **alors** (*b*))

cabane [kaban] *nf* **1.** *F* (small)
ramshackle house/flat/dump/shack
2. *P* prison*; **être en cabane,** to be
in clink/in the nick; **il a passé trois
ans en cabane,** he did three years
in the nick/*NAm* in (the) stir **3.** *P*

brothel* **4.** *P* **cabane bambou,**
striptease sideshow. (*Voir* **attiger** 3)

cabanon [kabanɔ̃] *nm* *F* **il est bon
à mettre au cabanon,** they ought to
lock him up/he's off his head.

cabe [kab] *nm* *P* = **cabot** 1, 2, 3.

cabèche, cabêche [kabɛʃ] *nf*,
caberlot [kabɛrlo] *nm* *O* *P*
head*/nut/bonce.

cabestron [kabɛstrɔ̃] *nm* *O* *P* (*a*)
mug/sucker/fall guy (*b*) fool*/
idiot/twit/clot.

cabinces [kabɛ̃s] *nmpl* *O* *P* WC*/
the bog(s).

cabochard, -arde [kabɔʃar,
-ard] *a&n* *F* stubborn/pig-headed
(person).

caboche [kabɔʃ] *nf* *F* **1.** head*/
nut **2.** intelligence*/savvy/gump-
tion **3.** **avoir la caboche dure** (*i*) to
be slow on the uptake/to be thick
(*ii*) to be stubborn/obstinate.

cabochon [kabɔʃɔ̃] *nm* *F* **1.** =
caboche 1 **2.** (*voiture*) sidelight.

cabombe [kabɔ̃b] *nf* *O* *P* candle;
glim; lamp; (electric) light/torch;
souffle la cabombe! put the light
out! **tenir la cabombe = tenir la
chandelle (chandelle** 11). (*Voir*
calbombe)

cabosse [kabɔs] *nf* *F* bruise/
bump; **se faire une cabosse,** to get
a bump.

cabot [kabo] *nm* *P* **1.** dog/pooch/
mutt; **sale cabot!** dirty dog/hound!
2. = **cabotin** **3.** (*mil*) corporal.

cabotin, -ine [kabotɛ̃, -in] *n* *F*
(*a*) inferior/third-rate actor *or*
actress; ham (*b*) show-off*.

cabotinage [kabɔtinaʒ] *nm F* (*a*) inferior acting/hamming (*b*) showing off.

cabotiner [kabɔtine] *vi F* (*a*) to act badly/to ham (*b*) to play-act (*c*) to play to the gallery.

caboulot [kabulo] *nm F* seedy *or* grotty pub/dive/doss-house.

cabris [kabri] *nmpl P* = **cabriolets.**

cabriole [kabri(j)ɔl] *nf F* **1.** faire une cabriole, to come a cropper **2.** faire la cabriole, to swing/to go with the tide **3.** faire des cabrioles, to have sex*/to sleep around.

cabriolets [kabri(j)ɔlɛ] *nmpl P* handcuffs*/cuffs.

caca [kaka] *nm F* (*langage enfantin*) **1.** excrement*/big job/poo/poo-poo; faire caca, to do a poo/to do poo-poo's; (*à un enfant*) tu as fait caca? have you done your duty?/have you done (your) big jobs? jette ça, c'est (du) caca, throw that away, it's nasty/dirty **2.** mettre à qn le nez dans son caca, to put s.o. (firmly) in his place/to rub s.o.'s nose in it.

cacade [kakad] *nf O P* **1.** mess/failure **2.** funk/climb-down.

cacafouiller [kakafuje] *vi O P* = **cafouiller.**

cacasse [kakas] *nf V* aller à la cacasse, to have sex*/to have it off.

cache-fri-fri [kaʃfrifri] *nm inv P* (*i*) very brief women's briefs/bikini briefs (*ii*) G-string. (*Voir* fri-fri)

cachemire [kaʃmir] *nm F* (waiter's) tea towel/*NAm* dish towel/cloth; duster.

cache-pot [kaʃpo] *nm inv P* (pair of) knickers.

cachet [kaʃɛ] *nm P* sum of money paid by a prostitute* to her pimp*.

cacheton [kaʃtɔ̃] *nm P* (*i*) fee (of private teacher, etc); (*artiste/comédien*) courir le cacheton, to look for work/a job (*ii*) sum of

money paid to a prostitute* (for her services) (*iii*) = **cachet.**

cachotterie [kaʃɔtri] *nf F* faire des cachotteries à qn, to keep/to hold things back from s.o.; to hold out on s.o.

cachottier, -ière [kaʃɔtje, -jɛr] *a&n F* secretive/cagey (person); quel cachottier vous faites! well, you are a sly one!

cacique [kasik] *nm F* **1.** candidate who comes first in an exam (*esp* for the *Ecole normale supérieure*) **2.** (*a*) important person*/big shot (*b*) employer/boss*.

cactus [kaktys] *nm P* **1.** problem/hitch/nuisance **2.** avoir un cactus dans la poche/dans le portefeuille, to be a miser*/to have short arms and deep pockets.

cadancher [kadɑ̃ʃe] *vi P* to die*.

cadavre [kadɑvr] *nm F* **1.** il y a un cadavre entre eux, they are linked by a crime; il y a un cadavre dans le placard, it's a bit of a mystery/we haven't got to the bottom of it **2.** empty (wine) bottle/empty/dead man/dead soldier **3.** unlucky gambler/jinxed player.

caddie [kadi] *nm F* truck; (supermarket) trolley.

cadeau, pl -eaux [kado] *nm* **1.** *F* c'est pas un cadeau!/c'est un cadeau! (*i*) he/she is really dull/a real pain! (*ii*) it's not (exactly) a piece of cake; il ne lui a pas fait de cadeau (*i*) he didn't spare him (*ii*) a fat lot of use he was to him; je te fais cadeau du reste, I'll spare you the details **2.** *P* un petit/p'tit cadeau, prostitute's fee.

cadenassé [kadnase] *a F* buttoned up/mum.

se cadenasser [səkadnase] *vpr F* to keep a secret/to keep mum/to button (up) one's lip.

cadène [kadɛn] *nf P* chain necklace.

cadènes [kadɛn] *nfpl,* **cadenet-**

tes [kadnɛt] *nfpl*, **cadennes** [kadɛn] *nfpl P* handcuffs*/cuffs.

cadet [kadɛ] *nm F* c'est le **cadet de mes soucis,** that's the least of my worries.

cador [kadɔr] *nm P* **1.** dog*/hound **2.** top dog/big shot/boss* **3.** expert/ace.

cadran [kadrɑ̃] *nm* **1.** *F* **faire le tour du cadran,** to sleep the clock round/round the clock **2.** *P* buttocks*.

cadre [kadr] *nm P* painting/canvass.

cafard, -arde [kafar, -ard] **I** *n F* **1.** smug, sanctimonious person **2.** (*a*) spy; informer* (*b*) sneak; tell-tale* **II** *nm F* **avoir le cafard,** to be depressed*/to have the blues/to be down in the dumps; **avoir un coup de cafard,** to be a bit down/to be feeling (a bit) blue; **il fiche le cafard à tout le monde,** he gets everyone down.

cafardage [kafardaʒ] *nm F* sneaking; tale-telling.

cafarder [kafarde] *F* **I** *vi* **1.** (*a*) (*i*) to spy (*ii*) to be an informer* (*b*) to sneak; to snitch/to tell tales/to tell on (s.o.) **2.** to feel depressed*/to have the blues **II** *vtr* **cafarder qn** (*i*) to spy on s.o.; to denounce/to inform* on s.o. (*ii*) to sneak/to split/to snitch on s.o.

cafardeur, -euse [kafardœr, -ǿz] *n F* sneak; tell-tale*.

cafardeux, -euse [kafardǿ, -ǿz] *F* **I** *a* depressed*/down in the dumps/browned off; **temps cafardeux,** depressing/miserable weather **II** *n* miserable person/miseryguts; **quel cafardeux!** what a misery!

caf'conc', caf'conce [kafkɔ̃s] *nm A P* (= *café-concert*) kind of old-time music-hall; café providing evening entertainment by artistes.

café [kafe] *nm P* **prendre le café du pauvre/des pauvres,** to have sex*

(after a meal at home, instead of coffee)/to make one's own entertainment. (*Voir* **fort 2**)

cafèt [kafɛt] *nf F* (*abbr* = *cafeteria*) coffee bar/café/caff.

cafeter [kafte] *vtr&i P* = **cafarder.**

cafeteur, -euse [kaftœr, -ǿz] *n P* = **cafardeur, -euse.**

cafetière [kaftjɛr] *nf P* **1.** (*i*) head*/nut/skull (*ii*) brains; **travailler de la cafetière,** to be mad*/to be round the bend; **un coup sur la cafetière,** a thump on the head; **en prendre un coup sur la cafetière,** to be on a downer; **se payer la cafetière de qn,** to make fun of s.o./to take the mickey out of s.o.; **bouillir de la cafetière,** to be overflowing with ideas **2.** sneak; tell-tale. (*Voir* **cresson 1** (*a*))

cafeton [kaftɔ̃] *nm A P* café/caff.

cafouillage [kafujaʒ] *nm F* mess/muddle/shambles; (*moteur, etc*) missing/misfiring.

cafouiller [kafuje] *vi F* to get into a mess/to make a mess of things; to muddle; to be all at sixes and sevens; to go to pieces; (*moteur, etc*) to miss/to misfire/to work in fits and starts; (*orateur*) (*i*) to talk incoherently/to burble/to splutter (*ii*) to swallow one's words (*iii*) to talk nonsense*/to talk a lot of hot air.

cafouilleur, -euse [kafujœr, -ǿz] *n*, **cafouilleux** [kafujǿ] *nm F* muddler/ham-fisted person/bungler.

cafouillis [kafuji] *nm F* muddle/mess/shambles.

cafouine [kafwin] *nf P* excrement*/dung.

cafter [kafte] *vtr&i P* = **cafeter.**

cafteur, -euse [kaftœr, -ǿz] *n P* = **cafeteur, -euse.**

cagade [kagad] *nf P* **1.** mistake*/blunder; **faire une cagade,** to slip up/to goof/to make a mess of things 2. diarrhoea*; defecation 3. intense fear*.

cage [kaʒ] *nf* 1. *P* prison*/coop/ pen; **mettre qn en cage**, to send s.o. to prison*/to put s.o. in the can; **cage à poules**, (communal) prison cell/cage 2. *F* **cage à poules/à mouches/à lapins**, tiny room/flat etc; poky hole/box/doll's house/ rabbit hutch 3. *O P* **cage à poules** = space behind glass doors in entrance hall of certain hotels from where prostitutes solicit 4. *F* **cage à poules**, climbing frame (in playground) 5. *F* ribs/rib-cage 6. *F* (*football*) goal (area); **le goal n'est pas sorti de la cage**, the goalie didn't come out of his goal.

cagée [kaʒe] *nf P* (*i*) vanful/vanload (*ii*) cageful of prisoners.

cagibi [kaʒibi] *nm F* 1. hut/shelter 2. lumber-room/cubby-hole/glory-hole.

cagna [kaɲa] *nf P* 1. (*a*) hut/lodgings (*b*) dug-out 2. room/pad/place/crash-out.

cagnard, -arde [kaɲar, -ard] *O F* I *a* idle/lazy* II *n* lazybones/good-for-nothing.

cagne [kaɲ] I *nf P* 1. useless individual 2. slut/trollop 3. broken-down horse/old nag 4. **avoir la cagne**, to feel lazy* II *nf P* (Arts) class preparing for the entrance exam to the *Ecole normale supérieure*. (*Voir* **khâgne**)

cagner [kaɲe] *vi P* to shirk/to swing the lead/to skive (off).

cagneux, -euse [kaɲø, -øz] *n P* student in a **cagne II**.

cagoinces, cagoinsses [kagwɛ̃s] *nmpl P* WC*/bog(s).

caguer [kage] *vi P* to defecate*/to (have a) crap.

cahier [kaje] *nm F* police record/form.

cahin-caha [kaɛ̃kaa] *adv F* se **porter cahin-caha**, to be so-so/to be fair to middling; **vivre cahin-caha**, to scrape a living/to get by; **leur ménage va cahin-caha**, they get by somehow.

cahoua [kawa] *nm P* = **caoua(h)**. (*Voir* **kawa**)

caïd [kaid] *nm P* 1. *P* leader (of gang, etc)/boss*/big chief/big shot/ hot shot; **jouer/faire son caïd**, to give oneself airs 2. *F* ace/expert/champion.

caille [kaj] I *nf F* girl*/chick; (*à un enfant, une femme*) **ma (petite) caille!** my pet! II *nf P* 1. **avoir qn/qch à la caille**, to hate* the sight of s.o./sth; to hate s.o.'s guts 2. **l'avoir à la caille**, to be furious; to be put out 3. **être à la caille** (*i*) to grouse/to grumble*; to be bloody-minded (*ii*) to be unlucky 4. **se retourner la caille**, to worry oneself sick. (*Voir* **œil**)

cailler [kaje] I *vtr&i P* **on caille/ ça caille**, it's bloody cold/it's (fucking) freezing/it's brass-monkey weather/it's (cold) enough to freeze the balls off a brass monkey II *vtr* 1. **se cailler le sang/le raisin/le mou**, to get worried stiff 2. *O* **cailler qn**, to hate the sight of s.o./to hate s.o.'s guts III *vpr* **se cailler** *P* **se cailler (les miches)**, to be (freezing) cold; **je me (les) caille**, I'm bloody freezing.

caillou, pl -oux [kaju] *nm P* 1. (*a*) head*; **caillou déplumé**, bald head; **ne pas avoir un poil sur le caillou**, to be bald* (*b*) intelligence*; **il passe pour avoir qch dans le caillou**, he's got brains 2. *O* (*couple*) **se sucer le caillou**, to kiss/ to neck 3. **battre le caillou** (*i*) to loaf about (the streets) (*ii*) to walk the streets in search of a job 4. stone object/ornament 5. *pl* **cailloux**, precious stones *esp* diamonds/sparklers.

caïman [kaimɑ̃] *nm F* senior master at the *École normale supérieure*.

caire [kɛr] *nm O P* money*/ackers/ shekels.

caisse [kɛs] **I** *nf* **1.** *P* head*; **bourrer la caisse à qn,** to stuff s.o.'s head full of lies, empty talk, etc; to lead s.o. up the garden path; **ne me bourre pas la caisse!** don't give me that rubbish! **se faire sauter la caisse,** to blow one's brains out **2.** *P* stomach*; **n'avoir rien au fond de la caisse,** to be starving/ravenous **3.** *P* chest; **être malade/souffrir de la caisse,** to be consumptive/to have a weak chest; **il s'en va de la caisse/il a la caisse qui se fait la malle,** his lungs are giving up the ghost/giving out **4.** *O P* **la caisse d'épargne,** mouth* **5.** *P* (*mil*) **(grosse) caisse,** prison*; **faire de la grosse caisse,** to be in clink **6.** *P* coffin/box **7.** *P* (*à l'église*) confessional (box) **8.** *F* (*a*) **passer à la caisse** (*i*) to get paid (*ii*) to be paid off (*b*) **faire la caisse,** to rob the till (*c*) **caisse noire,** slush fund **9.** *F* (old) car*/(old) banger/(old) wreck **10.** *P* (*moto, etc*) **rouler la caisse/ aller à fond la caisse,** to go all out/ to do a ton **11.** *F* **rouler la/sa caisse,** to show off*/to put on an act **12.** *F* **battre la grosse caisse,** to talk big **13.** *O F* **mettre qn en caisse,** to pull s.o.'s leg **II** *nm P* **c'est du caisse,** it's six of one and half a dozen of the other; it makes no odds/it's much of a muchness; **c'est jamais du caisse,** it's never the same. (*Voir* **quès**)

caiss(e)mar [kɛsmar] *nm O P* cashier.

caisson [kɛsɔ̃] *nm P* **1.** head*; **se faire sauter le caisson,** to blow one's brains out **2.** stomach*/ bread-basket.

calanche [kalɑ̃ʃ] *nf P* death; **(une) calanche vépé** (= *vp* = *voie publique*) (a) death on the public highway/the roads.

calancher [kalɑ̃ʃe] *vi P* to die*/to snuff it.

calbar(d) [kalbar] *nm P* (men's)

underpants; **il a rien dans le calbar(d),** he's got no guts/balls.

calbombe [kalbɔ̃b] *nf P* = **cabombe.**

calcer [kalse] *vtr V* **calcer une nana,** to have sex* with/to screw a girl.

calcif [kalsif] *nm P* (men's) underpants; **filer un coup dans le calcif,** to have sex*/to get one's leg over. (*Voir* **anguille**)

caldard [kaldar] *nm P* (*peu usuel*) = **calbard.**

cale [kal] *nf* **1.** *F* **être à fond de cale,** to be penniless*/to be on one's uppers **2.** *P* **être de la cale,** to be a homosexual* **3.** *P* **mettre une nana en cale,** to get a girl pregnant*/*esp NAm* to knock a girl up.

calé [kale] *a F* **1.** **être calé sur/en qch,** to be well-informed about sth/ to be good at sth; **être calé en maths,** to be good at maths; **c'est un type calé,** he's a bright/clever bloke **2.** difficult/complicated/ awkward/dodgy **3.** **ça c'est calé!** that's crafty!/that's clever! **4.** (= *recalé*) **être calé,** to fail (an exam) **5.** *A* rich*/well-off/well-to-do.

calebar(d) [kalbar] *nm P* (*peu usuel*) = **calbard.**

calebasse [kalbas] *nf P* **1.** head*/nut; **un coup sur la calebasse,** a thump on the head **2.** face*/mug **3.** big gawky woman **4.** *pl* sagging breasts; droopers.

calebombe [kalbɔ̃b] *nf P* = **cabombe.**

calecer [kalse] *vtr V* = **calcer.**

calecif [kalsif] *nm P* = **calcif.**

caleçon [kalsɔ̃] *nm P* prisoner's parcel.

caledard [kaldar] *nm P* (*peu usuel*) = **calbard.**

cale-dent(s) [kaldɑ̃] *nm P* snack.

calencher [kalɑ̃ʃe] *vi P* = **calancher.**

calendes [kalɑ̃d] *nfpl* F renvoyer qn/qch aux calendes grecques, to put s.o./sth off indefinitely.

calendo [kalɑ̃do] *nm*, **calendos(se)** [kalɑ̃dos] *nm* P **1.** Camembert cheese **2.** guard/ NAm conductor (of train).

caler [kale] **I 1.** *vtr&i* F (*voiture, moteur*) to stall **2.** *vi* F to back down/to climb down/to give up; to get cold feet; je cale, I give up **II** *vtr* **1.** F caler un malade sur des coussins, to prop a patient up on cushions **2.** P se caler les amygdales/les babines/les babouines/les badigoinces/les côtes/ les joues; se la caler/se les caler, to eat* heartily/to stuff oneself/to feed one's face/to get stuck in; ça cale l'estomac, it fills you up **III** *vpr* se caler F to settle comfortably (in an armchair, etc).

(se) caleter [(sə)kalte] *vi & pr* P = (se) calter.

caleur, -euse [kalœr, -øz] *n* P **1.** idler/loafer/shirker/skiver **2.** coward*/funk/fraidy cat.

calfouette [kalfwɛt] *nm* P = calbar(d).

calibre [kalibr] *nm* P pistol/ revolver*/shooter.

calots [kalo] *nmpl* P eyes*; rouler/ ribouler des calots, to roll one's eyes (in amazement)/to goggle; boiter des calots, to squint.

calotin [kalɔtɛ̃] F (*péj*) **I** *nm* (*a*) priest/clergyman*; ces fichus calotins, these blasted priests (*b*) (overzealous) churchgoer/bigot **II** *a* churchy.

calotte [kalɔt] *nf* F **1.** box on the ear/clout/smack/slap; flanquer une calotte à qn, to give s.o. a clout; se prendre une calotte, to get boxed round the ears **2.** (*péj*) la calotte, the clergy/the priesthood.

calotter [kalɔte] *vtr* P to steal*/to nick.

calouse [kaluz] *nf* P leg*; jouer des calouses, to walk.

calouser [kaluze] *vtr* O P calouser le bitume, to walk along the street/ to pound the pavement.

calpette [kalpɛt] *nf* P (wagging) tongue (of a gossip).

calsif [kalsif] *nm* P = calcif.

calter [kalte] *vi*, **se calter** [səkalte] *vpr* P to run away*/to clear off; je suis pressé, je calte I'm in a hurry, (I) must dash/I've got to split; je t'ai dit d'calter, I told you to get lost.

calva [kalva] *nm* F (*boisson*) calvados.

cam [kam] **I** *a inv* P (= *camouflé*) (*esp mil*) camouflaged **II** *nm* P (= *camelot*) street trader/hawker.

Camarde [kamard] *nf* O F (*esp littéraire*) la Camarde, death; baiser la Camarde, to die*/to meet one's maker.

camaro [kamaro] *nm* P friend*/ comrade/pal/buddy.

cambouis [kɑ̃bwi] *nm* P (*a*) le Cambouis = l'Intendance Militaire = approx the Royal Army Service Corps (now part of the Royal Corps of Transport) (*b*) un cambouis, a member of the Intendance Militaire.

cambrio [kɑ̃brio] *nm* P (= *cambrioleur*) burglar/housebreaker.

cambriole [kɑ̃briɔl] *nf* O P housebreaking/burgling.

Cambronne [kɑ̃brɔn] *Prnm* F le mot de Cambronne = merde! (*qv*); = four-letter(ed) word. (*Voir* mot 2)

cambrousard, -arde [kɑ̃bruzar, -ard], **cambroussard, -arde** [kɑ̃brusar, -ard] P **I** *a* (*a*) countrified (*b*) slow/awkward **II** *nm* peasant*/yokel/esp NAm hick.

cambrouse [kɑ̃bruz] *nf*, **cambrousse** [kɑ̃brus] *nf* P

(*campagne*) country; **au fin fond de
la cambrousse,** at the back of
beyond; **se paumer en pleine cambrousse,** to get lost in the middle of
nowhere.

cambuse [kɑ̃byz] *nf P* **1.** (*a*)
untidy house/hovel/dump/hole (*b*)
untidy room/hole/dump **2.** seedy
or sleazy pub; dive.

cambut [kɑ̃by] *nm P* **faire un
cambut,** to substitute/to switch imitation jewellery for real/false
money for good, etc; to pull a
switch. (*Voir* **chanstique**)

cambuter [kɑ̃byte] *P* **I** *vi* = **faire
un cambut** (**cambut**) **II** *vtr*
cambuter un jacquot, to crack a
safe.

cambuteur [kɑ̃bytœr] *nm P* person who makes the switch/the
exchange in a *cambut.* (*Voir*
cambut)

came [kam] **I** *nm P* (= *camelot*)
street trader/hawker **II** *nf* **1.** *P* (*a*)
drugs*/junk/dope; **priseur, -euse de
came,** junkie/junky (*b*) cocaine* **2.**
P (*a*) goods/merchandise/stuff (*b*)
shoddy goods/junk/trash **3.** *V*
envoyer/lâcher sa came, to ejaculate*/to come.

camé, -ée [kame] *P* (*drogues*) **I** *n*
drug addict*/dope addict/junkie/
junky **II** *a* under the influence of
drugs*/high (on drugs*)/doped up/
stoned; **il était camé jusqu'à l'os,** he
was bombed out of his mind.

camelote [kamlɔt] *nf F* (*a*) goods/
merchandise; **fais voir ta camelote!**
let's have a look at your stuff; **c'est
de la bonne camelote,** it's good stuff
(*b*) cheap shoddy goods; junk/
trash; **c'est de la camelote,** it's rub-
bish/trash; it's rubbishy/trashy.

camembert [kamɑ̃bɛr] *nm P* **1.**
traffic policeman's raised platform
2. circular machine-gun loader.

se camer [səkame] *vpr P* to take
drugs*; to be a drug addict*; to
get high/stoned (on drugs); **il se**

came à l'héro, he's on heroin*/he
gets high on H.

camion [kamjɔ̃] *nm* **1.** *P* girl* *or*
woman* with large breasts*/big tits
2. *F* **elle est belle comme un camion,** she's got a face like the back
(-end) of a bus.

camoufe [kamuf] *nf,* **camoufle**
[kamufl] *nf A P* candle; lamp;
(electric) light/torch.

camp [kɑ̃] *nm F* **ficher/***P* **foutre le
camp,** to run away*/to clear off/to
beat it; to bugger off; **fiche(z)(-moi)
le camp!** hop it!/get lost!* **fous(-
moi)/foutez(-moi) le camp!** sod off!/
bugger off!/piss off!/fuck off! **on
lève le camp,** let's split.

campagne [kɑ̃paɲ] *nf P* **1.** (*esp
prostituée*) **aller à la campagne,** to
go to prison* **2. emmener qn à la
campagne** (*i*) to lead s.o. up the
garden path (*ii*) to hold s.o. in contempt; **battre la campagne,** to be (a
bit) scatterbrained/to wander a bit
(in one's mind).

campêche [kɑ̃pɛʃ] *nm P* **bois de
campêche,** inferior champagne*.

camphre [kɑ̃fr] *nm O P* (*a*) alcohol (*b*) strong spirits*/rotgut.

camplouse [kɑ̃pluz] *nf,* **cam-
pluche** [kɑ̃plyʃ] *nf P* = **cam-
brous(s)e 1.**

campo(s) [kɑ̃po] *nm F* holiday/
day off/free time; **avoir campo,** to
have a day off (from school, work).

canadienne [kanadjɛn] *nf P* **une
canadienne en (peau de) sapin,** a
coffin/a wooden overcoat/a pine
overcoat.

canaque [kanak] *nm P* **1.** (*péj*)
Black*/negro/nigger **2.** French
Canadian/Canuck.

canard [kanar] *nm* **1.** *F* **marcher
comme un canard,** to waddle **2.** *F*
trempé comme un canard, drenched
(to the skin)/like a drowned rat **3.**
F **il fait un froid de canard,** it's
freezing cold **4.** *F* **mon petit
canard,** my darling*/ducks/ducky

5. *F* false rumour; hoax* **6.** *F* newspaper/rag/scandal sheet; **acheter un canard,** to buy a paper **7.** *F* difficult customer **8.** *F* (*musique*) false note; **il a fait un canard,** he hit a wrong note **9.** *F* a lump of sugar dipped in brandy or coffee **10.** *F* (*médecine*) speculum **11.** *P* (*i*) horse/nag (*ii*) broken-down hack **12.** *V* **baiser qn en canard,** to have sex* with s.o. dog(gie)-fashion/from behind. (*Voir* **patte 7; sirop 3**)

canarder [kanarde] *F* **I** *vtr* (*i*) to take pot-shots at people/to snipe at s.o. (*ii*) to kill s.o. (in this way) **II** *vi* (*a*) **canarder sur le compte de qn,** to spread false rumours about s.o. (*b*) to play/to sing a false note; to sing off key.

canardeur [kanardœr] *nm F* sniper.

canardier [kanardje] *nm F* rumour-monger/scandal-monger.

canasson [kanasɔ̃] *nm P* horse/nag/broken-down hack.

cancérette [kãserɛt] *nf F* cigarette*/cancer stick.

cancre [kãkr] *nm F* (*scol*) dunce/blockhead.

cané [kane] *a P* **1.** exhausted*/worn out **2.** dead.

caner [kane] *vi P* **1.** (*a*) to be afraid*/to have the jitters; **ne pas caner,** to keep one's pecker up (*b*) to be a coward*/to show the white feather; to climb down/to chicken out **2.** to die*/to kick the bucket **3.** to stay away/to skive (off) (from lectures, work, etc). (*Voir* **canner; décaner**)

caneur, -euse [kanœr, -øz] *P* **I** *a* cowardly*/yellow-bellied/chicken **II** *n* coward*/quitter.

canevas [kanva] *nm* **1.** *F* **broder le canevas,** to embroider a story **2.** *P* (*boxe*) canvas; **envoyer qn au canevas,** to floor s.o.

caniche [kaniʃ] *nm&f F* ce n'est/

c'est pas fait pour les caniches, it's not there as an ornament, it's meant to be used. (*Voir* **chien**)

canif [kanif] *nm F* **donner un coup/des coups de canif dans le contrat (de mariage),** to be unfaithful (to one's husband, wife).

canne [kan] **I** *nf* **1.** *P* **casser sa canne,** to die*/to peg out **2.** *pl P* legs*/pegs/pins; **mettre les cannes (en vitesse),** to run away*/to clear off; **être sur les cannes/avoir les cannes en vermicelle,** to be exhausted*/to be out on one's feet **3.** *F* **il a l'air d'avoir avalé sa canne,** he's as stiff as a poker/as a ram-rod; he's stiff and starchy. (*Voir* **parapluie**) **4.** *V* penis*/rod/prick; **avoir/tenir la canne,** to have an erection/to have a hard-on; **souffler dans la canne,** to fellate* s.o./to give s.o. a blow-job; **casser la canne,** to have sex*/to have it off/to get one's end away **II** *nm P* corpse*/stiff.

canné [kane] *a P* exhausted*/knocked up/knackered.

cannelles [kanɛl] *nfpl P* hand-cuffs*/bracelets.

canner [kane] *P* **I** *vi* to die*/to peg out **II** *vtr* to kill* (s.o.)/to knock (s.o.) off.

canon [kanɔ̃] *nm* **1.** *P* glass of wine **2.** *P* stomach*; **n'avoir rien à se mettre dans le canon,** to be starving/ravenous **3.** *V* **avoir une balle dans le canon,** to have an erection*/to have a loaded gun/to have a hard-on.

canonnier [kanɔnje] *a & nm F* (*football*) **(joueur) canonnier,** high goalscorer.

canotier [kanɔtje] *nm P* **travailler du canotier,** to be mad*/to be off one's rocker.

canou [kanu] *nm Belg V* female genitals*.

cantalou(p) [kãtalu] *nm O P* native of Auvergne/Auvergnat.

cantoche [kɑ̃tɔʃ] *nf P* canteen.

canulant [kanylɑ̃] *a F* boring.

canular, canulard[1] [kanylar] *nm F (i)* tall story *(ii)* practical joke/hoax*/leg-pull; **monter un canular à qn**, to hoax* s.o. *(iii)* students' rag.

canulard[2] *nm P* **1.** informer*/ grass **2.** male nurse.

canularesque [kanylarɛsk] *a F* faked/trumped-up (information, etc).

canule [kanyl] *nf F (pers, chose)* bore*/pest/pain.

canuler [kanyle] *vtr F* **1.** to bore* (s.o.)/to be a pest (to s.o.) **2.** to play a practical joke on (s.o.)/to hoax* (s.o.).

caoua(h) [kawa] *nm P* coffee. *(Voir* **cahoua**; **kawa**)

cap [kap] *a F (abbr = capable)* **t'es pas cap**, you haven't got it in you.

capa [kapa] *nf F (abbr = capacité)* **votre capa en droit**, your law diploma.

capet [kapɛ] *nm P* hat.

capiston [kapistɔ̃] *nm P (mil, marine)* captain.

capital [kapital] *nm P* virginity/maidenhead; **entamer le (petit) capital**, to deflower a virgin/to pick a girl's cherry/to be the first.

capitonnée [kapitɔne] *af F* **elle est bien capitonnée**, she's nice and plump/cuddly/well-padded/well-stacked.

capo [kapo] *nm* **1.** *F (mil)* (= **caporal**) corporal/corp. *(Voir* **kapo**) **2.** *P* **être capo**, to lose at gambling.

capon, -onne [kapɔ̃, -ɔn] *O F* **I** *a* cowardly/chicken **II** *n (a)* coward *(b)* sneak.

caponner [kapɔne] *vi O F (a)* to be a coward*/to be chicken *(b)* to sneak/to tell tales.

capote [kapɔt] *nf P* **capote anglaise**, condom*/French letter/frenchie/rubber (Johnny).

capout [kaput] *a&n F* = **caput**.

capsule [kapsyl] *nf P (casquette)* cap.

caput [kaput] *a&n F (a)* dead*/killed/done for *(b)* finished; **je suis caput**, I'm out of it/I've had it *(c)* **faire caput (à) qn**, to kill s.o. *(Voir* **kaput)**

caquer [kake] *vi P* to defecate*/to (have a) crap.

caquet [kake] *nm F* noisy chatter/gossiping/prattle; **rabattre le caquet à qn**, to shut s.o. up/to take s.o. down a peg (or two).

caquetage [kak(ə)taʒ] *nm F* noisy chatter(ing)/prattling/cackle.

caqueter [kak(ə)te] *vi F* to chatter*/to prattle/to cackle.

cara [kara] *nm O P (abbr = caractère)* character; **un mauvais cara**, a bad temper.

carabin [karabɛ̃] *nm F* **1.** medical student/medic(o) **2.** **carabin de la comète**, swindler*.

carabinade [karabinad] *nf F* medical students' rag.

carabine [karabin] *nf V* penis*.

carabiné [karabine] *a F* very strong/intense/a whale of a . . ./a father and mother of a . . .; splitting (headache); stinking (cold); stiff (drink, bill, etc); **une guigne carabinée**, an extraordinary run of bad luck; **une noce carabinée**, a rare old binge/a real piss-up; **une cuite carabinée**, a dreadful hangover; **un toupet carabiné**, a hell of a nerve/a bloody cheek.

carabiner [karabine] *vi F (jeux d'argent)* to lay an occasional stake.

carabinier [karabinje] *nm F* **arriver comme les carabiniers (d'Offenbach)**, to arrive too late/to miss the bus.

caraco [karako] *nm P* mistake*/blunder/boob.

carafe [karaf] *nf* **1.** *P* head*/nut **2.** *P* fool*/idiot/twit/nurd **3.** *F* **rester en carafe** (*i*) to be left in the lurch/to be left high and dry (*ii*) to be left out of it/to be left out in the cold; **ils m'ont laissé en carafe** (*i*) they left me high and dry/they left me in mid air (*ii*) they left me out of it; (*voiture*) to break down; **ma bagnole est restée en carafe,** my car conked out on me. (*Voir* **bouchon 6**)

carafon [karafɔ̃] *nm P* **1.** (*a*) head*/nut (*b*) (*cerveau*) **il n'a rien dans le carafon,** he's got no brains **2.** fool*/idiot/nurd.

carambolage [karɑ̃bɔlaʒ] *nm* **1.** (*aut*) (multiple) pile-up/crash **2.** *V* sex*/copulation.

caramboler [karɑ̃bɔle] *vtr* **1.** *F* to run/to crash/to plough into (a car); **cinquante voitures se sont carambolées sur l'autoroute,** there was a fifty car pile-up on the motorway **2.** *V* to have sex* with s.o.

carambouillage [karɑ̃bujaʒ] *nm,* **carambouille** [karɑ̃buj] *nf F* fraudulent conversion (for cash, of goods bought on credit).

carambouilleur [karɑ̃bujœr] *nm F* swindler*/fiddler/con man.

caramel [karamɛl] *nm P* (*drogues*) (*abcès provoqué par une piqûre avec une aiguille non stérilisée ou par des drogues impures*) ab/AB/ABC.

carante [karɑ̃t] *nf P* **1.** (*a*) table (*b*) (illicit) street-vendor's folding table **2. se mettre en carante** (*i*) to get angry*/to blow one's top (*ii*) to turn nasty/to cut up rough. (*Voir* **quarante**)

carapatage [karapataʒ] *nm P* hurried departure/quick exit.

se carapater [səkarapate] *vpr P* to run away*/to skedaddle/to split/to make a quick exit/to make tracks.

caraque [karak] *nf A P* dirty slut.

carat [kara] *nm* **1.** *F* **un sot à vingt-quatre/à trente-six carats,** a prize idiot **2.** *P* age; year; **un môme de treize carats,** a kid of thirteen; **prendre du carat,** to grow old/to get long in the tooth **3.** *P* **jusqu'au dernier carat,** (right) up to the last moment/up to the minute.

carbi [karbi] *nm P* **1.** coal/black stuff **2.** coalman/coalie/coaly **3.** *O* **aller au carbi/(aller) bosser au carbi,** (*esp pour un criminel*) to do unpleasant manual work/to get down to some hard work (for a change) **4.** money*/brass. (*Voir* **sac**)

carbonade [karbɔnad] *nf P* washing soda.

carboniser [karbɔnize] *vtr P* (*a*) **carboniser qn,** to ruin s.o.'s reputation/to discredit/to malign s.o.; to run s.o. down/to roast s.o. (*b*) **carboniser un coup,** to frustrate an attempt/to put the kibosh on sth.

carburant [karbyrɑ̃] *nm,* **carbure** [karbyr] *nm P* money*/dough/lolly.

carburer [karbyre] *vi P* **1.** *O* to pay*/to shell out **2.** to drink/to knock it back **3.** to work efficiently/to function well; **ça carbure,** it's going fine/it works like a treat; **carburer sec,** to drive very fast/to do a ton **4.** to think (hard)/to turn over in one's mind; **carbure un peu!** think it over!

carcan [karkɑ̃] *nm O P* (*esp turf*) broken-down old horse/nag/hack.

carder [karde] *vtr P* to scratch (s.o.). (*Voir* **cuir 3**)

cardinal [kardinal] *nm P* a klr made with red wine.

cardinales [kardinal] *nfpl O P* **avoir ses cardinales,** to have a period*/to have the reds.

cardinoche [kardinɔʃ] *nm F* = **cardinal.**

car(r)er [kare] *P* **I** *vtr* **1.** to conceal/to stash (sth) away **2.** to

steal*/to swipe/to lift (sth) **3.** to
place/to put (sth) somewhere; to
plonk (sth) down; **tu peux te le
car(r)er dans le train/dans le baba,**
you know where you can stick
that/you can stick that up your
arse/*NAm* ass **II** *vpr* **se car(r)er**
P to run away*/to skedaddle/to
make a quick exit.

caricature [karikatyr] *nf F* ugly
person/figure of fun; **quelle caricature!** what a fright!

carlets [karlɛ] *nmpl O P* **avoir ses
carlets,** to have a period*/to have
the flags out.

carlingue [karlɛ̃g] *nf P* **1.**
prison*/clink/stir **2.** (*WWII*) **la
Carlingue,** the Gestapo.

carluche [karlyʃ] *nf P* prison*/
clink/stir.

carme [karm] *nm A P* money*.

carmer [karme] *vtr&i O P* to pay*
up/to cough up.

carmouille [karmuj] *nf O P* pay-
ment/settling up.

carnaval [karnaval] *nm F* gro-
tesque person/figure of fun/guy/
scarecrow.

carne [karn] *nf*, **carogne** [karɔɲ]
nf P **1.** tough/inferior meat **2.**
old horse/nag/hack **3.** (*a*) bad-
tempered, cantankerous person;
(*femme*) bitch (*b*) good-for-nothing/
swine; **vieille carne,** old bag.

caroline [karɔlin] *nf P* **1.** *O* (*a*)
(passive) homosexual* (*b*) transves-
tite/TV **2.** (*drogues*) cocaine*/
coke.

carottage [karɔtaʒ] *nm F* (*a*) swin-
dling/cheating/diddling (*b*) nicking/
swiping.

carotte [karɔt] *nf F* **1.** hoax*/
swindle*; **tirer une carotte à qn** (*i*)
to try to hoax* s.o./to try to pull
the wool over s.o.'s eyes (*ii*) to did-
dle/to trick s.o. (out of sth); to do/
to con s.o. **2.** (*a*) (*billards*) **jouer/
tirer la carotte,** to leave nothing on
the table (*b*) (*tennis*) drop shot **3.**

les carottes sont cuites, it's all up;
ses carottes sont cuites, he's done
for/he's had it/he's had his chips.
(*Voir* **poil 10**)

carotter [karɔte] **I** *vtr F* **1.** to
steal*/to pinch/to nick **2.** **carotter qch à qn/qn de qch,** to do/to
swindle*/to diddle s.o. out of sth;
to con sth off s.o./to con s.o. out
of sth **3.** (*mil*) **carotter le service,**
to dodge duty; **carotter une permission,** to wangle some leave **II** *vi P*
(*a*) (*jeux d'argent*) to play for tri-
fling/piddling stakes (*b*) to jump
the queue/to gate-crash.

carotteur, -euse [karɔtœr, -øz]
n, **carottier, -ière** [karɔtje, -
jer] *n* **1.** *F* cheat/swindler*/trick-
ster/con artist/wangler **2.** *F*
malingerer*/shirker/skiver **3.** *P*
queue-jumper/gate-crasher.

caroubier [karubje] *nm P* =
caroubleur 1.

carouble [karubl] *nf P* **1.** duplicate key (used for robbery); skeleton key/screw **2.** lock.

caroubler [karuble] *vtr P* **1.** to
break into (a house, etc) with a
duplicate *or* skeleton key **2.** to put
(sth) under lock and key **3.** to
beat (s.o.) up*/to give (s.o.) a going
over **4.** to steal*/to swipe/to
pinch.

caroubleur [karublœr] *nm P* bur-
glar/*O* screwsman; picklock.

carpe [karp] *nf F* **1.** **faire la carpe,**
to pass out in (sheer) ecstasy/to go
into the seventh heaven **2.** **faire
des yeux de carpe (pâmée),** to show
the whites of one's eyes **3.**
regarder qn avec des yeux de carpe,
to make sheep's eyes at s.o.

carpette [karpɛt] *nf P* (*i*) weak/
feeble/flabby/spineless individual
(*ii*) quitter.

carrante [karɑ̃t] *nf P* = **carante
1.**

carre [kar] *nf P* **1.** hiding place;
mettre qch à la carre, to stash sth

away **2.** total stakes (at poker, etc) **3.** (*chambre*) rooms/digs/pad.

carré [kare] **I** *nm* P **1.** second-year student in a *grande école* or preparing for entry into a *grande école* **2.** four of a kind (at poker); **carré de valets,** four jacks **II** *a* F **1.** (*péj*) **tête carrée,** German **2. faire une tête carrée à qn,** to beat s.o. up*/to work s.o. over.

carreau, *pl* **-eaux** [karo] *nm* **1.** P eye*; **avoir un carreau à la manque,** to be blind in one eye **2.** P (*a*) monocle (*b*) *pl* **carreaux,** (large) glasses/specs/goggles **3.** P **en avoir un coup dans les carreaux,** to be drunk*/to be smashed out of one's head **4.** P (*a*) **le Petit Carreau,** the magistrates' court (= court of summary jurisdiction) (*b*) **le Grand Carreau,** the Crown Court (formerly the Assize Court) **5.** F **coucher qn sur le carreau,** to lay s.o. out/to flatten s.o./to send s.o. sprawling **6.** F **rester sur le carreau** (*i*) to be killed on the spot (*ii*) to be seriously wounded; to be laid out cold (*iii*) (*examen*) to be failed/ploughed **7.** F **se tenir à carreau,** to take every precaution/to be on one's guard; to lie low **8.** F **être sur le carreau,** to be out of work/on the dole.

carrée [kare] *nf* F (*a*) (*chambre*) room/flat; pad (*b*) (*mil*) barrack room.

carrelingues [karlɛ̃g] *nmpl* P glasses/specs.

carrer [kare] *vtr & vpr* P *Voir* **carer.**

carreur [karœr] *nm* P stakeholder (at poker, etc).

carreuse [karøz] *nf* P shoplifter.

carriole [karjɔl] *nf* F ramshackle old car*/jalopy.

carrosse [karɔs] *nm* O F **rouler carrosse,** to live in great style. (*Voir* **roue 3**)

carrossée [karɔse] *af* F **elle est bien carrossée,** she's got a good fig-ure/she's got everything in all the right places/she's well-stacked.

carrosserie [karɔsri] *nf* F (*pers*) build; **elle a une sacrée carrosserie,** she's big/large boned.

cartahu [kartay] *nm* P (*marine*) = leading seaman.

carte [kart] *nf* **1.** F **perdre la carte** (*i*) to lose one's bearings (*ii*) to get flustered **2.** F **c'était la carte forcée,** it was (a case of) Hobson's choice **3.** F **connaître/voir le dessous des cartes,** to be in the know/to have the low-down on sth **4.** P **carte (de France),** wet dream.

carton [kartɔ̃] *nm* **1.** F **rester/dormir dans les cartons,** to be shelved/pigeon-holed **2.** F **faire un carton,** to fire at s.o./to take a pot shot at s.o./to use s.o. for target practice **3.** P playing card; **battre les cartons,** to shuffle; **taper le carton,** to play cards **4.** V **faire/tirer un carton** (*a*) to have sex* with a woman/to get down to it; to have a quick screw/a quickie (*b*) (*homosexuels*) to have anal sex* with s.o.

cartonner [kartɔne] *vi* P **1.** O (*a*) to play cards (*b*) to be a compulsive card-player **2.** to break wind/to fart*.

cartonnier [kartɔnje] *nm* P card-sharp.

cartouse [kartuz] *nf* P card.

cas [kɑ] *nm* F **1. c'est bien le cas de le dire!** you said it!/and how!/you can say that again! **2. pas la peine d'en faire cas,** (it)'s not worth worrying about.

casaque [kazak] *nf* F **tourner casaque,** to make an about-face (in one's opinions, etc); (*politique, etc*) to change sides/to rat.

casaquin [kazakɛ̃] *nm* F **1. tomber sur le casaquin à qn,** to beat s.o. up*/to clobber s.o. **2. avoir qch dans le casaquin,** to be ill; (*vin*) **donner sur le casaquin,** to go to one's head.

casba(h)

casba(h) [kazba] *nf P* house/pad/
joint (esp brothel).

cascader [kaskade] *vi P* to serve a
prison sentence*/to do time/to do
bird.

cascadeur [kaskadœr] *nm F* (*a*)
stuntman (*b*) (*cirque*) acrobat.

case [kɑz] *nf P* **1.** house/pad **2.**
il a une case de moins/une case
(de) vide/une case qui manque; il
lui manque une case, he's mad*/
barmy/bonkers; he's not all there;
he's got a screw loose/missing **3.**
(= *casier judiciaire*) police record/
form.

caser [kaze] **I** *vtr* **1.** *F* caser qn,
to fix s.o. up with a job; il est bien
casé, he's got a good job/he's got
himself fixed up nicely **2.** *F* elle a
trois filles à caser, she's got three
daughters to marry off **3.** *V* (*a*) to
have sex* with s.o./to screw s.o. (*b*)
va te faire caser! fuck off! **II** *vpr*
se caser *F* **1.** to settle down/to
find somewhere to live **2.** to find a
job/to get fixed up with a job **3.**
to get married*/to settle down.

cash [kaʃ] *adv F* payer/casquer
cash, to pay cash (down); **100 balles cash**, 100 francs (cash) on the
nail/on the barrel.

casimir [kazimir] *nm P* waistcoat.

casingue [kazɛ̃g] *nm O*, **casino**
[kazino] *nm P* **1.** bar/pub/restau-
rant, etc **2.** handbag.

casque [kask] **I** *nm* **1.** *F*
Casques bleus, United Nations
(peace-keeping) troops **2.** *P* (*a*)
avoir/prendre son casque, to be
drunk*/to get drunk*/to get tanked
up (*b*) avoir le casque, to have a
hangover; j'en ai dans le casque,
I've got a bit of a head (from
drinking) **II** *nf P* donner le coup
de casque (*i*) = casquer 1 (*ii*) to
wrap up the sales talk.

casquer [kaske] *vi* **1.** *F* to pay*
up/to cough up/to foot the bill;
faire casquer qn de vingt francs, to

touch s.o. for twenty francs **2.** *P*
= cascader.

casquette [kaskɛt] *nf P* **1.** avoir
une casquette en peau de fesse, to
be bald* **2.** (*courses de chevaux*)
ramasser les casquettes, to come in
last **3.** *P* money lost at gambling
4. *P* prendre une casquette/être casquette, to be/to get drunk*; to get
tanked up.

casqueur, -euse [kaskœr, -øz] *n*
1. *F* the person who pays up/forks
out/foots the bill **2.** *P* cashier.

cassage [kasaʒ] *nm* **1.** *P* bur-
glary/house-breaking/breaking and
entering. (*Voir* **cassement**) **2.** *F*
cassage de gueule, punch-up.

cassantes [kasɑ̃t] *nfpl P* teeth*/
gnashers/choppers.

casse [kas] **I** *nm P* burglary/
break-in; faire un casse, to do a
place over **2.** robbery/heist **II** *nf*
F **1.** être bon pour la casse, to be
fit (only) for the scrap-heap **2.** il y
aura de la casse, there'll be trouble/
ructions/some rough stuff; faire de
la casse (*i*) to kick up a row/a
rumpus (*ii*) to smash a place up/to
do a place over **3.** (*mil*) casual-
ties/losses **4.** donner la casse à qn,
to dismiss s.o./to give s.o. the sack.

cassé [kase] *a* **1.** *F* qu'est-ce qu'il
y a de cassé? what's all the trou-
ble/hoo-ha about? qu'est-ce qu'il y
a encore de cassé? what's the trouble now? il y a quelque chose de
cassé, there's been a spot of bother.
(*Voir* **bras** 1) **2.** *F* (*sentimental*)
c'est cassé, it's over **3.** *P* drunk*.

casse-bonbons [kasbɔ̃bɔ̃] *nm
inv*, **casse-burettes** [kasbyrɛt]
nm inv, **casse-burnes**
[kasbyrn] *nm inv V* (*pers*) pest/
bloody nuisance/pain in the arse;
(*chose*) a bastard*/a sod.

casse-cou [kasku] *nm inv F* reckless person/daredevil.

casse-couilles [kaskuj] *nm inv*
V pest/bloody nuisance/pain in the
arse.

casse-croûte [kɑskrut] *nm inv*
1. *F* **casse-croûte de cheval**, straw
hat   2. *P* **se mettre au casse-croûte**,
to turn informer*.

casse-cul [kɑsky] *nm inv P* pest/
bloody nuisance/pain in the arse.

casse-dalle [kɑsdal] *nm inv P*,
casse-graine [kɑsgrɛn] *nm inv*
F 1. snack   2. = food counter (in
pub, etc); snack bar.

casse-gueule [kɑsgœl] *nm inv P*
1. strong spirits*/rotgut   2.
(*endroit*) hot spot; (*boîte, etc*) (low)
dive/crummy joint   3. reckless
undertaking; daredevil act(ion);
dicey/dangerous business.

cassement [kɑsmã] *nm P* =
cassage.

casse-noisettes [kɑsnwazɛt] *nm
inv V* 1. = **casse-bonbons**   2.
(*femme*) **faire casse-noisettes**, to
contract the vaginal muscles (during lovemaking)/to squeeze s.o.'s
nuts.

casse-olives [kɑsɔliv] *nm inv V*
= **casse-bonbons**.

casse-pattes [kɑspat] *nm inv P*
1. strong spirits*/rotgut   2. (*cyclisme*) breakneck descent.

casse-pieds [kɑspje] *F* **I** *nm inv*
(*pers*) (crashing) bore*/pest/nui-
sance/pain in the neck **II** *a*
(*chose*) **c'est rudement casse-pieds**,
it's a hell of a bore*/of a bind; it's
enough to give you a pain in the
neck. (*Voir* **pied 17**)

casse-pipe(s) [kɑspip] *nm P*
war; dangerous area; **il est reparti
au casse-pipe(s)**, he's gone back to
the front line; (*moto*) **aller au casse-
pipe(s)**, to ride very fast/to do a
ton. (*Voir* **pipe 2**)

casse-poitrine [kɑspwatrin] *nm
inv P* = **casse-pattes 1**.

casser [kɑse] **I** *vtr* 1. *P* **se la
casser**, to run away*/to do a bunk
2. *F* **ça ne casse rien**, there's nothing extraordinary about that/it's
nothing to write home about/it's no

great shakes; **il ne casse rien**, he's
no great shakes/he's no big deal
3. *F* **vouloir tout casser**, to go all
out/to pull all the stops out; **à tout
casser** (*i*) at full speed/without
restraint (*ii*) a hell of a ... /a helluva ...; no end of a ... /the
devil of a ... /a father and mother
of a ...; **un film à tout casser**, a
fantastic film/a great movie; **une
bringue à tout casser**, a hell of a
bender; **une attaque à tout casser**,
an all-out attack; **se faire applaudir
à tout casser**, to bring the house
down; **cet objet vaut 1000 balles à
tout casser**, this article is worth
1000 francs at the very most/at the
outside.   4. *P* **casser qch/casser ça
à qn**, to reprimand* s.o. severely/to
give s.o. a good telling-off; **qu'est-ce
qu'il va te casser quand il le saura!**
you won't half cop it when he finds
out!   5. *P* **la casser**, to die*/to kick
the bucket/to snuff it   6. *P* **la/les
casser à qn**, to bore* s.o. stiff/to
give s.o. a pain in the neck/to get
on s.o.'s wick; **tu me les casses!**
you're a bore*!/you're getting up
my nose!/stop bugging me!   7. *P*
ne pas en casser une, not to say a
word/to say nothing/to keep mum
8. *F* **il ne se casse pas**, he doesn't
put himself out much. (*Voir* **bail 2**;
baraque 2 (*a*); **bois 6**; **bonbons**;
bonnet 9; **burettes**; **burnes**;
canne 4; **cou 2**; **couille 1** (*a*);
croûte; **cruche[1] 2**; **cul 1**; **figure**;
graine 1; **gueule II 2**; **marmite**;
morceau 1, 2, 3; **nénette 4**; **nez**;
œuf; **oreille**; **patte 3, 7**; **pied 17**;
pot; **reins 2, 3**; **sucre 3**; **tête 5**)
II *vpr* **se casser** *P* to run away*/
to beat it/to split.

casserole [kɑsrɔl] *nf P* 1. police
informer*/copper's nark   2. (tinny)
old piano   3. (*voiture*) ramshackle
old banger   4. large old-fashioned
(silver) watch   5. worthless individ-
ual/washout/layabout   6. low-
class prostitute*/cheap whore/tart
7. (*a*) **passer qn à la casserole** (*i*) to
kill* s.o. (*ii*) to send s.o. flying/

sprawling (*iii*) **passer une nana à la casserole**, to rape/to gangbang a girl; (*brutalement*) to screw/to lay a girl (*b*) **passer à la casserole** (*i*) to get killed/bumped off (*ii*) to have a rough time (of it); to get the third-degree (*iii*) (*femme*) to get raped/gangbanged; to be laid/screwed (brutally) **8.** (*au théâtre, cinéma*) projector; spotlight.

casseur [kɑsœr] *nm* **1.** P burglar/house-breaker **2.** F **casseur d'assiettes**, swaggerer*; **porter son chapeau en casseur d'assiettes**, to wear one's hat at a rakish angle **3.** F scrap dealer.

cassis [kasis] *nm* P **1.** (*a*) head*/nut (*b*) brains; **il en a dans le cassis**, he's bright/he's no mug; **en avoir gros sur le cassis**, to be bitterly disappointed **2. cassis de lutteur**, heavy, rough red wine.

cassure [kasyr] *nf* P old actor.

castagne [kastaɲ] *nf* P **1.** brawl/free-for-all **2.** blow*; **coller/flanquer/foutre une castagne à qn**, to fetch s.o. a clout; to clobber/to thump s.o.

se castagner [səkastaɲe] *vpr* P to scuffle/to brawl; to have a punch-up.

castapiane [kastapjan] *nf* O P VD*/gonorrhoea/the clap.

castel [kastɛl] *nm* O P prison*.

castre [kastr] *nm* O P hospital.

casuel [kazɥɛl] **I** *nm* P (*esp prostituées*) **faire le casuel**, to hire a room by the hour **II** *a* P (*verrerie, etc*) easily broken/fragile.

catalogue [katalɔg] *nm* P penal code.

catalogué [katalɔge] *a&pp* F **c'est catalogué!** it's in the bag!/it's a (dead) cert!*

cataloguer [katalɔge] *vtr* F **cataloguer qn**, to size s.o. up/to suss s.o. out; **celui-là, je l'ai catalogué**, I've got him sussed out/I know where I stand with that one.

catastrophe [katastrɔf] *nf* F **1. en catastrophe** (*i*) panic stations/in a mad rush (*ii*) immediately/as a matter of the utmost urgency **2. c'est une vraie catastrophe, ce type-là!** that guy's/that bloke's a real drag!

catastrophé [katastrɔfe] *a* F **1.** (*plan, projet*) come to grief; (*avion, etc*) wrecked **2.** flabbergasted/dumbfounded/stunned/knocked all of a heap.

catastropher [katastrɔfe] *vtr* F **1.** to wreck (sth) **2.** to flabbergast* (s.o.)/to dumbfound (s.o.)/to knock (s.o.) sideways/to shatter (s.o.).

cat(e)au [kato] *nf* O **1.** F farm girl **2.** P = **catiche**.

catholique [katɔlik] *a* F straight; in order; genuine/kosher; **ce n'est pas (très) catholique**, I don't like the look/the sound of it; it looks/sounds fishy; **c'est un peu plus catholique**, that's more like it; **il n'est pas catholique**, he's a bit phoney/he's not altogether above-board/he's a bit shady.

catiche [katiʃ] *nf* O P (*a*) push-over/slut/tramp (*b*) prostitute*/whore/hooker/tart.

en catimini [ãkatimini] *adv phr* F on the sly.

catin [katɛ̃] *nf* O P = **catiche**.

cato [kato] *nf* O F P = **cat(e)au**.

causailler [kozɑje] *vi* O F to indulge in small talk/to chatter* (away)/to natter on.

causant [kozã] *a* F chatty/talkative; **il n'est guère causant**, he doesn't have much to say for himself/he doesn't waste his words.

causette [kozɛt] *nf* F little chat; **faire un bout/un brin de causette avec qn**, to have a (little) natter with s.o.

cautère [kotɛr] *nm* F **c'est un cautère sur une jambe de bois**, it's no earthly use/it's about as much use as an umbrella in a heatwave.

cavale [kaval] *nf P* **1.** escape (*esp* from prison)/getaway; **être en cavale,** to be on the run.

cavalendour [kavalɑ̃dur] *nm P* = **cave I 1.**

cavaler [kavale] **I** *vi* **1.** (*a*) *F* to run/to rush around; **cavaler cher,** to run hard (*b*) to run away* **2.** *P* to run after women/to chase skirt **II** *vtr P* **cavaler qn,** to bore*/to pester s.o.; **tu me cavales!** you're getting on my wick! (*Voir* **ciboulot 3**) **III** *vpr* **se cavaler** *P* to run away*/to clear off/to make a smart getaway/to make a run for it.

cavalerie [kavalri] *nf P* **1.** loaded dice/crooked dice; **envoyer la cavalerie,** to substitute loaded dice **2.** **de la grosse cavalerie** (*i*) stodgy food/stodge (*ii*) run-of-the-mill assortment/collection (of books, etc); **c'est de la grosse cavalerie,** it's the heavy stuff **3.** **la cavalerie de Saint-Georges,** English money/British gold (for subsidizing troops, for bribing the enemy, etc) **4.** false cheque, etc. (*Voir* **balancer 6**)

cavaleur [kavalœr] *nm P* womanizer*/Don Juan/Casanova/skirtchaser/ladies' man/wolf.

cavaleuse [kavaløz] *nf P* pushover/easy lay/tramp; **ce n'est qu'une petite cavaleuse,** she'll go after anything in trousers/she'll go to bed with anybody.

cave [kav] **I** *nm P* **1.** outsider (*ie* anyone not belonging to the **milieu**) **2.** (*a*) fall guy/mug/sucker (*b*) fool*/idiot/twerp/clot **3.** prostitute's (paying) customer. (*Voir* **descente 3**) **II** *a P* (*pers*) **1.** (looking) old/the worse for wear/decrepit **2.** **ce qu'il est cave!** (*i*) what a mug/a sucker (he is)! (*ii*) what a fool!/what a clot!

cavé [kave] *nm* = **cave II 1.**

caver [kave] *vtr P* to swindle*/to cheat/to diddle; **être cavé/se faire caver,** to be done.

cavette [kavɛt] *nf* **1.** *P* woman*

or girl* not belonging to the **milieu**; *esp* prostitute* without a pimp* **2.** *F* stupid* girl/dumb cluck.

caviar [kavjar] *nm F* passer au caviar = **caviarder.**

caviardage [kavjardaʒ] *nm F* (*i*) censoring (*ii*) censored passage (of book, newspaper article, etc).

caviarder [kavjarde] *vtr F* to censor/to blue-pencil (a passage in a book, newspaper, etc).

cavillon, onne [kavijɔ̃, -ɔn] *n P* fool*/little twerp.

cavouse, cavouze [kavuz] *nf P* cellar.

cavu [kavy] *nm P* buttocks*.

ce (cet), cette, *pl* **ces** [sə (sɛt), sɛt, se *or* sɛ], *unstressed dem a* (*a*) *F* eh bien, et cette jambe? well, how's that leg of yours? **et ce café, garçon?** what about that coffee, waiter? **ce cher Thomas!** good old Thomas! **cette question!** what a daft question!/what a thing to ask! (*b*) *P* **sur ce, salut!** OK fine, see you later! (*c*) *F* **je lui ai écrit une de ces lettres!** I wrote him such a letter! **vous avez de ces expressions!** the expressions you come out with! **j'ai une de ces faims!** I'm starving!/I'm ravenous!

cédule [sedyl] *nm P* schedule/timetable.

ceinture [sɛ̃tyr] *nf* **1.** *F* **se boucler/se mettre la ceinture; serrer sa ceinture (d'un cran)** (*i*) to tighten one's belt (another hole) (*ii*) to go without; **ceinture, mon vieux!/tu peux te mettre la ceinture, mon vieux!** you've had it, chum!/you can say goodbye to that, mate! **2.** *P* **s'en mettre/s'en donner plein la ceinture,** to eat* heartily/to have a good tuck-in/a good blow-out **3.** *P* **femme grosse à pleine ceinture,** woman in an advanced state of pregnancy.

ceinturer [sɛtyre] *vtr P* to arrest*/ to nab/to collar (s.o.).

cellot(t)e [sɛlɔt] *nf P* **1.** (prison) cell* **2.** faire de la cellot(t)e = faire de la cellule (**cellule**).

cellule [sɛlyl] *nf P* faire de la cellule, to go into hiding (from the police)/to go underground.

cencul [sãky] *nm O P* vice-principal (of *lycée*).

cent [sã] *num a F* **1.** je vous le donne en cent, I'll give you a hundred guesses/(I bet) you'll never guess (it) **2.** (*à l'hôtel, etc*) le numéro cent, the WC*/the loo. (*Voir* **coup 7, 12; mille**)

centrale [sãtral] *nf F* **1.** (= *maison, prison, centrale*) = county jail **2.** (= *École centrale*) = (university level) State school of engineering.

centre [sãtr] *nm* **1.** *P* name/handle/mon(n)nicker **2.** *V* female genitals*.

centriot [sãtri(j)o] *nm P* nickname.

centrouse, centrouze [sãtruz] *nf P* (= *maison, prison, centrale*) = county jail.

cep [sɛp] *nm P* nose*.

cerbère [sɛrbɛr] *nm F* (*a*) bad-tempered concierge (*b*) c'est un vrai cerbère, he's a grumpy old sod.

cerceau, *pl* **-eaux** [sɛrso] *nm* **1.** *F* avoir le dos en cerceau, to be round-shouldered **2.** *F* steering wheel (of car) **3.** *pl P* ribs.

cercle [sɛrkl] *nm P* cercle (de barrique), rib.

cercleux [sɛrklø] *F* **I** *nm* clubman; man about town **II** *a* clubbish.

cerf [sɛr, sɛrf] *nm* **1.** *F* (*a*) athletic type (*b*) good horseman **2.** *F* se déguiser en cerf, to run away*/to take to one's heels/to hare off **3.** *V* bander comme un cerf, to be horny/randy/ready for it.

cerise [s(ə)riz] *nf* **1.** *F* le temps des cerises, happy bygone days **2.**

P bad luck; avoir la cerise, to have (a run of) bad luck/to be down on one's luck; porter/ficher/foutre la cerise à qn, to bring s.o. bad luck/ to put a jinx on s.o. **3.** *P* head* **4.** face*; se taper la cerise, to eat* heartily/to feed one's face **5.** *P* se (re)faire la cerise (*i*) to pick oneself up/to get back on one's feet after an illness or a setback (*ii*) to do oneself proud **6.** *O P* ça lui fera la cerise! that'll teach him (a lesson)! **7.** *P* ramener sa cerise (*i*) to show off*/to shoot a line (*ii*) to grumble*/to grouse/to bellyache (*iii*) to turn up/to put in an appearance.

certals [sɛrtal] *nmpl A P* (= *certificats de licence*) diploma/degree.

certif [sɛrtif] *nm F* (*abbr* = *certificat d'études primaires*) certificate.

césarienne [sezarjɛn] *nf P* faire une césarienne, to steal* a wallet *or* purse, etc by slitting a pocket *or* bag, etc, with a razor blade, etc.

césarin [sezarɛ̃] *pron m P* he/him(self)/his nibs.

césarine [sezarin] *pron f P* she/her(self).

ceusses [søs] *dem pron m P* (**les**) ceusses qui (= *ceux qui*), those who.

cézig [sezig] *pron m P* he/him(self)/his nibs.

cézigos [sezigo] *pl pron m P* they/them(selves).

cézigue [sezig] *pron m P* he/him(self)/his nibs.

chabanais [ʃabanɛ] *nm P* **1.** *O* noise/row/din/racket/uproar **2.** *A* brothel*/knocking shop.

chabler [ʃable] *P* **I** *vtr* chabler qn (*i*) to attack* s.o./to set about s.o. (*ii*) to beat s.o. up*/to knock s.o. about **II** *vi* ça va chabler, there's going to be trouble/a riot/some aggro.

chabraque [ʃabrak] *P* **I** *a* (*a*) mad*/bonkers (*b*) (*femme*) (*i*) ugly (*ii*) loose(-living)/easy (*iii*) scatter-brained **II** *nf* (*a*) ugly woman/fright (*b*) trollop/slut (*c*) scatter-brain.

chafouin, -ine [ʃafwɛ̃, -in] *a&n F* weasel-faced/foxy-looking/sly-looking (person).

chagatte [ʃagat] *nf V* (*javanais de* **chatte**) female genitals*/cunt/pussy.

chagrin [ʃagrɛ̃] *nm P* **aller au chagrin** (*i*) to go to work (*ii*) to go in search of a job (*iii*) to lodge a complaint.

chahut [ʃay] *nm F* **1.** (*a*) noise/din/uproar*; **faire du chahut/en faire un chahut**, to kick up a row (*b*) horse-play/playing about **2.** rag/ragging.

chahutage [ʃaytaʒ] *nm F* **1.** horse-play/playing about **2.** (*a*) ragging (of teacher) (*b*) teasing (a girl) **3.** (*a*) booing (of a play, etc) (*b*) (*sports*) barracking.

chahuter [ʃayte] **I** *vi F* **1.** to kick up a row/to make a racket **2.** to indulge in horse-play/to lark about **3.** (*a*) to boo (*b*) to barrack **4. vol chahuté**, bumpy flight **II** *vtr* **1.** to knock (things) about/to send (things) flying **2.** to bump/to knock into (s.o.) **3.** (*a*) **chahuter un prof**, to rag a teacher (*b*) to tease (a girl).

chahuteur, -euse [ʃaytœr, -øz] **I** *a F* rowdy/disorderly/unruly **II** *n* (*a*) *F* rowdy; hooligan*/yob (*b*) *P* **chahuteur de macchabées**, undertaker's assistant.

chaille [ʃaj] *nf P* tooth.

Chaillot [ʃajo] *Prn F* **envoyer qn à Chaillot**, to send s.o. packing*/to send s.o. off with a flea in his ear.

chaillotte [ʃajɔt] *nf P* tooth.

chair [ʃɛr] *nf F* **1. un(e) marchand(e) de chair fraîche**, a white slaver **2. hacher qn menu comme chair à pâté/battre qn en chair à pâté** (*i*) to make mincemeat of s.o.

(*ii*) to beat s.o. within an inch of his life. (*Voir* **cuir 3**)

chaise [ʃɛz] *nf F* **rester le derrière entre deux chaises/s'asseoir entre deux chaises (le cul par terre)**, to fall between two chairs. (*Voir* **barreau**)

chaland [ʃalɑ̃] *nm F* **c'est un drôle de chaland**, he's a queer customer/an odd bod.

chaleur [ʃalœr] *nf P* **1. avoir les chaleurs**, to be afraid* **2.** (*pers*) **être en chaleur**, to be sexually excited*/to have the hots.

chaleureux [ʃalørø] *a P* afraid*/scared/cowardly/chicken.

chambard [ʃɑ̃bar] *nm F* **1.** disorder*/shambles; **quel chambard!** what a mess! **2.** row/din/racket; **faire du chambard**, to kick up a rumpus.

chambardement [ʃɑ̃bardəmɑ̃] *nm F* upheaval/upset; general reshuffle; **le grand chambardement social**, the great social revolution.

chambarder [ʃɑ̃barde] *F* **I** *vtr* **1.** (*a*) to ransack (a room, etc); **tout chambarder**, to turn everything upside down (*b*) to smash up (furniture, etc) (*c*) **chambarder les plans de qn**, to upset s.o.'s apple cart/to mess up s.o.'s plans **2.** to reorganize/to rearrange **II** *vi* **1.** to reorganize from top to bottom/to have a general reshuffle **2.** to kick up a row/a rumpus.

chambardeur, -euse [ʃɑ̃bardœr, -øz] *n F* **1.** hooligan*/yob **2.** revolutionary.

chambart [ʃɑ̃bar] *nm F* = **chambard**.

chambouler [ʃɑ̃bule] *vtr F* **1.** = **chambarder I 1 2. chambouler qn**, to give s.o. quite a turn/a nasty turn.

chambrer [ʃɑ̃bre] *vtr F* to tease*/to make fun of/to poke fun at (s.o.); **chambrer qn à froid**, to take the mickey out of s.o. (while keeping a straight face).

chameau, *pl* **-eaux** [ʃamo] **I** *nm* **1.** *P* (*homme*) beast/brute/sod/*NAm* son of a bitch/bastard*; (*femme*) bitch/(old) cow; ratbag; (*parfois*) **la chameau!** the bitch! **un vieux chameau,** an old so-and-so **2.** *F* **il est sobre comme un chameau,** he never drinks **3.** *P* gynaecological (examination) couch **II** *a P* **ce qu'il/qu'elle est chameau!** what a bastard* he/she is!

chamelle [ʃamɛl] *nf P* (*péj*) **1.** (*femme*) bitch/(old) cow **2.** prostitute*/(old) bag.

champ [ʃɑ̃] *nm F* **1.** **se sauver à travers champs,** to dodge a question/an issue; to change the subject **2.** **fou à courir les champs,** (as) mad as a hatter/as daft as a brush **3.** **le champ est libre,** the coast is clear/it's all clear **4.** **aller aux champs,** to go to the races/to go racing; **jouer le champ,** to play the field/to bet across the board **5.** **les Champs,** the Champs-Élysées (in Paris) **6.** **le champ de manœuvre,** (the) bed. (*Voir* **clef 2**; **refroidi**)

champ' [ʃãp] *nm,* **champe** [ʃãp] *nm P* champagne*/champers/bubbly.

champignard [ʃãpiɲar] *nm P* mushroom.

champignon [ʃãpiɲɔ̃] *nm F* **1.** (*aut*) accelerator (pedal); **appuyer sur/écraser le champignon,** to step on the gas/to step on it/to put one's foot down (on the floor) **2.** **le champignon,** dry rot.

champion [ʃãpjɔ̃] *a inv F* excellent*/champion.

chançard, arde [ʃãsar, -ard] *F* **I** *a* lucky/jammy **II** *n* lucky person/lucky blighter.

chance [ʃãs] *nf F* **1.** (ça c'est) **pas de chance!** that's hard luck!/tough luck! **(il) y a des chances!** most likely!/more likely than not! **joue ta chance!** have a go! **2.** **la faute à pas de chance,** nobody's fault.

chancetiquer [ʃãstike] *vi P* = **chanstiquer.**

chancre [ʃãkr] *nm F* **manger/bouffer comme un chancre,** to eat*/to stuff oneself like a pig.

chancrer [ʃãkre] *vi F* to eat*/to stuff oneself like a pig.

chandelier [ʃãdəlje] *nm* **1.** *F* **être sur le chandelier,** to be in a prominent position; **mettre qn sur le chandelier,** to put s.o. in the limelight **2.** *P* nose*.

chandelle [ʃãdɛl] *nf* **1.** *F* **souffler sa/la chandelle,** to die*/to snuff it **2.** *A F* **allons, la chandelle brûle,** come on, there's no time to lose **3.** *F* **je vous dois une fière chandelle,** you've saved my life **4.** *F* dandelion clock **5.** *P* (trickle of) snot; **une chandelle lui pend au nez,** his nose is running **6.** *P* bottle **7.** *P* single-column article (in newspaper) **8.** *P* (*aut*) spark plug **9.** *F* (*tennis*) **faire des chandelles,** to lob **10.** *F* **en voir trente-six chandelles,** to see stars (after a blow on the head, etc) **11.** *F* **tenir la chandelle** (*i*) to act as a go-between or decoy in a love affair (*ii*) to act as look-out in a love affair *or* to play gooseberry (*iii*) (*mari ou épouse*) to turn a blind eye (to the other's extramarital activities) **12.** *P* (*prostituée*) to work from a fixed patch.

chanson [ʃãsɔ̃] *nf F* **1.** **chansons (que tout cela)!** nonsense!/rubbish! **2.** **c'est toujours la même chanson,** it's always the same old story; **on connaît la chanson!** I've/we've heard that one before!/I've/we've heard it all before. (*Voir* **air III 3**)

chansonnette [ʃãsɔnɛt] *nf P* (*a*) harsh questioning (by police, etc)/(the) third degree/grilling (*b*) **avoir qn à la chansonnette/le faire à la chansonnette/pousser sa chanson-**

nette, to lead s.o. up the garden path/to have s.o. on.

chanstic, chanstique [ʃɑ̃stik] *nm P* **faire un chanstique** (*i*) = **faire un cambut (cambut)** (*ii*) to substitute loaded dice.

chanstiquer [ʃɑ̃stike] **I** *vtr&i P* to substitute/to switch imitation jewellery for real/false money for good, etc; to pull a switch **II** *vpr* **se chanstiquer** *P* **se chanstiquer en ...**¦to turn/to change into ....

chanter [ʃɑ̃te] **I** *vtr F* **qu'est-ce que vous me chantez là?** what's this fairy tale you're telling me?/what are you rabbiting on about? **II** *vi* **1.** *F* **si ça vous chante,** if you feel like it/if you fancy it; **je le ferai si ça me chante,** I'll do it if it suits me **2.** *F* **c'est comme si je chantais,** I'm just wasting my breath/I might as well be talking to myself **3.** *F* **faire chanter qn** (*i*) to compel s.o. to do sth (*ii*) to blackmail s.o.; **faire chanter qn sur un autre ton,** to make s.o. change his tune **4.** *F* **chanter plus haut,** to make a better offer/to go a bit higher/to up the bidding **5.** *P* to turn informer*/to squeal/to grass/ to shop.

chanterelle [ʃɑ̃trɛl] *nf F* **appuyer sur la chanterelle,** to hammer a point home/to rub it in.

chanvre [ʃɑ̃vr] *nm F* (*drogues*) **chanvre (indien),** hashish*/(Indian) hemp/hash.

chanvré [ʃɑ̃vre] *a F* (drogues) high on hash(ish)*.

chapardage [ʃapardaʒ] *nm P* stealing/pilfering/pinching; **menus chapardages,** petty thefts/pilfering.

chaparder [ʃaparde] *vtr P* to steal*/to pilfer/to pinch/to have light fingers.

chapardeur, euse [ʃapardœr, -øz] *P* **I** *a* thieving/pilfering/ pinching **II** *n* petty thief*/pilferer.

chapeau, *pl* **-eaux** [ʃapo] *nm*

1. *F* **chapeau!** (*a*) well done!/ bravo!/congrats!/hats off! (*esp TV*) **un coup de chapeau à ...!** hats off to ...! (*b*) (*iron*) great!/blinking marvellous! **2.** *P* **avoir le/aller au chapeau de paille,** to be sentenced (*i*) *A* to transportation with hard labour (*ii*) to preventive detention **3.** *P* ((*jeune*) *homme*) **perdre son chapeau de paille,** to lose his virginity **4.** **porter le chapeau** (*i*) *F* to take on (a) responsibility; to carry the can (*ii*) *P* to be (suspected of being) a police informer* (*iii*) to have a bad reputation **5.** *P* **travailler du chapeau,** to be mad*/off one's rocker **6.** *P* **(ne) t'occupe pas du chapeau de la gamine!** mind your own business! **7.** *F* (*aut*) **prendre un virage sur les chapeaux de roue(s),** to take/to screech round a bend at full speed **8.** *F* big (white) chief/boss* (of firm, etc) **9.** *P* **petit chapeau,** condom*/ French letter/rubber/Johnny. (*Voir* **baver II**)

chapeauter [ʃapote] *vtr F* **1.** to be in charge of/to be the head of (a department, etc) **2.** to write an introductory paragraph to (an article, etc) **3.** **chapeauter qn,** to give s.o. a (helping) hand/to put a word in for s.o.

chapelet [ʃaplɛ] *nm* **1.** *F* **défiler/ dévider son chapelet** (*i*) to pour one's heart out (*ii*) to speak one's mind/to have one's say **2.** *F* **un chapelet d'injures,** a string of insults/a stream of abuse **3.** *P* handcuffs*/cuffs.

Chapelouze [ʃapluz] *Prn P* **la Chapelouze,** the La Chapelle district in Paris).

chapiteau, *pl* **-eaux** [ʃapito] *nm P* head*.

chaque [ʃak] *pron F* (= *chacun*) **c'est quinze francs chaque,** they cost fifteen francs each.

char [ʃar] *nm P* **1. sans char?** no kid(ding)? **c'est pas du char!** I'm not kidding! **arrête ton char(, Ben**

Hur)! stop kidding!/come off it! **un sale char,** a dirty trick **2.** (*a*) **faire du char à qn,** to chat s.o. up/to flirt with s.o. (*b*) **faire des chars à son mari/à sa femme,** to be unfaithful to one's husband/wife; to two-time one's husband/wife **3. pousse ton char!** shift your carcass!

charabia [ʃarabja] *nm F* **1.** Auvergnat dialect **2.** gibberish/gobbledygook.

charbon [ʃarbɔ̃] *nm P* (*esp criminel*) **aller au charbon,** to do some unpleasant manual/hard work (for a change *or* out of necessity) instead of *or* as a front for one's normal shady activities. (*Voir* **sac**)

charcutage [ʃarkytaʒ] *nm P* bungled surgical operation/cock-up/butchery.

charcuter [ʃarkyte] *vtr P* **charcuter un malade,** to operate clumsily on a patient/to hack a patient about/to butcher a patient.

charcutier [ʃarkytje] *nm P* **1.** (clumsy) surgeon/butcher **2.** bungler/botcher.

Charenton [ʃarɑ̃tɔ̃] *Prn F* **c'est un pensionnaire de Charenton/il faut l'envoyer à Charenton,** he's mad*/he ought to be locked up/they ought to be put him in the loony bin; **un échappé de Charenton,** a madman/a loony/a nutter; **on se croirait à Charenton,** it's absolute bedlam/an absolute madhouse. (From Charenton, a town near Paris with a mental hospital.)

charge [ʃarʒ] *nf* **1.** *F* **il en a sa charge** (*i*) he's had as much as he can take (*ii*) he's very fat **2.** *F* (*a*) **faire une charge à qn,** to play a (nasty) trick on s.o. (*b*) **faire la charge de qn,** to take s.o. off/to take the mickey (out of s.o.) **3.** *P* (*drogues*) (*a*) effects from a drug; charge (*b*) marijuana*/grass.

chargé [ʃarʒe] *a P* **être chargé** (*a*) to be armed/to pack a gun (*b*) to have a criminal record/to have

form (*c*) to be drunk*/charged/bombed (*d*) to be high on drugs/stoned/bombed.

se charger [səʃarʒe] *vpr P* **1.** to arm oneself (with gun) **2.** to get drunk*/stoned **3.** to take a drug/to get stoned.

charibotage [ʃaribotaʒ] *nm P* adverse criticism/flak.

charibotée [ʃaribote] *nf P* **une charibotée de** ..., heaps/loads/piles of ...; **une charibotée d'injures,** a string of insults/a stream of abuse.

chariboter [ʃaribote] *vi P* **1.** to exaggerate*/to lay it on thick/to go a bit far **2.** to work without method/to muddle on **3.** to make a mess/a muddle.

Charlemagne [ʃarləmaɲ] *Prnm F* **faire Charlemagne,** to stop gambling when one is winning/to quit when the going's good.

charlemagner [ʃarləmaɲe] *vi F* = **faire Charlemagne** (**Charlemagne**).

Charles [ʃarl] *Prnm F* **tu parles, Charles!** now you're talking!

Charles-le-Chauve [ʃarlləʃov] *nm V* penis*/John Thomas; **faire sauter la cervelle à Charles-le-Chauve,** to masturbate*/to flog the bishop. (*Voir* **shampooing 2**)

Charlot [ʃarlo] *Prnm* **1.** *F* public executioner; **la bascule à Charlot** = the guillotine **2.** *F* (*cinéma*) Charlie Chaplin **3.** *F* happy-go-lucky individual; a joker; **quel charlot!** what a joker! **4.** *V* (*homme*) **amuser Charlot/s'amuser comme Charlot,** to masturbate*/to play with oneself.

charme [ʃarm] *nm F* **1. se porter comme un charme,** to be in the best of health/to be as fit as a fiddle **2. faire du charme,** to turn on the charm **3. chanteur de charme,** crooner.

charmeuses [ʃarmøz] *nfpl P* moustache*/tickler.

charmingue [ʃarmɛ̃g], **charmouille** [ʃarmuj] *a P* charming.

charnelle [ʃarnɛl] *nf P* (*péj*) girl* (regarded as a sex object)/bit of fluff.

charnière [ʃarnjɛr] *nf F* **nom à charnière** (*i*) double-barrelled name (*ii*) name containing the nobiliary particle *de*.

charognard [ʃarɔɲar] *nm P* **1.** butcher who sells tainted meat **2.** rotter*/louse/skunk.

charogne [ʃarɔɲ] *nf P* bastard*/sod.

charre [ʃar] *nm P* = **char.**

charrette [ʃarɛt] *nf F* car*. (*Voir* **roue 3**)

charriage [ʃarjaʒ] *nm P* **1.** con(fidence) trick **2.** leg-pulling; **passer qn au charriage**, to pull s.o.'s leg **3.** exaggeration/line-shooting **4.** (*a*) brutal attack (*b*) **charriage à la mécanique**, throttling/garotting.

charrier [ʃarje] **I** *vtr P* to poke fun at s.o./to take s.o. for a ride/to kid s.o.; **se faire charrier**, to have one's leg pulled **II** *vi* **1.** to joke; **sans charrier!** no kidding!/joking apart!/pull the other one! **2.** to overstep the mark/to lay it on a bit thick; **faut pas charrier!** that's going a bit far!/that's too much! (*Voir* **bégonias 1**)

charrieur, euse [ʃarjœr, -øz] *n P* joker/leg-puller; **c'est un charrieur** (*i*) he's always having people on (*ii*) he's a bit of a joker.

charron [ʃarɔ̃] *nm P* **aller/crier/gueuler au charron** (*i*) to cause a disturbance/to raise Cain/to raise hell/to scream blue murder (*ii*) to protest.

charronner [ʃarɔne] *P* **I** *vtr* to beat (s.o.) up*/to give (s.o.) a going-over **II** *vi* = **aller au charron (charron).**

chasse [ʃas] *nf* **1.** *F* **partir en chasse**, to go bargain-hunting **2.** *P* **peloton de chasse**, punishment squad/jankers brigade **3.** *P* **être en chasse**, to (try to) pick up/to get off with (women).

châsse [ʃas] *nm P* **1.** eye*; **cligner du châsse vers qn**, to wink at s.o.; **donner un coup de châsse(s) à qn**, to look at* s.o.; to give s.o. the glad eye; **avoir les châsses en portefeuille**, to have bags under one's eyes; **un(e) n'a qu'un châsse**, a one-eyed man/woman; **pisser des châsses**, to cry* **2.** **au châsse**, free/for nothing/on the house. (*Voir* **œil**)

chasse-coquin [ʃaskɔkɛ̃] *nm P* verger.

chasser [ʃase] *vi F* (*a*) to flirt (*b*) **elle chasse au mari**, she's on the look-out/on the hunt for a husband (*c*) **elle chasse le mâle**, she's on the prowl for a man. (*Voir* **brouillard 2** (*b*))

châsser [ʃase] *vtr P* to look* at/to clock.

châssis [ʃasi] *nm* **1.** *F* **c'est un beau châssis**, she's got a great figure/body; **vise le châssis!** get a load of that!/*NAm* check the chick out! **2.** *pl P* eyes*; **fermer les châssis**, to go to sleep*.

chat [ʃa] *nm* **1.** *P* (*a*) clerk of the court (*b*) examining magistrate (*c*) **chat fourré**, judge **2.** *V* female genitals*/pussy. (*Voir* **chatte 2**) **3.** *F* **arriver dès les chats**, to arrive home with the milk(-train) **4.** *F* **avoir un chat dans la gorge**, to have a frog in one's throat **5.** *F* **avoir d'autres chats à fouetter**, to have other fish to fry **6.** *F* **il n'y a pas de quoi fouetter un chat**, it's nothing to make a fuss/a song and dance about **7.** *F* **c'est pas fait pour les chats**, it's not there as an ornament, it's meant to be used. (*Voir* **chien II 3**) **8.** *F* **écriture de chat**, illegible scrawl **9.** *F* (*terme d'affection*) **mon (petit) chat**, my (little) darling*/my (little) pet/my (little) love. (*Voir* **chatte** 1) 10. F **(non,) c'est le chat!** it must have been the cat!/it was Mr Nobody I suppose! 11. **F pas un chat,** not a (living) soul 12. **F être comme chat sur braise,** to be like a cat on hot bricks/on a hot tin roof. (*Voir* **bouillie** (*b*))

châtaigne [ʃatɛɲ] *nf P* 1. blow*/ punch/clout; **passer à la châtaigne/ se ramasser une châtaigne,** to get beaten up 2. (*a*) brawl/punch-up/ scrap/fisticuffs (*b*) (*sports*) **jouer la châtaigne,** to play dirty/rough.

châtaigner [ʃatɛɲe] *vtr P* to hit/ to punch/to sock (s.o.); to exchange blows/to trade punches.

château, *pl* **-eaux** [ʃato] *nm P* 1. prison* 2. hospital.

Château-la-Pompe [ʃatolapɔ̃p] *nm F* (drinking) water*/Adam's ale.

chatouille [ʃatuj] *nf* 1. *F* **faire des chatouilles à qn,** to tickle s.o.; **craindre les chatouilles,** to be ticklish 2. *P* = **chtouille.**

chatouiller [ʃatuje] *vtr* 1. *F* **chatouiller les côtes à qn,** to give s.o. a good hiding 2. *P* **chatouiller une serrure,** to pick a lock. (*Voir* **dame 5**)

châtré [ʃatre] *a P* weak/spineless.

chatte [ʃat] *nf* 1. *F* **(petite) chatte,** darling*/pet 2. *V* female genitals*/pussy. (*Voir* **chat 2**; **bouffer 3**)

chaud [ʃo] I *a* 1. *F* **tenir les pieds chauds à qn,** to keep s.o. on the go 2. *F* **avoir la main chaude,** to have a run of luck (at gambling) 3. *F* enthusiastic/game; **il n'est pas chaud pour le projet,** he's not keen on the project 4. *F* **cela ne lui fait ni chaud ni froid,** it's all the same to him/he doesn't care about it one way or the other 5. *F* **ça va vous coûter chaud** (*i*) it'll cost you/you'll have to pay through the nose for it (*ii*) you'll pay/suffer for it 6. *F* **il fera chaud!** nonsense!*/never! **il**

fera chaud quand elle commencera à bosser! that'll be the day when she starts working! 7. *F* (*cri des garçons de café/de restaurant*) **chaud (devant)!** excuse me!/'scuse me!/ mind your backs! 8. *F* difficult/ tricky/dodgy/dic(e)y; risky; **on y va pas, c'est chaud,** we're not going there, it's too risky/it's hot 9. *P* lustful/hot; **être chaud de la pince/ de la pointe,** to be highly sexed/to be a randy devil. (*Voir* **lapin**) II *nm F* 1. **avoir les pieds au chaud,** to have a cushy job 2. **je crève de chaud,** I'm boiling (hot) 3. **il a eu chaud** (*i*) he was scared stiff/he got a nasty fright (*ii*) he had a narrow escape/a close shave.

chaude-lance [ʃodlɑ̃s] *nf,* **chaude-pince** [ʃodpɛ̃s] *nf,* **chaude-pisse** [ʃodpis] *nf P* VD*; **il a la chaude-pisse,** he's got the clap.

chaudron [ʃodrɔ̃] *nm* 1. *F* worn-out musical instrument, *esp* tinny old piano 2. *P* **écurer son chaudron,** to confess*/to come clean.

chauffage [ʃofaʒ] *nm F* cramming (for an exam).

chauffard [ʃofar] *nm F* (*conducteur*) (*i*) road hog; speed merchant; maniac (*ii*) hit-and-run driver.

chauffer [ʃofe] I. *vtr* 1. *F* **chauffer qn (en vue d'un examen),** to cram s.o. for an exam; **chauffer un examen,** to swot for an exam 2. *F* **il faut chauffer l'affaire,** we must strike while the iron is hot 3. *F* **chauffer un livre, un écrivain,** to promote/to plug a book, a writer 4. *F* **chauffer qn (à blanc)** (*i*) to get s.o. worked up (*ii*) to rouse/to incite s.o. (*Voir* **blanc II 2**) **chauffer une nana,** to get a woman sexually excited*/to get a woman going; (*théâtre*) **chauffer une scène,** to ginger up a scene; **chauffer une salle, l'auditoire,** to warm the place up/to get the audience going 5. *P* to steal*/to pinch; **on m'a chauffé mon portefeuille,** someone's pinched my wallet/*NAm* my pocketbook (*a*) to arrest*/to pinch; **se faire chauffer,** to get nicked (*b*) to catch (s.o.) redhanded. (*Voir* **four**) II *vi* **1.** *F* **ce n'est pas pour vous que le four chauffe,** it's not for you **2.** *P* **ça chauffe!** things are hotting up!/ things are getting a bit heated! **ça va chauffer!** there's going to be trouble!/there's trouble brewing!/ sparks are going to fly! (*Voir* **bain 5**)

chausser [ʃose] *vtr F* **ça me chausse (bien),** that suits me fine/ that suits me down to the ground.

chaussette [ʃosɛt] *nf P* **1.** (*voiture*) tyre **2. chaussettes à clous** (*i*) hobnailed boots (*ii*) plain-clothes policemen **3.** (*femme*) **mettre les chaussettes à la fenêtre,** not to have an orgasm*/not to come. (*Voir* **jus 2**)

chaussons [ʃosɔ̃] *nmpl P* **fabriquer/tresser des chaussons (de lisière),** to be in prison*/to be doing time.

chaussure [ʃosyr] *nf F* **1. trouver chaussure à son pied** (*i*) to find exactly what one is looking for (*ii*) to find a husband/a wife* (*iii*) to meet one's match/one's equal **2. avoir un pied dans deux chaussures,** to have two strings to one's bow **3. une chaussure à tout pied,** something quite ordinary/commonplace.

chauve [ʃov] *nm V* **chauve à col roulé,** penis*/John Thomas.

chbeb[1] [ʃbɛb] *a P* beautiful. (*Voir* **schbeb**[1])

chbeb[2], **chebeb** [ʃ(ə)bɛb] *nm O P* good-looking young homosexual. (*Voir* **schbeb**[2])

chéchia [ʃeʃja] *nm P* **travailler du chéchia,** to be mad*/off one's rocker.

chef [ʃɛf] *nm F* (*patron*) chief/boss; d'acc chef! OK, chief! (*as*) **un vrai chef,** a champion/an ace/the greatest.

chelem [ʃlɛm] *nm P* **être grand chelem,** to be penniless*/flat broke.

chelinguer [ʃlɛ̃ge] *vi P* = **chlinguer.**

chemin [ʃ(ə)mɛ̃] *nm F* **1. le chemin des écoliers,** the longest way round **2. il n'y va pas par quatre/ par trente-six chemins,** he goes straight to the point/he doesn't beat about the bush; **on vous cherche par les quatre chemins,** they're looking for you all over the place **3. être toujours sur les chemins/par voie et par chemin,** to be always gadding about **4. être en chemin de famille,** to be pregnant*/in the family way.

cheminée [ʃ(ə)mine] *nf* **1.** *P* halfbottle of red wine **2.** *V* (*sexe de la femme*) vagina*/flue.

chemise [ʃ(ə)miz] *nf* **1.** *F* **je m'en moque/m'en fiche comme de ma première chemise,** I couldn't care less*/I don't give two hoots (about it) **2.** *P* **compter ses chemises,** to be (sea)sick. (*Voir* **cul 10**)

chêne [ʃɛn] *nm P* man; **faire suer un chêne,** to kill* a man. (*Voir* **sueur**)

chenillon [ʃ(ə)nijɔ̃] *nm P* ugly girl*/woman*; slut.

chenoque [ʃ(ə)nɔk] *a & nm P* = **chnoque.**

chenu [ʃ(ə)ny] *a & nm O P* excellent*; **c'est du chenu,** that's firstrate.

chéquard [ʃekar] *nm F* (*péj, esp politique*) bribed backer (of an undertaking); influence peddler.

chèqueton [ʃɛktɔ̃] *nm P* cheque.

cher, *f* **chère** [ʃɛr] *a & adv* **1.** *F* **je l'ai eu pour pas cher,** I got it (on the) cheap **2.** *P* **je ne vaux pas cher,** I feel unwell*/I don't feel up to much. (*Voir* **cavalier 1** (*a*))

chercher [ʃɛrʃe] *vtr* **1.** *F* to blame (s.o.)/to pick on (s.o.); **tu l'as cherché!** you asked for it! **tu me cherches, et tu vas me trouver!** you're asking for it, and you'll get it if you're nǫt careful! **il me cherche,** he's trying to pick a quarrel with me **2.** *P* (*i*) **aller en chercher,** to earn money (*ii*) **aller les chercher,** to get money **3.** *P* **où vas-tu chercher ça?/qu'est-ce que tu vas chercher?** where did you get that idea from?/where did you dig that one up?/what are you getting at? **4.** *F* **ça va chercher dans les trois mille francs,** that'll fetch about three thousand francs; **elle va sûrement chercher dans les quarante berges,** she must be (at least) forty if she's a day **5.** *F* **ça va chercher loin,** that can have serious consequences; **ça ne va pas chercher loin,** it won't come to much. (*Voir* **bête 2; crosse; pou**)

chérer [ʃere] *vi P* = **cherrer.**

chéro(t) [ʃero] *F* (*a*) *a* rather dear/ too dear/pric(e)y (*b*) *adv* **ça vaut/ça fait chéro(t),** it's pretty expensive/ it's on the expensive side.

cherrer [ʃere] *vi P* **1.** to exaggerate*/to shoot a line/to talk big; **ne cherre pas!** come off it! **2.** to attack violently. (*Voir* **bégonias 1; mastic 2**)

chetard [ʃ(ə)tar] *nm P* (*a*) prison*/ stir (*b*) disciplinary cell.

chetouille [ʃ(ə)tuj] *nf P* VD*/the clap; **ramasser la chetouille,** to cop a dose.

cheval, *pl* **-aux** [ʃəval, ʃfal, -o] *nm* **1.** *F* **masculine woman/Amazon/woman*** built like a horse **2.** *F* **mémoire de cheval,** excellent memory; **fièvre de cheval,** raging fever **3.** *F* **c'est son cheval de bataille,** he flogs this subject to death; it's his hobby horse/his stock answer **4.** *F* **c'est pas un mauvais cheval,** he's not a bad (old) sort **5.** *F* **c'est un cheval à l'ouvrage/de labour/pour le travail,**

he's a glutton for work/a workaholic **6.** *F* **cela ne se trouve pas sous le pas d'un cheval/sous le sabot d'un cheval,** it's not easily come by; it doesn't grow on trees **7.** *P* **(vieux) cheval de retour,** old lag/jailbird **8.** *P* **becqueter/dîner/ manger avec les chevaux de bois,** to go without food/to go dinnerless **9.** *P* (*drogues*) heroin*/horse **10.** *F* (*a*) **être à cheval sur qch,** to be insistent about sth (*b*) **monter sur ses grands chevaux,** to get on one's high horse **11.** *F* **faire du cheval sur un tonneau,** to be bow-legged/ to have bandy legs. (*Voir* **boniment 2; remède 3; torchon 8**)

chevalier [ʃəvalje] *nm* **1.** *F* **chevalier d'industrie,** crook/swindler* **2.** *F* **les chevaliers de la gaule,** the knights of the rod/the angling fraternity **3.** *P* **chevalier de la guirlande,** convict **4.** *P* **chevalier de la lune,** burglar **5.** *P* **chevalier de la rosette/du prépuce-cul,** homosexual* **6.** *P* **chevalier de la piquouse,** drug addict*/junkie.

chevalière [ʃəvaljɛr, ʃfal-] *nf P* anus*/ring.

cheveu, *pl* **-eux** [ʃ(ə)vø] *nm* **1.** *P* **avoir mal aux cheveux/avoir le cheveu triste** (*i*) to have a bad head(ache) (*ii*) to have a hangover/ to feel a bit fragile **2.** *F* **il y a un cheveu,** there's a fly in the ointment/there's a hitch somewhere **3.** *P* **avoir un cheveu sur la langue,** to (have a) lisp **4.** *F* **se faire des cheveux (blancs),** to worry oneself stiff/to go grey with worry **5.** *F* **se prendre aux cheveux,** to come to blows/to have a set-to **6.** *F* **argument tiré par les cheveux,** far-fetched argument **7.** *P* **travailler du cheveu,** to be mad*/off one's rocker **8.** *F* **venir comme un cheveu/comme des cheveux sur la soupe,** to be most inappropriate/out of place; to be quite uncalled-for; **arriver comme un cheveu sur la soupe,** to arrive at an awkward moment/to turn up like a bad penny **9.** *F* trouver un cheveu dans le potage, to find something amiss 10. *F* y trouver un cheveu, to find a difference (for the worse) 11. *F* couper les cheveux en quatre, to split hairs. (*Voir* barbe II 3)

cheville [ʃ(ə)vij] *nf F* 1. se donner des coups de pied dans les chevilles, to blow one's own trumpet 2. il ne vous arrive/monte/vient pas à la cheville, he's not a patch on you/he's not in the same league as you 3. être en cheville avec qn, to be in collusion/in cahoots/in league with s.o. 4. vivre en cheville avec qn, to cohabit/to shack up with s.o.

se cheviller [səʃ(ə)vije] *vpr F* se cheviller avec qn = être en cheville avec qn (cheville 3).

chevilleur, -euse [ʃ(ə)vijœr, -øz] *n P* go-between; stooge/decoy.

chèvre [ʃɛvr] *nf P* 1. girl *or* woman of easy virtue; pushover/easy lay 2. prostitute*/whore.

chevreuil [ʃəvrœj] *nm P* 1. informer*/grass/squealer 2. peasant*.

chez [ʃe] *prep P* 1. non, mais chez qui? no damn fear!/not bloody likely!*/not if I know (anything about) it!/you must be joking! 2. *F* c'est bien de chez nous! that's typically French.

chiader [ʃjade] *P* I *vi* to work* hard/to swot; j'ai chiadé en latin, I did well in Latin II *vtr* j'ai chiadé mon thème, I made a good job of my prose.

chiadeur, -euse [ʃjadœr, -øz] *n P* hard worker; swot.

chialer [ʃjale] *vi F* 1. to cry*; to snivel; se mettre à chialer, to turn on the waterworks 2. to complain/to moan.

chiale-toujours [ʃjaltuʒur] *nm*, chialeur, -euse [ʃjalœr, -øz] *n F* 1. cry-baby; sniveller 2. moaner/grizzler.

chiant [ʃjɑ̃] *a V* irritating/sickening/bloody annoying; il est chiant, ce type-là! that bloke/that guy is a bloody nuisance/a real pain (in the arse/*NAm* ass).

chiard [ʃjar] *nm P* (*péj*) kid/brat.

chiasse [ʃjas] *nf V* 1. avoir la chiasse (*i*) to have diarrhoea*/the runs (*ii*) to be afraid*/to have the willies/to be shit-scared 2. quelle chiasse! what a bloody/sodding nuisance/drag!

chiasser [ʃjase] *vi V* to be afraid*/to be shit-scared/to be scared shitless.

chiasseur, -euse [ʃjasœr, -øz], chiasseux, -euse [ʃjasø, -øz] *V* I *a* cowardly/yellow(-bellied) II *n* coward*/yellow-belly.

chibis [ʃibi] *nm P* faire chibis, to escape/to do a bunk.

chibre [ʃibr] *nm V* penis*; un chibre mol, a limp prick.

chibrer [ʃibre] *vtr V* (*peu usuel*) to have sex*.

chic [ʃik] I *a F* c'est un chic type, he's a nice guy/a great bloke II *excl F* chic (alors)! fine!/great!/neat!

chicandier, -ière [ʃikɑ̃dje, -jɛr] *P* I *a* (*i*) quarrelsome* (*ii*) complaining/bellyaching (*b*) (*i*) quarrelsome person/awkward customer (*ii*) bellyacher.

chicard [ʃikar] *a O P* smart/stylish/chic.

chicha [ʃiʃa] *nm P* (*drogues*) (*verlan de haschisch*) hashish*.

chiche [ʃiʃ] I *a F* t'es pas chiche de le faire! you haven't got the guts to do it! II *excl F* 1. chiche! (*i*) you just try it!/I dare you! (*ii*) rats (to you)! 2. chiche (que tu ne le feras pas)! I bet you can't!/I bet you don't! chiche (que je le fais)! (I) bet you I can!/(I) bet you I will!

chichi [ʃiʃi] *nm F* fuss/to-do/carry-on; en voilà du chichi! what a fuss!/what a carry-on! **faire des chichis** (*i*) to make/to kick up a fuss (*ii*) to put on airs; **des gens à chichis**, affected people; snobs; **un type à chichis**, a prig/a poseur; **toutes sortes de chichis**, all kinds of complications/of snags.

chichite [ʃiʃit] *nf P* vague illness; imaginary illness.

chichiteur, euse [ʃiʃitœr, -øz], **chichiteux, euse** [ʃiʃitø, -øz] *a&n F* affected/snobbish; prissy/priggish; fussy; **c'est une femme chichiteuse**, she's a fusspot.

chicor(e) [ʃikɔr] *a O P* drunk*/blotto.

chicorée [ʃikɔre] *nf P* **1.** reprimand*/slating/telling-off **2. être chicorée**, to be drunk*/blotto **3. défriser la chicorée**, to flirt with/to chat up/to (try to) get off with a woman.

chicot [ʃiko] *nm F* stump (of tooth).

chié [ʃje] *a P* **c'est chié!** it's bloody good!/it's fucking amazing!

chie-dans-l'eau [ʃidãlo] *nm inv V* sailor/tarry arse.

chiée [ʃje] *nf V* **une chiée de ...**, a great quantity* of .../lots of .../oodles of .../lashings of .../bags of .../loads of .../stacks of ....

chie-en-lit [ʃiãli] *nm&f inv F* **1.** person who soils his/her bed **2.** *O* (*a*) (*i*) carnival/masquerade (*ii*) s.o. wearing a mask at a carnival (*b*) scarecrow/freak; **quelle chie-en-lit!** what a scarecrow! **3.** rabble; noisy disorder/havoc; **crier à la chie-en-lit**, to boo.

chien [ʃjɛ̃], *f* **chienne** [ʃjɛn] **I** *a* **1.** *F* **être chien**, to be mean*/stingy/tight-fisted; **être chien comme tout**, to be as mean as they come/as they make 'em **2.** *F* **être chien avec qn**, to be rotten to s.o./to be hard on s.o./to give s.o. a rough time **3.** *F* **avoir l'air chien**, to look like (a bit of a) swine/to look nasty **4.** *O P* **ça n'est pas tant chien**, it's not that bad **II** *n* **1.** *F* **il n'attache pas ses chiens avec des saucisses**, he's a skinflint/he's as mean* as they come **2.** *F* (*journ*) **faire des chiens écrasés/les chiens crevés/les chiens perdus**, to be a hack reporter; to be in charge of the accident column **3.** *F* **c'est pas fait pour les chiens**, it's not there as an ornament, it's meant to be used. (*Voir* **chat 7**) **4.** *F* **garder à qn un chien de sa chienne**, to have a grudge against s.o.; to have it in for s.o. **5.** *F* **avoir du chien**, to have charm/fascination; to be attractive/sexy; **il a du chien**, he's really something **6.** *F* **avoir un chien pour qn**, to be infatuated* with s.o./to have a crush on s.o. **7.** *F* (*locution populaire*) **les chiens aboient, la caravane passe**, = I don't care what Mrs Grundy says **8.** *F* **avoir un mal de chien** (*i*) to be in great pain (*ii*) to have the devil of a job (to do sth); **se donner un mal de chien**, to take great pains (with/over sth) **9.** *F* **vie de chien**, dog's life; **elle m'a fait mener une vie de chien**, she led me a dog's life; **quelle chienne de vie!** what a miserable life! **quel temps de chien!** what filthy weather! **métier/travail de chien**, drudgery; **être d'une humeur de chien**, to be in a vile mood/a filthy temper*; **avoir un caractère de chien**, to be a nasty/vile person; to be a nasty piece of work **10.** *P* **cette chienne de musique!** that bloody music! **11.** *F* **un coup de chien** (*i*) a sudden violent riot/clash/flare-up (*ii*) (*marine*) a sudden squall **12.** *F* **mon chien**, my darling*/my pet **13.** *F* **piquer un chien**, to take a nap **14.** *P* underling/subordinate/dogsbody; (*militaire*) **le chien de quartier/de caserne**, (company) sergeant-major; **chien du bord**, second officer **15.** *P* brandy **16.** *P* **chien vert**, jack of spades. (*Voir* **mordre 1**; **quille 4**)

chienchien [ʃjɛ̃ʃjɛ̃] *nm F* **1.** (*langage enfantin*) doggie/doggy; bowwow **2.** darling*/pet; **le chienchien à sa mémère,** mummy's little boy/little darling/little pet.

chiendent [ʃjɛ̃dɑ̃] *nm* **1.** *F* snag/difficulty/hitch **2.** *F* **arracher le chiendent,** to be kept hanging about; to be stood up **3.** *P* (*drogues*) marijuana*/grass/hay; **fumer le chiendent,** to smoke grass.

chienlit [ʃjɑ̃li] *nm&f F* = **chie-en-lit.**

chiennaille [ʃjɛnɑj] *nf F* rabble/riff-raff.

chiennerie [ʃjɛnri] *nf P* **1.** (*a*) beastliness/nastiness (*b*) filthy/dirty trick/sordidness **2.** meanness/tightfistedness.

chier [ʃje] *vi V* **1.** to defecate*/to shit/to crap; to have a crap/a shit **2. une gueule à chier dessus,** a repulsive face/a face like the back(-end) of a bus **3. il n'a pas chié la honte,** he's got nerve enough for anything **4. ça va chier (dur)!/ça va chier des bulles!/ça va chier des flammes!** now the shit's going to fly!/now there'll be a (hell of a) stink! **5. va chier!** get stuffed! **tu me fais chier!/(ne) me fais pas chier!** you make me sick!/you get on my bloody nerves!/don't give me that crap!/you're a pain in the arse! **envoyer chier qn,** to tell s.o. to bugger off/to piss off/to sod off; **va te faire chier!** bugger off!/sod off!/piss off! **se faire chier sérieux,** to be bored stiff/to be really pissed off! **qu'est-ce qu'on se fait chier ici!** God! it's bloody boring here!/we're really getting pissed off here! **6. ça, c'est chié!** nice work!/(that's) bloody good!/that's the stuff! **7. ça (ne) chie pas!** it doesn't matter a fuck! **8. y a pas à chier,** you can say what you bloody well/damn well like; there's no two ways about it **9. à chier,** no (bloody) good/rotten/hopeless **10. chier dans son fourreau,** to be afraid*/to

be shit-scared/to be scared shitless. (*Voir* **botte II 9; colle 7; colonne 1; confiture 5; matricule 2; poivre 2; pot**)

chierie [ʃiri] *nf V* sth that gets one down/a bloody nuisance; **quelle chierie!** what a bloody mess! **quelle chierie de temps!** what bloody awful weather!

chie-tout-debout [ʃitudbu] *nm&f inv V* tall thin person*/long streak of piss.

chieur, -euse [ʃjœr, -øz] *n V* (*pers*) **1.** stinker/bastard*/shit **2. chieur d'encre,** ink-slinger; pen-pusher.

chiffe [ʃif] **I** *nf F* **1. une chiffe (molle),** a spineless individual/a drip/a wet/a wimp **2. se sentir mou comme une chiffe,** to feel like a wet rag **3. la chiffe,** the rag-and-bone business; the junk business **II** *nm F* rag-and-bone man; junk dealer.

chiffon [ʃifɔ̃] *nm* **1.** *F* **parler/causer chiffons,** to talk (about) clothes/to talk dress/to talk fashion **2.** *P* handkerchief.

chiffonner [ʃifɔne] *vtr F* to worry/to annoy* s.o.; **ça me chiffonne,** that gets me/that bothers me; **qu'est-ce qui le chiffonne?** what's eating/bugging him?

chiffortin [ʃifɔrtɛ̃] *nm A P* rag-and-bone man; junk dealer.

chifftire, chiftir(e) [ʃiftir] *nm P* **1.** rag **2.** = **chiffortin.**

chignol(l)e [ʃiɲɔl] *nf F* **1.** old car*/banger/jalopy **2.** (any sort of) machine.

chignon [ʃiɲɔ̃] *nm P* **1.** head*/brains/intelligence; **elle n'a rien sous le chignon,** she's brainless **2.** (*femme*) **un chignon véreux,** a bitch. (*Voir* **crêpage; crêper**)

chinago [ʃinago] *a P* Chinese.

chinage [ʃinaʒ] *nm* **1.** *P* begging/cadging/scrounging **2.** *F* ill-natured criticism* (of s.o.) **3.** *F* practical joking/leg-pulling/ragging.

chine [ʃin] *nf P* **1.** cadging/ scrounging; **tabac de chine,** cadged tobacco **2.** peddling; door-to-door selling; **marchand à la chine,** street hawker.

chiner [ʃine] **I** *P vi* **1.** to hawk one's goods about **2.** to be in the rag-and-bone business **II** *vtr* **1.** *F* to criticize* (s.o.) severely/to pull (s.o.) to pieces/to run (s.o.) down **2.** *F* to make fun of (s.o.)/to pull (s.o.'s) leg/to have s.o. on **3.** *P* to cadge/to scrounge (sth).

chinetoc, chinetok, chinetoque [ʃintɔk] **I** *nm&f & a F* Chinese/chink; **bouffe chinetoc,** Chinese/chinky food **II** *nm P* bungler/botcher.

chineur, euse [ʃinœr, -øz] *n* **1.** *P* cadger **2.** *P* second-hand dealer **3.** *F* practical joker/leg-puller **4.** *F* (*a*) (carping) critic (*b*) scandalmonger.

chinois [ʃinwa] **I** *a F* (*a*) (*pers*) awkward/difficult (*b*) (*objet, chose*) over-elaborate/complicated/involved **II** *nm* **1.** *F* fellow/guy/bloke/ chap* (*esp* a stranger) **2.** *F* **c'est du (vrai) chinois (pour moi),** it's all Greek to me/it's double Dutch to me **3.** *F* **tremper ses chinois,** to get involved/implicated **4.** *F* **ça ne fait pas mes chinois,** that doesn't suit my book **5.** *V* penis*; **se battre/se polir le chinois,** to masturbate*/to toss off.

chinoiserie [ʃinwazri] *nf F* unnecessary complication; complicated formality; **chinoiseries (administratives),** red tape.

chiots [ʃjo] *nmpl P* = **chiottes (chiotte 3)**

chiotte [ʃjɔt] *nf P* **1.** (*péj*) (old) car*/jalopy/banger **2.** **c'est la chiotte/quelle chiotte!** it's a deadly bore/what a drag! **3.** *pl* WC*/ bog/*NAm* can/shithouse; (*mil*) **la corvée des chiottes,** latrine fatigue

4. aux chiottes! (*i*) go to hell! (*ii*) chuck it away! **aux chiottes, le patron!** to hell with the boss!/screw the boss! (*Voir* **courant 3**)

chipage [ʃipaʒ] *nm F* stealing; scrounging.

chipé [ʃipe] *a O F* **1. être chipé pour qn,** to be infatuated* with s.o./to have a crush on s.o. **2. elle n'est pas mal chipée,** she's not bad (looking).

chiper [ʃipe] *vtr F* **1.** to steal*/to pinch/to nick/to swipe (**qch à qn,** sth from s.o.) **2.** to catch/to cop (a cold, a disease).

chipette [ʃipɛt] *nf P* **ça ne vaut pas chipette,** that's worthless*/it's not worth a sausage.

chipeur, euse [ʃipœr, -øz] *F* **I** *a* thieving; scrounging **II** *n* petty thief*/sneak thief/pilferer; scrounger **III** *nm* man who steals another man's girl.

chipie [ʃipi] *F* **I** *nf* ill-natured/disagreeable woman; sourpuss/bitch; **vieille chipie,** old bat/old faggot; **une petite chipie,** a spiteful little minx **II** *af* catty/bitchy.

chipolata [ʃipɔlata] *nm or f P* (small) penis*/(*euph*) sausage.

chipotage [ʃipɔtaʒ] *nm F* **1.** haggling/quibbling (over trifles) **2.** time-wasting; fiddling about.

chipoter [ʃipɔte] *F* **I** *vi* **1.** to haggle/to quibble (over trifles) **2.** to nibble/to pick at one's food **3.** to waste time/to dilly-dally/to shilly-shally **II** *vtr* **ça me chipote,** it bothers me.

chipoteur, euse [ʃipɔtœr, -øz] *F* **I** *n* **1.** time-waster/s.o. who shilly-shallies **2.** haggler/quibbler/nit-picker **II** *a* **1.** time-wasting **2.** hair-splitting/nit-picking/picky **3.** choosy/fastidious.

chique [ʃik] *nf* **1.** *F* **c'est clair comme du jus de chique,** it's as clear as mud **2.** *P* **avaler sa chique/poser sa chique,** to die*/to kick the bucket **3.** *F* **avoir la chique** *(a)* to chew (a quid of) tobacco *(b)* to have a gumboil/a swollen cheek **4.** *F* **ça ne vaut pas une chique,** that's worthless*/it's not worth a brass farthing **5.** *F* **se sentir mou comme une chique,** to feel listless/like a wet rag; **il est mou comme une chique,** he's a drip/he's wet/he's a bit of a wimp **6.** *F (a)* **couper la chique à qn,** to cut s.o. short/to cramp s.o.'s style/ to cut in on s.o. *(b)* **en avoir la chique coupée,** to be flabbergasted *(c)* **couper la chique à quinze pas,** to have (very) bad breath **9.** *P* **avoir une chique,** to be drunk* **10.** *P* **pour la chique,** just for the fun of it/for the hell of it **11.** *V* **tirer sa chique,** to have sex*/to have it off/ to get one's end away; **cracher sa chique,** to ejaculate*/to shoot one's load.

chiqué [ʃike] *nm F* **1.** sham/ fake/phoney; **c'est du chiqué,** it's phoney/it's a fake; it's a put-up job; **tout ça, c'est du chiqué,** that's all eyewash; that's all make-believe; **c'est pas du chiqué,** it's straight from the horse's mouth; it's the real McCoy; **le/la faire au chiqué,** to sham/to make-believe; to put on an act **2.** fuss/to-do; **faire du chiqué,** to put on airs/to swank/to show off*; **un faiseur de chiqué,** a show-off*.

chiquement [ʃikmɑ̃] *adv F* **1.** *(s'habiller) (i)* smartly/stylishly *(ii)* nicely/decently **2.** splendidly/in first-class style.

chiquer [ʃike] *P* **I** *vi* **1.** to pretend/to sham; to make-believe; **chiquer à...,** to pretend to be...; **rien à chiquer!** nothing doing!*/no dice! **2.** **y a pas à chiquer!** there's no getting away from it!/there's no two ways about it! **II** *vtr* **1.** to eat*/to get stuck into (one's food) **2.** to fake/to cook (the books).

chiqueur, euse [ʃikœr, -øz] *n* **1.** *F* pretender/phoney **2.** *P*

swank/show-off* **3.** *P* glutton*/ guzzler/greedy-guts **4.** *P* small-time crook.

chlaff(e) [ʃlaf] *nm or f P* **aller au chlaff(e)/à (la) chlaff(e),** to go to bed*; **faire chlaff(e),** to sleep*; to be asleep/sleeping. (*Voir* **schlaf**)

chlass(e) [ʃlɑs] **I** *a P* drunk*/sozzled **II** *nm P* knife; dagger; chiv. (*Voir* **schlass(e) I, II**)

chleu(h) [ʃlø] *a&n P (WW II)* German*/Jerry.

chlingoter [ʃlɛ̃gɔte], **chlinguer** [ʃlɛ̃ge], **chlipoter** [ʃlipɔte] *vi P* to stink*/to pong; **chlingoter du bec,** to have foul breath. (*Voir* **schlinguer**)

chloff(e) [ʃlɔf] *nm or f P* = **chlaff(e).**

chmoutz [ʃmuts] *nm P (péj)* Jew*/ yid.

chnaps [ʃnaps], **chnique** [ʃnik] *nm F* inferior whisky or brandy; cheap spirits*/rotgut. (*Voir* **schnaps, schnick**)

chniquer [ʃnike] *vi P* to stink*/to pong.

chnoc, chnoque [ʃnɔk] *P* **I** *a* mad*/bonkers; gaga **II** *nm* fool*/ schmo(e)/schmuck; **un vieux chnoc,** a silly old fool/a doddering old idiot/an old fart. (*Voir* **schnock, schnoque**)

chnouf(fe) [ʃnuf] *nf P (drogues)* heroin*/H/junk. (*Voir* **schnouf(fe)**)

chnouffé, ée [ʃnufe] *n P (drogues)* heroin* addict/dope addict/junkie. (*Voir* **schnouffé**)

se chnouffer [səʃnufe] *vpr P (drogues)* to take heroin*; to be a heroin* addict/a junkie; to take dope. (*Voir* **se schnoufer**)

chochoter [ʃɔʃɔte] *vi P* to put on airs.

chochoteuse [ʃɔʃtøz] *af P* affected; finicky; genteel/(would-be) refined.

chochotte [ʃɔʃɔt] *nf* **1.** *F* **ma chochotte**, my darling*/my pet **2.** *P* (hypocritically) prudish woman; **faire sa chochotte**, to do a holier-than-thou act; **une vieille chochotte**, an old has-been **3.** *P (a)* effeminate young man (with exaggeratedly affected manerisms)/fairy/poofter *(b)* homosexual*.

choco [ʃɔko] *nm F* chocolate.

chocolat [ʃɔkɔla] *a inv P (a)* **être/faire chocolat**, to be done out of sth; to get swindled/rooked/cheated out of sth *(b)* **demeurer/rester chocolat**, to be left in the lurch; to be left stranded.

chocotter [ʃɔkɔte] *vi P* to be afraid*/to tremble with fear/to have the willies.

chocottes [ʃɔkɔt] *nfpl P* **1.** teeth*/ivories/gnasher/choppers **2. avoir/prendre les chocottes**, to be afraid*/to get the wind up/to have the jitters; **filer les chocottes à qn**, to put the wind up s.o.

choir [ʃwar] *vi F* **laisser choir (qn/qch)**, to drop/to get rid of/to dump (s.o./sth); **laisser choir ses potes**, to let one's mates down.

choléra [kɔlera] *nm P* disagreeable individual/nasty piece of work/poisonous character; *(chose, affaire)* nasty business.

chôme [ʃom] *nf P* unemployment.

chômedu, chôm'du [ʃomdy] *nm P* unemployed worker/person out of work; **être au chômedu**, to be unemployed/out of work/on the dole.

chômeur [ʃomœr] *nm P* glass of mineral water.

choper [ʃɔpe] *vtr P* **1.** to steal*/to pinch/to nick/to swipe (**qch à qn**, sth from s.o.) **2.** to catch/to cop; **il a chopé un rhume**, he caught a cold **3.** to arrest*; **se faire choper**, to get nabbed/done. (*Voir* biscuit 2)

chopeur, euse [ʃopœr, -øz] *P* **I**

a thieving; scrounging **II** *n* petty thief*/sneak thief/pilferer; scrounger.

chopin [ʃopɛ̃] *nm P* **1.** bit of luck/lucky break; windfall/godsend; **faire un (beau) chopin**, to clinch a good deal/to do a good piece of business **2.** (love) conquest/catch; **faire un (beau) chopin**, to make a good catch; to find a wealthy lover/a wealthy mistress **3.** *O* beautiful girl*; **cette fille, c'est un chopin**, that girl is a real beauty **4.** infatuation for/crush on (a girl/woman).

chopine [ʃopin] *nf* **1.** *F* bottle/glass (of wine, etc); **tu viens boire une chopine?** coming for a drink? **2.** *V* penis*/chopper.

chopiner [ʃopine] *vi P* to drink* heavily/to booze/to hit the bottle.

chopinette [ʃopinɛt] *nf F* small bottle, small mug(ful) (of wine, etc). (*Voir* **chopine 1**)

chopot(t)e [ʃopɔt] *nf* **1.** *P* (small) bottle (of wine, etc) **2.** *V* (large) penis*.

chose [ʃoz] **I** *a inv F* **être/se sentir tout chose/un peu chose**, to feel unwell*/out of sorts/under the weather; **vous avez l'air tout chose**, you look upset/as if something's happened/as if something's gone wrong **II** *nm&f F* **Monsieur Chose/Madame Chose**, Mr/Mrs What-do-you-callit; Mr/Mrs Thing-ummy; Mr What's-his-name/Mrs What's-her-name **III** *nm&f (euph pour remplacer des mots vulgaires)* **1. je vais te botter le chose**, I'll kick you up the you-know-where; **il a sorti son chose**, he's got his thingy out **2. être porté sur la chose**, to be fond of sex*/to like it/to like a bit of nooky.

chosette [ʃozɛt] *nf P* love-making.

chottes [ʃɔt] *nfpl P* = **chiottes (chiotte 3)**.

chou, *pl* **-oux** [ʃu] **I** *nm* **1.** *P* head*; brains/intelligence*; **en**

avoir dans le chou, to be intelligent/to have brains; **se casser/se creuser le chou,** to rack one's brains; **rentrer dans le chou à qn,** to attack s.o./to beat s.o. up*; **travailler du chou,** to be mad*/crazy/bonkers; **avoir le chou pourri,** to have funny ideas; **se monter le chou,** to get excited/to get (all) worked up   **2.** *F* **mon (petit) chou,** (my) darling*/my precious (one); **mon petit chou en sucre/en susucre,** sweetie-pie; **c'est un vrai chou!** he's a perfect darling! (*Voir* **chou II; choute**)   **3.** *P* **être dans les choux,** to be in a fix*/in a (pretty) pickle; (*plan, projet*) **finir dans les choux,** to fail/to come to grief; to be up the spout; (*courses*) **laisser les autres dans les choux,** to leave the rest of the field standing; **faire chou blanc,** to fail completely/to draw a (complete) blank; (*dans un jeu*) to fail to score   **4.** *F* **aller planter ses choux,** to retire and go and live in the country   **5.** *F* **faire ses choux gras,** to make one's pile/to feather one's nest; **faire ses choux gras de qch,** to make a handsome profit out of sth   **6.** *F* **faites-en des choux et des raves,** do just what you like with it/you can please yourself what you do with it   **7.** *P* **se taper le chou,** to have a good tuck-in/to have a good blow-out   **8.** *F* **chou pour chou,** taking one thing with another; **répondre à qn chou pour chou,** to answer s.o. pat   **9.** *F* **c'est chou vert et vert chou,** it's much of a muchness/it's six of one and half a dozen of the other.   **10.** *F* (*a*) **c'est bête comme chou,** it's as easy* as winkling/as falling off a log (*b*) **il est bête comme chou,** he's extremely stupid*/as thick as two (short) planks   **11.** *F* **manger les choux par les trognons,** to be dead and buried/to be pushing up the daisies. (*Voir* **feuille 1, 2; ramer I**) II *a* **ce que tu es chou!** you're a perfect darling! **ce serait**

chou! that'd be great!/nice! **c'est chou!** it's divine! (*Voir* **chou I 2**)

chouaga [ʃwaga] *a P* excellent*/first-rate/super/gorgeous.

chouaye [ʃwɛj] *adv P* = **chouïa 2, 3.**

choubiner [ʃubine] *P* I *vtr* to heat II *vi* **ça choubine,** everything's going well/going great guns; we're doing fine.

choubinette [ʃubinɛt] *nf P* small stove.

choucard(e) [ʃukar(d)] *a P* (*a*) pleasant (*b*) good-looking.

chouchou, *f* chouchoute [ʃuʃu, -ut] *n F* darling*/favourite/pet; **le chouchou de maman,** mummy's blue-eyed boy/mummy's little boy; **la chouchoute de papa,** daddy's darling (girl); **le chouchou du prof(esseur),** teacher's pet.

chouchouter [ʃuʃute] *F* I *vi* to pet/to caress/to fondle (s.o.); to pamper/to coddle (a child) II *vpr* **se chouchouter,** to have a cushy time.

choucroute [ʃukrut] *nf F* **petite choucroute,** curly head of hair. (*Voir* **pédaler 3**)

chouette [ʃwɛt] *F* I *a*   **1.** excellent*/first-rate/great/smashing; **une chouette cravate,** a snazzy tie   **2.** nice/pretty/good-looking/cute   **3.** honest/straight/decent   **4.** **être chouette,** to be duped/hoaxed/to be played for a sucker; to be done/had; **se faire chouette,** to be taken in/taken for a ride II *adv phr* **avoir qn à la chouette,** to like s.o./to have a soft spot for s.o.; to take a liking to s.o. III *excl* **chouette (alors)!** splendid!/fine!/super!/great!/smashing! IV *nm V* anus*; **prendre du chouette,** to be an active homosexual*; **donner/filer du chouette,** to be a passive homosexual*.

chouettement [ʃwɛtmɑ̃] *adv F* excellently/splendidly/fabulously.

chouettes [ʃwɛt] *nm or fpl* P **marcher sous ses chouettes**, to have one's (identity) papers in order.

chouettos(e) [ʃwɛtos] *a* P excellent*/great/super/marvellous; **c'est vraiment chouettos**, it's really terrific.

chou-fleur [ʃuflœr] *nm* **1.** F **avoir les oreilles en chou-fleur**, to have cauliflower ears **2.** *pl* P **choux-fleurs**, haemorrhoids/*N Am* hemorrhoids/piles.

chouflique [ʃuflik] *nm,* **choufliqueur** [ʃuflikœr] *nm* O P shoemaker/cobbler.

chouïa [ʃuja] P I *nm* **un chouïa de** ..., a little .../a small quantity of ... II *adv* **1. pas chouïa**, not much **2. vas-y chouïa!** go easy!/ steady on!

chouilla [ʃuja] *nm,* **chouille** [ʃuj] *nm* P = **chouïa 1.**

choumaque [ʃumak] *nm* P = **chouflique.**

choupaïa [ʃupaja] *a inv* P = **chouettos(e).**

choupette [ʃupɛt] *nf* F tuft of baby's hair tied with a bow.

choupiner [ʃupine] *vtr* F = **chouchouter.**

chouquette [ʃukɛt] *nf* P **1.** affected young woman **2.** *(a)* homosexual* *(b)* effeminate young man (with exaggeratedly affected mannerisms)/fairy/poofter; **il fait très chouquette**, he's rather camp.

chourave [ʃurav] *nf* P thieving.

chouravé [ʃurave] I *nm* P stolen goods II *a* P mad*.

chouraver [ʃuraver] *vtr* P to steal*.

chouraveur [ʃuravœr] *nm* P thief*.

chourin [ʃurɛ̃] *nm* O P knife; dagger.

chouriner [ʃurine] *vtr* O P to knife (s.o.)/to stab (s.o.) (to death); to cut (s.o.) up.

choute [ʃut] *nf* F **ma choute**, (my) darling*/my dear little girl. (*Voir* **chou 2**)

chouter [ʃute] *vtr* F = **chouchouter.**

chouterie [ʃutri] *nf* F caress(ing)/ fondling; cuddling.

chouya [ʃuja] *nm & adv* P = **chouïa.**

chpile [ʃpil] *nm* P gambling; **avoir beau chpile** *(i)* to have/to hold a good hand (at cards) *(ii)* to find it easy/to have no difficulty; **il avait beau chpile à faire cela**, it was a walkover/all plain sailing for him. (*Voir* **schpile**)

chpiler [ʃpile] *vi* P to gamble. (*Voir* **schpiler**)

chpileur [ʃpilœr] *nm* P gambler. (*Voir* **schpileur**)

chproum [ʃprum] *nm* P **1.** scandal/(scandalous) gossip/dirt; **faire du chproum**, to cause a scandal **2.** din/row/racket; **faire du chproum**, to kick up a row **3.** anger; **aller à chproum**, to lose one's temper/to flare up/to hit the roof. (*Voir* **schproum(e)**)

chrono [krɔno] *nm* F (= *chronomètre*) stop-watch; **il faisait du 360 chrono** (= *au chronomètre*) he was doing (a speed of) 360 km per hour.

chroumer [krume] *vi* P to thieve from cars in a police pound.

ch'tar, chtar(d) [ʃtar] *nm* P **1.** prison*/stir/clink; disciplinary cell. (*Voir* **schtar(d)**) **2.** blow*/ smack/sock/clout.

chtib(e) [ʃtib] *nm* P prison*. (*Voir* **schtib(e)**)

ch'timi [ʃtimi] *nm* P native of northern France/northerner. (*Voir* **schtim(m)i**)

chtouillard [ʃtujar] *nm* P person who has (got) VD*/the clap. (*Voir* **schtouillard**)

chtouille [ʃtuj] *nf* P VD*/the

clap; **ramasser la chtouille,** to cop a dose; **flanquer la chtouille à qn,** to give s.o. a dose. (*Voir* **schtouille**)

chtourbe [ʃturb] *nf P* trouble/ (spot of) bother; **dans la chtourbe,** in a fix*/a jam.

chtrasse [ʃtras] *nf P* room in a hotel, etc, used by a prostitute. (*Voir* **strasse 1**)

chut-chut [ʃytʃyt] *adv phr F* **à la chut-chut,** in strict confidence/on the QT/hush-hush.

chute [ʃyt] *nf F* **1. point de chute,** meeting place/rendezvous **2. chute de la phrase,** punch-line (of a joke).

chuter [ʃyte] *vi F* to fall/to come a cropper*; (*pièce*) to be a flop; (*fille, femme*) to go wrong/to allow herself to be seduced; (*cartes*) to lose; **chuter de trois levées,** to be three tricks down.

cibiche [sibiʃ] *nf P* cigarette*/fag/ ciggy. (*Voir* **sibiche**)

ciblot [siblo] *nm P* civilian/civvy; **en ciblot,** in civvies/in civvy clothes.

ciboule [sibul] *nf P* **1.** head* **2. entrer en ciboule,** to come in first.

ciboulot [sibulo] *nm P* head*; brains/intelligence*; **il en a dans le ciboulot,** he's got brains; **se creuser le ciboulot,** to rack one's brains; **il travaille du ciboulot,** he's got a screw loose; **tu me cours/tu me cavales sur le ciboulot,** you get on my nerves/on my wick; you send me up the wall.

cicatrice [sikatris] *nf F* female genitals*/gash/slit; **une affranchie de la cicatrice,** a girl who has lost her virginity.

ci-devant [sidvã] *nm&f inv F (hist)* old fog(e)y*/has-been/back-number.

cidre [sidr] *nm P* **1.** water **2. ça ne vaut pas un coup de cidre,** it's absolutely worthless*/it's not worth a sausage.

ciel [sjɛl] *nm* **1.** *F* **tomber du ciel** *(i)* to be a godsend *(ii)* to look blank; to have no idea what is going on **2.** *F* **il ne l'emportera pas au ciel,** he won't get away with it **3.** *P* **approcher du ciel à reculons,** to be guillotined **4.** *P* **monter au ciel/atteindre le septième ciel,** to have an orgasm*/to climax/ to come.

Cifelle [sifɛl] *Prn F* **la tour Cifelle,** the Eiffel Tower (in Paris).

ciflard [siflar] *nm P* (French dried) sausage. (*Voir* **sauciflard**)

cigare [sigar] *nm* **1.** *P* head*/ nut; **avoir mal au cigare,** to have a headache; **y aller du cigare,** to risk one's neck; to stick one's neck out; **travailler du cigare/être dérangé du cigare,** to be mad*/nuts/off one's block; **se remettre le cigare à l'endroit,** to pull oneself together; **couper le cigare à qn** *(a)* to guillotine s.o. *(b)* to interrupt s.o./to cut in on s.o. (talking) **2.** *P* intelligence*/brains; **avoir du cigare,** to be brainy **3.** *V* **cigare à moustache(s),** penis*.

cigler [sigle] *vtr&i P* to pay* (up)/ to settle. (*Voir* **sigler**)

cigogne [sigɔɲ] *nf* **1.** *F* tall, thin girl or woman; beanpole **2.** *P* **la Cigogne,** the Palais de Justice, the Préfecture de police (the headquarters of the Paris police).

cigotin [sigɔtɛ̃] *nm P* = **cigue.**

cigue [sig] *nm P* **1. avoir un cigue,** to be twenty years old; **il doit avoir deux cigues et un peu de mornifle,** he must be forty-two or forty-three years old **2.** twenty francs. (*Voir* **sigue**)

ciguer [sige] *vtr&i P* = **cigler.**

cil [sil] *nm P* **1. avoir les cils cassés,** to feel very sleepy; **plier les cils,** to go to sleep **2. jeter un cil à qn,** to make eyes at s.o.

cimetière [simtjɛr] *nm P* **rendre le cimetière bossu,** to be buried.

ciné [sine] *nm O F* cinema; **aller au ciné**, to go to the flicks/to the pictures/*NAm* to the movies.

cinéma [sinema] *nm F* **1.** **faire du cinéma** (*i*) to create a scene/to kick up a fuss (*ii*) to put on an act; **c'est du cinéma**, it's just show/it's all put on/it's all an act; **se faire son cinéma**, to make a fuss/a song and dance about something **2.** **se faire du cinéma/s'emmener au cinéma** (*i*) to have delusions/to imagine things (*ii*) to put on an act.

cinetoche [sintɔʃ] *nm P* cinema; **aller au cinetoche**, to go to the flicks/the pictures/*NAm* the movies.

cinglé, ée [sɛ̃gle] *a&n P* mad* (person); **il est raide cinglé**, he's stark raving mad/a complete nut/a nutter.

cinoche [sinɔʃ] *nm P* **1.** cinema; **le cinoche du coin**, the local fleapit; **aller au cinoche**, to go to the flicks/the pictures/*NAm* the movies **2.** **se faire du cinoche**, to have delusions/to imagine things.

cinoque [sinɔk] *a & nm&f P* = **cinglé(e)**.

cinq [sɛ̃, sɛ̃k] *num a inv & nm inv* **1.** *F* **il était moins cinq**, it was a narrow escape/a near thing/a close shave **2.** *F* **en cinq secs**, immediately*/in no time (at all)/in five seconds flat/in a couple of shakes **3.** *F* **faire cinq et trois font huit**, to limp/to dot and carry one **4.** *F* (*euph*) **le mot de cinq lettres/les cinq lettres = merde**. (*Voir* **Cambronne**) **dire les cinq lettres**, to use bad language/to use four-letter words; **répondre en cinq lettres à qn/dire cinq lettres à qn**, to tell s.o. to go to hell/to tell s.o. where to go/to tell s.o. where to get off **5.** *P* **y aller de cinq**, to shake hands; **je t'en serre cinq**, put it there! (*Voir* **écraser II 2**) **6.** *P* **les cinq à sept**, clandestine lovers; **un cinq à sept**, a quick one/a quick screw/a quickie (in daytime) **7.** *V* **faire**

cinq contre un, to masturbate*/to give (oneself/s.o.) a hand job/to toss off **8.** *F* **je vous reçois cinq sur cinq**, receiving you loud and clear/(*fig*) I get you/I see what you mean.

cinq-cinq [sɛ̃ksɛ̃k] *a O F* **c'est cinq-cinq**, it's great/super/fantastic.

cinq-en-cinq [sɛ̃kɑ̃sɛ̃k] *nm F* **un vigoureux cinq-en-cinq**, a hearty handshake.

cinquante-pour-cent [sɛ̃kɑ̃tpursɑ̃] *nm or f P* wife*/my better half.

cintrant [sɛ̃trɑ̃] *a P* very comical/screamingly funny*; **c'est cintrant!** it's a real scream!

cintré [sɛ̃tre] *a P* **être cintré**, to be mad*/nuts.

cipal, aux [sipal, -o] *nm P* (= *garde municipal*) member of the police in Paris *or* the local police.

cipale [sipal] *nf P* (*chemins de fer* = *voie principale*) main line.

cirage [siraʒ] *nm F* **être dans le cirage** (*i*) to be in a fix*/in a jam/in Queer Street (*ii*) to be in the dark/to be all at sea/to be in a complete daze (*iii*) to be depressed*/to have the blues (*iv*) (*aviation*) to be flying blind (*v*) to be drunk*; **être en plein cirage**, to be dead drunk*/completely blotto.

circuit [sirkɥi] *nm F* **1.** **être dans le circuit** (*i*) to be in the same line of business (*ii*) to be in the thick of it; **se faire un circuit**, to go on a pubcrawl/to do a tour of the nightclubs; to go pubbing/nightclubbing.

cirer [sire] *vtr F* **1.** (*scol*) **cirer un garçon**, to give a boy the bumps **2.** (**je n'en ai**) **rien à cirer!** I don't give a damn! (*Voir* **botte II 4, 5**)

cirque [sirk] *nm* **1.** *P* (*hum*) Chamber of Deputies **2.** *P* (*i*) commotion/fuss/scene/to-do (*ii*) chaos/bear garden **3.** *V* **mener le petit au cirque**, to have sex*.

cisaillé [sizɑje] *a P* **1.** penniless*; **cisaillé à zéro**, stony broke **2.** dumbfounded/flabbergasted.

cisailler [sizɑje] *vtr P* **1.** to fleece* (s.o.) (at gambling)/to clean (s.o.) out/to take (s.o.) to the cleaners **2.** to dumbfound/to flabbergast* (s.o.)/to knock (s.o.) sideways.

ciseaux [sizo] *nmpl V* **faire petits ciseaux/faire les ciseaux**, to insert simultaneously the index and middle fingers in the anus and vagina.

citoyen [sitwajẽ] *nm F* bloke/guy; **un drôle de citoyen**, a strange fellow/a queer customer.

citron[1] [sitrɔ̃] *nm P* head*/nut; intelligence*/brains; **se creuser/se presser le citron**, to rack one's brains; **se lécher le citron**, to kiss and cuddle.

citron[2], **Citron** *nf P* (*aut*) Citroën (*RTM*) (car).

citrouille [sitruj] *nf P* **1.** head*/nut **2.** fool*/idiot/twit; **avoir l'air citrouille**, to look like a prize idiot.

civ(e)lot [sivlo] *nm P* civilian/civvy; **en civ(e)lot**, in civvies/in civvy clothes.

clabaud [klabo] *nm F* = **clabaudeur, euse.**

clabaudage [klabodaʒ] *nm F* scandalmongering/malicious gossip/backbiting.

clabauder [klabode] *vi F* **1.** **clabauder sur/contre qn**, to say malicious things/to gossip about s.o. **2.** = **claboter.**

clabauderie [klabodri] *nf F* malicious gossip.

clabaudeur, euse [klabodœr, -øz] *n F* scandalmonger/backbiter.

claboter [klabɔte] *vi P* to die*/to peg out/to snuff it.

clac [klak] *nm* = **claque II 1, 2.**

clairon [klɛrɔ̃] *nm P* (*mil*) (automatic) rifle.

clam(e)cer [klamse] *vi P* to die*/to snuff it.

clampin, ine [klɑ̃pẽ, -in] *n F* **1.** loafer/layabout/skiver **2.** (young) show-off*/boaster.

clampiner [klɑ̃pine] *vi F* to hang about/to loaf about/to mooch around.

clam(p)ser [klɑ̃mse] *vi P* = **clam(e)cer.**

clandé [klɑ̃de] **I** *nm P* clandestine *or* illegal (*i*) brothel* (*ii*) gambling joint (*iii*) opium den (*iv*) café which serves (select) customers after hours **II** *nf P* prostitute* working in a clandestine/an illegal brothel*.

clandès [klɑ̃dɛs] *nm P* (*WWII*) black market.

claoui(e)s [kla(u)wi] *nmpl V* testicles*/goolies; **casser/râper les claoui(e)s à qn**, to bore* the balls off s.o./to give s.o. a pain in the arse/to get on s.o.'s tits.

claper [klape] *vi P* to eat*/to stuff oneself.

clapet [klapɛ] *nm P* mouth*; **fermer/boucler son clapet**, to shut* up/to pipe down; **elle a un de ces clapets!** she never stops talking!

clapette [klapɛt] *nf P* tongue/clapper.

clapier [klapje] *nm F* (*péj*) small (untidy) house or flat/dump/hole; rabbit hutch; *pl* **clapiers**, back streets/slums; **ça a fait jaser dans les clapiers**, it was the talk of the slums.

clapoter [klapɔte] *vi P* to die*.

clapper [klape] *vi P* = **claper.**

clapser [klapse] *vi P* to die*.

claquant [klakɑ̃] *a F* tiring/exhausting/killing.

claque [klak] **I** *nf* **1.** *F* **une tête à claques** (*i*) an unpleasant/unprepossessing face (*ii*) a cheeky-looking blighter; **c'est une tête à claques**, he's just asking for it **2.** *P* death; **il en a sa claque** (*i*) he's on his last legs/he's dead beat/he's all in (*ii*) he's fed up to the back teeth with it/he's had (more than) enough of it. (*Voir* **cliques**) **II** *nm P* **1.** brothel*/whorehouse **2.** gambling den.

claqué [klake] **I** *a* (*a*) *F* exhausted*/clapped out/shattered (*b*) *P* dead **II** *nm P* corpse*; **le jardin des claqués,** the cemetery/the boneyard; **la boîte aux claqués,** the mortuary.

claquedent [klakdɑ̃] *nm O P* **1.** = **claque II 1, 2 2.** half-starved person/miserable wretch.

claquefaim [klakfɛ̃] *nm A P* = **claquedent 2.**

claque-fric [klakfrik] *nm&f O P* spendthrift.

claque-merde [klakmɛrd] *nm or f P* mouth*; **ferme ton/ta claquemerde!** shut up!*/shut your face!

claquer [klake] **I** *vi P* (*a*) to die*; (*entreprise*) to go to pieces/to go bust; (*machine, appareil*) to pack up/to conk out/to go phut; **le moteur m'a claqué dans les mains,** the engine died on me; **il m'a claqué dans la main,** he's let me down at the last moment **II** *vtr F* **1.** to exhaust*/to wear (s.o.) out **2.** (*sport*) **se claquer un muscle,** to pull/to strain a muscle **3.** to spend* freely/to squander/to blow; **il claque tout son fric avec des putes,** he blows all his money on prostitutes. (*Voir* **bec 1**; **polichinelle 2** (*b*)) *F* (*a*) to tire oneself out/to work oneself to death/to kill oneself (with work)/to shatter oneself.

claquette [klakɛt] *nf P* tongue/clapper.

clarinette [klarinɛt] *nf* **1.** *A P* (*mil*) rifle **2.** *P* (burglar's) jemmy/NAm jimmy **3.** *P* **becqueter/bouffer des clarinettes,** to go hungry/to do without one's rations **4.** *V* **clarinette (baveuse),** penis*; **jouer un air de clarinette (baveuse),** to

fellate* (s.o.)/to give (s.o.) a blow-job.

class [klas] *adv P* = **classe II.**

classe [klas] **I** *nf F* **1.** **être de la classe,** to be due for (*i*) (*mil*) demob(ilization) (*ii*) retirement, etc **2. avoir la classe/une sacrée classe** (*i*) to be elegant*/to dress smartly (*ii*) to have brains/to be smart; **elle a de la classe/elle est classe,** she's got class/she's pretty classy **II** *adv P* enough; **j'en ai classe (et reclass(e)),** I'm fed up* with it/I've had (more than) enough of it/I'm fed up to the back teeth with it; **c'est classe!** that'll do!/that's enough!/give it a rest! **attends que ça soit classe!** wait till it's over!

classé [klase] *a F* **c'est un homme classé,** he's been sized up/sussed out.

classique [klasik] *a F* **le coup classique,** the same old trick/the usual stunt; **c'était le coup classique!** it was classic!

classiques [klasik] *nmpl P* **avoir ses classiques,** to have a period*/to have the monthlies.

se claveter [səklavte] *vpr P* = **se claquer.**

clavier [klavje] *nm P* set of false teeth.

clé [kle] *nf* = **clef.**

cleb(s) [klɛb(s)] *nm,* **clébard** [klebar] *nm P* dog*/hound/tyke/pooch/mutt.

cléber [klebe] *vtr P* to eat*.

clef [kle] *nf* **1.** *F* **mettre la clef sous la porte/sous le paillasson,** to sneak off/to do a moonlight flit/to do a bunk **2.** *F* (*i*) **prendre la clef des champs,** to run away*/to beat it (*ii*) to take to the country; **avoir la clef des champs,** to be free to roam **3.** *P* **... à la clef,** ... into the bargain/ ... with something tacked on (to it); **dîner avec du champagne à la clef,** dinner with champagne thrown in **4.** *P* **rendre ses clefs,** to die*/to cash in one's chips. (*Voir* **nager 3; portail**)

Cléopâtre [kleɔpɑtr] *Prnf* **1.** *F* **elle croit avoir le nez de Cléopâtre!** she thinks she's something (big)/the bee's knees! **2.** *V* **faire Cléopâtre,** to fellate* s.o./to suck cock.

cleps [klɛps] *nm P* = **cleb(s).**

clerc [klɛr] *nm F* **faire un pas de clerc** (*i*) to make a mistake* (through inexperience) (*ii*) to make a wrong move.

clergeon [klɛrʒɔ̃] *nm F* altar-boy.

cliche [kliʃ] *nf P* **1.** diarrhoea*; **avoir la cliche,** to have diarrhoea*/ to have the runs **2. avoir la cliche,** to be afraid*/to have the wind up/ to be in a blue funk.

cliché [kliʃe] *nm P* ugly face*/ugly mug.

clicher [kliʃe] *vtr P* (*phot*) to take a picture/to film; **cliche celle-là!** get that shot!/take that one!

clicli [klikli] *nm V* clitoris*/clit.

client [kli(j)ɑ̃] *nm* **1.** *F* man*/ chap/fellow/guy; **un sale client,** an ugly customer; **un drôle de client,** a weird sort of bloke/an odd bod **2.** *P* **merci, je ne suis pas client,** no thanks, you can count me out.

clignotants [kliɲɔtɑ̃] *nmpl P* eyes*/blinkers; **baver des clignotants,** to cry one's eyes out.

clille [klij] *nm P* client/customer/ punter (*esp* of prostitute); **clille de nuit,** all-nighter.

clinoche [klinɔʃ] *nf P* clinic/nurs-ing home.

clinquaille [klɛ̃kɑj] *nf P* money*/ cash.

clique [klik] *nf F* (*péj*) gang/ crowd/shower; **ramener sa clique,** to bring along all one's mates/bud-dies.

cliques [klik] *nfpl F* **prendre ses cliques et ses claques,** to pack up and clear out/to make off smartly.

cliquette [klikɛt] *nfpl* **1.** *P* ear*;

avoir du miel dans les cliquettes, to be deaf/hard of hearing **2.** *V* cli-toris*/button.

clito [klito] *nf*, **cliton** [klitɔ̃] *nm V* clitoris*/clit.

clochard [klɔʃar] *nm F* tramp*/ bum/down-and-out/*esp NAm* hobo.

cloche [klɔʃ] **I** *nf* **1.** *F* (*a*) tramp*/beggar; **c'est une cloche,** he's a down-and-out (*b*) **la cloche,** tramps/down-and-outs (in general); **être de la cloche** (*i*) to be a tramp/ a beggar/a down-and-out (*ii*) to have nowhere to sleep/to be home-less **2.** *P* (*a*) clumsy person (*b*) stupid* person; **quelle cloche!** what a clot! **sacrée cloche!** you poor dope!/you silly jerk! **vieille cloche!** poor old chap! **3.** *P* **sonner les cloches à qn,** to reprimand* s.o. severely/to tell s.o. off in no uncer-tain manner; **se faire sonner les cloches,** to be severely repri-manded*/to get a rocket **4.** *F* **déménager à la cloche (de bois),** to do a moonlight (flit) **5.** *F* **qui n'entend qu'une cloche n'entend qu'un son,** there are two sides to every question; **un (tout) autre son de cloche,** a quite different way of looking at things **6.** *F* **avoir des cloches aux mains,** to have blistered hands **7.** *P* **se (bien) taper la cloche,** to eat* heartily/to have a good blow-out **II** *a P* **1.** ugly **2.** stupid*; **ce que t'es cloche!** what a dope!/twit you are! **avoir un air cloche,** to look daft; **ça fait cloche,** that looks idiotic.

clocher [klɔʃe] *vi* **1.** *F* to go wrong; **qu'est-ce qui cloche?** what's the trouble? **il y a quelque chose qui cloche,** there's something the matter/something wrong; there's something not quite right **2.** *P* to listen.

clochettes [klɔʃɛt] *nfpl P* (*pers*) **avoir des clochettes au cul,** to be dirty/filthy.

clodo [klɔdo] *nm*, **clodomir**

[klɔdomir] *nm P* tramp/beggar/down-and-out/bum.

clone [klɔn] *nm P* (*homosexuels*) xerox queen.

clop(e) [klɔp] *P* I *nm* cigarette* end/fag-end; cigar butt II *nm or f* cigarette*/fag/cig(gy). (*Voir* **piqueur**)

clopin-clopant [klɔpĕklɔpɑ̃] *adv F* **aller clopin-clopant,** to limp along; to hobble about; **commerce qui va clopin-clopant,** business that has its ups and downs.

clopinettes [klɔpinɛt] *nfpl* 1. *P* (*a*) **des clopinettes,** nothing*/damn-all/sod-all (*b*) **des clopinettes!** nothing doing!*/no dice!/balls! 2. *V* testicles*/ballocks.

cloporte [klɔpɔrt] *nm & f P* 1. disgusting person/creep 2. door-keeper/hall porter; caretaker/janitor/concierge.

cloque [klɔk] *nf P* 1. fart 2. **être en cloque,** to be pregnant*/to be in the family way; **mettre une femme en cloque,** to get a woman pregnant/to get a woman in the family way/to put a woman in the (pudding) club.

cloquer [klɔke] *P* I *vtr* 1. (*a*) to give/to hand over/to fork out (*b*) to put; to bung/to chuck (*c*) to land (a blow) (*d*) **cloquer le naze,** to catch syphilis*/to cop a dose of syph; **cloquer le naze à qn,** to give s.o. syphilis*/to give s.o. a dose of syph 2. **se cloquer qch,** to treat oneself to sth; **se cloquer un godet,** to knock back a drink II *vi* to fart*. (*Voir* **paume**) III *vpr* **se cloquer** 1. to place/to plonk one-self (somewhere) 2. **se cloquer à poil,** to strip naked* 3. **je m'en cloque,** I couldn't care less*/I don't give a damn/I couldn't give a fart.

clou [klu] *nm* 1. *F* chief attraction/star turn/climax/highlight 2. *P* pawnshop/uncle's; **mettre qch au clou,** to pawn sth; **ses bagues sont au clou,** her rings are in hock 3. *F*

old/worn-out machine *or* instrument; **un vieux clou,** an old crock; (*vélo*) boneshaker; (*bagnole*) banger/heap/wreck 4. *P* (*mil*) cells/clink/glasshouse; **ficher qn au clou,** to run s.o. in/to put s.o. in the cooler 5. *P* jemmy/*NAm* jimmy; *pl* **clous,** burglar's tools 6. *P* **des clous!/des clous et du vent!** not (bloody) likely!*/no (blooming) fear!/nothing doing!*/not on your nelly! 7. *P* **bouffer des clous,** to go without food/to live on air 8. *F* **poser ses clous,** to down tools/to go on strike 9. *P* **pour des clous,** for nothing at all/for sweet FA 10. *P* **river son clou à qn,** to silence s.o.; **ça lui a rivé son clou,** that shut him up 11. *P* **il ne fiche pas/n'en fiche pas un clou,** he doesn't do a stroke (of work)/he does damn-all 12. *P* **ça ne vaut pas un clou,** it's worthless*/it's not worth a tinker's cuss; **je n'en donnerais pas un clou,** I wouldn't give a penny for it 13. *F* **arriver sur le clou,** to arrive on the dot/to be dead on time 14. *P* **clou de cercueil,** small cigar. (*Voir* **rouillé**)

clouant [kluɑ̃] *a P* amazing/staggering/stunning.

clouer [klue] *vtr P* **clouer qn,** to reduce s.o. to silence/to shut s.o. up*. (*Voir* **bec 1**)

coaltar [koltar] *nm P* 1. thick cheap red wine/plonk 2. **être dans le coaltar,** to be in a mess/in the soup; to be in a tight spot.

cocard [kɔkar] *nm P* black eye*/shiner.

cocarde [kɔkard] *nf P* 1. head*; **ce vin vous tape sur la cocarde,** this wine goes to your head 2. **avoir sa cocarde,** to be drunk*.

se cocarder [səkɔkarde] *vpr P* to get drunk*.

coccinelle [kɔksinɛl] *nf F* (*petite voiture Volkswagen*) Beetle (*RTM*).

coche [kɔʃ] *nm F* 1. **manquer/rater/louper le coche,** to miss one's chance/to miss the boat/to miss the buss 2. **faire la mouche du coche,** to buzz around/to be a busy- body.

cocher [kɔʃe] *nm P* **1.** (*aviation*) pilot **2.** (*musique*) conductor.

cochon, -onne [kɔʃ̃ɔ, ɔn] **I** *nm F* **1.** swine/dirty pig/filthy beast; **quel cochon!** what a swine!/what a bastard!* **2. jouer un tour de cochon à qn,** to play a dirty trick on s.o. **3.** (*a*) **travail de cochon,** botch job/slapdash piece of work (*b*) **il est adroit comme un cochon de sa queue,** he's ham-fisted; he's all fingers and thumbs **4. être amis/copains comme cochons,** to be as thick as thieves/to be great buddies **5. (et) cochon qui s'en dédit** (*i*) and to hell with anyone who says otherwise (*ii*) it's a deal **6. jouer un pied de cochon à qn,** to leave s.o. in the lurch **7. nous n'avons pas gardé les cochons ensemble!** don't be so familiar!/ don't take liberties (with me)! **je n'ai pas gardé les cochons avec lui!** he has no right to try it on with me! (*Voir* **cuivre**) **8. plein/soûl comme un cochon,** dead drunk*/ pissed as a newt **9. quel cochon de temps!** what filthy weather! **II** *nf F* slut **III** *a F* **1.** swinish/dirty/ disgusting/filthy; smutty (story); blue (joke) **2. ça, c'est cochon!** that's a dirty/a rotten trick! that's a rotten thing to do! **3. c'est pas cochon,** that's excellent*!/that's not at all bad! **mille francs, ce n'est pas cochon!** a thousand francs, that's pretty good!

cochonceté [kɔʃ̃ɔste] *nf P* **1.** smutty joke **2.** dirty trick.

cochonnaille(s) [kɔʃɔnaj] *nf(pl) F* (*charcuterie*) cooked meats (bought at a pork butcher's).

cochonner [kɔʃɔne] *vtr F* to bungle*/to botch (up)/to make a mess of (a piece of work, etc).

cochonnerie [kɔʃɔnri] *nf F* **1.**

(*a*) filthiness/filth (*b*) **dire des cochonneries,** to talk smut/obscenities; **raconter des cochonneries,** to tell dirty stories/blue jokes **2.** rubbish/trash/junk **3.** vile food/pigswill **4. faire une cochonnerie à qn,** to play a dirty trick on s.o./to do the dirty on s.o.

cocker [kɔkɛr] *nm P* **les avoir en oreilles de cocker,** to feel limp after making love/to feel shagged out.

cocktail [kɔktɛl] *nm F* (*a*) mixture of drugs (*eg* cocaine* and heroin*, barbiturates* and amphetamines*)/ cocktail (*b*) (*alcool*) **avaler un sacré cocktail,** to drink a hell of a mixture/to mix all sorts of drinks (at a party, etc); to mix the grape and the grain.

coco [koko, kɔ-] **I** *nm* **1.** *P* head*/nut; **avoir le coco fêlé/ détraqué,** to be mad*/to be off one's nut/to be as nutty as a fruitcake **2.** *P* stomach*; **se remplir le coco,** to eat* heartily/to stuff oneself/to have a good blow-out; **en avoir plein le coco,** to have a bellyful **3.** *P* throat/gullet; **dévisser le coco à qn,** to strangle s.o. **4.** *F* (*mot enfantin*) (*a*) cock/hen/chicken (*b*) egg/eggie **5.** *F* communist; **les cocos,** the commies/the reds **6.** *F* (*a*) (*type*) **un drôle de coco,** a strange fellow/an odd bod/a queer customer; **un vilain coco/un sale coco,** a nasty piece of work; (*iron et péj*) **c'est un gentil/un beau/un joli coco!** he's a nice one! (*b*) **mon (petit) coco,** my darling*/my pet **7.** *P* petrol; **mettre le coco,** to hurry* up/to step on the gas **II** *nf P* (*drogues*) cocaine*/coke/snow/ flake **III** *a F* old-fashioned/out of date.

cocoter [kɔkɔte] *vi P* to stink*/to pong.

cocotier [kɔkɔtje] *nm* **1.** *F* **gagner le cocotier,** to win the big prize/to hit the jackpot **2.** *F* **il descend de son cocotier,** he's a bit of a fool*

3. *F* **grimper au cocotier,** to fly into a temper **4.** *F* **radio cocotier,** bush telegraph **5.** *P* **buttocks***.

cocotte [kɔkɔt] *nf* **1.** *F* (*mot enfantin*) cock/hen/chicken/cock-a-doodle(-doo) **2.** *F* horse; **hue, cocotte!** gee up!/giddy up! **3.** *F* **ma (petite) cocotte,** my darling*/my pet/*esp NAm* honey(bunch)/sweetie(pie) **4.** *P* (*a*) kept woman* (*b*) prostitute*/tart/floozie **5.** *P* gonorrhoea*/clap **6.** *F* foot-and-mouth disease **7.** *F* inflammation of the eyelids.

cocotte-minute [kɔkɔtminyt] *nf P* prostitute* who gets through a succession of clients quickly.

cocotter [kɔkɔte] *vi P* to stink*/to pong.

cocu [kɔky] *nm F* **1.** cuckold **2.** **avoir une chance/une veine de cocu,** to have the devil's own luck; **cocu! you lucky devil! 3. et bien cocu qui s'en dédit!** (*i*) and to hell with anyone who says otherwise (*ii*) it's a deal.

cocufier [kɔkyfje] *vtr F* **1.** to be unfaithful to (one's husband) **2.** to seduce (s.o.'s) wife.

cœur [kœr] *nm F* **1.** (*a*) **joli cœur,** effeminate man, pansy (*b*) **faire le joli cœur,** to put on airs and graces **2. avoir le cœur bien accroché,** to have a strong stomach **3. avoir du cœur au ventre,** to be game/to have plenty of guts; **donner du cœur au ventre à qn,** to buck s.o. up/to put fresh heart into s.o.; **ça vous remettra du cœur au ventre,** that'll buck you up **4. avoir un cœur d'artichaut,** to fall in love with every pretty girl/handsome boy one meets **5. dîner/déjeuner par cœur,** to go without food **6. mettre cœur sur carreau,** to vomit*.

coffio(t) [kɔfjo] *nm P* safe/strong-box.

coffioteur [kɔfjɔtœr] *nm P* safe-breaker.

coffre [kɔfr] *nm* **1.** *F* chest/lungs/ wind; constitution; **avoir bon coffre,** to have a lot of puff **2.** *A P* prison*.

coffrer [kɔfre] *vtr P* to imprison*; **faire coffrer qn,** to put s.o. away inside; to run s.o. in; **se faire coffrer,** to get nicked.

cognard [kɔɲar] *nm,* **cogne** [kɔɲ] *nm P* (*gendarme*) policeman*/copper/cop.

Cogne-dur [kɔɲdyr] *attrib P* **la Maison Cogne-dur,** the police*/the cops.

cogner [kɔɲe] **I** *vtr F* **1.** (*a*) to strike/to hit/to thump (s.o.); to knock (s.o.) about; **se faire cogner par la police,** to get beaten up/done over by the police; **il cogne sa femme,** he knocks his wife about; **ça va cogner,** there's going to be trouble (*b*) *abs* **il cogne dur,** he's a hard hitter/he hits hard **2.** (*a*) **se cogner qch,** to treat/to help oneself to sth (*b*) **se cogner une corvée,** to lumber oneself with a thankless job (*c*) (*journ*) **se cogner une manif,** to cover/to report (on) a demo **3. se cogner la tête contre les murs,** to bang one's head against a brick wall **II** *vi P* **1.** to stink* **2. ça cogne,** the sun is beating down; it's pretty hot **III** *vpr* **se cogner 1.** *F* to come to blows/to have a fight*/to have a punch-up; **ils se sont cognés,** they had a punch-up/a fist-fight **2.** *V* to have sex*/to have a bang **3.** *P* **se cogner de qch,** to do without sth **4.** *P* **je m'en cogne,** I couldn't care less*/I don't give a damn.

cognerie [kɔɲəri] *nf P* police station*/cop shop.

cognon [kɔɲɔ̃] *nm P* fight*/punch-up/fist-fight.

cognoter [kɔɲɔte] *vi P* to stink*/ to smell/to pong (to high heaven).

coiffé [kwafe] *a F* **1. chien coiffé/ chèvre coiffée,** exceptionally ugly person/ugly duckling **2. être né coiffé,** to be born under a lucky star/with a silver spoon in one's mouth **3. être coiffé de qn,** to be infatuated* with s.o.; **être coiffé de qch,** to go for sth in a big way.

coiffer [kwafe] **I** *vtr* **1.** *F* to control/to be at the head of (an organization, etc) **2.** *F* (*sports*) to defeat; **coiffer d'une courte tête,** to beat by a short head; **se faire coiffer au poteau,** to be pipped at the post **3.** *F* **coiffer son mari,** to be unfaithful to one's husband **4.** *F* (*jeune fille*) **coiffer Sainte-Catherine,** to reach (the age of) 25 and remain unmarried **5.** *P* (*a*) to arrest* (s.o.); **je me suis fait coiffer par les flics,** I got nicked/nabbed by the fuzz (*b*) **coiffer le chapeau,** to carry the can. (*Voir* **chapeau 4**) **II** *vpr* **se coiffer** *F* **se coiffer de qn,** to become infatuated* with s.o.; **se coiffer de qch,** to go for sth in a big way.

coiffeur [kwafœr] *nm F* **le grand Coiffeur,** the executioner.

coin [kwɛ̃] *nm F* **1. la connaître dans les coins,** to know what's what/to know all the angles **2. en boucher un coin à qn,** to flabbergast* s.o.; **ça vous en bouche un coin!** that's flummoxed you! **3. dans le coin,** in these parts/round here; **est-ce que le patron est dans le coin?** is the boss about/around? **il habite dans le coin,** he lives (a)round here **4. le petit coin,** the smallest room/the loo/*NAm* the bathroom; **aller au petit coin,** to go to the loo/*NAm* the bathroom **5.** (*motocycliste*) **aller la poignée dans le coin,** to go at a terrific speed/to do a ton **6. se la prendre dans les coins,** to have sex*/to have a quick screw/to have a quickie in strange places.

coincé [kwɛ̃se] *a* **1.** *F* in a fix*/in a jam/stymied/up a gum tree **2.** *F* uneasy/not relaxed (in a sexual situation); sex-shy **3.** *P* (*homosexuels*) **homo/pédé coincé,** closet queen.

coincer [kwɛ̃se] **I** *vi P* to stink*/to pong **II** *vtr* **1.** *F* **coincer qn** (*i*) to corner s.o. (*ii*) to arrest* s.o./to nick s.o./to nab s.o. **III** *vpr* **se coincer** *V* **se coincer les couilles,** to get one's balls in a twist (esp by wearing tight trousers). (*Voir* **bulle II 1**)

coinceteau [kwɛ̃sto] *nm P* (*a*) (little) corner; district/manor; **dans le coinceteau,** in these parts/round here (*b*) sheltered spot.

coincoin [kwɛ̃kwɛ̃] *nm P* **1.** holder of the *Palmes académiques* **2.** priest*.

coinsteau, coinsto(t) [kwɛ̃sto] *nm P* = **coinceteau.**

coke [kok] *nf P* (*drogues*) cocaine*/coke.

col [kɔl] *nm F* **1. se hausser/se pousser du col,** to swank/to show off*/to put on airs **2. col bleu,** sailor/bluejacket **3. col(-)blanc,** white-collar worker **4. (faux) col,** head (of froth on glass of beer). (*Voir* **rabat 3**)

colbac, colbaque [kɔlbak] *nm P* neck; **sauter sur le colbac de qn,** to grab (hold of) s.o.

colbasse [kɔlbas] *nf P* room.

coletin [kɔltɛ̃] *nm P* = **coltin.**

colibar(d) [kɔlibar] *nm P* (*a*) parcel/package (*b*) (*argot des prisons*) (food) parcel.

colibri [kɔlibri] *nm P* **1.** untrustworthy acquaintance/rat/double-crosser **2.** tart/floozie.

colique [kɔlik] *nf* **1.** *F* (*pers ou chose*) bore*; **quelle colique!** what a drag!/what a bind! **2.** *F* **avoir la colique,** to be afraid*/to have the wind up/to be in a blue funk **3.** *V* **avoir des coliques bâtonneuses/cornues,** to have an erection*/to have a hard-on.

colis [kɔli] *nm* **1.** *F* girl* **2.** *P* prisoner (*esp* bound hand and foot with a rope) **4.** prostitute* 'posted' elsewhere by her pimp*.

collabo [kɔlabo] *nm P (esp WWII)* collaborator.

collage [kɔlaʒ] *nm F* = **colle 5.**

collant [kɔlɑ̃] **I** *a F (pers)* hard to get rid of; clinging; **ce qu'il est collant!** he's a real pain in the neck! **II** *nm P* thief*/sticky-fingers.

collante [kɔlɑ̃t] *nf F* letter giving notice of the date and place of an examination.

colle [kɔl] *nf* **1.** *F (pers)* (tenacious) bore*/sticker/clinger/leech **2.** *(scol) F (a)* oral test *(b)* detention; **ficher une colle à qn,** to keep s.o. in; **attraper deux heures de colle,** to be kept in for two hours/ to get two hours detention **3.** *F* poser/teaser; **poser/pousser une colle à qn,** to ask s.o. a sticky question/to stump s.o. **4.** *F (en entendant qch se casser)* **faites chauffer la colle!** that's right/go on, break up the happy home! **5.** *F* **ménage à la colle,** unmarried couple (living together); **être/vivre à la colle,** to live together/to live in sin/ to be shacked up with s.o. **6.** *F* **c'est de la colle,** that's all bunkum! **7.** *V* **chier dans la colle,** to exaggerate*/to bullshit. *(Voir* **pot***)*

coller [kɔle] **I** *vtr F* **1.** *(a)* to give/to land (a blow, etc); **coller son poing dans la figure de qn/ coller une tarte à qn,** to bash s.o. in the face/to sock s.o. on the jaw *(b)* to put/to place/to shove/to stick; **colle ça dans un coin,** stick it/plonk it/dump it in a corner; *(mil)* **coller qn au mur,** to stand s.o. up against a wall and shoot him *(c)* **coller qch à qn,** to foist/to palm off sth on (to) s.o.; **j'ai collé un PV,** I got/ picked up a parking ticket. *(Voir* **colloquer***)* **2. se coller qch,** to treat oneself to sth **3.** *(scol)* **coller un élève,** to keep a pupil in/to put a pupil in detention; *(à un examen)* to fail/to plough; **se faire coller,** to be failed/ploughed; to flunk (an exam) **4.** to stump/to floor (s.o.) **II** *vi* **1.** *F* **ça colle!** *(i)* agreed!*/

OK! *(ii)* that figures!/that makes sense! **ça colle?** how's tricks?/how goes it? *(Voir* **Anatole***)*; **ça ne colle pas,** there's something wrong/ there's something not quite right; that's no good; **ça ne colle pas avec lui,** I can't get on with him/we don't exactly hit it off; we don't see eye to eye **2.** *F (cyclisme, etc)* to keep close up behind the pacemaker; *(voiture)* **coller derrière,** to stay on s.o.'s tail **3.** *F* **elle lui colle au train,** she tags on to him/she clings on to him like a leech **4.** *V* to have sex* **III** *vpr* **se coller** *F* **1. se coller avec qn,** to live with s.o./to shack up with s.o. **2. se coller qn/qch,** to get stuck/landed/ lumbered with s.o./sth.

collet [kɔlɛ] *nm* **1.** *F* **être collet monté,** to be straight-laced/priggish; **elle est très collet monté,** she's a bit of a prig, really **2.** *P* **collet rouge,** *(à Paris)* auctioneer at the general auction rooms.

colletar [kɔltar] *nm P* = **coaltar.**

colleter [kɔlte] **I** *vtr F* to embrace/to hug (s.o.) **II** *vpr* **se colleter** *F* = **se coltiner.**

colletin [kɔltɛ̃] *nm P* = **coltin.**

colleur, -euse [kɔlœr, -øz] *n F* **1.** *(scol)* examiner **2.** bore*/pest/ pain.

collier [kɔlje] *nm* **1.** *F (a)* **donner un coup de collier,** to make a special effort/to put one's back into it; **il est franc du collier,** he's a hard worker/he won't give you any trouble *(b)* **reprendre le collier (du travail),** to go back to work/to get back into harness (after holiday, illness, etc); **reprendre le collier de misère,** to go back to the grind/to get back to (the) drudgery **2.** *P* **collier de corail,** haemorrhoids/ *NAm* hemorrhoids/piles.

collimateur [kɔlimatœr] *nm F* **avoir qn dans le collimateur,** to keep an eye on s.o./a close watch on s.o.

colloquer [kɔl(l)ɔke] *vtr* F **colloquer qch à qn,** to foist/to palm off sth on (to) s.o.

colo [kɔlo] *nm or f* F (= *colonie de vacances*) children's holiday camp/summer camp/summer school; **en colo,** at a holiday camp.

colombier [kɔlɔ̃bje] *nm* F **1. revenir au colombier,** to come back home/to come back to the nest **2.** (*théâtre*) **le colombier,** the gods.

colombin [kɔlɔ̃bɛ̃] *nm* **1.** *V* turd; **poser un colombin,** to defecate*/to (have a) crap; (*mil*) **être de colombin,** to be on latrine fatigue **2.** *P* **avoir les colombins,** to be afraid*/to be shit-scared **3.** *P* **des colombins!** not bloody likely!*/nothing doing!*/nuts!

colombine [kɔlɔ̃bin] *nf* P (*drogues*) cocaine*/coke.

colon [kɔlɔ̃] *nm* P **1.** colonel/the old man **2.** friend*/mate; **mon pauvre colon!** poor old chap!/poor blighter! **ben, mon colon!** (*i*) well, old cock! (*ii*) well, I'm damned!

colonne [kɔlɔn] *nf* V **1. il n'a pas chié la colonne (Vendôme),** he won't set the Thames on fire; he's no great shakes; **il croit qu'il a chié la colonne (Vendôme),** he thinks he's the cat's whiskers; he thinks the sun shines out of his arse **2.** penis/shaft; **se taper (sur) polir la colonne,** to masturbate*/to jerk off. (*Voir* **astiquer 4; branler II 4**)

coloquinte [kɔlɔkɛ̃t] *nf* P head*; **ça lui a tapé sur la coloquinte,** it drove him barmy/nuts.

colosse [kɔlɔs] *nm* **1.** *V* **égoutter son colosse/faire pleurer le colosse** (*i*) to urinate* (*ii*) to have an orgasm* **2.** *F* **être bâti comme un colosse,** to be built like a horse/to be a giant of a man.

coltin [kɔltɛ̃] *nm* P hard work/graft.

coltiner [kɔltine] **I** *vtr* F **se coltiner qch,** to take on sth disagreeable; to get landed/stuck/lumbered with sth; **c'est moi qui vais me col-** tiner toute cette vaisselle? have I really been lumbered with all that washing-up? **II** *vpr* **se coltiner** P **se coltiner avec qn,** to have a fight*/a punch-up with s.o.

comac [kɔmak], **comaco** [kɔmako], **comaque** [kɔmak] *a P* **1.** (*i*) (= **comme ça**) like that (*ii*) very big/huge/whopping **2.** broad-shouldered/hefty/beefy; athletic(-looking).

combien [kɔ̃bjɛ̃] *nm inv* F **le combien sommes-nous?** what's the date? **il y a un car tous les combien?** how often does the bus run? **tu es arrivé le combien?** where did you come (in your race)?

combientième [kɔ̃bjɛ̃tjɛm] *a&n* F **nous sommes le combientième aujourd'hui?** what's the date today? **tu as été reçu (le) combientième à l'examen?** where did you come in the exam?

combinard [kɔ̃binar] *P* **I** *nm* racketeer/spiv/smart Alec **II** *a* slick (operator).

combine [kɔ̃bin] *nf* **1.** *F* (*a*) racket/shady scheme/fiddle/trick; **une bonne combine,** a good wheeze; **gagner beaucoup d'argent au moyen de la combine,** to make a lot of money by fiddling; **tu es de la combine?** are you in on it?/are you with us? **je ne donne pas dans tes combines,** I'm not falling for your fancy tricks; **connaître les combines,** to be in the know; **des combines arabes,** complicated deals; **jouer une combine sûre,** to be on (to) a sure thing (*b*) knack; **(il) faut savoir la combine pour faire marcher ma radio,** to get my radio to work you've got to have the knack **2.** *P* (= *combinaison*) (woman's) slip.

combiner [kɔ̃bine] **I** *vtr* F to arrange/to cook up/to dream up **II** *vpr* **se combiner** F **ça ne se combine pas bien,** it doesn't look good/right.

comble [kɔ̃bl] *nm* F **ça, c'est le**

comédie   110   **compo**

comble/un comble! that's the limit!*/that's the last straw!/that takes the cake!/that takes the biscuit!/that beats everything!

comédie [kɔmedi] *nf F* **1. c'est une vraie comédie!** it's a laugh a minute! **2. c'est toujours la même comédie pour garer sa voiture,** it's always a real palaver trying to park your car **3. faire la comédie/faire une de ces comédies,** to make a scene/to kick up a fuss **4. jouer la comédie,** to sham/to play-act/to put on an act **5. être à la comédie,** to be out of work.

comète [kɔmɛt] *nf F* **tirer des plans sur la comète,** to dream up wild schemes; to build castles in the air/in Spain. (*Voir* **carabin 3**)

comingue [kɔmɛ̃g] *nf* commission/percentage; **tu prends combien de comingue?** how much do you get on it?

comm' [kɔm] *nf P* = **comingue.**

commande [kɔmɑ̃d] *nf P* **1.** police protection **2.** (*milieu, journ, etc*) job **3. une drôle de commande,** a strange/funny business **4. connaître la commande,** to be in the know **5. louper la commande,** to miss one's chance/the boat/the bus.

comme [kɔm] **I** *adv F* **1. comme ci comme ça,** (fair to) middling; so-so **2. c'est tout comme,** it comes to (much) the same thing; **il est nommé? – non, mais c'est tout comme,** has he been appointed? – no, but as good as **3. ... comme qui dirait ...,** ... so to speak ... / ... as you might say ... **4. j'ai comme une idée qu'il va venir ce soir,** I've a sort of idea that he'll come tonight **5. drôle comme tout,** terribly funny*; **rire comme tout,** to split one's sides laughing **6. à ce moment j'ai comme perdu la tête,** at that moment I sort of lost my head **7. ce n'est pas mal comme film,** it's not a bad film **9.** (= *comment*) **il y est arrivé Dieu sait comme,** he

managed it, God (alone) knows how; **voilà comme il est,** that's just like him/that's him all over **10. naturellement et comme de bien entendu!** absolutely! (*Voir* **autre**) **II** *nf O P* (= *commission*) commission/percentage. (*Voir* **comingue**)

comment [kɔmɑ̃] *adv F* **et comment!** and how!/not half!/you bet!/rather!/you said it! **ils ont été battus, et comment!** they were well and truly beaten/they were beaten and how!

commission [kɔmisjɔ̃] *nf F* (*a*) **faire une/sa petite commission,** to urinate*/to do a wee-wee/to go wee-wee(s)/to do (a) number one (*b*) **faire une/sa grosse commission,** to defecate*/to do number two(s)/to do big jobs.

commode [kɔmɔd] *nf P* piano/joanna.

communard [kɔmynar] **I** *nm P* (*boisson*) red wine and blackcurrant liqueur or syrup **II** *a P* **pif communard,** red nose*/bottle-nose.

compal [kɔpal] *nf P* (*scol*) = **compo.**

compas [kɔpa] *nm* **1.** *F* **allonger le compas,** to quicken one's pace **2.** *F* **avoir le compas dans l'œil,** to have a good eye (for measurements or distances) **3.** *pl P* legs*; **jouer des compas,** to run away*/to skedaddle.

compère [kɔpɛr] *nm F* **tout se fait par compère et commère,** it's all a put-up job.

compisser [kɔpise] *vtr P* to piss on (s.o./sth).

complet [kɔplɛ] *a F* **ça c'est complet alors!** that's the limit!*/that's all we needed!

complet-veston [kɔplɛvɛstɔ̃] *nm P* **se faire tailler un complet-veston,** to get beaten* up.

compo [kɔpo] *nf,* **compote**[1] [kɔpɔt] *nf P* (*scol*) composition/essay; test paper/revision test.

compote² *nf F* **1. mettre/réduire qn en compote,** to beat s.o. to a pulp; to make mincemeat of s.o. **2. avoir la tête en compote,** to have a splitting headache; **avoir les pieds en compote,** to have sore feet **3. pédaler dans la compote,** to make slow progress/to find the going difficult.

compotier [kɔ̃pɔtje] *nm* **1.** *F* **agiter les pieds dans le compotier,** to put one's foot in it/to drop a brick **2.** *P* head*.

comprenette [kɔ̃prənɛt] *nf F* understanding; **avoir la comprenette dure/difficile/lente; ne pas avoir la comprenette facile,** to be slow on the uptake/to be slow to catch on.

comprenoir [kɔ̃prənwar] *nm,* **comprenoire** [kɔ̃prənwar] *nf F* = **comprenette.**

compte [kɔ̃t] *nm F* **1. il a son compte/il en a pour son compte** (*i*) (*mort, fichu*) he's done for/he's had it; he's a gonner (*ii*) he's drunk*/he's had a skinful (*iii*) he's got what was coming to him; **j'ai eu mon compte,** I've had enough; **son compte est bon,** he's had it **2. en avoir son compte,** to get told off/to get hauled over the coals **3. un compte d'apothicaire,** an exorbitant bill **4.** (*femme*) **être laissée pour compte,** to be left on the shelf **5. tu te rends compte!** would you believe it!/can you imagine! **6. rendre des comptes,** to vomit*.

comptée [kɔ̃te] *nf P* (*a*) prostitute's earnings (to be handed over to her pimp*). (*Voir* **compteur 2** (*i*)) (*b*) racketeer's dues/take. (*Voir* **compteur 2** (*ii*))

compte-gouttes [kɔ̃tgut] *nm inv P* **fabriqué au compte-gouttes** (*i*) in very small quantities (*ii*) (*pers*) undersized*/short-arsed.

compteur [kɔ̃tœr] *nm P* **1. avoir un compteur à gaz dans le dos,** to be hunchbacked **2. relever le compteur** (*i*) (*souteneur*) to collect a

prostitute's earnings. (*Voir* **comptée** (*a*)) (*ii*) (*racketteur*) to collect one's dues/to haul in the take.

con [kɔ̃] I *nm V* **1.** female genitals*/cunt; **avoir le con en joie/être chaude du con,** to feel randy/to have the hots/to be asking for it **2.** fool*; stupid* bastard*/silly bugger/(silly) cunt/silly fucker; **le roi des cons,** a complete ass/a bloody idiot/a real jerk; **(quelle) bande de cons!** what a load of (bloody) idiots!/what a load of cretins! **pauvre con! poor sod! espèce de con!/tête de con!** you bloody fool!/you silly sod!/you stupid* bugger! **faire le con/jouer au con** (*i*) to play the bloody fool; to fart around; **va pas faire le con là-dedans!** don't go arsing about in there! **arrête de faire le con!** stop pissing about! (*ii*) to pretend to be stupid*/to act daft; **... à la con,** bloody silly ... /cockeyed ...; **idée à la con,** lousy idea/bloody stupid idea; **piège à cons,** swindle*/hoax. (*Voir* **attrape-cons**) **3.** contemptible person/creep/rotten bastard*/nasty piece of work/cunt/son of a bitch II *inv V* (*a*) **il est con comme la lune/comme un balai/comme un brêle/comme un panier,** he's as stupid* as they come/as daft as a brush; he's a bloody idiot/he's a prize cunt (*b*) **elle est rien con, ton histoire!** your story is all balls/a load of cobblers! **c'est trop con!** it's too bloody silly for words! **c'est drôlement con!** it's a load of crap!/it's fucking rubbish! **pas si con!** not such a bad idea!/a bloody good idea! (*Voir* **bite 3; conne** II)

conard [kɔnar] *nm & a V* = **connard.**

conasse [kɔnas] *nf V* = **connasse.**

concal [kɔ̃kal] *nm P* exam(ination).

concentre [kɔ̃sɑ̃tr] *nf P* (= *concentration*) gathering/group/band (of motorcyclists, etc).

concepige [kɔ̃spiʒ] *nm&f* P concierge/caretaker.

concierge [kɔ̃sjɛrʒ] *nm&f* F **1. quel(le) concierge!** what a chatterbox! **c'est une vraie concierge,** she's a terrible gossip **2. (ne) fais pas la concierge!** don't be nosy! **3. journal de concierge,** popular (news)paper/ = tabloid.

condé [kɔ̃de] *nm* P **1.** plainclothes detective **2.** (*a*) police permit (*b*) police protection; **avoir le/ du condé,** to be authorized to carry on a more or less illicit activity **3.** scheme/wheeze (for making easy money with minimum risk)/fiddle **4.** (*tuyau*) information*/tip(-off).

condisse [kɔ̃dis] *nf* P condition; circumstance.

conduite [kɔ̃dɥit] *nf* F **(s')acheter une conduite,** to turn over a new leaf/to mend one's ways. (*Voir* **Grenoble**)

coneau [kɔno] *nm&a* V = **connard I, II.**

confiture [kɔ̃fityr] *nf* **1.** F flattery **2.** F **de la confiture aux chiens,** cavi- ar(e) for the general **3.** F **mettre/réduire qn en confiture,** to pound s.o. to a jelly/to make mincemeat of s.o. **4.** P **être dans la confiture,** to be in a fix*/to be in a jam **5.** P **chier dans la confiture,** to exaggerate*/to bullshit **6.** P **opium**/treacle **7.** V passive homosexuality.

confortables [kɔ̃fɔrtabl] *nmpl* F carpet slippers.

confrérie [kɔ̃freri] *nf* P **la grande confrérie** (*i*) cuckolds/deceived husbands (in general) (*ii*) homosexuals* (in general)/pansyland.

cônir [konir] *vtr* P to kill*/to bump off.

conjungo [kɔ̃ʒɔ̃go] *nm* F marriage; **prononcer le conjungo,** to tie the knot; **mon conjungo,** my husband*/ my wife*/my better half.

connaissance [kɔnɛsɑ̃s] *nf* F girlfriend; boyfriend.

connaître [kɔnɛtr] *vtr* F **1. il la connaît (dans les coins),** he knows what's what/he knows what it's all about/he knows it inside out; **ça me connaît,** I know all about that/ you can't teach me anything about that; I'm an old hand/a dab hand at that; that's right up my street; **je ne connais que lui!** I know that only too well!/don't I know it! (*Voir* **bout** 4; **rayon**) **II** *vpr* **se connaître** F **il s'y connaît,** he's an expert/a dab hand; he knows his stuff/he knows what it's all about.

connard [kɔnar] **I** *nm* fool*/cunt/ stupid bastard/silly bugger **II** *a* stupid*/bloody silly.

connasse [kɔnas] *nf* V **1.** female genitals*/cunt **2.** = **con I 1, 2 3.** stupid bitch/silly cow/silly old bag **4.** (*a*) prostitute*/tart/hooker (*b*) freelance prostitute (not protected by a pimp).

conne [kɔn] **I** *nf* V prostitute* **II** *a f* V = **con II.**

conneau [kɔno] *nm & a* V = **connard I, II.**

connement [kɔnmɑ̃] *adv* V like a bloody fool.

connerie [kɔnri] *nf* V bloody nonsense*/balon(e)y/balls/crap; **quelle connerie!** balls!/what (a load of) crap!/cobblers! **faire une connerie,** to do sth bloody stupid; **il a encore fait une connerie,** he's fucked it up again; **c'est des conneries,** it's all cock/it's a load of balls; **(ne) dis pas de(s) conneries,** don't talk cock/balls/crap.

con(n)obler [kɔnɔble], **con(n)obrer** [kɔnɔbre] *vtr* P to know.

connu! [kɔny] *pp & excl* F = **ça me connaît (connaître 3).**

conomètre [kɔnɔmetr] *nm* V **faire péter le conomètre,** to be extremely stupid*/to be bloody silly.

conscrard [kɔ̃skrar] *nm* P (*argot de l'Ecole polytechnique*) conscript.

conscrit [kɔ̃skri] *nm* F (*a*) novice/greenhorn (*b*) (*argot de l'Ecole normale supérieure*) first-year student.

conséquent [kɔ̃sekɑ̃] *a* F big/important; **homme conséquent**, bigwig; **affaire conséquente**, important piece of business.

consigne [kɔ̃siɲ] *nf* F **avaler/manger la consigne**, to forget one's orders/one's instructions; to disregard one's orders/one's instructions.

consolation [kɔ̃sɔlasjɔ̃] *nf* **1.** F brandy; spirits*; **un petit verre de consolation**, a little drop of comfort **2.** P fellatio* *or* masturbation* instead of sex*.

consomme [kɔ̃sɔm] *nf* F (= *consommation*) drink (in a café, etc).

constipé [kɔ̃stipe] *a* F **1.** F miserly*. (*Voir* **morlingue**) **2.** F (*a*) serious-minded (*b*) sullen (*c*) uneasy/embarrassed/strained **3.** V **être constipé de l'entre-jambes/du calbard**, to be unable to get an erection*/a hard-on. (*Voir* **feuille 1**)

contact [kɔ̃takt] *nm* F (*pers*) contact/connection/informant (*esp* for drugs).

content [kɔ̃tɑ̃] *nm* P **avoir son petit content**, to have sex*.

contre [kɔ̃tr] *adv* F against/agin; **je suis contre**, I'm against it.

contrecarre [kɔ̃trəkar] *nf* F **1.** **faire une contrecarre à qn**, to put obstacles in s.o.'s way/to thwart s.o. **2.** rivalry.

contrecoup [kɔ̃trəku] *nm* F foreman/boss.

contredanse [kɔ̃trədɑ̃s] *nf* F police summons/(parking) ticket; **flanquer une contredanse à qn**, to book s.o./to give s.o. a ticket.

se contrefiche(r) [səkɔ̃trəfiʃ(e)] *vpr*, **se contrefoutre** [səkɔ̃-trəfutr] *vpr* P **je m'en fiche et (je) m'en contrefiche!/je m'en fous et (je) m'en contrefous!** I couldn't care less!*/I couldn't care bloody less!/I couldn't give a toss!

contremarque [kɔ̃trəmark] *nf* O F **une contremarque pour Bagneux/pour Pantin**, a doctor's prescription.

contremouche [kɔ̃trəmuʃ] *nf* P smuggling.

contrer [kɔ̃tre] *vtr* F to thwart/to cross (s.o.).

convalo [kɔ̃valo] P **I** *nm* convalescent **II** *nf* convalescence/sick leave.

converse [kɔ̃vɛrs] *nf* P conversation.

convoi [kɔ̃vwa] *nm* F **être du même convoi**, to be in the same boat.

convoque [kɔ̃vɔk] *nf* P summons.

cool [kul], **coolos** [kulos] *a* P cool; **il est très cool, ce mec**, he's a really cool guy/he's really laid-back.

coopé [kɔpe] *nf* F (*abbr* = *coopérative*) co-operative stores/co-op.

coordonnées [kɔɔrdɔne, kɔɔ-] *nfpl* F **donnez-moi vos coordonnées**, give me your address and phone number/give me your details.

cop [kɔp] *nm* P = **copain**.

copaille [kɔpaj] *nf* P despicable person/good-for-nothing/heel/louse. (*Voir* **balle 12**)

copain [kɔpɛ̃] *nm* F friend*/pal/mate/buddy; **être bons copains**, to be good pals/to be mates; **ils sont copains comme cochons**, they're great mates/very good buddies. (*Voir* **copine**)

copeaux [kɔpo, kɔ-] *nmpl* P **1.** **avoir les copeaux** (*i*) to have little or nothing; **des copeaux**, nothing* at all/not a damn thing/damn-all (*ii*) to be afraid*; **foutre les copeaux à qn**, to put the wind up s.o.

copie [kɔpi] *nf* P (*journ*) **pisser de la copie,** to churn it out; **pondre de la copie,** to write copy to order; **pisseur, -euse de copie,** hack writer. (*Voir* **pisse-copie**)

copier [kɔpje] *vtr* F **1. celle-là, tu me la copieras!** you won't catch me (out) again!/I'll know better next time!/I'll pay you back for that! **2. je la ferai copier, celle-là!** well, I like that!/that's a good one, that is!

copine [kɔpin] *nf* F (female) friend/girlfriend. (*Voir* **copain**)

copiner [kɔpine] *vi* F **copiner avec qn,** to become friendly with s.o./to be great mates with s.o.

copinerie [kɔpinri] *nf* F group of friends/gang.

coq [kɔk] *nm* F **des mollets de coq,** thin legs*/matchsticks.

coquard, coquart [kɔkar] *nm* P black eye*/shiner.

coque [kɔk] *nf* F **à la coque,** excellent*; **un dîner à la coque,** a slap-up dinner.

coquelicot [kɔkliko] *nm* P **1.** = **coquard 2. elle a ses coquelicots,** she's got a period*/she's got the curse.

coqueluche [kɔklyʃ] *nf* F **être la coqueluche de qn,** to be s.o.'s idol/great favourite/darling.

coquetier [kɔktje] *nm* F cup; **gagner/emporter le coquetier,** to win (the) top prize/to hit the jackpot.

coquette [kɔkɛt] *nf* V penis*/cock/prick.

coquetterie [kɔkɛtri] *nf* P **avoir une coquetterie dans l'œil,** to squint.

coqueur [kɔkœr] *nm* O P informer*/squealer/grass.

coquillage [kɔkijaʒ] *nm* P (girl's) virginity*/maidenhead/cherry.

coquillard [kɔkijar] *nm* P eye*; **je m'en bats/je m'en tamponne/je m'en tape le coquillard,** I couldn't care less*; I don't give a damn; to hell with it.

coquille [kɔkij] *nf* **1.** P prison* **2.** P = **coquillage.**

coquin [kɔkɛ̃] *nm* **1.** F (*hum*) (*a*) husband (*b*) fancy man **2.** F (*en Provence*) **coquin de sort!** hang it!/blow it!/damn it! **3.** P strong wine.

cor [kɔr] *nm* F **1.** he-man **2. emmaillotté dans un cor de chasse,** bandy-legged.

corbaque [kɔrbak] *nm* P crow; rook; raven.

corbeau [kɔrbo] *nm* P **1.** priest*/black coat **2.** body-snatcher/ghoul **3.** (*pers*) bird of ill omen **4.** writer of (anonymous) poison-pen letters **5.** rapacious person/shark.

corbi [kɔrbi] *nm* P (*abbr* = *corbillard*) hearse.

corde [kɔrd] *nf* F **1. être au bout de sa corde,** to be at the end of one's tether; **être à la corde** (*i*) to be at the end of one's tether (*ii*) to be penniless* **2. être sur la corde raide,** to be out on a limb/to walk the tightrope **3. sauter à la corde** (*i*) to tighten one's belt/to go without (food) (*ii*) to go/to do without **4. se mettre la corde au cou,** to get married*/to tie the knot/to get hitched/to get spliced **5. se mettre la corde pour . . .,** to give up all hope of . . . **6. ça sent la corde,** it looks suspicious/I don't like the look of it **7. tenir la corde,** to hold an advantage/to have the edge **8. il y va de la corde,** it's a hanging matter; **il ne vaut pas la corde pour la prendre,** he's not worth the rope to hang him with; **il a de la corde de pendu dans sa poche,** he has the devil's own luck **9. il pleut/il tombe des cordes,** it's raining cats and dogs; it's bucketing down **10.** (*aut*) **prendre un virage/un tournant à la corde,** to cut a corner close **11. ce n'est pas/ça ne rentre pas dans mes cordes,** it's not in my line/it's not my cup of tea; **c'est tout à fait dans mes cordes,** it's right up my street/it suits me fine.

corder [kɔrde] *vi P* **1.** to die* **2. corder avec qn,** to hit it off with s.o./to get on fine with s.o.

cormoran [kɔrmɔrɑ̃] *nm P* (*péj*) Jew*.

cornac [kɔrnak] *nm F* (tourist) guide. (*Voir* **cornaquer**)

cornanche [kɔrnɑ̃ʃ] *nf P* marked (playing-)card.

cornancher [kɔrnɑ̃ʃe] *P* **I** *vtr* to kill* **II** *vi* **1.** to play with marked cards **2.** to stink*.

cornaquer [kɔrnake] *vtr F* to guide/to shepherd (tourists). (*Voir* **cornac**)

cornard [kɔrnar] *nm F* deceived husband/cuckold.

corner [kɔrne] *vi* **1.** *F* **les oreilles ont dû lui corner,** his ears must have been burning **2.** *P* to stink*.

cornes [kɔrn] *nfpl F* **1. montrer les cornes,** to show fight **2. faire les cornes à qn,** to jeer at/to mock/ to make a face at s.o. **3. porter des cornes,** to be a cuckold/to wear horns; **faire porter des cornes à qn,** to cuckold s.o.

cornet [kɔrnɛ] *nm P* **1.** throat/gullet; **se rincer le cornet,** to have a drink*/to wet one's whistle **2.** stomach*; **se mettre qch dans le cornet/se remplir le cornet,** to eat* heartily/to have a good tuck-in.

cornette [kɔrnɛt] *nf F* **1.** woman whose husband is unfaithful to her **2.** (catholic) nun.

corniaud [kɔrnjo] *nm P* fool*/ clot/twit.

corniche [kɔrniʃ] *nf P* class preparing for Saint-Cyr military school.

corniches [kɔrniʃ] *nmpl P* first-year students at Saint-Cyr.

cornichon [kɔrniʃɔ̃] *nm* **1.** *P* novice/greenhorn **2.** *P* fool*/jerk

3. *P* telephone*/blower; **un coup de cornichon,** a (phone) call/a ring/a buzz **4.** *P* student preparing for Saint-Cyr military school **5.** *V* penis*/gherkin.

Cornouaille [kɔrnwaj] *Prnf O F* **aller en Cornouaille,** to be a cuckold/to wear horns.

corps [kɔr] *nm F* **1. il faut voir ce qu'il a dans le corps,** we'll have to see (*i*) what he's made of/what he's got in him (*ii*) what makes him tick **2. c'est un drôle de corps,** he's a strange creature/an odd bod.

corrida [kɔrida] *nf P* free-for-all/ punch-up; **quelle corrida!** what a carry-on/what a to-do! **ça a été une vraie corrida,** there was a lot of trouble/aggro.

corridor [kɔridɔr] *nm P* throat/ windpipe.

corser [kɔrse] **I** *vtr F* **1. corser une note,** to charge extortionately/ to stick sth (extra) on (the bill)/to rip (s.o.) off **2. corser un problème,** to make a problem harder to solve **3.** (*journ*) **corser la sauce,** to add spice to/to liven up a story **II** *vpr* **se corser** *F* **ça se corse/l'affaire se corse** (*i*) the plot thickens (*ii*) things are getting serious.

Corsic [kɔrsik] *nm,* **Corsico** [kɔrsiko] *nm P* Corsican.

corsif [kɔrsif] *nm P* corset.

cortausse [kɔrtos] *nf P* beating*/ severe thrashing/good hiding.

cossard [kɔsar] *P* **I** *a* lazy*/idle **II** *nm* lazybones/lazy bum/lazy slob.

cosse [kɔs] *nf P* **avoir la cosse/ avoir les pieds en cosses de melon,** to be/to feel lazy*; **tirer sa cosse,** to (sit around and) do nothing/to laze about/to do damn-all.

cossu [kɔsy] *a F* rich*/well-off/ well-to-do/flush.

costar(d) [kɔstar] *nm P* (*a*) man's suit; **se faire tailler un costar(d),** to get beaten up (b) **costar(d) de sapin,** coffin/wooden overcoat.

costaud, aude [kɔsto, -od], **costeau** [kɔsto], **costo, ote** [kɔsto, -ot] F I a hefty/beefy/ strapping (individual); solidly built (structure); tough (material, etc); (boisson) **ça c'est costaud!** that's strong!/that's got a kick in it! **je ne me sens pas costaud,** I don't feel too good/I feel a bit out of sorts II n strong/hefty/strapping person.

costume [kɔstym] nm P **se faire faire un costume en bois/en sapin,** to die*/to get fitted for a wooden overcoat. (Voir **Adam**; **Ève 2**)

cote [kɔt] nf F (a) reputation; **avoir une grosse cote,** to be highly thought of (b) favouritism/popularity; **avoir la cote (d'amour)/avoir la bonne cote/avoir une drôle de cote,** to be very popular.

côte [kot] I nf F **1. avoir les côtes en long,** to be lazy* **2. se tenir les côtes (de rire),** to laugh* uproariously/to split one's sides laughing **3. chatouiller/tanner les côtes à qn,** to give s.o. a good hiding **4. serrer les côtes à qn,** to keep s.o. at it; to keep s.o. up to scratch. (Voir **caler II 2**) II nf F **être à la côte,** to be penniless*/to be on one's beam ends.

côté [kote] nm F **être sur le côté** (i) to be laid up (ii) to be in a bad way.

cotelard [kɔtəlar] a P = **cottard.**

côtelette [kotlɛt, kɔ-] nf **1.** pl P ribs (of person); **sauver ses côtelettes,** to save one's skin **2.** pl O F mutton-chop whiskers. **3.** V **pisser sa/une côtelette,** to give birth to a baby.

coton [kɔtɔ̃] I a F difficult; complicated; **c'est coton,** it's a tough/ tricky job; it's a bit tricky II nm **1.** P trouble/difficulty; **il va y avoir du coton,** there's going to be trouble; **avoir un sacré coton pour ...,** to have the devil of a job to ...

2. F **filer un mauvais/un sale/un vilain coton,** to be in a bad way (in health or business) **3.** F **élevé dans le/dans du coton,** mollycoddled **4.** F fog/mist; (aviation) clouds **5.** F **se sentir tout en coton,** to feel flabby. (Voir **jambe 6**)

cottard [kɔtar] a P **1.** hefty/ husky/beefy/brawny **2.** (chose, problème) difficult/tough.

cotte [kɔt] nf P trousers*.

cou [ku] nm F **1. monter le cou à qn,** to kid s.o./to have s.o. on **2.** **casser le cou à qn,** to beat s.o. up*/to give s.o. a going over. (Voir **casse-cou**; **jambe 1**)

couchage [kuʃaʒ] nm P sex(ual intercourse)*.

couche [kuʃ] nf P **en avoir une couche/en tenir une couche,** to be an absolute fool*/a complete idiot/ really thick; **il en a/il en tient une couche!** he's really dumb/he's a real thickie.

couché, coucher[1] [kuʃe] nm P (prostituée) **avoir/faire un couché,** to have an all-night client/an all-nighter.

coucher[2] F I vi **coucher avec qn,** to have sex* with s.o./to sleep with s.o./to go to bed with s.o.; **coucher à droite et à gauche/avec n'importe qui,** to sleep/to screw around; to be an easy lay/a pushover II vtr **avoir un nom à coucher dehors** (avec un billet de logement)/**avoir un nom à coucher à la porte,** to have a name which is very difficult to pronounce. (Voir **adjudant**; **tête 20**) III vpr **se coucher 1.** F **va te coucher!** get lost!*/clear off! **2.** F (boxe) to take a dive **3.** P **elle se couche quand on lui dit de s'asseoir,** she'll go to bed with any Tom, Dick or Harry; she's an easy lay/a pushover.

coucherie [kuʃri] nf P sex(ual intercourse)*.

coucheur [kuʃœr] nm F **c'est un mauvais coucheur,** he's a cantankerous so-and-so/a bloody-minded sod/an awkward customer.

couci-couça [kusikusa], **couci-couci** [kusikusi] *adv F* so-so; **ça va couci-couça**, I'm fair to middling/not doing too badly.

coucou [kuku] *nm* **1.** *F* (*vieux véhicule, vieille machine*) (*i*) old plane/crate (*ii*) (old) banger/jalopy/ heap **2.** *O P* watch/tick-tock.

coude [kud] *nm F* **1. avoir mal au coude,** to be/to feel lazy **2. lâche-moi le coude!** stop bothering me! **3. lever/plier le coude,** to lift the elbow/to booze. (*Voir* **doigt 6; huile 1; se moucher 1**)

couenne [kwan] **I** *nf* **1.** *P* skin; **se gratter la couenne** (*i*) to scratch oneself (*ii*) to have a shave **2.** fool*/twit/clot **II** *a F* stupid*; **ce qu'il est couenne!** what a clot he is!/what a nurd!

couic [kwik] **I** *nm F* **1. faire couic,** to die*; **il n'a pas fait couic,** he just popped off **2. je n'y comprend/je n'y vois/je ne pige que couic,** I don't see/understand/get it at all; I can't make head or tail of it; I haven't the foggiest **II** *excl P* look sharp!

couillard [kujar] *a V* having large testicles*/big-balled/well-hung/well-equipped.

couille [kuj] *nf V* **1.** testicle*/ball; (*a*) **j'en ai plein les couilles,** I've had it up to here/I'm fucking fed up* (with it)/I'm pissed off (with it); **casser les couilles à qn,** to bore* s.o. rigid/to give s.o. a pain in the arse; **tu me casses les couilles/tu me fais mal aux couilles,** you give me (the) balls-ache (*b*) **avoir des couilles au cul,** to have guts/to have spunk/to have (a lot of) balls; **il n'a pas de couilles,** he's got no balls/no bottle (*c*) **c'est de la couille/c'est des couilles (en barre)!** that's balls!/that's bollocks!/that's a load of balls! **mes couilles!** balls!/ bollocks! **2. une couille molle,** a

wet/a drip/a wimp **3. partir/ tomber en couille,** to neglect onself/ to go to pot/to go downhill **4. ça, c'est couille!** that's a bugger!/that's a bastard! **5. je me ferai un porte-monnaie avec tes couilles!** I'll have your guts for garters! **6. baiser qn à couilles rabattues,** to make love to s.o. often and all over the place; to be always at it/on the go. (*Voir* **branler II 3; manche I 1; peau 22**)

couiller [kuje] *vtr P* to cheat*/to deceive*/to swindle*; **il s'est fait couiller,** he got done/had.

couillibi [kujibi] *nm P* fool*/twit/ clot.

couillon [kujɔ̃] *P* **I** *a* stupid*/ thick/dim; **être couillon comme la lune,** to be as thick as two short planks/to be a bloody idiot/to be a real jerk; **c'est drôlement couillon!** that's a load of cobblers! **c'est trop couillon!** it's too fucking daft for words! **II** *nm* (*a*) fool*/jerk/cre-tin; **espèce de couillon!** you bloody fool!/you silly fucker!/you stupid cunt! **faire le couillon,** to arse about/to fart about/to piss about. (*Voir* **attrape-couillons**) (*b*) (**et**) **couillon qui s'en dédit,** and to hell with anyone who says otherwise!

couillonnade [kujɔnad] *nf P* (*a*) nonsense*/rubbish/balon(e)y/crap/ shit; **quelle couillonnade!** what a load of tripe!/(what) balls!/bal-locks!/bullshit! **dire des couillon-nades,** to talk cock/to bullshit (*b*) **il en a fait une couillonnade,** he's made a balls(-up)/a cock(-up) of it (*c*) **en voilà une couillonnade!** what a bloody stupid thing to do!

couillonner [kujɔne] *P* **I** *vtr* (*a*) to make a fool/a sucker of (s.o.); to make a monkey out of (s.o.); **je me suis laissé couillonner,** I've been had/I've been done (*b*) to make a balls(-up) of sth; **du travail couil-lonné,** ballsed-up work/a balls-up **II** *vi* to fool around*/to arse about/to fart around/to piss about.

couillonnerie [kujɔnri] *nf P =* **couillonnade.**

couiner [kwine] *vi F* **1.** to cry*/to snivel/to whine/to whimper **2.** *(freins, pneus)* to squeal/to screech.

coulant [kulɑ̃] **I** *nm P* milk **II** *a F* easy-going; **homme coulant en affaires,** man who takes things in his stride.

coulante [kulɑ̃t] *nf V* **1.** diarrhoea*/the runs **2.** VD*/gonorrhoea*/clap.

coule [kul] *nf F* (*a*) **être à la coule** (*i*) to be in the know/to know what's what/to know the score/to be with it (*ii*) to be easy-going/laidback (*b*) **mettre qn à la coule,** to put s.o. wise/to show s.o. the ropes/to teach s.o. the tricks of the trade (*c*) **se mettre à la coule,** to get wise/to wise up (**de,** to)/to get with it.

coulé [kule] *a F* **c'est un homme coulé,** he's finished/done for/washed up; he's had it.

couler [kule] *vtr F* **1.** to discredit/to bring disgrace on (s.o.)/to ruin; **ce scandale l'a coulé,** this scandal has brought about his downfall/this scandal brought him down **2. se la couler douce,** to take it easy*/to have a good time/to have it easy.

couleur [kulœr] *nf F* **1.** lie/fib **2. affranchir/annoncer la couleur** (*i*) to have one's say/to state one's case; to show one's hand/to lay one's cards on the table (*ii*) to state one's choice of drink/to name one's poison; **faut pas changer de couleur,** don't mix your drinks **3. affranchir/éclairer qn sur la couleur,** to put s.o. in the know/to put s.o. wise **4. défendre ses couleurs,** to stick up for oneself **5. en dire de toutes les couleurs à qn,** to give s.o. a piece of one's mind; **on m'en dit de toutes les couleurs sur votre compte,** I've heard all sorts of (bad) things about you **6. en voir de toutes les couleurs,** to have a rough time of it; **en faire voir de toutes les couleurs à qn,** to lead s.o. a song and dance; **en avoir vu de toutes les couleurs,** to have been through the mill/to have had a rough time of it.

couloir [kulwar] *nm* **1.** *P* throat/gullet; **évacuer le couloir,** to vomit*/to throw up **2.** *V* **couloir à/aux lentilles,** anus*/arse(-hole)/*esp NAm* ass(-hole).

coup [ku] *nm F* **1. avoir le coup de/pour faire qch,** to have the knack of doing sth **2. boire un coup,** to have a drink; **il a bu un coup de trop,** he's had a drop too much/one too many **3. un sale coup,** a dirty trick; **ça, c'est un sale coup (pour la fanfare),** that's a blow!/that's a bit of bad luck! **4. écraser le coup,** to let bygones be bygones/to say no more about it **5. en avoir un coup,** to be mad*/insane **6. être dans le coup,** to be in the know; **mettre qn dans le coup,** to let s.o. in on the act **7. être aux cent coups,** to be worried stiff **8. être dans le coup** (*i*) to be in on sth/to be involved (*ii*) to know what's going on/to be with it (*iii*) to be onto sth; **être dans tous les coups,** to be in on everything/to have a finger in every pie **9. être là pour un coup,** to be on hand (to help s.o.)/to stand by (ready to help s.o.) **10. expliquer le coup,** to explain the situation/to gen s.o. up **11. faire le coup à qn,** to play a trick on s.o.; **si on cherche à vous faire le coup ...,** if people try it on with you ... **12. faire les cent/les quatre cents coups** (*i*) to live it up/to paint the town red/to have a ball (*ii*) to be capable of anything/to be up to all sorts of tricks **13. ne pas en faire/en ficher/***P* **en foutre un coup,** not to do a stroke of work/to do damn all/to sit on one's backside and do nothing **14. en jeter/en mettre un coup,** to put some guts/some vim/one's back into it; to buckle down to it; **mets-y un coup!** give it everything you've got! **15.** (*a*) (*cambriolage*) **monter un coup,** to set up/to pull (off) a job (*b*) **monter un coup contre qn,** to frame s.o.; **un coup monté,** a frame-up/a put-up job (*c*) **monter le coup à qn,** to (try to) deceive* s.o./to kid s.o./to have s.o. on; **ne me monte pas le coup!** don't give me that! **se monter le coup,** to kid oneself **16. tenir le coup,** to stick it out/to be able to take it **17. tenter le coup,** to chance it/to chance one's arm/to have a bash (at it)/to have a stab (at it); **ça vaut le coup,** it's worth a try; **ça ne vaut pas le coup,** it's not worthwhile/it's not worth it **18. prendre un coup de vieux,** to start to look old **19.** (*coït*) sex*/(a) screw; **un bon coup,** a good screw/a good lay. (*Voir* **balai; bambou; barre; blanc II 3; boule 1; carreau; châsse; chien; cidre; deux; discuter; épaule; ficher 1, 3; foudre; fourchette; foutre III 9; François; fusil 1; gueule I, 3; lapin; masse; massue; nez; patte; pied; pompe; pot; pouce 1; sabord; sabre; sens; soleil; tabac 1** (*c*)**; tampon; tirer 6; torchon 6; Trafalgar; veine**)

coupante [kupãt] *nf P* guillotine.

couparès [kuparɛs] *a P* penniless*/broke.

coupé [kupe] *a P* **être coupé (à blanc),** to be penniless*/to be skint.

coupe-chiasse [kupʃjas] *nm P* dispensing chemist.

choupe-choux [kupʃu] *nm inv* **1.** (*a*) *P* bayonet/pig-sticker (*b*) *F* cut-throat (razor) **2.** *O F* (*attrib*) **frère choupe-choux,** lay brother.

coupe-cigare [kupsigar] *nm P* guillotine.

coupe-lard [kuplar] *nm inv* knife.

coupe-la-soif [kuplaswaf] *nm F* (alcoholic) drink/thirst-quencher; snifter.

couper [kupe] *F* **I** *vtr* **1. couper** qn, to interrupt s.o./to cut s.o. short **2. la couper à qn,** to silence s.o./to reduce s.o. to silence; **ça te la coupe!** that stumps you!/that shuts you up!/beat that if you can! **II** *vi* **1. couper à qch,** to avoid/to dodge sth; **il ne coupera pas au service militaire,** he won't get out of his military service **2. ne pas couper dans qch,** not to be deceived/taken in by sth; **couper dedans,** to fall into the trap; **je n'y coupe pas,** I'm not falling for that. (*Voir* **chique 7; effet; sifflet 1; truc**) **III** *vpr* **se couper** *F* to contradict oneself (after having told a lie); to give oneself away; to let the cat out of the bag.

couperet [kuprɛ] *nm F* **passer au couperet,** to get the axe/the chop.

coupe-tif(f)es [kuptif] *nm inv F* hairdresser/barber.

Coupolard [kupɔlar] *nm F* member of the French Academy.

coupure [kupyr] *nf F* **1.** excuse/cover-up; **trouver une coupure,** to produce an alibi/to find a way out ·**2.** confidential piece of information*/tip-off **3. la coupure!** I'm not falling for that!

courailler [kuraje] *vi F* to run after women/girls; to chase skirt.

courailleur [kurajœr] *nm F* = **coureur.**

courant [kurã] *nm* **1.** *F* **courant (d'air)** (*i*) rumour/leak (*ii*) indiscretion **2.** *F* **se déguiser en courant d'air,** to make oneself scarce/to do a bunk **3.** *P* **faire courant d'air avec les chiottes,** to have foul breath.

courante [kurãt] *nf P* diarrhoea*/the runs/the trots.

courette [kurɛt] *nf F* = **courrette.**

coureur [kurœr] *nm F* **coureur de femmes/de filles/de jupes/de jupons,** womanizer*/skirt-chaser/wolf/Casanova.

coureuse [kurøz] *nf* P (*a*) girl*/woman* of easy virtue; a bit of a tart; easy lay/pushover (*b*) prostitute*/tart/hooker.

courge [kurʒ] *nf* P fool*/clot/berk/twit.

courgnole [kurɲɔl] *nf* P throat.

courir [kurir] I *vi* 1. F (*a*) **elle est toujours à courir**, she's always gadding about (*b*) to run after women/to chase skirt; **il ferait mieux de travailler au lieu de courir**, it'd be better if he did some work instead of running after women 2. F **il est bien loin s'il court encore**, he left ages ago 3. F **tu peux (toujours) courir!** nothing doing!*/no way! **laisse courir!** drop it!/give it a rest!/forget it! 4. P **courir qn**, to get on s.o.'s nerves/to bug s.o.; **tu me cours sur le haricot**, you get up my nose/you get on my wick II *vtr* F **courir les filles**, to chase after girls/to go chasing after skirt. (*Voir* **gueuse**; **poste**)

courrette [kurɛt] *nf* F 1. small journey/little trip 2. (*fuite*) **être en courrette**, to be on the run (from the police) 3. (*poursuite*) **faire une courrette à qn**, to pursue s.o./to be after s.o./to be on s.o.'s trail; **se faire faire la courette par qn**, to have s.o. on one's back.

courrier [kurje] *nm* F (*cartes*) Jack/knave.

course [kurs] *nf* F 1. (*pers*) **être à bout de course**, to be exhausted*/worn out/done in 2. **être dans la course**, to be in the know/to be with it; **il n'est pas dans la course**, he's out of it/he's not in the running. (*Voir* **bifteck 2**; **échalote**; **oignon**)

courser [kurse] *vtr* F **courser qn**, to chase s.o./to run after s.o.

coursette [kursɛt] *nf* F 1. **faire la coursette**, to run about (in vain) 2. **piquer une coursette**, to break into a run.

court-circuit [kursirkɥi] *nm* P sudden stabbing pain. (*pl* **courts-circuits**)

courtille [kurtij] *nf* P 1. **de la courtille**, on the short side (in length) 2. **être un peu de la courtille**, to be short of cash/to be hard up.

courtines [kurtin] *nfpl* P (*turf*) **les courtines**, (horse)racing/the races; **jouer aux courtines**, to have a bet on the horses/to have a flutter (on the gee-gees); **flamber dur aux courtines**, to gamble heavily at the races.

court-jus [kurʒy] *nm* P 1. short-circuit 2. = **court-circuit**. (*Voir* **penseuse**)

couru [kury] *a* F **c'est couru (d'avance)**, it's a cert*/a cinch; **c'était couru**, it was bound to happen.

cousin [kuzɛ̃] *nm* F 1. **un cousin à la mode de Bretagne**, a distant relation/a sort of relation 2. **ils sont grands cousins**, they're great friends/they hit it off well 3. **le roi n'est pas son cousin**, he thinks he's the cat's whiskers/the bee's knees 4. **recevoir ses cousins**, to have a period*/to have friends to stay.

cousu, ue [kuzy] F I *a* **cousu d'or**, rich*/rolling in it II *nf* (*a*) **une (toute) cousue**, a machine-made cigarette* (*b*) **une cousue main**, a hand-made cigarette*/a roll-your-own III *nm* **c'est du cousu main**, it's a cert*/a cinch/a sure bet/a sure thing.

couteau, *pl* -eaux [kuto] *nm* F **grand couteau** (*i*) top surgeon (*ii*) (*théâtre, cinéma*) leading role.

coûter [kute] *vi* F **pour ce que ça vous coûte!** as if it made any difference to you! (*Voir* **yeux**)

couture [kutyr] *nf* F 1. **battre qn à plate(s) couture(s)**, to beat s.o. hollow/to slaughter (an opponent)/to win hands down (at cards, etc) 2. **sur toutes les coutures**, from all sides/from every angle 3. gêné aux coutures (i) stiff/awkward/ill at ease (ii) in financial difficulties/ short of cash.

couvercle [kuvɛrkl] *nm* P **bouillonner/fermenter/frissonner du couvercle**, to be mad*/to flip one's lid.

couvert [kuvɛr] *nm* F 1. **mettre le couvert**, to prepare for a game of poker 2. **remettre le couvert**, to begin again/to start all over again.

couverte [kuvɛrt] *nf* F 1. blanket; **passer qn à la couverte**, to toss s.o. in a blanket 2. **tirer (toute) la couverte à soi**, to take the lion's share/to look after number one 3. cover-up/front; **son métier n'était qu'une couverte**, his profession was just a blind; **servir de couverte à qn**, to front for s.o.

couverture [kuvɛrtyr] *nf* F = **couverte 1, 2, 3**.

couvrante [kuvrɑ̃t] *nf* P = **couverte 1, 3**.

couyonner [kujɔne] *vtr&i* P = **couillonner**.

coxer [kɔkse] *vtr* P to arrest*/to nick.

crabe [krab] *nm* 1. F **le panier de crabes**, the rat race. (*Voir* **panier 2**) 2. P prison warder/screw 3. P (*mil*) (*a*) corporal (*b*) (*WWII*) old tank 4. P **un vieux crabe** (*i*) an old-timer (*ii*) a pig-headed/crabby old fool* 5. *pl* crab-lice/walking dandruff.

crac [krak] *nm* V female genitals*/slit/crack.

crachat [kraʃa] *nm* F 1. **se noyer dans un/dans son crachat**, to make a mountain out of a molehill 2. (*a*) decoration/medal/gong (*b*) ribbon/star/Grand Cross (of an order).

craché [kraʃe] *a* F (*a*) **c'est son père tout craché**, he's the (dead) spit/the spitting image of his father (*b*) **c'est lui tout craché!** that's him

all over!/that's just like him! (*Voir* **portrait** (*a*))

cracher [kraʃe] I *vi* 1. F **il ne faut pas cracher dessus**, it's not to be sneezed/sniffed at; **il ne crache pas sur le pinard**, he doesn't turn his nose up at plonk 2. F **cracher blanc**, to be very thirsty/to be parched 3. P to pay* (up)/to cough up. (*Voir* **bassin I 1** (*i*); **bassinet**) 4. P to confess*/to spit it out/to spill the beans. (*Voir* **bassin I 1** (*ii*); **bassinet**) II *vtr* P 1. to pay* up/to cough up; **j'ai dû cracher mille francs**, I had to cough up/fork out a thousand francs 2. to confess*; **crache-le!** out with it! (*Voir* **morceau 2**) 3. to drop (s.o.) (off); **je l'ai crachée chez elle en passant**, I dropped her (off) at her place. (*Voir* **air I 1**; **bénitier**; **feu 3**; **sac 11**; **son II 2**; **venin**) III *vpr* **se cracher** (*accident*) to crash/to have an accident (in one's car, etc).

cracheur, euse [kraʃœr, -øz] *n* P show-off*/swank.

crachoir [kraʃwar] *nm* F 1. **tenir le crachoir**, to monopolize the conversation/to do all the talking/to hold the floor 2. **tenir le crachoir à qn**, to play up to s.o.

crachouiller [kraʃuje] *vi* F to be always spitting; to splutter.

crack [krak] *nm* F (*a*) crack player/ace/wiz(ard) (*b*) star pupil.

cracra [krakra], **crade** [krad], **cradeau** [krado], **cradingue**, [kradɛ̃g], **crado** [krado], **cradoc** [kradɔk], **crados** [krados] *a inv* P dirty/lousy/filthy/crummy/grotty.

craigneux [krɛɲø], **craignos** [krɛɲos] *a* P **c'est craignos!** it's dreadful!/it's awful!/it stinks!

craindre [krɛ̃dr] *vi* P 1. to be wanted by the police/to be on the run 2. **ça craint!** it's dreadful!/it's awful!

crais! (crais!) [krɛ(krɛ)] *excl P* look out! (*Voir* **acrais!**)

cramé [krame] *nm P* **ça sent le cramé**, there's a smell of burning/ there's something burning.

cramer [krame] *vi P* **1.** to burn/to go up in smoke; **toute la baraque a cramé**, the whole place went up in flames **2.** to die*.

cramouille [kramuj] *nf V* female genitals*/pussy.

crampe [krɑ̃p] *nf P* **1. tirer sa/ une crampe**, to have sex*/to have it off **2. tirer sa crampe avec la Veuve**, to be guillotined.

crampette [krɑ̃pɛt] *nf P* **tirer sa crampette** = **tirer sa crampe** (**crampe 1**).

crampon [krɑ̃pɔ̃] *F* **I** *nm* (tenacious) bore*; limpet **II** *a* **ce qu'il est crampon!** what a bore*/drag he is!

cramponnant [krɑ̃pɔnɑ̃] *a F* pestering; **tu es cramponnant avec ta politique!** you're becoming a real pest with your politics!/your politics are a real drag!

cramponner [krɑ̃pɔne] *vtr F* **cramponner qn**, to bore* s.o./to pester s.o./to cling to s.o. (like a leech).

cram(p)ser [krɑ̃mse] *vi P* to die*.

cran [krɑ̃] *nm* **1.** *F* **avoir du cran**, to have guts **2.** *F* **baisser d'un cran**, to come down a peg (or two) **3.** *F* **être à cran**, to be on the point of losing one's temper/to be ready to explode; **j'avais les nerfs à cran**, my nerves were on edge; *P* **cela me foutait à cran**, that made him see red **4.** *F* **il ne me lâche pas d'un cran**, he won't leave me for a moment/I can't shake him off **5.** *P* (*mil*) **dix jours de cran**, ten days' CB/confined to barracks. (*Voir* **ceinture 1**)

crânage [krɑnaʒ] *nm F* snootiness.

crâne [krɑn] *nm* **1.** *F* **bourrer le crâne à qn**, to stuff s.o.'s head (up) with lies, etc; to (try to) lead s.o. up the garden path; to brainwash s.o.; **ne me bourre pas le crâne!** don't give me that (stuff)!/don't give me that old story! (*Voir* **bourrage**; **bourreur**) **2.** *F* **crâne de piaf** (*i*) = **crâneur 1** (*a*) (*ii*) fool*/ imbecile/bird-brain **3.** *P* (*argot policier*) **faire un crâne**, to make an arrest. (*Voir* **lessivage 2**)

crânement [krɑnmɑ̃] *adv F* **1. il s'en est acquitté crânement**, he did it without batting an eyelid **2. elle est crânement belle**, she's ravishing/ gorgeous.

crâner [krɑne] *vi F* to swank/to swagger/to show off*.

crâneur, euse [krɑnœr, -øz] *F* **I** *n* (*pers*) (*a*) show-off*/swank; toffee-nose; **faire le crâneur**, to swank/to show off* (*b*) stuffed shirt **II** *a* **il est un peu crâneur**, he puts it on a bit/he's a bit of a show-off*.

crapaud [krapo] *nm* **1.** *F* **avaler un crapaud** (*i*) to force oneself to do a very unpleasant task (*ii*) to swallow an insult **2.** *F* child*/kid/ brat **3.** *F* **crapaud de murailles**, stonemason **4.** *P* (*pers*) **un vilain crapaud**, a toad/a creep **5.** *P* purse **6.** *P* padlock **7.** *F* **faire un œil de crapaud mort d'amour**, to show the whites of one's eyes/to look like a dying duck in a thunderstorm.

crapautard [krapotar] *nm P* small purse; **constipé du crapautard**, miserly*.

crape [krap] *a&n P* = **crapule**.

crapoteux [krapotø] *a P* dirty/ filthy/crummy/grotty.

crapoussin [krapusɛ̃] *nm O P* undersized* person/shrimp; dwarf; freak.

crapser [krapse] *vi P* = **cram(p)ser**.

crapulados [krapylados] *nm P* = **crapulos**.

crapule [krapyl] *F* **I** *nf* rotter/ nasty piece of work/bastard*/toad; crook; *coll* scum **II** *a* nasty/dishonest (person, action).

crapulerie [krapylri] *nf F* dirty trick.

crapuleuse [krapylø̸z] *a P* **se la faire crapuleuse,** to go on a spree*/ on the razzle; to paint the town red.

crapulos [krapylos] *nm P* cheap cigar/stinkador/stinkaduro.

craquante [krakãt] *nf P* (wooden safety) match.

craque [krak] *nf* **1.** *F* (*a*) lie*/fib/ whopper (*b*) tall story **2.** *V* female genitals*/crack/slit.

craquer [krake] **I** *vtr P* **1.** to strike (a match) **2. faire craquer une crèche,** to burgle a house/to do a place over **II** *vi F* **1. plein à craquer** (*i*) chock-full/chock-a-block/chocker (*ii*) rich*/flush **2.** to tell lies/fibs **3.** (*pers*) to crack up.

craquette [kraket] *nf V* female genitals*/crack/slit.

craqueur, euse [krakœr, -ø̸z] *n F* fibber.

craquos [krakos] *nmpl P* spots/ pimples/*NAm* zits.

crasp' [krasp], **craspec** [kraspɛk], **craspect** [kraspɛ], **craspèque** [kraspɛk], **craspet** [kraspɛ], **craspignol** [kraspiɲɔl], **craspouillard** [kraspujar] *a P* filthy/crummy/ grotty.

crasse [kras] *nf F* **faire une crasse à qn,** to play a dirty trick on s.o./ to do the dirty on s.o.

crasserie [krasri] *nf F* **1.** sordidness/squalor **2.** avarice.

crasseux, euse [krasø̸, -ø̸z] **I** *a F* mean*/stingy **II** *n F* **1.** mean*/stingy person **2.** *nmpl F* **les crasseux,** the proles **3.** *P* comb.

crassouillard [krasujar] *a P* filthy/crummy/grotty.

crassouille [krasuj] *nf P* filth/ dirt.

cravacher [kravaʃe] *vi F* **1.** to make a desperate effort/to work like mad/to go like the clappers at sth **2.** to go at full speed/to belt along.

cravacheuse [kravaʃø̸z] *nf F* flagellator.

cravate [kravat] *nf* **1.** *F* head (of froth on glass of beer) **2.** *F* showing off; **c'est de la cravate!** it's all bluff!/it's just for show! **3.** *F* **faire une cravate à qn,** to put a neck-hold/a stranglehold on s.o. **4.** *F* **cravate de chanvre,** hangman's rope **5.** *P* **s'envoyer/s'en jeter/s'en mettre/se verser un (coup) derrière la cravate,** to knock back a drink/ to put one down the hatch/to sink one **6.** *P* **cravate à Charlot/à Gaston/à Gustave,** sanitary towel/*NAm* napkin.

cravater [kravate] **I** *vtr* **1.** *F* cravater qn, to kid/to hoodwink s.o.; to take s.o. for a ride **2.** *F* (*a*) to get (s.o.) in a neck-hold/a stranglehold (*b*) to collar (s.o.)/to grab s.o. by the neck **3.** *P* to arrest*/to nab/to collar (s.o.); **se faire cravater,** to get nabbed **4.** *P* to steal*/to pinch/to nick; **on m'a cravaté ma carte de crédit,** someone's swiped my credit card **II** *vi F* to exaggerate*/to shoot a line; to boast.

cravateur [kravatœr] *nm* **1.** *F* bluffer; boaster **2.** *P* counsel/barrister/brief.

cravetouse [kravtuz] *nf P* tie.

crayon [krɛjõ] *nm P* **1.** (financial) credit; **avoir du crayon,** to be in credit/in the black **2.** *pl* hair **3.** *pl* legs*; **agiter les crayons,** to run away*/to do a bunk/to scarper **4.** *P* walking-stick.

crayonner [krɛjɔne] *vi P* (*aut*) to accelerate/to put one's foot down.

cré [kre] *a inv P* (*abbr* = **sacré**) cré

nom de nom! hell! cré bon Dieu! (Jesus) Christ!

créature [kreatyr] *nf F* **1.** person/individual*; **c'est une bonne créature,** he's a good sort **2.** woman of easy virtue/floosie/tart.

crebleu! [krəblø] *excl P* (*abbr = sacrebleu*) damn it!

crèche [krɛʃ] *nf P* room; house/digs/pad.

crécher [kreʃe] *vi P* **1.** to live; **où que tu crèches?** where do you hang out? **2.** to go to bed*/to crash (out)/to kip down.

crédié! [kredje], **crédieu** [kredjø] *excl P* (*abbr = sacré nom de Dieu!*) (God) damn it (all)!

crédo [kredo] *nm P* (financial) credit.

crémaillère [kremajɛr] *nf F* **pendre la crémaillère,** to have/to give a house-warming (party); **à quand la crémaillère?** when's the house-warming (going to be)?

crème [krɛm] **I** *nm F* (= *café crème*) **un crème,** a (small) white coffee; **un grand crème,** a large white coffee **II** *nf F* **1. la crème,** the cream (of society)/the upper crust; the best **2. c'est de la crème,** it's a piece of cake; there's nothing to it; **c'est pas de la crème,** it's no easy matter; it's no walk-over.

crémerie [kremri] *nf F* **changer de crémerie,** to move on/to push off; **allez, on change de crémerie,** come-on, let's get out of here!/let's high-tail it out of here!

crénom! [krenɔ̃] *excl P* (*abbr = sacré nom de Dieu!*) = **crédié!**

crêpage [krepaʒ] *nm F* **crêpage de chignons,** fight*/set-to (between women).

crêpe [krɛp] *nf* **1.** *F* **se retourner comme une crêpe,** to change one's opinion completely; to do an about-face; to change sides; **je l'ai retourné comme une crêpe,** I soon changed his mind for him **2.** *F* **s'aplatir comme une crêpe,** to fall flat on one's face **3.** *F* **plaquer qn comme une crêpe,** to leave s.o. flat **4.** *F* (*voiture*) **faire la crêpe,** to turn turtle **5.** *F* fool*/idiot **6.** *P* beret.

crêper [krepe] *vpr F* (*femmes*) **se crêper (le chignon/la tignasse),** to fight/to have a set-to/to tear each other's hair out.

cresson [kresɔ̃] *nm* **1.** (*a*) *P* hair/thatch; **il n'a plus de cresson sur la fontaine/sur la cafetière/sur le caillou/sur la truffe,** he's lost his hair/he's bald* (*b*) *V* (*i*) (*femme*) pubic hair (*ii*) (*pour un homme*) **arroser le cresson,** to have sex* **2.** *P* money*; **le cresson ne pousse pas sans effort,** money doesn't grow on trees **3.** *P* **idem au cresson,** ditto. (*Voir* **brouter 1**; **marguerite 4**)

crétin, ine [kretɛ̃, -in] *F* **I** *n* fool*/cretin/moron; **quelle bande/quel tas de crétins!** what a shower!/what a bunch of morons! **II** *a* stupid*/cretinous/moronic.

creuser [krøze] **I** *vtr F* **1. ça vous creuse (l'estomac)/ça vous la creuse,** it gives you an appetite/it makes you feel peckish **2. se creuser la tête/le cerveau/la cervelle/le ciboulot/le citron/le navet,** to rack one's brains **II** *vpr* **se creuser** *F* **se creuser sur un problème,** to rack one's brains/to puzzle over a problem.

creux [krø] *F* **I** *nm* **avoir un creux (dans l'estomac),** to feel empty/peckish/ravenous **II** *a* **avoir le nez creux,** to be shrewd/far-sighted.

crevaille [krəvaj] *nf P* huge meal/feast/tuck-in/blow-out.

crevaison [krəvezɔ̃] *nf P* **1.** death **2.** exhaustion/extreme fatigue; **quelle crevaison** what a slog!/what a fag!

crevant [krəvɑ̃] *a P* **1.** boring/tiresome/deadly **2.** exhausting/killing; **ce boulot, c'est vachement crevant,** this job really kills you/is

really knackering **3.** very funny*/
side-splitting/killing; **c'était crevant**,
it was a real scream/it was (absolutely) priceless.

crevard, -arde [krəvar, -ard]
a&n P **1.** hungry/starving (person)
2. dying (person).

crevasse [krəvas] *nf V* female
genitals*/crack/slit.

crève [krɛv] *nf P* death; **attraper/
choper la crève** (*i*) to die* (*ii*) to
catch one's death (of cold).

crevé [krəve] *a P* **1.** dead **2.**
exhausted*/dead tired/shattered/
shagged-out/knackered.

crève-de-faim [krɛvdəfɛ̃],
crève-la-faim [krɛvlafɛ̃] *nm inv*
F half-starved person; down-and-
out.

crever [krəve] **I** *vi* **1.** *F* to have a
puncture **2.** *F* **crever de rire**, to
laugh* uproariously **3.** *P* (*pers*) to
die*/to snuff it; **qu'il crève!** to hell
with him! **tu peux (toujours) crever!**
get stuffed! **marche ou crève!** do or
die! **crever d'ennui**, to be bored to
death/bored out of one's mind; **je
crève de chaleur**, I'm baking/boil-
ing; **crever de faim**, to be starving/
famished; to be dying of hunger
II *vtr* **1.** *P* **crever la faim/la
crever/crever la dalle**, to be starv-
ing/famished **2.** *F* **crever qn**, to
work/to flog s.o. to death; to
knacker s.o. (*Voir* **tempérament 3**)
3. *F* **ça vous crève les yeux**, it's
staring you in the face/it's right
under your nose **4.** *P* to arrest*/to
bust (s.o.). (*Voir* **tas 2**) **5.** *P* to
wound **6.** *P* to kill **III** *vpr* **se
crever 1.** *F* **se crever (de travail)**,
to work oneself to death/to work
oneself into the ground/to kill oneself with work; **je me suis crevé là-
dedans pendant dix ans**, I slaved
away/flogged my guts out there for
ten years **2.** *P* **se faire crever**, to
get killed **3.** *F* **se crever (de rire)**,
to laugh* uproariously/to kill oneself (laughing)/to split one's sides

laughing/to piss oneself laughing
4. *F* **se faire crever**, to have a slap-
up meal/to have a good blow-out
5. *P* **tu t'en ferais crever!** get
stuffed!

cri [kri] *nm* **1.** *F* **le dernier cri**, the
latest fashion/the in-thing; **c'est le
dernier cri**, it's all the rage **2.** *F*
uproar; vehement protest; **faire du
cri/aller au(x) cri(s)**, to kick up a
fuss; **du cri sec/du drôle de cri**, a
hell of a row.

cric [kri(k)] *nm P* (poor-quality)
brandy/rotgut.

cricri [krikri] *nm F* **1.** (*insecte*)
cricket **2. cricri (ravageur)**, skinny/
wizened little female.

crin [krɛ̃] *nm F* **1.** (*a*) **être comme
un crin/être crin/être de mauvais
crin**, to be in a bad temper/in a
disagreeable mood; to be like a
bear with a sore head; to be cantankerous (*b*) **se faire des crins**, to
get (all) upset/to work oneself up
(into a state) **2. à tout crin/à tous
crins**, out-and-out/thoroughgoing
(revolutionary, etc) **3. avoir qn
dans le crin**, to be infatuated* with
s.o./to be gone on s.o. **4.** *pl* hair/
thatch; **se faire tailler les crins**, to
have one's hair cut. (*Voir* **peau 19**)

crincrin [krɛ̃krɛ̃] *nm F* screechy/
squeaky violin; fiddle; **racler le
crincrin**, to scrape on the fiddle.

se criquer [səkrike] *vi P* to run
away*/to clear off/to skedaddle/to
scarper.

crise [kriz] *nf F* (*a*) **piquer une
crise/attraper une crise de nerfs** (*i*)
to throw a fit; to have hysterics (*ii*)
to fly into a rage/to blow one's
top/to fly off the handle/to do
one's nut (*b*) **faire piquer une crise
(de nerfs) à qn**, to drive s.o. up the
wall.

crispant [krispɑ̃] *a F* irritating/
annoying/aggravating; **ce que tu es
crispant!** what a pain (in the neck)
you are!/you get on my wick!

cristi! [kristi] *excl P* (*abbr* = *sacristi!*) curse it!/damn it!/(damn and) blast it!

crob [krɔb] *a P* = **crobe.**

crobar [krɔbar] *nm P* sketch/drawing; **tu veux que je te fasse un petit crobar?** do I have to spell it out for you?

crobe [krɔb] *a P* (= *microbe*) tiny/titchy.

crocher [krɔʃe] **I** *vtr* **1.** *F* to grab; **je l'ai croché amicalement,** I took his arm in a friendly manner **2.** *F* to arrest*/to nab **3.** *P* to pick (a lock) **II** *vpr* **se crocher** *P* = **se crocheter.**

croches [krɔʃ] *nfpl P* hands*/hooks.

crochet [krɔʃɛ] *nm F* **1. vivre aux crochets de qn,** to live off s.o./to sponge off s.o. **2.** *pl* = **crocs 1, 2, 3.**

se crocheter [səkrɔʃte] *vpr P* **se crocheter (avec qn),** to come to blows (with s.o.)/to have a set-to (with s.o.)/to have a barney (with s.o.).

crochu [krɔʃy] *a F* **il a les doigts crochus/il a les pattes crochues/il les a crochues** (*i*) he's light-fingered/he's got sticky fingers (*ii*) he's miserly*/grasping/tight-fisted.

croco [krɔko] *nm F* crocodile (skin); **un porte-fafiots en croco,** a crocodile(-skin) wallet.

crocs [kro] *nmpl* **1.** *F* teeth*/fangs/gnashers; **avoir mal aux crocs,** to have toothache; **se laver les crocs au roquefort,** to have foul breath **2.** *F* **avoir les crocs,** to be starving/ravenous **3.** *P* **n'avoir plus mal aux crocs,** to die*/to peg out/to give up the ghost.

croire [krwar] **I** *vtr F* **1. je vous crois!/j'te crois!** you bet!/sure!/rather! **2.** (*intensif*) **quel temps, crois-tu!** did you ever see such weather! (*i*) what awful weather! (*ii*) what wonderful weather! **3.**

j'aime mieux le croire que d'y aller voir, I have my doubts but I'll take your word for it. (*Voir* **arriver 1**) **II** *vpr* **se croire** *F* **il se croit/s'en croit (un peu),** he thinks a lot of himself.

croître [krwatr] *vi F* **cela ne fait que croître et embellir** (*i*) (it's getting) better and better! (*ii*) (*iron*) it's getting worse and worse.

croix [krwa] *nf* **1.** *F* **mettre une croix dessus,** to consider it over and done with/to write sth off **2.** *F* **c'est/il faut la croix et la bannière pour ...,** it's the devil of a job to .../it's the very devil to ... **3.** *F* **il faut faire une croix (à la cheminée),** put out the flags!/mark it with a red letter! **4.** *P* **faire la croix des vaches à qn,** to mark s.o.'s cheek with a knife-scar or razor-cut (for informing on one's associates to the police, etc) **5.** *P* **gagner la croix de bois,** to be killed in action **6.** *F* **croix de bois, croix de fer(, si je mens je vais en enfer),** cross my heart (and hope to die). (*Voir* **boule 8**) **7.** *P* fool*/ignoramus/twit **8.** *P* (*prostituées*) a demanding client.

cromi [krɔmi] *nm P* (*verlan de micro*) microphone/mike.

croni [krɔni] *P* **I** *nm* corpse*; **le parc des cronis,** the cemetery*/the bone orchard **II** *a* dead.

cronir [krɔnir] *P* **I** *vtr* to kill* **II** *vi* to die*.

croquant [krɔkɑ̃] *nm F* (*péj*) **1.** peasant*/clodhopper/yokel/country bumpkin **2.** insignificant man/nonentity.

croquante [krɔkɑ̃t] *nf P* mouth*/cakehole/gob. (*Voir* **tabourets**)

croque [krɔk] **I** *nm F* **1.** (*péj*) = **croquant 1, 2 2.** = **croque-mort 3. pas un croque,** not a cent/not a brass farthing **II** *nf P* food*/eats/nosh.

croque-mort [krɔkmɔr] *nm F* undertaker's assistant; **avoir une**

figure de croque-mort, to have a face like an undertaker. (*pl* croque-morts)

croquemuche [krɔkmyʃ] *nm P* = croque-mort.

croqueneaux [krɔkno] *nm P* = croquenots.

croquenots [krɔkno] *nmpl P* big boots*/beetle-crushers.

croquer [krɔke] **I** *vtr* **1.** *P* to eat*/to scoff/to tuck into; **croquer un sandwich en moins de rien,** to wolf down a sandwich in no time **2.** *P* to squander (one's money, etc); to blue/to get through (money) **3.** *P* **croquer une poulette,** to have/to get a girl*/a bird **4.** *P* to arrest*/to nab (s.o.) **5.** *F* (*a*) **elle est jolie à croquer,** she's as pretty as a picture (*b*) **elle est gentille/mignonne à croquer,** she's a sweetie **6.** *V* (*fellation*) **se faire croquer,** to be sucked off. (*Voir* **marmot**) **II** *vi P* **1.** to eat*/to tuck in **2. en croquer** (*a*) to be a police informer*/to grass (*b*) to be a prostitute*/to be on the game (*c*) to be a homosexual*/one of them (*d*) to be a Peeping Tom/a voyeur **3. en croquer pour qn,** to be infatuated* with s.o./to have a crush on s.o.

croqueur [krɔkœr] *nm F* **croqueur de femmes,** womanizer*/Don Juan/wolf.

croqueuse [krɔkøz] *nf F* **une croqueuse de diamants,** an expensive mistress/a gold-digger.

croquignole [krɔkiɲɔl] *F* **I** *a* = croquignolet **II** *nf* **une croquignole,** a pretty girl/a bit of all right/a nice bit of stuff.

croquignoles [krɔkiɲɔl] *nfpl V* testicles*/nuts.

croquignolet, ette [krɔkiɲɔlɛ, -ɛt] *a F* dainty/(small and) pretty/sweet/cute.

croquis [krɔki] *nm F* **tu veux que je te fasse un petit croquis?** do I have to spell it out for you?

crosse [krɔs] *nf* **1.** *F* (*a*) **chercher des crosses à qn,** to pick a quarrel with s.o. (*b*) **prendre les crosses,** to stick up for s.o. **2.** *F* **se mettre/P se foutre en crosse,** to get angry **3.** *F* **lever/mettre la crosse en l'air** (*i*) to desert (*ii*) to surrender/to show the white flag **4.** *P* **autant/au temps pour les crosses!** start again!

crosser [krɔse] *P* **I** *vtr* **1.** to criticize* (s.o.)/to tell (s.o.) off; to pick a quarrel* (with s.o.) **2.** (*a*) to treat (s.o.) badly; to punish (s.o.); to beat (s.o.) **II** *vi* (*l'heure*) to strike **III** *vpr* **se crosser** *P* to wrangle; to scuffle.

crosseur [krɔsœr] *nm P* **1.** quarrelsome man **2.** = Attorney General.

crotte [krɔt] **I** *nf* **1.** *F* **ma (petite) crotte!** my darling!* **2.** *P* **c'est-il oui ou crotte?** is it yes or no?/are you going to or not? (*Voir* **merde I 14**) **3.** *P* **être à la crotte,** to be depressed*/to feel low/to have the hump **4.** *P* **il n'y a pas de quoi se rouler dans la crotte,** it's no laughing matter/it's not *that* funny **5.** *P* **ce n'est pas de la crotte,** it's not rubbish **6.** *F* **elle ne se prend pas pour de la crotte,** she thinks she's really something. (*Voir* **bique I 1; panier 8**) **II** *excl O P* (*euph de* **merde!**) shit!/damn (and blast) it!

crotter [krɔte] *vi P* to defecate*/to crap.

crougnat [kruɲa] *nm,* **crouilla(t)** [kruja] *nm,* **crouille** [kruj] *nm,* **crouilledouche** [krujduʃ] *nm P* (*péj*) Algerian/North African/Arab*/wog.

croulant [krulɑ̃] *P* **I** *nm* back-number/has-been; (*esp parents*) **les croulants,** the old people/the (old) folk(s); **c'est un croulant,** he's a square/he's an old fart/he's an old fogey* **II** *a* (*pers*) (*a*) old/ancient (*b*) old-fashioned/square/not with it.

croum(e) [krum] *nm P* credit (with a shop/a store, etc); **à croum(e),** on tick/on the cuff.

crouni [kruni] *nm & a P* = **croni.**

crounir [krunir] *P* **I** *vtr* to kill*/to do in/to bump off (s.o.) **II** *vi* to die*/to snuff it.

croupanche [krupɑ̃ʃ] *nm P* croupier.

croupe [krup] *nf F* (*esp femme*) buttocks*/behind/rear/rump; **tortiller de la croupe,** to wiggle/to sway one's hips (when walking).

croupion [krupjɔ̃] *nm F* **1.** (*a*) = **croupe** (*b*) **se décarcasser le croupion,** to put oneself out/to go to a lot of trouble **2.** (*cuisine*) parson's nose.

croupionner [krupjɔne] *vi F* to wiggle/to sway one's hips (when walking).

croustance [krustɑ̃s] *nf P* food*/grub/nosh.

croustillant [krustijɑ̃] *a F* (*a*) spicy/fruity (story, etc) (*b*) (*fille, femme*) sexy; **une petite femme croustillante,** a sexy little piece/number.

croustille [krustij] *nf O P* = **croustance.**

croustiller [krustije] *vi P* to eat/to nosh.

croustilleux, euse [krustijø, -øz] *a F* = **croustillant** (*a*).

croûte [krut] *nf F* **1. casser une croûte/casser la croûte/manger une croûte,** to have a snack/a bite/something (to eat); **viens casser la croûte avec moi,** come and have a bite to eat with me; **à la croûte!** (*i*) let's eat (*ii*) grub's up!/come and get it! **2. gagner sa croûte,** to earn one's living/one's bread and butter/to make a living. (*Voir* **miches 2** (*b*)) **3.** badly painted picture/daub **4. c'est une (vieille) croûte** (*i*) he's an old fogey*/he's an old fuddy-duddy/he's a stick-in-the-mud (*ii*) he's a twit/a clot **5.**

s'ennuyer/s'amuser comme une croûte derrière une malle, to be bored stiff/rigid; to be bored* to tears.

croûter [krute] *vi P* to eat/to feed (oneself, one's face)/to nosh; **de quoi croûter,** something to eat/a bite (to eat); **tu vas croûter ça,** take a bite of that/get that down you.

croûtier [krutje] *nm F* bad artist.

croûton [krutɔ̃] *nm F* **1.** = **croûtier 2.** = **croûte 4 3. s'ennuyer/s'amuser comme un croûton derrière une malle,** to be bored* stiff/rigid; to be bored* to tears.

cruche [kryʃ] **I** *nf* **1.** *F* fool*/idiot/twit/ass; **être bête comme une cruche,** to be thick/dense **2.** *P* **elle a cassé sa cruche,** she has lost her virginity*/her cherry **II** *a F* stupid*; **jamais je n'ai vu des gosses si cruches,** I've never seen such dumb kids.

cruchon [kryʃɔ̃] *nm F* = **cruche I 1.**

cube [kyb] *nm* **1.** (*scol*) *F* (*i*) third-year student in a class preparing for the *grandes écoles* or in a *grande école* (*ii*) pupil staying down for the third time **2.** *P* **gros cube,** 500 cc (plus) motor-bike; **les gros cubes,** the big bikes/heavy metal.

cuber [kybe] *vi* **1.** (*scol*) *F* to stay down for the third year **2.** *P* **ça cube/ça finit par cuber,** it's expensive/pric(e)y; it's going up; it mounts up.

cucu(l) [kyky] **I** *nm F* **le (petit) cucu(l),** buttocks*/bottom/backside/behind. (*Voir* **pan(-)pan**) **II** *a F* stupid*/daft; **ce qu'il est cucu(l)!** what a fool* he is!/he's daft; **il est cucu(l), ce film,** this film's stupid. (*Voir* **praline 4**)

cueille [kœj] *nf P* raid/bust/comb-out (by police).

cueillir [kœjir] *vtr* **1.** *F* (*a*) to arrest*; to round up (suspects); **se faire cueillir,** to be arrested/rounded up/hauled in/picked up (by the police) (*b*) **cueillir qn (au passage)**, to buttonhole s.o.; **se faire cueillir**, to get nabbed/caught **2.** **F où as-tu cueilli ça?** where did you dig that up from? **3.** *F* to collect (s.o.)/to pick (s.o.) up; **je passerai te cueillir demain soir**, I'll come and pick you up tomorrow evening **4.** *P* (*théâtre*) **se faire cueillir**, to get booed/hissed off the stage; to get the bird.

cuiller, cuillère [kɥijɛr] *nf* **1.** *F* **en deux/trois coups de cuiller (à pot)**, in less than no time/in two shakes (of a lamb's tail) **2.** *F* **être à ramasser à la (petite) cuiller** (*i*) to be badly hurt/smashed up (*ii*) to be exhausted* **3.** *F* **avaler sa cuiller**, to be scared stiff **4.** *F* **argenté comme une cuiller de bois**, penniless*/completely broke **5.** *F* (*tennis*) **servir à la cuiller**, to serve underhand **6.** *P* hand*; **serrer la cuiller à qn**, to shake hands with s.o.; **serre-moi la cuiller!** put it there! (*Voir* **dos**)

cuir [kɥir] *nm* **1.** *F* leather jacket; (*aviation*) (leather) flying suit; *pl* leathers **2.** *P* **un cuir/un fétichiste du cuir** (*i*) s.o. who is into leather/leather merchant (*ii*) (*homosexuels*) leather queen **3.** *F* (*a*) **faire un cuir**, to make an incorrect liaison (*eg il a fait une erreur* [ilafɛzynɛrœr]) (*b*) **il parlait sans cuirs**, his way of speaking didn't give him away **4.** *F* skin/hide; **tanner/carder le cuir à qn**, to give s.o. a good hiding; **se rôtir le cuir**, to sunbathe; **il a le cuir épais**, he's thick-skinned; **jurer entre cuir et chair**, to swear under one's breath.

cuirasse [kɥiras] *nf P* (*poitrine*) chest.

cuirassé [kɥirase] *a P* **cuirassé (à zéro)**, blind drunk*/blotto.

cuire [kɥir] *vi F* **on cuit dans cette salle**, it's boiling hot in this room; this room's like an oven. (*Voir* **dur I; dur II; jus 8; œuf**)

cuisinage [kɥizinaʒ] *nm F* ques-

tioning/interrogation/grilling/sweating (of prisoner, suspect) (with the object of forcing a confession).

cuisine [kɥizin] *nf F* **1.** = **cuisinage** **2.** underhand scheming/wangling/dirty work; **les petites cuisines du métier**, the little tricks of the trade; **la cuisine parlementaire**, parliamentary intrigue **3.** faking/cooking (of accounts, etc). (*Voir* **batterie**)

cuisiner [kɥizine] *vtr F* **1.** to question/to interrogate/to grill/to sweat (a prisoner, a suspect); to pump (s.o.) **2.** to cook up/to concoct (a scheme of revenge, etc) **3.** to fake/to tamper with (statistics, etc); **cuisiner des comptes**, to cook the books; **cuisiner une nomination pour qn**, to pull the wires/to pull a few strings in order to get s.o. an appointment.

cuisse [kɥis] *nf* **1.** *F* **se croire/croire qu'on est/s'imaginer sorti de la cuisse de Jupiter**, to think a lot of oneself/to have a high opinion of oneself; **elle se croit sortie de la cuisse de Jupiter**, she thinks she's really something/she thinks she's God's gift/she thinks she's the bee's knees **2.** *P* **avoir la cuisse hospitalière/facile/gaie/légère**, to be an easy lay/a pushover.

cuistance [kɥistãs] *nf P* **1.** cookery/cooking **2.** kitchen.

cuistancier, ière [kɥistãsje, -jɛr] *n*, **cuisteau**, *pl* **-eaux** [kɥisto] *nm*, **cuistot, ote** [kɥisto, -ɔt] *n P* cook.

cuit [kɥi] *a* **1.** *F* drunk*/juiced up/plastered **2.** *F* **un conservateur cuit et recuit**, a dyed-in-the-wool Conservative/a true blue Tory **3.** *F* **il a son pain cuit**, he's (financially) all right for the rest of his life; he's comfortably off **4.** *F* (*a*) (*pers*) ruined/done for/finished; **je suis cuit**, I'm done for/I've had it (*b*) (*chose*) ruined/kaputt; **ça c'est cuit**, that's had it/that's bitten the dust **5.** *F* **c'est du tout cuit**, it's a cert*/

it's a cinch/it's a walkover; it's all settled/it's in the bag; **ce n'est pas du tout cuit**, it's not all plain sailing; it's no pushover.

cuite [kɥit] *nf P* drunkenness; drunken bout; **prendre la/sa/une cuite; prendre une bonne/une forte cuite**, to get drunk*/canned/plastered; **avoir sa cuite**, to be dead drunk*/to be as pissed as a newt; **il a sa cuite**, he's completely smashed; **tenir une (bonne/forte) cuite**, to be/to have (had) a skinful; **cuver sa cuite**, to sleep oneself sober/to sleep it off; **le lendemain de cuite**, the morning after the night before.

se cuiter [səkɥite] *vpr P* to get drunk*/canned/paralytic/plastered/pissed.

cuivre [kɥivr] *nm F* **nous n'avons pas fait les cuivres ensemble!** don't take liberties (with me)!/don't try it on with me! (*Voir* **cochon 7**)

cul [ky] **I** *nm P* **1.** (*a*) backside/buttocks*/bottom/bum/*NAm* butt-/arse/*NAm* ass; **un coup de pied au cul**, a kick up the arse; **cul par-dessus tête**, head over heels/arse over tip/arse over tits/A over T; **faire tête à cul**, to go flying/to come a cropper*; **il en est tombé/il en est resté sur le cul**, he was flabbergasted/knocked sideways (*b*) **œil du cul/trou du cul**, anus*/arse-hole; **tu peux te le mettre/foutre au cul**, you can shove it/stick it up your arse; you know where you can stick it (*c*) **ne pas se manier le cul**, to sit on one's arse and do nothing; to do fuck-all/to do piss-all; **casser le cul à qn**, to bore* s.o. rigid/to give s.o. a pain in the arse/to get on s.o.'s tits **2. bas du cul/bout de cul**, undersized* person/short-arse **3.** stupid*/uncouth person; **un vieux cul**, a silly old bugger; **quel cul!** what a bloody fool! **c'est un vrai cul**, he's a right idiot/a real nurd **4. mon cul!** my foot!/my arse! **5. quel cul (il a)!** what amaz-

ing luck (he has)!/what a lucky blighter (he is)! **6. un gros cul** (*i*) a heavy goods vehicle (HGV) (*ii*) an HGV driver/a long-distance lorry-driver/a trucker **7. avoir qn au/dans le cul**, to be fed up/browned off with s.o.; **en avoir plein le cul**, to be fed up* (of it)/to be sick and tired (of it)/to be pissed off (with it); **l'avoir dans le cul**, to have had it; **il l'a dans le cul**, he's had it; that's screwed/fucked him up **8. avoir chaud au cul** (*i*) to be afraid*/to be in a blue funk/to be shit-scared (*ii*) (*esp femme*) to be (a bit of) hot stuff; to be randy; to be a bit of a nympho; to be asking for it **9. être à cul** (*i*) to have one's back to the wall (*ii*) to be penniless*/to be broke; **mettre qn à cul**, to clean s.o. out **10. être (comme) cul et chemise/être copains comme cul et chemise**, to be great buddies/mates; to be as thick as thieves **11. faire cul sec**, to down one's drink in one (go); **cul sec!** bottoms up!/down the hatch! **12. faire le cul de poule/faire la/sa bouche en cul de poule**, to purse one's lips; to pull a face/to pout **13. lécher le cul à qn**, to flatter* s.o./to lick s.o.'s arse. (*Voir* **lèche-cul**) **14. ça lui pend au cul (comme un sifflet de deux ronds)**, he's got it coming to him/he's (in) for it **15. je lui pisse au cul!** I couldn't give a toss (for him)!/he can go to hell!/he can get stuffed! **16. rire comme un cul**, to laugh without opening one's mouth **17. se crever le cul**, to work* hard/to slog away (at it)/to work one's arse off **18. traîner son cul/tirer au cul**, to shirk/to swing the lead/to skive off. (*Voir* **tire-au-cul**) **19. péter plus haut que son cul/que le cul** (*i*) to swank/to show off*/to put on airs (*ii*) to try to bite off more than one can chew/to set one's sights too high **20. se taper le cul par terre**, to roar with laughter/to be in stitches/to split one's sides laughing; **pas de quoi se taper le cul par terre!** it's no laughing matter! (*Voir* **astap(e)**) 21. **il chante comme mon cul,** he can't sing for toffee/for nuts 22. **avoir le cul sur selle** (*i*) to be in the saddle (*ii*) to be always sitting down 23. **faux cul** (*i*) deceitful/shifty person; shady customer (*ii*) hypocrite (*iii*) traitor/double-crosser 24. **papier cul,** toilet paper/loo paper/bum-fodder 25. **cause à mon cul, ma tête est malade,** bugger off/sod off, I don't want to know 26. (*a*) sex*; **histoires de cul,** sexy/porny/dirty stories; **il ne pense qu'au cul,** he's got sex on the brain/that's all he ever thinks about (*b*) women (in general)/skirt/crumpet (*c*) pornography/porn; **journal de cul,** tits and bums newspaper; **livre de cul,** porny book. (*Voir* **beurre 9**; **clochettes; feu 1, 6; pied 16**) **Il a** *V* stupid*/daft/wet; **ce qu'il est cul!** what a bloody idiot (he is)!/what a drip!

culbutant [kylbytɑ̃] *nm*, **culbute**[1] [kylbyt] *nf* O P trousers*/NAm pants.

culbute[2] *nf* F **faire la culbute** (*i*) (*pers*) to come a cropper*; (*ministère*) to fall/to collapse; (*entreprise*) to fail/to go bankrupt/to go bust (*ii*) to make a scoop/to make 100% profit (*iii*) to double one's stakes.

culbuté [kylbyte] *a* P **culbuté (à zéro),** (dead) drunk*/completely canned/paralytic.

culbuter [kylbyte] I *vtr* 1. P to convince (s.o.)/to win (s.o.) over 2. V **culbuter une femme,** to have sex* with a woman/to lay a woman II *vi* F = **faire la culbute** (**culbute**[2]).

culbuteur [kylbytœr] *nm* P **culbuteur de femmes,** womanizer*/ladykiller/wolf/Don Juan/Casanova.

cul-de-plomb [kydplɔ̃] *nm* P 1. clumsy clot 2. pen-pusher/petty bureaucrat 3. **c'est un cul-de-**

plomb, he's a lazy swine/he sits on his behind all day and does damn-all.

culeter [kylte] *vtr V* to have sex* with (s.o.).

culot [kylo] *nm* F 1. impudence*; **avoir du culot,** to be cheeky; to have plenty of cheek/of nerve; **avoir un culot monstre/un culot infernal/un sacré culot,** to have a hell of a cheek/to have the cheek of the devil; **vous en avez du culot!** you've got a nerve! **tu ne manques pas de culot!** you're a cool one!/you've got a (bloody) cheek! **y aller culot,** to bluff 2. (*dernier*) last chick hatched/last animal born (of litter); baby of the family; (*scol*) **culot (d'une promotion)** = wooden spoon/booby prize.

culotte [kylɔt] *nf* 1. P **avoir sa culotte,** to be drunk* 2. F (*a*) **prendre une culotte,** to get drunk* (*b*) **prendre/ramasser une culotte,** to lose heavily (at cards, etc)/to come a cropper*/to come unstuck 3. F **trembler/P faire/V chier dans sa culotte,** to be afraid*/to be scared stiff/to have the wind up; to wet/to piss oneself; to shit oneself 4. P **baisser/poser culotte,** to drop one's knickers/one's drawers 5. F **c'est la femme qui porte la culotte,** it's the wife who wears the trousers 6. F **jouer ses culottes,** to stake everything one has 7. F **je m'en moque comme de ma première culotte,** I couldn't care less; I don't give a damn 8. F **une vieille culotte de peau,** an old dugout/a Colonel Blimp 9. F (*certains ordres religieux*) **porter la culotte de zinc,** to conform to a rigorous discipline.

culotté [kylɔte] *a* F 1. impudent*/cheeky; **elle est culottée comme tout,** she's got a hell of a nerve/a bloody cheek; (*iron*) **vous n'êtes pas culotté, vous!** you don't want much, do you! 2. brave/

game **3.** (*livre, etc*) well-thumbed; rather the worse for wear.

se culotter [səkylɔte] *vpr P* to get drunk*.

cul-terreux [kytɛrǿ] *nm F* (*péj*) peasant*/clodhopper/country bumpkin/hick/yokel. (*pl* **culs-terreux**)

cumulard [kymylar] *nm F* (*péj*) holder of several (paid) jobs (etc)/ moonlighter.

cumuler [kymyle] *vi F* **il cumule,** he has more than one (paid) job/ he's a moonlighter/he's moonlighting.

cunu [kyny] *nm P* arithmetic; counting.

cunuter [kynyte] *vtr&i P* to count (numerically).

curaillon [kyrajɔ̃] *nm F* (*péj*) young priest; **petit curaillon de village,** (petty) parish priest.

curé [kyre] *nm* **1.** *F* **manger/P bouffer du curé,** to be violently anticlerical/to be a priest-hater **2.** *F* **avoir affaire au curé et aux paroissiens,** to be between the devil and the deep blue sea.

cure-dent(s) [kyrdɑ̃] *nm* **1.** *F* **venir en cure-dent(s),** to turn up at the end of a dinner/to gate-crash an evening party **2.** *P* knife **3.** *P* (*mil*) bayonet/toothpick **4.** *P* penis*/prick. (*pl* **cure-dents**)

curée [kyre] *nf F* **la curée,** the rat race; **se ruer à la curée (des places),** to join the rat race; **être âpre à la curée,** to be on the make.

cureton [kyrtɔ̃] *nm F* (*péj*) (*a*) parish priest (*b*) young priest.

curetot [kyrto] *nm,* **curetosse** [kyrtos] *nm P* = **cureton.**

curieux [kyrjǿ] *nm P* **1.** examining magistrate **2.** police superintendent.

cuterie [kytri] *nf P* stupidity.

cuti [kyti] *nf F* (*a*) (*médecine*) (*abbr* = *cuti-réaction*) skin test (*b*) **virer sa cuti,** to change one's way of life radically.

cuvée [kyve] *nf P* drinking bout/ drunken orgy/binge/bender/piss-up.

cuver [kyve] **I** *vtr F* **1. cuver son vin,** to sleep off the effects of wine/ to sleep oneself sober/to sleep it off **2. cuver sa colère,** to work off one's anger; to simmer down **II** *vi P* to laze about.

cyclard [siklar] *nm F* cyclist.

cyclo [siklo] *nm F* **1.** policeman on a bicycle **2.** (*abbr* = *cyclomoteur*) moped.

cyclope [siklɔp] *nm V* penis*; **faire pleurer le cyclope/égoutter son cyclope** (*i*) to urinate*/to have a slash/to take a leak (*ii*) to have an orgasm*/to ejaculate*/to come.

cygne [siɲ] *nm V* **baiser une femme en cygne,** to have sex* with a woman with her legs over her partner's shoulders/in the wheelbarrow position.

cynoque [sinɔk] *a P* mad*/crackers/bonkers. (*Voir* **sinoc, synoque**)

Cyrard [sirar] *nm F* cadet at the Saint-Cyr military school.

D

D [de] *nm F* **le système D** (= *système débrouille or système démerde: esp WWII*) (*a*) resourcefulness; wangling; fiddling (*b*) do-it-yourself.

dab, dabe[1] [dɑb] *nm P* **1.** father*/dad/pa; **mon vieux dab,** my old man. (*Voir* **beau-dab(e)**; **dab(e)s; grand-dab(e)**)) **2.** the boss*/the governor; **le Grand Dab,** God.

dabe[2] *nf P* mother*/mum/ma/old lady. (*Voir* **dab(e)s**)

dab(e)s [dɑb] *nmpl P* **mes dab(e)s,** my parents/the old folk(s)/my folks/mum and dad/ma and pa. (*Voir* **beaux-dab(e)s**)

dabesse [dabɛs] *nf P* = **dabe**[2]. (*Voir* **belle-dabesse**)

dabuche [dɑbyʃ] *nm P* **1.** = **dab 2.** = **dabe**[2] **3.** *pl* **dabuches** = **dab(e)s.**

dac! d'ac(c)! [dak] *int F* agreed!*/OK!/roger! **t'es d'ac?** OK with you?

dache, Dache [daʃ] *nm P* **envoyer qn à dache,** to send s.o. packing*/to send s.o. off with a flea in his ear; **va (le dire) à Dache!/va-t'en chez Dache!** go to hell!

dada [dada] *nm* **1.** *F* (*langage enfantin*) horse/gee-gee **2. aller à dada** (*i*) *F* (*langage enfantin*) to ride a cock-horse; to ride a horse/to ride a gee-gee (*ii*) *V* to have sex* with a woman/to ride a woman. (*Voir* **radada**) **3.** *F* hobby/fad; **chevaucher/enfourcher son dada,** to get on to one's pet subject/one's

hobby-horse **4.** *P* (*drogues*) mixture of heroin* and cocaine*.

dadais [dadɛ] *nm F* silly/awkward boy; **espèce de grand dadais!** you big lump!

daf, d'Af [daf] *nm P* = **bat' d'af.**

dal, dalle[1] [dal] *adv P* **que dalle,** nothing* at all/damn-all/sweet FA; **je n'y entrave/n'y pige que dalle,** I don't get it/I can't see what it's all about/I can't make head or tail of it; **je n'ai fichu que dalle aujourd'hui,** I've done damn all today.

dalle[2] *nf P* throat/gullet; **s'arroser/ se mouiller/se rincer la dalle,** to (have a) drink*/to wet one's whistle; **avoir la dalle en pente,** to have a permanent thirst/to like a drink; **se remplir la dalle,** to eat*.

dame [dam] **I** *nf* **1.** *F* **faire la (grande) dame,** to put on airs/to be all lah-di-dah **2.** *P* **vot'dame,** your wife*/your good lady/your missis **3.** *P* **ma petite dame** = missis/ honey/love/lovey/ducky/ducks **4.** *P* **une dame blanche,** a bottle of white wine **5.** *F* **dame de pique,** pack of cards; **chatouiller/taquiner/ faire valser la dame de pique,** to be fond of playing cards **6.** *P* (*a*) **aller à dame,** to fall/to come a cropper* (*b*) **envoyer qn à dame** (*i*) to send s.o. sprawling (*ii*) to spurn s.o. **7.** *P* **entrer en dame avec qn,** to strike up a conversation with s.o. **II** *int F* (*régional*) **dame ouais!** I should say so!

dame-pipi [dampipi] *nf F* (female) lavatory attendant. (*pl* **dames-pipi**)

damer [dame] *F* **I** *vtr* **1. damer le pion à qn,** to outwit s.o./to go one better than s.o. **II** *vi* to fall (over)/to come a cropper*.

damner [dɑne] *vtr F* **faire damner qn,** to drive s.o. crazy/to drink; **cela ferait damner un saint,** it's enough to make a saint swear.

danse [dɑ̃s] *nf* **1.** *P* thrashing/beating*; **donner/filer une danse à qn,** to give s.o. a good hiding; **ramasser une danse,** to get a good belting **2.** *F* **ouvrir la danse,** to start the ball rolling/to get things under way; **voilà la danse qui va commencer,** now we're in for it/the fun's just starting; there'll be fireworks.

danser [dɑ̃se] **I** *vtr P* **la danser,** to get a good hiding; **tu vas la danser!** you'll catch it!/you're in for it! **II** *vi F* **1. faire danser qn,** to lead s.o. a dance/to give s.o. a hard time (of it) **2. il ne sait sur quel pied danser,** he doesn't know which way to turn; he's all at sea; **avec lui on ne sait jamais sur quel pied danser,** you never know where you are with him. (*Voir* **anse 3; buffet 2; empêcheur**)

danseuse [dɑ̃søz] *nf F* (*à vélo*) **pédaler/rouler en danseuse,** to ride standing (up) on the pedals.

dansotter [dɑ̃sɔte] *vi F* to dance a bit (without really knowing how to).

dard [dar] *nm V* penis*/shaft/prick; **avoir du dard,** to be (very) sexually excited*; to be randy/horny.

dardillon [dardijɔ̃] *nm V* penis*/prick; **avoir le dardillon,** to have an erection*.

dare-dare [dardar] *adv F* in less than no time/like a shot/like the clappers/at the double/toot sweet.

dargeot [darʒo] *nm*, **dargif** [darʒif] *nm P* buttocks*; **faire fumer le dargeot à qn,** to give s.o. a good hiding.

daron [darɔ̃] *nm P* **1.** father*/old man **2.** boss*/(big white) chief **3.** *pl* **les darons,** parents/the old folk(s).

daronne [darɔn] *nf P* mother*/old lady.

darrac(q) [darak] *nm O* **1.** *P* hammer **2.** *V* penis*/tool/hammer.

datte [dat] *nf P* **1. ne pas en fiche(r) une datte,** to do nothing/to (sit on one's behind and) do damn-all **2. des dattes!** nothing doing!*/it's no go!/no dice! **ça c'est comme des dattes,** that's impossible.

daube [dob] *nf P* **1.** rotten meat **2.** syphilis* **3. c'est de la daube,** it's worthless*/it's not worth a sausage.

daubé [dobe] *a P* (*meubles, etc*) fake(d)/imitation.

dauffer [dofe] *vtr V* **dauffer qn,** to have anal sex* with s.o./to sodomize* s.o./to bugger s.o.

dauphin [dofɛ̃] *nm P* **1.** pimp*/ponce **2.** (burglar's) jemmy/*NAm* jimmy.

dé [de] *nm* **1.** *P* **lâcher les dés,** to throw in the towel/to throw in the sponge/to call it a day **2.** *P* **passer les dés,** to make peace/to make a peace offering **3.** *V* **dé à coudre,** anus*.

deb [dɛb] *a P* = **débile.**

débâcher [debaʃe] **I** *vi P* to pack up and leave **II** *vpr* **se débâcher** *P* to get up/to get out of bed.

débâcler [debakle] *vtr P* **débâcler la lourde,** to open the door.

débagoulage [debagulaʒ] *nm P* **1.** *O* vomiting **2.** (*orateur*) spouting (forth).

débagouler [debagule] *P* **I** *vi O* to vomit* **II** *vtr* **1.** to bring up (food)/to throw up **2.** to spout (nonsense, sales talk, etc).

déballage [debalaʒ] *nm* **1.** *F* show-down **2.** *P* (*femme*) make-up; **vaut mieux pas qu'il la voie au déballage,** it's best if he doesn't see her first thing before she puts her make-up on; **être volé au déballage,** to find the wrapping better than the goods **3.** *F* venting/pouring forth (of insults, one's feelings, etc).

déballé [debale] *a F* depressed*/discouraged/down in the mouth.

déballer [debale] *vtr & abs (a) F* to confess*; **allez, déballe!** come on, own up! *P* **déballer ses outils,** to confess*/to come clean; *F* **déballer (ce qu'on a sur le cœur),** to get it off one's chest *(b) F* **déballer ses connaissances,** to tell all one knows; **il a tout déballé sur la table,** he put all his cards on the table.

déballonné [debalɔne] *nm P* coward*/quitter.

se déballonner [sədebalɔne] *vpr P* **1.** to confess*/to come clean **2.** to funk it/to back out/to chicken out.

débander [debãde] *vi* **1.** *P* to be afraid* **2.** *V* to lose one's erection/to shrink/to go limp; **cela m'a fait débander rapide,** it was like a cold shower/it really put me off **3.** *P* to cease/to stop going; **sans débander,** to keep going/to keep it up.

débarbe [debarb] *nm,* **débarbot** [debarbo] *nm P* defence lawyer/mouthpiece.

débarboter [debarbɔte] **I** *vtr P* **débarboter qn,** to act as counsel for the defence for s.o./to be s.o.'s mouthpiece **II** *vpr* **se débarboter** *P* to get by/to manage; to shift for oneself.

débarbot(t)eur [debarbɔtœr] *nm P =* **débarbe.**

débarbouiller [debarbuje] **I** *vtr F* to get (s.o.) out of a scrape **II** *vpr* **se débarbouiller** *F* **1. qu'il se débarbouille,** let him sort it out for himself/let him shift for himself **2. le temps se débarbouille,** the weather's clearing up.

débarcade [debarkad] *nf P* release (from prison); discharge.

débardot [debardo] *nm P =* **débarbe.**

débarquement [debarkəmã] *nm P* start of a period*.

débarquer [debarke] **I** *vtr F* **débarquer qn,** to dismiss* s.o./to give s.o. the sack; **il faut le débarquer!** he's got to go! **II** *vi* **1.** *F* **débarquer chez qn,** to drop in on s.o. **2.** *F* **il débarque,** he's a novice; he's a bit green **3.** *P* **ça débarque/ils ont débarqué,** she's got her period*/she's got the curse. (*Voir* **Anglais**)

débauche [deboʃ] *nf F* **faire une (petite) débauche (de table),** to make a pig of oneself.

débauchée [deboʃe] *nf F* knocking-off time (after a day's work).

débaucher [deboʃe] **I** *vi F* to knock off (after a day's work) **II** *vpr* **se débaucher** *F* **laissez là vos livres et débauchez-vous un peu,** put your books away and have a bit of fun/let yourself go a little.

débecqueter [debɛkte] *vtr&i P =* **débecter.**

débectage [debɛktaʒ] *nm P* disgust/revulsion.

débectant [debɛktã] *a P* disgusting/revolting/sickening/nauseating.

débecter [debɛkte] *P* **I** *vi* to vomit*/to puke **II** *vtr* to disgust/to revolt/to sicken; **ça me débecte,** I can't stomach that/it makes me sick; **il me débecte,** he makes me (want to) puke **III** *vpr* **se débecter** *P* **je me débecte,** I'm bored* stiff.

déberlinguer [debɛrlẽge] *vtr P* to take s.o.'s virginity*/to pick s.o.'s cherry.

débile [debil] *a F* idiotic/feeble/moronic; **il est complètement débile,** he's an absolute moron.

débilitant [debilitã] *a F* saddening/depressing.

débinage [debinaʒ] *nm P* disparagement*/knocking/slamming/running down (of s.o.).

débine [debin] *nf F* **1.** être dans la débine, to be penniless*/to be down on one's luck/to be on one's beam-ends; tomber dans la débine, to go broke/to fall on hard times **2.** rout/disorderly retreat.

débiner [debine] **I** *vtr P* **1.** to disparage*/to run down/to knock (s.o.) **2.** débiner le truc, to give the game away/to spill the beans/to let the cat out of the bag **II** *vpr* **se débiner** *P* **1.** to make off/to make oneself scarce/to hop it **2.** to crack up/to break down/to go to pieces/to go downhill **3.** to run each other down/to knock each other.

débineur, -euse [debinœr, -øz] *n P* **1.** backbiter/knocker **2.** s.o. who lets the cat out of the bag/who spills the beans/who gives the game away.

déblayer [debleje] *vtr & abs* **1.** déblayer le terrain (*i*) *F* to pave/to clear the way; to lay the groundwork (for negotiations, etc); to clear the decks (*ii*) *P* to run away*/to beat it/to scarper/to do a bunk; déblaie! hop it!/push off!/scram! **2.** *F* (*théâtre*) déblayer (un rôle), to emphasize the main speeches in a role by rushing through the others.

débleuir [debløir] *vtr F* débleuir qn, to open s.o.'s eyes (to life)/to teach s.o. a thing or two/to put s.o. straight.

débloquer [debloke] *vi P* **1.** to vomit*/to puke (up) **2.** to defecate*/to have a crap **3.** débloquer (à pleins tubes), to talk rubbish/to talk cock/to talk crap; tu débloques! you're off your head/you're out of your mind!

déboisé [debwaze] *a P* bald*.

déboiser [debwaze] **I** *vtr P* se faire déboiser la colline, to get one's

hair cut **II** *vpr* **se déboiser** *P* to lose one's hair/one's thatch.

débonder [debɔ̃de] **I** *vtr F* débonder (son cœur)/se débonder le cœur, to pour out one's heart **II** *vi P* to defecate*.

débotté [debɔte] *nm F* au débotté, immediately* (on arrival)/at once/right away.

débouclage [debuklaʒ] *nm P* **1.** breaking open (of a door, a till, etc); blowing (of a safe) **2.** release (of a prisoner).

déboucler [debukle] **I** *vtr P* **1.** to break open (a door, safe, till, etc) **2.** to release (a prisoner) **II** *vpr* **se déboucler** *P* = **se débrider**.

déboucleur [debuklœr] *nm P* burglar; safe-breaker.

débouler [debule] *vi F* to leave/to be off; allons, il faut débouler, come on, we must shoot off/we've got to dash.

déboulonnage [debulɔnaʒ] *nm*, **déboulonnement** [debulɔnmɑ̃] *nm F* dismissal (from a post)/sacking/firing.

déboulonner [debulɔne] *vtr F* to dismiss*/to fire/to sack.

débourre [debur] *nf V* = **débourroir(s)**.

débourrer [debure] *vi* **1.** *V* to defecate*/to have a crap/to have a clear-out **2.** *P* to get over a hangover; avec tout ce que j'ai bu, je ne n'arriverai jamais à me debourrer, I'll never sober up after all this plonk. (*Voir* **froc 3**)

débourroir(s) [deburwar] *nm V* WC*/shithouse.

débousille [debuzij] *nf P* elimination of a tattoo.

déboussolé [debusɔle] *a F* confused/bewildered/lost; être tout déboussolé, to have lost one's bearings/to be all at sea.

déboutonnage [debutɔnaʒ] *nm F* unloading of one's mind/opening up of one's heart.

déboutonné [debutɔne] *a F* **1.** manger à ventre déboutonné, to eat* heartily/to gorge/to stuff oneself (with food) **2.** rire à ventre déboutonné, to laugh* uproariously/to roar with laughter.

se déboutonner [sədebutɔne] *vpr F* to unburden one's mind/to open up (one's heart)/to get it off one's chest.

se débrailler [sədebrɑje] *vpr F* la conversation se débraille, the conversation is getting rather close to the bone.

débrancher [debrɑ̃ʃe] *vtr P* to turn (s.o.) off; ça l'a vite débranché, it really turned him off/put him off.

débridage [debridaʒ] *nm P* = débouclage 1.

débrider [debride] *vtr* **1.** *P* = déboucler 1 **2.** *abs F* travailler huit heures sans débrider, to work eight hours non-stop/at a stretch.

débringué [debrɛ̃ge] *a P* slovenly.

débris [debri] *nm P* un vieux débris, an old fogey*/an old fuddy-duddy.

débrouillage [debrujaʒ] *nm F* resourcefulness; wangling.

débrouillard, arde [debrujar, -ard] *F* **I** *a* resourceful*/canny/smart **II** *n* resourceful person; c'est un débrouillard, he's got his wits about him/he's got plenty of gumption/he's a smart lad/he can look after himself.

débrouillardise [debrujardiz] *nf,* **débrouille** [debruj] *nf F* resourcefulness/smartness; wangling/fixing. (*Voir* **D**)

débrouiller [debruje] **I** *vtr F* débrouiller qn, to get s.o. out of a jam/a mess **II** *vpr* **se débrouiller** *F* to shift for oneself/to get by/to manage; qu'il se débrouille! let him

look after himself!/let him sort himself out! savoir se débrouiller, to know one's way around; se débrouiller tant bien que mal, to muddle through; se débrouiller pour avoir qch, to wangle sth; débrouillez-vous! that's your look-out! se débrouiller sur le voisin, to pass the buck/the baby.

déca [deka] *nm F* (= un café décaféiné) un déca, a (cup of) caffeine-free/decaffeinated coffee.

se décalcifier [sədekalsifje] *vpr F* (*hum*) (*homme*) to take one's (under)pants off. (*Voir* **calcif**)

décalqué [dekalke] *a F* c'est son père tout décalqué (*i*) he's the spitting image of his father (*ii*) he's a chip of(f) the old block.

décambuter [dekɑ̃byte] *vi P* **1.** (*a*) to come out/to emerge (*b*) to go out/to exit **2.** to run away*/to beat it.

décamper [dekɑ̃pe] *vi F* to run off/to bolt/to make oneself scarce/to clear out; décampe! clear off!/buzz off!/beat it! il a décampé, he's done a bunk/he's scarpered.

décaner [dekane] *vi P* to die*. (*Voir* **caner**)

décanillage [dekanijaʒ] *nm P* hurried departure/flight.

décaniller [dekanije] *vi P* **1.** = décamper **2.** décaniller (du page), to get out of bed/to show a leg.

décapant [dekapɑ̃] **I** *nm* poor quality liquor/rotgut **II** *a* (*vin, etc*) harsh.

décapiter [dekapite] *vtr F* to open/to uncork (a bottle).

décapitonnage [dekapitɔnaʒ] *nm P* undressing/stripping.

décapotable [dekapɔtabl] *a P* (*femme*) fond of taking off her clothes/ready and willing.

décapoter [dekapɔte] *vi P* (*femme*) to (do a) strip.

se décarcasser [sədekarkase] *vpr F (a)* to go to a (hell of a) lot of trouble/to put oneself out/to bend over backwards *(b)* to wear oneself out/to flog oneself to death; **je me suis décarcassé pour vous procurer ce billet,** I sweated blood to get you this ticket.

décarpillage [dekarpijaʒ] *nm P* **1.** sharing out/sorting out (of the proceeds of a robbery) **2.** undressing/stripping; **au décarpillage, il n'était pas beau,** he wasn't a pretty sight with no clothes on.

décarpiller [dekarpije] *vtr P* **1.** to sort out/to share out (the proceeds of a robbery) **2.** to undress *(esp* a woman).

décarrade [dekarad] *nf P* escape/flight/exit (from prison, etc).

décarrer [dekare] *vi P* **1.** to go out/to (make an) exit **2.** *(a)* to run away*/to make oneself scarce/to take off *(b)* to escape *(esp* from prison)/to go on the run **3. décarrer de belle,** to be acquitted/to beat the rap.

se décartonner [sədekartɔne] *vpr P* to grow old/to be getting on in years.

décati [dekati] *a F (a)* faded/wilted/old and worn; **elle n'est pas trop décatie,** she's not so dusty/she's worn quite well (considering) *(b) (visage)* wrinkled.

(se) décatir [(sə)dekatir] *vi & pr F* to show the effects of age; **elle commence à (se) décatir,** she's beginning to lose her looks.

décavage [dekavaʒ] *nm P* ruin/bankruptcy.

décavé, ée [dekave] **I** *a F* **1.** *(a)* ruined/done for/bankrupt *(b)* penniless*/(stony) broke **2. visage décavé,** pinched/haggard face **3.** = **décati II** *n F (a)* ruined person; bankrupt *(b)* s.o. who is penniless*/flat broke.

décesser [desese] *vtr&i F (se dit pour cesser)* **il ne décesse pas de se** plaindre, he never stops complaining.

déchanter [deʃɑ̃te] *vi F* to change one's tune/to come down a peg/to climb down; **il a fallu déchanter,** it was time to lose all our illusions.

déchard, arde [deʃar, -ard] *n P* hard-up individual/penniless* person; down-and-out.

décharge [deʃarʒ] *nf V* ejaculation/come.

décharger [deʃarʒe] *vi V* to ejaculate*/to shoot one's load. *(Voir* **plancher¹ 2)**

dèche [dɛʃ] *nf P* **1. être dans la dèche/être dans une dèche noire/tomber dans la dèche/battre la dèche,** to be penniless*/to be down on one's uppers/to be on one's beam ends **2.** *(dépense; faux frais)* expense(s).

décher [deʃe] *vtr P (a)* to pay* (up)/to dish out/to fork out *(b)* to spend *(c)* to pay for (something) *(d)* to lose (money).

déchet [deʃɛ] *nm F (pers)* dead loss/wash-out; **un vieux déchet,** a back-number/a has-been/an old fogey.

décheur, euse¹ [deʃœr, -øz] *a&n P* spendthrift/big spender.

décheux, euse² [deʃø, -øz] *a P* penniless*/stony broke/flat broke.

déchirer [deʃire] *vtr P* **la déchirer,** to die*. *(Voir* **false)**

déclouer [deklue] *vtr F* **déclouer qch,** to redeem sth/to take sth out of pawn.

décoconner [dekɔkɔne] *vi P* = **déconner.**

décocter [dekɔkte] *vi V* to defecate*/to have a crap.

décoction [dekɔksjɔ̃] *nf P* **1. une décoction (de coups de bâton),** a good thrashing/a beating*(-up) **2.** *F* **une sacrée décoction,** one hell of a concoction/mixture.

décoffrer [dekɔfre] *vi P* to give birth to a child.

décoller [dekɔle] **I** *vi* **1.** *F* **il ne décolle pas**, he just sticks there (like a leech)/he doesn't budge/you can't get rid of him **2.** *F* **six heures sans décoller**, six hours without a break/at a stretch **3.** *P* to die* **4.** *P (couple (marié))* to separate **5.** *P* **elle a drôlement décollé depuis sa maladie**, she's got terribly thin/she's gone to pieces/she doesn't look too good since her illness **6.** *F* to get high (on music, drugs, etc) **II** *vpr* **se décoller** *P* to grow thin (after an illness, etc)/to go to pieces/to go downhill.

décompte [dekɔ̃t] *nm F* **trouver du décompte à qch**, to be disillusioned by sth/to be disappointed in sth.

déconnage [dekɔnaʒ] *nm V* nonsense*/rubbish/tripe/cock/balls/crap/esp NAm* bull(shit).

déconner [dekɔne] *vi V* **déconner (à pleins tubes)**, to talk absolute nonsense*/to talk cock; **déconne pas!/arrête de déconner!** *(a)* cut the crap!/don't give me that bull/shit/crap/balls! *(b)* don't do anything stupid!/don't piss about!

déconneur, euse [dekɔnœr, -øz] *n V* s.o. who talks cock/bull-shitter; **quel déconneur, ce mec!** what a load of balls/crap that bloke/guy comes out with.

déconnographe [dekɔnɔgraf] *nm P* teleprinter/*NAm* teletypewriter.

déconnomètre [dekɔnɔmetr] *nm P* **1.** *(a)* radio (set) *(b)* television (set)/(idiot) box/(goggle) box **2.** telephone*/blower **3.** microphone/mike.

déconnophone [dekɔnɔfon] *nm P* mouth*; **fermer son déconnophone**, to shut one's trap.

décoqueter [dekɔkte] *vi V* = **décocter**.

décor [dekɔr] *nm F* **1.** *(voiture)* **entrer/rentrer/aller dans le(s) décor(s)**, to run/to smash into a wall, house, etc; to leave the road; **balancer/envoyer qn dans le(s) décor(s)**, to send s.o. flying **2.** **cela ne fera/ferait pas mal dans le décor**, that will/would suit me down to the ground **3.** **l'envers du décor**, the other side of the picture/of the coin.

découronner [dekurɔne] *vtr F* to debunk (s.o.).

se décramponner [sədekrã-pɔne] *vpr F* to shake s.o. off.

décrasser [dekrase] **I** *vtr F* **décrasser qn**, to smarten s.o. up/to lick s.o. into shape **II** *vpr* **se décrasser** *F (a)* to have the corners knocked off one; to smarten up; **décrasse-toi le cerveau!** come on, use your brain! *(b)* to go up in the world.

décrassing-room [dekrasiŋrum] *nm P* bathroom.

décrocher [dekrɔʃe] **I** *vtr* **1.** *F (a)* to get/to hook/to land; **décrocher le grand succès**, to make a big hit; **décrocher le gros lot**, to hit the jackpot; **ils ont décroché le contrat**, they landed the contract *(b)* to wangle; **il a décroché une bonne position**, he's wangled himself a nice job; **décrocher une augmentation**, to wangle/to land a rise **2.** *F* to redeem (sth)/to take (sth) out of pawn **3.** *P* **se faire décrocher**, get shot. *(Voir* **tableau 2**; **timbale 1**) **II** *vi* **1.** *F (a) (abandonner)* to give up/to drop out; **au bout d'une semaine de cours, il a décroché**, after a week, he gave up going to lectures *(b)* to retire (from one's job, an event, a place, a scene) **2.** *P* to eat* **3.** *P (drogues)* to stop taking drugs/to knock off the dope/to kick the habit.

décrochez-moi-ça [dekrɔ-ʃemwasa] *nm inv F* **1.** cheap secondhand garment; reach-me-down/hand-me-down; cast-off **2.** cheap secondhand clothes shop; **elle s'habille au décrochez-moi-ça,**

she gets her clothes from jumble sales/from the Oxfam shop.

(se) décrotter [(sə)dekrɔte] *vtr & pr F* **1.** = **(se) décrasser 2. se décrotter le nez,** to pick one's nose.

décuiter [dekɥite] **I** *vtr P* to sober (s.o.) up **II** *vpr* **se décuiter** *P* to sober up.

déculottée [dekylɔte] *nf P* **1.** heavy defeat; **prendre la déculottée,** to get thrashed/to get clobbered **2.** heavy loss (at gambling).

déculotter [dekylɔte] **I** *vtr P* **déculotter sa pensée,** to speak openly/freely **II** *vpr* **se déculotter** *P* to speak openly/freely.

dedans [dədɑ̃] *adv* **1.** *F* **mettre/P fiche(r)/flanquer/fourrer/foutre qn dedans,** to bamboozle s.o./to take s.o. in/to have s.o. on; **être mis dedans** (*i*) to be fooled/to be had/ to be taken in (*ii*) to be imprisoned/to be put inside; **jeter/fourrer qn dedans,** to send s.o. to prison*/ to put s.o. away **2. être dedans** (*i*) *F* to be in prison*/to be inside (*ii*) *P* to be drunk* **3.** *F* **rentrer dedans à qn,** to pitch into s.o./to lay into s.o./to go for s.o.; **je vais lui rentrer dedans,** I'm going to give him what for **4.** *P* (*a*) **donner/ entrer/rentrer dedans** qch, to knock/to crash/to bash/to smash into sth (*b*) **mettre une porte en dedans,** to break a door down/to break in **5.** *F* **mettre les pieds dedans,** to put one's foot in it; **je m'y suis foutu dedans,** I really boobed there **6.** *F* **marcher dedans,** to tread in (a dog's, etc) excrement/to put one's foot in some dog-shit/to tread in something nasty. (*Voir* **défourailler 1; donner 5; rentre-dedans**)

dédé [dede] *nm F* buttocks*/behind.

dédouaner [dedwane] **I** *vtr F* **dédouaner qn** (*i*) to give s.o. a clean bill of health (*ii*) to clear s.o.'s name (*iii*) to put s.o. in the picture; (*journ*) **il m'a dédouané,** he gave me

the (inside) story **II** *vpr* **se dédouaner** *F* to get out of trouble/out of a scrape/out of a jam.

def [dɛf] **I** *a P* (*abbr* = **défoncé**) **raide def,** (very) high/stoned (on drugs, drink); **ils étaient raide def,** they were completely zonked/ stoned/bombed out of their minds **II** *nf P* cap.

défarguer [defarge] **I** *vtr P* to clear (s.o.) of a charge/to put (s.o.) in the clear/to get (s.o.) off the hook **II** *vpr* **se défarguer** *P* **1. se défarguer de qch,** to get rid of sth (incriminating) **2. se défarguer sur le dos de qn,** to put the blame on s.o.; to pass the buck.

défargueur [defargœr] *nm P* witness for the defence.

se défausser [sədefose] *vpr P* = **défarguer II 1.**

se défendre [sədefɑ̃dr] *vpr* **1.** *F* to get along/to hold one's own/to manage; **je me défends pas mal,** I'm getting along quite nicely/I'm doing fine; **il se défend au tennis,** he's quite good at tennis **2.** *F* **elle se défend bien,** she wears (her age) well/she doesn't do badly for her age **3.** *P* (*prostituée*) to solicit*/to go on the game.

défense [defɑ̃s] *nf P* **1.** swindle; racket **2. avoir de la défense** = **se défendre 1.**

déferrer [defere] **I** *vtr F* **déferrer qn (des quatre pieds),** to disconcert s.o./to put s.o. out **II** *vpr* **se déferrer** *F* **c'est un mec qui ne se déferre pas facilement,** he's a bloke who's not easily put out.

deffe [dɛf] *nf P* = **def II.**

se défiler [sədefile] *vpr F* **1.** to run away*/to clear off/to beat it **2.** (*a*) to malinger*/to shirk; to skive (off)/to dodge the column (*b*) to back out (of sth unpleasant)/to duck out (of sth).

défilocher [defilɔʃe] *vtr P* **défilocher les haricots verts à qn,** to make a fool of s.o.

déflaque [deflak] *nf V* excrement*/shit.

déflaquer [deflake] *vi V* **1.** to defecate*/to shit **2.** to have an orgasm*/to come.

défonce [defɔ̃s] *nf P* **1.** (*drogues; état de stupeur*) high; **il était entre deux défonces,** he was between highs **2.** a good time*/a ball **3.** drudgery/hard work/grind.

défoncé [defɔ̃se] *a P* (*drogues*) high/stoned/bombed/tripping; **être défoncé,** to freak out; **il était complètement défoncé,** he was stoned out of his mind/he'd completely flipped.

défoncer [defɔ̃se] **I** *vtr P* **défoncer qn,** to beat s.o. to a pulp/ to work s.o. over/to rough s.o. up **II** *vpr* **se défoncer 1.** *P* to get drunk*/pissed **2.** *P* to get high/ stoned on drugs **3.** *V* to have sex* **4.** *P* **se faire défoncer,** to get severely beaten up/to get worked over **5.** *V* **se faire défoncer la rondelle,** to be sodomized*/to get one's ass fucked **6.** *P* **se défoncer pour faire qch,** to make an all-out effort to do sth.

défonceuse [defɔ̃søz] *nf V* penis*/chopper/tool; **être amputé de la défonceuse,** to lack virility.

déforme [defɔrm] *nf P* **être (un peu) en déforme,** to be (temporarily) out of luck (*esp* at gambling).

défourailler [defurɑje] *vtr&i P* **1.** to draw (a gun, knife, etc); **défourailler (dedans),** to pull the trigger/to shoot/to fire; to let s.o. have it **2.** to get out of prison*; to go on the run.

défrimer [defrime] *vtr P* to stare at (s.o.)/to look (s.o.) straight in the face.

défringuer [defrɛ̃ge] **I** *vtr P* to undress (s.o.) **II** *vpr* **se défringuer** *P* to undress/to get undressed/to take one's clothes off.

défrisé [defrize] *a F* **avoir l'air**

défrisé, to look down in the mouth/put out.

défrisement [defrizmɑ̃] *nm F* disappointment.

défriser [defrize] **I** *vtr F* to annoy* (s.o.); to disappoint (s.o.)/ to put (s.o.) out; **ça m'a beaucoup défrisé,** that really got me down **II** *vpr* **se défriser** *F* to lose heart; to feel put out.

défrusquer [defryske] **I** *vtr P* to undress (s.o.) **II** *vpr* **se défrusquer** *P* to undress/to get undressed/to take one's clothes off.

défunter [defœ̃te] *vi P* to die*/to kick the bucket.

dég [deg] *a P* = **dégueulasse.**

dégager [degaʒe] *vtr P* **1.** ça dégage! that's really great!/that's (pretty) amazing! **elle dégage,** she's really something/she's a bit of all right **2.** *int P* **dégage!** get lost!*/ buzz off!/scram!

dégaine [degɛn] *nf F* awkward gait/ungainly bearing/gawkiness; **vise la dégaine!** get a load of/just look at this freak!

dégauchir [degoʃir] *vtr* **1.** *F* **dégauchir qn,** to smarten s.o. up/to knock the rough edges off s.o./to lick s.o. into shape **2.** *P* to find/to get (a flat, etc).

dégelée [deʒle] *nf P* a beating*/a thrashing/a good hiding.

se dégeler [sədeʒle] *vpr F* (*pers*) to become less reserved/to thaw (out)/to loosen up.

déglingué [deglɛ̃ge] *a P* drunk*/ pissed.

déglinguer [deglɛ̃ge] *vtr F* to put out of order/to knock to pieces/to smash up/to bust up/to make a mess of.

dégobillade [degɔbijad] *nf P* vomit/spew/puke.

dégobillage [degɔbijaʒ] *nm P* vomiting/spewing/puking.

dégobiller [degɔbije] *vtr&i* P to vomit*/to throw up/to chuck up/to spew up/to puke (up).

dégobillis [degɔbiji] *nm* P vomit/spew/puke.

dégoiser [degwaze] *vtr&i* F (**en**) **dégoiser**, to talk* a lot/to rattle on/to rabbit on; to spout; **dégoiser tout**, to shoot one's mouth off; **dégoise! speak up! dégoiser sur qn/qch**, to run s.o./sth down; to go on about s.o./sth.

dégommage [degɔmaʒ] *nm* F dismissal/sacking/firing.

dégommer [degɔme] *vtr* F **1.** to dismiss* s.o./to give (s.o.) his marching orders/*NAm* walking orders; **se faire dégommer**, to get the sack/the push **2.** to oust (s.o.)/to push (s.o.) out **3.** to beat/to lick (s.o. at a game) **4.** to unearth; **où as-tu dégommé cette greluche?** where did you dig her up from?

dégonflade [degɔ̃flad] *nf*, **dégonflage** [degɔ̃flaʒ] *nm* F backing down/backing out/climbing down/getting cold feet/chickening out.

dégonflard, arde [degɔ̃flar, -ard], **dégonflé, ée** [degɔ̃fle] P **I** *a* cowardly*/yellow/chicken **II** *n* coward*/yellowbelly/quitter/chicken.

dégonflement [degɔ̃fləmɑ̃] *nm* F debunking (of hero, etc).

dégonfler [degɔ̃fle] **I** *vtr* F **dégonfler qn** (*i*) to take the wind out of s.o.'s sails (*ii*) to debunk (hero, etc) **II** *vpr* **se dégonfler** P **1.** to climb down/to back out/to have cold feet/to funk it/to chicken out/to lose one's bottle; **tu vas pas te dégonfler?** you're not going to chicken out?/(have you) lost your bottle? **2.** to confess*/to come clean/to get it off one's chest.

dégonfleur, euse [degɔ̃flœr, -øz] *a&n* P = **dégonflard, -arde**.

dégorger [degɔrʒe] *vi* V to ejaculate*/to come/to shoot one's load.

dégot(t)er [degɔte] **I** *vtr* F **1.** to find/to pick up/to dig up/to spot/to hit (up)on; **il a dégot(t)é ça chez un antiquaire**, he unearthed that in an antique shop; **je l'ai dégot(t)é chez sa mère**, I ran him to ground at his mother's **2.** (*a*) **dégot(t)er qn**, to oust (s.o.)/to supplant s.o./to knock s.o. off his perch (*b*) **dégot(t)er qn/qch**, to get the better of s.o./sth; to lick/to beat s.o./sth; **il vous dégot(t)e**, he's too clever for you/he's got you beat **II** *vi* P **1.** (*a*) **elle dégot(t)e bien** (*i*) she makes a good impression (*ii*) she looks good/I like the look of her (*b*) **qu'est-ce qu'elle dégot(t)e!** she's got something about her all right **2.** **ça dégot(t)e!** it's first-rate!

dégoulinade [degulinad] *nf* F drip/trickle (of paint, wine, etc).

dégoulinage [degulinaʒ] *nm* F dripping/trickling.

dégoulinante [degulinɑ̃t] *nf* P **1.** clock; watch **2.** run of bad luck.

dégouliner [deguline] *vi* F to trickle (down)/to drip (slowly, drop by drop).

dégoupillonner [degupijɔne] *vi* P to vomit*.

dégourdi [degurdi] *a* (*a*) F **il n'est pas dégourdi pour deux sous** (*i*) he's an old stick-in-the-mud (*ii*) he's a bit slow on the uptake (*b*) P **dégourdi comme un manche**, stupid*/thick (as two short planks)/dumb.

dégourdir [degurdir] **I** *vtr* F **dégourdir qn**, to sharpen s.o.'s wits; to put s.o. wise; **son séjour à Paris l'a dégourdi**, his stay in Paris has taught him a thing or two **II** *vpr* **se dégourdir** F **1.** (*a*) to grow smarter/to get with it/to wise up (*b*) to lose one's innocence/to learn a thing or two **2. se dégourdir la tête,** to get one's head together.

dégourrer [degure] *vtr P* **1.** to disgust; to dishearten **2.** to slander/to malign.

dégoûtance [degutɑ̃s] *nf P* = **dégoûtation.**

dégoûtant [degutɑ̃] *nm F* **un vieux dégoûtant,** a dirty old man.

dégoûtation [degutasjɔ̃] *nf P* disgusting person/thing.

dégoûté [degute] *a F* fastidious/finicky; fussy/choosy/picky; squeamish; **ne faites pas trop le dégoûté,** don't be too squeamish/don't turn your nose up at it! (*iron*) **vous n'êtes pas dégoûté(e)!** you don't want much, do you!

dégrafer [degrafe] **I** *vi P* to run away*/to sling one's hook **II** *vpr* **se dégrafer** *P* to give up/to withdraw; to cry off.

dégrainer [degrɛne] **I** *vtr P* **1.** to disparage* (s.o.)/to run (s.o.) down **2.** to seduce **3.** to get round (s.o.) **II** *vi P* (*a*) to knock off work (for the day) (*b*) to come out on strike.

dégraisser [degrɛse] **I** *vtr* **1.** *P* to steal* **2.** *F* to cut back on staff; **il faut dégraisser,** we've got to make some cutbacks/layoffs **II** *vpr* **se dégraisser 1.** *P* to be ruined **2.** *V* to have sex*.

dégraisseur [degrɛsœr] *nm P* tax collector.

dégréner [degrene] *vtr&i P* = **dégrainer.**

dégringolade [degrɛ̃gɔlad] *nf F* fall/tumble; **faire une dégringolade,** to come a cropper*; **quelle dégringolade après sa dernière situation!** what a comedown after his last job! **la dégringolade du franc,** the collapse of the franc.

dégringolée [degrɛ̃gɔle] *nf F* clutter (of people, things).

dégringoler [degrɛ̃gɔle] **I** *vtr&i F* to fall down/to tumble down; **il a dégringolé l'escalier,** he came tearing/clattering down the stairs/

he came a cropper* on the stairs **II** *vi F* (*a*) (*pers*) to come down in the world (*b*) (*affaires, etc*) to slump/to go to pieces **III** *vtr* **1.** (*a*) *F* **dégringoler l'administration,** to bring the government down (*b*) *P* to kill* (s.o.) **2.** *P* to lend (money) **3.** *P* to steal and hide (sth) quickly/to snatch and stash (sth).

dégrossi [degrosi] *a F* **un (individu) mal dégrossi,** a boor/a lout.

dégrossir [degrosir] **I** *vtr F* **dégrossir qn,** to smarten s.o. up/to lick s.o. into shape **II** *vpr* **se dégrossir** *F* to have the rough edges knocked off one; to smarten up/to acquire polish.

dégrouillard, arde [degrujar, -ard] *a&n F* = **débrouillard, -arde.**

se dégrouiller [sədegruje] *vpr F* to hurry* (up)/to get a move on/to get cracking; **allez, dégrouillez-vous!** come on, get a move on!/come on, get your finger out!

déguerpir [degɛrpir] *vi F* to run away*/to clear out/to beat it; **faire déguerpir qn,** to send s.o. off with a flea in his ear.

déguerpissement [degɛrpismɑ̃] *nm F* clearing off/clearing out/skedaddling.

dégueu [degø] *a P* (= **dégueulasse**) **c'est pas dégueu!** that's not bad!/that's pretty good!/that's great!

dégueulade [degølad, -gœ-] *nf P* vomit/spew/puke.

dégueulasse [degølas, -gœ-] *P* **I** *a* disgusting/repulsive/sickening; lousy; crappy; rotten; **un type dégueulasse,** a creep **II** *nm&f* disgusting/repulsive person; louse; creep; **c'est un petit dégueulasse!** he's a filthy little beast/sod!

dégueulasserie [degølasri, -gœ-] *nf P* (*a*) repulsiveness/vileness (*b*) **une dégueulasserie,** a vile/disgusting thing, etc.

dégueulatoire [degølatwar, -gœ-] *a P* revolting/sickening/sick-making/puke-making.

dégueulbi(f) [degølbi(f), -gœ-], **dégueulebite** [degølbit, -gœ-] *a V* = **dégueulasse**.

dégueulée [degøle, -gœ-] *nf P* **1.** vomit/spew **2.** une **dégueulée** (d'injures), a volley of abuse.

dégueulement [degølmɑ̃ -gœ-] *nm P* vomit(ing)/spew(ing).

dégueuler [degøle, -gœ-] *vtr&i P* **1.** to vomit*/to throw up/to puke (up)/to chuck up **2.** to speak/to say; **dégueule!** out with it!/spit it out! **dégueuler sur le compte de qn**, to criticize* s.o./to run s.o. down.

dégueulis [degøli, -gœ-] *nm P* vomiting/spewing/puking.

dégueuloir [degølwar] *nm P* mouth*/gob.

dégueulpif [degølpif, -gœ-] *a V* = **dégueulbi(f)**.

déguster [degyste] *vtr P* **déguster des coups**, to get a good hiding; **qu'est-ce qu'on a dégusté!** we didn't half catch/cop it!

se déhancher [sədeɑ̃ʃe] *vpr F* to sway/to wiggle one's hips when walking.

déharnacher [dearnaʃe] *vtr P* to undress (a woman).

dehors [dəɔr] **I** *nm P* (*prostituée*) **faire le dehors**, to walk the streets/to be a street-walker **II** *adv* **il est con dehors comme dedans**, he really is as stupid*/dumb/thick as he looks.

déhotter [deɔte] *P* **I** *vtr* **1.** to eject (s.o.)/to throw (s.o.) out/to turn (s.o.) out **2.** = **dégot(t)er I, 1 II** *vi* to run away*/to clear off/to beat it **III** *vpr* **se déhotter** *P* to hurry away/to get moving/to get a move on/to get cracking.

déjeté [deʒte, deʃte] *a F* (= **décatl**) **il/elle n'est pas déjeté(e)**, he's/she's well-preserved.

délinger [delɛ̃ʒe], **déloquer** [delɔke] **I** *vtr P* to undress (s.o.) **II** *vpr* **se délinger** *P* to undress/to get undressed/to strip off.

délourder [delurde] *vtr P* (*i*) to open (*ii*) to break down (a door). (*Voir* **lourde**; **lourder**)

démanché [demɑ̃ʃe] *a F* **1.** (*meuble*) rickety **2.** (*pers*) ungainly/hulking.

démancher [demɑ̃ʃe] **I** *vtr F* **démancher un complot**, to upset a plot. (*Voir* **trou 8**) **II** *vpr* **se démancher** *F* **se démancher pour obtenir qch**, to go to a lot of trouble/to put oneself out to get sth.

demander [dəmɑ̃de] *vtr F* **1. il ne demande que plaies et bosses**, he's always asking for trouble **2. je vous demande un peu!** I ask you!/did you ever! **3. faut pas lui en demander (trop)!** it's no use getting him to do it!/you mustn't ask too much of him! (*Voir* **heure**)

démangeaison [demɑ̃ʒɛzɔ̃] *nf F* **j'avais une démangeaison de lui demander s'il l'était**, I was itching to ask him whether he was.

démanger [demɑ̃ʒe] *vi F* (*a*) **la langue lui démangeait**, he was itching to speak; **la main me démangeait de lui flanquer une gifle**, my fingers were itching to give him a clout (*b*) **gratter qn où ça le démange**, to toady to s.o./to scratch s.o.'s back.

démantibuler [demɑ̃tibyle] **I** *vtr F* **démantibuler qch** (*i*) to put sth out of order (*ii*) to take sth to pieces/to bits (*iii*) to break sth up/to smash sth to pieces **II** *vpr* **se démantibuler** *F* to come to pieces/to break up/to fall apart.

se démaquer [sədemake] *vpr P* (*couple*) to separate/to break up/to split up.

déménager [demenaʒe] *F* **I** *vi* **1.** to be mad*; **il déménage**, he's off his head/he's got a screw loose **2.** to clear off/to do a bunk; **faire**

déménager qn, to chuck s.o. out; **allez, déménagez!** hop it!/scram! **3.** (*esp musique*) **ça déménage un max!** that's really great!/that's really something! (*Voir* **cloche I 4**) **II** *vtr* (*cambrioleurs*) **déménager la maison,** to strip the house (of its contents).

démerdard, arde [demɛrdar, -ard] **I** *a* **V** resourceful*/crafty/ shrewd **II** *n* resourceful* person; **c'est un démerdard,** he's a shrewd customer/there are no flies on him/ he's a crafty sod/he can look after himself; **c'est un démerdard à rebours,** he's a clumsy bugger.

démerde [demɛrd] **V I** *a* = **démerdard I II** *nf* (**système**) **démerde,** resourcefulness; wangling. (*Voir* **D**)

démerder [demɛrde] **I** *vtr* **V** **démerder qn,** to get s.o. out of a mess/out of the shit **II** *vpr* **se démerder** **V** **1.** (*a*) to get by/to manage (to get along)/to make out; **je me démerde,** I get by/I'm doing fine (*b*) to get out of a mess/out of the shit; **savoir se démerder,** to know how to get out of trouble/to know how to look after oneself; **démerde-toi!** get (yourself) out of that then! **2.** to hurry* up/to get one's arse into gear/to move it; **allez, démerde-toi!** come on, get your finger out!/come on, shift your arse! **3. se démerder de qch,** to get rid of sth.

démerdeur, euse [demɛrdœr, -øz] **V I** *a* = **démerdard, -arde II** *nm* lawyer/(defending) counsel.

demi [dəmi] *nm* **F** glass of beer/ = a half(-pint); **deux demis, s'il vous plaît!** two halves, please!

demi-cercle [dəmisɛrkl] *nm* **pincer/repincer qn au demi-cercle** (*i*) **F** to catch s.o. napping/off his guard/ on the hop (*ii*) **F** to get even with s.o./to fix s.o. (*iii*) **P** to arrest* s.o.

demi-cigue [dəmisig] *nm* **O P** ten

francs; ten-franc note. (*Voir* **cigue 2**) (*pl* **demi-cigues**)

démieller [demjɛle] **I** *vtr* **P** (*euph de* **démerder**) to get (s.o.) out of a fix*/a mess/a jam **II** *vpr* **se démieller** **P** to get out of a fix*/a mess/a jam.

demi-jambe [dəmiʒɑ̃b] *nf,* **demi-jetée** [dəmiʒəte] *nf,* **demi-livre** [dəmilivr] *nf* **P** fifty francs; fifty-franc note. (*pl* **demi-jambes, -jetées, -livres**)

demi-molle [dəmimɔl] *a phr* **P** **être/l'avoir en demi-molle,** to be unenthusiastic/not over-keen/half-hearted.

demi-plombe [dəmiplɔ̃b] *nf* **P** half an hour. (*Voir* **plombe**) (*pl* **demi-plombes**)

demi-porkesse [dəmipɔrkɛs] *nf* **P** = **demi-portion.** (*pl* **demi-porkesses**)

demi-portion [dəmipɔrsjɔ̃] *nf* **F** (*a*) undersized* person/half-pint/ shorty/short-ass/shrimp/weed/dead loss. (*pl* **demi-portions**)

demi-sac [dəmisak] *nm* **P** five hundred francs. (*pl* **demi-sacs**)

demi-sel [dəmisɛl] *nm* **P** **1.** petty criminal/small-time crook **2.** petty/small-time pimp*. (*pl* **demi-sels**)

demi-sigue [dəmisig] *nm* **P** = **demi-cigue.** (*pl* **demi-sigues**)

demi-tour! [dəmitur] *int* **P** hop it!/clear off!/beat it!

démo [demo] *nm&f* **F** demonstration cassette/record/tape; demo.

démoduler [demɔdyle] *vtr* **P** **démoduler qn,** to silence s.o./to shut s.o. up.

demoiselle [dəmwazɛl] *nf* **P** **1.** (*régional*) **comment va votre demoiselle?** how's your daughter? **2.** shy man; **il est comme une demoiselle au piano,** he's as gentle as a lamb/ as nice as pie **3.** (*turf*) filly **4.** half-bottle of red wine.

démolir [demɔlir] *vtr* **1.** *F* to thrash s.o. (to within an inch of his life)/to give (s.o.) the hiding of his life **2.** *P* to kill*/to bump off.

démolissage [demɔlisaʒ] *nm F* severe criticism*/slating/roasting/panning.

démonitisation [demɔnitizasjɔ̃] *nf F* discrediting (of politician, etc).

démonétiser [demɔnetize] *vtr F* to discredit (s.o.).

démonté [demɔ̃te] *a* (*a*) *F* temporarily without a car (*b*) *P* (*souteneur*) temporarily without a woman to live off.

démonter [demɔ̃te] *vtr F* to unnerve/to upset; **la nouvelle m'a complètement démonté,** I was really cut up/put out by the news; **il ne se laisse pas démonter,** he isn't easily flummoxed.

se démouscailler [sədemuskaje] *vpr P* = **se démerder 1.** (*Voir* **mouscaille**)

démouscailleur, euse [demuskajœr, -øz] *a&n P* = **démerdard, arde I, II.**

démurger [demyrʒe] **I** *vi P* to leave/to run off (in a hurry) **II** *vpr* **se démurger** *P* to hurry off/away.

déniaiser [denjɛze] *vtr F* **1.** to teach (s.o.) the ways of the world/to teach (s.o.) a thing or two **2.** to initiate (s.o.) sexually; **elle s'est fait déniaiser,** she's lost her virginity*/she's learnt a thing or two.

dénicher [deniʃe] *F* **I** *vtr* to find/to discover; **où as-tu bien pu dénicher ce vieux tacot?** where the devil did you dig up that old banger/crate? (*Voir* **filon 2**) **II** *vi* **dénicher sans tambour ni trompette,** to move off quietly, without attracting attention **III** *vpr* **se dénicher** *F* to find (a job, a flat).

dénicheur, euse [deniʃœr, -øz] *n F* searcher/ferreter (out); **dénicheur de talent(s),** talent scout;

headhunter; **dénicheur de merles** (*i*) rogue/cheat (*ii*) smart Alec.

se dénipper [sədenipe] *vpr P* to undress/to get undressed.

dent [dɑ̃] *nf* **1.** *F* **avoir la dent,** to be hungry*; **j'ai une de ces dents!** I'm so hungry I could eat a horse! **2.** *F* **avoir les dents longues** (*i*) to be very hungry*; to be famished/starving (*ii*) to be very ambitious; to be greedy/grasping **3.** *F* (*pers*) **avoir de la dent,** to be still young **4.** *F* (*cheval*) **avoir mal aux dents,** to be prevented from winning/to be pulled/to be nobbled **5.** *F* (*a*) **avoir la dent dure,** to be biting/sarcastic (*b*) **donner un coup de dent à qn,** to criticize* s.o. severely/to have a go at s.o. (*c*) **avoir/conserver/garder une dent contre qn,** to bear s.o. a grudge/to have it in for s.o. **6.** *F* (*a*) **être sur les dents** (*i*) to be exhausted* (*ii*) to be under pressure (from work or business) (*b*) **mettre qn sur les dents,** to work s.o. to death/to knock s.o. up **7.** *V* **se laver des dents,** to have cunnilingus*/to eat hair-pie. (*Voir* **poule 5**)

dentelle [dɑ̃tɛl] *nf F* **1.** **avoir les pieds en dentelle,** to refuse to agree to sth; to refuse to budge; to sit tight **2.** **faire dans la dentelle,** to be extra careful/to wear kid gloves; **il ne fait pas dans la dentelle,** he goes in feet first/he just dives straight in.

dentiste [dɑ̃tist] *nm P* **aller au dentiste,** to look for food/for something to eat.

se dépager [sədepaʒe], **se dépagnoter** [sədepaɲɔte] *vpr P* to get out of bed/to show a leg/to rise and shine.

dépannage [depanaʒ] *nm F* (*a*) tiding over/helping out; **tu pourrais pas me faire un petit dépannage?** could you just give me a hand?/could you do me a small favour? (*b*) fresh start (in one's career, etc).

dépanner [depane] vtr F **dépanner qn**, to tide s.o. over/to help s.o. out; to bail s.o. out; to get s.o. out of a difficulty/a hole; **j'ai oublié mon portefeuille, tu pourrais pas me dépanner?** I've forgotten my wallet, do you think you could drop me a few quid/a few bucks?

déparler [deparle] vi F **1.** to talk nonsense*; to ramble; to become incoherent/inarticulate through drink **2. il ne déparle pas,** he never stops talking.

départ [depar] nm F **piquer un départ,** to make a quick exit; to shoot off/to beat it.

se dépatouiller [sədepatuje] vpr P to get out of a fix*/a mess/a jam.

dépendeur [depɑ̃dœr] nm F **grand dépendeur d'andouilles,** tall and lanky good-for-nothing.

déphasé [defɑze] a F disoriented; (i) **je suis un peu déphasé aujourd'hui,** I'm just not with it today (ii) **il est complètement déphasé,** he's not all there/he's off his rocker.

dépiauter [depjote] **I** vtr F **1.** to skin (a rabbit, etc) **2.** to take (sth) to pieces **3.** to pull (a book, a play, a writer, etc) to pieces **II** vpr **se dépiauter** P to undress/to strip/to peel (off).

se dépieuter [sədepjøte] vpr P to get out of bed/to show a leg.

dépiquer [depike] vtr P to take (sth) out of pawn/out of hock.

déplanquer [deplɑ̃ke] P **I** vtr (a) to take (sth) out of its hiding-place (b) to take (sth) out of one's pocket (c) to take (sth) out of pawn **II** vi (a) to come out of hiding (b) to leave prison **III** vpr **se déplanquer** P to come out of hiding.

déplumé [deplyme] F **I** a (a) bald*; **c'est un mec d'une trentaine d'années un peu déplumé,** he's a balding thirty. (Voir **melon 1**) (b) penniless*/cleaned out/broke (c) **avoir l'air déplumé,** to look shabby/threadbare **II** nm bald(-headed)* person/baldie/baldy.

déplumer [deplyme] **I** vtr F **déplumer qn,** to clean s.o. out (at gambling) **II** vpr **se déplumer 1.** F to go bald*/to lose one's thatch **2.** P to get out of bed.

dépocher [depɔʃe] vtr F (a) to produce (sth) from one's pocket (b) to pay* up/to fork out (money)/to cough up.

se dépoisser [sədepwase] vpr P to extricate oneself (from financial difficulties, etc); to get out of a mess.

dépoivrer [depwavre] vi P to lay off the booze/to be on the waggon.

dépon(n)er [depɔne] **I** vtr P (a) to discourage (b) to disgust **II** vi V to defecate*/to drop one's load.

dépoter [depɔte] vtr (a) F (chauffeur de taxi) to drop off (a passenger) (b) F to exhume (a body) (c) P to give birth to/to drop (a baby). (Voir **géranium**)

dépotoir [depɔtwar] nm F **ma classe est le dépotoir de l'école,** I've got the dregs of the school in my class; V **son cul, c'est un vrai dépotoir,** she's been laid by just about everyone.

dépouille [depuj] nf P stealing/theft (of s.o.'s money, clothes, etc); mugging.

dépouiller [depuje] vtr P to steal (s.o.'s money, clothes, etc); to mug s.o.

déprime [deprim] nf F nervous depression; **il est en pleine déprime,** he's got the blues/he's really low.

dépucelage [depys(ə)laʒ] nm F deflowering (of a virgin); **son dépucelage c'était à 14 ans,** his/her first time was at 14; he/she had it for the first time at 14.

dépuceler [depys(ə)le] vtr **1.** F (a) to deflower (a virgin); **il s'est fait dépuceler par une pute,** he had

it with a prostitute the first time (*b*)
to open (a new packet of cigarettes,
etc); to cut (the pages of a book);
to christen (a bottle of wine, etc)
2. *P* **dépuceler sa gueule,** to be sea-
sick.

déquiller [dekije] *vtr F* **déquiller
qn** (*i*) to knock s.o. over/off his
pins (*ii*) to cripple s.o. (*iii*) to oust
s.o. from his/her job; to kick s.o.
out of their job.

der [dɛr] *n F* (*abbr = dernier(s),
-ière(s)*) (*i*) **le/la der (des der),** the
last (of all) (*ii*) **le der des der,** the
lowest of the low; **viens boire le der
des der,** let's have a last drink/let's
have one for the road; **la der des
der,** the war to end all wars. (*Voir*
tierce 2)

dérailler [deraje] *vi F* (*pers*) **1.** to
take the wrong turning/the wrong
path **2.** to talk rubbish/to talk
through one's hat **3.** to go off the
rails/to go (all) to pieces.

déramer [derame] **I** *vi P* to die*
II *vpr* **se déramer** *P* to commit
suicide/to do oneself in.

dérâté [derate] *nm F* **courir comme
un dérâté,** to run like mad/like the
clappers.

se dérâter [səderate] *vpr F* to run
like mad/like the clappers.

derche [dɛrʃ] *nm,* **derge** [dɛrʒ]
nm P **1.** (*a*) buttocks*; **papier à
derche,** toilet paper/bum-fodder;
avoir le feu au derche, to be in a
tearing hurry; **se magner le derche,**
to get a move on (*b*) anus*/
arsehole/*esp NAm* asshole **2. un
faux derche** (*i*) a shifty/shady customer (*ii*) a hypocrite (*iii*) a traitor/
a double-crosser.

dergeot [dɛrʒo] *prep & adv P*
behind.

dériper [deripe] *vi P* to run away*/
to clear off/to beat it.

dérive [deriv] *nf F* (*pers*) **aller à la
dérive,** to wander around aimlessly/
to drift.

derjo [dɛrʒo] *prep & adv P* behind;
le jardin est derjo, the garden's at
the back.

dernière [dɛrnjɛr] *nf F* **1. tu connais la dernière?** have you heard
the latest? **2.** (*turf*) **toucher la
dernière,** to back the winner of the
last race.

dérober [derɔbe] **I** *vi F* **1.** to
run away*/to make oneself scarce;
je ne pouvais pas dérober, I
couldn't slip off on the quiet **2.** to
dodge the issue/to back out **II** *vpr*
se dérober 1. *F* to deviate/to
leave the straight and narrow **2.** *P*
to go on the loose.

dérondir [derɔ̃dir] **I** *vtr P* to
sober (s.o.) up **II** *vpr* **se dérondir**
P to sober up/to get over one's
drink.

dérouillade [derujad] *nf,* **dé-
rouille** [deruj] *nf,* **dérouillée**
[deruje] *nf P* thrashing/beating(-
up); **prendre une/la dérouillade,** to
get a good hiding/belting; **passer
qn à la dérouille/filer une dérouillée
à qn,** to give s.o. a good hiding.

dérouiller [deruje] **I** *vtr* **1.** *F*
dérouiller qn, to rub the corners off
s.o./to lick s.o. into shape **2.** *P* to
thrash (s.o.) to beat (s.o.) up*/to
clobber (s.o.)/to work s.o. over **II**
vi P **1. (en) dérouiller,** to get pun-
ished; **qu'est-ce qu'il va dérouiller!**
he won't half cop it! **se faire dérouiller** (*i*) to get beaten up (*ii*) to
get killed/to get done in **2. qu'est-
ce que j'ai dérouillé!** I really went
through hell! **3.** (*a*) (*dans un
magasin*) to make the first sale of
the day (*b*) (*prostituée*) to pick up
the first client of the day. (*Voir*
jambe 2) **III** *vpr* **se dérouiller** *P*
to hurry* up/to get a move on.

dérouler [derule] *vi P* to (go on a)
pub-crawl/to go pub-crawling.

derrière [dɛrjɛr] *nm F* buttocks*/
behind/backside/bottom/*NAm*
fanny; **se lever le derrière le premier,** to get out of bed on the

wrong side; *P* **péter plus haut que son derrière** (*i*) to swank*/to show off*/to be snooty/to put on airs; **elle pète plus haut que son derrière,** she thinks she's really something/ the bee's knees (*ii*) to try to bite off more than one can chew; **se taper le derrière par terre/sur le coin d'un meuble,** to laugh* uproariously/to be in stitches; **il n'y a pas de quoi se taper le derrière par terre,** there's nothing to be jubilant about. (*Voir* **astap(e); botter 1; feu 1; se magner**)

désaper [desape] **I** *vtr P* to undress (s.o.) **II** *vpr* **se désaper** *P* to undress/to get undressed.

désargenté [dezarʒɑ̃te] *a F* (*a*) penniless*/out of money (*b*) short of money/cash.

désargenter [dezarʒɑ̃te] *vtr F* to clean s.o. out of money; **ces dépenses m'ont complètement désargenté,** these expenses have completely cleaned me out.

descendre [desɑ̃dr] **I** *vtr P* **1.** to kill*; **se faire descendre,** to get bumped off/done in **2. faire descendre,** to abort (an unborn child) **3.** to debunk; **descendre qn en flammes,** to shoot s.o. down in flames **4.** to down/to knock back (a drink) **II** *vi F* **mon dîner ne descend pas,** my dinner won't go down.

descente [desɑ̃t] *nf* **1.** *P* capacity for downing drink(s) (*esp* alcohol); big swallow **2.** *P* **descente de lit,** individual who would stoop to anything **3.** *F* **descente (de police),** (police) raid/bust **4.** *V* **descente à la cave/au barbu/au lac,** cunnilingus*/pearl-diving/muff-diving.

se désemplumer [sədezɑ̃plyme] *vpr F* to go bald*/to lose one's thatch.

se désentifler [sədezɑ̃tifle] *vpr P* to get divorced/to split up.

désert [dezɛr] *nm P* deserter.

déshabillage [dezabijaʒ] *nm F*

severe criticism*/dressing down; slating (of play, etc).

déshabiller [dezabije] *vtr F* **déshabiller qn** (*i*) to lay bare s.o.'s soul/s.o.'s innermost thoughts (*ii*) to criticize* s.o. severely/to give s.o. a dressing down; **déshabiller une pièce,** to slate a play.

désinto(x) [dezɛ̃tɔks] *nf P* (= *(une cure de) désintoxication*) detoxification/treatment for alcoholism *or* drug addiction; **faire une désinto(x),** to dry out.

se désopiler [sədezɔpile] *vpr F* to laugh* uproariously/to shake with laughter. (*Voir* **rate**)

désordre [dezɔrdr] *a P* disorganized/untidy.

désossé, ée [dezɔse] *a&n F* tall/ lanky (person).

désosser [dezɔse] *vtr F* (*a*) to break up/to strip down/to dismantle (a car, etc) (*b*) to dissect (a book, etc).

dessalé, ée [desale] *F* **I** *a* sharp/wide awake*/with it **II** *n* man/woman of the world; someone who has learnt a thing or two.

dessaler [desale] **I** *vtr F* **dessaler qn,** to put s.o. wise/to teach s.o. a thing or two/to open s.o.'s eyes **II** *vpr* **se dessaler** *F* to learn a thing or two/to learn the facts of life/to get with it/to wise up.

desserre [desɛr] *nf F* **être dur à la desserre,** to be mean*/close-fisted/ stingy.

dessin [desɛ̃] *nm F* **veux-tu que je te fasse un dessin?** do I have to spell it out for you (in words of one syllable)?/do you want a diagram?

dessouder [desude] *P* **I** *vtr* to kill*/to bump off/to do in **II** *vtr&i* **dessouder/la dessouder/se la dessouder,** to die*/to peg out.

dessous [dəsu] *nm* **1.** *F* **avoir le dessous,** to get the worst of it **2.** *F* **il y avait là un dessous que je ne**

comprenais pas, there was some mystery about it that I didn't understand **3.** *F* **être (tombé) dans le troisième/le sixième/le trente-sixième dessous** (*i*) to be penniless*/to be down and out (*ii*) to be completely discredited (*iii*) to be depressed*/down in the dumps **4.** *P* pimp's second woman **5.** *P* prostitute's fancy man. (*Voir* **carte 3**)

dessous-de-table [d(ə)sudtabl] *nm inv F* bribe/underhand commission/kickback/backhander.

dessus [dəsy] *adv F* **elle m'est tombée dessus (comme une furie),** she went off at me (something) alarming.

dételer [detle] *vi* **1.** *F* to take it easy*/to slow down/to ease up **2.** *F* to settle down (after a hectic life) **3.** *F* **sans dételer,** at a stretch/ straight off/without stopping **4.** *P* to leave one's wife*/to walk out on one's wife; to get a divorce/to get unhitched.

détente [detãt] *nf F* **être dur à la détente,** to be mean*/close-fisted/ stingy.

déterré [detɛre] *a F* **avoir une mine/une figure/une tête de déterré,** to look drawn and haggard/to look ghastly/to look like a living corpse/ to look like death (warmed up).

détrancher [detrãʃe] **I** *vtr P* **1. détrancher qn,** to distract s.o.'s attention **2. se faire détrancher,** to be spotted **II** *vpr* **se détrancher** *P* **1.** to look round; to turn round **2.** to change one's bet at the last moment.

détraqué [detrake] *a F* mad*; **être un peu détraqué,** to have a screw loose/to be a bit nutty/to be nuts.

(se) détraquer [sədetrake] *vpr F* (*pers*) to go (all) to pieces/to go off the rails.

détréper [detrepe] *vi P* (*camelots, etc*) to get rid of unlikely customers.

détroncher, se détroncher [(sə)detrɔ̃ʃe] *vtr & pr* = **(se) détrancher.**

deuche [døʃ] *nf,* **deudeuche** [dødøʃ] *nf F* (*aut* = *deux chevaux*) Citroën 2CV (*RTM*).

deuil [dœj] *nm* **1.** *F* **avoir les ongles en deuil,** to have dirty fingernails **2.** *F* **en faire son deuil,** to resign oneself to (the loss of) sth/to kiss sth goodbye **3.** *P* (*a*) **porter le deuil,** to lodge a complaint (*esp* with the police) (*b*) **aller au deuil,** to be in touch with the police (*c*) **il y a du deuil,** it's dangerous/ risky.

deusio [døzjo] *adv P* secondly.

deux [dø] *num a inv & nm* **1.** *F* **en moins de deux/deux coups les gros,** very quickly/immediately*/in no time at all/in two shakes (of a lamb's tail)/in two ticks **2.** *F* **c'est deux/ça fait deux,** that's two (completely) different things **3.** *F* **se casser en deux,** to double up (*i*) after a blow (*ii*) with laughter **4.** *P* **il était moins deux,** it was a close shave/a narrow shave/a near thing **5.** *P* (*souteneur*) **faire le coup de deux,** to live off two women. (*Voir* **attelé**) **6.** *V* **(de) mes deux!** balls!/ bollocks! **tiens, mes deux!** not bloody likely!*/not effing likely!/ not sodding likely! **7.** *P* **un deux soutados,** a cheap and inferior cigar/a stinkaduro.

deuxio [døzjo] *adv P* secondly.

deux-pattes [døpat] *nf P* = **deuche.**

deuzio [døzjo] *adv P* secondly.

dévalisé [devalize] *a F* (*magasin*) **être dévalisé,** to be sold right out of stock/to be cleaned out.

devant [dəvã] *nm* **1.** *F* **se faire arrondir le devant,** to become pregnant* **2.** *F* **bâtir sur le devant,** to develop a paunch/to get pot-bellied/to get a beer belly **3.** *P* male genitals*/bag of tricks.

devanture [dəvãtyr] *nf* **1.** *F* **lécher les devantures**, to go window-shopping **2.** *P* **faire la devanture**, to carry out a smash-and-grab raid **3.** *F* **se faire refaire la devanture** (*i*) to have a face-lift (*ii*) to get one's face bashed in **4.** *P* breasts*/boobs. (*Voir* **gondoler**)

déveinard [devɛnar] *nm F* (*a*) gambler, etc, whose luck is out (*b*) consistently unlucky man.

déveine [devɛn] *nf F* (run of) bad luck; **avoir la déveine/être en déveine/être dans la déveine**, to be out of luck/down on one's luck; to hit a bad patch.

dévider [devide] *vtr F* to reel off/ to ad-lib (a story, etc); **dévider le jars**, to talk slang.

dévisser [devise] **I** *vtr P* **1.** to injure (s.o.) (seriously) **2.** to kill* (s.o.) **3.** to find/to unearth/to dig up **4. dévisser le mironton**, to have a miscarriage. (*Voir* **billard 5**; **trou 8**) **II** *vi F* (*alpiniste*) to lose one's hold/to slip/to fall **III** *vpr* **se dévisser 1.** *F* **nom qui se dévisse** (*i*) double-barrelled name (*ii*) name with the nobiliary particle *de* **2.** *P* to leave*/to make tracks/to beat it **3.** *P* to die*.

dévorer [devɔre] *vtr V* to eat/to go down on (s.o.).

dévoreuse [devɔrøz] *nf P* hot stuff/red-hot mamma/hot number.

dézinguer [dezɛ̃ge] *vtr P* **1. dézinguer qch**, to smash sth up/to demolish sth **2. dézinguer qn**, to kill* s.o./to bump s.o. off.

diam(e) [djam] *nm P* diamond; *pl* **diam's, diames**, sparklers/rocks/ice.

diap [djap] *nf F* = **diapo**.

diapason [djapazɔ̃] *nm F* (*a*) **monter le diapason**, to raise one's voice (*b*) **baisser le diapason à qn**, to take s.o. down a peg (or two).

diapo [djapo] *nf F* (= *diapositive*) slide/transparency.

diche [diʃ] *nf P* headmistress.

dico [diko] *nm F* dictionary.

didi [didi] *nm,* **didine** [didin] *nf V* female genitals*/cunt.

didis [didi] *nmpl F* fingers.

didite [didit] *nf P* (*turf*) **faire didite**, to back/to have a bet on a horse that dead-heats.

Dieu [djø] *nm & int* **1.** *F* **Dieu merci!** thank goodness! **mon Dieu!/ grand Dieu!** heavens (above)!/dear me! **mon Dieu, mon Dieu!** good heavens!/really! **mon Dieu oui!** why, yes! **mon Dieu non!** well, no! **mon Dieu je n'en sais rien!** I'm sure I don't know! **pour l'amour de Dieu!** for goodness' sake!/for heaven's sake! **Dieu sait si j'ai travaillé**, God knows, I've worked hard enough **2.** *P* (*blasphèmes*) **bon Dieu (de bon Dieu)!/Dieu de Dieu!/(sacré) nom de Dieu!** God almighty!/my God!/Christ!/Jesus (Christ)!/Jeez(e)! **ce sacré bon Dieu d'idiot!** this goddam idiot! **ce n'est pas Dieu possible!** it ain't ruddy (well) possible!

digérer [diʒere] *vtr F* to swallow/to stomach (an insult, etc); **je ne digère pas ça**, I can't take that (sort of thing); that sticks in my stomach.

digeste [diʒɛst] *a F* (*nourriture*) easily digestible.

digestion [diʒɛstjɔ̃] *nf F* **lettre de digestion**, bread-and-butter letter.

digue [dig] *adv P* **que digue**, nothing* at all/damn all/sweet FA.

dig(ue)-dig(ue) [digdig] *nf P* **tomber en dig(ue)-dig(ue)** (*i*) to faint (*ii*) to have an epileptic fit.

dimanche [dimãʃ] *nm F* **il est né/ il est venu au monde un dimanche**, he was born tired; **c'est tous les jours dimanche!** every day's a holiday!/this is the life!

dinde [dɛ̃d] *nf F* (*a*) (*fille*) **petite dinde**, little goose/little softy; **quelles dindes que mes élèves cette année!** what a hopeless bunch of

girls I've got in my class this year!
(b) stupid woman; **prendre le thé avec un tas de vieilles dindes**, to take tea with a lot of old hens/old trouts.

dindon [dɛ̃dɔ̃] *nm* F fool*/clot/ prize idiot; **être le dindon de la farce**, to be the victim of a joke/to be the fall-guy/to be the mug.

dindonner [dɛ̃dɔne] *vtr* F **dindonner qn**, to fool s.o./to take s.o. in; to make a sucker/a mug of s.o.

dîne [din] *nf* P meal; food; **aller à la dîne**, to go and eat.

dingo(t), **ote** [dɛ̃go, -ɔt], **dingue**[1] [dɛ̃g] P **I** *a* (a) mad*/ bonkers/crackers/nuts (b) weird/ screwy (c) **être dingue de qn**, to be infatuated* with s.o./to be potty about s.o.; **elle en est dingue (de ce type)**, she's nuts/crazy about him **II** *n* crackpot/nutcase/screwball/ loony/nutter; **la maison/la baraque aux dingues**, the madhouse/the loony bin.

dingue[2] *nf* P jemmy/*NAm* jimmy.

dinguer [dɛ̃ge] *vi* P (a) **envoyer dinguer qch** (i) to chuck sth up (ii) to fling sth out/to chuck sth away (b) **envoyer dinguer qn** (i) to send s.o. packing*/to tell s.o. to get lost (ii) to send s.o. spinning/reeling (**contre**, against); to send s.o. flying.

dire [dir] *vtr* F **1. à qui le dites-vous?** you're telling me!/as if I didn't know!/don't I (just) know it! **2. ce n'est/c'est pas pour dire, mais ...**, you can say what you like, but ...; there's no getting away from it ... **3. ce n'est (pas tout) rien de le dire!** and no mistake!/you bet! **4. y a pas à dire**, there's no denying it/there's no getting away from it/ there's no two ways about it **5. je ne lui ai pas envoyé dire**, I told him (so) straight (to his face)/I let him have it straight **6. c'est moi qui vous le dis!** (you can) take my word for it!/need I say more?/say no more! **7. qu'il dit**, says he; so

he says; **que tu dis!** that's what *you* say!/*sez* you! (*Voir* **autre**; **comme I 3**)

direlot [dirlo] *nm* P = **dirlingue**.

dirigeoir [diriʒwar] *nm* P handle-bars (of bicycle).

dirlingue [dirlɛ̃g] *nm*, **dirlo(t)** [dirlo] *nm* P (= *directeur*) **1.** headmaster **2.** director.

disciplote [disiplɔt] *nf* P (*mil*) discipline; (= *Bat d'Af*) **compagnies de disciplote**, disciplinary companies (stationed formerly in North Africa).

disco [disko] *nf* F (*abbr* = *discothèque*) disco; **musique disco**, disco music; **danser disco**, to dance disco; to go disco dancing; **se fringuer disco**, to wear disco clothes/to dress disco.

discutailler [diskytaje] *vi* F (a) to argue the toss/to argufy (b) to chatter/to natter away; to rabbit on.

discuter [diskyte] *vtr* F **discuter le bout (de gras)/le coup (de gras)** (a) to argue the toss/to argufy (b) to talk about things in general; to have a good old natter/chinwag.

disputailler [dispytaje] *vi* F to wrangle/to bicker/to squabble (**sur**, about).

disputaillerie [dispytajri] *nf* F (petty) squabble; bickering.

disputailleur, **euse** [dispytajœr, -øz] F **I** *a* fond of bicker-ing; cantankerous **II** *n* squabbler.

disputer [dispyte] *vtr* F **disputer qn**, to tell s.o. off/to tick s.o. off.

disque [disk] *nm* **1.** F **changer de disque** (i) to change one's tune (ii) to change the subject; **change(z) de disque!** put another record on!/give it a rest! **2.** F **siffler au disque** (i) to whistle for sth (ii) to ask for sth in vain/to whistle for it **3.** V anus*; **casser le disque**, to have anal sex*/to sodomize; **se faire casser le disque**, to be buggered/

arse-fucked/*NAm* ass-fucked; to get one's arse/*NAm* ass fucked.

disserte [disɛrt] *nf F* (*scol*) (= *dissertation*) essay.

distingué [distɛ̃ge] *nm F* large glass of beer (one litre).

distinguo [distɛ̃go] *nm F* distinction; **faire le distinguo**, to make a subtle distinction.

distribe [distrib] *nf F* (*mil*) (= *distribution*) issue (of army rations).

distribution [distribysjɔ̃] *nf P* thrashing/beating (up).

dix [dis] *num a inv & nm inv* **1.** *F* **ça vaut dix!** (*i*) that's excellent*!/ ten out of ten! (*ii*) (*of story, etc*) that's a good one! **2.** *F* **je vous le donne en dix**, I'll give you ten guesses; you'll never guess **3.** *P* (*prisonnier*) **piquer le dix**, to pace up and down (in one's cell)/to get tired **4.** *F* **marcher à la dix heures dix**, to walk with one's feet turned out/with one's feet at a quarter to three **5.** *V* **dix (sous/ronds)**, anus*.

DKV [dekave] *a&n F P* = **decavé, ée.**

doc [dɔk] *F* **I** *nm* doctor/doc/medico **II** *nf* = **docu.**

doche [dɔʃ] *P* **I** *nf* mother*. (*Voir* **belle-doche**) **II** *nmpl* **les doches**, parents **III** *nfpl* **1.** (*a*) dice (*b*) teeth*; **boîte à doches**, domino box **2.** **avoir ses doches**, to have a period*/to be on the rag.

docu [dɔky] *nm F* (*a*) document(s)/info (*b*) documentary (film).

dodo [dodo] *nm F* (*a*) sleep/bye-bye(s); **faire dodo**, to go bye-byes (*b*) bed; **aller à dodo/aller au dodo/ aller faire dodo**, to go to bed/to go to beddy-byes.

dogue [dɔg] *nm F* **être d'une humeur de dogue**, to be in a vile mood/in a filthy temper; to be like a bear with a sore head.

doigt [dwa] *nm F* **1. être comme les doigts de la main**, to be hand in glove **2. mon petit doigt me l'a dit,** a little bird told me (so) **3. faire qch avec le petit doigt/les doigts dans le nez/***V* **les doigts dans le cul,** to do sth effortlessly/standing on one's head/with one's eyes shut; **gagner/arriver les doigts dans le nez,** to win by a mile/to romp home/to leave the rest standing **4. il ne fait rien de ses dix doigts,** he doesn't do a hand's turn **5.** (*a*) **cela se voit au doigt et à l'œil,** it's obvious/it's as plain as day (*b*) **obéir à qn au doigt et à l'œil,** to be at s.o.'s beck and call (*c*) **mener son personnel au doigt et à l'œil,** to have one's staff well trained/under one's thumb **6. se mettre/se fourrer/se ficher/se foutre le doigt dans l'œil, jusqu'au coude,** to be completely mistaken/to be (very) wide of the mark/to be barking up the wrong tree **7. recevoir sur les doigts,** to be reprimanded*/to be rapped over the knuckles **8. il s'en mord les doigts,** he bitterly regrets it/he's kicking himself **9. y mettre les doigts,** to steal*/to put one's hand in the till. (*Voir* **crochu; mordre; taper**)

se doigter [sədwate] *vpr P* (*femme*) to masturbate*/to finger oneself/to play with oneself.

dolluche [dɔlyʃ] *nm P* dollar/buck.

domb [dɔ̃b] *a P* = **dombi.**

dombeur [dɔ̃bœr] *nm P* (burglar's) jemmy/*NAm* jimmy.

dombi [dɔ̃bi] *a P* (*verlan de* **bidon**) **c'est dombi!** it's (a load of) rubbish/crap!

dominos [domino] *nmpl P* **1. (jeu de) dominos,** teeth*/ivories/choppers; **avoir mal aux dominos,** to have toothache **2.** (*drogues*) Durophet capsules/dominoes. (*Voir* **boîte 6**)

dondon [dɔ̃dɔ̃] *nf F* **grosse dondon/ forte dondon,** big lump of a girl/of a woman; big fat wench.

donne [dɔn] *nf P* **1.** alms **2.** generosity **3. être de la donne,** to lose money/to be a loser **4. ne pas être de la donne,** to be a miser*/to be miserly.

donné [dɔne] **I** *a&pp* F **c'est donné** (*i*) it's dirt-cheap (*ii*) it's a gift/it's a piece of cake **II** *nm* F **un donné,** an easy job/a piece of cake.

donner [dɔne] **I** *vtr* **1.** *P* **donner qn,** to denounce* s.o./to inform on s.o. **2.** *F* **je vous le donne en mille,** you can have as many guesses as you like; I bet you'll never guess **3.** *F* **on vous en donnera!** you don't want much, do you! **4.** *F* **se la donner de qn,** to mistrust s.o./to suspect s.o./to have one's suspicions about s.o. **5.** *F* **donner dedans,** to fall for it/to walk right into a trap. (*Voir* **œil**) **II** *vpr* **se donner** *F* **1. ça doit se donner,** it must be catching **2. s'en donner,** to have a good time; to give oneself a treat. (*Voir* **air I 3**)

donneur, euse [dɔnœr, -øz] *n* P (police) informer*/(copper's) nark/ grass.

donzelle [dɔ̃zɛl] *nf* F (*a*) (*péj*) girl*/young woman*/chick/bird (*b*) girl*/woman* of easy virtue; push-over/easy lay.

doré [dɔre] *a* F **1.** lucky **2. doré sur tranche,** excellent*.

dorer [dɔre] *vtr* V **se faire dorer,** to be buggered; **va te faire dorer!** get stuffed!

dormailler [dɔrmaje], **dor-masser** [dɔrmase] *vi* F to doze/ to snooze / to get some shut-eye.

dorme [dɔrm] *nf* P sleep/shut-eye; **aller à la dorme,** to go to bed*/to hit the sack.

dort-en-chiant [dɔrɑ̃ʃjɑ̃] *nm inv* V slowcoach/*NAm* slowpoke/daw-dler/weary Willie.

dorto [dɔrto] *nm* F (*scol*) (= *dortoir*) dormitory/dorm.

dorure [dɔryr] *nf* F **une vraie**

dorure, an easy* job/a cushy number.

doryphore [dɔrifɔr] *nm* F (*WWII*) German* soldier/Jerry.

dos [do] *nm* **1.** *P* **dos (vert)/dos fin,** pimp*/ponce **2.** *F* **j'en ai plein le dos,** I'm sick of it/I'm fed up* with it/I've had it up to here; **je le porte sur mon dos/il me scie le dos,** I've had (more than) enough of him; he bores me rigid **3.** *F* **avoir qn sur le dos,** to be saddled with s.o.; **mettre qch sur le dos de qn,** to saddle s.o. with sth **4.** *F* **l'avoir dans le dos,** to be duped/to be played for a sucker/to be had **5.** *P* **les avoir dans le dos,** to have the police* on one's track. (*Voir* **pied 18**; **reins 4**) **6.** *F* **je n'ai rien à me mettre sur le dos,** I haven't anything fit to wear/ I haven't a stitch to put on **7.** *F* (*a*) **elle est toujours dans mon dos,** she's always nagging at me/finding fault with me; she's always on my back (*b*) **elle est toujours sur mon dos,** she watches every move I make (*c*) **elle me tombe toujours sur le dos,** she's always jumping down my throat **8.** *F* (*pers*) **faire le gros dos** (*i*) to put on airs (*ii*) to bristle up **9.** *F* **il n'y va pas avec le dos de la cuiller** (*i*) he doesn't mince his words/he makes no bones about it/ (*ii*) he goes the whole hog/he stops at nothing **10.** *F* **passer la main dans le dos à qn,** to flatter* s.o.; **se passer la main dans le dos,** to pat oneself on the back **11.** *P* **filer/ donner/prendre du dos,** to be a homosexual **12.** *P* **faire un enfant dans le dos de qn,** to betray s.o.'s confidence **13.** *F* **être mort dans le dos,** to be frozen to death/perished with (the) cold. (*Voir* **bête I 5**; **sucre 3**)

dose [doz] *nf* **1.** *P* **j'en ai eu une dose/j'en ai eu ma bonne dose,** I've had more than my (fair) share of it **2.** *P* **en avoir/en tenir une dose,** to be an absolute fool*/to be as stupid as they come **3.** *P* **en prendre**

une **bonne dose**, to enjoy oneself immensely **4. avoir sa dose** (*i*) to have been badly beaten up (*ii*) to be dead **5.** *F* **forcer la dose**, to overdo it/to go too far; to pile on the agony **6.** *P* (*drogues*) dose/fix.

dossière [dɔsjɛr] *nf P* **1.** buttocks*; **jouer de la dossière**, to wiggle/to waggle one's behind (when walking); **remuer la dossière**, to hurry* (up)/to get cracking/to move it **2.** underpants with a slit in the back **3. prendre/refiler de la dossière**, to be a homosexual* **4. avoir de la dossière**, to have amazing luck/to have the luck of the devil.

douanier [dwanje] *nm P* glass of absinth(e).

doublage [dublaʒ] *nm P* double-cross(ing).

doublard [dublar] *nm P* **1.** head warder (in a prison) **2.** pimp's second woman **3.** prostitute's favourite client/john.

double [dubl] *nm P* **1.** = **doublard 2 2. mener/mettre qn en double**, to dupe s.o./to con s.o.; **se laisser mener en double**, to allow oneself to be played for a sucker.

doublé [duble] *nm F* **1. réussir un doublé**, to bring off a double **2. faire un doublé**, to give birth to twins.

doubler [duble] *vtr P* **1.** to double-cross (s.o.) **2.** to be unfaithful to (one's husband, one's wife) **3.** to steal*.

double-six [dubl(ə)sis] *nm P* **rendre le double-six à qn**, to be more than a match for s.o.

doubleur [dublœr] *nm P* thief.

double-zéro [dubləzero] *nm F* **c'est un double-zéro**, he's a dead loss/he's useless. (*pl* **doubles-zéros**)

doublure [dublyr] *nf P* **1.** figurehead/dummy/man of straw **2. les doublures se touchent**, I'm

penniless*/flat broke/skint **3.** = **doublard 2**.

douce [dus] **I** *nf* **1.** *P* (*drogues*) marijuana*/grass **2.** *O V* **se faire/se foutre une douce**, to masturbate*/to toss oneself off **II** *adv phr F* (*a*) **se porter à la douce**, to be so-so/fair to middling (*b*) **en douce (poil-poil)**, on the quiet/on the QT; between you me and the gatepost; **il a filé en douce**, he slipped off quietly; **vas-y en douce! glisser II 1**)

doucement [dusmɑ̃] *adv F* **1. vas-y doucement avec l'alcool**, go easy on the booze **2. ça m'a fait doucement rigoler**, I had a good laugh over it.

doucettement [dusɛtmɑ̃] *adv F* (*a*) gently; quietly (*b*) cautiously.

douche [duʃ] *nf F* **1. prendre une douche** (*a*) to get a soaking/to get soaked (to the skin) (*b*) to be let down **2. douche écossaise**, blowing hot and cold **3. je lui ai passé une bonne douche**, I gave him a good telling-off/I let him have it (good and proper).

douché [duʃe] *a&pp* **être douché** (*i*) *F* to be drenched/soaked to the skin (*ii*) *F* to be shaken (rigid) (*iii*) *P* to be fleeced (*iv*) *P* to have suffered a loss/to be let down (*v*) *P* to have got one's fingers burnt (in a speculation, etc).

doucher [duʃe] *vtr* **1.** *F* to cool off (s.o.'s enthusiasm for sth, etc) **2.** *F* **se faire doucher**, to get a soaking (from the rain) **3.** *P* to reprimand* (s.o.)/to tell (s.o.) off/to bawl (s.o.) out **4.** *P* to swindle*/to fleece (s.o.);to rip (s.o.) off.

doudou [dudu] *nf F* West Indian woman.

doudounes [dudun] *nfpl P* breasts*/boobs.

douillard, arde [dujar, -ard] *F* **I** *a* (*pers*) **1.** soft/cuddly/cosy **2.** rich*/loaded/rolling in it **3.** with a good thatch (of hair)/well-thatched **II** *n* **1.** soft person **2.** rich* person/moneybags **3.** well-thatched person; **douillards,** hair/thatch.

douille [duj] *nf P* **1.** money*/cash/dough **2.** *pl* **douilles,** hair/thatch; **se faire faucher les douilles,** to have a haircut/to get one's hair cut.

douiller [duje] *vtr&i P* to pay* (for); to fork out/to cough up; **ça douille!** that's pric(e)y!

douillettes [dujɛt] *nfpl V* testicles*/goolies.

doul(e) [dul] *nm P* **1.** hat*/titfer **2.** porter le/un doul(e) (*i*) to be wrongly accused/to take the rap (*ii*) to have a bad reputation (*iii*) to be (suspected of being) a police informer*.

doulos [dulos] *nm P* **1.** = **doul(e) 1, 2 2.** *pl* hair.

douloureuse [dulurøz] *nf F* **la douloureuse,** the bill/*esp NAm* the check (in hotel, restaurant, etc)/the damage/the bad news.

doux [du] *adv F* **filer doux,** to give in/to climb down/to knuckle under.

douze [duz] *nm F* **faire un douze,** to make a mistake*/to boob.

drag [drag] *nm P* (*drogues*) marijuana* cigarette/joint/reefer.

drage [draʒ] *nf P* **faire la drage,** to sell quack remedies.

dragée [draʒe] *nf P* bullet; **envoyer une dragée,** to fire a bullet/to shoot.

draguer [drage] *vtr&i F* to try to pick up/chat up/get off with s.o.; to chase skirt; (*homosexuels*) to cruise/to go cruising; **il est toujours en train de draguer les filles,** he's always trying to get off with the girls/with some chick or other.

dragueur [dragœr] *nm P* skirt-chaser; bloke/guy who's always chasing after the girls/who's always chatting up the girls/who's always

trying to make some girl or other; (*homosexuels*) s.o. who's cruising/who's trying to get off with s.o. else.

drap [dra] *nm F* **1.** être dans de beaux/vilains draps (*i*) to be in a fix*/in a fine (old) mess/in a pickle (*ii*) to be critically ill/in a bad way; **nous voilà dans de beaux draps!** we're really up the creek! **2.** tailler en plein drap (*i*) to be wasteful/extravagant (*ii*) to do just as one pleases.

drapeau, -eaux [drapo] *nm* **1.** *F* mettre son drapeau dans sa poche, to conceal one's opinions/to keep one's mouth shut **2.** *P* planter un drapeau, to leave without paying the bill **3.** *P* shirt.

drauper [dropɛr], **draupère** [dropɛr], **draupière** [dropjɛr] *nm P* (*verlan de* **perdreau**) policeman*.

dresser [drese] *vtr* dresser qn, to bring s.o. to heel/to make s.o. toe the line; **ça le dressera!** that'll show him where he gets off!

driver [drive] *vtr F* **1.** to drive (a car, etc) **2.** to run (a business).

drôle [drol] **I** *a F* (*a*) se sentir tout drôle, to feel queer/(a bit) funny/off colour/all peculiar (*b*) vous êtes drôle! qu'auriez-vous fait à ma place? don't be funny! what would you have done in my place? (*c*) un drôle de coco/de mec/de numéro/de paroissien/de type, a queer fish/an oddbod/a strange chap/a weird bloke/a funny fellow; une drôle d'odeur, a peculiar smell; quelle drôle d'idée! what a funny idea! **II** *adv P* ça m'a fait tout drôle de te voir là, I felt very odd/it gave me a funny feeling seeing you there.

drôlement [drolmɑ̃] *adv F* awfully/terribly/terrifically; **il fait drôlement froid,** it's jolly cold; **nous nous sommes drôlement amusés,** we had a smashing/fabulous time; **elle est drôlement bien,** she's gorgeous; **il a drôlement décollé,** he hasn't half changed; **et drôlement!** and how!

drôlet, ette [drolɛ, -ɛt], **drôlichon, onne** [droliʃɔ̃, -ɔn] *a F* funny/odd/queer/quaint.

(se) drop(p)er [(sə)drɔpe] *vi&pr P* to run away*; to beat it/to scarper.

dross [drɔs] *nm P* (*drogues*) residue in opium pipe/green mud.

drouille [druj] *nf P* (*a*) worthless goods; shoddy goods; trash/rubbish (*b*) unusable or unsaleable goods/left-overs.

drouilleur [drujœr] *nm P* buyer of clearance lines.

duce [dys] *nm P* **balancer/envoyer/expédier/faire le duce à qn,** to tip s.o. off*/to give s.o. a tip-off.

duch(e)nock [dyʃnɔk], **duch(e)noque** [dyʃnɔk], **ducon** [dykɔ̃], **duconneau** [dykɔno], **duconnard** [dykɔnar], **duconno** [dykɔno], **duconnoso** [dykɔnoso], **duconnosof** [dykɔnosɔf] *nm V* fool*/idiot/nit(wit)/twit/berk/jerk; silly sod; stupid bugger. (*Voir* **schnock**)

dudule [dydyl] *nm P* what's-his-name/what's-her-name/ what-do-you-call-him/what-do-you-call-her/thingamybob/thingy.

dur [dyr] **I** *a* **1.** *F* **être dur à cuire,** to be a tough nut (to crack); **il est dur à cuire,** he's a tough cookie **2.** *F* **il n'est pas dur!** he doesn't want much!/he's got a nerve! **3.** *P* **il n'est pas dur à piger,** he's quick on the uptake/he twigs on quickly/he cottons on quickly **4.** *V* (*a*) **l'avoir dur,** to have an erection*/to have a hard-on/to get it up (*b*) **l'avoir dur pour quelqu'un/en avoir dur pour quelqu'un,** to desire s.o. sexually/to be turned on by s.o./to be horny for s.o. (*Voir* **desserre**; **détente**; **dure**; **feuille 1**; **lâcher 2**; **respirer 1**) **II** *nm* **1.** *P* train: underground train/tube (train); **prendre le dur,** to go by train/by

tube; **brûler le dur,** to travel (on a train, on the tube) without paying **2.** *F* **un dur** (*i*) a nasty piece of work/a bastard*/a sod (*ii*) **un dur (à cuire)/un dur de dur,** a tough guy/a hard nut; **jouer au dur/jouer les durs (de durs),** to play the tough guy **3.** *P* (burglar's) jemmy/*NAm* jimmy **4.** *P* **le dur,** hard cash (as opposed to banknotes) **5.** *P* **les durs,** hard labour **6.** *P* **un verre de dur,** a glass of spirits*/a drop of the hard stuff. (*Voir* **dure; respirer 2**)

duraille [dyraj], **duraillon** [dyrajɔ̃] *a P* **1.** difficult/tough; **se lever tôt, c'est duraille,** it's a job to get up early **2.** miserly*/tight/stingy.

dure [dyr] *nf F* **1.** ground; **coucher sur la dure,** to sleep on the ground **2.** (*a*) **en dire de dures à qn,** to give s.o. a good telling-off/to bawl s.o. out (*b*) **il en a vu de dures,** he's had a bad/a hard/a rough time (of it); he's been through the mill (*c*) **en faire voir de dures à qn,** to give s.o. a bad/hard/rough time (of it); to put s.o. through it **3.** *adv phr* **à la dure,** violently; **il a été élevé à la dure,** he was brought up the hard way. (*Voir* **dur I, II**)

durer [dyre] *vi F* **1.** (*péj*) **est-ce qu'il dure toujours?** is he still alive? **2.** (*a*) **nous n'y pouvons plus durer,** we can't hold out/stick it out any longer (*b*) **il ne peut pas durer en place,** he can't stay put (a minute); he's like a cat on hot bricks/on a hot tin roof.

durillon [dyrijɔ̃], **durillot** [dyrijo], **duringue** [dyrɛ̃g] *a P* hard/tough/difficult.

duschnock [dyʃnɔk] *nm V* = **duch(e)nock.**

duvet [dyvɛ] *nm F* **1.** sleeping-bag **2. coucher sur le duvet,** to live in the lap of luxury.

dynamite [dinamit] *nf* **1.** *F* **n'y touche pas, c'est de la dynamite!**

don't touch it, it's dynamite! **2.** *P* (*a*) very strong drug or drink/dynamite/knock-out (*b*) very high-quality drug (*c*) marijuana* (*d*) heroin* (*e*) cocaine* (*f*) **marcher à la dynamite,** to be on drugs*.

dynamité, ée [dinamite] *P* **I** *a* high on drugs* **II** *n* drug addict*/junkie.

E

eau, *pl* **eaux** [o] *nf F* **1. marin d'eau douce,** dry-land sailor **2. il y a de l'eau dans le gaz** (*i*) there's trouble brewing; there's going to be trouble (*ii*) there's a snag in it somewhere **3.** (*a*) **clair comme l'eau de vaisselle,** as clear as mud (*b*) **clair comme de l'eau de roche,** perfectly clear/crystal clear **4. mettre de l'eau dans son vin,** to moderate one's opinions; to go easy/to ease off; to tone it down a bit **5.** (*projet, etc*) **tomber à l'eau; tourner/s'en aller/finir en eau de boudin,** to fall through/to fizzle out/to come to nothing/to end (up) in smoke **6. il n'a pas inventé l'eau chaude,** he's not very bright; he'll never set the Thames on fire **7.** (*a*) **eau plate,** ordinary (drinking) water (*b*) **eau à ressort/à pédale,** soda water (*c*) **eau d'affe,** brandy **8. avoir les eaux basses,** to be short of cash/out of funds; **les eaux sont basses,** I'm/he's hard up **9. à l'eau de rose** (*a*) harmless/inoffensive (*b*) milk-and-water; schmaltzy; gooey (sentimentality)/sugary/sticky/ soppy **10. un imbécile de la première eau/de la plus belle eau,** an out-and-out fool*/a complete idiot **11. tomber/lâcher de l'eau,** to urinate*. (*Voir* **bec 3; bénit 2; bidet; épée 2; revenir 3**)

ébaubi [ebobi] *a F* amazed/flabbergasted.

ébaubir [ebobir] *vtr F* to amaze/to flabbergast*.

éberlué [ebɛrlɥe] *a F* amazed/ flabbergasted/dumbfounded.

ébouriffant [eburifɑ̃] *a F* amaz-ing/startling (success, etc); **histoire ébouriffante,** preposterous story.

ébouser, ébouzer [ebuze] *vtr P* **1.** to overwhelm/to crush; to non-plus/to floor **2.** to kill*/to assassinate/to do in/*esp NAm* to blow away.

ébréché [ebreʃe] *a P* slightly drunk*/tipsy/merry.

écailler [ekaje] *vtr* to swindle*/to fleece (s.o.)/to clean (s.o.) out/to rip (s.o.) off.

échalas [eʃala] *nm F* **1.** tall/thin person; beanpole; **il est sec comme un échalas,** he's very skinny **2.** *pl* long/skinny legs*.

échalote [eʃalɔt] *nf P* **1.** anus* **2.** *pl* ovaries **3. pratiquer la course à l'échalotte,** to follow s.o. closely/ to breathe down s.o.'s neck.

échasses [eʃas] *nfpl F* long/ skinny legs*.

échassier [eʃasje] *nm F* tall/thin person.

échassière [eʃasjɛr] *nf P* prostitute* (who sits at the bar)/bar-girl/ hostess.

échauder [eʃode] *vtr F* to swin-dle*; **se faire échauder/être échaudé,** to get fleeced/to get one's fingers burnt/to be taken for a ride/to be ripped off.

échauffer [eʃofe] *vtr F* **échauffer les oreilles à qn,** to anger s.o./to rub s.o. up the wrong way.

échelle [eʃɛl] *nf F* **1. monter/ grimper à l'échelle** (*i*) to be taken in/to fall for something (*ii*) to get angry*/to flare up; **faire monter qn**

à l'échelle (i) to kid s.o./to have s.o. on; **c'est pas vrai, vous voulez me faire monter à l'échelle!** I don't believe it, you're pulling my leg!/ you're having me on! (ii) to make s.o. angry*/to get s.o.'s blood up/ to get s.o.'s goat **2. après ça, il faut/il n'y a plus qu'à tirer l'échelle,** that's the limit*/there's no point in carrying on; **après lui, il n'y a plus qu'à tirer l'échelle,** after what he's done we may as well give up.

s'échiner [seʃine] *vpr F* to work* oneself to death/to work oneself into the ground/to wear oneself out; **s'échiner à qch,** to slave away at sth/to slog one's guts out; **s'échiner à faire qch,** to break one's back doing sth.

échouer [eʃwe] *vi F* (*pers*) (*aboutir*) **il a échoué sur un banc de jardin public,** he ended up on a park bench.

éclairer [eklɛre, -ere] *vtr&i P* (a) **éclairer (la dépense),** to pay* up/to foot the bill (b) (*jeux d'argent*) to stake one's money/to lay it on the line; **les éclairer,** to show the colour of one's money.

éclat [ekla] *nm P* **c'est l'éclat!** it's really great!/it's (fucking) amazing!

s'éclater [seklate] *vpr F* **1.** (*drogues*) to have psychedelic visions/to trip **2.** to have a good time*/a ball (at a party, etc).

s'éclipser [seklipse] *vpr F* to run away*/to make oneself scarce/to do a disappearing act; **je me suis éclipsé(e) avant la fin,** I sneaked/ *NAm* snuck out before the end.

écluse [eklyz] *nf* **1.** *F* **lâcher/ ouvrir les écluses,** to start crying/to turn on the waterworks **2.** *P* **lâcher l'écluse,** to urinate*/to splash one's boots/to (have a) piddle/to take a leak.

écluser [eklyze] *P* **I** *vtr* **écluser un verre/un godet,** to knock back/to sink a drink; to put one down the

hatch/to have a swig **II** *vi* to urinate*.

écolo [ekɔlo] *nm or f F* (= *écologiste*) ecologist/ecofreak.

éconocroques [ekɔnɔkrɔk] *nfpl P* savings/economies.

écopage [ekɔpaʒ] *nm F* **1.** blow*/wound **2.** reprimand*/tell-ing-off/slating.

écoper [ekɔpe] **I** *vtr P* to drink* **II** *vi F* (a) to catch it/to cop it/to get it in the neck; **écoper de six mois de taule,** to cop six months inside; **il va écoper,** he's (in) for it/ he's got it coming to him/he'll cop it/he's for the high jump; **il a sale-ment écopé,** he got the book thrown at him (b) to be hit/ wounded.

écopeur [ekɔpœr] *nm F* victim; **c'est toujours moi l'écopeur,** I'm always the one who gets it in the neck/who takes the rap.

à écorche-cul [aekɔrʃ(ə)ky] *adv phr P* (a) **monter à écorche-cul,** to ride bareback; **descendre une pente à écorche-cul,** to go down a slope on one's backside (b) **il n'est venu qu'à écorche-cul,** we had to drag him here.

écorcher [ekɔrʃe] *vtr F* **1.** to murder (a language, etc) **2.** to overcharge/to fleece*; **il écorche ses clients,** he makes them pay through the nose/he rips them off **3.** **ça t'écorchera pas le derrière,** it won't bite you/it won't kill you.

écorcheur, euse [ekɔrʃœr, -øz] *n F* s.o. who overcharges/fleecer/ extortioner.

écorniflage [ekɔrniflaʒ] *nm F* cadging/scrounging/sponging.

écornifler [ekɔrnifle] *vtr O* to cadge/to scrounge (money, etc); to sponge; **écornifler une cibiche à qn,** to scrounge a fag off s.o.

écornifleur, euse [ekɔrniflœr, -øz] *n O F* cadger/scrounger/ sponger.

écosser [ekɔse] *vi O P* **1.** to pay* up/to shell out **2.** to spend lavishly; **elle m'en a fait écosser,** she cost me a pretty penny **3.** to work* hard; to do one's job **4.** to be a prostitute*/to solicit*/to be on the game.

écoutes [ekut] *nfpl,* **écoutilles** [ekutij] *nfpl P* ears*/lugholes.

écrabouillage [ekrabujaʒ] *nm,* **écrabouillement** [ekrabujmɑ̃] *nm F* crushing/squashing.

écrabouiller [ekrabuje] *vtr F* to crush/to squash; to reduce (s.o./ sth) to a pulp; to make mincemeat of (s.o.).

écrase-merde(s) [ekrɑzmɛrd] *nmpl P* big boots*/beetle-crushers.

écraser [ekrɑze] I *vi P* **1.** écrase! shut* up!/put a sock in it!/ give it a rest!/lay off! **2. en écraser,** to be a prostitute*/to be on the game **3. en écraser (dur),** to sleep like a log II *vtr* **1.** *P* **en écraser une (en lousdoc),** to let out a silent fart. (*Voir* **perle 5**) **2.** *P* **je t'en écrase cinq,** I shake your hand **3.** *F* **écraser l'affaire,** to hush something up. (*Voir* **champignon 1**; **coup 4**; **ivoire**; **planète**) III *vpr* **s'écraser** *P* to keep silent; to lie low/to keep a low profile.

écraseur, -euse [ekrɑzœr, -øz] *n F* rotten driver; road-hog.

écrémer [ekreme] *vtr P* to give sexual satisfaction to (s.o.)/to cream (s.o.) off/to bring s.o. off.

écroulé [ekrule] *a F* **être écroulé (de rire),** to be doubled up with laughter.

s'écrouler [sekrule] *vpr F* **s'écrouler dans un fauteuil,** to flop into/to collapse into an armchair.

écu [eky] *nm F* **avoir des écus,** to be rich*/to have pots of money*.

écumer [ekyme] *vtr F* **1. écumer la marmite/les marmites,** to scrounge/to sponge/to be a hanger-on **2. écumer les bars,** to go bar-hopping/to go on a pub crawl.

écumeur, -euse [ekymœr, -øz] *n F* **écumeur de marmite,** scrounger/ sponger/freeloader; hanger-on.

écumoire [ekymwar] *nf F* **1. en écumoire/comme une écumoire,** riddled with bullets **2. avoir la tête comme une écumoire,** to be scatterbrained/to have a brain like a sieve.

écureuil [ekyrœj] *nm F* **écureuil (à roulettes),** cyclist circling a racing track.

écurie [ekyri] *nf F* **1. entrer comme dans une écurie,** to come in without saying hallo/without introducing oneself **2. sentir l'écurie,** to be eager/in a hurry to get back home **3. c'est une vraie écurie,** it's a real pigsty.

édicule [edikyl] *nm F* (public) convenience/street urinal.

édredon [edrədɔ̃] *nm P* **faire l'édredon,** to steal* from a guest (at a hotel)/from a prostitute's client, etc, while he is asleep.

éducation [edykasjɔ̃] *nf P* **éducation anglaise,** flagellation/flag.

effacer [efase] I *vtr P* **1.** to kill*/to wipe out/to blow away **2.** to receive/to cop (a blow) **3.** to polish off/to knock back (food, drink). (*Voir* **gomme 2**) II *vpr* **s'effacer** *P* **1.** to die* **2. se faire effacer,** to do a disappearing act/to get the hell out of it.

effaroucher [efaruʃe] *vtr P* to steal*.

effet [efɛ] *nm F* **1. ça m'a coupé mes effets,** it took the wind out of my sails **2. ça m'a fait un drôle d'effet,** it gave me quite a turn **3. si c'est ça (tout) l'effet que ça te fait!** if that's the way you feel about it! **4.** (*esp autostoppeuse*) **faire des effets de cuisse,** to catch the driver's eye by showing/flashing one's legs.

effeuillage [efœjaʒ] *nm F* strip-tease.

effeuilleuse [efœjøz] *nf F* strip-tease artist/stripper.

égoïner [egɔine] *vtr* **1.** *P* **égoïner qn**, to evict s.o.; to throw/to kick/to boot s.o. out **2.** *V* to have sex* with (s.o.).

égorger [egɔrʒe] *vtr F* to fleece*/to rip off (a customer) (*b*) to ruin/to bleed dry (a creditor).

égout [egu] *nm P* mouth*/trap/kisser/gob.

s'égueuler [segœle] *vpr P* **s'égueuler à crier**, to shout oneself hoarse.

éjecter [eʒɛkte] *vtr F* (*a*) to throw out/to chuck out/to kick out (*b*) to dismiss*/to fire/to sack (s.o.); to give s.o. the push.

élastique [elastik] *nm F* **il les lâche avec un élastique**, he's really stingy/he's as mean as hell.

éléphant [elefã] *nm F* **1.** dry-land sailor/landlubber **2.** **il a une mémoire d'éléphant**, like an elephant he never forgets **3.** **comme un éléphant dans un magasin de porcelaine**, like a bull in a china shop.

élixir [eliksir] *nm P* **élixir de hussard**, hard liquor.

emballage [ãbalaʒ] *nm P* **1.** reprimand*/telling-off **2.** round-up/raid/bust (by the police).

emballarès [ãbalarɛs] *a P* arrested/nicked/run in.

emballé, ée [ãbale] *n F* enthusiast/fan. (*Voir* **emballer 1**)

emballement [ãbalmã] *nm F* (*a*) (transitory) enthusiasm/sudden craze (*b*) burst of energy (*c*) passing fancy.

emballer [ãbale] **I** *vtr* **1.** *F* to excite/to thrill (s.o.); to fire (s.o.) with enthusiasm; **ça ne m'emballe pas**, I can't work up much enthusiasm for that; that doesn't exactly

do a lot for me; **il ne m'emballe pas**, I don't go much on him; **être emballé par qn/qch**, to be (mad) keen on s.o./sth; to get carried away by sth **2.** *P* (*a*) to arrest* (s.o.)/to run (s.o.) in/to nick (s.o.) (*b*) to put (s.o.) in prison*/in the nick; **se faire emballer**, to get run in **3.** *P* to reprimand* (s.o.)/to tell (s.o.) off/to tell (s.o.) where he/she gets off; **se faire emballer**, to get told off **4.** *P* (*a*) to chat up/to sweet-talk/to get off with (s.o.)/to pick (s.o.) up; **emballer une nana**, to get off with/to pull a bird/a chick **II** *vpr* **s'emballer** *F* **1.** to be carried away (by excitement, enthusiasm, anger); **ne vous emballez pas!** cool it!/don't get excited!/don't get your knickers in a twist!/keep your hair on! **il s'emballe pour un rien**, he gets (all) worked up over nothing **2.** **s'emballer pour qn**, to fall madly in love with s.o./to fall for s.o.

emballes [ãbal] *nfpl P* **faire des emballes**, to make/to kick up a fuss.

emballeur [ãbalœr] *nm P* **1.** policeman* **2.** undertaker's assistant.

s'embaquer [sãbake] *vpr P* to lose/to be a loser (at the races, at gambling, etc).

embarbouiller [ãbarbuje] **I** *vtr F* to confuse/to muddle (s.o.) **II** *vpr* **s'embarbouiller** *F* to get muddled/confused/(all) mixed up.

embarquer [ãbarke] *vtr* **1.** *F* **il m'a embarqué dans l'avion**, he put me on the plane/he saw me onto the plane **2.** *F* **embarquer qn dans sa voiture**, to give s.o. a lift (in one's car) **3.** *F* **être embarqué dans une sale histoire**, to be mixed up in/to be involved in some nasty/dirty business **4.** *P* to arrest* (s.o.)/to run (s.o.) in; **se faire embarquer par les flics**, to get picked up by the cops **5.** *P* **embarquer**

une nana, to get off with/to pick up/to pull a girl/a chick/a bird.

embarras [ãbara] *nm F* faire de l'embarras/des embarras (*i*) to be fussy/to make a fuss; ne fais pas tant d'embarras! don't make such a song and dance about it! un faiseur/une faiseuse d'embarras, a fusspot (*ii*) to put on airs/to show off*.

embastiller [ãbastije] *vtr P* se faire embastiller, to be arrested*/to get run in.

embellemerdé [ãbɛlmɛrde] *a P* saddled with a troublesome mother-in-law.

embellie [ãbɛli] *nf F* stroke of luck; profiter de l'embellie, to make hay while the sun shines.

emberlificoter [ãbɛrlifikɔte] *vtr F* 1. to tangle (s.o.) up (in an argument, etc); to involve (s.o.) in difficulties/to get (s.o.) mixed up in something 2. to get round (s.o.)/to take (s.o.) in/to sweet-talk (s.o.).

emberlificoteur, euse [ãbɛrlifikɔtœr, -øz] *n F* hoaxer/duper; sweet-talker/soft-soaper.

embêtant [ãbɛtã] *F* I *a* annoying/aggravating; tiresome/boring; qu'il est embêtant, celui-là! what a pest!/what a pain!/he's a real nuisance! c'est bien embêtant! it's a real nuisance! II *nm* l'embêtant c'est que ..., the annoying thing is that .../the problem is that ...

embêté [ãbete] *a F* (*a*) bored*/fed up* (*b*) worried.

embêtement [ãbɛtmã] *nm F* 1. nuisance/annoyance/aggravation/bother; worry 2. chercher des embêtements, to look for trouble; avoir des embêtements, to be in a fix*.

embêter [ãbete] I *vtr F* (*a*) to annoy*/to be a nuisance to (s.o.); ne l'embête pas! stop pestering him!/leave him alone!/stop bugging him! il m'embête, he gets on my

nerves; I've got no time for him; ça m'embête de ... (*i*) I can't be bothered to ... (*ii*) I wish I didn't have to ...; ça m'embête d'arriver en retard, I hate being late (*b*) to bore* II *vpr* s'embêter *F* (*a*) to be worried; il ne s'embête pas, celui-là! you don't have to worry about him, he does pretty well for himself/his first priority is for number one; he's got a lot of nerve! (*b*) to be bored*; s'embêter comme une carpe/s'embêter ferme/s'embêter un bon coup/s'embêter à crever/s'embêter à mourir/s'embêter à cent sous de l'heure/s'embêter à cent francs de l'heure, to be bored stiff/rigid; to be bored to death/to tears.

embistrouiller [ãbistruje] *vtr P* to annoy*/to pester.

embobeliner [ãbɔbline], **embobichonner** [ãbɔbiʃɔne], **embobiner** [ãbɔbine] *vtr F* to get round (s.o.)/to take (s.o.) in/to lead (s.o.) up the garden path; se laisser embobeliner, to let oneself be hoodwinked/be taken in.

emboiser [ãbwaze] *vtr P* to get (a woman) pregnant*/to put (a woman) up the spout/*esp NAm* to knock (a woman) up.

emboîtage [ãbwataʒ] *nm F* (*théâtre*) booing/hissing; cat calls.

emboîter [ãbwate] *vtr* 1. *F* (*théâtre*) to boo/to hiss/to give (s.o.) the bird; se faire emboîter, to get the bird 2. *F* emboîter qn, to pull s.o.'s leg/*NAm* to razz s.o. 3. *P* (*a*) to arrest* (*b*) to send to prison*.

emboucané [ãbukane] *a P* fed up*/pissed off.

emboucaner [ãbukane] I *vtr P* 1. to irritate/to annoy*; tu m'emboucanes, you get on my tits/you're a pain in the arse/*NAm* ass 2. to stink (the place) out II *vpr* s'emboucaner *P* 1. to be *or* to get bored/pissed off/browned off **2.** to be poisoned.

embouché [ãbuʃe] *a* F **mal embouché** (*i*) foul-mouthed (*ii*) in a foul mood.

embourber [ãburbe] *vtr* P **1.** s'embourber du vin, to knock back/ to swill down wine **2.** s'embourber une femme, to have sex* with a woman; ils se sont embourbés, they had it away/they had it off.

embourremaner [ãburmane] *vtr* P to arrest*.

embouser [ãbuze] *vtr* P je l'embouse, he can get knotted/he can get stuffed/he can go to hell.

embrayer [ãbreje] **I** *vi* F **1.** to explain oneself/to say what one means **2.** to start work/to get cracking/to get down to it **II** *vtr* P embrayer une nénette, to have sex*/to have it off with a girl*.

embringuer [ãbrɛ̃ge] **I** *vtr* F **se laisser embringuer dans qch**, to get involved/mixed up in sth **II** *vpr* **s'embringuer** F **1.** s'embringuer dans qch, to get involved/mixed up in sth **2.** s'embringuer mal, to get off to a bad start.

embrouillage [ãbruja ʒ] *nm* F confusion/embarrassment.

embrouillamini [ãbrujamini] *nm* F confusion/disorder*/jumble.

s'embrouillarder [sãbrujarde] *vtr* F (*pers*) to get fuddled (with drink).

embrouille [ãbruj] *nf* P **1.** complete disorder*/muddle/jumble/hell of a mess **2.** shady transaction; **faire une embrouille à qn**, to do the dirty on s.o. **3.** l'Embrouille, the French Stock Exchange/the Bourse.

embrouilleur, euse [ãbrujœr, -øz] *n* **1.** F muddler **2.** P shady dealer.

embusqué [ãbyske] *nm* F (*a*) slacker/lead-swinger/skiver (*b*) shirker (from call-up or active service)/column-dodger.

embusquer [ãbyske] **I** *vtr* P to arrest*; **se faire embusquer**, to get nabbed **II** *vpr* **s'embusquer** F to shirk active service/to dodge the column.

éméché [emeʃe] *a* F slightly drunk*/merry/tipsy.

émécher [emeʃe] **I** *vtr* F émécher qn, to get s.o. slightly drunk*/ merry/tipsy **II** *vpr* **s'émécher** F to become slightly drunk*/to get tipsy/to get a bit pissed.

émeraudes [emrod] *nfpl* P (= hémorroïdes) piles.

emmanché [ãmãʃe] *nm & a* V **1.** (passive) homosexual*/fairy/*esp* NAm fag(got)/poof/queer **2.** (*imbécile*) berk/cretin; **espèce d'emmanché!** (you) silly prick!/you jerk!

emmancher [ãmãʃe] **I** *vtr* V to have anal sex* (with s.o.)/to sodomize* (s.o.)/to bugger s.o./to go in by the backdoor; **se faire emmancher**, to get one's arse/NAm ass fucked **II** *vpr* **s'emmancher** V to have anal sex* together/to arse-fuck/NAm ass-fuck/to shaft each other.

emmener [ãmne] *vtr* P **1.** être emmené en belle, to be taken for a ride (by gangsters, etc) **2.** je t'emmène à la campagne! go to hell!

emmerdant [ãmɛrdã] *a* P (bloody) annoying; bloody/damned boring; **ça c'est emmerdant!** it's a bloody nuisance!/that's a bastard! **tu es emmerdant**, you're a pain in the neck/you're a real drag.

emmerdation [ãmɛrdasjɔ̃] *nf* P = emmerdement.

emmerde [ãmɛrd] *nf* P annoyance/nuisance; drag; **avoir des emmerdes**, to have problems/to be in deep trouble/to be up shit-creek; **faire des emmerdes à qn**, to be a bloody nuisance to s.o./to be nothing but trouble for s.o.

emmerdé [ãmɛrde] *a P* être emmerdé, to be in the shit; **il est emmerdé jusqu'au cou,** he's right in the shit/he's up to his neck in shit.

emmerdement [ãmɛrd(ə)mã] *nm P* bloody/damned nuisance; **quel emmerdement!** what a bloody/sodding mess! **j'ai des emmerdements,** I've got problems; **il a des emmerdements avec sa femme,** he's having a bit of bother with his wife/he's got wife-trouble.

emmerder [ãmɛrde] **I** *vtr* **1.** to shit on/to crap on (sth) **2.** (*a*) to bore (s.o.) to death/to bore the pants off s.o./to bore the tits off (s.o.) (*b*) to get on s.o.'s nerves/s.o.'s wick; to bug/to pester s.o.; **tu m'emmerdes à la fin,** you're getting on my tits/you're getting up my nose; **je l'emmerde!** he can just go to hell!/bugger him!/he can fuck off!/sod him! **les voisins? je les emmerde!** the neighbours? they can just piss off!/sod the neighbours! **II** *vpr* **s'emmerder** *P* **1.** to be bored to tears/out of one's tiny mind; to be bored to death; to be really pissed off; **s'emmerder à cent sous de l'heure,** to be bored out of one's skull/shitless/rigid; **qu'est-ce qu'on s'emmerde ici!** God! it's boring here!/we're bored out of our tiny minds in this place! **2. ne pas s'emmerder,** not to worry about anything; to be doing very nicely thank you.

emmerdeur, euse [ãmɛrdœr, -øz] *n P* bloody nuisance/pest; **c'est un emmerdeur** (*i*) he's an irritating bastard*; he's a real headache; he's a pain in the arse/*NAm* ass (*ii*) he's a lousy sod/a shit/a creep.

emmieller [ãmjɛle] *vtr F* (*euph de* **emmerder**) to annoy*/to irritate; **tu m'emmielles!** you little so-and-so (I'd like to strangle you)!

emmistoufler [ãmistufle] *vtr F* (*rare*) to annoy*/to bug/to pester/ to worry/to bother. (*Voir* **mistoufle** 2)

emmitonner [ãmitɔne] *vtr F* **emmitonner qn,** to get round s.o./to sweet-talk s.o.; to soften/to sweeten s.o. up/to butter s.o. up.

emmouscaillement [ãmuskajmã] *nm P* (*rare*) = **emmerdement.**

emmouscailler [ãmuskaje] *vtr P* (*rare*) = **emmerder 2.**

emmoutarder [ãmutarde] *vtr A F* to annoy*/to irritate/to bug/to be a nuisance to (s.o.).

émos [emos] *nf O P* emotion; excitement; shock/turn.

émotion [emosjɔ̃] *nf F* **ça m'a fait une émotion,** it was a bit of a shock; it gave me quite a turn.

émotionnant [emosjɔnã] *a F* moving (story, etc); exciting; thrilling.

émotionner [emosjɔne] **I** *vtr F* to move/to affect (s.o.); to thrill (s.o.); to agitate (s.o.)/to upset (s.o.) **II** *vpr* **s'émotionner** *F* to get excited/to get worked up/to get into a state*.

empaffé [ãpafe] *P* **I** *a* (*a*) effeminate/poofy/queer (*b*) troublesome **II** *nm* (*a*) effeminate man; pansy/fairy (*b*) homosexual*/poof(ter)/*esp NAm* fag(got)/queer.

empaffer [ãpafe] **I** *vtr V* to have anal sex* with/to sodomize*/to bugger (s.o.); to screw s.o.'s arse/*NAm* ass. (*Voir* **paf II 2**) **II** *vpr* **s'empaffer** *P* to get drunk*. (*Voir* **paf I**)

empaillé, ée [ãpɑje] **I** *F a* stupid*/dim(-witted) **II** *n* (*a*) fool*/dope/dimwit (*b*) clumsy clot.

empalmer [ãpalme] *vtr F* to palm (card, coin, etc).

empalmeur [ãpalmœr] *nm F* card-sharper.

empapaouté [ãpapaute] *nm P* = **empaffé II.**

empapaouter [ãpapaute] *vtr P* = **empaffer.**

empaqueté [ɑ̃pakte] *nm P* = **empaillé II.**

empaqueter [ɑ̃pakte] *vtr P* **1.** to arrest* **2.** to send to prison* **3.** to fool (s.o.).

empaumer [ɑ̃pome] *vtr* **1.** *F* to dupe/to hoax*/to pull a fast one on (s.o.); **se faire empaumer/se laisser empaumer**, to be tricked/conned/taken in **2.** *P* to arrest*.

empêché [ɑ̃peʃe] *a F* **il est empêché de sa personne/il a l'air empêché**, he's awkward/he doesn't know what to do with himself.

empêcher [ɑ̃peʃe] *vtr F* **n'empêche**, all the same; so what?; makes no odds/same difference.

empêcheur [ɑ̃peʃœr] *nm F* **un empêcheur de danser en rond**, a spoilsport/a wet blanket/a real drag; **c'est un empêcheur de tourner rond**, he's the nigger in the woodpile.

empégaler [ɑ̃pegale] *vtr P* to pawn/to hock. (*Voir* **pégal(e)**)

empéguer [ɑ̃pege] *vtr P* = **empaumer 1.**

empeigne [ɑ̃pɛɲ] *nf P* **1. gueule d'empeigne** (*i*) ugly face*/ugly mug (*ii*) disagreeable person/sourpuss **2. marcher sur les empeignes**, to be down at heel/to be down on one's uppers.

empétardé [ɑ̃petarde] *nm P* (active) homosexual*.

empétarder [ɑ̃petarde] *vtr P* to have anal sex* with (s.o.); to screw/to fuck/to ball (s.o.'s) arse/*NAm* ass.

empiffrer [ɑ̃pifre] **I** *vtr F* to stuff/to cram (s.o. with food) **II** *vpr* **s'empiffrer** *F* to eat* greedily/to pig oneself/to stuff one's face.

empiler [ɑ̃pile] *vtr F* to swindle*/to con/to cheat/to do/to rook (s.o.); **se faire empiler**, to get done/to be had/to get ripped off.

empileur, -euse [ɑ̃pilœr, -øz] *n*

F swindler*/cheat/fraud/trickster/con man.

emplacarder [ɑ̃plakarde] *vtr P* to send to prison*.

emplafonner [ɑ̃plafɔne] *vtr P* **1.** to lay into (s.o.)/to beat (s.o.) up* **2.** to butt (s.o.) **3.** (*voiture*) to collide with/to run (smack) into/to smash into another vehicle).

emplâtre [ɑ̃platr] *nm* **1.** *F* spineless person; **c'est un emplâtre**, he's got no backbone **2.** *F* food that lies heavy on the stomach **3.** *F* (*a*) **mettre un emplâtre à sa fortune**, to patch up one's fortune (*b*) **c'est mettre un emplâtre sur une jambe de bois**, it's not the slightest use/it's no earthly use. (*Voir* **cautère**) **4.** *O P* blow*/punch/wallop; **coller un emplâtre sur la figure de qn**, to slap s.o. round the face.

emplâtrer [ɑ̃platre] *vtr P* **1.** to steal*/to nick/to knock off **2.** to lay into (s.o.)/to beat (s.o.) up*.

empoisonnant [ɑ̃pwazɔnɑ̃] *a F* annoying/irritating/aggravating; **c'est empoisonnant**, it's a damned nuisance.

empoisonné [ɑ̃pwazɔne] *a F* fed up*/sick and tired; **être empoisonné par qch**, to be plagued by/with sth; to be driven crazy/up the wall by sth.

empoisonnement [ɑ̃pwazɔnmɑ̃] *nm F* **quel empoisonnement que cette femme!** what a pest/pain that woman is! **cette affaire ne me donne que des empoisonnements**, I've had nothing but trouble from that business.

empoisonner [ɑ̃pwazɔne] **I** *vtr F* to bore*/to annoy*/to bug/to pester (s.o.); to drive s.o. up the wall **II** *vpr* **s'empoisonner** *F* (*a*) to get bored sick (*b*) to be driven up the wall (by s.o./sth).

empoisonneur, -euse [ɑ̃pwazɔnœr, -øz] *n F* deadly/crashing bore*; pain in the neck.

s'empoivrer [sãpwavre] *vpr P* to get drunk*.

emporter [ãpɔrte] *vtr P* **se faire emporter**, to get arrested/run in (by the police). (*Voir* **morceau 4**; **paradis**)

empoté, -ée [ãpɔte] *F* **I** *a* clumsy/awkward; **être empoté comme un casse-pot**, to be a clumsy clot; to be all thumbs **II** *n* (*a*) clumsy clot (*b*) dimwit/thickie; **espèce d'empoté!** you great idiot!/ you dumb cluck!

emproser [ãproze] *vtr P* = **empaffer.**

en [ã] *pron F* **il en est,** he's a homosexual*/he's one of them.

en-bourgeois [ãburʒwa] *nm inv P* plain-clothes policeman.

encadrer [ãkɑdre] *vtr* **1.** *F* **il a encadré un arbre,** he wrapped his car round a tree **2.** *P* **je ne peux pas l'encadrer,** I can't stand (the sight of) him **3.** *P* **tu peux le faire encadrer!** you know where you can stick it!/you can shove it up your arse! **4.** *P* to hit (s.o.) (repeatedly) in the face/about the head.

encaisse [ãkɛs] *nf F* (*boxe, etc*) **il est dur à l'encaisse,** he can take a lot of punishment.

encaisser [ãkɛse] *vtr* **1.** *F* (*a*) (*boxeur, etc*) **encaisser un coup,** to take a blow; **il a encaissé,** he took a hiding; **il sait encaisser,** he can take it (*b*) **il l'encaisse sans broncher,** he grins and bears it; **j'ai encaissé,** I put up with it **2.** *P* **je ne peux pas l'encaisser,** I can't stand (the sight of) him. (*Voir* **salade**)

encalbécher [ãkalbeʃe] *vtr P* (*rare*) to butt (s.o.).

encaldosser [ãkaldose] *vtr P* **1.** *A* to grab (s.o.) from behind **2. se faire encaldosser,** to be screwed from behind; to get one's arse/ *NAm* ass fucked/balled.

encanner [ãkane] *vtr P* to steal*.

encanneur, -euse [ãkanœr, -øz] *n P* crook/thief*.

encarrade [ãkarad] *nf P* entry; entering.

encarrer [ãkare] *vtr&i P* to enter.

enceintrer [ãsɛ̃tre] *vtr P* to make pregnant*.

enchariboter [ãʃaribɔte] *vtr P* (*rare*) **1.** to bore* (s.o.) **2.** to annoy*/to bug/to pester (s.o.).

enchaudelancer [ãʃodlãse] *vtr O P* **enchaudelancer qn,** to give s.o. VD*/the clap. (*Voir* **chaudelance**)

enchetarder [ãʃtarde], **enchetiber** [ãʃtibe] *vtr P* (*peu usuel*) **1.** to arrest*; **se faire enchetarder,** to get nabbed **2.** to put in prison*; **se faire enchetarder,** to get put inside/away.

enchoser [ãʃoze] *vtr P* **1.** to get pregnant*/to put (s.o.) up the spout/*esp NAm* to knock (s.o.) up **2.** = **emmerder I 1, 2.**

enchrister [ãkriste], **enchtiber** [ãʃtibe] *vtr P* to send to prison*/to put away.

encloquer [ãklɔke] *vtr P* to get (s.o.) pregnant*/to put (s.o.) up the spout/*esp NAm* to knock (s.o.) up.

encoinsta [ãkwɛ̃sta] *nm,* **encoinstas(s)** [ãkwɛ̃stas] *nm,* **encoinsto** [ãkwɛ̃sto] *nm P* door wedge (used by burglars to force a door).

encordé [ãkɔrde] *nm F* (*ecc*) Franciscan friar.

encorné [ãkɔrne] *nm F* deceived husband/cuckold.

encorner [ãkɔrne] *vtr F* to deceive/to cuckold (a husband).

encrister [ãkriste] *vtr P* = **enchrister.**

encroumé [ãkrume] *a P* in debt.

s'encroumer [sãkrume] *vpr P* to get into debt.

encroûtant [ãkrutã] *a F* soul-destroying (occupation, etc).

encroûté [ãkrute] *nm F* **(vieux, vieil) encroûté**, old fogey*/(old) fuddy-duddy.

s'encroûter [sãkrute] *vpr F* to get into a rut/to get stuck in one's ways/to stagnate/to become an old fogey*.

enculage [ãkylaʒ] *nm P* **enculage de mouches**, quibbling/hair-splitting/nit-picking.

enculé [ãkyle] *nm V* **1.** homosexual*/homo/fag(got)/queer **2.** fool*/cretin/silly sod/bloody fool/stupid bastard*/silly fucker; **bande d'enculés!** (what a) load of cretins!/(what a) load of bloody idiots!

enculer [ãkyle] *vtr* **1.** *P* **enculer les mouches**, to quibble/to split hairs/to nit-pick **2.** *V* (*a*) to have anal sex* with (s.o.)/to sodomize* (s.o.)/to bugger s.o./to screw s.o.'s arse/*NAm* ass; to buttfuck (s.o.); **va te faire enculer!** bugger off!/sod off!/fuck off!/go fuck yourself! (*b*) *abs* to be a homosexual*.

enculeur [ãkylœr] *nm* **1.** *V* = **enculé 2.** *P* **enculeur de mouches**, quibbler/hair-splitter/nit-picker.

endauffer [ãdofe] *vtr V* = **endoffer**.

endécher [ãdeʃe] *vtr P* **endécher qn**, to make s.o. short (of money); to put s.o. in an awkward financial situation.

endêvé [ãdɛve] *a O F* angry*/furious; provoked/aggravated.

endêver [ãdɛve] *vi F* **faire endêver qn**, to torment s.o./to drive s.o. wild/to get s.o.'s goat.

endoffer [ãdofe] *vtr V* to have anal sex* with (s.o.)/to screw (s.o.) from behind/to bugger (s.o.). (*Voir* **dauffer**)

endormant [ãdɔrmã] *a F* dull/boring/deadly.

endormeur, euse [ãdɔrmœr, -øz] *n* **1.** *F* crashing bore* **2.** *F* cajoler/sweet-talker **3.** *P* thief.

endormi [ãdɔrmi] *nm P* magistrate/judge/beak.

endormir [ãdɔrmir] **I** *vtr* **1.** *F* to bore* (s.o.) stiff **2.** *F* to cajole/to sweet-talk (s.o.) **3.** *F* (*boxe*) to knock out (an opponent) **4.** *P* to kill* **II** *vpr* **s'endormir** *F* **s'endormir sur une affaire**, to let sth drag on/to sit on sth. (*Voir* **mastic**; **rôti**[1])

endosses [ãdos] *nfpl P* **1.** shoulders; back **2.** **en avoir plein les endosses** (*i*) to be exhausted*/to be dead beat (*ii*) to be sick (and tired) of sth/to have had a bellyful of sth/to be browned off with sth.

endroit [ãdrwa] *nm* **1.** *F* **le petit endroit**, WC*/the loo/the smallest room **2.** *P* **le bon endroit**, (the) buttocks*.

enfance [ãfãs] *nf F* **c'est l'enfance de l'art**, it's very easy*/it's child's-play.

enfariné [ãfarine] *a F* **1.** **la langue/la bouche/la goule enfarinée/le bec enfariné**, mealy-mouth(ed) **2.** **être enfariné**, to be in a fix*.

enfifré [ãfifre] *nm P* homosexual*/poof/fag(got)/queer.

enfifrer [ãfifre] *vtr P* to have anal sex* with s.o./to bugger (s.o.).

enfilade [ãfilad] *nf F* run of bad luck.

enfilé [ãfile] *nm P* = **enfifré**.

enfiler [ãfile] **I** *vtr* **1.** *F* to swindle*/to cheat (s.o.) **2.** *F* (*a*) to knock back (a drink) (*b*) **s'enfiler un bon dîner**, to treat oneself to a good dinner; **s'enfiler un verre de bière**, to knock back a pint (of beer) (*c*) **s'enfiler une corvée**, to take on a rotten job (of work) **3.** *V* to have sex* with s.o.; **enfiler une nana**, to lay/to screw/to make a girl; **va te faire enfiler!** get stuffed!/go screw yourself! (*Voir* perle 3) **II** *vpr* **s'enfiler** *V* to have sex*/to make love; **s'enfiler une nana,** to screw/to ball/to make a girl.

enfileur, euse [ãfilœr, -øz] *n F* swindler*/cheat.

enflaquer [ãflake] *vtr O V* to shit(e) on/to crap on (sth).

enflé [ãfle] *nm F* fool*/clot/jerk; **espèce d'enflé!** you (blinking) idiot!/you dope!

enfler [ãfle] *vtr P* **1.** to swindle*/ to cheat (s.o.)/to double-cross (s.o.) **2.** to get (s.o.) pregnant*/to put (s.o.) in the club/to knock (s.o.) up.

enflure [ãflyr] *nf F* = **enflé.**

enfoiré [ãfware] *V* **I** *nm* **1.** homosexual*/poof/*esp NAm* fag(got)/queer **2. espèce d'enfoiré!** you stupid bugger!/you (stupid) prick!/you silly sod!/*esp NAm* you dumb shit! **II** *a* stupid*/dozy-arsed.

enfoirer [ãfware] *vtr V* to have anal sex* with (s.o.)/to screw (s.o.) from behind/to bugger (s.o.).

enfoncé [ãfɔ̃se] *a P* (a) beaten/ licked (b) cheated/swindled/rooked.

enfoncer [ãfɔ̃se] **I** *vtr* **1.** *F* to get the better of (s.o.)/to beat (s.o.) hollow/to lick (s.o.); **enfoncer qn dans les grandes largeurs,** to beat s.o. hollow/to hammer s.o. into the ground; **ça enfonce tout!** that beats everything!/that's got them all lick- ed **2.** *P* to accuse (s.o.)/to put the finger on (s.o.)/to blow the gaff on (s.o.) **3.** *F* **enfoncer une porte ouverte,** to come out with the obvi- ous; to flog a dead horse **II** *vpr* **s'enfoncer 1.** *V* to have sex*/to make love/to have it away **2.** *P* **s'enfoncer dans sa merde,** to be going downhill/to be on a bummer **3.** *F* **s'enfoncer qch dans le crâne,** to beat sth into one's head/to get sth into one's head.

enfonceur, euse [ãfɔ̃sœr, -øz] *n F* **enfonceur de porte(s) ouverte(s),**

s.o. who comes out with the obvi- ous. (*Voir* **enfoncer 3**)

enfouiller [ãfuje] *vtr P* to pocket.

enfouraillé [ãfuraje] *a P* armed with/carrying/packing a gun.

enfourailler [ãfuraje] **I** *vtr V* to have anal sex* with (s.o.)/to buttfuck (s.o.)/to bugger (s.o.) **II** *vpr* **s'enfourailler** *P* to arm oneself with a gun/to pack a gun.

enfournable [ãfurnabl] *a V* (*esp femme*) attractive/sexy; screwable/ fuckable.

enfourner [ãfurne] **I** *vtr* **1.** *F* **enfourner une affaire,** to start sth up/to get sth going/to get sth off the ground **2.** *F* to gobble (sth) up; to shove sth down/to stuff sth into (one's mouth, throat) **3.** *P* **enfourner un enfant à une femme,** to make a woman pregnant*/to put a bun in the oven/*esp NAm* to knock a woman up **II** *vpr* **s'enfourner** *F* **1.** to get into a fix*/to get mixed up in sth **2. s'enfourner dans une impasse,** to go down a blind alley.

engailler [ãgaje] *vtr P O* to deceive/to take in/to con.

engeance [ãʒãs] *nf F* mob/crew; **quelle engeance!** what a collection (of yobs, etc)! **triste engeance!** what a crew (of pathetic-looking charac- ters, etc)!

engelure [ãʒlyr] *nf P* (damned) nuisance/pain in the neck.

engerber [ãʒɛrbe] *vtr P* to arrest*.

engin [ãʒɛ̃] *nm V* penis*/tool.

englandé [ãglãde] *nm V* homosex- ual*/poof/fag(got).

englander [ãglãde] *vtr P* to swin- dle*/to cheat/to diddle; **se faire englander,** to get rooked.

engliche¹ [ãgliʃ] *a P* English.

Engliche² *nm&f P* Englishman*/ English woman/Brit.

engourdir [ãgurdir] *vtr P* to steal*.

engrainer [ãgrɛne] *vtr P* **1.** *O* to take on/to sign on (a worker) **2.** to con (s.o.) (**dans,** into).

engrais [ãgrɛ] *nm P* money*.

engraisser [ãgrɛse] *vtr P* **engraisser qn,** to give regular amounts of money to s.o.; (*prostituée et son souteneur*) **c'est elle qui l'engraisse,** she's his meal-ticket; **se faire engraisser,** to be kept.

engrosser [ãgrose] *vtr P* to get (s.o.) pregnant*/to get (s.o.) (into trouble)/to knock (s.o.) up.

engrosseur [ãgrosœr] *nm P* man who gets women pregnant*/gets girls into trouble/knocks girls up.

engueulade [ãgœlad] *nf P* (*a*) severe reprimand*/(good) telling-off/bawling out/bollocking; **recevoir une engueulade,** to get a rocket/to get a real bollocking; **envoyer une lettre d'engueulade à qn,** to write s.o. a stinker/a stinking letter (*b*) slanging match; **avoir une engueulade avec qn,** to have a slanging match/a huge row with s.o. (*Voir* **maison**)

engueulement [ãgœlmã] *nm A P =* **engueulade.**

engueuler [ãgœle] **I** *vtr P* **1.** to reprimand*/to bawl out; **se faire engueuler,** to get bawled out/to get a rocket/to get a (right) bollocking **2.** to insult. (*Voir* **poisson**) **II** *vpr* **s'engueuler** *P* **s'engueuler (ferme),** to have a slanging match; **s'engueuler avec qn,** to have a (flaming) row with s.o.

enguirlander [ãgirlãde] *vtr F* to reprimand* (s.o.)/to tell (s.o.) off/ to give (s.o.) a (good) dressing-down; **se faire enguirlander,** to get torn off a strip/to get a rocket.

énième [enjɛm] *a F* **pour la énième fois,** for the umpteenth time.

enjamber [ãʒãbe] *vtr V* **enjamber une femme,** to have sex* with a woman/to ride a woman; to get one's leg over.

enjambeur [ãʒãbœr] *nm V* womanizer*/highly-sexed male/lecher.

enlever [ãlve] *vtr F =* **enguirlander.** (*Voir* **ballon 1**)

enneigé [ãneʒe] *a P* high on cocaine*.

enquiller [ãkije] **I** *vtr&i P* to enter; **se faire enquiller dans une affaire,** to get involved in sth/ dragged into sth **II** *vpr* **s'enquiller** *P* to enter/to get in.

enquilleuse [ãkijøz] *nf P* woman thief*/shoplifter who hides stolen goods between her legs.

enquiquinant, ante [ãkikinã, -ãt] *a F* infuriating/irritating; **il est enquiquinant,** he's a pain in the neck/he gets up my nose.

enquiquinement [ãkikinmã] *nm F* (*a*) bore*/(terrible) nuisance/pest (*b*) pestering; **quel enquiquinement!** what a flipping/flaming/darned nuisance!

enquiquiner [ãkikine] **I** *vtr F* to bore*; to irritate/to annoy*/to aggravate/to pester/to bug; **je suis bien enquiquiné,** I've got problems **II** *vpr* **s'enquiquiner** *F* **s'enquiquiner (de qn/qch),** to be/to get bored with/fed up of/tired of (s.o./sth).

enquiquineur, euse [ãkikinœr, -øz] *F* **I** *a* infuriating/irritating **II** *n* (terrible) nuisance/pain in the neck.

enragé, ée [ãraʒe] *F* **I** *a* (*i*) **vie enragée,** wild/energetic life (*ii*) enthusiastic (sportsman, etc); **joueur enragé,** inveterate gambler/fanatic; **un facho enragé,** an out-and-out fascist **II** *n* **un(e) enragé(e) du football,** a football fanatic/a football nut; (*politique*) **les enragés,** the extremists. (*Voir* **vache**)

enrouler [ãrule] *vi F* (*cyclisme*) to pedal in an easy, relaxed manner.

s'enroupiller [sãrupije] *vpr P* to fall asleep/to flake out.

enseigne [ɑ̃sɛɲ] *nf F* **nous sommes tous logés à la même enseigne,** we're all in the same boat.

ensuqué [ɑ̃syke] *a O P* **1.** exhausted*/tired out/weary **2.** dazed/stupefied (*esp* under the influence of drugs).

entasseur, -euse [ɑ̃tɑsœr, -øz] *n F* miser*; hoarder.

entendu [ɑ̃tɑ̃dy] *a F* **comme de bien entendu,** naturally/of course; that goes without saying.

enterrement [ɑ̃tɛrmɑ̃] *nm F* **1.** **avoir une tête/une gueule d'enterrement,** to have a face as long as a fiddle; to look really down/gloomy; **ne fais pas cette tête d'enterrement!** don't look so miserable!/don't be such a misery! **2.** **c'est un enterrement de première classe,** that (thing) has been shelved for good.

enterrer [ɑ̃tɛre] *vtr F* **1.** **enterrer sa vie de garçon,** to have a stag party/a stag night **2.** **il nous enterrera tous,** he'll outlive the lot of us.

entiffer [ɑ̃tife] *vi P* to enter/to breeze in; to barge in.

entifler [ɑ̃tifle] *P* **I** *vi* = **entiffer** **II** *vtr* **entifler qn,** to marry s.o. (off) (avec, to) **III** *vpr* **s'entifler** *P* **1.** = **entiffer** **2.** to get married*.

entoiler [ɑ̃twale] *vtr P* to arrest*; **se faire entoiler,** to get nicked/run in.

entôlage [ɑ̃tolaʒ] *nm P* (*esp en parlant d'une prostituée*) stealing from/robbing/fleecing (a customer).

entôler [ɑ̃tole] *vtr P* (*esp en parlant d'une prostituée*) to rob/to steal (from)/to swindle*/to diddle; **entôler un clille,** to fleece*/to pull a fast one on one's customer/john.

entôleuse [ɑ̃tpløz] *nf P* prostitute* who robs/fleeces/swindles a customer.

entonner [ɑ̃tɔne] *F* (*rare*) **I** *vtr* to knock back (a drink) **II** *vi* to

booze/to tipple/to drink* like a fish.

entonnoir [ɑ̃tɔnwar] *nm P* **1.** throat/gullet **2.** stomach* **3.** **entonnoir à musique,** ear* **4.** hard drinker/drunkard*/boozer.

entortiller [ɑ̃tɔrtije] *vtr F* **entortiller qn,** to wheedle s.o./to cajole s.o./to get round s.o.; **elle sait l'entortiller,** she can twist him round her little finger.

entortilleur, -euse [ɑ̃tɔrtijœr, -øz] *n F* wheedler/cajoler/sweet-talker.

entourer [ɑ̃ture] *vtr P* to cheat/to deceive; to swindle*/to defraud.

entourloupe [ɑ̃turlup] *nf F* = **entourloupette.**

entourlouper [ɑ̃turlupe] *vtr F* **entourlouper qn,** to play a mean/rotten/dirty trick on s.o.; to swindle* s.o.

entourloupette [ɑ̃turlupɛt] *nf F* mean/rotten/dirty trick. (*Voir* **maison**)

entournures [ɑ̃turnyr] *nfpl F* **être serré/gêné aux entournures** (*i*) to be awkward/ill at ease (*ii*) to be in financial difficulties/short of cash.

entraîneur [ɑ̃trɛnœr] *nm F* decoy.

entraîneuse [ɑ̃trɛnøz] *nf F* hostess/bar-girl.

entraver [ɑ̃trave] *vtr P* to understand/to twig; **je n'entrave/je n'y entrave que couic/que dalle/que pouic,** I don't get it; I can't make head or tail of it; I haven't the foggiest/the faintest.

s'entre-cogner [sɑ̃trəkɔɲe] *vpr F* to have a fight/a punch-up.

entrée [ɑ̃tre] *nf* **1.** *F adv phr* **d'entrée (de jeu),** from the word go **2.** *V* **entrée des artistes,** anus*/backdoor. (*Voir* **service 3**)

entrejambes [ɑ̃trəʒɑ̃b] *nm P* **en avoir dans l'entrejambes,** to be well-hung/to have a nice bulge.

entremichon [ɑ̃trəmiʃɔ̃] *nm P* the cleft separating the two buttocks.

entrêper [ɑ̃trɛpe], **entréper** [ɑ̃trepe] *vtr P* (*camelot, etc*) to attract/to pull in (a crowd).

entripaillé [ɑ̃tripɑje] *a F* fat.

entrouducuter [ɑ̃trudykyte] *vtr V* to have anal sex* with (s.o.)/to bugger (s.o.)/to fuck (s.o.'s) ass.

entubage [ɑ̃tyباʒ] *nm P* swindling/doing/conning; swindle/con.

entuber [ɑ̃tybe] *vtr* **1.** *P* to swindle*/to do/to con; to dupe/to have on; **se faire entuber,** to be taken for a ride/to be had/to get ripped off **2.** *V* to have anal sex* with (s.o.)/ to sodomize* (s.o.)/to bugger (s.o.).

envapé [ɑ̃vape] *a P* under the influence of drugs; doped (up)/ charged (up).

enveloppe [ɑ̃vlɔp] *nf F* bribe*; **passer une enveloppe à qn,** to bribe s.o./to grease s.o.'s palm; **marcher à l'enveloppe,** to take a bribe/to go on the take.

envelopper [ɑ̃vlɔpe] *vtr P* **1.** to dupe/to hoax* (s.o.); **se faire envelopper,** to be taken in/to be taken for a ride/to be conned **2.** to arrest*; **se faire envelopper,** to get nicked **3.** to steal*/to pinch.

envers [ɑ̃vɛr] *adv phr P* **les avoir à l'envers,** to be lazy*/to sit about doing nothing.

enviandé [ɑ̃vjɑ̃de] *nm V* homosexual*/poof/fag(got).

enviander [ɑ̃vjɑ̃de] *vtr V* to have anal sex* with (s.o.)/to bugger (s.o.).

envie [ɑ̃vi] *nf F* (*esp langage enfantin*) **avoir envie,** to want to (do) wee-wee/to want a wee.

envoyer [ɑ̃vwaje] **I** *vtr* **1.** *P* **les envoyer,** to pay up*/to cough up/ to shell out. (*Voir* **soudure**) **2.** *P* **en envoyer une,** to take one's turn to tell a story, etc **3.** *P* (*a*) **envoyer qn en l'air** (*i*) to kill* s.o./ *esp NAm* to blow s.o. away (*ii*) to

send s.o. flying; to floor (an opponent) (*b*) **ça, c'est envoyé!** that's got him!/that's stumped him!/that's floored him! (*Voir* **bain 2; balader I; dinguer; dire 5; fumée 1; paître; se promener; rose II 2**) **II** *vpr* **s'envoyer 1.** *P* to wolf down/to scoff/to guzzle (food); to knock back (a drink); **s'envoyer un verre (de vin) (derrière la cravate),** to knock back a drink/a glass of wine **2.** *P* **s'envoyer la vaisselle,** to tackle the washing-up; to get landed/stuck with the washing-up; **s'envoyer tout le boulot,** to get on with/to get landed with the whole job **3.** *V* (*a*) **s'envoyer qn,** to have sex* with s.o.; **s'envoyer une nana,** to have it off with/to have it away with/to lay/to screw a girl/a bird/a chick (*b*) **s'envoyer en l'air** (*i*) to have sex*/to have it off/to have it away (*ii*) to have an orgasm*/to come (*iii*) to get high (on drugs, drink, etc) (*iv*) to commit suicide*/ to do oneself in.

épahules [epayl] *nfpl P* shoulders; **rouler des épahules,** to swagger/to throw one's weight around.

épais [epɛ] *a P* **j'en ai épais (sur la patate),** I've had (more than) enough of it/I'm fed up (to the back teeth) with it/I've had it up to here.

épaisseur [epɛsœr] *nf F* **se tirer d'épaisseur,** to manage to get out of a scrape.

éparpiller [eparpije] *vi P* **en éparpiller de première,** to sleep like a log.

épastrouillant [epastrujɑ̃] *a O F* = **épatant.**

épastrouiller [epastruje] *vtr O F* = **épater.**

épatamment [epatamɑ̃] *adv O F* stunningly/staggeringly/fabulously/ admirably.

épatant [epatɑ̃] *a O F* **1.** excellent*/first-rate/super/great; **c'est un type épatant,** he's a great guy; **ce**

n'est pas bien **épatant,** it's nothing to write home about **2.** *int* **épatant!** (that's) fine/great!

épate [epat] *nf* F **faire de l'épate** (*i*) to show off*/to swank/to put on airs (*ii*) to bluff (*iii*) to create a sensation/to make a splash; **faire des épates,** to make a fuss; **un faiseur d'épate,** a show-off.

épaté [epate] *a* F flabbergasted/amazed/dumbfounded/struck all of a heap.

épatement [epatmã] *nm* F amazement/stupefaction.

épater [epate] *vtr* F to flabbergast*/to amaze; **rien ne l'épate/il ne se laisse pas épater,** he isn't easily flummoxed; **épater la galerie,** to impress (the) onlookers/to show off*/to play for the gallery.

épaule [epol] *nf* F **1. donner un coup d'épaule à qn,** to help s.o. (out)/to give s.o. a helping hand **2. faire qch par-dessus l'épaule,** to do sth in a perfunctory manner **3. regarder qn par-dessus l'épaule,** to look down one's nose at s.o. **4. en avoir par-dessus les épaules,** to be fed up* (with sth); **j'en ai par-dessus les épaules,** I've had a bellyful (of it) **5. rouler les épaules,** to swagger.

épauler [epole] *vtr* F **épauler qn,** to help s.o. (out)/to give s.o. a helping hand/to give s.o. a leg-up; to back s.o. up.

épée [epe] *nf* F **1.** expert/ace **2. coup d'épée dans l'eau,** wasted/fruitless effort; **c'est un coup d'épée dans l'eau,** it's come to nothing.

épicemar(d) [épismar] *nm* P grocer.

épicerie [episri] *nf* F **changer d'épicerie,** to make a change (of surroundings, etc)/to move on/to get a change of air. (*Voir* **crémerie**)

épicier [episje] *nm* **1.** F s.o. indifferent to culture; philistine **2.** V

baiser qn en épicier, to make love to s.o. without enjoyment/mechanically.

épinards [epinar] *nmpl* P **aller aux épinards,** to be kept by a prostitute*. (*Voir* **beurre 5; graine 4**)

épingle [epɛ̃gl] *nf* **1.** F **tiré à quatre épingles,** in one's Sunday best/dressed up* to the nines **2.** F **tirer son épingle du jeu,** to get out of a tough situation unharmed/to get out while there's still time **3.** F **monter qch en épingle,** to make much of sth/to spotlight sth/to make a song and dance about sth **4.** V **ramasser des épingles,** to have anal sex*. (*Voir* **pelote 7; tête 19**)

épingler [epɛ̃gle] *vtr* **1.** F **épingler qn** (*i*) to arrest* s.o.; **se faire épingler,** to get nicked/nabbed (*ii*) to catch s.o. out.

épucheur, -euse [eplyʃœr, -øz] *n* **1.** F fault-finder **2.** P **éplucheuse de lentilles,** lesbian*.

épluchures [eplyʃyr] *nfpl* F **attention aux épluchures!** watch your step!/mind how you go!

époilant [epwalã] *a* A F surprising/astonishing; wonderful (news).

éponge [epɔ̃ʒ] *nf* **1.** P lung; **avoir les éponges mitées (à zéro)/bouffées aux mites,** to have tuberculosis/TB **2.** F **passons l'éponge (là-dessus),** let's say no more about it; let bygones be bygones **3.** F drunk(ard)*/soak **4.** P nymphomaniac/nympho.

éponger [epɔ̃ʒe] *vtr* **1.** F **éponger un retard,** to make up for lost time **2.** F to clean up (a large profit, etc) **3.** P **éponger qn,** to clean s.o. out (at gambling, etc)/to take s.o. to the cleaners **4.** V (*a*) (*prostituée*) to give sexual satisfaction to (a client) (*b*) **se faire éponger,** to have sex*.

époques [epɔk] *nfpl* F **avoir ses époques,** to have a period*/to have the curse; **elle a ses époques,** it's her time of the month.

époustouflant [epustuflɑ̃] *a F* amazing/staggering/stunning/terrific.

époustoufler [epustufle] *vtr F* to amaze/to astound/to flabbergast*.

épouvantail [epuvɑ̃taj] *nm F* **1.** bogey/bugbear/bugaboo **2. quel épouvantail!** what a fright!/what a mess!

éreintage [erɛ̃taʒ] *nm F* = **éreintement** 2.

éreintant [erɛ̃tɑ̃] *a F* exhausting/back-breaking/gruelling/killing (work, etc); **c'est éreintant!** it really takes it out of you!

éreinté [erɛ̃te] *a F* exhausted*/fagged (out)/bushed/whacked/shattered.

éreintement [erɛ̃tmɑ̃] *nm F* **1.** exhaustion **2.** (*critique*) savage attack/slating/panning; **éreintement avec des fleurs,** damning with faint praise.

éreinter [erɛ̃te] **I** *vtr F* **1.** to exhaust*/to tire (s.o.) out/to shatter s.o. **2.** to criticize* (author, s.o.'s character, etc) unmercifully; to slate/to pan/to roast/to pull to pieces (author, book, performance, etc) **II** *vpr* **s'éreinter** *F* **1.** to exhaust* oneself/to tire oneself out **2. s'éreinter à qch,** to slave away/to slog away at sth.

ergots [ɛrgo] *nmpl F* **monter/se dresser sur ses ergots,** to get on one's high horse.

ergotage [ɛrgɔtaʒ] *nm F* quibbling/hair-splitting/nit-picking.

ergoter [ɛrgɔte] *vi F* to quibble/to split hairs; **tu ne vas pas ergoter pour si peu,** don't be so finicky/choosy/picky.

erreur [ɛrœr] *nf P* **(y a) pas d'erreur!** that's right!/you're (so) right!/and no mistake!/no doubt (about it)!

s'esbigner [sɛzbiɲe] *vpr P* to clear off/to scarper/to do a bunk.

esbloquer [ɛzblɔke] **I** *vtr O P* to flabbergast*/to amaze/to astound **II** *vpr* **s'esbloquer** *O P* to be flabbergasted/dumbfounded.

esbrouf(f)ant [ɛzbrufɑ̃] *a F* amazing/astounding/staggering/unheard-of.

esbrouf(f)e [ɛzbruf] *nf F* (*a*) showing off; **faire de l'esbrouf(f)e** (*i*) to show off*/to put on airs (*ii*) to bluff; to shoot a line (*b*) **vol à l'esbrouf(f)e,** pocket-picking by hustling one's victim.

esbrouf(f)er [ɛzbrufe] *vtr&i F* (*a*) = **faire de l'esbrouf(f)e** (**esbrouf(f)e**) (*b*) **esbrouf(f)er qn,** to impress s.o./to take s.o. in/to bluff s.o. (by putting on airs, by blustering).

esbrouf(f)eur, euse [ɛzbrufœr, -øz] *F* **I** *a* (*a*) swanky/swanking (*b*) hectoring/hustling **II** *n* (*a*) swank/show-off* (*b*) hustler (*c*) bluffer (*d*) pickpocket* who hustles his/her victim; snatch-and-grab thief.

s'esbrousser [sɛzbruse] *vpr F* to run away*/to make a run for it/to make a break.

escagassant [ɛskagasɑ̃] *a P* difficult/tough.

escagasser [ɛskagase] *vtr P* (*régional*) **1.** to kill*/to bump off/to do in **2.** to beat (s.o.) up*/to do s.o. over **3.** to dumbfound/to flabbergast* (s.o.).

escalope [ɛskalɔp] *nf P* **1. rouler une escalope à qn,** to give s.o. a French kiss **2.** *pl* **escalopes,** ears* **3.** *pl* feet*.

escamper [ɛskɑ̃pe] *vi F* to run away*/to beat it/to clear off.

escampette [ɛskɑ̃pɛt] *nf F* **prendre la poudre d'escampette,** to run away*/to do a bunk/to take to one's heels.

escargot [ɛskargo] *nm P* (*rare*) telephone*.

escoffier [ɛskɔfje] *vtr A P* to kill*/to bump off.

s'escrimer [sɛskrime] *vpr F* s'escrimer à faire qch, to wear oneself out/to knock oneself out doing sth; to bite off more than one can chew.

esgourde [ɛsgurd] *nf P* ear*; **écarquillez vos esgourdes!** pin back your lugholes!

esgourder [ɛsgurde] *vtr P* (*i*) to hear (*ii*) to listen to.

esgourne [ɛsgurn] *nf A P* ear*.

espadoches [ɛspadɔʃ] *nfpl*, **espagas** [ɛspaga] *nmpl P* (= *espadrilles*) rope-soled sandals/espadrilles.

espèce [ɛspɛs] *nf* (*péj: pour renforcer une injure*) espèce de ... : *F* cette espèce d'idiot/cet espèce d'idiot, that silly fool*/that stupid idiot; *P* espèce de crétin!/espèce d'imbécile!/espèce d'andouille!/ espèce de con! you bloody fool! espèce de salaud! you bloody swine!/you bastard!

espingo [ɛspẽgo], **espingouin** [ɛspẽgwẽ] *P* I *a* Spanish II *nm* (*a*) Spanish (language) (*b*) un Espingo, a Spaniard*/a dago/a wop.

esquimau, *pl* **-aux** [ɛskimo] *nm F* choc-ice.

esquintant [ɛskẽtã] *a F* exhausting/back-breaking (work, etc).

esquinté [ɛskẽte] *a F* 1. exhausted*/all in/shattered/dead beat 2. (*santé, etc*) ruined.

esquintement [ɛskẽtmã] *nm F* 1. exhaustion 2. thrashing/beating/good hiding.

esquinter [ɛskẽte] I *vtr F* 1. to exhaust* (s.o.)/to tire (s.o.) out/to wear (s.o.) out/to knock (s.o.) up 2. (*a*) to kill* (s.o.)/to do (s.o.) in (*b*) to smash up (sth); to spoil/to damage; **s'esquinter les yeux**, to ruin one's eyes; **s'esquinter la santé**, to do in one's health; **esquinter une voiture**, to flog a car (to death)/to run a car into the ground; to smash up/to wreck a car. (*Voir*

tempérament 3) II *vpr* **s'esquinter** *F* 1. to tire/to wear oneself out (à faire qch, doing sth) 2. to get spoilt/damaged; **votre voiture s'esquinte en plein air**, your car's getting ruined standing in the open.

essence [esãs] *nf P* essence de panards, sweat on feet.

essorer [esɔre] *vtr P* 1. essorer qn, to clean s.o. out (of money)/to squeeze s.o. dry 2. (*prostituée*) to give sexual satisfaction (to a client).

essoreuse [esɔrøz] *nf P* 1. prostitute* 2. noisy motorbike.

estaf(f)ier [ɛstafje] *nm P* pimp*/ ponce.

estampage [ɛstãpaʒ] *nm F* (*a*) swindling/fleecing (*b*) swindle/con.

estampe [ɛstãp] *nf* 1. *P* = **estampage** 2. *F* (*euph; hum*) venez voir mes estampes japonaises, come up and see my etchings!

estamper [ɛstãpe] *vtr F* estamper qn, to swindle* s.o./to fleece s.o./to diddle s.o./to do s.o.; **se faire estamper**, to be done/rooked/ ripped off.

estampeur, euse [ɛstãpœr, -øz] *n F* swindler*/fleecer/shark; small-time crook.

estanco(t) [ɛstãko] *nm P* 1. shop 2. (*café*) = pub/bar.

estom' [ɛstɔm] *nm P* 1. stomach* 2. **le faire à l'estom'**, to put it over on s.o./to pull a fast one on s.o.; **faire qch à l'estom'**, to show a lot of guts 3. **avoir de l'estom'/avoir bon estom'** (*i*) to be brave*/to have guts (*ii*) to have plenty of cheek/a lot of nerve (*iii*) to be game.

estomac [ɛstɔma] *nm* 1. *F* avoir/ se sentir l'estomac dans les talons (*i*) to be famished/ravenous (*ii*) to be afraid*/to be in a blue funk 2. *F* avoir de l'estomac (*i*) to have guts (*ii*) to have plenty of cheek/a lot of nerve 3. *F* le faire à l'estomac, to pull a fast one on s.o.

4. *pl P* **estomacs,** (woman's) breasts*/lungs.

estomaquer [ɛstɔmake] *vtr F* **estomaquer qn,** to flabbergast*/to dumbfound s.o.; **ça m'a estomaqué(e),** it took my breath away/I was really staggered.

estom(m)e [ɛstɔm] *nm P* = **estom'.**

estourbir [ɛsturbir] *vtr P* to kill* (s.o.)/to bump (s.o.) off.

établi [etabli] *nm* **1.** *F* **aller à l'établi,** to go to work **2.** *P (prostituées)* bed.

étagère [etaʒer] *nf P* **étagère à mégot,** ear*.

étaler [etale] **I** *vi F* **en étaler,** to show off*/to swank/to put on airs **II** *vpr* **s'étaler** *F* **1.** to go sprawling/to come a cropper* **2.** to show off*/to swank/to put on airs **3.** to confess*.

état [eta] *nm F (a) (iron)* **être dans un bel état,** to be in a nice mess *(b)* **être dans tous ses états,** to be in a terrible state*/all worked up; **se mettre dans tous ses états,** to get all steamed up/het up.

état-major [etamaʒɔr] *nm F (boisson)* wine and lemon.

étau [eto] *nm V* female genitals*/ snatch.

éteignoir [etɛɲwar] *nm* **1.** *F (pers)* wet blanket **2.** *P* big nose* **3.** *P* top-hat **4.** *P* **c'est un vrai éteignoir de concupiscence,** she's as ugly as sin; she's a cock-freezer/a passion-killer.

étendre [etãdr] *vtr* **1.** *F* **étendre qn à un examen,** to fail/to plough/ to flunk s.o. in an exam; **se faire étendre à un examen,** to fail/to flunk an exam **2.** *P* to kill*; **se faire étendre,** to get killed/to be done in.

s'éterniser [setɛrnize] *vpr F* **1.** **s'éterniser chez qn,** to outstay one's welcome **2. pas la peine d'éterniser**

là-dessus, no point in crying over spilt milk.

éternuer [etɛrnɥe] *vi A P* **éternuer dans le sac/dans le son,** to be guillotined.

Étienne [etjɛn] *Prnm F* **à la tienne, Étienne!** cheers!*/good health!

étincelles [etɛsɛl] *nfpl F* **faire des étincelles** *(i)* to sparkle with wit *(ii)* to be very successful; **ça va faire des étincelles,** there'll be fireworks/ trouble; it's bad news.

étiquette [etikɛt] *nf P* ear*.

étoffe [etɔf] *nf F* **avoir de l'étoffe,** to have what it takes.

étoile [etwal] *nf* **1.** *P* **étoile filante,** part-time prostitute* **2.** *pl F* **voir les étoiles en plein midi,** to see stars (as the result of a blow, etc).

étouffage [etufaʒ] *nm P* stealing/ pinching/nicking.

étouffer [etufe] *vtr* **1.** *F* **ce n'est pas l'intelligence qui l'étouffe,** he's not overburdened with brains; **ce n'est pas la charité qui t'étouffe,** charity isn't exactly your strong point **2.** *F* **étouffer le coup,** to let bygones be bygones/to say no more about it/to forget old scores **3.** *F* **étouffer qch dans l'œuf,** to nip sth in the bud **4.** *F* **en étouffer un,** to knock back a drink **5.** *F (turf)* **étouffer un cheval,** to pull a horse **6.** *P* to steal*/to pinch/to nick.

étourdir [eturdir] *vtr P* to steal*.

étrangler [etrãgle] *vtr P* **en étrangler six,** to knock back six drinks one after the other. (*Voir* **pierrot 3**)

étrangleuse [etrãgløz] *nf P* (neck-)tie.

être [ɛtr] *vi F* **1. en être (comme un phoque),** to be a homosexual*/ to be one of them; **être pour hommes/être pour femmes,** to be a homosexual*/a lesbian*; to be gay **2. en être** *(i)* to belong to the police* *(ii)* to be a police informer* **3. l'être,** to be a cuckold **4. y être,** to understand; **tu y es?** d'you get me?/are you with me? **j'y suis,** I get the picture.

étrenne [etrɛn] *nf F* (*a*) **avoir l'étrenne de qch,** to be the first to use sth (*b*) **n'en avoir pas l'étrenne,** to get sth secondhand; to get s.o.'s cast-offs.

étrenner [etrɛne] *vi F* **tu vas étrenner!** you'll catch it!/you'll get it (in the neck)!

étrillage [etrijaʒ] *nm F* overcharging/fleecing.

étriller [etrije] *vtr F* **1.** to over-charge/to fleece* (s.o.); to rip (s.o.) off; **on s'est fait étriller à cet hôtel,** we got well and truly stung at that hotel **2. étriller qn aux échecs,** to wipe the floor with s.o. at chess **3.** to criticize* (s.o.) severely/to tear (s.o.) to pieces; to knock s.o. **4.** to thrash (s.o.)/to beat (s.o.) up*.

étripage [etripaʒ] *nm F* (*adversaires, etc*) tearing each other's guts out.

s'étriper [setripe] *vpr F* (*adversaires, etc*) to tear each other's guts out.

étron [etrɔ̃] *nm P* turd; **poser un étron,** to defecate*/to have a crap.

étuve [etyv] *nf F* sweltering (hot) room; **quelle étuve!** it's like an oven in here!

eulpif [ølpif] *a O P* smart/stylish/natty.

eustache [østaʃ] *nm F* (clasp-)knife/pig-sticker.

euzigs, euzigues [øzig] *pron P* them/themselves.

évaporé, ée [evapɔre] *F I a* (*pers, etc*) feather-brained/irresponsibe/flighty/giddy; **une blonde évaporée,** a dumb blonde **II** *n* **c'est une petite évaporée,** she's a featherbrain/a scatterbrain.

s'évaporer [sevapɔre] *vpr F* to vanish (into thin air)/to make oneself scarce.

Ève [ɛv] *Prnf F* **1. je ne le connais**

ni d'Ève ni d'Adam, I don't know him from Adam **2.** (*femme*) **dans le/en costume d'Ève,** naked*/in the altogether/in one's birthday suit. (*Voir* **Adam**)

s'exécuter [segzekyte] *vpr F* **1.** to pay* up **2.** to toe the line.

exhibo [egzibo] *nm F* (= *exhibitionniste*) dirty old man/flasher.

exister [egziste] *vi F* **ça n'existe pas!** (*i*) that's stupid!/that's absolute tripe! (*ii*) I don't believe it!

exo [egzo] *F I nm* (*scol*) (= *exercice*) exercise **II** *nf* (*exonérée*) theatre ticket free of entertainment tax.

expédier [ɛkspedje] *vtr F* **1.** to kill*/to do (s.o.) in/to bump (s.o.) off **2.** to ruin/to do for (s.o.) **3.** (*a*) **je l'ai expédié,** I got rid of him (*b*) to polish sth off; **s'expédier un verre,** to knock back a drink **4. c'est de l'expédié,** that was a quickie/a quick one!

expliquance [ɛksplikɑ̃s] *nf P* explanation.

s'expliquer [sɛksplike] *vpr* **1.** *F* **s'expliquer avec qn,** to have it out (man to man) with s.o.; **nous allons nous expliquer,** we'll sort this out together/we'll fight it out **2.** *P* (*argot du* **milieu**) to turn to prostitution/to become a prostitute*/to go on the game.

expo [ɛkspo] *F I nm* (= *exposé*) (*au lycée*) **faire un expo,** to give a talk (**sur,** on) **II** *nf* (= *exposition*) exhibition/show.

s'exterminer [sɛkstɛrmine] *vpr F* to work* one's guts out/to flog oneself to death (**à faire qch,** doing sth).

extra [ɛkstra] *F I a* excellent*/out of this world/something else/fantastic/terrific/great; **c'est extra!** that's great!/far out! **II** *nm* **c'est de l'extra,** it's extra-special; **s'offrir un petit extra,** to give oneself a small treat.

F

fabriquer [fabrike] *vtr* **1.** *F* to do/to be up to/to cook up; **qu'est-ce que tu fabriques?** what(ever)/what on earth are you up to? **qu'as-tu fabriqué avec mes clopes?** what on earth/what the hell have you done with my fags? **qu'est-ce qu'il peut bien fabriquer, maintenant?** what the heck is he up to now?/what's his game, this time? **2.** *P* to steal*/to pinch/to nick **3.** *P* to swindle*/to cheat/to diddle/to con; **je me suis fait fabriquer,** I've been done/had/taken for a ride **4.** *P* to arrest*; **être fabriqué/se faire fabriquer,** to get arrested/nicked; **il s'est fait fabriquer pour excès de vitesse,** he got done/he was busted for speeding; he got a speeding fine. (*Voir* **tas 2**)

Fac, fac [fak] *nf F* (= *la Faculté*) **la Fac,** (the) University; **quand j'étais à la fac/en fac,** when I was at university/at uni/at college/*esp NAm* in school.

façade [fasad] *nf F* face; **(re)faire sa façade,** to (tidy up one's) make up; to do one's face.

facho [faʃo] *a&n P* fascist; right-wing(er)/reactionary.

factionnaire [faksjɔnɛr] *nm P* **1. relever un factionnaire,** to have a drink (at the bar) **2.** turd. (*Voir* **sentinelle**)

fada [fada] *F* (*esp dial du midi*) **I** *a* stupid*/dumb/(a bit) nutty/nuts **II** *nm* fool*/nutter/crackpot.

fadasse [fadas] *a F* (*péj*) dull/insipid; **cette couleur est un peu**

fadasse, this colour/*NAm* color is a bit wishy-washy.

fade [fad] *nm* **1.** *P* share (of loot, etc)/cut/whack/split; **avoir/toucher son fade,** to get one's share/cut; **y aller de son fade/payer son fade,** to pay one's whack/to chip in with one's share **2.** *P* **avoir son fade** (*i*) to have one's fair share (of illness, bad luck, etc) (*ii*) to be drunk* **3.** *V* **prendre son fade,** to have an orgasm*/to come **4.** *F* (*drogues*) injection*/fix.

fadé [fade] *a P* **1.** (*facture, etc*) excessive/steep/stiff **2.** **être fadé** (*a*) to have had (more than) one's fair share (of illness, bad luck, etc); **avec trois rhumes, déjà, je suis drôlement fadé,** (*iron*) what with three colds already, my luck's really in/s.o.'s got it in for me (*b*) to be drunk*/tight/pissed (*c*) to have VD*/to have the clap/to have copped a dose (*d*) **il est fadé de son genre,** he's a prize specimen.

fader [fade] *vtr P* **1.** to give (s.o.) his share/whack/cut (of the loot, etc); **avec ça je ne serai pas fadé,** that's not a fair whack/(*iron*) whatever will I do with all that! **2.** to punish severely; **le juge l'a fadé,** the judge gave him a heavy (prison) sentence/threw the book at him **3.** to kill* (s.o.) **4.** to ruin/to spoil/to make a mess of **5.** to have an orgasm*/to come **6.** **se faire fader,** to get VD*/to get the clap/to cop a dose.

faf [faf] *a&n F* fascist; right-wing(er)/reactionary.

faffes [faf] *nmpl P* **1.** identity

papers; **maquiller les faffes,** to fake/ to forge identity papers; **taper aux faffes,** to check s.o.'s (identity) papers **2.** *A* banknotes.

fafiot [fafjo] *nm O P* **1.** banknote/ flimsy. **2.** *pl* identity papers.

faflard [faflar] *nm P* passport.

fafs [faf] *nmpl P* = **faffes.**

fagot [fago] *nm* **1.** *F* **une bouteille de vin de derrière les fagots,** a bottle of wine reserved for a special occasion **2.** *F* **un fagot d'épines,** a surly individual/a crosspatch **3.** *P* ex-convict/ex-con **4.** *P* homosexual*/fag(got) **5.** *F pl* **les fagots,** the woodwind (instruments).

fagotage [fagɔtaʒ] *nm F* **1.** (*a*) ridiculous way of dressing/peculiar get-up (*b*) dowdy/frumpish get-up **2.** botched piece of work/botch-up/ bungle.

fagoté [fagɔte] *a F* (**mal**) **fagoté,** badly dressed/dowdy/frumpish; **femme mal fagotée,** frump/scarecrow.

fagoter [fagɔte] **I** *vtr F* **1.** to botch/to bungle* (work) **2.** to dress (s.o.) like a scarecrow/badly **II** *vpr* **se fagoter** *F* to dress badly/ like a scarecrow; **comme les jeunes se fagotent de nos jours!** what dreadful clothes young people wear these days!

fagoteur, euse [fagɔtœr, -øz] *n F* botcher/bodger/bungler; **fagoteur de romans,** hack novelist.

faiblard [fɛblar] *a F* (*a*) weakish/ rather feeble; **ce vin est un peu faiblard,** this wine tastes like it's been watered down.

faible [fɛbl] *a P* **1. tomber faible,** to faint/to pass out **2. tomber faible sur qch,** to steal* sth/to knock sth off.

faignant, ante [fɛɲã, -ãt] *P* **I** *a* (*a*) idle/lazy* (*b*) cowardly **II** *n* (*a*) idler/slacker/loafer (*b*) coward*.

faillot [fajo] *nm P* = **fayot.**

faim [fɛ̃] *nf F* **1. j'ai une de ces faims!/je crève de faim!** I'm starving!/I'm ravenous! **2. il fait faim,** I feel peckish/I'm getting hungry **3. il s'est jeté dessus comme la faim sur le monde,** he threw himself into it unhesitatingly/like nothing on earth/like a man possessed.

fainéasse [fɛneas] *P* **I** *a* lazy*/ (bone) idle **II** *nm&f* idler/(lazy) bum/slacker.

faire [fɛr] *vtr* **1.** *F* **se laisser faire,** to be/to get taken in; **on ne me la fait pas!** you can't fool me! **faut pas me la faire!** don't try it on with me! **on t'a fait,** you've been had/ you've been done; someone's pulled a fast one over on you; **tu es fait, mon vieux!** you've had it, mate! **2.** *F* **ça fait chic/riche,** it looks smart/ posh **3.** *F* **la faire (à qn) à la vertu/à l'innocence,** to put on a virtuous/an innocent act (for s.o.'s benefit) **4.** *F* (*a*) to charge; **combien ça fait le demi?** how much is a half (of beer)? (*b*) to be worth; **une bagnole qui fait six mille francs,** a car that is worth six thousand francs **5.** *F* **savoir y faire,** to know the score/to be with it/to get by **6.** *F* **faire troisième/quatrième,** to come third/fourth **7.** *F* (*âge*) to look; **il faisait dans les vingt ans,** he looked about twenty; **elle fait très jeune,** she looks very young (for her age) **8.** *F* **j'ai de quoi faire,** I've got my work cut out **9.** *F* **ça commence à bien faire!** that's enough of that!/this is getting beyond a joke! **10.** *F* **faire l'Europe/l'Autriche,** to do Europe/ Austria **11.** *F* **faire (ses besoins),** to defecate*/to relieve oneself/to go; **un gosse qui fait dans sa culotte,** a kid who dirties/soils his pants **12.** *F* **c'est bien fait pour vous!** it serves you right!/you asked for it! **13.** *F* **être fait,** to be arrested; **il était fait comme un rat,** they had him cornered. (*Voir* **tas 2**) **14.** *P* to kill*/to do in **15.** *P* to steal*; **on m'a fait ma montre,** someone's pinched/nicked my watch **16.** *P* to seduce/to make/to have (s.o.) **17.** *P* (*prostituée*) **faire un client/un micheton,** to pick up and have sex* with a client; to do/ to turn a trick; **en faire,** to be a prostitute*/to be on the game **II** *vpr* **se faire 1.** *F* **ne pas s'en faire,** not to worry; **faut pas s'en faire!/ t'en fais pas!** don't worry (yourself) about it! **2.** *P* **se faire qn** (*a*) to put up with s.o.; **il faut se le faire!** (*i*) it's a hell of a drag! (*ii*) he's a real pain (in the neck)! (*b*) to have sex* with s.o.; **il se l'est faite,** he got laid/he got his end away.

faisan [fəzã, fɛzã] *nm P* = **faisandier.**

faisandé [fəzãde, fɛ-] *a F* **1.** fake/bogus/phon(e)y **2.** corrupt/ decadent (literature, style, etc).

faisander [fəzãde, fɛ-] *vtr P* to swindle*/to cheat/to con.

faisandier [fəzãdje, fɛ-] *nm P* unscrupulous person/swindler*/ crook/shark/con man.

faiseur [fəzœr] *nm F* fraud/swindler*/shark. (*Voir* **ange 1**; **embarras**)

falot [falo] *nm P* (*mil*) court-martial; **passer au falot,** to be court-martialled.

false [fals] *nm,* **falzar(d)** [falzar] *nm P* (pair of) trousers*/*esp NAm* pants/strides/keks/duds; **déchirer son false,** to fart* (loudly).

fameusement [faməzmã] *adv O F* famously/marvellously; **on s'est fameusement amusé(s),** we had a great time.

fameux, euse [famø, -øz] *a F* excellent*/first-rate; **un fameux menteur,** a hell of a liar; **une fameuse canaille,** an out-and-out/a downright bastard*; **ce n'est pas fameux,** it's not up to much/it's no great shakes; **pas fameux, ton boulot!** you're job's nothing to write home about.

familiale [familjal] *nf F* police *or* prison van/Black Maria*.

fan [fan] *nm F* fan; **club des fans,** fan club; **courrier des fans,** fan mail; **fan du foot,** football fan/nut.

fana [fana] *F* **I** *a* enthusiastic/ (dead) keen; **il est fana,** he's got it on the brain **II** *nm&f* fan; **fana de cinéma,** film buff; **un fana du flipper,** a pinball fanatic; **fana de rock,** rock freak.

fanal, *pl* **-aux** [fanal, -o] *nm P* stomach*.

fandard [fãdar] *nm P* = **fendard.**

fanfan [fãfã] *nm&f F* (= *enfant*) small child*/little boy/little girl.

fanfare [fãfar] *nf P* **c'est un sale coup pour la fanfare,** it's a hell of a blow.

fantabosse [fãtabɔs] *nm P* (*mil*) infantryman/foot-soldier/foot-slogger.

fantaise [fãtɛz] *nf F* (= *fantaisie*) fancy/imagination; **de fantaise,** fanciful/imaginary.

fantaisie [fãtezi] *nf P* fellatio*.

fantassin [fãtasɛ̃] *nm P* crablouse.

fantoche [fãtɔʃ] *nf P* = **fantaisie.**

faramineux, euse [faraminø, -øz] *a F* phenomenal/colossal; amazing/staggering; **prix faramineux,** steep/sky-high price(s); **un rhume faramineux,** a stinking cold.

farce [fars] *a O F* very funny*.

farci [farsi] *a P* fake(d).

farcir [farsir] **I** *vtr* **1.** *P* to deceive*/to trick/to con/to do the dirty on (s.o.) **2.** *P* to riddle (s.o.) with bullets/to fill (s.o.) with lead **II** *vpr* **se farcir 1.** *P* **se farcir qch** (*a*) to treat oneself to sth (*b*) to put up with sth; **ce bouquin, il faut se le farcir!** this book is such a drag/ is really heavy-going! (*c*) to steal* sth/to knock sth off **2. se farcir qn** (*a*) *P* to put up with s.o./to be stuck with s.o. (*b*) *V* to have sex* with s.o./to screw s.o.; **il se la**

farcirait bien, he'd love to make it with her; **se la farcir en vitesse,** to have a quick one/a quickie **3.** *P* to· serve a prison sentence*/to do time. (*Voir* **zizique**)

fard [far] *nm F* **piquer un fard,** to blush/to go red.

farfadet [farfadɛ] *nm P* foetus.

farfelu [farfəly] **I** *a F* weird/ nutty/crazy* **II** *nm* (*a*) insignificant person/nothing/jerk (*b*) nut/ nutter/weirdo.

farfouillement [farfujmã] *nm F* rummaging (about); groping.

farfouiller [farfuje] *vtr&i F* to rummage (about) (in, among); to grope (about, for, in); **farfouiller (dans) les affaires de qn,** to mess around with s.o.'s things; to meddle in s.o.'s business.

fargue [farg] *nm P* criminal charge/accusation; indictment.

farguer [farge] **I** *vtr P* to charge/ to accuse; to indict **II** *vpr* **se farguer** *P* to arm oneself with a gun/to be armed/to pack a gun.

fargueur [fargœr] *nm P* witness for the prosecution.

faridon [faridɔ̃] *nf O F* **1. faire la faridon,** to go on a spree*/on a binge/on a bender **2. être de la faridon,** to be penniless*/flat broke.

farine [farin] *nf F* **1. ce sont des gens de (la) même farine,** they're birds of a feather; they're all the same **2. rouler qn dans la farine,** to make a complete fool of s.o. **3. se les rouler dans la farine,** to laze about/to skive off.

fatma [fatma] *nf*, **fatmuche** [fatmyʃ] *nf P* (*péj*) woman*.

fauber(t) [fober] *nm P* **1.** tongue **2.** (*marine*) **passer le fauber(t) en ville,** to swan around in town.

faubourg [fobur] *nm P* buttocks*/ (shapely) posterior (*esp woman's*).

fauche [foʃ] *nf P* **1.** (petty) theft/

stealing/nicking; shoplifting **2.** stolen goods/haul/heist/loot.

fauché [foʃe] *a F* penniless*/dead broke; **fauché comme les blés,** a bit short/hard up/stony broke.

faucher [foʃe] *vtr* **1.** *F* to steal*/ to swipe/to nick; **qui a fauché mes clopes?** who's pinched my fags? **2.** *P* to guillotine (s.o.) **3.** *F* to clean (s.o.) out (at gambling).

faucheur [foʃœr] *nm P* **1.** thief **2.** executioner.

faucheuse [foʃøz] *nf P* guillotine.

Fauchman(n) [foʃman] *a P* = **fauché.**

faune [fon] *nf F* **la faune des cafés de Montparnasse,** the regular crowd of the cafés of Montparnasse/the Montparnasse set.

fauter [fote] *vi F* (*fille, femme*) to allow herself to be seduced; **ma chienne a fauté,** my dog's found herself a boyfriend.

fauteuil [fotœj] *nm F* (*cheval, etc*) **arriver/gagner (comme) dans un fauteuil,** to win easily/to romp home/to win hands down.

faux-col [fokɔl] *nm F* head (of froth on glass of beer).

faux-derche [fodɛrʃ] *nm P* (*i*) deceitful person/shifty customer (*ii*) hypocrite (*iii*) double-crosser.

faux-poids [fopwa] *nm inv P* (*i*) girl under age who looks older than she is; jailbait (*ii*) prostitute* under age.

faveur [favœr] *nf P* fellatio*.

favouille [favuj] *nf P* (= **fouille**) pocket.

fayot [fajo] *nm P* **1.** kidney bean/ haricot bean **2. aller becqueter des fayots,** to go to prison*/to do bird **3.** (*mil*) **faire fayot,** to re-enlist **4.** (*i*) swot (*ii*) eager beaver (*iii*) bootlicker/toady/creep.

fayotage [fajɔtaʒ] *nm P* (*péj*) bootlicking/toadying; sucking up to (one's boss, etc).

fayoter [fajɔte] *vi P* **1.** to be over-keen/to suck up to (s.o.); **tu es toujours à fayoter, salaud!** you're always sucking up to your boss, you creep! **2.** (*mil*) to re-enlist.

fée [fe] *nf P* (*drogues*) (*a*) **la fée blanche,** cocaine* (*b*) **la fée brune,** opium* (*c*) **la fée verte,** hashish*.

feignant, ante [fɛɲɑ̃, -ɑ̃t] *a&n P* = **faignant, ante.**

feignasse [fɛɲas] *a & nm&f P* = **fainéasse.**

feignasser [fɛɲase] *vi P* to laze about/to loaf about/to lounge about/to idle away one's time.

feignasson [fɛɲasɔ̃] *nm P* = **fainéasse.**

feinter [fɛ̃te] *vtr F* to deceive*/to dupe (s.o.)/to pull a fast one on (s.o.)/to take (s.o.) in; **t'es bien feinté!** you've been had/you've been taken for a ride.

fêlé [fɛle] *F a* slightly mad*/crack-ed; **il a le cerveau fêlé/la tête fêlée,** he's a bit cracked/he's got a screw loose/he's a bit funny in the head.

félouse [feluz] *nm P* North African (*esp* Algerian) soldier.

fêlure [fɛlyr] *nf F* **avoir une fêlure,** to be slightly mad*/a bit cracked/a bit touched (in the head).

femelle [fəmɛl] *nf F* (*péj*) woman*/female/creature; **ce n'est qu'une femelle,** after all, she's only a woman.

femme [fam] *nf* **1.** *F* **une petite femme,** a lady friend/a bit of skirt/a bit of fluff/a bit of stuff **2.** *F* **bonne femme** (*i*) wife*/old lady/missus (*ii*) woman (*iii*) *pl* **les bonnes femmes,** women (in general) **3.** *F* (*cartes*) queen **4.** *P* (*marine*) **femme du capitaine,** inflatable doll used for erotic purposes.

femmelette [famlɛt] *nf F* effeminate man/nancy-boy; sissy/weakling.

fendant [fɑ̃dɑ̃] *nm,* **fendard** [fɑ̃dar] *nm,* **fendart** [fɑ̃dar] *nm P* (*esp man's*) trousers/pants.

fend-la-bise [fɑ̃labiz] *nm P* someone in a tearing hurry.

se fendre [səfɑ̃dr] *vpr F* **1.** to be generous; to splash out (on sth); to shell out/to fork out/to cough up; **il ne s'est pas fendu** (*i*) he wasn't exactly what you'd call generous (*ii*) it didn't break him/it didn't cost him a penny **2.** **se fendre la gueule/la pêche/la pipe,** to laugh one's head off/to crack up/to crease oneself.

fendu [fɑ̃dy] *nm P* = **fendant.**

fendue [fɑ̃dy] *nf P* (*péj*) woman*.

fenêtre [fənɛtr] *nf* **1.** *F* **il faut passer par là ou par la fenêtre,** there's nothing else for it/there's absolutely no choice **2.** *F* **jeter son argent par la fenêtre,** to spend one's money like there was no tomorrow/to throw one's money down the drain **3.** *P* **mettre la tête/le nez à la fenêtre,** to be guillotined **4.** *F* **se mettre à la fenêtre,** to try to see one's opponent's cards **5.** *P* **boucher une fenêtre à qn,** to punch s.o. in the eye **6.** *P* (*prostituée*) **faire la fenêtre,** to solicit* from the window. (*Voir* **chaussette 3**)

fenêtrière [fənɛtrijer] *nf P* prostitute* who solicits from a window.

fente [fɑ̃t] *nf V* female genitals*/crack/slit.

féo [feo], **féodal** [feɔdal] *a P* great/super.

fer [fɛr] *nm* **1.** *F* **mauvais fer,** a dangerous fellow/an ugly customer/a heavy **2.** *P* **fer à souder,** large nose*/hooter **3.** *pl P* **fers,** tools used for safe-breaking.

fer-blanc [fɛrblɑ̃] *nm F* **en fer-blanc,** worthless*/shoddy/tinpot.

ferblanterie [fɛrblɑ̃tri] *nf O F* (*péj*) decorations/medals/gongs.

fermer [fɛrme] *vtr P* **ferme ta boîte!/ferme ta gueule!/ferme ta**

malle!/ferme ça!/ferme-la!/la ferme! shut up!*/belt up!/shut it/shut your face!/shut your trap!

fermeture [fɛrmətyr] *nf P* **fermeture! tu me cours!** shut* up! you get on my nerves!

ferraille [fɛrɑj] *nf F* small change; **je lui ai donné toute ma ferraille,** I gave him all my small change.

ferré [fɛre] *a F* **être ferré sur un sujet,** to be well up on sth/to know a subject inside out.

ferte [fɛrt] *nf P* **la bonne ferte,** fortune-telling; **taper/tirer la bonne ferte,** to tell fortunes.

fesse [fɛs] *nf P* **1.** *pl* **les fesses,** buttocks*/bottom/bum/*esp NAm* butt/arse/*esp NAm* ass; **poser ses fesses,** to sit down (on one's backside); **pousse tes fesses!** move up a bit!/shift your arse/*NAm* ass! **2. serrer les fesses** (*i*) to be afraid*/to get the wind up/to have the jitters/ to have cold feet (*ii*) to sit tight (*iii*) to be on one's guard (*iv*) **il est parti en serrant les fesses,** he went off with his tail between his legs **3. avoir chaud aux fesses** (*i*) to have a nasty fright (*ii*) to have the police hot on one's track **4. n'y aller que d'une fesse,** to set about it half-heartedly; **n'être assis que d'une fesse** (*i*) to be always on the go (*ii*) to be very nervous **5. prendre ses fesses à poignée,** to run like hell/to get the hell out (of somewhere) **6. occupe-toi de tes fesses!** mind your own bloody business! **7. mes fesses!** my arse/*esp NAm* my ass! **poli comme mes fesses,** downright/ bloody rude **8.** women/crumpet/ skirt*/a bit of the other; **y a de la fesse,** there's some skirt/crumpet knocking around **9.** (*a*) **magasin de fesses,** brothel* (*b*) **pain de fesses,** money earned by prostitution *or* pornography (*c*) porn; tits and bums; **magazine/revue de fesses,** porno/porny/dirty magazine/mag; **un film de fesses,** a dirty/porny film; a blue movie; *esp NAm* a

porno flick/a skin flick (*d*) **histoire de fesses,** sordid affair; **histoires de fesses,** cunt talk. (*Voir* **beurre 9; feu 1; peau 20**)

fessier [fesje] *nm F* buttocks*/ behind/arse/*esp NAm* ass.

feston [fɛstɔ̃] *nm F* **faire des festons en marchant = festonner.**

festonner [fɛstɔne] *vi F* (*ivrogne*) to stagger about/to lurch about.

fête [fɛt] *nf* **1.** *F* (*a*) **être à la fête,** to be as pleased as Punch/to be over the moon (*b*) **il n'était pas à la fête,** he was having a rough time (of it)/things weren't going too well for him **2.** *P* **faire sa fête à qn,** to beat s.o. up*/to work s.o. over; **ce sera/ça va être ta fête!** you'd better watch out!/you're in for it!/you'll get what's coming to you! **3.** *F* **il n'a jamais été/il ne s'est jamais vu à pareille fête,** he never had such a good time/he never enjoyed himself so much **4.** *F* **faire la fête,** to have a good time*/to live it up/to have a ball/to get one's rocks off.

feu [fø] *nm* **1.** *F* **avoir le feu quelque part/au derrière/***P* **au cul/aux miches/aux fesses,** to be in a tearing hurry/in a huge rush; to have ants in one's pants; **il courait comme s'il avait le feu au derrière,** you couldn't see him for dust; he went like greased lightning. (*Voir* **train 2**) **2.** *F* **avoir/donner le feu vert à qn,** to give s.o. the go-ahead/ the green light **3.** *P* **cracher/péter le feu,** to be full of go/to be full of beans **4.** *F* **il n'y a pas le feu,** no need to panic!/take your time! **il y a le feu sur le pont?** what's the big hurry?/what's the great rush? **5.** *P* revolver*/gun/shooter/piece **6.** *P* **avoir le feu au tambour/au cul,** to feel sexy/randy/horny.

feuille [fœj] *nf* **1.** *P* ear*/ lug(hole); **feuilles de chou,** big ears; **être dur de la feuille/être constipé des feuilles,** to be hard of hearing/ to be a bit deaf; **avoir les feuilles (de chou) ensablées** (*i*) to be hard of hearing (*ii*) not to take it in/to be a bit slow (to understand); (*musique*) **jouer à la feuille**, to play by ear **2.** *F* **feuille de chou**, newspaper/rag **3.** *P* **voir les feuilles/la feuille à l'envers**, to have sex* in the open air; to have a roll in the hay **4.** *V* **faire feuille de rose**, to have anal sex*/to lick (s.o.'s) anus*/to ream (s.o.'s) ass **5.** *F* **glisser dans les feuilles**, to confide a secret.

feuillées [fœje] *nfpl F* (*mil*) **les feuillées**, latrines.

fias [fjas] *nm P* **1.** (*souvent péj*) man*/fellow/bloke/guy **2.** anus*.

fiasc, fiasque [fjask] *nm F* (= *fiasco*) failure*/fiasco/flop.

fiasse [fjas] *nf P* (*souvent péj*) **1.** girl*/bird/chick/tart/judy **2.** *pl* **fiasses**, people.

fiaz(e) [fjaz] *nm P* = **fias 1, 2.**

ficelard [fislar] *nm F* an old hand/ a person who knows all the tricks of the trade.

ficelé [fisle] *a F* (*péj*) dressed up*/ got up; **mal ficelé**, untidily dressed; **elle est ficelée comme quat' sous**, she *does* look a mess/she looks like a sack of potatoes. (*Voir* **andouille 2**)

ficeler [fisle] *vtr F* **ficeler qn**, to dress s.o. up (badly, like a scarecrow); **qui donc vous a ficelé ainsi?** whoever got you up/rigged you out like that?

ficelier [fis(ə)lje] *a&nm F* **1.** (actor) who knows all the stage tricks **2.** (man) who lives by his wits/who knows the ropes.

ficelle [fisɛl] **I** *a F* cunning/wily/ smart **II** *nf O* **1.** *F* **une vieille ficelle**, an old hand/a wily (old) bird; a smooth operator **2.** *F* (*a*) (*truc*) **on voit bien la ficelle**, it's easy to see how it's done (*b*) **connaître les ficelles**, to know the ropes/to know the tricks of the trade (*c*) **tirer les ficelles**, to pull the strings/to run the show **3.** *pl*

F (*mil*) (NCO's *or* officer's) stripes/ gold braid **4.** *F* **casser la ficelle**, to get a divorce/to get unhitched **5.** *F* **faire ficelle**, to be quick about it/ to get a move on/to look sharp **6.** *pl P* handcuffs*/stringers **7.** *F* bootlace tie **8.** *F* **tirer sur la ficelle**, to exaggerate*/to stretch it a bit.

fichaise [fiʃɛz] *nf F* nonsense*/ rubbish/garbage/trash; **tout ça, c'est des fichaises**, that's a load of rot/bull/garbage.

fichant [fiʃɑ̃] *a O P* annoying/ aggravating; **que c'est fichant!** what a bloody/damned nuisance!

fiche, ficher [fiʃ, fiʃe] *vtr F* **1.** (= *faire*) **ne pas en ficher un coup/ ne pas en ficher une secousse/ne rien fiche(r)/ne pas en ficher lourd**, to do nothing/to skive off; **je n'ai rien fichu/aujourd'hui**, I haven't done a thing/a stroke all day. (*Voir* **dal**; **rame**) **qu'est-ce que ça fiche?** what does it matter?/who the hell cares? **ça ne fiche rien**, it doesn't matter a bit/a toss; **j'en ai rien à fiche**, I don't give a damn **2.** (= *mettre*) **fiche(r) qn dedans** (*i*) to fool* s.o./to take s.o. in; **on m'a fichu dedans**, I've been had (*ii*) to drop s.o. in it (*iii*) to put s.o. in prison*/to put s.o. inside; **fiche(r) qn dehors/en l'air**, to give s.o. the sack/to fire s.o.; to give s.o. their cards/the push. (*Voir* **air I 5**); **fiche(r) qn à la porte**, to throw/to chuck s.o. out; **ça fiche tout par terre/en l'air**, that ruins everything/ that messes everything up **3.** (= *donner*) **ficher un coup à qn**, to hit s.o./to clout s.o./to thump s.o.; **fiche-moi la paix!** (*i*) stop bugging me!/get lost!/shove off! (*ii*) shut up!*/belt up! **qui est-ce qui m'a fichu un imbécile pareil?** what have I done to be landed with such an idiot? **ça me fiche la déprime**, that gets me depressed/that makes me fed up; **ça m'a fichu un coup!** it hit me real(ly) hard! **qui est-ce qui m'a fichu ça?** how did I end up with

that? **4. va te faire fiche!** get the
hell out of here!/clear off!/go to
hell! **envoyer qn faire fiche,** to send
s.o. packing/to tell s.o. to clear off;
envoyer qch faire fiche, to chuck
sth up/to pack sth in; **fiche(r) le
camp,** to beat it/to do a bunk;
fiche-moi le camp! buzz off!/clear
off!/get lost! **5. je t'en fiche!** nothing of the sort!/not a bit of it!/not
at all!/not flipping likely! **vingt-cinq
ans je t'en fiche, elle a quarante ans
et mèche!** twenty-five, my foot –
she's forty if she's a day! **6. ça la
fiche mal,** that makes a lousy
impression **II** *vpr* **se ficher** *F* **1.
se ficher par terre** (*i*) to fling oneself on the ground/to the ground
(*ii*) to go sprawling/to come a
cropper* **2.** (*a*) **se fiche(r) de qn,**
to make fun of s.o./to pull s.o.'s
leg/to take the mickey out of s.o.;
vous vous fichez de moi, you're having me on/you're kidding me (*b*) **se
fiche(r) de qch,** to poke fun at sth;
ça, c'est se fiche(r) du monde! well,
of all the nerve!/what a (damned)
cheek! **je m'en fiche (pas mal)!/ce
que je m'en fiche!** I don't give a
damn!/I couldn't care less!*/a fat
lot I care! **je me fiche bien de ce
qu'on pense de moi,** I couldn't care
less what they think of me; **il se
fiche du quart comme du tiers,** he
doesn't give a damn for anything/
anybody; **je m'en fiche et m'en con-
trefiche/je m'en fiche comme de
l'an neuf/comme de l'an quarante/
comme de ma première chemise/
comme d'une guigne/comme un
poisson d'une pomme,** I couldn't
care less*!/I couldn't give a damn!/
I don't care two hoots! **3. se
ficher dedans,** to make a mistake*/
to put one's foot in it; **il s'est fichu
dedans,** he boobed **4. il peut se le
ficher quelque part!** he knows where
he can stick it!/he can stick it up
his arse/*NAm* ass!

fichets [fiʃɛ] *nmpl* P handcuffs*.

fichtre! [fiʃtr] *int* *F* **1.**
(*l'étonnement, l'admiration*) good

heavens!/good Lord!/well I never!
2. (*contrariété, douleur*) damn!/
blast!/hell!/Jeez! **3.** (*intensif*)
fichtre oui! rather!/I should say so!
fichtre non! no fear!/I should think
not! **je le sais fichtre bien!** don't I
know it!/I know it too damn well!
je n'en sais fichtre rien! I'm
damned if I know! **ça n'est fichtre
pas agréable de ...,** it's no joke to
.../it's no fun to ....

fichtrement [fiʃtrəmã] *adv* O F
(*intensif*) extremely/awfully/terribly;
hellishly; **il a fichtrement raison,**
he's dead right! **c'est fichtrement
bien,** it's damn(ed)/*NAm* darned
good; **c'est fichtrement loin,** it's a
hell of a long way/a damned long
way.

fichu [fiʃy] *a* *F* **1.** rotten/awful;
quel fichu temps! what filthy/lousy
weather! **une fichue idée,** a ridic-
ulous/stupid/lousy idea; **un fichu
embêtement,** a flipping/damn/*NAm*
darn nuisance **2. il est fichu,** he's
done for/he's had it/it's all up with
him; **c'est de l'argent (de) fichu,** it's
money down the drain; **ma montre
est fichue,** my watch has bitten the
dust/has had it/is bust **3. fichu
de,** likely to/capable of; **il est fichu
de partir avant que j'arrive,** it's just
like him to leave before I get
there/it's on the cards that he'll
leave before I get there; **il n'est
même pas fichu de faire ça,** he isn't
even up to/capable of doing that
4. (*a*) **être mal fichu** (*i*) to be badly
made/put together (*ii*) to feel tired*
(*iii*) to feel unwell*/under the
weather (*iv*) to be badly dressed/
badly turned-out. (*Voir* **as 2** (*ii*);
sou 1); **elle n'est pas mal fichue** (*i*)
she's quite well turned-out/quite
smart (*ii*) she's not bad-looking (*b*)
être bien fichu (*i*) to be well made
(*ii*) to be well-dressed/well turned-
out (*iii*) to be good-looking.

fichûment [fiʃymã] *adv* O F
extremely/awfully/terribly; **c'est
fichûment gentil à vous de m'écrire,**
it's jolly nice of you to write to me.

fiérot [fjero] F I a (a) stuck-up/
snooty (b) cocky II nm stuck-up
person/snob.

fiesta [fjɛsta] nf F celebration/
party; **faire la fiesta**, to go out on
the town/to live it up/to have a
ball.

fieu, pl -eux [fjø] nm (esp dial)
son/sonny; lad; **c'est un bon fieu,**
he's a good sort/a nice chap.

fifi [fifi] nm F 1. little boy*; **le fifi
à sa maman,** mummy's little boy
2. sparrow.

fifille [fifij] nf F little girl*; **la fifille
à son papa,** daddy's little girl.

fifine [fifin] nf P sanitary towel/
NAm napkin.

fifre [fifr] I indef pron P ne ...
que fifre, nothing* at all/not a
damn thing/sweet FA II nm 1. F
un grand fifre, a tall* thin person/a
beanpole 2. V **fifre à grelots,**
penis*.

fifrelin [fifrəlɛ̃] nm F **cela ne vaut
pas un fifrelin,** it's not worth a
(brass) farthing; **je n'ai pas un fifrelin,** I'm broke/I haven't a penny to
my name.

fifti, fifty [fifti] nm F half; **faire
fifti,** to go halves/fifty-fifty.

fifti-fifti [fiftififti] adv F half and
half/fifty-fifty.

figaro [figaro] nm 1. F (hum) barber 2. O P (garçons de café) **faire
figaro,** not to get a tip.

fignard [fiɲar] nm, **fignarès**
[fiɲarɛs] nm, **figne** [fiɲ] nm,
fignedé [fiɲde] nm, **fignolet**
[fiɲɔlɛ] nm P (a) buttocks*/arse/esp
NAm ass (b) anus*/arsehole/esp
NAm asshole.

figue [fig] nf 1. F **faire la figue à
qn,** to make an obscene gesture of
contempt at s.o. (by putting the
thumb between the fingers) 2. V
female genitals*/cunt 3. pl V testicles*/nuts; **avoir les figues molles,**
to feel sexually unexcited/to be
limp/to droop. (Voir **mi-figue**)

figure [figyr] nf F 1. (a) **casser la
figure à qn,** to push/to smash s.o.'s
face in; to beat s.o.'s head in (b) **se
casser la figure** (i) to come a cropper* (ii) to smash oneself up (in an
accident, etc) 2. **se payer la figure
de qn,** to take the mickey out of
s.o./to pull s.o.'s leg/to have s.o.
on 3. **faire triste figure,** to look
out of place/out of one's element/
like a fish out of water.

fil [fil] nm F 1. **avoir le fil,** to be
wide awake/to be all there/to be
with it 2. **avoir un fil à la patte** (i)
to have commitments/to be tied
down (ii) to be lumbered (with a
mistress); **se mettre un fil à la
patte/se laisser attacher un fil à la
patte,** to get married*/to get
hitched/to tie the knot 3. **donner
du fil à retordre à qn,** to give s.o. a
lot of trouble/to make life difficult
for s.o.; **il vous donnera du fil à
retordre,** you'll have your work cut
out with him/he'll give you a big
headache 4. **il n'a pas inventé le fil
à couper le beurre,** he won't set the
Thames on fire/he won't set the
world on fire/he's no superman/
he's nothing special 5. **avoir des
jambes comme des fils de fer,** to
have legs like matchsticks 6. **elle
est mince comme un fil,** she's a
mere slip of a girl/of a woman 7.
sécher sur le fil, to be stood up
8. **fil en quatre,** strong brandy 9.
être au bout du fil, to be on the
phone; to be at the other end of
the line; **donner un coup de fil à
qn,** to give s.o. a ring/a tinkle/a
buzz. (Voir **bobine 3**)

filaturer [filatyre] vtr F to shadow/
to tail (s.o.).

**fil-en-quatre, fil-en-six, fil-
en-trois** [filɑ̃katr, -ɑ̃sis, -ɑ̃trwɑ]
nm F strong spirits*/rotgut/hard
stuff.

filer [file] I vtr 1. F to give/to
hand over/to pass; **file-moi une
pipe,** slip me a fag; **en filer une
bonne à qn,** to clout s.o./to give

s.o. a good thump. (*Voir* **avoine**; **coton** II 2; **danse** 1; **dérouillée**; **doux**; **nœud**; **raclée**; **roustasse**; **sabre** 2; **toise** 1; **train**; **trempe**) 2. *P* **filer qn**, to tail/to shadow s.o. II *vi* 1. *F* **filer (en vitesse)**, to run away*/to beat it/to clear off; **filez!** clear off!/get lost!* **filer comme une flèche**, to shoot off/to dash off/to zoom off; **faut que je file**, must dash/fly; **il fila sur l'Amérique avec l'argent**, he skipped off to America with the money; **filer en douceur**, to slip away/to slope off. (*Voir* **anglaise**) 2. *V* **en filer**, to be a passive homosexual*. (*Voir* **chouette** II)

filet [filɛ] *nm F* **elle a le filet bien coupé**, she's got the gift of the gab/she's a real chatterbox.

filetouze [filtuz] *nm P* (= *filet*) string bag.

fileur, euse [filœr, -øz] *n F* 1. (*a*) shadow(er)/tail (*b*) informer*/snout/grass 2. racecourse spy (in search of winning tips).

filière [filjɛr] *nf F* **passer par/suivre la filière** (*i*) (*pers*) to work one's way up (from the bottom) (*ii*) (*demande d'emploi, etc*) to go through the usual (official) channels.

fille [fij] *nf* 1. *F* **elle est bonne fille**, she's rather naive 2. *F* prostitute*; **elle a des manières de fille**, she's a bit of a tart/a slut 3. *F* **courir les filles**, to be a womanizer*/a skirt-chaser/a bit of a lecher. (*Voir* **air** I 2)

fillette [fijɛt] *nf F* half-bottle (of wine).

filochard [filɔʃar] *a P* resourceful*/smart/canny.

filoche [filɔʃ] *nf P* **prendre qn en filoche/prendre la filoche de qn**, to shadow/to tail s.o.

filocher [filɔʃe] *vi P* 1. to shadow/to tail (s.o.) 2. *O* **filocher devant une corvée**, to shirk a

fatigue/a chore 3. to speed (along)/to belt along/to zip along.

filon [filɔ̃] *nm F* 1. (*a*) cushy job/cushy number/soft option; **les meilleurs filons**, the plum jobs/jobs for the boys (*b*) **avoir le filon**, to be sitting pretty 2. moneyspinner; **trouver le filon/trouver un bon filon/dénicher le bon filon**, to strike it rich/to strike it lucky/to strike oil.

fils [fis] *nm F* 1. boy/lad/chap/fellow; **c'est un bon fils**, he's a good sort (of chap) 2. **fils à papa** (*i*) young man with an influential father/rich man's son (*ii*) (young) playboy. (*Voir* **pute**)

fin [fɛ̃] I *nf* 1. *F* **tu es stupide à la fin!** you really are stupid! **il m'énerve, à la fin!** he's beginning to get on my nerves! 2. *P* **une fin de mois**, a part-time prostitute* 4. *F* **sentir la fin de saison**, to (begin to) feel old. (*Voir* **haricot** 3) II *a F* **j'avais l'air fin**, I looked a right idiot/a proper Charlie. (*Voir* **mouche** 4; **partie** 3 (*b*)) III *adv F* completely/absolutely; **fin soûl**, dead drunk*/plastered. (*Voir* **prêt** 1)

finasser [finase] *vi F* to outsmart; to resort to trickery; **finasser avec qn**, to play tricks on s.o.

fini [fini] *a F* 1. **un menteur fini**, an out-and-out liar; **un imbécile fini**, a complete/a downright idiot 2. **il est fini**, he's had it.

finir [finir] I *vtr P* **finir un client/son partenaire sexuel**, to bring a client/one's partner to orgasm*/to a climax; to bring off/to finish off a client/one's partner II *vpr* (*masturbation*) to finish oneself off/to bring oneself off.

finish [finiʃ] *adv & int P* out of the question!/never again!/that's it!/that's that!

fiole [fjɔl] *nf P* 1. head*; **se payer la fiole de qn**, to make a fool of s.o./to have s.o. on/to pull s.o.'s leg **2.** face*/mug; **j'en ai soupé de ta fiole!** I'm fed up with you!/I'm tired of looking at your ugly mug!/ I've had (just about) enough of you! **3.** self; **ma fiole,** myself; me; **sa fiole,** himself/herself; him/her.

fion [fjɔ̃] *nm* **1.** *F* **donner le (coup de) fion à qch** (*i*) to give/to put the finishing touch(es) to sth (*ii*) to clean/to tidy sth up **2.** *F* **avoir le fion pour faire qch,** to have the knack of doing sth **3.** *P* **coup de fion,** stroke of luck; **avoir du fion,** to be lucky; **avoir un fion du tonnerre,** to have the luck of the devil **4.** *P* **l'avoir dans le fion,** to be badly let down/to get a rotten deal **5.** *V* anus*/arsehole/*NAm* asshole/ ring.

fiotte [fjɔt] *nm P* **1.** man*/chap/ fellow/bloke **2.** (*occ f*) (*a*) effeminate man/pansy (*b*) homosexual*/ poof(ter)/fairy/fag(got).

fissa [fisa] *adv P* **faire fissa,** to be quick about it/to get a move on/to look sharp/to get one's finger out.

fiston [fistɔ̃] *nm F* son; youngster; **(mon) fiston,** my lad/my boy/ sonny.

fistot [fisto] *nm F* first-year naval cadet.

fistule [fistyl] *nf P* **avoir de la fistule,** to be lucky/to get a lucky break.

fixe [fiks] *nm F* (*drogues*) **un fixe,** an injection*/a fix; **se faire un fixe,** to shoot up.

fixé [fikse] *a F* **être fixé,** to know where one stands/to know the score.

fixer [fikser] *nm&f P* (*drogues*) drug addict*/fixer/junkie.

se fixer [səfikse] *vpr P* (*drogues*) to (have a) fix/to shoot up.

flac [flak] *nm P* **(il) y en a flac!** that's enough/I've had it up to here!/I'm sick to death of it!

flacdal(le) [flakdal] *a&nm P* soft/ spineless/gutless/weedy (person).

Flacmann [flakman] *Prn P* **aller chez Flacmann,** to defecate*. (*Voir* **flaquer 1**)

flacon [flakɔ̃] *nm* **1.** *F* (*a*) **prendre du flacon,** to be getting on (in years) (*b*) **avoir du flacon,** to be past one's prime/to be a bit long in the tooth; **plaisanterie qui a du flacon,** vintage joke; hoary old joke/chestnut **2.** *pl P* boots/shoes.

fla(-)fla [flafla] *nm F* **faire du fla(-)- fla/des flaflas,** to put on a show/ to flaunt oneself/to show off*.

flag [flag] *nm P* **être pris en flag/se faire piquer en flag** (= *en flagrant délit*), to be caught red-handed/in the act/with one's trousers/pants down.

flagada [flagada] *a inv F* **1.** (*pers*) exhausted*/fagged (out)/whacked **2. pantalon flagada,** baggy trousers.

flagda [flagda] *nm P* kidney bean/ haricot bean.

flagelle [flaʒɛl] *nf P* (sexual) flagellation/flag/fladge.

flageolet [flaʒɔlɛ] *nm* **1/** *V* penis*/stalk **2.** *V* clitoris*/clit **3.** *pl F* **flageolets,** matchstick legs.

flagre [flagr], **flague** [flag] *P* = **flag.**

Flahute [flayt] *nm&f P* (*a*) Fleming (*b*) (*cyclisme*) **des flahutes,** Belgian racers.

flambante [flɑ̃bɑ̃t] *nf P* **une flambante,** a match/a light.

flambard, arde [flɑ̃bar, -ard] *F* **I** *a* flashily dressed/overdressed (person) **II** *n* show-off*/swank; **faire le flambard,** to show off*/to swank.

flambe [flɑ̃b] *nf P* (*a*) gambling (*b*) (any) gambling game.

flambé [flɑ̃be] *a P* (*a*) (*au jeu*) ruined/done for/cleaned out/taken to the cleaners (*b*) (*pers*) **il est flambé,** he's had it/he's had his chips/he's done for.

flambeau [flɑ̃bo] *nm* P **avoir du flambeau,** to be lucky (*esp* at gambling).

flambée [flɑ̃be] *nf* F **une flambée,** a flash in the pan.

flamber [flɑ̃be] *vi* F (*a*) **flamber (dur),** to gamble (heavily). (*Voir* **courtines**) (*b*) to play cards 2. to squander/to spend heavily; **c'est de l'argent flambé,** it's money down the drain.

flambeur [flɑ̃bœr] *nm* F (*a*) (heavy) gambler (*b*) card player.

flan [flɑ̃] *nm* P 1. **à la flan** (*i*) *a phr* easy going/free and easy; **tes idées à la flan,** you and your lousy ideas (*iii*) *adv phr* in a slapdash fashion; **travail fait à la flan,** work/job done anyoldhow 2. **au flan,** at random/on the spur of the moment; **j'ai dit ça au flan,** I said that off the top of my head; **il est venu au flan,** he came on the off chance 3. **coup de flan,** unpremeditated crime; pilfering/shoplifting 4. (*a*) **du flan!** no chance!/nothing doing!*/not bloody likely!* (*b*) **c'est du flan!** it's a load of rubbish/hooey/codswallop! 5. **faire du flan,** to tell lies/to con s.o./to have s.o. on 6. **en rester comme deux ronds de flan,** to be flabbergasted; **elle en est restée comme deux ronds de flan,** she couldn't believe it/she was completely knocked out.

flanc [flɑ̃] *nm* 1. F **être sur le flanc** (*i*) to be laid up (*ii*) to be exhausted*/to be all in; **ce boulot m'a mis sur le flanc,** this job has worn me out 2. F **se battre les flancs,** to waste energy and achieve nothing/to beat one's head against a brick wall 3. P **tirer au flanc,** to shirk/to skive/to swing the lead; **tireur au flanc,** skiver/shirker.

flanchard, arde [flɑ̃ʃar, -ard] F I *a* 1. slightly unwell*/under the weather/off colour 2. cowardly*/yellow/chicken II *n* shirker/quitter/yellowbelly.

flanche [flɑ̃ʃ] *nm* P 1. crime; job/business; **monter un flanche,** to plan a burglary, etc/to pull a job 2. **aller au flanche,** to go gambling 3. (showman's) patter.

flancher [flɑ̃ʃe] *vi* F 1. to back down/to get cold feet/to chicken out; to lose one's bottle 2. to quit/to back out.

flancheur [flɑ̃ʃœr] *nm* P (*a*) (heavy) gambler (*b*) card-player.

flanelle [flanɛl] *nf* P **faire flanelle** (*i*) to loaf around/to mooch about (*ii*) to be an unprofitable customer (in a café, a brothel, etc).

flânocher [flɑnɔʃe] *vi* F to hang about/to loiter/to mooch (about)/to loaf (around)/to bum around.

flânocheur, euse [flɑnɔʃœr, -øz] *n* F dawdler/loafer/layabout.

flanquer [flɑ̃ke] I *vtr* F to throw/to chuck; **flanquer qch par terre,** to fling/to chuck/to plonk sth (down) on the ground/on the floor; **flanquer une gifle à qn,** to slap s.o. round the face/to clout s.o. round the ears; **flanquer un coup de pied à qn,** to kick s.o.; **flanquer qn à la porte** (*i*) to turn/to turf s.o. out; to throw/to chuck s.o. out (*ii*) to give s.o. the sack/to fire s.o./to give s.o. the push; **flanquer la trouille à qn,** to put the wind up s.o.; **flanquer la chtouille à qn,** to give s.o. VD*/the clap/a dose. (*Voir* **air I 5**; **gnon**) II *vpr* **se flanquer** F **se flanquer par terre** (*i*) to fling oneself to the ground (*ii*) to fall (over)/to fall flat on one's face/to come a cropper*. (*Voir* **air I 6**)

flanquette [flɑ̃kɛt] *nf* F (= *franquette*) **à la bonne flanquette,** simply/without ceremony; **venez dîner chez nous, ce sera à la bonne flanquette,** come for dinner, you'll have to take pot luck with us/it won't be anything special.

flapi [flapi] *a* F (*pers*) exhausted*/fagged out/washed out/shattered.

flaquedalle [flakdal] *a&nm P* = **flacdal(le)**.

flaquer [flake] *vi P* **1.** to defecate* **2.** to get cold feet/to chicken out/ to back out.

flash [flaʃ] *nm P* flash/bang (experienced by drug addicts).

flashant, -ante [flaʃɑ̃, -ɑ̃t] *a P* stunning/exceptionally good-looking; **c'est une fille flashante,** she really turns men on.

flasher [flaʃe] *vtr P* to turn on; **elle fait flasher les mecs,** she turns men on.

flasquer [flaske] *vi P* **1.** to defecate* **2. tu me fais flasquer!** you make me sick!/you're getting up my nose!

flaupée [flope] *nf P* = **flop(p)ée**.

flauper [flope] *vtr P* = **flop(p)er**.

flèche [flɛʃ] **I** *nm P* **1. je n'ai pas un flèche,** I haven't got a farthing/a cent/a bean **2.** trick/wangle **II** *nf* **1.** *O P* meat **2.** *P* gang **3.** *P* trick/dodge/fiddle.

flécher [fleʃe] *vi P* **flécher ensemble,** to work together/to team up/to gang up.

flémard, flemmard, -arde [flemar, -ard] *P* **I.** *a* lazy*/idle/ work-shy **II** *n* idler/slacker.

flémarder, flemmarder [flemarde] *vi P* to laze around/to sit around doing nothing; to bum around.

flème, flemme [flɛm] *nf P* laziness/slacking; **il a la flème,** he's feeling lazy/he doesn't feel like work(ing); **j'ai la flème de lire,** I don't feel like reading/I can't be bothered to read; **ça me donne la flème,** I can't be bothered (with it); **tirer sa flème,** to idle away one's time/to (sit and) do nothing/to bum around.

flemingite [flemɛ̃ʒit] *nf P* laziness; **il a une flemingite aiguë,** he's very lazy/he's a real slacker/he's a lazy sod.

fleur [flœr] *nf* **1.** *F* **s'envoyer des fleurs,** to give oneself a pat on the back/to blow one's own trumpet **2.** *F* **arriver/s'amener comme une fleur,** to drop in (on s.o.) unexpectedly **3.** *F* **être fleur bleue,** to be sentimentally amorous/(a bit of a) romantic **4.** (*a*) *F* gift/present; tip (*b*) *P* payoff (to police informer*, etc) (*c*) *P* cut/whack; share (of the loot) **5.** *F* **faire une fleur à qn** (*i*) to do s.o. a favour/a service (*ii*) to give s.o. a present (*iii*) to let s.o. off lightly **6.** (*a*) *F* **la fleur des pois,** the pick of the bunch/the cream of the crop (*b*) *P* **une fleur des pois,** a homosexual* **7.** *P* **être (à) fleur,** to be penniless*/broke **8.** *P* (*fille, femme*) **perdre sa fleur (d'oranger),** to lose one's virginity*/one's cherry. (*Voir* **macadam 1; nave 2** (*b*); **paf II 3**)

flibuster [flibyste] *vtr P* to steal*/ to pinch (sth).

flibusterie [flibystri] *nf P* stealing/pinching.

flibustier [flibystje] *nm P* thief*.

flic [flik] *nm P* policeman*/cop/copper/rozzer/*NAm* bull; **flic de la route,** speed cop; **voilà les flics,** here are the cops/the fuzz. (*Voir* **pavé**)

flicaille [flikaj] *nf coll P* **la flicaille,** the police*/the cops/the fuzz/*NAm* the bulls.

flicard [flikar] *nm P* **1.** policeman* **2.** informer*; snout/grass.

flingot [flɛ̃go] *nm P* rifle/shotgun.

flingot(t)er [flɛ̃gɔte] *vtr P* = **flinguer 1, 2, 3.**

flingue¹ [flɛ̃g] *nm P* (*a*) firearm/ gun/revolver*/shooter (*b*) rifle/shotgun.

flingue², flingué [flɛ̃ge] *a P* penniless*/bust/broke/cleaned out.

flinguer [flɛ̃ge] **I** *vtr P* **1.** to kill* (s.o.)/to gun (s.o.) down/to shoot (s.o.) dead/to bump (s.o.) off **2.** to have sex*/to lay (s.o.) **II** *vpr* **se**

flinguer to shoot oneself/to commit suicide*/to do oneself in.

flingueur [flε̃gœr] *nm* P killer/assassin/hit-man.

flippé [flipe] *a* P **1.** flipped out/high/freaked out (by a drug) **2.** **être flippé à mort,** to be doubled up with laughter/to be killing oneself laughing.

flipper [flipεr, flipœr] **I** *nm* F pinball (machine)/pin table **II** [flipe] *vi* P **1.** (*drogues*) to flip out/to freak out/to get high; **il a flippé,** he's flipped/he freaked out **2.** to be depressed*/down.

fliquaille [flikɑj] *nf coll* P = **flicaille.**

flique [flik] *nm* P = **flic.**

fliquer [flike] *vtr* P to carry out police surveillance/to police; **une société fliquée,** a police state.

fliquesse [flikεs], **fliquette** [flikεt] *nf* P policewoman.

flonger [flɔ̃ʒe] *vi* P to lurch/to stagger.

flop [flɔp] *nm* F (*théâtre, etc*) failure/flop; **sa pièce a fait flop,** his play flopped.

flop(p)ée [flɔpe] *nf* P **1.** large quantity/lashings/oodles/tons (of sth); crowd (of people); **elle a toute une flop(p)ée de gosses,** she's got a whole bunch of kids **2.** thrashing/beating.

flop(p)er [flɔpe] *vtr* P to thrash/to beat (up*).

flot [flo] *nm* F **être à flot** (*i*) to be rich*/flush (*ii*) to have one's head above water.

flottant [flɔtɑ̃] *nm* F track suit.

flottard [flɔtar] **I** *a* F watery/thin (sauce, etc); **du café flottard,** watery coffee/dishwater/gnat's piss **II** *nm* F naval cadet.

flotte [flɔt] *nf* F **1.** (*a*) (sea, river) water; **tomber dans la flotte,** to fall into the water/into the drink (*b*) (drinking) water*; **boire de la flotte,** to drink water/to have a drink of water (*c*) rain; **il tombe de la flotte,** it's raining/it's pouring **2.** (thin, watery) soup, sauce, coffee, etc **3.** **la Flotte,** the Naval Academy **4.** *pl* **des flottes de ...,** large numbers of ... /crowds of ...; oodles/lashings/tons of ....

flotter [flɔte] *v impers* F **il flotte,** it's raining/it's pouring.

flotteurs [flɔtœr] *nmpl* P (*a*) breasts*/boobs (*b*) falsies.

flouer [flue] *vtr* F to swindle*/to con (s.o.) (**de qch,** out of sth); **on m'a floué,** I've been had/done.

flouerie [fluri] *nf* F (*a*) swindle/con (trick) (*b*) swindling/cheating.

floueur, euse [fluœr, -øz] *n* F swindler*/cheat/con man/con artist.

flouse [fluz] *nm* P money*/cash/dough/bread.

flouser [fluze] *vi* P to fart*.

flouss [flus] *nm* P = **flouse.**

flousse [flus] *nf* P fart.

flouze [fluz] *nm* P = **flouse.**

flouzer [fluze] *vi* P = **flouser.**

flubard [flybar] **I** *nm* P **1.** (tele)phone* **2.** *pl* **flubards,** legs* **3.** coward* **II** *a* P frightened; cowardly*.

fluber [flybe] *vi* P to be afraid*.

flubes [flyb] *nmpl* P **avoir les flubes,** to be afraid*; to be a coward*/to be chicken; **ficher/flanquer/foutre les flubes à qn,** to put the wind up s.o.

flûtant [flytɑ̃] *a* P **c'est flûtant,** it's a damned/bloody nuisance.

flûte! [flyt] **I** *int* P damn!/blast (it)!/damn and blast!/blow it! **II** *nfpl* legs*/pins; **jouer/se tirer des flûtes,** to run away*/to beat it/to clear off.

flûter [flyte] *vi* F **1.** **je l'ai envoyé flûter,** I sent him packing/I told him where he could go **2.** c'est comme si je flûtais, I'm wasting my breath/I might (just) as well talk to myself/it's like talking to a brick wall.

focard [fɔkar] *a* P stupid*/daft.

focardise [fɔkardiz] *nf*, **focardité** [fɔkardite] *nf* P stupidity/foolishness.

fofolle [fɔfɔl] *af* F flighty/scatter-brained/nutty. (*Voir* **fou(-)fou**)

foie [fwa] *nm* 1. *F* **avoir les jambes en pâté de foie**, to have cottonwool legs 2. *P* **avoir les foies (blancs)**, to be afraid*/to be scared to death; to be a coward 3. *P* **manger/bouffer les foies à qn**, to make mincemeat of s.o.; to have s.o.'s guts for garters.

foin [fwɛ̃] *nm* 1. *F* money*; **quand il n'y a plus de foin dans le râtelier**, when the money runs out; **faire ses foins**, to make money; **mettre du foin dans ses bottes/dans ses sabots**, to feather one's nest; **avoir du foin dans ses bottes**, to be comfortably off/to have a nice little nest-egg put by 2. *F* beard; **le foin de la journée**, five-o'clock shadow 3. *P* **faire du foin** (*i*) to make a din/a (hell of a) noise/a racket (*ii*) to protest vehemently/to kick up a fuss/to make a scene; **faire un foin de tous les diables** (*i*) to make a terrific din (*ii*) to make a great song and dance (about sth)/to make a big stink (about sth)/to raise hell 4. *P* **coucher dans les foins**, to have a roll in the hay 5. *P* tobacco/baccy 6. *P* (*drogues*) marijuana*/hay. (*Voir* **bête II, 1**)

foirade [fwarad] *nf* P 1. **avoir la foirade** (*i*) to have diarrhoea*/the runs/the trots (*ii*) to be afraid*/to have the jitters/to be shitting oneself 2. disaster/failure*/flop.

foirage [fwaraʒ] *nm* P fiasco/failure*/washout; **c'est un vrai foirage**, it's a real flop.

foirailleur, -euse [fwarɑjœr, -øz] *n* P small-time reveller.

foire [fwar] I *nf* P **avoir la foire** = **avoir la foirade** (**foirade 1**) II *nf* F 1. crowd/crush 2. bedlam/bear-garden/madhouse 3. **faire la foire**, to let one's hair down/to paint the town red/to live it up/to have a ball/to get one's rocks off 4. **une foire d'empoigne**, free-for-all; rat-race 5. **la foire est sur le pont!** we've got to get a move on!/we must get cracking!

foirer [fware] *vi* 1. *P* = **avoir la foirade** (**foirade 1**); **foirer dans son fourreau**, to be shit-scared 2. *P* to defecate* 3. *F* to fail*/to flop/to come unstuck/to fall through.

foireur [fwarœr] *nm* P reveller.

foireux, -euse [fwarø, -øz] P *a&n* (*a*) (person) suffering from diarrhoea* (*b*) frightened/in a funk/jittery (*c*) **pièce foireuse**, play that flopped.

foiridon [fwaridɔ̃] *nf*, **foirinette** [fwarinɛt] *nf* F **faire la foiridon**, to go on a spree*/on a binge; to live it up.

foiron [fwarɔ̃] *nm* P buttocks*; **avoir le foiron flottant**, to wiggle one's hips (as one walks).

fois [fwa] *nf* 1. *F* **non mais des fois!** well, I like that!/don't make me laugh!/what d'you take me for?/do you mind! 2. *P* **des fois** (*i*) sometimes/now and then (*ii*) **des fois que vous le verriez/si des fois vous le voyez**, if by any chance you (should) happen to see him/just in case you (happen to) see him; **vous n'auriez pas des fois ...?** you haven't by any chance got ...?/you wouldn't happen to have ...?

foisonner [fwazɔne] *vi* P to smell bad/to stink*/to pong.

folichon [fɔliʃɔ̃] *a* F **ce n'est pas folichon**, it's not much fun/it's not very exciting.

folies [fɔli] *nfpl* F (*a*) **faire des folies**, to be extravagant/to splurge; **quel magnifique cadeau, vous avez fait des folies!** what a lovely present, you really shouldn't have done it! **ne faites pas de folies!** don't put yourself out! (*b*) **les folies de la jeunesse**, the follies of youth; **faire des folies**, to have a wild time/to have one's fling (*c*) (*fille, femme*) **faire des folies (de son corps)**, to sleep around.

folingue [fɔlɛ̃g] *a P* (slightly) mad*/loony/nuts/nutty.

folklo [fɔlklo] *a F* (*i*) eccentric*/offbeat/weird (and wonderful) (*ii*) old-fashioned.

folklore [fɔlklɔr] *nm F* **leur idée, c'est du folklore!** their idea can't be serious/is a load of rubbish!

follasse [fɔlas] *nf P* = **folle**[1].

folle[1] [fɔl] *nf P* homosexual*/queen. (*Voir* **fou**).

follingue [fɔlɛ̃g] *a P* = **folingue**.

foncer [fɔ̃se] *vi F* **1.** to speed along/to tear along/to belt along **2.** to throw oneself enthusiastically into sth/to charge into sth; **les flics ont foncé dans la foule**, the cops made a charge at the crowd; **quand je le vois, j'ai envie de lui foncer dedans**, each time I see him, he makes me so mad I could kill him **3. foncer dans le brouillard**, to go blindly ahead/to go ahead regardless.

fonceur, euse [fɔ̃sœr, -øz] *n F* dynamic/aggressive/go-ahead person.

fondant [fɔ̃dɑ̃] *nm P* (*drogues*) abscess caused by an unsterilized needle or by impure drugs/ab/AB/ABC.

fondre [fɔ̃dr] *vi F* **(se faire) fondre**, to slim; to train down; **tu as drôlement fondu**, you've really lost weight/got thin.

fondu [fɔ̃dy] **I** *a P* mad*/nuts/round the bend/bonkers **II** *nm F* **faire un fondu**, to drop out of circulation/to fade out of the picture.

fontaine [fɔ̃tɛn] *nf F* **ouvrir la fontaine**, to start crying/to turn on the waterworks. (*Voir* **cresson 1** (*a*); **wallace**)

foot [fut] *nm F* football; **jouer au foot**, to play football. (*Voir* **baby-foot**)

forçat [fɔrsa] *nm F* **les forçats de la route**, the competitors in the *Tour de France* cycle race.

forcé [fɔrse] *a F* **c'est forcé!** it's (just) got to happen!/there's no way round it!

forcir [fɔrsir] *vi F* to get fat; to put on weight.

format [fɔrma] *nm F* **1. un grand format** (*i*) a 10,000 franc note (in old francs) (*ii*) a five-hundred-franc note **2. ce type-là, c'est du grand format**, he's a big guy.

forme [fɔrm] *nf F* **être en pleine forme/avoir la forme**, to be in fine form/in the peak of condition; to be up to scratch; **tenir la forme**, to keep in trim.

formid [fɔrmid] *a F* = **formidable I**.

formidable [fɔrmidabl] **I** *a F* (*a*) great/super/terrific; **c'est formidable!** well I never! **elle est formidable**, she's fantastic/smashing/a smasher; **c'est un type formidable**, he's a great bloke/a really nice guy (*b*) incredible; **c'est tout de même formidable!** it's a bit much all the same!/that's the limit! **c'est formidable qu'elle ne puisse arriver à comprendre ça!** it's incredible (that) she can't understand that! **II** *nm F* **un formidable** = a pint (of beer).

formide [fɔrmid] *a F* = **formidable I**.

fort [fɔr] **I** *a F* **1.** clever/good (**en**, at) **2. c'est un peu fort (de café/en vinaigre)!** that's a bit much/a bit steep! **c'est (un peu) trop fort!/c'est plus fort que tout!** that's going too far!/that's too much!/that's coming it too strong! **3. en voilà une forte!/elle est forte, celle-là!** well I never!/that takes the cake!/that beats everything! **4. c'est plus fort**

que moi! I (simply) can't help it! (*Voir* **bouchon 7**; **cuite**; **gueule I, 2**; **thème**) II *adv* F (*a*) **y aller fort**, to exaggerate*/to lay it on (a bit) thick/to overdo it (*b*) **je ne vais pas fort**, I'm not feeling very well/I don't feel too good.

fortiche [fɔrtiʃ] *a & nm&f* P **1.** crafty/smart/clever/cunning (person); **il est fortiche**, he knows what's what; he knows the ropes/ he's on the ball **2.** strong/hefty/ burly (person); **c'est un fortiche**, he's a tough guy/a heavy **3. faire le fortiche**, to talk big.

fortif(e)s [fɔrtif] *nfpl* A P (*abbr* = *fortifications*) **les fortif(e)s**, the old defence works around Paris (formerly an habitual resort of criminals). (*Voir* **laf(f)es**)

fortune [fɔrtyn] *nf* F (*hommes*) **être en (quête de) bonnes fortunes**, to be on the make/after a bit; (to be trying) to get off with/to pull (a girl/a woman).

fosse [fos] *nf* F **avoir un pied dans la fosse/être au bord de la fosse**, to have one foot in the grave.

fossé [fose] *nm* F **sauter le fossé** (*i*) to take the plunge (*ii*) to get married*.

fossile [fɔsil, fɔ-] **I** *nm* F **un vieux fossile**, an old fossil/an old fogey/ (an old) has-been/an old fuddy-duddy **II** *a* fossilized/antiquated (ideas, etc).

se fossiliser [səfɔsilize, -fɔ-] *vpr* F to become an old fossil/fossilized; to get past it/to have had it.

fou, folle² [fu, fɔl] *a* F **1.** tremendous/enormous/fantastic; **un argent fou**, pots/loads/bags of money; **un monde fou**, a terrific/a huge crowd; **j'ai un mal fou à apprendre cette langue**, I'm having a really tough time with this language; **c'est un succès fou**, it's a smash hit/a tremendous success **2.** mad*/crazy; **t'es (pas) fou?** are you mad?/you must be out of your

mind! **3. c'est fou ce que …**, it's amazing/extraordinary how …; **c'est fou ce que c'est cher!** it costs the earth! **c'est fou ce qu'on s'amuse!** we're having a fantastic time! **c'est fou ce qu'elle est drôle!** she's a real scream!

fouaron [fwarɔ̃] *nm* P = **foiron**.

fouchtra [fuʃtra] **I** *a&nm* P (native, inhabitant) of Auvergne **II** *int* F = **fichtre!**

foudre [fudr] *nf* F **le coup de foudre**, love at first sight.

fouettard [fwɛtar] *nm* **1.** (*a*) F **le Père Fouettard**, the bog(e)yman (*b*) **un père fouettard** (*i*) F a very strict father (*ii*) P s.o. who likes to be dominated/beaten in sexual relations; passive flagellant **2.** P buttocks*; **botter le fouettard à qn**, to give s.o. a boot up the backside/ arse/*esp NAm* ass **3.** P **l'avoir dans le (père) fouettard**, to be swindled*/done/had/diddled; **se faire mettre dans le (père) fouettard**, to get the worst of it/to come off second best.

fouetter [fwete] *vi* P **1.** to stink* (to high heaven); **ça fouette ici**, it stinks in here **2.** to be afraid*/to get the wind up. (*Voir* **chat 5, 6**)

fou(-)fou [fufu] *am* F silly/foolish/harebrained/crazy. (*Voir* **fofolle**)

fou(i)gnedé [fu(i)ɲede] *nm* P (*a*) buttocks*/arse/*esp NAm* ass (*b*) anus*/arsehole/*esp NAm* arsehole.

fouille [fuj] *nf* P **1.** pocket; **en avoir plein les fouilles**, to be rich*/ flush/loaded **2. l'avoir dans la fouille**, to have it all sewn up; **c'est dans la fouille**, it's in the bag. (*Voir* **vaisselle**)

fouille-merde [fujmɛrd] *nm inv* P **1.** scandalmonger/muck-raker **2.** scavenger **3.** (private) investigator.

fouiller [fuje] **I** *vtr* V to have sex* with (s.o.)/to screw (s.o.)/to have it off (with s.o.) **II** *vpr* **se fouiller** P

1. se fouiller de qch, to (make) do without sth/to go without sth **2. tu peux te fouiller (si tu as des poches)!** (you can) go jump in the lake!/get stuffed!/get knotted!

fouillette [fujɛt] *nf P* **1.** pocket*. (*Voir* **fouille**) **2.** frisk; body search.

fouillouse [fujuz] *nf P* pocket*. (*Voir* **fouille**)

Fouilly-les-Chaussettes [fujilɛʃosɛt], **Fouilly-les-Coucous** [fujilɛkuku] *Prn F* = **Fouilly-les-Oies** (*a*).

Fouilly-les-Oies [fujilezwa] *Prn F* (*a*) imaginary out-of-the-way place; one-horse town/hick town; = Much-Binding-in-the-Marsh/ *NAm* Podunk. (*Voir* **Tripatouille-les-Oies**) (*b*) **sortir de Fouilly-les-Oies,** to come from the back of beyond/the sticks; *NAm* to come from the backwoods/the boondocks/the boonies; *Austr* to come from the backblocks.

fouinard [fwinar] **I** *a* (*a*) *F* inquisitive/nosy/snoopy/prying (*b*) *P* sly/sneaky **II** *nm F* nos(e)y parker/snoop(er).

fouinasser [fwinase] *vi P* = **fouiner 1.**

fouine [fwin] *nf F* **à figure de fouine,** weasel-faced/sly-faced; **c'est une vraie fouine,** he/she is very nosy/a nosy parker.

fouinedarès [fwindarɛs] *nm P* **1.** anus*. **2.** buttocks*.

fouiner [fwine] *vi* **1.** *F* (*a*) to ferret (about)/to nose about (*b*) to poke one's nose into/to mess about in other people's affairs; to snoop **2.** *P* to slink away/to slope off **3.** *P* to sneak/to rat (on s.o.).

fouineur, euse [fwinœr, -øz] *F* **I** *a&n* = **fouinard 1, 2 II** *n* bargain hunter.

foulant [fulã] *a F* tiring/exhausting/back-breaking; **ce n'est pas bien foulant,** it's a bit of a doddle/a soft option, really.

se fouler [səfule] *vpr F* **1.** to take pains (over sth)/to put oneself out (to do sth well) **2. il ne se foule pas/il ne se foule pas la rate/il ne se la foule pas,** he takes it easy/he doesn't exactly kill himself working/he doesn't overdo things; **il n'a pas à se fouler,** he doesn't have to flog himself to death/he's onto a cushy number. (*Voir* **méninges**)

foul(e)titude [fultityd] *nf F* **une foul(e)titude de ...,** a crowd/mass of ...; bags/heaps/loads/masses/ piles of ....

four [fur] *nm* **1.** *F* (*théâtre, etc*) failure/disaster/flop; **faire un four,** to flop; **la pièce a fait un four,** the play was a flop/the play flopped; **un four noir,** a complete washout **2.** *P* **chauffer le four,** to get drunk* **3.** *P* wide-open mouth; gape.

fouraille [furaj] *nf P* firearm/ shooter/piece.

fourailler [furaje] **I** *vtr V* to have sex* with (s.o.)/to screw (s.o.) (very quickly); **fourailler à la une,** to have a quick in-and-out job/a quickie; to bunny-fuck **II** *vi P* to use a firearm/to fire a gun.

fourbi [furbi] *nm F* **1.** (*mil*) kit/ gear **2.** belongings/gear/clobber/ stuff **3.** (*a*) rubbish; mess; bits and pieces; **je vais me débarrasser de tout ce fourbi,** I'm going to get shot of all this junk/I'm going to chuck this lot out (*b*) **(et) tout le fourbi,** the whole works*/the whole (kit and) caboodle; **habillé en jean, blouson noir et tout le fourbi,** dressed in jeans, black (leather) jacket, the lot/the whole works*/ you name it! (*c*) gadget*/contraption/whatsit/thingummyjig; **comment appelez-vous ce fourbi-là?** what's that thing called? **4.** peculiar/funny business; **un (vrai) fourbi arabe,** one hell of a mess; **un sale fourbi,** a rotten job; **c'est tout un fourbi,** it's quite a business **5.**

connaître le fourbi, to know what it's all about/to know all the tricks; **il connaît le fourbi**, he's no fool/he knows where it's at.

fourche [furʃ] nf 1. F **faire qch à la fourche**, to do sth anyoldhow 2. F **traiter qn à la fourche**, to treat s.o. roughly/badly 3. P **(voleur à la) fourche**, pickpocket*.

fourchette [furʃɛt] nf 1. F **il a un bon coup de fourchette/c'est une bonne fourchette/il joue bien de la fourchette**, he's got a good/healthy appetite 2. F **manger qch avec la fourchette du père Adam**, to eat sth with one's fingers 3. P **donner le coup de fourchette à qn**, to poke s.o. in the eyes (with the index and second fingers) 4. P **(voleur à la) fourchette**, pickpocket*; **vol à la fourchette**, pickpocketing/dipping.

fourgat [furga] nm P = **fourgue**.

fourgue [furg] nm P 1. receiver (of stolen goods)/fence 2. (drogues) pusher/dealer*/(the) man.

fourguer [furge] vtr P 1. (a) to sell/to flog (stolen goods) (b) to sell (sth) on the cheap (c) to palm (sth) off onto (s.o.) 2. to inform on*/to grass on (s.o.); to shop (s.o.) 3. (drogues) to push/to deal.

fourgueur [furgœr] nm P = **fourgue**.

fourlineur [furlinœr] nm P pickpocket*/dip.

fourmi [furmi] nf 1. F **avoir des fourmis dans les pattes**, to have pins and needles in one's legs; **j'ai des fourmis dans le pied**, my foot has gone to sleep 2. F **une fourmi blanche**, a busy and thrifty person/eager beaver 3. P **une fourmi rouge**, a woman traffic warden 4. P (drogues) (a) pusher/dealer* (b) addict (on a small scale). (Voir œuf 13)

fourneau, pl -eaux [furno] nm A P fool*.

fourré [fure] a F **être toujours fourré chez qn**, to be never off s.o.'s

doorstep/to be constantly (calling) at s.o.'s house; **être toujours fourré avec qn**, to hobnob with s.o. (Voir langue 9)

fourreau, pl -eaux [furo] nm P trousers*/esp NAm pants. (Voir chier 10; foirer 1)

fourrer [fure] I vtr 1. F (a) to cram/to stuff/to stick/to shove; **il a fourré la lettre dans sa poche**, he shoved the letter into his pocket; **fourre-toi ça dans la tête**, get that into your head (b) to place/to put; **il ne sait pas où il a fourré ses clés**, he doesn't know where he put his keys; **fourrez tout ça par terre!** dump all that lot on the ground! 2. F **fourrer qn dedans** (i) to cheat* s.o./to have s.o. on/to take s.o. in (ii) to put s.o. behind bars/to put s.o. inside 3. F **fourrer son nez partout**, to poke/to stick one's nose into everything 4. F **fourrer qn à la porte**, to turn/to turf s.o. out of the house 5. V to have sex* with s.o./to screw (s.o.)/to stuff (s.o.). (Voir doigt 6; tiroir 3) II vpr **se fourrer** F 1. (a) **je ne savais où me fourrer**, I (was so embarrassed that I) didn't know where to hide/where to put myself (b) **où est-il allé se fourrer?** where on earth has he got to?/what has he got himself into? 2. **chercher quelque trou où se fourrer**, to be looking for a job (without much hope of success) 3. **se fourrer dans la conversation**, to butt in 4. **s'en fourrer jusque-là**, to gorge oneself/to have a blow-out/to stuff one's face.

fourrure [furyr] nf V (femme) **humecter sa fourrure**, to urinate*/to (have a) piss.

foutaise [futɛz] nf P 1. rubbish/nonsense*/rot/bull(shit); **tout ça c'est de la foutaise/des foutaises**, that's a load of cods(wallop)/a load of old rubbish 2. **on s'est quitté(s) pour des foutaises**, we split up for no real reason/for sod all.

fouteur [futœr] *nm* V **fouteur de merde**, piss artist.

foutoir [futwar] *nm* P **1.** messy room, house, etc; pigsty/dump; **quel foutoir!** what a (bloody) shambles! **2.** brothel*/knocking shop.

foutral, als [futral] *a* P extraordinary/amazing.

foutraque [futrak] *a* O mad*/ bonkers/crazy.

foutre¹ [futr] **I** *nm* V semen*/ spunk/jism/cum **II** *int* V **foutre!** fuck (it)!/sod (it)!/bugger (it)!/shit!

foutre² **I** *vtr* **1.** P (*mettre*) **foutre qch par terre**, to chuck/to bung sth (down) on the ground; **foutre qn dehors/à la porte**, to kick s.o. out/ to give s.o. the boot/to give s.o. the push; V **ta lettre, tu peux te la foutre quelque part!** you know what you can do with your letter!/you can stick your letter up your arse/ *esp NAm* ass **2.** P (*donner*) **foutre un coup de pied à qn**, to give s.o. a kick up the arse/*esp NAm* ass; **ça m'a foutu le trac**, it gave me the creeps/the willies **3.** (*faire*) **il ne fout rien de la journée**, he just sits on his arse/ass all day long; he does bugger all; he just sods/bums around; **qu'est-ce que tu fous?** what the hell are you doing? **qu'est-ce qu'elle peut bien foutre là-dedans?** what the fuck is she doing in there? **4.** V **qu'est-ce que ça peut me foutre/qu'est-ce que j'en ai à foutre?** what the fuck's it got to do with me?/I don't give a fuck/a shit/a fart! **rien à foutre!** nothing doing!*/ not a chance in hell!/not a sodding chance! **5.** V **foutre le camp**, to fuck off/to bugger off/to sod off/to piss off; **foutez le camp!** fuck off!/ piss off!/sod off! **6.** V **fous-moi la paix!** (*i*) fuck off!/piss off!/sod off! (*ii*) shut up!*/lay off!/stop bugging me!/stop pissing me about! **va te faire foutre!** fuck off!/go fuck yourself!/screw you!/fuck you!/go screw yourself! **7.** V (*a*) **envoyer qn faire foutre**, to tell s.o. to fuck off

(*b*) **envoyer qch faire foutre**, to pack sth in (*c*) **tout foutre en l'air**, to bugger/to fuck/to screw everything up; **ça a tout foutu en l'air**, that's ballsed/*NAm* balled/bollocksed it up nicely **8.** P **ça la fout mal**, it's a bloody shame; that makes a lousy impression/that looks really bad **9.** P **en foutre un coup**, to work hard*/to work one's balls off/ *esp NAm* to work one's tail off **10. foutre la merde/le merdier dans qch**, to make a balls-up/a cock-up of sth; to balls sth up **11.** V **foutre qn**, to have sex* with s.o./to fuck s.o./to screw s.o. **II** *vpr* **se foutre** P **1. se foutre par terre** (*i*) to fling oneself on the ground (*ii*) to fall flat on one's face/to come a cropper* **2.** (*a*) **se foutre de qn** (*i*) to poke fun at s.o./to pull s.o.'s leg/to have s.o. on (*ii*) to mess s.o. about/around; **est-ce que vous vous foutez de moi?** are you trying to make me look stupid? **tu te fous de ma gueule?** are you taking the piss (out of me)?/what the hell do you take me for?/I'm not a complete arsehole/*esp NAm* asshole! (*b*) **se foutre de qch**, to poke fun at sth; **il s'en fout comme de l'an quarante/ comme de sa première chemise; il s'en fout pas mal/complètement; il s'en fout et s'en contrefout**, he couldn't give a damn/a fuck; **je me fous bien de ce qu'on pense de moi**, I don't give a damn what they think of me/they can think what they bloody well like about me; **ça, c'est se foutre du monde!** well, what a bloody/damn cheek/nerve! **3. se foutre dedans** (*i*) to put one's foot in it/to boob (*ii*) to cock sth up/to balls sth up/to fuck sth up **4. se foutre à faire qch**, to begin to do sth **5. s'en foutre plein la lampe**, to stuff one's face/to have a good blow-out/to pig out. (*Voir* **air I 6**)

foutrement [futr(ə)mã] *adv* P very/extremely; **c'est foutrement loin**, it's a bloody long way/it's damn far; **être foutrement con**, to be bloody stupid/damn thick; to be a fucking idiot.

foutrer [futre] *vi O V* (*homme*) to have an orgasm*/to come.

foutriquet [futrikɛ] *nm P* insignificant person/nobody/little squirt/little runt.

foutu [futy] *a P* **1.** (*a*) **être mal foutu** (*i*) (*appareil, etc*) to be badly made/designed; **ce stylo est très mal foutu,** this biro is useless (*ii*) (*pers*) to feel (bloody) tired*/shagged/knackered (*iii*) (*pers*) to feel unwell*/under the weather; **je suis vraiment mal foutu aujourd'hui,** I feel really lousy/dreadful today (*iv*) (*pers*) to be badly/untidily dressed (*v*) (*of pers*) to be ugly; **elle n'est pas mal foutue, cette nana,** she's not at all bad(-looking), that bird/chick (*b*) **être bien foutu** (*i*) to be well made; **c'est bien foutu, ce petit truc,** it's not bad, this little thingamyjig (*ii*) (*pers*) to be well-dressed (*iii*) (*pers*) to be good-looking; **il est vachement bien foutu, ce mec,** he's really something, that guy/bloke **2.** rotten/awful/lousy; **quel foutu temps!** what bloody awful/foul/lousy weather! **quelle foutue idée!** what a bloody stupid/pathetic/useless idea! **dans un foutu état,** in a terrible state; **un foutu imbécile,** a bloody idiot/a fucking idiot **3.** **il est foutu,** he's done for/he's had it; **c'est un type foutu,** he'll never get anywhere/he's finished; **la réunion est foutue,** the meeting's screwed up/buggered up; **ma montre est foutue,** my watch is bust/buggered; **c'est de l'argent (de) foutu,** it's money down the drain; **ce n'est pas la peine d'essayer, c'est foutu d'avance,** there's no point in trying/what's the use of trying, it's already fucked (up) **4. foutu de,** likely to/capable of; **il n'est même pas foutu de faire son lit,** he can't even make his own bed; **il est foutu de partir avant que j'arrive,** it's on the cards that he'll leave/he's bound to leave before I get there.

foutument [futymã] *adv P =* **foutrement.**

fracasser [frakase] *vtr O P* to burgle/*NAm* to burglarize.

fracasseur [frakasœr] *nm P* burglar.

fraîche [frɛʃ] *nf P* **1.** money*/cash/dough **2. une fraîche,** a bottle/carafe of water.

fraîchement [frɛʃmã] *adv F* **comment ça va? – comme le temps, fraîchement,** how are you? – not too hot/a bit chilly, like the weather.

frais¹, fraîche² [frɛ, frɛʃ] *a* **1.** *F* **frais comme l'œil/comme une rose,** as fresh as a daisy; **il n'est pas frais ce matin,** he doesn't look too hot this morning **2.** *P* **me voilà frais!/je suis frais (comme un porc)!** I'm in a fix*/I'm in a right old mess!/I'm really up the creek!

frais² *nmpl F* **1. arrêter les frais,** to give up/to throw in the sponge/the towel **2. aux frais de la princesse** (*i*) at the expense of the taxpayer/the government (*ii*) on the firm; on expenses (*iii*) on the house/buckshee.

fraise [frɛz] *nf* **1.** (*a*) *F* **aller aux fraises** (*i*) (*voiture*) to go off the road (by accident) (*ii*) (*hum, euph; amoureux*) to go for a walk in the woods (*b*) *P* **allez aux fraises!** get lost!*/go jump in a lake!/get knotted! **2.** *F* birthmark **3.** *P* **sucrer les fraises** (*i*) to tremble (all over)/to have the shakes (*ii*) to be gaga/to be old and doddery **4.** *P* face*/mug; **se sucrer la fraise/se refaire la fraise,** to make up/to powder one's nose **5.** *P* **ramener sa fraise** (*i*) to butt into the conversation/to put in one's oar (*ii*) to show off*/to talk big **6.** *P* **amener sa fraise,** to turn up/to put in an appearance/to show one's face **7.** *P* **envoyer qn sur les fraises,** to send s.o. packing*/to send s.o. off with a flea in his ear **8.** *P* nipple.

fraline [fralin] *nf P* = **frangine**.

framboise [frɑ̃bwaz] *nf V* clitoris*/clit.

franc [frɑ̃] *a F* safe/without risk; **c'est pas très franc**, it's a bit tricky/dodgy.

français [frɑ̃sɛ] *nm F* **vous ne comprenez pas le français?** = don't/can't you understand plain English?

la Franchecaille [lafrɑ̃ʃkɑj] *Prnf P* France.

franco [frɑ̃ko] **I** *a P* **1.** (*pers*) loyal/dependable **2.** = **franc II** *adv F* readily/unhesitatingly; **y aller franco**, to go straight to the point/to come right out with it; **vas-y franco!** go right ahead!

François [frɑ̃swa] *Prnm P* **faire le coup du père François à qn**, to strangle s.o./to throttle s.o.; to garrotte s.o.

francouillard [frɑ̃kujar] *nm P* franc.

frangibus [frɑ̃ʒibys] *nm P* brother/bruvver/bro'.

frangin [frɑ̃ʒɛ̃] *nm* **1.** *P* brother/bruvver/bro' **2.** *P* fellow*/chap/bloke/guy **3.** *P* friend*/mate **4.** *P* monk/friar **5.** *V* **petit frangin**, penis*.

frangine [frɑ̃ʒin] *nf P* **1.** sister/sis **2.** (*a*) girl*/bird/chick/sister (*b*) woman*/*esp NAm* dame/broad **3.** prostitute*/hooker/tart **4.** mistress **5.** lesbian*/lezzy/dyke **6.** nun.

frangipane [frɑ̃ʒipan] *nf* prostitute*/tart/hooker.

franquiste [frɑ̃kist] *nm P* receiver (of stolen goods)/fence.

fransquillon [frɑ̃skijɔ̃] *P* **I** *a* French/frog/froggish **II** *nm* Frenchman; **les Fransquillons**, the frogs/the froggies.

frappadingue [frapadɛ̃g] *a P* mad*/bonkers/barmy/nuts.

frappe [frap] *nf P* hooligan*/thug/yob/yobbo; **c'est une sale petite** frappe, he's a dirty/nasty little bastard*.

frappé [frape] *a P* mad*/crazy/loony/nuts.

frapper [frape] **I** *vtr P* to tap/to touch (s.o.) for money; to cadge (off s.o.)/to be on the cadge **II** *vpr* **se frapper** *F* to get flustered/to get into a state/to get worked up/to get panicky; **(ne) vous frappez pas!** don't panic! **ne te frappe pas le biscuit!** don't get worked up!/stay cool!

frégaton [fregatɔ̃] *nm F* naval commander.

frein [frɛ̃] *nm F* (*pers*) **mâcher/ronger son frein**, to champ (the bit)/to be raring to go.

frelot [frəlo] *nm P* (younger/kid) brother.

frelotte [frəlɔt] *nf P* **1.** (younger/kid) sister **2.** nun.

se fréquenter [səfrekɑ̃te] *vpr V* to masturbate*/to toss off/to play with oneself.

frère [frɛr] *nm* **1.** *F* friend*/mate/buddy; (*esp Black Sl*) (soul) brother; **tu es un frère**, you're a real pal/a brick; you're all right/OK **2.** *F* (*a*) **qu'est-ce qu'ils veulent, ces frères-là?** what do those blokes/guys want? (*b*) **vieux frère!** old chap!*/my old mate! **3.** *F* **un faux frère**, a traitor **4.** *F* **frère trois points**, freemason **5.** *P* **petit frère**, penis*/John Thomas; **dérouiller son petit frère**, to have sex*/to get one's end away.

frérot [frero] *nm F* (little/kid) brother.

frétillante [fretijɑ̃t] *nf* **1.** *P* tail **2.** *V* penis*.

frétillard [fretijar] *nm V* penis*.

fric [frik] *nm F* money*/bread/dough/lolly; **être bourré de fric**, to be loaded/rolling in it; **il pue le fric**, he's stinking rich; **aboule ton fric!** cough up/fork out! **ça m'a**

coûté plein de fric, it cost me a fortune/a hell of a lot.

fricassée [frikase] *nf F* **1.** thrashing/beating-up* **2.** **fricassée de museaux,** hugs and kisses; necking session.

fricasser [frikase] *vtr F* to squander/to blow (one's money).

fric(-)frac [frikfrak] *nm P* **1.** burglary/housebreaking; break-in; **faire un fric(-)frac,** to break in/to burgle/*NAm* to burglarize/to heist; **ils sont allés faire un fric-frac quelque part,** they've gone off to do a job some place **2.** burglar/cracksman. (*pl* **fric(-)frac(s)**)

fricfraquer [frikfrake] *vi P* = faire un fric(-)frac (**fric(-)frac 1**)

frichti [friʃti] *nm P* food*/grub/nosh/chow; meal; **être de frichti,** to be in charge of the cooking/to be chief cook.

fricot [friko] *nm F* **1.** grub/nosh/chow; cooking; **faire le fricot,** to do the cooking/to make the grub **2.** cushy job/soft number/soft option.

fricotage [frikɔtaʒ] *nm F* **1.** cooking **2.** underhand practice(s)/shady deal(ing); **c'est du fricotage,** it's a shady business/it's not above board.

fricoter [frikɔte] *vtr&i* **1.** *F* to cook; **elle fricote bien,** she's a good cook **2.** *F* to squander/to blow/to run through (money) **3.** *F* (*a*) to cook up; to wangle; **je me demande ce qu'il fricote,** I wonder what he's cooking up; **qu'est-ce que tu fricotes?** what are you up to? (*b*) to make a bit on the side/to make a fast buck; to fiddle (sth) **4.** *F* to shirk/(*mil*) to skrimshank **5.** *P* (*euph sexuel*) **ils fricotent ensemble ces deux-là,** those two are knocking around together.

fricoteur, euse [frikɔtœr, -øz] *n F* (*a*) wangler/fiddler (*b*) embezzler/swindler* (*c*) *nm* shirker/skiver/(*esp mil*) skrimshanker.

frictionnée [friksjɔne] *nf P*

thrashing/going over/roughing up/beating* up.

Fridolin [fridɔlɛ̃] *nm P* German*/Jerry/Fritz/Kraut.

fri-fri [frifri] *nm V* female genitals*; **cache fri-fri,** g-string.

frigo [frigo] **I** *a F* **il fait frigo,** it's freezing (cold) **II** *nm* **1.** refrigerator/fridge/*NAm* ice box; **mettre un projet au frigo,** to put a project into cold storage/to shelve a project.

frigorifié [frigɔrifje] *a F* (*pers*) **être frigorifié,** to be frozen stiff/to be frozen to death.

frimant, ante [frimã, -ãt] *n P* (*théâtre*) bit-player/extra/walker-on.

frime [frim] *nf F* **1.** (*a*) sham/pretence/put-on; **c'est de la frime,** it's all put on; that's just a lot of eyewash/hokum (*b*) **faire qch pour la frime,** to do sth for appearances' sake/for show **2.** *F* (*mere*) trifle **3.** (*a*) head* (*b*) face* (*c*) appearance/looks/(facial) expression **4.** (*théâtre*) **faire une frime/faire de la frime,** to have walk-on parts/to be an extra/to play bit parts **5.** **laisser qn en frime,** to abandon s.o./to leave s.o. high and dry/to leave s.o. in the lurch.

frimer [frime] *F* **I** *vi* **1.** to pretend; to put on an act/a show; to show off*; **qu'est-ce qu'elle vient nous frimer la gueule?** what kind of an act is she putting on? **frimer l'orgasme,** to pretend to have an orgasm/to make out **2.** **frimer bien,** to look good **II** *vtr* to look at*/to stare at.

frimeur [frimœr] *nm F* show-off*/poseur/poser.

frimousse [frimus] *nf F* (*usu petite fille*) (nice/cute/sweet little) face.

fringale [frɛ̃gal] *nf F* pang of hunger; **avoir la fringale,** to be ravenous/starving.

fringuer [frɛ̃ge] **I** *vtr P* to dress (s.o.); **bien fringué,** well-dressed; **fringué en jean,** wearing jeans **II**

vpr **se fringuer** *P* to dress oneself/ to get dressed; to do oneself up/to doll oneself up; **il s'est bien fringué pour sortir,** he'd got himself up all ready to go out.

fringues [frɛ̃g] *nfpl P* clothes*/ clobber/togs/gear; **fringues de coulisse,** (woman's) underwear.

fringueur [frɛ̃gœr] *nm P* second-hand clothes dealer.

frio [frio] *a P* **il fait frio,** it's freezing (cold)/it's brass monkey weather.

fripe [frip] *nf* **1.** *P* food*/grub/ nosh/chow; **faire la fripe,** to rustle up some food **2.** *pl F* **fripes,** secondhand clothes.

fripouillard [fripujar] *nm,* **fripouille** [fripuj] *nf F* (*a*) swindler*/trickster/con man (*b*) rotter/ swine/bastard*.

fripouillerie [fripujri] *nf F* (*a*) swindle*/con trick/dirty deal (*b*) swindling/cheating/double dealing.

friquet [frikɛ] *nm* **1.** *F* young whippersnapper **2.** *P* (*prison*) informer* **3.** *pl P* **Friquets,** German* soldiers/Jerries.

frire [frir] *vtr F* **1. je n'ai pas de quoi frire,** I've got nothing to eat **2. rien à frire!** nothing doing!*/not on your nellie!

frisco [frisko] *a&nm P* = **frisquet.**

Frisé [frize] *nm,* **Frisou,** *pl -* **ous** [frizu] *nm F* German* (soldier)/Jerry.

frisquet [friskɛ] *F* **I** *a* chilly/ nippy/parky; **il fait frisquet,** there's a nip in the air/it's a bit chilly **II** *nm* nip/chill in the air.

fristiquer [fristike] *vi P* to have a bite to eat*; to have a meal.

frit [fri] *a F* **on est frits,** we've had it/we're done for; our goose is cooked.

frite [frit] *nf P* **1.** face*; head; **vise un peu la frite qu'il a!** just take a dekko at his face! **2.** (*forme*) **il a la frite,** he's in great shape; **t'as pas**

la frite? don't you feel too good? **3.** blow*/slap (on buttocks) **4.** *pl* **tomber dans les frites,** to faint*/to pass out. (*Voir* **bouche 6**)

Fritz [frits] *P* **I** *a* German* (soldier)/Jerry **II** *nm* (*a*) German*/ Jerry/Fritz/Kraut; **les Fritz,** Jerry/ the Jerries (*b*) **le fritz,** (the) German (language).

Frizou, *pl* **-ous** [frizu] *nm F* German* (soldier)/Jerry.

froc [frɔk] *nm* **1.** *P* trousers*/pants **2.** *P* **déchirer son froc,** to fart* loudly **3.** *V* **chier/débourrer/ foirer/lâcher tout dans son froc,** to be afraid*/to be shit-scared/to be scared shitless **4.** *V* **pisser dans son froc,** to piss oneself laughing **5.** *P* **baisser son froc,** to humiliate oneself/to eat humble pie **6.** *pl P* clothes*.

frocard [frɔkar] *nm O P* **1.** monk/clergyman **2.** trousers*/ pants.

from [frɔm] *nm P* cheese.

fromage [frɔmaʒ] *nm* **1.** *F* cushy job/easy number/soft option; **il est dans un de ces fromages,** he's onto a really cushy number/he's got a really cushy job **2.** *F* **faire de ça un fromage/en faire tout un fromage,** to kick up a fuss about nothing/to make a song and dance about nothing **3.** *P* juryman/member of the jury **4.** *pl P* **fromages,** feet* **5.** *VV* smegma/cream cheese.

frome [frɔm] *nm,* **fromegi(e)** [frɔmʒi] *nm,* **frometegomme** [frɔmtəgɔm] *nm,* **frometon** [frɔmtɔ̃] *nm,* **fromgi** [frɔmʒi] *nm,* **fromgom** [frɔmgɔm] *nm,* **fromjo** [frɔmʒo] *nm,* **fromtegom** [frɔmtəgɔm] *nm,* **fromton** [frɔmtɔ̃] *nm P* cheese. (*Voir* **os 1**)

frotin [frɔtɛ̃] *nm P* = **frottin.**

frotte [frɔt] *nf P* **1. la frotte,** scabies/the itch; **la Frotte,** the Hôpital Saint-Louis, in Paris.

frottée [frɔte] *nf F* thrashing/beating/good hiding.

frotter [frɔte] **I** *vtr* **1.** *F* to thrash (s.o.)/to give (s.o.) a good hiding; **frotter les oreilles à qn,** to box s.o.'s ears **2.** *F* **frotter son nez dans qch,** to poke one's nose into sth **3.** *P* **en frotter une,** to smooch/to rub up against s.o. (*esp* when dancing a slow number) **4.** *V* to have sex* with (s.o.) **II** *vpr* **se frotter 1.** *P* to fight/to come to blows **2.** *F* **se frotter à qn,** to come up against s.o./to tangle with s.o.; **faut pas s'y frotter!** steer clear of him! **3.** *P* to smooch with/to rub up against (s.o.) when dancing (*esp* in the slow numbers) **4.** *V* to have sex*.

frotteuse [frɔtøz] *nf P* (safety) match.

frottin [frɔtɛ̃] *nm P* **faire une partie de frottin/faire un frottin,** to have a game of billiards.

frotting [frɔtiŋ] *nm P* (low-class/seedy) dance hall/dive.

frou-frou, froufrou [frufru] *nm O P* (burglar's) skeleton key. (*pl* **frous-frous, froufrous**)

froussard, arde [frusar, -ard] *a&n P* cowardly* (person)/chicken; **c'est un froussard/il est froussard,** he's a (bit of a) coward*.

frousse [frus] *nf P* fear; cowardice; **avoir la frousse,** to be afraid*/to have cold feet/to be scared stiff; **ficher/flanquer/foutre la frousse à qn,** to put the wind up s.o./to give s.o. the willies.

fruit [frɥi] *nm F* **un fruit sec** (*i*) a student who has failed to qualify for a profession/a dropout (*ii*) a failure*/a dead loss/a washout.

frusqué [fryske] *a P* dressed; **frusqué de/en noir,** dressed in/wearing black.

frusquer [fryske] **I** *vtr P* to dress/to clothe (s.o.) **II** *vpr* **se frusquer** *P* to get dressed/to put one's clothes on.

frusques [frysk] *nfpl P* clothes*; **mettre ses belles frusques,** to put one's glad rags on; **de vieilles frusques,** cast-offs; **apportez vos frusques de foot,** bring (along) your football clobber/gear.

frusquin [fryskɛ̃] *nm P* = **Saint-Frusquin** (*a*), (*b*).

fu-fute [fyfyt] *a P* = **fute-fute.**

fuite [fɥit] *nf F* **la fuite** (*i*) (*mil*) demob(ilization) (*ii*) (*scol*) the holidays.

se fuiter [səfɥite] *vpr P* to run away*/to scarper/to do a bunk.

fumant [fymɑ̃] *a F* wonderful/amazing/brilliant/terrific/sensational.

fumante [fymɑ̃t] *nf P* sock.

fumasse [fymas] *nf P* anger; **être (en) fumasse,** to be angry*/to be fuming/*esp NAm* to be mad/to be sore.

fumée [fyme] *nf* **1.** **balancer/envoyer la fumée** (*i*) *P* to shoot (a firearm)/to fire (*ii*) *V* to ejaculate*/to shoot (one's load) **2.** *V* (*fellation*) **avaler la fumée,** to give (s.o.) a blow-job/to give (s.o.) head.

fumelle [fymɛl] *nf P* (*a*) woman*/female (*b*) wife*.

fumer [fyme] *vi F* **1.** to be fuming/to be furious **2.** **ça fume!** things are warming up!/things are hotting up! **ça va fumer!** there'll be fireworks!/there'll be trouble!

fumeron [fymrɔ̃] *nm* **1.** *F* heavy smoker/chain-smoker **2.** *pl P* (*a*) legs*/pins (*b*) **avoir les fumerons,** to be afraid*/to have the jitters.

fumette [fymet] *nf P* **la fumette,** smoking/blowing (marijuana*, etc).

fumier [fymje] *nm P* despicable person/bastard*/louse/heel/shit/*esp NAm* son of a bitch; **espèce de fumier!** you bastard!/you sod!

fumiste [fymist] *F* **I** *nm* (*a*) practical joker/hoaxer (*b*) fraud/

phon(e)y **II** *a* **il est un peu fumiste,** he's a bit of a phon(e)y.

fumisterie [fymistəri] *nf* F practical joke/hoax*; **tout ça, c'est de la fumisterie!** that's a load of hooey!/it's a real con!

funérailles! [fynerɑj] *int* F (*dans le Midi*) **oh, funérailles!** oh blast!/oh no!/help!

furax(e) [fyraks], **furibard** [fyribar] *a* P furious/livid/hopping mad.

fusain [fyzɛ̃] *nm* P **1.** (cassocked) priest **2.** *pl* (*a*) **fusains,** legs* (*b*) **avoir les fusains,** to be afraid*/to have the wind up.

fusant [fyzɑ̃] *nm* P fart.

fuseaux [fyzo] *nmpl* F legs*; **il peut à peine se tenir sur ses fuseaux,** he can hardly keep on his pins.

fusée [fyze] *nf* P **lâcher une fusée,** to vomit*/to throw up/to puke.

fuser [fyze] *vi* P to fart*.

fusil [fyzi] *nm* **1.** F **coup de fusil,** exorbitant charge/overcharging/fleecing; **essuyer le/recevoir un coup de fusil,** to be fleeced/rooked/stung/ripped off **2.** F **changer son**

fusil d'épaule (*i*) to change jobs (*ii*) to change one's opinion(s); to switch sides **3.** F stomach*/bread-basket; **se bourrer le fusil,** to stuff oneself/to stuff one's face **4.** V **fusil à trois coups,** three-way lady (*ie* a prostitute who allows her clients to use her vagina, mouth and anus simultaneously).

fusiller [fyzije] *vtr* F **1.** to bungle*/to mess up/to make a botch-up of (sth); **fusiller sa bagnole,** to smash up one's car; to run one's car into the ground **2.** to fritter away/to blow (one's money); **se faire fusiller,** to lose at gambling; **fusiller une fortune au jeu,** to gamble away a fortune **3.** to overcharge/to fleece*/to rook (s.o.); to rip (s.o.) off **4.** (*a*) **fusiller qn du regard,** to look daggers at s.o. (*b*) (*journalisme*) **être fusillé par des photographes,** to be bombarded by photographers. (*Voir* **pavé 1**)

fut [fyt], **futal** [fytal] *nm* P trousers*/*esp NAm* pants; slacks; jeans.

fute-fute [fytfyt] *a* P smart/clever/sharp/on the ball; **elle n'est pas fute-fute,** she's not too bright.

G

gabarit [gabari] *nm F* (*usu péj*) **des gens de son gabarit,** people of his sort/people like him; **il fait un bon/ un sacré gabarit,** he's a great hulk of a man.

gabelou [gablu] *nm F* (*péj*) customs officer.

gâche [gɑʃ] *nf P* **une bonne gâche,** a cushy job/a soft option.

gâchette [gɑʃɛt] *nf F* **avoir la gâchette facile,** to be trigger-happy; **c'est une bonne gâchette,** he's/she's a good shot.

gadget [gadʒɛt] *int P* **gadget!** get lost!*/piss off!

gadiche [gadiʃ] *nf* = **gadin 2.**

gadin [gadɛ̃] *nm P* **1.** head*/nut **2.** fall; **(se) prendre/(se) ramasser un gadin,** to take a header/to come a cropper/to fall flat on one's face **3. y aller du gadin,** to be guillotined/executed **4.** cork (of a bottle).

gadoue [gadu] *nf P* **1.** mud/slime **2. je suis dans une belle gadoue!** I'm in a fine old mess! **3.** excrement*/shit **4.** prostitute*/tart.

gadouille [gaduj] *nf P* **1.** mud/ slime **2.** mess/disorder*/jumble/ muddle.

gadzarts [gadzar] *nm inv F* (= *gars des Arts*) student or former student of an *Ecole des Arts et Métiers* esp the *Ecole Nationale Supérieure des Arts et Métiers*.

gâfe [gɑf] *nm,* **gaffe¹** [gaf] *nm P* **1.** (*a*) look-out man (*b*) **faire gaffe,** to take care; to be on the look-out/to be on one's guard; **fais gaffe!** look out!/watch it!/(be) careful!/mind (out)! **fais gaffe à Marcel!** watch out for yourself with Marcel!/be on your guard with Marcel! **2.** prison warder/screw.

gaffe² *nf* **1.** *F* mistake*/gaff/boob; **faire une gaffe,** to make a mistake*/to drop a clanger/to put one's foot in it/to boob **2.** *P* **avaler sa gaffe,** to die*/to snuff it/ to kick the bucket.

gaffer [gafe] *P* **I** *vi* to act as lookout (man) **II** *vtr&i* to look (at)*/to observe; **gaffe un peu!** have a butcher's!/take a dekko!/get a load of this! **III** *vi F* to make a mistake*/to boob/to drop a clanger/to put one's foot in it.

gaffeur, -euse [gafœr, -øz] **I** *nm P* look-out man **II** *n F* blunderer; **c'est un drôle de gaffeur,** he's a blundering fool/he's always putting his foot in it.

gafouiller [gafuje] *vi P* = **gaffer I.**

gaga [gaga] *F* **I** *a inv* senile/gaga/ doddering **II** *nm* old dodderer/old fogey*.

gagneuse [gaɲøz] *nf P* (*a*) well-paid prostitute* (*b*) prostitute who is a good earner (for her pimp)/ good meal-ticket.

gai [ge] **I** *a* **1. un peu gai,** slightly drunk*/merry/tipsy **2.** homosexual*/lesbian*/gay; **une boîte gaie,** a gay club **II** *nm&f* homosexual*/ lesbian*/gay.

gail, gaille [gaj] *nm P* horse/nag.

galapiat [galapja] *nm O F* (*a*) loafer/layabout/good-for-nothing (*b*) rough/tough; **un petit galapiat,** a young tough/hooligan*.

gale [gal] *nf F* obnoxious person; (*homme*) creep/bastard*/nasty piece of work/*esp NAm* son of a bitch; (*femme*) bitch/cow.

galère [galɛr] *nf P* **1. monter une galère à qn,** to cook up an excuse; to have s.o. on/to try to pull the wool over s.o.'s eyes **2. c'est galère,** it's awful/dreadful; it's a bad scene.

galérien [galerjɛ̃] *nm F* **mener une vie de galérien,** to lead a dog's life.

galetouse, galetouze [galtuz] *nf P* **1.** = **galette 1 2.** mess tin/dixie.

galettard [galɛtar] *a P* rich*/loaded/rolling in it.

galette [galɛt] *nf* **1.** *P* money*/bread/dough; **avoir beaucoup de galette,** to be rich*/loaded; **épouser la grosse galette,** to marry into money **2.** *P* (*a*) nonentity/twit/twerp/nurd (*b*) clumsy clot **3.** *F* **plat comme une galette,** as flat as a pancake **4.** *pl P* **galettes,** flat breasts*/pancakes/gnat bites **5.** *V* **bouffer la galette,** to practise cunnilingus*/to eat s.o.

galetteux, euse [galɛtø, -øz] *a O P* = **galettard.**

galipette [galipɛt] *nf F* **1.** somersault; **faire la galipette,** to turn a somersault **2.** (*a*) **faire des galipettes,** to be up to one's tricks/to lark about (*b*) to have sex* (with s.o.)/to have a bit of fun.

galoche [galɔʃ] *nf P* **1. vieille galoche,** old fogey* **2.** kiss; **faire/rouler une galoche à qn,** to kiss s.o. passionately on the mouth/to give s.o. a French kiss.

galon [galɔ̃] *nm F* (*a*) **arroser ses galons,** to celebrate one's promotion (*b*) **prendre du galon** (*i*) to be promoted (*ii*) to move up in the world/to climb the ladder.

galonnard [galɔnar] *nm P* (*mil*) officer; **les galonnards,** the (top) brass/the brass hats.

galonné [galɔne] *nm P* (*mil*) (non-commissioned) officer.

galopard [galɔpar] *nm P* louse/cootie.

galopeuse [galɔpøz] *nf F* second hand (of clock, watch).

galopin [galɔpɛ̃] *nm F* small glass (= ¼ litre) of beer.

galoup [galu] *nm,* **galoupe** [galup] *nm P* ungentlemanly/unscrupulous behaviour/dirty trick; breach of trust; **faire un galoup à qn,** to do the dirty on s.o.

galtouse, galtouze [galtuz] *nf P* = **galetouse, galetouze.**

galuche [galyʃ] *nf P* Gauloise cigarette (*RTM*).

galure [galyr] *nm,* **galurin** [galyrɛ̃] *nm,* **galurot** [galyro] *nm P* hat*; titfer/lid; **porter le galure,** to be wrongly accused/to get the blame/to take the rap.

gamahuche [gamayʃ] *nf V* (*i*) fellatio*/blow-job/head (*ii*) cunnilingus*.

gamahucher [gamayʃe] *vi V* to have oral sex* (*i*) fellatio* (*ii*) cunnilingus*.

gamberge [gɑ̃bɛrʒ] *nf P* thought/reflection; daydream; **à la gamberge,** on second thoughts.

gambergeailler [gɑ̃bɛrʒaje] *vi P* to daydream; to have one's head in the clouds.

gamberger [gɑ̃bɛrʒe] **I** *vtr&i P* (*a*) to understand/to catch on (*b*) to think/to reflect (on) (*c*) to imagine/to get into one's head (**que . . .** , that . . .) (*d*) to daydream; to have one's head in the clouds **II** *vpr* **se gamberger** *P* to think hard; to worry.

gambette [gɑ̃bɛt] *nf P* leg*; **jouer/se tirer des gambettes,** to run away*/to scarper/to beat it.

gambille [gãbij] *nf P* **1.** (*a*) dance/hop (*b*) dance hall **2.** *pl* **gambilles,** legs*.

gambiller [gãbije] *vi P* to dance (to a lively rhythm)/to prance about/to jig about.

gamelle [gamɛl] *nf* **1.** *F* **manger à la gamelle,** to eat simply/to eat out of a tin **2.** *F* **s'accrocher une gamelle,** to go without (food) **3.** *P* **ramasser une gamelle,** to fall down/ to come a cropper*.

gamin [gamɛ̃] *nm F* **1.** (*a*) boy/ lad/kid/nipper; **un gamin de neuf ans,** a kid of nine (*b*) son; **mon gamin va aller en Angleterre,** my son's/my boy's going to England **2.** (*homme*) **il est très gamin,** he's very childish.

gamine [gamin] *nf* **1.** *F* (little) girl*/kid/nipper (*b*) daughter **2.** *P* **t'occupe du chapeau de la gamine!** mind your own business!

gamme [gam] *nf F* **toute la gamme!** the whole (damn) lot (of them)!

ganache [ganaʃ] *nf O* **1.** *P* (*pers*) (heavy) jaw **2.** *F* (*a*) fool*/idiot/ clot/dumb cluck (*b*) **vieille ganache,** old fool/silly old fogey*.

gano(t) [gano] *nm P* (*a*) hoard (of money, etc) (*b*) booty/loot (*c*) purse.

gapette [gapɛt] *nf P* (*casquette*) cap.

garage [garaʒ] *nm* **1.** *F* **mettre/ ranger (qn/qch) sur une voie de garage,** to shelve (s.o./sth) **2.** *P* (prostitute's term for a) hotel room.

garce [gars] *P* **I** *nf* (*a*) bitchy girl* *or* woman*; **sa mère est une de ces garces,** her mother is a real bitch/ cow (*b*) **fils de garce!** son of a bitch! (*c*) **une belle garce,** hot stuff*/ a bit of all right (*d*) prostitute*/ tart/scrubber (*e*) **quelle garce de vie!** what a hell of a life!/what a bloody awful life! **II** *a* bitchy; **ce qu'elle peut être garce!** what a bitch/a cow she can be! she can be really bitchy when she wants!

garde-à-vous [gardavu] *nm P* **être au garde-à-vous/avoir le gourdin au garde-à-vous,** to have an erection*/a hard-on.

garde-manger [gard(ə)mãʒe] *nm inv P* stomach*/bread-basket.

garde-mites [gard(ə)mit] *nm inv F* (*mil*) stores orderly.

gare [gar] **I** *nf F* **à la gare!** scram!/hop it!/beat it!/clear off!/ on your bike! **II** *int F* **gare!** watch out! **gare à tes pattes,** mind your legs*/feet*!

garer [gare] **I** *vtr F* to put by/to stash away (money, etc) **II** *vpr* **se garer** *F* **se garer des voitures,** to watch out for/to be careful of (the) traffic; **gare-toi de mon chemin!** steer clear of me!/keep out of my way!/get out of my way!

garga [garga] *nf,* **gargamelle** [gargamɛl] *nf,* **gargane** [gargan] *nf,* **garganelle** [garganɛl] *nf P* (*a*) throat/gullet (*b*) mouth*.

gargariser [gargarize] **I** *vtr P* **se gargariser le sifflet,** to have a drink*/to wet one's whistle **II** *vpr* **se gargariser** *F* **se gargariser avec/ de qch,** to be tickled to death/tick-led pink by sth.

gargarousse [gargarus] *nf P* = **garga.**

gargoine [gargwan] *nf P* throat; **se rincer la gargoine,** to wet one's whistle.

gargote [gargɔt] *nf F* cheap restau-rant *or* café.

gargoulette [gargulɛt] *nf,* **gargue** [garg] *nf P* (*a*) mouth* (*b*) throat/gullet.

garni [garni] *a P* **elle est bien garnie,** she's well-upholstered/well-stacked.

garno(t) [garno] *nm P* (*a*) lodg-ings/digs (*b*) hotel (*esp* used by prostitutes).

garouse [garuz] *nf P* (railway) sta-tion.

gars [ga] *nm F* **1.** boy/young man/lad/laddie; **un beau gars,** a fine/handsome young man; **bonjour, mon petit gars!** hello, young fellow/son(ny) **2.** man*/chap/guy/fellow; **eh les gars!** hey, (you) lads/guys! **un brave gars,** a good sort.

gaspard [gaspar] *nm P* **1.** rat **2.** **avaler le gaspard,** to receive Holy Communion.

gastro [gastro] *n P (CB)* (*a*) restaurant/café (*b*) meal; **gastro liquide,** drink; **gastro solide,** meal.

gâteau [gato] *nm F* **1.** **partager le gâteau,** to share/to split the profits/the loot **2.** **c'est du gâteau!** it's easy!*/it's a piece of cake!/it's a walkover! **3.** **papa gâteau** (*i*) overindulgent father/grandfather (*ii*) sugar daddy.

gâterie [gatri] *nf V* (*a*) fellatio*/blow job (*b*) cunnilingus*.

gau [go] *nm P* louse/cootie.

gauche [goʃ] **I** *adv phr F* **en mettre à gauche,** to put money by; **avoir un peu d'argent à gauche,** to have something put by for a rainy day **II** *nf F* **aller jusqu'à la gauche,** to go right on to the (bitter) end/to go the whole hog; **ils nous ont eu jusqu'à la gauche,** they cheated us right, left and centre. (*Voir* **arme; pied**)

gaucho [goʃo] *a&n inv P (pol)* leftist/lefty/Trot.

gaufre [gofr] *nf P* **1.** (peaked) cap **2.** face*; **se sucrer la gaufre,** to make up/to powder one's nose **3.** **ramasser une gaufre,** to fall flat on one's face/to come a cropper **4.** mistake*/error; **faire une gaufre,** to boob. (*Voir* **moule II**)

gaufrer [gofre] **I** *vtr P* to arrest*; **se faire gaufrer,** to be caught in the act/with one's pants down **II** *vpr* **se gaufrer** *P* **1.** to give oneself a treat; **on s'est bien gaufré!** we did ourselves proud; we had a rare old time **2.** to fall flat on one's face/to come a cropper.

gaule [gol] *nf V* penis*/rod; **avoir la gaule,** to have an erection*/to have a stiff(y). (*Voir* **chevalier 2**)

gaulée [gole] *nf P* beating* (up)/thrashing.

gauler [gole] *vtr* **1.** *P* to arrest*/to pinch/to nab; **se faire/se laisser gauler,** to get nicked **2.** *P* to steal*/to pinch/to knock off **3.** *V* to have sex* with (s.o.)/to knock (s.o.) off.

gavousse [gavus] *nf P* (*javanais de* **gousse**) lesbian*/lezzy/dyke.

gaye [gaj] *nm P* = **gail.**

gaz [gaz] *nm F* **1.** **(à) plein(s) gaz** (*i*) (*aut*) with one's foot down/on the floor (*ii*) at full speed/flat out/at a hell of a pace; **ouvrir/mettre les gaz,** to step on the gas/to put one's foot on the floor **2.** **allumer son gaz,** to wake up/to (sit up and) take notice **3.** **éteindre/fermer son gaz,** to die*/to snuff it **4.** **tuyau à gaz,** anus*/poop hole; **avoir des gaz,** to suffer from flatulence/from wind; **lâcher un gaz,** to break wind/to fart. (*Voir* **bec 7; eau**)

gazer [gaze] *vi* **1.** *F* to move at top speed/to belt along/to go like the clappers **2.** to go smoothly; **ça gaze?** how goes it?/how's tricks?; (everything) all right?/OK? **ça gaze!** everything's OK!/we're doing fine! **gazer au poil/à bloc,** to go (off) without a hitch **3.** *P* **ça va gazer!** there'll be trouble!/there'll be fireworks!/there's trouble brewing! **4.** *P* to stink*/to pong.

gazier [gazje] *nm P* **1.** geezer/bloke/guy **2.** homosexual*.

gazon [gazɔ̃] *nm* **1.** *P* hair/thatch; **n'avoir plus de gazon sur la plate-bande/sur la prairie/sur la terrasse,** to be as bald* as a coot; **se faire tondre le gazon,** to get one's hair cut **2.** *V* pubic hair/fringe/pubes; (*femme*) **mouiller son gazon,** to urinate*.

GDB [ʒedebe] *abbr P* (= *gueule de*

bois) **avoir la GDB,** to have a hangover.

gégène [ʒeʒɛn] *P* **I** *nm (mil)* general **II** *a* = **génial.**

gelé [ʒ(ə)le] *a P* **1.** gelé (à zéro), (dead) drunk*/(completely) canned/plastered **2.** c'est gelé, we've had it.

gelée [ʒ(ə)le] *nf P* gelée de coing, mess/fix*/hot water.

gencives [ʒɑ̃siv] *nfpl P* jaw(s); **un coup dans les gencives,** a punch on the jaw.

gendarme [ʒɑ̃darm] *nm* **1.** *F (a) (hareng saur)* red herring/Billingsgate pheasant *(b)* (Swiss) flat/dry sausage **2.** *F* **chapeau de gendarme,** (two-pointed) paper hat **3.** *F* bossy woman/battle-axe; **faire le gendarme,** to boss people about; to put one's foot down **4.** *F* **dormir en gendarme,** to sleep with one eye open **5.** *V* turd/calling card.

se gêner [səʒene] *vpr F* **1.** *(a)* **faut pas se gêner,** no need to ask *(b) (iron)* **il ne se gêne pas!** he's not backward in coming forward! **(ne) vous gênez pas!** don't mind me – make yourself at home! **2. (si) je vais me gêner!/avec ça que je vais me gêner!** you bet (your sweet life) I will!/you (just) see if I don't!

génial [ʒenjal] *a F* great/fantastic/marvellous; **c'est un mec génial,** he's a great bloke/guy; **une idée géniale,** a fantastic/an amazing idea/a crazy idea.

génisse [ʒenis] *nf P* cow/bitch (of a woman).

genou, *pl* **-oux** [ʒ(ə)nu] *nm F* **1. faire (un appel) du genou,** = to play footsy (under the table) **2. être sur les genoux,** to be exhausted*/ready to drop/flaked out **3. chauve comme un genou,** (as) bald* as a coot.

géo [ʒeo] *nf F (scol)* geography.

Georges [ʒɔrʒ] *nm F (aviation)* George/automatic pilot.

géranium [ʒeranjɔm] *nm P* **dépoter son géranium,** to die*/to drop off the twig.

gerbage [ʒɛrbaʒ] *nm P* prison sentence*/stretch/rap.

gerbe [ʒɛrb] *nf* **1.** *P* year in prison **2.** *V (femme)* masturbation*/fingerfuck/finger-job; **se filer une gerbe,** to bring oneself off.

gerbement [ʒɛrbəmɑ̃] *nm P* = **gerbage.**

gerber [ʒɛrbe] *P* **I** *vi* to vomit*/to throw up; **blèche à gerber,** as ugly as sin **II** *vtr (a)* **gerber qn à la passe/à la faux,** to condemn s.o. to death; **il a gerbé sept ans,** he's copped a seven-year stretch/he's doing seven years *(b)* **il est gerbé,** he's doing time/he's inside.

gerbier [ʒɛrbje] *nm P* judge/magistrate/beak.

gerce [ʒɛrs] *nf O P* prostitute*.

gésier [ʒezje] *nm P* stomach*/gut(s); **recevoir un coup dans le gésier,** to get one in the bread-basket; **ça m'est resté sur le gésier,** I couldn't stomach it.

gi! [ʒi] *int P* yes!/yeah!/OK!/roger! (*Voir* **gy 1**)

gibelet [ʒiblɛ] *nm F* **avoir un coup de gibelet,** to be a bit mad*/a bit cracked.

gibier [ʒibje] *nm* **1.** *F* **ce n'est pas de son gibier,** it's not (in) his line; it's not his cup of tea **2.** *P (prostituée)* **manger le gibier,** to keep (back) part of her earnings (from her pimp).

giboulée [ʒibule] *nf F* thrashing/good hiding.

giclée [ʒikle] *nf* **1.** *F* burst (of machine-gun fire) **2.** *V* (spurt of) semen*/sperm/spunk/come; **lâcher/tirer une giclée,** to ejaculate*/to come/to shoot one's load.

gicler [ʒikle] *vi P* **1.** *(arme à feu)* to go off **2.** *(pers)* to run away*/to beat it; **allez, gicle!** go on, hop it!/scram! (*Voir* **mirettes**) gicleur 209 gland

gicleur [ʒiklœr] *nm P* mouth*; **ferme ton gicleur!** shut up!*/shut your trap!

gidé [ʒide] *int P* = gi!

gidouille [ʒiduj] *nf P* 1. stomach*/belly 2. navel/belly-button.

gifle [ʒifl] *nf F* **une tête à gifles** = **une tête à claques** (**claque**).

gig [ʒig] *nm F* (*jazz, rock, etc*) gig/one-night stand.

gigal, *pl* **-aux** [ʒigal, -o] *nm O P* 1. slater 2. plumber.

gigo! [ʒigo] *int P* = gi!

gigolette [ʒigɔlɛt] *nf O P* 1. young girl* 2. (young) floozy/tart/scrubber; easy lay.

gigolo [ʒigɔlo] *nm F* 1. gigolo/fancy man 2. (*cartes*) jack.

gigolpince [ʒigɔlpɛ̃s] *nm P* = **gigolo 1.**

gigot [ʒigo] *nm F* 1. thigh 2. *pl* **gigots,** legs*.

gigoter [ʒigɔte] *vi F* 1. to wriggle about; **ne gigote pas!** don't fidget! 2. to dance/to shake a leg.

gigoteur, -euse [ʒigɔtœr, -øz] *n F* dancer.

gigue [ʒig] *nf F* 1. (**grande**) **gigue,** tall girl/beanpole 2. *pl* **gigues,** legs*.

gilboque [ʒilbɔk] *nm P* billiard table.

gilet [ʒilɛ] *nm* 1. *F* **pleurer dans le gilet de qn,** to pour out one's troubles to s.o./to cry* on s.o.'s shoulder 2. *P* stomach*; **se remplir le gilet,** to eat* heartily/to stuff oneself.

gileton [ʒiltɔ̃] *nm,* **gilogue** [ʒilɔg] *nm,* **gilton** [ʒiltɔ̃] *nm P* waistcoat.

gingin [ʒɛ̃ʒɛ̃] *nm F* 1. common sense; **avoir du gingin,** to have gumption 2. red wine/plonk/vino.

girafe [ʒiraf] *nf F* 1. tall/thin person 2. **peigner la girafe,** to waste one's time; to laze (about).

girelle [ʒirɛl] *nf O P* prostitute*.

girie [ʒiri] *nf O P* complaining/whining/bellyaching; **assez de giries!** stop moaning! **faire des giries** (*i*) to bellyache (*ii*) to put on airs.

girofle [ʒirɔfl] *a&nm P* (*i*) good-looking (*ii*) suave (person).

giroflée [ʒirɔfle] *nf P* **une giroflée (à cinq feuilles/à cinq branches),** a slap round the face.

girond [ʒirɔ̃] I *a P* (*esp femme*) good-looking; easy on the eye; **ce qu'elle est gironde!** she's a bit of all right! II *nm P* (passive) homosexual*.

gisquette [ʒiskɛt] *nf P* (*a*) woman*/bird/*NAm* dame/*NAm* broad (*b*) girl*/bird/chick/judy/tart.

giton [ʒitɔ̃] *nm F* (young, passive) homosexual*/catamite.

givré [ʒivre] *a P* 1. drunk*/sozzled/plastered 2. mad*/nuts/bonkers.

se givrer [səʒivre] *vpr P* to get drunk*/to get plastered.

glace [glas] I *nf P* **passer/se bomber devant la glace** (*i*) to stand a round (of drinks) (after losing a game) (*ii*) to be done out of one's share. (*Voir* **armoire**) II *nm P* = **glass(e).**

(à) glagla [aglagla] *adv phr P* **je les ai à glagla,** it's freezing; it's cold enough to freeze the balls off a brass monkey/it's brass monkey weather. (*Voir* **miches 1** (*b*))

glaglater [glaglate] *vi P* to be cold/freezing to death.

glaise [glɛz] *nf P* earth/ground; **il couche sur la glaise,** he sleeps on the bare ground.

glaiseux [glɛzø] *nm P* peasant*/hick/yokel/country bumpkin.

gland [glɑ̃] I *nm* 1. *P* fool*/clot/nit/twit 2. *V* penis*; **se taper sur le gland,** to masturbate*; **effacer le**

gland, to have sex*/to have it away **II** *a* **P** stupid*/daft.

glande [glãd] *nf* **1.** *F* **la glande,** mooning/lazing about; **la glande!** lazy so-and-so! **2.** *V* **se tirer sur la glande,** to masturbate*/to jerk off **3.** *P* **avoir les glandes,** to be jealous/green **4.** *P* **ça fout les glandes!** it gives you the creeps/the willies!

glander [glãde] *P* **I** *vi* to fritter away one's time/to moon about/to mooch around/to footle about; to mess around **II** *vtr* **qu'est-ce que tu glandes aujourd'hui?** what are you up to today?

glandeur, euse [glãdœr, -øz] *n* *P* idler/moocher/layabout; **quel glandeur, ce mec!** what a lazy so-and-so that bloke is!/what a skiver!

glandilleux, euse [glãdijø, -øz] *a* *P* difficult/dangerous/chancy/risky/dic(e)y/ticklish.

glandocher [glãdɔʃe] *vi* *P* = **glander I.**

glandouiller [glãduje] *vi* *P* **1.** = **glander I 2.** to wait/to hang about/to kick one's heels.

glandouilleur, euse [glãdujœr, -øz] *n* *P* = **glandeur, euse.**

glass(e) [glas] *nm* *P* **1.** (drinking) glass **2.** drink/snifter/snort; **payer un glass(e) à qn,** to buy/to stand s.o. a drink.

glaude [glod] *nf* *P* pocket.

glaviot [glavjo] *nm* *P* **1.** gob (of spit/phlegm) **2. se noyer dans un glaviot,** to make a mountain out of a molehill.

glavioter [glavjɔte] *vi* *P* to spit/to gob.

glisse [glis] *nf* *P* **faire de la glisse à qn,** to do s.o. out of his share of the loot; to hold out on s.o.

glisser [glise] **I** *vi* **1.** *P* **se laisser glisser,** to die*/to peg out **2.** *F* **ça glisse!** I don't care!/I don't give a damn! **laisse glisser!** don't take any notice!/don't pay any attention! **II**

vtr **1.** *F* **glisser qch en douce à qn,** to tell s.o. sth in confidence/confidentially **2.** *P* **glisser un fil,** to urinate*/to splash one's boots/to have a slash **3.** *V* to have sex* with (a woman)/to slip it to (a woman).

globe [glɔb] *nm* **1.** *P* stomach*; se **faire arrondir le globe,** to become pregnant*/to join the (pudding) club **2.** *F* **globes (arrondis),** (plump) breasts*/globes.

glu [gly] *nf* *F* **1.** (*pers*) **comme la glu** (*i*) boring/tedious (*ii*) annoying/irritating; **il est collant comme la glu,** you can't get rid of him; he bores you rigid **2. avoir de la glu aux doigts,** to have sticky fingers/to be light-fingered.

gluant [glyã] **I** *nm* *P* **1.** baby **2.** soap **II** *a* *P* (dead) boring; **il est gluant, ce mec,** you can't get rid of him; he bores you rigid.

gluau [glyo] *nm* *P* gob (of phlegm).

gluc(k) [glyk] *nm* *P* luck.

gnace [ɲas] *nm* *P* man*/fellow/bloke/guy.

gnaf [ɲaf] *nm* *P* **1.** cobbler **2.** bungler/botcher **3.** creep/bastard*/nasty piece of work/*NAm* son of a bitch.

gnangnan [ɲãɲã] *F* **I** *a inv* spineless/flabby/soppy/drippy/wet **II** *nm or f* (*a*) spineless person/sissy/wet/drip (*b*) dawdler/slowcoach **III** *nm* **du gnangnan,** drivel/rubbish.

gnard [ɲar] *nm* *P* = **gniard.**

gnaupe [ɲop] *nf* *P* (smoker's) pipe.

gniaf(fe) [ɲaf] *nm* *P* = **gnaf.**

gniangnian [ɲãɲã] *a&n* *F* = **gnangnan.**

gniard [ɲar] *nm* *P* **1.** child*/brat/kid/nipper **2.** = **gnace.**

gniasse [ɲas] *nm* *P* **1.** = **gnace 2. mon gniasse,** I/me/yours truly; **ton gniasse,** you; **son gniasse,** he/him; **vos gniasses,** you/you lot.

gniaule [ɲol] *nf P* = **gnole**.

gnière [ɲɛr] *nm P* = **gnace**.

gniol(l)e [ɲol] *nf P* = **gnole**.

gnion [ɲɔ̃] *nm P* = **gnon**.

gniouf [ɲuf] *nm & f P* = **gnouf I, II.**

gnognot(t)e [ɲɔɲɔt] *nf P* **1.** trash/rubbish/junk/tripe/crap; **ça, ce n'est pas de la gnognot(t)e!** (*i*) that's really something! (*ii*) it's no joke! **2.** trifle; **ça, c'est de la gnognot(t)e,** that's peanuts/that's just chicken feed.

gnole, gnôle [ɲol] *nf P* brandy; spirits*/rotgut/hard stuff/hooch/firewater; **un coup de gnole,** a wee dram/a drop of the hard stuff.

gnon [ɲɔ̃] *nm P* blow*/sock/thump; **filer/flanquer un gnon à qn,** to take a swipe at s.o.; **se flanquer un gnon,** to bang into sth/to bruise oneself; **sa bagnole a pris un gnon,** his car took a bash; his car got bashed in/smashed up.

gnouf [ɲuf] *P* **I** *nm* (*a*) prison*/clink/cooler/jug (*b*) police station*/cop shop (*c*) cell in a police station; lock-up (*d*) (*mil*) guardroom **II** *nf* **la Gnouf,** the *École normale des sciences.*

gnoufard [ɲufar] *nm P* **taupin,** *qv,* preparing for the *École normale supérieure.*

go [go] **I** *nm P* louse/cootie. (*Voir* **gau**) **II** *adv phr P* (*hum*) **allez, j'y go,** all right, I'll go/OK, I'm going.

Gob' [gɔb] *Prn P* **les Gob',** the Gobelins quarter (in Paris).

gobage [gɔbaʒ] *nm P* **1.** infatuation (**de,** for) **2.** snobbishness.

gobe-la-lune [gɔblalyn] *nm P* simpleton/sucker/mug.

gobelot(t)er [gɔblɔte] *vi F* to tipple/to drink*/to hit the bottle/to go on the booze.

gobe-mouches [gɔbmuʃ] *nm inv F* = **gobe-la-lune.**

gober [gɔbe] **I** *vtr* **1. gober des mouches,** to stand gaping; to have a vacant/stupid expression on one's face **2.** to swallow; **il a gobé tout ce qu'on lui a dit,** he fell for it hook, line and sinker; **et tu crois que je vais gober tout ça?** you really think I'm going to fall for that? (*Voir* **morceau**) **3.** to have a strong liking for (s.o.)/to go for (s.o.) in a big way; **je ne peux pas le gober,** I can't stand/stick him **II** *vpr* **se gober** *F* to have a big opinion of oneself/to fancy oneself; **elle se gobe énormément,** she thinks she's really something/she thinks she's the bee's knees.

se goberger [səgɔbɛrʒe] *vpr F* to pamper oneself/to indulge oneself.

gobette [gɔbɛt] *nf P* **1.** drink/booze; **payer la gobette,** to pay for the drinks **2.** (*en prison*) wine ration.

gobeur, euse [gɔbœr, -øz] *F* **I** *n* simpleton/sucker/mug; **gobeur de fausses nouvelles,** stupidly credulous person **II** *a* **il est très gobeur,** he'll swallow anything; he's easily taken in.

gobi [gɔbi] *nm P* negro/Black*.

godaille [gɔdaj] *nf F* feast/blow-out/tuck-in/nosh-up.

godailler [gɔdaje] *vi* **1.** *F* to tipple/to knock it back **2.** *F* (*a*) to (go on a) pub crawl/*NAm* to barhop **3.** *F* (*plan, projet, etc*) to go wrong/to fall through **4.** *V* to have an erection*/to have a hard-on **5.** *P* to be promiscuous/to sleep around.

godailleur [gɔdajœr] *nm F* **1.** tippler **2.** pub-crawler.

godailleux, euse [gɔdajø, -øz] *a P* (very) sexually excited*/randy/horny.

godant [gɔdɑ̃] *a P* sexually exciting/arousing/hot; **un film godant,** a film which really gets you going.

godasse [gɔdas] *nf P* (*a*) (big) boot (*b*) shoe.

gode [gɔd] **I** *nf F* ... à la gode = ... à la godille (**godille**) **II** *nm P* = **godemiché**.

godelureau, -eaux [gɔdlyro] *nm F* (*péj*) womanizer*/skirt-chaser; **c'est un godelureau,** he thinks he's God's gift to women.

godemiché [gɔdmiʃe] *nm P* dildo.

godenot [gɔdno] *nm F* misshapen *or* deformed little man; little runt/ squirt.

goder [gɔde] *vi* **1.** *P* to be (very) sexually excited*; to be ready for it; **goder pour qn,** to be horny/ randy for s.o.; to want s.o. (badly); **faire goder qn,** to give s.o. a sexual thrill/to turn s.o. on; **un film qui fait goder,** a film which really gets you going/turns you on **2.** *V* to have an erection*/to have a hard-on.

godet [gɔdɛ] *nm P* **1.** (drinking) glass **2.** glass(ful)/drink/jar; **basculer/écluser/s'envoyer/se cloquer/ se taper un godet,** to knock back a drink.

godeur, -euse [gɔdœr, -øz] *a P* (very) sexually excited*/horny/ randy/hot.

godiche¹ [gɔdiʃ] *nf P* fever/*esp* malaria.

godiche², godichon, -onne [gɔdiʃɔ̃, -ɔn] *F* **I** *a* (*a*) stupid*/ silly/thick/dumb; **je ne suis pas si godiche que j'en ai l'air,** I'm not as dumb as I look/I wasn't born yesterday (*b*) awkward/gawky; clumsy/ham-fisted **II** *nm&f* (*a*) fool*/simpleton/dope (*b*) **quelle godiche, cette fille!** what a lump (of a girl)!

godille [gɔdij] *nf F* ... à la godille (*i*) trashy/worthless* (*ii*) **faire qch à la godille,** to do sth for no particular reason; **travailler à la godille,** to work without method/anyoldhow.

godiller [gɔdije] *vi V* **1.** to have an erection*/to have a hard-on/to get it up **2.** to have sex*.

godilleur, -euse [gɔdijœr, -øz] *n V* highly-sexed man/woman; hot stuff; easy lay/good screw; (*homme*) pussy chaser/cunt chaser.

godillot [gɔdijo] *nm* **1.** *P* (big) boot/shoe; clodhopper **2.** *F* **parti godillot,** (political) party which follows the government line on everything.

godmiche [gɔdmiʃ], **godmiché** [gɔdmiʃe] *nm P* = **godemiché**.

godo [gɔdo] *nf P* lesbian*/lezzie/ dyke.

gogo [gogo] **I** *nm F* sucker/mug. (*Voir* **attrape-gogos**) **II** *adv phr F* **whisky à gogo,** whisky galore; **avoir de l'argent à gogo,** to have tons/ pots/loads of money.

gogs [gɔg] *nmpl*, **goguenards** [gɔgnar] *nmpl P* = **gogues**.

gogueneau, -eaux [gɔgno] *nm*, **goguenot** [gɔgno] *nm P* **1.** chamber pot*/po/jerry **2.** *pl* = **gogues**.

gogues [gɔg] *nmpl P* WC*/loo/ bog/*esp NAm* can/*esp NAm* John.

goguette [gɔgɛt] *nf F* **être en goguette,** to be on a binge/on a bender/out on the town.

goinfrade [gwɛ̃frad] *nf F* (bean)feast/blow-out/tuck-in/nosh-up.

goinfre [gwɛ̃fr] *nm F* glutton*/ greedyguts/guzzler/pig.

se goinfrer [səgwɛ̃fre] *F* **1.** (*a*) to drink like a fish (*b*) to eat like a pig/to make a pig of oneself **2.** to make a lot of money*/to coin it in/to make a pile.

gol [gɔl] *P* (= *mongolien*) **I** *a* stupid*/thick/moronic **II** *nm* moron/ cretin/nurd/jerk.

goldo [gɔldo] *nf P* Gauloise cigarette (*RTM*).

gomme [gɔm] *nf* **1.** *F* à la gomme (*i*) trashy/rubbishy/useless/hopeless; **une idée à la gomme,** a pathetic/useless idea (*ii*) without interest; **histoire à la gomme,** pointless story; **individu à la gomme,** hopeless person/dead loss **2.** *P* **gomme à effacer le sourire** (*i*) cosh (*ii*) (policeman's) rubber truncheon **3.** *P* **faire de la gomme/mettre (toute) la gomme** (*i*) to put on airs/to show off* (*ii*) to get a move on/to pull out all the stops/to step on it; **à toute gomme,** at full speed/flat out.

gommeux, -euse [gɔmø, -øz] *P* **I** *a* (*a*) flashy/overdressed (*b*) pretentious/snooty/snobbish **II** *n* (*a*) flashy dresser/overdressed person (*b*) member of high society/nob/toff; (*homme*) fop/dandy/*NAm* dude.

gonce [gɔ̃s] *nm P* (*rare*) = **gonze.**

goncesse [gɔ̃sɛs] *nf P* (*rare*) = **gonzesse.**

goncier [gɔ̃sje] *nm P* (*rare*) = **gonze.**

gondolant [gɔ̃dɔlɑ̃] *a F* very funny*/too funny for words/priceless/a scream.

gondole [gɔ̃dɔl] *nf P* taxi/cab.

gondoler [gɔ̃dɔle] **I** *vi P* **gondoler de la devanture,** to be pregnant*/to be in the (pudding) club **II** *vpr* **se gondoler** *F* to laugh* uproariously/to double up with laughter/to split one's sides laughing.

gonds [gɔ̃] *nmpl F* **sortir de ses gonds,** to get angry*/to fly off the handle/to blow one's top.

gone [gɔn] *nm*, **gonesse** [gɔnɛs] *nf F* (*dial lyonnais*) **1.** child*/brat/kid **2.** fellow/man*/guy/bloke.

gonflant [gɔ̃flɑ̃] *a F* = **gondolant.**

gonflé [gɔ̃fle] *a F* **1.** courageous; full of guts/balls **2.** rich*/flush/loaded **3.** cheeky; **t'es gonflé!** you've got a nerve/a cheek! **4.** **gonflé à bloc** (*i*) (*pers*) keyed up; in peak form (*ii*) (*pers*) full of beans/raring to go (*iii*) (*voitures*) **moteur gonflé,** souped-up engine.

gonfler [gɔ̃fle] **I** *vi F* to exaggerate*/to shoot a line/to lay it on a bit thick **II** *vtr* (*a*) *F* (*voitures*) **gonfler un moteur,** to soup up an engine (*b*) *P* **gonfler une femme,** to get a woman pregnant*/to put a woman in the club/to put a woman up the spout/*esp NAm* to knock a woman up.

gonse [gɔ̃s] *nm P* (*rare*) = **gonze.**

gonsesse [gɔ̃sɛs] *nf P* (*rare*) = **gonzesse.**

gonze [gɔ̃z] *nm P* man*/fellow/chap*/guy/bloke/dude.

gonzesse [gɔ̃zɛs] *nf P* woman*/girl*/bird/chick/lady.

gonzier [gɔ̃zje] *nm P* = **gonze.**

goret [gɔrɛ] *nm F* **1.** dirty child*; grubby/mucky little brat **2.** filthy pig; **manger comme un goret,** to eat* like a pig.

gorgeon [gɔrʒɔ̃] *nm F* **1.** (drinking) glass **2.** **se taper un gorgeon,** to knock back a drink.

gorgeonner [gɔrʒɔne] *vi V P* to have a drink*/to knock one back; to tipple.

Gorgonzola [gɔrgɔ̃zɔla] *nm F* **avoir les dents plombées au Gorgonzola,** to have bad breath.

gorille [gɔrij] *nm F* **1.** brute/thug; **espèce de gorille!** you big ape! **2.** bodyguard/strong-arm man/henchman/gorilla.

gosier [gozje] *nm F* **avoir le gosier en pente,** to have a permanent thirst; **avoir le gosier sec,** to be parched; **s'humecter le gosier,** to have a drink/to wet one's whistle.

gosse [gɔs] *nm&f* **1.** *F* kid/brat/nipper **2.** *F* young man/girl; **ma gosse (d'amour),** my girlfriend **3.** *F* **être beau/belle gosse,** to be a good-looking young man/girl **4.** *F* **gosse de riche,** rich man's son; spoilt (rich) brat/rich kid **5.** *FrC pl F* testicles*.

got [go] *nm P* louse/cootie. (*Voir* **gau**)

goualante [gwalɑ̃t] *nf P* (popular) song; **envoyer la goualante/pousser une goualante/y aller de sa goualante,** to sing a song.

gouale [gwal] *nm P* (*a*) blackmail (*b*) swindle*/racket/con **2. faire du gouale/aller au gouale,** to kick up a row/to make a big fuss.

goualer [gwale] *P* **I** *vtr&i* to sing (loudly) **II** *vtr* to blackmail (s.o.).

goualeur, -euse [gwalœr, -øz] *n P* **1.** (noisy) singer **2.** blackmailer.

gouape [gwap] *nf P* hooligan*/ yob(bo)/thug/nasty piece of work/ bastard*.

gouapeur [gwapœr] *nm P* layabout/(lazy) bum.

gouchotte [guʃɔt] *nf P* lesbian*.

goudou [gudu] *nf P* lesbian*/les/ lez/dyke.

gouge [guʒ] *nf F* **je n'ai pas une gouge,** I'm broke/I haven't got a penny.

gougnafier [guɲafje] *nm F* **c'est du travail de gougnafier/tu as fait ça comme un gougnafier,** you've messed/buggered it up.

gougne [guɲ] *nf,* **gougnette** [guɲɛt] *nf,* **gougnot(t)e** [guɲɔt] *nf P* = **gouine.**

gougnot(t)er [guɲɔte] **I** *vtr&i P* to be a lesbian*/to be gay/to be a dyke **II** *vpr* **se gougnot(t)er** *P* to practise lesbianism; **les deux filles se gougnottaient,** the two girls were having it away/bringing themselves off.

se gouiner [səgwine] *vpr P* to practise lesbianism.

gouine [gwin] *nf P* lesbian*/dyke/ les/lez.

goujon [guʒɔ̃] *nm* **1.** *F* (*pers*) **avaler le goujon** (*i*) to swallow/to take the bait (*ii*) to die*/to croak **2.** *F* **taquiner le goujon,** to fish for (sth/information) **3.** *P* young (inexperienced) pimp*.

goujonner [guʒɔne] *vtr F* to cheat*/to do (s.o.); **on vous a goujonné,** you've been had.

goule [gul] *nf P* **1.** (big) mouth* **2.** throat.

goulée [gule] *nf F* **1.** big mouthful/gulp **2. tirer une goulée,** to have a puff (of a cigarette)/to take a drag.

goulette [gulɛt] *nf P* = **goulot.**

goulot [gulo] *nm P* (*a*) throat/gullet; **se rincer le goulot,** to have a drink*/to wet one's whistle (*b*) **repousser du goulot,** to have bad breath.

goumi [gumi] *nm P* rubber cosh/ truncheon.

goupiller [gupije] **I** *vtr P* to arrange/to wangle/to fix (sth); **goupiller un truc,** to cook sth up; to knock sth together **II** *vpr* **se goupiller** *F* to happen/to work (out); **se goupiller bien,** to turn out well/to go off all right; **ça se goupille mal,** it's going badly.

goupillon [gupijɔ̃] *nm V* penis*; **mouiller le goupillon,** to have sex*/ to get one's end away. (*Voir* **sabre 2**)

goupiner [gupine] *P* **I** *vi* to work* hard/to slog (away) **II** *vtr* to steal*/to knock off/to pinch.

gourance [gurɑ̃s] *nf P* **1.** mistake*/bloomer/boob **2. avoir des gourances,** to be suspicious/to smell a rat.

gourbi [gurbi] *nm F* **1.** (*a*) dirty/ untidy lodgings *or* house; slum/ hovel/dump (*b*) (*mil*) funk-hole/fox-hole/dugout **2.** (*prisonniers, etc*) **faire gourbi,** to muck in together.

gourde [gurd] **I** *a F* stupid*/ gorm-less/thick **II** *nf* **1.** *F* fool*/thickie/*NAm* pumpkinhead/ dumbbell **2.** *P* head* **3.** *V* **gourde à poils,** penis*/meat.

gourdichon [gurdiʃɔ̃] *nm,* **gourdiflot** [gurdiflo] *nm P* = **gourde II 1.**

gourdin [gurdɛ̃] *nm V* (*a*) penis*/ chopper/shaft; **avoir le gourdin,** to have an erection* (*b*) **avoir du gourdin,** to womanize/to be a skirt-chaser/to be on the make; **avoir du gourdin pour une femme,** to be turned on by a woman/to be after a bit (of the other).

goure [gur] *nf P* fraud/con/decep-tion; **vol à la goure,** con(fidence) trick.

gourer [gure] **I** *vtr P* to cheat/to trick/to con/to take in/to pull a fast one on (s.o.) **II** *vpr* **se gourer** *P* **1.** (*a*) to be wrong; to make a mistake*/to boob; **il s'est gouré,** he boobed/he slipped up **2.** se **gourer de qn,** to mistrust s.o./to be suspicious of s.o.; **je m'en gourais,** I thought as much.

gourgandine [gurgɑ̃din] *nf A F* loose woman.

gourgandiner [gurgɑ̃dine] *vtr A F* **gourgandiner les femmes,** to womanize/to chase women.

gourrance [gurɑ̃s] *nf P* = **gourance.**

gourrer [gure] *vtr,* **se gourrer** [səgure] *vpr P* = **gourer, se gourer.**

gousse [gus] *nf P* **gousse (d'ail),** lesbian*.

se gousser [səguse] *vpr P* to practise lesbianism.

goût [gu] *nm P* **perdre le goût du pain,** to die*/to kick the bucket; **faire perdre/faire passer le goût du pain à qn,** to kill* s.o./to do s.o. in/to bump s.o. off.

goutte [gut] *nf* **1.** *F* nip (of brandy, etc); **boire une goutte,** to have a nip/a snort; **veux-tu de la goutte?** do you want a drop of the hard stuff? **il aime la goutte,** he's fond of a nip **2.** *F* **il a bu une goutte** (*i*) he was nearly drowned (*ii*) he suffered a heavy loss/he caught a packet **3.** *F* **se noyer dans une goutte d'eau,** to make a mountain out of a molehill **4.** *P*

faire la/sa goutte, uriner*/to take a leak/to splash one's boots.

goyau, aux [gwajo] *nm P* (cheap) prostitute*/old slag/scrubber.

grabasse [grabas] *a P* drunk*/ tight.

se grabater [səgrabate] *vpr P* to go to bed*/to hit the hay/to hit the sack.

grabuge [grabyʒ] *nm F* quarrel*; row/rumpus; **faire du grabuge,** to kick up a shindy/to create; **il va y avoir du grabuge,** there'll be trou-ble/there's gonna be some aggro.

gradaille [gradaj] *nf P* (*mil*) officers and N.C.O.s.

grade [grad] *nm F* **en prendre pour son grade/prendre qch pour son grade,** to be severely reprimanded*/ to get hauled over the coals; **il en a pris pour son grade!** he got what was coming to him!/he asked for it!

graille [graj] *nf P* food*/grub/ nosh; **à la graille!** grub's up!

grailler [graje] *vi P* to eat*/to nosh.

graillon [grajɔ̃] *nm P* gob (of phlegm).

graillonner [grajɔne] *vi F* to hawk up/to cough up phlegm/to gob.

grain [grɛ̃] *nm* **1.** *F* **être dans le grain,** to be in clover **2.** *F* **avoir un grain,** to be slightly mad*; **il a un grain,** he's not quite right in the head/he's a bit cracked/he's a bit nuts **3.** *F* **avoir son grain,** to be slightly drunk*/to be a bit tight **4.** *P* **grain de blé,** louse **5.** *V* **le grain de café,** clitoris*; **secouer son grain de café,** to finger oneself/to bring oneself off. (*Voir* **sel 1**)

graine [grɛn] *nf* **1.** *F* food*/grub; **casser la graine,** to have a bite (to eat) **2.** *F* **en prendre de la graine,** to take a leaf out of s.o.'s book **3.** *F* (*pers*) **monter/pousser en graine,** to grow older; to go to seed **4.** *F* (*mil*) **graine d'épinards**, gold braid on senior officers' epaulets/scrambled eggs **5.** (*a*) *F* **c'est de la mauvaise graine**, he's a bad lot (*b*) *F* **de la graine de bois de lit**, child*/tiny tot (*c*) *F* **de la graine de bagne**, jailbird (*d*) *P* **de la graine de con**, fool*/imbecile/bloody fool.

grainer [grɛne] *vi F* to eat*/to have a bite (to eat)/to nosh.

graissage [grɛsaʒ] *nm F* **graissage de patte**, bribe*/palm-greasing/backhander; kickback.

graisse [grɛs] *nf* **1.** *P* money*/bread/dough **2.** *P* **faire de la graisse**, to exaggerate*/to lay it on thick **3.** *P* **traîner sa graisse**, to hump one's fat (around); **amène ta graisse!** drag your carcass/your butt over here! **tire tes graisses!** get out of my way!/shift your arse/*NAm* ass! **4.** *P* cheating (at cards, etc) **5.** *P* **graisse d'abattage**, force/muscle power. (*Voir* **boniment 2**)

graisser [grɛse] **I** *vi P* to exaggerate*/to boast/to lay it on thick **II** *vtr F* **graisser la patte à qn**, to bribe s.o.; to grease/to oil s.o.'s palm; to make s.o. an offer they can't refuse. (*Voir* **botte II 4**)

grand-chose [grɑ̃ʃoz] *nm&f F* **un/une pas grand-chose**, a good-for-nothing; a poor sort; (*femme*) easy lay/a bit of a tramp.

grand-dab(e) [grɑ̃dab] *nm P* grandfather/grandad. (*Voir* **dab(e)**) (*pl* **grands-dab(e)s**)

grand-duc [grɑ̃dyk] *nm O F* **faire la tournée des grands-ducs**, to go on a spree*/to go out on the town/to live it up.

grand-mère [grɑ̃mɛr] *nf P* (*musique*) double bass.

grappillage [grapijaʒ] *nm F* (*a*) fiddling; making a fast buck (*b*) scrounging/cadging.

grappiller [grapije] *F* **I** *vi* (*a*) to fiddle; to make a fast buck/to make a bit on the side (*b*) to

scrounge/to cadge **II** *vtr* to scrounge/to sponge (a meal, etc).

grappin [grapɛ̃] *nm* (*a*) *P* hand*/hook (*b*) *F* **mettre le grappin sur qch, qn**, to lay one's hands on sth, s.o./to get one's hooks into sth, s.o./to grab sth, s.o. (*c*) *F* **mettre/poser le grappin sur qn**, to arrest* s.o./to pull s.o. in/to nick s.o.

gras, *f* grasse [grɑ, grɑs] **I** *a F* (*a*) **être gras à lard**, to be fat/porky (*b*) **être gras du bide**, to be fat/paunchy; to have a (beer) gut (*c*) **il n'y (en) a pas gras/ça n'est pas gras/c'est pas gras**, there's not much (of it)/that's not a lot (*d*) **se la faire grasse**, to live like a lord/to live off the fat of the land **II** *nm P* profit. (*Voir* **discuter**)

gras-double [grɑdubl] *nm F* paunch/pot belly/beer belly/spare tyre.

gratin [gratɛ̃] *F* **le gratin** (*a*) high society/the upper crust; **il fréquente le gratin**, he mixes with the nobs (*b*) the best/the pick of the basket/the cream.

gratiné [gratine] *a F* excessive/over the odds; **une addition gratinée**, an enormous/a huge bill; a rip-off; **prendre une cuite gratinée**, to get really plastered/rolling drunk*; **c'est gratiné!** it's a bit much!

gratouille [gratuj] *nf F* **1.** itch **2.** (*musique*) maraca.

gratouiller [gratuje] *F* **I** *vtr* to scratch **II** *vi* to itch.

grattante [gratɑ̃t] *nf P* **1.** hand*/mitt/paw **2.** match(stick).

gratte [grat] *nf* **1.** *F* perks/pickings; fringe benefits; **faire de la gratte**, to make a bit on the side **2.** (*médecine*) scabies/the itch **3.** *P* (*musique*) guitar; **jouer de la gratte**, to play the guitar/to strum at the guitar.

gratte-couenne [gratkwan] *nm P* barber/men's hairdresser.

grattée [grate] *nf P* thrashing/good hiding/beating*.

gratte-papier [gratpapje] *nm inv F* (*péj*) civil servant; pen-pusher.

gratter [grate] **I** *vtr F* **1.** (*auto, vélo*) to pass/to overtake (a competitor, another car, etc) **2. gratter le papier,** (*péj*) to scribble/to be a pen-pusher **3. gratter les fonds de tiroir,** to get a few perks/to make a bit on the side; **il n'y a pas grand-chose à gratter,** you won't make much out of that **4.** to scrape together (a sum of money) **II** *vi* **1.** *F* **un verre de qch qui gratte,** a glass of sth strong/of sth with a kick in it **2.** *P* to work* hard/to graft/to slog (away); **je gratte de 9 à 5,** I slave away from 9 to 5 **3.** *F* **en gratter pour qn,** to be infatuated* with s.o./to have a crush on s.o.; **gratter du pied,** to act the heavy lover. (*Voir* **couenne**; **jambon(neau)**; **pavé**) **III** *vpr* **se gratter 1.** *F* to hesitate/to think it over/to weigh up the pros and cons **2.** *P* **se gratter de qch,** to go without sth; **tu peux (toujours) te gratter!** nothing doing!/you can whistle for it!/not on your nelly! **3.** *P* **se faire gratter** (*a*) to get a shave/to get shaved (*b*) to get overtaken/to be passed (by another car, etc). (*Voir* **gratter I 1**)

gratteur, -euse [gratœr, -øz] *n F* (bad) violinist/fiddler.

grattiche [gratiʃ] *nf F* itch.

grattin [gratẽ] *nm F* **1.** = **gratin** **2. aller au grattin,** to go to work.

grattoir [gratwar] *nm F* razor.

grattouiller [gratuje] *vtr&i F* = **gratouiller.**

grattouse [gratuz] *nf F* = **grattiche.**

gravos, -osse [gravo, -os] *P* (*javanais de* **gros, grosse**) **I** *a* (big and) fat; tubby **II** *n* fat person/fatty/fatso.

grec [grɛk] *nm P* **1.** card-sharper; **faire le grec,** to manipulate the

cards, to work the broads **2. va te faire voir chez les Grecs!** go to hell!/piss off!/get stuffed!

à la grecque [alagrɛk] *adv phr P* **vol à la grecque,** con(fidence) trick/con.

greffier [grefje] *nm* **1.** *F* cat*/pussy(cat)/mog(gy) **2.** *V* female genitals*/pussy.

greffière [grefjɛr] *nf V* = **greffier 2.**

grègues [grɛg] *nfpl A F* **tirer ses grègues,** to run away*/to clear off/to make tracks.

grelot [grəlo] *nm* **1.** *F* **faire sonner son grelot,** to draw attention to oneself/to blow one's own trumpet **2.** *F* **attacher le grelot,** to take the initiative **3.** *P* **avoir les grelots,** to be afraid*; to have the shakes/the jitters; **flanquer/foutre les grelots à qn,** to put the wind up s.o. **4.** *F* (tele)phone*/blower; **filer/passer un coup de grelot à qn,** to give s.o. a ring/a tinkle **5.** *pl P* testicles*/nuts. (*Voir* **fifre II 2**)

grelotte [grəlɔt] *nf P* **avoir la grelotte,** to be afraid*/to be in a blue funk/to have the wind up.

grelotteur, -euse [grəlɔtœr, -øz] *n P* coward*/scaredy-cat/*esp NAm* fraidy cat.

greluche [grəlyʃ] *nf P* (young) woman*.

grenadier [grənadje] *nm* **1.** *F* tall/masculine woman **2.** *P* **tirer au grenadier,** to malinger/to swing the lead/to skive off.

Grenoble [grənɔbl] *Prn F* **faire à qn la conduite de Grenoble** (*i*) to give s.o. his marching orders/to give s.o. the (order of the) boot (*ii*) to make it hot for s.o./to give s.o. a rough time.

grenouillage [grənujaʒ] *nm F* **1.** (*a*) wangle; shady deal; fiddle (*b*) wangling/shady dealing(s)/wheeling and dealing **2.** scandalmongering/malicious gossip.

grenouillard [grənujar] *nm F* **1.** teetotaller **2.** cold-water fiend.

grenouille [grənuj] *nf* **1.** *F* **grenouille de bénitier,** excessively pious person/bigoted churchwoman **2.** *F* (*a*) (frog-shaped) money box (*b*) club money/funds (of a society, etc); **manger/bouffer/faire sauter la grenouille,** to make off with the cash-box/the kitty; to dip one's hand in the till **3.** *V* sperm/semen*/come; **grenouilles de bidet,** visible traces of semen; cum stains.

grenouiller [grənuje] *vi F* **1.** to be on the fiddle; to go in for shady dealing/to wheel and deal **2.** to go in for malicious gossip/to spread rumours; to bitch.

gribelle [gribɛl] *nf P* (*casquette*) cap. (*Voir* **grivelle**)

gribier [gribje] *nm,* **grifeton** [griftɔ̃] *nm P* = **griveton.**

griffard [grifar] *nm F* (pussy)cat*/mog(gy).

griffe [grif] *nf* **1.** *F* **donner un coup de griffe à qn,** to have a dig at s.o. **2.** *F* hand*; **serrer la griffe à qn,** to shake hands with s.o. **3.** *F* foot*; **aller à griffe,** to go on foot; to use/to go by Shank's pony; **taper des griffes,** to have smelly feet **4.** *P* **la Griffe,** the Army; military service.

griffer [grife] **I** *vtr* **1.** *F* (*a*) to seize/to catch/to grab (*b*) **griffer un bahut,** to catch a taxi **2.** *F* to steal*/to collar/to nab **3.** *P* **se griffer la tronche,** to put on one's make-up **II** *vpr* **se griffer** *V* to masturbate*/to take oneself in hand.

griffeton [griftɔ̃] *nm,* **grifton** [griftɔ̃] *nm P* soldier/infantryman/footslogger. (*Voir* **griveton**)

grignolet [griɲɔlɛ] *nm O P* bread.

grigou, *pl* **-ous** [grigu] *nm F* miser*/skinflint/tight ass.

grigri [grigri] *nm F* charm necklace.

gril [gri(l)] *nm F* **être sur le gril,** to be on tenterhooks; to be like a cat

on hot bricks/*NAm* on a hot tin roof.

grillante [grijɑ̃t] *nf P* cigarette*/fag/gasper.

grille [grij] *nf P* **1.** **grille d'égout,** set of false teeth **2.** **repeindre sa grille (en rouge),** to have a period*/to have the painters in/to have the decorators in/to have the reds.

griller [grije] **I** *vtr* **1.** *F* **griller une cigarette/***P* **en griller une,** to smoke a cigarette*/to have a smoke **2.** *F* (*sports*) **griller un concurrent,** to race past a competitor; to leave s.o. standing; to pip s.o. at the post **3.** *F* (*aut*) **griller le feu rouge,** to shoot/to jump the lights **4.** *P* (*a*) to criticize* (s.o.)/to run (s.o.) down/to knock (s.o.)/to pick (s.o.) to pieces (*b*) to denounce* (s.o.)/to put the finger on (s.o.)/to squeal on (s.o.) **5.** *P* (*a*) **il est grillé** (*i*) he's been found out/shown up; his cover's been blown (*ii*) he's ruined/done for; he's had it (*b*) **c'est une affaire grillée/c'est grillé,** it's up the creek/it's no go **II** *vpr* **se griller** *P* to lose one's reputation/one's credit/one's influence; to be discredited/done for/ruined.

grillot [grijo] *nm P* **1.** unscrupulous opportunist **2.** compromising document.

grimbiche [grɛ̃biʃ] *nf P* young woman*/babe/chick.

grimoire [grimwar] *nm O P* police record.

grimpant [grɛ̃pɑ̃] *nm P* trousers*/pants/strides.

grimper [grɛ̃pe] *vtr V* to have sex* with (s.o.)/to jump (s.o.)/to ride (s.o.). (*Voir* **arbre 1**)

grimpette [grɛ̃pɛt] *nf* **1.** *F* (short steep) climb **2.** *V* (*prostituées*) short time/quickie.

grimpouzer [grɛ̃puze] *vtr V* = **grimper.**

grinche [grɛ̃ʃ] *A P* **I** *nm* thief*/

burglar **II** *nf* theft/burglary; **vivre de la grinche,** to live by thieving.

grincher [gʀɛ̃ʃe] *vtr P* to steal*/to pinch/to nick.

gringue [gʀɛ̃g] *nm P* **faire du gringue à qn,** to make a pass at s.o./to give s.o. the come-on/to chat s.o. up/to try to pick s.o. up.

gringuer [gʀɛ̃ge] *vi P* to flirt/to make a pass at (s.o.)/to try it on with (s.o.)/to (try and) make out with (s.o.).

grinque [gʀɛ̃k] *nf P* food*/grub/ nosh.

griottes [gʀi(j)ɔt] *nfpl P* buttocks*/ bum/*esp NAm* butt/(pressed) hams/buns.

grippe-sou, *pl* **-sou(s)** [gʀipsu] *nm F* miser*/skinflint/tight ass.

grippette [gʀipɛt] *nf* **1.** *F* flu **2.** *V* female genitals*/snatch.

gris [gʀi] *a F* slightly drunk*/tipsy; **un peu gris,** a bit high/tight.

grisbi [gʀizbi] *nm P* money*/bread/ dough/ackers; **(ne) touchez pas au grisbi!** lay off the lolly!/hands off the dough!

grisol, *f* **-ole, grisolle** [gʀizɔl] *a P* dear/expensive/pric(e)y.

grive [gʀiv] *nf F* **soûl comme une grive,** as drunk* as a lord/as tight as a coot/as pissed as a newt **2.** *P* (*a*) the army (*b*) military service; **faire sa grive,** to do one's military service/to do one's stint in the army.

grivelle [gʀivɛl] *nf P* (*casquette*) cap. (*Voir* **gribelle**)

griveton [gʀivtɔ̃] *nm,* **grivier** [gʀivje] *nm P* soldier/infantryman/ footslogger. (*Voir* **griffeton**)

grognasse [gʀɔɲas] *nf P* (*péj*) **1.** (old) woman*; old bag/old bat/old bitch **2.** prostitute*/tart/floozie/ scrubber.

grognasser [gʀɔɲase] *vi P* to grumble*/to bitch.

grogne [gʀɔɲ] *nf F* grumbling/grou- sing/bitching.

groin [gʀwɛ̃] *nm* **1.** ugly mug **2.** nose/snout.

grôle [gʀol] *nm P* louse.

grole, grolle [gʀɔl] *nf P* boot/ shoe; **traîner sa grol(l)e/ses grol(l)es,** to laze about/to loaf around/to mess around/*NAm* to goof off.

grolles [gʀɔl] *nm* or *fpl P* **avoir les grolles,** to be afraid*/to have the willies; **flanquer/foutre les grolles à qn,** to put the wind up s.o.

gros, *f* **grosse** [gʀo, gʀos] **I** *n F* **1.** (*a*) large/fat person; **un gros plein de soupe,** a well-fed type/big fat lump (*b*) **eh bien, mon gros!** well, old man! **2.** rich/influential person; **les gros,** the nobs; the big shots **3.** **du gros qui tache/du gros (rouge),** ordinary red wine/plonk/ vino **4.** **faire son gros,** to defe- cate*/to do a number two **II** *nf P* prison*; **faire de la grosse,** to do time; **deux ans de grosse,** a two- year stretch. (*Voir* **bonnet**; **lé- gume**; **panse**; **papa**)

gros-cul [gʀoky] *nm P* **1.** shag (tobacco) **2.** heavy lorry/jugger- naut/HGV. (*pl* **gros-culs**)

grossium [gʀosjɔm] *nm P* impor- tant businessman/big shot/big bug/ bigwig.

à la grouille [alagʀuj] *adv phr P* all over the place; **les balancer à la grouille,** to spend* money like water/to live like a lord.

se grouiller [səgʀuje] *vpr F* to hurry* (up)/to get a move on/to get cracking; **grouille(-toi)!** look sharp!/move it!/get your finger out! **dis-lui de se grouiller,** tell him to step on it/to put a jerk in it.

grouillot [gʀujo] *nm F* (*a*) errand boy/messenger boy (*b*) subordinate/underling/minion (*c*) apprentice (*d*) rookie.

groulasse [grulas] *nf,* **groule** [grul] *nf A P* errand girl.

groumer [grume] *vi P* to grumble*/to grouse/to gripe.

groumeur, euse [grumœr, -øz] *a P* grumpy.

grouper [grupe] *vtr P* to arrest*/to pull (s.o.) in; **se faire grouper,** to get nicked **2.** to seize/to grab/to collar.

groupie [grupi] *nf P* groupie.

grue [gry] **I** *nf* (*a*) prostitute*/hooker/tart (*b*) *F* **grande grue,** great gawk of a woman **II** *a F* **une jeune femme très grue,** a very flashy young woman. (*Voir* **pied**)

guenipe [gǝnip] *nf A F* (*péj, rare*) slut/tart/scrubber/slag.

guenon [gǝnɔ̃] *nf* **1.** *F* ugly woman/hag/(old) bat/(old) bag **2.** *P* prostitute*/hooker/tart **3.** *P* **la guenon,** the wife*/the missis **4.** *P* (*drogues*) **avoir la guenon,** to be in need of drugs/to be strung out; **chasser la guenon,** to get the monkey off (one's back).

guenuche [gǝnyʃ] *nf F =* **guenon 1.**

guêpe [gɛp] *nf* **1.** *F* (*a*) nagging woman/nagger (*b*) (*homme*) persistent bore*/pain in the neck **2.** *F* **pas folle, la guêpe!** (I'm/she's/he's) not so daft/not such an idiot **3.** *P* = **guenon 4.**

guérite [gerit] *nf* (*ecc*) *F* confessional (box).

guêtres [gɛtr] *nfpl F* **tirer ses guêtres,** to run away*/to clear off/to beat it **2. traîner ses guêtres (partout)** (*a*) to loaf about/to mess around/*NAm* to goof off (*b*) to travel a lot; **il a traîné ses guêtres dans tous les coins,** he's been all over (the world)/he's been everywhere.

guette-au-trou [gɛtotru] *nm&f inv P* obstetrician; midwife.

gueugueule [gœgœl] *P* **I** *nf* pretty face **II** *a* (*fille, femme*)

attractive/good-looking; **ça c'est gueugueule!** she's a good looker!/that's a bit of all right!

gueulante [gœlɑ̃t] *nf P* uproar*/din; **pousser une gueulante** (*i*) (*colère, douleur*) to shout/to yell/to bawl; to yell one's head off/to shout one's mouth off (*ii*) to bawl/to belt out a song (*iii*) to give an almighty cheer/one hell of a cheer.

gueulard, arde [gœlar, -ard] *F* **I** *a* noisy/loud-voiced/loud-mouthed **II** *n* (*a*) loudmouth/bigmouth (*b*) glutton*/greedyguts (*c*) noisy baby; screaming kid/brat **III** *nf P* loudspeaker/loudhailer; Tannoy (*RTM*).

gueulardise [gœlardiz] *nf P* gluttony/greediness.

gueule [gœl] *nf* **I** *P* (*bouche*) **1. (vas-tu fermer) ta gueule!/ferme ta gueule!** shut up!*/belt up!; shut your mouth/trap/gob/face! **2. aller à la gueule,** to spout; to rabbit on; **être fort en gueule** (*i*) to be foulmouthed (*ii*) to be loud-mouthed/to shoot one's mouth off; **c'est un fort en gueule/une grande gueule,** he's got far too much to say for himself; he can't keep his trap shut; he's got a big mouth; **avoir de la gueule,** to have the gift of the gab **3. des coups de gueule,** shouting/bawling/slanging match; **donner de la gueule/donner un coup de gueule,** to shout one's mouth off; **jeter des injures à pleine gueule,** to bawl out abuse **4.** (*a*) **se soûler la gueule,** to get drunk*/pissed; **avoir la gueule de bois,** to have a hangover (*b*) **une fine gueule,** a gourmet; **être porté sur la gueule,** to be fond of eating and drinking; **s'en mettre plein la gueule/se taper la gueule,** to stuff one's face (*c*) **avoir la gueule ferrée/pavée,** to have a cast-iron stomach **5.** (*alcool, etc*) **emporter la gueule,** to burn one's throat/to take the roof off your mouth **II** *P* (*visage*) **1. gueule d'empeigne/gueule de**

raie/gueule à coucher dehors (avec un billet de logement dans sa poche), repulsive face/ugly mug; avoir une sale gueule, to have an ugly face; il a une sale/vilaine gueule, he looks like a nasty customer/a nasty piece of work 2. bourrer/casser la gueule à qn; rentrer dans la gueule à qn/foutre sur la gueule à qn, to bash s.o.'s head in/to beat s.o. up*/to work s.o. over; il se sont foutus sur la gueule, they had a punch-up; il s'est fait cassé la gueule, he got his face smashed in/he got beaten up/he got worked over; (mil) gueules noires (i) (coal) miners (ii) engine drivers 3. en faire une (sale) gueule/faire la gueule, to sulk/to pull a long face; il m'a fait la gueule, he's given me the cold shoulder 4. se payer/se foutre de la gueule de qn, to make fun of s.o./to poke fun at s.o./to have s.o. on/to pull s.o.'s leg; tu te fous de ma gueule, ou quoi? are you taking the piss, or what? 5. se ficher/se foutre la gueule par terre, to come a cropper*/to fall flat on one's face 6. se fendre la gueule, to laugh* uproariously/to split one's sides laughing 7. gueule d'amour, angelface 8. (terme d'affection) ma gueule, (my) darling*/(my) love III (usages variés) F avoir de la gueule, to have a certain something; ça a de la gueule, non? it's beautiful/that's really something, isn't it? ce chapeau a une drôle de gueule, that's a weird sort of hat; cette bagnole a de la gueule, that's some car/that car's really got something. (Voir enfariné 1; ramener)

gueulement [gœlmɑ̃] nm P shout/yell; il a poussé un gueulement de souffrance, he let out a yell of pain; pousser des gueulements, to make a hell of a din/to kick up a row; to shout one's mouth off.

gueuler [gœle] P I vi 1. to shout/to bawl/to holler; gueuler comme un sourd, to yell one's head

off; faire gueuler la radio, to turn the radio on full blast; sa télé gueule toujours, his telly/TV is still blaring away 2. to protest (noisily); arrête de gueuler! stop bitching!/stop bellyaching! II vtr to bawl out (a song, orders, etc). (Voir charron)

gueuleton [gœltɔ̃] nm P lavish meal/feast/nosh-up/tuck-in/blowout; tu parles d'un gueuleton/c'était un gueuleton à tout casser, that was one hell of a blow-out; nous avons fait un bon petit gueuleton, we did ourselves proud/we had a damn good meal.

gueuletonner [gœltɔne] vi P to eat* heartily/to have a good blowout/to have a good tuck-in.

gueuloir [gœlwar] nm 1. F (a) mouth* (b) throat 2. P = gueulard, arde III.

gueusaille [gøzɑj] nf F rabble/riff-raff/scum.

gueuse [gøz] nf F courir la gueuse, to chase skirt/to go out looking for a bit (of the other)/to be on the make.

gugusse [gygys] nm P 1. chap*/bloke/guy/geezer 2. (i) fool*/clot/twit (ii) crank/nut; faire le gugusse, to clown around/to loon about/to piss around. (Voir gus(se))

guibolles [gibɔl] nfpl P legs*; jouer des guibolles, to run away*/to scram; il (ne) tient pas sur ses guibolles, he's a bit shaky on his pins.

guichet [giʃɛ] nm 1. F (il est trop tard,) les guichets sont fermés! nothing doing!*/no go!/(it) can't be done!/no can do! 2. V le (petit) guichet, anus*/ring/hole.

guignard, arde [giɲar, -ard] F I a unlucky II n unlucky person.

guigne [giɲ] nf F bad luck; avoir la guigne, to be down on one's luck/to be jinxed; to have a run of bad luck; ficher/flanquer/fourrer/porter la guigne à qn, to bring s.o. bad luck/to jinx s.o.; **il porte (la) guigne,** he's bad luck/a jinx. (*Voir* **porte-guigne**)

guignol [giɲɔl] *nm* **1.** *F* eccentric/crank/nut; **faire le guignol,** to play the fool **2.** *pl P* **les guignols,** the police*/the fuzz **3.** *P* law court; magistrates' court; **passer au guignol,** to appear/to be up before the beak **4.** *F* (*théâtre*) prompt box.

guignon [giɲɔ̃] *nm F* bad luck; **c'est un abonné au guignon,** he's got rotten luck/he's got a jinx on him.

guili-guili [giligili] *nm F* **faire guili-guili à un gosse,** to tickle a kid under the chin.

guillotine [gijɔtin] *nf P* **1. guillotine sèche,** solitary (confinement) **2.** (*turf*) results board.

guimauve [gimov] *nf F* (*a*) sloppy/sentimental/icky poetry *or* song; **c'est de la guimauve, ta chanson,** your song's really soppy (*b*) **guimauve blonde,** insipid writing.

guimbarde [gɛ̃bard] *nf F* **vieille guimbarde,** ramshackle old car*/jalopy/(old) banger/(old) crock.

guimpe [gɛ̃p] *nf,* **guimpette** [gɛ̃pɛt] *nf P* (peaked) cap.

guinche [gɛ̃ʃ] *nm P* (*a*) (public) dance/hop/bop (*b*) (seedy) dance hall/dump/dive.

guincher [gɛ̃ʃe] *vi P* to dance/to bop/to jive.

guincheur, euse [gɛ̃ʃœr, -øz] *n P* dancer.

guindal, *pl* **-als** [gɛ̃dal] *nm P* = **godet 1, 2.**

guinde [gɛ̃d] *nf P* car*/motor/jam jar.

guise [giz] *nm V* penis*; **filer le coup de guise,** to have sex*/to have it off.

guiseau [gizo] *nm V* = **guise.**

guiser [gize] *vtr V* to have sex* (with s.o.)/to get one's leg over.

guisot [gizo] *nm* **1.** *P* leg* **2.** *V* penis*.

guitare [gitar] *nf* **1.** *F* **c'est toujours la même guitare,** it's (always) the same old story **2.** *F* (*fille, femme*) **avoir une belle guitare,** to have shapely hips **3.** *P* bidet.

guitoune [gitun] *nf P* **1.** (*a*) house/home/pad (*b*) (*mil*) funkhole/fox-hole/dugout **2.** (camping) tent **3.** electric guitar.

guizot [gizo] *nm* **1.** *P* leg* **2.** *V* penis*.

gun [gœn] *nm P* (*drogues*) hypodermic syringe*/gun/hypo.

gus(se) [gys] *nm P* **1.** fellow/guy/chap*/bloke; **qu'est-ce que c'est que ce gus(se)?** who's that character? **2.** eccentric* person/crank/nut.

gy [ʒi] *int & adv P* **1.** yes/yeah/OK/roger; **faire gy de la tête,** to nod (in agreement) **2. faire gy,** to be on the look-out; to be on one's guard; to keep one's eyes peeled/skinned.

gym [ʒim] *nf,* **gymn** [ʒimn] *nf,* **gymbour** [ʒimbur] *nf,* **gymbourique** [ʒimburik] *nf P* **1.** gymnastics; **il m'a fait faire une drôle de gym,** he really put me through my paces **2. au pas (de) gym,** at the double.

H

Les mots qui commencent par un h aspiré sont indiqués par un astérisque.
Words beginning with an aspirate h are shown by an asterisk.

*H [aʃ] *abbr* P **I** *nf* heroin*/H **II** *nm* hashish*/hash; **fumer du H,** to smoke hash/dope.

habillé [abije] *nm* P uniformed policeman*; **les habillés,** the boys in blue.

habitant [abitɑ̃] *nm* (*a*) P louse/cootie (*b*) F maggot (in fruit, etc).

hachès, hachesse [aʃɛs] *a* P (= *hors service*) (*i*) exhausted*/worn out/dead beat (*ii*) drunk*/paralytic/legless.

*hachoir [aʃwar] *nm* F **le Grand Hachoir,** the guillotine.

hafnaf [afnaf] *adv* P = **afanaf.**

*hallebardes [albard] *nfpl* F **il pleut/il tombe des hallebardes,** it's raining cats and dogs/it's tipping down/it's chucking it down.

halluciné(e) [alysine] *nm&f* F lunatic/nutcase/crackpot.

*hambourgeois [ɑ̃burʒwa] *nm* F (= *en bourgeois*) plain-clothes policeman*/CID officer. (*Voir* **bourgeois 2**)

hameçon [amsɔ̃] *nm* F (*pers*) **mordre à l'hameçon,** to rise to the bait.

*hanneton [antɔ̃] *nm* F **1.** avoir un hanneton dans le plafond/dans la boîte à sel, to have a bee in one's bonnet; **c'est un vrai hanneton,** he's completely scatterbrained **2. pas piqué des hannetons,** excellent*/first-rate; better than expected; **un rhume pas piqué des hannetons,** one hell of a cold; **il a reçu une raclée qui n'était pas piquée des hannetons,** he got a hiding he won't forget in a hurry.

*haquenée [akne] *nf* O F tall/gawky woman.

*hard [ard] *nm* F hard porn.

*hareng [arɑ̃] *nm* P **1.** pimp*/ponce **2.** (*a*) skinny horse/nag/hack (*b*) **sec comme un hareng,** as thin as a rake **3.** policeman*/detective **4. hareng saur,** German*/Jerry/kraut. (*Voir* **boniment 2; mare I; peau 21**)

*harengère [arɑ̃ʒɛr] *nf* F (*péj*) ignorant/foul-mouthed woman; fishwife.

*haricot [ariko] *nm* **1.** P **courir/taper sur le haricot à qn,** to bore* s.o. rigid/to give s.o. a pain (in the arse); to get on s.o.'s wick/up s.o.'s nose **2.** P **des haricots!** nothing doing!*/nuts!/not on your life!/not bloody likely!* **3.** P **c'est la fin des haricots,** that's the bloody limit*/that's the last straw/that's all we needed **4.** F (*a*) toes; feet*; **marcher sur les haricots à qn,** to tread on s.o.'s feet (*b*) **(jambes en) haricots verts,** skinny legs* **5.** P **les haricots verts,** the Germans*/the Krauts/the Jerries **6.** V clitoris*; (*femme*) **avoir le haricot à la portière,** to be (very) sexually excited*/randy/horny **7.** F **jouer pour des haricots** (*i*) to play for nothing*/for love (*ii*) to get nothing out of it/to come away empty-handed; **travailler pour des haricots,** to work for peanuts **8.** P **aller manger des haricots,** to go to prison* **9.** P **hôtel des haricots,** municipal prison. (*Voir* **défilocher**)

*haridelle [aridɛl] *nf* P **1.** bicycle/bike 2. old horse/old nag 3. tall/gawky woman.

***harnacher** [arnaʃe] **I** *vtr F* to rig out/to dress up (s.o.) **II** *vpr* **se harnacher** *F* to rig oneself out/to get togged up; **elle s'était harnachée en cow-boy pour attirer la clientèle,** she got dressed up in cowboy gear to attract custom.

***harnais** [arnɛ] *nmpl P* clothes*/gear/togs; **mettre les harnais,** to put one's glad rags on.

***harnaquer** [arnake] *vtr P* = **harnacher.**

***harnaqueur, -euse** [arnakœr, -øz] *n P* = **arnaqueur.**

***harpe** [arp] *nf P* **jouer de la harpe,** to be in prison*/to be doing time/to do bird.

***harpigner** [arpiɲe] **I** *vtr P* to take/to seize/to grab **II** *vpr* **se harpigner** *F* to come to blows/to have a punch-up.

***harpion** [arpjɔ̃] *nm P* foot*. (*Voir* **arpion**)

***harponner** [arpɔne] *vtr P* **1.** to arrest*/to nail/to nick; **se faire harponner,** to get nabbed/done **2.** to waylay/to collar (s.o.); **se faire harponner,** to get buttonholed.

***hasch** [aʃ] *nm P* (*drogues*) hashish*/hash; **ils fumaient du hasch,** they were smoking dope.

***haut** [o] *adv & nm F* **1. aller par haut et par bas,** to be sick and have diarrhoea* **2. le prendre de haut,** to put on airs/to be condescending towards s.o.; **le porter haut,** to have a high opinion/to think a lot of oneself.

***haute** [ot] *nf P* **la haute/les gens de la haute,** high society/the upper classes/the upper crust; **il a un petit accent de la haute,** his accent is very U/he has a very classy accent/he talks posh.

***hauteur** [otœr] *nf F* (*a*) **être à la hauteur** (*i*) (*pers*) to be capable/to know one's stuff; **je ne me sentais pas à la hauteur,** I didn't feel up to

it (*ii*) to be up to the mark/up to scratch; **dîner à la hauteur,** first class/slap-up meal (*b*) **ça, c'est à la hauteur!** that's the ticket!/sock it to them!

***Havre** [ɑvr] *nm F* **le Grand Havre,** heaven; paradise.

hebdo [ɛbdo] *nm F* (= *hebdomadaire*) weekly (paper, magazine).

hélico [eliko] *nm F* helicopter*/chopper.

hénaurme [henɔrm] *a F* enormous/ginormous.

Henriette [ɑ̃rjɛt] *Prnf P* (*drogues*) heroin*/henry.

herbe [ɛrb] *nf F* **1. manger l'herbe par la racine,** to be dead and buried/to be pushing up the daisies **2. sur quelle herbe avez-vous marché?** what's the matter with you?/what's eating you?/what's bugging you? **3.** (*jockey*) **brouter l'herbe,** to be unseated/to come a cropper* **4.** tobacco* **5.** marijuana*/grass/weed; **fumer de l'herbe,** to smoke grass **6. une mauvaise herbe,** a bad lot/a no-gooder. (*Voir* **blé 2**)

héro [ero] *nm or f P* (*drogues*) heroin*.

heure [œr] *nf F* **1. je (ne) te demande pas l'heure (qu'il est)!** I wasn't talking to you!/mind your own business! **je t'ai demandé l'heure qu'il est?** I didn't ask for your opinion!/who asked you? **2. s'embêter/s'emmerder à cent sous de l'heure,** to be bored* stiff/rigid/to death **3. faire l'heure,** to be punctual **4. l'heure du berger,** right time/moment for making love. (*Voir* **bouillon 5; quart 3**)

heureux, -euse [œrø, ørø, -øz] *a F* **il vit comme un imbécile heureux,** he lives in blissful ignorance.

***hic** [ik] *nm F* **voilà le hic!** that's the snag/the problem.

***hideur** [idœr] *nf F* (*esp femme*) **quelle hideur!** what a hideous sight!/what a fright!

hier [iɛr, jɛr] *adv F* **il est né d'hier,** he's still very green/he's a bit wet behind the ears; **je ne suis pas né d'hier,** I wasn't born yesterday/ what sort of a mug do you take me for?

***high** [aj] *a F* (*drogues*) high.

hippie, hippy [ipi] *a&n F* hippie/hippy.

hirondelle [irɔ̃dɛl] *nf F* **1.** cycle cop **2.** gatecrasher (*i*) at a (cocktail) party, etc (*ii*) (*théâtre*) at dress rehearsals, etc **3. avoir une hirondelle dans le soliveau,** to have bats in the belfry/to have a screw missing **4. les hirondelles volent bas,** there's trouble brewing **5. hirondelle d'hiver,** hot chestnut seller **6.** (*WWII*) **hirondelle de cimetière,** bomb.

histoire [istwar] *nf* **1.** *F* **c'est toujours la même histoire,** it's the same old story; **c'est dingue, cette histoire-là,** the whole thing's daft; **c'est de l'histoire ancienne,** it's ancient history **2.** *F* **c'est toute une histoire** (*i*) it's a long story (*ii*) it's one hell of a business **3.** *F* **la belle histoire!** is that all?/so what? **4.** *F* fib/story; **tout ça c'est des histoires!** that's a load of rubbish!/ *NAm* a bunch of hooey! **tu racontes des histoires!** you're pulling my leg!/you're having me on! **une histoire à dormir debout,** a tall story/a cock-and-bull story **5.** *F* (*a*) **faire des histoires/faire un tas d'histoires,** to kick up a fuss/a rumpus; **il a fait toute une histoire pour avoir cette bagnole,** he kicked up one hell of a fuss to get that car; **pas d'histoires!** don't let's have any bother!/come off it! **en voilà une histoire!** (*i*) what a lot of fuss!/ what a carry-on!/what a song and dance! (*ii*) what a rotten stroke of luck! (*b*) **avoir des histoires avec qn,** to be in s.o.'s black books/to be at loggerheads with s.o.; **(il) faut éviter d'avoir des histoires,** we've got to stay out of trouble (*c*) **chercher/ faire des histoires à qn,** to make trouble for s.o.; **s'attirer des his-**toires, to get into trouble; **cela s'est passé sans histoires,** it went like a dream/without a hitch **6.** *F* thingummy/thingumajig/whatcha(ma)-callit/whatsit/what's-its-name*; **qu'est-ce que c'est que cette histoire-là?** what's that (thing)? **7.** *F* **histoire de rire/de s'amuser/de se marrer,** just for a joke/just for fun/ just for the fun of it/for laughs; **ils ont volé cette tire, histoire de rigoler,** they stole that car for kicks; **j'y suis allé, histoire de faire qch,** I went just for the sake of (having) sth to do **8.** *F* **il a été renvoyé pour une histoire de femme,** he got the sack over some business with a woman/for carrying on with some woman **9.** *P* **avoir ses histoires,** to have a period*/to have the curse **10.** *P* male genitals*/private parts/privates.

hiviau, hivio(t) [ivjo] *nm P* winter.

holpif [ɔlpif] *a P* smart/stylish/ natty.

***homard** [ɔmar] *nm* **1.** *F* **rouge comme un homard,** (as) red as a beetroot **2.** *P* Englishman*.

homasse [ɔmas] *a F* (*femme*) mannish/butch.

homme [ɔm] *nm* **1.** *P* (*a*) husband; boyfriend; lover; **mon homme,** my old man (*b*) pimp* **2.** *F* (*a*) **je suis votre homme,** I'm your man (*b*) **ça c'est un homme!** that's what I call a man! **3.** *F* **dépouiller le vieil homme,** to turn over a new leaf **4.** *P* (*prostituée*) **être sous l'homme,** to be with a client/to be on the job. (*Voir* **barre 6**; **poids**)

hommelette [ɔmlɛt] *nf P* feeble man/(little) weed/wimp.

homme-orchestre [ɔmɔrkɛstr] *nm F* one-man band. (*pl* **hommes-orchestres**)

homo [ɔmo] *a&n F* homosexual*/ homo.

***honteuse** [ɔ̃tøz] *nf P* homosexual* who denies his true sexual feelings/who has not come out; closet queen.

horizontale [ɔrizɔ̃tal] *nf P* prostitute*/tart/hooker; **elle fait l'horizontale,** she earns her money on her back.

horloge [ɔrlɔʒ] *nf* **1.** *P* **la Grosse Horloge,** the Conciergerie (prison, in Paris) **2.** *F* **il a l'horloge détraquée,** he's got a dicky/a bad heart.

horreur [ɔrœr] *nf P* (*a*) obscenity; repulsive sexual behaviour; **il me proposa des horreurs,** he asked me to do sth really disgusting; **dire des horreurs,** to say obscene things (*b*) bizarre sexual behaviour (appreciated by partner).

host(e)au, hosto [ɔsto] *nm P* **1.** hospital **2.** (*mil*) prison*/glasshouse.

*****hotte** [ɔt] *nf P* **1.** (*a*) (old) car*/banger/jalopy (*b*) taxi/cab **2. en avoir plein sa hotte,** to be exhausted*/to be worn out.

*****hotu** [ɔty] **I** *nm P* nasty piece of work/heel/*esp NAm* son of a bitch **II** *a&nm* down-at-heel/shabby-looking (individual).

*****hourdé** [urde] *a* **1.** *F* stupid*/idiotic/daft **2.** *P* drunk*/stoned.

*****houri(e)** [uri] *nf P* (*souvent péj*) woman*.

houst(e)! [ust] *int P* = **oust(e) 1, 2.**

HS [aʃɛs] (*abbr* = *hors service*) *P* = **hachès, hachesse.**

*****hublot** [yblo] *nm P* **1.** lens (of pair of spectacles) **2.** *pl* **hublots,** eyes*/peepers; **il a les hublots ensablés,** he hasn't woken up yet.

huile [ɥil] *nf* **1.** *F* **huile de bras/de coude,** elbow grease **2.** *P* **huile (lourde),** important person*/VIP/bigwig; **les huiles,** the big shots/the top brass; **être/nager dans les huiles,** to have influence/to know the right people/to have pull/to

have clout **3.** *P* money* **4.** *P* **filer de l'huile,** to die in peace (having had the last rites). (*Voir* **baigner 1; pédaler 2; tronche**)

*****huit** [ɥit] *nm F* (*esp ivrogne*) **faire des huit,** to stagger/to lurch about (often while urinating).

huître [ɥitr] *nf P* **1.** fool*/mug/clot **2.** gob (of spit) **3. beurré/plein comme une huître,** very drunk*/pissed as a newt.

*****huit-reflets** [ɥir(ə)flɛ] *nm inv F* top hat/topper.

*****huppé** [ype] *a F* **1.** rich*/loaded/rolling in it; **c'est quelqu'un de très huppé,** he's gots pots/bags of money **2.** belonging to the smart set; posh/classy; **les gens huppés,** the nobs/the toffs.

*****hure** [yr] *nf P* **1.** head*/nut **2.** face*/mug; **se gratter/se ratisser la hure,** to (have a) shave.

*****hurf(e)** [œrf] *a P* elegant/posh/classy/snazzy. (*Voir* **urf(e)**)

*****hussard** [ysar] *adv phr F* **en hussard,** unceremoniously; *V* **baiser qn en hussard,** to make love to s.o. without preliminaries/to do away with the preliminaries/to get down to it. (*Voir* **élixir**)

à la *hussarde [alaysard] *adv phr V* **baiser/prendre qn à la hussarde,** to make love to s.o. without preliminaries/to get down to it.

hyper [ipɛr] *a F* (*a*) very/extremely/completely (*b*) excellent*/terrific/super/great.

hypo [ipo] *nm or f P* (*drogues*) hypodermic (needle*)/hypo/dropper.

à l'hypocrite [alipɔkrit] *adv F* **le feu est passé au rouge à l'hypocrite,** the light changed to red without warning.

hystérique [isterik] *a&nf F* nymphomaniac/nympho.

I

ici [isi] *adv F* **je vois ça d'ici** (*i*) I can just picture it (*ii*) I can see it coming.

icidé [iside], **icigo** [isigo], *FrC* **icite** [isit] *adv P* here.

idée [ide] *nf F* **1. il y a de l'idée,** you may have sth there; (*chose*) it's got a certain something **2.** very small quantity; **une idée d'ail,** just a hint of garlic **3. se faire des idées,** to imagine things; **je me suis fait des idées noires,** I was imagining all sorts of things/the worst; **ne vous faites pas d' idées,** don't get ideas (into your head) **4. j'ai dans l'idée que tu me roules,** I've got the feeling you're having me on **5. a-t-on idée de ...?** who ever heard of ...?/who would have thought it! **6. avoir de la suite dans les idées,** to be persistent; **il a de la suite dans les idées,** he doesn't give it a rest/give up.

idem [idɛm] *adv F* **idem au cresson,** the same thing; **elle a vingt ans et son ami idem,** she's twenty and so's her boyfriend.

idiot(e) [idjo, idjɔt] *n F* **espèce d'idiot!** you stupid idiot!/(you) silly twit! **arrête de faire l'idiot!** stop fooling around!/stop acting dumb!/stop acting the goat!

illico [iliko] *adv F* **illico (presto),** immediately*/right away/straight away/at once; **je suis sorti illico,** I left pronto/pretty sharpish.

illuse [ilyz] *nf F* (*abbr = illusion*) **se faire des illuses,** to get ideas/to imagine things.

image [imaʒ] *nf P* **(grande) image,** 100-franc note; *pl* **images,** banknotes (in general).

imbécile [ɛ̃besil] *nm&f F* **faire l'imbécile,** to act stupid*/to act dumb; to fool around/to act the goat.

imbitable [ɛ̃bitabl] *a P* incomprehensible; **c'est imbitable,** it's gibberish; it's all Greek. (*Voir* **biter 3**)

imbuvable [ɛ̃byvabl] *a F* (*pers*) insufferable/unbearable; (*film, etc*) (unbearably) awful/dreadful.

impair [ɛ̃pɛr] *nm F* (*a*) mistake*; **faire un impair,** to make a bloomer/a gaffe/a goof; to put one's foot in it/to boob (*b*) **faire un impair à qn,** to play a dirty trick on s.o./to do the dirty on s.o.

impayable [ɛ̃pɛjabl] *a F* very funny*/priceless; **vous êtes impayable!** you're a (real) scream!/*NAm* you're a riot!

impec [ɛ̃pɛk] *F* **I** *a* impeccable/perfect; **c'est impec!** great!/smashing!/amazing! **II** *adv* impeccably.

imper [ɛ̃pɛr] *nm F* (*abbr = imperméable*) raincoat/mac.

impossible [ɛ̃pɔsibl] *a F* **1.** (*pers*) impossible; **vous êtes impossible!** you're the bitter end! **2. à une heure impossible,** at an ungodly/unearthly hour; **rentrer à des heures impossibles,** to come home at all hours (of the night) **3.** (*proverbe*) **impossible n'est pas français,** everything's possible/there's no such word as impossible.

in [in] *a inv F* **être in** (*a*) (*être dans le coup*) to be in on sth (*b*) to be in fashion; **s'habiller in,** to wear the latest fashion.

incendier [ɛ̃sɑ̃dje] *vtr F* **1. incendier qn,** to reprimand* s.o. severely/to blow s.o. up/to tear s.o. off a strip; **se faire incendier,** to catch it/to get a rocket **2. incendier qn,** to ruin s.o.'s reputation/credit/influence; **ce scandale l'a définitivement incendié,** he's done for/all washed up after that scandal.

inco [ɛ̃ko] *a P* incorrigible/hopeless/past praying for.

incollable [ɛ̃kɔlabl] *a F* (*pers*) unbeatable; who can't be floored/faulted; **il est incollable sur l'histoire du cinéma,** you can't catch him out/beat him when it comes to films; he knows all there is to know about films.

incon [ɛ̃kɔ̃] *a&n P* (*pol, etc*) (= *inconditionnel*) unwavering (supporter); **c'est un incon du jazz,** he's a jazz fanatic/buff.

inconnoblé [ɛ̃kɔnɔble], **inconnobré** [ɛ̃kɔnɔbre] *a P* unknown.

s'incruster [sɛ̃kryste] *vpr F* to wear out/to overstay one's welcome; **quand on l'invite il s'incruste,** whenever he's invited he seems to take root/you just can't get rid of him; **je ne vais pas m'incruster ...,** don't let me/I mustn't take up any more of your time.

incurable [ɛ̃kyrabl] *a P* condemned to death; **c'est incurable!** it's hopeless!

indécrottable [ɛ̃dekrɔtabl] *a F* incorrigible/hopeless/past praying for; **un tire-au-flanc indécrottable,** a hopeless skiver/a lazy bum.

indérouillable [ɛ̃derujabl] *a P* **1.** stuck **2.** too ignorant to learn (a job, etc); **c'est un maladroit indérouillable,** he's a very clumsy/a hopeless worker **3.** sexually repulsive.

indic [ɛ̃dik] *nm P* (*abbr* = *indica-*

teur) police informer*/(copper's) nark/stool pigeon/grass.

indigestion [ɛ̃diʒɛstjɔ̃] *nf F* **j'en ai une indigestion,** I'm fed up* (to the back teeth) with it/I'm sick and tired of it.

indisposée [ɛ̃dispoze] *af F* (*euph*) **être indisposée,** to have a period*/to have the curse.

infectados [ɛ̃fɛktados] *nm P* cheap cigar/stinkweed/stinkador/stinkaduro.

info [ɛ̃fo] *nf P* (*presse*) (*abbr* = *information*) information/info.

infourgable [ɛ̃furgabl] *a P* unsaleable/unfloggable; **c'est infourgable ce truc,** you can't flog this thing anywhere/you can't give it away.

ino [ino] *a P* (*abbr* = *inoccupé*) unemployed.

inox [inɔks] *nm F* (= *inoxydable*) **(acier) inox,** stainless steel.

insinuante [ɛ̃sinɥɑ̃t] *nf P* (*drogues*) syringe*/hypo.

installer [ɛ̃stale] *vi P* **en installer,** to show off*/to swank; **il en installe un max, mais c'est du bidon,** he puts on a bold front, but it's all a bit of a sham.

installeur [ɛ̃stalœr] *nm F* show-off*/swank.

insti(t),-ite [ɛ̃sti(t)] *n F* (*abbr* = *instituteur*) (school)teacher/teach.

instrument [ɛ̃strymɑ̃] *nm V* penis*/tool.

insupporter [ɛ̃sypɔrte] *vtr F* **ce type m'insupporte,** I can't stand/stomach that bloke/guy.

intégrer [ɛ̃tegre] *vi F* (*scol*) **intégrer à une grande Ecole,** to get into a *grande Ecole*; **intégré à la Normale,** admitted to the *Ecole Normale*.

inter [ɛ̃tɛr] *nm* **1.** *P* tout/steer(er)/hustler **2.** *F* interpreter **3.** *F* (*téléphones*) (*abbr* = *interurbain*) trunks.

intox(e) [ɛ̃tɔks] *nf F* **1.** brainwashing; **ce n'est pas de**

l'information mais de l'intox(e), that's not objective info, that's plain propaganda 2. intoxication (through alcohol, drugs).

intoxico [ɛ̃tɔksiko] *nm&f F (a)* drunkard*/lush/soak (*b*) drug addict*/junkie.

introduire [ɛ̃trɔdɥir] *vtr* 1. *F* **l'introduire à qn,** to hoax s.o./to take s.o. in/to kid s.o. (along); **se la laisser introduire/se la faire introduire,** to let oneself be taken in/to be had 2. *P* **tu as réussi à l'introduire?** did you manage to screw her?

invalide [ɛ̃valid] *nm P* 20-centime coin.

invalo [ɛ̃valo] *nm&f F* invalid.

les Invaloches [lɛzɛ̃valɔʃ], **les Invalos** [lɛzɛ̃valo] *Prn P* the Invalides (quarter) (in Paris).

invitation [ɛ̃vitasjɔ̃] *nf F* **invitation à la valse,** (unwelcome) invitation to pay (*esp* the bill).

invite [ɛ̃vit] *nf F* invitation/invite.

invivable [ɛ̃vivabl] *a F* **avec sa pipe il devient invivable,** he's impossible to live with/he gets on my nerves smoking that pipe.

ioutre [jutr] *P (péj)* **I** *nm&f* Jew*/Jewess/yid **II** *a* Jewish. (*Voir* **youtre**)

isoloir [izɔlwar] *nm F* (public) urinal.

Italboche [italbɔʃ] *nm,* **Italgo** [italgo] *nm,* **Italo** [italo] *nm P (péj)* Italian*/Eyetie/wop.

itou [itu] *adv P* too/also/likewise; **et moi itou!** (and) me too!

Ivan [ivɑ̃] *Prn P* Russian*/Russkie; **les Ivans,** the Russians/the Commies.

IVG [iveʒe] *nf F (abbr = interruption volontaire de grossesse)* termination of pregnancy/abortion; **elle en est à sa 3ème IVG,** that's her third abortion.

ivoire [ivwar] *nm F* **écraser de l'ivoire/taquiner l'ivoire,** to play the piano/to tickle the ivories.

J

J [ʒi] *nm&fpl F (WWII)* (*d'après l'abbr que portaient les cartes de rationnement des jeunes adolescents en France à l'époque*) les J3, teenagers/young people.

jabot [ʒabo] *nm F* **1.** stomach*/belly; **se remplir le jabot**, to stuff oneself/to have a good blow-out **2.** **faire jabot/enfler le jabot/gonfler le jabot/se pousser du jabot**, to put on airs/to strut/to show off*.

jabotage [ʒabotaʒ] *nm F* chatter*/nattering/jabbering/jaw/yacketyyack.

jaboter [ʒabote] *vi F* **1.** to chatter*/to jabber/to rabbit **2.** to eat*/to fill one's belly/to stuff oneself/to pig oneself.

jaboteur, -euse [ʒabotœr, -øz] *n F* chatterbox*/gasbag/windbag.

jacasse [ʒakas] *nf F* chatterbox*; **ma concierge est une vieille jacasse**, my concierge is a real old gasbag.

jacasser [ʒakase] *vi F* to chatter*; **vous êtes là pour travailler, pas pour jacasser**, you're here to work, not to have a good natter; **assez jacassé!** put a sock in it!/stop gassing!

jacasserie [ʒakas(ə)ri] *nf F* (*a*) (endless) chatter*/jabbering/prattling/nattering (*b*) gossip.

jacasseur, -euse [ʒakasœr, -øz] *n*, **jacassier** [ʒakasje] *nm F* (*a*) chatterbox*/prattler; gasbag (*b*) gossip.

jack [ʒak] *nm P* = **jacques 7.**

jacot [ʒako] *nm* **1.** *P* (burglar's) jemmy/*NAm* jimmy **2.** *V* penis*/John Thomas **3.** *V* dildo **4.** *pl P* (*anat*) **jacots**, calves **5.** *P* = **jacques 7.**

jacques [ʒak] *nm* **1.** *P* (burglar's) jemmy/*NAm* jimmy **2.** *P* safe/peter **3.** *P* chamber pot*/jerry **4.** *V* penis*/John Thomas **5.** *V* un **jacques/un Monsieur Jacques**, a dildo **6.** *F* **faire le jacques/le Jacques**, to play the fool/to fool about/to act dumb **7.** *P* taximeter/clock.

jacquot [ʒako] *nm P V* = **jacot.**

jactance [ʒaktãs] *nf P* talk*/chat/conversation; **avoir de la jactance**, to have the gift of the gab; **ce type, c'est le roi de la jactance**, that bloke's got the gift of the gab.

jacter [ʒakte] *vi P* **1.** to talk* (at great length)/to gas; to (go) rabbit(ing) on **2.** to speak badly of (s.o.)/to slander/*NAm* to badmouth (s.o.); **la concierge jacte sur tous les locataires**, the caretaker goes on about all the tenants **3.** (*argot policier*) to confess*/to come clean/to give.

jacteur, -euse [ʒaktœr, -øz] *P* **I** *a* talkative/prattling/gossipy **II** *n* chatterbox*/gasbag/windbag.

jaffe [ʒaf] *nf P* (*i*) meal (*ii*) food*/grub/nosh; **à la jaffe!** grub's up!

jaffer [ʒafe] *vi P* to eat*.

Jag [ʒag] *nf F* (*aut*) Jaguar (*RTM*)/Jag.

jaja [ʒaʒa] *nm P* (red) wine/plonk; **écluser un jaja**, to knock back/to down a glass of vino. (*Voir* **patatrot**)

jalmince [ʒalmɛ̃s] *P* **I** *a* jealous/green **II** *nm&f* jealous person.

jalmincerie [ʒalmɛ̃s(ə)ri] *nf P* **1.** jealousy **2.** jealous person.

jamais [ʒamɛ] *adv F* **1.** mieux vaut tard que jamais, better late than never **2.** on ne sait jamais, you never know/just in case **3.** trois jours après jamais/au lendemain de jamais/à la Saint-Jamais, never; when pigs begin to fly/have wings.

jambard [ʒɑ̃bar] *nm P (pers)* bore*; pain (in the neck/in the arse/*NAm* the ass).

jambe [ʒɑ̃b] *nf* **1.** *F (a)* prendre ses jambes à son cou, to take to one's heels/to do a bunk *(b)* jouer des jambes, to run away*/to scarper **2.** *F* se dérouiller les jambes, to stretch one's legs **3.** *F* tenir la jambe à qn, to buttonhole/to corner s.o./to keep s.o. talking **4.** *F* tirer dans les jambes de qn, to play a dirty trick on s.o./to do the dirty on s.o.; to make life difficult for s.o. **5.** *F (a)* faire la belle jambe, to show off*/to swank/to strut about *(b)* ça vous fera une belle jambe! a fat lot of good that'll do you!/that won't get you very far! **6.** *F* avoir les jambes en coton/en laine/en papier mâché/en pâté de foie, to feel weak/wobbly on one's legs; j'ai les jambes comme du coton, my legs feel like (they're made of) jelly/cotton wool **7.** *F (a)* avoir les jambes en manches de veste/avoir des jambes Louis XV, to be bow-legged/bandy-legged *(b)* avoir des jambes comme des allumettes, to have legs like matchsticks/to have skinny legs **8.** *F* en avoir plein les jambes, to be worn out/bushed/whacked **9.** *(a)* *P* s'en aller sur une jambe, to stick to one drink; tu ne vas pas rentrer chez toi sur une jambe? you're not going to refuse a nightcap?/you must have one for the road *(b)* *F* ça se fait sur une jambe, you can do that standing on one leg; il a fait ses six semaines sur une jambe, he did those six weeks standing on his head/those six weeks were a

walkover for him **10.** *F (a)* faire qch par dessous/par dessus la jambe, to do sth/to work in a slipshod manner *(b)* traîter qn par dessous/par dessus la jambe, to treat s.o. badly/in an offhand manner **11.** *F* se jeter/être dans les jambes de qn, to get/to be (always) under s.o.'s feet **12.** *P* en aurai-je la jambe mieux faite? what good's that going to do me?/shall I be any the better for it? **13.** *P* ça vaut mieux qu'une jambe cassée/que de se casser la jambe, it's better than a kick in the pants/up the arse **14.** *P* la jambe! put a sock in it!/you're getting on my wick/stop being (such) a pain! **15.** *P* faire jambe de bois, to leave without paying/to do a flit; il a disparu en faisant jambe de bois, he left without paying the rent/he did a moonlight (flit) **16.** *O P* one hundred francs. (*Voir* demi-jambe) **17.** *V (femme)* lever la jambe, to be a pushover/to be an easy lay/to open one's legs for any one **18.** *V* une partie de jambes en l'air, a bit of slap and tickle/a bit of how's your father/a bit of the other; faire une partie de jambes en l'air, to have sex*/to have a screw/to have a fuck/to have a bit of the other **19.** *V* jambe du milieu/troisième jambe, penis*/middle leg/third leg. (*Voir* rond III 1; tricoter)

jamber [ʒɑ̃be] *vtr O F* jamber qn *(i)* to pester s.o./to annoy* s.o. *(ii)* to buttonhole s.o./to corner s.o./to keep s.o. talking.

jambon [ʒɑ̃bɔ̃] *nm P* **1.** gratter/racler du jambon, to play the guitar/the banjo, etc **2.** *pl* jambons, thighs.

jambon-beurre [ʒɑ̃bɔ̃bœr] *nm F* (buttered) ham roll *or* sandwich.

jambonneau [ʒɑ̃bɔno] **I** *nm* = jambon 1, 2 **II** *a* être jambonneau/n'avoir plus de chapelure sur le jambonneau, to be bald(-headed)*/to be as bald as a coot.

jambonner [ʒɑ̃bɔne] **I** *vi P* to play the guitar/the banjo, etc **II** *vtr* **1.** *P* **jambonner le blair à qn,** to thump/to bash s.o. on the nose **2.** *F* = **jamber.** (*Voir* **blair 1**)

janot [ʒano] *nm O F* **1.** fool*/simpleton/dupe. (*Voir* **jeannot**) **2.** janot tête-en-l'air, jaywalker.

jante [ʒɑ̃t] *nf F* **1.** se trouver sur les jantes, to be penniless*/to be down on one's uppers **2.** (*cyclisme*) être/rouler sur la jante, to be exhausted*/to be all in.

japonais [ʒapɔnɛ] *nmpl O P* money*.

japonaise [ʒapɔnɛz] *nf F* drink consisting of milk mixed with grenadine or strawberry syrup/ = milkshake.

jaquette [ʒakɛt] *nf* **1.** *F* tirer qn par la jaquette, to buttonhole s.o./ to stick to s.o. like a leech **2.** *P* il est de la jaquette (flottante)/il travaille de la jaquette, he's a homosexual*/he's gay/he's one of them **3.** *P* se faire la jaquette, to run away*/to scarper.

jar [ʒar] *nm P* = **jars.**

jardin [ʒardɛ̃] *nm* **1.** *F* faire du jardin, to criticize (s.o.)/to knock (s.o.)/to get at (s.o.)/to make digs (at s.o.) **2.** *P* aller au jardin (*a*) to work a fiddle/to swindle* (s.o.) (*b*) to indulge in sexual teasing *or* foreplay.

jardiner [ʒardine] *vtr O* **1.** *F* to criticize*/to run (s.o.) down/to knock s.o. **2.** *P* to tease (s.o.) sexually; to feel/to touch (s.o.) up.

jars [ʒar] *nm A P* (thieves', etc) slang/cant; **dévider/jaspiner le jars,** to talk slang/to talk the lingo.

jasante [ʒazɑ̃t] *nf O P* prayer.

jaser [ʒaze] *vi P* **1.** to chatter*/to gossip/to jabber; **ces deux vieilles commères passent leur temps à jaser,** those two gossips/old windbags do nothing but gas **2.** to divulge* a secret/to inform on s.o./

to talk; **en face des poulagas, il va jaser,** when he sees the cops, he's going to give us away/grass/talk **3.** *A* to pray.

jasper [ʒaspe] *vi P* **1.** to talk/to chatter* **2.** to divulge* a secret/to blab/to blow the gaff.

jaspillage [ʒaspijaʒ] *nm P* chatter(ing)*.

jaspiller [ʒaspije] *vi P* to talk/to chatter*. (*Voir* **bigorne 2**)

jaspilleur, -euse [ʒaspijœr, -øz] *P* **I** *n* chatterbox*/gasbag/windbag **II** *a* chattering.

jaspin [ʒaspɛ̃] *nm,* **jaspinage** [ʒaspinaʒ] *nm P* chatter(ing).

jaspiner [ʒaspine] *vi P* to talk/to chatter*.

jaspineur, -euse [ʒaspinœr, -øz] *P* (*rare*) **I** *a&n* = **jaspilleur, -euse II** *n* lawyer/barrister/brief.

jaune [ʒon] *nm F* **1.** strikebreaker/blackleg/scab **2.** sa femme le peint en jaune, his wife is unfaithful/is seeing another man/ has got s.o. on the side. (*Voir* **terre 2**)

jaunet, -ette [ʒonɛ, -ɛt] *n P* **I** (*de race jaune*) yellow skinned person/(*péj*) chink **II** *nm* gold coin.

jaunisse [ʒonis] *nf F* en faire une jaunisse (*i*) to be green with envy (*ii*) to be miffed/to have one's nose put out of joint (by sth/s.o.) (*iii*) (*en amour*) to be mad with jealousy; **il lui donne la jaunisse,** his carrying-on is making her/him sick with jealousy.

java [ʒava] *nf P* **1.** faire la java/ être en java, to have a good time*/ a rave-up/a ball; **partir en java,** to go on the razzle/to go out on the tiles **2.** (*a*) thrashing/good hiding; **la java des baffes,** beating* up/the third degree; **filer une java à qn,** to give s.o. a going-over/to work s.o. over/to beat s.o. up* (*b*) **emmener qn en java,** to take s.o. for a ride.

javanais [ʒavanɛ] *nm F* (*argot con-*

sistant à introduire dans un mot les syllabes **av** *ou* **va:** *donc* **jardin** *devient* **javardavin,** **jeudi** *devient* **javeudavi) c'est du javanais,** it's double Dutch.

javotte [ʒavɔt] *nf A F (esp femme)* chatterbox*/gossip.

jazz-tango [dʒaztãgo] *a P* être **jazz-tango,** to be bisexual/bi/AC-DC.

Jean [ʒã] *Prnm F* **1.** *(d'un enfant)* **comme un petit saint Jean,** naked*/ as God made us/in his birthday suit **2.** *(petit garçon)* **il fait son petit saint Jean,** he's on his best behaviour.

jean-fesse [ʒãfɛs] *nm inv A* = **jean-foutre** *(a).*

jean-foutre [ʒãfutr] *nm inv P (a)* unreliable person/good-for-nothing *(b)* nasty piece of work/sod/bastard* *(c)* fool*/twit/nurd.

jean-jean [ʒãʒã] *nm inv O F* stupid* individual/fool*/dope.

jean-le-gouin [ʒãləgwɛ̃] *nm inv P* (French) naval rating.

jeannot [ʒano] *nm F* **1.** fool*; simpleton. *(Voir* **janot 1)** **2.** cuckold/deceived husband **3.** **jeannot lapin,** bunny (rabbit).

Jean-nu-tête [ʒãnytɛt] *nm inv V* penis*/John Thomas.

jecte [ʒɛkt] *nf O P* tear(-drop).

je-m'en-fichisme [ʒmãfiʃism] *nm F* couldn't-care-less attitude.

je-m'en-fichiste [ʒmãfiʃist] *nm&f F* person who couldn't care less about anyone or anything.

je-m'en-foutisme [ʒmãfutism] *nm P* couldn't-give-a-damn attitude.

je-m'en-foutiste [ʒmãfutist] *nm&f P* person who doesn't give a damn/a shit about anyone or anything.

je-sais-tout [ʒ(ə)sɛtu] *a&nm inv* know-all; **un Monsieur Je-sais-tout,** Mr Know-all/Mr Know-it-all/(Mr) Clever-Dick.

jèse [ʒɛz] *nm P* Jesuit. *(Voir* **jèze)**

jésuite [ʒezɥit] *nm F (péj)* hypocrite.

jésus [ʒezy] *nm* **1.** *F (terme d'affection)* **mon jésus,** my (little) darling* **2.** *F* **être en Jésus,** to be stark naked*/starkers; **se mettre en Jésus,** to strip off **3.** *P* (young) passive homosexual*.

jetard [ʃtar] *nm P* = **ch'tar.**

jeté [ʒ(ə)te] *a F (a)* mad*/crazy; **il est complètement jeté avec ses idées modernistes,** he's completely nuts about all these modern ideas *(b)* drunk*.

jetée [ʒ(ə)te] *nf O P* hundred francs. *(Voir* **demi-jetée)**

jeter [ʒəte, ʃte] **I** *vtr* **1.** *F* to throw (s.o.) out/to chuck (s.o.) out; **se faire jeter,** to get thrown out **2.** *P* **ça, c'est jeté!** that's the stuff (to give 'em)! **3.** *P (a)* **en jeter,** to make a good impression; **en jeter à qn,** to impress s.o.; **elle en jette!** she's got what it takes!/she's got class!/she's really something!; **elle en jette, ta bagnole!** that's a really classy car you've got!/that's some car you've got there! *(b)* **la jeter mal,** to make/to give a bad impression; **la bien jeter,** to make/to give a good impression **4.** *F* **n'en jetez plus(, la cour est pleine),** give it a rest!/pack it in!/come off it! **5.** *P* **s'en jeter un,** to have a drink/to have one; **s'en jeter un dernier,** to have one for the road. *(Voir* **coup 14; cravate 5; dedans 1; jus 6; pierre; pommade 1; tête; venin)** **II** *vpr* **se jeter** *F* **se jeter dans qn,** to run right into s.o./to bang into s.o.

jeton [ʒətɔ̃, ʃtɔ̃] *nm* **1.** *F* **un faux jeton** *(i)* a shifty character *(ii)* a hypocrite; a double-dealer **2.** *F* **un vieux jeton** *(i)* an old person *(ii)* an old fogey*/a has-been/a back-number **3.** *P* punch/blow*; **prendre un jeton en pleine poire,** to get biffed/clouted/socked right on the nose **4.** *P* **avoir les jetons,** to be afraid*/to get the jitters; **donner/ flanquer les jetons à qn,** to put the wind up s.o./to give s.o. the willies; **ça me fout les jetons,** it gives me the creeps/it scares me shitless **5.** *P* **prendre/se payer un jeton (de mate)** (*i*) to be a voyeur/a Peeping Tom (*ii*) to watch an erotic/a porny display (secretly).

jettard [ʒətar] *nm P* = **ch'tar.**

jeu, *pl* **jeux** [ʒǿ] *nm F* **1.** (*a*) **vous avez beau jeu,** now's your chance (*b*) **il avait beau jeu à faire cela,** it was easy for him to do that; he had every opportunity to do that **2. jouer bon jeu bon argent** (*i*) to play it straight (*ii*) to mean business; **y aller bon jeu bon argent,** to come/to go straight to the point **3. faire le grand jeu à qn/sortir le grand jeu,** to give s.o. the works **4. nous sommes à deux de jeu,** two can play at that game; **ce n'est pas de jeu,** that's not fair/that's not on **5. serrer son jeu,** to take no risks/ to play it close to the chest. (*Voir* **épingle 2**)

jeudi [ʒǿdi] *nm F* **la semaine des quatre jeudis,** never; when pigs have wings/when Hell freezes (over); **tu risques d'attendre jusqu'à la semaine des quatre jeudis,** you'll end up waiting till the cows come home; **il vous le paiera la semaine des quatre jeudis,** it'll be a miracle if he pays you for it.

jeunabre, jeunâbre [ʒœnabr, -ɑbr] *P* **I** *a* young/youngish **II** *nm&f* youngster.

jeune [ʒœn] *a F* **1. son jeune homme,** her young man/her boyfriend **2.** not enough; **c'est un peu jeune/ça fait un peu jeune,** (*quantité*) it's a bit on the short side/on the small side; (*argent*) that's a bit tight/stingy; (*temps*) that's cutting it a bit fine.

jeunesse [ʒœnɛs] *nf F* **une jeunesse,** a girl*/a (little) bit of fluff.

jeunet, -ette [ʒœnɛ, -ɛt] *F* **I** *a* (*i*) young/youngish; **il est jeunet pour travailler dur,** he's a bit on the young side for hard work (*ii*) young and inexperienced/green/raw **II** *n* **un jeunet/une jeunette,** a young boy/girl; a mere lad/a slip of a girl.

jeunot, -otte [ʒœno, -ɔt] *F* **I** *a* = **jeunet I II** *nm* youth/(young) lad.

jèze [ʒɛz] *nm P* Jesuit. (*Voir* **jèse**)

ji [ʒi] *int & adv A P* **1.** yes/yeah/ OK/roger; **faire ji de la tête,** to nod in agreement **2. faire ji,** to be on the look-out; to be on one's guard. (*Voir* **gy; jy**)

jinjin [ʒɛ̃ʒɛ̃] *nm P* **1.** red wine/ plonk/vino **2. il n'a rien dans le jinjin,** he's empty-headed/he's got nothing up there/he's a bit dim.

job I [dʒɔb] *nm F* (*a*) job/work/ employment (*b*) soft/cushy job; safe job (*c*) temporary job; **c'est un job d'étudiant,** it's not a job for life/it's only temporary (*d*) cover- up/front/alibi* (for illegal activity) **II** [ʒɔb] *nm F* **1.** = **jobard I 2.** (*a*) **monter le job à qn** (*i*) to pull s.o.'s leg/to have s.o. on/to take s.o. in/to take s.o. for a ride (*ii*) to build up s.o.'s hopes (*iii*) to work on s.o.'s feelings; to work s.o. up/ to poison s.o.'s mind (**contre,** against) (*b*) **se monter le job** (*i*) to imagine things/to kid oneself (*ii*) to get excited/to work oneself up/to go off the deep end.

jobard, -arde [ʒɔbar, -ard] *F* **I** *n* **1.** mug/sucker **2.** madman/ madwoman/nutter/nut **II** *a* stupid*; naive.

jobarder [ʒɔbarde] *vtr* (*rare*) *F* **jobarder qn,** to hoax* s.o./to take s.o. for a ride/to have s.o. on.

jobarderie [ʒɔbard(ə)ri] *nf,* **jobardise** [ʒɔbardiz] *nf F* gullibility; **c'est de la jobarderie,** it's a

mugs' game; **commettre une
jobarderie,** to let oneself be taken
in/to be had.

jobré [ʒɔbre] *a* P mad*; **il est complètement jobré,** he's completely
nuts/he's off his head.

jockey [ʒɔke] *nm* **1.** F faire jockey, to be on a strict diet; **régime
jockey,** starvation diet **2.** P decoy
in gambling joint, etc/*NAm*
shill(aber).

joice [ʒwas] *a* P happy/cheerful/
pleased/joyful. (*Voir* **joisse**;
jouasse)

joint [ʒwɛ̃] **I** *nm* **1.** F (a) **trouver
le joint pour faire qch,** to hit on the
right way of going about sth; to
discover the trick/the knack of
doing sth; to come up with the
answer (b) (*drogues*) to find a
dealer/to get one's supplies/to
score **2.** V **aller au joint,** to have
sex*/to screw/to get one's end
away **II** *nm* P (*drogues*) mari-
juana* cigarette/joint; **fumer/tirer
un joint,** to smoke a joint.

joisse [ʒwas] *a* P = **joice.**

jojo [ʒɔʒɔ] F **I** *a* **1.** (a) nice/
pleasant; **c'est pas très jojo,** it's not
really/terribly nice (b) pretty/good-
looking (c) (*iron*) ugly/hideous;
**sans maquillage elle n'est pas telle-
ment jojo,** without all that make-up
she's not such a pretty sight **2. me
voilà jojo!** I'm in a fix*/I'm in a
fine old mess! **II** *nm* **1. c'est un
affreux jojo,** he's a horrible (little)
brat/kid **2. faire son jojo,** to
behave puritanically/to be all
goody-goody.

joli [ʒɔli] F **I** *a* (iron) fine/nice; **je
serais joli!** a fine mess I'd be in!
c'est pas joli, it's a poor show; **tout
cela c'est bien joli, mais ...,** that's
all very well, but ... **II** *nm* **c'est
du joli!** a nice mess (it is)!/it's a
disgrace! **il a encore fait du joli!** a
fine mess he's made of it again!
(*Voir* **coco 6** (a); **cœur 1**)

joliment [ʒɔlimɑ̃] *adv* F (*intensif*)

very/extremely; **joliment amusant,**
awfully funny; **il danse joliment
bien,** he's a jolly good/a great
dancer; **il a joliment raison!** he's
dead right! **on s'est joliment
amusé(s),** we had a great time/a
pretty good time.

jonc [ʒɔ̃] *nm* **1.** P money*; **avoir
du jonc,** to be rich*/not short of a
penny or two **2.** P gold **3.** P **se
peler le jonc,** to be chilled to the
bone **4.** P **foutre un coup de jonc,**
to steal* **5.** P **tu me pèles le jonc!**
you get on my bloody nerves!/you
get up my nose! **6.** V penis*.

joncaille [ʒɔ̃kaj] *nf* P **1.** money*
2. gold **3.** jewels.

jongler [ʒɔ̃gle] *vi* F **faire jongler qn
de qch,** to do s.o. out of what is
due to him.

Jordonne [ʒɔrdɔn] *Prn* F (=
j'ordonne) **c'est un monsieur/une
madame Jordonne,** he's/she's bossy/
a real bossy boots.

jordonner [ʒɔrdɔne] *vtr* F to boss
(s.o./people) about.

jornaille [ʒɔrnaj] *nf,* **jorne** [ʒɔrn]
nm A P day; daytime.

Joseph [ʒozɛf] *Prn* F self-right-
eous/smug young man; **faire son/le
Joseph,** to put on virtuous airs/to
play the innocent.

Joséphine [ʒozefin] *Prn* **1.** F
faire sa Joséphine (i) to play the
prude/to be all goody-goody (ii) to
put on airs (and graces) **2.** P
(*mil*) bayonet.

jouailler [ʒwaje] *vi* O F **1.** to
play a musical instrument badly
2. (*au jeu*) to play for small stakes.

jouasse [ʒwas] *a* P = **joice.**

jouer [ʒwe] *vtr* P **1. jouer qn,** to
fool* s.o. **2. les jouer,** to run
away*/to clear off/to beat it. (*Voir
air* I 2; **châtaigne 2** (b); **con** I 2;
feuille 1; **flûtes**; **jambe 1** (b);
rip(e))

joufflu [ʒufly] *nm* P buttocks*/
bum/*NAm* ass/*NAm* butt.

jouge 236 jus

jouge [ʒuʒ] *adv phr P* **en moins de jouge,** very quickly*/immediately/in no time (at all)/as quick as a flash.

jouir [ʒwir] *vi* 1. *F* (*iron; par antiphrase*) **ça l'a fait jouir!** I bet he enjoyed that! **quand je me suis mis le marteau sur les doigts j'ai joui,** I was overjoyed/ecstatic/over the moon when I hit my fingers with the hammer 2. *P* to have an orgasm*/to come.

jouissance [ʒwisɑ̃s] *nf P* orgasm*/climax.

jouissif, -ive [ʒwisif, -iv] *a F* very pleasurable; orgasmic.

joujou [ʒuʒu] *nm P* **faire joujou avec qn,** to have sex* with s.o.

jour [ʒur] *nm* 1. *F* (*pers*) **long comme un jour sans pain,** tall and thin 2. *F* **demain il fera jour,** tomorrow's another day 3. *F* (*femme*) **avoir ses jours,** to have a period*/to have the curse/to come on 4. *P* (*marchandises volées*) **ça craint le jour,** that stuff's hot. (*Voir* **soleil 4**)

jourdé [ʒurde] *nm,* **journaille** [ʒurnaj] *nf P* day.

journaleux [ʒurnalø] *nm F* (*péj*) journalist/hack.

journanche [ʒurnɑ̃ʃ] *nf,* **journe** [ʒurn] *nm or f P* day.

joyeuses [ʒwajøz] *nfpl V* testicles*/nuts.

joyeux [ʒwajø] *nm A P* (*mil*) soldier serving in a *bataillon d'Afrique*. (Voir **bat' d'Af**)

J't'arquepince [ʒtark(ə)pɛ̃s] *attrib P* (**ces messieurs de**) **la maison J't'arquepince,** the police*/the cops/the fuzz.

jucher [ʒyʃe] *vi A F* (*pers*) **où juchez-vous?** where do you live?/where do you hang out?

jugeot(t)e [ʒyʒɔt] *nf* 1. *F* common sense/gumption/savvy; **avoir de la jugeot(t)e,** to know what's what 2. *P* **passer en jugeot(t)e,** to stand for trial.

juif [ʒɥif] *nm* 1. *F* **le petit juif,** the funny bone 2. *P* (*péj*) miser*; **faire qch en juif,** to be mean/to be jewish about sth.

juivoler [ʒɥivɔle] *vtr O P* to overcharge/to rip off.

Jules, jules [ʒyl] *Prn & nm P* 1. chamber pot*/jerry 2. (*a*) (*i*) lover/fancy man (*ii*) boyfriend/bloke/guy (*b*) husband*; **mon jules,** my old man 3. pimp*/ponce 4. (*WWII*) German*/Jerry 5. (*drogues*) heroin*; cocaine* 6. **se faire appeler Jules,** to get reprimanded*/torn off a strip 7. lesbian. (*Voir* **Arthur**)

Julie, julie [ʒyli] *Prn & nf* 1. *F* **faire sa julie,** to be a prude/prudish/all goody-goody 2. *P* (*a*) (*i*) woman* (*ii*) wife*/old lady (*iii*) girlfriend; mistress (*b*) prostitute*/hooker 3. *P* (*drogues*) cocaine*; **de la julie du Brésil,** Brasilian coke.

Julot, julot [ʒylo] *Prn & nm P* 1. = **jules 2, 3, 4** 2. **un julot,** man*/chap*/bloke/guy (*esp* a stranger).

jumelles [ʒymɛl] *nfpl P* buttocks*/bum/*NAm* ass.

junk [dʒœk] *nm P* (*drogues*) heroin*/H.

junkie [dʒœki] *nm&f P* (*drogues*) drug addict*/junkie.

jupé [ʒype] *a P* drunk*.

jupon [ʒypɔ̃] *nm F* woman*/girl*/(bit of) skirt; **courir le jupon,** to run after girls *or* women/to chase skirt/to be on the make.

juponnard [ʒypɔnar] *nm F* womanizer*/skirt-chaser/wolf.

juponné [ʒypɔne] *a P* drunk*.

jus [ʒy] *nm* 1. *P* (dirty) water; **c'est clair comme du jus de boudin/de chique,** it's as clear as mud; **jus de grenouille,** water (as a drink); **jus de parapluie,** (rain)water; **tomber au jus,** to fall in the drink 2. *P* coffee; **jus de chapeau/de chaussette/de chique,** watery coffee/dishwater/

cat's piss; **au jus!** coffee time!/coffee's up! (*mil*) **c'est du dix au jus,** only ten days to demob; **soldat de 2ème jus** = private **3.** *P* (*a*) electric current/juice; **mettre le jus,** to switch on (*b*) petrol/juice/gas; **donner du jus,** to step on the gas/to step on it; **à plein jus,** at full throttle **4.** *P* (publisher's) blurb **5.** *P* a long speech; **faire un jus,** to spout on (at length) **6.** *P* **avoir du jus** (*i*) to be smart/elegant (*ii*) to have class; **jeter du/son jus** (*i*) to make a good impression (*ii*) to look classy/to have class **7.** *P* **ça vaut le jus,** it's worth it/it's worth the effort; **y mettre du jus,** to put one's back into it **8.** *F* **cuire/mariner/mijoter dans son jus,** to stew in one's own juice **9.** *F* **un français pur jus,** a hundred percent Frenchman/a typical Frenchman **10.** *F* **c'est le même jus,** it's the same thing; **c'est jus et verjus,** it's six of one and half a dozen of the other **11.** *P* **jus de sarment,** wine **12.** *P* nitroglycerine/soup **13.** *P* (*drogues*) heroin*/cocaine* **14.** *P* (*péj*) **jus de réglisse,** negro/Black* **15.** *V* semen*/sperm/spunk; **lâcher le jus,** to ejaculate*/to shoot one's load. (*Voir* **court-jus; tire-jus**)

jusqu'auboutisme [ʒyskobutism] *nm F* extremist attitude; (*politique*) hard line policy.

jusqu'auboutiste [ʒyskobutist]

nm&f F **1.** whole-hogger/all-outer; (*politique*) hard-liner **2.** diehard/last-ditcher/bitter-ender.

jusque [ʒysk(ə)] *prep F* **en avoir jusque-là,** to have had enough (of sth)/to be fed up* to the back teeth (with sth)/to have had it up to here.

juste [ʒyst] *a F* **ç'a été juste!** it was a tight squeeze! **arriver un peu juste,** to cut it a bit fine.

justice [ʒystis] *nf F* **des cheveux raides comme la justice,** dead straight hair.

jutant [ʒytã] *nm F* large pimple; **il a un jutant sur le pif,** he's got a big juicy spot/*NAm* zit on the end of his nose.

jute [ʒyt] *nm V* semen*/sperm/spunk.

juter [ʒyte] *vi* **1.** *P* to hold forth/to spout on **2.** *P* = **jus 6 3.** *V* to ejaculate*/to shoot (one's load).

juteux, euse [ʒytø, -øz] *P* **I** *a* (*a*) smart/classy/tarted up (*b*) **affaire juteuse,** juicy bit of business **II** *nm* (*mil*) (company) sergeant-major.

JV [ʒive] *abbr P* (*argot policier* = *jeune voyou*) young hooligan*/juvenile delinquent/young hoodlum.

jy [ʒi] *int & adv P* = **ji.**

K

kangourou [kɑ̃guru] *nm F* **1.** Australian*/Aussie **2. voler au kangourou,** to shoplift, hiding the stolen goods in one's clothes (as in a kangaroo pouch).

kapo [kapo] *nm O* (*mil WWII*) (*surveillant dans un camp de concentration*) German corporal. (*Voir* **capo 1**)

kasba(h) [kazba] *nf P* house/pad/joint.

kawa [kawa] *nm P* (a cup of) coffee.

kébour(g) [kebur] *nm*, **kébroc** [kebrɔk] *nm*, **kébrol** [kebrɔl] *nm O P* (*mil*) kepi/peaked cap.

képi [kepi] *nm P* (*mil*) **1. ramasser les képis,** to be promoted as a result of the death of one's superior(s)/to step into dead men's shoes **2.** (*ecc*) **képi à moustaches,** biretta.

kès [kɛs] *nm P* **c'est du kès,** it's six of one and half a dozen of the other; it makes no odds/it (all) comes to the same thing/it's much of a muchness; **c'est jamais du kès,** it's never the same.

khâgne [kaɲ] *nf P* (Arts) class preparing for the entrance exam to the *École normale supérieure.* (*Voir* **cagne**)

khâgneux, -euse [kaɲø, -øz] *n P* student in a **khâgne**.

kidnappinge [kidnapɛ̃ʒ] *nm P* kidnap(ping).

kif¹ [kif] *nm P* (*drogues*) marijuana*/kif/keef/kef/kief.

kif², kif-kif [kifkif] *a inv P* **c'est kif-kif (bourricot)/c'est du kif/** **c'est toujours du kif au même,** it's six of one and half a dozen of the other/it makes no odds/it (all) comes to much the same thing; **c'est pas du kif,** it's not the same thing at all/that's something quite different.

kiki [kiki] *nm P* **1.** (*a*) Adam's apple (*b*) windpipe; **serrer le kiki à qn,** to throttle s.o.; to wring s.o.'s neck **2.** (child's) penis*/willy. (*Voir* **quiqui**) **3. c'est parti mon kiki!** here we go!/off we go!/here goes!

kil(e) [kil] *nm*, **kilbus** [kilbys] *nm*, **kilo¹** [kilo] *nm P* **un kil de rouge** = a bottle of plonk/vino; **payer un kil à qn** = to stand s.o. a pint.

kilo² [kilo] *nm* **1.** *F* (*théâtre*) **en faire des kilos,** to overact/to overplay one's part **2.** *P* (*lycée*) **prendre un kilo,** to be punished/to get detention **3.** *V* **poser un kilo,** to defecate*/to have a crap.

kiné [kine] *F* **I** *nf* (= *kinésithérapie*) physiotherapy; **une séance de kiné,** a physio (session) **II** *nm&f* (= **kinésithérapeute**) physiotherapist/physio.

kino [kino] *nm O F* cinema; **j'vais au kino,** I'm going to the flics/to the pictures.

kir [kir] *nm F* (*boisson*) white wine and blackcurrant liqueur *or* syrup.

kit [kit] *nm P* (*drogues*) drug addict's instruments*/kit/artillery (for shooting up); **il avait toujours son kit sur lui pour une petite piquouse,**

he always had his kit with him for a quick fix.

Kiwi [kiwi] *nm F* New Zealand rugby player/kiwi.

klébard [klebar] *nm,* **klebs** [klɛbs] *nm P* dog*/hound/pooch/mutt. (*Voir* **clébard**; **clebs**)

knockout [knɔkut, nɔkaut], (*abbr*) **KO** [kɑo] *a P* (*a*) exhausted*/knocked out/done in/shattered (*b*) drunk*/pissed/paralytic (*c*) (*drogues*) stoned/high.

kopeck [kɔpɛk]. *nm F* **1.** (*a*) ne plus avoir un kopeck (en poche), to be penniless*/broke; je n'ai pas un kopeck, I haven't got a penny/I'm skint (*b*) *pl* kopecks, money*/bread/dough **2.** ça ne vaut pas un kopeck, it's not worth a farthing.

kroum(e) [krum] *nm P* = croum(e).

krounir [krunir] *vtr&i P* = crounir.

kyrielle [kirjɛl] *nf F* toute une kyrielle d'enfants, a whole hoard/tribe of children/kids; il leur a lancé à la figure toute une kyrielle d'injures, he shouted a whole stream of abuse at them/he was effing and blinding at them.

L

là [la] *adv* **1.** *F* (*a*) (*pers*) **être (un peu) là,** to be all there/to be no fool; to be wise/to be with it; **comme menteur il est un peu là,** he's a pretty good liar! **elle est un peu là** (*ii*) you can't miss her! (*b*) (*chose*) **être un peu là,** to be the real McCoy **2.** *F* **tout est là,** that's the whole point **3.** *P* **ils ne sont pas là** (*i*) there's no money (left) in the kitty (*ii*) I'm penniless*/skint **4.** *P* **je l'ai là,** I don't give a damn about him/I've had him up to here. (*Voir* **jusque; se poser 1, 2**)

lab [lab] *nm F* = **labo.**

labadé [labade] *adv,* **labago** [labago] *adv P* over there.

labo [labo] *nm F* laboratory/lab.

lac [lak] *nm* **1.** *F* (*a*) **être dans le lac** (*i*) (*pers*) to be done for/to be in the soup/to be up the creek; **je suis dans le lac,** I'm sunk (*ii*) (*projet, etc*) to be a failure/a flop; to fall through; **l'affaire est dans le lac,** it fell through/it came to nothing **2.** *V* female genitals*. (*Voir* **descente 4**)

lâchage [lɑʃaʒ] *nm F* dropping/running out on (s.o., a friend); jilting/chucking/throwing over (of boyfriend, girlfriend, etc).

lâcher [lɑʃe] *vtr* **1.** *F* (*a*) **lâcher son boulot,** to throw up/to chuck one's job; **lâcher la politique,** to give up/to drop politics (*b*) **lâcher qn,** (*amant*) to let s.o. down; to drop/to chuck s.o./to run out on s.o.; (*ami, etc*) to walk out on s.o./to leave s.o. in the lurch **2.** *F* **les** lâcher, to pay* up/to fork out; **être dur à les lâcher,** to be mean/stingy; **il ne les lâche pas,** he's really tight-fisted/he's a mean sod **3.** *P* **en lâcher un,** to let out a fart. (*Voir* **baskets 3; dé 1; écluse 1, 2; élastique; froc 3; fusée; gaz 4; morceau 2; paquet 5, 15; pédale 3; perle 4, 5; perlouse 2; rampe 1; valse; vent**)

lâcheur, -euse [lɑʃœr, -øz] *n F* unreliable person/s.o. who lets you down; quitter; **on ne voit plus votre ami, c'est un lâcheur,** we haven't seen your friend for ages, he's deserted us.

lacsatif [laksatif] *nm,* **lacsé** [lakse] *nm,* **lacsif** [laksif] *nm P* **1.** handbag **2.** 100-franc note. (*Voir* **sac 1**)

lacson [laksɔ̃] *nm P* package; **lacson de pipes,** cigarette packet.

ladé [lade] *adv P* (*a*) there (*b*) here.

laf(f)es [laf] *nfpl A P* **les laf(f)es,** the old defence works around Paris (formerly an habitual resort of criminals. (*Voir* **fortif(e)s**)

laga [laga], **lago** [lago], **laguche** [lagyʃ] *adv P* = **ladé.**

laine [lɛn] *nf F* **1. manger la laine sur le dos à qn,** to fleece s.o. **2. jambes en laine,** weak/wobbly legs*; **avoir des jambes en laine,** to be exhausted*/to be out on one's feet. (*Voir* **jambe 6**)

lait [lɛ] *nm* **1.** *F* (*a*) (*pers*) **boire du (petit) lait,** to take it all in eagerly/to lap it up; **avaler qch comme du petit lait,** to be tickled pink by sth (*b*) (*boisson*) **ça se boit comme du**

petit lait, it slips down nicely 2. *P* lait de chameau/de panthère/de tigre, pastis. (*Voir* pain 7; soupe 2; vache)

laitue [lɛty, le-] *nf* 1. *P* novice prostitute*; prostitute under age 2. *V* female genitals*/fruit basket 3. *V* (*femme*) pubic hair/minge fringe/pubes; mouiller sa laitue, to urinate*.

laïus [lajys] *nm F* speech/lecture; faire/piquer un laïus, to speechify/ to hold forth; on a eu droit à son laïus, we had to sit and listen to his lecture; ce n'est que du laïus, it's just talk/waffle/a lot of hot air.

laïusser [lajyse] *vi F* to make a (long) speech; to speechify/to hold forth.

lambda [lãbda] *a P* ordinary/com- monplace; le pékin lambda, the man in the street/Mr Average.

lambin, ine [lãbɛ̃, -in] *F* I *a* slow/dawdling II *n* slowcoach/ *NAm* slowpoke/dawdler.

lambiner [lãbine] *vi F* to dawdle/ to take one's time (about sth); to footle around/to mess about.

lamdé [lamde] *nf P* (*largonji de dame*) (*a*) lady (*b*) wife*/old lady.

lame [lam] *nf P* 1. knife/chiv 2. pisser des lames de rasoir (en tra- vers) (*i*) to experience pain when urinating/to piss pins and needles (*ii*) to have VD*/to have the clap.

lamedé [lamde] *nf P* = lamdé.

lamedu [lamdy] *nm P* goods.

lamefé [lamfe] *nf P* = lamfé.

lamer [lame] *vtr P* to stab/to knife/ to stick (s.o.).

lamfé [lamfe] *nf P* (*a*) woman* (*b*) wife*/old lady.

laminoir [laminwar] *nm F* faire passer qn au laminoir, to give s.o. a hard time (of it)/to put s.o. through the mill.

lampe [lãp] *nf P* 1. stomach*; s'en mettre/s'en coller/s'en foutre/

s'en taper plein la lampe, to eat* heartily/to have a good blow-out/ to (have a good) tuck-in/to pig oneself 2. lampe à souder (*i*) (*avions*) turbojet (*ii*) (*mil*) machine- gun/tommy-gun.

lampée [lãpe] *nf F* swig (of wine, etc); vider un verre d'une lampée, to down a drink in one go.

lamper [lãpe] *vtr F* to gulp down/ to swig (down)/to knock back (a drink).

lampion [lãpjɔ̃] *nm* 1. *F* l'air des lampions/les lampions, rhythmical stamping of feet to indicate impa- tience 2. *P* eye* 3. *P* un coup dans le lampion, a drink/a swig; boire un lampion, to knock one back 4. *P* = lampe 1.

lampiste [lãpist] *nm F* scapegoat/ fall guy/mug; s'en prendre au lampiste, to bully/to take it out on one's subordinate(s).

lance [lãs] *nf P* 1. rain 2. water; boire de la lance, to have a drink of water 3. urine; jeter de la lance, to urinate*/to have a slash 4. VD* 5. (*drogues*) syringe*/ hypo.

lancé [lãse] *a F* slightly drunk* and talkative.

lancecailler [lãskaje] *vi O P* to urinate*.

lance-parfum [lãsparfɛ̃] *nm inv P* machine-gun/tommy-gun.

lance-pierre [lãspjɛr] *nm P* 1. rifle 2. il les lâche/les envoie au lance-pierre, he's tight with his money; you have to drag the money out of him 3. être nourri avec un lance-pierre, to be on a strict diet; manger avec un/au lance-pierre, to bolt down one's food (*esp* a small amount).

lancequinade [lãskinad] *nf P* steady downpour (of rain).

lancequine [lãskin] *nf P* 1. rain 2. water 3. urine.

lancequiner [lɑ̃skine] *vi P* **1.** to rain; **lancequiner à pleins tubes**, to rain cats and dogs/to chuck it down/to piss down **2.** *O* to weep/ to cry one's eyes out **3.** to urinate*/to piss.

lancer [lɑ̃se] *vi F* **ma dent me lance**, my tooth's giving me stabbing pains/shooting pains; my tooth's giving me hell.

lanciner [lɑ̃sine] *vtr O F* to bore* (s.o.).

langouse [lɑ̃guz] *nf P* tongue; **filer une langouse à qn**, to give s.o. a French kiss.

langouste [lɑ̃gust] *nf P* prostitute*.

langue [lɑ̃g] *nf* **1.** *F* **langue verte**, slang **2.** **avaler sa langue** (*i*) *P* to die* (*ii*) *P* to yawn one's head off (*iii*) *F* **tu as avalé/perdu ta langue?** has the cat got your tongue? **3.** *F* **avoir la langue bien pendue**, to have the gift of the gab **4.** *F* (*réponse à une devinette*) **donner/jeter sa langue au(x) chat(s)**, to give up; **je donne ma langue au chat!** go on, I'll buy it!/I give up! **5.** *F* **s'en mordre la langue**, to regret bitterly having spoken; to kick oneself **6.** *F* (*pers*) **tirer la langue**, to show signs of exhaustion/to be near the end of one's tether **7.** *F* **faire tirer la langue à qn**, to keep s.o. waiting/hanging about **8.** *F* **il n'a pas la/sa langue dans sa poche**, he's a great talker/he's never at a loss for words/he's never stuck for sth to say **9. faire une langue (fourrée) à qn** (*a*) *P* to give s.o. a French kiss (*b*) *V* (*cunnilinctus*) to suck s.o.('s cunt)/to go down on s.o. **10.** *V* **donner sa langue au chat**, to eat fur pie. (*Voir* **bœuf II 3; cheveu 3**)

languetouse, languetouze [lɑ̃gətuz] *nf*, **languette** [lɑ̃gɛt] *nf* **1.** *P* tongue **2.** *V* (*occ*) clitoris*/ clit. (*Voir* **langouse**)

lanlaire [lɑ̃lɛr] *attrib F* **envoyer qn faire lanlaire**, to send s.o. packing*/ to tell s.o. to get lost.

lansquine [lɑ̃skin] *nf*, **lansquiner** [lɑ̃skine] *vi P* = **lancequine, lancequiner**.

lanterne [lɑ̃tɛrn] *nf* **1.** *P* window **2.** *P* eye*. (*Voir* **pisser 3**) **3.** *P* stomach*; **se taper sur la lanterne**, to be hungry* **4.** *F* **être la lanterne rouge**, to come last (in a race, etc); = to win the wooden spoon; (*à l'école*) to be bottom of the class **5.** *F* (*a*) **éclairer sa lanterne**, to explain one's point (of view) (*b*) **éclairer la lanterne de qn**, to put s.o. straight.

lanterner [lɑ̃tɛrne] *F* **I** *vi* to waste (time)/to dilly-dally/to dawdle **II** *vtr* **1.** to bother/to pester/ to annoy* (s.o.) **2.** to keep (s.o.) waiting.

lanternière [lɑ̃tɛrnjɛr] *nf O P* brothel-keeper/madam(e).

lantiponnage [lɑ̃tipɔnaʒ] *nm O F* idle/frivolous talk.

lantiponner [lɑ̃tipɔne] *vi F O* to talk in an idle/frivolous way.

lap(e) [lap] *nm & adv P* nothing*; **que lap(e)**, nothing* at all/damn all/sweet FA; **bonnir lap(e)**, not to utter a word; to keep mum; **je n'y pige que lap(e)**, I can't make head nor tail of it; **un bon à lap(e)**, a good-for-nothing/a layabout.

lape-verres [lapvɛr] *nm P* drunkard*/tippler/boozer/soak.

lapin [lapɛ̃] *nm* **1.** *F* (*a*) **c'est un rude/un fameux/un fier lapin** (*i*) he's a great bloke/guy; he's a brick (*ii*) he's smart; he's quite a lad (*iii*) he's got plenty of nerve (*b*) **un drôle de lapin**, a queer customer/an odd character (*c*) **un sacré lapin**, a hell of a twit (*d*) **mon vieux lapin**, old chap/old man/old thing/old cock **2.** *F* **mon petit lapin**, my darling*/my dear/my pet **3.** *F* **lapin de gouttière**, (alley) cat/moggy **4.** *F* **faire le coup du lapin à qn**, to kill s.o. (by a blow to the neck from behind) **5.** *P* **poser un lapin (à qn),** to fail to turn up/to stand s.o. up; **becqueter du lapin,** to be let down/ to be stood up **6.** *P* **un chaud lapin,** a highly-sexed man/hot stuff/ a bit of a lad/a randy sod **7.** *P* **sentir le lapin,** to smell fuggy/ sweaty. (*Voir* **peau 10**; **pet**)

lapine [lapin] *nf* **1.** *F* (*a*) **une (mère) lapine,** a woman with many children (*b*) **une mère lapine,** an over-conscientious mother/a mother hen **2.** *P* **une chaude lapine,** a highly-sexed girl*/woman*; a nympho/hot stuff; **c'est une chaude lapine,** she's a bit of all right; she'd jump into bed with anyone; she'd fall for anything in trousers **3.** *P* (*péj*) **lapine de couloir,** maid(servant); chamber-maid.

lapiner [lapine] *vi P* (*pers*) (*péj*) to keep on having children/to have one child after another/to breed like a rabbit.

lapinisme [lapinism] *nm F* **1.** (*péj*) excessive fertility (in a woman) **2.** population explosion.

lapinoche [lapinɔʃ] *nm,* **lapinski** [lapinski] *nm,* **lapinskoff** [lapinskɔf] *nm P* rabbit/bunny(-rabbit).

lapp(e) [lap] *nm & adv P* = **lap(e).**

laps [laps] *nm P* rabbit/bunny(-rabbit).

lapuche [lapyʃ] *nm & adv P* = **lap(e).**

laquépem [lakepɛm] *nm P* (*largonji de* **paquet**) packet.

larbin [larbɛ̃] *nm F* (*usu péj*) servant/flunkey; waiter (in a café).

larbine [larbin] *nf F* (*usu péj*) maid.

larbinos [larbinos] *nm P* flunkey.

lard [lar] *nm* **1.** *F* (se) **faire du lard,** to become fat (through idleness); to put on (a lot of) weight; **être gras à lard,** to be as fat as a pig **2.** *P* (*pers*) **un gros lard,** a big (fat) slob **3.** *P* **rentrer dans/sauter sur le lard**

à qn, to attack s.o./to go for s.o. **4.** *P* **prendre tout sur son lard,** to assume complete responsibility/to take the rap/to carry the can **5.** *F* **ne pas savoir si c'est du lard ou du cochon,** to be unable to tell one thing from the other/to be unable to tell butter from margarine/not to know one end of a horse from another **6.** *P* skin; **se gratter le lard,** to have a scratch; **se racler le lard,** to have a shave **7.** *P* = **lardon.** (*Voir* **saloir**)

larder [larde] *vtr P* **larder qn,** to get on s.o.'s nerves.

lardeuss(e) [lardøs] *nm,* **lardif** [lardif] *nm,* **lardingue** [lardɛ̃g] *nm P* overcoat.

lardoir [lardwar] *nm,* **lardoire** [lardwar] *nm F* **1.** sword **2.** knife/chiv.

lardon [lardɔ̃] *nm P* young child*/ kid/brat; **faire un lardon,** to have a baby (boy).

lardoss(e) [lardos] *nm P* overcoat.

lardu [lardy] *nm P* **1.** police station* **2.** police superintendent **3.** policeman*; **les lardus,** the police*/ the cops/the fuzz.

larfeuil(le) [larfœj] *nm P* wallet.

large [larʒ] **I** *nm F* **1.** **être au large,** to be rich*/well off; **en ce moment, on n'est pas au large,** we're a bit broke/things are a little tight, at the moment **2.** **prendre le large/tirer au large,** to run away*/ to clear off/to beat it **II** *a F* **l'avoir large,** to be lucky. (*Voir* **mener**)

largement [larʒəmɑ̃] *adv F* **il en a eu largement (assez),** he's had (more than) enough.

largeot [larʒo] *a F* widish/broadish.

largeur [larʒœr] *nf F* **dans les grandes largeurs,** thoroughly/with a vengeance/in a big way.

largonji [largɔ̃ʒi] *nm O P* butchers' slang (in which words were altered by substituting **l** for the first letter and adding the original first letter and **é, em, i, oque, uche,** etc, to the end; thus **largonji** = **jargon**).

largue [larg] *nf P* prostitute*/tart.

larguer [large] *vtr P* **1.** to set (s.o.) free/to release (a prisoner, etc) **2.** to give (s.o.) up; to drop (s.o.); **tu devrais larguer cette môme,** you should chuck/ditch/dump that girl **3.** to give/to hand over (sth); to throw sth out; **j'ai largué toutes mes vieilles frusques,** I've chucked out all my old clothes. (*Voir* **amarres; voile 2**)

larme [larm] *nf F* **1. le faire aux larmes,** to cry/to turn on the waterworks; **y aller de sa (petite) larme,** to shed a little tear **2. prendre une larme de rhum dans son café,** to have a drop of rum in one's coffee.

larméleauté [larmelote] *nm P* (*largonji de marteau*) hammer.

larmichette [larmiʃɛt] *nf P* **une larmichette de rhum** (*i*) a tiny drop (*ii*) a drop more (rum); a wee dram (of rum).

larron [larɔ̃] *nm F* **s'entendre/ s'accorder comme larrons en foire,** to be as thick as thieves.

larteaumic [lartomik] *nm P* (*largonji de marteau*) hammer.

larton [lartɔ̃] *nm P* bread; **larton savonné,** white bread.

lartonnier [lartɔnje] *nm P* baker.

larve [larv] *nf F* spineless person/ wet/drip.

lasagne [lazaɲ] *nf,* **lasane** [lazan] *nf P* **1.** letter/note **2.** wallet/*NAm* bill fold.

lascar [laskar] *nm P* (fine, clever, lazy, etc) character/customer; **quel lascar!** what a lad!/he's a lad! **un rude lascar,** a tough guy/a tough customer; **c'est un drôle de lascar,** he's a queer customer/he's a bit of a rogue; **sacrés lascars, va!** you're a fine bunch!

Latin [latɛ̃] *Prn F* (= *le Quartier latin*) **le Latin,** the Latin quarter (in Paris). (*Voir* **le Quartier**)

latronpem [latrɔ̃pɛm] *nm P* (*largonji de* **patron**) boss*/chief.

latte [lat] *nf P* **1.** boot; shoe **2. un coup de latte,** a kick/a boot (up the arse/*esp NAm* ass); **filer un coup de latte (à qn),** to cadge (money off s.o.) **3. traîner ses lattes,** to be poverty-stricken/to be down and out. (*Voir* **traîne-lattes 2**) **4. marcher à côté de ses lattes,** to be penniless*/to be down on one's uppers **5.** ski **6. un deuxième latte,** a private (soldier).

latter [late] *vtr P* **1.** to kick/to boot (s.o.) **2.** to tap (s.o. for money).

lattoche [latɔʃ] *nf P* boot; shoe.

laubé, laubiche [lobe, lobiʃ] *a P* (*largonji de* **beau**) beautiful.

lauchem [loʃɛm] *a P* (*largonji de* **chaud**) hot.

lavabe [lavab] *nm F* (= *lavabo*) WC*/lavatory/loo.

lavage [lavaʒ] *nm F* **1.** pawning **2.** selling-off; **faire un lavage de . . .** , to sell off . . . (*esp* one's personal belongings or stolen goods) **3. lavage de cerveau,** brainwashing **4.** = **lavasse.** (*Voir* **tête 7**)

lavasse [lavas] *nf F* (*boisson*) tasteless stuff/dishwater/catlap; **du café! c'est de la lavasse!** (you call that) coffee! it's dishwater!/it's gnat's piss!

lavdu [lavdy] *a&nm P* = **lavedu.**

lavé [lave] *a P* penniless*/cleaned out/broke.

lavedu [lavdy] *P* **I** *a* (*a*) rotten/ lousy (*b*) ugly **II** *nm* (*a*) victim of a swindle/fall guy; mug/sucker (*b*) fool*/idiot/clot.

lavement [lavmã] *nm P* **1.** (*chose ou pers*) bore*/drag **2. partir**

comme un lavement, to run away*/ to be off like a shot.

laver [lave] *vtr* **1.** *F* to launder (money); **laver un chèque,** to forge a cheque (by altering it) **2.** *F* to sell (cheap or at a loss)/to sell off (*esp* one's own belongings or stolen goods)/to turn (sth) into cash **3.** *F* **se laver le bout du nez,** to give oneself a cat's lick **4.** *V* (*fellation*) **se laver les dents,** to give (a man) a blow-job/head. (*Voir* **pied 15**; **tête 7**)

lavette [lavɛt] *nf P* **1.** tongue **2.** spineless person/drip/washout/ wimp; **son mari, c'est une vraie lavette,** her husband's a real drip.

laveur [lavœr] *nm P* receiver (of stolen goods)/fence.

lavure [lavyr] *nf F* **lavure (de vaisselle) = lavasse.**

laxé [lakse] *nm P* **1.** 100-franc note. (*Voir* **lacsé 2**) **2.** linen.

laxon [laksɔ̃] *nm P* linen.

lazagne [lazaɲ] *nf,* **lazane** [lazan] *nf P* = **lasa(g)ne.**

lazaro [lazaro] *nm P* (*a*) prison* (*b*) prison cell (*c*) cell in a police station.

laziloffe [laziləf] *a&nm P* = **lazziloffe.**

lazingue [lazɛ̃g] *nm P* = **lasa(g)ne.**

lazziloffe [laziləf] *P* **I** *a* syphilitic/poxy/siffy **II** *nm* syphilis*/syph.

leaubé, leaubiche [lobe, lobiʃ] *a P* = **laubé, laubiche.**

léchage [leʃaʒ] *nm F* **léchage de vitrines,** window-shopping.

léchard, arde [leʃar, -ard] *n P* flatterer*/bum-licker/arse-crawler/ *NAm* ass-crawler.

lèche [lɛʃ] *nf P* **la lèche,** flattery*/ arse-licking/*NAm* ass-licking; **faire (de) la lèche à qn,** to flatter* s.o./to suck up to s.o.; to lick s.o.'s boots/ s.o.'s arse/*NAm* s.o.'s ass.

léché [leʃe] *a F* **c'est du travail léché,** that's a good job done/a careful job.

lèche-bottes [lɛʃbɔt] *nm inv P* flatterer*/bootlicker/toady.

lèche-carreaux [lɛʃkaro] *nm F* = **lèche-vitrines.**

lèche-cul, lèche-motte [lɛʃky, -mɔt] *nm inv V* flatterer*/ arse-licker/*NAm* ass-licker.

lécher [leʃe] **I** *vtr F* **1.** il s'en léchait les doigts/les pouces/les babines, he smacked his lips/licked his chops over it **2.** lécher les vitrines, to go window-shopping. (*Voir* **devanture 1**) **3.** lécher les bottes/les genoux/les pieds à qn, to lick s.o.'s boots/to creep; *V* **lécher le cul à qn,** to suck up to s.o.; to arse-lick/*NAm* to ass-lick (s.o.). (*Voir* **amygdales 1**) **II** *vpr* **se lécher** *F* to kiss.

lèche-train [lɛʃtrɛ̃] *nm inv P* flatterer*/arse-licker/*NAm* ass-licker/toady.

lécheur, euse [leʃœr, -øz] *n P* lécheur (de bottes), flatterer*/bootlicker/*esp NAm* apple-polisher.

lèche-vitrines [lɛʃvitrin] *nm F* window-shopping; **faire du lèche-vitrines,** to go window-shopping.

lecture [lɛktyr] *nf P* (*prostituée*) **être en lecture,** to be with a client/ to be on the job.

légionnaire [leʒɔnɛr] *nm P* bottle of red wine.

légitime [leʒitim] *nf P* **ma légitime,** my wife*/the missis/the boss.

légobiffin [legobifɛ̃] *nm* (*mil*) *P* soldier of the Foreign Legion; legionary. (*Voir* **biffin 2**)

légume [legym] *nf P* **1.** (grosse) légume, important person*/VIP/ bigwig/big shot; (*mil*) high-ranking officer; **les grosses légumes,** the top people; (*mil*) the top brass/the brass hats **2.** **perdre ses légumes** (*i*) (*femme*) to have a period* (*ii*) to be incontinent/to wet oneself (with fright).

légumier [legymje] *nm* P VIP's car.

lentilles [lãtij] *nfpl* 1. P eyes* 2. V **mangeuse de lentilles**, lesbian*. (*Voir* **couloir** 2; **éplucheur, euse** 2)

Léon [leɔ̃] *Prnm* F **vas-y, Léon!** have a go, Joe!

lerche [lɛrʃ], **lerchem** [lɛrʃɛm], **lerchot** [lɛrʃo] P I *adv* **il n'y avait pas lerche de crème sur le gâteau**, there wasn't much cream on the cake; **c'est pas lerche**, that's not much; **y en a pas lerche**, there isn't much (of it) II *a* dear/expensive/pric(e)y; **une brique pour ça, c'est lerche**, a million for that, it's a bit much/that's a bit steep.

lesbombe [lɛsbɔ̃b] *nf* A P prostitute*.

lésé(e) [leze] *nf* A P woman*; *esp* wife *or* mistress of a pimp*.

lessivage [lɛsivaʒ] *nm* F 1. selling-off. (*Voir* **lavage** 2) 2. **lessivage de crâne**, brainwashing.

lessive [lɛsiv] *nf* F 1. selling-off. (*Voir* **lavage** 2) 2. heavy loss (at cards, etc)/clean-out 3. (*esp pol*) purge/clean-up 4. **une lessive pour les prisonniers politiques**, an amnesty for political prisoners.

lessivé [lɛsive] *a* 1. F ruined (financially)/cleaned out/taken to the cleaner's; **je me suis fait lessiver au poker**, I got cleaned out at poker 2. P exhausted*/completely washed out/shattered/dead beat.

lessiver [lɛsive] *vtr* F 1. to sell/to flog 2. (*fin*) to launder money 3. (*a*) to polish off (an opponent); **se faire lessiver**, to get licked (*b*) to kill* (s.o.)/to wipe (s.o.) out 4. to ruin (financially)/to clean (s.o.) out/to take (s.o.) to the cleaner's; **être lessivé** (*i*) to lose one's shirt (on a horse, etc) (*ii*) to be out of the running. (*Voir* **tête** 7)

lessiveur [lɛsivœr] *nm* P receiver (of stolen goods)/fence. (*Voir* **laveur**)

lessiveuse [lɛsivøz] *nf* P 1. steam locomotive 2. machine-gun.

se lester [səlɛste] *vpr* F **se lester (l'estomac)**, to eat* heartily/to have a good feed/to stuff oneself.

lettre [lɛtr] *nf* F 1. **faire des lettres/être en lettres**, to study arts subjects 2. **passer comme une lettre à la poste**, to go smoothly/without any problems/without a hitch/like clockwork. (*Voir* **cinq** 4)

leudé [lœde] *nm* P two-franc coin.

leur [lœr] *nm* F **ils continuent à faire des leurs**, they're still getting up to their old tricks; **ils ont encore fait des leurs**, they've been up to their old tricks again. (*Voir* **sienne** 1)

leur(s)zig(ue)s [lœrzig] *pron* P they/them/themselves.

levage [ləvaʒ] *nm* P picking up (of man or woman in the street, etc); (*prostituée*) **faire un levage**, to make a pick-up/to get a trick.

lever [ləve] I *vtr* P 1. to arrest* (s.o.)/to pick (s.o.) up/to run s.o. in 2. to steal*/to lift 3. **lever un mec**, (*femme*) to pick up a bloke/guy (in the street, in a bar, etc); (*prostituée*) to make a pick-up/to get a trick; (*homme*) **lever une femme**, to pick up/to get off with/to make out with a woman. (*Voir* **ancre**; **coude** 3; **jambe** 17; **pied**) II *vi* P to have an erection*; **quand je vois ses miches, je lève**, I get a hard-on when I see her tits.

leveur [ləvœr] *nm* P thief*/tea leaf.

leveuse [ləvøz] *nf* P prostitute*.

levrette [ləvrɛt] *nf* V **baiser qn en levrette**, to have sex*/to make it doggie-fashion/doggie-style (with s.o.).

lévrier [levrije] *nm* F police spy/sleuth/bloodhound.

levure [ləvyr] *nf* P **se faire la levure**, to run away*/to make a quick exit/to do a bunk.

lézard [lezar] *nm F* **1.** idler/lounger/layabout **2. faire le lézard/prendre un bain de lézard** = **lézarder 2.**

lézarder [lezarde] *vi F* **1.** to idle/to laze about/to lounge about **2.** to sunbathe/to bask in the sun/to soak up the sun.

liard [ljar] *nm O F* **1. il n'a pas un (rouge) liard,** he's penniless*; he hasn't a halfpenny to his name **2. couper un liard en deux/en quatre,** to be very stingy/tightfisted.

Liban [libã] *nm P (drogues)* Lebanese hashish*/Leb.

lichailler [liʃaje] *vi P* to drink*/to tipple/to booze.

lichard [liʃar] *nm P* tippler.

liche [liʃ] *nf P* nip/wee dram/snort/snifter.

lichedu [liʃdy] *nm P* **1.** nasty piece of work/bastard* **2.** policeman*.

licher [liʃe] *P* **I** *vtr* **1.** to lick; to slobber; **se licher la gueule,** to kiss/to snog **2.** to knock back (a drink, etc) **II** *vi* to drink* heavily/to booze/to tipple.

lichette [liʃɛt] *nf P* thin, small slice (of bread, meat, etc)/nibble/taste.

licheur, -euse [liʃœr, -øz] *n O P* heavy drinker/tippler/boozer.

lichoter [liʃote] *vi P* to drink*/to tipple/to booze.

lieute [ljøt] *nm F (mil, marine, etc)* lieutenant/lieut.

lieux [ljø] *nmpl F* WC*; **où sont les lieux?** where's the loo/*NAm* the bathroom?

lièvre [ljɛvr] *nm* **1.** *F* **il a une mémoire de lièvre,** he's got a memory like a sieve **2.** *F* **c'est vous qui avez levé le lièvre,** you started it **3.** *F* **c'est là que gît le lièvre,** that's the crucial point/the crux of the matter **4.** *F* **prendre le lièvre au gîte,** to catch s.o. napping **5.** *F* **courir deux/plusieurs lièvres à la fois,** to try to do two things/too many things at once **6.** *F* **nous courons le même lièvre,** we're both after the same thing **7.** *P (femme)* easy lay/pushover **8.** *F (courses, etc)* front runner/pacemaker; **il a fait le lièvre sur le 1er tour,** he set the pace on the first lap.

ligedu [liʒdy] *nm P* = **lichedu 1, 2.**

lignard [liɲar] *nm O F* **1.** *(mil)* infantryman/footslogger **2.** hack writer/penny-a-liner.

ligne [liɲ] *nf* **1.** *F (journaliste, écrivain)* **tirer à la ligne,** to pad out an article **2.** *F* **c'est dans ma ligne!** that's right up my street! **c'est bien dans sa ligne!** that's him all over! **3.** *P (drogues)* cocaine* (arranged in lines *or* strips and taken up by means of a tube).

ligodu [ligɔdy], **ligoduji** [ligɔdyʒi] *adv & int P (peu usuel)* yes/OK.

ligote [ligɔt] *nf P* (length of) cord/rope *(esp* for tying s.o. up).

ligoter [ligɔte] *vtr P* to read.

lili-pioncette [lilipjõsɛt] *nf P (drogues)* morphine*/Aunt Emma.

limace [limas] *nf P* **1.** shirt/dicky dirt **2.** *(péj)* woman*/bit of skirt/bit of fluff **3.** *pl* **limaces,** lips.

limande [limãd] *nf* **1.** *P* slap in the face **2.** *P* prostitute* **3.** *F (femme)* **être plate comme une limande,** to be as flat as a pancake/as a board **4.** *F* **faire la limande,** to bow and scrape/to crawl/to kowtow **5.** *P (motos)* **rouler en limande,** to ride crouched forwards on one's bike.

limasse [limas] *nf,* **lime** [lim] *nf P* = **limace 1.**

limé [lime] *a&pp F* **un (verre de) blanc limé,** (a glass of) white wine diluted with lemonade.

limer [lime] **I** *vtr&i V (homme)* **limer (qn),** to have sex* (with s.o.)/to grind/to have a bit of in and

out/to get one's end away **II** *vpr*
se limer *V* to masturbate*/to jack
off/to jerk off.

limier [limje] *nm F* sleuth/blood-
hound.

limogeage [limɔʒaʒ] *nm F* (*a*)
(*mil*) superseding/bowler-hatting (of
a senior officer) (*b*) dismissal (of a
government official, etc).

limoger [limɔʒe] *vtr F* (*a*) (*mil*) to
supersede (a senior officer)/to
bowler-hat (s.o.) (*b*) to dismiss (a
government official, etc).

limonade [limɔnad] *nf* **1.** *F* être
dans la limonade (*i*) to be in a fix*
(*ii*) to keep a (small) bar/to be in
the (drinks) trade **2.** *P* tomber
dans la limonade, to fall into the
water/into the drink.

limonadier [limɔnadje] *nm F* pub-
lican/bar-keeper/keeper of a small
pub.

limouse, limouze [limuz] *nf P*
1. shirt **2.** file (for smoothing
metal).

linge [lɛ̃ʒ] *nm F* **1.** (il) faut laver
son linge sale en famille, don't wash
your dirty linen in public **2.** avoir
du linge (*i*) to be well-dressed/to
have a good wardrobe (*ii*) to be
well-off **3.** du beau linge (*i*) a
good-looker/a bit of all right (*ii*)
fashionable society/(the) jet set.

lingé [lɛ̃ʒe] *a F* être bien lingé, to
be well-dressed.

linger [lɛ̃ʒe] **I** *vtr F* to dress/to rig
out **II** *vpr* se linger *F* to get
dressed up*/togged up.

lingre [lɛ̃gr] *nm P* (*a*) knife/razor
(used as an offensive weapon)/chiv
(*b*) (surgeon's) scalpel.

lingue [lɛ̃g] *nm P* **1.** = lingre **2.**
(= lingot) gold bar/ingot.

linguer [lɛ̃ge] *vtr P* to stab (s.o.)
with a knife or razor.

linguot [lɛ̃go] *nm P* = lingre.

lino [lino] **I** *nm F* linoleum/lino

II *F* (*a*) *nf* Linotype (machine) (*b*)
nm&f Linotype operator/linotypist.

linotte [linɔt] *nf F* tête de linotte,
empty-headed/featherbrained per-
son.

lion [ljɔ̃] *nm F* avoir mangé/bouffé
du lion, to be on the rampage.

lionne [ljɔn] *nf F* une lionne, a
fashionable woman.

lipper [lipe] *vi O P* **1.** to eat* **2.**
to drink.

liquette [likɛt] *nf P* shirt/dicky
dirt.

liquider [likide] *vtr* **1.** *F* to get
rid of (s.o.) **2.** *P* to kill* (s.o.)/to
liquidate (s.o.)/to wipe (s.o.) out; se
faire liquider, to get done in/
bumped off.

lisbroquer [lisbrɔke] *vi P* to uri-
nate*/to (have a) piss.

Lisette [lizɛt] *Prnf F* pas de ça,
Lisette! (let's have) none of that!/
come off it!

lispoquer [lispɔke] *vi P* = lisbroquer.

lisse [lis] *a P* être lisse, to be a
fool*.

lissépem [lisepɛm] *vi P* (*largonji
de* pisser) to urinate*/to piss/to
pee.

lisses [lis] *nfpl P* stockings; lisses
en soie noire, black silk stockings.

litanies [litani] *nfpl F* (*aéronau-
tique*) checklist; débiter les litanies,
to run through the checklist.

litron [litrɔ̃] *nm P* litre (of wine); il
ne tient pas son litron, he can't take
his drink/he can't hold his liquor.

lixdré [liksdre] *a&nm P* (*largonji de*
dix) ten.

lobé [lɔbe] *am P* good-looking. (*Voir*
laubé)

locdu [lɔkdy] *a&n P* = loquedu.

loche [lɔʃ] **I** *nm or f P* (*a*) taxi-
driver/cabby (*b*) taxi/cab **II** *nf P*
= loque 1 **III** *nf P* ear*.

loco [lɔko] *nf F* (*abbr* = locomotive)

engine/loco; **faire la loco,** to smoke like a chimney.

lof [lɔf] *nm F* **revenir au lof,** to give in/to knuckle under.

loffe [lɔf] *a F* = **loufoque I.**

loffiat [lɔfja] *nm P* = **louf(f)iat II.**

loge [lɔʒ] *nf F* **être aux premières loges,** to have a ringside seat/to have a grandstand view.

loger [lɔʒe] *vtr P (police)* to track (s.o.) down. (*Voir* **enseigne**)

loi [lwa] *nf F* **1. avoir la loi** (*i*) to have the upper hand (*ii*) to get the best of it **2. faire la loi,** to lay down the law; **les enfants ne font pas la loi ici!** kids don't run this place!

loific [lwafik] *nm P (largonji de* **foie**) liver.

à loilpé [alwalpe], **à loilpuche** [alwalpyʃ] *a phr P (largonji de* **à poil**) naked*/starkers.

loinqué [lwɛ̃ke] **I** *adv P* far off/a long way away **II** *nm P (largonji de* **coin**) corner.

lolo [lolo] *nm* **1.** *F (mot enfantin)* milk **2.** *F* **c'est du lolo!** it's nice! **3.** *P pl* lolos, breasts*/tits/Bristols/ milk bottles/jugs. (*Voir* **boîte 6**)

loloches [lɔlɔʃ] *nmpl P* breasts*/ milk bottles/tits/Bristols. (*Voir* **soutien-loloches**)

long, longue [lɔ̃, lɔ̃g] *F* **I** *a* **les avoir longues** (*i*) to be ravenously hungry* (*ii*) to be extremely ambitious **II** *adv phr* **de longue,** uninterruptedly/on end **II** *nm* **1.** cigar **2. avoir les côtes en long,** to be extremely (*i*) lazy (*ii*) tired **3. y aller de tout son long,** to go at it hammer and tongs. (*Voir* **bras 2; jour 1; nez**)

longe [lɔ̃ʒ] **I** *nf P* year (of prison sentence); **il me reste cinq longes à tirer,** I've got five years left to do **II** *nf F* **marcher sur sa longe,** to get into a fix*/to get (all) tied up.

longuet, -ette [lɔ̃gɛ, -ɛt] *a F*

rather long/longish (book, time, etc); (a bit) on the long side.

longueur [lɔ̃gœr] *nf F* **être sur la même longueur d'ondes,** to be on the same wavelength; **être sur une autre longueur d'ondes,** to be way off beam/to be way out.

lopaille [lɔpɑj] *nf,* **lopart** [lɔpar] *nm,* **lope** [lɔp] *nf,* **lopette** [lɔpɛt] *nf P* **1.** bastard*/nasty piece of work/*NAm* son of a bitch; **sale petite lope,** dirty little bugger **2.** (*i*) homosexual*/pansy/queer/ *NAm* fag(got) (*ii*) coward*; **cette lopette s'est carapatée dès le début de la bagarre,** the little poofter pissed off as soon as the fighting started.

loque [lɔk] *nf* **1.** *F (pers)* **être comme une loque,** to be as limp as/ to feel like a wet rag **2.** *pl P* loques, clothes*/clobber/gear.

loqué [lɔke] *a P* dressed/togged up.

loquedu [lɔkdy] *P* **I** *a* worthless*/rotten **II** *nm* **1.** (*a*) good-for-nothing/layabout/bum (*b*) mean(-looking)/dangerous *or* unpleasant man; bastard*/louse/ *NAm* son of a bitch **2.** *O* mad*/ bonkers/crackers.

loquer [lɔke] **I** *vtr P* to dress **II** *vpr* **se loquer** *P* to get dressed/to put one's clothes on.

lorgne [lɔrɲ] *nf P (cartes)* ace.

lot [lo] *nm* **1.** *F* **gagner/décrocher le gros lot,** to strike it lucky; to hit the jackpot **2.** *P (fille, femme)* **un beau petit lot,** a dish/a bit of all right/a nice bit of stuff.

loto [lɔto, lo-] *nm F* **rouler/ribouler des lotos,** to roll one's eyes (in amazement)/to goggle. (*Voir* **boule 7**)

loubac [lubak] *a A P* mad*/ bonkers.

loubar(d) [lubar] *nm P* (young) hooligan*/yob/yobbo/thug; rocker; **des loubards de banlieue,** (young) thugs/hooligans (often on motorbikes) who terrorize people in the suburbs/= hell's angels/bikers.

loubarde [lubard] *nf F* = **loupiot(t)e²**.

loubé [lube] *nm P* (*largonji de* **bout**) **1.** a small amount/a wee bit/a smidgen **2. mettre les loubés,** to run away*/to clear off.

loubiats [lubja] *nmpl P* beans.

(en) loucedé [ãlusde], **(en) loucedoc** [ãlusdɔk] *adv phr P* (*largonji de* **en douce**) on the quiet/on the q.t./on the sly; **lorgner qn en loucedoc,** to eye s.o. up/to give s.o. the glad eye.

louchante [luʃɑ̃t] *nf P* the moon.

louche [luʃ] *nf P* hand*/flipper/mitt/paw; **serrer la louche à qn,** to shake hands with s.o.; **filer la louche à qn,** to give s.o. a helping hand/to lend a hand; **mettre la louche au panier,** to feel up/to touch up (a woman).

louchébem, louchébème [luʃebɛm] *nm P* = **loucherbem 1, 2.**

loucher [luʃe] *vi F* **loucher vers/sur qch,** to look longingly at sth/to have one's eyes on sth/to eye sth (up).

loucherbem, loucherbème [luʃebɛm] *nm P* **1.** butcher **2.** form of **largonji,** but more complex.

louchon, -onne [luʃɔ̃, -ɔn] *n P* **1.** cross-eyed person; squint-eyes **2. la louchonne,** the moon.

louf [luf], **loufetingue** [luftɛg] *a F* = **loufoque I.**

louffe [luf] *nf P* fart; **lâcher une louffe,** to (let out a) fart*.

louf(f)er [lufe] *vi P* to (let out a) fart*.

louf(f)iat [lufja] *nm* **1.** *P* waiter (in a café) **2.** *P* rotter; boor; slob **3.** *F* (*marine*) lieutenant.

loufoque [lufɔk] *F* **I** *a* (*pers*) mad*/cracked/bonkers/a bit

touched (in the head)/nuts; (*histoire, etc*) crazy/daft **II** *nm&f* crackpot/crank/screwball/nut/nutter.

loufoquerie [lufɔkri] *nf F* (*a*) eccentricity; barminess/craziness (*b*) crackbrained action/crazy thing to do.

louftingue [luftɛg] *a F* = **loufoque I.**

louise [lwiz] *nf P* **lâcher une louise,** to (let out a) fart*.

louisette [lwizɛt] *nf F* the guillotine.

Louis-Quinze [lwikɛz] **I** *Prn F* **avoir des jambes Louis-Quinze,** to have bandy legs/to be bandy(-legged) **II** *nf P* **une Louis-Quinze** (*i*) mistress/lover (*ii*) prostitute*.

loulou, loulout(t)e [lulu, -ut] **I** *nm&f F* dear/darling*/love **II** *nm P* (*a*) bastard*/nasty piece of work (*b*) yob(bo)/hooligan*; **je me suis fait volé par une bande de loulous,** I was robbed/mugged by a gang of thugs.

loup [lu] *nm* **1.** *F* **mon petit loup! mon gros loup!** my darling!*/my pet!/my love! **2.** *F* (*a*) mistake*/miscalculation (*b*) **ça marche pas, y a un loup quelque part,** there must be something wrong (with it) because it isn't working **3.** *F* (*théâtre*) fluff/fluffed entrance **4.** *F* **un vieux loup de mer,** an old sea-dog/an old salt **5.** *P* **elle a vu le loup** (*i*) she knows a thing or two (*ii*) she's lost her virginity*/her cherry; she's fallen off the apple tree. (*Voir* **péter**)

loupage [lupaʒ] *nm F* (*a*) bungling (*b*) botched work (*c*) flaw/defect.

loupague [lupag], **loupaque** [lupak] *nm A P* louse/cootie.

loup-cervier [lusɛrvje] *nm O F* profiteer/shark. (*pl* **loups-cerviers**)

loupe [lup] *nf F* **1.** (*a*) bungling/botching (*b*) defect/flaw **2.** idleness/laziness/slackness.

loupé [lupe] *F* **I** *a* (*a*) botched/ bungled (work) (*b*) (*machine, etc*) defective (*c*) (*fichu*) **pas besoin de s'en faire, c'est loupé,** there's no point in getting all het up about it, it's up the spout **II** *nm* (*a*) slip/ mistake* (*b*) defect/flaw.

loupel [lupɛl] *nm,* **loupenne** [lupɛn] *nm P =* **loupague.**

louper [lupe] *F* **I** *vi* to misfire; to go haywire; **ça n'a pas loupé,** that didn't miss; that hit the mark/that must've gone home **II** *vtr* (*a*) to bungle*/to botch (a piece of work); to make a mess of sth; **il a loupé son coup,** he botched it/he messed it up (*b*) to miss (one's turn/train/ opportunity); to fail/to flunk (exam); (*théâtre*) to fluff (one's lines, entrance); (*aviation*) **louper son atterrissage,** to crashland; **cette affaire m'a fait louper les vacances,** that business put paid to/messed up/wrecked my holidays. (*Voir* **coche 1; commande 5**)

loupeur, -euse [lupœr, -øz] *n F* bungler/botcher.

loupiau [lupjo] *nm,* **loupiot, - iot(t)e¹** [lupjo, -jɔt] *n F* small child*/brat/kid.

loupiot(t)e² *nf F* (*a*) small light; torch; flash-light (*b*) electric light (bulb).

lourd [lur] **I** *a F* **avoir le bras lourd,** to be rich*/loaded **II** *adv F* **il n'en reste pas lourd,** there's not much left/there aren't many left; **je ne donnerais pas lourd de ...,** I wouldn't give much for ...; **gagner lourd,** to earn good money; **je ne suis pas payé lourd,** I'm not paid much **III** *nm* **1.** *F* fool*/ idiot/clot/nitwit **2.** *P* peasant*/ yokel/hick **3.** *P* (*drogues*) opium*/ mud.

lourde [lurd] *nf P* **1.** door; **boucler la lourde,** to shut the door; **casser la lourde/mettre la lourde en dedans,** to burgle/*NAm* to burglar- ize/to break in; **mettre qn à la lourde,** to show s.o. the door/to kick s.o. out **2.** strong drug/pow- erful narcotic.

lourder [lurde] *vtr P* **1.** to shut (a door) **2. lourder qn** (*i*) to show s.o. the door/to throw s.o. out/to kick s.o. out (*ii*) to dismiss* s.o./to give s.o. the push.

lourdeur [lurdœr] *nm P* burglar/ house-breaker.

lourdier, -ière [lurdje, -jɛr] *n P* doorkeeper/concierge/caretaker.

lourdingue [lurdɛ̃g] *a P* **1.** stu- pid*/thick/dim **2.** (*a*) heavy; **c'est drôlement lourdingue à trimbal(l)er,** it's bloody heavy to lug around (*b*) **en avoir lourdingue sur la con- science,** to have a load on one's mind.

(en) lousdé [ɑ̃lusde], **(en) lousdoc** [ɑ̃lusdɔk] *adv phr P =* **(en) loucedé, (en) loucedoc.**

loustic [lustik] *nm F* **1.** joker/ comedian; **faire le loustic,** to fool around/to act the goat **2.** bloke/ *esp NAm* guy; **c'est un drôle de loustic,** he's a strange character; he's an oddball; he's a funny bloke/*esp NAm* guy.

loute [lut] *nf F =* **louloute.**

lovés [love] *nmpl P* money*/loot/ bread.

luc [lyk] *nm P* (*inversion de* **cul**) (*i*) anus* (*ii*) buttocks*.

le Lucal [ləlykal], **le Luco** [ləlyko] *Prn F* the Luxembourg gar- dens (in Paris).

lucarne [lykarn] *nf* **1.** (*a*) *P* eye*/ peeper (*b*) *V* **lucarne enchantée,** anus*/round eye **2.** *P* monocle.

luisant [lɥizɑ̃] *nm A P* **1. le luisant,** the sun **2.** *pl* **luisants,** pat- ent leather shoes.

luisante [lɥizɑ̃t] *nf P A* **la luisante,** the moon.

luisard [lɥizar] *nm A P* **le luisard,** the sun.

luisarde [lɥizard] *nf A P* **la luisarde,** the moon.

lundi [lœ̃di] *nm F* **faire/fêter le lundi,** to take Monday off; **faire lundi,** to take the day off. (*Voir* **Saint-Lundi**)

lune [lyn] *nf* **1.** *P* buttocks*/bum/ NAm* butt; **faire voir la lune (en plein jour),** to show one's buttocks/ to moon **2.** *F* whim; mood; **il est dans une bonne lune,** he's in one of his good moods **3.** *F* **avoir (un quartier de) la lune dans la tête,** to be mad*/loony/moonstruck **4.** *F* **être dans la lune,** to be starry-eyed/ to be wool-gathering/to be miles away/to be day-dreaming/to have one's head in the clouds **5.** *F* **tomber de la lune,** to be unaware of what's going on/to look blank **6.** *F* **faire voir la lune à qn en plein midi/en plein soleil,** to fool s.o./to lead s.o. up the garden path **7.** *F* **je vous parie la lune que ...,** I bet you anything you like that ... **8.** *P* **elle a vu la lune** (*i*) she knows a thing or two (*ii*) she has lost her virginity*/her cherry **9.** *V* **se faire taper dans la lune,** to be sodomised/to get one's ass fucked. (*Voir* **chevalier 4; con II** (*a*))

luné [lyne] *a F* **être bien/mal luné,** to be in a good/bad mood.

lunette [lynɛt] *nf P* **mettre la tête à la lunette,** to be guillotined.

luron [lyrɔ̃] *nm F* **c'est un gai/un joyeux luron,** he's one of the lads; he's a bit of a lad; he's quite a lad.

luronne [lyrɔn] *nf F* (*a*) strapping girl (*b*) tomboy; **c'est une luronne,** she's not a bit shy (of men)/she's not backward in coming forward.

lustucru [lystykry] *nm F* **1.** fool*/simpleton/nurd **2. (le père) Lustucru,** the bogeyman.

lutainpème [lytɛ̃pɛm] *nf A P* (*largonji de* **putain**) prostitute*.

luttanche [lytɑ̃ʃ] *nf P* (*a*) wrestling (*b*) contest/fight/struggle.

M

M [ɛm] *nf P* **1.** (= **merde**) turd/crap **2.** (*drogues*) morphine*/shit.

maboul, -oule [mabul] *P* **I** *a* mad*/crazy/nuts/round the bend/bonkers **II** *n* loony/nut(ter)/crackpot.

maboulisme [mabulism] *nm*, **maboulite** [mabulit] *nf P* madness.

mac [mak] *nm P* **1.** pimp*/ponce/mack **2.** boss/governor/guv.

macab [makab] *nm P* corpse*/stiff. (*Voir* **macchab(e)**)

macache [makaʃ] *int O P* (c'est) macache (et midi sonné)!/macache bonnot! not (bloody) likely*!/no fear!/nothing doing!/not on your Nellie!

macadam [makadam] *nm P* **1.** fleur de macadam, prostitute*/streetwalker; faire le macadam, to solicit*/to walk the streets/to be on the game **2.** faire/piquer un macadam, to feign/to fake an accident (in order to claim insurance, etc).

macadamiste [makadamist] *nm&f P* s.o. who fakes an accident (in order to claim insurance, etc).

macaron [makarɔ̃] *nm* **1.** *F* (*a*) rosette (of a decoration) (*b*) (*insigne*) badge (on official car) **2.** (*voiture*) steering wheel; manier le macaron, to take the wheel **3.** *P* blow*/punch/clout; filer un macaron à qn, to clout s.o.

macaroni [makarɔni] *nm* **1.** *F* rambling speech **2.** *P* Italian*/Eyetie/wop **3.** *V* penis*; s'allonger le macaroni, to masturbate* **4.** *P*

telephone wire/spaghetti **5.** *pl P* macaronis, long, thin legs*.

macchab(e) [makab] *nm*, **mac(c)habée** [makabe] *nm P* corpse*/stiff. (*Voir* **chahuteur II** (*b*); **trottinette 2**)

mâcher [maʃe] *vtr F* **1.** mâcher de haut, to eat without appetite **2.** mâcher à vide, to live on daydreams. (*Voir* **frein**)

machin [maʃɛ̃] *n* **1.** *F* (*a*) (*pers*) (monsieur, madame) Machin, (Mr, Mrs) what's-his-name/what's-her-name/what-d'you-call-him/ what-d'you-call-her; machin, Thingum(m)ybob/thingy (*b*) (*thg*) what's-its-name*/thing(amy)/whatcha-(ma)callit/whatsit; contraption/gadget (*c*) (*péj*) vieux machin, old fogey*; espèce de vieux machin! you old fool! **2.** *P* penis*/tool/thingy/instrument.

machin-chose [maʃɛ̃ʃoz] *nm*, **machin-chouette** [maʃɛ̃ʃwɛt] *nm F* = **machin** (*b*).

machine [maʃin] *nf* **1.** *F* thing/gadget/contraption **2.** *F* (*fille, femme*) what's-her-name/what-d'you-call-her/thingy **3.** *F* machine à confetti, ticket punch **4.** vehicle/plane/bike/machine **5.** *P* (*a*) (*livre*) publication (*b*) (*pièce, film, etc*) production/show **6.** *P* machine à coudre/à percer/à secouer le paletot, machine-gun; tommy-gun **7.** *pl V* machines, testicles*. (*Voir* **bosseler; raccourcir**)

machiner [maʃine] *vi F* to do/to be up to; qu'est-ce que tu

machines? what are you up to/
cooking up?

machinette [maʃinɛt] *nf P* pickpocket*.

machin-truc [maʃɛ̃tryk] *nm F* =
machin (*b*). (*Voir* **truc**)

mâchon [mɑʃɔ̃] *nm P* big meal/
blow-out/tuck-in.

machotte [matʃɔt] *nf P* active
homosexual*.

mâchouiller [mɑʃuje] *F* **I** *vtr&i*
to eat without appetite **II** *vtr* to
chew away at (sth).

mâchuré [mɑʃyre] *a P* drunk*.

se mâchurer [səmɑʃyre] *vpr P* to
get drunk*.

macque [mak] *nf,* **macquesée**
[makze] *nf P* (woman) brothel
owner; madam(e).

macreuse [makrøz] *nf F* **avoir du
sang de macreuse,** to be cool, calm
and collected.

macrotin [makrɔtɛ̃] *nm P* (=
maquereautin) young pimp*.

madame [madam] *nf F* **1.**
(woman) brothel owner/madam(e)
2. jouer à la madame, to put on
airs (and graces).

madame-pipi [madampipi] *nf P*
(lady) WC*/lavatory attendant.
(*Voir* **pipi 1** (*a*))

Madeleine [madlɛn] *Prn F* **pleurer
comme une Madeleine,** to cry one's
eyes out/to cry buckets.

maganer [magane] *vtr FrC P* **1.**
to beat (s.o.) up*/to work (s.o.)
over/to do (s.o.) in **2.** to damage/
to bash (up)/to prang (a car).

magase, magaze [magaz] *nm P*
shop/store.

(se) magner [s(ə)maɲe] *vtr&pr P*
**se magner (le derche/le derrière/les
fesses/le mou/le popotin/la ron-
delle/le train),** to hurry* up/to get
a move on/to get cracking/to pull
one's finger out.

magnes [maɲ] *nfpl P* **faire des**

magnes (*i*) to put on airs/to show
off* (*ii*) to kick up a fuss (*iii*) to
make difficulties/to put difficulties
in the way.

magnéto [maɲeto] *nm F* (=
magnétophone) tape recorder.

magnificat [magnifikat, maɲifika]
nm F **le magnificat est plus long
que les vêpres,** your slip's showing/
Charlie's dead.

mago [mago] *nm P* shop/store.

magot [mago] *nm F* savings/nest
egg/pile; **avoir un joli magot,** to
have a nice little nest egg put by;
épouser un gros magot, to marry
into money.

magouille [maguj] *nf P* (*a*) wan-
gle/shady deal(s) (*b*) wangling/
shady dealing(s)/wheeling and dealing (*c*) **il y a de la magouille,** I'm
being cheated here; s.o.'s having me
on/not playing straight.

magouiller [maguje] *vtr F* to wan-
gle/to wheel and deal/to get up to
some shady business/to (work a)
fiddle.

magouilleur [magujœr] *nm F*
wangler/shady dealer/wheeler-
dealer/fiddler.

mahomet [maɔmɛ(t)] *nm P* the
sun.

mahous(s), mahousse [maus]
a P = **maous(s), maousse.**

maigrichon, -onne [mɛgriʃɔ̃, -
ɔn], **maigriot, -otte** [mɛgrijo, -
ɔt] *a F* thin/skinny (person).

mailloche [majɔʃ] *a P* big/strong/
hefty/beefy.

main [mɛ̃] *nf* **1.** *F* **passer la main,**
to stand aside/to step down/to
make way for s.o. else **2.** *F*
homme de main, hired assassin/
hired gun **3.** *P* **faire une main
tombée à qn,** to pat s.o.'s bottom/
to touch s.o. up **4.** *P* (*prostituée*)
être en main, to be with a client/to
be on the job. (*Voir* **baladeur;
chaud I 2; doigt 1; dos 10;
malheureux 4; se moucher 1;**

palmé; panier 8; péter 9; poil 3; sac; tour I 3)

se maintenir [səmɛ̃tnir] *vpr F* **ça va? – ça se maintient,** how goes it? – so-so/not so bad/bearing up.

maire [mɛr] *nm F* **passer devant le maire,** to get married*/to get hitched.

mairie [mɛri, me-] *nf F* **se marier à la mairie du 21ᵉ (arrondissement)/se marier derrière la mairie,** to live together.

maison [mɛzɔ̃] *nf* **1.** *F* **maison close/maison (à gros numéro),** brothel*; **maison de passe,** hotel, etc, used by prostitutes and their clients/call joint; **maison d'abattage,** cheap brothel/cat-house; (*prostituée*) **travailler en maison,** to work in a licensed brothel **2.** *P* **la maison tire-bouchon/tire-bouton** (*a*) liaison between two lesbians (*b*) lesbians in general/gay women **3.** *P* exceptional; huge; first-rate; **une bagarre maison,** an almighty row/one hell of a fight; **une châtaigne maison,** a hell of a clout; **une engueulade maison,** a real ticking-off/a right ballocking; **une entourloupette maison,** a very dirty trick **4.** *F* **la (Grande) Maison** (*i*) the police* (*ii*) the headquarters of the (Paris) police/the Central Police Headquarters. (*Voir* **J't'arquepince; parapluie 5; pébroc 2; poulaga** (*c*))

mal [mal] **I** *adv F* **1. pas mal** (*i*) not (at all) bad; **il (n')est pas mal ce tableau,** this picture's quite good (*ii*) **elle n'est pas mal,** she's quite good-looking/not (at all) bad (*iii*) **je m'en fiche pas mal!** a fat lot I care! I couldn't care less! **il en était pas mal fâché,** he wasn't half cross about it/it really bugged him **2.** (*a*) **pas mal de ...,** quite a lot of .../quite a bit of .../a good deal of ...; quite a few ...; **y a pas mal de choses à faire,** there's quite a lot/a hell of a lot of things to do (*b*) **j'ai pas mal envie de rester,** I've a good mind/half a mind to stay

(*c*) **nous sommes pas mal à dîner ce soir,** we're rather a lot for dinner this evening **3. tu vas mal, toi!** you're exaggerating!/you're stretching it a bit! **4. se trouver mal sur qch,** to appropriate sth/to make off with sth. (*Voir* **blanchi**) **II** *nm* **1.** *F* **il n'y a pas de mal/***P* **y a pas d'mal,** don't mention it! **2.** *F* (*a*) **se donner un mal de chien pour faire qch,** to bend over backwards to do sth (*b*) **sans se faire de mal,** without taking too much trouble/without overdoing it.

malabar [malabar] *F* **I** *a* strapping/hefty/beefy/butch **II** *nm* hefty chap/strapping fellow/beefy guy/muscle man.

malade [malad] *a F* **1. vous voilà bien malade!** poor chap!/poor thing!/poor you! **2. t'es pas (un peu) malade?** have you gone mad*?/you must be out of your (tiny) mind!/are you off your rocker?

maladie [maladi] *nf F* **1. il en fera une maladie,** he'll have a fit (when he finds out); he's not going to be very happy about it **2. maladie de neuf mois,** pregnancy.

malaga [malaga] *nm O P* **un malaga de boueux,** a glass of red wine.

malagauche [malagoʃ], **malapatte** [malapat] *O F* **I** *a* awkward/clumsy/ham-fisted **II** *nm&f* awkward person/clumsy clot/butterfingers.

mal-baisé(e) [malbeze] *nm&f V* frustrated/badly-laid person; **les mal-baisées,** unsatisfied wives/women.

malchançard [malʃɑ̃sar] *nm F* unlucky person/unlucky blighter.

maldonne [maldɔn] *nf F* **il y a maldonne,** there's (been) a mistake somewhere; something's wrong somewhere.

mâle [mɑl] *nm V* (*femme*) **aller au mâle/prendre du mâle/se farcir du mâle,** to have sex*/to get laid.

mal-en-pattes [malɑ̃pat] *nm inv*
F **c'est un mal-en-pattes,** he's a
clumsy oaf; he's all fingers and
thumbs.

malfrappe [malfrap], **malfrat**
[malfra], **malfrin** [malfrɛ̃] *nm P*
hooligan*/thug/yob.

malheur [malœr] *nm F* **1.** (*iron*)
le beau malheur!/le grand malheur!
there's no harm in that!/what's all
the fuss about? **2. jouer de
malheur,** to be out of luck **3. (ne)
parle pas de malheur!** God forbid!/
have a heart! **4. ces formulaires de
malheur!** these blasted forms! **5.
faire un malheur** (*a*) to do something desperate; to commit murder;
se faire un malheur, to commit suicide*; **s'il entre ici je fais un
malheur!** if he comes in here I'll do
something desperate; I'll kill him;
I'll kill myself (*b*) (*théâtre, etc*) to
be a hit/a huge success.

malheureux, -euse [malœrø,
-øz] *a F* **1.** trivial/paltry; **vous
faites des histoires pour cinq
malheureux francs!** you're making
all this hoo-ha over a measly five
francs! **2. te voilà enfin, ce n'est
pas malheureux!** here you are at
last, and about time too! **3. si
c'est pas malheureux!/c'est-y pas
malheureux!** isn't it a shame!/it's a
crying shame!/it's too bad! **4.
avoir la main malheureuse** (*i*) to be
unlucky (*ii*) to be clumsy/awk-
ward/hamfisted. (*Voir* **pierre**)

malice [malis] *nf* **1.** *F* **la belle
malice!** there's nothing very clever
in that! **2.** *P* **se faire malice tout
seul,** to masturbate*. (*Voir* **sac 15**)

malin [malɛ̃] *F* **I** *a* (*a*) (*iron*) **c'est
malin!** that *is* clever (of you) (*b*)
c'est pas malin, that's not very diffi-
cult/there's nothing very clever in
that **II** *nm* (*a*) **un malin/un petit
malin/un gros malin,** a smart guy/a
smart Alec(k) (*b*) **faire le/son malin,**
to try to be clever/smart; to show
off*.

malle [mal] *nf* **1.** *P* mouth*; **ferme

ta malle! shut up!*/shut your
trap!/pack it in! **2.** *P* (*mil*) guardroom **3.** *P* **boucler sa malle,** to
die*/to snuff it **4.** *F* **faire sa
malle/ses malles,** to be at death's
door **5.** *F* **faire la malle à qn,** to
walk out on s.o./to leave s.o. in the
lurch **6.** *F* **(se) faire la malle,** to
run away*/to scarper/to do a bunk
7. *F* **porter sa malle,** to be hunch-
backed/to have a hump **8.** *F*
malle à quatre nœuds, handkerchief
containing one's savings, etc.

maller [male] *vi P* to run away*/to
scarper/to do a bunk. (*Voir* **malle
6**)

mallette [malɛt] *nf F* **1. faire mallette et paquette,** to (pack one's
bags and) clear out **2. mallette à
quatre nœuds = malle à quatre
nœuds (malle 8**).

mallouser, mallouzer
[maluze] *vi P* = **maller.**

malpoli [malpɔli] *a F* impolite.

maltouze [maltuz] *nf P* **pastiquer
la maltouze,** to smuggle.

malva [malva] *adv P* (*verlan de va
mal*) it's going badly; **aller chez
malva,** (*événement, situation*) to go
badly/to be bad; (*pers*) to be in
poor health; **il va chez malva,** he's
not doing so well/he's going to the
dogs.

mamelu, -ue [mamly] *a&n P*
(woman) with large breasts; **c'est
une grosse mamelue,** she's got huge
tits.

mamie [mami] *nf F* grandmother/
gran/grannie/granny/nana.

mamours [mamur] *nmpl F* **faire
des mamours à qn,** to fondle/to
caress s.o.; **se faire des mamours,** to
kiss and cuddle/*O* to canoodle/to
bill and coo.

manchard [mɑ̃ʃar] *nm P* beggar.

manche [mɑ̃ʃ] **I** *nm F* **1.** *P* fool*;
c'est un manche, he's a (clumsy)
clot/a twit; **il raisonne comme un
manche,** he can't think straight; **il

conduit comme un manche (à couilles), he's a hopeless driver; he can't drive for toffee/for nuts; il se débrouille/s'y prend comme un manche, he goes about things in a cockeyed/hamfisted way. (*Voir* dégourdi (*b*)) 2. *F* manche à balai (*i*) tall, thin person/beanpole (*ii*) (*avions*) joystick (*iii*) con comme un manche à balai, as daft as a brush/ a real twit/a real jerk 3. *F* être du côté du manche, to be on the strongest/the winning side 4. *F* tomber sur un/le manche, to come up against/to hit a snag 5. *V* avoir le manche, to have an erection*/a stiff(y)/a rod. (*Voir* astiquer 4; branler I) II *nf F* (*a*) *coll* la manche, beggars (*b*) faire la manche, to beg/to go on the cadge (*c*) faire la/une manche à qn, to go round with the hat for s.o./to have a whip-round for s.o. (*Voir* jambe 7; paire 1)

manchette [mɑ̃ʃɛt] *nf F* 1. mettre des manchettes pour faire qch, to make elaborate preparations before doing sth 2. *pl* handcuffs*/ cuffs 3. (*bière*) head.

manchot [mɑ̃ʃo] *a F* 1. il n'est pas manchot (*i*) he's clever with his hands (*ii*) he's no fool/there are no flies on him 2. (*iron*) t'es pas manchot, non? haven't you got hands?

manchouillard [mɑ̃ʃujar] *a&nm P* one-armed/one-handed (man).

mandagat [mɑ̃daga] *nm P* (= *mandat*) money order/postal order.

mandal(l)e [mɑ̃dal] *nf P* slap round the face; filer une mandal(l)e à qn, to give s.o. a clout.

mandarin [mɑ̃darɛ̃] *nm F* intellectual/highbrow/egghead/academic.

mandarines [mɑ̃darin] *nfpl P* very small breasts*/pimples/gnat('s) bites.

mandibules [mɑ̃dibyl] *nfpl P* jaws; jouer des mandibules, to eat*/

to nosh; se faire les mandibules sur qch, to chew sth.

mandole [mɑ̃dɔl] *nf P* = mandal(l)e.

mandoline [mɑ̃dɔlin] *nf* 1. *P* machine-gun 2. *P* (*a*) round bedpan (*b*) bidet 3. *V* (*femme*) jouer de la mandoline, to masturbate*/to play with oneself/to finger oneself.

mandrin [mɑ̃drɛ̃] *nm V* penis*; avoir le mandrin, to have an erection*.

manettes [manɛt] *nfpl P* 1. ears*/lugs 2. pedals (of bicycle); appuyer/pousser sur les manettes, to pedal away 3. à fond les manettes, very quickly*/at full throttle/at full speed 4. perdre/lâcher les manettes, to lose all self-control/to get flustered/to get all balled up.

mangav [mɑ̃gav] *nm P* beggar.

mangave [mɑ̃gav] *nf P* begging/ beggary; il est à deux doigts de la mangave, he's within an inch of the gutter/he's almost been reduced to begging.

mangeaille [mɑ̃ʒaj] *nf F* food*/ grub/nosh. (*Voir* bâfrer 2)

mange-merde [mɑ̃ʒmɛrd] *nm inv P* miser*/skinflint.

manger [mɑ̃ʒe] *vtr* 1. *F* manger de la prison, to do time/to do a stretch 2. *P* en manger, to be a police informer*/to grass 3. *V* to have oral sex* with s.o./to eat (s.o.) 4. *F* manger à la table qui recule, to go without food 5. *P* il va s'en manger une, he'll get what's coming to him/he'll get his. (*Voir* bête II 1; boire; consigne; morceau 2; nez 11; pif 6; pissenlit; poisson 2; pouce 2; râtelier 1)

mange-tout [mɑ̃ʒtu] *nm inv F* 1. squanderer/spendthrift 2. *pl* (*WWII*) Germans.

mangeur [mɑ̃ʒœr] *nm* 1. *F* mangeur de curés, violently anticlerical person. (*Voir* bouffeur) 2. *P*

mangeur de crucifix, sanctimonious hypocrite **3.** *P* **mangeur de blanc,** pimp*/ponce; white slaver.

mangeuse [mãʒøz] *nf P* **mangeuse d'hommes/mangeuse de santé,** highly-sexed woman/hot lay/easy lay/nympho.

(se) manier [s(ə)manje] *vtr&pr P* = **(se) magner.**

manières [manjɛr] *nfpl F* **1. faire des manières,** to be affected/to put on airs; **pas tant de manières!** come off it! **2. en voilà des manières!/voyez manières!** fine manners you have, I must say!/that's a nice way to behave!/talk about manners!

manieur [manjœr] *nm F* **manieur de fonte,** weight-lifter.

manif [manif] *nf P* (*abbr* = *manifestation*) (public) demonstration/demo.

manigance [manigãs] *nf F* (*a*) underhand dealing/undercover deal/fiddle; fiddling; hanky-panky/jiggery-pokery; goings-on; *O* **il y a quelque manigance sous roche,** there's something fishy going on (*b*) *pl* underhand practices/wire-pulling.

manigancer [manigãse] **I** *vtr F* to scheme/to plot; to wangle/to work (sth) underhand; **qu'est-ce qu'il manigance?** what's he up to?/what's his (little) game?/what's he cooking up? **II** *vpr* **se manigancer** *F* je me demande ce qui se **manigance,** I wonder what's going on; I wonder what's cooking; **il se manigance quelque chose,** there's something in the wind.

manipes [manip] *nfpl F* (*scol*) (= *manipulation*) practical work (*esp* in chemistry, physics).

manitou [manitu] *nm F* **le (grand) manitou,** the big boss/the big shot/the big white chief; **être le manitou de l'affaire,**to run/to boss the show.

manivelle [manivɛl] *nf P* **1.** (*aut*) steering wheel **2. s'achever à la manivelle,** to masturbate*.

mannezingue [manzɛ̃g] *nm P* publican/landlord; bartender. (*Voir* **zingue 2**)

manoche [manɔʃ] *nf F* (French card game of) *manille.*

manouche [manuʃ] *P* **I** *nm&f* gipsy/gippo **II** *nm* Romany/gipsy lingo.

manque [mãk] *nm P* **1.** (*drogues*) **être en (état de) manque,** to suffer from withdrawal symptoms*/to need a fix; to have/to be in cold turkey **2. manque de pot!** hard luck!/bad luck! **3.** (*pers ou chose*) **à la manque** (*i*) unreliable. (*Voir* **nière 2**) (*ii*) poor/worthless*/useless/third-rate; **un(e) modelliste à la manque,** a would-be dress designer; **un artiste à la manque,** a second-rate artist; **une idée à la manque,** a hopeless/half-baked idea.

manquer [mãke] *vtr F* **(il ne) manquait plus que ça!** that's the last straw!

maous(s), maousse [maus] *a P* (*a*) huge/enormous/tremendous/whacking/great (*b*) (*pers*) hefty/tremendously strong (*c*) slap-up/stupendous.

mappemondes [mapmɔ̃d] *nfpl P* (large) breasts*/globes.

maq [mak] *nm P* = **maquereau.**

maqua [maka] *nf P* = **maquerelle.**

maque [mak] *nm P* = **maquereau.**

maqué [make] *a P* **être maqué avec qn,** to be living (in sin) with s.o./to be shacked up (with s.o.)

maquer [make] **I** *vtr P* to exploit (s.o.)/to swindle* (s.o.)/to con (s.o. out of sth) **II** *vpr* **se maquer** *P* se **maquer avec qn,** to live (in sin) with s.o./to shack up with s.o.

maquereau [makro] *nm P* pimp*/ponce/mack.

maquereautage [makrotaʒ] *nm P* living off a prostitute*/procuring/pimping.

maquereauter [makrote] *vi P* to procure/to live off the earnings of a prostitute*/to pimp.

maquereautin [makrotɛ̃] *nm P* (*a*) young inexperienced pimp* (*b*) small-time pimp*.

maquerellage [makrɛlaʒ] *nm P* = **maquereautage**.

maquerelle [makrɛl] *nf*, **maquesée** [makze] *nf P* (woman) brothel owner; madam(e).

maquillage [makijaʒ] *nm* **1.** *F* (*a*) forging/faking; fiddling; doctoring (*b*) disguising/faking-up (of stolen car) **2.** *P* self-inflicted injury (in order to claim insurance, etc).

maquille [makij] *nf F* **1.** = **maquillage 1** (*b*) **2.** marking (of playing cards).

maquiller [makije] **I** *vtr F* to fake up (a car, a picture, etc); to forge/to doctor (a cheque); to fiddle (the accounts); to distort/to cover up (the truth); **ils ont maquillé la voiture,** they did a paint-job on the car; **qu'est-ce que tu maquilles?** what are you up to? (*Voir* **brème 1**; **faffes 2**) **II** *vpr* **se maquiller 1.** *P* (*a*) to malinger/to fake an illness (*b*) to inflict a wound, an injury on oneself (in order to claim insurance, etc) **2.** *F* = **se manigancer**.

maquilleur, euse [makijœr, -øz] *n F* cheat/swindler*; forger (of cheques); fiddler (of accounts); faker-up (of stolen cars).

marabout [marabu] *nm P* naval chaplain.

marant [marɑ̃] *a&nm* = **marrant I, II.**

marasquin [maraskɛ̃] *nm P* blood.

maravédis [maravedi(s)] *nm O F* **je n'ai pas un maravédis,** I'm penniless*/I haven't a brass farthing.

marca, marcat [marka] *nm P* market.

marchand [marʃɑ̃] *nm F* **1.** marchand de barbaque/de bidoche/de viande, white-slaver **2.** marchand de lacets (*i*) gendarme (*ii*) plain clothes policeman **3.** marchand de participes, teacher/schoolmaster/pedant **4.** marchand de puces, junk dealer; old-clothes man **5.** marchand de soupe (*i*) proprietor of a poor/a seedy restaurant (*ii*) ce n'est qu'un marchand de soupe, he's only interested in making a profit/he's only in it for the money **6.** être le mauvais marchand de qch, to be the loser by sth.

marchande [marʃɑ̃d] *nf* **1.** *F* marchande de plaisir/d'amour, prostitute* **2.** *P* marchande d'ail, lesbian*/les/dyke.

marchandise [marʃɑ̃diz] *nf* **1.** *F* vanter/étaler/faire valoir sa marchandise (*i*) to make the most of oneself (*ii*) (*fille, femme*) to show off the goods/her charms; to show what she's got **2.** *P* male genitals*/bag of tricks/the goods **3.** *P* excrement*/shit/crap; **mettre les pieds dans la marchandise,** to tread in the shit **4.** *P* drugs*/the goods.

marché [marʃe] *nm F* marché aux puces, flea market.

marcher [marʃe] *vi F* **1.** je marche (avec vous)! I'm on!/agreed!/count me in! (je ne) marche pas! nothing doing!*/(you can) count me out! je ne marche pas à moins de 100 francs, nothing doing under 100 francs; ça n'a pas marché, it didn't work/it didn't come off; il a marché, he fell for it/he swallowed it; il n'a pas marché, he wasn't having any **2.** faire marcher qn (*i*) to order s.o. about/to push s.o. around (*ii*) to fool s.o./to pull s.o.'s leg/to lead s.o. up the garden path; **on vous a fait marcher,** you've been had. (*Voir* **dix 4**)

marcheur [marʃœr] *nm* **1.** *F* vieux marcheur, dirty old man **2.** *P* housebreaker/burglar.

marcheuse [marʃøz] *nf* **1.** *F* (*théâtre*) walker-on/extra; **rôle de marcheuse,** walk-on part/bit part **2.** *P* prostitute*/street-walker.

marchis [marʃi] *nm P* (*mil*) = **margis.**

marcot(t)in [markɔtɛ̃] *nm P* month. (*Voir* **marqué II**)

marde [mard] *nf FrC P* (= **merde**) **1.** shit/crap **2.** **fou comme de la marde,** crazy*/nuts*/crackers **3.** **manger de la marde,** to have a lot of problems/to be in a fix*/to be in the shit/to be in it.

marder [marde] *vtr P* **marder qn,** to look at* s.o./to stare at s.o.

mardeux [mardø] *nm FrC P* (= **merdeux**) shit/creep/jerk/bastard*.

mardoche [mardɔʃ] *nm P* Tuesday.

mare [mar] **I** *nf* **la mare aux harengs,** the Herring Pond/the Atlantic. (*Voir* **pavé 7**) **II** *adv P* = **marre.**

marée [mare] *nf F* **marée noire,** oil slick.

se marer [səmare] *vpr F* = **se marrer.**

margis [marʒi] *nm P* (*mil*) (= *maréchal des logis*) sergeant (in the cavalry or artillery)/sarge.

margotin [margɔtɛ̃] *nf,* **margoton** [margɔtɔ̃] *nf P* woman of easy virtue/easy lay/pushover.

margouillis [marguji] *nm F* **1.** slush/slime/mud; mess **2.** **mettre qn dans le margouillis,** to put s.o. in a fix*.

margoulette [margulɛt] *nf P* **1.** face*/mug; **casser la margoulette à qn,** to smash s.o.'s face in/to spoil s.o.'s beauty for him **2.** mouth*/ kisser.

margoulin [margulɛ̃] *nm F* **1.** (*bourse*) petty speculator **2.** dishonest tradesman/swindler*/shark **3.** black marketeer/spiv **4.** black-

mailer **5.** bungler/botcher/bodger; **il a fait ça comme un margoulin,** he bungled/botched it.

marguerite [margərit] *nf* **1.** **effeuiller la marguerite** (*i*) *F* to play 'she loves me, she loves me not' (*ii*) *P* to have sex* **2.** *P* condom*/ French letter/*NAm* rubber **3.** *P* helicopter*/chopper **4.** *P* **une marguerite,** a white hair; **avoir des marguerites dans le cresson,** to have some white hairs (on one's head)/to have some silver threads among the gold.

Marianne [marjan] *Prnf F* the (French) Republic; **travailler pour Marianne,** to be expecting (a baby).

marida [marida] **I** *nm P* marriage/holy deadlock; **aller au marida,** to get married*/hitched **II** *a inv P* married/hitched/spliced.

se marida [səmarida] *vpr P* **se marida avec qn,** to get married* to s.o.; **je me suis marida,** I've got hitched.

maridat [marida] *nm P* = **marida I.**

Marie-Chantal [mariʃɑ̃tal] *Prnf F* **c'est une Marie-Chantal,** she's a rich, empty-headed little snob/a Mayfair nitwit/ = a Sloane ranger/ a bright young thing.

Marie-couche-toi-là [marikuʃtwala] *nf inv P* woman of easy virtue/pushover/easy lay/ scrubber/tart.

mariée [marje] *nf* **1.** *F* **la mariée est trop belle,** it's too good to be true; **il se plaint que la mariée est trop belle/il trouve la mariée trop belle,** he doesn't know how lucky/ how well off he is **2.** *P* pint (of beer) **3.** *P* **voiture de la mariée,** police *or* prison van/Black Maria*.

Marie-graillon [marigrajɔ̃] *nf inv P* slut/tart/scrubber.

Marie-Jeanne [mariʒan] *nf P* (*drogues*) (*a*) marijuana*/Mary Jane (*b*) marijuana* cigarette/joint/ reefer.

marie-louise [marilwiz] *P* **I** *nf*
fart. (*Voir* **louise**) **II** *nm or f* (*mil*)
un(e) marie-louise, a young, newly-
promoted officer/an angel-face.

Marie-pisse-trois-gouttes
[maripistrwɑgut] *nf inv P* very
young girl*.

Marie-salope [marisalɔp] *nf* **1.**
F mud dredger **2.** *P* (*a*) slut/
scrubber/tart (*b*) prostitute*/tart
3. *P* (*mil*) field kitchen **4.** *F* (*boisson*) bloody Mary.

marine [marin] *nf P* **travailler pour
la marine**, to be constipated.

mariner [marine] *vi F* **1.** to wait/
to hang about/to kick one's heels
2. laisser mariner qn, to let s.o.
stew in his own juice.

mariol(e), mariolle [marjɔl] *F*
I *a* clever/smart/cunning **II** *nm*
faire le mariol(e), to show off*.

marjo [marʒo] *nm&f P* (= *margi-
nal*) drop out; hippie; second-class
citizen.

marle[1] [marl] *a&nm P* =
mariol(e).

marle[2]**, marlou** [marlu],
marloupatte [marlupat],
marloupin [marlupɛ̃] *nm P* pro-
curer/pimp*/ponce.

marloupinerie [marlupinri] *nf*,
marlouserie [marluzri] *nf P* sly
trick/cunning dodge.

marmaille [marmɑj] *nf F* (*coll*)
children/kids; **la marmaille sortait
de l'école**, the kids were coming out
of school.

marmailleux [marmɑjø] *a F*
swarming with children/full of kids.

marmelade [marmǝlad] *nf F* **1.**
(*a*) **en marmelade**, in a frightful
mess; **quelle marmelade!** what a
mess!/what a shambles! (*b*) **avoir
les pieds en marmelade**, to have
very sore feet*; **mettre qn en
marmelade**, to make mincemeat of
s.o./to beat s.o. to a pulp **2. être
dans la marmelade**, to be in a fix*/
in the soup/in a jam.

marmitage [marmitaʒ] *nm P* (*mil*)
heavy bombardment/heavy shell-
ing/pounding.

marmite [marmit] *nf* **1.** *P* (*mil*)
heavy shell **2.** *P* prostitute* supporting her pimp*; meal ticket **3.**
P **la grande marmite** = the county
gaol **4.** *P* **(nez en) pied de
marmite**, (large) flat nose*/pug-nose
5. *F* **faire bouillir la marmite**, to
earn one's bread and butter; **casser
la marmite**, to quarrel with one's
bread and butter. (*Voir* **écumer**;
écumeur)

marmiter [marmite] *vtr P* **1.** (*mil*)
to bombard (trenches, etc) with
heavy shells **2.** (*prison*) **se faire
marmiter**, to get caught infringing
regulations.

marmot [marmo] *nm F* **1.** kid/
brat/nipper **2. croquer le marmot**,
to be kept waiting/to be kept hanging about.

marmouset [marmuzɛ] *nm F* **1.**
undersized* person/shorty/shrimp/
pipsqueak **2.** kid/nipper.

marner [marne] *vi P* to work*
hard/to slog (away).

marneur [marnœr] *nm P* hard
worker/grafter.

maronnant [marɔnɑ̃] *a F* = **marronnant**.

maronner [marɔne] *vi F* = **marronner**.

marotte [marɔt] *nf F* **1.** hobby/
fad; **flatter la marotte de qn**, to
play up to s.o. **2. avoir une
marotte pour qn**, to be infatuated
with s.o./to be sweet on s.o.

marqua, marquas [marka] *nm
P* market.

marqué [marke] **I** *a F* **c'est un
homme marqué**, he's a marked man
II *nm P* (*a*) month (*b*) one month's
imprisonment; moon; **tirer six marqués de ballon**, to do a six-month
stretch.

marque-mal [markmal] *nm inv F*

suspicious-looking character/shady customer.

marquer [marke] *vi F* **marquer mal/bien,** to give/to make a bad/a good impression. (*Voir* **midi**)

marquet [markɛ] *nm P* = **marqué II.**

Marquis [marki] *nm F* (*locution populaire*) **après vous, Marquis – non, après vous, Prince,** after you, Claude. – no, after you, Cecil.

marquise [markiz] *nf* **1.** *P* madam(e) (of a brothel) **2.** *F* (*iron*) **tout va très bien, Madame la Marquise!** oh yes, things couldn't be going better!/everything's just fine!

marquotin [markɔtɛ̃] *nm P* month.

marquouse [markuz] *nf P* **1.** mark (on a playing card) **2.** scar/tattoo (mark).

marquouser [markuze] *vtr P* **1.** to mark (playing cards) **2.** to tattoo.

marrade [marad] *nf F* fun (and games)/lark.

marraine [marɛn] *nf P* female witness for the prosecution.

marrant [marɑ̃] **I** *a&nm F* **1.** very funny*/funny ha-ha; **il est marrant!/quel marrant!** he's a (real) scream! **vous êtes marrant, vous alors!** you're the limit! **il n'est pas marrant,** he's a drip; he's as dull as ditchwater/he's not much fun **2.** (*étrange*) odd/funny/strange/funny peculiar **II** *nm V* anus*.

marre [mar] *adv P* **1.** (*a*) **avoir marre de qch/en avoir marre,** to be fed up* with sth/to have had enough of sth/to be cheesed off with sth/to be sick of sth; **(il) y en a marre!** I've had a bellyful of it/a basinful of it! **j'en ai marre,** I'm fed up (to the back teeth) with it/I've had it up to here (*b*) **avoir marre de qn,** to be fed up with s.o./to be bored* stiff with s.o./to be sick of s.o./to be browned off with s.o. **2.**

c'est marre!/en voilà marre/un point, c'est marre! and that's all there is to it!/enough said!/and that's that!/enough's enough.

se marrer [səmare] *vpr F* to laugh* uproariously/to split one's sides laughing; to have a good laugh; **elle se marrait un bon coup,** she was in stitches; **tu me fais marrer** (*i*) you make me laugh (*ii*) that's a laugh; you can't kid me; **on va se marrer,** we're going to have a good time/a ball.

marron [marɔ̃] **I** *nm P* (*a*) blow*/clout; **coller/flanquer/foutre un marron à qn,** to fetch/to land s.o. a clout; **fous-lui un marron!** thump him!/give him one! (*b*) **secouer la poêle à marrons à qn,** to beat s.o. up*/to give s.o. a going-over/to knock the living daylights out of s.o. **II** *a* **1.** *F* (*a*) (*médecin*) unlicensed/clandestine (*b*) sham/shady **2.** *P* **faire qn marron,** to arrest* s.o.; **être (fait) marron,** to be arrested; **se faire faire marron,** to get nabbed/nicked **3.** *P* **être (fait) marron,** to be duped/to be had/to be taken in/to be taken for a ride. (*Voir* **paumer 2**; **tas 2**) **III** *nm P* victim/mug/sucker/fall-guy/patsy.

marronnant [marɔnɑ̃] *a F* boring/tiresome/annoying; **que c'est marronnant!** what a bore*/bind/drag!

marronner [marɔne] *vi F* **1.** to grumble*/to grouse; **marronner des jurons,** to mutter (oaths under one's breath) **2.** to be very angry*/to be furious; **faire marronner qn,** to get s.o.'s back up **3.** to wait around/to hang about/to kick one's heels.

Marsiale [marsjal] *Prnf P* Marseille(s); **un de la Marsiale,** a native of Marseille(s)/someone from Marseilles.

marsouin [marswɛ̃] *nm* **1.** *F* marine/*NAm* leatherneck **2.** *F* sailor **3.** *V* penis*.

marteau [marto] **I** *a F* mad*; **il est un peu marteau,** he's not all there, he's a bit cracked/he's a bit nutty **II** *nm* **1.** *F* **graisser le marteau,** to bribe the doorman/the porter; to grease the doorman's/the porter's palm **2.** *F* **avoir un coup de marteau,** to be (slightly) mad* **3.** *V* **marteau à boules,** penis*/chopper.

Martigue [martig] *a&n P* (native) of Marseille(s).

maso [mazo] *F* (= *masochiste*) **I** *a* masochistic **II** *nm&f* masochist. (*Voir* **sado**)

masque [mask] *nf P* bad luck.

massacrant [masakrɑ̃] *a F* **être d'une humeur massacrante,** to be in a vile/a foul mood; to be in a filthy temper.

massacre [masakr] *nm F* **il a une tête de massacre,** he's got an unpleasant/a horrible face; he's no oil painting.

massacrer [masakre] *vtr F* (*a*) to bungle*/to botch/to bodge/to make a hash of (sth) (*b*) to murder (a piece of music); to murder/to massacre (a language) (*c*) to ruin (clothes).

massacreur, -euse [masakrœr, -øz] *n F* bungler/botcher/bodger.

masse [mas] **I** *nf F* **une grande masse de marchandises,** a whole mass of goods; **des masses de ...,** masses of ...; **il (n')y en a pas des masses,** there isn't/aren't an awful lot **II** *nf F* **coup de masse** = **coup de massue** (**massue**).

masser [mase] *vi P* **1.** to work* hard/to keep at it **2.** to exaggerate*.

massue [masy] *nf F* **coup de massue** (*i*) staggering blow/shattering news/bombshell (*ii*) overcharging/fleecing (at hotel, restaurant, etc)/daylight robbery/rip-off.

mastard [mastar] *a P* (*a*) very big/enormous/huge/whacking (great) (*b*) tremendously strong.

mastègue [mastɛg] *nf P* (*a*) food* (*b*) meal.

mastéguer [mastege] *vi P* (*a*) to eat* (*b*) to chew.

mastic [mastik] *nm P* **1.** muddle; **tu parles d'un mastic!** talk about a mess! **2.** **cherrer dans le mastic,** to exaggerate*/to boast/to talk big/to lay it on thick **3.** **s'endormir sur le mastic,** to dawdle over one's work/to fall asleep on the job **4.** **péter dans le mastic,** to drop one's work **5.** (*a*) thick soup (*b*) **bouder le mastic,** to pick at one's food.

masticotte [mastikɔt] *nf P* **avoir une bonne masticotte,** to have the gift of the gab.

mastiquer [mastike] *vtr P* to eat*.

mastoc [mastɔk] *a inv & nm F* heavy/loutish/lumpish (man).

mastodonte [mastodɔ̃t] *nm F* (*a*) (*véhicule*) juggernaut (*b*) (*pers*) colossus/hulking great brute (*c*) (*chose*) whopper.

mastroquet [mastrokɛ] *nm P* = publican; keeper of a pub or wine bar. (*Voir* **troquet**)

m'as-tu-vu [matyvy] *nm inv F* **1.** swank/show-off*; **faire le m'as-tu-vu,** to prance around; to camp it up **2.** conceited actor.

mat [mat] **I** *a P* exhausted*/dead beat **II** *a F* finished; **c'est mat,** it's all over.

mat' [mat] *nm P* morning; **à quatre plombes du mat',** at four am/four in the morning.

matador [matadɔr] *nm F* (*milieu*) tough guy; big shot; magnate.

mataf [mataf] *nm P* sailor*.

mataguin [matagɛ̃] *nm P* (*javanais de* **matin**) morning.

matave [matav] *nm P* = **mataf.**

mate [mat] **I** *nm P* = **mat'** **II** *nf P* door.

matelas [matla] *nm P* **1.** well-filled wallet/wad (of banknotes); **avoir le matelas,** to be rich*/to be rolling (in it) **2.** hoard (of money); savings/nest egg.

mater [mate] *vtr P* (*a*) to watch closely/to keep an eye on (s.o./sth) (*b*) to look at*/to take a dekko at/ to have a gander at (s.o./sth); **mate-moi ça!** get a load of that! (*c*) to be a peeping Tom/a voyeur. (*Voir* **jeton 5**)

matère [matɛr] *nf P* = **maternelle.**

matérielle [materjɛl] *nf F* **la matérielle,** the necessities of life; **gagner/faire sa matérielle,** to make a living/to keep the wolf from the door.

maternelle [matɛrnɛl] *nf O P* mother*/mater; **la maternelle,** my old lady.

mateur [matœr] *nm P* voyeur/Peeping Tom.

math(s) [mat] *nf(pl) F* maths; **fort en math(s),** good at maths/*NAm* math.

matheux, -euse [matø, -øz] *n F* (*occ péj*) keen mathematician/maths wizard.

mathurin [matyrɛ̃] *nm F* sailor.

matière [matjɛr] *nf F* **avoir de la matière grise,** to be clever/brainy/ smart.

matin [matɛ̃] *nm F* **1. un de ces (quatre) matins/un beau matin,** one of these (fine) days **2. être du matin,** to be an early riser/early bird.

maton [matɔ̃] *nm P* **1.** policeman* **2.** (male) prison warder/screw.

matonne [matɔn] *nf P* (female) prison warder/screw.

matos [matos] *nm P* **1.** man*/ bloke/guy/*NAm* dude **2.** (= *matériel*) equipment/gear.

matou [matu] *nm* **1.** *F* **c'est un vilain matou,** he's an unpleasant character/a nasty bit of work **2.** *P* lover/fancy man/boyfriend.

matouser, matouzer [matuze] *vtr P* = **mater.**

matraquage [matrakaʒ] *nm P*

matraquage (publicitaire), plugging (of commercials, etc on radio, television).

matraque [matrak] *nf* **1.** *F* **coup de matraque,** barefaced overcharging (in restaurant, etc) **2.** *P* **mettre la matraque** (*i*) to lay the winning card(s) (*ii*) to take drastic measures; to use forceful tactics **3. avoir la matraque** (*i*) (*cartes*) to hold a winning hand (*ii*) *V* to have an erection*.

matraquer [matrake] *vtr P* **1.** to overcharge/to fleece/to rip off (one's customers) **2.** to inflict a stiff penalty on (s.o.); to punish* (s.o.) severely.

matraqueur [matrakœr] *nm P* dirty player (at football, etc); hacker.

matricule [matrikyl] *nm P* **1. annoncer son matricule,** to fart **2. ça va barder/ça va chier, pour ton matricule!** you're (in) for it!/you've got it coming to you!/you'll cop it!

matuche [matyʃ] *nm P* **1.** = **maton 1, 2 2.** *pl* **matuches,** loaded dice.

matz [mats] *nm P* chap*/guy/bloke.

la Maub(e) [lamob] *Prn F* (*i*) place Maubert (*ii*) the Maubert district (in Paris). (*Voir* **la Mocobo**)

mauresque [mɔrɛsk] *nm F* (*boisson*) pastis with orgeat.

mauvaise [movɛz] *af F* **1. l'avoir mauvaise,** to be indignant/annoyed **2. je la trouve mauvaise,** I don't find that at all funny.

mauviette [movjɛt] *nf F* frail-looking/sickly-looking individual; **elle mange comme une mauviette,** she doesn't eat enough to keep a sparrow alive.

max [maks] *nm P* (= *maximum*) (*a*) **il en a pris un max,** he copped the maximum (*b*) **il déconne un max,** he's a real joker (*c*) **j'en ai vu un max, de ces films,** I've seen lots/ loads of those films.

maxée [makse] *nf P* brothel owner; madame. (*Voir* **macquesée**)

maxi [maksi] **I** *nm or f F* maxi (skirt, coat) **II** *nm P* (= *maximum*) (*a*) **je suis bon pour le maxi,** I'm sure to get the maximum sentence (*b*) (*esp aut; fig*) **donner/taper le maxi,** to go all out/to step on it/ to put one's foot down.

mazette [mazɛt] **I** *nf F* **c'est une mazette** (*i*) he's hopeless (at games, at sport) (*ii*) he's a spineless individual/he's a dead loss **II** *int O F* (*admiration, étonnement*) **mazette!** good Lord!/well I never!/my goodness!

mec [mɛk] *nm P* **1.** pimp*/ponce **2.** (*a*) fellow*/guy/chap/bloke; **un drôle de mec,** an odd character/a funny bloke; **un sale/vilain mec,** a nasty piece of work; **un petit mec,** a little twerp; **pauv' mec!** poor sod! **t'es un pauv' mec!** you're a jerk/a sod/a bastard*! **c'est un bon mec,** he's a nice bloke/an ace guy (*b*) **le mec des mecs/le grand Mec,** God (*c*) tough guy; **un mec à la redresse,** a thug (*d*) husband*; boyfriend; lover; **mon mec,** my man/my bloke/my guy. (*Voir* **rousse 1**)

mécanique [mekanik] *nf* **1.** *F* gadget **2.** *pl P* shoulders; **rouler les mécaniques,** to swagger/to show off*; to throw one's weight around **3.** *F* **c'est de la belle mécanique** (*i*) (*voiture*) that's a nice-looking machine (*ii*) (*femme*) she's got a great chassis.

mécano [mekano] *nm F* mechanic/ grease monkey.

méchamment [meʃamɑ̃] *adv P* very/extremely/fantastically/terrifically; **un type méchamment bien,** a hell of a nice guy.

méchant [meʃɑ̃] **I** *a* **1.** *F* **ce n'est pas bien méchant,** there's no (great) harm in it/it's not too serious **2.** *P* terrific/fantastic **II** *nm F* **faire le méchant,** to be/to turn nasty; to be difficult.

mèche [mɛʃ] **I** *nf F* (*a*) **vendre la mèche,** to divulge a secret*/to give the game away/to let the cat out of the bag/to spill the beans/to blow the gaff (*b*) **éventer la mèche** (*i*) to get wind of a secret (*ii*) = **vendre la mèche II** *nf inv F* **1.** **être de mèche avec qn,** to be in collusion/ in league/in cahoots with s.o.; to be hand in glove with s.o. **2.** **et mèche!** and a bit more (besides)!/ and the rest! **elle a trente ans et mèche,** she's thirty if she's a day/ she's the wrong side of thirty. (*Voir* **toutiche** (*b*)) **3.** **(il n'y a) pas mèche,** not a (ghost of a) chance/ nothing doing*/no way **4.** **on n'y voit (pas) mèche,** you can't see a thing.

mécol, mécolle [mekɔl] *pron P* I/me/myself/yours truly. (*Voir* **mézigo**)

mecqueton, mecton [mɛktɔ̃] *nm P* **1.** (*a*) young pimp* (*b*) small-time pimp* **2.** (*jeune voyou*) (young) petty criminal **3.** (*petit mec*) twerp/jerk. (*Voir* **mec**)

médaille [medaj] *nf F* **porter la médaille** (*i*) to be framed (*ii*) to carry the can.

médicale [medikal] *nf P* **sortir en médicale,** to be released (from prison, etc) on medical grounds/to get a medical discharge.

médoche [medɔʃ] *nf,* **méduche** [medyʃ] *nf P* medal; decoration.

Méduse [medyz] *Prnf F* **c'est la tête de Méduse,** it's petrifying/ paralysing.

meetinge [mitɛ̃ʒ] *nm P* (*esp pol*) meeting/rally/meet.

meffe [mɛf] *nf P* (*verlan de femme*) girl*/woman; bird/chick/*NAm* broad.

mefus [mefy(s)] *nf P* = **meffe.**

meg [meg] *nm P* = **mégot.**

mégachiée [megaʃje] *nf V* **une mégachiée de ...,** a fantastic quantity of ... /loads and loads of .... (*Voir* **chiée**)

mégaphone [megafɔn] *nm* P exhaust (pipe) (*esp* of motorbike).

mégot [mego] *nm* P (*a*) cigarette-end*/butt/fag-end/dog-end; **boîte à mégots**, ash tray (*b*) cigar stump (*c*) cigarette*/fag/cig. (*Voir* **étagère**)

mégotage [megɔtaʒ] *nm* P **1.** (*mesquinerie*) scrimping/skimping **2.** small-time activities/chicken-feed.

mégot(t)er [megɔte] *vi* P **1.** to go around picking up cigarette-ends* **2.** (*a*) to live meanly/to scrimp/to skimp (*b*) **ne pas mégot(t)er sur qch**, not to be stingy/mean with sth **3.** to be a small-time operator/a small-timer.

mégot(t)eur, euse [megɔtœr, -øz], **mégot(t)eux, euse** [megɔtø, -øz], **mégot(t)ier, ière** [megɔtje, -jɛr] *n* P **1.** person who picks up cigarette-ends*; down-and-out/bum/tramp **2.** small-time operator/small-timer **3.** skinflint/penny-pincher/tight-ass.

mélanco [melɑ̃ko] *a* P melan-choly/mournful/gloomy.

se mélanger [səmelɑ̃ʒe] *vpr* P to have sex*.

mélasse [melas] *nf* F **être dans la mélasse** (*i*) to be in a fix*/to be in a jam/to be up a gum-tree (*ii*) to be penniless*/to be broke/to be cleaned out.

mêlé-cass(e), mêlécasse [melekɑs] *nm* F cassis (blackcurrant liqueur) and water mixed with cognac or vermouth; **voix de mêlé(-)cass(e)**, thick/hoarse/husky voice (of a drunkard).

mêler [mele] **I** *vtr* F **vous avez bien mêlé les cartes!** a nice mess you've made of it! **II** *vpr* **se mêler** F **de quoi je me mêle!/de quoi tu te mêles!** what's it got to do with you?/who asked you? **mêlez-vous de vos oignons!** mind your own business!

mêle-tout [mɛltu] *nm&f inv* F busy-body/nosy parker.

méli-mélo [melimelo] *nm* F mish-mash/hotchpotch/muddle/jumble (of facts, etc); **tout est méli-mélo**, everything's ballsed up. (*pl* **mélis-mélos**)

mélo [melo] **I** *nm* F (= *mélodrame*) melodrama/blood-and-thunder drama/tear-jerker **II** *a* F (= *mélodramatique*) melodramatic/over-the-top.

melon [məlɔ̃] *nm* P **1.** head*; **avoir le melon déplumé,** to be bald(headed)* **2.** (*péj*) Arab*/wog **3.** freshman (at Saint-Cyr) **4.** *pl* **melons,** (large) breasts*/melons. (*Voir* **cosse**)

membre [mɑ̃br] *nm* **1.** F **se saigner aux quatre membres,** to work* oneself to the bone **2.** P (= *membre viril*) penis*/member.

membré [mɑ̃bre] *a* P well-hung/well equipped.

membrer [mɑ̃bre] *vi* F to work* hard/to slog (away).

membrineuse [mɑ̃brinøz] *nf* P tongue/clapper.

même [mɛm] *adv* **1.** F **mais tout de même!** but dash it all!/but hang it all! **2.** F **ah! tout de même, vous voilà!** so you've turned up at last! **3.** P **je l'avais prévenu, même que je lui avais écrit,** I told him – I even wrote to him. (*Voir* **pareil**)

mémé, mémée [meme] *nf* F **1.** grandma/granny/nan(n)a **2.** old woman/old dear. (*Voir* **orties**)

mémère [memɛr] *nf* F **1.** grandma/granny/nan(n)a **2.** mother/mummy; **un beau chien-chien à sa mémère**, mummy's sweet little doggy **3.** (*péj*) **une grosse mémère**, a blowsy middle-aged or elderly woman. (*Voir* **orties**)

ménage [menaʒ] *nm* F **1.** homo-sexual liaison (between two males or two females) **2.** (unmarried) couple.

mendès [mɛ̃dɛs] *nm P* (*a*) milk (*b*) glass of milk.

mendiche [mɑ̃diʃ] *nm*, **mendigo(t)** [mɑ̃digo] *nm P* beggar/down-and-out.

mendigoter [mɑ̃digɔte] *vtr&i P* to beg.

mener [m(ə)ne] *vtr F* **ne pas en mener large**, to be in a tight spot; to have one's heart in one's boots; **il n'en menait pas large**, he'd had the fear of God put into him. (*Voir* **barque**; **bateau I 2**; **belle 2**; **cirque 3**; **double 2**)

ménesse [menɛs] *nf P* **1.** woman* **2.** (*compagne*) wife*; mistress; girlfriend; lover.

mengave [mɑ̃gav] *nf P* begging. (*Voir* **mangave**)

Ménilmuche [menilmyʃ] *Prn P* Ménilmontant (in Paris).

méninges [menɛ̃ʒ] *nfpl F* (*a*) **se casser/creuser/se fatiguer/se masturber/se retourner/se torturer les méninges**, to rack one's brains; **il ne se foule pas les méninges**, he doesn't exactly overwork/overtax his brain; **casse-toi les méninges!/fais (un peu) travailler tes méninges!** use your loaf! (*b*) **on a visité des musées pour se stimuler les méninges**, we did a few museums/we got a bit of culture.

méningite [menɛ̃ʒit] *nf F* **il ne s'est pas donné une méningite**, he didn't exactly overtax his brain.

menotte [mənɔt] *nf F* (child's) little hand/donny.

menouille [mənuj] *nf P* money*/cash; change.

mentale [mɑ̃tal] *nf*, **mentalité** [mɑ̃talite] *nf F* (*a*) **avoir une bonne mentale** (*i*) to be reliable (*ii*) to have a normal outlook (on life) (*iii*) to follow accepted beliefs, etc (*b*) **avoir une mauvaise/une sale mentale** (*i*) to be unreliable (*ii*) to have an unhealthy outlook (on life) (*iii*) to reject accepted beliefs, etc

(*c*) (*iron*) **belle mentalité!/jolie mentalité!** what a nice mind you've got!/what a charming way of looking at things you have!

menterie [mɑ̃tri] *nf F* fib/story.

menteuse [mɑ̃tøz] *nf P* **1.** tongue/clapper **2. la Grande Menteuse**, the Press.

méquer [meke] *vtr P* to order (s.o.) about.

mequeton [mɛktɔ̃] *nm P* = **mecqueton**.

mer [mɛr] **I** *a P* (= *merveilleux*) marvellous/great/super. (*Voir* **mérovingien**) **II** *nf F* **1. ce n'est pas la mer à boire**, it's quite easy*; nothing to it! **2.** (*voiture*) **tenir la mer**, to hold the road well.

mercanti [mɛrkɑ̃ti] *nm F* profiteer/shark.

mercenaire [mɛrsənɛr] *nm F* **travailler comme un mercenaire**, to work* like a horse (for next to nothing); to work for peanuts.

mercure [mɛrkyr] *nm F* **avoir du mercure aux fesses**, to have ants in one's pants.

merdaille [mɛrdɑj] *nf coll P* **1.** dirty brats/ragamuffins **2.** riff-raff; scum.

merdailleux [mɛrdɑjø] *nm*, **merdaillon** [mɛrdɑjɔ̃] *nm P* **1.** dirty (little) brat/street arab/street urchin **2.** dirty dog/dirty beast; skunk; stinker/shit.

merde [mɛrd] **I** *nf P* **1.** excrement*/shit/crap **2.** (*a*) (*chose*) crap (*b*) (*pers*) **une (grosse) merde/une grossière merde**, a turd/a shit **3. laisser tomber qn comme une merde**, to drop s.o. like a piece of shit **4. traîner qn dans la merde**, to treat s.o. like dirt; to drag s.o. through the mire **5. il fait sa merde/il ne se croit pas une merde/il ne se prend pas pour de la merde**, he thinks he's really something/he thinks he's the cat's whiskers/the bee's knees; he thinks the sun shines out of his arse **6. il a de la merde dans les yeux** (*i*) he can't see a thing (*ii*) he can't see further than his nose **7. l'avoir à la merde,** to be in a foul mood/in a filthy temper* **8.** (*a*) **être dans la merde,** to be in a (hell of a) fix*/to be in the shit/to be up shit creek (without a paddle); **on n'est pas dans la merde, tiens!** we're really up the creek now!/we're in a bloody mess! (*b*) **mettre/foutre qn dans la merde,** to land/to drop s.o. in the shit **9. merde pour ...,** to hell with ...; **merde pour le boulot!** stuff the job! **10. semer la merde,** to cause chaos and confusion **11. il y a de la merde au bout du bâton,** it's a terrible state of affairs; it's a shitty set-up **12. avoir un œil qui dit merde à l'autre,** to be cross-eyed/to (have a) squint **13.** (*drogues*) (*a*) heroin*; morphine*; shit (*b*) hashish*/shit **14. (c'est-il) oui ou merde?** (is it) yes or no? **15. mouche à merde,** (house-)fly/blue-bottle **16. ça sent la merde,** it stinks (to high heaven). (*Voir* **foutre²** I **10**) **II** *int P* (*a*) **merde (alors)!/merde et contre-merde!/et puis merde!/merde de merde!/mille merde!** shit!/bugger it!/damn and blast it! (*b*) **ah! merde, ce que c'est beau!** shit! it's bloody beautiful!/Christ! it's really nice! (*Voir* **bordel 4**)

merder [mɛrde] *vi P* to fall through/to come to nothing/to fizzle out; **j'ai complètement merdé à l'examen,** I screwed up the exam.

merdeux, euse [mɛrdø, -øz] *P* **I** *a* (*a*) dirtied/soiled (*b*) filthy/nasty/shitty **II** *n* (*pers*) (*a*) dirty swine; bugger; turd; *f* dirty bitch (*b*) **un petit merdeux,** a little squirt/a dirty (little) bugger/a (little) shit; **une petite merdeuse,** a stuck-up little bitch **III** *nm* **faire le merdeux,** to have a very high opinion of oneself; **il fait le merdeux,** he thinks the sun shines out of his arse. (*Voir* **bâton 3**)

merdier [mɛrdje] *nm P* (*a*) **je suis dans un sacré merdier,** I'm in a bloody mess/in a hell of a fix* (*b*) **on n'est pas encore sorti de ce merdier,** we're not out of the shit yet (*c*) **foutre le merdier quelque part,** to balls sth up. (*Voir* **foutre²** I **10**)

merdique [mɛrdik] *a P* **1.** very difficult; **ce problème de math est complètement merdique,** this maths/NAm math problem is bloody difficult/a real bastard **2.** of poor quality; not up to the mark; **c'est plutôt merdique comme système,** it's a really shitty/crappy system; **ce film est complètement merdique,** this film is trash/shit/really crappy.

merdouille [mɛrduj] *nf P* **1.** excrement*/shit **2.** clumsiness/awkwardness/cackhandedness.

merdouiller [mɛrduje], **merdoyer** [mɛrdwaje] *vi P* to flounder/to be all at sea/to get all tied up; to get into a bloody mess.

mère [mɛr] *nf* (*a*) *F* (*occ péj*) **la mère Thomas,** old Mrs Thomas/old mother Thomas (*b*) *P* **et dites donc, la petite mère!** well, missis!/well, ducks!/well, old girl!

mère-maca [mɛrmaka] *nf P* (= *mère maquerelle*) madam(e) of a brothel. (*pl* **mères-maca**)

mère-pipi [mɛrpipi] *nf P* (female) lavatory attendant. (*pl* **mères-pipi**)

mère-poule [mɛrpul] *nf F* over-indulgent mother/mother hen.

mérinos [merinos] *nm P* **laisser pisser le mérinos,** to bide one's time/to wait till the moment is ripe/to let things take their (normal) course.

merlan [mɛrlɑ̃] *nm* **1.** *P* hairdresser/barber **2.** *P* pimp*/ponce/nookie bookie **3.** *P* **faux merlan,** petty criminal/small-time operator/small-timer **4.** *F* **faire des yeux de merlan frit** (*i*) to roll one's eyes heavenwards/to show the whites of one's eyes; to look like a dying

duck in a thunderstorm (*ii*) to gaze
ecstatically (at s.o.).

merle [mɛrl] *nm F* **1.** (*pers*) **jaser
comme un merle,** to chatter like a
magpie/to go rabbiting on **2.** (*a*)
un fin merle, a cunning person/a
crafty specimen (*b*) **un vilain merle/**
(*iron*) **un beau merle,** a nasty piece
of work; an awkward customer; **sif-
fle, beau merle!** just wait till I get
you!/I'll get you in the end! (*Voir*
dénicheur)

merlette [mɛrlɛt] *nf P* (young)
prostitute* soliciting on behalf of
another.

merlifiche [mɛrlifiʃ] *nm P* showman; mountebank.

merlins [mɛrlɛ̃] *nmpl P* legs*.

merluche [mɛrlyʃ] *nf P* (*péj*) **1.**
woman* **2.** wife*.

mérovingien [merɔvɛ̃ʒjɛ̃] *a P* =
mer I.

mésigue [mezig] *pron P* =
mézigue.

messe [mɛs] *nf F* **1. dire/tenir/
faire des messes basses,** to carry on
a conversation in an undertone; **je
n'aime pas les messes basses,** I
don't like people whispering to
each other **2. je ne répète pas la
messe pour les sourds/je n'aime pas
chanter la messe pour les sourds,** I
don't like having to say the same
thing twice.

messieurs-dames [mesjødam]
nmpl F **bonjour, messieurs-dames,**
good morning sir, madam; morning
all! **entrez messieurs-dames,** come
in, sir, madam; come in, ladies and
gentlemen.

métallo [metalo] *nm F* metallurgist;
metal-worker; steel-worker.

météo [meteo] *F* **I** *nm* meteorolo-
gist/weather man; (*TV*) **Monsieur
météo,** the weather man **II** *nf* (*a*)
weather report (*b*) weather centre;
Met office (*c*) **la météo est bonne,**
(they say) the weather will be fine/
it's looking good.

métèque [metɛk] *nm F* (*péj*) for-
eigner; dago; wog; wop.

métier [metje] *nm F* **1. il est du
métier** (*i*) he's in the same line (of
business) (*ii*) he knows all the
tricks of the trade/all the angles
2. vous faites là un vilain métier!
that's a dirty game you're playing
3. faites votre métier! mind your
own business!/get on with your
own job! **4. quel métier!** what a
life!

mètre [mɛtr] *nm F* **piquer un cent
mètres,** to run away*/to beat it/to
clear off.

métro [metro] *nm* **1.** *P* one
gramme of cocaine* **2.** *P* **avoir un
métro de retard,** to be slow to
understand things/to be slow on
the uptake **3.** *F* (*locution populaire*)
métro, boulot, dodo, = work, rest
and no play; = the boredom of
everyday life/the daily grind.

mettable [metabl] *a P* desirable/
sexy; screwable; **une femme mettable,** an easy lay; **elle est mettable,**
she's a bit of all right.

metteur, -euse [metœr, -øz] *n F*
metteur en l'air, killer/assassin;
murderer/murderess.

mettre [mɛtr] *vtr* **1. le mettre à qn**
(*i*) *F* to fool s.o.; **se le faire mettre,**
to be taken for a ride; **il vous l'a
bien mis!** he made a right mug out
of you! (*ii*) *P* to have sex* with
s.o.; **se faire mettre,** to get laid **2.**
F (*boxe*) **les mettre avec qn,** to have
a bout with s.o. **3.** *P* **les mettre,**
to make oneself scarce/to do a
bunk. (*Voir* **air I 7; bocal 3; boîte
3, 5; bout 6; coup 6, 14; dedans
1; doigt 6, 9; paquet; veilleuse;
voile 2**) **II** *vpr* **se mettre** *F* **1.
s'en mettre jusque-là,** to eat* heart-
ily/to tuck in/to have a blow out/
to make a pig of oneself. (*Voir*
lampe 1) **2. se mettre avec qn/se
mettre ensemble,** to cohabit/to
shack up with s.o.; **ils se sont mis
ensemble,** they're living together **3.
il se met bien,** he does himself well/

he does himself proud. (*Voir* **bain 1** (*b*); **s'ôter**; **table 2**)

meubles [mœbl] *nmpl F* (*pers*) **faire partie des meubles**, to be part of the furniture/to be a permanent fixture.

meuf [mœf] *nf P* (= *femme*) girl*/ woman*; bird/chick; **sa meuf**, his old lady.

meule [mœl] *nf P* **1.** (motor)bike **2.** *pl* **meules**, buttocks*/buns/*NAm* fanny **3.** *pl* teeth* **4.** **mouiller la meule**, to have one's first drink of the day.

meumeu [mømø] **I** *a P* excellent*/first-rate/super **II** *nf F* (*langage enfantin*) cow/moo cow/moo moo.

meunier [mønje] *nm F* cockroach.

meurt-de-faim [mœrdəfɛ̃] *nm inv*, **meurt-la-faim** [mœrlafɛ̃] *nm inv F* down-and-out; **recevoir un salaire de meurt-de-faim**, to get paid starvation wages/to be on the breadline.

meurt-de-soif [mœrdəswaf] *nm inv F* heavy drinker/alky/(real) boozer/thirsty mortal.

mézig [mezig], **mézigo** [mezigo], **mézigue** [mezig] *pron P* I/me/ myself/yours truly. (*Voir* **tézig(ue), cézig(ue)/sezig(ue), no(s)- zig(ue)s, vo(s)zig(ue)s, euzig(ue)s/leur(s)zig(ue)s**)

miam-miam! [mjamjam] *int F* yum-yum!

miauler [mjole] *vi F* (*pers*) to grouse; to whine/to bellyache.

miché [miʃe] *nm P* **1.** (*a*) prostitute's client*/trick/meal* ticket/John (*b*) homosexual prostitute's client/ trick **2.** mug/sucker.

se micher [səmiʃe] *vpr P* to disguise oneself.

miches [miʃ] *nfpl P* **1.** (*a*) buttocks*/buns/bum/*NAm* butt/*NAm* fanny; **pincer les miches à une femme**, to pinch a woman's bottom/to goose a woman (*b*) **poser**

ses miches, to sit down (on one's backside)/to plonk one's arse down somewhere; **serrer les miches** (*i*) to be on one's guard/to be wary (*ii*) to sit tight (*iii*) to get the wind up; **avoir les miches à zéro/avoir les miches à glagla/avoir les miches qui font bravo**, to be dead scared/to be in a blue funk/to be scared shitless; to have cold feet; **avoir chaud aux miches**, to have a nasty fright; **il est parti en serrant les miches**, he went off with his tail between his legs; **on se caille les miches**, it's brass-monkey weather (*b*) **occupe-toi de tes miches!** mind your own bloody business! **2.** (*a*) breasts*/boobs/Bristols (*b*) (*femme*) **gagner sa croûte avec ses miches**, to prostitute oneself/to earn a living on one's back. (*Voir* **feu 1**)

michet [miʃɛ] *nm*, **micheton** [miʃtɔ̃] *nm P* = **miché 1, 2.**

michetonner [miʃtɔne] *vi P* **1.** to pay s.o. to have sex*; to pay a prostitute*/a homosexual* to have sex* **2.** (*femme*) to prostitute oneself (on a casual basis).

michetonneuse [miʃtɔnøz] *nf P* (*a*) (part-time) prostitute* (*b*) woman of easy virtue/easy lay/ pushover; slut (*c*) kept woman.

michette [miʃɛt] *nf P* lesbian prostitute.

michto [miʃto] *a P* **c'est michto**, it's fine.

mickey [miki] *nm P* adulterated drink/Mickey Finn. (*Voir* **balançoire**)

micmac [mikmak] *nm F* **1.** (= **manigance**) funny business **2.** jumble/mess **3.** complication/fuss.

micro [mikro] *nm* **1.** *F* microphone/mike; **micro clandestin**, bug; **parler au micro**, to talk into the mike **2.** *P* mouth*; **ferme ton micro!** shut up!*

microbe [mikrɔb] *nm F* **1.** **attraper un microbe**, to catch a bug; **garde tes microbes!** keep your germs to yourself! **2.** (*a*) small boy/(tiny) tot/nipper (*b*) under-sized* person/little runt.

midi [midi] *nm* **1.** *F* **ne pas voir clair en plein midi,** to be blind to the obvious/the facts **2.** *F* **chercher midi à quatorze heures,** to look for difficulties where there are none; to complicate the issue/things **3.** *F* **c'est midi (sonné)!** not likely!*/no fear!/not on your nellie! **4.** *V* **marquer midi,** to have an erection*/to get it up. (*Voir* **étoiles**)

midinette [midinɛt] *nf O F* shop girl/dressmaker's apprentice.

mie [mi] **I** *nf P* **1. une mie de pain,** someone with no go (in him, her) **2. à la mie de pain,** worthless*/no good/not worth a damn **3.** (*a*) **mie de pain mécanique,** louse/cootie (*b*) **mie de pain à ressorts,** flea **II** *nf A F* (*fille, femme*) loved one/lady love.

miel [mjɛl] **I** *nm* **1.** *F* **c'est du (pur) miel,** it's (dead) easy*/it's a piece of cake **2.** *V* excrement*/shit. (*Voir* **cliquette 1**) **II** *int P* **miel!** damn!/blast!/damn and blast!/sugar!/shit!

miette [mjɛt] *nf F* **1. je ne m'en fais pas une miette,** it doesn't bother me in the slightest **2. et des miettes,** and the rest/and a bit more besides.

mi-figue [mifig] *a phr F* **mi-figue, mi-raisin,** neither one thing nor the other; half of one thing and half another.

mignard, arde [miɲar, -ard] *n F* small child*/kid.

mignonnettes [miɲɔnɛt] *nfpl P* photographs sold in the streets (of Paris, etc) purporting to be 'dirty postcards'.

mijoter [miʒɔte] **I** *vtr F* **mijoter un complot,** to hatch a plot; **qu'est-ce que tu mijotes dans ton coin?** what are you hatching up over there?/what are you cooking up? **il mijote des conneries,** he's up to no good

II *vpr* **se mijoter** *F* **qu'est-ce qui se mijote?** what's up?/what's going on? **je sais qu'il se mijote quelque chose,** I know there's something in the wind.

milieu [miljø] *nm F* **le milieu/les gens du milieu,** the (French) under-world; gangland.

mille [mil] *nm inv F* **1. des mille et des cents,** pots of money* **2. mettre/taper dans le mille** (*i*) to be successful/to come out on top (*ii*) to be spot on/to score a bulls-eye/to hit the nail on the head/to get it in one. (*Voir* **donner 2**)

mille-feuille(s) [milfœj] *nm* **1.** *P* **c'est du mille-feuille(s),** it's dead easy*/it's a cinch **2.** *V* female genitals*/crumpet/fur pie **3.** *P* wad of ten 100-franc notes.

milliasse [miljas] *nf F* enormous quantity*; huge sum (of money).

millimètre [milimɛtr] *nm F* **faire du millimètre,** to economize/to skimp.

mille-pattes [milpat] *nf P* (*CB*) lorry/truck/HGV/juggernaut/rig.

milord [milɔr] *nm O F* immensely rich* man.

mimi [mimi] **I** *a* sweet/darling/pre-cious/cute **II** *nm* **1.** *F* (*a*) **mon petit mimi,** my darling*/my pet. (*Voir* **mimine 1**) (*b*) (*à un enfant*) **fais un gros mimi à ta maman,** give mummy a nice big kiss **2.** *F* pussy (cat*) **3.** *V* female genitals*/pussy/*Brit* fanny; **faire mimi,** to have cunnilingus*/to eat hairpie.

mimine [mimin] *nf* **1.** *F* **ma petite mimine,** my darling*/my pet. (*Voir* **mimi II 1** (*a*)) **2.** *pl P* **mimines,** hands*.

minable [minabl] *F* **I** *a* (*pers*) shabby/seedy-looking*/grotty; (*meubles, voiture, etc*) shabby(-look-ing)/tatty/grotty/crummy; **un salaire minable,** a crummy wage/a pittance/peanuts **II** *n* (*pers*) hope-less/useless individual; a dead loss;

un tas de minables, a pathetic bunch/a useless lot.

mince! [mɛ̃s] *int F* (*a*) (**ah!**) **mince alors!** (*i*) well, I'll be blowed!/just fancy that!/well I never!/good Lord!/crikey!/you don't say! (*ii*) drat!/blast!/damn! (*b*) **mince de rigolade!** what a lark!/what a giggle!

mine [min] *nf F* **1. faire mine de rien,** to look as if nothing had happened; **mine de rien, il t'a tiré les vers du nez!** he pumped you so casually, you didn't know he was doing it! **mine de rien, il est pas si con que ça!** you wouldn't think it, but he's not as dumb as he looks! **mine de rien et bouche cousue!** mum's the word! **2.** (*iron*) **nous avons bonne mine maintenant!** *don't* we look foolish! **t'as bonne mine!** get away with you!/go on!/I'm not impressed! **j'ai bonne mine maintenant que je lui ai dit le contraire,** I'm going to look good, now that I've told him something (quite) different.

mine-babines [minbabin] *nf FrC P* mouth organ/harmonica/(mouth) harp.

minet, -ette [minɛ, -ɛt] *n* **1.** *F* **mon minet/ma minette,** my darling*/my pet **2.** *F* fashionable/sophisticated/chic young man *or* young woman; trendy **3.** *F* pussy (cat*)/kitty **4.** *V* female genitals*/pussy; **faire minette,** to have cunnilingus*/to pearl-dive.

mini [mini] *nm&f F* **1.** mini (skirt,etc) **2.** *f* (*aut*) mini (*RTM*).

minon [minɔ̃] *nm F* **1.** pussy (cat*)/mog(gy)/kitty **2.** fluff.

minot [mino] *nm F* child*/kid/brat/nipper.

minou [minu] *nm* **1.** *F* pussy (cat*)/mog(gy) **2.** *V* female genitals*/pussy.

minouche [minuʃ] *nf F* darling/pet.

minouse [minuz] *nf P* (pair of) (woman's) pant(ie)s/briefs/knickers.

minus [minys] *nm inv,* **minus habens** [minysabɛ̃s] *nm inv F* **1.** fool*/clot/twit/moron; **c'est un minus,** he's not very bright/he's moronic **2.** freshman/fresher; *occ* = **bizut(h).**

minute [minyt] **I** *nf P* (*pers*) **se poser là cinq minutes,** to be hefty/on the beefy side **II** *int F* **minute (papillon)!** just a minute!/hold on!/hang on!/half a mo!/not so fast!/hold your horses!

mioche [mjɔʃ] *nm&f F* **1.** small child*/mite/kiddy; **bande de mioches,** band of little urchins/of tiny tots **2. faire descendre le mioche,** to bring about an abortion.

mirand [mirã] *a P* short-sighted/half-blind.

mirante [mirãt] *nf P* mirror.

mirer [mire] *vtr P* to look (closely) at; **mire un peu celle-là!** get a load of/take a dekko at her!

mirettes [mirɛt] *nfpl P* eyes*/peepers (*a*) **gicler des mirettes,** to cry (*b*) **en mettre plein les mirettes à qn,** to hoodwink s.o./to pull the wool over s.o.'s eyes.

mirifique [mirifik] *a F* excellent*/marvellous/terrific/fabulous.

mirifiquement [mirifikmã] *adv F* excellently/marvellously/terrifically/fabulously.

mirliton [mirlitɔ̃] *nm V* **souffler dans le mirliton,** to fellate* (s.o.)/to give (s.o.) a blow-job/to give s.o. head.

miro [miro] *a P* myopic/short-sighted; **il est miro,** he's as blind as a bat.

mirobolant [mirɔbɔlã] *a F* stupendous/astounding/splendiferous/staggering news (etc).

miron [mirɔ̃] *nm P* cat/pussy/mog(gy).

mironton [mirɔ̃tɔ̃] **I** *a&nm F* odd

(character)/strange (individual); **un drôle de mironton,** an odd bod/a weirdo. (*Voir* **dévisser 5**) II *nmpl* P mirontons, eyes*.

mise [miz] *nf* F **faire une mise en scène à qn,** to hoax* s.o./to fool* s.o. (*Voir* **air I 7**)

miser [mize] *vtr* **1.** F on ne peut pas miser là-dessus, you can't count on it/bank on it. (*Voir* **tableau 4** *(a)*) **2.** V **miser qn,** to have sex* with s.o./to lay s.o./to ball s.o. **3.** V va te faire miser! get stuffed!

misère [mizεr] *nf* F **1.** cent francs? une misère! a hundred francs? a mere trifle! **2.** quelle misère! what a (rotten) life! **3.** ça vous tombe dessus comme la misère sur le pauvre monde, it happens to you before you know what's going on/it comes like a bolt from the blue **4.** faire des misères à qn, to tease s.o. unmercifully/to put s.o. through it. (*Voir* **collier 1** *(b)*)

mistenflûte [mistãflyt] *nm* O F what's-his-name*/what-d'you-call-him.

misti [misti] *nm* F (*cartes*) jack of clubs.

mistigri(s) [mistigri] *nm* F (pussy) cat/puss/moggy.

miston [mistɔ̃] *nm* P **1.** child*/kid/nipper **2.** prostitute's client/trick/John/meal ticket.

mistonne [mistɔn] *nf* P (*péj*) woman*; girl*.

mistouflard [mistuflar] *nm* P pauper/down-and-out.

mistoufle [mistufl] *nf* **1.** P poverty; être dans la mistoufle, to be down and out/to be very hard up **2.** F faire des mistoufles à qn, to pester/to annoy*/to tease s.o.

mistron [mistrɔ̃] *nm* P (*cartes*) (game of) *trente et un.*

mitaines [miten] *nfpl* F **1.** boxing gloves; croiser les mitaines, to box; to have a punch-up **2.** y aller avec des mitaines, to go at it with kid

gloves **3.** dire qch sans mitaines, to say sth bluntly; to blurt sth out; je n'ai pas pris de mitaines pour le lui dire, I didn't mince my words with him.

mitan [mitã] *nm* P **1.** middle/centre; au mitan de la place, in the centre of the square; en plein mitan, smack in the middle/a bull's-eye **2.** = **milieu.**

mitard [mitar] *nm* P **1.** disciplinary cell/punishment cell (in prison)/cooler **2.** faire du mitard, to lie low/to hole up.

mitarder [mitarde] *vtr* F se faire mitarder, to be put in solitary confinement/to get solitary/to get put in the cooler.

mite [mit] I *nf* P **1.** j'ai la mite aux yeux, my eyes are (all) gummed up **2.** bouffé aux mites, mad*/bonkers II *nm* P = **mitard 1.**

miter [mite] *vi* P to cry*/to grizzle.

miteusement [mitøzmã] *adv* F shabbily (dressed).

miteux, euse [mitø, -øz] F I *a* shabby/seedy(-looking)/down at heel; tatty/crummy/grotty (furniture, etc); ragged/tattered (clothes) II *n (a)* shabby person/ragbag *(b)* child*/kid/brat III *nf* woman easily given to tears/crybaby.

miton [mitɔ̃] *nm* F cat/pussy/mog(gy).

mitonnard [mitɔnar] *nm* P = **mitan 1, 2.**

mitraille [mitrɑj] *nf* F small change/small coins.

mitrailler [mitrɑje] *vtr* F les photographes mitraillent les délégués, the photographers are clicking away at the delegates.

mitrailleuse [mitrɑjøz] *nf* P **1.** chatterbox*/babbling brook **2.** automatic stamping machine.

mob [mɔb] *nf* F (= *Mobylette*) light motor-cycle; moped/pot-pot.

mobilard [mɔbilar] *nm F* (= *gendarme mobile*) policeman belonging to a special mobile squad.

mochard [mɔʃar] *a P* (*a*) pretty ugly (*b*) pretty lousy/pretty awful.

moche [mɔʃ] *a F* (*a*) ugly; **moche comme un pou/moche à faire peur/ moche à pleurer**, as ugly as sin; **ce qu'il est moche!** he's really ugly/ he's got a face like the back of a bus! (*b*) rotten/lousy; **la pluie pendant les vacances, c'est moche**, it's rotten/foul if it rains when you're on holiday; **c'est moche ce qu'il a fait**, that's a lousy/nasty trick he played; **qu'en dis-tu? – c'est moche!** what do you think of it? – it stinks!/it's disgusting! **être moche avec qn**, to treat s.o. badly/to be rotten to s.o. (*c*) poor/shoddy (work); **c'est moche, le travail que t'as fait**, it's pretty abysmal/awful, this work you did.

mochement [mɔʃmɑ̃] *adv F* (*a*) in an ugly way (*b*) in a rotten/lousy way (*c*) poorly/shoddily.

mocheté, *occ* **mochetée** [mɔʃte] *nf F* (*a*) ugly woman/fright/hag/ (old) bag; **c'est une mocheté, celle-là!** she's as ugly as sin/she's got a face like the back of a bus! (*b*) **ce costume! a-t-on jamais vu une mocheté pareille?** have you ever seen such a lousy suit?

mochetingue [mɔʃtɛ̃g], **mocheton, -onne** [mɔʃtɔ̃, -ɔn] *a P* = **moche**.

moco, Moco [mɔko] *nm P* native/inhabitant (*i*) of Marseille(s) (*ii*) of Toulon (*iii*) of Provence.

la Mocobo [lamɔkɔbo] *Prn F* = (*i*) the place Maubert (*ii*) the Maubert district (in Paris). (*Voir* **la Maub(e)**)

mœurs [mœrs] *nfpl P* (= *la brigade (de la police) des mœurs*) **les mœurs**, the vice squad. (*Voir* **mondaine**)

mohican [mɔikɑ̃] *nm V* penis*.

moinaille [mwanɑj] *nf coll F* (*péj*) monks in general.

moineau, *pl* **-eaux** [mwano] *nm* 1. *F* (*a*) *O* **un drôle de moineau**, a strange fellow/a funny old bird; **un sale moineau/un vilain moineau**, a bad lot/a heel/a louse (*b*) **c'est un épouvantail à moineaux**, he's/she's a real scarecrow; he's/she's enough to frighten off the birds (*c*) **tirer/brûler sa poudre aux moineaux** (*i*) to waste one's efforts (*ii*) to spend one's money recklessly (*d*) **avoir une cervelle de moineau**, to be feather-brained/empty-headed. (*Voir* **perchoir**) 2. *P* penis*; **filer un coup de moineau à qn**, to have sex* with s.o.

moinerie [mwanri] *nf F* (*péj*) 1. = **moinaille** 2. monastery/friary.

moins [mwɛ̃] *F* **I** *adv phr* (*a*) **tu n'es pas malade, au moins?** I hope you're not ill/you're not ill, are you?/I can take it you're not ill? (*b*) **c'est bien le moins!** it's the least he/she can do! **II** *prep* **il était moins une/moins deux/moins cinq**, it was a near thing/a close shave/a close call/a narrow escape. (*Voir* **deux 4**)

mois [mwa] *nm F* 1. **treizième mois**, Christmas bonus 2. **oublier les mois de nourrice**, to pretend to be younger than one really is/to be mutton dressed up as lamb 3. **avoir ses mois**, to have a period*; **elle a ses mois**, it's her time of the month. (*Voir* **trente-six**)

moisi [mwazi] *a F* **pas moisi**, strong/robust.

moisir [mwazir] *vi F* (*a*) to hang about/to be kept waiting; **il a pas moisi longtemps ici**, he didn't hang around/he didn't need to be told to go (*b*) **moisir en prison**, to rot in prison; **on moisit à travailler dans ce bureau**, you stagnate/vegetate working in this office.

moite [mwat] *a P* 1. **les avoir moites**, to be afraid*/to be in a blue funk/to wet oneself/to be shitting oneself 2. **être moite**, to say nothing/to keep quiet/to stay mum.

moiter [mwate] *vi P* to be afraid*/ to wet oneself/to be pissing oneself. (*Voir* **moite 1**)

moitié [mwatje] *nf F* **ma (chère/ douce) moitié** (*i*) my wife*/my better half (*ii*) my husband*/my better half.

mol(l)ard [mɔlar] *nm P* gob (of spit *or* phlegm).

mol(l)arder [mɔlarde] *vi P* to spit/to gob/to hawk up phlegm.

mollasse [mɔlas], **mollasson, onne** [mɔlasɔ̃, -ɔn] *F* **I** *a&n* flabby/spineless/gutless (person) **II** *n* **un grand mollasse/une grande mollasse/mollassonne**, a great lump (of a man/woman).

molletogommes [mɔl(ə)tɔgɔm], **molletons** [mɔltɔ̃] *nmpl P* calves (of legs).

mollo(-mollo) [mɔlo(mɔlo)], **mollot** [mɔlo] *adv P* **y aller mollo(-mollo)**, to act cautiously; **vas-y mollo(-mollo)!** (take it) easy!/ easy does it!/easy now!

mollusque [mɔlysk] *nm F* **c'est un mollusque**, he's got no go in him; he's got no backbone/he's a drip/ he's a bit wet.

molosse [mɔlɔs] *P* **I** *a* huge/ colossal (man) **II** *nm* huge man; colossus/giant.

moltegommes [mɔltəgɔm] *nmpl*, **moltogommes** [mɔltɔgɔm] *nmpl P* = **molletogommes.**

momaque [mɔmak] *nf*, **mômaque** [momak] *nf A P* little girl.

môme [mom] **I** *nm&f* (*a*) *F* child*/kid/brat (*b*) *F* young boy/ young girl* (*c*) *P* **il est encore tout môme**, he's still only a kid **II** *nm P* **faire descendre le môme**, to bring about an abortion; **pisser un môme**, to give birth (to a baby) **III** *nf P* **1.** woman*; **une jolie môme**, a nice bit of stuff/a nice piece of skirt/a nice bit of crumpet **2.** (*a*) mistress (*b*) (gangster's, pimp's) moll.

momi [mɔmi] *nf P* = **mominette.**

momichon [mɔmiʃɔ̃] *nm*, **mômichon** [momiʃɔ̃] *nm P* child*/kid/brat.

momignard, arde [mɔmiɲar, -ard], **mômignard, arde** [momiɲar, -ard], **mominard, arde** [mɔminar, -ard], **môminard, arde** [mominar, -ard] *nf P* young child*/little kid.

mominette [mɔminɛt] *nf P* small glass of absinthe *or* pastis.

monacos [mɔnako] *nmpl A P* money*/dough.

mondaine [mɔ̃dɛn] *nf P* (*police*) **la mondaine**, the vice squad. (*Voir* **mœurs**)

monde [mɔ̃d] *nm* **1.** *F* (*a*) **en faire (tout) un monde**, to make a lot of fuss/to make a song and dance about it (*b*) **se faire un monde/des mondes de qch**, to make a mountain out of a molehill **2.** *F* **se croire le centre du monde**, to think no small beer of oneself/to think one is the cat's whiskers **3.** *F* **ça (alors), c'est un monde!** well, that's the limit*/the last straw! **4.** (*a*) *F* **se moquer/se ficher/*P* se foutre du monde**, not to give a damn about anyone/anything; **elle se fout du monde**, she's got a bloody/damn cheek/nerve! **ils se foutent du monde**, they don't give a toss; **c'est se moquer du monde!** it's the height of impertinence! (*b*) **vous vous moquez du monde!** you're joking! **5. c'est le monde à l'envers!** what *is* the world coming to!/it's a mad/ crazy world (we live in)! (*Voir* **balcon**)

moniche [mɔniʃ] *nf V* female genitals*.

monnaie [mɔnɛ] *nf F* **1.** (*esp femme*) **commencer à rendre la monnaie**, to begin to grow old; **rendre la monnaie**, to be old and ugly **2. payer qn en monnaie de singe**, to let s.o. whistle for his money **3.**

par ici, la monnaie! give me the money!/come on, cough up!/give!

monseigneur [mõsɛɲœr] *nm F* (burglar's) jemmy/*NAm* jimmy.

monsieur [məsjø] *nm F* **1. faire le (gros) monsieur,** to act big **2. un joli/un vilain monsieur,** a bad lot/a nasty piece of work.

monstre [mõstr] *F* **I** *a* huge/enormous/whopping/whacking (great); **un sandwich monstre,** a huge sandwich/a whopper **II** *nm* **1.** (*a*) **se faire un monstre/des monstres de tout,** to make mountains out of molehills **2.** *O* **te voilà, petit monstre!** there you are, you little monster! **3. quel monstre, cette bagnole!** what a powerful beast that car is!

mont [mõ] *nm F* **promettre monts et merveilles à qn,** to promise s.o. the earth.

montage [mõtaʒ] *nm P* frame-up/put-up job/fit-up.

montagne [mõtaɲ] *nf F* (*a*) **se faire une montagne de rien,** to make a mountain out of a molehill (*b*) **se faire une montagne de qch/s'en faire (toute) une montagne,** to make heavy weather of sth (*c*) **c'est la montagne qui accouche d'une souris,** what a lot of fuss about nothing!

montant [mõtã] *nm P* **1.** ladder **2.** *pl* **montants,** trousers*/*NAm* pants.

monte [mõt] *nf P* (*prostituées*) **une monte,** a short time/a quick job/a quickie.

monté [mõte] *a* **1.** *F* **il était monté,** he was (all) worked up; his blood was up; **il est monté contre moi,** he's furious with me; he's got a down on me. (*Voir* **tête**) **2.** *F* slightly drunk*/tipsy/merry **3.** *P* (*a*) (*homme*) **être bien monté/monté comme un âne/monté comme un cheval/comme une mule,** to be well-developed/well-equipped/well-hung/hung like a bull (*b*) (*iron*)

vous voilà bien monté! that's a nice mess you've landed yourself in! (*Voir* **bourrichon**; **collet 1**; **coup 15**)

monte-en-l'air [mõtɑ̃lɛr] *nm inv F* cat-burglar/climber.

monter [mõte] **I** *vi F* **faire monter qn** (*i*) to take a rise out of s.o. (*ii*) to make s.o.'s blood boil/to get s.o. all worked up. (*Voir* **cheval 10** (*b*); **échelle 1**; **soupe**) **II** *vtr* **1.** *F* **monter qn contre qn,** to set s.o. against s.o./to egg s.o. on against s.o. **2.** *P* (*prostituée*) **monter un client** (*i*) to have sex* with a client/to turn a trick (*ii*) to have a short time/a quickie with a client (in a hotel room); **tu montes, chéri?** do you want a good time, love/honey? **3.** *P* to have sex* with (s.o.)/to jump/to mount/to climb (s.o.). (*Voir* **bateau I 1**; **bourrichon**; **cou 1**; **coup 15**; **tête 13**) **III** *vpr* **se monter** *F* to flare up/to fly off the handle/to lose one's cool; **elle se monte pour un rien/pour des riens,** she gets all worked up over nothing.

montgolfière [mõgɔlfjɛr] *nf* **1.** *P* nymphomaniac/nympho **2.** *pl V* testicles* **3.** *pl V* breasts*/balloons.

Montparno [mõparno] *Prn F* (*i*) the Montparnasse quarter (*ii*) the boulevard du Montparnasse (in Paris).

montrouze [mõtruz] *nf P* watch/ticker.

Mont Valo [mõvalo] *Prn F* Mont Valérien (near Paris).

monumental, -aux [mɔnymãtal, -o] *a F* huge/enormous; **d'une bêtise monumentale,** incredibly stupid*.

moral [mɔral] *nm F* **avoir le moral,** to be in high spirits/to feel on top of the world; **avoir le moral à zéro,** to be right down in the dumps; to be really depressed*/low/down;

remonter le moral à qn, to cheer s.o. up/to buck s.o. up.

morbac, morbaque [mɔrbak] *nm P* **1.** crab(-louse)/pubic louse **2.** (*a*) child*/brat (*b*) (*pers*) little squirt/little runt.

morceau, -eaux [mɔrso] *nm F* **1.** manger/casser un morceau, to have a bite (to eat)/to have a snack. (*Voir* **pouce 2**) **2.** bouffer/casser/cracher/lâcher/manger le morceau, to confess*; to turn informer*/to grass **3.** casser le morceau à qn/en casser un morceau à qn, to give s.o. a piece of one's mind/to let s.o. have it straight **4.** emporter le morceau (*i*) to succeed; to win out; to get one's own way (*ii*) to be very cutting (in one's remarks) **5.** gober le morceau, to swallow the bait/to fall for it (hook, line and sinker) **6.** (*a*) un morceau de femme, a (mere) slip of a woman (*b*) (*fille, femme*) un beau morceau, a nice bit of stuff/a bit of all right **7.** (*gros sexe*) avoir un morceau, to be well-hung.

morcif [mɔrsif] *nm P* (= *morceau*) piece/morsel.

mordante [mɔrdɑ̃t] *nf P* (*lime*) file.

mordants [mɔrdɑ̃] *nmpl P* scissors.

mordicus [mɔrdikys] *adv F* stubbornly/tooth and nail; défendre mordicus son opinion, to stick to one's guns.

mordre [mɔrdr] *vtr & ind tr* **1.** *F* quel chien l'a mordu? what's biting him?/what's bugging him?/what's got into him? **2.** *F* il ne mord pas à l'espagnol, he can't get on with Spanish/he hasn't taken to Spanish; je ne peux pas y mordre, it's beyond me **3.** *F* ça mord? any luck? **4.** *F* ça ne mord pas (*i*) (don't worry,) it won't bite (you) (*ii*) nothing doing/(you can) count me out **5.** *F* c'est à se les mordre/à se la mordre (*i*) it's very funny*!/it's a scream! (*ii*) it's appalling!/it's maddening! **6.** *P* to understand;

tu mords? (do you) get it? **7.** *P* to look at* (s.o./sth) closely; mords(-moi-ça)!/mordez(-moi-ça)! just look at that!/take a dekko at that!/get a load of that! **8.** *adv phr P* ... à la mords-moi le doigt/le chose/le nœud/l'œil (*i*) ridiculously (*ii*) hesitantly/hit-or-miss (*iii*) in a dodgy/peculiar sort of way. (*Voir* **doigt 8**; **pouce 7**; **truc**)

mordu, -ue [mɔrdy] *F* **I** *a* (*a*) être mordu du théâtre, to be mad on/(dead) keen on the theatre; mordu du foot, crazy/mad/nuts about football (*b*) être mordu pour qn, to be madly in love with s.o.; to be crazy/wild/mad about s.o. **II** *n* enthusiast/fan; c'est un mordu du flipper/du jogging, he's pinball/jogging crazy; he's nuts/crazy about pinball/jogging; he's a pinball/jogging nut; he's been bitten by the pinball/jogging bug.

moré [mɔre] *nm P* brother.

morfal(e) [mɔrfal] *nm P* = **morfalou.**

morfaler [mɔrfale] *P* **I** *vi* to stuff oneself (with food) **II** *vtr* to wolf (one's food) (down); morfaler sa mangeaille, to shovel food into one's mouth **III** *vpr* se morfaler *P* to stuff oneself (with food)/to (make a) pig (of) oneself.

morfalou [mɔrfalu] *nm P* **1.** glutton*/greedyguts/pig **2.** grasping person/grabber.

morfic [mɔrfik] *nm P* = **morpion 1.**

morfier [mɔrfije], **morfiler** [mɔrfile], **morfiller** [mɔrfije] *vtr&i* **1.** *P* to eat* **2.** *V* to have cunnilingus* (with)/to go down (on)/to eat.

morfler [mɔrfle] *vtr P* (*a*) to get/to cop (a punishment/a prison sentence); morfler le maxi, to get the maximum sentence (*b*) faire morfler qn, to put s.o. through it/to give s.o. the works.

morgane [mɔrgan] *nf P* salt.

morganer [mɔrgane] *vtr P* **1.** (*i*) to eat* (*ii*) to chew (*iii*) to bite **2.** to denounce* (s.o.)/to blow the whistle on (s.o.).

moricaud, aude [mɔriko, -od] *F* **I** *a* dark-skinned **II** *n* (*péj*) Black*/darkie/wog/spade.

morlingue [mɔrlɛ̃g] *nm P* purse; wallet; **être constipé/dur du morlingue; avoir un hérisson/un piège à loups/des oursins dans le morlingue,** to be miserly*/stingy/tight-fisted/tight-assed.

morniflard [mɔrniflar] *nm P* purse.

mornifle [mɔrnifl] *nf P* **1.** (*a*) money* (*b*) small change **2. flanquer/refiler une mornifle à qn,** to land s.o. a backhander (in the face) **3.** jibe/dig (at s.o.) (*Voir* **cigue 1**)

mornifleur [mɔrniflœr] *nm P* counterfeiter/forger.

morph [mɔrf] *nf P* (*drogues*) (= *morphine*) morphine*/shit.

morphal(e) [mɔrfal] *nm P* = **morfal(e).**

morphaler [mɔrfale] *vtr, i & pr P* = **morfaler I, II, III.**

morphalou [mɔrfalu] *nm P* = **morfalou.**

morphiller [mɔrfije] *vtr&i P V* = **morfil(l)er 1, 2.**

morphino [mɔrfino] *nm&f P* (= *morphinomane*) morphine* addict/junkie.

morpion [mɔrpjɔ̃] *nm* **1.** *F* crab(-louse)/pubic louse **2.** *P* child*/brat **3.** *F* (*jeu*) = noughts and crosses/*NAm* tick tack toe.

mort [mɔr] **I** *a F* **1.** (*a*) **c'est mort/elle est morte** (*i*) let's call it a day (*ii*) it's all over (and done with) (*iii*) it's hopeless (*b*) **encore une de morte!/elle est morte!** that's another day's work done! **2.** (*a*) (*chaussures etc*) worn out; useless (*b*) (*bouteille*) empty/dead. (*Voir* **dos 13**) **II** *nm F* **1. la place du mort,** the front passenger seat/*esp NAm Austr* the death seat **2. faire le mort** (*i*) to lie low (and say nothing) (*ii*) (*cartes*) to play dummy **III** *nf F* **ce n'est pas la mort (d'un homme),** it's not all that difficult. (*Voir* **vache**) **IV** *adv phr P* extremely; **freiner à mort,** to jam on the brakes; *V* **bander à mort,** to have a terrific/a throbbing erection*/hard-on.

mortibus [mɔrtibys] *a P* dead/stiff/cold.

morue [mɔry] *nf P* prostitute*/tart/slut.

morveux, euse [mɔrvø, -øz] *F* **I** *a* snotty-nosed/with a runny nose **II** *n* (*a*) (annoying) child*/brat (*b*) raw/green kid; **c'est un morveux,** he's still wet behind the ears (*c*) **un petit morveux,** a snotty-nosed kid/a little jerk/a little runt (*d*) **les morveux veulent moucher les autres,** it's like Satan reproving sin; **quand on est morveux on se mouche,** do your own dirty business.

moscoutaire [mɔskuter] *nm&f F* (*péj*) moscoutaire, communist/commie/bolshie.

mot [mo] *nm F* **1. pas un mot à la reine mère!** mum's the word!/keep it under your hat! **2. mot de cinq lettres** (= **merde**), = four-letter(ed) word. (*Voir* **Cambronne**) **3. un (petit) mot,** short letter/note/a few lines.

motal [mɔtal] *nf P* motorbike.

motard [mɔtar] *nm F* **1.** motorcyclist; biker/bikie **2.** police motor-cyclist/cycle cop.

moto [mɔto] *nf F* motor-bike/bike; **casque de moto,** skid lid.

motobécane [mɔtobekan] *nf F* (light) motor-cycle/bike.

motocyclard [mɔtɔsiklar] *nm F* (*a*) = **motard 1, 2** (*b*) dispatch rider.

motorisé [mɔtɔrize] *a F* **êtes-vous motorisé?** have you got a car?/are you mobile?/have you got wheels?

motte [mɔt] *nf* **1.** *P* **faire la motte,** to go halves/to go dutch **2.** *V* anus* **3.** *V* (*a*) female genitals*/beaver/cunt (*b*) female pubis/mons veneris. (*Voir* **astiquer 4**)

motus [mɔtys] *int F* **motus (et bouche cousue),** mum's the word!/keep it under your hat!

mou, molle [mu, mɔl] **I** *a F* **1.** flabby/spineless/wet (individual) **2. pâte molle/cire molle,** person you can twist round your little finger. (*Voir* **chiffe I 1, 2; chique 6**) **II** *adv P* **y aller mou,** to act cautiously; **vas-y mou!** mind how you go!/easy does it!/go easy!/take it easy! **III** *nm P* **1.** human flesh/body; **rentrer dans le mou à qn,** to attack s.o./to beat s.o. up*/to work s.o. over **2. bourrer le mou à qn,** to have s.o. on/to lead s.o. up the garden path; **c'est du mou!** it's a lot of eyewash/it's a load of bull! (*Voir* **crâne; bourre-mou**) **3. gonfler le mou,** to exaggerate*/to shoot a line **4. bout de mou,** penis*/meat/muscle/gristle **5. les mous,** the lungs **6.** paper money/notes.

mouchard [muʃar] *nm F* **1.** (*a*) sneak/tell-tale (*b*) police informer*/snout/grass **2.** detective*/dick **3.** spy-hole (in door, prison cell, etc) **4.** (*dans un camion, etc*) tachograph/spy in the cab.

mouchardage [muʃardaʒ] *nm F* (*i*) spying; sneaking (*ii*) grassing; **mouchardage électronique,** telephone tapping; bugging.

moucharde [muʃard] *nf P* moon.

moucharder [muʃarde] *vtr F* (*a*) to spy (on)/to sneak (on) (s.o.) (*b*) to denounce* (s.o.)/to grass (on s.o.).

mouche [muʃ] *nf F* **1.** (= **mouchard 1**) **faire la mouche,** to turn informer **2. quelle mouche vous pique?** what's biting you?/

what's bugging you?/what's got into you? **3. tuer les mouches au vol/à quinze pas,** to have bad breath **4. c'est une fine mouche,** he's/she's a crafty little so-and-so; he/she knows what he's/she's after. (*Voir* **coche 2; enculer 1; merde 15**)

moucher [muʃe] **I** *vtr* **1.** *F* **moucher qn,** to tell s.o. off/to put s.o. (firmly) in his place; **se faire moucher,** to get put in one's place; **il a été mouché de belle façon,** he really got told where to get off **2.** *P* **moucher qn,** to beat s.o. up*/to work s.o. over; **se faire moucher,** to get injured/damaged **4.** *P* **mouche ton nez!** mind your own business! (*Voir* **morveux II** (*d*)) **II** *vpr* **se moucher 1.** *F* **il ne se mouche pas de la main gauche/du coude/du pied** (*i*) he thinks an awful lot of himself (*ii*) he does things in great style/he doesn't do things by halves (*iii*) he lays it on (a bit) thick **2.** *P* **je m'en mouche!** I couldn't care less!*/I don't give a damn!

moucheron, onne [muʃrɔ̃, -ɔn] *n F* child*/kid/brat/sprog.

mouchique [muʃik] *a P* **1.** ugly/hideous **2.** disreputable; notorious.

mouchodrome [muʃɔdrom] *nm P* bald* head/skating rink.

mouchoir [muʃwar] *nm F* **1. le mouchoir d'Adam,** one's fingers **2.** (*sport*) **arriver dans un mouchoir (de poche),** to make a close finish.

moudre [mudr] *vtr P* **en moudre,** to be(come) a prostitute*; to be/to go on the game.

la Mouffe [lamuf] *Prn F* the rue Mouffetard (and district) (in Paris).

mouffeter [mufte] *vi P* = **mouf(f)ter.**

mouf(f)let, ette [muflɛ, -ɛt] *n P* child*/kid/sprog; **avoir un mouf(f)let dans le tiroir,** to be pregnant*/to have a bun in the oven.

mouf(f)ter [mufte] *vi P* to blab/to blow the gaff; **ne pas mouf(f)ter/ne rien mouf(f)ter**, to keep mum.

mouillé [muje] *a* **1.** *F* **il est mouillé dans cette affaire**, he's in it up to his neck **2.** *P* **il fait mouillé**, it's wet/it's raining. (*Voir* **poule 4**)

mouiller [muje] **I** *vi P* (*a*) **mouiller pour qn**, to be infatuated* with s.o./to have a crush on s.o./to have a thing about s.o. (*b*) (*femme*) to be sexually excited*; to be randy/horny/juicy **2.** *F* **il mouille/ça mouille**, it's raining/it's pelting down **3.** *P* to pay up*/to cough up **II** *vtr* **1.** *P* **en mouiller**, to talk (away) nineteen to the dozen/to rabbit on **2.** *P* **mouiller qn**, to compromise s.o./to implicate s.o. **3.** *P* **mouiller le goupillon**, to have sex*/to dip one's wick **III** *vtr&i P* **mouiller (son froc)**, to be afraid*/to have the willies; **les mouiller**, to be scared stiff/to have the wind up/to be in a blue funk. (*Voir* **dalle²**; **meule 4**) **IV** *vpr* **se mouiller 1.** *F* to compromise oneself; to implicate oneself (in a shady business, deal, etc); to stick one's neck out/to get one's feet wet; **il ne veut pas se mouiller**, he doesn't want to get mixed up in it **2.** *F* to commit oneself/to let oneself in for sth **3.** *P* to bet heavily.

mouilles [muj] *nfpl P* buttocks*.

mouillette [mujɛt] *nf P* **1.** tongue **2. aller à la mouillette** = **se mouiller 1.**

mouisant [mwizɑ̃] *nm P* (*scol*) poverty-stricken student.

mouisard [mwizar] *nm P* poverty-stricken person/down-and-out; **c'est un mouisard**, he's hit hard times.

mouise [mwiz] *nf P* **être dans la mouise**, to be penniless*/to be very hard up/to (have) hit hard times.

moujingue [muʒɛ̃g] *nm P* **1.** child*/kid/brat/sprog **2. tricoter le moujingue**, to bring about an abortion.

moukala [mukala] *nm P* revolver*/gun/piece/shooter.

moukère [mukɛr] *nf P* (*a*) (*péj*) woman*/bint (*b*) wife* (*c*) mistress (*d*) prostitute*/*esp NAm* hooker/tart.

moule [mul] **I** *nf* **1.** *P* (*a*) drip/wet/wimp (*b*) fool*/twerp/dope/jerk **2.** *V* female genitals*; **avoir la moule qui bâille**, to be sexually excited*/randy/horny **3.** *P* **avoir les moules**, to be afraid*/to have the wind up/to have the willies **4.** *P* **avoir de la moule**, to be very lucky **II** *nm P* **moule à gaufre(s)** (*i*) fool*/prize idiot/jerk (*ii*) pock-marked face.

mouler [mule] *vtr P* **1. en mouler**, to be a prostitute*/to solicit*/to be on the game **2.** to leave (sth) behind/to abandon (sth) **3. mouler un bronze**, to defecate*/to have a crap.

moulin [mulɛ̃] *nm* **1.** *F* engine (of car, plane, etc) **2.** *F* **moulin à paroles** (*i*) tongue (*ii*) chatterbox*/gasbag/windbag **3.** *P* (*mil*) **moulin à café**, machine-gun **4.** *F* **avoir un moulin qui tourne/des moulins qui tournent**, to have a profitable source of income **5.** *P* pimp*'s mistress/fancy piece.

mouliner [muline] *vi F* **1.** (*cycliste*) to pedal along at a steady pace **2.** to chatter*/to talk (away) nineteen to the dozen.

moulinette [mulinɛt] *nf* **1.** *P* sub-machine-gun; tommy-gun **2.** *F* (*i*) tongue (*ii*) chatterbox*.

moulu [muly] *a F* (*i*) exhausted*/dead beat (*ii*) aching all over.

mouniche [muniʃ] *nf V* female genitals*.

mouquère [mukɛr] *nf P* = **moukère**.

mourant [murɑ̃] *a F* **1.** very funny*/killing/creasing **2.** exasperating/maddening.

mourir [murir] *vi* **1.** *F* c'est à mourir de rire, it's very funny*/it's absolutely killing **2.** *P* tu t'en ferais mourir! nothing doing!/not blooming likely!/no fear!/not (bloody) likely*!

mouron [murɔ̃] *nm P* **1.** se faire du mouron, to get worried/to worry oneself sick/to get into a state*; te fais pas de mouron pour moi! don't worry about me! **2.** hair; ne plus avoir de mouron sur la cage, to be as bald* as a coot **3.** (woman's) pubic hair/pubes; beaver.

(se) mouronner [(sə)murɔne] *vi&pr P* to worry oneself sick.

mouscaille [muskɑj] *nf* **1.** *P* mud/dirt/gunge **2.** *V* excrement/ shit/crap **3.** *P* être dans la mouscaille, to be in a fix*/to be up to one's neck in it/to be in the shit **4.** *P* avoir qn à la mouscaille, to hate s.o.'s guts.

mousmé(e) [musme] *nf P* (*a*) young woman* (*b*) mistress (*c*) (young and pretty) prostitute*.

moussante [musɑ̃t] *nf P* beer/ ale/lager.

mousse [mus] *nf P* **1.** se faire de la mousse, to worry oneself sick **2.** beer/lager.

mousseline [muslin] *nf P* (*drogues*) morphine*.

mousser [muse] *vi* **1.** *F* to fume (with anger)/to blow one's top/to fly off the handle **2.** faire mousser qn (*i*) *F* to rile s.o./to get s.o.'s goat (*ii*) *F* to crack s.o. up/to build s.o. up (to be pretty amazing) (*iii*) *V* to masturbate* s.o./to cream s.o. off **3.** se faire mousser (*i*) *F* to show off*/to blow one's own trumpet; to think one is the cat's whiskers (*ii*) *V* se faire mousser le créateur, to masturbate*/to bring oneself off/to cream one's jeans.

mousseux [musø] *nm P* soap.

moussu [musy] *a P* hairy.

moustachue [mustaʃy] *nf P*

(*homosexuels*) masculine/butch/ macho homosexual.

moustique [mustik] *nm P* (troublesome) child*/brat/pest.

moutard [mutar] *nm F* (*a*) small boy/kid/brat (*b*) *pl* les moutards, the kids.

moutarde [mutard] *nf F* **1.** la moutarde lui est montée au nez, he lost his temper/he went off the deep end **2.** c'est (comme) de la moutarde après dîner, it's like closing the stable door after the horse has bolted; it's come a day after the fair **3.** s'amuser à la moutarde, to waste one's time on trifles. (*Voir* pesant)

moutardier [mutardje] *nm* **1.** *F* il se croit le premier moutardier du pape, he's grown too big for his boots **2.** *P* buttocks*.

moute [mut] *af A F* (*rare*) beautiful; nice/sweet.

mouton [mutɔ̃] *nm* **1.** *F* un mouton à cinq pattes, something very rare; chercher le mouton à cinq pattes, to look for the impossible **2.** *F* (*esp prisons*) police informer*/(copper's) nark/grass/ snout **3.** *pl F* moutons, fluff (under bed, etc) **4.** *P* laisser pisser le mouton, to bide one's time. (*Voir* mérinos)

moutonner [mutɔne] *vtr F* **1.** to spy on/to inform against (a prisoner) **2.** to sound (s.o.) out/to pump (s.o.).

m'sieu [msjø] *nm F* (= *monsieur*) mister/Mr; sir.

m'sieurs-dames [msjødam] *nmpl F* = **messieurs-dames.**

muche [myʃ] *nf F* hiding place.

mucher [myʃe] *vtr F* to hide.

mud [myd] *nm P* (*drogues*) opium*/ mud.

Muette [myɛt] *nf F* (*mil*) la grande Muette, the Army.

muf(f)e [myf] *nm P* = **mufle 1, 2.**

muffée [myfe] *nf P* **1.** prendre une (bonne) muffée, to get drunk*/to tie one on; avoir la muffée/une muffée, to be dead drunk*/to be (completely) plastered. (*Voir* tenir 2) **2.** y en a une muffée, there's tons of it/there's any amount of it.

mufflée [myfle] *nf P* = **muffée.**

mufle [myfl] *nm P* **1.** face*/mug **2.** bastard*/nasty piece of work/*esp NAm* son of a bitch; espèce de mufle! what a slob/lout/jerk!

muflée [myfle] *nf P* = **muffée.**

mule [myl] *nf F* ferrer la mule (*i*) to make illicit profits* (when buying for others); to make a bit on the side (*ii*) to take a bribe (for obtaining an interview for s.o.). (*Voir* tête 4)

mur [myr] *nm* **1.** *F* faire le mur (*i*) to slip out/away; to skive off (*ii*) (*mil*) to go over the wall **2.** *F* être logé entre quatre murs, to be in prison*/inside **3.** *F* se heurter contre un mur, to come up against a brick wall **4.** *F* c'est pire que (de) parler à un mur, it's like talking to a brick wall **5.** *F* (il) y a de quoi se taper la tête contre les murs, it's enough to drive you up the wall **6.** *P* pickpocket's accomplice who acts as a shield while the theft is carried out.

mûr [myr] *a* **1.** *F* habit mûr, coat that has seen better days **2.** *P* drunk*/high/stewed/pissed. (*Voir* vert I 2)

muraille [myrɑj] *nf F* être logé entre quatre murailles, to be in prison*/inside. (*Voir* mur 2)

se murdinguer [səmyrdɛ̃ge] *vpr P* = **se mûrir.**

mûre [myr] *nf P* blow*/punch; sock (in the face).

se mûrir [səmyrir] *vpr P* to get drunk*.

museau, eaux [myzo] *nm F* **1.** face*; joli petit museau, sweet/cute little face; vilain museau, ugly mug; se poudrer le museau, to powder one's face/one's nose **2.** mouth* **3.** nose*. (*Voir* fricassée 2)

musette [myzɛt] *nf P* **1.** c'est dans la musette, it's a cert*/it's in the bag **2.** il a reçu une raclée qui n'était pas dans une musette/il en a pris plein sa musette, he got a hiding he won't forget in a hurry.

musicien [myzisjɛ̃] *nm P* **1.** flatterer* **2.** crook/underhand dealer **3.** *pl* musiciens, beans.

musico(t) [myziko] *nm P* musician.

musique [myzik] *nf* **1.** *F* connaître (un peu) la musique, to know what's what/to know the score **2.** *P* flattery*/blarney **3.** *F* blackmail **4.** *F* réglé comme du papier à musique, as regular as clockwork **5.** *F* (*a*) faire de la musique/en faire une musique, to kick up a row/to raise a rumpus; ils faisaient une musique enragée, they were making a hell of a din/racket; baisse un peu ta musique! pipe down, will you! (*b*) ses parents ont fait une musique énorme, her parents made an awful fuss about it **6.** *F* c'est une autre musique, that's another matter/that's a different kettle of fish **7.** *P* cross-examination.

musiquette [myzikɛt] *nf* **1.** (*péj*) music of sorts; amateur music **2.** *P* blackmail.

la Mutu [lamyty] *Prn F* the Palais de la Mutualité (in Paris).

mystère [mistɛr] *nm F* **1.** mystère et boule de gomme! I haven't a clue!/search me! **2.** y a pas de mystère, quoi! it's as simple as that!/there's no two ways about it!

N

na! [na] *int* F (*mot d'enfants*) so there!/ya boo sucks! **j'irai pas, na!** I'm not going, so there!/I'm not going and that's that!

nada [nada] *adv* P **1.** no **2.** nothing*.

nage [naʒ] *nf* F **être (tout) en nage/ se mettre en nage,** to be bathed in sweat/dripping with sweat.

nageoire [naʒwar] *nf* P **1.** *pl* **nageoires,** sidewhiskers/sideboards **2.** arm/fin/flipper.

nager [naʒe] *vi* F **1.** to be out of one's depth; **je nage complètement,** I'm all at sea; **en maths, il nage complètement,** he's completely lost/ he's hopeless at maths **2.** **savoir nager,** to know the ropes/to be clued up; to know the score **3.** **il nage comme un caillou/comme un chien de plomb/comme une clef,** he swims like a brick.

nana [nana] *nf* P **1.** (*a*) woman*/ girl*/bird/chick; **la vraie nana,** the goods (*b*) girlfriend; **sa nana,** his bird/his chick/his woman **2.** prostitute*. (*Voir* **peau 3**)

nanan [nanɑ̃, nɑ̃nɑ̃] *nm* F **c'est du nanan!** (*i*) yum-yum! (*ii*) it's a piece of cake!/it's money for old rope!/ it's a walkover!/it's a doddle!

nanar [nanar] *a&nm* P **c'est (du) nanar,** it's worthless*/it's no good/ it's useless; **ce film est un vieux nanar,** this film is a load of old rubbish/a dead loss.

nanard [nanar] P **I** *a* stupid*/ silly/soft **II** *n* fool*/dope/nana.

nanti [nɑ̃ti] *a* F **être bien mal nanti(e),** to have a bad wife*/husband*.

Nantoche [nɑ̃tɔʃ] *Prn* F Nanterre (*suburb of Paris*).

nap [nap] *nm* F (= *napoléon*) (*a*) (*à l'origine*) twenty-franc gold piece (bearing the effigy of Napoleon I) (*b*) (any) gold piece.

naph [naf] *nf* P = **naphtaline.**

naphtalinard [naftalinar] *nm* P (*mil*) retired army officer recalled to active duty/dugout/retread.

naphtaline [naftalin] *nf*, **naphte** [naft] *nf* P (*drogues*) (*a*) cocaine*/ coke (*b*) *occ* heroin*.

napo [napo] *nm* P Neapolitan.

nappe [nap] *nf* F **1.** **mettre la main sur la bonne nappe,** to strike it rich **2.** **trouver la nappe mise,** to marry into a fortune.

naquer du fla [nakedyfla] *vi* A P (= *largonji de flaquer*) to defecate*.

narc [nark] *nm* P (*drogues*) narcotic; *pl* **narcs,** drugs/dope/junk.

nardu [nardy] *nm* P police superintendent/super.

narines [narin] *nfpl* F **en prendre plein les narines,** to be snubbed.

narquin [narkɛ̃] *nm* P safe-cracker. (*Voir* **arquin**)

narzo [narzo] *nm* P (*verlan de zonard*) layabout; yob/yobbo/hooligan*.

nase [naz] **I** *nm* P nose* **II** *a* P = **naze² 1, 2.**

naseau, -eaux [nazo] *nm* P (*a*) nose* (*b*) *pl* nostrils.

nasi [nazi]ˉ*a* *P* = **nazi(coté).**

nasque [nask] *nf* *P* **prendre une nasque,** to get drunk*; **ils ont pris une nasque de première,** they got completely pissed/plastered/smashed.

nasse [nas] *nf* *F* (*a*) **être dans la nasse,** to be in a fix*/a mess/a jam (*b*) **tomber dans la nasse,** to fall into a trap; to get stymied.

se natchaver [sənatʃave] *vpr* *P* to run away*/to beat it/to scram/to skedaddle.

nattes [nat] *nfpl* *F* **faire des nattes,** to get into a tangle/to get muddled/to get tied up in knots/to lose the thread (of one's ideas).

nature [natyr] **I** *nf* *F* **1.** disparaître/s'évanouir/se perdre dans la nature, to vanish into thin air **2.** (*aut*) partir/se retrouver dans la nature, to run/to smash into a wall, tree, etc **3.** envoyer/expédier qn dans la nature, to send s.o. packing*/to turf s.o. out **4.** lâcher qn dans la nature, to give s.o. his head/to give s.o. a free rein **5.** c'est une (vraie) force de la nature, he's as strong as an ox; he's a giant of a man **6.** c'est une nature, he's a natural/he's a real personality **7.** c'est une petite nature, he's a bit wet/a bit of a drip **8.** il n'est pas aidé par la nature, he's stupid* (from birth)/he's a natural idiot **II** *a inv* *F* **1.** ça fera plus nature, that'll look more natural **2.** (*pers*) (*a*) natural/open/frank/uninhibited (*b*) gullible/easily taken in **3.** (*boisson, etc*) neat **III** *adv* *P* naturally/of course.

naturlich(e) [natyrliʃ] *adv* *P* naturally/of course.

navaler [navale] *vi* *P* (*a*) to run (at full pelt) (*b*) to run away*/to beat it. (*Voir* **cavaler 1** (*a*))

navdu [navdy] *nm* *P* = **navedu.**

nave [nav] *nm* *P* **1.** (*individu n'appartenant pas au* **milieu**) outsider **2.** (*a*) victim of a swindle*/ fall guy/mug/sucker (*b*) (**essence de**) **nave/(fleur de) nave,** fool*/idiot/twerp/clot **3.** (*film, etc*) tripe/rubbish.

navedu [navdy] *nm* *P* = **nave 1, 2.**

navet [navɛ] *nm* **1.** *F* trashy/third-rate novel; rubbishy/trashy/third-rate film; tripe; (*pièce*) pure ham **2.** *P* **des navets!** nothing doing!/not bloody likely!* **3.** *P* idiot/clot **4.** *P* **se creuser le navet,** to rack one's brains **5.** *P* **le champ de navets,** the cemetery* **6.** *P* **il a du sang de navet,** he's got no guts/no spunk.

naveton [navtɔ̃] *nm,* **navetot** [navto] *nm* *P* fool*/idiot/twerp/ clot.

navette [navɛt] *nf* *P* **1.** head* **2.** stupid woman.

naviguer [navige] *vi* *F* (*a*) to move around/to travel about (from one place to another); **il a beaucoup navigué,** he's knocked about a bit/ he's been around (*b*) **il sait naviguer,** he knows the ropes/the score.

naz [naz] *nm* *P* nose*.

naze[1] [naz] *P* **I** *nm* **1.** nose* **2.** syphilis*/syph/pox; **il a chopé le naze,** he's copped a dose (of syph) **II** *nm&f* s.o. infected with syphilis*/syphilitic/sypho. (*Voir* **cloquer 1** (*d*))

naze[2], **nazebroque** [nazbrɔk] *a* *P* **1.** syphilitic/syphed up/poxy **2.** worthless*/rubbishy/useless; **ce n'est pas de la marchandise naze,** it's none of your poxy rubbish; **ma moto est complètement naze,** my bike's conked out/packed up.

nazi(coté) [nazi(kɔte)] *a* *P* syphilitic/syphed up.

naziqué [nazike] *a* *P* syphilitic/ siffy/syphed up.

naziquer [nazike] *vtr* *P* to infect (s.o.) with syphilis*/to give (s.o.) a dose.

nécro [nekro] *nf*, **nécrops** [nekrɔps] *nf P* (*a*) post-mortem/ autopsy (*b*) (*esp journal*) obituary.

nèfles [nɛfl] *nfpl* **1.** *F* **avoir qch pour des nèfles**, to get sth dirt-cheap/for a song/for peanuts **2.** *P* **des nèfles!** nothing doing!/no (blooming) fear!/not bloody likely!*

négatif [negatif] *adv F* no/negative.

négifran [neʒifrɑ̃] *nf P* (*verlan de* **frangine**) sister/sis.

nègre [nɛgr] **I** *nm* **1.** *P* (*péj*) Black*/nigger/niggra/blackman **2.** *F* ghost-writer; devil (of barrister); (general) dogsbody; **il me faut un nègre**, I want s.o. to do the donkey work **3.** *F* **fais comme le nègre!** carry on(, sailor)!/keep it going!/ don't stop! **4.** *F* **parler petit nègre**, to talk pidgin French **5.** *V* (*péj*) **noir comme dans le trou du cul d'un nègre**, as black as a nigger's/*Austr* an abo's arsehole. (*Voir* **bosser**) **II** *a inv F* **propos nègre blanc**, double talk.

négresse [negrɛs] *nf P* **1.** flea **2.** bottle of red wine; **éternuer sur/ étouffer/étrangler/éventrer une négresse**, to down/to knock back a bottle of plonk/a bottle of vino.

négrier [negrije] *nm F* harsh task-master/slave-driver.

négro [negro] *nm P* (*péj*) Black*/ negro/nigger.

neige [nɛʒ] *nf* **1.** *P* (*drogues*) cocaine*/snow/white stuff **2.** *V* **une trompette à la neige**, fellatio*/ blow-job/head.

neiger [neʒe] *vi F* **il a neigé sur sa tête**, he's got white hair.

nénés [nene] *nmpl P* breasts*/tits/ knockers/boobs/Bristols; **des nénés de chez Michelin**, falsies.

nénesse [nenɛs] *nf P* (*a*) woman* (*b*) wife*.

nénette [nenɛt] *nf P* **1.** (young) woman*/girl*/chick/bird; **nénette ronronnante**, sex kitten; **vas-y, nénette!** attagirl! **2.** head* **3.**

travailler de la nénette, to be mad*/off one's rocker **4. se casser la nénette** (*i*) to rack one's brains (*ii*) to be frustrated (*iii*) to come a cropper*; **il ne se casse pas la nénette**, he doesn't exert himself/he doesn't put himself out; **j'en ai pardessus la nénette**, I'm sick and tired of it/I've had it up to here/I've had a bellyful of it.

nénuphar [nenyfar] *nm V* female genitals*.

nerf [nɛr] *nm* **1.** *F* **taper sur les nerfs à qn**, to get on s.o.'s nerves **2.** *F* **mets-y du nerf!** [nɛrf] put some go/some guts/some vim into it! **3.** *P* **je n'ai pas un nerf (dans la fouille)**, I'm penniless*/I haven't got a bean. (*Voir* **pelote 2**)

nervi [nɛrvi] *nm F* gangster/hood-lum.

nespasien [nɛspazjɛ̃] *nm F* (*hum*) person who makes excessive use of *n'est-ce pas?* in speaking/= a 'you-knower'.

nettoyage [nɛtwajaʒ] *nm F* **1. nettoyage (à sec)**, cleaning out (financially) **2.** (*cambrioleur, etc*) **nettoyage d'une maison**, stripping bare (of a house) **3.** rifling (of s.o.'s pockets) **4.** (*mil, police, etc*) mopping-up (operation).

nettoyer [nɛtwaje] *vtr F* **1. nettoyer qn (à sec)**, to clean s.o. out (financially)/to take s.o. to the cleaners; **je suis nettoyé**, I'm cleaned right out/I'm completely broke **2.** (*cambrioleur, etc*) **nettoyer une maison**, to strip a house bare **3. nettoyer un homme**, to rifle a man's pockets **4.** (*mil, police, etc*) to mop up **5.** to kill* (s.o.) off/to eliminate (s.o.)/to wipe (s.o.) out/to blow (s.o.) away.

neuf [nœf] *a F* **quoi de neuf?** what's the news?/what's new? **rien de neuf**, (there's) no news.

neuil(le) [nœj] *nf P* night.

Neuneu[1] [nønø], **Neuneuille** [nønœj] *Prn F* Neuilly-sur-Seine (*suburb of Paris*); **aller à la fête à Neuneu,** to dress up/to put on one's best bib and tucker.

neuneu[2] [nønø] *nm F* **la bombe à neuneu,** the neutron bomb.

neveu [nəvø] *nm F* **un peu, mon neveu!** not half!/you bet!/I should jolly well think so! (*Voir* **Bretagne**)

nez [ne] *nm* **1.** *F* **ça lui pend au nez,** he's got it coming to him; he's (in) for it; **qui sait ce qui nous pend au nez?** who knows what's in store for us? **2.** *F* **ton nez remue!/ton nez branle!** you're fibbing! **3.** *F* **je l'ai dans le nez,** I can't stand him; he gets up my nose/up my nostrils **4.** *F* **si on lui pressait/pinçait/tordait le nez il en sortirait du lait; on lui presserait/pincerait le nez qu'il en sortirait encore du lait,** he's still wet behind the ears; he's still a bit green **5.** *F* (*a*) **se salir/se piquer le nez,** to get drunk*/to hit the bottle/to go on the booze (*b*) **avoir un (petit) coup dans le nez/avoir un coup de trop dans le nez/avoir le nez piqué,** to be drunk*. (*Voir* **verre 1**) **6.** *F* (**en**) **faire un nez/faire un drôle de nez/faire un sale nez,** to look disgruntled; to pull a long face; **vise un peu le nez qu'il fait!** just look at the face he's pulling! **7.** *F* **se promener le nez au vent,** to be on the lookout for (*i*) opportunities (*ii*) bargains **8.** *F* **à vue de nez,** at a guess/at a rough estimate; **faire qch à vue de nez,** to do sth in a rough and ready way. (*Voir* **pifomètre**) **9.** (*a*) *F* **cela n'est pas pour ton nez!** that's not for (the likes of) you! (*b*) *P* **mouche ton nez!** mind your own business! **10.** *F* **se casser/se cogner le nez** (*i*) to find nobody at home (when calling at a house) (*ii*) to be frustrated (*iii*) to fail (in business); to come a cropper **11.** *F* **se manger/se bouffer le nez** (*i*) to quarrel*/to wrangle; to be always getting at each other (*ii*) to fight/to scrap **12.** *F* **avoir bon nez/avoir le nez creux/**

avoir le nez fin/avoir du nez (*i*) to be shrewd/*esp NAm* cute/smart (*ii*) to have a flair/a nose for a bargain **3.** *F* **ça va nous retomber sur le coin du nez (comme un sifflet de deux ronds/de deux sous),** we're sure to get the blame for it; you'll have to carry the can for it **14.** *F* **avoir le nez trop long,** to be (too) nosy/to be a Nosy Parker **15.** *P* **saigner du nez,** to be afraid*/to have the wind up/to be in a blue funk. (*Voir* **caca 2; doigt 3; fourrer I 3; laver 3; marmite 4; pleuvoir; ver**)

niac [njak], **niacoué** [njakwe] *a&nm P* Indochinese; viet; chink.

niagué [njage], **niaqué** [njake] *a P* Chinese*/chink.

niaiser [njɛze] *vtr FrC P* to waste one's time/to mess around/to loaf about.

niaiseux, -euse [njɛzø, -øz] *a FrC F* stupid*/dumb/dense/thick.

niard [njar] *nm P* **1.** child*/kid/brat **2.** man*/chap*/fellow/bloke/guy. (*Voir* **gniard**)

niasse [njas] *nm P* **1.** = **niard 2 2. mon niasse,** I/me/yours truly; **ton niasse,** you; **son niasse,** he/him.

nib [nib] *adv & pron inv A P* nothing*; **nib!** my foot!/get lost!*/nothing doing! **nib de nib/nib de rien,** nothing at all/sweet Fanny Adams; **un bon à nib,** a good-for-nothing/a layabout; **nib de tif(fe)s,** bald*.

nibards [nibar] *nmpl P* breasts*.

nibe! [nib] *excl P* silence!/quiet!

nibé [nibe] *nm A P* **1.** trifling matter/trifle **2.** small-scale robbery.

nicdouille [nikduj] *a & nm&f F* = **niguedouille.**

nicher [niʃe] *vi F* to live; **où nichez-vous?** where do you hang out? **Malte, où est-ce que ça se niche?** where the hell is Malta on the map?

niches [niʃ] *nmpl P* breasts*.

nichons [niʃɔ̃] *nmpl P* breasts*/ tits/boobs; **faux nichons,** falsies.

nickel [nikɛl] *a P* **c'est nickel(-nickel)!/c'est drôlement nickel!** *(i)* that's great!/that's absolutely marvellous! *(ii)* *(impeccable)* it's spick and span/as clean as a new pin.

nickelé [nikle] *a F* **1. avoir les pieds nickelés** *(i)* to refuse to agree to sth/to refuse to budge/to sit tight *(ii)* to be lucky **2. avoir la tête nickelée,** to be bald(-headed)*.

nicodème [nikɔdɛm] *nm F* fool*/ twit/dummy.

niçois [niswa] *a P* (*au poker, etc*) **être niçois,** not to increase one's stake/to stand pat/to stay put.

nième [ɛnjɛm] *a* **1.** *F* **pour la nième fois,** for the umpteenth time **2.** *P* **être nième** [njɛm], to suffer from withdrawal symptoms*/to need a fix/to be (in) cold turkey.

nien [njɛ̃] *nm,* **nienne** [njɛn] *nf P* yearning for drugs; withdrawal symptoms/cold turkey.

niente [njɑ̃t] *nf P* nonentity/nothing/nobody.

nière [njɛr] *nm P* **1.** chap*/fellow/ bloke/guy **2.** accomplice/confederate; **un nière à la manque,** an unreliable accomplice. (*Voir* **gnière**)

niflette [niflɛt] *nf P* (*drogues*) **1.** cocaine*/coke/nose candy **2.** heroin*/H.

nigaudinos [nigodinos] *nm P* fool*/clot/twit/prize idiot/jerk.

niguedouille [nigduj] *F* **I** *a* stupid*/idiotic **II** *nm&f* fool*/idiot/ imbecile.

nini [nini] *nm F* fool*/ninny/twerp/ jerk.

niole [njɔl] *nf,* **niôle** [njol] *nf P* brandy/spirits*/rotgut/hard stuff/ hooch/firewater; **un coup de niole,** a wee dram/a drop of the hard stuff. (*Voir* **gnôle**)

Niort [njɔr] *Prn P* **aller à Niort/bat-** tre **à Niort,** to swear blind that one is innocent.

nippé [nipe] *a F* dressed/rigged out/togged up.

nipper [nipe] **I** *vtr F* (*habiller*) to rig (s.o.) out/to tog (s.o.) up/to kit (s.o.) out/to get (s.o.) up (in sth) **II** *vpr* **se nipper** *F* to rig oneself out/to tog oneself up/to get oneself up (in sth).

nippes [nip] *nfpl F* (old) clothes*/ gear/clobber.

nique [nik] *nf F* **faire la nique à qn,** to cock a snook at s.o./to thumb one's nose at s.o.

niquedouille [nikduj] *a & nm&f F* = **niguedouille.**

niquer [nike] *vtr P* **1.** to have sex* with (s.o.)/to screw (s.o.)/to have it off with s.o. **2. se faire niquer par qn,** to be taken in/to get done/to be conned/to get screwed by s.o.

nisco! [nisko] *excl P* nothing doing!/not (bloody) likely!*

niston, onne [nistɔ̃, -ɔn] **I** *n P* **1.** child*/kid; boy/girl. (*Voir* **fiston**) **2.** (*prisons*) passive homosexual*/wife **II** *a P* = **niçois.**

nitouche [nituʃ] *nf F Voir* **Sainte-Nitouche.**

nivet [nivɛ] *nm F* bribe/backhander/illicit profits* (in business).

nobler [nɔble] **I** *vtr P* to know/to be acquainted with (s.o.) **II** *vpr* **se nobler** *P* to be called/named (so-and-so).

noblesse [nɔblɛs] *nf P* **la noblesse,** the (French) underworld/gangland. (*Voir* **milieu**)

nocdu [nɔkdy] *a P* ugly.

noce [nɔs] *nf* **1. faire la noce** *(i)* *F* to have a good time*/to live it up*/to have a ball/to go on a spree/to go on a binge/to go on a bender; **usé par la noce,** worn out with living it up *(ii)* *P* to become a prostitute*/to go on the game **2.** *F* **il n'avait jamais été à pareille(s)**

noce(s) (*i*) he'd never had such a good time/he was having the time of his life/he'd never had it so good (*ii*) (*iron*) he'd never seen such a shambles/such an unholy mess **3.** *F* **je n'étais pas à la noce,** I was feeling very uneasy/I wasn't at all happy; I was having a bad time/a rough time.

nocer [nɔse] *vi F* to go on a spree/to live it up*/to have a ball/to have a wild time.

noceur, -euse [nɔsœr, -øz] *n F* dissipated/debauched person; reveller*/fast liver/hell-raiser/hellbender.

nœud [nø] *nm* **1.** *P* **(tête de) nœud,** fool*/idiot/nut/nurd **2.** *P* **mon nœud!** my foot!/my Aunt Fanny!/my arse!/*esp NAm* my ass! **3.** *P* **filer son nœud** (*i*) to die*/to kick the bucket (*ii*) to run away*/to clear off/to do a bunk **4.** *V* penis*/knob; **se baigner le nœud,** to have sex*/to dip one's wick/to get one's end away **5.** *V* **sacré bavard de mon nœud!** you bloody ballsaching gasbag! (*Voir* **malle 8**; **mallette 2**; **mordre 8**; **peau 19**)

noie [nɔj] *nf*, **noille** [nɔj] *nf P* night.

noir [nwar] **I** *a P* **1.** **(soûl) noir,** (dead) drunk*/plastered/sloshed/blotto **2.** **avoir son pédigrée noir,** to have a black police record/to have form. (*Voir* **œil 20**; **série 1**) **II** *nm* **1.** *F* **avoir le noir/broyer du noir/voir tout en noir,** to be depressed/to have the blues/to be down in the dumps **2.** *F* **(petit/grand) noir,** (small/large cup of) black coffee **3.** *F* **acheter qch au noir,** to buy sth on the black market; **faire du noir,** to be a black marketeer; **travailler au noir,** to moonlight **4.** *P* (*drogues*) opium*/black stuff/tar **5.** *P* ex-prisoner/ex-con/old lag.

noircicaud, noircicot [nwarsiko] *a P* slightly drunk*/tipsy/half-seas-over.

noircif [nwarsif] *nm F* **le noircif =** **noir II 3.**

noircir [nwarsir] **I** *vtr F* **1.** **noircir du papier,** to write something down **2.** **noircir le tableau,** to take a gloomy view/to look on the black side (of things) **II** *vpr* **se noircir** *P* to get drunk*/to have one over the eight/to get sloshed.

noire [nwar] *nf* **1.** *F* **il est dans ses noires,** he's in one of his black moods **2.** *P* night **3.** *P* opium*/black stuff/tar.

noirot [nwaro] *nm P* taxi-driver/cabbie on night shift.

noisette [nwazɛt] *V* **1.** clitoris*/clit **2.** *pl* **noisettes,** testicles*/nuts **3.** **avoir en chaud aux noisettes,** to have had a close shave/a close call.

noite [nwat] *nf P* night.

noité [nwate] *a P* **être bien noité,** to have a shapely posterior; **elle est salement bien noitée,** she's got a real cute ass.

noix [nwɑ] **I** *nf* **1.** *P* fool*/nut(case) **2.** *P* **vieille noix** (*i*) old fogey*/old codger (*ii*) (*hum*) old fruit/old bean/old thing/old chap* **3.** *P* head*/nut **4.** *P* **à la noix (de coco/de veau),** worthless*/useless/lousy/crappy/shitty; **des boniments à la noix,** empty talk/eyewash/bull; **un film à la noix,** a dreadful/an awful film; **une idée à la noix,** a useless/pathetic/lousy idea; **un travail à la noix,** a trashy piece of work; **faire qch à la noix de coco,** to bungle* sth/to balls sth up **5.** *V pl* testicles*/nuts; **tu me casses les noix/tu me fais mal aux noix,** you get on my nerves/you're getting on my tits/you give me (the) balls-ache **6.** *P* buttocks*; **une belle paire de noix,** a shapely posterior/a cute ass; **serrer les noix** (*i*) to be on one's guard/to watch it (*ii*) to sit tight/to be afraid*/to have the wind up/to have the jitters; **il a les noix qui font bravo,** he's got the wind up/he's lost his bottle; **il est parti en serrant les noix,** he went off with his tail between his legs **II** *a inv* **P avoir l'air noix,** to look an absolute fool*; **ce que tu es noix!** you're hopeless!

nom [nɔ̃] *nm* F **1. nom de nom!/ nom d'un nom!/nom d'un chien!/ nom d'un (petit) bonhomme!/nom d'une pipe!/nom de deux!/nom d'un tonnerre!/tonnerre de nom!** *etc,* good heavens!/my goodness!/flip me!/flipping heck!/blimey!/for heaven's sake!/blow it!/hang it (all)! **nom de Dieu!** my God!/Jesus (Christ)!/Christ (Almighty)!/Jeez!/ damn!/bloody hell! **2. ça n'a pas de nom!** (*i*) it's unspeakable! (*ii*) it's incredible! (*Voir* **charnière**; **coucher²** II; **se dévisser 1; rallonge 1; tiroir 1; tonnerre II**)

nombril [nɔ̃bri] *nm* F **il se prend pour le nombril du monde,** he thinks he's God's gift (to mankind)/he thinks he's the bee's knees.

nonnette [nɔnɛt] *nf* F bandaged finger/dolly.

nono [nɔno] *a inv* F (*mil*) **zone nono,** unoccupied zone.

nonosse [nɔnos] *nm* F (*mot enfantin*) bone.

Noraf [nɔraf] *nm* P = **Nordaf(e)s.**

nord [nɔr] *nm* F **perdre le nord** (*i*) to lose one's bearings/to be all at sea (*ii*) to lose one's head/to get (all) confused/to go (all) to pieces (*iii*) to go mad*/to go (clean) round the bend.

Nordaf(e)s [nɔraf] *nmpl* P Arabs of *or* from North Africa (*esp* Algerians).

Normale [nɔrmal] *Prnf* F (= *l'école normale supérieure*) the highest educational institution (of university level) which prepares the intellectual élite of France for the higher posts in teaching and other professions.

Normand [nɔrmɑ̃] *nm* F **1.** don-

ner/faire une réponse de Normand/ répondre en Normand, to give an evasive/non-committal answer **2. faire le trou normand,** to have a drink/a glass of spirits (*esp* calvados) between courses (of a meal) **3. c'est un fin Normand,** he's a shrewd fellow **4. (et) Normand qui s'en dédit!** and to hell with anyone who says otherwise!

Norm' Sup' [nɔrmsyp] *Prnf* F = **Normale.**

noszig(ue)s [nozig] *pron* P we/ us/ourselves. (*Voir* **mézig(ue), tézig(ue), cézig(ue)/sézig(ue), vo(s)zig(ue)s, euzig(ue)s, leur(s)zig(ue)s**)

notaire [nɔtɛr] *nm* F **c'est comme si le notaire y avait passé,** his word is as good as his bond.

note [nɔt] *nf* F **1. donner la note** (*i*) to call the tune (*ii*) to set the tone **2. chanter sur une autre note/changer de note,** to change one's tune/to alter one's tone **3. piquer une bonne/une mauvaise note,** to get a good/a bad mark **4. forcer la note,** to overdo it. (*Voir* **saler 1** (*b*))

nôtres [notr] *nfpl* F **nous avons bien fait des nôtres,** we've played quite a few tricks of our own/we had a few things up our sleeves.

nouba [nuba] *nf* P **faire la nouba,** to celebrate/to go on a spree/to go on a bender/to paint the town red/ to live it up*/to have a ball.

nougat [nuga] *nm* P **1. du nougat/ un vrai nougat/du vrai nougat,** an easy job/a cushy number; **c'est du nougat,** it's easy*/a walkover/a doddle **2. toucher son nougat,** to get one's share/one's whack/one's cut (of the proceeds, profits, etc) **3.** *pl* **nougats,** feet*; legs*.

nougatine [nugatin] *nf* P **de la (vraie) nougatine,** an easy job/a cushy number; **c'est de la nougatine,** it's easy*/a walkover/a doddle.

nouille [nuj] *nf* **1.** *F* dope; **c'est une nouille,** he's/she's a drip; he's/she's got no guts; **quelle nouille!/ espèce de nouille!** what a jerk/drip/nurd! **ce que c'est nouille, ton idée!** what a pathetic idea! **2.** *pl P* (*CB*) interference/background fizz/garbage.

nounou [nunu] *nf F* (*mot enfantin*) nanny.

nounours [nunurs] *nm F* (*mot enfantin*) **1.** teddy(bear) **2.** fur coat.

nourrisson [nurisɔ̃] *nm F* (*iron*) (any) dependant; another mouth to feed.

nouvelles [nuvɛl] *nfpl F* (*a*) **j'ai de vos nouvelles!** I've heard about your goings-on! (*b*) **vous m'en direz/donnerez des nouvelles,** you'll be as pleased as Punch with it; I'm sure you'll like it; **goûtez ça, vous m'en direz des nouvelles,** just you taste that/get a load of that(, and tell me what you think about it)! (*c*) **vous aurez de mes nouvelles,** you haven't heard the last of this; I'll give you something to think about; I'll give you what-for!

nouzailles [nuzɑj] *pron P* = **nos-zig(ue)s.**

noyaux [nwajo] *nmpl F* **rembourré avec des noyaux de pêche,** hard and lumpy.

noye [nɔj] *nf P* night.

noyé [nwaje] *a F* **1/** (*vin, pastis, etc*) watered down/drowned **2.** (*pers*) out of one's depth/hopelessly at sea.

nozig(ue)s [nozig] *pron P* = **noszig(ue)s.**

nuitard [nɥitar] *nm P* worker on night shift.

nuiteux [nɥitø] *nm P* worker, *esp* taxi-driver who works at night.

nullard, -arde [nylar, -ard] *F* **I** *a* useless/hopeless/pathetic **II** *n* (*a*) stupid* person/dunce/dummy/thickie (*b*) hopeless person/washout/dead loss.

nullité [nylite] *nf F* (*a*) stupid person/dunce (*b*) hopeless person/washout/dead loss.

numéro [nymero] *nm F* **1.** (*a*) **un (drôle de) numéro** (*i*) an eccentric* (person)/a weirdie/a weirdo (*ii*) an odd/strange/funny person; an odd bod (*iii*) an amusing person/a funny bloke (*b*) **un vieux numéro,** an old stick-in-the-mud/a back number/a has-been/an old fogey* (*c*) **je connais le numéro,** I know his sort/I've got his number/I've got him sized up **2.** ... **numéro un,** best; **tenue numéro un,** best clothes; **ennemi public numéro un,** public enemy number one **3.** **il aime faire son (petit) numéro,** he likes going through his same old routine/he likes going through with his (little) act **4.** **(maison à) gros numéro,** brothel*/knocking shop/whorehouse **5.** **numéro cent,** WC* **6.** (*menace*) **je retiens votre numéro!** you haven't heard the last of this!/I've got your number! **7.** **filer le/un bon numéro (à qn),** to give (s.o.) a valuable piece of information/a good tip **8.** **tirer le bon numéro,** to draw the winning ticket; **j'ai tiré un bon numéro,** I did well when I married him/her; I picked a winner (when I married him/her).

nunu [nyny] *nm P* nudist; **une plage à nunu,** a nudist/naturist beach.

O

obitus [ɔbitys] *nm O P* death.

obligado [ɔbligado] *adv P* **faire qch obligado**, to do sth under compulsion/to be forced into doing sth.

occase [ɔkaz] *nf P* **1.** opportunity; **profiter de l'occase**, to make the most of sth; **louper/rater l'occase**, to miss the chance/to miss out on sth; **je ferai ça à l'occase**, I'll do it if I get the chance **2.** bargain/good buy/snip **3.** **d'occase**, secondhand; **bagnole d'occase**, used car; **tuyaux d'occase**, stale news.

occasion [ɔkazjɔ̃] *nf P* **faire d'occasion**, to look old/shop-worn.

l'occup(e) [lɔkyp] *nf P* (*WWII*) German occupation.

s'occuper [sɔkype] *vpr P* **1.** **(ne) t'occupe pas (du pot de chambre)**, don't worry!/never mind!/not to worry! **2.** **(ne) t'occupe (pas) (du chapeau de la gamine)!** mind your own business! (*Voir* **oignon 4**)

œil, *pl* **yeux** [œj, jø] *n* **1.** *F* **taper de l'œil**, to feel sleepy/drowsy **2.** *F* **taper/donner dans l'œil de/à qn**, to take s.o.'s fancy **3.** *F* **tourner de l'œil** (*i*) to faint*/to pass out (*ii*) to die* **4.** *F* **je m'en bats l'œil**, I don't care a hoot/I don't give a damn **5.** *F* (*a*) **à l'œil**, free/gratis*/on the house/buckshee; **entrer à l'œil**, to get in for nothing (*b*) **avoir l'œil**, to be given credit/tick **6.** *F* **il a les yeux plus grands que le ventre/que la panse**, he's bitten off more than he can chew **7.** *F* **jeter un œil**, to have a glance/a look; **risquer un œil**, to take a peep/to

have a look-see **8.** *F* (*a*) **faire les yeux doux à qn**, to make (sheep's/goo-goo) eyes at s.o. (*b*) **faire de l'œil à qn** (*i*) to give s.o. the glad eye/to eye s.o. up (*ii*) to wink at s.o. **9.** *F* **faire les gros yeux à qn/regarder qn d'un œil noir**, to give s.o. a black look **10.** *F* **en mettre plein les yeux à qn**, to bluff s.o./to hoodwink s.o. **11.**(*a*) *F* **l'avoir dans l'œil**, to be duped/to be done (in the eye) (*b*) *P* **se mettre le doigt dans l'œil (jusqu'au coude)**, to be completely mistaken/to be right up the pole/to be on the wrong track; to stick one's foot in it **12.** *F* (*et*) **mon œil!** my foot!/my Aunt Fanny! **13.** *F* **faire qch pour les beaux yeux de qn**, to do sth for the love of s.o. **14.** *F* **il n'a pas les/ses yeux dans la/sa poche** (*i*) he's very observant; he keeps his eyes skinned/peeled (*ii*) he's got his wits about him/he knows the score/he's very clued up **15.** *F* (*a*) **ouvrir l'œil (et le bon)**, to be on the lookout/to keep an eye on things; to keep one's eyes peeled; to keep a weather eye open (*b*) **avoir/tenir qn à l'œil; avoir l'œil sur qn**, to keep an eye/a close watch on s.o. **16.** *F* **avoir l'œil américain**, to be wide awake*/on the alert **17.** *F* (*a*) **coûter les yeux de la tête**, to cost the earth/to cost a packet (*b*) **payer les yeux de la tête**, to pay the earth (for sth)/to pay through the nose (for sth) **18.** *F* **il n'a pas froid aux yeux**, he's got plenty of cheek/he's not backward at coming forward **19.** *F* **ouvrir des yeux ronds**, to be wide-eyed (with amazement)/to be flabbergasted* **20.** *F* **avoir un œil à la caille/un œil poché/un œil au beurre noir,** to have a black eye*/a shiner **21.** *F O* **ça a de l'œil,** that looks good/smart; it's got sth; **cela manque d'œil,** it lacks style/sth **22.** *F* **être très sur l'œil,** to be very strict **23.** *F* **ne dormir que d'un œil,** to cat-nap **24.** *F* **taper dans l'œil de qn,** to take s.o.'s fancy **25.** *F* **se rincer l'œil,** to get an eyeful (of a woman's charms) **26.** *V* **œil de bronze/œil du cul,** anus*/round eye. (*Voir* **bras** 4; **carpe** 2; **crapaud** 7; **doigt** 5, 6; **frais**[1] 1; **merlan** 4; **merde I** 6, 12; **pisser** 3; **trou** 7; **zut** (*d*))

œillet [œjɛ] *nm* **1.** *V* anus* **2.** *pl P* **œillets,** eyes*; **gicler des œillets,** to cry*/to weep/to cry one's eyes out.

œuf [œf], *pl* **œufs** [ø] **1.** *P* **espèce d'œuf!** silly fool*! **fais pas l'œuf,** don't behave like an idiot **2.** *P* **aux œufs,** excellent*/first-class **3.** *F* **avoir l'œuf colonial,** to be pot-bellied/to have a gut/to have a beer-belly **4.** *P* **casser son œuf/ses œufs,** to have a miscarriage **5.** *P* **œufs sur le plat,** flat breasts*/pimples/gnat bites; **elle a des œufs sur le plat,** she's as flat as a board/as a pancake **6.** *P* **l'avoir dans l'œuf** (*i*) to be duped/hoaxed/conned/had (*ii*) to fail/to come a cropper* **7.** *F* **marcher (comme) sur des œufs,** to tread/to skate on thin ice **8.** *P* **plein comme un œuf** (*i*) chock-full/chock-a-block/chocker (*ii*) dead drunk*/as high as a kite **9.** *P* **rond comme un œuf,** as drunk* as a lord/as pissed as a newt **10.** *F* **c'est comme l'œuf de Colomb,** it's easy once you've thought of it **11.** *P* **va te faire cuire un œuf!** get lost!*/go to hell!/go and boil your head! **12.** *pl P* testicles* **13.** *F* **avoir des œufs de fourmis sous les pieds,** to have ants in one's pants **14.** *F* **tête/face d'œuf,** idiot*/nurd/twerp/jerk.

offense [ɔfɑ̃s] *nf F* **y a pas d'offense!** don't mention it!/that's quite all right!

officemar(d) [ɔfismar] *nm P* officer.

officiel [ɔfisjɛl] *F* **I** *a* genuine/authentic **II** *nm* **de l'officiel,** the real McCoy/the real thing/the genuine article **III** *int* **officiel!/officiel Jules!** (it's) no joke!/straight up!/there's no getting away from it!/it's for sure!

oie [wa] *nf F* **1. une oie blanche,** an innocent young girl* **2. ne faites pas l'oie!** don't be silly!/don't be an idiot!/don't be such a silly goose! **3. envoyer qn ferrer des oies,** to send s.o. on a fool's errand. (*Voir* **boniment** 2)

oignard [waɲar] *nm,* **oigne** [waɲ] *nm* **1.** *V* anus* **2.** *pl P* buttocks* **3.** *pl P* feet*.

oignon [ɔɲɔ̃] *nm* **1.** *F* **en rang d'oignons,** strung out in a row/single file **2.** *pl P* buttocks* **3.** *P* luck; **avoir l'oignon qui décalotte,** to have all the luck **4.** *F* **ce n'est/c'est/ce ne sont pas mes oignons,** it's none of my business; **occupe-toi/mêle-toi de tes oignons!** mind your own business! **5.** *F* **aux petits oignons,** excellent*/first-class; **soigner qn aux petits oignons,** to treat s.o. (*i*) with loving care/with kid gloves (*ii*) (*iron*) harshly **6.** *P* **pratiquer la course à l'oignon,** to follow s.o. closely/to dog s.o.'s footsteps/to breathe down s.o.'s neck **7.** *P* (*turf*) also-ran/hack/stumer **8.** *F* pocket watch **9.** *V* **petits oignons,** testicles*/balls/goolies **10.** *V* anus*; **tu peux te le carrer à l'oignon!** you can stick it up your arse/*esp NAm* ass!

oiseau, *pl* **-eaux** [wazo] *nm* **1.** *F* **un drôle d'oiseau,** an odd sort of chap/a strange bird/a queer fish; **un vilain oiseau,** a shady customer; a nasty piece of work **2.** *F* **aux oiseaux,** excellent*/super **3.** *P* **donner des noms d'oiseaux à qn,** to insult s.o./to call s.o. rude names **4.** *P* (child's) penis*/willy.

oiselle [wazɛl] nf O F innocent young girl*.

oison, onne [wazɔ̃, -ɔn] n F credulous person; mug/sucker.

olive [ɔliv] nf **1.** P bullet/slug **2.** P changer ses olives d'eau, to urinate*/to go and see a man about a dog/to splash one's boots **3.** pl V testicles*/goolies/nuts.

olpette [ɔlpɛt], **olpiche** [ɔlpiʃ], **olpif** [ɔlpif] a P smart/stylish/natty.

ombre [ɔ̃br] nf **1.** P être à l'ombre, to be in prison*/to be inside; mettre qn à l'ombre, to put s.o. away **2.** F il y a une ombre au tableau, there's something wrong somewhere; there's a fly in the ointment **3.** P marche à l'ombre! get out of my way!/piss off!

omelette [ɔmlɛt] nf **1.** F (broken) mess/shambles **2.** P omelette soufflée, pregnant* woman.

onze [ɔ̃z] num a inv & nm inv F prendre/aller par le train onze/le train d'onze heures, to walk*/to go on foot/to go by Shank's pony/to foot it. (Voir **bouillon 5**)

op [ɔp] nm P (drogues) opium*.

opé [ɔpe] nf F (= opération) (police) operation.

opérer [ɔpere] vtr P opérer qn de qch, to cheat/to swindle*/to diddle/to do/to con s.o. out of sth.

or [ɔr] nm F **1.** or noir, oil/black gold **2.** c'est de l'or en barres (i) it's as safe as the Bank of England/as safe as houses (ii) he's as straight as a die **3.** c'est en or, it's easy*/it's a piece of cake **4.** un caractère d'or/en or, a lovely nature; j'ai une femme en or, my wife's a real treasure/is worth her weight in gold; une idée en or, a marvellous/great/fantastic idea; (théâtre) un rôle en or, a great/marvellous part; une occasion en or, an opportunity not to be missed; a (great) bargain **5.** l'avoir en or, to be lucky **6.** rouler sur l'or, to be

rich*/to be rolling in it. (Voir **cousu I**; **pont**)

orange [ɔrɑ̃ʒ] **I** nf **1.** P balancer/payer une orange à qn, to hit/to slap s.o. **2.** P avoir des oranges sur l'étagère, to have small/hard breasts* **II** nm F l'orange, amber traffic light; prendre l'orange bien mûr, to jump the lights.

orchestre [ɔrkɛstr] nm P déboucher son orchestre, to defecate*/to have a crap. (Voir **homme-orchestre**)

ordure [ɔrdyr] nf V utterly despicable person; ordure! you shit(bag)!/you rat! (femme) you bitch!

oreille [ɔrɛj] nf F **1.** il s'est (bien) fait tirer l'oreille/il s'est fait un peu tirer l'oreille, he needed quite a bit of persuading; il ne s'est pas fait tirer l'oreille, he didn't need to be asked twice **2.** fendre l'oreille à qn, to put (an officer, official, etc) on the retired list **3.** casser les oreilles à qn (i) to deafen s.o. (with noise) (ii) to drive s.o. mad (with questions, etc) **4.** dormir sur les deux oreilles (i) to sleep* soundly/like a log (ii) to feel safe and secure (about sth). (Voir **cocker**; **échauffer**; **frotter 1**; **secouer 3**)

orges [ɔrʒ] nfpl F faire ses orges, to make one's pile/one's stack.

orme [ɔrm] nm F donner à qn un rendez-vous sous l'orme, to make s.o. wait till doomsday/till the cows come home.

ornichon [ɔrniʃɔ̃] nm A P chicken.

ornie [ɔrni] nf A P hen/chicken.

orphelin [ɔrfəlɛ̃] nm **1.** P (a) cigarette-end*/dog-end (b) cigar stump **2.** F odd item (book, plate, etc) from a set **3.** V turd.

orphelines [ɔrfəlin] nfpl V testicles*.

orties [ɔrti] nfpl F faut pas pousser mémé/mémère dans les orties! don't overdo it!/don't push your luck too far!/don't flog it to death!

os [ɔs, *pl* o] *nm* **1.** *F* difficulty/
snag/hitch; **il y a un os (dans le
frometon),** there's been a hitch;
tomber sur un os, to come up
against a snag **2.** *F* (*a*) **c'est un os,**
he's a dangerous customer (*b*) **c'est
un os dur à ronger,** it's a hard nut
to crack **3.** *F* **ça vaut l'os!** that's
worthwhile! **4.** *F* **c'est le même os,**
it all comes down to the same
thing in the end **5.** *F* (*a*) **se casser
les os,** to come a cropper*/to fail
(*b*) **casser/rompre les os à qn,** to
beat s.o. up*/to work s.o. over **6.**
P (*a*) **refiler un os à qn,** to sell s.o.
a pup/to palm sth off onto s.o. (*b*)
l'avoir dans l'os, to be diddled/to
be taken in/to be done/to be had
7. *P* money; **gagner son os,** to earn
one's living **8.** *P* (*projet, etc*)
tourner en os de boudin, to fail*/to
fall through/to fizzle out/to come
to nothing **9.** *P* **chez les têtes en
os,** in the cemetery*/in the bone-
yard **10. os à moelle** (*i*) *P* nose*;
faire juter l'os à moelle, to use
one's fingers instead of a handkerchief (*ii*) *V* penis*; **avoir l'os,** to
have an erection*/to have a bone-
on/to have a hard-on; **faire juter
l'os à moelle/se taper sur l'os,** to
ejaculate*/to shoot one's load;
rogner l'os, to perform fellatio*/to
give (s.o.) a blow-job **11.** *F* **amène
tes os,** come (over) here/drag your
carcass over here. (*Voir* **paquet;
pisser 8**)

oseille [ozɛj] *nf P* **1.** money*;
faire son oseille, to get rich* **2. la
faire à l'oseille à qn,** to (try to) pull
a fast one (over) on s.o./to make a
sucker (out) of s.o. **3.** ... **à
l'oseille,** bogus/phon(e)y/trashy/
worthless* **4. faire à l'oseille,** to
make-believe/to put on an act **5.
avoir mangé de l'oseille,** to be
angry*.

oseillé [ozɛje] *a P* rich*/loaded.

osier [ozje] *nm P* money*; **avoir un
champ d'osier,** to be very rich*/to
be rolling in it.

osselets [ɔslɛ] *nmpl P* **courir sur
les osselets à qn,** to keep a close
watch on s.o./to keep tabs on s.o.;
ne me cours pas sur les osselets,
stop pestering/bugging me.

ost(e)au, osto [ɔsto] *nm P* hospital. (*Voir* **hosto**)

ostiner [ɔstine] *vi FrC F* to go on
saying the opposite; to be awk-
ward/difficult (about sth).

ostrogot(h) [ɔstrɔgo] *nm F* rough,
uncouth man; barbarian; **quel
ostrogot(h)!** what a savage! **un drôle
d'ostrogot(h),** a weirdo.

s'ôter [sote] *vpr F* **ôte-toi de là!** get
out (of here)!/get out of the way!
ôte-toi de là que je m'y mette!
that's my place if you don't mind!/
shift yourself and make room for
me!

ôticher [otiʃe] *vtr P* to seduce.

oua(h)-oua(h) [wawa] *nm F*
(*mot d'enfant*) dog*/bow-wow/
doggy(-woggy).

ouais! [wɛ] *int F* (*oui*) yeah; (*iron*)
oh yeah!

ouallou! [walu], **ouate!** [wat] *int
P* not a bit of it!/nothing of the
kind!/don't you believe it!/rubbish!

ouatères [watɛr] *nmpl F* WC*/
loo/*NAm* john.

ouatte! [wat] *int P* = **ouate!**

oubli [ubli] *nm F* **marcher à l'oubli,**
to feign ignorance/to pretend one
doesn't know.

oublier [ublije] **I** *vtr F* **1. oublier
de respirer,** to die*/to snuff it **2.
fais-toi oublier!** get out of my
sight!/get lost!*/make yourself
scarce! **II** *vpr* **s'oublier** *F* (*enfant,
chien etc*) to urinate*/to forget one-
self/to wet oneself.

oubliettes [ublijɛt] *nfpl F* **mettre/
jeter qch aux oubliettes,** to consign
sth to oblivion/to shelve sth indefinitely.

ouf! [uf] *int F* **ouf!** phew! **avant de
pouvoir dire ouf!** before you could

say Jack Robinson; **il n'a pas dit ouf!** he didn't say a word.

oui-da! [wida] *int O F* yes, indeed!/yes, of course!/*NAm* yes, sirree!

ouiouine [wiwin] *nf P* sanitary towel/*NAm* napkin.

ouistiti [wistiti] *nm P* **1.** chap*/ fellow/bloke/guy **2.** the boss's son **3.** skeleton key.

ourdé [urde] *a P* drunk*; **ourdé à zéro**, blind drunk*.

ourdée [urde] *nf P* **il tient une bonne ourdée,** he's dead drunk*/ he's pissed out of his mind/he's completely plastered.

ours [urs] *nm* **1.** *F* manuscript that has gone the rounds (of the publishers)/that has been repeatedly rejected **2.** *F* white elephant **3.** *P* (*mil*) glasshouse **4.** *P* **avoir ses ours,** to have one's period*/to have the curse **5.** *F* grumpy person/old bear.

ourson [ursõ] *nm P* baby.

ousque, ous'que [uskə] *adv P* (= *où est-ce que*) where; **ous'qu'il est?** where is he? **c'est là ousque je suis né,** that's where I was born.

oust(e)! [ust] *int P* **allez oust(e)!** (*i*) come on/get a move on!/look sharp! (*ii*) hop it!/scram!/get out of my road!

outil [uti] *nm* **1.** *P* **un drôle d'outil,** a clumsy clot/a tool **2.** *P* (*a*) knife (*b*) gun (*c*) *pl* weapons **3.** *V* penis*/tool **4.** *P* **déballer ses outils** (*i*) to confess*/to open up (*ii*) to take one's trousers off and expose one's genitals/to flash; **remballer ses outils,** to put one's trousers (back) on again.

outillé [utije] *a P* (*homme*) **bien outillé,** well-equipped/well-hung/ well-endowed.

outiller [utije] *vtr P* to knife/to stab (s.o.).

ouverture [uvɛrtyr] *nf P* **avoir l'ouverture retardée,** to be slow on the uptake.

ouvrage [uvraʒ] **I** *nm P* (*cambriolage, coup*) job. (*Voir* **boîte 6**) **II** *nf F* **c'est de la belle ouvrage,** that's a nice piece of work; (*iron*) that's a nice mess (you've got us into).

ouvrier [uvrije] *nm P* burglar/ housebreaker.

ouvrir [uvrir] *vtr P* **1.** **l'ouvrir,** to confess*/to open one's trap/to open up **2.** **l'ouvrir sur qn,** to criticize* s.o./to run s.o. down/to knock s.o.

ovale [ɔval] *nm P* (*fille, femme*) **avoir un bel ovale,** to have a shapely posterior/a cute ass.

P

pac [pak] *nm P* = **pac(k)son**.

pacha [paʃa] *nm F* **1.** **mener une vie de pacha/faire le pacha**, to (sit back and) take it easy; to live like a lord **2.** (*marine*) **le pacha**, the captain/the old man.

packson [paksɔ̃] *nm*, **pacqsif** [paksif] *nm*, **pacqson** [paksɔ̃] *nm*, **pacque** [pak] *nm*, **pacqueson** [paksɔ̃] *nm*, **pacsif** [paksif] *nm*, **pacson** [paksɔ̃] *nm P* **1.** parcel/package **2.** (*turf*) **toucher le packson**, to make a lot of money/to make a packet **3.** pack(et) of cigarettes *or* tobacco **4.** (*drogues*) sachet *m*/dose *f* of heroin*.

paddock [padɔk] *nm P* bed*; **être au paddock**, to be in bed.

se paddocker [səpadɔke] *vpr P* to go to bed*/to hit the hay/to hit the sack/to crash out.

padoc [padɔk] *nm P* = **paddock**.

se padoquer [səpadɔke] *vpr P* = **se paddocker**.

paf [paf] **I** *a inv P* drunk*; **complètement paf/paf à rouler**, dead drunk*/plastered/pissed/sloshed **II** *nm* **1.** *P* **tomber sur un paf**, to hit a snag **2.** *V* penis* **3.** *P* **beau comme un paf (en fleur)** (*i*) dressed in new clothes/a new outfit (*ii*) all tarted up. (*Voir* **terrine 2** (*b*))

se paffer [səpafe] *vpr P* to get drunk*.

pagaïe [pagaj] *nf*, **pagaille** [pagaj] *nf*, **pagale** [pagal] *nf F* **1.** muddle/jumble/confusion/chaos; quelle pagaïe! what a mess!/what a shambles! **en pagaïe**, in disorder/in a mess; **une belle pagaïe**, an abolute muddle/a right old shambles; **c'est la pagaïe dans la cuisine**, the kitchen looks like a bomb's hit it **2.** **il y en a en pagaïe**, there's lots/loads of it; there are masses of them; **avoir de l'argent en pagaïe**, to have bags of money*/to be rolling in it.

pagailleur, euse [pagajœr, -øz] *n F* muddler/messer.

pagailleux [pagajø] *a F* (*a*) in a muddle/in a mess/in a shambles; shambolic; cluttered (up) (*b*) (*pers*) messy.

pagaye [pagaj] *nf F* = **pagaille**.

page¹ [paʒ] *nf* **1.** *F* **être à la page** (*i*) to be up-to-date/to be with it (*ii*) to be in the know/in the picture; **mettre qn à la page**, to bring s.o. up-to-date; to put s.o. in the picture/to gen s.o. up; **se mettre à la page**, to keep up with the times **2.** **tourner la page** (*i*) *F* to let bygones be bygones (*ii*) *V* to turn over a new leaf (*iii*) *V* to be a homosexual* (*iv*) *V* to have anal sex* with s.o./to screw s.o. from behind.

page² *nm*, **pageot** [paʒo] *nm P* bed*; **aller/se filer/se mettre au page**, to go to bed*/to hit the hay/to hit the sack. (*Voir* **décaniller 2**)

se pageoter [səpaʒɔte] *vpr P* to go to bed*/to hit the sack/to crash out.

pager [paʒe] **I** *vi P* to sleep/to kip

down/to get some shut-eye **II** *vpr* **se pager** *P* to go to bed*.

pagne [paɲ] *nm*, **pagnot** [paɲo] *nm P* bed*.

se pagnot(t)er [səpaɲɔte] *vpr P* to go to bed*/to get into bed/to turn in/to crash out/to hit the sack.

pagouze [paguz] *nf P* salary; wages; pay.

paie [pɛj] *nf F P* = **paye.**

paillarde [pajard] *nf F* bawdy/ dirty/coarse story *or* joke etc; **chanter des paillardes,** to sing dirty songs/rugby songs.

se paillarder [səpajarde] *vtr F* (a) to have a good time*/to have a ball (b) to have a good laugh.

paillasse [pajas] *nf P* **1.** stomach*/belly; **crever/trouer la paillasse à qn,** to knife s.o. in the guts **2.** (a) (cheap) prostitute*/tart (b) easy lay/pushover/scrubber/tart.

paillasson [pajasɔ̃] *nm P* **1.** *P* (a) = **paillasse 2** (b) **mener une vie de paillasson,** to lead a fast/ debauched life **2.** *F* (*péj*) servile person/doormat **3.** *F* old tennis racket. (*Voir* **clef 1**)

paille [pɑj] *nf* **1.** *F* **être sur la paille,** to be in extreme poverty/to be down and out **2.** *F* **voilà une paille que je ne t'ai vu!** it's ages since I last saw you! **3.** *F* **il demande un million: une paille!** he's asking a million: a mere trifle!/ that's peanuts!/that's chicken feed! **4.** *F* **avoir/tenir une paille,** to be drunk* **5. faire des pailles à ...** = **faire des paillons à ... (paillon).** (*Voir* **chapeau 2, 3**)

paillon [pɑjɔ̃] *nm P* **faire un paillon/des paillons à son mari/à sa femme,** to be unfaithful to one's husband*/wife*; to cheat on one's husband*/wife*; to have a bit on the side.

pain [pɛ̃] *nm* **1.** *F* **avoir du pain sur la planche,** to have one's hands

full/to have a lot on one's plate **2.** *F* (*pers*) **bon comme du bon pain/ bon comme le pain,** good-hearted/ good-natured **3.** *F* **je ne mange pas de ce pain-là,** I don't go in for that sort of thing!/that's not my cup of tea! **4.** *F* **se vendre/ s'enlever comme des petits pains,** to sell/to go like hot cakes **5.** *F* **il n'a pas inventé les pains à cacheter,** he'll never set the Thames/the world on fire **6.** *P* blow*/punch; **coller/flanquer/foutre un pain (sur la gueule) à qn,** to hit s.o. in the face/to sock s.o. on the jaw **7.** *V* **pain au lait,** penis* **8.** *pl V* **petits pains/pains au lait,** buttocks*/buns **9.** *V* **pain blanc/frais/des Jules,** prostitution/pimps' bread and butter; **manger du pain blanc,** to procure/to live off a prostitute's earnings/to pimp. (*Voir* **bénit 1; cuit 3; fesse 9** (b); **goût; planche 4**)

paire [pɛr] *nf* **1.** *F* **ça, c'est une autre paire de manches,** that's another story/that's a different kettle of fish/that's a whole new ball game **2.** *P* (a) **se faire la paire,** to clear off/to do a bunk/to beat it (b) **dîner à la paire,** to leave without paying for one's meal **3.** *P* **avoir une paire de lunettes contre le soleil,** to have two lovely black eyes **4.** *F* (*pers*) **les deux font la paire,** they make a fine pair **5.** *V* testicles*; **avoir une belle paire/en avoir une paire,** to have guts/to have balls/to have spunk.

paître [pɛtr] *vi F* **envoyer paître qn,** to send s.o. packing*/to tell s.o. to get lost/to tell s.o. where to go; **va paître ailleurs!** clear off!/get lost!*

paix [pɛ] *nf P* **ficher/foutre la paix à qn,** to leave s.o. alone/in peace; **fiche-moi/fous-moi la paix!** leave me alone!/stop bugging me!/get lost!*/ go to hell!/piss off!

pajot [paʒo] *nm P* = **pageot.**

se pajoter [səpaʒɔte] *vpr P* = **se pageoter.**

pakson [paksɔ̃] *nm P* = **pacson.**

palace [palas] *a* P excellent*/first-rate*. (*Voir* **palas(s), pallas**)

palanquée [palɑ̃ke] *nf* P une palanquée de ..., lots*/loads/lashings/oodles of ....

palas(s) [palas] P **I** *a* (*chose*) good/great; nice; beautiful; **une idée palas(s)**, a great/smart/fantastic idea **II** *nm* **1.** (*boniment*) patter/hot air/gas/yackety-yak; **du palas(s) (en tartine)**, boloney/bull(shit)/eyewash **2. faire du palas(s)**, to swank/to show off* **3.** (*a*) **faire du palas(s) à qn**, to try to get round s.o./to try and coax s.o./to fast-talk s.o. (*b*) **faire du palas(s) à une femme**, to chat a woman up/to sweet-talk a woman/to try to get off with a woman.

palasser [palase] *vi* P (*a*) to ad-lib (*b*) to gas/to yack/to rabbit (on)/to bunny.

palasseur [palasœr] *nm* P compulsive talker/windbag/gasbag.

pâle [pɑl] **I** *a* P **1.** (*mil*) se faire porter pâle (*i*) to go sick/to report sick (*ii*) to sham sick/to malinger*/to skive off **2. être pâle des genoux** (*i*) to be exhausted*/on one's knees (*ii*) to have a hangover **II** *nm* P corpse*/stiff.

paletot [palto] *nm* P **1. le dernier paletot/le paletot de sapin,** coffin/wooden overcoat; **se faire faire un paletot sans manches/un paletot de sapin,** to die*/to put on a wooden overcoat **2. tomber/sauter sur le paletot à qn,** to sail into s.o./to jump (on) s.o. **3. prendre tout sur le paletot,** to carry the can/to take the rap **4. avoir qn sur le paletot,** to be saddled with s.o.; **il a les flics sur le paletot,** he's got the cops on his heels/on his back/breathing down his neck; he's on the run from the cops **5. mettre la main sur le paletot à qn,** to arrest* s.o./to collar s.o. (*Voir* **machine 6**)

palette [palet] *nf* P **1.** hand*/mitt **2.** shoulder-blade **3.** kneecap.

pâlichon, -onne [pɑliʃɔ̃, -ɔn] *a* F palish/rather pale; (*pers*) peaky/sickly.

palissandre [palisɑ̃dr] *nm* P avoir la bouche/la gueule en palissandre, to have a hangover.

pallaque [palak] *nf* P prostitute*.

pallas(s) [palas] *a&nm* P = **palas(s)**.

palmé, -ée [palme] **I** *n* F holder of the *Palmes académiques* **II** *a* F avoir les mains palmées/P les avoir palmées, to be workshy.

palombe [palɔ̃b] *nf* P woman*; girl*; bird/chick.

palper [palpe] **I** *vtr* F to receive/to earn/to win (money); qu'est-ce qu'on a pu palper comme pognon! we were raking it in/making money hand over fist! j'ai jamais palpé aux courses, I've never won anything on the horses **II** *vpr* se palper F tu peux te palper! nothing doing!*/you've got another thing coming!/(you can) take a running jump!/you can go (and) fly a kite!

palpitant [palpitɑ̃] *nm* P heart/ticker.

palpouser [palpuze] *vtr* P = **palper.**

paltoquet [paltɔkɛ] *nm* F (*a*) non-entity; (pompous) idiot (*b*) A boor.

paluche [palyʃ] *nf* P hand*/mitt; écraser les paluches, to shake hands; s'emmêler les paluches, to play (the piano, etc) badly/to keep hitting wrong notes.

palucher [palyʃe] **I** *vtr* P to finger/to fondle/to caress/to feel up/to touch up (a woman) **II** *vpr* se palucher **1.** P to imagine/to kid oneself **2.** V to masturbate*/to take oneself in hand.

pana [pana] *nm* P = **panne 3** (*a*), **6.**

panache [panaʃ] *nm* F **1. avoir**

son **panache**, to be slightly drunk*/ to be a bit tight/to be rather tiddly **2. faire panache**, (*cycliste, etc*) to take a header; to be pitched over the handlebars; (*voiture*) to turn a somersault/to overturn; **faire un panache complet**, to turn right over/to turn turtle.

panade [panad] *nf* **1.** *F* **être dans la panade** (*i*) to be in a fix*/to be in the soup (*ii*) to be penniless*/to be down and out **2.** *P* spineless individual/drip/wet.

panais [panɛ] *nm* **1.** *P* shirt-tail **2.** *P* **des panais!** not bloody likely!* **3.** *V* penis*/root; **dégraisser/dé-rouiller/planter/tremper son panais**, to have sex*/to dip one's wick.

Panam(e) [panam] *Prnm P* Paris.

panard [panar] *nm* **1.** *P* foot*/hoof; *pl* plates (of meat); **avoir les panards enflés**, to have swollen feet **2.** *P* **j'en ai plein les panards**, I'm sick and tired of it/I'm cheesed off with it **3.** *P* share (of booty)/cut/whack/split. (*Voir* **fade 1**) **4.** *V* **prendre son panard**, to have an orgasm*/to come. (*Voir* **essence**)

pandore [pɑ̃dɔr] *nm A F* policeman*.

pane [pan] *nf F* = **panne 6.**

pané [pane] *a P* = **panné.**

panet [panɛ] *nm P V* = **panais 1, 3.**

panetière [pantjɛr] *nf F* cockroach/black beetle.

panetot [panto] *nm P* = **paletot.**

panier [panje] *nm* **1.** *F* **panier à salade**, police *or* prison van/Black Maria*/*esp* NA*m* paddy waggon **2.** *F* **c'est un panier de/aux crabes** (*i*) they're always fighting amongst themselves/they're all at each other's throats (*ii*) it's a rat race **3.** *P* job lot (of books, etc) **4.** *P* side-car (of motor-bike) **5.** *F* **on peut les mettre dans le même panier**, they're all as bad as each other **6.** *F* **c'est un panier percé**,

he spends money like water **7.** *F* **le dessus du panier**, the pick of the bunch; the cream; **le fond du panier**, the bottom of the barrel; the dregs **8.** *P* **panier (à crottes)**, buttocks*/bottom/ass; **mettre la main au panier** (*i*) to feel/to pinch a (woman's) bottom; to goose (a woman) (*ii*) to feel (s.o.) up/to touch (s.o.) up/to try to get off with s.o. **9.** *V* female genitals*/cunt; **descendre au panier**, to have oral sex* with a woman/to go down on a woman; **se faire défoncer le panier**, to have sex*/to have it away/to get balled. (*Voir* **anse 3**; **con II** (*a*))

paniquard [panikar] *F* **I** *a* scaremongering/alarmist **II** *nm* scaremonger/alarmist.

panne [pan] *nf F* **1.** (*pers*) **être en panne**, to be stuck/to have come to a standstill **2.** (*a*) **laisser qn en panne**, to leave s.o. in the lurch/to let s.o. down (*b*) **elle est en panne de cigarettes**, she's (run) out of cigarettes **3.** (*a*) (*théâtre*) (*i*) small part/bit part (*ii*) bad actor/actress; bit (part) actor/actress **4.** worthless*/useless object, etc; (*tableau*) daub; (*brocante*) unsaleable object/ = white elephant; (*pers*) hopeless/useless individual; **son patron le traite comme de la pan(n)e**, his boss treats him like dirt/badly **5.** lapse of memory **6.** poverty; **dans une panne noire**, terribly hard-up/stony-broke.

panné [pane] *a F* penniless*/flat broke/down and out.

panoplie [panɔpli] *nf P* male genitals*/cricket set; **sortir sa panoplie**, to expose oneself/to flash.

panosse [panɔs] *nm P* **1.** fool*/idiot/clot/twerp **2.** stick-in-the-mud **3.** mug/sucker.

panouillard [panujar] *nm P* **1.** = **panosse 1, 2, 3 2.** (*théâtre*) bit actor.

panouille [panuj] *nf P* **1.** = **panosse 1, 2, 3 2.** small part/bit part.

pan(-)pan [pãpã] *nm F* **faire pan(-)- pan (cucul) à un enfant**, to smack a child's bottom/to give a child a smack-botty. (*Voir* **zizi 1**)

panse [pãs] *nf* **1.** *F* stomach*/belly; **grosse panse**, paunch*/pot-belly/(beer) gut **2.** *P* (*a*) **se faire crever la panse**, to get knifed in the guts (*b*) **bouffer à s'en faire crever la panse**, to stuff one's guts/to blow one's guts out **3.** *O F* **il n'a pas fait une panse d'a**, he hasn't done a stroke of work/he's done damn-all. (*Voir* **œil 6**)

pansu, -ue [pãsy] *a&n F* paunchy*/tubby/pot-bellied (person).

pante [pãt] *nm P* **1.** fellow*/chap/bloke/guy; **un drôle de pante**, an odd character/an oddball **2.** mug/sucker.

panthère [pãtɛr] *nf P* **1. ma panthère**, my wife*/the missis **2. lait de panthère**, pastis.

pantouflard [pãtuflar] *nm F* stay-at-home/home-bird.

pantoufle [pãtufl] *nf F* (*pers*) dead loss/washout; **quelle pantoufle!** he's hopeless! **2. il joue comme une pantoufle**, he can't play for nuts/for toffee **3. raisonner comme une pantoufle**, to talk through one's hat **4.** civilian job **5.** (*a*) sum of money which may be demanded from any graduate of a *grande école* who does not remain in the service of the state (*b*) graduate of a *grande école*.

pantoufler [pãtufle] *vi F* **1.** to talk through one's hat/to talk cock **2.** (*a*) to take it easy/to put one's feet up (*b*) to lead a quiet life **3.** (*officier*) to take a civilian job; (*fonctionnaire*) to go into non-governmental employment.

pantoute [pãtut] *adv FrC P* not at all/no way.

pantre [pãtr] *nm P* = **pante 1, 2.**

Pantruchard, -arde [pãtryʃar, -ard] *n P* Parisian.

Pantruche [pãtryʃ] *Prnm P* Paris.

panuche [panyʃ] *nf P* **être dans la panuche** = **être dans la panade (panade 1).**

pap [pap] *nm F* (= (*noeud*) *papillon*) bow tie/dicky (bow).

papa [papa] *nm* **1.** *F* **à la papa**, in a quiet/simple/homely way; **faire l'amour/baiser à la papa**, to make love in a slow, leisurely fashion; **on a fait le voyage à la papa**, we took it nice and easy **2. un gros papa**, a banknote of any large denomination **3. de papa**, old-fashioned/behind the times/antiquated; **le football de papa**, football as it used to be played **4.** (*cartes*) **les quatre papas**, the four kings. (*Voir* **fils 2; gâteau 3**)

papaout [papau(t)] *nm P* homosexual*.

pape [pap] *nm F* **aller à Rome sans voir le pape**, to narrowly lose (a game, etc). (*Voir* **téléphoner 2**)

papeau [papo] *nm P* hat*/titfer.

papelard [paplar] *nm F* **1.** (*a*) (piece of) paper (*b*) letter (*c*) (official) document **2.** *pl* (*a*) identity papers (*b*) business papers (*c*) newspapers **3.** police record/form.

papier [papje] *nm* **1.** *F* (*journalisme*) **faire un papier**, to write copy/to do an article/to do a piece (for a newspaper) **2.** *F* (*a*) **avoir un bon papier/avoir le papier**, to have a good record/a good reputation (*b*) police record; **il avait un papier chez la police**, he had form **3.** *F* **connaître le papier**, to be well-informed (**de**, about) **4.** *F* (*turf, etc*) **faire le papier**, to study form; **faire son papier**, to make out one's bet **5.** *F* **papier à douleur**, unpaid bill **6.** *F* **un papier**, a ten-franc note **7.** *F* **rayez ça de vos papiers**, don't count on it **8.** *F* **être dans les petits papiers de qn**, to be in s.o.'s good books **9.** *pl* P playing cards. (*Voir* **cul 24**; **musique 4**; **torchette**)

papillon [papijɔ̃] *nm* **1.** P **papillon d'amour**, crab(-louse)/pubic louse **2.** F (parking) ticket **3.** P **avoir les papillons noirs = broyer du noir (noir II 1)**. (*Voir* **minute II**)

papognes [papɔɲ] *nfpl* P hands*.

papotage [papɔtaʒ] *nm* F (*a*) chattering; gossiping (*b*) chatter/gossip.

papoter [papɔte] *vi* F to gossip; to chatter*; to go babbling on.

papouille [papuj] *nf* P caress/tickle/squeeze/cuddle; (*péj*) **faire des papouilles à qn**, to paw s.o.

papouiller [papuje] *vtr* P to caress/to cuddle/to hug/(*péj*) to paw (s.o.).

paquelin [pak(ə)lɛ̃] *nm* P = **pacson**.

pâquerette [pɑkrɛt] *nf* **1.** F **cueillir les pâquerettes**, to wander about idly/to moon about/to waste time **2.** F (*voiture*) **aller aux pâquerettes**, to run off the road **3.** V female genitals*. (*Voir* **tige 2**)

Pâques [pɑk] *nm* F **1. remettre qch à Pâques ou à la Trinité**, to put sth off indefinitely **2. faire Pâques avant les Rameaux**, to consummate a marriage before the ceremony/to have sex* before marriage/to jump the gun.

paquesif [paksif] *nm*, **paqueson** [paksɔ̃] *nm* P = **pacsif, pacson**.

paquet [pakɛ] *nm* **1.** F **avoir son paquet** (*i*) to get one's (just) deserts (*ii*) to get a good hiding (*iii*) to be reprimanded*; **il a eu son paquet**, I told him what I thought of him (*iv*) to meet with disappointment (*v*) to be dead drunk*/to have had a skinful **2.** F **donner son paquet à qn** (*i*) to dismiss* s.o./to give s.o. his/her cards (*ii*) to give s.o. a piece of one's mind **3.** F **faire son paquet/faire ses paquets** (*i*) to pack

up (and go); to pack one's bags (*ii*) to prepare for death/to prepare to meet one's maker **4.** F **faire des paquets sur/contre qn**, to speak ill of s.o. **5.** F **lâcher/dire son paquet à qn**, to let fly at s.o./to let s.o. have it/to give s.o. a piece of one's mind **6.** F **risquer le paquet** (*i*) to risk it/to chance it; to stick one's neck out (*ii*) to go the whole hog **7.** F **toucher un joli paquet**, to make/to win a packet **8.** F **(y) mettre le paquet**, to go all out/to pull out all the stops/to give it all one's got **9.** F (*pers*) (*i*) **quel paquet!** what a lump! (*ii*) **être fichu comme un paquet de linge sale**, to be got up like a guy/done up like a dog's dinner (*iii*) **c'est un paquet d'os**, he's (nothing but) a bag of bones/he's all skin and bones; **c'est un paquet de nerfs**, he's a bundle of nerves **10.** P **elle va bientôt déposer son paquet**, her baby's due any time now; **faire descendre le paquet**, to bring about an abortion **11.** P male genitals*/privates/cricket set **12.** P stock *or* supply of (illegal) drugs **13.** P **paquet touristique**, package trip/holiday **14.** P **lâcher le paquet**, to confess*/to spill the beans/to blow the gaff **15.** (*a*) P **lâcher/envoyer le paquet**, to shoot/to fire (a gun); **ils lui ont lâché le paquet dans le dos**, they emptied their guns into him (*b*) V **envoyer/lâcher son paquet**, to have an orgasm*/to ejaculate*/to shoot one's load **16.** V **paquet de tabac**, woman's pubic hair/beaver.

paqueté [pakte] *a FrC* P drunk*/canned/plastered.

se paqueter [səpakte] *vpr FrC* P to get drunk*/plastered.

para [para] *nm* F (*mil*) (= *parachutiste*) paratrooper/para.

parachuter [paraʃyte] *vtr* F to pitchfork (s.o. into a job, etc).

parade [parad] *nf* P **défiler la parade**, to die*.

paradis [paradi] *nm F* **1.** (*théâtre*) **le paradis**, the gods **2. vous ne l'emporterez pas en paradis!** you won't get away with it!/I'll get even with you!

paradouze [paraduz] *nm P* paradise.

paralance [paralɑ̃s] *nm P* umbrella*/brolly.

parano [parano] *a F* (= *paranoïde*) **il est parano**, he's paranoid/obsessed; he's got it on the brain.

parapluie [paraplɥi] *nm* **1.** *F* **il a l'air d'avoir avalé un parapluie**, he's very stiff and starchy **2.** *P* **porter le parapluie**, to bear the responsibility/to carry the can/to take the rap **3.** *P* **fermer son parapluie**, to die* **4.** *P* alibi*/cover/front **5.** *P* **la Maison Parapluie**, the police*; the cop shop. (*Voir* **sirop 3**)

paratonnerre [paratɔnɛr] *nm F* (*pers*) screen/decoy/cover (*eg* to divert the suspicions of a jealous husband, etc).

paravent [paravɑ̃] *nm F* **1.** = **paratonnerre 2. Chinois de paravent**, strange-looking person; figure of fun.

parcours [parkur] *nm P* venture/undertaking.

pardaf [pardaf] *nm*, **pardess** [pardəs] *nm P* overcoat.

pardessus [pardəsy] *nm P* **pardessus sans manche/de sapin**, coffin/wooden overcoat; **se faire faire un pardessus en sapin**, to die*. (*Voir* **paletot 1**)

pardeuss(e) [pardøs] *nm P* overcoat.

pardi! [pardi] *int F* (*a*) good Lord!/good heavens! (*b*) of course! naturally!

pardingue [pardɛ̃g] *nm P* overcoat.

pardon! [pardɔ̃] *int P* **1. pardon! t'y vas fort!** steady on! **2.** (*admiration, etc*) **le père était déjà costaud, mais alors le fils, pardon!** the

father was a hefty bloke, but as for the son, well! **pardon! c'est pas de la camelote**, it's far from being trash.

pardoss(e) [pardos] *nm P* overcoat.

paré [pare] *a P* **1.** rich*; **être paré**, to have a fat bank account **2. un boulot paré**, a cushy job.

pare-brise [parbriz] *nmpl P* spectacles/specs/glasses.

pare-choc(s) [parʃɔk] *nmpl P* breasts*/knockers/bumpers.

pare-flotte [parflɔt] *nm inv P* umbrella*.

pareil [parɛj] *P* **I** *nm* **c'est du pareil au même**, it all comes to the same thing/it's much of a muchness/it's as broad as it's long **II** *adv* **(et) moi pareil!** so do I!/me too!

pare-lance [parlɑ̃s] *nm P* umbrella*.

parentaille [parɑ̃taj] *nf F* (*péj*) **toute la parentaille**, the whole crowd of relations; the whole blessed family.

parenthèses [parɑ̃tɛz] *nfpl F* **avoir les jambes en parenthèses/P pisser entre parenthèses**, to be bow-legged/bandy(-legged).

parfum [parfœ̃] *nm P* **être au parfum**, to be well-informed/to be in the know/to know the score; **mettre qn au parfum**, to inform s.o. about sth/to put s.o. in the know/to wise s.o. up/to tip s.o. off*/to put s.o. in the picture/to gen s.o. up/to give s.o. the low-down.

parfumer [parfyme] *vtr P* = **mettre au parfum** (**parfum**).

Parigot, -ote [parigo, -ɔt] *a&n P* Parisian.

parler [parle] **I** *vi F* **1. tu parles (, Charles)!** (*i*) now you're talking!/that's more like it! (*ii*) you're telling me!/you bet!/not half!/rather! (*iii*) what a hope!/no chance!/you have to be joking!/what do you take me for?/oh yeah? 2. (a) **bonne cuisinière, tu parles!** elle n'est pas fichue de faire cuire un œuf! good cook my foot! she can't even boil an egg! (b) **tu parles d'une rigolade!** talk about a lark!/it was a right giggle! 3. **trouver à qui parler,** to meet one's match **II vpr se parler A F** (dial) to be courting.

parlote [parlɔt] nf F (idle) talk/(empty) chatter*/hot air.

parloter [parlɔte] vi F to chatter*/to gossip/to have a natter.

paroisse [parwas] nf F 1. **changer de paroisse** (i) to move (house) (ii) to change one's local (pub) 2. **porter des chaussettes de deux paroisses,** to be wearing odd socks.

paroissien [parwasjɛ̃] nm F man*/chap*/fellow/bloke/guy; **c'est un drôle de paroissien,** he's a strange character/an odd bloke/a funny guy.

parole [parɔl] nf & int F **parole (d'homme)!** word of honour!/cross my heart! **ma parole!** upon my word!/well I never!

paroli [parɔli] nm F (turf) bet.

parpagne [parpaɲ] nf P **aller à la parpagne,** to go into the country(side).

parpaing [parpɛ̃] nm P punch/thump (in the face).

parrain [parɛ̃] nm P 1. lawyer/barrister/counsel 2. pl **parrains,** (male) witnesses (for the prosecution) 3. (mafia) godfather.

partant [partɑ̃] nm F **je suis partant,** (you can) count me in; **je ne suis pas partant,** (you can) count me out.

parti [parti] a F (**un peu**) **parti,** slightly drunk*/tipsy/woozy; **à moitié parti,** half-seas over/half-gone; **complètement parti,** sloshed/plastered/stoned.

particulier [partikylje] nm F **quel drôle de particulier!** what a strange chap!/what a funny bloke!

particulière [partikyljɛr] nf F **sa particulière,** his sweetheart/his steady (girlfriend)/his regular.

partie [parti] nf F 1. F **vous avez la partie belle,** now's your chance/the ball's in your court 2. **P une partie de traversin,** a nap/a snooze/forty winks 3. (a) **une partie carrée** (i) F a double date (ii) P (a sex) orgy involving two couples/a foursome; = wife-swapping (b) P **une partie fine,** (a sex) orgy 4. F **les parties (honteuses, nobles),** male genitals*/private parts/privates 5. F (boum) party. (Voir **bordelaise; jambe 18**)

partousard, arde [partuzar, -ard] n P person who takes part in an orgy.

partouse [partuz] nf P (collective sex) orgy; daisy chain; **partouse à la bague,** daisy chain; **partouse carrée,** orgy for two couples/foursome; = wife-swapping.

partouser [partuze] vi P to take part in an orgy.

partouzard, arde [partuzar, -ard] n P = **partousard, arde.**

partouze [partuz] nf P = **partouse.**

partouzer [partuze] vi P = **partouser.**

pas [pɑ] **I** nm F 1. **mettre qn au pas,** to make s.o. toe the line/to bring s.o. to heel 2. **sauter le pas,** to take the plunge **II** adv 1. P (a) **pas?** = n'est-ce pas? (b) **y a pas,** there's no denying it/there's no getting away from it/there's no two ways about it (c) **pas vrai?** that so?/right? **c'est foutu ton truc, pas vrai?** it's all screwed up, isn't it?/you've ballsed it! go on, admit it! 3. F **il connaît Londres comme pas un,** he knows London better than anyone; **il est menteur comme pas un,** he's a terrible liar 4. F **il est pas mal, ce mec-là,** he's not at all bad, that bloke/he's a pretty good-looking guy.

passe [pas] I *nf* **1.** *F* **vous êtes en bonne passe,** you're in a strong position; it's all plain sailing for you **2.** *P* period of time spent with a prostitute* and paid for by the client/trick; **chambre de passe,** bedroom (*esp* in a hotel) let by the hour; **hôtel de passe,** hotel which lets out rooms by the hour to prostitutes; **maison de passe,** brothel*/whorehouse/call joint/knocking shop; **passe bourgeoise,** straightforward sex with a prostitute*/a quick (in and out) job/a quickie; (*prostituée*) **être en passe,** to be with a client/to be on the job; **faire une passe,** to do/to turn a trick; (*hôtelier*) **faire la passe,** to let out rooms to prostitutes (by the hour) **3.** *P* **passe anglaise,** gambling game with dice; **rouler la passe,** to shake the bones II *nm* *F* **1.** pass key/master key **2.** passport.

passe-lacet [paslasɛ] *nm* *F* **raide comme un passe-lacet,** penniless*/broke to the wide.

passer [pase] I *vi* **1.** *F* **il faut passer par là ou par la porte/par la fenêtre,** it's a case of Hobson's choice/there's no alternative/love it or leave it/like it or lump it **2.** **y passer** (*i*) *F* to die*; **il a bien failli y passer,** he nearly kicked the bucket (*ii*) *P* to be done for/to be a goner (*iii*) *F* to go through the mill/to have a hard time of it (*iv*) *P* to be made love to/to have it (off)/to get screwed (*v*) *F* **tout le monde y passe,** it happens to everyone/we all have to go through it (*vi*) **j'y ai passé/j'y suis passé,** I've been through it **3.** *F* to faint/to pass out II *vtr* **1.** *F* **qu'est-ce que je vais lui passer!/qu'est-ce qu'il va se faire passer!** I shan't half tell him off!/he won't half cop it! **2.** *P* **le faire passer,** to bring about a miscarriage. (*Voir* **arme; as 6; banque 1; casserole 7; châtaigne 1; de 2; main 1; piano; pogne 1;**

pommade 1; savon; suif; tabac 1; travers)

passe-sirop [pasiro] *nm inv P* telephone mouthpiece.

passeur, -euse [pasœr, -øz] *n F* smuggler (of drugs, refugees, etc); **passeur fourmi,** drug dealer*/pusher.

passe-volant [pasvɔlã] *nm F* uninvited guest/gatecrasher.

passion [pasjɔ̃] *nf F* **un homme/une femme à passions** (*i*) a sex(ual) pervert/a perve (*ii*) hot stuff (sexually)/a good lay/a good screw/a good fuck.

passoire [paswar] *nf F* **1.** memory like a sieve **2.** spendthrift **3.** (*gardien de but*) **c'est une passoire,** he lets them all through.

pastag(u)a [pastaga] *nm P* pastis.

pastèque [pastɛk] *nf* **1.** *P* **envoyer une pastèque,** to fire (a gun, etc) **2.** *P* buttocks* **3.** *V* female genitals*.

pastille [pastij] *nf P* **1.** bullet **2.** blow*/clout **3.** anus*; **être de la pastille,** to be a homosexual*/one of them; **se faire défoncer la pastille,** to get one's arse/*NAm* ass screwed **4.** **lâcher une pastille,** to fart* **5.** **venir en pastilles de Vichy,** to gate-crash a dinner party **6.** *P* (*CB*) microphone/mike/lollipop.

pastiquer [pastike] *vtr&i P* to smuggle. (*Voir* **maltouze**)

pastiquette [pastikɛt] *nf P* = **passe I 2, 3.**

pastiqueur, -euse [pastikœr, -øz] *n P* smuggler.

pastis [pastis] *nm F* muddle/mess/confusion; awkward situation; **être dans le pastis,** to be in a fix*/in a jam; **être dans un drôle de pastis,** to be in an awful mess/a real shambles.

pasto [pasto] *nm P* blind alley/dead end/cul-de-sac.

pastoche [pastɔʃ] *nf P* fart.

patachon [pataʃɔ̃] *nm* F **mener une vie de patachon,** to have a good time/to live it up*/to go the pace.

patafioler [patafjɔle] *vtr O P (esp dial)* **que le bon Dieu te patafiole!** go to hell! **que le diable le patafiole! to hell with him!**

patapouf [patapuf] *nm* F **un gros patapouf,** fat* lump (of a man); fatso/fatty/fat slob.

patate [patat] *nf* **1.** F potato/spud/tater **2.** P head*; **avoir qch sur la patate,** to have something on one's mind **3.** P heart; **en avoir gros/lourd sur la patate,** to have plenty to be worried about/to be upset about (sth) **4.** P peasant* **5.** P fool*/clot/twit **6.** P large nose*/beak **7.** P blow*/punch/wallop/clout **8.** P hole in sock **9.** P **des patates!** not (bloody) likely*/no (blooming) fear!/nothing doing! **10.** P **sentir la patate,** to sound fishy/to smell a rat **11.** F **avoir la patate** (a) = **avoir la frite (frite 2)** (b) to be lucky.

patati [patati] *adv* F **et patati et patata,** and so on and so forth/and all the rest of it.

patatras [patatra] *int* F crash! **et patatras le voilà par terre!** and down he went with a wallop!

patatrot [patatro] *nm* P **faire (un) patatrot/jouer du jaja au patatrot,** to run away*/to beat it/to do a bunk/to scarper.

pâte [pɑt] *nf* F **1. une bonne pâte,** a kind and simple soul **2. tomber en pâte** (i) to fall over/to come a cropper* (ii) to faint*/to pass out. (*Voir* **mou I 2**)

pâté [pɑte] *nm* **1.** F **avoir les bras en pâté de foie,** to have arms like matchsticks **2.** V **boîte à pâté,** anus*/shit-hole.

pâtée [pɑte] *nf* **1.** F food*/grub/swill **2.** F beating*/thrashing/good hiding; **son père lui a collé une pâtée maison,** his father beat the living daylights out of him.

patelin [patlɛ̃] *nm* F (a) native village/birthplace (b) small village; **ce n'est qu'un petit patelin!** what a (godforsaken) dump!

patente [patɑ̃t] *nf FrC* F gimmick.

pater [patɛr] *nm* P father*/the old man/pater/pop.

paternel [patɛrnɛl] *nm* F **le paternel,** father*/the old man.

patin [patɛ̃] *nm* P **1.** tongue; **rouler un patin (à qn),** to give s.o. a French kiss **2.** *pl* **patins,** shoes; **traîner ses patins,** to loaf around **3. chercher des patins (à qn),** to pick a quarrel* (with s.o.) **4. prendre/porter les patins de qn,** to stick up for s.o. (in a quarrel or fight) **5. faire le patin,** to shoplift.

patinage [patinaʒ] *nm* F pawing (s.o.)/monkeying about (with s.o.)/touching (s.o.) up.

patiner [patine] *vtr* F to paw (*esp* a woman)/to monkey about with (s.o.)/to touch up (s.o.).

patoche [patɔʃ] *nf* P hand*/paw.

patouillard [patujar] *nm* F (*maritime*) (old) tub.

patouille [patuj] *nf* **1.** F mud/slush/goo **2.** F (a) water (b) sea **3.** P gentle caress/squeeze/cuddle.

patouiller [patuje] **I** *vi* F to splash/to flounder (in the mud) **II** *vtr* P = **patiner.**

patouilleux, -euse [patujø, -øz] *a* F (a) muddy/slushy (b) choppy (sea).

patraque [patrak] **I** *a* F unwell*/out of sorts; **je me sens tout patraque,** I feel a bit under the weather; **avoir le cœur patraque,** to have a dicky heart **II** *nf* **1.** P (wrist-)watch **2.** F chronic invalid; old crock **3.** F broken-down machine.

patriotard [patriɔtar] *nm* F (*péj*) blatant patriot/flag-wagger/jingoist.

patron [patrɔ̃] *nm* F **le patron** (i) the boss*/the (big white) chief (ii) my husband*/my old man (iii) police superintendent (iv) chief commissioner of (the Paris) police.

patronne [patron] nf F **la patronne** (i) the proprietress/the boss (ii) my wife*/the missis/the old lady.

patte [pat] nf F 1. leg*; **à quatre pattes**, on all fours; **aller à pattes**, to go on foot/to leg it; **traîner la patte** (i) to limp along (ii) to lag behind; **jouer des pattes/se tirer des pattes/tricoter des pattes**, to run away*/to clear off/to beat it; (pers) **il retombe toujours sur les pattes**, he always falls/lands on his feet; **se fourrer dans les pattes de qn**, to get under s.o.'s feet 2. hand*/paw/mitt; **bas les pattes!** (i) hands off!/keep your paws to yourself!/paws off! (ii) no fighting here!/no fisticuffs here! **avoir le coup de pattes**, to be clever with one's hands/to have the knack (of sth) 3. **casser les pattes à qn**, to put a spoke in s.o.'s wheel 4. **se faire faire les pattes/être fait aux pattes** (i) to be caught/to get nabbed (ii) to be taken prisoner/to be run in 5. **faire qch aux pattes**, to steal*/to pinch/to nab sth 6. (a) **pattes d'araignée** (i) spidery handwriting (ii) long, thin fingers (b) **faire des pattes d'araignée à qn**, to caress s.o.'s body (esp the genitals) delicately with the tips of one's fingers 7. (a) **ça ne casse pas trois pattes à un canard**, there's nothing extraordinary about that; **il n'a jamais cassé trois pattes à un canard**, he won't set the world on fire 8. **donner un coup de patte à qn**, to have a (sly) dig at s.o. 9. (femme) **mettre la patte**, to put on/to use a sanitary towel/NAm a sanitary napkin/a tampon. (Voir **graissage**; **graisser 2**)

pattoches [patɔʃ] nfpl large hands*/mitts/paws.

patuche [patyʃ] nf P licence (to exercise a trade or profession); **se**

faire inscrire à la patuche, to take out a licence.

paturons [patyrɔ̃] nmpl P feet*; **jouer des paturons**, to run away*/to skedaddle.

paulard [polar] nm V **(gros) paulard**, penis*/John Thomas.

paumaquer [pomake] vtr P = **paumer** (all senses).

paumard, -arde [pomar, -ard] n P loser.

paume [pom] nf P **se faire cloquer la paume**, to be sentenced to preventive detention.

paumé, ée [pome] I a P 1. penniless*/stony broke 2. exhausted*/flaked out II n P moral and physical wreck/derelict/down-and-out/drop-out.

paumer [pome] I vtr P 1. (a) to lose (money at gambling) (b) to lose (an object, one's hair, etc) 2. to arrest*; **paumer qn marron**, to catch s.o. red-handed; **se faire paumer**, to get nabbed 3. (a) to steal*/to pinch/to swipe; **se faire paumer**, to be diddled 4. to catch (an illness, a disease) 5. to waste (one's time). (Voir **rat 4**) II vpr **se paumer** P 1. to get lost/to lose one's way 2. to go down in the world/to go to the dogs/to become a down-and-out/to drop out.

pauvreté [povrəte] nf F **se jeter là-dessus/sur les biscuits comme la pauvreté sur le monde**, to jump unhesitatingly at sth/to do sth like there was no tomorrow.

pavé [pave] nm F 1. **fusiller le pavé**, to blow one's nose (in the street) with one's fingers 2. **malheureux come un pavé de bois** (i) as unhappy as can be (ii) utterly destitute 3. **gratter le pavé**, to be desperately poor; to scrape a living from the gutter; to be on the breadline 4. **battre le pavé** (i) to loaf about the streets/about town (ii) to tramp the streets (in search of work, etc) 5. **clair comme un**

pavé dans la gueule d'un flic, perfectly clear/patently obvious **6.** il n'a plus de pavé dans la cour, he's toothless/he hasn't got a tooth left in his head **7.** un pavé dans la mare, a (nice) bit of scandal **8.** ten thousand francs (one million old francs) **9.** prendre le haut du pavé, to lord it (over s.o.); ici, c'est lui qui tient le haut du pavé, he's the big white chief around here **10.** battre/faire le pavé, to be a prostitute*/a streetwalker; to be on the game. (*Voir* brûler 3)

paver [pave] *vtr F* **1.** avoir le gosier pavé, to have a cast-iron throat **2.** la ville en est pavée/les rues en sont pavées, you can find it/them everywhere; it's/they're common as dirt.

paveton [pav(ə)tɔ̃] *nm P* paving stone; être sur le paveton, to be in the gutter/on the breadline.

pavillons [pavijɔ̃] *nmpl P* ears*/flaps/flappers.

pavoiser [pavwaze] *vi* **1.** *F* to rejoice/to put out the flags **2.** *P* (*a*) to have a black eye (*b*) *O* (*boxe*) to be bleeding from the nose **3.** *P* to show off*/to parade oneself/to swagger **4.** *P* to blush/to go red **5.** *P* to have a period*/to fly the flag **6.** *P* to get into debt.

pavot [pavo] *nm P* buttocks*.

pavoule [pavul] *nf P* prostitute*.

pavton [pavtɔ̃] *nm P* = **paveton.**

pavute [pavyt] *nf P* (*javanais de* pute) prostitute*.

pax [paks] *nm P* air passenger.

paxon [paksɔ̃] *nm P* = **packson 4.**

paye [pɛj] *nf* **1.** *F* c'est une mauvaise paye, he's a bad/a slow payer **2.** *P* ça fait une paye/il y a une paye qu'on s'est vus, it's been ages/donkey's years since we met; il y en a pour une paye, it'll take ages/years.

payer [peje, pɛ-] **I** *vi F* ça paye (*i*) it's profitable/it brings in a good return (*ii*) it's very funny*/priceless/a laugh a minute **II** *vtr F* **1.** s'en payer (une tranche), to have a good time*/a good laugh/a ball **2.** tu me le paieras!/tu vas me payer ça! you'll pay for that!/I'll get my own back (on you) for that! **3.** se payer qch (*i*) to treat oneself to sth (*ii*) to have to put up with sth **4.** j'ai payé pour le savoir, I've learned it/I know it to my cost; (*fig*) je l'ai payé cher, I paid dearly for it. (*Voir* figure 2; monnaie 2; place 2; poire 7; portrait (*c*); tête 8)

pays¹ [pe(j)i] *nm F* **1.** battre du pays, to wander from one's subject; to ramble/to waffle (on) **2.** il est bien de son pays! well, he *is* green!

pays², payse [pe(j)i, pe(j)iz] *n F* fellow-countryman/-countrywoman; nous sommes pays, we're from the same parts/the same place/the same village.

paysage [peizaʒ] *nm F* cela fait bien dans le paysage, it's just right/it's just the ticket.

PBI [pebei] *abbr F* (= *pas de bouches inutiles*) (we will have) no unwelcome guests!

pd, PD [pede] *abbr P* (= *pédé(raste)*) homosexual*/queer/poof(ter)/fag(got). (*Voir* pédé)

peau, *pl* **peaux** [po] *nf* **1.** *F* bouffer à s'en faire crever la peau du ventre, to eat* an enormous amount/to stuff one's guts/to pig oneself **2.** *F* manger la peau sur le dos à qn, to starve s.o. **3.** *F* une nana en peau, a girl in a low-cut dress/showing a lot of cleavage **4.** *F* faire peau neuve, to turn over a new leaf **5.** *F* la peau lui démange, he's itching for trouble **6.** *F* avoir qn dans la peau, to be infatuated* with s.o./to be crazy about s.o.; il l'a dans la peau, he's madly in love with her/he's got her under his skin **7.** *F* se sentir mal dans sa peau, to feel uncomfortable; se sentir bien dans sa peau, to feel very much at ease **8.** *F* avoir la peau trop courte, to be lazy* **9.** *F* **traîner sa peau,** to loaf about **10.** *F* **communiste en peau de lapin,** would-be communist **11.** *F* **peau d'âne,** diploma; sheepskin **12.** *F* **peau de banane,** plot (against s.o.)/trap (set to catch s.o. out) **13.** *P* (*a*) **faire/ trouer la peau à qn,** to kill* s.o./to bump s.o. off (*b*) **se faire (crever) la peau,** to commit suicide*/to do oneself in (*c*) **risquer sa peau,** to risk one's life **14.** *P* **avoir la peau de qn,** to kill* s.o.; **j'aurai ta peau!** I'll get you! **15.** *P* **il ne sait pas quoi faire de sa peau,** he doesn't know where to put himself **16.** *P* **travailler pour la peau,** to work for nothing*; to have one's trouble for nothing; **il n'a eu que la peau,** he got nothing (out of it)/he didn't get a sausage **17.** *P* **porter la peau à qn,** to excite s.o. sexually/to turn s.o. on/to work s.o. up **18.** *P* **péter dans sa peau,** to be too big for one's boots **19.** *P* **la peau!/ peau de balle (et balai de crin)!/ peau de balle et variété!/peau de nœud!/peau de zob(i)!** (*i*) nothing*/ nix (*ii*) nothing doing!*/my Aunt Fanny!/no fear!/nuts! **la peau de mes burnes!** no chance!/no dice!/ no way! (*Voir* **balpeau** (*i*), (*ii*); **zébi(e)**) **20.** *P* (*a*) **vieille peau** (*i*) ageing prostitute* (*ii*) old trout/old bag/old hag (*fille*) **peau (de chien),** tart/scrubber (*c*) **une peau de vache** (*i*) (*homme*) a bastard*/a lousy bum/a sod/*esp NAm* a son of a bitch (*ii*) (*fille, femme*) a bitch/a cow; **sa mère est une vraie peau de vache,** her mother is a real cow (*d*) **une peau de fesses,** a nasty piece of work/a despicable character; **peau de fesses!** (you) scum! **21.** *P* **une peau d'hareng** (*i*) un uncompromising person/a hard nut (*ii*) a useless individual/a drip/a wet **22.** *P* (*a*) (*maritime*) **peau de couille,** oilskin (*b*) **peau de bête,** fur coat **23.** *P* (*a*) **peau de saucisson,** inferior merchandise; junk/rubbish (*b*) **à la peau de toutou,** useless/worthless*;

trashy/rubbishy. (*Voir* **tanner**; **zobi 2**)

peaufiner [pofine] **I** *vtr F* to be finicky/to be picky/to niggle over (a piece of work) **II** *vpr* **se peaufiner** *F* to make up/to do one's face; to put on one's make-up/one's warpaint.

peausser [pose] *vi P* to (go to) sleep*/to kip down/to crash out.

peaussier [posje] *nm F* skin specialist/dermatologist.

peau-rouge [poruʒ] *nm F* hooligan*/hoodlum/rough/lout/thug/ yob; **ces peaux rouges terrorisaient tout le quartier à la nuit tombée,** those yobbos terrorized the whole neighbourhood at night.

pébroc, pébroque [pebrɔk] *nm P* **1.** umbrella, brolly. (*Voir* **sirop 4**) **2. la Maison Pébroc,** the police* **3.** cover/front/alibi*; **servir de pébroc à qn,** to front for s.o.; **son métier n'était qu'un pébroc,** his profession was just a blind.

pêche [pɛʃ] **I** *nf P* **aller à la pêche,** to be out of work **II** *nf* **1.** *P* blow*; **balancer/filer/flanquer/ foutre une pêche à qn (en pleine poire),** to punch s.o. in the face/to take a swing at s.o. **2.** *P* (*a*) face* (*b*) head*; **sucer la pêche à qn,** to kiss s.o.; **se fendre la pêche,** to laugh* uproariously/to kill oneself laughing; **nous nous fendions la pêche,** we were in stitches **3.** *P* **avoir la pêche,** to be in high spirits/to feel on top of the world **4.** *V* turd; **poser/déposer une pêche/sa pêche,** to defecate*/to drop one's load.

pêchecaille [pɛʃkaj] *P* **I** *nf* fishing **II** *nm* fisherman/angler.

pêcher [peʃe] *vtr F* **où as-tu pêché ça?** where did you get hold of that?/where did you pick that up?/ who told you that?

pecnaud [pekno] *nm P* peasant*. (*Voir* **péquenaud**)

pécole [pekɔl] *nf P* gonorrhoea*/ the clap.

pécore [pekɔr] **I** *nf F* (*a*) silly girl/woman; *esp NAm* dumb cluck/ dumb broad (*b*) stuck-up girl/ woman **II** *nm P* peasant*/yokel.

pécufier [pekyfje] *vtr P* to write (a report, etc).

pécul [peky] *nm P* (*a*) toilet paper/ loo paper/bum-fodder (*b*) old paper(s); bumf.

pécune [pekyn] *nf P* money*.

pédale [pedal] *nf* **1.** *F* **perdre les pédales,** to lose all self-control/to get flustered/to get all balled up; **tu perds les pédales,** you're slipping/ you're cracking up; **il a perdu les pédales,** he's going mad/nuts; he's lost his marbles **2.** *P* homosexual*/queer/poof/poove/*esp NAm* fag(got); **une pédale,** a homo(sexual); **la pédale,** gay men (in general)/pansyland; **être de la pédale,** to be a queer/to be gay/to be one of them **3.** *F* **lâcher les pédales** (*i*) to be at death's door (*ii*) to give up/to throw in the towel.

pédaler [pedale] *vi P* **1.** (*a*) to rush along, to go full blast (*b*) to run away*/to beat it **2. pédaler dans l'huile/dans le beurre,** to go smoothly/without a hitch; to make good progress **3. pédaler dans la choucroute/dans la semoule/dans le yaourt** (*i*) to find the going difficult/to make slow progress (*ii*) to be unable to speak clearly/to mumble (*iii*) to be all mixed up/confused.

pédalo [pedalo] *nm,* **pédé** [pede] *nm,* **pédéro** [pedero] *nm P* homosexual*/queer/*esp NAm* fag(got)/poof/poove.

pédesouille, pédezouille [pedzuj] *nm P* = **pedzouille.**

pedigree, pédigrée [pedigre] *nm P* police record (of criminal)/ pedigree/form.

pédoc, pédoque [pedɔk] *nm P* homosexual*/gay.

pedzouille, pédzouille [pɛdzuj, pe-] *nm P* (*a*) peasant*/ country bumpkin/yokel/hick/rube (*b*) clumsy lout/oaf.

pégal(e) [pegal] *nm P* pawnshop.

pègre [pɛgr] *nm P* thief*/swindler*/crook/gangster.

pégreleux [pɛgr(ə)lø] *nm P* small-time thief*/petty crook.

pégrer [pegre] *vtr P* **se faire pégrer,** to get nabbed/nicked.

pégriot [pegri(j)o] *nm P* petty thief*/pilferer; small-time crook; (young) delinquent/hooligan*.

peigne [pɛɲ] *nm P* (burglar's) crowbar/jemmy/*NAm* jimmy.

peigne-cul [pɛɲky] *nm,* **peigne-derche** [pɛɲdɛrʃ] *nm P* (*pers*) (*a*) miser*/skinflint/tight-ass (*b*) creep/yob/lout/jerk. (*pl* **peigne-culs, peigne-derches**)

peignée [peɲe] *nf F* **1.** thrashing/ beating*(-up); **ficher une peignée à qn,** to give s.o. a good hiding **2.** fight/scrap/set-to.

se peigner [səpeɲe] *vpr F* (*esp entre femmes*) to (have a) fight/a scrap; to tear each other's hair out.

peigne-zizi [pɛɲzizi] *nm P* (*pers*) creep/lout/jerk. (*pl* **peigne-zizis**)

peinard, -arde [pɛnar, -ard] *P* **I** *a* (*a*) **boulot peinard,** cushy job/ soft option; **père peinard,** easygoing man; **vie peinarde,** easy life/ soft option; **être peinard,** to have it easy*/to have a bit of peace/to play it cool; to be laid-back; **on sera bien peinards ici,** we'll be OK here/we'll get a bit of peace here; **rester/se tenir peinard,** to take things easy/to lie doggo/to keep one's nose clean; **tiens-toi peinard,** keep quiet/take it easy/stay cool/ play it cool (*b*) **être peinard,** to be well off **II** *nm* easy-going man; **faire qch en (père) peinard,** to be in no hurry to do sth/to take it easy*; **il est sorti en peinard,** he slipped out quietly/on the quiet.

peinardement [pɛnardəmɑ̃] *adv* P (*a*) quietly/slyly/on the sly/on the quiet/on the QT (*b*) in a leisurely fashion (*c*) without any fuss.

peinardos [pɛnardos] *P* I *a* easy*/cushy/soft; easy-going/laid-back II *adv* in a leisurely fashion

peine-à-jouir [pɛnaʒwir] *nm inv* P s.o. who has difficulty in reaching orgasm/frigid person.

peintre [pɛtr] *nm* P **avoir les peintres,** to have a period*/to have the painters in.

peinture [pɛtyr] *nf* F **je ne peux pas le voir en peinture,** I can't bear the sight of him; I hate the sight of him; I can't stick him.

peinturlurer [pɛtyrlyre] *vtr* F to paint (a building, etc) in all the colours of the rainbow.

pékin [pekɛ̃] *nm* F civilian; **en pékin,** in civvies/in civvy street.

pelé [p(ə)le] I *nm* F **il n'y avait que trois pelés et un tondu/que trois pelés et quatre tondus/que trois teigneux et un pelé,** there were only a few odd bods/a few odds and sods/a handful II *a* F (*pers*) fleeced/cleaned out.

peler [p(ə)le] I *vtr* 1. F **peler qn** (*i*) to strip s.o. (of all his property, etc)/to take s.o. to the cleaners/to clean s.o. out (*ii*) to fleece* s.o./to diddle s.o. 2. P **qu'est-ce qu'il me pèle, ce mec!** that bloke/guy really gets up my nose/gets on my tits! II *vi* P **je pèle (de froid),** I'm freezing (cold). (*Voir* **jonc 3, 5**)

pèlerin [pɛlrɛ̃] *nm* 1. F (long-distance) traveller 2. F (*a*) man*/chap/fellow/bloke/type (*b*) eccentric* (person)/queer customer/odd (sort of) fellow 3. P policeman* 4. P umbrella*/brolly.

pèlerinage [pɛlrinaʒ] *nm* V **faire un pèlerinage aux sources,** to have cunnilingus* (with a woman)/to go down on s.o.

pèlerine [pɛlrin] *nf* O P policeman* (in Paris).

pelle [pɛl] *nf* 1. F **ramasser une pelle** (*i*) to fall off (a horse, a bicycle, etc)/to take a spill (*ii*) to come a cropper* 2. P **rouler une pelle à qn,** to give s.o. a French kiss 3. F **à la pelle,** in big quantities/in large numbers/in profusion; **remuer l'argent à la pelle,** to be very rich*/to be rolling in it 4. P **en prendre plus avec son nez qu'avec une pelle,** to be smelly*/to stink*/to pong.

pello [pɛlo] *nm* P = **pelot, pélot.**

pelloche [pɛlɔʃ] *nf* P (*phot*) (roll of) film.

pellot [pɛlo] *nm,* **pelo** [pəlo] *nm,* **pélo** [pelo] *nm* P = **pelot, pélot.**

pelops! [pəlɔps] *int* P not (bloody) likely!*/no fear!/not on your nellie!

pelot [pəlo] *nm,* **pélot** [pelo] *nm* P **sans un pelot,** penniless*; **je n'ai pas un pelot,** I'm flat broke/I haven't got a bean.

pelotage [p(ə)lɔtaʒ] *nm* 1. P cuddling; (heavy) necking/petting; pawing; feeling up/touching up; **partie de pelotage,** necking session/snogging session; **y a du pelotage!** she's a bit of all right; **pas de pelotage avant le mariage!** no sampling the goods! 2. F flattery*/soft soap/fast talk.

pelote [p(ə)lɔt] *nf* 1. F **faire/arrondir sa (petite) pelote,** to make one's pile/to feather one's nest 2. F **avoir les nerfs en pelote,** to be on edge/jumpy/jittery; **mettre les nerfs en pelote à qn,** to set s.o.'s nerves on edge 3. P (*mil*) **la pelote,** the defaulters' squad; **faire la pelote,** to do punishment drill 4. P **envoyer qn aux pelotes,** to send s.o. packing*/to send s.o. away with a flea in his ear; **va aux pelotes!** go to hell!/screw you! 5. *pl* P breasts*/boobs; **pelotes à épingles,** large droopy breasts 6. *pl* P testicles*/balls 7. F **une pelote d'épingles,** a bad-tempered person/a crosspatch/ a prickly individual.

peloter [p(ə)lɔte] **I** *vtr* **1.** *P* **peloter une nana,** to cuddle a girl; to neck with/to feel up/to touch up a girl; to paw a girl/to maul a girl about **2.** *F* to flatter* (s.o.)/to butter (s.o.) up/to suck up to (s.o.) **II** *vpr* **se peloter** *P* to pet/to neck/ to snog; **ça se pelote là-dedans,** there's some (heavy) petting/there's a real snogging session going on in there.

peloteur, euse [p(ə)lɔtœr, -øz] *n* **1.** *P* cuddler/(heavy) necker/snogger/petter **2.** *F* flatterer*/soft-soap artist/fast-talker.

pelousard, arde [p(ə)luzar, -ard] *n* *F* racegoer/horse-racing enthusiast.

pelure [p(ə)lyr] *nf* **1.** *F* (*a*) overcoat/fur coat (*b*) clothes*/gear/ clobber; **enlever sa pelure,** to undress/to peel off **2.** *P* **une (vraie) pelure,** a stupid* person/a fool*/a bonehead **3.** *P* prepared statement (in writing)/(press) handout **4.** *pl P* **pelures,** tyres (of racing cycle).

pénard, arde [penar, -ard] *a&nm P* = **peinard 1, 2.**

penco [pãko] *nm P* (*scol*) boarder.

pendantes [pãdãt] *nfpl P* **1.** earrings **2.** testicles*; **un coup de pied aux pendantes,** a kick in the balls/ goolies.

pendard [pãdar] *nm* **1.** *F* rogue/ rotter/good-for-nothing **2.** *pl P* (large) drooping breasts*.

pendeloques [pãdlɔk] *nfpl*, **pendentifs** *nmpl V* testicles*/ danglers.

pendouiller [pãduje] *vi P* to hang loosely/to dangle.

pendule [pãdyl] *nf* **1.** *F* taximeter/clock **2.** *F* **remonter la pendule à qn contre qn d'autre,** to work s.o. up against s.o. else **3.** *P* **en faire/ en chier une pendule,** to make a big

fuss about nothing **4.** *P* (woman's) buttocks*/arse/*NAm* ass/fanny.

pénible [penibl] *a F* (*pers*) difficult; **ce qu'il est pénible!** he's a real nuisance/a pain in the neck! **ce qu'elle est pénible!** she's impossible/she's the limit!

péniche [peniʃ] *nf P* **1.** large car* **2.** *pl* big boots*/boats/tugboats/ canal boats **3.** *pl* (big) feet*.

péno [peno] *nm P* (*football;* = *pénalty*) penalty.

pensarde [pãsard] *nf P* (*peu usuel*) head*; **c'est un intello, il en a dans la pensarde,** he's got brains.

penscu [pãsky] *nm P* (*scol*) boarder.

pense-bête [pãsbɛt] *nm F* memory jogger/aide-mémoire.

penser [pãse] *vtr&i F* **1.** (*a*) **penses-tu!/pensez-vous!/tu penses!/ vous pensez!** not (bloody) likely!*/ not on your (sweet) life!/don't you believe it! **est-ce qu'il a donné un bon pourboire? – tu penses!** did he give a good tip? – you must be/ you have to be joking! (*b*) **tu n'y penses pas!/vous n'y pensez pas!** (surely) you don't mean it!/you're not serious!/you've got to be joking! **2. bande de ce que je pense!** you shower of so-and-sos! **marcher dans ce que je pense,** to tread in dog's muck; **il peut se le mettre où je pense,** you know where he can stick/stuff it!/you know what he can do with it! **il lui a flanqué un coup de pied où je pense,** he booted him up the you-know-where **3. il ne pense qu'à ça,** he's got a one-track mind/a dirty mind.

penseuse [pãsøz] *nf P* head*; **court-jus dans la penseuse,** migraine.

pensio [pãsjo] *nm F* boarder.

pente [pãt] *nf* **1.** *P* **avoir la dalle/ le gosier en pente,** to have a perpetual thirst/to be a heavy drinker/ to be a real boozer; **avoir sa pente,** to be drunk*/juiced-up **2.** *F* **être**

sur la pente du mal, to be going downhill/to the dogs; **être/glisser sur la mauvaise pente** (*i*) to be in a bad way (*ii*) to be past hope/ beyond recovery.

pépé [pepe] *nm F* grand(d)ad/ grandpa.

pépée [pepe] *nm* **1.** *F* (*mot d'enfant*) doll(y) **2.** *P* (*a*) girl*/ doll/bird/chick; **une belle pépée,** a nice bit of stuff/fluff; **quelle jolie pépée!** she's a bit of all right! (*b*) (*péj*) dolly-bird/dolly-girl (*c*) **courir les petites pépées,** to chase skirt; to chat up/to try to get off with the girls **3.** *P* (*a*) prostitute*/pro/ hooker (*b*) woman*/girl* (of easy virtue); easy lay/pushover.

pépère [pepɛr] **I** *nm F* **1.** grandfather/grandpa/grand(d)ad **2.** *occ* father*/dad/daddy **3.** easy-going old codger/old softy; **c'est un gros pépère** (*i*) he's a big old softy (*ii*) (*enfant*) he's a nice, chubby little lad **II** *a F* (*a*) **une somme pépère,** a nice fat sum (of money); **un gueuleton pépère,** a good blowout; **un sandwich plus que pépère,** a huge/whopping great sandwich (*b*) **un petit coin pépère,** a cosy little spot/a snug little corner; **un petit boulot pépère(-maous),** a cushy job/ a cushy billet/a soft option (*c*) (*pers*) easy-going/laid-back **III** *adv F* **1.** **jouer pépère,** to play nicely/ not to play rough **2.** (*aut*) **rouler pépère,** to jog along/to tootle along.

pépète, pépette[1] [pepɛt] *nf P* **de la pépète/des pépètes/pépettes,** money*/lolly/dough/bread.

pépette[2] *nf P* = **pépée 2.**

pépie [pepi] *nf F* **1.** **avoir la pépie,** to have a perpetual thirst/to like a drink **2.** **elle n'a pas la pépie,** she never stops talking/she's not stuck for words/she's got the gift of the gab.

pépin [pepɛ̃] *nm* **1.** *F* hitch/snag; **avoir un pépin,** to be in trouble*/in

difficulties; to hit a snag/to have a spot of bother **2.** *F* **avoir un/le pépin pour qn,** to be infatuated* with s.o./to have a crush on s.o. **3.** *P* **avoir avalé le pépin,** to be pregnant* **4.** *P* umbrella*/brolly **5.** *P* parachute. (*Voir* **timbale 2**)

pépinière [pepinjɛr] *nf F* nursery (of young actors, up-and-coming ballet dancers, etc); breeding-ground (of anarchists, etc).

pépite [pepit] *nf F* **il n'a plus une pépite,** he's penniless*/he hasn't a farthing.

pépon [pepɔ̃] *nf P* (= **pompe**) **pépons,** shoes; sneakers/pumps.

péquenaud, péquenot [pekno] *nm*, **péquenouille** [pekənuj] *nm P* peasant*/clodhopper/country bumpkin/hick.

péquin [pekɛ̃] *nm F* civilian. (*Voir* **pékin**)

percal(e) [pɛrkal] *nm P* tobacco/ baccy/snout; **il se fume bien, ton percal,** that's a nice bit of baccy.

percée [pɛrse] *nf F* illegal frontier-crossing.

percer [pɛrse] *P* **I** *vtr* **percer qn,** to kill* s.o.; to put a bullet/a knife through s.o. **2.** **va te faire percer!** (go and) get stuffed! **II** *vi* (*cyclisme*) to have a puncture.

perche [pɛrʃ] *nf F* **1.** **une grande perche,** a tall, thin person*/a beanpole **2.** **tendre la perche à qn,** to give s.o. a helping hand/to help s.o. out.

percher [pɛrʃe] *F* **I** *vi* to live/to hang out; **où perchez-vous?** where do you hang out? **je perche au troisième,** I live (up) on the third floor; **où ça perche, ce trou-là?** where on earth is this place? **II** *vtr* **percher un vase sur une armoire,** to stick a vase on top of a wardrobe **III** *vpr* **se percher** *F* (*a*) **il est allé se percher à Montmartre,** he's gone to live at the top of Montmartre (*b*) **tâchez de vous percher de manière à dominer la foule,** try and find somewhere so that you can see over the heads of the crowd.

perchoir [pɛrʃwar] *nm F* **perchoir à moineaux**, bow-tie/dicky-bow/ dicky/butterfly bow.

perco [pɛrko] *nm F* (coffee) percolator.

percuté [pɛrkyte] *a P* mad*/ bonkers/touched (in the head).

perdre [pɛrdr] *vtr F* **1. elle l'a perdu**, she's lost her virginity*/she's lost her cherry/she's lost it **2. il n'en a pas perdu une**, he saw everything/he didn't miss a thing.

perdreau, *pl* **-eaux** [pɛrdro] *nm P* (a) plain-clothes policeman; detective (b) policeman*.

père [pɛr] *nm* **1.** *P* **le père presseur**, the taxman **2.** *V* (a) **le père frappart**, penis* (b) **repartir avec son père frappart sous le bras**, to return empty-handed. (*Voir* **fouettard 1, 3**; **François**; **peinard I, II**)

perfo [pɛrfo] *nf F* **1.** card punch **2.** key-punch operator/punch girl.

périf [perif] *nm P* (= *le périphérique*) (Paris) ring road.

périmé [perime] *nm F* (*pers*) backnumber/old fogey*/old has-been/ old fart.

périodique [perijɔdik] *nm P* filter(-tip) cigarette*.

périscope [periskɔp] *nm F* **un coup de périscope**, a discreet look, glance (at sth/s.o.).

perle [pɛrl] **I** *nf* **1.** *F* (*pers*) jewel/ gem/pearl/treasure **2.** *F* (*scol, etc*) howler/gem; **c'est une perle**, it's a peach **3.** *F* (**passer son temps à**) **enfiler des perles**, to idle one's time away/to footle about **4.** *P* **lâcher la perle**, to die*/to kick the bucket **5.** *P* **lâcher une perle**, to (let out a) fart*/to blow off; **écraser une perle**, to fart* silently **6.** *V* female genitals* **7.** *P* prostitute* who will perform unnatural acts/who is game for anything **II** *nm P* = **perlot.**

perlimpinpin [pɛrlɛ̃pɛ̃pɛ̃] *nm F* **1. tout ça, c'est de la poudre de perlimpinpin**, that's boloney/that's (a load of) codswallop **2. un perlimpinpin**, a dash/a soupçon (of sth).

perlot [pɛrlo] *nm P* tobacco/baccy/ snout.

perloter [pɛrlɔte] *vi P* (*boxe*) to pack a punch.

perlouse, perlouze [pɛrluz] *nf P* **1.** pearl **2.** fart; **lâcher une perlouse**, to (let out a) fart*/to blow off/to let (one) off.

perm(e) [pɛrm] *nf P* (= *permission*) **1.** (*mil*) leave **2.** (*mil*) pass **3.** (*scol*) free period.

pernaga [pɛrnaga] *nm,* **perniflard** [pɛrniflar] *nm,* **pernifle** [pɛrnifl] *nm P* Pernod (*RTM*).

péronnelle [perɔnɛl] *nf F* silly half-wit (of a girl)/silly goose/*NAm* dumb chick.

le Pérou [lɔperu] *Prnm F* **gagner le Pérou**, to make a fortune; **ce n'est pas le Pérou** (*i*) it's not exactly a fortune/it's not very much (money); it's not highly paid (*ii*) it's nothing to write home about/it's no great shakes; **pas pour tout l'or du Pérou**, not for all the tea in China.

à perpète, perpette [apɛrpɛt] *adv phr P* for ever (and ever)/for life; **jusqu'à perpète**, till the cows come home; **être condamné à perpète**, to get a life sentence/to get life; **il habite à perpète**, he lives at the back of beyond; **c'est à perpète-les-ouilles**, it's miles away.

perquise [pɛrkiz] *nf P* (= *perquisition*) house search (by police)/raid.

perroquet [pɛrɔkɛ] *nm* **1.** *F* (*pers*) chatterbox*/parrot **2.** *F* (a) pastis with mint (b) absinth(e); **asphyxier/avaler/étrangler un perroquet**, to drink a glass of (*i*) pastis with mint (*ii*) absinthe **3.** *P* (*mil*) sniper **4.** *P* counsel/barrister/brief. (*Voir* **soupe 1**)

perruche [pεryʃ, pe-] *nf F* talkative woman/chatterbox*/gas bag/windbag.

perruque [pεryk, pe-] *nf* **1.** *F* **une vieille perruque,** an old fogey*/an old has-been **2.** *P* hair; **il a une perruque en peau de fesse,** he's as bald* as a coot **3.** *P* **faire de la perruque,** to do sth on the side/on the quiet; to moonlight.

perruquemar [pεrykmar] *nm P* hairdresser/barber.

persiennes [pεrsjεn] *nfpl F* spectacles/specs/glasses.

persil [pεrsi] *nm P* **1.** **aller au persil/faire son persil** (*i*) to walk the streets/to go on the game (*ii*) (*homme*) to pick up a prostitute* (*iii*) to show off*/to parade oneself (in order to attract attention *or* admirers) **2.** **aller au persil,** to go to work **3.** (*a*) hair under the armpits (*b*) pubic hair; (*femme*) **arroser le persil,** to urinate*.

persiller [pεrsije] *vi P* (*prostituée*) to walk the streets/to solicit*/to go on the game.

persilleuse [pεrsijøz] *nf P* prostitute*/pro/hooker.

pervenche [pεrvɑ̃ʃ] *nf F* = traffic warden.

pesant [pəzɑ̃] *nm F* (*histoire, blague, etc*) **valoir son pesant de cacahuètes/de moutarde,** to be very funny*/to be worth a guinea a minute.

pescal(e) [pεskal] *nm P* **1.** fish **2.** (*maquereau*) pimp*/nookie bookie.

pèse [pεz] *nm P* = **pèze.**

pèse-brioches [pεzbri(j)ɔʃ] *nm inv P* bathroom scales.

pesetas, pésetas [pezeta] *nfpl,* **pésètes, pésettes** [pezεt] *nfpl P* money*.

péseux, -euse [pezø, -øz] *a P* rich*/rolling in it.

pessigner [pesiɲe, pε-] *vtr P* **pessigner une lourde,** to break down/in a door.

peste [pεst] *nf F* (*esp enfant*) pest/damn nuisance; **petite peste,** little pest/little horror.

pestouille [pεstuj] *nf P* bad luck.

pet [pε(t)] *nm P* **1.** fart; **faire/lâcher un pet,** to (let out) fart*/to blow off; **vouloir tirer des pets d'un âne mort,** to try to get blood out of a stone; **ça ne vaut pas un pet (de lapin),** it's absolutely worthless*/it's not worth a fart; **il n'a pas un pet** [pε] **de bon sens,** he hasn't got an ounce of common(-sense) **2.** (*a*) **il va y avoir du pet** (*i*) there's trouble brewing; there's going to be trouble (*ii*) there's going to be a juicy bit of scandal (*b*) **faire du pet,** to kick up a row **3.** danger; **il n'y a pas de pet,** it's OK/there's no danger; **pas de pet que ...,** there's no danger that ... **4.** **fleurer/flurer le pet à qn,** to pick a quarrel* with s.o. **5.** **porter le pet** (*i*) to lay a charge (against s.o.) (*ii*) to lodge a complaint with the police **6.** accomplice; **faire le pet,** to keep a look-out/to be on the watch; **pet!** look out! **7.** **filer/partir comme un pet (sur une toile cirée),** to run away*/to scarper/to take to one's heels/to sling one's hook/to do a bunk **8.** **avoir un pet de travers,** to feel unwell* **9.** [pε] (*a*) **je lui ai flanqué un pet,** I punched him/I socked him one (*b*) **ta voiture a pris un pet,** your car's taken a bash.

pétanqueur [petɑ̃kœr] *nm P* homosexual*/queer/fag(got).

pétant [petɑ̃] *a P* **à cinq heures pétantes,** on the stroke of five/at five sharp/at five on the dot.

Pétaouchnok, Pétaouchnoque, Pétaousch- nock [petauʃnɔk] *Prn F* imaginary faraway place.

pétarader [petarade] *vi P* to be very angry*/to be hopping mad.

pétard [petar] *nm* **1.** *F* row/din/uproar*; **faire du pétard,** to kick up a row/to make a hell of a lot of noise; **un coup de pétard,** a rumpus/a racket/a hullabaloo **2.** *P* buttocks*/behind/bum/*NAm* butt; **se manier/se magner le pétard,** to hurry*/to get a move on/to get cracking/to shift one's arse/*NAm* to shift one's fanny **3.** *P* gun/firearm/revolver*/shooter **4.** *F* **être en pétard,** to be very angry*/to be in a flaming temper/ *esp NAm* to be really mad; **se mettre/se filer/se foutre en pétard,** to get angry*/to blow one's top/to do one's nut; **mettre qn en pétard,** to make s.o. angry*/to put s.o. in a huff/to get up s.o.'s nose **5.** *P* **aller au pétard/porter le pétard,** to lodge a complaint with the police/ *NAm* to put in a beef **6.** *F* **faire du pétard,** to indulge in malicious gossip/to spread rumours **7.** *P* **sans un pétard,** penniless*; **je n'ai pas un pétard,** I'm flat broke/I haven't got a bean **8.** = **pet 3 9.** *F* snag/hitch; **le pétard c'est que..., **the big problem is (that) ... **10.** *P* (*drogues*) marijuana cigarette*/joint/reefer.

pétarder [petarde] **I** *vi* **1.** *F* to kick up a row/to make a big stink/to kick up one hell of a fuss **2.** *P* to lodge a complaint with the police/*NAm* to put in a beef **II** *vpr* **se pétarder** *F* to quarrel*/to wrangle.

pétardier, ière [petardje, -jɛr] *P* **I** *a* (*a*) quarrelsome/argumentative (*b*) noisy/rowdy **II** *n* (*a*) bickerer/squabbler/awkward customer (*b*) noisy individual/noisy sod (*c*) scandalmonger.

pétase [petaz] *nm P* hat*.

pétasse [petas] *nf P* **1.** fear/fright/funk; **avoir la pétasse,** to be afraid*/to be in a blue funk **2.** mess/fix*/jam **3.** buttocks* **4.**

(*péj*) woman*/bint **5.** prostitute*/tart/scrubber/floozy **6.** homosexual*/queer/poof/homo.

pète [pɛt] *nm P* buttocks*/bum/*NAm* butt.

pété [pete] *a P* drunk*; **pété à mort,** dead drunk*/pissed (to the eyeballs)/stewed.

pétée [pete] *nf V* **1.** **tirer une pétée,** to have sex*/to get one's end away **2.** **filer une pétée,** to have an orgasm*/to come (off).

pet-en-l'air [pɛtɑ̃lɛr] *nm inv F* (man's) short indoor jacket; bumfreezer.

péter [pete] **I** *vi* **1.** *F* (*chaise, etc*) to break/to give way; (*corde, etc*) to snap; **la tête me pète,** my head feels as if it's going to burst **2.** *F* **il faut que ça pète (ou que ça dise pourquoi),** it's got to work/it has to happen (come what may) **3.** *F* **péter la santé,** to be bursting with health **4.** *P* to break wind/to fart* **5.** *P* **elle me fait péter les boutons de braguette,** she really turns me on/gets me going; she makes me (feel) randy/horny; she gives me a rise/a hard-on **6.** *P* **envoyer péter qn,** to tell s.o. to clear off; **elle l'a envoyé péter,** she told him to go to hell/to bugger off **7.** *P* **péter dans la soie** (*i*) to show off*/to swank (*ii*) to dress luxuriously (*iii*) to be rich*/to be rolling in it **8.** *P* **manger à s'en faire péter la sous-ventrière,** to eat* till one is ready to burst/to stuff one's guts/to really pig oneself; **rire à se péter la sous-ventrière,** to laugh uproariously/to split one's sides laughing **9.** *P* **péter dans la main à qn** (*i*) (*pers*) to let s.o. down/to fail to keep one's promise to s.o. (*ii*) (*projet, idée, plan*) to fail*/to fall through/to come to nothing/to fizzle out; **ça m'a pété dans la main,** it fell through/it didn't work out **10.** *P* to kick up a (hell of a) row/to make a big fuss; **ça va péter (sec)!** there's going to be a hell of a stink!/there's going to be a big bust-up! **11.** *P* **arriver/gagner en pétant,** to win easily/to romp home **II** *vtr* **1.** *F* **péter le feu/du feu/des flammes,** to be bursting with energy/to be full of beans **2.** *P (a)* **péter la faim/la péter,** to be ravenously hungry* *(b)* **viens au rade, je la pète,** let's go to the pub, I'm dying for a drink **3.** *P* **se péter la gueule,** to do oneself an injury; to come a cropper* **4.** *P* **péter une lourde,** to break down a door **5.** *P (femme)* **avoir vu péter le loup,** to have lost one's virginity*. (*Voir* **conomètre; cul I 19; derrière 2; mastic 4**) **III** *vpr* **se péter** *P* se péter (la tête), to blow one's mind (on drugs).

pète(-)sec [pɛtsɛk] *nm F* disciplinarian/martinet.

péteur, euse[1] [petœr, -øz] **I** *n* *P* **1.** farter **2.** ill-mannered oaf/lout/boor **3.** coward* **II** *nf P* motor-bike.

péteux, euse[2] [petø, -øz] *P* **I** *n* *(a)* coward*/yellowbelly *(b)* snob/show-off* *(c)* bastard*/rotter/stinker/creep **II** *a (a)* cowardly*/yellow/in a funk *(b)* pretentious/snobby/snooty *(c)* rotten/lousy (individual).

pètezouille [pɛtzuj] *nm P* = **pedzouille.**

petiot, ote [pətjo, -ɔt] *a&n F* tiny/wee/titchy/diddy (child); **un petiot/une petiote,** a tiny tot.

petit [pəti] **I** *a&nm F* **un petit coup de rouge,** a nice drop of red wine; **s'en jeter un petit (blanc),** to down a glass of (white) wine **II** *n* **1.** *F* **bonjour, mon petit,** good morning, my dear **2.** *F (argent)* **faire des petits,** to increase; to bear interest **3.** *P* anus*; **prendre du petit,** to have anal sex*/to go in by the backdoor **4.** *P* buttocks*. (*Voir* **cirque 3; coin 4; endroit 1; frère 5; noir II 2; salé**)

petite [pətit] *nf P* **1.** mettre en petite *(i)* to steal*; to shoplift *(ii)* to hide/to stash away (the proceeds of a robbery, etc); **j'ai un peu de pèze en petite,** I've got something put away for a rainy day **2.** **une petite,** a small glass of pastis *or* absinthe **3.** *(drogues)* **prendre une petite,** to take a fix (*esp* of heroin*).

petit-nègre [pətinɛgr] *nm F* **parler petit-nègre,** to talk pidgin French.

pétochard [petɔʃar] *P* **I** *a* cowardly*/yellow/chicken **II** *nm* coward*/yellowbelly/chicken.

pétoche [petɔʃ] *nf P* fear/(blue) funk; **avoir la pétoche,** to be afraid*/to have the wind up/to be scared shitless.

pétoire [petwar] *nf F* **1.** (child's) pop-gun **2.** gun/firearm/revolver*/peashooter **3.** moped/pot-pot/put-put.

peton [pətɔ̃] *nm F (mot enfantin)* tiny foot/tootsie(-wootsie)/tootsy(-wootsy).

pétouille [petuj] *nf P* **1.** = **pétoche 2.** = **pétrin.**

pétoulet [petulɛ] *nm P* buttocks*; **avoir le pétoulet à zéro,** to be afraid*/to be in a blue funk/to be scared shitless.

pétouze [petuz] *nf P* = **pétard.**

pétrin [petrɛ̃] *nm F* **être dans le pétrin/dans un beau pétrin,** to be in a fix*/in the soup/up the creek/in a tight spot; **se mettre dans le pétrin,** to get into a fix*/into a mess; **mettre qn dans le pétrin,** to get s.o. into a fix*/to land s.o. in a fine mess; to drop s.o. in it; **un beau pétrin!/un joli pétrin!** here's a fine mess!

pétrole [petrɔl] *nm F* hard liquor/strong spirits*/rotgut.

pétrousquin [petruskɛ̃] *nm P* **1.** *O* = **pedzouille 2.** buttocks*/bum/*NAm* butt/*NAm* fanny; **tomber sur son pétrousquin,** to sit down with a bump/to land up on one's arse/*NAm* ass **3.** civilian/ civvy **4.** fellow/chap*/bloke/guy.

pétrus [petrys] *nm O P* buttocks*.

pétun [petœ̃] *nm A P* tobacco/ baccy.

pétuner [petyne] *nm A P* to smoke.

petzingue [pɛtzɛ̃g] *nm P =* **pétard.**

petzouillard [pɛtzujar] *nm*, **petzouille** [pɛtzuj] *nm P =* **pedzouille.**

peu [pø] *adv & nm F* **1. un peu (, mon neveu)!** rather!/not half!/you bet/I should say so! **2. c'est un peu bien!** that's jolly good!/that's really great! **3. ça, c'est un peu fort!** that's a bit much! **4. ah! non, très peu (pour moi)!**/**ah! non, très peu de ce genre!** not for me!/not blooming likely!/I'm not having any!/count me out! **5. viens un peu!** come here! **6. un peu beaucoup,** far too much.

peuchère! [pøʃɛr] *int F (dial du Midi)* blast!/strewth!

peuple [pœpl] *nm F* **il y avait du peuple,** there was quite a crowd/ there were a lot of people.

peur [pœr] *nf F* **vous n'avez pas peur!** you've got a nerve!/you don't want much, do you?/you're not backward in coming forward, are you? (*Voir* **bleu I 2**)

pèze [pɛz] *nm P* money*/dough/ bread/lolly; **être au pèze,** to be very rich*/to be rolling in it; **un vieux tout à fait au ' pèze,** a stinkingly rich old man; **fusiller son pèze,** to blow a hole in one's money/to blow one's dough.

pfui! [pfɥi] *int F* phooey!

PG [peʒe] *abbr F (= prisonnier de guerre)* prisoner of war/POW.

phalanges [falɑ̃ʒ] *nfpl P* hands*.

phalangettes [falɑ̃ʒɛt] *nfpl P* fingers.

phalzar [falzar] *nm P* (pair of)

trousers*/*NAm* pants. (*Voir* **falzar(d)**)

pharamineux, -euse [faraminø, -øz] *a F* fantastic/colossal. (*Voir* **faramineux**)

phare [far] *nm F* **piquer un phare,** to blush/to go red.

pharmaco [farmako], **pharmago** [farmago] *nm P (= pharmacien)* chemist.

pharo [faro] *nm F (= pharaon)* faro (*card game*).

phéno [feno] *a A F* phenomenal; prodigious/amazing.

phénomène [fenɔmɛn] *nm F* outlandish character; freak/weirdo.

philo [filo] *nf F (scol)* philosophy.

philosophailler [filɔzɔfaje] *vi F (péj)* to philosophize.

phonard [fɔnar] *nm O P* **1.** telephone* **2.** telephonist.

phonarde [fɔnard] *nf O P* (telephone) operator.

phono [fɔno] *nm O F (= phonographe)* gramophone.

phoque [fɔk] *nm P* **1. les avoir à la phoque,** to be lazy*/to be workshy **2.** homosexual*. (*Voir* **être 1**)

photographier [fɔtɔgrafje] *vtr F* **photographier qn,** to identify s.o.; **se faire photographier,** to be spotted.

phrasicoter [frazikɔte] *vi F* to speechify/to hold forth.

phrasicoteur [frazikɔtœr] *nm F* speechifier/spouter/waffler.

PHS [peaʃɛs] *nm F (= (réunion) pour hommes seulement)* stag party; stag dinner; stag night.

piaf [pjaf] *nm P* **1.** (*a*) sparrow (*b*) (any) bird **2. un drôle de piaf,** a strange individual/a queer bird **3.** (*rare*) policeman*. (*Voir* **crâne 2**)

piaillard, -arde [pjɑjar, -ard] *a&n F* squawking/screeching/ squealing (person).

piaille [pjɑj] *nf F* bad luck.

piailler [pjaje] *vi F* to squawk/to screech/to squeal; to chatter*.

piailleur, euse [pjɑjœr, -øz] *n F* = **piaillard, arde.**

piane-piane [pjanpjan] *adv F* very slowly/very softly/nice and gently; **vas-y piane-piane!** gently does it!/go easy!

piano [pjano] *nm* **1.** *F* **piano du pauvre/piano des pauvres/piano à bretelles,** accordion **2.** *P (drogues)* **piano du pauvre,** hashish* **3.** *P* **passer au piano/jouer du piano,** to have one's fingerprints taken **4.** *P (comptoir de café)* bar. (*Voir* **zinc**) **5.** *P* **touches de piano,** teeth*/ivories; **il n'a plus de ratiches dans son piano,** he's got no teeth left **6.** *P* **vendre des pianos,** to talk nonsense*/to talk a lot of hot air **7.** *V* **jouer du piano,** to fart*.

piastre [pjastr] *nf FrC F* dollar.

piaule [pjol] *nf P* room/pad/digs; **ma piaule,** my place.

se piauler [səpjole] *vpr P* to go home/to turn in/to make tracks.

pibloque [piblɔk] *nf P* concierge/caretaker/*esp NAm* janitor.

pibouic [pibwik] *nm P (musique)* clarinet.

à pic [apik] *adv phr F* (*a*) **arriver/tomber à pic,** to come/to happen at the right moment/in the nick of time; **ça tombe à pic,** it couldn't have come at a better time/it worked out just right (*b*) **répondre à pic,** to answer pat.

picaillon [pikajɔ̃] *nm P* (*a*) money*/cash; **j'ai plus un picaillon,** I haven't got a penny (*b*) *pl* **picaillons,** small change; cash; money*; **avoir des picaillons,** to be rich*/to be rolling in it.

pichet [piʃɛ] *nm P* wine.

pichoun [piʃun] *a F* small/little/tiny/wee/titchy. (*Voir* **pitchoun**)

pichpin [piʃpɛ̃] *nm P* = **pitchpin.**

pichteau   [piʃto]   *nm,*

pichtegorme [piʃtəgɔrm] *nm,*
pichtegorne [piʃtəgɔrn] *nm,*
pichto   [piʃto]   *nm,*
pichtogorme [piʃtɔgɔrm] *nm,*
pichtogorne [piʃtɔgɔrn] *nm P* ordinary (red) wine/plonk/vino.

pick-up [pikœp] *nm P* **travailler du pick-up,** to talk nonsense*.

picoler [pikɔle] *vi P* to drink* heavily/to hit the bottle/to tipple/to (go on the) booze; **je me suis mis à picoler,** I hit the bottle/I went on the booze.

picoleur [pikɔlœr] *nm P* heavy drinker/drunkard*/tippler/boozer; **c'est un grand picoleur,** he's a real boozer/he can't half knock it back.

picolo [pikɔlo] *nm P* wine/plonk/vino.

picot [piko] *nm P* fool*/idiot.

picotin [pikɔtɛ̃] *nm F* **pas un picotin,** not a bean/not a cent.

picouse [pikuz] *nf P* = **piquouse.**

picouser [pikuze] *vtr P* = **piquouser.**

picrate [pikrat] *nm P* poor-quality wine/plonk/vino.

pictance [piktɑ̃s] *nf P* alcoholic drink/liquor.

pictancheur [piktɑ̃ʃœr] *nm P* heavy drinker/drunkard*/tippler/boozer.

pictancher [piktɑ̃ʃe], **picter** [pikte] *vi P* to drink* heavily/to hit the bottle/to go on the booze/to tipple.

picton [piktɔ̃] *nm P* ordinary red wine; **boire un coup de picton,** to knock back some wine.

pictonner [piktɔne] *vi P* = **picoler.**

pie [pi] *nf F* chatterbox*; **jaser comme une pie,** to chatter* away (nineteen to the dozen); **elle est bavarde comme une pie (borgne),** she's a terrible chatterbox*/she's got the gift of the gab.

pièce [pjɛs] *nf* **1.** *F* **on n'est pas aux pièces,** we're not in any hurry/ there's no rush **2.** *O F* **jouer une pièce à qn,** to play a trick/a joke on s.o.; to pull s.o.'s leg **3.** *F* **pièce rapportée/pièce collée,** outsider/odd man out **4.** *F* **mettre qn en pièces,** to slander s.o./to pull s.o. to pieces **5.** *P* **pièce de dix ronds/pièce de dix sous,** anus*; **il a perdu sa pièce de dix ronds/de dix sous,** he's a homosexual*/he's queer **6.** *P* **pièce humide,** syringe*/hypo; **artilleur de la pièce humide,** male nurse. (*Voir* **service**)

pied [pje] *nm* **1.** *F* (*a*) **se lever du pied gauche,** to get out of bed on the wrong side; **je suis parti du pied gauche avec lui,** we started off on the wrong foot/I got off to a bad start with him **2.** *F* **faire du pied à qn** (*i*) to give s.o. a kick (as a warning) (*ii*) to play footsie with s.o. (*Voir* **genou** 1) **3.** *F* **mettre les pieds dans le plat,** to make a mistake*/to put one's foot in it/to drop a brick/to drop a clanger **4.** *F* **il ne sait sur quel pied danser,** he doesn't know which way to turn/ he's in a real quandary **5.** *F* **lever le pied,** to abscond/to bolt/to flit/ to welsh; **un financier qui lève le pied,** a fly-by-night **6.** *F* **se tirer des pieds** (*i*) to run away*/to beat it/to clear off (*ii*) to get out of a scrape **7.** *F* **sortir/s'en aller les pieds devant,** to die*/to go out feet first **8.** *F* **ça lui fera les pieds/des pieds!** that'll serve him right!/that'll teach him (a lesson)! **c'est bien fait pour ton pied/pour tes pieds!** it serves you right! **9.** *F* **sécher sur pied/faire le pied de grue,** to be kept waiting/to be kept hanging about/to kick one's heels; **on m'a laissé faire le pied de grue dans la salle d'attente,** I was left to sweat it out in the waiting room **10.** *F* **faire un pied de nez à qn,** to thumb one's nose at s.o./to cock a snook at s.o. **11.** *F* **mettre qn à pied,** to dismiss* s.o./to fire s.o./to give s.o.

the sack **12.** *F* **jouer un pied de cochon à qn,** to play a dirty trick on s.o.; to let s.o. down badly **13.** *F* **c'est le coup de pied de l'âne,** that's the unkindest cut of all **14.** *F* **il ne se donne pas des coups de pied,** he's always giving himself a pat on the back; he's always blowing his own trumpet **15.** *P* **(aller) se laver les pieds** (*i*) to be sentenced to hard labour (*ii*) to receive a stiff* sentence **16.** *P* **il y a des coups de pied au cul qui se perdent,** some people are past praying for; there's no hope for some people **17.** *P* **casser les pieds à qn** (*i*) to bore* s.o. stiff; **il me casse les pieds,** he's a terrible bore*/he bores me rigid/he's a real drag (*ii*) to put a spoke in s.o.'s wheel **18.** *P* **avoir les pieds dans le dos/dans les reins,** to have the police* on one's track/ on one's tail. (*Voir* **dos** 5; **reins** 4) **19.** *P* **j'en ai le pied/j'en ai mon pied,** I'm fed up with it/I've had it up to here **20.** *P* (*a*) **pied de biche,** (burglar's) jemmy/*NAm* jimmy (*b*) **faire le pied de biche,** to canvass from house to house/from door to door (*c*) **tirer le pied de biche,** to beg from house to house **21.** *P* (*mil*) **pied de banc,** NCO (*esp sergeant*) **22.** *P* (*a*) fool*/idiot; **quel pied!** what a twerp!/what a jerk! (*b*) **il joue comme un pied,** he can't play for nuts/for toffee; **il conduit comme un pied,** he's a shocking driver **23.** *P* **avoir/toucher son pied,** to share out the spoils **24.** *P* (*a*) kick/thrill (from drugs); **prendre son pied,** to get a kick out of sth/ to get one's rocks off; **j'ai pris mon pied,** it was a real gas/I got a real kick (out of it)/it really turned me on; **c'était le pied!** it was great/fantastic/a gas!/it really blew my mind! **25.** *V* **prendre son pied** (*i*) to have sex*/to have it away/to get one's leg over (*ii*) to have an orgasm*/to come **26.** *P* **coup de pied de Vénus,** dose of VD*/the clap. (*Voir* **bête** II 1; **bouquet** 3;

chaud I 1; chaud II 1; **chaussure** 1, 2, 3; **dentelle**; lécher 3; **marmite** 4; **se moucher** 1; **nickelé**)

pied-de-figuier [pjedəfigje] *nm* P (*péj*) Arab/wog. (*pl* **pieds-de-figuier**)

pied-noir [pjenwar] *nm&f* F Algerian-born Frenchman/woman. (*pl* **pieds-noirs**)

piège [pjεʒ] *nm P* **1. piège (à poux)** (*i*) beard (*ii*) comb **2.** bookmaker/bookie **3.** prison* **4. piège à nichons**, bra/titholder **4. piège à filles** (*i*) attractive man*/good-looker (*ii*) stylish nice-looking car (used to attract women). (*Voir* **con** I 2 (*iii*); **morlingue**)

piéger [pjeʒe] *vi P* **1.** to be a bookmaker; to take bets **2. se faire piéger**, to be had/to be conned.

pierre [pjεr] I *nf* **1.** *F* **jeter la pierre à qn**, to criticize* s.o./to run s.o. down **2.** *F* **malheureux comme les pierres** (*i*) as unhappy as can be/thoroughly miserable (*ii*) penniless*/stony broke **3.** *F* **pierre de taille**, miser*/skinflint **4.** *pl P* jewels/sparklers/stones II *Prnm F* **Pierre et Paul; Pierre, Paul et Jacques**, Tom, Dick and Harry.

pierreuse [pjerøz] *nf P* prostitute*/street-walker.

pierrot [pjεro] *nm* **1.** *F* (*a*) country bumpkin (*b*) fool*/twit (*c*) **un drôle de pierrot**, a strange fellow*/an odd chap **3.** *P* **étrangler un pierrot**, to drink/to knock back a glass of white wine.

piétaille [pjetaj] *nf P* (*mil*) **la piétaille**, the infantry/footsloggers/PBI (= poor bloody infantry).

piétard [pjetar] *nm P* pedestrian.

piéton [pjetɔ̃] *nm P* **1.** traffic policeman* **2.** tramp/*esp NAm* hobo.

pieu [pjø] *nm P* **1.** bed; **se mettre au pieu**, to go to bed*/to kip

down/to crash out/to hit the hay; **bath au pieu**, good in bed/(a) good screw **2.** bottle of red wine.

pieuter [pjøte] I *vi P* to (go to) sleep*/to hit the sack II *vpr* **se pieuter** *P* to go to bed*.

pieuvre [pjœvr] *nf F* (*pers*) parasite/limpet/leech/hanger-on.

pif [pif] *nm P* **1.** (large) nose*/conk/hooter **2. ça lui pend au pif**, he's got it coming to him; he's (in) for it; **qui sait ce qui nous pend au pif?** who knows what's in store for us? **3. je l'ai dans le pif**, I can't stand him/he gets up my nose **4.** (*a*) **se salir/se piquer le pif**, to get drunk* (*b*) **avoir un (petit) coup dans le pif/avoir un coup de trop dans le pif/avoir le pif sali/avoir le pif piqué**, to be drunk* **5. au pif**, at a rough guess; **faire qch qu pif**, to do sth by guesswork **6. se casser/se cogner le pif** (*i*) to find nobody at home (when calling at a house) (*ii*) to be frustrated (*iii*) to fail (in business); to come a cropper* **6. se manger/se bouffer le pif** (*i*) to quarrel*; to be always getting at each other (*ii*) to fight/to scrap. (*Voir* **communard**)

piffard [pifar] *nm P* **1.** large nose* **2.** man with a large nose.

piffer [pife] I *vtr P* **je (ne) peux pas le piffer**, I can't stand (the sight of) him/he gets up my nose II *vpr* **se piffer** *P* **ils ne peuvent pas se piffer**, they can't stand each other/they hate each other's guts.

piffeur [pifœr] *nm P* man with a flair for nosing out things.

piffomètre [pifɔmɛtr] *nm P* = **pifomètre**.

piffre [pifr] *nm P* glutton*/greedy person/greedy-guts.

se piffrer [səpifre] *vpr P* to eat* greedily/to gorge oneself/to stuff one's guts/to pig oneself.

pifomètre [pifɔmɛtr] *nm P* **au pifomètre**, at a rough estimate/at a rough guess; **calculer au pifomètre**, to guesstimate; **aller au pifomètre,** to play it by ear.

pige [piʒ] *nf P* **1.** year (of age, of prison sentence); **à/pour soixante piges il n'est pas mal,** he's not bad for sixty **2. faire la pige à qn,** to go one better than s.o./to leave s.o. standing **3.** freelance journalism; **être payé à la pige,** to be a penny-a-liner/to be paid by the line.

pigeon [piʒɔ̃] *nm F* **1. loger comme/avec les pigeons,** to live in an attic **2.** (*pers*) sucker; **plumer un pigeon,** to fleece a mug/a sucker **3. il fait un croquis comme un pigeon avec sa queue!** he can't draw for nuts!

pigeonneau, *pl* **-eaux** [piʒɔno] *nm F* (*pers*) mug/sucker/easy mark.

pigeonner [piʒɔne] *vtr F* to swindle*/to cheat; to dupe/to take (s.o.) in; to fleece; **je me suis laissé/fait pigeonner,** I've been had/done.

pigeonnier [piʒɔnje] *nm F* (*théâtre*) the gods.

piger [piʒe] *vtr P* **1.** to steal*; **piger la conversation de qn,** to ace in on s.o.'s conversation **2.** to understand*; **il n'a pas pigé,** it hasn't registered with him/he hasn't twigged/the penny hasn't dropped; **je n'y ai rien pigé,** I couldn't make head or tail of it; **tu piges?** get it?/you dig? **je pige,** I get it; I get the drift; **piger rapidement,** to be quick on the uptake; **piges-tu la combine?** do you see what they're up to?/do you see their little game? **je ne pige rien aux maths,** I haven't a clue about maths/maths is like double-dutch to me **3.** to look* at/to have a butchers at (sth); **pige-moi ça!** just look at that!/get a load of that!/take a dekko at that! **4.** (*a*) **piger un rhume,** to catch a cold (*b*) **piger cinq ans de prison,** to cop a five-year stretch **5.** to spot (the winner of a race) **6. se faire piger,** to get nabbed. (*Voir* **dal**)

pigette [piʒɛt] *nf P* **depuis pas mal de pigettes,** for a number of years. (*Voir* **pige 1**)

pigiste [piʒist] *nm&f F* freelance journalist/freelance(r).

pignole [piɲɔl] *nf V* masturbation; **se taper une pignole,** to masturbate*/to toss oneself off.

pignoter [piɲɔte] *vi P* to pinch and scrape.

pignouf [piɲuf] *nm P* **1.** lout/yob/layabout/hooligan*/thug **2.** miser*/skinflint/tight-ass.

pilant [pilɑ̃] *a P* very funny*.

pile [pil] **I** *nf F* **1.** thrashing; **donner/flanquer une pile à qn** (*i*) to give s.o. a thrashing/to beat s.o. up* (*ii*) to get the better of s.o./to beat s.o. (in a race, etc) **2. recevoir une pile,** to suffer a crushing defeat **II** *adv F* in the nick of time/bang on time; **s'arrêter pile,** to stop dead/to come to a dead stop; **arriver pile,** to arrive on the dot; **vous tombez pile,** you've come just at the right moment/you timed it just right; **à six heures pile,** on the dot of six.

piler [pile] *F* **I** *vtr* to thrash (s.o.)/to beat (s.o.) up*; **être à piler,** to deserve/to need a good hiding; **notre équipe s'est fait piler,** our team was licked/got thrashed **2. la piler,** to be famished **II** *vi* **1.** to brake abruptly/to jam on the brakes **2.** to toil away/to slog. (*Voir* **poivre 1**)

pilier [pilje] *nm* **1.** *F* (*péj*) **pilier de bar/de café/de bistrot,** frequenter of pubs; bar lounger; **c'est un vrai pilier de bar,** he's always propping up the bar/he seems to live in the pub **2.** *pl P* fat/solid/sturdy legs*; **être ferme sur ses piliers,** to be steady on one's pins.

pills [pils] *nmpl P* (*drogues*) LSD* pills.

piloches [pilɔʃ] *nfpl P* teeth*/choppers/grinders.

piloirs [pilwar] *nmpl P* fingers.

pilon [pilɔ̃] *nm P* **1.** beggar/bum; faire le pilon, to beg **2.** leg*.

pilonner [pilɔne] *vi* **1.** *P* to beg/ to sponge **2.** *F* to work* hard/to slog away/to do a bit of hard grind.

pilonneur [pilɔnœr] *nm P* beggar/ bum.

pilule [pilyl] *nf F* **1.** dorer la pilule, to sugar the pill **2.** prendre la pilule, to be thwarted/rebuffed; to come to grief; l'équipe de foot a pris une pilule, the football team got thrashed.

piment [pimɑ̃] *nm P* nose*.

pinaillage [pinɑjaʒ] *nm P* quibbling/hair-splitting/nit-picking.

pinailler [pinɑje] *vi P* to quibble/ to split hairs; to be finicky/picky.

pinailleries [pinɑjəri] *nfpl P* = pinaillage.

pinailleur, -euse [pinɑjœr, -øz] *n P* quibbler/hair-splitter/nit-picker; finicky person/fusspot.

pinard [pinar] *nm F* wine/plonk/ vino.

pinarium [pinarjɔm] *nm P* brothel*.

pince [pɛ̃s] *nf* **1.** *P* hand*/paw/ mitt; serrer la pince à qn, to shake hands with s.o.; serre-moi la pince! tip us your fin/your flipper! **2.** *P* foot*; à pince(s), on foot; aller à pinces/se taper la route à pinces, to foot it/to hoof it/to leg it **3.** *F* (burglar's) jemmy/*NAm* jimmy **4.** *pl P* handcuffs*/cuffs **5.** *P* pinces d'Adam, fingers **6.** *P* gare la pince! mind you don't get nabbed/ pinched! **7.** *V* female genitals*/ snatch **8.** *V* (*homme*) être (un) chaud de la pince, to be hot stuff/a randy sod; to be always ready for it; to sleep around; (*femme*) être chaude de la pince, to be hot stuff; to be continually randy/horny; to be a bit of a nympho; to sleep around **9.** *P* bonne pince! well done!

pinceau, *pl* -eaux [pɛ̃so] *nm* **1.** *P* (*a*) foot* (*b*) leg*; affûter des pinceaux, to walk **2.** *P* se laver les pinceaux (*i*) to be sentenced to hard labour (*ii*) to receive a stiff sentence **3.** *P* s'embrouiller/ s'emmêler les pinceaux, to get into a muddle/to get tied up in knots **4.** *V* penis*.

pince-cul [pɛ̃sky] *nm P* (*a*) rowdy party/dance/*NAm* shindig (*b*) (low-class) dance hall/dive. (*pl* pince-cul(s))

pincée [pɛ̃se] *nf F* une bonne pincée (de billets), a good wad of notes.

pince-fesses [pɛ̃sfɛs] *nm inv P* = pince-cul.

pincer [pɛ̃se] *vtr F* **1.** to arrest*; se faire pincer, to get nabbed/ nicked/pinched; il s'est fait pincer en sautant de la fenêtre, the police collared him as he jumped out of the window **2.** pincer un rhume, to catch/to get a cold **3.** en pincer pour qn/être pincé pour qn, to be infatuated* with s.o./to be crazy about s.o./to have a crush on s.o. **4.** to understand/to see; tu pinces? get it? (*Voir* nez 4)

pincettes [pɛ̃sɛt] *nfpl* **1.** *F* il n'est pas à prendre avec des pincettes (*i*) he's like a bear with a sore head (*ii*) I wouldn't touch him with a barge-pole **2.** *P* legs*; tricoter des pincettes (*i*) to dance (*ii*) to run like mad; affûter des pincettes/se tirer des pincettes, to run away*/to beat it/to clear off.

pine [pin] *nf V* penis*/cock/prick; il est revenu avec la pine sous le bras, he didn't make out/he couldn't get it up.

piné [pine] *a P* successful.

piner [pine] *vtr V* to have sex* (with s.o.)/to have it away with s.o./to screw s.o.

pinette [pinɛt] *nf V* (*rare*) sex*/ quickie/quick screw.

pineur, -euse [pinœr, -øz] *n V* = **pinailleur, -euse 2.**

pingler [pɛ̃gle] *vtr P* to arrest*/to collar/to nab/to cop/to nick. (*Voir* **épingler**)

pinglots [pɛ̃glo] *nmpl*, **pingots** [pɛ̃go] *nmpl P* feet*.

pingouin [pɛ̃gwɛ̃] *nm P* **1.** Spaniard*. (*Voir* **Espingouin**) **2.** *pl* feet* **3.** policeman* **4.** (*homme*) (**habillé**) **en pingouin**, in evening dress/in a penguin suit **5.** (*a*) (*individu*) bloke/guy (*b*) (*compagnon*) (boy)friend.

pingouinche [pɛ̃gwɛ̃ʃ] *nm P* Spaniard*.

pingre [pɛ̃gr] *F* **I** *a* miserly*/ mean/stingy; **il est pingre comme tout**, he's as mean as can be **II** *nm&f* miser*/skinflint/tight-ass.

pingrerie [pɛ̃grəri] *nf F* stinginess/ meanness.

pinoche [pinɔʃ] *a P* excellent*/ super/first-rate.

pinocher [pinɔʃe] *vtr&i* **1.** *P* (*homme*) to be promiscuous/to sleep around/to screw around **2.** *F* to quibble/to split hairs; to be finicky/picky.

pinte [pɛ̃t] *nf F* **se faire/s'offrir/se payer une pinte de bon sang**, to have a good time/a good laugh.

pinté [pɛ̃te] *a P* **être pinté**, to be dead drunk*/smashed/plastered/ pissed.

pinter [pɛ̃te] *P* **I** *vi* to tipple/to booze **II** *vtr* to swill/to knock back (beer, wine) **III** *vpr* **se pinter** *P* to get drunk*.

pin-up [pinœp] *nf inv F* pin-up.

piochage [pjɔʃaʒ] *nm F* hard work; swotting.

pioche [pjɔʃ] *nf F* hard work/slog/ grind. (*Voir* **tête 4**)

piocher [pjɔʃe] **I** *vtr F* to study hard at (sth)/to swot at (sth);

piocher son espagnol, to mug up one's Spanish **II** *vi* (*a*) *F* to study hard/to swot (*b*) *F* **il faut tout le temps piocher**, it's a constant grind (*c*) *P* **pioche (dans le plat)!** dig in!

piocheur, -euse [pjɔʃœr, -øz] *n F* hard worker/swot/slogger.

piocre [pjɔkr] *nm P* louse.

pioger [pjɔʒe] *vi P* to live/to hang out.

piole [pjɔl] *nf P* = **piaule.**

pion [pjɔ̃] **I** *nm* **1.** *F* (*scol*) = junior master; = prefect; *NAm* = monitor **2.** *P* **pas un pion**, not a cent/not a bean; **je ne donnerais pas un pion pour l'acheter**, I wouldn't give a penny for it. (*Voir* **damer**) **II** *a P* drunk*/plastered/ smashed.

pioncer [pjɔ̃se] *vi P* to sleep/to kip down/to doss down; to get some kip/some shut-eye; **pioncer ferme**, to be fast asleep/to be dead to the world; **pioncer un bon coup**, to have a good snooze/a good kip.

pionceur, -euse [pjɔ̃sœr, -øz] *n P* sleeper/snoozer.

pionnard [pjɔnar] *nm P* drunk(ard)*/boozer/tippler.

se pionnarder [səpjɔnarde] *vpr P* to get drunk*.

pionne [pjɔn] *nf F* (*scol*) = assistant mistress; = (girl) prefect; *NAm* = (girl) monitor.

se pionner [səpjɔne] *vpr P* to get drunk*.

pionneur, -euse [pjɔnœr, -øz] *n F* (*scol*) tell-tale/sneak.

pioupiou [pjupju] *nm O P* (young) infantryman/foot-soldier. (*pl* **pioupious**)

pipard [pipar] *nm P* pipe-smoker.

pipe [pip] *nf* **1.** *P* cigarette*/ cig(gy)/fag. (*Voir* **lacson**) **2.** *P* **casser sa pipe**, to die*/to kick the bucket/to snuff it **3.** *F* **mettez ça dans votre pipe!** put that in your pipe and smoke it! **4.** *P* **se fendre**

la pipe, to laugh* uproariously/to split one's sides laughing; **nous nous fendions la pipe,** we were in stitches **5.** *P* **prendre la pipe/ remporter une pipe,** to get badly caught out/to come to grief/to come a cropper; to lose out on a deal/to get stung **6.** *V* **fellatio*; faire/tailler une pipe à qn,** to give s.o. a blow-job/to blow s.o./to suck s.o. off/to suck s.o.'s cock/to give s.o. head; **prise de pipe,** blow-job/ head; **une bouche à tailler des pipes,** a real cocksucker's mouth. (*Voir* **nom 1; tête 9**)

pipelet, pipelette [piplɛ, piplɛt] *n F* (*a*) concierge/porter/caretaker (of block of flats, etc) (*b*) nosey and gossipy person/nosey parker.

piper [pipe] **I** *vtr* **1.** *F* **piper qn,** to trick s.o./to catch s.o.; **se faire piper,** to get caught/to be tricked **2.** *P* to arrest*; **se faire piper,** to get nabbed/nicked **3.** *P* **je (ne) peux pas le piper,** I can't stand/ stick/stomach/bear him (at any price); he really gets up my nose **4.** *F* **il n'a pas pipé/il n'a pipé mot,** he kept silent; he didn't say a word/a dicky bird **5.** *V* **piper qn,** to give s.o. fellatio*/to blow s.o./to give s.o. a blow-job/to suck s.o. off **II** *vi P* to be a pipe-smoker.

piperlot [pipɛrlo] *nm P* (pipe) tobacco.

pipette [pipɛt] *nf P* **1.** cigarette* **2.** vol à la pipette, stealing petrol (from cars) by siphoning it off **3.** ça ne vaut pas pipette, that's worth-less*/it's not worth a sausage. (*Voir* **tripette**)

pipeur, euse [pipœr, -øz] *n* **1.** *F* swindler*; cheat **2.** *V* fellator/ cocksucker/head artist/dick licker.

pipi [pipi] *nm* **1.** *F* (*a*) **faire pipi/ faire un petit pipi,** to urinate*/to wee-wee/to piddle/to pee; **aller faire pipi,** to spend a penny/to pay a call/to go for a pee; **j'ai envie d'aller faire pipi,** I want to go to the loo/*NAm* the bathroom/*NAm*

the john (*b*) urine*/wee(-wee); **il a fait pipi dans sa culotte,** he's wet himself/he's had an accident; **il y a du pipi de chien sur le tapis,** the dog's made a puddle/the dog's weed/the dog's pissed on the carpet. (*Voir* **dame-pipi**) **2.** *P* **du pipi de chat** (*i*) (*boisson*) poor-quality wine, etc/cat's piss/gnat's piss; **ce café, c'est du pipi de chat,** this coffee's like dishwater/this coffee is as weak as piss (*ii*) (*film, roman, etc*) rubbish/tripe.

pipi-room [pipirum] *nm F* WC*; **où sont fourrés les pipi-room?** where the hell is the loo/*NAm* the john in this place?

Pipo [pipo] *P* **I** *Prnf* **la Pipo,** the *École polytechnique* (in Paris) **II** *nm* **un Pipo,** a student at the *École polytechnique.*

piquage [pikaʒ] *nm F* arrest. (*Voir* **piquer 1**)

pique [pik] *nf F* **être à cent piques au-dessus de qn,** to be vastly superior to s.o./to be ten times better than s.o.; **il est à cent piques au-dessous de son frère,** he isn't a patch on his brother. (*Voir* **dame 5**)

piqué, ée [pike] *F* **I** *a* slightly mad*/cracked/nuts/screwy/loony **II** *n* crack-brained person/nut(ter); **c'est une vieille piquée,** the old girl's a bit touched in the head. (*Voir* **hanneton 2; ver**)

pique-assiette [pikasjɛt] *nm&f inv F* scrounger/sponger/parasite/ freeloader/hanger-on.

pique-fesse [pikfɛs] *nf P* nurse.

pique-gâteau [pikgato] *nm,* **pique-gaufrette** [pikgofrɛt] *nm P* nose*.

pique-lard [piklar] *nm P* flick knife.

pique-pouces [pikpus] *nm,* **pique-prunes** [pikpryn] *nm P* tailor.

piquer [pike] *vtr* **1.** *F* **faire piquer son chien**, to have one's dog put down/put to sleep **2.** *F* to steal*/ to pinch/to swipe (**qch à qn**, sth from s.o.); **je ne l'ai pas volé, je l'ai piqué sur un chantier**, I didn't steal it, I found it lying around; **il a fallu qu'on pique une tire pour y aller**, we had to nick a car to get there **3.** *P* to arrest*; **se faire piquer**, to get nabbed; **il s'est fait piqué**, he got nicked/picked up **4.** *P* to tattoo; **se faire piquer**, to get tattooed **5.** *P* to stab/to knife (s.o.) **6.** *V* to have sex* with (a woman) **7.** *F* **piquer les cartes**, to cheat at cards (by marking them). (*Voir* **assiette 4**; **départ**; **dix 3**; **macadam 2**; **mouche 2**; **nez 5**; **sèche²**; **tas 4**; **truc**) **II** *vpr* **se piquer** *F* to take drugs; to give oneself a fix/to fix (up)/to shoot up; **il se pique**, he's a drug addict/a junkie/a fixer.

piqueton [piktɔ̃] *nm P* ordinary red wine. (*Voir* **picton**)

piquette [pikɛt] *nf P* **1.** = **piqueton 2.** **ça n'était pas de la piquette**, that was no small matter **3.** **prendre/ramasser une piquette** (*i*) to get beaten up/to get a good hiding (*ii*) to get thrashed/licked/hammered.

piqueur [pikœr] *nm P* **1.** (*a*) pickpocket/dip (*b*) thief; **piqueur de troncs**, man who steals from a church collecting-box **2.** **piqueur de clopes**, man who goes around picking up cigarette* ends.

piquouse [pikuz] *nf P* (*drogues*) shot/injection*/fix/shoot; **faire une piquouse à qn**, to give s.o. a fix; **se faire une piquouse**, to give oneself a fix/to shoot up. (*Voir* **chevalier 6**)

piquouser [pikuze] *vtr P* **piquouser qn**, to give s.o. an injection/a jab/a shot/(*drogues*) a fix.

piquouze [pikuz] *nf P* = **piquouse.**

piquouzer [pikuze] *vtr P* = **piquouser.**

pirater [pirate] *vtr F* to record/to copy fraudulently (records, films, videos, etc); **des cassettes piratées**, pirated cassettes.

pire [pir] *adv A P* **tant pire!** (= *tant pis!*) never mind!/it can't be helped!

pirouette [pirwɛt] *nf F* **répondre par des pirouettes**, to reply (to sth serious) with a joke.

piscine [pisin] *nf F* **en pleine piscine**, in a frightful mess.

pissant [pisɑ̃] *a P* very funny*.

pissat [pisa] *nm P* **pissat (d'âne)**, poor-quality wine, etc; cat's piss/ gnat's piss.

pisse [pis] *nf P* piss; **c'est de la pisse d'âne, ta bière!** your beer's as weak as piss!

pisse-copie [piskɔpi] *nm&f P* hack writer/penny-a-liner. (*Voir* **copie**)

pissée [pise] *nf P* (*a*) downpour (of rain) (*b*) **une bonne pissée**, a good piss.

pisse-froid [pisfrwa] *nm inv P* (*pers*) cold fish; wet blanket.

pissement [pismɑ̃] *nm P* pissing/ peeing.

pissenlit [pisɑ̃li] *nm P* **manger les pissenlits/bouffer du pissenlit par la racine**, to be dead and buried/to be pushing up the daisies.

pisser [pise] **I** *vi* **1.** *P* to urinate*/to piss/to pee; **avoir envie de pisser**, to want to (have a) piss/to be bursting (for a pee); **il est allé pisser un coup**, he's gone for a piss/a slash; **pisser dans sa culotte**, to wet one's pants/knickers **2.** *P* **une bouteille qui pisse**, a leaking bottle **3.** *P* **pisser des châsses/de l'œil/de la lanterne**, to cry (one's eyes out) **4.** *P* **pisser entre parenthèses**, to be bandy(-legged) **5.** *P* **laisse pisser!** let it ride!/forget it! **6.** *P* **ne se sentir plus pisser**, to feel like a million/to feel on top of the world **7.** *P* **en faire pisser à qn**, to put s.o. through it/to put s.o. through the mill **8.** *V* **pisser son os,** to have an abortion **9.** *V* **envoyer pisser qn,** to tell s.o. to piss off **10.** *V* **faire pisser qn,** to make s.o. piss himself laughing; **il nous raconte des blagues à faire pisser,** his jokes are so good (that) they make you piss yourself **11.** *V* **c'est moi qui pisse contre le mur,** I'm the one in charge around here; I'm (the) boss here **12.** *V* (*pluie*) **ça pisse dur/il pleut comme une vache qui pisse,** it's pissing down/it's bucketing down/it's chucking it down **13.** *P* **avoir autant d'effet que pisser dans la mer,** to stand as much chance as a fart in a windstorm; **c'est comme si je pissais sur un bec (de gaz),** I might as well save my breath; it's a sheer waste of time; it's like banging your head against a brick wall. (*Voir* **copie**; **côtelette 3**; **cul 15**; **froc 3**; **lame 2**; **mérinos**; **môme 2**; **mouton 4**; **sang 7**; **violon**) II *vpr* **se pisser** *V* to piss oneself/to kill oneself laughing.

pissette [pisɛt] *nf P* **1.** (*aut*) windscreen washer **2.** fire-hose nozzle.

pisseur, euse[1] [pisœr, -øz] *n P* **I** **c'est un pisseur,** he keeps disappearing for a piss/for a pee; he's got a weak bladder **II** *nf* **pisseuse** (*a*) baby girl; young girl*; little brat (*b*) woman*/bird/bint (*c*) slut/tart/scrubber. (*Voir* **copie**)

pisseux[1]**, euse**[2] [pisø, -øz] *a P* (*a*) smelling of urine/piss/pee (*b*) stained with urine/piss stained/pee stained (*c*) filthy/tatty/scruffy (*d*) (*couleur*) faded/washed-out/wishy-washy; **jaune pisseux,** dingy yellow.

pisseux[2] *nm P* **1.** inexperienced young man; **je ne vais pas laisser ce petit pisseux me donner des conseils,** I'm not going to let that little runt/jerk give me advice **2.** clumsy and dirty/scruffy worker who bungles everything; **espèce de pisseux!** you jerk!/you clumsy idiot!

pisse-vinaigre [pisvinɛgr] *nm inv P* grumbler/grouser/groucher.

pissoir(e) [piswar] *nm P* urinal/pisshouse/loo/*NAm* can/*NAm* john/(*homosexuels*) cottage.

pissoter [pisɔte] *vi P* to be for ever pissing.

pissotière [pisɔtjɛr] *nf,* **pissotoire** [pisɔtwar] *nf P* (public) urinal/cottage; (*homosexuels*) **faire les pissotières,** to go cruising in urinals/to go john cruising/to go cottaging.

pissouse, pissouze [pisuz] *nf P* = **pisseuse**[1].

pistache [pistaʃ] *nf P* **prendre une pistache,** to get drunk*; **il tient une belle pistache,** he's dead drunk/he's pissed out of his mind.

se pistacher [səpistaʃe] *vpr P* to get drunk*/pissed.

pistage [pistaʒ] *nm F* (*police, etc*) shadowing/tailing (suspect).

pistard [pistar] *nm F* (*cyclisme*) track racer.

piste [pist] *nf F* **être en piste,** to be in the running.

pister [piste] **I** *vtr F* to track/to trail (s.o.); to shadow/to tail (a suspect, etc); **pister des clients,** to tout for customers **II** *vpr* **se pister** *F* to make tracks/to get going/to get moving/to get a move-on.

pisteur [pistœr] *nm F* **1.** (nightclub, etc) tout **2.** (police) spy/tail/shadow.

pistoche [pistɔʃ] *nf F* (*scol*) **la pistoche,** the (swimming) pool/the baths.

pistolache [pistɔlaʃ] *nm P* pistol/revolver*.

pistole [pistɔl] *nf F* cell (in prison).

pistolet [pistɔlɛ] *nm F* **1.** **un drôle de pistolet,** an odd (sort of) chap/a strange bloke/a queer fish **2.** bed pan/bottle.

piston [pistɔ̃] *nm* **1.** *F* **avoir du piston,** to get s.o. to use his influence on one's behalf; to know the right people; to have friends in the right places; to have backstairs influence; **il est arrivé à coups de piston,** he succeeded because he knows the right people/through the old boy network; **faire obtenir une place à qn au piston,** to pull a few strings/wires in order to get s.o. a job **2.** *F (musique) (a)* cornet *(b)* cornet-player **3.** *P (mil, etc)* (= *capiston*) captain **4.** *P (i)* candidate for *(ii)* student at the *École Centrale.*

pistonnage [pistɔnaʒ] *nm F* backstairs influence/string-pulling/wire-pulling/pull.

pistonner [pistɔne] *vtr F* **pistonner qn,** to use one's influence to help s.o.; to pull strings/wires for s.o.; to back s.o.; **il s'est fait pistonner,** he got s.o. to pull strings for him.

pistonneur, euse [pistɔnœr, -øz] *n F* influential backer; friend at court/string-puller.

pitaine [pitɛn] *nm* (= *capitaine*) *P (a) (mil)* captain/cap *(b)* (sea) captain/cap'n.

pitancher [pitɑ̃ʃe] *vtr P* = **pictancher.**

pitancheur [pitɑ̃ʃœr] *nm P* = **pictancheur.**

pitchoun [pitʃun], **pitchounette** [pitʃunɛt] *a F* small/little/tiny/wee/titchy. (*Voir* **pichoun**)

pitchpin [pitʃpɛ̃] *nm P* **c'est du (vrai) pitchpin,** it's easy*/it's a sure bet/it's a doddle. (*Voir* **pichpin**)

piton [pitɔ̃] *nm P* (big) nose*.

pitou [pitu] *nm P* soldier/private/raw recruit.

pitre [pitr] *nm F* **faire le pitre,** to clown (around)/to act the fool.

pitrerie [pitrəri] *nf F* (piece of) clowning; buffoonery.

pivase [pivaz] *nm A P* nose*/conk.

pive [piv] *nm*, **piveton** [pivtɔ̃] *nm P (a)* wine/plonk *(b)* poor-quality wine.

pivoine [pivwan] *nf P* **piquer sa pivoine,** to blush/to go (bright) red.

pivoiner [pivwane] *vi P* to blush/to go (bright) red.

pivois [pivwa] *nm P* = **pive.**

pivoter [pivɔte] *vi F* **faire pivoter qn,** to boss s.o. about.

pivots [pivo] *nmpl F* legs*.

pivre [pivr] *nm P* = **pive.**

PJ [peʒi] *abbr F* (= *Police Judiciaire*) **la PJ** = CID (Criminal Investigation Department).

placage [plakaʒ] *nm F* = **plaquage.**

placard [plakar] *nm P* **1.** *(a)* prison*; **foutre qn au placard,** to throw/to bung s.o. in jail/in clink *(b)* prison cell **2.** *(homosexuels)* **sortir du placard,** to come out of the closet.

placarde [plakard] *nf P* **1.** public square **2.** *(au marché)* **une bonne placarde,** a good pitch **3.** (cushy) job **4. louer des placardes,** to book seats **5.** hide-out/hide-away/hiding place/hidey-hole.

placarder [plakarde] **I** *vtr P* **1.** to place/to find a job for (s.o.) **2.** to hide (sth)/to stash (sth) away **II** *vpr* **se placarder** *P* to get/to fix oneself up with a job.

placardier [plakardje] *nm P* tout.

place [plas] *nf P* **1. place d'armes,** stomach* **2. c'était à payer sa place,** I wouldn't have missed it for anything **3.** *(prostituée)* to look for a client/to solicit* (at the door of a hotel, etc).

placé [plase] *a F (a)* **il a le cœur bien placé,** his heart is in the right place *(b)* **elle a des rondeurs bien placées,** she comes out in (all) the right places.

placeur [plasœr] *nm P* tout.

placoter [plakote] *vi FrC F* to gossip/to chatter*/to gas.

plafond [plafɔ̃] *nm F* **1.** head*; **se faire sauter le plafond,** to blow one's brains out **2. être bas de plafond,** to be stupid*/thick/dim/dumb. (*Voir* **bas-de-plafond**) **3. sauter au plafond** (*i*) to jump for joy (*ii*) to flare up/to blow one's top/to hit the roof. (*Voir* **araignée**)

plafonnard [plafɔnar] *nm P* = **plafond 1.**

à plaga [aplaga] *adv phr P* = **plat II** (*all senses*).

plaie [plɛ] *nf F* (*pers*) pest/menace; **quelle plaie!** what a nuisance! (*Voir* **demander 1**)

plaisir [plezir] *nm F* **au plaisir!** nice seeing you!

plan [plɑ̃] *nm* **I** *F* **laisser qn en plan,** to leave s.o. stranded/to leave s.o. in the lurch/to walk out on s.o./to ditch s.o.; **laisser qch en plan,** to leave sth unfinished/to leave off in the middle of sth/to drop sth; **rester en plan,** to be stranded/to be left in the lurch/to be left out in the cold/to be ditched/to be left high and dry **II** *nm P* **il n'y a pas plan!**/**y a pas plan!** (there's) nothing doing!/it's no go! **y a plan pour sortir d'ici?** is there any way out of here? **III** *nm P* metal tube containing precious objects, etc, hidden in the anus.

planche [plɑ̃ʃ] *nf F* **1.** (*a*) (*scol*) blackboard; **passer à la planche,** to go up to the blackboard (*b*) oral (test) **2.** (*théâtre*) **brûler des planches,** to act with fire; to put a lot into one's performance; **balayer les planches,** to act in the curtain-raiser **3. il y a du travail sur la planche,** there's plenty of work to be done/there's a lot to do. (*Voir* **pain 1**) **4. une vraie planche à pain,** a flat-chested woman; **être plate comme une planche à pain**/**à repasser,** to be as flat as a board/as a pancake **5. s'habiller de quatre planches**/**être entre quatre planches,** to be dead (and buried)/to be wearing a wooden overcoat/to be six foot under **6.** (*aut*) **mettre le pied sur la planche,** to accelerate/to put one's foot down/to step on the gas **7.** ski.

plancher¹ [plɑ̃ʃe] *nm F* **1. le plancher des vaches,** dry land/terra firma **2. débarrasser**/**décharger**/**vider le plancher,** to clear out/to beat it; **videz(-moi) le plancher!** get lost!*/beat it!/hop it!/scram! **3. rouler pied au plancher,** to drive with one's foot on the floor/to drive flat out.

plancher² *vi F* to be called up to demonstrate or write something on the blackboard; **il a dû plancher devant un parterre de spécialistes,** he had to spout/make his little speech in front of a group of experts.

plané [plane] *a F* **faire un vol plané,** to fall (heavily)/to come a cropper*/to pitch down (head first).

planer [plane] *vi F* to be under the influence of a drug; to feel exhilarated (after taking a drug); (*drogues*) to be high/to be stoned; **planer à trois mille mètres,** to be floating on cloud nine.

planète [planɛt] *nf P* **1.** (*avion*) **écraser la planète,** to crash **2.** (*drogues*) **être sur sa planète,** to be high/to be stoned.

plan-plan [plɑ̃plɑ̃] *a P* (*a*) quiet/tranquil (*b*) easy (going)/leisurely/laid-back; **amour plan-plan,** gentle/leisurely/tender lovemaking. (*Voir* **plon-plon**)

planque [plɑ̃k] *nf* **1.** *F* soft/cushy job; safe berth; soft option; **ce fut une ruée pour la distribution des planques,** there was a rush to find jobs for the boys; **une bonne planque si on a de la veine!** nice work if you can get it! **son nouveau boulot, c'est la planque,** he's got a dead cushy new job/his job's a real doddle **2.** *P* (*a*) hiding place/hide-out/hide-away/hidey-hole (*b*) (*mil*) funk-hole **3.** *P* savings/nest-egg/stash **4.** *P* (*prostituées*) sum of money put on one side for a prostitute's own use and held back from her pimp **5.** *P* police surveillance/obbo/stake-out; **être en planque,** to be under surveillance/under observation by the police; **la baraque était en planque,** the police had the place staked out; **le flic faisait la planque devant l'immeuble,** the cop was on watch in front of the building. (*Voir* **attigé**)

planqué [plɑ̃ke] *nm P* (*a*) slacker/skiver/lead-swinger; s.o. who has landed himself with a cushy job (*b*) (*mil*) shirker (from call-up or active service)/column-dodger; funker.

planquer [plɑ̃ke] **I** *vtr P* **1.** (*a*) to hide (sth)/to stash (sth) (away); **il a planqué la came dans ses chaussettes,** he stashed the dope in his socks (*b*) to put (money) by (*c*) to plant (stolen goods) **2.** to place/to put/to stick/to shove (sth somewhere) **II** *vi* to put (somewhere) under surveillance/to stake out (a place)/to keep (somewhere) under observation **III** *vpr* **se planquer** *P* **1.** (*a*) (*s'abriter*) to take cover/shelter; to hide (oneself) (*b*) to go into hiding/to go to ground/to lie low; **elle s'est planquée chez des amis,** she's hiding out/she's lying low with (some) friends **2.** to park oneself/to plonk oneself down (somewhere).

planquouse [plɑ̃kuz] *nf P* = **planque.**

planquouser [plɑ̃kuze] *vtr&pr P* = **planquer I, II.**

plante [plɑ̃t] *nf P* **une belle plante,** a fine specimen (of humanity).

planté [plɑ̃te] *a F* **ne la laissez pas plantée là,** don't leave her standing there; **ne reste pas planté là! dis qch!** don't just stand there like a stuffed dummy, say sth!

planter [plɑ̃te] **I** *vtr* **1.** *F* **planter là qn** (*i*) to leave s.o. in the lurch; **je ne vous planterai pas là,** I won't let you down (*ii*) to jilt s.o. (*iii*) to walk out on s.o. **2.** *F* to put/to stick/to shove; **planter ses miches sur une chaise,** to plonk one's arse/*NAm* ass/*NAm* fanny down on a chair **3.** *P* to stab (s.o.)/to knife (to death) **4.** *V* (*a*) to have sex* (with a woman)/to screw (a woman) (*b*) (*homosexuels*) to have anal sex* (with s.o.); **il aime bien planter les mecs,** he likes screwing men. (*Voir* **chou I 4**; **drapeau 2**) **II** *vpr* **se planter** *F* **1.** (*aut*) to go off the road (into a ditch, etc) **2.** (*théâtre*) to forget one's lines/to get stuck **3.** to make a mistake*/to go wrong (in one's calculations, etc) **4.** to fail; **il s'est planté à l'examen,** he failed/he flunked the exam.

planton [plɑ̃tɔ̃] *nm F* **faire le planton,** to hang about (waiting).

plaquage [plakaʒ] *nm F* chucking/ditching/dumping/jilting (*esp* of lover); **alors, toi et ton mec, c'est un plaquage en règle?** so it's all over/finished between you two, is it?/so you've really chucked him, have you?

plaqué [plake] *nm F* **c'est du plaqué,** it's false/phon(e)y/fake.

plaquer [plake] *F* **I** *vtr* **1.** (*a*) to leave (s.o.) in the lurch/to ditch (s.o.) (*b*) to jilt (s.o.); **elle a plaqué son mari,** she's walked out on her husband; **il l'a plaquée, son mec,** her bloke's dropped her/chucked her/given her the push **2.** **avoir envie de tout plaquer,** to feel like chucking everything up/packing everything in **II** *vi* to give up; to throw in the sponge/the towel.

plaquouse [plakuz] *nf F* (red) spot/patch/blotch (on the skin).

plaquouser [plakuze] *vtr&i* = **plaquer.**

plastron [plastrɔ̃] *nm F* chest (of human body).

plastronner [plastrɔne] *vi* F to pose/to strut/to show off*/to put on airs.

plastronneur, -euse [plas-trɔnœr, -øz] *n* F (*pers*) (*a*) show-off*/swank/pose(u)r (*b*) stuffed shirt.

plat [pla] I *nm* 1. F mettre les petits plats dans les grands, to spare no expense/to go to town on (sth) 2. F en faire (tout) un plat (à qn), to make a great fuss/a song and dance about sth (to s.o.); to pile it on; il n'en a pas fait un plat, he made no bones about it 3. P il en fait un plat! it's boiling hot!/it's a real scorcher! 4. P faire du plat à qn (*i*) to flatter* s.o./to butter s.o. up (*ii*) to sweet-talk s.o./to chat s.o. up/to try to get off with s.o./to try and make out with s.o. 5. P plat de nouilles, fool*/idiot/twerp/drip. (*Voir* **nouille**) 6. *pl* P plats, faked dice 7. F puiser dans le plat, to help oneself/to dig in. (*Voir* **œuf**; **pied** 3; **repiquer** II 2) II *adv phr* F 1. être à plat (*i*) to be exhausted*/all in; j'étais complètement à plat, I was completely run down/I felt quite washed out; cette maladie l'a mis à plat, this illness has really knocked him out (*ii*) (*aut, etc*) to have a flat (tyre) 2. en mettre à plat, to save/to put by/to stash away (money).

platane [platan] *nm* F embrasser un platane, to wrap a car round a tree.

plateaux [plato] *nmpl* P loaded dice.

plates-bandes [platbɑ̃d] *nfpl* F marcher sur/piétiner les plates-bandes de qn, to poach on s.o.'s preserves/to poke one's nose into s.o.'s business; (ne) marchez pas sur mes plates-bandes, mind your own business/keep out of my patch.

platine [platin] *nf* O P tongue; avoir une fameuse platine, to have the gift of the gab; quelle platine! what a gasbag!/what a windbag!

plato [plato] *nm* P platonic love.

plâtrage [plɑtraʒ] *nm* F c'est du plâtrage, tout ça, that's (all) a load of rubbish/hooey.

plâtre [plɑtr] *nm* 1. F essuyer les plâtres, to be the first to try out sth new; on a dû essuyer les plâtres au début, we had a few teething troubles in the beginning 2. P money*; être (plein) au plâtre, to be rich*; se faire un petit plâtre, to make a little bit on the side.

(se) plâtrer [(sə)plɑtre] *vtr&pr* F se plâtrer (le visage), to plaster one's face with make-up/to put on one's warpaint.

plat-ventre [plavɑ̃tr] *nm inv* F 1. (*natation*) belly-flop 2. faire un plat-ventre, to come a cropper/to fall flat on one's face.

plein [plɛ̃] I *a* F drunk*; plein comme un boudin/une bourrique/un fût/une huître/un œuf/une outre/un Polonais/une vache, dead drunk*/drunk as a lord/tight as a drum/high as a kite/pissed as a newt. (*Voir* **andosses** 2; **as** 5; **botte** 2; **cul** I 7; **dos** 2; **plâtre** 2; **tube**) II *nm* P faire le plein, to eat* heartily/to stoke up III *adv* P tout plein, very much/a lot; tout plein de gens, any number of people/loads of people; y avait plein de fric dans le portefeuille, there was plenty of money*/bread/dough in the wallet/*NAm* billfold; elle est mignonne tout plein, she's terribly sweet; she's a real sweetie. (*Voir* **œil** 10)

pleur [plœr] *nm* F bureau des pleurs, complaints office; allez vous plaindre ailleurs, ici ce n'est pas le bureau des pleurs! go and complain somewhere else!

pleurer [plœre] *vi* F 1. pleurer pour avoir qch, to demand sth; je veux ça ou je pleure! give it (to) me or I'll scream! 2. (*a*) il est bête à pleurer, he's unbelievably stupid*/he's as thick as two short planks (b) **c'est bête à en pleurer** (i) it's as easy* as winking (ii) it's quite idiotic. (*Voir* **colosse; cyclope; vache**)

pleurnichard, -arde [plœrniʃar, -ard] n F cry-baby/sniveller/whiner.

pleuvasser [plœvase], **pleuviner** [plœvine] v impers F to drizzle.

pleuvoir [plœvwar] v impers **1.** F **il pleut tant qu'il peut,** it's raining hard/it's pelting down. (*Voir* **corde 9; hallebardes; seau; vache**) **2.** P **un nez dans lequel il pleut/où il pleut dedans,** a turned-up nose/a pug-nose **3.** P **il pleut!** (i) not (bloody) likely*!/not on your life! (ii) watch it!/look out! **4.** F (a) **elle ramasse du fric comme s'il en pleuvait,** she's raking it in (b) **à la manif, il y avait des flics comme s'il en pleuvait,** there were police absolutely everywhere/you couldn't move for cops at the demo.

pleuvoter [plœvɔte] v impers F = **pleuvasser.**

pli [pli] nm F **1. ça ne fait pas un pli** (i) that's fine/perfect (ii) it's all plain sailing (iii) no doubt about it **2. mettre qn au pli,** to make s.o. toe the line/to bring s.o. to heel **3. les enfants prennent aisément de mauvais plis,** children easily get into bad habits.

plomb [plɔ̃] nm F **1. ça te mettra du plomb dans la tête,** that'll steady you down a bit/knock some sense into you **2. avoir du plomb dans l'aile** (i) to be ill/to be in a bad way (ii) to be in difficulties (iii) to be about to die*/to be on the way out.

plombard [plɔ̃bar] nm P plumber.

plombe [plɔ̃b] nf P hour; **voilà cinq plombes,** it's striking five now; **à cinq plombes pile,** on the dot of five; **ça fait une plombe que j'attends,** I've been waiting a whole hour/a solid hour for you.

plombé [plɔ̃be] a P infected with syphilis/siffy/pox-ridden/poxy.

plomber [plɔ̃be] **I** vtr P **1.** to infect (s.o.) with syphilis*/to give (s.o.) the pox/to give s.o. a dose; **se faire plomber,** to cop a dose (of the pox); **il s'est fait plomber,** he's got syph **2.** to shoot (s.o.)/to fill (s.o.) with lead/to drill (s.o.) full of holes; **elle l'avait plombé, le mec, avec son propre flingue,** she'd shot the bloke/esp NAm guy with his own gun **II** vi P **1.** A (heure) to strike **2.** O to stink*/to pong; **plomber du goulot,** to have bad breath; **ça plombe dans cette baraque,** it stinks in here.

plonge [plɔ̃ʒ] nf F washing up (esp in restaurant); **j'ai dû faire la plonge dans un resto à Paris pour gagner le fric nécessaire,** I had to be a washer-up/I had to wash dishes in a Parisian restaurant to get the money together.

plongeon [plɔ̃ʒɔ̃] nm F **faire le plongeon** (i) to make up one's mind (to do sth)/to take the plunge (ii) to bow deeply/to give a low bow (iii) to lose a great deal of money.

plonger [plɔ̃ʒe] vi **1.** F to do the washing-up/to wash dishes (esp in restaurant) **2.** F to lose a great deal of money **3.** P **il a plongé,** he's been sent to prison*/sent down; he's been put inside/away **4.** P to disappear/to escape (from the police, etc); **il a plongé en Suisse,** he went into hiding in Switzerland.

plongeur [plɔ̃ʒœr] nm F washer-up/bottle-washer (esp in restaurant).

plon-plon [plɔ̃plɔ̃] a P = **plan-plan.**

plote [plɔt] nf P **envoyer qn aux plotes** = **envoyer qn aux pelotes (pelote 4).**

plouc, plouk [pluk] nm P **1.** peasant*/country bumpkin/NAm

hick 2. stupid* person/fool*/twit/
nit/clot/cloth-head.

ploum [plum] *nm P* 1. = **plouc 1**
2. native of Auvergne/Auvergnat.
(*Voir* **Auverploum**)

plouque [pluk] *nm P* = **plouc 1,
2.**

plouquesse [plukɛs] *nf P* peasant*/country bumpkin. (*Voir* **plouc
1**)

pluche [plyʃ] *nf F* **la pluche**, peel-
ing (of potatoes); (*mil, etc*) **les
pluches**, spud-bashing.

pluie [plɥi] *nf F* 1. **il n'est pas né/
tombé de la dernière pluie**, he
wasn't born yesterday; there are no
flies on him 2. **en mettre un à
l'abri de la pluie**, to down a drink/
to knock one back 3. **faire la pluie
et le beau temps**, to be the boss/to
rule the roost; **c'est lui qui fait la
pluie et le beau temps ici**, he's the
big white chief around here.

plumaison [plymɛzɔ̃] *nf F* fleec-
ing/ripping off (of s.o.).

plumard [plymar] *nm P* bed*; **aller
au plumard/se fourrer au plumard**,
to go to bed*/to hit the hay/to hit
the sack/to crash out.

se plumarder [səplymarde] *vpr P*
to go to bed*/to turn in/to hit the
hay/to hit the sack/to kip down/to
crash down.

plume [plym] I *nm P* bed*; **il est
resté au plume, le veinard!** he
stayed in bed, the lucky devil! II
nf 1. *F* **y laisser des plumes**, to
lose money (*esp* at gambling); **il y a
laissé des plumes/il a perdu des
plumes**, he lost out on it/he didn't
get off scot-free/he got his fingers
burnt 2. *F* **craindre pour ses
plumes/avoir chaud aux plumes**, to
go about in fear of one's life 3. *F*
voler/voltiger dans les plumes à qn,
to attack s.o./to go for s.o. 4. *F*
passer à la plume, to get beaten up;
passer qn à la plume, to beat s.o.
up*/to work s.o. over 5. *pl F*
hair; **perdre ses plumes**, to go

bald*/to lose one's thatch 6. **P**
wing (of aircraft) 7. *P* (burglar's)
jemmy/*NAm* jimmy 8. *P* **tirer une
plume de l'aile à qn**, to blackmail
s.o./to put the screws on s.o. 9. *V*
fellatio*; **tailler une plume (à un
mec)**, to give head to/to blow/to
suck off/to give a blow-job to (a
bloke/a guy); **ce qu'il préfère, c'est
qu'on lui taille une plume**, he really
gets off when you give him a blow-
job/he likes you to suck him off.

plumeau, *pl* **-eaux** [plymo] 1.
F **un vieux plumeau**, an old stick-
in-the-mud/an old fuddy-duddy 2.
P (*boisson*) glass of champagne*;
avoir/tenir son plumeau, to be
(slightly) drunk*/tipsy 3. *P* (*a*) **va
chez Plumeau** go to hell!/get lost!*
(*b*) **envoyer qn chez Plumeau**, to
chuck/to turf s.o. out. (*Voir*
Plumepatte) 4. *V* **foutre un coup
de plumeau (à une femme)**, to have
sex* with/to screw/to fuck (a
woman).

plumée [plyme] *nf* 1. *F* fleecing/
ripping off (of s.o.) 2. *P* thrash-
ing/beating-up/(good) hiding.

Plumepatte [plympat] *Prn P*
envoyer qn chez Plumepatte, to
chuck/to turf s.o. out. (*Voir*
plumeau 3 (*b*))

plumer [plyme] I *vtr F* to fleece*
(s.o.); **se faire plumer**, to get
fleeced/cleaned out; **je me suis fait
plumer**, I got done/had; I was
taken for a ride; I got diddled.
(*Voir* **pigeon 2**) II *vpr* **se plumer**
P 1. to fight/to have a set-to 2.
to go to bed*/to hit the sack.

plumet [plymɛ] *nm P* **avoir/tenir
son plumet**, to be (slightly) drunk*/
tiddly.

plumier [plymje] *nm P* violin/fid-
dle.

PLV [peɛlve] *abbr F* (= *pour la vie*)
for ever (and ever)/for life.

pluviner [plyvine] *v impers F* =
pleuvasser.

pneu [pnø] *nm F* **crever son pneu,** to die*.

pochard, -arde [pɔʃar, -ard] *n P* drunk(ard)*/boozer/alkie.

pocharder [pɔʃarde] *O* **I** *vtr P* to make (s.o.) drunk* **II** *vpr* **se pocharder** *P* to get drunk*.

pocharderie [pɔʃardəri] *nf O P* boozing/heavy drinking.

pochardise [pɔʃardiz] *nf O P* habitual drinking/drunkenness/boozing.

poche [pɔʃ] **I** *nm F* (= *livre de poche*) paperback **II** *F* **1. c'est dans la poche,** it's a cert*/it's in the bag **2. faire les poches à qn,** to pick s.o.'s pockets; to go through s.o.'s pockets **3. mettez ça dans votre poche (et votre mouchoir (par-)dessus)!** put that in your pipe and smoke it! **4. s'en mettre plein les poches,** to make a fortune **5. mettre qn dans sa poche,** to twist s.o. round one's little finger; **il te mettrait dans sa poche,** he'd make mincemeat of you/he'd have you for breakfast/he'd wipe the floor with you **6. en être de sa poche,** to be out of pocket (by it)/to lose out; **j'y ai été de ma poche,** I had to pay* up/to cough up. (*Voir* **se fouiller 2; langue 8; œil 14**).

pocher [pɔʃe] *vtr F* **pocher l'œil à qn/P pocher qn,** to give s.o. a black eye*; **P la ferme, ou je te poche un œil,** if you don't belt up I'll give you a black eye.

pochetée [pɔʃte] *nf P* fool*/prize idiot/twit/twerp/berk; **il en a une pochetée,** he's as daft as a brush/he's a complete arse(hole)/*esp NAm* ass(hole).

pochon [pɔʃɔ̃] *nm P* black eye*/shiner.

poème [pɔɛm] *nm F* **c'est un poème!** it's a beaut(y)!/it's priceless!

pogne [pɔɲ] *nf* **1.** *P* hand*/mitt; **passer la pogne,** to give up/to hand over (to s.o.); **passe la pogne!** let's shake hands (and make peace)! **2.** *P* **avoir les pognes retournées,** to be lazy/to be bone idle **3.** *P* (*a*) grip; **un homme à pogne/de pogne** (*i*) a strong man/a muscle-man (*ii*) a masterful man (*b*) **être à la pogne de qn,** to be under s.o.'s thumb; **à ma pogne,** in my power. (*Voir* **poigne**) **4.** *P* **prendre la pogne,** to take the initiative **5.** *P* **y mettre la pogne,** to steal*/to nick/to pinch sth **6.** *V* **se faire une pogne,** to masturbate*/to take oneself in hand/to give oneself a hand-job **7.** *P* = **pognon.**

se pogner [səpɔɲe] *vpr V* to masturbate*/to take oneself in hand/to give oneself a hand-job/to toss oneself off.

pognon [pɔɲɔ̃] *nm P* money*/lolly/bread/dough; **avoir du pognon/être au pognon,** to be rich*/to be rolling in it/to have plenty of dough.

poids [pwa] *nm F* **1. il ne fait pas le poids,** he isn't up to it/he's not up to scratch **2.** (*a*) **avoir du poids** (*i*) to be getting on in years (*ii*) to have influence; to carry weight; **c'est un homme de poids** (*i*) he's getting on a bit/he's a bit long in the tooth (*ii*) he's important/he's a big noise/he's a bigwig (*b*) **prendre du poids,** to age/to grow old **3.** (*pers*) **un poids mort,** a dead loss; (*employé*) someone who does not pull his weight/a passenger. (*Voir* **faux-poids; sanctuaire**)

poigne [pwaɲ] *nf F* (hand-)grip/grasp; **un homme à poigne** (*i*) a strong man/a muscle-man (*ii*) a firm-handed/masterful man; **montrer de la poigne,** to be equal to the situation; **il manque de poigne,** he lacks grip. (*Voir* **pogne 3**)

poignet [pwaɲe] *nm* **1.** *P* **ne pas se fouler le poignet,** to take it easy*/to raise no sweat **2.** *P* **se casser le poignet/les poignets sur qch,** to steal*/to pinch sth/to whip sth **3.** *V* **épouser/fréquenter/se taper la veuve poignet,** to masturbate*/to toss off/to jack off/to be married to the five-fingered widow.

poil [pwal] *nm* **1.** *P* **à poil,** naked*/starkers/in the altogether/in one's birthday suit; **se mettre/se foutre à poil,** to strip **2.** *F* (*a*) **au poil!** super!/great!/fantastic! **ça me va au poil,** that suits me down to the ground/that suits me to a T; **au (petit) poil/au quart de poil,** dead accurate/spot on/right on the button; **à un petit poil près/***P* **à un poil de cul près/à un poil de grenouille près,** as near as dammit; **un poil plus vite,** a tiny bit faster (*b*) **j'ai eu mon train, mais au poil!** I caught my train, but only just! **3.** *F* **avoir un (sacré) poil (dans la main),** to be workshy/to be bone-idle **4.** *P* **avoir du poil (aux yeux/au cul),** to have courage*; **il a du poil,**he's got guts/balls; **un brave à trois poils,** a guy with real guts **5.** *F* **ne plus avoir un poil de sec** (*i*) to be sweating buckets/like a pig (*ii*) to be scared stiff/to have the wind up **6.** *F* **chercher des poils sur l'œuf,** to split hairs **7.** *F* mood/temper; **être de mauvais poil,** to be in a bad mood **8.** *P* (*a*) **tomber sur le poil à/de qn; dresser le poil à/de qn; ficher/flanquer/foutre un poil à qn,** to attack* s.o./to lay into s.o./to go for s.o. (*b*) **avoir la police sur le poil,** to be hunted by the police/to have the police on one's back **9.** *F* (*a*) **reprendre du poil (de la bête),** to pick up/to perk up/to get back on one's feet (after an illness or a setback) (*b*) **reprendre du poil de la bête,** to take a hair of the dog (that bit you) **10.** *F* **poil de brique/poil de carotte/poil de Judas,** redhead/carrot-top/ginger **11.** *F* **faire le poil à qn** (*i*) to diddle s.o. out of his money/to fleece* s.o./to rip s.o. off (*ii*) to beat/to lick s.o.; to get the better of s.o. **12.** *V* (*femme*) **se compter les poils,** to masturbate*/to touch oneself up.

poilant [pwalɑ̃] *a P* screamingly

funny*/killing; **c'était poilant,** it was a real killer.

se poiler [səpwale] *vpr P* to laugh* uproariously/to split one's sides laughing/to kill oneself laughing/to piss oneself (laughing).

poil-poil [pwalpwal] *adv F* **ça colle poil-poil,** that's just the job/that's just what we need/that'll do (the trick) nicely. (*Voir* **douce II** (*b*))

à poilpuche [apwalpyʃ] *adv P* naked*/starkers. (*Voir* **poil 1**)

poilu [pwaly] **I** *a P* **1.** brave/courageous*/gutsy/balls(e)y. (*Voir* **poil 4**) **2. c'est poilu** (*i*) it's super/great (*ii*) it's extremely funny*/killing **II** *nm F* **1.** French soldier (in the First World War) **2.** he-man/a really butch guy.

point [pwɛ̃] *nm* **1.** *F* **un point, c'est tout!** and that's that!/and that's all there is to it!/and there's an end to it!/period!/full stop! **2.** *F* **être mal en point,** to be in a bad way; **être plus mal en point,** to be worse off **3.** *F* **commencer à rendre des points,** to age/to grow old **4.** *P* franc **5.** *P* **avoir un point de côté,** to be sought by the police/to be on the run **6. point noir** (*i*) *F* (*sur la route*) black spot (*ii*) *V* anus*/ring hole. (*Voir* **chute 1**)

pointe [pwɛ̃t] *nf* **1.** *F* **s'asseoir sur la pointe des fesses,** to sit on the edge of a chair **2.** *F* **avoir une pointe de vin,** to have had a drop too much; **avoir sa pointe,** to be (slightly) drunk* **3.** *P* (*a*) **être de la pointe,** to be (*i*) a womanizer*/a skirt-chaser (*ii*) a lecher/a sex maniac (*b*) (*homme*) **être chaud/dur de la pointe** (*i*) to like sex*; to be continually randy/horny (*ii*) to be obsessed by sex* (*c*) **tomber pour la pointe,** to be arrested* for a sexual offence; **les mecs de la pointe,** the sexual offenders/sex maniacs (serving a prison sentence) (*d*) **être de la pointe,** to be an active homosexual*; **il est de la pointe bic,** he likes (to screw) Arabs **5.** *O V* **pousser**

sa pointe, to have sex* **6.** *P* knife.

pointé [pwɛ̃te] *a* **1.** *P* arrested/detained/rounded up (by the police) **2.** *V* (passive) homosexual. (*Voir* **zéro¹** 2)

pointer [pwɛ̃te] **I** *vtr* **1.** *V* (*a*) to have (*esp* anal) sex* (with a woman) (*b*) (*homosexuel actif*) to have anal sex*/to screw (s.o.'s) ass/to go in by the back door **2.** *P* **se faire pointer,** to be arrested*/to get nabbed **II** *vpr* **se pointer** *P* (*pers*) to turn up/to appear on the scene/to show up.

pointeur [pwɛ̃tœr] *nm* **1.** *P* great womanizer*/Don Juan/*V* cunt chaser **2.** *V* active homosexual*.

pointure [pwɛ̃tyr] *nf* *F* **tu ne fais pas la pointure,** you're not up to it.

poire [pwar] **I** *nf* **1.** *F* **faire sa poire (anglaise),** to put on airs/to give oneself airs; to fancy oneself **2.** *F* **garder une poire pour la soif,** to put something by for a rainy day **3.** *F* **couper la poire en deux,** to split the difference; to compromise **4.** *F* **la poire est mûre,** the moment is ripe **5.** *P* **ma poire,** I/me/myself/yours truly. (*Voir* **pomme**) **6.** *P* mug/sucker; **une poire blette,** a complete sucker/a real mug; **est-ce que tu me prends pour une poire?** what sort of a sucker do you take me for? **l'impôt des poires,** the mugs' tax (*ie* income tax); **être la poire,** to be the mug/the fall guy **7.** *P* head*; **se payer la poire de qn** (*i*) to swindle* s.o./to play s.o. for a sucker (*ii*) to ridicule s.o./to take the mickey out of s.o. **8.** *P* face*/mug (*a*) **sucer la poire à qn,** to kiss s.o.; **je les ai vus en train de se sucer la poire,** I saw them snogging away (*b*) **une pêche en pleine poire,** a blow on the mouth/one right in the kisser (*c*) **il a une bonne poire** (*i*) he looks a nice sort of bloke/guy (*ii*) he looks a bit of a mug **9.** *V* fellatio*; **prendre en poire,** to give head to/to

suck off (a man) **II** *a P* **être poire,** to be over-indulgent; to be a mug/a sucker.

poireau, *pl* **-eaux** [pwaro] *nm* **1.** *P* mug/sucker/easy mark **2.** *P* **faire le poireau** = **poireauter 3.** *F* **le Poireau,** decoration (*le Mérite agricole*) awarded to farmers, etc **4.** *V* penis*; **s'agiter/se chatouiller/faire glouglouter le poireau,** to masturbate*/to flog the bishop **5.** *V* (*fellation*) **souffler dans le poireau,** to give a blow-job to s.o./to suck s.o. off **6.** *P* (*musique*) clarinet.

poireauter [pwarɔte] *vi P* to be kept waiting/to be kept hanging about/to kick one's heels; **faire/laisser poireauter qn,** to keep s.o. waiting/to keep s.o. hanging about; **j'ai poireauté deux heures après l'autobus,** I hung around for two hours waiting for the bus to turn up.

poirer [pware] **I** *vtr P* to catch/to nab (s.o.); **se faire poirer,** to get nabbed/nicked; **je me suis fait poirer à pomper à l'examen,** I got caught cheating in the exam **II** *vpr* **se poirer** *P* to have a good time.

poiroter [pwarɔte] *vi P* = **poireauter.**

poiscaille [pwaskɑj] *nm,* **poiscal** [pwaskal] *nm P* **1.** fish **2.** pimp*/sweet man/nookie bookie.

poison [pwazɔ̃] *nm P* (*pers*) pest; **cet enfant est un petit poison,** this child's a little horror; (*chose*) damn nuisance/drag; **quel poison ce travail!** what a bind this work is!

poissant [pwasɑ̃] *a F* **1.** sticky; (*pers*) clinging; **il est poissant,** he's like a leech; I can't shake him off **2.** unlucky/bringing bad luck.

poissard [pwasar] *nm F* unlucky bloke/guy.

poissarde [pwasard] *nf F* vulgar, foul-mouthed woman; **langage de poissarde,** Billingsgate; **parler comme une poissarde,** to talk common/like a fishwife.

poisse [pwas] **I** *nf F* **1.** bad luck; tough luck; **avoir la poisse,** to be unlucky; to have tough luck; **porter (la) poisse à qn,** to bring s.o. bad luck; **jour de poisse,** bad day (at the races, etc); **quelle poisse!** just my luck!/tough luck!/rotten luck! (*Voir* **porte-poisse**) **2.** bore*/fag; **quelle poisse!** what a bind! **c'est vraiment la poisse!** it's a real drag! **3.** (*pers*) bore*/pain in the neck/menace/nuisance/drag **II** *nm P* **1.** pimp* **2.** hooligan*/good-for-nothing/layabout/yob(bo) **3.** thief*/sticky-fingers/tea leaf.

poisser [pwase] *vtr P* **1.** *O* to steal*/to pinch/to swipe **2.** to arrest*; **se faire poisser,** to get nabbed/nicked/run in **3.** to bore* (s.o.) stiff/rigid; **tu me poisses avec tes problèmes,** you're a real pain with all your problems; **poissez-en d'autres/un autre, moi je ne marche pas!** go and tell that to somebody else, I don't want to know.

poisson [pwasɔ̃] *nm* **1.** *F* **faire des yeux de poisson frit,** to stare (vacantly) into space **2.** *F* **donner à manger aux poissons,** to be sea-sick/to feed the fishes **3.** *F* **gros poisson,** big business man/big shot **4.** *P* **attraper/engueuler/enguirlander qn comme du poisson pourri,** to tell s.o. off/to tear s.o. off a strip/to bawl s.o. out/to give s.o. a bollocking **5.** *P* pimp* **6.** *P* **changer le poisson/les poissons/son poisson (d'eau),** to urinate*/to take a leak/to splash one's boots **7.** *F* **noyer le poisson,** to confuse the issue deliberately/to use delaying tactics. (*Voir* **bocal 3; se ficher 2; queue 4**)

poisson-lune [pwasɔ̃lyn] *nm F* **avoir une figure de poisson-lune,** to be moon-faced.

poitringle [pwatrɛ̃gl] **I** *a P* tubercular/consumptive **II** *nf* (*poitrine*) chest; **il lui a donné un coup en pleine poitringle,** he thumped him right in the chest.

poivrade [pwavrad] *nf P* boozing; **en avoir une poivrade,** to be drunk*/boozed up/juiced up.

poivre [pwavr] **I** *nm* **1.** *F* **piler du poivre,** to talk scandal/to backbite **2.** *P* **chier/jeter du poivre,** to escape (*esp* from the police); to throw s.o. off the track **3.** *P* brandy **II** *a P* = **poivré 1.**

poivré [pwavre] *a P* **1.** drunk*/plastered/smashed/sozzled **2.** infected with syphilis*/syphed-up/pox-ridden/siffy; **il était poivré,** he had syph/he was a sypho **3.** expensive; **la note est poivrée,** the bill is a bit on the high side/a bit over the top.

poivrer [pwavre] **I** *vtr P* **1.** to make (s.o.) drunk; **se poivrer la gueule,** to get drunk*/pissed/plastered; **il sont là-bas en train de se poivrer la gueule,** they're over there getting steadily sloshed/stoned (out of their tiny minds) **2.** to infect (s.o.) with syphilis*/to give (s.o.) a dose; **se faire poivrer,** to cop a dose (of the pox)/to get syph **II** *vpr* **se poivrer** *P* **1.** to get drunk*/plastered/smashed/stoned **2.** to cop a dose of syph(ilis)*/of the pox.

poivrier [pwavrije] *nm P* thief* who robs drunks/*NAm* lush roller; **vol au poivrier,** robbing of drunks/*NAm* lush rolling.

poivrière [pwavrijɛr] *nf F* the road; **je ne vois pas le bout de cette poivrière,** this road's never-ending/I'll never get there (at this rate).

poivrot [pwavro] *nm P* drunk(ard)*/esp NAm* lush/alkie/wino/boozer.

se poivroter [səpwavrote] *vpr P* to get drunk*/pickled/sozzled.

poix [pwa] *nf F* **avoir de la poix aux mains,** to have sticky fingers (when it comes to money).

poke [pɔk] *nm F* (*cartes*) poker; **taper un poke jusqu'à l'aube,** to play poker till dawn.

Pola(c)k [pɔlak] *nm P* (*péj*) Pole/
Polack.

polar [pɔlar] **I** *nm F* detective
novel/whodunit **II** *n F* (*scol*) swot.

polard [pɔlar] *nm V* penis*/stick/
shaft/pole.

police [pɔlis] *nf P* (*prostituée*) **faire
ses polices,** to report regularly (for
a health check).

polichinelle [pɔliʃinɛl] *nm* **1.** *F*
(*a*) ugly, misshapen person (*b*) figure of fun; **faire le polichinelle,** to
act the buffoon/to lark about (*c*)
mener une vie de polichinelle, to
have a good time*/to lead a fast
life/to go the pace (*d*) **un secret de
polichinelle,** an open secret/every-
body's secret **2.** *P* (*a*) **avoir un
polichinelle dans le tiroir,** to be
pregnant*/to have a bun in the
oven/*esp NAm* to be knocked up
(*b*) **claquer le polichinelle,** to bring
on an abortion.

politesse [pɔlitɛs] *nf* **1.** *P* **faire
une politesse à une femme,** to give
(sexual) pleasure to a woman/to do
a woman a favour **2.** *V* **faire une
politesse à un homme,** to give a
man a blow-job; to do a man a
favour.

politicaille [pɔlitikaj] *nf,* **politi-
caillerie** [pɔlitikaj(ə)ri] *nf F*
(*péj*) political manoeuvring; peanut
politics.

politicailler [pɔlitikaje] *vi F* (*péj*)
to indulge in political manoeuvring.

politicailleur [pɔlitikajœr] *nm,*
politicard [pɔlitikar] *nm F* (*péj*)
political manoeuvrer/bad politician.

polka [pɔlka] *nf P* **1. jouer la
polka des mandibules,** to eat*
(quickly and voraciously) **2.**
woman*/bird/*NAm* dame/*NAm*
broad **3.** pimp's woman **4.** buttocks*.

polker [pɔlke] *vi P* to stink* (to
high heaven)/to pong/to whiff.

pollop(e)! [pɔlɔp] *int P* =
polop(e)!

polochon [pɔlɔʃɔ̃] *nm P* bolster;
bataille (à coups) de polochons, pillow fight; **partie de polochon,** nap/
snooze; **dormir avec son polochon,**
to sleep alone/to sleep with one's
pillow.

Polonais [pɔlɔnɛ] *nm F* **soûl
comme un Polonais,** dead drunk*/
as drunk as a lord/pissed as a
newt.

polope! [pɔlɔp] *int P* **1.** look
out!/watch out!/careful! **2.** nothing doing!/no dice!/you'll be
lucky!/not bloody likely*!

poltron [pɔltrɔ̃] *nm O P* fart.

poly [pɔli] *nm F* (*étudiants*) photo-
copied lecture (notes).

polychiée [pɔliʃje] *nf V* = **chiée.**

polycope [pɔlikɔp] *nm F* = **poly.**

pomaquer [pɔmake] *vtr P* to lose
(money, one's hair, etc).

pommade [pɔmad] *nf F* **1.** flattery*/soft soap; **jeter/passer (de) la
pommade à qn,** to flatter s.o./to
butter s.o. up; to lay it on thick;
couper dans la pommade, to fall for
flattery* **2. être dans la pommade,**
to be in a fix*/in a jam.

pommadeur, -euse [pɔmadœr,
-øz] *n F* flatterer*/soft-soap artist/
fast talker.

pommadin [pɔmadɛ̃] *nm O P* **1.**
dandy/toff **2.** hairdresser/barber.

pomme [pɔm] **I** *nf* **1.** *F* **quand
j'étais haut comme trois pommes,**
when I was just a kid/when I was
knee high to a grasshopper **2.** *F*
pomme d'Adam, Adam's apple **3.**
F **tomber dans les pommes,** to
faint*/to pass out **4.** *F* simpleton/
mug/sucker; **pauvre pomme!** you
poor sucker! **c'est une pomme à
l'eau,** he's/she's a real clot/twerp/
jerk/nurd **5.** *P* **aux pommes,**
excellent*/first-rate; **c'est aux pommes!** it looks good!/*Austr* she'll be
apples! **une nana aux pommes,** a
good-looking bird/chick; a doll **6.**
P **des pommes!** not (bloody)

likely!*/ no (blooming) fear!/nothing doing! **7.** *P* (*théâtre*) **recevoir des pommes cuites,** to get the bird **8.** *P* **pomme de terre,** hole in one's sock **9.** *P* head*/nut; **avoir une pomme d'escalier,** to be as bald* as a coot **10.** face*/mug **11.** *P* **ma pomme,** I/me/myself/yours truly; (*également:* **ta pomme, sa pomme, votre pomme, nos pommes, vos pommes, leurs pommes**). (*Voir* **sucer I 2**; **sucre 7**) **II** *a P* simple/naive/green.

pommé [pɔme] *a F* (*a*) absolute/complete/utter (fool, etc) (*b*) downright/out-and-out (blunder, etc) (*c*) excellent*/first-rate; slap-up (meal).

pompage [pɔ̃paʒ] *nm V* fellatio*/blow-job/head.

pompard [pɔ̃par] *nm P* = **pompelard.**

pompe [pɔ̃p] *nf* **1.** *F* **avoir le/un coup de pompe,** to be exhausted*/fagged out/shattered/shagged out/pooped; **j'ai le coup de pompe (de onze heures),** I've got that sinking feeling **2.** *F* **à toute(s) pompe(s),** very quickly*/at full speed/as fast as possible/flat out **3.** *F* **faire des pompes,** to do push-ups/press-ups **4.** *P* (*a*) *pl* **pompes,** big boots*/big shoes/beetle-crushers; **j'ai des pompes aspirantes,** my shoes have got holes in them/my shoes let in water (*b*) **un coup de pompe au derrière,** a kick up the backside **5.** *P* **marcher à côté de ses pompes,** to feel out of sorts **6.** *P* **balancer/filer un coup de pompe à qn,** to borrow (money) from s.o./to get a sub off s.o./to cadge off s.o. **7.** *P* (*mil*) **un soldat de deuxième pompe**/*nm* **un deuxième pompe,** a private. (*Voir* **Château-la-Pompe**)

pompé [pɔ̃pe] *a P* exhausted*/pooped/shattered/fagged (out).

pompe-l'air [pɔ̃plɛr] *nm F* s.o. who gets on other people's nerves/a pain in the neck.

pompelard [pɔ̃p(ə)lar] *nm P* fireman.

pompe-la-sueur [pɔ̃plasɥœr] *nm F* (*patron d'entreprise, etc*) workhorse; slave-driver.

pomper [pɔ̃pe] **I** *vtr* **1.** *F* to pump (s.o.) (for information) **2.** *F* to borrow money from (s.o.)/to tap (s.o.) for money/to cadge off s.o. **3.** *F* to exhaust* (s.o.); **je suis pompé,** I'm shattered/fagged/pooped; **tu me pompes l'air,** you're wearing me out/you're getting on my nerves/I'm getting fed up with you; **elle me pompe, cette nana!** she's a real drag/pain, that girl! **4.** *F* **pomper de l'air,** to talk a lot/to go blathering on/to chunter away/to rabbit on **5.** *V* **pomper (le dard à) qn,** to fellate* s.o./to suck s.o. off/to give s.o. head/to give s.o. a blow-job **6.** *P* **va te faire pomper!** get lost!*/go screw yourself!/go fuck yourself! **II** *vi* **1.** *P* **pomper (dur),** to drink* heavily/to (go on the) booze/to tipple **2.** *F* to swot **3.** *F* to copy from s.o./to crib from s.o./to cheat.

pompette [pɔ̃pɛt] *a F* slightly drunk*/tipsy/half-seas-over.

pompeuses [pɔ̃pøz] *nfpl P* lips; **elle a des pompeuses à tailler des pipes,** she's got a real cock-sucker's mouth.

pompier [pɔ̃pje] *nm* **1.** *F* **fumer comme un pompier,** to smoke like a chimney **2.** *V* **faire un pompier,** to fellate* (s.o.)/to suck cock/to give head.

pomplard [pɔ̃plar] *nm* **1.** *P* fireman **2.** *V* fellatio*; **faire un pomplard à qn,** to give s.o. a blow-job/to give s.o. head/to suck s.o. off.

pompon [pɔ̃pɔ̃] *nm F* **1.** *O* **avoir son pompon,** to be slightly drunk*/tipsy/half-seas-over **2.** **à lui le pompon!** (*i*) he's streets ahead! (*ii*) he takes the cake! **ça, c'est le pom-**

pon! that's the limit!*/that's the last straw!

pomponette [pɔ̃pɔnɛt] *nf P* **boire à la pomponette,** to down a drink in one/at one go.

pondeuse [pɔ̃døz] *nf F (hum)* **c'est une bonne pondeuse,** she's got lots of children/she breeds well/she breeds like a rabbit.

pondre [pɔ̃dr] **I** *vtr F (journ, etc)* to produce/to give birth to/to turn out (an article, a poem, a speech, etc); **il les pond en série,** he churns them out by the dozen **II** *vtr&i* to give birth (to a child).

ponette [pɔnɛt] *nf P (a)* gangster's moll; pimp's woman *(b)* (young) prostitute*.

pont [pɔ̃] *nm F* **1.** *(jour chômé entre deux jours fériés)* **faire le pont,** to take the intervening working day(s) off; to take an extra day off; to make a long weekend of it **2. faire un pont d'or à qn,** to make s.o. a lucrative offer to entice him to change his job; **on lui a fait un pont d'or,** they made it worth his while/they made him an offer he couldn't refuse **3. pont arrière,** buttocks*/rear end.

ponte [pɔ̃t] **I** *nf A P* gambling **II** *nm* **1.** *F* important person*/big shot **2.** *P* gambler/punter; **un gros ponte,** a heavy gambler **3.** *P* drugs trafficker/dealer*/pusher.

ponter [pɔ̃te] *vi P* to gamble.

pontifier [pɔ̃tifje] *vi F* to pontificate/to lay down the law.

Pont-Neuf [pɔ̃nœf] *Prn F* **se porter comme le Pont-Neuf,** to be as fit* as a fiddle.

pop [pɔp] *nm P (drogues)* shot of a drug *(esp* heroin)/fix*/shoot; **se mettre un pop,** to shoot up.

Popaul [pɔpɔl] *nm V* penis*/John Thomas; **égouter Popaul,** to urinate*/to take a leak; **emmener Popaul au cirque,** to have sex*/to get one's end away; **étrangler**

Popaul, to masturbate*/to beat the meat/to flog the bishop; **imperméable à Popaul,** condom*/rubber/mac.

la Popinque [lapɔpɛ̃k] *Prn F* the Popincourt district (in Paris).

Popofs [pɔpɔf] *nmpl P* **les Popofs,** the Russians*/the Rus(s)kies/the Reds.

Popol [pɔpɔl] *nm V* = **Popaul.**

popote [pɔpɔt] **I** *a inv F* homely; stay-at-home; **elle est vachement popote,** she's never out of the kitchen; she's always busy about the house **II** *nf* **1.** *F (a)* **faire la popote,** to do the cooking *(b)* kitchen; *(mil, etc)* canteen *(c)* **faire popote (ensemble),** to mess together **2.** *P* drug addict's instruments*/ artillery/arsenal.

popotier [pɔpɔtje] *nm F* canteen manager; *(mil)* mess officer.

popotin [pɔpɔtɛ̃] *nm P (a)* buttocks*/bottom/*NAm* fanny/*NAm* butt *(b)* **(se) remuer/se trémousser le popotin,** to dance/to shake a leg *(c)* **tortiller du popotin,** to swing/to wiggle one's hips (when walking) *(d)* **se manier/se magner le popotin,** to hurry* (up); **magne-toi le popotin!** get a move on!/shift your arse/ *NAm* ass!/pull your finger out!

popu [pɔpy] **I** *a F* popular; common/vulgar **II** *nm F* = **populo.**

populo [pɔpylo] *nm F (a)* the (common) people/*(péj)* the rabble/riff-raff/hoi polloi *(b)* crowd/mob; **c'est plein de populo là-dedans,** it's really packed/chocker in there.

poque [pɔk] *nf FrC P* bruise/bump.

poquer [pɔke] *vtr FrC P* to bash (sth) in/to dent (sth).

porcelaine [pɔrsəlɛn] *nf F* bidet.

porcherie [pɔrʃəri] *nf F (fig)* pigsty/shambles.

porcif(e) [pɔrsif] *nf,* **porsiffe** [pɔrsif] *nf,* **porcive** [pɔrsiv] *nf P (a)* portion/part *(b)* portion of food (for one person).

porno [pɔrno] *F* **I** *a* pornographic/ porno/porny/blue/dirty; **blague porno,** dirty/porny joke; **film porno,** blue/porno movie/film; **revue porno,** dirty/porny mag(azine) **II** *nm* **le porno,** pornography/porn; **lire des pornos,** to read porny/dirty books, magazines, etc; **porno doux/ dur,** soft/hard porn. (*Voir* **hard; soft**)

portail [pɔrtaj] *nm V* female genitals*; **essayer la clef dans le portail,** to rape (s.o.).

porte [pɔrt] *nf F* **1. à la porte!** out!/get out! (*Voir* **fiche(r) 2; flanquer**) **2.** (*fig*) **vous vous êtes trompé de porte,** you've come to the wrong place **3. trouver porte de bois,** to find nobody at home **4. aimable comme une porte de prison,** like a bear with a sore head **5.** (*a*) **habiter à la porte de qn,** to live next door to s.o. (*b*) **c'est la porte à côté,** it's only a hop, skip and a jump from here **6. se ménager une porte de sortie,** to give oneself a let-out/a safety clause **7. il n'était pas derrière la porte le jour de la distribution,** he wasn't there when God gave out common sense/he's not terribly bright/he's not all there. (*Voir* **bagatelle; clef 1; enfoncer 3**)

porté [pɔrte] *a F* **1. c'est bien porté,** it's the right thing to do; **c'est mal porté,** it's bad form **2. être porté sur la bouche,** to be fond of one's food; **être porté sur la bouteille,** to like a drink; to be a bit of a boozer/an alky. (*Voir* **article 2; bagatelle; chose II 3; truc**)

porte-bif(f)etons [pɔrt(ə)biftɔ̃] *nm inv,* **porte-fafiots** [pɔrt(ə)fafjo] *nm inv P* wallet. (*Voir* **biffeton 3; fafiot 1**)

porte-coton [pɔrt(ə)kɔtɔ̃] *nm inv F* second fiddle; dogsbody.

porte-cravate [pɔrt(ə)kravat] *nm inv P* neck.

portefeuille [pɔrt(ə)fœj] *nm F* **1.**

lit en portefeuille, apple-pie bed **2. ferme ton portefeuille, c'est moi qui paie,** your fly's undone; you're showing your medals **3. œil en portefeuille,** a black eye*/a shiner.

porte-flingot [pɔrt(ə)flɛ̃go] *nm inv,* **porte-flingue** [pɔrt(ə)flɛ̃g] *nm inv P* bodyguard/henchman/ gorilla. (*Voir* **flingot**)

porte-guigne [pɔrt(ə)giɲ] *nm inv F* (*pers*) jinx/jonah/bad luck. (*Voir* **guigne**)

porteluque [pɔrt(ə)lyk] *nm P* wallet.

portemanteau [pɔrt(ə)mɑ̃to] *nm* **1.** *P* shoulders **2.** *P* **poser un portemanteau,** to knife s.o. in the back **3.** *V* **avoir un portemanteau dans le pantalon,** to have an erection*/a hard-on.

portemince [pɔrt(ə)mɛ̃s] *nm P* wallet.

porte-monnaie [pɔrt(ə)mɔnɛ] *nm V* **porte-monnaie à moustaches,** female genitals*/cunt/beaver.

porte-pipe [pɔrt(ə)pip] *nm inv P* mouth*; **en avoir un coup dans le porte-pipe,** to be drunk*/to be juiced up.

porte-poisse [pɔrt(ə)pwas] *nm inv F* (*pers*) jinx/jonah/bad luck. (*Voir* **poisse I 1**)

porter [pɔrte] **I** *vtr F* **1. en porter** (= *porter des cornes*) to be a cuckold; **elle lui en fait porter depuis des années,** she's been unfaithful to him/she's had a bit on the side/ she's had a fancy-man for years. (*Voir* **culotte 5**) **II** *vpr* **se porter** *P* **un(e) ... qui se porte bien,** a rare old ...; **recevoir un savon qui se porte bien,** to get a telling-off one won't forget in a hurry.

porteur [pɔrtœr] *nm P* accomplice.

porteuses [pɔrtøz] *nfpl* hands*/ mitts/paws.

porte-viande [pɔrt(ə)vjɑ̃d] *nm inv P* (first-aid) stretcher. (*Voir* **viande 1, 2**)

Portigue [pɔrtig] *nm&f P* Portuguese.

portillon [pɔrtijɔ̃] *nm F* **ça se bouscule au portillon,** he's spluttering/he can't get his words out (fast enough)/he's having trouble getting his words out.

porto(s) [pɔrto(s)] *a&nm P* Portuguese.

portrait [pɔrtrɛ] *nm P* face*; (*a*) **le portrait tout craché de son vieux,** the dead spit/the spitting image of his old man (*b*) **abîmer le portrait à/de qn,** to spoil s.o.'s beauty (for him)/to smash s.o.'s face in; **il s'est abîmé le portrait,** he's messed his face up; **se faire abîmer le portrait,** to get one's face bashed in/to get worked over; **rectifier/rentrer dans le portrait à qn,** to hit s.o. hard in the face / to sock s.o. on the jaw/ to smash s.o.'s face in/to lay into s.o. (*c*) **se payer le portrait de qn,** to make fun of s.o.; to take the mickey/the piss out of s.o.

portugaises [pɔrtygɛz] *nfpl P* ears*; **dessable tes portugaises!** pin back your lugholes! **avoir les portugaises ensablées** (*i*) to be deaf (*ii*) to fail to understand/to be a bit slow on the uptake.

pose [poz] *nf F* **la faire à la pose,** to show off*/to be a bit of a pose(u)r/to put on airs.

poser [poze] **I** *vi* **1.** *F* **faire poser qn,** to keep s.o. waiting/hanging about **2.** *F* **je ne pose pas à l'ange,** I don't pretend to be an angel **3.** *P* to work the three-card trick **II** *vtr* **1.** *F* **ça vous pose,** it gives you status/standing; it makes you look big/good **2.** *P* **poser ça là,** to down tools; to stop work(ing). (*Voir* **chique 2; kilo²; lapin 5; pêche II 4; portemanteau 2; prune**) **III** *vpr* **se poser** *P* **1.** se poser là, to be excellent*/first-class; **il se pose là comme gaffeur,** when it comes to putting one's foot in it he takes some beating **2.** **il se pose (un peu) là** (*i*) he's a hefty bloke/

he's a giant (*ii*) he's just right for the job.

poseur [pozœr] *nm P* card-sharper who works the three-card trick.

posséder [pɔsede] *vtr F* to fool* (s.o.)/to pull a fast one on (s.o.); to diddle/to con (s.o.); **je me suis fait posséder,** I've been had.

possible [pɔsibl] *a F* (*a*) **possible!** it's (quite) possible/very likely/(it) could well be (*b*) **pas possible!** impossible!/you can't mean it!/you don't say!/no way!

poste [pɔst] **I** *nm F* **toujours solide/fidèle au poste,** still going strong/still alive and kicking **II** *nf O F* **aller un train de poste/courir la poste,** to hurry* (up)/to get a move on.

postère [pɔstɛr] *nm P* buttocks*/ behind/bum/*NAm* butt/*NAm* fanny.

postérieur [pɔsterjœr] *nm F* buttocks*/posterior/backside/behind.

postiche [pɔstiʃ] *nf* **1.** *F* (*esp* door-to-door salesman's) spiel; sales talk; **il travaille à la postiche,** he's got a good line in sales talk/patter/ fast talk **2.** *P* **faire une postiche à qn,** to pick a quarrel with s.o.; **sa femme va lui faire une postiche,** his wife's going to give him hell.

posticheur [pɔstiʃœr] *nm F* door-to-door salesman, etc/fast-talker.

postillon [pɔstijɔ̃] *nm* **1.** *F* **envoyer/lancer des postillons,** to splutter (when speaking) **2.** *O V* **donner le postillon/faire postillon,** to insert the index finger into s.o.'s anus*/to finger-fuck.

postillonner [pɔstijɔne] *vi F* to splutter (when speaking).

pot [po] *nm* **1.** *F* **pot de colle,** boring person/bore*/pain in the neck; **c'est une julie pot de colle, cette nana,** she's a damned nuisance **2.** *F* **c'est le pot au noir** (*i*) it's a wretched business (*ii*) it's a hopeless muddle **3.** *F* **être invité à un**

pot, to be invited for a drink/for a jar/for drinks; **allons boire/prendre un pot,** let's go and have a drink **4.** F **payer les pots cassés,** to be left holding the baby/to carry the can/to take the rap **5.** F **c'est le pot de terre contre le pot de fer,** he's met more than his match **6.** F **tourner autour du pot,** to shilly-shally/to beat about the bush **7.** F **sourd comme un pot,** as deaf as a post **8.** F **découvrir le pot aux roses** [potoroz], to get to the bottom of sth; **quand le pot aux roses sera découvert,** when the balloon goes up/when the news breaks **9.** A F **être à pot et à rot,** to be bosom friends **10.** F **faire son pot,** to make a fortune/to make one's pile **11.** F **pot à tabac,** tubby little person/pot-bellied person **12.** P luck; **un coup de pot,** a stroke of luck/a lucky break; **avoir du pot,** to be lucky/in luck; to have a lucky break; **manquer de pot,** to be unlucky/out of luck; **manque de pot!/pas de pot!** hard luck!/rotten luck!/bad luck!/too bad! **un pot de cocu/un pot d'enfer/un pot du tonnerre,** the luck of the devil **13.** P (*au jeu*) **le pot,** the kitty/the pot **14.** P **bousculer le pot de fleurs/**V **chier dans le pot,** to exaggerate*/to shoot a line **15.** P (*drogues*) marijuana*/pot **16.** P buttocks*/bum/arse/*NAm* ass/*NAm* fanny; **se manier le pot/se magner le pot,** to hurry* (up)/to shift one's arse/to get one's finger out **17.** P **casser le pot à une jeune fille,** to rob a girl* of her virginity*/to take a girl's cherry **18.** V anus*; **pot d'échappement,** arsehole/*NAm* asshole/poop chute/exhaust pipe; **casser le pot,** to have anal sex*; **se faire casser le pot,** to be buggered/to have one's arse/*NAm* ass fucked **19.** P **j'en ai plein le pot,** I'm fed up* with it/I'm sick and tired of it. (*Voir* **cuiller 1**; **s'occuper**; **yaourt**)

potable [pɔtabl] *a* F bearable/toler- able; **un bouquin qui est tout**

juste potable, a book which is just about readable; **travail potable,** average sort of work. (*Voir* **buvable**)

potache [pɔtaʃ] *nm* F schoolboy/schoolkid (attending a *collège* or *lycée*).

potage [pɔtaʒ] *nm* **1.** A F **pour tout potage,** altogether/all in all/all told **2.** F **servir le potage à la seringue,** to live parsimoniously **3.** P **être dans le potage,** to be utterly confused/to be all at sea/to be in a daze **4.** P **envoyer/expédier le potage à qn,** to kill* s.o.

potard [pɔtar] *nm* P chemist; chemist's assistant; pharmacy student.

potasser [pɔtase] F **I** *vtr* to study hard at (sth)/to swot up (sth)/to cram for (sth); **potasser son espagnol,** to mug up one's Spanish; **potasser un examen,** to work hard* for an exam **II** *vi* to study hard/to swot/to cram.

potasseur [pɔtasœr] *nm* F hard worker; swot/slogger.

potauf [pɔtof] *nm* P = **pot-au-feu I, 3.**

pot-au-feu [pɔtofø] **I** *nm inv* **1.** F **faire aller le pot-au-feu,** to keep the pot boiling **2.** F stay-at-home woman **3.** P prostitute* supporting a pimp*/meal-ticket **II** *a inv* F (*a*) stay-at-home (woman) (*b*) plain/homely (person).

pot-de-vin [podvɛ̃] *nm* F bribe*/hush money/backhander; **donner un pot-de-vin à qn,** to grease s.o.'s palm/to make it worth s.o.'s while. (*pl* **pots-de-vin**)

pote [pɔt] *nm&f* P friend*/mate*/pal/buddy; **écoute-moi, mon pote!** listen, mate!/bud! **il est allé boire un coup avec les potes,** he went for a drink with the lads/with his mates/with his buddies.

poteau, *pl* **-eaux** [pɔto] *nm* **1.** F **le poteau,** the execution post (for s.o. about to be shot); **mettre qn au poteau,** to put s.o. against the wall

2. *P* = **pote 3.** *P* **avoir son poteau,** to be drunk* **4.** *F* **avoir des (jambes comme des) poteaux,** to have legs like tree trunks.

potée [pɔte] *nf F* **une potée de ...,** a large quantity* of ...; heaps/ loads/piles of ...; **j'en ai une potée,** I've got masses/tons/pots.

poteuf [pɔtœf] *nm P* = **pot-au-feu I 3.**

potin [pɔtɛ̃] *nm F* **1.** row/uproar*/ rumpus; **un potin d'enfer/de tous les diables,** a hell of a racket/the devil of a row; **faire du potin** (*i*) to kick up a row/a racket (*ii*) to make a fuss/to make trouble **2.** (*a*) (piece of) gossip/scandal; **ça a fait du potin,** it made quite a stir (*b*) *pl* **potins,** gossip/scandal/tittle-tattle (*c*) **prendre les potins de qn,** to get news of/about s.o.

potinage [pɔtinaʒ] *nm F* (piece of) gossip/scandal/tittle-tattle.

potiner [pɔtine] *vi F* to gossip/to talk scandal/to tittle-tattle.

potinier, -ière [pɔtinje, -ɛr] *F* **I** *a* gossipy **II** *n* gossip(er)/scandal-monger **III** *nf* **potinière,** gos-sipmonger/gossip-shop.

potiron [pɔtirɔ̃] *nm F* member of the jury (of an Assize Court).

potron-ja(c)quet [pɔtrɔ̃ʒakɛ] *nm,* **potron-minet** [pɔtrɔ̃minɛ] *nm A F* **dès potron-ja(c)quet/dès potron-minet,** at the crack of dawn.

pou, *pl* **poux** [pu] *nm* **1.** *F* **sale comme un pou,** filthy/filthy dirty **2.** *F* **laid/moche comme un pou,** as ugly as sin **3.** *F* **fier/orgueilleux comme un pou,** as proud as a pea-cock **4.** *F* **écorcher un pou pour en avoir la peau,** to be very miserly*/ stingy **5.** *P* **chercher des poux à qn,** to pick a quarrel* with s.o./to be forever picking on s.o. **6.** *P* (*WWII*) member of the Maquis. (*Voir* **bicher 2; piège 1**)

pouacre [pwakr] *a & nm&f A F* **1.** unwashed/dirty/filthy (person) **2.** mean/miserly*/stingy (person).

pouacrerie [pwakrəri] *nf A F* **1.** dirt/filth **2.** meanness/miserliness/ stinginess.

se poualer [səpwale] *vpr P* = **se poiler.**

poubelle [pubɛl] *nf F* ramshackle old car*/old crock/jalopy/heap; **où as-tu garé ta poubelle?** where did you park your old heap of junk/ that old pile of scrap metal?

pouce [pus] *nm* **1.** *F* (*a*) **donner un coup de pouce à qn/à qch,** to give s.o./sth a push; to influence s.o.; **avoir un coup de pouce,** to have influence/to have friends in the right places/to have pull (*b*) **donner le coup de pouce à qch,** to give the finishing touch(es) to sth/ to finish sth off (*c*) **faire/filer le coup de pouce** (*i*) (*commerçant*) to give short weight/to jiggle the scales (*ii*) to raise the price/to up the ante **2.** *F* **manger sur le pouce,** to have a quick snack/a quick bite (to eat); **lire un livre du pouce,** to skim through a book **3.** *F* **se tourner les pouces/tourner ses pouces,** to twiddle one's thumbs/to idle around; **ne pas se fouler le pouce/les pouces,** to take it easy*/ to laze about **4.** *F* **mettre les pouces,** to give in/to surrender/to knuckle under; (*scol*) **pouce!** pax!/ give in!/truce! **5.** *F* **et le pouce (avec)!/et puis le pouce!** and a bit over!/and a bit more!/and the rest! **6.** *F* **sur le pouce** (*i*) gratis*/buck-shee/on the house (*ii*) off the cuff **7.** *F* **s'en mordre les pouces,** to bit-terly regret it/to kick oneself **8.** *F* **être malade du pouce,** to be miserly*/tight-fisted **9.** *P* (*pers*) **trois pouces et le cul tout de suite,** all body and no legs **10.** *F* **serrer les pouces à qn,** to bully s.o. (into doing sth)/to put the screws on s.o./to clamp down on s.o. **11.** *F esp FrC* **faire du pouce/voyager sur le pouce,** to hitch(-hike)/to thumb a lift **12.** *F* **tenir/serrer les pouces pour qn,** to keep one's fingers crossed for s.o./to wish s.o. luck. (*Voir* **lécher 1**)

poucettes [pusɛt] *nfpl P* handcuffs*.

pouche [puʃ] *nm P* (*CB*) = **pushpull**.

poudre [pudr] *nf* 1. *F* **il n'a pas inventé la poudre**, he won't set the Thames/the world on fire 2. *F* **jeter de la poudre aux yeux**, to blind s.o. to the true facts; **c'est de la poudre aux yeux**, it's only window-dressing; it's just bluff/it's all eyewash 3. *F* (*a*) **être (vif) comme la poudre**, to be very touchy (*b*) **cette affaire sent la poudre**, it's a dodgy business/the balloon could go up at any moment 4. *P* (*drogues*) heroin*. (*Voir* **escampette; moineau** (*c*))

poudrée [pudre] *nf P* road/highway.

poudrette [pudrɛt] *nf P* (*drogues*) cocaine*/snow.

pouet-pouet [pwɛpwɛ], **pouette-pouette** [pwɛtpwɛt] **I** *a O P* so-so; fair to middling **II** *attrib P* **faire pouet-pouet**, to make up to s.o.

pouf [puf] **I** *nm P* 1. **faire (un) pouf**, to go off without paying (one's bill, one's debt) 2. (seedy) brothel*/whorehouse/knocking shop **II** *nf P* = **pouffiasse**.

pouffant [pufã] *a F* very funny*; **dans ce rôle il est pouffant**, in that part he's a real scream.

(se) pouffer [(sə)pufe] *vpr&i F* to burst out laughing/to guffaw.

pouffiasse [pufjas] *nf P* (*péj*) 1. (*grosse femme*) fat slob (of a woman)/fat bag 2. immoral woman*/slut/scrubber 3. (low-class) prostitute*/cheap hooker/cheap tart.

pouic [pwik] *adv P* **que pouic**, nothing*/not a damn thing. (*Voir* **entraver**)

pouilladin [pujadɛ̃], **pouillas-**

son [pujasɔ̃] *P* **I** *a* down and out **II** *nm* down-and-out/no-hoper.

poulaga [pulaga] *nm P* (*a*) policeman*/cop (*b*) (plain-clothes) detective (*c*) **la Maison Poulaga**, the police*/the fuzz.

poulaille [pulɑj] *nf P coll* **la poulaille** (*a*) the police*/the law/the fuzz (*b*) (*théâtre*) people/audience who frequent the **poulailler**.

poulailler [pulɑje] *nm F* 1. (*théâtre*) the gods/*NAm* peanut gallery 2. **poulailler ambulant**, police van/Black Maria*.

poulardin [pulardɛ̃] *nm*, **poulardos** [pulardos] *nm P* = **poulaga** (*a*), (*b*), (*c*).

poulasse [pulas] *nf P* = **pouffiasse**.

poule [pul] *nf* 1. *P* (*a*) woman*/bird/chick (*b*) kept woman; **sa poule**, his little bit of fluff/stuff; his mistress (*c*) prostitute*; **poule de luxe**, high-class prostitute; call girl (*d*) brothel* owner/madam 2. *F* **ma (petite) poule!** my pet!/my darling!* 3. *P* (*a*) *coll* **la poule**, the police*/the fuzz; **il a la poule aux miches**, he's got the cops on his back/breathing down his neck (*b*) **une fausse poule**, a bogus policeman*/a phon(e)y cop 4. *F* (*pers*) **une poule mouillée**, a wet/a drip/a wimp 5. *F* **quand les poules auront des dents**, when pigs have wings/when the cows come home 6. *F* (*hum*) **ce n'est pas à la poule à chanter devant le coq**, a wife should not tell her husband what to do.

Pouleman(n) [pulman], **Poulemince** [pulmɛ̃s], **Pouleminche** [pulmɛ̃ʃ], **Pouleminse** [pulmɛ̃s] *nm P* **la Maison Pouleman(n)** (*a*) the police*/the cops (*b*) Police headquarters.

poulet [pulɛ] *nm* 1. *F* (*terme d'affection*) **mon (petit) poulet**, my pet/(my) sweetie/sweetheart/*esp NAm* sugar 2. (*a*) *F* **c'est du**

poulet! it's easy!*/it's a cinch! (*b*) *P* **et mon cul, c'est du poulet!** get lost!*/no way!/no such luck!/you have to be joking! **3.** *A P* love letter/billet doux **4.** *A P* horse/nag **5.** *P* (*a*) policeman*/copper/cop (*b*) (plain-clothes) detective.

poulette [pulɛt] *nf* **1.** *F* (*a*) (young) girl*/pretty young thing; bird/chick/doll (*b*) **ma poulette,** my darling*/my pet **2.** *P* passive homosexual*/nancy boy/poofter.

pouliche [puliʃ] *nf* **1.** *F* = **poulette 1** (*a*), (*b*), (*c*) **2.** *P* **pouliche faux-poids** (*a*) girl under age who looks older than she is; jailbait (*b*) prostitute* under age; chicken dinner.

Poulman(n) [pulman] *nm P* = **Pouleman(n).**

poulo [pulo] *nm P* (*théâtre*) the gods/*NAm* peanut gallery.

pouloper [pulɔpe] *vi P* to gallop along; to run hard.

poulot, otte [pulo, -ɔt] *n F* (*à un enfant*) (my) pet/(my) darling*/ (my) love.

poulotter [pulɔte] *vtr F* to pamper/to (molly)coddle.

poulton [pultɔ̃] *nm P* = **poulo.**

poultoque [pultɔk] *nm P* policeman*.

poupée [pupe] *nf F* **1.** girl*/ (baby) doll; **cette poupée,** that girl*/bird/chick **2.** (*a*) finger bandage (*b*) bandaged finger/dolly.

pouponner [pupɔne] *vi F* to be pregnant*.

poupoule [pupul] *nf F* **ma poupoule,** my darling*/my pet.

pour [pur] **I** *prep F* **1. c'est pour de bon/pour de vrai,** I mean it/I'm serious/it's for real **2. moi, je suis pour,** I'm for it **3. être pour hommes,** to be a homosexual*; **être pour femmes,** to be a lesbian* **II** *nm O P* **c'est du pour!** it's a pack of lies!/it's a load of crap! **c'est pas du pour!** it's the gospel truth!

pourceau, *pl* **-eaux** [purso] *nm F* (*péj*) (*pers*) swine/bastard*.

pourliche [purliʃ] *nm P* gratuity/ tip.

pourri [puri] **I** *a F* **1.** (*esp enfant*) thoroughly spoilt **2. être pourri d'argent,** to be very rich*/to be stinking rich **3. il n'est pas pourri,** he's fighting fit* **4. elle n'est pas pourrie,** she's not bad/she's a bit of all right/she's a nice bit of stuff **II** *nm P* **1.** rotter/slob/creep; **pourri!** you swine!/you bastard*! **bande de pourris!** you sods!/you (lousy) bastards! **2.** *Belg* idler/loafer/ lazybones/layabout.

pourriture [purityr] *nf F* rotter/ bastard*; **pourriture!** you swine!/ (you) creep!

poursoif [purswaf] *nm P* gratuity/ tip.

pourvoyeur, euse [purvwajœr, -ǿz] *n F* (*drogues*) dealer*/pusher.

pouské [puske] *nm P* (*argot des gitans*) revolver*/gun.

poussa(h) [pusa] *nm F* (*péj*) paunchy*/pot-bellied man.

pousse-au-crime [pusokrim] *nm inv F* strong wine; strong spirits*; mother's ruin.

pousse-au-vice [pusovis] *nm inv P* aphrodisiac.

pousse-ballon [pusbalɔ̃] *nm inv F* poor football player/ball pusher.

pousse-bière [pusbjɛr] *nm inv F* (*boisson*) chaser.

pousse-café [puskafe] *nm inv F* (after-dinner) liqueur.

pousse-cailloux [puskaju] *nm inv F* infantryman/foot-slogger.

pousse-canule [puskanyl] *nm inv P* male nurse/medical orderly.

pousse-dehors [pusdəɔr] *nm inv F* (alcoholic) drink taken early in the morning; early-morning nip.

pousser [puse] **I** *vtr F* **en pousser une,** to sing a song. (*Voir* **goualante**) **II** *vi* to exaggerate*; to overdo it; **faut pas pousser!** that's a bit much!/that's (going it) a bit strong! (*Voir* **bouchon 12; char 3; laïus; orties; va-comme-je-te-pousse (à la)**) III *vpr* **se pousser** *F* **pousse-toi!** move up!/ shove up!

poussette [pusɛt] *nf F* (*drogues*) syringe*/hypo.

poussier [pusje] *nm P* = **pucier²**.

poussière [pusjɛr] *nf F* **1.** cela m'a coûté dix francs et des poussières, it cost me ten francs plus/ten and a bit francs **2.** (*musique*) **faire des poussières,** to play some false notes. (*Voir* **rentrer 2**)

poussin [pusɛ̃] *nm F* **1.** (*a*) young child (*b*) **mon poussin,** my pet/my darling*/my little chickabiddy **2.** (*mil, etc*) (first-year) officer cadet.

PPH [pepeaʃ] *abbr P* (= *passera pas l'hiver*) **un PPH,** an old man (or s.o. considered to be 'ancient' by the younger generation)/a square/ an old fart.

(au) p.p.p.d.c. [opepepedese] *abbr P* (= *au plus petit poil du cul*) (*a*) absolutely super!/really great! (*b*) dead accurate/spot on/right on the button.

praline [pralin] *nf* **1.** *P* blow*/ wallop **2.** *P* bullet/slug **3.** *V* clitoris*; **avoir la praline en délire,** to be on the point of orgasm **4.** *P* **ça paraît un peu (cucul) la praline,** it seems (*i*) a bit out-of-date/old hat (*ii*) rather silly/a bit cuckoo; **il fait un peu cucul la praline,** he's a bit of a twit/a wimp.

pravise [praviz] *nf,* **pravouse** [pravuz] *nf P* (*drogues*) dose of cocaine* *or* morphine*.

prêchi-prêcha [preʃipreʃa] *F* **I** *int* stop preaching!/don't go on (and on) about it! **II** *nm inv* **1.** sermonizing/preachifying **2.** **c'est un prêchi-prêcha,** he's/she's forever going on at us.

précieuses [presjøz] *nfpl P* testicles*/family jewels.

Préfectance [prefɛktɑ̃s] *nf P* (= *Préfecture*) (Paris) police headquarters.

prem [prɛm, prɔm], **prems** [prɔms] *a & nm&f F* (*scol*) first; **je suis prem(s) en maths,** I'm top in maths.

première [prɔmjɛr] *a phr P* **de première,** excellent*/first-class; **un mec de première,** a really great bloke/ guy. (*Voir* **bourre II 4**)

prendre [prɑ̃dr] **I** *vtr* **1.** *F* **qu'est-ce que tu vas prendre!** you're (in) for it!/you'll catch it! **qu'est-ce que j'ai pris!** I didn't half catch/cop it! **2.** *F* **j'en prends et j'en laisse,** I take things as they come/I take things in my stride; **avec lui, il faut en prendre et en laisser,** you can't believe everything he says/you've got to take what he says with a pinch of salt **3.** *F* **en prendre,** to get rich*/to make a pile **4.** *F* **où prends-tu ça?** how do you make that out?/where do you get that idea from? **5.** *P* (*homosexuels*) **celui qui en prend,** passive partner **II** *vi F* **ça ne prend pas (avec moi)!** that won't work with me!/it won't wash with me! **ce truc-là prend toujours,** that trick always works/ it's a sure bet.

presse [prɛs] *nf P* (*prostituée*) **être sous presse,** to be with a client/to be on the job.

presto [prɛsto] *adv F* immediately*/pronto/pdq. (*Voir* **illico; subito**)

prêt [prɛ] *a F* **une femme tout prête,** a woman of loose morals/a push-over/an easy lay.

prétentiard, -arde [pretɑ̃sjar, -ard] *F* **I** *a* pretentious **II** *n* pretentious/conceited person; **quel prétentiard!** what a conceited little jerk!/he really does think a lot of himself!

preu [prø] *a&nm inv F* (*scol*) (the) first; top.

prévence [prevɑ̃s] *nf P* (= *detention préventive*) detention on suspicion/detention awaiting trial; **mettre en prévence**, to take into custody/to hold (s.o.) (on suspicion).

prévent [prevɑ̃] *nm F* (= *préventorium*) observation sanatorium.

prévette [prevɛt] *nf P* = **prévence**.

prévôt [prevo] *nm P* (*en prison*) privileged prisoner.

priante [priɑ̃t] *nf P* **1.** prayer **2.** church service.

primeur [primœr] *nf* **1.** *F* virginity*/maidenhead **2.** *P* very young prostitute (*esp* under age).

prise [priz] **I** *af P* **être prise**, to be pregnant* **II** *nf P* **1.** (*drogues*) small quantity of cocaine* sniffed up the nose/snort of coke **2.** stench/stink/pong. (*Voir* **bec 6**)

priseur [prizœr] *nm P* **1.** nose*/ conk **2.** (*drogues*) **priseur de cocaïne/de coke**, cocaine*/coke sniffer.

privé [prive] *nm F* private detective*/(private) dick.

prix [pri] *nm F* **1. un prix de Diane**, a very pretty girl*/woman*; a smasher/a bit of all right/a nice bit of stuff **2. un prix à réclamer**, an ugly woman; **cette fille, c'est un vrai prix à réclamer**, she'll never be a candidate for Miss World **3. ce n'est pas un prix de vertu**, she's/ he's no angel. (*Voir* **beurre 6**)

pro [pro] *nm inv F* (= *professionnel*) pro.

problo [problo], **probloc**, **probloque** [problok] *nm&f P* landlord/landlady (of rented flat/ NAm apartment, etc); **le problo réclame son loyer**, the landlord's asking for the rent. (*Voir* **proprio 1**; **propriote**)

probzi [probzi], **probzo** [probzo] *nm P* maths problem.

proc [prok] *nm*, **procu** [proky] *nm P* (= *procureur de la République*) = public prosecutor.

prof [prof] *nm&f F* (*scol, etc*) (= *professeur*) (*a*) master/mistress; **le/ la prof de maths**, the maths teacher (*b*) **prof de fac(ulté)** (*i*) prof(essor) (*ii*) lecturer.

professionnelle [profesjonɛl] *nf F* prostitute*/pro.

profiter [profite] *vi F* **1.** (*enfant, plante, etc*) to thrive/to grow; **ça lui a bien profité, ces vacances**, his holiday did him a world of good **2.** (*étoffe, vêtements*) to wear well; (*plat, salaire*) to go a long way.

profonde [profɔ̃d] *nf P* pocket; **en avoir plein les profondes**, to be rich*/loaded.

projo [proʒo] *nm P* (*cinéma, etc*) (= *projecteur*) projector.

prolo [prolo] *nm P* (= *prolétaire*) proletarian/prole; **tes fringues font prolo**, you look like a real pleb in those clothes.

prolongé [prolɔ̃ʒe] *a F* **jeune fille prolongée**, girl who is taking a long time to get married; old maid.

promenade [promnad] *nf F* (*a*) easy job/cinch/doddle (*b*) **promenade (de santé)**, easy victory/walkover.

(se) promener [(sə)promne] *vtr&pr F* **1.** (*a*) **envoyer qn (se) promener/envoyer promener qn**, to send s.o. packing*/to tell s.o. to clear off; **va te promener!** get out!/ go jump in the lake!/go take a running jump! (*b*) **envoyer tout promener**, to give everything up/to chuck everything **2. il laisse promener ses affaires partout**, he leaves his things lying all over the place/all over the shop.

promis, ise [promi, -iz] *nm&f O F* fiancé(e)/intended/betrothed.

promo [promo] *nf F* (= *promotion*) **1.** (*scol*) year/class; **la promo de '68**, the class of '68 **2.** (*marketing, etc*) (sales) promotion; **en promo**, on (special) offer.

prompto [prɔ̃to] *adv P* immediately*/pronto.

propé [prɔpe] *nf A F* (= *propédeutique*) **(l'année de) propé**, an intermediate year of study at the start of a degree course in arts or science.

propre [prɔpr] **I** *a* **nous voilà propres!** we're in a fine (old) fix*!/ this is a nice mess we've got ourselves into! **II** *nm* **ça, c'est du propre!/en voilà du propre!** well, that's a real mess!/that's a complete shambles!

proprio [prɔpri(j)o] *nm P* **1.** (= *propriétaire*) proprietor/owner/landlord. (*Voir* **problo, probloc, probloque**; **propriote**) **2.** (= *propriété*) **venez faire le tour du proprio**, come on, I'll show you round the place.

propriote [prɔpri(j)ɔt] *nf P* propietress/owner/landlady. (*Voir* **proprio 1**; **problo, probloc, probloque**)

prose [proz] *nm*, **prosinard** [prɔzinar] *nm P* = **proze, prozinard.**

protal [prɔtal] *nm F* (*scol*) head (of *lycée*). (*Voir* **proto, provo**)

protescul [prɔtǝsky] *nm P* (*péj*) Protestant.

proto [prɔto] *nm F* (*scol*) head (of *lycée*). (*Voir* **protal; provo**)

prout [prut] *nm P* fart*; **lâcher un prout**, to (let out) a fart.

prouter [prute] *vi P* to fart*.

prouteur, -euse [prutœr, -øz] *a P* afraid*/frightened; cowardly/yellow.

prove [prɔv] *nf*, **provise** [prɔviz] *nf P* (= *provision*) **chèque sans prove**, dud cheque/bouncer.

provisoire [prɔvizwar] *nf F* **être en provisoire**, to be (out) on conditional discharge.

provo [prɔvo] *nm F* (*scol*) head (of *lycée*). (*Voir* **protal; proto**)

proxémac [prɔksemak] *nm*, **proxo** [prɔkso] *nm P* pimp*/procurer.

proze [proz] *nm*, **prozinard** [prɔzinar] *nm P* **1.** buttocks*; **se magner le proze**, to get a move on/ to pull one's finger out; **l'avoir dans le proze**, to be cheated/had/done **2.** luck; **faut avoir du proze pour faire ça**, you need a bit of luck to do that.

prune [pryn] *nf* **1.** *F* **aux prunes** (*i*) last summer (*ii*) next summer (*iii*) never **2.** *F* **pour des prunes**, for nothing*/for peanuts; **ça compte pour des prunes**, that doesn't count for anything; **je ne veux pas me déranger pour des prunes**, I'm not going to put myself out for nothing **3.** *P* **des prunes!** not (bloody) likely!*/no fear!/nothing doing!/not on your life!/no chance! **4.** *P* bullet/slug **5.** *P* blow*; slap; **avoir de la prune**, to pack a punch **6.** *P* (*contravention*) **se faire coller une prune**, to be booked/to get a ticket **7.** *P* **se fendre la prune**, to laugh* uproariously/to split one's sides laughing; **on se fendait la prune**, we were in stitches **8.** *P* **avoir sa prune**, to be drunk* **9.** *V* **déposer/poser une prune**, to defecate*/to drop one's load **10.** *pl V* **prunes**, testicles*/ nuts.

pruneau, *pl* -eaux [pryno] *nm* **1.** *P* bullet. (*Voir* **prune 4**) **2.** *P* blow*. (*Voir* **prune 5**) **3.** *P* **des pruneaux!** not (bloody) likely!* (*Voir* **prune 3**) **4.** *F* **pour des pruneaux**, for nothing*. (*Voir* **prune 2**) **5.** *pl V* testicles*. (*Voir* **prune 10**) **6.** *P* quid of tobacco **7.** *P* bruise(-mark); black eye*/ shiner.

prunelle [prynɛl] *nf F* **jouer de la**

prunelle, to ogle (at s.o.)/to make (sheep's) eyes (at s.o.); **je m'en bats la prunelle,** I don't give a damn.

prusco(t) [prusko] *nm* P Prussian.

Prusse [prys] *Prnf* F **1.** travailler **pour le roi de Prusse,** to work for nothing*/for love **2. aller voir le roi de Prusse,** to go to the loo/to spend a penny/to have a look at the plumbing.

pschtt [pʃt] *nm* F *(scol)* **faire un pschtt,** to show one's admiration and approval.

pschutteux [pʃytø] *a* P smart/stylish.

pseudo [psødo] *nm* F **1. c'est du pseudo,** it's pseudo/fake/phon(e)y/bogus **2.** pseudonym.

psy [psi] *nm* F **1.** (= *psychiatre*) psychiatrist/shrink **2.** (= *psychiatrique*) mental patient/psycho.

psycho [psiko] *nf* F (= *psychologie*) **il fait de la psycho,** he's doing/studying psychology.

puant [pɥɑ̃] I *nm* P abscess caused by an unsterilized needle or by impure drugs; ab/AB/ABC II *nm* P cheese III *a* F objectionably conceited/bumptious.

pub [pyb] *nf* F (= *publicité*) publicity; **faire de la pub,** to advertise; **il est dans la pub,** he's in advertising.

puce [pys] *nf* F **1. les puces,** flea market. *(Voir* **marché; marchand 4) 2.** undersized* person/little squirt/shrimp **3. charmer ses puces,** to have a drink before going to bed/to have a nightcap **4. chercher des puces,** to go through sth with a fine tooth-comb **5. chercher des puces à qn,** to provoke s.o. **6. avoir la puce à l'oreille,** to be uneasy/suspicious; **ça m'a mis la puce à l'oreille,** it made me suspicious/it made me smell a rat **7. secouer ses puces,** to stretch oneself (out) **8. secouer les puces à qn** *(i)* to give s.o. a good hiding *(ii)* to tell s.o. off **9. saut de puce,** quick flight (in an aircraft)/hop **10.**

(cartes) **les puces,** the three aces **11.** *(terme d'affection)* **ma puce,** my darling*/my pet/my love.

puceau [pyso] *nm* F (male) virgin.

pucelage [pys(ə)laʒ] *nm* F virginity*.

pucier [pysje] *nm* **1.** F junk dealer in a flea market **2.** P bed*/fleabag/bug-trap; **dix heures de pucier,** ten hours' kip.

pue-la-sueur [pylasɥœr] *nm inv* P *(péj)* manual worker. *(Voir* **pompe-la-sueur)**

pull [pul, pyl] *nm* F pullover/jumper.

pullupper [pulɔpe] *vi* P = **pouloper.**

punaise [pynɛz] *nf* **1.** F **punaise de sacristie/de confessionnal,** bigoted churchwoman **2.** P *(a)* woman of easy virtue; pushover/easy lay/scrubber *(b)* A prostitute*/tart/tramp **3.** P shrew/vixen; bitch **4.** P *(WWII)* **punaises vertes,** German soldiers/Jerries. *(Voir* **soufflet 2)**

punch [pœnʃ] *nm* F dynamism; **manquer de punch,** to lack punch.

punich [pyniʃ], **puniss** [pynis] *nf* P *(scol)* punishment.

pur [pyr] *nm* F **un pur,** an uncompromising politician, etc/a hard-liner/a dry.

pure [pyr] *nf* P *(drogues)* heroin* *or* cocaine* with a high degree of purity.

purée [pyre] *nf* **1.** P **balancer la purée,** to fire/to shoot a gun, etc **2.** V **balancer/envoyer/jeter/lâcher la/sa purée,** to have an orgasm*/to come/to shoot one's load **3.** F **être dans la purée,** to be penniless*/broke/skint; **être dans la purée noire,** to be on one's beam ends/in a real fix* **4.** F *(brouillard)* **purée de pois,** peasouper **5.** P drink of absinthe **6.** P **purée!** *(i)* hell!/blast!/darn! *(ii)* you jerk!/you nurd!

purge [pyrʒ] *nf P* thrashing/good hiding; **coller/donner/filer une purge à qn,** to beat s.o. up*/to work s.o. over; **prendre la purge** (*i*) to get beaten up (*ii*) (*sports*) to get thrashed/licked/hammered.

purotin [pyrɔtɛ̃] *nm P* person living in abject poverty; down-and-out(er).

pus [py] *adv P* (= *plus*) **y a pus!** (= *il n'y en a plus*) (it's) no go!

pusher [puʃœr] *nm or f P* (*drogues*) dealer*/pusher.

push-pull [puʃpul] *nm P* (*CB*) **push-pull (à roulettes),** car*/push-pull.

putain [pytɛ̃] *nf P* **1.** (*a*) prostitute*/whore/tart (*b*) **enfant de putain!/fils de putain!** you son of a bitch! **2. cette putain de guerre!** this bloody war! **leur putain de bagnole!** their bloody/*NAm* goddamn/sodding car! **3. petite putain!** you little sod! **4.** *int* (bloody) hell!/blast!/dammit! **putain de bordel de merde!** sodding/pissing/fucking hell!/bugger it!/sod it!

putasse [pytas] *nf V* prostitute*/whore.

putasser [pytase] *vi V* to be a prostitute*/to solicit*/to be on the game; **il envoie sa femme putasser,** he sends his wife out on the game.

putasserie [pytasri] *nf V* **1.** whoring **2.** living as a prostitute* **3. quelle putasserie!** what a bloody mess!

putassier, -ière [pytasje, -jɛr] *P* **I** *a* whorish/tarty; **langage putassier,** filthy/dirty language **II** *nm* whoremonger/woman chaser.

pute [pyt] *nf* **1.** *V* prostitute*/whore/hooker/tart; **fils de pute!** you son of a bitch! **à la pute,** tarty/whorish **2.** *P* (*cartes*) **les putes,** (the) four queens.

putinerie [pytinri] *nf,* **putinisme** [pytinism] *nm A P* **1.** (habitual) prostitution **2.** lewdness/debauchery.

pyjama [piʒama] *nm F* **faire du pyjama,** to stay at home (in order to save money).

Q

quarante [karɑ̃t] *nf P* **1.** (*a*) table (*b*) (illicit) street-vendor's folding table/fly-pitcher's stand **2.** se mettre en quarante (*i*) to get angry*/to blow one's top (*ii*) to turn nasty/to cut up rough (*iii*) to square up (for a fight). (*Voir* **carante; se ficher 2** (*b*))

quarante-quatre [karɑ̃tkatr] *nm inv* **1.** *F* (*médecin à ses patients*) dites quarante-quatre! say ninetynine!/say ah! (*Voir* **trente-trois**) **2.** *P* un quarante-quatre maison, a good kick in the pants.

quart [kar] *nm* **1.** *P* (*a*) police station; il est au quart, he's down the station/the cop shop (*b*) police superintendent. (*Voir* **quart-d'œil**) **2.** *F* (*prostituée*) faire le quart, to walk her beat **3.** *F* (*a*) passer un mauvais/un fichu/un sale quart d'heure, to have a rough time of it/ to go through some awkward moments; faire passer un mauvais quart d'heure à qn, to give s.o. a bad time/to put s.o. through it (*b*) le quart d'heure de Rabelais, the hour of reckoning (*c*) pour le quart d'heure, for the time being **4.** *F* les trois quarts du temps, most of the time **5.** *F* partir au quart de tour, to set off at an easy pace **6.** *P* quart de beurre, gold bar/ingot. (*Voir* **se ficher 2** (*b*); **poil 2** (*a*); **tiers**)

quart-de-brie [kardəbri], **quart-de-rire** [kardərir] *nm P* big nose*/conk. (*pl* quarts-de-brie; quarts-de-rire)

quart-d'œil [kardœj] *nm P* police superintendent. (*Voir* **quart 1** (*b*))

Quartier [kartje] *Prn F* (= *le Quartier latin*) le Quartier, the Latin quarter (in Paris). (*Voir* **Latin**)

quat'crans [katkrɑ̃] *nm P* (*mil*) very strict NCO. (*Voir* **cran 5**)

quatre(-z-)yeux [katrəzjø, katrjø], **quat'zyeux**[1] [katzjø] *nmpl F* entre quatre(-z-)yeux, in private/between you and me; between you, me and the gatepost/ lamp-post.

quat'zyeux[2] [katzjø] *a&nm P* (*péj*) bespectacled (person)/four-eyes.

québri [kebri] *nf P* (*verlan de* **brique**) ten thousand (new) francs.

quelque chose [kɛlkəʃoz] *indef pron m inv F* **1.** prendre quelque chose, to get a bashing/to cop it; tu vas prendre quelque chose! you'll catch it! (*Voir* **grade**) **2.** il a quelque chose, there's something the matter with him **3.** vous y travaillerez quelque chose comme deux ans, you'll be at it for about two years **4.** il lui manque un petit quelque chose, he's slightly lacking somewhere; he's got a screw loose **5.** aller faire quelque chose, to go to the loo/*NAm* the bathroom.

quelquefois [kɛlkəfwa] *adv F* in case; quelquefois qu'il serait arrivé, in case he'd arrived.

quelque part [kɛlkəpar] *adv* **1.** *F* aller quelque part, to go to the WC*/the loo/*NAm* the bathroom **2.** *F* donner à qn un coup de pied quelque part, to give s.o. a kick up the backside; tu veux mon pied quelque part? do you want my foot up your backside? **3.** *P* **je l'ai quelque part!** I don't give a damn about him! **je les ai quelque part!** you know where you can stick 'em! **quant à ton offre généreuse, moi je me la mets quelque part,** as for your generous offer, you can stick it; **il peut se le/la mettre quelque part!** he can stuff it (up his arse)! **les ordres du patron, moi je me les mets quelque part,** I don't give a toss about the boss's orders.

quelqu'un [kɛlkœ̃] *indef pron* **1.** *F* **elle se croit déjà quelqu'un,** she thinks she's really something; **ils sont quelqu'un dans leur village,** they're somebodies/big fish in their own village **2.** *P* **c'est quelqu'un, ça alors!** (*i*) that's (really) something! (*ii*) that's a damn nuisance!/ that's a bit much!

quèn [kɛn] *a P* exhausted*/dead beat/shagged out/shattered.

quenaude [kənod] *nf P* pipe.

quener [kɛne] *vi P* to have sex*/to have it away/to screw.

quenotte [kənɔt] *nf F* (*langage enfantin*) tooth/toothy-peg.

quenottier [kənɔtje] *nm F* dentist.

quèque [kɛk] *a & adv F* (= *quelque*) **quèque chose = quelque chose**; **quèque part = quelque part.**

quéquette [kekɛt] *nf V* (child's) penis*/willy/wee-wee.

quès [kɛz] *nm P* **c'est du quès,** it's six of one and half a dozen of the other/it makes no odds/it's as broad as it's long/it's much of a muchness; **c'est jamais du quès,** it's never the same. (*Voir* **kes**)

qu'est-ce que [kɛskə] *interr pron* **1.** *P* (= *combien*) (*a*) **qu'est-ce que vous êtes de personnes ici?** how many of you are there here? (*b*) (*excl*) **qu'est-ce qu'il fait beau!** isn't the weather gorgeous! **qu'est-ce qu'on rigole!** what a laugh! **2.** *F* (= *pourquoi*) **qu'est-ce que tu avais besoin d'aller lui dire ça?** what did

you want to go and say that to him for?

qu'est-ce qui [kɛski] *interr pron F* **1.** (= *ce qui*) **je vous demande un peu qu'est-ce qui lui prend?** whatever's got into him! **2.** (= *qui*) **je ne savais pas qu'est-ce qui était là,** I didn't know who was there.

question [kɛstjɔ̃] *nf F* **1. question boulot, je me débrouille,** as far as work goes, I get on all right **2. c'te question!/quelle question!** what a thing to ask!

quétaine [keten] *a FrC P* **1.** old-fashioned/dated; past it **2.** cheap and nasty/rubbishy.

queue [kø] *nf* **1.** *V* penis*/cock/ prick **2.** *F* **il s'en retourna la queue entre les jambes/la queue basse,** he went off with his tail between his legs **3.** *P* **faire des queues à son mari/à sa femme,** to be unfaithful to one's husband/ wife; to cheat on one's husband/ wife; to have a bit on the side **4.** *F* (*a*) (*aut*) **queue de poisson,** wobbling (on greasy road); **faire une queue de poisson (à qn),** to cut in (on s.o.)/to cut (s.o.) up (*b*) **finir en queue de poisson,** to come to nothing/to fizzle out/to peter out **5.** *P* **pas la queue d'un/d'une,** not a sign of one/not a blessed one/not a sausage; **n'en avoir pas la queue d'un,** to be penniless*/skint **6.** *F* **ajouter des queues aux zéros,** to cook the books **7.** *F* **n'avoir ni queue ni tête,** to be pointless; **une histoire sans queue ni tête,** a story that one cannot make head or tail of/a real cock-and-bull story **8.** *P* (*prisons*) **queue de cervelas,** daily walk in the prison yard/exercise period **9.** *F* **tenir la queue de la poêle,** to be in charge/to run the show/to rule the roost **10.** *F* **laisser une queue,** to pay only part of a bill; to settle only part of a debt **11.** *P* **rond comme une queue**

de pelle, dead drunk*/(completely) pissed/smashed/plastered.

queue-de-rat [kødra] nf V **faire queue-de-rat,** to fail to have an orgasm*; **il a fait queue-de-rat,** he went limp/he didn't come/he couldn't manage it/he didn't get his rocks off.

queue-de-vache [kødvaʃ] a inv F **cheveux queue-de-vache,** mousy(-coloured) hair.

queutage [køtaʒ] nm V fornication/screwing/fucking.

queutard [køtar] V I nm (obsédé sexuel) (i) womanizer*/wolf/randy bugger/cunt chaser; **c'est un queutard,** he's sex mad/he'd screw anything on two legs (ii) dirty old man II a sexually obsessed/sex mad/cunt struck.

queuter [køte] vi 1. P to miss; **ça n'a pas queuté,** that went home 2. to fornicate/to screw/to fuck/to get one's end away.

quibus [kɥibys] P money*/the readies/the wherewithal.

qui c'est qui [kisɛki] P = **qui est-ce qui.**

qui est-ce qui [kiɛski] interr pron m sg F **je ne sais pas qui est-ce qui vous a dit ça,** I don't know who told you that.

quillard [kijar] nm F (mil) soldier who is about to be or who has just been demobbed.

quille [kij] nf 1. F **la quille** (i) (mil) demobilisation/demob (ii) (scol) holidays/vacation/hols/vac 2. P leg*/pin; **il ne tient pas sur ses quilles,** he's a bit shaky on his pins; **jouer des quilles,** to skedaddle/to leg it; **être sur ses quilles,** to be in good health/in fine form 3. F **être planté comme une quille,** to be rooted to the spot 4. F **être reçu comme un chien dans un jeu de quilles,** to be given a chilly welcome; to be made as welcome as a dog on a putting green 5. P **quille**

à la vanille, girl* 6. O P penis*; **abattre la quille,** to have sex*/to get one's end away.

quiller [kije] I vtr P to cheat*/to trick/to swindle*/to con (s.o.) II vi P to run away*/to beat it/to leg it.

quimper [kɛ̃pe] P I vi 1. (a) to fall/to take a header (b) to fall into a trap (c) to be victimized 2. to be sentenced; **quimper chéro,** to get a stiff sentence/to get the book thrown at one 3. to die*/to snuff it II vtr 2. **laisser quimper qn,** to abandon s.o./to drop s.o./to ditch s.o. 2. to arrest* 3. to seduce/to get off with (a woman) 4. to urinate*/to (have a) piss.

quincaille [kɛ̃kɑj] nf F 1. copper coins/copper(s) 2. jewels.

quincaillerie [kɛ̃kɑjri] nf F 1. medals/decorations 2. cheap jewellery 3. (informatique) hardware 4. weapons/firearms; hardware/ironmongery.

Quincampe [kɛ̃kɑ̃p] Prn F **la Quincampe,** the rue Quincampoix (in Paris).

quine [kin] adv P **j'en ai quine,** I'm fed up* with it/I've had enough (of it)/I've had it.

quinquets [kɛ̃kɛ] nmpl P eyes*/lamps/peepers; **allumer ses quinquets,** to open one's eyes; **rouler/ribouler des quinquets,** to roll one's eyes (with amazement)/to goggle/to gawp; **faux quinquets,** spectacles/glasses/specs.

quinquin [kɛ̃kɛ̃] nm P **petit quinquin,** native of northern France.

quinte [kɛ̃t] nf P **attraper quinte et quatorze (et le point),** to catch VD* (i) syphilis*/syph/the pox (ii) gonorrhea*/the clap.

quinteux, -euse [kɛ̃tø, -øz] a F (pers) crotchety.

quintuplée [k(ɥ)ɛ̃typle] nf P hand*/bunch of fives.

quiqui [kiki] *nm P* **1.** (*a*) Adam's apple (*b*) windpipe; **serrer le quiqui à qn,** to throttle s.o.; to wring s.o.'s neck **2.** (child's) penis*/willy/wee-wee. (*Voir* **kiki**)

quoi [kwa] **I** *rel pron* **1.** *P* **de quoi (je me mêle)?/non, mais, de quoi?** what was that?/what did you say?/did you say something? **2.** *F* **avoir de quoi,** to be comfortably off/to be worth a bob or two; **il a de quoi,** he's not short of a bob or two **3.** *F* **(il n'y a) pas de quoi!** don't mention it!/a pleasure!/cheers! (*b*) **il n'y a pas là de quoi être fier,** that's nothing to be proud of/nothing to crow about **II** *int F* **enfin, quoi, c'est la vie!** well, such is life! **il est mort, quoi!** he's dead and that's that!

R

rab [rab] *nm P* (*esp mil*) extra; a bit more; a drop more; **y a du rab,** there's second helpings/(some) seconds/(some) extras; **tu n'as pas un(e) clope en rab?** can you spare a cig?/can I bum a fag? **un petit rab?** would you like a drop more? **faire du rab,** to do a bit of extra work (without extra pay). (*Voir* **rabiot**)

rabat [raba] *nm F* **1.** tout **2.** pimp*/ponce **3. rabat de col/de cope,** bribe*/backhander; hush money; **faire un rabat de col/de cope à qn,** to bribe s.o./to give s.o. a backhander/to grease s.o.'s palm.

rabatteur [rabatœr] *nm F* = **rabat 1, 2.**

rabatteuse [rabatøz] *nf F* procuress.

rabattre [rabatr] *vi P* to return/to come back. (*Voir* **caquet**)

rabe [rab] *nm P* = **rab.**

rabiau [rabjo] *nm,* **rabiauter** [rabjote] *vtr&i,* **rabiauteur, - euse** [rabjotœr, -øz] *nm&f P* = **rabiot, rabioter, rabioteur, -euse.**

rabibochage [rabibɔʃaʒ] *nm F* (*a*) patching up/botching up (of sth) (*b*) patching up (of a quarrel)/ making it up.

rabibocher [rabibɔʃe] **I** *vtr F* **1.** (*a*) to patch (sth) up/to botch sth up/to make sth do (*b*) to patch up (a quarrel); to patch things up/to make it up (with s.o.) **2.** to put (a gambler) back on his feet **II** *vpr* **se rabibocher** *F* to become reconciled/to make it up/to patch things up/to kiss and make up.

rabiot [rabjo] *nm P* **1.** (*a*) second helping; seconds/left-overs; **en rabiot,** going begging; **qui veut du rabiot?** who wants some more/ seconds? (*b*) illicit profits*/pickings/graft; **se faire du rabiot,** to make a bit on the side **2.** (*a*) extra work; **faire du rabiot,** to work over(time)/to do a bit extra (*b*) (*mil*) extra period of service (owing to imprisonment, etc).

rabiotage [rabjɔtaʒ] *nm* (*mil*) *P* scrounging.

rabioter [rabjɔte] *P* **I** *vi* **1.** to make illicit profits*/to fiddle/to make a bit on the side **2.** to scrounge surplus food, etc **II** *vtr* to scrounge; to wangle; (*mil*) **j'ai rabioté deux jours de perm,** I've wangled two extra days' leave.

rabioteur, euse [rabjɔtœr, -øz] *n P* **1.** person who makes a bit on the side/fiddler **2.** scrounger; wangler.

râble [rɑbl] *nm F* **1.** (*a*) (*dos*) back (*b*) (*épaules*) shoulders **2. il m'a sauté sur le râble/il m'est tombé sur le râble** (*i*) he jumped on me (*ii*) he cornered me/he buttonholed me.

râbler [rɑble] *vtr P* to attack* (s.o.)/to go for (s.o.)/to set about (s.o.).

rabobiner [rabɔbine] *vtr P* to patch (sth) up.

raboin [rabwɛ̃] *nm P* = **rabouin¹ 1, 2.**

raboter [rabɔte] *vtr P* **raboter l'argent de qn,** to steal* s.o.'s money; to do s.o. out of his/her money.

rabouin, ine [rabwɛ̃, -in] **I** *n P* gipsy/gippo **II** *nm P* **le Rabouin**, the Devil/Old Nick.

raccord [rakɔr] *nm F* **faire un raccord**, to touch up one's makeup/to freshen up (one's face).

raccourcir [rakursir] *vtr A P* to guillotine/to behead/to top (s.o.); **la machine à raccourcir**, the guillotine.

raccroc [rakro] *nm F* **faire le raccroc** (*i*) to tout (*ii*) (*prostituée*) to solicit*/to walk the streets/to hustle.

raccrocher [rakrɔʃe] **I** *vtr F* **1.** (*camelot, vendeur, etc*) to stop (s.o. in the street, etc); (*prostituée*) to accost (passer-by)/to hustle **2.** to grab hold of/to latch on to (sth) (again) **II** *vpr* **se raccrocher** *F* (*au jeu, etc*) to recoup one's losses.

raccrocheuse [rakrɔʃøz] *nf F* prostitute*/street-walker/hooker.

race [ras] *nf F* **quelle (sale) race!** what a collection!/what a pathetic bunch!/what a load of jerks!

racine [rasin] *nf* **1.** *F* (*pers*) **prendre racine**, to cling like a leech/like a limpet; to take root **2.** *pl P* **racines**, toes.

racket [rakɛt] *nm F* racket.

racketter [rakɛtɛr] *nm*, **raketteur** [rakɛtœr] *nm F* racketeer.

raclé [rakle] *a F* penniless*/(flat) broke.

raclée [rakle] *nf F* **1.** thrashing/good hiding; **donner/filer/flanquer/** *P* **foutre une raclée à qn**, to give s.o. a good hiding/to beat s.o. up*/to work s.o. over; **recevoir sa raclée en homme**, to take one's punishment like a man **2.** (*sport, etc*) (decisive) defeat (in a game)/good hiding; **ils ont pris une sacrée raclée à la demi-finale**, they got hammered/thrashed/licked in the semi-final.

racler [rakle] **I** *vtr F* **1. racler qn**, to clean s.o. out (at gambling)/to

take s.o. to the cleaners **2. racler les fonds de tiroir**, to scrape the barrel **II** *vpr* **se racler** *P* to (have a) shave; **se faire racler**, to get shaved. (*Voir* **cuir 3**)

raclette [raklɛt] *nf P* **1.** squad car; **coup de raclette**, police raid/round-up; bust **2.** (*aut*) windscreen wiper.

racloir [raklwar] *nm P* razor.

raclure [raklyr] *nf P* despicable individual/scum(bag)/louse/son of a bitch; *V* **raclure de pelle à merde**, shit/bastard*/mother-fucker.

radada [radada] *nm P* **1.** buttocks* **2. aller au radada**, to have sex*/to make love/to have it away. (*Voir* **rondibé**)

radar [radar] *nm F* **aujourd'hui je marche au radar**, I'm not really with it today.

rade [rad] **I** *nm P* **1.** (*i*) (*comptoir*) bar (*ii*) (*débit*) bar/pub; **allez, on va boire un coup au rade**, come on, let's go to the pub for a drink **2.** road/street; pavement; (*prostituées, etc*) **faire le rade**, to solicit*/to tout for custom; to hustle **II** *nf F* (*a*) **demeurer/rester en rade** (*i*) to be left in the lurch/high and dry/standing (*ii*) to be left out of it/to be left out in the cold (*b*) **laisser qn en rade** (*i*) to leave s.o. in the lurch/high and dry (*ii*) to leave s.o. out of it/to leave s.o. out in the cold (*c*) **sa bagnole est tombée en rade**, her/his car's broken down/conked out.

rader [rade] *vi P* (*prostituée*) to solicit*/to walk the streets/to pound the pavement/to hustle.

radeuse [radøz] *nf P* prostitute*/streetwalker/hooker.

radin, e [radɛ̃, -in] *P* **I** *a* mean*/stingy/tight-fisted/penny-pinching **II** *nm* miser*/skinflint/tight-ass.

radiner [radine] **I** *vi P* to arrive*/to turn up/to show up/to blow in; (*en hâte*) to rush over; (*revenir*) to rush back/to dash back **II** *vpr* **se**

radiner *P* **alors, tu te radines!** so you decided to show up! **il s'est radiné à huit heures,** he showed up/rolled up at eight.

radinerie [radinri] *nf P* miserliness/stinginess/tightfistedness/penny-pinching.

radis [radi] *nm* **1.** *F* **je n'ai pas un radis,** I'm penniless*/I haven't got a bean; **je ne dépense pas un radis de plus,** I'm not spending a penny more **2.** *F* **ça ne vaut pas un radis,** it's worthless*/it's not worth a sausage/*NAm* a dime **3.** *P* **des radis!** nothing doing!/no fear!/not (bloody) likely!*/no way! **4.** (*péj*) **radis noir** (*a*) priest* (*b*) Black*/negro **5.** *pl P* (*a*) feet* (*b*) toes. (*Voir* **bouchon 7**)

radoter [radɔte] *vtr F* **qu'est-ce qu'il radote?** what's he rambling/drivelling on about?

raffiot [rafjo] *nm F =* **rafiau.**

raffolement [rafɔlmɑ̃] *nm F* infatuation (**de,** for).

raffoler [rafɔle] *vi F* (*a*) **raffoler de qn,** to be infatuated* with s.o./to be gone on s.o./to have a thing about s.o. (*b*) **raffoler de qch,** to be mad (keen) on sth/to be nuts about sth; **je n'en raffole pas,** I'm not crazy about it.

raffut [rafy] *nm F* noise/row/racket; **faire du raffut** (*i*) to kick up a row (*ii*) to kick up a fuss/a stink; **un raffut du diable/de tous les diables,** a devil of a row/one hell of a row.

rafiau, *pl* **-aux** [rafjo] *nm*, **rafiot** [rafjo] *nm F* (*bateau*) (vieux) **rafiau,** old tub.

rafistolage [rafistɔlaʒ] *nm F* (*a*) patching up/botching up; making (sth) do (for the moment).

rafistoler [rafistɔle] *vtr F* (*a*) to patch up/to botch up/to make (sth) do (for the moment) (*b*) to get (sth) going again; **leur ménage s'est rafistolé,** they've patched things up/they're having another go at it.

rafût [rafy] *nm F =* **raffut.**

ragaga [ragaga] *nm P* **faire du ragaga,** to waste one's time (doing something useless)/to piss about/to fart about.

rageant [raʒɑ̃] *a F* infuriating.

rager [raʒe] *vi F* **cela me fait rager!** it's infuriating!/it makes me mad!

ragnagnas [raɲaɲa] *nmpl P* **avoir ses ragnagnas,** to have one's period*/to have the curse.

ragot [rago] *nm F* (*a*) piece of ill-natured gossip/tittle-tattle (*b*) *pl* **ragots,** ill-natured gossip/tittle-tattle.

ragoter [ragɔte] *vi F* to gossip maliciously/to tittle-tattle.

ragougnasse [raguɲas] *nf F* poor-quality food/pigswill.

raidard [rɛdar] *a P* penniless*/(stony) broke.

raide [rɛd] **I** *a* **1.** *P* drunk*/tight/stoned/plastered **2.** *P* **être raide,** to be penniless*; **raide comme une barre/raide à blanc/raide comme la justice/raide comme un passe-lacet,** stony broke/skint **3.** *F* (*a*) **une histoire raide,** a tall story/a tale that's a bit hard to swallow; **il en raconte de raides,** he's always spinning some yarn or other/some cock-and-bull story (*b*) **il lui faisait des propos assez raides,** he made some pretty suggestive remarks to her (*c*) **ça c'est un peu raide!/elle est raide, celle-là!** (*i*) that's a bit far-fetched/a bit hard to swallow! (*ii*) that's a bit much/a bit steep! (*d*) **il en a vu de(s) raides,** he's had some strange experiences/he's seen a thing or two/he's been around **4.** *F* **être sur la corde raide,** to be on a tightrope **5.** *P* (*mil*) **se (faire) porter raide,** to report sick **6.** *V* **être raide,** to have an erection*/to be as stiff as a poker **II** *adv* **1.** *F* **être raide fou,** to be raving mad*/to be (stark staring) bonkers **2.** *P* (*esp drogues*) **être raide def,** to be stoned/bombed out of one's mind. (*Voir* **def**; **défoncé**) **III** *nm* O P **1. boire du raide**, to drink neat spirits **2.** ten-franc note.

raidi [rɛdi] *a* P drunk*/stoned/plastered.

raidillard [rɛdijar] *nm* O P ten-franc note.

raidillon [rɛdijɔ̃] *nm* O P neat spirits*/rotgut.

raidir [rɛdir] *vi* P **1.** to die* **2. se faire raidir**, to get cleaned out (at gambling).

raie [rɛ] *nf* **1.** F buttocks* **2.** P **se magner la raie**, to get a move on/to get one's finger out **3.** P **pisser à la raie à qn**, to despise s.o.; **je te/vous pisse à la raie!** two fingers to you! **4.** P **taper dans la raie (à qn)**, to sodomise* (s.o.) **5.** A V female genitals*.

raiguisé [rɛgize] *a* P cleaned out (at gambling).

raisin [rɛzɛ̃] *nm* P **1.** blood/claret **2. avoir du raisin**, to be courageous*/to have guts **3. avoir qn dans le raisin**, to be infatuated* with s.o./to have a crush on s.o. **4. prendre un coup de raisin**, to get angry*/mad.

raisiné [rɛzine] *nm* P (= **raisin 1**) **faire du raisiné**, to have a nosebleed.

rajouter [raʒute] *vtr* F **en rajouter**, to lay it on thick; **n'en rajoute pas!** don't exaggerate!/come off it!

râlage [rɑlaʒ] *nm* F **1.** being in a bad temper **2.** grumbling*/grousing.

râlant [rɑlɑ̃] *a* F maddening/infuriating.

raléger [raleʒe] *vi* P = **ralléger**.

râler [rɑle] *vi* F **1.** to be very angry*/to be in a foul temper; **râler comme un pou/râler ferme/râler sec**, to be hopping mad **2.** to grumble*/to grouse/to gripe.

râleur, euse [rɑlœr, -øz],

râleux, euse [rɑlø, -øz] F **I** *a* **il est terriblement râleur**, he's always grumbling/bellyaching/griping about something **II** *n* grumbler/grouser/bellyacher.

ralléger [raleʒe] *vi* P to turn up/to show up/to breeze in/to blow in; (*revenir*) to get back.

rallonge [ralɔ̃ʒ] *nf* **1.** F **nom à rallonge**, double-barrelled name **2.** F bribe*/backhander **3.** F **demander une/de la rallonge (au patron)**, to ask for a rise/*esp* NAm a raise **4.** P (flick-)knife/switchblade/shiv.

rallonger [ralɔ̃ʒe] *vtr* P to stab/to knife (s.o.).

ramarrer [ramare] *vi* P to meet up (with s.o.) again.

ramasser [ramase] *vtr* **1.** P to arrest* **2.** P to reprimand* **3.** P **se faire ramasser** (*i*) to be arrested*/to get picked up/to get nicked (by the police) (*ii*) to be reprimanded*/ticked off (*iii*) (*scol*) to fail an exam (*iv*) (*théâtre, etc*) to be a flop **4.** F **ramasser un rhume**, to catch/to pick up a cold **5.** F **ramasser un PV/une contredanse**, to get a ticket. (*Voir* **billet 3**; **bûche I 4**; **cuiller 2**; **culotte 2** (*b*); **gadin 2**; **pelle 1**; **traînard**; **valdingue II 2**; **veste**) **II** *vpr* **se ramasser** P **se ramasser par terre**, to fall (down)/to come a cropper*.

ramassis [ramasi] *nm* F (*péj*) (*a*) untidy heap/pile/assortment (of things) (*b*) bunch/crowd (of people).

ramastiquer [ramastike] *vtr* P = **ramasser**.

rambin [rɑ̃bɛ̃] *nm* P **1. faire du rambin à qn** (*i*) to flatter* s.o./to butter s.o. up (*ii*) to make up to s.o./to try and get off with s.o./to sweet-talk s.o. **2.** excuse; **marcher au rambin**, to try to make amends/to wriggle out (of sth)/to try to get out (of sth).

rambiner [rãbine] *P* **I** *vtr* **1.** rambiner le coup/l'affaire, to reach a peaceful settlement/to sort things out; ça devrait rambiner vos affaires, that should put things straight for you **2.** to put new life into (s.o.)/to cheer (s.o.) up/to buck (s.o.) up **II** *vi* to become reconciled/to make peace; il vaut mieux rambiner, it's better to patch things up.

rambineur, euse [rãbinœr, -øz] *n P* **1.** peace-maker/patcher-up (of quarrels) **2.** flatterer*/fast talker.

rambot [rãbo] *nm P* appointment/meeting/date/rendezvous.

rambour [rãbur] *nm P* **1.** appointment/meeting/date/rendezvous; on avait rambour chez lui, we had a meeting/we'd arranged to meet at his place **2.** *pl* rambours, information*/gen; il nous a fourni tout un tas de rambours sur elle, he gave us a whole load of info/a hell of a lot of info/the low-down on her.

ramdam(e) [ramdam] *nm P* uproar*/noise/din/row: faire du ramdam(e) (*i*) to make a din/to kick up a row (*ii*) to grumble*/to bellyache (*iii*) to protest; arrêtez ce ramdam! stop this racket!/cut it out!

rame [ram] *nf P* avoir la rame, to be lazy*/bone idle; ne pas (en) faire/fiche(r)/foutre une rame, to sit around and do nothing; to footle about; il n'en fout pas une rame, he doesn't do a stroke; he does damn-all/fuck-all/piss-all; he just pisses around.

ramée [rame] *nf P* = rame.

ramenard, arde [ramnar, -ard] *P* **I** *a* self-important **II** *n* swank/show-off*; bigmouth/loudmouth.

ramener [ramne] **I** *vtr P* ramener sa gueule/la ramener (*i*) to butt into the conversation/to stick in one's oar (*ii*) to shove one's opinions down people's throats (*iii*) to grumble*/to grouse/to gripe/to bellyache (*iv*) to protest (*v*) to show off*/to think a lot of oneself/to come the acid. (*Voir* fraise 5) **II** *vpr* se ramener *F* to arrive*/to turn up/to roll up/to show up/to blow in; alors, tu te ramènes? are you coming, then?

rameneur, euse [ramnœr, -øz] *n P* show-off*; line-shooter.

ramer [rame] **I** *vtr F* il s'y entend comme à ramer des choux, he hasn't a clue/he hasn't got the slightest; he doesn't know which end of a cow you get the milk from **II** *vi* **1.** *P* bien ramer, to work* hard/to slog away **2.** to get tired* **3.** *V* to have sex*/to dip one's wick/to get one's end away.

ramier [ramje] *nm* **1.** *F* lazybones/(lazy) bum **2.** prostitute*.

ramolli, ie [ramɔli] *F* **I** *a* soft (in the head)/half-witted **II** *n* dodderer.

se ramollir [səramɔlir] *vpr F* to go/to get soft (in the head).

ramollo(t) [ramɔlo] **I** *a F* il est un peu ramollo(t), he's gone a bit soft in the head/a bit gaga **II** *nm* **1.** *F* un vieux ramollo(t), a dodderer/a has-been/an old fogey*/an old fuddy-duddy **2.** *V* se taper un ramollo(t), to masturbate*.

ramoner [ramɔne] *vtr* **1.** *P* to reprimand* (s.o.)/to haul (s.o.) over the coals/to bawl s.o. out; je l'ai ramoné de la belle façon, I didn't half tell him off **2.** *P* (*au jeu*) to clean (s.o.) out/to take (s.o.) to the cleaners **3.** *V* to have sex* with (s.o.).

rampant [rãpã] *nm* **1.** *F* (*aviation*) les rampants, the ground staff/the kiwis **2.** *P* taxi/cab.

rampe [rãp] *nf* **1.** *P* lâcher la rampe, to die*/to kick the bucket **2.** *F* (*a*) tenir bon/dur la rampe, to be still going strong (*b*) tiens bon/dur la rampe! (*i*) hold onto your hat!/hold tight!/*esp NAm* hang in there! (*ii*) look after yourself!/keep your pecker up!/*esp NAm* hang in there!

ramponneau, *pl* **-eaux** [rãpɔno] *nm P* blow*; **flanquer un ramponneau à qn,** to thump/to hit s.o. (*esp* in a fight).

ramponner [rãpɔne] *vtr P* to thump/to hit (s.o.).

rancard [rãkar] *nm P* **1.** information*/info/tip-off/low-down/gen **2.** = **rancart 2.**

rancarder [rãkarde] **I** *vtr P* **1.** to tip (s.o.) off*/to give s.o. the low-down/to gen s.o. up; to put (s.o.) wise **2.** to make an appointment/a date with (s.o.)/to arrange to meet s.o. **II** *vpr* **se rancarder** *P* to get the info/to get genned up (on sth); **je me suis rancardé sur le patron,** I got the low-down/the gen on the boss.

rancart [rãkar] *nm F* **1.** mettre/filer/flanquer qch/qn au rancart, to discard sth; to shelve sth; to retire (officer, official); **nous avons filé son projet au rancart,** we've got rid of/got shot of/slung out his idea; **elle est au rancart,** she's on the shelf **2.** appointment/meeting/date/rendezvous; **elle a rancart avec son mec,** she's got a date with/she's meeting her bloke/guy.

rangé [rãʒe] *a F* **être rangé (du côté) des voitures,** to settle down; **ce voleur est rangé des voitures,** this thief* has reformed/gone straight.

rangemane [rãʒman] *nm A P* = **rangeur.**

rangemaner [rãʒmane] *vtr A P* **1.** to swindle*/to cheat/to con (s.o.) **2.** to beat (s.o.) up*/to knock (s.o.) about/to work (s.o.) over.

rangeur [rãʒœr] *nm A P* swindler*/cheat/con artist.

ranquiller [rãkije] *vtr&i F P* = **renquiller.**

rantanplan [rãtãplã] *nm P* **faire qch au rantanplan,** to use bluff/to try it on.

raousse! [raus] *int P* get out!

raousser [rause], **raouster** [rauste] *vtr P* to turf (s.o.) out.

rapapillotage [rapapijɔtaʒ] *nm,* **rapapilloter** [rapapijɔte] *vtr,* **se rapapilloter** *vpr F* = **rabibochage, rabibocher, se rabibocher.**

râpé [rɑpe] *a P* **c'est râpé,** it's no good/it's done for/it's had it/it's a flop.

râper [rɑpe] *vtr* **1.** *P* **les râper à qn,** to bore* s.o. rigid; **il me les râpe,** he's a dreadful bore*/he's a real pain. (*Voir* **pied 19**) **2.** *V* to have sex* with (a woman)/to have it away with (a woman).

râpeuse [rɑpøz] *nf P* tongue.

rapiat, -ate [rapja, -at] *F* **I** *a* miserly*/stingy/tight **II** *n* miser*/skinflint.

rapide [rapid] *nm F* **c'est un rapide,** he's quick on the uptake/he's smart/he catches on quick; there are no flies on him.

rapido(s) [rapido(s)] *adv P* very quickly*/at the double/quick as a flash/pdq/pronto.

rapière [rapjer] *nf O P* knife/dagger.

rapiérer [rapjere] *vtr O P* to knife/to stab/to stick (s.o.).

rapio [rapjo] *adv P* = **rapido(s).**

raplapla(t) [raplapla] *a F (pers)* exhausted*; washed out/frazzled.

rappliquer [raplike] **I** *vi P* to return/to rush back/to dash back; **rappliquer à la maison,** to make tracks (for home); **il a rappliqué à minuit,** he rolled in at midnight; **rappliquer sur qn,** to make a beeline for s.o. **II** *vpr* **se rappliquer** *P* = **rappliquer.**

rapport [rapɔr] *nm* **1.** *F* **rapport à ...,** because of ... /on account of

...**/about** ...; **je ne dirai rien, rapport à ton père,** I won't say anything because of your father **2.** *F* (*esp scol*) **faire des rapports,** to be a sneak/to tell tales **3.** *P* (*prostituée*) **être d'un bon rapport,** to be a good earner/a good meal-ticket (for her pimp).

rapporter [rapɔrte] *vi F* (*esp scol*) to (be a) sneak/to be a tell-tale; **il est toujours à rapporter,** he's always telling tales; **rapporter sur le compte de qn,** to tell on s.o.

rapporteur, -euse [rapɔrtœr, -øz] *n F* (*esp scol*) tell-tale/sneak.

râpure [rɑpyr] *nf P* bore*/drag; awful grind.

raquedal [rakdal] *nm P* miser*/skinflint.

raquer [rake] *vtr P* to pay* up/to cough up; **c'est moi qui ai dû raquer,** I had to fork out/shell out the cash; **ils te feront raquer jusqu'au dernier sou,** they'll screw you for every penny you've got.

rarranger [rarɑ̃ʒe] *vtr P* **se faire rarranger** (*i*) to be swindled/diddled/overcharged (*ii*) to get hurt/wounded (*iii*) to get told off/ticked off (*iv*) to catch VD*/to cop a dose.

ras [rɑ] *a* **1.** *F* miserly*/mean/stingy/tight **2.** *P* **en avoir ras le bol,** to be fed up* (to the back teeth) with sth/to have had one's fill of sth; **j'en ai ras le bol,** I've had it up to here. (*Voir* **bol 4; ras-le-bol**)

rasant [rɑzɑ̃] *a F* (very) boring (person, speech, etc); **qu'il est rasant, ton vieux!** your old man's a real bore*/drag/pain!

ras-de-bitume [rɑdəbitym], **rasduc** [radyk], **ras-du-cul** [radyky] *nm&a P* undersized* (person)/(little) runt/pipsqueak.

rase [rɑz] *nm P* **1.** priest* **2.** prison chaplain.

rase-bitume [rɑzbitym] *nm P* = **ras-de-bitume.**

rase-pet [rɑzpɛ] *nm inv P* (**veston**) **rase-pet,** (man's) short jacket; bumfreezer.

raser [rɑze] **I** *vtr F* **1. demain on rase gratis,** that'll be the day! **2.** to bore* (s.o.); **ça me rase,** this bores me to tears/this bores me rigid **II** *vpr* **se raser** *F* to be bored* (stiff).

raseur, -euse [rɑzœr, -øz] *n F* (*pers*) bore*; **ce qu'elle est raseuse!** she's a real pain/drag!

rasibe [rɑzib] *nm P* razor.

rasibus [rɑzibys] *F* **I** *adv* (*a*) **couper rasibus,** to cut it close/fine (*b*) **la balle me passa rasibus de l'oreille,** the bullet grazed my ear **II** *int* (*a*) **rasibus!** nothing doing! (*b*) ... **et puis rasibus!** ... and then it was all over!

rasif [rɑzif] *nm P* razor.

ras-le-bol [rɑlbɔl] *nm P* complete dissatisfaction *or* disgust; **'68 dans les facs, c'était le ras-le-bol,** students in '68 had just about had enough (of everything). (*Voir* **bol 4; ras 2**)

ras-le-cul [rɑl(ə)ky] *nm P* = **ras-le-bol.**

rasoir [rɑzwar] *F* **I** *a* boring; **ce que c'est rasoir!** what a bore/bind/drag! **II** *nm* (*pers ou chose*) bore*/drag; **qu'il est rasoir!** what a pain in the neck!

rassembler [rasɑ̃ble] *vtr P* **se faire rassembler,** to be reprimanded*/ticked off.

rassis [rasi] *nm V* **se coller/se taper un rassis,** to masturbate*.

rasta[1] [rasta] *nm&f P* (= *rastafari*) (*a*) rastafarian/rasta; **la musique rasta,** rasta music (*b*) (*péj*) negro*/black.

rasta[2] *nm*, **rastacaille** [rastakaj] *nm*, **rastaquouère** [rastakwɛr] *nm F* (*péj*) flashy foreign adventurer (*esp* from South America).

rat [ra] *nm* **1.** *F* (*a*) voir les rats, to have persecution mania (*b*) voir les rats bleus, to see pink elephants/to have the DT's **2.** *P* c'est un rat, he's a miser*; être/vivre comme un rat, to be miserly*/mean/stingy **3.** *F* être fabriqué/fait/paumé comme un rat, to be caught out/to be cornered/to be done for **4.** *F* s'embêter/s'ennuyer comme un rat mort, to be bored* stiff **5.** *F* mon petit rat, my darling*/my pet **6.** *F* rat de bibliothèque, bookworm **7.** *F* rat d'église, assiduous churchgoer **8.** *F* rat d'hôtel, (flashy) hotel thief **9.** *F* petit rat (d'Opéra), young female ballet-dancer (still attending dancing classes and used as an extra) **10.** *P* il a bouffé du rat, you can't see him for dust **11.** *F* (*péj*) face de rat, repulsive face/ratface **12.** *P* (*péj*) (*Maghrébin*) North African; Arab*/wog.

rata [rata] *nm P* (*a*) stew (*b*) nous avons eu un maigre rata, we had a lousy meal (*c*) ne pas s'endormir sur le rata, to be alert/wide awake; not to fall asleep on the job. (*Voir* ratatouille 1)

ratagasse [ratagas] *nm P* = ratage.

ratage [rataʒ] *nm F* failure; misfire; failing/missing.

ratatiner [ratatine] *vtr P* **1.** to kill*/to bump off **2.** to destroy/to smash up **3.** to beat (s.o.) up*/to work (s.o.) over.

ratatouille [ratatuj] *nf P* **1.** (*a*) stew (*b*) poor-quality food/pigswill **2.** thrashing/beating-up*/pasting.

ratatouiller [ratatuje] *vi P* (*moteur*) to miss/to misfire/to splutter.

rate [rat] *nf F* se dilater/se désopiler la rate, to have a good laugh/to split one's sides laughing. (*Voir* se fouler)

raté¹ [rate] *a P* pock-marked (face).

raté², **ée** *n F* (*pers*) failure*/washout.

râteau, *pl* **-eaux** [rato] *nm P* **1.** comb/bug-rake **2.** être sur les râteaux, to be exhausted*.

râtelier [ratəlje] *nm F* **1.** manger au râtelier de qn, to live at s.o.'s expense/to scrounge off s.o.; manger à deux râteliers (*i*) to have two strings to one's bow (*ii*) to have a foot in both camps; manger à plusieurs râteliers/à tous les râteliers, to take one's profit where one finds it; to make the most of what comes along **2.** remettre ses armes au râtelier, to leave the service **3.** false teeth/dentures. (*Voir* foin 1)

rater [rate] *vtr F* il n'en rate pas une! he's always putting his foot in it!/he's always making a mess of things!

ratiboiser [ratibwaze] *vtr P* **1.** (*a*) ratiboiser qch à qn, to do s.o. out of sth; to nick/to pinch sth from s.o. (*b*) ratiboiser sur les notes de frais, to fiddle the expenses **2.** (*esp au jeu*) to fleece (s.o.)/to clean (s.o.) out/to take (s.o.) to the cleaners **3.** to kill* (s.o.)/to bump (s.o.) off **4.** le voilà ratiboisé, he's done for/he's had it/he's had his chips **5.** se faire ratiboiser les tif(fe)s, to get a haircut.

ratiche¹ [ratiʃ] *nf P* **1.** knife/chiv/shiv **2.** church **3.** *pl* ratiches, teeth*/gnashers.

ratiche² *nm*, **ratichon** [ratiʃɔ̃] *nm P* (*péj*) priest*.

ratichonne [ratiʃɔn] *nf P* (*péj*) nun.

ratier [ratje] *nm P* prisoner.

ratière [ratjɛr] *nf P* prison*.

ratissage [ratisaʒ] *nm F* les flics étaient en train de faire une ratissage du quartier, the cops were combing the area/doing a house to house search.

ratissé [ratise] *a P* **1.** ruined/done for **2.** penniless*/broke to the wide.

ratisser [ratise] *vtr* **1.** *F* to arrest*; **la police les a ratissés,** the police* nabbed/nicked the whole lot of them **2.** *F* to search/to comb (a district); **la police a ratissé tout le quartier,** the police searched/combed the entire district **3.** *P* to fleece* (s.o.)/to clean (s.o.) out/to take (s.o.) to the cleaners **4.** *P* to kill* (s.o.). (*Voir* **hure 2**)

raton [ratɔ̃] *nm* **1.** *F* **mon petit raton,** my darling*/my pet **2.** *P* (*péj*) North African; Arab*/wog. (*Voir* **rat 12**)

raton(n)ade [ratɔnad] *nf P* (*a*) (*à l'origine*) (*esp en Algérie*) punitive raid against the Arabs; Arab-bashing (*b*) (*par extension*) brutal action by a majority group against a minority group.

ratonner [ratɔne] *vi P* (*homosexuels*) to go cruising for Arab partners.

ratonneuse [ratɔnøz] *vi P* (*homosexuels*) homosexual attracted by Arabs.

raugmenter [rɔgmɑ̃te] *P* **I** *vtr* to increase/to put up the price of (sth) **II** *vi* (*les prix*) to increase/to go up.

ravagé [ravaʒe] *a F* **il est complètement ravagé!** he's quite mad*!/he's nuts!

ravalement [ravalmɑ̃] *nm F* (*péj*) **elle fait son ravalement,** she's putting on her makeup/her war-paint.

ravelin [ravlɛ̃] *nm F* (*a*) secondhand/used car (*b*) vintage car.

ravelure [ravlyr] *nf P* ugly old hag/old bag/old bat.

ravet [ravɛ] *nm F* cockroach/black beetle.

ravigotant [ravigɔtɑ̃] *nm F* pick-me-up/tonic/bracer.

ravigoter [ravigɔte] **I** *vtr F* to cheer (s.o.) up/to buck (s.o.) up; **un** petit verre va le ravigoter, a drop of spirits will put new life into him/will perk him up **II** *vpr* **se ravigoter** *F* to cheer up/to buck up.

ravissant [ravisɑ̃] *nm F* sissy/pansy.

ravito [ravito] *nm F* (= *ravitaillement*) food supplies/stocks; **aller au ravito,** to go shopping.

rayon [rɛjɔ̃] *nm F* **1. c'est (de) mon rayon,** that's right up my street/that's just my cup of tea; **ce n'est pas (de) mon rayon,** that's not in my line (of country)/that's not in my department **3. en connaître un rayon,** to know a lot; to be in the know; to be an old hand (at it); to know the score; to know the ropes **4. en filer un rayon,** to put some vim/one's back/a jerk into it; to go all out; **il en a mis un rayon,** he pulled out all the stops/he really got down to it.

rayonner [rɛjɔne] *vi V* to have an orgasm*/to come.

razif [razif] *nm P* razor.

razis [razi] *nm P* = **rase 1, 2.**

réac [reak] *a & nm&f F* (*pol*) (= *réactionnaire*) reactionary.

rébec(c)a [rebɛka] *nm P* **faire du rébec(c)a** (*i*) to grumble*/to grouse/to gripe/to bellyache (*ii*) to kick up a row/a rumpus/a shindy; **(il) va y avoir du rébec(c)a,** there'll be trouble; there'll be a hell of a noise/racket; **il a fait du rébec(c)a pour avoir ça,** he kicked up a real fuss to get that.

rebectage [rəbɛktaʒ] *nm P* **1.** getting back to normal (health, etc); getting back on one's feet (financially, etc) **2.** reconciliation/making it up **3.** petition for a reprieve.

se rebecquer [sərəbɛke], **se rebéquer** [sərəbeke] *vpr F* (*a*) to answer back (*b*) to protest (*c*) to be up in arms (about sth).

rebe(c)queur, euse [rəbɛkœr, -øz] *a&n F* insolent/impertinent/ bolshy (person).

rebec(que)tant [rəbɛktɑ̃] *a P* (*a*) appetizing (*b*) encouraging (*c*) (sth) that cheers you up/bucks you up.

rebec(que)ter [rəbɛkte] *P* **I** *vtr* **1.** to buck (s.o.) up **2.** to reconcile (people) **II** *vi* **1.** to become reconciled/to make it up **2.** to buck up/to start feeling better **III** *vpr* **se rebec(que)ter** *P* **1.** to pick up (physically, financially) **2.** to become reconciled/to make it up; to put things right.

rebec(que)teur [rəbɛktœr] *nm P* doctor/doc/medico.

rebichoter [rəbiʃɔte] *vtr P* to identify/to spot (s.o./sth).

rebiffe [rəbif] *nf F* **1.** vengeance **2. faire de la rebiffe/aller à la rebiffe,** to take offence/to get one's back up/to bristle up; to be up in arms (about sth).

rebiffement [rəbifmɑ̃] *nm F* bristling up; indignant refusal to obey.

rebiffer [rəbife] *F* **I** *vtr* **rebiffer qn,** to snub s.o./to give s.o. the cold shoulder **II** *vi* **rebiffer (au truc),** to begin again; to have another go/another shot (at sth). (*Voir* **repiquer II** 3) **III** *vpr* **se rebiffer** *F* to take offence/to bristle up; **faire rebiffer qn,** to get s.o.'s back up; **se rebiffer contre qch,** to be up in arms against sth/to kick against sth/to hit back at sth.

rebiquer [rəbike] *vtr* **1.** *P* **ça me rebique,** it gets on my nerves/it gets me down/that gets me **2.** *F* **elle a les cheveux qui rebiquent,** her hair is curling up/sticking up.

rebondir [rəbɔ̃dir] *vi P* **envoyer rebondir qn,** to send s.o. packing/to tell s.o. to clear off/to give s.o. the push.

rebouiser [rəbwize] *vtr P* to kill* (s.o.)/to do (s.o.) in/to bump s.o. off.

récal [rekal] *a P* (= *récalcitrant*) recalcitrant/rebellious/obstinate/ bolsy.

recalage [rəkalaʒ] *nm F* failure (in an exam).

recalé, ée [rəkale] *a&n F* failed (candidate); **les recalés,** the failures/the flunkers.

recaler [rəkale] **I** *vtr F* **1.** to fail* (s.o. in an exam); **être recalé/ se faire recaler,** to be failed/to flunk **2.** to set (s.o.) up again/to put new life into (s.o.); to set (tradesman, etc) on his feet again **II** *vpr* **se recaler** *F* to get back on one's feet again/to get a new lease of life/to recover one's health.

recaser [rəkɑze] *vtr F* **1.** to find another job for (s.o.) **2.** to rehouse/to resettle (s.o.) **3. elle cherche à se recaser,** she's looking for another husband/a replacement.

recharger [rəʃarʒe] *vtr&i F* to refill (glasses) (for another round of drinks); to set them up again.

réchauffage [reʃofaʒ] *nm F* dishing up/rehashing (of sth old as new).

réchauffante [reʃofɑ̃t] *nf P* wig.

réchauffé [reʃofe] *nm F* rehash/ stale news; **c'est du réchauffé,** we've heard that (news, joke, etc) before; that's ancient history/that's old hat.

rechoper [rəʃɔpe] *vtr P* to catch (s.o.) again; to get another go at (s.o.); **je le rechoperai au tournant,** I'll find a way of getting even with him.

récidiver [residive] *vi F* to do sth again.

recluse [rəklyz] *nf,* **récluse** [reklyz] *nf P* (= *reclusion, réclusion*) solitary confinement/solitary.

reco [rəko] *nf F* (*mil*) recce.

recoller [rəkɔle] **I** *vi P* **ça recolle maintenant,** they've made it up/ they're friends again **II** *vpr* **se recoller** *P* **ils se sont recollés,**

they're living together again/they're giving it another go.

reconnobler [rəkɔnɔble], **reconnobrer** [rəkɔnɔbre] *vtr P* (= *reconnaître*) to recognize.

récré [rekre] *nf F* (*scol*) (= *récréation*) recreation/playtime/break.

recta [rɛkta] *F* **I** *a inv* punctual; **ils sont recta et font un gros travail,** they arrive on the dot and get through a lot of work **II** *adv* (*a*) punctually/on the dot/bang on time (*b*) **payer recta,** to pay on the nail (*c*) **ça me conduirait recta au ridicule,** that would make me look ridiculous straight away/straight off/for a start.

rectifier [rɛktifje] *vtr P* **1.** to kill*; **se faire rectifier,** to get bumped off/done in **2.** to swindle*/to cheat/to fleece*/to rip off. (*Voir* **portrait** (*b*))

rectifieur [rɛktifjœr] *nm P* killer; executioner.

récupération [rekyperasjɔ̃] *nf F* scrounging/cadging.

récupérer [rekypere] *vtr F* to scrounge/to cadge.

rédimer [redime] *vtr P* **1.** to kill*/to bump off **2.** to destroy/to smash **3.** to beat (s.o.) up*/to work (s.o.) over.

redingote [rədɛ̃gɔt] *nf P* **redingote de sapin,** coffin/wooden overcoat.

redresse [rədrɛs] *nf P* **1.** c'est un **type à la redresse** (*i*) he knows just what he's doing/he's on the ball/he knows the score (*ii*) he's a tough guy/he's got guts **2. mettre qn à la redresse,** to reprimand* s.o./to blow s.o. up/to give s.o. a good telling-off.

redresser [rədrɛse] **I** *vtr P* **1.** to reprimand*/to blow (s.o.) up **2.** to look* at/to take a dekko at (s.o./sth) **3.** to recognize/to identify/to spot **II** *vi V* to have an erection*/a hard-on.

reefer [rifɛr] *nm F* (*drogues*) marijuana cigarette*/reefer.

refaire [rəfɛr] **I** *vtr F* **1.** (*au café, au pub, etc*) **à refaire!** same again! **2.** to swindle*/to do/to diddle (s.o.); **on t'a refait,** you've been done; **être refait,** to be had; **je suis refait de vingt francs,** I've been done out of twenty francs; **il ne faut pas me la refaire!** don't try it on with me! **4.** to steal*; **on m'a refait mon porte-monnaie,** someone's pinched/swiped my purse. (*Voir* **cerise** 5) **II** *vpr* **se refaire** *F* **1.** (*a*) to get back on one's feet (physically, financially)/to pick up again; **il s'est bien refait,** he's made a good recovery (*b*) **à mon âge on ne peut pas se refaire,** at my age you can't change your ways; **tu ne me referas pas!** you won't change me! **2.** to retrieve/to recoup one's losses; to make/to stage a comeback.

réfectionner [refɛksjɔne] *vtr F* to do up (a house, etc).

refil(e) [rəfil] *nm P* **1. aller au refil(e)/être au refil(e)** (*i*) to vomit*/to throw up (*ii*) to pay* up; to pay back **2. faire un refil(e),** to make a loan **3.** goods sold (in a shop).

refiler [rəfile] **I** *vtr P* **1. refiler qch à qn** (*i*) to give sth (back) to s.o./to pass sth on to s.o./to slip s.o. sth; **elle m'a refilé ses vieilles fringues,** she handed her old clothes down to me (*ii*) to fob/to palm sth off on s.o.; **se faire refiler qch,** to get fobbed/palmed off with sth; **il m'a refilé sa grippe,** he gave me his flu **2. la refiler,** to sleep (out) in the open. (*Voir* **tubard** I) **II** *vi P* **en refiler,** to be a homosexual*/to be one of them. (*Voir* **jaquette** 2)

refouler [rəfule] *vi P* (*a*) to stink* (*b*) to have foul breath.

refourgue [rəfurg] *nf P* selling of stolen goods to a receiver/a fence.

refroidi [rəfrwadi] *nm P* corpse*/

stiff; **champ/jardin/parc des re-froidis,** cemetery*/bone orchard; **musée des refroidis,** mortuary/ morgue. (*Voir* **boîte 6**)

refroidir [rəfrwadir] *vtr P* to kill* (s.o.)/to make cold meat of (s.o.)/ to bump (s.o.) off.

refus [rəfy] *nm F* **ce n'est pas/c'est pas de refus,** I won't say no to that/I don't mind if I do.

refuser [rəfyze] *vtr F* **il ne se refuse rien,** he does himself proud; he doesn't stint himself.

régalade [regalad] *nf F* (*a*) treating (s.o.)/doing (s.o.) proud (*b*) treat.

régalant [regalɑ̃] *a F* **cela n'est pas régalant,** that's no joke/that's not at all funny*/what's so funny* about that?

régaler [regale] **I** *vtr* **1.** *F* **c'est moi qui régale,** it's my treat/it's my shout/this one's on me **2.** *P* to pleasure (a woman) (sexually) **II** *vpr* **se régaler 1.** *F* **se régaler de qch,** to treat oneself to sth; **on s'est bien régalé(s)** (*i*) we thoroughly enjoyed it/we had a great time (*ii*) we had a slap-up meal; we did ourselves proud **2.** *V* to have an orgasm*.

regardant [rəgardɑ̃] *a F* (*économe*) careful (with one's money); stingy.

regarder [rəgarde] *vtr F* **1. regardez-moi ça!** just look at that!/ get a load of that! **2. (non, mais) tu ne m'as pas regardé!/tu m'as bien regardé?** what do you take me for?/d'you think I'm a mug? **3. ça te regarde!** mind your own damn business!

régime [reʒim] *nm F* **régime jockey,** strict diet.

reginglard [rəʒɛ̃glar] *nm F* wine (*esp* a local wine with a somewhat sharp taste).

reglinguet [rəglɛ̃gɛ] *nm F* = **reginglard.**

réglo [reglo] *P* **I** *a inv* (*a*) (*pers*) straight/on the level; **c'est un type réglo,** he's an all-right guy/he's straight-up/he's on the level (*b*) (*papiers*) in (good) order **II** *adv* **il s'est conduit réglo avec moi,** he's acted straight with me/he was on the level with me.

regonfler [rəgɔ̃fle] *vtr F* to cheer (s.o.) up/to buck (s.o.) up/to bolster (s.o.) up; to put new life into (s.o./sth); **il est regonflé à bloc,** he's back on top of the world/he's back to his old self again; **ça m'a regonflé,** that's put me back on my feet.

regriffer [rəgrife] *vtr P* to take back.

régul(e) [regyl], **régulier, -ière¹** [regylje, -jɛr] *a P* = **réglo 1** (*a*).

régulière² *nf P* **ma régulière** (*i*) the wife*/the missis/the old lady (*ii*) the woman I live with/my better half/my old lady (*iii*) my steady girlfriend.

reine [rɛn] *nf P* homosexual*/ queen. (*Voir* **tante**)

reins [rɛ̃] *nmpl* **1.** *F* **il a les reins solides,** he's a man of substance **2.** *F* **il ne se cassera pas les reins à travailler,** he won't kill himself working **3.** *F* **casser les reins à/de qn** (*i*) to kill* s.o. (*ii*) to break s.o./ to ruin s.o. **4.** *P* **les avoir dans les reins,** to have the police* on one's track. (*Voir* **dos 5**; **pied 18**) **5.** *P* **être chaud des reins,** to be highly sexed/randy/horny. (*Voir* **chaud I 9**) **6.** *F* **avoir qch sur les reins,** to be saddled/landed with sth.

relâche [rəlɑʃ] *nf P* **faire relâche,** to have one's period*.

relance [rəlɑ̃s] *nf P* **1.** borrowing **2. aller à la relance,** to go gunning for s.o. **3. faire une relance,** to have another go/to take a second bite at the cherry.

relancer [rəlɑ̃se] *vtr* **1.** *P* to borrow **2.** *F* **relancer qn,** to pester s.o./to badger s.o.; to chase after s.o.

relarguer [rəlarge] *vtr P* to release/to set free.

relax(e) [rəlaks, rilaks] *a F* relaxed; **elle est très relax,** she's very easy-going/laid-back.

relègue [rəlɛg] *nf P* preventive detention.

relingé [rəlɛ̃ʒe] *a P* (*a*) wearing new clothes (*b*) wearing different clothes.

reluire [rəlɥir] *vi* 1. *F* **manier/ passer la brosse à reluire,** to flatter* s.o./to soft-soap s.o. 2. *F* to enjoy oneself immensely/to have a ball 3. *V* to have an orgasm*/to get one's rocks off.

reluisant [rəlɥizɑ̃] *a F* **cela n'est pas très reluisant,** it's not all that wonderful.

reluquer [rəlyke] *vtr F* 1. **reluquer qn,** to leer at s.o./to give s.o. the glad eye 2. **reluquer qch,** to covet sth/to have one's eye on sth.

rem [rɛm] *nf P* (*verlan de mère*) mother*/(the) old lady/(the) old girl.

remballer [rɑ̃bale] *vtr F* = **rembarrer.** (*Voir* **outil 4**)

rembarrer [rɑ̃bare] *vtr F* (*a*) to snub (s.o.); to put (s.o.) (firmly) in his place (*b*) to go for (s.o.)/to jump down (s.o.'s) throat/to bite (s.o.'s) head off; **se faire rembarrer,** to get sat on.

rembiner [rɑ̃bine] I *vtr P* = **rambiner** I, 1, 2 II *vpr* **se rembiner** *P* = **rambiner** II.

rembo [rɑ̃bo] *nm P* rendezvous. (*Voir* **rambot**)

rembour [rɑ̃bur] *nm P* 1. rendezvous. (*Voir* **rambour**) 2. **aller au rembour,** to pay* up; to pay back/ to settle up.

rembrayer [rɑ̃breje] *vi F* to start work again.

remède [rəmɛd] *nm* 1. *P* revolver*/persuader 2. *P* **un remède d'amour/un remède contre l'amour** (*i*) a woman as ugly as sin/ a perfect fright/an eyesore (*ii*) an old bitch/an old slag 3. *F* **remède de cheval,** drastic remedy/kill or cure remedy; **remède de bonne femme,** old wives' tale.

remesurer [rəməzyre] *vi P* to vomit*.

remettre [rəmɛtr] *vtr F* 1. (*a*) **remettons ça!** (*i*) let's have another go!/let's begin again! (*ii*) (*aussi* **remettons-nous ça!**) let's have another drink!/let's set 'em up again! (*b*) **voilà qu'elle remet ça!** she's at it again! 2. **en remettre (un peu),** to exaggerate*/to lay it on (a bit) thick.

remise [rəmiz] *nf F* **être sous la remise,** to be on the shelf.

remiser [rəmize] I *vtr P* 1. **remiser qn (à sa place),** to put s.o. (firmly) in his place/to take s.o. down a peg or two 2. to superannuate (s.o.)/to put (s.o.) out to grass 3. to give (s.o.) up/to drop (s.o.)/to chuck (s.o.)/to walk out on (s.o.) II *vi F* 1. to take it easy*/ to slow up/to ease up 2. to settle down (after a merry life).

remontant [rəmɔ̃tɑ̃] *nm F* pickme-up/bracer/tonic.

remonte [rəmɔ̃t] *nf P* procuring girls for brothels/talent hunting.

remoucher [rəmuʃe] *vtr P* 1. to tell (s.o.) off/to put (s.o.) firmly in his place; **se faire remoucher,** to get told off/to get sat on 2. to recognize/to identify; to spot 3. to look* at (s.o./sth).

se rempiffer [sərɑ̃pife] *vpr P* to put on weight.

rempilé [rɑ̃pile] *nm F* (*mil*) reenlisted soldier.

rempiler [rɑ̃pile] *vi F* (*mil*) to reenlist/to sign on again.

rempli [rɑ̃pli] *a F* rich*/loaded.

se remplir [sərɑ̃plir] *vpr F* **se remplir (les poches),** to get rich*/to make a packet.

se remplumer [sərãplyme] *vpr F*
(*pers*) **1.** to pick up again (physically, financially) **2.** to put on
weight (again).

remue-fesses [rəmyfɛs] *nm inv*
P (any kind of) dance.

renâcler [rənɑkle] *vi F* (*a*) to show
reluctance (in doing sth); to hang
back; **renâcler à la besogne,** to be
workshy; **il a accepté en renâclant,**
he accepted grudgingly (*b*) **renâcler
à un plat,** to turn one's nose up at
a dish.

renâcleur [rənɑklœr] *nm F* **1.**
grumbler* **2.** shirker.

renard [rənar] *nm* **1.** *F* strike-
breaker/blackleg/scab **2.** *F* **tirer
au renard,** to malinger/to be workshy **3.** *P* **cracher/écorcher/faire/
lâcher/piquer un renard; aller au
renard,** to vomit*/to throw up.

renarder [rənarde] *vi P* to vomit*/
to throw up.

renaud [rəno] *nm P* **1. être en
renaud,** to be very angry* (**contre
qn,** with s.o.); to be in a foul temper*/to be hopping mad; to see
red; **filer/mettre qn en renaud,** to
make s.o. furious **2.** violent pro-
test/row; **y a du renaud,** there's a
hell of a row (going on); **chercher
du renaud à qn,** to pick a quarrel*
with s.o./to have a bone to pick
with s.o.

renaude [rənod] *nf P* **faire de la
renaude** = **renauder.**

renauder [rənode] *vi P* to grumble*/to complain/to beef/to bellyache.

renaudeur, -euse [rənodœr,
-øz] *n P* grumbler/griper/belly-
acher.

rencard [rãkar] *nm P* **1.** information*/gen/info **2.** = **rencart.**
(*Voir* **rancard**)

rencarder [rãkarde] *vtr P* **1. rencarder qn,** to give s.o. the informa-
tion/to gen s.o. up/to fill s.o. in
2. = **rencarter.** (*Voir* **rancarder**)

rencart [rãkar] *nm P* **1.** = **ren-**

card 2. rendezvous/date/meeting;
filer un rencart à qn, to make/to
get/to fix a date with s.o.

rencarter [rãkarte] *vtr P* to
arrange to meet (s.o.)/to make a
date with (s.o.).

rencontre [rãkɔ̃tr] *nf* **1.** *F* **le
faire à la rencontre,** to pretend that
it is a chance meeting **2.** *P* **faire
qn à la rencontre,** to butt s.o. in
the chest.

se rencontrer [sərãkɔ̃tre] *vpr F*
comme on se rencontre! it's a small
world! **comme cela se rencontre!**
how lucky!/how things do happen!

rendème [rãdɛm] *nm inv P* =
rendez-moi.

rendève [rãdɛv] *nm P* rendezvous.

rendez-moi [rãdemwa] *nm inv P*
vol au rendez-moi, theft which
involves giving change for a
(bank)note which one then takes
back surreptitiously/ringing the
changes.

rendre [rãdr] *vtr F* **ça rend!** it
works!/it does the trick! **ça n'a rien
rendu,** it was a waste of time. (*Voir*
tripes)

rengaine [rãgɛn] *nf F* **c'est
toujours la même rengaine/la vieille
rengaine,** it's always the same old
story; **c'est sa rengaine,** he's always
harping on that subject.

rengainer [rãgene] *vtr F* **rengainer
toujours la même histoire,** to be
always harping on the same string.

rengracier [rãgrasje], **ren-
grâcir** [rãgrasir] *vi P* **1.** to back
down/to (beat a) retreat/to chicken
out **2.** to keep quiet/to stay out of
the picture **3.** to cool down **4.** to
come to terms.

reniflant [rəniflã] *nm P* nose*/
sniffer/smeller.

renifle [rənifl] *nf P* **la renifle,** the
police*/the fuzz.

renifler [rənifle] **I** *vtr* **1.** *P* **je
(ne) peux pas le renifler,** I can't
bear/stick/stomach him (at any
price) **2.** *F* **il sait renifler une**

bonne affaire, he's got a (good) nose for a bargain **3.** *P* **renifler le coup,** to sense (the) danger; to smell a rat **II** *vi* **1.** *F (a)* **renifler sur qch,** to sniff at/to turn one's nose up at sth *(b) (pers)* **renifler sur l'avoine,** to be off one's food **2.** *P* **ça renifle,** it stinks/pongs.

reniflette [rəniflɛt] *nf* **1.** *F* **avoir la reniflette,** to have the sniffles **2.** *P (drogues)* cocaine*/nose candy.

reniquer [rənike] *vi P* to grumble*/to grouse/to gripe; to object.

renquiller [rãkije] **I** *vtr* **1.** *F* to put (sth) back in one's pocket; **renquille ton argent, c'est moi qui paie,** put your money away, it's/this one's on me **2.** *F* **renquiller son compliment,** to say no more/to shut up* **II** *vi* **1.** *P (mil)* to re-enlist **2.** *P* to come back/to return.

renseignements [rãsɛɲmã] *nmpl P* **aller aux renseignements,** to feel (a woman's bottom)/to goose (a woman)/to touch (a woman) up.

rentes [rãt] *nfpl P (prostituée à son client)* **tu penses à mes rentes?** how about a little present?

se rentoiler [sərãtwale] *vpr P* to put on weight again/to put weight back on.

rentre-dedans [rãtrədədã] *nm P* **faire du rentre-dedans à une femme,** to make amorous advances to/to make a pass at woman; to get off with/to make out with a woman.

rentrer [rãtre] *vi F* **1.** **les jambes me rentrent dans le corps,** I'm exhausted*/I can hardly keep on my feet **2.** **faire rentrer qn dans la poussière/en terre/cent pieds sous terre** *(i)* to reprimand* s.o. severely/to tell s.o. where they get off *(ii)* to humiliate s.o./to drag s.o. through the mud **3.** **rentrer dans qn,** to pitch into s.o./to go for s.o./ to have a go at s.o. *(Voir* **chou I 1; dedans 3, 4** *(a)*; **lard 3; mou III 1; portrait** *(b))*

renversant [rãvɛrsã] *a F* stagger-ing/stunning/amazing/astounding (news, etc).

renversée [rãvɛrse] *nf P* **partir en renversée,** to go on a spree*/to go on a bender/to paint the town red.

renverser [rãvɛrse] *vtr F* to amaze/to flabbergast*/to astound/ to stagger (s.o.). *(Voir* **vapeur)**

rep [rɛp] *nm P (verlan de père)* father*/(the) old man/(the) guv'nor.

repapilloter [rəpapijɔte] **I** *vtr F* to reconcile (people); to make it up **II** *vpr* **se repapilloter** *F* se repapilloter avec qn, to become reconciled with s.o./to make it up with s.o.

réparouze [reparuz] *nf P* repair; repairing.

repassage [rəpasaʒ] *nm P* **1.** murder/killing/bumping off/doing in **2.** swindling/cheating/diddling; double-crossing.

repasser [rəpase] **I** *vtr P* **1.** to kill*/to murder/to bump off/to do in **2.** *O* to swindle*/to cheat/to diddle; to double-cross; **être repassé,** to be done out of one's fair share (of the loot) **II** *vi F* **vous repassez!** you've got another thing coming! **pour ça, tu repasseras!** you've got a hope!/no chance!/nothing doing!*/no way! *(Voir* **planche 4)**

repaumer [rəpome] *vtr P* to grab back/to snatch back.

repérer [rəpere] **I** *vtr* **1.** *F* to spot/to pick out; to track down; **repérer qn dans la foule,** to spot s.o./to pick s.o. out in the crowd; *(turf, etc)* **il a le flair pour repérer les gagnants,** he's got a knack of picking winners **2.** *F* **tu vas nous faire repérer!** you'll get us caught! **3.** *P* to keep (s.o.) under surveillance/to keep a close watch on (s.o.) **II** *vpr* **se repérer** *F (a)* **se repérer dans une ville,** to find one's way about in a town *(b)* **je n'arrive pas à me repérer dans ce problème,** I can't make head or tail of this problem.

repiquer [rəpike] **I** *vtr P* to re-arrest; **se faire repiquer**, to be recaptured **II** *vi* **1.** *F* to recuperate/to get back on one's feet again **2.** *F* **repiquer à un plat**, to have a second helping **3.** *P* **repiquer (au truc)** (*i*) to begin again; to have another go/another shot (*ii*) to go back to one's old ways (*iii*) to re-enlist; **repiquer au tapin**, to go back on the game.

répondant [repɔ̃dɑ̃] *nm* **avoir du répondant** (*i*) *F* to have money put by (for a rainy day) (*ii*) *P* (*femme*) to be overweight.

répondre [repɔ̃dr] *vi F* **je vous en réponds!** you bet!/rather!/you can take my word for it!

repousser [rəpuse] *vi P* (*a*) to stink*/to smell foul (*b*) to have bad breath. (*Voir* **goulot** (*b*))

repoussoir [rəpuswar] *nm F* (*esp femme*) **c'est un repoussoir**, she's terribly ugly/an eyesore; she's got a face like the back of a bus.

représentation [rəprezɑ̃tasjɔ̃] *nf F* **être toujours en représentation**, to be always showing off/putting on an act.

requimpe [rəkɛ̃p] *nf O P* full-length coat.

requimpette [rəkɛ̃pɛt] *nf O P* (short) jacket.

requin [rəkɛ̃] *nm F* shark/shady dealer*/swindler.

requinquant [rəkɛ̃kɑ̃] *F* **I** *nm* tonic/pick-me-up/reviver **II** *a* (drink, etc) that bucks you up/that puts you to rights.

requinquer [rəkɛ̃ke] **I** *vtr F* **1.** (*a*) to smarten (s.o.) up/to spruce (s.o.) up (*b*) to give (a place) a face-lift/to posh up (a place) **2.** to buck (s.o.) up; (*boisson*) **ça vous requinque**, it's got a kick in it **II** *vpr* **se requinquer** *F* **1.** (*a*) to smarten oneself up (*b*) to get a new set of clothes **2.** to perk up (after an illness).

resco [rɛsko] *nm P* poor-quality café/restaurant; cheap eating-house.

respectueuse [rɛspɛktɥøz] *nf O P* prostitute*/tart.

respirante [rɛspirɑ̃t] *nf P* **1.** mouth* **2.** (*drogues*) cocaine*/nose candy.

respirer [rɛspire] *vtr P* **1. dur à respirer**, incredible/hard to swallow **2. un dur à respirer**, a tough guy/a hard nut to crack.

respirette [rɛspirɛt] *nf P* (*drogues*) cocaine*/nose candy.

resquillage [rɛskijaʒ] *nm F* **1.** gatecrashing **2.** wangling/fiddling.

resquille [rɛskij] *nf F* **faire de la resquille = resquiller 1, 2.**

resquiller [rɛskije] *vtr & abs F* **1.** to gatecrash; to get in without paying **2.** to wangle/to fiddle.

resquilleur, -euse [rɛskijœr, -øz] *n f F* **1.** uninvited guest/gate-crasher; **roi des resquilleurs**, champion gatecrasher **2.** (*a*) wangler (*b*) cheat* (*c*) queue-jumper (*d*) fare dodger.

ressaut [rəso] *nm P* **1.** (*a*) **mettre/foutre qn à ressaut**, to get on s.o.'s nerves/to drive s.o. mad/to get s.o.'s goat (*b*) **aller/être à ressaut**, to lose one's temper/to flare up **2. faire du ressaut**, to rebel/to revolt/to be up in arms (about sth).

ressauter [rəsote] *vi P* (*a*) to protest/to rebel/to be up in arms (*b*) **faire ressauter qn**, to provoke s.o. (to anger)/to make s.o. blow his stack.

ressauteur [rəsotœr] *nm P* rebel/agitator; barrack-room lawyer.

ressent [rəsɑ̃] *nm P* warning; **aller au ressent/porter le ressent**, to alert the police*.

se ressentir [sərəsɑ̃tir] *vpr P* (*a*) **s'en ressentir pour qch**, to feel fit for sth/to feel up to sth; **je ne m'en ressens pas de faire ça**, I don't feel up to doing that (*b*) **s'en ressentir pour qn**, to have a liking for s.o./to be keen on s.o./to be struck on s.o.

ressort [rəsɔr] *nm F* **le grand ressort**, heart/ticker.

restau [rɛsto] *nm F* restaurant; **restau-U**, university restaurant/canteen. (*Voir* **RU**)

rester [rɛste] *vi F* **y rester**, to be killed (on the spot); **cette fois, tu vas y rester!** this time your number's up!/you've had it this time! (*Voir* **carafe 3**; **flan 6**; **plan I** (*c*))

restif [rɛstif] *nm P* restaurant.

resto [rɛsto] *nm F* restaurant.

resucé, ée [rəsyse] *F* **I** *a* stale (news, etc) **II** *nf* **resucée** (*a*) rehash (of book, etc) (*b*) **une resucée**, a drop more; **(on en boit) une petite resucée?** (how about) another little drink?/how about another?

retailler [rətɑje] *vi P* to hesitate/to pull back.

rétamé [retame] *a P* **1.** drunk*/tight/zonked; **il était complètement rétamé**, he was (completely) pissed **2.** exhausted*/worn out/pooped/knackered **3.** penniless*/skint/flat broke.

rétamer [retame] **I** *vtr P* **1.** to get (s.o.) drunk*; **se (faire) rétamer**, to get drunk/to get pissed **2.** to exhaust* (s.o.)/to knock (s.o.) out/to knacker (s.o.) **3.** to clean (s.o.) out (at gambling)/to take (s.o.) to the cleaners **II** *vpr* **se rétamer** *P* **1.** to fall down/to come a cropper* **2.** to flunk/to fail*; **je me suis rétamé à mon exam**, I flunked my exam.

retape [rətap] *nf F* **1.** (*a*) (*prostituée*) **faire la retape**, to solicit*/to hustle/to be on the game; **être à la retape**, to be on the beat (*b*) **faire de la retape**, to tout (around)/to hustle; to go scouting for customers, volunteers, etc **2.** cheap/vulgar publicity.

retaper [rətape] **I** *vtr* **1.** (*a*) to patch up/to do up (an old house, etc); to repair/to fix (up) (in a perfunctory way); to straighten (bed) (*b*) **se retaper les cheveux**, to straighten one's hair **2.** to buck (s.o.) up/to cheer (s.o.) up; **prends ça, ça te retapera**, drink that, it'll set you up (again); **se retaper le moral**, to buck up/to (begin to) feel better **3.** to fail (a candidate in an exam) **II** *vpr* **se retaper** *F* **1.** to perk up (after an illness)/to get back on one's feet/to get back to one's old self **2.** to recover from a financial setback/to get back on one's feet.

retapissage [rətapisaʒ] *nm P* **passer au retapissage**, to submit to an identification parade.

retapisser [rətapise] *vtr P* to identify/to recognize; **il a été retapissé par les flics**, he was spotted/clocked by the cops.

retenir [rət(ə)nir] *vtr F* (*a*) **je te retiens!** I'll get my own back on you for that!/I shan't forget you in a hurry! (*b*) **je la retiens, celle-là** (*i*) I'll get my own back for that! (*ii*) that's a good one, that is! (*c*) **pour le tact, je te retiens!** talk about tact!

retoquer [rətɔke] *vtr F* to fail* (a candidate in an exam).

retourne [rəturn] *nf F* **avoir les bras à la retourne**/*P* **les avoir à la retourne**, to be lazy*/to be (bone) idle; to be work-shy. (*Voir* **bras 1**)

retourné [rəturne] *a* **1.** *P* **les avoir retournés**, to be lazy*. (*Voir* **bras 1**) **2.** *F* **être tout(e) retourné(e)**, to be all of a dither/to be all shook up.

retourner [rəturne] **I** *vtr F* (*bouleverser*) to shake/to shock (s.o.); **ça m'a tout retourné(e)**, that gave me quite a turn. (*Voir* **crêpe 1**) **II** *vi P* **en retourner**, to take to prostitution/to go on the game. (*Voir* **sang**) **III** *vpr* **se retourner**

F **1. il sait se retourner,** he can take care of himself; he'll get by; he's never at a loss; **il saura bien se retourner,** he'll manage all right **2. s'en retourner (à un endroit),** to go back (to a place); to make one's way back; **il s'en retourna sans dire un mot,** he went off without saying a word.

rétro [retro] *nm* F (= *rétroviseur*) driving mirror/rear-view mirror.

retrousser [rətruse] *vtr* P **1.** to earn (money) (*esp* dishonestly); **il en a retroussé,** he made a penny or two **2. elle en retrousse,** she lives on her charms.

se retrouver [sərətruve] *vpr* F **1.** (*rentrer dans ses frais*) **s'y retrouver** (*i*) to break even (*ii*) to make a profit out of sth; to make something out of sth **3. on se retrouvera!** I'll get my own back!/I'll get even with you!

réussi [reysi] *a* F **c'est réussi, ça!** (*i*) a nice mess you've made of that! (*ii*) very clever!

réussir [reysir] F **I** *vi* **les huîtres ne me réussissent pas,** oysters don't agree with me; I'm allergic to oysters; **les vacances, ça ne lui a pas réussi,** his holiday/vacation didn't do him any good **II** *vtr* **réussir le coup** (*i*) to do the trick; **je n'ai pas réussi le coup,** I didn't bring it off (*ii*) (*iron*) to make a fine mess of it.

revenant [rəvnɑ̃] *nm* F stranger; **quel revenant vous faites!/mais c'est un revenant!** hello, stranger!/look who's back from the dead!

revendre [rəvɑ̃dr] *vtr* F **1. en revendre à qn,** to outwit s.o.; to take s.o. in **2. avoir de qch à revendre,** to have plenty to spare; **on en a à revendre,** we've got loads going begging.

revenez-y [rəvnezi] *nm inv* F **1. un revenez-y de tendresse,** a renewal of affection **2. il m'a joué un vilain tour, mais je l'attends au revenez-y,** he has played a dirty

trick on me, but (just) wait till he tries it again! **3.** (*plat, etc*) **avoir un (petit) goût de revenez-y,** to taste more-ish.

revenir [rəvnir] *vi* **1.** F **je n'en reviens pas!** I just can't get over it!/well, I never!/that's amazing! **2.** F **n'y revenez plus!** don't do it again! **3.** F **le voilà revenu sur l'eau,** he's found his feet again; **cette question est revenue sur l'eau/ sur le tapis,** this question has cropped up again **4.** P (= *venir*) **je reviens de le voir,** I've just seen him.

réverbère [reverber] *nm* P (*femme, prostituée*) **être sous les réverbères,** to be on the streets.

reviens [rəvjɛ̃] *nm* F **mon livre s'appelle reviens!** make sure you give my book back to me!

réviso [revizo] *nm&f* F (*pol*) revisionist.

revoici [rəvwasi] *prep* F **me revoici!** here I am again!/(it's) me again! **me revoici sans le sou!** here I am – broke again! **nous revoici à Noël,** it's Christmas again.

revoilà [rəvwala] *prep* F **le revoilà!** there he is again!

revoyure [rəvwajyr] *nf* P **à la (bonne) revoyure!** so long!/(I'll) be seeing you!/see you!

revue [rəvy] *nf* F **1. nous sommes de revue,** we'll meet again (before long) **2. je suis encore de la revue** (*i*) I'm (in) for it again/I'm for the high jump again (*ii*) I've been swindled again/I've been had again.

rez-de-chaussée [redʃose] *nm inv* F (*journ*) article in the lower half of the page.

se rhabiller [sərabije] *vpr* **1.** F (*comédien, joueur médiocre*) **il peut aller se rhabiller,** he might as well give up **2.** P **va te rhabiller!** shut up!*/belt up!/get lost!* **3.** P **se faire rhabiller,** to be swindled/done/had.

rhume [rym] *nm P* **prendre qch pour son rhume,** to be reprimanded*/to get hauled over the coals; **qu'est-ce qu'il a pris pour son rhume!** he didn't half get told off!/ he didn't half cop it!

ribambelle [ribɑ̃bɛl] *nf F* (*usu péj*) long string (of names, insults, etc); **toute une ribambelle de gosses,** a whole load/crowd/bunch of kids.

ribarbère [ribarbɛr] *nm A P* revolver*.

ribote [ribɔt] *nf F* (*a*) binge/ bender/booze-up; **faire (la) ribote,** to go on a spree/on a bender; to have a booze-up; **être en ribote** (*i*) to be drunk*/tight (*ii*) to be out on the town/to be on a binge.

riboter [ribɔte] *vi F* to go on a spree*; to have a booze-up.

riboteur, -euse [ribɔtœr, -øz] *F* **I** *a* boozy **II** *n* heavy drinker/ boozer.

ribouis [ribwi] *nm O P* **1.** boot; shoe (*esp* poor quality) **2.** cobbler **3.** foot*.

ribouldingue [ribuldɛ̃g] *nf O P* spree; **faire la ribouldingue,** to go on a spree*/to paint the town red.

ribouldinguer [ribuldɛ̃ge] *vi O P* = **faire la ribouldingue (ribouldingue).**

riboule [ribul] *nf P* **partir en riboule,** to go on a spree*/to go out on the town.

ribouler [ribule] *vi F* **ribouler des calots/des lotos/des quinquets,** to roll one's eyes (in amazement)/to goggle.

riboustin [ribustɛ̃] *nm P* revolver*.

ricain, -aine [rikɛ̃, -ɛn] *P* **I** *a* American*/Yank(ee) **II** *nmpl* **Ricains,** Americans/Yanks.

ric-à-rac [rikarak], **ric-à-ric** [rikarik], **ric et rac** [rikɛrak] *F* **I** *a* il est **ric-à-rac,** he's very strict **II** *adv* (*a*) punctually (*b*) strictly/ rigorously (*c*) to the last penny; **payer ric-à-rac,** to pay on the nail

(*d*) barely/narrowly; **c'était ric-à-rac,** it was touch and go/a bit tight.

richard, -arde [riʃar, -ard] *n F* rich* person/moneybags; **c'est un gros richard,** he's rich*/he's rolling in it/he's absolutely loaded.

riche [riʃ] **I** *a F* (*a*) excellent*; **une riche idée,** a splendid idea; **comme offre ce n'est pas riche,** it's not much of an offer (*b*) **ça fait riche!** it looks posh! **II** *adv phr V* **baiser qn à la riche,** to have anal sex* with s.o./to brown s.o.

ric-rac [rikrak] *a & adv F* = **ric-à-rac.**

rideau [rido] **I** *nm P* **1.** (*a*) (*voiture*) **tomber en rideau,** to break down/to conk out (*b*) (*pers*) **être en rideau,** to have come to a standstill/to be stuck **2. faire rideau/ passer au rideau,** to be done out of sth **II** *int P* (that's) enough!/that'll do!/cut it out!

rider, ridère [raidɛr] *P* **I** *a* smart/elegant/distinguished-looking; well-dressed **II** *nm* (*a*) elegantly dressed man (*b*) (man's) snazzy suit.

rien [rjɛ̃] **I** *indef pron F* (*a*) **ce n'est pas rien!** that's quite something! (*b*) **pour trois fois rien,** for next to nothing (*c*) **il sait deux fois rien,** he knows nothing about anything; he's dead ignorant (*d*) (*iron*) **rien que ça!** is that all! **II** *adv P* (*intensif*) very/not half; **elle est rien laide!** she's as ugly as sin! **elle est rien bath!** she's a stunner!/she's a bit of all right! **c'est rien bath!** it's simply terrific! **ce serait rien chouette!** that'd be great! **il fait rien froid!** it ain't half cold!/it's bloody cold! **il est rien salaud,** he's a real sod/a filthy bastard*/a son-of-a-bitch.

rien-du-tout [rjɛ̃dytu] *F* **I** *nf inv* woman of easy virtue*/pushover/tart **II** *nm inv* (*a*) a nobody/a nothing* (*b*) a bastard*/a nasty piece of work/a creep.

rif(e), riff(e) [rif] *nm P* **1.** (*a*) fire; **mettre/coller le rif(e) à qch,** to set fire to sth (*b*) light (from a lighter); **tu as du rif(e)?** (have you) got a light? **2.** (*a*) argument/quarrel*; **chercher du rif(e) à qn,** to pick a quarrel with s.o. (*b*) fight/brawl/punch-up (*esp* between rival gangs); **il cherchent le rif,** they're looking for trouble/for action **3.** (*mil*) war(fare); front; firing line; **aller/monter au rif(e),** to go off to war; to get into the thick of the fighting; to get into the firing line **4. mettre qn en rif(e),** to make s.o. angry*/to get s.o.'s goat (up) **5.** revolver*/shooter. (*Voir* **d'autor**; **sirop 9**)

rif(f)auder [rifode] *vtr P* (*a*) to set fire to/to burn (*b*) to cook/to heat up (food).

se riffer [sərife] *vpr P* to fight/to have a punch-up.

rifflette [riflɛt] *nf* = **riflette**.

rififi [rififi] *nm P* **1.** scuffle/brawl/free-for-all; **faire du rififi,** to fight/to have a punch-up; **chercher le rififi,** to look for trouble/for aggro **2.** money*.

riflard [riflar] *nm F* umbrella*/brolly.

rifle [rifl] *nm P* **1.** = **rif 1** (*a*) **2.** revolver*.

rifler [rifle] *vtr P* **1.** to set fire to (sth)/to burn (sth) **2.** to pick a quarrel* with (s.o.) **3.** to steal*; to rifle.

riflette [riflɛt] *nf P* **1.** revolver* **2.** (*mil*) war(fare); front (line); **partir pour la riflette,** to go off to war; to get into the thick of the fighting; to get into the firing line; **on en a marre de la riflette,** we're sick of the fighting. (*Voir* **rif 3**)

riflo(t) [riflo] *a P* elegant/expensively dressed; snazzy; **avoir des goûts de riflos,** to have expensive tastes.

rigolade [rigɔlad] *nf F* (*a*) fun/fun and games/lark; **une partie de rigo**lade, a bit of fun/a bit of a laugh; a rare old time; **tout ça, c'est de la rigolade,** that's just tomfoolery/that's just for fun; **prendre qch à la rigolade,** to laugh sth off; **il prend tout à la rigolade,** he won't take anything seriously/he thinks it's all one big joke; **ce n'est pas de la rigolade,** it's no laughing matter/there's nothing to laugh about (*c*) **c'est de la rigolade/c'est une vraie rigolade** (*i*) it's child's play/it's a cinch (*ii*) it's a right giggle/a real joke (*iii*) it's a real con.

rigolard, arde [rigɔlar, -ard] *F* **I** *a* (*a*) funny*/comical (*b*) full of fun; fond of a joke/a lark **II** *n* joker; **c'est un rigolard,** he likes a laugh.

rigolboche [rigɔlbɔʃ] *a P* = **rigolo 1.**

rigoler [rigɔle] *vi F* (*a*) to laugh*/to joke; **tu rigoles!** you're joking!/you're kidding!/you're not serious, are you? (*iron*) **tu me fais rigoler!** you slay me!/you make me laugh! **ne me fais pas rigoler,** don't make me laugh! **pour rigoler,** for fun/for a laugh; **je ne rigolais pas,** I was serious/I wasn't kidding/it's no joke; **histoire de rigoler un coup,** it's good for a laugh/for a joke (*b*) to have fun/to enjoy oneself; **ils ont bien rigolé hier soir,** they had a good time/a good laugh last night.

rigoleur, euse [rigɔlœr, -øz] *F* **I** *a* fond of a laugh/a joke/a lark **II** *n* joker; **c'est un rigoleur,** he's always ready (*i*) for a joke (*ii*) with a joke.

rigolo, ote [rigɔlo, -ɔt] *F* **I** *a* (*a*) funny*/comical; **c'était d'un rigolo!** it was a scream!/it was too funny for words!/it was a (real) killer! **ce n'était pas rigolo,** it was no joke; **c'est rigolo!** what a lark!/what a giggle! (*b*) odd/peculiar/surprising; **tiens, c'est rigolo ce truc-là,** that thing's a bit odd/a bit funny (*c*) **fille rigolote,** good-time girl **II** *n* **1.** joker/comedian; **c'est un rigolo,**

ton père, your father's a real scream **III** *nm* **1.** revolver*/gun/shooter/piece **2.** (burglar's) jemmy/*NAm* jimmy.

rigouillard [rigujar] *a A P* = **rigolard 1.**

rigoustin [rigustɛ̃] *nm O P* revolver*/gun.

rikiki [rikiki] *a&nm F* = **riquiqui.**

rilax(e) [rilaks] *a P* = **relax(e).**

rima [rima] *nm P* (*verlan de mari*) husband*/the old man.

rince [rɛ̃s] *nf P* **remettre la rince,** to have another round of drinks; to set them up again.

rincé [rɛ̃se] *a P* **1.** exhausted*/washed out **2.** (*a*) done for (*b*) cleaned out (at gambling).

rince-cochon [rɛ̃skɔʃɔ̃] *nm inv P* white wine and mineral water drunk to relieve a hangover; = hair of the dog.

rincée [rɛ̃se] *nf F* **1.** heavy shower; **j'ai pris une rincée,** I got caught in a downpour/I got soaked **2.** thrashing/beating*(-up).

rince-gueule [rɛ̃sgœl] *nm inv P* (after dinner) liqueur *or* spirits.

rincer [rɛ̃se] *vtr* **1.** *F* to drench; **se faire rincer,** to get drenched/soaked (in the rain); **2.** *P* to clean (s.o.) out (at gambling); **se faire rincer,** to get cleaned out/to get taken to the cleaners **3.** *P* to stand (s.o.) a drink; **c'est lui qui rince,** the drinks are on him/he's buying **4.** to thrash (s.o.)/to beat (s.o.) up*; **se faire rincer,** to get beaten up/to get worked over **5.** *P* **se rincer les amygdales/le bec/la dalle,** to have a drink; to wet one's whistle; to knock back a drink. (*Voir* **œil 25**)

rincette [rɛ̃sɛt] *nf,* **rinçonnette** [rɛ̃sɔnɛt] *nf P* = **rince-gueule.**

rinçure [rɛ̃syr] *nf F* **de la rinçure (de bouteilles/de bidet),** poor quality *or* weak wine/beer; dishwater/cat's piss/gnat's piss.

ringard [rɛ̃gar] *P* **I** *a* (*pièce, etc*) poor-quality/hammy/mediocre; (*individu*) hopeless/useless; old-fashioned/behind-the-times/passé **II** *nm* **1.** mediocre actor/ham **2.** good-for-nothing; nonentity **3.** person with old-fashioned *or* out-of-date ideas, etc; square.

ringardise [rɛ̃gardiz] *nf P* old-fashioned ideas; squareness.

rip [rip] *nm P* **jouer rip,** to make off/to run away*/to skedaddle.

ripaille [ripɑj] *nf F* feast/spread/tuck-in; **faire ripaille,** to have a good blow-out.

ripailler [ripɑje] *vi F* to have a good blow-out.

ripailleur, euse [ripɑjœr, -øz] *n F* carouser/reveller*/merry-maker.

ripans [ripɑ̃] *nmpl P* **mettre les ripans,** to slam the brakes on/to put the anchors on.

ripatonner [ripatɔne] *vi P* **1.** to walk*/to go by Shanks's pony/to foot it **2.** to run away*/to beat it/to blow/to hop it.

ripatons [ripatɔ̃] *nmpl P* **1.** (old, well-worn) boots/shoes **2.** feet*/dogs/tootsies; **jouer des ripatons/se tirer des ripatons,** to run away*/to leg it.

ripe [rip] *nm P* = **rip.**

riper [ripe] *vi P* **1.** to slip away/to slope off; to make oneself scarce; **allez ripez!** clear off! **2.** to steal*/to pinch **3.** to clean (s.o.) out; to rip (s.o.) off.

ripincelle [ripɛ̃sɛl] *nm* (*mil*) *F* = **riz-pain-sel.**

ripolin [ripɔlɛ̃] *nm P* make-up/face-paint/war-paint.

ripopée [ripɔpe] *nf F* **1.** weak wine; poor-quality wine; slops/dishwater **2.** hotchpotch/hash-up (of ideas, theories, etc).

ripopo [ripɔpo] *a P* (*sport*) badly played/fluffed (shot, etc).

ripou [ripu] a P (verlan de **pourri**) **elle n'est pas ripou,** she's not bad/ she's a bit of all right.

riquette [rikɛt] nf P diarrhoea*/ Bombay cruds/the runs.

riquiqui [rikiki] F I a (portion, etc) undersized/puny/measly; **il est tout riquiqui,** he's only pint-sized II nm **1.** undersized* person/little squirt/shrimp/little runt **2.** (the) little finger/pinkie **3.** poor-quality brandy or spirits* (of any kind)/ rotgut; **un petit verre de riquiqui,** a little drop of spirits/a wee dram.

rire [rir] vi **1.** F un(e) ... **pour rire,** an apology for a ... **2.** P **c'était pour de rire,** it was only my little joke; it was only (done) for a laugh.

rital, pl **-als** [rital] P (péj) I a Italian II nm **Rital,** Italian*/Eye-tie/Wop.

ritournelle [riturnɛl] nf F **1. c'est toujours la même ritournelle** (i) he's always harping on the same string (ii) it's always the same old story **2.** (publicité) jingle.

rivette [rivɛt] nf P (active) homo-sexual*.

rixer [rikse] vi P (CB) to stop trans-mitting/QRX.

riz-pain-sel [ripɛ̃sɛl] nm inv F (mil) soldier or officer in the French Army Service Corps.

roberts [robɛr] nmpl P breasts*/ boobs/tits; **roberts de chez Miche-lin,** falsies; **une belle paire de roberts,** a nice pair of knockers.

robine [robin] nf FrC P methylated spirits/meths.

robinet [robinɛ] nm **1.** F **tenir le robinet,** to hold the purse-strings **2.** F **ouvrir le robinet,** to start cry-ing/to turn on the waterworks **3.** F **fermer le robinet,** to shut up*/to put a sock in it **4.** F (pers) **un robinet d'eau tiède,** a drivelling bore* **5.** V **robinet d'amour,** penis*.

robineux [robinø] nm FrC P drunk(ard)*/wino/alky/meths drinker.

rodéo [rodeo] nm P (collective) rape/gangbang.

rôdeuse [rodøz] nf F prostitute*/ street-walker/hooker/hustler.

rogne [roɲ] nf F **1.** bad temper*; **être en rogne,** to be in a bad tem-per/in a huff; **se mettre/se ficher/**P **se foutre en rogne,** to get angry*/to get hot under the collar/to get shirty; **mettre/ficher/**P **foutre qn en rogne,** to make s.o. angry*; **ça me fiche en rogne,** that makes me see red/that really makes me mad **2.** **chercher rogne/des rognes à qn,** to pick a quarrel* with s.o.

rogner [roɲe] I vi F **1.** to be angry*/to be in a temper **2.** to grumble*/to grouse II vtr F **rogner les ailes à qn,** to clip s.o.'s wings. (Voir **os 10**)

rogneux, -euse [roɲø, -øz] F I a angry*/furious/in a temper II n bad-tempered person/crosspatch.

rognonnement [roɲɔnmɑ̃] nm F grumbling*/grousing/griping.

rognonner [roɲɔne] vi F to grum-ble*/to grouse/to gripe.

rognons [roɲɔ̃] nmpl V testicles*/ nuts/balls.

rognure [roɲyr] nf P (low-class) prostitute*/slag/cheap tart.

rogomme [rogɔm] nm P spirits*/ liquor/booze; **voix de rogomme,** husky/beery voice (of a drunkard).

roi [rwa] nm F **1. un morceau de roi,** a pretty woman*/a dish/a tasty piece **2. travailler pour le roi de Prusse,** to work for nothing/to do sth for love/to get nothing out of it **3. aller où le roi va à pied/va seul/ va en personne; aller voir le roi de Prusse,** to go to the WC*/to the loo/NAm to the bathroom; to have a look at the plumbing **4.** (a) **le roi des fromages/des vins,** a really good cheese/wine (b) **le roi des**

imbéciles, a complete idiot*/a prize idiot; **c'est le roi des cons**, he's a complete arsehole/*NAm* asshole; he's a real nurd/jerk; **le roi des salauds**, a first-class bastard*/a real sod.

romaine [rɔmɛn] *nf P* **être bon comme la romaine** (*i*) to be done for/to be certain to get it in the neck (*ii*) to be pushed into sth unpleasant/to get lumbered with sth.

romance [rɔmãs] *nf P* **piquer une romance**, to go to sleep*/to go to bed*.

romano [rɔmano] *nm F* gipsy/romany/gippo.

rombier [rɔ̃bje] *nm P* fellow*/chap/guy/bloke.

rombière [rɔ̃bjɛr] *nf P* (*péj*) **1.** (*a*) woman* (*b*) pretentious and ridiculous (middle-aged) woman (*c*) **une vieille rombière**, an old hag/an old bag/an old trout/an old bat **2.** brothel owner/madam.

roméo [rɔmeo] *nm F* (= *rhum et eau*) rum and water (drink).

rompre [rɔ̃pr] *vtr P* **ça me les rompt**, it gets on my (bloody) nerves/on my tits. (*Voir* **tête 5**)

ronchon [rɔ̃ʃɔ̃] *nm&f inv F* grumbler/grouser.

ronchonneau, *pl* **-eaux** [rɔ̃ʃono] *nm F* = **ronchon(n)ot 2.**

ronchonnement [rɔ̃ʃɔnmã] *nm F* grumbling*/grousing/griping.

ronchonner [rɔ̃ʃɔne] *vi F* to grumble*/to grouse/to gripe.

ronchon(n)ot [rɔ̃ʃɔno] *nm F* **1.** (*mil*) griping (old) army officer **2.** grumbler/grouser/griper.

rond [rɔ̃] **I** *a P* drunk*; **rond comme une barrique/comme une bille/comme un boudin/comme une boule**, dead drunk*/as high as a kite; **il est fin rond**, he's as pissed as a newt **II** *adv F* **ça ne tourne pas rond**, it's not working properly;

there's sth wrong/up; **elle ne tourne plus rond**, she's potty/crackers; she's off her head; she's a bit touched **III** *nm* **1.** *F* **faire les ronds de jambe**, to crawl/to bow and scrape_ **2.** *P* **(en) être/(en) rester comme deux ronds de flan**, to be flabbergasted*/dumbfounded/struck dumb/knocked out (by sth) **3.** *P* **il n'a pas le/un rond**, he's penniless*/he's completely broke; **j'ai plus un rond sur moi**, I'm completely skint; **je l'ai eu pour pas un rond**, I got it for nothing **4.** *P* **il n'est pas ambitieux pour un rond/pour deux ronds**, he's not the least bit ambitious **5.** *F* **faire des ronds dans l'eau**, to be idle/to twiddle one's thumbs **6.** **le rond/la pièce de dix ronds**, anus*/ring/ring-piece/round eye; **donner/prendre/refiler du rond**, to be a homosexual*/to be an arse-bandit. (*Voir* **baver II**)

rond-de-cuir [rɔ̃dkɥir] *nm F* (*a*) clerk (*esp* in government service); pen-pusher; **vieux rond-de-cuir**, old stick-in-the-mud (*b*) bureaucrat. (*pl* **ronds-de-cuir**)

rondelle [rɔ̃dɛl] *nf V* **1.** anus*/ring/ring-piece/round eye; **se manier/se magner la rondelle**, to hurry* (up)/to pull one's finger out/to shift one's arse/*NAm* ass; **être de la rondelle**, to be a homosexual*/to be an arse-man/*NAm* ass-man; **casser la rondelle**, to have anal sex*/to go in by the back door **2.** **baver sur les rondelles à qn**, to get on s.o.'s nerves/on s.o.'s tits; to give s.o. a pain in the arse.

rondibé [rɔ̃dibe] *nm V* **rondibé (du radada)** = **rondelle 1.**

rondin [rɔ̃dɛ̃] *nm* **1.** *V* turd; **poser un rondin**, to defecate*/to (have a) crap **2.** *pl P* breasts*/tits.

rondir [rɔ̃dir] **I** *vtr P* to make (s.o.) drunk*/to tie one on (s.o.) **II** *vpr* **se rondir** *P* to get drunk*/to have one over the eight.

rondouillard, -arde [rɔ̃dujar, -ard] *F* **I** *a* (small and) fat; plump/ chubby/podgy/dumpy **II** *n* fat person*/fatso/fatty.

rondouille [rɔ̃duj] *a F* = **rondouillard I.**

ronflaguer [rɔ̃flage] *vi P* **1.** to snore **2.** to sleep.

ronfle [rɔ̃fl] *nf P* sleep; **aller à la ronfle,** to go to sleep*.

ronfler [rɔ̃fle] *vi P* **1.** (*a*) to sleep (*b*) **ronfler avec qn,** to sleep with s.o./to go to bed with s.o. **2.** il **faut que ça ronfle,** we must speed things up; we must get things moving; we'd better pull our finger(s) out; **où ça ronfle,** where it's at.

ronflette [rɔ̃flɛt] *nf P* sleep/ snooze/doze/nap; **faire/piquer/ pousser une ronflette,** to have forty winks/to get some shut-eye.

ronfleur [rɔ̃flœr] *nm P* **1.** telephone*/blower **2. envoyer le ronfleur à qn,** to tip s.o. off/to give s.o. the low-down.

ronflon [rɔ̃flɔ̃] *nm P* = **ronflette.**

rongeur [rɔ̃ʒœr] *nm P* (*a*) taximeter/clock (*b*) taxi-driver/cabbie (*c*) taxi/cab.

ronibus [rɔnibys] *nm P* bus.

roploplo(t)s [rɔplɔplo] *nmpl P* breasts*/tits/knockers.

Rosalie [rozali] *nf P* (*mil*) bayonet/ toothpick/(meat-)skewer.

rosbif [rɔzbif] *P* **I** *a* English **II** *nm* Englishman*/woman; limey; **les rosbifs,** the Brits.

rose [roz] **I** *a F* **1. ce n'est pas bien rose, cette histoire-là,** it's a pretty horrific story **2. elle n'avait pas la vie bien rose,** she didn't have an easy time of it; her life wasn't exactly a bed of roses **II** *nf* **1.** *F* **cela ne sent pas la rose/les roses,** that doesn't smell at all nice; that smells nasty/that stinks **2.** *F* **envoyer qn sur les roses,** to send s.o. packing*/to tell s.o. to clear off **3.** *F* **ce n'était pas des roses,** it

wasn't all plain sailing **4.** *P* **tante rose,** period*. (*Voir* **bouton 1**; **eau 9**; **feuille 4**; **pot 8**)

roseaux [rozo] *nmpl P* **se faire couper les roseaux,** to have one's hair cut.

rosette [rozɛt] *nf V* anus*; amateur **de rosette,** (active) homosexual*.

rossard [rosar] **I** *a P* **1.** lazy*/ idle **2.** spiteful/catty/bitchy **II** *nm P* = **rosse II 1, 2.**

rosse [rɔs] **I** *a P* **1.** (*a*) objectionable/beastly/nasty/horrid (person); **professeur rosse,** swine of a teacher (*b*) (*pers, esp femme*) catty/bitchy (*c*) smutty (song, etc); low-down/ rotten/lousy (trick, etc) **II** *nf P* **1.** objectionable person/rotter/ toad/nasty piece of work/(mean) bastard* **2.** *O* (*mauvais cheval*) old nag.

rossée [rose] *nf F* **une (bonne) rossée,** a thrashing/a beating*(-up)/a good hiding.

rosser [rose] *vtr F* **rosser qn,** to thrash s.o./to beat s.o. up*/to give s.o. a good hiding; to lick s.o./to hammer s.o.

rosserie [rɔsri] *nf F* **1.** nastiness/ rottenness/bitchiness **2.** (*a*) nasty/ dirty/rotten trick; smutty story; double cross; **faire une rosserie à qn,** to do the dirty on s.o. (*b*) snide/spiteful/catty/bitchy remark.

rossignol [rɔsiɲɔl] *nm F* **1.** unsaleable article/white elephant/ piece of junk; (*voiture*) bottler/ palm-tree/square-wheeler; **des rossignols,** old (unsaleable) stock; **écouler/passer un rossignol à qn,** to sell s.o. a pup; **on vous a refilé un rossignol,** you've been had/done **2.** skeleton key/picklock/screw **3.** bung (of barrel) **4. rossignol à glands,** pig.

rot [ro] *nm P* belch/burp; **faire/ lâcher un rot,** to belch/to burp; **faire faire son rot à un bébé,** to burp a baby/to get a baby's wind up.

rotations [rɔtasjɔ̃] *nfpl P* **avoir des rotations,** to belch/to burp.

roter [rɔte] *vi P* **1.** to belch/to burp **2. en roter** (*i*) to have a rough/tough time of it/to go through the mill (*ii*) to be angry*/furious/all steamed up (*iii*) to work* hard/to slave away (at sth) **3. en roter des ronds de chapeau,** to be flabbergasted*/to be struck all of a heap.

roteur, euse [rɔtœr, -øz] *P* **I** *n* (*pers*) belcher **II** *nf* **roteuse,** bottle of champagne*.

rôti [roti] **I** *nm F* **s'endormir sur le rôti** (*i*) to dawdle over one's work/to fall asleep on the job (*ii*) to be half-hearted in one's love-making/to have one's mind on other things/to fall asleep on the job **II** **a P être rôti** (*i*) to be done for; to have lost one's reputation/one's credit; **tout est rôti,** it's no go (*ii*) to have been betrayed/to have been sold down the river.

rotin [rɔtɛ̃] *nm F* **je n'ai pas un rotin,** I'm penniless*/flat broke; I haven't got a bean.

rôtissoir [rotiswar] *nm,* **rôtissoire** [rotiswar] *nf P* crematorium.

rotoplo(t)s [rɔtɔplo] *nmpl P* breasts*/tits/knockers.

rototos [rɔtɔto] *nmpl P* **1.** breasts*/knockers **2. faire des rototos,** to belch/to burp.

rotules [rɔtyl] *nfpl F* **être sur les rotules,** to be exhausted*/to be on one's last legs/to be fagged out; **mettre qn sur les rotules,** to exhaust* s.o./to wear s.o. out.

roubignolles [rubiɲɔl] *nfpl V* testicles*/balls/nuts; **j'en ai plein les roubignolles,** I'm fed up* to the back teeth (with it)/I've had a bellyful (of it).

roublard, arde [rublar, -ard] *F* **I** *a* crafty/cunning/artful (person); **elle est roublarde,** she's up to every trick **II** *n* crafty person; artful/cunning devil; **un fin roublard,** a cunning old fox; **c'est un roublard,** he knows a trick or two; he's a wily old bird/he's a crafty (old) beggar.

roublarderie [rublardəri] *nf F* = **roublardise 1.**

roublardise [rublardiz] *nf F* **1.** cunning/craftiness **2.** piece of cunning/of trickery; sly/crafty/cunning trick.

rouchie [ruʃi] *nf P* (low-class) prostitute*/cheap tart/scrubber/floozy.

roucouler [rukule] *vi F* (*amoureux*) to bill and coo.

roudoudou [rududu] *nm O* **1.** *F* (kind of) sweet/*NAm* candy **2.** *P* fellow/chap*/guy/blighter; **un vieux roudoudou,** an old fogey*.

roue [ru] *nf F* **1. mettre des bâtons dans les roues,** to put a spoke in s.o.'s wheel; to throw a spanner in the works **2.** (*cyclisme*) **prendre la roue de qn/être dans la roue de qn/sucer la roue de qn,** to follow s.o. closely/to get right behind s.o./to be on s.o.'s tail **3. la cinquième roue du carrosse/de la charrette,** an entirely useless person/thing; (*dans une entreprise*) passenger **4. être dans la roue,** to be with it/to know the ropes **5. en roue libre,** laid-back; free-wheeling **6. il est parti sur les chapeaux de roue,** he left in a big rush.

rouflaquette [ruflakɛt] *nf F* **1.** kiss curl **2.** *pl* side-whiskers/side-burns.

rouge [ruʒ] *nm* **1.** *F* **un coup de rouge,** a glass of red wine; **gros rouge,** coarse red wine/plonk **2.** *F* red/communist/commie **3.** *P* **envoyer le rouge,** to shoot **5.** *P* **mettre le rouge** (*i*) to break off with s.o. (*ii*) to create a disturbance.

rougeole [ruʒɔl] *nf P* **avoir la rougeole,** to be a member of the Legion of Honour.

rougnotter [ruɲɔte] *vi P* to stink*/to smell (to high heaven).

rouillarde [rujard], **rouille** [ruj] *nf P* bottle (of wine, etc).

rouillé [ruje] *a P* être tombée sur un clou rouillé, to be pregnant*.

rouiller [ruje] *vi P* (*prostituée*) to be without work/without a client; to be resting.

roulant [rulɑ̃] **I** *a F* very funny* (joke, sight, etc); **c'est roulant!** it's a scream!/it's a killer! **il est roulant!** he's a real scream! **II** *nm* **1.** *F* travelling salesman/rep **2.** *F* **les roulants** (*i*) train crews (*ii*) lorry *or* bus crews, etc **3.** *P* taxi/cab.

roulante [rulɑ̃t] *nf* **1.** *F* (*mil*) field kitchen **2.** *P* car* **3.** *pl P* **roulantes**, (game of) bowls.

rouleau, *pl* **-eaux** [rulo] *nm* **1.** *F* (*a*) être au bout de son rouleau, to be at the end of one's tether (*b*) c'est le bout du rouleau pour lui, it's all up with him/it's curtains for him **2.** *pl V* rouleaux, testicles*; avoir mal aux rouleaux, to have VD*; baver sur les rouleaux à qn/casser les rouleaux à qn, to get on s.o.'s nerves/on s.o.'s wick/on s.o.'s tits; to give s.o. a pain in the arse/ *NAm* ass **3.** *F* changer de rouleau (*i*) to change one's tune (*ii*) to change the subject; change(z) de rouleau! put another record on!

roulée [rule] **I** *af F* (*femme*) bien roulée, with a good figure/with curves in all the right places/well-stacked **II** *nf* **1.** *F* hand-rolled cigarette*/roll-up **2.** *P* donner une roulée à qn, to beat s.o. up*/to work s.o. over.

rouler [rule] **I** *vtr* **1.** *F* **rouler qn** (*i*) to swindle*/to rook/to diddle/to do s.o.; **se faire rouler,** to be conned/done/had; **il m'a roulé de mille francs,** he did me out of a thousand francs (*ii*) (*vaincre*) to beat/to lick/to hammer s.o. **2.** *F* **rouler les cafés,** to go from one café/bar to another; to go pub-crawling **3.** *F* **en rouler une,** to (hand-)roll a cigarette* **4.** *P* **se les rouler,** to (sit about and) twiddle one's thumbs/to have a cushy time/to do damn all. (*Voir* **bosse 2; caisse 10; escalope 1; mécanique 2; patin 1; pelle 2; saucisse**) **II** *vi F* **1.** **ça roule!** (*i*) it's going fine/things are going well/everything's OK (*ii*) it's a deal!/I'm on! **ça roule?** how goes it?/how's tricks?/everything OK? **ça roule entre eux,** they get on (very) well together/they hit it off well **2.** **rouler (un peu partout),** to knock about (the world)/to be a rolling stone; **j'ai roulé,** I've been around/I've knocked about (a bit)/I've been places. (*Voir* **bosse 2** (*a*)) **3.** to lead a fast life **4.** to throw the dice/to roll the bones **5.** to talk a lot/too much; to shoot one's mouth off; to sound off. (*Voir* **danseuse; jante 2; or 6**) **III** *vpr se* **rouler** *F* **se rouler (par terre),** to laugh* uproariously/to fall about laughing; **il y a de quoi se rouler (de rire),** it's a real scream/a killer. (*Voir* **crotte I 4**)

roule-ta-bille [rultabij] *nm inv,* **roule-ta-bosse** [rultabɔs] *F* (*pers*) rolling stone/drifter.

rouletaille [rultaj] *nf P* (game of) roulette.

roulette [rulɛt] *nf* **1.** *F* dentist's drill **2.** *F* **ça marche/ça va comme sur des roulettes,** everything's going/working smoothly; things are going like clockwork/like a house on fire **3.** *P* **les roulettes; les vaches/les guignols à roulettes** (*i*) policemen* on bicycles/cycle cops (*ii*) police motorcyclists/cycle cops.

rouleur, euse [rulœr, -øz] **I** *n F* **1.** cheat/diddler/con artist/swindler*; s.o. who always gets the best of the bargain **2.** (*pers*) (*a*) rolling stone/drifter (*b*) **rouleur de cafés/de cabarets,** pub-crawler **3.** s.o. who talks too much/who shoots his mouth off **4.** **rouleur**

(de mécaniques), s.o. with superior airs/conceited person; show-off*/ pose(u)r **II** *nf P* (low-class) prostitute*/(cheap) tart/scrubber/slut **III** *nf FrC P* hand-rolled cigarette*/ roll-up.

roulottage [rulɔtaʒ] *nm F* stealing from parked vehicles.

roulotte [rulɔt] *nf F* **vol/P chourave à la roulotte,** stealing from parked vehicles; **voleur/P chouraveur à la roulotte,** thief* who steals from parked vehicles.

roulotter [rulɔte] *vi F* = **rouler II 1, 5.**

roulottier [rulɔtje] *nm F* thief* who steals from parked vehicles.

roulure [rulyr] *nf P* (*péj*) prostitute*/tart/slut.

roupane [rupan] *nf P* **1.** (*a*) (woman's) dress (*b*) clothing **2.** (town) policeman's uniform.

roupanner [rupane] *vtr P* **se les roupanner,** to twiddle one's thumbs/to do damn-all.

roupes [rup] *nfpl,* **roupettes** [rupet] *nfpl* **1.** *P* car wheels **2.** *V* testicles*/balls.

roupie [rupi] *nf P* **1.** drop of running mucus/snot; dewdrop; **avoir la roupie,** to have a runny nose **2. roupies de café,** coffee slops/coffee dregs **3.** (*a*) **de la roupie de sansonnet/de singe,** worthless* stuff/ rubbish/tripe; **c'est de la roupie de sansonnet,** it's strictly for the birds; it's a load of old rubbish (*b*) **c'est pas de la roupie de sansonnet/de singe,** it's not bad; it's none of your cheap rubbish **4. une vieille roupie,** an old hag/bat/trout.

roupignolles [rupiɲɔl] *nfpl V* testicles*.

roupillade [rupijad] *nf F* nap/ doze/snooze/forty winks.

roupiller [rupije] *vi F* to (go to) sleep*/to have a kip/to get some shut-eye.

roupilleur, -euse [rupijœr, -øz]

F **I** *a* sleepy/drowsy **II** *n* sleeper/snoozer.

roupillon [rupijɔ̃] *nm F* sleep/nap/ snooze; **piquer un roupillon,** to have forty winks/to grab some shut-eye/ to have a kip.

roupillonner, roupionner [rupijɔne, rupjɔne] *vi F* = **roupiller.**

rouquemoute [rukmut] *nm&f P* **1.** redhead/carrot-top **2.** (rough) red wine/plonk.

rouquin, -ine [rukɛ̃, -in] **I** *a F* red-haired/carroty(-haired)/ginger- (-haired) **II** *nm&f* redhead/carrot-top/copper-nob **III** *nm P* (rough) red wine.

rouquinos [rukinos] *a P* red. (*Voir* **bada 1**)

rouscaille [ruskaj] *nf P* (*a*) complaint/grouse/beef (*b*) grumbling*/ bellyaching/beefing/bitching.

rouscailler [ruskaje] *vi P* to grumble*/to grouse/to bitch/to gripe/to bellyache/to beef.

rouscailleur, -euse [ruskajœr, -øz] *P* **I** *a* grouchy/(always) grumbling* **II** *n* grumbler/grouser/bellyacher/grump.

rouspétance [ruspetɑ̃s] *nf F* (*a*) resistance/protest/opposition; **pas de rouspétance!** don't answer back! **faire de la rouspétance,** to be obstreperous/to moan about sth (*b*) grumbling*/grousing/griping/bellyaching.

rouspéter [ruspete] *vi F* (*a*) to resist/to protest/to show fight; **il n'a pas rouspété,** he went like a lamb (*b*) to grumble*/to grouse/to gripe/to bellyache.

rouspéteur, -euse [ruspetœr, -øz] *F* **I** *a* (*a*) quarrelsome*; obstreperous (*b*) grouchy **II** *n* (*a*) quarrelsome person; obstreperous person; difficult person (*b*) grumbler/grouser/griper/bellyacher.

rouspignolles [ruspiɲɔl] *nfpl V* testicles*. (*Voir* **roubignolles**)

Rousqui [ruski] *nm P* = **Rousski.**

rousse [rus] *nf P* **1.** *coll* la rousse, the police*/the law/the fuzz; **un mec de la rousse,** a policeman*/a rozzer **2. faire de la rousse = rousser.**

rousser [ruse] *vi P* to grumble*/to grouse/to gripe/to bellyache.

roussi [rusi] *nm F* **ça sent le roussi,** there's trouble brewing; there's danger ahead; we're in for a rough time.

roussin [rusɛ̃] *nm P* **1.** policeman* **2.** police informer*; (copper's) nark.

Rousski [ruski] *nm P* Russian*/Russki.

roustaflettes [rustaflɛt] *nfpl V* testicles*.

roustasse [rustas] *nf,* **rouste** [rust] *nf,* **roustée** [ruste] *nf P* severe thrashing/good hiding/beating*(-up); **filer/flanquer une roustasse à qn,** to beat s.o. up*/to give s.o. a good hiding/to thrash s.o.

rouster [ruste] *vtr P* to thrash (s.o.)/to beat (s.o.) up*.

rousti [rusti] *a P* done for/ruined.

roustir [rustir] *vtr P* **1.** to swindle* (s.o.)/to cheat (s.o.)/to diddle (s.o.) **2.** to steal*; to rob **3.** (*rôtir*) to burn/to roast.

roustisseur, euse [rustisœr, -øz] *n P* **1.** cheat/swindler*/con artist **2.** sponger/scrounger.

roustissure [rustisyr] *nf P* **de la roustissure/des roustissures,** worthless* stuff/trash/junk/tripe.

roustons [rustɔ̃] *nmpl V* testicles*/balls; **baver sur les roustons à qn,** to get on s.o.'s nerves/on s.o.'s wick; to give s.o. a pain in the arse.

routard [rutar] *nm P* traveller on foot; hiker.

routier [rutje] *nm F* **vieux routier,** old campaigner/old trouper/old stager/old hand.

routière [rutjɛr] *nf P* tart/floozie/tramp.

royalement [rwajalmɑ̃] *adv F* (*a*) s'amuser royalement, to enjoy oneself immensely/to have a whale of a time (*b*) je m'en fiche royalement, I couldn't care less* (about it)/I couldn't give two hoots for it.

RU [ɛry] *nm F* (*abbr* = *restaurant universitaire*) university restaurant/canteen. (*Voir* **restau**)

ruban [rybɑ̃] *nm P* **1.** road; **se taper un bon bout de ruban,** to walk a fair way/quite a distance **2.** pavement; (*prostituées*) **faire le ruban,** to walk the streets/to hustle; **il a envoyé sa femme sur le ruban,** he sent his wife out on the game/on the streets.

rubaner [rybane] *vi P* (*prostituées*) to walk the streets/to be on the game/to hustle.

rubis [rybi] *nm F* (*i*) *O* **faire rubis sur l'ongle,** to drink to the last drop (*ii*) **payer rubis sur l'ongle,** to pay (down) to the last halfpenny.

ruche [ryʃ] *nf P* **1.** nose* **2. se taper la ruche,** to eat* heartily/to tuck it away.

rudement [rydmɑ̃] *adv F* **c'était rudement bon,** it was jolly/awfully/damned good; **je suis rudement fatigué,** I'm dog-tired/I'm dead beat; **vous avez rudement bien fait,** you certainly did the right thing.

rupin, ine [rypɛ̃, -in] *P* **I** *a* (*a*) excellent*/first-rate (*b*) elegant/smart (*c*) luxurious/plush (*d*) (filthy) rich*/loaded/flush **II** *nm* rich* person; **c'est un rupin,** he's rolling in it; **les rupins,** the rich, the well-to-do; the filthy/the stinking rich.

rupiner [rypine] *vi P* **1.** to do well (in an exam); **il a rupiné,** he's done a good paper; he's given a good answer **2. ça rupine,** everything's fine/OK.

rupinos [rypinos], **rupinskoff**
[rypɛ̃skɔf] *a A P* = **rupin I.**
Ruscoff, Ruskoff [ruskɔf, -ry-]
nm P Russian*/Russki.

rustine [rystin] *nf P (pers)* bore*/
button-holer/leech.

S

sabbat [saba] *nm F* **faire un sabbat de tous les diables,** to make an awful lot of noise/a terrible racket; **c'est le sabbat déchaîné,** it's (all) hell let loose.

sable [sabl] *nm F* **1.** (*a*) **être (mis) sur le sable,** to be left high and dry/in the lurch (*b*) **être sur le sable** (*i*) to be penniless*/to be down and out (*ii*) to be out of work **2.** (*train*) **aller dans le sable,** to go off the rails/to be derailed.

sabler [sable] *vtr F* to drink*; **sabler le champagne,** to celebrate with champagne.

sableur, euse [sablœr, -øz] *n O F* hard drinker/drunkard*/boozer.

sabord [sabɔr] *nm* **1.** *F* **mille sabords!** shiver my timbers! **2.** *pl P* **les sabords,** eyes*/peepers; **coup de sabord,** searching glance; **donner un coup de sabord à qch,** to give sth the once over.

sabot [sabo] *nm* **1.** *F* **je vous vois/ je vous entends venir avec vos gros sabots,** I can see what you're after/ it's pretty obvious what your little game is/I can see you coming (a mile off) **2.** *F* (*a*) bungler/botcher (*b*) **travailler comme un sabot,** to botch/to bodge one's work; to bungle* sth; to botch/to louse things up (*c*) **jouer comme un sabot,** to play very badly/to be a hopeless player; **il joue comme un sabot,** he can't play for toffee **3.** *F* **raisonner comme un sabot,** to talk through one's hat **4.** *F* **dormir comme un sabot,** to sleep* like a log **5.** *F* **il ne reste pas/il n'a pas les deux pieds dans le même sabot** (*i*) he

doesn't remain idle for long/he gets on with the job (*ii*) he knows what's what; he knows the score; there are no flies on him **6.** *P* useless rubbish/junk; dud violin; old tub (of a ship); ramshackle old car*, bicycle, etc **7.** *P* **casser le sabot à une jeune fille,** to deflower a girl/to pick a girl's cherry. (*Voir* **foin 1**)

sabotage [sabɔtaʒ] *nm F* (*a*) botching/bodging/bungling (of work) (*b*) botched piece of work.

saboter [sabɔte] *F* **I** *vi* to botch one's work **II** *vtr* to botch/to bodge/to bungle* (work); to make a bad job of (sth)/to louse things up; to murder (a song, etc).

saboteur, euse [sabɔtœr, -øz] *n F* bungler/botcher/bodger.

saboulade [sabulad] *nf*, **saboulage** [sabulaʒ] *nm*, **saboulement** [sabulmɑ̃] *nm F* reprimand*/telling-off/dressing-down/ rocket.

sabouler [sabule] **I** *vtr F* to reprimand* (s.o.)/to tell (s.o.) off/to blow (s.o.) up/to give (s.o.) a rocket **II** *vpr* **se sabouler** *F* **1.** to dress up (in fine clothes) **2.** to make oneself up/to put on the war-paint.

sabre [sabr] *nm* **1.** *F* **le sabre et le goupillon,** the Army and the Church **2.** *V* penis*; **filer le/un coup de sabre,** to have sex*/to get one's end away.

sabrer [sabre] *vtr* **1.** *F* to bungle*/to botch/to bodge/to make a mess of (sth) **2.** *F* to make drastic cuts in/to cut great chunks out of (a play, a manuscript, etc) **3.** *F* to criticize* (s.o.)/to run (s.o.) down/ to knock (s.o.) **4.** *P* **sabrer une fille,** to have sex* with a girl; **il la sabre,** he's knocking her off; **sabrer qn à la verticale,** to give s.o. a knee trembler/to give s.o. a stand-up job/to have it (off) standing up **5.** *P* to kill*/to eliminate/to knock off/to bump off.

sabreur [sabrœr] *nm* **1.** *F* bungler/botcher/bodger; **sabreur (de besogne),** slapdash worker **2.** *P* fornicator.

sac [sak] *nm* **1.** *F* (*a*) (*i*) a hundred francs (*ii*) a thousand francs (*iii*) ten francs (*b*) **avoir le (gros) sac/ être au sac,** to be (stinking) rich*/ to have stacks (of money); **il y a le sac,** they've got pots of money/ they're absolutely loaded (*c*) **faire/ gagner son sac,** to make one's pile (*d*) **épouser un sac/le gros sac,** to marry a rich girl/to marry (into) money **2.** *F* **sac à viande** (*i*) shirt (*ii*) sleeping bag **3.** *F* (*pers*) **sac d'os,** bag of bones **4.** *F* **un sac (de nœuds),** a muddle **5.** *F* (*boxe*) **travailler le sac,** to practise with the punchbag **6.** *F* **sac percé,** spendthrift **7.** *F* **sac à vin,** drunkard*/ boozer/(old) soak/alky; **il en a plein son sac/il a son sac,** he's drunk*/he's had a skinful **8.** *F* **mettez ça dans votre sac!** put that in your pipe and smoke it! **9.** *F* **prendre qn la main dans le sac,** to catch s.o. red-handed/in the act/ with his hand in the till **10.** *F* **l'affaire est dans le sac/c'est dans le sac,** it's a (dead) cert*/it's in the bag **11.** *F* **cracher/éternuer dans le sac,** to be guillotined **12.** *F* **ficelé/ fichu comme mon sac,** dressed like a guy/tramp/scarecrow **13.** *F* **sac à malice,** bag of tricks; **avoir un nouvel expédient dans son sac à malice,** to have another card up one's sleeve; **c'est un sac à malice,** he's always got something else up his sleeve **14. vider son sac** (*i*) *F*

to get it off one's chest/to make a clean breast of it (*ii*) *P* to empty one's bowels/to have a clear-out **15.** *P* **il a reçu une raclée qui n'était pas dans un sac,** he got a hiding he won't forget in a hurry **16.** *P* stomach* **17.** *P* **sac à charbon/à carbi,** priest*. (*Voir* **tour I 1**)

sac(c)agne [sakaɲ] *nf*, **sac(c)aille** [sakɑj] *nf P* knife/ chiv/sticker; **donner un coup de sac(c)agne à qn,** to stab s.o.

sac(c)agner [sakaɲe] *vtr P* to stab/to knife/to chiv (s.o.).

sachets [saʃɛ] *nmpl P* socks.

sacouse [sakuz] *nm P* handbag.

sacquer [sake] **I** *vtr F* to dismiss* (s.o.)/to give s.o. the sack; **être sacqué,** to get the sack **II** *vpr* **se sacquer** *P* to go to bed*/to hit the sack.

sacré [sakre] *a P* damn(ed)/ bloody/*NAm* goddam(n); **votre sacré chien,** that bloody dog of yours/your blasted dog; **sacré imbécile!** you bloody fool! **il a un sacré pot,** he's damn lucky/he's got the luck of the devil; **c'est un sacré menteur,** he's one hell of a liar/a bloody liar; **sacré nom de Dieu!** (God) damn it (all)! **sacré nom d'un chien!/sacré nom de nom!** damn and blast (it)!/bloody hell! (*Voir* **baiseuse**)

sacrément [sakremɑ̃] *adv P* damn(ed)/bloody; **il fait sacrément froid,** it's damn(ed) cold/bloody cold/jolly cold.

sacrer [sakre] *vi O F* to curse and swear/to eff and blind.

sado [sado] *F* (= *sadique*) **I** *a* sadistic **II** *n* sadist.

safran [safrɑ̃] *nm O P* **aller au safran,** to throw one's money away/ to chuck one's money about.

sagouin, ine [sagwɛ̃, -in] *F* **I** *a* dirty/slovenly/filthy **II** *n* slovenly individual/filthy pig/slob; (*femme*) slut; (*homme*) swine/slob.

saïdi [saidi] *nm O P* (*péj*) North African/Arab* (*esp* living in France); wog. (*Voir* **sidi** 1)

saignant [sɛɲɑ̃] *a F* tough/full of grit.

saignée [seɲe] *nf F* **faire une saignée à qn,** to extort money from s.o./to bleed s.o.

saigner [seɲe] *vtr* **1.** *F* to extort money from (s.o.); **ils l'ont saigné à blanc,** they've cleaned him out/bled him white **2.** *P* (*a*) to kill* (s.o.) with a knife/to stab (s.o.) to death (*b*) **ça va saigner!** there's trouble brewing!/there's going to be trouble!/there'll be some aggro! (*Voir* **barder** 2)

saindoux [sɛ̃du] *nm P* (*mil*) corporal/corp.

sainfoin [sɛ̃fwɛ̃] *nm P* **en faire un sainfoin,** to make a lot of noise/to kick up (a hell of) a row.

saint [sɛ̃] *F* **I** *a* **toute la sainte journée,** the whole blessed day **II** *nm* (*a*) **prendre un air de petit saint,** to look as though butter wouldn't melt in one's mouth (*b*) **c'est un petit saint (de bois),** he's a little prig (*c*) **mieux vaut s'adresser à Dieu qu'à ses saints,** it's better to go straight to the top.

saint-bernard [sɛ̃bɛrnar] *nm inv F* **c'est un vrai saint-bernard,** he's a good Samaritan.

Saint-Crépin [sɛ̃krepɛ̃] *nm F* **1. prendre la voiture de Saint-Crépin,** to walk*/to go by Shanks's pony **2. tout son saint-crépin,** all one's worldly goods.

Saint-Cyr [sɛ̃sir] *Prnm F* (*d'après l'école militaire de Saint-Cyr*) **il ne faut pas être sorti de Saint-Cyr pour ...,** you don't have to be a genius to ....

Sainte-Anne [sɛ̃tan] *Prn* (*jadis hôpital psychiatrique à Paris*) *F* **être bon/fait/mûr pour Sainte-Anne,** to be raving mad*/to be fit for the loony-bin; **un échappé de Sainte-Anne,** a nutcase/a loony/a nutter.

Sainte-Barbe [sɛ̃tbarb] *nf F* **1. c'est la Sainte-Barbe,** it's an awful bore/a real drag. (*Voir* **barbe** 1) **2.** *O* **faire sauter la Sainte-Barbe,** to put fire to/to light the powder keg; **faites sauter la Sainte-Barbe!** let everything go to hell!

sainte-nitouche [sɛ̃tnituʃ] *nf F* **elle fait la sainte-nitouche/elle a l'air d'une sainte-nitouche/elle a un air de sainte-nitouche,** she looks as if butter wouldn't melt in her mouth.

Sainte-Touche [sɛ̃ttuʃ] *nf F* pay day.

Saint-Fric [sɛ̃frik] *nm P* money*/dough/ackers.

saint-frusquin [sɛ̃fryskɛ̃] *nm P* (*a*) **tout le saint-frusquin,** the whole bag of tricks*/the whole (damn) lot/the whole (kit and) caboodle (*b*) **tout son saint-frusquin,** all one's worldly goods.

Saint-Ger [sɛ̃ʒɛr] *Prn F* the Saint-Germain-des-Prés district (in Paris).

Saint-Glinglin [sɛ̃glɛ̃glɛ̃] *nf F* **à la Saint-Glinglin,** never (in a month of Sundays); when pigs (begin to) fly; **jusqu'à la Saint-Glinglin,** till the cows come home; till hell freezes over.

Saint-Jean [sɛ̃ʒɑ̃] *nm O F* **1. en Saint-Jean,** naked*/in the altogether/in one's birthday suit **2. employer toutes les herbes de la Saint-Jean,** to leave no stone unturned.

Saint-Lago [sɛ̃lago] *Prn P* (the prison of) Saint-Lazare.

Saint-Lundi [sɛ̃lœdi] *nf F* **faire la Saint-Lundi,** to take Monday off. (*Voir* **lundi**)

Saint-Martin [sɛ̃martɛ̃] *nf O F* **c'est la Saint-Martin,** it's the same thing; it comes to the same thing.

saint-truc [sɛ̃tryk] *nm P* **tout le saint-truc,** the whole bag of tricks*/the whole (kit and) caboodle/the works.

salade [salad] *nf* **1.** *F* **salade (russe),** jumble/mix-up/hotchpotch; (*journ*) bad copy/messy article; **mettre tout en salade,** to mix everything up/to get things into a muddle/to throw everything into confusion; **elle fait une salade!** she gets everything mixed up! **quelle salade!** what a mess!/what a muddle! **2.** *F* **vendre sa salade,** to work at one's job; to make a living **3.** *F* sales talk; **savoir vendre sa salade,** to have the gift of the gab/to have a good line in sales patter; **bon(n)ir sa salade à qn,** to hand out the sales patter/spiel/talk to s.o.; **encaisser des salades,** to swallow it **4.** *P* **faire un brin de salade,** to leave without paying; to welsh **5.** *P* **passer une salade à qn,** to reprimand* s.o./to tear s.o. off a strip **6.** *pl P* (*a*) scandal; backbiting (*b*) lies (*c*) nonsense*; **tout ça c'est des salades!** that's a lot of poppycock! **arrête/avale/rencaisse tes salades!** shut up*!/belt up!/give it a rest! (*Voir* **panier 3**)

saladier [saladje] *nm P* **1.** fast talker/line-shooter; glib salesman **2.** fusspot **3.** trouble-maker/stirrer **4.** mouth*; **taper du saladier,** to have foul breath.

salamalec [salamalɛk] *nm F* salaam; bowing and scraping; **faire des salamalecs à qn,** to bow and scrape to s.o.; to kowtow to s.o.

salaud, aude [salo, -od] *n P* **1.** *O* dirty/filthy individual; slut; **petit salaud!** you dirty little beast! **2.** bastard*/swine/sod; (*femme, rare*) bitch; **un beau salaud,** a dirty/filthy bastard; a shit; (*affectueusement*) **dis, mon salaud!** listen, you old bugger! **petit salaud!** you little bastard! **espèce de salaud!** you rotten swine!/you bastard! **le dernier des salauds/un salaud de première/le roi des salauds,** an out-and-out/a downright bastard*; **ça c'est un tour de salaud,** that's a lowdown/dirty trick.

salauderie [salodri] *nf P* **1.** dirty/mean/lowdown trick **2.** *usu pl* filthy language.

sale [sal] *a F* **1.** (*a*) rotten/nasty/dirty/filthy; **sale type,** bastard*/swine/nasty piece of work; **il a une sale gueule,** he looks really mean/he looks like a nasty piece of work; **sale bête,** dirty dog; **sale fasciste!** filthy Fascist!/Fascist pig! **c'est une sale affaire,** it's a dirty business; **il m'a joué un sale tour/un sale gag,** he did the dirty on me (*b*) rotten/beastly (weather) (*c*) (*prix, etc*) exorbitant/stiff (*d*) (*blague, histoire*) blue/spicy/fruity/dirty **2.** **c'est pas sale!** it's pretty good!/it's not bad at all! (*Voir* **coup 3**)

salé [sale] **I** *a F* (*a*) spicy (story); blue/dirty (joke); **en raconter de salées,** to tell smutty stories *or* jokes (*b*) (*prix*) exorbitant/stiff (*c*) (*peine de prison*) stiff/(unduly) severe **II** *nm P* **un (petit) salé/un morceau de salé,** a (newborn) baby; a little brat; **avoir un (petit) salé dans le tiroir,** to be pregnant*/to have a bun in the oven.

salement [salmã] *adv P* (very) badly; **être salement touché,** to be terribly badly wounded; **être salement fatigué,** to be exhausted*/to be dead-beat; **salement difficile,** bloody difficult; **ça va nous rendre salement service,** it'll be jolly useful.

saler [sale] *vtr* **1.** *F* (*a*) to overcharge/to fleece*/to rip off (customers) (*b*) **saler la note,** to stick it on/to bump up (the bill); **on nous a salés,** we were stung/we had to pay through the nose **2.** **saler qn,** to be harsh with s.o./tough on s.o.; **on l'a salé,** he got a stiff sentence/they threw the book at him.

saleté [salte] *nf* **1.** *F* (*a*) dirty trick; **faire une saleté à qn,** to do the dirty on s.o. (*b*) smutty remark; blue/dirty joke **2.** *P* rotten bastard*/rotten sod/nasty piece of work/*NAm* son of a bitch.

salière [saljɛr] *nf F* hollow above the collar bone/salt cellar.

saligaud, aude [saligo, -od] *n P* = **salaud, aude.**

salingue [salɛ̃g] *P* **I** *a* dirty/filthy **II** *n* filthy/disgusting person.

salir [salir] *vtr P* **tu la salis!** you're exaggerating!/you're laying it on (a bit) thick! (*Voir* **nez 5**)

salisson [salisɔ̃] *nf F* (*dial*) dirty/untidy young girl.

salivard [salivar] *nm O F* chatterbox*/gasbag/windbag.

salive [saliv] *nf F* **1.** **perdre/gaspiller/user sa salive,** to waste one's breath **2.** **dépenser beaucoup de salive,** to talk a lot*/to talk nineteen to the dozen **3.** **avaler/ravaler sa salive,** to be stumped (for an answer).

salle [sal] *nf P* **1.** **salle à manger,** mouth*; **salle à manger démontable,** set of false teeth **2.** **des plaisanteries de salle de garde,** dirty/blue jokes. (*Voir* **tabourets**)

saloir [salwar] *nm P* **mettre le lard/la viande au saloir,** to go to bed*.

salon(n)ard, arde [salɔnar, -ard] *n F* social climber; s.o. who frequents social functions in the hope of making profitable contacts.

salonnier [salɔnje] *nm F* (*journ*) journalist who specializes in the arts *or* social functions, etc.

salop [salo] *nm,* **salopard** [salɔpar] *nm P* (dirty) bastard*/swine/sod/NAm son of a bitch. (*Voir* **salaud 2**)

saloparde [salɔpard] *nf O P* = **salope.**

salope [salɔp] *nf P* **1.** bitch/cow; slut/tart; **cette petite salope,** that little slut/bitch; **c'est une vieille salope ce type,** that bloke's/that guy's a real bastard*/louse **2.** prostitute*/tart.

saloper [salɔpe] *vtr P* to botch/to

bungle*/to make a mess of (sth); to muck (sth) up/to bugger sth up.

saloperie [salɔpri] *nf P* **1.** = **salaud, aude 2.** (*a*) filth/filthiness; **saloperie de temps!** filthy/disgusting weather! (*b*) **dire des saloperies,** to talk smut/filth (*c*) **faire une saloperie à qn,** to play a dirty trick on s.o./to do the dirty on s.o. **2.** rubbish/trash; **c'est de la vraie saloperie,** it's absolute rubbish/junk **3.** botched piece of work/bungle/botch-up.

salopiat [salɔpja] *nm,* **salopiau(d)** [salɔpjo] *nm,* **salopin** [salɔpɛ̃] *nm,* **salopiot** [salɔpjo] *nm P* = **salaud.**

salsif(i)s [salsif(i)] *nmpl P* **1.** fingers; **une poignée de salsif(i)s,** a punch/a bunch of fives **2.** toes.

salut! [saly], **salutas!** [salytas] *int F* (*a*) **salut (la compagnie)!** (*i*) hello/hi (everybody/everyone/*esp NAm* you guys)! (*ii*) so long/cheers/bye (everybody)! (*b*) **bonjour, salut!** hello, how are you? (*c*) **et puis salut!** right, that's it!/I quit!/I've had it!

sana [sana] *nm F* sanatorium/san.

sanctuaire [sɑ̃ktɥɛr] *nm F* **peser qch au poids du sanctuaire,** to examine sth thoroughly.

sandos [sɑ̃do] *nm F* = **sans-dos.**

sandwich [sɑ̃dwi(t)ʃ] *nm F* **être pris en sandwich,** to be caught/stuck/jammed/sandwiched (between two things, two people).

sandwicher [sɑ̃dwi(t)ʃe] *vtr F* to sandwich; **il était sandwiché entre deux femmes,** he was sandwiched between two women.

sang [sɑ̃] *nm* **1.** *F* **attraper le coup de sang/en prendre un coup de sang** (*i*) to burst a blood vessel (*ii*) to become very angry*/to hit the roof; **il a failli crever d'un coup de sang,** he nearly bust a blood vessel **2.** *F* **avoir du sang dans les veines,** to have guts **3.** *F* **avoir qch dans le sang,** to be mad*/crazy/nuts about sth; **il l'a dans le sang,** he's got it in his blood **4.** *F (a)* **se faire du mauvais sang/se cailler le sang/se faire du sang noir,** to worry/to fret; **ne vous faites pas de mauvais sang à mon sujet,** don't worry your head about me *(b)* **se dévorer/se manger/ se miner/se ronger/se tourner le(s) sang(s),** to worry oneself sick **5.** *F* **suer sang et eau** [sɑ̃keo], to sweat blood **6.** *F* **ça m'a tourné/retourné les sangs,** it gave me quite a turn/it upset me no end **7.** *P* **pisser du sang** *(i)* to bleed like a stuck pig *(ii)* to sweat one's guts out **8.** *P (a)* **bon sang (de bon sang)!/bon sang de bon Dieu!** damn and blast (it)!/(bloody) hell! *(b)* **bon sang d'imbécile!** you bloody fool! *(Voir* **navet 6; pinte)**

sanglier [sɑ̃gli(j)e] *nm P* **1.** *(péj)* priest* **2.** ash tray.

se sanguiner [səsɑ̃gine] *vpr P* to get drunk*.

sans [sɑ̃] *prep* **1.** *F* **pourquoi porter des lunettes si tu y vois sans?** why wear glasses if you can see without? **2.** *P* **des lettres de lui? voilà trois mois qu'on est sans,** letters from him? we haven't had any for three months. *(Voir* **un I 2)**

sans-châsses [sɑ̃ʃas] *a P* blind. *(Voir* **châsse 1)**

sans-dos [sɑ̃do] *nm inv F* high stool/bar stool.

sans-le-sou [sɑ̃lsu] *nm&f inv F* penniless* person; down-and-out.

sans-loches [sɑ̃lɔʃ] *a P* deaf. *(Voir* **loche III)**

sans-mirettes [sɑ̃miret] *a P* blind. *(Voir* **mirettes)**

sansonnet [sɑ̃sɔnɛ] *nm A P* gendarme. *(Voir* **roupie 3)**

sans-soin [sɑ̃swɛ̃] *nm&f inv F* careless person.

Santaga [sɑ̃taga] *Prn F* **la Santaga,** the Santé prison (in Paris). *(Voir* **santoche II)**

santé [sɑ̃te] *nf F* **1. avoir une** petite santé, to have poor health/to be delicate; **soigner sa petite santé,** to mollycoddle oneself **2. il en a une santé!/il a une certaine santé!** he's got a nerve!/I like his cheek! *(Voir* **mangeuse)**

santiags [sɑ̃tjag] *nfpl F (bottes mexicaines)* Mexican (style) boots.

santoche [sɑ̃tɔʃ] **I** *nf P* health **II** *Prn F* **la Santoche,** the Santé prison (in Paris). *(Voir* **la Santaga)**

santonner [sɑ̃tɔne] *vtr P* = **sataner.**

saoul [su], **saoulard** [sular], **saouler** [sule], *etc* = **soûl, soûlard, soûler,** *etc.*

sape [sap] **I** *nf F (mil)* **la sape,** army engineers/sappers **II** *nmorf P* prison sentence; **sape de gonzesse,** light sentence **III** *nf P* **1. la sape,** the clothing industry **2.** *pl* **sapes,** clothes*/gear/threads.

sapé [sape] *a P* **bien sapé,** well-dressed.

sapement [sapmɑ̃] *nm P* = **sape II.**

saper [sape] **I** *vtr P* to convict/to sentence (s.o.); **être sapé,** to be sentenced **II** *vtr P* to dress; **être bien sapé,** to be well-dressed **III** *vpr* **se saper** *P* to get dressed.

saperlipopette! [sapɛrlipɔpɛt], **saperlotte!** [sapɛrlɔt] *int O F* good heavens!/heavens above!/good gracious!

sapeur [sapœr] *nm* **1.** *F (pers)* **fumer comme un sapeur,** to smoke like a chimney **2.** *P* **avaler le sapeur,** to take Holy Communion. *(Voir* **tablier 2)**

sapin [sapɛ̃] *nm* **1.** *F* coffin; **sentir le sapin,** to have one foot in the grave; **toux qui sent le sapin,** churchyard cough **2.** *P* taxi/cab. *(Voir* **costar(d); paletot 1)**

saprelotte! [saprəlɔt], **sapristi!** [sapristi] *int O F* good heavens!/good Lord!

saquer [sake] *vtr F* = **sacquer.**

sarbacane [sarbakan] *nf P* rifle.

sarcif [sarsif] *nm*, **sarcigol** [sarsigɔl] *nm P* sausage/banger.

sarco [sarko] *nm P* coffin.

sardine [sardin] *nf* **1.** *F* (*mil*) NCO's stripe **2.** *pl P* **les sardines,** the fingers **3.** *V* **égoutter sa sardine,** to urinate*.

sardoche [sardɔʃ] *nf P* sardine.

sarrasin [sarazɛ̃] *nm P* (*typo*) non-union worker; blackleg.

sarrasiner [sarazine] *vi P* (*typo*) to work at non-union rates.

satané [satane] *a F* (*intensif*) blasted/damn(ed)/confounded/cursed; **satané temps!** beastly weather! **c'est un satané menteur,** he's a damn(ed) liar.

sataner [satane] **I** *vtr P* **sataner qn,** to beat s.o. up*/to knock the stuffing out of s.o./to work s.o. over **II** *vpr* **se sataner** *P* to (have a) fight/a set-to/a punch-up; to set about each other.

saton [satɔ̃] *nm P* blow*; kick.

satonner [satɔne] *vtr P* = **sataner.**

satyre [satir] *nm F* **1.** sex maniac; dirty old man **2.** flasher.

sauce [sos] *nf* **1.** *F* rain; shower; **recevoir une sauce,** to get soaked **2.** *F* **allonger/rallonger la sauce,** to pad out a book; to spin out a story **3.** *F* **on le met à toutes les sauces,** he's given all kinds of different jobs to do; **je ne sais à quelle sauce le mettre,** I don't know what use to make of it/of him **4.** *F* **un repas à trente francs sans la sauce,** a thirty-franc meal without extras/with no frills **5.** *F* (*a*) **gâter la sauce,** to spoil the whole business/the whole show (*b*) **qu'il en boive la sauce,** he'll have to put up with the consequences **6.** *F* **être dans la sauce,** to be in a fix*/to be in the soup **7.** *F* (*mus*) **faire de la sauce,** to impro-

vise **8.** *F* (*aut*) (*i*) petrol (*ii*) diesel (oil); **mettre toute la sauce,** to step on the gas; **rajouter de la sauce,** to accelerate/to put one's foot down **9.** **balancer/envoyer la sauce** (*i*) *P* to fire (a gun, a burst of machine-gun fire, etc) (*ii*) *V* to ejaculate*/to shoot one's load. (*Voir* **accommoder 2**)

saucée [sose] *nf F* **1.** (*a*) downpour (*b*) **attraper/recevoir une saucée,** to get drenched/to get soaked (to the skin) **2.** reprimand*/telling-off/rocket.

saucer [sose] *vtr F* **1.** to drench/to soak (to the skin); **l'orage nous a saucés,** we got wet through in the storm; **se faire saucer,** to get drenched/to get soaking wet **2.** to reprimand*/to tell (s.o.) off/to blow (s.o.) up; **se faire saucer,** to get a rocket.

sauciflard [sosiflar] *nm P* sausage/banger.

saucisse [sosis] *nf* **1.** *F* (*mil*) (*a*) observation balloon; barrage balloon (*b*) trench mortar shell **2.** *F* **il ne les attache pas avec des saucisses,** he's very mean. (*Voir* **chien II 1**) **3.** *F* fool*/idiot/silly sausage **4.** *P* **rouler les saucisses,** to have one's fingerprints/one's dabs taken **5.** *P* **rouler des saucisses,** to exchange French kisses/to have a snogging session.

saucisson [sosisɔ̃] *nm* **1.** *P* = **saucisse 3** **2.** *P* (*péj*) woman*/old bag/old bat. (*Voir* **peau 23**)

saucissonné [sosisɔne] *a F* dressed in tight-fitting clothes/got up like a sausage.

saucissonner [sosisɔne] **I** *vtr* **1.** *F* to tie up like a sausage **2.** *P* to arrest* **II** *vi F* to have a snack/to picnic; **nous avons saucissonné dans le train,** we had a snack on the train.

saucissonneur, -euse [sosisɔnœr, -øz] *n F* picnicker.

saumâtre [somɑtr] *a* F **1.** (*pers*) bitter/sour **2.** (*a*) **l'avoir saumâtre,** to be indignant/annoyed (*b*) **je la trouve saumâtre,** I think that's a bit much; I don't find that at all funny; I don't go a bundle on that.

saumure [somyr] *nf* P sea/the briny.

sauré [sore] *nm,* **sauret** [sorɛ] *nm* O P **1.** pimp*/ponce/mack/sweet man/nookie bookie **2.** gendarme.

saut [so] *nm* F **1. faire le saut,** to make a decision/to take the plunge **2.** (*a*) **faire le saut en l'air,** to be hanged/to swing (*b*) **faire le grand saut,** to die*/to (take a) leap into the (great) unknown **3. faire un saut chez qn,** to pop round to s.o.'s house/to drop in on s.o.

saute-au-crac [sotokrak] *nm inv* V **c'est un saute-au-crac,** he's obsessed/he's got a one-track mind; he's cunt-struck; he'd screw anything in a skirt. (*Voir* **crac**)

saute-au-paf [sotopaf] *nf inv* V nymphomaniac/nympho; **c'est une saute-au-paf,** she'd jump into bed with anyone. (*Voir* **paf II 2**)

sautée [sote] *nf* F **grande sautée,** tall, thin person*; beanpole.

sauter [sote] I *vtr* **1.** F **je la saute,** I'm starving/ravenous **2.** P to arrest*; **se faire sauter,** to get nabbed/nicked **3.** P to have sex* with (s.o.)/to have/to jump; **elle s'est fait sauter,** she got laid/screwed/jumped **4.** F **se faire sauter (la cervelle),** to blow one's brains out II *vi* **1.** F to get angry*/to hit the roof **2.** F **il faut que ça saute!/(allez,) et que ça saute!** jump to it!/make it snappy!/look sharp! **3.** P **sauter du train en marche,** to practise coitus interruptus/to withdraw (before ejaculation). (*Voir* **fossé; pas I 2**)

sauterelle [sotrɛl] *nf* F tall girl/beanpole.

sauteur, euse [sotœr, -øz] *n* I F unreliable person/waverer II

nm P womanizer*; **un sacré sauteur,** a really good lover/a hell of a good lay III *nf* P **1.** bottle of champagne* **2.** flea **3.** (*a*) prostitute*/tart (*b*) easy lay/pushover; **une sacrée sauteuse,** a good screw.

sauvage [sovaʒ] I *a* F **grève sauvage,** wildcat strike II *nm* P **1.** (*esp criminel*) lone wolf/loner **2. se mettre en sauvage,** to strip (right) off.

(à la) sauvette [alasovɛt] *adv phr* F ready to cut and run/ready to beat it quickly; (*camelots*) **vendre à la sauvette,** to sell goods in the street illicitly/without having a licence.

savate [savat] *nf* F **1.** clumsy person/bungler/botcher; **quelle savate! what a clumsy clot! 2. traîner la savate,** to be down and out/down on one's uppers/on one's beam ends.

savater [savate] *vtr* F to bungle*/to botch/to bodge (up).

savetier [savtje] *nm* F clumsy person/bungler/botcher.

saveur [savœr] *nf* P **coup de saveur,** (searching) glance; **donner un coup de saveur à qch,** to take a butcher's at sth/to get an eyeful (of sth).

savoir [savwar] *vtr* F **1. je n'ai pas à le savoir,** I don't want to know/it's got nothing to do with me **2. est-ce que je sais(, moi)?** don't ask me!/I haven't a clue!/no idea! **3. il en sait des choses,** he knows a thing or two/he knows what's what/he's got his wits about him. (*Voir* **un**)

savon [savɔ̃] *nm* F **1.** (severe) reprimand*; **donner/flanquer/passer un savon à qn,** to reprimand* s.o./to tear s.o. off a strip/to bawl s.o. out; **recevoir un savon,** to be reprimanded*/to catch it/to get a rocket **2. être comme un savon,** to be stark naked*.

savonnage [savɔnaʒ] *nm* F reprimand*/telling-off/bawling-out.

savonner [savɔne] *vtr* F **savonner (la tête à) qn,** to reprimand* s.o./to tell s.o. off/to give s.o. a (good) dressing down; **se faire savonner (la tête),** to get told off.

savonnette [savɔnɛt] *nf* F (*aut*) bald tyre.

saxo [sakso] *nm* F saxophone/sax.

sbire [zbir] *nm* A F (*péj*) **1.** (officious) policeman* **2.** prison warder/screw.

scaphandre [skafɑ̃dr] *nm* P **scaphandre de poche,** (contraceptive) sheath/condom*/rubber/Johnnie.

schbeb¹ [ʃbɛb] *a* P beautiful. (*Voir* **chbeb¹**)

schbeb², **schebeb** [ʃ(ə)bɛb] *nm* P good-looking young homosexual*. (*Voir* **chbeb²**)

schib [ʃib] *nm* A P **1.** prison* **2.** policeman*.

schlaf [ʃlaf], **schlaff(e)** [ʃlaf] *nm or f* P **aller au schlaf/à (la) schlaf,** to go to bed*; **faire schlaf,** to sleep; to be sleeping. (*Voir* **chlaff(e)**)

schlague [ʃlag] *nf* P flogging.

schlaguer [ʃlage] *vtr* P to flog.

schlass(e) [ʃlas] **I** *a* P drunk*/sozzled **II** *nm* P knife; dagger; chiv. (*Voir* **chlass(e) I, II**)

schlingoter [ʃlɛ̃gɔte], **schlinguer** [ʃlɛ̃ge], **schlipoter** [ʃlipɔte] *vi* P to stink*; **schlingoter du bec,** to have foul breath. (*Voir* **chlingoter, chlinguer, chlipoter**)

schlof(f), **schloff(e)** [ʃlɔf] *nm or f* P = **schlaf.**

schloffer [ʃlɔfe] *vi* P to sleep*.

schmecter [ʃmɛkte] *vi* P to stink*/to pong.

schmit [ʃmit] *nm* P gendarme.

schnaps [ʃnaps] *nm*, **schnick** [ʃnik] *nm* F inferior whisky or brandy; cheap spirits*/rotgut. (*Voir* **chnaps, chnique**)

schnock, schnoque [ʃnɔk] P **I** *a* mad*/bonkers; gaga **II** *nm* fool*/blockhead/*NAm* schmo(e)/schmuck; **vieux schnock,** silly old fool/old dodderer/old goat. (*Voir* **chnoc, chnoque**)

schnouf(fe) [ʃnuf] *nf* P (*drogues*) (*i*) heroin* (*ii*) dope/junk. (*Voir* **chnouf(fe)**)

schnouffé, ée [ʃnufe] *n* P (*drogues*) heroin* addict; junkie. (*Voir* **chnouffé**)

se schnouffer [səʃnufe] *vpr* P (*drogues*) to take heroin*; to be a heroin addict/to be a junkie. (*Voir* **se chnouffer**)

schnouper [ʃnupe] *vi* P to be a dipsomaniac/a dipso/an alky.

schpile [ʃpil] *nm* P gambling; **avoir beau schpile** (*a*) to have/to hold a good hand (at cards) (*b*) to find it all plain sailing; to have a good chance/a good opportunity; **il avait beau schpile à faire cela** (*i*) it was easy for him to do that (*ii*) he had every opportunity to do that. (*Voir* **chpile**)

schpiler [ʃpile] *vi* P to gamble. (*Voir* **chpiler**)

schpileur [ʃpilœr] *nm* P gambler. (*Voir* **chpileur**)

schpromm [ʃprɔm] *nm*, **schproom** [ʃprum] *nm*, **schproum(e)** [ʃprum] *nm* P **1.** scandal/(scandalous) gossip/dirt; **faire du schpromm,** to cause a scandal **2.** din/row/racket; **faire du schpromm,** to kick up a row **3.** anger; **aller à schpromm,** to lose one's temper/to hit the roof. (*Voir* **chproum**)

schtar(d) [ʃtar] *nm*, **schtib(e)** [ʃtib] *nm*, **schtilibem** [ʃtilibɛm] *nm* P prison*/stir; disciplinary cell/cooler. (*Voir* **ch'tar 1; chtib(e)**)

schton [ʃtɔ̃] *nm* P blow*/punch/slug. (*Voir* **jeton 3**)

schtim(m)i [ʃtimi] *nm* P native of northern France/northerner. (*Voir* **ch'timi**)

schtouillard [ʃtujar] *nm* P person with VD*/the clap. (*Voir* **chtouillard**)

schtouille [ʃtuj] *nf* P VD*/(the) clap; **ramasser la schtouille**, to cop a dose; **flanquer la schtouille à qn**, to give s.o. a dose. (*Voir* **chtouille**)

sciant [sjɑ̃] *a* F boring; **il est sciant** (*i*) he's a damn nuisance (*ii*) he's a terrible bore.

scie [si] *nf* F (*chose ou pers*) bore*/bind; nuisance; **quelle scie!** what a bore!/what a bind!

Sciences-Po [sjɑ̃spo] *nfpl* F = École supérieure des Sciences politiques.

scier [sje] *vtr* **1.** P (*a*) to dismiss*/to get rid of (s.o.) (*b*) to jilt/to throw over/to chuck (s.o.) (up) **2.** F (se faire) scier à la base, to be dumbfounded/bowled over; **ça m'a scié (à la base)**, I was staggered. (*Voir* **bois 15; dos 2**)

scion [sjɔ̃] *nm* P knife/chiv/sticker; dagger; **donner un coup de scion à qn**, to stab s.o.

scionner [sjɔne] *vtr* P to stab/to knife/to chiv (s.o.).

sciure [sjyr] *nf* F **avoir de la sciure dans le tronc**, to be a fool*/an idiot; to be wood from the neck upwards.

score [skɔr] *nm* P prison sentence*/time.

scoubidou [skubidu] *nm* P **1.** contraption/gadget **2.** (*stérilet*) coil/loop.

scoumoune [skumun] *nf* P persistent bad luck.

scribe [skrib] *nm* F (*péj*) clerk/pen-pusher.

scribouillage [skribujaʒ] *nm* F (*a*) scribbling (*b*) work written in poor/slapdash style; scribble.

scribouillard, arde [skribujar, -ard] *n* F (*péj*) clerk/pen-pusher.

scribouiller [skribuje] **I** *vi* F (*a*) to be a pen-pusher (*b*) to scribble; to write in poor/slapdash style **II** *vtr* P to write (a letter, etc).

scribouilleur, euse [skribujœr, -øz] *n* F scribbler/pen-pusher.

scro(n)gneugneu, *pl* **-eux** [skrɔɲøɲø] *nm* F (*a*) cantankerous old soldier; Colonel Blimp (*b*) *int* grumble, grumble ...!/moan, moan ...!

scroum [skrum] *nm* P = **schproum(e)**.

seau, *pl* **seaux** [so] *nm* F **1. il pleut/il tombe à (pleins) seaux; il tombe des seaux**, it's raining hard/it's raining cats and dogs/it's bucketing down/it's pelting down **2. être dans le seau**, to be in a fix*/to be in the soup.

Sébasto [sebasto] *Prn* F **le Sébasto**, the boulevard de Sébastopol (in Paris). (*Voir* **Topol**)

sec *f* **sèche¹** [sɛk, sɛʃ] **I** *a* F **1. l'avoir sec** (*i*) to be very thirsty/parched. (*Voir* **gosier**) (*ii*) to be very angry*/furious/fuming (*iii*) to be indignant/annoyed **2.** (*esp scol*) **rester sec**, to be stumped (for an answer) **3. consultation sèche**, free consultation. (*Voir* **cri 2**) **II** *adv* F **1. aussi sec**, immediately*/straight away **2. quinze mille balles sec**, a cool fifteen thousand quid/nicker **3. les envoyer sec**, to pay* up/to fork up **4.** *adv phr* **être à sec** (*i*) to run out of words/ideas; to dry up (*ii*) to be penniless*/to be broke/to be skint; **mettre qn à sec**, to clean s.o. out/to take s.o. to the cleaners. (*Voir* **péter I, 10**) **III** [sɛk] *nf* F (= *seconde(s)*) **en cinq sec(s)**, very quickly*/in two shakes (of a lamb's tail)/in (next to) no time.

sécateur [sekatœr] *nm* P (*péj*) **baptisé au sécateur**, Jewish*.

seccotine [sɛkɔtin] *nf* O F (*pers*) tenacious bore*.

séchage [seʃaʒ] *nm* F (*scol*) cutting/skipping (of lectures).

sèche² *nf* 1. F (*scol*) **piquer une sèche,** to be stumped/to dry up (at an oral exam) 2. P cigarette*/fag/ cig(gy); **griller une sèche,** to smoke a fag; **piquer une sèche,** to cadge/to bum a fag.

séché [seʃe] *a* P dead; **il est séché,** he's a goner/he's had it/he's done for.

sécher [seʃe] I *vtr* 1. F **sécher un verre/un pot,** to knock back/to swig (down) a drink 2. F (*a*) (*scol*) **sécher un cours,** to miss/to skip/to skive off a lecture (*b*) **sécher une réunion,** to cut a meeting 3. F **sécher un candidat,** to fail a candidate 4. P **sécher un type,** to kill* s.o./to bump s.o. off 5. P **la sécher,** to be very thirsty/parched II *vi* 1. F to be stumped/to be floored; to dry up (*esp* in an exam) 2. P (*pers*) to smoke. (*Voir* **fil 7**; **pied 9; tas 3**)

séchoir [seʃwar] *nm* P prison.

séco [seko] *a&nm* F = **sécot.**

secor [səkɔr] *a&nm* P (*verlan de corse*) Corsican.

sécot [seko] F I *a* lean/lanky/ skinny II *nm* **un petit sécot,** a skinny little bloke/*esp* NAm guy.

secouée [səkwe] *nf* F 1. reprimand*/telling off 2. great quantity*; **il y en avait une secouée,** there were heaps/loads/tons of them.

secouer [səkwe] I *vtr* 1. F to shake (s.o.) up/to make (s.o.) sit up and listen 2. F to reprimand* (s.o.)/to tear (s.o.) off a strip. (*Voir* **puce 8**) 3. F **secouer les oreilles à qn,** to give s.o. a flea in his ear 4. P to steal* 5. P to arrest* 6. P **(j'en ai) rien à secouer!** I don't give a damn! (*Voir* **puce 7**) II *vpr* **se secouer** F to get a move on/to get moving; to shake oneself out of it/ to snap out of it; **secoue-toi!/ secouez-vous!** get cracking!/look alive!/make it snappy!

secouette [səkwɛt] *nf* V (act of) masturbation*/wanking/tossing off.

secousse [səkus] *nf* F **en donner/ en mettre/***P* **en foutre une secousse,** to work* hard/to (really) get down to it; **il n'en fiche pas une secousse,** he doesn't do a stroke (of work)/he doesn't do a hand's turn.

la Sécu [laseky] *abbr* F (= *la Sécurité sociale*) = the National Health Service (NHS).

seg [sɛg] *nm* F 1. (*scol*) second/ junior master 2. (*marine*) executive officer.

sègue [sɛg] *nf* V masturbation*/ wank/hand-job; **se taper une sègue,** to toss off/to jack off/to wank.

seins [sɛ̃] *nmpl* P 1. **tu me fais mal aux seins!** you get on my (bloody) nerves!/you get on my tits! 2. **se tâter le sein,** to worry (about one's health); **arrête de te tâter le sein,** stop worrying about it/don't let it get you down.

sel [sɛl] *nm* F 1. **lancer/mettre son grain de sel; y aller de son grain de sel,** to make uncalled-for remarks/ to chip in/to chime in; **il met son grain de sel dans tout,** he's always sticking his nose into what doesn't concern him 2. (*a*) (*iron*). **c'est fin comme du gros sel,** very clever! (*b*) **cela ne manque pas de sel,** it's quite clever/witty really.

sélect (*f* **sélect** *or* **sélecte**) [selɛkt] *a* F select/high-class/posh (gathering); **le monde sélect,** high society.

self [sɛlf] *nm* F self-service store *or* restaurant.

sellette [sɛlɛt] *nf* F **être sur la sellette,** to be on the carpet; **mettre/ tenir qn sur la sellette,** to have s.o. on the carpet.

semer [səme] *vtr* F (*a*) to get rid of/to shed/to shake off/to give the slip to (s.o.); **semer une connaissance,** to drop an acquaintance (*b*) (*courses*) to leave (a competitor) behind/to outdistance (s.o.). (*Voir* **merde I 10**)

semi [səmi] *nmorf F* (= (*camion*) *semi-remorque*) articulated lorry/artic.

semou [səmu] *nf P* (*verlan de* **mousse**) beer.

semoule [səmul] *nf* **1.** *P* **être dans la semoule**, to be in a fix*/a jam. (*Voir* **pédaler 3**) **2.** *V* **envoyer/lâcher la semoule**, to ejaculate*/to shoot one's load.

sens [sãs] *nm P* **un coup de sens unique**, a drink of red wine.

sensass [sãsas] *a F* sensational/terrific/smashing/super; **un type sensass**, a great bloke/*esp NAm* guy.

sent-bon [sãbɔ̃] *nm inv*, **sentibon** [sãtibɔ̃] *nm inv F* scent/perfume; **sentir le sent-bon**, to smell nice.

sentiment [sãtimã] *nm F* **le faire au sentiment à qn/avoir qn au sentiment**, to play on s.o.'s (better) feelings; **vous ne m'aurez pas au sentiment**, that won't work with me/you won't get me that way.

sentinelle [sãtinɛl] *nf P* **1. relever une sentinelle**, to have a drink (at the bar) **2.** turd. (*Voir* **factionnaire**)

sentir [sãtir] *F* **I** *vtr* **1. je ne peux pas le sentir**, I can't bear/stand/stick (the sight of) him; I just can't stomach him. (*Voir* **blairer I** (*b*)) **II** *vi* **ça ne sent pas bon**; **ça sent mauvais**, I don't like the look of it/it's (a bit) fishy; it stinks **III** *vpr* **s'en sentir** *F* **je ne m'en sens pas**, I don't feel like it; I'm not (very) keen on it.

serbillon [sɛrbijɔ̃] *nm O P* **faire/envoyer le serbillon à qn** = **faire/envoyer le serre à qn** (**serre**).

sergot [sɛrgo] *nm O P* policeman*.

série [seri] *nf* **1.** *F* **série noire**, run of bad luck; chapter of accidents **2.** *P* (*femme*) **passer en série**, to be raped by several men in succes-

sion/to be gangbanged; **passage en série**, group rape/gang bang.

sérieux [serjø] *nm F* litre glass of beer.

serin [s(ə)rɛ̃] *F* **I** *a* stupid*/idiotic (person) **II** *nm* fool*/nitwit/nit/twit.

seriner [s(ə)rine] *vtr F* **seriner qn/seriner qch à qn**, to drum sth into s.o. (by constant repetition).

seringue [s(ə)rɛ̃g] *nf P* **1.** (*a*) firearm; rifle; pistol (*b*) submachine-gun **2.** (*mus*) trombone **3.** (*pers*) bore* **4. chanter comme une seringue**, to sing out of tune/off key **5. coup de seringue**, sudden feeling of tiredness; sinking feeling. (*Voir* **potage 2**)

seringuer [s(ə)rɛ̃ge] *vtr P* **seringuer qn**, to shoot s.o./to riddle s.o. with bullets/to fill s.o. with lead.

serpent [sɛrpã] *nm* **1.** *F* **un serpent à lunettes**, person wearing spectacles; four-eyes **2.** *P* gob (of spit, phlegm) **3.** *F* (*journ, hum*) **serpent de mer** = silly season story.

serpillière [sɛrpijɛr] *nf P* (girl's, woman's) dress.

serre [sɛr] *nm P* **faire/envoyer le serre à qn**, to warn s.o. (by a signal); to give s.o. the tip-off/to tip s.o. the wink.

serré [sɛre, se-] *a F* miserly*/tight(-fisted). (*Voir* **entournures**)

serrer [sɛre, se-] **I** *vtr P* **1.** to arrest*; **se faire serrer**, to get nabbed/nicked **2.** to rob s.o./to pick s.o.'s pocket **3.** to strangle (s.o.) **4.** to exaggerate*/to overstate (sth) **5. se la serrer** (*i*) to shake hands (*ii*) to tighten one's belt/to go without (food). (*Voir* **ceinture 1**; **cinq 5**; **fesse 2**; **jeu 5**; **pince 1**; **pouce 12**; **vis**) **II** *vpr* **se serrer** *F* to reduce one's expenses; to cut down on inessentials.

sert [sɛr] *nm P* = **serre**.

servi [sɛrvi] *a&pp P* **être servi** (*i*) to be arrested* (*ii*) to be sent to prison*.

service [sɛrvis] *nm* **1.** *F* **faire du service**, to be over-zealous/to be over-keen **2.** *P* **service trois pièces**, male genitals*/bag of tricks/cricket set **3.** *V* **entrée de service**, anus*/ back door.

service-service [sɛrvissɛrvis] *a F* **être service-service**, to be a stickler for rules and regulations; to go by the book; **service-service! duty is duty!/rules are rules!**

serviette [sɛrvjɛt] *nf P* **coup de serviette**, (police) raid/bust.

servietter [sɛrvjɛte] *vtr P* to round up (suspects, etc) (in a police raid).

seug [sœg] *nm P* = **seg 1, 2.**

seulabre [sœlɑbr] *a P* alone/on one's tod.

seulet, ette [sœlɛ, -ɛt] *a F* alone/ lonely; **je suis bien seulette,** I'm all on my own/on my lonesome.

sexe, sexy [sɛks, sɛksi] *a F* sexy; **elle est sexe,** she's a sexy girl/a bit of all right/a nice bit of stuff/a sexy piece.

sézig, sézigue [sezig] *pron P* him(self)/her(self)/oneself; his nibs. (*Voir* **cézig(ue), mézig(ue), no(s)zig(ue)s, vo(s)zig(ue)s, euzig(ue)s, leur(s)zig(ue)s**)

shake [ʃek] *nm F* milkshake/shake.

shampooing [ʃɑ̃pwɛ̃] *nm* **1.** *P* **passer un shampooing à qn,** to reprimand* s.o./to give s.o. a dressing-down/to give s.o. a rocket **2.** *V* **shampooing maison/shampooing à Charles-le-Chauve,** fellatio*/blow-job.

shit [ʃit] *nm P* **1.** hashish*/shit **2.** heroin*/shit.

shoot [ʃut] *nm P* (*drogues*) injection*/shot/fix; **se faire un shoot,** to shoot up/to fix (up).

shooté [ʃute] *nm P* (*drogues*) drug addict*/junkie/fixer.

se shooter [səʃute] *vpr P* (*drogues*) to inject oneself with a drug/to shoot up/to fix (up).

shooterie [ʃutri] *nf P* (*drogues*) place where drug addicts go to shoot up/shooting gallery.

shooteuse [ʃutøz] *nf P* (*drogues*) hypodermic needle*/hyp(e)/hypo/ dropper; **enragé de la shooteuse,** heroin* addict/junkie/fixer.

sibiche [sibiʃ] *nf P* cigarette*/fag. (*Voir* **cibiche**)

SIDA [sida] *abbr F* (= *syndrome immuno-déficitaire acquis*) acquired immune deficiency syndrome/ AIDS.

sidérant [siderɑ̃] *a F* staggering/ shattering (piece of news, etc).

sidéré [sidere] *a F* dumbfounded/ staggered/flabbergasted*; **j'en suis resté sidéré,** I was completely shattered (by the news).

sidérer [sidere] *vtr F* to dumb-found/to flabbergast*/to stagger (s.o.)/to strike (s.o.) all of a heap/ to shatter (s.o.).

sidi [sidi] *nm P* (*péj*) **1.** North African/Arab* (*esp* living in France); wog **2.** man*/chap*/guy; **un drôle de sidi,** an odd sort of bloke.

siècle [sjɛkl] *nm F* **il y a un siècle que je ne vous ai vu,** I haven't seen you for ages/for yonks.

sienne [sjɛn] *nf F* **1. faire des siennes,** to be up to one's tricks; **il a encore fait des siennes,** he's been up to his tricks again. (*Voir* **leur**) **2. y aller de la sienne,** to make one's contribution (of stories, songs, etc)/to join in.

sifflard [siflar] *nm P* (French) sausage/banger. (*Voir* **sauciflard**)

sifflé! [sifle] *int P* rubbish!/boo!

siffler [sifle] **I** *vtr* **1.** *P* to swig/to knock back (a drink) **2.** *P* **siffle-**

le! come on, out with it!/shoot!/ give! **3.** *F* **se faire siffler (par la police),** to be pulled up (by the police) **4.** *F* **siffler une fille,** to give a girl a wolf-whistle/to wolf-whistle at a girl **II** *vi F* **c'est comme si je sifflais,** I'm wasting my breath/I might (just) as well be talking to myself/I might (just) as well save my breath.

sifflet [siflɛ] *nm P* **1.** throat; **couper le sifflet à qn** (*i*) to cut s.o.'s throat (*ii*) to shut s.o. up; to take the wind out of s.o.'s sails (*iii*) to take s.o.'s breath away; **serrer le sifflet à qn,** to strangle s.o./to throttle s.o./to wring s.o.'s neck; **se rincer le sifflet,** to wet one's whistle*/to knock one back. (*Voir* **nez 13**)

sifflot(t)e [siflɔt] *nf P* syphilis*/ syph.

sigler [sigle] *vtr&i P* to pay* (up)/ to settle. (*Voir* **cigler**)

sigma [sigma] *nm P* syphilis*.

signé [siɲe] *a&pp F* **c'est signé,** it's easy to guess who did that/it's clear to see who's behind that/it's written all over it.

sigue [sig] *nm P* **1. avoir un sigue,** to be twenty years old; **avoir deux sigues et un peu de mornifle,** to be forty-two or forty-three years old **2.** *O* twenty francs. (*Voir* **cigue**)

silencieux [silɑ̃sjø] *nm* **1.** *P* revolver* **2.** *V* **se taper un silencieux,** to masturbate*.

singe [sɛ̃ʒ] **1.** *F* ape/imitator **2.** *F* ugly person; fright; scarecrow **3.** *P* **le singe,** the boss/the guv'nor **4.** *P* (*mil*) **du singe,** corned beef/bully beef. (*Voir* **monnaie 2**)

singerie [sɛ̃ʒ(ə)ri] *nf F* **monter une singerie (à qn),** to lead (s.o.) up the garden path/to pull a fast one (on s.o.).

singesse [sɛ̃ʒɛs] *nf F* (*péj*) ugly girl*/woman*; fright; scarecrow.

sinoc, sino(c)que [sinɔk],

sino(c)qué [sinɔke] *a P* mad*/ bonkers. (*Voir* **synoque**)

sinoquet [sinɔkɛ] *nm O P* head*.

siouplaît, siouplé [sjuple] = *s'il vous plaît.*

siphon [sifɔ̃] *nm P* head*.

siphonné [sifɔne] *a F* mad*/ crazy/batty/crackers; **il est complètement siphonné,** he's absolutely nuts/as nutty as a fruit cake.

siphonner [sifɔne] *vi P* to talk through one's hat/to talk rubbish/ to talk cock.

sirop [siro] *nm P* **1.** alcoholic drink; **avoir un coup de sirop,** to be drunk*; to have had a drop too much/one too many; **sortir du sirop,** to sober up **2. sirop de bois tordu,** wine **3. sirop de grenouille(s)/de canard/de parapluie,** water*/Adam's ale; **tomber au sirop,** to fall into the water/the drink; **sirop (de pébroc, de pébroque),** rain(water) **4. tomber dans le sirop,** to faint/to pass out **5. je l'ai eu au sirop,** I led him up the garden path; I put one over on him **6. ça ne vaut pas un coup de sirop,** that's worthless*; it's not worth a sausage **7. être dans le sirop** (*i*) to be in a fix*/in a jam/in a spot of bother (*ii*) to feel dop(e)y/muzzy/woozy **8.** gambling den/joint; dive **9.** (*drogues*) **sirop de rif,** speedball* **10.** (human) blood (from a wound) **11. sirop de corps d'homme,** sperm/ semen*/love juice/come.

siroter [sirɔte] *vtr P* to drink* heavily/to booze/to tipple.

siroteur, -euse [sirɔtœr, -øz] *n F* tippler/drunkard*/heavy drinker/ boozer/alky.

sita [sita] *nm F* (*à Paris*) dust cart (*from 'Société industrielle de transports automobiles'*).

situasse [sityas] *nf P* (= *situation*) social position/status.

situation [situɑsjɔ̃] *nf F* **être dans une situation intéressante,** to be pregnant*/to be in an interesting condition.

situer [situe] *vtr F* **situer qn,** to size s.o. up/to suss s.o. out.

six-à-neuf [sizanœf] *nm P* sixty-nine (simultaneous oral sex by two partners). (*Voir* **soixante-neuf**)

(à la) six-quatre-deux [alasiskatdø] *adv phr F* **faire qch à la six-quatre-deux,** to do sth in a slapdash manner; to dash sth off; to do sth all anyhow; **travail à la six-quatre-deux,** slapdash work.

skating [sketiŋ] *nm F* **un skating à mouches,** a bald head*/a skating rink.

sked [skɛd] *nm P* (= *disque*) record/disc/album.

skoumoune [skumun] *nf P* bad luck/tough luck. (*Voir* **scoumoune**)

slalom [slalɔm] *nm F* **faire du slalom entre les voitures,** to dodge in and out among the cars; **conduire à Paris c'est un drôle de slalom,** driving in Paris is one hell of an obstacle race.

smala(h) [smala] *nf F* large family; **elle est partie au bord de la mer avec toute sa smala(h),** she's gone off to the seaside with all her tribe.

smicard, arde [smikar, -ard] *n F* person receiving the *SMIC* (= *salaire minimum interprofessionnel de croissance*)/worker on statutory minimum wage.

smigard, arde [smigar, -ard] *n A F* person receiving the *SMIG* (= *salaire minimum interprofessionnel garanti,* now replaced by SMIC)/worker on guaranteed minimum wage.

smok [smɔk] *nm F* (= *smoking*) dinner-jacket/*NAm* tuxedo.

snack(-bar) [snak(bar)] *nm F* snack bar.

snif(f) [snif] *nm P* (*drogues*) cocaine*/(nose) candy.

sniffer [snife] *vi P* to take drugs (*esp* cocaine*) nasally; to sniff/to snort (coke); **sniffer de la colle,** to sniff glue.

sniffeur, euse [snifœr, -øz] *n P* (glue) sniffer; cocaine snorter/sniffer.

snob [snɔb] *a F* smart/posh; **ça fait très snob,** that's very posh/very with it/very U.

snobard, arde [snɔbar, -ard] *n F* (*péj*) snob.

snober [snɔbe] *vtr F* (*péj*) **snober qn,** to look down on s.o.; to give s.o. the cold shoulder/the brush-off.

snobinard, arde [snɔbinar, -ard] *n F* (*péj*) a bit of a snob.

snobinette [snɔbinɛt] *nf F* (*péj*) pretentious/stuck-up young woman; little snob.

soce [sɔs] *nf P* (= *société*) gathering; gang; **bonsoir la soce!** (good)night all!

social [sɔsjal] *nm P* friend*/mate/pal/buddy.

socialo [sɔsjalo] *nm F* socialist/lefty.

sœur [sœr] *nf P* **1.** (*a*) girl-friend; mistress (*b*) any girl* *or* woman* friend/sister; **c'est une sœur,** she's a real friend **2.** effeminate young man/pansy **3.** (*a*) **et ta sœur!** (*to which the answer is often* **elle bat le beurre (et quand elle battra la merde tu viendras lécher le bâton))** (*i*) what do you take me for?/who (the hell) do you think I am? (*ii*) not bloody likely!*/get lost!/take a running jump! (*b*) **et ma sœur, elle en a!** pull the other one (= leg), it's got bells on!

sœurette [sœrɛt] *nf F* **1.** little sister **2.** girl*/woman*; **alors, sœurette?** what's on, honey?/how about it, love?

soft [soft] *nm F* soft porn.

soie [swa] *nf P* avoir qn sur la soie, to have s.o. on one's track/on one's trail. (*Voir* **péter I 7**)

soif [swaf] *nf F* 1. il fait soif! (*i*) it's thirsty weather! (*ii*) it's thirsty work! 2. jusqu'à plus soif, to the very end.

soiffard, arde [swafar, -ard] *F* I *a* (*i*) (s.o. who is) always ready for a drink (*ii*) (s.o.) who drinks too much II *n* (*i*) thirsty mortal (*ii*) drunk(ard)*/boozer.

soiffer [swafe] *vi F* to drink* heavily/to (hit the) booze.

soiffeur, euse [swafœr, -øz] *n F* heavy drinker/drunk(ard)*/boozer/old soak.

soigné [swaɲe] I *a P* excellent*/first-class/first-rate*; **une raclée soignée**, a hell of a beating*; **un rhume soigné**, a rotten cold/a stinker II *nm F* (*iron*) voilà du soigné! that's a fine piece of work!

soigner [swaɲe] *vtr F* 1. soignez-le bien(, pas d'indulgence)! give him the works!/give him the full treatment! 2. il faut te faire soigner! you must be mad*!/you need your head seeing to!/you need your head examined!

soin-soin [swɛ̃swɛ̃] *F* I *a* excellent*/great/first-rate/super II *adv* excellently/superbly/beautifully/marvellously.

soissonnais [swasɔnɛ] *nm V* soissonnais (rose), clitoris*.

soixante-neuf [swasɑ̃tnœf] *nm P* sixty-nine (simultaneous oral sex by two partners). (*Voir* **six-à-neuf**)

sokète [sokɛt] *nf Belg F* faire une sokète, to have a nap/to get a bit of shut-eye/to have a kip.

soleil [solɛj] *nm* 1. *F* piquer un soleil, to blush/to flush; un coup de soleil, a sudden blush/flush (of confusion) 2. *P* avoir un coup de soleil, to be tipsy/(be)fuddled (with drink) 3. *F* user le soleil, to laze

about 4. *P* (*marchandises volées*) ça craint le soleil, those goods are hot/that stuff's hot. (*Voir* **jour 4**) 5. *P* a million francs 6. *F* c'est le soleil de janvier, he's a feeble sort of bloke.

solide [solid] *nm F* chercher le solide; songer/viser au solide, to have an eye to the main chance/to look to the main chance.

sombre [sɔ̃br] *a F* un sombre imbécile/crétin, a complete fool*/a prize idiot/a real cretin.

son [sɔ̃] I *poss a F* il/ça sent son policier d'une lieue, you can tell he's a detective a mile away; he's got detective written all over him II *nm* 1. *P* les son et lumière, the old folks/the old fogeys; il est tout à fait son et lumière, he's past it 2. *P* cracher/éternuer dans le son, to be guillotined 3. *O F* faire l'âne pour avoir du son, to pretend to be stupid in order to find sth out. (*Voir* **boule 2, 3**)

sonnage [sɔnaʒ] *nm P* borrowing; tapping (for money); cadging.

sonnanche [sɔnɑ̃ʃ] *nf P* bell.

sonné [sɔne] *a* 1. *F* mad*/cracked/nutty 2. *F* (*a*) stunned (by a blow)/groggy (*b*) (*boxe*) punch-drunk 3. *P* sentenced/condemned; il est sonné, he's had it.

sonner [sɔne] *vtr P* 1. sonner qn (*i*) to kill* (*ii*) to stun s.o. by banging his head against a wall/on the pavement, etc 2. to beat (s.o.) up*/to work (s.o.) over 3. to flabbergast* (s.o.)/to knock (s.o.) flat (with astonishment) 4. on ne vous a pas sonné(e)! who asked you (to butt in)?/mind your own business! 5. se faire sonner, to be severely reprimanded*/to get a rocket. (*Voir* **cloche I 3**)

sonneur [sɔnœr] *nm F* 1. dormir comme un sonneur (de cloches), to sleep like a log; ronfler comme un sonneur, to snore like a pig 2.

sono 400 sou

boire comme un sonneur, to drink like a fish.

sono [sɔno] *nf F* (= *sonorisation*) **la sono était pourrie,** the sound (system) wasn't working/the PA (system) was up the creek.

sonore [sɔnɔr] *nm V* **le mettre au sonore,** to have anal sex*.

Sophie [sɔfi] *Prn F* (*fille*) **faire sa Sophie** (*i*) to behave prudishly/to be (all) goody-goody (*ii*) to show off*/to put on airs.

sorbonnard, arde [sɔrbɔnar, -ard] *F* (*péj*) **I** *a* **esprit sorbonnard,** niggling turn of mind **II** *n* student *or* lecturer at the Sorbonne.

sorbonne [sɔrbɔn] *nf P* head*; **je paumerai la sorbonne,** I'll lose my head.

sorcier [sɔrsje] *a F* **ce n'est pas (bien) sorcier,** there's nothing very difficult about that!/you don't have to be a magician to do that!

sorcière [sɔrsjɛr] *nf F* **une vieille sorcière,** an old hag/an old trout/an old witch.

sorgue [sɔrg] *nf P* evening; night.

sorlots [sɔrlo] *nmpl P* boots; shoes.

sort [sɔr] *nm F* **faire un sort à un repas,** to eat up/to make short work of a (whole) meal; **faire un sort à une bouteille de vin,** to polish off a bottle of wine.

sortable [sɔrtabl] *a F* **il n'est pas sortable,** you can't take him (out) anywhere.

sortie [sɔrti] *nf F* **1.** outburst/tirade; **faire une sortie à/contre qn,** to pitch into s.o./to lash out at s.o.; **elle est capable de n'importe quelle sortie devant les gens,** she's capable of saying anything in front of other people **2. ils sont de sortie,** they're missing/they're nowhere to be found. (*Voir* **porte 6**)

sortir [sɔrtir] **I** *vtr F* **1.** to dismiss*/to expel (s.o.); **se faire sortir,** to get thrown out/chucked out **2.**

to say/to come out with (a remark, etc); (*plaisanterie*) **il nous en a sorti une bien bonne,** he came out with a good one **II** *vi* **1.** *F* **d'où sortez-vous?** (*i*) don't you (even) know that?/where have you been all this time? (*ii*) where are your manners?/where were you brought up? **2.** *F* (= *venir de* ...) (*a*) **sortir de faire qch,** to have just done sth; **je sors de le voir,** I've just seen him (*b*) **merci (bien)! je sors d'en prendre,** I've had quite enough of that (already), thank you!/you won't find me doing that again (in a hurry)! **3.** *F* **je ne sors pas de là/je n'en sors pas,** I stick to that; that's my firm conviction; you won't make me change my mind; **il n'y a pas à sortir de là,** you can't get away from that/there's no getting away from it **4.** *F* **j'ai trop à faire, je n'en sors pas,** I'm completely swamped/ploughed under (with work) **5.** *P* **en sortir,** to leave prison*/to be released (from prison). (*Voir* **trou 2**) **6.** *P* (*a*) **sortir avec une femme,** to sleep with a woman (*b*) **sortir avec (une fille/un garçon),** to go out with/to go steady with/to date (a girl/a boy). (*Voir* **aller 10**) **III** *vpr* **s'en sortir** *F* to make ends meet/to get by.

sossot, otte [sɔso, -ɔt] *a P* stupid*/daft/twittish.

sou [su] *nm F* **1.**(*a*) **fichu comme quatre sous,** dressed like a guy/any old how; **je n'en donnerais pas quatre sous,** I wouldn't give you a thank-you for it **2. en être/en rester comme deux sous de frites,** to be flabbergasted* **3. être près de ses sous,** to be mean/miserly*/tight-fisted **4. être sans le sou,** to be penniless*; **il n'a pas le premier sou,** he hasn't a penny to his name **5.** (*a*) **il n'est pas ambitieux pour deux sous/pour un sou,** he's not in the least ambitious (*b*) **il n'a pas pour deux sous de courage,** he hasn't an ounce of courage.

soua-soua [swaswa] *a inv P* excellent*/first-rate/out of this world. (*Voir* **soin-soin**)

souche [suʃ] *nf F* fool*/idiot/nitwit/blockhead.

soucoupe [sukup] *nf* **1.** *F* soucoupe volante, flying saucer **2.** *pl P* soucoupes, ears*/flaps.

soudure [sudyr] *nf* **1.** *F* faire la soudure, to bridge the gap/to tide (one) over **2.** *P* money*; envoyer la soudure, to pay* up/to fork out.

soufflant, ante [suflɑ̃, -ɑ̃t] **I** *a* *F* amazing/astounding; ça, c'est soufflant, it's breathtaking **II** *nm P* revolver*; pistol **III** *nf P* trumpet.

souffle [sufl] *nm F* impudence/cheek; il ne manque pas de souffle! he's got a nerve/a flipping cheek!

soufflé [sufle] *a F* **1.** être soufflé, to be flabbergasted*/dumbfounded/struck all of a heap **2.** impudent/cheeky; t'es soufflé toi! you've got a nerve!

souffler [sufle] **I** *vtr F* **1.** souffler qn, to take s.o. aback/to flabbergast* s.o.; son culot nous a soufflés, his cheek took our breath away/staggered us **2.** souffler qch à qn (*i*) to swindle* s.o. out of sth (*ii*) to whisper sth to s.o./to have a word in s.o.'s ear about sth **II** *vi F* (*a*) tu peux souffler dessus, you can whistle for it (*b*) il croit qu'il va y arriver en soufflant dessus, he thinks he can do it just like that/without having to do anything. (*Voir* **canne I 4**; **chandelle 1**; **mirliton**)

soufflerie [sufləri] *nf P* lungs.

soufflet [suflɛ] *nm* **1.** *pl F* soufflets, lungs **2.** *P* soufflet à punaises, concertina/accordeon.

soufrante [sufrɑ̃t] *nf P* (sulphur-tipped) match.

souhaits [swɛ] *nmpl F* (*se dit à qn qui vient d'éternuer*) à vos souhaits! bless you!

souk [suk] *nm P* shambles; faire le

souk/faire un sacré souk, to have a wild party.

soûl [su] *F* **I** *a* drunk*; raisonnement de femme soûle, stupid talk/incoherent nonsense*. (*Voir* **bourrique 6**; **cochon 8**; **grive**; **Polonais**; **vache**) **II** *nm* boire/manger/rire/chanter tout son soûl, to drink/to eat/to laugh/to sing to one's heart's content; s'amuser tout son soûl, to enjoy oneself to the full; en avoir tout son soûl, to have all that one wants.

soulager [sulaʒe] **I** *vtr F* soulager qn de qch, to steal* sth from s.o./to relieve s.o. of sth **2.** *V* soulager qn, to bring s.o. to orgasm*/to bring s.o. off/to help s.o. out **II** *vpr* se soulager **1.** *F* to urinate*/to relieve nature **2.** *V* to masturbate*/to bring oneself off.

soûlant [sulɑ̃] *a P* boring/tedious; il est soûlant, his talking makes my head spin.

soûlard, arde [sular, -ard] *n P* drunk(ard)*/boozer/alky; un vieux soûlard, an old soak.

soûlardise [sulardiz] *nf P* drunkenness.

soûlaud, aude [sulo, -od] *n P* = soûlard, arde.

soûler [sule] **I** *vtr F* soûler qn, to make/to get s.o. drunk* **II** *vpr* se soûler *F* to get drunk*; ils se sont soûlés la gueule, they got pissed; se soûler de paroles, to become intoxicated by the sound of one's own voice.

soûlerie [sulri] *nf P* **1.** drunkenness **2.** drinking bout*/binge/bender/piss-up.

soulever [sulve] *vtr F* **1.** to steal*/to lift (s.o.'s purse, etc) **2.** to seduce/to get off with (a woman) **3.** ça me soulève le cœur, that turns my stomach/disgusts me.

souliers [sulje] *nmpl F* être dans ses petits souliers (*i*) to be ill at ease (*ii*) to be in an awkward/embarrassing situation.

soûlographe [sulɔgraf] *nm P* = **soûlard.**

soûlographie [sulɔgrafi] *nf P* = **soûlerie 1, 2.**

soûlot [sulo] *nm P* = **soûlard.**

soupapes [supap] *nfpl P* lungs.

soupe [sup] *nf* **1.** *F* **soupe au perroquet,** bread soaked in wine **2.** *F* **monter/s'emporter comme une soupe au lait,** to fly off the handle/ to go off the deep end. (*Voir* **soupe-au-lait**) **3.** *F* (*esp mil*) grub/nosh/chow; **être de soupe,** to be on cookhouse fatigue; **à la soupe!** grub's up!/come and get it! **aller à la soupe,** to (go and) have dinner/a meal **4.** *F* (*couple*) **manger la soupe à la grimace,** to sulk (after a quarrel*); **recevoir la soupe à la grimace,** to get a poor welcome (from one's wife on returning home) **5.** *F* **trempé comme une soupe,** drenched (to the skin)/like a drowned rat **6.** *F* **un gros plein de soupe** (*i*) a fat/pompous ass; a bighead/a big slob (*ii*) bigwig/big shot/big noise **7.** *F* (*théâtre*) **servir la soupe,** to play small roles/to take bit parts **8.** *F* (*ski*) soft snow **9.** *P* **par ici la bonne soupe!** (*i*) come and get ·it (*ie* come and get a good hiding)! (*ii*) that's the way to make money! (*Voir* **cheveu 8; marchand 5**)

soupe-au-lait [supolɛ] *nf inv F* fiery-tempered person; **c'est une soupe-au-lait,** he's/she's liable to fly off the handle/to ⸍ go off the deep end at any moment.

souper [supe] *vi F* **j'en ai soupé,** I'm fed up* (with it/him/her, etc); I've had enough/a bellyful (of it/ him/her, etc). (*Voir* **fiole 2**)

souquer [suke] *F* **I** *vtr* to thrash (s.o.)/to beat (s.o.) up* **II** *vi* to work* hard/to exert oneself/to flog oneself (to death).

sourdine [surdin] *nf* **1.** *F* **mettre la sourdine,** to shut up*/to pipe down/to put a sock in it **2.** *P* **la sourdine,** the secret police.

sourdingue [surdɛ̃g] *a&nm&f P* deaf (person).

souricière [surisjɛr] *nf* **1.** *F* police trap **2.** *P* police station/ lock-up.

sourire [surir] *nm P* **sourire de la vache,** knife cuts in both cheeks starting from the corner of the mouth (used on prostitutes who give information to the police, etc). (*Voir* **croix 4**)

souris [suri] *nf* **1.** *P* (*péj*) woman*/bird/chick/dame/broad **2.** *F* **petite souris** (*i*) busy little old lady (*ii*) mousy little woman **3.** *F* **souris de sacristie,** bigoted churchwoman **4.** *P* **souris d'hôtel,** (female) hotel thief.

sous-cul [suky] *nm P* (*a*) seat mat/bottom mat (*b*) (padded) cushion (to sit on).

sous-fifre [sufifr] *nm F* underling/ second fiddle/second-stringer/dogsbody.

sous-lieute [suljøt] *nm F* (*mil*) second lieutenant.

sous-mac [sumak] *nf P* chief assistant to brothel keeper; brothel hostess.

sous-main [sumɛ̃] *adv phr F* **en sous-main,** behind the scenes.

sous-maq, sous-maque[1] [sumak] *nf P* = **sous-mac.**

sous-maque[2] *nm P* deputy governor (of a prison).

sous-marin [sumarɛ̃] *nm P* **1.** swindler*/crook/shark **2.** worker sent to spy on other workers *or* who has secret motives for working in his job; s.o. who does not appear on the payroll.

sous-maxe [sumaks] *nf P* = **sous-mac.**

sous-off [suzɔf] *nm F* (*mil*) non-commissioned officer/non-com/ NCO.

sous-ventrière [suvɑ̃trijɛr] *nf P* manger à se faire péter la sous-ventrière, to stuff one's guts/to have a (good) blow-out.

sous-verge [suvɛrʒ] *nm inv F* underling/second fiddle/(general) dogsbody.

soutien-loloches [sutjɛ̃lɔlɔʃ] *nm P* bra/tit-holder. (*Voir* loloches)

souvent [suvɑ̃] *adv P* plus souvent! no fear!/not (bloody) likely!*/not on your life! plus souvent que j'irais! you won't catch me going!/ no way am I going!

spé [spe] *nm P* = spécial.

'spèce [spɛs] *nf P* 'spèce de ... = espèce de ....

spécial, *pl* **-aux** [spesjal, -o] **I** *nm P* **1.** (*homme*) filer/prendre du spécial, to be a homosexual* **2.** (*femme*) faire le spécial, to be a backside special **II** *a* **1.** *F* c'est un peu spécial, it's rather odd/queer **2.** *P* (*euph*) mœurs spéciales, homosexuality; avoir des goûts spéciaux, to have homosexual tendencies/to be that way inclined.

spécialo [spesjalo] *nm F* specialist.

speed [spid] *nm P* (*drogues*) amphetamine*/speed.

speedé [spide] *a P* être speedé (*i*) (*drogues*) to be on amphetamines*/ speed; to be speeding (*ii*) to be very excited/nervous/strung out; il bosse trop, il est complètement speedé, he works so much he's like a bag of nerves/it's like he's on speed.

sport [spɔr] *nm F* **1.** il y aura du sport!/nous allons voir du sport! there'll be some fun now!/there'll be some action now!/now for the fireworks! **2.** c'est du sport, it's difficult and dangerous.

stal [stal] *nm&f F* (= staliniste) commie/red/ = trot.

steak [stɛk] *nm P* gagner son steak, to earn one's living. (*Voir* bifteck 2)

step [stɛp] *nm P* nose*; step à trier (les lentilles)/à repiquer les choux, big nose.

stick [stik] *nm P* (*drogues*) marijuana* cigarette/joint.

stomba [stɔ̃ba] *nf P* (*verlan de* baston) fight/punch-up/fisticuffs.

stop [stɔp] *nm F* faire du stop, to hitch(-hike)/to thumb (a lift); to backpack; aller à Paris en stop, to hitch (it)/to thumb it to Paris; un camion nous a pris en stop, we hitched/thumbed a lift on a lorry.

stoppeur, -euse [stɔpœr, -øz] *n F* hitch-hiker/hitcher; backpacker.

stoqué [stɔke] *a FrC P* être stoqué sur qn, to have a crush on s.o./to be nuts about s.o./to have a thing about s.o.

store [stɔr] *nm P* eyelid; baisser les stores, to close one's eyes.

strasse [stras] *nf P* **1.** (*a*) room (*b*) room in a hotel, etc, used by a prostitute* **2.** street; road.

strippeuse [stripøz] *nf*, **stripteaseuse** [striptizøz] *nf F* stripper/*NAm* nudie.

stropiat [strɔpja] *nm P* cripple (real or sham).

stuff [stœf] *nm P* (*drogues*) drugs*/ dope/junk.

stup [styp] *nm P* (*drogues*) narcotic; *pl* stups, drugs/dope/junk; (*police*) la Brigade des stups/les Stups, the Drug(s) Squad.

suant [sɥɑ̃] *a P* boring.

suante [sɥɑ̃t] *nf P* week.

sub [syb] *nm P* (*verlan de bus*) bus.

subito [sybito] *adv F* subito (presto) (*i*) all of a sudden (*ii*) immediately*/at once/pronto/in a jiffy.

subodorer [sybɔdɔre] *vtr F* (*pers*) to suspect/to get wind of (sth); to sense (danger, etc); il a subodoré quelque chose, he smelt a rat.

subtiliser [syptilize] *vtr F* to steal*/to sneak/to swipe; ils m'ont subtilisé ma montre, they've pinched my watch.

sucer [syse] I *vtr* **1.** *F* **sucer qn (jusqu'au dernier sou/jusqu'à la moelle des os),** to suck s.o. dry/to bleed s.o. white/to take s.o.'s last penny **2.** *P* **sucer la pomme à qn,** to kiss s.o. (*Voir* **caillou 2**; **poire I 8** (*a*)) **3.** *V* (*fellation, cunnilinctus*) to suck (s.o.) off/to go down on s.o./to eat s.o. **II** *vi P* to drink* to excess/to (hit the) booze.

sucette [sysɛt] *nf P* (*CB, etc*) microphone/mike/lollipop.

suçon [sysɔ̃] *nm F* love-bite/hickey.

sucrage [sykraʒ] *nm* prison sentence/stretch/rap/time.

sucre [sykr] *nm* **1.** *F* **c'est du (vrai) sucre,** it's easy*/it's a cinch/it's a doddle **2.** *F* **un vrai sucre,** a pet/a poppet **3.** *F* **casser du sucre sur le dos/sur la tête de qn,** to speak ill of s.o./to run s.o. down/to knock s.o. **4.** *F* **il a été tout sucre et tout miel,** he was as sweet as could be; he was all honey **5.** *P* (*drogues*) (*a*) LSD*/sugar (lump) (*b*) heroin*/cocaine* *or* morphine* in powdered form; sugar **6.** *F* (*théâtre*) **recevoir son morceau de sucre,** to be applauded the moment one first appears on stage **7.** *P* **sucre de pomme,** jemmy/*NAm* jimmy. (*Voir* **bout 9**)

sucrée [sykre] *nf F* **faire la sucrée,** to put on demure airs; **elle fait la sucrée,** she acts as though butter wouldn't melt in her mouth.

sucrer [sykre] I *vtr P* **1.** to arrest*; **se faire sucrer,** to get nabbed **2.** to steal*. (*Voir* **fraise 3, 4**) **II** *vpr* **se sucrer** *F* (*a*) to get rich*; to feather one's nest (*b*) to take the lion's share.

sucrette [sykrɛt] *nf F* **aller à la sucrette,** to compromise with one's conscience.

suée [sɥe] *nf P* **1.** fright/scare **2.** hard work/sweat/grind/slog.

suer [sɥe] I *vi* **1.** *F* **faire suer qn,** to bore* s.o. stiff; **se faire suer,** to be cheesed off/browned off; **tu me fais suer!** you get on my nerves!/you're a pain in the neck! **2.** *P* **envoyer suer qn,** to send s.o. packing*/to send s.o. off with a flea in his ear **II** *vtr P* **1. en suer une,** to (have a) dance **2. faire suer le burnous,** to overwork people/to be a slavedriver. (*Voir* **sang 5**)

sueur [sɥœr] *nm P* **sueur de chêne,** killer. (*Voir* **chêne**)

suif [sɥif] *nm P* **1.** reprimand*; **donner/flanquer/passer un suif à qn,** to reprimand* s.o./to tear s.o. off a strip **2. chercher du suif,** to be out for a fight; **chercher du suif à qn,** to pick a quarrel* with s.o.; **être en suif,** to be at loggerheads **3.** uproar; **faire du suif,** to kick up a row **4.** scandal **5. se faire du suif,** to worry/to fret **6. faire en suif,** to cheat (at cards) **7. jeter du suif,** to be elegantly dressed; to put on one's glad rags.

suiffard [sɥifar] *nm P* **1.** elegantly dressed man; toff/dandy/swell **2.** cheat (at cards). (*Voir* **suif 6**)

suiffée [sɥife] *nf P* beating*/thrashing/good hiding.

suiffer [sɥife] I *vtr P* **1.** to reprimand* (s.o.) severely **2.** to pick a quarrel* with (s.o.) **II** *vpr* **se suiffer** *P* to quarrel*.

suiffeur, euse [sɥifœr, -øz] *n P* quarrelsome* person/troublemaker.

suisse [sɥis] *nf F* **boire en suisse/faire suisse/picoler en suisse** (*i*) to drink on one's own (without treating the company) (*ii*) to be a secret drinker.

suite [sɥit] *adv phr F* (= *tout de suite*) at once/immediately*.

sulfater [sylfate] *vtr P* **sulfater qn,** to shoot/to kill* s.o. with a submachine-gun.

sulfateuse [sylfatøz] *nf P* submachine-gun.

sulfureux [sylfyrø] *nm P* absinth(e).

sultane [syltan] *nf P* mistress.

sup [syp] *a inv F* (= *supplémentaire(s)*) supplementary/extra; **une heure sup,** an hour's overtime.

super [sypɛr] *F* **I** *a* excellent*/super/terrific/great* **II** *nm* (*aut*) (= *supercarburant*) = four star (petrol).

super-banco [sypɛrbãko] *a F* **la question super-banco,** the sixty-four thousand dollar question.

super-class [sypɛrklas] *a F* excellent*/fantastic/really great/amazing/far out.

supérette [sypɛrɛt] *nf F* small supermarket/mini-market.

superlifique [sypɛrlifik] *a O F* splendiferous.

supin [sypɛ̃] *nm F* (*scol*) = **surgé.**

suppositoire [sypozitwar] *nm F* **suppositoire d'autobus,** bubble car.

supprimer [syprime] **I** *vtr F* **supprimer qn,** to kill* s.o./to liquidate s.o./to remove s.o./to bump s.o. off **II** *vpr* **se supprimer** *F* to commit suicide*.

sûr [syr] *F* **I** *a* **c'est sûr et certain,** it's absolutely certain/it's a dead cert*; **c'est du sûr,** it's a good tip/it's good info; **pour sûr!** sure!/of course! **pour sûr que c'est pas facile!** of course it's not easy! **bien sûr?** you really mean it? **II** *adv* surely; **pas sûr!** perhaps not!

surbine [syrbin] *nf O P* (police) surveillance.

surbiner [syrbine] *vtr P* (*esp police*) to keep (s.o.) under surveillance; to watch/to keep a close eye on (s.o.).

surboum [syrbum] *nf F* party. (*Voir* **boum**)

Sûrepige [syrpiʒ] *nf P* (= *Sûreté*) Criminal Investigation Department/CID; *approx* = New Scotland Yard.

surface [syrfas] *nf* **1.** *F* **en boucher une surface à qn,** to flabbergast* s.o.; to knock s.o. sideways/all of a heap; **ça vous en bouche une surface!** that's flummoxed you! **2.** *P* **il a de la surface,** he's comfortably off/he's not short of a penny or two.

surgé [syrʒe] *nm,* **surgeot** [syrʒo] *nm,* **surgo** [syrgo] *nm F* (= *surveillant général*) vice-principal/deputy head(master); senior master.

surin [syrɛ̃] *nm P* knife/dagger/chiv.

suriner [syrine] *vtr P* to knife (s.o.); to stab (s.o.) to death; to chiv(e) (s.o.).

surineur [syrinœr] *nm P* knifer/chive-man/knife merchant.

surpatte [syrpat] *nf F* = **surboum.**

surprenante [syrprənãt] *P* **I** *nf* illegal and faked lottery **II** *adv phr* **à la surprenante,** unawares/by surprise.

surrincette [syrɛ̃sɛt] *nf P* a second after-dinner liqueur/another liqueur/a refill. (*Voir* **rincette**; **rince-gueule**)

surtout [syrtu] *conj phr F* **surtout que ...,** (e)specially as ....

survé [syrve] *nm F* = **surgé.**

survolté [syrvɔlte] *a F* (*a*) excited/worked up/(all) het up (*b*) **une affaire survoltée,** a souped-up job.

survolter [syrvɔlte] *vtr F* **survolter une foule,** to get a crowd worked up.

susucre [sysykr] *nm F* (*langage enfantin*) sugar.

swing [swiŋ] *a O F* hip/with it; **une jeune fille swing,** a with-it chick; **les gens swing,** hip-cats; **une robe swing,** a fashionable dress.

sympa [sɛ̃pa] *a F* (= *sympathique*) likeable/attractive/congenial; **être très sympa,** to be nice; **elle est très sympa, cette prof,** that teacher's really nice/very friendly.

synoque [sinɔk] *a* P mad*/crackers/bonkers. (*Voir* **cynoque**; **sinoc, sino(c)que, sino(c)qué**)

syphilo [sifilo] P I *nf* syphilis*/ syph II *nm* person suffering from syphilis*; syphilitic/siffo.

syphlotte [siflɔt] *nf* P syphilis*/ syph/siff/(the) pox.

système [sistɛm] *nm* F **taper/courir sur le système à qn,** to get on s.o.'s nerves/on s.o.'s wick. (*Voir* **D**)

T

tabac [taba] *nm F* **1.** *(a)* *(esp police)* **passer qn à tabac**, to beat s.o. up*/to work s.o. over/to do s.o. over; **passage au tabac**, beating* up/working over; **les flics l'ont passé à tabac**, the cops worked him over/beat him up *(b)* **il y a du tabac**, we're in for a spot of bother; there's going to be some aggro/action/trouble *(c)* **(un coup de) tabac**, a fight*/a punch-up *(d)* **faire un tabac** *(i)* to kick up a fuss/to make a song and dance about sth *(ii)* *(théâtre)* to be a success/a hit **2.** *(a)* **un mauvais tabac**, a bad business *(b)* **se donner un tabac terrible**, to give oneself no end of trouble **3.** **c'est le même tabac**, it's the same thing; **ce n'est pas le même tabac**, that's quite a different matter/*NAm* that's a whole new ball game **4.** *O* **tabac de Chine**, OP (= other people's) tobacco. (*Voir* **blague 3; paquet 16; pot 11**)

tabassage [tabasaʒ] *nm F* beating* up (of s.o.)/going over/working over/doing over; fight*/punch-up; third degree.

tabassée [tabase] *nf F* beating* (up)/(good) thrashing/pasting; fight*/punch-up; trouble/aggro.

tabasser [tabase] **I** *vtr F* to beat (s.o.) up*/to work (s.o.) over/to give (s.o.) a going over; to give (s.o.) the third degree **II** *vpr F* **se tabasser** to (have a) fight/to have a punch-up.

tabellion [tabeljɔ̃] *nm F* (*hum*) limb of the law; lawyer.

tabernacle [tabεrnakl] *nm O V* female genitals*.

table [tabl] *nf* **1.** *F* **sous la table**, secretly/under the table **2.** *P* **se mettre/passer à table** *(i)* to confess*/to come clean *(ii)* to grass/to snitch; to shop (s.o.); **manger à la grande table**, to be a police* informer/a copper's nark/a snout. (*Voir* **manger 4**)

tableau, eaux [tablo] *nm F* **1.** *(vieille femme)* **un vieux tableau**, a painted old hag/mutton dressed as lamb **2.** **décrocher ses tableaux**, to pick one's nose **3.** *(a)* **jouer/miser sur les deux tableaux**, to lay odds both ways/to hedge (one's bets) *(b)* **jouer/miser sur le même tableau**, to put all one's eggs in one basket **4.** **cela fera bien dans le tableau/cela ne ferait pas mal dans le tableau**, that will/would suit me down to the ground. (*Voir* **ombre 2**)

tablettes [tablεt] *nfpl F* **mettre qch sur ses tablettes**, to make a note of sth; **rayez cela de vos tablettes**, you can forget that.

tablier [tablije] *nm* **1.** *F* **rendre son tablier**, to leave (one's job)/to give in one's notice/to ask for one's cards **2.** *V* **tablier de forgeron/de sapeur**, (woman's) pubic hair/mount of Venus **3.** *F* **ça lui va comme un tablier à une vache**, it looks ridiculous on him/her.

tabourets [taburε] *nmpl P* teeth*/choppers; **n'avoir plus de tabourets dans la salle à manger/dans la croquante**, to have no teeth.

tac [tak] *nm P* taxi/cab.

tacot [tako] *nm F* (ramshackle) old

car*/banger/old crock/jalopy; **quel tacot!** what a wreck!/what a heap!

taf [taf] *P* **I** *nm* **1.** fear/funk; **avoir le taf,** to be afraid*/to get the wind up **2.** share (of the loot)/cut; **aller au taf,** to share out the spoils/to divvy up **3.** (*a*) **aller au taf,** to go to work (*b*) (*prostituée*) **faire le taf,** to solicit*/to be on the job **4.** **prendre son taf,** to ejaculate*/to come/to shoot one's load **II** *nf* **1.** *O* cigarette*/fag **2.** puff/drag on a cigarette*.

tafanar(d) [tafanar] *nm P* buttocks*/arse/*esp NAm* ass.

taffe [taf] *nm&f P* = **taf**.

taffer [tafe] *vi P* to be afraid*/to get the wind up.

taffeur, -euse [tafœr, -øz] *O P* **I** *a* cowardly*/yellow **II** *n* coward*/chicken/yellowbelly.

tailler [taje] **I** *vtr* **1.** *F* **tailler de la besogne à qn,** to make work for s.o. **2.** *P* **en tailler une avec qn,** to have a chat*/a chinwag/a natter with s.o.; to chew the fat with s.o. (*Voir* **bavette**) **3.** *P* **tailler (la route),** to run away*/to beat it/to clear off. (*Voir* **basane 3**; **drap 2**; **pipe 6**; **plume II 9**) **II** *vpr* **se tailler** *P* to run away*/to scarper/ to beat it.

tal [tal] *nm A P* buttocks*.

tala [tala] *F* **I** *nm&f* (militant) Roman Catholic student (*esp* at the Ecole normale supérieure) (*from* 'ceux qui vont **à la** messe') **II** *a* sanctimonious.

talbin [talbɛ̃] *nm P* banknote/greenback; **quelques talbins,** a few quid.

talc [talk] *nm P* cocaine*/talc.

talmouse [talmuz] *nf O F* blow*/ punch/wallop.

talochage [talɔʃaʒ] *nm F* slapping (round the face); clouting (on the head).

taloche [talɔʃ] *nf F* slap (round the face); clout (on the head); **filer une**

taloche à qn, to slap s.o. round the face.

talocher [talɔʃe] *vtr F* to slap (s.o.) (round the face); to clout (s.o.) (on the head); to box (s.o.'s) ears.

talon [talɔ̃] *nm P* (*femme*) **avoir les talons courts,** to be an easy lay/a pushover. (*Voir* **estomac 1**)

tam [tam] *nm P* = **tam-tam**.

tambouille [tãbuj] *nf P* cooking/ cookery; food*/chow/nosh/grub; **faire la tambouille,** to make/to get (the) grub; **quelle tambouille!** what muck!

tambour [tãbur] *nm F* **1.** **raisonner comme un tambour (mouillé),** to talk through one's hat/to talk drivel **2.** **marcher comme un tambour,** to fall for it (like a mug) **3.** **il n'y a pas de quoi faire passer le tambour de ville,** it's nothing to make a song and dance about; it's nothing to write home about. (*Voir* **feu 6**)

tampax [tãpaks] *nm or f P* filter tip(ped) cigarette*.

tampon [tãpɔ̃] *nm F* **1.** **coup de tampon,** violent blow*/punch/ thump; **coups de tampon,** brawl/ punch-up **2.** *pl* **tampons,** fists **3.** (*mil*) orderly/batman.

tamponnage [tãpɔnaʒ] *nm,* **tamponnement** [tãpɔnmã] *nm F* beating*-up/good hiding.

tamponner [tãpɔne] **I** *vtr* **1.** *F* **tamponner qn,** to beat s.o. up*/to give s.o. a good hiding/to knock s.o. about **2.** *P* **tamponner une nana/une nénette,** to have sex* with a girl; (*fille*) **se faire tamponner,** to get laid **II** *vpr* **se tamponner 1.** *F* to come to blows/to have a punch-up **2.** *P* **je m'en tamponne,** I couldn't care less*; I don't give a damn; to hell with it. (*Voir* **coquillard**)

tamponnoir [tãpɔnwar] *nm P* sani- tary towel/*NAm* napkin; rag.

tam-tam [tamtam] *nm F* (*a*) (vulgar/loud) publicity; ballyhoo (*b*) row/fuss; **faire du tam-tam (à propos de qch/autour de qch)**, to make a great to-do/to make a song and dance/to kick up a rumpus (about sth).

tandem [tɑ̃dɛm] *nm F* pair (of criminals, etc); duo/couple/twosome.

tangent, -ente¹ [tɑ̃ʒɑ̃, -ɑ̃t] **I** *a* **1.** *P* **c'est tangent** (*i*) it's as near as dammit (*ii*) it's touch and go **2.** *F* **être tangent à un examen**, to narrowly fail an exam **II** *n F* candidate who came very near the pass mark/borderline case **III** *nf F* **1.** invigilator (at an exam) **2.** sword (of student at the *Ecole polytechnique*) **3. prendre la tangente/s'échapper par la tangente/filer par la tangente** (*i*) to fly off at a tangent; to dodge the question/to wriggle out (of sth) (*ii*) to make a quick getaway/to beat it.

tango [tɑ̃go] *nm F* (*boisson*) beer with grenadine syrup added/(sort of) shandy.

tannant [tanɑ̃] *a P* boring; annoying/irritating; **il est tannant**, he drives me mad; he's a pest/a (damned) nuisance.

tannée [tane] *nf F* thrashing/(good) hiding/tanning.

tanner [tane] *vtr* **1.** *F* **tanner (la peau à) qn**, to thrash s.o./to tan the hide off s.o./to give s.o. a (good) hiding. (*Voir* **côte I 3**; **cuir 3**) **2.** *F* **tanner les oreilles à qn au sujet de qch**, to din to/to drum sth into s.o. **3.** *P* to bore* (s.o.); to pester/to badger (s.o.); to annoy*/to irritate (s.o.); to drive s.o. up the wall/mad.

tanneur [tanœr] *nm P* cadger/sponger/scrounger.

tant [tɑ̃] *adv* **1.** *F* **il pleut tant qu'il peut**, it's raining like anything/it's raining cats and dogs **2.** *F* **vous m'en direz tant!** (*i*) you don't say! (*ii*) now I see!/now I understand!

3. *F* **un Docteur Tant pis**, a pessimist; **un Docteur Tant mieux**, an optimist **4.** *P* **tant qu'à** (= *quant à*), as for; **tant qu'à ça, je m'en fous**, as for that, I don't give a damn; **tant que vous y êtes, prenez-en deux**, take two, while you're about it. (*Voir* **pire**)

tante [tɑ̃t] *nf P* **1.** homosexual*/fairy/queen/poof(ter)/*esp NAm* fag(got)/nancy-boy **2.** (*insulte*) **espèce de tante!** you poofter! **3. quelle tante!** what a bore (he is)!/what a pest (he is)! **4. chez ma tante**, at the pawn-broker's/in hock **5. si ma tante en avait, elle s'appellerait mon oncle**, if my aunt had balls she'd be my uncle **6.** (*CB*) **Tante Victorine**, television (set)/TV. (*Voir* **Bretagne**; **rose II 4**)

tantine [tɑ̃tin] *nf F* auntie/aunty.

tantinette [tɑ̃tinɛt] *nf* = **tante 1**.

tantouse, tantouze [tɑ̃tuz] *nf P* (ageing) homosexual*. (*Voir* **tante 1**)

tapage [tapaʒ] *nm P* cadging; tapping/touching (of s.o. for money).

tapanard [tapanar] *nm P* buttocks*.

tapant [tapɑ̃] **I** *a F* **arriver tapant/à l'heure tapante**, to arrive dead on time/bang on time/on the dot **II** *nm P* (smelly) cheese.

tape [tap] *nf P* failure/setback/knock; **quelle tape!** what a flop! **ramasser/prendre une tape** (*i*) to come a cropper (*ii*) to flop.

tapé [tape] *a P* **1.** mad*/bonkers/crackers **2.** excellent*/first-rate; **une réponse tapée**, a smart answer; **ça, c'est (bien) tapé!** that's a good one!/nice work!

tape-à-l'œil [tapalœj] *F* **I** *a inv* flashy/showy/loud/tarty **II** *nm* **du tape-à-l'œil**, flashy stuff; **c'est du tape-à-l'œil**, it's all for show.

tapecu(l), tape-cul [tapky] *nm F* **1.** (ramshackle) car*; banger/

jalopy; (vélo) boneshaker 2. train that stops at every station 3. faire du tapecu(l), to trot (on horseback).

tapée [tape] nf F great quantity*/ large number (of things, people); une tapée de marmots, a swarm of brats; j'en ai une tapée, I've got heaps/tons/plenty.

taper [tape] I vtr F taper la carte, to play cards; taper une belote/en taper une, to play/to have a game of belote 2. F (aut) taper du 200, to clock 200 kilometres an hour; to hit the 200 mark 3. F taper qn de cent francs, to tap/to touch s.o. for a hundred francs; to cadge a hundred francs off s.o. 4. F se faire taper sur les doigts, to take the rap 5. P se taper/s'en taper le derrière/ le cul par terre, to split one's sides laughing/to kill oneself laughing. (Voir astap(e); colonne 2; gueule I 4 (b); lampe 1; tête 22) II vi 1. F (soleil) to beat down; ça tape! it's a scorcher! 2. F (a) taper sur qn, to abuse/to knock s.o.; on lui a tapé dessus, they pitched into him (b) (mil) taper sur un objectif, to give a target a pasting; to strafe an objective 3. F taper ferme, to slog 4. P to stink*; ça tape ici! what a stink! taper des pieds, to have smelly feet*. (Voir nerf 1; œil 1, 2; système; tas 4; ventre) III vpr se taper 1. F se taper de qn, to make fun of s.o./to poke fun at s.o.; je me/m'en tape de lui, I couldn't give a damn about him 2. F se taper de qch (i) to be deprived of sth/to (have to) do without sth; je me tape de tout ça! I couldn't give a damn about all that! 3. F se taper qch (i) to treat oneself to sth (nice); se taper un double whisky, to treat oneself to a double whisky. (Voir cloche I 7; gueuleton) (ii) to have to do sth (unpleasant); se taper 20 kilomètres à pied, to have to do 20 kilometres on foot; se taper le ménage, to get landed/lumbered with the house-work 4. P tu peux te taper! noth-

ing doing!*/no way!/you can whis-tle for it!/take a running jump! 5. V se taper une femme, to have sex* with/to lay/to screw a woman. (Voir colonne 2)

tapette [tapɛt] nf P 1. homosex-ual*/fairy/pansy/nancy boy/esp NAm fag(got); c'est une vraie tapette, he's a real poof(ter); bar à tapettes, gay bar 2. tongue/clap-per; avoir une fameuse/une sacrée tapette; avoir une de ces tapettes, to be a dreadful chatterbox*; to have the gift of the gab.

tapeur, euse [tapœr, -øz] n F 1. third-rate pianist 2. cadger/ sponger/scrounger.

tapin [tapɛ̃] nm P 1. prostitute*/ hooker/tart; faire le tapin/aller au tapin/descendre sur le tapin, to be a prostitute*/a street-walker/to be on the game 2. work/job; aller au tapin, to go to work.

tapinage [tapinaʒ] nm P prostitu-tion; être au tapinage, to solicit*/to be on the game.

tapiner [tapine] vi P 1. (prostituée) to walk the streets (looking for cli-ents)/to solicit*/to be on the game; to be on the job 2. to work.

tapineuse [tapinøz] nf P prosti-tute*/street-walker/hooker.

tapir [tapir] nm F (scol) 1. private lesson 2. pupil who takes private lessons.

tapiriser [tapirize] vtr F (scol) to coach.

tapis [tapi] I a P être tapis, to be penniless*/to be broke II nm 1. F discussion de marchands de tapis, haggling 2. F sur le tapis, on the carpet/under consideration 3. P faire un tapis, to kick up a row/to make a fuss 4. P = tapis-franc. (Voir revenir 3)

tapis-franc [tapifrɑ̃] nm A P low drinking-den/gambling joint; dive; hangout (for criminals).

tapissage [tapisaʒ] *nm P* **passer au tapissage**, to submit to an identification parade.

tapisser [tapise] *vtr P* to identify/ to recognize/to clock (s.o.); **il s'est fait tapissé par les flics**, he was spotted by the cops/the cops got a make on him.

tapisserie [tapisri] *nf F* **faire tapisserie**, to be a wallflower (at a dance); to sit on the sidelines.

tapuscrit [tapyskri] *nm F* typed manuscript.

taquemart [takmar] *nm P* taxi/ cab. (*Voir* **tac**)

taquet [takɛ] *nm O F* blow*/ punch; **prendre un taquet dans la gueule**, to get a clout on the jaw.

tarabuster [tarabyste] *vtr F* **1.** (*a*) to annoy*/to worry/to pester/to bug (s.o.) (*b*) **se tarabuster l'esprit**, to rack one's brains **2.** to reprimand* (s.o.)/to blow (s.o.) up.

taratara! [taratara] *int F* nonsense*!/bunkum!/fiddlesticks!

taraudée [tarode] *nf F* thrashing/ beating*(-up)/pasting/(good) hiding.

tarauder [tarode] *vtr F* **1.** to thrash/to beat (up)*/to lay into (s.o.) **2.** to annoy*/to pester/to bug (s.o.).

tarbouif [tarbwif] *nm P* nose*/ hooter.

tarde [tard] *nf P* night.

tarderie [tardri] *nf P* (*femme*) **une (vraie) tarderie**, an old hag/an old bag; (*chose, idée, etc*) unpleasantness; problem; **cette robe c'est une vraie tarderie**, that dress is a real eyesore/a perfect mess.

tardillon, -onne [tardijɔ̃, -ɔn] *n F* last child/baby (of the family).

tardingue [tardɛ̃g] *a&nf P* ugly (woman).

tarebouif [tarbwif] *nm P* = **tarbouif.**

targette [tarʒɛt] *nf P* **1. coup de** targette, loan; **filer un coup de targette à qn**, to borrow from s.o./ to cadge off s.o./to touch s.o. (for sth) **2.** *pl* **targettes**, shoes/boots; **coup de targette**, kick.

tarif [tarif] *nm F* maximum penalty (for crime, etc).

tarin [tarɛ̃] *nm P* **1.** nose*/conk **2. se casser/se cogner le tarin** (*i*) to find nobody at home (when calling at a house) (*ii*) to fail (in business); to come a cropper* **3. avoir qn dans le tarin**, to detest s.o.; **je l'ai dans le tarin**, he gets up my nose **4. se salir/se piquer le tarin**, to get drunk*; to hit the bottle; **avoir un (petit) coup dans le tarin/avoir un coup de trop dans le tarin/avoir le tarin sali**, to be drunk*.

tarpé [tarpe] *nm P* (*verlan de* **pétard**) cigarette* de marijuana/ joint/reefer.

tartavelle [tartavɛl] *a&nf P* ugly (woman).

tarte [tart] **I** *a F* **1.** (*pers*) stupid*/daft; ridiculous **2.** ugly; lousy/crummy; ridiculous; **un film tarte**, rotten/stupid film; **chapeau tarte**, ridiculous hat **II** *nf* **1.** *F* (*théâtre, etc*) custard pie (thrown at s.o.) **2.** *F* **c'est de la (vraie) tarte**, it's easy*/it's a piece of cake; **la vie ce n'est pas de la tarte**, life's not always a bed of roses **3.** *P* slap/ smack **4.** *P* **se fendre la tarte**, to laugh* a lot/to be in stitches.

Tartempion [tartɑ̃pjɔ̃] *nm F* (*pers*) (*a*) thingummy/what's-his-name/so-and-so (*b*) any Tom, Dick or Harry.

tarter [tarte] *vtr P* **tarter qn**, to slap s.o.'s face; to punch s.o. in the face.

tartignol(l)e [tartiɲɔl] *a P* = **tarte I 1, 2.**

tartinage [tartinaʒ] *nm P* borrowing/cadging/scrounging.

tartine [tartin] *nf* **1.** *F* long, rambling speech, letter, article, etc; screed; **il m'a débité toute une tar-**

tine (*i*) he came out with this really long story (*ii*) he lectured me at great length/he seemed to go on for ever; **en faire une tartine/faire des tartines sur qch,** to waffle on about sth **2.** P shoe/boot **3.** *pl* P feet*. (*Voir* **palas(s) II 1**)

tartiner [tartine] **I** *vi* **1.** F to ramble (on)/to waffle (on)/to be long-winded **2.** P to borrow (*esp* money) **II** *vpr* **se tartiner** P **1.** to look the worse for wear **2. je m'en tartine! I** don't give a damn!/ I couldn't care (bloody) less!*

tartinier [tartinje] *nm* F long-winded, rambling, speaker *or* writer.

tartir [tartir] *vi* **1.** P **envoyer tartir qn,** to tell s.o. to get lost/to bugger off; to give s.o. the bum's rush **2.** P **se faire tartir,** to be bored* stiff/ to be fed up to the back teeth **3.** V to defecate*/to (have a) shit/to (have a) crap.

tartiss(es) [tartis] *nm or f pl,* **tartissoires** [tartiswar] *nm or f pl.* V WC*/craphouse/crapper/ shithouse.

tartissure [tartisyr] *nf* V stain, dirty mark (of excrement on underclothes).

tartouillard [tartujar], **tartouille** [tartuj] *a* P = **tarte I 1, 2.**

tartouse [tartuz], **tartouzard** [tartuzar], **tartouze** [tartuz] *a* P = **tarte I 1, 2.**

tas [tɑ] *nm* F **1. sur le tas,** immediately*/straight away **2. prendre qn sur le tas,** to catch s.o. in the act/ red-handed; **être crevé/fabriqué/fait marron/piqué sur le tas,** to be caught in the act/to be caught red-handed **3. sécher sur le tas,** to wait in vain/to be hung up **4. piquer dans le tas,** to help oneself; to take one's choice/to take one's pick; **taper/cherrer dans le tas,** to strike out blindly; to take on all comers/to take what comes **5.** (*prostituée*) **faire le tas,** to solicit*/

to walk the streets/to be on the game; to hook/to hustle **6.** ugly girl*/woman*; **quel tas!** what a mess (she is)!/what a fright! **7. tas de ferraille/de boue/de tôle,** broken-down car*/old banger/wreck/ heap (of scrap metal) **8.** large quantity*; **un tas de mensonges,** a pack of lies; **(il) y en a des tas (et des tas),** there's heaps/bags/loads of them; **j'ai un tas de choses à faire,** I've (got) loads of things to do; **quel tas de gens!** what a collection!/what a crew! **tas de crétins!** bunch of idiots! **tas de salauds!** you bastards!

tasse [tɑs] *nf* **1.** F **la grande tasse,** the sea/the drink/the briny/Davy Jones's locker; **boire (à) la grande tasse,** to be drowned at sea; **boire/ prendre une tasse,** to get a mouthful (when swimming) **2.** F (*entreprise, affaire, etc*) **boire la tasse,** to come a cropper*/to fail/to come unstuck/to go under **3.** P **en avoir sa tasse,** to be (thoroughly) fed up* (with sth)/to have had it (up to here) **4.** P **tasse (à thé),** street urinal (*esp* one frequented by homosexuals)/cottage/tea room(s); **faire les tasses,** to cottage/to go cottaging/to go john cruising **5.** P glass of wine.

tassé [tɑse] *a* F (*a*) full/complete/ whole; **livre de 1000 pages bien tassées,** book with a good/of at least 1000 pages; **deux heures (bien) tassées,** two whole/solid hours (*b*) **un grog bien tassé,** a stiff grog.

tasseau, *pl* **-eaux** [tɑso] *nm* P = **tassot.**

tassée [tɑse] *nf* F large quantity*. (*Voir* **tas 8**)

tasser [tɑse] **I** *vtr* P **1. qu'est-ce que je lui ai tassé!** I gave him what for!/I didn't half let him have it! **2. qu'est-ce qu'il s'est tassé au dîner!** he didn't half put it away at dinner! **II** *vpr* **se tasser** F to settle down; to blow over; **(tout) ça se tassera/finira (bien) par se tasser,** it will (all) sort itself out; it'll all come out in the wash; **tout finit par se tasser,** everything comes out all right in the end.

tasseuse [tasøz] *nf P* homosexual* who frequents urinals/who hangs about in loos/*NAm* johns (looking for partners).

tassot [taso] *nm P* nose*; **se sécher le tassot,** to blow/to wipe one's nose.

tata [tata] *nf* **1.** *F (mot enfantin)* auntie/aunty **2.** *F* **Madame Tata,** Mrs Busybody **3.** *P* homosexual*/queen/fairy/poof.

tatane [tatan] *nf P* boot; shoe; **filer un coup de tatane dans les burnes à qn,** to kick s.o. in the balls.

tâter [tate] **I** *v ind tr F* **1. vous en tâterez,** it'll come your way one of these days/you'll get your chance **2. il a tâté de la prison,** he's done time/he's been inside **II** *vpr* **se tâter 1.** *F* **se tâter (avant de faire qch),** to think it over/to weigh up the pros and cons (before doing sth) **2.** *P* **va te faire tâter!** get lost!*/beat it!/go (and) jump in the lake!/go play with yourself!

tâteuse [tatøz] *nf P* skeleton key.

tati [tati] *nf F P* = **tata 1, 4.**

tatoué [tatwe] *nm P* **un tatoué,** a tough guy.

tatouille [tatuj] *nf P (a)* thrashing/beating*(-up) *(b)* defeat/licking.

tatouiller [tatuje] *vtr P (a)* to thrash/to beat (s.o.) up* *(b)* to defeat/to lick.

taulard, -arde [tolar, -ard] *P* **I** *n* prisoner; convict; old lag/jailbird **II** *a* **mes Noëls taulards,** the Christmases I spent in prison*/in clink.

taule [tol] *nf P* **1.** prison*; **en taule,** in the nick; **aller en taule,** to go to prison; **faire de la taule,** to do time/to do a stretch; **il a fait de la taule,** he's been inside/he's done bird; *(mil)* **six semaines de taule,** six weeks' detention/six weeks in the glasshouse; **la Grande Taule,** the Central Police Headquarters **2.** *(a)* house; *(voleurs)* drum/gaff; **rappliquer à la taule,** to return home/to make tracks *(b)* room/pad **3.** brothel*/knocking shop.

taulier [tolje] *nm P* **1.** proprietor/owner/keeper (of pub, lodging house, brothel, etc) **2.** boss*/guv'nor/chief.

taulière [toljɛr] *nf P* brothel owner/madam(e).

taupe [top] *nf* **1.** *F* **partir pour le/s'en aller au royaume des taupes,** to die* **2.** *F (a) (mil)* **guerre de taupes,** mine warfare *(b) (espionnage)* mole **3.** *F (scol)* second-year class preparing for the *Ecole polytechnique (b)* special maths class **3.** *P* **vieille taupe,** old hag/old bag/old bat **4.** *P* prostitute*/tart.

taupin [topɛ̃] *nm F (scol) (a)* student reading for the *Ecole polytechnique (b)* student in special maths class.

taxer [takse] *vtr P* to steal*/to knock off.

taxi [taksi] *nm* **1.** *F* taxi/cab driver; **il est taxi,** he's a cabby **2.** *F (véhicule)* car; plane **3.** *P* agent/go-between **4.** *P* prostitute*.

t'chi [tʃi] *adv phr P* **que t'chi,** nothing* at all/damn all/sweet FA/sod-all.

tchin-tchin [tʃintʃin] *int F* cheers!*/cheerio!/chin-chin!

teb [tɛb] *nf P (verlan de* **bite***)* penis*/cock/prick/tool.

técolle [tekɔl] *pron P* you.

tefu [tefy] *nf P (a)* motorbike/bike *(b)* mobylette/moped.

téhon [teɔ̃] *nf P (verlan de honte)* shame.

teigne [tɛɲ] *nf F (femme)* shrew/vixen; cow.

teigneux [tɛɲø] *nm P* **1.** nasty individual/rotter/louse **2. j'en**

mangerais sur la tête d'un teigneux, I (simply) adore it. (*Voir* **pelé I**)

teint [tɛ̃] *nm* F **bon teint** (*i*) authentic/genuine/kosher (*ii*) staunch; **catholique bon teint,** staunch catholic.

teinté [tɛ̃te] *a* P drunk*/sloshed.

teintée [tɛ̃te] *nf* P (*a*) drunkenness (*b*) binge.

télé [tele] *nf* F (*a*) television/TV/telly/*NAm* tube; **je l'ai vu à la télé,** I saw it on the box (*b*) television set/TV/telly/goggle-box/idiot-box.

télégraphe [telegraf] *nm* O (*a*) F **faire le télégraphe,** to wave one's arms about; to gesticulate (wildly) (*b*) P **faire le télégraphe à qn,** to warn s.o. (by a signal); to give s.o. the tip-off/to tip s.o. off*.

télémuche [telemyʃ] *nm* P telephone*/blower.

téléphone [telefɔn] *nm* **1.** F **téléphone arabe,** grapevine/bush telegraph **2.** P WC; **aller au téléphone,** to go to the toilet/to pay a call.

téléphoner [telefɔne] *vtr&i* **1.** F **c'était téléphoné,** it was easy to see what was coming; you could have told a mile off what was going to happen next **2.** P **téléphoner au pape,** to defecate* **3.** V (*fellation*) **téléphoner dans le ventre,** to give head/to give (s.o.) a blow-job.

télévise [televiz] *nf* F = **télé.**

téloche [telɔʃ] *nf* P = **télé.**

tème [tɛm] *nm* P **faire tème** = **faire thème (thème 2).**

tempérament [tɑ̃peramɑ̃] *nm* **1.** F **avoir du tempérament,** to be highly sexed/to be hot-blooded **2.** P **tu en as un tempérament!** you've got a nerve! **3.** P **se crever/s'escrimer/s'esquinter le tempérament,** to knock oneself up.

température [tɑ̃peratyr] *nf* F **prendre la température,** to see how things stand/to suss things out.

templier [tɑ̃plije] *nm* F **1. jurer comme un templier,** to swear like a trooper/to eff and blind (all over the place) **2. boire comme un templier,** to drink* heavily/to drink like a fish.

temps [tɑ̃] *nm* F **1. il fera beau temps quand je ferai cela,** it'll be a long time before I do that **2. en deux temps trois mouvements,** immediately*/in no time/in two shakes (of a lamb's tail) **3. prendre/se payer/s'en payer/passer du bon temps,** to have a good time/to have fun. (*Voir* **tirer 5**)

tendeur [tɑ̃dœr] *nm* P highly-sexed man; womanizer*/gash-hound.

tendre [tɑ̃dr] *nm* F **avoir un tendre pour qn,** to have a soft spot for s.o.

tendron [tɑ̃drɔ̃] *nm* **1.** O F young, innocent girl **2.** P (*homosexuels*) **se faire un tendron,** to have sex* with a young boy/to have a chicken dinner.

tenir [tənir] *vtr* **1.** F **tenir un bon rhume,** to have a stinking cold **2.** P **en tenir une,** to be drunk*/to have one tied on; **qu'est-ce qu'il tient (comme cuite/comme muffée)!** he's dead drunk*!/he's completely sozzled! **3.** P **en tenir/en tenir une (couche),** to be an absolute fool*/to be very stupid*. (*Voir* **couche 1**) **4.** F **en tenir pour qn,** to be infatuated* with s.o./to have a crush on s.o./to fancy s.o. (*Voir* **crachoir 1, 2; mer 3**)

tentiaire [tɑ̃sjɛr] *nf* P (= *maison pénitentiaire*) penitentiary/(reformatory) prison*.

terre [tɛr] *nf* V **terre jaune,** anal sex*/sodomy/buggery. (*Voir* **rentrer 2**)

terre-neuve [tɛrnœv] *nm* F **faire le terre-neuve,** to help lame ducks.

terreur [tɛrœr] *nf* F gangster/thug; **jouer les terreurs,** to act tough/to play the tough-guy.

terrible [tɛribl] **I** *a* F terrific/extraordinary/fantastic/great/out of this world; **c'était pas bien terrible,** it wasn't anything special; **c'est un type terrible,** he's terrific/incredible **II** *adv F* fantastically/terribly; **ça chauffe terrible,** it's going really well/it's really great/it's going great guns.

terriblement [tɛribləmã] *adv F* (*intensif*) terribly/dreadfully; **terriblement en retard,** terribly late.

terrine [tɛrin] *nf P* **1.** face*/mug; **se fendre la terrine,** to laugh* a lot/to split one's sides laughing; **nous nous fendions la terrine,** we were in stitches **2.** head* (*a*) **souffrir de la terrine,** to have headaches (*b*) **terrine de gelée d'andouille!/terrine de gelée de paf!** you bloody fool!/you stupid* bugger!

têtard [tɛtar] *nm P* **1.** baby (boy)/kid/brat **2.** drunkard*/heavy drinker/boozer/alky **3.** **être têtard** (*i*) to be a mug/a sucker; to be the fall guy/the patsy; **faire qn têtard,** to dupe s.o./to take s.o. in; to make a sucker out of s.o. (*ii*) to be arrested*/to be nabbed **4.** horse fit only for the knacker's yard.

têtarer [tɛtare] *vtr A P* **têtarer qn** = **faire qn têtard** (**têtard 3** (*i*)).

tétasses [tetas] *nfpl P* (large, pendulous) breasts*/big tits.

tête [tɛt] *nf* **1.** *F* **une grosse tête,** an intellectual/a highbrow/an egghead **2.** *F* **faire la/sa tête,** to sulk/to make a face; **(en) faire une tête,** to pull a long face; to look glum/grim; **faire une drôle de tête,** to look quite put out **3.** *F* **c'est une tête de bois,** he's a blockhead/he's wood from the neck up **4.** *F* **c'est une tête de cochon/de mule/de pioche/***P* **de lard,** he's/she's pigheaded; he's/she's as stubborn as a mule **5.** *F* **casser/rompre la tête à qn,** to annoy*/to pester s.o.; to get on s.o.'s nerves **6.** *F* **j'en ai par-dessus la tête!** (*i*) I've had enough (of it)!/I'm fed up (with it)!/I've had it up to here! (*ii*) I'm up to my eyes in it! **7.** *F* **laver/lessiver/**

savonner la tête à qn, to reprimand* s.o. severely/to tear s.o. off a strip; **lavage de tête,** reprimand*/ticking-off/bawling-out **8.** *F* **se payer la tête de qn** (*i*) to take the mickey out of s.o. (*ii*) to fool s.o./to pull a fast one on s.o. **9.** *F* **tête de pipe,** picture of s.o. (*eg* in a newspaper); **avoir une tête de pipe,** to have a funny face/to look odd **10.** *F* **avoir qch derrière la tête,** to have a secret plan/to have sth up one's sleeve **11.** *F* **tête d'oreiller** (= **taie d'oreiller**), pillowcase/pillow-slip **12.** *F* **avoir une bonne tête** (*i*) to look a decent (sort of) chap (*ii*) to look a bit of a mug (*iii*) to have one's head screwed on the right way **13.** *F* **monter la tête à qn,** to work on s.o.'s feelings/s.o.'s emotions; to poison s.o.'s mind; to work s.o. up (**contre,** against); **il avait la tête montée,** he was (all) worked up; his blood was up **14.** *F* **jeter qch à la tête de qn,** to foist sth on s.o. **15.** *P* **faire à qn une grosse tête,** to box s.o.'s ears/to give s.o. a thick ear **16.** *P* **tomber sur la tête,** to go mad*/crackers/bonkers; **il est tombé sur la tête,** he's mad*/he was dropped on his head when he was young; **je ne suis pas tombé sur la tête,** I'm not daft **17.** *P* **tête d'imbécile!** (you) idiot!/(you) clot! **18.** *P* **se taper la tête,** to eat* heartily/to have a good tuck-in/to have a good blow-out **19.** *P* **petite tête** (**d'épingle**), young fellow/young lad; (*terme d'affection*) **comment ça va, petite tête?** how goes it, my boy/laddie? **20.** *P* **avoir une tête à coucher dehors (avec un billet de logement dans sa poche),** to have a very ugly face*/to have a face that would stop a clock. (*Voir* **carré II; claque 1; cul 1, 25; enterrement 1; gifle; linotte 1; nœud 1; œil 17; un; veau**)

téter [tete] *vi F* to drink* heavily/to booze/to knock it back/to swill it down.

tétère [tetɛr] *nf*, **téterre** [tetɛr] *nf*
P head*.

tétés [tete] *nmpl* P breasts*/tits/tit-
ties.

tétines [tetin] *nfpl* P (pendulous)
breasts*.

tétonnière [tetɔnjɛr] *a&nf* F big-
bosomed (woman).

tétons [tetɔ̃] *nmpl* P breasts*/tits/
titties.

tettes [tɛt] *nfpl* F (woman's) nip-
ples/teats.

teuch [tœʃ] *nm* P (*drogues*) (*verlan
de* **shit**) hashish*/shit.

teuche [tœʃ] *nf* P (*verlan de*
chatte) female genitals*/pussy/
beaver.

teuf-teuf [tœftœf] *nm* F **1.** (*mot
d'enfant*) train/puffer (train)/puff-
puff/chuff-chuff/chuffer **2.** (*a*) (*mot
d'enfant*) car*/brum-brum (*b*) ramshackle old car*/banger/jalopy.

tévé [teve] *nf* F (*a*) television/telly/
TV (*b*) television set/TV set/telly.
(*Voir* **télé 1, 2**)

texto [tɛksto], **textuel** [tɛkstɥɛl],
textuo [tɛkstɥo] *adv* P word for
word; verbatim.

tézig(ue) [tezig] *pron* P you/your-
self. (*Voir* **mézig(ue), cézig(ue)/
sézig(ue), no(s)zig(ue)s,
vo(s)zig(ue)s, euzig(ue)s/
leur(s)zig(ue)s**)

thala [tala] *a&n* F = **tala.**

thé [te] *nm* P **1. marcher au thé** (*i*)
to drink* heavily/to be a
drunk(ard) (*ii*) (*drogues*) to smoke
marijuana*/grass **2. prendre le
thé,** to be a homosexual*. (*Voir*
tasse 4; théière 2)

théâtreux, -euse [teatrø, -øz] *n*
F (*péj*) actor/actress with little talent; actor/actress of sorts.

théière [tejɛr] *nf* P **1.** head* **2.**
= **tasse (à thé) (tasse 4).**

thème [tɛm] *nm* **1.** F **c'est un fort
en thème,** he's a swot/a bit of an
egghead **2.** P **faire thème,** to keep

mum; to keep one's trap shut (and
mind one's own business).

thésard, -arde [tezar, -ard] *n* F
student preparing a thesis.

Thomas, thomas [tɔma] *nm* P
chamber-pot*/jerry.

thunard [tynar] *nm* P = **thune**
(*a*).

thunarder [tynarde] *vi* P **1.** to
pinch and scrape **2.** to play for
small stakes/for peanuts.

thune [tyn] *nf* A P (*a*) five-franc
piece (*b*) **je me suis retrouvé sans
une thune,** I found myself penniless* (*c*) **je n'en donnerais pas deux
thunes,** I wouldn't give tuppence
for it.

thunette [tynɛt] *nf* A P = **thune**
(*a*).

à tic [atik] *adv phr* F **prendre qn à
tic,** to take a dislike to s.o.

ticket [tikɛ] *nm* P **1. un drôle de
ticket,** an odd character/a strange
person*/a strange (sort of) chap/a
funny bloke/a queer fish **2.** nym-
phomaniac/nympho **3. prendre un
ticket** (*i*) to be a voyeur/a Peeping
Tom; to get an eyeful (*ii*) to watch
a pornographic show. (*Voir* **jeton**)
4. (*a*) 1000 (old) franc note (*b*) 10
(new) franc note **5. avoir/faire un
ticket avec qn,** to make a hit with
s.o. (of the opposite sex)/to get off
with s.o./to click with s.o. (*Voir*
touche 1)

tickson, ticson [tiksɔ̃] *nm* P **1.**
(railway, theatre, etc) ticket **2.** =
**ticket 4 3. faire un tickson avec
qn** = **faire un ticket avec qn (ticket
5**).

tic-tac [tiktak] *nm* P revolver*.

tiédasse [tjedas] *a* F lukewarmish.

tienne [tjɛn] *poss pron f* F **1. à la
(bonne) tienne!** cheers*!/here's mud
in your eye!/skol! **2. tu as encore
fait des tiennes!** you've been up to
your old tricks again!

tierce [tjɛrs] *nf* P **1.** gang (of
criminals, etc) **2. avoir tierce**

belote et dix de der, to be fifty (years old).

tiers [tjɛr] *nm* F (*a*) **devoir au tiers et au quart**, to owe money right and left (*b*) **consulter le tiers et le quart**, to consult all and sundry (*c*) **je me moque du tiers comme du quart**, I don't give a damn about anyone or anything.

tiffes [tif] *nmpl* P = **tifs.**

tif(f)ier [tifje] *nm* P hairdresser/barber.

tifs [tif] *nmpl* P hair/thatch. (*Voir* **nib**)

tige [tiʒ] *nf* **1.** F (*a*) **vieille tige**, old chap*/old boy (*b*) (*aviation*) **les vieilles tiges**, pilots who got their licence before 1914 **2.** F **des tiges de pâquerettes**, thin, spindly legs*/matchsticks **3.** P cigarette* **4.** shoe; boot **5.** (*usu m*) policeman*. (*Voir* **brouter 2**)

tignasse [tiɲas] *nf* F shock/mop (of hair). (*Voir* **crêper**)

tilleul [tijœl] *nm* **1.** F (*boisson*) red and white wine mixed **2.** P **se faire élaguer les tilleuls**, to get one's hair cut/to be scalped.

tilt [tilt] *adv* P **faire tilt** (*i*) to hit the mark; to be spot on (*ii*) to have an inspiration/a sudden thought; **et puis tout à coup, ça a fait tilt**, and then, suddenly, it clicked.

timbale [tɛ̃bal] *nf* F **1. décrocher la timbale**, to win the prize; to hit the jackpot; to bring home the bacon **2. avoir un pépin dans la timbale**, to be slightly mad*/to have a screw loose.

timbre [tɛ̃br] *nm* F head*; **avoir le timbre fêlé/avoir un coup de timbre**, to be slightly mad*/to be a bit cracked/to have a screw missing.

timbré [tɛ̃bre] *a* F **1.** slightly mad*/cracked/dotty/potty **2.** **du papier timbré** (*i*) a summons (*ii*) an (unpleasant) official communication.

tinche [tɛ̃ʃ] *nf* P (*a*) **faire la tinche**, to beg (*b*) **faire la/une tinche à qn**,

to go round with the hat for s.o./to have a whip-round for s.o.

tinée [tine] *nf* P large quantity*/lots/bags; **il y en a une tinée**, there's tons of it.

tinette [tinɛt] *nf* P **1.** (*a*) old car*/(old) banger/jalopy (*b*) vintage car (*c*) old motorbike **2. faire une tinette sur qn**, to criticize* s.o./to knock s.o./to drag s.o.'s name through the mud **3.** *pl* **tinettes**, WC*/loo/*NAm* john.

tintin [tɛ̃tɛ̃] F **I** *nm* **faire tintin**, to (have to) go without; to be done out of sth; to get nothing* **II** *int* (**c'est**) **tintin!** nothing doing!*/no go!/not a hope!

tintouin [tɛ̃twɛ̃] *nm* F **1.** din/racket/shindig **2.** worry/trouble/bother; **donner du tintouin**, to give trouble; **elle me donne bien du tintouin**, she's a headache; **quel tintouin ces gosses!** what a worry the kids are! **3. tout le tintouin**, the whole bag of tricks*.

tiquer [tike] *vi* F **il n'a pas tiqué**, he didn't turn a hair; **sans tiquer**, without batting an eyelid; **cela le fera tiquer!** that'll shake him!/that'll give him a jolt! **tiquer sur qch**, to react unfavourably to sth/to jib at sth.

tirage [tiraʒ] *nm* F **1.** difficulty/trouble; **il y a du tirage entre eux**, they don't hit it off **2. le premier tirage**, the first time/the first go/the first shot.

tiraillement [tirajmɑ̃] *nm* F disagreement/wrangling/friction.

tirailler [tiraje] *vtr* F to annoy*/to plague/to pester/to bug (s.o.).

tiraillerie [tirajri] *nf* F **1.** wrangling/friction **2.** plaguing/pestering.

tirailleur [tirajœr] *nm* F freelance (journalist).

tirants [tirɑ̃] *nmpl* P stockings.

tire [tir] *nf* **1.** F (**vol à**) **la tire**, pickpocketing; **voleur à la tire**, pickpocket*/dip/dipper; **faire la tire,** to be a pickpocket/to pick pockets **2.** *P* (*a*) car* (*b*) taxi/cab.

tire-au-cul [tiroky] *nm inv P* malingerer*/lazy bastard*/lazy sod/ skiver.

tire-au-flanc [tiroflɑ̃] *nm inv F* malingerer/shirker/skiver/lead-swinger/lazy bum.

tirebouchonnant [tirbuʃɔnɑ̃] *a F* very funny*/hilarious/killing (joke, etc).

se tirebouchonner [sətir-buʃɔne] *vpr F* to laugh* uproariously/to crease oneself/to double up with laughter.

tire-bouton [tirbutɔ̃] *nm P* **la maison tire-bouton,** (the world of) lesbians*/lesbianism; **un ménage tire-buton,** a couple of lesbians.

tirée [tire] *nf F* **1.** long distance (still to be covered); **il y a encore toute une tirée,** there's still a long haul/trek ahead **2.** **une tirée de ...,** lots of ... /heaps of ... / loads of ....

tire-fesses [tirfɛs] *nm inv F* drag lift/ski tow/ski lift.

tire-jus [tirʒy] *nm inv P* handkerchief*/nose-wipe/snot rag.

(à) tire-larigot [atirlarigo] *adv phr F* **boire à tire-larigot** (*i*) to drink by pouring wine (etc) from a height into one's mouth (*ii*) to drink* heavily/like a fish; **s'en donner à tire-larigot,** to drink/to eat to one's heart's content; to have one's fill.

tirelire [tirlir] *nf* **1.** *P* face* and mouth*/mug; **bouche de tirelire,** satchelmouth; **se fendre la tirelire** (*i*) to laugh (all over one's face) (*ii*) to break into a broad smile **2.** *P* head*/bonce **3.** *P* stomach*/belly/ guts **4.** *V* female genitals*.

tire-l'œil [tirlœj] *nm inv F* eye-catching feature/eye-catcher.

tire-moelle [tirmwal] *nm inv P* handkerchief*/snot rag/nose rag.

tire-môme(s) [tirmom] *nf P* mid-wife.

tire-pognon [tirpɔɲɔ̃] *nm inv F* one-arm(ed) bandit/fruit machine.

tirer [tire] **I** *vtr* **1.** *F* **ça tire!** it's stiff/tough going! **2.** *F* **être tiré à quatre,** to be worried stiff **3.** *P* to steal*/to pinch/to swipe/to knock off **4.** *F* **six mois à tirer,** six months to go/to do/to get through; **en voilà encore un(e) de tiré(e)!** that's another year (day, month, etc) gone! **5.** *P* **tirer de la prison/tirer son temps,** to serve a prison* sentence/to do time/to do bird; **tirer sept ans,** to get seven years/to do a seven-year stretch; **deux longes à tirer,** two years to do **6.** *V* (*a*) **se tirer son/un coup,** to masturbate*/to toss off (*b*) (*homme*) **tirer son/un coup,** to have sex*/to get one's end away. (*Voir* **couverte 2; couverture; crampe 1, 2; crampette; cul 18; échelle 2; ficelle II 2** (*c*)**, 7; flanc 3; ligne 2; renard 2; ver**) **II** *vpr* **se tirer 1.** *F* to come to an end; **ça se tire,** the end's in sight; it's nearly finished; it'll soon be over now; **ça s'est bien tiré?** did everything go off well?/did everything turn out all right? **2.** *P* (*pers*) to run away*/to beat it/to clear off/to make tracks; **bon, faut que je me tire,** right, must go!/OK, I'm off! **tirez-vous de là!** hop it!/clear off! (*Voir* **flûtes II; patte 1; pied 6; ripatons 2**)

tireur [tirœr] *nm* **1.** *F* pickpocket*. (*Voir* **tire 1**) **2.** *F* **tireur au flanc = tire-au-flanc 3.** *P* **tireur au cul = tire-au-cul.**

tiroir [tirwar] *nm* **1.** *F* **nom à tiroir** (*i*) double-barrelled name (*ii*) name with a handle to it **2.** *P* stomach*. (*Voir* **mouf(f)let; polichinelle 2** (*a*)**; salé²**) **3.** *P* **fourrer un corps dans le tiroir,** to place a corpse* in the coffin/to box a corpse.

tisane [tizan] *nf P* **1.** wishy-washy drink/catlap/gnat's piss/dish-water

2. severe thrashing/beating*; **filer une tisane à qn,** to beat s.o. up*.

tisaner [tizane] *vtr P* **tisaner qn,** to give s.o. a thrashing/to beat s.o. up*.

tisanier [tizanje] *nm P* male nurse.

titi [titi] *nm P* **1.** street arab/cheeky urchin/cocky little kid **2. titi négro** = pidgin English.

titine [titin] *nf,* **tititine** [tititin] *nf P* machine-gun.

toboggan [tɔbɔgã] *nm P* **se graisser le toboggan,** to drink* heavily/to booze/to hit the bottle.

toc [tɔk] **I** *a inv* **1.** *F* worthless*/sham/rubbishy/trashy **2.** *F* **être un peu toc,** to be slightly mad*/to be a bit touched **3.** *P* ugly **4.** *P* stupid*/dozy/gormless **5.** *P (pers)* dangerous/vicious **II** *nm* **1.** *F* fake/sham/imitation (gold, jewellery, etc); **bijoux en toc,** imitation jewellery; **c'est du toc!** it's a sham!/it's phon(e)y!/it's rubbish!/it's junk! **2.** *P* **marcher sous un toc/sous des tocs,** to go about with false identity papers **3.** *P* **manquer de toc,** to lack self-confidence/to lack nerve; **il ne manque pas de toc,** he's pretty sure of himself **III** *int P* **(et) toc!** so there!/put that in your pipe (and smoke it)!

tocade [tɔkad] *nf F* = **toquade.**

tocant [tɔkã] *nm P* heart/ticker.

tocante [tɔkãt] *nf P* watch/ticker.

tocard, arde [tɔkard] *P* **I** *a* = **toc I II** *n (a) (turf)* (rank) outsider; stumer *(b) (pers)* hopeless case/dead loss.

tocasse [tɔkas], **tocasson** [tɔkasɔ̃] *a P* = **toc I.**

tocbombe [tɔkbɔ̃b] *a,* **toctoc** [tɔktɔk] *a inv P* mad*/daft/dotty/potty.

toile [twal] *nf* **1.** *F* **se mettre/se filer/se glisser dans les toiles,** to go to bed*/to get between the sheets **2.** *P* **déchirer la toile,** to fart* loudly **3.** *P* **se faire/se payer une**

toile, to go to see a film; to go to the cinema/the flics.

toise [twaz] *nf P* thrashing/good hiding; **filer une toise à qn,** to beat s.o. up*/to clobber s.o.; **se filer des toises,** to fight/to have a punch-up.

toison [twazɔ̃] *nf F* mop/shock (of hair).

toiture [twatyr] *nf P* head*; **onduler de la toiture,** to be mad*/to have a screw loose; **varloper la toiture,** to have a haircut/to get one's barnet cut.

tôlard, arde [tolar, -ard] *a&n P* = **taulard, arde 1, 2.**

tôle [tol] *nf P* = **taule** *(all senses).*

se tôler [sətole] *vpr P* to laugh* uproariously.

tôlier [tolje] *nm P* **1.** = **taulier 1, 2 2.** superintendent of police.

tôlière [toljɛr] *nf P* = **taulière.**

tomate [tɔmat] *nf* **1.** *F* **être (rouge) comme une tomate,** to be as red as a beetroot **2.** *P (boisson)* pastis with grenadine **3.** *P* rosette of the Legion of Honour **4.** *P* face* **5.** *P* head* **6.** *P* red nose* **7.** *P* **des tomates!** nothing doing!*/no fear!/not (bloody) likely!* **8.** *P* fool*/idiot/twit; **avoir l'air tomate,** to look stupid* **9.** *P* **en être/en rester comme une tomate,** to be flabbergasted* **10.** *P* **grouille-toi la tomate!** hurry up!/get a move on!/move it! **11.** *P* **avoir ses tomates,** to have a period*/the curse.

tombeau, *pl* **-eaux** [tɔ̃bo] *nm F* **1. il me mettra/conduira au tombeau** *(i)* he'll outlive me *(ii)* he'll be the death of me **2.** *(pers)* **c'est un vrai tombeau,** his lips are sealed/he won't breathe a word about it **3. à tombeau ouvert,** at breakneck speed.

tomber [tɔ̃be] **I** *vtr P* **1.** to floor (s.o.)/to knock (s.o.) down **2.** to have sex* with (a woman)/to lay (a woman); **il les tombe toutes,** they all fall for him; he's a real Casanova/a real ladies' man/a wolf **3.** (*prostituée*) to pick up (a client)/to score/to turn a trick. (*Voir* **eau 11**; **veste**) **II** *vi* **1.** *F* **les bras m'en tombent,** I'm flabbergasted*/amazed **2.** *F* **laisser tomber qn** (*i*) to let s.o. down; to hang s.o. up (*ii*) to drop s.o./to ditch s.o. **3.** *F* **laisse tomber!** forget it!/drop it!/give it a rest! **4.** *F* **qu'est-ce qui/qu'il tombe!** it's pouring!/it's raining cats and dogs! **5.** *P* (*a*) to be arrested* (*b*) to be condemned (*c*) to be sentenced. (*Voir* **bec 7**; **dessus**; **eau 5**; **manche I 4**; **paletot 2**; **pomme 3**; **tête 16**)

tombeur [tɔ̃bœr] *nm F* **1.** womanizer*; **(grand) tombeur (de femmes/de filles),** sexually aggressive man; ladykiller/wolf/Don Juan/Casanova.

tondre [tɔ̃dr] *vtr F* **1.** to fleece* (s.o.); to take s.o. to the cleaners/to clean s.o. out; **se laisser tondre (la laine sur le dos),** to get fleeced **2.** **se faire tondre,** to get one's hair cut **3.** **j'ai d'autres chiens à tondre,** I've got other fish to fry.

tondu [tɔ̃dy] *a F* **être tondu (à zéro),** to be penniless*/cleaned out.

tonneau, *pl* **-eaux** [tɔno] *nm F* **1.** **du même tonneau,** of the same kind; alike; **ce sont gens du même tonneau,** they're birds of a feather; **c'est du même tonneau,** it's much of a muchness; it's six of one and half a dozen of the other **2.** (*voiture*) **faire un tonneau,** to roll over; to turn turtle. (*Voir* **cheval 11**)

tonnerre [tɔnɛr] *F* **I** *nm* **être fait comme un coup de tonnerre,** to be badly made **2.** ... **du tonnerre,** wonderful/terrific/great; **il fera un médecin du tonnerre/du tonnerre de Dieu/du tonnerre du diable/de tous les tonnerres,** he'll make a bloody good/a fantastic doctor; **un repas du tonnerre (de Dieu),** a fantastic/terrific meal; **un nom du tonnerre de Dieu,** a hellishly difficult name to pronounce **3.** **au tonnerre de**

Dieu, a long way away/very distant **II** *int* **tonnerre!/tonnerre de Dieu!/tonnerre de chien!/mille tonnerres (de Brest)!** by thunder!/heavens above!/good heavens! (*Voir* **nom 1**)

tonton [tɔ̃tɔ̃] *nm F* **1.** uncle **2.** *P* (*CB*) **Tonton Victor,** television (set)/TV.

tonus [tɔnys] *nm F* energy/dynamism.

topaze [tɔpaz] *nm P* grafter.

topo [tɔpo] *nm F* **1.** (*a*) (*journ*) (popular) article (*b*) exposé/report/breakdown; **faire un topo sur ...,** to hold forth on ...; **c'est toujours le même topo,** it's always the same old story **2.** (*mil*) staff officer/brass hat.

Topol [tɔpɔl] *Prn F* **le Topol,** the boulevard de Sébastopol (in Paris). (*Voir* **Sébasto**)

toquade [tɔkad] *nf F* (passing) craze/fad; infatuation; **avoir une toquade pour qn,** to be infatuated* with s.o./to have a crush on s.o.

toquant [tɔkɑ̃] *nm F* heart/ticker. (*Voir* **tocant**)

toquante [tɔkɑ̃t] *nf F* watch/ticker. (*Voir* **tocante**)

toquard [tɔkar] *a&n P* = **tocard.**

toqué [tɔke] *a F* **1.** (slightly) mad*/cracked/round the bend; **il est un peu toqué,** he's a bit touched in the head/he's got a screw loose/he's a bit of a nutcase **2.** **être toqué de qn,** to be infatuated* with s.o./to have a crush on s.o./to be nuts about s.o.; **il est toqué de la télé,** he's got telly on the brain.

se toquer [sətɔke] *vpr F* **se toquer de qn,** to become infatuated* with s.o.; to be crazy*/nuts about s.o.

torché [tɔrʃe] *a F* **bien torché,** well done/(pretty) good; **mal torché,** botched/bungled. (*Voir* **bouchon 11**)

torche-cul [tɔrʃky] *nm inv P* (*a*) toilet paper/loo paper/bog paper/bumf (*b*) trashy book/article (fit only for use as toilet paper) (c) newspaper/rag.

torchée [tɔrʃe] *nf P* **1.** fight*/scrap **2.** beating*/thrashing/good hiding.

torcher [tɔrʃe] **I** *vtr* **1.** *F* to dash off/to knock off (an article, etc); to do (sth) in a hurry; **elle a bientôt torché son rapport,** she soon got through her report **2.** *P* **ce bouquin est drôlement bien torché,** this book's damn well written **3.** *F* to botch/to mess up (a job, etc) **4.** *P* **se faire torcher,** to get a good hiding; to get beaten up **II** *vpr* **se torcher** *P* **1.** to wipe one's backside/bum/arse/*NAm* ass **2.** to fight/to have a punch-up **3.** **je m'en torche!** I don't give a damn!/I couldn't give a toss! **tu peux te torcher!** take a running jump!/go (and) jump in the lake!

torchette [tɔrʃɛt] *nf O F* **papier torchette,** toilet paper/loo paper.

torchon [tɔrʃɔ̃] *nm* **1.** *P* slovenly woman/slut; **être fait comme un torchon,** to be dressed like a slut **2.** *P* toilet paper/bum-fodder/bumf/bog roll **3.** *F* (*journal*) rag **4.** *F* badly written article/rubbish/tripe **5.** *F* **il ne faut pas mélanger les torchons et les serviettes,** we mustn't get our values mixed **6.** *P* **se donner/se filer/se flanquer un coup de torchon,** to fight/to have a set-to/to have a bit of an argy-bargy **7.** *F* **le torchon brûle (chez eux),** they don't hit it off (together)/they're always at each other's throats **8.** *V* **être à cheval sur un torchon,** to have a period*/to have the rag °out/to be on the rag **9.** *O P* (*théâtre*) **lever le torchon,** to raise the curtain.

torchonner [tɔrʃɔne] *vtr F* = torcher 2, 3.

tordant [tɔrdɑ̃] *a F* very funny*/creasing/side-splitting.

tord-boyau(x) [tɔrbwajo] *nm F* poor-quality brandy/rotgut.

tordre [tɔrdr] **I** *vtr A P* to kill* **II** *vpr* **se tordre** *F* **se tordre (de rire)/rire à se tordre,** to laugh* a lot/to split one's sides laughing/to fall about (laughing); **c'était à se tordre,** it was a (perfect) scream/a real killer; **il y a de quoi se tordre,** it's enough to make a cat laugh.

tordu, -ue [tɔrdy] **I** *a* **1.** *F* **être (complètement) tordu,** to be (quite) mad*/loony/nuts **2.** *F* (*pers*) twisted/warped/bent **3.** *P* **avoir la gueule tordue,** to be as ugly as sin. (*Voir* **sirop** 2) **II** *n* **1.** *F* **c'est un tordu/une tordue,** he's/she's (quite) mad*/a nutter/a loony; **les tordus,** the lunatic fringe **2.** *P* **des tordus sans intérêt,** a bunch of dreary gits.

torgn(i)ole [tɔrɲɔl] *nf P* (*a*) blow*/punch/slap (round the face) (*b*) beating*/thrashing/good hiding.

torgn(i)oler [tɔrɲɔle] *vtr P* **torgn(i)oler qn,** to slap s.o. round the face; to hit s.o. (on the head)/to give s.o. a clout.

torieux! [tɔrijø] *int FrC P* damn and blast!/hell's bells!/bloody hell!

tornif [tɔrnif] *nm P* handkerchief*/nose-wipe/snot-rag.

torpille [tɔrpij] *nf P* professional beggar; **marcher à la torpille,** to live by begging.

torpiller [tɔrpije] *vtr* **1.** *F* to torpedo (s.o.'s plans, etc) **2.** *P* to borrow money from (s.o.)/to tap (s.o.) for money/to cadge off s.o. **3.** *V* to have sex* with (s.o.).

torpilleur [tɔrpijœr] *nm P* **1.** scrounger/cadger/sponger **2.** beggar **3.** door-to-door salesman **4.** (**en**) **faire/en chier un torpilleur,** to attach too much importance to sth; to overdo sth; to make a fuss about sth.

torsif [tɔrsif] *a P* very funny*.

tortillard [tɔrtijar] *nm* **1.** *F* (*a*) local railway (*b*) slow train (that stops at every station) **2.** *P* deformed cripple **3.** *P* espresso coffee.

tortiller [tɔrtije] **I** *vtr P* to wolf down/to bolt down/to make short work of (food) **II** *vi* **1.** *P* to eat* like a horse; **il tortille bien,** he's got an appetite like a horse **2.** *F* to quibble; **il n'y a pas à tortiller (du cul pour chier droit),** it's got to be done/there's no getting out of it; there's no getting away from it. (*Voir* **croupe**)

tortore [tɔrtɔr] *nf P* food*/grub*/ nosh.

tortorer [tɔrtɔre] *vtr&i P* to eat*/to nosh.

tôt [to] *adv F* **c'est pas trop tôt!** and about time too!

total [tɔtal] *nm F* **ils se sont chamaillés et, total, les voilà brouillés,** they've had a row and, to cut a long story short, they're no longer on speaking terms.

totale [tɔtal] *nf P* (*med*) total hysterectomy.

toto [tɔto] *nm* **1.** *P* (head) louse/ cootie **2.** *F* **vas-y, toto!** attaboy!

totoche [tɔtɔʃ] *nf F* darling.

Totor [tɔtɔr] *nm V* penis*; **dérouiller Totor,** to have sex*/to get one's end away.

totote [tɔtɔt] *nf F* darling*.

toubib [tubib] *nm F* doctor/doc/ quack/medico; (*mil*) MO (= medical officer).

toubibaille [tubibɑj] *nf F* (*péj*) **la toubibaille,** the medical fraternity.

touche [tuʃ] *nf* **1.** *F* **faire une touche avec qn; avoir une/la touche avec qn,** to make a hit with s.o. (of the opposite sex)/to get off with s.o./to click with s.o./to make out with s.o.; **essayer de faire une touche avec qn,** to make a pass at s.o./to try to get off with s.o. **2.** *F* **rester sur la touche,** to stay on the sidelines/out in the cold; **ce mot reste sur la touche,** this word is not yet generally accepted **3.** *F* (*péj*) appearance/look(s); **je n'aime pas sa touche,** I don't like the look of

him; **quelle (drôle de) touche!** what a sight!/what a mess! **il en a une touche!** what a strange-looking character!/what a weirdo! **4.** *P* **touches de piano,** teeth*/ivories **5.** *P* puff at/on a cigarette; drag **6.** injection*/shot/jab (of a drug, etc) **7.** *V* **se faire une touche,** to masturbate*/to play with oneself.

touché [tuʃe] *a P* (slightly) mad*/ (a bit) touched in the head.

touche-à-tout [tuʃatu] *F* **I** *a* (*a*) (person) who can't keep his hands off things (*b*) meddling/interfering **II** *nm&f* (*a*) meddler/busybody (*b*) Jack of all trades (and master of none).

toucher [tuʃe] *F* **I** *vi* **1. toucher beau,** to touch lucky **2.** to steal*/ to pick pockets **II** *vtr* **pas touche!** don't touch!/mustn't touch. (*Voir* **air II 1** (*a*); **fade 1**; **pied 23**) **III** *vpr* **se toucher 1.** *P* **je m'en touche,** I couldn't care less*/I don't give a damn **2.** *V* to masturbate*/ to play with oneself.

touche-pipi [tuʃpipi] *nm P* **jouer à touche-pipi** (*i*) (*enfants*) to play mummies and daddies/doctors and nurses (*ii*) to have a (heavy) petting session; not to go all the way.

touffe [tuf] *nf P* **1. onduler/travailler de la touffe,** to be mad*/to have a screw loose **2.** pubic hair.

touf(f)iane [tufjan] *nf P* (*drogues*) (*a*) opium* (*b*) opium pipe.

toupet [tupɛ] *nm F* impudence*/ cheek; **quel toupet!** what a cheek!/ what a nerve! **il a eu le toupet de faire ça,** he had the cheek/the gall/ the nerve to do that.

toupie [tupi] *nf* **1.** *F* **vieille toupie,** (silly) old bag/old bat/old trout **2.** *P* head*/nut.

toupiller [tupije] *vi F* to bustle about/to buzz about (*esp* in the house).

tour [tur] **I** *nm* **1.** *F* **avoir plus d'un tour dans son sac,** to have more than one trick up one's sleeve

2. *F* **faire un petit tour,** to urinate*/ to go and see a man about a dog/ to pay a call **3.** *F* **en un tour de main,** as quick as a flash/like lightning **4.** *F* **quand viendra mon tour,** when my turn comes (to die)/when my number's up **5.** *P* **tour de bête,** promotion by seniority. (*Voir* **bâton I 1; cadran 1; cochon I 2; proprio 2; sale 1** (*a*)) **II** *nf F* **la Tour pointue,** the Paris Police headquarters.

tourlourou [turluru] *nm A P* (*mil*) infantryman/foot-soldier/foot-slogger.

tourlousine, tourlouzine [turluzin] *nf P* (*a*) blow*/punch (*b*) thrashing/beating*(-up)/good hiding.

tournailler [turnɑje] *F* **I** *vi* (*a*) to keep wandering round and round (*b*) to hang about/to prowl (about); **tournailler autour d'une femme,** to hang around/to bother a woman **II** *vtr* to twiddle (sth) round and round.

tournanche [turnɑ̃ʃ] *nf P* = **tournée 1, 2, 3.**

tournanché [turnɑ̃ʃe] *a P* **une petite brune bien tournanchée,** a shapely little brunette/a little brunette with a lovely figure.

tournant [turnɑ̃] *nm F* **1.** avoir/ choper/pincer/rattraper qn au **tournant** (*i*) to arrest* s.o. (*ii*) to get one's own back on s.o.; to get s.o. by the short and curlies; **attendre un concurrent au tournant,** to be waiting for (an opportunity to catch) a rival; **je l'aurai au tournant!** I'll get even with him yet! **2. faire un (drôle de) tournant à qn,** to play a dirty trick on s.o./to do the dirty on s.o. **3.** (*a*) **savoir prendre le tournant,** to know how to cope with a situation (*b*) **être dans un sale tournant,** to be in a fix*/to be in a (right old) mess.

tournante [turnɑ̃t] *nf P* key.

tourne [turn] *nf F* (*cartes*) turned-up card (indicating trumps)/turn-up.

tournebouler [turnəbule] *vtr F* to upset (s.o.)/to mix (s.o.) up/to put (s.o.'s) head in a whirl.

tournée [turne] *nf* **1.** *F* **payer/ offrir une tournée,** to stand a round (of drinks); to pay for/to stand drinks all round; **c'est ma tournée,** it's my round/my shout; the drinks are on me; **c'est la tournée du patron,** the drinks are on the house **2.** *P* thrashing; **flanquer une tournée à qn,** to thrash s.o./to beat s.o. up*/to give s.o. a good hiding. (*Voir* **grands-ducs**)

tournicoter [turnikɔte] *vi F* to wander round and round/up and down.

tourniquer [turnike] *F* **I** *vi* (*a*) = **tournicoter** (*b*) to hover (round) **II** *vtr* to twiddle (sth) round and round/to twiddle about with sth.

tourniquet [turnikɛ] *nm P* (*mil*) **passer au tourniquet,** to be court-martialled.

tournoyer [turnwaje] *vi F* to shilly-shally; to quibble.

tourte [turt] **I** *a F* stupid*/thick/ dense/dumb; **elle est belle mais plutôt tourte,** she's pretty but rather thick **II** *nf* **1.** *F* fool*/clot/thickie **2.** *F* **en rester comme une tourte,** to be flabbergasted*/to be knocked all of a heap **3.** *P* slap/smack.

tourtières [turtjɛr] *nfpl P* (*musique*) cymbals.

tousser [tuse] *vi O F* **1.** to grumble*/to grouse; to protest **2.** (*iron*) **il n'est pas poivré, non, c'est que je tousse!** he's not drunk, oh no – not much! **tu ne connais pas la rue Madeleine? – non, c'est que je tousse! j'y demeure,** do you happen to know the rue Madeleine? – do I know it? I only live there!

tout [tu] *F* **I** *pron* **1. et tout et tout,** and all the rest of it/and so on and so forth **2. il a tout du délégué d'atelier,** he's the epitome of a shop steward **3. drôle comme tout,** very funny*; **rire comme tout,** to laugh* a lot/like anything; **il est bête comme tout,** he's really stupid*/a real moron **II** *nm* **ce n'est pas le tout, ça!** that's a long way from what's wanted/that's not good enough!

tout-fou [tufu] *F* **I** *am* mad*/bonkers **II** *nm* (prize) idiot/nutcase/nutter.

toutiche [tutiʃ], **toutime** [tutim] *nm P* (*a*) (**tout**) **le toutiche,** the whole lot/the (whole) works/the whole bag of tricks* (*b*) **et tout le toutiche/(le) toutiche et la mèche,** and so on and so forth.

tout-le-monde [tuləmɔ̃d] *nm F* **Monsieur Tout-le-monde,** the man in the street/the average man/Mr Average.

toutou [tutu] *nm F* (*a*) (*esp mot d'enfant*) dog/doggie/doggy/bow-wow; **viens, mon toutou!** come on, little doggy (*b*) **filer comme un toutou,** to let oneself be easily led; to be as meek as a lamb. (*Voir* **boniment 2; peau 23**)

Tout-Paris [tupari] *nm F* Parisian smart set; **il connaît son Tout-Paris à fond,** he knows everybody who is anybody in Paris.

à tout-va [atuva] *adv phr F* abundantly/copiously.

toxico [tɔksiko] *nm&f P* (= *toxicomane*) drug addict*/dope addict/junkie/junky/druggy.

trac [trak] *nm F* fear/fright/funk; (*théâtre*) stage fright; (examination) nerves; **avoir le trac/se prendre de trac,** to be afraid*/to have the wind up; **filer le trac à qn,** to put the wind up s.o. (*Voir* **traquer**)

tracassin [trakasɛ̃] *nm* **1. avoir le tracassin** (*i*) *F* to worry/to fret (*ii*) *F* to have the fidgets **2.** *V* penis*; **avoir le tracassin,** to have an erection*.

tracer [trase] **I** *vi P* to move

quickly/to get a move on; to speed/to belt along; **allez, trace!** come on, get a move on! **II** *vpr* **se tracer** *P* to leave hurriedly/to clear off/to scarper.

tracsir [traksir] *nm*, **traczir** [trakzir] *nm P* = **trac.**

traduc [tradyk] *nf F* (*scol*) crib.

Trafalgar [trafalgar] *Prnm F* **un (coup de) Trafalgar,** a sudden catastrophe/an unexpected disaster; a (dirty) trick.

trafiquer [trafike] *vtr P* **qu'est-ce que tu trafiques?** what the hell are you up to?

train [trɛ̃] *nm* **1.** *P* buttocks*/bum/*NAm* butt; **un coup de pied dans le train,** a kick up the arse/*NAm* ass. (*Voir* **se magner, (se) manier**) **2.** *P* **avoir le feu au train,** to be in a tearing hurry/a great rush; to have ants in one's pants. (*Voir* **feu 1**) **3.** *P* **se crever/se casser le train,** to work* hard/to flog oneself to death **4.** *P* **être en train,** to be tipsy; **il était un peu en train,** he'd had a drop (too much) **5. être dans le train,** to be up-to-date/to be in the swim/to be with it **6.** *P* **filer le train à qn/coller qn au train/coller au train de qn,** to follow s.o. closely/to trail s.o./to dog s.o.('s footsteps) **7.** *F* uproar*/noise/din/row; **faire du train/faire un train de tous les diables,** to kick up (a hell of) a row **8.** *P* (*hétérosexuel ou homosexuel*) **faire le petit train,** to take part in an orgy/a daisy chain. (*Voir* **onze; tremblement**)

traînailler [trɛnɑje] *F* **I** *vtr* (*a*) **traînailler la jambe,** to drag one's leg (*b*) to keep on repeating (sth); to repeat (sth) over and over again **II** *vi* to wander (aimlessly) about; to loaf around.

traînard [trɛnar] *nm P* **faire/ramasser un traînard,** to fall heavily/to come a cropper*.

traîne [trɛn] *nf F* **être à la traîne,** to be late; to lag behind; **arriver à la traîne,** to turn up late.

traînée [trɛne, trene] *nf P* (low-class) prostitute*/(cheap) floozy/slut/(cheap) tart.

traîne-la-patte [trɛnlapat] *nm inv F* **1.** tramp/hobo/bum **2.** slacker/weary Willie/skiver.

traîne-lattes [trɛnlat] *nm inv P* **1.** tramp/hobo/bum **2.** person in dire poverty/down-and-out.

traîne-malheur [trɛnmalœr] *nm inv,* **traîne-misère** [trɛnmizɛr] *nm inv F =* **traîne-lattes 2.**

traîne-patins [trɛnpatɛ̃] *nm inv F =* **traîne-lattes 1, 2.**

traîne-pattes [trɛnpat] *nm inv F =* **traîne-la-patte.**

traîne-sabots [trɛnsabo] *nm inv,* **traîne-savates** [trɛnsavat] *nm inv,* **traîne-semelles** [trɛnsəmɛl] *nm inv F =* **traîne-lattes 1, 2.**

traîneur [trɛnœr] *nm F (peu usuel)* **traîneur de cafés,** pubcrawler.

traineux [trɛnø] *nm FrC F* **1.** person who leaves things *or* litter all over the place; untidy/messy person **2.** slowcoach/*NAm* slowpoke.

trainglot [trɛ̃glo] *nm P (mil)* soldier in the French Army Service Corps.

train(-)train [trɛtrɛ̃] *nm F* **le train(-)train (quotidien) de la vie,** the ordinary humdrum daily routine; the daily grind; **rien qui sort du train(-)train des événements ordinaires,** nothing out of the ordinary; **aller son petit train(-)train/s'en aller de son train(-)train habituel,** to jog along/to trundle along (in one's own little way).

trait [trɛ] *nm F* **faire des traits à sa femme/à son mari,** to be unfaithful/to cheat on one's wife/one's husband.

tralala [tralala] *nm F* **1.** faire du tralala, to make a great show/to splash out; **sans tralala,** without fuss/without standing on ceremony **2.** être sur son tralala/en grand tralala, to be all dressed up/to be dressed up to the nines **3.** et tout le tralala, and all the rest/and so on and so forth.

tranche [trɑ̃ʃ] *nf* **1.** *F* s'en payer une tranche (*i*) to have the time of one's life/to have a great time/to have a ball (*ii*) to have a good laugh; s'en payer une (bonne) tranche, to let oneself go/to let one's hair down **2.** *P* fool*/idiot; faire la tranche, to play the fool/to act the goat; en avoir une tranche, to be as daft as they come. (*Voir* couche 1) **3.** *P* = tronche.

tranche-montagne [trɑ̃ʃmɔ̃taɲ] *nm F* boaster/show-off*; d'un air de tranche-montagne, blusteringly.

trancher [trɑ̃ʃe] *vtr V* to have sex* with (a woman). (*Voir* troncher)

tranchouillard [trɑ̃ʃujar] *nm P* = tranche 2.

trans [trɑ̃s] *a O P* excellent*/sensational/out of this world.

transbahutement [trɑ̃sbaytmɑ̃] *nm F* transferring; transporting; épuisé par le transbahutement de ses bagages, worn out with carting/humping his luggage around.

transbahuter [trɑ̃sbayte] **I** *vtr F* (*a*) to shift/to hump around/to cart around; transbahuter une armoire, to shift a wardrobe; impossible de transbahuter tout ce bazar! it's just impossible to shift all this stuff! si je n'avais pas à me transbahuter! if only I didn't have to move/to shift! transbahuter des touristes d'un musée à l'autre, to shepherd tourists from one museum to another **II** *vpr* se transbahuter *F* to shift oneself (about)/to traipse around.

transfo [trɑ̃sfo] *nm F* (= *transformateur*) transformer.

transparent [trɑ̃sparɑ̃] *a F* tu n'es pas transparent, you're (standing) in my light; you'd make a better door than a window.

transpiration [trãspirasjɔ̃] *nf P* **passer à la transpiration,** to (have a) dance.

transpoil [trãspwal] *a P* = **trans.**

tran(-)tran [trãtrã] *nm F* = **train-train.**

trapanelle [trapanɛl] *nf F (aviation)* glider.

trappe [trap] *nf P* mouth*; **boucle la trappe!** shut up!*/shut your trap!

trapu [trapy] *a F (scol)* clever/brain; **être trapu en math,** to be bright at maths/*NAm* math; **ce problème est trapu,** that's a sticky problem.

traquer [trake] *vi F* to be afraid*; *(théâtre)* to get stage fright. *(Voir* **trac)**

traquette [trakɛt] *nf P* **avoir la traquette/prendre les traquettes,** to be afraid*/to get the wind up. *(Voir* **trac)**

traqueur, euse [trakœr, -ǿz] *F* **I** *a* cowardly*/chicken/yellow **II** *n* coward*/chicken/bottler.

traquouse [trakuz] *nf P* = **traquette.**

trav [trav] *nm P* = **travelo(t).** *(Voir* **travs)**

travail [travaj] *nm P* **1.** *(cambrioleur)* **faire un petit travail,** to break into/to do a safe **2.** *(prostituée)* **aller au travail,** to go (out) on the beat/on the game.

travailler [travaje] *vi P (prostituée)* **aller travailler,** to go (out) on the beat/on the game. *(Voir* **bigoudi; canotier; chapeau 5; chou I 1; pick-up; touffe 1)**

travailleuse [travajǿz] *nf P* **une bonne travailleuse,** a prostitute* profitable to her pimp; good earner/good meal-ticket.

travelo(t) [travlo] *nm P (a) (travesti)* drag; **en travelo(t),** in drag *(b)* transvestite/drag queen/TV.

travers [travɛr] *nm F* **1. prendre**

par le travers, to take a short cut **2. être en plein travers,** to be dead out of luck **3. passer au travers** *(i)* to get away with it; to beat the rap *(ii)* to draw a blank *(iii) (vendeur, prostituée)* not to have a customer.

traversin [travɛrsɛ̃] *nm F* **faire un coup de traversin,** to go to sleep*/to have a nap/to get some shut-eye. *(Voir* **partie 2)**

de travioc [dətravjɔk] *adv phr P* = **de traviole.**

de traviole [dətravjɔl] *adv phr P* crooked/(all) on one side/lopsided/askew/skew-whiff; **son chapeau était tout de traviole,** his hat was all askew; **le monde va de traviole,** the world's all cock-eyed/all upside down.

travs [trav] *nmpl P* (= *travaux forcés)* **les travs (à perpète),** penal servitude (for life).

tref [trɛf] *nm,* **trèfle** [trɛfl] *nm P* **1.** *O* tobacco/baccy **2.** crowd/mob **3.** money*/lolly/dough **4.** *O* **passer qn au tref,** to beat s.o. up*/to work s.o. over **5.** **as de trèfle,** anus*/arsehole/*NAm* asshole.

tremblement [trãbləmã] *nm F* **tout le tremblement (et son train),** the whole bag of tricks*/the whole shooting-match/the (whole) works/the whole kit and caboodle.

tremblote [trãblɔt] *nf P* **avoir la tremblote** *(i)* to have the jitters *(ii)* to have the shivers/the shakes.

trempe [trãp] *nf,* **trempée** [trãpe] *nf P* beating*/thrashing/good hiding; **filer une trempe à qn,** to beat s.o. up*/to work s.o. over/to clobber s.o.

tremper [trãpe] *vi P* **tremper dans un coup,** to be involved in a crime; to be a party to/an accessory to a crime. *(Voir* **baigneur 3; bain 6** *(c);* **biscuit 3)**

trente [trãt] *nm inv F* **se mettre sur son trente et un,** to put one's glad rags on/to get (all) dolled up/to get dressed up to the nines.

trente-six [trãtsi(s), -siz] *F* **I** *a*
1. umpteen; **avoir trente-six raisons
de faire qch,** to have umpteen reasons for doing sth **2. faire les
trente-six volontés de qn,** to dance
attendance on s.o./to be at s.o.'s
beck and call **II** *nm* **1. le trente-
six** = the CID **2. tous les trente-
six du mois,** once in a blue moon.
(*Voir* **chandelle 10; chemin 2**)

trente-sixième [trãtsizjɛm]
a&nm inv F umpteenth. (*Voir* **dessous 3**)

trente-trois [trãttrwa] *nm inv F*
dites trente-trois! say ninety-nine!
(*Voir* **quarante-quatre 1**)

trèpe, trêpe [trɛp] *nm,* **trêple**
[trɛpl] *nm P* crowd/mob.

trésor [trezɔr] *nm* **1.** *F* **mon trésor,**
(my) darling*/(my) treasure; **sa
secrétaire est un vrai trésor,** his secretary is a real treasure **2.** *F* **il a
dépensé des trésors pour cette
affaire,** he spent a fortune over this
business **3.** *V* anus*.

tréteau, *pl* **-eaux** [treto] *nm P*
horse/nag.

triage [trijaʒ] *nm P* **à chaque triage,**
each time; **le premier triage,** the
first time; **plusieurs triages,** several
times.

triangle [triãgl] *nm F* (*cache-sexe*)
G-string.

tricard [trikar] *nm P* **I** *nm* ex-con-
vict prohibited from entering specified areas **II** *a&nm* (worker, etc)
sent to Coventry.

triche [triʃ] *nf F* trick; trickery;
cheating (*esp* at cards); **c'est de la
triche,** that's cheating; that's not
fair.

trichoter [triʃɔte] *vi F* to cheat/to
fiddle.

trichoterie [triʃɔtri] *nf F* cheat-
ing/fiddling.

tricoter [trikɔte] *vi F* **tricoter des
jambes/des gambettes/des pincettes**
(*i*) to dance (*ii*) to run away/to
make off/to clear off.

tricotin [trikɔtɛ̃] *nm V* **avoir le
tricotin,** to have an erection*. (*Voir*
trique 5)

trictrac [triktrak] *nm P* shady deal.

trifouillage [trifujaʒ] *nm F* **1.**
rummaging (about) **2.** fiddling
about; meddling; tampering.

trifouiller [trifuje] *vtr&i F* **1.** to
rummage about (in a drawer, etc)
2. to fiddle about/to mess about;
to tamper with/to meddle (with).

Trifouillis-les-Oies [trifu-
jilezwa] *Prn F* = **Tripatouille-les-
Oies.**

trimar(d) [trimar] *nm P* **1.** road/
highway; **battre le trimar(d)/être
sur le trimar(d),** to be on the road;
to be a tramp **2.** (*pers*) tramp/
NAm hobo/bum.

trimarder [trimarde] *vi P* **1.** to be
on the road; to be a tramp **2.** =
trimer.

trimardeur, euse [trimardœr,
-ɸz] *P* **I** *nm&f* tramp/vagrant/
vagabond/*NAm* hobo/bum **II** *nf*
prostitute*/streetwalker/hooker/
tart.

trimbal(l)age [trɛ̃balaʒ] *nm F*
dragging about/lugging about (of
parcels, etc); trailing about/around
(of children, etc).

trimbal(l)ement [trɛ̃balmã] *nm
F* = **trimbal(l)age.**

trimbal(l)er [trɛ̃bale] **I** *vtr* **1.** *F*
to carry about/to drag about/to lug
about (sth); **il trimbal(l)e toujours
sa famille avec lui,** he always has
his family in tow **2.** *P* **qu'est-ce
qu'il trimbal(l)e!** what a fool*!/what
a clot! **II** *vpr* **se trimbal(l)er** *F* to
wander around; to drag oneself
along/to trail (along).

trime [trim] *nf P* drudgery/slog;
hardship; **une vie de trime,** a hard
life/a rotten life.

trimer [trime] *vi F* **trimer (dur)/tri-
mer comme un mercenaire,** to
work* hard/to slog away (at sth);
quand on a trimé toute une vie,

when one has slaved away all one's life; **faire trimer qn,** to keep s.o. at it/to keep s.o.'s nose to the grindstone.

trimeur [trimœr] *nm F* hard worker/slogger/drudge.

tringle [trɛ̃gl] **I** *a P* silly **II** *nf* **1.** *P* **se mettre la tringle,** to go without/to tighten one's belt **2.** *P* **travailler pour la tringle,** to work for (next to) nothing/for peanuts **3.** *P* **j'en ai tringle,** I'm sick and tired of it/I'm fed up (to the back teeth) with it **4.** *V* penis*/rod; **avoir la tringle,** to have an erection*; **il est de la tringle,** he likes sex*/he's continually randy/he's got a one-track mind; (*coït*) **un coup de tringle,** a screw/a fuck.

tringler [trɛ̃gle] *vtr V* to have sex* (with)/to screw/to fuck/to get one's end away.

tringlette [trɛ̃glɛt] *nf V* (*coït*) (quick) screw/fuck.

tringleur [trɛ̃glœr] *nm,* **tringlomane** [trɛ̃glɔman] *nm V* man* who is fond of sex*; fucker/screwer.

tringlodrome [trɛ̃glɔdrom] *nm V* = **baisodrome.**

tringlot [trɛ̃glo] *nm P* = **trainglot.**

trinquée [trɛ̃ke] *nf F* drinking (in company); **j'aime la trinquée au bistrot avec les potes,** I like having a drink at the pub with friends.

trinquer [trɛ̃ke] *vi* **1.** *F* to drink* (*esp* heavily); to booze; **on a trinqué ensemble,** we had a few (together) **2.** *P* to get the worst of sth/to get it in the neck/to cop it; to get a punishment/a thrashing/a prison sentence, etc; to take the rap; **trinquer de six mois de taule,** to get six months inside; **s'en tirer sans trinquer,** to get off scot-free.

trinqueur [trɛ̃kœr] *nm F* drunkard*/(heavy) drinker/tippler/boozer.

trip [trip] *nm P* (*drogues*) trip (*esp*

on LSD*); **faire un trip,** to get high; **redescendre d'un trip,** to come down from a trip/to stop tripping.

tripaille [tripɑj] *nf* **1.** *F* offal/innards/guts **2.** *P* flabby breasts*.

tripatouillage [tripatujaʒ] *nm* **1.** *F* rummaging (about); tinkering/tampering; fiddling about/messing about; fiddling (of an election) **2.** *P* pawing/feeling up/touching up (*esp* of a woman).

Tripatouille-les-Oies [tripatujlezwa] *Prn F* (imaginary) out-of-the-way place; one-horse town; = Much-Binding-in-the-Marsh/*NAm* Podunk. (*Voir* **Fouilly-les-Oies**)

tripatouiller [tripatuje] *vtr* **1.** *F* to rummage about in (a drawer, etc) **2.** *F* to fiddle/to fix (an election, etc); to tinker/to tamper with (sth); to fiddle about with/to mess about with (sth) **3.** *P* to paw/to feel up/to touch up/to grope (*esp* a woman).

tripatouilleur [tripatujœr] *nm P* (*a*) man who (habitually) paws/touches up/monkeys about with women; groper (*b*) fiddler.

Tripatouillis-les-Oies [tripatujilezwa] *Prn F* = **Tripatouille-les-Oies.**

tripe [trip] *nf* **1.** *F* **avoir la tripe républicaine,** to be an out-and-out republican **2.** *pl P* **tripes,** guts/innards; **rendre/dégueuler tripes et boyaux,** to vomit*/to be as sick as a dog/to spew one's guts up; **je sentais mes tripes se retourner,** I felt my stomach heaving; **mettre les tripes au soleil/à l'air à qn,** to rip s.o. up (with a knife, etc) (*c*) (*théâtre*) **jouer avec ses tripes,** to play a role/a part with gut-feeling/to put one's guts into sth.

triper [tripe] *vi P* (*drogues*) to take a trip (*esp* LSD*)/to trip.

tripette [tripet] *nf F* **ça ne vaut pas tripette,** that's worthless*/it's not worth a sausage.

tripeur, euse [tripœr, -øz] *n P* (*drogues*) tripper (*esp* on LSD*).

tripotage [tripɔtaz] *nm F* **1.** messing about/fiddling about **2.** underhand/shady/crooked deal; skulduggery; (election) fiddle; **tripotage financier**, market jobbery; **tripotages de caisse**, tampering with/fiddling the cash.

tripotailler [tripɔtaje] *vtr F* (*péj*) = **tripoter** (*all senses*).

tripotée [tripɔte] *nf P* **1.** thrashing/(good) hiding/belting/beating*(-up); **flanquer une tripotée à qn**, to knock s.o. about **2. une tripotée de ...**, a large number/quantity* of ...; lots of ..., crowds of ....

tripoter [tripɔte] *F* **I** *vi* **1.** to mess about/to fiddle about; **tripoter dans un tiroir**, to rummage about in a drawer **2.** to engage in underhand deals/shady deals/shady business; **tripoter dans l'immobilier**, to get involved in some shady property deals **II** *vtr* **1.** to mess about with/to fiddle with (sth); **ne tripote pas mes outils!** don't play around with my tools! **2. qu'est-ce que vous tripotez là?** what are you getting up to (there)? **3.** to deal dishonestly with (money) **4. tripoter qn**, to paw s.o./to monkey around with s.o./to touch s.o. up/to grope s.o.; **ne me tripotez pas comme ça!** don't paw me like that! **III** *vpr* **se tripoter 1.** *F* **il se tripote quelque chose**, there's something fishy going on **2.** *V* to masturbate*/to play with oneself.

tripoteur [tripɔtœr] *nm F* **1.** man who touches up women/groper **2.** (*a*) mischief-maker/schemer (*b*) shady dealer/fiddler; swindler*/shark.

tripoteux [tripɔtø] *nm FrC F* = **tripoteur 1.**

triquard [trikar] *nm P* = **tricard I.**

trique [trik] *nf* **1.** *P* prohibition from entering specified areas/bar.

(*Voir* **tricard 1**) **2.** *F* cudgel/heavy stick; **avoir recours à la trique**, to use big stick methods/to get out the big stick **3.** *F* **sec/maigre comme un coup de trique**, as thin as a rake **4.** *F* **mener qn à la trique**, to rule s.o. with a rod of iron **5.** *V* penis*/shaft/rod; **avoir la trique**, to have an erection*/a hard-on/a rod on.

triqué [trike] *a V* **être triqué**, to have an erection*.

triquée [trike] *nf O P* thrashing/beating*(-up)/belting; **filer une triquée à qn**, to give s.o. a (good) hiding.

triquer [trike] *vi V* to have an erection*/a hard-on; to get it up.

trisser [trise] *vi P* to run away*/to beat it/*NAm* to hightail it/to clear off.

se trisser [sətrise], **se trissoter** [sətrisɔte] *vpr P* = **trisser.**

tristouillard [tristujar], **tristouillet, ette** [tristujɛ, -ɛt], **tristounet, ette** [tristunɛ, -ɛt] *a P* rather sad.

trogne [trɔɲ] *nf F* face*; **une trogne d'ivrogne**, a beery mug.

trognon [trɔɲɔ̃] **I** *a F* dear/nice/sweet; **ce qu'il/qu'elle est trognon!** what a cute little boy/girl! **II** *nm* **1.** *F* darling*/pet/sweetie/cutie; **un petit trognon comme toi**, a nice little chap like you; a sweet little (slip of a) girl like you **2. jusqu'au trognon**, to the (bitter) end; well and truly; up to the neck; **avoir qn jusqu'au trognon**, to take s.o. in completely **3.** *P* head*; **se casser le trognon**, to rack one's brains; **y aller du trognon**, to risk one's neck; **dévisser le trognon à qn**, to strangle s.o. **4.** *P* face*/mug.

trombe [trɔ̃b] *nf* **1.** *F* **entrer/sortir en trombe**, to burst in/out; to dash in/out; to sweep in/out (like a whirlwind) **2.** *P* = **tromé.**

trombine [trɔ̃bin] *nf P* **1.** head*/ bonce/nut **2.** face*/mug.

trombiner [trɔ̃bine] *vtr V* **trombiner une femme,** to have sex* with a woman.

tromblon [trɔ̃blɔ̃] *nm* **1.** *P* (*i*) *O* broad-topped high hat (*ii*) (any) hat* **2.** *P* (any) unwieldy *or* old-fashioned-looking firearm **3.** *V* **filer un coup de tromblon,** to have sex*.

tromblonard [trɔ̃blɔnar] *nm P* face*; **se casser le tromblonard,** to fall flat on one's face/to come a cropper*.

tromboner [trɔ̃bɔne] *vtr V* **tromboner une femme,** to have sex* with a woman.

tromé [trɔme] *nm P* (*verlan de métro*) underground/metro/tube.

trompe [trɔ̃p] *nf O P* **1.** face* **2.** head*.

trompe-la-mort [trɔ̃plamɔr] *nm&f inv F* (*a*) death-dodger (*b*) aged, sick person (*c*) daredevil.

trompette [trɔ̃pɛt] *nf* **1.** *F* **c'est la trompette du quartier,** he's/she's the local gossip **2.** *P* face* **3.** *P* mouth* **4.** *P* nose*/hooter; **avoir le nez en trompette,** to have a turned-up nose.

trompinette [trɔ̃pinɛt] *nf P* small nose*.

tronc [trɔ̃] *nm* **1.** *P* head*; **se casser le tronc,** to worry **2.** *P* **se taper le tronc,** to eat* heartily/to have a good tuck-in/a good blow-out **3.** *P* (*péj*) **tronc (de figuier),** Arab*/wog. (*Voir* **sciure**)

tronche [trɔ̃ʃ] *nf P* **1.** head*; **filer un coup de tronche à qn,** to (head-)-butt s.o.; **se casser la tronche,** to rack one's brains; **se payer la tronche de qn,** to make fun of s.o./ to take the mickey out of s.o. **2.** face*; **se taper la tronche,** to eat* heartily/to feed one's face **3.** **tronche (à l'huile),** fool*/twerp/clot; **tronche plate!** (you) clothhead!

troncher [trɔ̃ʃe] *vtr V* **troncher une femme,** to have sex* with a woman. (*Voir* **trancher**)

troncheur [trɔ̃ʃœr] *nm V* man who has sex/screw(er)/fucker.

trône [tron] *nm F* lavatory/loo seat/throne; **il est sur le trône,** he's (sitting) on the throne/he's on the loo.

troquet [trɔkɛ] *nm P* (*a*) *A* (*patron de café*) = publican; keeper of a pub or wine bar. (*Voir* **mastroquet**) (*b*) (*petit café*) = pub/(wine) bar; **une tournée de troquets,** a pub-crawl.

trot [tro] *nm F* **au trot,** at the double; **allez-y, et au trot!** go on, and be quick about it!

trotte [trɔt] *nf F* (*a*) distance/ stretch/run; **il y a une bonne trotte d'ici là/ça fait une bonne trotte,** it's a good way from here; **faire une bonne trotte,** to go a good long way (to see s.o., etc); **tout d'une trotte,** at a stretch/without stopping.

trotter [trɔte] **I** *vi F* **elle est toujours à trotter,** she's always on the go **II** *vpr* **se trotter** *P* (*a*) to go (away)/to be off/to make tracks (*b*) to run away*/to clear off (in a hurry).

trotteuse [trɔtøz] *nf P* prostitute*/ streetwalker/*esp NAm* hooker.

trottinant [trɔtinɑ̃] *nm P* = **trottinet.**

trottinet [trɔtinɛ] *nm P* foot*.

trottinette [trɔtinɛt] *nf* **1.** *F* (small) car; runabout **2.** *P* **trottinette à macchabs,** hearse/meat wag(g)on.

trottoir [trɔtwar] *nm F* **1.** (*prostituée*) **faire le trottoir,** to solicit*/to walk the streets/to be a street-walker; to hook/to hustle; **fille de trottoir,** streetwalker; **elle fait le trottoir,** she's on the game **2.** (*théâtre*) **le grand trottoir,** the classical repertory (of the French stage).

trou [tru] *nm* **1.** *F* place; **habiter un petit trou (mort/paumé/perdu),** to live in a dead-and-alive hole/dump; to live at the back of beyond; **un petit trou pas cher,** a little place that's not too dear **2.** *P* prison*/nick/clink/jug; **on l'a mis au trou,** they put him away/he was put inside **3.** *P* grave; **on l'a mis dans le trou,** they buried him; **être dans le trou,** to be dead and buried **4.** *F* **boire comme un trou,** to drink like a fish; *P* **avoir un trou sous le nez,** to be a heavy drinker **5.** *F* **boucher un trou,** to pay off a debt; **faire un trou pour en boucher un autre,** to rob Peter to pay Paul; **cela servira à boucher un trou,** that'll (help to) tide us over **6.** *F* **faire son trou,** to get on (in the world); to make a name for oneself **7.** *F* **avoir les yeux en face des trous,** to be all there; *P* **t'as donc pas les yeux en face des trous?** don't you get it?/can't you see?/are you blind? **8.** *V* **trou du cul/trou de balle,** anus*/arsehole/*NAm* asshole; **un vieux trou de balle,** an old fogey*; **(petit) trou du cul!** (you) bloody fool!*/(you) jerk!/(you) arsehole!/*NAm* (you) asshole! **jusqu'à la Saint-trou-du-cul,** till doomsday/till the cows come home; **avoir le trou du cul qui fait bravo,** to be very frightened/in a blue funk; to be shit-scared/to be scared shitless; **se démancher/se décarcasser/se dévisser le trou du cul pour faire qch,** to make every effort/to go all out (to do sth); to shift one's arse/*NAm* ass **9.** *P* (*aviation*) **il a fait un trou dans l'eau,** he's gone for a Burton **10.** *F* **trou normand,** glass of Calvados (drunk between two courses of a meal) **11.** *P* (*drogues*) **se faire des trous,** to shoot up/to fix/to fill oneself full of holes.

troubade [trubad] *nm P* private/(infantry) soldier/squaddie.

trouduc [trudyk] *n V* (= *trou du cul*) bloody fool*/jerk/nurd; **petit**

trouduc! you arsehole/*NAm* asshole!

trouffion [trufjɔ̃] *nm P* = **trou-fion.**

troufignard [trufiɲar] *nm V* anus*/arse(hole).

troufigner [trufiɲe] *vi V* to stink*.

troufignon [trufiɲɔ̃] *nm V* anus*/arse(hole)/*NAm* ass(hole).

troufion [trufjɔ̃] *nm P* (infantry) soldier/private/squaddie.

trouillard, arde [trujar, -ard] *P* **I** *a* cowardly*/windy/yellow(-bellied) **II** *n* coward*/funk/chicken/bottler.

trouille [truj] *nf P* cowardice; **avoir la trouille,** to be afraid*/to have the wind up; **flanquer/ficher/foutre la trouille à qn,** to put the wind up s.o./to scare the pants off s.o.; **une trouille verte/noire,** a blue funk; **tu n'as pas la trouille!** you've got a nerve!/you're not backward in coming forward!

trouiller [truje] *vi P* to be afraid*/to get the wind up/to lose one's bottle.

trouillomètre [trujɔmɛtr] *nm P* **avoir le trouillomètre à zéro,** to be in a blue funk/to be scared stiff/to be scared shitless.

trousse-couilles [truskuj] *nm P* (men's) underpants*/nut chokers.

trousser [truse] *vtr* **1.** *F* **il est toujours à trousser les jupons,** he's always chasing after women/he's forever chasing skirt/he's always after a bit of the other **2.** *V* to have sex* with (a woman); **elle s'est fait trousser,** she got laid **3.** *F* to get through/to polish off (work, business, a meal).

trousseur [trusœr] *nm F* **trousseur de jupons,** womanizer*/skirt-chaser/ladies' man.

truander [tryɑ̃de] *vtr P* to swindle*/to con/to do (s.o.).

truc [tryk] *nm* **1.** *F* (*a*) trick/dodge/wheeze/caper; **les trucs du métier,** the tricks of the trade (*b*) knack; **avoir le truc,** to have the knack; **prendre le truc pour faire qch,** to get the hang of it **2.** (*a*) *F* what's-its-name*/thingummyjig/thingy; **passe-moi ce truc-là,** give me that thing/that what-you-macal-lit (*b*) *P* (*pers*) thingy/what's-his-name*/thingummybob (*c*) *F* (*chose*) **j'ai un truc à te dire,** I've got something to tell you; **il y a un tas de trucs à faire,** there's loads of things to do (*d*) *F* **ça, c'est pas mon truc,** that's not my (sort of) thing at all/that's not my cup of tea **3.** *F* **couper/mordre dans le truc,** to fall into the trap/to fall for it **4.** *F* **lâcher/débiner le truc,** to let the cat out of the bag **5.** *P* **piquer au truc,** to have a go; **repiquer au truc,** to have another shot **6.** *O P* prostitution; **faire le truc,** to solicit*/to be on the game **7.** *P* **être porté sur le truc,** to be fond of sex*/to like it a lot/to have a one-track mind.

trucage [tryka3] *nm P* = **truquage.**

trucider [tryside] *vtr P* to kill*/to bump off/to do away with (s.o.).

trucmuche [trykmyʃ] *nm P* what's-its-name*/thingy/thingum-myjig.

truffard [tryfar] *nm A P* soldier.

truffe [tryf] *nf P* **1.** (bulbous) nose* **2.** idiot*/twit/clot/nurd/jerk.

trumeau [trymo] *nm F* **vieux trumeau,** ugly old woman*/old hag/old bat.

truquage [tryka3] *nm P* fixing/rigging/faking/fiddling; doctoring.

truqué [tryke] *a P* faked/rigged/fixed; **c'est truqué,** it's a con/a fix.

truquer [tryke] *vtr P* to fake/to fix/to fiddle/to rig; **il avait truqué les cartes,** he'd fixed the cards; **truquer une élection,** to rig an election.

truqueur [trykœr] *nm P* (male) homosexual prostitute.

truqueuse [trykøz] *nf P* (low-class) prostitute*/(cheap) tart/(cheap) floozy.

truster [trœste] *vtr F* to monopolize (s.o./sth)/to keep (s.o./sth) to oneself.

tsoin-tsoin [tswɛ̃tswɛ̃] *a F* = **soin-soin.**

tubard¹ [tybar] *nm P* (*turf*) tip; **refiler un tubard à qn,** to give s.o. a tip/to put s.o. onto a good horse/to put s.o. onto sth hot.

tubard², arde [tybar, -ard] (= *tuberculeux*) **I** *a* suffering from TB **II** *nm&f* person suffering from TB/TB case.

tubardise [tybardiz] *nf F* tuberculosis/TB.

tube [tyb] *nm* **1.** *O F* top hat/topper **2.** *O P* stomach* **3.** *P* telephone*/blower; **filer/passer un coup de tube à qn,** to give s.o. a bell/a buzz/a tinkle **4.** *P* = **tubard¹ 5.** *P* = **tubard², arde 6.** *F* hit song/record; **tube de l'été,** summer hit/chart-topper **7.** *P* **débloquer/déconner à plein(s) tube(s),** to talk utter nonsense*/a load of rubbish/(a load of) shit; to bullshit **8.** *V* penis*; **se faire souffler dans le tube,** to be given a blow-job/to be sucked off.

tuber [tybe] *vtr P* **1.** (*turf*) to give s.o. a good tip/to put s.o. onto a good horse **2.** to telephone (s.o.).

tubeur [tybœr] *nm P* (*turf*) tipster.

tuile [tyil] *nf* **1.** *F* (unexpected) mishap/accident/blow; **quelle tuile!** what a blow!/what a drag! **une tuile imprévue,** a bolt from the blue **2.** *P* one million francs *or* centimes.

turbin [tyrbɛ̃] *nm P* **1.** work*/slog/grind/graft; **aller au turbin,** to go to work; **se remettre au turbin,** to get back to the daily grind/the slog **2.** (*cambriolage, etc*) job; **aller au turbin,** to pull (off) a job **3.**

faire un vache turbin/un drôle de turbin à qn, to do the dirty on s.o./ to play a dirty trick on s.o. **4.** prostitution; **aller au turbin,** to go on the game.

turbine [tyrbin] *nf V* **turbine à chocolat,** anus*.

turbiner [tyrbine] *vi P* **1.** to work* hard/to flog oneself (to death)/to slog away at sth **2.** (*prostituées*) to solicit*/to be on the game.

turbineuse [tyrbinøz] *nf P* prostitute*.

turf [tyrf] *nm P* **1.** prostitution/ prostitute's beat; **(fille de) turf,** prostitute*; **aller au/sur le turf,** to go on the beat/the game; to walk the streets **2.** work/job; **c'est pas mon turf,** it's none of my business/ nothing to do with me.

turfer [tyrfe] *vi P* (*prostituées*) to solicit*/to be on the game/to hustle.

turfeuse [tyrføz] *nf P* prostitute*.

turlu [tyrly] *nm P* telephone*.

turlupiner [tyrlypine] *vtr F* to bother/to worry/to annoy*; **qu'est-ce qui te turlupine?** what's eating you?/what's bugging you?

turlutte [tyrlyt] *nf V* fellatio*; **faire une turlutte à qn,** to give s.o. a blow-job/to give s.o. head.

turne [tyrn] *nf P* (*chambre, logement*) room/digs/place/pad.

tutoyer [tytwaje] *vtr F* **se faire tutoyer,** to get reprimanded*/told off/ticked off.

tutu [tyty] *nm* **1.** *F* = **tubard²** **2.** *P* (*vin ordinaire*) wine/plonk/vino

3. *P* telephone* **4.** *V* anus*; *P* (*langage enfantin*) bottom/botty.

tutu-panpan [tytypɑ̃pɑ̃] *nm F* smack-bottom/smack-botty. (*Voir* **cucul**)

tutute [tytyt] *nf P* wine/plonk/vino.

tututter [tytyte] *vi P* to drink* wine/to tipple.

tuyau [tɥijo] *nm F* **1.** tip/hint/ advice; **il m'a donné quelques tuyaux sur l'affaire,** he gave me the low-down/some gen/a few tips on that business **2.** *P* (*turf*) tip/cert; **marchand de tuyaux,** tipster; **un tuyau de première main,** a dead cert/a tip straight from the horse's mouth **3.** *P* (*a*) *A* **tuyau de poêle,** top-hat/topper (*b*) **(pantalon) tuyau de poêle,** drainpipe trousers/drainpipes **4.** *P* **la famille tuyau de poêle,** homosexuals (in general)/ pansyland **5.** *F* **à pleins tuyaux = à plein(s) tube(s) (tube 7).**

tuyauter [tɥijote] *vtr F* **tuyauter qn,** to inform s.o./to give s.o. a tip*/to put s.o. in the know/to gen s.o. up/to give s.o. the low-down; **être bien tuyauté,** to be in the know.

type [tip] *nm P* **1.** man*/bloke/ guy; **un chic type,** a great guy/ bloke; **un sale type,** a bastard*/a sod/*esp NAm* a son of a bitch; **t'es un pauvre type!** you poor bastard*!/you poor sod!/you're a real jerk!

typesse [tipɛs] *nf P* (*esp péj*) woman*/bird/chick/female.

typo [tipo], **typote** [tipɔt] *n F* (= *typographe, typographie*) (*a*) compositor/comp (*b*) (*erreur*) typo.

U

u [y] *a* F (université); **cité U** = (students') hall(s) of residence. (*Voir* **restau**)

un, une [œ̃, yn] F I *num a&n* **1. il était/c'était moins une,** it was a narrow escape/a close shave/a near thing; **s'en tirer à moins une,** to have a narrow squeak **2. être sans un,** to be penniless*/to be (dead/stony) broke **3. ne faire ni une ni deux,** not to think twice about it/to make no bones about it; **sans faire ni une ni deux,** without hesitation/without more ado **4. l'un(e) dans l'autre,** taking one thing with another/on average/by and large **5. et d'un(e)!** so much for that (one)!/that settles that! **d'abord et d'une,** to begin with/for a start/to kick off with **6.** (*journal*) **la une,** the front page/page one; **cinq colonnes à la une,** front page spread/banner headline; **événement qui fait la une,** front page news/news which hits the headlines **7. de deux choses l'une,** it's one thing or the other/either ..., or ... II *indef pron* **tu n'en as même pas une de voiture,** you haven't even got a car III *indef art* **il a fait une de ces têtes,** you should have seen his face! **tu m'as fait une de ces peurs!** you gave me such a fright! IV *indef pron avec 'en'* **en boucher un** (*coin*) **à qn,** to flabbergast* s.o.; **en griller une** (*cigarette*), to smoke a cigarette*; **je n'ai pas pu en placer une,** I couldn't get a word in edge- ways. (*Voir* **bander 2; bonir; pas II 3; rater**)

unif [ynif] *nm* F uniform.

unique [ynik] *a* F **il est unique!** (*i*) he's priceless! (*ii*) he's the (absolute) limit! **voilà qui est unique!** who ever heard such nonsense!

unité [ynite] *nf* P ten thousand (new) francs.

urf(e) [œrf] *a* O P elegant/smart/posh/snazzy.

urger [yrʒe] *vi* F to be urgent; **ça urge!** it's urgent!/it can't wait!/it's got to be done quickly! **y'a rien qui urge,** there's no great hurry.

usine [yzin] *nf* P **1. aller à l'usine,** to go to work **2.** (*aut*) **usine à gaz,** carburettor **3. qu'est-ce que c'est que cette usine?** what sort of a place/dump is this?

usinage [yzinaʒ] *nm* P exploitation/sweating (of labour).

usiner [yzine] P I *vtr* to exploit/to sweat (s.o./work-force) II *vi* (*a*) to work* hard/to slog (away); **ça usine ici!** we're hard at it in here! (*b*) (*prostituée*) to go on the beat/on the game.

utilité [ytilite] *nf* F (*théâtre*) actor/actress; **les utilités,** the small/minor parts; **jouer les utilités** (*i*) (*théâtre*) to play bit parts (*ii*) (*fig*) to play second fiddle/a minor role (in an enterprise, etc).

V

va [va] *excl P* **1.** (*précédant une injure*) **va donc, petit con!** get lost, you little jerk!/nurd! **2.** (*intensif*) **je t'aime bien, va!** of course I love you! **3. va pour ...**, OK for ... /it's OK with me; **va pour le prix**, the price is fine.

vacciné [vaksine] *a F* **1. être vacciné avec une aiguille de phono**, to talk* a lot/to chatter* away (nineteen to the dozen) **2.** to be hardened/immune (to sth); **tu peux y aller, je suis vacciné!** do what you like, it won't affect me! **3. être majeur(e) et vacciné(e)**, to know all about the birds and the bees/to know what's what/to know the score.

vachard [vaʃar] *a P* **1.** mean/ nasty/rotten; **ce que tu peux être vachard, des fois!** you can be a real bastard* at times! **2.** difficult; **il est plutôt vachard, ce problème**, it's a bit of a bastard/sod this problem.

vachardise [vaʃardiz] *nf P* meanness/nastiness.

vachasse [vaʃas] *nf P* (*péj*) (large, ugly) woman*/slob/bag/(fat) cow.

vache [vaʃ] **I** *a P* **1.** (*pers*) mean/ nasty/rotten; **ce qu'il peut être vache**, he can be a real bastard*/a rotten swine; **elle est vache, sa femme**, his wife's a real bitch/cow; **il a été vache comme tout avec moi**, he was really mean/rotten to me **2.** (*chose*) rotten/nasty; **un coup vache**, a dirty trick; **ça, c'est vache!** that's a filthy trick! **II** *nf* **1.** *P* (*homme*) bastard*/swine/sod; (*femme*) bitch/cow; **sale vache!** you

bastard!/you filthy swine!/you sod! **bande de vaches!** you swine!/you lousy bastards! **2.** *P* policeman*/ cop; **les vaches**, the cops/the fuzz/ *NAm* the bulls; **mort aux vaches!** down with the cops!/death to the fuzz! **vache à roulettes**, motorcycle cop **3.** *P* **vache à lait**, mug/sucker **4.** *P* **manger/bouffer/se taper de la vache enragée**, to rough it/to have a hard time of it **5.** *F* **le plancher des vaches**, dry land/terra firma **6.** *F* **pleurer comme une vache**, to cry one's eyes out **7.** *F* **il pleut comme (une) vache qui pisse**, it's chucking it down/it's pissing down **8.** *P* **plein comme une vache**, dead drunk*/loaded/pissed **9.** *P* **coup en vache**, an underhand trick/a dirty trick; **faire un coup en vache à qn**, to do the dirty on s.o. **10.** *P* (*excl*) **oh la vache!** (*i*) damn!/blast!/ hell!/sod! (*ii*) (*admiration*) blimey!/ I'll be damned!/wow!/Christ! **11.** *P* **un(e) vache de problème**, one hell of a problem/a really sticky problem; **une vache de moto**, one hell of a (motor)bike/a really amazing bike. (*Voir* **peau 20** (*c*) (*ii*))

vachement [vaʃmɑ̃] *adv P* **1.** (*très*) **c'est vachement bon**, it's damned/bloody good; **j'ai vachement soif**, I'm bloody thirsty/I could really do with a drink; **t'es vachement con**, you're a bloody idiot* **2.** *O* in a mean way; **il m'a répondu vachement**, he replied nastily.

vacherie [vaʃri] *nf P* **1.** dirty/ mean/rotten trick; **faire une vacherie à qn**, to play a nasty trick on s.o./to do the dirty on s.o.; **dire des**

vacheries à qn, to be bitchy/nasty to s.o. 2. **cette vacherie de temps!** this bloody/*NAm* goddamn weather! **c'est une vraie vacherie ce machin-là!** it's a load of junk!/it's absolute rubbish!/(a load of) crap!

vachère [vaʃɛr] *nf O P* police bus.

vachetement [vaʃtømɑ̃] *adv P* = **vachement.**

va-comme-je-te-(la-)pous-se [vakɔmʒtə(la)pus] *adv phr F* **à la va-comme-je-te-(la-)- pousse,** anyoldhow/all anyhow/in a slapdash way.

vacs [vak(s)] *nfpl F* (= *vacances*) holidays/hols/vacation/vac.

va-de-la-gueule [vadlagœl] *nm P* bigmouth/loudmouth.

vadrouille [vadruj] *nf F* **être en vadrouille,** to rove around/to roam around/to prowl around; to loaf around; **partir en vadrouille,** to go out for a bit of a wander/a bit of fun.

vadrouiller [vadruje] *F* I *vi* to wander about/to knock around/to loaf around II *vpr* **se vadrouiller** (*a*) to loaf around/to knock about (*b*) to gad about/to gallivant.

vadrouilleur [vadrujœr] *nm F* gadabout/gallivanter.

vague [vag] *nf P* pocket.

vaguer [vage] *vtr P* **vaguer qn,** to go through s.o.'s pockets/to frisk s.o.

vaisselle [vɛsɛl] *nf P* 1. **vaisselle de fouille,** pocket money; **se faire un peu de vaisselle de fouille,** to make a bit of pocket money/to get oneself a bit of cash together 2. (*lesbiennes*) **laver la vaisselle,** to have cunnilingus*.

valda [valda] *nf P* 1. bullet/slug 2. *O* green traffic light.

valdingue [valdɛ̃g] *P* I *nf* 1. suitcase/case; **faire la valdingue,** to do a bunk/to make tracks/to scarper 2. **la Grande Valdingue,** death II *nm* 1. (*cartes*) jack 2.

ramasser un **valdingue,** to come a cropper*/to fall flat on one's face.

valdinguer [valdɛ̃ge] *vi P* 1. to come a cropper*/to go sprawling/to fall flat on one's face 2. (*a*) **envoyer valdinguer qn** (*i*) to send s.o. packing*/to send s.o. off with a flea in his ear/to tell s.o. to get lost (*ii*) to send s.o. spinning/reeling (*b*) **envoyer valdinguer qch,** to fling/to chuck sth away.

valise [valiz] *nf F* 1. **faire la valise,** to run away*/to scarper/to clear off 2. **avoir des valises sous les yeux,** to have rings/bags under one's eyes. (*Voir* **malle**)

valiser [valize] *vtr F* (*a*) to run away*/to do a bunk (*b*) to walk out on (s.o.) (*c*) to throw/to boot/to kick (s.o.) out.

valoche [valɔʃ] *nf*, **valouse** [valuz] *nf P* (suit)case.

valouser [valuze] *vtr P* (*a*) to walk out on (s.o.) (*b*) to throw (s.o.) out; **il l'a valousée,** he kicked her out/booted her out/got rid of her.

valse [vals] *nf P* 1. **envoyer la valse/lâcher les valses lentes,** to pay* up 2. **faire la valse à qn,** to walk out on s.o. 3. **inviter qn à la valse,** to ask s.o. to step outside (for a fight); **filer une valse à qn,** to beat s.o. up*/to thrash s.o.

valser [valse] *vi F* 1. to throw/to fling/to chuck; **envoyer valser qn,** to send s.o. packing*/to tell s.o. to buzz off; **envoyer valser qch,** to send sth flying 2. **faire valser l'argent/les faire valser,** to spend money like water.

valseur [valsœr] *nm* 1. *P* buttocks*/arse/*NAm* ass 2. *V* anus*; **filer du valseur** (*i*) to have anal sex*/to be ass-fucked (*ii*) to be a passive homosexual* 3. *P* trousers*/*NAm* pants/strides/duds.

valseuses [valsøz] *nfpl V* testicles*/balls/nuts.

valtouse [valtuz] *nf P* (suit)case.

vamper [vɑ̃pe] *vtr F* to vamp/to
flirt; **elle essayait de le vamper,** she
was flirting with him/she was trying to get off with him.

vanne [van] *nf P* **1.** witty but sar-
castic remark/(nasty) crack/dig/
jibe; **lancer une vanne à qn,** to
make a dig at s.o./to knock s.o. **2.**
dirty trick **3.** spot of bother/trou-
ble **4.** *pl* **lâcher les vannes,** to urinate*.

vanné [vane] *a P* exhausted*/dead
beat/shagged out/knackered.

vanneau, *pl* **-eaux** [vano] *nm*
1. *O P* = **vanne 1, 2, 3 2.** *pl F*
bargain goods.

vanner [vane] **I** *vtr P* to exhaust*/
to tire out/to shatter/to knacker
II *vi* **1.** to boast*/to brag/to talk
big **2.** to make a (nasty) crack/to
knock/to have a dig (at s.o./sth)
III *vpr* **se vanner** *P* to become
exhausted*; **se vanner à la bourre,**
to have too much sex*/too much of
the other/to shag one's arse off.

vanneur, -euse [vanœr, -øz] *n P*
boaster/bragger/show-off*/big
mouth.

vannot [vano] *nm* **1.** *P* = **vanne
1, 2, 3 2.** *pl O F* bargain goods.

vanterne [vɑ̃tɛrn] *nf P* window.

vape [vap] *nf P* **1. être (complètement) dans les vapes/être en pleine
vape** (*i*) to be dopey/woozy/in a
daze (*esp* after drugs *or* when tired,
etc) (*ii*) to have one's head in the
clouds **2. tomber dans les vapes,**
to faint/to pass out **3. sentir/
renifler/respirer la vape,** to suspect
sth fishy/to smell a rat.

vapeur [vapœr] *nf P* **renverser la
vapeur,** to urinate*.

vaporisateur [vaporizatœr] *nm O
P* machine gun/tommy gun.

varlot [varlo] *nm P* customer who
buys nothing (in a shop) and
annoys the staff in the process/
browser.

vase [vaz] *P* **I** *nf* **1.** rain **2.**

water **II** *nm* **1.** *O* (*a*) anus* (*b*)
buttocks* **2.** luck; **avoir du vase,**
to be lucky/jammy.

vaseliner [vazline] *vtr F* to flatter*/to butter (s.o.) up.

vaser [vaze] *vi P* to rain.

vaseux, -euse [vazø, -øz] *a F*
1. unwell*/under the weather/off-
colour; tired/washed out; **se sentir
vaseux** (*i*) to feel unwell* (*ii*) to
have a hangover **2.** (*confus*)
woolly/muddle-headed/hazy.

vasouillard, -arde [vazujar, -
ard] *a F* (*propos, explication, idée,
etc*) woolly/airy-fairy/muddled;
(*pers*) woolly-minded/muddled-
headed.

vasouiller [vazuje] *vi F* (*a*) to
struggle/to flounder; to be floored/
stumped (*b*) to make a mess of sth/
to balls (sth) up.

va-te-faire-fiche [vatfɛrfiʃ] *adv
phr F* **à la va-te-faire-fiche,** any-
oldhow/in a slapdash way.

va-te-laver [vatlave] *nf P* slap/
blow*; **flanquer une va-te-laver à
qn,** to slap s.o. round the face/
head.

veau [vo] *nm P* **1. (tête de) veau,**
fool*/clot/clod/*NAm* dumb cluck
2. (*a*) prostitute* (who doesn't put
herself out too much) (*b*) frigid
woman **3.** (*turf*) outsider; (*mauvais
cheval*) nag **4.** slow vehicle/
jalopy/banger/heap/crate.

vécés [vese] *nmpl F* WC*/loo/*NAm*
bathroom/*NAm* john.

veilleuse [vɛjøz] *nf P* **1.** *F* **étein-
dre/souffler sa veilleuse,** to die*/to
snuff it **2.** *F* **mettre qch en veilleuse,** to shelve sth/to keep sth
ticking over **3.** *P* **la mettre en veilleuse,** to shut up*/to button one's
lip; **mets-la en veilleuse!** put a sock
in it!/pipe down! **4.** *F* **se mettre
en veilleuse,** to keep a low profile/
to drop out of circulation/to lie
low.

veilleux [vɛjø] *nm P* (*pers*) night-owl.

veinard, -arde [vɛnar, -ard] *F* **I** lucky/jammy **II** *nm&f* lucky person/lucky devil; **le veinard!** (the) jammy so-and-so/(the) jammy sod!/the lucky beggar!

veine [vɛn] *nf F* luck; **coup de veine**, stroke of luck/lucky break; **pas de veine!** bad luck!/hard luck! **avoir de la veine**, to get a lucky break/to hit lucky; **il a de la veine**, he's a lucky devil/a jammy so-and-so. (*Voir* **cocu** 2)

vélo [velo] *nm F* bicycle/cycle/bike.

vélodrome [velɔdrom] *nm F* **un vélodrome à mouches**, a bald head*/a skating rink.

velours [vəlur] *nm P* **1.** profit/winnings/takings; **jouer sur du velours**, to stake only one's winnings/to play on (the) velvet; **rouler sur le velours**, to be winning/on a winning streak **2. c'est du velours**, it's very easy*/a piece of cake.

vendange [vɑ̃dɑ̃ʒ] *nf P* (*produit d'un cambriolage*) loot/swag/takings.

vendanger [vɑ̃dɑ̃ʒe] *vi P* to burgle/*NAm* to burglarize/to steal*.

vendre [vɑ̃dr] *vtr F* to denounce* (s.o.)/to shop (s.o.)/to squeal on (s.o.)/to grass (on s.o.).

vendu [vɑ̃dy] *nm F* double-crosser/rat/grass/*esp NAm* fink; **va donc, eh, vendu!** you traitor!/you rat!

venin [vənɛ̃] *nm V* **cracher/filer/jeter/lâcher son venin**, to ejaculate*/to come/to shoot one's load.

vent [vɑ̃] *nm* **1.** *F* **du vent**, nothing*; **ce n'est que du vent**, it's all hot air/wind/nonsense; **envoyer du vent**, to tell lies/tall stories **2.** *P* **du vent!** clear off!/buzz off!/get lost!* **3.** *F* **jouer du vent**, to run away*/to clear off **4.** *F* **lâcher un vent**, to fart/to break wind/to blow off **5.** *F* **perdre son vent**, to waste one's breath **6.** *F* **avoir du vent**

dans les voiles, to be drunk* **7.** *F* **être dans le vent**, to be with it/to know where it's at/to be trendy.

ventilateur [vɑ̃tilatœr] *nm P* helicopter*/chopper.

ventre [vɑ̃tr] *nm F* **1. avoir qch dans le ventre**, to have guts/to have balls/*NAm* to be ballsey; **savoir ce que qn a dans le ventre**, to see what sort of stuff s.o. is made of **2. prendre du ventre**, to get a potbelly/a gut **3. se serrer le ventre**, to tighten one's belt **4. taper sur le ventre à qn**, to dig/to poke s.o. in the ribs **5. tu me fais mal au ventre!** you make me feel sick!/you make me (want to) puke!

ventrée [vɑ̃tre] *nf O F* **une ventrée**, a bellyful.

Vénus [venys] *Prn P* **recevoir un coup de pied de Vénus**, to get VD*/to cop a dose.

ver [vɛr] *nm F* **1. nu comme un ver**, stark naked*/starkers **2. pas piqué des vers**, first rate*/not (half) bad/one hell of a .... (*Voir* **hanneton** 2) **3. tirer les vers du nez à qn**, to worm sth out of s.o./to pump s.o. **4. tuer le ver**, to take hair of the dog/an eye-opener/an alcoholic pick-me-up.

verdâtres [vɛrdɑtr] *nmpl A P* (*WWII*) German* soldiers/Jerries.

verdine [vɛrdin] *nf P* gypsy's caravan.

véreux [verø] *nm F* old offender/old lag.

verjot [verʒo] *a O P* lucky/jammy.

verlan, verlen [vɛrlɑ̃] *nm F* (**code**) verlan/verlen, backslang.

verni [vɛrni] *a P* lucky; **être verni**, to be lucky/to get a break; **il est verni**, he's a jammy devil.

vérole [verɔl] *nf P* syphilis*/syph; **attraper/choper la vérole**, to get the pox **2.** problem/difficulty; **quelle vérole!** what a drag!

vérolé [verɔle] *a P* **1.** syphilitic; **il**

est **vérolé,** he's got the pox **2.** (*appareil*) rubbishy/poxy.

verre [vɛr] *nm F* **1.** avoir un verre de trop/avoir un verre dans le nez, to have had one too many/one over the eight; **boire un petit verre,** to have a snort/a snifter **2.** manier **qn comme du verre cassé,** to handle s.o. with kid gloves **3.** se noyer dans un verre d'eau, to make a mountain out of a molehill; **une tempête dans un verre d'eau,** a storm in a teacup.

Versigo [vɛrsigo] *Prn P* Versailles.

vert [vɛr] **I** *a* **1.** *P* (*a*) tricked/ deceived; **être vert,** to be conned (*b*) furious/angry*/mad; **il en était vert,** he was as mad as hell **2.** *F* (*a*) saucy/spicy (story); **en raconter des vertes et des pas mûres,** to tell spicy/smutty/dirty jokes (*b*) **en avoir vu des vertes et des pas mûres,** to have been through the mill/to have been through a lot; **en faire voir des vertes et des pas mûres à qn,** to give s.o. a bad time/a hard time **II** *nm F* se mettre au vert, to take a break/a rest from sth **III** *nf P* **1.** spicy/saucy/ smutty story **2.** *A* absinth(e).

verts-de-gris [vɛrdəgri] *nmpl P* (*WWII*) German* soldiers/Jerries.

vesse [vɛs] *nf F* (silent, smelly) fart.

vesser [vɛse] *vi F* to fart*/to blow off; **vesser du bec,** to have bad breath.

vessie [vɛsi] *nf F* **prendre des vessies pour des lanternes,** to be easily taken in/to believe that the moon is made of green cheese; **il vous ferait prendre des vessies pour des lanternes,** he'd talk black into white/he'd pull the wool over your eyes.

veste [vɛst] *nf F* **1.** failure*/setback; **ramasser/remporter une veste,** to fail*/to come a cropper **2.** **tourner/retourner sa veste,** to change one's colours/one's tune **3.**

tomber la veste, to take one's coat off/to slip off one's jacket.

véto [veto] *nm F* (= *vétérinaire*) veterinary surgeon/vet; *NAm* animal doctor.

veuve [vœv] *nf* **1.** *F* la Veuve, the guillotine **2.** *F* la veuve sapin, coffin **3.** *P* fréquenter/se taper la veuve poignet, to masturbate*/to flog the bishop/to beat the dummy.

viande [vjãd] *nf P* **1.** (human) body/carcass; **bouge ta viande!** move your carcass!/shift! **amène ta viande!** drag your carcass over here!/get your arse/*NAm* ass over here! (*Voir* **porte-viande**) **2.** viande (froide), corpse/stiff **3.** *P* girl*/woman*; bird/chick; **sa viande,** his girlfriend/old lady/bit of stuff. (*Voir* **bout 10; marchand 1; sac 2; saloir**)

se viander [savjãde] *vpr P* (*en moto*) to come a cropper*/to smash oneself up/to break one's neck.

vibure [vibyr] *nf F* à toute vibure, very quickly*/at full speed/like greased lightning.

vice [vis] *nm F* **1.** il a du vice/c'est une boîte à vice (*i*) he's a sly/ crafty/sharp customer; he's a smart alec; (*en affaires*) he's a shark (*ii*) he's cheeky; **il ne manque pas de vice,** he's got plenty of cheek/he's a cheeky devil **2.** *O* aller au vice, to visit a prostitute*.

vicelard, -arde [vislar, -ard] *P* **I** *a* (*a*) sly/cunning (*b*) depraved **II** *n* (*a*) sly/cunning person/sharp customer (*b*) un vieux vicelard, an old reprobate/an awkward customer.

viceloque [vislɔk] *a P* **1.** sly/ cunning **2.** depraved.

vicelot [vislo] *nm P* **1.** sly customer **2.** sexually depraved man/ sex maniac.

vidage [vidaʒ] *nm F* **1.** dismissal/ sacking (from job) **2.** chucking out (from pub, etc).

vidange [vidɑ̃ʒ] *nf P* **faire la/une vidange,** to urinate*/to take a leak.

vidé [vide] *a F* **1.** exhausted*/tired out/worn out **2.** penniless*/broke/ cleaned out **3.** dismissed/sacked/ fired.

vider [vide] *vtr F* **1. vider les lieux/le plancher,** to beat it/to make oneself scarce **2.** to dismiss* (s.o.)/to give (s.o.) the sack **3.** to exhaust* (s.o.)/to wear (s.o.) out **4.** to ruin (s.o.)/to clean (s.o.) out/ to squeeze (s.o.) dry **5.** to throw out/to boot out/to chuck out (s.o.); **se faire vider** (*i*) to be dismissed/ sacked/fired (*ii*) to get thrown out/ booted out/chucked out (of a club, a café, etc). (*Voir* **sac 14**)

videur [vidœr] *nm F* chucker-out/ bouncer.

vie [vi] *nf* **1.** *F* **faire la vie/mener la vie,** to live it up/to have a good time **2.** *F* **faire une vie/faire la vie à qn,** to make a scene/to kick up a fuss **3.** *F* **enterrer sa vie de garçon,** to give a stag party **4.** *F* **une vie de chien,** a dog's life.

vié, vier [vje] *nm O P* penis*.

vieille [vjɛj] *nf F* **1. la vieille,** mother*/the old lady **2.** (*vieille femme; femme quelconque*) **ma vieille,** old girl.

viergeot, -otte [vjɛrʒo, -ɔt] *n O F* virgin.

vieux [vjø] **I** *nm F* **1.** father*/the old man/the guv'nor **2. mes vieux,** my parents/my (old) folks **3. mon vieux,** old chap*/(my) old mate/ (my) old pal **4.** (*patron*) boss*/ chief/guv'nor **5. prendre un coup de vieux,** to age/to get old **II** *a* (*intensif*) **vieux con/crétin, va!** (you) old idiot!/(you) old bastard*!/you silly cunt!

vif [vif] *nm F* **être pris sur le vif,** to be caught in the act/to be caught red-handed.

vigne [viɲ] *nf F* **être dans les vignes du Seigneur,** to be drunk*/well away/loaded.

vilain [vilɛ̃] *nm F* **il y aura/il va y avoir du vilain,** there's going to be some trouble/there's some trouble brewing.

villégiature [vileʒjatyr] *nf P* **être en villégiature,** to be in prison*/in clink.

Villetouse [viltuz] *Prn P* La Villette (quarter in Paris).

vinaigre [vinɛgr] *nm F* **1. faire vinaigre,** to hurry* up/to get a move on **2. ça tourne au vinaigre,** things have taken a turn for the worse **3. crier au vinaigre** (*i*) to get angry* (*ii*) to call for help/to scream blue murder.

vinasse [vinas] *nf F* (poor quality) wine/cheap plonk.

vingt [vɛ̃] *num a F* **vingt-deux!** watch out!/watch it! **vingt-deux, v'là les flics!** beat it, here come the cops!

vioc [vjɔk], **viocard** [vjɔkar] *a&nm P* = **vioque, vioquard.**

violette [vjɔlɛt] *nf* **1.** *F* (*a*) gift/ present; **faire une violette à qn,** to do s.o. a favour (*b*) (*pourboire*) tip **2.** *P* **avoir les doigts de pied en bouquet de violettes,** to have an orgasm*/to come. (*Voir* **fleur 5**)

violon [vjɔlɔ̃] *nm* **1.** *P* prison*/ jug/clink; **être au violon,** to be in the nick; **jouer du violon,** to escape (*esp* from prison)/to do a bunk **2.** *P* **boîte à violon,** coffin **3.** *P* **payer les violons,** to pay the expenses/to pay the piper **4.** *F* **c'est comme si je pissais dans un violon,** it's like talking to a brick wall.

vioquard [vjɔkar] **I** *a P* old/ aged/ancient **II** *nm P* old person/ old timer; grandad/grandpa.

vioque [vjɔk] *nm&f P* **1.** old person/old timer **2. mes vioques,** my parents/my (old) folks; **mon/ma vioque,** my old man/lady.

vioquer [vjɔke] *vi P* to age/to get old.

vioquerie [vjɔkri] *nf P* old age.

vipère [viper] *nf* P **vipère broussail-leuse**, penis* **2. avoir une vipère dans le porte-monnaie**, to be miserly*/tight-fisted; to have a death adder in one's pocket.

virage [viraʒ] *nm* F **choper qn au virage**, to get one's own back on s.o. (*Voir* **tournant**)

virer [vire] *vtr* F **1.** to dismiss*/to sack/to fire; **se faire virer**, to get the boot/to get kicked out. (*Voir* **cuti**)

vis [vis] *nf* **serrer la vis à qn** (*i*) F to put the screw(s) on s.o./to pressur-ize s.o. (*ii*) P to strangle s.o.

visage [vizaʒ] *nm* F **1. épouser un visage**, to marry a pretty face **2. trouver visage de bois**, to find nobody at home.

viscope [viskɔp] *nf* F (*casquette à visière*) peaked cap.

vise-au-trou [vizotru] *nm&f inv* P obstetrician; midwife.

viser [vize] *vtr* P to look at/to clock; **vise moi ça!/vise un peu ça! get a load of that!/just take a dekko at that!

vision [vizjɔ̃] *nf* F **avoir des visions**, to kid oneself/to delude oneself; to be seeing things.

visite [vizit] *nf* F **avoir de la visite**, to have a period*/to have visitors.

vissé [vise] *a* P **être mal vissé**, to be in a filthy temper/in a vile mood.

visselot [vislo] *nm* P = **vicelot**.

visser [vise] *vtr* F **1.** to put the screw(s) on (s.o.) **2. être vissé sur sa chaise**, to be glued to one's seat; **il y semble vissé**, it looks as though there's no shifting him.

visu [vizy] *nm* P (*CB*) meeting/eye-ball; **se faire un visu**, to lay an eye-ball (on s.o./sth)/to eyeball (s.o./sth).

vit [vi] *nm* V penis*; **rouge comme un vit de noce**, terribly shy/bashful.

vite-fait [vitfɛ] *nm* F (*boisson, coït*

rapide) a quick one/a quickie; **tirer un (coup) vite-fait**, to have a quick poke/a quick screw/a quick in-and-out job.

vivoter [vivɔte] *vi* F to live from hand to mouth/to just get by.

vivre [vivr] *vi* F **1. apprendre à vivre à qn**, to teach s.o. manners/a lesson **2. se laisser vivre**, to take it easy.

voile [vwal] *nf* **1.** F **avoir du vent dans les voiles**, to be (slightly) drunk*/to be tipsy/to be merry **2.** P **mettre/lever/larguer les voiles**, to run away*/to scarper/to do a bunk **3.** P **marcher à voiles et à vapeur**, to be bisexual/bi; to be AC/DC/ambidextrous; to swing both ways.

voir [vwar] **I** *vtr* P **va voir ailleurs si j'y suis! get lost!*/take a running jump! va te faire voir (par/chez les Grecs)! get stuffed!/go screw yourself! **II** *adv* P **dites voir!** just tell me!/get on with it! **écoutez voir!** just listen to this!/get a load of this! **montre voir!** give us a look! **regarde voir!** just take a dekko!

voiture-balai [vwatyrbalɛ] *nf* F last bus, tube, etc (at night).

volaille [vɔlɑj] *nf* **1.** A P (*péj*) prostitute* **2.** P (*coll*) **la volaille**, the police*/the cops. (*Voir* **poulet**)

volante [vɔlɑ̃t] *nf* P (*police*) **la volante**, the flying squad/the swee-ney.

volée [vɔle] *nf* F thrashing/hiding/beating*.

voler [vɔle] **I** *vtr* P **il ne l'a pas volé**, he asked for it/it serves him right **II** *vi* P **1. voler dans les plumes**, to attack s.o./to go for s.o. **2. il vole bas** (*i*) he's not very intel-ligent*/not a very bright spark (*ii*) he's no high flyer.

volet [vɔle] *nm* F **mettre les volets à la boutique**, to die*/to shut up shop.

volière [vɔljɛr] *nf* A P brothel*.

volo [vɔlo] *nf F* (= *volonté*) à volo, at will/ad lib; as you like.

voltigeur [vɔltiʒœr] *nm F* (*locution populaire*) à tout à l'heure, voltigeur! – à bientôt, mon oiseau! See you later, alligator! – In a while, crocodile!

volume [vɔlym] *nm F* **1.** faire du volume, to throw one's weight around **2.** écrire des volumes, to write reams.

vo(s)zig(ue)s [vozig] *pron P* you/yourselves.

vôtre [votr] *poss pron* à la bonne vôtre, cheers!/good health!

vouzailles [vuʒaj] *pron P* = **vo(s)zigues.**

voyage [vwajaʒ] *nm* **1.** *F* faire le grand voyage, to die* **2.** *P* (*drogues*) faire un voya- ge, to take a trip/to trip; il est du/il fait un voyage, he's on a trip/he's tripping **3.** *V* y aller du voyage/de son voyage, to ejaculate*/to come; emmener qn en voyage, to give s.o. an orgasm*.

voyager [vwajaʒe] *vi P* (*drogues*) to get high/to trip.

voyante [vwajɑ̃t] *nf A F* passer à la voyante, to be guillotined.

vrai [vrɛ] **I** *a F* **1.** pas vrai? right?/OK? c'est pas vrai! oh no!/it's not possible! **2.** un vrai de vrai/le vrai de vrai, the real thing/the genuine article/the real McCoy **II** *nm F* **1.** un vrai de vrai, a genuine person; c'est un vrai de vrai, he's genuine/he's for real/he's all right **2.** c'est pour de vrai, it's for real.

vrille [vrij] *nf* lesbian*/les/dyke.

vu, vue [vy] **I** *a F* **1.** c'est tout vu, it's all settled; vu? agreed? c'est bien vu?/c'est vu? OK?/all right?/got it?/all clear? **2.** on aura tout vu! wonders will never cease! **3.** ni vu ni connu! keep it under your hat!/mum's the word! (*Voir* **m'as-tu vu**) **II** *nf P* **1.** à vue de nez, at a rough guess/roughly **2.** en mettre plein la vue à qn, to hoodwink s.o./to have s.o. on.

vulgos [vylgos] *a P* vulgar/coarse/crude.

vurdon [vyrdɔ̃] *nm P* gypsy's caravan.

W

wagon [vagɔ̃] *nm A P* prostitute*.

wagon(n)ets [vagɔnɛ] *nmpl F* **recharger les wagon(n)ets,** to buy another round of drinks; to set 'em up again.

wallace [valas, wa-] *nf F* **(fontaine) Wallace,** drinking fountain.

waterloo [watɛrlo] *nm F* **1.** rout/defeat **2. en plein waterloo,** dead out of luck.

waters [watɛr, -v-] *nmpl F* WC*/toilet/loo/*NAm* john. (*Voir* **ouatères**)

watrin [watrɛ̃] *nm P* (pair of) trousers.

weekendard [wikɛndar] *nm F* weekend holiday-maker/weekender.

whisky [wiski] *nm P* **whisky soviétique,** (glass of) red wine.

X

X, x [iks] *nm F* **1.** (*a*) **l'X,** the *École polytechnique* (in Paris); **un X,** a student at the *École polytechnique* (*b*) **un fort en x/une tête à x,** a gifted mathematician/s.o. who is good at maths **2. je vous l'ai dit x fois,** I've told you a thousand times/any number of times **3. avoir les jambes en x,** to be knock-kneed.

Y

y [i] **I** *adv* F (*a*) **ah, j'y suis!** ah, now I understand!/I've got it!/I'm with you! **vous y êtes!** you've got it!/you've hit the nail on the head! **tu y es?** (*i*) do you get it?/have you twigged? (*ii*) are you ready? **vous n'y êtes pas du tout** (*i*) you're not with it at all (*ii*) you're wide of the mark/you're not very warm (*b*) **il n'y est plus,** he's not all there (*c*) **je voudrais (bien) t'y voir!** I'd like to see *you* do it!/see if you can do it better! **II** *pron inv* P (= *lui*) **dites-y que je suis venu,** tell him I've come; **demandez-y s'il en a,** ask him if he's got any. (*Voir* **dire** 4) **III** *pers pron* P (= *il, ils*) he; they; **y chiale,** he's blubbering; **y chialent,** they're blubbering; **c'est-y pas vrai?** isn't that right/so?

ya [ja] *nm* P (*abbr*) = **yatagan.**

yakas [jaka] *nmpl* P eyes*.

yaouled [jaulɛd] *nm* P (young) Arab* (*esp* of the Arab community in Paris).

yaourt [jaurt] *nm* F (*aut*) **pot de yaourt,** bubble car.

yatagan [jatagɑ̃] *nm* P knife/chiv.

yeuter [jøte] *vtr* P = **zyeuter.**

yeux [jø] *nmpl Voir* **œil.**

yéyé [jeje] **I** F *a inv* (*années 60*) pop; **chanteur, -euse yéyé,** pop singer; **chanson yéyé,** pop song **II** *nm* 1. **le yéyé,** pop music 2. *f* **yéyette** [jejɛt] pop-mad teenager.

youde [jud] **I** *nm&f* P (*péj*) Jew*/yid **II** *a* P (*péj*) jewish.

youdi [judi] *nm* P (*péj*) Jew*/Yid.

youpin, ine [jupɛ̃, -in], **youtre** [jutr] P (*péj*) **I** *nm&f* Jew*/Jewess/yid/sheeny **II** *a* Jewish.

youvance [juvɑ̃s] *nm* P (*péj*) Jew*/yid/heeb.

youvoi [juvwa] *nm* P (*verlan de voyou*) hooligan*/yob(bo).

youyou [juju] *nm&f* P Yugoslav.

yoyo [jɔjo] *nm* P set of (master) keys.

yoyoter [jɔjɔte] *vi* P **yoyoter de la mansarde,** to be slightly mad*/to have a screw loose/to have bats in the belfry.

Yvans [ivɑ̃] *nmpl* P Russians*/Russkies.

Z

zacharie [zakari] *nm P* skeleton.

zaiber [zebe] *vtr V* (*verlan de*
baiser) to have sex*/to screw/to
have it away.

zan [zã] *nm P* liquorice. (*Voir* **bout**
7 (*b*))

zanzi [zãzi] *nm P* dice game played
in bars for drinks.

zarbi [zarbi] *nm P* (*verlan de*
bizarre) eccentric*/strange/odd person; oddball/weirdo/weirdie.

zaz(ou) [zaz(u)] *nm F* **un costume**
zaz(ou), a zoot suit.

zeb [zɛb] *nm V* penis*.

zébi(e) [zebi] *nf P* **peau de zébi(e)**
(*i*) trash/rubbish/junk (*ii*) nothing*/damn all/sod all.

zèbre [zɛbr] *nm F* **1.** (*individu*)
character/bloke/*esp NAm* guy; **un**
drôle de zèbre, a weird character/
an oddball/a funny guy; **qu'est-ce**
que c'est que ces zèbres-là? who are
those jokers? **faire le zèbre**, to play
the fool **2.** (*CB*) name/handle.

zef(f) [zɛf] *nm F* wind/breeze.

zèle [zɛl] *nm F* **faire du zèle**, to be
an eager beaver; to overdo it; **pas**
de zèle! don't overdo it!

zep [zɛp] *nm P* (*verlan de* **pèze**)
money*/brass/dough/the ready.

zéph [zef] *nm*, **zèphe** [zɛf] *nm F*
wind/breeze.

zéphir(e), zéphyr(e) [zefir] *nm*
A P (formerly) soldier of the **bat'**
d'Af.

zéro [zero] **I** *nm F* (*pers*) (*a*) **un**
vrai zéro/un zéro à gauche/un zéro
en chiffre/un zéro fini, a nonentity/

a complete washout/a dead loss/a
nobody/*esp NAm* a no-no (*b*) **c'est**
un pur zéro (dans l'équipe), he's just
a passenger (in the team)/he's just
there for the ride **2.** *F* (*scol*) **un**
zéro pointé, a nought/a zero (in
exam, etc) **3.** *F* **être à zéro/avoir**
le moral à zéro, to be depressed*/
to be low/to feel down/to be down
in the dumps **4.** *F* **partir de/à**
zéro, to start from scratch **5.** *P*
les avoir à zéro, to be afraid*/to be
in a blue funk/to be scared shitless
6. *P* **bander à zéro**, to be/to get
highly excited; to be/to get all
worked up **7.** *P* **le zéro**, the anus*
II *int P* nothing doing! **zéro pour la**
question! no way!/not bloody
likely!*/not on your life!

zetoupar [zetupar] *nf P* (*verlan de*
partouze) orgy.

zézette [zezɛt] *nf P* tot of
absinth(e).

ziber [zibe] *vtr* **1.** *P* to do (s.o.)
out of (sth)/to screw (s.o.) **2.** *V* =
zaiber.

zic [zik], **zicmu** [zikmy] *nf P*
(*verlan de musique*) music.

zieuter [zjøte] *vtr P* = **zyeuter.**

zig [zig] *nm O P* fellow/chap*; **un**
bon zig, a decent sort of bloke/a
great guy; **un drôle de zig**, a
weirdo/a screwball; a queer fish.

zigomar [zigɔmar] *nm*,
zigoteau, zigoto [zigɔto] *nm*
P **1.** odd character; **c'est un drôle**
de zigomar, he's a queer customer.
(*Voir* **zig**) **2.** **faire le zigoto**, to
play the fool/to show off*; **fais pas**
le zigoto! don't try it on with me!

zigouigoui [zigujguj] *nm V* penis*.

zigouiller [ziguje] *vtr P* (*a*) to knife (s.o.)/to cut up (s.o.) (*b*) to kill*/to murder; **toute la bande a été zigouillée,** the whole lot of them were wiped out.

zigouince [zigwɛ̃s] *nf A P* prostitute*.

zigue [zig] *nm P* = **zig.**

zigué [zige] *a P* bald(-headed)*.

ziguer [zige] *vtr P* **ziguer qn,** to clean s.o. out/to take s.o. to the cleaners (at cards, etc).

zinc [zɛ̃g] *nm F* **1.** bar/counter (of public house); **prendre un verre sur le zinc,** to have a drink at the bar **2.** (*esp vieil avion*) plane/crate; **vider le zinc,** to bale out. (*Voir* **culotte 9**)

zingue [zɛ̃g] *nm P* **1.** = **zinc 1 2.** = publican/landlord; bartender.

zinzin [zɛ̃zɛ̃] **I** *nm F* **1.** noise/ row/uproar*/rumpus **2.** thingummy/what's-its-name*/what-do-you-call-it **3.** c'est un zinzin, he's mad*/bonkers/nuts **4.** violin/fiddle **II** *a* mad*/cracked/nuts/ loopy.

zizi [zizi] *nm* **1.** *V* (*i*) penis* (*ii*) female genitals*; **faire zizi pan(-)-pan,** to have sex* **2.** *P* whatsit/ what's-its-name*/thingummy.

zizique [zizik] *nf P* music; **se farcir de la zizique,** to go to a concert; **en avant la zizique!** here we go!/off we go!/let it rip!

zob [zɔb] *nm V* **1.** penis* **2.** (**mon**) **zob!** my arse!/*NAm* my ass!/my foot!/nuts!/balls! (*Voir* **peau 19**)

zobi [zɔbi] *nm* **1.** *V* penis* **2.** *P* **peau de zobi** (*i*) trash/rubbish/junk (*ii*) nothing*/damn all/sweet FA.

zomblou [zɔ̃blu] *nm P* (*verlan de blouson*) blouson.

zonard, -arde [zonar, -ard] *n* **1.** homeless person/down-and-out **2.** hooligan*/yob/thug; delinquent. (*Voir* **narzo**)

zone [zon] *nf F* **1.** **la Zone,** slum area/shanty town (on the outskirts of any large town); **chez eux c'est la Zone,** they're desperately poor **2.** *excl* (*péj*) **la zone!** poor thing!/ poor sod!

zoner [zone] **I** *vi P* **1.** to hang about/to mooch about/to mess around/*NAm* to goof off **2.** (*drogues*) to get high/to trip **3.** (*homosexuels*) to cruise/to go cruising **II** *vpr* **se zoner** *P* to go to bed*/to turn in/to hit the sack.

zonga [zɔ̃ga] *nm P* (*verlan de gazon*) (*drogues*) marijuana*/grass.

zonier, -ière [zonje, -jɛr] *n F* = **zonard, -arde.**

zou! [zu] *int F* **allez zou!** shoo!/hop it!

zouave [zwav] *nm F* **faire le zouave** (*a*) to brag/to show off*; **ne fais pas le zouave,** don't try it on (with me) (*b*) to play the fool. (*Voir* **dache**)

zouaviller [zwavije] *vi P* = **faire le zouave (zouave).**

zouzou [zuzu] *nm P* = **zouave.**

zozo [zozo] *nm O F* **1.** mug/sucker **2.** fool*/idiot/clot/nit.

zozor [zozɔr] *nm A P* **du zozor,** money*.

zozores [zozɔr] *nfpl P* ears*.

zozoter [zozɔte] *vi F* to lisp.

zozotte [zozɔt] *nf A F* **ma zozotte!** my darling!*/my pet!

zut [zyt] *int F* (*a*) **zut (alors)!** damn!/dash it!/darn it!/blow it! (*b*) (**et puis**) **zut!** rubbish!/fiddlesticks! **zut pour vous!** go to blazes!/get lost!* **dis-lui zut de ma part!** tell him to go to hell! (*c*) I can't be bothered! (*d*) **avoir un œil qui dit zut à l'autre,** to be cross-eyed/to (have a) squint.

zyeuter [zjøte] *vtr P* to have a look at (sth)/to take a butcher's/to have a dekko/to have a squint at sth; **zyeute-moi ça!** get a load of that!/ get an eyeful of that!

zygue [zig] *nm P* = **zig.**

Index of English
Slang Synonyms

afraid, to be: *see* **coward, to be a.**

agreed! ace; all right; check! done! fair enough! fucking A; I'll buy it! I'll go along with that! I'm game! I'm on! It's OK by me! OK! ok! okay! okey-doke! okey-dokey! right-ho! right-o(h)! right on! righty-(h)o! Roger! roger! that suits me to a T! yeah! yep! you're on!

alibi: blind; cover; front.

American: septic tank; Yank; Yankee.

amphetamines: A; bam; blackbirds; black and tan; black and white (minstrel/nigger); blues; bombida; bombido; candy; chalk; dex; dexie; dexo; dexy; double blue; drivers; forwards; garbage; green dragon; greenies; jelly baby; jolly beans; leaper; lid popper(s); lift pill; peach; root; sparkle plenty; speed; speedball; sweeties; thrust; truck drivers; uppers; uppies; wake-up; (old lady) white; whitey; white; zoom.

amyl nitrate: amy; amyl; amys; pearls; poppers; popsy; snapper.

anal sex, (to have): to be done brown; brown job; to brown; chain gang; to cornhole; daisy chain; to do; to do it dog-fashion/ doggy fashion/dogways; to do it Greek style/like the Greeks/the Greek way; to earn one's brown wings; to finger fuck; to fist fuck; fist-fucking; floral arrangement; to get one's brown wings; to Greek;

to have a cup of tea; to Oscar; to ram; to ream; to ream s.o.'s (ass) out; to screw; to tongue s.o. out.

angry: aer(e)ated; bummed out; fuming; furious; hacked off; hopping mad; humpy; livid; mad; porky; red-assed; sick; smoky; sore; wild.

angry, to be: to be hot under the collar/in a huff/in a stew/in a wax; to blow a fuse/a gasket; to blow one's lid/one's stack/one's top/one's wig; to blow up; to burn; to cop the needle/the spike; to cut up nasty/rough/ugly; to do one's block/lolly/nut; to flare up; to flip one's lid/one's noodle/one's raspberry/one's top; to fly off the handle; to fly up in the air; to get all steamed-up/all worked up; to get one's blood up/one's dander up/one's gage up/one's Irish up/ one's monkey up; to get one's rag out; to get mad/narked/shirty; to get s.o.'s back up; to get s.o.'s goat; to get the needle/the spike; to go ape; to go off crook; to go spare; to go through the ceiling/the roof; to go up in the air; to have a fit; to have kittens; to have the rats; to hit the ceiling/the roof; to lose one's rag/shirt/wool; to nearly have a baby; to see red; to spit; to throw a fit; to wig out. (*See* **temper**)

annoy, to: to aggravate; to be a pain in the arse/ass/neck; to bug; to crease; to devil; to dig; to faze; to get s.o.'s back up; to get s.o.'s goat; to get in s.o.'s hair; to get on s.o.'s tits/wick/willy; to get up s.o.'s nose; to get under s.o.'s skin; to give s.o. balls ache; to give s.o. a pain in the arse/ass/neck; to give s.o. the nadgers/the pip; to gripe s.o.; to needle; to peeve; to pester; to plague; to play up; to ride; to tread on s.o.'s toes; to turn off.

anus: arse; arsehole; ass; asshole; backdoor; brown; brownie; bumhole; bung-hole; cornhole; ding; dinger; fart-hole; gig; gonga; hole; jack; Khyber; poop chute; poop hole; ring; ring hole; ring-piece; round eye; shit-hole; tokus.

Arab: wog.

arm: fin; flipper: wing.

arrest, to: to bag; to bust; to collar; to cop; to do; to get; to gobble; to grab; to haul in; to hoist; to hook; to knock off; to lag; to lift; to lumber; to nab; to nail; to nick; to pick up; to pinch; to pluck; to pull in; to put the snatch on; to rap; to run in; to snatch; to tag; to touch; to yank.
(*See* **imprison, to**)

arrested, to be: to be *or* to get busted/done/nabbed/narked/nicked/picked up/run in.

arrive, to: to blow along; to blow in; to breeze in; to get in under the wire; to land; to make the scene; to lob in; to pop in, to pop up; to roll along; to roll up; to show up; to turn up (out of the blue); to weigh in.

attack s.o., to: to crack down on; to go for; to lay into; to light into; to pile into; to rip into; to sail into; to set about; to wade into; to walk into.

Australian: Aussie; Ozzie; Wallaby.

bag of tricks, the whole: (and) all that jazz; all the rest of it; and what have you; the whole bang shoot; the whole boiling; the whole kit (and caboodle); the whole set-up; the whole shebang; the whole shooting match; the whole works.

bald-head(ed person): baldie; baldy; billiard-ball; skating-rink; as bald as a coot/an egg.

barbiturates: barbies; barbs; blue heavens; double blue; downers; goofball; goofers; green and blacks; peanuts; phenie; purple hearts; rainbows; red birds; red devils; red jackets; reds; sleeper; stumbler; yellow-jacket.

bastard: basket; beggar; bitch; bleeder; bugger; effer; (old) fart; fatherfucker; fink; fucker; gink; heel; jerk; MF; mother; motherfucker; muhfuh; nasty piece of work; no-gooder; nogoodnik; pig; pisspot; quandong; rat; ratbag; ratfink; roughneck; sao; scumbag; shit; shit-ass; shit-bag; shite; shithead; shitheel; shitpot; shitstick; skunk; slag; slob; so-and-so; s.o.b.; sod; sonofabitch; son of a bitch; sonovabitch; stinker; stinkpot; swine; toerag; tough; tripehead; turd; tyke; worm; wrong'un.
(*See* **hooligan**)

beating(-up): belting; dusting; hammering; hiding; knuckle sandwich; lambasting; larruping; licking; milling; paddy-whack; pasting; shellacking; smack-botty; tanning; third degree; thrashing; towelling; walloping; whacking; whopping; working over.

beat up, to: to bash (about); to bash s.o.'s face/head in; to bash the living daylights out of s.o.; to bat; to batter; to beat hollow; to beat the living daylights out of s.o.; to beat the piss/the shit out of s.o.; to belt; to brain; to bust (s.o.'s ass); to cane; to clobber; to clock; to clonk (s.o. on the head); to clout; to clump; to cream; to crown; to do; to do over; to dot (s.o. one); to do up; to duff up; to dust s.o.'s jacket (for him); to dust up; to flatten; to floor; to give it to s.o.; to give s.o. a (good) going-over; to give s.o. a belt/a licking/a milling/a thick ear/a walloping/a working over; to give s.o. the horrors/the once-over; to go over; to have a scrap; to kick s.o.'s head in; to knock s.o.'s block off/s.o.'s teeth in; to knock hell out of s.o.; to knock s.o. silly/for six; to knock s.o. to kingdom come; to knock s.o. into the middle of next week; to knock the bejesus/the living day-lights/the stuffing out of s.o.; to knuckle; to KO; to lace into; to lambaste; to lam (into); to larrup; to lather; to lay into; to lay one on s.o.; to leather; to let s.o. have it; to mug; to murder; to paste; to pay; to plaster; to plug; to pound s.o. into a jelly; to put the boot in; to put the leather in; to rough up; to rub out; to scrap; to shellac(k); to skelp; to slam; to slaughter; to slog; to slug; to smack; to smash s.o.'s face in; to smash up; to sort out; to stick one on s.o.; to stoush; to swipe; to take a swipe at s.o.; to tan s.o.'s hide; to thrash; to total; to towel; to whip; to whop; to wipe the floor with; to work over.

bed: doss; feather(s); flea-bag; flop; hay; kip; letty; pit; rack; sack; shake-down; Uncle Ned.
bed, to go to: to doss (down); to get between the sheets; to go to kip; to hit the hay; to hit the pad; to hit the roost; to hit the sack; to kip (down); to rack out; to sack out; to shake down; to turn in.
(*See* **sleep, to go to**)

Benzedrine (*RTM*): bean; benny; benz; copilots; drin; (old lady) white.

betray, to: *see* **divulge a secret, to.**

Black: boogie; coon; darkey; darkie; darky; dinge; fade; jig; jigaboo; Jim Crow; jungle bunny; nig; nigger; nignog; nigra; Sambo; schwartz; shine; smoke; snowball;

soul brother; soul sister; spade; Uncle Tom; wog.

Black Maria: cop-wag(g)on; hurry-up wag(g)on; jam sandwich; meat wag(g)on; milk wag(g)on; paddy-wag(g)on.

bloody (*euphemisms or substitutes for*): bally; blanketty; blasted; blazing; bleeding; blessed; blinking; blithering; blooming; damned; darn; darned; deuced; dratted; effing; flaming; flipping; frigging; fucking; goddamn; goddamned; motherfucking; ruddy; sodding.

blow: backhander; bang; bash; belt; biff; bonk; clip (round the ear); clump; conk; crack; cuff; facer; finisher; flattener; fourpenny one; haymaker; lefthander; right-hander; slog; slug; smasher; sock; swipe; thump; wallop; whack; wipe.

boots, big: beetle-crushers; boats; bovver-boots; canal boats; clodhoppers; daisy-roots; DM's; Doc Martens; tugboats.

bore, to: to bore s.o. to death/to tears; to bore s.o. rigid/stiff; to bore the balls off s.o.; to bore the hind legs off a donkey; to give s.o. a pain in the arse; to get on s.o.'s tits.
(*See* **annoy, to**)
bore: bind; buttonholer; clinger; clinging vine; drag; fixture; hanger-on; pain in the neck; (bloody) nuisance; pest; plague; schmo; schmock; schmoe; sticker; zombie.
bored, to be: to be bored rigid/stiff; to be bored to death/to tears; to be chocker.
(*See* **depressed**)
boring: deadly; draggy; dullsville; killing; rotten; yawny.

boss: chief; gaffer; gov; (the) governor; guv; (the) guv'nor; the man; the old man; skip; skipper.

brave: *see* **courageous.**

breasts: balloons; bazookas; bazooms; beauties; boobies; boobs;

bouncers; bristlers; bristols; bubbies; bumpers; cans; charms; dairies; diddies; droopers; dumplings;
falsies; fainting fits; gay deceivers;
globes; gnat bites; hammocks;
headlights; jugs; knockers; lungs;
maraccas; marshmallows; melons;
milk-bottles; milk-shop; ninnies;
norgies; norgs; norkers; norks; pancakes; pimples; pippins; shakers;
shelf-kit; swingers; tale of two cities; threepenny bits; tits; titties;
udders; upholstery.

bribe: backhander; commission;
dirty money; drop; dropsy; earner;
fix; grease; hush money; kickback;
loot; lug; oil; palm-grease; palm-
oil; pay-off; payola; schmier;
straightener; sugar; sweetener; (the)
take; taste; velvet.
bribe, to: to grease s.o.'s palm;
to square; to straighten; to sugar;
to sweeten.
bribe, to accept a: to be on
the take; to get a backhander; to
make a bit on the side; to take
one.
(*See* **profits, illicit**)

brothel: bawdy house; bed house;
blue house; cat house; honky-tonk;
hook shop; jag house; joy-house;
knocking shop; massage parlour;
meat-house; molly-shop; parlour;
red-light house; shebang; stew;
timothy; whorehouse; whore-shop.

bungle, to: to arse up; to ball(s)
up; to bitch (everything up); to
blow; to bodge up; to bog up; to
bollix (up); to bollocks; to boob;
to botch; to bugger up; to cock up;
to fluff it; to foul (things) up; to
fuck; to goof up; to gum up (the
works); to hash (up); to jigger up;
to knock up; to louse (things) up;
to make a balls/a balls-up/a ball-
up/a bog/a bollocks/a cock-up/a
mess/a muck of; to mess up; to
muck up; to muff.

buttocks: arse; arsehole; ass;
asshole; backside; behind; bottom;
botty; bum; butt; can; cheeks;

ding; dinger; dish; end; fanny;
jacksie; Keester; posterior; prat;
rear(-end); sit-me-down; sit-upon;
stern; tail; tokus.

cannabis: charas; charash; dagga;
(Indian) hay; (Indian) hemp; (the)
herb; India; india; locoweed;
maconha; manicure; mutah; ton.
(*See* **marijuana**)

car: banger; Beetle; bomb;
boneshaker; bottler; buggy; bus;
caddy; chevvy; crate; crock; doodle-bug; drag; heap (of junk); Jag;
jalopy; jam-jar; Limmo; limo;
motor; palm-tree; Roller; Rolls;
rust bucket; square-wheeler; (tin-)-
Lizzie; wheels; (old) wreck.

cat: kitty; mog; moggie; moggy;
puss.

cemetery: bone-orchard; bone-
yard.

cert, it's a: *see* **easy, very.**

chamber-pot: daisy; guzunder;
jemima; jerry; jordan; latrine-buck-
et; latrine-pail; pisspot; po; pottie;
potty; smoker; thunder-mug; tinkler.

champagne: bubbly; cham(p);
champers; fizz; giggle-water;
shampers; the widow.

chap, old: old bean; buddy;
chum; fruity-pie; old fruit; old
man; old pal; old thing.
(*See* **man**)

chat; chattering: bunny;
cackle; chinfest; chinwag; clack;
clackety-clack; confab; gas(sing);
hot air; jabber(ing); jaw; natter;
nattering; patter; prattling; verbal;
yabber; yack; yak; yackety-yack;
yap; yapping; yatter.
chat to; to chatter: to
bunny; to chew the fat/the rag; to
clack; to confabulate; to have a
bull session/a bunny/a chinwag/a
confab/a natter; to gas; to gossip;
to jabber; to jaw; to jive; to natter
(on); to poodle on; to prattle; to
rabbit; to schmoose; to schmooze;

to talk away nineteen to the dozen; to yabber; to yack; to yak; to yammer; to yap; to yatter.
(*See* **talk volubly, to**)

chatterbox: babbling brook; bag of wind; blabbermouth; flapjaw; gabber; gasbag; gasser; parrot; pitcher; spruiker; windbag; to have the gift of the gab.

cheat, to: *see* **fool, to; swindle, to.**

cheated, to be: *see* **fooled, to be; swindled, to be.**

cheers!: bottoms up! bung-ho! cheerio! chin chin! down the hatch! good health! happy days! here's looking at you! (here's) mud in your eye! skin off your nose!

child: brat; chick; chit; dustbin (lid); godfer; God forbid; holy terror; kid; kiddie; kiddy; mischief; mite; nip; nipper; saucepan lid; (young) shaver; snip; sprog; tiddler; toddler; (tiny) tot.

Chinese: Chink; Chinky; gook.

cigarette: burn; cancer-stick; cig; ciggie; ciggy; coffin-nail; drag; fag; faggeroo; gage; gasper; oily-rag; roll-up; roll-your-own; root; smoke; spit and drag; tab; twirl.
(*See* **marijuana cigarette**)

cigarette-end: bumper; dead soldier; dog-end; fag-end; nicker; roach (of marijuana cigarette); old soldier; snipe; tab-end.

clergyman: bible-basher; bible-puncher; black coat; devil-dodger; dog-collar brigade; God man; holy Joe; Joe; sin shifter; sky-pilot.

clitoris: button; clit.

clothes: cast-offs; clobber; drag; duds; gear; get-up; glad rags; hand-me-downs; rags; rig-out; rig-up; slops; threads; togs; turnout; vines.

cocaine: angel; bernice; bernies; Big C; big bloke; C; candy; Cecil; cee; Charley (coke); coke; cokey; cokie; cokomo; corine; flake; girl; heaven/gold dust; kokomo; nose-candy; powder; snow; talc; white cross; white stuff; whizz-bang.

coffin: concrete/pine/wooden overcoat.

condom: bag; French letter; French safe; frenchie; frenchy; (rubber) johnnie; mac; mack; packet of three; rubber; safe; scumbag; skin.

confess, to: *see* **divulge a secret, to.**

corpse: cold meat; dead meat; dead 'un; goner; stiff.

courage, to have; courageous, to be: to be game; to have backbone; to have balls; to have grit; to have guts; to have (plenty of) go; to have intestinal fortitude; to have spunk; to have what it takes; to keep one's pecker up; to stand the gaff.

coward: bottler; chicken; cissy; fraidy cat; funk; funker; patsy; quitter; ring-tail; scare-baby; scaredy-cat; sissy; yellowbelly.

coward, to be a; cowardly, to be: to back down; to be dead scared/in a blue funk/(a bit) green about the gills/gutless/jittery/panicky/pucker-assed/scared shitless/scared stiff/shit-scared/spunkless/windy/yellow/yellow-bellied; to be shitting oneself/wetting oneself; to bottle; to bug out; to chicken out; to fink; to freeze; to funk it; to get cold feet/the wind up; to go soft; to have a yellow streak; to have butterflies (in one's stomach/tummy); to have the chills/the collywobbles/the heebie-jeebies/the horrors/the jim-jams/the jitters/the screaming-meemies/the shakes/the squitters/the willies; to have no guts; to have ring-flutter; to hit the panic button; to lose one's bottle; to nearly have a baby/kittens; to psych out; to punk out; to push the panic button; to show the white feather; to turn chicken/milky; to wet oneself/one's pants.

crazy: *see* **mad.**

criticism, (severe): backbiting; bitching; coating; cutting up; dressing-down; flak; knocking; lambasting; lamming; panning; razz; roast; roasting; running down; slamming; slating.
(*See* **reprimand**)

criticize, to (severely): to backbite; to bad-mouth; to bitch; to chip at; to crab; to cut up; to cut to pieces; to do dirt on; to drag s.o.'s name through the mud; to give s.o. a coating/a dressing down; to hammer; to have a dig at; to have a go at; to haul up; to jump on s.o.; to jump down s.o.'s throat; to knock; to lambaste; to lash; to lay into; to pan; to pick on; to pull to pieces; to put down; to put the poison in; to rap over the knuckles; to razz; to roast; to run down; to run into the ground; to slag off; to slam; to slate; to snap at s.o.; to snap s.o.'s head off; to tear to pieces; to wade into.
(*See* **reprimand, to (severely)**)

cropper, to come a: to come a gutzer/a mucker/a purler; to fall flat on one's face; to go for a burton; to go kerplunk; to go sprawling; to take a flier; to take a header.
(*See* **fail, to**)

cunnilingus: cannibalism; kipper feast; muff-diving; pearl diving.
to practise cunnilingus: to dive into the bushes; to eat; to eat furpie/hairpie; to French; to go down on; to muff; to pearl-dive; to suck (off); to tongue; to whistle in the dark.
person who practises cunnilingus: cannibal; cuntlapper; muff-diver; pearl-diver.

darling: angel-face; chickabiddy; cutie; dearie; deary; duck; ducks; ducky; hon; honey; honeybunch; lamb; love; lovey; pet; poppet; pre-cious; sweet; sweetie; sweetie-pie; sweety; sweety-pie; treasure.

dead: cold; done for; pushing up the daisies; six feet under; stiff.

dealer: *see* **drugs; swindler.**

deceive, to: *see* **fool, to.**

defecate, to: to cack; to crap; to do big jobs; to do number two(s); to do one's duty; to do a poo; to do sth no one else can do for you; to drop one's load; to go for a crap/a shit/a pony (and trap)/a tom tit; to go to the bog/to the loo; to have a clear-out/a crap/a shit/a shite; to perform; to poo; to relieve nature; to relieve oneself; to shit.

denounce, to: *see* **divulge a secret, to; inform on, to.**

depressed: blue; brassed off; browned off; cheesed off; chocker; chuffed; creased; cut up; down; downbeat; down in the doldrums/in the dumps/the mouth; gutted; low.
to be depressed: to be in an indigo mood/in low water; to be on a bummer/on a downer/on a low; to feel grim; to flip; to have the blues/the hip/the hump/the mizzers/the pip.

detective: *see* **police.**

diarrhoea: Bombay cruds; collywobbles; the gripe; Montezuma's revenge; the runs; the screamers; shitters; the shits; the tom tits; the trots; the turistas.

die, to: to be carried out feet first; to be on the way out; to be six feet under; to be with one's fathers; to cash in one's chips; to check out; to choke; to come to the end of the line; to conk out; to cop it; to croak; to drop off the twig; to get fitted for a wooden overcoat; to give up the ghost; to go; to go for a burton; to go off the hooks; to go out feet first; to go to glory; to go west; to have bought a packet; to have bought it; to have had it;

to kick off; to kick the bucket; to meet one's maker; to pack up; to pass in one's marbles; to peg out; to pip out; to pop off; to quit it; to quit the scene; to shut up shop; to slip the painter; to snuff it; to snuff out; to sprout wings; to take a leap into the great unknown; to take off; to turn up one's toes.

dismiss, to: to axe; to boot (out); to bounce; to can; to chuck out; to ditch; to fire; to give s.o. the air/the axe/the bird/the boot/ the bullet/the chop/the chuck/the (old) heave-ho/the one-two/the order of the boot/the pink slip/the push/the sack/the shaft/the shove/ the tin-tack; to give s.o. his/her cards/marching orders/walking orders; to kick out; to kiss off; to lay off; to pack s.o. in/out; to pitch s.o. out; to put the skids under; to roust out; to sack; to shaft; to show s.o. the door; to sling out; to throw s.o. out (on his ear); to turf out; to write s.o. off. (*See* **packing, to send s.o.**)
dismissed, to be: to be fired; to be thrown out on one's ear; to get the air/the axe/the bird/the (order of) the boot/the bullet/one's cards/the chop/the kick/the push/the sack/the shove/ the tin-tack; to get one's marching orders/one's walking orders; to get kicked out.

disparage, to: *see* **criticize, to (severely).**
disparagement: *see* **criticism, (severe).**

divulge a secret, to: to belch; to blab (one's mouth off); to be a blab(ber)mouth; to blow the gaff; to blurt it out; to come clean; to cough up; to dob in; to give the game/show away; to let the cat out of the bag; to nark; to open up; to peach (on s.o.); to pool; to put the squeal in; to sell s.o. down the river; to shice; to shoot one's face/ mouth off; to shoot the works; to sing (like a canary); to snitch; to

spill one's guts/the beans; to squawk; to squeal; to talk. (*See* **inform on, to**)

dog: bitser; bow-wow; doggy; Heinz 57; hound; mutt; pooch; tyke.

done for: it's all over with s.o.; it's all up with s.o.; it's curtains for s.o.; to have bought it; caput; come unstuck; dished; down-and-out; finished; a goner; gone to pot; the game's up; kaput; to have 'had it; to have had one's chips; s.o.'s number is up; sunk; up a gum tree; wiped out. (*See* **fix, to be in a**)

dress up, to: to doll up; to dud up; to ponce oneself up; to posh oneself up; to put on one's best bib and tucker; to put on one's glad rags; to put on one's Sunday best; to rig out; to spruce (oneself) up; to tart oneself up; to titivate; to tog oneself up.
dressed up, all: all dolled up; all poshed up; all togged up; done up like a spiced pig; dressed (fit) to kill; dressed like a dog's dinner; dressed up/got up to the nines/to the teeth/to the knocker; in full fig; in one's best bib and tucker; in one's glad rags; in one's Sunday best; in one's monkey-suit; jazzed up; la-di-da(h); looking the business; looking (like) a million dollars; natty; posh; ritzy; sharp; slinky; snappy; snazzy; swish; tarted up; tasty.

drink, (heavily) to: to bash it; to be on the booze/on the bottle/ on the grog/on it; to booze; to down a pint/a few jars; to drink like a fish; to get bevvied; to get some elbow practice; to get tanked up; to go on the beer/the booze/ the bottle/the grog/the shicker; to go for a pot; to have a bevvy/a few jars/one for the road/a slug/a snort; to hit the booze/the bottle/ the sauce; to keep the damp out; to knock one back; to lap it up; to lift the little finger; to lubricate (one's throat); to lush; to pen and ink; to shift a pint; to sink a pint; to slug; to sluice one's ivories; to snatch a quick one; to souse; to sozzle; to sup up; to swig; to tank up; to tie one on; to tie on a load; to toss off a pint; to wet one's whistle.

(alcoholic) drink: black and tan; black velvet; booze; electric soup; firewater; gage; grog; (the) hard stuff; hoo(t)ch; juice; junglejuice; lubrication; moonshine; mother-in-law; never-fear; plonk; rat poison; red biddy; red-eye; rot gut; sauce; shicker; snakebite; tanglefoot; tiddl(e)y; turps; varnish; Vera Lynn; vino.

alcoholic drink, an: bevvy; bracer; drappie; drappy; drop (of the hard stuff); eye-opener; snifter; snort; snorter; (a drop of) tiddl(e)y; tincture; tot; wee dram.

inferior drink: bilge(-water); cat-lap; cat's piss; dishwater; gnat's piss; hogwash; washing-up water.

drugs: dope; junk; nasties; shit; stuff.

drugs, to use: to be on dope/ on the needle/on speed/on a trip; to blast; to blow; to crank up; to dabble; to dope up; to fix (up); to get off (on dope); to go on a jag; to have the weekend habit; to jolt; to joy-pop; to mainline; to pop (pills); to shoot up; to skin-pop; to speed; to spike; to switch on; to take; to take off; to trip (out); to use; to wag out.

drugs, under the influence of: blasted; blocked; bombed (out); boxed; brought down; canned; charged up; cooked up; crashed out; dosed up; flipped (out); floating (on cloud nine); flying high; freaked out; full; funked out; geed up; geezed up; gone; gowed up; high; hooked; hopped up; hyped up; jacked up; junked up; knocked out; lit up; loaded; off/on the habit; on; on dope/on speed/on a trip; potted;

ripped; schnockered; smashed; snowed; spaced out; spiked; stoned; strung out; switched on; tead-up; tripped out; turned on; twisted; up; wasted; wired; zoned; zonked.

drugs, withdrawal symptoms from: to be cold turkey; to be hung up/sick/strung out; to be waiting for the man; to have a chinaman/a monkey on one's back; to have the chuck habit/the horrors; to need a fix; yen sleep; yen-yen.

drug addict: AD; ad; cokehead; cotton freak; cubehead; DA; dabbler; dip; dope addict; dope fiend; doper; dopehead; druggie; druggy; fixer; freak; goof; hard-liner; hay-head; head; hophead; hyp(e); hypo; joy-popper; junkie; mainliner; pothead; skinpopper; snowbird; speedball; tea blower; tea head; user; viper; voyager; weedhead.

drug addict's equipment/instruments: artillery; biz; (the) business; fit; gear; gimmick; joint; kit; layout; machinery; tools; works.

needle/syringe: dropper; hyp(e); hype-stick; hypo; jabber; machine; nail; point; spike.

injection: dig; fix; hyp(e); hypo; jab; jab-off; jag; jolt; mosquito bite; ping; pop; shoot; skinpopping; Tom Mix; wake-up.

drugs, dealer of: bagman; candy man; carrier; Chino; connection; connector; connexion; dealer; deckman; dope peddler/pusher; fixer; junkie; kickman; the man; mule; operator; ounce man; powder monkey; pusher; sandman; travel-agent; viper.

drunk, (to be): arseholed; bagged; barrelled up; bevvied; blind (drunk); (Harry) blinders; blotto; boiled; boozed (up); bottled; boxed; canned; corked; crashed; crocked; cut; dagged; dead drunk; dead to the world;

edged; elephants; far gone; floating on cloud nine; full; fuzzled; fuzzy; gaged; gassed; geezed up; glassy-eyed; gone; grilled; groggy; half-cut; half-pissed; half-seas over; half-stewed; hammered; happy; helpless; high (as a kite); in one's cups; jagged; jolly; juiced up; knocked out; legless; liquored up; lit-up; loaded; lubricated; lushed up; merry; muzzy; paralytic; pickled; pie-eyed; pissed (up); pissed as arseholes/as a newt; pixilated; plastered; potted; ploughed; raunchy; rigid; ripped; rotten; screwed; shaved; shellacked; shickered; shot; slewed; sloppy; sloshed; smashed; snaped; soaked; soused; sozzled; spifflicated; sprung; squiffy; steaming; stewed; stiff; stinking (drunk); stinko; stoned; stunned; tanked up; teed up; three/four sheets in/to the wind; tiddl(e)y; tight (as a newt); tipsy; under the influence; under the table; well away; well-oiled; whittled; woozy; zonked; zoned.

drunk(ard): alkie; alko; alky; bar-fly; boozer; dipso; dosser; juice-head; lush; piss-artist; pisspot; piss-tank; rumdum; rumhound; rummy; rumpot; soaker; souse; sozzler; tank; tippler; wino.

dumbfound, to: *see* **flabbergast, to.**

dupe, to: *see* **fool, to.**

dupe: *see* **fool.**

duped, to be: *see* **fooled, to be.**

ears: ear-holes; flappers; flaps; lobs; lugholes; lug'oles; lugs; tabs.

easy, very: a (dead) cert; child's play; a cinch; cushy; dead easy; a doddle; as easy as ABC/as pie/as winking; a gift; in the bag; jammy; kid's stuff; like falling off a log; money for jam/for old rope; nothing to it; a piece of cake; a piece of piss; plain sailing; a pushover; a romp; a snack; a snap; a snip; a sure bag; a sure thing; a walkover.

easy, to take it: to be sitting pretty; to bludge; to bugger about/around; to coast along; to diddle away one's time; to dilly dally; to doddle it; to fake off; to goof off; to hang loose; to have a cushy/an easy/a soft time of it; to kill time; to lay up; to lead a soft life; to live the life of Riley; to lollop around; to loosen up; to mess about/around; to mooch about/around; to piddle about/around.

eat (greedily), to: to demolish; to dig in; to eat like a horse/a pig; to feed one's face; to fill one's belly; to get stuck in; to gorge; to have a (good) blow-out/a (good) feed/a (good) tuck-in; to hog it; to make a pig of oneself; to nosh; to pig oneself; to pig out; to put on the nosebag; to scoff; to shovel it down; to stodge; to stoke up; to stuff one's face/one's guts/oneself; to tie on the nosebag; to tuck in; to tuck it away; to wolf.

eccentric (person): card; case; caution; character; crank; dag; freak; funny; goofball; kook; kooky; oddball; odd specimen; out-to-lunch; queer cove/cuss/customer/fish/specimen; ratbag; rum one; screwball; wacky; weirdie; weirdo; weirdy.

ejaculate, to: to come (off); to cream (one's jeans); to drop one's load; to fire; to fire in the air; to fire blanks; to get one's nuts off; to jet the juice; to shoot (one's load).

English: Brit; limey; Pom; Pommy.

erection, to have an: to be horny/hot/randy; to be as stiff as a poker; to crack a fat; to get it up; to get the jack; to get hot nuts; to get a raise; to have a bar on/a beat on/a bone-on/a hard-on; to have a biggie/a bone/a boner/a horn/a rod/a stand/a stiff/a stiffy; to have the hots; to have lead in one's pencil; to have a loaded gun; to have it up; to raise a beam; to raise it; to rise to the occasion; to stay.

458

(*See* **penis**)

exaggerate, to: to be a bit much; to bullshit; to come it (a bit) strong; to come the acid; to gild the lily; to go a bit (too) far; to go over the top; to jazz; to lay it on thick; to lay it on with a shovel/with a trowel; to overdo it; to pile it on; to shit; to soup up; to spin a yarn; to stretch it a bit far; to talk big; to talk in telephone numbers.

excellent: ace; amazing; bad; bang-up; beaut; a bit of all right; bonzer; boss; champion; classy; corking; crackerjack; daisy; dandy; ducky; fab; famous; fantastic; far-out; first class; first rate; a gas; gear; golden; gorgeous; great; groovy; hunky-dory; jake; keen; kill; magic; neat; nifty; not at all bad; OK; out of sight; out of this world; really great; rip-snorting; scrumptious; sensational; smashing; something else; spanking; stunning; super; superduper; superfly; ten out of ten; terrific; tickety-boo; tip-top; topping; top-flight; top-hole; top-line; top-notch; whizzo; wicked; wizard.

(*See* **first-rater**)

excite, to (sexually): to cock tease; to give s.o. the come-on; to lead on; to prick tease; to switch on; to turn on; to work up.

excited, sexually: fruity; horny; hot; juiced (up); randy; sex crazy; sexed up; sex mad; shag-happy; switched on; turned on; worked up.

excrement: big jobs; cack; crap; hocky; macaroni; muck; poo; poo-poo; pony (and trap); Richard; shit; turd.

exhaust, to: to bust a gut; to conk out; to knacker; to knock up; to take it out of s.o.; to wear out.

exhausted, to be: to ache/to be aching all over; all in; beat; buggered; burned out; bushed; busted; clapped out; cooked; creased; dead-beat; dead-tired; dead on one's feet; dished up; done for/in/up; to drag-ass; dragged-out; to drop; fagged out; fit to drop; flaked out; flat out; frazzled; fucked; half-dead; (Harry) flakers; to have had it; jiggered; knackered; knocked out; knocked up; at one's last gasp; on one's last legs; out on one's feet; pegged out; played out; pooped out; ready to drop/flop; rooted; shagged; shot; sold out; stonkered; tuckered; used up; washed out; washed up; whacked; whipped; worn to a frazzle.

exhausting: back-breaking; fagging; gruelling; killing; knacker-ing; shattering; tiring.

expletives: balls! blast it! bleeding hell! blimey! bloody hell! blow it! blow me! bollocks! bother! botheration! buggeration! bugger it! bugger you! bull! by George! by God! by Golly! by gum! by jiminy! by jingo! by Jove! Christ (Almighty)! cor blimey! crumbs! dammit! damn! damn and blast! darn! darnation! darn it! dash (it all)! doggone it! drat it! flipping hell! for Christ's sake! for crying out loud! for goodness sake! for heaven's sake! for Pete's sake! for the love of Mike! fuck a duck! fucking hell! fuck it! fuck me! Gawd 'elp us! Gawd love us! Geeze! glory be! God Almighty! goddamm it! good God!/good gracious! good grief! good heavens! good Lord! goodness! goodness me! goodness gracious me! gorblimey! Gordon Bennett! gosh! great Scott! hang it! hang up! heaven forbid! heck! hell! hell's bells (and buckets of blood)! holy cats/cow/fuck/mackerel/ Moses/ shit/ smoke! jeez(e)! Jeez(e)! Jesus (Christ)! Jesus fucking Christ! like buggery! lord love a duck! lumme! lummy! my foot! my Gawd! my God!/my hat! pissing hell! shit! shit a brick! shite! shit me! shucks! sodding hell! sod it! strewth! strike a light! strike me pink! stone the crows! struth! tarnation! well, I'm blowed/buggered! what the deuce/the devil/the heck!

eye, a black: an eye in mourning; a painted peeper; a shiner; (*both eyes*) to have one's eyes in full mourning.
   eye, to give s.o. a black: to black s.o.'s eye; to bung s.o.'s eye up; to put s.o. in mourning.
   eyes: blinkers; glims; lamps; lights; mince-pies; mincers; minces; peepers.

face: boat (race); chevy (chase); clock; coupon; dial; dial-piece; kisser; lug; map; mug; mush; muzzle; pan; phiz; phizog.

fail, to: to bomb; to catch a cold; to come unstuck; to be washed up; to fall down on a job; to fall flat on one's face; to fall through; to fizzle out; to flop; to fold; to go down like a ton of bricks; to go down the drain/the pan; to go kaput; to go kerflooie; to go phut; to go smash; to go to the dogs/to the wall; to go up the flue; to lay an egg; to pull the plug (on sth/s.o.); to put the skids under sth.
   to fail s.o. in an examination: to flunk; to pip; to plough.
   failure: bomb; brodie; bummer; bust; dead duck; dead loss; dud; fizzle; fivver; flop; flopperoo; frost; muff; oil-can; washout.

faint, to: to black out; to chuck a dummy; to flake out; to go out like a light; to keel over; to pass out.

fart, to: to blow off; to drop one's guts; to let off.
   fart: raspberry.

fat person: dumpling; fatso; podge; porky; roly-poly.

father: da; dad(da); daddio; daddy; (the) gov; (the) governor; guv; (the) guv'nor; the old man; pa; pop; poppa.

fed up, to be: to be brassed off; to be chocker; to be chuffed; to be jack (of sth); to be peed off; to be pissed off; to be poxed off; to be sick (and tired) of sth; to be sick of the whole layout; to be teed off; to have had a basinful/a bellyful/a gutful; to have had it up to here. (*See* **bored, to be**)

feet: beetle-crushers; dogs; hoofs; paddlers; plates of meat; tootsies; tootsie-wootsies; tootsy; trotters.

fellate s.o., to; to have fellatio: to blow; to eat; to French; to give (s.o.) head; to give (s.o.) a head-job; to give (s.o.) a pipe-job; to gobble; to go down on (s.o.); to plate; to root; to suck cock; to suck off; to tongue.
   fellatio: cannibalism; cock-sucking; the French way; head; head job; knob job; pipe job; root; skull job; snow job; zipper dinner.
   fellator: cannibal; cock-sucker; dick licker; gobbler; jaw queen; knob-gobbler; rooter.

fellow: see **chap, old; man.**

female genitals: ass; beaver; box; bush; (the) business; cleft; clout; cookie; cooze; crack; crease; crumpet; cunt; doughnut; fanny; fig; fish bowl; fish pond; fish shop; fish tank; flue; fruit basket; furburger; fur pie; futz; gash; gig; glue factory; glue pot; goods; hairburger; hairpie; hole; jazz; jelly-roll; jing-jang; keester; Lady Jane; manhole; minge; mink; monkey; muff; organ grinder; pee slit; piece of ass; pouch; prat; puka; puss; pussy; quiff; quim; scratch; slit; slot; snapper; snatch; split beaver; split tail; tail; twack; twammy; twat.

fight: aggro; bovver; dust-up; hoedown; mill; mix-up; punch-up; rough house; rough stuff; rough-up; row; rumble; scrap; set-to; stoush. (*See* **quarrel**)

first-rate: see **excellent.**

first-rater: ace; beaut; corker; cracker; daisy; dish; dream; dreamboat; eyeful; fizzer; gas; the greatest; hot cack; humdinger; hunker; knockout; looker; the mostest; peach; rattler; rip-snorter; smasher; stunner; whacker; whammy; whopper; wow.

fit, (to feel): to be as fit as a fiddle/as right as rain; to be full of beans/full of get up and go/full of pep/full of piss and vinegar/full of vim; to be fighting fit; to be in cracking form/in fat city/in good nick/in high gear/in the pink; to be up to the mark; to be zingy/zippy; to feel chipper; to feel on the top of the world; to have (a lot of) ginger; to have lead in one's pencil.

fix, to be in a: to bat on a sticky wicket; to be for the high jump; to be gone a million; to be in a fine old/a right old how-do-you-do; a pretty kettle of fish; to be in a bad patch/in a bad way/in a hole/in a hot spot/in a jam/in a mess/in a pickle/in a scrape/in a (tight) spot; to be in hot water/in schtuck; to be in the muck/in the shit/in the soup; to be on the hook; to be stuck up a gum tree; to be up shit creek without a paddle/up the creek/up the smoke. (*See* **done for; penniless**)

flabbergast, to: to amaze; to bowl over; to floor; to jigger; to knock all of a heap/down with a feather/flat/out/sideways; to shatter; to stagger; to strike all of a heap; to stun; to take the wind out of s.o.'s sails; to throw; to wow.

flabbergasted: amazed; bowled over; floored; jiggered; knocked all of a heap; knocked out; knocked sideways; shattered; staggered; stunned; thrown.

flatter, to: to apple-polish; to be all over s.o.; to blarney; to butter s.o. up; to creep; to flannel; to hand s.o. a sweet line; to kiss ass; to lay it on thick; to lay it on with a trowel; to lick s.o.'s boots; to play up to s.o.; to polish the apple; to scratch s.o.'s back; to shine up to; to slime; to slobber over (s.o.); to smarm all over s.o.; to soft-soap; to spiel; to suck around; to suck up to s.o.; to sugar s.o. up; to sweeten s.o. up; to sweet-talk; to tell the tale.

flatterer: apple-polisher; arsecrawler; arse-creeper; arse-kisser; arse-licker; ass crawler; ass kisser; ass licker; back scratcher; back slapper; boot-licker; bumsucker; cock-sucker; crawler; creep; flanneller; kiss-ass; oddball; pink-eye; slick customer; slim(e)y; smarmer; soft-soap artist; spieler; suckass; sweet-talker; toady.

flattery: apple-polishing; applesauce; arse-crawling; arse-licking; back-scratching; blarney; butter; eyewash; flannel; goo; moody; mush; oil; sawder; slime; snow-job; soft soap; spiel; sugar; sweet-talk.

fleece, to: *see* **swindle, to.**

fogey, old: back number; blimp; has been; old codger; old crock; old dodderer; old dodo; old dugout; old fart; old fossil; old fuddy-duddy; old geezer; old goat; old stick-in-the-mud.

food: chow; chuck; din-dins; dub; eats; extras; grub; hash; moosh; resurrection pie; scoff; seconds; slops; stodge; swill; tack; tuck; tucker; victuals.

fool: arse; ass; arsehole; asshole; barmpot; berk; Berkeley Hunt; bird brain; blithering idiot; blockhead; bohunk; bonehead; boob(y); boof-head; bungalow; bunny; cabbage-head; (proper) Charley; chinless wonder; chowderhead; chucklehead; chuff; chump; clit; clodhopper; cloghead; clot; coot; cretin; cripple; cuckoo; cunt; daftie; dafty; damfool; deadhead; deadneck; dick; dickhead; dill; dimwit; dingbat; dope; dozy-arsed bastard;

dozy twit; drip; drongo; droob; drube; duffer; dumb ass/bunny/cluck/jerk; dumbdumb; dumdum; dumbo; dummy; dumpling; easy mark; (silly) fart; fathead; featherbrain; goose; Herbert; Hooray Henry; jay; jerk; jughead; juggins; klutz; knucklehead; lamb; lughead; lummox; lump; lunkhead; meathead; mental eunuch; moron; motherfucker; mug; muggins; musclehead; mush; muttonhead; nana; nebbish; nerd; nignog; nincompoop; nit; nitwit; nong; noodle; nurd; patsy; pea(-)head; pigeon; pillock; pinhead; piss-artist; pisser; poon; poonce; prat; prick; prize idiot; puddinghead; pumpkinhead; Richard Cranium; sap(head); sawney; scatterbrain; schlemiel; schlemihl; schmo; schmock; schmoe; schnook; shower; silly (sausage); soft touch; spare; spastic; steamer; steaming idiot; stupe; sucker; thickhead; thickie; tit; tool; turniphead; twat; twerp; twirp; twit; wally; wanker; wet; wolly; yap; yo-yo; zombie.

fool s.o., to: to bitch (s.o. out of sth); to bite; to cattle; to cod; to diddle; to do (s.o. out of sth); to do the dirty on s.o.; to do s.o. down; to do the dirty on s.o.; to dope s.o.; to double cross; to euchre s.o.; to fake s.o. out; to fox s.o.; to goof s.o.; to goose s.o.; to have s.o. on; to hornswoggle; to hose; to jew s.o.; to jive s.o.; to kid s.o. (along); to lead s.o. up the garden path; to make s.o. look a chuff/a right monkey; to make a monkey/a sucker out of s.o.; to play games with s.o.; to play s.o. for a sucker; to pull a fast one on s.o.; to pull a gag on s.o.; to pull s.o.'s leg; to pull the wool over s.o.'s eyes; to pull s.o.'s pisser; to put the bite on s.o.; to put it/one across s.o.; to sell s.o. a pup; to spoof; to string s.o. along; to suck s.o. in; to swing a fast one on s.o.; to take s.o. in; to take s.o. for a

ride; to take the Michael/the mickey/the mick/the mike/the piss; to take a rise out of s.o.; to two-time. (*See* **swindle, to**)

to fool around: to fart(-arse) about/around; to footle about; to fuck about/around; to horse about/around; to jack around; to lark about; to mess about/around; to monkey about/around; to muck about/around; to piddle about/around; to play about/around; to ponce about/around; to skylark; to sod about/around.

foot: *see* **feet.**

French (person): Frog; Froggie; Froggy.

friend: bud; buddy; chum; cobber; cock; cocker; cock-sparrow; mate; mucker; old China; pal; pard; pardner; side-kick; sport.

funny, very: creasing; a gas; a guinea a minute; a hoot; a killer; killing; priceless; rich; a riot; a scream; screamingly funny; side-splitting; rollicking; too funny for words.

gadget: *see* **what's-its-name.**

German: Fritz; Heinie; Hun; Jerry; Kraut; Krauthead; squarehead.

get lost! beat it! bollocks to you! bugger off! bugger you! buzz off! damn you! drop dead! frig off! fuck off! get knotted/rooted/screwed/stuffed! get the hell out of here! get your tail out of here! git! go (and) jump in the lake! go and play marbles! go fly a kite! go fuck/screw yourself! go tell it to the Marines! go to blazes/to buggery/to hell! hop it! knackers (to that)! knickers! lay off! leggo! naff off! not on your nellie! nuts (to you)! on your bike! piss off! ponce off! push off! put that in your pipe and smoke it! rats to you! save it! scat! scoot! scram! screw you! screw that! shag off! skip it! sod off! stick it! stow it! stuff it! two fingers! up your gig! up yours! vamoose! (you can) stick it up your flue/up your gonga/up your jumper! you can shove that right up your arse! you know what you can do with that! you know where you can shove/stick that!

girl: babe; baby; bint; bird; bit of all right/crumpet/fluff/skirt/stuff/tail; bobby-dazzler; bobby soxer; broad; brush; chick; corker; cracker; crumpet; cunt; cutie; cutey; dame; dish; doll; dolly; dolly-bird; eager beaver; female; filly; flapper; fluff; flychick; fox; foxy lady; frail job; frill; gal; gel; girlie; hammer; jail bait; Jane; Judy; lovely; lulu; mamma; mink; moll; mouse; nice bit of cunt/goods/homework/stuff; peach (of a girl); piece (of ass/goods); pin-up; potato peeler; quail; queen; raver; scrubber; sex kitten; sheila; shiksa; smasher; sugar; tart; tomato; wench.

gonorrhoea: blue balls; clap; knob rot.
   to have gonorrhoea: to cop/to catch/to get a dose; to get dosed up; to have the clap; to piss pins and needles.

glutton: greedy guts; guzzler; hog; pig; piggy; (walking) dustbin.

goodbye! bung ho! bye! cheers! chin chin! see you! so long! ta-ta! tatty-bye! toodle-oo! toodle-pip!

good time: ball; bash; bat; beanfeast; beer-up; bender; blast; blinder; binge; booze-up; do; fling; fuck-about; gas; gig; hell bender; high jinks; jollies; jolly-up; knees-up; lark; piss-about; piss-up; rave-up; shivoo; thrash; wing-ding; whing-ding.
   to have a good time: to barhop; to beat it up; to be on cloud nine; to be on the loose; to be out on the tiles/the town; to blow one's mind; to get a kick out of sth; to get off on sth; to get one's rocks off; to go on a binge/ on the racket/on the razzle(-dazzle); to go to town; to have a ball/ a high old time/a rare old time/a whale of a time; to hit the high spots; to lead a fast life; to live it up; to make whoopee; to paint the town red; to push the boat out.

gratis: buckshee; for free; freebie; on credit; on the cuff; on the house; on the nod; on tick.

grudge against, to have a: to crowd s.o.; to give s.o. the finger; to have a down on s.o.; to have a monkey on one's back; to have it in for s.o.; to have/to get one's knife into s.o.; to put the freeze on s.o.; to send s.o. to Coventry.

grumble, to: to beef; to belly-ache; to bitch; to bleat; to brass off; to chunter on; to crab; to create; to gripe; to grizzle; to grouch; to grouse; to have a beef about sth; to mizzle; to moan and groan; to whinge; to yap; to yawp.
   grumbling: belly-aching; beefing; griping; grousing.

hand: breadhooks; bunch of fives; daddle; dooks; dukes; fin; fist; flapper; flipper; forks; grappling hooks; hooks; lugs; mauler; meat hooks; mitt; oliver twist; paw.

handcuffs: bracelets; cuffs; darbies; pinchers; snitchers; stringers.

handkerchief: billy; hankie; hanky; nose-rag; nose-wipe(r); sniffer; sniff rag; snitch rag; snot-rag; wipe(r).

hashish: afghan; block; brick; candy; chunks; cube; hash; hemp; muggles; red Leb; shit.
   (*See* **cannabis**)

hat: cadie; cady; kelly; lid; sky-piece; stove-pipe; tile; titfer; topper.

head: attic; bean; beezer; block; bonce; brain box; chump; conk; crumpet; dome; headpiece; loaf; napper; nob; noddle; noggin; noodle; nut; onion; think-box; thinker; think-piece; top-knot; Uncle Ned; (upper) storey.

helicopter: chopper; dust-off; whirly-bird.

heroin: Big H; birdie-powder; boy; courage pills; crap; dojee; dojie; doojee; doojer; dooji; dynamite; elephant; H; Henry; heroin; horse; jack; junk; needle(-)candy; rocks; rock-candy; salt; scag; scat; scot; shit; shmeck; shmee; skag; smack; speedball (heroine and cocaine); stuff; sugar; white cross; white stuff; (old lady) white.

hoax: blarney; booby-trap; bunk(um); catch; clap-trap; cock-and-bull story; eyewash; flummery; gag; guff; hanky-panky; hooey; humbug; jiggery-pokery; leg-pull; plant; sell; spoof; swizz; swizzle; take-in; take-on; yarn. (*See* **swindle**)

hoax, to: *see* **fool, to; swindle, to.**

homosexual: angel; arse-bandit; ass-bandit; arse-man; ass man; aunt; auntie; aunty; bait; beef-bandit; brown-hatter; bum-boy; bummer; bum-rubber; butch; catch; chocolate lover; coal-burner; cock-handler; cock-pusher; cock-sucker; cornholer; creampuff; cruiser; dick licker; dirt track rider; drag queen; fag; faggot; fairy; fart-catcher; fist fucker; flit; flower; flute(r); freak; fruit; fruit-cake; gay; ginger beer; girl; gobbler; gonif; gonof; gonoph; gooser; gussie; homo; hoof; hustler; jock(er); jockey; joey; knob-gobbler; lilly; limp-wrist; lizzie; maricon; Mary; mola; mutton fancier; nance; nancy-boy; nellie; nelly; oddball; pansy; pitch; pix; ponce; poof; pooftah; poofter; poonce; poove; popcorn; poufdah; pouff; punk; quean; queen; queenie; queer; quince; rough-trade; shirt-lifter; short-arm bandit; sissy; skippy; sod; softy; sonk; steamer; sweet; swish; third-sexer; toilet queen; tonk; treacle; turd-burglar; turd-snipper; twink; wolf; wonk.

homosexual (*adj*): bent; camp; gay; ginger; kinky; lacy; left-handed; light-footed; limp-wristed; pansified; poofy; poncy; possodeluxe; queer; wonky.

to be a homosexual: to be one of them.

hooligan: biker; good-for-nothing; goon; gorilla; greaser; hood; hoodlum; layabout; lout; nasty piece of work; punk; rough; ted; teddy-boy; thug; tough guy; yob; yobbo.

hungry, to be: to be empty; to be famished; to be/to feel peckish; to be ravenous; to be starving.

hurry (up), to: to ball the jack; to barrel ass; to beetle off; to be nippy; to buck up; to burn; to burn up the tarmac; to do sth double-quick/in double-quick time; to get a hump on/a hustle on/a move on/a shift on/a wiggle on; to get going; to get one's skates on; to get weaving; to give sth the gun; to go flat out; to have a burn-up; to look lively/snappy; to make it snappy; to pull one's finger out; to put one's foot/toe down; to run like blazes; to shift; to shift one's carcass; to shake a leg; to snap it up; to step on it; to step on the gas; to stir one's stumps; to tear along; to whack up the pace; to whizz; to whoosh; to zap along; to zip along.

husband: better half; hubby; old man; other half.

immediately: *see* **quickly, very.**

important person: big Brother; big bug; big cheese; big gun; biggy; big hitter; big man; big noise; big shot; big-time operator; big-timer; big white chief; bigwig; boss of the show; the brass; brasshat; fat cat; high-up; Mr Big; (his) nibs; nob; the nobs; silvertail; somebody; top brass; top dog; tycoon; VIP.

imprison, to: to bang up; to bolt up; to box; to cage; to can; to clap in jail; to jug; to lag; to lock up; to nick; to put away; to put in the can/in clink; to send down/up; to shop.
(*See* **arrest, to**)

impudence: back-chat; brass; buck; cheek; face; gall; lip; mouth; neck; nerve; once-a-week; sass; sauce.

impudent, to be: to be brassy/ cheeky/cocky/cool/flip/fresh/gutsy/ lippy/ nervy/sassy/saucy/snippy; to be a cool hand/a cool one/a cool customer; to have a hell of a cheek/nerve; to have a neck/a nerve; to sauce s.o.

individual: *see* **chap; man.**

infatuated, to be: to be bats about; to be batty over; to be crazy about/over; to be dippy about; to be gone on; to be goofy over; to be head over heels; to be hipped/hooked on; to be hot for; to be hung up on; to be mad/nuts/ nutty about; to have a pash on; to be potty about; to be sold on; to be sent; to be shook/soft on; to be swept off one's feet by; to be sweet on; to be struck on; to be wild about; to carry a torch for; to dig; to fall for; to fancy; to go gaga over; to go for sth in a big way; to have a pash on; to have a soft spot for; to have a thing about; to have it bad for; to have s.o. under one's skin; to le(t)ch for/about; to queer for; to rave; to take a shine to; to think the world of.

inform on, to: informer, to be an: to blow the gaff on; to blow the whistle on; to come copper; to do the Royals; to finger; to fink; to grass; to lolly; to nark; to turn nark; to nose on s.o.; to put in the G; to put the finger on; to rat on s.o.; to sell out; to shop s.o.; to skunk; to sneak on s.o.; to snitch; to split on s.o.; to squeal on s.o.; to tell on; to top off; to turn snitch.
(*See* **divulge a secret, to**)

information, to give: dope; gen; guff; (hot) tip; lowdown; oil; poop; SP; steer; tip-off; to give s.o. the lowdown/the SP/the wire; to put s.o. in the picture; to put s.o. on to sth; to put s.o. wise; to tip s.o. off; to tip s.o. the wink.

informer, police: canary; copper's nark; finger; fink; grass; grasser; nose; rat; sneak; snitch; snout; splitter; squealer; stooge; stoolie; stool-pigeon; supergrass; top-off; Uncle.

intelligence: brains; common; grey matter; gumption; horse-sense; savvy.

Irish: harp; Mick; Paddy; Pat.

Italian: dago; ding; Eyetie; macaroni; spaghetti; wop.

Japanese: Jap; Nip.

Jew: four-by-two; hebe; heeb; Ikey (Mo); Jaybird; Jewboy; kike; mockie; mocky; sheenie; sheeny; shonk; Yid.

kill (s.o.), to: to blow away; to bump off; to cream; to croak; to do for; to do in; to drill holes in s.o.; to erase; to fill full of lead; to fit with a concrete overcoat; to get; to give the works; to gun down; to hit; to ice; to kiss off; to knock off; to liquidate; to make a hit; to off; to pip; to plug; to polish off; to pop off; to put a hole through (s.o.); to put away; to put on the spot; to rap; to rip off; to rub out; to score; to scrag; to shut up; to snuff out; to take for a ride; to wipe out.

killer: head hunter; hit man; liquidator; red man; torpedo; trigger man.
(*See* **suicide, to commit**)

laugh uproariously, to: to be

doubled-up; to be in fits (of laughter); to be in hysterics/in stitches; to be tickled pink/to death; to crease oneself; to double up; to hoot; to kill oneself laughing; to laugh like a drain; to laugh one's head off; to piss oneself laughing; to scream; to split one's sides laughing; to wet oneself.

lazy, to be: to be bone-idle; to be born tired; to be a bummer/a lazybones/a lazy bum; to be dozy; to bum around; to be workshy. (*See* **easy, to take it; malinger, to**)

leave, to: *see* **run away, to.**

legs: drumsticks; gams; matchsticks; pegs; pins; shanks; stalks; stilts; stumps.

lesbian: amy-john; bull-dagger; bull-dyke; butch; charley; dike; dyke; fairy lady; fairy queen; fanny tickler; fem; finger artist; jasper; kinky; les; lesbie; lesbo; lessie; lez; lezo; lezzie; Marge; Mary; minty; queer; quim queer; tootsie.

less, couldn't care: I couldn't care/I don't give a bean/a damn/a fart/a fig/a fuck/a hang/a monkey's/a rap/a sausage/a tinker's cuss/a (tinker's) toss/tuppence/a tuppenny damn/a tuppenny fuck/ two hoots.

lie: corker; cracker; crock of shit; fairy tale; fib; jazz; jive; pork pie; rouser; story; tall story; tall tale; whopper; yarn.
to lie: to be full of wind; to fib; to jazz; to jive; to madam; to pitch/to pull/to spin a yarn; to tell stories.
(*See* **fool (s.o.), to**)

life, to lead a soft: *see* **easy, to take it.**

limit! that's the: that beats the Dutch; that beats everything; that's a bit much/a bit off/a bit rich/a bit steep/a bit thick! that's all we needed! that's the absolute limit! that's the bloody limit! that's the last straw! that takes the biscuit/ the cake!

look at, to: to bad eye; to clock; to dig; to do a double take; to eyeball; to gander; to geek; to get an eyeful/a load of; to gig; to give s.o. the glad-eye/the once-over; to goof at; to have a butcher's/a dekko/a gander/a look-see/a mike/a shufty/ a squint at; to keep one's eyes open/peeled/skinned; to keep tabs on; to lamp; to lay an eyeball on; to make (goo-goo) eyes at; to screw; to squint; to take a dekko/a gander/a screw/a slant at.
look: butcher's; eyeball; flash; gander; geek; gig; glad-eye; look-see; once-over; shufty; squint.

LSD: acid; blue heaven; candy; the chief; D; sugar; trip; twenty-five; (instant) zen.

mad: bananas; barmy; bats; batty; bonkers; bug-house; buggy; bugs; cracked; crackers; crackpot; cuckoo; crazy; daft; doolally (tap); doodle-alley; dotty; far gone; gaga; kooky; loco; loony; loopy; mental; mishugah; moony; not quite all there; nutty (as a fruit cake); off one's chump/head/nut/onion/rocker/trolley; off-the-wall; pixilated; plumb crazy; potty; psycho; queer; scatty; screwy; stark raving bonkers; touched; unglued; wacky; wig; yarra.
to be/to go mad: to be living in cloud-cuckoo land; to be out of one's tiny mind; to be weak in the upper story; to crack up; to freak out; to go haywire; to go off the hooks/off the rails; to go round the bend/round the twist; to go up the pole/up the wall; to have bats in the belfry/attic; to have a screw/a slate/a tile loose; to lose one's marbles.
mad person: headcase; loony; nut; nutcase; nutter; screwball.

male genitals: block and tackle; bulge; crown jewels; goods; marriage prospects; meat and two veg; privates; three-piece suite.

malinger, to: to bludge; to dodge the column; to goldbrick; to have lead in one's arse; to scrimshank; to shirk; to skive (off); to skrimshank; to swing the lead; to swing it.

malingerer: bludger; column-dodger; dodger; goldbrick; lead-swinger; scrimshanker; shirker; skiver; skrimshanker; slowcoach; slowpoke.

man: baby; beggar; bird; blighter; bloke; bod; bugger; buster; cat; cookie; dude; egg; fella; feller; galoot; gee; geezer; gent; get; gink; git; goof; guy; jockey; John; joker; josser; lug; mac; mate; merchant; mush; turkey; wallah.

marijuana: baby; bambalacha; bang; bhang; bo-bo; boo; brick; canapa; charas; charash; duros; dynamite; fu; gage; ganga; gangster; ganjah; ganji; gauge; (Acapulco) gold; gow; grass; greefo; green; grefa; griffo; gunji; gunny; (Indian) hay; joy-smoke; juana; juane; juanita; keef; kief; love-weed; (sweet) lucy; M; marjie; marjorie; Mary; Mary Ann(e); Mary Jane; Mary Warner; Mexican red; moocah; mota; muggles; Panama red; plant; pot; rope; salt and pepper; splay; stum; tampi; tea; weed; weed-tea; yesca.

marijuana cigarette: ace; African woodbine; birdwood; bomber; burn; dubee; duby; gangster; giggle smoke weed; greefa; grefa; griffa; gyve; jay; jive stick; joint; jolt; joystick; ju; ju-ju; kick-stick; killer; mezz; muggles; pod; pot; rainy-day woman; reefer; rope; sausage; smoke; spliff; stick (of gage/of tea); twist.

married, to get: to do the double act; to get hitched; to get hooked; to get spliced; to jump the broomstick/the hurdle; to take the big leap/the plunge; to tie the knot.

masturbate, to: to ball off; to bash the bishop; to be married to the five-fingered widow; to beat off; to beat the dummy/the meat; to blow; to bring oneself off; to cream off; to diddle; to finger oneself; to finger fuck; to flog the bishop/the dummy/one's donkey; to frig; to fuck off; to get a grip on oneself; to get it off; to have a ball-off; to hank; to hold oneself; to hot-rod; to jack off; to jap off; to jerk off; to jerk one's gherkin; to milk; to play with oneself/with one's instrument/with one's pecker; to play with hank; to pound off; to pound the meat; to pull off; to pull one's plonker/one's pudding/one's wire; to rub (it) off; to rub up; to screw off; to strangle one's grannie; to stroke the lizard; to toss (oneself) off; to varnish the cane; to wank (oneself) off; to whank.

masturbation: do-it-yourself; finger job; finger fuck; hand job; one off the wrist; rub-up; toss(-off); wank; whank; wire-pulling.

masturbator: hand artist; sausage grappler; wanker; whanker; wire-puller.

mescaline: cactus; mesc; peyote.

mess, in a: *see* **fix, in a.**

miser: cheapskate; meanie; meany; penny-pincher; piker; skinflint; tight-arse; tight-ass; trot artist; trotter.

miserly: careful (with one's money); close-fisted; jewish; mean; measly; mingy; penny-pinching; snotty; stingy; tight; tight-arsed; tight-assed; tight-fisted.

to be miserly: to have a reach impediment; to have a death adder in one's pocket; to have short arms and deep pockets; to skin a turd; to throw one's money about like a man with no arms.

mistake: ball-up; balls(-up); bish; bloomer; bodge-up; boner; boob;

booboo; clanger; cock-up; gaffe; howler; screw-up.

to make a mistake: to ball it; to balls sth up; to be off base; to be (way) off beam; to be up the pole; to boob; to drop a brick/a clanger/a stumer; to get one's wires crossed; to goof off; to make a balls(-up)/a ball-up/a bodge-up/a booboo/a cock-up/a gaffe/a goof/a (right) mess/a slip-up; to put one's foot in it; to screw (sth) up; to slip up.

money: ackers; bar; beans; bees and honey; bit; bluey; bob; brass; bread; buck; bundle; century (note); chink; copper(s); daughter; dibs; dimmock; do-re-mi; dosh; dough; dross; dust; earners; filthy lucre; fin; five; fiver; five spot; folding stuff; font; G; gelt; gilt; gold; goodies; gorilla; grand; green-back; greenies; half-a-dollar; jack; jack's alive; kale; lettuce; lolly; looka; loot; mazuma; moola(h); monkey; (the) necessary; (the) needful; nest-egg; nicker; oncer; oner; poppy; quid; quiff; ready; readies; rhino; sausage and mash; scratch; shekels; sobs; sov; spondu-licks; sugar; tenner; ten-spot; tin; velvet; white; (the) wherewithal.

mood, to be in a bad: *see* **angry, to be.**

morphine: Aunt Emma; birdie-powder; block; joy-powder; Miss Emma; morf; morph; snow; white cross; white stuff; whizz-bang.

mother: ma; mamma; mom; mum; muvver; (my) old girl; (my) old lady; (my) old woman.

moustache: drooper; (face) fun-gus; handlebar moustache; tash; tickler.

mouth: bazoo; box of dominoes; cakehole; chops; gob; kisser; mush; north and south; puss; rat-trap; satch; satchel mouth; trap; yap.

naked: in one's birthday suit; in the altogether; in the buff; in the raw; stark bollock-naked; starkers; without a stitch on.

negro: *see* **Black.**

nonsense: all my eye (and Betty Martin); apple sauce; balderdash; ballyhoo; baloney; balls; bilge; blah-blah; blarney; blather; blether; bollocks; boloney; bosh; bull; bull-shine; bullshit; bumf; bum-fodder; bunkum; cherry ripe; claptrap; cock; codswallop; crap; eyewash; fanny; fiddlesticks; flam; flapdoodle; flim-flam; flummery; fudge; gammon; garbage; guff; hocky; hogwash; hokey pokey; hokum; holly-golly; hooey; horse shit; hot air; jazz; junk; malarkey; moonshine; muck; mush; piffle; pigwash; piss; poppycock; rot; shit; spoof; squit; stuff (and nonsense); swill; taurus excretus; tommy rot; tosh; trash; tripe; twaddle; waffle.

to talk nonsense: to be full of shit; to crap on; to flip one's lip; to jive; to shuck; to shoot one's mouth off; to spoof; to talk a lot of junk; to talk a load of rot; to talk like a nut; to talk nuts/pif-fle/rot/shit; to talk through the back of one's neck; to talk wet.

nose: beak; beezer; bill; boko; conk; hooter; horn; neb; nozzle; s(ch)nozz; s(ch)nozzle; schnozzola; sneezer; sniffer; snitch; snoot; snout.

not (bloody) likely!; noth-ing doing!: balls! can't be done! count me out! no chance! no can do! no dice! no fear! no go! no sale! no soap! no such luck! no way! not a chance in hell! not a sodding chance! not a hope! not effing likely! not sodding likely! not on your life/on your nellie/on your sweet life! not if I know anything about it! take a running jump! **(***See* **get lost!)**

nothing: bugger-all; chicken feed; chicken shit; damn all; FA; Fanny Adams; fat lot; fleabite; fuck-all;

nix; not a droob; not a sausage; nowt; piss-all; sod-all; sweet FA; sweet Fanny Adams; sweet fuck-all; zilch.

opium: black stuff; can; chef; dopium; dreams; dream wax; goma; gow; green ashes/mud; hop; ice-cream; mud; O; pen-yen; poppy; tar; treacle; twang; yenshee.
opium pipe: bamboo.
oral sex: *see* **cunnilingus; fellatio.**
orgasm, to have an: to come; to come off; to cum; to finish off; to get (it) off; to get one's rocks off; to go off; to pop.
(*See* **ejaculate, to**)

packing, to send s.o.: to bounce s.o.; to choke s.o.; to give s.o. the air/the brush off/the bum's rush/his marching orders/the raspberry; to railroad; to send s.o. to the devil; to send s.o. off with a flea in his ear; to sling out; to tell s.o. where he gets off; to tell s.o. to fuck off/to piss off/to sod off.
(*See* **dismiss s.o., to**)

paunch: beer belly; beer gut; belly; bread basket; corporation; Derby Kelly; pod; podge; pot; pot-belly; tub; tummy.
(*See* **stomach**)

pawn, to; in pawn: to dip; to hock; to lumber; to put in hock/in pop; to put up the spout; at my uncle's; at the hockshop; in hock; in pop; up the spout.

pay (up), to: to ante (up); to brass up; to chip in; to cough up; to dab down; to dish out; to do the necessary; to foot the bill; to fork out; to pay cash on the nail; to pitch in; to plonk out; to shell out; to splash out; to stand sam; to stand the racket; to stump up.

PCP: angel dust.
peasant: bushwhacker; chew-

bacon; clod; clodhopper; country bumpkin; hayseed; hick; hillbilly; jaybird; joskin; mossback; redneck; rube; shitkicker; swedey.

penis: bayonet; bazooka; bone; (the) business; chopper; cock; dick; dickory dock; dicky; dong; donker; donkey; doodle; end; gear stick; gherkin; gun; hammer; Hampton (wick); hot rod; instrument; jack; jigger; jing-jang; jock; John Thomas; joint; joystick; knob; (middle/third) leg; lizard; lob; meat; nob; (the) old man; one-eyed trouser snake; organ; pecker; peenie; pencil; Perce; Percy; persuader; peter; pisser; plonker; poker; prick; putz; ramrod; rig; rod; roger; root; sausage; schlong; shaft; short-arm; stalk; stick; stiffy; tail; tassel; thing; thingy; tonk; tool; twinkle; Uncle Dick; wally; wanger; weapon; weeny; whang(er); wiggy; willie; willy; winkle; yang; yard.

penniless: boracic (lint); broke; broke to the wide; cleaned out; dead broke; down on one's uppers; hard-up; in low water; in queer street; light; on one's ass; on one's beam ends; on the bread line; on the outer; on the rory; peppermint; pink lint; piss-poor; played out; shit poor; short; skint; stony (broke); tapped out.
to be penniless: to feel the pinch; not to have a bean/a brass farthing/a cent/a sausage.
(*See* **fix, to be in a**)

period, to have a: to be on the rag; to come on; to fall off the roof; to fly the flag; flowers; to have the curse; to have the month-lies; to have mum nature; to have the decorators/the painters in; to have one's relations to stay; to have the rag on/out; to have the reds; joey; the wet season.

pervert, to be a: dirty old man; to have a dirty/filthy mind; filthy sod; flasher; to be kinky; perve; secko; sex fiend; sexo.

pimp: bludger; bully; easy rider; fancy man; flesh peddler; hustler; mack; mackerel; mackman; nookie; bookie; ponce; white slaver.

pocket: cly; keester; kick; pit; poke; sky-rocket.

police: boys in blue; bulls; button men; (the) cops; (the) Force; (the) filth; (the) fuzz; (the) law; (the) ·Man; monarch; New York's finest; old Bill; pigs; SPG; sweeney; Uncle.

policeman, (uniformed): blue-bottle; bobby; cop; copper; flatfoot; flattie; flatty; fuzz; man in blue; old Bill; pig; swedey; woodentop.

policeman (*general term*): bobby; bogey; bull; cop; copper; fed; filth; fuzz; grasshopper; nab; oink; old Bill; paddler; peeler; pig; rozzer; scuffer; swedey.

detective: dick; eye; fly-ball; fly-bob; fly-bull; fly-cop; fly-dick; fly-mug; gumshoe; private eye; Richard; snoop; tail; tec.

police station: bridewell; cop-shop; factory; hoosegow; lock-up; nick; warehouse.
(*See* **Black Maria**)

pregnant, to be: to be clucky/expecting; to be in a delicate condition/in the club/in the family way/in pool/in poke/in trouble/in the pudding club; to be knocked up/preggers; to be up the duff/up the spout; to have a bun in the oven.

to make pregnant: to get in the club/in the family way/into trouble; to knock up; to put up the duff/up the spout.

priest: *see* **clergyman.**

prison: bird; boob; can; CB; cala-boose; calaboosh; chok(e)y; clink; cooler; glasshouse; hoosegow; jail; jankers; jigger; Joe Gurr; jug; klink; lock-up; (the) nick; pen;

pokey; quad; quod; shop; shovel; slammer; slams; sneezer; stir; tank.

to be in prison: to be banged up; to be behind bars; to be bolted up; to be in bird; to be inside; to do bird; to do time.
(*See* **imprison, to**)

prison cell: bing; bird-cage; chok(e)y; coffin; cooler; flowery dell; hole; lock-up; Peter (Bell); slot; think tank; wishing well.

prisoner: con; first-timer; fresh fish; jailbird; jaybird; (old) lag; lifer; polisher; toe-ragger; yardbird.

prison sentence: bender; bird-lime; bit; carpet (bag); drag; fistful; five fingers; five spot; hair-cut; handful; hard (labour); lag-ging; pontoon; porridge; rap; spot; stretch; ten-spot; ticket; time; wooden one.

prison warder: flue; fuzz; screw; twirl.

profits, illicit: bit on the side; commission; earner; graft; gravy; perks; pickings; rake-off.
(*See* **bribe**)

prostitute: alley cat; bag(gage); bat; blister; brass; broad; bunny; call-girl; chippy; chromo; cruiser; doxy; endless belt; fancy woman; flat-backer; flesh peddler; floosie; floosy; floozie; floozy; forty-four; fruit; hello-dearie; hooker; hustler; joy-girl; meal ticket; moll; pig-meat; possum; pro; pross; prossie; prossy; prostie; prosty; puta; quickie; quicky; scrubber; slag; street-walker; tom; tomato; tart; tramp; trollop; wench; working girl.

prostitute's client: casual; john; one-nighter; one-night job; punter; trade; trick.

prostitution: the business; the game; the turf.
(*See* **solicit, to**)

pub: battle-cruiser; beer joint; boozer; clip-joint; joint; local; nightspot; nineteenth hole; rubadub; rubbity; watering hole.

quantity, a great: bags; a barrel of; dozens of; ever so much; heaps; a hell of a lot; lashings; loads; lots; lousy with; no end of; oodles; piles; pots; stacks; tons; umpteen; wad.

quarrel: argle-bargle; argy-bargy; barney; breeze; bull and cow; donnybrook; dust-up; flare-up; hassle; hoedown; rhubarb; row; ruck; rumpus; scrap; screaming match; slanging match; split-up; up-and-downer; upper-and-downer; yike.

to quarrel: to argufy; to be bolshy/obstropolous; to go for s.o.; to hassle; to have an argy-bargy with s.o.; to make the fur fly; to pal out; to pick a bone with s.o.; to queer oneself with; to row; to tangle; to yike.
(*See* **fight**)

quickly, very: as quick as dammit; as soon as dammit; asap; at a cracking pace; at a fair old lick; at a fast mince; before you can say Jack Robinson; chop chop; to fire on all cylinders; hubba hubba; in a jiff; in a jiffy; in a twinkling; in nothing flat; in quick order; in two shakes (of a lamb's tail); in two ticks; licketysplit; like the clappers; like fury; like greased lightning; like a house on fire; like mad; like a shot; like a streak of piss; nippy; pdq; pretty damn quick; pronto; (a bit) sharpish.

ready, absolutely: all buttoned up; all set; all sewn up; all shipshape; all taped; all teed up; all wrapped up.

reprimand: bawling out; blowing-up; calling-down; coating; dressing-down; rap; raspberry; roasting; rocket; slating; strafing; talking-to; telling-off; ticking-off; wigging.

reprimand, to: to ball out; to bawl out; to bite s.o.'s head off; to blow s.o. up; to call down; to carpet; to chew s.o.'s balls/ears/head off; to chew s.o.'s ass out; to come down on s.o. like a ton of bricks; to cuss; to dish it out; to dress down; to eat s.o.'s head off; to give (s.o.) a balling out/a ballocking/a bawling out/a coating/a going-over/a jawing/a mouthful/a kick in the pants/a piece of one's mind/a rocket/stick/what-for; to give it to s.o. (hot and strong); to go crook; to haul s.o. over the coals; to have s.o. on the carpet/on the mat; to jaw s.o. out; to jump on s.o.; to lambaste; to let s.o. have it; to lead off at; to light into; to pitch into; to play old Harry with; to put s.o. through his facings; to read the riot act; to ream s.o./s.o.'s ass out; to send s.o. away with a flea in his ear; to sit on s.o.; to slap down; to slate; to strafe; to tear s.o. off a strip; to tell s.o. where to get off; to tick s.o. off; to wipe the floor with s.o.

reprimanded, to be: to be on the carpet; to carry the can; to catch it; to cop it; to get a bawling-out/a bollocking/a talking-to/a telling-off/a ticking-off/a wigging; to get a kick in the pants/a lot of stick/a slice of tongue-pie; to get hauled over the coals; to get hell; to get one's ass chewed out/one's head bitten off.

resourceful: all there; cagey; clever-clever; cleverclogs; a clever Dick; clever guts; cute; deep; dodgy; downy; fly; know-all; know-it-all; mustard; nifty; shrewd; slick; smart; smart-arsed; smart-assed; snak(e)y; snide; snidey; swift; wide; wise.

resourceful person: cleverclogs; clever Dick; clever guts; dodger; finagler; flyboy; know-all; know-it-all; shrewdie; slyboots; smart arse; smart ass; smarty pants; smooth operator.

to be resourceful: to be up to every move; to be on the ball; to be/to get on with it; to get wise; to have the suss; to know a thing or two; to know all the tricks of the trade/all the wrinkles; to know the drill/the ropes; to know one's p's and q's; to know one's way about; to know what's what; to wise up.

revolver: artillery; barker; biscuit; gat; heat; heater; pea-shooter; persuader; piece; rod; roscoe; Saturday night special; sawn-off; shooter; shooting-iron; six-shooter; squirter; tool.

rich: cashed up; doughy; filthy rich; flush; in the money; loaded; plush; rolling in it; stinking (rich); stinking with money; well-fixed; well-heeled; well-lined; well-off; well-stacked.

to be rich: to be in the chips/ in the heavy/in the money; to be on easy street; to be worth a packet; to coin it in; to feather one's nest; to have a barrel of money/ stacks (of money); to make a bomb; to make a packet; to make one's pile; to make money hand over fist; to rake it in.

ropes, to know the: *see* **resourceful, to be.**

rot: *see* **nonsense.**

rot, to talk: *see* **nonsense, to talk.**

rotten: awful; beastly; cheesy; chronic; corny; crappy; crummy; dud; foul; ghastly; lousy; mingy; mouldy; mucky; no bloody good; poxy; pukeish; pukey; putrid; rancid; ropey; shocking; shoddy; stinking.

rotter: *see* **bastard.**

run away, to: amscray; to beat it; to belt off; to blow; to breeze off; to bugger off; to bug out; to buzz off; to check out; to cheese it; to clear off; to clear out; to dash; to do a bunk/a disappearing act/a fade/a guy/a mick(e)y/a mike/a slope; to drag-ass; to fade; to flit; to fuck off; to get moving/rolling; to go through; to hare off; to haulass; to have it away for the hurry-up; to hightail it; to hit the road/ the track/the trail; to hive off; to hook; to hotfoot it; to kick off; to lam (out); to leg it; to make oneself scarce; to make tracks; to mizzle; to mosey off; to nick off; to nip off; to pack up; to pee off; to piss off; to ponce off; to pop off; to pull out; to push off; to quit the scene; to rat off; to run out on s.o.; to scarper; to scoot; to scram; to screw; to shag-ass; to shag off; to ship out; to shit off; to shoot off/through; to shove off; to skedaddle; to skip off; to slide off; to slope off; to smoke (off); to sneak out; to sod off; to split; to split out; to take a powder; to take stoppo; to take off; to toddle off/ along; to tommy; to tool off; to turn tail; to vamoose; to waltz off.

Russian: commie; commy; red; Russky.

sack, to: *see* **dismiss, to.**

sailor: jack; Jack tar; tar; jolly; leather-neck; matlow; pongo; (old) salt; shellback.

Scotsman: Jimmy; Jock; Mac; Sawney.

self-conceited, to be: *see* **show off, to.**

semen: baby-juice; bullets; come; cum; cream; crud; hocky; jism; jissom; jizz; juice; load; love juice; scum; spunk.

sex, to have: to ball; to bang; to be at it; to bed; to be in a leg-over position; to be on the job; to bunny fuck; to crack it; to diddle; to dig; to dip one's wick; to do; to do a knee-trembler; to do the naughty; to feature with s.o.; to finger fuck; to frig; to fuck; to futz; to get into s.o.'s pants; to get (it) in; to get it off; to get it up; to get one's leg over; to get one's black/red wings; to give s.o. the bullets; to give it to s.o.; to give a length; to give s.o. a thigh sandwich; to go to bed with; to go enders with (a woman); to go the naughty; to grab a piece of cake; to grind; to have a bang/bayonet practice/a chicken dinner/a bit of crumpet/a bit of the other/a bit on the side/a bit of spare/a bit of stray/a dry fuck/a dry hump/a grind/a jump/a lay/a nibble/a poke/a quick one/a quickie/a screw/a shag/a taste/a wham-bam; to have it; to have s.o.; to have it away with; to have it off with; to have one's banana peeled/one's nuts cracked; to have a roll in the hay/a tumble; to honeyfuck; to horse; to hose; to hump; to jazz; to jerk; to join the mounties; to knock off; to knock a slice off; to lay; to make it; to make out; to nail; to nut; to open one's legs for s.o.; to perform; to plant; to plug; to poke; to pound; to pull; to pull a train; to put the hooks on s.o.; to ram; to ride; to rock; to roger; to roll; to root; to rub off; to scrape; to screw; to see the sky through the trees; to shaft; to shag; to skip; to sleep about/around/with s.o.; to slip s.o. a length; to snatch a quick one; to stick it in; to stuff; to tear it off; to tear off a piece of ass; to thread; to trick; to tup; to wham; to work; to yard.

sex: bang; bed; belt; bit of crumpet; bit of tail; bit of the other; bit on the side; business; daisy chain; dry fuck; dry hump; finger-fuck; fuck; fucking; gash; grind; half and half; heing and sheing; how's your father; honey-fucking; hump; jazz; jig-a-jig; jig-jig; jing-jang; jump; knee-trembler; lay; naughty; nookie; nooky; pull; quick one; quickie; ride; roll; root; screw; screwing; shag; slap and tickle; snatch; thrash; wham-bam.
(*See* **anal sex; oral sex**)

shirt: dicky dirt; flesh-bag; shift; shimmy.

show off, to: to be too big for one's boots; to be big-headed; to big-note oneself; to be snotty-nosed/uppity; to ego trip; to fancy oneself; to gam; to go on an ego trip; to play to the gallery; to put on the dog/a front/the ritz; to skite; to splurge; to swank; to talk big; to think no end of oneself; to think one is the bee's knees/the cat's whiskers/the big I am/hot shit/really it; to throw one's weight around; to toss (oneself) off; to walk tall.

show off: bighead; bit-note man; blowhard; dazzle-dasher; four-flusher; ho-daddy; lair; line-shooter; poser; skite; swank; swanky; swellhead.

shut up, to: to belt up; to button one's mouth/lip; to dummy; to hold one's guts; to ice; to keep mum; to keep one's gob shut; to keep one's trap shut; to pipe down; to shush; to squelch; to wrap up.

shut up! belt up! button your lip/your mouth! can it! cheese it! chuck it! cut the cackle! cut it out! cut out the fancy stuff! cut the crap! drop dead! drop it! dry up! give it a rest! knock it off! nark it! none of your lip! pack it in! pack it up! pipe down! put a sock in it! shut your face/your gob/your row! shut it! stow it! turn it up! wrap it up!
(*See* **get lost!**)

silence s.o., to: to choke s.o. off; to give s.o. a clincher; to put the damper on; to put the kibosh on s.o.; to score off s.o.; to settle s.o.'s hash; to shut s.o. up; to sit upon s.o.; to squash s.o.

sleep, to go to: to be out like a light; to crash down/out; to doss down; to drop off; to get some shut-eye; to go (to) bye-byes; to go to kip; to grab some shut-eye; to have forty-winks/a kip/a nap/a snooze; to hit the sack; to nod off; to pad down; to plough the deep; to zizz.

sodomise, to: see **anal sex (to have)**.

solicit, to: to be on the game/on the streets/on the turf; to go (john) cruising; to hustle; to kerb crawl; to kerb cruise; to mack; to peddle ass; to score; to swing a bag; to tote; to trade; to trick (a john); to turn a trick; to walk the streets; to whore.

Spaniard: dago; wop.

spectacles: bins; glims; goggles.

spend, to: to blow; to get through; to go to town; to lay out; to play ducks and drakes with one's money; to piss away (one's money); to run through; to shoot the works; to splash out; to throw good money after bad; to throw money down the drain; to throw one's money about.

spirits, strong: see **(alcoholic) drink**.

spree, to be/to go on a: see **good time, to have a**.

state, in a: all of a dither; all of a doodah; all of a flutter; all of a jitter; all at sea; all shook up; dithery; edgy; flummoxed; nervy; rattled; uncool; uptight.

to be in a state: to be in a flap/in a lather/in a stew/in a tizwas/in a tizzy; to be rattled/strung-up; to flap; to go off the rails; to go to pieces; to go into a tail-spin; to have the fidgets/the jitters/the twitters; to sweat; to work oneself up into a lather.

steal, to: to bag; to bone; to case a joint; to dip; to do over; to do a case/a job/a villainy; to finger; to half-inch; to have it away with; to heist; to hoist; to hook; to jump; to knock off; to knock over; to lift; to make (away with); to move; to nab; to nick; to nip; to pinch; to pull a job; to put one's mitts on sth; to reef; to ring the changes; to rip off; to roll; to scale; to screw a gaff; to scrounge; to shop; to snaffle; to snatch; to sneak; to snipe; to stick up; to swipe; to take off; to turn over; to walk away with; to walk off with; to whip; to whizz; to win.

stolen: (fell) off the back of a lorry; hot; knocked off. (See **theft; thief**)

stink, to: to honk; to hoot; to hum; to niff; to be niffy; to be nifty; to pen and ink; to pong; to whiff; to be whiffy.

stomach: bread-basket; belly; Derby Kell(y); tummy. (See **paunch**)

stupid, extremely: chuckle-headed; cretinous; (as) daft/dim as they come; daffy; dense; dilly; dim; dimwitted; dippy; dopey; dozy; drippy; dumb; fat; fatheaded; featherbrained; flatheaded; goofy; gormless; half-baked; jerky; klutzy; obtuse; plain daft/dumb; priceless; puddled; sappy; soft (in the head); soppy; slow on the uptake; squitty; thick; thick as a plank/as two short planks; thickheaded; thickskulled; wet; wood from the neck up; wrongheaded.

suicide, to commit: to blow one's brains out; to bump oneself off; to do away with oneself; to do oneself in; to take the easy way out.

suit, to: that suits me down to the ground; that suits my book; that suits me to a T; that's just what the doctor ordered; that's right up my street; that's just my cup of tea; that's right up my alley.

swank, to: see **show off, to**. **swank(er):** see **show off**.

swindle, to: to be on a fiddle; to burn; to chisel; to con; to cross; to diddle; to do out of; to fit up; to fleece; to flimflam; to fob; to frame; to frig; to fuck; to gazump; to goldbrick; to grift; to gyp; to nick; to pull a fast one; to rip off; to rook; to rush; to screw; to sell a pup; to set up; to shaft; to sharp;

to skin; to slip one over on s.o.; to snow; to sting; to swizzle; to take s.o. for a ride; to twist; to tuck up; to wangle; to work a fiddle.

swindle: (the old) army game; clip-game; cross; daylight robbery; fiddle; fit-up; fix; flim-flam; frame-up; hustle; racket; ramp; razzle-dazzle; rip off; sell; skin game; sting; swizz; swizzle; wangling.

swindler: chiseller; con artist; con man; crook; diddler; double-crosser; fiddler; fixer; flimflammer; frigger; gazumper; goldbricker; griffer; gyp; highbinder; racketeer; rorter; scalper; shark; sharp; sharpie; shortchange artist; skin artist; spieler; twister; wangler.

syphilis: knob rot; pox; siff; syph.
to have syphilis: to be a sypho/a syphy; to be poxed up/siffy/syphy/syphed up.

talk volubly, to: *see* **chat, to.**

talkativeness: *see* **chat; chattering.**

tall, thin person: bag of bones; bean-pole; big gawk; drain pipe; flag-pole; long streak of piss; string-bean.

tease, to: *see* **annoy, to.**

teeth: choppers; dominoes; fangs; gnashers; grinders; ivories; mashers; pearlies; snappers; toothy-pegs.

telephone: bell; blower; buzzer; Darby and Joan; dog and bone; horn; Mike Malone.
to telephone: to give s.o. a bell/a buzz/a tinkle; to get on the blower to s.o.

television: boob tube; box; goggle-box; idiot box; idiot's lantern; telly; the tube.

temper, to be in a bad: to be crabby/niggly/shirty/stroppy; to be in a right old paddy; to be like a bear with a sore head; to have one's shirt out; to be on the war-path.

(*See* **angry, to be**)

testicles: bag of tricks; balls; bal-locks; bollix; bollocks; chestnuts; cobblers; cods; danglers; dusters; family jewels; futures; goolies; jocks; knackers; maracas; marbles; marriage gear/prospects; marshmallows; Niagaras; nuts; orchestras; pills; stones; two-piece.

tired: *see* **exhausted.**

tramp: bindle stiff; bo; bum; bummer; dosser; down-and-out; drifter; fink; floater; scruff; stiff; sundowner; swagman.

trousers: bags; daks; drainpipes; kecks; keks; pants; slacks; strides.

umbrella: brolly; gamp; gingham; mush.

underpants: drawers; jockeys; nut chokers; underdaks.

undersized (person): half-pint; knee-high to a grasshopper; lightweight; lofty; pint-sized; pip-squeak; runt; sawn-off; short-arse; shorty; shrimp; tich; titch.

unwell, to be/to feel: to come over (all) funny/(all) queer; crook; dicky; funny; groggy; knocked-up; laid-up; liverish; off-colour; off one's oats/one's feed; offish; to have an off day; on one's last legs; one degree under; out of sorts; poorly; queer; rough; seedy; shaky; sick as a parrot; umpty; uncle Dick; under the weather.

uproar, an: barney; bear garden; circus; hoo-ha(a); hoop-la; hullaba-loo; kerfuffle; kick-up; racket; rough-house; row; ruck(us); rumpus; scream; shemozzle; shindig; shindy; (a big) stink.
to make an uproar: to be bolshy/obstropolous/rowdy; to kick up a dust/fuss/row; to make the fur fly; to play old Harry; to raise Cain; to raise (merry) Hell; to raise hell/a big stink.

urinate, to: to do wee-wees; to do number one; to do small jobs; to diddle; to go to the gents/the loo; to go for a leak/for a piddle/ for a piss/for a strain; to have a Jimmy Riddle/a pee/a piss/a run-out/a slash/a squirt/a wee-wee; to have a look at the plumbing; to let fly; to pay a call/a visit; to pee; to piddle; to piss; to point Percy at the porcelain; to pop outside; to see a man about a dog; to shed a tear for Nelson; to siphon the python; to splash one's boots; to spring a leak; to squeeze the lemon; to tiddle; to tinkle; to turn on the waterworks; to water the horses; to widdle.
urine: pee; piddle; piss; wee; wee-wee.

vagina: *see* **female genitals.**
VD: *see* **gonorrhea; syphilis.**
virginity: cherry; maidenhood.
  to lose one's virginity: to fall off the apple tree; to lose one's cherry.

vomit, to: to barf; to be as sick as a dog; to chuck up; to chunder; to cry Ruth; to feed the fishes; to fetch up; to go for the big spit; to have a technicolour yawn; to heave (one's guts up); to honk (one's chuff); to puke (up); to ralph up; to shoot the cat; to sick up; to spew (one's guts up); to throw a map; to throw up; to York.

walk, to: to foot it; to foot-slog; to go for a toddle; to hoof it; to leg it; to pad it; to ride Shanks's pony/Shanks's mare.

WC: bathroom; bog; can; cottage; craphouse; crapper; dike; dub; dunny; (the) Gents; Jane; (the) john; karzy; khazi; (the) ladies; lav; (the) little boy's/little girl's room; (the) loo; pisser; pisshouse; powder-room; privy; shit-house; shouse; (the) smallest room; tea house; tea room; throne-room; trizzer.

weep, to: to be a cry-baby; to blub; to grizzle; to put on a/the (big) sob-act; to turn on the waterworks.

what's-his-name; what's-her-name: doings; thing; thingamy; thingum(e) bob; thingummy; what-do-you-call-him; whatcha-(ma)callit; whatsit.

what's-its-name: (the) doings; doo-da; doodah; doofer; doohickey; doojigger; gimmick; gubbins; jigger; oojamaflip; oojie; thingamy; thingamybob; thingamyjig; thingum(e)bob; thingummy; thingy; whatcha(ma)callit; what-do-you-call-it; whatnot; whatsit.

wife, (my): my ball and chain; my better half; cheese and kisses; headache; (the) light of my life; the litle woman; (the) main squeeze; the missus; the missis; my old duchess; my old Dutch; my old girl; my old lady; my old woman; my other half; my sparring partner; my trouble and strife.
(See **husband***)*

woman: bird; broad; cat; dame; fem; female; floosie; floosy; floozie; floozy; hen; Judy; mamma; potato peeler; queen; sheila; skirt.
(pej) bagage; bat; bint; bitch; cow; crow; gash; hagbag; hellcat; scrubber; shagbag; tart; tramp.
  attractive woman: bit of all right; bit of stuff; crumpet; fox; foxy lady; hot lay/mamma/piece/ stuff; mover; nice bit of stuff; nympho; piece of ass/crumpet/ skirt; sex bomb; sexpot.
  (ugly) old woman: old bat; old biddy; old crow; old faggot; old trout.
(See **girl***)*

womanizer, to be a: a bit of a lad; Casanova; to be cunt-struck; fast worker; to be a fast one with the girls; filthy sod; gash-hound; hound-dog; jelly-roll; lady-killer; one for the ladies; petticoat chaser;

ram; skirt-chaser; skirt-hunter; smoothie; smoothy; tail-man; wolf.

work hard (at), to: to be an eager beaver; to be snowed under; to bust a gut; to dig; to do one's damnedest/darnedest; to flog oneself to death; to get down to a bit of hard grind; to go at it tooth and nail; to grind; to kill oneself with work; to knock oneself out; to peg away; to piss blood; to plug away; to put in a bit of hard graft; to shag one's arse off; to sweat blood; to sweat one's guts out; to work like the devil; to work like a dog/a nigger; to work like shit/like stink.

worthless: crap; crappy; a dead loss; diddly (shit); duff; fit for/good for the scrap heap; measly; mouldy; nbg; NBG; no earthly use; no great shakes; not much cop; not worth a cracker/a crumpet/a damn/a nickel/a rap; not worth shucks/tuppence; poxy; shitty; tin-pot; the pits; tuppenny-ha'penny; trashy; a washout.